About Ingredien

Unless recipes specify otherwise:

Flour called for is all-purpose flour, sifted before measuring.

Baking powder is double-acting baking powder.

Butter is salted butter.

Sour cream is the commercial type.

Eggs are large eggs.

Brown sugar is measured firmly packed.

Garlic cloves are of medium size.

Herbs and spices are dried.

All measures are standard, all measurements level.

OVEN TEMPERATURES

Below 300° F. = very slow

300° F. = slow

325° F. = moderately slow

350° F. = moderate

375° F. = moderately hot

400-25° F. = hot

450-75° F. = very hot

500° F. or more = extremely hot

FAHRENHEIT/CELSIUS (CENTIGRADE) SCALE

	Boiling Point F.	*Boiling Point* C.	
(of Water)	212°	100°	(of Water)
	200°	93.3°	
	190°	87.8°	
	180°	82.2°	
	170°	76.7°	
	160°	71.1°	
	150°	65.6°	
	140°	60°	
	130°	54.4°	
	120°	48.9°	
	110°	43.3°	
	100°	37.8°	
	90°	32.2°	
	80°	26.7°	
	70°	21.1°	
	60°	15.6°	
Freezing Point	50°	10°	Freezing Point
	40°	4.4°	
(of Water)	32°	0°	(of Water)

Conversion Formula:
Fahrenheit to Celsius (Centigrade):
Subtract 32 from Fahrenheit reading, divide by 1.8.

The DOUBLEDAY COOKBOOK

The DOUBLEDAY COOKBOOK

Complete Contemporary COOKING

Jean Anderson and Elaine Hanna

ILLUSTRATIONS BY MEL KLAPHOLZ
PHOTOGRAPHS BY WILL ROUSSEAU

Doubleday & Company, Inc.
GARDEN CITY, NEW YORK

Library of Congress Cataloging in Publication Data

Anderson, Helen Jean, 1929–
The Doubleday cookbook: complete contemporary cooking

Includes index.
1. Cookery.   I. Hanna, Elaine, joint author.
II. Title.
TX651.A57   641.5
ISBN 0-385-09088-9
Library of Congress Catalog Card Number 75–1000

ACKNOWLEDGMENTS

We are greatly indebted to the following companies for providing equipment to use in the testing and development of recipes:

General Electric Company, Housewares Division, Bridgeport, Connecticut (for portable appliances); *KitchenAid, The Hobart Manufacturing Company,* Troy, Ohio (dishwashers and heavy-duty electric mixers); *Ronson Corporation,* Woodbridge, New Jersey (electric cook-and-stir blenders); *The West Bend Company,* West Bend, Wisconsin (small electric appliances, cookware, and bakeware); and *Whirlpool Corporation,* Benton Harbor, Michigan (gas and electric ranges).

We also wish to thank the following for their gracious co-operation and for supplying quantities of valuable information:
Agricultural Extension Service, University of Wyoming; Aluminum Association; American Dietetics Association; American Home Economics Association; American Institute of Baking; American Lamb Council; American Meat Institute; American Museum of Natural History; American Mushroom Institute; American Spice Trade Association; Bourbon Institute; Brooklyn Botanic Garden; California Foods Research Institute; Cling Peach Advisory Board; Council on Foods and Nutrition, American Medical Association; Dried Fruit Association of California; Fishery Council; Florida Board of Conservation; Florida Citrus Commission; Food and Nutrition Board, National Academy of Sciences, National Research Council; French National Federation of Regional Committees for Promotion and Development of Agricultural Products; French National Wines Committee; Gas Appliance Manufacturers' Association; Glass Container Institute; Idaho Potato and Onion Commission; Madeira Wine Association; Maine Department of Sea and Shore Fisheries; Metal Cookware Manufacturers Association; Maryland Department of Economic Development; Massachusetts Department of Fisheries and Game; National Apple Institute; National Broiler Council; National Canners Association; National Coffee Association; National Dairy Council; National Electrical Manufacturers Association; National Fisheries Institute; National Live Stock and Meat Board; National Macaroni Institute; National Turkey Federation; New York Botanical Garden; New York State College of Agriculture, Cornell University; New York State College of Human Ecology, Cornell University; New York State Cooperative Extension Service; North Carolina Agricultural Extension Service; Nutrition Foundation;

Pan-American Coffee Bureau; Porto Wine Institute; Potato Growers Association
of California; Poultry and Egg National Board; Rice Council; Roquefort
Association; Tea Council of the U.S.A.; Shrimp Association of the Americas;
United Fresh Fruit and Vegetable Association; U. S. Department of
Agriculture; U. S. Department of Health, Education and Welfare; U. S.
Department of the Interior, Fish and Wildlife Service; Washington State
Apple Commission; Wine Advisory Board; Wine Institute; Wisconsin
Conservation Department

We wish to thank Hammacher Schlemmer, 147 East 57th Street, New York,
New York 10022, for providing the accessories for the photographs.

CONTENTS

viii CONTENTS

RECIPE SECTION

LIST OF COLOR ILLUSTRATIONS

following page 224

I. LOW-CALORIE RECIPES:

Potage Saint-Germain
Steamed Globe Artichoke and Steamed Asparagus
Beef Sukiyaki, Low-Calorie Fillets of Flounder en Papillote, and Steak Tartare
Poached Meringue Ring with Dessert Cardinal Sauce

following page 344

II. LOW-COST RECIPES:

Minestrone Milanese
Tourtière, Country Captain, and Fisherman's Baked Shells
Home-baked breads and rolls

following page 464

III. QUICK AND EASY RECIPES:

Quick Fish Stew
Spaghetti with Butter, Cream, Parmesan, and Mushrooms
Confetti Corn, Baked Eggs in Tomatoes, and Osaka Skillet Broccoli
Baked Alaska and Cherries Jubilee

following page 584

IV. VARIATIONS ON BASIC RECIPES:

"Frosted Tomatoes, Belgian-Style Tomatoes, and Tomatoes Finlandia
Roast Beef Leftovers: Yukon Stew, Beef Stuffed Vegetables, and Beef Curry
Butterscotch Parfait, Chocolate Ice Cream and Hot Fudge Sauce, and
    Strawberry Ice Cream Soda

following page 728

V. HOMESPUN AMERICAN FAVORITES:

Indoor Clambake
Baked Country Cured Ham with Baking Powder Biscuits

Acknowledgment

We wish to thank Hammacher Schlemmer, 147 East 57th Street, New York, New York 10022, for providing the accessories for the photographs.

The
DOUBLEDAY
COOKBOOK

INTRODUCTION

What makes this cookbook different?

Here, for the first time, is a comprehensive cookbook that provides calorie counts for every recipe (and keys all low-calories recipes ⚖), that features hundreds of budget-stretching (¢) and timesaving (⌧) recipes. Here, too, is a book that explains what it will mean to cook using metric measurements (as Americans may soon be doing), that emphasizes savory recipes (soups, meats, poultry, seafoods, vegetables, and salads) instead of sweets because of our increasing awareness of good nutrition.

The book's purpose is to assemble between two covers the most complete, up-to-date information available about food and cooking. To be the cook's— *every* cook's—book. To answer her most pressing questions, no matter how rudimentary (What kind of potato boils best? What kind of apple makes the best pie?), to assist with menu planning, to provide background information on the selection, preparation, storage, and serving of food, wines, and spirits.

This isn't a book devoted to fundamentals alone. It is a book filled with new and unusual recipes.

Those blasé about food insist there are no new recipes. We believe that there are. Certainly there are new-to-print recipes, and it is these that we have concentrated upon, although we have not forsaken those recipes essential to a basic cookbook. These, however, are offered, not as ends in themselves, but as foundations of innumerable variations, points of embarkation for the beginner.

There are recipes for those who yearn for involvement with the raw materials of cooking, who long to make soup the old-fashioned way or feel a yeast dough respond to their touch. There are recipes for busy women who must put a good meal on the table fast. And there are culinary tours de force for the occasional showpiece dinner.

The recipes come from many sources: from our own imaginations (particularly those showing how to short-cut time-consuming routines by using convenience foods); from friends and relatives; from centuries-old handwritten receipt files; from regional inns, restaurants, and hotels around the world. There are recipes from Latin America, Asia, and Africa as well as from Europe, each as true to the original as it was possible to make it given American ingredients and implements.

Every recipe has been tested—retested whenever necessary—so that every specific might be included: number of servings (figured in average-size portions); pan, casserole, or mold size whenever that size is important to the recipe's success; exact cooking times and temperatures together with descriptions of what a particular recipe should look, taste, or feel like when "done." And, lest the cook mistake a natural cooking phenomenon for failure, she is alerted to any surprises she may encounter as she prepares a particular recipe. She is also advised how to rescue such genuine failures as curdled hollandaise or runny jelly.

Leftovers, instead of being lumped together in a single chapter, have been placed where they will be most useful—following a robust turkey, for example, or a giant ham. And, to help the cook budget her time, recipes that can be partially made ahead of time are so indicated along with the point at which they may be refrigerated or frozen and the final touches each requires before being served.

This book, more than ten years in the writing, has not been built upon a gimmick. Its intent, simply, is to be a contemporary guide to good cooking and eating, to teach the *whys* of cooking as well as the *hows*.

Its purpose is to coax the timid into the kitchen, to motivate the indifferent, and to challenge accomplished cooks into realizing their creative potential. In short, to share the fun of cooking as well as the fundamentals, to offer something of value to all who cook as well as to those who have not yet learned how.

HOW TO USE THIS BOOK

All recipes in this book call for specific products by their generic (general descriptive) names, not the brand names; "quick-cooking rice," for example, is the fully precooked minute variety, "liquid hot red pepper seasoning" is the fiery bottled sauce made with tabasco peppers.

Whenever the name of a recipe is capitalized (Medium White Sauce, for example, or Flaky Pastry I), the recipe is included elsewhere in the book; consult Index for page numbers.

Whenever a method or technique is marked with an asterisk,* ("build a moderately hot charcoal fire,*" for example), how-to information is described in full detail elsewhere in the book; see Index for page numbers.

Three symbols are used throughout the book to key recipes:

⚖=Low-Calorie
¢=Budget
⧖=Quick and Easy

Specific sizes of pan, casserole, or mold are given whenever those sizes are essential to the success of a recipe.

Unless a recipe specifies alternate ingredients, do not make substitutions— margarine for butter, for example; oil for shortening; syrup for sugar. *And never substitute the new soft margarine for regular margarine or the new no-sift flour for sifted all-purpose flour.*

Suggestions for garnishes, seasonings, and leftovers are included within each chapter wherever appropriate.

Preheat oven or broiler a full 15 minutes before using. *Tip:* Have oven checked frequently for accuracy (many utility companies provide this service free of charge).

Use middle oven rack for general baking and roasting; whenever a higher or lower rack position is essential, recipe will so direct.

"Cool" as used in recipes means to bring a hot food to room temperature; "chill" means to refrigerate or place in an ice bath until chilled throughout.

Read each recipe through carefully before beginning it, making sure that all necessary ingredients and utensils are on hand and that instructions are clear.

Recipe yields are given in average-size servings or portions. A recipe that "Makes 4 Servings," for example, will feed 4 persons of *average* appetite.

An Explanation of How the Calorie Counts Were Calculated: Calorie counts for average-size servings are set down in round numbers (130 calories per serving instead of 128.5). Also, whenever recipes call for variable amounts (1–2 tablespoons, ¼–½ cup), the count is figured using the first, or lower, quantity only. Finally, if a recipe suggests alternative ingredients, the calorie count is based upon the principal ingredient, not the alternative.

About Ingredients

Unless recipes specify otherwise:
Flour called for is all-purpose flour, sifted before measuring.
Baking powder is double-acting baking powder.
Butter is salted butter.
Sour cream is the commercial type.
Eggs are large eggs.

Brown sugar is measured firmly packed.

Garlic cloves are of medium size (about like the first joint of the little finger).

Herbs and spices are dried.

Pepper is black pepper, preferably freshly ground.

"Celery stalk" means 1 branch of a bunch; some recipe books call the branch a "rib," the bunch a "stalk." As used here, "stalk" and "rib" are synonymous.

All measures are standard, all measurements level.

CHAPTER 1

THE FUNDAMENTALS OF COOKING

ABOUT SELECTING POTS AND PANS

Housewares departments offer so many glamorous lines of cookware it is difficult to choose which is best. That porcelain-lined, double-weight copper asparagus steamer with brass handles *is* stunning. But is it necessary? Not at $69.98 unless you are rich and fond of steamed asparagus ($69.98 will buy many of the basics of the beginning kitchen). The point is to buy what utensils you will use frequently, then to add the more specialized items as you need them. Quality counts and should not be sacrificed for the sake of a pretty pot. Here are some shopping tips to guide you when buying.

Look for:
– Utensils durable enough to withstand daily use without wearing thin, denting, warping, chipping, pitting, cracking, or discoloring.
– Medium to heavyweight cookware, sturdily constructed with flat bottoms, straight or gently flared sides, and snug (but easy-to-remove) lids. *Note:* Decorative enamelware is sometimes too lightweight to cook food without scorching it.
– Well-balanced skillets and saucepans that will stand squarely on burners whether lids are on or off (always test for tippiness with the lids off).
– Easy-to-clean utensils with rounded corners and no ridges, protruding rivets, or crevices to catch and hold bits of food.
– Utensils with firmly mounted, heatproof handles and knobs.
– Utensils that can be hung or nested to save space.

Some Specifics about Different Kinds of Cookware

Aluminum: People still shy away from aluminum, believing the old wives' tale that it poisons food. *Not so.* Aluminum is one of the best all-around cooking materials available. It is inexpensive; a quick, even conductor of heat, sturdy enough to take daily wear and tear, yet lightweight enough to handle comfortably. It is stamped into lightweight and medium-weight saucepans, kettles, and bakeware and cast into heavy skillets, kettles, and griddles. Moreover, it is available plain or colored (anodized). Some people insist that aluminum gives tomatoes and other acid foods a metallic taste, yet just as many disagree. Aluminum, however, is not entirely fault free: It darkens and pits when exposed to alkaline or mineral-rich foods or when left to soak in sudsy water; it must be scoured frequently and, if anodized, cannot be washed in a dishwasher. *Cleaning Tip:* To brighten drab aluminum, boil an acid solution (2 tablespoons cream of tartar or 1 cup vinegar to each 1 quart water) in utensil 5–10 minutes, then scour with a soap pad, rinse, and dry.

Stainless Steel: Extremely sturdy and long suffering. Stainless steel's greatest shortcoming is that it is a poor conductor of heat and must be bonded to a good conductor—usually copper or aluminum —if it is to cook properly (even thus, it is better for stove-top cooking rather than baking). Sometimes pan bottoms only are clad with copper or aluminum, sometimes the entire utensil is 2-ply (stainless steel inside and aluminum outside), and sometimes it is 3-ply (a copper, carbon steel, or aluminum core sandwiched between 2 layers of stainless steel). Stainless steel cookware costs more than aluminum but is easier to clean and slower to dent or scratch. It *will* heat-streak if permitted to boil dry, but unless it is seriously discolored it can be brightened with one of the special stainless-steel cleansers.

Cast Iron: The work horse of days past and still the favorite for frying chicken and baking popovers and corn sticks because of its ability to absorb and hold heat. But cast iron is leaden and cumbersome and unless well seasoned or enameled (as much of it now is) it is likely to rust; unenameled cast iron should never be used for liquid recipes— they will taste of rust. Most modern cast-iron cookware is preseasoned and ready to use, but the old-fashioned ware must be seasoned before using. *To Season* (or reseason): Wash and dry utensil, rub with unsalted shortening, and heat uncovered 2 hours in a 350° F. oven. *Cleaning Tip:* Use soap instead of synthetic detergents so that a utensil's seasoning will last through several washings, then dry over lowest burner heat; store uncovered to prevent beads of "sweat" from collecting and rusting the iron.

Copper: The choice of gourmets because of its ability to transmit the merest flicker of heat evenly, slowly, constantly. But, to do the job well, the copper must be heavy gauge (thin decorator sets look good—*but do not cook well*), and, to be safe for cooking, copper utensils must be lined with tin and retinned whenever copper begins to show through. Copper, unquestionably, makes the handsomest pots and pans, but it is luxury priced, quick to scar, and pesky to clean and polish. Miraculous as commercial copper cleaners are, they must nevertheless be applied with plenty of elbow grease. An additional shortcoming of copper cookware: Most of it is made with metal handles and knobs, meaning that you must use potholders constantly.

Enameled Metals (also called *Agateware, Graniteware,* and *Enamelware*): Metal utensils coated inside and out with thin layers of porcelain. Available in dazzling colors and decorator patterns, enamel utensils are nonporous and inert (unreacting in the presence of acid or alkaline foods) and for that reason are well suited to pickling and preserving. They are, however, easily chipped, cracked, scratched, and stained. *Cleaning Tip:* To float charred foods magically off the bottoms of enamel pots, boil a baking soda solution in the pots several minutes (2–3 tablespoons baking soda to each quart water).

Nonstick Finishes: These are improving all the time. Originally so delicate they required special nylon implements and "soft" scouring pads, they are now hardier, less easily scratched or scraped. They permit virtually fat-free cooking (a blessing to the calorie and cholesterol conscious) and require little more cleaning than a quick sponging. They cannot, however, take intensive heat, should not be used for broiling.

Flameproof Glass: Good all-around stove-top and ovenware, inert like enamelware, easy to clean. Relatively sturdy although the glass will break if dropped or subjected to abrupt temperature changes.

Freezer-to-Stove Ceramic Ware: A Space

Age material, inert, extremely durable. The ideal container for freezer-to-oven-to-table casseroles. Still fairly expensive and as yet available only in a limited choice of colors and styles.

Earthenware: Clay bakeware, glazed until nonporous, nonabsorbent; it may be high-fired and hard, low-fired and crumbly. Expert cooks insist that earthenware alone, because of its ability to release heat slowly, can impart to baked beans, *cassoulet,* and other long-simmering oven dishes the proper mellowness and consistency. Earthenware must be handled gingerly, however, cooled thoroughly before it is washed lest its glaze crack, exposing the clay underneath; the clay will pick up flavors, then pass them along—*stale*—to each subsequent dish. *Warning:* Within the last few years, certain Mexican pottery glazes were found to be poisonous. Play it safe. Use Mexican pottery for decoration, *not* for cooking or eating.

Selecting and Caring for Knives

Fine knives are the cook's best friends—sturdily constructed, well balanced and designed knives that can be honed to long-lasting razor keenness. It is the dull knife that cuts the cook, rarely the sharp one, because the dull knife must be forced. Good knives are expensive, but justifiably so because they will perform well over a period of years. What distinguishes the fine knife from the inferior? Here are a few indicators:
– Choose knives that feel comfortable in the hand. Top quality knives have handles of close-grained hardwood, rubbed to satiny smoothness; they will not warp, split, or splinter. Shoddy knives may have handles of soft wood (usually painted) or molded out of some synthetic (often rough around the seams).
– Look for blades well anchored in handles. In fine knives, blades extend to the tops of the handles and are held fast by 2 or 3 broad, double-headed rivets lying flush with the handle. Cheaper blades may be sunk only halfway into the handle, held by 1 or 2 small wire rivets or simply glued in place.
– Insist upon forged carbon steel knives, budget permitting. They are the choice of chefs and gourmets because of their fine, hard smoothness that will take and keep a keen cutting edge. They *will* stain and rust, however, unless washed and dried as soon as they are used. Stainless steel, made stainproof and rustproof by the addition of chromium and nickel, is softer, quicker to dull.
– Select knives with well-shaped blades. The *forged,* tapering from both blunt edge to sharp and handle to point, are choicest. *Stamped blades,* cut out of uniformly thick metal, usually indicate poor quality; *beveled blades,* cut from metal thicker on one edge than the other, taper from blunt side to sharp but not from handle to point—popular construction for medium-priced knives.

Hollow-ground blades, also in the medium price range, have broad, concave cutting surfaces; they are adept at slicing but easily damaged. *Shopping Tip:* If a brand name is stamped on a knife blade, the knife is probably a good one; manufacturers of inferior merchandise don't bother.

Some Knife Care Tips:
– Treat knives with respect, washing and drying them as soon as they are used, gently scouring off any darkened spots with metal soap pads. Do not wash in the dishwasher, do not soak; either can loosen rivets, rot handles and rust blades.
– Always use knife on a cutting surface softer than the blade—hardwood is ideal, makes the knife last longer.
– Store knives in a knife rack, never jammed into a drawer where the blade may be bent or nicked (and the cook injured).
– Use knives strictly for slicing, cutting, and chopping, never for prying off lids and bottle tops; it's damaging to the knife, dangerous, too.
– Sharpen knives frequently. Because each person tends to hold a blade to the

steel or stone at a slightly different angle, it's best if the same person does all the knife sharpening—the knives will last longer.

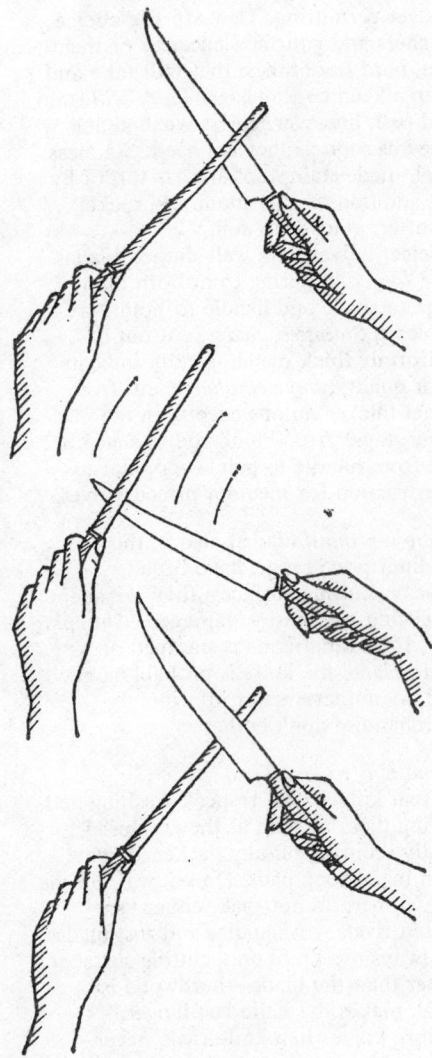

How to Sharpen a Knife

To sharpen on an electric sharpener, follow manufacturer's instructions.

The Beginning Kitchen: Equipment Needed

SAUCEPANS, KETTLES, SKILLETS (WITH LIDS)
1 pint, 1½ and 3 qt. saucepans
2 or 3 qt. double boiler
1 gallon kettle
12″ or 15″ roaster (with rack)
1–1½ gal. Dutch oven
7″ and 10″ skillets
6–8 cup coffeepot
2 or 3 qt. teakettle

OVENWARE
9″×5″×3″ loaf pan
13″×9″×2″ loaf pan
2 (8″ or 9″) round cake pans
8″ or 9″ square pan
2 (8″ or 9″) piepans
10″ tube pan
Muffin pan
Cookie sheet

BOWLS, CASSEROLES
Nest of mixing bowls
1½–2 and 3 qt. casseroles (with lids)
4–6 custard cups or ramekins

MEASURERS
Measuring spoons
Dry measure set
1 cup and 1 pt. liquid measuring cups

UTENSILS
Long-handled cooking spoons (one slotted)
Wooden spoon
Ladle
Large and small cooking forks
Large and small spatulas
Rubber spatula
Pancake turner
Tongs
Can and bottle openers, corkscrew
Large and small, coarse and fine sieves
5-cup flour sifter
Colander
Funnel
Salt and pepper shakers
4-sided grater
Bulb baster
Rotary beater
Reamer
Pastry blender

2″ chopping knife
ry shears
rted cookie cutters
l cutting board
e, steel, or knife sharpener
slicer
on baller
ger-corer
vers, poultry pins
mp deveiner

RMOMETERS
ndy
ep fat

ALL APPLIANCES
tomatic coffee maker
ectric mixer
ectric blender
ectric skillet or Dutch oven

he Gourmet Kitchen

o the Intermediate Kitchen, add as
eeded:

AUCEPANS, KETTLES,
SKILLETS (WITH LIDS)
Sauté pan
Butter warming set
Steamer basket
Fish poacher
Clam steamer
Stock pot
Large round and oval cocottes
Terrine
Polenta pot
Oval fish skillet
Wok set
Omelet pan
Crepe pan
Paella pan
Heavy griddle
Chafing dish
Fondue set
Espresso set
Turkish coffeepot
China teapot

OVENWARE
Pizza pans
Flan rings
Tart and tartlet tins
Assorted round and oval au gratin pans
Brioche pans

Tiered cake pan set
Corn stick pans
Popover pans

BOWLS, CASSEROLES, MOLDS
Nest of soufflé dishes
Scallop shells
Pots de crème
Large earthenware crock or bowl for
    marinating
Copper beating bowl
Assortment of plain and decorative
    molds: for salads, ice cream bombes,
    mousses, steamed puddings
Coeur à la crème basket
Pâté en croûte mold

UTENSILS
Wire skimmer
Extra wooden spoons, whisks, ladles,
    rubber spatulas
Mortar and pestle
Salt mill
Nutmeg grater
Spaghetti tongs
Porcelain onion grater
Cutlet bat
Meat cuber-pounder
Wooden mallet
Escargots plates, holders
Full set of pastry bags, decorative tips
Butter curler, paddles
Extra pastry brushes
Tapered French pastry pin
Springerle pin
Pastry board
Marble slab
Tortilla press
Krumkake iron
Rosette iron
Preserving, jelly making, freezing, and
    canning equipment (see those chapters
    for details)
Cream horn tins

CUTLERY
Full sets of cookie, aspic, truffle cutters
Oyster knife
Clam knife
Fluting knife
Filleting knife
Boning knife
Tomato knife
Meat cleaver
Fish scaler

Potato masher
Garlic crusher
Rolling pin, stockinette, pastry cloth
Cookie and cake racks
Potholders, hot pads
Clock and timer

CUTLERY
2 paring knives
Slicing knife
8″ chopping knife
Bread knife
Vegetable peeler
Carving set
Corer
Kitchen shears
Cutting board
Biscuit cutter
Ice pick

THERMOMETERS
Oven
Meat

SMALL APPLIANCES
Toaster
Waffle iron or griddle
Portable electric mixer (optional)

FOR STORAGE
Canisters with scoops
Towel and paper dispensers
Graduated refrigerator containers

SINK ACCESSORIES
Drainer, drainboard
Garbage pail
Sponges, scourers
Dishpan, dish towels
Vegetable and bottle brushes

The Intermediate Kitchen

To the Beginning Kitchen add:

SAUCEPANS, KETTLES,
SKILLETS (WITH LIDS)
1, 2, *and* 3 or 4 qt. saucepans
4 qt. pressure saucepan
Egg poacher
Steamer
Deep fat fryer
2 or 3 qt. Dutch oven
12″ skillet
10″ heavy iron skillet
5″ or 6″ skillet

OVENWARE
Jelly-roll pan
Extra 9″×5″×3″ l
Extra 8″ or 9″ squa
Extra muffin pans, ‹
9″ or 10″ spring for

BOWLS, CASSEROLES,
Extra mixing bowls
1½ or 2 qt. soufflé dis
1½ or 2 qt. au gratin
2 or 3 qt. bean pot
6–8 cup ring mold
4–6 individual gelatin m

MEASURERS
Extra measuring spoons
Extra dry measures
1 qt. liquid measure
Ruler
Scale

UTENSILS
Mixing fork
Slotted pancake turner
Extra wooden spoons
Balloon whip
1 or 2 wire whisks
Food mill
Meat grinder
Rotary grater
Pepper mill
Potato ricer
Pot strainer
Jar opener
Ball scoop
Wide-mouth funnel
Garlic basket
Salad basket
Tea sieve
1 cup flour sifter
V-shaped poultry rack
Extra cake, cookie racks
Pastry bag and decorative tips or ca
  decorating set
Pastry wheel
Pastry brush
Cookie press
Cake and pie keepers
Cheesecloth
Needle and thread
Asbestos flame tamer

CUTLERY
Extra paring knives
Grapefruit knife

10″-
Pou
Ass‹
Sm‹
Sto
Egg
Me
We
Sk‹
Sh›

TH
C‹
D‹

SN
A
E
E
E

Curved chopper and chopping bowl
Cherry pitter
Zester
Lemon stripper
Bean frencher
Mandolin cutter
Pasta machine
Long and short larding needles
Skewers in assorted lengths
Nutcracker set
Lobster crackers

SMALL APPLIANCES

Heavy duty mixer with attachments
  including dough hook
Ice-cream freezer (hand or electric)
Electric food chopper-grinder
Electric coffee grinder
Quantity automatic coffee maker
Electric can opener-knife sharpener
Electric hot trays
Rotisserie
Electric bun warmer
Electric ice crusher
Electric toaster-oven
Electric knife

Some Cooking Terms Defined

The language of food, so clear cut and routine to experienced cooks, often bewilders the beginner. Defined here are the more common general terms; elsewhere in the book, in the sections where they most apply, are the more specific terms—*muddle*, for example, a bar technique, is defined in the beverages chapter; *soft ball*, a test used in making candy, is explained in that chapter.

adjust: To taste before serving and increase seasoning as needed.
agneau: The French word for "lamb."
à la: A French idiom loosely translated to mean "in the style of." *À la maison*, for example, is "as prepared at this house or restaurant, the house specialty," and *à la bourguignonne* ("as prepared in Burgundy"—with Burgundy wine).
à la king: Cut up food, usually chicken or turkey, in cream sauce, often with slivered pimiento and sliced mushrooms added.

à la mode: As used in America, pie or other dessert topped with a scoop of ice cream. In French cuisine, braised meat smothered in gravy.
al dente: An Italian phrase meaning "to the tooth," used to describe pasta cooked the way Italians like it—tender but still firm.
allumette: The French word for "match," used to describe food cut in matchstick shapes; also a slim, bite-size puff pastry hors d'oeuvre.
amandine: Made or served with almonds.
à point: A French phrase used to describe food cooked just to the point of doneness.
au gratin: A dish browned in oven or broiler, usually topped with buttered bread crumbs or grated cheese or both. *Gratiné* means the same thing.
au jus: Food, usually roast beef, served in its own juices.

baba: A sweet yeast cake, studded with raisins and dried fruit, saturated with brandy, kirsch, or rum (*baba au rhum*).
bain marie: French for a "steam table" or "hot water bath" (which see).
bake: To cook by dry oven heat.
ball: To cut into balls.
barbecue: To cook in a hot spicy sauce, often over a grill; also the food so cooked and the grill used for cooking it.
bard: To tie bacon, suet, or fatback around lean meats to prevent their drying out in cooking. For barding instructions, see Some Special Ways to Prepare Meat for Cooking in the meat chapter.
Bar-le-Duc: A red or white currant preserve named for Bar-le-Duc, France, where it is made.
baste: To ladle or brush drippings, liquid, butter, or sauce over food as it cooks, the purpose being to add flavor and prevent drying.
batter: An uncooked mixture, usually of eggs, flour, leavening, and liquid, that is thin enough to pour.
batterie de cuisine: A French phrase used to describe all the implements, utensils, and paraphernalia of cooking.
beard: To cut the hairy fibers off

unshucked mussels.

beat: To mix briskly with a spoon, whisk, rotary or electric beater using an over-and-over or round-and-round motion.

beignet: The French word for "fritter."

beurre: The French word for "butter." *Beurre manié* is a mixture of butter and flour, kneaded until smooth, that is added as a thickener to sauces and stews. *Beurre noir* is butter heated until dark brown; *beurre noisette,* butter heated until the color of amber.

bien fatigué: A French term meaning "wilted"; it is used to describe salad greens dressed with hot dressing, then tossed until properly limp.

bind: To stir egg, sauce, or other thick ingredient into a mixture to make it hold together.

bisque: A creamed soup, usually with a shellfish base.

blanch: To immerse briefly in boiling water to loosen skins or to heighten and set color and flavor.

blaze (flame, flambé): To set a match to liquor-drenched food so that it bursts into flames.

blend: To mix two or more ingredients together until smooth.

boeuf: The French word for "beef."

boil: To heat liquid until bubbles break at the surface (212° F. for water at sea level); also to cook food in boiling liquid.

bone: To remove bones.

braise: To brown in fat, then to cook covered on the topstove or in the oven with some liquid.

bread: To coat with bread crumbs.

brine: To preserve in a strong salt solution; also the solution itself.

brown: To cook at high heat, usually on the topstove in fat, until brown; also to set under a broiler until touched with brown.

bruise: To partially crush—as a clove of garlic in a mortar and pestle—to release flavor.

brûlé, brûlée: The French word for "burned," used in cooking to describe foods glazed with caramelized sugar.

brunoise: A French cooking term used to describe finely diced or shredded vegetables, usually a mixture of them cooked in butter or just enough stock to moisten. *Brunoise* is used to flavor soups and sauces.

brush: To apply butter, liquid, or glaze with a brush.

butterfly: To split food down the center, almost but not quite all the way through, so that the two halves can be opened flat like butterfly wings.

café: The French word for "coffee."

candy: To preserve in or glaze with sugar syrup.

caramelize: To heat sugar until it melts and turns golden brown; also to glaze food with caramelized sugar. *Caramel* is liquid, browned sugar used to flavor and color gravies and sauces.

chapon: A chunk or cube of bread, rubbed with oil and garlic, that is tossed with green salads to impart a subtle garlic flavor; it is discarded before serving. For still subtler flavor, the chapon can simply be rubbed over the salad bowl before the greens are added.

chiffonade: A soup garnish composed of finely cut vegetable strips (commonly lettuce and sorrel).

chill: To let stand in the refrigerator or crushed ice until cold.

chop: To cut into small pieces with a knife or chopper; chopped foods are more coarsely cut than the minced.

clarify: To make cloudy liquid clear, usually by heating with raw egg white, then straining through cloth. For instructions, see Some Basic Soup-Making Techniques in the soup chapter.

clove (of garlic): One small almond-sized segment of the head or bulb of garlic.

coat: To dip in crumbs, flour, or other dry ingredient; also to cover with sauce or aspic.

coat a spoon: A doneness test for custards and other cooked egg-thickened mixtures; when the egg has thickened (cooked) sufficiently, it will leave a thin, custardlike film on a metal spoon.

cocotte: The French word for "casserole"; *en cocotte* simply means "cooked in a casserole." *Cocottes* can be whopping or just large enough to serve one person.

coddle: To poach in water just below the boiling point.

combine: To mix together two or more ingredients.

cool: To bring hot food to room temperature.

coq: The French word for "cock" or "rooster."

core: To remove the core.

cream: To beat butter or other fat either solo or with sugar or other ingredients until smooth and creamy.

crème: The French word for "cream."

crimp: To seal the edge of a pie or pastry with a decorative edge.

croûte: The French word for "crust" or "pastry." Something prepared *en croûte* is wrapped in or topped with a crust.

crumble: To break up with the fingers.

crush: To reduce to crumbs.

cube: To cut into cubes.

cure: To preserve meat, fish, or cheese by salting, drying, and/or smoking.

cut in: To mix shortening or other solid fat into dry ingredients until the texture is coarse and mealy.

deep-fat-fry: To cook by immersing in hot (usually about 360° F.) deep fat.

deglaze: To scrape the browned bits off the bottom of a skillet or roasting pan, usually by adding a small amount of liquid and heating gently; this mixture is added to the dish for flavor.

degrease: To skim or blot grease from a soup, sauce, or broth or, easier still, to chill it until the grease rises to the top and hardens; it can then be lifted off.

demi-glace: A rich brown sauce or gravy made by boiling down meat stock.

devil: To mix with hot seasonings (commonly mustard and cayenne).

dice: To cut into fine cubes, usually ⅛"–¼".

dilute: To weaken or thin by adding liquid.

disjoint: To separate at the joint, most often poultry or small game.

dissolve: To pass a solid (sugar, salt, etc.) into solution; also to melt or liquefy.

dot: To distribute small bits (usually butter or other fat) over the surface of a food.

dough: A pliable raw mixture, usually containing flour, sugar, egg, milk, leavening, and seasoning, that is stiff enough to work with the hands.

dragées: Candy shot used in decorating cookies, cakes, and candies. Silver dragées are the hard BB-like shot.

drain: To pour off liquid.

draw: To remove the entrails of poultry, game, or fish; to eviscerate.

dredge: To coat lightly with flour, confectioners' sugar, or other powdery ingredient.

dress: To draw or eviscerate; also to add dressing to a salad.

drippings: The melted fat and juices that collect in the pan of meat, poultry, or other food as it cooks.

drizzle: To pour melted butter, syrup, sauce, or other liquid over the surface of food in a very fine stream.

drop: To drop from a spoon, as cookie dough onto a baking sheet.

dust: To coat very lightly with flour, confectioners' sugar, or other powdery mixture. Dusted foods are more lightly coated than the dredged.

duxelles: A thick, almost pastelike mixture of minced sautéed mushrooms, sometimes seasoned with shallots, salt, and pepper, that is mixed into sauces, stuffings, and other recipes.

en brochette: Food cooked on a skewer.

en papillote: Food cooked in oiled parchment or in a packet.

entree: The main course of a meal.

essence, extract: Concentrated flavoring.

eviscerate: To remove entrails, to draw.

filet, fillet: A boneless piece of meat or fish. *Fillet* is the English spelling, *filet* the French; *filet* is also the spelling used to identify beef tenderloin (*filet mignon*).

filter: To strain through several thicknesses of cloth.

finish: To garnish a dish before serving, to add the finishing touches.

flake: To break into small pieces with a fork.

flambé: See *blaze.*

flour: To coat with flour.

fluff: To fork up until light and fluffy; also a spongy gelatin dessert.

flute: To make a decorative edge on pies or pastries; to crimp. Also to cut mushrooms or other small vegetables into fluted or scalloped shapes.

fold: To mix using a gentle over-and-over motion. Also, literally, to fold rolled-out pastry into a neat package as when making puff pastry.

fold in: To mix a light ingredient (beaten egg white, whipped cream) into a heavier one using a light over-and-over motion so that no air or volume is lost.

forcemeat (farce): Finely ground meat, poultry, or fish often combined with ground vegetables, bread crumbs, and seasonings used in making stuffings, *quenelles,* and croquettes.

fouet: The French word for the "balloon whip" or "whisk."

freeze: To chill until hard and icy.

French-fry: To cook in deep hot fat (see *deep-fat-fry*).

fricassee: A way of braising cut-up chicken and small game. The pieces are dredged and browned, then cooked, covered, in liquid or sauce, often in the company of vegetables. Food can be fricasseed on top of the stove or in the oven.

frizzle: To fry thinly sliced meat at intense heat until crisp and curled.

fromage: The French word for "cheese."

frost: To spread with frosting or coat with sugar; also to chill until ice crystals form, as when frosting mint julep cups.

frothy: Light and foamy.

fry: See *panfry*.

fumet: A concentrated stock used as a base for sauces.

garnish: To decorate a dish before serving. The *garniture* is the decoration.

gâteau: The French word for "cake."

giblets: The heart, liver, and gizzard of fowl and small game.

glace: The French word for "ice cream."

glacé: A French word used to describe candied or sugared food; *marrons glacés,* for instance, are candied chestnuts.

glace de viande: A rich brown meat glaze made by boiling meat stock down until dark and syrupy; it is added to sauces and gravies for flavor and color.

glaze: To cover food with a glossy coating, most often syrup, aspic, melted jellies or preserves. Also to brush pastry

with milk or beaten egg to make it glisten.

grate: To cut food into small particles by passing through a grater.

grease: To rub with grease.

grease and flour: To rub with grease, then dust lightly with flour. *Note:* Most pans need greasing only, but those in which extra-sweet or fruit-heavy batters will be baked will probably require greasing *and* flouring to keep the cake or bread from sticking.

grill: To broil on a grill, commonly over charcoal.

grind: To reduce to fine particles or paste by putting through a grinder.

grissini: Slim Italian bread sticks.

hot water bath, water jacket: A large kettle in which preserving jars are processed, also a pan of water in which a dish of custard or other apt-to-curdle dish is placed during baking. *Note:* If the water in the kettle boils, it becomes a *boiling water bath.*

husk: To remove the coarse outer covering, as when husking corn. Also, the covering itself.

ice: To spread with icing; also, to chill until hard and icy.

infusion: Hot liquid in which tea, coffee, herbs, or spices have been steeped.

jell (also gel): To congeal with gelatin. Also, to cook into jelly.

jelly-roll style: A flat piece of meat, fish, or cake rolled up around a filling.

julienne: Food cut into small match-stick-like strips.

knead: To work with the hands in a rhythmic pressing-folding-turning pattern until smooth and satiny.

kosher: Food prepared or processed according to Jewish ritual law.

lait: The French word for "milk."

lard: To insert bits of lard or other fat into lean meat to keep it moist and succulent throughout cooking. Also, the rendered fat of hogs.

leaven: To lighten the texture and increase the volume of breads, cakes, and cookies by using baking powder, soda, or yeast, which send gases bubbling through the batter or dough during baking. Angel cakes and sponge cakes are leavened by the air beaten into the egg whites.

legumes: A protein-rich family of plants that includes beans, peas, lentils, and peanuts.

let down: To dilute by adding liquid.

liaison: A thickening agent (flour, cornstarch, arrowroot, egg, or cream) used to thicken soups and sauces or bind together stuffings and croquettes.

line: To cover the bottom and sides of a pan or mold with paper, a layer of cake or crumbs before adding the food to be cooked, chilled, or frozen.

macerate: To soak fruits in spirits.

marinate: To steep meat, fish, fowl, vegetables, or other savory food in a spicy liquid several hours until food absorbs the flavoring. Technically, *macerating* and *marinating* are the same; *macerate*, however, applies to *fruits*, *marinate* to savory food. The steeping medium is called a *marinade*.

marmite: A tall French stock pot, often made of earthenware.

marrow: The soft buttery substance found in the hollows of bones; gourmets consider it a delicacy. *Marrow spoons* are the long, slender-bowled spoons designed specifically for digging the marrow out of bones.

mash: To reduce to pulp, usually with a potato masher.

mask: To coat with sauce or aspic.

matzo: The flat unleavened bread traditionally eaten by Jews during Passover.

mealy: Resembling meal in texture; as used to describe baked potatoes, it means that they are light and crumbly, almost flaky.

meat glaze: See *glace de viande*.

medallion: Small coin-shaped pieces of meat, commonly beef.

melt: To liquefy by heating.

mince: To cut into fine pieces. Minced foods are more finely cut than the chopped.

mirepoix: A mixture of minced sautéed vegetables—traditionally carrots, celery, and onions—used in French cooking to flavor sauces, stuffings, stews, and other savory dishes.

mix: To stir together using a round-and-round motion.

mocha: The combined flavors of coffee and chocolate.

moisten: To dampen with liquid.

mold: To cook, chill, or freeze in a mold so that the food takes on the shape of the mold. To *unmold* simply means to remove from the mold.

mortar and pestle: An old-fashioned implement, still basic to the gourmet kitchen. The mortar is a bowl-shaped container, usually made of porcelain or wood, the pestle a heavy blunt instrument of the same material used for pulverizing seasonings against the walls of the mortar.

mound: To stand in a mound when taken on or dropped from a spoon; the term is used to describe the consistency of gelatin-thickened mixtures.

mull: To heat fruit juice (frequently cider or grape juice), wine, ale, or other alcoholic beverage with sugar and spices.

nap: To coat with sauce.

noisette: A small round slice of meat, usually lamb.

nonpareilles: Another name for dragées or candy shot used in decorating cakes, cookies, and candies.

oeuf: The French word for "egg."

oie: The French word for "goose."

pain: The French word for "bread."

panbroil: To cook in a skillet over direct heat with as little fat as possible; drippings are poured off as they accumulate.

panfry: To cook in a skillet *with* some fat *without* pouring off drippings. The French word for it is *sauté*.

parch: To dry corn or other starchy vegetable by roasting.

pare: To cut the peeling from fruits or vegetables.

paste: A smooth blend of fat and flour or other starch thickener. Also, any food pounded to a paste. Also, a dough, specifically that of puff or *choux* pastry.

peel: To remove the peeling from fruits

or vegetables by pulling off rather than cutting away.

pepper: To season with pepper.

pickle: To preserve in brine or vinegar.

pinch: The amount of salt, sugar, herb, or spice, etc., that can be taken up between the thumb and forefinger, less than ⅛ teaspoon.

pipe: To apply a frilly border, usually of frosting or mashed potatoes, by squirting through a pastry bag fitted with a decorative tip.

pit: To remove pits.

plank: To broil on a wooden plank.

pluck: To pull the feathers from poultry.

plump: To soak raisins or other dried fruit in liquid until they soften and plump up.

poach: To cook submerged in simmering liquid.

poisson: The French word for "fish."

pone: Flat and round or oval in shape, as a corn pone.

popadam: Thin, crisp, deep-fat-fried East Indian wafers eaten with curry.

poulet: The French word for "chicken."

pound: To flatten with a mallet or cutlet bat.

preheat: To bring oven or broiler to required temperature before adding food.

prick: To pierce with the tines of a sharp fork. Pricking is necessary to keep pie shells from shrinking and warping during baking, also to free fat underneath the skin of ducks and geese as they roast.

proof: To set a yeast mixture in a warm, dry spot to rise.

purée: To grind to paste either by pressing through a food mill or whirling in an electric blender.

quenelles: Soufflé-light, poached forcemeat dumplings sauced and served as is or used to garnish meat or fish platters.

ragout: A hearty brown stew.

ramekin: A small baking dish big enough for one portion, commonly made of earthenware.

réchauffé: A French cooking term meaning "reheated."

reconstitute: To restore milk or other dehydrated food to a liquid or moist state by mixing in water.

reduce: To boil down rapidly until volume is reduced and flavors concentrated.

refresh: To plunge hot food (most often vegetables) into ice water to set the color and flavor. Just before serving the food is warmed in butter or sauce.

render: To heat lard or other animal fat so that it melts away from connective tissue and other solid particles. Rendered lard is smooth and creamy, almost pure fat and an excellent shortening for pastries. Another term for *render* is *try out.*

rib: One branch (stalk) of a bunch of celery. *Note:* In some cookbooks, stalk means the entire bunch or head of celery; as used here, however, stalk and rib are synonymous.

rice: To put through a ricer.

rissole: A filled sweet or savory deep-fat-fried pie or turnover.

roast: To cook uncovered in the oven by dry heat.

roe: Fish eggs.

roll out: To roll into a thin flat sheet with a rolling pin.

roux: A butter and flour paste, sometimes browned, sometimes not, used as a thickener for soups and stews. It is the soul of Creole cooking.

rusk: A crisp brown piece of bread, usually twice baked to make it extra light and dry; it may be sweet or plain.

salpicon: Mixed cubed foods served in a sauce or dressing.

salt: To season with salt.

sambal: Any of the many condiments served with curry.

sauce: To combine or cover with sauce.

sauté: See *panbroil.*

scald: To heat a liquid, most frequently milk or cream, just short of the boiling point until bubbles begin to gather around the edge of the pan. Also, to plunge tomatoes or peaches, etc., into boiling water to loosen their skins; to blanch.

scale: To remove scales from fish.

scallop: To bake in cream or a cream sauce underneath a bread crumb topping.

score: To make shallow knife cuts over the surface of food, usually in a crisscross pattern.

scrape: To scrape the skin from a fruit or vegetable with a knife.

sear: To brown meat quickly, either in a very hot oven or in a skillet over high heat, to seal in the juices.

season: To add salt, pepper, herbs, spices, or other seasonings.

seasoned flour: Flour seasoned with salt and pepper.

seed: To remove seeds.

serrate: To cut a decorative zigzag border into food, pastries, for example, using a zigzag pastry wheel, or orange, lemon, or grapefruit halves or baskets.

set, set up: To congeal, as when thickened with gelatin.

shell: To remove the shells—most commonly of eggs, nuts, or shrimp.

shirr: To cook whole eggs in ramekins with cream and sometimes a topping of buttered bread crumbs.

short: An adjective used to describe pastry or cookies made crumbly or flaky by a high proportion of shortening.

shred: To cut in small, thin strips or shreds, usually by pressing through a grater.

shuck: To remove the shells of clams, oysters, mussels, or scallops; also to remove husks from corn.

sieve: To strain liquid through a sieve; also the strainer itself.

sift: To pass flour or other dry ingredient through a fine sieve or sifter.

simmer: To heat liquid to about 185° F., just until bubbles begin to form; also to cook food in simmering liquid.

singe: To burn hairs off the skin of plucked poultry.

skewer: To thread small chunks of food on long metal or wooden pins; also the pin itself.

skim: To scoop fat, froth, or other material from the surface of a liquid with a spoon.

skin: To remove the skin of poultry, game, or fish.

sliver: To cut in fine, thin pieces, usually no more than ½″ long and a fraction of that wide.

snip: To cut in fine pieces or to gash with scissors.

soak: To let stand in liquid.

soft peaks: Descriptive phrase used to describe a mixture beaten until peaks will form but curl over at the top instead of standing up straight.

spit: To cook on a spit.

sponge: A frothy gelatin dessert; also the puffy yeast culture used to leaven bread.

steam: To cook, covered, *over* a small amount of boiling liquid so that the steam formed in the pan does the cooking.

steep: To let tea leaves, coffee grounds, herbs, or spices stand in hot liquid until their flavor is extracted.

sterilize: To kill microorganisms of spoilage by boiling or subjecting to steam under pressure.

stew: To cook submerged in simmering liquid; also the food so cooked.

stiff but not dry: Term used to describe egg whites beaten until they will stand in stiff but moist and glistening peaks.

stir: To mix with a spoon or whisk using a round-and-round motion.

stir-fry: Oriental method of briskly tossing or stirring foods as they fry.

stock: The broth strained from stewed or boiled meats, seafood, poultry, or vegetables.

strain: To separate liquids from solids by passing through a sieve.

stud: To insert whole cloves, slivers of garlic, or other seasoning over the surface of food.

stuff: To fill with stuffing.

swirl: To whirl liquid gently in a pan; also to ease a new ingredient—an egg, for example—into swirling liquid.

syrupy: Of the consistency of syrup; the term is applied most often to partially congealed gelatin. When syrupy, it is ready to whip or use as a glaze.

tahini: Sesame seed paste, a popular ingredient of Middle Eastern recipes.

tenderize: To make tender, especially meat, either by pounding or scoring to break up connective tissues or by adding a chemical tenderizer or acidic marinade to soften them.

terrine: An earthenware container used

for baking pâté and other minced or ground meat mixtures. Also the dish so cooked.

thick and lemony: A not particularly apt phrase used to describe stiffly beaten egg yolks; at this consistency they are more nearly the color and texture of mayonnaise.

thicken: To thicken a liquid by adding flour or other starch thickener, by adding eggs or by boiling down.

thin: To dilute by adding liquid.

timbale: A custard-thickened mixture of meat, poultry, fish, or vegetables usually baked in a small mold or ramekin or served in a crisp timbale (rosette) case (see breads chapter for recipe).

toast: To brown bread by heating.

toast points: Small triangular pieces of toast.

toss: To mix by flipping or turning food over and over as when dressing a green salad or combining stuffing ingredients.

treacle: The English word for "molasses."

truss: To tie poultry or other food into a compact shape before roasting.

try out: See *render*.

turn: To flute or scallop food, especially mushrooms or other small round vegetables. Also, literally, to turn food over as it cooks or steeps.

veau: The French word for "veal."

viande: The French word for "meat."

vin: The French word for "wine."

volaille: The French word for "poultry."

whey: The watery liquid that separates from the solid curds when milk or cream curdles.

whip: To beat until stiff, usually with a whisk, rotary or electric beater.

whisk: A handy beating implement made of looped wires.

wok: A broad, bowl-shaped Oriental pan particularly suited to stir-frying because of its thin metal construction, round bottom and high sides. Set upon a metal ring or collar, it can be used on American burners.

work: To mix slowly with the fingers, to knead.

zest: The colored part of citrus rind used as a flavoring; also the oil pressed from it.

How to Measure Ingredients

Although "born cooks" can produce success after success without measuring a thing, most of us fail whenever we resort to such haphazard methods. We must not only measure but *measure correctly*, a special skill in itself.

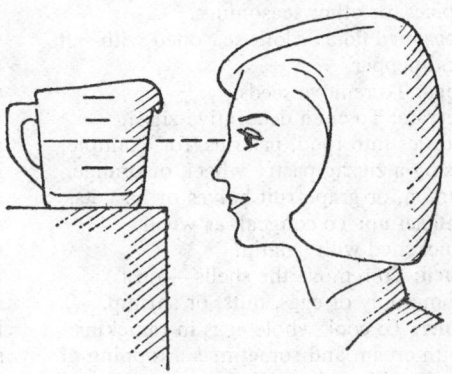

Liquids, Oils
Stand cup on level surface, fill to mark, stoop to check quantity at eye level.

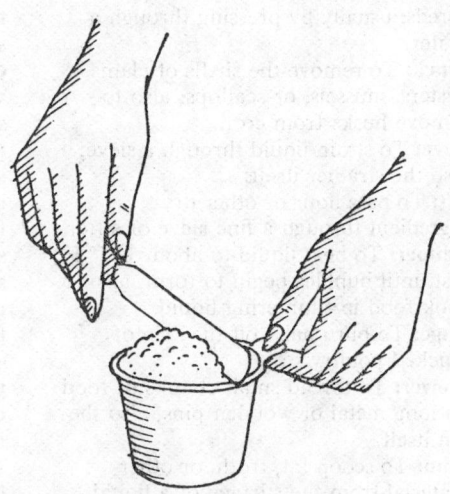

Dry Ingredients, Crumbs, Minced/ Grated Foods
Sift flour, confectioners' sugar *before* measuring (granulated sugar, too, if lumpy); pile food lightly in measure without tapping cup or shaking contents down; level off as shown.

Exception: Brown sugar must be packed firmly into measure; if lumpy, roll between sheets of wax paper with a rolling pin before measuring.

Melted Fats
If fat is soft, measure as directed for solid fat, then melt and use. If fat is brittle and hard, melt, estimating as nearly as possible amount you'll need, then measure as directed for oils.

Tips: Measure syrups, molasses, honey, other sticky liquids in lightly greased cups *or* dry measures (so surface can be leveled off); scrape measure out well with a rubber spatula.

Solid Fats
Pack, a little at a time, in a dry measure cup, pressing out air pockets; level off, then scrape cup out well with rubber spatula.
Note: The old water-displacement method is no longer considered accurate.

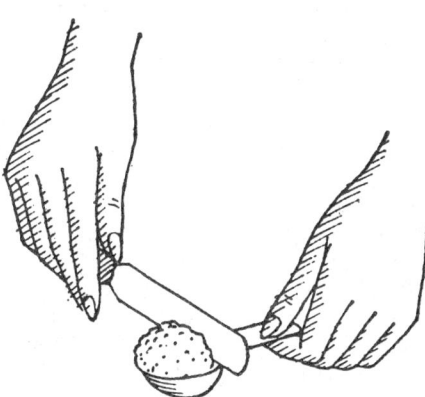

How to Use Measuring Spoons

How to Measure Pans

All recipes in this book specify baking pan, casserole, or mold size when that size is essential to the success of a recipe. Modern containers usually have their vital statistics (length, width, depth, and volume) stamped on the bottom. If not, here is the correct way to take them.

Linear Measurements: For length, width, and diameter, measure pan across the top, inside edge to inside edge. For depth, stand ruler in pan, noting distance from rim to bottom.

Volume: Pour water into container, using a measuring cup, and record how many cups or quarts are needed to fill it.

Tip: Once measurements are taken, scratch them on the outside of the container so that they need not be retaken.

The Techniques of Chopping, Mincing, Slicing

A skilled chef wields his knife with all the grace of a swordsman, and to the novice his knife seems swordlike. Its weight and size, however, speed the cutting. Those timid about knives often choose knives too small for the job. For all round use, an 8″ blade is best; for bulkier, tougher foods, a 10″ blade and for small foods a 4″–6″ blade. Here are the basic cutting techniques, applicable with only minor adjustments to all kinds of food. Work slowly at first; speed will come.

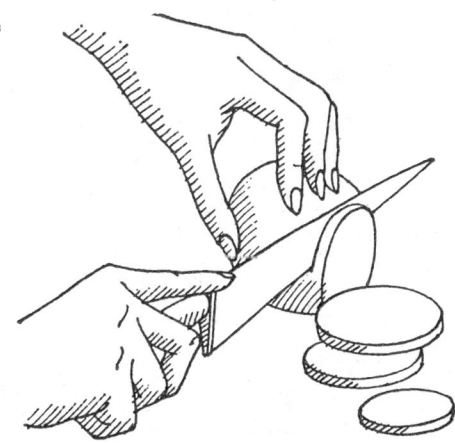

To Slice Food
Peel; halve lengthwise or cut a thin slice off bottom so food is steady on cutting board. Slice straight through in thickness desired.

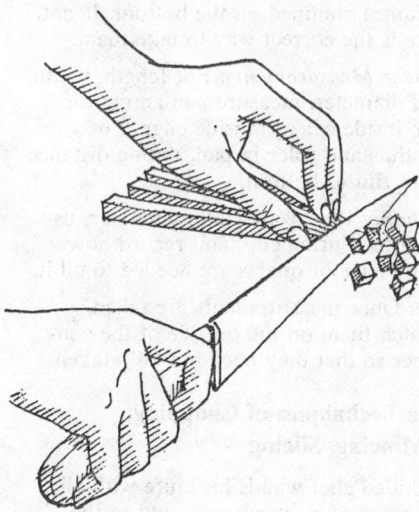

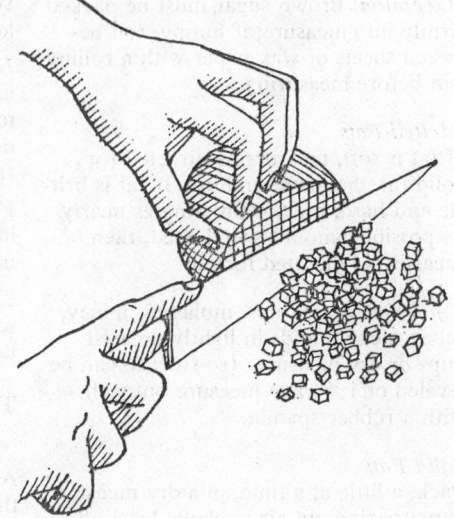

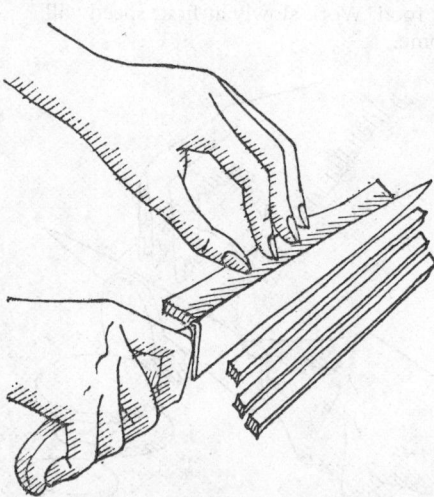

To Cube and Dice
Peel and slice—½"–1" for cubes,
⅛"–¼" for dice. Stack slices and cut
in strips of the same thickness, then
gather several strips together and cut
crosswise into uniform cubes.

To Chop and Mince Solid Foods
Peel, halve lengthwise, place cut side
down on board and, cutting almost—but
not quite—through food, make evenly
spaced vertical and horizontal cuts in a
crisscross pattern—about ¼" apart for
chopped foods, closer together for
minced, then slice straight through.

To Mince or Dice Celery
Make a series of cuts the length of the
stalk without cutting clear through the
end, then slice crosswise into desired
widths. If stalks are thick, they should
be split lengthwise first, again almost but
not quite through the end. *Note:* Carrots,
thinly sliced lengthwise, can be similarly
minced.

To Snip Herbs with Scissors
Bunch chives, dill tops, or other wispy
herbs together, then cut straight across
with scissors at ⅛" intervals—or more
or less.

To Grate Rind, Onion, Hard Cheese
Rub in short quick strokes over fine side
of grater onto wax paper; brush grater
with a pastry brush to free clinging bits.

To Cut in Strips, Julienne
Peel and slice—¼" thick for regular
strips, ⅛" for julienne; stack 3–4 slices
and cut in ⅛" strips. For julienne, cut
strips in uniform lengths as desired.

To Shred Cabbage
Quarter, core, then slice fine or grate on
coarse side of grater.

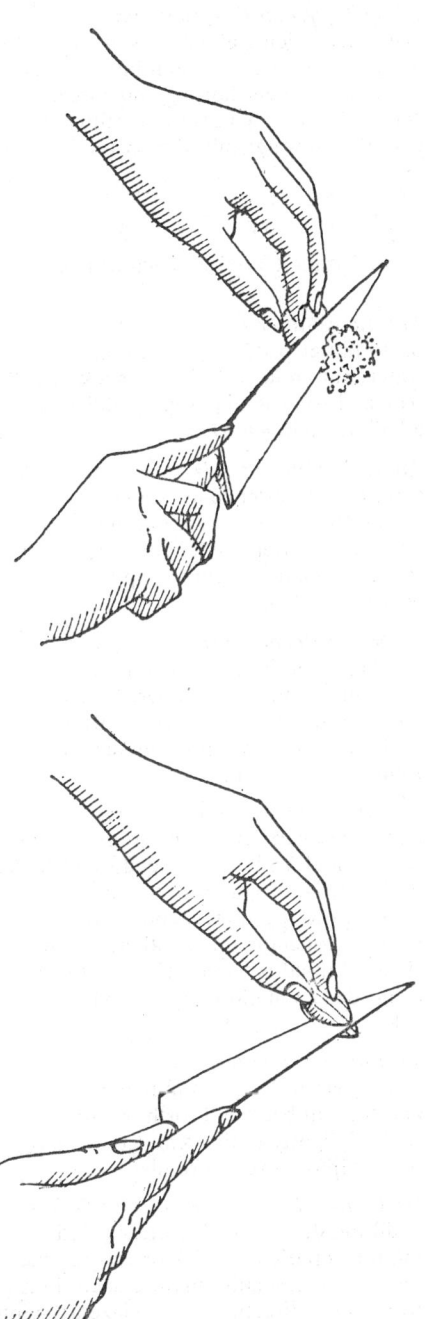

To Chop and Mince Leafy Foods
Bundle leaves together and slice straight across, then, anchoring knife point to board with 1 hand, move knife up and down over leaves in an arc as though it were hinged to board, again and again to desired fineness.

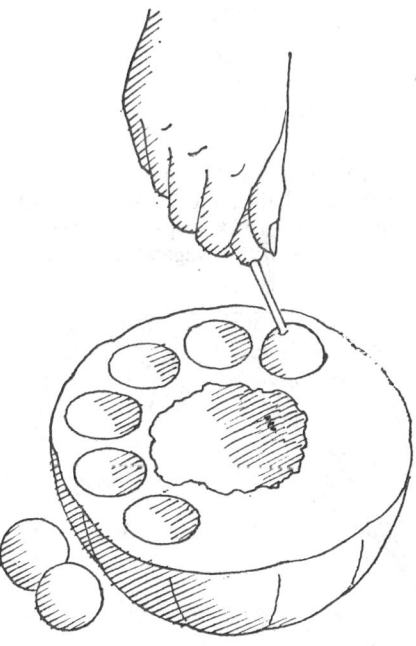

Tip: Garlic, shallots, and other small foods are less apt to slip if *lightly* salted.

To Make Melon or Vegetable Balls
Peel vegetable; halve and seed melon. Press ball cutter firmly straight into food, rotate until embedded, then twist out and remove ball.

To Use a Chopping Bowl
Coarsely cut or break up food, place in bowl, then chop vigorously with curved chopper.

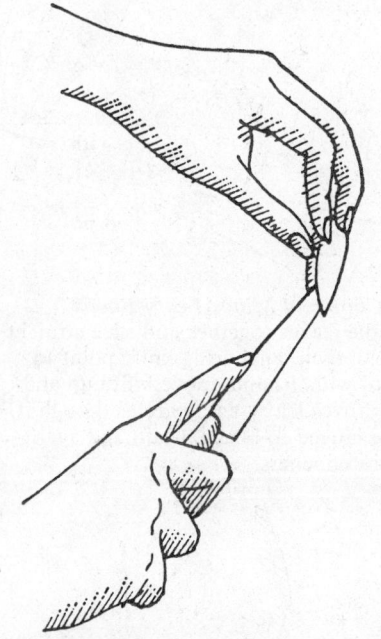

To Sliver or Shave Almonds
Blanch, peel, halve, and while still moist cut lengthwise in ⅛″ strips. To shave, cut lengthwise with a vegetable peeler.

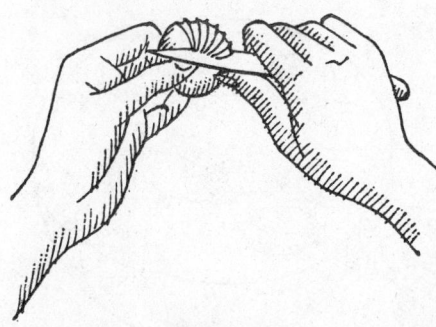

To Flute Mushrooms
Holding mushroom cap in left hand and paring knife rigidly in right, rotate mushroom toward you and against *stationary* blade, making fluted indentations from crown to bottom.

To Make Onion Chrysanthemums
Peel, then, slicing about ¾ way down toward root end, cut onion into ⅛″ sections. Hold under hot tap and spread "petals" gently. Tint rose or yellow, if you like, in water mixed with food coloring.

Some Other Cooking Techniques

To Make Butter Balls
Scald butter paddles and chill in ice water; cut an ice cold butter stick in ½″ pats and roll each between paddles into a ball; drop in ice water to "set."

To Make Butter Curls
Chill butter curler in ice water; also chill butter (in refrigerator). Pulling toward you, draw curler full length of butter stick, scooping out curl; drop in ice water to "set" curl.

To Make Bacon Curls
Fry bacon until limp, spear 1 end with a fork, and wind around tines. Continue frying until brown and crisp, turning frequently so bacon is evenly cooked. Remove from fork.

To Line Pans with Ladyfingers
Cut ladyfingers lengthwise in long, slim wedges and arrange, rounded sides down, over bottom of pan in a sunburst pattern, fitting close together. Stand ladyfingers upright, touching one another, around sides. If mold is flared, trim ladyfingers as needed to fit close together around sides.

To Line Pans with Crumbs
Butter pan well, spoon in fine crumbs, and tilt pan back and forth, rotating and shaking lightly until evenly coated all over. Tip out excess crumbs.

To Glaze Molds and Pans with Gelatin
Chill mold; prepare any clear gelatin mixture (Basic or Quick or Easy Aspic or any other gelatin mixture according to package directions). To glaze a 1-pint mold, you'll need about 1 cup; for a 1–1½-quart mold, about 1 pint. Chill gelatin until thick and syrupy, pour into chilled mold, and tilt back and forth,

rolling around until bottom and sides are evenly coated. Tip out excess and keep its consistency syrupy. Quick-chill mold until gelatin is tacky. Continue pouring in gelatin, building up layers, until desired thickness is reached; 2–3 layers will glaze most mixtures, but for spiky foods add an extra layer or 2. Fill mold and chill until firm. Unmold very carefully, using only the briefest dip in hot water—glaze will quickly melt.

Note: Numerous other cooking techniques (seeding and juicing of tomatoes, for example, separating eggs, etc.) are included elsewhere in the book in the sections where they seem most appropriate. Consult Index for page numbers.

Some Preparation Short Cuts, Cooking Tips and Tricks

Preparation:
– To anchor wax paper to a counter (when rolling dough or grating food), dampen counter, then press paper to it.
– To deaden the clattery sound of a rotary beater, stand bowl on a folded, dampened dishcloth or towel.
– To strain stock or other liquid through "cloth" when there is none, substitute paper toweling (but *not* the new super-absorbent type).
– To roll bread or cracker crumbs *neatly,* seal bread or crackers inside a plastic bag, then roll with a rolling pin. Or crush in an electric blender, instead.
– To melt small amounts of chocolate, place in a custard cup and stand in a small pan of simmering water.
– To fill without incident small, easily tipped-over molds, stand them in muffin pans.
– To prevent fish or meat ball mixtures from sticking to your hands as you shape the balls, rinse hands frequently in cold water.
– To avoid overcoloring foods, add liquid food coloring with an eyedropper, paste color by daubing on the end of a toothpick.
– To prevent slippery foods from slipping as you slice or chop, dip fingers in salt.

It also may help to lightly salt the cutting board.
– To measure out ½ egg, beat 1 whole egg, then spoon out ½ (add remaining ½ to a sauce or scrambled eggs).
– To crush whole cardamom seeds if you have no mortar and pestle, remove puffy white outer shell, then pulverize dark inner seeds by placing in the bowl of a spoon, fitting another spoon on top and grinding the 2 together. *Note:* Other small seeds—cumin, coriander, etc.—can be ground the same way.
– To expedite peeling of boiled potatoes, score lightly around middle before cooking; afterward, simply spear potatoes with a fork ånd peel skin back from the score marks.
– To "frost" grapes, brush lightly with beaten egg white, then dip in granulated sugar and dry on a cake rack.
– To peel an onion zip-quick, cut a thin slice off top or bottom, then pull away papery outer skin.

Cooking and Baking:
– To brighten beets and red cabbage, add 1 tablespoon cider vinegar or lemon juice to the cooking water.
– To scald milk without scorching it, heat in a very heavy saucepan or top of a double boiler over just boiling water until tiny bubbles appear at edges of milk.
– To help keep sour cream from curdling, bring to room temperature before adding to hot mixtures and never allow to boil.
– To keep butter from burning during frying or sautéing, mix 2-to-1 with cooking oil or use clarified butter.*
– To soften hard, dry brown sugar, heat uncovered in a 200° F. oven until dry and crumbly, then pulverize in an electric blender.
– To prevent food from overbrowning as it bakes, wrap in foil with the shiny side out.
– To keep cooked, drained spaghetti from clumping when it must be held a few minutes, toss lightly with 1 tablespoon warm olive or other cooking oil.

– To prevent pancakes from sticking to the griddle, sprinkle it lightly with salt instead of greasing.
– To douse a small burner or oven fire, sprinkle with baking soda or salt.
– To soothe a superficial burn, hold under cold running water, rub with cold, heavy cream or apply a baking soda–water paste.
– To test oven temperature when gauge is broken, preheat oven 15 minutes, then place a sheet of white paper (typewriter bond is a good weight) on center rack for 5 minutes; if paper blackens, oven is 500° F. or more; if it turns deep brown, oven is 450°–500° F.; if golden brown, oven is 400°–450° F.; if light brown 350°–400° F.; and if a pale biscuit color, 300° F. or less.

Serving and Storing:
– To clean spills from serving dishes before carrying them to the table, wipe with cotton swabs or swab sticks.
– To keep plastic food wrap from sticking to itself, store in refrigerator.

COMMON CAN SIZES

Note: Cans of the same size do not necessarily weigh the same—depends on what's inside. Meats and seafoods are canned in such a variety of shapes and sizes they are not included here; nor are bantam jars of baby foods. Read labels carefully.

Industry Term	Approx. Net Weight	Approx. Cups	Approx. Servings	Type of Food
6 oz.	6 oz.	¾	4–6	Frozen juice concentrates.
8 oz.	8 oz.	1	1–2	Fruits, vegetables, ready-to-heat-and-eat dishes.
Picnic	10½–12 oz.	1¼	2–3	Condensed soups; fruits, meats, fish, vegetables, prepared dishes.
12 oz. vacuum	12 oz.	1½	3–4	Vacuum-pack corn.
No. 300	14–16 oz.	1¾	3–4	Pork and beans, meat dishes, cranberry sauce, blueberries.
No. 303	16–17 oz.	2	4	Fruits, vegetables, some meat products, ready-to-serve soups.
No. 2	1 lb. 4 oz. or 1 pt. 2 fl. oz.	2½	5	Juices, ready-to-serve soups, pineapple, apple slices, some ready-to-serve recipes; no longer popular for fruits, vegetables.
No. 2½	1 lb. 13 oz.	3½	7	Fruits, pumpkin, sauerkraut, tomatoes, spinach, and other greens.
No. 3 cyl. or 46 fl. oz.	3 lb. 3 oz. or 1 qt. 14 fl. oz.	5¾	10–12	Economy "family-size" fruit and vegetable juices, pork and beans; institution-size condensed soups, some vegetables.
No. 10	6½–7¼ lbs.	12–13	25	Institution-size fruits, vegetables.

— To build up a supply of ice cubes, remove from trays when frozen hard and very dry, bundle into large plastic bags and store in freezer. If dry enough when removed from trays, cubes will not stick to one another.

— To apportion vegetables evenly—and quickly—for a crowd, use an ice-cream scoop; No. 10 size=½ cup; No. 12=¾ cup.

— To cover a cake frosted with a soft or fluffy icing, stick toothpicks in top and sides, then drape foil or plastic food wrap over toothpicks.

— To keep fruit pies as fresh-tasting as possible, cover with foil or plastic food wrap and store at room temperature, then warm uncovered 10 minutes in a 350° F. oven before serving.

— To loosen a sticking crumb crust, set piepan on a hot damp cloth and hold cloth ends against sides of pan 1–2 minutes.

— To cut extra-fresh soft bread in thin slices, dip knife in boiling water, shaking off extra drops, then slice.

Cleaning:
— To remove the smell of onions or garlic from hands, rinse hands in cold water, rub with salt or baking soda, rinse again, then wash with soap and water.

— To remove stains from fingers, rub with a cut lemon.

OVEN TEMPERATURES

Below 300° F.=very slow
300° F.=slow
325° F.=moderately slow
350° F.=moderate
375° F.=moderately hot
400–425° F.=hot
450–475° F.=very hot
500° F. or more =extremely hot

Conversion Formulas:
Fahrenheit to Centigrade: Subtract 32 from Fahrenheit reading, multiply by 5, then divide by 9. For example: 212° F.— 32=180×5=900÷9=100° C.
Centigrade to Fahrenheit: Multiply centigrade reading by 9, divide by 5 and add 32. For example: 100° C.×9=900÷5= 180+32=212° F.

FAHRENHEIT / CENTIGRADE SCALE

Boiling Point F.		Boiling Point C.
(of Water) 212°	– – –	–100° (of Water)
200°	– – –	93.3°
190°	– – –	87.8°
180°	– – –	82.2°
170°	– – –	76.7°
160°	– – –	71.1°
150°	– – –	65.6°
140°	– – –	60°
130°	– – –	54.4°
120°	– – –	48.9°
110°	– – –	43.3°
100°	– – –	37.8°
90°	– – –	32.2°
80°	– – –	26.7°
70°	– – –	21.1°
60°	– – –	15.6°
Freezing 50°	– – –	10° Freezing
Point 40°	– – –	4.4° Point
(of Water) 32°	– – –	0° (of Water)

What It Will Mean to Cook with Metric Measures

If America adopts the metric system of measurements as expected, how will the change affect your cooking? First of all, don't throw away your cookbooks, because the conversion will not be immediate. Best predictions, in fact, are that it will take the big industries ten years at least to adopt the metric system, and consumers many, many years more. Metric weights and measures will be taught in the grades, so school children may well master the system before their parents. (Some corporations have already printed for classroom use booklets describing the metric system and how it works; others have devised slide-rule-type converters for instant calculations.)

What, exactly, is the metric system? A way of measuring, far simpler than our own, because it is based on the decimal system with larger measures being subdivided into units of ten.

Food researchers have always used the metric system because it is more precise than American weights and measures.

European cooks use it, too, and have found nothing mystifying or complicated about it (they, in truth, would be baffled by our own system of pounds and ounces, yards and inches, which are not based on logical units of ten).

In recipes, the principal difference between our present way of measuring and the metric is that dry ingredients like flour and sugar are weighed rather than measured in a cup. It's an easier, more efficient method because the flour can be sifted directly onto a piece of wax paper on a scale, the dial indicating exactly when the proper amount of flour has been added. Meats, fruits, and vegetables, whether sliced, diced, or whole, will be called for by weight rather than by cup, and, of course, they will be sold in supermarkets by the kilogram instead of the pound.

Small measures—tablespoons, teaspoons, and fractions thereof—are not likely to change. Indeed, the European system of calling for a soupspoon of sugar or a coffee spoon of vanilla is less accurate than our own, so hang onto your measuring spoons.

In the metric system, liquids are measured in measuring cups, but the calibrations are marked in liters, ½ liters, ¼ liters, and milliliters instead of in cups. Again, the system is more refined because each liter is subdivided into 10 deciliters, each deciliter into 10 centiliters, each centiliter into 10 milliliters. One advantage is immediately obvious: there will be no more such cumbersome measurements as ½ cup plus 1 tablespoon, or 1 cup minus 3 teaspoons.

To simplify the switch to metric, manufacturers of scales and measuring cups are expected to (and some already do) use dual markings, showing quantities in liters and cups for liquids, grams and ounces for weights. If there are gourmet kitchen shops in your area, you will find there already food scales and cups calibrated in both metric and U.S. measures.

To give you an idea of how the metric system works, we have included in the pages that follow a table of Metric Weights and Measures as well as conversion tables for weights, fluid and linear measures, the ones most apt to affect the cook.

METRIC WEIGHTS AND MEASURES

FLUID MEASURES

10 milliliters = 1 centiliter
10 centiliters = 1 deciliter
10 deciliters = 1 liter
10 liters = 1 decaliter
10 decaliters = 1 hectoliter
10 hectoliters = 1 kiloliter

CUBIC MEASURES

1000 cubic millimeters = 1 cubic centimeter
1000 cubic centimeters = 1 cubic decimeter
1000 cubic decimeters = 1 cubic meter

WEIGHTS

10 milligrams = 1 centigram
10 centigrams = 1 decigram
10 decigrams = 1 gram
10 grams = 1 decagram
10 decagrams = 1 hectogram
10 hectograms = 1 kilogram

LINEAR MEASURES

10 millimeters = 1 centimeter
10 centimeters = 1 decimeter
10 decimeters = 1 meter
10 meters = 1 decameter
10 decameters = 1 hectometer
10 hectometers = 1 kilometer

METRIC EQUIVALENTS OF U. S. WEIGHTS AND MEASURES

WEIGHTS (AVOIRDUPOIS)

5 grams = 1 teaspoon (approx.)
28.35 grams = 1 ounce
50 grams = 1¾ ounces
100 grams = 3½ ounces
227 grams = 8 ounces
1000 grams (1 kilogram) = 2 lbs. 3¼ oz.

FLUID MEASURES

1 deciliter = 6 tablespoons + 2 teaspoons
¼ liter = 1 cup + 2¼ teaspoons

½ liter=1 pint+4½ teaspoons
1 liter=1 quart+4 scant tablespoons
4 liters=1 gallon+1 scant cup
10 liters=2½ gallons+2½ cups (approx.)

LINEAR MEASURES

2½ centimeters=1 inch
1 meter (100 centimeters)=39⅓ inches

Some Abbreviations Used In European Cookbooks: g.=gram; kg.=kilogram; cm.= centimeter; c.=cuiller (spoon), usually qualified by type (coffee spoon, soupspoon, or tablespoon); dl.=deciliter.

TABLE OF EQUIVALENTS

Note: All measures are level.

Pinch or dash=less than ⅛ teaspoon
3 teaspoons=1 tablespoon
2 tablespoons=1 fluid ounce
1 jigger=1½ fluid ounces
4 tablespoons=¼ cup
5 tablespoons+1 teaspoon=⅓ cup
8 tablespoons=½ cup
10 tablespoons+2 teaspoons=⅔ cup
12 tablespoons=¾ cup
16 tablespoons=1 cup
1 cup=8 fluid ounces
2 cups=1 pint
2 pints=1 quart
⅘ quart=25.6 fluid ounces
1 quart=32 fluid ounces
4 quarts=1 gallon
2 gallons (dry measure)=1 peck
4 pecks=1 bushel

SOME FRACTIONAL MEASURES

½ of ¼ cup=2 tablespoons
½ of ⅓ cup=2 tablespoons+2 teaspoons
½ of ½ cup=¼ cup
½ of ⅔ cup=⅓ cup
½ of ¾ cup=¼ cup+2 tablespoons
⅓ of ¼ cup=1 tablespoon+1 teaspoon
⅓ of ⅓ cup=1 tablespoon+2⅓ teaspoons
⅓ of ½ cup=2 tablespoons+2 teaspoons
⅓ of ⅔ cup=3 tablespoons+1⅔ teaspoons
⅓ of ¾ cup=¼ cup

SOME DRY WEIGHTS (AVOIRDUPOIS)

4 ounces=¼ pound
8 ounces=½ pound
16 ounces=1 pound

Some Emergency Substitutions

In a pinch, any of the following ingredient substitutions can be made successfully *except* in temperamental cakes, breads, cookies, or pastries.

Leavening:
– 1½ teaspoons phosphate or tartrate baking powder=1 teaspoon double-acting baking powder.
– ¼ teaspoon baking soda+½ teaspoon cream of tartar=1 teaspoon double-acting baking powder.
– ¼ teaspoon baking soda+½ cup sour milk=1 teaspoon double-acting baking powder *in liquid mixtures;* reduce recipe content by ½ cup.

Thickening:
– 1 tablespoon cornstarch=2 tablespoons all-purpose flour.
– 1 tablespoon potato flour=2 tablespoons all-purpose flour.
– 1 tablespoon arrowroot=2½ tablespoons all-purpose flour.
– 2 teaspoons quick-cooking tapioca= 1 tablespoon all-purpose flour (use in soups only).

Sweetening, Flavoring:
– 1¼ cups sugar+⅓ cup liquid=1 cup light corn syrup or honey.
– 3 tablespoons cocoa+1 tablespoon butter=1 (1-ounce) square unsweetened chocolate.
– ⅛ teaspoon cayenne pepper=3–4 drops liquid hot red pepper seasoning.

Flour:
– 1 cup sifted all-purpose flour−2 tablespoons=1 cup sifted cake flour.
– 1 cup+2 tablespoons sifted cake flour =1 cup sifted all-purpose flour.
– 1 cup sifted self-rising flour=1 cup sifted all-purpose flour+1¼ teaspoons baking powder and a pinch of salt; when using, substitute measure for measure for all-purpose flour, then omit baking powder and salt in recipe.

Dairy:

– ½ cup evaporated milk + ½ cup water
= 1 cup whole milk.

– 1 cup skim milk + 2 teaspoons melted
butter = 1 cup whole milk.

– 1 cup milk + 1 tablespoon lemon juice
or white vinegar = 1 cup sour milk (let
stand 5–10 minutes before using).

– ¾ cup milk + ¼ cup melted butter =
1 cup light cream.

Eggs:

– 2 egg yolks = 1 egg (for thickening
sauces, custards).

– 2 egg yolks + 1 tablespoon cold water =
1 egg (for baking).

– 1½ tablespoons stirred egg yolks = 1
egg yolk.

– 2 tablespoons stirred egg whites = 1 egg
white.

– 3 tablespoons mixed broken yolks and
whites = 1 medium-size egg.

Miscellaneous:

– 1 cup boiling water + 1 bouillon cube
or envelope instant broth mix = 1 cup
broth.

– 1 teaspoon beef extract blended with
1 cup boiling water = 1 cup beef broth.

– 1 cup fine bread crumbs = ¾ cup fine
cracker crumbs.

– ½ cup minced, plumped, pitted prunes
or dates = ½ cup seedless raisins or dried
currants.

– 6 tablespoons mayonnaise blended with
2 tablespoons minced pickles or pickle
relish = ½ cup tartar sauce.

SOME USEFUL EQUIVALENTS

Food	Weight or Amount	Approximate Equivalent Volume or Number
Fruits		
Apples	1 pound	3–4 medium (2½–3 cups sliced)
Apricots (fresh)	1 pound	5–8 medium (2–2½ cups sliced)
Apricots (dried)	1 pound	4½ cups cooked
Bananas	1 pound	3–4 medium (1¼–1½ cups mashed)
Berries (except strawberries)	1 pound	2 cups
Cherries	1 quart	2 cups pitted
Cranberries	1 pound	1 quart sauce
Dates (unpitted)	1 pound	2 cups pitted
Dates (diced, sugared)	1 pound	2⅔ cups
Figs (dried)	1 pound	3 cups chopped, 4 cups cooked
Grapes	1 pound	2½–3 cups seeded
Lemons	1 pound	5–6 medium (1 cup juice)
	1 lemon	3 T. juice, 2 t. grated rind
Limes	1 pound	6–8 medium (⅓–⅔ cup juice)
	1 lime	1–2 T. juice, 1 t. grated rind
Oranges	1 pound	3 medium (1 cup juice)
	1 orange	⅓ cup juice, 1 T. grated rind
Peaches, pears	1 pound	4 medium (2–2½ cups sliced)
Peaches (dried)	1 pound	4 cups cooked
Prunes	1 pound	4 cups cooked
Raisins (seedless)	1 pound	3 cups
Raisins (seeded)	1 pound	2½ cups
Rhubarb	1 pound, cut up	2 cups cooked
Strawberries	1 pint	1½–2 cups sliced

Food	Weight or Amount	Approximate Equivalent Volume or Number
Vegetables		
Beans, peas (dried)	1 pound	2¼–2½ cups raw, 5–6 cups cooked
Cabbage	1 pound	4½ cups shredded
Green peas in the pod	1 pound	1½ cups shelled peas
Limas in the pod	1 pound	¾–1 cup shelled limas
Mushrooms	½ pound	3 cups sliced, 1 cup sliced sautéed
Onions (yellow)	1 medium	½ cup minced
Pepper (sweet green or red)	1 large	1 cup minced
Potatoes (Irish)	1 pound	3 medium, 1¾ cups mashed
Dairy, Fats		
Milk (whole, skim, buttermilk)	1 quart	4 cups
Milk (evaporated)	13 oz. can	1⅔ cups
	5¾ oz. can	¾ cup
Milk (sweetened, condensed)	14 oz. can	1⅓ cups
Cream, sour cream	½ pint	1 cup
Cheese (Cheddar, process)	½ pound	2 cups grated
Cheese (cottage)	½ pound	1 cup
Cheese (cream)	3 oz. package	6 tablespoons
Butter, margarine (not whipped)	1 pound	2 cups
	1 (¼ lb.) stick	½ cup
	⅛ (¼ lb.) stick	1 tablespoon
Lard	1 pound	2 cups
Eggs (whole)	4–6	1 cup
Egg whites	10–12	1 cup
Egg yolks	13–14	1 cup
Cereal, Pasta		
Buckwheat groats	1 cup raw	4 cups cooked
Bulgur wheat	1 cup raw	4 cups cooked
Corn meal	1 pound	3 cups
	1 cup raw	4 cups cooked
Cornstarch	1 pound	3 cups
Flour (all purpose)	1 pound	4 cups, sifted
Flour (cake)	1 pound	4½–5 cups, sifted
Flour (whole-wheat)	1 pound	3½ cups, unsifted
Oats (rolled)	1 pound	5 cups
	1 cup raw	1¾ cups cooked
Pasta:		
Macaroni	1 pound	4 cups raw, 8 cups cooked
Noodles	1 pound	6 cups raw, 7 cups cooked
Spaghetti	1 pound	4 cups raw, 7–8 cups cooked
Rice (regular)	1 pound	2¼ cups raw; 6¾ cups cooked
Rice (converted)	14 ounces	2 cups raw; 8 cups cooked
Rice (quick-cooking)	14 ounces	4 cups raw; 8 cups cooked
Rice (brown)	12 ounces	2 cups raw; 8 cups cooked
Rice (wild)	1 pound	3 cups raw; 11–12 cups cooked

Food	Weight or Amount	Approximate Equivalent Volume or Number
Breads, Crackers, Crumbs		
Bread	1 slice, fresh	1 cup soft crumbs or cubes
	1 slice, dry	⅓ cup dry crumbs
Soda crackers	28	1 cup fine crumbs
Graham crackers	15	1 cup fine crumbs
Chocolate wafers	19	1 cup fine crumbs
Vanilla wafers	22	1 cup fine crumbs
Sugar, Salt, Coffee		
Coffee (ground)	1 pound	3⅓ cups grounds
Salt	1 pound	2 cups
Sugar (granulated)	1 pound	2 cups
Sugar (superfine)	1 pound	2¼–2½ cups
Sugar (brown)	1 pound	2¼–2⅓ cups
Sugar (confectioners')	1 pound	4½ cups, sifted
Nuts, Candy		
Candied fruit and peel	1 pound	3 cups chopped
Coconut	1 pound	5–6 cups flaked or shredded
Unshelled Nuts:		
Almonds	1 pound	1¼ cups nut meats
Brazil nuts	1 pound	1½ cups nut meats
Peanuts	1 pound	2 cups nuts
Pecans	1 pound	2¼ cups nut meats
Walnuts	1 pound	1¾ cups nut meats
Shelled almonds, pecans, peanuts, walnuts	1 pound	4–4½ cups nut meats
Shelled Brazil nuts	1 pound	3 cups nut meats
Marshmallows	¼ pound	16 regular size

serving dishes in baking pans of hot water.

– Cut pies or cakes or dish up desserts about 1 hour ahead, then cover and, if needed, refrigerate or set in freezer.

A Quantity Purchasing Guide

The difficulty in feeding dozens of people, obviously, is knowing how much food to buy. No two people eat alike; some stuff themselves with seconds and thirds while others simply sit around and pick at their plates. For that reason, dieticians have learned that the most accurate way of computing large amounts of food needed is by multiplying out average-size servings (¼ pound helpings of meat, for example, ½ cup portions of vegetables). Most quantity recipe yields are given in numbers of servings or portions, not in numbers of persons they will serve. The shopping guide below has been computed the same way and will provide enough food for 48 "average-size" portions. In a pinch (or on a tight budget), these amounts will serve 48 persons. But in this day of abundance, most people find average-size servings skimpy. Thus, the quantities of food in the following guide will serve 30–35 hungry men and women amply, slightly fewer if it's a stag affair, slightly more if a ladies' lunch. *Tip:* When buying a number of roasts or birds, choose those of similar size and shape so that they will cook in the same length of time.

Food	Approx. Quantity Needed for 48 Servings
BEVERAGES	
Fruit juice	4 (46 ounce) cans
Coffee (instant)	1 (4 ounce) jar+3 T.
Coffee (ground)	1¼ lbs.
Tea (instant)	1½ cups
Tea (bags)	4 doz.
Tea (leaf)	¼ lb.+3 T.
Coffee cream	1½ qts.
Sugar cubes	1 lb.
Lemon (for tea)	6 large

MEAT, POULTRY	
Beef Roast (bone-in)	35 lbs.
Beef Roast (boneless)	25 lbs.
Hamburger (ground chuck)	12–16 lbs.
Ham (bone-in)	20–24 lbs.
Ham (boneless)	12–16 lbs.
Frankfurters	10–12 lbs.
Broiler-Fryers, Roasting Chickens	35–40 lbs.
Turkey (roast)	35–40 lbs.
Cooked Boneless Turkey Roast, Roll	9–10 lbs.
Uncooked Boneless Turkey Roast, Roll	16 lbs.

VEGETABLES	
Frozen	4 (2½ lb.) pkgs. *or* 16 (10 ounce) pkgs.
Canned	2 (6½–7¼ lb.) cans (the No. 10 size)

SALADS	
Lettuce hearts	12 medium heads
Lettuce leaves	6 medium heads
"Deli" Vegetable salad (ready mixed)	2 gals.
"Deli" potato salad	1½ gals.
"Deli" fruit salad	1 gal.

PASTA AND RICE	
Spaghetti, noodles	6–8 lbs.
Rice (regular)	4½ lbs.
Rice (converted)	2½ (28 ounce) pkgs.
Rice (quick-cooking)	2½ (28 ounce) pkgs

RELISHES	
Cranberry sauce	6 (1 lb.) cans
Olives	2 qts.
Mustard	1 qt.
Ketchup	3 (14 ounce) bottles
Carrots (for strips)	2 lbs.

Food	Approx. Quantity Needed for 48 Servings
SANDWICHES: See Sandwiches in Quantity in the chapter on sandwiches.	

DESSERT	
Canned fruit	2 (6½–7¼ lb.) cans
Ice cream	2 gal. or 8–9 (1 qt.) bricks

MISCELLANEOUS	
Sliced bread	1 pullman loaf+1 (1 lb.) loaf
French bread	3 (18″) loaves
Butter, margarine	1½ lbs.
Cottage cheese	6 lbs.
Potato chips	2 lbs.

About Cooking Out of Doors

Some Tips on Buying Outdoor Grills:
– Make the first grill a basic one; then, if family enjoyment justifies the splurge, buy a more luxurious model next time with all the extras—rotating windshield, motorized spit, automatic timers, temperature gauge, warming oven, deep fat fryer, storage shelves, cutting board, and counters.
– Choose sturdy, easy-to-clean-and-regulate equipment. Grills should be constructed of heavy, rust-resistant metal and contain adjustable fire beds and grids.
– Select a grill that suits the family's needs and size. The cooking area should be large enough to accommodate enough food for everyone at once but not so large there are vast empty spaces through which heat will escape, thus wasting fuel. For flexibility, choose a roll-around or fold-up grill; for permanence an all-weather gas or electric model.

Basic Cooking Tools Needed:
Long-Handled 2-Pronged Fork
Long-Handled Spatula or Turner
Long-Handled Basting Brush
Large and Small Tongs
Sharp Knife
Sturdy Meat Thermometer

Handy Extras:
Long-Handled Hinged Grill (for small foods)
Basket Broiler (for cut-up chicken, etc.)
Long Skewers (preferably with wood handles)
Cast-Iron Skillet
Kettle

Basic Fire Tools Needed:
Charcoal Tongs and Poker
Rake for Leveling Coals
Scoop for Adding and Removing Coals
Insulated Gloves
Sprinkler Can (for dousing flare-ups)
Bucket of Sand (for putting out grease fires)

Handy Extras:
Electric Fire Starter
Bellows

How to Build a Charcoal Fire:
(*Note:* Charcoal comes in a number of forms, but the briquettes are handiest to use; store in a dry place.)
– Lay fire ahead of time; light ½ hour before cooking if grill and amount of food to be cooked are small, 1 hour ahead if grill and food quantity are large.
– If firebox lacks dampers, line with foil to catch drips and simplify cleaning. If grill is a large one, arrange a layer of sand or coarse gravel on bottom before adding charcoal; it will insulate grill and save fuel.
– For General Purpose Grilling: Pile or spread enough briquettes to equal or slightly exceed surface area of food to be cooked and, if possible, make the layer deep enough to last throughout cooking.
– For Spit Cooking: Mound a deep bed of briquettes toward the back of the grill so that there is room in front for the drip pan and so that the spit, positioned to turn toward the back of the grill, will send drippings into the pan instead of the coals causing flare-ups.
Note: Fires for spit cooking should be hot or moderately hot.
– Using a fire starter, preferably the one the grill manufacturer recommends, light the briquettes. Commercial starters come

in liquid, jelly, and treated paper form. In addition, there are electric and gas starters. Never use gasoline or kerosene —they will ruin the flavor of the food. *Caution: Never add starter after a fire is lighted, even if the coals look dead; there's danger of a flash fire or explosion.*

— Let briquettes burn down to glowing coals covered with fine white ash, rearranging as necessary to provide more even heat and replenishing, as needed, by adding fresh briquettes around the fringes.

— Before adding food, test fire temperature as follows:

Type of Fire	Grill Thermometer Reading	"Hand Test" (Maximum Time Hand Can Be Held at Grill Level before Being Removed)
Moderate	300° F.	5 seconds
Moderately Hot	325° F.	4 seconds
Hot	350–75° F.	2–3 seconds

Note: Fire temperatures for grilling different kinds of food are recommended wherever appropriate in recipes throughout the book.

— *To Cool a Hot Fire:* Close grill dampers, spread coals out over fire bed in a checkerboard pattern. If still too hot, shovel some coals into a sand bucket, and if that doesn't cool the fire, remove any food on grill, sprinkle coals lightly with water and when steam subsides return food to grill.

— *To Heat Up a Cool Fire:* Open dampers, stir coals, knocking off the white ash, then cluster in center of grill; tuck a few charcoal chips underneath hot coals and add fresh briquettes around the edges.

— *For a Fresh Woodsy Fragrance:* Toss a few dampened hardwood chips onto the coals, preferably hickory, apple, or pear; avoid pine or resinous woods, which will send a turpentine flavor through the food. *Note:* For special savor, scatter dried sage, thyme, or rosemary *lightly* over the coals; especially good with chicken or lamb.

Note: Outdoor cooking times are extremely variable, being affected by outdoor temperature, gusts of wind, type of grill and charcoal used. Usually, it is possible to speed or slow grilling by raising or lowering the grids or spit. If

not, cool or heat up the fire as directed earlier. The grilling times included in the meat, poultry, and seafood chapters should be used as guides only.

Caution: Make sure coals are out before leaving a grill; cover with sand or, if you want to save partially burned charcoal, scoop coals into water, then fish out and spread to dry.

About Pit Cooking

Unless you have a strong back and willing crew, save pit roasting for the pros. It is heavy work. But for a simple clambake on the beach: Dig a saucer-shaped hole about 2 feet deep and 4–5 feet across, line with nonporous rocks, build a bonfire on top, and let it burn about 3 hours until rocks are sizzling hot. Rake coals away, brush ashes aside, then blanket rocks with about 6 inches of seaweed, preferably the succulent rockweed, which will provide lots of steam. Next, layer in the food, beginning with unshucked clams and mussels, then adding corn in the husk, unpeeled potatoes and peeled onions, whole lobsters, disjointed young chickens,

separating the layers with more rockweed. Add a final blanket of rockweed,
cover all with a damp tarpaulin, and
weight down with sand. Let steam
1–3 hours, 1 hour if shellfish only are
being cooked, 2½–3 if vegetables and
chicken are being cooked along with the
shellfish. Then dig up and enjoy!

About Camp and Galley Cooking

Cooking at a campsite is scarcely
roughing it these days. Nor is cooking in
a minuscule galley aboard a bobbing
inboard. There are compact, fully
portable camp stoves that run on
gasoline or liquid propane (LP), fold-up
stoves fueled by canned heat, gimbal
stoves guaranteed not to tilt when the
boat does, making it possible to bake and
broil on location as well as heat things
up. Moreover, there are portable refrigerators and freezers (gas or electricity
powered, some of which can be plugged
in wherever there are outlets), not to
mention a rash of insulated, welterweight
carryalls that will keep hot foods hot,
cold foods cold, and frozen foods frozen
during hours of transit. It is impractical
here to do more than generalize, not
only because space is limited but also
because new items are being introduced
faster than they can be described.
Suffice it to say that nearly anything
that can be cooked at home can also be
cooked on location, as a stroll through
a sporting goods store or catalogue
quickly proves.

CHAPTER 3

THE LARDER

Today's larder includes the cupboard, the pantry, the refrigerator, the freezer, and the spice shelf. Storing it efficiently demands skill. Before setting out for the market, familiarize yourself with the ingredients you use and need most.

ABOUT INGREDIENTS

Science continues to revolutionize cooking *and* eating; each year supermarket shelves grow longer, accommodating new products that bewilder the shopper with an infinite variety of choices. What is the best buy? The all-purpose, the presifted, or the self-rising flour? Corn, peanut, olive, safflower, or blended vegetable oil? The following list is intended to explain the differences between certain basic ingredients. Other ingredients—and some not so basic—can be found elsewhere in the book in chapters where they are most frequently used: yeast in the breads chapter, for instance, and baking powders in the section on cakes (consult the Index for page numbers).

Dairy Products

Milk: Nearly all milk sold today is *pasteurized.* (*Certified milk,* sometimes sold locally, is raw milk handled and bottled under strict sanitary conditions.) *Pasteurized milk* has been heated, then quick-cooled to destroy microorganisms of spoilage, thereby improving keeping qualities. It is available in a variety of fluid forms.

Fluid Milks

Homogenized Milk: Uniformly smooth rich milk that will stay uniformly smooth and rich (no cream floating to the top) because the butter particles have been broken up and dispersed evenly throughout.

Skim Milk: Whole milk with 98–99 per cent of the butterfat removed.

Fortified Milk: Whole or skim milk enriched with vitamins (commonly A and D) and/or minerals and protein.

Flavored Milk: Chocolate or other flavored whole, skim, or partly skim milk. Such milks often have sugar, salt, and stabilizers added. (Also available powdered as drink mixes.)

Buttermilk: Originally the residue left after churning butter, but today a simulated version, usually made with skim milk and flecked with butter.

Acidophilus Milk: A particularly tart buttermilk, acid but easy to digest. A powdered form is sold at drugstores.

Low-Sodium Milk: A special diet milk in which 90 per cent of the sodium has been replaced by potassium. The fluid form is available only in limited amounts, primarily on the West Coast. Powdered and canned varieties are stocked by drugstores.

Yogurt: Whole or partially skimmed milk fermented into a thick creamy curd; plain yogurt is high in protein and calcium, relatively low in calories (about 120 per cup). Also available in a variety of flavors.

Canned Milks

Evaporated Milk: Homogenized milk with about 60 per cent of the water removed and vitamin D added. Mixed ½ and ½ with water, it has the consistency and food value of whole milk, for which it may be substituted. Use full strength to increase the creaminess of sauces and soups, to coat chicken or chops before crumbing or breading, to top fruits and puddings.

Sweetened Condensed Milk: A sticky-sweet evaporated blend of whole milk and sugar, usually used to sweeten beverages, to make candy, ice creams, and other desserts.

Powdered Milks

Nonfat Dry Milk: Whole milk from which almost all water and butterfat have been removed, processed to dissolve rapidly in liquid. To reconstitute, follow package directions. One cup milk powder will make about 3 cups fluid milk, best when covered and refrigerated overnight to develop full flavor. Reconstituted dry milk can be substituted for the fresh; as powder, it can be added to hamburgers, meat loaves, and mashed potatoes to enrich flavor and nutritive value. *Whole Dry Milk Powder* is also available, but in limited quantities. Because of its butterfat content, it must be kept refrigerated.

Cream and Cream Substitutes

Heavy (Whipping) Cream: Rich and thick (35–40 per cent butterfat) and thicker still after a brief stretch in the refrigerator.

Light (Coffee) Cream: With half the butterfat (18–20 per cent) of heavy cream, light cream is a better all-purpose

cream, the choice for creaming coffee and tea. It will not whip.

Half-and-Half: A ½ and ½ mixture of milk and light cream (12–15 per cent butterfat). It will not whip but can be substituted for light cream in puddings and ice creams to shave calories a bit.

Sour Cream: A thick, silky-smooth commercial product made by souring light cream (it has the same butterfat content). A newer entry is *Half-and-Half Sour Cream* made from a ½ and ½ mixture of milk and light cream. It has about half the calories of regular sour cream.

Powdered (Instant) Cream: A mixture of dehydrated light cream and milk solids, with stabilizer added. Use as label directs.

Pressurized Whipped Cream: Sweetened cream, emulsifiers, and stabilizer in an aerosol can that whip into snowy drifts at the touch of a button.

Cream Substitutes: Nondairy products in liquid, powder, and pressurized form, usually composed of hydrogenated vegetable oils, sugar, emulsifiers, and preservatives. Depending upon form, these may be used in beverages, in cooking, and as dessert toppings.

Fats and Oils

Butter: Federal requirements demand that butter be 80 per cent butterfat. In addition, it is federally graded as to flavor, color, texture, and body, the finest quality being US Grade AA (or US Grade Score 93, the figure representing the grader's quality points). The remaining grades, in descending order, are A (US Score 92), B (Score 90), and C (Score 89). The AA and A are the grades most commonly available. Butter may be (and often is) artificially colored; it may be *salted* or *unsalted,* often called *sweet butter,* though true sweet butter is any butter—salted or unsalted—churned from sweet cream instead of sour. The newest form of butter is the *whipped,* which has simply been beaten full of air to soften it into a better spreading consistency. Whipped butter is lighter in weight than standard butter—6 sticks per pound as opposed to 4—and it must not be substituted for standard butter in recipes.

Margarine: A butter substitute compounded of vegetable (primarily soybean) and animal oils. To make margarine taste more like butter, cream and milk are sometimes added; to make it look more like butter, yellow food coloring is blended in. Margarine is frequently fortified with vitamins A and D and may contain preservatives and emulsifiers as well. Specialty margarines include *diet spreads,* the polyunsaturated, the *soft* and the *whipped* and a *no-burn* variety. *Note:* Margarine has slightly greater shortening power than butter and should not be substituted for it in temperamental cake, cookie, or pastry recipes.

Vegetable Shortening: Fluffy-soft all-purpose cooking fats made by pumping hydrogen into vegetable oils; usually snow white but sometimes tinted yellow. These are particularly good for deep fat frying because of their high smoking point; superior, too, for making pastries, cookies, and cakes. Do not refrigerate because the shortening may break down.

Lard: Pork fat, rendered and clarified. It is often hydrogenated and stabilized with emulsifiers and preservatives so that no refrigeration is needed (read label carefully and store as directed). Because lard has subtle meat flavor and a more brittle texture than other shortenings, it is particularly suited to making pastries.

Cooking and Salad Oils: The two are the same *except* that certain oils—olive, for one—taste better in salads than others and, having relatively low smoking points, are poor choices for deep fat frying. Oils are pressed from myriad vegetables, nuts, seeds, and fruits. The best all-round cooking-salad oils are *corn, cottonseed, peanut,* and *soybean* or blends of these. Lightest of all is the nearly colorless *safflower oil,* favored by the cholesterol conscious. Among the other oils available are *coconut, palm,*

sesame (a dark, heavy Oriental favorite), *sunflower seed, walnut,* and *almond oils.* To Mediterranean Europe, however, oil is olive oil. No other will do. *Virgin olive oil,* highly esteemed by connoisseurs, is unrefined oil from the first pressing. Subsequent pressings yield coarser, stronger oils, sometimes with a greenish cast (a sure sign of strong flavor). The most delicate of all is the champagne-pale (and champagne-priced) olive oil of France, best reserved for very special salads. Italy, Spain, and Greece all produce good all-round olive oils—straw-colored, aromatic, but not overly strong. Whenever possible, buy olive oil by the can rather than by the bottle so that it's shielded from the light and does not go stale. If you have neither the taste nor the pocketbook for pure olive oil, mix ½ and ½ with another vegetable oil. It's best not to refrigerate olive oil—or, for that matter, other oils; they will harden and turn cloudy. However, if you buy large bottles and use oil only occasionally, you may want to refrigerate the oil to keep it from turning rancid. When using, measure out only what you need and let come to room temperature—most of the cloudiness will disappear. *Cooking Tip:* When sautéing with olive oil, keep the heat a shade lower than usual to reduce spattering.

Wheat Flours

The milling industry is well into the Age of Specialization, grinding out flours in a variety of textures and types. The plain, white general-purpose flours, as required by the *Federal Enrichment Program,* have had B vitamins (thiamine, riboflavin, and niacin) and iron added so that their food value equals that of whole wheat flour. Some millers further enrich their flours by adding vitamins A and D and calcium.

All-Purpose Flour: The everything flour, equally good for baking cakes, pies, breads, and cookies, for thickening sauces and gravies, and for dredging foods to be fried. It is milled from hard and soft wheats and is *enriched.*

Bread Flour: An *enriched* hard wheat flour with a high content of the protein (gluten) needed to give bread its framework.

Cake Flour: An *unenriched* superfine flour milled from soft wheat. Too delicate for general use, it produces cakes of exceedingly fine and feathery grain.

Pastry Flour: Neither as coarse as all-purpose flour nor as fine as cake flour, pastry flour has just enough body to produce flaky-tender piecrusts. It is not as widely distributed as it once was. Most people today use all-purpose flour for pastry.

Self-Rising Flour: Enriched all-purpose flour to which baking powder and salt have been added. It can be substituted for all-purpose flour in recipes that call for baking powder and salt; to use, measure out the quantity of flour called for and omit the baking powder and salt. *Note:* To be effective, self-rising flour must be strictly fresh.

Presifted Flour: A timesaving, *enriched,* all-purpose flour that does not require sifting before measuring *except* for tall and tender cakes or other critical (easily-thrown-off-balance) recipes.

Instant-Type Flour: The sauce and gravy specialist, a granular white flour that blends into hot or cold liquids without lumping. It needs no sifting before measuring. Use for thickening only, not for baking or dredging, *except* as label instructs. *Not enriched* as a rule.

Whole Wheat Flour (Graham Flour): Unrefined, unbleached flour containing the iron- and vitamin B-rich wheat bran and germ. Never sift.

Gluten Flour: High-protein, low-starch (and low-calorie) flour milled from hard wheat; it is used to make gluten and other "slimming" breads.

Bran, Cracked Wheat, Wheat Germ Flours: All-purpose flours to which bran, cracked wheat, or wheat germ has been added; do not sift. Because of their coarse textures, these flours are particularly suitable for breads.

Note: Other wheat products (semolina, etc.) are discussed along with other grains in the chapter on cereals and rice.

Other Flours

Cereals other than wheat—*barley, buckwheat, corn, oats, rice,* and *rye*—are also milled into rough and smooth flours. They are available at specialty food stores, primarily, and most of them bake into supremely good breads. In addition, there are *noncereal flours: potato, soy,* and *lima bean, peanut, cottonseed, tapioca,* and *carob* (the St.-John's-bread of the Mediterranean). These, however, with the exception of potato flour, which makes exceptionally fine angel cake and is a splendid thickener of sauces and gravies, are seldom used solo but blended with other flours or foods to boost flavor and nutritive value.

Note: As a thickener, potato flour, like cornstarch and arrowroot, will thin down if overheated.

Thickeners

Arrowroot: Extracted from a tropical tuber once used to treat arrow wounds, this delicate, flavorless starch thickens without turning cloudy. Use it when a glistening, jewel-like glaze is needed.

Cornstarch: Fine white starch ground from the hearts of dried corn. It has about twice the thickening power of all-purpose flour, *but will thin down after thickening if overstirred or overcooked and will refuse to thicken at all if mixture is too acid or too sweet.* Handle carefully, as label directs.

Flour: See all-purpose and instant-type flours.

Note: Additional information on starch thickeners can be found in the chapter on sauces, gravies and butters.

Leavenings

Baking Powders: See the chapter on cakes.

Baking Soda: Pure bicarbonate of soda used to leaven acid batters and doughs (those containing molasses, sour milk or buttermilk, vinegar).

Cream of Tartar: A fine white powder crystallized from grape acid used in commercial baking powders. It will also whiten and "cream" candies and frostings, increase the volume and stability of beaten egg whites.

Yeasts: See the chapter on breads.

Sugars and Syrups

Granulated (White) Sugar: Highly refined, free-pouring, 99 1 per cent pure all-purpose sugar crystallized from sugar cane or beets. As a convenience, it is also pressed into cubes.

Superfine (Castor) Sugar: Extra-fine-grain, quick dissolving sugar. A boon to drink mixing, it also makes unusually good cakes and frostings.

Confectioners' (10X, Powdered) Sugar: Pulverized sugar mixed with cornstarch; particularly suited to making uncooked candies and frostings. Always sift before measuring.

Brown Sugar: Soft, molasses-flavored crystals left behind after the refining of granulated sugar. Brown sugar has a higher mineral content than granulated sugar. The *light brown* is more delicate than the *dark*. Newest form: free-pouring granules.

Raw Sugar: Sugary residue left in the vat after molasses is run off. It is crude, course-grained, and brown. It contains more minerals, notably potassium, then refined sugar. Potassium, however, is not a mineral apt to be lacking in the normal diet.

Maple Sugar: Crystallized, concentrated maple syrup.

Two Special Sugars, Both Decorative: Rock Candy, several-carat-big sugar crystals on a string; *colored granulated sugars.*

Noncaloric Sweeteners: Liquid, tablet, and powdered calorie-free sugar substitute (saccharine).

Corn Syrups: Light and *dark syrups* made from hydrolyzed cornstarch.

Maple Syrup: The concentrated sap of the sugar maple tree. Also available: *Maple Blended Syrup,* a mixture of maple and other syrups, and *Buttered Maple Syrup.*

Molasses: Available in many grades from the smooth, sweet, dark amber syrup extracted directly from sugar cane juices to the rougher, browner, not-so-sweet by-products of sugar refining. *Blackstrap,* the darkest and coarsest and least sweet of all, amounts to the dregs; it is not, as some believe, a nutritional powerhouse because some of its minerals are not assimilable by the body. Any grade of molasses can be *sulfured* or *unsulfured* depending upon whether sulfur was used in the sugar refining. The unsulfured is preferable because of its lighter color and more full-bodied cane-sugar flavor.

Sorghum: A molasses-like syrup extracted from sorghum.

Honey: Flower nectar that has been processed and condensed by bees. Flavors vary according to the flowers bees have fed upon; among those considered especially choice are heather honey, sourwood, rosemary, and the famous Hymettus (from the wild thyme carpeting the slopes of Mt. Hymettus near Athens). Honey may be liquid and golden, creamy and brown, or still in the comb. Do not refrigerate; the honey will turn grainy. Honey averages about 20 calories more per tablespoon than granulated sugar, but contains only the merest traces of vitamins and minerals despite faddist claims to the contrary.

Chocolate and Cocoa

Unsweetened Chocolate: The bitter, all-purpose, unadulterated chocolate rendered out of ground, roasted cocoa beans.

Semisweet Chocolate: Bitter chocolate sweetened with sugar and softened somewhat with extra cocoa butter. It is ideal for dipping because it melts smoothly and rehardens without streaking. Also now available as *semisweet chocolate bits*. Because they are lightly glazed, they hold their shape during baking.

Milk Chocolate: A blend of chocolate, sugar, and powdered milk meant to be eaten out-of-hand. The newest form: lightly glazed *milk chocolate bits,* similar to the semisweet but sweeter, milder, milkier.

Dark German (Sweet Cooking) Chocolate: Sweetened pure bitter chocolate, darker and more brittle than the semisweet because it lacks the extra cocoa butter.

No-Melt Unsweetened Chocolate: A pudding-thick blend of cocoa, vegetable oil, and preservatives ready to mix into candies, frostings, and batters. Each 1-ounce packet equals 1 (1 ounce) square unsweetened chocolate.

Swiss White Chocolate: Sweetened cocoa butter.

Cocoa: All-purpose chocolate powder ground from roasted cocoa beans. It contains virtually no cocoa butter, therefore fewer calories and saturated fats.

Dutch-Type Cocoa: Cocoa processed with alkali to mellow the flavor and darken the color.

Instant Cocoa Mixes: Assorted blends of cocoa, sugar, flavorings, emulsifiers, and sometimes milk powder processed to dissolve instantly in beverages.

Salt

Table (Cooking) Salt: A fine salt manufactured from rock salt and brine. It may be *iodized* (have sodium or potassium iodide added as a goiter preventive) or *plain;* often contains desiccants to keep it free-flowing.

Kosher Salt: Originally a coarse salt made under rabbinical supervision but more commonly today a generic term meaning any coarse natural sea salt. Alternate names are *Dairy, Cheese,* and *Flake Salt.*

Pickling Salt: Pure fine-grain salt with no additives.

Rock (Ice Cream) Salt: Coarse, crude salt used in freezing ice cream.

Flavored Salts: The repertoire is lengthy, including combinations of dehydrated vegetables and salt, charcoal and salt, assorted herbs, spices, and salt.

Pepper See The Herb and Spice Shelf.

Commercial Condiments, Sauces, and Seasonings

Worcestershire Sauce: A secret, spicy blend of soy sauce, shallots, anchovies, vinegar, garlic, molasses, and other ingredients designed to pep up meats and savory dishes.

Soy Sauce: Salty brown sauce extracted from lightly fermented soybeans.

Steak Sauce: A generic name for various thick brown bottled sauces concocted specifically to serve over broiled steaks and chops.

Liquid Hot Red Pepper Seasoning: Another generic name used to identify the incendiary sauces made of tabasco peppers, vinegar, and salt. Use drop by drop.

Liquid Gravy Browner: A blend of caramel, vegetable protein, vinegar, salt, and other flavorings used to brown gravies and sauces and impart a lusty meaty flavor.

Prepared (Wet, Bottled) Mustards: There are dozens of blends, some sunny and mild, some brown and spicy, some superhot.

The Milds: Prepared Mild Yellow Mustard (the old hot-dog favorite); *Prepared Spicy Yellow* (or *Brown*) *Mustard* (spicy but not fiery); *Dijon* and *Bordeaux* (spicy French wine-flavored mustards); *Dijon-type* (in the style of—but not necessarily from—Dijon), and *Creole* (a pungent beige blend showing tiny flecks of spice).

The Hots (all peppery and brown): *English, Düsseldorf, German,* and

Bahamian Mustard. Pretty hot stuff, too, is the American horseradish-mustard mixture.

Note: A discussion of whole and powdered mustards follows in the Herb and Spice Chart.

Some Marketing Tips

– Make a shopping list, setting down first any staples in low supply, then adding those foods needed in preparing the week's meals. Consider seasonal specials —both nonperishables or "freezables"— and buy in bulk whenever storage space permits.
– Buy only what quantities your family can use without waste or what can be stored properly in cupboard, pantry, refrigerator, or freezer.
– Read package labels carefully. By law they must include: net weight, all ingredients, including such additives as vitamins, minerals, preservatives, emulsifiers, artificial sweetener, flavoring, and coloring; identification of dietetic properties (sugar-free or sugar-reduced, low sodium, etc.). The latest ruling states that, if any food contains more artificial flavoring than natural, the name of the food must indicate that fact (i.e., Maple-Flavor Syrup rather than Maple Syrup). Helpful labels may also list proportions of saturated, monounsaturated, and polyunsaturated fats and calorie counts; they may indicate number of servings, provide descriptions of the food (diced, sliced, whole, etc.), and offer a recipe. When buying, suit the style of the food to the use: Why pay more for fancy whole tomatoes if they will be made into sauce?
– When buying "instants," and prepared foods, consider whether the extra cost is worth the time saved.
– Reject bulging or leaking cans; dented ones are all right provided they do not bulge or leak. Also reject soft or uneven packages of frozen food, ripped or torn packages of cereals, flours, pasta, breads, and crackers.
– When you discover a food that is

spoiled or less than top quality, return it to the grocer. Most markets welcome valid complaints because they are then able to trace and correct the difficulty.
– Hurry all food home, unload and store properly, using the following charts as guides.

About Storing Food in the Freezer

Note: Packaging and preparation tips are covered fully in the chapter on canning and freezing. Also what to do if the power should fail and freezer should be off for some hours.

General Tips:
– Check commercial frozen foods before storing, overwrapping any torn or damaged packages in foil or plastic food wrap.
– If package has been badly damaged and food exposed, use food as soon as possible.
– Date packages as they go into the freezer and use the oldest ones first.
– Update freezer inventory with every new addition.

About Storing Food in the Refrigerator

General Tips:
– Clean refrigerator out regularly, preferably before marketing.
– Store new supplies behind the old so the old will be used first.
– Group often used foods together in accessible spots. If possible, reserve a special corner for leftovers.
– *If power fails,* keep refrigerator door shut; food will remain cool several hours.

About Storing Meats, Poultry, Seafood:
– Never wash before storing.
– Always remove market wrapping from fresh uncooked meats, poultry, or seafood and *rewrap loosely* in wax paper or foil unless directed otherwise.
Exception: Prepackaged meats to be cooked within 2 days.
– Store in coldest part of refrigerator (it varies from model to model; check manufacturer's instruction booklet).

MAXIMUM RECOMMENDED STORAGE TIME FOR FROZEN FOODS AT 0° F.

Because the type of food and packaging and the number of times a freezer is opened all affect the keeping quality of frozen foods, storage times can only be approximate. Use foods *before* maximum time is up; they are unlikely to spoil immediately afterward, but their quality will deteriorate rapidly.

Food	Storage Time in months
Fresh, uncooked meats	
Beef, veal, lamb roasts, steaks, and chops	12
Ground beef, veal, lamb	4–6
Beef, veal, lamb liver, heart, and kidneys	3–4
Pork roasts, chops	4–6
Ground pork, fresh sausage meat	1–3
Pork liver	1–2
Smoked and Cured Meats	
Ham, slab bacon, frankfurters	1–3
Sausages	1–2
Cooked Meats	
Beef, veal, and lamb roasts	4–6
Pork roasts	2–4
Stews, meats in gravy or sauce, meat loaves and balls, meat pies, hash	2–4
Fresh, Uncooked Poultry	
Chicken	12
Turkey, duckling, goose, game birds	6
Giblets	2–3
Cooked Poultry	
Chicken	4–6
Turkey, duckling, goose	2–4
Fresh, Uncooked Seafood	
Lean, white fish	4–6
Oily, gamy fish	3–4
Shucked clams, oysters, scallops, shrimp	3–4
Cooked Seafood	
Fish (all kinds)	1–2
Crab and lobster meat	2–3
Shrimp	1–2
Shellfish in sauce (Newburg, thermidor, etc.)	1
Vegetables	12
Herbs	6
Dairy Products	
Butter	6–8
Cream (whipped)	3–4
Hard cheeses	6–8
Ice cream, sherbet, ices	1–2

Food	Storage Time in months
Margarine	12
Eggs (Yolks, Whites)	12
Breads	
Baked yeast breads and rolls	6–8
Baked quick breads	2–4
Sandwiches (avoid mayonnaise or cream cheese based spreads, jelly or hard-cooked-egg fillings)	2–3 weeks
Cakes and Cookies	
Baked cakes and cookies (unfrosted)	6–8
Baked cakes and cookies (frosted or filled)	2–4
Cookie Dough	2–4
Pastries	
Unbaked pie shells	6–8
Unbaked pies (fruit or mince)	6–8
Baked pies (fruit or mince)	2–4

Note: The storage chart includes only those homemade cakes and pastries suitable for home freezing. There are, of course, commercially frozen cheesecakes, cream and custard pies—silky-smooth ones—but food companies use stabilizers unavailable to the home cook.

About Storing Vegetables, Fruits:
– Wash only if chart recommends it.
– Unless chart directs otherwise, vegetables to be stored in the hydrator should be put in perforated plastic bags, those to be stored on shelves in plain plastic bags.

About Storing Leftover, Cooked Foods:
– Quick-cool hot food (in an ice or ice water bath) and package airtight.
– Remove any stuffing from meat, poultry, or seafood and wrap separately.
– Leftover canned foods can be covered and stored in the can 3–4 days,

MAXIMUM RECOMMENDED STORAGE TIME FOR REFRIGERATED FOOD

Note: Use following times as a guide only, checking highly perishable foods every day or so. Refrigerator load, how often door is opened, food packaging all affect storage time.

Food	Special Storage Tips	Storage Time
Fresh, Uncooked Meats		
Roasts		5 days
Steaks, chops		3–5 days
Ground meat, stew meat		2 days
Variety meats		1–2 days
Cured and Smoked Meats		
Ham (roasts), Bacon	Leave in original wrapper or wrap loosely in plastic food wrap. Store canned hams as labels direct.	1 week
Sliced ham, luncheon meats, sausages		2–3 days
Frankfurters		4–5 days
Cooked Meats, Leftovers		3–4 days

Food	Special Storage Tips	Storage Time
Fresh, Uncooked Poultry	Store giblets separately in a plastic bag.	2–3 days
Cooked Poultry, Leftovers	Remove stuffing and wrap airtight separately.	2 days
Fresh, Uncooked Seafood		
Fish	Clean and dress* before storing. Wrap loosely.	1–2 days
Live lobsters, crabs	Have claws pegged and animals packed in seaweed in double-thick moistureproof bag. Pop bundle into a large plastic bag and refrigerate. Do not cover animals with water; they will die.	6–8 hours
Shrimp	Store shelled or unshelled in plastic bags.	1–2 days
Clams, mussels, oysters, scallops	Store the unshucked in plastic bags, the shucked in their liquor in airtight containers.	1 day
Smoked and Pickled Fish		1–2 weeks
Cooked Seafood, Leftovers		1–2 days
Raw Vegetables		
Artichokes, beans, broccoli, Brussels sprouts, cauliflower, chayotes, eggplant, fennel, peas (in the pod), peppers	Remove any blemished leaves, stalks.	3–5 days
Asparagus	If limp, remove ½″ stems; stand in cold water 1 hour.	3–4 days
Beets, carrots, parsnips	Remove all but 1″ tops; rinse if dirty.	2 weeks
Cabbage, cardoons, celeriac, Celery	Remove blemished leaves, stalks; wash celery if dirty.	3–7 days
Corn on the cob	Store in the husk in plastic bags.	1 day
Cucumbers, summer squash	Wipe if very dirty.	1 week
Leeks, scallions, salsify	Trim roots, unusable tops; rinse salsify.	3–7 days
Lettuces, all salad greens, spinach, dark leafy greens	Wash and dry well. Do not break up salad greens until salad-making time.	3–8 days
Mushrooms	Do not trim or wipe; cover loosely.	1 week
New potatoes, breadfruit	*Note:* Potatoes need not be refrigerated, but cold storage makes them stay sweet longer.	1 week
Okra	Wash if very dirty; dry.	3–4 days
Plantain (dead ripe only)	*Note:* Ripen the green at room temperature.	1–2 days
Tomatoes (dead ripe only)	Store unwrapped, uncovered. *Note:* Slightly underripe tomatoes can be ripened in the refrigerator; takes 8–12 days.	2–3 days

Food	Special Storage Tips	Storage Time
Cooked Vegetables, Left-overs		2–4 days
Fresh, Ripe Fruits	(all except avocados, bananas, melons, pineapple, stored at room temperature)	
Berries	Discard bruised berries; cover loosely.	2–3 days
Soft fruits	Discard damaged fruits; cover loosely or store in perforated plastic bags.	3–7 days
Firm fruits	Same as for soft fruits.	1–2 weeks
Leftover Raw or Cooked Fruits	Store airtight.	3–5 days
Fruit Juices (fresh, canned, frozen)	Store in airtight containers.	5–7 days
Dairy Products		
Fresh milk, cream, buttermilk	Store in original or airtight nonmetal container.	3–4 days
Sour cream, yogurt	Same as for milk.	1 week
Canned milk	After opening, store covered in original container.	10 days
Cottage, cream, process cheese, spreads	Store airtight in original container.	1–3 weeks
Semi-hard and hard, mild and strong cheese	Butter cut edges to prevent drying; double wrap in foil or plastic food wrap. For long storage, wrap in vinegar-moistened cheesecloth (keep cloth moist). Cut off mold (it is harmless, merely unattractive).	3–9 months
Cheese scraps	Grate and store in an airtight jar.	2–3 weeks
Butter	Store in original wrapper in "butter keeper section."	1–2 weeks
Eggs		
Whole raw	Store small end down, covered, in egg keeper or carton.	10 days
Raw whites, broken eggs	Store in airtight nonmetal container.	1 week
Raw yolks	Cover with cool water and store in airtight jar.	2–3 days
Hard cooked	Store in the shell or shelled and individually wrapped in foil or plastic food wrap. Label eggs "cooked."	10 days
Miscellaneous Foods		
Brown sugar	To keep moist, store box in airtight plastic bag in hydrator.	3–6 months
Coffee (ground)	Store airtight in original can.	3–4 weeks
Custards	Quick-cool, cover, and refrigerate at once.	1 day
Custard and cream cakes and pies	Quick-cool, cover loosely with plastic food wrap, and refrigerate at once.	3–5 days

Food	Special Storage Tips	Storage Time
Drippings	Store in tightly covered can or jar.	2 months
Gravies, sauces	Quick-cool, cover, and refrigerate at once.	2–3 days
Lard	Store in original carton or wrapped airtight. *Note:* New types need no refrigeration; read label carefully.	2 weeks– 2 months
Maple syrup (genuine without preservative)	After opening, store airtight.	2–4 months
Margarine	Store in original wrapper.	2–4 weeks
Nuts (shelled)	Store in airtight jar.	3–4 months
Leftover cooked rice, cereal, pasta, puddings, gelatins	Cool rapidly and store tightly covered.	3–4 days
Relishes, ketchup, pickles, mayonnaise	After opening, store airtight.	2–3 months

About Storing Food in Cupboard or Pantry

"Pantry" is a marvelously old-fashioned word, calling to mind trips to Grandmother's house with its bright shelf parade of home-preserved foods. But a pantry is not a thing of the past. It is as essential today as a refrigerator or freezer. Ideally, it should be a step away from the kitchen—big and airy, reasonably cool, dry, and dark. Cupboard shelves, too, should be well ventilated, cool, dry, and dark.

General Tips:
– Keep pantry and cupboards scrupulously clean, protecting shelves with spill-resistant, easy-to-clean coated paper or vinyl shelf liners. Reline shelves frequently and in the interim wipe regularly with a weak vinegar-water solution to keep ants, roaches, and silverfish at bay.
– Check often for food spoilage (bulging or leaky cans, frothing bottles), for mice (tattered packages are a sure sign if there are also droppings), weevils, roaches, ants, or silverfish. *When Pests Attack:* Clear the shelves, destroying any infested foods (flours, cornstarch, cereals, nuts, raisins, and meals are favorite breeding grounds). Transfer uninfested foods to large screw-top jars (the quart and half-gallon preserving

jars are perfect for flours, meals, cereals, nuts, raisins, etc.). Burn old shelf liners; thoroughly vacuum floors, shelves, walls; spackle all holes, cracks, and crevices, then scrub down the entire pantry with the vinegar-water solution. Use an appropriate insecticide—*following label directions carefully*—then let pantry or cupboards stand open several days before restocking with food.
– Be especially selective about the shelf to be used for storing tea, coffee, flavorings, and leavenings. It should be extra cool, dry, and dark.
– When adding supplies to pantry or cupboard, place the new behind the old so that the old will be used first.
– Seal opened packages airtight (*bug-tight*), either by transferring contents to large preserving jars or by overwrapping in plastic bags and closing with rubber bands or "twisters."
– Get rid of market bags and cartons as soon as they're emptied. *Never* save, *never* store in cupboards. They're an open invitation to roaches, weevils, silverfish, ants. But most of all to roaches. These pests are fond of the glue used in manufacturing bags and cartons and females seek out the snug dark folds and crevices in which to lay their eggs. A market bag or carton, seemingly free of roaches, may in fact harbor hundreds of soon-to-hatch eggs.

SHELF LIFE OF PANTRY AND CUPBOARD ITEMS

Food	Special Storage Tips	Maximum Recommended Storage Time in a Cool, Dark, Dry Place
Canned Foods Fruits and vegetables	Cover and refrigerate after opening.	3 years
All other canned foods		1–2 years
Honey, Preserves, Jams, Jellies, Pickles, Condiments	Refrigerate pickles and condiments after opening.	1 year or more
Vinegar, Bottled Salad Dressings, Peanut Butter	Refrigerate salad dressings and peanut butter after opening.	6 months
Syrups, Molasses	Store tightly capped; discard if moldy.	Indefinitely
Vegetable Oil, Shortening	Store tightly capped; never refrigerate.	6–12 months
Freeze-Dried Foods	After opening, rewrap airtight or as label directs.	Indefinitely or as label states.
Dehydrated Foods (Milk, Potatoes, etc.)	Store in original packages, closing snugly after each use.	6 months
Dried Fruits, Vegetables, and Fish	After opening, store in airtight jars or overwrap package in plastic food wrap.	1 year or longer
Cereals, Pasta Breakfast cereals, Flour, corn meal, Pasta, cornstarch, Rice, wild rice	Tightly reseal after each use; for long storage, transfer to large screw-top jars.	2–3 months 2–3 months 3–6 months Indefinitely
Sugar Granulated, confectioners' Brown	Store airtight. Store in airtight canister with an apple slice; or store in refrigerator (see refrigerator storage chart).	3–6 months 3–6 months
Leavenings Baking powder, soda, cream of tartar Yeast (dried)	Store airtight away from stove or heat. Store airtight away from all heat.	6 months Until package expiration date

Food	Special Storage Tips	Maximum Recommended Storage Time in a Cool, Dark, Dry Place
Mixes (Cake, Cookie, Pudding, Soup)		6 months
Beverages		
Coffee beans	Store in airtight tin.	1 month
Coffee, ground	(See About Storing Food in the Refrigerator.)	
Instant, freeze-dried	Store airtight away from stove.	6 months; 3–4 weeks after opening
Tea	Store airtight away from stove.	1 year; 2–3 weeks after opening
Cocoa, drink mixes	Store airtight.	6 months
Nuts, etc.		
Unshelled nuts	Store in perforated plastic bags (for storage of *shelled nuts,* see About Storing Food in the Refrigerator).	6 months
Popcorn (Unpopped)	Store airtight.	1 year
Popcorn (Popped)	Store in plastic bags.	2 weeks
Coconut	Store airtight; refrigerate after opening.	6 months
Flavorings		
Extracts	Store tightly capped, away from stove.	6 months
Salt	Store *near* stove to help keep dry.	1 year or longer
Pepper	Use whole corns in pepper mill.	1 year or longer
Food Colorings	Store tightly capped.	1 year or longer
Breads (All Kinds)	Store in original wrapper or plastic food wrap in ventilated breadbox.	2–4 days
Crackers (All Kinds)	Store tightly sealed in original package or in airtight canisters.	1–2 months
Cakes and Cookies	See cake and cookie chapters for storage details.	
Pies and Pastries	Store loosely covered with foil or plastic food wrap in a pie saver. (*Note:* Custard and cream pies and pastries must be refrigerated.)	3–4 days

Food	Special Storage Tips	Maximum Recommended Storage Time in a Cool, Dark, Dry Place
Vegetables		
Dasheens	Store in perforated boxes or	1 week
Kohlrabi	bins in a very cool, dark, dry	2 weeks
Onions	place with plenty of air cir-	1–4 weeks
Potatoes (Irish)	culating. Check vegetables	1 month
Potatoes (sweet), yams	frequently and discard any	1 week
Pumpkin, rutabaga	that are sprouting or soften-	1 month
Turnips	ing.	1 week
Winter squash		1–3 weeks

The Herb and Spice Shelf

Man has always cherished herbs and spices. Squabbled and fought over them, too. And journeyed to the ends of the earth. The discovery of America, everyone knows, was a happy accident; what Columbus was really after was a direct sea route to the spice treasures of the East.

To primitive man, herbs and spices were magic plants possessing powers of creation, regeneration, and immortality. Much later, kings counted their wealth in peppercorns, gladiators munched fennel to bolster their courage, and prophets wore crowns of laurel to sharpen their "vision." Up until the Middle Ages, mothers strung necklaces of cloves for their children to keep evil spirits away and tucked sprigs of dill in their own buttonholes Still later, Englishmen devoured pounds of sage each spring, believing "He that would live for aye must eat sage in May."

Today we attribute no magic to herbs and spices other than their power to uplift mundane fare. What are these aromatics so indispensable to mankind? What, in fact, is an herb? A spice? Generally speaking, an herb is the leaf of tender, fragrant annuals and biennials that grow in temperate climates. Spices are the more pungent roots, barks, stems, buds, fruits, and leaves of tropical or subtropical plants, usually perennials. Crossing boundaries are the aromatic seeds, produced by both herb and spice plants.

Some General Tips on Buying, Storing, and Using Herbs and Spices

– Buy in small amounts and store no longer than 1 year; flavors fade fast. Toss stale herbs onto hearth or charcoal fires to scent the air.

– Try using whole spices, grinding or grating them as needed. They are far more aromatic than the preground. Whole spices can also be used to season soups, stocks, and stews. You'll need about 1½ times more whole spices than ground, so adjust recipe accordingly. Tie spices in cheesecloth and simmer along with soup or stew or whatever, then lift out before serving.

– Store herbs and spices tightly capped away from direct sunlight in a cool, dry place.

– Use herbs and spices sparingly, discriminatingly, never combining too many in a single recipe. Be particularly cautious about hot peppers.

– Crush dried herbs between your fingers as you add; body heat will intensify their flavor. Always taste for seasoning *after* herbs or spices have been warmed through.

– If an herb or spice is unfamiliar, taste *before* adding. The best way—though you may not want to go to the trouble—is to blend with a little softened cream cheese or butter, then to let stand at room temperature several minutes so that the seasoning's flavor will develop fully.

– When herbs or spices are being added "cold" to cold dishes—dips and spreads, for example—allow flavors to mature and ripen about ½ hour at room tem-

perature before serving. Or warm the
seasoning in a little butter over low
heat before adding—especially advisable
for raw-tasting chili and curry powders.
– Use fresh herbs as often as possible;
they are so much more fragrant than
the dry and are being stocked in greater
and greater variety by big city grocers.
Better still, grow your own (tips for
growing and using fresh herbs are included at the end of this section).
– Use a light hand with garlic powders
and juices; they gather strength on the
shelf. Remember, too, that a crushed
clove of garlic has 2–3 times the impact
of a minced one.

– *If a dish is overseasoned, try one or
more of the following remedies:*
• Strain out bits of herb or spice.
• Simmer a raw, peeled, quartered potato in mixture 10–15 minutes, then
remove; it will absorb some of the excess
flavor.
• Reduce amount of salt (if it has not
already been added) and stir in a little
sugar or brown sugar.
• Thicken gravy or stew with a flour or
cornstarch and water paste.
• If mixture is overly sweet, sharpen
with about 1 teaspoon lemon juice or
vinegar.
• Serve mixture well chilled; cold numbs
the palate.
• Prepare a second batch—*unseasoned*—
and combine with the first.

– *When making recipes in quantity, adjust seasonings as follows:*

Quantity Being Made	Herb and Spice Adjustment
2 times the recipe	Use 1½ times amounts called for
3 times the recipe	Use 2 times amounts called for
4 times the recipe	Use 2½ times amounts called for

AN HERB AND SPICE CHART

Note: Because detailed herb and spice uses are included in the Seasoning Charts in the Meat, Poultry, Seafood, Game, and Vegetable chapters, suggestions here will be general.

Herb or Spice	Description	Popular Forms	Essential to		Easy to Grow
			Basic Herb/Spice Shelf	Gourmet Herb/Spice Shelf	
Allspice	*Spice.* Berry of a Caribbean tree with combined flavor of cinnamon, cloves, and nutmeg. Use primarily for cakes, cookies, pies, puddings, breads.	Dried whole; powdered	X	X	
Anise	*Aromatic seed.* Licorice-flavored cousin to the carrot; used in candies, liqueurs, Scandinavian and German breads, pastries, cookies, beef stews.	Dried whole; powdered		X	
Basil	*Herb.* Bitter, clove-flavored relative of mint. Good with any tomato dish, especially Italian.	Dried crushed or ground leaves; fresh	X	X	X
Bay leaves (Laurel)	*Herb.* Woodsy, faint flavor of cinnamon-sarsaparilla; bitter when overused; good with veal, fowl, fish.	Dried whole; powdered	X	X	
Capers	*Herb.* Tart flower buds of Mediterranean caper bush; superb with eggs, seafood, veal, tomatoes. Choicest are tiny, tender *nonpareil.*	Pickled or brined whole		X	
Cardamom	*Spice.* Lemony-gingery seeds, especially popular in Scandinavia for breads, cakes, cookies.	Dried whole; powdered		X	
Caraway	*Aromatic seed.* Delicately licorice, nutty. Used in rye bread, German and Nordic cheeses; good with cabbage and sauerkraut.	Whole dry seeds		X	

53

AN HERB AND SPICE CHART (continued)

Herb or Spice	Description	Popular Forms	Essential to Basic Herb/Spice Shelf	Essential to Gourmet Herb/Spice Shelf	Easy to Grow
Celery seed	*Aromatic seed.* Concentrated celery flavor.	Whole dry seeds; powdered	X	X	
Chervil	*Herb.* Delicate, sweet, parsley-licorice flavor; component of *fines herbes*. Excellent with seafood, green salads.	Dried whole or ground leaves; fresh		X	X
Chives	*Herb.* The most delicate onion; wispy green tops; all-purpose herb for savory dishes.	Minced dried, frozen, freeze-dried; fresh	X	X	X
Cinnamon	*Spice.* Sweet, slightly "hot" bark of the cassia tree. Used primarily for cookies, cakes, pies, puddings, spicy beverages.	Sticks; powdered	X	X	
Cloves	*Spice.* Pungent flower buds of the clove tree. Used mainly in cakes, pies, puddings, spicy sauces and drinks.	Whole dried buds; powdered	X	X	
Coriander	*Aromatic seed.* Nutty seed of a plant of the parsley family; principal seasoning of Latin American sausages, meat dishes. Fresh leaves *(cilantro)* also used.	Whole dried seeds; powdered		X	
Cumin	*Aromatic seed.* Similar to caraway but more medicinal; one of the chief ingredients of chili and curry powders. Good with cabbage, sauerkraut, in meat loaves.	Whole dry seeds; powdered		X	
Dill	*Herb.* Lemony-tart; enhances seafoods, egg and cheese dishes, salads, cucumbers, tomatoes.	Dried whole and powdered seeds; weed (dried leaves); fresh	X	X	X

Name	Description	Forms available			
Fennel (Finocchio)	*Herb.* Feathery, faintly licorice member of the parsley family. Superb with seafood; a favorite Scandinavian flavoring for sweet breads, pastries, cakes, cookies.	Dried whole and powdered seeds, leaves; fresh bulbs		X	X
Fenugreek	*Aromatic seed.* Bitter red-brown seeds with a burnt sugar taste. A component of curry powder, imitation maple flavoring, chutney.	Whole dry seeds; powdered		X	
Filé powder	*Herb.* Dried sassafras leaves; flavor woodsy, root beer-like. Used to flavor and thicken gumbos, other Creole dishes.	Powder		X	X
Garlic	See Specialty Onions (vegetable chapter).	Fresh bulbs; powder; salt; juice	X	X	
Geranium	*Herb.* Many flavors (rose, lemon, apple), all good in confactions, jellies, fruit compotes. A particularly fragrant, pretty garnish.	Fresh potted plants		X	X
Ginger	*Spice.* Biting but sweet root of an Asian plant. One of the most versatile spices, essential to Oriental sweet-sour dishes, pickles, cakes, cookies, pies.	Dried whole and cracked roots; crystallized; preserved; powdered; fresh	X	X	
Horseradish	*Herb.* Peppery white root with a turnip-like flavor. Used primarily to add zip to sauces, dips, spreads, salad dressings.	Prepared (bottled); fresh	X	X	
Juniper	*Aromatic berry.* Dried, smoky-blue, resinous, bitter-sweet berry of the juniper bush. Used to flavor gin, game, salmon, goose, duck, pork.	Dried whole berries		X	X
Lemon verbena	*Herb.* Sweet lemon-flavored leaves; best used to flavor or garnish fruit salads, desserts.	Fresh potted plants		X	X

AN HERB AND SPICE CHART (continued)

| Herb or Spice | Description | Popular Forms | Essential to | | Easy to Grow |
			Basic Herb/Spice Shelf	Gourmet Herb/Spice Shelf	
Mace	*Spice.* Fibrous husk of nutmeg; flavor similar but milder. All-purpose spice, equally at home in savory and sweet dishes.	Dried blades; powdered	X	X	
Marjoram	*Herb.* Mild cousin of oregano with musky-mellow, almost nutty bouquet. Particularly good with veal, lamb, fowl, potatoes, and tomatoes.	Dried whole leaves; powdered	X	X	X
Mint	*Herb.* More than 30 varieties: peppermint and spearmint (the two most popular), apple, lemon and orange, etc. Best in jellies, confections, fruit salads, and desserts, as a pretty, perky garnish.	Whole, crushed and powdered dried leaves; as extracts, oils; fresh	X	X	X
Mustard	*Spice.* Bitter and biting; *two main types* are relatively mild *White* and extra-strong *Brown* or *Oriental.* Used primarily in zippy sauces, pickles, salad dressings, deviled foods. Of the prepared, the Dijon-type, made with wine, is considered choicest.	Whole dried or powdered seeds; variety of prepared (bottled) blends.	X	X	X
Nasturtium	*Herb.* Leaves of the popular flower, peppery and tart, not unlike watercress. Use in salads. Blossoms also good in salads, as garnishes.	Fresh		X	X
Nutmeg	*Spice.* Mellow, sweet-nutty seed of the nutmeg tree. Like mace, an all-purpose spice, equally good with sweets and meats, fruits and vegetables.	Dried whole seeds; ground	X	X	
Oregano	*Herb.* Wild marjoram with a bitter, marigold-like flavor. An Italian favorite for spaghetti sauces, pizza, other tomato-rich dishes.	Dried whole or crushed leaves; powdered	X	X	X

	Description	Form available			
Paprika	*Spice.* Ground dried pods of fleshy, mild-to-slightly-hot Capsicum peppers, native to Latin America but now the soul of Hungarian cooking. The Hungarian sweet rose paprika is the reddest, sweetest, mildest. *Note:* All paprika is extremely high in vitamin C.	Ground	X	X	
Parsley	*Herb.* There are dozens of varieties, but the two most popular are the curly and the somewhat stronger Italian or plain-leaf. A multipurpose herb, a component of *fines herbes* and *bouquet garni.*	Fresh; flakes (dried leaves)	X	X	X
Pepper (true)	*Spice.* "The Master Spice," once as rare and costly as gold. There are three types, all from the same tropical vine: the pungent *BLACK* (dried, unhusked, immature berries), the milder *WHITE* (dried inner white cores of ripe berries), and the *GREEN* (unripe whole berries). The white is preferable for seasoning light soups and sauces, the green for those who want a less peppery black pepper.	Black dried peppercorns; cracked, ground, seasoned, and lemon-flavor black pepper; whole and ground white pepper; whole dried and liquid-packed green peppercorns		X	
Peppers (Capsicums)	*Spice.* Not true peppers but a large group of New World pods called "peppers" by Columbus because they were as fiery as the Indian pepper. Capsicums are both red and green, mild and hot (the hot are collectively called *Chili Peppers*). There are dozens of Capsicums, all important to Latin American cuisine, but the following are the most available. *Popular Red Peppers:* *Cayenne* (ground hot red pepper); plump, sweet, scarlet *Ancho;* sharper, browner, elongated *Mulato;* long skinny, torrid *Pasilla;* and the tiny incendiary *Pequin.* *Popular Green Peppers:* The superhot *Serrano* and *Jalapeño* and the milder, though sometimes hot *Poblano.*	Ground (cayenne); crushed and whole dried pods; canned and pickled whole pods; fresh whole pods; liquid hot red pepper seasoning *CAUTION:* Never rub eyes when working with hot peppers — pain is excruciating. Always wash hands well when preparations are done. (*Note:* To "cool" hot peppers, rinse well, remove seeds, stems, veins, then soak 1 hour in lightly salted cold water.)	X	X	

57

AN HERB AND SPICE CHART (continued)

Herb or Spice	Description	Popular Forms	Essential to		Easy to Grow
			Basic Herb/Spice Shelf	Gourmet Herb/Spice Shelf	
Poppy seed	*Aromatic seed.* Tiny, nutty, silver-blue seeds of the poppy (they contain no opium). Good in breads, pastries, cakes, salads, with noodles.	Whole seeds		X	
Rocket (rugula)	See Other Salad Greens in the salad chapter.	Fresh			X
Rosemary	*Herb.* Heady, lemony-resinous, needle-like leaves. Good with lamb, green peas, pork.	Dried whole or powdered leaves		X	X
Saffron	*Spice.* Expensive, dried orange stigmas of the saffron crocus. (It takes 225,000 hand-plucked stigmas to yield 1 pound, hence the high price). Flavor is medicinal, the key seasoning of Paella, Spanish breads, cakes, *To Use:* Soak strands in tepid water, then use this infusion to flavor and color recipes.	Dried whole stigmas; powdered		X	
Sage	*Herb.* Musky, lime-scented silver-green leaves; the identifiable herb of poultry seasoning and stuffings.	Dried whole, crushed and powdered leaves	X	X	X
Savory	*Herb.* There are two savories, the delicate, aromatic *Summer Savory* and the more bitter *Winter Savory*. The *Summer* is the better herb, especially delicious with eggs and cheese.	Dried whole and powdered leaves		X	X
Sesame seed (benne)	*Aromatic seed.* Small flat pearly seeds, nutty with a tinge of bitterness. Good in breads and pastries, toasted in salads. (*Note:* These stale and go rancid quite rapidly; buy as needed.) *To Toast:* Warm uncovered in piepan 10-15 minutes at 350° F., stirring often until golden, or 1-2 minutes in a heavy skillet over moderate heat.	Whole seeds		X	

Name	Description	Available forms			
Shallots	See Specialty Onions (vegetable chapter).	Fresh	X		
Tarragon	*Herb.* Succulent, licorice-flavored green leaves. Superlative with seafood, eggs, crisp green salads. Component of *fines herbes*.	Dried whole and powdered leaves; fresh sprigs	X	X	X
Thyme	*Herb.* All-round meat, fowl and fish herb with a vaguely minty, vaguely tea-like flavor. Customarily included in a *bouquet garni*. Particularly fragrant is lemon thyme.	Whole dried or powdered leaves	X	X	X
Turmeric	*Spice.* Deep yellow-orange root of an Asian plant related to ginger. Dried and ground, it becomes an integral part of curry powder, the "yellow" of mustard. Turmeric alone has a thin, flat, medicinal taste. Used primarily in pickles, chutneys, curries.	Powdered	X		
Vanilla bean	*Aromatic seed capsule.* Long black seed pod of a wild Mexican orchid, sweet and perfume-like.	Beans; extract	X	X	
Woodruff	*Herb.* Sweet-musky woodland herb, the leaves of which are used in the *Maibowle* (Rhine wine afloat with strawberries).	Fresh	X	X	

Some Less Used Herbs and Spices

Achiote: Small red seeds of a Latin American tree similar to and and used as a substitute for saffron in Mexican cooking.

Angelica: Sweet, succulently stalked member of the parsley family, most often available candied and used as a decoration in confectionery.

Borage: Medicinal-tasting European herb used in teas and other beverages.

Burnet: A leafy cucumber-flavored herb, excellent in salads.

Costmary: Minty but bitter herb used in making ale; good used *sparingly* in salads.

Horehound: A bitter herb aromatic of tobacco, once popular for flavoring candies and cough drops.

Hyssop: An astringent variety of mint used in liqueurs; scatter a few leaves into green salads for bite.

Lavender: "The old ladies' herb," the clean and lemony perfumer of bureaus and closets. Few people cook with lavender, but a leaf or two, minced into a fruit cup or salad, injects a pleasing, elusive scent.

Lemon balm: Crisp lemony-minty leaves that double nicely for mint.

Lovage: A celery-flavored herb, particularly compatible with fowl and game.

Marigold: The pungent garden variety; use sparingly to pep up salads, poultry stuffings. The flower stamens can be dried and substituted for saffron.

Rose hips: The tart, crab-apple-like fruit of the rose; delicious boiled into jelly or minced into venison or rabbit stews. Extremely high in vitamin C.

Rue: An old-fashioned acrid herb used in minute quantities to perk up fruit cups and salads.

Sweet cicely: A kind of chervil often— but erroneously—called myrrh because both have a faintly licorice-parsley flavor. True myrrh is an aromatic gum.

Sweet flag: An iris with cinnamon-and-ginger-flavored rhizomes used in seasoning confections and puddings.

The Herb Blends

Bouquet garni: A bouquet of herbs— fresh parsley and thyme plus a bay leaf —bundled together, simmered in soups, stews, stocks, or other liquid recipes, then fished out before serving. The French way to prepare the bouquet is to wrap the parsley around the two other herbs, but Americans may prefer to tie all three in a tiny cheesecloth bag (imperative, by the way, if dry spices are used so that they don't float out and overseason the dish). A bouquet garni may contain other seasoners—a celery stalk, perhaps, a garlic clove— but it must begin with parsley, thyme, and bay leaf. Food companies now market dried blends called *bouquet garni* which should be used as labels direct.

Fines herbes: A French favorite— minced fresh or dried chervil, tarragon, parsley, chives, and sometimes basil, sage, marjoram, fennel, or oregano employed as a multipurpose seasoner. Particularly good in salads. Now available bottled.

Poultry seasoning: All the good poultry and poultry stuffing seasoners—sage, marjoram, powdered onion, pepper, and sometimes thyme—premixed and ready to use.

The Spice Blends

Barbecue spice: Zippy blend of chili peppers, cumin, garlic, cloves, paprika, sugar, and salt created specifically for barbecued foods but also good mixed into salad dressings, meat loaves and patties, egg, cheese, and potato dishes.

Charcoal seasoning: A smoky mix of powdered charcoal, herbs, spices, salt, and sometimes sugar and monosodium glutamate designed to impart a charcoal-broiled flavor.

Chili powder: Ground chili peppers, cumin seeds, oregano, garlic, salt, and occasionally cloves, allspice, and onion

—the staples of Mexican and Tex-Mex cooking.

Cinnamon sugar: Simply that, cinnamon and sugar premixed and ready to sprinkle onto hot buttered toast, waffles, pancakes, or fresh-from-the-oven breads.

Crab boil (*shrimp spice*): Peppercorns, crumbled bay leaves, dried red peppers, mustard seeds, chips of dried ginger, and other whole spices suitable for seasoning boiled crab and shrimp.

Curry powder: An Occidental invention; Indian cooks would never dream of using curry powder, but grind their own spices, varying the combinations according to the food to be curried. Commercial curry powders contain as many as 16 to 20 spices, predominantly cinnamon, cloves, cumin, fenugreek, ginger, turmeric, red and black pepper, the quantity of pepper determining the curry's "hotness."

Tip: When adding curry powder to a cold dish (such as a dip or spread), always warm it a few minutes first in butter over low heat to mellow the "raw" taste.

A HOMEMADE CURRY POWDER

Makes about ¼ cup

2 tablespoons ground coriander
1 tablespoon ground turmeric
1 teaspoon each ground cumin,
*   fenugreek, ginger, and allspice*
½ teaspoon each ground mace and
*   crushed dried hot red chili peppers*
¼ teaspoon each powdered mustard
*   and black pepper*

Work all ingredients together in a mortar and pestle until well blended. Store airtight.

Curry paste: A blend of curry powder, ghee (clarified butter), and vinegar available in gourmet shops. Use in place of curry powder, allowing about 1–2 tablespoons paste to season a curry for 6 persons.

Pickling spice: Mixture of mustard and coriander seeds, white and black peppercorns, whole cloves and allspice, whole hot red chili peppers, broken cinnamon sticks and bay leaves, chunks of gingerroot; versatile enough to use for a variety of pickles, preserves, and condiments.

Pie spices:

Apple pie spice: Blend of cinnamon, nutmeg, and sometimes allspice.

Pumpkin pie spice: Mixture of cinnamon, ginger, nutmeg, allspice, and cloves.

Pizza spice: A garlicky, oniony blend similar to Barbecue spice compounded specifically for pizza toppings.

Quatre-épices: A French blend of 4 spices—cloves, ginger, nutmeg, and white pepper—used as an all-purpose seasoner for meats and vegetables, soups and sauces. *To Make:* Mix together 5 tablespoons ground cloves and 3 tablespoons *each* ground ginger, nutmeg, and white pepper. Store airtight. Particularly good on carrots, turnips, and parsnips, broiled steaks and chops.

Seasoned salt: The formula varies from processor to processor, but essentially an aromatic blend of salt, spices, and herbs that can be used as an all-purpose seasoning.

Some Herb and Spice Substitutions

Because a number of herbs and spices taste somewhat the same, the following can be interchanged in a pinch (substitute measure for measure):

Herbs
Basil and Oregano
Caraway and Anise
Celery Seeds and Minced Celery Tops
Chervil and Parsley
Chervil and Tarragon
Fennel and Anise
Fennel and Tarragon
Oregano and Marjoram
Sage and Thyme

Spices
Allspice and *equal parts* Cinnamon,
    Cloves, and Nutmeg

Chili Peppers and Cayenne
Commercial Curry Powder and
   Homemade Curry Powder
Nutmeg and Mace

About Other Additives

Monosodium glutamate (MSG; the
ajinomoto of Japanese cuisine): Neither
herb nor spice, this white crystalline
vegetable extract must nonetheless be
included because of its popularity as a
flavor enhancer. Long an Oriental
standby, it is tasteless, yet has the mysterious power of freshening and developing other foods' flavors. *Note:* MSG has
recently come under medical scrutiny,
some researchers believing overdoses
cause giddiness, fainting spells.

Meat tenderizers: These are discussed
fully in the meat chapter (see The Ways
of Tenderizing Meat).

About Growing Herbs at Home

Herbs are easy to grow, even on apartment window sills, provided their pots
are big enough. Mini hothouse sets won't
do except for sprouting seeds. Those
herbs particularly suited to home growing are so marked in the Herb and Spice
Chart.

Successful herb gardening is a vast and
complex subject, requiring a book in itself. What we include here—in a most
general way—are growing tips applicable to the majority of herbs. Persons
seriously interested in growing herbs can
obtain firsthand advice from county
agricultural extension agents, local nurs-
ery and botanical garden staffs.

Some General Herb-Growing Tips:
– Transplant seedlings when they're
about 2″ high and their leaves are turning a hearty green. Pick a sunny patch
of ground, preferably one that will be
shaded part of the day.
– Allow plenty of space between plants,
especially important with such ramblers
as mint and tarragon, which will quickly
overrun pot or yard.

– When using pots, choose big ones
(about 6″ across the top), made of clay
or other porous material. Drop about 1″
coarse gravel or ceramic chips into the
bottoms to ensure good drainage, then
fill with moderately rich soil; the commercial "planting mix" works well for
most herbs.
– Root herbs in pots or ground, not too
deep or they will die, then loosely pack
damp soil around stems. Water lightly.
– Stand potted herbs in a bright window, eastern exposure if possible, so that
plants will catch the early morning light
but be spared the searing noonday sun.
Herbs in southern windows may need to
be shaded part of the day; watch closely
for signs of "burning" or browning.
– Water herbs whenever soil *feels* dry,
hosing liberally with a fine spray or, in
the case of potted herbs, adding water
from the top until it trickles through to
the saucer below. *Note:* If more than
¼″ water accumulates in a saucer, tip
out; herbs do not like their feet wet.
Above all, beware of overwatering; it's
more likely to kill than underwatering.
– About every week to 10 days, spray
herb foliage lightly with water.
– Keep an eagle eye out for aphids (pale,
wingless, pinhead-size insects), which
are fond of tender-sweet herbs like
tarragon and chervil, also for equally
small and pesky white flies which prefer
basil. The best way to keep both at bay
is by rinsing herbs frequently with cool
water, paying particular attention to the
undersides of leaves where the insects
gather to lay eggs. Insecticides are risky
from a plant as well as a human
standpoint. Delicate herbs simply cannot
withstand repeated sprayings. Use
insecticides only as a last resort, choosing
those safe for food crops, administering
with utmost caution and following label
directions to the letter.
– To prolong the growing season of
annuals, nip off flower buds as they
appear.
– Thin herbs as needed, transplanting
"weeded out" plants in separate pots or
plots where they will have plenty of
growing room.

About Using Fresh Herbs:

— Cut and use herbs often; snipping promotes growth. To cut, reach down near the soil and snip each stalk separately with scissors. Resist the temptation (especially strong with chives) to shear the tops right off in a crew cut. Also avoid cutting too deeply into woody stems. (*Note:* Herbs are said to be at their headiest just before blooming, also early in the day when touched with dew. *But* herbs are rarely used first thing in the mornng, so it makes more sense to cut them when they are needed.)

— Wash herbs gently, swishing them up and down in cool water, then drain, shaking lightly or patting dry on paper toweling.

— Mince herbs as they are needed and in quantities needed. If herbs are tender, mince stems and all; otherwise, use the leaves only. Wispy herbs like dill, chives, and fennel are most efficiently minced by gathering a dozen or so strands or tops together, then snipping straight across with scissors. A chopping knife makes short shrift of larger, coarser herbs.

— To store unused fresh herbs, wrap stalks loosely in damp paper toweling and tuck into the hydrator or stand stalks upright in ¼″ cold water in a wide-mouth preserving jar, screw on lid and refrigerate. (*Note:* Minced herbs store poorly; better to freeze them—see About Freezing Herbs in the chapter on canning and freezing.)

— When substituting fresh herbs for the dry, double or triple the quantity called for, tasting as you add until the flavors seem well balanced. Fresh herbs are far more subtle than the dry.

How to Dry Fresh Herbs:

— Pick prime leaves, preferably just before herbs bloom and early in the morning as soon as the dew has evaporated.

— Wash herbs gently and pat dry on paper toweling.

— Spread out on a cheesecloth-covered cookie rack and dry outdoors in a warm shady spot (bring inside at night), in a dry, airy room *or* in a 200° F. oven. Drying times will vary according to humidity and herb variety; test leaves often for crumbliness.

— When herbs are dry and crumbly, remove any twigs and stems and pack leaves whole in airtight jars. Or, if you prefer, crush with a rolling pin between sheets of wax paper, then bottle airtight.

CHAPTER 4

MENU PLANNING, TABLE SETTING, AND SERVICE

Keeping menus varied and nutritious, at the same time pleasing the family without shattering the budget, is not as complicated as it may seem. Planning meals is rather like mastering a formula in that, once the technique is learned, it becomes automatic. Here, then, are the rules.

Points to Consider in Planning Menus

Plan Ahead: Work out several days' menus at a time (a week's, if possible) so that you can vary foods from meal to meal and day to day, take advantage of local or seasonal "specials," do the major marketing in a single trip, and use leftovers ingeniously. You'll save time and money.

Balance Meals Nutritionally: Think of each meal in relation to the other two of the day so that the quota of Basic Four Food Groups is met. Bear in mind, too, any dietary problems—diabetes (low carbohydrate diet), high blood pressure, or heart disease (often necessitating a low-cholesterol diet), obesity (low-calorie diet), and food allergies. (Read the information on nutrition, Eat Well, Keep Well, in the Appendix.)

Stick to the Budget: Shop prudently so the family will eat well *throughout* the week, "well" meaning happily, heartily, and wholesomely. On a tight budget meats are the first to go. High protein foods, of course, are essential to good health. If bargain meats are beyond the budget, substitute such protein-rich foods as dried peas, beans, lentils, and cheese.

Few meats are actually bargains, but in most areas and seasons, chicken, turkey, pork, and ham cost less than beef, veal, and lamb. Best buys, invariably, are organ meats—chicken or turkey gizzards (sometimes mere pennies a pound), pork liver, beef heart. Hamburger is a good buy, too, not because it's cheap but because it can be stretched so easily with cereal, bread crumbs, pasta, and rice, which *are*. Bony, gristly cuts are usually economical—beef or lamb shanks, oxtail, pigs' feet. Well prepared, they are also tender and savory.

Abide by Family Likes and Dislikes: No point in buying what the family won't eat. Each family member no doubt has idiosyncrasies, and though it's impossible to delight everyone at every meal, you can avoid those foods any member dislikes intensely and include each week one of his favorites. This same common sense applies to party menus. Unless you know your guests' tastes to be sophisticated, don't startle them with raw pickled fish or a heady tripe stew. Stick to the reliables—beef, poultry, pork, and ham—but prepare them new ways. Another important company dinner consideration is any physical or religious dietary restrictions guests may have. Ask and plan accordingly (see Some Dietary Taboos).

Consider the Season: Not only because of the availability and economy of foods in season but also because of the weather's affect on appetites. Cold weather sharpens them, hot weather just the reverse. Winter meals, thus, can be heavier, spicier than summer meals. And, of course, hotter.

Suit the Meal to the Occasion: Folksy foods—meat loaves, pasta, thick vegetable-strewn soups—are perfect for family or informal suppers; dressy dinners demand something more elegant, a roast fowl, perhaps, a delicately sauced fish, or a wine-laced French stew. For a buffet, food should be bite-size or at least tender enough to cut with a fork. No one wants to tackle an unboned piece of chicken or a not so tender chop while balancing a plate on his lap.

Be Artistic: The look of a meal counts as much as the taste because, no matter how beautifully cooked, an all-white or all-brown meal comes off badly. It *looks* drab. Think of a menu as an artist does a canvas, assembling a variety of colors and textures, shapes and flavors into a pleasing whole. Avoid too many rich foods within a meal or too many bland, too many spicy or too many insipid, too many tart or too many sweet. Strike for balance and harmony.

SOME DIETARY TABOOS

Faith	Forbidden foods
Catholic (Continental U.S. Only)	Meat or poultry on Ash Wednesday or Good Friday
Eastern Orthodox	Meat or poultry on *any* Wednesday or Friday or during Lent
Orthodox Jewish	Any nonkosher meat or fowl, any animal blood, eggs with blood spots Pork, ham, or pork products (lard, etc.) Shellfish, snails, eels, turtles Birds of prey, scavengers, rabbit Meat and dairy foods at the same meal Canned milk, salted butter (not customary, though not actually forbidden)
Moslem	Pork, alcohol. Certain sects also prohibit the eating of beef and beef products.
Hindu	Beef, veal, pork, fertile eggs. Hindu vegetarians are forbidden all meat, fish, fowl, and eggs. Some are so strict they will eat neither blood-colored vegetables nor those that grow underground because a worm or other small animal may have been injured as the vegetable was uprooted.
Vegetarian	Strict vegetarians refuse all animal foods (meat, fowl, fish, eggs, milk, cheese, etc.). The less strict will eat dairy products.

Note: The best policy, always, is to ask the prospective guest in advance what foods he is denied, thereby saving embarrassment all around.

MENUS FOR MOST OCCASIONS

Note: In the Menus That Follow, Any Dish Marked with an asterisk (*) Is In-cluded in the Recipe Sections of the Book. For Page Numbers, See the Index.

FOUR SUNDAY BREAKFASTS

Orange Juice
Panfried Canadian Bacon*
Apple Pancakes* with Butterscotch Syrup*
Old-Fashioned Hot Chocolate*   Coffee

Broiled Grapefruit*
Broiled Sausage*   Egg in a Nest*
Buttered Toast   Peach Preserves
Milk   Coffee

Fresh Sliced Peaches
Benedict-Style Eggs*
Blueberry Muffins*
Maple Milk*   Milk   Coffee

Fresh Fruit Cocktail
Kedgeree*
Bannocks*
Old-Fashioned Apple Jelly*
Milk   Tea   Coffee

MORNING COFFEE

Coffees, like teas, can be plain or fancy. If the group is small, keep the menu short and limit the choice of breads to 2 or 3. If the group is large, offer a greater variety, perhaps 4–5 breads and 2 cakes.

BASIC MENU PATTERN

Fresh Fruit Juice
An Assortment of Breads and Cakes
Jams   Jellies   Preserves   Honey   Butter
Coffee   Hot Chocolate and/or Tea
Cream   Milk   Sugar

For Simple Coffees: Choose 1 item from 2 different columns below.
For Elaborate Coffees: Choose 1 bread, 2–3 sweet breads, and 1 cake, varying the flavors and textures.

Breads	*Sweet Breads*	*Cakes*
Any Muffins	Any Coffee Cake	Any Upside-Down Cake
Brioche*	Any Fruit Nut Bread	Applesauce Cake*
Croissants*	Cinnamon Raisin Pinwheels*	Gingerbread*
Sally Lunn*	Danish Pastry*	Pound Cake*
Toast or any Sweet	Hot Cross Buns*	Orange, Date, and Nut Loaf*
or Spicy Toast	Old-Fashioned Yeast-Raised	Spice Cake*
Toasted English Muffins	Doughnuts*	Real Sponge Cake* (baked
	Panettone*	in muffin pans as cupcakes)
	Stollen*	

TWO WINTER BRUNCHES

Bloody Marys*   Tomato Juice
Sausage Ring* Filled with Scrambled Eggs*
Baked Mushroom Caps Stuffed with Hazelnuts*
Hilda's Yorkshire Scones*   Peach Preserves
Coffee   Tea

———

Whiskey Sours*   Fruit Juices
Creamed Finnan Haddie* in Puff Pastry Shells
Braised Chicken Livers with Parsley Gravy*
Baked Tomatoes*
Coffee   Cocoa   Tea

———

TWO SUMMER BRUNCHES

Orange Blossoms*   Screwdrivers*
Chicken Mayonnaise*
Cold Sliced Smithfield Ham   Baking Powder Biscuits*
Old-Fashioned Applesauce*   Pickled Peaches*
Cucumber Aspic*
Hot Coffee   Iced Coffee

———

Chilled Champagne   Chilled Dry Sherry
Honeydew Melon Wedges
Turkey and Mushroom Crepes*
Chilled Salmon Mousse*   Sauce Verte*
Zucchini in À La Grecque Marinade*
Bakery Croissants
Hot Coffee   Iced Coffee   Hot Tea   Iced Tea

A LADIES' WINTER LUNCHEON

Fresh Tomato Soup*
Quiche Bourbonnaise*
Asparagus Vinaigrette*
Coeur à la Crème*
Coffee

A LADIES' SUMMER LUNCHEON

Iced Clear Mushroom Broth*
Crab Louis* in Avocado Shells
Croissants
Meringue Star Shells* Filled with Lime Milk Sherbet*
Iced Tea

FIVE FAST LUNCHES

Mickey's Mac and Meat*
Tossed Green Salad
Italian Bread Sticks
Fruit Cocktail   Pound Cake
Milk   Coffee

———————

Hot Beef Consommé* (made ahead of time)
Individual Muffin Pizzas*
Applesauce   Cookies
Milk   Coffee

———————

Quick Chicken or Turkey à la King*   Toaster Waffles
Olives   Gherkins   Radishes
Orange Sherbet Topped with Sliced Bananas
Milk   Coffee

———————

Tomato-Vegetable Bouillon* (made ahead of time)
Fried Fish Sticks in Hot Dog Rolls   Tartar Sauce
Peaches and Cream   Cookies
Milk   Coffee

———————

Welsh Rabbit*
Broiled Tomatoes*   Dill Pickles
Butterscotch Pudding
Milk   Coffee

FIVE LUNCH-BOX MENUS

Cold Southern Fried Chicken*
Chilled Container of Old-Fashioned Potato Salad*
Orange or Tangerine
Butterscotch Brownies*
Milk

If for Adults:
Add: Thermos of clear Beet Soup*
Carrot and Celery Sticks
Substitute: Coffee or Tea for Milk

Cranberry Juice
Sliced Baked Ham* in Baking Powder Biscuits*
Apple Turnovers*   Cheddar Cubes
Milk

If for Adults:
Substitute: Coffee or Tea for Milk

Thermos of Chili*
Crackers   Corn Chips
Sweet Green Pepper and Carrot Sticks
Pear or Apple
Grandmother's Soft Ginger Cake*
Milk

If for Adults:
Substitute: Coffee or Tea for Milk

Cornish Pasties*
Chilled Container of Jiffy Deviled Eggs*
Cherry Tomatoes
Spicy Applesauce*
Dropped Oatmeal Chippies*
Milk

If for Adults:
Add: Thermos of clear or Sherried Mushroom Broth*
Substitute: Coffee or Tea for Milk

Bologna-Cheese or Ham Loaf* Sandwiches
Chilled Container of Creamy Sweet-Sour Coleslaw*
Quick Peach Crisp*
Milk

If for Adults:
Add: Thermos of Quick Asparagus Soup*
Dill Pickles
Substitute: Cold Sliced Ham Loaf* with Sour Cream-Mustard Sauce* for sandwiches
Coffee or Tea for Milk

AFTERNOON TEA

Afternoon tea may be nothing more than tea and cookies, or it may be a lavish British-style ritual with assorted sandwiches, cakes, cookies and pastries. Use the following menu patterns as a guide.

BASICS

Milk   Cream   Tea   Sugar   Lemon Slices

Party Sandwiches*

For a Simple Tea Choose 1
{
- Chicken and Avocado*
- Cream Cheese and Watercress*
- With Date Filling*

For a Formal Tea Choose 2-3
{
- Egg Salad*
- Potted Salmon*
- Salmon-Caper*
- Tongue and Chutney*
- Whitstable*
}

Sweet Breads, Cakes

For a Simple Tea Choose 1
{
- Any Fruit Nut Bread
- Boston Brown Bread*
- Kugelhupf*
- Light or Dark Fruit Cake

For a Formal Tea Choose 2
- Petits Fours*
}

Cookies

For a Simple Tea Choose 1
{
- Brandy Snaps*
- Butter Stars*
- Florentines*
- Kourabiedes*

For a Formal Tea Choose 2-3
- Madeleines*
- Maude's Cookies*
- Meringue Kisses*
- Scottish Shortbread*
- Spritz*
}

Pastries

For a Formal Tea Choose 1
{
- Chocolate Eclairs*
- Cream Horns*
- Cream Puffs*
- Meringues Chantilly*
- Tart Shells filled with Strawberry Jam
}

Welcome Extras: Salted Nuts, Mints

For a Special Occasion Tea: Substitute a decorated White Wedding Cake,* Royal Fruit Wedding Cake,* or other favorite cake for one of the choices above, using it as a centerpiece and asking the honoree to cut the first piece.

PICNICS

Note: Hot foods travel well in thermos jugs, cold foods packed in ice or cans of chemical dry ice in foam or insulated carryalls. Handy gourmet accessories: a chafing dish, an ice bucket for chilling wines, silver, napkins, portably sturdy wineglasses and plates.

A COOL WEATHER FAMILY PICNIC

Quick New England-Style Clam Chowder*   Crackers
Boston Baked Beans*   Cocktail Sausages
Crisp Apples   Cheddar Cheese Wedges
Gingerbread*
Spiced Orange Tea Mix*

A WARM WEATHER FAMILY PICNIC

Circassian Chicken*
Marinated Tomatoes and Artichokes*
Dill Pickles   Ripe and Green Olives
Buttered rolls
Thelma's 1, 2, 3, 4, Cake*
Beer   Easy Lemonade Mix*

A COOL WEATHER GOURMET PICNIC

Hot Buttered Rum*
Mugs of Minestrone Milanese*
Savory Meat Balls* Served from Chafing Dish
Ripe and Green Olives
Garlic Buttered Italian Bread
Ripe Pears   Brie and Port du Salut
Espresso*

A WARM WEATHER GOURMET PICNIC

Iced Vodka   Chilled Champagne
Chilled Billi-Bi*
Caviar Stuffed Hard-Cooked Eggs
Sausage and Pastry Rolls*
Assorted Danish Sandwiches*
Vanilla Pots de Crème*
Petits Fours*
Coffee

FOUR BACK-YARD BARBECUES

Guacamole*   Taramasalata*   Corn Chips   Crackers
Charcoal-Broiled Hamburgers*   Charcoal-Broiled Frankfurters
Buns   Relishes   Chili Sauce   Mustard   Sliced Bermuda Onions
Three Bean Salad*   German Macaroni Salad*
Assorted Ice Creams
Sweet Lemon Loaf*
Soft Drinks   Beer   Coffee

———

Andalusian Gazpacho*
Charcoal-Broiled Sirloin Steak Stuffed with Mushrooms*
Charcoal-Baked Potatoes*   Sour Cream-Almond Sauce*
Corn on the Cob
Grapefruit and Avocado Salad*
Biscuit Tortoni*
Sangria*   Coffee

———

Oysters or Clams on the Half Shell*
(*Rioja Red or Chianti*)
Charcoal Spit-Roasted Loin of Pork*
South American Hot Barbecue Sauce*
Charcoal-Baked Butternut Squash*
Beans Lyonnaise*
Caribbean Compote*   Pecan Crisps*
Coffee

———

Antipasto*
(Chilled *Vinho Verde* or *Portuguese Rosé*)
Charcoal-Broiled Portuguese-Style Chicken or Turkey*
Scalloped Potatoes*
Ratatouille*
Basket of Fresh Fruit   Crackers   Assorted Cheeses
Coffee

———

FOUR FORMAL DINNERS

Clam Juice on the Rocks*
(Chilled *Meursault* or *Montrachet*)
Duckling à l'Orange*
Wild Rice
Buttered Green Beans
Poached Meringue Ring* with Algarve Apricot Sauce*
Demitasse*

———

Coquilles St. Jacques à la Parisienne*
(Chilled *Graves Médoc* or *Cabernet Sauvignon*)
Tournedos of Beef*   Béarnaise Sauce*
Bulgur-Mushroom Kasha*
Minted Green Peas*
Green Grapes and Sour Cream*
Demitasse*

———

Cucumber Velouté*
Pomerol or *Échézeaux* (for lamb), chilled *Moselle* (for pork)
Crown Roast of Lamb or Pork*
Carrots Vichy*
Danish-Style New Potatoes*
Cherries Jubilee*
Coffee

———

Melon and Ham*
(Chilled *Chablis* or *Montrachet*)
Paupiettes of Sole with Rosy Sauce*
Snow Peas and Scallions*
Mushroom Risotto*
Classic Pots de Crème au Chocolat*
Coffee

FOUR INFORMAL DINNERS

Sangria*
Paella*
Garlic French Bread*
Sliced Avocado and Lettuce Salad
Rum Flan*
Coffee

———

Won Ton Soup*
Lobster Cantonese*
Boiled Rice
Lichees in Port Wine*   Almond-Orange Icebox Cookies*
Tea

———

Caponata*   Crackers
(Chilled *Soave*)
Chicken and Mushroom Stuffed Manicotti*
Spinach and Cucumber Salad
Lemon Granité*   Florentines*
Espresso*

———

Cheese Fondue*
(*Kirsch,* midway through the fondue)
Sliced Smoked Ham, German Salami, Thuringer   Dill Pickles
Apples and Pears
Coffee

THREE HOLIDAY MENUS

EASTER DINNER

Sherried Mushroom Broth*
Ham en Croûte*
(*Volnay* or Chilled *Rosé*)
Curried Hot Fruit Compote*
Buttered Boiled New Potatoes
Steamed Asparagus*   Hollandaise Sauce*
Charlotte Russe*
Milk   Coffee   Tea

THANKSGIVING DINNER

Crudités*
Tomato Bouillon*
(Chilled *Chablis* or *Soave*)
Roast Turkey with Oyster or Savory Sausage Stuffing*
Turkey Gravy*   Cran-Apple Relish*
Orange-Candied Sweet Potatoes*
Brussels Sprouts with Chestnuts*
Creamed Onions*
Herb Biscuits*
Old-Fashioned Pumpkin Pie*
Milk   Coffee   Tea

CHRISTMAS DINNER

Shrimp Cocktail*
(Chilled *Traminer, Riesling,* or *Rhine* wine)
Roast Goose with Sage and Onion Dressing*
Braised Chestnuts*   Giblet Gravy*
Spicy Applesauce*
Green Beans in Mustard Sauce*
Molded Cranberry-Pecan Salad*
Plum Pudding* with Brandy or Rum Sauce*
Milk   Coffee   Tea

A STAG DINNER

Oysters Remick*
(*St. Emilion*)
Broiled Porterhouse Steak with Madeira-Mushroom Sauce*
Stuffed Baked Potatoes*
Caesar Salad*
Country-Style Apple Pie*
Coffee

A LATE SUPPER

Bouillabaisse*
Garlic French Bread*
Romaine and Radish Salad
Fruit and Cheese
Coffee   Tea

A SMORGASBORD MENU

GROUP I

Scandinavian Herring Salad   Rollmops*   Herring in Sour Cream*
Aquavit

GROUP II

Smoked Salmon   Easy Tuna Salad*   Cold Boiled Shrimp*
Iced Beer

GROUP III

Cold Roast Beef   Decorative Jellied Veal Loaf*
Country-Style Liver Pâté*
Wilted Cucumbers*   Pickled Red Cabbage*   Herbed Potato Salad*
Iced Beer

GROUP IV

Swedish Meat Balls in Mushroom Gravy*
Sage and Cider Scented Roast Fresh Ham*
Danish-Style New Potatoes*
Iced Beer

GROUP V (DESSERT)

Cheese Board (Danish Blue, Crema Dania)
Fruit Salad   Almond Tarts (Swedish Sandbakelsen)*
Coffee

Note: Aquavit is served with the first group only, chilled beer with all the rest (except dessert). Pumpernickel, rye bread, and sweet butter should accompany all savory courses.

Tips on Serving Smorgasbord:
– Stand table well away from wall so traffic around it will flow freely.
– Group hot and cold foods separately without crowding, elevating some, if you

like, on linen-draped boxes. Set hot dinner plates near hot foods, cold plates near cold foods.

— To avoid jam-ups, arrange napkins and silver on a separate small table nearby.
— Replenish dishes as needed—in the kitchen, not at the table.

Tips on Eating Smorgasbord: Take herring only the first time at the table, then make a return trip for each successive group. In fine restaurants, a fresh plate is used for each new group (though not for return trips within any group), but such lavish use of plates may not be practical at home.

RIJSTTAFEL

In Indonesia, *rijsttafel* (rice table) may consist of 4 or 40 different dishes, depending upon the number of servants available (traditionally, there was one boy to handle each dish). The most practical way to serve rijsttafel in America is as a buffet, carefully charted to avoid traffic jams. Center the table with a gigantic bowl of rice, then cluster around it the various hot dishes (on burners or in chafing dishes). Nearby, set a stack of deep plates or shallow soup plates and, on a small table within easy reach, the silver rolled up in napkins. Condiments and salads are best placed at opposite ends of the buffet table, and dessert is served separately. How does one tackle this mountain of food? The Indonesian way is to cover the plate with rice, then to add dabs of this and that around the rice as neatly as paints on a palette. The trick is to keep the different dishes from getting scrambled so, if necessary to avoid overloading a plate, return to the table again and again à la smorgasbord. Chilled beer is the perfect rijsttafel beverage.

Hot Boiled Rice
Shrimp with Cucumbers and Snow Peas*　　Chicken Sate*
Indonesian Spiced Beef*　　Sweet and Sour Pork*　　Lamb and Dhal Curry*
Radish Salad*　　Hot Sweet-Sour Bean Sprout Salad*

CONDIMENTS

Toasted Coconut　　Salted Peanuts　　Pickled Hot Peppers
Shrimp Puffs (chips or wafers)　　Raw Cucumber Sticks
Plum Sauce*　　Chutney　　India Relish

DESSERT

Fresh Pineapple Boats*
Coffee　　Tea

A SUMMER COCKTAIL PARTY

Menu	For 12	Quantities Needed For 24	For 50
Pretty Party Pâté*	1 recipe	2×the recipe	3×the recipe
Melba rounds	2 dozen	4 dozen	8 dozen
Cold Marinated Shrimp*	2×the recipe	4×the recipe	8×the recipe
Crisp Cucumber Rounds Tokyo Style*	2×the recipe	4×the recipe	8×the recipe
Garlicky Cocktail Almonds*	1 recipe	2×the recipe	3×the recipe
Beer Cheese Spread*	Not needed	1 recipe	2×the recipe
Caponata*	Not needed	2×the recipe	3×the recipe
Crackers	Not needed	5–6 dozen	10–12 dozen

A WINTER COCKTAIL PARTY

Menu	For 12	Quantities Needed For 24	For 50
Chutney-Nut Meat Balls*	1 recipe	2×the recipe	4×the recipe
Rumakis*	2×the recipe	4×the recipe	8×the recipe
Quiche Tartlets*	1 recipe	2×the recipe	3×the recipe
Spiced Olives*	1 recipe	2×the recipe	3×the recipe
Garlic Nibbles*	Not needed	Not needed	1 recipe
Taramasalata*	Not needed	Not needed	4×the recipe
Sesame seed crackers	Not needed	Not needed	5–6 dozen

Note: For tips on calculating the amount and kind of liquor needed, see the chapter on beverages.

TWO INFORMAL SUMMER BUFFETS

Menu	For 12	Quantities Needed For 24	For 50
Chicken or Turkey Loaf* (cold)	2×the recipe	3×the recipe	4×the recipe
Tomatoes Stuffed with Easy Tuna Salad*			
Tomatoes	1 dozen	2 dozen	50
Easy Tuna Salad	1 recipe	2×the recipe	3×the recipe
Jiffy Deviled Eggs*	2×the recipe	3×the recipe	4×the recipe
Jellied Garden Vegetable Salad*	2×the recipe	3×the recipe	6×the recipe
Herbed Potato Salad*	2×the recipe	3×the recipe	6×the recipe
Danish Meat Balls*	Not needed	Not needed	4×the recipe
Buttered Noodles (cook by package directions)	Not needed	Not needed	4 lbs. (raw)
Fresh Peach Crisp*	2×the recipe	4×the recipe	8×the recipe
Coffee (see How to Make Coffee for a Crowd, beverage chapter)			

Menu	For 12	Quantities Needed For 24	For 50
Glazed and Decorated Cold Ham*	4 lbs. boneless ham 6 lbs. bone-in ham	6 lbs. boneless 8 lbs. bone-in	12 lbs. boneless 16 lbs. bone-in
Macaroni and Shellfish Salad*	2×the recipe	3×the recipe	8×the recipe
Bean and Beet Salad*	3×the recipe	6×the recipe	12×the recipe
Tomato Aspic*	2×the recipe	4×the recipe	8×the recipe
Parker House Rolls*	1½ dozen	2½ dozen	5½ dozen
Ambrosia*	2×the recipe	4×the recipe	8×the recipe
Florentines*	1 recipe	2×the recipe	4×the recipe

Coffee (see How to Make Coffee for a Crowd, beverage chapter)

TWO FORMAL SUMMER BUFFETS

Menu	For 12	Quantities Needed For 24	For 50
Smoked Salmon	2¼ lbs.	4¾ lbs.	9½ lbs.
Pâté-Filled Ham in Aspic*	1 recipe	1 recipe	2×the recipe
Chaud-Froid of Chicken Breasts*	3×the recipe	6×the recipe	10×the recipe
Avocado Mousse*	2×the recipe	4×the recipe	6×the recipe
Shellfish and Saffron Rice Salad*	Not needed	Not needed	4×the recipe
Lemon Fluff*	2×the recipe	4×the recipe	5×the recipe
Gingered Honeydew Melon*	Not needed	Not needed	5×the recipe

Coffee (see How to Make Coffee for a Crowd, beverage chapter)

Menu	For 12	For 24	For 50
Fresh Fruit Cocktail	1½ qts.	3 qts.	6 qts.
Whole Salmon in Aspic*	1 recipe	1 recipe	2×the recipe
Country Captain*	1 recipe	2×the recipe	3×the recipe
Boiled Rice* (see How to Cook Rice, cereals and pasta chapter)	3×the recipe	5×the recipe	7×the recipe
Wilted Cucumbers*	3×the recipe	6×the recipe	10×the recipe
Russian Salad*	2×the recipe	4×the recipe	8×the recipe
Strawberries Romanoff*	3×the recipe	6×the recipe	8×the recipe
Meringues Chantilly*	Not needed	Not needed	2×the recipe or 4 dozen bakery meringues

Coffee (see How to Make Coffee for a Crowd, beverage chapter)

TWO INFORMAL WINTER BUFFETS

Menu	For 12	Quantities Needed For 24	For 50
Lamb Curry*	2×the recipe	4×the recipe	7×the recipe
Nut Rice*	3×the recipe	5×the recipe	7×the recipe
Coulibiac*	1 recipe	1 recipe	2×the recipe
Parsley Sauce*	3×the recipe	5×the recipe	7×the recipe
Cherry Tomatoes	1 qt.	2 qts.	1 gal.

Menu	Quantities Needed For 12	For 24	For 50
Waldorf Salad*	3×the recipe	6×the recipe	12×the recipe
Imperial Peach Mold*	2×the recipe	4×the recipe	8×the recipe
Coffee (see How to Make Coffee for a Crowd, beverage chapter)			
Lasagne*	1 recipe	2×the recipe	3×the recipe
Beef Stew for a Crowd*	½ recipe	1 recipe	2×the recipe
Tossed green salad Choice of dressings	3 qts. prepared salad greens	6 qts. greens	3 gals. greens
Tutti-Frutti Ice Cream*	2×the recipe	4×the recipe	8×the recipe
Almond-Orange Icebox Cookies*	½ recipe	1 recipe	1 recipe
Coffee (see How to Make Coffee for a Crowd, beverage chapter)			

TWO FORMAL WINTER BUFFETS

Menu	Quantities Needed For 12	For 24	For 50
Consommé Madrilène* (in punch cups)	3×the recipe	6×the recipe	12×the recipe
Melba toast	1 dozen	2 dozen	4½ dozen
Moussaka*	2×the recipe	2×the recipe	4×the recipe
Artichoke Hearts Vinaigrette*	3×the recipe	6×the recipe	12×the recipe
Rosy King Crab Bake*	2×the recipe	4×the recipe	6×the recipe
Buttered noodles (cook by package directions)	1½ lbs. (raw)	2½ lbs.	4 lbs.
Hot Fruit Compote*	2×the recipe	4×the recipe	8×the recipe
Lemon Wafers*	1 recipe	1 recipe	2×the recipe
Coffee (see How to Make Coffee for a Crowd, beverage chapter)			
Veal Marengo*	2×the recipe	3×the recipe	6×the recipe
Shrimp Creole*	2×the recipe	3×the recipe	5×the recipe
Risi e Bisi*	3×the recipe	6×the recipe	12×the recipe
Hearts of lettuce Choice of dressings	3 qts. lettuce	6 qts. lettuce	3 gals. lettuce
Viennese Fruit Flan*	2×the recipe	4×the recipe	7×the recipe
Coffee (see How to Make Coffee for a Crowd, beverage chapter)			

About Parties for Young People

Preschool Children have limited tastes and appetites and are happy with a few fancily cut sandwiches spread with peanut butter or cream cheese and jelly, ice cream (preferably a choice of vanilla and strawberry or chocolate), a decorated yellow or white cake (or cupcakes), a milk or fruit drink, and perhaps a few cookies and hard candies.

Preteens have outgrown the pastel confectionery of small children's parties and prefer heftier fare: sundaes, sodas, and shakes (particularly if they can concoct their own), more sophisticated cakes (Burnt Sugar,* Coconut Cream,* Devil's Food,* Angel Food,* Spice*). Moreover, their parties are as apt to be suppers as midafternoon affairs. Always popular: charcoal-broiled hot dogs and hamburgers, Heroes,* Sloppy Joes,* fried chicken, Spaghetti and Meat Balls in Tomato Sauce,* potato salad, coleslaw, Boston Baked Beans.*

Teen-agers today are about three times as worldly as their parents were at the same age. Many have traveled, if not abroad, at least to big cities where there are ethnic restaurants. They have sampled Smorgasbord, whole repertoires of pasta and Chinese classics, Shish Kebabs,* Beef Stroganoff,* chili (not the canned but the fiery Texas type), Tacos,* and very possibly Paella,* Moussaka,* Bouillabaisse,* Borsch,* tempura, Sukiyaki,* and Teriyaki.* Let your own teen-ager help plan the menu. He or she knows what's *in* and *out*.

A PRESCHOOL BIRTHDAY PARTY

Basic White* or Basic Three-Egg Butter Cake*
with Basic Butter Cream, Cherry or Berry Butter Cream Frosting*
Vanilla Ice Cream*　　　Berry Ice Cream*
Mints　　Roasted Peanuts
Easy Pink Lemonade*

A PRETEEN BIRTHDAY BARBECUE

Charcoal-Broiled Hot Dogs and Hamburgers
Buns　　　Relishes　　　Mustard　　　Ketchup　　　Onions
Old-Fashioned Potato Salad*
Creamy Sweet-Sour Coleslaw*
Chocolate Freezer Ice Cream*
Devil's Food Cake* with White Mountain Frosting*
Milk　　　Iced Tea

A TEEN BIRTHDAY SUPPER

Cold Marinated Shrimp*
Guacamole*　　　Crackers　　　Corn Chips
Ripe and Green Olives
Pizza* with a Choice of Toppings
Marinated Roasted Peppers*
Tossed Green Salad　　　Choice of Dressings
Biscuit Tortoni
Lemon Chiffon Cake* with Lemon Butter Cream Frosting*
Milk　　　Soft Drinks

AN EASTER EGG ROLL

Hard-Cooked Eggs　　　Easter Egg Dyes and Decals
Candy Easter Eggs　　　Salted Nuts
Easy Yellow Cupcakes* with Basic Butter Cream Frosting*
Assorted Ice-Cream Sodas*

A HALLOWEEN PARTY

Hot Buttered Popcorn*　　　Popcorn Balls*
Candied Apples*　　　Molasses Taffy*　　　Sugared Nuts*
Tea Punch*

Table Setting and Service

Formal dinners have gone the way of servants, which is to say *away*. Entertaining today is casual, convivial, and most Americans prefer it that way. Few hostesses object to kibitzers in their kitchens; in fact, many welcome helping hands. Modern tables, reflecting the breakdown of rules, are more apt to wear denims, paisley, and bandanna prints than snowy damasks and linens—except for the most formal affairs. Service, too, is relaxed, being dictated more by convenience than convention.

What most Americans have adopted is *English Service,* far from stuffy although the name suggests it. This, simply, is a relaxed family-style service in which the host dishes up food at the table and passes it clockwise around the table, ladies first.

When there are several courses, a *Compromise Service* works well. Appetizers, soups, and desserts are dished up in the kitchen and brought to the table, the entrée is served at table English style.

Russian Service is fussy, formal, and out of the question for anyone lacking a battery of servants to pass platters or plates of food to each guest.

Table-Setting Tips:

Linens: Make sure tablecloth has plenty of overhang, 15"–18" all around. Place napkins, folded into rectangles, to the left of the forks with the long, open sides facing plates or, if there is no first course, perpendicularly down the center of covers (place settings) or plates.

Flatware: Forks to the left, knives and spoons to the right, lined up in order of use (from the outside in) with handles in a straight line about 1" from table edge. Two exceptions: The small cocktail fork, which is placed to the right, on the outside, and the butter spreader, laid horizontally across the bread-and-butter plate. Forks and spoons are arranged

How to Set Tables

Breakfast

Lunch

Informal Dinner

Semiformal Dinner

Small Buffet

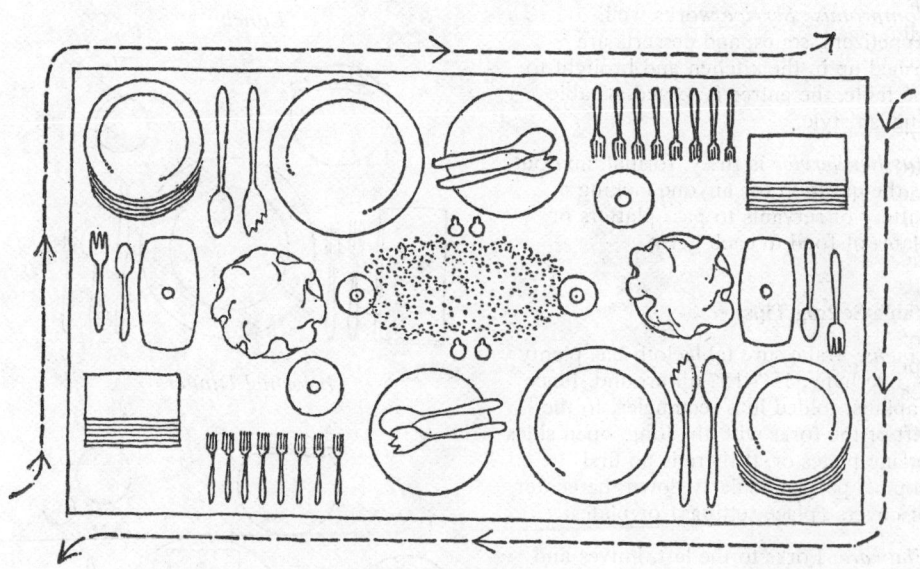

Large Buffet

prongs and bowls up, knives with cutting edges toward plates. It's best not to place more than 3 pieces of silver on each side of a plate. If the dinner is a fairly formal one, bring in dessert silver as dessert is served.

Cover (Individual Place Setting): To avoid crowding guests at a table, allow at least 30″ from the center of one cover to the next.

Service Plates: These add a handsome, gracious touch. Use plates that are at least 10″ across, place in the center of each cover, and use as an underliner for the appetizer and soup. Remove before bringing in the entree.

Glasses: The water tumbler should stand just above the point of the dinner knife, wine goblets slightly to the right of it. If two wines are being served, both wineglasses should be on the table at the start of the meal.

Finger Bowls: Too pretentious for casual dinners, finger bowls do still appear at formal affairs. They are presented before dessert, bracketed by dessert fork and spoon on doily-lined dessert plates. *To Use:* Set fork and spoon on table to left and right of plate, finger bowl and doily on table just above and to the left of the plate.

Flower Arrangements and Centerpieces: Keep them simple and keep them low so that guests aren't peering into a jungle of blossoms and greenery. Avoid strongly perfumed flowers, also those known to cause allergies.

Candles: Use in the evening only and place strategically so guests aren't forced to stare directly into a flame.

Place Cards: When there are too many guests at dinner to direct personally to their places, place cards do the job well. Use small white or ivory cards and letter simply Mr. Brown, Miss Green, or in the case of two Mr. Browns or Miss Greens, Mr. Josiah Brown, Mr. Everett Brown, Miss Abigail Green, Miss Eleanor Green. Center cards just above each cover.

Serving and Clearing Tips:

– Remove serving dishes first, then plates, flatware, and glasses, beginning with the hostess and moving to the right around the table. *Exception:* If the hostess herself is clearing, she should begin with the guest to her right and proceed around the table, taking up her own plate last. When a table is properly cleared, the centerpiece alone should remain.

– Serve and remove plates from the left, using the left hand, glasses from the right with the right hand. Work quickly, quietly, *never* reaching in front of a guest. *Note:* If two are waiting table, plates may be taken from the right as new ones are added from the left.

– Fill water or wineglasses as they stand on the table; never lift them.

– Crumb a table only if necessary, whisking crumbs onto a small plate with a napkin.

– When serving coffee at the table, bring in cups and saucers empty, placing them to the guests' right. Coffee spoons should be on the saucers, behind the cups with their handles parallel to the cup handles.

Seating Tips:

– The host and hostess sit at opposite ends of a table. To the host's right sits the lady guest of honor, to his left the lady of next importance. The male guests of first and second importance are seated to the hostess's right and left. Remaining seats are filled as the hostess chooses— man, woman, man, woman—but never with husbands and wives together.

– To avoid confusion, the hostess should direct each guest to his seat.

A WEEK'S BUDGET MENUS

	Breakfast	Lunch	Supper
Sunday	Fruit Cocktail Whole Wheat Pancakes* Maple Syrup Butter Grilled Sausages Milk Coffee	Baked Ham* Orange-Flavored Mashed Yams* Scalloped Cabbage* Corn Sticks* Butterscotch Tapioca Pudding* (makes enough for 2 meals) Old-Fashioned Ginger Biscuits* (makes enough for 2 meals) Milk Coffee	Vegetable Soup Hot Buttered Popcorn* Oranges Tangerines Cookies Cocoa
Monday	Stewed Fruits Scrambled Eggs Whole Wheat Toast Milk Coffee	Spaghetti and Meat Balls in Tomato Sauce* Lettuce Hearts Oil and Vinegar Dressing Garlic Bread* Fruit Cheese Milk Coffee or Tea	Boston Baked Beans* (with some leftover ham added) (makes enough for 2 meals) Waldorf Salad* Butterscotch Tapioca Pudding* Sugar Cookies* (makes enough for 2 meals) Milk Coffee or Tea
Tuesday	Cranberry Juice Grilled Leftover Sliced Ham Fried Corn Meal Mush* Butter Syrup Milk Coffee	Chicken-Noodle Soup* Cheese Crackers* Spicy Applesauce* (makes enough for 2 meals) Cookies Milk Coffee or Tea	Tomato Juice Economy Meat Loaf* (makes enough for 2 meals) Baked Potatoes* Lemon-Glazed Carrots* Old-Fashioned Bread and Butter Pudding* Milk Coffee or Tea

84

Wednesday

Orange Juice
Buttered Hominy Grits
Grilled Sausage Patties
Milk   Coffee

Fruit Cocktail
Hot Meat Loaf Sandwiches
Carrot and Celery Sticks
Cookies
Milk   Coffee

Cranberry Juice Cocktail
Quick Tuna Surprise*
Caraway Coleslaw with Creamy Oil
and Vinegar Dressing*
Easy Date and Walnut Pudding*
(makes enough for 2 meals)
Milk   Coffee

Thursday

Half Grapefruit
French Toast*
Butter   Jam   Honey
Cocoa   Coffee

Golden Split Pea Soup with Ham*
(makes enough for 2 meals)
Buttered Whole Wheat Toast
Sliced Tomatoes
Cookies
Milk   Coffee

Crudités*
Tamale Pie*
Lettuce Hearts   French Dressing
Ambrosia*
Sugar Cookies*
Milk   Tea or Coffee

Friday

Tomato Juice
Skillet Egg and Potato Breakfast*
Milk   Coffee

Ambrosia-Fruit Cup
Baked Bean Sandwiches
Creamy Sweet-Sour Coleslaw*
Old-Fashioned Ginger Biscuits*
Milk   Coffee

Jambalaya*
Buttered Green Beans
Hot Corn Bread*
Pineapple Upside-Down Cake*
Milk   Coffee or Tea

Saturday

Hominy, Beans and Salt Pork*
Buttered Whole Wheat Muffins*
Spicy Applesauce*
Milk   Coffee

Tomato-Cheese Rabbit*
Tossed Green Salad
Ice Cream   Sugar Cookies*
Milk   Coffee

Golden Split Pea Soup with Ham*
Cheese Biscuits*
Molded Fruit Salad
Easy Date and Walnut Pudding*
Milk   Tea or Coffee

A WEEK'S MENUS FOR A 1200-CALORIE-A-DAY DIET

Note: Portions are average size unless otherwise indicated; T. = 1 tablespoon, t. = teaspoon.

	Monday	Calories	Tuesday	Calories
Breakfast	Tomato Juice (1/2 cup)	23	Orange Juice (1/2 cup)	55
	Boiled or Poached Egg	80	Ready-to-Eat High-Protein Cereal (1 cup with 1 t. sugar,	170
	Slice Whole Wheat Toast, 1 t. butter	98	1/2 cup skim milk)	95
	Black Coffee or Tea with Lemon	0	1/2 Toasted English Muffin, 2 t. jelly	0
		201	Black Coffee or Tea with Lemon	320
Lunch	Cold Roast Beef and Tomato Sandwich (2 thin slices		Beef Broth (1 cup)	35
	lean beef, 1/2 tomato, mustard or horseradish)	278	Cottage Cheese (1 cup, uncreamed)	195
			1/2 Tomato on Lettuce (topped with minced scallions,	
	Apple	70	1 T. Tangy Low-Calorie Salad Dressing*)	45
	Skim Milk (1 cup)	90	1 (2") piece Angel Food Cake* (unfrosted)	120
		438	Black Coffee or Tea with Lemon	0
				395
Dinner	Sautéed Calf's Liver*	280	Egg Roll (packaged)	53
	Riced Boiled Medium Size Potato	100	Chicken Chow Mein*, 1/3 cup Boiled Rice	292
	Low-Calorie Asparagus*	40	Pineapple Chunks (1/2 cup water-pack)	64
	Low-Calorie Sherbet	65	Vanilla Wafer (1)	20
	Black Coffee or Tea with Lemon	0	Black Coffee or Tea with Lemon	0
		485		429
Anytime Snack	1 Cup Skim Milk	90	1/2 Cup Skim Milk	45
Total Day's Calories:		1214		1189

86

	Wednesday	Calories	Thursday	Calories
Breakfast	1/2 Grapefruit	55	Tomato Juice (1/2 cup)	23
	1 Slice French Toast (fried in 1 t. butter, sprinkled with 1 t. confectioners' sugar)	198	Boiled or Poached Egg	80
			Slice Whole Wheat Toast, 1 t. butter	98
	Black Coffee or Tea with Lemon	0	Black Coffee or Tea with Lemon	0
		253		201
Lunch	Tuna Sandwich (1/3 cup water-pack tuna mixed with minced celery, onion, lemon juice)	270	Clam Chickee*	20
	Carrot and Celery Sticks	25	Chef's Salad (2 oz. cheese, 1 oz. lean ham, Low-Calorie Thousand Island Dressing*)	305
	Sliced Canned Peaches (1/2 cup water-pack)	38	Melba Toast (2 slices)	32
	Skim Milk (1 cup)	90	Skim Milk (1 cup)	90
		423		447
Dinner	Broiled (4 oz.) Herb Burger*	247	Cabbage Rolls and Sauerkraut*	270
	On 1/2 Toasted Bun	70	Poppy Seed Noodles* (1/2 cup)	100
	Skillet Mushrooms*	30	Fruit Cocktail (1/2 cup water-pack)	72
	Low-Calorie Green Beans*	35	Vanilla Wafer (1)	20
	Broiled 1/2 Tomato	18	Black Coffee or Tea with Lemon	0
	Low-Calorie Gingered Orange Fluff* with Low-Calorie Dessert Topping*	39		462
	Black Coffee or Tea with Lemon	0		
		439		
Anytime Snack	1 Cup Skim Milk	90	1 Cup Skim Milk	90
Total Day's Calories:		1205		1200

A WEEK'S MENUS FOR A 1200-CALORIE-A-DAY DIET (continued)

	Friday	Calories	Saturday	Calories
Breakfast	Peach Nectar (1/2 cup)	60	1/2 Grapefruit	55
	Ready-to-Eat High Protein Cereal (1 cup with 1 t sugar, 1/2 cup skim. milk)	170	Boiled or Poached Egg	80
			Slice Whole Wheat or Enriched Bread Toast, 1 t butter	98
	Black Coffee or Tea with Lemon	0	Black Coffee or Tea with Lemon	0
		230		233
Lunch	Tomato Cocktail*	35	Open-Face Grilled Cheese and Bacon Sandwich	269
	Scrambled Egg Sandwich (2 eggs scrambled in 2 t butter, seasoned with chives)	333	Wilted Cucumbers*	40
			Seedless Grapes (2/3 cup)	47
	Skim Milk (1 cup)	90	Skim Milk (1 cup)	90
		458		446
Dinner	Low-Calorie Fillets of Flounder en Papillote*	180	Steak Florentine* (4 oz.)	310
	Medium-Size Parsleyed Potato	100	Boiled Chopped Spinach	23
	Low-Calorie Boiled Carrots*	40	Strawberries Grand Marnier*	100
	Gingered Honeydew Melon*	65		
	Black Coffee or Tea with Lemon	0	Black Coffee or Tea with Lemon	0
		385		433
Anytime Snack	1/2 Cup Skim Milk	45	2 Medium-Size Carrots	40
	1 Small Banana	81	1/2 Cup Skim Milk	45
Total Day's Calories:		1199		1197

	Sunday	Calories
Brunch	1/2 Medium-Size Cantaloupe	60
	Low-Calorie Sautéed Kidneys* with Skillet Mush-	
	rooms and 1/2 Broiled Tomato	278
	OR	
	2 Poached Eggs and 2 Slices Grilled Bacon	
	Toasted English Muffin, 2 t. butter	206
	Black Coffee or Tea with Lemon	0
		544
Mid-	1 Medium-Size Apple	70
Afternoon	1 Cup Skim Milk	90
Snack		160
Dinner	1/2 Lemon-Broiled Chicken* (small)	290
	Low-Calorie Cauliflower*	35
	Frozen French-Style Green Beans and Mushrooms	
	(1/2 cup)	26
	Green Grapes and Sour Cream* (made with yogurt)	138
	Black Coffee or Tea with Lemon	0
		489
Total Day's Calories:		1193

CHAPTER 5

BEVERAGES

ALCOHOLIC BEVERAGES

The French are master chefs, the Viennese master confectioners, but when it comes to mixing drinks, Americans are the masters. So many drinks—hard and soft—are American inventions: ice-cream sodas, fizzy colas and floats, not to mention cocktails (and cocktail parties). We drink, perhaps, a greater variety of beverages than any other people and are constantly concocting new ones. Moreover, we have developed a European fondness for fine wines and choice brews and an adventurous spirit in sampling exotic liqueurs.

About Beers and Ales

Beer and ale are closely related fermented malt beverages, brewed in different ways. The technical differences matter not so much here as the results. *Ale* tastes more strongly of hops than beer, particularly *stout* and *porter,* which are heavy, dark, and bittersweet.

The most popular *beer* is bubbly, golden *lager,* a light brew held in the cask until cleared of sediment (*lager* is from *lagern,* the German word meaning *to store*). It is carbonated (hence the bubbles), bottled or canned, and pasteurized. *Draught beer* is drawn straight from the cask and not pasteurized. American lagers average 3.2–5 per cent alcohol, European lagers slightly more. *Bock beer,* available in spring, is a dark, sweetish, heavy lager brewed from dark-roasted malt. *Pilsner* is pale lager, originally from Pilsen, Czechoslovakia, made with natural mineral water.

About Serving Beers and Ales: The ideal temperature for serving beer is said to be 40° F., cool but not as cold as Americans like it. Europeans frown upon the American practice of serving ice cold beer, insisting that it destroys the flavor. Should beer be poured so that there is no head? Depends on personal preference. Connoisseurs insist upon a creamy head about 1″ thick because it proves the beer isn't flat and seals in the flavor. To achieve a good head, tilt glass and pour enough beer gently down the side to ⅓ full, then stand glass upright and pour beer straight in. To minimize head, continue filling tilted glass.

About Wines

The subject of wine (by definition the fermented juice of freshly pressed grapes) is nearly inexhaustible, and in a basic cookbook there simply is not room to do more than capsulize. Whole volumes have been devoted to wines, indeed to single wines.

APÉRITIF WINES AND WINE-BASED DRINKS

Wine (those served before meals)	Appropriate Glass	How To Serve
Byrrh	6-ounce old-fashioned glass	on the rocks
Dry Champagne (Brut)	9-ounce tulip goblet	well chilled
Dry Sherry (Fino or Manzanilla)	6-ounce sherry glass	well chilled
Dubonnet or Dubonnet Blonde	6-ounce sherry glass	well chilled
Lillet (similar to vermouth, made of white wine, brandy, herbs)	6-ounce old-fashioned glass or sherry glass	on the rocks or well chilled
Vermouth (dry and sweet)	6-ounce old-fashioned glass or sherry glass	on the rocks or well chilled

The Types of Wine:

TABLE WINES

(Natural wines served with meals; they have an alcoholic content of 10–14 per cent.)

Dry Red Wines:

French:

Bordeaux (called claret by the British): Many experts consider these the finest of all table wines. When good, they are rich, fragrant, full-bodied. Bordeaux include *Médoc, Pomerol, Saint-Emilion, Graves.* Outstanding chateaux are *Château Lafite-Rothschild, Château Latour, Château Mouton-Rothschild.*

Burgundy: Another superb group of French wines, heavier than Bordeaux and more robust. Some better known red Burgundies are *Beaujolais, Eché-zeaux, Volnay, Pommard, Beaune,* and, three of the best: *Chambertin, Romanée-Conti,* and *La Tâche.*

Loire Valley Wine: Chinon, Anjou (both light bodied and well balanced).

Rhône Valley Wine: Châteauneuf-du-Pape, Côte Rôtie (heady and rich), and Hermitage (generously full flavored).

Italian: Popular imports are *Barbera, Barbaresco, Bardolino* (much like Chianti but smoother), *Barolo* (which some consider Italy's greatest dry red wine), *Chianti* (the best may not come in the *fiasco,* or straw-covered bottle; look for the neckband imprinted with the black rooster), *Lambrusco* (a crackling red) and *Valpolicella* (delicate).

Spanish and Portuguese: Both countries produce good—if sometimes rough—red table wines. Most readily available are the Spanish *Rioja* and Portuguese *Dão.*

American: California vineyards produce first-rate dry red wines, notably *Cabernet Sauvignon* (a Bordeaux-type), *Pinot Noir* (similar to Burgundy), *Gamay, Zin-fandel, Barbera,* and *Grignolino.*

Dry White Wines:

French:

Bordeaux: Graves (both dry and semidry).

Burgundy: Chablis (light and very dry), *Meursault* (soft, flowery, feminine), *Montrachet* (Dumas declared that Montrachet "should be drunk while kneeling") and *Pouilly-Fuissé* (dry but fruity).

Loire Valley Wine: Muscadet (very dry), *Pouilly-Fumé* and *Sancerre* (both still and dry), and *Vouvray* (still or crackling, dry or semidry).

Alsatian Wine: Gewürztraminer (fruity, almost gingery), *Riesling* (dry and elegant), *Sylvaner* (fresh, light, and fruity), and *Traminer* (similar to *Gewürztraminer* but subtler).

Italian: Brolio Bianco (light), *Est! Est!! Est!!!* and *Orvieto* (dry or semidry), *Frascati, Soave* (very light and smooth), *Verdicchio* (dry or semidry with a touch of bitterness).

German: The noble grape of Germany is the Riesling, hence the varietal name Reisling may appear on labels of both Rhine and Moselle wines. To tell Rhine wines from the Moselle at a glance, look at the bottle. Both come in tall slim bottles but the Rhine bottle is brown, the Moselle green.

Rhine Wine: The choicest are from the Rheingau, a 20-mile stretch on the right bank of the Rhine between Wiesbaden and Rüdesheim. Ones to seek out are *Hochheimer* (called hock by the British), *Rüdesheimer,* and *Johannisberg* (Schloss Johannisberg may be Germany's most famous vineyard). The *Rheinhessen,* just across the river from the Rheingau, produces the popular *Liebfraumilch,* not a single wine but a blend. It is produced throughout the Rheinhessen, thus can be very good (look for such labels as Blue Nun, Hans Christof, Crown of Crowns), or it can be disappointing. Rhine wines, generally, are pleasantly light and dry.

Moselle Wine: The best are from the *Mittel* (*Middle*) *Moselle* and include *Piesporter, Bernkastler* (Bernkasteler Doktor is perhaps the most renowned), *Kroever, Zeltinger,* and *Wehlener.*

Steinwein: One of the best wines from Franconia (valleys of the Main and its tributaries), this light wine comes in the squatty *Bocksbeutel* instead of the tall, graceful bottles of Rhine and Moselle wines. There are other wines from Franconia, but Steinwein is best known to Americans.

Spanish and Portuguese: As with the Spanish table reds, *Rioja* is the name to look for in white table wines. Probably the best known Portuguese white wine is *vinho verde,* a tart young green wine, best drunk very cold.

American: California vintners produce excellent dry white wines. Some to try: *Semillon* and *Sauvignon Blanc* (similar to but drier than Sauternes), *Chardonnay* and *Pinot Blanc* (chablis types), *Riesling, Traminer, Sylvaner,* and *Grey Riesling.* A number of Eastern vineyards also produce creditable Rieslings.

Rosé Wines:

There are fewer good rosé wines than dry reds or whites. The best imports are *Tavel* and *Anjou* from France, *Mateus* from Portugal. California also has good rosés: *Grenache* and *Gamay.*

DESSERT WINES

(Sweet, still, or fortified wines that are especially compatible with dessert; fortified wines are those that have had spirits added, often brandy, to bring the alcoholic content up to about 20 per cent).

Sauternes: People quibble as to whether these white Bordeaux are table or dessert wines. They are sweetish, however, and connoisseurs prefer them with dessert, particularly fruit. Among the greats are *Château d'Yquem* and *Château La Tour-Blanche.*

Madeira: There are many Madeira wines, all fortified, all classified according to sweetness. The driest is *Sercial,* then *Verdelho,* then *Boal* and, sweetest of all, *Malmsey. Rainwater Madeira* is a blend, which though light in color can be fairly rich or dry. Madeira, by the way, is a superb wine to use in cooking, especially in soups, sauces, and desserts. Sercial is also popularly served with turtle soup.

Port, Porto: True Porto comes from Porto, Portugal, and is a far cry from domestic imitations, which are spelled simply port. Some are exquisitely light and golden, some tawny and mellow, some thick and sweet. All are fortified. The classifications of port are: *Ruby* (fruity, sweeet, young red wine), *Tawny* (aged in wood and amber in color), *Vintage* (wine of a single excellent year, carefully aged and costly), *Crusted* (aged port, not necessarily of one vintage; *crusted* refers to the sediment that accumulates in the bottle. These wines should be decanted so that the sediment doesn't land in the glass).

Sherry: The best known of the dessert wines, sherries come from Jerez, Spain, after which they are named. They are fortified but mellower, nuttier than either the ports or Madeiras. *Dry sherries* are *Fino, Manzanilla,* and *Vino de Pasto* (these are best served cold as apéritifs); the *medium dry* is *Amontillado* (very nutty and a good all-purpose sherry); and the *sweet* are *Amoroso, Oloroso,* and *Brown. Cream sherry* is a very sweet *Oloroso.*

Tokay: White or amber sweet Hungarian wine from Tokay grapes. Tokays are also made in California.

Other Dessert Wines: Málaga (from Spain), *Marsala* (from Sicily), *Mavrodaphne* (from Greece, and *Muscatel* (Greece, Spain, and Portugual produce good ones). These are generally very sweet, some quite syrupy and raisiny.

Champagne and Other Sparkling Wines

Champagne: True champagne comes from the ancient province of Champagne around Rheims, and it and only it can be sold as "Champagne" in France and most of Europe. This is the reason why domestic champagne is labeled "California Champagne" or "Ohio" or "New York State Champagne." (Some of the domestics are very good, too.) Champagne is a white wine made from the Pinot Noir and Pinot Chardonnay grapes, twice fermented—once before bottling, once afterward (which produces the bubbles). All champagnes are blends, usually made from both varieties of Pinot grapes. When the white grapes alone (Chardonnay) are used, the results are a lighter champagne called *blanc de blanc.* Depending upon the amount of sweetening added *after* the first fermentation, champagne may be dry or sweet. The terms used to denote degree of sweetness are: *brut* or, in the case of California champagne, *natur* (the driest), *extra dry* (not as dry as brut), *demi-sec* (fairly sweet), and *sec* or *doux* (quite sweet). Pink champagne is simply champagne made from pressings allowed to stay on the skins a bit longer than usual (the pigment in the *pinot noir* grape skins pinkens the juice). When should champagne be served? It is the one wine that can be served at any time of the day, any course of the meal. The sweeter champagnes, however, are more suited to dessert.
Tip on Opening Champagne Bottles: Don't pop the cork, ease it out slowly and steadily so you don't shake up the champagne.

Other Sparkling Wines: There are many bubbling red and white wines, but sparkling Burgundy is the one Americans know best (Americans like it, the French don't). It is produced in much the same way as champagne except that the wine used is red Burgundy. France also makes a sparkling *Anjou* (rosé) and a sparkling *Vouvray* (dry or semidry white). Portugal makes some bubbling rosés, Germany some sparkling whites, Italy, too, including the famous *Asti Spumante.* California makes a version of nearly every sparkling French wine.

COOKING WINES

The idea of "cooking wine" is an absurd holdover from the days of prohibition. Cooking wines are "salted" so they won't be drunk. It is pointless to buy them, because the best wines to cook with are "drinking" wines (except, of course, those that cost the earth).

Some Terms and Techniques Having to do with Wines

The Language of Wine Labels: Because so many wines are imported and their labels written in foreign languages, the beginner has trouble decoding the message. The labels carrying the most meaningful information are those of French and German wines. Here then, are some of the common label terms and what they mean:

Appellation Contrôlée: A French term meaning that the wine was produced where it says it was, a guarantee of place of origin, so to speak, entitling the wine to a regional name—Bordeaux, for example, or Burgundy (the more specific the regional name, by the way, the better the wine will probably be). It further means that the traditional standards of the locale were upheld in the production of the wine.

Cave: The French word for *wine cellar; cave* on a label is not a guarantee of quality.

Clos: The French word for *vineyard;* if a label contains the phrase *"clos de"* followed by the name of a vineyard, it means the wine was produced at the local vineyard, and if the vineyard (and vintage) is a good one, the wine should be good.

Crus Classés: In 1855 the vineyards of Médoc and Sauternes in Bordeaux were classified according to excellence, and 62 were rated *Grands Crus* (great growths), a designation many Bordeaux labels still carry. Within the *Grands Crus* were five subdivisions, from the first and finest (*Premiers Crus*) through second, third, and fourth to fifth growths. Some bottles still display *Premiers Crus* on their labels, meaning they were the finest of the 1855 classification. Wines marked *Crus Exceptionnels* were in the category just below the *Grands Crus,* and those marked *Crus Bourgeois* and *Crus Artisans,* etc., were lower still. Since 1855, however, vineyards have changed hands, qualities have changed, and there is much pressure for a new system, of classification that will give credit where credit is due today. The new system, however, has not been determined, so the 1855 terms still hold.

Kabinet: A German label term meaning that the grower guarantees this particular wine to be the highest quality.

Mise en Bouteilles au (or *du*) *Château:* A French term meaning *estate-bottled.* Because most wine-producing châteaux are in Bordeaux, this particular phrase appears primarily on Bordeaux wines. With Burgundies, the equivalent phrase is *Mise en* (or *du*) *Domaine.* Other French phrases meaning estate-bottled are *Mise en Bouteille par le Propriétaire* or, more simply, *Mise à la Propriété.* The German equivalents: *Abfüllung, Kellerabfüllung,* and *Schlossabzug.*

V.D.Q.S. An abbreviation on French labels for *Vins Délimités de Qualité Supérieure.* It merely means that the wine has been produced according to government regulation and is not an indication of quality.

Other Wine Terms and Techniques:

Claret: The British name for red Bordeaux table wines.

Decant: To pour from one container to another. Aged wines need to be decanted so that any sediment stays in the original bottle. Decanting also is important for many dry red wines because it aerates them and brings out their full flavor.

Dry: A term meaning not sweet.

Lees: Sediment in a liquor or wine.

Marc: The grape skins and seeds left in the press after the juice has been run off. It is used to make *marc,* a potent *eau de vie.*

May Wine: Light German spring wine punch flavored with woodruff. Also called *Maibowle.* Some May wine is bottled.

Must: Pressed grape juice before and during fermentation.

Room Temperature: Ideally 60° F. and the temperature at which most dry red table wines are at their best.

Solerization: A process used in making Madeira and sherry in which casks of certain vintages are stacked, one on top of the other, the oldest being at the bottom. During the blending of the wines, a little from each tier is added in carefully worked-out proportions. When the bottom casks are empty, they are refilled from those directly above. Not all Madeira and sherry are made by this process, but those that are are marked *Solera*.

Varietal Wine: A wine named for the variety of grape from which it was made. *Riesling* is a varietal wine and so are *Semillon, Pinot Noir* and *Gamay* from California.

Vin Blanc: French for *white wine*.

Vin Rouge: French for *red wine*.

Vin du Pays: Local wine and the one to drink when traveling abroad. Much of it cannot be sampled out of its own locale, and much of it is very pleasant indeed.

Vins Ordinaires: Ordinary table wines, red or white, usually served in a carafe. These are the wines served in many French *bistros* and inns.

Vintage: Considerable fuss is made about vintage, more perhaps than is justified, because in off years wine of a great vineyard is likely to be better than that of a so-so vineyard in a great year. Vintage refers to the year's crop, and grapes, like other crops, experience good years and bad. Vintage matters most with French and German wines where weather is more changeable than in warmer, sunnier climes (vintage means little with Italian, Spanish, California, and Portuguese wines—except for Porto).

About Starting a Wine Cellar

People who enjoy wine usually keep a supply on hand; some even go to the expense of building temperature-controlled rooms so that the wines will mature properly. Wines are "alive," and if they are to mature properly, certain conditions must be met.

Temperature: Wine should not be subjected to abrupt temperature changes, so store well away from radiators, air conditioners, and drafts. Though the ideal "cellar" climate is about 55° F., wines will not suffer noticeably at temperatures up to 70° F. if those temperatures are constant. They are apt to deteriorate, especially the more perishable whites, in superheated apartments or where there are sudden changes from hot to cold.

Light: Keep wines in a dim or dark spot; intense light—natural or artificial—is damaging.

Vibration: Wines should mature undisturbed, the bottles lying on their sides so that the corks do not dry out and admit destructive bacteria or mold. This means no vibration from dishwashers, laundry, or other household equipment and no picking up and inspecting by family, friends, or neighbors.

The cellar, of course, need not be a cellar. It can be a closet shelf in a skyscraper apartment if conditions are right. What is the best way to buy wines? You'll save by buying by the case, also by buying good vintages young. Most wines, dry reds particularly, are better with a few years' maturity. When a vintage is good, buy labels you like as soon as they are available, then put them away for several years. Choice French wines can increase tenfold in price within a few years.

About Bottle Shapes and Sizes: Certain types of wines are sold in certain types of bottles, and as you come to know wines, you'll be able to recognize the wine by glancing at the bottle. Sizes vary, too. The best bottle sizes to buy are those that you will use up in the course of an evening. The standard bottle size for most still wines is 24–26 ounces, enough for 2–3 people at dinner if one wine only is being served. Many are available in half bottles or pints containing 12.5 ounces, enough for 1–2 persons. A number of domestic wines are bottled by the gallon and half gallon (a money saver when a great many people are to be served). For general use, however, the standard bottle size is best.

CHAMPAGNE BOTTLE SIZES

Size	Capacity	Glassfuls
Split (also called Nip or Baby)	6 oz.	2 (3 oz.)
Pint	½ bottle or quart	3 (4 oz.)
Bottle or Quart	26 oz.	6 (4 oz.)
Magnum (a double bottle)	52 oz.	13 (4 oz.)
Jeroboam (a double magnum)	4 bottles or quarts	26 (4 oz.)

About Serving Wines

When a wine is to be served and what it is to accompany determine the type that should be served. But the rules aren't as rigid as they once were, and the old business about red wines with red meats and white wines with white meats shouldn't be taken as law. A full-bodied red wine complements rare roast beef, it's true, but that same wine might not pair as happily as a dry white wine with *pot-au-feu* or other boiled beef dishes. What you choose, then, is largely a matter of personal preference and common sense. Obviously, a rich dry red wine would be inappropriate with delicate white fish. And a fragile white would do nothing for venison. It would be foolish to lavish a fine wine on meat loaf, but equally so to downgrade filet mignon with a poor one. Generally speaking, white wines are the best choices for seafood, the humbler wines accompanying the humbler fish. The wine that goes best with poultry depends upon how the poultry was cooked—that in a white sauce calls for white wine, but *coq au vin* or chicken with a robust tomato sauce will team better with red wine. With experience, one begins to know instinctively happy partnerships of food and wine. And a good way to gain that experience is by eating in fine restaurants and asking the sommelier (wine steward) what he recommends with your choice of menu.

When Two Wines Are to Be Served: The rules again are fairly simple: white wine before red, young wine before old, and dry wine before sweet. *Tip:* Avoid serving wine with salad or other vinegary food—the vinegar deadens the palate to the taste of the wine.

About Wineglasses: Few people have room today to store several kinds of wineglasses, so the best idea is to have an all-purpose glass and, shelf space permitting, a special tulip goblet for champagne. The all-purpose glass should be large—anywhere from 10 to 20 ounces, stemmed, round-bowled, and of clear, thin uncut crystal or glass (the better to appreciate the color of the wine).

About Wine-Serving Temperatures: Red wines should be served at room temperature provided the room isn't sweltering. To wine connoisseurs, room temperature is 60° F.—a bit cool for those used to heated houses—but a red wine served at a room temperature in the 70°'s will still be good. White and rosé wines should be chilled before serving, not so much that they lose flavor, just enough to enhance them (about 40–45° F.). Two to three hours in the refrigerator should do it. Don't try to quick-chill wine in the freezer— too much danger of its freezing. Champagnes should be served well chilled and so should sparkling Burgundies. *Note:* When chilling wine in an ice bucket, rotate bottle frequently so wine chills evenly.

About Uncorking and Pouring Wines: First of all, get a proper corkscrew— one that gently lifts out the cork—and learn to use it before tackling a fine wine. To open a bottle, cut around the metal covering over the cork about 1" below the top of the bottle and peel off;

wipe mouth of bottle with a dry, clean napkin. Center tip of corkscrew in cork and twist into cork, using the proper technique for the particular corkscrew, then *ease* cork out. Don't pop the cork or jerk it out—doing so unsettles the wine.

Red wines should be uncorked about an hour before serving so that they have a chance to "breathe" and develop full flavor. If the wine is an old one with sediment in the bottle, decant carefully into a clean, dry decanter and leave unstoppered. Or, if wine is very old and precious, cradle gently in a wine basket (its purpose is to keep wine as nearly as possible in its cellar position so that a minimum of sediment is stirred up). White and rosé wines should be uncorked just before serving. Wrapping a wine bottle in a white linen napkin is unnecessary unless the wine has been chilled in an ice bucket and is dripping. If in doubt about the quality of a wine, pour a little into your own glass and sample before serving guests (this is routinely done by sommeliers in restaurants). When pouring, never fill each glass more than ⅓–½ (another reason for having large wineglasses; the air space in the glass allows you to swirl the wine, bringing out its full bouquet). *Tip:* As you finish pouring wine into a glass, twist bottle slightly as you lift it to prevent dripping.

About Leftover Wines: Once opened, wines quickly turn to vinegar. White wines will keep refrigerated several days, red and fortified wines somewhat longer (uncork the leftover red wine and let it stand at room temperature about an hour before serving). If the wine should turn to vinegar, don't despair. Use it to dress salads.

About Whiskies and Liquors

All whiskies are liquor but all liquors aren't whiskey, the difference being that whiskey is distilled from grain mash (rye, corn, barley, wheat) and liquor from a variety of things—grain, sugar cane (rum), cactus (tequila), potatoes (vodka—although much of today's vodka is made of grain). Another clarification: *Whiskey* is the common spelling, *whisky* the British (used for scotch and Canadian whisky). Here, then, is a quick alphabet of popular liquors:

Aquavit: Potent, colorless Scandinavian liquor distilled from grain mash or potatoes, usually flavored with caraway. It is drunk ice cold, neat, sometimes with a beer chaser.

Arrack: A strong rumlike liquor distilled from fermented coconut juice. It is popular in Indonesia, Asia, and the Middle East.

Blended Whiskey: A blend, ⅕ 100-proof straight whiskey, ⅘ other whiskies and neutral spirits. Blended whiskies must be at least 80 proof, but they are almost always light and smooth.

Bourbon: The American liquor—amber brown, rich, and smooth—distilled from a fermented mash of rye, corn, and malted barley. *Straight bourbon* is distilled from a mash containing at least 51 per cent corn; *blended bourbon* is a whiskey blend containing at least 51 per cent straight bourbon. *Sour mash* is a type of bourbon made by fermenting each new load of mash with "working yeast" from the previous batch. Rather like sour dough bread, for which yeast starters are kept alive and used over and over, each successive dough replenishing the starter.

Canadian Whisky: Liquor distilled from blends of rye, corn, wheat, and barley. It is similar to rye and bourbon but smoother and lighter.

Corn Whiskey: Liquor distilled from fermented corn mash. To qualify as *straight corn whiskey,* it must contain at least 51 per cent corn. Corn whiskey is, of course, the *white lightning* or *moonshine* of Southern bootleggers.

Gin: Distilled neutral grain spirits, crisp, colorless, and lightly flavored with juniper. There are two types: *London dry gin,* the type Americans know, and *Dutch* or *Holland gin* (*Jenever* or *Geneva*), a heavier, stronger variety which the Dutch drink neat.

Irish Whiskey: An Irish liquor distilled from grain, primarily barley. It is dry and light, has none of the smokiness of scotch.

Rum: Liquor distilled from sugar syrup or molasses. Made primarily in the Caribbean, rum can be light and soft, it can be golden, amber, or rich dark brown, and it can be full-bodied. Darkest of all is *Demerara* rum, made from sugar cane grown along the Demerara River in British Guiana.

Rye: Whiskey distilled wholly or partly from rye mash. Its flavor is similar to bourbon, but many people find it smoother, more full bodied. *Rock and Rye* is rye flavored with rock candy, lemon, and orange.

Schnapps (also *Snaps*): A generic word meaning in Holland and Germany any strong dry colorless liquor such as gin, in Scandinavia (except Finland) aquavit, and in Finland vodka.

Scotch: A well-aged blend of grain and malt whiskies made in Scotland. The smoky flavor comes from the peat fires over which the malted barley is dried.

Sour Mash: See Bourbon.

Southern Comfort: Bourbon mixed with peach liqueur and fresh, peeled, and pitted peaches, then aged several months. It is sweeter, mellower than bourbon but has a deceptive kick.

Straight Whiskey: Pure, unblended grain whiskey from 80 to 110 proof that has been aged at least two years. The term is usually used in conjunction with bourbon or rye.

Tequila: A colorless or pale yellow liquor, usually 100+ proof, distilled from the fermented juice of the agave cactus.

Vodka: Highly distilled, charcoal filtered, colorless liquor distilled from fermented grain mash or potatoes. Vodka is unaged, flavorless, odorless and ranges from about 65 to 98 proof.

About Brandies and Liqueurs

These are usually served after meals or used in mixing drinks.

Absinthe: A bitter licorice-flavored liqueur made with wormwood and herbs. Because of the harmful effects of wormwood, absinthe was banned in France in 1915 and subsequently by many other countries including the United States.

Advokaat: A creamy egg liqueur.

Anis: Clear anise (licorice) liqueur popular in France and Spain. It is mixed with water (which turns it milky) and drunk as an apéritif.

Anisette: Clear sweet liqueur aromatic of anise seeds; unlike anis, it is drunk neat as a cordial.

Applejack: The American version of apple brandy.

Apricot Liqueur: A liqueur made from apricots; syrupy and fragrant.

Armagnac: See Brandy.

B&B: A half-and-half mixture of Benedictine and brandy, available bottled.

Benedictine: A sweet, fruity, herby liqueur made originally by Benedictine monks at the abbey of Fécamp in France. Though laymen today make Benedictine, they carry on in the tradition of the monks, using their secret recipe.

Brandy: Technically, distilled wine or other fermented fruit juice, well aged, usually in wood. There are many brandies: *Cognac* (one of the choicest, made in Cognac, France), *Armagnac* (another fine dry French brandy, this one from Armagnac), *Calvados* (the fine apple brandy of Normandy), and *Marc* (or *Grappa*), distilled from the grape skins, pulp, and seeds left in the wine press after the juice has been drained off.

Chartreuse: A brandy-based liqueur made by monks of the monastery of La Grande Chartreuse near Grenoble, France. Pale green or golden in color, it is flavored with hyssop, angelica, balm, cinnamon, and other herbs and spices.

Cherry Heering: A Danish cherry liqueur.

Cherry Suisse: A Swiss cherry-chocolate liqueur.

Cognac: See Brandy.

Cointreau: A choice French orange-flavored liqueur.

Crème: Crème liqueurs have been sweetened, are thick and syrupy. The list of them is long, but among the better known are: *Crème d'Ananas* (pineapple), *Crème de Banane* (Banana), *Crème de Cacao* (chocolate), *Crème de Café* (coffee), *Crème de Cassis* (black currant), *Crème de Fraise* (strawberry), *Crème de Framboise* (raspberry), *Crème de Menthe* (mint—both a white and green are available), *Crème de Roses* (rose), *Crème de Vanille* (vanilla) and *Crème de Violette* (violet).

Curaçao: An orange-flavored liqueur made on the Caribbean island of Curaçao from the dried rind of bitter (Seville) oranges.

Danziger Goldwasser: A German herb- and orange-flavored liqueur adrift with flecks of gold leaf (they are harmless to drink).

Drambuie: Pale, amber scotch-based liqueur sweetened with heather honey and flavored with herbs.

Eau de Vie: "Water of life," a colorless, potent liqueur distilled from fermented fruit juices and/or skins and pits. If the fruit is the grape (as in Marc, see Brandy), the *eau de vie* is a brandy. If a fruit other than grape, it is technically not brandy. *Kirsch* and *framboise,* for example, are *eaux de vie* but not brandies.

Forbidden Fruit: An American brandy-based liqueur flavored with shaddock (a variety of grapefruit).

Fraise: A French *eau de vie* made from strawberries.

Framboise: A French *eau de vie* made from raspberries.

Galliano: A spicy, golden Italian liqueur.

Grand Marnier: A French cognac-based liqueur flavored with orange.

Grappa: An Italian *eau de vie* made from grape skins and seeds left in the wine press (see Brandy).

Irish Mist: A liqueur distilled from Irish whiskey and sweetened with heather honey.

Kahlúa: A syrupy Mexican liqueur made of coffee and cocoa beans.

Kirsch: A crisp, colorless cherry *eau de vie.* Also called *Kirchwasser.*

Kümmel: A colorless German liqueur aromatic of caraway seeds.

Maraschino: An Italian wild cherry liqueur.

Marc: See Brandy.

Metaxa: A heavy, dark, sweet Greek brandy.

Ouzo: A clear licorice-flavored Greek brandy, mixed with water and drunk as an apéritif. Like anis, it turns cloudy when mixed with water.

Parfait Amour: A perfumy lavender liqueur.

Pernod: Yellow, licorice-flavored liqueur much like absinthe except that it contains no wormwood. Mixed with water, it is a favorite French apéritif.

Pisco: A Peruvian grape brandy.

Poire William: Clear, colorless pear *eau de vie,* the finest of which contains a ripe pear inside the bottle.

Prunelle: Brown, brandy-based French liqueur flavored with sloes (bitter plums).

Quetsch: An Alsatian *eau de vie* made of fermented purple plum juice.

Raki: A fiery anise-flavored spirit popular in Greece, Turkey, and the Middle East.

Ratafia: A fruit liqueur, often homemade.

Sambuca Romana: An Italian anise (licorice) liqueur; not very sweet.

Slivovitz: A plum brandy made in Hungary and the Balkans.

Sloe Gin: A liqueur made by steeping sloes (small tart plums) in gin.

Strega: A flowery golden Italian liqueur.

Tia Maria: A heavy rum-based, coffee-flavored West Indian liqueur.

Triple Sec: A clear, orange-flavored liqueur much like Curaçao.

Vandermint: A Dutch chocolate-mint liqueur.

A MISCELLANY OF ALCOHOLIC BEVERAGES

These do not fit neatly into any of the preceding categories, yet are commonly used today.

Falernum: Not really a liqueur but a colorless West Indian lime-almond-ginger syrup, about 6 per cent alcohol. It is used in mixing many "tropical" drinks.

Grenadine: Pink pomegranate syrup, sometimes containing alcohol.

Hard Cider: Fermented apple cider; it often has quite a kick.

Pimm's Cup: There are four Pimm's Cups, all cordial-like drink mixes, said to have been originated by a bartender at Pimm's Restaurant in London. Because of popular demand, the mixes were bottled. Pimm's No. 1 is a gin-based mix, No. 2 a whisky-based mix, No. 3 rum-based, and No. 4 brandy-based. All are commonly used in mixing cocktails.

Pulque: The fermented sap of the agave cactus and practically the national drink of Mexico. Pulque is thick, sweetish and looks rather like buttermilk.

Sake: People often call this Japanese fermented rice drink wine; technically, it isn't because wine is fermented grape juice. Sake is nearer beer because both are fermented grain drinks; however, sake's alcoholic content at 20 per cent is well above that of conventional beers. In Japan, sake is served warm in doll-size china cups, usually at the start of a meal. *Mirin* is another rice drink, similar to sake but sweeter. It is used more for cooking than drinking.

Vermouth: Vermouth is not so much wine as a wine-based drink, heavily infused with herbs. Dry vermouth is pale (the best comes from France), sweet Vermouth is dark or light and usually Italian. Dry vermouth is integral to martinis, sweet vermouth to manhattans.

Bitters

These are used in making cocktails, also taken as apéritifs, liqueurs, and medicine (many bitters are said to be good for digestion). Bitters are made of aromatic seeds, herbs, barks, and plants from carefully guarded recipes. Many have high alcoholic content, all are bitter or bittersweet.

Abbott's Aged Bitters: American bitters prepared for more than a hundred years by the Abbott family in Baltimore.

Amer Picon: Popular French bitters.

Angostura: Probably the best known of all bitters, these were created by a German doctor in Trinidad.

Boonekamp: Famous Dutch bitters.

Campari: Italy's most popular bitters, drunk everywhere mixed with club soda (campari sodas are now bottled in Italy the way colas are here).

Fernet Branca: Another popular Italian bitters, this one heavy and dark and more often used for medicinal purposes than for mixing drinks.

Orange Bitters: Bitters made from the dried peel of Seville (bitter) oranges.

Unicum: Popular bitters made in Hungary.

Equipping and Stocking the Home Bar

Basic Equipment Needed:
Jigger, Measuring Cup
Ice Bucket

Cocktail Shaker
Large Mixing Glass
Muddler, Stirring Rods, Long-Handled
  Spoons
Flat Bar Strainer
Paring Knife, Vegetable Peeler
Lemon Squeezer
Corkscrew, Can and Bottle Openers
Ice Pick and Tongs
Bag and Mallet for Crushing Ice
Ice Scoop
Note: Descriptions of the commonly
used cocktail and highball glasses are
included in the Drink Chart that follows.

Some Useful Extras:
Electric Blender
Electric Juicer
Electric Ice Crusher
Electric Portable Mixer

Basic Supplies Needed:
Liquor: bourbon, brandy, gin, light rum,
rye, scotch, vodka
Mixers: Sweet and dry vermouth,
aromatic bitters, ginger ale, club soda,
tonic water, bitter lemon, cola, tomato
juice

Staples: Sugar (superfine and confectioners'), maraschino cherries, cocktail
olives, cocktail onions, cocktail toothpicks

Perishables: Lemons, limes, oranges,
fresh mint, horseradish

Some Useful Extras:
Apple brandy
Benedictine
Campari
Canadian whisky
Crème de cacao
Crème de menthe
Grenadine
Irish whiskey
Lime juice (bottled)
Liquid hot red pepper seasoning
Mineral water (bottled)
Orange bitters
Port (tawny)
Rum (medium and dark)
Sherry (fino, amontillado and cream)
Triple Sec
Worcestershire Sauce

How to Buy Liquor for a Party

Almost all liquor is available in pints,
fifths, quarts, and half gallons. It's
usually wise to buy by the quart or half
gallon (you have more liquor in fewer
bottles and you may also be able to save
a little money). If the party is small and
you know your guests well, you probably
also know what each drinks and can
order accordingly. If a party is large, be
guided by the drinking habits and fads in
your area. In some communities, people
drink a great deal of scotch and gin but
little else; in others (the South, for
example), people prefer bourbon. Order
a good supply of the two or three
popular liquors, then also buy a few
bottles of the next most popular—just in
case. Here, then, is a guide to ordering.

DRINK CALCULATOR

For a Dinner Party

No. of Guests	Approx. Drink Consumption	Liquor Needed
4	8–12	1 fifth
6	12–18	1 quart
8	16–24	2 fifths
12	24–36	2 quarts
20	40–60	4 fifths
40	80–120	7 quarts

For a Cocktail Party

No. of Guests	Approx. Drink Consumption	Liquor Needed
4	12–16	1 quart
6	18–24	2 fifths
8	24–32	2 fifths
12	36–48	3 fifths
20	60–80	5 fifths
40	120–160	9 quarts

Note: To be safe, substitute quarts wherever
fifths are mentioned. It is always good to
have a little reserve liquor.

Some Terms and Techniques of Drink Mixing

Bottled in Bond: This phrase is not a
mark of quality in whiskey. It merely
means that certain government regula-

DRINK CHART
(Each Recipe Makes 1 Serving)

Tips for Making Better Drinks:
— Measure all ingredients carefully.
— Use the freshest and best ingredients possible.
— *Shaking* is for cloudy drinks. Shake drinks in a cocktail shaker — *vigorously* — to blend.
— *Stirring* is for clear drinks. Use a glass pitcher and glass stirrer.
— Use clean ice that has been stored away from foods (ice absorbs odors). *To crush,* wrap cubes in a dish towel and pound with a hammer; or use an ice crusher. *To crack,* tap ice block with ice cracker. *To shave,* pull ice shaver (a gadget rather like a wood plane) across ice block.
— Use *superfine* sugar (not confectioners' or granulated); use domino-shape sugar cubes; 1 small cube equals about 1/2 domino cube.
— Add liquor last when mixing with fruit juice, milk, cream or egg.
— Mix drinks to order and serve as soon as they're made in chilled glasses.

Drink	Approx. Calories per Serving	Type of Glass	Best Time to Serve	Kind and Amount of Liquor	Ice
Alexander (Brandy or Gin)	225	4½ or 6 oz. cocktail glass	After dinner	1½ oz. brandy or gin	1/2 cup cracked ice
Americano	120	8 oz. highball glass	Before or between meals	2 oz. sweet vermouth	2-3 ice cubes
B & B	100	2 oz. liqueur glass	After dinner	1/2 oz. brandy	—
Bacardi	190	4½ oz. cocktail glass	Before meals	2 oz. Bacardi rum	1/2 cup cracked ice
Black Russian	245	6 oz. old-fashioned glass	Before meals	2 oz. vodka	2 ice cubes
Black Velvet	280	12 oz. tankard or beer glass	Between meals	1 (6-6½ oz.) split chilled dry champagne	—
Bloody Mary	140	5 oz. Delmonico or juice glass	Before meals	1½ oz. vodka	1/2 cup cracked ice
Bullshot	135	6 oz. old-fashioned glass	Before or between meals	1½ oz. vodka.	2 ice cubes
Campari Soda	40	8 oz. highball glass	Before or between meals	1 oz. Campari	2 ice cubes
Champagne Cocktail	180	6-8 oz. champagne goblet	Before meals	Chilled champagne to fill glass	—
Collins (basic recipe)	230	10-12 oz. collins glass	Before or between meals	2 oz. liquor (gin for Tom Collins, blended whiskey for John Collins, rum for Rum Collins, etc.)	3/4-1 cup cracked ice
Crème de Menthe Frappé	100	2-2½ oz. sherry glass	After dinner	1 oz. green crème de menthe	1/4 cup crushed ice
(Note: Any liqueur may be prepared as a frappé; prepare as directed, substituting another liqueur for crème de menthe.)					
Cuba Libre	285	12 oz. collins glass	As a midafternoon cooler	2 oz. rum	3-4 ice cubes

Note: Calorie counts for all alcoholic beverages that follow were computed on the basis of 100-proof liquor. By using a lower proof, you can reduce the number of calories somewhat:

Proof (all liquors)	Measure	Number of Calories
80	1 fluid ounce	65
86	1 fluid ounce	70
90	1 fluid ounce	73
100	1 fluid ounce	82

Other Liquid or Liqueur	Seasonings	How to Mix	Garnishes
1/2 oz. heavy cream 3/4 oz. crème de cacao	—	Shake all ingredients with ice and strain into glass.	Sprinkling of nutmeg
Club soda to fill glass	1 oz. Campari	Place ice, vermouth, and Campari in glass, fill with soda and stir to mix.	Twist of lemon peel
1/2 oz. Benedictine	—	Pour Benedictine in glass, then pour in brandy.	—
Juice of 1/2 lime	3-4 dashes grenadine 1/2 teaspoon sugar	Shake all ingredients with ice and strain into glass.	—
1 oz. coffee liqueur	—	Stir all ingredients with ice in glass.	—
3/4 cup chilled stout	—	Pour champagne and stout simultaneously into tankard.	—
1/3 cup tomato juice 1 teaspoon lemon juice	2 dashes Worcestershire 1-2 dashes liquid hot red pepper seasoning Pinch each salt and cayenne	Shake all ingredients with ice and strain into glass.	—
Beef consommé to fill glass	Salt to taste	Place vodka and ice in glass, fill with consommé, season, and stir.	Twist of lemon peel
Club soda to fill glass	—	Place ice and Campari in glass and pour in soda.	—
—	1 lump sugar 2-3 dashes aromatic bitters	Place sugar in glass, drop bitters on sugar, and pour in champagne.	Twist of lemon peel
Juice of 1 lemon Club soda to fill glass	1 teaspoon sugar	Place juice, sugar, ice, and liquor in glass, fill with soda, and stir.	Cocktail cherry Slice of lemon
—	—	Fill glass with ice and pour liqueur evenly over all. Insert straws.	—
Juice of 1/2 lime Chilled cola to fill glass	—	Place juice, ice and rum in glass, fill with cola, and stir to mix.	Small lime wedge

103

Drink	Approx. Calories per Serving	Type of Glass	Best Time to Serve	Kind and Amount of Liquor	Ice
Daiquri (plain)	185	4½ oz. cocktail glass	Before meals	1 oz. light rum	1/2 cup cracked ice
Daiquiri (frozen)	185	6-8 oz. champagne goblet	Before meals	2 oz. light rum	1/2 cup shaved or crushed ice
Eggnog	435	12 oz. collins glass	As a between-meals refresher	2 oz. brandy, light rum, sherry, or port	1/2 cup cracked ice
French 75	245	8 oz. highball glass	Before meals	2 oz. gin	1/2 cup cracked ice
Gibson (see Martini)					
Gimlet	210	4½ oz. cocktail glass	Before meals	2 oz. gin or vodka	1/2 cup cracked ice
Gin or Vodka and Tonic	170 (with 1½ oz. liquor) 210 (with 2 oz. liquor)	8 oz. highball glass	Before meals or between meals	1½-2 oz. gin or vodka	3 ice cubes
Gin or Sloe Gin Fizz	150 with gin 110 with sloe gin	8 oz. highball glass	Before or between meals	1½ oz. gin or sloe gin	1/2 cup cracked ice 2 ice cubes
Gin Rickey	130	8 oz. highball glass	Before or between meals	1½ oz. gin	2-3 ice cubes
Grasshopper	250	4½ oz. cocktail glass	After dinner	1 oz. white crème de cacao	1/2 cup cracked ice
Grog	190	8 oz. mug	Anytime as a cold-weather bracer	2 oz. dark rum or brandy	—
Hot Buttered Rum	235	8 oz. mug	Anytime as a cold-weather bracer	2 oz. dark rum	—
Hot Toddy	170	6 oz. old-fashioned glass	Anytime as a cold-weather bracer	1½ oz. dark rum, brandy, bourbon, rye, or scotch	—
Irish Coffee	290	6-8 oz. mug or cup	Anytime as a cold-weather bracer	1½ oz. Irish whiskey	—
Kir	200	8 oz. wineglass	Before meals		2 ice cubes

Other Liquid or Liqueur	Seasonings	How to Mix	Garnishes
Juice of 1/2 lime	3/4 teaspoon sugar	Shake all ingredients with ice and strain into glass.	—
Juice of 1/2 lime	3/4 teaspoon sugar 3-4 dashes Maraschino	Buzz all ingredients with ice in an electric blender at high speed about 1 minute until fluffy; spoon into glass, insert short straws.	—
1 cup milk	1 egg 2 teaspoons sugar	Shake all ingredients with ice and strain into glass.	A sprinkling of nutmeg
Juice of 1 lemon Chilled champagne to fill glass	1 teaspoon sugar	Place lemon juice, sugar, and gin in glass and stir to mix; add ice and pour in champagne.	—
Juice of 1/2 lime or 1 tablespoon bottled lime juice	1½ teaspoons Triple Sec	Shake all ingredients with ice and strain into glass.	—
Quinine water to fill glass	1 lime wedge	Squeeze lime wedge over glass, then drop in; add gin, ice, quinine water; stir slightly.	—
Juice of 1/2 lemon Club soda to fill glass	1 teaspoon sugar	Shake all ingredients but soda with cracked ice and strain over ice cubes in glass. Fill with soda and stir.	—
Juice of 1/2 lime Club soda to fill glass	—	Squeeze lime over glass and drop in, add ice, gin, and soda, and stir.	—
1 oz. green crème de menthe 3/4 oz. heavy cream	—	Shake all ingredients with ice and strain into glass.	—
Juice of 1/2 lemon Boiling water to fill mug	1 lump sugar 1 lemon slice 2 cloves 1/2 cinnamon stick	Place lemon juice, rum, and seasonings in mug, fill with boiling water, and stir to mix.	—
1 teaspoon brandy Boiling water to fill mug	1 teaspoon light brown sugar 4 cloves 1 strip orange peel 1 teaspoon unsalted butter 1 cinnamon stick	Place rum and brandy in mug, add sugar, cloves and orange peel; place butter on a spoon in mug and pour boiling water over butter; stir with cinnamon stick.	—
Boiling water to fill glass	1 lemon slice stuck with 3 cloves 1/4 cinnamon stick 1 teaspoon sugar	Put rum and seasonings in glass, insert metal spoon, and slowly pour in water; stir to mix.	—
1/2-3/4 cup hot strong black coffee	2 teaspoons sugar	Pour coffee into mug, add whiskey and sugar and stir; let whipped cream slide over a metal spoon to float on coffee. Do not stir.	2 tablespoons *very* lightly whipped cream
6 oz. Chablis or other dry white wine 1/2 oz. crème de cassis	1 strip lemon peel	Place ice, wine and crème de cassis in glass, twist lemon peel over glass, and drop in. Stir gently.	—

DRINK CHART (continued)

Drink	Approx. Calories per Serving	Type of Glass	Best Time to Serve	Kind and Amount of Liquor	Ice
Manhattan (regular)	200	4½ oz. cocktail glass	Before meals	2 oz. rye	1-2 ice cubes
Manhattan (dry)	190	4½ oz. cocktail glass	Before meals	2 oz. rye	1-2 ice cubes
Margarita	175	4½ oz. cocktail glass (dip rim in lime juice, then in salt to "frost")	Before meals	2 oz. tequila	1/2 cup cracked ice
Martini (*Note:* Connoisseurs keep both gin and vermouth in the refrigerator.)					
Regular	142	4½ oz. cocktail glass	Before meals	1½ oz. gin or vodka	2-3 ice cubes
Dry	138	4½ oz. cocktail glass	Before meals	1½ oz. gin or vodka	2-3 ice cubes
Extra dry	135	4½ oz. cocktail glass	Before meals	1¾ oz. gin or vodka	2-3 ice cubes
Gibson	175	4½ oz. cocktail glass	Before meals	2 oz. gin or vodka	2-3 ice cubes
Milk Punch	385	12 oz. collins glass	As a between-meals refresher	2 oz. brandy, bourbon, rum, rye, or Irish whiskey	1/2 cup cracked ice
Mint Julep	185	10-12 oz. collins glass or silver julep cup	Anytime as a refresher	2 oz. bourbon	2 cups cracked ice
Mist					
Scotch	165	6 oz. old-fashioned glass	Before meals for Scotch and Irish mist, after dinner for heather mist	2 oz. scotch	1/2 cup shaved ice
Heather	220	6 oz. old-fashioned glass		2 oz. Drambuie	1/2 cup shaved ice
Irish	165	6 oz. old-fashioned glass		2 oz. Irish whiskey	1/2 cup shaved ice
Moscow Mule	220	8 oz. pewter or silver mug	Before or between meals	2 oz. vodka	2-3 ice cubes
Negroni	170	10-12 oz. collins glass	Before or between meals	1 oz. gin	2-3 ice cubes
Old-Fashioned	135 (with 1½ oz. liquor) 175 (with 2 oz. liquor)	6 oz. old-fashioned glass	Before meals	1½-2 oz. blended whiskey or, if you specify it, rye, scotch, bourbon, or rum	1-2 ice cubes
Orange Blossom	155	4½ oz. cocktail glass	Before meals	1½ oz. gin	1/2 cup cracked ice
Pimm's Cup	160	10-12 oz. collins glass	Before or between meals	2 oz. Pimm's No. 1	2-3 ice cubes
Pink Lady	195	4½ or 6 oz. cocktail glass	Before meals	2 oz. gin	1/2 cup cracked ice

Other Liquid or Liqueur	Seasonings	How to Mix	Garnishes
3/4 oz. sweet vermouth	—	Stir rye and vermouth gently with ice, strain into glass, and garnish.	Cocktail cherry
3/4 oz. dry vermouth	—		Twist of lemon peel
Juice of 1/2 lime	2-3 dashes Triple Sec or curaçao	Shake all ingredients with ice and strain into glass.	—
1/2 oz. extra dry vermouth	—	Stir gin or vodka and vermouth very gently with ice, strain into glass, and garnish.	Green olive
1/3 oz. extra dry vermouth	—		Twist of lemon peel
1/4 oz. extra dry vermouth	—		Twist of lemon peel
1/4 oz. extra dry vermouth	—		2-3 cocktail onions
1¼ cups cold milk	1 teaspoon sugar	Shake all ingredients with ice and strain into glass.	Sprinkling of nutmeg
—	12 large tender mint leaves 1 teaspoon sugar	Place leaves and sugar in glass and muddle, pressing leaves against sides of glass to extract flavor; discard mint. Pack glass with ice and let stand 1-2 minutes to "frost" outside; slowly pour in bourbon, rotating glass; garnish and serve with straws. SIP SLOWLY!	3-4 sprigs mint
—	—	Fill glass with ice, drizzle in whiskey or liqueur, and garnish.	Twist of lemon peel
—	—		Twist of lemon peel
—	—		Twist of lemon peel
Juice of 1/2 lime Ginger beer to fill mug	—	Place ice in mug, add lime and vodka; stir, then fill with ginger beer.	Slice of lime
1 oz. Campari 1 oz. sweet vermouth Club soda to fill glass	—	Place ice, gin, Campari, and vermouth in glass, fill with soda and stir.	Slice of orange
1 teaspoon club soda	1/2 lump sugar saturated with 1-2 dashes aromatic bitters; for an extra good drink, also add 2 drops scotch and 3 drops curaçao.	Place sugar and soda in glass, add ice and whiskey, stir, and garnish.	Twist of lemon peel Slice of orange Maraschino cherry
1 oz. orange juice	1 teaspoon sugar	Shake all ingredients with ice and strain into glass.	—
Lemon soda to fill glass	—	Place ice, garnishes, and Pimm's in glass, fill with soda, and stir.	Slice of lemon Strip of cucumber peel
Juice of 1/2 lemon 3-4 dashes apple brandy	3-4 dashes grenadine 1 egg white	Shake all ingredients with ice and strain into glass.	—

Drink	Approx. Calories per Serving	Type of Glass	Best Time to Serve	Kind and Amount of Liquor	Ice
Pisco Sour	165	5 oz. Delmonico or juice glass	Before meals	1½ oz. Pisco brandy	1/2 cup cracked ice
Planter's Punch	190 (without orange juice) 220 (with orange juice)	10-12 oz. collins glass	Before or between meals	2 oz. dark rum	1/2 cup cracked ice, shaved ice to fill glass
Port Wine Cooler	130	12 oz. collins glass glass	Before or between meals	1/2 cup dry port wine	Crushed ice to 1/2 fill glass
Pousse-Café	95	1 oz. liqueur glass	After dinner	1 teaspoon grenadine 1 teaspoon green crème de menthe 1 teaspoon yellow Chartreuse 1 teaspoon Triple Sec 1 teaspoon brandy	—
Rob Roy	190 (with dry vermouth) 200 (with sweet vermouth)	4½ oz. cocktail glass	Before meals	2 oz. scotch	1/2 cup shaved or cracked ice
Rum Swizzle	190	8 oz. highball glass	Before or between meals	2 oz. rum	1/2 cup crushed ice
Salty Dog	230	8 oz. highball glass	Before meals	2 oz. vodka	2 ice cubes
Screwdriver	300	12 oz. collins glass	Before meals	2 oz. vodka	1/2-2/3 cup crushed ice
Side Car	230	4½ oz. cocktail glass	After dinner	1½ oz. brandy	1/2 cup cracked ice
Singapore Sling	260	12 oz. collins glass	Before or between meals	2 oz. gin	3/4 cup cracked ice
Sour (basic recipe)	190	5 oz. Delmonico or juice glass or 6 oz. sour glass	Before meals	2 oz. rye, bourbon, scotch, rum, brandy, or gin	1/2 cup cracked ice
Spritzer	90	12 oz. collins glass	With or between meals	1/2 cup Rhine wine	3/4 cup cracked ice
Stinger	245	4½ oz. cocktail glass	After dinner	1¾ oz. brandy	1/2 cup cracked ice
Vermouth Cassis	190	8 oz. wineglass	Before meals	—	2 ice cubes
Zombie	450	12 oz. collins glass	Before meals	1½ oz. light rum 1½ oz. dark rum 1½ oz. Demerara rum	1/2 cup cracked ice 4 ice cubes

Other Liquid or Liqueur	Seasonings	How to Mix	Garnishes
Juice of 1/2 lemon	1 egg white 1 teaspoon sugar	Shake all ingredients with ice and strain into glass.	—

Juice of 1/2 lemon or lime
Juice of 1/2 orange
(optional)
	1/2 oz. Falernum or
	1 teaspoon sugar
		Shake all ingredients with cracked ice and strain into glass filled with shaved ice, garnish, add straws.	1/2 orange slice
			1 stick fresh
			    pineapple
			Maraschino
			    cherry
			Mint

1/2 cup ginger ale	—	Place ice in glass, add wine and ginger ale, and stir to mix.	—
—	—	Pour grenadine into glass and let stand a few seconds. Gently place a glass stirrer in grenadine and very slowly pour in each liqueur down along stirrer in order listed so each floats on the other.	—

3/4 oz. sweet or dry vermouth	Dash aromatic bitters	Stir scotch and vermouth with ice and bitters and strain into glass. Add garnishes.	Strip of lemon
			    peel
			Maraschino
			    cherry

Juice of 1/2 lime Club soda to fill glass	1 teaspoon sugar 3-4 dashes aromatic bitters	Stir lime juice, rum, seasonings, and ice in a pitcher until it "frosts," strain into glass, and add soda.	—
Grapefruit juice to fill glass	Pinch salt	Place all ingredients in glass and stir.	—
Orange juice to fill glass	—	Place all ingredients in glass and stir.	—
Juice of 1/2 lime 1 oz. Cointreau	—	Shake all ingredients with ice and strain into glass.	—

Juice of 1/2 lemon or lime
1 oz. cherry brandy or
    liqueur
Club soda to fill glass
	2-3 drops Benedictine
	2-3 drops brandy
		Place ice, juice, gin, cherry brandy and soda in glass and stir; with a medicine dropper, add Benedictine, then brandy by inserting halfway into glass. Float orange slice on top and place cherry in center.	Thin orange slice
			Maraschino
			    cherry

Juice of 1/2 lemon	1 teaspoon sugar
	2 dashes aromatic
	    bitters
		Shake all ingredients with ice and strain into glass. Add garnishes.	Small orange wedge
			Maraschino
			    cherry

Club soda to fill glass	—	Place all ingredients in glass and stir.	—
1 oz. white crème de menthe	—	Shake all ingredients with ice and strain into glass.	—
4 oz. dry vermouth 1/2 oz. crème de cassis 2 oz. chilled club soda	Twist of lemon peel	Place ice in glass, pour in vermouth, twist lemon peel over glass and drop in. Add crème de cassis, club soda and stir gently.	—
Juice of 1/2 lime 1 tablespoon apricot liqueur 1 tablespoon pineapple juice	1½ teaspoons Falernum	Shake all ingredients with cracked ice, strain into glass, add ice cubes and garnishes. Insert straws and SIP VERY SLOWLY!	Thin orange slice Mint sprigs

tions have been met, that the whiskey is at least four years old and 100 proof, that it was produced by a single distiller, and that it will be stored in a bonded warehouse until federal excise taxes have been paid by the distiller (this usually is done as the whiskey is ready to be shipped to the retailer).

Dash: A bar measure—6–8 drops or ⅙ teaspoon.

Fifth: ⅘ of a quart or 25.6 fluid ounces.

Frost: To chill a glass until frost forms on the outside.

To Frost Rims of Glasses: Dip rims of glasses in lemon, lime, or orange juice or in lightly beaten egg white, then in sugar or salt to frost (salt for margaritas, sugar for most sweet fruit drinks), then let dry 3–4 minutes until sugar hardens.

Jigger (or *Shot*): A bar measure—1½ ounces. A large jigger is 2 ounces.

Muddle: To mix together ingredients, lightly bruising and mashing with a pestlelike muddler.

Neat: A way of drinking liquor—in straight shots without ice.

On the Rocks: Descriptive term for a drink served with ice cubes.

Pony: A bar measure—1 ounce.

Proof: The measure of alcoholic content of liquor; in the U.S., proof is exactly twice the percentage of alcohol. Thus, something marked 100 proof is 50 per cent alcohol.

Shake: To blend by shaking vigorously in a covered shaker. Shaking produces a cloudy drink, stirring a clear one.

Standing: A term used to describe a cocktail, usually martini, served without ice.

Stir: To mix, using a long-handled spoon or stirring rod in a gentle circular motion. The purpose is to mingle ingredients, not to agitate them.

Twist: A twisted piece of lemon or orange rind, usually about 1½″ long and ¼″ wide. The technique is to twist the rind over the drink to extract the oil, then to drop the rind into the drink.

Up: A term used to describe a cocktail served without ice.

V.S.: An abbreviation often seen on liquor labels. It stands for *very superior*. Others are: *V.S.O.* (*very superior old*), *V.V.O.* (*very, very old*) and *V.V.S.* (*very, very superior*).

NUMBER OF (1½ oz.) DRINKS IN:

Bottle Size	1 Bottle	2 Bottles	4 Bottles	6 Bottles	8 Bottles	10 Bottles
Fifth (25.6 oz.)	17	34	68	102	136	170
Quart (32 oz.)	21	42	84	126	168	210

Note: When serving martinis or manhattans, allow 1 bottle of vermouth to 3 quarts of liquor.

⊠ SANGRIA

A Spanish wine and fruit drink, cooling
on a hot summer day.
Makes 8–10 servings

1 (24-oz.) bottle dry red wine
1 orange
1 lemon or lime
1 pint club soda
6–8 ice cubes
1 peeled, sliced peach or ⅓ cup
  stemmed ripe strawberries or ⅓ cup
  raspberries (optional)

Pour wine into a large pitcher. Using a
vegetable peeler, peel rinds from orange
and lemon in long spirals and add to
wine; add juice from the orange and ½
the lemon. Stir in soda, add ice and the
peach. Let stand 5 minutes, then serve in
large wine goblets. About 100 calories
for each of 8 servings, 80 calories for
each of 10 servings.

ROYAL EGGNOG

This recipe is a modern version of an old
family favorite. In copper-plate script at
the side was noted, "For cases of
Exhaustion. If the case is not serious,
half the quantity of brandy may be used.
Give every *hour* in cases of extreme
weakness!"
Makes about 36 servings

12 eggs, separated
1½ cups sugar
1 quart milk
1 quart brandy or 1 pint each whiskey
  and brandy
1 quart light cream
¾ cup light rum (optional)
½ teaspoon nutmeg

Cover and refrigerate egg whites until
needed; beat yolks until thick in a large
bowl; add sugar, a little at a time, and
beat until pale and fluffy. Slowly beat in
milk, alternately with brandy; cover and
chill 3–4 hours. About ½ hour before
serving, take egg whites from refrigerator. Just before serving, beat yolk
mixture well, add cream and, if you like,
rum. Whip egg whites to soft peaks and
fold into yolk mixture. Pour into a
well-chilled punch bowl and sprinkle

with nutmeg. (*Note:* So that eggnog will
be fresh for late arrivals or "seconds,"
whip up only ½ of the egg whites and
mix with ½ of the yolk mixture. Mix the
remainder when needed.) About 220
calories per serving if optional light rum
is used, 205 calories per serving if rum is
not used.

⊠ EASY RUM AND COFFEE NOG

Makes 16–20 servings

2 quarts vanilla ice cream
1 quart hot strong coffee
1 quart light rum
¼ teaspoon nutmeg

Place ice cream in a metal bowl, pour in
coffee, and stir until ice cream is
melted. Mix in rum, pour into punch
bowl, and sprinkle with nutmeg. About
300 calories for each of 16 servings,
240 for each of 20 servings.

Nonalcoholic Beverages

About Coffee

When Muhammadanism spread through
Arabia forbidding Moslems to drink
alcoholic beverages, the faithful turned
to something else with "kick." That
something was coffee. The Arabs
introduced coffee to the Turks, who
glorified it with coffeehouses, then
Turkish invaders carried coffee into
Europe. Coffee came to the New World
with the colonists; the first coffee plant
was brought over by a Dutchman about
fifty years later, and from it, the story
goes, the Latin American coffee industry
began.

Today Latin and South America are top
coffee producers along with Indonesia
(especially Java and Sumatra), Yemen,
Hawaii, and a number of Caribbean
islands. Coffee varieties often take their
names from the areas where they're
grown—Colombian coffee, for example,
Brazilian, Puerto Rican, Arabian Mocha,
Blue Mountain Jamaican. Most popular
brands are skillful blends because coffee
made from a single variety is insipid;

indeed, it takes many different coffees to produce rich, well-rounded flavor. It is possible, however, to buy beans of a particular variety—Mocha or Colombian—and have them ground or mixed to order. The best plan is to try a number of brands and blends until you hit upon the one you like.

About Roasts: If variety and blend determine the flavor of coffee, so, too, does the roast, which can vary from *light* and *cinnamon* through *medium, high, city,* and *French* to *Italian* (nearly black and the roast to use for demitasse and espresso). The darker the roast, incidentally, the less the caffeine.

About Grinds: Coffee can be bought in the bean, the best way to buy it if you have a coffee mill, because coffee stays fresh in the bean far longer than it does after being ground. Once ground—and exposed to the air—coffee stales fast. That's why it is best to buy only a pound at a time and to store in the refrigerator once the tin is opened. There are three grinds of coffee available today:

Regular Grind	Use for Percolators
Drip Grind	Use for Drip or Old-Fashioned Coffeepots
Fine Grind	Use for Vacuum Coffee Makers (*Note:* Drip grind may also be used)

In addition, there is the fine powdery coffee used in making Turkish coffee, but it is available only at gourmet groceries or Middle Eastern shops and must be especially sought out.

About Decaffeinated Coffee: Caffeine is a stimulant that affects many people adversely, so it was inevitable that someone would discover a way of extracting most of the caffeine from coffee. Decaffeinated coffees are widely available in all standard grinds, also as instant coffee.

About Coffee with Chicory: Chicory—the same one used for salads—has a long brown root, which, when roasted and ground, can be brewed into a bitter dark

drink. When Napoleon banned the importation of coffee, the French hit upon mixing their dwindling reserves with roasted chicory, and they do yet, though there is no shortage of coffee. Coffee with chicory is strong and bitter but popular still around New Orleans.

About Instant Coffees: In the beginning, these seemed feeble imitations of freshly brewed coffee. But research has perfected the process so that modern instant coffees are very good indeed. One of the advantages—in addition to instant cups of coffee—is that the powder or granules can be used in recipes as easily as cocoa. So popular have the instants become that there is now instant espresso.

About Freeze-Dried Coffees: These are the newest and best instant coffees because they taste remarkably like freshly brewed coffee. They are made by flash-freezing strong, fresh coffee, then drawing off the ice crystals by a special vacuum process that does not affect the flavor of the coffee as heat dehydrating does (this is the method used for conventional instants). Freeze-dried crystals can also be used in recipes if the mixture they're being added to is liquid or at least moist—the crystals dissolve on contact.

About Coffee Substitutes: These (Postum, to name one) are made of dark roasted cereals and are good for those unable to take any coffee at all. They are available as ground or instant types.

How to Make Coffee

In an Old-Fashioned Pot: Measure coffee (*drip grind*) into pot, allowing 1 standard coffee measure or 2 level tablespoons for each serving, add cold water (¾ cup for each 2 tablespoons coffee), and stir. Set over moderately high heat, cover, and when mixture bubbles up once, remove from heat and add 3–4 tablespoons cold water to settle grounds. Set pot over low heat and steep 5 minutes—do not allow to boil. To serve, pour through a very fine small strainer into cups.

In a Percolator: Measure cold water into pot, allowing ¾ cup for each serving. Set percolator basket in place in pot, measure *regular grind* coffee into it, using 1 standard coffee measure or 2 level tablespoons for each ¾ cup water. Cover with lid. Set pot over moderately high heat and, when coffee begins to perk (when it bubbles in glass lid dome) and turns pale amber, turn heat to moderately low and let coffee perk gently 6–8 minutes. Remove basket of grounds, stir coffee, and serve. Keep hot over low heat but do not let coffee boil.

In a Drip Pot:

Filter-Flask Type: Roll filter paper into a cone and stick into neck of flask. In a saucepan or teakettle, measure amount of cold water needed—¾ cup for each serving—and bring to a boil over high heat. Meanwhile, measure *drip grind* coffee into filter cone, allowing 1 standard coffee measure or 2 level tablespoons for each ¾ cup water. Set flask on a burner topped with an asbestos flame tamer, but do not turn burner on. When water boils, take from heat, let bubbling subside and pour over coffee grounds; stir once, then let drip through. Lift out paper of grounds, turn on burner heat (to low) and let coffee steep 1–2 minutes. Pour and serve.

Conventional Drip Pot: Measure amount of cold water needed—¾ cup per serving—into a teakettle or saucepan and bring to a boil. Meanwhile, rinse coffeepot with scalding hot water. Fit basket into bottom part of pot and measure in *drip grind* coffee, allowing 1 standard coffee measure or 2 level tablespoons for each ¾ cup water. Fit upper compartment over basket and set pot on a burner (not turned on). When water boils, take from heat, let bubbling subside, and pour into upper compartment, cover, and let water drip through. When about ½ of the water has dripped through, turn burner under pot to low. When all water has dripped through, lift off upper compartment and

basket of grounds. Stir coffee, let mellow 1–2 minutes over low heat, then serve.

In a Vacuum-Style Coffee Maker: For each cup of coffee wanted, measure ¾ cup cold water into lower compartment. Fit filter into upper bowl and measure in *fine or drip grind* coffee—1 standard coffee measure or 2 level tablespoons for each ¾ cup water. Set pot over high heat and, when water comes to a full rolling boil, insert upper part of coffee maker into bottom, using a slight twist to ensure a tight seal. When water rises into top part, stir well and turn heat to low. Let brew bubble in top part 2–3 minutes, then remove coffee maker from heat (this creates a vacuum, causing coffee to plunge into lower part of coffee maker). When coffee has filtered back into lower part, lift off top part. Keep coffee hot over low heat.

In an Automatic Coffee Maker: Follow manufacturer's instructions closely, experimenting with the mild-strong control until you achieve the brew you like.

In an Espresso Pot: These aren't espresso pots (true espresso is made by passing steam under pressure over the coffee grounds) but Italian-style drip pots. But they make espresso-like coffee and are easy to use. For each serving use 6 tablespoons cold water (in a standard measuring cup, 6 tablespoons is midway between the ⅓ and ½ cup marks) and 1 standard coffee measure or 2 level tablespoons of *French or Italian roast drip grind* coffee. Place water in middle part of pot, grounds in middle basket; fit all parts of pot together, cover and set over moderately high heat. When water comes to a full boil, turn pot upside down, turn heat off, and let coffee drip through. Serve in demitasse cups with a twist of lemon and, if you like, sugar. But never cream. To be really Italian, skip the lemon, too. (*Note:* Some Italian housewares shops sell home-size espresso machines; use according to manufacturer's directions.)

HOW TO MAKE COFFEE FOR A CROWD

Number of Servings	Coffee Needed (Regular Grind)	Water Needed
20	½ pound	1 gallon
40	1 pound	2 gallons
60	1½ pounds	3 gallons

Tie coffee in a muslin or cheesecloth bag large enough to hold at least twice the quantity you're using, drop into a kettle of just boiling water, reduce heat immediately so water no longer boils, and let stand 10–12 minutes. Plunge bag up and down several times, then remove. Keep coffee hot over low heat but do not allow to boil. (*Note:* If you're making coffee for more than 60, set up 2 kettles.) To clear coffee, add 1–2 eggshells to each kettle.

Quantity Instant Coffee: From 2 ounces instant coffee you can make 20 cups of coffee. Simply empty coffee powder or granules into a large kettle and for each 2 ounces add 1 gallon simmering water. Stir, let steep a few minutes, then serve. *Note:* Always add the hot water to the coffee, never the other way around.

HOW TO MAKE COFFEE OVER A CAMPFIRE

The principle is the same as for quantity coffee, the amount is simply smaller. Use the following proportions:

Number of Servings	Coffee Needed (Regular Grind)	Water Needed
2	¼ cup	1½ cups
4	½ cup	3 cups
6	¾ cup	4½ cups
8	1 cup	6 cups
10	1¼ cups	7½ cups
12	1½ cups	9 cups

Tie coffee in a large muslin or cheesecloth bag. Bring water to a boil in a large pot over glowing coals, drop in bag of coffee, pull pot to side of fire where water will stay hot but not boil. Let steep 10–12 minutes, swish bag of grounds up and down 2–3 times, then lift out. *Note:* If you have no bag for grounds, simply place loose grounds in bottom of pot, pour in water, and set over coals. When water bubbles up just once, stir well, transfer pot to edge of fire, add about ¼ cup cold water to settle grounds, and let steep 8–10 minutes.

Some Tips for Making Better Coffee

— Buy only a week's supply of coffee at a time and, once the can is opened, store tightly covered in the refrigerator.

— Do not mix any stale coffee with a freshly opened tin.
— If you buy coffee in the bean, grind it as you need it (and keep grinder spotless). Whole roasted beans will keep their flavor about 1 month.

– Use the proper grind of coffee for your coffee maker.

– Keep coffee maker spanking clean. This means washing after each use with soap and water, getting at spouts and crevices with a small bottle brush, rinsing well in hot water, and drying thoroughly. Occasionally pot may need to be scoured (though those with metal-plated insides should never be). If you prefer, remove stains with one of the commercial preparations instead of the scouring pad.

– Store coffee maker unassembled so air can circulate.

– Measure coffee and water carefully, using 1 standard coffee measure or 2 level tablespoons for each ¾ cup water. *Note:* If you like really strong coffee, use 3 level tablespoons for each ¾ cup water; if you prefer it weak, use 2 scant tablespoons for each ¾ cup water.

– Always use cold water when making coffee; hot tap water tastes flat. Also use naturally soft (or chemically softened) water; hard water gives coffee an unpleasant metallic taste.

– Never allow coffee to boil—it becomes a bitter potion. The most desirable temperature for brewing coffee is between 185° F. and 205° F.

– Use a coffee maker of the right size for the amount of coffee you need. All coffee makers should be used to at least ¾ of their capacity, so if you often make small amounts, keep a special small pot for just that purpose.

– Remove coffee grounds from the coffee maker as soon as the coffee is brewed.

– Keep coffee hot until it is served. Reheated coffee tastes stale.

– Serve coffee as soon after making as possible; don't try to keep hot longer than 1 hour because coffee deteriorates rapidly on standing.

Some Variations on Coffee

Demitasse: This is simply extra-strong black coffee served in small (demi, or half-size) cups. To make, use one of the standard methods, substituting a dark

French or *Italian* roast for the regular *or* increasing, the amount of regular roast coffee to 3–4 level tablespoons per ¾ cup of water.

Iced Coffee: Brew demitasse using one of the basic methods. Fill tall glasses with ice and pour in hot demitasse. Or, if you prefer, brew regular strength coffee and cool. Serve over ice or, for stronger coffee, over coffee ice cubes (coffee frozen in ice cube trays).

Café au Lait: This is the traditional breakfast beverage throughout Europe. Brew demitasse by one of the basic methods. At the same time, heat an equal quantity of milk to scalding. Pour milk into a pitcher and fill cups by pouring the hot milk and coffee simultaneously and adding about equal amounts of each.

Mocha: Brew demitasse by one of the basic methods. Also make an equal amount of any favorite cocoa. Then serve as you would *café au lait,* pouring equal amounts of black coffee and cocoa into each cup.

Café Royal: Prepare demitasse. Pour a cup, place a sugar lump on an after-dinner coffee spoon, add a little cognac and blaze. When sugar melts, stir into coffee. *Note:* This is best, perhaps, as a do-it-yourself drink, each person preparing his own.

Viennese Coffee:

Hot: Brew strong coffee and mix with an equal quantity of hot milk or light cream. Pour into a tall glass, sweeten to taste, and top with a float of whipped cream.

Frosted: Brew strong coffee. Place a scoop of vanilla ice cream in a tall glass, slowly pour in coffee, top with whipped cream, and dust with confectioners' sugar.

Café Diable (Makes 6 servings): Here's a showy after-dinner drink. Place 6 sugar lumps, 8 cloves, ½ cinnamon stick, a 1″ strip of lemon rind, and ⅓ cup cognac in a chafing dish but do not mix. Blaze cognac with a match, then stir. Add 1 quart very strong hot coffee, heat about 1 minute, ladle into cups, and serve.

⚖ **TURKISH COFFEE (KAHVESI)**

Dark, pungent Turkish coffee is now sold in gourmet shops along with special cone-shaped Turkish coffeepots. The special pot isn't essential—a long handled saucepan, deep enough to swish the grounds around, works nearly as well. This coffee should be made in small amounts—no more than 3–4 servings at a time.
Makes 3 servings

1 cup water
1 tablespoon sugar
2 tablespoons Turkish coffee or pulverized Italian roast coffee

Heat water and sugar uncovered in a Turkish coffeepot (*cezve*) or small saucepan over moderately high heat, stirring occasionally until sugar dissolves. Gradually add coffee, swirling or stirring, then heat almost to boiling and let foam up; remove from heat and let foam subside. Return to heat and repeat foaming and settling 2 more times. Keep swirling coffee as it heats. Spoon a little foam into demitasse cups, then half fill with coffee. (*Note:* To settle grounds quickly, add 1–2 drops cold water just before serving.) 18 calories per serving.

⚖ **CAPPUCCINO**

This popular Italian coffee drink is thought to have been named for Capuchin monks, who wear coffee-brown robes.
Makes 4–6 servings

1 pint hot espresso
1 cup scalding hot milk
Cinnamon or nutmeg (optional)
4–6 cinnamon sticks (optional)

Beat espresso and milk in a heated bowl until frothy; pour into cups. (*Note:* The correct size is something between a demitasse and a regular coffee cup, but either of these will do just as well.) Sprinkle lightly with cinnamon, add cinnamon sticks for stirring, and serve. Set out the sugar bowl for those who want it. About 40 calories for each of 4 servings, 27 for each of 6 servings.

⊠ **BAHAMIAN COFFEE**

Brown sugar and cinnamon make the difference.
Makes 4 servings

1 quart milk
¼ cup instant coffee powder
¼ cup firmly packed dark brown sugar
4 cinnamon sticks

Bring milk to a simmer over moderate heat, stir in coffee and sugar, and when dissolved heat uncovered 1–2 minutes; do not boil. Serve in tall mugs with cinnamon stick stirrers. About 215 calories per serving.

About Tea

All teas can be divided into three groups: *black,* fermented teas, obtained principally from India, Ceylon, and Taiwan; *green,* unfermented teas (most come from Japan, though in days past China was the leading exporter); and *oolong,* semifermented teas from Taiwan.

Black Teas: Americans know these best. They produce fragrant, amber brews, the blend (most contain as many as 20 different teas) determining flavor; it may be brisk and strong, nutty, fruity, flowery, even winelike. Popular black teas include *Assam,* a robust tea from northeast India (when blended with Ceylon tea, it is called *Irish Breakfast Tea*); *Darjeeling,* from the Himalayas, more delicate and, some people insist, India's finest tea; *Earl Grey* (a full-bodied blend of Taiwan teas); *English Breakfast* (choice, mellow blend of India and Ceylon teas); *Lapsang Souchong* (a strong, smoky Taiwan tea); and *Sumatra* (an Indonesian tea commonly used in blends).

Black tea leaves are graded as to size. The largest are *souchong,* second largest *orange pekoe* or simply, *pekoe.* Smaller, cut or broken leaves are called *broken orange pekoe* or *broken pekoe souchong* (these make especially aromatic tea). *Fannings* are smaller still and used for tea bags.

Green Teas: These astringent yellow-green brews are beloved by Orientals. The four principal sizes are *gunpowder* (so called because, on drying, the tiny leaves roll into balls), *imperial* (slightly larger balls), *young hyson* (longer, twisted leaves), and *hyson* (the longest, most loosely twisted). Japanese green teas are *basket-fired* (dried in bamboo baskets over charcoal until deep olive brown), *pan-fired* (dried in iron pans over coals), or *natural leaf* (coarse leaves pan-fired for short periods of time). Basket-fired is considered choicest.

Oolong Teas: These semifermented teas combine the mellowness of black teas with the tang of the green; they make deceptively light-colored brews. *Formosa Oolong* is the mildest and most popular. *Note:* For an exceptionally good pot of tea, mix 1 teaspoon *Formosa Oolong* with your favorite black tea blend; if, for example, you need 6 teaspoons tea, use 1 teaspoon Formosa Oolong and 5 teaspoons black tea.

Scented Teas: Teas, particularly Oolong, are often mixed with dried flowers or herbs. Among the common blends are *Jasmine* and *Peppermint* teas.

Instant Teas: These are pulverized black teas mixed sometimes with malto-dextrin, which preserves their flavor. They are available plain or mixed with sugar and lemon and dissolve in both hot or cold water.

Tea-Like Beverages:

Tisanes: When England taxed tea, colonial American women swore off it and began making infusions of raspberry leaves, sage, and a variety of other herbs, seeds, and flowers. Many of these tisanes remain popular today, and a number—peppermint, verbena, sassafras, linden, rose hips, camomile—can be bought as "tea bags."

Maté: Also known as Paraguay tea, these are the dried leaves of the young shoots of a variety of holly. They brew into a strangely smoky, oily drink that tastes a little like green tea.

Yaupon: Along the southeastern Atlantic seaboard grow the stunted, gnarled yaupon trees, an evergreen of the holly family. American Indians used to gather and dry the leaves, then brew them into a strong drink that was used in purification rites. A milder version, yaupon tea, is still made on North Carolina's Outer Banks. And very good it is.

About Buying Tea

As with coffee, the best way to determine the tea you like best is to experiment, trying first one blend, then another. Most popular blends are available both by the half pound or pound as loose tea or in tea bags. Teas keep far better than coffee, but they should be stored tightly covered and far away from foods whose flavors they might absorb.

How to Make Tea

Hot Tea: Use a china, heatproof glass, or porcelain pot rather than a metal one (metal makes tea taste metallic). Scald the pot with boiling water. For each serving, use ¾ cup water and 1 teaspoon (*not* measuring teaspoon) loose tea (or 1 tea bag). Place required quantity of water—*cold water*—in a saucepan or teakettle and bring to a full boil. Meanwhile, place tea in teapot. Pour boiling water directly over tea, let steep 3–5 minutes. Stir and serve with lemon, sugar, and, if you like, milk or cream. *Note:* Tea, like coffee, should never boil. If tea is too strong (color is less an indicator than flavor), simply weaken with additional boiling water.

VARIATIONS:

Spiced Tea: Prepare as directed but add 6–8 cloves and a cinnamon stick to the teapot along with the tea.

Iced Tea: Prepare hot tea as directed but use 1½ teaspoons tea to each ¾ cup water. Pour hot tea into tall glasses filled

HOW TO MAKE HOT TEA FOR A CROWD

Number of Servings	Tea Needed	Water Needed
20	2 oz. (7 tablespoons) loose tea OR 20 tea bags	3 cups
40	¼ lb. (1 cup—2 tablespoons) loose tea OR 40 tea bags	1½ quarts
60	6 oz. (1¼ cups+1 tablespoon) loose tea OR 60 tea bags	2 quarts+1 cup

Bring water to a rolling boil in a saucepan (not aluminum). Remove from heat, add tea, stir, cover, and brew 5 minutes. Scald teapot and strain tea into pot. To serve: Pour about 2 tablespoons tea into each cup and fill with piping hot freshly boiled water, adjusting strength by varying amount of tea. (*Note:* For a quantity Tea Punch, see the Party Punch Chart.)

with ice cubes. Add lemon and sugar to taste, sprig with mint, if you wish, and serve. *To Make a Pitcherful* (8–10 servings): Bring 1 quart cold water to a full boil in a large enamel or heatproof glass saucepan, remove from heat, add ⅓ cup loose tea (or 15 tea bags) and let steep 4–5 minutes. Stir well, then strain through a very fine sieve into a pitcher containing 1 quart ice water. Pour into tall glasses filled with ice. *Note:* If you refrigerate tea while it is still hot, it will cloud. To clear, stir in a little boiling water.

⚖ RUSSIAN-STYLE TEA

Russians serve tea in slim heatproof glasses instead of cups—a 6- to 8-ounce size is about right.
Makes 6 servings

2 quarts boiling water (about)
8 teaspoons black tea (Indian or Ceylon)
Thinly sliced lemon
Strawberry or raspberry jam (optional)
Lump sugar

Have water boiling furiously and keep boiling throughout the tea service (use a samovar if you have one). Pour a little boiling water into a teapot to warm it, swish around, and pour out. Place tea in teapot, add 1½ cups boiling water, cover, and let steep 3–5 minutes. Strain tea into a second warmed teapot and keep warm. To serve, pour about ¼ cup tea into each glass and add boiling water to fill; adjust amount of tea according to strength desired. Pass lemon, jam, and sugar. (*Note:* Russians often stir a spoonful of jam into their tea or place a lump of sugar in their mouths and drink the tea through it.) About 40 calories per serving if optional jam is used, 18 calories per serving if jam is not used.

⚖ ▨ SPICED ORANGE TEA MIX

Makes enough for 40 servings

1 cup powdered orange-flavored beverage mix
¼ cup instant tea powder
1 (3-ounce) package sweetened lemonade mix
1 cup sugar
1 teaspoon cinnamon
½ teaspoon cloves

Mix all ingredients and store airtight. To make 1 cup spiced orange tea, place 1 tablespoon mix in a cup, pour in 1 cup boiling water, and stir until dissolved. About 30 calories per serving.

Some Tips for Making Better Milk Drinks

– For richer flavor, use evaporated milk or a ½ and ½ mixture of evaporated and fresh milk (especially good in chocolate drinks).
– To reduce calories, use skim or reconstituted nonfat dry milk instead of whole milk—their calorie content is approximately half that of whole milk.
– To prevent "skin" from forming on hot milk or hot milk drinks, stir often with a wire whisk.
– Use a low heat for hot milk or chocolate drinks—both scorch easily.
– Never try to mix cocoa or cinnamon directly with milk or other liquid; blend first with an equal quantity of sugar.
– When combining milk and an acid fruit juice, slowly mix fruit juice into milk rather than vice versa—less chance of curdling.

Some Garnishes for Milk Drinks (choose garnishes compatible in flavor with the drink):
Dustings of cinnamon, cinnamon-sugar, nutmeg, instant cocoa mix, or confectioners' sugar (all drinks)
Grated or shaved chocolate (for chocolate, mocha, or butterscotch drinks)
Grated orange or lemon rind (for fruit-milk drinks)
Marshmallows (especially good for cocoa)
Whipped cream fluffs (all drinks)
Cinnamon stick stirrers (good with chocolate and fruit-milk drinks)
Peppermint stick stirrers (good with cold chocolate drinks)
Fruit kebab stirrers (whole fresh berries, grapes, melon balls, cherries, or pineapple chunks threaded on long wooden skewers—good with fruit-milk drinks)

⊠ SOME QUICK MILK DRINKS

Each makes 1 serving
Pour 1¼ cups cold milk into a 12-ounce glass and blend in any of the following:

Chocolate Milk: 2–3 tablespoons chocolate syrup and ¼ teaspoon vanilla. 270 to 300 calories per serving, depending on amount of chocolate syrup used.

Mocha Milk: 2 tablespoons chocolate syrup, 1 teaspoon instant coffee powder blended with 1 tablespoon tepid water and ¼ teaspoon vanilla. 270 calories per serving.

Vanilla Milk: 1 tablespoon superfine sugar and 1 teaspoon vanilla. 245 calories per serving.

Butterscotch Milk: 2–3 tablespoons butterscotch syrup and ¼ teaspoon vanilla. 252 to 272 calories per serving, depending on amount of syrup used.

Maple Milk: 3–4 tablespoons maple syrup. 350 to 400 calories per serving, depending on amount of syrup used.

Milk and Honey: 3–4 tablespoons honey and a pinch nutmeg or mace. 392 to 456 calories per serving, depending on amount of honey used.

Molasses Milk: 3–4 tablespoons molasses. 350 to 400 calories per serving, depending on amount of molasses used.

Honey-Molasses Milk: 2 tablespoons each honey and molasses. 428 calories per serving.

Melba Milk: 3–4 tablespoons Melba Sauce. 320 to 360 calories per serving, depending on amount of Melba Sauce used.

Pour 1 cup cold milk or buttermilk into a 12-ounce glass and blend in either of the following:

Peachy Milk: ⅓–½ cup puréed frozen peaches and ⅛ teaspoon almond extract. About 245 calories per serving.

Berry Milk: ⅓–½ cup sieved puréed frozen strawberries or raspberries. About 235 calories per serving.

To Make Malted Milk: Prepare any of the Quick Milk Drinks as directed but add 2 tablespoons malted milk powder (plain or chocolate depending upon flavor of drink) and beat well. (*Note:* 2 tablespoons malted milk will increase total calories per serving by about 115 calories.)

⊠ SOME MILK SHAKES

The electric blender whips up shakes best, but a rotary or portable electric mixer works fairly well. A milk shake becomes a "frosted" when ice cream is beaten in, a "float" when a scoopful is dropped in after beating.
Each makes 1 serving

Pour 1 cup cold milk into blender container and blend in any of the following:
Banana Milk Shake: 1 small very ripe peeled and well-mashed banana and ¼ teaspoon vanilla. Serve sprinkled with cinnamon or nutmeg. About 240 calories per serving.
Berry Milk Shake: ⅓ cup puréed strawberries or raspberries, 3–4 tablespoons berry preserves and, if you like, 1–2 drops red food coloring. About 310 to 360 calories per serving, depending on amount of preserves used.
Chocolate Milk Shake: 2–3 tablespoons chocolate syrup or Cocoa Syrup. 230 to 265 calories per serving, depending on amount of syrup used.
Caramel Milk Shake: 2 tablespoons Caramel Syrup and ¼ teaspoon maple flavoring. About 260 calories per serving.
Coffee Milk Shake: 2 teaspoons each instant coffee powder and sugar. About 190 calories per serving.
Mocha Milk Shake: 2 tablespoons chocolate syrup and 1 teaspoon each instant coffee powder and sugar. About 250 calories per serving.
Orange Milk Shake: ⅓ cup orange juice. About 200 calories per serving.

To Make Frosted Milk Shakes: Add 1–2 scoops of an appropriate ice cream to milk along with flavoring and blend until thick and creamy and no lumps of ice cream remain. Some good combinations: Chocolate Milk Shake and coffee ice cream; Banana Milk Shake and butterscotch ice cream; Orange Milk Shake and pistachio ice cream. (*Note:* For each scoop of ice cream used, add 150 calories.)

To Make Malted Milk Shakes: Add 1–2 tablespoons malted milk powder to any milk shake recipe before blending, then blend as directed. (*Note:* Chocolate malted milk powder is especially good in the Chocolate, Caramel, Coffee, and Mocha Milk Shakes.) For each tablespoon of malted milk powder used, add 58 calories.

⊠ BASIC ICE CREAM SODA

As good as the corner drugstore ever made.
Makes 1 serving

¼ cup cold milk or light cream
2 scoops vanilla or any flavor ice cream
Chilled club soda (or ginger ale, cola, or other favorite carbonated drink)
Garnishes (optional): whipped cream, maraschino cherry

Pour milk into a 12-ounce glass, add 1 scoop ice cream, pour in a little soda, and stir briskly, mashing ice cream. Add second scoop of ice cream, fill with soda, stir again, and garnish. 340 calories per serving if made with milk, 420 if made with light cream (optional garnishes not included). Add 25 calories for each tablespoon of whipped cream used, 17 calories for each cherry.

VARIATIONS:

Chocolate Ice Cream Soda: Mix milk with 2–3 tablespoons chocolate syrup, then proceed as directed, using chocolate or vanilla ice cream. Add 50 calories to basic ice cream soda calorie counts for each tablespoon chocolate syrup used.

Mocha Ice Cream Soda: Prepare Chocolate Ice Cream Soda but use coffee ice cream. Calorie counts the same as for chocolate ice cream soda.

Coffee Ice Cream Soda: Mix milk and 1 teaspoon instant coffee powder, then proceed as directed, using coffee ice cream. 340 calories per serving.

Strawberry or Raspberry Ice Cream Soda: Mix milk with ¼ cup crushed strawberries or raspberries or 2–3 tablespoons strawberry or raspberry syrup and proceed as directed, using vanilla, strawberry, or raspberry ice cream. Garnish with a berry instead of cherry. About 370 calories for the strawberry soda made with fresh berries, about 420 if made with syrup. About 390 calories for the raspberry soda made with berries, 420 made with syrup.

Cherry Ice Cream Soda: Mix milk with 2–3 tablespoons cherry preserves or cherry sundae topping, then proceed as directed, using vanilla or cherry ice cream. 440 to 490 calories per serving, depending on amount of preserves used.

Peach, Pineapple, or Apricot Ice Cream Soda: Mix milk with ¼ cup puréed peaches, pineapple, or apricots, then proceed as directed, using a compatible flavor of ice cream. About 450 calories per serving for the peach and pineapple sodas, 460 per serving for the apricot.

Lemon or Orange Ice Cream Soda: Mix milk with 2–3 tablespoons frozen lemonade or orange juice concentrate, then proceed as directed, using lemon or orange ice cream or sherbet. About 395 calories per serving for the lemon soda made with ice cream, 295 calories if made with sherbet. About 385 calories per serving for the orange soda made with ice cream, 285 if made with sherbet.

☒ ICE CREAM FLOATS

These are quick, fun, and so easy that very young children can make them. The combinations are as broad as the imagination—all you need are a variety of ice creams or sherbets and carbonated beverages or fruit juices.
For Each Serving: Drop a hefty scoop of ice cream or sherbet into a tall glass, add a little carbonated drink or fruit juice, stir briskly, mashing ice cream slightly, then pour in enough carbonated drink or fruit juice to fill glass. Fancier variations can be made by mixing in a little chocolate or fruit syrup or by adding an extra scoop of ice cream at the end. Calorie counts, obviously, will vary according to ingredients used. But as a minimum for a float made with sherbet

and carbonated fruit drink, you can figure about 230 calories per serving. For a float made with ice cream and carbonated fruit drink, you can figure about 280 calories per serving.

☒ 500-CALORIE MEAL-IN-A-GLASS

A high-protein formula that can be used in place of solid food. Good for those unable to take solids; also good—between meals—for those on weight-gaining diets. Use the 250-calorie version as a quick breakfast or lunch.
Makes 1 serving

1 cup cold milk
2 eggs
2 teaspoons sugar
½ cup vanilla ice cream, softened slightly
¼ teaspoon vanilla
Nutmeg

Beat together all ingredients except nutmeg until frothy, using an electric blender, rotary or electric mixer. Pour into a chilled tall glass and dust with nutmeg.

VARIATIONS:

⚖ **250-Calorie Meal-in-a-Glass:** Beat together ¾ cup cold skim milk, 1 egg, ½ cup ice cream, and ¼ teaspoon vanilla; omit sugar.

Chocolate 500-Calorie Meal-in-a-Glass: Prepare as directed but substitute chocolate ice cream for vanilla, omit sugar, and add 1 teaspoon cocoa.

Coffee 500-Calorie Meal-in-a-Glass: Prepare as directed but substitute coffee ice cream for vanilla and add 1–2 teaspoons instant coffee powder.

LIQUORLESS EGGNOG

Makes 6 servings

4 eggs, separated
½ cup sugar
2 cups cold milk
1 cup cold light cream
1½ teaspoons vanilla
⅛ teaspoon salt
¼ teaspoon nutmeg

Beat egg yolks and ¼ cup sugar until

thick and cream colored; gradually add milk, cream, vanilla, salt, and ⅛ teaspoon nutmeg and beat until frothy. Beat egg whites with remaining sugar until soft peaks form and fold in. Cover and chill until serving time. Mix well, pour into punch bowl, and sprinkle with remaining nutmeg. About 250 calories per serving.

¢ ⊠ HOT COCOA

Inexpensive, easy, and good.
Makes 1 cup

1 tablespoon cocoa
1 tablespoon sugar
Pinch salt
⅓ cup water
⅔ cup milk

Mix cocoa, sugar, and salt in a small saucepan, slowly stir in water. Heat and stir over moderately low heat until mixture boils, then boil slowly, stirring constantly, 2 minutes. Add milk and heat to scalding but do not boil. About 190 calories per serving.

VARIATIONS:

Cocoa for a Crowd (Makes 12 servings): Mix ¾ cup cocoa with ¾ cup sugar and ½ teaspoon salt in a large saucepan. Gradually stir in 1 quart warm water, set over low heat, and heat, stirring now and then, 8–10 minutes. Add 2 quarts milk and heat to scalding. Serve in mugs, sprinkled, if you like, with cinnamon or nutmeg or topped with marshmallows. About 190 calories per serving not including marshmallows (for each used, add 25 calories).

Iced Cocoa: Prepare cocoa as directed, then cool, stirring occasionally. Pour over ice cubes, top with a dollop of whipped cream, and sprinkle with cinnamon. About 190 calories per serving, plus 25 calories for each tablespoon of whipped cream used.

⊠ RICH-QUICK COCOA

Like Old-Fashioned Hot Chocolate but quicker.
Makes 2 servings

1½ cups milk
2 tablespoons cocoa
2 tablespoons sugar
⅛ teaspoon salt
¼ teaspoon butter or margarine
¼ teaspoon vanilla

Bring milk to a simmer; meanwhile, blend cocoa and sugar. Mix a little hot milk into cocoa mixture, return to pan, add remaining ingredients, and heat and stir 1–2 minutes to blend flavors. Pour into mugs or cups and serve. About 210 calories per serving.

VARIATIONS:

Hot Mocha: Prepare as directed but substitute 1 tablespoon instant coffee powder for 1 tablespoon cocoa and omit butter. About 190 calories per serving.

Caramel Coffee: Prepare as directed but substitute 4 teaspoons instant coffee powder for cocoa and omit salt, butter, and vanilla. About 175 calories per serving.

OLD-FASHIONED HOT CHOCOLATE

The kind Grandmother used to make—dark and rich.
Makes 4–6 servings

2 (1-ounce) squares unsweetened chocolate
1 cup water
¼ cup sugar
Pinch salt
3 cups milk
⅓ cup heavy cream

Heat and stir chocolate, water, sugar, and salt in the top of a double boiler over simmering water until chocolate melts. Slowly stir in milk and heat uncovered to serving temperature. Meanwhile, whip cream. Serve in mugs or cups topped with whipped cream. About 340 calories for each of 4 servings, 225 for each of 6 servings.

Some Tips for Making Better Fruit Drinks

– Use freshly squeezed, unstrained juice whenever possible.
– Freeze some of the fruit juice or drink mixture to use as "ice cubes"—prevents drinks from watering down as the ice melts.
– When making punch in quantity, use a large ice block in punch bowl rather than crushed or cubed ice; it melts more slowly, waters the punch down less.
– For extra-tangy fruit drinks, add a little grated orange, lemon, or lime rind.
– When a recipe calls for both fruit juice and rind, grate the rind first, then cut open fruit and squeeze.
– Save syrup drained from canned or frozen fruits to use in fruit drinks.
– Try sweetening drinks with honey or light corn syrup instead of sugar—they dissolve more easily and make drinks mellower.
– For really sparkling drinks, add ginger ale or other carbonated beverage just before serving.
– Have drink ingredients well chilled before mixing together.
– Avoid putting tinted ice cubes in colorful fruit drinks that might gray the drinks as they melt; pink cubes, for example, in green limeade will turn the limeade khaki.
– Avoid heavy, awkward garnishes that make beverages difficult to drink.

Some Garnishes for Fruit Drinks
(choose those compatible in flavor with the drink):
Plain or fancily cut orange, lemon, or lime slices or wedges
Spirals of orange, lemon, or lime rind
Cocktail cherries, fresh cherries or berries
Pineapple chunks or melon balls
Fruit kebabs (grapes, cherries, melon balls, whole berries, or pineapple chunks threaded alternately on long wooden skewers)
Pineapple stick stirrers (simply, long, thin sticks of pineapple)

Cinnamon stick stirrers (for hot drinks)
Orange or lemon slices stuck with cloves (for hot drinks)

⊠ SOME QUICK COOLERS

For best results, have fruit juices, ginger ale, club soda, colas, etc., well chilled before mixing coolers.
Each makes 1 serving

Ginger-Grapefruit Cooler: Put 3–4 ice cubes in a 12-ounce glass, then fill, using equal quantities grapefruit juice (or pineapple, orange, tangerine, grape, or cranberry juice) and ginger ale. Sprig with mint and, if you like, add a slice of orange or lime. Calories per serving: 88 for the ginger-grapefruit cooler, 110 for the orange, grape and pineapple, 100 for the tangerine, and 125 for the cranberry.

Caribbean Cooler: Half fill a 12-ounce glass with crushed ice, add 1/3 cup each pineapple and orange juices, then fill with cola. Add a maraschino cherry and an orange slice. About 130 calories per serving.

Minted Apple-Lime Cooler: Bruise 2 mint leaves with 1/2 teaspoon sugar in a 12-ounce glass. Add apple juice or cider to half fill and mix well. Add 1 tablespoon lime juice and 2–3 ice cubes and mix again. Fill with ginger ale and add a wedge of lime. About 110 calories per serving.

Cranberry Sparkle: Put 3–4 ice cubes in a 12-ounce glass, then fill, using equal quantities cranberry juice, lemonade, and club soda. About 90 calories per serving.

Orange-Milk Cooler: Mix 1/2 cup each milk or skim milk and orange juice in a 12-ounce glass. Add ice cubes and fill with any fruit-flavored carbonated beverage. About 170 calories per serving if made with milk, 140 if made with skim milk.

⏃ **Orange-Tea Cooler:** Mix 2 teaspoons instant tea powder with 1/2 cup orange juice in a 12-ounce glass. Add 2 ice cubes and fill with club soda or ginger ale. Sprig with mint. About 55 calories per serving.

Wine Cooler: Half fill a 12-ounce glass with crushed ice, then fill with equal quantities sweet or dry red or white wine and ginger ale or club soda. About 95 calories per serving if made with ginger ale, 50 calories per serving if made with club soda.

Shandy Gaff: Mix equal quantities cold beer and lemon soda. Do not add ice. About 95 calories per serving.

⊠ EASY LEMONADE MIX

A handy mix to have on hand in the refrigerator (also handy to have on long car trips). Whenever anyone wants a glass of lemonade, all he has to do is add water and ice and stir.
Makes about 1½ quarts, enough for 2 dozen glasses of lemonade

1 quart lemon juice
1 cup sugar
2 cups light corn syrup

Stir all ingredients together until sugar dissolves. Pour into screw-top jar, cover, and store in refrigerator. To serve, shake well and pour ¼ cup mix into a 12-ounce glass, add ice, fill with water or club soda, and stir well. *Note:* This mix keeps well several weeks. To make in a pitcher, allow ¼ cup mix to 1 cup ice water. About 125 calories per serving.

VARIATIONS:

⊠ **Easy Limeade Mix:** Substitute 1 quart lime juice for lemon juice; if you like, add a few drops green food coloring. About 125 calories per serving.

⊠ **Easy Orangeade Mix:** Substitute 1 quart freshly squeezed orange juice for lemon juice, omit sugar, and reduce corn syrup to 1½ cups; proceed as directed but use ½ cup mix per serving. Makes 12 servings at about 155 calories each.

⊠ **Easy Orange Crush:** Substitute 3 cups orange juice for lemon juice and add 1 cup each pineapple juice, crushed pineapple, and lemon juice; omit sugar.

Use ½ cup mix per serving. Makes 12 servings at about 215 calories each.

⊠ **Easy Pink Lemonade:** Prepare Easy Lemonade Mix and add ¾ cup grenadine syrup; if you like, add a few drops red food coloring. Use ¼ cup mix per serving. (*Note:* Cranberry juice gives a nice color, too, but makes a tarter drink: Mix 1 quart cranberry juice with the Easy Lemonade Mix and use ½ cup mix per serving.) About 150 calories per serving if made with grenadine. Makes 30 servings if made with cranberry juice at about 120 calories each.

⊠ **Easy Grape Lemonade:** Pour ½ cup Easy Lemonade Mix into an ice-filled 12-ounce glass, fill with grape juice, and stir well. About 210 calories per serving.

MINTY LEMON-LIME FROST

Makes 4 servings

A little sugar for frosting glasses
½ cup sugar
½ cup boiling water
¼ cup firmly packed minced fresh mint
½ cup lime juice
2 tablespoons lemon juice
3 cups cold water
2–3 drops green food coloring
4 mint sprigs (garnish)

Frost* rims of 4 (12-ounce) glasses with sugar and chill until ready to use. Stir sugar with boiling water and mint until dissolved, cool 10 minutes, and strain into a large pitcher. Add fruit juices, cold water, coloring, and about 6 ice cubes; mix well. Place 3 ice cubes in each glass, fill with juice mixture, and sprig with mint. About 105 calories per serving.

CRANBERRY SHRUB

Shrubs are a colonial holdover. Originally spiked with rum or brandy, they are today an acid fruit juice served on the rocks or mixed with water or club soda. They make refreshing apéritifs, especially if served with scoops of tart sherbet.
Makes 8 servings

1 quart cranberry juice
2 cups sugar
Rind of 1 lemon (cut in thin strips)
½ cup white vinegar or ⅔ cup lemon
  juice
1 quart water or club soda (optional)
1 pint tart fruit ice or sherbet
  (optional)

Simmer cranberry juice, sugar, and rind, uncovered, in a saucepan (not aluminum) 10 minutes, stirring now and then. Off heat, mix in vinegar; cool, pour into a bottle, cover, and refrigerate. Serve as is on the rocks in punch cups or small glasses. *Or* half fill a tall glass with shrub, add ice, and fill with water or club soda. *Or* pour into punch cups and top each serving with a scoop of tart fruit ice. About 350 calories per serving if made with sherbet or fruit ice, about 295 if made without.

VARIATIONS:

Raspberry or Blackberry Shrub: Crush 2 quarts ripe berries with 2 cups sugar, cover, and let stand overnight. Press through a cheesecloth-lined sieve, extracting as much juice as possible. Omit lemon rind but mix in vinegar. Taste for sweetness and, if too tart, add a bit more sugar, stirring until dissolved. Store and serve as directed. About 380 calories per serving without fruit ice, about 435 per serving with.

Cherry or Currant Shrub: Simmer 2 quarts tart, pitted red cherries, red or black currants, covered in a large saucepan (not aluminum) with 2 cups sugar and ⅓ water, stirring now and then, until mushy. Cool, cover, and let stand overnight. Press through a cheesecloth-lined sieve, extracting as much juice as possible. Omit lemon rind but add vinegar. Taste for sweetness and adjust as needed. Store and serve as directed. About 275 calories per serving without fruit ice, 350 calories per serving with.

Spiked Shrub: Prepare any of the 3 shrubs as directed, omitting sherbet; mix in 1 fifth light rum or brandy. Pour into bottles, cover, and store in a cool

place at least 1 week before serving. Serve as is over crushed ice or mixed ½ and ½ with club soda in tall glasses with plenty of ice. Makes 16 servings at about 280 calories each if made with cranberry shrub and club soda, about 325 calories per serving if made with raspberry or blackberry shrub, and about 270 calories per serving if made with cherry or currant shrub.

⚗ ⊠ **TOMATO COCKTAIL**

Makes 4 servings

1 pint tomato juice
2 tablespoons lemon juice
1 tablespoon sugar
1 tablespoon minced yellow onion
1 bay leaf, crumbled
Pinch pepper

Mix all ingredients, cover, and chill 1–2 hours. Strain and serve in juice glasses. About 35 calories per serving.

VARIATIONS:

⚗ ⊠ **Tomato-Celery Cocktail:** Prepare as directed but add ½ cup diced celery and substitute 1 tablespoon cider vinegar for 1 tablespoon of the lemon juice. About 35 calories per serving.

⚗ ⊠ **Spicy Tomato Cocktail:** Prepare as directed but add 1 teaspoon prepared horseradish, 1 crushed clove garlic, ½ teaspoon Worcestershire sauce and substitute minced scallions for yellow onion. About 35 calories per serving.

⚗ ⊠ **Tomato Bouillon** (Makes 4–6 servings): Prepare as directed but omit lemon juice and sugar and add 1 cup beef broth or consommé and ½ teaspoon Worcestershire sauce. Serve on the rocks in small old-fashioned glasses. 43 calories for each of 4 servings, 30 for each of 6 servings.

⚗ ⊠ **Tomato-Clam Cocktail** (Makes 8 servings): Prepare as directed, then mix in 2 (8-ounce) bottles clam juice and 3–4 dashes liquid hot red pepper seasoning. Makes 8 servings at about 30 calories each.

Some Easy Appetizer Beverages

Serve in 4- to 6-ounce glasses on small plates lined with paper coasters. Suitably garnished, these can substitute for appetizer or soup courses. Pass them around before the meal or serve at the table. The following recipes all make 4 servings.

⊠ ⚖ **Clam Juice on the Rocks:** Mix 2 cups chilled clam juice with 2 tablespoons lemon juice, 1 tablespoon minced chives, 1 teaspoon Worcestershire sauce, and 2–3 drops liquid hot red pepper seasoning. If you like, add ¼ cup light cream and ⅛ teaspoon garlic salt. Serve on the rocks. About 20 calories per serving without cream.

⊠ ⚖ **Clam Chickee:** Mix 1 cup each chilled clam juice and chicken broth. Season to taste with celery salt and top each serving with a dollop of sour cream; sprinkle with salt and paprika. *Variation:* Substitute madrilène for chicken broth. About 20 calories per serving without cream.

⊠ ⚖ **Sauerkraut Juice Cocktail:** Mix 2 cups chilled sauerkraut juice with 2 tablespoons lemon juice, ½ teaspoon prepared horseradish, and ¼ teaspoon bruised caraway seeds. About 10 calories per serving. Or use 1 cup each sauerkraut juice and tomato juice. About 15 calories per serving. Serve with a slice of lemon.

⊠ ⚖ **Bullseye:** Mix 1 (10½-ounce) can chilled condensed beef bouillon and 1 cup chilled tomato-vegetable juice; serve with a twist of lemon peel. About 20 calories per serving.

⊠ ⚖ **Hen's Eye:** Mix 1 cup each chilled chicken broth and tomato juice; serve sprinkled with minced chives and sieved hard-cooked egg yolk. About 20 calories per serving.

⊠ **Pineapple-Grapefruit Frappé:** Blend 1 cup each unsweetened pineapple and grapefruit juice, 2 tablespoons lime juice, ¼ cup honey, and 1 unbeaten egg white in an electric blender at high speed ½ minute. Add 6–7 crushed ice cubes, a bit at a time, continuing to blend until thick and frothy. Pour out and serve. About 120 calories per serving.

⊠ **Red Orange Cocktail:** Mix 1 cup each chilled cranberry juice and orange juice; to each serving add a melon ball, berry, or cherry stuck on a cocktail pick. About 75 calories per serving.

⚖ **Vegetable Juice Cocktail:** In an electric blender, at high speed, purée 3 peeled and coarsely chopped medium-size carrots, 3 radishes, 3 scallions, ¼ cup each celery leaves and watercress, 1 canned beet that has been diced, ½ cup beet liquid, and 1½ cups ice water. Cover and refrigerate 1 hour, strain, mix in 1 teaspoon salt and ⅛ teaspoon pepper. If you like, mix in 2–3 tablespoons vegetable pulp and serve. About 20 calories per serving.

⚖ **Quick Yogurt Kholodnyk:** Peel, seed, and purée 1 medium-size cucumber with ½ cup ice water in an electric blender at high speed. Mix in 1 cup yogurt (or buttermilk), ½ teaspoon lemon juice, ¼ teaspoon salt, a pinch cayenne pepper, and 1–2 teaspoons snipped fresh dill. Cover and chill ½ hour. If a little thick, thin with ice water or cold milk. About 30 calories per serving made with buttermilk, 40 calories per serving made with yogurt.

SOME DECORATIVE ICES AND ICE RINGS FOR PUNCH BOWLS

Note: Chilled, boiled water makes clearer ice than water straight out of the tap. To unmold decorative ice blocks, dip in hot—not boiling—water. Boiling water may crack the block.

Float: Half fill a metal loaf pan, metal bowl, decorative gelatin or ring mold with cold boiled water; freeze solid. Arrange washed strawberries, pineapple chunks or rings, black and/or green grapes, melon balls, lemon, lime or orange slices, drained maraschino cherries on ice in a decorative pattern; add ¼" cold boiled water and freeze. Fill mold with cold boiled water and freeze. Unmold and float in punch bowl.

Christmas Wreath: Arrange 1 dozen each red and green maraschino cherries and a few mint leaves in a decorative pattern in the bottom of a 5-cup ring mold. Carefully pour in 1″ cold boiled water and freeze solid. Fill with cold boiled water and freeze. Unmold and float in punch bowl.

Wedding Ring: Pour 1″ cold boiled water in any large ring mold and freeze solid. Arrange rinsed sweetheart roses close together on ice, add ½″ cold boiled water, and freeze. Fill ring with more water and freeze. Unmold and float in Champagne Punch.

Ice Bowl: Half fill a 3-quart metal bowl with cold boiled water; set a 1-quart metal bowl inside larger bowl, weighting down so it will stay in center; freeze solid. Remove weights from small bowl, fill with hot water, then lift small bowl out. Unmold ice bowl by dipping large bowl in hot water, float right side up in punch bowl and fill with fresh flowers or fruit. (*Note:* Ice bowl can also be set in a deep platter and used as a container for ice cream or fruit desserts. It can be made ahead of time and stored in the freezer.)

Party Ice Cubes: Half fill ice cube trays with cold boiled water; freeze solid. Into each cube, place a cherry, berry, wedge of pineapple, lemon, lime, or orange, or a mint leaf. Fill with cold boiled water and freeze. (*Note:* Water can be tinted with food coloring, a colorful fruit liqueur, maraschino or cranberry juice, but it will color the punch as it melts.)

Iced Fruits: Rinse and dry any pretty chunky fruits and freeze solid on foil-lined baking sheets. (*Note:* Frozen cherries and grapes tend to sink to the bottom of a punch bowl; berries, pineapple rings, peach halves, citrus slices, and melon balls float.) To use iced fruits, simply peel off foil and drop into punch bowl. They will keep punch cool without diluting it.

PARTY PUNCH CHART

Note: Whenever possible, buy punch ingredients in large containers — gallons or magnums of wine or magnums of champagne instead of fifths, institution size cans of fruit juice. You'll have to order ahead, but you'll save money. Unless you have use of an institutional kitchen and its giant kettles, do not try to mix punch for 100 at one time; make 2 batches for 50 or, if necessary, 4-5 batches for 2 dozen (especially important if punch mixture must be heated at any time).

NONALCOHOLIC PUNCHES	Quantities For			
	1 Dozen	2 Dozen	50 People	100 People
Autumn Apple Punch				
Apple juice	1½ quarts	3 quarts	1½ gallons	3 gallons
Cinnamon sticks	2	4	8	16
Whole cloves	8	1 dozen	1½ dozen	2 dozen
Pineapple juice	1⅓ cups	1½ pints	1½ quarts	3 quarts
Lemon juice	1/2 cup	1 cup	1 pint	1 quart
Orange juice	1 pint	1 quart	2 quarts	1 gallon
Ginger ale	1 (28-oz.) bottle	2 (28-oz.) bottles	4 (28-oz.) bottles	8 (28-oz.) bottles

Place 1-2 quarts apple juice in a large kettle (not aluminum); tie spices in cheesecloth, add to kettle, and simmer uncovered 15 minutes; discard spice bag. Mix spiced juice with remaining fruit juices. To serve, place a large block of ice in a large punch bowl, add fruit juice and ginger ale. (*Note:* For large quantities, mix batches as needed, using 1 bottle ginger ale to each 2½ quarts fruit juice mixture.) About 55 calories per 4-ounce serving.

Hot Party Mocha				
Unsweetened chocolate	4 (1-oz.) squares	1/2 pound	1 pound	2 pounds
Sugar	1 cup	1 pound	2 pounds	4 pounds
Water	1/2 cup	1 cup	1 pint	1 quart
Instant coffee powder	2 teaspoons	4 teaspoons	8 teaspoons	1/3 cup
Cinnamon	1/4 teaspoon	1/2 teaspoon	1 teaspoon	2 teaspoons
Heavy cream	1/2 cup	1 cup	1 pint	1 quart
Scalding hot milk	2½ quarts	5 quarts	2½ gallons	5 gallons

Heat and stir chocolate, sugar, water, coffee, and cinnamon in a heavy saucepan over low heat until chocolate melts; cover and cool. Beat cream to soft peaks and fold into chocolate mixture. To serve, pour chocolate mixture into a large silver punch bowl, add hot milk, and stir to mix. (*Note:* For large quantities, mix chocolate mixture and hot milk as needed to fill punch bowl, allowing about 1¼ cups chocolate mixture to 2½ quarts milk.) About 180 calories per 4-ounce serving.

Hot Spiced Cider				
Apple cider	3 quarts	1½ gallons	3 gallons	6 gallons
Light brown sugar	1 pound	2 pounds	4 pounds	8 pounds
Cinnamon sticks	3	6	1 dozen	2 dozen
Whole cloves	1 dozen	1½ dozen	2 dozen	3 dozen

Place cider and sugar in a large kettle (not aluminum); tie spices in cheesecloth, add, and simmer uncovered 15 minutes; discard spice bag. Serve from a silver punch bowl or large coffee or teapot. About 115 calories per 4-ounce serving.

	Quantities For			
	1 Dozen	2 Dozen	50 People	100 People

Hot Spicy Grape Juice

Oranges	1	2	4	8
Whole nutmegs, cracked	2	3	5	8
Whole cloves	1 dozen	1½ dozen	2 dozen	3 dozen
Cinnamon sticks	2	4	8	16
Grape juice	2 quarts	1 gallon	2 gallons	4 gallons
Boiling water	1 quart	2 quarts	1 gallon	2 gallons
Lemon juice	1/2 cup	1 cup	1 pint	1 quart
Sugar	1 cup	1 pound	2 pounds	4 pounds

With a vegetable peeler, cut rind from oranges in long strips; tie in cheesecloth with spices; save oranges to use another time. Place spices and remaining ingredients in a very large heavy kettle (not aluminum) and simmer, uncovered, stirring occasionally 10-15 minutes; discard spice bag. Serve hot from a large silver punch bowl. About 75 calories per 4-ounce serving.

Jubilee Punch

Orange juice	1½ quarts	3 quarts	1½ gallons	3 gallons
Lemon juice	1½ cups	3 cups	1½ quarts	3 quarts
Maraschino cherries (and liquid)	1/3 cup	2/3 cup	1½ cups	3 cups
Sparkling white grape juice	2 (1-qt.) bottles	4 (1-qt.) bottles	8 (1-qt.) bottles	16 (1-qt.) bottles

Mix orange and lemon juice with cherries. To serve, place a large block of ice in a large punch bowl, add fruit mixture, then pour in grape juice. (*Note:* For large quantities, mix batches as needed, using about equal quantities fruit mixture and grape juice.) About 65 calories per 4-ounce serving.

Lemonade or Limeade

Sugar	3 cups	3 pounds	6 pounds	12 pounds
Water	2½ quarts	5 quarts	2½ gallons	5 gallons
Lemon or lime juice	3 cups	1½ quarts	3 quarts	1½ gallons
Fresh mint sprigs	1 dozen	2 dozen	50	100

Heat sugar and water in a large kettle (not aluminum), stirring until sugar dissolves; cool to room temperature and mix in lemon juice. To serve, place a large block of ice in a large punch bowl and pour in lemonade. Sprig glasses with mint. About 90 calories per 4-ounce serving.

Pineapple-Raspberry Cream Punch

Pineapple juice	1 quart	2 quarts	1 gallon	2 gallons
Ginger ale	2 (28-oz.) bottles	4 (28-oz.) bottles	8 (28-oz.) bottles	16 (28-oz.) bottles
Vanilla ice cream	1 quart	2 quarts	1 gallon	2 gallons
Raspberry sherbet	1 quart	2 quarts	1 gallon	2 gallons

Pour pineapple juice and ginger ale over ice cream and sherbet and stir until melted and blended. About 95 calories per 4-ounce serving.

PARTY PUNCH CHART (continued)

	1 Dozen	2 Dozen	50 People	100 People
			Quantities For	

Tea Punch

	1 Dozen	2 Dozen	50 People	100 People
Superfine sugar	1 cup	1 pound	2 pounds	4 pounds
Oranges, sliced	2	4	8	16
Lemons, sliced	6	9	1 dozen	1½ dozen
Hot strong tea	1 quart	2 quarts	1 gallon	2 gallons
Boiling water	1 quart	2 quarts	1 gallon	2 gallons
Ginger ale	2 (28-oz.) bottles	4 (28-oz.) bottles	8 (28-oz.) bottles	16 (28-oz.) bottles

Place all but last ingredient in a large, heavy kettle (not aluminum) and stir, bruising fruit slightly, until sugar dissolves; cover and cool 1-2 hours. To serve, place a large block of ice in a large punch bowl, then fill, adding about equal quantities tea mixture and ginger ale. About 50 calories per 4-ounce serving.

Three Fruit Punch

	1 Dozen	2 Dozen	50 People	100 People
Superfine sugar	1/3 cup	2/3 cup	1⅓ cups	2⅔ cups
Grapefruit juice	1½ cups	3 cups	1½ quarts	3 quarts
Orange juice	1½ cups	3 cups	1½ quarts	3 quarts
Apricot or peach nectar	2 quarts	1 gallon	2 gallons	4 gallons
Finely grated orange rind	1½ teaspoons	1 tablespoon	2 tablespoons	1/4 cup
Club soda	1 (28-oz.) bottle	2 (28-oz.) bottles	4 (28-oz.) bottles	8 (28-oz.) bottles
Oranges, sliced (garnish)	1	1	2	3

Place sugar and grapefruit juice in a large kettle (not aluminum) and stir until sugar dissolves. (*Note:* For large quantities, you may need to heat slightly; do not boil; cool to room temperature.) Mix in all but last 2 ingredients. To serve, place a large block of ice in a large punch bowl, then fill, adding 1 bottle club soda for each 2¾ quarts fruit juice mixture. Float orange slices on top and replenish, as needed, with fresh slices. About 60 calories per 4-ounce serving.

ALCOHOLIC PUNCHES

Champagne Punch

	1 Dozen	2 Dozen	50 People	100 People
Lemon juice	2/3 cup	1⅓ cups	2½ cups	1 quart
Superfine sugar	1/3 cup	2/3 cup	1¼ cups	1 pound
Cranberry juice	3 cups	1½ quarts	3 quarts	1½ gallons
Champagne	3 (26-oz.) bottles	6 (26-oz.) bottles	12 (26-oz.) bottles	24 (26-oz.) bottles
Ginger ale	1 (28-oz.) bottle	2 (28-oz.) bottles	4 (28-oz.) bottles	8 (28-oz.) bottles
Brandy (optional)	1/2 cup	1 cup	1 pint	1 quart

Stir lemon juice and sugar together in a large kettle (not aluminum) until sugar dissolves. (*Note:* For large quantities, you may need to heat gently to dissolve sugar; do not boil; cool to room temperature.) Mix in cranberry juice. To serve, place a large block of ice or decorative ice ring* in a large punch bowl; add fruit juice mixture, champagne, ginger ale, and, if you like, brandy; mix gently. (*Note:* For large amounts, mix in batches as needed, using 2 quarts fruit juice mixture to 4 bottles champagne, 2 bottles ginger ale, and 1 cup brandy.) About 100 calories per 4 ounce serving made with brandy, 90 calories per 4-ounce serving made without brandy.

PARTY PUNCH CHART (continued)

	Quantities For			
	1 Dozen	**2 Dozen**	**50 People**	**100 People**

Claret Cup

Red Bordeaux wine	3 (24-oz.) bottles	6 (24-oz.) bottles	12 (24-oz.) bottles	24 (24-oz.) bottles
Superfine sugar	3/4 cup	1½ cups	3 cups	3 pounds
Nutmeg	1/2 teaspoon	1 teaspoon	1½ teaspoons	1 tablespoon
Maraschino liqueur	1/4 cup	1/2 cup	1 cup	1 pint
Club soda	3 (28-oz.) bottles	6 (28-oz.) bottles	12 (28-oz.) bottles	24 (28-oz.) bottles
Unpeeled cucumber, sliced thin	1 small	1 large	2 large	3 large
Borage sprigs (optional garnish)	3-4	5-6	8-10	12-15

Stir wine and sugar together in a large punch bowl until sugar dissolves. (*Note:* For very large quantities, heat 1-2 bottles wine with sugar, stirring constantly, in a large saucepan (not aluminum) until sugar dissolves; do not boil; cool completely.) Mix nutmeg and maraschino liqueur into wine mixture. To serve, place a large block of ice in a large punch bowl and fill by pouring in equal quantities wine mixture and club soda; stir lightly. Float cucumber slices on top and, if you like, sprig with borage. Replenish cucumber and borage as needed. About 60 calories per 4-ounce serving.

Fish House Punch

Superfine sugar	1½ cups	3 cups	3 pounds	6 pounds
Water	1 cup	1 pint	1 quart	2 quarts
Lemon juice	1 quart	2 quarts	1 gallon	2 gallons
Dark Jamaican rum	2 quarts	1 gallon	2 gallons	4 gallons
Brandy	1 quart	2 quarts	1 gallon	2 gallons
Peach brandy	1/2 cup	1 cup	1 pint	1 quart

Heat and stir sugar and water in a large saucepan over moderate heat until sugar dissolves; cool to room temperature. Mix sugar syrup with remaining ingredients in a large punch bowl and let "ripen" at room temperature 2 hours. Add a large block of ice and let stand 1/2 hour longer. Mix gently and serve. (*Note:* For large quantities [for 50 or 100], mix in batches for 2 dozen and omit ripening time.) About 275 calories per 4-ounce serving.

(*continued foll. page*)

PARTY PUNCH CHART (continued)

	Quantities For			
	1 Dozen	2 Dozen	50 People	100 People

Glögg

	1 Dozen	2 Dozen	50 People	100 People
Oranges	1	2	4	8
Whole cloves	8	16	2 dozen	3 dozen
Cardamom seeds	1 tablespoon	2 tablespoons	1/4 cup	1/2 cup
Cinnamon sticks	2	4	8	16
Water	1 pint	1 quart	2 quarts	1 gallon
Sugar	1 cup	1 pound	2 pounds	4 pounds
Seedless raisins	1 cup	2 cups	1 pound	1½ pounds
Whole blanched almonds	1 cup	2 cups	1 pound	1½ pounds
Dry port or red Bordeaux wine	2 (24-oz.) bottles	4 (24-oz.) bottles	8 (24-oz.) bottles	16 (24-oz.) bottles
Aquavit or vodka	2 fifths	3 quarts	6 quarts	12 quarts

With a vegetable peeler, cut rind from oranges in long strips; tie in cheesecloth with spices; save oranges to use another time. Place spice bag in a large kettle (not aluminum), add water and sugar, and simmer uncovered, stirring until sugar is dissolved, 5-10 minutes. Add raisins and almonds and simmer 3-5 minutes; cool slightly, mix in wine and aquavit, then cool, cover, and store overnight. To serve, remove spice bag and heat glögg to steaming, but not boiling. Pour into a large silver punch bowl and ladle into mugs or heatproof punch cups, adding a few raisins and almonds to each serving. About 255 calories per 4-ounce serving.

Mulled Wine

	1 Dozen	2 Dozen	50 People	100 People
Whole cloves	1 dozen	1½ dozen	2 dozen	3 dozen
Cinnamon sticks	4	8	16	2¼ dozen
Water	3 cups	1½ quarts	3 quarts	1½ gallons
Sugar	1 cup	1 pound	2 pounds	4 pounds
Lemons, sliced thin	2	4	8	16
Red Bordeaux or Burgundy wine	3 (24-oz.) bottles	6 (24-oz.) bottles	12 (24-oz.) bottles	24 (24-oz.) bottles

Tie spices in cheesecloth, place in a large kettle (not aluminum), add water and sugar, and simmer uncovered 10 minutes, stirring now and then. Add lemons, bruise slightly, and let stand off heat 10 minutes. Add wine and slowly bring to a simmer; do not boil. Pour into a large silver punch bowl or ladle into heatproof mugs. About 100 calories per 4-ounce serving.

Orange Blossom Cup

	1 Dozen	2 Dozen	50 People	100 People
Orange juice	1 quart	2 quarts	1 gallon	2 gallons
Rhine, Moselle or Riesling wine	2 (24-oz.) bottles	4 (24-oz.) bottles	8 (24-oz.) bottles	16 (24-oz.) bottles
Light rum	1 quart	2 quarts	4 quarts	8 quarts
Superfine sugar (optional)	1/4 cup	1/2-2/3 cup	1 cup	1 pound
Oranges, sliced thin	1	2	3	4

Mix juice, wine and rum; taste and add sugar if needed. (*Note:* If quantities are large, you may have to heat mixture slightly so sugar will dissolve. Cool well.) To serve, place a large block of ice in a large punch bowl, pour in punch and float orange slices on top, replenishing them as needed. About 170 calories per 4-ounce serving made with sugar, about 165 calories per serving made without sugar.

	Quantities For			
	1 Dozen	**2 Dozen**	**50 People**	**100 People**
Party Daiquiris				
Cracked ice	3 cups	1½ quarts	3 quarts	1½ gallons
Frozen limeade or lemonade concentrate or frozen daiquri mix	1 (6-oz.) can	2 (6-oz.) cans	4 (6-oz.) cans	8 (6-oz.) cans
White or light rum	1 fifth	2 fifths	3 quarts + 1 cup	6½ quarts

(*Note:* Make in batches for 1 dozen.) Place all ingredients in a 1/2 gallon jar that has a tight-fitting lid (mayonnaise jars are good) and shake vigorously about 1/2 minute until frothy. Strain into cocktail glasses and serve at once. About 205 calories per 4-ounce serving.

Party Milk Punch				
Superfine sugar	1/4 cup	1/2 cup	1 cup	1 pound
Bourbon, rye or blended whiskey	1 pint	1 quart	2 quarts	4 quarts
Ice cold milk	3½ quarts	7 quarts	3½ gallons	7 gallons
Nutmeg	1/4 teaspoon	1/4 teaspoon	1/2 teaspoon	3/4 teaspoon

Mix all but last ingredient in a large kettle, ladle over an ice block in a large punch bowl, and sprinkle with nutmeg. About 120 calories per 4-ounce serving.

Quick Party Eggnog				
Chilled eggnog mix	2 quarts	4 quarts	8 quarts	16 quarts
Light rum	1 fifth	2 fifths	3 quarts	6 quarts
Heavy cream	1 pint	1 quart	2 quarts	4 quarts
Nutmeg	1/4 teaspoon	1/4 teaspoon	1/2 teaspoon	3/4 teaspoon

Mix eggnog and rum; whip cream to soft peaks and fold in; cover and chill 1 hour. Ladle into a large punch bowl and sprinkle with nutmeg. (*Note:* For large amounts, make up in batches for 2 dozen, keep cold, and refill punch bowl as needed.) About 250 calories per 4-ounce serving.

CHAPTER 6

APPETIZERS AND HORS D'OEUVRE

The cocktail party may be an American invention, but the practice of nibbling while drinking goes back to the Greeks and Romans. (Nibbling is perhaps the wrong word because these early gluttons stuffed themselves.)

Appetizers today are served with more restraint, their purpose being to whet the appetite and set the tone of the meal—unless, of course, cocktails only are being served, in which case appetizers are there to temper the drinking (or at least the effects of it).

The difference between hors d'oeuvre and appetizers isn't as sharply defined as it once was. Hors d'oeuvre, meaning "outside the work," is a French phrase used to describe the hot or cold savories served at the start of a meal. In France hors d'oeuvre, often a selection of tart foods, are served at the table. In America hors d'oeuvre have come to mean the finger foods passed around with cocktails. Appetizer is a more encompassing word, including not only hors d'oeuvre but also any beverage or savory food served before the meal.

Making appetizers appeals to the drama in most of us—a fine thing as long as they don't upstage the foods to follow or prove so irresistible that guests overeat. The best practice is to keep appetizers tantalizing but simple.

Some Recipes Included Elsewhere in This Book That Can Double as Appetizers

Scattered throughout the book, and particularly in the meat, poultry, seafood, and vegetable sections, are many recipes that can be served as appetizers. Some are good cocktail fare, others more appropriately served at table as a first course. For page numbers, see the Index. Among those that are particularly good are:

MEAT AND POULTRY APPETIZERS

Hot

Meat balls (make bite-size and use sauces or gravies as dips)
Creamed meats or poultry (serve in bite-size tart shells or croustades)
Any small sautéed or glazed sausages
Balinese Beef on Skewers
Barbecued, Luau, or Chinese-Style Spareribs
Dolma
Herb Stuffed Kidney and Bacon Rolls
Marrow Bones
Party Pasties

Sautéed Chicken Livers
Teriyaki Hors d'Oeuvre
Yakitori

Cold
Tart, spreadable meat salad
Danish Liver Loaf
Sausage and Pastry Rolls (good cold or hot)
Scotch Eggs (good cold or hot)
Steak Tartare

SEAFOOD APPETIZERS

Hot
Bite-size batter-fried or breaded fish or
    shellfish
Bite-size fish or shellfish balls or croquettes
Bite-size sautéed or broiled fish or shellfish
Creamed or scalloped seafood served in tart
    shells, Carolines, scallop shells or ramekins
Any of the escargot recipes
Any savory baked stuffed clams or oysters
    such as Casino, Florentine, Originata,
    Remick, Rockefeller, etc.

Either of the following clam recipes: Clams
    Bulhão Pato, Clams Marinière
Any of the following mussels recipes: Filey
    Bay Mussels, Marseille-Style, Marinière
Any of the following oyster recipes: Angels
    or Devils on Horseback, Oysters Baked in
    Mushroom Caps
Any of the following scallops recipes: Co-
    quilles St. Jacques à la Parisienne or à la
    Provençale, Scallops en Brochette
Any of the following shrimp recipes: Gin-
    gery Chinese Shrimp, Japanese Butterfly
    Shrimp, Scampi, Shrimp Rumaki
Brandade de Morue

Cold
Cold marinated, pickled, or spiced fish or
    shellfish such as Pickled Herring, Ceviche,
    Escabeche, Rollmops, Sashimi
Cold curried fish or shellfish
Cold smoked raw or marinated fish
Any savory, spreadable fish or shellfish
    salad (chop the ingredients a little more
    finely than usual)
Armenian Mussels stuffed with Rice, Cur-
    rants, and Piñon Nuts
Clams or oysters on the half shell

CHEESE AND EGG APPETIZERS

Hot
Any fondue or rabbit
Cheese or Egg Croquettes
Crostini alla Mozzarella
Quiche Lorraine
Scotch Woodcock

Cold
Basic Stuffed Eggs
Deviled Eggs and Jiffy Deviled Eggs
Eggs in Aspic
Egg Salad
Pickled Eggs
Rosemary Eggs

VEGETABLE APPETIZERS

Hot
Braised Artichokes Provençal
Leek Pie
Pissaladière
Roman Artichokes Stuffed with Anchovies

Cold
Pickled vegetables
Tart, cold, marinated vegetables or vegetable
    salads (à la Grecque, Vinaigrette, Sweet-
    Sour, etc.)
Celery Victor
Tabbouleh

BREAD APPETIZERS

Hot
Savory Party Biscuits (Herb, Onion, Bacon,
    Cheese, etc.)
Blini
Pizza or Quick Pizza (make bite-size or cut
    in small squares)
Tortillas (make miniatures and fill with
    Texas Red)

Cold
Savory Party Sandwiches
Savory toast (Chive, Herb, Curry, Garlic,
    Cheese, etc.) (good cold or hot)
Cheese Crackers
Melba Toast

About Pâté

There are dozens of *pâtés,* all liver and/or meat pastes of one kind or another. Most luxurious is *pâté de foie gras,* made of the livers of force-fed geese, seasoned with spices and sometimes brandy or Madeira. It is sold canned, also fresh, by the pound (the fresh must be kept refrigerated until ready to be served; the canned need not and, in fact, actually mellows and ages on the shelf like fine wine). *Pâté de foie gras truffé* has had truffles added, sometimes minced and mixed throughout but more often in a row down the middle of the pâté. *Pâté de foie d'oie* contains about 25 per cent pork liver, 75 per cent goose liver. Some other famous pâtés:

à la Meau: Meat pâté made of game; it usually contains some liver.

à la Périgueux: A truffled meat-liver pâté made of poultry and game.

à la Rouennaise: Duckling pâté.

d'Amiens : Pâté made of duckling and other livers.

Lorraine: Meat pàté made from a mixture of veal, pork, and game.

Pâté en Croûte: Pâté baked in a crust (the crust need not be eaten).

Pâté Maison: The specialty of the particular restaurant. These usually contain a mixture of livers (poultry, calf, pork), also some ground meat.

Terrine: A mixture of liver and game or poultry leftovers baked in and served from a terrine (small earthenware dish).

How to Serve Pâté

All pâtés should be served cold (chill cans at least 24 hours before opening). When the pâté is to be served as a spread with cocktails, unwrap or slide out of can (dip can briefly in hot water, if necessary, to loosen pâté, or open both ends of can and push pâté out). Center pâté on a small serving plate and smooth fat layer with a spatula. Serve with melba rounds or hot buttered toast triangles and a pâté knife for spreading.

To Glaze Pâté with Aspic: This adds a festive touch. Scrape fat layer from block of pâté, then smooth surface. Make about 1 pint aspic, using beef or chicken broth,* and chill until syrupy. Spoon 2–3 layers of aspic over pâté, 1 at a time, and chill until tacky before adding next layer. Decorate top of pâté with herb sprigs, pimiento and truffle cutouts, seal under a final layer of glaze, and chill until firm. Also chill any leftover aspic, then chop and wreathe around plate of pâté.

If pâté is to be served at the table as a first course, slice ¼"–½" thick (do not remove fat layer) and overlap 2–3 slices (depending on size and richness) on each plate. Add a ruff of lettuce, if you like, provide pâté spreaders, and pass hot buttered or unbuttered toast triangles.

How Much Pâté Is Enough? Depends on the richness, but generally, ⅛–¼ pound per person is ample.

COUNTRY-STYLE LIVER PÂTÉ

Makes 16–18 servings

1 medium-size yellow onion, peeled and
    coarsely chopped
1 pound calf's liver, trimmed of
    membrane and veins and cubed
½ cup light cream
2 eggs, separated
2 teaspoons salt
¼ teaspoon pepper
¼ teaspoon ginger
Pinch allspice
¼ cup melted bacon drippings, butter, or
    margarine

Preheat oven to 300° F. Purée onion in an electric blender at high speed, add liver, a little at a time, puréeing until creamy; strain through a fine sieve. Mix in cream; lightly beat yolks and add along with remaining ingredients. Beat egg whites to soft peaks and fold in. Spoon into a well-greased 9"×5"×3" loaf pan, set in a hot water bath, and bake uncovered 1–1¼ hours until a knife inserted in the center comes out clean. Cool pâté upright in pan on a wire rack, cover, and chill at least 12 hours. Invert on a platter and serve. About 95 calories for each of 16 servings, 85 for each of 18 servings.

VARIATIONS:

Pretty Party Pâté: Prepare, chill and unmold pâté; trim so loaf is about ¼″ smaller all around than its pan. Make a clear aspic by dissolving 1 envelope unflavored gelatin in 3 cups hot beef consommé. Pour ⅔ cup aspic into a clean 9″ × 5″ × 3″ loaf pan and chill until tacky; keep remaining aspic warm. Arrange truffle, radish, and/or lemon rind cutouts, tarragon or parsley sprigs in desired design on aspic, spoon a little warm aspic on top, and chill until tacky. Fit pâté loaf into pan, fill to brim with aspic, and chill until firm; also chill any remaining aspic; unmold. Chop extra chilled aspic and use to garnish platter along with radish roses and watercress sprigs. About 105 calories for each of 16 servings, 95 for each of 18 servings.

Smoky Liver Pâté Spread: Cream ½ loaf Country-Style Liver Pâté with ½ pound soft Braunschweiger (link liver spread available at supermarkets). If you like, pack into a small bowl, decorate with truffle cutouts and tarragon leaves, and seal with ¼″ clear aspic. Chill until firm and serve from bowl without inverting. About 145 calories for each of 16 servings, 130 for each of 18 servings.

EASY CHICKEN LIVER PÂTÉ

Makes 6–8 servings

1 pound chicken livers, halved at the natural separation
3 tablespoons butter or margarine
2 (3-oz.) packages cream cheese, softened to room temperature
3–4 tablespoons brandy
1 teaspoon salt (about)
⅛ teaspoon pepper
⅛ teaspoon nutmeg
2 teaspoons finely grated yellow onion

Glaze:
1 (10½-oz.) can madrilène or beef consommé
1 teaspoon unflavored gelatin
Cutouts of truffle and pimiento; parsley or tarragon sprigs (decoration)

Brown livers in butter in a skillet over moderately high heat 4–5 minutes; transfer to an electric blender cup with drippings and scraped-up browned bits, add all remaining ingredients except glaze, and blend at high speed until smooth. Taste for salt and adjust as needed. Spoon into a small shallow serving bowl (about 1-pint size) and chill 2–3 hours. For glaze: Heat madrilène and gelatin over low heat, stirring constantly, until gelatin dissolves. Chill until thick and syrupy; spoon a thin layer on top of pâté and chill until tacky. Decorate with truffle and pimiento cutouts and herb sprigs. Add more madrilène to seal in design and chill until firm. Serve with melba rounds. About 290 calories for each of 6 servings, 215 for each of 8 servings.

¢ ⊠ LIVER-CHEESE PÂTÉ

Makes about 1½ cups

½ pound smoked liverwurst
1 tablespoon steak sauce
1 tablespoon dry sherry
1 (3-oz.) package cream cheese, softened to room temperature

Mash liverwurst with a fork in a small bowl. Blend in remaining ingredients and serve as a spread for crackers or Melba toast. About 45 calories per tablespoon.

PÂTÉ CORNUCOPIAS

Makes 8 servings

8 thin slices lean boiled ham or prosciutto, cut about 4″ long and 2″ wide
1 (8-oz.) can pâté de foie gras or 1 recipe Liver-Cheese Pâté, or Smoky Liver Pâté Spread at room temperature
2–3 tablespoons minced parsley

Shape ham slices into small cornucopias,

secure with toothpicks, and fill centers with pâté. Chill 2–3 hours. Just before serving, remove toothpicks and sprinkle pâté with parsley. About 145 calories per serving.

VARIATION:

Spread ham with pâté, roll up jelly-roll style, and secure with toothpicks. Chill as directed. Dip each end of rolls in parsley, remove toothpicks, and serve. About 145 calories per serving.

About Caviar

At $50 or more a pound, fresh caviar is hardly the everyday appetizer, and any meal beginning with it had better be elegant. What determines the quality of caviar and rockets the price sky high is the size of the eggs (caviar is the roe of sturgeon or similar fish, lightly salted). Costliest is from the *beluga* sturgeon that swims in the Caspian Sea, surrounded by Russia and Iran. The eggs are giant size, sometimes as big as peas; they are soft and translucent and range in color from silvery gray to black. Next come *osetra* (medium-size caviar, usually gray or gray green) and *sevruga* (smaller gray grains; one in 2,000 sevruga sturgeon has golden roe, so rare a delicacy that any found in Iran is reserved for the Shah). Still smaller grained are *sterlet* and *ship* caviars. (*Note:* Malossol is not a kind of caviar but a way of preserving it by salting.)

There are other caviars: tiny, gritty black *lumpfish caviar* (usually from the Baltic Sea), *red caviar* (salmon roe), and orange carp roe, or *tarama*. These are not nearly so choice or costly as sturgeon caviar.

Fresh caviar is extremely perishable and must be kept refrigerated from the instant it is taken from the fish until the moment it is served. Malossol and pasteurized caviar, packed in small jars, are less perishable but may need refrigeration (read labels carefully). Pressed caviar, also less perishable than the fresh, has been treated in an acid solution, then brined, drained, and pressed. None of these are a match for the fresh.

How to Serve Caviar

The only way to serve fresh caviar, gourmets insist, is from its own tin, imbedded in crushed ice with nothing more to accompany than buttered toast points and, perhaps, lemon wedges, each guest helping himself. Anything more is lily gilding. Others, however, like to accompany caviar with small bowls of minced onion, chopped hard-cooked egg white, sieved egg yolks, and occasionally a bowl of sour cream and plate of sliced pumpernickel. It's a matter of taste. The classic "caviar" drinks are chilled fine dry champagne or icy cold vodka drunk neat from liqueur glasses.

The less princely caviars are best used for making hors d'oeuvre and canapés, dips, spreads, and salad dressings and a variety of other recipes. They also make colorful garnishes.

How much caviar per person? 1 to 2 ounces, depending on your bank balance.

About Smoked Salmon

Another elegant, expensive appetizer. The salmon is raw but salted and smoked so that it has a cool velvety texture, a rosy, translucent look, and a delicately balanced woodsy-sea flavor. Smoked salmon should never seem oily or show grains of salt; taste before buying, rejecting any that is over-poweringly salty or smoky. The choicest smoked salmon comes from Scotland, but that from Nova Scotia, Norway, Denmark, and the Columbia River area is very good too. Lox is Jewish smoked salmon, slightly saltier than the regular, and a breakfast favorite with cream cheese and bagels.

The best way to buy smoked salmon is from the center cut, sliced thin but not so thin the slices tear (allow about 3 ounces per person). Like most seafoods, smoked salmon is perishable and must be kept refrigerated.

There are other smoked fish; sturgeon, which is very like salmon and best served like it; whitefish, eel, and trout, which need to be skinned and boned before serving. In addition, there are many canned smoked fish and shellfish, best served as cocktail tidbits or minced and mixed into dips and spreads.

How to Serve Smoked Salmon

The more simply the better. Trim away ragged edges (save to mix into scrambled eggs or make into a spread or dip with cream cheese and mayonnaise). Overlap slices neatly (about 3 per portion) on small chilled plates. Garnish with lemon wedges and sprinkle, if you like, with capers; set out the pepper mill. Or, if you prefer, forgo the capers and pass a cruet of olive oil and small dishes of minced yellow onion and hard-cooked egg.

Another way to serve smoked salmon is on cut-to-fit, thin slices of pumpernickel spread with unsalted butter. Cut bite size, these make luxurious canapés.

Crudités

Crudités is simply a French term for crisp, raw vegetables eaten out of hand as appetizers. Any colorful combination can be used; in fact, the more colorful the better. Choose tenderest young vegetables, pare only if necessary, then cut into easy-to-eat sticks or chunks. Certain vegetables—cherry tomatoes, radishes, button mushrooms, etc.—are naturally bite-size and best left whole with a sprig of stem to make dipping easier. Group vegetables spoke-fashion on a bed of crushed ice and center with a bowl of kosher or seasoned salt (makes a very low-calorie appetizer), or, if you prefer something heartier, serve with a savory dressing or dip. Some good vegetable choices:

TO SERVE IN LONG (2"–3") SLIM STICKS
Carrots
Celery and celeriac
Cucumbers (peel only if waxed)
Fennel
Scallions
Sweet green and/or red peppers
Turnips
Zucchini

TO SERVE WHOLE
Asparagus tips
Brussels sprouts (tiny ones)
Button mushrooms
Cherry tomatoes
Endive leaves
Radishes

TO SERVE IN BITE-SIZE CHUNKS
Broccoli and cauliflowerets

SOME APPROPRIATE DIPS
(see Index for page numbers)
Any flavored mayonnaise
Avocado Dressing
Cold Béarnaise
Cold Ravigote Sauce
Green Goddess Dressing
Horseradish Cream Sauce
Russian Dressing
Green Sauce (Salsa Verde)
Sour Cream-Anchovy, -Chive, or -Curry
  Sauce
Sour Cream-Roquefort Dressing
Tapenade
Thousand Island Dressing

About Antipasto

Antipasto, an Italian word meaning "before the meal," is simply a combination plate of raw, cooked, or pickled vegetables, meats and fish, hard-cooked eggs and cheese served at the table as an appetizer and eaten with a fork. Any colorful, tart combination, artfully arranged, is appropriate. One of the best ways to serve antipasto is to load a giant platter and let each guest help himself. Have the foods as nearly bite size as possible, or at least easy to serve (thin slices of cheese and meat, for example, should be rolled into tubes or cornucopias, hard-cooked eggs halved or quartered). Serve with cruets of olive oil and red wine vinegar.

Some Popular Components of Antipasto

(Many are available at supermarkets, others at Italian groceries.)

Meats: Thinly sliced prosciutto or boiled ham, salami, pastrami, dry hot Italian sausages

Fish: Oil-packed tuna, sardines, or anchovies

Eggs: Hard cooked, deviled, or stuffed

Cheese: Thinly sliced provolone, mozzarella, or Gorgonzola

Vegetables: Caponata; any dried bean or chick-pea salad; marinated or pickled beets or artichoke hearts; green or ripe olives; radishes; celery or carrot sticks; fennel or celery hearts; pickled hot green or red peppers; roasted sweet green or red peppers; oil-packed pimientos; cherry tomatoes

About Serving Cheeses as Appetizers

The best cheeses to serve before dinner are pungent or rich ones that are not likely to be overeaten. Bland cheeses may seem a better choice, but they aren't because guests tend to keep nibbling them until their appetites are gone.

Two kinds of cheese, usually, are sufficient. Place well apart on a large cheese board or, failing that, on two small ones. Let stand at room temperature at least an hour before serving, longer if cheeses are particularly hard or cold—they need plenty of time to soften and mellow.

If the cheeses are to be fully appreciated, they should be served with unsalted, unseasoned crackers. Serve the crackers on a separate plate, not ringed around the cheeses. And provide a separate knife for each cheese so the flavors don't get mixed.

For a full rundown on the kinds of cheese and additional tips on serving them, see the chapter on eggs and cheese.

Nuts as Appetizers

Salted and seasoned nuts may be served as cocktail nibbles, but avoid putting out so many guests overeat. Supermarkets carry dazzling varieties of ready-to-serve cocktail nuts, some of them very good. None, however, can compare with those you roast or deep-fry yourself (see chapter on candies and nuts for directions).

About Hollowed-out Stuffed Vegetables

These make attractive and neat-to-eat cocktail tidbits. Simply hollow out cherry tomatoes, radishes, raw baby zucchini or carrots, cucumbers and fill with red or black caviar, any savory cocktail spread, or tart spreadable cheese, any savory egg, seafood, meat, or poultry salad, chopping ingredients for these a little more finely than usual. Long vegetables like cucumbers, zucchini, and carrots can be hollowed out, stuffed, chilled, then sliced ¾"–1" thick. Others should be filled shortly before serving. A number of vegetables—mushroom caps, celery stalks, small artichoke bottoms— are tailor made for stuffing, no need to hollow out. The only precautions to take when stuffing vegetables: make the vegetables bite size and the filling firm enough to stay inside them.

About Canapés

Canapés are decorative open-face sandwiches small enough to eat in a bite or two. Whether hot or cold, they should look neat and freshly made, never fussed over (or left over). The best are salty or savory, colorful and appetizing.

Canapés can be nothing more than a bread cutout spread with a savory filling (any of the following spreads are suitable, also any egg, seafood, meat, or chicken salad, provided the ingredients are minced instead of chopped). Canapés can be much more elaborate, rather like mini Danish sandwiches, spread first with a savory butter or mayonnaise, then mounted with a dab of caviar, sliver of smoked salmon, or *pâté de foie gras*, round of cucumber or cherry tomato or hard-cooked egg, cluster of tiny Danish shrimp. The spread is essential—to keep the bread from drying out (or the topping from seeping in) and to hold the canapé together.

Any firm-textured bread, thinly sliced and cut in fancy shapes, makes a good base for canapés (white bread, brown, pumpernickel, rye, French, or Italian bread). It can be toasted or not or fried golden brown in butter. Other good canapé foundations or "couches" (*canapé* is French for "couch") are crisp bland crackers, melba toast, piecrusts cut in fancy shapes, Puff Pastry shaped into tiny patty shells, or Choux Pastry into doll-size puffs (see Carolines).

How Many Canapés Are Enough? Better figure on 3–4 per person. Put out a variety—2 or 3 different kinds, perhaps 1 hot and 2 cold.

Some Canapé Spreads

Any of the savory butters and mayonnaises given in the sandwich and sauce chapters can be used. Very moist spreads should be applied shortly before serving, otherwise the bread becomes soggy. Others, however, may be put on ahead of time. (*Tip:* It's easier to spread the bread, then cut into fancy shapes.) Slices can be divided into trim squares, rectangles, or triangles or cut with small decorative cookie cutters. For a professional touch, spread canapés with one kind of spread, then pipe on a decorative border or design using another spread of contrasting color but compatible flavor.

(*Note:* Only creamy spreads should be put through pastry tubes; any containing bits of solid food will merely clog the works.)

How Much Spread Is Needed? 1 cup should do about 8 dozen canapés—if thinly applied.

Roquefort Spread (Makes About ¾ Cup): Cream together 4 ounces Roquefort or blue cheese, ¼ cup each unsalted butter and softened cream cheese, and 2 tablespoons brandy. For quick flavor variations: Substitute Stilton and port, Cheddar and sherry, or Caerphilly and stout for the Roquefort and brandy. About 40 calories per canapé including bread.

Caviar Spread (Makes About ⅓ Cup): Blend ¼ cup unsalted butter with 3 tablespoons black caviar, 1 teaspoon lemon juice, and ¼ teaspoon finely grated onion. About 30 calories per canapé including bread.

Sardine Spread (Makes About ½ Cup): Blend together ¼ cup each unsalted butter and mashed, skinless, boneless sardines; season to taste with lemon juice and pepper. About 30 calories per canapé including bread.

Some Canapé Suggestions

Shrimp: Spread bread or toast rounds with Caper Butter, top with tiny Danish shrimp and a rosette of Tartar Sauce or curlycue of pimiento. About 30 calories per canapé.

Sardine: Spread a cracker (any bland kind) with Herb Butter, top with 2–3 boneless, skinless sardines and a red onion ring filled with sieved hard-cooked egg yolk. About 35 calories per canapé.

Russian: Spread pumpernickel squares with Russian Dressing, cover with cut-to-fit slices of smoked turkey or ham, and garnish with alternating rows of pimiento-stuffed olives and minced hard-cooked egg white. About 40 calories per canapé.

Ham or Tongue: Spread crackers or bread rounds with unsalted butter, top with cut-to-fit slices of Swiss cheese and ham or tongue, and garnish with overlapping slices of radish and dill pickle. About 40 calories per canapé.

Chicken: Spread bread or toast rectangles with Anchovy Butter, top with cut-to-fit slices of chicken, and garnish with a fluff of Green Mayonnaise and a rolled anchovy fillet. About 35 calories per canapé.

Smoked Oyster: Spread crackers with softened cream cheese, top with smoked oysters, and garnish with a border of Caviar Mayonnaise and a twisted lemon slice. About 30 calories per canapé.

Tuna and Parmesan: Top butter-fried toast rounds with hot creamed tuna, sprinkle with grated Parmesan, and broil until golden. Serve straight from the broiler. About 40 calories per canapé.

Broiled Anchovy: Spread toast rounds with any cheese spread, broil until bubbly, and top with crossed anchovy fillets. About 40 calories per canapé.

Hot Chicken Liver: Top fried toast rounds with hot sautéed, chopped chicken livers, crisp bacon crumbles, a cherry tomato slice, and a cucumber twist. About 50 calories per canapé.

Aspic: Cover bread slices with cut-to-fit slices of cold meat, poultry, or fish fillets, glaze with thin layers of aspic made from meat, poultry, or fish stock,* and chill until tacky. Cut in small squares, triangles, or rectangles, decorate, if you like, with herb sprigs, pimiento slivers or olive slices, and seal under a thin glaze of aspic. Chill well before serving. About 40 calories per canapé.

Stuffed Rolls: Cut ends from long, skinny loaves of French or Italian bread, scoop out soft insides and fill with any savory, not-too-soupy spread or seafood, egg, meat, or chicken salad. Wrap in foil and chill 6–8 hours. Slice thin and serve. About 40 calories per slice.

About Garnishing Canapés
Any sandwich garnish, done on a doll's scale, will work (see About Sandwich Garnishes).

About Party Sandwiches
These are covered fully in the chapter on sandwiches.

¢ ⊠ **CURRIED CUCUMBER PARTY ROUNDS**

Makes about 3 dozen canapés

Curry Mayonnaise:
1¼ cups mayonnaise
1–2 tablespoons curry powder
½ teaspoon Worcestershire sauce
¼ teaspoon garlic powder
¼ teaspoon onion powder
2–3 dashes liquid hot red pepper seasoning
3 dozen thin rounds pumpernickel bread about 1½"–2" in diameter
1 medium-size cucumber, sliced ⅛" thick (do not peel)

Mix first 6 ingredients together until fluffy; spread liberally on each pumpernickel round and top with a cucumber slice. About 85 calories per canapé.

⚖ ⊠ **CRISP CUCUMBER ROUNDS TOKYO STYLE**

This is such a good recipe it's difficult to believe there are only two ingredients. Makes 4–6 servings

1 (6-ounce) bottle Japanese soy sauce, chilled well
2 medium-size cucumbers, chilled well, peeled, and sliced ½" thick

Pour soy sauce into a small, deep mixing bowl, add cucumbers, and toss lightly to mix. Cover and chill 2 hours. To serve, transfer to a serving bowl and set out a separate small container of toothpicks.

VARIATION:

Substitute 2½ cups of almost any crisp raw vegetable for the cucumbers: short carrot sticks, bite-size cauliflowerets, whole radishes or water chestnuts, small chunks of celery, or a combination of these.

About 2 calories per cucumber round. The other raw vegetables will run approximately the same per piece.

⚖ PROSCIUTTO-STUFFED MUSHROOM HORS D'OEUVRE

Makes 3½–4 dozen hors d'oeuvre

1 (3-ounce) package cream cheese,
    softened to room temperature
½ (2-ounce) tube anchovy paste
¼ pound prosciutto, finely chopped
1 tablespoon capers
1 tablespoon minced parsley
1 tablespoon minced watercress
½ teaspoon Worcestershire sauce
3–4 tablespoons light cream
1 pound 1" mushrooms, stemmed and
    peeled (save stems to use later)

Mix cheese, anchovy paste, prosciutto, capers, parsley, watercress, and Worcestershire, adding enough cream to give mixture the consistency of *pâté*. Stuff mushroom caps, heaping mixture in center, cover, and refrigerate until about ½ hour before serving. Let come to room temperature, then serve with cocktails. About 20 calories per hors d'oeuvre.

⚖ MELON AND HAM

A popular European first course.
Makes 4 servings

6 ounces paper-thin slices prosciutto,
    Bayonne, or Westphalian ham, well
    chilled
½ ripe honeydew, casaba, or crenshaw
    melon, well chilled
Freshly ground pepper

Cut rind from melon, remove seeds, and slice lengthwise into thin crescents. Alternate slices of ham and melon on chilled plates and pass the pepper mill. About 50 calories per serving.

VARIATIONS:

⚖ **Figs or Mangoes and Ham:** Prepare as directed, substituting thinly sliced, peeled ripe figs or mangoes for the melon. About 50 calories per serving.

⚖ **Melon and Ham Tidbits:** Cut peeled and seeded melon in ¾" cubes, wrap in thin strips of ham, and secure with toothpicks. Serve as cocktail food; pass a pepper mill. About 20 calories per serving.

⚖ MARINATED MUSHROOMS

Makes 4–6 servings

1 cup water
½ cup olive or other cooking oil
½ cup lemon juice or white vinegar
1 clove garlic, peeled and bruised
1 teaspoon thyme
1 teaspoon tarragon
1 bay leaf
1 teaspoon salt
½ teaspoon peppercorns
1 pound button mushrooms, wiped clean

Simmer all ingredients except mushrooms uncovered 5 minutes. Add mushrooms, boil 1 minute, then cool, cover, and refrigerate overnight. Remove from refrigerator about ½ hour before serving, mix well, and serve in marinade or drained and speared with toothpicks. About 50 calories for each of 4 servings, 40 calories for each of 6 servings.

VARIATION:

Marinated Artichoke Hearts: Substitute 1 (1-pound) can drained artichoke hearts for the mushrooms (halved if large) and proceed as directed. (*Note:* Quartered artichoke bottoms are good this way, too.) About 70 calories for each of 4 servings, 50 for each of 6 servings.

¢ ARMENIAN BEAN APPETIZER

A good addition to antipasto.
Makes 4–6 servings

¼ cup olive oil
2 tablespoons lemon juice
¾ teaspoon salt (about)
⅛ teaspoon white pepper
1 clove garlic, peeled and crushed
3 tablespoons minced parsley
2 cups cooked, drained dried pea beans
    or navy beans, flageolets, or
    cannellini

Beat oil with lemon juice and salt until creamy, mix in pepper, garlic, and 2 tablespoons parsley. Pour over beans, mix lightly, cover, and marinate 3–4 hours in refrigerator, stirring now and then. Remove from refrigerator, stir well, let stand at room temperature 15–20 minutes, then serve sprinkled with remaining parsley either as a first course in lettuce cups with lemon wedges or spooned onto sesame seed wafers. About 275 calories for each of 4 servings, 185 calories for each of 6 servings.

VARIATION:

¢ **Turkish Bean Appetizer:** Prepare as directed but add 1 tablespoon minced fresh dill and 1 teaspoon minced fresh mint. Serve topped with paper-thin, raw onion rings. About 275 calories for each of 4 servings, 185 calories for each of 6 servings.

COLD MARINATED SHRIMP

Makes 6 servings

1 pound boiled, shelled, and deveined medium-size shrimp
⅓ cup tart salad dressing (French, Tarragon French, Lorenzo, Spanish Vinaigrette) or, if you prefer, Sauce Verte
1 clove garlic, peeled, bruised, and stuck on a toothpick
1 tablespoon snipped fresh dill or 1 teaspoon dried dill

Mix all ingredients, cover, and chill 6–8 hours, tossing shrimp in marinade now and then. Drain shrimp, discarding garlic, and serve with toothpicks (marinade can be saved and used again with other shellfish). About 75 calories per serving.

VARIATIONS:

Cold Marinated Scallops: Prepare as directed but substitute 1 pound poached or, if tiny, *raw* bay scallops for shrimp; chill only 4 hours. About 70 calories per serving.

Cold Marinated Oysters: Poach 1½ pints shucked oysters in their liquor 3–4 minutes just until edges ruffle, drain (save liquor for soup) and marinate as directed for shrimp. About 65 calories per serving.

Cold Marinated Mussels: Steam open 2 dozen mussels and shuck*; marinate as directed for shrimp. About 85 calories per serving.

◁▷ **Low-Calorie Marinated Cold Shellfish:** Prepare any of the above recipes as directed using a low-calorie French, Italian, or herb dressing. About 65 calories per serving for shrimp, 60 for scallops, 55 for oysters, and 75 for mussels.

PICKLED TRIPE

Pickled tripe can be kept 3–4 days in the refrigerator; if held longer, the flavor becomes unpleasantly strong.
Makes 4–6 servings

1½ pounds honeycomb tripe
2 cups cold water
1 teaspoon salt
1 small yellow onion, peeled and coarsely chopped
1 bay leaf, tied in cheesecloth with 5–6 peppercorns
1 cup white vinegar

Prepare tripe for cooking* and cut in 2″ squares. Place in a large kettle with all but last ingredient, cover, and simmer about 2 hours until very tender. Remove cheesecloth bag and add vinegar. Spoon into a large wide-mouthed jar and cover with vinegar mixture. (*Note:* if there is not enough to cover tripe, make up with a ½ and ½ mixture of water and white vinegar.) Cover tightly and store in refrigerator. Serve cold as an appetizer course or cut in smaller pieces and serve on an hors d'oeuvre tray. About 180 calories for each of 4 servings, 120 calories for each of 6 servings.

⊠ SPICED OLIVES

Makes about 3 cups

1 (6½-ounce) can large unpitted ripe olives, drained
1 (6½-ounce) jar large unpitted green olives, drained
2 cups French Dressing
4 thick lemon slices
1 tablespoon mixed pickling spices
2 large cloves garlic, peeled and bruised

Place all ingredients in a large wide-mouthed jar with a tight-fitting lid. Cover tightly and shake well. Store in refrigerator at least 2 days before serving; shake jar from time to time. Drain liquid from olives (save it for another batch), remove lemon slices and garlic. Serve with toothpicks. 15 to 20 calories per olive, depending on size.

⊠ DILL AND GARLIC OLIVES

Makes about 1 pint

2 (8½-ounce) jars unpitted green olives
1 clove garlic, peeled and crushed
2 tablespoons olive oil
3 large sprigs fresh dill

Empty olives and their juice into a small bowl, add remaining ingredients, and toss to mix. Cover and chill at least 24 hours before serving. 15 to 20 calories per olive, depending on size.

¢ SAUTÉED SPICED CHICK-PEAS

Serve warm as a cocktail nibble instead of salted nuts.
Makes 8–10 servings

1 pound dried chick-peas, washed, boiled, and drained
¼ cup olive or other cooking oil
1½ teaspoons chili powder
1 teaspoon garlic salt
Salt

Pat chick-peas dry between several thicknesses paper toweling. Heat oil in a large heavy skillet over moderate heat ½ minute. Add about ⅓ of the chick-peas and sauté, stirring constantly, until pale golden. Add ½ teaspoon chili powder and sauté 1–2 minutes longer, stirring constantly until peas are slightly crisp (reduce heat if peas brown too fast). Remove peas with a slotted spoon and drain on paper toweling; keep warm. Sauté remaining peas the same way, adding chili powder as directed; drain on paper toweling. Add garlic salt and toss lightly to mix. Taste, then salt as needed. About 210 calories for each of 8 servings, 170 calories for each of 10 servings.

VARIATION:

Sauté peas as directed but omit chili powder and garlic salt. Instead, toss with seasoned salt to taste. About 210 calories for each of 8 servings, 170 calories for each of 10 servings.

⚖ DRY-ROASTED HERBED MUSHROOMS

An unusual appetizer and oh! so low in calories.
Makes 4–6 servings

½ teaspoon garlic salt
1 pound medium-size mushrooms, wiped clean and sliced thin
1 teaspoon seasoned salt
½ teaspoon oregano
½ teaspoon powdered rosemary

Preheat oven to 200° F. Sprinkle 2 lightly oiled baking sheets with garlic salt and arrange mushrooms 1 layer deep on sheets. Mix seasoned salt and herbs and sprinkle evenly over mushrooms. Bake, uncovered, about 1½ hours until dry and crisp but not brown. Cool slightly and serve as a cocktail nibble. (Note: Store airtight; these absorb moisture rapidly.) About 30 calories for each of 4 servings, 20 for each of 6.

⚖ ¢ ⊠ CURRIED COCKTAIL MELBAS

Makes 40 Melbas

8 slices firm-textured white bread
⅓ cup melted butter or margarine
¼ teaspoon garlic powder
¼ teaspoon onion powder
1½ teaspoons curry powder
3–4 drops liquid hot red pepper seasoning

Preheat oven to 300° F. Trim crusts from bread. Mix butter with remaining ingredients and, using a pastry brush, brush over 1 side of each slice. Cut each slice into 5 thin strips, arrange on an ungreased baking sheet, and bake uncovered 25–30 minutes until golden brown and crisp. Serve hot or at room temperature. About 25 calories per Melba.

⊠ ¢ GARLIC NIBBLES

Makes about 5 quarts

1 (11-ounce) package crisp corn chips
2 cups toasted honeycombed wheat
  cereal
2 cups toasted bite-size, checkered corn
  cereal
¾ pound shelled pecans
1 (2½-ounce) package cheese tidbits
1 (10-ounce) package small cheese-
  flavored crackers
1 cup butter or margarine
2 teaspoons garlic salt
1 teaspoon salt
2 tablespoons steak sauce
4–5 drops liquid hot red pepper
  seasoning

Preheat oven to 250° F. Place chips,
cereals, pecans, and crackers in 1 or 2
large, shallow roasting pans and toss
lightly to mix. Heat butter and remaining
ingredients over moderate heat 2–3
minutes until butter is melted, pour
evenly over nibble mixture, and toss to
mix. Bake uncovered 1 hour, stirring
occasionally; cool in pans. Mixture will
keep 2–3 weeks if stored airtight. About
75 calories per ¼ cup.

¢ GARLIC-CHEESE CRISPS

Makes about 2½ dozen

1 cup sifted flour
2 teaspoons garlic salt
⅓ cup butter or margarine, chilled
1 cup coarsely grated sharp Cheddar
  cheese
1 tablespoon Worcestershire sauce
1–2 teaspoons ice water (optional)

Preheat oven to 400° F. Mix flour and
garlic salt in a bowl and cut butter in
with a pastry blender until mixture
resembles coarse meal; add cheese and
toss well. Sprinkle Worcestershire sauce
over mixture and toss lightly and quickly
with a fork. Ingredients should just hold
together; if not, add ice water. Shape
into ¾" balls and arrange 2" apart on
ungreased baking sheets; flatten each to a
thickness of about ¼". Bake 10 minutes;
reduce oven temperature to 300° F.,
and bake 10 minutes longer until golden

and crisp. Cool on wire racks before
serving. About 45 calories per crisp.

VARIATION:

Prepare as directed but mix in 2
tablespoons minced pimiento, onion, or
ham along with the cheese. About 45
calories per crisp.

⟐ ¢ CHEESE CRACKERS

Makes 6–7 dozen

1½ cups sifted flour
1 teaspoon salt
⅛ teaspoon paprika
⅛ teaspoon cayenne pepper
½ cup chilled margarine (no substitute)
½ pound sharp Cheddar cheese, coarsely
  grated
2½–3 tablespoons ice water

Mix flour, salt, paprika, and cayenne in a
shallow bowl and cut in margarine with a
pastry blender until mixture resembles
coarse meal. Add cheese and toss to mix.
Sprinkle water evenly over surface, 1
tablespoon at a time, mixing lightly with
a fork; dough should just hold together.
Divide dough in half and shape each on a
lightly floured board into a roll about 9"
long and 1½" in diameter; wrap in foil
and chill well. About 10 minutes before
crackers are to be baked, heat oven to
375° F. Slice rolls ¼" thick, space 1"
apart on ungreased baking sheets, and
bake 10 minutes until golden; transfer at
once to wire racks to cool. Store airtight.
Serve at room temperature or, if you
prefer, reheat about 5 minutes at 350° F.
About 30 calories per cracker.

SHRIMP TOAST

Makes 6–8 servings

1 (4½-ounce) can shrimp, drained and
  minced very fine
2 tablespoons minced water chestnuts
3 scallions, minced (white part only)
1 teaspoon minced gingerroot
1 teaspoon cornstarch
1 teaspoon dry sherry
¼ teaspoon sugar
¼ teaspoon salt
2 egg whites, lightly beaten

4 thin slices firm-textured, day-old white bread, trimmed of crusts
Peanut or other cooking oil for deep fat frying

Mix all but last 2 ingredients. Begin heating oil in a deep fat fryer with a basket and deep fat thermometer over moderately high heat. Pile shrimp mixture on bread, dividing total amount evenly, and spread just to edges; press down lightly. Cut each slice into 4 triangles. When oil reaches 350° F., place 2 or 3 triangles, spread sides up, in fryer basket, lower into oil, and fry about 1 minute until golden and puffed. (*Note:* Triangles should automatically flip over; if not, turn to brown evenly.) Drain on paper toweling and keep warm in a 250° F. oven while you fry the rest. Serve hot. About 115 calories for each of 6 servings, 85 calories for each of 8 servings.

QUICHE LORRAINE TARTLETS

Serve warm as hors d'oeuvre.
Makes 1½ dozen

1 recipe Flaky Pastry II

Filling:
¾ cup coarsely grated Gruyère or Swiss cheese
¼ cup crumbled crisply cooked bacon
2 eggs, lightly beaten
¾ cup light cream
½ teaspoon salt
Pinch white pepper
Pinch nutmeg
Pinch cayenne pepper

Preheat oven to 425° F. Prepare pastry, divide in half, and roll out 1 piece at a time into a circle about ⅛″ thick. Cut with a 3″ biscuit cutter and line fluted or plain tart tins about 2½″ in diameter. Set tins on baking sheets. Dividing total amount evenly, sprinkle cheese and bacon into pastry shells. Mix remaining ingredients and pour into shells. Bake on center oven rack 10 minutes, remove from oven, and let stand 2 minutes. Meanwhile, reduce oven to 350° F. Return tartlets to oven and bake 5 minutes until filling is puffed and pastry

golden. Cool in tins 2–3 minutes, then lift from tins and cool slightly on a wire rack. Serve warm. (*Note:* Tartlets may be baked ahead of time, then cooled and refrigerated until shortly before serving. Reheat on a baking sheet 5–8 minutes at 350° F.) About 210 calories per tartlet.

VARIATION:

Any quiche Lorraine variations (see Eggs and Cheese) can be prepared as tartlets instead of full-size pies.

BEEF BOREKS

Phyllo pastry leaves (sheets) are sold by Middle Eastern groceries and bakeries.
Makes 25–30 servings

½ (1-pound) package phyllo pastry leaves, at room temperature (refrigerate remainder to use another time)
½ cup (about) melted butter (no substitute)

Filling:
½ pound ground beef chuck
1 small yellow onion, peeled and minced
1 clove garlic, peeled and crushed
2 tablespoons tomato purée
1 egg yolk, lightly beaten
1 tablespoon minced parsley
½ teaspoon salt
⅛ teaspoon pepper
⅛ teaspoon cinnamon
⅛ teaspoon allspice

Unroll pastry, arrange leaves in an even stack, then halve lengthwise *and* crosswise, making 4 stacks about 8″×6″. Pile stacks on top of each other and cover with cloth to prevent drying. Prepare filling: Brown beef 5 minutes over moderately high heat, add onion and garlic, and continue cooking until meat is no longer pink; drain off drippings. Off heat, mix in remaining ingredients; cool to room temperature. Preheat oven to 350° F. Lift 1 pastry leaf to a flat surface so short side faces you and brush with butter. Place a rounded ½ teaspoon filling 1″ from bottom and slightly off center and fold as shown; brush with melted butter, then fold over and over into a small, neat triangle. Fill and fold remaining boreks the same way.

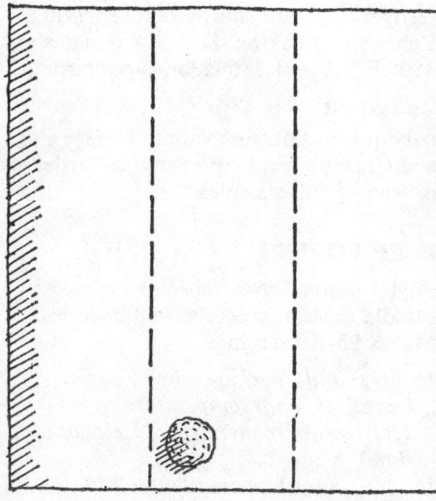

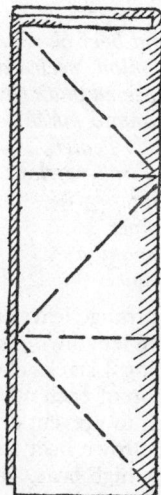

Space 1″ apart on buttered baking sheets, brush with melted butter, and bake about 25 minutes until well browned. Serve hot. (*Note:* These can be made up to the point of baking several hours ahead of time; cover and refrigerate until needed.) About 125 calories for each of 25 servings, 105 calories for each of 30 servings.

VARIATIONS:

Spinach and Mozzarella Boreks: Prepare as directed but use the following filling instead of the beef: Thaw 1 (10-ounce) package frozen chopped spinach and drain well; mince spinach very fine, mix in ¼ pound finely minced mozzarella cheese, ¼ cup finely grated Parmesan, ½ teaspoon salt, and ⅛ teaspoon pepper. About 105 calories for each of 25 servings, 90 calories for each of 30 servings.

Cheese Boreks: Prepare as directed but substitute the following filling for the beef: Mix 1 (3-ounce) package softened cream cheese with 1 cup each crumbled feta and cottage cheeses, 1 lightly beaten egg yolk, ½ teaspoon salt, ⅛ teaspoon pepper, and 1 tablespoon minced fresh dill, chives, or parsley. About 135 calories for each of 25 servings, 115 calories for each of 30 servings.

PIROSHKI

A Russian favorite.
Makes about 25 servings

Yeast Dough:

1 cup scalded milk
1 tablespoon sugar
1½ teaspoons salt
¼ cup butter, margarine, or lard
¼ cup warm water (105–15° F.)
1 package active dry yeast
2 eggs, lightly beaten
5 cups sifted flour (about)

Glaze:

¼ cup melted butter or margarine or 2 egg yolks beaten with 2 tablespoons cold water

Filling:

½ pound ground beef chuck or a ½ and ½ mixture of lean ground pork and beef
1 small yellow onion, peeled and minced
1 tablespoon flour
½ cup beef broth
¾ teaspoon salt
⅛ teaspoon pepper
1 hard-cooked egg, peeled and minced
1 teaspoon minced parsley

Mix milk, sugar, salt, and butter in a small bowl, stirring until sugar dissolves; cool to lukewarm. Pour warm water into a large warm bowl, sprinkle in yeast, and stir until dissolved. Add eggs to milk mixture, stir into yeast, add 3 cups flour and beat until smooth. Mix in enough additional flour, a little at a time, to make a soft dough. Mixture will be sticky but should leave sides of bowl reasonably clean. Knead on a lightly floured board until satiny and elastic, 8–10 minutes, adding as little extra flour as possible. Shape into a smooth ball, place in a large greased bowl, turning to grease all over. Cover with cloth and let rise in a warm spot until doubled in bulk, about ¾ hour. Punch down, and let rise again until doubled in bulk. Meanwhile, prepare filling: Brown meat over moderately high heat 5 minutes, add onion, and continue browning until no pink remains. Remove meat and onion to a bowl with a slotted spoon, blend flour into drippings and brown lightly. Slowly add broth, salt, and pepper and heat, stirring, until thickened. Mix into meat along with egg and parsley; cool. When dough has risen a second time, punch down, turn onto lightly floured board, and knead lightly 2 minutes. Quarter dough, then cut each quarter into 12 equal pieces. Roll each piece into a ball,

then flatten into a round about ¼″ thick with a lightly floured rolling pin. Place a scant teaspoon of filling in center of rounds, moisten edges with cold water, and fold as shown, pinching edges to seal.

Arrange seam side down 2″ apart on ungreased baking sheets, cover, and let rise 15 minutes. Meanwhile, preheat oven to 375° F. Brush *piroshki* with glaze and bake 20–25 minutes until well browned. Serve hot. About 160 calories per serving.

VARIATIONS:

Liver and Bacon Piroshki: Prepare as directed, using the following filling instead of the beef: Brown ½ pound calf or beef liver in 2 tablespoons bacon drippings over high heat 3–4 minutes; grind fine along with 1 peeled small yellow onion. Mix in 4 slices cooked, crumbled bacon, ½ cup soft bread crumbs soaked in ½ cup milk, ¾ teaspoon salt and ⅛ teaspoon pepper. About 170 calories per serving.

Mushroom Piroshki: Prepare as directed but instead of beef filling use the following: Sauté 2 pounds minced mushrooms and 1 minced yellow onion in ¼ cup butter over moderately high heat 4–5 minutes. Off heat, mix in 1 cup soft bread crumbs, ⅓ cup sour cream, 2 minced, peeled, hard-cooked eggs, 1 teaspoon salt, ⅛ teaspoon pepper, and 1 tablespoon minced parsley or fresh dill. About 165 calories per serving.

Easy Piroshki: Substitute 2 (8-ounce) packages refrigerated crescent rolls for the yeast dough. Unroll packages, 1 at a time, do *not* separate at perforations but pinch together to make an unbroken sheet of dough. Roll out about ⅛″ thick on a lightly floured board, cut with a 2½″ biscuit cutter, fill, fold, seal, and bake as directed. About 160 calories per serving.

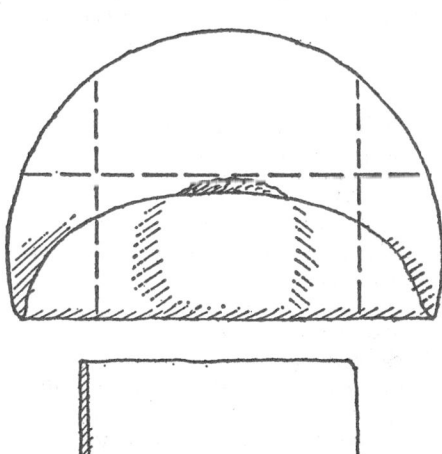

⊠ EASY PIGS IN BLANKETS
Makes 8–10 servings

*1 (8-ounce) package refrigerated
crescent rolls*
*2 tablespoons prepared mild yellow
mustard (about)*
*2 (5½-ounce) packages cocktail
frankfurters*

Preheat oven to 375° F. Unroll and
separate crescent rolls and roll out, 1 at a
time, on a lightly floured board to a
thickness of ⅛″; spread lightly with
mustard and cut in strips about 3″ long
and 1¼″ wide (you should get 4 strips
from each roll). Wrap frankfurters in
strips, sealing ends with cold water,
arrange seam sides down, 2″ apart, on
ungreased baking sheets and bake 10–12
minutes until golden. Serve hot with or
without a bowl of mild mustard or chili
sauce as a dip. About 230 calories for
each of 8 servings, 185 calories for each
of 10 servings.

⊠ PIGS IN POKES
Makes 8–10 servings

*2 (5½-ounce) packages cocktail
frankfurters*
½ cup chili sauce
16 bacon slices, halved crosswise

Preheat broiler. Dip franks in chili sauce,
then wrap in bacon, securing with
toothpicks. Broil 4″ from the heat,
turning frequently, 3–5 minutes until
bacon is crisp and browned. Serve hot
with toothpicks. About 200 calories for
each of 8 servings, 160 calories for each
of 10 servings.

⊠ HOT GLAZED COCKTAIL
SAUSAGES
Makes 6–8 servings

Glaze:

1 cup tomato purée
3 tablespoons cider vinegar
⅓ cup firmly packed light brown sugar
1½ teaspoons chili powder
1 clove garlic, peeled and crushed

*2 (5½-ounce) packages cocktail
frankfurters*

Mix glaze ingredients in a skillet and
simmer uncovered 2–3 minutes, stirring
now and then. Add frankfurters and
simmer uncovered, stirring occasionally,
about 10 minutes until lightly glazed.
Pour into a chafing dish and serve with
toothpicks. About 225 calories for each
of 6 servings, 170 calories for each of 8
servings.

VARIATIONS:

⊠ **Orange and Mustard-Glazed Cocktail
Sausages:** Prepare as directed but
substitute the following glaze for that
above: 1 cup orange juice, ⅓ cup
medium dry sherry or ginger ale, 3
tablespoons each sugar and molasses, and
4 teaspoons spicy brown prepared
mustard. About 235 calories for each of
6 servings, 180 calories for each of 8
servings.

⊠ **Cocktail Sausages Glazed with Plum
Sauce:** Prepare as directed but substitute
1 recipe Plum Sauce for the glaze above.
About 230 calories for each of 6
servings, 175 calories for each of 8
servings.

⊠ **Sweet-Sour Cocktail Sausages:** Prepare as directed but substitute ½ recipe
Sweet-Sour Sauce for the above glaze.
About 230 calories for each of 6
servings, about 175 calories for each of
8 servings.

¢ HOT SPICY MEAT BALLS
Makes about 12 servings

Meat Balls:

1 pound ground beef chuck
*1 medium-size yellow onion, peeled and
finely grated*
1 teaspoon garlic salt
1 tablespoon steak sauce
¼ teaspoon pepper
*⅛ teaspoon crushed dried hot red chili
peppers*
*¾ cup soft white bread crumbs soaked in
¼ cup cold water*
1 egg, lightly beaten
2 tablespoons cooking oil (for browning)

Sauce: (optional)

3 tablespoons flour
2 tablespoons pan drippings
1½ cups beef broth
2 tablespoons tomato paste
2 tablespoons dry red wine or 1
   tablespoon red wine vinegar
⅛ teaspoon pepper

Mix all meat ball ingredients except oil and shape in 1″ balls. Brown well in oil, a few balls at a time, 5–7 minutes in a heavy skillet over moderately high heat; remove to paper toweling with a slotted spoon. Drain all but 1 tablespoon drippings from pan, add balls, turn heat to low, cover, and simmer 10–15 minutes, adding about 2 tablespoons water, if needed, to keep balls from sticking. Serve hot on toothpicks with or without a savory dip (Béarnaise, Chinese-Style Sweet-Sour, and Plum Sauce are particularly good). Or, if you prefer, serve in the above sauce: Brown and drain balls as directed; before returning to pan, blend flour into drippings, add remaining ingredients, and heat and stir until thickened. Add meat balls, cover, and simmer 10–15 minutes. Serve from a chafing dish with toothpicks. About 160 calories per serving.

VARIATIONS:

Roman Meat Balls: For the meat balls, use ½ pound each ground beef chuck and hot or sweet Italian sausages removed from casings; stir-fry 10 minutes over moderately high heat until cooked through. Drain off drippings and cool meat slightly; then mince. Mix with ingredients called for but omit hot red peppers; add 3 tablespoons grated Parmesan and substitute ¾ teaspoon salt for garlic salt. Shape into 1″ balls, brown and cook as directed. About 170 calories per serving.

Chutney-Nut Meat Balls: To the meat ball mixture add ⅓ cup minced walnuts or toasted almonds. Proceed as directed, simmering in the sauce to which ⅓ cup well-drained, minced chutney has been added. About 180 calories per serving.

Chili Meat Balls: Prepare meat balls as directed, omitting hot red chili peppers and adding 1 tablespoon chili powder and 2 tablespoons chili sauce. Also prepare sauce, blending 1 teaspoon chili powder into drippings along with flour. About 160 calories per serving.

Blue Cheese Meat Balls: Prepare meat balls as directed, omitting hot red chili peppers and adding 3–4 tablespoons crumbled blue cheese. Serve without sauce but pass Sour Cream-Roquefort Dressing as a dip. About 165 calories per serving.

RUMAKIS (HOT BACON AND CHICKEN LIVER HORS D'OEUVRE)

Makes about 6 servings

6 chicken livers, quartered
1 (6-ounce) bottle Japanese soy sauce
¼ cup sake or medium dry sherry
½ clove garlic, peeled and crushed
2 (½″) cubes fresh gingerroot, peeled and crushed
8 water chestnuts (about), each cut in 3 thin slivers
¾ cup light brown sugar
½ pound lean bacon, each strip halved crosswise

Marinate chicken livers in refrigerator in a mixture of soy sauce, sake, garlic, and ginger about 12 hours or overnight. Make a slit in the center of each piece of liver, insert a sliver of water chestnut, and roll in brown sugar; wrap each in a piece of bacon and secure with a toothpick. Place *rumakis* in a piepan, add marinade, cover, and marinate 2–3 hours longer in refrigerator, turning occasionally in marinade. Preheat oven to 400° F. Drain marinade from rumakis and reserve. Roast rumakis uncovered ½–¾ hour, pouring off drippings as they accumulate and basting often with marinade until nicely glazed and brown. About 320 calories per serving.

SIZZLING CHICKEN LIVERS

Makes 6 servings

¼ cup soy sauce
2 tablespoons dry sherry or sake
1 tablespoon dark brown sugar
1 clove garlic, peeled and quartered
½ pound chicken livers, halved at the
  natural separation
1 tablespoon cornstarch blended with ¼
  cup canned condensed beef broth
1–2 tablespoons flour
2 tablespoons peanut or other cooking oil

Mix soy sauce, sherry, sugar, and garlic in a bowl, add livers, cover, and marinate in refrigerator 1–2 hours. Drain marinade into a small saucepan; discard garlic. Bring to a simmer, blend in cornstarch paste, and heat, stirring constantly, until thickened and clear; transfer to a small chafing dish and keep warm. Dredge chicken livers in flour and stir-fry in oil 3–4 minutes until lightly browned. Transfer to chafing dish and heat 1–2 minutes. Serve from chafing dish with toothpicks for spearing livers. About 120 calories per serving.

About Dips and Spreads

There's something convivial about dips and spreads. Dips are an American invention, and a very good one, too. Spreads are not, though Americans have certainly enlarged the repertoire. The main caution to bear in mind when preparing either is to keep them the right consistency: dips should be thick enough not to dribble or splash, spreads soft enough to spread easily without tearing the bread or breaking the crackers. Another good practice: Make dips and spreads ahead of time so that their flavors will mellow.

In addition to the recipes that follow, a number of salad dressings and sauces make excellent dips:

Dressings to Use as Dips *(see Salad Chapter for Recipes):*	*Particularly Good with:*
Avocado Dressing	Vegetables
Blender Garlic-Roquefort Dressing	Vegetables
California-Sour Cream Dressing	Vegetables
Camembert Cream Dressing	Vegetables
French Dressing (and Variations)	Vegetables, Seafood
Fresh Herb Dressing	Vegetables
Garlic-Herb Dressing	Vegetables, Seafood
Green Goddess Dressing	Vegetables
Green Mayonnaise	Vegetables
Low-Calorie Yogurt Dressing	Vegetables
Old-Fashioned Cooked Dressing	Vegetables
Russian Dressing	Vegetables, Seafood
Sauce Verte	Vegetables
Shallot Dressing	Vegetables, Seafood
Sour Cream Dressing	Vegetables, Seafood
Sour Cream-Roquefort Dressing	Vegetables
Thousand Island Dressing (and Variations)	Vegetables, Seafood
Wine Dressing	Vegetables, Seafood

Sauces to Use as Dips
(see Sauces Chapter for Recipes):

Particularly Good with:

Béarnaise	Meat, Seafood, Vegetables
Caper and Horseradish	Seafood, Vegetables
Chinese-Style Sweet-Sour	Meat, Seafood
Cocktail	Seafood
Cold Ravigote	Vegetables
Easy Sour Cream (and Variations)	Meat, Seafood, Vegetables
Fin and Claw Cocktail	Seafood
Green Sauce	Vegetables
Gribiche	Seafood
Hollandaise (and Variations)	Meat, Seafood, Vegetables
Hot Chinese Mustard	Meat
Mayonnaise (and Variations)	Meat, Seafood, Vegetables
Pineapple-Pepper Sweet-Sour	Meat
Plum Sauce	Meat
Tapenade	Vegetables
Tartar	Seafood, Vegetables
Tempura	Seafood

▨ DILLY DEVILED HAM DIP

Makes about 1 pint

1 cup sour cream
1 (8-ounce) package cream cheese,
softened to room temperature
2 (2¼-ounce) cans deviled ham
1 tablespoon minced onion
2 teaspoons prepared spicy brown
mustard
1 tablespoon minced dill pickle

Beat all ingredients together with an electric mixer or rotary beater until smooth and creamy. Cover and let stand at room temperature 1 hour before serving to blend flavors. About 48 calories per tablespoon.

▨ CREAM CHEESE, BACON AND HORSERADISH DIP

Makes about 1½ cups

½ cup milk or light cream
1 (8-ounce) package cream cheese,
softened to room temperature
1 tablespoon prepared horseradish
1 teaspoon Worcestershire sauce
⅓ cup crisp, crumbled bacon

Blend milk and cheese until smooth, mix in remaining ingredients, cover, and let stand at room temperature 1 hour before serving. About 65 calories per tablespoon.

▨ CLAM AND CREAM CHEESE DIP

Makes about 1½ cups

1 (8-ounce) package cream cheese,
softened to room temperature
¼ cup light cream
1 tablespoon lemon juice
1 tablespoon Worcestershire sauce
¼ teaspoon prepared horseradish
¼ teaspoon salt
Pinch white pepper
1 (8-ounce) can minced clams, drained

Blend cream cheese and cream until smooth, mix in remaining ingredients, cover, and chill 1–2 hours to blend flavors. About 80 calories per tablespoon.

VARIATION:

Deviled Clam Dip: Prepare as directed, reducing cream to 2 tablespoons and adding 2 tablespoons spicy brown mustard, 1 tablespoon grated onion, ¼ crushed clove garlic, and ⅛ teaspoon liquid hot red pepper seasoning. About 78 calories per tablespoon.

⬚ SHERRIED GREEN CHEESE DIP

A particularly good dip for small celery sticks.
Makes about 2 cups

8 ounces sharp Cheddar cheese spread, softened to room temperature
6 ounces Roquefort cheese, softened to room temperature
¼–⅓ cup medium-dry sherry

With an electric mixer beat cheeses and ¼ cup sherry until smooth; if you like a softer dip, add more sherry. Cover and let stand 1 hour at room temperature to blend flavors before serving. About 50 calories per tablespoon.

¢ ⬚ ZINGY SOUR CREAM DIP

Makes about 1½ cups

1 cup sour cream
2 tablespoons mayonnaise
¼ cup finely grated Parmesan cheese
1 teaspoon onion juice
½ teaspoon Worcestershire sauce
½ teaspoon prepared horseradish
½ teaspoon prepared spicy brown mustard
¼ teaspoon salt

Mix all ingredients together, cover, and chill 1–2 hours before serving. About 35 calories per tablespoon.

⬚ CURRY DIP

Good as a dip for crisp sticks of celery, carrot, or finocchio.
Makes about 2½ cups

2 (8-ounce) packages cream cheese, softened to room temperature
⅓ cup milk
1 tablespoon Worcestershire sauce
¼ teaspoon liquid hot red pepper seasoning
1 tablespoon curry powder
1 tablespoon finely grated yellow onion
½ teaspoon salt

Beat all ingredients together with an electric mixer or rotary beater until creamy. Cover and chill several hours. Let stand ½ hour at room temperature before serving. If mixture still seems a bit stiff for dipping, thin with a little milk. About 45 calories per tablespoon.

⬚ GUACAMOLE

Makes about 1 pint

2 ripe medium-size avocados
1 tablespoon lemon juice
1 teaspoon minced scallion
2 tablespoons mayonnaise
½ teaspoon crushed dried hot red chili peppers
¼ teaspoon salt

Halve avocados lengthwise and remove pits; scoop flesh into a small bowl, sprinkle with lemon juice, and mash with a fork. Mix in remaining ingredients, place a piece of plastic food wrap directly on surface, and chill 1–2 hours. Stir well and serve as a dip for crisp corn chips. About 30 calories per tablespoon.

GUACAMOLE WITH TOMATO

Makes about 1 pint

1 small firm tomato, peeled, cored, seeded, and coarsely chopped
Juice of ½ lemon
2 ripe medium-size avocados
1 tablespoon grated onion
1 tablespoon olive oil
½–1 small pickled hot green chili pepper, drained, seeded, and minced
½ teaspoon salt

Spread chopped tomato out on several thicknesses of paper toweling, cover with more toweling, and pat until almost all moisture is absorbed. Place lemon juice in a small bowl; halve avocados lengthwise, remove pits, scoop flesh into bowl, and mash with a fork (mixture should be quite lumpy). Mix in tomatoes and remaining ingredients. Place a small piece of plastic food wrap directly on surface of guacamole and let stand at room temperature 1 hour to blend flavors. Stir well and serve with crisp corn chips. About 30 calories per tablespoon.

⚖ ¢ ☒ CHILI DIP

Makes 3 cups

1 (11-ounce) can condensed chili-beef
  soup
¾ cup canned condensed beef
  consommé
1 cup sour cream
¼ teaspoon chili powder
½ teaspoon Worcestershire sauce
2–3 drops liquid hot red pepper
  seasoning

Mix together all ingredients, cover, and chill 2 hours to blend flavors. Stir well and serve with corn chips. About 15 calories per tablespoon.

☒ BLACK BEAN DIP

Makes about 2¾ cups

2 (8-ounce) packages cream cheese,
  softened to room temperature
1 (1-pound) can black beans, drained
  well and puréed
¼ cup minced onion
1 clove garlic, peeled and crushed
2 tablespoons dry sherry
¼ teaspoon liquid hot red pepper
  seasoning
¼ teaspoon salt

Place all ingredients in a small mixing bowl and beat with an electric mixer or rotary beater until smooth; cover and chill 2–3 hours. Let stand at room temperature about 20 minutes before serving so mixture is a good dipping consistency. About 35 calories per tablespoon.

EGGPLANT DIP

Makes about 1 quart

2 (1-pound) eggplants, peeled and cut
  in 1" cubes
1 medium-size yellow onion, peeled and
  coarsely chopped
½ clove garlic, peeled and crushed
⅔ cup olive oil
3 (3-ounce) packages chive-flavored,
  softened cream cheese

3 tablespoons tarragon vinegar
Juice of ½ lemon

Sauté eggplants, onion, and garlic in oil in a heavy kettle over moderately high heat 12–15 minutes, stirring frequently, until lightly browned; purée, a little at a time, in an electric blender at high speed. Blend cheese with remaining ingredients, add purée and beat until smooth. Cover and chill several hours. Serve as a dip for sesame seed crackers or Euphrates bread. About 38 calories per tablespoon.

BEER CHEESE SPREAD

This spread is best if allowed to age about a week in the refrigerator before using.

Makes about 1 quart

1 pound mild Cheddar cheese, finely
  grated
1 pound sharp Cheddar cheese, finely
  grated
¼ cup finely grated Bermuda onion
½ clove garlic, peeled and crushed
¼ cup ketchup
1 tablespoon Worcestershire sauce
⅛ teaspoon liquid hot red pepper
  seasoning
1 (12-ounce) can beer

Let cheeses soften at room temperature at least 1 hour. Mix in all remaining ingredients except beer, then, using an electric mixer, beat in the beer, a little at a time; continue beating until light and fluffy. Chill well before serving. About 50 calories per tablespoon.

☒ GARLIC CHEESE BALL

Makes 8 servings

½ pound sharp Cheddar cheese, grated
  fine
1 (8-ounce) package cream cheese,
  softened to room temperature
2 cloves garlic, peeled and crushed
Pinch salt
⅓ cup minced pecans or walnuts or ¼
  cup finely chopped fresh parsley or
  2–3 tablespoons paprika (optional)

Using your hands, mix cheeses, garlic, and salt until thoroughly blended, then shape into a ball. If you wish, roll in the nuts, parsley, or paprika to coat evenly. Wrap in foil and chill 2–3 hours to mellow. Serve at room temperature as a spread for crisp crackers. (*Note:* This cheese ball may also be frozen.) About 245 calories per serving.

⌧ CHIVE CHEESE

Makes about 1 cup

2 (*3-ounce*) *packages cream cheese,* *softened to room temperature*
¼ *cup minced chives*
¼ *cup light cream*
¼ *teaspoon salt*
⅛ *teaspoon white pepper*

Cream all ingredients together until smooth and use as a spread for crackers or stuffing for raw mushroom caps, celery stalks, or endive spears. About 60 calories per tablespoon.

⌧ TARAMASALATA (GREEK FISH ROE DIP)

This thick, creamy Greek appetizer is made with *tarama* (pale orange carp roe). Greek and Middle Eastern groceries sell it, but if unavailable use red caviar.
Makes about 1 cup

¼ *cup tarama* (*carp roe*) *or red caviar*
2 *tablespoons lemon juice*
2 *slices white bread, trimmed of* *crusts, soaked in cold water and* *squeezed dry*
½ *cup olive oil*
¼ *cup cooking oil*
¼ *teaspoon onion juice*

Blend *tarama,* lemon juice, bread, and olive oil in an electric blender at high speed 1 minute, scrape any unbroken roe from blender blades, and blend again ½ minute. Add vegetable oil and blend ½ minute. Stir in onion juice and serve at room temperature as a dip for raw vegetables or unsalted crackers. Or use as a spread for pumpernickel rounds or Melba toast. About 110 calories per tablespoon.

¢ ⌧ EGG-DILL SPREAD

Makes about 1 pint

5 *hard-cooked eggs, peeled and minced*
⅓ *cup melted butter or margarine*
1 *teaspoon prepared Dijon-style mustard*
1 *tablespoon minced fresh dill*
1 *tablespoon white wine vinegar*
½ *teaspoon salt*
½ *teaspoon Worcestershire sauce*
⅛ *teaspoon pepper*
2–3 *dashes liquid hot red pepper* *seasoning*

Mix all ingredients together and use as a cocktail spread. Especially good on small squares of pumpernickel. About 30 calories per tablespoon.

⌧ DEVILED HAM COCKTAIL SPREAD

Makes about 1¼ cups

1 (*3-ounce*) *package cream cheese,* *softened to room temperature*
2 (*3-ounce*) *cans deviled ham spread*
½ *teaspoon Worcestershire sauce*
1 *teaspoon lemon juice*
1 *tablespoon grated onion*

Blend all ingredients together and use as a spread for crackers or stuffing for celery stalks, raw mushroom caps, or hollowed-out cherry tomatoes. About 40 calories per tablespoon.

⌧ MOCK LIPTAUER SPREAD

Genuine Liptauer is a soft, sharp Hungarian cheese mixed with herbs, spices, and capers. Here's a zippy substitute, delicious spread on pumpernickel.
Makes about 1 cup

2 (*3-ounce*) *packages cream cheese,* *softened to room temperature, or* ¾ *cup cottage cheese, pressed through a* *fine sieve*
¼ *cup soft butter or margarine*
2 *teaspoons minced capers*
1½ *teaspoons anchovy paste*
½ *teaspoon caraway seeds*
1 *teaspoon minced chives*
1 *teaspoon grated onion*
¼ *teaspoon salt*
½ *teaspoon paprika*

Blend ingredients together, pack into a crock, cover, and chill 3–4 hours before serving. About 45 calories per tablespoon.

⚖ ¢ CAPONATA (SICILIAN EGGPLANT SPREAD)

Refrigerated, this will keep about a week. Bring to room temperature before serving.
Makes about 3 cups

4 tablespoons olive oil
1 small eggplant, cut in 1" cubes but not peeled
1 medium-size yellow onion, peeled and minced
⅓ cup minced celery
1 cup tomato purée
⅓ cup coarsely chopped, pitted green and/or ripe olives
4 anchovy fillets, minced
2 tablespoons capers
2 tablespoons red wine vinegar
1 tablespoon sugar
½ teaspoon salt (about)
¼ teaspoon pepper
1 tablespoon minced parsley

Heat 3 tablespoons oil in a large, heavy saucepan 1 minute over moderately high heat, add eggplant and sauté, stirring now and then, 10 minutes until golden and nearly translucent. Add remaining oil, onion, and celery and stir-fry 5–8 minutes until pale golden. Add remaining ingredients except parsley, cover, and simmer 1¼–1½ hours until quite thick, stirring now and then. Mix in parsley, cool to room temperature, taste for salt and adjust as needed. Serve as a spread for crackers. About 17 calories per tablespoon.

About Cocktails

These are not alcoholic cocktails but chilled fruits or seafoods served at the start of a meal. They are easy to prepare and can be quite glamorous, depending upon the presentation.

Fruit Cocktails

Tart fruits (grapefruit, oranges, grapes, pineapple) are the best appetite whetters. They may be fresh, frozen, or canned (or a combination), they can be served solo, mixed together, or teamed with blander fruits such as bananas, peaches, pears, avocados, apples, apricots, melons, or berries. Fruits, of course, should be peeled whenever the skin is hard or thick, cored or sectioned, seeded and cut in bite-size chunks, then chilled several hours. They may be spiked with champagne or dry wine, grenadine or crème de menthe or sprigged with fresh mint, rose geranium, or lemon verbena (if these leaves are tucked into the fruits before chilling, their bouquet will permeate the fruit). If fruits are not naturally tart, drizzle with lemon, lime, orange, or cranberry juice or with ginger ale.

Fruit cocktails may be simply served in stemmed goblets, more elaborately presented by dishing into small bowls and imbedding in larger bowls of crushed ice or by mounding into grapefruit or orange shells, avocado or mango halves. Serve unadorned or crown with scoops of fruit ice or sherbet dabs of tart fruit jelly. The main point to bear in mind when making fruit cocktails: Keep the fruit mixtures tart and light, varied and colorful.

FRUIT JUICE COCKTAILS

(These are included in the beverage chapter.)

SEAFOOD COCKTAILS

Shrimp cocktail is America's favorite, especially when the shrimp are plump and tender, cooked in a fragrant court bouillon and served well chilled on beds of crushed ice with a horseradish-hot cocktail sauce. Other cold, cooked shellfish make delicious cocktails, too—lobster, crab, Alaska king crab, tiny bay scallops, especially with Green Dressing. Full instructions for preparing and cooking shellfish are included in the seafood chapter, also directions for serving oysters and clams on the half shell, for pickling shrimp and oysters. Here, too, are recipes for Escabeche (Mexican Pickled Fish), Ceviche (Peruvian Raw Pickled Fish), and a number of other unusual cold fish dishes that can double as appetizers.

Seafood cocktails are routinely served in small stemmed glasses with ruffs of greenery and dabs of cocktail sauce. They're far more appealing arranged on beds of crushed ice or piled into avocado, papaya, or mango halves. However served, seafood cocktails should be accompanied by a tart rather than a rich dressing. And the portions should be small.

CHAPTER 7

SOUPS

With so many soups coming out of cans and boxes, few of us bother to make them the old-fashioned way. Too bad, because we're missing the friendliness of the soup kettle singing on the back of the stove. Such headiness it sends through the house, such promise of goodness. Making soup, time consuming as it may be (and it isn't always), *is* virtually effortless because the kettle can bubble away unattended.

The varieties of soup are nearly endless (as supermarket shelves testify), but basically there are four types: *thin clear soups, cream soups, thick vegetable and/or meat soups,* and *sweet or dessert soups.* Within these categories are the hot and the cold, the delicate and the husky, some of which are closer to stews than soups (certain of these—Bouillabaisse, Philadelphia Pepper Pot, Ukrainian-Style Borsch—are included in meat or seafood chapters; for page numbers, see the Index). There has always been some confusion about the difference between bouillons and consommés, bisques and other creamed soups, so to clarify:

A Quick Dictionary of Soups

Bisque: A rich creamed soup, usually of puréed crab, lobster, shrimp, or other shellfish.

Bouillon, Broth, Stock: Used interchangeably, all three terms mean the rich, savory liquid made by simmering meat, fish, or poultry with vegetables and seasonings in water. *Bouillon,* from the French verb *bouillir* (to boil) is sometimes made of a combination of meats; *broths and stocks,* however, are usually made of one meat only. *Brown stocks* are brewed from beef and beef bones and *white stocks* from veal.

Chowder: A lusty fish or shellfish soup, usually made with milk and often made with vegetables.

Consommé: A rich, clarified meat or poultry broth. *Double consommé* is simply double strength, made either by boiling down regular consommé or by using a higher proportion of meat and bones to liquid. *Jellied consommé* is just that; if rich enough, consommé will jell naturally when chilled; weaker consommés must be fortified with gelatin.

Madrilène: A sparkling, clear, ruby blend of beef or chicken consommé and tomatoes. When chilled, as it usually is before serving, madrilène jells slightly.

Potage: The French word for *soup;* as used today, it often means a creamed vegetable soup, especially a thick one.

Velouté: A soup enriched with egg yolks and cream.

Some Basic Soup-Making Techniques

How to Clarify Broths: For each quart, allow 1 egg white and 1 crushed eggshell. Beat egg white until soft peaks form, stir into cooled broth along with shell, set over lowest heat, and heat, stirring with a whisk, until mixture foams up. Remove from heat, stir once, then let stand undisturbed 1 hour at room temperature. Line a sieve with a fine dish towel wrung out in cold water, set over a deep bowl, and ladle in broth, egg, shell and all, taking care not to stir up sediment in bottom of pan. Let drip through undisturbed. Remove any specks of fat from clarified liquid by blotting up with a paper towel. *Note:* An easier way to clarify is simply to pour the broth through the cloth-lined sieve, but for jewel-clear liquid, use the egg white and shell.

How to Color Stocks and Broths: Mix in a little commercial gravy browner or, for more delicate flavor, caramelized sugar (it won't make the broth sweet):

Caramelized Sugar: Melt 1 cup sugar in a very heavy saucepan (not iron) over lowest heat, stirring. When dark brown, remove from heat and cool to room temperature. Add 1 cup boiling water, drop by drop, stirring all the while. Return to low heat and heat, stirring, until caramelized sugar dissolves.

How to Color Soups: The tiniest drop of food color can brighten vegetable cream soup, especially a green or red one.

How to Degrease Soups: The easiest way is to chill the soup, then lift off the hardened fat. Second best: skim off as much fat as possible, then blot up the rest by spreading paper toweling flat on the surface of the soup.

How to Dilute Soups: When held too long on the stove or chilled, soups often need thinning before serving. Thin cream soups with milk or light cream; meat, poultry, or fish soups with meat, poultry, or fish broth; vegetable soups with a meat or chicken broth or, if the soup contains tomatoes, with tomato juice.

Cabbage and dried bean soups can be thinned with beer.

How to Reduce Soups: Boil uncovered until reduced to desired strength.

How to Thicken Soups:

With Flour (best for cream soups): For each 1 cup soup, add any of the following:
– 1 tablespoon flour blended with 2 tablespoons cold water, milk, or broth
– 2 tablespoons rice, potato, soya, peanut, or wheat germ flour blended with ¼ cup cold water, milk, or broth
– 1 tablespoon flour blended with 1 tablespoon softened butter or margarine

Method: Blend a little hot soup into thickening agent, then quickly return to soup and heat, stirring, until thickened and smooth. For best flavor, let soup mellow 5–10 minutes after thickening.

With Raw Cereal (best for meat or vegetable soups): For each 1 cup soup, add any one of the following:
– 1 teaspoon medium pearl barley
– 1 teaspoon rice
– 1 teaspoon oatmeal

Method: About 1 hour before soup is done, mix in cereal, cover, and simmer, stirring now and then.

With Raw Potato (best for meat and vegetable soups; excellent for those with wheat and/or egg allergies): Allow 3 tablespoons grated raw potato for each cup soup; mix in 15–20 minutes before soup is done and cook, stirring now and then.

With Raw Egg (best for cream soups): For each 1 cup soup, add any one of the following:
– 2 egg yolks, lightly beaten
– 1 whole egg, lightly beaten

Method: Blend a little hot soup into egg, return to soup, set over *lowest* heat, and cook, stirring briskly, about 2 minutes until slightly thickened and no raw taste of egg remains; do not boil. *Note:* For easier blending, beat egg or yolks with about 2 tablespoons cold milk or broth or, for added zip, dry sherry.

With Hard-Cooked Egg (excellent for dried bean soups): For each 2 cups soup, mix in 1 finely chopped hard-cooked egg just before serving. *Note:* If you prefer, scatter egg on top of each portion instead of mixing in.

With Pasta (best for consommés, meat and vegetable soups): Pasta doesn't thicken soup so much as give it body. Any thin spaghetti or macaroni, broken in short lengths, or tiny pasta shapes such as *stellette* (stars), *semini* (seeds), or alphabet letters will work. Depending on how hearty a soup you want, add 1–2 tablespoons uncooked pasta per cup. The pasta can be cooked in the soup (use package directions as a guide) or separately and added just before serving (this is the method to use when a clear broth is wanted).

With Bread Crumbs (good for meat or vegetable soups): Allow 1–2 tablespoons soft or dry bread crumbs per cup of soup and mix in just before serving.

Some Tips for Making Better Soups

– Most soups taste better if made 1–2 days ahead of time; reheat just before serving.
– Use vegetable cooking water in making soups, also in thinning condensed canned soups.
– Best bones to use for stocks: shin, marrow, neck, oxtail.
– Best bones to use for jellied stocks: veal knuckles.
– Whenever a soup tastes bland, add a little salt and pepper. Sometimes that's all that's needed to bring out the flavor.
– Use bouillon cubes or powders to strengthen weak soups.
– Cool soups uncovered and as quickly as possible.
– Always taste a cold soup before serving and adjust seasonings as needed; cold foods dull the taste buds and usually need more seasoning than hot foods.
– When a soup is flavored with wine or beer, reduce the salt slightly.
– Always add wine to soup shortly

before serving and do not let soup boil.
– Use a light hand in adding wine to soup—¼–⅓ cup per quart is usually enough. Too much wine will merely make the soup bitter.
– If a soup is to be reduced (boiled down), add the salt at the very end.
– If a soup seems *slightly* salty, add a peeled, halved raw potato and simmer about 15 minutes; it will absorb some of the salt. Remove the potato before serving.
– To mellow tomato soup, add 1 tablespoon sugar or light brown sugar.
– To give vegetable cream soups more character, purée the vegetables in a food mill; a blender will reduce them to "pap."

About Pressure Cooking Soups

Soups suffer when cooked under pressure so use the pressure cooker only when necessary and only for making stocks. For best results, use 15 pounds pressure and process meat bones and stock 40 minutes, poultry 20 minutes, and vegetables 5. Release pressure and finish cooking over low heat. To reach their peak of flavor, meat stocks may take as much as 1 hour of slow simmering, poultry stocks about ½ hour, and vegetable stocks 15 minutes. This method seems to produce stocks that don't taste of the pressure cooker.

About Serving Soups

How to Choose a Soup: Soups can be the prelude to an elegant meal or, in the case of a family-style lunch or supper, the meal itself. Soup served as a first course should set the tone of the meal and complement what's to follow. Thus, if the main course is rich or spicy, the soup should be light or bland (never serve a cream soup with a creamed entree). If the main course is roast meat or fowl, the soup may be richer, a bisque, perhaps, or a cream vegetable soup. Pay attention to flavors, too, never duplicating within a meal. Soup should be the counterpoint, offering a contrast of flavor, texture, color, and sometimes temperature (a steaming soup is splendid before cold salmon, a cool vichyssoise before broiled steak). Cool soups, obviously, are welcome on blistery days, warm soups in winter.

How to Figure Number of Servings: As a general rule, 1 quart soup will make 6 first course servings, 4 main course.

How to Choose the Proper Soup Bowl and Spoon: The kind of soup and the formality of the meal both dictate which to use. Here's a list of popular soup bowls and spoons together with tips for using each:

Type of Soup Bowl	Appropriate Spoon	Appropriate Soup
Bouillon cup	Teaspoon	Bouillon, consommé, or other thin, clear soup that can be drunk
Double-eared bouillon cup	Round-bowled soupspoon	Bouillon, consommé, or other thin, clear soup that can be drunk
Oriental soup bowl	Teaspoon	Clear Oriental soups such as Won Ton or Egg Drop
Soup plate	Round- or Oval-bowled soupspoons	Chowders, thick meat, poultry, or vegetable soups
Marmite	Any soupspoon	Baked or broiled soups
Multipurpose American soup bowls	Any soupspoon	Any soup
Mugs	———	Any hot or cold soup that can be drunk
Glasses	———	Any cold soup that can be drunk

About Tureens: When a meal is informal and soup the main course, a tureen adds a note of importance; it also keeps the soup hot for "seconds."

Some Tips on Serving Soups

Hot Soups: Have the soup steaming hot and ladle into heated soup bowls.

Cold Soups: Have soup well chilled and serve in chilled bowls. For a festive touch, bed the soup bowls in larger bowls of crushed ice or, if the soup is a thin one, serve in glasses on the rocks.

Some Ways to Garnish Soups

Clear Soups (Hot)
Avocado slices or cubes
Chiffonade (butter-sautéed shreds of lettuce or sorrel)
Crumbled French-fried onions
Cubed, peeled, seeded tomato
Dumplings (liver, marrow, farina)
Gnocchi
Julienne strips of cooked meat or vegetables or brunoise (butter-sautéed shreds of carrot, leeks, and celery)
Lemon, lime, or orange slices
Matzo balls
Minced fresh chives, chervil, dill, mint, parsley, or tarragon

Pasta (Kreplach, Nockerln, Spätzle,
Viennese soup "peas," Won Tons)
Quenelles (especially for fish broth)
Royale Custard
Sliced, cooked beef marrow
Slivered pimiento or sliced green or ripe
olives

Clear Soups (Cold or Jellied)
Avocado slices or cubes
Cubed, peeled, seeded tomato
Cubed, peeled, or unpeeled cucumber
Lemon, lime, or orange slices or wedges
Minced fresh chives, chervil, dill, fennel,
mint, parsley, tarragon, or watercress
Minced radishes or scallions
Sour cream sprinkled with one of the
minced herbs listed above

Cream Soups (Hot or Cold)
Bacon crumbles
Croutons (plain or seasoned)
Crumbled French-fried onions
Crumbled or grated cheese
Finely grated lemon or orange rind
Minced cashews, peanuts, pistachio or
piñon nuts or slivered blanched or
toasted almonds
Minced fresh chives, chervil, dill, fennel,
mint, parsley, tarragon, or watercress
Minced or thinly sliced truffles
Paprika, chili or curry powder
Poppy or caraway seeds
Sliced ripe or green olives
Slivered pimiento

Thick Vegetable, Meat, or Fish Soups
Bacon crumbles
Croutons (plain or seasoned)
Grated sharp cheese
Lemon or orange slices (especially for
fish soups)
Minced chives, dill, parsley, or
watercress
Sliced frankfurters or sautéed pepperoni
(especially for dried pea or bean
soups)

¢ ⚖ **ALL-PURPOSE STOCK**

Before freezers and refrigerators there
was the stock pot. It's still a good way to
use meat and vegetable leftovers,
vegetable cooking water, celery tops,
mushroom stems, tomato peelings, and
other vegetable parings.
Makes about 1 quart

*2–3 cups finely chopped mixed leftover
lean meat and vegetables*
1 pound beef, veal, or lamb bones
2 quarts water
1 bouquet garni,* tied in cheesecloth
Salt
Pepper

Simmer leftovers, bones, water, and
bouquet garni covered in a large, heavy
kettle 2–3 hours; add salt and pepper to
taste. Strain through a fine sieve, cool,
chill, and skim off fat. Store in
refrigerator or freezer and use as a base
for soups, stews, and sauces. About 35
calories per cup.

⚖ **CHICKEN BROTH (STOCK)**

The perfect base for soups and stews.
Makes about 2 quarts

*1 (5½–6-pound) stewing hen, cleaned
and dressed*
2 quarts water
*1 medium-size yellow onion, peeled and
quartered*
1 stalk celery (include tops)
1 medium-size carrot, peeled
2 sprigs parsley
1 bay leaf
6 peppercorns
1½ teaspoons salt

Place hen, giblets, and all remaining
ingredients in a large heavy kettle,
cover, and simmer 1½–2 hours until hen
is tender; lift hen and giblets from broth
and cool. *Note:* For more tender giblets,
remove after 15–20 minutes' simmering.
Strain broth, cool, then chill and skim
off fat; save fat, if you like, clarify* and
keep on hand to use in cooking. Discard
chicken skin, remove meat from bones,
and save to use in recipes calling for
cooked chicken meat. About 40 calories
per cup.

BEING CREATIVE WITH CANNED SOUPS

Canned soups are good mixers. Take one flavor, blend in a second or third, add an herb or spice, and you've a whole new recipe. There are endless combinations. Invent your own or try any of the following; all are based on standard soup can sizes (they range from 10 ounces to about 1 pound). Simply heat and stir soups, liquid and seasonings 5-10 minutes (do not boil), garnish and serve.

Canned Soup Combinations	Liquid to Add	Seasonings	Garnish	Number of Servings
Cream of Asparagus + Cheddar cheese	2 soup cans milk	Pinch nutmeg or mace	Coarsely grated Cheddar	4-6
Cream of Asparagus + cream of chicken	2 soup cans milk	1-2 T. curry powder	Coarsely chopped, roasted, blanched peanuts	4-6
Bean with Bacon + tomato bisque	1 soup can water	1-2 T. chili powder, pinch garlic salt	Bacon crumbles	6-8
Black bean + mushroom + beef broth (clear)	1/4 cup dry sherry	1/4 t. each thyme, crushed dried chili peppers, and garlic powder	Minced hard-cooked egg and minced parsley	4-6
Cream of Celery + chicken broth	1 soup can light cream and 1/4 cup dry white wine	1 T. curry powder, 2 T. minced chutney	Grated orange or lemon rind, toasted slivered almonds	4-6
Chicken with Rice + escarole	3/4 cup water and 1/4 cup dry white wine	1 t. lemon juice, pinch thyme and nutmeg	Minced escarole, parsley, or watercress	4-6
Cheddar Cheese + cream of mushroom	1½ soup cans milk, 1/3 soup can dry white wine	Pinch each savory, thyme, and mace	Sliced canned mushrooms, paprika	4-6
Cheddar Cheese + tomato	2 soup cans milk	1 T. minced onion, pinch each basil and oregano	Minced chives and pimiento slivers	4-6

164

Soup Combination	Liquid	Seasoning	Garnish	Servings
Clam Chowder + tomato bisque	2 soup cans water	1 bay leaf, a pinch basil	Minced chives or parsley, croutons	4-6
Green Pea + tomato	2 soup cans milk	Pinch savory or mint, 1/2 t. grated orange rind	Croutons or orange slices	4-6
Green Pea + tomato + beef broth or consommé	1 soup can milk, 1/3 soup can dry sherry			4-6
Green Pea + cream of mushroom + beef broth	1 soup can water, 1/3 soup can dry white wine	Pinch thyme and savory	Sliced canned mushrooms	4-6
Green Pea + Cheddar cheese + chicken or beef broth	1 soup can milk, 1/3 soup can dry white wine	1 T. mint flakes, 1 t. grated orange rind	Whipped cream and grated orange rind	6
Green Pea + cream of chicken	2 soup cans milk	1-2 T. creamy peanut butter	Minced roasted, blanched peanuts	4-6
Mushroom + tomato + beef broth (clear)	1/2 soup can water, 1/4 cup dry red wine or sherry	Pinch thyme	Sliced, peeled, seeded tomato, minced parsley	4-6
Mushroom + escarole (clear)	1/2 cup water and 1/4 cup dry white wine	1 bay leaf, 1 uncrushed clove garlic (remove before serving)	Lemon slices	4
Mushroom + minestrone + beef broth (clear)	1/4 cup dry white wine		Minced parsley	4-6
Pepper Pot + tomato	2 soup cans water	1 bay leaf, 1/8 teaspoon crushed dried chili peppers		4-6
Shrimp or Lobster + tomato bisque	2 soup cans milk or light cream, 1/4 cup dry sherry	Pinch tarragon or chervil, 1 t. grated orange rind	Danish shrimp, orange slices, or grated orange rind	4-6
Turkey Noodle + cream of celery or mushroom	2 soup cans milk or light cream, 1/4 cup dry white wine	Pinch each sage and thyme	Grated Parmesan or Cheddar	4-6
Vichyssoise + tomato bisque	2 soup cans milk	Pinch each thyme and basil	Minced French-fried onions or bacon crumbles	4-6

VARIATIONS:

¢ ⚖ **Economy Chicken Broth:** Proceed as directed, using 4–5 pounds chicken backs and wings instead of the hen and simmering about 1 hour. About 40 calories per cup.

⚖ **Delicate Chicken Broth:** Proceed as directed, using 4 quarts water instead of 2. About 20 calories per cup.

⚖ **Turkey Broth:** Prepare as directed, substituting 1 (6-pound) turkey for the hen. About 40 calories per cup.

⚖ ¢ CHICKEN GIBLET STOCK

Use as a base for soups, sauces and gravies.
Makes about 1 pint

Giblets and neck from 1 chicken, washed
2 cups cold water
½ small yellow onion, peeled and coarsely chopped
½ stalk celery
½ carrot, peeled
1 bay leaf
2 peppercorns
½ teaspoon salt (about)

Simmer giblets and remaining ingredients, covered 15 minutes. Remove liver and reserve, also remove heart if it is tender. Re-cover and simmer remaining giblets until tender, 1–2 hours, replenishing water as needed. Strain stock, taste for seasoning and adjust as needed; chill and skim off fat. Mince giblets and, if you like, meat from neck. Save to use in gravy or sauce recipes or mix into recipes calling for cooked chicken meat. About 40 calories per cup.

VARIATIONS:

⚖ **Turkey Giblet Stock** (Makes about 1 quart): Cook turkey giblets and neck as directed for chicken, using 1 quart water and doubling all remaining ingredients. About 40 calories per cup.

⚖ **Giblet Stock from Other Poultry and Game Birds:** Prepare as directed for Chicken Giblet Stock, adjusting quantity of water and seasonings to number of giblets. About 50 calories per cup.

⚖ **Quantity Giblet Stock:** For each additional pint of stock needed over and above what basic recipe makes, use 1 pint chicken broth, 2–3 chicken livers, ¼ yellow onion, peeled, ½ stalk celery, and ½ bay leaf. Simmer as directed, removing 1 liver after 15 minutes (so stock will not be overly strong of liver). Simmer remaining giblets 1–2 hours, replenishing liquid with chicken broth as needed. Strain and season to taste as directed. Mince giblets and add to stock or save to use in other recipes. About 40 calories per cup.

¢ ⚖ BEEF BROTH (STOCK)

A rich brown broth to use in making soups and sauces.
Makes about 3 quarts

4–5 pounds beef shin- and marrowbones, cracked (a ½ and ½ mixture is best)
1 large yellow onion, peeled and coarsely chopped
2 leeks, washed, trimmed, and coarsely chopped
2 medium-size carrots, peeled and coarsely chopped
2 stalks celery, coarsely chopped
5 quarts water
2–3 sprigs parsley or a bouquet garni,* tied in cheesecloth
6 peppercorns
1 bay leaf, crumbled
1 tablespoon salt (about)

Bring all ingredients to a boil in a large heavy kettle, turn heat to low, skim off froth, cover, and simmer 4–5 hours; check pot occasionally and add extra water if needed. Skim off fat, then strain stock through a sieve lined with a double thickness of cheesecloth; pour into a clean kettle and boil rapidly uncovered until reduced to about 3 quarts. Taste for salt and adjust as needed. Cool, then chill; lift off solidified fat. Stock is now ready to use in recipes. Store in refrigerator or freezer. About 35 calories per cup.

VARIATIONS:

¢ ⚖ **Brown Beef Stock:** Roast bones uncovered in a shallow roasting pan in a

425° F. oven ¾–1 hour until brown. Meanwhile, stir-fry onion, leeks, carrots, and celery in 2 tablespoons beef drippings or margarine in kettle 12–15 minutes over moderate heat until well browned. Add bones, 4 quarts water, and remaining ingredients. Drain fat from roasting pan, add remaining water, stirring to scrape up browned bits; pour into kettle and proceed as directed. About 50 calories per cup.

♏ **Double-Strength Beef Broth:** Brown bones as for Brown Beef Stock (above). Also brown 2 pounds boned beef chuck, shank, or neck, cut in 1″ cubes, in 2 tablespoons beef drippings or margarine in a large kettle; add vegetables, brown, then proceed as above. *Note:* Boned beef may be saved after cooking and used in hash, stuffing, or sandwich spreads. About 45 calories per cup.

♏ **Veal (White) Stock:** Prepare like Beef Broth (above), using 2 veal shanks and 4–5 pounds veal bones or a ½ and ½ mixture of veal and beef bones. About 40 calories per cup.

♏ BEEF CONSOMMÉ

Richer than Beef Broth and delicious hot or cold.
Makes about 1 quart

1 quart Beef Broth or Double-Strength Beef Broth
½ pound very lean ground beef
½ medium-size carrot, peeled and minced
1 small yellow onion, peeled and minced
½ stalk celery, minced

Simmer all ingredients, covered, 1 hour; strain through a fine sieve lined with cheesecloth, cool, chill, and remove all fat. Clarify,* taste for salt, and adjust as needed. Serve hot or cold. About 35 calories per cup.

VARIATIONS:

♏ **Double Consommé:** Prepare as directed; after clarifying, boil rapidly, uncovered, until reduced by half. If you like, stir in ½ cup dry sherry or Madeira. Serve hot or cold. About 45 calories per cup without sherry, 60 calories with.

♏ **Consommé Royale:** Prepare one recipe Royale Custard (made with beef consommé), cut in fancy shapes, and float a few pieces in each soup bowl. About 55 calories per cup.

♏ **Jellied Consommé:** Prepare consommé as directed and chill 1 cup about 2 hours to test firmness. If firm, no extra gelatin is needed. If semifirm, mix 1 envelope unflavored gelatin into consommé; if liquid, 2 envelopes. Heat, stirring, until gelatin dissolves, then cool and chill until firm. Before serving, break up consommé with a fork. Serve in chilled bowls or bowls set in larger bowls of crushed ice. Sprinkle with minced chives, scallions, or parsley and garnish with lemon wedges. About 45 calories per cup if made with one envelope gelatin, 50 calories per cup made with 2 envelopes gelatin.

♏ BEEF TEA

A very concentrated beef broth that makes a bracing midafternoon refresher. It's nourishing, good for convalescents.
Makes about 1 pint

1 pound very lean beef, ground twice
2 cups water
¾ teaspoon salt (about)

Place meat and water in the top of a double boiler over simmering water, cover, and simmer 2 hours, stirring now and then. Strain through a fine sieve lined with a double thickness of cheesecloth. Add salt, taste, and add more if needed. Cool, chill, and remove fat. Store in refrigerator and heat whenever desired; do not boil when reheating. About 30 calories per cup.

VARIATION:

♏ **Raw Beef Tea:** This must be made fresh each time, so it's best to make small amounts. Place ½ pound beef and 1 cup cold water in an electric blender and buzz at high speed 30 seconds. Cover and let stand at room temperature ½ hour. Strain through a fine sieve lined with cheesecloth, stir in ¼ teaspoon salt, and serve as is or slightly chilled. About 40 calories per cup.

⚖️ ¢ EASY FISH STOCK

Bones of haddock, halibut, and/or pike produce a fragrant stock. Use for making seafood soups and sauces.
Makes 2 quarts

2 quarts cold water
1 pound fishbones, heads and trimmings
1 tablespoon salt

Place all ingredients in a kettle, cover, and simmer 1 hour. Strain liquid through a fine sieve and use for poaching fish, making soups or sauces. (*Note:* This stock freezes well.) About 5 calories per cup.

¢ ⚖️ VEGETABLE STOCK

Use this stock as a base for vegetable soups or sauces.
Makes about 3 quarts

2 large yellow onions, peeled and minced
2 cups coarsely chopped, scrubbed, unpeeled carrots
2 cups coarsely chopped celery (include some tops)
2 cups coarsely chopped, unpeeled tomatoes
2 cups coarsely chopped mushrooms (include stems)
2 leeks, washed, trimmed, and coarsely chopped
1 cup coarsely chopped cabbage or cauliflower heart and trimmings (optional)
4 sprigs parsley
2 bay leaves, crumbled
6 peppercorns
4 teaspoons salt (about)
1 gallon water

Simmer all ingredients in a large covered kettle 2 hours; check liquid occasionally and add water as needed to maintain level at about 3 quarts. Strain stock through a fine sieve and measure; if you have more than 3 quarts, boil rapidly, uncovered, to reduce; if less than 3 quarts, add boiling water to round out measure. Taste for salt and adjust as needed. Cool, then store in refrigerator or freezer. About 15 calories per cup.

⚖️ CONSOMMÉ MADRILÈNE

Madrilène should be made with sun-ripened tomatoes, but since they are scarce, this recipe substitutes canned purée.
Makes 4 servings

2 cups tomato purée
1 quart beef consommé or fat-free chicken broth
1 teaspoon minced chives
1 teaspoon minced parsley
⅛ teaspoon cayenne pepper
¼ cup dry sherry or Madeira wine (optional)
1 tablespoon slivered pimiento (optional)

Mix purée, consommé, chives, parsley, and cayenne in a saucepan, cover, and heat over lowest heat 15 minutes; mixture should barely simmer. Strain through a fine sieve lined with several thicknesses of cheesecloth. For a sparkling madrilène, let drip through undisturbed. Bring liquid to a boil and, if you like, stir in sherry and pimiento. About 35 calories per serving.

VARIATION:

⚖️ **Jellied Consommé Madrilène:**
Prepare as directed. Heat 1 envelope unflavored gelatin in ⅓ cup water over moderate heat, stirring until dissolved. Stir into madrilène, add sherry and, if you like, pimiento. Taste for salt and adjust as needed. Cool, then chill until firm. Break madrilène up with a fork, ladle into chilled bowls, garnish with minced chives or watercress and lemon wedges, and serve. About 45 calories per serving.

⚖️ BASIC ASPIC

Clear aspic is sometimes used to coat or glaze party food—a whole ham, for example, poached fresh salmon, a *chaud-froid,* meat or poultry, or vegetable canapés. Any clear meat, poultry, vegetable, or fish stock can be used. (*Note:* A recipe for Court Bouillon and directions for clarifying it are included in the fish chapter.)
Makes about 1 quart

1 quart clarified Beef Broth, Brown
Beef Broth, Veal (White) Stock,
Chicken Broth, or Vegetable Stock*
*1–2 envelopes unflavored gelatin
(optional)*
¼–½ cup cold water (optional)

First, determine broth's jelling power by
chilling 1 cup. If it sets up firmly, it will
need no gelatin; if soft, it will need 1
envelope gelatin, if soupy, 2 envelopes.
(*Note:* Vegetable stock will always need
the full amount of gelatin.) Soften
required amount of gelatin in cold water
—¼ cup cold water to each envelope
gelatin—then add to broth (including
that chilled for jelling test) and heat and
stir over low heat until dissolved. To
prevent bubble formation, stir gently; do
not beat. Chill until thick and syrupy.
(*Note:* To quick-chill, set over ice cubes.)
Aspic is now ready to use for glazing
foods or as recipes direct.

If made without gelatin, the same calorie
count as broth or stock from which it
was made, if made with 1 envelope
gelatin, add 7 calories per cup, if made
with 2 envelopes gelatin, add 14 calories
per cup.

VARIATIONS:

▨ ⚖ **Quick and Easy Aspic:** Slowly
heat 1 envelope unflavored gelatin and 3
cups beef consommé or madrilène,
stirring until dissolved. If you like, mix in
2–3 tablespoons medium-dry sherry. 50–
60 calories per cup, depending on
amount of sherry used.

▨ ⚖ **Quick and Easy Light Aspic:**
Soften 1 envelope unflavored gelatin in
1½ cups cold water, then heat and stir
until dissolved. Add 1 (10½-ounce) can
beef consommé or madrilène. About 40
calories per cup.

⚖ ¢ **GAME SOUP**

When a game bird has been eaten down
to the bones, it's time for game soup.
Makes 4 servings

*Carcass, skin, meat scraps, and any
giblets from 1–2 pheasants or wild
ducks or 2–3 grouse, partridges, quail,
or pigeons*

5 cups cold water
*1 medium-size yellow onion, peeled and
stuck with 3 cloves*
1 medium-size carrot, peeled and diced
1 stalk celery, minced
½ small turnip, peeled and diced
1 bouquet garni,* tied in cheesecloth
¼ cup medium dry sherry
1½ teaspoons salt (about)
¼ teaspoon pepper

Break up carcass and place with skin,
scraps, and giblets in a large saucepan.
Add all but last 3 ingredients, cover, and
simmer over lowest heat 1½–2 hours.
Check liquid occasionally and add a little
water if necessary. Strain liquid through
a fine sieve lined with cheesecloth; skim
off fat. Measure liquid and add water or
chicken broth as needed to make 1 quart.
If there is more than 1 quart liquid,
reduce by boiling rapidly uncovered.
Heat soup to serving temperature, stir in
sherry, salt, and pepper, taste for salt and
adjust as needed. About 30 calories per
serving.

¢ ⚖ ▨ **CHICKEN NOODLE SOUP**

Makes 4 servings

1 quart Chicken Broth
1 cup fine noodles
1 cup diced cooked chicken meat
Salt
Pepper
2 teaspoons minced parsley

Bring broth to a boil in a large saucepan,
add noodles and chicken, and simmer,
uncovered, about 10 minutes until
noodles are tender. Taste for salt and
pepper and adjust as needed. Stir in
parsley and serve. About 70 calories per
serving.

VARIATION:

¢ ⚖ ▨ **Chicken and Rice Soup:** Prepare as directed, substituting ⅓ cup
uncooked rice for the noodles and cooking 15–20 minutes until rice is tender.
Season and serve as directed. About 70
calories per serving.

¢ ⚖ ⊠ EGG DROP SOUP

Makes 4 servings

1 quart Chicken Broth
1 scallion, minced (optional)
½ teaspoon sugar
1 teaspoon soy sauce
2 tablespoons cornstarch blended with ¼
*   cup cold water*
1 egg, lightly beaten with 1 tablespoon
*   cold water*

Heat broth and, if you like, scallion to
boiling in a heavy saucepan over
moderate heat. Mix in sugar, soy sauce,
and cornstarch paste and heat, stirring
constantly, until slightly thickened. Bring
mixture to a full boil, remove from heat
and drizzle in egg mixture, stirring
constantly. Ladle into hot bowls and
serve. About 75 calories per serving.

WON TON SOUP

Fresh squares of noodle dough called
won ton skins or wrappers can usually
be bought in Chinese groceries. They
should be refrigerated in foil or saran
and used within 4–5 days. If you're
unable to buy them, here's how to make
your own.
Makes 8 servings

Won Ton Dough:

1½ cups sifted flour
1 teaspoon salt
1 egg, lightly beaten with 3 tablespoons
*   cold water*

Filling:

¼ pound very lean uncooked pork,
*   ground twice, or ½ cup minced cooked*
*   chicken meat or shrimp*
2 water chestnuts, minced
2 scallions, minced
1 teaspoon grated fresh gingerroot or ⅛
*   teaspoon ginger*
1 teaspoon soy sauce
½ teaspoon salt
Pinch pepper

Broth:

2 quarts+1 cup chicken broth
½ cup julienne strips of cooked chicken
*   meat or roast pork (optional)*

For dough, sift flour with salt, add egg
mixture all at once, and stir briskly with
a fork until dough holds together; turn
onto a lightly floured board and knead
2–3 minutes until smooth. Cover and let
rest ½ hour. Dust board and rolling pin
lightly with cornstarch and roll dough as
thin as possible into a square about 16";
cut in 2½" squares. Mix filling
ingredients. Arrange noodle squares on
counter, spoon about ½ teaspoon filling

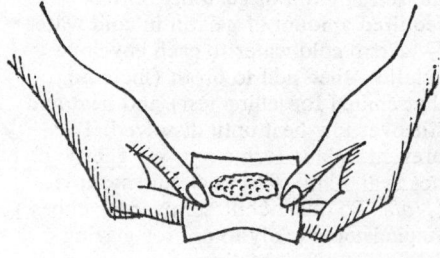

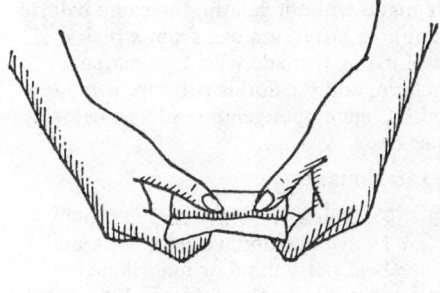

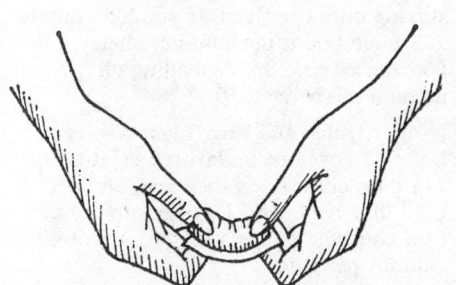

onto each, a little above center, then
roll, as shown, sealing by moistening
edges with cold water. Bring broth to a
boil in a large kettle, drop in 6–8 won
tons, and boil, uncovered, 5 minutes;
lift out won tons and cover with a damp
towel. Cook remaining won tons the
same way. When all won tons are done,

return to broth and simmer, uncovered, 1 minute. Ladle broth into soup bowls, add 3 won tons to each, and serve. If you like, float a few strips chicken or pork in each bowl. About 145 calories per serving with pork-filled won ton (add 20 calories per serving if optional roast pork is added to broth). About 120 calories per serving for chicken or shrimp filled won ton (add 12 calories per serving if optional cooked chicken is added to broth).

⚖ CLEAR TURTLE SOUP

Turtle meat is available fresh in some big cities; elsewhere it is sold frozen and canned. All three forms may be used for this soup.
Makes 6 servings

2 pounds turtle meat, cut in ½" cubes
2 medium-size yellow onions, peeled and minced
2 stalks celery, minced
1 medium-size carrot, peeled and minced
1 cup canned tomatoes
1 bay leaf, crumbled
2 sprigs parsley
1 beef soupbone, cracked
2 quarts water or 1 pint turtle broth and 1½ quarts water
2 teaspoons salt (about)
¼ teaspoon pepper
⅓ cup dry sherry or Madeira wine
6 thin slices lemon

If using fresh or frozen turtle meat, parboil,* save broth, then proceed as follows. Place all ingredients except sherry and lemon in a heavy kettle, cover, and simmer 1 hour until meat is tender. Lift out 1 cup turtle meat, cut in ¼" cubes, and reserve. Simmer remaining mixture, covered, 2 hours longer; check pot occasionally and add a little more water, if necessary. Strain liquid through a fine sieve lined with a double thickness of cheesecloth; skim off fat, measure broth, and, if less than 1½ quarts, add enough boiling water to round out measure; if more than 1½ quarts, boil rapidly uncovered to reduce. Add reserved turtle meat and sherry, simmer 2–3 minutes, taste for salt and

adjust as needed. Ladle into soup bowls, float a lemon slice in each, and serve. (*Note:* The turtle meat strained out of the soup can be added to a stock pot, to vegetable soups, or to stews.) About 40 calories per serving.

VARIATION:

Home-Style Turtle Soup: Simmer all ingredients except sherry and lemon in a covered kettle 3 hours until turtle is tender. Stir in sherry and serve. Omit lemon. About 260 calories per serving.

⚖ ☒ MOCK TURTLE SOUP

Makes 4 servings

1 (8-ounce) bottle clam juice
2 (10½-ounce) cans condensed beef consommé
4 peppercorns
⅛ teaspoon thyme
⅛ teaspoon marjoram
¼ cup sweet Madeira or sherry

Combine clam juice and consommé in a saucepan. Tie peppercorns and herbs in cheesecloth and add. Cover and simmer 15 minutes; discard cheesecloth bag, stir in wine, ladle into soup cups, and serve. About 70 calories per serving.

⚖ TOMATO VEGETABLE BOUILLON

This Southern recipe has been handed down for generations. Rumor has it that it was Robert E. Lee's favorite soup.
Makes 4 servings

6 large ripe tomatoes, peeled, seeded, and coarsely chopped
1 medium-size yellow onion, peeled and coarsely chopped
1 stalk celery, coarsely chopped
2 carrots, peeled and coarsely chopped
½ sweet green pepper, cored, seeded, and coarsely chopped
1 pint water
1 bay leaf
1 tablespoon sugar
¼ cup dry sherry
1 teaspoon salt (about)
Pinch pepper

Place vegetables, water, bay leaf, and

sugar in a large saucepan, cover, and
simmer ½ hour. Strain through a fine
sieve and return to pan. Add sherry, salt
to taste, and pepper. Serve steaming
hot. About 80 calories per serving.

⚖ CLEAR MUSHROOM BROTH

Glorious when made with morels,
chanterelles, or other edible wild
mushrooms.
Makes 6 servings

*1 pound mushrooms, wiped clean and
minced*
*1½ quarts beef bouillon or consommé,
skimmed of any fat*
*1 small sprig each thyme, parsley, and
marjoram, tied in cheesecloth
(optional)*
½ teaspoon finely grated onion
6 thin slices lemon

Place all ingredients except lemon in a
large saucepan (not aluminum), cover,
and simmer over lowest heat 1 hour,
using an asbestos flame tamer, if
necessary, to keep bouillon just
trembling. Taste for salt and adjust as
needed. Cool broth and chill overnight.
Strain through a sieve lined with a
double thickness of cheesecloth. Serve
cold or piping hot with a lemon slice
floating in each soup bowl. About 35
calories per serving.

VARIATION:

⚖ **Sherried Mushroom Broth:** Prepare
as directed; just before serving, stir in
¼–⅓ cup medium-dry sherry and, if
you like, 2–3 very thinly sliced raw
mushrooms or 1 thinly sliced truffle.
About 45 calories per serving.

⚖ CLEAR BEET SOUP

Makes 4 servings

*2 (1-pound) cans sliced beets, drained
(reserve liquid)*
1½ cups beef consommé
1 teaspoon red wine vinegar
⅛ teaspoon celery seeds
1 sprig fresh dill or ¼ teaspoon dill weed
*1 tablespoon cornstarch blended with
1 tablespoon cold water*
¼ cup heavy cream (optional)

Measure 1½ cups beet liquid and pour
into a saucepan; dice enough beets to
make 1 cup and set aside (save remaining
beets and beet liquid to serve as a
vegetable). Add consommé, vinegar,
celery seeds, and dill to pan, cover, and
heat over lowest heat 10 minutes;
mixture should just tremble; strain.
Return to pan, stir in cornstarch paste,
and heat over moderate heat, stirring,
until mixture is slightly thickened and
clear. Off heat, stir in diced beets.
Ladle into soup bowls, float 1 tablespoon
cream on top of each, and serve. About
40 calories per serving without the
cream, 95 calories with.

VARIATION:

⚖ **Jellied Clear Beet Soup:** Heat
mixture as directed, strain, and set
aside. Omit cornstarch paste and cream.
Instead, heat 1 envelope unflavored
gelatin in ⅓ cup water over moderate
heat, stirring until gelatin dissolves.
Mix into soup, add beets, cover, and
chill until thick and syrupy. Stir well,
re-cover, and chill until firm. Just before
serving, break up mixture with a spoon.
Ladle into chilled bowls and top, if you
like, with sour cream and a sprinkling
of minced chives or dill. Garnish with
lemon or lime wedges. About 40
calories per serving without sour cream.
Add 30 calories per serving for each
tablespoon of sour cream topping used.

⚖ FRENCH ONION SOUP

If broth is pale, color a rich amber
brown with liquid gravy browner or
caramelized sugar.*
Makes 4 servings

*½ pound Spanish or yellow onions,
peeled and sliced paper thin*
2 tablespoons butter (no substitute)
*1 quart beef broth, bouillon, or
consommé*
⅛ teaspoon pepper

Stir-fry onions in butter in a large,
heavy saucepan over low heat 10–15
minutes until pale golden. Add broth
and pepper, cover, and simmer 20–25
minutes, stirring occasionally, until

onions are very tender. Taste for salt and add if needed. Serve steaming hot with French bread. About 110 calories per serving.

VARIATION:

French Onion Soup Au Gratin: Prepare soup as directed and, while it simmers, preheat oven to 400° F.; also lightly toast 4 slices French bread. Ladle soup into 4 ovenproof soup bowls (individual casseroles or marmites are perfect), float a piece of toast in each, and sprinkle generously with grated Parmesan cheese. Bake, uncovered, 5–7 minutes until cheese is lightly browned and bread puffed up. Serve at once. About 200 calories per serving.

¢ ⚖ **TURNIP SOUP**

Makes 4 servings

½ pound turnips, peeled and cut in small dice
1 small yellow onion, peeled and minced
2 cups chicken or beef broth
2 cups water
1 teaspoon salt
2 teaspoons Worcestershire sauce
1 teaspoon soy sauce
1 teaspoon minced chives
1 tablespoon slivered pimiento

Simmer all ingredients except chives and pimiento in a covered saucepan over moderately low heat 20–25 minutes. Stir in chives and pimiento and serve. About 35 calories per serving.

VARIATIONS:

¢ ⚖ **Rutabaga Soup:** Prepare as directed, substituting 2 cups diced, peeled rutabaga for turnip and increasing cooking time slightly, about 5–10 minutes. Same calories as turnip soup.

¢ ⚖ **Parsnip Soup:** Substitute 2 cups diced, peeled parsnips for turnips and proceed as recipe directs. Good with a little grated Parmesan sprinkled on top. About 70 calories per serving.

⚖ ¢ **GERMAN TAPIOCA SOUP**

A good way to use up tag ends of chicken or turkey.
Makes 4 servings

½ cup pearl or large pearl tapioca
1 cup cold water
5 cups beef broth or bouillon
¼ cup tomato purée
1 bay leaf
¼ cup slivered cooked chicken or turkey (preferably white meat)

Soak tapioca in water at least 3 hours or overnight. Pour broth into a saucepan, add tapioca and any remaining soaking water, tomato purée, and bay leaf. Cover and simmer about 1 hour until tapioca is clear and no raw starch taste remains; check liquid occasionally and add a little extra water if too thick. Remove bay leaf, stir in chicken, heat 2–3 minutes longer, and serve. About 130 calories per serving.

DE LUXE CREAM OF VEGETABLE SOUP

Thickened with cream and egg, not flour.
Makes 4 servings

1½ cups diced raw vegetable (asparagus, celery, peas, broccoli, spinach, carrots, onion, cauliflower, zucchini, or mushrooms)
2 tablespoons butter (no substitute)
1 pint chicken broth
1 teaspoon finely grated onion
1 cup heavy cream
2 egg yolks, lightly beaten

Stir-fry vegetable in butter in a heavy saucepan over moderately low heat about 10 minutes until wilted, not brown. Add broth and onion, cover, and simmer 10–15 minutes until vegetable is very soft. Put through a food mill or purée in an electric blender at low speed. Pour into the top of a large double boiler and set over simmering water. Mix cream and egg yolks and stir into soup; heat, stirring constantly, until slightly thickened. Taste for salt and pepper and adjust as needed. Serve piping hot. From about 320–55 calories per serving, carrot and pea soups highest.

BASIC PROPORTIONS FOR CREAMED VEGETABLE SOUPS
(Makes 6 servings)

Variety	Butter	Flour	Liquid	Cooked Vegetable Purée	Salt	White Pepper	Optional Seasonings
Artichoke (globe and Jerusalem), asparagus, celery, endive Calories per serving: 150-60 for artichoke soup, 140-50 for asparagus, celery, or endive soup	3 T.	3 T.	1 pint each milk and chicken or vegetable broth	2½ cups	1 t.	1/8 t.	Pinch each thyme and nutmeg and 1/4 cup dry white wine
Broccoli, cauliflower, onion, leek, Brussels sprouts, cabbage, kale About 110-20 calories per serving	3 T.	3 T.	1 pint each milk and beef, chicken, or vegetable broth	2 cups	1 t.	1/8 t.	Pinch each cardamom and mace and 1/4 cup grated mild Cheddar or Gruyère
Carrot, green pea Calories per serving: 120-30 for carrot soup, 135-45 for green pea soup	2 T.	2 T.	1 pint each milk and chicken or vegetable broth	2 cups	1 t.	1/8 t.	1 t. grated orange rind, pinch rosemary, nutmeg, or savory or 1 T. minced fresh tarragon or chervil
Parsnip, turnip, rutabaga Calories per serving: about 160 for parsnip, 130 for turnip or rutabaga	2 T.	2 T.	1 pint each milk and beef or chicken broth	2 cups	1 t.	1/8 t.	Pinch each cinnamon, allspice and ginger
Potato, tomato			SEE SPECIAL RECIPES THAT FOLLOW				

174

Variety	Butter	Flour	Liquid	Cooked Vegetable Purée	Salt	White Pepper	Optional Seasonings
Spinach, cress, sorrel About 140 calories per serving	3 T.	3 T.	1 pint each milk and chicken broth	2½ cups	1 t.	1/8 t.	2 T. each grated onion and lemon juice or curry powder, pinch nutmeg
Summer squash About 170 calories per serving	3 T.	3 T.	3 cups milk and 1 cup beef or chicken broth	3 cups	1 t.	1/8 t.	1/4 cup minced onion, 1/4 t. each savory and oregano, pinch cinnamon or mace
Winter squash, sweet potato, pumpkin, yam Calories per serving: about 180 for pumpkin soup, 190 for winter squash, and 235 for yam or sweet potato	2 T.	1 T.	1 pint each milk and chicken broth	2 cups	1 t.	1/8 t.	1/4 cup each orange juice and honey, 1/4 t. each cinnamon, ginger, and cloves

METHOD: Melt butter in a large, heavy saucepan over moderate heat, blend in flour, add liquid, and heat, stirring, until mixture boils; turn heat to low, smooth in purée and seasonings, cover, and let mellow 5-10 minutes to blend flavors. Serve hot or chill and serve cold. (*Note:* For a silky-smooth soup, strain through a fine sieve, then heat to serving temperature or chill.)

VARIATIONS: In addition to the all-of-a-flavor soups above, many vegetables team well. To prepare, follow basic proportions above, using a 1/2 and 1/2 mixture of any of the following purées:

Carrot and Jerusalem artichoke
Carrot and celery
Carrot and green pea
Carrot and parsnip
Carrot and turnip
Carrot and rutabaga

Carrot and winter squash
Carrot and pumpkin
Carrot and sweet potato or yam
Celery and green pea
Celery and spinach
Celery and summer squash

Onion and carrot
Onion and green pea
Onion and spinach
Onion and celery
Onion and summer squash
Onion and pumpkin

CREAM OF ALMOND SOUP

Serve hot or icy cold.
Makes 4 servings

1 stalk celery, minced
1 clove garlic, peeled and crushed
2 tablespoons butter or margarine
3 cups chicken broth
⅔ cup finely ground blanched almonds
⅛ teaspoon mace
1 cup heavy cream
1–2 tablespoons toasted, slivered
 almonds

Stir-fry celery and garlic in butter in a
heavy saucepan 4–5 minutes over
moderate heat until limp; add broth,
ground almonds, and mace, cover, and
simmer 30–40 minutes, stirring
occasionally. Remove from heat and let
stand at room temperature 1 hour.
Purée in an electric blender at low
speed or press through a fine sieve.
Return mixture to saucepan, smooth in
cream, and heat uncovered, stirring
occasionally, 2–3 minutes; do not boil.
Taste for salt and add if needed. Ladle
into hot bowls, sprinkle with toasted
almonds, and, if you like, dust with
paprika. *Or* chill well and serve cold.
About 440 calories per serving.

▣ QUICK ASPARAGUS SOUP

Makes 4 servings

1 (10-ounce) package frozen cut
 asparagus
⅓ cup boiling water
2 tablespoons butter or margarine
¾ teaspoon salt
Pinch white pepper
1 pint milk
1 tablespoon dry vermouth

Place asparagus, water, butter, salt, and
pepper in a small saucepan and simmer
uncovered, stirring occasionally, 15–20
minutes until asparagus is tender; purée,
a little at a time, in an electric blender
at low speed. Return to pan, add milk,
and heat 3–5 minutes, stirring occasionally. Stir in vermouth and serve hot or
chill and serve cold. About 150 calories
per serving.

CREAM OF ASPARAGUS SOUP

Makes 6 servings

2 pounds asparagus, washed, trimmed,
 and cut in 2″ chunks
1 cup chicken broth
2 tablespoons butter or margarine
2 tablespoons flour
1 cup milk
1 cup heavy cream
1½ teaspoons salt (about)
⅛ teaspoon white pepper

Simmer asparagus, covered, in chicken
broth 10–15 minutes until very tender.
Note: If you want to garnish soup with
a few tips, remove 10–12 when crisp
tender and reserve. Put asparagus and
liquid through a food mill or purée, a
little at a time, in an electric blender at
low speed. Melt butter in saucepan over
moderate heat, blend in flour, add milk
slowly, stirring until smooth. Mix in
purée and cream and heat, stirring
occasionally, until hot but not boiling.
Add salt to taste and pepper. Ladle into
bowls and, if you wish, garnish with
asparagus tips. About 240 calories per
serving.

VARIATION:

Chilled Cream of Asparagus Soup: Use
2½ pounds asparagus to make purée and
1 pint light cream instead of milk and
heavy cream. Prepare as directed, cool,
cover, and chill 2–3 hours. Taste for salt
and pepper and adjust as needed before
serving. About 245 calories per serving.

▣ CURRIED AVOCADO SOUP

Makes 6 servings

2 (10½-ounce) cans condensed chicken
 broth
1 teaspoon grated onion
¼ garlic clove, peeled and crushed
2 teaspoons curry powder
2 ripe medium-size avocados
2 teaspoons lemon juice
1 cup milk or light cream

Simmer broth, onion, garlic and curry
powder uncovered in a small saucepan
8–10 minutes. Halve avocados lengthwise, remove pits, scoop out flesh, and

purée in electric blender at low speed with lemon juice and 1 cup hot broth. Add to broth in pan, stir in milk, and heat, stirring occasionally, 2–3 minutes. Serve hot or chill and serve cold. About 225 calories per serving if made with light cream, 175 per serving if made with milk.

CREAMY CARROT SOUP

Delicately seasoned with cloves and rosemary.
Makes 4–6 servings

6–8 medium-size carrots, peeled and cut in 2" chunks
2 medium-size yellow onions, peeled and quartered
2 sprigs parsley
3 whole cloves
¼ teaspoon rosemary
2 (10½-ounce) cans condensed chicken broth
1 pint milk
⅛ teaspoon pepper
2 tablespoons minced parsley

Place carrots, onions, parsley, cloves, rosemary and chicken broth in a saucepan, cover, and simmer 45–50 minutes until carrots are very soft; remove cloves and parsley and discard. Put mixture through a food mill or purée, a little at a time, in an electric blender at low speed. Return to pan, stir in milk and pepper, and heat, stirring, 2–3 minutes. Serve hot or chill and serve cold. Garnish each portion with a little minced parsley. About 155 calories for each of 4 servings, 105 for each of 6.

CHESTNUT SOUP

In the Pyrenees chestnut soup is sometimes enriched with leftover scraps of game bird; use it if you have it, or bits of turkey, goose, duck, or chicken.
Makes 6 servings

1 medium-size yellow onion, peeled and minced
1 stalk celery, minced
2 tablespoons butter or margarine
1 tablespoon flour

1 pint chicken broth or water
1 pound shelled, peeled chestnuts
6 cups milk
1 cup heavy cream
½–¾ cup minced, cooked chicken, goose, turkey, duck, or game bird (optional)
1½ teaspoons salt
⅛ teaspoon white pepper
⅛ teaspoon mace
⅓ cup croutons

Stir-fry onion and celery in butter in a large, heavy saucepan over moderately low heat 5–8 minutes until pale golden. Sprinkle with flour, mix well, then slowly stir in broth. Add chestnuts, cover, and simmer about ½ hour until very soft. Put through a food mill or purée in an electric blender at low speed; return to pan and set over moderate heat. Add all remaining ingredients except croutons and heat, stirring, about 5 minutes; do not allow to boil. Taste for salt and adjust; ladle into soup bowls and pass croutons separately. (*Note:* This soup will be mellower if made the day before and reheated in the top of a double boiler.) About 515 calories per serving if made with chicken broth, 500 per serving if made with water. Add 25 calories per serving if optional poultry meat is used.

⊠ CREAM OF CORN SOUP

Makes 6 servings

1 small yellow onion, peeled and minced
3 tablespoons bacon drippings
1 (10-ounce) package frozen whole kernel corn, thawed and chopped fine, or 1 can (1 pound) whole kernel corn, drained and chopped fine
2 tablespoons minced celery leaves
3 tablespoons flour
1 pint milk
1 cup light cream
1½ teaspoons salt (about)
Pinch pepper
Paprika

Stir-fry onion in drippings in a large saucepan over moderate heat 8–10 minutes until golden. Mix in corn and celery leaves and stir-fry 3–5 minutes.

Blend in flour, add milk and cream, and heat, stirring constantly, until thickened and smooth. Add salt to taste and pepper. Serve piping hot, topped with a blush of paprika. About 250 calories per serving.

CUCUMBER VELOUTÉ

Makes 4–6 servings

6 tablespoons butter or margarine
2 medium-size yellow onions, peeled and coarsely chopped
3 medium-size cucumbers, peeled, seeded, and diced
1 teaspoon salt
⅛ teaspoon white pepper
Pinch mace
2 (13¾-ounce) cans chicken broth
2 tablespoons flour
2 eggs yolks, lightly beaten
1 cup light cream
2 tablespoons minced parsley

Melt 4 tablespoons butter in a large skillet over moderate heat, add onions and cucumbers, and sauté, stirring, 8–10 minutes until onions are golden. Stir in salt, pepper, mace, and broth, cover, and simmer 15 minutes until vegetables are soft. Put through a food mill or purée, a bit at a time, in an electric blender at low speed. In a large saucepan, melt remaining butter over moderate heat. Blend in flour, add purée, and heat, stirring constantly, until thickened and smooth. Spoon a little hot mixture into yolks, then return all to saucepan. Mix in cream, reduce heat to lowest point, and warm 1–2 minutes longer, stirring; do not boil. Serve hot or cold garnished with minced parsley. About 395 calories for each of 4 servings, 265 for each of 6.

LUXE CREAM OF MUSHROOM SOUP

Makes 4 servings

¾ pound mushrooms, wiped clean and minced
2 tablespoons butter (no substitute)
1 tablespoon cornstarch
1½ cups chicken broth
1½ cups light cream
½ teaspoon salt (about)
⅛ teaspoon white pepper
1 teaspoon Worcestershire sauce

Stir-fry mushrooms in butter in a heavy saucepan over low heat 5–7 minutes until limp; blend in cornstarch, add broth, and heat, stirring, 3–4 minutes. Cover and simmer over lowest heat 12–15 minutes, stirring occasionally. Purée half the mixture in an electric blender at low speed or put through a food mill; return to pan. Add remaining ingredients and heat, stirring, 2–3 minutes. Taste for salt and adjust as needed. About 285 calories per serving.

VARIATION:

⚖ **Low-Calorie Cream of Mushroom Soup:** Omit butter and cornstarch; simmer mushrooms in broth, then proceed as recipe directs, substituting skim milk for cream. About 40 calories per serving.

⚖ **POTAGE SAINT-GERMAIN**

This soup should be made with fresh young peas, but if they're unavailable, use the frozen. Restaurants sometimes use dried split peas—very good but not authentic.
Makes 4 servings

2 cups cooked green peas, drained
2 cups White Stock or a ½ and ½ mixture of water and beef bouillon
½ teaspoon minced fresh chervil or ¼ teaspoon dried chervil
1 tablespoon butter (no substitute)
¼ cup croutons

Set aside 1 tablespoon peas; put the rest through a food mill or purée in an electric blender at high speed, adding a little stock if necessary. Mix purée and stock and strain through a fine sieve, pressing solids to extract as much liquid as possible. Pour into a saucepan, add chervil and butter, and heat, stirring now and then, about 5 minutes until a good serving temperature. Taste for seasoning and adjust as needed. Stir in reserved peas, ladle into bowls, and sprinkle with croutons. About 115 calories per serving.

BOULA-BOULA

Makes 4 servings

2 cups fresh or frozen green peas
1 cup boiling water
½ teaspoon salt
2 cups clear turtle soup
¼ cup medium-dry sherry
⅓ cup heavy cream

Simmer peas in water with salt about 8 minutes until tender; put through a food mill or purée in an electric blender at low speed; press through a fine sieve. Return to pan, add turtle soup and sherry, and heat slowly, stirring occasionally, 5 minutes. Meanwhile, preheat broiler; also whip cream until soft peaks will form. Place 4 ovenproof soup bowls or *marmites* on a baking sheet, fill with soup, and top with whipped cream. Broil 4″ from heat about 1 minute until flecked with brown. Serve at once. About 155 calories per serving.

VARIATION:

☒ **Quick Boula-Boula:** Heat together 1 (10½-ounce) can condensed cream of pea soup, 1 soup can water, 1 (12-ounce) can turtle soup, and ¼ cup medium-dry sherry, stirring now and then, until piping hot. Ladle into bowls, top with drifts of sour cream, and serve. About 145 calories per serving.

☒ CREAMY PEANUT SOUP

A fragrant soup that makes a nice change of pace.
Makes 6 servings

2 tablespoons butter or margarine
2 tablespoons flour
1 teaspoon salt
¼ teaspoon cayenne pepper
Pinch nutmeg
1 pint milk
1 pint light cream
1 cup creamy peanut butter
¼ cup tawny port or dry sherry

Melt butter in a large saucepan over moderate heat, blend in flour and seasonings, add milk and cream, and heat, stirring constantly, until thickened and smooth. Add peanut butter and continue to heat, stirring, until melted. Mix in wine and serve. About 525 calories per serving.

VICHYSSOISE I

Deliciously bland and silky.
Makes 6 servings

2 tablespoons butter or margarine
3 large leeks, washed, trimmed, and sliced thin
2 scallions, washed, trimmed, and sliced thin
1 small yellow onion, peeled and sliced thin
1 pound potatoes, peeled and sliced thin
2½ cups chicken broth
1½ teaspoons salt
Pinch white pepper
1 pint heavy cream
2 tablespoons minced fresh chives

Melt butter in a large kettle over moderate heat, add leeks, scallions, and onion, and sauté, stirring, 8–10 minutes until golden. Stir in all remaining ingredients except heavy cream and chives, cover, and simmer 45 minutes until vegetables are mushy; press all through a fine sieve. Return to kettle, add heavy cream, and heat and stir just until mixture boils. Remove from heat and put through sieve once again. Cool to room temperature, cover, and chill several hours. Serve very cold, topped with chives. About 415 calories per serving.

VICHYSSOISE II

Sour cream gives this vichyssoise a certain zing. It's not quite as calorie-laden as Vichyssoise I.
Makes 8 servings

¼ cup unsalted butter
5 large leeks, washed, trimmed, and sliced thin
2 medium-size yellow onions, peeled and sliced thin
2 pounds Irish potatoes (Maine or Eastern are best), washed, peeled, and sliced thin

1 (10½-ounce) can condensed chicken
  broth
1 (10½-ounce) can condensed beef
  consommé
2 cups water
2 teaspoons salt
1 pint milk
1 pint light cream
1 cup sour cream
¼ cup minced fresh chives

Melt butter in a large kettle over
moderate heat, add leeks and onions,
and sauté, stirring, 8–10 minutes until
golden. Add potatoes and stir-fry 2–3
minutes. Stir in broth, consommé, water
and salt, cover, and simmer 45–50
minutes until vegetables are mushy.
Remove from heat and press all through
a fine sieve. Return purée to kettle, add
milk and light cream, and heat, stirring,
until mixture just boils. Remove from
heat, cool slightly, then smooth in sour
cream. Put through sieve once again.
Cool to room temperature, cover, and
chill several hours. Serve very cold with
a sprinkling of minced chives. About 385
calories per serving.

PUMPKIN SOUP

Makes 4–6 servings

1½ cups pumpkin purée
3 cups chicken broth
1 tablespoon flour
1 teaspoon salt
¼ teaspoon ginger
¼ teaspoon nutmeg
¾ cup milk or light cream
1 teaspoon minced chives
2 egg yolks, lightly beaten

Heat pumpkin and chicken broth in top
of a double boiler over direct heat to a
simmer. Blend flour, salt, ginger, and
nutmeg with ¼ cup milk, mix into
pumpkin, and heat, stirring, 3–4 minutes.
Cover, set over simmering water, and
cook 20 minutes, stirring occasionally;
mix in chives. Beat egg yolks lightly with
remaining milk, add to soup, cook, and
stir 5 minutes over simmering water,
then serve. (Note: The flavor of this
soup improves on standing. Just be sure
to reheat slowly in the top of a double

boiler and to stir well.) Depending
upon whether soup is made with milk or
light cream, 130–195 calories for each
of 4 servings, 90–130 for each of 6.

SORREL-CRESS SOUP

Serve icy cold as a refreshing first
course.
Makes 6 servings

1 medium-size yellow onion, peeled and
  minced
¼ cup butter or margarine
⅓ cup minced sorrel
1 cup minced watercress
3 tablespoons flour
1 cup light cream
1 (10½-ounce) can condensed chicken
  broth
1 pint milk
3 eggs, lightly beaten
1½ teaspoons salt
⅛ teaspoon white pepper

Stir-fry onion in 2 tablespoons butter in
a small skillet over moderate heat 8–10
minutes until golden. Off heat, stir in
sorrel and watercress. Melt remaining
butter in a saucepan over moderate heat
and blend in flour. Add cream, chicken
broth, and 1 cup milk and heat, stirring
constantly, until thickened and smooth.
Mix a little hot sauce into eggs, pour into
pan, and heat and stir 1 minute; remove
from heat. Purée onion-sorrel mixture
with remaining milk in an electric
blender at high speed, then stir into hot
mixture. Season with salt and pepper,
cool to room temperature, cover, and
chill several hours before serving.
About 285 calories per serving.

¢ ⚖ ⊠ QUICK CREAM OF TOMATO SOUP

Makes 6 servings

⅓ cup minced yellow onion
2 tablespoons butter or margarine
2 tablespoons flour
½ teaspoon basil
½ teaspoon oregano
1¼ teaspoons salt
⅛ teaspoon pepper
1 tablespoon tomato paste

1 tablespoon light brown sugar
1 (10½-ounce) can condensed beef
  consommé
1 cup milk
1 (1-pound 12-ounce) can tomatoes (do
  not drain)

Stir-fry onion in butter in a large heavy
saucepan 3–5 minutes until limp, blend
in flour, herbs, salt, and pepper, then
stir in tomato paste, light brown sugar,
consommé, and milk and heat, stirring
constantly, until thickened and smooth.
Put tomatoes through a food mill or
purée, a little at a time, in an electric
blender at low speed; add to pan and
simmer, uncovered, 12–15 minutes—do
not allow to boil. Ladle into soup bowls
and serve piping hot. About 130
calories per serving.

MUSHROOM-TOMATO BISQUE

Makes 6 servings

½ pound mushrooms, wiped clean and
  minced
4 tablespoons butter or margarine
1 cup chicken broth
1 (1-pound 12-ounce) can tomatoes (do
  not drain)
1 small yellow onion, peeled and minced
2 tablespoons sugar
1 clove garlic, peeled and crushed
¼ teaspoon white pepper
2 tablespoons flour
1 cup heavy cream
2 teaspoons salt
Pinch baking soda

Stir-fry mushrooms in 2 tablespoons
butter in a large saucepan over
moderately high heat 2–3 minutes until
golden; add broth, cover, and simmer
15 minutes. Put through a food mill or
purée in an electric blender at low speed;
set aside. Put tomatoes, onion, sugar,
garlic, and pepper in the same saucepan,
cover, and simmer ½ hour; purée, a little
at a time, in an electric blender at low
speed, then strain through a fine sieve
and reserve. Melt remaining butter in
the top of a double boiler over direct
heat, blend in flour, then mix in cream
and cook, stirring, until smooth and
thickened. Set over simmering water, add

mushroom and tomato purées, salt and
soda, and heat, stirring, about 5 minutes.
About 285 calories per serving.

⊠ COLD CLAM BISQUE

Makes 6 servings

2 (8-ounce) cans minced clams (do not
  drain)
1 pint light cream
1 teaspoon Worcestershire sauce
⅛ teaspoon liquid hot red pepper
  seasoning
¼ teaspoon salt (about)
1 tablespoon minced chives

Purée clams with their liquid in an
electric blender at high speed until
smooth. Add ½ the cream, the
Worcestershire sauce, and liquid hot
red pepper seasoning and buzz about 5
seconds at low speed to blend. Pour into
a large bowl, add remaining cream, and
salt to taste. Chill 2–3 hours and serve
sprinkled with chives. About 210 calories
per serving.

SHELLFISH BISQUE

Makes 6 servings

¼ cup minced yellow onion
¼ cup minced carrot
3 tablespoons butter or margarine
1 pound cooked lobster, shrimp, or crab
  meat, well picked over and minced
⅓ cup dry white wine
2 cups water, Easy Fish Stock, or Rich
  Court Bouillon
1 pint heavy cream
2 egg yolks, lightly beaten
½ teaspoon salt (about)
⅛ teaspoon white pepper
¼ cup medium-dry sherry or brandy
  (optional)

Stir-fry onion and carrot in butter in a
heavy saucepan over moderately low
heat 5 minutes until onion is limp; add
shellfish and stir-fry 2–3 minutes. Add
wine and water, cover, and simmer 10
minutes. Remove from heat and let
stand ½ hour to blend flavors. Put
mixture through a food mill or purée in
an electric blender at low speed. Pour
into the top of a large double boiler, set
over simmering water, add cream and

heat, stirring, 5 minutes. Mix a little hot bisque into yolks, return to pan, and heat, stirring constantly, until no raw taste of egg remains. Add seasonings and, if you like, sherry; taste for salt and adjust if needed. Serve hot or chill and serve cold. (*Note:* For a pretty garnish, reserve about ¼ of the minced shellfish and scatter over each portion.) About 330 calories per serving without optional sherry or brandy. Add 10 calories per serving if sherry is used, about 25 calories per serving if brandy is used.

BILLI-BI

A delicate mussel soup delicious hot or cold.
Makes 4 servings

5 dozen mussels in the shell, prepared for cooking*
2 medium-size yellow onions, peeled and minced
2 stalks celery, minced
½ pound mushrooms, wiped clean and minced (include stems)
¼ cup minced parsley
⅛ teaspoon pepper
2½ cups water or 2 cups water and ½ cup Easy Fish Stock
1 cup dry white wine
1 cup light cream

Place mussels in a large, heavy kettle with all but last ingredient, cover, bring to a boil over moderate heat, then reduce heat and simmer 3 minutes until mussels open. With a slotted spoon lift out mussels and reserve to serve as a separate course or at another meal. Strain cooking liquid through a fine sieve lined with a triple thickness of cheesecloth, pour into a clean saucepan, and boil rapidly, uncovered, until reduced by about half. Turn heat to low, stir in cream, and heat and stir until piping hot. Taste for salt, adjust as needed and serve. Or chill well and serve cold. About 215 calories per serving.

⊠ CREAM OF CHICKEN OR TURKEY SOUP

Makes 4 servings

1 quart chicken or turkey broth
1 cup heavy cream
¼ teaspoon salt (about)
⅛ teaspoon white pepper
⅛ teaspoon nutmeg or mace
1 tablespoon minced parsley or chives

Bring broth to a simmer and slowly mix in cream. Add salt to taste, pepper, and nutmeg. Cover and let mellow over lowest heat about 10 minutes. Serve hot or icy cold, topped with minced parsley. About 250 calories per serving.

VARIATIONS:

⊠ **Potage à la Reine:** Prepare cream soup as directed, using chicken broth. Ladle into bowls but do not scatter with parsley. Instead, float about ¼ cup julienne strips of cooked white chicken meat in each bowl. About 280 calories per serving.

⊠ **Chicken or Turkey Velouté:** Melt 4 tablespoons butter in a large, heavy saucepan and blend in 4 tablespoons flour. Add broth and cream and heat, stirring constantly, until thickened and smooth; mix in all seasonings. Blend a little hot soup into 3 lightly beaten egg yolks, return to saucepan, set over lowest heat, and warm, stirring constantly, 1–2 minutes until no raw taste of egg remains; do not allow to boil. Serve hot topped with minced parsley. About 430 calories per serving.

⚖ AVGOLEMONO SOUP (GREEK CHICKEN-LEMON SOUP)

Makes 4 servings

1 quart chicken broth
¼ cup uncooked rice
Pinch mace or nutmeg
3 egg yolks
Juice of 1 lemon
Salt
Pepper

Place broth, rice, and mace in a large saucepan, cover, and simmer 25–30 minutes until rice is very tender. Beat yolks with lemon juice; spoon a little hot broth into egg mixture, return to pan, and heat over lowest heat 1–2 minutes, stirring constantly, until no taste of raw egg remains; do not boil. Taste for salt and pepper and season as needed. About 130 calories per serving.

SENEGALESE SOUP

A cream of chicken soup spiked with curry and chutney.
Makes 4 servings

2 tablespoons butter or margarine
2 tablespoons flour
1 tablespoon curry powder
2 (13¾-ounce) cans chicken broth
2 tablespoons minced chutney
1 cup julienne strips of cooked chicken (preferably white meat)
2 egg yolks lightly beaten with ½ cup heavy cream
4 teaspoons minced chives

Melt butter in a heavy saucepan over moderate heat, blend in flour and curry powder, add broth, and heat, stirring, until mixture boils. Reduce heat, add chutney and chicken, and heat, stirring now and then, 5–10 minutes to blend flavors. Spoon a little hot broth into egg mixture, pour into pan, set over lowest heat, and cook, stirring constantly, 1–2 minutes until no taste of raw egg remains; do not boil. Ladle into soup bowls, sprinkle with chives, and serve. About 310 calories per serving.

CHEDDAR CHEESE SOUP

Makes 6 servings

2 tablespoons butter or margarine
2 tablespoons flour
6 cups milk
1 clove garlic, peeled and bruised (optional)
1½ cups coarsely grated sharp Cheddar cheese
1 cup dry white wine or water
2 egg yolks, lightly beaten
¼ cup heavy cream
1 teaspoon salt (about)
⅛ teaspoon white pepper

Pinch nutmeg
⅓ cup finely grated mild Cheddar cheese

Melt butter in the top of a double boiler set over simmering water. Blend in flour, then slowly stir in milk; add garlic if you wish. Heat uncovered, stirring frequently, 10 minutes; mix in cheese and stir until melted; add wine. Mix egg yolks and cream, stir a little hot mixture into yolks, return to pan, and heat, stirring constantly, until no raw taste of egg remains. Remove garlic, mix in salt, pepper, and nutmeg, taste for salt and adjust as needed. Ladle into bowls, sprinkle with the mild Cheddar and serve. About 390 calories per serving if made with wine, about 360 per serving if made with water.

¢ OXTAIL SOUP

Makes 6 servings

2 pounds oxtail, cut in 1"–1½" chunks and trimmed of excess fat
½ cup unsifted flour plus 2 tablespoons
2 tablespoons beef drippings or cooking oil
2 medium-size yellow onions, peeled and minced
2 quarts water, or 6 cups water and 1 pint beef broth or bouillon
2 tablespoons ketchup
2 teaspoons salt
¼ teaspoon pepper
1 bay leaf
½ teaspoon thyme
3 cloves
2 sprigs parsley
2 medium-size carrots, peeled and diced
1 stalk celery, diced
⅓ cup dry sherry or port wine (optional)

Dredge oxtail in ½ cup flour, then brown in drippings in a large, heavy kettle over high heat; drain on paper toweling. Turn heat to moderate and stir-fry onions 8–10 minutes until golden; sprinkle in remaining flour, mix well, and brown lightly. Slowly add water, stir in ketchup, salt, and pepper, also bay leaf tied in cheesecloth with thyme, cloves, and parsley. Return oxtail to kettle, cover, and simmer 3 hours until meat is fork tender; cool and skim off fat; remove cheesecloth bag. Separate meat from bones, cut in bite-size pieces, and return to kettle along with carrots and celery. Cover and simmer 10–15 minutes until carrots are tender; if you like, mix in sherry. Serve as is *or* strain kettle liquid, serve as a first course, and follow with oxtail and vegetables. About 310–320 calories per serving depending upon whether made with water only or with broth and water. Add about 15 calories per serving if optional wine is used.

VARIATION:

¢ **Clear Oxtail Soup:** Prepare as directed, browning oxtail without dredging and omitting all flour and ketchup from recipe. About 50 calories *less* per serving than oxtail soup.

¢ **SCOTCH BROTH**

Makes 6–8 servings

2 pounds lean neck of mutton or lamb (with bones), cut in 2" chunks
2 medium-size yellow onions, peeled and minced
2 cups diced, peeled carrots
½ medium-size rutabaga, peeled and cut in small dice
2 leeks or 4 scallions, washed, trimmed, and coarsely chopped
½ cup medium pearl barley
1 gallon water
1 tablespoon salt (about)
¼ teaspoon pepper
2 tablespoons minced parsley

Place all ingredients except parsley in a large kettle, cover, and bring to a boil. Skim froth from surface, reduce heat, cover, and simmer 2–2½ hours, stirring now and then, until lamb is tender. Cut meat from bones in small pieces, if you like, and return to kettle or leave meat on bones. Stir, taste for salt and adjust as needed. Sprinkle with parsley and serve in deep bowls. About 415 calories for each of 6 servings, 315 for each of 8.

RUSSIAN BORSCH

Makes 6–8 servings

3½ quarts water

2 pounds beef shank bone with some meat attached
½ pound ham hock
1 pound lean pork shoulder in 1 piece
2 bay leaves, crumbled
8 peppercorns
4 sprigs parsley
2 carrots, peeled and cut in 1" chunks
2 leeks, washed, trimmed, and cut in 2" chunks
2 stalks celery, cut in 2" chunks
2 pounds beets, washed, trimmed, and peeled
1 pound yellow onions, peeled and cut in thin wedges
3 cloves garlic, peeled and crushed
1 (6-ounce) can tomato paste
¼ cup white wine vinegar
1 tablespoon salt
¼ teaspoon pepper
2 cups thickly sliced cabbage
1 cup sour cream
¼ cup minced fresh dill

Place water, bones and meat, bay leaves, peppercorns, parsley, carrots, leeks, and celery in a large, heavy kettle, cover, and simmer, stirring occasionally, 3–3½ hours until meats almost fall from bones. Trim meat from bones and cut in bite-size pieces; set aside. Strain broth, discarding vegetables and seasonings, then chill several hours until fat rises to top and hardens; lift off fat and discard. Thinly slice all beets but 1, grate it, mix with ½ cup cold water, and reserve. Return strained broth to kettle, add sliced beets, onions, garlic, tomato paste, vinegar, salt, and pepper, cover, and simmer, stirring occasionally, 2 hours. Add reserved meat, cabbage, grated beet, and beet water and simmer, covered, 15–20 minutes until cabbage is crisp tender. Ladle into large soup bowls, top each serving with a float of sour cream, and sprinkle with dill. About 585 calories for each of 6 servings, 440 for each of 8.

¢ ⚜ ☒ **QUICK BORSCH**

Although no quick borsch can match the old-fashioned variety that simmers long and slow on the back of the stove, this one comes close. It contains less than

one-fourth the calories of Russian borsch.
Makes 6 servings

2 tablespoons butter or margarine
1 medium-size yellow onion, peeled and sliced thin
1½ cups finely sliced cabbage
2 (10½-ounce) cans condensed beef consommé
4 (8-ounce) cans julienne beets (do not drain)
2 tablespoons tarragon vinegar
1 tablespoon tomato paste
½ teaspoon salt
Pinch pepper
¼ cup sour cream
2 tablespoons minced fresh dill or parsley

Melt butter in a large saucepan over moderately high heat, add onion and cabbage, and sauté, stirring occasionally, 8–10 minutes until cabbage is nearly tender. Add consommé and ½ the beets; purée remaining beets in an electric blender at low speed and add to pan along with vinegar, tomato paste, salt, and pepper. Simmer, uncovered, 15 minutes. Ladle about ½ cup borsch liquid into a small bowl and blend in sour cream; return to pan and smooth into borsch. Ladle into large, flat soup bowls and serve hot with a sprinkling of minced fresh dill or chill well and serve cold. About 140 calories per serving.

⚔️ ☒ **COCKALEEKIE**

This old Scottish cock and leek soup used to be rich as a stew. Today you're more apt to be served the following version— with or without prunes.
Makes 4 servings

1 pound leeks, washed, trimmed, halved lengthwise, and sliced ⅛″ thick (include some green tops)
1 tablespoon butter or margarine
1 quart chicken broth
½ teaspoon salt
⅛ teaspoon pepper
½ cup diced, cooked chicken meat
4–6 whole or coarsely chopped pitted prunes (optional)
1 teaspoon minced parsley

Stir-fry leeks in butter in a saucepan over moderately low heat 2–3 minutes. Add all remaining ingredients except parsley, cover, and simmer 10 minutes. Sprinkle with parsley and serve. About 100 calories per serving without the optional prunes, 132 calories per serving with the prunes.

WATERZOOIE (BELGIAN CHICKEN SOUP)

Extra rich!
Makes 8 servings

1 (6–7-pound) hen or capon, cleaned and dressed
¼ cup unsalted butter, softened to room temperature
5 large leeks, washed, trimmed, and cut in large chunks
5 large stalks celery, cut in large chunks (include tops)
2 large carrots, peeled and cut in large chunks
2 medium-size yellow onions, each peeled and stuck with 2 cloves
6 sprigs parsley
½ teaspoon thyme
¼ teaspoon nutmeg
6 peppercorns
1 bay leaf, crumbled
2 quarts chicken broth
1 cup dry white wine (optional)
4 egg yolks lightly beaten with ¾ cup heavy cream
1 lemon, sliced thin
2 tablespoons minced parsley

Preheat broiler. Rub chicken well with butter and broil 4″–5″ from heat, turning often, about 20 minutes until lightly browned. Transfer chicken to a large, heavy kettle, add giblets and all but last 3 ingredients, cover, and simmer 1–1½ hours until chicken is tender. Lift chicken and giblets from broth, cool until easy to handle, peel off skin and discard; separate meat from bones and cut in large chunks; mince giblets. Meanwhile, continue simmering vegetables, covered, in broth. When chicken is cut up, strain broth and skim off fat. Return broth to kettle, add cut-up chicken and giblets, cover, and heat 5 minutes. Mix a little hot broth into yolk mixture, return to kettle, and warm over lowest heat 2–3 minutes; do not boil. Ladle into soup bowls, top each portion with a lemon slice and scattering of parsley and serve. About 870 calories per serving without optional wine, about 885 per serving if wine is used.

MULLIGATAWNY SOUP

A curried chicken and tomato soup.
Makes 6 servings

3 tablespoons butter or margarine
1 small yellow onion, peeled and minced
1 medium-size carrot, peeled and diced fine
1 stalk celery, diced fine
½ green pepper, cored, seeded, and minced
¼ cup unsifted flour
1 tablespoon curry powder
¼ teaspoon nutmeg
3 cloves
2 sprigs parsley
1 quart chicken broth
1 teaspoon salt
⅛ teaspoon pepper
1 cup chopped tomatoes
1 cup cooked, diced chicken
½ cup heavy cream
1 cup boiled rice

Melt butter in a large saucepan, add onion, carrot, celery, and green pepper, and stir-fry 8–10 minutes until onion is golden. Blend in flour, curry powder, and nutmeg; add cloves, parsley, broth, salt, pepper, and tomatoes, cover, and simmer 1 hour. Strain broth; pick out and discard cloves and parsley; purée vegetables in an electric blender at low speed or put through a food mill. Smooth purée into broth, return to heat, add chicken and cream, and heat, stirring, 5–10 minutes to blend flavors. Add rice, heat and stir 2–3 minutes longer, then serve. About 285 calories per serving.

NEW ENGLAND CLAM CHOWDER

Makes 6 servings

1 pint shucked clams, drained (reserve liquid)
⅓ cup diced salt pork
1 medium-size yellow onion, peeled and minced
2 cups diced, peeled potatoes
½ cup water
2 cups milk
1 cup light cream
1 teaspoon salt (about)
⅛ teaspoon white pepper
⅛ teaspoon paprika

Pick over clams, removing any shell fragments; leave whole or, if you prefer, mince or grind medium fine. Lightly brown salt pork in a large, heavy saucepan over moderate heat, lift out, and reserve. Stir-fry onion in drippings 5–8 minutes until pale golden, add potatoes, water, clam liquid, and salt pork. Cover and simmer 10–12 minutes until potatoes are nearly tender, stirring occasionally. Add clams, milk, cream, salt, and pepper, cover, and simmer 5 minutes to heat through; do not boil. Ladle into hot bowls, dust with paprika, and serve. About 310 calories per serving.

⊠ QUICK NEW ENGLAND-STYLE CLAM CHOWDER

Makes 6–8 servings

2 small yellow onions, peeled and minced
3 tablespoons butter or margarine
2 (10½-ounce) cans minced clams (do not drain)
2 cups diced, peeled potatoes
1 teaspoon salt
⅛ teaspoon white pepper
2 cups milk
1 cup light cream
¼ teaspoon paprika

Stir-fry onions in 2 tablespoons butter in a large saucepan over moderate heat 5–8 minutes until pale golden. Drain liquid from canned clams into pan, add potatoes, salt, and pepper, cover, and simmer 10–12 minutes until potatoes are nearly tender, stirring occasionally. Add clams, milk, and cream, cover, and simmer 5–7 minutes just to heat through. Add remaining butter, stir until melted.

Ladle into hot soup bowls, sprinkle with paprika, and serve with hard rolls or crisp crackers. About 300 calories for each of 6 servings, 225 for each of 8.

¢ NEW ENGLAND FISH CHOWDER

Makes 4 servings

3 tablespoons butter (no substitute)
1 medium-size yellow onion, peeled and minced
3 medium-size Irish potatoes, peeled and cut in ¼″ cubes
½ cup hot water
1 pound haddock or cod fillets
2 cups milk
1 teaspoon salt
⅛ teaspoon white pepper
Paprika (garnish)

Melt 2 tablespoons butter in a large, heavy saucepan over low heat. Add onion and sauté 8–10 minutes, until golden, *not brown*. Add potatoes and water, cover, and simmer 10 minutes; add fish, cover, and simmer 10 minutes longer. (*Note:* Adjust burner so mixture *simmers;* if it boils, fish may overcook and become watery.) Off heat, flake fish with a fork, add milk, salt, and pepper; cover and let stand 1 hour at room temperature to blend flavors. Reheat slowly, stirring frequently, about 10 minutes. *Do not allow to boil.* Ladle into soup bowls, sprinkle lightly with paprika, and dot with remaining butter. Serve with oyster crackers or hot crusty bread. About 365 calories per serving.

VARIATION:

For extra richness, substitute ½ cup light or heavy cream for ½ cup of the milk. About 410 or 450 calories per serving, depending upon whether light or heavy cream is used.

⚖ MANHATTAN CLAM CHOWDER

Manhattan-style clam chowder may contain sweet green pepper and/or corn, but it *always* contains tomatoes. New England Clam chowder never does.
Makes 8 servings

1 medium-size yellow onion, peeled and minced
2 tablespoons butter, margarine, or bacon drippings
1½ cups diced, peeled carrots
½ cup diced celery
2 cups diced, peeled potatoes
1 (1-pound 12-ounce) can tomatoes (do not drain)
2 cups water or Easy Fish Stock
1½ teaspoons salt
⅛ teaspoon pepper
1 pint minced fresh or canned clams, drained (reserve liquid)
Drained clam liquid + enough bottled clam juice to total 1 pint
1 tablespoon minced parsley

Stir-fry onion in butter in a large, heavy kettle over moderate heat 5–8 minutes until pale golden. Add remaining vegetables (breaking up the tomatoes), water, salt, and pepper. Cover and simmer 15 minutes. Off heat, add clams and clam liquid, cover, and let stand ½ hour to blend flavors. Return to heat and simmer about 5 minutes, sprinkle with parsley, and serve. About 140 calories per serving.

VARIATION:

Prepare as directed, reducing carrots to 1 cup and adding ½–¾ cup diced, seeded, cored sweet green pepper or whole kernel corn. About 140 calories per serving if made with green pepper, 150 per serving if made with corn.

⚖ ☒ 10-MINUTE MANHATTAN-STYLE CLAM CHOWDER

Not only quick but low-caloric, too.
Makes 4 servings

1 (10½-ounce) can minced clams (do not drain)
1 (10¾-ounce) can condensed vegetable soup
1 soup can cold water
½ teaspoon celery flakes
⅛ teaspoon thyme

Drain clam liquid into a large saucepan; set clams aside. Add all remaining ingredients except clams, cover and simmer 5 minutes. Stir well, add clams, and heat, uncovered, 1–2 minutes, stirring occasionally. Ladle into hot soup bowls and serve with chowder crackers. About 85 calories per serving.

MATELOTE (FISH STEW WITH WINE)

Matelotes are usually made with fresh water fish—except in Normandy.
Makes 6 servings

¾ pound small white onions, peeled
2 tablespoons olive or other cooking oil
½ pound mushrooms, sliced thin
2 cloves garlic, peeled and crushed
1 bouquet garni,* tied in cheesecloth
Pinch nutmeg
Pinch cinnamon
1 teaspoon salt (about)
¼ teaspoon pepper
1 quart dry red or white wine
2 cups Easy Fish Stock
1 pound carp, pike, or other lean fresh water fish, cleaned, dressed, and cut in 2" chunks
1 pound catfish or whitefish, cleaned, dressed, and cut in 2" chunks
1 pound eel, skinned, cleaned, dressed, and cut in 1" chunks
¼ cup brandy
2 tablespoons butter or margarine
2 tablespoons flour
½ pound boiled crayfish or shrimp, shelled and deveined
⅓ cup croutons

Sauté onions in oil in a large burner-to-table kettle over moderately high heat, turning frequently, 10 minutes until golden. Add mushrooms and garlic and stir-fry 2–3 minutes. Add *bouquet garni,* seasonings, wine, and stock, cover, and simmer 10 minutes; add fish. Warm brandy in a small pan, blaze with a match, and pour flaming over fish. Cover and simmer 10–15 minutes until fish just flakes. Drain 2–3 cups liquid from kettle and reserve; melt butter in a saucepan over moderate heat, blend in flour, add reserved liquid, and heat, stirring, until slightly thickened; add crayfish, stir all into kettle, taste for salt and add more if needed. Scatter croutons over soup and serve. About 370 calories per serving.

VARIATION:

Matelote Normandy Style: Substitute halibut or haddock for the carp, mackerel or tuna for the catfish, and apple cider for the wine. Prepare as directed; just before serving, stir in ½ cup heavy cream. Garnish with 1 dozen each steamed mussels and soft clams in the shell; omit croutons. About 575 calories per serving.

¢ DRIED BEAN SOUP

This soup freezes well.
Makes 12 servings

1 pound dried beans (any kind), washed and sorted
1 gallon cold water, or 1 quart cold water and 3 quarts beef, chicken, or turkey broth
2 medium-size yellow onions, peeled and coarsely chopped
3 carrots, peeled and diced
2 stalks celery, diced
2 cloves garlic, peeled and crushed (optional)
1 tablespoon bacon drippings, margarine, or cooking oil
2 teaspoons salt (about)
¼ teaspoon pepper
2 tablespoons minced parsley

Soak beans* in 1 quart water overnight or use the quick method. Drain, measure soaking water, and add enough cold water to total 3 quarts. Place beans and water in a large, heavy kettle with all but last 3 ingredients, cover, and simmer about 1½ hours until very soft. Put half of mixture through a food mill or purée, a little at a time, in an electric blender at low speed. Return to kettle and heat until bubbly. Add salt and pepper, tasting and adjusting salt as needed. Sprinkle with parsley and serve. About 155 calories per serving if made with water only, 190 per serving if made with broth and water.

VARIATIONS:

¢ **Savory Dried Bean Soup:** Prepare as directed, adding a ham bone or pig's knuckle, chunk of salt pork or bacon, or leftover roast bone to the pot. Other good additions: leftover meat, gravy, and vegetables, medium-dry sherry or Madeira to taste. About 190 calories per serving if made with water only, 225 per serving if made with broth and water.

¢ **Rosy Dried Bean Soup:** Prepare as directed, smoothing 1½ cups tomato purée into soup shortly before serving. About 200 calories per serving if made with water only, 235 per serving if made with broth and water.

Creamy Dried Bean Soup: Cook beans as directed, using 2 quarts water instead of 3. After puréeing, blend in 1 quart light cream and heat to serving temperature; do not boil. About 325 calories per serving.

¢ HEARTY CHICK-PEA AND SAUSAGE SOUP

Makes 8–10 servings

1 pound dried chick-peas, washed and sorted
3 quarts cold water (about)
1 small lean ham bone with some meat attached
2 sprigs parsley
½ pound chorizos, pepperoni, or other hot sausage, skinned and sliced ½" thick
2 medium-size yellow onions, peeled and coarsely chopped
2 cloves garlic, peeled and crushed
2 medium-size carrots, peeled and sliced thin
½ teaspoon oregano
¼ teaspoon thyme
¼ teaspoon coriander
1½ teaspoons salt (about)
⅛ teaspoon pepper (about)

Soak chick-peas overnight in 1 quart water or use the quick method.* Drain, measure soaking water, and add cold water to total 3 quarts. Place peas, water, ham bone and parsley in a large, heavy kettle, cover, and simmer 1 hour. Meanwhile, brown *chorizos* in a large, heavy skillet; lift out with a slotted spoon and reserve. Stir-fry onions, garlic, and carrots in drippings 10–12 minutes over

moderate heat to brown lightly, stir in remaining ingredients (but not sausages) and add to chick-peas. Re-cover and simmer 1–1½ hours until peas are mushy. Lift out ham bone, cut off any meat and reserve; discard parsley. Purée kettle mixture, a little at a time, in an electric blender at low speed or put through a food mill. Return all to kettle; add ham and sausages and heat, stirring, 10–15 minutes to blend flavors. Taste for salt and pepper and adjust as needed. Serve hot. About 370 calories for each of 8 servings, 295 for each of 10.

¢ OLD-FASHIONED BLACK BEAN SOUP

Makes 6 servings

1 pound dried black beans, washed and sorted but not soaked
3 quarts cold water
2 medium-size yellow onions, peeled and minced
2 cloves garlic, peeled and crushed
3 tablespoons bacon drippings
2 medium-size tomatoes, peeled, cored, seeded, and chopped
¾ teaspoon oregano
½ teaspoon crushed dried hot red chili peppers
¼ teaspoon thyme
2 teaspoons salt
⅛ teaspoon black pepper
½ cup dry sherry
2 hard-cooked eggs

Place beans and water in a very large, heavy kettle, cover, and simmer 1¼–1½ hours until almost tender. Meanwhile, stir-fry onions and garlic in drippings in a heavy skillet over moderate heat 8–10 minutes until golden, stir in tomatoes, all herbs and spices, and set aside. When beans are almost tender, stir in skillet mixture, cover, and simmer 1½–2 hours longer until beans are mushy. Put mixture through a food mill or purée by pressing through a fine sieve. Return to pan, add salt, black pepper, and sherry, and heat, stirring frequently, 5–10 minutes to blend flavors. Peel eggs, sieve the yolks, and mince the whites. Ladle soup into large bowls, sprinkle with yolks and

whites, and serve. About 395 calories
per serving.

¢ EASY BLACK BEAN SOUP

Makes 4 servings

1 cup minced Spanish or Bermuda onion
2 cloves garlic, peeled and crushed
2 tablespoons butter or margarine
½ teaspoon crushed coriander seeds
¼ teaspoon oregano
⅛ teaspoon thyme
¼ cup dry sherry
1 (10½-ounce) can condensed beef consommé
2 (1-pound) cans black beans (do not drain)
1 bay leaf, crumbled

Stir-fry onion and garlic in butter in a
large saucepan over moderate heat 8–10
minutes until golden. Blend in herbs and
sherry and heat 1–2 minutes, then add
remaining ingredients and simmer,
uncovered, stirring occasionally, ½–¾
hour until flavors are well blended. Ladle
into soup bowls and serve. About 475
calories per serving.

¢ LAMB, PEPPER, AND BARLEY SOUP

Makes 8–10 servings

1 lamb shank, cracked, or a meaty leg or shoulder bone from a leftover roast
1 cup medium pearl barley, washed
1 cup dried green split peas, washed and sorted
2 medium-size yellow onions, peeled and minced
1 clove garlic, peeled and crushed
1 sweet green pepper, cored, seeded, and minced
3½ quarts cold water
4 teaspoons salt (about)
¼ teaspoon pepper

Place all ingredients in a large, heavy
kettle, cover, and simmer 2 hours,
stirring occasionally. Cut meat from
bones and return to kettle. Taste for
salt and adjust if necessary. Serve hot
with crusty bread or crisp crackers.
(*Note:* This soup keeps well in the
refrigerator about 1 week. It also freezes

well.) About 255 calories for each of
8 servings, 200 for each of 10.

¢ GOLDEN SPLIT PEA SOUP WITH HAM

A Norwegian favorite, hearty enough to
serve as a main course.
Makes 8–10 servings

2 medium-size yellow onions, peeled and coarsely chopped
2 tablespoons bacon drippings, butter, or margarine
2 cups diced, cooked ham
1 pound yellow split peas, washed and sorted
3 quarts water
⅛ teaspoon rosemary
1 tablespoon salt
¼ teaspoon pepper

Stir-fry onions in drippings 5–8 minutes
in a large saucepan over moderate heat
until pale golden. Add ham and stir-fry
5 minutes. Add remaining ingredients,
cover, and simmer 1 hour, stirring
occasionally. Serve steaming hot with
buttery chunks of garlic bread. About
305 calories for each of 8 servings, 245
for each of 10.

VARIATION:

Lentil and Ham Soup: Prepare as
directed, substituting 1 pound lentils for
the peas and simmering ¾ hour until
tender, not mushy. Calorie counts the
same as for split pea soup.

¢ MINESTRONE MILANESE

Italians like minestrone made with red
kidney beans; Americans more often use
navy or pea beans. Either makes a husky
main-dish soup.
Makes 10 servings

½ pound dried red kidney, navy, or pea beans, washed and sorted
2 cups water
1 large yellow onion, peeled and minced
1 clove garlic, peeled and minced
⅓ cup diced salt pork
2 tablespoons olive or other cooking oil
3 quarts beef broth or water or a ½ and ½ mixture of water and beef bouillon

2 medium-size carrots, peeled and diced
2 medium-size potatoes, peeled and
   diced
2 cups finely shredded cabbage
½ cup minced celery
⅓ cup tomato paste
2 teaspoons minced fresh basil or 1
   teaspoon dried basil
¼ teaspoon thyme
2 teaspoons salt (about)
¼ teaspoon pepper
2 small zucchini, diced (optional)
1 tablespoon minced parsley
1 cup ditalini or elbow macaroni
⅓ cup grated Parmesan cheese

Soak beans overnight in water or use the quick method,* drain. Stir-fry onion, garlic, and salt pork in oil in a large, heavy kettle 5–8 minutes over moderate heat until onion is pale golden. Add beans and broth, cover, and simmer 1 hour. Add all remaining ingredients except zucchini, parsley, *ditalini*, and Parmesan, cover, and simmer 1 hour, stirring now and then. Add zucchini, parsley, and ditalini, cover, and simmer 15–20 minutes longer until ditalini is tender. Taste for salt and adjust as needed. Stir Parmesan into soup or, if you prefer, pass separately. About 240 calories per serving if made with water alone, 260 if made with broth and water, 285 if made with broth alone.

⚖ ARTICHOKE SOUP

An unusually delicate soup. Good hot or cold.
Makes 4 servings

2 cups globe artichoke hearts (fresh,
   frozen, or drained canned)
2 tablespoons butter or margarine
1 cup milk
2 cups water
1 teaspoon salt
⅛ teaspoon white pepper
1 clove garlic, peeled and speared with
   a toothpick
½ cup beef consommé
1 teaspoon minced parsley

If artichokes are fresh, parboil 20–25 minutes and drain. If frozen, thaw just enough to separate. Quarter hearts, then

slice thin crosswise. Stir-fry in butter in a saucepan (not aluminum) over moderately low heat 5 minutes; do not brown. Add all but last 2 ingredients, cover, and simmer over lowest heat 20 minutes. Discard garlic, purée about half the mixture in an electric blender at low speed or put through a food mill; return to pan. Add consommé and heat to serving temperature, stirring now and then. Serve hot sprinkled with parsley. About 125 calories per serving.

VARIATION:

⚖ **Cold Artichoke Soup:** Slice artichokes but do not fry; omit butter. Simmer as directed, then purée and proceed as above. About 80 calories per serving.

⊠ ¢ CABBAGE SOUP

A simple soup that can be used as the foundation of a variety of unusual European soups. Four of the best are included here as easy variations.
Makes 6 servings

2 cups finely shredded green cabbage
1 medium-size yellow onion, peeled and
   minced
¼ cup butter or margarine
6 cups beef broth, bouillon, or
   consommé
½ teaspoon salt
¼ teaspoon pepper
½ cup finely grated Cheddar or
   Parmesan cheese or ½ cup sour cream

Stir-fry cabbage and onion in butter in a large, heavy saucepan over moderately low heat until cabbage is wilted, not brown. Add broth, salt, and pepper, cover, and simmer 15–20 minutes until cabbage is tender. Ladle into soup bowls, sprinkle with cheese or top with sour cream, and serve. About 165 calories per serving.

VARIATIONS:

¢ **German Cabbage Soup:** Prepare as directed and just before serving thicken with 2 tablespoons flour blended with ¼ cup cold water. Also stir in 1 tablespoon caraway seeds and 2 tablespoons butter or margarine; omit cheese or sour cream topping. About 170 calories per serving.

¢ **French Cabbage Soup:** Prepare as directed, increasing broth to 2 quarts and adding at the same time 1 cup each diced peeled potatoes and carrots and 1 peeled and crushed clove garlic. Top with croutons instead of cheese or sour cream. About 190 calories per serving.

¢ **Basque Cabbage Soup:** Prepare as directed, increasing broth to 2 quarts and adding at the same time 1 cup cooked dried limas and 1 peeled and crushed clove garlic. Top each serving with ¼ teaspoon vinegar instead of cheese or sour cream. About 195 calories per serving.

¢ **Russian Sauerkraut Soup:** Prepare as directed, substituting 2 cups drained sauerkraut for cabbage and adding 1 (1-pound) undrained can tomatoes, breaking tomatoes up. Top each serving with sour cream. About 190 calories per serving.

☒ ¢ **CORN CHOWDER**
Makes 6 servings

6 slices bacon, diced
2 medium-size yellow onions, peeled and chopped
1 medium-size sweet green pepper, cored, seeded, and chopped
2 (10-ounce) packages frozen whole kernel corn
3 cups milk
2 teaspoons salt
⅛ teaspoon pepper
⅛ teaspoon nutmeg

Brown bacon in a very large skillet over moderate heat and drain on paper toweling. Stir-fry onions and green pepper in drippings 8–10 minutes until onions are golden. Add corn, cover, and simmer 10–12 minutes. Uncover, break up any frozen bits of corn, and simmer, uncovered, 5 minutes, stirring occasionally. Add remaining ingredients and simmer 5 minutes. Ladle into soup bowls and top each serving with bacon. About 225 calories per serving.

☒ ¢ **BASIC POTATO SOUP**
Makes 6 servings

1 small yellow onion, peeled and minced
2 tablespoons butter or margarine
2 cups diced, peeled potatoes
2 cups cold water or chicken broth
1 teaspoon salt
½ teaspoon celery salt
1 cup milk
1 cup light cream
⅛ teaspoon white pepper
1 tablespoon minced parsley, chives, or dill

Stir-fry onion in butter in a heavy saucepan over moderate heat 5 minutes until limp; add potatoes, water, salt, and celery salt, cover and simmer 10–15 minutes until potatoes are nearly tender. Add milk, cream, and pepper and simmer, uncovered, stirring occasionally, 3–5 minutes until potatoes are done. Sprinkle with parsley and serve. About 190 calories per serving if made with water, 210 if made with broth.

VARIATIONS:

¢ **Potato Soup au Gratin:** Prepare soup as directed, ladle into flameproof bowls, top each with a little grated Cheddar or Parmesan cheese and a sprinkling of nutmeg or paprika, and broil quickly to brown. About 220 calories per serving if made with water, 240 if made with broth.

¢ **Mashed Potato Soup:** Prepare as directed, substituting 2 cups seasoned mashed potatoes for the diced and simmering 10 minutes altogether, beating with a whisk now and then. About 210 calories per serving if made with water, 230 if made with broth.

¢ **Cream of Potato Soup:** Prepare as directed; purée in an electric blender at low speed or put through a food mill. Serve hot or cold. Same calorie counts as Basic Potato Soup.

⊠ JIFFY POTATO-ONION SOUP

Makes 6 servings

2 cups milk
2 (13¾-ounce) cans chicken broth
1 (1⅜-ounce) package dry onion soup mix
1 tablespoon parsley flakes
1 (5-serving size) envelope instant mashed potatoes
⅓ cup crisp, crumbled bacon (optional garnish)

Heat milk, chicken broth, onion soup mix, and parsley flakes, uncovered, over moderately high heat, stirring occasionally, until mixture boils. Remove from heat and gradually add instant mashed potatoes, stirring briskly. Return to heat and warm 2–3 minutes longer, beating with a wire whisk. Ladle into soup bowls and top, if you like, with bacon crumbles. About 185 calories per serving without optional bacon garnish. Add about 15 calories per serving if bacon crumbles are used.

¢ CALDO VERDE (PORTUGUESE GREEN SOUP)

If Portugal has a national dish it is *caldo verde,* a tweedy green soup that bubbles on stoves across the country (including those of Lisbon's more sophisticated restaurants). Basically, it's a potato soup, spiked with onions and garlic and textured with shreds of kale or cabbage and spinach.
Makes 8–10 servings

3 medium-size yellow onions, peeled and coarsely chopped
2 cloves garlic, peeled and crushed
⅓ cup olive oil
6 potatoes, peeled and diced
1 gallon water
1 medium-size cabbage, cored and sliced thin
1 pound fresh spinach, washed, trimmed, and sliced thin
3 tablespoons salt
¼ teaspoon pepper

Sauté onions and garlic in oil in a large, heavy kettle 8–10 minutes over moderate heat until golden, stirring occasionally.

Add potatoes and sauté, stirring, 10 minutes. Add water and simmer, uncovered, 2 hours, stirring now and then. Add remaining ingredients and continue simmering, uncovered, 45 minutes, stirring occasionally. Ladle into large soup bowls and serve. About 190 calories for each of 8 servings, 155 for each of 10.

¢ ITALIAN-STYLE SPINACH AND RICE SOUP

Accompanied by garlic bread and sliced tomatoes, this makes a refreshing, light lunch.
Makes 6–8 servings

2 medium-size yellow onions, peeled and coarsely chopped
2 tablespoons butter or margarine
4 (13¾-ounce) cans chicken broth
½ cup uncooked rice
2 (10-ounce) packages frozen chopped spinach, thawed
2 teaspoons salt
¼ teaspoon nutmeg
⅛ teaspoon pepper

Stir-fry onions in butter in a large saucepan over moderate heat 8–10 minutes until golden. Add broth and bring to a boil. Stir in rice and boil, uncovered, 10 minutes until rice is about half done. Add remaining ingredients and simmer 12–15 minutes longer until rice is done. Ladle into soup bowls and serve. About 170 calories for each of 6 servings, 130 for each of 8.

¢ ⚒ FRESH TOMATO SOUP

Makes 6 servings

2 medium-size yellow onions, peeled and quartered
1 stalk celery, cut in 2" chunks
1 (10½-ounce) can condensed beef consommé
6 large ripe tomatoes, peeled, cored, and quartered
1 tablespoon butter or margarine
2 teaspoons salt
⅛ teaspoon pepper
2 tablespoons minced fresh chives or dill

Place onions, celery, and consommé in

a large saucepan, cover, and simmer 45 minutes until onions are mushy. Add tomatoes, cover, and simmer 15–20 minutes until tomatoes have reduced to juice; cool 10 minutes, then put through a food mill or purée, a little at a time, in an electric blender at low speed. Return to pan, add butter, salt, and pepper, and simmer uncovered 5 minutes. Serve hot or cold garnished with minced chives. About 75 calories per serving.

¢ ⚖ **ANDALUSIAN GAZPACHO (COLD SPANISH VEGETABLE SOUP)**

Glorious on a hot summer day. And almost a meal in itself.
Makes 6 servings

¾ cup soft white bread crumbs
3 tablespoons red wine vinegar
2 cloves garlic, peeled and crushed
¼ cup olive oil
1 large cucumber, peeled, seeded, and cut in fine dice
1 sweet green pepper, cored, seeded, and minced
8 large ripe tomatoes, peeled, cored, seeded, and chopped fine
1 cup cold water
½ teaspoon salt
⅛ teaspoon pepper

Place bread crumbs, vinegar, garlic, and oil in a small bowl and mix vigorously with a fork to form a smooth paste; set aside. Mix all remaining ingredients in a large mixing bowl, then blend in bread paste. Cover and chill at least 24 hours before serving. Serve icy cold in soup bowls as a first course or as a midafternoon refresher. For a special touch, bed the soup bowls in larger bowls of crushed ice and garnish with sprigs of fresh dill or basil or, failing that, watercress or parsley. About 130 calories per serving.

⚖ **BASIC FRUIT SOUP**

Slavs and Scandinavians sometimes serve a hot or cold fruit soup before the main course; berries, cherries, and plums are the favored "soup fruits."

Makes 4 servings

1 pint berries, washed and stemmed (strawberries, raspberries, blueberries, boysenberries, blackberries, or gooseberries)
1 pint water or a ½ and ½ mixture of water and dry white wine
¼ cup sugar (about)
2 teaspoons lemon juice
1 tablespoon cornstarch blended with 2 tablespoons cold water
Heavy cream, sour cream, or buttermilk (optional topping)

Simmer berries in water in a covered saucepan 10 minutes until mushy; put through a food mill or purée in an electric blender at low speed, then press through a fine sieve. Return purée to pan, add remaining ingredients, and heat to a boil, stirring. Taste for sugar and add more, if needed. Serve hot or cold, topped, if you like, with cream. From about 70–120 calories per serving if made with water only, 130–55 if made with water and wine (strawberries and gooseberries are the lowest in calories). Add 50 calories per serving for each tablespoon heavy cream topping used, 30 calories for each tablespoon sour cream, and 5 calories for each tablespoon buttermilk.

VARIATIONS:

⬚ **Quick Berry Soup:** Substitute 2 (10-ounce) packages thawed frozen berries or 1 (1-pound) undrained can berries for the fresh. Do not cook; purée and sieve, then add enough water to make 1 quart. Heat with sugar (just enough to taste), lemon juice, and cornstarch paste as directed. About 115–30 calories per serving, depending on kind of berries used.

Spiced Fruit Soup: Prepare as directed, adding ½ teaspoon cinnamon and ¼ teaspoon each nutmeg and cloves along with sugar. Calorie counts the same as Basic Fruit Soup.

Curried Fruit Soup: Prepare as directed, adding 2 teaspoons curry powder along with sugar. About 10 calories more per serving than Basic Fruit Soup.

Sweet-Sour Fruit Soup: Prepare as directed, increasing sugar to 5 table- spoons and adding, at the same time, 3 tablespoons red or white wine vinegar. About 10 calories more per serving than Basic Fruit Soup.

Plum Soup: Substitute 1 pound purple plums for berries and simmer 25–30 minutes until mushy; cool slightly, pit, then purée and proceed as for the Basic Fruit Soup. About 160 calories per serving without optional cream topping.

COOL HUNGARIAN CHERRY SOUP

Although Hungarians traditionally serve this cold soup *before* the entree, you may find it too sweet for an appetizer. If so, serve as a hot weather dessert.
Makes 4–6 servings

2 (1-pound 1-ounce) cans pitted dark sweet cherries (do not drain)
1 cup sour cream
¼ cup superfine sugar
¼ cup tawny port or cream sherry (optional)

Drain cherry liquid into a mixing bowl, add sour cream, sugar, and, if you like, the wine, and stir until well blended. Add cherries, cover, and chill 3–4 hours before serving. About 380 calories for each of 4 servings, 255 for each of 6.

¢ ⚖ APPLE SOUP

Serve as a first course or light dessert.
Makes 4–6 servings

1 pound greenings or other tart cooking apples, peeled, cored, and sliced thin
3 cups water
1 teaspoon grated lemon rind
2 teaspoons lemon juice
½ cup sugar (about)
½ teaspoon cinnamon
¼ teaspoon nutmeg
1 cup sour cream blended with ½ cup milk (optional)

Place all but last ingredient in a saucepan, cover, and simmer about 20 minutes until apples are mushy. Put through a food mill or purée in an

electric blender at low speed; taste for sugar and add more if needed. Serve hot or cold with a little of the sour cream mixture drizzled on top, if you like. About 145 calories for each of 4 servings, 100 for each of 6 without optional sour cream topping. Add 25 calories per serving for each tablespoon of topping used.

VARIATION:

Russian Apple Soup: Prepare as directed, using 2 cups water and 1 cup red Bordeaux wine for cooking the apples. Before puréeing, add ¼ cup red or black currant jelly and stir until melted. Purée and serve hot or cold with or without cream topping. About 235 calories for each of 4 servings, 160 for each of 6 without sour cream topping.

WINE SOUP WITH SNOW EGGS

Germans serve this heady Rhine wine soup as a first course; you may prefer it as dessert.
Makes 4–6 servings

2 tablespoons butter (no substitute)
2 tablespoons flour
1 pint Rhine wine
1 pint water
3–4 tablespoons sugar
1 cinnamon stick
1 (2") strip lemon rind
2 egg yolks, lightly beaten

Snow Eggs:
1 egg white
1 tablespoon sugar
1 teaspoon sugar mixed with ¼ teaspoon cinnamon

Melt butter in a heavy, shallow saucepan about 8" in diameter over moderately low heat. Blend in flour, slowly stir in wine, water, and sugar; add cinnamon and lemon rind. Heat slowly, stirring, until slightly thickened. Simmer, uncovered, over lowest heat 5 minutes. Meanwhile, beat egg white and sugar until soft peaks form; set aside. Mix a little soup into yolks, return to pan, and heat, stirring, 1–2 minutes; do not boil. Taste for sugar and add more if needed. Remove lemon rind and cinnamon stick.

Lift pan off burner, drop egg white onto soup by teaspoonfuls, and let stand undisturbed 5 minutes. To serve, carefully lift out 4–5 snow eggs with a slotted spoon and set aside so you can get a soup ladle into pan without breaking any eggs. Ladle soup into hot bowls, float 2–3 snow eggs in each, and dust lightly with cinnamon sugar. Also good served cold. About 230 calories for each of 4 servings, 155 for each of 6.

BEER SOUP (ØLLEBRØD)

Beer soup, or *Øllebrød* (ale and bread), as the Danes call it, is not often sampled by tourists because it's more often served at home than in restaurants.
Makes 4 servings

4 slices dark Danish rye bread or
  pumpernickel
1 (12-ounce) bottle Danish or German
  dark ale or malt beer
6–8 tablespoons sugar
2 teaspoons lemon juice
Heavy cream

Break bread into small pieces and mix with beer. Cover and chill at least 4 hours or overnight; transfer to a saucepan and heat over moderately low heat, stirring constantly, 5–10 minutes until the consistency of applesauce. Press through a fine sieve or purée in an electric blender at low speed. Return to pan and bring to serving temperature. Mix in 6 tablespoons sugar and the lemon juice; taste for sweetness, and add more sugar if desired. Serve piping hot with plenty of cream poured over each serving. About 180–200 calories per serving, depending on amount of sugar used. Add 50 calories per serving for each tablespoon of heavy cream topping used.

Soup Dumplings, Garnishes, and Trimmings

Note: For additional dumpling recipes, also recipes for plain and flavored croutons, see the chapter on breads.

¢ VIENNESE SOUP "PEAS"

An unusual soup garnish that can be made ahead of time.
Makes about 1 cup, enough to garnish 8 soup servings

½ cup sifted flour
1 teaspoon salt
1 egg, lightly beaten
¼ cup milk
Shortening or cooking oil for deep fat
  frying

Mix flour, salt, egg, and milk and beat until smooth. Heat shortening in a deep fat fryer over high heat until deep fat thermometer registers 375° F. Drizzle batter from the end of a teaspoon into hot fat to form small "peas" and fry 30–40 seconds until golden. Scoop out with a slotted spoon and drain on paper toweling. Fry only a few "peas" at a time so you don't crowd pan. Serve sprinkled on top of any soup. These may be made ahead, stored airtight, then reheated. Simply spread out on a baking sheet, set uncovered in a 400° F. oven, and let warm 4–5 minutes. About 60 calories for each of 8 servings.

ROYALE CUSTARD

Makes enough to garnish 6 soup servings

1 egg plus 2 egg yolks, lightly beaten
½ cup beef consommé, chicken broth,
  or milk
⅛ teaspoon salt
Pinch cayenne pepper

Preheat oven to 325° F. Mix all ingredients and pour into a well-buttered, shallow baking dish or pie plate 6″–7″ in diameter. (*Note:* Custard should be about ½″ deep.) Set dish on a rack in a large, shallow baking pan, pour in hot water to a depth of ½″, and bake, uncovered, 25 minutes or until a knife inserted midway between rim and center comes out clean. Lift custard from water bath and cool upright in its baking dish on a wire rack. Cut in small cubes or diamonds or into fancy shapes with truffle cutters. Float in consommé or other clear soup as a garnish, allowing 3–4 cubes or cutouts per serving. About

45 calories per serving made with milk, 40 made with chicken broth and 38 made with beef broth.

VARIATIONS:

Indian Royale Custard: Prepare custard using chicken broth; whisk in ½ teaspoon curry powder, then bake as directed. The same calorie counts as royale custard.

Vegetable Royale Custard: Prepare custard with chicken broth or milk, smooth in 2 tablespoons puréed cooked spinach, green peas, tomatoes, or asparagus and bake as directed. Add about 1 calorie per serving to above counts for vegetable royale custard made with spinach or asparagus, 2 calories per serving for that made with tomatoes, and 3 calories per serving for that made with green peas.

MARROW DUMPLINGS

Makes 2 dozen

¼ cup uncooked beef marrow, scraped from marrowbones (at room temperature)
½ cup cracker meal or crumbs
1 tablespoon minced parsley
¾ teaspoon salt
½ teaspoon grated lemon rind
⅛ teaspoon pepper
2 eggs, lightly beaten

Cream marrow until smooth, blend in remaining ingredients, mix well, and let stand 10 minutes. Shape into 1″ balls. Drop into just boiling soup or stew and simmer, uncovered, 4–5 minutes. Do not cook more than 1 layer of dumplings at a time. Serve in soup or with stew, allowing 3–4 dumplings per serving. About 30 calories per dumpling.

¢ FARINA DUMPLINGS

Good in any clear meat or vegetable soup.
Makes 2 dozen

1 cup milk
¼ cup uncooked farina or cream of wheat
1 egg, lightly beaten
1 tablespoon butter or margarine
½ teaspoon salt
⅛ teaspoon white pepper

Heat milk almost to boiling over moderate heat, stir in farina and heat, stirring constantly, 2–3 minutes until thick. Off heat, beat in remaining ingredients. Cool to room temperature. Drop by ½ teaspoon into 2–3 quarts *just* boiling soup, cover, and simmer 4–5 minutes. Do not cook more than one layer of dumplings at a time; remove first batch with a slotted spoon and keep warm while you cook the rest. Serve 3–4 dumplings in each bowl of soup. About 20 calories per dumpling.

LIVER DUMPLINGS

Makes 2 dozen

¼ pound calf, beef, or lamb liver, sliced ¼″–½″ thick
½ cup water
1 egg, lightly beaten
1½ cups soft white bread crumbs
2 tablespoons light cream
¾ teaspoon salt
⅛ teaspoon pepper
¼ teaspoon marjoram or thyme
1 teaspoon minced parsley
¼ cup minced yellow onion
½ clove garlic, peeled and crushed (optional)
1 tablespoon butter or margarine

Simmer liver, uncovered, in water 5 minutes; drain and put through finest blade of a meat grinder. Mix in egg, crumbs, cream, salt, pepper, marjoram, and parsley. Stir-fry onion and, if you like, garlic in butter 3–5 minutes over moderate heat until limp; stir into liver. Drop mixture by ½ teaspoonfuls and cook, uncovered, a few dumplings at a time, in 2–3 quarts just boiling clear meat or vegetable soup 3–4 minutes. Lift dumplings out with a slotted spoon and keep warm while you cook the rest. Serve a few dumplings in each bowl of soup. About 25 calories per dumpling.

¢ POTATO DUMPLINGS

Makes 2 dozen small soup dumplings,
1 dozen stew dumplings

3 medium-size potatoes, boiled in their
  skins, drained, and peeled
1 egg, lightly beaten
⅓ cup sifted flour
1½ teaspoons salt
⅛ teaspoon white pepper
¼ teaspoon nutmeg (optional)
½ cup croutons

Return potatoes to their pan and dry
uncovered, 1–2 minutes over lowest
heat; mash or rice. Beat in all remaining
ingredients except croutons. Shape into
1″ or 2″ balls, push a crouton into
center of each 1″ ball, 2–3 into larger
balls. Drop into just boiling soup or stew
and cook uncovered, allowing 5–7
minutes for the 1″ balls and 10–12 for
the 2″ balls. (*Note:* Don't crowd
dumplings; they should be in a single
layer, so cook half at a time if
necessary.) Use the 1″ dumplings to
garnish soup, the 2″ for stew. About
25 calories for each soup dumpling, 50
calories for each stew dumpling.

¢ MATZO BALLS

Matzo meal can be bought in kosher
groceries and delicatessens.
Makes 1½ dozen

2 eggs, lightly beaten
½ cup matzo meal
1 teaspoon salt
¼ teaspoon ginger, cinnamon, or nutmeg
  (optional)
3 tablespoons cold water

Mix all ingredients, cover, and refrigerate ½ hour. Drop by rounded teaspoonfuls on top of just boiling chicken broth
or other clear soup, cover, and cook at
a slow boil 15–20 minutes. Serve at
once. About 20 calories per matzo ball.

VARIATIONS:

Mary's Matzo Balls: Reduce water to
2 tablespoons and add 2 minced, sautéed
chicken livers and 2 teaspoons minced
parsley to ingredients called for. Butter
hands, roll into 1″ balls, then cook as
directed. About 30 calories per ball.

Precooked Matzo Balls: Prepare matzo
ball mixture, then cook as directed in
boiling salted water instead of soup
(for this amount you'll need about 3
quarts water and 2 tablespoons salt).
Lift from salted water with a slotted
spoon and add 2–3 matzo balls to each
bowl of chicken broth or clear soup.
Same calorie count as matzo balls.

KREPLACH

These meat-filled egg noodles, served in
clear soups, are a Jewish favorite. The
noodle dough should be rolled slightly
thicker than for ribbon noodles so the
filling won't poke through.
Makes about 1½ dozen

Egg Noodle Dough:
¾ cup sifted flour
½ teaspoon salt
1 egg, lightly beaten

Filling:
½ cup cooked minced chicken, chicken
  livers, or beef
1 tablespoon chicken or beef broth
1 teaspoon grated onion
½ teaspoon salt
⅛ teaspoon pepper

Make dough first: Sift flour with salt,
add egg, and mix with a fork until
mixture holds together. Knead on a
lightly floured board 2–3 minutes until
satiny. Cover and let rest 30 minutes.
Roll thin into a square about 12″, then
cut in 2½″ squares. Mix filling ingredients and drop about ½ teaspoonful on
the center of each noodle square.
Dampen dough edges with cold water,
fold noodle over to form a triangle, then
press edges together with tines of a fork.
Let *kreplach* stand uncovered on a
lightly floured surface 20 minutes; turn
and let stand 20 minutes longer. Cook,
uncovered, at a slow boil 10–15 minutes
in chicken broth, clear soup, or salted
water (for this amount you'll need 3–4
quarts; if using water, add 2 tablespoons
salt). Serve kreplach in chicken or beef
broth or other clear soup, allowing 2–3
per bowl. About 35 calories each.

CHAPTER 8

MEAT

Meat always gets star billing. It's the dish around which all others are planned, the one for which wines are chosen, the one that sets the tone of a meal. It's the most expensive part of our diet, the most universally well liked, the most versatile, and certainly one of the most nutritious. Meat thus deserves a worthy role and the best possible supporting cast. It needs skillful and imaginative handling, preferential treatment sometimes, and kid glove care always.

HOW TO FIND QUALITY IN MEAT

Your guarantee of wholesomeness is the federal inspector's seal, a round purple stamp about the size of a silver dollar on beef, somewhat smaller on veal, lamb,

and pork. All meat entered in interstate commerce must be federally inspected and passed before it can be sold. This means that the animals have been found free of disease and that the slaughterhouse handling them has met U. S. Department of Agriculture sanitation standards. About 80 per cent of the meat sold in this country is federally inspected; most of the remaining 20 per cent is state or city inspected.

Look next for the *grade or degree of excellence*. Meat may be graded federally (these grades vary from animal to animal and will be discussed separately under Beef, Veal, Lamb, and Pork), or it may be graded by a packing house. The equivalent of U. S. Prime or Choice, for example, might be labeled Premium by one packer and Star, Puritan, or Certified by others. Packer grading is more often done with ham than other meats.

About Aging

Only beef, lamb, and mutton ribs and loins of high quality are aged, the purpose being to make them as flavorful and tender as possible. They may be *dry aged* (held 3 to 6 weeks at low temperature and humidity), *fast aged* (held 2 days or less at 70° F. and rather high humidity), or *vacuum packaged* (covered with a moisture-vaporproof film that stays on from packer to buyer). Most dry-aged and vacuum-packaged meat goes to hotels and restaurants; what we buy is usually fast aged or unaged—except in transit from slaughterhouse to our own homes (considerable tenderizing takes place during this period of 6 to 10 days). Because many people prefer more well-aged meat, especially beef, butchers often age it in their own coolers.

The Food and Calorie Value of Meat

All meat is a high quality protein food supplying substantial amounts of B vitamins, iron, and phosphorous; most is moderate or moderately high in calories, but, considering its high nutritive value, is a wise choice for calorie counters. Food and calorie values of meat vary considerably from animal to animal, also from cut to cut.

The Cuts of Meat

All cuts can be fitted into two categories: *the tender* and the *less tender*. Learning which are which isn't difficult once you remember that exercise and age are what toughen meat. The most frequently exercised parts of the animal, therefore —legs, neck, shoulder, rump, flank— will be far tougher than the seldom exercised rib and loin; old cows will be more sinewy than pampered young heifers or steers. Diagrams of the various cuts appear in the sections on Beef, Veal, Lamb, and Pork, as well as rules and recipes for preparing them.

How to Make the Most of Your Meat Dollar

– Learn the cuts of meat and cook them properly. Why buy relatively expensive top round for stew when neck, shank, and chuck are not only cheaper but better?
– Buy in quantity, by the side if you have a freezer. If not, buy large cuts and divide them up as follows (below):
– Make the most of leftovers (see suggestions in each of the meat sections).
– Take advantage of supermarket specials.
– Steer clear of luxury cuts—steaks, chops, rib roasts—and concentrate upon less expensive pot roasts, Swiss steaks, shanks, and stews.

Original Cut	First Meal	Second Meal
10″ Beef rib roast	Rib roast	Deviled Short Ribs
Whole ham	Ham steak	Roast ham
Square shoulder of lamb	Blade chops	Shoulder roast

The Ways of Tenderizing Meat

Down the centuries cooks have devised ingenious ways of softening up not-so-tender cuts both mechanically and chemically.

Mechanical tenderizing merely means breaking up tough meat fibers by *pounding, cubing, scoring, or grinding.*

Chemical tenderizing means softening tough fibers with an *enzyme, acid marinade, or moist heat cooking.* Using enzymes isn't as new as it may seem, because Latin American women have been tenderizing meat with papaya juice for ages (many modern tenderizers are simply crystalline forms of its enzyme, papain). The majority of today's tenderizers are the instant type, so read directions carefully before using. Marinating, on the other hand, isn't as effective a tenderizer as originally thought because the juices of the marinade hardly penetrate meat at all in contrast to papain. Far more effective is the moist heat cooking that follows marination.

Some Special Ways to Prepare Meat for Cooking

To Bard: To tie sheets or strips of fat around lean cuts so they won't dry out during cooking.

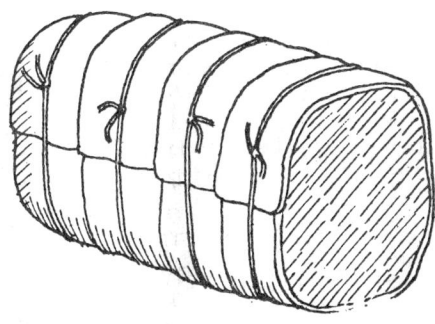

Commonly barded meats are whole beef tenderloin, filet steaks and tournedos;
lean veal roasts; venison and game birds; poultry. Suet and bacon are recommended for beef and veal; bacon for pheasant and chicken; fatback or salt pork for venison and wild game birds.
Note: Many butchers will do the barding for you.

To Bone: To remove bones (have butcher do it whenever possible). *Filleting* refers to boning small pieces like steaks and chops. (*Note:* Base cooking times on *boned* weight.)

To Butterfly: To cut small boneless chops horizontally through the center, cutting almost but not quite through so that they can be opened flat like a book.

To French: To remove meat from rib ends of lamb, veal, or pork chops or crown roasts and to garnish with paper frills or small fruits.

To Lard: To insert long strips of chilled fat (lardoons) into lean meats with a larding needle. If the cut is large, strips the length of it are drawn through the center with a long-bladed larding needle.

When cuts are small, short lardoons are drawn through the surface in a technique called *piquing*. Piquing needles are fairly small, not unlike yarn needles. Piquing can also be done without a needle: make small slits at intervals over surface of meat, tuck in small cubes of fat and, if you like, garlic slivers and herbs.

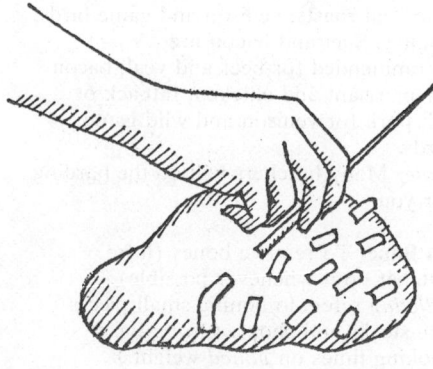

Piquing

Meats often larded: beef rump and round roasts; veal leg roasts; whole beef liver and heart. Good larding fats are fatback, salt pork, fat trimmed from pork loin or fresh ham. *Note:* Always chill fat well before larding—makes the going easier. To make salt pork less salty, blanch lardoons quickly in boiling water, drain, and chill.

To Shape (also known as **To Skewer and Tie**): To make meat as compact as possible by inserting small skewers and pulling together with cord. The purpose is to make meat cook as evenly as possible.

To Slash: To cut outer fat of steaks and chops at regular intervals so they won't curl as they cook.

To Trim: To cut excess fat from outer layer of steaks and chops; most are best with fat trimmed to a thickness of ¼″.

Should Meat Come to Room Temperature before Cooking?

Many home economists say not, but we think meat cooks more evenly, becomes more juicily tender if allowed to stand at room temperature about 2 hours before cooking. But there are exceptions: naturally thin cuts like flank steak, which are broiled only until rare (having them well chilled safeguards against overcooking); highly perishable meats such as hamburger, liver, kidneys, heart, and sweetbreads.

The Ways of Cooking Meat

What every cook hopes for is as succulent and tender a piece of meat as possible. Since naturally tender cuts cannot be made more tender by cooking (only less so), the object is to preserve every ounce of original tenderness. This is best done (with a few exceptions, which will be discussed as we come to them) by *dry heat cooking*. The less tender cuts, on the other hand, can be made more tender if cooked by *moist heat*. Here are the basic methods of each (with variations).

Dry Heat Cooking:

Roasting: There are two schools of thought about roasting meat. American cooking experts generally recommend a continuous low heat (300–25° F.) to reduce shrinkage and sputtering and to produce exquisitely juicy, evenly cooked roasts; classically trained chefs favor searing to brown both the roast and the pan juices. We prefer the low heat method but include both so you can take your pick. Whichever you use, place meat on a rack in a shallow roasting pan (so that it doesn't stew in its own juice); do not cover, do not baste (roast fat side up so drippings run down over meat), and do not add any liquid. Recommended for all large tender cuts of beef, veal, lamb, pork, and ham.

VARIATIONS:

Spit Roasting: Meat turned on a spit in an oven or rotisserie or over a charcoal fire will generally take about 5 minutes less per pound than oven-roasted meat. To cook evenly, the meat must turn smoothly throughout cooking, which means that it must be perfectly balanced at all times. Best ways to ensure balance: choose blocky, compact cuts or, if spitting more than one piece of meat, counterbalance as needed with extra metal skewers. Despite all precautions, a roast may become unbalanced during cooking because it loses weight—unevenly—via drippings;

keep an eye on the spit and rebalance roast if necessary. Newest rotisseries are equipped with "compensators" that adjust the spit to a roast's changing weight and keep it turning smoothly. Rotisseries, incidentally, cook at varying speeds, so it's wise to consult the manufacturer's timetable. Also read his directions before buying a big roast— if too big, it won't stay balanced.

Smoke Roasting: This centuries-old Chinese way of cooking meat is becoming increasingly popular. Properly done, it requires special equipment so that the meat hangs behind and above the fire and cooks in a cloud of smoke. (Inquire in local gourmet or patio shops about Chinese smoke ovens or about directions for building your own L-shaped smoke oven.) Without special equipment you can still give steaks and roasts a deliciously smoky flavor by tossing packaged aromatic wood chips on a charcoal fire or, if these are unavailable, green hardwood prunings, water-soaked shavings or sawdust (1 hour is usually long enough for the soaking). *Caution:* Never use pine or other resinous woods that will make the meat taste of turpentine.

Pit Roasting: When French explorers saw American Indians roasting whole deer and buffalo in earthen pits, they called it *barbe à queue,* meaning that the animals were cooked from "beard to tail." We now use their phrase to describe all meat cooked in pits, both open and closed. Most pit barbecuing is too complicated to try in your own back yard, so for anything grander than a clambake, hire a professional. Best bets for back-yard barbecues: beef rump or pork loin.

Broiling: Cooking in a broiler, 2″–5″ from the heat (depending on thickness of cut). The meat should be placed on a rack in a broiler pan, browned on one side, turned with tongs (so savory juices aren't lost), and browned on the other side. Do not salt *until after browning*— salt draws moisture to the surface of the meat and prevents browning. Recommended for tender beef and ham steaks, lamb chops, ground beef and lamb, but not for pork or veal chops, no matter how tender. Pork must always be cooked until well done, and at broiling temperature it may toughen and dry. Veal, being lean and delicate, also tends to dry out. Both should be braised.

VARIATIONS:

Charcoal Broiling (Grilling): Browning over glowing coals instead of under a broiler. Cooking times vary considerably, depending on amount of wind and outdoor temperature.

Campfire Broiling: Essentially the same as charcoal broiling except that the fuel is wood and the fire a bit cooler.

Hibachi Broiling: This is charcoal broiling on a doll's scale (most hibachis, whether round or square, measure only 10″–16″ across). But these sturdy little Japanese braziers put out a lot of heat and are perfect for grilling chops, small steaks, and such hors d'oeuvre as Teriyaki and Rumaki. Use long bamboo skewers, thoroughly water-soaked so that they won't burn.

Panbroiling: Cooking, uncovered, in a heavy skillet over moderate to moderately high heat without any fat or liquid (if meat is especially lean, lightly oil or salt skillet to prevent sticking). Cook until nicely browned on both sides and at desired doneness, turning often with tongs. Pour off drippings as they collect (this is one of the principal differences between panbroiling and frying). With the exception of extra-large steaks that are too unwieldy for skillet cooking, any cuts suitable for broiling can be panbroiled. *Browning Tips:* To brown well, meat must be dry on the surface; wipe with a damp cloth, if necessary, and do not salt until after cooking.

Frying: There are two methods:

Panfrying (Sautéing): The technique is virtually the same as for panbroiling *except* that the meat is cooked in a small amount of fat. Recommended for lean veal and lamb chops, for cube steaks and lean ground meat patties.

Deep Fat Frying: Cooking by immersing in very hot fat (usually 300–80° F. on a deep fat thermometer). For best results, use a deep fat fryer with wire basket. Recommended for small breaded cuts or croquettes.

Moist Heat Cooking:

Braising: Whether used for pot roasts, Swiss steaks, or fricassees, the technique is the same. Meat is browned in a heavy skillet or kettle in a little fat, then covered and simmered until tender over low heat or in a slow oven with a small amount of liquid (the fat is usually poured off after browning). Recommended for pork and veal chops, also for marginally tender steaks and roasts.

Cooking in Liquid (Stewing): Here's the way to tenderize the toughest cuts. Most of them (corned beef and smoked pork excepted) will taste better if browned in a little fat before being covered with liquid (water, stock, wine, or a combination) and left to simmer slowly in a covered kettle until fork tender. As with braising, the simmering can be done on top of the stove or in the oven.

New Ways to Cook Meat

Infrared Cooking: Many of the modern, portable, plug-in broilers, roasters, and rotisseries cook by infrared heat, which produces richly browned, extra-juicy steaks, chops, and roasts a shade quicker than conventional ovens. For greatest efficiency, bring meat to room temperature before cooking and preheat unit thoroughly. Each of these units operates somewhat differently, so follow the manufacturer's directions.

"Radar" or Microwave Cooking: Heralded as the ovens of tomorrow, these units cook with supersonic speed by generating heat inside the food itself (oven walls, racks, and cooking utensils all remain cool). When the first models appeared some twenty-five years ago, they cost thousands of dollars; today they cost only a little more than conventional ovens. New models have built-in electric units that brown meat as it cooks; originally, though foods cooked jet-quick, they came from the oven unbrowned and unappetizing.

About Cooking Frozen Meat

To defrost or not to defrost? It really doesn't make any difference. The advantage of defrosting is that the meat will cook more quickly; the advantage of not defrosting is that, if plans change and the meat cannot be cooked on schedule, all is not lost (thawed frozen meat should not be refrozen).

How to Defrost: Leave meat in its wrapper and set it in the refrigerator or on the counter top (a large roast will take 4–7 hours per pound to defrost in the refrigerator, roughly half that at room temperature; a steak 1″ thick will take 12–14 hours to thaw in the refrigerator, 3–4 hours at room temperature). Never defrost meat in warm water unless it is to be cooked in liquid. Once defrosted, meat can be cooked exactly like fresh meat.

How to Cook Solidly Frozen Meat:

Roasts: Unwrap, place on a rack in a shallow roasting pan, and begin roasting just as you would a fresh roast. When meat has partially thawed, remove from oven and insert meat thermometer in center of roast, not touching bone. Return to oven and continue roasting to desired temperature. *Note:* Solidly frozen roasts will take 1½–2 times as long to cook as the fresh.

Steaks, Chops, and Hamburgers:

To Broil: Place 1″–2″ farther away from heat than recommended for fresh meat and increase total cooking time 1½–2 times.

To Charcoal-Broil: Cook 5″–6″ above moderately hot coals, turning often, about ½ again as long as you would fresh meat.

To Panbroil or Panfry: Brown both sides quickly in a very hot skillet before surface has a chance to thaw (once thawing starts and juices run out, the meat will not brown). Reduce heat to moderately low and cook as you would fresh meat, but turning oftener. Cook 1½–2 times as long.

Meat Loaves: Cook exactly like fresh loaves but 1½–2 times as long. If loaf contains raw pork, insert meat thermometer when loaf is soft enough to do so and continue cooking to 185° F.

Meats to Be Breaded: Thaw just until surface is soft so that breading will stick; then proceed as for fresh meat, increasing cooking time by 1½–2.

Commercially Frozen Meat: Follow package directions.

About Pressure Cooking Meat

Meat cooked under pressure loses flavor, succulence, and attractiveness, so pressure-cook only when absolutely necessary to save time and then only for pot roasts or Swiss steaks that aren't apt to fall apart. Techniques vary from cooker to cooker, so follow the manufacturer's directions. In general, meat will suffer less if cooked at 10 pounds pressure than at 15.

About Reheating Meat

Roasts, the most often leftover cuts, are also the most difficult to rehabilitate. Ideally, they should be transformed into entirely new dishes (see leftover recipes in beef, veal, lamb, and pork sections), but if such is not possible, any of these simple techniques will make warmed-over meat presentable:
– Slice very thin, place on heated plates, and top with hot gravy or sauce.

– Preheat oven to 300° F. Place roast on a rack in a shallow roasting pan and set, uncovered, on upper rack; place a pan of water underneath and heat 25–30 minutes.
– Preheat oven to 350° F. Slice meat thin, layer into a shallow, ungreased casserole with just enough gravy, pan juices, or sauce to cover, cover with foil, and heat 20 minutes. If you prefer, heat slices in gravy, juices, or sauce in a covered skillet about 5 minutes over moderately low heat.

About Meat Stocks

Many of the world's great recipes depend upon stocks, gentle brews of bones, meat trimmings, herbs, and vegetables. Some stocks are simple, others elaborate; some delicate, others concentrated; some dark, some light. Almost all can simmer unattended on the back of the stove. For recipes, see the chapter on soups.

How to Render Fat

Clean, sweet lard (rendered pork fat) and suet (beef kidney fat) are excellent for browning meats and vegetables because they're economical and impart a mellow, meaty flavor. Lard is also such a superior pastry fat that many cooks will use no other.

Suitable Fats to Render: Beef kidney fat; pork kidney fat, clear plate, and fatback.

General preparation: Cut fat into strips 1″ wide, remove any skin, then cut in 1″ cubes. Trim out any meat particles (these burn quickly and can give rendered fat an acrid flavor). Leave fat as cubes or put through coarse blade of meat grinder.

Stove-Top Method: Place prepared fat in a large, heavy skillet and add a little cold water to keep fat from browning before it melts (½ cup should be sufficient for 1–2 pounds fat). Heat uncovered over moderately low heat, stirring frequently, until all fat is melted, about 10 minutes. If you are rendering pork fat, the *cracklings* (cellular membranes in which the fat was held) will soon crispen and brown and rise to the surface. Skim them off and press out any remaining lard (save cracklings for Crackling Bread; they're also good to munch like potato chips). Strain melted fat through a double thickness of cheesecloth and cool until firm. For especially fine grain, cover and chill quickly in the refrigerator. Spoon solidified fat into small crocks or glass jars, cover with lids, and store in a cool, dry, dark, well-ventilated place. Top quality lard or suet, properly stored, should keep 6–12 months.

Oven Method: Preheat oven to 250° F. Spread prepared fat over the bottom of a large, shallow pan, set uncovered in oven and let try out (melt), stirring occasionally. Skim off any cracklings, then strain, cool, and store as above.

To Clarify Rendered Fat: Place prepared fat in a large, heavy saucepan, add boiling water to cover, then boil slowly, uncovered, 10–15 minutes, stirring frequently. Cool 10 minutes, strain through several thicknesses of cheesecloth, cool, and chill without disturbing; lift off clear top layer of fat; discard liquid underneath and scrape off and discard sediment and semiliquid layer on bottom of fat. Store fat in a cool, dry, dark, airy spot.

To Clarify Meat Drippings: Let drippings solidify, then chop coarsely, place in a heavy saucepan with water to cover, and proceed as directed for clarifying rendered fat.

How to Use Meat Thermometers

Meat thermometers, unfortunately, have not kept abreast of America's changing tastes. Rare roast beef, if you go by the thermometer, has an internal temperature of 140° F. Not so. To rare

beef enthusiasts, that is medium rare, perhaps even medium. Nearer the mark is 125° F. Readings for lamb are high, too. According to the thermometer, lamb should be cooked to 170° F., well done, indeed, and a disappointment to those who like it juicily pink (130–35° F.). A few thermometers have readings as low as 130° F.; for most 140° F. is the cutoff point. If you are especially fond of very rare meat, try to obtain the new spot-check thermometer (inserted into meat only as it approaches doneness) or the type of thermometer used by food researchers with a 0–220° F. scale (Griffith Labs of Rahway, New Jersey, make them; or inquire through a local gourmet shop or home economics department about obtaining one).

There are two basic types of meat thermometers: the spring-type and the mercury type, the latter preferred by some cooks because of its more detailed scale. Both are used the same way:

For Oven Roasting:
– Hold thermometer against side of meat so you can gauge location of bone, fat, and gristle.
– Insert thermometer in center of largest lean muscle, not touching bone, fat, or gristle.

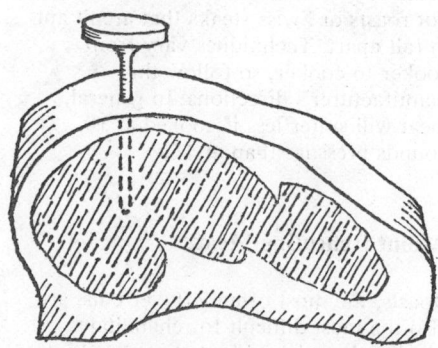

Place meat in oven with scale facing door so that you can read temperatures at a glance.

For Spit Roasting:
– Insert thermometer into end of cut and parallel to spit so that it touches neither

bone nor spit. If necessary, adjust angle slightly so thermometer will clear grill, hood, or oven walls as spit turns.

– When stopping rotisserie, see that thermometer comes to rest as far from heat as possible; otherwise it may break.

BEEF

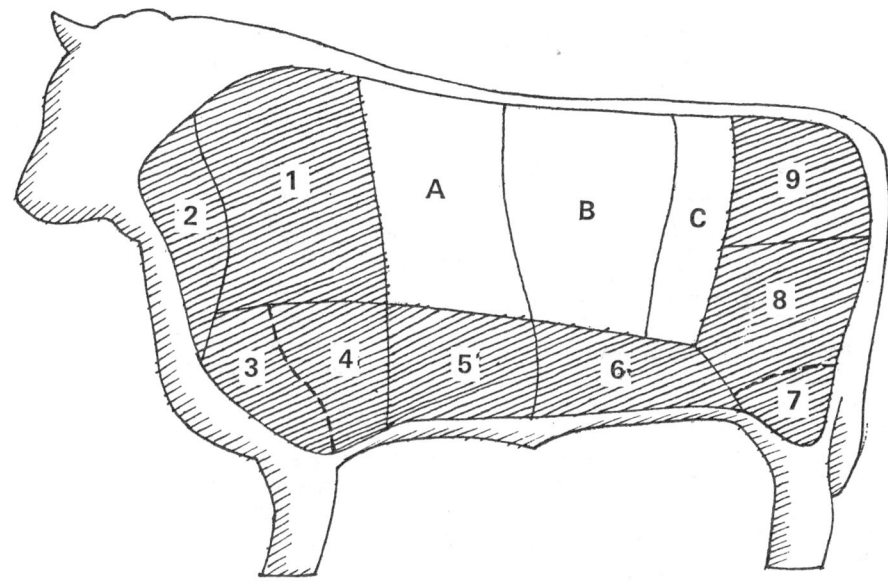

Note: Unshaded parts are the tender cuts. Shaded parts are not-so-tender.

THE TENDER CUTS:
  A. Rib
       Roasts (rib, rib eye, or Delmonico)
       Steaks (rib, rib eye, or Delmonico)
  B. Loin
       Steaks (club, T-bone, porterhouse)
       Tenderloin
  c. Sirloin
       Sirloin steaks

THE NOT-SO-TENDER CUTS:
  1. Chuck (shoulder)
       Pot roasts
       Swiss-style steaks (blade, arm)
       Stew beef
       Ground beef
  2. Neck
       Stew beef

3. Shank
     Stew beef
     Shank crosscuts
4. Brisket
     Corned beef
5. Plate
     Short ribs
     Stew beef
     Ground beef
6. Flank
     Flank steak
     London broil
7. Heel of Round
     Stew beef
8. Round
     Pot roasts
     Steaks (top, eye, and bottom round)
     Ground beef
9. Rump
     Pot roasts

T-bones sizzling on a back-yard grill . . .
hamburgers with all the trimmings . . .
prime ribs bathed in their own natural
juices—they're so American it's difficult
to believe cattle are not native to
America. The first arrived in Florida
with the Spaniards about four hundred
years ago, rangy beasts of burden to the
settlers, but to Indians a refreshing
change from game. In a way, Indians
were responsible for the birth of
America's beef industry because they
moved these cattle across the Mississippi
into the grasslands beyond, where they
thrived. Strangely, white men preferred
pork and chicken to beef and may
never have prized beef if Civil War
shortages hadn't driven them to eat it.
Suddenly longhorns were in demand,
the rush was on, and with it the hell-for-
leather days of cowboys and cattle
barons and hundred-mile drives to
market. Soon there were railroads, and
beef, no longer driven to market, grew
fat and lazy and succulent and tender.
Ranchers quickly learned that penned
steers were tenderer still and those fed
corn and grain the most flavorful.
Today beef production is highly
scientific. And beef, itself, is our No. 1
meat.

How to Recognize Quality in Beef

Look first for the *federal inspector's
round purple stamp* (see discussion at
beginning of this chapter), second for
grade, which is based on *conformation*
(proportion of meat to bone), *quality*
(marbling or distribution of fat in lean,
color and texture of lean, fat and bone)
and *cutability* (amount of usable meat).
If beef has been graded by a federal
agent, you will see his stamp, a series
of shield-shaped purple emblems
running the length of the carcass (the
purple dye is harmless):

U.S. Prime: The finest young beef,
well marbled and blanketed with a
creamy layer of fat. Little prime beef
reaches the supermarket—it's the grand
champion steer or heifer bought by
prestige butchers, hotels, and restaurants.

U.S. Choice: Finely grained, well-
marbled beef just a shade under prime.
Available at good markets across the
country.

U.S. Good: The most widely available
grade. This meat hasn't quite the well-
marbled look of higher grades, but
many people prefer its somewhat
chewier texture.

U.S. Standard: Here's an economical,
all-purpose beef. Its steaks and roasts,
though not the juiciest, are quite
acceptable. The meat is not particularly
well marbled, and the outer fat covering
is apt to be skimpy.

The four lowest grades—*U.S.
Commercial, Utility, Canner, and
Cutter*—are of little concern here
because they're rarely sold in retail
stores. Packers use them for making
sausages, frankfurters, and other process
meats.

*How to Tell Quality When the Grade
Doesn't Show on the Cut:* Tender, young
beef will be bright cherry red, the fat
creamy white and the chine (backbone)
spongy and red. Older beef will be
darker red, its fat yellowish and bones
flinty. An orange cast to the fat suggests
the animal was range fed and that its
meat may be tough.

Note: When first cut, beef will be dark
purple-brown. This doesn't mean it's
spoiled, old, or tough, merely that it
hasn't been exposed to the air (oxygen
gives beef its vivid red color).

About Tendered Beef

By injecting live animals with an enzyme
called papain, meat packers cannot
only assure tenderness of roasts and
steaks, but they can also make certain
cuts of round, rump, and chuck so
tender they can be broiled or roasted.
Such beef is sold as *"tendered beef"* and
is accompanied by cooking instructions.
Follow them because tendered beef
usually cooks more quickly than
untendered beef.

ROAST BEEF

The Top Tender Cuts

Standing Ribs: There are 3 different rib roasts, named for the part of the rib from which they come:

First-Rib Roast (5–8 pounds): Also sometimes called the *11th-and-12th-rib roast,* this cut is from the loin end of the rib. It's the most desirable and expensive rib roast because of its large, meaty center muscle, called the rib eye.

Center-Rib Roast (5–8 pounds): The mid-rib cut with a slightly smaller eye and slightly lower cost.

Sixth-and-Seventh-Rib Roast (5–8 pounds): From the chuck or shoulder end of the rib, this roast may not be so tender as the first two.

3 Styles for Standing Ribs: Each rib roast can be cut 3 ways:

10″ Standing Rib: The ribs are 10″ long, the backbone still intact. There's little advantage in having such long ribs because they provide almost no meat. Better to have them cut off and to cook as short ribs.

7″ Standing Rib: Probably the best style; 3″ of ribs have been sawed off and the backbone removed.

6″ Standing Rib: The newest look in rib roasts, a bit too "sawed off," perhaps, to be graceful, but a good choice for spit roasting because it is easy to balance on the spit.

Boned and Rolled Rib Roast (4–6 pounds): All rib roasts can be boned and rolled; they are easier to carve than standing ribs but take longer to cook. Some say they lack the rich, beefy flavor of standing ribs.

Rib Eye or Delmonico Roast (3–6 pounds): The boneless, meaty rib eye.

Whole Tenderloin or Filet (see Tenderloin).

Sirloin (8–12 pounds): The granddaddy of roasts adored by the English. Few American butchers will sell sirloin as roast because it's much more in demand as steak. *Boneless sirloin,* however, is becoming more and more popular, particularly in the Northeast.

Marginally Tender Roasts

These less expensive cuts are "iffy" roasts —tender enough to roast *if* from prime, choice, or tendered beef. When in doubt about them, braise.

Sirloin Tip (3–5 pounds): A chunky, lean, triangular cut.

Standing or Rolled Rump (4–7 pounds): Often underrated, this blocky, hind-quarter cut has unusually good flavor.

Top Round (3–6 pounds): Though usually reserved for steaks, top round can be left whole and roasted. It's a single, large lean muscle, the tenderest one of the round.

Eye Round (2½–5 pounds): Probably the "iffiest" cut of all. Eye round looks like whole tenderloin, but there the resemblance ends; it will be tender enough to roast only if of tiptop quality.

How to Roast Beef

Suitable Cuts: Standing Rib, Boned and Rolled Rib, Rib Eye, Sirloin and, if top quality, Sirloin Tip, Standing and Rolled Rump, Top and Eye Round. Bear in mind that boneless roasts will take about 10 minutes per pound longer to cook than bone-in roasts; also that small roasts take proportionately longer to cook than large roasts.

Amount Needed: The bigger the roast, the better it will be. Standing ribs should weigh at least 5 pounds and be 2 ribs wide; boned and rolled ribs should be no less than 4 pounds. To figure number of servings, allow ⅓–½ pound boneless roast per person; ¾ pound bone-in roast.

General Preparation for Cooking: Let roast stand at room temperature 1½–2 hours if possible. Season, if you like, with salt and pepper (salt penetrates only ¼″, so it makes little difference whether a roast is salted before or after cooking). For extra savor, rub roast with a cut clove of garlic or suitable herb (see Sauces, Gravies, and Seasonings for Roast Beef). Some cooks also like to flour a roast and start it at a high temperature to help seal in juices and give it a nice brown crust, but tests have shown it's wasted effort as far as sealing in the juices is concerned.

Continuous Low Heat Method: Preheat oven to 300° F. Place roast fat side up in a large, shallow roasting pan; all but standing ribs should be put on a rack so they're kept out of the drippings (with standing ribs, the ribs themselves act as a rack). Insert meat thermometer in lean in center of roast, not touching bone. Do not cover roast; do not add liquid to pan; do not baste roast as it cooks. Using times and temperatures in Roast Beef Chart as a guide, roast to desired degree of doneness. Transfer roast to heated platter, let "rest," if you like, then serve Au Jus or with Pan Gravy.

Searing Method: Preheat oven to 450° F. Insert meat thermometer and place in pan as for low heat method. Roast, uncovered, 25 minutes, reduce heat to 300° F. (leaving oven door open will quickly bring temperature down), and continue roasting to desired doneness. Bone-in roasts will take about 16 minutes per pound for rare (125–30° F.), 18 for medium rare (140–45° F.), 20–22 for medium (155–60° F.), and 25–27 for well done (165–70° F.); boneless roasts will require 8–10 minutes longer per pound for each degree of doneness. Transfer roast to heated platter, garnish, and serve.

How to Spit-Roast Beef

Always make sure a roast *stays* balanced and turns evenly throughout cooking. If you plan to let roast "rest" 15–20 minutes before serving, remove from spit when thermometer is 5–10° below desired doneness.

Best Cuts: A 6″ or 7″ Standing Rib or a Boned and Rolled Rib.

Amount Needed: For best results, the

standing rib should weigh 5–8 pounds, the boned and rolled rib 4–6.

General Preparation for Cooking: If using the standing rib, have butcher remove backbone. Let roast stand at room temperature 1½–2 hours if possible. Season or not, as you like.

In Rotisserie or Oven: Preheat unit. Insert spit on bias so meat is balanced; tighten holding forks. Insert meat thermometer in center of largest lean muscle, touching neither bone nor the spit. Attach spit to rotisserie and roast to desired doneness. Standing ribs will take 12–14 minutes per pound for rare (125–30° F.), 15–17 for medium rare (140–45° F.), 18–20 for medium (155–60° F.), and 21–23 for well done (165–70° F.). Boned and rolled roasts will take about 10 minutes longer per pound for each degree of doneness.

Over Charcoal: Prepare a moderately hot charcoal fire.* Balance roast on spit as above and insert thermometer. Adjust fire bed height so coals are 6″ from spit, then roast to desired doneness, using approximately same times as for rotisserie. Watch thermometer closely— it's the truest indicator of doneness.

VARIATION:

Spit-Barbecued Beef: Marinate roast in refrigerator 12–24 hours in 1 pint Barbecue Sauce for Beef, turning 2–3 times. Let come to room temperature in marinade, then spit-roast as above. During last ¾ hour of cooking, baste often with marinade. Serve with Barbecue Gravy for Beef.

ROAST BEEF CHART

American tastes are changing. Those who like rare roast beef like it *really* rare, about 125–30° F. on a meat thermometer, not 140° F., as many cookbooks recommend. To rare beef buffs, 140° F. is medium rare, perhaps even medium. It depends on one's definition of rare. If you like beef juicy and red (not pink), try taking it from the oven when the thermometer reads 120–

25° F. and letting it "rest" at room temperature 15–20 minutes before carving. Letting beef rest is good practice no matter how you like it cooked—the roast will be juicier, easier to carve. Because a roast will continue cooking as it rests, it should be brought from the oven when the thermometer is 5–10° below desired doneness.

About Using the Chart
– Times can only be approximate, since shape of cut, amount of fat and bone, the way the meat was aged, and internal temperature all affect roasting time. So does size; proportionately, large roasts

take less time to cook than small ones. Timetables, thus, are most useful in telling you when to put a roast in the oven so that you can gauge meal preparation time. For the truest test of doneness, use a meat thermometer.
– Times are for roasts that have stood at room temperature 1½–2 hours, then roasted at a constant low temperature (300° F.).
• To roast at 325° F. (the outer fat covering will be slightly crisper), allow about 2 minutes less per pound.
• For refrigerated roasts, allow 2–3 minutes more per pound.

Cut	Weight in Pounds	Approximate Minutes per Pound at 300° F.	Meat Thermometer Temperature
Standing Ribs			
Rare	5–8	17–19	125–30° F.
Medium rare	5–8	20–22	140–45° F.
Medium	5–8	23–25	155–60° F.
Well done	5–8	27–30	165–70° F.
Boned and rolled Rib roasts	4–6	Add about 8–10 minutes per pound to each of the times given for standing ribs —and keep a close eye on the meat thermometer.	
Sirloin			
Rare	8–12	16–20	125–30° F.
Medium rare	8–12	20–22	140–45° F.
Medium	8–12	23–25	155–60° F.
Well done	8–12	26–30	165–70° F.

Note: The following cuts should be roasted only if prime, choice, or "tendered." Some beef connoisseurs also feel that they are better cooked to medium or well done.

Cut	Weight in Pounds	Minutes per Pound	Meat Thermometer
Sirloin tip (a boneless roast)			
Rare	3–5	28–30	125–30° F.
Medium rare	3–5	30–33	140–45° F.
Medium	3–5	34–38	155–60° F.
Well done	3–5	40–45	165–70° F.
Standing rump			
Rare	5–7	20–22	125–30° F.
Medium rare	5–7	23–25	140–45° F.
Medium	5–7	26–28	155–60° F.
Well done	5–7	29–32	165–70° F.
Boned and rolled Rump roast	4–6	Add 5–8 minutes per pound to each of the times given for standing rump, but use meat thermometer as the most accurate indicator.	

Cut	Weight in Pounds	Approximate Minutes per Pound at 300° F.	Meat Thermometer Temperature
Top round (a chunky, boneless cut)			
Rare	3–6	28–30	125–30° F.
Medium rare	3–6	30–33	140–45° F.
Medium	3–6	34–38	155–60° F.
Well done	3–6	40–45	165–70° F.

Note: Because of their long, narrow shape, rib eye (Delmonico) and eye round will cook more evenly at 350° F. than 300° F. The same is true of all small roasts (under 3 pounds).

Rib eye and eye round			
Rare	3–6	12	125–30° F.
Medium rare	3–6	14	140–45° F.
Medium	3–6	16	155–60° F.
Well done	3–6	18–20	165–70° F.

SAUCES, GRAVIES, AND SEASONINGS FOR ROAST BEEF

For Cooking: Seasonings, Herbs, Spices	For Hot Roast Beef: Gravies	Sauces
Garlic	Au jus (unthick-	Bordelaise
Mustard	ened pan gravy)	Bourguignonne
Oregano	Mushroom	Espagnole
Parsley	Pan gravy	Figaro (roast
Rosemary	Sour cream	tenderloin)
Thyme	Wine	Périgueux
		Hot horseradish
		Smitane (roast
		tenderloin)

For Hot or Cold Roast Beef: Condiments	For Cold Roast Beef: Sauces
Horseradish	Cumberland
Ketchup or chili	Cold ravigote
sauce	Rémoulade
Mustard	Sour cream-
Pickles (bread and	horseradish
butter, dill,	Tartar
green tomato)	Whipped horse-
	radish

How to Carve a Standing Rib Roast:
Lay roast, large side down, on platter; if
wobbly, cut slice off bottom to level.
Steady roast by inserting carving fork
below top rib; with a short-bladed knife,
cut down along ribs to loosen meat.
With a carving knife, cut across face of
roast to ribs, making slices ⅛″–¼″
thick and lifting each off as it is cut.

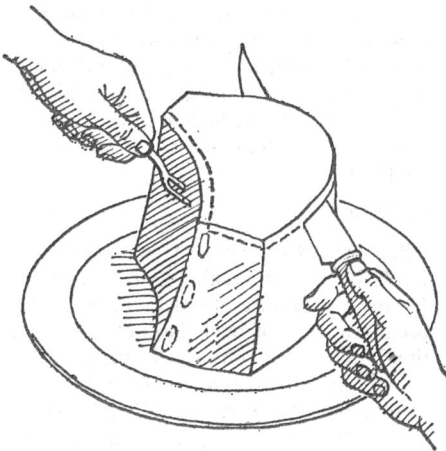

**How to Carve a Boned and Rolled Rib
  Roast:**
If roast seems firm (and carver is
experienced) remove strings in kitchen.
Otherwise, leave on lest roast fall apart.
Lay roast on its side on platter. Steady
with fork, and cut straight down through
roll into ⅛″–¼″ slices, removing strings
as you go. When through carving, turn
roast cut side up so juices won't run out.

Some Garnishes for Roast Beef Platters
(in addition to parsley fluffs and
watercress sprigs)

The point in garnishing is to make a
roast look as good to eat as it is. Group
vegetables around platter, alternating
colors, or wreathe them prettily around
roast, using only enough to enhance the
roast, not so many that you overwhelm
it and make carving difficult.

Artichoke Bottoms: boiled and buttered;
Artichoke Bottoms Stuffed with

Vegetables; Artichoke Bottoms
Princesse.

Artichoke Hearts: boiled and buttered.

Asparagus Tips: boiled and buttered.

Brussels Sprouts: boiled and buttered.

Carrots: Buttered Baby Carrots;
Carrots Rosemary; Lemon-Glazed
Carrots; Carrots Vichy.

Celery Hearts: boiled and buttered.

Fruits: broiled apricot or peach halves;
spiced crab apples.

Mushrooms: sautéed button mushrooms,
mushroom caps, or sliced mushrooms;
Baked Mushroom Caps Stuffed with
Hazelnuts.

Onions: Glazed Onions; Pan-Braised
Onions; Stuffed Onions.

Parsnips: Currant or Caramel-Glazed
Parsnips; Roasted Parsnips.

Pickles: mustard; watermelon rind.

Potatoes: Franconia, Château,
Parisienne, Dauphine, or Shoestring
Potatoes; cones of Duchess Potatoes;
Parsleyed, Herbed, or Lemon-Glazed
New Potatoes; Danish-Style New
Potatoes.

Tomatoes: raw cherry tomatoes or
tomato wedges; Stuffed Tomatoes.

Turnips: Glazed or Roasted Turnips;
Turnips Stuffed with Risotto.

Yorkshire Pudding: baked in individual
ramekins.

ROAST BEEF REVISITED

(How to Use Up Leftovers)

⚖ **BEEF MIROTON**

Here's an unusually good way to use up leftover roast beef.
Makes 4 servings

1 medium-size yellow onion, peeled and minced
1 tablespoon beef drippings, butter, or margarine
2 tablespoons flour
1 cup beef broth
1 cup leftover beef gravy
2 tablespoons red wine vinegar
½ cup dry red or white wine (optional)
1 tablespoon tomato paste
8 slices leftover roast beef
1 tablespoon minced parsley

Sauté onion in drippings over moderate heat 8–10 minutes until golden; blend in flour, slowly add broth, and cook, stirring, until thickened. Mix in all remaining ingredients except beef and parsley, then heat, stirring, 2–3 minutes. Pour about ⅓ of the sauce into a shallow, ungreased 1½-quart casserole, lay beef on top, overlapping slices, and add remaining sauce. Cover and refrigerate 1 hour. Preheat oven to 350° F. Bake, covered, 15–20 minutes until bubbly. Sprinkle with parsley and serve. About 230 calories per serving.

¢ **BEEF CROQUETTES**

Makes 4 servings

2 cups cubed leftover lean cooked beef
1 large yellow onion, peeled and quartered
2 tablespoons butter or margarine
¼ cup unsifted flour
1 cup strong beef broth or stock
1¼ teaspoons salt
⅛ teaspoon pepper
1 tablespoon steak or Worcestershire sauce
1 egg, lightly beaten
¾ cup toasted fine bread crumbs
¼ cup cooking oil

Grind beef with onion, using fine blade of meat grinder. Melt butter over moderately high heat, mix in flour, and brown *lightly,* stirring. Slowly add broth and heat, stirring, until thickened; add salt, pepper, and steak sauce and mix into ground meat. Spread in a shallow dish, cover, and chill until easy to work. Shape into 8 sausage-like rolls, dip in egg, then in crumbs; dry on a wire rack 10 minutes. Brown croquettes in oil in a large, heavy skillet over moderate heat 5–7 minutes, turning often; drain on paper toweling and serve. Good with gravy, Tomato, Mushroom, or Madeira Sauce. About 380 calories per serving (without sauce).

VARIATIONS:

Other Meat Croquettes: Use leftover lamb, pork, ham, veal, or chicken or a ½ and ½ mixture of chicken and ham or tongue instead of beef. Do not brown the flour, and use chicken broth instead of beef broth. Otherwise mix and cook as directed above. About 380 calories per serving for lamb, pork, ham or veal croquettes, 330 calories per serving for chicken croquettes.

Deep-Fat-Fried Croquettes: Shape meat mixture into 16 balls, dip in egg and crumbs, and deep-fry in a basket 2–3 minutes in 375° F. fat. Drain and serve. About 380 calories per serving.

Dressed-Up Croquettes: Add any 1 of the following to croquette mixture: 1 tablespoon prepared mustard or horseradish; ¼ cup minced ripe olives; ½ cup chopped, sautéed mushrooms; 2 tablespoons chili sauce, minced capers, dill pickle, or sweet green pepper; 1 crushed clove garlic; 1 teaspoon parsley flakes, oregano, marjoram, curry, or chili powder; 1 teaspoon mint flakes (for lamb); 1 teaspoon dill (for veal or lamb). About 385 calories per serving for croquettes made with olives or mushrooms; all others 380 calories per serving.

¢ **Budget Croquettes:** Add 1½ cups cooked rice or mashed potatoes to croquette mixture, shape into 12 rolls, and brown as directed. Makes 6 servings. About 400 calories per serving.

¢ **PARSLEYED BEEF PINWHEELS**

Makes 6 servings

Pastry:

2 cups packaged biscuit mix
½ teaspoon salt
1 tablespoon minced parsley
⅔ cup milk

Stuffing:

2 cups coarsely ground cooked beef
¾ cup condensed cream of mushroom, celery, or tomato soup
3–4 scallions, minced fine
1 tablespoon steak sauce

Preheat oven to 400° F. Mix pastry ingredients lightly with a fork, knead 8–10 times on a floured board, and roll into a 6″×10″ rectangle. Mix all stuffing ingredients and spread over pastry, leaving ½″ margins all round. Roll from the long side so you have a roll 10″ long. Transfer to an ungreased baking sheet with a wide spatula and bake, uncovered, 30 minutes until lightly browned. Slice and serve with hot leftover gravy or Quick Mushroom Gravy. About 410 calories per serving (without gravy).

VARIATION:

¢ **Beef Stuffed Crepes** (6–8 servings): Preheat oven to 350° F. Instead of making pastry, prepare 1 recipe Crepes for Savory Fillings. Prepare stuffing as directed, adding ½ cup milk or cream. Place a little stuffing in the center of each crepe and roll up. Lay crepes seam side down, close together, in a single layer in a buttered 8″×8″×2″ pan. Bake, uncovered, 20–30 minutes until heated through. If you like, sprinkle with grated cheese and brown quickly under broiler. Serve with hot leftover gravy, Quick Mushroom Gravy, or Tomato or Cheese Sauce. About 265 calories for each of 6 servings (without gravy), 200 calories for each of 8 servings (without gravy).

Some Additional Ways to Use Up Leftover Roast Beef

¢ **Beef, Macaroni, and Tomato Casserole** (6 servings): Mix together ½ pound boiled, drained macaroni, 1½ pints canned tomato or meatless spaghetti sauce, 2–3 cups diced cooked beef, and 1 drained (4-ounce) can sliced mushrooms. Season to taste with garlic or onion salt and pepper. Spoon into a greased 2½-quart casserole, top with grated cheese, and bake uncovered about 30 minutes at 375° F. until bubbly. About 660 calories per serving.

¢ **Beef Creole** (4 servings): Stir-fry 1 minced large yellow onion, 1 minced sweet green pepper, and 1 cup minced celery in 3 tablespoons drippings or butter in a large, heavy skillet over moderate heat 8–10 minutes until onion is golden. Add 1 (10-ounce) package frozen sliced okra, 1 (10-ounce) package frozen whole kernel corn, 1 (1-pound) can tomatoes, 1–2 teaspoons chili powder, and 2 cups diced cooked beef. Cover and simmer 15 minutes. Stir in ¼ teaspoon gumbo filé and salt and pepper to taste and serve over boiled rice. About 330 calories per serving.

Spicy Breaded Beef Slices (Number of servings flexible): Cut roast into ¼″ slices and trim off fat. Spread slices out on a large platter, sprinkle with salt and pepper, and drizzle with about 2 tablespoons red wine vinegar; let stand 20–30 minutes. Dip slices in flour, then in 1 egg lightly beaten with 2 tablespoons milk or cream, then in dry bread crumbs to coat evenly. Brown on both sides in 2–3 tablespoons butter or oil in a large skillet over moderately high heat; serve with Rémoulade or Tomato Sauce. About 260 calories per medium-size (3-ounce) slice (without sauce).

¢ **Beef and Potato Cakes** (4–6 servings): Mix together 2 cups mashed potatoes, 1½ cups coarsely ground cooked beef, 1 lightly beaten egg, 1 teaspoon onion flakes, and salt and pepper to taste. Shape into patties, dust lightly with flour, and brown in 2 tablespoons butter 2–3 minutes on each side over moderate heat. (*Note:* Finely crumbled leftover hamburgers can be used in place of roast.) For extra zip, mix in any of the following: 1 tablespoon minced parsley, chives, prepared mustard, horseradish, chili sauce, or ketchup. About 285 calories for each of 4 servings, 205 calories for each of 6 servings.

▨ **Quick Beef Paprika** (4 servings): Stir-fry ½ cup each minced yellow onion and mushrooms in 2 tablespoons butter, margarine, or drippings in a heavy skillet 8–10 minutes over moderate heat until onion is golden. Blend in 1–2 tablespoons paprika and ½ cup light cream and simmer, uncovered, 5 minutes. Add 2 cups cubed cooked beef, cover, and simmer over lowest heat 10–15 minutes until beef is heated through and flavors blended. Season to taste with salt and pepper, smooth in 1 cup sour cream, and serve over buttered noodles or boiled rice. (*Note:* Veal may be substituted for the beef.) About 400 calories per serving.

Beef Curry (4–6 servings): Stir-fry 1 minced yellow onion and chopped sweet apple in ¼ cup meat drippings or oil 8 minutes until golden; blend in 5 tablespoons flour, 3 tablespoons curry powder, 1 teaspoon salt, 1 pint beef broth (use part gravy if you have it), 1 cup water (or vegetable cooking water or tomato juice), and 1 tablespoon Worcestershire sauce and heat, stirring, until thickened. Add 3–4 cups cubed cooked beef, cover, and simmer 20 minutes. Let stand off heat ¾–1 hour, if possible, to blend flavors, then reheat just before serving. Serve with boiled rice, chutney, a green salad, and buttery chunks of garlic bread. (*Note:* Recipe may also be made with lamb or veal.) About 410 calories for each of 4 servings, 270 calories for each of 6 servings.

¢ **Beef, Mushroom, and Noodle Casserole** (6 servings): Mix together ½ pound boiled, drained noodles, 2 (10½-ounce) cans cream of mushroom soup blended with 1 cup milk, 1 undrained (4-ounce) can sliced mushrooms and 3 cups julienne strips of cooked beef. Season to taste with garlic or onion salt and pepper. Spoon into a greased 2½-quart casserole, top with about ⅓ cup butter-browned bread crumbs, and bake, uncovered, 30–40 minutes at 350° F. until bubbly. (*Note:* Dish is also good made with leftover roast veal.) About 600 calories per serving.

¢ **Beef and Vegetable Pie** (4–6 servings): Mix 2 cups cubed cooked beef with 2 cups mixed leftover vegetables— any compatible combination: peas and carrots, corn and green or lima beans, potatoes with almost anything. Stir in 1½ cups thin leftover gravy or 1 (10½-ounce) cream of potato or celery soup thinned with ¾ cup water and, for extra flavor, 1 minced yellow onion and ½ minced sweet green pepper sautéed in a little butter until limp. Spoon into a greased 6-cup casserole or deep pie dish, cover with Flaky Pastry I, Rough Puff Pastry, or Biscuit Topping for Casseroles, and bake, uncovered, 35–40 minutes at 425° F. until lightly browned. (*Note:* Lamb or veal can be used instead of beef.) About 690 calories for each of 4 servings, 460 calories for each of 6 servings.

¢ **Beef Stuffed Vegetables** (4 servings): Prepare 4 large tomatoes, sweet green peppers, or yellow onions for stuffing.* Stir-fry 1 minced yellow onion, 2 minced stalks celery, ¼ pound chopped mushrooms, and 1 crushed clove garlic in ¼ cup drippings or butter 8–10 minutes over moderate heat until onion is golden. Off heat mix in 1½ cups each soft white bread crumbs and coarsely ground cooked beef and ¾ cup leftover gravy or tomato sauce. Stuff vegetables, stand upright in an ungreased 1-quart casserole, and pour in gravy, beef broth, or tomato juice to a depth of ½″. Bake, uncovered, 30–45 minutes at 375° F. until tender. (*Note:* Veal, lamb, or ham can be used in place of beef.) About 345 calories per serving.

¢ **Barbecued Beef and Potatoes** (Number of servings flexible): Prepare

1 recipe Barbecue Gravy for Beef.
Arrange sliced beef in an ungreased
shallow casserole and top with drained,
canned whole potatoes. Pour in gravy
almost to cover and bake, uncovered,
about 20 minutes at 350° F. until heated
through. (*Note:* Leftover roast pork can
be prepared the same way.) Recipe too
flexible for a meaningful calorie count.

¢ **Beef Chow Mein or Chop Suey** (4
servings): Stir-fry 1 minced large yellow
onion or bunch scallions in 2 tablespoons
oil 5 minutes over moderate heat in a
large skillet; add 2 cups diced cooked
beef and stir-fry 5 minutes longer.
Prepare 2 (1-pound) cans chow mein or
chop suey vegetables (without meat) by
package directions and when hot stir in
skillet mixture and 1 tablespoon soy
sauce. Simmer, uncovered, 2–3 minutes
and serve over chow mein noodles or
boiled rice. (*Note:* Pork can be
substituted for the beef.) About 270
calories per serving.

¢ **Roast Beef Hash** (4–6 servings): Stir-
fry 1 minced yellow onion in 2
tablespoons meat drippings in a large,
heavy skillet over moderate heat 8–10
minutes until golden. Add 2 cups diced
roast beef, 2–3 cups diced boiled
potatoes, 1 teaspoon salt, ¼ teaspoon
pepper, ½ cup evaporated milk, and 1
minced large dill pickle. Spread hash
evenly in skillet, leave uncovered, and
brown over moderately low heat without
stirring 30–40 minutes until underside is
crusty. Fold over in half as you would an
omelet and slide onto a heated platter.
Serve with dill pickles, chili sauce, or
ketchup. (*Note:* This recipe can be
halved easily. It can also be made with
corned beef, canned or processed meats,
tongue, leftover lamb, pork, veal, or
ham.) About 365 calories for each of 4
servings, 245 calories for each of 6
servings.

¢ **Yukon Stew** (6 servings): In a large
saucepan place 2 cups cubed cooked
beef, 1 pound each peeled and parboiled
whole baby carrots, new potatoes, and
small white onions *or* 1 (1-pound) can
each drained whole baby carrots and

whole potatoes and 1 (1-pound) can
undrained small white onions. Add
leftover gravy, beef broth, or water
almost to cover (if using water, add a
beef bouillon cube for extra flavor; also,
if you like, 2 tablespoons tomato paste,
1–2 tablespoons Worcestershire or steak
sauce). Cover and simmer 15 minutes
over moderate heat; stir in 3 tablespoons
flour blended with ¼ cup cold water and
heat, stirring, until thickened. Taste for
salt and pepper and adjust as needed.
Serve as is or, if you like, top with
Dumplings and finish cooking as
dumpling recipe directs. Or, ladle into
small individual casseroles, top with
pastry or Biscuit Topping for Casseroles,
and bake about 25–30 minutes at
425° F. until brown. (*Note:* Lamb or
veal can be used instead of beef.) About
355 calories per serving with dumplings,
pastry, or biscuit topping, 255 calories
per serving without.

Sliced Cold Beef: Slice beef about ¼″
thick, trim of fat, and top with any
recommended cold sauce (see Sauces,
Gravies, and Seasonings for Roast Beef).
Recipe too flexible for a meaningful
calorie count.

Sliced Hot Beef: Slice beef about ¼″
thick, trim of fat, and layer into a
shallow, ungreased casserole. Add just
enough hot sauce to cover (see Sauces,
Gravies, and Seasonings for Roast Beef),
cover with foil, and heat 20 minutes at
350° F. Or, if you prefer, heat beef in
sauce about 5 minutes in a covered
skillet over moderately low heat. Recipe
too flexible for a meaningful calorie
count.

Hot Roast Beef Sandwiches: Heat meat
in any suitable sauce as for Sliced Hot
Beef (above) and serve, open face, on a
slice of toast or bread. Or, heat beef
slices in a little broth, drain, and
sandwich between toasted hamburger
buns spread with mustard, relish,
chutney, or any condiment you wish.
Recipe too flexible for a meaningful
calorie count.

To Make the Most of Very Small Amounts:

– Cube beef or cut in julienne strips and toss into hearty salads (chef's salad, dried bean, egg, potato, pasta, or rice salads).

– Cube and use to stretch budget casseroles (dried bean, pasta, rice, mixed vegetables).

– Cube and substitute for raw beef in soups and broths (add bones, whenever possible, to enrich flavor). Or dice fine and add to vegetable soups—homemade or canned.

– Add lean scraps and bones to stock pot.

– Grind fine and make into sandwich spreads by mixing with softened cream cheese, mayonnaise and/or mustard, or horseradish.

– Grind fine, mix with any seasoned butter, a little minced onion or capers, mustard or other spicy condiment and use as a cocktail spread.

– Grind fine and add to any savory stuffings.

– Grind small scraps fine, simmer with water to cover, purée in a blender, strain and use as a base for making gravy.

– Cut into small thin slices, trim of fat, and layer into custard cups, adding thinly sliced cooked carrots between layers, if you like. Fill to brim with Basic Aspic or Jellied Consommé Madrilène and chill until firm. Unmold on salad greens and serve with mayonnaise or any suitable cold sauce (see Sauces, Gravies, and Seasonings for Roast Beef).

BEEF TENDERLOIN

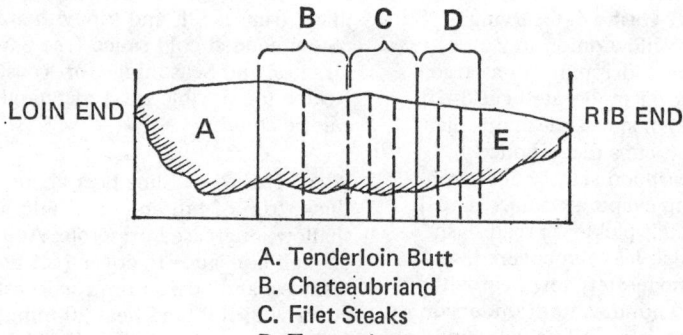

A. Tenderloin Butt
B. Chateaubriand
C. Filet Steaks
D. Tournedos
E. Filet Mignon

Butter-smooth, boneless, and so tender you scarcely need a knife to cut it, tenderloin is the Rolls-Royce of beef. It can be roasted, sliced into steaks, and broiled or sautéed, cubed for Stroganoff or Fondue Bourguignonne, even ground for Steak Tartare.

Though we tend to think of filet mignon as any small tenderloin steak, it is actually the smallest of four. Choicest is the 2"–3" *chateaubriand,* cut from the chunky center of the tenderloin; it should weigh at least 1 pound before trimming and serve 2–3. Next in line are the individual *filet steaks,* 3"–3½" in diameter and usually cut 1"–2" thick.

Third are the *tournedos* or *medallions of beef,* about 1" less in diameter but cut similarly thick. Finally come the *filets mignons* from the thin rib end. *Mignon* means *dainty* or *tiny*, and these, rarely seen in supermarkets, are often no more than 1½″ across. All tenderloin deserves special treatment, both in the cooking (always serve rare or medium rare) and in the presentation.

A word about grade: It is sometimes difficult to buy prime, even choice tenderloin because butchers don't like to strip it from top grade animals—it's too integral a part of T-bones and porterhouse steaks. Little matter, however, because tenderloin from a good grade animal will be very nearly as tender.

ROAST WHOLE BEEF TENDERLOIN

Tenderloin isn't the easiest cut to roast because it tapers sharply at one end. For best results, tuck the skinny end under before barding (or buy only the plump part of the tenderloin) and roast just until rare or medium rare. Many butchers, incidentally, will do the barding for you.
Makes 8–12 servings

Suet for barding
1 whole beef tenderloin (about 4–6
   pounds), trimmed of fat and
   connective tissue
3–4 tablespoons softened unsalted butter
   or Garlic Butter
1½ teaspoons salt
¼ teaspoon pepper

Suggested Garnishes:
Stuffed Mushrooms
Broiled tomato halves
Shoestring Potatoes
Watercress or parsley sprigs

Suggested Sauce:
Béarnaise or Madeira

Bard tenderloin* with suet, then let stand at room temperature 1½–2 hours if convenient. Meanwhile, preheat oven to 450° F. Rub exposed tenderloin ends with 2 tablespoons butter, insert meat thermometer in center of meat, and roast, uncovered, on a rack in a shallow roasting pan 6–7 minutes per pound for rare (125–30° F.), 8–9 minutes for medium rare (140–45° F.). Remove suet covering during last 10–15 minutes and brush tenderloin well with remaining butter so it will brown nicely. Transfer to steak board or hot platter, cover loosely, and let "rest" 5 minutes. Sprinkle with salt and pepper and garnish with 2 or more of the suggested garnishes. Slice ½″–1″ thick and serve with Madeira, Béarnaise, or other suitable sauce (see chart of Sauces, Gravies, and Seasonings for Roast Beef, also for Steaks). About 420 calories for each of 8 servings (without sauce), 375 for each of 12 servings (without sauce).

To Roast a Half Tenderloin (4–6 servings): Choose a 2–3 pound tenderloin of as uniform thickness as possible. Bard and tie as above, insert thermometer, and roast at 450° F., using above times as a guide. About 420 calories for each of 4 servings, 375 calories for each of 6 servings (without sauce).

To Spit-Roast Whole Beef Tenderloin:

In Rotisserie or Oven: Preheat unit. Balance barded tenderloin on spit by skewering lengthwise; tighten holding forks, attach to rotisserie, and broil 25–30 minutes for rare, 35–40 for medium rare or according to the manufacturer's time table. Remove suet and brown quickly under broiler. Season and serve. Same calorie counts as roast whole beef tenderloin.

Over Charcoal: Prepare a hot charcoal fire.* Balance barded tenderloin on spit as above, attach to rotisserie, adjust height so spit is 6″ from coals, and broil 30–35 minutes for rare, 40–45 for medium rare. Remove suet for last 10 minutes and brush often with melted unsalted butter. Season and serve. Same calorie counts as roast whole beef tenderloin.

VARIATIONS (All have approximately the same number of calories per serving as roast whole beef tenderloin not including sauce, except for last two variations. They run about 100 calories higher per serving):

Beef Tenderloin Rosemary: Bard and roast tenderloin as directed up to point of removing suet. When suet is removed, sprinkle tenderloin with ½ teaspoon crushed rosemary, 1 teaspoon salt, and ¼ teaspoon coarsely ground pepper. Finish roasting as directed, basting often with Burgundy (you'll need about ⅔ cup in all). When serving, top each portion with some of the Burgundy pan drippings.

Beef Tenderloin Madeira: Before barding, marinate tenderloin in 1 pint medium-dry Madeira 4–8 hours in the refrigerator; remove from marinade, pat dry, bard, and roast as directed. Serve with Madeira Sauce (use marinade in preparing sauce).

Spicy Marinated Beef Tenderloin: Before barding, marinate tenderloin 4–8 hours in refrigerator in 1½ cups moderately sweet port or Madeira mixed with ½ cup tarragon vinegar, 1 thinly sliced yellow onion, and ¼ teaspoon each cinnamon, nutmeg, and ginger. After marinating, bard and roast as directed. When making gravy, use strained marinade for the liquid.

Savory "Stuffed" Tenderloin: Before barding, cut tenderloin almost—but not quite—through in 1″ slices (it's the same technique used in preparing garlic bread, cutting to, but not through, the bottom crust). Spread tenderloin slices with a savory butter (see chart of Sauces, Butters, and Seasonings for Steaks), reshape, pressing slices together, and tie with string to secure. Bard and roast as directed.

Truffled Tenderloin: Slice tenderloin as for Savory "Stuffed" Tenderloin, spread slices with softened butter, and sprinkle with a little finely minced truffles (you'll need 2–3). Reshape tenderloin, tie with ¼ teaspoon coarsely ground pepper, bard, and roast as directed. Serve, if you like, with Madeira Sauce.

ROAST TENDERLOIN OF BEEF SMITANE

Makes 4–6 servings

1 (2–3-pound) beef tenderloin of uniform thickness, trimmed of fat and connective tissue
1 small yellow onion, peeled and minced
1 carrot, peeled and minced
1 stalk celery, minced
2 tablespoons butter or margarine
1 tablespoon finely grated lemon rind
4–5 slices fat bacon or thin strips salt pork
1¼ cups sour cream
Paprika

Suggested Garnish:
Stuffed Mushrooms
Watercress or parsley sprigs

Let tenderloin stand at room temperature 1½–2 hours if convenient. Meanwhile, stir-fry onion, carrot, and celery in butter over low heat about 10 minutes until tender but not brown; mix in lemon rind. Preheat oven to 450° F. Spread vegetable mixture over tenderloin, lay bacon slices on top, and insert meat thermometer in center. Roast uncovered on a rack in a shallow roasting pan 6–7 minutes per pound for rare (125–30° F.) and 8–9 for medium rare (140–45° F.). Remove bacon and vegetables and discard. Transfer tenderloin to a steak board or hot platter and keep warm. Skim fat from drippings, smooth in sour cream, and warm gently, but do not boil, 1–2 minutes. Garnish beef with stuffed mushrooms and cress, top with some of the sauce, and sprinkle with paprika. Pass remaining sauce. About 520 calories for each of 4 servings, 345 calories for each of 6 servings (without garnish).

PRINCE OF WALES BEEF TENDERLOIN

Makes 4–6 servings

1 (2–3-pound) beef tenderloin of uniform thickness, trimmed of fat and connective tissue
1 (4-ounce) can pâté de foie gras
3–4 truffles, finely chopped

1 small yellow onion, peeled and minced
1 carrot, peeled and minced
1 stalk celery, minced
¼ cup minced cooked ham
2 tablespoons butter or margarine
¼ teaspoon thyme
½ bay leaf, crumbled
Suet for barding or 4–5 thin strips salt
   pork
1 cup tawny port

Suggested Garnish:
Sautéed mushroom caps
Sliced truffles
Watercress or parsley sprigs

Let tenderloin stand at room temperature
1½–2 hours if convenient. Preheat oven
to 450° F. Cut tenderloin almost—but
not quite—in half lengthwise so 1 long
side acts as a hinge and tenderloin can be
opened flat like a book. Spread ½ of
tenderloin with pâté, leaving a narrow
margin all around; sprinkle other side
with chopped truffles, close tenderloin,
and sew shut with stout thread; set aside.
Stir-fry onion, carrot, celery, and ham in
butter 10 minutes over low heat until
vegetables are tender but not brown; mix
in thyme and bay leaf. Spread vegetable
mixture over tenderloin, then bard and
tie* or cover with strips of salt pork.
Insert meat thermometer and roast,
uncovered, on a rack in a shallow
roasting pan just until thermometer
reaches 120° F. Discard suet, skim fat
from drippings, and push vegetables
from tenderloin down into pan. Add port
and continue roasting uncovered until
thermometer reads 125–30° F. Transfer
tenderloin to a hot platter, remove
thread, and top with strained pan juices.
Garnish with mushrooms, truffle slices,
and watercress and serve. About 470
calories for each of 4 servings, 310
calories for each of 6 servings (without
garnish).

TENDERLOIN OF BEEF
WELLINGTON

For best results, use the plump center
portion of the tenderloin. Delicious with
Périgueux or Madeira Sauce.
Makes 6 servings

1 (3-pound) beef tenderloin of uniform
   thickness, trimmed of fat and
   connective tissue
1 recipe Rough Puff Pastry
3 tablespoons minced shallots or scallions
¾ pound mushrooms, wiped clean and
   minced
6–7 tablespoons softened unsalted butter
2 tablespoons brandy or dry Madeira
   wine
½ teaspoon salt
⅛ teaspoon pepper
1 (2-ounce) can pâté de foie gras at
   room temperature

Glaze:
2 egg yolks lightly beaten with 2
   tablespoons cold water

Let tenderloin stand at room temperature
1½–2 hours if convenient. Meanwhile,
prepare pastry and, after final folding
and sealing, wrap and chill. Stir-fry
shallots and mushrooms in 3 tablespoons
butter over moderately low heat 5
minutes; add brandy and simmer,
uncovered, until liquid evaporates; mix in
salt and pepper and cool. Preheat oven
to 450° F. Place tenderloin on a rack in
a shallow roasting pan and spread with
butter (include ends). Roast, uncovered,
10 minutes, brushing with more butter
after 5 minutes; remove from oven and
cool ½ hour. Reduce oven to 425° F.
Roll pastry into a rectangle big enough
to wrap tenderloin (about 8" × 15");
save scraps to use as decoration. Brush
center and margins of pastry with glaze;
spread a strip of mushroom mixture just
the size of the tenderloin across center of
pastry, leaving 1½" margins at ends.
Spread pâté on top of tenderloin, then
place pâté side *down* on mushroom
mixture. Bring pastry ends up on top of
meat and pinch firmly to seal; fold pastry
ends in and pinch. Place seam side down
on an ungreased baking sheet, cut 3
steam vents in top of pastry, and insert
meat thermometer through center hole
into meat. Prick pastry lightly in a
crisscross pattern and decorate with
small pastry shapes cut with truffle
cutters. Brush with glaze, covering pastry
cutouts lightly and taking care not to

cover steam holes. Bake in top ⅓ of oven about 25 minutes until lightly browned and thermometer reaches 125° F. (rare) or 140° F. (medium rare). (*Note:* If pastry browns before meat is done, reduce oven to 350° F.) When done, lift to a hot platter and let "rest" 5 minutes. To serve: Cut off 1 end of pastry, then cut straight across through pastry and meat, making slices ¾"–1" thick. About 700 calories per serving.

VARIATIONS:

Easy Beef Wellington: Prepare mushroom mixture and roast tenderloin 10 minutes as directed. Substitute 1 (8-ounce) package refrigerated crescent roll dough for Rough Puff Pastry. Open dough and spread flat, halve crosswise but do not separate into individual rolls. Fit halves together on a lightly floured board so you have a rectangle about 9"×14"; pinch margins and perforations together so you have an unbroken sheet of dough. If necessary, roll lightly to enlarge slightly, then wrap and bake tenderloin as directed. About 700 calories per serving.

Beef en Croûte: Substitute a 3-pound eye round of beef for tenderloin and have fat trimmed to ⅛". Do not spread with butter. Roast 15 minutes at 450° F., then proceed as directed for Tenderloin of Beef Wellington or Easy Beef Wellington. About 700 calories per serving.

BROILED WHOLE BEEF TENDERLOIN

Makes 8–12 servings

Suet for barding
1 whole beef tenderloin (about 4–6 pounds), trimmed of fat and connective tissue
2–3 tablespoons softened unsalted butter or Parsley-Lemon or Herb Butter (optional)
1½ teaspoons salt
¼ teaspoon pepper

Suggested Garnishes:
2–3 tablespoons Maître d'Hôtel, Parsley-Lemon, or Herb Butter
¾ pound sautéed button mushrooms
1½ dozen cherry tomatoes
Watercress sprigs

Suggested Sauce:
Béarnaise

Bard and tie tenderloin.* Let stand at room temperature 1½–2 hours if convenient. Preheat broiler. Place tenderloin on broiler rack and broil 6" from heat 30–40 minutes, giving it a quarter turn every 8–10 minutes, until rare or medium rare (make a small slit near center to test doneness). Discard suet covering and, if you like, spread tenderloin with softened butter. Brown under broiler 3–4 minutes, turning every minute. Transfer to steak board or heated platter, sprinkle with salt and pepper, and top with Maître d'Hôtel Butter. Surround with garnishes and pass Béarnaise Sauce. For more sumptuous dinners, use more elaborate trimmings (see Classic Garnishes for Steaks, also chart of Sauces, Butters, and Seasonings for Steaks). About 395 calories for each of 8 servings (without sauce), 265 calories for each of 12 servings (without sauce).

To Charcoal Broil: Prepare a moderately hot charcoal fire.* Broil barded tenderloin 5" from coals 25–30 minutes for rare, 35–40 for medium rare, turning frequently. Remove suet for last 10 minutes of broiling. Approximately the same number of calories per serving as broiled whole beef tenderloin.

To Charcoal Barbecue: Marinate unbarded tenderloin in 1 pint Barbecue Sauce for Beef 4–8 hours in refrigerator, turning occasionally. Pat dry, bard, and charcoal broil as above. After removing suet, turn often, brushing with barbecue sauce. Serve with Barbecue Gravy for Beef. Approximately the same number of calories per serving as broiled whole beef tenderloin (without sauce).

VARIATION:

Beef Tenderloin à la Bourguignonne: Marinate unbarded tenderloin in refrigerator 4–8 hours in 2 cups red Burgundy blended with ¼ cup olive oil, ½ crushed clove garlic, and 1 teaspoon Dijon-style mustard, turning occasionally. Broil by recipe above; after suet is removed, brush with marinade instead of butter and brown under broiler. Pour ¼ cup warmed Burgundy (or marinade) over meat, slice, and serve with Bourguignonne Sauce. About 400 calories for each of 8 servings, 270 calories for each of 12 servings.

FLAMING CHATEAUBRIAND MAÎTRE D'HÔTEL

Before ovens were reliable, chateaubriand was broiled, sandwiched between two other steaks, so it would be evenly pink throughout. No one worried if the outer steaks charred black—the chateaubriand was what mattered. Today we can cook it perfectly (which means never more than medium rare) without sacrificing two good steaks. Makes 2–3 servings

1 (3" thick) chateaubriand
1 clove garlic, peeled and halved (optional)
4 tablespoons unsalted butter, softened to room temperature
½ cup brandy, warmed
½ teaspoon salt
⅛ teaspoon pepper

Garnishes:
2 tablespoons Maître d'Hôtel Butter
½ recipe Château Potatoes

Suggested Sauce:
Chateaubriand or Béarnaise

Preheat broiler. If you like, rub meat well with garlic. Spread with 2 tablespoons butter. Melt remaining butter and set aside. Broil chateaubriand 5" from heat 12–14 minutes on each cut side for rare and 15–17 for medium rare, basting 1–2 times with melted butter. Transfer to chafing dish or skillet set over low heat, add brandy, warm briefly, and blaze with a match. Spoon flaming brandy over steak and before flames die ease steak onto steak board or hot platter. Sprinkle

with salt and pepper, top with Maître d'Hôtel Butter, and surround with potatoes. Pass sauce separately. To serve, cut in thin slices across the grain. About 585 calories for each of 2 servings, 390 calories for each of 3 servings.

VARIATION:
Bard* chateaubriand before broiling; remove suet covering 7–10 minutes before end of cooking so meat will brown nicely. The same number of calories per serving as Flaming Chateaubriand Maître d'Hôtel.

FILET STEAKS, TOURNEDOS, AND FILETS MIGNONS

It should be re-emphasized that the filet steaks here are what we commonly (and incorrectly) call filets mignons—tenderloin steaks 3–3½" across. The filets mignons really are *mignons,* dainty chunks cut from the thin end of the filet (see Cuts of Tenderloin illustration). All cooking times are for steaks that have stood at room temperature 1½–2 hours. Allow 1 1"–2" thick filet steak per person; 1–2 1"–2" tournedos, and, depending on size, 2–3 filets mignons.

To Panfry (Sauté): Wrap a strip of bacon or suet around edge of each steak, if you like, and tie with string or secure with toothpicks. Warm a little butter and oil (for 4 steaks, 2 tablespoons butter and 1 of oil are about right) in a heavy skillet over moderately high heat, add steaks, and brown, uncovered, 3–4 minutes on a side for very rare, 5–6 for rare, and 7–8 for medium rare (to test for doneness, press steak in center with your finger—unlike raw filet, which is soft, it should feel slightly resilient). If you plan to leave bacon on, turn steaks on end and brown lightly. Transfer to a hot platter, remove strings or toothpicks and, if you like, bacon. Sprinkle with salt and pepper and serve with pan juices or a suitable sauce (see chart of Sauces, Butters, and Seasonings for Steaks). Small mushroom caps, which can be sautéed in the pan right along with the steaks, make a delicious garnish.

To Panbroil (filet steaks only): Bacon-wrap or not, as you wish. Brown filets, uncovered, in a lightly greased or salted heavy skillet over moderately high heat 3–4 minutes on a side for very rare, 5–6 for rare, and 7–8 for medium rare; pour off any drippings as they collect.

To Broil: Preheat broiler. Place bacon-wrapped steaks on lightly greased broiler rack and broil 3″ from heat 4–5 minutes on a side for very rare, 6–7 for rare, and 8–9 for medium rare. If you wish, brush both sides of steaks lightly with melted butter before broiling. (*Note:* A good way to broil very small mignons is à la shish kebab on long metal skewers with strips of bacon inter-twined. They'll take slightly less time to broil than larger tenderloin steaks.) About 350 calories per 1″ steak if broiled or panbroiled, slightly more if panfried.

Some Easy Ways to Dress Up Filets and Tournedos

Marinated Filets or Tournedos: Marinate steaks 8 hours in refrigerator in a good homemade French or herb dressing or in Japanese Steak Sauce. Remove from marinade, let stand at room temperature 1 hour, then bacon-wrap and broil as directed, brushing often with marinade.

Surprise Filets or Tournedos: Make small pockets in raw steaks (work from outer edge, cutting a horizontal slit deep into center of each). Place 1 teaspoon pâté in each pocket and, if you like, ¼ teaspoon minced truffle. Or tuck a small lump Roquefort or blue cheese in each. Close with toothpicks, wrap with bacon or suet, and panfry or broil.

Savory Filets or Tournedos: Just before serving, rub steaks with a dab of flavored butter (see chart of Sauces, Butters, and Seasonings for Steaks).

Filets or Tournedos in Wine: Panfry 4 steaks and transfer to a hot platter. Heat ¼ cup dry red wine, Madeira, or port with ¼ teaspoon tarragon, chervil,

chives, or rosemary in skillet, stirring, until bubbly. Pour over steaks and serve.

Filets or Tournedos in Minute Sauce: Panfry 4 steaks and transfer to a hot platter. Add 2 tablespoons lemon juice, 1 tablespoon Worcestershire sauce, and ½ teaspoon Dijon-type mustard to skillet and heat, stirring, until bubbly; pour over steaks.

Flaming Filets or Tournedos: Broil or panfry 4 steaks, then transfer to a chafing dish set over low heat. Add ⅓–½ cup warmed cognac, heat 1 minute, and blaze with a match. Spoon flaming cognac over steaks and season with salt and pepper. If you like, swirl in 1 table-spoon Maître d'Hôtel Butter when flames subside.

Filet or Tournedo "Canapés": Odd as these combinations may sound, they're delicious:
– Serve steaks on broiled thick tomato slices; top with pâté, Duxelles, or Mus-tard Sauce.
– Serve steaks on grilled pineapple rings and top with Sauce Diable.
– Serve steaks on grilled avocado crescents (brush with lemon and sauté 1–2 minutes in butter); top with Sauce Diable or Brown Curry Sauce.
– Serve steaks on butter-browned, breaded eggplant rounds and top with Tomato Sauce.

Some Classic Ways to Serve Tournedos (and Filets)

À la Béarnaise: Panfry 4–6 steaks, arrange in a circle on a hot platter, mound Château Potatoes in center, and drizzle steaks with Béarnaise; pass extra sauce.

À la Bordelaise: Top panfried steaks (any number you wish) with ½″ slices poached marrow (see Marrowbones) and a little minced parsley. Serve with Bordelaise Sauce.

À la Clamart: On a hot platter arrange panfried steaks, tiny buttered new po-tatoes, and boiled artichoke bottoms

I. LOW-CALORIE RECIPES

Potage Saint-Germain – Steamed Globe Artichoke – Beef Sukiyaki –
Poached Meringue Ring

Potage Saint Germain (page 178)

Steamed Globe Artichoke (page 772); and Steamed Asparagus (page 777)

Beef Sukiyaki (page 227); Low-calorie Fillets of Flounder en Papillote (page 558); and Steak Tartare (pages 227-28)

Poached Meringue Ring with Dessert Cardinal Sauce (pages 1058 and 1065)

filled with buttered or Puréed Green Peas. Quickly boil and stir ⅓ cup dry white wine in steak skillet to reduce by ½, pour over steaks, and serve.

Chasseur: Before cooking steaks, sauté ½ pound sliced mushrooms and 2 tablespoons minced shallots or scallions in 2 tablespoons butter over moderate heat 5 minutes; set aside. Panfry 6 steaks, place each on a fried crouton round, and keep warm on a hot platter. Pour fat from steak skillet, add ½ cup beef stock and 2 teaspoons tomato paste, and boil rapidly, stirring, until reduced by half. Mix in ¼ cup Madeira blended with 2 teaspoons cornstarch and heat, stirring, until thickened and clear. Add mushrooms and 1 tablespoon minced parsley (or 1 teaspoon each minced parsley, tarragon, and chervil), pour over steaks, and serve.

Choron: Serve panfried steaks on fried crouton circles and garnish with boiled artichoke bottoms filled with buttered green peas or asparagus tips. Mix 1 cup Béarnaise Sauce with 2 tablespoons tomato paste and spoon a little over each steak.

Henri IV: Panfry 4–6 steaks, place on fried crouton rounds, and drizzle with pan juices deglazed with ¼ cup Madeira. Arrange in a ring on a hot platter, top each steak with a hot artichoke bottom filled with Béarnaise, and decorate with truffle slices. Mound Château or Parisienne Potatoes in center and pass extra Béarnaise.

Rossini: Serve panfried steaks on fried crouton rounds topped with ¼″ slices *pâté de foie gras,* decorative truffle slices, and a little Madeira Sauce. (*Note:* Pâté will be more attractive if lightly dusted with flour and sautéed briefly in a little butter over low heat.) Garnish with Château Potatoes and watercress; pass extra sauce.

FONDUE BOURGUIGNONNE

Picture a group of friends gathered round, spearing chunks of steak and cooking them in a bubbling pot of oil; picture an array of sauces and condiments, there for the dunking, and you have the idea of Fondue Bourguignonne. It's a merry Swiss dish that's perfect for a small party. Everything can be prepared well in advance and set out at the last minute.
Makes 6 servings

3 pounds beef tenderloin or boneless sirloin, trimmed of fat and cut in 1″ cubes
3 cups (about) cooking oil (a ½ and ½ mixture of peanut and corn oil is especially good) or 3 cups Clarified Butter

Sauces: Prepare 2 or more, choosing with an eye to variety. Any hot sauces can be reheated in the top of a double boiler or hot water bath minutes before serving. Some sauces traditionally served: Aurore, Béarnaise (a must), Cumberland, Diable, Mustard, Rémoulade, Sour Cream-Horseradish. Not traditional but good: Brown Curry, Madeira, Smitane, and Teriyaki sauces.

Condiments: Choose 3 or more, again for variety: spicy and mild mustards, chutney, tomato or mushroom ketchup, horseradish, olives, pickled onions, or mushrooms.

Special Equipment: You'll need a fondue bourguignonne pot, a deep metal or enameled-metal pot as distinguished from the heavy, shallow, ceramic cheese fondue dish (preferably the 2-quart size) with a stand and alcohol burner, fondue forks and long bamboo skewers.

How to Set the Table: Place fondue stand and burner in the center of the table. At each place provide 2 salad plates (1 for the raw chunks of beef, the other for sauces), 2–3 bamboo skewers, and a fondue fork in addition to dinner knife, fork, spoon, and napkin.

How to Serve: In the kitchen, half fill fondue pot with oil and heat slowly on the stove until a cube of bread will sizzle; set over lighted alcohol burner on dining table. Arrange a small mound of steak cubes on 1 of the salad plates at each place and garnish with watercress or parsley. Surround burner with small bowls of sauces and condiments; set out salt shaker and pepper mill. (*Note:* Pour any particularly liquid sauces into small ramekins and set 1 on each sauce plate.)

How to Eat Fondue Bourguignonne:
Each guest first spoons an assortment of sauces and condiments onto his empty plate. Then, using a long bamboo skewer, he spears a chunk of filet, plunges it into the fondue pot, and cooks it the way he likes it (allow 5–10 seconds for rare, 10–15 for medium, and 20 for well done). More than 1 chunk of meat can be cooked at a time, but it's important to regulate the burner so the oil bubbles vigorously—but does not sputter—each time a new chunk is added. To help reduce sputter, keep a small chunk of bread in the oil, replenishing whenever it threatens to burn. After cooking a piece of steak, the person transfers it to his fondue fork, dunks it in a sauce or condiment, and eats it.
Caution: Some recipes recommend using 2 fondue forks, 1 for cooking, the other for dunking and eating. But, if you forget to switch forks (and it's easy to do so), you can get a nasty mouth burn. So play it safe and use bamboo skewers.

What to Serve with Fondue Bourguignonne: Since the fondue table will be crowded, it's best to follow with a separate salad course—a cold green bean or crisp tossed salad is ideal. As for wine, uncork a good red Burgundy or Bordeaux. About 475 calories per serving (without sauces).

BEEF STROGANOFF

A true Stroganoff has very little sour cream and no mushrooms, tomato paste, or paprika. What makes it special is the spicy mustard. It's best made with beef tenderloin, but if your budget won't allow it, use sirloin.
Makes 4 servings

1½ pounds beef tenderloin or boneless sirloin, trimmed of fat and cut in 2″ × ½″ strips

¼–½ teaspoon salt (depending upon saltiness of broth and mustard)
¼ teaspoon pepper
1 medium-size Bermuda onion, peeled and sliced ¼″ thick
4 tablespoons butter or margarine
2 tablespoons flour
1 cup strong beef stock or canned condensed beef broth
1 teaspoon prepared Dijon-type mustard
¼ cup sour cream at room temperature

Spread beef strips out on heavy brown paper and sprinkle evenly with salt and pepper. Toss to mix, spread out again, top with onion slices and let stand 2 hours at room temperature. Melt 2 tablespoons butter in a large, heavy skillet over moderately low heat and blend in flour. Mix in stock and heat, stirring, 3–5 minutes until thickened. Blend in mustard and remove sauce from heat. In a second large skillet, melt remaining butter over moderately high heat, add beef and onion, and brown quickly—this will take about 10 minutes. Add browned beef *but not the onion* to the sauce, set over moderate heat, cover, and simmer, stirring once or twice, 15 minutes (onion can be saved for hamburgers or stew). Remove from heat, stir in sour cream, and serve. About 440 calories per serving.

⚔ TERIYAKI-STYLE TENDERLOIN

Makes 4 servings

1½ pounds beef tenderloin in 1 piece

Marinade:

¾ cup Japanese soy sauce
¼ cup mirin, sake, or medium-dry sherry
1 tablespoon light brown sugar (only if sake or sherry is used)
2 teaspoons finely grated fresh gingerroot or 1 tablespoon minced preserved ginger

Place tenderloin in a large bowl. Mix marinade ingredients, pour over meat, cover, and let stand at room temperature 1½–2 hours, turning meat several times. Remove meat from marinade and broil 4″ from the heat about 15 minutes, turning every 3 minutes and basting with marinade. (*Note:* This cooking time is for a medium-rare *teriyaki.* If you like it rarer, reduce cooking time to about 10–12 minutes, if more well done, increase it to 17 minutes.) To serve, cut in thin slices and top with a little marinade. About 290 calories per serving.

VARIATION:

⚖ **Teriyaki Hors d'Oeuvre:** Cut tenderloin into ¾″–1″ cubes and marinate as directed; drain, reserving marinade. Broil 4″ from heat 1–2 minutes, turn, baste with marinade, and broil 1–2 minutes longer. Skewer with toothpicks or bamboo skewers. Or, if you have a hibachi, set out the raw marinated cubes, long metal skewers, or fondue forks and let everyone broil their own teriyaki. Makes about 6–8 servings. About 185 calories for each of 6 servings, 140 calories for each of 8 servings.

⚖ **BEEF SUKIYAKI**

Sukiyaki is a good choice for a small dinner because all ingredients can be cut up well in advance (cover and refrigerate until the last minute), because it can be cooked quickly at the table in an electric skillet and because it needs nothing more than rice to accompany. Made the Japanese way, it contains *dashi,* a broth made of dried bonito flakes (packets are sold in Oriental groceries), *sake,* the fermented rice drink, *shirataki,* yam noodles, and soybean cake. The shirataki and bean cake can be omitted if necessary, the dashi replaced by beef broth and the sake by sherry. Some people make sukiyaki with *mirin,* a sweet sake, and omit the sugar. You can achieve the same effect by using a sweeter sherry and adding only enough sugar to "mellow" the sukiyaki. It should never taste sweet.

Makes 4 servings

1 (2″) cube suet
1 cup paper-thin slices Spanish onion

6 scallions, trimmed and halved lengthwise
3 stalks celery, cut diagonally into thin slices
1 (8-ounce) can bamboo shoots, drained and sliced thin
1¼ pounds beef tenderloin or boneless sirloin, sliced paper thin
½ pound mushrooms, wiped clean and sliced thin
⅔ cup canned shirataki (optional)
1 soybean cake, cut in 1½″ cubes (optional)
1 quart washed, sorted spinach leaves
½ cup dashi or canned beef broth
½ cup sake or medium-dry sherry
½ cup Japanese soy sauce
3 tablespoons light brown sugar

Heat a large, heavy skillet over high heat 1 minute or set an electric skillet on highest heat; when good and hot, spear suet with a cooking fork and rub over bottom to grease; discard suet. Reduce heat to moderate, add onion, scallions, and celery, and stir-fry 5–8 minutes until lightly wilted; lay bamboo shoots, beef, mushrooms, *shirataki,* bean cake, and spinach on top. Mix *dashi* with sake, soy sauce, and sugar and pour over all. Cover and steam 3–4 minutes. Uncover and toss lightly as you would a salad, then simmer, uncovered, 2–3 minutes longer. Serve with rice. About 350 calories per serving (without rice).

⚖ **STEAK TARTARE**

What we call steak tartare the French call steak *à l'Américaine*—a tribute to our superb beef. Strangely, our name for the dish comes from their way of serving it—with tartar sauce. But Americans prefer to use raw egg yolks and to mix in an assortment of condiments.
Makes 4 servings

1½ pounds beef tenderloin or sirloin steak, trimmed of all fat and finely ground
4 raw egg yolks
1 teaspoon minced chervil (optional)
1 medium-size yellow onion, peeled and minced
2 tablespoons minced parsley

Lightly shape beef into 4 patties, place each on a chilled plate, and, using the back of a spoon, press a hollow in the center of each. Slide a raw egg yolk into each hollow and, if you like, sprinkle with chervil. Pass remaining ingredients in small bowls or arrange in separate mounds around each patty so that everyone can mix in whatever— and as much of it as they like—along with the egg yolk. Set out salt and pepper. Some other optional accompaniments: cayenne pepper, Worcestershire sauce, lemon wedges, anchovy fillets, hot buttered toast—either plain or spread with anchovy paste. About 350 calories per serving.

STEAKS

Sumptuous, succulent, often whopping— these are the cuts Americans do better than anyone else. The tender steaks come from the rib and loin sections, the marginally tender from the round, rump, chuck, flank, and plate. (Refer to Beef Chart.)

The Tender Steaks
Choicest of the choice are the T-bone, porterhouse, and pinbone sirloin because they contain large chunks of butter-smooth tenderloin. All tender steaks should be cut at least 1″ thick and will be juicier if closer to 2″; all are well enough marbled with fat that they can be cooked without additional fat. Broil or charcoal broil any of the following, and, except for sirloins, which are too hefty to handle easily in a skillet, panbroil.
Rib and boneless rib steaks
Delmonico or rib eye steak
Club steak
T-bone steak
Shell steak (T-bone minus the tenderloin)
Porterhouse steak
Strip steak (porterhouse minus the tenderloin)

Sirloin steaks (pinbone, flat bone, wedge bone, and boneless)
Note: Butchers sometimes remove the pinbone from the pinbone sirloin, grind the tail end and tuck it in where the bone was; this simplifies carving. Some also grind the long, lean tail of the porterhouse and tuck it underneath the tenderloin.

The Marginally Tender Steaks
If from prime or tendered beef, some of these lean "budget" steaks will be tender enough to broil; others will need all the help they can get (i.e., pounding, scoring, marinating, braising). Being leaner than the tender steaks, they are also somewhat lower in calories and cholesterol; their texture is firmer, their flavor more robust.

The Broilables (IF from top quality or tendered beef):
Top and eye round steaks
Tip or sirloin tip steak
Rump steak
Skirt steak fillet
Flank and flank steak fillets
Boneless blade and blade chuck steak

Petite steak
Minute steak } *Note:* Though tender enough to broil, these steaks are so thin they should be panfried as quickly as possible in butter or drippings.
Cube steak

The Unbroilables: Blade steak (when not first cut), arm steak, and bottom round are the cuts to braise: to use for Swiss steak, to stuff and roll, to smother with onions and mushrooms and rich brown gravy. *Note:* Any of the broilables listed above become unbroilables when cut from lower grades of beef.

How to Cook

Amount Needed: ⅓–½ pound boneless steak per person, ½–¾ pound in bone-in steak.

General Preparation for Cooking: If steaks seem unusually moist, wipe with a damp cloth so they will brown nicely. Trim off all but ¼″ outer fat and slash at 1″ intervals to keep steaks from curling. Rub with pepper, if you like, also garlic, but not salt (salt draws moisture to the surface and slows browning). Let steaks stand at room temperature 1½–2 hours before cooking if convenient. (*Note:* Naturally thin cuts like flank steak, also thinly cut minute, petite, or cube steaks, should be refrigerated until just before cooking so that the quick, intense heat does not carry them beyond the point of tenderness—medium rare.)

Cooking Tips

— Whenever in doubt about the tenderness of a steak, sprinkle each side with unseasoned meat tenderizer, pierce deeply all over with a sharp fork, and let stand as package directs.
— Always turn steaks with tongs to avoid piercing them and losing savory juices.
— When broiling, panbroiling, or panfrying marginally tender steaks, never cook beyond medium rare (longer cooking will merely toughen and dry them).
— When carving large, marginally tender steaks, cut across the grain in thin slices, holding the knife at a slight angle (this breaks up long, coarse fibers).

To Panfry (Sauté): Recommended for minute, petite, and cube steaks; skirt fillets, boneless blade steak, tip steak, top and eye round cut about 1″ thick. Warm 1–2 tablespoons butter, margarine, drippings, or cooking oil in a large, heavy skillet over moderately high heat about 1 minute, add steaks, and brown on both sides. Minute, petite, and cube steaks will take only 1–2 minutes per side; the other steaks about 3 minutes per side for very rare, 4 for rare, and 5 for medium rare. Season and serve.

To Panbroil: Recommended for all tender steaks except large sirloins; for top and eye round, tip and boneless blade steaks. If steaks seem especially lean, grease or salt skillet *lightly;* heat over moderately high heat about 1 minute, add steaks, and cook, uncovered, turning occasionally and pouring off drippings as they accumulate, until browned on both sides and at desired doneness (use times below as a guide). Season and serve. (*Note:* Do not add water or other liquid to skillet.)

To Broil: Recommended for all tender steaks; also for top quality or tendered skirt fillets, chuck and boneless blade steak, top and eye round, tip and rump steaks. (*Note:* Flank steak requires a bit different technique [see London Broil].) If steaks are very lean, brush lightly with melted butter. Preheat broiler. Rub rack with drippings or oil and, to save a messy clean-up, line broiler pan with foil. Place steak on rack and set in broiler so fat edge of steak is toward back of oven (this reduces spattering). Adjust height and broil to desired doneness as directed in Steak Broiling Chart (below), turning steak only once. Season and serve.

VARIATION:

Planked Steak: A festive way to serve broiled steak is on an oak or hickory plank (most housewares departments sell them), wreathed with Duchess Potatoes, sautéed mushroom caps, and grilled tomatoes. Planks, usually rectangular or oval, should be at least 1″ thick and from 15″–18″ long. Most are seasoned by the manufacturer (see his directions), but, if not, here's *how to season a plank* yourself: brush top and sides with bland cooking oil, place on a sheet of foil on oven rack, and let stand in a 275° F. oven 1–1½ hours. Remove from oven and wipe well with paper toweling— plank is now ready *to use* (see Planked Steak with Vegetables). *To care for plank:* wipe thoroughly with paper toweling immediately after using, then wash quickly in warm, sudsy water, rinse in cool water, pat dry, then allow to dry completely. Store, loosely wrapped, in a cool, dry place. (*Note:* If any part of plank is exposed during broiling, brush lightly with oil and cover with foil to prevent charring.)

To Charcoal Broil: Recommended for all tender steaks; also for top quality or tendered tip, rump, chuck, and boneless

APPROXIMATE TOTAL PANBROILING TIMES

Steak Thickness	Very Rare	Rare	Medium Rare	Medium	Well Done
	Minutes	Minutes	Minutes	Minutes	Minutes
1"	6–7	8–10	11–12	13–14	15–16
1½"	8–10	11–12	13–14	15–17	18–20
2"	13–15	16–17	18–19	20–22	25–30

blade steaks. Prepare charcoal fire.* For steaks 1"–1¾" thick, it should be hot (350–75° F. on grill thermometer) or of an intensity to make you remove your hand after 2–3 seconds at grill level. For steaks 2" thick or more, it should be moderately hot (325° F.) or enough to make you withdraw your hand after 4 seconds. Spread enough glowing coals evenly over fire bed to equal area of meat and to last throughout cooking. Lightly grease grill with fat trimmed from steak, place steak on grill, adjust height, and broil as directed in Steak Broiling Chart. Turn only once during cooking. Season and serve.

VARIATION:

Marinated Steaks: Marginally tender steaks will be juicier if marinated 4 hours in refrigerator in Barbecue Sauce for Beef, Japanese Steak Sauce, or any good Italian, herb, or garlic dressing. Bring steak to room temperature in marinade, lift out, and pat dry. Grill as directed, brushing often with marinade.

To Braise: Here's the most sure-fire way of cooking marginally tender steaks. Braising isn't one recipe, but many— Beef Birds, Swiss Steak, Chicken, and Country-Fried Steaks are all braised. You'll find these and other ways of braising steaks among the recipes that follow.

To Test Steaks for Doneness:

Bone-in steaks: Make a small slit near bone and check color of meat.

Boneless steaks: Make a small slit near center of steak to determine color.

Thick steaks (more than 2½"): Insert meat thermometer in center of largest lean muscle, not touching bone. A very rare steak will be 120° F., a rare one 130° F., a medium-rare one 140° F., a medium one 150° F., and a well-done one 160–70° F.

How to Give Steak Extra Flavor
(Choose 1 Method Only.)

Before Cooking:
— Marinate steak 4 hours in refrigerator in Barbecue Sauce for Beef or Japanese Steak Sauce (or any good herb, Italian, or garlic dressing). Let come to room temperature, lift from marinade, pat dry, and broil, brushing often with marinade.
— Rub each side of steak with a cut clove garlic.
— Rub each side of steak with a compatible herb or spice (see Sauces, Butters, and Seasonings for Steaks).
— Spread both sides of steak with 1 small grated yellow onion that has been blended with 2 tablespoons Dijon mustard and 2 teaspoons cooking oil or softened butter.
— Brush both sides of steak with 1 tablespoon soy sauce that has been mixed with 1 tablespoon each steak sauce, Worcestershire sauce, and chili sauce.

— **Hungarian Steak:** Rub 2 teaspoons paprika (preferably the Hungarian sweet rose) into each side of steak, then cook by desired method. Top with sautéed onion rings, given the merest blush of paprika, and serve.

STEAK BROILING CHART

Times (for steaks that have stood at room temperature 1½-2 hours) are approximate since shape and size of cut, amount of fat and bone, type of oven or grill all affect broiling time. In outdoor charcoal broiling, wind is also a factor.

Steak	Thickness	Oven or Fire Temperature	Distance from Heat	Approximate Minutes per Side				
				Very Rare	Rare	Medium Rare	Medium	Well Done
Oven Broiling								
Top and eye round, tip and rump steaks, skirt fillets, chuck and boneless blade steak; all tender steaks except bone-in sirloins.	1"	broil	2"	3	4	5	6	7
	1½"	broil	3"	6	7	8	9	10-12
	2"	broil	4"	14	15	16	17	18-19
Pinbone, wedge bone, and flat bone sirloin	1"	broil	3"	7	8	9	10	11-13
	1½"	broil	4"	10	11	12	13	14-15
	2"	broil	5"	18	19	20	21	22-24
Charcoal Broiling								
Tip, rump, chuck and boneless blade steaks; all tender steaks.	1"	hot	4"	3	4-5	6	7-8	9-10
	1½, 1¾"	hot	4"	4	5-6	7-8	9-10	12-15
	2"	moderately hot	5"	6-7	8-9	10-12	14-16	18-20
	2½"	moderately hot	5"	10-12	13-15	16-18	20-22	23-25

NOTE: Directions and times for broiling tenderloin steaks, flank steak, and hamburgers are given in the discussion of each, since each requires a somewhat different technique.

231

During Cooking:
– While broiling, brush or baste with Madeira, port, sherry, dry red or white wine, brandy, dark rum, or bourbon.
– While broiling, brush or baste with any barbecue sauce.
– While charcoal broiling, toss any of the following directly onto coals: 2–3 sprigs fresh sage or 1 tablespoon dried sage, a dozen bay leaves, 1 tablespoon cracked juniper berries.
– During last minutes of broiling or pan-broiling, brush lightly with Herb, Chive, Garlic, Mustard, or Anchovy Butter.

– **Roquefort Steak:** During last half minute of broiling, spread top of steak with 2–3 tablespoons Roquefort or blue cheese that have been creamed with 2 tablespoons softened butter.

After Cooking:
– Just before serving, top with 3–4 tablespoons flavored butter (see Sauces, Butters, and Seasonings for Steaks).
– Just before serving, top with a ½ and ½ mixture of sautéed, minced yellow onions and mushrooms.
– Just before serving, top with the following: ½ cup each minced mushrooms and yellow onions that have been sautéed 10 minutes in butter with ¼ cup each minced celery and sweet red or green pepper and 1 crushed clove garlic.
– Serve steak with a suitable sauce (see Sauces, Butters, and Seasonings for Steaks).

– **Flaming Steak:** Warm ⅓ cup brandy, bourbon, rye, or dark rum, pour over hot steak, and flame, spooning flaming liquid over steak until flames subside. If you like, flame at the table.

– **Steak Mirabeau:** Broil steak to desired doneness. Lay 9–10 anchovy fillets over steak in a crisscross pattern, dot with 2–3 tablespoons Anchovy Butter and ¼ cup sliced pitted ripe olives. Broil 20–30 seconds to melt butter and serve.

– **Steak Lyonnaise:** Panbroil steak, transfer to hot platter, and smother with sautéed yellow onions (about ½ cup is right for a 2-serving steak). To skillet add 1 tablespoon red wine vinegar, 2 tablespoons dry white wine, and ½ cup Rich Brown Sauce or canned beef gravy. Heat 2–3 minutes, stir in 1 tablespoon minced parsley, pour over steak, and serve.

– **Drunken Steak:** Panbroil steak and transfer to hot platter. To skillet add 2 tablespoons butter and ⅓ cup brandy, dark rum, or bourbon and heat 1–2 minutes, scraping up browned bits. Pour over steak and serve.

Some Simple Garnishes for Steak (in addition to parsley or watercress sprigs):

Artichoke Bottoms: boiled and buttered; Artichoke Bottoms Stuffed with Vegetables; Argenteuil Style; Artichoke Bottoms Princesse.

Artichoke Hearts: boiled and buttered; Artichokes Du Barry.

Celery: braised; boiled buttered celery hearts.

Cucumbers: boiled and buttered; Sautéed Cucumbers; Braised Vegetable-Stuffed Cucumbers.

Belgian Endive: braised.

Mushrooms: sautéed button mushrooms, mushroom caps, or sliced mushrooms; Baked Mushroom Caps Stuffed with Hazelnuts.

Onions: Glazed Onions; Pan-Braised Onions; Sautéed Onions; French Fried Onion Rings; Stuffed Onions.

Potatoes: Parsleyed Potatoes; French Fried Potatoes; Shoestring Potatoes; Duchess Potatoes; Herbed or Lemon-Glazed New Potatoes; Danish-Style New Potatoes.

Rice: Croquettes.

Tarts: small pastry shells filled with small or diced vegetables in Béchamel or Medium White Sauce, Risotto, or *pâté de foie gras*.

Tomatoes: raw cherry tomatoes; Fried Tomatoes or Green Tomatoes; Fried Tomatoes Provençale; Broiled Tomatoes; Deviled Tomatoes; Stuffed Tomatoes.

SAUCES, BUTTERS, AND SEASONINGS FOR STEAKS

Sauces		Butters	Seasonings, Herbs, Spices	Condiments
Béarnaise	Herb	Anchovy	Marchands	Chervil	Horseradish
Bordelaise	Japanese	Bercy	de vin	Chives	Mustard
Bourguignonne	steak sauce	Chive	Mustard	Garlic	Soy sauce
Brown sauce	Lyonnaise	Curry	Pimiento	Ginger	Steak sauce
fines herbes	Madeira	Garlic	Shallot	Mustard	Teriyaki
Chasseur	Madeira-	Herb	Tarragon	Parsley	sauce
Chateaubriand	mushroom	Horseradish	Tomato	Rosemary	Worces-
Choron	Marchands	Maître		Tarragon	tershire
Colbert	de vin	d'hôtel			sauce
Diable	Périgueux				
Dijonnaise	Poivrade				
	Salsa friá				
	Shallot				
	Smitane				

Some Classic Garnishes for Steak:

À la Bouquetière: Surround steak with small clusters of diced cooked carrots, turnips, Parisienne Potatoes, buttered green peas, beans, and cauliflowerets.

À la Bourguignonne: Decorate platter with Pan-Braised Onions and sautéed button mushrooms; serve with Bourguignonne Sauce.

À la Châtelaine: Surround steak with Braised Chestnuts, Château Potatoes, and artichoke bottoms filled with Soubise Sauce.

À la Clamart: (see Some Classic Ways to Serve Tournedos).

À la Dauphine: Surround steak with Dauphine Potatoes.

À la Duchess: Surround with Duchess Potatoes.

À la Jardinière: Exactly the same as Bouquetière except that carrots and turnips are cut with a ball cutter instead of being diced; serve with Hollandaise Sauce.

À la Tyrolienne: Surround steak with sautéed tomato wedges and top with sautéed onion rings.

Au Vert-Pré: Surround steak with Shoestring Potatoes and watercress sprigs; top with dabs of Maître d'Hôtel Butter.

Richelieu: Surround steak with Stuffed Tomatoes (use cherry tomatoes), Butter-Braised Hearts of Lettuce, and Château Potatoes.

Note: Any of these classic garnishes may also be used to garnish Broiled Whole Beef Tenderloin, broiled or panbroiled filet steaks, tournedos, or filets mignons.

How to Carve Porterhouse and Sirloin Steaks:

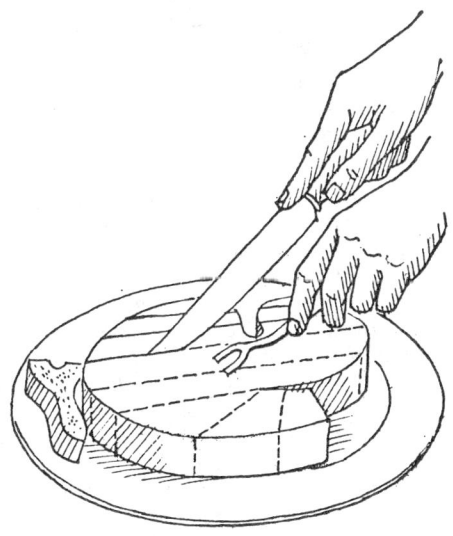

Steady steak with carving fork, cut around bone with a small carving knife and lift out. Cut straight across steak in ¾″–1″ slices. If steak is very thick, slant knife slightly (so less juice is lost). See that each person is served some of the tenderloin.

PLANKED STEAK WITH VEGETABLES

Unlike small or quick-cooking cuts that can be broiled altogether on a plank, sirloin steaks should be ½–¾ done before being set on plank because plank chars easily.
Makes 6 servings

1 (3–4-pound) sirloin steak, cut 1½″ thick
Salt
Pepper
1 recipe Duchess Potatoes (hot)
1 egg beaten with 1 tablespoon cold water (glaze)
2 tablespoons Maître d'Hôtel Butter or other flavored butter (see Sauces, Butters, and Seasonings for Steaks)

Garnishes (choose 1 or 2):

1 pound mushroom caps, sautéed
3 tomatoes, halved and broiled
1 recipe French-Fried Onion Rings or 1 (8-ounce) package frozen French-fried onion rings, cooked by package directions
2 cups boiled, buttered green peas
12 boiled, buttered whole baby carrots or 12 boiled, buttered broccoli flowerets

Trim all but ¼″ fat from steak and slash at 1″ intervals. Let steak stand at room temperature 1½–2 hours if convenient. Preheat broiler. Broil steak on lightly greased rack on 1 side following times in Steak Broiling Chart. Meanwhile, lightly oil plank and place on rack below steak to heat. Turn steak, season lightly with salt and pepper, and broil exactly ½ remaining recommended time. Transfer to plank, pipe a border of potatoes around plank, and brush potatoes lightly with egg glaze. Return steak to broiler and broil to desired doneness. If potatoes brown too fast, cover loosely with foil. (*Note:* Placing foil underneath plank

helps keep it clean.) Season steak with remaining salt and pepper and top with dabs of Maître d'Hôtel Butter. Arrange garnish between steak and potatoes, set plank in its holder or on a tray, and serve. About 700 calories per serving with a garnish of mushrooms and tomatoes.

To Plank Small Steaks (2 Servings): Substitute 2 (1″–1½″) rib, Delmonico, club, or T-bone steaks for sirloin. Broil on 1 side, transfer to plank, pipe with potatoes, and broil to desired doneness. Garnish and serve. About 700 calories per serving with a garnish of mushrooms and tomatoes.

SIRLOIN STEAK STUFFED WITH MUSHROOMS

Makes 8–10 servings

1 flat bone sirloin steak, cut 2½″–3″ thick (about 7 pounds)
1½ teaspoons salt
¼ teaspoon pepper
¼ cup dry port or red wine, warmed

Stuffing:

1 medium-size yellow onion, peeled and minced
⅓ cup butter or margarine
1 pound mushrooms, wiped clean and chopped fine
2 cups soft white bread crumbs
½ clove garlic, peeled and crushed
¼ teaspoon pepper
1½ teaspoons oregano
2 teaspoons minced parsley

Garnish:

2 recipes French-Fried Onion Rings

With a sharp knife, make a deep horizontal pocket in steak; slash fat edge at 1″ intervals and set steak aside while you prepare stuffing. Stir-fry onion in butter over moderate heat 5–8 minutes until pale golden; add mushrooms and brown over high heat 3–4 minutes. Off heat mix in remaining ingredients. Preheat broiler. Place stuffing in steak pocket and sew or skewer edges shut (to make more secure, tie steak with string, just as if wrapping a package). Broil on a lightly greased rack 5″ from heat about 20 minutes per side for rare, 22 for medium, and 24 for well done (before turning, sprinkle with ½ the salt and pepper). Transfer steak to steak board or heated platter, remove string and skewers, sprinkle with remaining salt and pepper, and, to show that steak is stuffed, cut off 2–3 slices, making them ⅓″ –½″ thick. Drizzle wine over steak, tipping board so it mingles with steak juices. Arrange some onion rings on top of steak and pass the rest. Top each serving with a ladling of steak juices. About 880 calories for each of 8 servings, 705 calories for each of 10 servings.

To Charcoal Broil: Prepare a moderately hot charcoal fire*; stuff steak as directed and broil on lightly greased grill 5″ from coals 15 minutes per side for rare, 18 for medium rare, 20 for medium, and 25 for well done.

.

CARPETBAG STEAK

This steak is best when broiled the Australian way—until medium rare or medium well—so the oysters have just enough time to cook. If you like rare steak, simmer the oysters, uncovered, in their liquor 3–4 minutes before stuffing the steak. Drain them well, pat dry on paper toweling, then proceed as recipe directs.
Makes 8–10 servings

1 flat bone sirloin steak, cut 2½″–3″
*   thick (about 7 pounds)*
¼ teaspoon pepper
1½ dozen small oysters, drained
1½ teaspoons salt

Garnishes:

Broiled tomato halves
Maître d'Hôtel Butter

Preheat broiler. With a sharp knife, make a deep horizontal pocket in steak; slash fat edge at 1″ intervals. Rub pocket with pepper and stuff with oysters. Sew opening shut with stout thread and broil steak on a lightly greased rack 5″

from heat 21 minutes on a side for medium rare, 22 for medium, and 23 for medium well (before turning, sprinkle with half the salt). Transfer steak to steak board or heated platter and sprinkle with remaining salt; remove thread. Surround with broiled tomato halves and top with pats of Maître d'Hôtel Butter. To serve, cut down through steak, making slices about ½″ thick. About 850 calories for each of 8 servings, 680 calories for each of 10 servings.

STEAK AU POIVRE

The quantity of pepper here is minimal for this classic steak. The best way to crush peppercorns is in a mortar and pestle or to place in a small plastic bag and roll with a rolling pin or pound with a soft drink bottle.
Makes 4 servings

4 teaspoons peppercorns, crushed
4 (1″-thick) club or Delmonico steaks
Cooking oil
1 teaspoon salt
4 small pats Maître d'Hôtel Butter
2–3 tablespoons brandy

Trim fat on steaks to ¼″ and slash at 1″ intervals. Sprinkle ½ teaspoon pepper on each side of each steak and press in well with the heel of your hand; let stand at room temperature ½ hour. Brush a large, heavy skillet with oil and heat over high heat 1 minute. Reduce heat to moderately high, add steaks, and panbroil, turning often, a total of 6 minutes for very rare, 8–10 for rare, 11–12 for medium rare, 13–14 for medium, and 15–16 for well done. Transfer to a hot platter, sprinkle with salt and top with butter pats. Pour brandy into skillet, stirring to scrape up brown bits, and heat 1 minute. Pour over steaks and serve. About 540 calories per serving.

To Broil: Preheat broiler. Prepare steaks as directed and broil 2″ from heat on lightly greased rack to desired doneness (use times in Steak Broiling Chart). Omit brandy; sprinkle with salt, top with butter, and serve.

To Charcoal Broil: Prepare a hot char-coal fire*; prepare steaks as directed and broil on lightly greased grill 4″ from heat to desired doneness (see Steak Broiling Chart). Omit brandy; sprinkle with salt, top with butter, and serve.

VARIATION:

Steak au Poivre Flambé: Panbroil steaks as above, transfer to chafing dish, and sprinkle with salt; omit butter. Pour ½ cup brandy into skillet, scrape up brown bits, and pour over steaks. Heat until mixture bubbles, blaze with a match, and spoon flames over steak. Serve when flames subside. About 480 calories per serving.

STEAK ALLA PIZZAIOLA

Makes 2 servings

2 *Delmonico, boneless shell or strip steaks, cut ¾″ thick*
1 *teaspoon olive oil*
¼ *teaspoon salt*
Pinch pepper
2 *teaspoons minced parsley*

Sauce:

2 *medium-size ripe tomatoes, peeled, cored, and coarsely chopped*
1 *clove garlic, peeled and crushed*
½ *teaspoon oregano*
2 *tablespoons olive oil*
½ *teaspoon salt*
⅛ *teaspoon pepper*

Rub steaks lightly with olive oil and set aside while you make the sauce. Place all sauce ingredients in a small skillet and simmer uncovered over moderately low heat, stirring occasionally, about 30 minutes until most of the liquid has evaporated. Quickly brown steaks on 1 side in another skillet over moderately high heat, turn, sprinkle lightly with salt and pepper. When second side is brown, turn again, season with remaining salt and pepper, top with sauce, cover, and simmer over lowest heat just 5 minutes. Sprinkle with parsley and serve. About 660 calories per serving.

☒ STEAK DIANE I

Some people like a touch of mustard in their steak Diane sauce, some don't. We offer both recipes here.
Makes 2 servings

2 (½-*pound*) *Delmonico steaks, cut ½″ thick*
2 *tablespoons unsalted butter*
2 *tablespoons minced shallots*
2 *tablespoons warmed cognac* (*optional*)
½ *teaspoon salt*
⅛ *teaspoon pepper*
1 *tablespoon minced parsley*
1 *tablespoon minced chives*
2 *teaspoons Worcestershire sauce*
2 *teaspoons steak sauce*

Trim outer layer of fat on steaks to ¼″ and slash at 1″ intervals; pound steaks between waxed paper with a meat mallet until ¼″–⅓″ thick. Melt butter in a large, heavy skillet over moderate heat and sauté shallots 3–4 minutes until pale golden; push to side of skillet. Raise burner heat to moderately high, add steaks, and brown 2–3 minutes on a side. If you like, turn heat to low, pour cognac over steaks, and flame. Transfer steaks to a heated platter and sprinkle with salt and pepper. Stir remaining ingredients into skillet drippings and heat, scraping up brown bits, about 1 minute. Pour over steaks and serve. About 580 calories per serving.

VARIATION:

☒ **Steak Diane II** (with mustard): Pound and brown steaks as directed; remove to platter. Blend into drippings along with above ingredients ¼ cup dry sherry and 1–2 teaspoons prepared Dijon-style mustard; boil up quickly to reduce slightly, pour over steaks, and serve. About 610 calories per serving.

STEAK FLORENTINE

Makes 2–3 servings

1 *porterhouse steak, cut 1½″ thick*
1 *clove garlic, peeled and cut in thin slivers*
⅛ *teaspoon pepper*
1 *tablespoon olive oil*

½ teaspoon salt
Lemon wedges

Rub each side of steak well with garlic, pepper, and oil and let stand at room temperature 2 hours. Heat a large, heavy griddle over moderately high heat about 1 minute and brown steak quickly on both sides. Reduce heat to moderately low and cook steak 10–12 minutes on a side for very rare, 12–14 for rare, 15–17 for medium, and 18–20 for well done. Season with salt and serve with lemon wedges. About 465 calories for each of 2 servings, 310 calories for each of 3 servings.

VARIATION:

⊠ **Minute Steaks Florentine** (2 Servings): Rub both sides of 2 minute steaks with garlic, pepper, and oil and let stand at room temperature 10 minutes. Heat a lightly oiled skillet 1 minute over moderately high heat and brown steaks quickly, about 1 minute on each side. Season with salt and serve with lemon wedges. About 465 calories per serving.

⊠ **PANNED CHUCK STEAKS ROSEMARY**

These steaks should only be served rare or medium rare—longer cooking makes them tough.
Makes 4 servings

4 (1¼"–1½" thick) small boneless blade chuck steaks
¾ teaspoon unseasoned meat tenderizer
½ cup butter or margarine
¼ teaspoon powdered rosemary
1 teaspoon salt
¼ teaspoon pepper
1 tablespoon Worcestershire sauce
1 teaspoon prepared mild yellow mustard
1 tablespoon hot water

Sprinkle both sides of each steak with tenderizer and pierce deeply with a sharp fork at ½" intervals. Lightly brown ¼ cup butter in a large, heavy skillet over moderate heat and stir in rosemary. Add steaks and brown about 2 minutes on a side for very rare, 3 for rare, and 4 for medium rare. Season

with salt and pepper, transfer to heated platter, and keep warm. Melt remaining butter in the skillet, add remaining ingredients, and cook and stir 1 minute; pour sauce over steaks and serve. About 600 calories per serving.

"CHARCOAL" BROILED CHUCK STEAK

When buying blade steak for this recipe, make sure it is the first cut or that nearest the rib; it will be tender enough to broil, but other blade steaks may not be. To help preserve tenderness, serve rare.
Makes 4 servings

1 (3½–4-pound) blade chuck steak, cut 1" thick and trimmed of excess fat
1½ teaspoons unseasoned meat tenderizer
½ teaspoon seasoned salt
1 teaspoon charcoal seasoning
¼ teaspoon pepper

Slash fat edges of steak at 1" intervals, then brush each side with a little water. Mix remaining ingredients, pat ½ on 1 side of steak and pierce meat deeply at ½" intervals. Turn steak, sprinkle with remaining mixture, and pierce as before. Cover steak loosely and let stand about ¼ hour. About 10 minutes before you're ready to broil steak, preheat broiler. Broil 2" from heat 3–4 minutes on a side for very rare, 5 for rare, and 6 for medium rare. About 480 calories per serving.

⊠ HOT STEAK SANDWICHES

Not really sandwiches, but juicy little steaks served on butter-browned bread, these are quick, easy, and *good!*
Makes 2 servings

2 (¼"-thick) small individual-size minute or cube steaks (they should be about the size of a slice of bread)
1–2 tablespoons butter or margarine
½ teaspoon salt
Pinch pepper
2 slices firm-textured white bread

Brown steaks quickly on 1 side in 1 tablespoon butter in a heavy skillet over moderately high heat (this will take about 1 minute). Turn, sprinkle with a little salt and pepper, and brown second side 1 minute. Season second side, remove steaks from skillet, and keep warm. If drippings seem scanty, add remaining butter to skillet. Quickly brown bread on both sides in drippings. Place 1 steak on each toasted bread slice and serve. About 430 calories per serving.

BALINESE BEEF ON SKEWERS (SATE)

One part of the 20 or 30 dish Indonesian *rijsttafel* (rice table) is *sate*—salty-spicy beef cubes grilled over charcoal. By themselves, with their sauce or soy sauce as a dip, these make exotic cocktail fare; with rice, an original main dish.
Makes 4 entree servings, enough hors d'oeuvre for 6–8

1½ pounds boneless sirloin steak, cut in ¾" cubes

Marinade:

1 teaspoon coriander seeds, crushed
1 teaspoon curry powder
⅛ teaspoon ginger
1 medium-size yellow onion, peeled and minced
1 clove garlic, peeled and crushed
1 tablespoon lime or lemon juice
3 tablespoons soy sauce
⅛ teaspoon pepper

Sauce:

3 tablespoons minced yellow onion
2 tablespoons cooking oil
1 teaspoon lemon juice
¼ cup peanut butter (creamy or crunchy)
1 cup hot water
Pinch hot red chili peppers (optional)

Place beef in a bowl. Mash coriander in a mortar and pestle with curry, ginger, onion, garlic, and lime juice, add to beef with soy sauce and pepper and knead well. Cover and chill 6–8 hours, turning meat 1 or 2 times in marinade. Meanwhile, prepare sauce: sauté onion in oil 5–8 minutes over moderate heat until pale golden, add remaining ingredients,

and simmer, uncovered, 10 minutes; cool and reserve. For cooking sate, prepare a hot charcoal fire* or preheat broiler. Skewer beef cubes on bamboo or metal skewers, not too close together, and broil 3"–4" from heat, turning often and basting with marinade 7–10 minutes for rare, 12 for medium, and 15 for well done. Warm sauce, uncovered, over low heat. Serve with rice, topped with some of the sauce; or as a cocktail snack. About 495 calories per entree serving (without rice); about 330 calories for each of 6 hors d'oeuvre servings, 250 calories for each of 8 hors d'oeuvre servings.

VARIATIONS:

Chicken or Pork Sate: Substitute ¾" cubes of white chicken meat or lean pork for beef and prepare as directed, broiling at least 15 minutes until well done (this is particularly important for pork; if necessary, place skewers 5" from heat so pork cooks through without drying out). About 415 calories for each of 4 entree servings made with chicken, 535 calories made with pork.

Beef Sate Padang Style: Instead of using marinade above, grind 1 teaspoon caraway seeds in a mortar and pestle with ½ teaspoon each turmeric and curry powder, 1 minced yellow onion, 1 crushed clove garlic, a pinch hot red chili peppers, and 1 tablespoon lime or lemon juice; add 3 tablespoons soy sauce and ½ cup coconut liquid or Coconut Milk. Pour marinade over beef, then marinate and broil as directed above. About 400 calories for each entree serving.

⊠ LONDON BROIL

The best way to make London broil tender is to serve it rare and to cut it *across the grain* in thin slices.
Makes 6 servings

1 (2½–3-pound) flank steak, trimmed of excess fat
1½ teaspoons salt
¼ teaspoon pepper

Preheat broiler. Score both sides of steak in a crisscross pattern, making

cuts ⅛″ deep and 1″ apart. Broil on
an oiled rack 2″–3″ from heat 4 minutes, turn with tongs, and broil 4 minutes
longer. Transfer to a board or platter
with a well (so juices will collect) and
season with salt and pepper. Carve
across the grain, slanting knife slightly,
into slices ⅛″–¼″ thick. Top each
portion with some of the juices and, if
you like, pass Madeira-Mushroom Sauce.
About 400 calories per serving.

To Charcoal Broil: Prepare a hot charcoal fire*; score steak as directed and
broil on lightly greased grill 3″ from
coals about 3–4 minutes per side. Season
and serve.

VARIATION:

Marinated Broiled Flank Steak: Marinate a scored flank steak in refrigerator
in any meat marinade or thin barbecue
sauce 4–6 hours. Remove from
marinade and broil or charcoal broil,
basting frequently with marinade. Slice
and serve. About 400 calories per
serving.

BACON-WRAPPED FLANK STEAK PINWHEELS

Makes 4 servings

*1 (2-pound) flank steak, trimmed of
 excess fat*
*2 tablespoons butter or margarine,
 softened to room temperature*
1 teaspoon unseasoned meat tenderizer
¼ teaspoon salt
¼ teaspoon pepper
1 teaspoon caraway seeds
2 teaspoons oregano
6–8 slices bacon

Preheat broiler. Score 1 side of steak in
a crisscross pattern, making cuts ⅛″
deep and 1″ apart, then spread with
butter and sprinkle with tenderizer.
Pierce meat deeply all over with a sharp
fork, sprinkle with salt, pepper, caraway,
and oregano and roll, jelly-roll style,
starting from a long side: secure with
skewers. Slice crosswise into rolls 1½″
thick, wrap a bacon slice around each,
and resecure with skewers. Broil on a
lightly greased rack 3″–4″ from heat 5

minutes on each side, then bake, uncovered, 5 minutes at 350° F. (no need to
preheat oven). (*Note:* If bacon doesn't
crispen, turn pinwheels on edge and
broil to brown.) Good with broiled tomato halves topped with broiled mushroom caps. About 740 calories per
serving.

VARIATION:

**Stuffed Flank Steak Pinwheels (Makes 6
servings):** Score steak, spread with
butter, sprinkle with tenderizer, and
pierce as recipe directs. Sprinkle with
salt and pepper but omit caraway seeds
and oregano. Spread about 2 cups any
well-seasoned meat or poultry stuffing to
within 1″ of edges, then roll jelly-roll
style, secure with skewers, slice, and
wrap with bacon as directed. Broil 5
minutes on a side, 3″–4″ from the heat,
then bake, uncovered, 10 minutes at
350° F. About 575 calories per serving.

PORTUGUESE VEGETABLE-BRAISED FLANK STEAK

Flank steak smothered with a thick
tomato-carrot-onion-green-pepper gravy.
Makes 4 servings

*1 (2-pound) flank steak, trimmed of
 excess fat*
2 tablespoons flour
2 tablespoons olive oil or cooking oil
1 medium-size carrot, peeled and minced
*½ medium-size sweet green pepper,
 cored, seeded, and minced*
2 stalks celery, minced
*1 medium-size yellow onion, peeled and
 minced*
1 (10½-ounce) can condensed beef broth
1 teaspoon salt
¼ teaspoon pepper
2 tablespoons tomato paste
1 teaspoon lemon juice

Score each side of steak in a crisscross
pattern, making cuts ⅛″ deep and 1″
apart. Using the rim of a heavy saucer,
pound flour into both sides of steak (use
1 tablespoon altogether). Brown steak
well on both sides in oil in a heavy kettle
over moderately high heat; lift out and
set aside. Add carrot, green pepper,
celery, and onion to kettle and stir-fry

8–10 minutes until onion is golden. Add remaining flour and cook and stir 1 minute; stir in remaining ingredients, return steak to kettle, cover, and simmer about 1½ hours until tender. To serve, transfer steak to heated platter and, slanting the knife, slice crosswise into thin strips. Pour some of the gravy (with vegetables) over steak. Pass the rest in a gravy boat. About 600 calories per serving.

HERB-STUFFED FLANK STEAK

The herb-bread stuffing makes two pounds of steak do the job of three.
Makes 6 servings

1 (2-pound) flank steak, trimmed of excess fat
1 medium-size yellow onion, peeled and minced
½ cup finely chopped celery
¼ cup butter or margarine
2 cups soft white bread crumbs
1½ teaspoons salt
¼ teaspoon pepper
1 tablespoon minced parsley
¼ teaspoon thyme
¼ teaspoon marjoram
¼ teaspoon sage
2 tablespoons beef drippings or cooking oil
2 cups beef broth or dry red wine
3 tablespoons flour mixed with 3 tablespoons cold water

Preheat oven to 325° F. Score 1 side of steak in a crisscross pattern, making cuts ⅛″ deep and 1″ apart. Sauté onion and celery in butter over moderately low heat 8 minutes until pale golden; off heat, mix in crumbs, 1 teaspoon salt, ⅛ teaspoon pepper, and the herbs. Sprinkle unscored side of steak with remaining salt and pepper and spread stuffing to within 1″ of edges, patting down firmly. Roll jelly-roll style, starting from a short side, and tie well with string (around the roll and end over end). Brown roll in drippings in a Dutch oven over moderate heat 7–10 minutes, add broth, cover, and bake 1½ hours until tender. Transfer meat to a platter and remove strings. Mix flour-water paste into pan liquid

and heat, stirring, until thickened. Cut steak crosswise into thick slices and serve with gravy. About 580 calories per serving.

VARIATION:

Argentine Stuffed Flank Steak: Score steak as directed above, then prepare the following stuffing: remove casings from ½ pound *chorizo* or other garlic-flavored sausage and sauté the meat, breaking it up, 5 minutes over moderately high heat. Add ½ cup minced celery and 4 minced scallions and sauté 5 minutes longer. Off heat mix in ½ cup soft white bread crumbs, ¼ cup minced parsley, ½ teaspoon salt, and 1 lightly beaten egg. Spread on steak as directed above, then roll, brown, and bake as directed. Serve with a peppery chili sauce. About 595 calories per serving.

RUSSIAN-STYLE POT STEAK

Flank makes as flavorful a "Stroganoff" as more expensive steak.
Makes 4 servings

1 (2–2¼-pound) flank steak, trimmed of excess fat and cut crosswise into strips ½″ × 1½″
⅔ cup unsifted flour
1 teaspoon salt
¼ teaspoon pepper
3 tablespoons bacon drippings
2 medium-size yellow onions, peeled and coarsely chopped
1 large carrot, peeled and coarsely grated
1 tablespoon minced parsley
1 tablespoon paprika
1 (10½-ounce) can condensed beef broth
⅔ cup water
½ cup sour cream

Dredge meat by shaking a few strips at a time in a paper bag with flour, salt, and pepper. Heat bacon drippings in a heavy kettle over moderately high heat about 1 minute, add beef, and brown well on all sides, about 15 minutes. Reduce heat to moderate, add onions, carrot, parsley, and paprika, and sauté, stirring, 8–10 minutes until onions are golden. Add broth and water, cover, and simmer slowly 1–1½ hours until meat is tender. Mix in sour cream and serve with boiled new potatoes or buttered noodles. About 725 calories per serving.

⚖️ CHINESE BEEF AND PEPPERS

If you want to double this recipe, use two skillets instead of one giant one so the vegetables don't overcook and lose their crisp-tender delicacy.
Makes 2 servings

2 tablespoons peanut or other cooking oil
1 small yellow onion, peeled and minced
1 sweet green pepper, cored, seeded, and cut in 1" squares
1 teaspoon Chinese black beans, rinsed (optional)
1 clove garlic, peeled and crushed
1 thin slice gingerroot or ⅛ teaspoon ginger
1 tomato, peeled, seeded, and cut in 6 wedges
½–¾ pound flank steak, trimmed of fat and cut across the grain in slices ⅛" thick
1 teaspoon dry sherry
½ teaspoon salt
½ teaspoon sugar
1 teaspoon soy sauce

Heat oil in a large skillet or *wok* over high heat ½ minute, add onion, green pepper, black beans, garlic, and ginger, and stir-fry 2 minutes. Add tomato and stir-fry 1 minute. Reduce heat to moderately high and push vegetables to side of pan; add beef and stir-fry 1 minute, sprinkling in sherry. Mix remaining ingredients, sprinkle over beef, and stir-fry ½ minute. Serve over boiled rice or Chinese Fried Rice.

VARIATIONS:

⚖️ **Chinese Beef with Snow Peas:** Substitute ¼ pound snow pea pods and, if you like, ¼ pound thinly sliced mushrooms for onion and green pepper; stir-fry as directed. Add 1 (4-ounce) can drained, thinly sliced water chestnuts in place of tomato, stir-fry 1 minute, then proceed as recipe directs.

⚖️ **Chinese Beef with Broccoli and Bean Sprouts:** Substitute ½ pound parboiled, thinly sliced broccoli for onion and green pepper and stir-fry as directed. Add ½ (1-pound) can well-drained bean sprouts along with tomato and proceed as recipe directs.

⚖️ **Chinese Beef and Cabbage:** Substitute ½ pound shredded Chinese cabbage for green pepper, proceed as recipe directs.

All versions: About 340 calories per serving (without rice).

BEEF BIRDS (ROULADES)

Makes 6 servings

12 (5"×3"×¼") slices beef round pounded thin as for scaloppine
Salt
Pepper
Flour (for dredging)
¼ cup beef or bacon drippings or cooking oil
⅔ cup finely chopped celery (optional)
½ cup thinly sliced mushrooms (optional)
2 cups beef broth
3 tablespoons flour blended with 3 tablespoons cold water

Stuffing:

1 large yellow onion, peeled and minced
2 tablespoons beef or bacon drippings
½ cup finely chopped mushrooms
2 cups soft white bread crumbs
½ cup water
1 egg, lightly beaten
½ teaspoon salt
⅛ teaspoon pepper
2 tablespoons minced parsley

Sprinkle beef with salt and pepper and set aside while you prepare stuffing. Sauté onion in drippings over moderate heat 5–8 minutes until pale golden, add mushrooms and stir-fry 1–2 minutes; off heat mix in remaining ingredients. Spoon about 2 tablespoons stuffing on each piece meat, roll, and tie well with string. Dredge rolls in flour and brown, a few at a time, in drippings in a Dutch oven 5–7 minutes over moderate heat; drain on paper toweling. If you wish, add celery and mushrooms and stir-fry

2–3 minutes. Drain all but 1 tablespoon drippings from kettle, return meat, add broth, cover, and simmer 1½ hours until tender (or bake 1½ hours at 350° F.). Transfer rolls to serving dish and remove strings. Mix flour-water paste into kettle and heat, stirring, until thickened. Serve with gravy and buttered noodles. About 410 calories per serving.

VARIATIONS:

⚖ **German Rouladen:** Salt and pepper beef as directed, then, instead of making stuffing, lay a thin strip dill pickle on each piece beef, also 2 teaspoons each capers and minced onion and ½ strip bacon. Roll, tie, and cook as recipe directs. About 310 calories per serving.

Italian Braciuolini: Salt and pepper beef as directed, then make the following filling instead of one given above: Brown ½ cup minced onion and ½ pound ground beef chuck or sweet Italian sausage meat in 2 tablespoons olive oil 5–8 minutes over moderately high heat: drain off drippings. Off heat mix in 1 cup soft white bread crumbs, ½ teaspoon salt, ⅛ teaspoon pepper, 1 lightly beaten egg, and ½ teaspoon oregano or basil. Spoon filling onto meat, roll, tie, and proceed as recipe directs. (*Note:* If you like, cook rolls in a thin tomato sauce instead of broth, omitting chopped celery and mushrooms.) Good with Gnocchi or any buttered pasta. About 420 calories per serving.

Paupiettes à la Bourguignonne: Prepare rolls as directed, then cook in 1 cup dry red wine and 1 cup beef broth with 1 peeled clove garlic and ⅛ teaspoon thyme (omit celery and mushrooms). About 10 minutes before serving, thicken gravy as directed and add 1 recipe Pan-Braised Onions and 1 recipe Sautéed Mushrooms. About 545 calories per serving.

Beef Birds with Sour Cream Gravy: Prepare rolls by basic recipe above but omit flour-water paste; stir in 1 cup sour cream just before serving. About 480 calories per serving.

OLD-FASHIONED SWISS STEAK

Makes 4–6 servings

¼ cup unsifted flour
1½ teaspoons salt
¼ teaspoon pepper
1 (3–4-pound) blade or arm steak, cut about 2" thick
3 tablespoons beef or bacon drippings or cooking oil
1 large yellow onion, peeled and minced
2 stalks celery, minced
2 small carrots, peeled and minced
1 (1-pound) can tomatoes (do not drain) or 1 (1-pound) can Spanish-style tomato sauce
1½ cups beef broth or hot water

Mix flour, salt, and pepper and sprinkle about 2 tablespoons on 1 side of meat; pound with a meat mallet or edge of heavy saucer. Turn meat and pound in remaining flour the same way. Melt drippings in a Dutch oven over moderately high heat 1 minute and brown meat well, about 5 minutes on each side. Remove meat and set aside. Sauté onion, celery, and carrots in remaining drippings 8 minutes until golden. Return meat to kettle, spoon vegetables on top, add tomatoes and broth. Cover and simmer 1½–2 hours until tender, basting meat once or twice. Cut into portions, top with vegetables and gravy, and serve. About 640 calories for each of 4 servings, 590 calories for each of 6 servings.

To Bake: Prepare as directed but, instead of simmering on top of stove, cover and bake 2–2½ hours in a 350° F. oven.

EASY SWISS STEAK

Makes 4–6 servings

1 (3–4-pound) blade or arm steak, cut about 2" thick
2 cloves garlic, peeled and crushed
¼ teaspoon pepper
1 (1⅜-ounce) package dry onion soup mix
1 (6-ounce) can tomato paste
⅓ cup dry white wine

Preheat oven to 350° F. Place steak on a large double thickness of foil and rub each side with garlic and pepper; pat on soup mix. Combine tomato paste and wine and spread on top side only. Wrap foil around steak, place in a shallow roasting pan, and bake 2–2½ hours until tender. Unwrap, carve into thin slices, and top each serving with drippings. About 540 calories for each of 4 servings, 360 calories for each of 6 servings.

ESTERHÁZY STEAK

Steak, mushrooms, onion, celery, and carrot in a tart sour cream-caper gravy. Worth every calorie-packed forkful!
Makes 2–4 servings

1 pound top round, cut ¼" thick and pounded thin as for scaloppine
⅓ cup unsifted flour
1 teaspoon salt
⅛ teaspoon pepper
3 tablespoons butter, margarine, or meat drippings
1 carrot, peeled and minced
2 medium-size mushrooms, wiped clean and minced
1 stalk celery, minced
1 small yellow onion, peeled and minced
1 tablespoon minced parsley
1 cup beef stock or broth
1 tablespoon minced capers
1 cup sour cream

Cut steak into pieces about 4" square. Mix flour, salt, and pepper and rub well into both sides of each piece of steak; reserve 1 tablespoon seasoned flour. Brown steak on both sides in butter in a large, heavy skillet over moderately high heat, push to side of skillet, add all minced vegetables and parsley, and stir-fry 5–8 minutes. Blend in reserved seasoned flour. Turn heat to low, add broth, cover, and simmer 40–45 minutes until steak is tender. Mix in capers, then smooth in sour cream and heat (but do not boil) about 1 minute. Serve hot with boiled potatoes or buttered noodles. About 980 calories for each of 2 servings, 490 calories for each of 4 servings.

CHICKEN-FRIED STEAK

Prepared much the same way as the famous Southern "batter-fried" chicken.
Makes 2–4 servings

1 pound top or bottom round, cut ¼" thick and pounded thin as for scaloppine
½ cup unsifted flour
2 eggs lightly beaten with 3 tablespoons milk
1 cup fine dry bread crumbs or cracker meal
4–5 tablespoons lard, meat drippings, butter, or margarine
1 teaspoon salt
⅛ teaspoon pepper

Cut steak into 3" squares; dust well with flour, dip in egg, then in crumbs to coat evenly. Heat 3 tablespoons lard in a large, heavy skillet over moderately high heat and brown steak 2–3 minutes on a side, adding more lard as needed. When all pieces are browned, sprinkle with salt and pepper, turn heat to low, cover, and cook about 45 minutes until tender. About 950 calories for each of 2 servings, 475 calories for each of 4 servings.

COUNTRY FRIED STEAK

The Middle Western way to make a "tough" steak tender.
Makes 2–4 servings

1 pound bottom round, cut ¼" thick
1 teaspoon salt
⅛ teaspoon pepper
⅓ cup unsifted flour
3 tablespoons beef or bacon drippings, butter, or margarine
⅔ cup water

Cut steak into pieces about 3" square, sprinkle each side with salt and pepper, and rub generously with flour. Place between several thicknesses wax paper and pound well with the blunt side of a meat cleaver or edge of a heavy saucer. Heat drippings about 1 minute in a large, heavy skillet over moderately high heat and brown steak quickly on both sides. Turn heat to low, add water, cover, and simmer 30–40 minutes until steak is tender. When serving, top each portion with pan gravy. About 700 calories for each of 2 servings, 350 calories for each of 4 servings.

VARIATIONS:

Country Fried Steak with Onion: Season, pound, and brown steak as directed, then remove from skillet. In the drippings stir-fry 1 thinly sliced large yellow onion 8–10 minutes until golden brown; remove from skillet temporarily. Return meat to skillet, pile onions on top, add water, cover, and simmer as directed. About 720 calories for each of 2 servings, 360 calories for each of 4 servings.

Country Fried Steak with Mushrooms: Season, pound, and brown steak as above; remove from skillet. Stir-fry ½ pound thinly sliced mushrooms in drippings 5 minutes until limp and remove; return meat to skillet, spoon mushrooms on top, add water, cover, and simmer as directed. About 730 calories for each of 2 servings, 365 calories for each of 4 servings.

GROUND BEEF

How ground beef is to be used determines how it should be ground. For light, juicy hamburgers, it should be coarsely ground, one time only. For meat balls and meat loaves, where firmer textures are desirable, it can be finely ground two or three times. Generally speaking, the more finely—and often—meat is ground, the more compact it will be when cooked.

What kind of hamburger should you buy? Again, it depends on use. Also budget. Here are the three most popular kinds:

Regular Hamburger (ground trimmings, usually from shank, plate, and brisket): The cheapest ground beef, also the fattest (often ¼ to ⅓ fat), which means it will

shrink considerably during cooking as the fat melts and drippings run off.

Ground Chuck: Probably the best all round hamburger meat. It has just enough fat (about 15%) to make it juicy, an excellent flavor, and a moderate price.

Ground Round: The most expensive "hamburger," also the leanest, meaning it may dry out if cooked much beyond medium rare (when having round ground to order, make sure the butcher adds about 2 ounces suet for each pound lean). Ground round is a good choice for calorie counters—a ¼ pound *broiled* patty averages about 220 calories.

⊠ HAMBURGERS

Though it's usually recommended that meat be brought to room temperature before cooking, hamburger is an exception because of its great perishability. Cooking times given here are for meat refrigerated until ready to use. Makes 3–4 servings

1 pound ground beef
1 teaspoon salt
⅛ teaspoon pepper

Shape beef *lightly* into 3 plump patties or 4 slim ones and cook by one of the methods below; season with salt and pepper just before serving.

To Panfry (Sauté): Especially recommended for lean meat. Brown hamburgers uncovered in 1–2 tablespoons cooking oil, butter, margarine, or drippings in a large, heavy skillet over moderately high heat; plump patties will take about 5 minutes on a side for rare, 6 for medium, and 7 for well done, thin patties about 1 minute less per side for each degree of doneness. While hamburgers cook, do not press down or "spank" with a pancake turner—you'll only force out succulent juices. About 355 calories for each of 3 servings, 265 for each of 4 servings.

⊠ ⚖ *To Panbroil:* Recommended for dieters, also for meat heavily flecked with fat. Lightly brush a large, heavy skillet with oil or sprinkle with salt; heat

1 minute over moderately high heat, add hamburgers, and brown, uncovered, using the same cooking times as for panfrying. Pour off drippings as they accumulate. About 320 calories for each of 3 servings, 240 calories for each of 4 servings.

⊠ ◁ᖬᐅ *To Broil:* Recommended for dieters and fatty hamburger meat. Preheat broiler; broil hamburgers 3″ from heat on a lightly greased broiler rack. Plump patties will take 5–6 minutes on a side for rare, 7 for medium, and 8–9 for well done, thin patties about 1 minute less per side in each instance. About 320 calories for each of 3 servings, 240 calories for each of 4 servings.

◁ᖬᐅ *To Charcoal Broil:* Recommended for plump patties only. Prepare a moderately hot charcoal fire.* Lay hamburgers on a lightly greased grill and broil 4″ from the heat about 4–5 minutes on a side for rare, 6 for medium, and 7–8 for well done. About 320 calories for each of 3 servings, 240 calories for each of 4 servings.

To Braise: Brown patties quickly in a lightly greased large, heavy skillet over high heat, turn heat to low and pour in 1–1½ cups liquid (dry red wine; broth; gravy; tomato juice, soup, or sauce; cream of mushroom, cheese, or celery soup), cover, and simmer slowly 15–20 minutes. Serve topped with the cooking liquid. About 350 calories for each of 3 servings (cooked in broth, wine, or tomato juice), 265 calories for each of 4 servings. Burgers cooked in gravy, sauce, or soup will run approximately 65–100 calories more for each of 3 servings (depending on richness), 50–75 calories more for each of 4 servings.

⊠ 20 VARIATIONS ON HAMBURGERS

All amounts based on recipe above

Cheeseburgers: Shape patties as directed, brown on 1 side, and season lightly; turn, season again, top with a thin slice American cheese and cook to desired doneness. About 420 calories for each of

3 servings, 315 calories for each of 4 servings.

Blue Cheese Burgers: Shape meat into 6 thin patties; in the center of 3 place a scant teaspoon blue cheese spread. Top with remaining patties and pinch edges to seal. Cook as directed, season with ¼ teaspoon salt and ⅛ teaspoon pepper and serve. About 370 calories per serving.

Surprise Burgers: Shape meat into 6 thin patties; in the center of 3 place a scant teaspoon of any of the following: minced onion, dill pickle, or capers; sweet pickle relish; grated Cheddar or Swiss cheese. Top with remaining patties and pinch edges to seal. Cook and season as directed. About 320 calories per serving made with onion, capers or pickle, 370 if made with cheese.

Stuffed Burgers: Shape beef into 6 thin patties, top 3 with scant tablespoons leftover mashed potatoes or turnips, boiled rice or pilaf, leftover cooked peas, beans, corn, diced beets, or carrots. Top with remaining patties, pinch edges to seal, cook and season as directed. About 330 calories per serving.

Herb Burgers: Into beef mix 1 tablespoon minced chives and ¼ teaspoon each sage and marjoram or thyme; shape into patties, cook and season as directed. About 320 calories for each of 3 servings, 240 calories for each of 4 servings.

Dilly Burgers: Into beef mix 1 tablespoon each sour cream, minced chives, fresh dill, and capers; shape into patties, cook as directed, and season with ½ teaspoon salt and ⅛ teaspoon pepper. About 330 calories for each of 3 servings, 245 calories for each of 4 servings.

Deviled Burgers: Mix beef with 2 tablespoons each cold water and spicy brown prepared mustard, 1 teaspoon each grated onion and Worcestershire sauce, ½ teaspoon salt, and 2–3 dashes liquid hot red pepper seasoning. Shape and cook as directed but do not season. About 320 calories for each of 3 servings, 240 calories for each of 4 servings.

Curry Burgers: Into beef mix 2 tablespoons grated onion, 1 tablespoon curry powder, 1 teaspoon garlic salt, ⅛ teaspoon cayenne pepper, and a pinch each ginger and cinnamon. Shape and cook as directed but do not season. About 320 calories for each of 3 servings, 240 calories for each of 4 servings.

Chili Burgers: Into beef mix 1 tablespoon each grated onion, chili sauce, chili powder, ½ teaspoon garlic salt, and ⅛ teaspoon cayenne pepper. Shape and cook as directed but do not season. About 320 calories for each of 3 servings, 240 calories for each of 4 servings.

Barbecue Burgers: Into beef mix 1 tablespoon each ketchup, Worcestershire sauce, red wine vinegar, chili powder, ¼ teaspoon salt, and ⅛ teaspoon cayenne pepper. Shape and cook as directed but do not season. About 325 calories for each of 3 servings, 245 calories for each of 4 servings.

Pizza Burgers: Shape meat into 4 patties and broil 3 minutes on a side. Sprinkle lightly with salt. Top each patty with 1–2 tablespoons canned pizza sauce, a thin slice mozzarella cheese, a sprinkling oregano, and, if you like, crushed hot red chili peppers. Return to broiler and broil just until bubbly. About 310 calories per serving.

Teriyaki Burgers: Mix beef with 2 tablespoons each soy sauce, dry sherry, and minced sautéed scallions, ½ crushed clove garlic, 1 teaspoon grated fresh gingerroot, and ⅛ teaspoon pepper. Shape and cook as directed but do not season. About 325 calories for each of 3 servings, 245 calories for each of 4 servings.

Burgundy Burgers: Mix 1 minced scallion into beef, also 2 tablespoons Burgundy wine, ½ crushed clove garlic, ½ teaspoon salt, and a pinch pepper. Shape and cook as directed but do not season. About 3 minutes before serving, add ½ cup Burgundy to skillet and continue cooking, basting often. Serve topped with pan juices. About 325 calories for each of 3 servings, 245 calories for each of 4 servings.

Mushroom Burgers: Mix beef with 2 tablespoons minced sautéed onion and ⅓ cup minced sautéed mushrooms, 1 teaspoon salt, and ⅛ teaspoon pepper. Shape and cook as directed but do not season. About 325 calories for each of 3 servings, 245 calories for each of 4 servings.

Pepper Burgers: Mix beef with 2 tablespoons each minced sautéed green pepper and onion, 1 teaspoon salt, and ⅛ teaspoon pepper. Shape and cook as directed but do not season. About 325 calories for each of 3 servings, 245 calories for each of 4 servings.

Bacon Burgers: Mix beef with ¼ cup each minced sautéed onion and crisp bacon bits. Shape into patties, cook and season as directed. About 420 calories for each of 3 servings, 315 calories for each of 4 servings.

Nut Burgers: Mix beef with 2 tablespoons minced onion, ⅓ cup finely chopped pecans, piñon nuts, toasted almonds or walnuts, and 2 teaspoons minced parsley. Shape, cook and season as directed. About 410 calories for each of 3 servings, 310 calories for each of 4 servings.

Burgers au Poivre: Shape into 4 patties, sprinkle each side of each with ¼ teaspoon coarsely ground pepper and press into meat with the heel of your hand. Let stand at room temperature 20–30 minutes. Panfry hamburgers in 2 tablespoons butter 3–4 minutes on a side; remove to a hot platter, sprinkle with salt, and keep warm. To drippings add 1 tablespoon each butter, minced parsley, and cognac and heat 1–2 minutes, stirring to get up any brown bits. Spoon over burgers and serve. About 315 calories per serving.

Burgers Diane: Shape into 4 patties and panfry in 2 tablespoons unsalted butter about 4 minutes on a side; remove from skillet, season with ½ teaspoon salt and ⅛ teaspoon pepper, and keep warm. To skillet add 3 tablespoons dry sherry, 1 tablespoon each unsalted butter, minced chives, parsley, and cognac and 1 teaspoon each Worcestershire sauce and prepared spicy brown mustard. Heat 1–2 minutes, stirring with a wooden spoon to scrape up brown bits, pour over burgers, and serve. About 320 calories per serving.

⊿⊿ ¢ **Budget Burgers:** To extend 1 pound ground beef so it will serve 6, mix in 1 lightly beaten egg and any of the following, then shape, cook and season as directed:
– 1 cup mashed, drained cooked beans (navy, kidney, pinto, or chick-peas). About 225 calories per serving.
– 1 cup mashed potatoes, boiled rice, bulgur wheat, or pilaf and, if mixture seems a little dry, 1–2 tablespoons broth, milk, tomato juice, or water. About 175 calories per serving.
– 1 cup crushed potato chips or corn-flakes. About 200 calories per serving.
– 1 cup cracker meal or poultry stuffing mix and ¼–⅓ cup broth, milk, or tomato juice. About 275 calories per serving.
– 1 cup soft bread crumbs or crumbled corn bread and ¼–⅓ cup broth, milk, or tomato juice. About 215 calories per serving.
– ½ cup each minced celery and finely grated carrot and 2 tablespoons finely grated onion. About 175 calories per serving.
– 1 cup finely diced boiled potatoes, ½ cup diced, drained cooked beets, and 2 tablespoons grated onion. About 195 calories per serving.

⊠ ¢ BEEF LINDSTROM

Here's a delicious way to use up leftover boiled beets and potatoes.
Makes 4–6 servings

1 pound ground beef
⅔ cup minced boiled beets, well drained
1 cup minced boiled potatoes
1 tablespoon finely grated onion
2 teaspoons minced capers
2 egg yolks, lightly beaten
2 tablespoons light cream

¼ teaspoon salt
Pinch pepper
2–3 tablespoons butter or margarine

Mix beef with all ingredients except butter, cover, and chill several hours until firm enough to shape. Shape into small rectangular patties about 3″ long and 1″ wide, then brown 5–7 minutes in butter in a large, heavy skillet over moderately high heat. To avoid crowding skillet, do about half the patties at a time, setting browned ones, uncovered, in a 250° F. oven to keep warm while you brown the rest. About 375 calories for each of 4 servings, 250 calories for each of 6 servings.

SALISBURY STEAK

Makes 2–4 servings

½ recipe Mushroom Gravy
1 pound ground beef
1 teaspoon salt
⅛ teaspoon pepper

Prepare gravy by recipe and keep warm. Shape beef into 2 flat oval patties and panbroil in a large, lightly greased skillet over moderately high heat 5–6 minutes on each side for rare, 7 for medium, and 8–9 for well done. Sprinkle with salt and pepper, smother with mushroom gravy, and serve. About 580 calories for each of 2 servings, 290 calories for each of 4 servings.

⊠ ¢ SLOPPY JOES

Makes 6 servings

1 teaspoon beef drippings or cooking oil
1 pound ground beef
1 medium-size yellow onion, peeled and chopped fine
½ cup ketchup
½ cup chili sauce
1 tablespoon Worcestershire sauce
1 teaspoon salt
⅛ teaspoon pepper
⅓ cup water
6 hamburger buns, warmed

Brush a skillet with drippings and warm over moderate heat ½ minute. Add beef and onion and sauté 10 minutes, stirring frequently. Add all remaining ingredients except buns and simmer, uncovered, 10 minutes. Spoon mixture between split buns and serve. About 320 calories per serving.

VARIATIONS:

⊠ ⚖ ¢ **Sloppy Josés:** Substitute 1 cup canned Spanish-style tomato sauce for ketchup and chili sauce; prepare and serve as directed. About 280 calories per serving.

⊠ ¢ **Sloppy Franks:** Add 1–2 teaspoons chili powder to meat mixture, simmer as directed, and spoon over hot dogs in hot dog buns. About 460 calories per serving.

⊠ ¢ **Cheesy Joes:** Lightly toast bottom half of each hamburger bun, top with a slice of cheese (American, Cheddar, Swiss, etc.), and toast until cheese begins to melt. Spoon meat mixture over cheese, add bun lids, and serve. About 420 calories per serving.

⚖ ¢ ECONOMY MEAT LOAF

Makes 6 servings

1½ pounds ground beef
1 cup rolled oats
2 teaspoons salt
¼ teaspoon pepper
1 teaspoon prepared spicy yellow
  mustard
1 teaspoon prepared horseradish
1 large yellow onion, peeled and chopped
  fine
¾ cup milk or skim milk
¼ cup cold water

Preheat oven to 350° F. Using your hands, mix all ingredients together thoroughly. Pack into an ungreased 9″×5″×3″ loaf pan. Bake, uncovered, 1 hour. Loosen loaf from pan, drain off drippings (save for gravy), invert on a heated platter, and serve. About 225 calories per serving.

JOHN'S SAGEY MEAT LOAF

Makes 8 servings

3 pounds ground beef
1 cup finely chopped Bermuda or Spanish
  onion

1 clove garlic, peeled and crushed
1 cup coarse soda cracker crumbs
3 eggs
¼ cup dry white vermouth
¼ cup water
2 teaspoons minced fresh sage or ½
  teaspoon dried sage
¼ teaspoon parsley flakes
¼ teaspoon thyme
¼ teaspoon marjoram
1½ teaspoons salt
⅛ teaspoon pepper

Preheat oven to 325° F. Mix all ingredients thoroughly, using your hands, and pack into an ungreased 9″×5″×3″ loaf pan. Bake, uncovered, 1 hour and 25 minutes or until loaf begins to pull from sides of pan. Remove from oven and let stand 5 minutes. Pour off any drippings, turn loaf onto a warmed platter, and serve. About 435 calories per serving.

¢ BEEF AND PORK LOAF

Makes 6–8 servings

¾ cup lukewarm milk
1 egg, beaten
1½ cups soft white bread crumbs
1 pound ground beef
1 pound ground lean pork
1 large yellow onion, peeled and minced
⅓ cup minced gherkins
1 tablespoon salt
¼ teaspoon pepper
1 tablespoon Worcestershire sauce

Preheat oven to 350° F. Combine milk and egg, add crumbs, and let stand 5 minutes; mix thoroughly with remaining ingredients, turn into an ungreased shallow roasting pan, and shape into a loaf. Bake, uncovered, 1½ hours, basting off excess drippings (save for gravy). Transfer loaf to a heated platter and let stand 5 minutes before cutting. Serve hot with gravy, Sweet-Sour Sauce, or Mushroom Gravy. Or chill and serve cold with Mustard Sauce. About 435 calories for each of 6 servings, 325 calories for each of 8 servings.

SPICY MEAT LOAF

Makes 6–8 servings

2½ pounds ground beef
1 (8-ounce) package poultry stuffing mix
1 (1⅜-ounce) package dry onion soup mix
1 pint sour cream
½ cup tomato juice
1 clove garlic, peeled and crushed
1 tablespoon Worcestershire sauce
1 teaspoon oregano
⅛ teaspoon pepper
1 egg, beaten

Preheat oven to 325° F. Mix all ingredients, using your hands, and pack into an ungreased 9″×5″×3″ loaf pan. Bake, uncovered, 1 hour and 15 minutes. Let loaf cool upright in its pan 10 minutes, then turn onto a heated platter and serve. About 730 calories for each of 6 servings, 550 calories for each of 8 servings.

¢ POT-ROASTED BEEF AND VEGETABLE ROLL

Makes 4 servings

1 pound ground beef
1 teaspoon salt
⅛ teaspoon pepper
2 tablespoons bacon drippings or margarine
2 cups beef broth
2–3 tablespoons flour blended with 2 tablespoons cold water

Stuffing:

1 small yellow onion, peeled and minced
⅓ cup finely chopped celery
1 small carrot, peeled and finely grated
1 tablespoon bacon drippings or margarine
¾ cup soft white bread crumbs
1 egg, lightly beaten
2 tablespoons minced parsley
1 teaspoon salt
⅛ teaspoon pepper

Mix beef, salt, and pepper and roll with a rolling pin between 2 sheets waxed paper to a rectangle about 7″×10″, keeping edges as straight as possible. Prepare stuffing: sauté onion, celery, carrot in drippings over moderate heat 5 minutes and mix in remaining ingredients. Spread over beef, leaving ½″ margins all round, then roll, jelly-roll style, pinching edges to seal. Brown roll in 2 tablespoons drippings in a heavy kettle over moderate heat 5 minutes, turning frequently and gently. Remove roll and pour off all but 1 tablespoon drippings. Place roll seam side down on a rack, return to kettle, add 1 cup broth, cover, and simmer 40 minutes. Lift roll and rack from kettle, transfer roll to a platter and keep warm. Add remaining broth to kettle, mix in flour-water paste, and heat, stirring, until thickened. Pour a little gravy over meat roll and pass the rest. About 410 calories per serving.

VARIATION:

About ½ hour before serving, add any of the following to kettle: peeled, halved new potatoes or turnips, carrots cut in 2″ chunks, peeled small white onions. Arrange vegetables on platter with meat and keep warm while making gravy. Recipe too flexible for a meaningful calorie count.

⚖ ¢ STUFFED GREEN PEPPERS

Makes 6–8 servings

8 medium-size sweet green peppers
1 pound ground beef
1 medium-size yellow onion, peeled and chopped fine
1 teaspoon garlic salt
½ teaspoon salt
¼ teaspoon pepper
1½ cups cooked rice (hot or cold)
2½–3 cups canned marinara or Spanish-style tomato sauce

Prepare peppers for stuffing.* Sauté beef in a lightly greased heavy skillet over moderate heat 10 minutes until no longer pink, stirring to break up chunks; transfer to a bowl with slotted spoon. Drain all but 2 tablespoons drippings from skillet, add onion and sauté 8–10 minutes, stirring occasionally, until golden. Mix onion and all remaining ingredients except sauce into meat; stuff each pepper loosely, filling to within ¼″ of the top. Stand peppers in a deep saucepan so they touch and support each other. Pour in sauce so it surrounds peppers but does not touch the filling. Cover and simmer slowly 1 hour until peppers are tender. Lift peppers to a heated platter, top with some of the sauce, and pass the rest. About 260 calories for each of 6 servings, 195 calories for each of 8 servings.

¢ BAKED PEPPERS STUFFED WITH BEEF AND RED KIDNEY BEANS

Makes 6 servings

6 large sweet green or red peppers
1 pound ground beef
1 large yellow onion, peeled and minced
1 (10½-ounce) can condensed cheese soup thinned with 1¼ cups water
1 (6-ounce) can tomato paste
2 teaspoons salt
2 teaspoons chili powder
¼ teaspoon pepper
1 (1-pound) can red kidney beans (do not drain)
⅓ cup hot water

Prepare peppers for stuffing and parboil.* Stir-fry beef, without adding any fat, in a large, heavy skillet over moderate heat 10 minutes until no longer pink, breaking up large clumps. Add onion and stir-fry 5 minutes. Mix in remaining ingredients except beans and water; then stir in beans and simmer, uncovered, ½ hour, stirring now and then. Preheat oven to 375° F. Arrange peppers upright in an ungreased small casserole so they touch and support each other; fill with skillet mixture. Pour water into casserole and bake, uncovered, about 45 minutes until peppers are fork tender. (Note: Any leftover stuffing can be heated and spooned over peppers.) About 365 calories per serving.

¢ PICADILLO

Spicy, a little bit sweet, a little bit salty, picadillo is Mexican minced meat. Serve as is, use as a filling for meat pies, or for making Chiles Rellenos.
Makes 4–6 servings

1 large yellow onion, peeled and minced
1 clove garlic, peeled and crushed
1 tablespoon olive oil
1 pound ground beef
½ (6-ounce) can tomato paste
1 canned jalapeño chili, seeded and minced, or ¼ teaspoon crushed hot red chili peppers
⅓ cup minced raisins
¼ teaspoon oregano
⅛ teaspoon cinnamon
Pinch cloves
¾ teaspoon salt
Pinch black pepper
¼ cup minced blanched almonds

Sauté onion and garlic in oil in a large, heavy skillet over moderate heat 8–10 minutes until golden. Add meat and sauté 3–5 minutes, breaking up any clumps. Blend in tomato paste, add remaining ingredients, and heat, stirring, 5 minutes to blend flavors. About 395 calories for each of 4 servings, 265 calories for each of 6 servings.

CHILES RELLENOS (MEXICAN STUFFED PEPPERS)

For real chiles rellenos, you need dark green poblano chilis. These aren't often available fresh in this country, and even if they were, many of us would find them too hot. Sweet green peppers may be substituted and so may the canned mild green chilis (better get two cans because the chilis are very fragile and difficult to stuff).
Makes 6 servings

6 poblano chilis, or 6 small sweet green peppers, or 12 Italian elle peppers, or 2 (1-pound 10-ounce) cans peeled, roasted mild green chilis, drained
1 recipe Picadillo (recipe above)
Shortening or cooking oil for deep fat frying

Coating:
½ cup unsifted flour
4 eggs, separated

Sauce:
1 small yellow onion, peeled and minced
1 clove garlic, peeled and crushed

2 tablespoons olive oil
½ (6-ounce) can tomato paste
1 (8-ounce) can tomato sauce
1 (13¾-ounce) can chicken broth
1 teaspoon sugar
½ teaspoon salt
Pinch pepper

If using fresh peppers, toast and peel
(see Marinated Roasted Peppers for
how to do it). If using canned chilis,
rinse gently in cold water and remove
seeds. Drain peppers on paper toweling.
Prepare *picadillo* and cool to room
temperature. Sauté onion and garlic for
sauce in oil in a large skillet over
moderate heat 8–10 minutes until
golden; mix in remaining ingredients,
turn heat to low, and let sauce simmer,
uncovered, until you're ready for it.
Begin heating shortening or oil in a deep
fat fryer over moderately high heat
(use a deep fat thermometer). Stuff
chilis with picadillo and set aside while
you prepare coating. Beat yolks and
whites, separately, until thick, then fold
yolks into whites. Roll stuffed chilis in
flour, then dip in egg. When fat reaches
375° F., fry chilis, a few at a time,
2–3 minutes until golden. Drain on
paper toweling, add to tomato sauce,
and warm, uncovered, about 5 minutes.
Serve chilis topped with the sauce.
About 445 calories per serving.

VARIATION:

Chiles Rellenos con Queso: These chilis
are made just like traditional *rellenos*
except that they're stuffed with cheese
instead of picadillo. Use small peppers—
either Italian *elle* or canned chilis—and
prepare for stuffing as above. Fill with
softened cream cheese, coarsely grated
sharp Cheddar, or Monterey Jack
(you'll need about ½ pound). Then
proceed as recipe directs, dipping chilis
in flour and beaten egg, deep frying
until golden, and warming in tomato
sauce. About 320 calories per serving if
made with cream cheese or Monterey
Jack, 330 calories per serving if made
with Cheddar.

POLISH STUFFED CABBAGE ROLLS WITH LEMON SAUCE

A friend gave us this old family recipe.
Makes 4 servings

1 medium-size cabbage, trimmed of
    coarse outer leaves
1½ quarts boiling water
3½ teaspoons salt
1 large yellow onion, peeled and minced
¼ cup butter or margarine
1 pound ground beef
½ cup uncooked rice
¼ teaspoon black pepper
2 tablespoons lemon juice
2 tablespoons flour blended with
    2 tablespoons cold water
⅛ teaspoon white pepper

Place cabbage, water, and 1 teaspoon
salt in a large kettle and boil,
uncovered, 3–4 minutes until leaves are
pliable. Drain, reserving 2½ cups cooking
water. Cool cabbage in a colander under
cold running water until easy to handle,
drain well, core, and remove 12 whole
outer leaves (discard any with holes).
Cut base of large white vein from each
leaf and discard; spread each leaf flat.
(*Note:* Save rest of cabbage to use later.)
Stir-fry onion in 2 tablespoons butter
over moderate heat 5–8 minutes until
transparent and mix with beef, rice,
2 teaspoons salt, and the black pepper.
Put a spoonful of the mixture on the
center of each leaf, fold sides in over
filling, and roll up loosely. Secure with
toothpicks. Arrange rolls 1 layer deep in
a large kettle, add reserved cabbage
water, lemon juice, and remaining
butter. Cover and simmer 1 hour. Lift
rolls to a serving dish and keep warm.
Mix flour paste into kettle and cook and
stir over moderate heat 3–4 minutes
until liquid thickens slightly; add
remaining salt and the white pepper.
Pour some of the sauce over rolls and
pass the rest. About 440 calories per
serving.

SWEDISH MEAT BALLS I

Swedish meat balls are sometimes made
of one meat only, but more often with
a combination of beef, pork, and/or

veal. Some recipes call for mashed potatoes (a dandy way to use up leftovers), others don't. For smorgasbord, the balls are tiny (about ½") and served *without* sauce; for entrees they're larger and awash in pale cream gravy.
Makes 4–6 servings

Meat Balls:

1 medium-size yellow onion, peeled and minced
1 tablespoon butter or margarine
1 pound boned beef chuck, ground twice
¼ pound boned lean pork shoulder, ground twice
1½ teaspoons salt
¼ teaspoon pepper
Pinch nutmeg (optional)
¾ cup fine dry bread crumbs
¼ cup milk
¼ cup water
1 egg, lightly beaten
2 tablespoons butter or margarine (for browning meat balls)

Gravy:

2 tablespoons butter or margarine
2 tablespoons flour
1¼ cups light cream
½ teaspoon salt
Pinch white pepper

Sauté onion in butter 3–5 minutes over moderate heat until limp; mix well with remaining meat ball ingredients and shape into ¾"–1" balls. Brown, ⅓ of balls at a time, in butter in a large, heavy skillet 8–10 minutes over moderate heat until well done; drain on paper toweling. (*Note:* The ½" smorgasbord balls will cook in 5–8 minutes.) Drain drippings from skillet and add butter for gravy. When melted, blend in flour, add cream, and heat, stirring, until thickened. Season, add meat balls, simmer uncovered 5 minutes, shaking pan occasionally, and serve.

VARIATIONS:

Swedish Meat Balls II (with potatoes): When mixing meat balls, add 1 cup cold mashed potatoes; reduce bread crumbs to ¼ cup and water to about 2 tablespoons (add only enough to make balls shape easily). Shape and cook as directed.

Swedish Meat Balls in Mushroom Gravy: Mix, shape, and brown meat balls as above; in drippings sauté ½ pound sliced mushrooms 4–5 minutes; add to balls. Make gravy as directed, adding meat balls and mushrooms at the same time.
All versions: about 700 calories for each of 4 servings, 470 calories for each of 6 servings.

SAVORY MEAT BALLS

Because this recipe freezes well and is dressy enough for a party, it's a good one to make in quantity (2 or 3 times the recipe) and keep on hand.
Makes 4 servings

1 pound ground beef
1 teaspoon garlic salt
¼ teaspoon pepper
1 tablespoon Worcestershire sauce
1 small yellow onion, peeled and minced
¾ cup soft white bread crumbs
¼ cup milk
1 egg, lightly beaten
2 tablespoons bacon drippings or cooking oil

Gravy:

3 tablespoons flour
1½ cups water
1 beef bouillon cube
1 tablespoon tomato paste
¼–½ teaspoon salt
⅛ teaspoon pepper

Mix beef, garlic salt, pepper, Worcestershire sauce, and onion thoroughly. Soften bread crumbs in milk 5 minutes, then mix into meat along with egg. Using ¼ cup as a measure, shape into balls. Brown well in drippings in a large, heavy skillet over moderate heat about 10 minutes. (*Note:* To avoid crowding pan, brown in 2 batches.) Remove to a paper-towel-lined bowl. For the gravy: Drain all but 2 tablespoons drippings from skillet, blend in flour, and brown lightly over moderate heat, stirring constantly. Add water and bouillon cube and cook and stir until thickened. Mix in all remaining ingredients, add meat balls, cover, and simmer 15 minutes. Serve with buttered wide noodles, rice, or mashed potatoes. About 390 calories per serving.

¢ DANISH MEAT BALLS (FRIKADELLER)

If you like a light, fluffy meat ball, use the club soda in the meat mixture instead of milk.
Makes 4–6 servings

½ pound boned beef chuck, ground 2–3 times
½ pound boned lean pork shoulder, ground 2–3 times
1 medium-size yellow onion, peeled and minced
1 teaspoon salt
¼ teaspoon pepper
1 tablespoon minced parsley
¼ cup unsifted flour
½ cup plus 2 tablespoons club soda or milk
¼ cup butter or margarine

Mix beef, pork, onion, salt, pepper, and parsley well; sprinkle flour over meat, add club soda or milk, and mix again, then beat hard with a wooden spoon. (Mixture will be quite soft.) Heat butter in a large, heavy skillet over moderate heat 2 minutes until bubbly. Using a measuring tablespoon, drop 4–5 spoonfuls meat mixture into skillet, shaping into small balls. (To prevent mixture from sticking, dip spoon in cold water.) Brown balls 8–10 minutes, turning with a pancake turner so they cook evenly. Because they contain pork, they must be cooked through *with no sign of pink* in the middle. Drain on paper toweling and keep warm while you brown the rest. Serve hot with boiled potatoes or Danish-Style New Potatoes and pickled beets or red cabbage. Or serve cold with potato salad or as a *smørrebrød*, sliced on buttered rye bread. About 390 calories for each of 4 servings, 260 calories for each of 6 servings.

MEAT BALL STROGANOFF

Makes 4 servings

Meat Balls:
1 pound ground beef
¾ cup soft white bread crumbs
1 small yellow onion, grated fine
1 egg
2 tablespoons light cream
1 teaspoon salt
Pinch pepper
2 tablespoons butter or margarine (for browning)

Sauce:
2 tablespoons butter or margarine
1 medium-size yellow onion, peeled and coarsely chopped
¼ pound mushrooms, wiped clean and sliced very thin
2 tablespoons paprika
3 tablespoons flour
1 (10-ounce) can condensed beef broth
¼ cup water
1 tablespoon prepared Dijon-style mustard
½ cup sour cream

Mix all meat ball ingredients except butter and shape into 1″ balls; brown on all sides in butter in a large, heavy skillet over moderately high heat; drain on paper toweling. In the same skillet, melt butter for sauce and stir-fry onion 8–10 minutes over moderate heat until golden. Add mushrooms and sauté, stirring occasionally, about 5 minutes until lightly browned. Blend in paprika and flour, add broth and water slowly, and heat, stirring constantly, until thickened; smooth in mustard. Return meat balls to skillet, cover, and simmer over low heat 20 minutes. Mix in sour cream, heat and stir about 1 minute, but do not boil. Serve over buttered wide noodles. About 540 calories per serving (without noodles).

⊠ ¢ MICKEY'S MAC AND MEAT

If you have neither time nor money, here's the main dish to make.
Makes 4 servings

1 large yellow onion, peeled and minced
2 tablespoons beef drippings, butter, or
   margarine
1 pound lean ground beef
1 cup elbow macaroni, boiled by package
   directions
1 (10½-ounce) can condensed tomato
   soup
1 teaspoon salt
⅛ teaspoon pepper
1 (10-ounce) package frozen cut green
   beans or green peas (optional)

Stir-fry onion in drippings in a heavy
saucepan over moderately high heat 8
minutes until golden. Add beef and
brown well. Mix in all remaining
ingredients except beans or peas. Cover,
turn heat to low, and simmer 20
minutes. Serve hot or, if you wish, mix in
beans or peas, cover, and simmer 7–10
minutes until just tender. About 490
calories per serving if made with green
peas, 450 per serving if made with beans,
and 440 per serving if made without
either.

KÖNIGSBERGER KLOPS (GERMAN MEAT BALLS IN LEMON-CAPER SAUCE)

Makes 4 servings

Meat Balls:

1 medium-size yellow onion, peeled and
   chopped fine
1 tablespoon butter or margarine
2 slices white bread soaked in ½ cup
   cold water and squeezed almost dry
½ pound ground beef
½ pound ground lean pork
2 medium-size potatoes, boiled and riced
6 anchovies, chopped fine
1 egg, lightly beaten
1 teaspoon salt
⅛ teaspoon pepper
¼ cup unsifted flour

Sauce:

¼ cup butter or margarine
¼ cup unsifted flour
2 cups beef broth
2 tablespoons capers
2–3 tablespoons lemon juice

Sauté onion in butter over moderate

heat 8–10 minutes until golden, then
mix with remaining meat ball
ingredients except flour. Shape into 1″
balls and roll lightly in flour. Simmer
meat balls, half at a time, 5–7 minutes
in salted water (about 2 teaspoons salt
to 2 quarts water). Meanwhile, make
the sauce: melt butter in a large saucepan
over moderate heat, blend in flour, slowly
add broth, and cook, stirring, until
thickened. Add capers, lemon juice to
taste, and meat balls, cover, and simmer
5–10 minutes. Serve with boiled
potatoes. About 570 calories per serving.

SWEET-SOUR BEEF BALLS WITH PINEAPPLE AND PEPPERS

Makes 4 servings

1 pound ground beef
½ teaspoon salt
¼ teaspoon pepper
1 clove garlic, peeled and crushed
2 tablespoons soy sauce
2 tablespoons cooking oil
2 medium-size sweet green peppers,
   cored, seeded, and chopped fine
1 small carrot, peeled and cut diagonally
   into paper thin slices
½ cup boiling water
1 chicken bouillon cube
⅔ cup pineapple juice
¼ cup red wine vinegar
2 tablespoons sugar
1 (13½-ounce) can pineapple chunks
   (do not drain)
2 tablespoons cornstarch mixed with ⅓
   cup cold water

Mix together beef, salt, pepper, garlic,
and 1 tablespoon soy sauce and, using a
rounded tablespoon as a measure, shape
into balls. Brown balls, ⅓ at a time, in
oil in a large, heavy skillet over moderate
heat 4–5 minutes, then drain on paper
toweling. Pour all but 2 tablespoons
drippings from skillet, add green peppers
and carrot, and stir-fry 2–3 minutes. Mix
in remaining soy sauce and all other
ingredients except cornstarch paste, add
beef balls, cover, and simmer 10
minutes. Stir in cornstarch paste and
simmer, stirring, 2–3 minutes until
slightly thickened. Serve over hot boiled

rice or Chinese Fried Rice. About 415 calories per serving (without rice).

¢ MARJORIE'S SAVORY BEEF AND RICE

Makes 4 servings

1 teaspoon beef drippings or cooking oil
1 pound ground beef
1 large yellow onion, peeled and minced
1 cup uncooked rice
1 (1-pound) can tomatoes (do not drain)
1 (10½-ounce) can condensed tomato soup
1 teaspoon salt
⅛ teaspoon pepper

Brush the bottom of a heavy saucepan with drippings, add beef, and brown well over moderately high heat, stirring frequently. Push beef to one side of pan, add onion, and sauté 5 minutes until transparent. Mix in remaining ingredients. Cover, reduce heat to low, and simmer, stirring frequently, 30–40 minutes until rice is tender and flavors blended (keep an eye on the pot because mixture tends to stick). Serve hot as a main course. (*Note:* If you double the recipe, increase simmering time to about 50 minutes.) About 470 calories per serving.

SHEPHERD'S PIE

Makes 4 servings

1 large yellow onion, peeled and chopped fine
1 sweet green pepper, cored, seeded, and coarsely chopped (optional)
2 tablespoons beef or bacon drippings or cooking oil
1¼ pounds ground chuck
1 beef bouillon cube
½ cup boiling water
1 tablespoon cornstarch mixed with 2 tablespoons cold water
1¼ teaspoons salt
¼ teaspoon pepper
1 tablespoon steak sauce
3 cups hot seasoned mashed potatoes

Preheat oven to 400° F. Sauté onion and green pepper in drippings in a large skillet over moderate heat 10 minutes until onion is golden. Add beef and sauté, breaking meat up with a spoon, about 10 minutes, until lightly browned; drain off fat as it accumulates. Dissolve bouillon cube in water, add to cornstarch mixture, then stir into skillet along with salt, pepper, and steak sauce. Heat, stirring, 1–2 minutes. Spoon into an ungreased 1½-quart casserole, spread potatoes over surface and roughen with a fork. (*Note:* Recipe may be prepared to this point ahead of time; cool, cover, and chill. Bring to room temperature before proceeding.) Bake, uncovered, 25–30 minutes, then broil 4" from heat 2–3 minutes to brown. About 490 calories per serving.

VARIATION:

Substitute 3 cups finely ground leftover cooked beef or lamb for the ground chuck; stir-fry 2–3 minutes with sautéed onion and green pepper, then proceed as recipe directs. About 500 calories per serving.

⚔ ¢ TAMALE PIE

Makes 6 servings

Crust:

1 quart water
2 teaspoons salt
1 cup yellow corn meal

Filling:

1 medium-size yellow onion, peeled and coarsely chopped
½ sweet green pepper, cored, seeded, and coarsely chopped
1 tablespoon cooking oil or bacon drippings
1 pound lean ground beef
1 clove garlic, peeled and crushed
1 tablespoon chili powder
¾ teaspoon salt
¼ teaspoon oregano
Pinch pepper
1 (8-ounce) can tomato sauce

Topping:

2 tablespoons finely grated Parmesan cheese

Preheat oven to 350° F. Bring water

and salt to a boil in a large saucepan, very gradually add corn meal, beating constantly so it doesn't lump. Turn heat to low and continue cooking and stirring about 5 minutes until quite thick. Spread ⅔ of mush in the bottom of a buttered 9″×9″×2″ pan and set aside; keep rest warm. For the filling, stir-fry onion and green pepper in oil in a large skillet over moderate heat 8–10 minutes until onion is golden; mix in meat, garlic, chili powder, salt, oregano, and pepper and stir-fry 5 minutes longer, breaking up clumps of meat. Mix in tomato sauce and simmer, uncovered, about 5 minutes; spoon over mush in pan, top with remaining mush, spreading as evenly over all as possible. Sprinkle with Parmesan and bake, uncovered, 30 minutes. Let stand at room temperature 10 minutes, then cut into large squares and serve. About 275 calories per serving.

¢ CHILI

Makes 10–12 servings

4 medium-size yellow onions, peeled and coarsely chopped
3 cloves garlic, peeled and crushed
¼ cup olive or other cooking oil
1 teaspoon oregano
2 bay leaves, crumbled
2 pounds ground beef
¼ cup chili powder
1 (1-pound 12-ounce) can tomatoes (do not drain)
3 (1-pound 4-ounce) cans red kidney beans (do not drain)
2 teaspoons salt
3 tablespoons cider vinegar
⅛–¼ teaspoon crushed hot red chili peppers

Sauté onions and garlic in the oil in a large, heavy kettle over moderate heat, stirring occasionally, 10 minutes until golden. Add oregano, bay leaves, and beef and sauté, breaking up meat, 10 minutes until beef is no longer pink. Add 2 tablespoons chili powder, tomatoes, 2 cans kidney beans and simmer, uncovered, over low heat, stirring occasionally, 1½ hours. Add

remaining chili powder and kidney beans along with salt, vinegar, and red peppers. Simmer, stirring now and then, 15 minutes longer. Serve hot, or cool and freeze for future use. About 450 calories for each of 10 servings, 375 calories for each of 12 servings.

TEXAS RED (CHILI)

The "bowl of red" Texans adore isn't what most of us think of as chili; it has no beans, tomatoes, or onions and is simply a torrid blend of beef, chili peppers, and herbs.
Makes 6 servings

3 pounds boned beef chuck, cut in 1½″ cubes and trimmed of all fat
1 tablespoon rendered suet or cooking oil
6 dried ancho chili peppers or 6 tablespoons chili powder (anchos are the large red chilis, full-flavored but not fiery)
5 cups cold water
1 tablespoon oregano
1 tablespoon crushed cumin seeds
2 teaspoons salt
1–2 teaspoons cayenne pepper (depending on how hot you can take chili)
2 cloves garlic, peeled and crushed
2 tablespoons masa harina (available in Latin groceries) or 2 tablespoons corn meal

Put meat through coarse blade of meat grinder, then brown, a little at a time, in suet in a heavy skillet over moderately high heat; lift to a large, heavy kettle with a slotted spoon and set aside. Wash peppers in cold water, discard stems and seeds. Tear peppers into 2″ pieces, place in a small saucepan with 2 cups water, cover, and simmer 20 minutes; drain, reserving cooking water. Peel skin from peppers and purée with pepper water in an electric blender at high speed or put through a food mill. (Wash hands well after handling peppers and avoid touching face while working with them.) Mix pepper purée into beef, also remaining water, and bring to a boil over high heat. (*Note:* If using chili

powder instead of peppers, simply place
in kettle with beef and full amount of
water.) Adjust heat so mixture stays at
a slow simmer, cover, and cook 30
minutes. Stir in all remaining ingredients
except *masa harina*, cover, and simmer
45 minutes. Mix in masa harina, cover,
and warm over lowest heat 30 minutes
longer, stirring occasionally so mixture
doesn't stick. If chili seems thick, thin
with ⅓–½ cup boiling water. About
460 calories per serving.

¢ CORNISH PASTIES

Cornish children take pasties to school
for lunch (with their initials pricked out
in the crust), and farmers munch them at
apple-picking time. Although seasonings
vary from town to town, the basic
ingredients remain the same—beef,
potatoes, and onions wrapped up in flaky
pastry.
Makes 1 dozen

Pastry:

4 cups sifted flour
2 teaspoons salt
1½ cups chilled shortening or 1 cup
  shortening and ½ cup lard
½ cup ice water (about)
1 egg, lightly beaten with 1 tablespoon
  cold water (glaze)

Filling:

1 pound ground beef round
3 cups (¼″) raw potato cubes
½ cup minced yellow onion
2 teaspoons salt
¼ teaspoon pepper

Mix flour and salt in a large bowl and cut
in shortening with a pastry blender until
the texture of coarse meal. Sprinkle
water over surface, a tablespoon at a
time, mixing briskly with a fork after
each addition. Pastry should *just* hold
together; wrap in foil and chill while
you prepare and mix filling ingredients
together. Preheat oven to 450° F. Shape
pastry into 3 balls and roll, 1 at a time,
on a lightly floured pastry cloth into a
13″ square; using a 5″–6″ saucer as a
guide, cut 4 rounds from each square.
Brush edges of rounds with glaze, spoon

a little filling onto lower ½ of each
round, then fold upper ½ over. Press
edges together and crimp with a fork.
Cut 2–3 small slits in top of each pastie
and brush with glaze, being careful not
to seal slits. Bake 15 minutes, reduce
heat to 350° F., and bake 30 minutes
longer until lightly browned. Serve warm
or cold. (*Note:* To reheat pasties, set
uncovered in a 350° F. oven 10–15
minutes.) About 500 calories per pastie.

VARIATION:

¢ **Party Pasties:** Prepare as recipe
directs, then cut circles with a biscuit
cutter. Fill and seal as above. Bake
uncovered 10 minutes at 450° F., then
15–20 minutes at 350° F. Makes about
2 dozen. About 250 calories per pastie.

BEEF AND MUSHROOM PIROG (RUSSIAN MEAT PIE)

Makes 4 servings

1 recipe Sour Cream Pastry
2 teaspoons milk (glaze)

Filling:

1 medium-size yellow onion, peeled and
  minced
2 tablespoons butter or margarine
½ pound mushrooms, wiped clean and
  coarsely chopped
¾ pound ground beef
1 teaspoon salt
⅛ teaspoon pepper
½ cup sour cream

Prepare pastry by recipe, wrap loosely
in waxed paper, and chill while you
make the filling. Sauté onion in butter
over moderate heat 5–8 minutes until
pale golden. Add mushrooms and stir-fry
2 minutes, add beef, breaking up with a
fork, and brown 5–7 minutes. Off heat,
stir in salt, pepper, and sour cream and
cool to room temperature. Preheat
oven to 400° F. Divide pastry in half,
shape into 2 balls, and roll, 1 at a time,
on a lightly floured board into 9″ × 14″
rectangles. Lop 1 pastry over rolling pin
and transfer to an ungreased baking
sheet; brush edges with cold water.
Spread filling over pastry, leaving ½″
margins all round. Cut 3 V-slits near

center of second pastry, place on top of filling, press edges to seal, and crimp. Brush pastry with milk to glaze and bake, uncovered, 50–60 minutes until golden. Cut into large squares and serve. About 720 calories per serving.

POT ROASTS

In addition to the marginally tender roasts discussed earlier, these are the favorite cuts for pot roasting (see Beef Chart). Cooked slowly, with some liquid, they can be surprisingly tender.

Inside Chuck Roll
Blade Pot Roast
Arm Pot Roast
English (Boston) Cut
Rolled Shoulder Roast
Fresh Brisket
Rolled Plate
Rolled Neck
Bottom Round
Heel of Round

How to Pot Roast Beef

Pot roast isn't one recipe but dozens. Any sizable cut that is browned, then cooked slowly in a tightly covered pot with a small amount of liquid is pot roasted. Here are some favorites.

POT ROAST

Mashed potatoes are particularly good with this pot roast because of its rich brown gravy.
Makes 6–8 servings

1 (4-pound) boned and rolled beef roast (rump, chuck, sirloin tip, bottom or eye round)
2 tablespoons beef drippings or cooking oil
1 small yellow onion, peeled and minced
2½–3 teaspoons salt
½ teaspoon pepper (about)
¼ cup cold water
3 cups beef stock, water, or a ½ and ½
mixture of condensed beef broth and water
6 tablespoons flour

Brown beef well on all sides in drippings in a heavy kettle over moderately high heat; remove to a bowl. Stir-fry onion in drippings 8–10 minutes until golden; return beef to kettle and sprinkle with 1 teaspoon salt and ¼ teaspoon pepper. Add water, reduce heat to low, cover, and simmer 3 hours until tender, turning meat occasionally (check pot frequently and add 1–2 tablespoons cold water if needed, but no more). When beef is tender, transfer to a heated platter, cover loosely and keep warm. Skim all but 1–2 tablespoons fat from drippings, add 2 cups stock to kettle, and stir to scrape up browned bits. Blend remaining stock with flour and stir slowly into kettle; heat, stirring, until thickened. Reduce heat, cover, and simmer 2–3 minutes; add remaining salt and pepper to taste. Slice pot roast (not too thin) and serve with gravy. About 615 calories for each of 6 servings, 460 calories for each of 8 servings.

VARIATIONS:

Oven Pot Roast: Preheat oven to 350° F. In a large, flameproof casserole, brown beef and onion as directed; add seasonings and ½ cup water. Cover tight (if lid does not fit snugly, cover with foil) and bake 3 hours until meat is tender. Prepare gravy as directed and serve. About 615 calories for each of 6 servings, 460 calories for each of 8 servings.

Electric Skillet Pot Roast: Make sure roast will fit in covered skillet before starting. Set control at 350° F., brown meat and onion as directed, add salt, pepper, and water, cover, and simmer at 200–12° F. 3 hours until meat is tender. Prepare gravy as directed and serve. About 615 calories for each of 6 servings, 460 calories for each of 8 servings.

Pressure Cooker Pot Roast: Brown beef and onion in open pressure cooker; add seasonings, ½ cup water (or amount of liquid manufacturer recommends). Seal cooker, bring to 10 pounds pressure and cook 15 minutes per pound (meat cooked at 10 pounds pressure will be more tender than that cooked at 15). Reduce pressure, open cooker, remove meat, and keep warm. Prepare gravy in open cooker, using method above. About 615 calories for each of 6 servings, 460 calories for each of 8 servings.

Burgundy Pot Roast: Rub beef with 1 peeled and cut clove garlic; brown it and onion as directed. Substitute ½ cup Burgundy for the water, add 1 crumbled bay leaf, cover, and simmer. When making gravy, use ½ cup Burgundy and 2½ cups stock. About 645 calories for each of 6 servings, 485 calories for each of 8 servings.

German-Style Pot Roast: Cook pot roast as directed. When making gravy, reduce flour to 3 tablespoons, add 6–8 crushed gingersnaps and 2 tablespoons dark brown sugar. For the liquid, use ¼ cup red wine vinegar and 2¾ cups stock. About 620 calories for each of 6 servings, 465 calories for each of 8 servings.

Yankee Pot Roast: About 50 minutes before roast is done, add 6 medium-size, peeled, halved potatoes, 8 peeled small carrots, 1 pound peeled small white onions, 1 small rutabaga, peeled and cut in 1″ cubes, and ½ cup beef broth. Sprinkle vegetables with 1 teaspoon salt, cover and simmer until meat and vegetables are both tender. Arrange vegetables around meat on platter and keep warm; make gravy as directed and serve. About 755 calories for each of 6 servings, 570 calories for each of 8 servings.

Barbecued Pot Roast: Rub raw beef roast with a mixture of 1 teaspoon paprika and 1 teaspoon chili powder, then proceed as recipe directs. Use drippings to make Barbecue Gravy for Beef instead of basic pot roast gravy above. About 615 calories for each of 6 servings, 460 calories for each of 8 servings.

Pot Roast with Sour Cream-Horseradish Gravy: Prepare beef and gravy according to recipe; just before serving, stir 1 (8-ounce) undrained can sliced mushrooms into gravy; remove from heat, blend in 1 cup sour cream and 2 tablespoons prepared horseradish, and serve. About 690 calories for each of 6 servings, 525 calories for each of 8 servings.

BEEF À LA MODE (FRENCH POT ROAST)

When preparing beef à la mode, the French lard the meat to make it more tender and flavorful. American beef, however, is so well marbled with fat it doesn't need larding. The outer covering of fat should be no more than ¼″ thick. Makes 8–10 servings

Marinade:

2 cups dry red wine
1 medium-size yellow onion, peeled and sliced thin
1 large carrot, peeled and sliced thin
2 stalks celery, coarsely chopped (include tops)
1 clove garlic, peeled and minced
2 bay leaves, crumbled
½ teaspoon thyme
¼ teaspoon pepper
¼ teaspoon nutmeg
6 cloves
1 bouquet garni,* tied in cheesecloth

Pot Roast:

1 (5-pound) boned and rolled beef roast (rump, chuck, sirloin tip, or eye of round)
¼ cup beef or bacon drippings or lard
2 teaspoons salt
¼ cup brandy
2 calf's feet, blanched* and split, or 1 large veal knuckle, cracked
2 cups dry red wine or a ½ and ½ mixture of wine and beef broth
2 tablespoons cornstarch or arrowroot mixed with 2 tablespoons cold water (optional)

Place marinade ingredients in a large bowl (not metal) and mix well; add beef, cover, and refrigerate 24 hours, turning beef 3–4 times. Remove beef from marinade and let stand on a wire rack ½ hour; pat dry with paper toweling. Reserve marinade. Preheat oven to 325° F. Heat drippings in a large Dutch oven over moderately high heat 1 minute, add beef and brown well on all sides, 10–15 minutes; add reserved marinade and all remaining ingredients except cornstarch mixture. Cover and bring to a boil; transfer to oven and simmer, covered, about 3½ hours until tender, turning beef every hour. Transfer beef to a heated platter and remove strings. Strain gravy (save calf's feet if you wish—there's meat on them), skim off fat, and boil rapidly 5–10 minutes to reduce to about 3 cups. Taste for salt and pepper and adjust if needed. If you prefer a thickened gravy, stir in cornstarch paste and heat, stirring, until thickened. Pour a little gravy over beef and pass the rest. To serve, slice meat, not too thin, across the grain. About 700 calories for each of 8 servings, 555 calories for each of 10 servings.

VARIATION:

Beef à la Mode with Vegetables: About 1 hour before beef is done, add 16 peeled whole baby carrots and 16 peeled small white onions to the pot, cover, and continue cooking until beef and vegetables are tender. Remove carrots and onions with a slotted spoon, arrange around beef on platter, and sprinkle with minced parsley. Prepare gravy as directed above and serve. About 710 calories for each of 8 servings, 570 calories for each of 10 servings.

BEEF À LA MODE IN ASPIC

Start this recipe two days before you plan to serve it.
Makes 8–10 servings

1 recipe Beef à la Mode
Beef à la Mode cooking liquid plus enough strong beef stock or broth to total 6 cups
3 envelopes unflavored gelatin

Optional Decoration:
Thin slices truffles cut in fancy shapes
Hard-cooked egg white cut in fancy shapes
Sprays fresh tarragon, chervil, or dill

Garnishes:
Chopped aspic
Watercress sprigs
Radish roses

Prepare beef à la mode as directed but do not thicken cooking liquid; combine instead with enough stock to total 6 cups. Cool meat, remove strings, and trim off fat; wrap in foil and chill overnight. Next day, mix gelatin into 1 cup of the stock; bring remaining stock to a simmer, stir in gelatin mixture, and simmer, stirring, until dissolved. Clarify aspic* if you like. Cool slightly, pour a ¼" layer aspic in an ungreased 9" × 5" × 3" loaf pan and chill until almost firm but still tacky. Meanwhile, chill remaining aspic over a bowl of ice until syrupy. Carve beef into thin slices. If you like, arrange truffle and egg cutouts and herb sprays on aspic layer in a decorative design. Cover with meat, overlapping slices and building up layers to fill pan to within ½" of top. Pour in aspic to cover meat completely; chill remainder (it will be chopped and used to garnish platter). Cover meat loosely and chill until firm, at least 6 hours. To serve, unmold on a cold platter, surround with coarsely chopped aspic, and garnish with watercress and radishes. Serve with Rémoulade or Ravigote Sauce and a cold *macédoine* of vegetables.

VARIATIONS:

Beef à la Mode in Wine Aspic: Substitute ⅓ cup medium dry sherry or Madeira for ⅓ cup stock when making aspic (particularly good if aspic is clarified).

À la Mode from Leftovers: Make aspic with canned condensed beef bouillon, allowing 1 envelope gelatin for each pint. Layer aspic and beef into loaf pan as directed, reducing amount of aspic according to quantity of leftover beef.

All versions: about 705 calories for each of 8 servings, 565 calories for each of 10 servings.

SAUERBRATEN

Begin this recipe three days before you plan to serve it.
Makes 10 servings

1 (5-pound) boned and rolled beef roast (rump, chuck, bottom or eye round)
2 medium-size yellow onions, peeled and sliced thin
1 stalk celery, coarsely chopped (include tops)
1 large carrot, peeled and sliced thin
3 cloves
3 peppercorns
2 bay leaves
2 cups dry red wine or red wine vinegar
3 cups cold water
1 tablespoon salt
½ teaspoon pepper
2 beef marrowbones (about 1 pound)
¼ cup cooking oil
½ cup beef drippings, lard, or margarine
½ cup unsifted flour
12 gingersnaps, crumbled
1–2 tablespoons sugar

Place beef, vegetables, cloves, peppercorns, and bay leaves in a large bowl. Bring wine, water, salt, and pepper to a boil and pour over beef. Cover and refrigerate 3 days, turning beef in marinade twice a day. About 3 hours before you're ready to serve, remove beef from marinade and pat dry with paper toweling; reserve marinade. Brown beef and marrowbones well in oil in a large kettle over moderate heat, about 15 minutes. (*Note:* If bones brown before meat, remove temporarily.) Add marinade, cover, and simmer 1½ hours, turn meat, re-cover, and simmer 1–1½ hours longer until tender; transfer to a large platter and keep warm. Strain marinade and discard vegetables; scoop marrow from bones, sieve, and add to marinade. Heat drippings in a heavy saucepan over moderate heat, blend in flour and brown 1–2 minutes. Stir in marinade, reduce heat to low, and cook, stirring, until thickened. Mix in gingersnaps and sugar to taste. Carve meat at the table—not too thin or slices will crumble—and serve with plenty of gravy. Or carve in the kitchen, arrange slices slightly overlapping on a platter, and pour some of the gravy down the center; pass the rest. Serve with Potato Dumplings, Spätzle, or boiled potatoes.
About 570 calories per serving (without dumplings, spätzle, or potatoes).

POT-AU-FEU

Most countries have their favorite meal-in-a-pot. In France it's Pot-au-Feu, in Italy Bollito Misto, in Spain Olla Podrida, in Argentina Puchero. What goes into the pot depends on what the housewife has in her garden and barnyard. How the dish is served depends largely on whim—sometimes the broth is a first course; sometimes everything is eaten together like a stew.
Makes 10–12 servings

1 (4-pound) boned and rolled beef roast with a very thin outer covering of fat (chuck, rump, or bottom round is best to use)
2 pounds beef or veal marrowbones, cracked
1 gallon cold water
5 teaspoons salt
¼ teaspoon pepper
2 bouquets garnis,* tied in cheesecloth
2 bay leaves
1 medium-size yellow onion, peeled and stuck with 6 cloves
2 stalks celery, cut in 2" lengths
1 (4-pound) stewing chicken, cut up (include giblets)
2 pounds carrots, peeled and cut in 2" lengths
2 pounds turnips or 1 (2-pound) rutabaga, peeled and cut in 1" cubes
2 bunches leeks, trimmed and cut in 2" lengths, or 1 pound small white onions, peeled
1–2 tablespoons minced parsley (garnish)

Place beef on a rack in a 2½-gallon kettle, add bones, water, seasonings, yellow onion, celery, and giblets, cover, and bring to a boil over moderate heat. Skim off froth, reduce heat, cover, and simmer 1 hour. Add chicken, cover, and simmer 2½ hours until beef and chicken are nearly tender. Add carrots and turnips (also white onions if using instead of leeks) and simmer 15 minutes; add leeks, if using, and simmer 15 minutes longer until vegetables and meats are tender. About 555 calories for each of 10 servings, 465 calories for each of 12 servings.

To Serve Broth and Meats Separately: Remove strings from beef and place in the center of a large platter with chicken; wreathe with vegetables, top with a little broth, sprinkle with parsley, and keep warm in a very slow oven. Skim fat from broth, strain, taste for salt and pepper, and adjust if needed. Scoop marrow from marrowbones, spread on slices of French bread, float a slice in each bowl of broth, and serve. Follow broth course with the meat and vegetables, carving the beef against the grain. Pass a little extra broth for spooning over each portion.

To Serve Pot-au-Feu as a Stew: When meats are tender, cut into small slices and serve in soup bowls with vegetables, plenty of the broth, and a sprinkling of parsley.

Traditional Accompaniments for Pot-au-Feu: Coarse (kosher-style) salt, gherkins, mustard, horseradish, and crusty French bread. Boiled potatoes are appropriate too.

To Make Ahead: Prepare pot-au-feu 1 day in advance—but no more—cool, cover, and refrigerate. Lift off fat, then cover and reheat very slowly. Leftover broth, incidentally, is excellent for gravies, brown sauces, and soups (especially onion).

To Halve the Recipe: Use a 2-pound beef roast and a 2½–3 pound whole frying chicken; halve all other ingredients and prepare as directed, reducing simmering time for the chicken to about 1 hour. All other simmering times will remain the same.

VARIATIONS:

Polish-Style Boiled Dinner: Omit chicken, add giblets from 3–4 chickens along with beef and 1 (1–1½-pound) *kielbasa* sausage ring (prick skin to prevent bursting) along with the turnips and carrots. When serving, cut sausage into thick chunks. About 575 calories for each of 10 servings, 470 calories for each of 12 servings.

Bollito Misto: Add 1 (2–3-pound) fresh or smoked beef tongue to kettle along with beef, then proceed as recipe directs. When serving, remove skin and small bones from tongue, then slice. Accompany with boiled potatoes and pass 2 or more of the following: Green Sauce, Béarnaise, Tomato Sauce, prepared mustard or horseradish. About 655 calories for each of 10 servings (without sauce), 565 calories for each of 12 servings.

OLLA PODRIDA (SPANISH ONE-DISH DINNER)

Ideally, *podrida* should simmer in an earthenware pot (*olla*), but a good heavy kettle works almost as well.
Makes 8 servings

1 pound dried chick-peas, washed and sorted
1 gallon plus 1 quart cold water
1 (2-pound) boned and rolled beef roast (chuck, rump, or bottom round)
1 (2-pound) smoked boneless pork shoulder butt
1 pound beef or veal marrowbones, cracked
½ pound salt pork (optional)
2 teaspoons salt
¼ teaspoon pepper
2 bay leaves
1 bouquet garni,* tied in cheesecloth
2 cloves garlic, peeled and crushed
1 medium-size yellow onion, peeled
1 (3-pound) frying chicken, cut up
1 pound chorizos (Spanish sausages) or other garlic-flavored sausages or blood sausages
1½ pounds carrots, peeled and cut in 2" lengths

1 bunch leeks, trimmed and cut in 2"
   lengths
1 medium-size cabbage, trimmed and
   cut in 8 wedges and cored
4 hot boiled medium-size potatoes,
   peeled and quartered

Soak chick-peas in 1 quart cold water
overnight or use the quick method.*
Drain, tie loosely in cheesecloth, and
place in a 3-gallon kettle with beef, pork
butt, bones, salt pork, remaining water,
salt, pepper, bay leaves, *bouquet garni*,
garlic, and onion. Cover and bring to a
boil over moderate heat. Skim froth
from surface, reduce heat, cover, and
simmer 1¼ hours. Add chicken and
simmer covered 45 minutes; add
sausages and carrots and simmer,
covered, 15 minutes, then add leeks and
cabbage and simmer, covered, 15
minutes longer or until all meats and
vegetables are tender. Lift chick-peas to
a vegetable dish, discard cheesecloth,
and keep warm. Lift meats and chicken
to a large heated platter, cut strings, and
discard bones; wreathe with vegetables,
tuck potatoes in here and there and
keep warm. Skim broth of fat, strain,
taste for salt and pepper and adjust as
needed. Ladle a little broth over chick-
peas, also meats and vegetables, and
serve with spicy and/or mild mustard
and extra broth. If you prefer, serve
broth separately as a first course,
keeping meats and vegetables warm in a
very slow oven. About 1,000 calories
per serving.

VARIATION:

Puchero (Argentine One-Dish Dinner):
Omit chick-peas and pork shoulder butt;
use a 3-pound beef roast or 5 pounds
short ribs, cut in serving size pieces, and
simmer as directed above. Add chicken,
sausages, and vegetables as directed, also
2 pounds pumpkin or winter squash,
peeled and cut in 2" chunks (these go
into the pot with the carrots). About 5
minutes before *puchero* is done, add 4
ears sweet corn, husked and cut in 2"
lengths. Serve in large soup bowls,
including plenty of sliced meat,
vegetables, and broth. Accompany with

boiled sweet potatoes (you'll need 4,
peeled and halved). About 800 calories
per serving.

BOILED BRISKET OF BEEF WITH PARSLEY DUMPLINGS

Makes 6–8 servings

1 (4-pound) lean beef brisket
3 quarts cold water
1 large yellow onion, peeled
2 stalks celery, cut in 2" lengths
1 tablespoon salt
¼ teaspoon pepper
2 beef bouillon cubes
1 recipe Quick Dumplings
2 tablespoons minced parsley

Place beef on a trivet in a large kettle,
add all remaining ingredients except
dumplings and parsley, cover, and bring
to a boil over moderately high heat.
Skim froth from surface, then simmer
covered 3½–4 hours until fork tender.
Just before meat is done, prepare
dumplings by recipe, adding parsley to
dry ingredients. Lift meat to a heated
platter and keep warm. Skim broth of
fat and bring to a boil. Drop dumpling
mixture by rounded tablespoonfuls on
top of broth; simmer, uncovered, 10
minutes, cover tight, and simmer 10
minutes longer. Remove dumplings with
a slotted spoon and arrange around
meat. Carve meat, not too thin, across
the grain. If you wish, pass a little broth
in a gravy boat, or serve with
Horseradish Sauce or Caper and
Horseradish Sauce. Save remaining broth
and use as stock.

VARIATION:

Boiled Brisket of Beef with Vegetables:
Omit dumplings. Cook your choice of
vegetables along with the beef—small
whole carrots, cubed turnips or
rutabagas, leeks, small white onions,
halved or quartered parsnips, halved
potatoes, cabbage wedges, timing their
additions to the pot so that they—and
the beef—will be done at the same time.
Wreathe meat with vegetables and serve.
Both versions: about 665 calories for
each of 6 servings, 500 calories for each
of 8 servings.

STEWS

Stew beef comes from the sinewy, well-exercised parts of the animal (see Beef Chart) and can be cut small or left in a single large chunk. In general, the front half of the animal provides more good stew meat than the hind—these fore cuts seem to have slightly more fat, also more of the connective tissue that cooks down into gelatin, making the meat lusciously moist and tender. Ask for chuck, neck, brisket, plate, or shank.

OLD-FASHIONED BEEF STEW

Makes 4–6 servings

2 pounds boned beef chuck or bottom
    round, cut in 1½" cubes
½ cup unsifted flour
2 teaspoons salt
¼ teaspoon pepper
2–3 tablespoons beef drippings or
    cooking oil
1½ pounds small white onions, peeled
6–8 medium-size carrots, peeled and cut
    in 1" chunks
1 pound small turnips, peeled and
    halved, or 1 pound parsnips, peeled
    and cut in 2" chunks (optional)
1 bay leaf
2 cups beef broth, water, dry red wine,
    or beer
1 tablespoon minced parsley

Dredge beef by shaking in a paper bag with flour, 1 teaspoon salt, and ⅛ teaspoon pepper; then brown, a few pieces at a time, in 2 tablespoons drippings in a large, heavy kettle over moderately high heat; transfer to a bowl. Brown onions in remaining drippings 8–10 minutes, stirring occasionally, and remove to bowl. Drain drippings from kettle, return beef and onions, and add all remaining ingredients except parsley. Cover and simmer 1½–2 hours until beef is tender. (Note: You can prepare recipe to this point early in the day or, better still, the day before. Cool, cover, and refrigerate,

or freeze for future use. Reheat slowly, stirring often.) Sprinkle with parsley and serve. About 700 calories for each of 4 servings, 470 calories for each of 6 servings.

VARIATIONS:

Beef and Vegetable Stew: About 15–20 minutes before serving, stir in 2 cups fresh or frozen green peas, whole kernel corn, or diced celery (or a combination of these), cover, and simmer until tender. About 760 calories for each of 4 servings, 510 calories for each of 6 servings.

Beef Stew with Mushrooms: With the beef, onions, and carrots simmer ½ pound sliced mushrooms that have been lightly browned in butter. About 705 calories for each of 4 servings, 470 calories for each of 6 servings.

Beef Stew with Dumplings: About 30 minutes before serving, make Dumplings, add to stew, cover, and cook according to dumpling recipe. About 875 calories for each of 4 servings, 585 calories for each of 6 servings.

BEEF STEW FOR A CROWD

This recipe should be started a day before it's to be served.
Makes about 25 servings

12 pounds boned beef chuck or bottom
    round, cut in 1½" cubes
2 cups sifted flour
2 tablespoons salt (about)
½ teaspoon pepper
¾ cup beef drippings or cooking oil
2 quarts liquid (use liquid from canned
    onions, below, and round out with a
    ½ and ½ mixture of water and canned
    condensed beef broth or dry red wine)
2 beef bouillon cubes
4 tablespoons tomato paste
4 bay leaves
5 (1-pound) cans small white onions,
    drained (reserve liquid)
5 (1-pound) cans whole baby carrots,
    drained
2 tablespoons liquid gravy browner
¾ cup sifted flour blended with ¾ cup
    cold water (if needed to thicken gravy)

Dredge beef by shaking a few pieces at a time in a paper bag with flour, 1 tablespoon salt, and the pepper. For cooking the stew, use 2 2-gallon kettles. Brown beef a little at a time, using 2 tablespoons drippings in each kettle; transfer to a bowl with a slotted spoon. Continue, adding more drippings as needed, until all beef is browned. This will take about ¾ hour. Turn heat to low, return beef to kettles, then add to *each:* 1 quart liquid, 1 bouillon cube, 2 tablespoons tomato paste, and 2 bay leaves. Cover and simmer 1½–2 hours until meat is tender, stirring occasionally. Cool, cover kettles, and chill overnight. Next day, skim off fat. About 1 hour before serving, set kettles on lowest heat and warm slowly. About ¾ hour before serving, add onions and carrots, dividing them between the 2 kettles, cover and cook over moderate heat until tender. Mix in gravy browner, taste for salt, and adjust as needed. If stew seems thin, add half the flour-water to each kettle and heat, stirring, until thickened. Serve over buttered wide noodles, rice, or whole boiled potatoes. About 605 calories per serving (without noodles, rice, or potatoes).

¢ BEEF AND PEPPER STEW IN RED WINE

Makes 6 servings

2 pounds boned beef chuck, cut in 1½"
  cubes
3 medium-size yellow onions, peeled and
  coarsely chopped
2 cloves garlic, peeled and crushed
1 (13¾-ounce) can beef broth
1½ cups water
⅔ cup dry red wine
¼ teaspoon salt
Pinch pepper
6 medium-size sweet green peppers,
  cored, seeded, and cut into eighths

Brown beef all at once without any fat in a large, heavy kettle over high heat 15–20 minutes, stirring so all sides brown well. Reduce heat to moderate, add onions and garlic, and sauté, stirring, 8–10 minutes until golden. Add all remaining ingredients except peppers, cover, and simmer slowly 1½ hours until meat is almost tender. Add peppers, pushing them down into stew, cover, and simmer 30–45 minutes longer until beef is tender. Serve hot over boiled rice. About 390 calories per serving (without rice).

BEEF AND BLACK BEAN STEW WITH PIÑON NUTS

Makes 6 servings

2½ pounds boned beef chuck, cut in
  1½" cubes
¼ cup olive oil
2 medium-size yellow onions, peeled
  and cut in thin wedges
2 cloves garlic, peeled and crushed
1 teaspoon paprika
1 bay leaf, crumbled
½ teaspoon thyme
½ teaspoon salt
⅛ teaspoon pepper
2 large ripe tomatoes, peeled, cored, and
  cut in thin wedges
⅔ cup dry white wine
1 cup boiling water
2 (1-pound) cans black beans (do not
  drain)
¾ cup shelled piñon nuts

Brown meat in oil, a little at a time, in a large, heavy kettle over high heat; remove to a bowl and reserve. Add onion and garlic to kettle, reduce heat to moderate, and stir-fry 8–10 minutes until golden. Mix in paprika, herbs, salt, pepper, and tomatoes and stir-fry about 5 minutes until tomatoes have released most of their juice. Return meat to kettle, add wine and water, cover, and simmer 1 hour. Stir in 1 can beans and the nuts, cover, and simmer ½–1 hour longer until meat is tender. Add remaining beans, cover, and simmer 15–20 minutes to blend flavors. (*Note:* If stew seems thick, thin with ¼–½ cup boiling water.) Serve over boiled rice. About 805 calories per serving (without rice).

STEWED CHUNKS OF BEEF IN WHITE WINE-VEGETABLE GRAVY

Makes 6–8 servings

2 large carrots, peeled and minced
2 stalks celery, chopped fine
2 leeks, sliced (include tender green tops)
2 medium-size yellow onions, peeled and minced
2 cloves garlic, peeled and crushed
¼ cup olive oil
3 pounds boned beef chuck, rump, or top round cut in 1" cubes
3 medium-size tomatoes, peeled, cored, seeded, and coarsely chopped
¾ cup dry white wine
2 tablespoons minced parsley
1 bay leaf
1 teaspoon salt
⅛ teaspoon pepper

Sauté carrots, celery, leeks, onions and garlic in oil in a large, heavy kettle, stirring occasionally, over moderately high heat 10–12 minutes until golden brown; remove to a bowl. Brown beef in kettle, a few pieces at a time, over high heat. Turn heat to low, return sautéed vegetables to kettle, add remaining ingredients, cover, and simmer 1½–2 hours until beef is tender. Uncover, raise heat to moderate and boil 10–15 minutes, stirring often, to reduce gravy. Serve over boiled potatoes or wide buttered noodles. About 625 calories for each of 6 servings, 470 calories for each of 8 servings (without potatoes or noodles).

BOEUF À LA BOURGUIGNONNE I

There are many variations of Beef Bourguignonne, each slightly different. Some call for cognac, others currant jelly, but all are basically the same— chunks of stew beef simmered in red wine (traditionally Burgundy) with herbs and onions. We offer two recipes. The first cooks in the oven, the second on top of the stove. Both will be better if made a day ahead and reheated slowly before serving. Both freeze well.
Makes 6 servings

1 (¼-pound) piece bacon, trimmed of rind and cut in 1" × ¼" × ¼" strips
1 quart water
1 tablespoon olive oil
3 pounds boned beef chuck, cut in 1½" cubes and patted dry on paper toweling
1 large yellow onion, peeled and sliced thin
1 large carrot, peeled and minced
1 teaspoon salt
⅛ teaspoon pepper
2 tablespoons flour
2 cups red Burgundy or other dry red wine
1⅓ cups strong beef stock or 1 (10½-ounce) can condensed beef broth
1 tablespoon tomato paste
2 cloves garlic, peeled and crushed
2 (4") sprigs fresh thyme or ½ teaspoon dried thyme
2 (4") sprigs parsley
1 bay leaf, crumbled
1 recipe Pan-Braised Onions
1 pound mushrooms, wiped clean and sliced ¼" thick
2 tablespoons butter or margarine

Preheat oven to 500° F. Simmer bacon, uncovered, in water 10 minutes; drain, pat dry, then brown in oil in a large, heavy skillet over moderately high heat about 5 minutes; drain on paper toweling. Brown beef in skillet in bacon drippings, a few pieces at a time, and drain on paper toweling. Reduce heat to moderate, add onion and carrot to skillet, and stir-fry 8–10 minutes until onion is golden. Place beef and bacon in an ungreased 3-quart casserole, add onion and carrot, and toss to mix. Sprinkle with salt, pepper, and flour and toss again. Set, uncovered, in oven 3–5 minutes; remove, stir well, and set in oven 3–5 minutes longer (this helps brown flour and seal in meat juices). Remove casserole from oven and reduce oven temperature to 325° F. Stir wine, stock, tomato paste, and garlic into casserole. Tie thyme, parsley, and bay leaf into cheesecloth and drop into casserole. Cover casserole, set in oven, and simmer 2½–3 hours until beef is tender. Meanwhile, prepare onions and reserve; also stir-fry mushrooms in butter over moderate heat 8–10 minutes until tender; set aside. When beef is tender, remove it and bacon bits to a large bowl with a slotted spoon; keep warm. Discard cheesecloth bag. Put casserole liquid through a fine sieve, pressing with a wooden spoon to purée vegetables; return to casserole and boil, uncovered, about 5 minutes to reduce slightly. Return beef and bacon to casserole. Add onions and mushrooms, distributing them well, cover, and simmer slowly about 5 minutes. Serve hot with boiled new potatoes or noodles, a crisp green salad, and a red Burgundy wine. About 840 calories per serving (without potatoes or noodles).

BOEUF À LA BOURGUIGNONNE II

Slightly lower in calories than Boeuf à la Bourguignonne I.
Makes 8 servings

1 (½-pound) piece lean bacon, trimmed
of rind and cut in 1" × ¼" × ¼"
strips
1 quart water
4 pounds boned beef chuck or rump,
cut in 1½" cubes and patted dry on
paper toweling
1 tablespoon olive oil
2 carrots, peeled and sliced thin
2 medium-size yellow onions, peeled and
sliced thin
3 tablespoons flour
1 teaspoon salt
¼ teaspoon pepper
⅘ quart Beaujolais or other dry red
wine
3 (10½-ounce) cans condensed beef
broth
2 cloves garlic, peeled and crushed
2 (4") sprigs fresh thyme or ½ teaspoon
dried thyme
1 bay leaf, crumbled
1 recipe Pan-Braised Onions
1 pound mushrooms, wiped clean and
sliced ¼" thick
2 tablespoons butter or margarine

Simmer bacon, uncovered, in water 10 minutes. Drain and pat dry, then brown in a large, heavy kettle over moderately high heat 5 minutes; drain on paper toweling. Brown meat in bacon drippings, a few pieces at a time, and drain on paper toweling. Add oil to kettle, reduce heat to moderate, and stir-fry carrots and onions 8–10 minutes until golden. Return beef and bacon to kettle, add flour, salt, and pepper, and toss to mix. Add wine, broth, garlic, thyme, and bay leaf, cover, and simmer, stirring occasionally, 1½–2 hours until beef is tender. Meanwhile, prepare Pan-Braised Onions and set aside. Also sauté mushrooms in butter 8–10 minutes until golden; set aside. When beef is tender, remove thyme sprigs; add mushrooms and onions, cover, and simmer 10–15 minutes longer. If stew seems thick, thin with about 1 cup boiling water. Serve with boiled new potatoes, noodles, or rice, a crisp green salad, and dry red wine. About 810 calories per serving (without potatoes, noodles, or rice).

CARBONNADE FLAMANDE (FLEMISH BEEF-BEER STEW)

Beer gives this nut-brown stew its unusual malty flavor.
Makes 6 servings

2 tablespoons butter or margarine
6 medium-size yellow onions, peeled and
sliced thin
2 cloves garlic, peeled and crushed
½ cup unsifted flour
1 tablespoon salt
¼ teaspoon pepper
3 pounds boned beef chuck, cut in
1½" cubes and trimmed of excess fat
⅛ teaspoon nutmeg
¼ teaspoon thyme
2 (12-ounce) cans beer
1 tablespoon sugar or light brown sugar
(optional)

Melt butter in a large, heavy kettle over moderate heat, add onions and garlic, and sauté, stirring occasionally, 10 minutes until golden; drain on paper toweling. Place flour, salt, and pepper in a heavy brown paper bag and dredge beef, a few cubes at a time, by shaking in the mixture. Brown beef, a little at a time, in kettle over high heat, adding more butter as needed. Reduce heat to moderate, return beef, onions, and garlic to kettle, add all remaining ingredients except sugar, cover, and simmer slowly, stirring occasionally, about 2 hours until beef is fork tender. Skim any fat from gravy. Taste gravy and if it seems a trifle bitter stir in sugar. Simmer, uncovered, about 10 minutes longer, then serve with tiny boiled new potatoes and tall glasses of well-chilled beer. About 645 calories per serving (without potatoes).

BEEF CATALAN

Frenchwomen in the Pyrenees make a marvelous beef stew that's as much Spanish as French. Some add rice to the pot, others white kidney beans; some use a heavy hand with spices, other a light touch. This is a flexible recipe, so you can adjust the ingredients to suit your taste.
Makes 8–10 servings

1 (¼-pound) piece bacon, trimmed of rind and cut in ¼" cubes
4 pounds boned beef rump or chuck, cut in 1½" cubes and patted dry on paper toweling
1 tablespoon olive oil
3 medium-size yellow onions, peeled and sliced thin
2 cloves garlic, peeled and crushed
4 medium-size carrots, peeled and cut in 2" chunks
½ pound small turnips, peeled and quartered
1 (1"×3") strip orange peel (orange part only)
1 stick cinnamon
3 cloves
1 bay leaf, crumbled
2 (4") sprigs fresh thyme or ½ teaspoon dried thyme
3 ripe tomatoes, peeled, seeded, juiced, and coarsely chopped
2 cups dry red wine
1⅓ cups strong beef stock or 1 (10½-ounce) can condensed beef broth
2 (1-pound 4-ounce) cans cannellini (white kidney beans), drained

2½ teaspoons salt
⅛ teaspoon pepper
3 tablespoons minced parsley

Preheat oven to 325° F. Brown bacon in a large, heavy kettle over high heat and drain on paper toweling. Brown beef in drippings, a few cubes at a time, over moderately high heat; remove to a bowl and reserve. Add oil to kettle and stir-fry onions, garlic, carrots, and turnips 10–12 minutes until onions are golden. Tie orange peel, cinnamon, cloves, bay leaf, and thyme in cheesecloth and add to kettle along with bacon, beef, tomatoes, wine, and stock. Cover kettle, set in oven, and simmer 2½–3 hours until beef is tender. Discard cheesecloth bag. (*Note:* Recipe can be made up to this point well ahead of time. Cool, cover, and refrigerate or freeze for use later. Bring to room temperature before proceeding or, if frozen, thaw gently over low heat, stirring frequently.) Add remaining ingredients except parsley and bake, uncovered, 30 minutes, stirring 1 or 2 times. Mix in parsley and serve over hot fluffy rice or Saffron Rice. About 780 calories for each of 8 servings (without rice), 625 calories for each of 10 servings.

HUNGARIAN GOULASH

Though traditionally made with beef, *gulyás*, the Hungarian national dish, can be prepared with any meat or game. Here's a basic version with four popular variations.
Makes 4–6 servings

1¼ cups finely chopped yellow onion
1 sweet green pepper, cored, seeded, and chopped fine
¼ cup lard, butter, or margarine
2 pounds boned beef chuck, shin, or bottom round, cut in 1½" cubes
2 tablespoons paprika (use the Hungarian sweet rose if possible)
1½ teaspoons salt
¼ teaspoon pepper
1 teaspoon cider vinegar
2 cups beef stock, broth, or water

Sauté onion and green pepper in lard in

a kettle over moderate heat 5–8 minutes until onion is pale golden; drain on paper toweling. Add meat to kettle and brown well over moderately high heat. Turn heat to low, add paprika, and stir 1–2 minutes. Return onion mixture to kettle, add remaining ingredients, cover, and simmer 1½–2 hours until meat is tender. Serve with Nockerln or buttered noodles. About 380 calories for each of 4 servings (without Nockerln or noodles), 255 calories for each of 6 servings.

VARIATIONS:

Transylvanian Goulash: About ½ hour before goulash is done, add 1 pound drained sauerkraut, cover, and simmer until meat is tender. Mix in 1 cup sour cream and serve. About 500 calories for each of 4 servings, 335 calories for each of 6 servings.

Yugoslav Goulash: Sauté 1 clove peeled, crushed garlic with onion and green pepper, then proceed as directed, substituting 1 (1-pound 12-ounce) can undrained tomatoes for beef stock. If you prefer, use 1 cup beef stock and 1 (8-ounce) can tomato sauce. About 380 calories for each of 4 servings, 255 calories for each of 6 servings.

Savory Goulash: Prepare as directed, adding 1 teaspoon caraway seeds or marjoram and/or 1 clove peeled, crushed garlic along with other seasonings. About 380 calories for each of 4 servings, 255 for each of 6 servings.

¢ ⟐ **Budget Goulash:** Add 4 peeled, quartered potatoes ½ hour before beef is done, cover, and simmer until tender. Makes 6 servings. About 305 calories per serving.

COUNTRY-STYLE UKRAINIAN BORSCH

Old country-style borsch, the national dish of the Ukraine, always has a good chunk of meat cooking along with the vegetables. A mild tartness is characteristic—beet or rye *kvas* (liquid from fermented beets or rye yeast batter) used to be traditional, but nowadays lemon, vinegar, even sorrel leaves or rhubarb juice are substituted. Makes 12–14 servings

1 (2-pound) boned and rolled beef roast (chuck, bottom round, or rump), trimmed of fat
1 (2-pound) smoked boneless pork shoulder butt
1 gallon cold water
2–4 teaspoons salt
1 bouquet garni,* tied in cheesecloth with 1 peeled clove garlic and 6 peppercorns
2 medium-size yellow onions, peeled and coarsely chopped
2 carrots, peeled and cut in julienne strips
2 cups finely chopped celery
8 medium-size boiled beets, peeled and diced or cut in julienne strips
1 (1-pound 12-ounce) can tomatoes (do not drain)
4 cups finely shredded cabbage
2 cups boiled dried white beans or 1 (1-pound 4-ounce) can cannellini beans (do not drain)
3–4 tablespoons lemon juice
2 tablespoons snipped fresh dill (optional)
1 pint sour cream (optional garnish)

Place meats, water, 2 teaspoons salt, cheesecloth bag, and onions in a 3-gallon kettle, cover, and bring to a boil over moderate heat. Skim froth from surface, reduce heat, re-cover, and simmer 2–2½ hours until meats are nearly tender. Add carrots and celery, cover, and simmer 20 minutes; add beets, tomatoes (cut them up), and cabbage, cover, and simmer 20 minutes longer. Remove cheesecloth bag and gently stir in beans and lemon juice. (*Note:* Recipe may be prepared to this point a day or so ahead; cool, cover and chill.) Heat slowly to boiling, taste for salt and pepper and adjust as needed. Stir in dill if you like. Ladle into deep soup bowls, serve with a slice or 2 of meats, and top with dollops of sour cream. About 505 calories for each of 12 servings, 435 calories for each of 14 servings.

VARIATIONS:

Borsch Stew: Instead of using large chunks of beef and pork, use 2 pounds each boned chuck and pork shoulder butt, cut in 1½″ cubes. Otherwise, prepare as directed. If you prefer, use 3–4 pounds beef shank or bone-in soup meat in place of the chuck. About 505 calories for each of 12 servings, 435 calories for each of 14 servings.

⚖ ¢ **Economy Borsch:** Omit all meats; substitute strong beef stock for half the water called for, and simmer vegetables as directed. Makes 12 servings. About 205 calories per serving.

Beef and Bacon Borsch for 6 Persons: Use 2 pounds boned beef chuck cut in 1½″ cubes and substitute 3–4 slices diced, lean smoked bacon for the pork shoulder butt; halve all other ingredients and prepare as recipe directs. Cooking times will be about the same. About 450 calories per serving.

OLD-FASHIONED STEAK AND KIDNEY PIE

Mashed or boiled potatoes and Brussels sprouts or carrots are traditional with steak and kidney pie.
Makes 6 servings

1 pound beef kidney, free of membrane and fat
2 cups cold water mixed with 1 teaspoon salt
2½ pounds lean, boned beef chuck or bottom round, cut in 1½″ cubes
¼ cup rendered suet, beef drippings, or cooking oil
3 medium-size yellow onions, peeled and minced
3 tablespoons flour
1 (10½-ounce) can condensed beef broth
1 cup cold water
2 teaspoons salt
¼ teaspoon pepper
1 bouquet garni,* tied in cheesecloth (optional)

Pastry:
1 recipe Flaky Pastry I
1 egg yolk mixed with 1 tablespoon cold water (glaze)

Soak kidney in salt water 1 hour, drain, and pat dry on paper toweling; remove cores and cut kidney in 1″ cubes. Brown beef, a little at a time, in suet in a large, heavy kettle over high heat; remove and reserve. Brown kidney, stirring, and add to beef. Turn heat to moderate, add onions and stir-fry 8–10 minutes until golden; mix in flour and brown 1–2 minutes. Return meat to kettle, add all but pastry ingredients, cover, and simmer 1½–2 hours until tender. Discard *bouquet garni* if used. Transfer to an ungreased 2-quart casserole that measures about 9″ across. (*Note:* If you have a pie funnel, place in center of casserole before adding meat; it will help prop up crust and keep pie from boiling over.) Preheat oven to 425° F.

Roll pastry into a 10″ circle and make 3 V-slits in center. Moisten casserole rim, top with pastry, roll edges under until even with rim, press down to seal and crimp. Brush pastry with glaze, making sure not to cover slits. Bake in top ⅓ of oven (with foil under casserole to catch drips) 10–12 minutes, reduce heat to 350° F., and bake 25 minutes longer until nicely browned. To serve, cut wedge-shaped pieces of pastry and arrange on top of each helping of meat.

VARIATION:

Just before serving, insert a small funnel in a V-slit and pour in 1–2 tablespoons dry sherry.

Both versions: about 945 calories per serving.

BAKED CASSEROLE OF BEEF AND ONIONS

Makes 4–6 servings

2 pounds boned beef chuck, cut in 1½″ cubes
½ cup unsifted flour
2 teaspoons salt
¼ teaspoon pepper

3 tablespoons beef drippings or cooking
oil
2 large yellow onions, peeled and sliced
thin
1 bay leaf, crumbled
2½ cups canned condensed beef broth or
1 cup broth and 1½ cups dry red wine
or beer

Preheat oven to 350° F. Dredge beef
by shaking in a paper bag with flour, ½
teaspoon salt, and ⅛ teaspoon pepper.
Brown, a few pieces at a time, in
2 tablespoons drippings in a shallow
flameproof 2-quart casserole over
moderately high heat; remove to a bowl.
Stir-fry onions in remaining drippings
8–10 minutes until well browned. Return
beef to casserole, add remaining salt
and pepper and all other ingredients,
cover and bake 1½–2 hours until tender.
Serve with mashed potatoes, boiled
noodles, or plenty of crusty bread for
getting up the gravy. About 645
calories for each of 4 servings (without
potatoes, noodles, or bread), 430
calories for each of 6 servings.

VARIATIONS:

Skillet Beef Stew: A large electric
skillet cooks this stew perfectly. Brown
beef at 350° F., then sauté onions at the
same temperature. Add remaining
ingredients, cover and simmer 1 hour at
200° F. until tender; stir occasionally.
About 645 calories for each of 4
servings, 430 calories for each of 6
servings.

Farmhouse Beef Casserole: Prepare and
bake casserole as directed. Spread
Farmhouse Potato Topping over surface,
roughen with a fork, and broil 4″ from
the heat 3–4 minutes until touched with
brown. About 900 calories for each of
4 servings, 600 calories for each of
6 servings.

¢ **FARMHOUSE MEAT AND
POTATO PIE**

Makes 6 servings

Pastry:

2 cups sifted flour
1 teaspoon salt
⅓ cup chilled shortening
⅓ cup chilled lard
4–5 tablespoons ice water
1 egg yolk mixed with 1 tablespoon cold
water (glaze)

Filling:

1½ pounds boned beef chuck, cut in
1″ cubes
½ cup unsifted flour
2 teaspoons salt
3 medium-size potatoes, peeled and
sliced ½″ thick
1 large yellow onion, peeled and sliced
thin
¼ teaspoon pepper
1⅔ cup beef stock or 1 cup canned
condensed beef broth and ⅔ cup water

Preheat oven to 425° F. Sift flour and
salt for pastry into a bowl and cut in
shortening and lard with a pastry
blender until the texture of oatmeal.
Sprinkle ice water over surface, a
tablespoon at a time, mixing briskly with
a fork after each addition. Pastry should
just hold together. Wrap in foil and
chill while you prepare the filling. Dredge
beef by shaking in a paper bag with
flour and 1 teaspoon salt. Place beef in
an ungreased shallow 1½-quart casserole
with a wide rim. Layer potatoes and
onion on top, sprinkling pepper and
remaining salt between layers. Pour
stock over all. Roll pastry into a circle
about 3″ larger in diameter than the
casserole and cut a strip 1″ wide from
around outer edge. Moisten casserole
rim with cold water and lay strip on rim;
moisten strip. Cut 2–3 decorative holes
near center of pastry circle; place on top
of filling and press edges into pastry
strip. Trim pastry even with rim and
crimp. Brush with glaze, avoiding
decorative edge. Bake 15 minutes,
reduce heat to 350° F., and bake 1¼
hours longer until meat is tender (test
by poking a skewer through decorative
hole). Serve hot with a crisp green salad.

About 680 calories per serving.

PRUNE AND SWEET POTATO TZIMMES

Jewish New Year would not be complete without the sweet-but-savory, meat-and-vegetable stew called *tzimmes*. Honey, symbolic of the wish for sweetness throughout the New Year, is the traditional sweetener.

Makes 4 servings

1½–2 pounds boned beef chuck, cut in 1" cubes
3 tablespoons rendered chicken fat, shortening, or cooking oil
1 medium-size yellow onion, peeled and chopped fine
1 quart cold water
1½ teaspoons salt
¼ teaspoon pepper
¼ teaspoon cinnamon
3 medium-size sweet potatoes, peeled and cut crosswise in 1" slices
½ pound pitted prunes
½ cup honey
1 tablespoon shortening
2 tablespoons flour

Brown beef in fat in a heavy kettle over moderately high heat; transfer to a bowl. Stir-fry onion in drippings 8–10 minutes over moderate heat until golden; return beef to kettle, add water, salt, and pepper, cover, and simmer slowly ¾ hour. Add all but last 2 ingredients, cover partially, lid askew, and simmer ¾ hour longer until meat is tender. Shake pan, do not stir, to prevent sticking. Melt shortening in a small skillet over moderate heat, blend in flour and brown slowly 3–4 minutes; mix in 1 cup kettle liquid, then return all to kettle and *shake,* but do not stir, to distribute (mixture should be thick, not soupy). Heat 1–2 minutes and serve. About 830 calories per serving.

VARIATION:

Carrot Tzimmes: Omit prunes and add 4–5 carrots, peeled and sliced 1" thick. If you like, substitute Irish potatoes for the sweet. Otherwise, prepare as directed. About 715 calories per serving.

INDONESIAN SPICED BEEF

Makes 4–6 servings

2 medium-size yellow onions, peeled and coarsely chopped
2 cloves garlic, peeled and crushed
3 tablespoons peanut oil
1 flank steak (about 2–2¼ pounds), cut crosswise into strips ½" × 1½"
1 (2") stick cinnamon
6 cloves
2 tablespoons paprika
1 tablespoon crushed coriander seeds
1–2 teaspoons cayenne pepper (depending on how hot you like things)
1 teaspoon turmeric
1 teaspoon ginger
¼ teaspoon cumin
4 medium-size new potatoes, peeled and cut in ½" cubes
2 cups Coconut Milk
1½ teaspoons salt

Stir-fry onions and garlic in oil in a heavy kettle over moderate heat 8–10 minutes until golden; remove to a bowl. Raise heat to high and brown meat, a few pieces at a time; transfer to paper toweling to drain. Reduce heat to low, return meat, onions, and garlic to kettle and mix in all remaining ingredients. Cover and simmer, stirring occasionally, about 1½ hours until meat is tender. Serve hot over fluffy boiled rice. About 740 calories for each of 4 servings (without rice), 495 calories for each of 6 servings.

BOMBAY-STYLE CURRIED BEEF

India has hundreds of curries, some hot (the Madras), some not so hot (the Bombay). Either is usually accompanied by popadams (crisp-fried paper-thin pancakes available in specialty food shops), and two or three sambals (side dishes).

Makes 4–6 servings

2 pounds boned lean beef chuck or bottom round, cut in 1" cubes
3 tablespoons beef drippings, butter, or margarine

2 large yellow onions, peeled and
minced
2 cloves garlic, peeled and crushed
2 tablespoons curry powder
1½ cups hot water
⅔ cup tomato sauce
1 teaspoon salt
1 cup yogurt, at room temperature
(optional)

Sambals (choose 2 or 3):

Bombay Duck (salty, dried fish sautéed
or baked till crisp)
Sweet chutney
Sour pickles (mango, walnut, red
cabbage, cucumber, onion, beet)
Red or green chili peppers
Minced onions or scallions
Chopped salted peanuts or almonds

Not traditional but good (choose 1 or 2):

Flaked coconut, raisins, chopped hard-
cooked eggs, a mixture of grated
orange and lemon or lime rind, minced
parsley

Brown beef, a few pieces at a time, in
drippings in a heavy kettle over
moderately high heat; remove to a bowl.
Stir-fry onions and garlic in kettle 8–10
minutes over moderate heat until
golden; mix in curry powder and heat
1 minute. Return beef to kettle, mix in
all remaining ingredients except yogurt,
cover, and simmer 1½–2 hours until
meat is tender. Remove from heat and,
if you wish, stir in yogurt. Serve over
boiled rice with a variety of sambals.
About 605 calories for each of 4
servings, 405 calories for each 6 servings
(without rice or sambals).

¢ BRAISED OXTAIL WITH CARROTS

Makes 6–8 servings

4 pounds oxtail, cut in 1½" chunks and
trimmed of excess fat
2 tablespoons cooking oil
2 medium-size yellow onions, peeled and
chopped fine
3 cups hot water or 1 (12-ounce) can
beer and 1½ cups water or 2 cups
water and 1 cup dry red wine
1 (8-ounce) can tomato sauce

½ teaspoon celery seeds
1 bay leaf, crumbled
1 tablespoon minced parsley
1 teaspoon Worcestershire sauce
1½ teaspoons salt
⅛ teaspoon pepper
6–8 medium-size carrots, peeled and
sliced ½" thick
2 tablespoons flour blended with 2
tablespoons cold water

Brown oxtail in oil in a large, heavy
kettle over high heat and drain on
paper toweling. Reduce heat to moderate, add onions to kettle and sauté,
stirring, 8–10 minutes until golden.
Return meat to kettle, add remaining
ingredients except carrots and flour-
water paste, cover, and simmer over low
heat 3 hours until meat is tender. Cool
and skim off fat. (Note: Recipe can be
prepared to this point a day or so ahead
of time. Cool, cover, and refrigerate or
freeze for future use. Bring to room
temperature before proceeding, or if
frozen thaw gently over low heat,
stirring frequently.) Add carrots,
cover, and simmer 20 minutes until
tender. Mix in flour-water paste and
heat, stirring, until thickened. Serve
over buttered noodles. About 515
calories for each of 6 servings (without
noodles), 385 calories for each of 8
servings.

MARROWBONES

If you don't have long, narrow marrow
spoons for getting the marrow out of the
bones, use iced-tea spoons—they work
just as well.
Makes 2 servings

3 pounds beef marrowbones, cut in 2"–
3" lengths and trimmed of fat
2 tablespoons cooking oil
1 quart water
1 teaspoon salt
⅛ teaspoon black pepper
2 slices hot unbuttered toast, halved
diagonally
⅛ teaspoon white pepper (optional)

Brown bones well in oil in a large
kettle over moderate heat. To keep
marrow from falling out of bones as they

simmer, wrap each in cheesecloth, or lay bones flat in kettle and handle *very gently*. Add water, salt, and black pepper, cover, and simmer over low heat 1 hour. Using a slotted spoon, lift bones to heated plates. Remove cheesecloth, if used, and serve marrowbones with toast. If you prefer, scoop marrow from bones before serving, spread on toast, and sprinkle with white pepper. Serve hot as an appetizer. (*Note:* Marrow can also be cut into slices about ¼″ thick and floated in hot consommé as a garnish.) Calorie data unavailable for marrow.

Short Ribs

It's curious that pork spareribs should be such a favorite and their beef counter-part, short ribs, so often slighted. These 3″ rib ends (see Beef Chart) are budget priced and, when braised and skillfully seasoned, unusually good eating.

¢ BRAISED SHORT RIBS OF BEEF

Makes 4 servings

3½–4 *pounds beef short ribs, cut in 3″ pieces*
2 *tablespoons cooking oil or beef drippings*
1 *medium-size yellow onion, peeled and sliced thin*
¼ *pound mushrooms, wiped and sliced*
1 *large carrot, peeled and sliced thin*
1 *teaspoon salt*
¼ *teaspoon pepper*
1 *cup beef broth*
2 *tablespoons flour blended with 2 tablespoons cold water*
¼ *teaspoon liquid gravy browner*

Brown ribs slowly (about 15–20 minutes) in oil in a large kettle over moderately low heat. Add onion, mushrooms, carrot, salt, pepper, and broth, cover, and simmer 1½ hours until meat is tender. Transfer ribs to a deep serving dish and keep warm. Purée vegetables and cooking liquid in an electric blender at low speed or put through a food mill; return to kettle. Mix in flour-water

paste and gravy browner and cook, stirring, until thickened. Pour some gravy over short ribs and serve (remaining gravy can be passed in a gravy boat). About 490 calories per serving.

¢ DEVILED SHORT RIBS

Makes 4 servings

4 *pounds beef short ribs, cut in serving size pieces*

Marinade:
¼ *cup prepared spicy brown mustard*
¼ *cup prepared mild yellow mustard*
1 *cup dry white wine*
½ *cup beef broth*
2 *tablespoons Worcestershire sauce*
2 *tablespoons finely grated yellow onion*
1 *clove garlic, peeled and crushed*
½ *teaspoon salt*
¼ *teaspoon pepper*

Place ribs in a large, deep bowl; beat all marinade ingredients together until smooth and pour over ribs. Cover and refrigerate at least 12 hours, turning ribs now and then. Drain, reserving marinade. Preheat oven to 425° F. Place ribs on a rack in a roasting pan and roast, uncovered, 15–17 minutes until browned; turn and brown 15–17 minutes longer. Reduce oven tempera-ture to 325° F. Transfer ribs to a second roasting pan (do not use rack), top with ¾ cup marinade, cover with foil, and bake 2–2½ hours until tender. Just before serving, heat remaining marinade and serve as a hot sauce with the ribs. About 520 calories per serving.

¢ SHORT RIBS AND CHICK-PEAS IN TOMATO SAUCE

Makes 6 servings

3 *pounds beef short ribs, cut in serving size pieces*
½ *cup unsifted flour*
1 *teaspoon salt*
¼ *teaspoon pepper*
3 *tablespoons cooking oil*
2 *medium-size yellow onions, peeled and sliced thin*
1 *clove garlic, peeled and crushed*

1 bay leaf, crumbled
¼ teaspoon oregano
½ cup dry red wine
1 (6-ounce) can tomato paste
1½ cups water
2 (1-pound 4-ounce) cans chick-peas,
  drained
1 tablespoon minced parsley

Dredge ribs, a few at a time, by shaking
in a paper bag with flour, salt, and
pepper, then brown in oil, a few at a
time, in a large, heavy kettle over
moderately high heat and drain on
paper toweling. Add onions, garlic, bay
leaf, and oregano to kettle and stir-fry
8–10 minutes until onions are golden
brown. Return ribs to kettle, reduce heat
to low, add wine, tomato paste, and
water, cover, and simmer 1½–2 hours,
stirring occasionally, until ribs are
tender. Add chick-peas and parsley
and simmer, uncovered, stirring now and
then, 10–15 minutes longer to blend
flavors, then serve. About 455 calories
per serving.

Other Forms of Beef

Corned Beef: Brisket (and sometimes
plate or rump) cured either in brine or
by having brine pumped through the
arterial system. Old-fashioned corned
beef is salty and gray-pink, newer,
milder types rosy red; both are available
by the half or whole brisket. Newest
entry is corned beef for oven roasting;
it comes in two flavors: mild cure and
spicy garlic (wrappers give full
instructions for oven and spit roasting).
Also available: canned corned beef and
sandwich slices in pliofilm packages.
Allow ⅓–½ pound corned beef per
person.

Chipped Beef (also called *Dried Beef*):
Tissue-thin slices of salty dried beef;
allow 1–2 ounces per person.

Beef-Bacon Slices: Rather like pastrami
without the spices, these slices of cured
beef are cooked just like bacon. Allow
3–4 slices per person.

Smoked Sliced Beef: Ready-to-eat
sandwich meat made by pressing
coarsely ground beef into rounds or
squares, curing, smoking, and cooking.
Allow 1–2 slices per person.

Jerky or Jerked Beef: The original
dried beef. These salty, leathery strips
and chunks are still a great favorite
among American Indians and Mexicans
(Latin groceries are the best place to
buy them).

Freeze-Dried Beef: Not much beef is
being freeze-dried as yet, though the
process may eventually revolutionize our
lives. Freeze-dried meat requires very
little storage space and no refrigeration.
To date it is being used primarily in soup
mixes and camp foods, also by
astronauts.

¢ NEW ENGLAND BOILED DINNER

Makes 6 servings

4 pounds corned brisket of beef, wiped
  with damp paper toweling
2 quarts cold water
6 peppercorns and 1 bay leaf tied in
  cheesecloth
6 medium-size carrots, peeled and
  halved crosswise
6 medium-size potatoes, peeled and
  halved
1 small rutabaga, peeled and cut in
  6 wedges
1 medium-size cabbage, trimmed of
  coarse leaves, cored, and cut in
  6 wedges

If necessary, tie brisket into a neat
shape; place in a very large kettle, add
water and cheesecloth bag, cover, and
bring to a boil over high heat. Reduce
heat to low and simmer 10 minutes;
uncover and skim off any scum. Re-cover
and simmer about 4 hours until tender.
Remove cheesecloth bag; transfer meat
to a platter, cover loosely with foil and
keep warm. (*Note:* Meat can be
refrigerated at this point and held 1–2
days; let come to room temperature
before proceeding.) Bring kettle liquid
to a boil and taste; if not too salty, add

carrots, potatoes, and rutabaga, cover, and boil 20 minutes; add meat and cabbage, cover, and cook 15–20 minutes longer. If liquid is too salty, cook carrots, potatoes, and rutabaga, covered, in about 2″ lightly salted water 20 minutes, add meat and cabbage, and proceed as above. Drain vegetables and make a border around a very large platter; place meat in center. Serve with horseradish, mustard, or mustard pickles. To be really traditional, add a plate of Rhode Island Jonnycake and serve apple dumplings for dessert. About 730 calories per serving.

¢ CORNED BEEF AND CABBAGE

Some people say the only way to make good corned beef and cabbage is to cook the two together, but *don't* if the beef cooking water seems greasy and/or salty—boil the cabbage separately. When carving corned beef, make the slices thick or thin but always slice *against* the grain.

Makes 6–8 servings

*4 pounds corned brisket of beef, wiped
  with damp paper toweling*
2 quarts cold water
6 peppercorns
6 whole allspice
1 bay leaf
*1 medium-size yellow onion, peeled and
  quartered*
*1 medium-size cabbage, trimmed of
  coarse outer leaves, cored, and cut in
  8 wedges*

If necessary, tie brisket into a neat shape; place in a very large kettle with water, peppercorns, allspice, bay leaf, and onion, cover, and bring to a boil over high heat. Reduce heat to low and simmer 10 minutes; uncover and skim off any scum. Re-cover and simmer about 4 hours until tender. Taste cooking water and, if it seems delicate enough, add cabbage, cover, and simmer 15–20 minutes until crisp tender. Otherwise, place cabbage in a separate kettle, add about 2″ lightly salted boiling water, cover, and boil 15–20 minutes; drain. Arrange beef on a heated large platter and surround with cabbage wedges. Serve with boiled potatoes and a mustard or horseradish sauce. About 590 calories for each of 6 servings, 440 calories for each of 8 servings.

¢ HOMEMADE CORNED BEEF HASH

Makes 4 servings

*1 medium-size yellow onion, peeled and
  chopped fine*
*2 tablespoons any meat drippings,
  butter, or margarine*
2 cups diced, cooked corned beef
2 cups diced, cooked cold potatoes
2 teaspoons Worcestershire sauce
1 tablespoon minced parsley
⅛ teaspoon pepper
4 Poached Eggs

Stir-fry onion in drippings in a large, heavy skillet over moderate heat 5–8 minutes until transparent. Stir in corned beef and potatoes; sprinkle evenly with Worcestershire sauce, parsley, and pepper. Pat hash down with a broad spatula and cook, uncovered, without stirring, 10–12 minutes until a brown crust forms on the bottom. Turn, using 2 broad spatulas, and brown flip side 8–10 minutes. To serve, cut in 4 equal portions and top each with a poached egg. About 390 calories per serving.

¢ ⊠ CORNED BEEF AND POTATO PUFF

Makes 4 servings

1 (12-ounce) can corned beef
1 tablespoon steak sauce
2 cups hot mashed potatoes
¼ cup heavy cream
Pinch nutmeg
4 Fried Eggs

Break up corned beef with a fork, place in a flameproof 1½-quart casserole, and brown lightly over moderate heat, stirring constantly. Mix in steak sauce. Beat potatoes with cream and nutmeg and spread over beef. Brown 2–3 minutes under the broiler, 4″–5″ from the heat, top with eggs, and serve. About 525 calories per serving.

¢ ⚖ **RED FLANNEL HASH**

Makes 4–6 servings

1 (12-ounce) can corned beef, minced
2 large boiled potatoes, peeled and
*   chopped fine*
1 cup minced, cooked beets
1 medium-size yellow onion, peeled and
*   minced*
Pinch pepper
3 tablespoons butter, margarine, or
*   bacon drippings*

Mix corned beef, potatoes, beets, onion, and pepper well. Melt butter in a heavy 9″ or 10″ skillet over moderately low heat, add hash, and let cook slowly about 35–40 minutes until a crisp brown crust forms on the bottom. Turn carefully and brown flip side 10–15 minutes or, if you prefer, instead of browning second side, fold as an omelet and serve. Accompany, if you like, with Sour Cream Horseradish Sauce or top each serving with a poached egg. About 335 calories for each of 4 servings (without sauce or poached egg), 225 calories for each of 6 servings.

VARIATIONS:

Oven-Browned Red Flannel Hash: Mix corned beef, potatoes, beets, and pepper and set aside. Stir-fry onion in butter 8–10 minutes in a large, heavy skillet over moderate heat until golden. Add beef mixture and stir-fry about 5 minutes. Transfer to a greased 9″ piepan and drizzle with 2 tablespoons melted butter mixed with 2 tablespoons light cream. Brown under broiler, 4″ from heat, 5–6 minutes and serve. About 400 calories for each of 4 servings, 270 calories for each of 6 servings.

Hamburger Red Flannel Hash: Substitute 1 pound ground lean beef chuck for the corned beef, mix with potatoes, beets, onion, 1 teaspoon salt, and the pepper. Brown in a skillet as in basic recipe above, or brown in the oven as in first variation. For skillet-browned hash, about 355 calories for each of 4 servings, 235 calories for each of 6 servings. For oven-browned hash, about 420 calories for each of 4 servings, 280 calories for each of 6 servings.

¢ ▨ **CREAMED CHIPPED BEEF**

Makes 4 servings

1 (4-ounce) package chipped beef
¼ cup butter or margarine
¼ cup unsifted flour
2 cups milk
Pinch pepper

Separate beef slices and tear into medium-size shreds; taste and if too salty cover with boiling water and let stand 1 minute; drain well. Melt butter in a saucepan over moderate heat, add beef, and heat, stirring occasionally, 2–3 minutes until lightly frizzled. Off heat, blend in flour, then milk. Return to heat and cook, stirring constantly, until thickened and smooth. Add pepper, taste for salt and add if needed. Serve over slices of dry toast. About 265 calories per serving (without toast).

VARIATIONS:

Parsleyed Chipped Beef: Just before serving, mix in 2 tablespoons minced parsley. About 265 calories per serving (without toast).

Chipped Beef Curry: Prepare as directed up to point of adding flour; mix in flour, also 1–2 tablespoons curry powder, 1 teaspoon Worcestershire sauce, and ¼ teaspoon each garlic and onion powders. Proceed as directed and serve over boiled rice or toast. About 265 calories per serving (without rice or toast).

Chipped Beef in Cheese Sauce: Prepare as directed; add ¼ pound mild processed cheese, 1 tablespoon Worcestershire sauce, and 2–3 dashes liquid hot red pepper seasoning. Heat, stirring, until smooth and serve over buttered noodles or dry toast. About 365 calories per serving (without noodles or toast).

Chipped Beef, Cheese, and Olives:
Prepare Chipped Beef in Cheese Sauce
and just before serving stir in ½ cup
thinly sliced pimiento-stuffed green
olives. About 375 calories per serving
(without toast).

Chipped Beef "Chili": Prepare Chipped
Beef in Cheese Sauce, then mix in
1 tablespoon each chili powder and
ketchup. Serve over toast or boiled dried
kidney beans. About 365 calories per
serving (without toast or beans).

Barbecued Chipped Beef: Prepare
Chipped Beef "Chili," increasing amount
of ketchup to 3 tablespoons and adding
2 tablespoons cider vinegar. Serve over
toast. About 365 calories per serving
(without toast).

⊠ CREAMED CHIPPED BEEF AND MUSHROOMS

Extra rich and filled with meat.
Makes 4–6 servings

2 (4-ounce) packages chipped beef
½ pound mushrooms, wiped clean and
  sliced thin
1 clove garlic, peeled and crushed
  (optional)
2 tablespoons butter or margarine
2 (10½-ounce) cans condensed cream
  of mushroom soup
1 cup cold water
⅛ teaspoon white pepper
½ cup sour cream

Separate beef slices and tear into
medium-size shreds; taste and if too salty
cover with boiling water and let stand
1 minute; drain thoroughly. Sauté
beef, mushrooms, and, if you like, the
garlic in the butter in a large skillet over
moderately high heat 3–4 minutes until
mushrooms are golden; set aside. In a
saucepan mix soup and water and heat,
uncovered, over moderate heat until
almost boiling. Add skillet mixture and
remaining ingredients and heat, but do
not boil, 2–3 minutes. Serve over toast
or chow mein noodles. About 530
calories for each of 4 servings (without
toast or noodles), 355 calories for each
of 6 servings.

VEAL

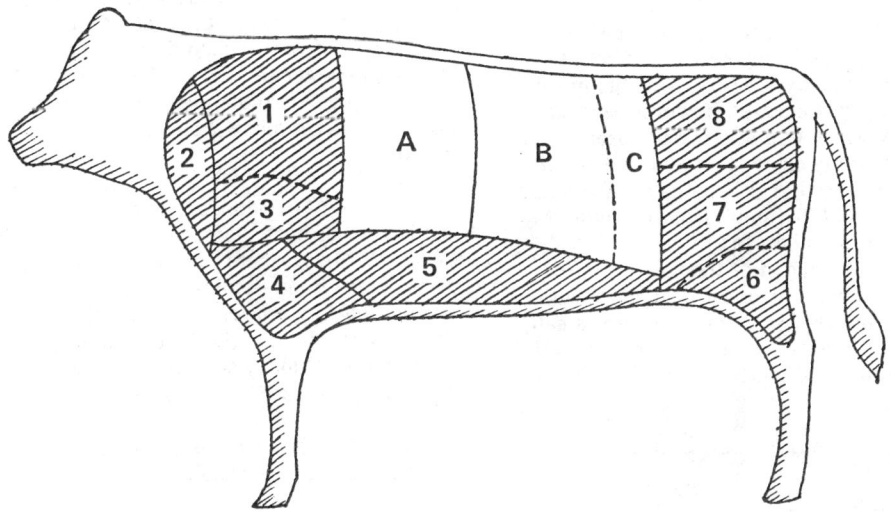

Note: Unshaded parts are the tender cuts. Shaded parts are not-so-tender.

THE TENDER CUTS:
  A. RIB
      Roasts (rib, crown)
      Chops (rib, boneless rib)
  B. LOIN
      Roasts
      Chops (loin, kidney)
  C. SIRLOIN
      Roasts
      Steaks

THE NOT-SO-TENDER CUTS:
  1. SHOULDER
      Blade roasts
      Blade steaks
      Stew veal
      Ground veal

2. NECK
    Stew veal
3. ARM
    Arm roasts
    Arm steaks
4. SHANK
    Shank crosscuts
5. BREAST
    Roasts for stuffing
    Riblets (stew veal)
6. HEEL OF ROUND
    Stew veal
7. ROUND (LEG)
    Cutlets, scaloppine
    Round steaks
    Roasts
8. RUMP
    Roasts

Compared to juicy red steaks or prime ribs, veal seems colorless, characterless. Americans tend to treat it as junior-grade beef, a mistake because veal is too lean and delicate to fling on a grill or pop in the oven. It needs coddling in butter, stock, or sauce, enhancing with herbs, rounding out with vegetables or other meats. European recipes prove how very good veal can be. *Wiener Schnitzel,* for example, tender and moist under its crispy brown crust, sagey *saltimbocca,* creamy *blanquette de veau.*

Unfortunately, the veal beloved by Europeans—velvety white meat of suckling calves—isn't available in this country. Recently, however, certain Eastern supermarkets have been selling something close to it: *plume de veau,* pale-fleshed veal from calves fed a dry skim milk formula. It hasn't quite the flavor of calves fed mother's milk, but it's miles ahead of the rosy grass-fed veal most of us must be content with. Technically, veal is the meat of a calf 5 to 12 weeks of age. After that, until it matures into beef, its meat is of no use.

How to Recognize Quality

Look for the top federal grades (USDA PRIME, CHOICE, and GOOD), also for federally inspected (wholesome) meat. The lean should be firm, velvety, and moist; it will have no marbling of fat and practically no outer fat covering. The color of the lean varies, depending upon the animal's age and diet. Very young milk-fed veal will be grayish-white with only the faintest blush of pink; older grass or grain-fed veal will be pink, rosy, and sometimes quite red (once an animal begins nibbling grass, its flesh begins to redden). The bones of veal should be spongy and red inside and what fat there is, creamy, sweet, and firm.

Roast Veal

Loin and Rib Roasts: The most luxurious veal roasts.

Rib Roast (4–6 pounds): Very lean, very expensive. There's usually more demand for rib as chops than as roasts.

Crown Roast (8 pounds up): This custom-made showpiece contains 2 or more rib sections bent into a circle. Rib ends are frenched (stripped of meat) and the trimmings ground and piled in the center of the crown (remove this ground meat before roasting the crown because it slows cooking time; some of the ground meat can be mixed with the stuffing or all of it can be saved and used for loaves or patties). To determine the size of crown roast you need, figure 2 chops per person.

Loin Roast (4–6 pounds): The equivalent of beef short loin (steak row). With veal there's more demand for loin as chops—junior steaks containing tiny nuggets of tenderloin. In England, the favorite loin roast is that with the kidney still attached (it nestles just underneath the ribs).

Rolled Loin (3–5 pounds): Boned and rolled loin; good for stuffing.

Double Loin or Saddle (8–12 pounds): Right and left loins, still intact.

Sirloin Roast (3–4 pounds): A very tender roast from the part of the animal between the loin and rump.

Rolled Double Sirloin (5–6 pounds): Right and left sirloin roasts, boned and rolled.

Shoulder Roasts: Moderately priced and perfect for braising: arm roast (4–5 pounds), blade roast (4–5 pounds), and rolled shoulder (3–5 pounds; good for stuffing).

Leg Roasts: After rib and loin, these are the most tender and expensive. Good for roasting or pot roasting: Standing rump (4–6 pounds), rolled rump (3–5 pounds), center leg (3–4 pounds), and shank half of leg (5–8 pounds).

Breast: A thin 3–5-pound bony cut that's best when stuffed. Also available boned and rolled (3–4 pounds).

How to Roast Veal

Because veal is so lean and delicate, it shouldn't be shoved in the oven and left to roast all by itself. It has no fat to baste it as it cooks, no marbling to make it juicy, thus will dry out if not barded, larded, and/or basted throughout cooking. Veal also suffers from searing and should only be roasted at a constant low temperature (325° F.). The best veal is that roasted with some liquid in the company of vegetables (see individual recipes that follow). Unlike beef or lamb, which are best served rare, veal does not reach its peak of flavor until it is well done (160° F. on a meat thermometer) and its juices run clear. Meat thermometers still mark 170° F. as the proper degree of doneness for veal, and some cookbooks even recommend cooking it to 175° F. or 180° F., but at that temperature it will be quite gray, dry, and tough. Try the lower temperature, then let the roast "rest" at room temperature 15–20 minutes before carving to allow its juices to settle. It will have the merest tinge of pink and be supremely tender and succulent.

Best Cuts: For simple oven roasting, leg, rib and bone-in or rolled loin or rump are the most suitable but they must be well barded—or at least draped with bacon or slices of salt pork—if they are to be juicy.

Amounts Needed: 4–5 pounds is a good all-round weight for bone-in roasts, 3–4 pounds for the boneless. To determine number of servings, allow ½–¾ pound bone-in roast per person, ⅓–½ pound boneless roast.

General Preparation for Cooking: If the veal is very young and lean, have butcher bard* the roast well. You can do it yourself or, if roast has some fat, merely lay strips of bacon (unsmoked is best) or salt pork over it. It's a good idea to blanch the bacon or salt pork quickly in boiling water so that its flavor

doesn't overpower the more delicate one of the veal. To simplify carving of rib or loin roasts, ask butcher to loosen backbone. Rub roast well with pepper and, if you like, salt. For extra savor, also rub with a cut clove of garlic and/or compatible herb or spice (see Sauces, Gravies, and Seasonings for Veal). Before roasting, let roast stand at room temperature 1½–2 hours if possible.

Continuous Low Heat Method: Preheat oven to 325° F. Place roast fattest side up on a rack in a shallow roasting pan and insert thermometer in center, not touching bone. Roast, uncovered, 30–35 minutes per pound for bone-in roasts, about 40 for rolled roasts or until thermometer reaches 160° F. For extra juiciness and flavor, baste every 15–20 minutes with melted butter or with a ½ and ½ mixture of melted butter and dry red or white wine. Remove roast from oven and let stand 15–20 minutes before serving (it will continue cooking slightly). Serve *au jus* or with Pan Gravy.

VARIATIONS:

Barbecue-Style Roast Veal: Do not bard. Marinate roast in All-Purpose Barbecue Sauce 24 hours in refrigerator. Lift from sauce and roast as directed, basting every 15 minutes with some of the sauce.

Roast Veal with Anchovies: Do not bard. Make tiny slits over roast and insert thin garlic slivers (2 cloves should be enough). Mix minced celery, minced peeled onions and minced carrots (2 of each) in a shallow open roasting pan and lay roast on vegetables. Drape fillets from 1 (2-ounce) can anchovies over veal and pour oil from can over all. Top with 4–5 slices bacon. Insert thermometer and roast as directed; discard bacon but reserve anchovies. Strain cooking liquid into a saucepan, pressing out as much as possible. Mash anchovies and add along with 1 tablespoon anchovy paste and 1 cup Veal (White) Stock, beef or chicken broth. Heat and serve as sauce.

Cream Roasted Veal: In a shallow open roasting pan, mix together 2 peeled and sliced onions, 2 peeled and sliced carrots, 1 cup minced parsley, and 2 minced cloves garlic. Place roast on vegetables, pour ½ cup heavy cream over meat, and roast as directed, basting every ½ hour with ¼ cup lukewarm heavy cream. When roast is done, strain pan juices and pass as gravy.

About Spit-Roasting Veal: Because of its leanness veal is a poor choice for spits and rotisseries; cooked thus, it will toughen and dry out.

Some Glazes for Roast Veal

Veal is a particularly versatile meat, so experiment with some of the glazes and flavor combinations that follow to see which appeal to your family most. About ½ hour before roast is done, spread or drizzle any of the following over it and continue cooking as directed, basting once or twice with pan drippings:
– 1 cup sherry, port, Madeira, dry red or white wine, or apple cider.
– 1 cup beer, ale, or stout.
– 1 cup *marinara* sauce or clam juice.
– 2 peeled and chopped medium-size yellow onions simmered ½ hour in 2 cups milk.
– ½ cup soy sauce mixed with ½ cup ketchup.
– ½ cup honey mixed with ½ cup chianti or dry vermouth.
– 1 cup grape, apple, red or black currant, or quince jelly, chopped.
– 1 (8-ounce) can whole or jellied cranberry sauce.

How to Carve Veal Roasts:
Rib: See How to Carve a Standing Rib Roast.

Leg or Rump: See How to Carve Leg of Lamb.

Loin: See How to Carve a Pork Loin Roast.

Some Garnishes for Roast Veal Platters
(in addition to parsley and watercress)

Because roast veal lacks the rich brown color of roast beef, it profits, particularly, from judicious garnishing. Choose two vegetables from the list below, striving for contrast of color, size, texture, and shape, then group or cluster around roast as artistically as possible. If you are feeling ambitious, try cutting one of the vegetables into fancy shapes. Add only enough garnish to showcase the roast, not so much that the roast is overwhelmed and carving becomes difficult.

Artichoke Bottoms: boiled and buttered; Artichoke Bottoms Stuffed with Vegetables; Artichoke Bottoms Princesse.

Artichoke Hearts: boiled and buttered.

Asparagus Tips: boiled and buttered.

Brussels Sprouts: boiled and buttered.

Carrots: Buttered Baby Carrots; Carrots Rosemary; Lemon-Glazed Carrots; Carrots Vichy.

Celery Hearts: boiled and buttered.

Crab Apples: whole canned or spiced.

Green Beans: Green Beans Amandine; Green Beans with Mushrooms.

Lima Beans: boiled and buttered; Baby Limas with Pecans.

Macédoine of Vegetables (hot).

Mushrooms: sautéed button mushrooms; mushroom caps or slices; Baked Mushroom Caps Stuffed with Hazelnuts.

Onions: Pan-Braised Onions; Stuffed Onions.

Orange Cups or Baskets: filled with hot or cold cranberry sauce or hot buttered peas.

Parsnips: Currant-Glazed Parsnips, Caramel-Glazed Parsnips, or Roasted Parsnips.

Pickles: Bread and Butter, Dill, Mustard; also pickled mushrooms or red cabbage.

Potatoes: Parsleyed, Herbed, Lemon-Glazed, or Danish-Style New Potatoes; also Franconia, Château, Parisienne, Dauphine, Shoestring, and cones of Duchess Potatoes.

Snow Peas: boiled and buttered; Snow Peas and Water Chestnuts.

Tomatoes: raw cherry tomatoes or tomato wedges; Stuffed Tomatoes; Broiled Tomatoes.

SOME SAUCES, GRAVIES, AND SEASONINGS FOR VEAL

FOR COOKING		FOR HOT ROASTS		FOR STEAKS AND CHOPS	
Seasonings, Herbs, Spices		*Sauces*	*Gravies*	*Sauces*	*Butters*
Allspice	Mace	Avgolemono	Au jus (un-	Aurore	Anchovy
Basil	Marjoram	Hot horseradish	thickened	Béarnaise	Bercy
Bay	Nutmeg	Light curry	pan gravy)	Bordelaise	Chive
Leaves	Oregano	Marinara	Mushroom	Chasseur	Herb
Cardamom	Paprika	Paloise	Pan gravy	Choron	Horseradish
Chili	Parsley	Parsley	Sour cream	Duxelles	Lemon
Powder	Rosemary	Portugaise		Madeira	Maître d'hôtel
Chives	Sage	Smitane		Mustard	Noisette
Cinnamon	Shallots	Soubise		Robert	Shallot
Cloves	Summer	Tarragon			Tomato
Curry	Savory	Tomato			Tuna
Powder	Tarragon	Velouté			Watercress
Dill	Thyme	Zingara			
Garlic	Truffles				
Lemon					

FOR HOT OR COLD VEAL	FOR COLD ROASTS
Condiments	*Sauces*
Applesauce	Aioli
Chutney	Anchovy
Cranberry sauce	mayonnaise
Horseradish	Chaud-froid
Mushrooms	Cumberland
(pickled)	Mayonnaise
Mustard	Sour cream-
Peaches (bran-	cucumber
died or pickled)	Sour cream-
Pickles (bread	horseradish
and butter,	Tuna
dill, mustard)	mayonnaise
Preserved kumquats	
Spiced fruits (crab	
apples, peaches,	
pears)	

ROAST VEAL STUFFED WITH WALNUTS AND MUSHROOMS

Makes 8 servings

1 (4-pound) veal leg, shoulder, or rump roast, boned but not rolled (save bones for Veal Stock)
1 teaspoon salt
⅛ teaspoon pepper
6 slices bacon

Stuffing:

⅔ cup finely chopped yellow onion
2 cloves garlic, peeled and crushed
2 tablespoons butter or margarine
2 cups finely chopped mushrooms
¾ cup toasted bread crumbs
1½ cups toasted walnuts, chopped fine
¼ teaspoon powdered rosemary
1 tablespoon minced parsley
1 teaspoon salt
¼ teaspoon pepper
2 eggs, lightly beaten

Preheat oven to 325° F. Lay veal cut side up and flatten slightly with a meat mallet; sprinkle with salt and pepper. Prepare stuffing: Sauté onion and garlic in butter over moderate heat 5–8 minutes until pale golden, add mushrooms, and sauté 3–4 minutes longer. Off heat, mix in remaining stuffing ingredients. Spread stuffing on veal almost to edges and roll; tie securely in several places and set on a rack in a shallow, open roasting pan. Cover with bacon, insert meat thermometer in center of meat, making sure it doesn't rest in stuffing. Roast, uncovered, 35–40 minutes per pound until thermometer reads 160° F. Lift meat from pan, discard bacon, and let roast "rest" 15–20 minutes. Remove string and slice about ½" thick. Serve with Pan or Au Jus Gravy. About 520 calories per serving (without gravy).

VARIATIONS:

Omit stuffing above and use 3 cups of any of the following stuffings: Oyster; Sage and Mushroom; Sage and Onion; Herbed Bread or prepared stuffing mix. Calories per serving: about 595 if made with Oyster Stuffing; about 560 if made with Sage and Mushroom Stuffing; 545 made with Sage and Onion Dressing; about 580 if made with Herbed Bread Stuffing or prepared stuffing mix.

Sauerkraut Stuffed Veal: Season veal as directed. Mix 1 (1-pound) drained can sauerkraut with 2 sautéed minced yellow onions, 1 sautéed minced sweet green pepper, 2 cups dry white bread crumbs, 1 teaspoon salt, ¼ teaspoon pepper, and 1 lightly beaten egg. Spread stuffing on veal and proceed as recipe directs. About 350 calories per serving.

⚖ **Neapolitan Roast Stuffed Veal:** Season veal with pepper only. Mix ¼ cup each anchovy paste and minced parsley with 3 crushed cloves garlic, 2 tablespoons each lemon juice and minced capers, 1 tablespoon grated lemon rind, 2 teaspoons prepared mild yellow mustard, and ¼ teaspoon pepper. Spread ½ mixture on veal, roll, and tie; spread remainder on top of veal, cover with bacon, and roast as directed. About 300 calories per serving.

Veal Roast Stuffed with Ham: Sprinkle veal with pepper only, spread with 1 cup deviled ham or 2 cups ground ham mixed with ⅓ cup heavy cream; lay 6–8 bacon slices lengthwise over filling, then roll, tie, and roast as directed, basting frequently during last ½ hour with chianti. About 415 calories per serving.

BRAISED VEAL ROAST WITH VEGETABLE GRAVY

Makes 8 servings

1 (4–5-pound) boned and rolled veal shoulder or rump (save bones for Veal Stock)
2 tablespoons cooking oil

*2 large yellow onions, peeled and
    coarsely chopped*
1–2 cloves garlic, peeled and crushed
1 carrot, peeled and chopped fine
1 stalk celery, chopped fine
1 bouquet garni,* tied in cheesecloth
2 teaspoons salt
¼ teaspoon pepper
⅓ cup cold water
¼ cup unsifted flour
*3 cups Veal Stock or a ½ and ½ mixture
    of beef and chicken broths*
*1–2 teaspoons liquid gravy browner
    (optional)*

Brown veal well in oil in a heavy kettle
over moderate heat; add all but last 3
ingredients, cover, and simmer 2½–3
hours until tender, turning meat once. If
pot cooks dry before veal is done, add
2–3 tablespoons cold water. Transfer
veal to platter and keep warm. Discard
bouquet garni; purée vegetables and any
remaining kettle liquid in an electric
blender at low speed. Blend flour with 1
cup stock. Add remaining stock and
purée to kettle and bring to a boil. Stir
in flour paste and cook, stirring, until
thickened. Cover and simmer 2–3
minutes; taste for seasoning and adjust.
For a darker gravy, add browner. Slice
roast about ¼" thick and serve with
plenty of gravy. About 350 calories per
serving.

VARIATIONS:

Oven Pot Roast:

Electric Skillet Pot Roast:

} Follow
variations
under Pot
Roast in
the Beef
section.

Pressure Cooker Pot Roast: Brown veal
and onion in oil in open pressure cooker;
add all but last 3 ingredients, seal
cooker, bring pressure to 10 pounds, and
cook 10 minutes per pound. Reduce
pressure, open cooker, remove veal and
keep warm. Prepare gravy in open
cooker using basic method above.

All cooking methods above: about 350
calories per serving.

Herbed Veal Pot Roast with Wine Gravy:
Add 1 teaspoon oregano, basil, marjoram,
or thyme along with other seasonings.
Simmer roast in ⅓ cup dry red or white
wine instead of water. For gravy, use
1½ cups of the same wine and 1½ cups
stock. About 390 calories per serving.

Veal Pot Roast in Tomato Sauce:
Simmer roast in 1 cup tomato sauce
instead of ⅓ cup water. When making
gravy, use 1½ cups each tomato juice
and stock. Just before serving, smooth in
¼ cup grated Parmesan cheese. About
385 calories per serving.

Veal Pot Roast with Vegetables: Prepare
roast as directed; about 45 minutes
before it is done, add ½ cup additional
stock and any or a combination of the
following: 16 small white onions and
new potatoes, both peeled; 1 small peeled
rutabaga cut in 1½" cubes; 8 peeled
parsnips, small whole turnips or leeks,
24 peeled whole baby carrots. Season
vegetables with 1 teaspoon salt, cover,
and simmer until meat and vegetables
are tender. Prepare gravy as directed.
Wreathe vegetables around meat and
serve. About 510 calories per serving.

Veal Pot Roast with Wine and Olives:
Follow basic recipe but simmer roast on
a trivet with ⅓ cup dry red wine instead
of water. When making gravy, strain
vegetables from cooking liquid; use 1 cup
each dry red wine and stock and omit
flour. Stir in ½ cup chopped pitted ripe
olives, heat about 5 minutes, and serve.
About 400 calories per serving.

Veal Pot Roast with Avgolemono Sauce:
Cook veal on a trivet by basic recipe
above, but omit onions, carrot, and
celery. For sauce, see Lamb Pot Roast
with Avgolemono Sauce. About 355
calories per serving.

VEAL SHOULDER BRAISED WITH ROSEMARY AND VERMOUTH

Once you've browned the meat and onions, you need only keep half an eye on the pot. This roast literally cooks itself.
Makes 6 servings

1 (3½-pound) boned and rolled veal
    shoulder roast
½ teaspoon salt
¼ teaspoon pepper
2 tablespoons flour
¼ cup cooking oil
4 medium-size yellow onions, peeled and
    cut in thin wedges
1 clove garlic, peeled and crushed
¼ teaspoon summer savory
1 (4″) sprig fresh rosemary or ¼
    teaspoon crushed dried rosemary
1 (4″) sprig fresh thyme or a pinch
    dried thyme
1 cup dry white vermouth
1½ cups water

Rub veal well with salt, pepper, and flour and brown well on all sides in oil in a large, heavy kettle over moderately high heat. Reduce heat to moderate, add onions and garlic, and stir-fry 8–10 minutes until golden. Add remaining ingredients, cover, and simmer slowly 2–2½ hours until tender, turning veal about every hour. To serve, carve into slices about ¼″ thick and top with the juices, which will have cooked down into a rich brown gravy. About 480 calories per serving.

BRAISED VEAL ROAST WITH BREAD AND GREEN PEPPER STUFFING

Makes 8 servings

1 (4-pound) veal leg, rump, or shoulder
    roast, boned but not rolled (save bones
    for Veal Stock)
2 tablespoons cooking oil
1 teaspoon salt
1½ cups Veal Stock or ¾ cup each beef
    broth and water

Stuffing:

1 medium-size yellow onion, peeled and
    minced
1 medium-size sweet green pepper,
    cored, seeded, and minced
3 pimientos, seeded and coarsely
    chopped
2 tablespoons butter or margarine
3 cups soft white bread crumbs
1 teaspoon minced fresh basil or ½
    teaspoon dried basil
1 teaspoon garlic salt
⅛ teaspoon pepper

Spread veal flat, cut side up, and let stand while you prepare stuffing. Sauté onion, green pepper, and pimientos in butter in a large, heavy skillet over moderate heat 5–8 minutes until onion is pale golden. Off heat mix in remaining stuffing ingredients; spread over veal almost to edges, roll, and tie securely in several places. Brown veal in oil in a heavy kettle over moderately high heat; sprinkle with salt. Place a rack under veal, add stock, and simmer slowly about 2 hours until tender, basting every 20–30 minutes with cooking liquid. Or cover and bake 2 hours at 325° F. Let veal "rest" 10 minutes, remove strings, and serve. Skim fat from cooking liquid and serve as gravy. When carving, make slices ¼″–½″ thick. About 400 calories per serving.

VARIATIONS:

Substitute 3 cups of any of the following stuffings for that above: Oyster; Sausage and Mushroom; Rice and Mushroom; Sage and Onion; Herbed Bread or prepared stuffing mix. Calories per serving: about 460 calories per serving if made with Oyster Stuffing; 480 if made with Sausage and Mushroom Stuffing; 455 with Rice and Mushroom Stuffing; 415 with Sage and Onion Dressing; 445 if made with Herbed Bread Stuffing or prepared stuffing mix.

Braised Veal Roast Verde: Omit above stuffing; instead, mix together 2 tablespoons soft butter, 1 cup each minced Italian parsley and raw spinach, and 1 crushed clove garlic. Spread on veal, roll, tie, and proceed as directed. Just before serving, mix ¼ cup each minced chives, dill pickles, and capers into cooking liquid. About 345 calories per serving.

⚔ BRAISED STUFFED BREAST OF VEAL WITH RED CURRANT GRAVY

Makes 6 servings

3–4 pounds breast of veal, boned but not rolled (use bones for Veal Stock)
1 small clove garlic, peeled and crushed
¼ teaspoon pepper
¼ cup bacon or beef drippings
1½ cups Veal Stock or ¾ cup each beef broth and water

Stuffing:

1½ cups soft white bread crumbs
1 medium-size yellow onion, peeled and minced
1 teaspoon summer savory
1 teaspoon sage
1 tablespoon minced parsley
1 teaspoon salt
¼ teaspoon pepper
1 teaspoon celery seeds
1 egg, lightly beaten

Gravy:

¼ cup unsifted flour blended with ½ cup cold Veal Stock
Veal cooking liquid
¼ cup red currant jelly

Rub veal inside and out with garlic and pepper. Mix stuffing and spread on cut side of veal almost to edges; roll and tie securely in several places. Brown veal all over in drippings in a heavy kettle over moderate heat. Place a rack under meat, add stock, cover, and simmer about 2 hours until tender. Lift meat to platter and let "rest" while you make the gravy. Blend flour paste into cooking liquid and heat, stirring, until thickened. Smooth in jelly, taste for salt and pepper and adjust. Remove strings from veal, slice ¼"–½" thick, and top with some of the gravy. Pass the rest. About 235 calories per serving.

VARIATION:

⚔ **Braised Stuffed Breast of Veal with Vegetable Gravy:** Stuff, roll, and tie veal as directed. Brown 2 minced, peeled carrots and 2 minced, peeled small yellow onions in drippings before browning veal; add veal and brown, then proceed as directed. When making gravy, purée vegetables and cooking liquid in an electric blender at low speed, return to kettle, thicken with flour paste as directed but omit jelly. About 210 calories per serving.

VEAL ORLOFF

If you want to show off, here's the recipe to do it with. It's a complicated four-part affair, but fortunately it *can* be made ahead. Perfect accompaniments: a fragrant green salad and chilled white Burgundy.

Makes 6 servings

2 carrots, peeled and coarsely grated
2 medium-size yellow onions, peeled and coarsely chopped
¼ cup butter or margarine
1 (3-pound) boned and rolled veal loin or rump roast (ask butcher to prepare roast carefully and tie tightly)
1½ teaspoons salt
⅛ teaspoon pepper
1 cup dry vermouth

Filling:

½ pound mushrooms, wiped clean and minced
2 tablespoons minced shallots
6 tablespoons butter or margarine
3 tablespoons rice, parboiled 5 minutes in 1 quart water and drained
2 medium-size yellow onions, peeled and sliced thin
1 cup sauce (given below)

Sauce:

4 tablespoons butter or margarine
6 tablespoons flour
½ teaspoon salt
Pinch white pepper
Pinch nutmeg
Strained veal cooking liquid plus enough heavy cream to total 2½ cups

Topping:

Remaining Sauce
3 (1-ounce) packages Gruyère cheese,
  grated fine
2 egg yolks
Paprika (garnish)

Stir-fry carrots and onions in butter in a heavy kettle over moderately high heat about 5 minutes until golden; add roast and brown lightly on all sides. Add salt, pepper, and vermouth, cover, and simmer slowly 1½–2 hours until tender.

While roast cooks, begin filling: Sauté mushrooms and shallots in 4 tablespoons butter over lowest heat about 30 minutes until all moisture has evaporated. At the same time, let drained rice and onions cook, covered, in 2 tablespoons butter in a very heavy skillet or flameproof casserole over lowest heat about ½ hour until very soft but not brown. Check skillet now and then and add 1–2 tablespoons water if they threaten to scorch. When veal is done, lift from kettle and let cool 15–20 minutes.

For the sauce: Melt butter in a saucepan, blend in flour and seasonings, add veal cooking liquid-cream mixture, and heat, stirring, until thickened and smooth.

To complete the filling: Mix 1 cup sauce into rice and onions, purée in an electric blender at low speed, then combine with mushrooms and shallots.

To prepare topping: Whisk 2 packages grated Gruyère into remaining sauce, heating and stirring until melted. Mix a little hot sauce into egg yolks, return to sauce, and remove from heat at once.

To assemble Orloff: Discard strings from roast and slice about ¼″ thick; spread slices with filling in order they were cut and overlap on a large (about 14″) flameproof platter. Pour topping over slices, sprinkle with remaining Gruyère, and add a blush of paprika. (*Note:* Recipe may be prepared up to this point several hours ahead, covered, and refrigerated until about ¾ hour before serving.)

For final cooking: Preheat oven to 375° F. Set platter, uncovered, on upper oven rack and bake 25–30 minutes until sauce is bubbly and touched with brown. Serve at once. About 945 calories per serving.

VITELLO TONNATO (COLD ROAST VEAL IN TUNA-MAYONNAISE SAUCE)

Perfect for a summer luncheon, especially with slices of full-flavored, vine-ripened tomatoes and a well-chilled dry Graves or Soave.
Makes 6–8 servings

1 (3-pound) boned and rolled veal rump
  roast
2 tablespoons olive oil
2 medium-size yellow onions, peeled and
  sliced thin
2 stalks celery, sliced thin
1 carrot, peeled and sliced thin
2 cloves garlic, peeled and quartered
3 large sprigs parsley
1 (4″) sprig fresh thyme or ½ teaspoon
  dried thyme
1 (2-ounce) can anchovy fillets, drained
1 (7-ounce) can white meat tuna,
  drained and flaked
¾ cup dry vermouth
1 teaspoon salt
¼ teaspoon pepper

Tuna-Mayonnaise Sauce:

2 cups puréed kettle mixture
Juice of 1 lemon
1 cup mayonnaise (about)
2 tablespoons drained capers
2 tablespoons minced parsley
Lemon wedges

Lightly brown roast in oil in a heavy kettle over moderately high heat; add remaining ingredients (except sauce), cover, and simmer slowly 2 hours, turning veal after 1 hour. Lift veal to a large bowl; purée kettle mixture in an electric blender at low speed or put through a food mill. Pour over veal, cover, and chill 24 hours, turning veal occasionally. Lift veal from purée and wipe off excess. Measure 2 cups purée and blend with lemon juice and enough mayonnaise to give it the consistency of thin cream sauce. (*Note:* Remaining purée can be used as the liquid ingredient in tuna or salmon loaves.) Slice veal about ¼" thick, arrange, overlapping, on a large platter, spooning a little sauce over each slice; re-cover and marinate several hours in refrigerator. Just before serving, ladle a little more sauce over all, sprinkle with capers and minced parsley. Set out lemon wedges and pass remaining sauce. About 840 calories for each of 6 servings, 630 calories for each of 8 servings.

For a Milder, Less Rich Sauce: Cook veal as directed; *strain* kettle liquid, then boil uncovered until reduced to about 1½ cups. Pour over veal, cover, and marinate as directed. Lift veal from marinade and slice; combine marinade with mayonnaise and lemon as above, spoon over veal, proceed and serve as directed. About 725 calories for each of 6 servings, 545 calories for each of 8 servings.

⚔ JELLIED VEAL LOAF

Makes 6 servings

1½ pounds veal shoulder or rump, cut in 2" cubes
1½ pounds veal bones
1 medium-size yellow onion, peeled
1 medium-size carrot, peeled
1 stalk celery
2 teaspoons salt
¼ teaspoon peppercorns and 2 sprigs parsley, tied in cheesecloth
2 quarts cold water

Place all ingredients in a large kettle, cover, and bring to a boil over high heat. Skim froth from surface, turn heat to low, and simmer 1½–2 hours until veal is tender. Cool 30 minutes, lift veal from broth with a slotted spoon, and cool until easy to handle. Slice each piece of meat ¼" thick against the grain and reserve. Meanwhile, simmer bones, broth, and vegetables, covered, 2 hours longer. Strain broth through a cheesecloth-lined sieve, discard bones and vegetables. If you like, clarify* broth; boil rapidly, uncovered, until reduced to about 1

quart; cool until syrupy. Fold meat into broth, ladle into an ungreased 9"×5"×3" loaf pan and chill until firm. Unmold on a bed of lettuce and decorate with radish roses and cherry tomatoes. When serving, slice fairly thick. About 200 calories per serving.

VARIATION:

⚔ **Decorative Jellied Veal Loaf:** Prepare as directed up to point of folding meat into syrupy broth. Pour a ¼" layer of syrupy broth in loaf pan and chill until tacky. Arrange a decorative layer of sliced hard-cooked egg, tomato "petals," and scallion stems on jellied broth and seal with a thin layer of broth; chill until tacky. Fold meat into remaining broth and spoon carefully into pan. Chill until firm. About 215 calories per serving.

Some Ways to Use Up Leftover Roast Veal

Veal Balls in Lemon Broth (4 servings): Mix together 1½ cups finely ground leftover veal, ½ cup fine soft white bread crumbs, 1 egg, 1 minced scallion, 2 tablespoons heavy cream, 1 teaspoon each anchovy paste and minced parsley, ¼ teaspoon salt, and a pinch pepper; shape into ½" balls. Bring 2 (13¾-ounce) cans chicken broth to a simmer, stir in the juice of ½ lemon, then add veal balls. Cover and simmer 25 minutes. Sprinkle with 1 tablespoon minced parsley and serve in soup bowls. About 310 calories per serving.

Veal-Tuna Salad (4 servings): Mix 1 cup finely diced veal with 1 (7-ounce) drained can tuna, 1 minced yellow onion, 1 tablespoon each capers, minced fresh parsley and dill, the juice of ½ lemon, and ⅓–½ cup mayonnaise (just enough for good consistency). Serve in lettuce cups or use as a sandwich spread. About 340 calories per serving.

Veal-Mushroom Ramekins (4 servings): Stir-fry ½ cup minced mushrooms and 2 tablespoons minced shallots in 1 tablespoon butter 5 minutes; mix with

1½ cups finely ground leftover veal, ½ cup heavy cream, ¼ teaspoon dill weed, and a pinch each pepper and nutmeg. Fold in 4 egg whites beaten with ¼ teaspoon salt until soft peaks form. Spoon into 4 buttered custard cups and top with 2 tablespoons cracker meal mixed with 1½ teaspoons each melted butter and grated Parmesan. Set in a shallow baking pan, pour 1½ cups hot water around cups, and bake uncovered ½ hour at 350° F. Brown quickly under broiler, if you like, and serve. About 410 calories per serving.

Quick Veal Paprika:

Veal, Mushroom, and Noodle Casserole:

Veal and Vegetable Pie:

Veal Stuffed Vegetables:

Roast Veal Hash:

Yukon Stew:

Veal Curry:

Follow recipes given in Some Additional Ways to Use Up Leftover Roast Beef, substituting veal for beef.

Sliced Cold Veal: Slice veal about ¼" thick and top with any recommended cold sauce (see Sauces, Gravies, and Seasonings for Veal).

Sliced Hot Veal: Slice veal about ¼" thick and layer into a shallow greased casserole. Add just enough hot sauce or gravy to cover (see Some Sauces, Gravies, and Seasonings for Veal), cover with foil, and heat 20 minutes at 350° F. Or heat veal slices in sauce about 5 minutes in a covered skillet over moderately low heat.

Hot Roast Veal Sandwiches: Heat veal slices in a suitable sauce or gravy in a skillet as for Sliced Hot Veal (above). Serve open face on toast, buns, or bread.

To Make the Most of Very Small Amounts: See suggestions given for beef.

Veal Steaks and Chops

If you think of these simply as slices of the veal roasts described earlier, you won't have much difficulty keeping them straight. An arm steak, for example, is a slice of arm roast, a rib chop a slice of the rib, a sirloin a slice of the sirloin, and so on. The smaller cuts, logically, are the chops, the larger ones steaks. (Refer to Veal Chart.) The most popular are:
Blade steak
Arm steak
Rib chops (plain and Frenched)
Loin chops (plain, kidney, noisettes, or medallions)
Sirloin steak
Round steak (sometimes called cutlet)
Cube steak
Frozen veal steaks (plain or breaded)

How to Cook

Amounts Needed: Rib and loin chops are best cut about 1" thick; other steaks and chops range from ½" to 1". Allow 1–2 rib or loin chops per person, 1 cube or frozen veal steak. Steaks will generally serve 2 and sometimes as many as 4, depending on how thick they're cut. Allow about ½–¾ pound bone-in chop or steak per person, ⅓–½ pound boneless.

General Preparation for Cooking: If meat seems moist, wipe with a damp cloth so it will brown well. Sprinkle with pepper but not salt (it prevents browning) and for extra savor, rub with a cut clove garlic and/or compatible herb such as sage, thyme, or marjoram (see Some Sauces, Gravies, and Seasonings for Veal). Let chops or steaks stand at room temperature 1½–2 hours before cooking if convenient.

Cooking Methods Not Recommended: Broiling, panbroiling, charcoal broiling. Veal chops and steaks are too lean to cook without some fat and/or liquid; moreover, they shrivel, toughen, and dry under intense broiler heat.

To Panfry (Sauté): Best for chops and steaks cut ½"–¾" thick, also for cube and frozen veal steaks. Heat 1–2 tablespoons butter, drippings, or cooking oil in a large, heavy skillet over moderately high heat about ½ minute, add chops or steaks and brown well on both sides, turning frequently. Cube and frozen steaks will need only 3–5 minutes altogether; ½"–¾" steaks and chops will take 20–30 minutes and, once browned, should finish cooking over fairly low heat. Do not cover and do not add liquid.

VARIATIONS:

Dredged Chops or Steaks: Dip meat in seasoned flour (about ⅓ cup unsifted flour, 1 teaspoon salt and ¼ teaspoon pepper), then cook as directed.

Herbed Chops or Steaks: Dip meat in ⅓ cup unsifted flour mixed with 1 teaspoon each salt and a compatible herb such as sage, marjoram, rosemary, or thyme and ¼ teaspoon pepper. Cook as directed.

Hungarian-Style Chops or Steaks: Dip meat in ⅓ cup unsifted flour mixed with 2 tablespoons paprika, 1 teaspoon salt, and a pinch pepper. Cook as directed.

Breaded Chops or Steaks: Sprinkle both sides of meat lightly with salt and pepper, dip in ⅓ cup unsifted flour, then in 1 egg lightly beaten with 1 tablespoon cold water, finally in 1 cup fine dry bread crumbs (for extra flavor, use seasoned crumbs). To make breading stick, let breaded chops dry on a cake rack 15 minutes before browning. Cook as directed, doubling amount of butter used. Drain well on paper toweling before serving.

To Braise: Here's the very best way to cook veal chops and steaks because it allows them to cook through and at the same time remain juicily tender. Brown chops or steaks 3–4 minutes on a side over moderately high heat in 1 tablespoon butter, drippings, or cooking oil; add about ½ cup water to skillet, cover and simmer slowly over low heat

or in a preheated 350° F. oven until cooked through. Chops will take 30–45 minutes, depending on thickness; steaks 50–60. (*Note:* Cube or frozen veal steaks will need only 10–15 minutes in all, noisettes about 20.)

For Extra Savor: Substitute any of the following for water called for above: medium dry white or red wine, rosé, sherry, Madeira, dry vermouth, or apple cider; tomatoes (or juice or sauce); orange, apple, or mixed fruit juices; milk, buttermilk, or light cream; barbecue or meatless spaghetti sauce; chicken or beef broth; ½ (10½-ounce) can condensed onion, cream of celery, mushroom, tomato, or asparagus soup.

Some Variations on Braised Veal Chops and Steaks
(All Quantities Based on Enough Chops or Steaks for 4 Persons)

Portuguese-Style: Brown meat as directed and pour off drippings; season *lightly,* add ¾ cup each tomato purée and liquid drained from canned ripe olives, 1 tablespoon olive oil, ½ cup sliced pitted ripe olives, 1 minced medium-size yellow onion, 1 crushed clove garlic, and ¼ teaspoon crushed juniper berries. Cover and simmer as above. About 360 calories per serving.

⚖ **Flambéed with Endives:** Brown meat as directed and pour off drippings; season, add ¼ cup cognac and flame, spooning liquid over chops. Add ⅓ cup beef broth, 4 small whole endives, and ⅛ teaspoon garlic powder. Cover and simmer as directed. Transfer meat and endives to a platter, add ¼ cup heavy cream to skillet, and simmer 1–2 minutes, stirring. Pour over meat and serve. About 285 calories per serving.

Budapest-Style: Brown meat as directed, season, and add ½ cup chicken broth. Top each chop with 1 sweet green pepper ring and 1 whole split, seeded pimiento (steaks should be completely covered with pepper and pimiento).

Cover and simmer as directed. Transfer to platter and keep warm. To skillet add 2 tablespoons grated onion, ½ cup heavy cream, and ¼ cup milk and simmer 2–3 minutes. Blend 1 tablespoon flour with ¼ cup milk, add to skillet, and cook, stirring, until slightly thickened. Season to taste, pour over chops, and serve. About 415 calories per serving.

Smothered Chops or Steaks: Brown 2 sliced medium-size yellow onions along with meat and pour off all but 1 tablespoon drippings; season and add 1 (10½-ounce) can condensed cream of mushroom, celery, or chicken soup thinned with ⅓ cup milk. Cover and simmer as directed. About 425 calories per serving.

En Casserole: Sauté together 2 slices minced bacon, 1 minced medium-size yellow onion, and 1 diced carrot over moderate heat 5 minutes until onion is pale golden; transfer all to an ungreased 1½-quart casserole. Brown meat as directed and add to casserole. Sprinkle all lightly with salt and pepper, add 1 *bouquet garni** and ½ cup dry white wine. Cover and oven-simmer as directed. Uncover during last 15 minutes so juices will cook down. If you like, add 6–8 peeled small white onions or new potatoes before baking. About 390 calories per serving.

In Orange Sauce: Brown 2 slices bacon in a skillet, remove, and crumble. To drippings add 1 tablespoon butter and brown chops as directed; season with salt and pepper. Add bacon, ¾ cup orange juice, and 1 tablespoon slivered orange rind. Cover and simmer as directed. Transfer meat to platter, add ¼ cup heavy or light cream to pan juices and heat 1–2 minutes, stirring (do not boil). Pour sauce over meat and serve. If you like, substitute ¼ cup grapefruit juice for ¼ cup of the orange juice. Proceed as directed and garnish platter with orange and grapefruit sections. About 415 calories per serving.

⚖ **Dijonnaise:** Brown meat as directed but do not pour off drippings. Season chops and top with ¼ cup minced shallots or scallions and 2 tablespoons minced parsley. Add ½ cup beef broth, cover, and simmer as directed. Transfer meat to a platter and keep warm. To skillet add ¼ cup beef broth and 1 tablespoon Dijon mustard. Heat and stir 1–2 minutes, pour over meat, and serve. About 290 calories per serving.

With Basil Butter: Cream ¼ cup butter until light and mix in 2 tablespoons minced fresh basil. Brown meat as directed, drain off drippings, then season meat and spread top side with basil butter. Add ⅓ cup chicken broth, cover, and simmer as directed. Transfer meat to platter; quickly boil skillet liquid to reduce to ¼ cup. Spoon over meat, sprinkle with chopped pistachio nuts, and serve. About 330 calories per serving.

Calcutta-Style: Brown meat as directed, lift out and set aside. In drippings sauté 1 minced medium-size yellow onion 5–8 minutes until pale golden; add 1 tablespoon curry powder and cook and stir 1–2 minutes. Add ½ cup dry white wine or chicken broth, return meat to pan, season lightly with salt and pepper, cover, and simmer as directed. About 10 minutes before meat is done, add 1 peeled, thinly sliced ripe small mango (or, if out of season, 2 peeled, thinly sliced peaches and ¼ cup raisins). Cover and simmer until meat is tender. About 320 calories per serving.

Lyonnaise: Brown meat as directed, lift out, and set aside. In drippings sauté 3 thinly sliced large yellow onions 8–10 minutes until golden. Return meat to pan, season, and pile some onions on top. Add ⅓ cup chicken broth and 1 tablespoon vinegar. Cover and simmer as directed. Sprinkle with minced parsley and serve. About 315 calories per serving.

À la Crème: Brown meat as directed, season, then drain off drippings. Add ½ cup dry white wine, Madeira, or dry sherry, cover, and simmer as directed. Transfer meat to a platter and keep warm. Quickly boil down skillet liquid to ¼ cup, mix in 1 cup light cream and ½ cup Velouté or Medium White Sauce, a dash of nutmeg, and 1 teaspoon lemon juice; simmer (but do not boil) 2–3 minutes. Spoon some sauce over meat and pass the rest. If you like, scatter minced truffles, toasted slivered almonds, or minced scallions or chives over meat and add a blush of paprika. About 485 calories per serving.

Chasseur (Hunter's Style): Brown meat as directed, lift out, and set aside. In pan drippings sauté 6 minced shallots or scallions and ½ pound sliced mushrooms 4–5 minutes until golden. Return meat to pan, season, add ½ cup dry white wine, cover, and simmer as directed. Transfer meat to platter and keep warm. To pan liquid, add 1 cup beef gravy, 1 tablespoon tomato paste, and 2 teaspoons each minced chervil and tarragon. Quickly bring to a boil, spoon some sauce over meat, and pass the rest. About 340 calories per serving.

À la Bourguignonne: Brown meat as directed, lift out, and set aside. Drain off drippings; add 2 slices bacon to skillet, brown, remove, and crumble. In drippings sauté ½ pound thinly sliced mushrooms 4–5 minutes until golden; return meat and bacon to pan, season lightly, add ⅔ cup red Burgundy wine and 1 pound Pan-Braised Onions. Cover and simmer as directed. Transfer meat and vegetables to a deep dish. Thicken pan liquid with 1 tablespoon *beurre manié.** Spoon some gravy over meat and pass the rest. About 445 calories per serving.

With Sour Cream-Cheddar Sauce: Cook meat as directed and transfer to a deep platter. Smooth 1 cup sour cream and ⅓ cup grated sharp Cheddar cheese into pan and simmer over low heat until cheese melts; stir constantly. Season to taste with onion and garlic salt, pour over meat, and serve. About 435 calories per serving.

Noisettes of Veal in Champagne-Cream Sauce: Brown meat as directed and season; pour off drippings, add ½ cup champagne, cover, and simmer about 20 minutes until meat is tender. Add ¼ cup heavy cream, 2 tablespoons diced pimiento, and, if you like, 2 thinly sliced truffles. Warm 1–2 minutes longer and serve. About 360 calories per serving.

Some Classic Garnishes for Veal Chops and Steaks

À la Française: Lift chops or steaks to a hot platter and wreathe with Peas à la Française.

À la Piémontaise: Bread and sauté chops as directed and serve on a bed of Risotto alla Milanese. Pass Tomato Sauce.

À la Provençale: Transfer chops or steaks to platter and keep warm. To skillet add ¼ cup dry white wine, 1 cup tomato sauce, and ¼ crushed clove garlic; heat, stirring, 2–3 minutes to get up browned bits. Pour over chops and garnish with cherry tomatoes that have been stuffed with a ½ and ½ mixture of sautéed minced mushrooms and scallions, topped with grated Parmesan and lightly browned under broiler. Sprinkle all with minced parsley and serve.

À la Jardinière: ⎫
Au Vert-Pré: ⎬ see Some Classic Garnishes for Steak.

Rossini: ⎱ see Some Classic Ways to Serve Tournedos.

À la Bretonne: ⎫
Parmentier: ⎬ see Some Classic Garnishes for Lamb Chops.

SAGE-SCENTED VEAL CHOPS STUFFED WITH PROSCIUTTO HAM

Makes 4 servings

4 veal rib chops, cut 1½" thick
4 paper-thin slices prosciutto ham
4 thin slices Gruyère cheese about 1½"
    wide and 2" long
1 clove garlic, peeled and halved
2 tablespoons butter or margarine
2 bay leaves
4 (4") sprigs fresh sage or 1 teaspoon
    dried leaf sage tied in cheesecloth
½ cup dry white wine
¼ teaspoon salt
Pinch pepper

Cutting from the curved outer edge, make a deep pocket in each veal chop. Flatten out each slice of *prosciutto,* top with a slice of Gruyère and wrap envelope style. Insert a prosciutto-Gruyère package in each veal pocket and close with toothpicks. Rub both sides of chops with garlic, then brown in butter in a large, heavy skillet over moderately high heat 2–3 minutes on each side. Add bay leaves, top each chop with a sage sprig (or drop cheesecloth bag of dried sage into skillet), pour in wine, cover, and simmer slowly 45–50 minutes until chops are just cooked through. Remove sage, bay leaves, and toothpicks, sprinkle chops with salt and pepper, and serve with some of the pan drippings spooned over each portion. About 470 calories per serving.

HOTEL OASIS VEAL CHOPS

These Roquefort-flavored chops were a specialty of the Hotel Oasis near Palma, Majorca.
Makes 4 servings

4 loin veal chops, cut ¾" thick
½ cup homemade French Dressing
1 tablespoon finely grated lemon rind
1 tablespoon crumbled Roquefort
    cheese
¼ cup unsifted flour
1 egg, lightly beaten with 2 tablespoons
    milk

¾ cup fine toasted bread crumbs
3 tablespoons olive or other cooking oil

If chops have long, thin "tails," curl around thick portions and secure with toothpicks. Mix French dressing, lemon rind, and Roquefort, mashing cheese well; pour into a shallow enamel pan or glass baking dish, add chops and arrange in a single layer. Cover and chill 6–8 hours, turning chops in marinade 1 or 2 times. Dip chops in flour, then in egg, then in crumbs to coat evenly. Sauté in oil in a large heavy skillet 15–20 minutes on each side over moderately low heat. Drain on paper toweling and serve. About 405 calories per serving.

Veal Cutlets (Scallops)
(Refer to Veal Chart)

What the Italians call *scaloppine,* the Germans *Schnitzel,* the French *escalopes de veau,* and the English *collops* are veal cutlets or scallops to us —small, thin, boneless slices, usually from the veal leg but sometimes from the loin or rib. The choicest are those from the top round. All cutlets should be cut across the grain and slightly on the diagonal, always very thin—¼"–⅜" —and trimmed of any filament and fat.

Usually they are pounded to between ⅛" and ¼" thick (recipes here specify whether to pound or not). Most butchers will do the pounding, but, if not, you can easily do it yourself. Simply slip cutlet between two sheets of wax paper and flatten with a cutlet bat, rolling pin, or the side of a meat cleaver. Three or four resounding whacks per side per cutlet should do the job.

Though there are dozens of ways to prepare cutlets, almost all are variations on two basic cooking methods: *panfrying* (or *sautéing*) and *braising* (browning in fat, then finishing in a small amount of liquid or sauce). If you've never cooked cutlets before, don't attempt more than four or six at a time. Use as quick and light a hand as possible and rush the cutlets to the table the instant they're done.

ESCALOPES DE VEAU À LA CRÈME (SAUTÉED VEAL CUTLETS IN HEAVY CREAM SAUCE)

You'll note that this recipe calls for boiling the heavy cream to thicken and enrich the cutlet sauce. When, exactly, *can* cream be boiled without curdling and when can't it be? If the sauce is bland, light or heavy cream can be safely boiled. But if the sauce is acid (containing tomatoes, for example, or vinegar), the cream should not be boiled. Sour cream, being naturally acid, should never be boiled.

Makes 4 servings

1½ pounds veal round, sliced ¼" thick
*   and pounded thin as for scaloppine*
2 tablespoons butter or margarine
1 tablespoon cooking oil
2 tablespoons minced scallions or shallots
⅓ cup dry vermouth
½ cup beef broth
1 cup heavy cream
½ teaspoon salt
⅛ teaspoon pepper

Wipe cutlets dry with paper toweling so they will brown. Heat butter and oil in a large, heavy skillet over moderately high heat until a cube of bread will sizzle. Brown cutlets, a few at a time, 3–4 minutes on each side, using tongs to turn. Drain on paper toweling and keep warm at back of stove. Pour all but 2 tablespoons drippings from skillet, reduce heat to moderate, add scallions, and stir-fry 2–3 minutes. Add vermouth and broth and boil rapidly, stirring to get up browned bits, until reduced to about ¼ cup. Add cream and boil, stirring, until reduced by ½. Sprinkle cutlets with salt and pepper, return to skillet and warm 1–2 minutes, basting with sauce. Taste sauce, adjust salt and pepper if needed, and serve. About 575 calories per serving.

VARIATION:

Sautéed Veal Cutlets and Mushrooms in Cream Sauce: Brown cutlets and prepare sauce as directed. At the same time, stir-fry ½ pound thinly sliced mushrooms in 2 tablespoons butter and 1 tablespoon oil in a separate skillet 3–5 minutes until lightly browned. Add to cream sauce and cook and stir 1–2 minutes. Add cutlets, warm, and serve as directed. About 670 calories per serving.

ESCALOPES DE VEAU À LA ZINGARA (SAUTÉED VEAL CUTLETS WITH TONGUE, HAM, AND MUSHROOMS)

Makes 4 servings

1½ pounds veal round, sliced ¼" thick
*   and pounded thin as for scaloppine*
1 teaspoon salt
¼ teaspoon pepper
½ cup unsifted flour
5 tablespoons butter or margarine
½ cup Madeira wine
¾ cup Rich Brown Sauce (Demi-Glace)
1 tablespoon tomato paste
⅓ cup julienne strips of cooked smoked
*   tongue*
⅓ cup julienne strips of cooked ham
⅓ cup julienne strips of mushrooms
1 truffle, cut in fine julienne

Sprinkle both sides of cutlets with salt and pepper, then dredge in flour. Heat 3 tablespoons butter in a large, heavy skillet over moderately high heat until a bread cube will sizzle, and brown cutlets, a few at a time, 3–4 minutes on a side, using tongs to turn. Drain on paper toweling and keep warm at back of stove. Add Madeira to skillet and simmer, stirring to get up browned bits, until reduced by half. Blend in Rich Brown Sauce and tomato paste and simmer, stirring occasionally, until thickened and the consistency of gravy. Meanwhile, in a separate skillet, sauté tongue, ham, mushrooms, and truffle in remaining butter 2–3 minutes. Add to sauce and warm 1–2 minutes. To serve, place cutlets on a hot platter and top each with a heaping spoonful of the skillet mixture. About 590 calories per serving.

☒ PICCATE (ITALIAN-STYLE SAUTÉED VEAL SCALLOPS)

Makes 2 servings

¾ pound veal round, sliced ¼" thick and pounded thin as for scaloppine
¾ teaspoon salt
⅛ teaspoon pepper
⅓ cup unsifted flour
1 tablespoon olive oil
1 tablespoon butter
2 tablespoons lemon juice
2 teaspoons minced parsley

Sprinkle both sides of veal with salt and pepper, and cut in pieces about 3" square. Dredge veal squares in flour, shaking off excess so they're lightly dusted. Heat oil and butter in a heavy skillet over moderately high heat about 1 minute, add veal, and brown 1–2 minutes on a side; drain on paper toweling. Add lemon juice and parsley to skillet and stir quickly to get up browned bits. Return veal, warm 1–2 minutes, basting with lemon-parsley mixture, and serve. About 335 calories per serving.

WIENER SCHNITZEL (BREADED VEAL CUTLETS)

The Viennese say a *Wiener Schnitzel* is perfect if the crust is crisp, amber brown, and puffed here and there so that you can slip a knife between it and the cutlet. Here's the trick: Bread each cutlet *just* before cooking, drop into hot (but not smoking) fat, and brown, turning one time only. *Do not* dry the breaded cutlets 15–20 minutes on a rack before cooking (the breading will stick fast and refuse to puff). Cook only as many cutlets at a time as you need and serve at once.

Makes 4 servings

1½ pounds veal round, sliced ¼" thick and pounded thin as for scaloppine
2 teaspoons salt (about)
¼ teaspoon pepper (about)
⅓ cup clarified butter*

⅓ cup lard
½ cup unsifted flour
2 eggs, beaten until frothy
1 cup fine dry bread crumbs
Lemon wedges (garnish)

Sprinkle both sides of cutlets with salt and pepper. If they seem too large to handle easily or to fit in your skillet, halve them (the Viennese like whopping Schnitzels that hang over the edges of their plates, but if you're an inexperienced Schnitzel cook, it's better to work with smaller pieces). Begin heating butter and lard in a very large, heavy skillet over moderately high heat. Dip cutlets in flour, then eggs and crumbs, each time shaking off excess (they should have a thin, even, all-over crumb coating). To test fat temperature, drop in a cube of bread; when fat bubbles vigorously about it, carefully add cutlets, allowing plenty of space between them. Brown on 1 side, 3–4 minutes, turn with tongs, and brown other side. Drain well on paper toweling and serve at once with lemon wedges. Bread and brown seconds as people ask for them. About 425 calories per serving.

VARIATIONS:

Schnitzel à la Holstein: Prepare Wiener Schnitzel as directed. Top each cutlet with a fried egg, drape 2 anchovy fillets over egg in an X-pattern, and sprinkle, if you like, with drained capers. About 520 calories per serving.

Parsleyed Schnitzel: Season cutlets, dredge in flour, dip in egg, then in crumbs mixed with 1 tablespoon minced parsley. Brown as directed and serve with lemon. About 425 calories per serving.

Cheese Schnitzel: Season cutlets, dredge in flour, dip in egg, then in crumbs mixed with 1 tablespoon finely grated Parmesan cheese. Brown as directed and serve with lemon. About 430 calories per serving.

Sardellenschnitzel (Anchovy Schnitzel): Season cutlets with pepper but not salt, then spread each thinly with Anchovy Butter, leaving ¼″ margins all round. Fold cutlets over, secure with toothpicks, bread and brown as for Wiener Schnitzel. Remove toothpicks and serve with lemon. About 475 calories per serving.

Schnitzel Cordon Bleu: Season cutlets with pepper and a very little salt. Cut small pieces of thinly sliced Swiss cheese and Westphalian or *prosciutto* ham so they're about ½ the size of cutlets. Lay 1 slice ham on ½ of each cutlet, top with cheese, then fold cutlet over and pound 1 or 2 times between waxed paper to seal. Bread and brown as for Wiener Schnitzel and serve with lemon. About 475 calories per serving.

Parisian Schnitzel: Season cutlets, dredge in flour, dip in egg but not in crumbs. Brown as for Wiener Schnitzel and serve with lemon. About 375 calories per serving.

Naturschnitzel (Plain Schnitzel): Season cutlets, dredge in flour, but do not dip in egg or crumbs. Brown as directed in 3–4 tablespoons clarified butter* and serve with lemon. About 355 calories per serving.

Rahmschnitzel (Cream Schnitzel): Season cutlets, cut in strips 2″–3″ × 1½″ and dredge in flour only. Brown in 3–4 tablespoons clarified butter,* remove from skillet, and drain on paper toweling. Pour off drippings; add 1 cup beef consommé to skillet and boil rapidly, stirring to scrape up browned bits, until reduced by half. Add 1 cup light cream and boil uncovered, stirring, until reduced by half. Turn heat to low, return veal to skillet, warm 2–3 minutes, stirring, and serve. About 490 calories per serving.

Paprika Schnitzel: Season cutlets and sprinkle both sides well with paprika. Cut into strips and proceed as for *Rahmschnitzel.* Just before returning veal to skillet, swirl in 2 tablespoons sour cream. Add veal, warm 2–3 minutes (but do not boil), stirring occasionally. About 380 calories per serving.

⊠ VEAL SCALOPPINE ALLA MARSALA

Makes 4–6 servings

2 pounds veal round, sliced ¼″ thick and
*   pounded thin as for scaloppine*
½ teaspoon salt
⅛ teaspoon pepper
3 tablespoons butter or margarine
3 tablespoons beef consommé
⅓ cup Marsala wine

Sprinkle veal with salt and pepper and let stand at room temperature 10–15 minutes. Brown a few pieces at a time, 2–3 minutes on a side, in butter in a large, heavy skillet over moderately high heat; remove to a heated platter and keep warm. Add consommé and wine to skillet and boil, uncovered, 1–2 minutes, stirring to get up browned bits. Pour over *scaloppine* and serve. About 460 calories for each of 4 servings, 310 calories for each of 6 servings.

VARIATIONS:

⊠ **Veal Scaloppine with Parsley:** After sprinkling scaloppine with seasonings, dredge lightly in flour. Brown as directed, remove to a heated platter and keep warm. Stir 1 tablespoon each lemon juice and minced parsley into skillet along with consommé and wine and boil, uncovered, as above. Pour over veal and serve. About 470 calories for each of 4 servings, 320 calories for each of 6 servings.

⊠ **Veal Scaloppine with Parsley and Prosciutto:** Dredge and brown scaloppine as for variation above and set aside. In drippings, stir-fry ¼ cup finely slivered *prosciutto* ham; spoon over scaloppine. Add parsley, lemon juice, consommé, and wine to skillet, boil uncovered as above, pour over scaloppine and serve. About 470 calories for each of 4 servings, 320 calories for each of 6 servings.

☒ **Veal Scaloppine with Mushrooms:** Lightly brown ½ pound thinly sliced mushrooms in 2 tablespoons butter; remove from heat and set aside. Prepare Scaloppine alla Marsala as directed. Just before serving, add mushrooms to wine in skillet, warm 1–2 minutes, pour over scaloppine, and serve. About 525 calories for each of 4 servings, 355 calories for each of 6 servings.

VEAL PARMIGIANA

Makes 4 servings

½ cup toasted fine bread crumbs
¼ cup finely grated Parmesan cheese
1¼ teaspoons salt
⅛ teaspoon pepper
1 pound veal round, sliced ¼" thick and pounded thin as for scaloppine
1 egg, lightly beaten
⅓ cup olive oil
2 cups Italian Tomato Sauce or 1 (15½-ounce) jar meatless spaghetti or pizza sauce
½ pound mozzarella cheese, coarsely grated

Preheat oven to 375° F. Mix crumbs, Parmesan, salt, and pepper. Dip veal in egg, then in crumbs to coat evenly (pat crumbs onto veal so they stick firmly). Arrange veal on a wire rack and let dry 10–12 minutes so coating will adhere during cooking. Heat oil in a large, heavy skillet over moderately high heat about 1 minute, add half of veal, and brown 1–1½ minutes on a side; drain on paper toweling. Brown remaining veal the same way. Arrange veal in a single layer in an ungreased shallow 2-quart casserole or au gratin pan, top with sauce and mozzarella. Bake, uncovered, ½ hour until cheese melts and sauce is bubbly.

Serve with a crisp romaine salad, chunks of hot garlic bread, and chianti. About 475 calories per serving.

SALTIMBOCCA

Prosciutto is very salty, making additional salt in the recipe unnecessary. Makes 4–6 servings

2 pounds veal round, sliced ¼" thick and pounded thin as for scaloppine
¼ pound prosciutto ham, sliced paper thin
2 tablespoons minced fresh sage or 1 teaspoon dried sage
⅛ teaspoon pepper
3–4 tablespoons butter or margarine
¼ cup dry white wine

Veal slices should be about 4"×4"; if extra long, halve crosswise. Trim prosciutto slices so they're roughly the same size. Sprinkle 1 side of each veal slice with sage and pepper; top with prosciutto slice and toothpick in place. Melt butter in a large skillet over moderately high heat and brown veal quickly on both sides. Transfer to a heated platter, remove toothpicks, and keep warm. Add wine to skillet, let boil, uncovered, 1–2 minutes, scraping with a wooden spoon to get up any brown bits; pour over veal and serve. About 515 calories for each of 4 servings, 345 calories for each of 6 servings.

BOCCONCINI (ITALIAN BRAISED VEAL AND CHEESE)

Makes 4 servings

1½ pounds veal round, sliced ¼" thick and pounded thin as for scaloppine
½ pound Swiss cheese
½ teaspoon minced fresh sage or ¼ teaspoon dried sage
⅛ teaspoon pepper
2 tablespoons butter or margarine
¼ cup dry white wine
1 tablespoon lemon juice
½ teaspoon salt

Halve veal slices lengthwise; cut thin strips of cheese about ½" smaller all round than veal, lay one strip on each veal slice, roll jelly-roll style, and secure with toothpicks. Place rolls in a piepan, sprinkle with sage and pepper, cover, and chill several hours. Melt butter in a large, heavy skillet over moderate heat, add veal rolls, and brown well on all sides, about 5–10 minutes. Add remaining ingredients, cover and simmer 18–20 minutes until veal is tender. Serve with a generous ladling of pan juices. About 530 calories per serving.

VEAL AND PEPPERS

Makes 4–6 servings

2 pounds veal round, sliced ¼" thick and pounded thin as for scaloppine
¼ cup olive oil
2 tablespoons minced shallots
1 medium-size yellow onion, peeled and minced
1 clove garlic, peeled and crushed
¾ cup dry white wine
1½ teaspoons minced fresh sage or ¼ teaspoon dried sage
½ teaspoon minced fresh marjoram or ¼ teaspoon dried marjoram
2 medium-size sweet green peppers, cored, seeded, and cut lengthwise in strips 1" wide
Juice of ½ lemon
1 teaspoon salt
⅛ teaspoon pepper

Cut veal crosswise into strips 1½" wide. Heat oil in a large, heavy skillet over moderately high heat 1 minute, add veal, and brown as quickly as possible. Remove from skillet and set aside. Reduce heat to moderate, mix in shallots, onion, and garlic, and stir-fry about 8 minutes or until golden. Return veal to skillet, stir in remaining ingredients, cover, and simmer 12–15 minutes until tender. Serve with boiled rice. About 565 calories for each of 4 servings (without rice), 380 calories for each of 6 servings.

VEAL BIRDS

Makes 4 servings

1½ pounds veal round, sliced ¼" thick and pounded thin as for scaloppine
1 teaspoon salt
⅛ teaspoon pepper
2 tablespoons butter or margarine
½ cup chicken broth or dry red or white wine
½ cup beef broth
1 tablespoon flour blended with 1 tablespoon cold water

Stuffing:

2 slices bacon
1 medium-size yellow onion, peeled and minced
1 clove garlic, peeled and crushed (optional)
¼ pound mushrooms, wiped clean and chopped fine
1 cup soft white bread crumbs
1 tablespoon minced parsley
¼ teaspoon basil

Prepare stuffing first: Brown bacon in a small skillet over moderate heat, remove, crumble, and reserve. Sauté onion and, if you like, garlic in drippings 5–8 minutes until pale golden, add mushrooms and sauté 2–3 minutes longer. Off heat mix in bacon and remaining stuffing ingredients. Cut veal into slices that measure about 3"×5".

Sprinkle one side of veal slices with salt and pepper, place a small dab of stuffing in center of each, roll, and secure with toothpicks. Brown rolls, ½ at a time, in butter in a large skillet or flameproof casserole over moderately high heat 5–10 minutes. Add chicken broth, cover, and simmer over low heat or in a preheated 350° F. oven 20–25 minutes until veal is tender. Transfer rolls to a deep dish and keep warm. Add beef broth and flour paste to skillet liquid and heat, stirring, until thickened. Pour over rolls and serve. About 430 calories per serving.

VARIATIONS:

Veal Birds in Wine-Cream Sauce: Stuff, roll, and brown veal birds as directed. Add ½ cup dry sherry, Madeira, or apple cider, cover, and simmer until tender. Remove rolls to a deep platter and keep warm. Quickly boil down pan liquid to ¼ cup, smooth in ½ cup heavy cream, and heat 1–2 minutes. Pour over veal and serve. About 555 calories per serving.

Veal Birds "in the Soup": Stuff, roll, and brown veal birds as directed. Add 1 (10½-ounce) can condensed cheese, cream of mushroom, chicken, celery, or tomato soup thinned with ⅓ cup milk, cover, simmer until tender, and serve. About 530 calories per serving.

Ham- and Dill-Stuffed Veal Birds: Reduce bread crumbs in stuffing mixture to ½ cup and add ½ cup minced ham and ¼ teaspoon thyme. *Spread* each veal slice with a little stuffing, add 1 long, slim dill pickle wedge, then roll and cook as directed. About 450 calories per serving.

Veal Birds Stuffed with Anchovies and Olives: Omit mushrooms from stuffing mixture and add 6–8 minced anchovy fillets and ¼ cup minced pimiento-stuffed olives. Do not salt or pepper veal slices; spread each with 1 tablespoon anchovy paste, add a dab of stuffing, then roll and cook as directed. Garnish with lemon slices and capers. About 450 calories per serving.

Russian Veal Birds (Bytky): Sauté ¼ pound ground lean pork along with onion; omit garlic and mushrooms from stuffing. Stuff, roll, and brown birds as directed; remove from skillet. Sauté ½ pound thinly sliced mushrooms in drippings 3–5 minutes, return birds to skillet, add chicken broth, and simmer as directed. Remove birds to a deep platter

and keep warm. Smooth 1 cup sour cream and 1 tablespoon Worcestershire sauce into skillet, warm (but do not boil) 1–2 minutes, pour over birds, and serve. About 630 calories per serving.

Prosciutto-Stuffed Veal Birds with Avocado: Omit stuffing and do not salt or pepper veal slices; spread each with 1 teaspoon prepared spicy brown mustard, cover with trimmed-to-size slices *prosciutto*, then roll and cook as directed. Transfer rolls to a deep dish and keep warm. Blend ½ cup heavy cream into pan liquid and add 1 thinly sliced, peeled, and pitted *firm* avocado. Warm gently 1–2 minutes, pour around veal, garnish with sieved hard-cooked egg yolk and serve. About 580 calories per serving.

VEAL BIRDS WITH CHICKEN LIVER STUFFING
Makes 4 servings

1½ pounds veal round, sliced ¼" thick and pounded thin as for scaloppine
2 tablespoons butter or margarine
1 (13¾-ounce) can chicken broth
1 tablespoon flour blended with 1 tablespoon cold water
1 cup sour cream (at room temperature)
¼ cup toasted slivered almonds

Stuffing:

½ pound chicken livers
¼ cup unsifted flour
1 medium-size yellow onion, peeled and minced
1 clove garlic, peeled and crushed
2 tablespoons butter or margarine
¾ cup soft white bread crumbs
¼ teaspoon sage
¼ teaspoon thyme
1 teaspoon salt
⅛ teaspoon pepper
1 tablespoon minced parsley
1 egg, lightly beaten

Prepare stuffing first: Dredge livers in flour and sauté with onion and garlic in butter over moderately high heat 5 minutes; turn heat to low and cook 1–2 minutes longer. Cool slightly, chop livers medium fine, and return to skillet; mix in remaining stuffing ingredients. Place a small amount of stuffing in center of each veal slice, roll, and secure with toothpicks. Brown rolls, half at a time, in butter in a large skillet over moderately high heat, add broth, cover, and simmer 20–25 minutes until tender. Lift rolls to a shallow casserole and keep warm. Blend flour paste into skillet liquid and heat, stirring, until thickened. Smooth in sour cream, warm 1–2 minutes, and pour over veal. Sprinkle with almonds and serve. About 720 calories per serving.

VEAL CUTLETS OSCAR

Makes 4 servings

4 veal cutlets, cut ½″ thick
4 tablespoons butter or margarine
1 teaspoon salt
⅛ teaspoon pepper
⅓ cup dry white wine
½ pound fresh lump or backfin crab meat, carefully picked over
½ recipe Buttered Asparagus Tips
1 recipe Béarnaise Sauce

Brown cutlets, half at a time, in 2 tablespoons butter in a large, heavy skillet over moderately high heat 5–10 minutes. Sprinkle with salt and pepper, add wine, cover, and simmer about 20 minutes until tender. In a separate small skillet, sauté crab in remaining butter 3–4 minutes (do not brown). Arrange veal on platter and spoon crab over each cutlet. Pour veal cooking liquid into crab skillet and boil rapidly, uncovered, to reduce to ¼ cup; pour over crab. Top each portion with a few asparagus tips and arrange rest around platter. Drizzle with Béarnaise and pass the rest. Good with Château Potatoes.

VARIATION:

Veal Cutlets with Lobster: Prepare as directed, substituting lobster for crab.

Both versions: About 480 calories per serving.

⚖ TERRINE OF VEAL AND HAM

Makes 4–6 servings

1 pound veal round, sliced ¼″ thick and pounded thin as for scaloppine
1 teaspoon salt
¼ teaspoon pepper
4 scallions, minced
6 ounces lean boiled ham, sliced ⅛″ thick
1¾ cups fat-free chicken broth (about)
1 envelope unflavored gelatin
¼ cup cold water

Preheat oven to 325° F. Cover bottom of a 9″ piepan with one layer of veal slices fitted as close together as possible and trimmed as needed so they don't overlap; sprinkle lightly with salt, pepper, and scallions and top with one layer of ham. Continue building up layers until all meat is used up. Pour in ⅔ cup chicken broth, cover with foil, and bake about 1 hour until veal is tender.

Remove from oven and weight meat down with a very heavy plate so that layers will stick together, forming a single circle; cool to room temperature. Carefully drain broth from pan and strain through cheesecloth; add enough additional broth to measure 1¾ cups.

Mix gelatin and water in a small saucepan and heat and stir over low heat until gelatin dissolves; stir into broth. Pour a ¼″ layer of broth aspic in a *clean* 9″ piepan and chill until almost firm. (If you like, arrange a decorative layer of carrot, radish, pimiento, or egg white cutouts on top and seal with a thin layer of aspic; chill again until tacky.)

Carefully slide veal-ham circle onto gelatin so that it is centered and cover with remaining aspic. Chill several hours until firm. To serve, unmold on a bed of greens and cut into wedges as you would a pie. Pass Mustard Mayonnaise Sauce or any creamy dressing. About 305 calories for each of 4 servings, 205 calories for each of 6 servings (without sauce).

GROUND VEAL

The logical cuts to grind are the sinewy, economical ones—*flank, breast, shank,* and *neck*—though some people insist upon the lean delicacy of shoulder (at half again the price). Ground veal does not make very good loaves or patties—too lean—and will be better if mixed ½ and ½ or 2 to 1 with ground pork, beef, lamb, or sausage meat or if mixed with enough vegetables or liquid to keep it moist. Once through the grinder is usually enough for veal unless you want extra-firm loaves or patties. In that case, have it ground twice.

A popular item in many supermarkets is something called *mock chicken legs,* ground veal shaped into a "drumstick" around a wooden skewer. Braised or panfried, these taste very much like chicken. Also popular are *choplets,* ground veal shaped like very thin loin chops (they're best panfried like Cube Steaks).

SAVORY VEAL AND VEGETABLE BURGERS

Makes 4 servings

1 pound ground veal
½ pound ground pork
1 small yellow onion, peeled and grated
1 carrot, peeled, parboiled, and grated
1½ teaspoons salt
¼ teaspoon pepper
2 teaspoons Worcestershire sauce
2 tablespoons butter or margarine
⅓ cup beef broth
1 tablespoon tomato paste

Mix all but last 3 ingredients and shape into 4 burgers about 1″ thick. Brown both sides well in butter in a heavy skillet over moderately high heat, about 5–7 minutes altogether. Turn heat to low, add broth mixed with tomato paste, cover, and simmer 15–20 minutes, basting every 5 minutes, until cooked through. Serve topped with skillet gravy. About 345 calories per serving.

VARIATIONS:

Veal and Mushroom Burgers: When mixing burgers, omit grated onion and add 1 small minced onion and ¼ pound chopped mushrooms sautéed in 2 tablespoons butter until limp. Shape and cook burgers as directed. Just before serving, add ¼ pound sliced sautéed mushrooms to gravy and warm 1–2 minutes. About 410 calories per serving.

Almond-Veal Burgers: Add ½ cup coarsely chopped toasted almonds to burger mixture; proceed as recipe directs. Smooth ½ cup sour cream into gravy just before serving. About 510 calories per serving.

LEMON VEAL LOAF

Makes 6–8 servings

5 slices firm-textured white bread
¾ cup milk
2½ pounds ground veal
1 medium-size yellow onion, peeled and minced
2 eggs
1 cup sour cream
1 tablespoon minced parsley
1 tablespoon minced fresh dill or 1 teaspoon dried dill
1 tablespoon minced capers
1 teaspoon finely grated lemon rind
¼ teaspoon thyme
¼ teaspoon salt
⅛ teaspoon pepper

Preheat oven to 350° F. Let bread soak in milk 10 minutes. Mix all ingredients together well and pat into a lightly greased 9″×5″×3″ loaf pan. Bake, uncovered, 1 hour; drain off drippings. Let loaf cool in its pan 15–20 minutes before slicing. Serve warm or chill and serve cold. Especially good with Lemon Sauce or Sour Cream-Horseradish Sauce. About 485 calories for each of 6 servings, 365 calories for each of 8 servings.

VIENNESE VEAL LOAF

Ground veal, pork, and ham make this loaf moist and flavorful.
Makes 8–10 servings

2 pounds veal, ground twice
1 pound lean pork, ground twice
¾ pound lean cooked ham, ground fine
2 large yellow onions, peeled and minced
18 soda crackers, rolled to fine crumbs
  (about 1½ cups)
2 teaspoons salt
1 teaspoon white pepper
1½ teaspoons poultry seasoning
1 tablespoon Worcestershire sauce
2 eggs, lightly beaten

Preheat oven to 375° F. Using your hands, mix all ingredients together well and shape in a shallow, lightly greased roasting pan into a loaf about 9″ × 3″. Bake, uncovered, about 1¾ hours or until a knife inserted in center of loaf comes out clean. (*Note:* If loaf seems to brown too fast, cover with foil. Transfer loaf to a heated platter, cover loosely with foil, and let "rest" 10 minutes before slicing.) If you wish, make Pan Gravy with the drippings or Mushroom Gravy. About 520 calories for each of 8 servings, 415 calories for each of 10 servings.

VEAL LOAF STUFFED WITH EGGS

Makes 6–8 servings

2 pounds ground veal
¼ pound ground very fat pork
¾ cup soft white bread crumbs
2 teaspoons salt
¼ teaspoon pepper
1 tablespoon finely grated lemon rind
½ cup evaporated milk
2 eggs, lightly beaten
3 large hard-cooked eggs, shelled
¼ cup melted butter, margarine, or
  bacon drippings

Preheat oven to 350° F. Mix veal, pork, crumbs, salt, pepper, lemon rind, milk, and beaten eggs thoroughly. Pack ⅓ into a greased 9″ × 5″ × 3″ loaf pan; arrange hard-cooked eggs lengthwise down center of meat mixture and pack in remaining mixture; brush lightly with butter. Bake, uncovered, basting occasionally with melted butter, 1–1¼ hours or until lightly browned and loaf pulls slightly from sides of pan. Let stand 10

minutes before inverting on platter. Serve hot with Tomato or Mustard Sauce; or serve cold with mayonnaise or suitable cold sauce (see Some Sauces, Gravies, and Seasonings for Veal). About 475 calories for each of 6 servings, 355 calories for each of 8 servings.

BUTTERMILK VEAL BALLS IN GRAVY

Makes 4–6 servings

Meat Balls:

1 pound ground veal
¼ pound ground pork
¾ cup fine dry bread crumbs
1 small yellow onion, peeled and grated
  fine (optional)
¼ cup buttermilk
1 teaspoon garlic salt
¼ teaspoon pepper
2 tablespoons bacon drippings or cooking
  oil

Gravy:

3 tablespoons flour
1 cup chicken broth
1 cup beef broth

Thoroughly mix all meat ball ingredients but bacon drippings and shape into 1″ balls. Brown balls, about half at a time, 10 minutes in drippings in a large, heavy skillet over moderate heat; remove to a bowl. For gravy, blend flour into drippings, add broths, and cook and stir until thickened. Return meat balls, cover, and simmer 15 minutes. About 390 calories for each of 4 servings, 260 calories for each of 6 servings.

VARIATIONS:

Veal Balls with Onions and Sour Cream: Prepare and brown meat balls as recipe directs; remove to a bowl. Sauté 3 thinly sliced large yellow onions in drippings 8–10 minutes until golden. Return meat balls to skillet, add 1 cup chicken broth, cover, and simmer 15 minutes. Drain pan liquid into 1 cup sour cream, whisk together, and return to skillet. Heat (but do not boil) 1–2 minutes. Serve over noodles, rice, or mashed potatoes. 525

calories for each of 4 servings (without noodles, rice, or potatoes), 350 calories for each of 6 servings.

Veal and Beef Balls (6 servings): In making balls use ¾ pound each ground veal and beef; add 1 lightly beaten egg along with all other ingredients, then shape and cook as recipe directs. About 530 calories for each of 4 servings, 355 calories for each of 6 servings.

Blue Cheese-Veal Balls: In making balls, increase buttermilk to ½ cup and add 2 ounces crumbled blue cheese; proceed as recipe directs. About 445 calories for each of 4 servings, 295 calories for each of 6 servings.

Veal and Chicken Balls: Omit pork when making balls and add 1 cup finely ground leftover cooked chicken, 2 tablespoons melted butter, and 1 lightly beaten egg; shape and brown as directed. Drain off all pan drippings, add 1 (10½-ounce) can cream of chicken soup thinned with ⅓ cup milk, cover, and simmer 15 minutes. 490 calories for each of 4 servings, 320 calories for each of 6 servings.

The Lesser Cuts of Veal
(See Veal Chart)

From these so-called "tough cuts" come some of the most famous veal dishes— blond *blanquette de veau* (a white French veal stew which the French make with *tendron*, the part of the breast containing the "false ribs" or cartilage, which cooks down to gelatinous tenderness), tomatoey brown *Marengo*, not to mention luscious Italian *Osso Buco* made with veal shanks. Hardly poor man's fare. All any of the following lesser cuts need in order to become fork tender is gentle stewing or braising in the company of liquid, vegetables, and herbs:

Fore and hind shanks
Breast and riblets
City chicken (chunks of veal shoulder on wooden skewers)
Stew meat
Neck
Brisket rolls and pieces
Heel of round

VEAL PAPRIKASH
Makes 4 servings

2 pounds boned veal shoulder, cut in 1″ cubes
2 tablespoons butter or margarine
2 medium-size yellow onions, peeled and minced
1 clove garlic, peeled and crushed
2 tablespoons paprika (the Hungarian sweet rose paprika is best)
½ teaspoon salt
⅛ teaspoon pepper
½ cup dry white wine
1 tomato, peeled, cored, seeded, and coarsely chopped
1 cup sour cream

Brown veal, a few pieces at a time, in butter in a large, heavy kettle over high heat; remove to a bowl. Add onions and garlic to kettle, reduce heat to moderate, and stir-fry 8–10 minutes until golden. Return veal to kettle, mix in all remaining ingredients except sour cream, cover, and simmer slowly 1½–2 hours until veal is tender. Mix in sour cream and serve over buttered wide noodles or *Nockerln*. About 585 calories per serving (without noodles or nockerln).

WIENER (VIENNESE) GOULASH
Makes 4 servings

1½ cups thinly sliced yellow onions
4 tablespoons butter, margarine, or shortening
2 pounds boned breast of veal, cut in 1″ cubes
2 tablespoons paprika
1 teaspoon salt
Pinch pepper
1 cup water (about)
1 cup sour cream at room temperature

Fry onions in 2 tablespoons butter 10–12 minutes over moderate heat in a heavy kettle until lightly browned; remove and set aside. Brown meat well on all sides in remaining butter over moderately high heat. Return onions to kettle and shake paprika over all to redden. Add salt, pepper, and water, cover, and simmer over very low heat 1½–2 hours until meat is tender; add a little more water from time to time, if needed, to keep kettle from cooking dry. When meat is tender, smooth in sour cream. Serve with boiled potatoes. About 600 calories per serving (without potatoes).

BLANQUETTE DE VEAU (FRENCH WHITE VEAL STEW)

When veal stew meat is simmered without first being browned (as in a *blanquette*), it produces an ugly scum. The best preventive: Cover veal with cold water, bring to a simmer, and cook 2 minutes. Rinse veal *and* kettle well, then begin recipe.
Makes 4 servings

2 pounds boned veal shoulder, cut in 1"
cubes and blanched to remove scum
(see above)
1 large yellow onion, peeled and stuck
with 4 cloves
1 carrot, peeled
1 stalk celery
1 leek, trimmed of roots (optional)
1½ teaspoons salt
⅛ teaspoon white pepper
1 bouquet garni,* tied in cheesecloth
1 bay leaf
3 cups cold water
2 tablespoons butter or margarine
3 tablespoons flour
2 egg yolks, lightly beaten
12 small white onions, boiled
½ pound button mushrooms, lightly
sautéed
Pinch nutmeg
1–2 tablespoons lemon juice
2 teaspoons minced parsley

Place veal, vegetables, all seasonings, and water in a kettle, cover, and simmer slowly 1½ hours until veal is tender. Remove veal to a bowl with a slotted spoon; strain broth and discard vegetables. Rinse and dry kettle, add butter, and melt over moderate heat, blend in flour, slowly add broth, and heat, stirring, until thickened. Return veal to kettle, cover, and simmer 5–10 minutes. Blend a little sauce into yolks, then return to kettle. Add onions and mushrooms; heat and stir 2–3 minutes but do not boil. Off heat, mix in nutmeg and lemon juice. Ladle into a deep platter and sprinkle with parsley. Good with buttered noodles. About 530 calories per serving.

For a Richer Blanquette: Add 1–2 veal knuckles to pot when making blanquette. *Or* use 1 pound veal shoulder cubes and 1½–2 pounds neck, breast, or riblets. Simmer until bones slip easily from meat; discard bones, return meat to sauce, and finish as directed. About 625 calories per serving.

BALKAN VEAL AND CHESTNUT STEW

Except for shelling the chestnuts, you'll find this unusual veal stew a breeze to prepare.
Makes 4–6 servings

2 tablespoons butter or margarine
2 pounds boned veal shoulder, cut in 1"
cubes
1 medium-size yellow onion, peeled and
coarsely chopped
1 clove garlic, peeled and crushed
1 (13¾-ounce) can chicken broth
½ cup dry white wine
1 (4") sprig fresh thyme or ¼ teaspoon
dried thyme
1 teaspoon salt
⅛ teaspoon pepper
1 pound shelled, peeled chestnuts*

Melt butter in a large, heavy kettle over moderately high heat, add veal, and brown well on all sides, 8–10 minutes. Reduce heat to moderately low, add onion and garlic, and stir-fry 5 minutes. Add all remaining ingredients except chestnuts, cover, and simmer 1 hour; add chestnuts, cover, and simmer 30 minutes longer until chestnuts and veal are tender. Serve over rice or Bulgur Pilaf with a spicy Yugoslav traminer wine or a white Greek retsina. About 670 calories for each of 4 servings, 450 calories for each of 6 servings (without rice or pilaf).

VEAL MARENGO

Makes 6 servings

3 pounds boned veal shoulder, cut in 1½" cubes
¾ cup unsifted flour
¼ teaspoon pepper
1 tablespoon plus ½ teaspoon salt
⅓ cup olive oil
2 medium-size yellow onions, peeled and coarsely chopped
1 clove garlic, peeled and crushed
1⅔ cups dry white wine
½ cup water
1 (6-ounce) can tomato paste
½ teaspoon thyme
½ teaspoon tarragon
½ teaspoon finely grated orange rind
½ pound button mushrooms, wiped clean and trimmed of coarse stems
2 tablespoons minced parsley

Preheat oven to 325° F. Dredge veal by shaking in a paper bag with flour, pepper, and 1 tablespoon salt, then brown, a few cubes at a time, in a little of the oil in a large heavy skillet over moderately high heat; add additional oil as needed. Transfer veal to a 3-quart oven-to-table casserole. Stir-fry onions and garlic in skillet 8–10 minutes until golden, add wine, water, tomato paste, thyme, tarragon, and remaining salt, and boil uncovered about 2 minutes. Mix in orange rind and pour into casserole. Cover and bake 2 hours. (*Note:* Casserole can be prepared to this point 1–2 days ahead. Cool, cover, and refrigerate until about 3 hours before serving. Bring to room temperature before proceeding.) Mix in mushrooms, cover, and bake ½ hour at 325° F. Stir in parsley and serve with boiled rice or buttered wide noodles. About 550 calories per serving (without rice or noodles).

VEAL AND SHRIMP IN LEMON-WINE SAUCE

Makes 6 servings

3 pounds boned veal shoulder, cut in 1" cubes
3 cups boiling water
1¼ teaspoons salt
2 medium-size yellow onions, peeled and sliced thin
2 carrots, peeled and sliced thin
3 sprigs parsley
1 sprig dill
Rind of 1 lemon cut in long strips (use a vegetable peeler)
3 tablespoons butter or margarine
3 tablespoons flour
Juice of ½ lemon
3 tablespoons dry vermouth
⅛ teaspoon white pepper
¼ teaspoon cardamom
1 pound small shrimp, boiled, shelled, and deveined
1 medium-size cauliflower, divided into flowerets, boiled, and drained (it should be hot)

Simmer veal in salted boiling water 2–3 minutes; strain stock and set veal aside. Rinse kettle well, return veal and stock.

Add vegetables, parsley, dill, and lemon rind, cover, and simmer slowly 1½ hours until veal is tender. Remove veal; strain stock and discard vegetables. In the same kettle, melt butter over moderate heat, blend in flour, add stock, and heat, stirring, until thickened. Add lemon juice, vermouth, pepper, and cardamom and let boil, uncovered, about 5 minutes to reduce slightly. Turn heat to low, add veal and shrimp, and simmer, covered, 10–15 minutes to blend flavors.

To serve, mound cauliflower in center of a platter and top with veal, shrimp, and plenty of sauce. About 535 calories per serving.

VEAL RIBLETS PARMIGIANA

Makes 4 servings

3–3½ pounds veal riblets
¼ cup unsifted flour
3 tablespoons olive or other cooking oil
½ teaspoon salt
¼ teaspoon pepper
⅛ teaspoon garlic powder
1 (15-ounce) can tomato sauce
⅓ cup beef broth
3 tablespoons finely grated Parmesan
  cheese
¼ pound mozzarella cheese, coarsely
  grated or thinly sliced

Preheat oven to 350° F. Dredge riblets in flour and brown, a few at a time, in oil in a large skillet over moderately high heat. Transfer to an ungreased 2½-quart casserole, sprinkle with salt, pepper, and garlic powder. Drain all but 1 tablespoon oil from skillet, add tomato sauce and broth, stir to scrape up brown bits, and pour over riblets. Sprinkle with Parmesan, cover, and bake about 1 hour until riblets are tender. Uncover, scatter mozzarella on top, and broil 4" from heat 2–3 minutes until cheese melts and is speckled with brown. Serve with Polenta or buttered noodles. About 530 calories per serving (without Polenta or noodles).

BRAISED VEAL RIBLETS

Makes 4 servings

3–3½ pounds veal riblets
¼ cup unsifted flour
2 tablespoons butter or margarine
1 tablespoon cooking oil
2 tablespoons flour
1 cup beef broth
1 cup cold water
¾ teaspoon salt
⅛ teaspoon pepper
1 large yellow onion, peeled and sliced
  thin
1 pound carrots, peeled and cut in 2"
  chunks (optional)
¼ teaspoon grated lemon rind
1 teaspoon minced parsley

Dredge riblets in flour and brown, a few at a time, in butter and oil in a heavy

kettle over moderately high heat; drain on paper toweling. Blend 2 tablespoons flour into drippings, slowly add broth and water, stirring until smooth. Return meat to kettle, season with salt and pepper, add onion and carrots. Cover and simmer 1 hour until veal is tender; check liquid from time to time and add a little water if necessary. Just before serving, stir in lemon and parsley. Serve with crusty bread or mashed potatoes. About 430 calories per serving (made without carrots), about 470 calories per serving (made with carrots).

OSSO BUCO (ITALIAN-STYLE BRAISED VEAL SHANKS)

Osso buco owes its unique flavor to gremolata, a mixture of lemon rind, parsley and garlic added just before serving.
Makes 4 servings

4 pounds veal shanks, cut in 3" lengths
½ cup unsifted flour
1 tablespoon salt
¼ teaspoon pepper
⅓ cup olive oil
2 cloves garlic, peeled and crushed
1 medium-size yellow onion, peeled and
  minced
2 large carrots, peeled and cut in small
  dice
1 stalk celery, chopped fine
½ cup dry white wine
1 (13¾-ounce) can chicken broth
1 tablespoon minced fresh basil or
  1 teaspoon dried basil
1 bay leaf, crumbled
Pinch thyme

Gremolata:

1 tablespoon minced parsley
2 teaspoons finely grated lemon rind
1 clove garlic, peeled and minced

Dredge veal by shaking in a heavy paper bag with flour, salt, and pepper, then brown in oil, a few pieces at a time; remove and reserve. Add garlic, onion, carrots, and celery to kettle and sauté 5–8 minutes until pale golden. Add wine and boil rapidly, uncovered, 4–5 minutes until reduced by half. Return veal to kettle, arranging so marrow cannot fall out, and add all remaining ingredients except gremolata. Cover and simmer 1¼–1½ hours until veal is tender but not falling off the bones. Mix gremolata and sprinkle over shanks, cover, and simmer 5–10 minutes longer. Serve, spooning vegetables and cooking liquid over veal. Or, if you prefer, purée vegetables and cooking liquid until smooth; spoon a little over veal and pass

the rest in a sauceboat. Risotto alla Milanese is the traditional accompaniment. About 930 calories per serving.

VARIATION:

Braised Veal Shanks with Tomato Sauce: Prepare recipe as directed, reducing amount of chicken broth to ½ cup and adding, at the same time, 1 (1-pound) undrained can tomatoes. About 950 calories per serving.

LAMB AND MUTTON

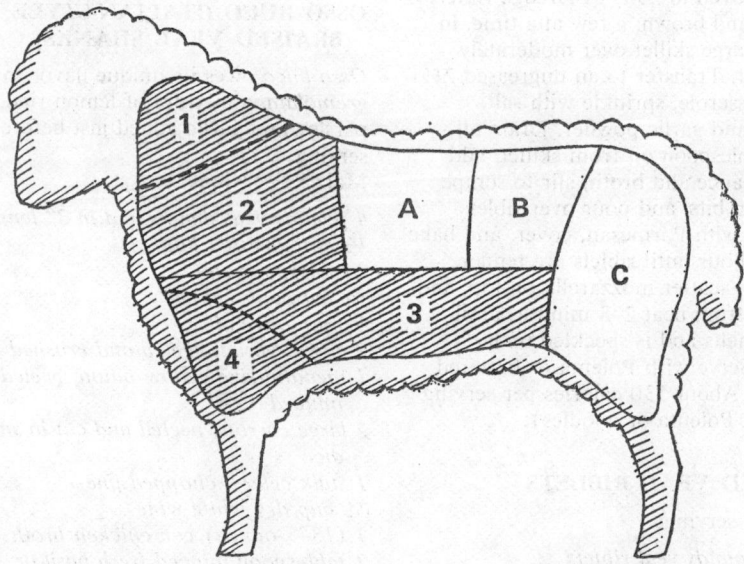

Note: Unshaded parts are the tender cuts. Shaded parts are not-so-tender.

THE TENDER CUTS:
  A. RIB
     Roasts (rib, crown)
     Chops (rib, Frenched rib)
  B. LOIN
     Roasts (loin, double loin)
     Chops (loin, kidney or English)
  C. LEG
     Leg of lamb or mutton
     Leg chop or steak
     Cubes for kebabs

THE NOT-SO-TENDER CUTS:
  1. NECK
     Neck slices
  2. SHOULDER
     Roasts (rolled, cushion, square
        shoulder)
     Chops (blade, arm)
     Stew lamb or mutton
     Ground lamb or mutton
  3. BREAST
     Roasts for stuffing
     Riblets (stew lamb or mutton)
  4. SHANK
     Lamb or mutton shanks

Though adept at cooking beef and pork, we often approach lamb with uncertainty. Many of us don't like it (or think we don't), perhaps because cookbooks have for years insisted that lamb be cooked well done. Not true. Anyone who has tasted baby lamb roasted the French way—until juicily pink and not an instant longer—is quickly converted. How delicate this lamb is, and how delicious. Almost every foreign country prizes lamb as highly (or more highly) than beef, not surprising when you consider that lamb (or one of its early ancestors) was man's first meat.

Technically, lamb is a young sheep under 1 year of age. *Baby or milk-fed lamb* is 6–8 weeks old, *"spring" lamb* 3–5 months old, and *lamb* 6 months to 1 year. When lamb reaches its first birthday, it becomes *yearling mutton;* at age 2, it's full-scale *mutton. Pré-salé lamb,* the French favorite, is lamb grazed on the *prés salés* (salt marshes) of Brittany and Normandy.

In the old days, lamb was available primarily in spring, hence the name "spring" lamb. Today, however, it is available the year round.

How to Recognize Quality

Buy top grades (USDA PRIME, CHOICE, or GOOD), also meat that has been federally inspected (found wholesome). It will have velvety-pink-to-red lean (the older the animal, the redder the meat), firm creamy fat and bones that are spongy and red inside. Mutton is dark red with flinty bones and brittle fat.

About the Fell: The outer fat of lamb has a thin, papery covering called the *fell,* which has caused some controversy. Should it be removed before cooking? Some gourmet cooks say yes, because it gives even youngest lamb a strong flavor. Others say it should be left on legs of lamb because it helps them hold their shape during roasting, seals in juices, and speeds cooking. We've tried both ways and can't see enough difference to justify the fuss. On other cuts of lamb, especially small ones, peel the fell off *before* cooking.

About the Musk Glands: Buried in the leg of lamb (near the hock joint) and in the shoulder are large, yellowish "musk" glands (so called because people once thought they gave lamb a musky off-flavor). They don't, but they *are* conspicuous, particularly in young lamb, so most butchers routinely remove them. If your butcher hasn't, simply snip them out yourself.

A Word About the Cuts of Lamb and Mutton: They are the same in both animals, the only real difference being that in mutton they're larger, less tender (especially neck, leg, breast, and other well-exercised muscles), and more strongly flavored. The majority of recipes in this book call for lamb simply because American preferences are for it, but mutton can be substituted in any of the recipes that are braised or stewed.

Roast Lamb

LEG: The most popular Lamb roast and one of the most expensive, leg of lamb is cut the following ways:
Full (whole) leg (6–10 pounds)
Sirloin half of leg (4–5 pounds)
Shank half of leg (3–5 pounds)
Center leg (3–5 pounds)
Boned and rolled leg (3–5 pounds)

LOIN AND RIB ROASTS: All are expensive and supremely tender:
Sirloin (2–2½ pounds)
Loin (2–2½ pounds)
Saddle or double loin (4–5 pounds)
Rolled double loin (3–4 pounds)
Rib or rack (2½–3 pounds)
Crown roast (rib roasts bent and tied into a circle; 6 pounds up)

SHOULDER AND BREAST: More economical but less tender:
Square shoulder (4–6 pounds)

Precarved shoulder (a trimmed shoulder, cut into chops and tied back into original shape; about 5 pounds)
Cushion shoulder (the one to stuff; 3–5 pounds)
Rolled shoulder (3–5 pounds)
Breast (1½–2 pounds)
Boned and rolled breast (also good to stuff; 1½ pounds)

How to Roast Lamb

People are of many minds about the best way to roast lamb. Some prefer a constant low temperature, some a constant moderately high temperature, others a combination of high and low, which is the French way. Still others treat each cut differently: baby lamb, they say, is best roasted fast at a very high temperature, spring lamb at a lower one. Here are the three most popular methods and the preferred cuts for each.

(*Note:* Meat thermometers (many cookbooks, too) still advise cooking lamb to 170° F. or 180° F., but at those temperatures it will be depressingly gray and dry. For those who like it juicily pink, 140–45° F. is just about perfect. Some, of course, prefer it really rare (130–35° F.), others more well done. Try cooking a lamb roast to one of the lower temperatures; if it isn't to your liking, roast a bit longer.) Always let roast "rest" 15–20 minutes before carving so juices have a chance to settle.

Cooking times given here can only be approximate, since shape of cut, proportion of fat and bone, internal temperature at time of roasting all affect over-all time. The truest test of doneness is the meat thermometer.

Amount Needed: Allow ⅓–½ pound boned lamb per serving, ½–¾ pound bone-in lamb.

Preparation for Cooking: Legs need none (unless you elect to remove the fell); shoulders and loin should have the fell peeled off and fat trimmed to ⅛″. Let roast stand at room temperature 1½–2 hours if convenient. Rub, if you like, with salt and pepper (salt only penetrates ¼″ so it really doesn't matter whether roast is salted before cooking or not).

To Give Roast Extra Flavor:

– Rub with 1 of the following: 2 tablespoons curry powder or Dijon-style mustard; 1 teaspoon marjoram, thyme, rosemary, summer savory, or dill.
– Make tiny slits over surface of fat and insert thin garlic slivers in each, or crushed mint, sage, or basil leaves.
– Mix ¼ cup mild yellow mustard with 2 tablespoons soy sauce, 2 crushed cloves garlic, 1 tablespoon sugar, and ¼ teaspoon ginger; spread over roast.
– Marinate roast 24 hours in refrigerator in dry red wine, Teriyaki Sauce, All-Purpose Barbecue Sauce, or other aromatic marinade, turning occasionally. Drain and roast as directed, basting often with marinade during last ½ hour.

Continuous Low Heat Method (for leg of lamb, loin, saddle, and boneless roasts): Preheat oven to 325° F. Place roast fat side up on a rack in a shallow roasting pan (loin and rib roasts usually don't need racks because ribs hold them out of drippings). Insert meat thermometer in center of largest lean muscle, not touching bone. If roast is small, insert very carefully on an angle so that thermometer is secure. Do not add water, do not cover. Roast, without basting, as follows: 12–13 minutes per pound for rare (130–35° F.), 14–16 for medium rare (140–45° F.), 18–20 for medium (150–60° F.), and, if you must have it well done, 20–25 minutes per pound (160–65° F.). (*Note:* Boneless roasts, also small (3–4-pound) roasts, will take *slightly* (3–5 minutes) longer per pound for each degree of doneness.) Let roast "rest" 15–20 minutes before carving.

Continuous Moderately High Temperature (good for all but baby lamb): Pre-

heat oven to 375° F. Place roast in pan
and insert thermometer as above. Do
not cover, do not add liquid. Roast,
without basting, 11–13 minutes per
pound for rare (130–35° F.), 13–15 for
medium rare (140–45° F.), 16–18 for
medium (150–60° F.), 18–20 for well
done (160–65° F.), and about 3 minutes
longer per pound for boneless roasts
for each degree of doneness. Let roast
"rest" 15–20 minutes before carving.

Searing (French) Method (good for all
cuts): Preheat oven to 450° F. Place
roast in pan and insert thermometer as
above; do not cover or add liquid. Sear
15 minutes, reduce heat to 350° F. and
roast, without basting, 10–12 minutes
per pound for rare (130–35° F.), 12–14
for medium rare (140–45° F.), 14–16
for medium (150–60° F.), 16–18 for
well done (160–65° F.), and slightly
longer per pound for each degree of
doneness for boneless roasts. Let "rest"
before carving.

About Baby Lamb: Because baby lamb
is so delicate and tender, it's best roasted
quickly in a very hot oven, 450° F.
Place fat side up on a rack, insert meat
thermometer, do not add water, and do
not cover. Roast 10–15 minutes per
pound until medium rare (140–45° F.).
It's most succulent and flavorful at this
temperature and should not be served
more well done.

About Mutton: Loin, rack, and leg are
the best cuts to roast, and searing is the
best method. Follow directions for lamb
above.

Some Glazes for Roast Lamb

Half an hour before roast is done,
spread or drizzle any of the following
over surface and continue cooking as
directed, basting every 10 minutes.
– ½ cup melted mint, apple, grape, or
red currant jelly.
– ½ cup warmed orange or lime marmalade.

– ½ cup minced chutney heated with ½
cup apple juice, red wine, or water.
– ¼ cup mint, apple, grape, or red currant jelly heated with ¼ cup honey or
firmly packed light brown sugar and ⅛
teaspoon each nutmeg and cinnamon.
– ¼ cup firmly packed light brown sugar
and ¼ teaspoon cinnamon heated in 1
cup apple juice or cider until dissolved.
– ½ cup chili sauce mixed with ¼ cup
cider vinegar and 1 teaspoon chili
powder.

**Some Easy Variations on Oven-Roasted
Lamb**

À la Bordelaise (for large roasts cooked
by Continuous Low Heat Method): For
each person, place ⅓ cup potato balls in
pan with lamb, drizzle with 3–4 tablespoons oil or melted butter, and roast,
uncovered, 40 minutes, turning balls occasionally. Add 6–8 button mushrooms
for each person, toss with potatoes, and
continue roasting 15–20 minutes until
meat is done. Garnish meat with drained
vegetables, then sprinkle with the following: ¼ cup soft white bread crumbs that
have been sautéed in 2 tablespoons butter with 1 crushed clove garlic and 1
tablespoon minced parsley.

À la Boulangère (for large roasts cooked
by Continuous Low Heat Method):
Begin roasting lamb as directed; meanwhile, stir-fry 2 cups coarsely chopped
yellow onion in ¼ cup butter over moderate heat until pale golden; sprinkle
with ½ teaspoon salt and ⅛ teaspoon
pepper. When roast has only ¾ hour
more to cook, take from oven and lift
from pan, rack and all. Make a bed of
onions in pan, place roast on top, and
continue roasting to desired doneness.
When serving, spoon some onions on top
of roast and wreathe the rest around
platter. Pass Pan Gravy.

À la Bretonne: Roast lamb by one of
the methods above and serve with 1
recipe Boiled Dried White Beans, cooked
as directed, but with the following
changes: to the pot add 1 large yellow
onion, peeled and stuck with 3 cloves,

2 peeled cloves garlic, 2 bay leaves, and 2 parsley sprigs. When beans are tender, drain, remove onion, garlic, bay leaves, and parsley and toss with 3 tablespoons melted butter, 1 crushed clove garlic, 2–3 tablespoons lamb drippings, and 1 tablespoon each tomato paste and minced parsley. Lamb can be wreathed with the beans or the two can be served separately.

À la Provençale: Buy a large, full leg of lamb, make tiny slits over surface, and tuck in anchovy fillets and thin garlic slivers; rub well with summer savory and thyme and let stand at room temperature 3 hours. Roast by one of the methods above but baste often with 1½ cups lamb stock or beef broth mixed with ½ cup each melted butter and dry vermouth. While roast "rests," boil pan drippings and any remaining basting mixture 3–5 minutes to reduce, stir in 2 tablespoons minced parsley, and pour into a sauceboat. Accompany roast with Boiled Dried White Beans dressed with olive oil and garlic.

Arni Psito (Greek-Style Roast Lamb): Make small slits over surface of roast and tuck in thin garlic slivers (use 3 cloves garlic in all). Brush roast with 2 tablespoons olive oil or melted butter and drizzle with the juice of 2 lemons. Roast by one of the methods above and, when half done, add 2 cups boiling water to pan, 1 teaspoon salt, ⅛ teaspoon pepper. Continue roasting uncovered until tender. Skim pan liquid of fat and serve over lamb as sauce.

Neapolitan Roast Lamb: Make small slits over surface of roast and tuck in thin garlic slivers (use 3 cloves). Marinate lamb 24 hours in refrigerator in 2 cups dry red or white wine mixed with 1 minced small yellow onion, 2 tablespoons finely grated lemon rind, and 1½ teaspoons powdered rosemary. Lift meat from marinade, brush with 2 tablespoons olive oil, and roast as directed, basting often with strained marinade. Use marinade in making Pan Gravy.

Roast Lamb Bonne Femme: Choose a large, full leg of lamb and place in pan as directed. For each person add to pan: 1 halved, peeled medium-size potato and 3 peeled small white onions drizzled with ¼ cup oil or melted bacon drippings. Sprinkle with 1 teaspoon salt and ⅛ teaspoon pepper and roast, uncovered, turning once or twice. These will take 1–1¼ hours to cook, so gauge accordingly. Drain on paper toweling and wreathe around roast on platter.

Roast Lamb in Buttermilk (for roasts cooked by Continuous Low Heat Method): Marinate roast in 1 quart buttermilk and 1 cup minced yellow onion 24 hours in refrigerator, turning occasionally. Transfer to roasting pan, strain buttermilk over lamb, and roast as directed, basting every half hour. If pan boils dry, add a little more buttermilk or boiling water.

Oven-Barbecued Roast Lamb: Marinate lamb in All-Purpose Barbecue Sauce 24 hours in refrigerator, turning occasionally. Lift from marinade and roast by one of the basic methods, basting every 15 minutes with barbecue sauce.

Roast Lamb with Dill-Crumb Topping: Roast lamb by one of the basic methods and about ½ hour before it is done, remove from oven and brush with 1 tablespoon melted butter; then pat on: 2 cups fine soft bread crumbs tossed with 2 tablespoons each minced dill, parsley, and melted butter, 1 crushed clove garlic, and ¼ teaspoon pepper. Return to oven and roast, uncovered, to desired doneness.

Taverna-Style Roast Leg of Lamb: Choose a 5–6-pound short leg of lamb and trim off all outer covering of fat. Rub well with the juice of 1 lemon. Make tiny slits over surface and tuck in thin garlic slivers (use 2 cloves). Mix together 2 finely crumbled bay leaves, 1 teaspoon thyme, and ¼ teaspoon each oregano and pepper and rub over lamb; pour the juice of 1 lemon over all.

Let stand in a cool place 24 hours. Roast lamb by Continuous Moderately High Temperature method for exactly 1 hour (the roast will be quite rare). Remove from oven and let rest 15–20 minutes before serving.

How To Spit-Roast Lamb

Best Cuts: Leg, rolled shoulder, double loin, loin, saddle, or rack.

Amount Needed: The same as for Roast Lamb *but* avoid small roasts; 4–5 pounds is a good size (except for racks and loins that weigh only 2½–3).

Preparation for Cooking: The same as for oven roasting. When saddle, loin, or rack is to be spit-roasted over charcoal, have butcher leave flank on and roll up and tie.

In Rotisserie or Oven: Preheat unit. Balance roast carefully on spit: full and half legs should be skewered from butt to shank end with spit running parallel to bone; all boneless cuts are spitted lengthwise straight through the center; spit loin, rack, and saddle end to end straight through the middle so they are well balanced. Tighten holding forks. Insert meat thermometer in center of largest lean muscle, making sure it touches neither spit nor bone, also that it will not hit any part of rotisserie as it turns. The best way is to insert the thermometer on an angle or in the end of the roast. Attach spit to rotisserie and roast 5″–6″ from heat according to manufacturer's timetable or 5 minutes less per pound than recommended for lamb roasted the Continuous Low Heat Method. Keep a close eye on the thermometer and remove lamb when it registers about 5° below desired doneness. Remove roast from spit and let "rest" 15–20 minutes before carving.

Over Charcoal: Prepare a moderate charcoal fire.* Balance meat on spit and insert thermometer as for rotisserie.

(*Note:* Saddle, loin, and rack of lamb should be roasted only where heat can be regulated by lowering or raising spit.) Attach spit to rotisserie, place drip pan in center, and push coals to the front and back of it. Roast lamb 6″–7″ from coals, using rotisserie roasting times as a guide. Check thermometer regularly and use it as the true indicator of doneness.

VARIATIONS (*for rotisserie or charcoal spit roasting*):

– Marinate roast in All-Purpose Barbecue Sauce overnight, then spit-roast as directed, basting often with sauce during last ½ hour of cooking.
– Brush roast frequently with ¼ cup Garlic Butter mixed with 2 tablespoons olive or other oil.
– The day before roasting lamb, purée 2 large yellow onions, coarsely chopped, in an electric blender at high speed with ⅓ cup water and 2 peeled cloves garlic. Pour over roast, cover, and refrigerate 24 hours, turning often. Lift roast from marinade, scrape off excess, and rub roast with 2 tablespoons paprika (preferably the sweet rose type). Spit and roast as directed.

Some Garnishes for Roast Lamb Platters
(in addition to parsley and watercress sprigs)

Group or wreathe around lamb roast as prettily as possible one or two of the following, selecting garnishes of contrasting color and shape:

Artichoke Bottoms: boiled and buttered; filled with puréed sweet green peas or spinach.

Asparagus Tips: boiled and buttered.

Brussels Sprouts: boiled and buttered.

Carrots: Buttered Baby Carrots; Carrots Rosemary; Lemon-Glazed Carrots.

Endives: Braised Belgian Endives.

Fruits: broiled apricot or peach halves filled with dabs of red currant jelly.

Mushrooms: sautéed button mushrooms; Baked Mushroom Caps Stuffed with Hazelnuts.

Onions: Glazed Onions; Pan-Braised Onions; Stuffed Onions.

Parsnips: Currant or Caramel-Glazed

Parsnips; Roast Parsnips.

Potatoes: Parsleyed, Herbed, Lemon-Glazed, or Danish-Style New Potatoes.

Tomatoes: Stuffed Tomatoes.

Turnips: Glazed or Roasted Turnips; Turnips Stuffed with Risotto.

SAUCES, GRAVIES, AND SEASONINGS FOR ROAST LAMB

For Cooking Seasonings, Herbs, Spices		For Hot Roasts Gravies	Sauces
Basil	Oregano	Au jus (Un-	Brown curry
Bay Leaf	Paprika	thickened	Fresh mint
Cinnamon	Parsley	pan gravy)	Garlic
Curry powder	Rose geranium	Pan gravy	Mustard hol-
Dill	Rosemary		landaise
Garlic	Saffron		Paloise
Ginger	Sage		Périgueux
Juniper berries	Summer Savory		Poivrade
Lemon	Tarragon		Quick lemon-
Marjoram	Thyme (espe-		caper
Mint	cially wild thyme)		
Mustard	Turmeric		

For Hot or Cold Roasts Condiments	For Cold Roasts Sauces
Chutney	Anchovy mayonnaise
Hot mustard fruits	Cumberland
Jellies (apple, crab	Herb mayonnaise
apple, mint, red	Indienne
currant, rose	
geranium)	

How to Carve Leg of Lamb:

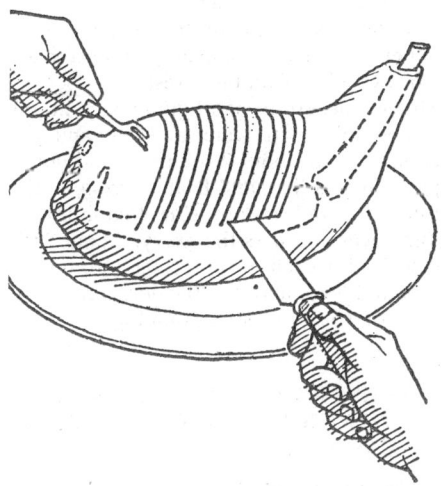

Place leg on platter so plump, meaty portion is away from carver. Cut 2–3 thin slices from near side to form a base. Stand roast on base and, beginning at shank end, cut straight down to bone. Free slices by running knife down along shank bone. Lift out and transfer to platter.

French Method

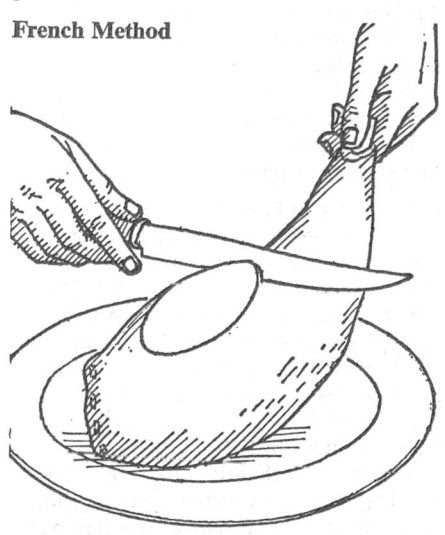

So very easy. Simply lift leg bone with hand, then with a carving knife carve the length of the leg, parallel to the bone, in thin slices.

⚖ CROWN ROAST OF LAMB

This spectacular roast deserves a fine red Bordeaux, a Médoc, perhaps, or Saint-Emilion.
Makes 6–8 servings

*1 (12–16 rib) crown roast of lamb
   (about 4–6 pounds) (Note: Have
   butcher remove backbone and french
   ribs.)*
¼ teaspoon pepper
*Chicory (pale inner leaves) and
   watercress sprigs (garnish)*
Seedless green grapes (garnish)

If butcher has filled crown with ground trimmings, remove (save for lamb burgers). Let roast stand at room temperature 1½–2 hours if convenient. Preheat oven to 325° F. Place roast, rib ends up, in a large, shallow roasting pan (no need for a rack) and rub with pepper. Force a large foil ball into crown so it won't cook out of shape; cover rib ends with foil; insert meat thermometer between 2 ribs, not touching bone. Roast, uncovered, 12–15 minutes per pound for rare (130–35° F. on thermometer), 15–17 for medium rare (145–50° F.), 18–20 for medium (150–60° F.), and 20–25 for well done (160–70° F.). Transfer to a hot platter and let "rest" 15–20 minutes. Put paper frills on rib ends or, if you prefer, pitted green olives or preserved kumquats. Fill crown with chicory and cress and decorate base with clusters of grapes. Good with Château Potatoes and Peas à la Française. About 250 calories for each of 6 or 8 servings.

To Stuff: Before roasting, fill crown with 2 cups stuffing (Rice and Mushroom, Pecan-Bulgur Wheat, and Herbed Bread Stuffings are especially good). Cover stuffing loosely with foil and roast as above, allowing about 5 minutes longer per pound; uncover stuffing for last ½ hour of cooking. Calories for each of 6 servings: About 420 with Rice and Mushroom Stuffing; 445 with Pecan-Bulgur Wheat Stuffing; and 410 with Herbed Bread Stuffing. Calories for each of 8 servings: 400 with Rice and Mushroom Stuffing; 420 with Pecan-

Bulgur Wheat; and 395 with Herbed
Bread Stuffing.

To Carve: Separate into chops by slicing
down along ribs.

VARIATION:

**Crown Roast of Lamb Filled with
Vegetables:** Omit chicory and cress and
fill crown with any of the following:
buttered green peas mixed with pearl
onions or sliced mushrooms or Green
Peas with Mint and Orange; Rice Pilaf;
Brussels Sprouts Véronique or Brussels
Sprouts with Chestnuts; Puréed or
Braised Chestnuts or Sautéed
Mushrooms. For approximate calorie
counts, add to the 250 calories per
serving of the unfilled crown roast, the
calories per serving given for each of the
recipes listed above (see Index for page
numbers).

SWEDISH-STYLE ROAST LEG OF
LAMB

Could this recipe have been invented by
a thrifty Swedish housewife who hated
to throw out the leftover breakfast
coffee? Perhaps. Although there is no
pronounced coffee taste, the coffee does
enrich both the color and the flavor of
the lamb.
Makes 8–10 servings

1 (6–8-pound) leg of lamb
2 teaspoons salt
¼ teaspoon pepper
1½ cups hot strong coffee
½ cup light cream
1 tablespoon sugar
*1 large carrot, peeled and coarsely
    grated*
1½ cups hot water
3 tablespoons red currant jelly
*2 tablespoons flour blended with ¼ cup
    cold water (optional)*

Preheat oven to 325° F. Rub lamb well
with salt and pepper and place fat side
up on a rack in a shallow roasting pan;
insert meat thermometer in center of
leg, not touching bone. Roast,
uncovered, using times given for
Continuous Low Heat Method as a
guide. About 1 hour before roast is done,
mix coffee, cream, and sugar and pour
over lamb; sprinkle carrot into pan.
Continue roasting lamb to desired
doneness, basting frequently. Transfer to
a heated platter and let "rest."
Meanwhile, strain pan liquid and skim off
fat; combine with water and jelly and
cook and stir about 2 minutes. Add flour
paste, if you like, and heat, stirring, until
thickened and smooth. Carve lamb into
thin slices and pass the gravy. About 555
calories for each of 8 servings (from a
6-pound leg), about 570 calories for
each of 10 servings (8-pound leg).

ROAST LEG OF LAMB STUFFED
WITH RICE, PIÑON NUTS, AND
CURRANTS
Makes 6–8 servings

1 (6-pound) leg of lamb

Stuffing:

2 tablespoons olive oil
½ cup uncooked rice
*1 medium-size yellow onion, peeled and
    minced*
1 clove garlic, peeled and crushed
3 tablespoons minced parsley
1 tablespoon minced mint
¼ cup dried currants
½ cup piñon nuts
1 cup chicken broth
1 teaspoon salt
¼ teaspoon pepper

Ask butcher to bone leg of lamb, leaving
about 2″ of leg bone in at the narrow
end (this makes the leg handsomer and
easier to stuff). Preheat oven to 325° F.
For stuffing, heat oil 1 minute in a
saucepan over moderately high heat,
add rice, onion, and garlic, and stir-fry
2–3 minutes until rice is golden. Mix in
remaining ingredients, cover, and simmer
8–10 minutes until all moisture is
absorbed. Cool slightly. Spoon stuffing
into leg, then sew or skewer cavity shut.
Place leg in a large shallow roasting pan
and roast, uncovered, 3 hours. To carve,
cut straight across in ½″ slices. About
830 calories for each of 6 servings, 620
calories for each of 8 servings.

HERB STUFFED ROLLED LEG OF LAMB

Makes 6–8 servings

1 (6-pound) leg of lamb, boned and opened flat but not rolled

Stuffing:

¼ cup minced parsley
3 cloves garlic, peeled and crushed
1 tablespoon minced fresh basil or 1 teaspoon dried basil
1 tablespoon olive oil
1 tablespoon softened butter
1 tablespoon lemon juice
1 teaspoon salt
¼ teaspoon pepper

Preheat oven to 325° F. Peel fell from lamb and discard; spread lamb out fat side down on counter. Mix stuffing and spread over lamb leaving ½″ margins; roll jelly-roll style and tie round at 2″ intervals. Place on a rack and roast, uncovered, 3 hours. Serve as is with Pan Gravy (when making, use dry red wine for ½ the liquid) or with hot Caper Sauce. About 465 calories for each of 6 servings, 350 calories for each of 8 servings.

LEG OF LAMB BRAISED WITH ONIONS, CARROTS, AND TOMATOES

Although we don't think of leg of lamb as a cut to braise, it is savory and succulent prepared this way. The vegetables cook down into a rich, rosy gravy.
Makes 6 servings

1 (3–4-pound) half leg of lamb
2 tablespoons cooking oil
2 medium-size yellow onions, peeled and minced
2 carrots, peeled and diced
2 stalks celery, chopped fine
1 bouquet garni,* tied in cheesecloth
1 (10½-ounce) can beef bouillon
1 (1-pound) can tomatoes (do not drain)
1½ teaspoons salt
¼ teaspoon pepper

Preheat oven to 325° F. Brown lamb well in oil in a Dutch oven over moderately high heat; remove from kettle. Stir-fry onions, carrots, and celery in drippings over moderate heat 5–8 minutes until onions are pale golden; return meat to kettle, add remaining ingredients, cover, and bring to a simmer. Transfer to oven and bake, covered, 1½–2 hours until tender, basting 2–3 times. Lift meat to a hot platter; purée vegetables and drippings in an electric blender at low speed or put through a food mill. Warm gravy, taste for seasoning and adjust if needed. Pour a little gravy over meat and pass the rest. About 525 calories per serving.

VARIATION:

Braised Mutton: Substitute a half leg of mutton for lamb; prepare as directed, baking about 35–40 minutes per pound until tender. About 555 calories per serving.

SICILIAN-STYLE BRAISED LEG OF LAMB

Makes 6 servings

1 (4-pound) half leg of lamb
2 tablespoons cooking oil
2 tablespoons flour
1½ teaspoons minced fresh sage or ½ teaspoon dried sage
½ teaspoon minced fresh rosemary or ⅛ teaspoon dried rosemary
2 cloves garlic, peeled and crushed
1 teaspoon salt
¼ teaspoon pepper
½ cup red wine vinegar
½ cup hot water
3–4 anchovy fillets, minced

Preheat oven to 325° F. Brown lamb lightly all over in oil in a Dutch oven over moderately high heat. Sprinkle flour, herbs, and garlic over lamb and continue browning 2–3 minutes, turning lamb frequently. Add all remaining ingredients except anchovies, cover, and bring to a simmer. Transfer to oven and simmer, covered, 1½–2 hours until tender; baste 2–3 times. Lift meat to platter; stir anchovies into drippings and serve as a gravy. About 495 calories per serving.

ROAST STUFFED CUSHION SHOULDER OF LAMB

Makes 6–8 servings

1 (4-pound) cushion shoulder of lamb
1 teaspoon salt
⅛ teaspoon pepper
2–3 cups stuffing (Rice Pilaf, Rice and Mushroom Stuffing, Pecan-Bulgur Wheat, Rice and Kidney, Black Olive and Onion, and Bread and Apricot Stuffing are very good, but prepared packaged stuffing may also be used)

Preheat oven to 325° F. Skewer all but one side of roast shut, sprinkle pocket with salt and pepper, stuff loosely, and close with skewers. Place roast fat side up on a rack in a shallow roasting pan and roast, uncovered, about 2 hours until tender. Lift meat from pan and let "rest" 15–20 minutes before serving. To carve, cut across the grain in slices ½" thick. Serve with Au Jus or Pan Gravy. (Note: For an extra-special touch, glaze roast during last ½ hour of cooking [see Some Glazes for Roast Lamb].) Approximate calories for each of 6 servings: about 850 if made with Rice Pilaf; 805 with Rice and Mushroom Stuffing; 835 with Pecan-Bulgur Wheat Stuffing; 825 with Rice and Kidney Stuffing; 815 with Black Olive and Onion Stuffing; and 845 with Bread and Apricot Stuffing. Approximate calories for each of 8 servings; 640 if made with Rice Pilaf; 605 with Rice and Mushroom Stuffing; 630 with Pecan-Bulgur Wheat Stuffing; 620 with Rice and Kidney Stuffing; 610 with Black Olive and Onion Stuffing; and 635 with Bread and Apricot Stuffing.

EASY ATHENIAN BRAISED LAMB SHOULDER

Cook in an electric skillet if you like.
Makes 6 servings

1 (3-pound) rolled lamb shoulder
2 tablespoons olive oil or cooking oil
1 medium-size yellow onion, peeled and coarsely chopped
1 clove garlic, peeled and crushed (optional)
2 teaspoons salt
¼ teaspoon pepper
1 teaspoon rosemary, oregano, marjoram, or thyme (optional)
⅓ cup cold water
3 cups lamb stock or a ½ and ½ mixture of beef broth and cold water
6 tablespoons flour
½–1 teaspoon liquid gravy browner (optional)

Brown lamb well all over in oil in a heavy kettle over moderate heat; add onion, garlic, seasonings and water, cover, and simmer slowly about 2½ hours. Keep an eye on the pot and add about ¼ cup extra water if liquid boils away. When lamb is tender, lift to a platter and keep warm. Drain all but 1–2 tablespoons drippings from kettle, add 2 cups stock, stirring to scrape up browned bits. Blend flour and remaining stock in a shaker jar, pour into kettle, and heat, stirring, until thickened. If you like a dark gravy, add gravy browner. Slice roast about ¼" thick and serve with plenty of gravy.

VARIATIONS:

To Oven Braise: Preheat oven to 350° F. Brown lamb as directed in a large, flameproof casserole, add onion, garlic, seasonings, and water, cover, and bake 2½–3 hours as directed. Prepare gravy as above and serve.

To Braise in Electric Skillet: Set control at 350° F. Brown lamb as directed, add onion, garlic, seasonings, and water; reduce heat to 212° F. and simmer 2–2½ hours until tender. Make gravy and serve.

All versions above: about 580 calories per serving.

Braised Lamb Roast with Avgolemono Sauce: Brown and simmer lamb until tender, using basic method above. When making gravy, omit flour-stock paste. Add the 3 cups stock to kettle and bring to a simmer. Beat 3 egg yolks lightly, add the juice of 1 lemon, and slowly beat in 1 cup hot stock; return all to kettle. Simmer, stirring constantly, 1–2 minutes but do not boil. Serve over lamb as you would gravy. About 585 calories per serving.

Braised Lamb Roast with Tomato Sauce:
Brown lamb, add onions and seasonings,
but substitute ⅓ cup tomato juice for the
water; simmer as directed until tender.
When making gravy, use 1 (8-ounce) can
tomato sauce and 2 cups stock and
reduce flour to ¼ cup. About 590
calories per serving.

Braised Lamb Roast with Vegetables:
Prepare basic recipe above and, when
lamb has only ¾ hour longer to cook,
add 2 dozen peeled whole baby carrots,
12 peeled new potatoes, and 12 small
peeled turnips. Sprinkle with 1 teaspoon
salt, add ½ cup additional stock, cover,
and continue simmering until meat and
vegetables are tender. Lift meat to a hot
platter, wreathe with vegetables, and
keep warm. Prepare gravy as directed.
About 730 calories per serving.

CHARCOAL SPIT-ROASTED BREAST OF LAMB

Makes 6 servings

6 pounds lean breast of lamb

Marinade:

2 cups dry red wine
2 cloves garlic, peeled and crushed
1 medium-size yellow onion, peeled and
* sliced thin*
1 teaspoon powdered rosemary
¼ teaspoon pepper

Place lamb in a large, shallow bowl; mix
marinade, pour over lamb, cover, and
marinate 24 hours in refrigerator.
Prepare a moderate charcoal fire.* Lift
meat from marinade and weave spit in
and out of ribs to balance; tighten
holding forks. Attach spit to rotisserie
and roast 7″–8″ from coals 1 hour,
basting frequently with strained
marinade. Lower spit 1″–2″ nearer
coals and roast 20–30 minutes longer,
basting, until tender and richly browned.
About 470 calories per serving.

VARIATION:

**Greek-Style Spit-Roasted Breast of
Lamb:** Omit marinade; instead, mix the
following basting sauce: ¼ cup melted
butter or margarine, 2 tablespoons olive

oil, 2 cloves garlic, crushed, and 2
tablespoons lemon juice. Spit-roast breast
as above, basting every 15–20 minutes.
Season with salt and pepper before
serving. About 500 calories per serving.

APRICOT-GLAZED STUFFED BREAST OF LAMB

Makes 4 servings

*1 (1¾-pound) breast of lamb (have
  butcher crack ribs to simplify carving)*

Stuffing:

¼ cup minced onion
½ cup diced celery
½ cup coarsely chopped piñon nuts
3 tablespoons butter or margarine
¼ cup dried currants
½ cup diced dried apricots
¼ cup uncooked rice
¾ cup water
1 tablespoon minced parsley
1 tablespoon dry white wine

Glaze:

¼ cup dried apricots
1½ cups water

Preheat oven to 350° F. Carefully make
a pocket in lamb breast by inserting a
small sharp knife at one end and freeing
meat from ribs; repeat on opposite end
so pocket runs length of breast. For
stuffing, stir-fry onion, celery, and nuts in
butter in a large, heavy skillet 8–10
minutes over moderate heat until golden.
Mix in fruits and rice and stir-fry 2–3
minutes. Add water, cover, and simmer
8–10 minutes until all moisture is
absorbed. Mix in parsley and wine and
cool to room temperature. Meanwhile,
simmer glaze ingredients, uncovered,
about 15–20 minutes; purée at low speed
in an electric blender and add enough
water to bring measure to 2 cups. Fill
lamb breast with stuffing, poking it into
all corners; toothpick shut and lace with
fine string to seal. Place breast in a
shallow roasting pan, pour in glaze, and
bake uncovered 2 hours, basting with
glaze every 20 minutes. Remove
toothpicks and lacings and serve. To
carve, cut straight across between ribs.
About 600 calories per serving.

SPIT-ROASTED WINE-STEEPED LAMB CHUNKS

Makes 4 servings

¼ cup olive or other cooking oil
½ cup dry red wine or red wine vinegar
¼ teaspoon thyme
⅛ teaspoon seasoned pepper
2½–3 pounds boned leg of lamb, cut in 2" chunks
1 teaspoon salt
Watercress sprigs (garnish)

Mix oil, wine, thyme and pepper in a large bowl. Add lamb, toss well to mix, cover, and chill 8 hours or overnight, turning lamb in marinade 2 or 3 times. Drain off marinade and reserve. Arrange lamb on spit by skewering each chunk through the middle; avoid crowding. Attach spit to rotisserie and broil 25–30 minutes for rare, 30–35 for medium, 40–45 for well done. Meanwhile, add ½ teaspoon salt to marinade and heat uncovered to simmering. Keep hot and baste lamb 2–3 times during cooking. Transfer lamb to a heated platter, sprinkle with remaining salt, sprig with cress, and serve.

VARIATIONS:

Skewered Minted Lamb: Omit thyme from marinade and add 2 tablespoons finely chopped fresh mint or 1 tablespoon dried mint, ⅓ cup firmly packed light brown sugar, and 1 teaspoon finely grated lemon rind. Proceed as recipe directs.

Garlic Skewered Lamb: Add 2 cloves garlic, peeled and crushed, and 1 tablespoon finely grated onion to marinade and proceed as directed. (*Note:* For a subtle difference of flavor, vary wine used in marinade: Burgundy, rosé, sauterne, and dry sherry or Madeira are all good.)

All versions: about 520 calories per serving.

TURKISH LAMB SHISH KEBABS

Developed by early travelers who would spear chunks of meat and warm them over campfires, shish kebabs are today sophisticated international fare. They can be made of beef, lamb, ham, venison, chicken, liver, even lobster, shrimp, or scallops. Broil them in the oven or, better yet, over a charcoal fire. Makes 6 servings

Marinade:

1 cup olive oil
½ cup lemon juice
2 cloves garlic, peeled and crushed
¼ teaspoon pepper
1 teaspoon oregano

Kebabs:

4 pounds boned leg of lamb, cut in 1½" cubes
3 sweet green peppers, cored, seeded, and cut in 2" squares
1 pound small white onions, peeled and parboiled
1 pound medium-size mushrooms, wiped clean and stemmed
3 large, firm tomatoes, quartered (do not peel or core)
1 teaspoon salt

Mix marinade in a large bowl, add lamb, toss to mix, cover, and chill 8 hours or overnight, turning lamb 2 or 3 times. Drain off marinade and reserve. Alternate lamb, green peppers, and onions on skewers, beginning and ending with lamb; for best results, put mushrooms and tomatoes on separate skewers (so they won't overcook). Add ½ teaspoon salt to marinade and brush some of it over vegetables. Arrange lamb skewers on a broiling rack or, if you have the necessary gadget, attach to rotisserie spit. Broil 3"–4" from heat 15–20 minutes for rare, 20–25 for medium, and 25–30 for well done, turning frequently so kebabs cook evenly and brushing occasionally with marinade. About 10 minutes before meat is done, lay mushroom and tomato skewers on broiler rack, brush with marinade, and broil, turning frequently, until lightly browned. Sprinkle meat with remaining salt and serve kebabs with boiled rice, bulgur wheat, or Bulgur Pilaf.

VARIATIONS:

Charcoal-Broiled Shish Kebabs: Prepare a moderately hot charcoal fire* and broil kebabs 4″ from coals, using times given above as a guide.

Beef Kebabs: Substitute sirloin or top round for the lamb and broil about 5 minutes less than times given above for rare, medium, or well done.

All versions: about 685 calories per serving.

ROAST LAMB REVISITED

(How to Use Up Leftovers)

⊠ CRISPY BREADED LAMB SLICES

Makes 2 servings

¼ cup unsifted flour
¼ cup ice water
1 egg, lightly beaten
4 thick slices leftover roast lamb
⅓ cup toasted, seasoned bread crumbs
2 tablespoons cooking oil

Blend flour and water until smooth, add egg and mix well but do not beat. Dip lamb slices in batter, then in crumbs to coat evenly and thickly; let stand on rack at room temperature 5 minutes. Sauté lamb about 3–4 minutes on each side in oil in a skillet over moderate heat, turning frequently until golden brown. Reduce heat to low and cook 1–2 minutes longer. Serve with Tartar, Whipped Horseradish, or Quick Lemon-Caper Sauce. About 515 calories per serving (without sauce).

LAMB AND EGGPLANT CASSEROLE

A very good way to use up leftover roast lamb.
Makes 4 servings

2 small yellow onions, peeled and chopped fine
1 clove garlic, peeled and crushed
2 tablespoons cooking oil
1 medium-size eggplant, peeled and cut in rounds ¼″ thick
1½ teaspoons salt

1 (1-pound 4-ounce) can Italian plum tomatoes (do not drain)
¼ teaspoon pepper
½ cup uncooked rice
8 medium-thick slices leftover roast lamb, trimmed of fat
2 tablespoons minced parsley

Stir-fry onions and garlic in oil in a deep, flameproof 2½-quart casserole over moderate heat 8 10 minutes until golden. Layer eggplant into casserole, working onion mixture into spaces between slices. Sprinkle with ½ teaspoon salt. Spoon tomatoes over eggplant, sprinkle with ½ teaspoon salt and ¼ teaspoon pepper. Cover and simmer slowly 30 minutes until eggplant is tender. Sprinkle in rice and top with lamb, pressing slices down slightly into mixture underneath; sprinkle with remaining salt. Cover and simmer 20 minutes; uncover and sprinkle with parsley. To serve, place 2 lamb slices on each plate and top with spoonfuls of rice-eggplant-tomato mixture. About 450 calories per serving.

¢ CURRIED LAMB LEFTOVERS

Makes 2 servings

2 tablespoons butter, margarine, or cooking oil
1 large yellow onion, peeled and minced
1 small tart apple, peeled, cored, and coarsely chopped
1 clove garlic, peeled and crushed
2 teaspoons curry powder
2 tablespoons dried lentils
1 cup canned tomatoes (include liquid)
1 cup hot water
1 teaspoon salt
1½ cups lean leftover cooked lamb, cut in ½″ cubes

Heat butter in a saucepan over moderate heat 1 minute, add onion and sauté about 8 minutes until golden. Add apple, garlic, and curry powder and stir-fry 1 minute. Add all remaining ingredients, reduce heat to low, cover, and simmer about 45 minutes, stirring frequently. Serve hot over boiled rice and accompany, if you like, with chutney and chopped scallions. About 515 calories per serving.

¢ LEFTOVER LAMB PILAF

Makes 4 servings

1 cup uncooked rice
1 large yellow onion, peeled and minced
2 tablespoons butter or margarine
2 cups chicken or beef broth
1 teaspoon salt
⅛ teaspoon pepper
⅓ cup seedless raisins
2 cups coarsely chopped, lean leftover
   roast lamb
2 tablespoons cooking oil
1 cup leftover gravy or canned beef
   gravy
2 tablespoons tomato paste
¼ teaspoon ginger
1 clove garlic, peeled and crushed
½ teaspoon seasoned salt

In a 2-quart saucepan stir-fry rice and onion in butter over moderate heat 3–4 minutes until rice is pale golden. Add broth, salt, pepper, and raisins, partially cover, and simmer about 20 minutes until rice is barely tender and all liquid absorbed. Meanwhile brown lamb lightly in oil over moderate heat, add all remaining ingredients, cover, and simmer until rice is tender. Toss lamb mixture into rice, using 2 forks. Serve with chutney. About 560 calories per serving.

ARTICHOKES STUFFED WITH LAMB

Makes 6 servings

6 large globe artichokes, parboiled and
   drained

Stuffing:

2 cups ground leftover cooked lamb
1 medium-size yellow onion, peeled and
   minced
2 tablespoons cooking oil
1 cup soft white bread crumbs
1 egg, lightly beaten
⅓ cup leftover gravy or chicken or beef
   broth
2 tablespoons minced parsley
1 teaspoon salt
⅛ teaspoon pepper
1 tablespoon lemon juice

Topping:

½ cup coarse white bread crumbs tossed
   with 2 tablespoons melted butter or
   margarine

Preheat oven to 325° F. Remove chokes from artichokes,* then arrange artichokes upright and close together in an ungreased casserole. Brown lamb and onion in oil in a heavy skillet over moderate heat 10–12 minutes; off heat mix in remaining stuffing ingredients; fill artichoke centers and top each with buttered crumbs. Pour hot water around artichokes to a depth of 1"; cover and bake 45–50 minutes. Serve with Hollandaise Sauce. About 315 calories per serving (without sauce).

¢ LAMB AND LASAGNE CASSEROLE

Makes 6 servings

1 (1-pound) can tomato sauce
1 (6-ounce) can tomato paste
1 cup hot water
1½ teaspoons salt
¼ teaspoon pepper
2 teaspoons oregano
2 teaspoons basil
1 clove garlic, peeled and crushed
1 medium-size yellow onion, peeled and
   chopped fine
3 cups ground, lean cooked lamb
1 cup cottage cheese or ricotta cheese
½ cup sour cream
½ pound lasagne noodles, cooked by
   package directions and drained
¼ cup grated Parmesan cheese

In a saucepan mix tomato sauce, paste, water, salt, pepper, herbs, garlic, onion, and lamb. Simmer uncovered, stirring occasionally, ½ hour. Preheat oven to 350° F. Combine cottage cheese and sour cream. In an 8" or 9" square greased baking dish layer in noodles and meat sauce, beginning and ending with noodles and adding dabs of cottage cheese mixture on each sauce layer. Sprinkle with Parmesan and bake, uncovered, 30 minutes; raise temperature to 400° F. and bake 10 minutes longer to brown. Cut in squares and serve. About 480 calories per serving.

SAVORY LAMB BURGERS

A good leftover dish.
Makes 2 servings

*1 cup coarsely ground, lean leftover
    roast lamb*
*2 scallions, chopped fine (include green
    tops)*
1 medium-size dill pickle, chopped fine
*1 (2-ounce) can mushrooms, drained and
    chopped fine*
1 tablespoon chili sauce
½ teaspoon salt
⅛ teaspoon pepper
¼ teaspoon prepared horseradish
¼ cup coarse cracker crumbs
*1 tablespoon light cream or leftover
    gravy*
2 tablespoons butter or margarine

Mix lamb with all remaining ingredients
except butter. Shape into 2 patties,
cover, and chill 1 hour. Melt butter in a
skillet over moderate heat, add lamb
patties, and sauté 8–10 minutes, turning
frequently until browned on both sides
and heated through. About 390 calories
per serving.

⚔ ¢ THRIFTY SCOTCH BROTH

Makes 6–8 servings

*2 medium-size yellow onions, peeled and
    coarsely chopped*
*3 medium-size carrots, peeled and cut in
    small dice*
*½ medium-size rutabaga, peeled and cut
    in small dice*
½ cup medium pearl barley, washed
3½ quarts cold water
*Leftover lamb roast, leg or shoulder
    bone with a little meat attached*
4 teaspoons salt
¼ teaspoon pepper
1 tablespoon minced parsley

Place all ingredients except parsley in a
large (at least 1½-gallon) kettle, cover,
and simmer 1½–2 hours. Cut meat from
bones in small pieces and return to kettle.
Stir, taste for salt, and adjust as needed.
Sprinkle with parsley and serve. About
210 calories for each of 6 servings, 160
calories for each of 8 servings.

Some Additional Ways to Use Up Leftover Roast Lamb

Lamb and Zucchini Casserole (4
servings): Stir-fry 3 cups sliced zucchini
with ½ cup chopped onion, ¼ cup
minced sweet green pepper, and 1 crushed
clove garlic in 3 tablespoons olive oil in
a large, heavy skillet 8–10 minutes over
moderate heat until golden. Add 2 cups
canned tomatoes, 1 teaspoon salt, and ¼
teaspoon each oregano and pepper and
simmer, uncovered, 10 minutes. Stir in 2
tablespoons flour blended with 3
tablespoons cold water and heat, stirring,
until thickened. Place 1 cup cubed
cooked lamb in a greased 1½-quart
casserole, spread ½ vegetable mixture on
top, and sprinkle with ½ cup grated
Cheddar cheese. Add another 1 cup
cubed lamb, the remaining vegetable
mixture, and ½ cup grated cheese. Top
with ½ cup butter-browned bread crumbs
and bake, uncovered, 20 minutes at
350° F. until bubbly. About 570 calories
per serving.

¢ Lamb and Lima Stew (4 servings):
Brown 2 cups cubed cooked lamb in
2 tablespoons bacon drippings or butter
with 1 medium-size chopped onion 8–10
minutes in a heavy saucepan. Add
1 (10-ounce) package frozen baby lima
beans, 1 (1-pound) can tomatoes,
1 teaspoon salt, and ¼ teaspoon each
thyme, basil, and pepper. Cover and
simmer 30–40 minutes, stirring
occasionally, until beans are tender.
About 370 calories per serving.

¢ Lamb and Black-Eyed Pea Salad
(4 servings): Place 2 cups each diced
cooked lamb and cold, cooked, drained
black-eyed peas in a bowl. Add 2
tablespoons each minced parsley and
onion and dress with a good garlic,
herb, or Italian dressing. Let stand
30 minutes, toss again, and serve.
About 375 calories per serving.

Shepherd's Pie: See Shepherd's Pie Variation in the beef section.

Lamb and Vegetable Pie:
Lamb Stuffed Vegetables:
Roast Lamb Hash:
Yukon Stew:
} Follow recipes given in Some Additional Ways to Use Up Leftover Roast Beef, substituting lamb for beef.

Sliced Cold Lamb: Slice lamb about ¼" thick, trim of fat, and top with any recommended cold sauce (see Sauces, Gravies, and Seasonings for Roast Lamb).

Sliced Hot Lamb: Slice lamb about ¼" thick, trim off fat, and layer into an ungreased shallow casserole. Add just enough hot sauce to cover (see Sauces, Gravies, and Seasonings for Roast Lamb), cover with foil, and heat 20 minutes at 350° F. If you prefer, warm lamb in sauce about 5 minutes in a covered skillet over moderately low heat.

To Make the Most of Very Small Amounts: Follow suggestions given for beef, substituting lamb for beef.

Lamb Chops and Steaks

The choice is far broader than most of us suspect, and so is the price range. Rib and loin chops are the T-bones and porterhouse of the lamb world. Far better buys are the meatier arm and blade chops cut from the shoulder and lamb steak, which is cut from the leg. (*Note:* Mutton chops and steaks are the same except that they are slightly larger and less tender.) Here, then, are some of the popular varieties:

Loin chops (plain or kidney—with the lamb kidney in the center of the chop)
Rib chops (plain, double, or Frenched— with the meat stripped from the rib ends and paper frills slipped on as decoration)

Noisettes (trimmed eye of loin or rib)
Sirloin chop (the equivalent of sirloin steak)
Shoulder chops (arm, blade, boneless, Saratoga—boned and rolled)
Leg steak
Cube steak (knitted together from lamb trimmings)

How to Cook

Amount Needed: Allow ⅓–½ pound boneless chops or steaks per person, ½–¾ pound of the bone-in. Loin and rib chops are best cut 1"–1½" thick, others ¾"–1".

General Preparation for Cooking: Peel fell from outer fat and trim fat to about ⅛"; slash at 1" intervals to prevent curling. If meat seems moist, wipe with a damp cloth so it will brown well. Rub with pepper, if you like, also garlic and/ or compatible herb (see Sauces, Butters, and Seasonings for Lamb Chops and Steaks) but not salt—it draws moisture to surface and prevents browning. Let chops or steaks stand at room temperature 1½–2 hours if convenient.

To Panfry (Sauté): Especially good for noisettes, cube and leg steaks, shoulder chops. Heat 1–2 tablespoons butter or cooking oil in a heavy skillet over moderately high heat about 1 minute, add chops and brown well on both sides, turning frequently with tongs. Cube steaks will take only 3 minutes altogether, noisettes 5–8, leg steaks and shoulder chops 8–12, depending upon whether you like pinkish or well-done meat. Season and serve.

VARIATION:

Panfried Lamb Chops or Steaks with Minute Sauce: After cooking chops or steaks, transfer to a heated platter and keep warm. Drain all but 1 tablespoon drippings from skillet and add 2 tablespoons butter, 1 tablespoon hot water, 1 teaspoon Worcestershire sauce, and ½ teaspoon lemon juice. Heat 1 minute, swirling mixture round, spoon over meat, and serve.

To Panbroil: Recommended for loin, rib, arm, blade, and sirloin chops, also leg steaks. If chops seem very lean, lightly grease or salt skillet to keep meat from sticking. Heat over moderately high heat ½–1 minute, add chops and cook, uncovered, using times below as a guide. Turn frequently with tongs and pour off drippings as they accumulate. Season and serve.

To Broil: Recommended for the same cuts as panbroiling. Preheat broiler; line broiler pan with foil to eliminate messy clean-ups; lightly grease rack. Place chops on rack, fat edges toward back to prevent spattering. Adjust height and broil to desired doneness using times in Lamb Chop and Steak Broiling Chart as a guide. Turn chops only once during cooking, using tongs. Season and serve.

APPROXIMATE TOTAL PANBROILING TIMES (IN MINUTES)

Chop Thickness	Rare	Medium Rare	Medium	Well Done
1"	5–7	8–9	10–12	12–14
1½"	7–8	9–10	12–13	14–16
2" (English chop)	8–9	10–12	13–15	16–18

LAMB CHOP AND STEAK BROILING CHART

Times (for chops or steaks at room temperature) are *approximate* because shape of chop, amount of fat and bone affect cooking time; outdoors, wind and temperature do too.

Oven Broiling

Cut	Thickness	Oven or Fire Temperature	Distance from Heat	Approximate Minutes per Side for Rare	Medium	Well Done
Loin, rib, and sirloin chops; 2" English chops	1"	Broil	2"	4–5	6	7
	1½"	Broil	2"	6	7	8
	2"	Broil	3"	8	9	10–12
Arm and blade chops; leg steaks	¾"	Broil	3"	Not recommended	5	6–7
	1"	Broil	3"		6	8–10
Mutton rib and loin chops	1"	Broil	3"	Not recommended	8	9–10
	1½"	Broil	3"		10	12–14

Charcoal Broiling

Cut	Thickness	Oven or Fire Temperature	Distance from Heat	Rare	Medium	Well Done
Loin, rib, and sirloin chops; 2" English chops	1"	Hot	4"	5–6	7	8
	1½"	Hot	4"	7	8–9	10
	2"	Moderately hot	5"	8–10	10–12	12–14
Arm and blade chops; leg steaks	¾"	Moderately hot	4"	Not recommended	6	7–8
	1"	Moderately hot	4"		7	10
Mutton rib and loin chops	1"	Moderately hot	4"	Not recommended	10	11–12
	1½"	Moderately hot	5"			13–15

VARIATION:

Planked Chops: Especially good for 1"–1½" thick rib or loin chops. Preheat broiler and prepare plank (see Planked Steak for details). Place chops close together on plank (cover any exposed areas of wood with foil to prevent charring) and broil 2" from heat 4–5 minutes. Remove from broiler, season lightly with salt and pepper, and turn. Pipe a border of Duchess Potatoes around chops and brush lightly with Egg Glaze. Return to broiler and broil 4–5 minutes longer. Serve on plank, topping each chop with a dab of Maître d'Hôtel Butter. Garnish with broiled mushroom caps and/or tomato halves.

To Charcoal Broil: Recommended for the same cuts as panbroiling. Prepare charcoal fire.* For steaks or chops 1"–1½" thick it should be hot (350–75° F. on grill thermometer) or of an intensity to make you remove your hand from grill level after saying, "Mississippi" 3 times. For 2" chops or steaks it should be moderately hot (325° F.) or 4 Mississippis by the hand test. Spread glowing coals over fire bed to equal area of meat to be broiled, adjust height, and broil according to Lamb Chop and Steak Broiling Chart (above). Place a drip pan under meat to reduce flare-ups. Season and serve.

To Braise: Especially good for lamb and mutton arm, blade and leg chops about 1" thick. Brown chops 2–3 minutes on a side over moderately high heat in a large heavy skillet lightly brushed with butter, drippings or oil; pour off all drippings. Season chops with salt and pepper, add a small amount of water (⅓ cup is about right for 4 chops), cover and simmer slowly over low heat or cover and bake in a preheated 350° F. oven ¾–1 hour until tender.

For Extra Savor: For the ⅓ cup water, substitute beer or dry vermouth; tomato juice, sauce or canned tomatoes; beef broth or onion soup; apple cider or juice or All-Purpose Barbecue Sauce.

Some Variations on Braised Lamb Chops

All quantities based on enough chops for 4 persons

Italian-Style: Rub chops with a cut clove garlic, then brown as directed. Season, add 1 cup meatless spaghetti sauce, cover, and simmer or bake until tender.

With Vegetables: Brown chops as directed and arrange in an ungreased roasting pan. Add 4 peeled, quartered potatoes, 4 peeled, quartered turnips, 12 peeled small white onions, and 2 stalks celery cut in 2" lengths. Add 1 cup beef broth, sprinkle with 1 teaspoon salt and ¼ teaspoon pepper, cover, and ovenbraise as directed above ¾–1 hour until chops and vegetables are tender. Baste 1–2 times during cooking. Sprinkle with 1 tablespoon minced parsley just before serving.

With Wine and Herbs: Rub chops with a cut clove garlic and ¼ teaspoon rosemary or with ¼ teaspoon each basil and oregano. Brown as directed, season with salt and pepper, then cover and braise in ½ cup dry red or white wine until tender.

To Bake: Recommended for arm, blade, or leg chops cut ½"–¾" thick. Preheat oven to 350° F. Place steaks in a foil-lined shallow baking pan, sprinkle each with ⅛ teaspoon salt or garlic salt and a pinch pepper. Bake, uncovered, 30 minutes, turn sprinkle again with salt and pepper, and bake, uncovered, 30 minutes longer until tender.

VARIATION:

Baked Barbecued Lamb Chops: Omit seasonings, cover chops with 1 cup All-Purpose Barbecue Sauce or any favorite barbecue sauce, and bake, uncovered, as directed.

To Test Lamb Chops and Steaks for Doneness:

Bone-In Cuts: Make a small slit near bone to determine color of lean. Rare lamb will be rosy and juicy, medium faintly tinged with pink, and well-done gray-brown.

Boneless Cuts: Make a small cut in center of lean and check color.

How to Give Lamb Chops and Steaks Extra Flavor

Before Panfrying, Panbroiling, Broiling or Charcoal Broiling:
— Marinate chops or steaks 4 hours in refrigerator in All-Purpose Barbecue Sauce or any good garlic, herb, or Italian dressing. Let come to room temperature in marinade, pat dry, and cook. If broiling or grilling, brush often with marinade.
— Brush both sides of chops or steaks with a little soy sauce or Teriyaki Sauce and let stand about 15 minutes.
— Rub both sides of chops or steaks with a little olive oil and crushed garlic and let stand 15–20 minutes.
— Rub both sides of chops or steaks with a little crushed fresh gingerroot and garlic and let stand 15–20 minutes.

During Broiling or Charcoal Broiling:
— While broiling arm or blade chops, leg chops or steaks, brush often with the following mixture: ¼ cup melted butter, 2 tablespoons cooking oil, 1 tablespoon lemon juice, and ¼ teaspoon garlic powder.
— While charcoal broiling, toss any of the following onto the coals: 2–3 sprigs fresh sage, basil, or rosemary or 1 tablespoon of the dried; a dozen bay leaves or 1 tablespoon cracked juniper berries.
— During last minutes of broiling or grilling, brush lightly with Herb, Chive, Garlic, Lemon, or Anchovy Butter.

After Panfrying or Panbroiling:
— Serve with Tomato Sauce and garnish platter with Stuffed Tomatoes.

— Lamb Chops Financière: Transfer chops to platter. Drain drippings from skillet, add ¼ cup Madeira, and cook and stir until reduced by half. Add 1 cup Rich Brown Sauce and bring to a boil. Serve chops on heart-shaped slices of butter-browned toast and top with sauce.

— Lamb Chops à la Mexicaine: Transfer chops to platter. To skillet add 1 cup Rich Brown Sauce, 2 tablespoons each red wine vinegar and slivered orange rind (orange part only) and simmer 2 minutes. Spoon over chops and serve, garnished with Baked Bananas.

Some Simple Garnishes for Lamb Chops

Artichoke Bottoms: boiled and buttered; filled with Macédoine of Vegetables, buttered green peas, boiled flageolets, navy or pea beans.

Brussels Sprouts: boiled and buttered.

Mushrooms: sautéed button mushrooms, mushroom caps, or sliced mushrooms; Mushroom Caps Stuffed with Hazelnuts.

Onions: Glazed Onions; Pan-Braised Onions; Stuffed Onions.

Peaches and Pears: broiled halves; halves filled with red currant or mint jelly; pickled, spiced, or brandied peaches or pears.

Potatoes: Duchess, Shoestring, French-Fried; Parsleyed, Herbed, Lemon-Glazed, or Danish-Style New Potatoes.

Tomatoes: raw cherry tomatoes; Broiled Tomatoes, Stuffed Tomatoes.

Some Classic Garnishes for Lamb Chops

À la Bretonne: Arrange chops in a circle on a large platter and fill center with boiled flageolets, navy or pea beans and sprinkle with minced parsley and any pan drippings.

À la Niçoise: Arrange chops in a circle on a large platter, fill center with Château Potatoes, and surround with buttered French-style green beans and whole sautéed cherry tomatoes (do not peel). Pass Tomato or Portuguese Sauce.

Dubarry: Place chops on an ovenproof serving dish and surround with boiled cauliflowerets. Top cauliflower with Mornay Sauce, sprinkle with Parmesan cheese, and broil 2"–3" from heat 2–3 minutes until freckled with brown.

Parmentier: Garnish chops with Hashed Brown Potatoes.

Talleyrand: Transfer chops to a platter and keep warm. To skillet add 2 tablespoons butter, ¼ pound chopped mushrooms, and 4 diced truffles; stir-fry 2–3 minutes over moderate heat until mushrooms are golden. Add ¼ cup dry sherry and 1 cup heavy cream and heat, stirring, 1–2 minutes. Pour over chops. Fill center of platter with thick Onion Sauce.

À la Clamart:
Chasseur: } see Some Classic Ways to Serve Tournedos.
Rossini:

SAUCES, BUTTERS, AND SEASONINGS FOR LAMB CHOPS AND STEAKS

Sauces		Butters		Seasonings, Herbs, Spices		Condiments
Béarnaise	Périgueux	Anchovy	Maître	Basil	Mustard	Chutney
Bontemps	Portugaise	Bercy	d'hôtel	Bay leaf	Oregano	Mustard
Bordelaise	Réform	Chive	Noisette	Dill	Paprika	Soy sauce
Brown	(mutton	Garlic	Parsley	Garlic	Parsley	Teriyaki
Chateaubriand	chops)	Herb	Shallot	Ginger	Rosemary	sauce
Choron	Romaine	Lemon	Tomato	Juniper	Sage	Worces-
Madeira	Soubise			berries	Tarragon	tershire
	Tomato			Lemon	Thyme	sauce
				Marjoram		
				Mint		

ENGLISH MIXED GRILL

Makes 2 servings

2 loin lamb chops, cut 1¼" thick and trimmed of excess fat, or 2 filet mignons, cut 1¼" thick
2 slices bacon (optional)
2 medium-size pork sausages
1 cup water
⅓ cup melted butter or margarine
½ pound calf's liver, cut in 1" strips
4 lamb kidneys, trimmed of fat, membranes, and cores
6 medium-size mushroom caps, wiped clean
2 medium-size ripe tomatoes, halved crosswise (do not peel)
1¼ teaspoons salt (about)
¼ teaspoon pepper
2 small pats Maître d'Hôtel Butter
2 sprigs watercress (garnish)

Preheat broiler. Coil "tail" around each chop and secure with a toothpick. Or, if using filets, wrap a bacon slice around each and secure. Simmer sausages uncovered in the water 8 minutes; drain and pat dry on paper toweling. Arrange chops or steaks on a lightly greased broiler rack and brush with melted butter. Broil 3" from heat for 3 minutes. Arrange sausages, liver, kidneys, mushrooms, and tomatoes around chops, brush with melted butter, and broil 5 minutes. Sprinkle all with half the salt and pepper, then turn. Brush again with melted butter and broil 2–3 minutes for a rare mixed grill, 3–4 minutes for medium, and 5–6 for well done; sprinkle with remaining salt and pepper. To serve, arrange chops in center of a heated platter, top each with a pat of Maître d'Hôtel Butter, and surround with sausages, liver, kidneys, mushrooms, and tomatoes. Garnish with cress and accompany with Shoestring Potatoes or French-Fried Potatoes. (*Note:* These ingredients just fit comfortably on a standard broiler rack, so if you want to double the recipe, you'll have to use 2 broilers or broil the components separately.) About 1040 calories per serving (without Maître d'Hôtel Butter or garnish).

SHERRIED LAMB CHOPS STUFFED WITH MUSHROOMS AND TRUFFLES

Makes 4 servings

4 rib lamb chops, cut 1¼" thick and trimmed of excess fat
1 slice bacon
1 cup finely chopped mushrooms
1 tablespoon fine, dry white bread crumbs
2 truffles, coarsely chopped
1 teaspoon minced parsley
¼ teaspoon minced garlic
1 teaspoon butter or margarine
½ teaspoon salt
⅛ teaspoon pepper
¼ cup medium dry sherry
¼ cup beef broth

Starting at the rib bone, cut a pocket in each chop. Prepare stuffing: Fry bacon in a small skillet until crisp, drain on paper toweling, crumble, and reserve. Pour off all but 1 tablespoon bacon drippings, then stir-fry mushrooms 2–3 minutes over moderately high heat until golden. Off heat, mix in bacon, crumbs, truffles, parsley, and minced garlic; spoon into chop pockets (no need to use toothpicks or skewers to seal in stuffing). Brown chops over moderately high heat in a skillet brushed with butter as follows: 5–6 minutes on each side for rare, 6–7 for medium, 7–8 for well done. Use tongs for turning chops and drain off fat as it accumulates. Sprinkle with salt and pepper, transfer to a hot platter and keep warm. Drain drippings from skillet, add sherry and broth, and heat, stirring to scrape up any brown bits. Boil, uncovered, until reduced by half, pour over chops, and serve. About 300 calories per serving.

LAMB CHOPS WITH ZUCCHINI EN PAPILLOTE

Makes 4 servings

4 shoulder lamb chops, cut ½" thick and trimmed of excess fat
1 teaspoon celery salt
⅛ teaspoon pepper
1 teaspoon minced chervil
2 medium size yellow onions, peeled and sliced thin
4–6 medium-size zucchini, quartered lengthwise
4 medium-size carrots, peeled and cut in strips 2" long and ½" wide
4 small potatoes, peeled and sliced ¼" thick (optional)
1 teaspoon salt

Preheat oven to 350° F. Cut 4 (16") squares of heavy duty foil. Place a chop on each, sprinkle with celery salt, pepper, and chervil; top with vegetables and sprinkle evenly with salt. Wrap tight and bake on a baking sheet 50–60 minutes until chops are tender. Serve in packets. About 415 calories per serving.

GROUND LAMB

Unquestionably the best cut of lamb to grind is shoulder because it has a good ratio of lean to fat, good flavor and texture. Second best are trimmings from shank and neck. Because lamb is finely grained, it needs to be ground one time only unless you want an unusually compact loaf or patty; if so, have the lamb ground twice. Like other ground meats, ground lamb is highly perishable and should be refrigerated until you're ready to use it. Ground lamb is leaner than most ground beef, more delicate in flavor, and usually slightly lower in cost.

⊠ LAMB BURGERS

To be at their best, lamb burgers should be cooked until medium or well done. Makes 3–4 servings

1 pound ground lean lamb shoulder
1 teaspoon salt
⅛ teaspoon pepper

Lightly shape lamb into 3 plump or 4 slim patties and cook by one of the methods below; season with salt and pepper just before serving.

To Panfry (Sauté): Recommended for lean meat. Brown patties uncovered in 1–2 tablespoons cooking oil, butter, margarine, or drippings in a large, heavy skillet over moderately high heat. Plump patties will take about 5 minutes on a side for medium and 6 for well done, thin patties about 1 minutes less per side for each degree of doneness. To keep patties juicy, avoid spanking or pressing down with a pancake turner as they cook. About 365 calories for each of 3 servings, 270 calories for each of 4 servings.

⚖ **To Panbroil:** Recommended for dieters, also for meat heavily flecked with fat. Lightly brush a large, heavy skillet with oil or sprinkle with salt; heat 1 minute over moderately high heat, add burgers, and brown, uncovered, using cooking times given for panfrying. Pour off drippings as they accumulate. About 265 calories for each of 3 servings, 200 calories for each of 4 servings.

⚖ **To Broil:** Recommended for dieters and fatty meat. Preheat broiler. Broil patties 3″ from heat on a lightly greased broiler rack. Plump patties will take about 6 minutes on a side for medium and 7–8 for well done, thin patties about 1 minute less per side in each instance. About 265 calories for each of 3 servings, 200 calories for each of 4 servings.

⚖ **To Charcoal Broil:** Recommended for plump patties only. Prepare a moderately hot charcoal fire.* Broil patties on a lightly greased grill 4″ from heat about 4–5 minutes on a side for medium and 6–7 for well done. About 265 calories for each of 3 servings.

To Braise: Brown patties quickly in a lightly greased large, heavy skillet over high heat, turn heat to low, and pour in 1–1½ cups liquid (water; dry red, rosé or white wine; broth or gravy; tomato juice, soup, or sauce; cream of mushroom, celery, or asparagus soup). Cover and simmer slowly 15–20 minutes. Serve patties with cooking liquid. About 365 calories for each of 3 servings (if braised with water), 270 calories for each of 4 servings.

Some Variations on Lamb Burgers
(all amounts based on recipe above)

Lamb and Sausage Burgers: Mix ½ pound cooked, drained sweet or hot sausage meat with lamb; shape into 6 patties, cook and season as directed. (Makes 6 patties.) About 355 calories per patty.

⚖ **Smothered Barbecue Burgers:** Mix lamb with 1 cup soft white bread crumbs, ½ cup milk, 1 teaspoon salt, ¼ teaspoon chili powder, and ⅛ teaspoon pepper. Form into 6 patties and brown quickly in a lightly greased large, heavy skillet over high heat. Turn heat to low. Mix 2 tablespoons each Worcestershire sauce and sugar with 1 cup cider vinegar, ½ cup ketchup, and 1 tablespoon minced onion; pour over patties, cover, and simmer 10–15 minutes. Serve patties topped with plenty of sauce. (Makes 6 patties.) About 240 calories per patty.

Lamb Burgers in Foil: Shape lamb into 4 patties; place each on a large square of heavy foil, top with thinly sliced potatoes, carrots, celery, and onion, season with salt and pepper, and wrap tight. Place on a baking sheet and bake 45–50 minutes at 350° F. until vegetables are tender; or grill 5″–6″ from a moderately hot charcoal fire 30–40 minutes, turning packages every 10 minutes. (Makes 4 servings.) About 480 calories per serving.

Hawaiian Lamb Burgers: Shape lamb into 4 patties and panbroil 3 minutes on each side; remove from skillet; drain off drippings. Drain syrup from 1 (13½-ounce) can pineapple chunks, add cold water to make 1 cup liquid, and blend in 2 tablespoons cornstarch. Add ¼ cup each cider vinegar and dark brown sugar, 2 tablespoons soy sauce, and ¼ teaspoon ginger. Pour into skillet and heat, stirring until thickened. Add patties, pineapple chunks, and 1 cup minced sweet green pepper. Cover and simmer 15 minutes. Top patties with sauce and flaked coconut and serve. (Makes 4 servings.) About 365 calories per serving (without coconut), 440 calories per serving (with coconut).

Russian Lamb Burgers: Mix ¼ cup minced onion and 2 tablespoons minced chives into lamb; shape into 4 patties, cook and season as directed. When serving, top each patty with a generous dollop of sour cream and 1 tablespoon red or black caviar. (Makes 4 servings.) About 315 calories per serving.

Crowned Lamb Burgers: Shape, cook and season lamb burgers as directed. Just before serving, top with any of the following:

– Minced ripe or pimiento-stuffed green olives
– Applesauce and chopped fresh mint
– Horseradish, sour cream, and capers
– Cranberry sauce and/or crushed pineapple
– Pickled red cabbage or minced pickled beets and sour cream
– Sautéed minced onions and mushrooms
– Sautéed minced sweet green and/or red peppers and onions

Note: See 20 Variations on Hamburgers; all can be made with ground lamb instead of beef.

¢ MOUSSAKA

Traditionally, *moussaka* has three layers —fried eggplant, a spicy meat mixture, and a custard-like sauce—but thrifty cooks often slip in an extra layer of leftover vegetables. The list of ingredients is long, but if you begin at the bottom and work up, you shouldn't have any trouble preparing this Greek and Turkish favorite.
Makes 8–10 servings

Bottom Layer:
2 medium-size eggplants
1 teaspoon salt
⅔ cup olive oil (about)
¼ cup fine dry bread crumbs

Middle Layer:
4 medium-size yellow onions, peeled and minced
2 cloves garlic, peeled and crushed
3 tablespoons olive oil
2 pounds ground lamb shoulder or beef chuck
¼ cup tomato paste
½ cup dry red wine
½ teaspoon oregano
¼ teaspoon cinnamon
1 bay leaf, crumbled
2 teaspoons salt
⅛ teaspoon pepper
¼ cup minced parsley
¼ cup fine dry bread crumbs
2 eggs, lightly beaten
¼ cup grated Parmesan cheese

Top Layer:
6 tablespoons butter or margarine
6 tablespoons flour
⅛ teaspoon nutmeg
⅛ teaspoon white pepper
1 teaspoon salt
3 cups milk
¼ cup grated Parmesan cheese
4 egg yolks, lightly beaten

Peel thin strips of skin lengthwise from eggplants every ½″ so you have a striped effect, then cut in rounds ½″ thick. Sprinkle rounds with salt and weight down between paper toweling 1 hour. Meanwhile, lightly oil a 14″×10″×2″ pan and pat crumbs over bottom; set aside. Now begin middle layer: stir-fry onions and garlic in oil in a large, heavy skillet over moderate heat 8–10 minutes until golden. Add meat and brown, breaking up any chunks, 10–15 minutes. Turn heat to low, mix in all but last 4 ingredients, and simmer uncovered, stirring occasionally, 15 minutes. Off heat, stir in parsley and crumbs; cool to room temperature and mix in eggs and Parmesan. By now, eggplants should be ready to fry. Brown rounds well on both sides, doing only 3–4 at a time and using 2 tablespoons oil—no more—for each batch; drain on paper toweling and arrange in pan in a double layer, fitting rounds as close together as possible. Spread meat sauce evenly over all. (Note: Recipe can be prepared to this point a day ahead and refrigerated. Bring to room temperature before proceeding.) Now begin final layer: melt butter in top of a double boiler over direct heat, blend in flour, nutmeg, pepper, and salt. Add milk and heat, stirring, until thickened; remove from heat. Mix Parmesan with yolks, then stir in a little of the hot sauce; return all to sauce, set over simmering water, and heat, stirring constantly, 2 minutes. Cool to room temperature. Preheat oven to 325° F. Spread sauce over meat and bake moussaka, uncovered, 1½ hours until topping is puffy and lightly browned. Remove from oven, let stand 10 minutes, then cut in large squares and serve. About 820 calories for each of 8 servings, 655 calories for each of 10 servings.

BRAISED LAMB PATTIES IN TOMATO PURÉE

Makes 4 servings

Patties:

1 pound ground lean lamb shoulder
1 medium-size yellow onion, peeled and minced
1 egg, lightly beaten
½ cup soft white bread crumbs
2 tablespoons minced parsley
1 teaspoon paprika
1 teaspoon salt

⅛ teaspoon pepper
½ cup flour (for dredging)
3 tablespoons butter or margarine (for browning)

Tomato Purée:

3 large ripe tomatoes, peeled, cored, seeded, and minced
⅓ cup apple cider
1 tablespoon minced parsley
¾ teaspoon salt
⅛ teaspoon pepper

Preheat oven to 350° F. Mix all but last 2 patty ingredients and shape into 4 patties. Dredge in flour and brown both sides in butter in a heavy skillet over moderately high heat. Transfer patties to an ungreased shallow baking pan and set aside. In same skillet, simmer all purée ingredients about 5 minutes, stirring often, to blend flavors. Pour over patties and bake, uncovered, 30–35 minutes until bubbly. About 405 calories per serving.

¢ LEBANESE LAMB PIE (KIBBEH)

Makes 6–8 servings

Top and Bottom Layers:

2 cups bulgur wheat
2⅔ cups simmering water
1 medium-size yellow onion, peeled and minced
1 pound finely ground lamb shoulder
1 teaspoon salt

Middle Layer:

1 medium-size yellow onion, peeled and minced
1 clove garlic, peeled and crushed
2 tablespoons olive oil
1 pound finely ground lamb shoulder
1 teaspoon salt
½ teaspoon cinnamon
⅛ teaspoon cardamom
Pinch pepper
1 cup coarsely chopped piñon nuts
½ cup dried currants or coarsely chopped raisins

Topping:

¾ cup melted butter or margarine
Yogurt

Preheat oven to 350° F. Soak bulgur wheat in water 20 minutes and drain well. Put onion and lamb through fine blade of meat grinder several times until reduced to paste; grind bulgur wheat until smooth and pasty and knead into lamb mixture along with salt. Pat ½ of mixture over the bottom of an oiled 13″×9″×2″ pan and set aside. For middle layer, stir-fry onion and garlic in oil 8–10 minutes in a large, heavy skillet over moderate heat; add lamb, salt, spices, and pepper and heat, stirring, about 10 minutes, breaking up any clumps of meat. Off heat, mix in nuts and currants; spread over wheat layer in pan. Pat remaining wheat mixture over all and press down firmly. Score top in a crisscross pattern and drizzle butter over surface. Bake, uncovered, 30–40 minutes until lightly browned. Cool slightly, cut into large squares, and served topped with dollops of yogurt. About 975 calories for each of 6 servings, 730 calories for each of 8 servings.

⚖ DOLMA (STUFFED GRAPE LEAVES)

Brined or preserved grape leaves can be found in Greek, Turkish, or gourmet groceries.
Makes 6 servings

1 (1-pound) jar grape leaves
1 quart warm water (about)
Juice of 2 lemons

Stuffing:
1 pound ground lean lamb shoulder
½ cup uncooked rice
½ cup minced yellow onion
1 teaspoon salt
¼ teaspoon allspice
⅛ teaspoon pepper
⅓ cup water
1 tablespoon minced parsley

If grape leaves seem salty, rinse well in warm water; sort leaves, selecting the most perfect to stuff; save the rest. Mix stuffing ingredients thoroughly. Place a grape leaf vein side up and stem end toward you on the counter; near the base put 1 heaping teaspoon stuffing. Fold right and left sides over stuffing and roll up—rolls should be quite tight so they won't unroll during cooking. Repeat until all stuffing is gone (you should have about 4 dozen rolls). Place a cake rack in a large, heavy kettle (it should be about 9″ in diameter) and on it make a bed of the imperfect leaves. (These are merely to cushion the *dolma* and are discarded after cooking.) Arrange rolls very close together in neat rows in a single layer on top of leaves, place a dinner plate on top to weight down slightly. Pour in enough warm water to reach plate, cover, and simmer 35 minutes. Pour in lemon juice, re-cover, and simmer 15 minutes longer. When serving, pass lemon slices. About 230 calories per serving.

¢ LAMB STUFFED CABBAGE ROLLS

Makes 4–6 servings

1 medium-size cabbage, trimmed of coarse outer leaves
1½ quarts boiling water
1 teaspoon salt
2 cups tomato juice or sauce
1 bay leaf
1 clove garlic, peeled

Stuffing:
1 cup crumbled hard rolls
⅓ cup cold water
1 pound ground lean lamb shoulder
1 medium-size yellow onion, peeled and minced
1 egg, lightly beaten
1 teaspoon grated lemon rind
1 teaspoon chili powder (optional)
1½ teaspoons salt
¼ teaspoon pepper

Preheat oven to 325° F. Boil cabbage in salted water 3–4 minutes until leaves are pliable; cool in a colander under cold running water until easy to handle, drain well, core, and remove 12 whole outer leaves (save rest to use later). Cut base of large vein from each leaf and discard; spread leaves flat. For stuffing, soak rolls in water 5 minutes, squeeze as dry as possible, and mix with remaining stuffing ingredients. Put a spoonful stuffing on center of each leaf, fold sides in, and roll loosely; fasten with toothpicks. Layer rolls in an ungreased Dutch oven, add tomato juice, bay leaf, and garlic, cover, and bring to a boil. Transfer to oven and bake 1 hour, uncover and bake ½ hour longer. (*Note:* If using tomato sauce, check consistency and add a little water if too thick.) Remove garlic and bay leaf before serving. About 370 calories for each of 4 servings, 245 calories for each of 6 servings.

VARIATIONS:

¢ **Cabbage Rolls and Sauerkraut:** Prepare rolls as directed and layer into Dutch oven with 1 (1-pound 14-ounce) drained can sauerkraut. Add tomato juice, bay leaf, and garlic and bake as directed. About 405 calories for each of 4 servings, 270 calories for each of 6 servings.

¢ **Nova Scotia Cabbage Rolls:** Omit rolls, water, egg, and chili powder from stuffing and add ½ cup rolled oats and ¾ cup sour cream. After peeling off the 12 leaves, coarsely chop remaining cabbage. Prepare and arrange cabbage rolls in Dutch oven as directed, top with chopped cabbage and tomato juice (omit bay leaf and garlic). Cook as recipe directs. About 630 calories for each of 4 servings, 420 calories for each of 6 servings.

¢ HERBED LAMB LOAF

Makes 4–6 servings

1¼ pounds ground lean lamb shoulder
1 medium-size yellow onion, peeled and
   minced
⅓ cup minced green pepper
2 eggs
2 cups packaged stuffing mix
1 tablespoon minced parsley
¼ teaspoon thyme
½ teaspoon salt
⅛ teaspoon pepper
¾ cup lamb, beef, or chicken stock

Preheat oven to 350° F. Mix all ingredients well, using your hands, and shape into a loaf in a greased shallow roasting pan. Bake, uncovered, ¾–1 hour until loaf is firm to the touch and nicely browned. Serve as is or with Tomato Sauce. About 495 calories for each of 4 servings, 330 calories for each of 6 servings.

¢ CURRIED LAMB AND CARROT LOAF

Makes 6 servings

1½ pounds ground lean lamb shoulder
1 cup very finely grated carrots
1 medium-size yellow onion, peeled and
   minced
½ cup minced celery
3 tablespoons minced chutney
1½ cups corn bread stuffing mix
1 medium-size tart apple, peeled, cored,
   and minced
2 eggs
⅓ cup water
¼ cup minced parsley
2 tablespoons curry powder
1¼ teaspoons salt
¼ teaspoon cinnamon
⅛ teaspoon pepper

Preheat oven to 350° F. Mix all ingredients thoroughly with your hands and pack into a greased 9″×5″×3″ loaf pan. Bake, uncovered, 50–60 minutes until loaf pulls from sides of pan and is firm in center. Pour off any drippings. Let loaf stand upright in pan 5 minutes before inverting and turning out. About 420 calories per serving.

LAMB BALLS EN BROCHETTE

Makes 6 servings

1 cup soft white bread crumbs
⅔ cup evaporated milk
1 egg, lightly beaten
¾ teaspoon garlic salt
¾ teaspoon celery salt
¼ teaspoon pepper
¼ teaspoon cinnamon (optional)
1½ pounds ground lean lamb shoulder
12 cherry tomatoes
6 preserved kumquats
12 mushroom caps, wiped clean

Basting Sauce:

¼ cup cider vinegar
¼ cup salad oil

2 tablespoons dark brown sugar
1 tablespoon steak sauce

Soak crumbs in milk 5 minutes; mix with egg, seasonings, and lamb. Shape into 1½" balls and chill several hours. Preheat broiler. Arrange lamb balls on long skewers, not close together. Alternate tomatoes, kumquats, and mushroom caps on separate skewers. Mix basting sauce. Broil lamb balls 4" from heat, turning and basting frequently, for 10 minutes. Add vegetable skewers and continue broiling 5 minutes, turning and basting lamb and vegetables frequently with sauce. This version and variation: about 430 calories per serving.

VARIATION:

Use 1½ teaspoons minced fresh mint in lamb ball mixture; omit cinnamon.

¢ TURKISH LAMB BALLS
BAKED IN TOMATO SAUCE

Makes 4–6 servings

Lamb Balls:

1½ pounds ground lean lamb shoulder
1 medium-size yellow onion, peeled
  and minced
1 clove garlic, peeled and crushed
½ cup cracker meal
2 eggs, lightly beaten
1¼ teaspoons salt
¼ teaspoon cinnamon
⅛ teaspoon anise
⅛ teaspoon pepper
3 tablespoons olive oil

Sauce:

1 (8-ounce) can tomato sauce
1 cup water

Preheat oven to 350° F. Mix all lamb ball ingredients except oil, using your hands, and shape into 2" balls. Brown balls well on all sides in oil in a large, heavy skillet over moderately high heat; drain on paper toweling. Transfer balls to an ungreased shallow 2-quart casserole. Mix tomato sauce and water, pour over balls, and bake uncovered

30–45 minutes until bubbly. Serve with rice or boiled potatoes. About 555 calories for each of 4 servings (without rice or potatoes), 370 calories for each of 6 servings.

¢ CRISPY LAMB-STUFFED
BULGUR BALLS

Good as an hors d'oeuvre as well as a main course.
Makes 4 servings

1 cup bulgur wheat
2 cups boiling water
¾ teaspoon salt

Stuffing:

¼ pound ground lean lamb shoulder
1 small yellow onion, peeled and minced
1 tablespoon olive oil
1 tablespoon minced parsley
¾ teaspoon salt
⅛ teaspoon pepper

Coating:

2 eggs beaten with 2 tablespoons milk
⅔ cup unsifted flour

Shortening or cooking oil for deep fat
  frying

Stir bulgur wheat into boiling salted water, cover, and simmer about 8 minutes until all moisture is absorbed. Remove from heat and leave covered while you prepare filling. Stir-fry lamb and onion in olive oil about 10 minutes over moderate heat until lamb is no longer pink. Off heat mix in remaining stuffing ingredients; cool slightly. To roll balls, knead 1 heaping tablespoon bulgur until it holds together, shape into a small ball, then with your index finger, make a well in center; spoon in about ¼ teaspoon stuffing and reshape into a ball to seal. Repeat until all bulgur is used up—you should have about 2 dozen balls; refrigerate them while you heat shortening. When shortening reaches 365° F. on deep fat thermometer, dip balls in egg, roll in flour, then fry 3–4 minutes until golden brown. Drain on paper toweling and serve piping hot. About 340 calories per serving.

The Lesser Cuts of Lamb
(See Lamb and Mutton Chart)

"Lesser," in this case, means less expensive and less appreciated, but no less tender or delicious when properly prepared:

Neck slices and chunks
Shanks (fore and hind)
Riblets
Stew meat (the best comes from the shoulder)

¢ **ECONOMY LAMB STEW**

A rich brown lamb and vegetable stew that costs very little to make.
Makes 4 servings

2–2½ pounds lean neck of lamb, cut in
1½" cubes, or 2 lamb shanks, each
cracked into 3 pieces
2 tablespoons cooking oil
3 medium-size yellow onions, peeled
and coarsely chopped
6–8 medium-size carrots, peeled and
halved crosswise
2 medium-size turnips, peeled and
quartered
½ teaspoon minced garlic
½ teaspoon salt
¼ teaspoon pepper
1 teaspoon basil
½ teaspoon parsley flakes
2 cups water
¼ cup unsifted flour blended with ¼ cup
cold water

Brown meat well, a few pieces at a time, in oil in a large, heavy kettle over moderately high heat; transfer to a bowl. In the same kettle, stir-fry onions until golden, about 8–10 minutes. Return lamb to kettle, add all remaining ingredients except flour-water paste, cover, and simmer 1¾ hours until lamb is tender. Mix in flour paste and heat, stirring, until thickened. Serve over boiled noodles with a crisp green salad. About 420 calories per serving.

VARIATION:

¢ **Economy Lamb and Potato Stew:**
Prepare stew as directed and about ¾ hour before it is done add 4–5 peeled and halved potatoes. Cover and continue cooking until potatoes and lamb are both tender. About 525 calories per serving.

CASSOULET (FRENCH-STYLE BAKED BEANS WITH LAMB, PORK, AND GOOSE)

If the following recipe seems long and involved, it is. There just isn't any short cut to a good cassoulet. There are dozens of versions, all based on dried white beans cooked with a combination of meats. Here's one of the best.
Makes 8 servings

1½ pounds dried white beans (Great
Northern or navy), washed and sorted
3 quarts cold water (about)
½ pound salt pork with rind left on
1 carrot, peeled
1 medium-size yellow onion, peeled and
stuck with 6 cloves
1 bouquet garni* and 3 peeled cloves
garlic, tied in cheesecloth
1 pound boned pork shoulder, cut in
1" cubes and trimmed of excess fat
1 pound boned lamb or mutton shoulder,
cut in 1" cubes and trimmed of
excess fat
2 tablespoons lard, goose, duck, or
bacon drippings
2 medium-size yellow onions, peeled and
minced
1 ham shank with some meat attached
(leftover is fine)
1 meaty pork hock
1 clove garlic, peeled and crushed
1 cup beef broth
½ cup tomato purée
½ pound Kielbasa, Cotechino, or other
garlicky pork sausage
½ pound mild pork sausage
½ preserved goose (leg and breast,
obtainable in gourmet shops) or
½ roast goose or 1 small roast duckling
2 teaspoons salt (about)
¼ teaspoon pepper (about)
1 clove garlic, peeled and halved
1 cup soft white bread crumbs
2 tablespoons melted goose, duck, or
bacon drippings

Soak beans in 1½ quarts water overnight or use the quick method.* Drain, measure soaking water, and add enough cold water to total 1½ quarts. Simmer beans, covered, with salt pork, carrot, onion, and cheesecloth bag 1 hour; do not drain. In another kettle brown pork and lamb, a few pieces at a time, in lard over moderately high heat; transfer to a bowl. Stir-fry onions in remaining drippings 8–10 minutes over moderate heat until golden. Return meat to kettle, add ham shank, hock, garlic, broth and tomato purée. Cover and simmer ½ hour, add sausages, and simmer, covered, ½ hour longer. Off heat add preserved goose, scraped of excess fat, and let stand 15 minutes. Preheat oven to 300° F. Cut all meats from bones in bite-sized pieces; slice sausages ½" thick. Discard whole onion, carrot, and cheesecloth bag. Cut rind from salt pork; slice rind thin and dice the salt pork. Taste beans for salt and pepper and adjust as needed. Rub the inside of a deep 6-quart earthenware casserole or bean pot with the cut garlic, add salt pork rind, then layer in beans, salt pork, and all meats, beginning and ending with beans and sprinkling each layer with a little pepper. Pour in meat and bean broths. (*Note:* You may prepare recipe to this point early in the day or even the day before. Cover and refrigerate until about 4 hours before serving; let come to room temperature.) Top with crumbs and drizzle with melted drippings. (*Note:* For a less rich mixture, skim fat from broths before adding.) Bake, uncovered, 1½–2 hours until a brown crust forms on top of beans. Serve with a crisp green salad and a dry red or rosé wine. About 990 calories per serving.

NAVARIN OF LAMB PRINTANIER (FRENCH LAMB STEW)

Makes 6 servings

2 pounds boned lean lamb shoulder, cut in 1½" cubes
½ pound lean neck of lamb (with bones), cut in 1½" cubes
2 tablespoons butter or margarine
1 tablespoon sugar

3 tablespoons flour
3 cups meat stock or a ½ and ½ mixture of chicken broth and water
¾ cup tomato purée
2 teaspoons salt
¼ teaspoon pepper
1 bouquet garni,* tied in cheesecloth
1 clove garlic, peeled and crushed
12 small white onions, peeled
12 baby carrots, peeled
12 small new potatoes, peeled
4 turnips, peeled and quartered
1 pound fresh green peas, shelled, parboiled, and drained
½ pound fresh green beans, halved, parboiled, and drained

Preheat oven to 325° F. Brown lamb, a few pieces at a time, in butter in a large, heavy skillet over moderately high heat. Sprinkle last batch with sugar and let brown slightly, then transfer all to a Dutch oven. Lightly brown flour in skillet, slowly stir in stock, tomato purée, 1 teaspoon salt, and the pepper, and heat, stirring, until smooth; pour over meat. Add *bouquet garni* and garlic, cover, and bake 45 minutes. Add onions, re-cover, and bake 15 minutes. Add carrots, potatoes, and turnips, pushing them down into gravy, sprinkle with remaining salt, cover, and bake 30 minutes. Add peas and beans, cover, and bake 5–7 minutes. Ladle into a deep platter, pass the gravy separately, and serve with crusty bread. About 640 calories per serving.

LAPP LAMB STEW

Makes 8 servings

4 pounds boned lean lamb shoulder, cut in 1½" cubes
2 tablespoons butter or margarine
3½ cups water
4 stalks fresh dill
2 scallions, trimmed of roots
2 tablespoons cider vinegar
½ teaspoon salt
⅛ teaspoon pepper
¼ cup unsifted flour blended with ⅓ cup cold water

Brown lamb, a few cubes at a time, in

butter in a large, heavy kettle over moderately high heat; transfer to paper toweling to drain. Return lamb to kettle, add all remaining ingredients except flour-water paste, cover, and simmer slowly 1½–2 hours until lamb is tender. Lift lamb from liquid and set aside. Put liquid, scallions, and dill through a food mill or purée, a little at a time, in an electric blender at low speed. Return liquid to kettle, raise heat to moderate, mix in flour-water paste, and heat, stirring constantly, until thickened and smooth. Return lamb to kettle and heat uncovered, stirring occasionally, about 5 minutes longer. Serve hot with boiled new potatoes. About 540 calories per serving (without potatoes).

LAMB AND DHAL (DRIED PEA) CURRY

Makes 6–8 servings

3 pounds boned lamb shoulder, trimmed
    of excess fat and cut in 1" cubes
1 tablespoon curry powder
1 pint yogurt
¼ cup butter or margarine
3 medium-size yellow onions, peeled and
    sliced thin
2 cloves garlic, peeled and crushed
1 pound yellow split peas
10 thin slices gingerroot
1 green chili pepper, sliced thin
    (include seeds)
2 sticks cinnamon
6 cloves
1 tablespoon powdered cumin
1 tablespoon crushed coriander seeds
2 teaspoons powdered cardamom
2 teaspoons powdered turmeric
½–1 teaspoon cayenne pepper
    (depending on how hot you like your
    curry)
1 (6-ounce) can tomato paste
1 quart water
1½ teaspoons salt

Place lamb in a large bowl, sprinkle with curry, and toss to mix; stir in yogurt and let stand at room temperature 1 hour. Melt butter in a large, heavy kettle over moderate heat, add onions

and garlic, and sauté, stirring, 12–15 minutes until golden brown. Add all but last 3 ingredients and heat, stirring, 2–3 minutes. Stir in meat-yogurt mixture, tomato paste, water, and salt, cover, and simmer slowly 1½–2 hours until lamb is tender, stirring now and then. Serve over boiled rice and accompany with chutney. About 880 calories for each of 6 servings, 660 calories for each of 8 servings (without rice).

VARIATION:

Lamb Curry: Prepare as directed but omit split peas and reduce water to 2 cups. About 650 calories for each of 6 servings, 490 calories for each of 8 servings.

GREEK LAMB AND ARTICHOKE STEW

Makes 6 servings

3 pounds boned lamb shoulder, trimmed
    of excess fat and cut in 1" cubes
2 tablespoons olive oil
2 medium-size yellow onions, peeled
    and coarsely chopped
3 tablespoons flour
3 cups water
1 (9-ounce) package frozen artichoke
    hearts, thawed
Juice of 1 lemon
1 tablespoon minced mint
½ teaspoon salt
⅛ teaspoon pepper
3 egg yolks, lightly beaten

Brown lamb a little at a time in the oil in a large, heavy kettle over moderately high heat; drain on paper toweling. Stir-fry onions in drippings 10 minutes until lightly browned. Return lamb to kettle, sprinkle with flour, and toss to mix; add water, cover, adjust heat so mixture stays at a slow simmer, and cook 1½ hours until lamb is nearly tender. Add artichokes and lemon juice, cover, and simmer 20–25 minutes until tender. Mix in mint, salt, and pepper, taste and adjust seasonings if necessary. Ladle as much liquid from kettle as possible, briskly stir a little into egg yolks, then combine with remaining liquid; drizzle over lamb and artichokes, shake kettle slightly to distribute mixture, but do not stir. Serve over boiled rice. About 640 calories per serving (without rice).

COUSCOUS (NORTH AFRICAN LAMB STEW)

Couscous is not only the name of the cooked wheat cereal over which the stew is served but the name of the stew itself.

Makes 4–6 servings

Stew:

2 pounds boned lamb shoulder, cut in 1" cubes
2 tablespoons olive oil
2 tablespoons butter or margarine
1 (2½-pound) broiler-fryer, cut up
3 medium-size yellow onions, peeled and coarsely chopped
1 clove garlic, peeled and crushed
4 ripe tomatoes, peeled, cored, seeded, and coarsely chopped
½ teaspoon thyme
¼ teaspoon saffron
1 bay leaf, crumbled
6 cups chicken broth or water
2 medium-size sweet green peppers, cored, seeded, and cut in thin strips
6 medium-size carrots, peeled and cut in 1" chunks
1 tablespoon salt (about)
¼ teaspoon pepper
1 (1-pound 4-ounce) can chick-peas, drained
2 cups coarsely grated or sliced cabbage

Couscous:

1 recipe Boiled Couscous (Note: Use 1 cup of stew liquid and 3 cups chicken broth.)

Hot Sauce:

1 cup stew liquid
2 tablespoons tomato paste
1 teaspoon paprika
½–1 teaspoon crushed dried hot red chili peppers
¼ teaspoon coriander
⅛ teaspoon cumin

Prepare stew first: Brown lamb in oil and butter in a large, heavy kettle over moderately high heat; drain on paper toweling. Also brown and drain chicken. Add onions and garlic to kettle and brown 10–12 minutes; add tomatoes and herbs and cook and stir 2–3 minutes. Return lamb and chicken to kettle, add broth, green peppers, carrots, salt, and pepper, cover, and simmer ½ hour. Remove chicken, cover, and refrigerate. Continue cooking stew until lamb is nearly tender, about ½ hour. Remove 2 cups liquid from kettle and refrigerate (1 cup will be used for the Boiled Couscous, 1 for the Hot Sauce). Cool stew, chill, and skim off fat. (*Note:* Recipe can be prepared to this point a day or 2 in advance.) When ready to proceed, boil couscous as directed, using 1 cup of the reserved kettle liquid. Return chicken to stew and add chick-peas and cabbage. Place boiled couscous in a large colander lined with a triple thickness of dampened cheesecloth, set over kettle à la double boiler, cover with foil, and simmer stew slowly ½–¾ hour until meats are very tender and flavors well blended. Meanwhile, mix remaining reserved cup kettle liquid with all hot sauce ingredients and keep warm over lowest heat. To serve: Mound boiled couscous on a large platter and top with stew. Pass hot sauce separately, letting each person take as much or little as he wants. About 1520 calories for each of 4 servings, 1015 calories for each of 6 servings.

¢ RAGOUT OF MUTTON AND BEANS

Makes 6 servings

¼ pound salt pork, cut in small dice
2 pounds boned mutton shoulder, trimmed of excess fat and cut in 1" cubes
2 large yellow onions, peeled and minced
1 teaspoon sugar
1 tablespoon flour
1 cup cold water
1 clove garlic, peeled and crushed (optional)
1 pound dried white, pink, or red kidney beans, boiled 1 hour but not drained

Preheat oven to 325° F. Brown salt pork in a large, heavy skillet over moderate heat, lift out with slotted spoon and reserve. Brown mutton, a few pieces at a time, in drippings over moderately high heat, transfer to a bowl. Sauté onions in same skillet 8–10 minutes until golden; sprinkle with sugar and allow to caramelize slightly. Blend flour into skillet, add water, and heat, stirring, 1–2 minutes. Off heat return meat and salt pork to skillet. Place beans and their cooking liquid in an ungreased 1-gallon casserole or bean pot, add skillet mixture, and stir lightly. Cover and bake 1½–2 hours until meat is tender. About 575 calories per serving.

MOROCCAN LAMB BAKE

Makes 4 servings

⅔ cup seedless raisins
⅓ cup dry sherry
¼ cup chicken or beef broth
2 pounds boned lean lamb shoulder, cut in 1" cubes
3 tablespoons olive oil
2 medium-size yellow onions, peeled and coarsely chopped
1 clove garlic, peeled and crushed
1 teaspoon salt
½ teaspoon crushed hot red chili peppers
½ teaspoon turmeric
½ teaspoon oregano
¼ teaspoon thyme
⅛ teaspoon cinnamon
2 large ripe tomatoes, peeled, cored, seeded, and chopped
2 tablespoons minced parsley

Topping:

1 (4-ounce) package frozen French-fried onion rings, cooked by package directions
½ cup toasted blanched almonds
½ cup toasted blanched filberts

Soak raisins in sherry and broth 1 hour at room temperature. Preheat oven to 350° F. Brown lamb well in oil in a large, heavy skillet over moderately high heat; add onions and garlic and stir-fry about 8 minutes until lightly browned. Add remaining ingredients except parsley and topping, bring to a simmer, and stir

in raisins and soaking liquid. Transfer to an ungreased 2-quart casserole, cover tight, and bake 2 hours until tender. Check occasionally and if mixture seems dry add about ¼ cup hot water. When done, stir in parsley and arrange onion rings on top. Mix nuts in a small bowl and let each person scatter some over his portion. Serve with rice. About 975 calories per serving.

¢ IRISH STEW

Prepare this stew early in the day or even a day ahead so flavors will blend and fat can be skimmed off.
Makes 4 servings

5 medium-size potatoes, peeled and halved
2½ pounds lean neck of lamb (with bones)
3 large yellow onions, peeled and sliced thin
4 teaspoons salt
¼ teaspoon white pepper
1 quart cold water
2 tablespoons minced parsley (optional)

Layer potatoes, lamb, and onions into a 4-quart kettle with a tight-fitting lid, beginning and ending with potatoes. Add salt, pepper, and water, cover, and simmer about 2 hours until lamb is tender. Cool and refrigerate, covered, at least 3 hours. When ready to serve, skim fat from surface and discard. Heat stew, covered, over low heat until piping hot. Ladle into heated soup bowls, including plenty of the liquid. Sprinkle with parsley, if you wish, and serve. About 745 calories per serving.

VARIATION:

¢ Irish Stew with Dumplings (traditional in some parts of Ireland): Prepare and chill stew as directed. Skim off fat, then bring to a simmer over low heat. Make Dumplings by recipe, add to stew, cover, and cook as dumpling recipe directs. About 920 calories per serving.

¢ LAMB NECK SLICES BRAISED WITH LIMAS AND CARROTS

Makes 4 servings

3 pounds lamb neck slices, cut 1" thick
and trimmed of excess fat
⅓ cup unsifted flour
1½ teaspoons salt
½ teaspoon pepper
3 tablespoons butter or margarine
1 large yellow onion, peeled and sliced
thin
⅔ cup lamb or beef stock
2 tablespoons dry white wine
1 teaspoon finely grated lemon rind
⅛ teaspoon rosemary
1 (10-ounce) package frozen baby lima
beans (do not thaw)
4 carrots, peeled and sliced thin
1 tablespoon minced parsley

Dredge neck slices in a mixture of flour, salt, and pepper, then brown in butter in a large, heavy skillet over moderately high heat; remove and set aside. Brown onion in drippings 10–12 minutes over moderate heat. Return lamb to skillet, pull onions on top, and add stock, wine, lemon rind, and rosemary. Cover and simmer slowly 35–40 minutes. Break up block of frozen limas by hitting package against edge of counter, scatter limas in and around neck slices, also carrots. Re-cover and simmer slowly 20–25 minutes longer until lamb and vegetables are tender. Sprinkle with parsley and serve. About 590 calories per serving.

¢ NECK OF LAMB IN DILL SAUCE

Makes 4 servings

2½ pounds lean neck of lamb (with
bones), cut in 2" chunks
1 large yellow onion, peeled and
chopped fine
1½ teaspoons seasoned salt
⅛ teaspoon white pepper
1 tablespoon snipped fresh dill, tied in
cheesecloth
3 cups cold water
2 tablespoons butter or margarine
3 tablespoons flour

2 egg yolks, lightly beaten
1 tablespoon lemon juice
1–2 teaspoons snipped fresh dill
(garnish)

Place lamb, onion, seasoned salt, pepper, cheesecloth bag, and water in a 1-gallon kettle, cover, and simmer 1¾–2 hours until lamb is tender. Drain off broth, cool, skim off fat and reserve. Melt butter in a large saucepan over moderate heat, blend in flour, slowly add reserved broth, and heat, stirring constantly, until thickened. Add meat to sauce and simmer, covered, 10 minutes. Blend a little sauce into egg yolks, then return to pan. Heat and stir 2–3 minutes but do not boil. Off heat stir in lemon juice. Taste for salt and pepper and adjust. Sprinkle with remaining dill just before serving. Good with boiled potatoes, crusty bread and asparagus, green peas, or broccoli. About 425 calories per serving.

VARIATION:

¢ **Breast of Lamb in Dill Sauce:** Substitute 3 pounds lean breast of lamb, cut in serving-size pieces, for neck. Proceed as recipe directs but reduce simmering time to about 1½ hours. About 450 calories per serving.

LANCASHIRE HOT POT

Every town in Lancashire, England, has *its* version of Hot Pot. Here's one of the oldest.
Makes 4 servings

2½ pounds lean neck of mutton or
lamb (with bones), cut in 2" chunks
1 sheep's kidney or 2–3 lamb kidneys,
trimmed of fat, membranes, and
cores and sliced ¼" thick (optional)
2 large yellow onions, peeled and
coarsely chopped
5–6 medium-size potatoes, peeled and
sliced ¾" thick
4 medium-size carrots, peeled and cut
in 2" chunks (optional)
1 quart cold water (about)
4 teaspoons salt
¼ teaspoon pepper

Preheat oven to 325° F. Layer lamb,

kidney, onions, potatoes, and carrots in an ungreased deep 4-quart casserole; end with a layer of potatoes arranged as close together as possible. Pour in 3 cups water mixed with salt and pepper, then add enough additional water to come to bottom of potato layer. Cover with a buttered piece of foil. Bake 1 hour, uncover, and bake 1 hour longer until meat is tender and potatoes are browned on top. Serve with pickled red cabbage. About 550 calories per serving.

¢ **BARBECUED LAMB RIBLETS**

Makes 4 servings

3 pounds lamb riblets or spareribs, cut in serving size pieces
1 lemon, sliced thin
2 cups water
1 large yellow onion, peeled and sliced thin
2 tablespoons Worcestershire sauce
2 small cloves garlic, peeled
1 teaspoon salt
¼ teaspoon pepper
¼ cup chili sauce
2 cups barbecue sauce

Place all ingredients but barbecue sauce in a large, heavy kettle, cover, and simmer 1½ hours. Drain (save liquid for soups, gravies, etc.) and arrange riblets in a shallow roasting pan. Pour in barbecue sauce and let stand at room temperature 2 hours, turning ribs occasionally. Preheat oven to 325° F. Bake riblets, uncovered, 45 minutes, basting and turning often in sauce until browned, glazed, and tender.

VARIATION:

¢ **Charcoal Barbecued Lamb Riblets:** Prepare riblets as directed up to point of baking. Meanwhile, prepare a moderately hot charcoal fire.* Lift riblets from barbecue sauce, shaking off excess, and broil 4"–5" from coals, turning and basting frequently, about 20 minutes until browned, glazed, and tender. Watch closely to avoid scorching.

Both versions: about 875 calories per serving.

¢ **ROAST LAMB SHANKS**

Makes 4 servings

4 lamb shanks, each cracked into 3 pieces
1½ teaspoons unseasoned meat tenderizer
2 cloves garlic, peeled and slivered
2 tablespoons melted butter or margarine
2 tablespoons olive or other cooking oil
2 tablespoons lemon juice

Preheat oven to 325° F. Sprinkle shanks evenly with tenderizer and pierce deeply with a fork. Make 4 or 5 slits over meaty part of each shank and tuck in garlic slivers. Place shanks on a rack in a shallow roasting pan; mix butter, oil, and lemon juice and brush over shanks. Roast, uncovered, 1–1¼ hours until tender, brushing frequently with butter mixture. Serve hot with Mint Sauce or Rose Geranium Jelly. About 380 calories per serving.

¢ **CHARCOAL BARBECUED LAMB SHANKS**

Makes 4 servings

4 lamb shanks, each cracked into 3 pieces
Marinade:
½ cup cider vinegar
½ cup bottled thick French dressing
2 tablespoons Worcestershire sauce
2 teaspoons garlic salt
¼ teaspoon pepper
¼ teaspoon liquid gravy browner

Lay shanks in a large, shallow casserole. Blend all marinade ingredients by shaking in a jar; pour over shanks. Cover and refrigerate 4–6 hours, turning shanks 2–3 times. Prepare a moderately hot charcoal fire.* Place each shank on a piece of heavy foil, add 2 tablespoons marinade and wrap tight. Arrange shanks on grill, not too close together, and cook 3" from coals 1¼–1½ hours, turning 3–4 times with tongs. Unwrap 1 shank and test for tenderness—meat should just begin to separate from bone.

If not, rewrap and cook a few minutes longer. When tender, unwrap shanks. Lightly grease grill, place shanks directly on grill, and cover loosely with foil wrappings. Brown 5–7 minutes, turning 1 or 2 times. (*Note:* A low fire is best for the final browning, so scatter the coals if fire seems too hot.) About 390 calories per serving.

¢ BRAISED LAMB SHANKS

Makes 2 servings

2 lamb shanks, each cracked into
* 3 pieces*
2 tablespoons meat drippings or cooking
* oil*
¾ teaspoon salt
½ cup liquid (water, dry white or rosé
* wine, beer, cider, or beef consommé)*
1 bouquet garni,* tied in cheesecloth

Brown shanks well in drippings in a heavy kettle over moderate heat; pour off drippings, add remaining ingredients. Cover and simmer about 1½ hours, turning shanks once or twice, until tender. Or cover and bake about 1½ hours at 325° F. Skim liquid of fat and serve as gravy. About 370 calories per serving.

VARIATIONS:

¢ **Braised Lamb Shanks with Vegetables:** Sauté 1 coarsely chopped yellow onion along with shanks; add 4 carrots, 1 rutabaga and/or 4 turnips, all peeled and cut in large chunks, along with water, then proceed as directed. Increase salt slightly. About 420 calories per serving.

Braised Lamb Shanks with Sour Cream and Capers: Cook shanks as directed and lift to a deep platter. Skim fat from broth, mix in ½ cup sour cream and 2 tablespoons capers. Spoon a little sauce over shanks and pass the rest. About 490 calories per serving.

¢ **Braised Lamb Shanks with Gremolata:** Sauté 1 minced yellow onion along with shanks; add 1 peeled and diced carrot with water and simmer as directed. About 10 minutes before serving, mix Gremolata, which consists of: 1 tablespoon minced parsley, 1 small crushed clove garlic, and 2 teaspoons grated lemon rind; sprinkle over shanks. Thicken broth, if you like, before serving. About 400 calories per serving.

Piñon- and Rice-Stuffed Lamb Shanks: Braise shanks as directed until very tender and bones are loose; cool until easy to handle, then carefully push bones out; save broth. Mix ¾ cup cooked seasoned rice with 1 tablespoon minced parsley, 2 tablespoons coarsely chopped piñon nuts, and 1 minced scallion. Stuff shanks with mixture and arrange in an ungreased shallow baking dish. Add broth and bake, uncovered, 15–20 minutes at 350° F. About 490 calories per serving.

¢ ⚒ BOMBAY LAMB SHANKS

Makes 2 servings

2 small lamb shanks, each cracked into
* 3 pieces*

Marinade:

1 medium-size yellow onion, peeled and
* coarsely chopped*
½ cup yogurt
½ teaspoon curry powder
¼ teaspoon garlic powder
½ teaspoon poppy seeds, crushed in a
* mortar and pestle*
1 teaspoon salt
¼ teaspoon pepper
¼ teaspoon ginger
¼ teaspoon cinnamon
1 tablespoon lemon juice

Place lamb shanks in a large, deep bowl. Blend marinade ingredients in an electric blender at high speed 1 minute, then pour over shanks. Cover and chill 3–4 hours, turning shanks 1 or 2 times. Prepare a moderately hot charcoal fire.* Place each shank on a large square of heavy foil, top with ¼ cup marinade, and wrap tight. Reserve remaining marinade. Lay shanks on grill, not too close together, and cook 3″ from coals 1¼ – 1½ hours, turning 3–4 times with tongs. Unwrap 1 shank and test for tenderness

—meat should begin to separate from bone. If it doesn't, rewrap and cook a little longer. When tender, unwrap shanks and lay directly on grill. Broil 5–7 minutes, brushing occasionally with marinade and turning shanks so they brown evenly. About 250 calories per serving.

PORK

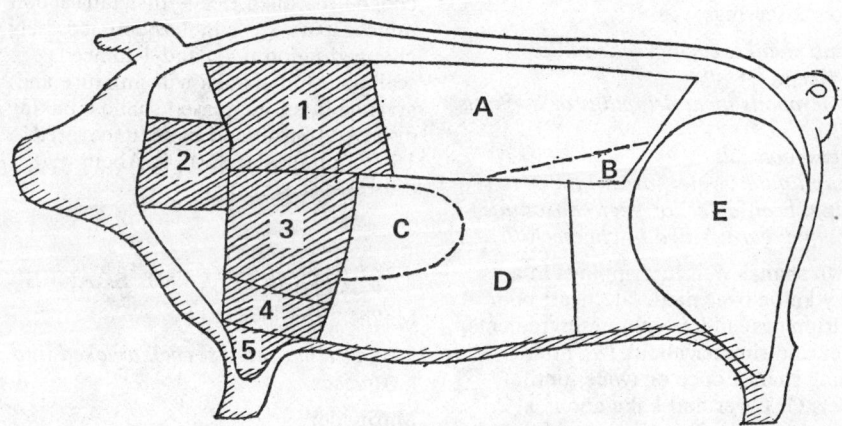

Note: Unshaded parts are the tender cuts. Shaded parts are not-so-tender.

THE TENDER CUTS:
A. LOIN
    Roasts (blade loin, center loin, crown, sirloin)
    Chops (rib, loin, blade, sirloin)
    Canadian bacon
    Back ribs
    Fat back
B. TENDERLOIN
C. SPARERIBS
D. BACON
    Bacon
    Salt pork
E. HAM (LEG)
    Hams (fresh and cured)
    Ham steaks

THE NOT-SO-TENDER CUTS:
1. BOSTON BUTT (SHOULDER)
    Roasts
    Steaks (blade, cube)
    Stew pork
    Ground pork
    Fat back
    Lard
2. JOWL
3. PICNIC
    Roasts (arm, fresh and smoked picnic)
    Steak (arm)
    Stew pork
    Ground pork
    Sausage
4. HOCK
    Fresh and smoked hock
5. FEET
    Fresh pigs' feet (trotters)
    Pickled pigs' feet

II. LOW-COST RECIPES

Minestrone Milanese – Tourtière – Home baked breads

Minestrone Milanese (pages 190-91)

Tourtière (page 373); Country Captain (page 496); and Fisherman's Baked Shells (pages 700-01)

Home Baked Breads and Rolls (pages 940-88)

Thanks to breeders who are producing leaner, trimmer hogs, today's pork has about ⅓ fewer calories and ⅕ more protein than yesterday's. It remains one of our most nutritious meats, also one of the most economical and versatile.

How to Recognize Quality in Pork
The federal grades of pork (US 1, 2, 3, Medium, and Cull) are seldom used because the quality of pork varies less than that of beef, veal, or lamb. To be sure of good quality, look for finely grained, beige-pink lean with some marbling (very young pork will be nearly white with little marbling) and a snowy outer covering of fat. Look, too, for the federal inspector's round seal, which guarantees wholesomeness.

About Cooking Pork
The cardinal rule of pork cookery: *always cook until well done* (this is to kill the microscopic parasites that cause trichinosis, a serious, sometimes fatal illness). Not long ago cookbooks recommended cooking pork to an internal temperature of 185° F., but researchers have now proved that trichinae (the disease causers) are killed at about 140° F. The new recommended internal temperature for pork roasts is 170° F. But, if you prefer ivory-hued pork with juices that run clear, by all means cook to 180° F. *Caution:* Wash hands well after handling raw pork (especially ground pork) and never taste pork until after it is cooked.

Roast Pork

Pork is the most roastable of all meats because almost everything except the head, feet, and tail can be roasted. The choicest roasts come from the loin, the next best from the shoulder and ham.

Loin Roasts: It is possible to buy whole pork loins but not very practical; they are too cumbersome for home ovens. For extra-large parties, it is easier to cook two smaller roasts (side by side) than to tackle one giant.

Center Loin Roast (3–5 pounds): The preferred loin roast because of its sizable tenderloin.

Sirloin Roast (3–4 pounds): Second best; it may contain some tenderloin.

Blade Loin Roast (3–4 pounds): It has the shoulder blade (hence its name) but no tenderloin.

Half Loin Roast (5–7 pounds): Half the loin plus either the sirloin or blade loin.

Rolled Loin (3–5 pounds): Any of the above, boned and rolled.

Crown Roasts: Showy, super deluxe roasts made by removing the backbone from 1 or 2 half loins and shaping into a circle. Rib ends are frenched and garnished with paper frills or small fruits. Butchers sometimes grind the trimmings and pile them in the center of the crown. This ground meat should be removed because it slows roasting (mix with the dressing you're using to stuff the roasted crown, or save for meat loaf). Smallish crowns contain 10–14 ribs, large ones may have 24 or more ribs and weigh 10 pounds or more; all must be specially ordered. To determine the size you need, figure 2 ribs per person.

Tenderloin (¾–1½ pounds): A long, lean muscle equivalent to beef filet or tenderloin. Boneless and luxury priced. Roast *or* braise.

Shoulder Roasts: Meaty, moderately priced cuts of excellent flavor.

Boston Butt (4–6 pounds): A blocky cut from the shoulder of pork. Also called *Boston Shoulder.* It is often available boned and rolled.

Fresh Picnic (5–8 pounds): Also called *Picnic Shoulder;* the lower part of the shoulder; it contains some shank.

Cushion-Style Picnic (3–5 pounds): Boned but not rolled; perfect for stuffing.

Rolled Fresh Picnic (3–5 pounds): Boned and rolled picnic.

Arm Roast (3–5 pounds): The top part of the picnic; it has no shank.

Fresh Hams: Hams are the hind legs of pork, and fresh ones are those that have not been cured and smoked. These make superlative roasts:

Whole Ham (10–14 pounds)
Whole Boneless Ham (7–10 pounds)
Half Hams: Butt Portion (5–7 pounds); Shank Portion (5–7 pounds)

How to Roast Pork

Suitable Cuts: All fresh hams, loin and shoulder roasts. Because tenderloin and crown roasts are such luxurious cuts, there are separate recipes for each.

Amounts Needed: Pork roasts should weigh at least 3 pounds and will be juicier if 4 or more. To figure number of servings, allow ⅓ pound boneless roast per person and ½ pound bone-in roast.

General Preparation for Cooking: To simplify carving of loin roasts, have butcher loosen backbone. With the exception of fresh hams, whose crisp roasted skin some people enjoy, roasts should have any skin removed and the outer fat layer trimmed to ½". If skin is left on ham, score every ½". Let roast stand at room temperature 1½–2 hours if possible. Rub surface, if you like, with a little pepper and, for extra flavor, a cut clove garlic and/or compatible herb (see Sauces, Gravies, and Seasonings for Pork).

Continuous Low Heat Method: Preheat oven to 325° F. Place roast fat side up in a large, shallow roasting pan; all but bone-in loin roasts should be placed on a rack; bone-in loins can be arranged so ribs act as a rack. Insert meat thermometer in center of roast, not touching bone; if roast is stuffed, make sure thermometer is as near center as possible, but in meat, not stuffing. Roast, uncovered, until well done, without adding liquid to pan and without basting (use times in Roast Pork Chart as a guide). Transfer roast to heated platter, let "rest," if you like, 15–20 minutes to allow juices to settle and facilitate carving. Then serve.

Searing Method (recommended for loin roasts only): Preheat oven to 450° F. Insert meat thermometer and place roast in pan as for low heat method (above). Set roast in oven, reduce heat to 350° F. and roast, uncovered, 30–35 minutes per pound or until thermometer registers 170° F. Do not add water and do not baste.

Roast Pork Chart (*opposite*)
Times (for roasts that have stood at room temperature 1½–2 hours, then roasted at a constant 325° F.) are merely approximate because size and shape of cut, proportion of fat and bone, internal temperature before roasting all affect cooking time.
– To roast at 350° F., allow 1–2 minutes less per pound and watch meat thermometer closely.
– For refrigerated roasts, allow 2–3 minutes more per pound.

How to Spit-Roast Pork

Best Cuts: Boned and rolled loin roasts. Small bone-in loins (with backbone removed) can be spit-roasted if carefully balanced and checked frequently for balance during cooking. Not recommended for spit-roasting, except over charcoal, where heat can be closely controlled by raising and lowering spit: hams and shoulder roasts (they are too chunky and/or irregularly shaped to cook evenly).

Amount Needed: Rolled roasts should weigh 4–5 pounds, bone-in roasts at least 3 if they are to be succulent and tender.

General Preparation for Cooking: Trim outer fat to ½" and, if possible, let roast stand at room temperature 1½–2 hours. Season or not, as you like.

In Rotisserie or Oven: Preheat unit. Insert spit lengthwise through center of roast so roast is balanced; tighten holding forks. Insert meat thermometer in center of largest lean muscle, touching neither bone nor the spit. Attach spit to rotisserie

Cut	Weight in Pounds	Approximate Minutes per Pound at 325° F.	Meat Thermometer Temperature
Loin			
Center loin roast	3–5	30	170° F.
Sirloin and blade loin	3–4	40	170° F.
Half loin roast	5–7	35	170° F.
Rolled loin roast	3–5	40–45	170° F.

(*Note:* The following shoulder roasts and fresh hams will be more flavorful if roasted to 185° F.)

Cut	Weight in Pounds	Approximate Minutes per Pound at 325° F.	Meat Thermometer Temperature
Shoulder			
Boston butt	4–6	40	170° F.
Rolled Boston butt	3–4	45–50	170° F.
Fresh picnic	5–8	30	170° F.
Cushion-style picnic	3–5	35	170° F.
Rolled fresh picnic	3–5	40	170° F.
Arm roast	3–5	35–40	170° F.
Fresh Hams			
Whole ham	10–14	25	170° F.
Whole boneless ham	7–10	35	170° F.
Half ham (butt or shank portion)	5–7	30–35	170° F.

and roast 30 minutes per pound for bone-in roasts, 35–40 minutes per pound for rolled roasts. Thermometer should register at least 170° F. and, if you like no traces of pink, 180° F. Remove roast from spit and let "rest" 15–20 minutes before carving.

Over Charcoal: Prepare a moderate charcoal fire toward back of grill.* Balance meat on spit: Loins should be spitted lengthwise, straight through the center; bone-in hams with spit parallel to leg bone; rolled shoulder or hams on the bias. Tighten holding forks. Insert meat thermometer in center of roast, making sure it does not touch spit or bone; also make sure it will not hit anything as spit turns; attach spit to rotisserie. Because pork is rather fat, it is more likely to cause flare-ups than beef, veal, or lamb. To reduce flare-ups: Adjust height of spit so it is 7"–8" from coals, have spit turn away from you, and place a drip pan toward front of grill, where it will catch drips (metal TV dinner trays make dandy drip pans, so does a triple-thick rectangle of heavy foil with its edges turned up). When roast is ½ done, lower spit 1"–2". Roast, using this chart as a guide:

Cut	Weight in Pounds	Approximate Minutes per Pound over a Moderate Fire	Meat Thermometer Temperature
Bone-in loin roasts	3–7	25–35	170° F.
Rolled loin roast	3–5	30–35	170° F.
Boston butt	4–6	35–40	170° F.
Rolled Boston butt	3–4	40	170° F.
Fresh picnic	5–8	25–30	170° F.
Rolled fresh picnic	3–5	35	170° F.
Whole ham	10–14	25–30	170° F.
Whole boneless ham	7–10	30–35	170° F.
Half ham (butt or shank portion)	5–7	30–35	170° F.

VARIATION:

Spit-Barbecued Pork: Marinate roast in refrigerator 8–12 hours in 2 cups All-Purpose Barbecue Sauce, turning occasionally. Lift from sauce and pat dry with paper toweling. Spit-roast as directed, brushing often with barbecue sauce during last ½ hour of cooking.

Some Glazes for Roast Pork

About 30 minutes before roast is done, spread or drizzle any of the following over surface and continue cooking as directed, basting once or twice:
– 1 (8-ounce) can whole or jellied cranberry sauce.
– 1 cup apricot, pineapple, peach, or cherry preserves.
– 1 cup orange, lemon, or ginger marmalade.
– 1 cup black currant, red currant, apple, or cranberry jelly.
– 1 cup maple syrup, honey, or molasses.
– 1 cup firmly packed light or dark brown sugar mixed with ¼ cup sherry, Madeira, port, or fruit juice (cranberry, orange, apricot, apple, pineapple, or grape).
– ½ cup firmly packed dark brown sugar mixed with 1 cup orange juice and 1 tablespoon each lemon juice and prepared spicy brown mustard.
– 1 cup apple juice or cider mixed with ¼ teaspoon each cinnamon, ginger, and cloves.
– ½ cup soy sauce mixed with ¼ cup maple or dark corn syrup and, if you like, 2–3 tablespoons cognac.
– 1–1½ cups beer or stout.
– 1½ cups creamy or crunchy peanut butter.

How to Carve a Pork Arm Roast:
Separate large lean muscles from one another by making cuts at natural divisions and around the bones. Cut each large muscle across the grain into thin slices.

How to Carve Fresh Hams: These are carved in the same way as cured hams (see carving instructions in Ham and Other Cured Pork).

How to Carve a Pork Loin Roast:

If butcher hasn't removed backbone, do so before setting roast on platter. Lay roast on platter so curved rib section will face the carver. Insert fork in top of roast and slice by cutting down along each rib.

How to Carve a Picnic Shoulder:

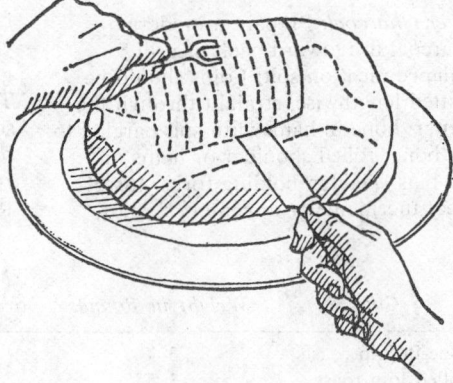

Cut a slice off side of picnic, then turn picnic so it rests on cut surface. At a point near elbow, cut straight down to armbone, then along bone; lift off this boneless piece; slice. Cut meat from both sides of armbone and cut each into thin slices.

SAUCES, GRAVIES, AND SEASONINGS FOR PORK

For Cooking: Seasonings, Herbs, Spices		*For Hot Roasts, Chops and Steaks:*	
		Sauces	Gravies
Anise	Ginger	Barbecue	Au jus (unthick-
Bay leaf	Juniper berries	Charcutière (espe-	ened pan gravy)
Caraway	Lemon	cially chops, steaks)	Mushroom
Chervil	Lime	Chinese barbecue	Pan gravy
Chili powder	Mace	sauce	Sour cream
Chives	Nutmeg	Diable	
Cinnamon	Orange	Horseradish	
Cloves	Oregano	Hot mustard	
Coriander	Parsley	Madeira (especially	
Curry powder	Rosemary	chops, steaks)	
Dill	Sage	Molé	
Fennel	Thyme	Mustard	
Garlic		Orange	
		Piquante	
		Plum	
		Poivrade	
		Robert	
		Sweet-sour	
		Tomato	

For Hot or Cold Pork: Condiments	*For Cold Roasts:* Sauces
Applesauce	Cumberland
Chutney	Salsa fría
Cranberry sauce	Sour cream-
Horseradish	horseradish
Mustard	Whipped
Peaches (brandied	horseradish
or pickled)	
Pickles (bread and	
butter, dill, green	
tomato, mustard,	
sweet, watermelon	
rind)	
Preserved kumquats	
Relishes (corn, pepper,	
sweet pickle)	
Spiced fruits (crab	
apples, peaches,	
pears)	
Soy sauce	

Some Garnishes for Roast Pork Platters (in addition to parsley fluffs and watercress sprigs)

Choose one or two fruits and/or vegetables of contrasting but compatible color and flavor and group or cluster around roast as artfully as possible.

Apples: Baked or Cinnamon Apples; Fried Apple Rings.

Apricots: whole canned or spiced; broiled halves with or without a dab of tart red jelly in the hollow; Blue Cheese Stuffed Apricots.

Bananas: Sautéed Halved Bananas.

Brussels Sprouts: boiled and buttered.

Carrots: Buttered Baby Carrots; Carrots Rosemary; Lemon-Glazed Carrots; Carrots Vichy.

Crab Apples: whole canned or spiced.

Grapes: small clusters of green and/or red grapes.

Onions: Glazed Onions; Pan-Braised Onions; Stuffed Onions.

Orange Cups or Baskets: filled with candied yams or whipped sweet potatoes; buttered green peas or hot cranberry sauce.

Parsnips: Currant or Caramel-Glazed Parsnips; Roasted Parsnips.

Peaches and Pears: broiled halves; halves filled with Spicy Applesauce or cranberry sauce; pickled, spiced, or brandied peaches or pears.

Pickles: green tomato, mustard, and watermelon rind.

Pineapple: broiled chunks or rings; Pineapple and Grape Kebabs.

Potatoes: Parsleyed, Herbed, Lemon-Glazed, or Danish-Style New Potatoes.

Preserved Fruits: figs or kumquats.

Squash: Spicy Mashed Squash in Orange Cups.

Sweet Potatoes: Orange-Candied Sweet Potatoes or Yams.

Tomatoes: raw cherry tomatoes or tomato wedges; Deviled Tomatoes; Stuffed Tomatoes.

Turnips: Glazed or Roasted Turnips; Turnips Stuffed with Risotto.

ROAST PORK À LA BOULANGÈRE

Pork roasted as an old-time French baker's wife would do it, on a buttery bed of onions and potatoes. It's a good choice for a party because it's the sort of dish everyone likes.
Makes 8–10 servings

1 (5-pound) pork center loin roast
3 cloves garlic, peeled and crushed
3½ pounds medium-size potatoes
2 cups coarsely chopped onions
⅓ cup minced parsley
¼ cup melted butter or margarine
1 teaspoon minced fresh marjoram or ½ teaspoon dried marjoram (optional)
1 tablespoon salt
¼ teaspoon pepper

Preheat oven to 350° F. Place pork fat side up in a very large, shallow roasting pan and rub well with garlic. Insert meat thermometer in center of roast, not touching bone. Roast, uncovered, 1 hour. Meanwhile, peel potatoes and slice very thin, letting slices fall into a large bowl of cold water (to prevent darkening, keep potatoes submerged until you're ready to use them). When pork has roasted 1 hour, remove from pan and set aside; pour off all drippings. Drain potatoes well and place in roasting pan, add all remaining ingredients and toss to mix. Place pork fat side up on top of potatoes. Raise oven temperature to 400° F. and roast, uncovered, 1–1½ hours longer or until thermometer registers 170° F. Stir potatoes from time to time and, if they seem dry, sprinkle with a little chicken broth. To serve, center pork on a large heated platter and wreathe with potatoes. About 620 calories for each of 8 servings, 495 calories for each of 10 servings.

CZECH-STYLE ROAST LOIN OF PORK WITH PARSNIP-SOUR CREAM SAUCE

Makes 6–8 servings

1 large parsnip, peeled, trimmed of
  woody central core, and coarsely
  grated
1 stalk celery, coarsely chopped
2 medium-size yellow onions, peeled and
  coarsely chopped
1 cup water
1 cup dry white wine
1 (4-pound) boned and rolled pork loin

Sauce:

Pan drippings and chopped vegetables
2 tablespoons butter or margarine
2 tablespoons flour
1 cup sour cream
2 teaspoons salt
⅛ teaspoon white pepper

Preheat oven to 325° F. Place parsnip, celery, and onions in a large, shallow roasting pan and toss lightly to mix. Pour in water and wine and lay pork fat side up on vegetables. Insert meat thermometer in center of pork. Roast, uncovered, 40–45 minutes per pound or until thermometer registers 170° F. Lift roast from pan and let "rest" while you prepare the sauce. Purée pan drippings and vegetables, a few at a time, in an electric blender at low speed or put through a food mill. Melt butter in a saucepan over moderate heat and blend in flour. Add purée and heat, stirring, until thickened and smooth. Blend in remaining ingredients and heat, stirring, 1–2 minutes until satiny. Do not boil. Carve pork into slices ¼″ thick and top each serving with sauce. About 755 calories for each of 6 servings, 570 calories for each of 8 servings.

ROAST LOIN OF PORK STUFFED WITH APPLES AND PRUNES

Makes 4–6 servings

1 (3–3½-pound) pork loin roast (blade
  loin, center loin, or sirloin)
1 tart apple, peeled, cored, and sliced
  thin
7–8 pitted prunes, halved

1 teaspoon sugar
1 teaspoon salt
⅛ teaspoon pepper
1 recipe Pan Gravy
¼ cup currant jelly

Preheat oven to 325° F. With a sharp knife, cut down between ribs to backbone to form 8–9 chops. Force chops apart slightly and tuck a few apple slices and 2 prune halves between each. Using string, tie loin tightly together to seal in stuffing. Mix sugar, salt, and pepper and rub over roast. Place fat side up on a rack in a shallow roasting pan (loin roasts don't usually require racks, but it's a good idea to use one here because of the juiciness of the stuffing). Roast, uncovered, about 40 minutes per pound until well done (it is difficult to use a meat thermometer because of the way roast is cut, but, to be sure meat is done, insert thermometer in center of 1 chop, not touching bone; it should read 170° F.). Transfer to a heated platter, remove strings, and keep warm. Make Pan Gravy, blend in currant jelly, and serve. About 670 calories for each of 4 servings, 450 calories for each of 6 servings.

BAUERNSCHMAUS

Bauernschmaus is the Austrian Farmer's Feast traditionally eaten after winter hog killing. It should be served with tall steins of well-chilled beer.

Makes 8 servings

1 (4-pound) pork center loin roast
1 (3-pound) smoked shoulder butt
1 recipe Bread Dumplings
1 recipe Caraway Sauerkraut
1 pound frankfurters
1 recipe Pan Gravy

About 3 hours before serving, begin roasting pork loin by basic recipe*; also begin simmering smoked shoulder butt.* Meanwhile, make dumpling batter and chill. About 40 minutes before serving, begin Caraway Sauerkraut recipe, adding frankfurters along with sauerkraut and simmering all together. At the same time, simmer dumplings in boiling water as recipe directs. While sauerkraut and dumplings cook, lift pork loin and shoulder butt to serving platter and let "rest"; also make Pan Gravy from roast drippings. To assemble Bauernschmaus, pile well-drained sauerkraut and frankfurters in the center of a very large platter, arrange slices of loin roast and shoulder butt around the edge, and tuck dumplings in here and there. Pass gravy separately.

VARIATION:

If you prefer, broil frankfurters instead of cooking with sauerkraut and drape over sauerkraut just before serving; use 6–8 baked pork chops in place of the loin roast.

Both versions: about 1295 calories per serving.

CROWN ROAST OF PORK

Makes 10 servings

1 (20-rib) crown roast of pork (about 7–8 pounds) (Note: Make sure butcher removes backbone and frenches rib ends.)
¼ teaspoon pepper
1 recipe Pecan-Bulgur Wheat Stuffing or 1½ quarts any stuffing
10 spiced crab apples or preserved kumquats (garnish)
Parsley or watercress sprigs (garnish)

If butcher has filled center of roast with ground rib trimmings, remove and save for meat loaf. Let roast stand at room temperature 1½–2 hours if possible. Preheat oven to 325° F. Arrange roast, rib ends up, in a large, shallow roasting pan (no need for a rack) and rub with pepper. Insert a meat thermometer between 2 ribs in center of meat, making sure it does not touch bone. Cover rib ends with foil to keep them from charring. Roast, uncovered, 2 hours; spoon stuffing into hollow in center of roast, cover loosely with foil, and roast 1½ hours longer. Remove all foil and roast 15–20 minutes longer or until thermometer registers 170° F. Using 2 pancake turners, transfer roast to heated platter and let "rest" 15–20

minutes. Place crab apples or kumquats on alternate rib ends and wreathe base with parsley or cress. Serve as is or with Pan Gravy. About 590 calories per serving.

For a Smaller Crown Roast (6–8 servings): Order a 12–16-rib crown roast (5–6 pounds) and prepare exactly like larger roast. Allow about 35 minutes per pound roasting time. About 615 calories for each of 6 servings (from a 12-rib roast), 640 calories for each of 8 servings (from a 16-rib roast).

How to Carve a Crown Roast: With a very sharp, rather small carving knife, slice down between each rib and remove chops 1 at a time. Serve 2 chops—and some stuffing—to each person.

PORK TERIYAKI

Makes 4 servings

2 pounds lean boned pork loin, cut in 1″ cubes

Marinade:

½ cup Japanese soy sauce
½ teaspoon ginger
1 tablespoon sugar
1 tablespoon dark brown sugar
¼ cup sake or dry sherry
1 clove garlic, peeled and minced
1 small yellow onion, peeled and minced

Place pork in a large bowl; combine all marinade ingredients, pour over pork, mix well, cover, and refrigerate 4–6 hours. Preheat oven to 400° F. Drain marinade from pork and reserve. Line a roasting pan with foil, place a wire rack in pan and arrange pork on rack. Roast, uncovered, 35–40 minutes, turning often and basting frequently with marinade, until pork is tender and cooked through. Serve with boiled or Chinese Fried Rice. About 470 calories per serving (without rice).

ROAST WHOLE PORK TENDERLOIN

Makes 4 servings

1 (1½-pound) pork tenderloin
1 clove garlic, peeled and slivered
¼ teaspoon pepper
2 strips bacon (optional)
1 teaspoon salt

Preheat oven to 325° F. Make 6–8 tiny slits over surface of pork and insert a garlic sliver in each; rub well with pepper. Place tenderloin on a rack in a shallow roasting pan and insert meat thermometer in center. If meat seems lean, lay bacon strips on top. Roast, uncovered, about 1 hour until thermometer registers 170° F. Remove bacon for last 20 minutes of roasting so meat will brown. Transfer tenderloin to a hot platter, sprinkle with salt, and let "rest" 15 minutes. To serve, cut into slices ¼"–½" thick. If you like, make Pan Gravy. About 380 calories per serving.

VARIATIONS:

Roast Stuffed Whole Pork Tenderloin:
Split tenderloin lengthwise, not quite all the way through so that one long side acts as a hinge, and spread flat like a book. Spread 1 cut side with 1–1½ cups Herbed Bread Stuffing or Sage and Onion Dressing, close, and tie in several places to hold in stuffing. Season and roast as directed above. About 435 calories per serving.

Orange-Glazed Whole Pork Tenderloin:
Prepare tenderloin and begin roasting as directed. Meanwhile prepare glaze by mixing ¼ cup orange juice with ¼ cup firmly packed light brown sugar. When tenderloin has roasted ½ hour, brush with a little glaze. Continue roasting as directed, brushing once or twice more with glaze. (*Note:* Any of the glazes recommended for pork or ham can be used in place of the orange glaze.) About 390 calories per serving.

Oven-Barbecued Pork Tenderloin:
Prepare a marinade by mixing ½ cup light corn syrup with ¼ cup each soy sauce and ketchup, 2 tablespoons each Worcestershire sauce and cider vinegar, 1 teaspoon powdered mustard, and 1 crushed clove garlic. Place tenderloin in a large bowl with marinade, cover and chill 8 hours or overnight, turning occasionally. Lift meat from marinade and roast as directed above, omitting slivered garlic. Baste with marinade every 15 minutes. About 380 calories per serving.

Rosy Chinese-Style Pork Tenderloin:
Heat and stir ½ cup each soy sauce and sugar, 1 cup water, and 8–10 drops red food coloring in a small saucepan over moderate heat until sugar dissolves. Place tenderloin in a large bowl, add saucepan mixture, cover, and chill 8 hours or overnight, turning meat occasionally. Lift meat from marinade, roll in 1 cup sifted cornstarch, and roast as directed, omitting garlic slivers. Baste with marinade every 15 minutes. About 380 calories per serving.

BRAISED WHOLE PORK TENDERLOIN WITH MUSHROOM GRAVY

Makes 4 servings

1 (1½-pound) pork tenderloin
1⅓ cups water
3 bay leaves
1 (4") sprig fresh thyme or ¼ teaspoon dried thyme

Gravy:

4 tablespoons butter or margarine
½ pound mushrooms, wiped clean and sliced thin
3 tablespoons flour
Drippings from pork tenderloin
1 cup water
¼ cup dry white wine
1 teaspoon salt
⅛ teaspoon pepper

Brown tenderloin well on all sides in a large, heavy skillet over moderately high heat. This will take about 10 minutes. Reduce heat to moderately low, add water, bay leaves, and thyme, cover, and simmer about 1 hour until pork is fork tender. Discard bay leaves and thyme sprig; drain liquid from skillet and reserve. Remove pork and keep warm while you make the gravy. Melt 2 tablespoons butter in the skillet and sauté mushrooms about 5 minutes over moderate heat until tender. Remove to a small plate. Melt remaining butter, blend in flour, and heat, stirring, 3–5 minutes until *roux* turns a rich amber brown. Add drippings and water and heat, stirring, until thickened and smooth. Add mushrooms, wine, salt, and pepper and continue to cook and stir 2–3 minutes. To serve, carve tenderloin crosswise into slices 1″ thick, arrange on a platter, and smother with mushroom gravy. About 530 calories per serving.

BRAISED PORK TENDERLOIN FILLETS

Makes 4 servings

8 slices pork tenderloin, cut 1½″–1¾″ thick
½ cup unsifted flour
1 teaspoon salt
¼ teaspoon pepper
2 tablespoons cooking oil
¼ cup water, dry white wine, or apple juice

Dredge fillets by shaking in a paper bag with flour, salt, and pepper; brown 4 minutes on each side in oil in a heavy skillet over moderately low heat. Add water, cover and simmer 30 minutes until fork tender and no trace of pink remains. Serve with Pan Gravy, Mustard Sauce, or other suitable sauce (see Sauces, Gravies, and Seasonings for Pork). About 470 calories per serving (without gravy or sauce).

VARIATIONS:

Pork Fillets Charcutière: Dredge and brown fillets as recipe directs, add 1 cup Charcutière Sauce instead of water, cover, and simmer as directed. Serve on a mound of hot mashed potatoes; pass extra Charcutière Sauce. About 690 calories per serving.

Breaded Pork Fillets: Dip fillets in flour, then in 1 egg beaten with 1 tablespoon

cold water, then in seasoned bread crumbs to coat evenly; let dry on a rack at room temperature 10 minutes. Brown in ¼ cup cooking oil, drain off all but 1 tablespoon drippings, add water, cover, and simmer until tender and well done. Uncover, raise heat to moderate, and cook 1–2 minutes, turning frequently, to crispen crumb coating. About 500 calories per serving.

STUFFED ROAST SHOULDER OF PORK

Makes 8 servings

1 (4-pound) cushion-style picnic shoulder (ask butcher to give you the bones)
1 teaspoon salt
⅛ teaspoon pepper
1 quart (about) Herbed Bread, Apple and Pecan, or other savory stuffing or 1 (8-ounce) package poultry stuffing mix prepared by package directions

Preheat oven to 325° F. Trim outer fat on shoulder to ½″, sprinkle cavity with salt and pepper, and loosely spoon in stuffing. Skewer edges shut every 1″–1½″ and lace with string; place fat side up on a rack in a shallow roasting pan and insert meat thermometer in center, making sure it does not rest in stuffing. Roast uncovered about 35 minutes per pound or until thermometer reaches 170° F. Let roast "rest" 15–20 minutes at room temperature before carving. Serve as is or with Au Jus Gravy, using stock made from bones.

To Glaze: About ½ hour before roast is done, top with a suitable glaze (see Some Glazes for Roast Pork) and finish roasting as directed, basting once or twice. Calories per serving: about 565 calories if made with Herbed Bread Stuffing; 585 calories with Apple and Pecan Stuffing, and 540 calories made with prepared poultry stuffing mix.

VARIATION:

Stuffed Roast Loin of Pork: Have butcher bone a 4-pound center loin roast and make a pocket the length of it for stuffing. Trim fat, then salt and pepper pocket as above; fill loosely with stuffing (you'll need about 2½ cups), skewer and lace opening shut. Roast as directed, allowing about 35 minutes per pound or until thermometer registers 170° F. Calories per serving: about 640 if made with Herbed Bread Stuffing; 420 if made with Apple and Pecan Stuffing, and 385 made with prepared poultry stuffing mix.

SAGE AND CIDER SCENTED ROAST FRESH HAM

If skin is left on a fresh ham during roasting, it will become bubbly brown and crunchy. When carving, slice into thin strips and include one or two with each portion. Eat pork skin with your fingers—it's far too crisp to catch with a fork.

Makes 10–12 servings

1 (5–7-pound) fresh half ham (shank or butt portion)
3¾ cups apple cider
1 tablespoon powdered sage
2½ teaspoons salt (about)
¼ teaspoon pepper
5 tablespoons flour blended with ½ cup cold water

Preheat oven to 325° F. Leave skin on ham and score at ½″ intervals or, if you prefer, remove and trim fat to ½″. Place ham on a rack in a shallow roasting pan. Moisten surface with ¼ cup cider, sprinkle evenly with sage and, if you've left skin on, with 1 teaspoon salt. Insert meat thermometer in center of ham, not touching bone. Roast, uncovered, 30–35 minutes per pound or until thermometer reaches 170° F. After 1 hour's roasting, pour 1 cup cider over ham. Continue to roast, basting occasionally with pan drippings. When ham is done, transfer to hot platter and let "rest." Remove rack from roasting pan, add remaining cider, set over moderate heat, and heat, scraping browned bits from bottom. Mix in flour paste and heat, stirring, until thickened and smooth. Add remaining salt and the pepper. Strain gravy before serving. About 390 calories for each of 10 servings, 325 calories for each of 12 servings.

PORK "POT ROAST" WITH APPLE GRAVY

This isn't the usual way of preparing pork roast, but it's a good one because it requires so little attention.

Makes 8–10 servings

1 (5–7-pound) fresh ham or 1 (4-pound) rolled Boston butt or fresh picnic
1 teaspoon salt
¼ teaspoon pepper
¼ cup cold water

Gravy:
6 tablespoons flour
1½ cups water
1½ cups apple juice
1½ teaspoons salt
¼ teaspoon pepper
⅛ teaspoon liquid gravy browner

If ham has skin on, remove; trim fat to ½″. Render fat trimmings in a large, heavy kettle over moderately low heat; discard trimmings and pour off all but 2 tablespoons drippings. Raise heat to moderate, add pork and brown all over, about 15 minutes. Add salt, pepper, and water, cover, and simmer 3½–4 hours until cooked through. Transfer to a hot platter and keep warm while making gravy. Drain off all but 1–2 tablespoons drippings; blend in flour, then remaining gravy ingredients and heat, stirring and scraping brown bits from bottom, until thickened; cover and simmer 2–3 minutes; taste and adjust seasonings if needed. Slice roast, not too thin, and serve with plenty of gravy. Potato Pancakes and red cabbage go well with this. About 465 calories for each of 8 servings, 370 calories for each of 10 servings.

To Cook in the Oven: Preheat oven to 325° F. Prepare pot roast as directed but simmer in oven instead of on top of stove. Check kettle occasionally to see that liquid simmers but does not boil; reduce temperature to 300° F. if needed.

VARIATIONS:

Country Inn Pork Pot Roast: About 1 hour before pork is done, add ½ cup water, 6–8 peeled, halved potatoes, 8 peeled small carrots, 1 pound peeled small white onions or 1 small rutabaga, peeled and cut in 1″ cubes. Sprinkle vegetables with 1 teaspoon salt and ⅛ teaspoon pepper, cover, and simmer until tender. Transfer meat and vegetables to heated platter and keep warm while making gravy as directed. About 645 calories for each of 8 servings, 520 calories for each of 10 servings.

Barbecued Pork Pot Roast: Marinate pork in any zippy barbecue sauce 24–28 hours. Pat meat dry and rub with 1 tablespoon chili powder. Brown as recipe directs, add ¼ cup barbecue sauce along with water called for, cover, and simmer as directed, turning meat once or twice. If you like, serve with additional barbecue sauce. About 485 calories for each of 8 servings, 385 calories for each of 10 servings.

Cranberried Pork Pot Roast: Brown pork, then add 1 cup whole or jellied cranberry sauce along with water, cover, and simmer as directed. Transfer pork to a hot platter, top with cooked-down pan juices, and keep warm; make Pan Gravy in a separate saucepan. About 510 calories for each of 8 servings, 405 calories for each of 10 servings.

Extra-Savory Pork Pot Roast: Make 8–10 tiny slits over surface of roast and tuck a thin garlic sliver in each (use 1 clove garlic in all). Brown as directed and simmer 2 hours. Transfer pork to a rack in a shallow roasting pan, spread with ¼ cup prepared mild yellow mustard, and bake, uncovered, at 300° F. 1 hour. Score fat in a diamond pattern, stud with cloves, and pat on ½ cup light brown sugar. Bake 1 hour longer, basting occasionally with pan drippings. Serve hot or cold. About 465 calories for each of 8 servings, 370 calories for each of 10 servings.

CHOUCROUTE GARNIE (SAUERKRAUT WITH MEAT)

Serve a well chilled Riesling or Traminer wine with this Alsatian classic. Or beer.
Makes 8 servings

1 large yellow onion, peeled and minced
2 tablespoons lard or butter
2 pounds sauerkraut, drained
1 tart apple, peeled, cored, and coarsely chopped
1 teaspoon juniper berries, tied in cheesecloth
1 (¼-pound) piece fat bacon or salt pork
2½–3 cups dry white Alsatian or other wine
1 (4-pound) center cut pork loin roast or (3-pound) boned and rolled loin
8 knackwurst
8 bratwurst or frankfurters

Preheat oven to 300° F. Sauté onion in lard in a heavy kettle over moderate heat 5–8 minutes until pale golden. Add kraut, apple, juniper berries, bacon, and wine; cover and bring to a simmer, then transfer to oven and bake 1 hour. Meanwhile, trim fat on loin to ¼″ and brown, fat side first, in a heavy skillet over moderate heat about 10 minutes; pour off drippings as they accumulate. When kraut has baked 1 hour, add pork, re-cover, and bake 1¾ hours longer. Check pot occasionally and add more wine if it seems dry; mixture should be moist but not soupy. Add sausages and bake 15 minutes until tender; remove cheesecloth bag. Pile sauerkraut on a large platter, top with bacon, sausages, and sliced pork. Serve with boiled potatoes sprinkled with minced parsley. About 1015 calories per serving (without potatoes).

VARIATIONS:

Substitute 6–8 small meaty pork hocks for pork loin and add to sauerkraut along with wine and apple; otherwise, prepare as directed. About 1015 calories per serving.

Substitute 1½ pounds Kielbasa (Polish sausage) or Cotechino (Italian sausage) for either of the German sausages and add to sauerkraut along with wine and apple. About 1015 calories per serving.

About ½ hour before serving, stir a stout jigger of kirsch into kettle. About 1040 calories per serving.

ROAST PORK REVISITED

(How to Use Up Leftovers)

¢ SLICED PORK AND BAKED BEAN CASSEROLE

A delicious way to revive leftover roast pork.
Makes 4 servings

8 slices leftover roast pork, cut ¼" thick
2 tablespoons bacon drippings or cooking oil (about)
1 large yellow onion, peeled and minced
1 medium-size sweet green pepper, seeded, cored, and minced
¼ teaspoon powdered mustard mixed with 1 tablespoon cold water
1 (1-pound 5-ounce) can baked beans in tomato sauce
1 tablespoon Worcestershire sauce
¼ cup chili sauce
3 tablespoons dark brown sugar

Preheat oven to 350° F. Trim excess fat from pork, dice enough of it to measure 2 tablespoons, and render in a skillet over moderate heat. Measure drippings and add enough bacon drippings to total 2 tablespoons. Sauté onion and green pepper in the drippings 8–10 minutes until golden, stirring occasionally. Mix in mustard, beans, and remaining ingredients; spoon half into an ungreased 2-quart casserole. Arrange pork slices on beans, top with remaining beans, cover, and bake ½ hour until bubbly. About 560 calories per serving.

⚖ SUBGUM (10-INGREDIENT) PORK CHOW MEIN

Makes 4 servings

¼ cup blanched, slivered almonds
2 tablespoons cooking oil
1½–2 cups diced leftover roast pork, trimmed of fat
½ pound mushrooms, wiped clean and sliced thin
1½ cups shredded celery cabbage or finely chopped celery
2 cups chicken broth
1 teaspoon salt
2 tablespoons cornstarch blended with ¼ cup cold water
1 (4-ounce) can bamboo shoots, drained and sliced thin
1 (1-pound) can bean sprouts, drained

Stir-fry almonds in oil in a *wok* or heavy skillet 1–2 minutes over moderately high heat until golden; drain on paper toweling. Pour oil from skillet, add pork, mushrooms, and cabbage, and stir-fry 2 minutes. Add broth, salt, and cornstarch mixture and heat, stirring, until thickened. Add remaining ingredients and cook and stir 2–3 minutes. Serve over heated chow mein noodles topped with almonds. About 330 calories per serving.

To Make with Raw Pork: Cut ½ pound pork tenderloin or loin across the grain into ⅛"×⅛"×2" strips. Stir-fry almonds as directed and drain. Add pork to skillet and stir-fry 1–2 minutes; add vegetables and proceed as recipe directs. About 300 calories per serving.

VARIATION:

⚖ **Pork Lo Mein:** Boil and drain ½ pound Chinese egg noodles or spaghettini by package directions. Omit almonds. Stir-fry pork, mushrooms, and cabbage in oil 2 minutes, add ½ cup broth, salt, and cornstarch mixture, and heat, stirring, until thickened. Instead of adding bamboo shoots and bean sprouts, top with noodles, cover, and simmer 3–4 minutes. Serve with soy sauce. About 330 calories per serving.

⚔ CHAR SHU DING (DICED ROAST PORK WITH CHINESE VEGETABLES)

Makes 4–6 servings

2 tablespoons cooking oil
1 cup minced yellow onion
1½ cups coarsely shredded celery
  cabbage
½ pound mushrooms, wiped clean and
  sliced thin
¼ pound snow pea pods
2 stalks celery, cut in thin diagonal slices
1 sweet green or red pepper, cored,
  seeded, and cut in long, thin strips
2 cups diced or sliced leftover roast pork
2 cups chicken broth
3 tablespoons soy sauce
½ teaspoon MSG (monosodium
  glutamate)
¼ teaspoon sugar
2 tablespoons cornstarch blended with ¼
  cup cold water
1 (1-pound) can bean sprouts, drained
1 (3-ounce) can water chestnuts,
  drained and sliced thin
⅓ cup toasted, slivered almonds

Heat oil in a wok or large, heavy skillet over moderately high heat 1 minute; add onion, celery cabbage, mushrooms, pea pods, celery, and green pepper and stir-fry 3–4 minutes (do not brown). Add pork and stir-fry 1 minute, then broth, soy sauce, MSG, sugar, and cornstarch mixture and cook, stirring, until thickened. Toss in bean sprouts and water chestnuts and heat 1–2 minutes. Taste for salt and adjust as needed. Serve over boiled rice and top each portion with toasted, slivered almonds. About 300 calories for each of 4 servings, 195 calories for each of 6 servings.

¢ ⚔ ▣ CHOP SUEY

Tag ends of peas, beans, or carrots cluttering up the refrigerator? Toss them into chop suey. This one can also be made with leftover beef or lamb.
Makes 4 servings

2 tablespoons cooking oil
1 cup minced yellow onion
4 stalks celery, cut in thin diagonal
  slices
1 sweet green or red pepper, cored,
  seeded, and cut in long, thin strips
2 cups diced or sliced leftover roast
  pork
2 cups chicken broth
3 tablespoons soy sauce
¼ teaspoon sugar
2 tablespoons cornstarch blended with
  ¼ cup cold water
1 (1-pound) can bean sprouts, drained

Heat oil in a wok or large, heavy skillet over moderately high heat 1 minute, add onion, celery, and green pepper, and stir-fry 3–4 minutes (do not brown). Add pork and stir-fry 1 minute, then all remaining ingredients except bean sprouts; cook and stir until thickened. Add sprouts and toss 1–2 minutes. Taste for salt and adjust as needed. Serve over boiled rice or chow mein noodles. About 270 calories per serving.

To Make with Raw Pork: Slice lean tenderloin or loin across the grain into strips 2″ long and ⅛″ wide; stir-fry 1 minute in oil, then add onion, celery, and green pepper and proceed as directed. About 240 calories per serving.

Some Additional Ways to Use Up Leftover Roast Pork

¢ ⚔ **Chinese Pork-Fried Rice** (4 servings): Stir-fry 1½ cups minced leftover pork, 1 minced small yellow onion, and 1 crushed clove garlic in 2 tablespoons peanut oil in a large, heavy skillet over moderately high heat 5–8 minutes until lightly browned. Stir in 1 cup uncooked rice and stir-fry 3–4 minutes. Add 1 drained (4-ounce) can sliced mushrooms, 1¾ cups water, 2 tablespoons soy sauce, and a pinch pepper. Bring to a boil, cover, and simmer slowly 25 minutes until rice is tender. Top, if you like, with strips of scrambled egg. About 275 calories per serving (without egg).

¢ **Creamed Pork and Peas** (4 servings): Stir-fry 1 minced small yellow onion in

2 tablespoons butter in a large, heavy skillet over moderate heat 8–10 minutes until golden; mix in 1 (10½-ounce) can cream of celery soup, 2 tablespoons heavy cream, 1 teaspoon each paprika and Worcestershire sauce, 1½ cups diced cooked pork, and 1 (10-ounce) package frozen green peas. Cover and simmer 10–12 minutes, breaking up block of peas after 5 minutes. Taste for salt and pepper and season as needed. Serve over biscuits or toast. About 340 calories per serving (without biscuits or toast).

⚖ **Cubed Pork and Olives in Sour Cream** (2 servings): Melt 2 tablespoons butter in a saucepan over moderate heat and blend in 2 tablespoons flour, 1 teaspoon paprika, and ½ teaspoon each garlic salt and onion salt. Add 1 cup water and 1 tablespoon lemon juice and heat, stirring, until thickened. Add 1½ cups cubed cooked pork and ½ cup sliced, pitted ripe olives, cover, and simmer 5–10 minutes to blend flavors. Off heat, mix in ⅓ cup sour cream. Serve over boiled rice. About 235 calories per serving (without rice).

¢ ⚖ **Pork, Rice, and Vegetable Casserole** (4–6 servings): Mix 3 cups cooked rice with 2 cups each diced cooked pork and mixed, diced leftover vegetables. Stir in 1 (10½-ounce) can cream of celery, mushroom, tomato, or asparagus soup thinned with 1 cup milk. Spoon into a buttered 2-quart casserole, cover, and bake 30–40 minutes at 400° F. *Optional Topping:* Just before serving, scatter ¼–⅓ cup buttered bread crumbs or grated Cheddar cheese over casserole and broil quickly to brown. About 475 calories for each of 4 servings (without topping), 310 calories for each of 6 servings.

Barbecued Pork and Potatoes:

Roast Pork Hash:

Follow recipes given in Some Additional Ways to Use Up Leftover Roast Beef, substituting pork for beef.

Sliced Cold Pork: Slice pork about ¼″ thick, trim of fat, and top with any recommended cold sauce (see Sauces, Gravies, and Seasonings for Pork).

Sliced Hot Pork: Slice pork about ¼″ thick, trim of fat and layer into an ungreased shallow casserole. Add just enough hot sauce (see Sauces, Gravies, and Seasonings for Pork) to cover, cover with foil, and heat 20 minutes at 350° F. Or, if you prefer, heat pork in sauce 5 minutes in a covered skillet over moderately low heat.

Hot Roast Pork Sandwiches: Heat meat and a suitable sauce in a skillet as for Sliced Hot Pork (above) and serve, open face, on toast or bread.

To Make the Most of Very Small Amounts: See suggestions given for beef.

Suckling Pig

Suckling pigs call to mind the days of Jolly Olde England, where whole pigs were spitted in open hearths, and the luaus of Hawaii, where they are pit-roasted on the beach. They are not often prepared in modern America, although they were popular at colonial feasts. Suckling pigs are 6 to 8 weeks old and weigh from 10 to 20 pounds. There is little meat on them, but what there is approaches pâté in richness. Some people like to munch the richly browned skin, but for most tastes it is too leathery. Suckling pigs must always be especially ordered, sometimes as much as a week or two ahead. The best size is in the 14- to 18-pound range—large enough to contain some meat, small enough to fit in most home ovens. To figure number of servings, allow about 1¼ pounds pig per person (most of the weight is bone). *Tip:* To keep the pig cool until roasting time (you can't get a suckling pig in the refrigerator unless you clear virtually everything else out), place in an extra-large roasting pan and set on a porch or just outside the door (suckling pig is cold weather food, so the outdoor temperature should be just about right unless it's below freezing; in that case, you'll have to make accommodations inside). Turn a large washtub upside down over the pig and weight down with bricks or large rocks to remove temptation from neighborhood dogs.

Suckling pig should be reserved for the most festive occasions. When inviting guests, tell them what you plan to serve —some people are squeamish about seeing a whole pig on a platter.

ROAST SUCKLING PIG

Makes 10–12 servings

1 (15-pound) suckling pig, dressed
1 tablespoon salt
1 teaspoon pepper
1 recipe Chestnut Mushroom Stuffing or 1 recipe Brandied Wild Rice, Corn Bread, and Chestnut Stuffing
¼ pound butter, softened to room temperature

Garnishes:

1 small red apple or 1 lemon
1 pint fresh cranberries
12 laurel or English ivy leaves

Preheat oven to 350° F. Wipe pig inside and out with a damp cloth and dry with paper toweling. Rub inside well with salt and pepper. Lay pig on its side and stuff loosely; wrap remaining stuffing in foil and refrigerate. Close cavity with skewers and lace together to close. Place a large, sturdy rack in an extra-large shallow roasting pan; lay a triple thickness of foil diagonally on top, allowing plenty of overhang. Lift pig onto foil so it, too, is diagonal to the pan, bend hind legs forward and front legs backward into a "praying" position so pig crouches. Turn up foil edges, forming a "pan" to catch drips. Rub pig with butter; cover ears and tail with bits of foil and force a foil ball about the size of an apple into the mouth. Roast uncovered, brushing occasionally with butter, 18 minutes per pound. Meanwhile, string cranberries and leaves into 2 garlands. Save 2 cranberries for pig's eyes. About 1 hour before serving, place foil package of stuffing in oven to heat. When pig is done, lift carefully to an extra-large platter; remove skewers,

lacing, and foil. Place an apple or lemon in pig's mouth, 1 cranberry in each eye (secure with toothpicks) and lay garlands around neck. Place extra stuffing in a separate dish and skimmed drippings in a gravy boat.

To Spit Roast over Charcoal: Prepare a very large, moderate charcoal fire.* Prepare and stuff pig as above, truss legs to body in kneeling position, and insert spit lengthwise through center of pig so it is balanced; use at least 4 holding forks, 2 at each end, to secure pig on spit. Arrange coals in a circle and place a drip pan in the center. Attach spit to rotisserie, adjust height so spit is 7"–8" from coals, and roast pig 15–18 minutes per pound. Arrange on platter and garnish as above.

How to Carve Suckling Pig: Set platter on table so pig's head is to left of carver. First, remove the hams or hind legs, then divide pig into chops by cutting along the backbone, then down along each rib. See that each person receives both chops and ham or leg meat. Roast suckling pig and spit-roasted suckling pig: about 1135 calories for each of 10 servings if made with Chestnut Mushroom Stuffing; 1330 calories per serving if made with Brandied Wild Rice, Corn Bread, and Chestnut Stuffing; about 945 calories for each of 12 servings if made with Chestnut Mushroom Stuffing; 1110 calories per serving if made with Brandied Wild Rice, Corn Bread, and Chestnut Stuffing.

Pork Chops and Steaks

The easiest way to learn these small cuts is to relate them to the roasts from which they come (see Pork Chart). A blade chop, for example, is simply a slice of the blade loin; a loin chop, a slice of center loin; a sirloin chop, a slice of sirloin, and so on. As with roasts, the most expensive chops and steaks are those from the loin, the most economical those from the Boston butt or picnic:

Blade Chop: A moderate sized, moderate-priced chop from the blade loin roast.

Rib Chop: A smallish, moderate-to-expensive chop from the rib end of the center loin. It is usually cut 1 rib thick.

Butterfly Chop: A double rib chop, made by removing the rib bone, cutting the meat almost in half horizontally, and opening flat like a book. It's fairly expensive and must be ordered.

Loin Chop: The choicest pork chop. It is cut from the heart of the center loin roast, usually 1 rib thick, and contains a plump nugget of tenderloin. Expensive as pork chops go.

Top Loin Chop: A loin chop with the tenderloin removed. Fairly expensive.

Sirloin Chop: A chop from the sirloin roast; any cut from the part bordering the loin may contain a tag end of tenderloin. Moderately expensive.

Tenderloin Slices: These are to pork what filet is to beef—boneless, butter-smooth, luxury-priced steaks. A whole pork tenderloin weighs only ¾–1½ pounds, so a single slice is scarcely a mouthful.

Blade Steak: A slice of Boston butt containing the shoulder blade; 1 blade steak will usually serve 2. Economical.

Arm Steak: A meaty slice of the picnic, large enough for 2. Economical.

Leg Steak: Also called pork cutlet, this is simply a slice of fresh ham, usually from the butt portion; 1 leg steak will serve 2. Moderate.

Porklet: The pork equivalent of cube steak. It's a small boneless shoulder steak that's been tenderized by cubing. Economical.

How to Cook

Amounts Needed: All pork chops and steaks should be at least ½" thick and will be more attractive and succulent if cut ¾"–1"; those to be stuffed should be 1¼"–1½" thick.

Tenderloin Slices: Allow 2–3 (¼"–½") slices per person.

Rib, Loin, and Top Loin Chops: Allow 1–2 per person.

Blade, Butterfly, and Sirloin Chops; Porklets: Allow 1 per person.

Blade, Arm, and Leg Steaks: Allow 1 for each 2 persons.

General Preparation for Cooking: If meat seems moist, wipe with a damp cloth so it will brown nicely. Trim off all but ¼" outer fat; rub with pepper if you like, also garlic and/or a compatible herb (see Sauces, Gravies, and Seasonings for Pork) but not with salt (chops and steaks should not be salted until after browning). Let stand at room temperature 1½–2 hours before cooking if convenient.

To Broil or Panbroil: Not recommended; by the time chops and steaks have cooked through at this intense heat, they will be dry, tough, and stringy.

To Panfry (Sauté): Recommended only for very thin pork chops or steaks (those ½" or less) and then only as a change of pace from braised chops (see recipes that follow).

To Braise: Here's the preferred method for preparing all pork chops and steaks because it allows them to cook thoroughly without toughening and drying. Brown chops or steaks 5 minutes on a side over moderately high heat in a skillet brushed with oil; pour off all drippings. Sprinkle lightly with salt and pepper, add a small amount of water (⅓ cup is about right for 4 chops or 2 steaks), cover, and simmer slowly over low heat or in a preheated 350° F. oven 50–60 minutes until well done.

To test for doneness: Make a small slit near bone (or, if meat is boneless, in the center); flesh should show no traces of pink. Or, pierce meat with a sharp fork near center; if juices run clear with no tinges of pink, meat is well done. Serve as is or with Pan Gravy or Country Gravy.

For Extra Savor: Substitute any of the following for the water called for above: tomato juice or sauce or undrained, canned tomatoes; pineapple, orange, apple, or mixed fruit juices; milk, buttermilk, or light cream; barbecue or meatless spaghetti sauce; undrained, canned crushed pineapple; chicken or beef broth; ginger ale; beer or dry white wine; ½ (10½-ounce) can condensed onion, black bean, cream of celery or mushroom, tomato, or tomato and rice soup.

Some Variations on Braised Pork Chops and Steaks
(all quantities based on enough chops or steaks for 4 persons)

Smothered Pork Chops or Steaks: Brown meat as directed above; pour off drippings, season meat, and add 1 (10½-ounce) can condensed cream of mushroom, celery, or chicken soup thinned with ⅓ cup milk. Cover and simmer as directed.

Hawaiian-Style Steaks or Chops: Brown meat as directed; pour off drippings and season meat. Top each steak with 2 pineapple rings, each chop with 1, add ½ cup syrup from can or ½ cup pineapple juice, and sprinkle with 2–3 tablespoons light brown sugar. Cover and simmer as directed. When done, remove meat and pineapple rings to a hot platter and keep warm. To pan juices add 1¼ cups pineapple juice blended with 1 teaspoon cornstarch and heat, stirring, until thickened and clear. Spoon some sauce over meat and pass the rest.

Italian-Style Pork Chops or Steaks: Rub both sides of chops or steaks with a cut clove garlic, then brown as directed in a skillet brushed with olive oil; pour off drippings and season meat. Pour in 1 cup meatless or mushroom spaghetti sauce, cover, and simmer as directed.

Hungarian-Style Pork Chops or Steaks: Rub chops or steaks with 1–2 teaspoons paprika, brown as directed, and remove from skillet. In drippings stir-fry

1 minced medium-size yellow onion 5–8 minutes over moderate heat until pale golden. Return chops to skillet, season with salt and pepper, add ½ cup beef broth and 1 bay leaf. Cover and simmer as directed. Transfer chops to a platter, blend 1 cup sour cream into pan juices, heat 1 minute but do not boil. Pour over meat and serve.

Indiana Pork Chops or Steaks: Brown meat as directed; pour off drippings and season meat. Top each chop with a ¼″ slice yellow onion and a thin slice lemon (use 2–3 of each on steaks). Mix ½ cup ketchup, ½ cup water, and 2 tablespoons each dark brown sugar and Worcestershire sauce, pour over meat, cover, and simmer as directed. Uncover during last 15 minutes so juices will cook down.

Herbed Pork Chops or Steaks in Wine: Rub chops or steaks with a mixture of ¼ teaspoon each powdered rosemary, sage, and garlic powder and let stand at room temperature 15 minutes. Brown as directed; pour off drippings from skillet and season meat with salt and pepper. Add ½ cup dry white wine, cover, and simmer as directed. Transfer meat to a hot platter and keep warm. Boil down pan juices until reduced to 2–3 tablespoons; spoon over meat and serve.

Braised Pork Chops or Steaks with Dressing: Brown chops as directed; pour off drippings and season meat. Top each chop or steak with 2–3 tablespoons poultry stuffing mix prepared by package directions, add ½ cup condensed cream of mushroom, celery, or chicken soup thinned with ½ cup water, cover, and simmer as directed. Uncover for last 5 minutes.

Orange-Lemon Pork Chops or Steaks: Brown meat as directed and pour off drippings. Top each with a ¼″ thick slice peeled, seeded orange and lemon. Mix 1 teaspoon salt, ⅛ teaspoon pepper, ¼ cup firmly packed light brown sugar, and ¾ cup orange juice; pour over meat, cover, and simmer as directed.

Apple-Raisin Pork Chops: Brown chops as directed; pour off drippings and season meat. Top each with a ½″ thick slice cored tart apple (peeled or unpeeled) and fill centers with seedless raisins. Pour in ⅓ cup apple juice or cider, cover, and simmer as directed.

Pork Chops with Sherried Applesauce: Brown chops as directed; pour off drippings and season meat. Arrange in a lightly greased 2-quart casserole. Mix 1 (1-pound) can applesauce with ½ cup medium-dry sherry or port and ¼ teaspoon each ginger, cinnamon, and nutmeg. Spoon ½ of applesauce mixture over chops and bake, uncovered, as directed 30 minutes. Turn chops, top with remaining applesauce, and bake, uncovered, 30 minutes longer or until thoroughly cooked.

Pork Chop-Corn Scallop: Brown chops as directed; pour off drippings and season meat. Arrange in a lightly greased 2-quart casserole. To skillet in which chops were browned, add ½ cup boiling water and heat 1–2 minutes, scraping up browned bits; pour over chops. Mix 1 (1-pound) can cream-style corn with 1½ cups soft bread crumbs, 3 tablespoons each prepared mild yellow mustard and finely grated onion, ¼ teaspoon salt, and a pinch pepper. Spoon mixture on top of each chop, mounding it up, and bake, uncovered, as directed, but without turning.

To Bake Pork Chops: Preheat oven to 350° F. Arrange chops in a lightly greased shallow roasting pan or casserole and bake, uncovered, ½ hour; drain off drippings. Sprinkle with salt and a pinch pepper, turn, and bake uncovered ½ hour longer or until no trace of pink remains. Transfer to a hot platter, sprinkle with salt and pepper. Serve as is or with Pan Gravy or Country Gravy.

For Extra Savor: About 10 minutes before chops are done, top each with any 1 of the following: 2 tablespoons apple jelly or whole cranberry sauce; ½ peach filled with red currant jelly; 1 pineapple ring or 2 tablespoons pineapple chunks sprinkled with 1 teaspoon light brown sugar. Or spread each chop with 1 tablespoon mustard (mild or spicy) or 1 tablespoon peanut butter (crunchy or creamy).

Some Variations on Baked Pork Chops (all quantities based on enough chops for 4 persons)

Plum-Glazed Pork Chops: Arrange chops in pan as directed. Mix ½ cup plum jelly with 1 tablespoon each red wine vinegar and liquid gravy browner, 1 teaspoon salt, ½ teaspoon ginger, and ⅛ teaspoon pepper. Spoon over chops and bake uncovered, without turning, 1 hour or until cooked through.

Orange-Glazed Pork Chops: Bake chops ½ hour, drain off drippings, and turn. Mix 1 teaspoon salt and ⅛ teaspoon pepper with ½ cup orange juice, ¼ cup firmly packed light brown sugar, and 1 teaspoon prepared mild yellow mustard; pour over chops and bake, uncovered, ½ hour longer until cooked through. Remove chops to a hot platter and keep warm. Mix 1 teaspoon cornstarch with 1 tablespoon cold water, stir into pan juices along with 1 tablespoon grated orange rind. Set over moderate heat and cook, stirring, until thickened and clear. Stir in 1 peeled, seeded, and sectioned orange, spoon over chops, and serve.

Pineapple-Glazed Pork Chops: Follow Orange-Glazed Pork Chops recipe above; substitute pineapple juice for orange, omit rind, and use 1 cup pineapple tidbits instead of orange sections.

Pork Chops 'n' Sweet Potatoes: Bake chops as basic recipe directs; 20 minutes before they are done, arrange 1 (1-pound) drained can sweet potatoes or yams around chops, brush with 2 tablespoons melted butter, and sprinkle with 2 tablespoons dark brown sugar. Continue baking as directed until done, basting potatoes once with pan juices.

Pork Chops and Sauerkraut: Bake chops as recipe directs 30 minutes; remove from pan and drain off drippings. Empty 1 (1-pound) can undrained sauerkraut into pan and arrange over bottom; lay chops on top, season with salt and pepper, and sprinkle, if you like, with paprika. Bake, uncovered, 30 minutes longer until chops are done.

Pork Chops and Baked Beans: Bake chops as recipe directs; 20 minutes before they are done remove from pan. Empty 1 (1-pound) can baked beans into pan, stir in 1 tablespoon each prepared mild yellow mustard, dark brown sugar, and Worcestershire sauce. If you like, also add 1 (8-ounce) drained can pineapple tidbits. Top with chops and continue baking, uncovered, 20 minutes longer or until chops are done.

Carolina Pork Chops: Place chops in pan, top with 1¼ cups All-Purpose Barbecue Sauce, bake, basting occasionally with sauce, 1 hour until done.

BRAISED PORK CHOPS AND ONIONS ROSEMARY

Makes 4 servings

4 loin pork chops, cut 1" thick and trimmed of excess fat
¾ cup unsifted flour
1 teaspoon salt
⅛ teaspoon pepper
1 tablespoon butter or margarine
2 medium-size yellow onions, peeled and sliced thin
¾ cup dry white vermouth
¾ cup water
2 (4") sprigs fresh rosemary or ¼ teaspoon dried rosemary

Preheat oven to 350° F. Dredge chops by shaking in a paper bag with flour, salt, and pepper. Melt butter in a heavy Dutch oven over moderately high heat and brown chops well on both sides, about 8–10 minutes. Remove from heat, lay onion slices over chops, pour in vermouth and water, and lay rosemary sprigs on top (if using dried rosemary, sprinkle evenly over all). Cover and bake 1 hour or until chops are tender. Remove herb sprigs and serve, topping each portion with onions and a generous ladling of pan juices. About 365 calories per serving.

VARIATION:
Substitute fresh or dried sage or thyme for the rosemary and prepare as directed.

GRUYÈRE-GLAZED PORK CHOPS

These chops are so rich one per person is enough.
Makes 4 servings

4 loin pork chops, cut 1" thick and trimmed of excess fat
1 tablespoon olive or other cooking oil
1 tablespoon butter or margarine
½ teaspoon salt
⅛ teaspoon pepper
½ cup dry white wine, apple cider, or apple juice
1½ cups finely grated Gruyère cheese
1 tablespoon prepared Dijon-style mustard
¼ cup heavy cream or evaporated milk

Preheat oven to 350° F. Brown chops 4–5 minutes on a side in oil and butter in a large flameproof casserole over moderately high heat; drain off all fat. Sprinkle with salt and pepper, add wine, and bake uncovered 50–60 minutes until chops are tender. Meanwhile, blend together cheese, mustard, and cream (mixture will not be smooth). When chops are tender, spread top of each with cheese mixture and broil 3" from heat 2–3 minutes until lightly speckled with brown. (*Note:* Casserole liquid can be served in a gravy boat or saved for stock.) About 525 calories per serving.

⚖ CALIFORNIA-STYLE PORK CHOPS

Makes 4 servings

½ teaspoon cloves
1 clove garlic, peeled and crushed
4 teaspoons olive or other cooking oil
1 teaspoon finely grated lemon rind
½ teaspoon salt
⅛ teaspoon seasoned pepper
4 loin pork chops, cut 1" thick and trimmed of excess fat
1 tablespoon frozen orange juice concentrate
½ cup ginger ale

Mix cloves, garlic, 3 teaspoons oil, lemon rind, salt, and pepper and brush on both sides of chops; let stand at room temperature 1 hour. Preheat oven to 350° F. Brush bottom of a shallow flameproof 2-quart casserole with remaining oil and heat over moderately high heat 1 minute. Add chops and brown 4–5 minutes on each side; drain off all fat. Mix orange concentrate and ginger ale and pour over chops. Transfer casserole to oven and bake, uncovered, 50–60 minutes until chops are tender and cooked through. About 320 calories per serving.

CREOLE PORK CHOPS

Makes 4 servings

4 loin or rib pork chops, cut 1" thick and trimmed of excess fat
1 teaspoon cooking oil
1 teaspoon salt
⅛ teaspoon pepper
¼ teaspoon paprika
2 tablespoons butter or margarine
1 medium-size yellow onion, peeled and minced
1 medium-size sweet green pepper, cored, seeded, and minced
1½ cups canned tomatoes, coarsely chopped (include some liquid), or 1½ cups tomato sauce
¼ teaspoon sugar
2–3 drops liquid hot red pepper seasoning

Preheat oven to 350° F. Brown chops 5–7 minutes on each side over moderately low heat in a skillet brushed with oil. Transfer to a lightly greased 2½-quart casserole; sprinkle with salt, pepper, and paprika. Pour off all but 1 tablespoon drippings from skillet, add butter, and sauté onion and green pepper over moderate heat 8–10 minutes until onion is golden. Add remaining ingredients and simmer, uncovered, 10 minutes, stirring occasionally. Pour sauce over chops, cover, and bake 50–60 minutes until fork tender. Good with Saffron Rice.

VARIATION:

Creole Pork Steaks: Substitute 2 (¾") blade or arm steaks for chops and proceed as directed, allowing at least 1 hour baking time.

Both versions: about 395 calories per serving.

BARBECUED PORK CHOPS

This dish freezes well; double or triple recipe, if you like, then let chops cool in sauce before packing in freezer containers.
Makes 4 servings

4 rib or loin pork chops, cut 1" thick and trimmed of excess fat
1 teaspoon cooking oil

Chuck Wagon Barbecue Sauce:

½ cup ketchup
½ cup cider vinegar
¾ cup water
1 medium-size onion, peeled and minced
1 clove garlic, peeled and crushed
1 tablespoon chili powder
1 tablespoon Worcestershire sauce
¼ cup firmly packed light brown sugar
1 teaspoon salt
¼ teaspoon pepper

Preheat oven to 350° F. Brown chops well on each side 8–10 minutes over moderately high heat in a skillet brushed with oil; transfer to a small roasting pan or casserole. Meanwhile, simmer all sauce ingredients 20 minutes, stirring frequently. Pour sauce over chops and bake, uncovered, 1 hour or until tender. Turn chops once during baking. About 360 calories per serving.

PORK CHOPS WITH GARLIC-CRUMB STUFFING

Makes 6 servings

6 rib pork chops, cut 1¼" thick and trimmed of excess fat
1 teaspoon cooking oil
1 teaspoon salt
¼ teaspoon pepper
⅓ cup boiling water, chicken or beef broth

Stuffing:

1 small yellow onion, peeled and minced
¼ cup minced celery
2 cloves garlic, peeled and crushed
1 tablespoon cooking oil
1 cup poultry stuffing mix
¼ cup hot water
*1 small tart apple, peeled, cored, and
  chopped fine*
¼ teaspoon salt
⅛ teaspoon pepper

Preheat oven to 350° F. Starting at rib
bone, cut a pocket in each chop.
Prepare stuffing: stir-fry onion, celery,
and garlic in oil over moderate heat
5–8 minutes until pale golden. Off heat
mix in remaining ingredients and spoon
into chop pockets (no need to use
toothpicks or skewers to seal in stuffing).
Brown chops well on each side, about
8–10 minutes, over moderately high
heat in a skillet brushed with oil.
Transfer to an ungreased shallow
roasting pan, sprinkle with salt and
pepper, add boiling water, cover, and
bake 1–1¼ hours or until tender. About
450 calories per serving.

VARIATIONS:

Oyster-Stuffed Pork Chops: Cut pockets
in chops as above and fill with well-
drained, coarsely chopped fresh oysters
(you'll need about 1⅓ cups; save broth).
Toothpick openings shut if oysters seem
to slide out. Proceed as directed,
substituting oyster broth for boiling
water. About 390 calories per serving.

Spinach-Stuffed Pork Chops: Stuff
chops with about 1½ cups well-drained,
cooked, minced spinach, then proceed
by basic recipe above. About 370
calories per serving.

Substitute 1⅓ cups Sage and Onion
Dressing; Pecan-Bulgur Wheat Stuffing;
Rice and Mushroom Stuffing, or any
favorite for that given above. Proceed
as directed. Calories per serving: about
500 if made with Sage and Onion
Dressing; 520 with Pecan-Bulgur Wheat
Stuffing; and 505 with Rice and
Mushroom Stuffing.

PORK CHOP AND WILD RICE CASSEROLE

Makes 4 servings

*1 medium-size yellow onion, peeled and
  coarsely chopped*
1 carrot, peeled and coarsely grated
3 tablespoons butter or margarine
*1 cup wild rice, cooked by package
  directions*
*1 teaspoon minced fresh sage or ¼
  teaspoon dried sage*
Pinch nutmeg
1¾ teaspoons salt
*4 loin pork chops, cut 1" thick and
  trimmed of excess fat*
¾ cup unsifted flour
2 teaspoons paprika
¼ teaspoon pepper
½ cup dry white wine

Preheat oven to 350° F. Sauté onion
and carrot in 2 tablespoons butter in a
heavy skillet over moderate heat 8–10
minutes until golden, stirring occasionally; mix in rice, sage, nutmeg, and
¾ teaspoon salt. Spoon into a lightly
greased 2-quart casserole and set aside.
Dredge chops by shaking in a heavy
paper bag with flour, paprika, pepper,
and remaining salt. Brown chops
5 minutes on a side in 1 tablespoon
butter in same skillet over moderately
high heat; pour off drippings. Lay
chops on top of rice, pour wine over all,
cover, and bake about 1 hour or until
chops are cooked through. About 545
calories per serving.

SKILLET PORK CHOPS AND RICE

Makes 4 servings

*4 loin or rib pork chops, cut 1" thick
  and trimmed of excess fat*
1 teaspoon cooking oil
2 teaspoons salt
¼ teaspoon pepper
1 cup uncooked rice
*1 (10½-ounce) can condensed beef or
  chicken broth or onion soup*
1 cup hot water

Brown chops well on each side, about
8–10 minutes, over moderately high
heat in a skillet brushed with oil. Pour

off all but 1 tablespoon drippings, sprinkle chops with half the salt and pepper. Scatter rice over chops and sprinkle with remaining salt and pepper. Add broth and water, cover, and simmer 50–60 minutes until chops are tender. About 415 calories per serving.

To Bake: Brown chops as directed, transfer to a 2-quart ungreased casserole, season, add remaining ingredients, cover and bake 1 hour at 350° F. until chops are tender.

VARIATIONS:

Baked Pork Chops, Peppers, and Rice: Brown chops as directed and transfer to an ungreased 2-quart casserole. In drippings stir-fry 2 diced sweet green peppers and 1 thinly sliced yellow onion 5–8 minutes over moderate heat until onion is pale golden. Mix in rice, spoon over chops, add seasonings, broth, and water; cover and bake 1 hour at 350° F. until chops are tender. About 435 calories per serving.

Spanish Pork Chops and Rice: Prepare variation above through point of stirring rice into skillet mixture. Mix in 1 crushed clove garlic and spoon over chops; add 1 (1-pound 12-ounce) can undrained tomatoes (break them up with a fork) instead of broth and water or use 1 (1-pound) can Spanish-style tomato sauce and ½ cup hot water. Season, cover, and bake 1 hour at 350° F. until chops are tender. About 470 calories per serving.

EASY PORK CHOP CASSEROLE

Makes 4 servings

4 loin or rib pork chops, cut 1" thick and trimmed of excess fat
1½ teaspoons salt
3–4 medium-size potatoes, peeled and sliced ½" thick
2 large yellow onions, peeled and sliced ¼" thick
⅛ teaspoon pepper
1 (10½-ounce) can condensed cream of celery, mushroom, or chicken soup

⅔ cup water or ⅓ cup water and ⅓ cup milk

Preheat oven to 350° F. Arrange chops in a lightly greased 2½-quart casserole. Sprinkle with ¾ teaspoon salt, top with potatoes, onions, remaining salt, and the pepper. Blend soup and water and pour into casserole; cover and bake 1 hour. If you like, brown 2–3 minutes under broiler just before serving. About 435 calories per serving.

VARIATIONS:

Pork Chop and Green Pepper Casserole: Arrange chops in casserole; omit potatoes and top instead with 3 sweet green peppers, cored, seeded, and cut in wide strips; season. Use tomato soup instead of celery, thin with ⅔ cup water, and pour over chops, or use 1½ cups tomato sauce (do not thin). Cover and bake. About 370 calories per serving.

Pork Chop and Mixed Vegetable Casserole: Arrange chops in casserole; on top of them layer 3 peeled sliced potatoes, 1 seeded, cored, sliced green pepper, 2 peeled and sliced large yellow onions, and 1 cup whole kernel corn; season. Mix 1 (10½-ounce) can vegetable soup with ½ cup water and pour over all. Cover and bake as directed. About 475 calories per serving.

SWEET-SOUR PORK, POTATO, AND ONION CASSEROLE

Makes 4 servings

4 loin pork chops, cut 1" thick and trimmed of excess fat
1 teaspoon cooking oil
2 large yellow onions, peeled and sliced ¼" thick
⅓ cup cider vinegar
⅓ cup firmly packed light brown sugar
¾ cup fruit juice (orange, pineapple, apple, or a combination)
1 tablespoon Worcestershire sauce
1¼ teaspoons salt
¼ teaspoon pepper
1 tablespoon cornstarch mixed with 1 tablespoon cold water
4 large potatoes, peeled and quartered lengthwise

Preheat oven to 375° F. Brown chops 8–10 minutes on each side over moderately high heat in a skillet brushed with oil, then transfer to an ungreased 2½-quart casserole. Sauté onions in drippings 8–10 minutes until golden and spread over chops. Add remaining ingredients to skillet and heat, stirring, until slightly thickened. Pour sauce over chops, tucking potatoes in here and there. Cover and bake ¾–1 hour until chops and potatoes are tender.

VARIATION:

Substitute root beer for the fruit juice —believe it or not, it's good. Both versions: about 480 calories per serving.

PANFRIED PORK CHOPS

Though it's not generally recommended that pork chops be panfried, they can be prepared this way if cut quite thin (no more than ½″ thick) and cooked very gently. Made by the following recipe, they are surprisingly tender and moist. Makes 4 servings

8 loin or rib pork chops, cut ½″ thick
and trimmed of excess fat
1 teaspoon cooking oil
1 teaspoon salt
¼ teaspoon pepper

Country Gravy (optional):

3 tablespoons flour
1½ cups milk
¾ teaspoon salt (about)
⅛ teaspoon pepper

Brown chops 2–3 minutes on each side over moderate heat in a large, heavy skillet brushed with oil. (*Note:* If necessary, use 2 skillets to avoid crowding pan.) Turn heat to low and cook chops, uncovered, 10–15 minutes, turning frequently until no trace of pink remains. Sprinkle with salt and pepper, transfer to a hot platter, and keep warm while making gravy. Drain all but 2 tablespoons drippings from skillet, blend in flour and brown lightly over moderately low heat. Add milk gradually and heat, stirring, until thickened. Season to taste with salt and pepper. Spoon some gravy over chops

before serving, if you like, or pass separately. About 345 calories per serving.

VARIATIONS:

Country-Fried Pork Chops: Dredge chops, 1 at a time, by shaking in a heavy paper bag with ¾ cup unsifted flour, the salt, and pepper. Brown, increasing amount of oil to 1 tablespoon, then finish cooking as directed. Serve with Country Gravy. About 370 calories per serving.

German-Style Breaded Pork Chops: Dip chops in ½ cup unsifted flour to coat evenly, then in 1 egg beaten with 1 tablespoon cold water, then in 1 cup toasted, seasoned bread crumbs. Let dry on a rack at room temperature 10 minutes. Panfry as directed, using 2 tablespoons cooking oil. Serve with Country Gravy and boiled potatoes or buttered noodles. (*Note:* If you prefer, use crushed cornflakes or cracker meal instead of crumbs for breading chops.) About 405 calories per serving.

Italian-Style Breaded Pork Chops: Dip chops in ½ cup unsifted flour to coat, then in 1 egg beaten with 1 tablespoon cold water, then in ¾ cup toasted, seasoned bread crumbs mixed with ¼ cup grated Parmesan cheese. Let dry on a rack at room temperature 10 minutes. Panfry as directed in 2 tablespoons olive oil over very low heat to avoid scorching crumb coating. Serve with hot Tomato Sauce. About 415 calories per serving (without tomato sauce).

SWEET AND SOUR PORK

Makes 2 servings

⅓ cup soy sauce mixed with ⅓ cup
sugar
¾ pound boned lean pork loin, trimmed
of fat and cut in ¾″ cubes
Shortening or cooking oil for deep fat
frying
¼ cup sifted cornstarch
2 tablespoons cooking oil
1 clove garlic, peeled and minced
1 medium-size sweet green pepper,
cored, seeded, and cut in 1″ squares

1 medium-size carrot, peeled and cut in julienne strips
1 cup chicken broth
¼ cup cider vinegar
2 tablespoons sugar
2 tablespoons soy sauce
1½ teaspoons cornstarch blended with 1 tablespoon cold water
2 pineapple rings, cut in ¾" cubes

Heat soy sauce mixture, stirring, until sugar dissolves; pour over pork, cover, and chill 4–8 hours, turning meat occasionally. Begin heating fat for deep fat frying over high heat; insert wire basket and deep fat thermometer. Lift meat from marinade with slotted spoon, roll in cornstarch, and let dry 5 minutes. When fat reaches 350° F., fry cubes 2–3 minutes until golden brown; drain in basket and keep warm. Heat 2 tablespoons oil in *wok* or heavy skillet over moderate heat 1 minute, add garlic, pepper, and carrot, and stir-fry 2–3 minutes; do not brown. Mix in broth, vinegar, sugar, and soy sauce, cover, and simmer 2–3 minutes. Add cornstarch mixture, pineapple, and pork and heat, stirring, until slightly thickened. Serve over boiled rice or Chinese Fried Rice; pass extra soy sauce. About 635 calories per serving (without rice).

VARIATION:

Sweet and Sour Spareribs: Substitute 1½ pounds 3" spareribs for pork loin; cut into individual ribs, cover with water, and simmer 35–45 minutes until just tender. Drain, marinate, dredge, and fry as directed (watch ribs carefully while frying, they brown quickly). Proceed as recipe directs, adding spareribs to skillet with cornstarch mixture and pineapple. About 635 calories per serving.

Spareribs, Back Ribs, and Country-Style Backbone

These bony cuts provide as good eating as any other part of the hog. Spareribs used to be budget fare—but no more; they've grown far too popular to remain poor man's meat. The lesser known back ribs and country-style backbone are still good buys, however, and can be substituted for spareribs in any of the following recipes.

How to Cook

Amounts Needed: Allow ¾–1 pound ribs per person. Always choose ribs that are meaty between the bones and that have a thin covering of meat over the bones.

General Preparation for Cooking: If ribs are to be spit-roasted, leave in 1 piece; otherwise, cut in serving size chunks 2-ribs wide. Marinate, if you like, in a piquant sauce—the ribs will be better for it.

To Roast:

Continuous Low Heat Method: Preheat oven to 325° F. Place ribs on a rack in a shallow roasting pan and roast, uncovered, about 30 minutes per pound until well done. (*Note:* Because of thinness and boniness of ribs, it is practically impossible to get an accurate meat thermometer reading. To test for doneness, make a cut near the center of a meaty section; if no pink remains, ribs are done.)

Searing Method: Preheat oven to 450° F. Place ribs on a rack in a shallow roasting pan and roast, uncovered, 30 minutes; drain off all drippings. Reduce heat to 325° F. and roast, uncovered, about 20 minutes per pound longer or until well done.

To Spit-Roast:

In Rotisserie or Oven: Preheat unit. Balance ribs on spit by weaving rod in and out; attach to rotisserie and roast about 20 minutes per pound until well done.

Over Charcoal: Build a moderate charcoal fire.* Balance ribs on spit, attach to rotisserie, adjust height so spit is 4"–5" from coals, and roast about 20 minutes per pound until well done (place drip pan under ribs to reduce flare-ups).

VARIATION:

Spit-Barbecued Ribs: Marinate ribs in refrigerator 12–24 hours in 2 cups All-Purpose or other barbecue sauce, turning 2–3 times. Lift from marinade, shake off excess, and spit-roast as above, basting often with sauce during last 15–20 minutes.

To Braise: Here is the best way to cook ribs because the meat becomes extra juicy, extra flavorful, and so tender it practically falls off the bones. Technically, oven-barbecued ribs are braised because they cook with a small amount of liquid; so are ribs prepared by any of the other following recipes.

CHINESE-STYLE SPARERIBS

Sweet-sour and soy-glazed.
Makes 4 servings

4 pounds (3" long) lean spareribs, cut in serving size pieces

Sauce:

1 cup soy sauce
1 cup sugar
1 cup water
6 cloves garlic, peeled and crushed
¼ cup Hoi Sin sauce (available in Chinese groceries) or ¼ teaspoon ginger

Place ribs in a large, deep bowl. Simmer sauce ingredients 2–3 minutes, stirring, until sugar dissolves; pour over ribs, cover, and chill overnight, turning ribs occasionally. Preheat oven to 350° F. Arrange ribs in shallow roasting pan and pour in sauce. Bake, uncovered, 2 hours, turning ribs every ½ hour and basting with sauce, until fork tender and glossy brown. Serve with hot mustard and plum sauce. About 560 calories per serving.

LUAU SPARERIBS

Superb finger food! Honey gives these spareribs a mellow, *slightly* sweet flavor.
Makes 6 servings

5 pounds spareribs, cut in serving-size pieces
2 cups water

Sauce:

½ cup kettle broth
½ cup ketchup
⅓ cup honey
⅓ cup soy sauce
2 tablespoons dry sherry
2 small slices fresh gingerroot, peeled and crushed, or ½ teaspoon ginger
1 clove garlic peeled and crushed

Place ribs in a very large, heavy skillet or roaster, add water, cover, and simmer 1 hour; drain, reserving ½ cup kettle broth. Spread ribs out on a large tray. Mix kettle broth with remaining sauce ingredients and pour over ribs; cover and refrigerate 8 hours, turning 1–2 times. When ready to cook, preheat broiler or, if you prefer, prepare a moderate charcoal fire.* Broil or grill ribs 4"–5" from heat, basting continually with sauce and turning often until all sauce is gone and ribs are crisply brown. This will take about 15 minutes. About 405 calories per serving.

FAVORITE BARBECUED SPARERIBS

Richly glazed but not too spicy.
Makes 6 servings

5 pounds spareribs, cut in serving-size pieces

Sauce:

1 cup firmly packed light brown sugar
¼ cup Worcestershire sauce
⅓ cup soy sauce
¼ cup cider vinegar
¼ cup chili sauce
½ cup ketchup
2 teaspoons prepared mild yellow mustard
2 cloves garlic, peeled and crushed
⅛ teaspoon pepper

Preheat oven to 350° F. Place ribs in a large, shallow roasting pan and bake, uncovered, ¾ hour. Drain off all drippings. Mix sauce ingredients, pour over ribs, and bake uncovered 1¼–1½ hours longer, turning and basting every 20 minutes until tender and richly browned. (*Note:* For even better flavor, marinate ribs in sauce in turned-off oven 3–4 hours after first ¾ hour of baking and drain off drippings; then bake 1½ hours longer as directed.)

VARIATIONS:

Favorite Charcoal-Barbecued Spareribs: Wrap ribs in a double thickness heavy foil and bake 1½ hours at 350° F. Unwrap and drain off drippings. Marinate ribs in sauce 1–2 hours at room temperature; meanwhile, prepare a moderate charcoal fire.* Remove ribs from sauce, lay on grill about 4″ from coals, taking care not to crowd them, and broil 20 minutes, basting frequently with sauce and turning often.

Both versions: about 405 calories per serving.

OVEN BARBECUED COUNTRY-STYLE SPARERIBS

For those who like their barbecue "hot."
Makes 4 servings

4 pounds spareribs, cut in serving size pieces

Sauce:

⅓ cup orange juice
⅓ cup lemon juice
⅓ cup ketchup or chili sauce
⅓ cup molasses
1 tablespoon Worcestershire sauce
1 clove garlic, peeled and crushed
1 teaspoon powdered mustard
1 teaspoon salt
1 teaspoon prepared horseradish
3 drops liquid hot red pepper seasoning

Topping:

2 lemons, sliced thin

Preheat oven to 450° F. Place ribs in a large, shallow roasting pan and roast, uncovered, 30 minutes, turning once. Remove from oven and drain off all fat. Turn oven off. Mix all sauce ingredients together and pour over ribs. Top with sliced lemons, cover loosely with foil, and let stand at room temperature 2–3 hours. Preheat oven to 325° F. Return ribs to oven and roast, uncovered, about 1 hour until tender and well browned, basting frequently with sauce in pan. Remove lemon slices and serve. About 480 calories per serving.

PAPRIKA SPARERIBS WITH CARAWAY SAUERKRAUT

Spareribs the German way, oven-baked on a bed of chopped apple and sauerkraut.
Makes 4 servings

3 pounds spareribs, cut in serving-size pieces
1½ teaspoons salt
1 teaspoon paprika
⅛ teaspoon pepper
1 (1-pound) can sauerkraut (do not drain)
1 large tart apple, peeled, cored, and coarsely chopped
1 teaspoon caraway seeds

Preheat oven to 350° F. Arrange spareribs meaty side up in a single layer in a large roasting pan; sprinkle evenly with salt, paprika, and pepper. Roast, uncovered, ½ hour, turn, and roast ½ hour longer; drain off all drippings. Mix sauerkraut, apple, and caraway seeds and place *under* spareribs. Return to oven and roast, uncovered, 1 hour, turning ribs occasionally. To serve, pile sauerkraut in the center of a large hot platter and surround with spareribs. Good with noodles and sour cream. About 380 calories per serving (without noodles and sour cream).

BAKED SPARERIBS WITH APPLE-CELERY STUFFING

Because the flavor of pork is not unlike that of chicken, you can, if you like, substitute your favorite poultry stuffing for the Apple-Celery Stuffing. You might also try the Apple-Celery Stuffing for chicken. It's delicious.
Makes 4 servings

3 pounds spareribs, cut in chunks 3 or 4 ribs wide
1 teaspoon salt ·
¼ teaspoon pepper

Apple-Celery Stuffing:

1 cup soft white bread crumbs
½ cup finely chopped apple
¼ cup minced celery
2 tablespoons minced yellow onion
1 tablespoon minced parsley
⅛ teaspoon cinnamon
½ teaspoon salt
⅛ teaspoon pepper
1 egg, lightly beaten

Preheat oven to 350° F. Toss together all stuffing ingredients. Turn half the ribs hollow side up and spread evenly with stuffing; top with remaining ribs, meaty side up, to make "sandwiches," then tie each securely with string. Place ribs in a shallow roasting pan and sprinkle with half the salt and pepper. Bake, uncovered, 1 hour and drain off drippings; turn ribs, sprinkle with remaining salt and pepper, and bake 1 hour longer or until tender and well browned. Transfer to a hot platter, remove strings and serve. About 405 calories per serving.

VARIATION:
Substitute 2 cups any bread or rice stuffing for the Apple-Celery Stuffing.

GROUND PORK

Because of the danger of trichinosis, some local laws forbid butchers to grind raw pork (if the machine isn't thoroughly cleaned after grinding pork, the next batch of meat to go through may become contaminated; this is especially dangerous with beef, which is so often eaten rare). If you grind pork yourself, wash each grinding part thoroughly in hot soapy water, then rinse well in boiling water and wipe dry with a clean soft cloth.

The best cuts of pork to grind are shoulder, picnic, or lean trimmings from the side or belly. The more times and the more finely pork is ground, the more compact it will be when cooked. For a light-textured loaf, coarsely grind, once. For pork balls, where a firmer texture is preferable, grind fine, two or three times.

PORK AND VEAL RING

Makes 6 servings

1 pound ground lean pork
1 pound ground veal
4 slices white bread, trimmed of crusts
½ cup milk
1 medium-size yellow onion, peeled and grated fine
2 tablespoons finely grated lemon rind
1 teaspoon poultry seasoning
1 tablespoon salt
¼ teaspoon pepper
1 egg, lightly beaten

Preheat oven to 350° F. Mix pork and veal. Cut bread into small cubes, soak in milk 5 minutes, then mix with meat and all remaining ingredients. Pack into a lightly greased 5-cup ring mold and bake, uncovered, 1 hour. Let stand 5 minutes; loosen edges and pour off drippings (save for gravy). Turn ring out on a hot platter and fill center, if you like, with mashed potatoes or yams or any creamed vegetable. Pass gravy or Mushroom Gravy. About 330 calories per serving.

To Bake as a Loaf: Pack mixture into a lightly greased 9" × 5" × 3" loaf pan or shape into a loaf in a lightly greased, shallow roasting pan. Bake as directed.

PORK BALLS IN SOUR CREAM GRAVY

Makes 4 servings

Pork Balls:

1 pound ground pork shoulder
¼ cup sifted flour
1 medium-size yellow onion, peeled and finely grated
¼ teaspoon sage
½ teaspoon finely grated lemon rind
1 teaspoon salt
⅛ teaspoon pepper
½ cup soft white bread crumbs
1 egg, lightly beaten
¼ cup ice water

Gravy:

2 tablespoons bacon drippings or cooking
  oil
3 tablespoons flour
¾ cup water
¾ cup milk
1 cup condensed beef broth or chicken
  broth
½ cup sour cream

Toss together all ingredients for meat balls, then, using a rounded tablespoon as a measure, roll into small balls. Brown well in drippings in a large skillet over moderately low heat 10 minutes, remove with slotted spoon and keep warm. Drain off all but 2 tablespoons drippings, blend in flour and brown lightly. Slowly add water, milk, and broth and heat, stirring, until thickened; simmer uncovered 2–3 minutes. Mix in sour cream, return pork balls to skillet, and warm 5 minutes over lowest heat; do not boil. Serve over boiled rice or buttered noodles. About 470 calories per serving (without rice or noodles).

VARIATIONS:

Curried Pork Balls: Omit sage from meat balls but add ½–1 teaspoon curry powder. When making gravy, blend ½ teaspoon curry powder into drippings along with flour; omit sour cream. Otherwise, prepare as directed. Serve with chutney. About 410 calories per serving.

Pork and Peanut Balls: Omit sage from meat balls but add ¼ cup finely chopped toasted peanuts. Proceed as directed. About 530 calories per serving.

¢ TOURTIÈRE

Tourtière is a spicy pork pie traditionally served by French Canadians at *réveillon,* the Christmas feast following midnight mass. Some tourtières contain beef, but the most authentic are made entirely of pork.
Makes 6–8 servings

Filling:

1½ pounds ground lean pork
1 teaspoon salt

¼ teaspoon celery salt
¼ teaspoon pepper
⅛ teaspoon cloves
½ teaspoon savory
1 small bay leaf, crumbled

Pastry:

1 recipe Flaky Pastry II

Sauté pork in a large skillet over moderate heat, breaking it up with a fork, until no pink remains. Turn heat to low, stir in all remaining filling ingredients, cover, and simmer 15 minutes. Uncover and simmer 10 minutes longer until liquid reduces to about ⅓ cup. Drain liquid into a small bowl and chill. Cool meat to room temperature. Meanwhile, prepare pastry as directed; roll and fit half into a 9″ piepan; reserve the rest for the top crust. Preheat oven to 450° F. Skim fat from reserved liquid, then mix liquid into meat and spoon into pie shell. Moisten pastry edges with cold water. Roll top crust and cut decorative steam vents near the center. Top pie with crust, seal pastry edges and crimp. Bake 10 minutes, then reduce heat to 350° F. and bake 30–35 minutes longer until pastry is lightly browned. Cut into wedges while still warm and serve with bread and butter pickles or sweet pickle relish. (*Note:* Baked tourtières can be cooled to room temperature, wrapped airtight, and frozen. To serve: Thaw, then reheat, uncovered, for ½ hour in a 350° F. oven.) About 415 calories for each of 6 servings, 310 calories for each of 8 servings.

The Cuts of Pork to Stew

Europeans, the old saying goes, "eat everything about a pig but its squeal." We aren't so imaginative (or adventurous?) but do enjoy hocks, feet, and sinewy trimmings when well prepared.

Hocks: The fleshy, upper portion of a hog's front legs.

Pigs' Feet: Also called *trotters,* these are the feet and ankles of pigs. They are bony, full of gristle and tendons, but if stewed or pickled, the meat becomes tender and the gristle cooks down into gelatin. The forefeet are more delicate than the hind (these aren't often sold). Have your butcher clean and prepare pigs' feet for cooking.

Stew Meat: The best parts of pork to use for stew are belly (well trimmed of fat), shoulder (Boston butt), and picnic because of their well-developed flavor and firm texture.

¢ PORK AND RED CABBAGE RAGOUT

Makes 6 servings

3 pounds boned pork shoulder, cut in 1½" cubes and trimmed of excess fat
3 medium-size yellow onions, peeled and coarsely chopped
1 medium-size tart apple, peeled, cored, and diced
Leaves from 2 stalks celery
4 cloves
6 peppercorns
2 (13¾-ounce) cans chicken broth
1 cup dry red wine
2 teaspoons salt
½ small red cabbage, trimmed, cut in slim wedges, and parboiled
1½ cups sour cream

Brown pork, a few pieces at a time, in a large, heavy kettle over high heat (you won't need any fat) and drain on paper toweling. Reduce heat to moderate, add onions and apple, and stir-fry 8–10 minutes until golden. Return pork to kettle. Tie celery leaves, cloves, and peppercorns in cheesecloth and add to kettle along with broth, wine, and salt. Cover and simmer 1¾ hours until pork is almost tender. Add cabbage wedges, pushing them down into stew, re-cover, and simmer 15–20 minutes longer until pork and cabbage are tender. Discard cheesecloth bag. Remove stew from heat; using a slotted spoon, lift cabbage from kettle and wreathe around a large, deep platter; pile meat in center and keep warm. Blend sour cream into kettle liquid and heat and stir 1–2 minutes (do not boil). Ladle over cabbage and pork and serve. About 675 calories per serving.

¢ SPICY PORK AND TURNIP STEW

Makes 6 servings

3 pounds boned pork shoulder, cut in 1½" cubes and trimmed of excess fat
5 large turnips, peeled and cut in ½" cubes
2 medium-size yellow onions, peeled and coarsely chopped
1 clove garlic, peeled and crushed
4 whole allspice
6 peppercorns
4 cloves
4 sprigs parsley
1 (13¾-ounce) can chicken broth
½ cup dry white wine
1 cup water
1 teaspoon salt
2 tablespoons flour blended with 3 tablespoons cold water

Brown pork well on all sides in a large, heavy kettle over high heat (you won't need any fat). Reduce heat to low, add turnips, onions, and garlic, and stir-fry with pork 5 minutes. Tie spices and parsley in cheesecloth and add along with all remaining ingredients except flour-water paste, cover, and simmer 2 hours until pork is tender. Remove pork and turnips with a slotted spoon and set aside; discard cheesecloth bag. Strain cooking liquid, return to kettle, mix in flour-water paste, and heat, stirring constantly, until thickened. Remove pork and turnips to kettle and heat, uncovered, 5 minutes longer, stirring occasionally. Serve with boiled potatoes or sweet potatoes. About 550 calories per serving (without potatoes).

⚔ ¢ PORK HOCKS WITH SAUERKRAUT

Pork hocks and sauerkraut can be served with or without the cooking liquid; in either case boiled potatoes and crusty bread are traditional accompaniments.

Makes 4 servings

6 meaty pork hocks
1 quart cold water
1 medium-size yellow onion, peeled and sliced thin
2 bay leaves
10 peppercorns
2 sprigs parsley or 1 teaspoon dried parsley
Leaves from 2 stalks celery, coarsely chopped, or ½ teaspoon celery salt
1 (1-pound 11-ounce) can sauerkraut, drained

Scrub hocks well under cold running water; scrape skin with a sharp knife to remove any hairs. Place hocks in a 1½-gallon kettle with water and onion. Tie bay leaves, peppercorns, parsley, and celery leaves in cheesecloth and add to kettle (if using celery salt, mix with kettle liquid). Cover and bring to a boil over moderate heat; uncover and skim off froth. Reduce heat to low and simmer, covered, 2–2½ hours until meat is very tender. Discard cheesecloth bag. Cool, cover, and chill several hours until fat rises to surface and hardens. When ready to serve, skim off fat (broth will be jellied), add sauerkraut, cover, and heat slowly until piping hot. About 300 calories per serving.

⚖ ¢ STEWED PIGS' FEET (BASIC METHOD)

Before they can be used in recipes, pigs' feet require careful, preliminary stewing. Allow 1–2 pigs' feet per person and have butcher clean and prepare them for cooking.

Stock (enough for 4–6 pigs' feet):

1½ quarts water
¾ cup dry white wine
2 carrots, peeled and sliced thin
2 stalks celery, sliced thin
2 medium-size yellow onions, peeled and each stuck with 2 cloves
1 bouquet garni,* tied in cheesecloth
1 tablespoon salt
4 peppercorns

Wash pigs' feet well in cool water, then tie each tightly in cheesecloth so it will keep its shape. Place in a large, heavy kettle with stock ingredients, cover, and bring to a simmer over moderate heat. Adjust heat so stock stays at a slow simmer and cook, covered, 4–5 hours until feet are very tender. Cool in liquid, drain well (save broth for soups and stews), and remove cheesecloth. Use in any of the following recipes. About 255 calories per pig's foot.

VARIATIONS:

¢ ⚖ **Pickled Pigs' Feet:** Prepare by recipe above, but use 3 cups each cider vinegar and water for stewing instead of 1½ quarts water. When feet are tender, cool in liquid, drain, and chill well. Remove cheesecloth and serve cold with Spanish Vinaigrette Sauce. About 255 calories per pickled pig's foot.

¢ ⚖ **Stewed Calf's Feet:** First, blanch feet. *To blanch calf's feet:* Wash and scrub well in cool water, place in a large, heavy kettle, cover with cold water, cover, and bring to a boil. Drain, rinse feet in cold water, and wash kettle. Return feet to kettle, add stock ingredients listed for Stewed Pigs' Feet (above), and proceed as recipe directs. About 140 calories per calf's foot.

⚖ ¢ PIGS' FEET IN SCALLION AND JUNIPER SAUCE

Makes 4 servings

6 pigs' feet, stewed (see Index)

Sauce:

⅓ cup minced scallions
2 tablespoons butter or margarine
⅔ cup white wine vinegar
6 juniper berries, crushed
Pinch nutmeg
Pinch pepper
1¼ cups stock (use that from stewing pigs' feet)
2 tablespoons flour blended with 3 tablespoons cold water

After stewing pigs' feet, cool in stock just until easy to handle; drain, remove cheesecloth and keep feet warm while preparing sauce. Sauté scallions in butter in a small saucepan 8–10 minutes, stirring occasionally, over moderate heat until golden; add vinegar, juniper berries, nutmeg, and pepper and boil, uncovered, to reduce. When almost all vinegar has evaporated, add stock. Mix in flour paste and heat, stirring, until thickened and smooth. Pour sauce over pigs' feet and serve. About 290 calories per serving.

VARIATION:

Instead of making Scallion and Juniper Sauce, serve pigs' feet with Mustard, Diable, or any other suitable sauce (see Sauces, Gravies, and Seasonings for Pork).

HAM AND OTHER CURED PORK
(See Pork Chart)

Whether served as a festive holiday ham, glistening under an amber glaze, a cool, spicy loaf, or a grilled steak, ham runs beef a close second as America's favorite meat. Although we think of any cured pork as ham, it is technically the hind leg only, and it can be fresh as well as cured. We are concerned here with all the cured and smoked cuts, the bacons and butts, picnics and jowls as well as the hams. Here's a quick dictionary to those commonly used:

Aged Hams: Heavily cured and smoked hams that have been hung from one to seven years. They are usually covered with mold (it washes off and does not mean the meat is spoiled).

Country Cured Hams: Hams (and sometimes other cuts of pork) that have been dry-cured (preserved in a mixture of dry salt and seasonings), smoked slowly over fragrant hardwood fires, and aged at least six months. The meat is mahogany colored, salty, and firm. America's most famous country hams are the Virginia, Smithfield, Tennessee, Georgia, and Kentucky; each is salty and firm of flesh, each has a distinctive flavor, determined by breed of hog, feed, and seasonings used in the curing. Most country cured hams are uncooked, although fully cooked ones are now available. Read labels carefully.

Cured Hams: Curing is a method of preserving, not of cooking. Large processors cure hams by soaking in brine or, more recently, by pumping brine through the meat. Cured hams may or may not be smoked and may or may not be cooked.

Cured and Smoked Hams: Hams that have been brined and smoked—but not cooked unless labels clearly say so.

Cook-Before-Eating Hams: This is the term commonly used to identify uncooked or partially cooked hams. It's a good term because the shopper knows at a glance that the meat must be cooked before serving.

Fully Cooked Hams: Hams so labeled can be eaten straight from the wrapper; they will develop richer flavor, however, if baked until meat thermometer reads 130° F.

Ready-to-Eat Hams: The same as fully cooked hams.

Smoked Ham or Pork: Meat that has been cured, then smoked, but not necessarily cooked.

Sugar Cured Hams: Hams cured in brine or dry salt mixed with brown sugar or molasses.

Tendered or Tenderized Hams: These terms are often misinterpreted to mean "cooked hams." They are really only sales words and mean little.

Uncooked Hams: Raw hams that must be thoroughly cooked before eating. They may be cured or cured and smoked.

How to Recognize Quality in Ham and Other Cured Pork

Large cuts often—but not always—carry the round federal inspector's seal guaranteeing wholesomeness of meat. Quality is less easily determined because little pork is federally graded and because the appearance of cured pork ranges from the pale pink of processed hams to the offputting moldiness of aged country cured hams. Both may be of top quality. Your best assurance is to buy reputable brands.

Standard Processed Hams

These tender, cured packing-house hams are usually smoked (but not always). They may be fully cooked or uncooked; labels should clearly state which.

Whole Ham:

Bone-In (8–24 pounds): The full hind leg of the hog.

Semiboneless (6 pounds up): A ham from which the troublesome hip (aitch) and shank bones have been removed to simplify carving. The leg bone remains in, helping ham hold its compact oval shape, but skin and excess fat have been removed. Also sold as half hams or by the slice.

Boneless (6–14 pounds): A boned and rolled ham.

Half Ham:

Butt Portion (4–12 pounds): Also called Full Butt, this is the choice meaty, rump half of the ham, more expensive than the shank portion.

Shank Portion (4–12 pounds): Also known as Full Shank. This leg half of the ham is bonier and less expensive than the butt half.

Semiboneless (4 pounds and up): Half a semiboneless ham (see above).

Boneless (3–7 pounds): Half a boned and rolled ham (see above).

Ham End: This is what's left of a ham after the center slices or steaks have been removed. The Butt End is meaty but contains the cumbersome hipbone; the Shank End tapers sharply and may be too skimpy to roast.

Specialty Hams

Domestic:

Smithfield: So many country cured hams claim to be the prized Smithfield hams that the Virginia General Assembly has adopted a statute: "Genuine Smithfield hams are cut from carcasses of peanut-fed hogs, raised in the peanut belt of the State of Virginia or the State of North Carolina, and cured, treated, smoked and processed in the town of Smithfield in the State of Virginia." What makes these hams so special is their firm, mahogany-hued flesh and smoky-salty flavor. Most must be cooked long and slow before eating, though some are now sold fully cooked. Available only as whole hams (12–14 pounds is a good size) through gourmet butchers or via mail order.

Virginia: Like Smithfield hams, these country cured hams are firm of flesh and salty of flavor. They may be from hogs fattened on peanuts, or those allowed to forage for acorns, nuts, and aromatic roots. Whole hams are available uncooked or fully cooked from gourmet butchers, also by mail order.

Canned Ham: Boned, skinned, trimmed, ready-to-eat hams. They are cured but not necessarily smoked and weigh from 1½–10 pounds (the larger the ham, the better). Though fully cooked, canned hams will have better flavor if baked or sliced and panfried. Some come with special glazes—honey, champagne, pineapple (we've found that, to be really well glazed, most need a little longer in the oven than can directions recommend). Some require refrigeration, so read label carefully and store accordingly.

Imported: (*Note:* Because trichinosis is not a problem in Europe, many European hams are eaten raw.)

Bayonne Ham: Dry-cured ham from Béarn or the Basque country of France. Many are cured in the town of Bayonne (hence the name), many simply cured with Bayonne salt. The hams are raw and the Basques like to eat them that way on buttered slabs of rough peasant bread. Available in gourmet groceries.

Irish Ham: The best known come from Belfast. They may be bone-in or boneless, pickled or brined; what gives them their unique flavor is the smoking over peat fires. Irish hams must be soaked, scrubbed, and simmered, then baked before eating (prepare like Country Cured Ham). Available in specialty food shops.

Prosciutto: What we call *prosciutto* is really Parma ham (*prosciutto* is simply the Italian word for *ham*). These hams come from Parma, Italy, are exquisitely seasoned, salt cured, air dried, and pressed so that their rosy brown flesh is unusually firm. Prosciutto is most often sliced tissue thin and eaten raw as an appetizer but can be used in recipes. Available in gourmet groceries, also in cold cut counters of many metropolitan supermarkets.

Westphalian Ham: A salty, reddish German ham similar to prosciutto that comes from hogs fed sugar beet mash. It, too, is sliced paper thin and eaten raw. Available in specialty food shops.

York Ham: An English ham with mild flavor and delicate pink meat. Like Irish ham, it must be cooked before eating (use recipe for Country Cured Ham). When served hot, York ham is traditionally accompanied by Madeira Sauce.

Canned Ham: The most readily available imported canned hams are the York, Prague, and Polish, all mild-cured, all skinless and boneless. Also available in specialty food shops are canned prosciutto and Westphalian hams.

How to Bake Ham

Note: What we call baked ham is really roasted; it has simply been the American habit to speak of ham as baked the same way we speak of a meat loaf or potato as baked although these, too, are technically roasted.

Suitable Cuts: Any of the standard processed hams, canned hams, or country cured hams. Each requires a somewhat different technique, however.

Amount Needed: The bigger the ham, the more succulent it will be. To figure number of servings, allow ⅔ pound per person for a bony ham (shank portion), ⅓–½ pound for other bone-in hams; ¼–⅓ pound boneless ham; also ¼–⅓ pound *net weight* canned ham per person.

General Preparation for Cooking (standard processed hams only): Remove skin, if still on, by slipping a sharp knife underneath and peeling off. Trim fat to ½″. Let ham stand at room temperature 1½–2 hours before cooking, if convenient.

Uncooked (Cook-Before-Eating) Ham: Follow manufacturer's cooking directions or prepare as follows. Preheat oven to 325° F. Place ham on a rack in a shallow roasting pan (whole hams should be fat side up, half hams cut side down). Insert meat thermometer in center, not touching bone. Bake, uncovered, until thermometer reads 160° F. Whole or boneless hams will take approximately 18–20 minutes per pound, half hams 22–24. Transfer ham to heated platter and let "rest" 15–20 minutes before carving. Serve hot or cold.

To Glaze (see Some Glazes for Baked Hams):

Liquid Glazes: Begin basting ham after 15–20 minutes in oven and continue basting at 15–20-minute intervals throughout cooking. About ½ hour before ham is done (no sooner or cuts will spread too much), remove from oven and score fat in a large crisscross pattern, making cuts ⅛″ deep. Stud with cloves or decorate (see On Decorating and Garnishing Hams). Return ham to oven and finish cooking, basting frequently. For a browner glaze, finish cooking at 425° F.

Thick Glazes: Bake ham as directed but do not baste. About ½ hour before ham is done, remove from oven and score. Stud with cloves (avoid intricate decorations because glaze will cover them up). Pat or spread on glaze, return ham to oven, and finish cooking, basting if glaze recipe calls for it. For a richly brown glaze, finish cooking at 425° F.

Ready-to-Eat Hams: If wrapper gives cooking directions, follow them. If not, use procedure for uncooked hams above, but bake only until thermometer registers 130° F. Whole and boneless hams will require about 12–15 minutes per pound, half hams about 18–20. Glaze and decorate as above and serve hot or cold.

Canned Hams: If ham is accompanied by baking directions, use them. If not, prepare as follows. Preheat oven to 325° F. If ham has a heavy fat covering (few canned hams do), trim to ½″. Place ham flattest side down on a rack in a shallow roasting pan. (*Note:* If using a round canned ham, cut a thin slice off bottom so ham won't roll about pan.) Insert meat thermometer in center of ham and bake, uncovered, about 20 minutes per pound or until thermometer registers 130° F. Glaze and decorate as above and serve hot or cold.

Country Cured Hams: A day or two before you plan to serve ham, place in a very large oval kettle, sawing off hock, if necessary, to fit ham in. If ham is very salty, salt crystals will be visible. Cover with cool water and let stand 24 hours at room temperature, changing the water 3–4 times. If ham is not salty, change soaking water 1–2 times. Next day, scrub ham well under running tepid water to remove any mold and pepper.

Wash well again in tepid water. Place ham on a rack in the same large kettle, add cool water to cover, cover, and bring to a boil over high heat. Skim froth from surface, re-cover, adjust heat so water stays at a slow simmer, and cook 25–30 minutes per pound or until fork tender and bone feels loose; cool ham in cooking liquid. Preheat oven to 350° F. Lift ham from liquid, peel off rind, and trim fat to ½″. Score in a crisscross pattern and stud with cloves. Pat on a thick glaze (Brown Sugar and Bread Crumbs is the traditional glaze for Smithfield and Virginia hams). Place ham glaze side up on a rack in a shallow roasting pan and bake, uncovered, 45 minutes or until glaze is nicely browned. Transfer ham to serving platter and let cool at least 20 minutes before serving. In the South, these hams are served at room temperature (or chilled), but almost never hot. When carving, slice paper thin.

How to Spit-Roast Ham

Best Cuts: Ready-to-Eat Hams, especially skinless, boneless rolls (whole, half, or quarter); semiboneless hams can be spit-roasted if carefully balanced. *Not recommended:* uncooked hams (heat is too intense to ensure thorough cooking) and bone-in hams (they are too irregularly shaped to cook evenly).

Amount Needed: ¼–⅓ pound boneless or semiboneless ham per person. Do not try to spit-roast less than a quarter ham roll.

General Preparation for Cooking: Remove any casing; most ham rolls have little outer fat, so trimming is unnecessary. Tie roll as you would a parcel so it will hold its shape during cooking. Let stand at room temperature 1½–2 hours if convenient.

In Rotisserie or Oven: Preheat unit. Insert spit lengthwise through center of ham to balance, tighten holding forks. Insert meat thermometer in center, not touching spit. Attach to rotisserie and roast, using manufacturer's or the following timetable: 10–12 minutes per pound for whole ham rolls, 15–17 for half rolls, and 20 for quarter rolls. Thermometer should read 130° F. Let ham "rest" 15–20 minutes before carving. *To Glaze:* About ½ hour before ham is done, baste with any liquid glaze and continue basting often (see Some Glazes for Baked Hams).

Over Charcoal: Prepare a moderate charcoal fire toward back of grill.* Balance ham on spit and insert thermometer as above, attach spit to rotisserie 6"–7" from coals. Place drip pan at front of fire. Roast, using manufacturer's times or those for rotisserie roasting. Glaze, if you like, as above.

Some Glazes for Baked Hams

Basically, there are two kinds of glaze: (1) liquids that are basted on throughout cooking and (2) thick or dry mixtures that are patted or spread on about ½ hour before ham is done.

Liquid (Baste-On Glazes): (*Note:* Hams basted with beer, champagne, wine, and fruit juice will be glossier if rubbed with a mixture of ¼ cup light brown sugar and 1 teaspoon powdered mustard before cooking.)

Cranberry-Horseradish: 1 (1-pound) can cranberry jelly, melted and mixed with ¼ cup prepared horseradish.

Cider-Sweet Pickle: 1½ cups apple cider mixed with ¾ cup sweet pickle juice.

Champagne or Wine (sherry, port, Madeira, sweet red or white wine).

Beer, Ale, or Stout.

Rum (dark or light).

Fruit Juices: Apple, apricot, cranberry, grape, orange, pineapple. Also good: syrup from canned or pickled peaches or pears.

Syrups: Maple, pancake, light or dark corn syrup, molasses, strained honey.

Thick Glazes:

Brown Sugar and Bread Crumbs: 1 cup firmly packed light brown sugar mixed with ½ cup fine soft white bread crumbs and 1½ teaspoons powdered mustard. Particularly good with Smithfield or Virginia hams.

Mustard: 1 cup firmly packed light brown sugar mixed with ¼ cup prepared mustard (any type) and 2 tablespoons cider vinegar or 3 tablespoons honey, molasses, maple syrup, or dark or light corn syrup.

Cinnamon and Cloves: ¾ cup sugar mixed with ½ teaspoon cloves and ¼ teaspoon cinnamon. Sprinkle evenly over ham and baste with orange or pineapple juice or apple cider.

Sherry or Port: Brush ham with a little warmed light corn syrup, then pat on light brown sugar to a thickness of ¼". Slowly drizzle 1 cup sweet sherry or port over all and finish cooking, basting with additional sherry or port.

Peanut Butter: Spread 1–1½ cups creamy or crunchy peanut butter over ham.

Brown Sugar: Brush a little warmed light or dark corn syrup, molasses, or honey over ham, then pat on light or dark brown sugar to a thickness of about ¼".

Marmalade: Warm orange, lemon, or ginger marmalade slightly and spread evenly over ham.

Preserves: Use apricot, pineapple, peach, pear, or cherry preserves, sieve or purée in a blender at high speed, warm slightly, and spread evenly over ham.

Jelly: Use black or red currant, apple, or cranberry. Melt jelly, then brush over ham every 10 minutes during last ½ hour of baking.

On Decorating and Garnishing Hams

Hams glazed with syrup, fruit juice, wine, or jelly will look more festive if decorated. Use fruits and/or nuts, keeping the design simple. To make design stick to ham, brush surface with warmed corn syrup, honey, or molasses, then simply press on decoration. Larger designs, made with peaches or apricots, have a tendency to slither off, so toothpick in place (be sure to remove toothpicks before carving). It's a good idea to remove any decorations before storing leftover ham because they deteriorate rapidly and may spoil the ham.

Garnishes for Hot Ham Platters:

Spiced, pickled, or brandied peaches
Brandied figs
Orange cups filled with candied yams, whipped sweet potatoes, buttered green peas, or hot cranberry sauce
Fried Apple Rings
Sautéed Pineapple Rings
Sautéed Halved Bananas

Garnishes for Cold Ham Platters:

Chopped aspic (preferably fruit or meat)
Avocado slices and shredded romaine
Lemon cups filled with cold cranberry sauce or tart jelly
Seedless green grapes and crab apples
Whole spiced crab apples and watercress
Preserved kumquats and parsley or watercress

How to Carve a Whole Bone-In Ham:

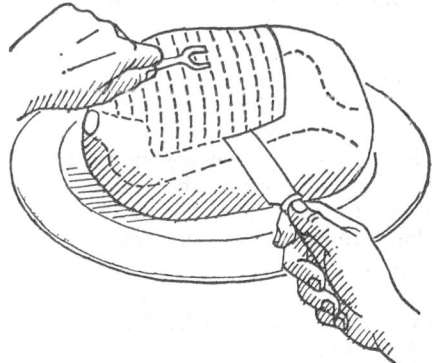

Place ham on platter, fat side up with shank to carver's right. Cut 2–3 slices parallel to leg from thin side (if ham is from left leg, thin side will face carver; if from a right leg, it will be on the far side). Cut straight down from top to bone in thin slices, then release slices by running knife along bone.

How to Carve a Semiboneless Whole Ham:

Stand ham on its side and slice from right to left, cutting down to leg bone. Loosen slices by cutting along bone.

How to Carve a Shank Half Ham:

Turn platter so shank is on left; turn ham so thickest side is up, then cut along bone and lift out boneless "cushion,"

which is the top half of the ham. Place "cushion" cut side down and cut straight through in thin slices. Cut around leg bone and remove; turn ham so flat side is down and slice straight through as with "cushion."

How to Carve a Butt Half Ham:

Place ham face down on platter, cut down along hip (aitch) bone, and remove large boneless chunk from side of ham. Place boneless chunk cut side down and slice straight through. Steady remaining ham with fork, slice across to bone, and loosen each slice with tip of knife.

BAKED PECAN-STUFFED HAM

Makes 18–20 servings

1 (10–12-pound) bone-in or semiboneless cook-before-eating ham
1 gallon cold water (about)
½ cup cider vinegar
½ cup firmly packed dark brown sugar

Stuffing:

2 medium-size yellow onions, peeled and minced
1 cup minced celery
3 tablespoons bacon drippings or cooking oil
2 cups soft white bread crumbs
¼ cup cracker crumbs
¼ teaspoon salt
¼ teaspoon pepper
2 tablespoons minced parsley
1 cup finely chopped pecans
2 eggs, lightly beaten

Topping:

1 cup firmly packed light brown sugar
½ cup soft white bread crumbs
1½ teaspoons powdered mustard

Place ham on a rack in a very large kettle, add water *just* to cover, also vinegar and sugar. Cover and simmer 1½ hours. Meanwhile prepare stuffing: Stir-fry onions and celery in drippings over moderate heat 5–8 minutes until pale golden; off heat mix in remaining ingredients. When ham is tender, cool in broth until easy to handle. Begin preheating oven to 325° F. Lift ham from kettle and place lean side up on counter. With a sharp knife, cut down to and along shank bone; remove all bones (save for stock or soup). Fill cavity with stuffing, skewer shut, and, if you like, tie around with string. Place ham fat side up on a rack in a shallow roasting pan and bake, uncovered, 1¼ hours. Mix topping, pat over ham, and bake 15–20 minutes longer. Remove skewers and string, transfer ham to platter, and serve. Also good cold. About 615 calories for each of 18 servings, 555 calories for each of 20 servings.

To Halve Recipe: Use a 5–6-pound shank portion half ham. Simmer in 2½ quarts water with ⅓ cup each vinegar and dark brown sugar for 1 hour. Halve stuffing recipe. Bone, stuff, and bake ham as above, reducing time to 1 hour. Cover with topping and bake 15–20 minutes longer. About 620 calories for each of 9 servings, 555 calories for each of 10 servings.

HAM EN CROÛTE (HAM IN PASTRY)

For a spectacular buffet, serve ham wrapped in pastry. Use boneless ham (to simplify carving) and one that's pear-

SAUCES, GRAVIES, AND SEASONINGS FOR HAM
AND OTHER CURED PORK

For Cooking Seasonings, Herbs, Spices		For Hot Hams and Ham Steaks Sauces	Gravies
Allspice	Lemon	Hot mustard	Pan Gravy
Bay leaf	Mace	Madeira	Red Eye Gravy
Celery salt	Mustard	Mustard	
Cinnamon	Nutmeg	Orange	
Cloves	Orange	Parsley	
Curry powder	Parsley	Périgueux	
Dill	Sage	Plum	
Ginger	Thyme	Portugaise	
Horseradish		Raisin	
		Robert	
		Sweet-sour	
		Yorkshire	

For Hot or Cold Hams Condiments	For Cold Hams Sauces
Applesauce	Cumberland
Chutney	Cranberry
Horseradish	Dijonnaise
Mustard	Hot mustard
Peaches (brandied, pickled)	Mustard
Pears (brandied, pickled)	Robert
Pickles (bread and butter, dill, green tomato, mustard, watermelon rind)	Sour cream-horseradish
	Spicy cranberry
	Tartar
	Whipped horse-radish
Preserved kumquats	
Relishes (corn, pepper)	
Spiced fruits (crab apples, peaches, pears)	
Soy sauce	

shaped (so the ham will look more like ham).
Makes 16–18 servings

1 (8–10-pound) boneless, ready-to-eat ham

Pastry:

6 cups sifted flour
2 teaspoons salt
2 teaspoons baking powder
½ teaspoon powdered mustard
¼ teaspoon sage
1½ cups vegetable shortening
2 tablespoons lemon juice
1½ cups ice water (about)

Glaze:

2 egg yolks lightly beaten with 2 tablespoons cold water

Bake ham by basic method* but do not glaze. About 20 minutes before it is done, make pastry: sift dry ingredients and cut in shortening until mixture resembles coarse meal. Briskly fork in lemon juice and just enough ice water to hold pastry together. Remove ham from oven and raise temperature to 425° F. Halve pastry and roll half on a lightly floured board into a rectangle about 20″×12″ and ¼″ thick. Ease onto an ungreased large baking sheet; place ham on pastry with fat side up. Roll remaining pastry into a similar rectangle, lay over ham and trim edges so they just meet those of bottom pastry (this will be about halfway up sides of ham). Moisten edges with water and pinch into a smooth seam. Cut a vent in top of pastry near center; brush pastry with glaze. Cut decorative leaves and flowers from pastry trimmings and arrange on pastry; glaze. Bake, uncovered, in top ⅓ of oven 35–45 minutes until richly browned. When half done, check glaze and patch up any uneven spots with remaining glaze. Remove ham from oven, transfer to platter, and let "rest" 10–15 minutes. To serve, carve straight through as you would any boneless ham. Include some pastry with each serving. This ham is good hot or cold. About 850 calories for each of 16 servings, 755 calories for each of 18 servings.

To Halve Recipe: Use a 4–5-pound boneless half ham; halve pastry recipe, roll into a single rectangle, drape over ham, and pinch edges together underneath. Glaze and bake as directed. (Makes 8–10 servings). About 850 calories for each of 8 servings, 680 calories for each of 10 servings.

HAM IN ASPIC

Makes 10–12 servings

1 (5-pound) canned ham

Aspic:

2 envelopes unflavored gelatin
3 (10½-ounce) cans condensed beef consommé or madrilène
½ cup medium-dry sherry

Decoration:

2–3 truffles or pitted ripe olives, sliced thin
Small watercress, parsley, or tarragon sprigs
Thin slices cooked carrot or hard-cooked egg white cut in fancy shapes

Remove ham from can and chill well. Slowly heat gelatin in consommé, stirring, until dissolved; add sherry and cool over ice cubes until syrupy. Set ham on a rack over a tray, spoon on a light, even glaze of aspic. Dip decorations in aspic and arrange on ham; chill until firm. Give ham 3 more light glazes of aspic, chilling each well. (*Note:* To keep aspic syrupy, melt briefly over warm water, then return to ice bath.) Use overflow aspic on tray if reasonably clear. When final ham glaze is firm, transfer ham to platter and refrigerate. Pour remaining aspic into a shallow pan and chill until firm. To serve, cube extra aspic and arrange around base of ham. About 670 calories for each of 10 servings, 560 calories for each of 12 servings.

VARIATION:

Pâté-Filled Ham in Aspic: Have butcher cut ham lengthwise into ½″ slices, then tie together. For filling, mix 3 cups canned liver pâté, ⅓ cup heavy cream, 2 tablespoons prepared mild yellow mustard, 1 teaspoon Worcestershire sauce, and, if you like, 2–3 tablespoons cognac (filling should be a good spreading consistency). Untie ham carefully and thinly spread both sides of slices with filling; reshape ham and tie in several places. Wrap in foil and chill overnight; reserve remaining pâté. Next day, remove strings (ham should now hold its shape). "Frost" ham with reserved pâté and chill 2–3 hours. (*Note:* If pâté seems stiff, warm briefly over warm water.) Glaze and decorate ham as above. When serving, slice crosswise. About 820 calories for each of 10 servings, 685 calories for each of 12 servings.

Smoked Picnics and Butts
(See Pork Chart)

Smoked Picnic (4–10 pounds): Also called *Picnic Ham*, this bone-in, lower shoulder portion, when cured and smoked, tastes very much like ham. It is available uncooked, fully cooked and canned (canned picnics are boned, skinned, and trimmed).

Smoked Boneless Shoulder Butt (1–4 pounds): This long, slim boneless roll is a good choice for small families; it has a mild, smoky-sweet flavor.

How to Cook

Amounts Needed: Allow ⅓–½ pound smoked boneless shoulder butt or canned picnic (net weight) per person, ¾ pound smoked picnic.

Note: Fully cooked smoked picnics can be prepared by recipe for Ready-to-Eat Hams, canned picnics by that for Canned Hams. Though uncooked smoked picnics and shoulder butts can be baked like Uncooked Hams, they will be juicier if prepared by the following method.

General Preparation for Cooking: Remove skin from picnic (butt won't have any) and trim fat to ½".

Basic Method: Place picnic or butt on a rack in a large, heavy kettle and add just enough cold water to cover. Put lid on kettle and bring to a boil; adjust heat so water stays at a slow simmer, then cook 15 minutes per pound. Let meat cool 10 minutes in cooking water. Preheat oven to 325° F. Transfer meat to a rack in a shallow roasting pan and insert meat thermometer in center, not touching bone. Bake uncovered, allowing 25 minutes per pound for the picnic, 30–35 for the butt or until meat thermometer reaches 170° F. *To Glaze:* Smoked picnics may be glazed like Baked Ham. Smoked butts have a very skimpy covering of fat and do not glaze well;

they can, however, be drizzled with honey, maple syrup, or molasses and baked 10–15 minutes at 425° F. to make them glisten. Transfer meat to a heated platter and let "rest" 15–20 minutes before carving. Serve hot or cold.

VARIATIONS:

Simmered Boneless Shoulder Butt: Place butt in kettle and add water as directed; cover and simmer 50 minutes per pound until tender. Lift from liquid, cool 10 minutes, then slice and serve with boiled vegetables and, if you like, Mustard or Horseradish Sauce.

Pickled Smoked Shoulder Butt: Place butt in kettle and add water as directed; add 1 tablespoon mixed pickling spices, 1 peeled clove garlic, and ½ cup cider vinegar. Simmer and bake as directed in Basic Method.

⊠ SKILLET HAM, PINEAPPLE, AND PEPPERS
Makes 6 servings

3 cups diced cooked ham
2 tablespoons butter or margarine
1 (8-ounce) can pineapple tidbits (do not drain)
2 medium-size sweet green peppers, cored, seeded, and cut in ¼" strips
½ cup firmly packed light brown sugar
2 tablespoons cornstarch
½ cup chicken broth
½ cup cider vinegar
2 tablespoons soy sauce
2 pimientos, diced

In a large skillet stir-fry ham in butter 3–5 minutes over moderately high heat until lightly browned. Add pineapple and green peppers and stir-fry 3–4 minutes until peppers are crisp-tender. Mix sugar, cornstarch, broth, vinegar, and soy sauce, stir into skillet, and heat, stirring, until thickened. Add pimientos and serve over boiled rice. About 310 calories per serving (without rice).

⊠ CREAMED HAM

Makes 4 servings

¼ cup butter or margarine
¼ cup unsifted flour
⅛ teaspoon pepper
¼ teaspoon powdered mustard
1 cup milk
½ cup light cream
1½ cups slivered or diced cooked ham
2 tablespoons minced pimiento (optional)
½ teaspoon salt

Melt butter in a large saucepan over moderately low heat, blend in flour, pepper, and mustard; slowly add milk and cream and heat, stirring until thickened. Add remaining ingredients, adjusting salt to taste. Serve over toast, waffles, muffins, or hot biscuits or in pastry shells or "fluffed up" baked potatoes. About 375 calories per serving (without toast, waffles, muffins, biscuits, pastry shells, or potatoes).

VARIATIONS:

Creamed Ham and Eggs: Add 4 quartered hard-cooked eggs along with ham. About 455 calories per serving.

Creamed Ham and Mushrooms: Add 1 drained (4-ounce) can sliced mushrooms along with ham. About 385 calories per serving.

Creamed Ham, Cheese, and Olives: Add ¼ cup extra milk to sauce. Add ½ cup grated sharp Cheddar cheese and ¼ cup sliced pimiento-stuffed green olives with ham. About 500 calories per serving.

Creamed Ham and Vegetables: Add ¼ cup extra milk to sauce; also 1½–2 cups any leftover vegetable (corn, peas, cut asparagus, lima beans, broccoli, and cauliflowerets are particularly good). About 435 calories per serving.

HAM, POTATO, AND GREEN PEPPER CASSEROLE

Makes 4 servings

1 quart thinly sliced, peeled potatoes
3 cups (½") cooked lean ham cubes
½ medium-size sweet green pepper, cored, seeded, and chopped fine
3 scallions, chopped fine (include green tops)
2 tablespoons bacon drippings, butter, or margarine
3 tablespoons flour
¾ teaspoon powdered mustard
2 cups milk
1½ teaspoons salt
⅛ teaspoon white pepper

Preheat oven to 375° F. Arrange half the sliced potatoes in a greased 2-quart casserole. Toss ham, green pepper, and scallions together and scatter over potatoes; top with remaining potatoes. Melt drippings in a small saucepan over moderate heat, and blend in flour and mustard. Slowly add milk and heat, stirring constantly, until smooth and thickened. Mix in salt and pepper. Pour sauce evenly over potatoes, cover, and bake 1 hour. Uncover and bake 30 minutes longer until potatoes are fork tender and golden. About 530 calories per serving.

EASY HAM AND CORN CASSEROLE

Makes 4 servings

2 cups diced cooked ham
1 small yellow onion, peeled and grated fine
1 small sweet green pepper, cored, seeded, and minced
1 (1-pound) can cream-style corn
1 (8-ounce) can whole kernel corn, drained
½ cup light cream

Topping:

1½ cups packaged seasoned bread cubes or croutons
¼ cup melted butter or margarine
1 tablespoon Worcestershire sauce

Preheat oven to 350° F. Mix all ingredients except topping and spoon into a buttered 1½-quart casserole. Sprinkle with bread cubes; mix butter and Worcestershire sauce and drizzle on top. Bake, uncovered, 30 minutes until bubbly and brown. About 535 calories per serving.

HAM TETRAZZINI

Makes 6 servings

5 tablespoons butter or margarine
½ pound mushrooms, wiped clean and sliced thin
¼ cup finely chopped yellow onion
¼ cup unsifted flour
2 cups chicken broth
1¼ cups light cream
1 cup grated sharp Cheddar cheese
1½ teaspoons salt
⅛ teaspoon pepper
1 teaspoon lemon juice
3 cups cubed cooked ham
½ pound macaroni, cooked by package directions
¼ cup finely grated Parmesan cheese

Preheat oven to 400° F. Melt butter in a large saucepan over moderate heat and stir-fry mushrooms and onion 5 minutes until onion is pale golden. Blend in flour slowly add broth and cream, and heat, stirring, until thickened. Add all remaining ingredients except ham, macaroni, and Parmesan and cook, stirring, until cheese melts. Off heat mix in ham and drained macaroni and toss to mix. Spoon into a greased 2-quart casserole, top with Parmesan, and bake uncovered 25–30 minutes until bubbly and lightly browned. About 615 calories per serving.

VARIATION:

Ham and Tongue Tetrazzini: Reduce ham to 2 cups and add 1 (6-ounce) jar tongue, diced; proceed as directed. About 630 calories per serving.

¢ HAM AND EGG SHORTCAKE

Makes 4–6 servings

3 tablespoons butter or margarine
3 tablespoons flour
2 cups milk
2 cups diced cooked ham
4 hard-cooked eggs, peeled and quartered
½ teaspoon salt (about)
¼ teaspoon pepper
1 teaspoon prepared spicy brown mustard (optional)
1 tablespoon minced parsley

Topping:

½ cup sifted flour
½ cup yellow corn meal
¼ teaspoon salt
1–2 tablespoons sugar
2 teaspoons baking powder
1 egg, lightly beaten
2 tablespoons melted butter or margarine
½ cup milk

Preheat oven to 400° F. Melt butter in a saucepan over moderate heat and blend in flour; slowly add milk and heat, stirring, until thickened. Off heat add remaining ingredients except topping, taste for salt and adjust as needed. Spoon into a greased 9"×9"×2" pan or a 2-quart casserole. For topping, mix flour, corn meal, salt, sugar, and baking powder in a bowl. Combine egg, butter, and milk, add to dry ingredients, and beat with a rotary beater *just* until smooth. Spoon on top of ham mixture and bake, uncovered, 30 minutes until golden. Cut into squares and serve. About 630 calories for each of 4 servings, 420 calories for each of 6 servings.

¢ HAM SHANK STEW WITH DUMPLINGS

Best made the day before with dumplings added during reheating.
Makes 4–6 servings

½ pound dried whole green peas or lima beans, washed and sorted
2½ quarts cold water (about)
½ pound dried split green peas, washed and sorted
1 ham shank with some meat attached (leftover is fine)
2 medium-size carrots, peeled and diced
2 medium-size yellow onions, peeled and minced
1 teaspoon salt (about)
¼ teaspoon pepper
1 tablespoon dark brown sugar
1 tablespoon cider vinegar
¼ teaspoon thyme (optional)
1 clove garlic, peeled and crushed
1 recipe Quick Dumplings or Biscuit Dumplings
1 tablespoon minced parsley

Soak whole peas or limas in 2 cups water overnight or use the quick method.* Drain, measure soaking water, and add enough cold water to make 2½ quarts. Add all remaining ingredients except dumplings and parsley, adjusting salt to taste. Cover and simmer 1½–2 hours until peas are tender. Remove meat from ham shank, cut into bite-size pieces, and return to kettle. Mix dumplings and drop by tablespoonfuls on top of just boiling stew; simmer, *uncovered,* 10 minutes, cover tightly, and simmer 10 minutes longer. Sprinkle with parsley and serve in soup bowls. About 595 calories for each of 4 servings, 395 calories for each of 6 servings.

HAM LOAF

An all-ham loaf will not slice as well as one made with part ham and part pork or veal.
Makes 6 servings

1½ pounds ground smoked ham
½ pound ground lean pork or veal shoulder
2 eggs, lightly beaten
1½ cups soft white bread crumbs
1 cup milk
1 large yellow onion, peeled and minced (optional)
¼ teaspoon pepper
½ teaspoon celery salt
½ teaspoon powdered mustard

Preheat oven to 350° F. Mix all ingredients, pack into a lightly greased 9"×5"×3" loaf pan, and bake uncovered 1 hour. Remove from oven and let "rest" 5 minutes. Drain off drippings, then turn loaf out on platter. Make Pan Gravy with some of the drippings or serve loaf with Mustard or Raisin Sauce. Or chill well and serve cold with Mustard or Sour Cream-Horseradish Sauce. About 445 calories per serving (without sauce or gravy).

VARIATIONS:

Ham Loaf Ring: Pack ham loaf mixture in a greased 5-cup ring mold instead of a loaf pan and bake as directed. When serving, fill center with mashed sweet potatoes or buttered green peas and mushrooms. About 445 calories per serving (without vegetables).

Spicy Ham Loaf: Add ¼ cup minced parsley and ⅛ teaspoon each cloves, cinnamon, and nutmeg to loaf mixture and proceed as directed. About 445 calories per serving.

Caramel-Glazed Ham Loaf: Sprinkle bottom of loaf pan with ⅓ cup firmly packed light brown sugar and ½ teaspoon cloves before packing in meat; bake as directed. About 490 calories per serving.

Tomato-Glazed Ham Loaf: Substitute 1 cup tomato juice for milk when mixing loaf. Proceed as directed, basting loaf frequently with tomato juice throughout baking. About 10 minutes before loaf is done, top with 1 cup Tomato Sauce. Continue baking, and serve with additional Tomato Sauce. About 435 calories per serving.

Orange-Glazed Ham Loaf: Substitute 1 cup orange juice for milk when mixing loaf. Shape mixture into a loaf in a lightly greased shallow roasting pan; bake, uncovered, as directed but baste often during last ½ hour with Orange Glaze. *To make glaze:* mix ¼ cup firmly packed light brown sugar with 1 tablespoon cornstarch; add 1½ cups orange juice and heat, stirring, until thickened and clear. (*Note:* Any leftover glaze can be served with loaf as a sauce.) For extra tang, mix in 2 teaspoons slivered orange rind (orange part only). About 485 calories per serving.

Individual Ham Loaves: Shape ham mixture into 6 small loaves and place in a lightly greased, large shallow roasting pan. Mix 1 (8-ounce) can tomato sauce, 2 tablespoons cider vinegar, ½ cup firmly packed light brown sugar, and ½ cup water and pour over loaves. Bake uncovered ¾ hour, basting frequently. About 525 calories per serving.

SWEET-SOUR HAM AND HAMBURGER LOAF

An unlikely combination of meats that is surprisingly good.
Makes 6 servings

1 pound ground smoked ham
1 pound hamburger or ground beef chuck
1 cup soft white bread crumbs
½ cup milk
½ cup cold water
2 eggs, lightly beaten
1 small yellow onion, peeled and grated fine
⅛ teaspoon liquid hot red pepper seasoning
¾ teaspoon salt

Sauce:

1 cup firmly packed light brown sugar
½ cup cider vinegar
½ cup boiling water
1 tablespoon prepared spicy brown mustard

Preheat oven to 350° F. Mix all loaf ingredients and shape into a loaf in a shallow roasting pan lined with lightly greased foil. Mix sauce and pour over loaf. Bake uncovered, basting frequently, 1 hour. Remove from oven and let stand 5 minutes. Transfer to platter, using 2 pancake turners, and serve. About 530 calories per serving.

⚖ TOP HAT HAM SOUFFLÉ

Makes 4 servings

¼ cup butter or margarine
¼ cup sifted flour
½ teaspoon salt
⅛ teaspoon white pepper
Pinch cayenne pepper
1 cup milk
4 eggs, separated
1 cup ground cooked ham

Preheat oven to 350° F. Melt butter in a saucepan over moderate heat, blend in flour, salt, and peppers; slowly add milk and heat, stirring, until thickened. Beat yolks lightly, mix in a little of the hot sauce, then return all to pan. Cook, stirring constantly, 1–2 minutes but do not boil. Off heat, mix in ham; cool to room temperature. Beat egg whites until fairly stiff peaks form, then fold into ham mixture. Spoon into an ungreased 1½-quart soufflé dish. To form top hat, insert a table knife in soufflé mixture about ½″ deep and 1″ from edge of dish and draw a circle concentric to dish. Bake, uncovered (without opening oven door), 35–45 minutes until puffed and golden. Serve at once. About 325 calories per serving.

VARIATION:

⚖ **Ham and Cheese Soufflé:** Reduce amount of butter to 3 tablespoons then proceed as recipe directs, adding ¾ cup ground ham and ⅓ cup grated sharp Cheddar cheese to hot sauce. Fold in egg whites and bake as directed. About 350 calories per serving.

BAKED SWEET AND SOUR HAM BALLS

Makes 4 servings

Meat Balls:

½ pound ground smoked ham
½ pound ground lean pork
1 cup soft white bread crumbs
½ cup milk
½ teaspoon garlic salt
⅛ teaspoon pepper
1 egg, lightly beaten

Sauce:

1 cup firmly packed light brown sugar
¼ cup cider vinegar
½ cup pineapple juice
1 teaspoon powdered mustard

Preheat oven to 325° F. Mix all meatball ingredients and shape into 16 balls about 1″ in diameter. Arrange in a greased shallow baking pan. Mix sauce ingredients in a saucepan, bring to a boil, and cook, stirring constantly, 2–3 minutes. Pour sauce over meat balls and bake, uncovered, 1 hour, basting frequently. About 535 calories per serving.

BAKED HAM AND ASPARAGUS ROLLS IN CHEESE SAUCE

Makes 4 servings

16 stalks steamed asparagus
8 thin slices boiled ham
2 tablespoons butter

Sauce:

3 tablespoons butter or margarine
3 tablespoons flour
1½ cups milk
¾ cup heavy cream
¾ cup coarsely grated Gruyère, Swiss,
* or Cheddar cheese*
1 teaspoon salt
⅛ teaspoon white pepper
2 tablespoons finely grated Parmesan
* cheese*

Preheat oven to 425° F. Roll 2 stalks asparagus in each ham slice and secure with toothpicks. Sauté rolls in butter over moderate heat 2 minutes, then arrange in an ungreased shallow 1½-quart casserole. To make sauce, melt butter in a saucepan, blend in flour, slowly add milk, and cook, stirring, until thickened. Mix in remaining ingredients except Parmesan and heat, stirring, until cheese melts. Pour sauce over rolls, sprinkle with Parmesan, and bake uncovered 15 minutes. About 650 calories per serving.

VARIATIONS:

Endive-Stuffed Ham Rolls: Substitute 8 boiled Belgian endives for asparagus, roll each in a ham slice, and proceed as directed. About 650 calories per serving.

Broccoli-Stuffed Ham Rolls: Substitute 8 slim broccoli spears for asparagus, roll each in a ham slice, and proceed as directed. About 650 calories per serving.

Banana-Stuffed Ham Rolls: Substitute 8 lengthwise banana halves for asparagus, roll each in a ham slice, and proceed as directed. About 700 calories per serving.

Pineapple-Cream Cheese Ham Rolls: Spread each ham slice with a little softened cream cheese and roll around a pineapple spear; proceed as directed. About 665 calories per serving.

HAM THE SECOND TIME AROUND
(How to Use Up Leftovers)

⚖ ¢ HAM TIMBALES

Makes 4 servings

1 cup milk
1 cup soft white bread crumbs
2 tablespoons butter or margarine
1 tablespoon finely grated yellow onion
½ teaspoon salt
⅛ teaspoon pepper
⅛ teaspoon cloves
2 eggs, lightly beaten
1 cup ground cooked ham

Preheat oven to 325° F. Mix all but last 2 ingredients in a saucepan and bring to a boil, stirring constantly. Off heat, stir a little hot mixture into eggs, then return to pan. Mix in ham. Spoon into 4 well-greased custard cups and set in a shallow baking pan; pour in enough water to come halfway up cups. Bake, uncovered, 35–45 minutes or until a knife inserted in center comes out clean. Loosen edges of timbales and invert gently on a hot platter. Good with hot Mushroom or Tomato Sauce. About 255 calories per serving (without sauce).

¢ CRUSTY-CRUMB HAM CROQUETTES

Makes 4 servings

¼ cup butter or margarine
¼ cup sifted flour
1 cup milk
3 scallions, minced
⅛ teaspoon pepper
1 teaspoon prepared mild yellow mustard
1 teaspoon finely grated lemon rind
* (optional)*
¼ cup minced sweet green pepper
* (optional)*
1 egg, lightly beaten
1½ cups ground cooked ham
½ teaspoon salt (about)
1 egg lightly beaten with 1 tablespoon
* cold water*
⅓ cup toasted seasoned bread crumbs
¼ cup cooking oil

Melt butter in a large saucepan over moderate heat, blend in flour, slowly add milk, and heat, stirring, until thickened. Add scallions, pepper, mustard, and, if you like, lemon rind and green pepper. Spoon a little sauce into beaten egg, then return to saucepan. Mix in ham and salt to taste; then chill until easy to shape. Roll into 8 balls about 2″ in diameter, dip in egg-water mixture, then in crumbs to coat evenly. Let dry on a rack at room temperature 5 minutes. Heat oil in a large, heavy skillet over moderately high heat about 1 minute, then fry balls 3–4 minutes, turning frequently, until browned on all sides. Drain on paper toweling and serve. Good with Hot Mustard or Parsley Sauce.

To Deep-Fat-Fry: Prepare balls as directed; heat fat in a deep fat fryer to 380° F., add balls a few at a time, and brown about 2 minutes; drain well and serve.

Both versions: About 410 calories per serving (without sauce).

¢ ⚖ BOK CHOY (CHINESE CABBAGE AND HAM)

Makes 4 servings

1 medium-size Chinese or celery cabbage, trimmed and cored
1½ teaspoons salt
2 tablespoons cooking oil
½ cup cooked ham strips (about ⅛″ thick and 3″ long)
1 tablespoon cornstarch
1 cup chicken broth

Shred cabbage fine, cover with cold water, mix in 1 teaspoon salt, and let crispen 30 minutes; drain thoroughly. Heat oil in a large, heavy skillet or *wok* over moderately high heat 1–2 minutes. Add cabbage and ham and stir-fry 2–3 minutes until cabbage just wilts. Mix cornstarch, chicken broth, and remaining salt, add to skillet, and cook, stirring constantly, 2 minutes until mixture thickens slightly. Serve with boiled rice. About 155 calories per serving (without rice).

¢ HAM-TUNA-NOODLE CASSEROLE

Makes 4 servings

¼ cup butter or margarine
¼ cup sifted flour
2 cups milk
1½ teaspoons salt
¼ teaspoon pepper
1 tablespoon Worcestershire sauce
1 cup diced cooked ham
1 (7-ounce) can white or light tuna, drained and flaked
1 (4-ounce) can sliced mushrooms, drained
½-pound box thin noodles, cooked by package directions

Topping:

1 cup soft white bread crumbs mixed with 3 tablespoons melted butter or margarine

Preheat oven to 350° F. Melt butter in a saucepan over moderate heat and blend in flour; slowly add milk and heat, stirring, until thickened. Off heat mix in remaining ingredients except topping. Spoon into a lightly buttered 2-quart casserole and sprinkle topping over surface. Bake, uncovered, 30 minutes. About 615 calories per serving.

VARIATIONS:

¢ **Ham and Green Pea Casserole:** Prepare as directed, omitting tuna and adding 1 (10-ounce) package frozen green peas, cooked by package directions. For extra zip, mix ½ cup grated sharp cheese into sauce before adding remaining ingredients. About 565 calories per serving.

¢ **Ham and Mushroom Casserole au Gratin:** Instead of making white sauce with butter, flour, and milk, use 1 (10½-ounce) can cream of mushroom soup thinned with ¾ cup milk. Substitute ½ cup grated sharp Cheddar cheese for topping and bake as directed. About 635 calories per serving.

¢ **Ham-Noodle Casserole:** Prepare as directed, omitting tuna and increasing amount of ham to 2 cups. About 590 calories per serving.

Some Additional Ways to Use Up Leftover Ham

Creamed Ham and Potatoes (4 servings): In a large skillet mix 4 cups diced raw potatoes, 1½ cups chopped ham, ¼ cup minced yellow onion, 1 tablespoon flour, 1 teaspoon salt, and ⅛ teaspoon pepper; add 1 cup each milk and light cream, cover, and simmer, stirring occasionally, 20–30 minutes until potatoes are tender. Taste for salt and adjust as needed. Serve over toast, muffins, biscuits or waffles. About 415 calories per serving (without toast, muffins, biscuits, or waffles).

⊠ **Quick Creamed Ham** (4 servings): In a saucepan mix 1 (10½-ounce) can condensed green pea, mushroom, or celery soup, ½ cup milk, 1½ cups chopped or slivered ham, 2 tablespoons coarsely chopped pimiento, and ¼ teaspoon powdered mustard. Cover and simmer 10 minutes, stirring occasionally. If you like, stir in 4 quartered hard-cooked eggs. Serve over toast, muffins, biscuits, or waffles. About 295 calories per serving (without eggs, toast, muffins, biscuits, or waffles).

⊠ ¢ **Chinese Ham and Rice** (4 servings): Sauté 1½ cups slivered ham, 1 diced sweet red pepper, and 3 minced scallions in 2 tablespoons cooking oil 2–3 minutes over moderate heat. Add 1 (4-ounce) can water chestnuts, drained and sliced thin, and 3 cups cold cooked rice; stir-fry 4–5 minutes until rice is lightly browned. Stir together (do not beat) 2 eggs and 1 tablespoon soy sauce and mix into rice; heat, stirring, until eggs are just set. Serve with extra soy sauce. About 335 calories per serving.

Ham and Egg Pie (6 servings): Line a 9″ piepan with pastry and sprinkle with ¾ cup minced ham. Break 5–6 eggs on top, sprinkle with ½ teaspoon and ⅛ teaspoon pepper, and top with ¾ cup minced ham. Cover with pastry, crimp, and cut steam vents near center. Brush with glaze if you like (1 egg beaten with 1 tablespoon cold water). Bake ½ hour at 425° F. until lightly browned. Serve hot or cold. About 490 calories per serving.

¢ ⊠ **Ham and Baked Beans** (2 servings): Mix 1 (1-pound) can baked beans, 1 cup cubed or slivered ham, 2 tablespoons molasses, 1 tablespoon prepared mild yellow mustard, and 1 teaspoon prepared horseradish. Simmer, covered, 15–20 minutes until bubbly, or spoon into an ungreased 1-quart casserole, cover, and bake ½ hour at 350° F. About 505 calories per serving.

Ham en Brochette (Number of servings flexible): Alternate 2″ ham cubes on long skewers with any of the following: canned pitted apricots, cling peach halves, preserved kumquats, spiced crab apples, pineapple or banana chunks, parboiled sweet red and green pepper squares, boiled white onions, canned potatoes, mushroom caps, unpeeled tomato wedges, large pitted ripe olives. Brush lightly with melted butter and broil 5″–6″ from heat, turning often, until ham is lightly browned. Recipe too flexible for a meaningful calorie count.

⊠ ¢ **Ham and Potato Pie** (4 servings): Mix 1½ cups minced ham with 2 cups mixed cooked vegetables, succotash, or creamed corn in a buttered 1½-quart casserole. Cover with 2 cups seasoned mashed potatoes, roughen surface with fork, and bake uncovered ½ hour at 425° F. until touched with brown. About 500 calories per serving.

Ham and Egg Cakes (4 servings): Mix 1½ cups ground ham, 4 minced hard-cooked eggs, 1 cup soft white bread crumbs, 1 beaten egg, ½ teaspoon salt, ⅛ teaspoon pepper, and 2 tablespoons minced parsley. Shape into 4 flat cakes, dust with flour, and sauté 2 minutes on a side in 2 tablespoons butter over moderate heat. About 320 calories per serving.

Ham and Cheese Heroes (Number of servings flexible): Split thin loaves of French bread or hard rolls lengthwise, spread with Garlic Butter, prepared mild yellow mustard, and a ½ and ½ mixture of ground ham and grated cheese (Cheddar, Swiss, or Gruyère).

Top with other half of loaf, wrap in foil, and bake 20 minutes at 350° F. Recipe too flexible for a meaningful calorie count.

⊠ **Barbecued Ham Slices** (4 servings): Cut 8 thick slices of ham and arrange in a greased shallow baking dish. Mix together ¼ cup each chili sauce and firmly packed dark brown sugar, 1 tablespoon each prepared mild yellow mustard and cider vinegar; spread over ham and bake, uncovered, 20 minutes at 350° F. About 335 calories per serving.

Potted Ham (Makes about 1½ cups): Mix 1 cup finely ground lean ham with 2 sieved hard-cooked egg yolks, ¼ cup soft butter, and ⅛ teaspoon powdered mustard. Beat until well blended, pack into a crock or jar, and cover with ⅛″ clarified butter.* Refrigerate and use as a canapé or sandwich spread. About 70 calories per tablespoon.

⚖ **Ham Mousse** (4 servings): Mix 1 envelope unflavored gelatin and ½ cup pineapple juice or cold water and heat slowly, stirring until dissolved. Add 2 cups ground ham, 1 teaspoon prepared mild yellow mustard, 1 teaspoon prepared horseradish, and, if you like, 2 tablespoons diced pimiento. Cool to room temperature. Fold in 1 stiffly beaten egg white and ½ cup heavy cream, whipped. Spoon into an ungreased 1-quart mold and chill until firm. (*Note:* Chicken or tongue may be used in place of ham.) About 290 calories per serving.

Ham Stuffed Vegetables
Ham Hash
} Follow recipes given in Some Additional Ways to Use Up Leftover Roast Beef, substituting ham for beef.

Ham, Olive, and Egg Salad (4 servings): Mix 2 cups cubed ham, 3 quartered hard-cooked eggs, 1 cup diced celery, ½ cup sliced pimiento-stuffed green olives, 2 minced gherkins, and ¾ cup mayonnaise. About 585 calories per serving.

Ham and Chicken Salad (4 servings): Mix 1½ cups each cubed ham and chicken with 1 cup diced celery, 2 tablespoons each minced dill pickle, parsley, and grated yellow onion, and ¾ cup mayonnaise. About 555 calories per serving.

Ham and Tongue Salad (4 servings): Mix 1½ cups each cubed ham and tongue with 1 cup diced celery, 2 tablespoons each sweet pickle relish and prepared mild yellow mustard, and ¾ cup mayonnaise. About 625 calories per serving.

Ham Waldorf Salad (4 servings): Mix 2 cups each diced ham and diced unpeeled red apple, 1 cup diced celery, ½ cup coarsely chopped pecans or walnuts, 1 cup mayonnaise, and 2 tablespoons lemon juice. About 745 calories per serving.

Ham in Avocado (4 servings): Dip 2 peeled, pitted, and halved avocados in lemon juice to prevent darkening; stuff with 1½ cups ground ham mixed with enough Thousand Island Dressing to moisten. Garnish with seeded grapes and grapefruit sections. About 380 calories per serving.

Ham in Peaches (Number of servings flexible): Mix equal quantities of diced ham and cottage cheese and use to stuff cling peach halves. Recipe too flexible for a meaningful calorie count.

To Make the Most of Very Small Amounts:
– Mix ½ cup ground ham to dry ingredients for Quick Dumplings; finish mixing and cook as directed.
– Mix ½ cup ground or finely diced ham to dry ingredients for biscuits, muffins, or corn bread; finish mixing and bake as directed.
– Cube ham or cut in julienne strips and toss into hearty salads (chef's salad, dried bean, egg, potato, pasta, rice, or fruit salad).
– Dice or cut ham in julienne strips and add to Scalloped Corn, Corn Gumbo,

Corn Pie, or Corn Fritters.
– Dice ham and add to Hashed Brown Potatoes, Rice Pilaf, Deluxe Macaroni and Cheese, any meat sauce for spaghetti, any budget casserole.
– Grind ham fine and use in making sandwich fillings or savory stuffings (for ideas, see Some Additional Ways to Use Up Leftover Roast Beef).
– Dice ham or grind coarsely and add to omelets or scrambled eggs, waffle or pancake batter.

What to Do with Ham Bones:
– Add to the pot when cooking any dried beans, peas, or lentils.
– Add to the pot when cooking fresh mustard greens, spinach, turnip greens, green or wax beans, black-eyed peas.
– Use in making dried pea, bean, or lentil soup, Corn Chowder, or Quick Cream of Tomato Soup. Or add trimmings to canned or packaged soups.

Ham Steaks and Slices
(See Pork Chart)

Ham Steak: Also called *Ham Center Slice,* this large oval slice from the middle of the ham is the equivalent of beef round or veal cutlet. Cut thick, it can be baked; cut thin, broiled, panbroiled, grilled, panfried, or braised. Available uncooked and ready-to-eat.

Ham Butt Slice: Cut a little higher on the ham than the center slice, this steak is not quite so large or expensive. Available uncooked or ready-to-eat.

Smoked Picnic Slice: This large oval slice resembles ham steak but is not as tender or expensive. Available uncooked or ready-to-eat.

How to Cook

Amounts Needed: A ham steak or slice cut ½″ thick will serve 2–4; cut 1″–2″ thick, it will serve 4–6. To figure by weight: allow ⅓–½ pound per person.

General Preparation for Cooking: Remove any rind, trim off all but ¼″ outer fat, then slash fat edge at 1″ intervals to prevent curling.

To Panfry (*Sauté*): Recommended only for very lean ham steaks and slices ¼″–¾″ thick. *Uncooked ham:* Brown, uncovered, in 1 tablespoon bacon drippings or cooking oil in a large, heavy skillet over moderately low heat, allowing 3 minutes per side for ¼″ thick steaks, 4–5 minutes per side for ½″ steaks, and 6 minutes per side for ¾″ steaks. Season with pepper and, if needed, salt. *Ready-to-eat ham:* Prepare like uncooked ham but brown about half as long on each side.

VARIATION:

Mustard Ham Steak: Before cooking, spread 1 side of ham with 1½ tablespoons mild yellow mustard and sprinkle with pepper. Place ham in skillet mustard side down and brown as directed. Before turning, spread top with 1½ tablespoons mustard and sprinkle with pepper; turn and brown as before.

To Panbroil: Recommended for steaks and slices ¼″–¾″ thick. If ham seems lean, grease or salt skillet *lightly;* heat over moderately low heat 1 minute, add ham steak, and cook, using panfrying times as a guide. Turn with tongs and drain off drippings as they collect.

VARIATION:

Ham Steak in Sour Cream-Onion Gravy: Panbroil steak as directed, remove to a heated platter, and keep warm. In drippings sauté 2 thinly sliced large yellow onions 8–10 minutes over moderate heat until golden; smooth in 1 cup sour cream, ⅓ cup milk, and ¼ teaspoon paprika. Heat and stir (but do not boil) 1–2 minutes over low heat. Pour over ham and serve.

To Broil: Recommended for ham steaks or slices ½″–1½″ thick. Preheat broiler. Rub rack with drippings or oil and line pan underneath with foil. Place ham on rack, fat edge to back to reduce sputtering, then adjust height and broil using times in chart below as a guide. Use tongs for turning. For extra flavor, brush steaks often during cooking with a liquid glaze (see Some Glazes for Baked Hams).

To Charcoal Broil: Recommended for ham steaks or slices ½"–1½" thick. Build a moderately low charcoal fire.* Lightly grease grill with drippings or oil, place ham on grill, adjust height from coals, and broil according to chart. If you like, brush often during cooking with a liquid glaze (see Some Glazes for Baked Hams).

Ham Steak Broiling Chart

Times (for steaks refrigerated until ready to be broiled) are approximate at best because size and shape of cut, amount of fat and bone, type of oven or grill all affect broiling time. In outdoor cooking, wind and temperature must also be considered.

To Braise: Especially good for uncooked ham steaks and slices about 1" thick. Brown both sides of steak quickly in a lightly greased large, heavy skillet over moderately high heat; pour off drippings. Add 1 cup liquid (water; orange, pineapple, apple, or apricot juice; apple

cider; beer, sherry, port, Madeira, champagne, sweet or dry red or white wine), cover, turn heat to low, and simmer until done. *Uncooked hams* will take about 20 minutes (turn after 10); *ready-to-eat hams* 5–10 minutes in all.

VARIATIONS:

Ham Steak Virginia: Braise steak as directed, using water for the liquid; remove ham to a heated platter and keep warm. Stir ½ cup medium-dry sherry and ¼ cup firmly packed light brown sugar into skillet and heat, stirring, over moderate heat until sugar dissolves. Blend 2 tablespoons flour with ¼ cup cold water, mix into skillet, and heat and stir until thickened. Return steak to skillet, turn heat to low, and simmer uncovered 5–7 minutes, basting and turning frequently. Serve on a bed of Creamed Spinach.

Tomato-Smothered Ham Steak: Brown steak on both sides and drain off drippings. Sprinkle with 1 teaspoon instant minced onion and top with 1 (1-pound) can tomato sauce or spaghetti sauce with mushrooms. Cover and simmer, using

Oven Broiling

Cut	Thickness	Oven or Fire Temperature	Distance from Heat	Approximate Minutes per Side
	½"	Broil	3"	4
Uncooked	¾"	Broil	3"	7
Ham steaks	1"	Broil	4"	9
	1½"	Broil	4"	10–12
	½"	Broil	3"	3–5 total (do not turn steak)
Ready-to-eat	¾"	Broil	3"	3
Ham steaks	1"	Broil	4"	5
	1½"	(not recommended)		

Charcoal Broiling

	½"	Moderately low	4"	5
Uncooked	¾"	Moderately low	4"	6–8
Ham steaks	1"	Moderately low	5"	10
	1½"	Moderately low	5"	12
	½"	Moderately low	4"	3–4
Ready-to-eat	¾"	Moderately low	4"	4–5
Ham steaks	1"	Moderately low	4"	5–6

times in basic recipe for braising as a guide.

Ham Steak in Port Wine Sauce: Brown steak on both sides and drain off drippings. To skillet add ¾ cup water, ⅓ cup tawny port wine, and 1 tablespoon soy sauce. Cover and simmer until done as directed above. Lift ham to a heated platter and keep warm; boil wine sauce, uncovered, 2–3 minutes until reduced to about ½ cup. Pour over ham and serve.

To Bake: Recommended for 1½″–2″ thick ham steaks and slices. Preheat oven to 325° F. Place ham on a rack in a shallow roasting pan. If you like, stud surface with cloves and top with a thin glaze (see Some Glazes for Baked Hams). Bake uncovered, basting occasionally with glaze, if used, until tender. *Ready-to-eat hams* need only 30–35 minutes, regardless of thickness. Time *uncooked hams* as follows: 1–1¼ hours for a 1½″ steak, 1½–1¾ hours for a 2″ steak.

VARIATIONS:

Marinated Ham Steak: Marinate steak in refrigerator overnight in ½ cup dry red wine or red wine vinegar mixed with ½ cup pineapple juice and ½ teaspoon ginger. Place ham and marinade in baking pan and bake as directed, basting often.

Chinese-Style Ham Steak: Marinate steak in refrigerator overnight in ⅓ cup soy sauce mixed with ¼ cup firmly packed light brown sugar, ¼ cup cider vinegar, 1 crushed clove garlic, and 1 teaspoon powdered mustard. Place ham and marinade in pan and bake as directed, basting often.

Chutney-Glazed Ham Steak: Mix 1 cup minced chutney with ¼ cup firmly packed light brown sugar and ⅓ cup water; spread over ham and bake as directed.

Ham Steak with Bing Cherry Sauce: Place ham directly in pan (omit rack) and set aside. Mix 2 tablespoons sugar, 1 tablespoon cornstarch, and ½ cup cold water and heat, stirring, until thickened.

Off heat add 1 (1-pound) can pitted Bing cherries (do not drain), pour over steak, and bake as directed.

Barbecued Ham Steak: Place ham in pan without rack, top with 1 cup All-Purpose Barbecue Sauce, and bake as directed.

Baked Stuffed Ham Steak (6–8 servings): Use 2 (1″ thick) *ready-to-eat ham* steaks instead of 1 thick steak; spread 1 steak evenly with 1½–2 cups Sage and Onion or Corn Bread Stuffing or with packaged stuffing prepared by directions. Top with second steak and skewer together in several places. Bake uncovered 45 minutes.

BAKED HAM AND SWEET POTATOES

Makes 4–6 servings

4 medium-size sweet potatoes, parboiled, peeled, and halved
4 pineapple rings or 1 cup pineapple chunks or tidbits
1 ready-to-eat ham steak, cut ¾″ thick (about 2 pounds)
6 cloves
2 tablespoons light brown sugar
½ cup pineapple juice

Preheat oven to 350° F. Arrange potatoes in an ungreased 2½-quart casserole, cover with pineapple, and top with ham. Stud ham with cloves and sprinkle with sugar. Pour pineapple juice over all and bake, uncovered, 30–40 minutes.

VARIATION:

Use 2½ cups cubed cooked ham instead of steak; substitute ⅛ teaspoon powdered cloves for whole cloves and mix with sugar. Otherwise, prepare as directed.

Both versions: About 780 calories for each of 4 servings, 520 calories for each of 6 servings.

⊠ COUNTRY-FRIED HAM WITH RED EYE GRAVY

Country-Fried Ham with Red Eye Gravy

is one of those generations-old Southern recipes that probably seemed too simple to write down. It isn't really. To have any success, you must use country-cured ham, a heavy iron skillet, and just the right amount of heat—too much and the ham will scorch, too little and it won't brown. Some say coffee gives the gravy its red color, but most country cooks simply simmer the gravy, scraping up any browned bits, till it turns red-brown on its own.
Makes 2–4 servings

1 teaspoon bacon drippings or lard
1 center slice country-cured ham, cut
  ¼″ thick
⅔ cup cold water
1 tablespoon hot strong coffee (optional)

Place a heavy iron skillet over moderately low heat and heat 1 minute; add drippings and, when melted, place ham in skillet. Fry, turning often, until ham is nicely browned on both sides; this will take about 15 minutes. Remove ham to a heated platter and keep warm. Add water to skillet and continue heating, stirring and scraping up browned bits, 3–5 minutes until gravy turns red-brown; add coffee if you like. Spoon a little gravy over ham and pass the rest. Serve with grits. About 570 calories for each of 2 servings (without grits), 285 calories for each of 4 servings.

Bacon, Salt Pork, and Jowl
(See Pork Chart)

"The leaner, the better" doesn't apply to bacon because fat is what gives bacon its woodsy-sweet flavor and tender crispness. Ideally, bacon should be half to two thirds fat—snowy and firm with wide, evenly distributed streakings of bright pink lean. (Because of its high fat content, bacon stores poorly, so don't buy more than a week's supply at a time.) The flavor of bacon, like that of ham, varies according to the breed of animal, feed, cut, method of curing and smoking. Your best assurance of quality is to buy brands you trust.

Slab Bacon: Cured and smoked side of pork. It's cheaper than presliced bacon and, according to some people, has better flavor. Butchers will slice it for you or you can do it yourself.

Sliced Bacon: Slab bacon that has been trimmed of rind, sliced, and packaged. Available as:

Regular Sliced: The best all-round bacon, not too thick, not too thin. There are 16–20 slices per pound.

Thick Sliced: A shade thicker than regular-sliced bacon, this has an old-fashioned, hand-sliced look. About 12–16 slices per pound.

Thin Sliced: Good for sandwiches, serving with eggs or crumbling into bacon bits, but too thin and fragile to do the sort of wrapping *rumakis* need. About 35 slices per pound.

Canned Sliced: A convenience food for campers and apartment dwellers with pint-sized refrigerators, these canned precooked bacon slices need no refrigeration and can be heated in minutes. 1 can (18–20 slices) =1 pound fresh bacon.

Ends and Pieces: These penny-saving scraps are great for soups, sandwiches, salads.

Bacon Crumbles or Bits: Crisp, cooked bits of bacon ready to toss into salads, soups, and casseroles. Usually bottled in small amounts.

Country-Cured Bacon: Also called *Country-Style Bacon,* this is salty, heavily smoked bacon. Often it comes from the same hogs as Smithfield or Virginia hams. More expensive than ordinary bacon and available by the slab or slice in gourmet food shops.

Irish Bacon: This Irish equivalent of country-cured bacon is a doubly long strip containing both the "streaky" we usually think of as bacon and the lean eye of loin used for Canadian bacon. For shipping, the two are cut through to the rind just below the ribs, then folded together compact-style. Whether you buy Irish bacon by the slab or have it sliced to order, you will get both parts. Like country-cured bacon, Irish bacon is heavily salted and smoked; it is more expensive than standard bacon and is available in gourmet shops.

Canadian Bacon: Sometimes called *Back Bacon*, this is the boneless, lean eye of loin, cured and smoked. In flavor and texture it resembles ham more than bacon and is best when cooked like ham. Available presliced or in rolls, also canned as *Pork Loin Roll.*

Smoked Loin Chops: A fairly new item closely related to Canadian bacon. These are simply cured and smoked loin chops. They're presliced and packaged with full cooking directions.

Jowl: Also called *Bacon Square,* this is the fleshy cheek of the hog trimmed into 5″–8″ squares, cured and smoked. It is boneless, fatter than bacon, and, except for that which is country-cured, budget priced. Use as you would bacon.

Salt Pork: Sometimes known as "white bacon," salt pork comes from the side of the hog. It is mostly fat (though that of top quality contains a handsome streak of lean); it is cured *but not smoked* and used primarily for seasoning. Frequently, people confuse salt pork with *fat back;* they are not at all the same. Fat back is fresh (uncured, unsmoked) fat from the back of the hog used for cooking and making lard.

How To Cook

Amounts Needed: Allow 2–4 slices bacon or Canadian bacon per person. When buying Canadian bacon by the roll, figure ¼–⅓ pound per person.

General Preparation for Cooking: Remove any rind. Irish and country-cured bacon, because of their saltiness, will profit by 5–10 minutes simmering in water before being broiled, panbroiled, or baked. Drain well, pat dry, then follow basic methods.

To Panfry (Sauté): Especially recommended for sliced Canadian bacon. Melt about 1 teaspoon bacon drippings in a heavy skillet over moderately low heat, add bacon, and cook 4–5 minutes on a side until delicately browned.

To Panbroil: Good for all but Canadian bacon, which is too lean to cook without additional fat. Take bacon straight from refrigerator and place unseparated slices in a cold skillet. Set over moderate heat and cook, turning often with tongs and separating slices as they heat, 6–8 minutes until crisp and brown. Spoon off drippings as they collect and drain bacon well on paper toweling before serving.

To Broil: Recommended for all but Canadian bacon. Preheat broiler. Take bacon straight from refrigerator and arrange slices on broiler rack so fat edges overlap slightly. Broil 4″ from heat 2–3 minutes on a side until crisp and golden. Use tongs to turn and watch closely. Drain on paper toweling before serving.

To Bake:

Bacon: Here's the way to cook bacon for a crowd. Preheat oven to 400° F. Lay cold bacon strips, fat edges overlapping, on a large cookie rack set in a shallow roasting pan. Bake, uncovered, 12–15 minutes without turning until crisp and brown.

Canadian Bacon: Buy a roll of Canadian bacon weighing at least 2 pounds. Slip off casing and place roll fat side up on a rack in a shallow roasting pan. Insert meat thermometer in center. Preheat oven to 325° F. and bake, uncovered, about 35 minutes per pound or until meat thermometer registers 160° F. For an extra-juicy bacon, add 1 cup liquid to pan before baking (chicken stock, orange, apple, or pineapple juice, beer) and bake as directed, basting often. For more festive ways to bake Canadian bacon, see recipes that follow.

To Spit-Roast (for Canadian bacon rolls only; for best results, choose one weighing 3–4 pounds):

In Oven or Rotisserie: Preheat unit. Insert spit straight through roll, end to end, attach to rotisserie and insert meat thermometer in center so it does not touch spit. Roast about 25 minutes per pound or until thermometer registers 160° F. Baste every 15–20 minutes, if you like, with orange, apple, or pineapple juice or with a thin glaze (see Some Glazes for Baked Hams).

Over Charcoal: Build a moderate charcoal fire.* Balance roll on spit and insert meat thermometer as above; attach to rotisserie and adjust height so spit is 4″–5″ from coals. Roast about 25 minutes per pound or until thermometer registers 160° F., basting, if you like, with orange, apple, or pineapple juice or with a thin glaze (see Some Glazes for Baked Hams).

How to Save and Use Bacon Drippings
Collect drippings in a tall coffee tin; when full, spoon drippings into a deep saucepan, add 1 cup water, and sprinkle 2–3 tablespoons flour on top (this is to make any sediment settle). Bring to a boil over moderate heat without covering or stirring. Remove from heat, cool slightly, strain through a double thickness of cheesecloth, and pour into a large jar. Cover and store in refrigerator. Use in place of butter or margarine for frying and sautéing, also for seasoning vegetables.

BAKED GINGER-GLAZED CANADIAN BACON

Makes 4–6 servings

1 (2-pound) roll ready-to-eat Canadian bacon
1½ cups ginger marmalade
¼ cup brandy

Have butcher remove casing from bacon, slice ⅛″–¼″ thick, and tie together into original shape. Preheat oven to 325° F. Place bacon fat side up on a rack in a shallow roasting pan. Mince any large pieces of ginger in marmalade, then mix all with brandy; spread half over bacon. Bake, uncovered, ½ hour; spread with remaining marmalade and bake ½ hour longer. Transfer to a hot platter, remove

strings, and serve with English or Dijon-style mustard.

VARIATION:
Substitute orange or lime marmalade or chopped mango or peach chutney for ginger marmalade; proceed as directed.

All versions: About 890 calories for each of 4 servings, 595 calories for each of 6 servings.

BAKED YAMS, APPLES, AND CANADIAN BACON

Makes 4 servings

4 medium-size yams, parboiled, peeled, and sliced ½″ thick
2 tart apples, peeled, cored, and cut in ¼″ rings
½ teaspoon salt
8 slices ready-to-eat Canadian bacon, cut ¼″ thick
1 teaspoon prepared hot mustard
¼ cup firmly packed light brown sugar
2 tablespoons butter or margarine

Preheat oven to 375° F. Layer yams and apples into a buttered 2½-quart casserole, sprinkling with salt as you go. Spread each side of bacon slices lightly with mustard and arrange on top, overlapping spoke fashion. Sprinkle with sugar and dot with butter. Bake uncovered 30 minutes until yams are tender and bacon lightly glazed. About 565 calories per serving.

¢ HOG JOWL AND BLACK-EYED PEAS

An old Southern custom, practiced yet in some communities, is to eat hog jowl and black-eyed peas on New Year's Day. Brings good luck, they say.
Makes 6 servings

1 pound dried black-eyed peas, washed and sorted
2 quarts cold water
1 (½-pound) piece country-cured hog jowl
1 small dried hot red chili pepper
Salt to taste

Soak peas overnight in 1 quart water or use the quick method.* About 1 hour

before peas have finished soaking, scrub
jowl well under running tepid water;
place in a large, heavy kettle with 1
quart water and the chili pepper. Cover
and bring to a boil, adjust heat so water
stays at a slow simmer, and cook 1 hour.
Add peas and their soaking water to
kettle, cover, and simmer about 2 hours
longer until peas and jowl are both
tender. Check pot occasionally and, if
mixture seems thick, thin with about ½
cup hot water. Taste for salt and season
as needed; discard chili pepper. Cut jowl
into thin slices, return to kettle, and
warm 5–10 minutes. Serve in soup bowls,
making sure each person gets some of
the jowl. About 355 calories per serving.

¢ SCALLOPED SALT PORK AND
POTATOES

A good budget main dish.
Makes 4–6 servings

½ pound salt pork, trimmed of rind and
  cut in small dice
Salt pork drippings and enough bacon
  drippings to total ¼ cup
1 quart thinly sliced, peeled potatoes
  (you'll need 4–5 medium-size potatoes)
1 large yellow onion, peeled and sliced
  thin
2 tablespoons flour
¼ cup minced parsley
⅛ teaspoon pepper
1½ cups light cream

Preheat oven to 350° F. Stir-fry salt
pork 8–10 minutes in a large, heavy
skillet over moderate heat until lightly
browned. Pour off drippings and reserve,
adding bacon drippings as needed to
measure ¼ cup. In a buttered 2-quart
casserole, build up alternate layers of
potatoes, onion, and salt pork, beginning
and ending with potatoes. Drizzle each
onion layer with drippings, then sprinkle
with flour, parsley, and pepper. Pour in
cream, cover, and bake 1–1½ hours until
potatoes are tender. Broil quickly, if you
like, to brown; then serve. About 615
calories for each of 4 servings, 410
calories for each of 6 servings.

¢ CREAMED SALT PORK IN
POTATO NESTS

Makes 4 servings

1 pound salt pork, trimmed of rind and
  cut in small dice
1 quart boiling water
Salt pork drippings and enough bacon
  drippings to total ¼ cup
¼ cup unsifted flour
⅛ teaspoon sage
Pinch nutmeg
Pinch pepper
1 pint light cream
2 tablespoons minced parsley
Salt to taste
4 cups hot seasoned mashed potatoes

Place salt pork in a saucepan, add boiling
water, and simmer uncovered 5 minutes;
drain well and pat dry on paper toweling.
Stir-fry salt pork in a large, heavy skillet
over moderate heat 8–10 minutes until
lightly browned; pour off drippings and
reserve, adding enough bacon drippings
to measure ¼ cup. Transfer salt pork to
hot plate and set, uncovered, in a
250° F. oven to keep warm (no need to
preheat oven). Return drippings to skillet,
blend in flour, sage, nutmeg, and pepper;
add cream slowly and heat, stirring, until
thickened and smooth. Mix in parsley,
taste for salt and add as needed. Mound
1 cup mashed potatoes on each of 4
serving plates, flatten slightly, and make
a well in the center. Fill with salt pork,
top with some of the cream sauce, and
pass the rest. About 900 calories per
serving.

VARIETY MEATS

These are the other edible parts of beef,
veal, lamb, and pork, the organ meats
such as heart, liver, kidneys, sweetbreads,
brains, tongue, and tripe. Europeans,
considering them the choicest parts of
the animal, lavish attention upon them,
but we, alas, too often pass them up in
favor of steaks, chops, and roasts. Organ
meats are the most nutritious of all meats
because they contain concentrated

sources of certain minerals and vitamins. They are lean and thus low-calorie, but they are, for the most part, cholesterol-rich (particularly liver, kidney, and brain) and should be minimal in the diets of those with high cholesterol blood levels.

Because there is less demand for variety meats (with the exception, perhaps, of calf's liver) than for steaks, roasts, and chops, they are cheaper than the popular cuts. Moreover, correctly prepared, variety meats are surprisingly tender, delicately flavored, and good.

BRAINS

Though gourmets have long been lyrical about brains, likening their fragile texture to that of cooked mushrooms, their flavor to the most delicate white fish, they are not everyone's dish. It's the *idea* of eating brains that puts people off. If you've never tasted them, a good way to begin is by ordering *Cervelles au Beurre Noir* (Brains in Black Butter Sauce) or perhaps Brains Vinaigrette in some fine French restaurant. Delicious.

The choicest brains are those from calves or lambs; pork and beef brains have stronger flavor and less delicate texture. All brains are highly perishable (always cook within 24 hours) and for that reason are a special order item. When ordering, insist that the brains be *absolutely fresh.* Recently, frozen brains have been appearing in supermarket counters and, though they haven't quite the character of fresh brains, they are a very good substitute when the fresh aren't available. Always follow package directions when preparing.

Like sweetbreads (with which they can often be used interchangeably in recipes), brains are easily torn or broken. They require extra-gentle handling, careful cleaning and soaking, and sometimes blanching before they can be used in recipes.

Amount Needed: Allow ¼–⅓ pound brains per serving. Lamb and pork brains

usually weigh about ¼ pound each, calf brains ½ pound, and beef brains ¾ pound.

To Prepare for Cooking: Wash brains carefully in cold water, then place in a large bowl and cover with acidulated water (1 tablespoon lemon juice or white vinegar and 1 teaspoon salt to 1 quart water) and soak 1½ hours. Drain, very gently peel off as much thin outer membrane as possible (it clings tightly and is almost transparent). Soak for another 1½ hours in fresh acidulated water, changing the water 1–2 times; drain and again peel off as much membrane as possible. Also cut away opaque white bits at base of brains. (*Note:* If membrane is not peeled off before cooking, any blood trapped underneath will leave brown streaks, marring the brains' creamy color.)

To Blanch: Gourmets disagree as to whether brains should be blanched before cooking. If they are to be braised, blanching serves no real purpose and actually leaches out some of the subtle flavor. If they are to be sautéed, blanching will help make them firm, make them easier to slice and handle. To blanch, place brains in a saucepan (not aluminum), add acidulated water to cover, and simmer uncovered over low heat. Lamb brains will need only 15 minutes, pork and calf brains about 20, and beef brains about 30. Drain well, cover with ice water, and let stand until cold. Drain again and pat dry on paper toweling.

Some Classic Garnishes for Brains (see Some Classic Garnishes for Sweetbreads)

⚔️ **SAUTÉED BRAINS**

Makes 4 servings

1¼ pounds brains
½ cup unsifted flour
1 teaspoon salt
¼ teaspoon pepper
¼ cup butter or margarine
8 small unbuttered toast triangles
  (optional)

Suggested Sauces:

Bordelaise
Diable
Madeira

Prepare brains for cooking and blanch as directed.* Make sure they are quite dry. Slice ½″ thick and dredge lightly in a mixture of flour, salt, and pepper. Heat butter in a large, heavy skillet over moderate heat and sauté brains 3–4 minutes on each side until nicely browned. Drain on paper toweling. Serve as is with 1 of the sauces suggested above or, if you like, on toast triangles. About 250 calories per serving (without sauce or toast).

VARIATIONS:

Cervelles au Beurre Noir (Brains in Black Butter Sauce): Prepare Sautéed Brains as directed, remove from skillet and keep warm. Place ½ cup Clarified Butter in a clean small skillet and heat, moving pan continuously, over low heat just until butter begins to brown. Mix in 2 tablespoons white vinegar or lemon juice and 1 tablespoon minced parsley. Pour over brains and serve. If you like, sprinkle brains with 2 tablespoons drained capers before adding butter. About 450 calories per serving.

⊲⊳ **Breaded Brains:** Prepare, slice, and dredge brains as above, then dip in 1 egg lightly beaten with 1 tablespoon cold water and finally in fine dry bread crumbs or cracker meal. Sauté in butter as directed and serve with Lemon Butter. About 260 calories per serving (without lemon butter).

Broiled Brains
(See Broiled Sweetbreads)

BRAINS VINAIGRETTE

Makes 4 servings

1¼ pounds brains
1 quart cold water
1 tablespoon white vinegar or lemon juice
1 teaspoon salt
¼ teaspoon peppercorns and 1 bouquet garni, tied in cheesecloth*
½ small yellow onion, peeled
1 small carrot, peeled

Vinaigrette Dressing:

¼ cup white wine vinegar
¼ teaspoon salt
⅛ teaspoon white pepper
¾ cup olive oil

Prepare brains for cooking.* Place in a large enamel, stainless-steel, or teflon-lined saucepan with all but dressing ingredients and simmer, uncovered, 20–25 minutes. Meanwhile, prepare dressing by shaking all ingredients in a shaker jar. When brains are cooked, lift out with a slotted spoon, halve, and arrange on a hot platter. Drizzle with about ½ cup dressing and pass the rest.

To Serve Cold: Cool brains in cooking liquid, then drain and chill well. Slice ½″ thick, drizzle with dressing, and serve.

Hot or cold: About 340 calories per serving.

COQUILLES OF BRAINS MORNAY

Makes 4 servings

1¼ pounds brains
2 cups hot Mornay Sauce
⅓ cup fine dry bread crumbs mixed with 2 tablespoons melted butter or margarine (optional topping)

Prepare brains for cooking and blanch as directed*; cut in small dice. Preheat oven to 350° F. Mix brains with sauce and spoon into lightly buttered scallop shells or ramekins. Top, if you like, with buttered crumbs. Set on a baking tray and bake, uncovered, 15 minutes, then brown quickly under broiler and serve. About 445 calories per serving.

VARIATION:

Coquilles of Sweetbreads Mornay: Prepare as directed, substituting sweetbreads for brains. About 405 calories per serving.

BRAIN TIMBALES

Makes 6 servings

2 pounds brains
6 slices bacon, fried until crisp and
  crumbled
2 tablespoons soft white bread crumbs
1 teaspoon grated yellow onion
1 teaspoon salt
⅛ teaspoon white pepper
3 eggs, lightly beaten
1½ cups heavy cream
6 toast rounds spread with Anchovy
  Butter

Prepare brains for cooking and blanch as directed*; cube, then purée in an electric blender at low speed or press through a fine sieve. Preheat oven to 350° F. Mix brains with all but last ingredient and spoon into well-buttered ramekins, filling ⅔ full. Set ramekins in a shallow baking pan, add water to pan to a depth of about 1½ inches, cover loosely with buttered foil, and bake 30–40 minutes until timbales are just firm. Remove ramekins from water bath and cool 5 minutes. To unmold, run a spatula around edge. Unmold each timbale carefully on a toast round and serve. About 405 calories per serving.

VARIATIONS:

Sweetbread Timbales: Substitute sweetbreads for brains and prepare as directed. About 385 calories per serving.

⊴⊳ **Timbales au Gratin:** Prepare timbales as above, then top each with buttered bread crumbs mixed with a little Parmesan cheese (about ⅓ cup buttered crumbs in all, 1 tablespoon Parmesan). Bake, uncovered, in water bath and serve in ramekins. About 300 calories per serving.

HEART

The hearts of beef, veal, pork, and lamb are all good to eat. They're chewy and muscular, taste a little bit like liver, and, when stuffed and braised or stewed,

make a very good meal indeed. If you are lucky enough to find very young lamb or veal hearts, you can simply slice and sauté them as you would calf's liver. All hearts are highly perishable, highly nutritious. They're also low in calories and, because there is little demand for them, budget priced. Better order ahead. Hearts are not routinely stocked at neighborhood markets.

Amount Needed: Allow about ½ pound per serving. Beef hearts run large—from 3–5 pounds—and make a good choice for a large family; veal hearts weigh ¾ pound and are perfect for 2 (if they don't have big appetites); pork hearts weigh about ½ pound, and lamb hearts between ¼ and ½.

To Prepare for Cooking: Wash heart well in tepid water, remove all fat, halve lengthwise and cut out vessels and large tubes. Leave halves joined if heart is to be stuffed, otherwise, cut up as individual recipes direct. If heart seems especially muscular, soak 1–2 hours in sour milk or acidulated water (1 tablespoon vinegar or lemon juice and 1 teaspoon salt to 1 quart water) to tenderize.

To Simmer (Stew): Place heart halves in a deep pot and add broth or salted water to cover (1 teaspoon salt for each quart water). Cover and simmer until tender, about 3–4 hours for beef heart, 2–2½ for pork and veal hearts. Serve with Pan Gravy or a suitable sauce (see Some Herbs and Seasonings/Sauces and Butters for Variety Meats). (*Note:* Lamb hearts should not be simmered; they're better if braised or sautéed.) To give simmered hearts extra flavor, add an onion, carrot, celery stalk, and parsley sprigs to the pot.

To Pressure Cook (not recommended for lamb hearts): Prepare heart for cooking; do not stuff. Brown heart in bacon drippings in open cooker, add ½ cup water or stock (or amount of liquid manufacturer recommends). Seal cooker, bring to 10 pounds pressure, and cook 15–20 minutes per pound or according to manufacturer's timetable (meat cooked at 10 pounds pressure will be more tender than that cooked at 15). Reduce pressure, open cooker, remove heart, and keep warm. Prepare Pan Gravy in open cooker.

¢ SAUTÉED HEARTS

Only young lamb or veal hearts will be tender enough to sauté.
Makes 4 servings

2 pounds lamb or veal hearts
3 tablespoons butter or margarine
¼ teaspoon salt
Pinch pepper
Pinch nutmeg (optional)
4 slices buttered toast (optional)
1 tablespoon minced parsley (optional)

Prepare hearts for cooking,* halve lengthwise, and slice ¼"–½" thick. Melt butter in a large, heavy skillet over moderately high heat, let it foam up, then subside. Add hearts, reduce heat to moderate, and stir-fry 2–3 minutes. Season and serve, if you like, on buttered toast sprinkled with parsley. About 340 calories per serving.

VARIATIONS:

Sautéed Hearts and Mushrooms: Prepare and slice hearts as above. Stir-fry ½ pound thinly sliced mushrooms in butter 3–4 minutes over moderately high heat; push to side of skillet, add hearts, and sauté as directed. Season and serve. About 355 calories per serving.

Mixed Fry: Prepare and slice 1 veal heart as directed above; cut ¼ pound calf's liver into thin strips; prepare 2 lamb kidneys for cooking* and sauté halves in 2 tablespoons butter 3–4 minutes over moderate heat, turning often with tongs. Remove from skillet and slice. Raise heat to high, add heart, liver, and kidney, and stir-fry quickly 2–3 minutes. Season with salt and pepper and, if you like, 1 tablespoon each lemon juice and minced parsley. Serve as is or on buttered toast. About 350 calories per serving.

⚖ **Low-Calorie Sautéed Hearts:** Reduce quantity of hearts to 1½ pounds; prepare as directed, using 2 tablespoons butter instead of 3. Omit buttered toast. About 260 calories per serving.

¢ CHICKEN-FRIED HEART

Makes 4 servings

2 pounds pork or beef heart
½ cup unsifted flour
1 teaspoon salt
¼ teaspoon pepper
¼ teaspoon thyme
¼ cup butter, margarine, or bacon
  drippings
½ cup hot water

Prepare heart for cooking* and slice ½" thick. Dredge in a mixture of flour, salt, pepper, and thyme and brown quickly on both sides in butter in a large, heavy skillet over moderately high heat. Add water, cover, turn heat to very low, and simmer 1½–2 hours until tender. Check skillet occasionally and add a little more water if needed. About 390 calories per serving.

VARIATION:

⚖ **Low-Calorie Chicken-Fried Heart:** Reduce quantity of heart to 1½ pounds; prepare as directed, using 2 tablespoons butter instead of ¼ cup. About 285 calories per serving.

¢ BRAISED STUFFED HEART

Makes 6 servings

1 (4–5-pound) beef heart
1 teaspoon salt
¼ teaspoon pepper
2 tablespoons butter or margarine
2 cups beef broth
2 tablespoons flour blended with 2
  tablespoons cold water

Stuffing:

1 cup minced yellow onion
⅓ cup minced carrot
2 tablespoons minced celery
2 tablespoons butter or margarine
1½ cups cooked rice
2 tablespoons minced parsley
1 teaspoon poultry seasoning

Prepare heart for cooking* and pat dry on paper toweling. Rub inside and out with salt and pepper and let stand while you prepare stuffing. Stir-fry onion, carrot, and celery in butter in a heavy skillet over moderate heat 8–10 minutes until golden; mix with remaining stuffing ingredients. Spoon loosely into heart cavity and close opening with poultry pins and string or sew up with needle and thread. Brown heart all over in 2 tablespoons butter in a heavy kettle over moderate heat. (*Note:* Use tongs for turning so you don't pierce heart and lose precious juices.) Add broth, cover, and simmer slowly about 3 hours until tender, turning 1–2 times during cooking. Check pot occasionally and add a little water if necessary. Lift heart to a heated platter, remove pins, string or thread and keep warm. Stir flour paste into kettle liquid and heat, stirring constantly, until thickened and smooth. Taste for salt and pepper and adjust if needed. To serve: slice heart crosswise, not too thin, and pass gravy. About 510 calories per serving.

VARIATION:

Substitute 2 cups Sage and Onion Dressing, Cornbread and Sausage Stuffing, or other savory stuffing for that above and proceed as directed. About 485 calories per serving if made with Sage and Onion Dressing, 640 calories per serving if made with Cornbread and Sausage Stuffing.

¢ CASSEROLE OF VEAL HEARTS AND VEGETABLES

Makes 4 servings

2 pounds veal hearts
⅓ cup unsifted flour
1 teaspoon salt
¼ teaspoon pepper
3 tablespoons bacon drippings or cooking oil
1 large yellow onion, peeled and minced
1 cup water
¼ cup tomato paste
1 tablespoon Worcestershire sauce
4 carrots, peeled and cut in 2" chunks
3 turnips, peeled and quartered
3 stalks celery, cut in 2" chunks
1 tablespoon minced parsley

Preheat oven to 350° F. Prepare hearts for cooking* and quarter. Dredge in a mixture of flour, salt, and pepper and brown in drippings in a heavy skillet over moderate heat 3–4 minutes; transfer to an ungreased 2½-quart casserole. Stir-fry onion in drippings 5–8 minutes until pale golden, stir in water, tomato paste, and Worcestershire sauce, and pour into casserole. Tuck vegetables in here and there, cover, and bake 1½–2 hours until hearts are tender. Uncover, sprinkle with parsley, and serve. About 355 calories per serving.

¢ BALMORAL HEART PATTIES

Good in hamburger buns.
Makes 4 servings

1 pound sliced beef or veal heart, trimmed of large vessels
2 scallions
½ cup quick-cooking oatmeal
¼ cup evaporated milk
1¼ teaspoons salt
¼ teaspoon pepper
1 tablespoon Worcestershire sauce
2 tablespoons minced parsley
3 tablespoons bacon or beef drippings, butter, or margarine
1 cup beef gravy (homemade or canned)

Put heart through finest blade of food grinder along with scallions; mix in oatmeal, milk, salt, pepper, Worcester-shire sauce, and parsley, cover, and chill 1 hour. Shape into 4 plump patties and brown slowly in drippings in a heavy skillet over moderate heat; reduce heat to low and cook, uncovered, turning frequently, 10–12 minutes until cooked through but not dry. Transfer to a hot platter and keep warm. Heat gravy in skillet drippings and serve with patties. About 345 calories per serving.

KIDNEYS

The kidneys of all meat animals are edible, but those of lamb and veal are the most cherished because of their delicacy and tenderness; either can be broiled or sautéed. Beef and pork kidneys are another matter; being muscular and strongly flavored, they're best when braised or stewed. All kidneys are a high-protein, low-calorie food and an excellent source of iron and B vitamins. When buying kidneys, always make sure they smell sweet and fresh.

Amount Needed: Allow ⅓–½ pound kidneys per person. Lamb kidneys are so tiny (only 1½–3 ounces each) that you'll need 2–3 per person. Veal kidneys average ½–¾ pound and will usually serve 1 to 2. Beef kidneys weigh about 1 pound and pork kidneys ¼ pound.

To Prepare for Cooking: Because of their delicacy, lamb and veal kidneys should never be washed. Peel off any outer fat, the thin membrane, and then cut out the knobs of fat and tubes underneath; the job will be easier if the kidneys are first halved lengthwise. Beef and pork kidneys should be washed well in tepid water, then split and trimmed of fat and tubes.

⚖ SAUTÉED KIDNEYS

Only lamb or veal kidneys are delicate enough to sauté. And even these are a bit tricky. If sliced, the kidneys will send a lot of juice out into the skillet so that they "stew" rather than sauté. The best method is the one that follows—sautéing the kidneys halves, then slicing and returning briefly to the skillet. Kidneys, by the way, do not brown so much as turn an even gray-beige. They're best slightly rare.
Makes 4 servings

1½ pounds lamb or veal kidneys
3 tablespoons butter or margarine
¼ teaspoon salt
Pinch pepper
1 tablespoon lemon juice (optional)
1 tablespoon minced parsley (optional)

Prepare kidneys for cooking.* Melt butter in a large, heavy skillet over moderately high heat, let it foam up, then subside. Add kidneys and sauté,

turning often with tongs. Veal kidneys will need 8–10 minutes, lamb kidneys only 3–5. Remove from skillet and slice about ¼" thick (lamb kidneys may also be simply quartered). Return kidneys to skillet and warm about 2 minutes, shaking skillet. Season and, if you like, sprinkle with lemon juice and parsley. Serve as is or with suitable sauce (see Some Herbs and Seasonings/ Sauces and Butters for Variety Meats). About 275 calories per serving (without sauce).

VARIATIONS:

⚖ **Sautéed Kidneys and Mushrooms:** Prepare kidneys as above and set aside. Stir-fry ½ pound thinly sliced mushrooms in butter 3–5 minutes over moderately high heat, push to side of skillet, add kidneys, and proceed as directed. About 290 calories per serving.

Sautéed Kidneys in Onion and Wine Sauce: Prepare and sauté whole kidneys as above; remove from skillet and keep warm. In drippings stir-fry 2 tablespoons minced scallions 3–4 minutes, add ½ cup dry vermouth and boil rapidly to reduce by ½. Add 1 tablespoon each lemon juice and minced parsley. Slice kidneys, return to skillet, and season. Warm, shaking skillet, 1–2 minutes and serve. About 330 calories per serving.

⚖ **Low-Calorie Sautéed Kidneys:** Reduce amount of butter to 2 tablespoons and prepare as directed. About 230 calories per serving.

⚖ BROILED KIDNEYS

Lamb and veal kidneys are the most suitable for broiling, and they must be basted often with melted butter and broiled only until rare or medium if they are to remain moist and tender.
Makes 4 servings.

1½ pounds lamb or veal kidneys
⅓ cup melted butter or margarine
½ teaspoon salt
⅛ teaspoon pepper
4 slices buttered toast, trimmed of
  crusts and halved diagonally (optional)

1 tablespoon lemon juice (optional)
1 tablespoon minced parsley (optional)

Preheat broiler. Prepare kidneys for cooking.* Place on lightly greased broiler rack and brush well with melted butter. Broil 3″ from heat, brushing often with melted butter, about 4–5 minutes on a side for rare and 5–7 for medium. Serve, if you like, on toast points sprinkled with lemon juice and parsley. Or serve with Bordelaise or other suitable sauce (see Some Herbs and Seasonings/Sauces and Butters for Variety Meats). About 250 calories per serving (without toast or sauce).

VARIATIONS:

⚖ **Marinated Broiled Kidneys:** Prepare kidneys as above, then marinate 3–4 hours in refrigerator in French, Italian, garlic, or herb dressing. Broil as directed, brushing often with dressing instead of butter. About 235 calories per serving.

⚖ **Breaded Broiled Kidneys:** Prepare kidneys as above. Dip in melted butter, then in fine dry bread crumbs. Broil as directed, basting often with melted butter. About 270 calories per serving.

⚖ **Lamb Kidney en Brochette:** Prepare kidneys as above. Alternate on skewers with mushroom caps (you'll need about 12 altogether), weaving strips of bacon in and out. Broil 3″ from heat, turning often, 12–15 minutes until bacon is browned. Season and serve. About 265 calories per serving.

⚖ **Low-Calorie Broiled Kidneys:** Prepare as directed, using low-calorie French, Italian, garlic, or herb dressing for basting instead of butter. Omit buttered toast slices. About 200 calories per serving.

⚖ **BRAISED KIDNEYS**

Beef and pork kidneys come from mature animals, thus they tend to be tough. The most successful way to tenderize them is to brown them, then to cook, covered, with a small amount of liquid.
Makes 4 servings

1½ pounds beef or pork kidneys
½ cup unsifted flour
1 teaspoon salt
¼ teaspoon pepper
3 tablespoons butter, margarine, or
* bacon drippings*
½ cup liquid (water, beef broth, dry red
* or white wine, tomato juice)*

Prepare kidneys for cooking,* halve lengthwise, and slice crosswise ¼″ thick. Dredge in a mixture of flour, salt, and pepper, then brown on both sides in butter in a large, heavy skillet over moderately high heat. Turn heat to low, add liquid, cover, and simmer slowly about 20 minutes until tender. About 290 calories per serving.

VARIATION:

Prepare and dredge kidneys as above. Before browning, stir-fry 1 minced small yellow onion in butter; push to side of skillet, add kidneys and proceed as directed. Sprinkle with 1 tablespoon minced parsley before serving. About 300 calories per serving.

⚖ **Low-Calorie Braised Kidneys:** Prepare as directed, reducing amount of butter to 2 tablespoons and using water as the liquid. About 250 calories per serving.

CHAFING DISH KIDNEYS WITH SHERRY

Makes 4 servings

1½ pounds lamb kidneys
2 tablespoons butter or margarine
¼ cup medium-sweet sherry or Madeira
⅛ teaspoon pepper

Sauce:

2 slices bacon, chopped fine
1 small yellow onion, peeled and minced
½ clove garlic, peeled and minced
1 small carrot, peeled and cut in small
* dice*
2 ripe tomatoes, peeled, seeded and
* chopped fine*
¾ cup beef bouillon

Prepare kidneys for cooking* and halve lengthwise. Sauté rapidly in butter in a skillet over moderately high heat

2 minutes and set aside while you prepare sauce. Stir-fry bacon, onion, garlic, carrot, and tomatoes in a skillet over moderately high heat 5–8 minutes, add bouillon, cover, and simmer 10 minutes. Purée in an electric blender at low speed or put through a food mill. (*Note:* If preparing this at table, place sauce and all remaining ingredients near chafing dish.) Turn burner flame to high, spoon kidneys and any drippings into chafing dish, and stir-fry 2 minutes; lower flame, add sherry, and cook and stir 2 minutes. Add pepper and sauce and heat, stirring, just until it bubbles. Serve over buttered noodles or boiled rice. About 345 calories per serving (without noodles or rice).

HERB STUFFED KIDNEY AND BACON ROLLS

Makes 2 servings

3 lamb kidneys
½ cup soft white bread crumbs
1 tablespoon minced chives
1 tablespoon minced parsley
1 teaspoon chervil
⅛ teaspoon garlic powder
⅛ teaspoon pepper
2 tablespoons softened butter or
*   margarine*
6 slices bacon, halved

Preheat oven to 425° F. Prepare kidneys for cooking* and quarter. Mix crumbs with herbs, garlic powder, pepper, and butter. Spread each ½ bacon slice with herb mixture and roll up with a piece of kidney inside; secure with toothpicks. Arrange on a rack in a shallow baking pan and bake, uncovered, about 25 minutes, turning frequently until bacon is crisp. Remove toothpicks and serve with vegetables or on buttered toast. About 445 calories per serving (without vegetables or toast).

⊠ KIDNEYS EN COCOTTES

Makes 2 servings

3 slices bacon
¾ pound lamb kidneys
1 teaspoon minced chives

2 eggs
2 tablespoons light cream
Pinch salt
Pinch paprika

Preheat oven to 350° F. Brown bacon in a small skillet over moderate heat; drain on paper toweling and reserve. Prepare kidneys for cooking* and cut in 1" cubes; sauté in bacon drippings over moderately high heat 3–4 minutes until lightly browned. Using a slotted spoon, transfer kidneys to 2 buttered individual ramekins, sprinkle with chives and crumbled bacon. Break each egg into a cup and slide into ramekin; add 1 tablespoon cream to each. Set ramekins in a water bath and bake uncovered 12–14 minutes until egg white is just set. Sprinkle with salt and pepper and serve. About 460 calories per serving.

DEVILED KIDNEYS

Makes 4 servings

1½ pounds lamb kidneys
2 tablespoons prepared mild yellow
*   mustard*
¼ cup heavy cream
1 tablespoon steak sauce
⅛ teaspoon pepper
⅓–½ cup packaged Italian-style bread
*   crumbs*
¼ cup melted butter or margarine
4 slices hot buttered toast

Preheat oven to 325° F. Prepare kidneys for cooking.* Mix mustard, cream, steak sauce, and pepper; dip each kidney in mustard mixture, then in bread crumbs to coat evenly. Arrange in a buttered shallow baking dish and drizzle a little melted butter over each kidney. Bake, uncovered, 25 minutes until tender, basting with extra melted butter as needed to brown crumbs evenly. Serve on hot buttered toast with pan drippings ladled over kidneys. About 440 calories per serving (without toast).

⊠ KIDNEYS IN SOUR CREAM

Makes 4 servings

1½ pounds lamb kidneys
3 tablespoons butter or margarine
2 tablespoons lemon juice
4 scallions, minced (include green tops)
¾ teaspoon seasoned salt
¼ teaspoon pepper
½ teaspoon summer savory
1½ cups sour cream
1 tablespoon minced parsley

Prepare kidneys for cooking* and slice thin. Stir-fry rapidly in butter in a heavy skillet over moderate heat 3–4 minutes until pink color almost disappears. Turn heat to low, stir in all remaining ingredients except parsley. Heat, stirring, 1–2 minutes, sprinkle with parsley, and serve. Good with hot buttered noodles or boiled rice. About 460 calories per serving (without noodles or rice).

⊴⊵ BRAISED VEAL KIDNEYS AND MUSHROOMS

Makes 4 servings

1½ pounds veal kidneys
¼ cup unsifted flour
3 tablespoons bacon drippings, butter, or margarine
½ pound button mushrooms, wiped clean
½ cup water, beef broth, or dry red wine
½ teaspoon salt
⅛ teaspoon pepper

Preheat oven to 350° F. Prepare kidneys for cooking* and halve lengthwise. Dredge in flour and brown lightly in 2 tablespoons drippings in a heavy skillet over moderately high heat 2–3 minutes. Transfer to an ungreased 1½-quart casserole; brown mushrooms in remaining drippings 2–3 minutes and add to kidneys. Drain off all but 1 tablespoon drippings from skillet, add water, and stir to scrape up brown bits; pour into casserole. Sprinkle with salt and pepper, cover, and bake 45 minutes until tender. About 280 calories per serving.

VARIATIONS:

Braised Veal Kidneys with Vegetables:
Small new potatoes, 1″ chunks of carrots, turnips, or rutabagas or parboiled white onions can be cooked along with the kidneys in the same casserole; add a little extra salt and pepper. Recipe too flexible for a meaningful calorie count.

⊴⊵ **Low-Calorie Braised Veal Kidneys:**
Prepare as directed, reducing amount of drippings to 2 tablespoons and using water as the liquid. About 250 calories per serving.

¢ CLARA'S KIDNEY STEW

Makes 4 servings

1½ pounds veal or beef kidneys
2 cups cold water
1 teaspoon salt
½ cup unsifted flour
⅛ teaspoon pepper
3 tablespoons beef or bacon drippings or cooking oil
1½ cups beef broth
1 bay leaf, crumbled
1 tablespoon flour blended with 1 tablespoon cold water
1 tablespoon minced parsley

If beef kidneys are used, soak in cold water mixed with 1 teaspoon salt 1 hour; drain well and pat dry on paper toweling. Prepare kidneys for cooking* and cut into ¾″–1″ cubes. Dredge lightly in mixture of flour, salt, and pepper. Sauté, half of kidneys at a time, 3–4 minutes in drippings in a heavy skillet over moderately high heat; remove with a slotted spoon to a large, heavy saucepan. Add broth to skillet, stir brown bits from bottom, and pour over kidneys. Add bay leaf, cover, and simmer until tender, about 15–20 minutes for veal kidneys, 35–40 for beef. Thicken gravy, if you like, by blending in flour paste and heating and stirring until thickened. Taste for seasoning and adjust if necessary. Sprinkle with parsley and serve. Good with boiled potatoes or hot buttered noodles. About 305 calories per serving.

Other Kidney Recipes
Old-Fashioned Steak and Kidney Pie (see Beef)
Beef, Kidney, Mushroom, and Oyster Pie (see Beef)
English Mixed Grill (see Lamb)

LIVER

Liver to most people is calf's liver (or, to be more accurate, veal liver), but beef, pork, and lamb liver are good, too, especially lamb liver, which is tender enough to sauté and which can be substituted for calf's liver in the recipes that follow. Unfortunately, it is not often available. Beef and pork liver have a strong flavor but when ground into loaves or braised can be quite savory and succulent. All liver is a potent source of iron, vitamin A, and most of the B vitamins, all is low in calories.

Because of its popularity, calf's liver is rather expensive; it is now available packaged in frozen slices as well as fresh. Lamb, beef, and pork livers are reasonably priced. All liver is highly perishable and should be cooked within 24 hours of purchase. Top quality calf's liver will be rosy red, moist, and quivery (so tender, someone said, you can push your thumb through it). Lamb liver will be equally delicate but redder, beef and pork liver deep red-brown and fairly firm.

Amount Needed: Allow ¼ –⅓ pound liver per serving. Beef liver weighs about 10 pounds; pork liver about 3; veal liver averages 2½ pounds, and lamb liver 1.

To Prepare for Cooking: Liver needs very little preparation. Simply peel off covering membrane (so liver won't shrivel and curl during cooking), then cut out any large vessels.

Cooking Tip: Because of its quivery texture, liver is difficult to grind raw. To make the job easier, cut into strips, sauté briefly in butter or drippings to firm, then grind.

⟐⟐ ⊠ SAUTÉED CALF'S LIVER

Liver is best on the rare side—faintly pink with rosy juices. If overcooked, it becomes tough and dry.
Makes 2 servings

2 tablespoons butter or margarine
¾ pound calf's liver, sliced ¼" thick
Pinch nutmeg (optional)
Pinch summer savory (optional)
¼ teaspoon salt
⅛ teaspoon pepper

Melt butter in a large, heavy skillet over moderately high heat, let it foam up, then subside. Add liver and brown 2–3 minutes per side for rare, 3–3½ for medium. Sprinkle both sides with seasonings and serve. About 280 calories per serving.

VARIATIONS:

⟐⟐ **Calf's Liver and Onions:** Stir-fry 1 thinly sliced small Bermuda onion in butter 5–8 minutes over moderate heat until pale golden. Push to side of pan, raise heat to moderately high, add liver and brown as directed. Season and serve topped with onions. About 300 calories per serving.

Calf's Liver and Bacon: Omit butter; brown 4 slices bacon in a large skillet over moderately high heat and drain on paper toweling. Pour off all but 1 tablespoon drippings, add liver, brown and season as directed. Serve topped with bacon. About 380 calories per serving.

Calf's Liver Burgundy: Stir-fry 1 thinly sliced small Bermuda onion and 1 crushed clove garlic in 2 tablespoons olive oil 5–8 minutes over moderate heat until pale golden. Push to side of pan, add liver, raise heat to moderately high, and brown as directed. Season with salt and pepper, lift to a hot platter and keep warm. Add ¼ cup Burgundy or other dry red wine to skillet, boil 1 minute, pour over liver, and serve. About 325 calories per serving.

Calf's Liver in Mustard Sauce: Sauté liver as directed above, remove to a heated platter and keep warm. To skillet add ¼ cup beef broth and ⅓ cup heavy cream and boil rapidly, uncovered, to reduce by half. Off heat smooth in 2 teaspoons Dijon-style mustard and 1 teaspoon minced parsley. Pour over liver and serve. About 425 calories per serving.

⚖ ⌛ BROILED LIVER

Lamb's and calf's livers are the only ones suitable for broiling.
Makes 4 servings

1¼ pounds lamb's or calf's liver, sliced ½″ thick
⅓ cup melted butter or margarine
½ teaspoon salt
⅛ teaspoon pepper

Preheat broiler. Place liver on a lightly greased broiler rack and brush well with melted butter. Broil 4″ from heat 2–3 minutes per side for rare and 4 minutes per side for medium, brushing frequently with melted butter. Season and serve as is or topped with a compatible butter or sauce (see Some Herbs and Seasonings/Sauces and Butters for Variety Meats). About 280 calories per serving.

VARIATION:

⚖ **Low-Calorie Broiled Liver:** Broil as directed, using low-calorie Italian or French dressing for basting instead of butter. About 200 calories per serving.

¢ BRAISED LIVER

Here's the way to make beef or pork liver succulent.
Makes 4 servings

1 small Bermuda onion, peeled and minced
3 tablespoons bacon drippings
1¼ pounds beef or pork liver, sliced ¼″–½″ thick and cut in strips 4″ long and 1″ wide
½ cup unsifted flour
1 teaspoon salt
¼ teaspoon pepper
1 cup beef broth (about) or a ½ and ½ mixture of broth and dry red or white wine
1 tablespoon minced parsley

Stir-fry onion in 2 tablespoons drippings in a large, heavy skillet over moderate heat 10–12 minutes until lightly browned; lift out with a slotted spoon and set aside. Add remaining drippings to skillet. Dredge liver in a mixture of flour, salt and pepper and brown, a few pieces at a time, in drippings. Return all liver and onion to skillet, add broth, cover, and simmer over lowest heat about 45 minutes until tender. Check skillet occasionally and add a little extra broth if necessary. When liver is done, lift to a heated platter, smother with skillet gravy, and sprinkle with parsley. About 370 calories per serving.

VARIATION:

⚖ **Low-Calorie Braised Liver:** Prepare as directed, reducing amount of drippings to 2 tablespoons and using water as the liquid ingredient. About 325 calories per serving.

⚖ ⌛ CALF'S LIVER ALLA VENEZIANA

Makes 2 servings

2 medium-size yellow onions, peeled and minced
2 tablespoons butter or margarine
1 tablespoon olive oil
3 tablespoons dry vermouth
¼ teaspoon salt
Pinch pepper
⅔ pound calf's liver, sliced ¼″–½″ thick and cut in strips about 2″ long and 1″ wide
1 tablespoon lemon juice
1 tablespoon minced parsley

Stir-fry onions in butter and oil in a large heavy skillet 5–8 minutes over moderate heat until pale golden; add vermouth, salt and pepper and simmer 1–2 minutes to reduce. Raise heat to moderately high, add liver, and stir-fry quickly 3–5 minutes, just until redness disappears (liver will not brown). Add lemon juice and parsely and serve. About 305 calories per serving.

⚖ ☒ **CALF'S LIVER AND BACON EN BROCHETTE**

Makes 4 servings

1¼ pounds calf's liver, sliced ¼"–½"
  thick and cut in strips 4" long and
  1½" wide
8 slices bacon
2 tablespoons melted bacon drippings,
  butter, or margarine
1 tablespoon steak sauce

Preheat broiler. Thread liver on long
skewers, interweaving with bacon; do
not crowd pieces. Lay skewers across a
shallow baking tray and brush with a
mixture of drippings and steak sauce.
Broil 4"–5" from heat 6–8 minutes,
turning frequently and brushing with
sauce mixture until bacon is crisp and
liver lightly browned. Serve on or off the
skewers. About 290 calories per serving.

VARIATION:

⚖ **Japanese-Style Liver en Brochette:**
Marinate liver strips 2–4 hours in
refrigerator before broiling in following
mixture: 2 tablespoons each peanut oil
and soy sauce, 1 tablespoon steak sauce,
¼ cup dry sherry, 1 teaspoon grated
gingerroot, and ½ crushed clove garlic.
Skewer with bacon and broil as directed,
brushing frequently with marinade.
About 295 calories per serving.

**CALF'S LIVER WITH
PROSCIUTTO AND PARSLEY**

Makes 4 servings

1¼ pounds calf's liver, sliced ¼"–½"
  thick
¾ cup unsifted flour
1½ teaspoons salt
¼ teaspoon pepper
¼ cup butter or margarine
¼ cup julienne strips of prosciutto ham
3 tablespoons minced yellow onion
½ teaspoon summer savory or sage
3 tablespoons minced parsley
1 tablespoon flour (use that from
  dredging liver) blended with ½ cup
  beef broth
½ cup dry Marsala wine
1 tablespoon lemon juice
Lemon wedges (garnish)

Dredge liver lightly in a mixture of flour,
salt and pepper and sauté in butter in a
large, heavy skillet over moderately high
heat, about 2–3 minutes per side for rare,
3½ for medium. Remove liver and keep
warm. Turn heat to moderately low, add
prosciutto, onion, savory, and parsley
to skillet, and stir-fry 5–8 minutes until
onion is pale golden. Mix in flour paste
and remaining ingredients and heat,
stirring, until thickened. Return liver to
skillet, heat 1–2 minutes, then serve
garnished with lemon wedges. About 365
calories per serving.

¢ ☒ **GINGERY CHINESE-STYLE
LIVER**

Budget fare if made with pork liver.
Makes 4 servings

1¼ pounds pork, lamb, or calf's liver,
  sliced ¼"–½" thick and cut in strips
  3" long and ½" wide
3 tablespoons peanut or other cooking
  oil
½ teaspoon ginger
¼ teaspoon pepper
½ cup thinly sliced bamboo shoots
¼ cup soy sauce
2 tablespoons hot water
½ teaspoon sugar
3 cups hot cooked rice
4 scallions, minced

Stir-fry liver in oil in a *wok* or heavy
skillet over high heat 2–3 minutes until
lightly browned. Reduce heat, sprinkle
with ginger and pepper, and stir-fry 1
minute. Add all but last 2 ingredients and
heat, stirring, until bubbling. Spoon over
rice, sprinkle with scallions, and serve.
About 415 calories per serving.

¢ ⚖ **BRAISED BEEF LIVER
WITH TOMATO-MUSHROOM
GRAVY**

Makes 8 servings

2½ pounds young beef liver, in 1 piece
¼ cup sifted flour
2 teaspoons salt
¼ teaspoon pepper
¼ cup bacon drippings, butter, or
  margarine

1 medium-size yellow onion, peeled and
    sliced thin
¼ cup minced mushrooms
¾ cup beef bouillon
1 bay leaf, crumbled
1 tablespoon tomato paste

Peel any outer membrane from liver,
then wipe liver with damp paper
toweling; dredge in a mixture of flour,
salt and pepper and brown well on all
sides in drippings in a large, heavy
kettle over moderate heat about 5
minutes. Liver will swell as it browns but
don't be alarmed. Turn heat to low, add
all remaining ingredients except tomato
paste, cover, and simmer 1½ hours until
liver is tender, turning halfway through
cooking. Lift liver to a platter and keep
warm. Stir tomato paste into gravy;
strain gravy and pour over liver. About
325 calories per serving.

¢ FINNISH CHOPPED LIVER AND RICE CASSEROLE

Finns serve wild mushrooms, cucumbers
in sour cream, and buttered home-baked
rye bread with this dish. Made with beef
liver, it's a budget dish.
Makes 4 servings

1¼ pounds beef or calf's liver, sliced
    ¼"–½" thick
3 tablespoons butter or margarine
1 large yellow onion, peeled and minced
1½ cups uncooked rice
2 cups boiling water
1 cup milk
1 cup seedless raisins
2 teaspoons salt
¼ teaspoon pepper
¼ teaspoon marjoram
2 tablespoons dark brown sugar or
    molasses

Preheat oven to 350° F. Sauté liver in
butter in a skillet over moderately high
heat 3–4 minutes until browned; cool
slightly and chop fine. Brown onion in
drippings 8–10 minutes and reserve.
Simmer rice, water, and milk together in
a saucepan with lid askew about 15
minutes until rice is barely tender; turn
into a buttered 1½-quart casserole, add
liver, onion, and remaining ingredients,

and toss well with 2 forks. Bake
uncovered, 20–30 minutes until all
liquid is absorbed. About 585 calories
per serving.

¢ DANISH LIVER LOAF

Serve hot with bright crisp vegetables or
cold on dark rye bread with pickled
beets.
Makes 6 servings

¼ pound salt pork, trimmed of rind and
    diced
1 pound beef liver, trimmed of
    connective tissues and tubes and cut in
    strips about 2" wide
1 medium-size yellow onion, peeled and
    minced
1 (10½-ounce) can condensed beef broth
2 dozen soda crackers, crumbled (about
    1½ cups)
½ teaspoon thyme
1 tablespoon minced parsley
¼ teaspoon pepper
1 teaspoon dark brown sugar
½ teaspoon ginger
2 eggs, lightly beaten

Preheat oven to 400° F. Fry salt pork in
a heavy skillet over moderately low heat
5 minutes until pale golden and rendered
of all drippings; remove with a slotted
spoon and reserve. Sauté liver in
drippings over moderate heat 5–7
minutes, until lightly browned; remove
and reserve. Sauté onion in drippings
5–8 minutes until pale golden and reserve
in skillet. Pour broth over crackers and
let stand. Grind liver and salt pork
together, using fine blade of meat
grinder, then mix thoroughly with onions
and drippings, crackers and broth, and all
remaining ingredients. Spoon into a
lightly greased 9"×5"×3" loaf pan
and bake, uncovered, on center rack 40
minutes until firm. Cool upright in pan
on rack 20 minutes; invert on serving
platter and turn out. Serve hot or cold
but slice fairly thick. About 335 calories
per serving.

SWEETBREADS

Of all the variety meats, sweetbreads are considered the most delectable. Certainly they're the most luxurious (they cost about the same as fine steak).

What are they? Technically, the thymus gland of young animals, a big double-lobed gland consisting of the large, smooth, choice *kernel* or *heart sweetbread,* located in the breast, and the smaller, more irregular *throat sweetbread.* The two, spoken of as a pair, are linked by a tube, which should be removed. Sweetbreads are ultrafragile, creamy-smooth, and faintly nutty; they resemble brains in flavor and texture and can be used interchangeably with them in many recipes. Most sweetbreads sold in this country are the milky-white, finely-grained veal sweetbreads. Lamb sweetbreads are sometimes available but are too small to be very practical; also available: yearling beef sweetbreads (rougher and redder) and pork sweetbreads (stronger flavored and a favorite with Europeans for pâtés and soufflés). No matter what animals sweetbreads come from, they will be from young ones (the thymus gland disappears with maturity).

You may also run across something called *beef breads,* not true sweetbreads but the pancreas gland of beef. Though stronger in flavor and coarser in texture, these do resemble sweetbreads and can be prepared like them.

All sweetbreads are extremely perishable; if they are not to be served on the day they're bought, they should be blanched and refrigerated and, even then, served within 24 hours. Recently, frozen sweetbreads have been available, an excellent choice because they needn't be prepared immediately (always cook by package directions). Restaurants get most of the fresh sweetbreads, so give your butcher plenty of notice. And insist that the sweetbreads be *absolutely fresh.*

Amount Needed: Because sweetbreads are so rich, ¼–⅓ pound is about as much as a person can handle comfortably. A pair of veal sweetbreads averages ¾–1 pound, lamb sweetbreads ¼ pound, and yearling beef sweetbreads about 1½ pounds. Pork sweetbreads run around ¾ pound, but unless you raise your own hogs, you aren't likely to find them.

To Prepare for Cooking: Wash sweetbreads gently in cold water, then place in a large bowl and cover with cold acidulated water (1 tablespoon lemon juice or white vinegar and 1 teaspoon salt to 1 quart water) and soak 1½ hours. The sweetbreads will turn white. Drain, gently peel off as much thin outer membrane as possible; it clings stubbornly and is almost transparent, so have patience. Soak for another 1½ hours in fresh acidulated water, changing it 1 or 2 times; drain once more and peel away what membrane you missed the first time. Separate the 2 lobes from the tube (some people like to add it to the stock pot).

To Blanch: Connoisseurs are of two minds about blanching. Some recommend it no matter how the sweetbreads are to be cooked, others insist that it's necessary only when the sweetbreads are to be broken into smaller pieces and sautéed. Blanching does steal away some of the delicate flavor, but it also firms up the sweetbreads and makes them easier to handle. Perhaps a good rule of thumb: If sweetbreads are to be braised whole, don't blanch. Otherwise, do. Place the sweetbreads in a large enamel, stainless-steel, flameproof glass, or teflon-lined saucepan, add acidulated water to cover, and simmer, uncovered, 15 minutes over lowest heat (young beef sweetbreads and beef breads (the pancreas) will need about 25 minutes). Drain, cover with ice water, and let stand until cold. Drain well and pat dry on paper toweling. Some cooks like to place sweetbreads between paper towels and weight with heavy plates to get out excess moisture; not a bad idea when they're to be sautéed. The sweetbreads are now ready to sauté or use in recipes. To divide into smaller pieces, gently break apart at the natural separations.

Some Classic Garnishes for Sweetbreads
Note: Many of these are the same as for tournedos, steaks, and lamb chops.

À la Nantua: Arrange sautéed sweet-breads in a circle on a large platter. Fill center with tiny puff pastry shells (half regular size) filled with tiny boiled shrimp in Suprême Sauce and sprinkled with slivered truffles. Pass extra Suprême Sauce.

St. Germain: Serve sautéed or broiled sweetbreads on individual patties of Hashed Brown Potatoes; drizzle with Béarnaise Sauce.

À la Financière: Prepare Braised Sweetbreads as directed, transfer to crisp, fried rounds of white bread, and set in center of a hot large platter. Scatter 1 minced truffle and ¼ cup slivered smoked tongue over sweetbreads and drizzle with Financière Sauce. Garnish with 4 Chicken Quenelles, ¼ pound sautéed button mushrooms, 2 sliced sautéed lamb's kidneys, and 1 dozen pitted green olives (blanch quickly in boiling water if they seem extra salty). Add sprigs of watercress and serve.

À la Clamart:
Choron: } see Some Classic Ways to Serve Tournedos.
Rossini:

À la Jardinière: } see Some Classic Garnishes for Steaks.

Talleyrand: } see Some Classic Garnishes for Lamb Chops.

⚤ **SAUTÉED SWEETBREADS**

The following recipes are all for veal sweetbreads, but lamb or young beef sweetbreads may be substituted.
Makes 4 servings

1¼ pounds sweetbreads
½ cup unsifted flour

1 teaspoon salt
¼ teaspoon pepper
¼ cup butter or margarine

Suggested Sauces:
Béarnaise
Beurre Noir
Diable
Madeira

Prepare sweetbreads for cooking and blanch as directed.* Leave whole or halve at the natural separation and pat very dry on paper toweling. Dredge lightly in a mixture of flour, salt, and pepper, then sauté in butter in a large, heavy skillet over moderate to moderately high heat 3–4 minutes on a side until nicely browned. Drain on paper toweling and serve with 1 of the sauces suggested above. About 215 calories per serving (without sauce).

VARIATIONS:

⚤ **Breaded Sweetbreads:** Prepare and blanch sweetbreads as directed,* halve at the natural separation, and pat dry on paper toweling. Dredge in seasoned flour as above, dip in 1 egg lightly beaten with 1 tablespoon cold water and then in fine dry bread crumbs or cracker meal. Sauté in butter as directed and serve with Maître d'Hôtel Butter. About 285 calories per serving (without butter).

Sautéed Sweetbreads and Mushrooms: Prepare and blanch sweetbreads as directed*; divide into small pieces but do not dredge. Sauté with ½ pound wiped, sliced mushrooms in 3 tablespoons butter over moderate heat 6–8 minutes until browned. While sweetbreads are sautéing, make a thin Velouté Sauce: melt 2 tablespoons butter in a saucepan, blend in 2 tablespoons flour, add 1 cup veal or chicken stock, and heat, stirring, until thickened. Mix ⅓ cup heavy cream with 1 egg yolk, stir slowly into sauce, and heat and stir 1 minute (do not boil). Season with ½ teaspoon salt and a pinch white pepper. Spoon sweetbreads and mushrooms onto unbuttered toast triangles and smother each serving with sauce; pass any remaining sauce. About 415 calories per serving.

⚖️ **Sautéed Sweetbreads and Prosciutto:** Prepare sweetbreads as directed but sauté quickly just to brown, about 5 minutes. Add 3 tablespoons each minced chives and parsley, ¼ cup each minced prosciutto ham and apple cider or chicken broth. Put lid on skillet askew and simmer 5 minutes, shaking pan occasionally. About 260 calories per serving.

⚖️ **BROILED SWEETBREADS**

Makes 4 servings

1¼ pounds sweetbreads
½ cup melted butter or margarine
½ teaspoon salt
⅛ teaspoon pepper

Prepare sweetbreads for cooking and blanch as directed,* halve at the natural separation, and pat very dry on paper toweling. Preheat broiler. Place sweetbreads on lightly greased broiler rack and brush well with melted butter. Broil 5″ from heat 2–3 minutes until lightly browned, brushing 1 or 2 times with butter; turn and broil 2–3 minutes longer, again brushing with butter. Season and serve as is or with a suitable sauce (see Some Herbs and Seasonings/ Sauces and Butters for Variety Meats). About 215 calories per serving.

VARIATIONS:

⚖️ **Broiled Brains:** Prepare basic recipe above or any of the variations below as directed, substituting brains for sweetbreads. About 255 calories per serving.

⚖️ **Savory Broiled Sweetbreads:** Prepare sweetbreads as above, then dredge in ⅓ cup unsifted flour mixed with ½ teaspoon salt and ¼ teaspoon each pepper and summer savory. Broil as directed, brushing often with melted butter or a ½ and ½ mixture of melted butter and Madeira wine. About 240 calories per serving.

⚖️ **Broiled Breaded Sweetbreads:** Prepare sweetbreads as above, dip in melted butter, then in fine dry bread crumbs or cracker meal. Broil as directed, brushing often with melted butter. For extra flavor, use seasoned crumbs. About 240 calories per serving.

⚖️ **Sweetbreads and Bacon en Brochette:** Prepare sweetbreads as above, but break into chunks about the size of walnuts; wrap each in ½ slice bacon and secure with a toothpick. Place on skewers, not too close together, and brush with melted butter. Broil 6″ from heat, turning often and brushing with pan drippings or extra melted butter, about 15 minutes until golden brown. *For Extra Flair:* Alternate mushroom caps on skewers with bacon-wrapped sweetbreads and broil as directed. About 315 calories per serving.

⚖️ **BRAISED SWEETBREADS**

An elegant way to present braised sweetbreads is wreathed on a platter around buttered potato balls, baby carrots, and asparagus tips; drift with minced parsley just before serving. Makes 4 servings

1¼ pounds sweetbreads
1 carrot, peeled and sliced thin
1 large yellow onion, peeled and sliced thin
¼ cup butter or margarine
½ cup unsifted flour
1 teaspoon salt
¼ teaspoon pepper
1 cup dry white wine or chicken broth
1 bay leaf
¼ teaspoon thyme
3 sprigs parsley
2 tablespoons dry sherry

Prepare sweetbreads for cooking* but do not blanch. Preheat oven to 350° F. Pat sweetbreads dry on paper toweling; leave whole or, if very large, divide into bite-size pieces. Stir-fry carrot and onion in butter in a large, flameproof casserole 8–10 minutes over moderate heat until golden. Dredge sweetbreads lightly in flour mixed with salt and pepper. Push carrot and onion to side of casserole, add sweetbreads, and sauté 2–3 minutes on each side until golden. Add all remaining ingredients except sherry, transfer casserole to oven, cover, and bake ¾ hour (25–30 minutes if sweetbreads are in small pieces). Lift sweetbreads to a heated platter and keep warm. Purée vegetables and casserole liquid in an electric blender at low speed or put through a food mill. Bring purée to a simmer, add sherry, pour over sweetbreads, and serve. About 310 calories per serving.

VARIATIONS:

Braised Sweetbreads on Ham: Prepare sweetbreads as directed and serve on thin slices of broiled ham. About 370 calories per serving.

Braised Brains: Prepare as directed, substituting brains for sweetbreads. About 350 calories per serving.

CREAMED SWEETBREADS

Makes 4 servings

1¼ pounds sweetbreads
¼ cup butter or margarine
¼ cup unsifted flour
2 cups milk
¾–1 teaspoon salt
⅛ teaspoon white pepper
¼ cup heavy cream
4 frozen puff pastry shells, baked by package directions, or 4 slices buttered toast, trimmed of crusts and halved diagonally

Prepare sweetbreads for cooking and blanch as directed.* Melt butter in the top of a double boiler over direct heat, blend in flour, slowly add milk, and heat, stirring, until thickened. Mix in salt, pepper, and cream. Set over simmering water, break sweetbreads into small pieces, and mix gently into sauce, using a rubber spatula. Heat, uncovered, stirring occasionally, 5–10 minutes. Serve in pastry shells or on toast. About 555 calories per serving.

VARIATIONS:

Creamed Brains: Substitute brains for sweetbreads and prepare as directed. (*Note:* Brains may also be used in any of the variations that follow.) About 595 calories per serving.

With Truffles: Just before serving, fold in 1 thinly sliced truffle. About 555 calories per serving.

With Mushrooms: Add ¼ pound sautéed, thinly sliced mushrooms along with sweetbreads. About 565 calories per serving.

With Ham, Tongue, or Chicken: Add an extra ¼ cup heavy cream and ½ cup diced lean boiled ham, tongue, or cooked white chicken meat along with sweetbreads; taste for salt and adjust as needed. About 635 calories per serving.

With Sherry or White Wine: Just before serving, stir in 2 tablespoons medium-dry sherry or white wine. About 600 calories per serving.

With Chestnuts or Almonds: Add ½ recipe Boiled Chestnuts or ⅓ cup toasted, slivered almonds along with sweetbreads and proceed as directed. About 625 calories per serving.

Herbed with Eggs: Add 3 quartered hard-cooked eggs and 1 tablespoon each minced chives and parsley along with sweetbreads and proceed as directed. About 615 calories per serving.

With Oysters: Add 1 dozen small oysters (fresh or frozen) along with sweetbreads and proceed as directed. About 600 calories per serving.

Au Gratin: After simmering sweetbreads in sauce, turn into a buttered 1½-quart casserole, top with ¼ cup fine buttered bread crumbs, and brown quickly under broiler. About 625 calories per serving.

Florentine: Prepare creamed sweetbreads as directed and set aside. Butter 6 scallop shells or ramekins and spoon ¼ cup hot puréed or minced spinach into each. Fill with creamed sweetbreads and pipe a border of Duchess Potatoes around the edge. Brush with egg glaze and brown lightly under broiler. Serve sprinkled with diced pimiento or frizzled julienne strips of ham. About 600 calories per serving.

In a Spinach Ring: Prepare 1 Spinach Ring, fill with creamed sweetbreads, and serve. About 715 calories per serving.

⚔ **SWEETBREAD SOUFFLÉ**

Makes 6 servings

1 pound sweetbreads
¼ cup butter or margarine
¼ cup sifted flour
1 cup milk
¾ teaspoon salt
⅛ teaspoon pepper
⅛ teaspoon nutmeg
4 eggs, separated

Prepare sweetbreads for cooking and blanch as directed.* Chop fine, measure out 1⅓ cups, and save any remaining sweetbreads to toss into scrambled breakfast eggs. Melt butter in a saucepan over moderate heat, blend in flour, slowly add milk, and heat, stirring constantly, until thickened and smooth. Add all seasonings. Beat egg yolks lightly, spoon a little hot sauce into them, then return to saucepan. Turn heat to low and cook, stirring, 1–2 minutes (do not boil). Off heat, mix in sweetbreads, lay a piece of wax paper directly on surface, and cool to room temperature. Meanwhile, preheat oven to 350° F. Beat egg whites until soft peaks form, and fold into sauce. Spoon into an ungreased 1½-quart soufflé dish and bake, uncovered, on center rack 40–50 minutes until puffed and golden. Serve at once. About 225 calories per serving.

TONGUE

Next to tripe and heart, tongue is one of the most muscular variety meats and needs special treatment to tenderize it. Beef tongue is available fresh, corned, pickled, and smoked and, in some parts of the country, ready-to-serve. Veal tongue is usually sold fresh, but lamb and pork tongues, being smaller, are almost always precooked, ready-to-eat meats.

Amount Needed: Beef tongues weigh 2½–5 pounds, veal tongues about 2 pounds, pork tongues 1 pound and lamb tongues barely ¼ pound. Allow ⅓–½ pound per serving.

To Simmer and Prepare for Use in Recipes:

Fresh Tongue: Wash well in cool water, place in a large stainless-steel, enamel, or teflon-lined kettle, and cover with salted water (1 teaspoon salt to 1 quart water). For extra savor, add ½ unsliced lemon, 1 peeled yellow onion stuck with 3–4 cloves, 1–2 stalks celery (include tops), 1–2 bay leaves, and a large sprig each parsley and thyme. Cover, bring to a boil, and skim off froth. Re-cover and simmer slowly until tender: veal tongue will take 2–2½ hours, beef tongue 3–4. Plunge tongue into cold water to loosen skin, lift out, and pat dry. Slit skin lengthwise on underside of tongue from root to tip and peel off; cut away root, small bones, and gristle. If tongue is to be served cold, it will be more flavorful if chilled in its own broth. Tongue is now ready to use in recipes or to serve sliced hot or cold. Good with Mustard, Madeira, or Raisin Sauce (also see Some Herbs and Seasonings/Sauces and Butters for Variety Meats).

Smoked or Pickled Tongue: Soak 2–3 hours in cold water before simmering, then proceed as for fresh tongue.

To Parboil (use in recipes that call for cooking tongue ¾–1 hour or longer): Simmer as directed but reduce cooking time to 2 hours for beef tongue, 1½ hours for veal tongue. Proceed with preparation as directed.

PARISIAN-STYLE BRAISED SLICED BEEF TONGUE

Makes 6–8 servings

1 (3–3½-pound) fresh or smoked beef tongue

Sauce:

3 slices lean bacon, diced
1 carrot, peeled and diced
3 scallions, sliced thin
1 stalk celery, diced
4 mushrooms, wiped clean and minced
1 clove garlic, peeled and crushed
1 cup beef broth

1 cup water
⅛ teaspoon pepper
¼ cup dry sherry or cognac (optional)

Parboil tongue, remove skin, root, bone, and gristle,* and slice ⅜"–½" thick (begin at large end, slicing straight through, but as you approach small end, hold knife slightly at an angle). Prepare sauce: Stir-fry bacon and vegetables in a heavy skillet over moderate heat 8–10 minutes to brown lightly, add remaining sauce ingredients, cover, and simmer ½ hour. Cool slightly and purée in an electric blender at slow speed or put through a food mill. Pour sauce into a deep, heavy skillet, add tongue slices, cover, and simmer 45 minutes until tongue is very tender. Serve with lots of sauce. (*Note:* For even richer flavor, let tongue slices marinate in sauce overnight in refrigerator before simmering.)

VARIATION:

Substitute veal tongue for beef and proceed as directed. Ready-to-eat lamb or pork tongues may also be used but need only be sliced and warmed 10–15 minutes in the sauce.

Both versions: about 435 calories for each of 6 servings, 325 calories for each of 8 servings.

PICKLED TONGUE

Makes 6–8 servings

1 (3–3½-pound) fresh beef tongue
2½ quarts cold water
1 cup cider vinegar
2 tablespoons pickling spice, tied in
  cheesecloth

Wash tongue, place in a large, heavy kettle with all ingredients, cover, and bring to a boil. Skim froth from surface, re-cover, and simmer 3–4 hours until tender. Cool tongue in broth until easy to handle, lift out, skin, cut away root, bones, and gristle. Strain and skim broth.

To Serve Hot: Place tongue in a clean kettle, add broth, cover, and reheat 8–10 minutes over moderately low heat. Lift out, drain and serve with Mustard Sauce. *To Glaze:* Instead of warming

tongue in broth, place on a rack in a shallow, open roasting pan, spread with 1 cup firmly packed light brown sugar mixed with ¼ cup cider vinegar and 1 tablespoon honey or light corn syrup. Bake, uncovered, 15–20 minutes at 350° F., basting often with mixture until glazed. (*Note:* Minced chutney or chopped tart fruit jellies can be used to glaze tongue as can Plum or Sweet-Sour Sauce or any of the thin ham glazes [see Some Glazes for Baked Hams].)

To Serve Cold: Simmer tongue as directed; skin, cut away root, bones, and gristle. Return tongue to strained, skimmed broth, cover, and chill several hours. Remove from broth, slice thin, and serve with Mustard or Sour Cream-Horseradish Sauce.

Hot or cold: about 380 calories for each of 6 servings (without sauce), 280 calories for each of 8 servings.

TONGUE, HAM, AND EGG CASSEROLE

Makes 6 servings

6 thick slices cooked tongue
6 thick slices boiled ham
3 hard-cooked eggs, shelled and sliced
2 cups Medium White Sauce
⅓ cup buttered white bread crumbs or
  crushed cornflakes or potato chips

Preheat oven to 350° F. Layer tongue, ham, and eggs into an ungreased, shallow 1½-quart casserole, pour in white sauce, top with crumbs, and bake uncovered ½ hour; brown quickly under broiler and serve. About 455 calories per serving.

VARIATIONS:

– Spread 1 (1-pound) jar creamed spinach and ¼ pound sliced sautéed mushrooms between tongue and ham layers, then proceed as recipe directs. About 510 calories per serving.
– Substitute any cheese sauce for white sauce. About 535 calories per serving.
– Substitute corned beef, a mild salami, bologna, or luncheon meat for ham. About 455 calories per serving.

⊠ DEVILED TONGUE

Makes 4 servings

2 tablespoons prepared spicy brown
  mustard
2 tablespoons steak sauce
8 thick slices cooked tongue
1 egg, lightly beaten with 1 tablespoon
  cold water
½ cup toasted seasoned bread crumbs
3 tablespoons butter or margarine

Mix mustard and steak sauce and spread
evenly on both sides of tongue slices;
let stand 10 minutes. Dip tongue in egg
and crumbs to coat thickly. Brown in
butter, a few slices at a time, in a heavy
skillet over moderate heat. Serve
sprinkled with a few drops tarragon
vinegar or, if you prefer, with Diable
Sauce. About 430 calories per serving
(without sauce).

TONGUE MOUSSE

Makes 8 servings

¼ cup butter or margarine
6 tablespoons flour
1½ cups milk
½ cup light cream
3 eggs plus 2 egg whites, lightly beaten
4 cups finely ground cooked, smoked, or
  canned tongue (you'll need about
  2 pounds)
1½ cups soft white bread crumbs
1 teaspoon salt (about)
⅛ teaspoon white pepper
2 teaspoons prepared mild yellow
  mustard

Preheat oven to 350° F. Melt butter in
a saucepan over moderate heat, blend in
flour, then slowly stir in milk and cream,
and heat, stirring until smooth and
thickened. Off heat blend in eggs, a
little at a time, mixing well after each
addition. Fold in tongue and remaining
ingredients, taste for salt and adjust as
needed. Spoon into a well-buttered 1½-
quart mold, cover with a buttered piece
of foil, and bake in a water bath 1–1¼
hours until center of mousse is just firm
to the touch. Remove from water bath
and let stand 10 minutes before

unmolding. To unmold: Run a spatula
around edge of mousse to loosen, then
invert. Serve hot, garnished with
buttered peas or asparagus tips, or cool,
cover loosely, chill, and serve on a bed
of watercress. About 475 calories per
serving.

JELLIED BEEF TONGUE

Makes 6–8 servings

1 (3–3½-pound) fresh or smoked beef
  tongue
1½–2 pounds beef or veal bones,
  cracked
1 medium-size yellow onion, peeled
1 carrot, peeled
1 stalk celery
1 tablespoon salt (if using fresh tongue)
¼ teaspoon peppercorns
2 bay leaves
2½ quarts cold water

Wash tongue, place in a large, heavy
kettle with all ingredients, cover, and
bring to a boil. Skim froth from surface,
re-cover, and simmer 3–4 hours until
tender. Cool tongue in broth until easy
to handle, lift out, skin, cut away root,
bones, and gristle. Cover loosely and
cool. Meanwhile, continue simmering
bones, uncovered, in broth 1 hour
longer. Strain broth through a cheesecloth-lined sieve, cool, and skim off all
fat. Return stock to kettle, boil rapidly,
uncovered, until reduced to about 1½
quarts, then clarify* if you like. Cut off
smaller ⅓ of tongue and tuck, rounded
side out, into hollow on underside of
larger piece so that the 2 almost form
a circle. Fit tongue into a bowl just large
enough to hold it and fill to the brim
with broth. Chill several hours until firm,
then unmold on a bed of greens. Good
with Mustard Mayonnaise. About 375
calories for each of 6 servings, 280
calories for each of 8 servings.

VARIATIONS:

Tongue in Rosé Aspic: Instead of using
recipe above, simmer tongue by basic
method*; remove skin, root, bones, and
gristle. For the aspic: Simmer 2 cups
fat-free chicken broth with a *bouquet*

garni,* tied in cheesecloth, ½ hour; strain and clarify.* Mix in 4 cups rosé wine, 1–2 drops red food coloring, 2–3 drops liquid hot red pepper seasoning, and salt to taste. Mix 4 envelopes unflavored gelatin with 1 cup cold water, heat slowly, stirring, until gelatin dissolves; stir into wine mixture. Cut tongue as directed above and fit into bowl; cover with aspic and chill until firm. (*Note:* Any remaining aspic may be chilled, then chopped and used to garnish tongue platter.) About 475 calories for each of 6 servings, 360 calories for each of 8 servings.

Jellied Sliced Beef Tongue: Prepare either of the above recipes up to point of cutting tongue. Slice tongue thin and layer into a 2-quart decorative mold. Fill with aspic and chill until firm. Unmold and serve as directed. Calorie counts the same as for the recipes above.

TRIPE

Tripe is the lining of the stomach of meat animals, and that considered choicest is *honeycomb tripe,* the lining of the second stomach of beef. Also good are *pocket tripe,* the lower end of the second stomach, and *plain* or *smooth tripe,* which is not honeycombed and not so delicate. Tripe is available pickled, canned, and fresh. Fresh tripe is always sold partially cooked but needs still further cooking.

Amount Needed: Allow ¼–½ pound tripe per person, depending upon whether it is simply prepared or served in a rich sauce.

To Prepare for Cooking: Pull or cut all fat from tripe and discard; wash well in cold water. Pickled tripe, though thoroughly cooked, usually needs to be soaked in cold water 1–2 hours before using.

To Simmer: All fresh tripe must be simmered until tender before it can be eaten or used in many recipes (those

that follow tell when it must be simmered). Cut tripe into manageable pieces so it will be easier to handle and cook more evenly. Place in a large, deep kettle (not aluminum or tripe will discolor) and cover with lightly salted water (1 teaspoon salt to each quart of water). Cover and simmer gently 1½– 2 hours until tender. Tripe can now be cut in 2″ squares and served hot in bowls with some of the broth; it can be cooled in its own broth, drained, chilled, and eaten with a sprinkling of vinegar. Or it can be used in recipes (cut up as individual recipes specify).

⚖ **FRIED TRIPE**

Makes 4–6 servings

2 pounds tripe
2 eggs, lightly beaten
¾ cup toasted seasoned bread crumbs
¼ cup cooking oil
Lemon wedges

Prepare tripe for cooking and simmer.* Drain, pat very dry on paper toweling, and cut in 2″ squares or strips. Dip in egg and crumbs to coat thickly and let dry 5 minutes on a rack at room temperature. Heat oil in a large heavy skillet over moderately high heat 1 minute and fry tripe, a few pieces at a time, 1–2 minutes until crisp and golden brown. Drain on paper toweling and set, uncovered, in a 250° F. oven to keep warm while you fry the rest. Serve with lemon wedges. About 290 calories for each of 4 servings, 190 calories for each of 6 servings.

CREAMED TRIPE AND ONIONS

Makes 4 servings

2 pounds honeycomb tripe
3 medium-size yellow onions, peeled and sliced thin
3 cups milk
½ teaspoon salt
⅛ teaspoon white pepper
2 tablespoons butter or margarine
3 tablespoons flour blended with ¼ cup cold milk

Prepare tripe for cooking and simmer.*

Meanwhile, simmer onions, covered, in
milk over low heat 20 minutes until
tender. When tripe is done, drain, cut
in 2" squares, and add to onions along
with salt and pepper. Cover and let stand
off heat 1–2 hours to blend flavors.
About 10 minutes before serving, warm
to serving temperature over low heat.
Add butter and flour paste and heat,
stirring, until thickened. Serve in soup
bowls with crusty chunks of bread.
About 350 calories per serving.

⚖ **TRIPE LYONNAISE**

Makes 4 servings

2 pounds honeycomb tripe
6 tablespoons butter or margarine
2 large yellow onions, peeled and sliced
   thin
1 tablespoon minced parsley
1 tablespoon white vinegar
Salt
Pepper

Prepare tripe for cooking and simmer.*
Drain, pat dry on paper toweling, and
cut in 2" squares. Stir-fry in 3 tablespoons butter in a large, heavy skillet
over moderate heat about 2 minutes
until golden; drain on paper toweling
and keep warm. In a separate skillet
stir-fry onions in remaining butter
8–10 minutes over moderate heat until
golden. Mix tripe and onions, sprinkle
with parsley and vinegar, and mix again.
Taste for salt and pepper and season as
needed. Toss again and serve. Good
spooned over hot mashed potatoes.
About 290 calories per serving.

⚖ **TRIPE MAÎTRE D'HÔTEL**

Makes 4 servings

2 pounds honeycomb tripe
1 cup cold water
1 cup beef broth
1 cup dry white wine
½ teaspoon salt
1 bouquet garni,* tied in cheesecloth
   with 3 thick lemon slices
2 egg yolks, lightly beaten
⅛ teaspoon nutmeg
⅛ teaspoon cayenne pepper

Prepare tripe for cooking* and cut in
strips 2" long and ¾" wide. Place in a
large kettle (not aluminum) with water,
broth, wine, salt and bouquet garni,
cover and simmer 1½–2 hours until
tender. Transfer tripe to a deep platter
with a slotted spoon and keep warm.
Boil broth, uncovered, over high heat
until reduced to about 1 cup; discard
cheesecloth bag. Mix a little hot broth
into yolks, then return to broth. Set over
lowest heat and cook 1–2 minutes until
slightly thickened (do not boil). Mix in
nutmeg and cayenne, taste for seasoning
and adjust. Pour over tripe and serve.
About 210 calories per serving.

⚖ **TRIPES À LA MODE DE
CAEN**

This steaming marmite of tripe flavored
with apple brandy comes from
Normandy but is the favorite of all
France.
Makes 8 servings

4 pounds tripe
4 small yellow onions, peeled and
   coarsely chopped
4 carrots, peeled and cut in small dice
4 leeks, coarsely chopped
1 calf's foot, cleaned, split and sawed
   in 3–4 pieces (these are a bit
   difficult to find, but most gourmet or
   kosher butchers will either have them
   or order them)
3 cloves garlic, peeled
1 bouquet garni,* tied in cheesecloth
2 teaspoons salt
¼ teaspoon white pepper
⅛ teaspoon allspice
2 quarts cold water
2–3 thin sheets barding suet (you'll need
   enough to cover the kettle you're
   making the tripe in)
½ cup calvados or aged cider

Pastry:

1½ cups sifted flour
½ cup cold water

Preheat oven to 300° F. Prepare tripe
for cooking,* cut in 3" squares, and set
aside. Mix vegetables in a large kettle
and lay calf's foot on top. Add tripe,

SOME HERBS AND SEASONINGS/SAUCES AND BUTTERS FOR VARIETY MEATS

Brains/Sweetbreads	Heart	Kidneys	Liver	Tongue	Tripe
Herbs/Seasonings:	*Herbs/Seasonings:*	*Herbs/Seasonings:*	*Herbs/Seasonings:*	*Herbs/Seasonings:*	*Herbs/Seasonings:*
Bay leaf	Bay leaf	Basil	Bay leaf	Bay leaf	Bay leaf
Chervil	Garlic	Bay leaf	Lemon	Chervil	Cloves
Garlic	Parsley	Garlic	Parsley	Cloves	Garlic
Lemon	Sage	Lemon	Nutmeg	Garlic	Lemon
Mace	Tarragon	Oregano	Rosemary	Lemon	Mace
Nutmeg	Thyme	Parsley	Sage	Orange	Parsley
Parsley		Shallots	Savory	Parsley	Sage
Tarragon	*Sauces/Butters:*	Thyme	Shallots	Tarragon	Thyme
Thyme	Bordelaise		Thyme	Thyme	
	Chasseur	*Sauces/Butters:*			*Sauces/Butters:*
Sauces/Butters:	Madeira	Bercy Butter	*Sauces/Butters:*	*Sauces/Butters:*	(for fried tripe
Albuféra	Maître d'Hôtel	Bordelaise	Bercy Butter	Chasseur	only):
Allemande	Butter (sliced,	Diable	Bordelaise	Diable	Diable
Aurore	sautéed heart)	Duxelles	Diable	Duxelles	Piquante
Béarnaise	Mushroom	Herb	Herb	Hot Horseradish	Rémoulade
Beurre Noir		Madeira	Italienne	Madeira	Tartar
Bordelaise		Maître d'Hôtel	Maître d'Hôtel	Mustard	Tomato
Caper Butter		Butter	Butter	Piquante	
Diable		Mustard	Mustard	Poivrade	
Duxelles		Tortue	Piquante	Raisin	
Financière			Robert	Romaine	
Italienne				Sauce Bercy	
Madeira				Tortue	
Maître d'Hôtel				Vinaigrette	
Butter					
Noisette Butter					
Paprika					
Parsley-Lemon					
Butter					
Périgueux					
Piquante					
Poulette					
Régence					
Robert					
Soubise					
Suprême					
Talleyrand					
Tomato					

garlic, *bouquet garni,* seasonings, and water. Lay suet over all to cover, then place lid on kettle. Prepare pastry by mixing flour and water until sticky. Turn out on a heavily floured board, knead 1 or 2 times, then roll into a rope long enough to go around kettle. Use rope like putty to seal kettle lid to kettle. Set kettle on lowest oven rack and bake 6–7 hours. Discard pastry and suet; spoon tripe into a large tureen with a slotted spoon. Cut meat from calf's foot and add to tripe. Strain kettle liquid, discarding vegetables, garlic and bouquet garni. Strain and skim off fat, then bring to a boil and stir in Calvados. Ladle over tripe and serve. Good with crusty bread or boiled potatoes. About 160 calories per serving (without bread or potatoes).

⚔ **PHILADELPHIA PEPPER POT**

Begin this recipe one or even two days before you plan to serve it. Though called a soup, pepper pot is hearty enough to serve as a main dish. It was invented at Valley Forge by a chef in George Washington's army.
Makes 8–10 servings

1 meaty veal shank
2 pounds beef marrowbones, cracked
5 quarts cold water
2 tablespoons salt (about)
1 teaspoon peppercorns
2 large yellow onions, peeled and minced
1 bouquet garni,* tied in cheesecloth
2 pounds tripe
3 medium-size potatoes, peeled and cut in ½" cubes
1 teaspoon marjoram
2 tablespoons minced parsley
1 recipe Dumplings

Simmer shank and marrowbones, covered, in 2 quarts water with 1 tablespoon salt, ½ teaspoon peppercorns, the onions, and *bouquet garni* 3–4 hours. Meanwhile, prepare tripe for cooking* and cut in 2" squares. Place in a large kettle (not aluminum) with remaining water, salt, and peppercorns, cover, and simmer

2 hours until very tender; lift from broth and set aside; strain and save broth. When bones have simmered 3 hours, lift from broth; cut meat from shank and add to tripe; scoop out marrow, chop coarsely and also add to tripe; refrigerate. Strain broth, combine with tripe broth and refrigerate overnight. Next day place broth in a large kettle (not aluminum), add tripe and meat, potatoes and marjoram, cover, and simmer 10 minutes. Add parsley, taste for salt and adjust as needed. Prepare dumplings, bring broth to a boil and drop in dumplings from a tablespoon (make 1 for each person). Simmer, uncovered, 10 minutes, then cover and simmer 10 minutes longer. To serve, ladle out steaming bowls of soup and float a dumpling in each. About 235 calories for each of 8 servings, 185 calories for each of 10 servings.

SAUSAGES
(See Quick Alphabet of Sausages.)

How to Cook Fresh Sausages

Because they contain pork, sausages, whether smoked or not, must be thoroughly cooked before they're eaten. Many, especially large ones, will require a combination of methods—steaming or simmering *plus* panfrying, broiling, or grilling if they are to be done inside by the time they are brown outside.

Amount Needed: ¼–⅓ pound sausage per person.

General Preparation for Cooking: Very little. Bulk sausage must be shaped into balls or patties, sausage rolls sliced. The biggest question concerns links. Should they be pricked before cooking? Opinions vary, but probably the best rule to follow: American sausages, no; European sausages, yes (they're moister and may burst if not pricked).

To Simmer:

Links: Place sausages in a saucepan, add just enough lightly salted boiling water—or beer or ale—to cover, cover, and simmer 10–30 minutes, depending on size, until cooked through. *To Test:* Remove 1 sausage and cut into center; it should show no traces of pink. (*Note:* If links are to be browned after simmering, they will need to be simmered only 8–10 minutes.)

Bulk Sausage: Roll into ¾"–1" balls, drop into lightly salted boiling water, cover, and simmer 10–15 minutes until cooked through. These are best served in a Medium White Sauce, made using ½ and ½ sausage cooking water and heavy cream. Flavor with a little dry white wine and nutmeg. Let sausages warm in sauce about 5 minutes before serving to mellow flavors.

To Steam (for links only): Place links on a rack in a saucepan, add 1–1½ cups boiling water (it should not touch sausages), cover, and steam 15–20 minutes until cooked through. (*Note:* Very chunky sausages may take as long as ½ hour.) If sausages are to be browned later, reduce steaming time to 10–15 minutes.

To Panfry (*Sauté*) (for small links only): Strictly speaking, this is a combination of simmering and panfrying, but since it is all done in one skillet, it is called panfrying. Place sausages in a cold skillet, add ¼ cup water, cover, and simmer 5–10 minutes, depending on size. Uncover and brown slowly over moderately low heat, turning often with tongs. (*Note:* Swiss and German women drain off the simmering water, then brown sausages slowly in 1–2 table-spoons butter or lard. Sometimes before browning, they pat sausages dry and dredge lightly in flour—gives a crisper finish. When sausages are simmered first, they need only be browned in butter.)

To Panbroil (for patties and slices): Slice a sausage roll ½" thick or shape bulk sausage into patties about ½" thick and 3" across. Place patties in a cold skillet, set over moderate heat, and cook 15–20 minutes until cooked through. Turn only once during cooking; do not press down or spank with spatula.

To Braise (links and patties): Brown sausages slowly in 1–2 tablespoons butter in a large, heavy skillet over moderate heat, add ½ cup liquid (water, beer or ale, dry white wine, tomato juice or sauce, barbecue sauce, apple or pineapple juice, ginger ale plus 1–2 tablespoons soy or *teriyaki* sauce), cover, and simmer 15 minutes.

To Bake:

Sausage Roll: Preheat oven to 375° F. Leave roll whole, place on a rack in a shallow roasting pan, and insert meat thermometer in center. Roast uncovered, without basting, 45 minutes to 1 hour or until thermometer reads 185° F. Serve as is or with Pan Gravy or Tomato Sauce.

Links: Preheat oven to 400° F. Spread links out in a shallow roasting pan and roast, uncovered, 25–30 minutes, turning often with tongs so they brown evenly.

To Broil (for links that have been simmered or steamed first): Preheat broiler. Brush sausages well with melted butter or oil, place on a greased broiler pan, and broil 3" from heat, turning often with tongs, 5–8 minutes until nicely browned.

To Charcoal Broil (for links that have first been simmered or steamed): Prepare a moderate charcoal fire.* Brush sausages with melted butter or oil, place on lightly greased grill, and broil 3" from heat, turning often with tongs, 5–8 minutes until well browned on all sides.

Some Easy Ways to Dress Up Sausage Patties

All make 4 servings

Baked Sausage and Apples: Shape 1 pound bulk sausage into 4 patties and brown well on both sides over moderate heat. Transfer to an ungreased 6-cup casserole. Peel, core, and thinly slice 4 tart apples; toss with ¼ cup firmly packed light brown sugar, ¼ teaspoon cinnamon, a pinch nutmeg, and the juice of ½ lemon. Spread over patties. Top with ¼ cup fine buttered bread crumbs and bake, uncovered, at 350° F. about ½ hour until lightly browned and bubbly.

Baked Sausage and Sweet Potatoes: Shape and brown patties as above; transfer to an ungreased 6-cup casserole, top with 1 (9-ounce) package frozen sweet potatoes or Hawaiian-style sweet potatoes (with pineapple), cover, and bake ½–¾ hour at 350° F. until bubbly.

Smothered Sausage Patties: Shape and brown patties as in first variation; transfer to an ungreased 6-cup casserole, top with 1 (10½-ounce) can cream of mushroom, celery, or tomato soup thinned with ⅓ cup milk and bake, uncovered, ½ hour at 350° F. until bubbling. (*Note:* 2 cups canned or Pan Gravy can be substituted for the soup.)

Barbecued Sausage Patties: Follow Smothered Sausage Patties recipe preceding but bake in 2 cups All-Purpose Barbecue Sauce instead of soup.

Sausage Patties Creole: Shape and brown patties as in first variation; transfer to an ungreased 6-cup casserole. Drain all but 2 tablespoons drippings from skillet, add 1 minced medium-size yellow onion, 1 crushed clove garlic, and ⅓ cup minced sweet green pepper, and stir-fry 8–10 minutes until onion is golden. Add 1 (1-pound) can drained, chopped tomatoes, ½ teaspoon salt, and a pinch each marjoram and thyme. Heat, stirring, 5 minutes. Pour over sausages and bake, uncovered, ½–¾ hour at 350° F. until sauce is thick and bubbly.

Sauerkraut and Sausage: Shape and brown patties as in first variation; remove to an ungreased 6-cup casserole. Top with 1 (1-pound) can undrained sauerkraut, sprinkle lightly with paprika, and bake uncovered 30 minutes at 350° F.

South Pacific Sausage Patties: Shape and brown patties as in Baked Sausage and Apples; remove from skillet and set aside. Pour all but 2 tablespoons drippings from skillet, add 1 minced medium-size yellow onion, ½ sweet green pepper cut in small thin slivers, and stir-fry 5–8 minutes until onion is pale golden. Return patties to skillet, pull onions and peppers on top, add 1 (13½-ounce) drained can crushed pineapple and 1 tablespoon soy sauce, cover, and simmer 30 minutes. Uncover and, if mixture seems too liquid, simmer uncovered about 5 minutes longer to reduce.

Sausage "Sandwiches": Shape 1 pound bulk sausage into 8 thin patties of equal size. Top 4 with a thin layer of seasoned mashed potatoes, yams, or drained crushed pineapple. Top with remaining patties and crimp edges to seal. Brown both sides well over moderate heat. If patties are stuffed with mashed potatoes, add 1½ cups Pan Gravy (or canned), cover, and simmer ½ hour. If stuffed with yams or pineapple, add ½ cup apple cider, pineapple juice, or crushed pineapple, cover, and simmer ½ hour.

Some Simple Ways to Spice Up Sausage Links

All make 4 servings

Note: Use fresh or country-style pork sausage links instead of European varieties unless otherwise specified.

Braised Sausages, Apples, and Onions: Brown 1 pound sausage links slowly in 1–2 teaspoons butter or bacon drippings in a large, heavy skillet over moderate heat; remove and drain. In drippings, stir-fry 1 thinly sliced Bermuda onion 5–8 minutes until pale golden; add 1 (1-pound 4-ounce) drained can sliced apples, 1 tablespoon lemon juice,

2 tablespoons light brown sugar, ¼ teaspoon cinnamon, and a pinch each cloves and nutmeg; toss to mix. Return sausages to skillet, pushing down into apples, cover, and simmer ½ hour.

Baked Sausages and Beans: Brown 1 pound sausage links as in recipe above. Prepare ½ recipe Easy Brandied Beans up to point of baking. Lay sausages on beans, pushing them down slightly, and bake as directed.

Country-Fried Sausage and Potatoes: Slice ½ pound country-style sausage links ½″ thick and brown well in 2 tablespoons butter or oil. Add 1 chopped medium-size yellow onion, 4 raw potatoes, peeled and sliced thin, cover, and cook 8–10 minutes. Uncover and stir-fry 10–15 minutes until nicely browned. Season with ½ teaspoon salt, a pinch each pepper and thyme and serve.

Sausage Succotash: Slice ½ pound sausage links ½″ thick and brown well in 1–2 tablespoons bacon drippings; drain on paper toweling. Prepare 1 recipe Quick Succotash as directed up to point of adding corn. Add sausage along with corn, and finish cooking as directed.

Italian-Style Sausage and Black Beans: Begin 1 recipe Brazilian Black Beans, substituting ½ pound fresh Italian-style pork sausage for bacon. Cut sausage casings and remove meat; stir-fry in 1 tablespoon olive oil 3–5 minutes, breaking up clumps; remove to paper toweling with a slotted spoon. Brown onions and garlic in drippings as recipe directs, add sausage along with remaining ingredients and proceed as directed.

Sausage and Vegetable Gumbo: Begin 1 recipe Vegetable Gumbo but substitute ½ pound sausage links for bacon; cut in ½″ slices and brown well in 1 tablespoon butter. Add onion and celery, sauté as directed, then proceed according to recipe.

Baked Sausages and Sweets:
Barbecued Sausages:
South Pacific Sausages:
Sauerkraut and Sausages:
} Follow variations given for sausage patties, substituting 1 pound sausage links for 1 pound bulk sausage. Brown links well in a small amount of butter or drippings, then proceed as recipes direct.

How to Heat and Serve Fully Cooked Sausages

Frankfurters and Other Fully Cooked Link Sausages: Franks, wieners, and knackwurst can be prepared by any of the methods below; to determine best ways of preparing the more unusual sausages, consult Quick Alphabet of Sausages, then follow directions below. (*Note:* American sausages are best *not* pricked before cooking, but the chunky, moist European sausages should be lest they burst.)

To Simmer: Cover with simmering water or, for richer flavor, with beer or a ½ and ½ mixture of water and dry white wine and *simmer* (not boil) 5–8 minutes until heated through. Or cover with simmering liquid, remove from heat, and let stand, covered, 8–10 minutes. (*Note:* If beer or wine-water mixture is used, save for making soups or stews.)

To Steam: Arrange sausages 1 layer deep on a rack in a saucepan or vegetable steamer, add 1 cup boiling water, cover, and heat 8 minutes over moderate heat. Water should stay at a slow boil.

To Panfry (*Sauté*): Brown sausages in 1–2 tablespoons butter, margarine, meat drippings, or cooking oil in a heavy skillet over moderate heat 3–5 minutes, turning frequently. If you prefer, halve lengthwise and brown about 2 minutes on each side.

To Broil: Brush sausages well with oil, melted butter or margarine and broil on lightly greased broiler rack 3″ from heat 4–5 minutes, turning often until evenly browned (use tongs for turning). Or split, brush with butter, and broil about 2 minutes per side.

To Charcoal Broil: Prepare a moderately hot charcoal fire.* Lay sausages in a single layer on a lightly greased grill and broil 4″–5″ from heat 3–4 minutes, turning frequently with tongs, until lightly browned. (*Note:* Sausages can also be wrapped in heavy foil —not individually but in a single large package— and steamed on the grill 12–15 minutes.)

To Roast Over a Campfire: Let fire burn down to glowing coals. Spear sausages crosswise on long-handled forks or peeled sticks (no more than 2–3 per fork or stick) and roast 3″ from coals, turning frequently, 4–5 minutes until lightly browned.

Andouille: Usually this sausage is simply sliced and eaten cold, but it can be browned in butter or drippings. Slice ¼″–½″ thick and brown in 2–3 tablespoons butter or bacon drippings in a large, heavy skillet over moderate heat about 2–3 minutes on each side. Or brush with melted butter or drippings and broil 4″ from heat about 2 minutes on each side.

Blood Sausages: These come in different sizes and shapes, each requiring somewhat different treatment. The *small links* may simply be left whole and browned in 2–3 tablespoons bacon drippings or butter in a large, heavy skillet 3–5 minutes; turn frequently with tongs. The *large round ring* is best braised: Brown 5–7 minutes in 2–3 tablespoons bacon drippings or butter in a large, heavy skillet over moderately low heat, add 1 cup water or stock, cover, turn heat to low, and simmer about ½ hour until heated through. *Fat chunky rolls* like *Zungenwurst* can be sliced ¼″–½″ thick, peeled of casings, and, if you like, dredged lightly in flour (helps reduce spattering). Brown in 2–3 tablespoons butter or bacon drippings in a large, heavy skillet over moderately low heat 3–4 minutes on each side. *Berliner Blutwurst,* another variety, should be covered with boiling water and allowed to stand 20 minutes (keep lid on pot). Remove, slice, and serve. Or, if you like, gently brown hot slices in about 2 tablespoons butter in a large, heavy skillet over moderately low heat 2–3 minutes per side.

Leberkäse: This delicate German liver pâté is nearly always served hot. Slice about ½″ thick and place slices on a rack over boiling water in a vegetable steamer or in the top of a double boiler. Cover and steam 25–30 minutes until heated through. Or slice 1″ thick and sauté slowly in about 3 tablespoons butter in a large, heavy skillet with 1 thinly sliced yellow onion. Keep heat low and allow about 5 minutes per side; handle with care, using a pancake turner to turn slices.

Scrapple: Slice ¼″–½″ thick or cut in finger-shaped sticks; dredge lightly in flour and brown in 3–4 tablespoons butter or bacon drippings in a large, heavy skillet over moderate heat until crisply browned. Slices will take 3–5 minutes per side, fingers slightly less time but more frequent turning.

¢ **BASIC HOMEMADE SAUSAGE MEAT**

Makes 6 pounds; about 2 dozen patties

4½ pounds lean pork (trimmings, head meat, etc.)
1½ pounds fat pork (cheek, jowl, trimmings, etc.)
3 tablespoons salt
1 tablespoon pepper
1 tablespoon sage

Coarsely grind lean and fat pork together, mix with remaining ingredients, and grind 2 more times. Shape into patties about 3″ across and ½″ thick, wrap each in foil or saran and freeze until firm. For cooking instructions, see How to Cook Fresh Sausages.

To Make Links: First of all, you need a sausage stuffing attachment for your meat grinder or electric mixer. Second you need casings (butchers can usually get them for you). Ask either for sheep casings or small artificial casings about ¾"–1" in diameter; they come in continuous rolls and can be bought by the pound or yard. For the quantity of sausage above, you'll need about 3½ yards. Sheep and other natural casings are usually packed in salt and must be soaked about 1 hour in cold water to dissolve out the salt and soften the casings. Attach a moist casing to stuffer as electric mixer manufacturer directs, then force sausage into it. Every 3"–4", press casing together and twist around once to form links. If you alternate direction of twisting (i.e., twisting clockwise one time and counterclockwise the next), the links will stay linked. Tying each with string in a square knot is foolproof. Work carefully, trying not to tear or break casings. Freeze sausages or store in refrigerator (don't try to keep fresh sausages in refrigerator more than a few days; they're highly perishable).

About 140 calories per *cooked* sausage link; about 370 calories per *cooked* sausage patty.

VARIATIONS:

Mixed Sausage: Prepare basic recipe as directed, but instead of using all pork use 3 pounds lean beef or veal, 2 pounds lean pork, and 1 pound fat pork. About 135 calories per *cooked* sausage link; about 340 calories per *cooked* sausage patty.

Hot Italian-Style Pork Sausage: Omit sage from basic recipe above and add the following: 1 medium-size chopped yellow onion, 1 minced clove garlic, 2 teaspoons paprika, 1 tablespoon crushed dried red chili peppers, 2 teaspoons fennel seeds, ½ teaspoon each crushed bay leaf and thyme, ¼ teaspoon crushed coriander, and ½ cup dry red wine. Put through coarse blade of grinder twice to blend, then stuff into small casings as directed

above, twisting into links every 6" or so. Or do as the Italians do and make one long continuous rope of sausage, coiling it like a garden hose. Freeze or refrigerate. To use, simply cut off the amount you need (see How to Cook Fresh Sausages). About 140 calories per *cooked* sausage link.

Sweet Italian-Style Pork Sausage: Follow recipe for Hot Italian-Style Pork Sausage (above) but reduce amount of crushed dried red chili peppers to 1 teaspoon. About 140 calories per *cooked* sausage link.

Fresh Chorizos (Hot Spanish Sausages): Follow basic recipe above but omit sage and use all lean pork. Add the following: 1 tablespoon oregano, 6 minced cloves garlic, ⅓ cup chili powder, 1 teaspoon ground cumin, 1 tablespoon crushed dried red chili peppers, and ⅔ cup vinegar. Put through coarse blade of grinder twice to blend, then stuff into casings as directed for Italian-style sausages above. About 140 calories per *cooked* sausage link.

⚖ ¢ **SCRAPPLE**

At hog-butchering time the Pennsylvania Dutch cook any pork scraps with corn meal into a mush called scrapple. This version isn't the original, but it's good.
Makes 6 servings

2 large meaty pork hocks
¼ pound lean pork trimmings
1½ quarts water
1½ teaspoons salt
¼ teaspoon pepper
¾ teaspoon sage
1⅓ cups yellow corn meal

Scrub hocks well under cold running water; scrape skin with a sharp knife to remove any hairs. Place hocks in a large, heavy kettle with water and salt, cover, and simmer 2–2½ hours until meat nearly falls from bones. Lift meat from kettle, discard skin and bones, and coarsely grind meat. Strain broth and skim off fat; wash and dry kettle. Measure 1 quart broth into kettle, add ground meat, pepper, and sage, and bring to a boil. Mix corn meal into remaining cold broth, then add slowly to boiling broth, stirring constantly so it doesn't lump. Continue cooking and stirring until thickened. Turn heat to lowest point, set kettle on an asbestos flame tamer, cover, and let cook about ½ hour. Taste for seasoning and adjust if necessary. Spoon mixture into an ungreased 9"×5"×3" loaf pan, cover with foil, and chill until firm. To serve, unmold, slice, and panfry following directions given under How to Heat and Serve Fully Cooked Sausages. About 290 calories per serving.

SAUSAGE RING

Makes 6 servings

2 pounds sausage meat
1 cup soft white bread crumbs
1 teaspoon sage
¼ teaspoon nutmeg
¼ teaspoon cloves
2 eggs, lightly beaten
½ cup milk

Preheat oven to 350° F. Mix all ingredients, using your hands. Form into a ring 6"–7" in diameter in a lightly greased shallow roasting pan. Bake, uncovered, 45 minutes until well browned; remove drippings as they accumulate with a bulb baster. If you like, serve with Pan Gravy or hot Tomato Sauce. Or fill center with Scrambled Eggs or Creamed Mushrooms. About 550 calories per serving (without gravy or sauce, Scrambled Eggs, or Creamed Mushrooms).

SCOTCH EGGS

These eggs are also good quartered and served cold as an appetizer. They are not as difficult to make as they may sound, and the only trick in making the sausage coating stick to the eggs is to make certain the shelled hard-cooked eggs are thoroughly dry.
Makes 4 servings

Shortening or cooking oil for deep fat frying

4 hard-cooked eggs, shelled and patted dry on paper toweling
1 pound sausage meat
⅓ cup unsifted flour
1 egg, lightly beaten with 1 tablespoon cold water
½ cup toasted seasoned bread crumbs

Preheat oven to 400° F. Begin heating shortening in a deep fat fryer over moderately high heat (use basket and deep fat thermometer). Meanwhile, divide sausage into 4 equal parts and mold each around an egg, making as firm and smooth as possible. Dredge lightly in flour, dip in egg, and roll in crumbs to coat evenly. When fat reaches 350° F., fry eggs, 2 at a time, 2–3 minutes until golden brown; drain on paper toweling. Place eggs in an ungreased pie tin and bake, uncovered, 10–15 minutes until sausage is cooked thoroughly. Halve each egg lengthwise and serve hot. Or cool and serve on a bed of crisp salad greens. About 505 calories per serving.

¢ SAUSAGE, MUSHROOM, AND RICE CASSEROLE

Makes 4 servings

1 pound fresh sausage links (American style, hot or sweet Italian), frankfurters, or kielbasa
2 cups cooked rice
1 (8-ounce) can mushroom stems and pieces (do not drain)
1 (10½-ounce) can condensed cream of mushroom soup
⅓ cup milk or water
⅓ cup fine cracker crumbs
2 tablespoons finely grated Parmesan cheese
2 tablespoons melted butter or margarine

Preheat oven to 350° F. Simmer fresh sausages 8 minutes and drain. Cut sausages in ½" chunks and toss with rice, mushrooms, soup, and milk. Spoon into a buttered 1½-quart casserole; mix crumbs, cheese, and melted butter and scatter over top. Bake, uncovered, ½ hour, brown quickly under broiler, and serve. About 645 calories per serving.

¢ TOAD IN THE HOLE (SAUSAGES IN YORKSHIRE PUDDING)

Makes 4–6 servings

1 cup sifted flour
1 teaspoon salt
1 cup milk
½ cup cold water
3 eggs, lightly beaten
1 pound fresh sausage links
¼ cup water
¼ cup melted beef or bacon drippings or vegetable shortening
2 cups hot beef gravy (homemade or canned)

About 40 minutes before serving time, make batter: mix flour and salt in a bowl, add milk, a little at a time, beating with a rotary or electric beater until smooth. Add water and eggs and beat until bubbly. Cover loosely and set aside ½ hour in a cool place (do not refrigerate). Preheat oven to 450° F. Simmer sausages in water in a covered skillet 8 minutes; drain well on paper toweling. Beat batter until bubbles appear on surface. Pour drippings into a 13½″×9″×2″ baking pan and heat in oven 1–2 minutes until smoking hot. Pour batter into pan and arrange sausages on top here and there. Bake, uncovered, on center oven rack 15–20 minutes until well browned, well risen, and crisp. Cut into large squares and serve piping hot with gravy. About 710 calories for each of 4 servings, 475 calories for each of 6 servings.

¢ KIELBASA-CANNELLINI CASSEROLE

Makes 6 servings

2 tablespoons olive oil
1 kielbasa sausage (about 1½ pounds), cut in ¼″ rounds
2 medium-size yellow onions, peeled and chopped fine
2 cloves garlic, peeled and crushed
⅓ cup minced parsley
½ teaspoon fennel seeds, crushed
1 teaspoon coriander seeds, crushed
1 teaspoon oregano
1 teaspoon salt
⅛ teaspoon pepper
2 (1-pound) cans zucchini in tomato sauce (do not drain) or 1 pound fresh zucchini, sliced and sautéed in butter, plus ¾ cup tomato sauce
2 (1-pound 4-ounce) cans cannellini (white kidney beans), drained
1 (6-ounce) can tomato paste

Preheat oven to 350° F. Heat oil in a large, heavy skillet over moderately high heat about 1 minute, add sausage and brown on both sides; drain on paper toweling. Add onions and garlic to skillet and sauté, stirring, 5–8 minutes until golden. Mix in parsley, herbs, salt, and pepper. Return sausage to skillet, add all remaining ingredients, and toss lightly to mix. Transfer to an ungreased shallow 3-quart casserole and bake, uncovered, 1½ hours, stirring occasionally. Serve as main dish. About 610 calories per serving.

SAUSAGE AND PASTRY ROLLS

Good party fare, these can be made ahead and refrigerated or frozen. Cool after baking, wrap, and freeze or refrigerate. To serve, bring to room temperature, then reheat, uncovered, in a 350° F. oven 10–15 minutes.

Makes 4–6 servings

Pastry:

1 recipe Extra Short Pastry
1 egg lightly beaten with 1 tablespoon cold water (glaze)

Filling:

1 pound sausage meat
2 tablespoons soft white bread crumbs
½ teaspoon salt
⅛ teaspoon pepper
2 tablespoons finely grated yellow onion (optional)

Preheat oven to 425° F. Prepare pastry, wrap in foil, and chill while you make the filling. Sauté sausage in a heavy skillet over moderately low heat 10–12 minutes, breaking up meat with a fork and spooning off fat as it accumulates. Transfer to a bowl, add remaining ingredients, and mix well with your hands. Roll half the pastry on a lightly floured cloth into a strip about 3"×15"; brush margins with glaze. Spoon half the filling down center of pastry in a narrow strip. Fold pastry edges over so you have a roll 1½"×15". Press edges together and crimp with a fork. Cut into 3" lengths, make small steam vents in the top of each roll, and arrange 1½" apart on an ungreased baking sheet. Roll, fill, and cut remaining pastry the same way. Brush rolls lightly with glaze, taking care not to cover vents, and bake uncovered 20 minutes until lightly browned. Cool slightly on wire racks. Serve warm as a light entree with relish or chutney or as buffet finger food. About 785 calories for each of 4 servings, 520 calories for each of 6 servings.

BIGOS (POLISH HUNTER'S STEW)

If the following recipe seems intricate, consider the original, once served at royal Polish hunts. It fed around 100 and included ducks, venison, hare (and anything else the hunters had bagged) *plus* Polish sausage, beef, lamb, pork, and chicken—each cooked in a *separate pot*. This version, at least, puts everything into one pot.
Makes 6–8 servings

¼ pound salt pork, trimmed of rind and diced
½ pound lean boned beef chuck, cut in 1" cubes
½ pound lean boned pork shoulder, cut in 1" cubes
½ pound lean boned lamb shoulder, cut in 1" cubes
1 (3–3½-pound) frying chicken, cut up
2 large yellow onions, peeled and minced
1 carrot, peeled and split lengthwise
2 stalks celery
2 stalks parsley
6 peppercorns tied in cheesecloth with 1 bay leaf
1 cup beef broth (about—just enough to keep meats from sticking)
¼ pound dried mushrooms
2 pounds sauerkraut
1 kielbasa sausage, sliced ½" thick

1 tablespoon sugar
½ teaspoon salt
3 tablespoons flour blended with ¼ cup cold water
½ cup dry Madeira wine

Brown salt pork in a large, heavy kettle over moderately high heat; remove and set aside. In drippings brown each meat separately; drain on paper toweling. Also brown and drain chicken, adding a little bacon drippings if necessary. Lightly brown onions, return meats to kettle, lay chicken pieces on top, and scatter with salt pork cubes. Add carrot, celery, parsley, cheesecloth bag, and broth, cover, and simmer 1 hour, adding a little extra broth if necessary. Meanwhile, prepare mushrooms for cooking.* Pour their soaking water over sauerkraut, cut mushrooms in thin strips and mix with kraut. Remove vegetables and cheesecloth bag from kettle and discard. Lift out chicken, cut meat from bones, and return to kettle. Add sauerkraut mixture and remaining ingredients and toss carefully to mix. Cover and simmer ½–¾ hour until all meats are tender. Serve with mashed or boiled potatoes. About 755 calories for each of 6 servings, 565 calories for each of 8 servings.

▨ SOME HOT DOG QUICKIES

Note: Luncheon meats, bologna, mild salamis, and cold cuts can be substituted in any of the recipes calling for sliced or diced frankfurters.

California Splits: Split franks lengthwise, not quite all the way through, and spread half of them with seasoned mashed potatoes or sweet potatoes; top with unspread franks, pressing together like sandwiches. Spread with mild yellow mustard, lay a slice of American or Swiss cheese over each, and bake uncovered 15 minutes at 400° F.

Corny Dogs: Make a batter with ½ cup yellow corn meal, 1 cup sifted flour, 1 teaspoon salt, ¼ teaspoon baking powder, 1 cup milk, and 1 egg; beat until smooth. Dip franks in batter to coat, then fry in deep fat (375° F.) until browned, 2–3

minutes. Drain on paper toweling and
dip in mustard as you eat.

Souper Doggies: Make slits the length of
frankfurters, insert strips of cheese the
same length. Place in a buttered shallow
casserole, sprinkle with ¼ cup minced
onion, and pour in 1 (10½-ounce) can
cream of mushroom, celery, tomato, or
asparagus soup. Bake, uncovered, ½
hour at 350° F.

Texas Hounds: Serve hot dogs in buns
smothered with Texas Red or other chili.

Some Additional Hot Dog Quickies

– Sauté franks whole, roll up in pancakes
or crepes, and eat out of hand, using
mustard as a dip.
– Alternate cocktail franks or Vienna
sausages on skewers with cherry
tomatoes, whole canned potatoes, and
sweet green and red pepper squares.
Broil 4"–5" from heat about 5
minutes, turning often and brushing
with All-Purpose Barbecue Sauce until
lightly browned.
– Alternate cocktail franks or Vienna
sausages on skewers with preserved
kumquats, sweet green and red pepper
squares, and pineapple chunks and broil
4"–5" from heat about 5 minutes,
turning often and brushing with Plum or
Sweet and Sour Sauce.
– Split franks lengthwise, fill with any
cheese spread, and broil in buttered
buns until browned and bubbly.
– Split franks lengthwise, fill with hot
seasoned mashed potatoes mixed with
mustard to taste, place in buns, drizzle
with melted butter, sprinkle with finely
grated cheese, and broil quickly to
brown.
– Cut franks in chunks and layer into a
casserole of sauerkraut or pickled red
cabbage sprinkled with poppy seeds and
bake uncovered ½ hour at 350° F.
– Cut in chunks and layer into a casserole
of canned baked beans, creamed corn,
ravioli or spaghetti in sauce, or Spanish
rice and bake, uncovered, ½ hour at
350° F.

– Chop fine, mix into leftover mashed
potatoes, and fry as potato cakes.
– Slice thin and scatter on Pizza.
– Slice thin and fold into scrambled
eggs or omelets.
– Slice thin and simmer until hot in 1
(10½-ounce) can split pea soup
blended with 1 (10½-ounce) can cream
of tomato soup and 2 teaspoons curry
powder.
– Slice thin and float in hot vegetable,
tomato, potato, or split pea soup.
– Slice thin and toss into potato or
macaroni salad.
– Slice thin or dice and add to meatless
spaghetti sauce; serve over spaghetti or
macaroni.
– Slice thin and use to stretch leftover
meat dishes, stews, soups, and casseroles.

What Goes On a Hot Dog Except Mustard, Onions, and the Usual?

– Pickled Red Cabbage
– Hot German Potato Salad
– Carolina Coleslaw
– Wilted Cucumbers
– Creamed Onions
– Batter-fried onion rings
– A ½ and ½ mixture of sautéed minced
mushrooms and onions
– Hot sauerkraut
– A ½ and ½ mixture of minced ripe and
pimiento-stuffed olives
– Equal parts peeled, seeded, chopped
tomatoes, minced onion, and sweet green
pepper sautéed in a little butter until
"wilted"
– Sour cream, minced onion, and caviar
– Baked beans
– Minced chutney and tiny Cheddar
cheese cubes
– Equal parts minced pineapple, celery,
and sweet pickle relish
– Spaghetti sauce (with or without meat)
– Sweet-Sour or Plum Sauce
– Any cheese spread
– Any of the sauces or condiments
recommended for ham (see Sauces,
Gravies, and Seasonings for Ham and
Other Cured Pork)

QUICK ALPHABET OF SAUSAGES

FRESH SAUSAGES (uncured, unsmoked, uncooked). Cook thoroughly before eating (specific recipes follow).

Name	Description	How to Prepare	Good Accompaniments
Bockwurst	Delicate German veal sausage made in spring at bock beer time; aromatic of onion and/or chives, parsley, nutmeg.	Panfry.	Bock beer.
Bratwurst	Chunky German veal and pork sausage usually seasoned with coriander or caraway, lemon, and ginger. Now being sold precooked as well as fresh.	Panfry, using beer or ale for the initial simmering; drain and brown in butter.	Hashed Brown Potatoes.
Chipolata	Small Italian pork and rice sausages sometimes called "little fingers." Seasonings: chives, thyme, coriander.	Panfry. The French use chipolatas to garnish large roasts and poultry.	Potatoes, roasts, poultry.
Fresh Pork Sausage	The American favorite, a mixture of ground fresh pork and pork fat, seasoned with pepper and sage. It is made under federal inspection, cannot contain more than 3 per cent added moisture or 50 per cent fat. Comes in bulk (loose for patties), links and rolls. *Country Style* is a coarser grind. *New Entry:* Brown 'n Serve links and patties.	*Links:* Simmer, steam, panfry, braise, bake and if first simmered or steamed, broil or charcoal broil. *Patties:* Panbroil, braise, *Roll:* Bake.	Eggs, grits, cooked apples, potatoes, dried beans and lentils.
Fresh Italian-style Pork Sausage	The pizza sausage, hot or sweet; usually made in continuous ropes. One type, *cotechino*, is made with pork skins.	Panfry or braise; use in casseroles and, removed from casings, in spaghetti sauce.	Lentils, dried beans, spaghetti.
Fresh Thuringer	Finely ground pork-veal sausage aromatic of coriander, celery seed, and ginger. Now available "scalded" as well as fresh.	If not "scalded," braise or simmer and brown in butter. Good in Cassoulet.	Potatoes, dried beans.
Loukanika	Greek lamb and pork sausage seasoned with orange rind. Greeks usually cut them in 1" chunks, grill and serve as *meze* (hors d'oeuvre).	Panfry or simmer and broil or charcoal broil.	Fried eggs, tomatoes, rice.

434

Toulouse	Small, coarse-textured French pork sausage; seasoned with garlic and white wine.	Braise or panfry; use in Cassoulet and other casseroles or remove from casing and use in stuffings.	Lentils, dried beans.
Weisswurst	Unusually delicate, small white German sausage made of veal, cream, and eggs. Traditionally served après-midnight at Oktoberfest with rye rolls and sweet German mustard.	Steam.	Rye rolls, sweet mustard, pretzels, beer.

FRESH SMOKED SAUSAGES. Cook thoroughly before eating.

Bauernwurst (farmer sausage)	A highly seasoned, super hot dog from Germany; usually coarse of texture.	Steam or simmer, then brown in butter or broil	Sauerkraut.
Country-style Fresh Pork Sausage	A smoked version of fresh country-style sausage; it may be all pork or a combination of pork and beef. Usually sold in links.	Simmer, steam, panfry, braise, bake and, if first simmered or steamed, broil or charcoal broil.	Eggs, grits, apples, potatoes, dried beans.
Romanian Sausage	A lean pork sausage stuffed into casings and flavored with garlic and ginger.	Steam or simmer, then brown in butter or broil.	Potatoes, cabbage.

COOKED SAUSAGES. Usually these are made of fresh meats, though sometimes from cured. They are fully cooked and safe to eat as is, but most will improve if heated through before serving.

Andouillette	Small tripe or chitterling sausages that are a specialty of Normandy.	The French way is to make a few shallow slits in sausage and to sauté in butter or to broil or grill, brushing with melted butter.	Mashed or Lyonnaise Potatoes.
Blood Sausage	A large dark sausage made of pig's blood and cubes of pork fat. Occasionally you may find uncooked ones, but most are fully cooked. Certain German varieties are smoked as well.	Uncooked ones must be simmered, then sliced and browned; cooked ones need only be sliced and browned lightly in butter.	Mashed potatoes, sauerkraut.

435

QUICK ALPHABET OF SAUSAGES (continued)

Name	Description	How to Prepare	Good Accompaniments
Boudins Blancs	Very delicate, very expensive white French sausages made of pork, chicken, cream, eggs, onions, and fine bread crumbs.	Sauté gently in butter or brush with melted butter and broil just to heat.	Mashed potatoes.
Cotto	A soft, cooked Italian salami, usually sold sliced as a sandwich meat.	Use for sandwiches.	Bread, mustard, dill pickles.
Leberkäse	Not a sausage so much as a smooth German pork liver pâté eaten hot instead of cold.	Slice and heat over boiling water in a vegetable steamer or sauté gently in butter.	Steamed: rye bread and mustard. Sautéed: fried onions.
Liver Sausages	Large creamy-smooth links, some highly spiced. Usually made of pork liver mixed with pork and/or veal. American varieties may or may not be smoked; German types almost always are. Liver sausages can be fairly firm or soft enough to spread.	Use as sandwich filling or as a spread for crackers.	Bread (especially rye) and crackers.
Scrapple	The Pennsylvania Dutch invented this pork and corn meal mush combination as a way to use up the odds and ends of hog butchering. Scrapple comes in chunky rolls, both canned and in packages in supermarket meat coolers.	Slice and brown in butter or bacon drippings.	Eggs, grits, fried apples, cabbage, potatoes.

COOKED, SMOKED SAUSAGES: Some (*andouille, Bierwurst*, bologna, the German liver sausages) are eaten as is; others (mainly the frankfurter types) will be better if heated through. Specific directions follow.

Name	Description	How to Prepare	Good Accompaniments
Andouille	The large French tripe or chitterling sausage is the big brother of *andouillettes*. Unlike them, it is more often sliced thin and eaten cold as an hors d'oeuvre. Occasionally it is sliced and sautéed gently in butter.	Slice and serve cold as an appetizer or heat slices by sautéing in butter.	When sautéed: mashed potatoes.

436

Berliner Blutwurst	A smoked variation of blood sausage (see Cooked Sausages) containing bacon cubes.	Heat in boiling water, then slice; or, after heating, sauté in butter with onion and apple rings.	Cranberry sauce, sautéed onions and apples.
Berliner Bockwurst	A smoky red Berlin sausage, not unlike our hot dog. It's a favorite late night snack, served steaming from street-corner stands.	Steam or heat in boiling water, then serve.	Sauerkraut; also any of our hot dog trappings.
Bierwurst	A soft, cooked German salami, usually sold sliced as sandwich meat. Garlicky.	Use in making sandwiches.	Beer and bread.
Bologna	The original Bolognese sausage is *mortadella*, a plump, creamy link studded with cubes of fat. True mortadella is air-dried briefly, putting it into the cervelat family. American mortadella is simply fat-studded American bologna — a creamy, pink pork-beef blend with lots of garlic. There are many types: *large, ring, stick* (slightly coarser), *chub* (an ultra smooth mix of beef, pork, and bacon), *Schinkenwurst* (ham bologna), *Lebanon* (a sour, briefly air-dried type from Lebanon, Pa.), all-beef bologna and a delicate veal bologna.	Use in sandwiches, salads, and soups; also see suggestions that follow.	Swiss or American cheese, lettuce, sliced tomatoes, all kinds of bread, mustard, and mayonnaise.
Frankfurters and Wieners	Frankfurters came from Frankfurt, wieners from Vienna; today they're 100 per cent Americanized as hot dogs. Some are all beef (the Kosher), but most are 60 per cent beef and 40 per cent pork. Casings are natural, artificial or non-existent (as in skinless franks). *Vienna sausages* are wieners cut in short links and canned. Most popular frankfurter sizes: *regular* (9-10 franks per lb.), *dinner* (5 per lb.), *foot-long* (4 per lb.) and *cocktail* (26-28 per lb.). New entries: *smoked frankfurters* (called *Smoked Links* and sometimes just *Smokies*), *cheese frankfurters*.	See recipes and suggestions that follow.	Almost anything savory.

437

QUICK ALPHABET OF SAUSAGES (continued)

Name	Description	How to Prepare	Good Accompaniments
German Liver Sausages (liverwursts)	The list is long, but among those especially worth seeking out: *Braunschweiger* (mild and creamy), *Hildesheimer Streichleberwurst* (all calf's liver), *Zwiebelwurst* (with browned onion in it), *Trufflewurst* (with truffles), *Sardellenwurst* (with anchovies).	All are ready-to-eat and best served cold with bread or crackers.	Bread (especially rye), crackers.
Kielbasa	A large garlicky Polish sausage, mostly pork but sometimes with veal or beef. Once available only fresh, *Kielbasa* is now being processed by American packers and sold "fully cooked" or "scalded." Check the labels.	Steam or simmer to heat; cook with sauerkraut; use in stews and casseroles.	Sauerkraut, dried peas, beans, and lentils.
Knackwurst (or knockwurst or knoblauch)	Short chunky German frankfurter highly seasoned with garlic. There's also a Bavarian version called *Regensburger*.	Simmer or steam to warm or cook with sauerkraut. Can be substituted for hot dogs.	Sauerkraut, any of our hot dog condiments.
Strasbourg Liver Sausage	A French liver sausage with pistachio nuts.	Ready-to-eat; use as an appetizer.	Bread, crackers.
Strasbourg Sausage	Sort of a smoked, French hot dog.	Simmer, steam or use in Choucroute Garnie.	Sauerkraut
Tongue Sausage	A large sausage made of tongue and other meats. Available sliced and in links.	Ready-to-eat; use in making sandwiches.	Cheese, bread, mustard, mayonnaise, pickles.

438

Zungenwurst	A German blood sausage made with tongue and studded with diced fat.	Slice and brown in butter.	Sauerkraut, mashed potatoes.
A SPECIALTY SAUSAGE: This one defies categorizing.			
Mettwurst	A very soft, very fat German pork sausage, bright red in color and aromatic of coriander and white pepper. It is cured and smoked *but not cooked* and it is eaten raw. Because of its spreadability, it is also called *Schmierwurst* (*schmier* meaning *smear*).	Use as a spread for bread.	Bread.

SALAMIS AND CERVELATS (SUMMER SAUSAGES)

These are the original sausages, developed ages ago when salting, drying, and smoking were the only ways to preserve meat. The Italians came up with salamis, the Germans, cervelats. Both are mixtures of chopped pork and/or beef and secret blends of herbs and spices. With few exceptions (cooked kosher salami), both are raw and eaten that way (curing, drying, and smoking render them safe).

For all their similarities, the two are different. Salamis are laden with garlic, cervelats have none; salamis are rarely smoked, cervelats commonly are; salamis are rather coarse of texture; cervelats, generally fine. Salamis are air-dried from 1 to 6 months and thus are usually hard, dry, and shriveled. Cervelats can be dry but more often they are softer and moister—*semidry* is the trade term—having spent only 2 to 5 days in the drying room or smokehouse. Salamis need not be stored in the refrigerator (though they'll keep there almost forever), cervelats should be.

There are dozens of different salamis and cervelats, most of them named after the towns where they are made, as well as other hard peppery links classified as *dry sausages*. Here are some of the more popular.

Salamis

Italian:

Calabrese: A red hot type from Southern Italy.

Campagnole: Rough-textured, spicy peasant salami.

Genoa: One of the best; quite fat and studded with whole peppercorns.

Milano: Finely grained, fairly delicate, flavored with pepper and white wine.

Pepperoni: Small, dry salami-like sausage available both sweet and hot.

Soppressata: A flat oval salami—peppery, gingery, *garlicky!*

German:

Hard Salami: A lean Italian type without all the garlic.

Hungarian: Called simply Hungarian salami, it is mild, often smoked.

French:

Arles: Coarsely grained Provençal sausage with a crisscross cording.

Lyon: Fine, all-pork salami in large casings.

American:

Alessandri, Alpino: Italian types made of pork and beef.

Frizzes: Also Italian style; sweet and peppery types are made, both scented with anise. The sweet is corded with blue string, the hot with red.

Italian: Another American-Italian salami, this one coarsely chopped pork mixed with minced beef, whole peppercorns, and red wine or grape juice.

Kosher: Soft, cooked all-beef salami made under rabbinical supervision. Available sliced and whole.

Cervelats

German:

Cervelatwurst: Finely minced beef and pork, lightly smoked, mildly seasoned with mustard, red and black pepper, sugar, and salt. Semidry.

Farmer Cervelat: Rather soft, small link of coarsely chopped beef and pork in equal proportion. *Farmer Sausage* is a bigger, beefier, smokier version.

Gothaer, Göttinger: Two hard, dry cervelats, one from the town of Gotha, the other from Göttingen.

Holsteiner: Sort of a super Farmer Sausage, heavily smoked; ring-shaped.

Thuringer: Here's the favorite. Often called simply *Summer Sausage,* it's salty but mild, fairly soft. Coriander is the noticeable spice.

Italian:

Mortadella: (see Bologna under Cooked, Smoked Sausages).

Swedish:

Göteborg: A large cardamom-flavored, coarsely textured pork cervelat, smoked and air-dried.

Swiss:

Landjäger: Very smoky, dry, wrinkled black cervelat, pressed into small sticks instead of rolls. It is made of beef and pork.

Other Dry Sausages

Chorizos: Small, hard, dry Spanish sausages, flavored with pimiento, garlic, and red pepper. Especially good with chick-peas, black beans, and other dried peas and beans.

Linguiça: Small, slim Portuguese sausages, saturated with garlic and paprika. A favorite ingredient in Portuguese and Brazilian soups, stews, and casseroles.

Some Ways to Use Salamis and Cervelats

Note about Slicing: A good general rule is "the firmer the sausage, the thinner the slice."

Thin Slices:
– In Antipasto or on hors d'oeuvre trays.
– With a savory spread as open-face sandwiches.
– In sandwiches, solo with mustard or mayonnaise, or in tandem with Swiss, American, or cream cheese.
– In making Pizza or Quick Pizzas.
– In Grilled Cheese Sandwiches.
– Wrapped around small chunks of pineapple, peach, pear, banana, mango or preserved kumquat, skewered and broiled under bastings of Sweet-Sour Sauce.

– Shaped into cornucopias, filled with a savory cheese spread, and served as cocktail snacks.

Diced or Minced (¼ –⅓ cup is enough in each instance):
– Teamed with boiled rice, mashed or Stuffed Baked Potatoes, Lyonnaise or Hashed Brown Potatoes, Macaroni and Cheese.
– Added to Chinese-Style Snow Peas, Green Beans Provençal, Neapolitan Beans with Parmesan, Hopping John, Chick-Pea Pilaf, any boiled dried beans, spinach or other greens dressed with oil and vinegar.
– Added to stuffings for poultry or pork.
– Mixed with cheese, onion, garlic, or other savory dips and spreads.
– Added to Cheese or Mushroom Soufflé.

Julienne Strips (⅓ –½ cups is enough):
– In crisp green salads.
– In scrambled eggs or omelets.

LUNCHEON AND OTHER SPECIALTY MEATS

The list is long—and *lengthening*. It includes the familiar canned luncheon loaves and the huge array of cold cuts (many of them borderline sausages) found in supermarket counters. New flavor combinations are arriving almost daily: liverwursts studded with pistachio nuts, ham, or cheese; sandwich meats with olives, pimiento, or cheese. There are peppered meat loaves, honey loaves, pickle and pimiento loaves, plain loaves, and old-fashioned Dutch loaves, not to mention souse and headcheese. The majority of these specialty meats are simply sliced and eaten cold—as is, in sandwiches or cocktail snacks. But they can be used in recipes. And they can be served with flair. See recipes and suggestions that follow, also ideas given in Some Hot Dog Quickies and Some Ways to Use Salamis and Cervelats.

⚖ GLAZED BAKED LUNCHEON MEAT LOAF

Makes 4 servings

1 (12-ounce) can luncheon meat
12 cloves

Glaze:

⅓ cup firmly packed light brown sugar
2 tablespoons cider vinegar
1 teaspoon powdered mustard
⅛ teaspoon allspice

Preheat oven to 350° F. Lay luncheon meat on its side and score top lightly in a crisscross pattern; stud with cloves. Place in a shallow open roasting pan; mix glaze and spread over loaf. Bake, uncovered, about ½ hour until lightly glazed, basting occasionally with glaze runoff. Slice and serve. About 310 calories per serving.

VARIATIONS:
– Cutting almost but not all the way through, divide loaf into 8 equal slices. Into each cut tuck a thin slice of canned pineapple, American cheese, or Spanish onion. Omit cloves but glaze and bake as directed. (*Note:* Loaves with onion or cheese slices may be topped with 1 cup Tomato Sauce or All-Purpose Barbecue Sauce instead of glaze and baked as directed.)
– Score luncheon loaf but omit cloves. Toothpick small chunks of canned pineapple, peaches, or apricots over top, glaze, and bake as directed.
– Omit glaze above and substitute 1 of the following: ⅓ cup maple, light, or dark corn syrup; orange, lemon, or ginger marmalade; any barbecue sauce; apple cider or pineapple juice (these 2 good with crushed pineapple topping); bake as directed.
– Omit glaze above and substitute any recommended for Baked Ham, using about half as much; bake as directed.

All recipe variations too flexible for meaningful calorie counts.

INDONESIAN FRUIT AND MEAT BAKE

Makes 6 servings

1 (12-ounce) can luncheon meat, diced
2 cups cooked shell macaroni, well drained
1¼ cups drained pineapple tidbits
½ cup peeled, sliced seedless green grapes
3 tablespoons butter or margarine
3 tablespoons flour
2 teaspoons curry powder
½ teaspoon ginger
1 teaspoon salt
¼ teaspoon pepper
1 (13-ounce) can evaporated milk
⅓ cup flaked coconut

Preheat oven to 350° F. Mix meat, macaroni, pineapple, and grapes in an ungreased 1½-quart casserole; set aside. Melt butter in a saucepan over low heat, blend in flour, curry powder, ginger, salt, and pepper; add milk and heat slowly, stirring constantly, until thickened and smooth. Add to casserole and toss lightly to mix. Sprinkle with coconut and bake, uncovered, 25–30 minutes until browned and bubbly.

VARIATION:

Substitute 1¾ cups finely diced frankfurters, Vienna sausages, or bologna for luncheon meat.

Both versions: about 420 calories per serving.

¢ MEATY PEPPER-CORN BAKE

Makes 6 servings

1 (12-ounce) can luncheon meat, diced
2 tablespoons bacon drippings
¼ cup minced yellow onion
⅓ cup minced green pepper
1 (17-ounce) can cream-style corn
1½ cups coarse cracker crumbs
2 tablespoons melted butter or margarine
1 cup evaporated milk or heavy cream
½ teaspoon salt
⅛ teaspoon pepper

Preheat oven to 350° F. Stir-fry meat in drippings until lightly browned; add onion and pepper and stir-fry 5 minutes.

Mix in corn. Spoon half of mixture into a greased shallow 2-quart casserole or *au gratin* dish; top with half crumbs, then remaining corn mixture. Toss rest of crumbs with melted butter and scatter over top. Mix milk, salt, and pepper and pour over all. Bake, uncovered, 30–40 minutes until touched with brown. About 425 calories per serving.

¢ LUNCHEON CHEESE BAKE

Makes 4–6 servings

4 slices white bread
2 tablespoons softened butter or margarine
2 teaspoons prepared spicy brown mustard
1½ cups diced luncheon meat
1 cup cubed processed American cheese
3 eggs, lightly beaten
1½ cups milk
1 teaspoon salt
⅛ teaspoon white pepper

Preheat oven to 350° F. Spread bread with butter and mustard and cut in ½" cubes. Toss with meat and cheese in a buttered 1½-quart casserole. Mix eggs, milk, salt, and pepper and pour into casserole. Bake, uncovered, 50 minutes until puffed and browned. About 520 calories for each of 4 servings, 345 calories for each of 6 servings.

¢ CURRIED LUNCHEON MEAT HASH

Makes 4 servings

2 cups diced, cold, cooked potatoes
2 cups diced luncheon meat
¼ cup minced yellow onion
½ teaspoon celery salt
⅛ teaspoon pepper
⅓ cup mayonnaise or salad dressing
1 tablespoon curry powder
3 tablespoons butter, margarine, or cooking oil

Mix all ingredients except butter in a bowl, cover, and let stand at room temperature ½ hour. Heat butter in a heavy skillet over moderate heat about 1 minute, add mixture, press down, and brown about 15 minutes. Cut hash "cake" in half, turn each over, and brown other side the same way. Serve with chutney. About 480 calories per serving.

LUNCHEON SALAD STUFFED ROLLS

Makes 1 dozen

1 (12-ounce) can luncheon meat, cubed
6 hard-cooked eggs, shelled and quartered
1 sweet green pepper, cored, seeded, and cut in thin strips
1 (4-ounce) can pimientos
1 (8-ounce) jar pimiento-stuffed olives, drained
1 small yellow onion, peeled and quartered
2 tablespoons prepared mild yellow mustard
1 cup mayonnaise or salad dressing (about)
2 tablespoons steak sauce
12 hot dog or hamburger buns, split and spread with softened butter or margarine

Preheat oven to 325° F. Put meat, eggs, green pepper, pimientos, olives, and onion through fine blade of meat grinder; mix with mustard, mayonnaise, and steak sauce (mixture should be consistency of cottage cheese, so add more mayonnaise if needed). Fill buns with stuffing, close and wrap each in foil. Bake ½ hour and serve. About 420 calories per roll.

BOLOGNA TURNOVERS

Makes 6 servings

½ pound bologna, diced
1 (8-ounce) can mixed vegetables, drained
2 cups canned beef gravy
1 (9¼-ounce) piecrust stick
1 egg, lightly beaten with 1 tablespoon cold water

Preheat oven to 425° F. Mix bologna, vegetables, and about ¾ cup gravy—just enough to moisten mixture. Prepare pastry by package directions and roll thin; cut out 6 (6″) circles (use rerolls, too). Spoon stuffing on half of each circle, dividing amount evenly. Fold pastry over stuffing and crimp edges with a fork to seal. Place turnovers on an ungreased baking sheet, slash tops in 2 or 3 places, and brush with egg glaze, taking care not to cover slits. Bake, uncovered, 25–30 minutes until golden brown. Heat remaining gravy and serve with turnovers. About 380 calories per serving.

⊿⊅ ¢ DEVILED EGG AND BOLOGNA CASSEROLE

Makes 6 servings

6 hard-cooked eggs, shelled and halved lengthwise
3 tablespoons mayonnaise
2 teaspoons prepared mild yellow mustard
1 teaspoon cider vinegar
¼ teaspoon garlic salt
Pinch white pepper
6 slices bologna
1 (10½-ounce) can cream of celery, mushroom, or asparagus soup
½ cup milk
¼ teaspoon onion juice
1 pimiento, seeded and chopped fine
1 tablespoon minced parsley

Preheat oven to 350° F. Mash egg yolks and mix with mayonnaise, mustard, vinegar, garlic salt, and pepper; stuff whites with mixture and put back together, forming "whole" eggs. Place each egg on a bologna slice, bring sides up in center to form bundles and toothpick in place. Place bologna-egg bundles in an ungreased 1½-quart casserole. Mix soup, milk, onion juice, and pimiento and pour over eggs. Bake, uncovered, 25–30 minutes. Remove toothpicks, sprinkle with parsley, and serve. About 255 calories per serving.

⊠ Quick Tricks with Luncheon and Other Specialty Meats

Note: Though listed under sausages, the packaged, sliced American bologna is really a cold cut and can be used in any of the following ways.

– Lay a thin slice of luncheon meat or a cold cut on a large square of heavy foil, spread with your favorite cheese spread, top with another meat slice, and continue building up layers until you have a stack about 1"–1½" high. Drizzle with melted butter or, for more flavor, All-Purpose Barbecue Sauce or Sweet-Sour Sauce. Wrap and bake 20–30 minutes at 350° F. To serve, cut straight through in slices about 1" wide. Serve, if you like, with additional sauce. (4 servings).
– Mix 1 (8-ounce) package poultry stuffing mix with 2 tablespoons melted butter and just enough water to make it hold together; press into the bottom and up the sides of a buttered 9"×9"×2" baking pan to form a "crust" and bake, uncovered, 10 minutes at 400° F. Mix 1½ cups diced luncheon meat or cold cuts with 1½ cups Medium White or Cheese Sauce and ¾ cup drained, canned mixed vegetables. Spoon into crust and bake, uncovered, ½ hour at 350° F. Serve at the table by cutting in large squares. (4–6 servings.)
– When making Eggs Benedict, use thinly sliced luncheon or cold cuts instead of ham.
– Make Scalloped Potatoes with Ham as directed, substituting diced luncheon meat or cold cuts for the ham.
– Make Creamed Chipped Beef or Creamed Chipped Beef and Mushrooms, substituting minced luncheon meat or cold cuts for chipped beef; increase salt as needed.
– Shape cold cuts into cornucopias, fill with hot, seasoned, mashed sweet potatoes, drizzle with pineapple juice or honey, and brown quickly under broiler.
– Fry thin bologna slices in a hot, lightly greased skillet until they curl into "cups"; fill with creamed onions, potatoes, peas, or mixed vegetables; with puréed peas or spinach; with Hot Macédoine of Vegetables, Hot German Potato Salad, fluffy, seasoned mashed potatoes, or sweet potatoes.

CHAPTER 9

GAME AND GAME BIRDS

Cooking game is no more mysterious than roasting beef, frying chicken, or stewing lamb. It's just that the "bag" is often brought home whole and the average woman is shocked numb at the idea of skinning or plucking and butchering. Well, cleaning game isn't as neat as peeling a potato, but fortunately the messiest job (eviscerating) will probably have been done in the field. As for the rest—skinning, aging, cutting up a carcass—there are butchers in most parts of the country who will do these jobs for you—even if you have shot the game yourself; some will even package and label cuts for the freezer. In many big cities, gourmet markets sell fresh game in season and frozen game year round. More and more game (especially rabbit and buffalo) and game birds (ducks, geese, and pheasant) are being raised for the table. Still, in rural areas, you may have to go after your own game or befriend someone who does.

About Quality

Game bought from a reputable market will have been federally inspected (to ensure wholesomeness) and because of the fussiness of game fanciers, will usually be of high quality as well. But that which your husband or neighbor shoots may not be. Three factors determine quality: *age of the animal* (the younger, the better), *diet*, and *care the kill was given in the field* (more potentially good game is lost through sloppy field handling than for any other reason). As soon as an animal or bird is shot, it should be eviscerated (especially important on warm days), and large animals must also be bled. The process is too complicated to include here; the best way to learn is firsthand from an experienced hunting guide or secondhand from a detailed hunting manual. As for the age of the animal, hunting guides can quickly judge (usually by looking at an animal's teeth or bird's beak, feet, or breastbone), and so can most butchers. Diet, obviously, is more difficult to determine because a wild creature will eat what it must in order to survive. Still, there are clues. Certain species prefer certain kinds of food. As a general rule, vegetarians are better flavored than meat or fish eaters. Where an animal or bird is bagged can also suggest what it's been eating. For example, a deer shot in an evergreen thicket may have nibbled evergreen berries and thus taste of them. Here again, an experienced hunter can advise you. He can also show you how to sniff the ruffled feathers of a duck or goose to determine whether it's been eating fish. And he can judge the general health of an animal or bird by examining the fur or feathers.

How do you determine quality of game in a store? Much the way you do for any other meat. Venison and other red meat should be moist (not wet) and velvety with a clean fresh smell. Birds and small game should also be moist, their flesh springy to the touch, of good color and odor with little or no shot damage.

About Food Value

Game and game birds are high protein foods; most are lean because they are well exercised.

FURRED GAME

Large Animals: Choicest is venison, the meat of deer and other antlered animals. Buffalo, now being raised for the table, has a fine "beefy" flavor. Some people like bear, which tastes like pork and, like it, must be cooked until well done because of the danger of trichinosis (see Pork). There is very little wild boar around; most of that sold in this country is shipped in frozen from Europe. Cuts of large game are much like those of other meat animals (see Beef, Lamb, and Pork Charts), the tenderest coming from the little-exercised rib and loin, the toughest from the neck, leg, rump, and flank.

About the Heart and Liver: These delicacies are often eaten in camp by hunters because they don't travel well. They should be removed from the carcass immediately, plunged into cold water to remove the animal heat, then kept cool. Prepare as you would beef or calf's heart and liver.

Small Animals: More rabbit is eaten in this country than all other furred game put together. It has light, delicate meat, much like that of chicken, and is a popular supermarket item. Squirrel is popular quarry too, though gamier and darker fleshed. Gamier still, and less often eaten, are opossum, raccoon, and muskrat. Butchers may be less inclined

to dress small game that you have bagged yourself than the large, so you may have to do it yourself. The eviscerating and bleeding, as mentioned earlier, should have been done in the field; what remain are the skinning and final dressing.

To Skin Rabbits and Squirrels: Note: Always wear rubber gloves. Though it's unlikely an animal is diseased, tularemia, an infectious disease transmitted to man through cuts and scratches can't be discounted altogether. The surest way to tell if an animal is diseased is by looking at its liver; a healthy liver will be dark red, moist, and velvety, a diseased liver splotched with white. Though thorough cooking will make a diseased animal safe to eat, most people prefer not to chance it.

The first step in skinning is to hang the animal upside down by its legs and to make incisions in the skin as shown opposite.

Next, begin peeling skin from flesh, working from the feet toward the head —with a rabbit, the job's as easy as taking off gloves. Squirrels are more difficult because their skin is more firmly attached to the flesh. You will have to work more slowly, freeing skin as needed with a knife. (*Note:* Raccoons and muskrats require slightly different techniques; opossums are not skinned at all but scraped free of hairs after being scalded. A good hunting manual will describe each process in detail.)

Final Dressing: Remove the scent or musk glands located in the fat underneath the forelegs (the equivalent of the armpit) and in the small of the back. These are small yellow kernels that can be flicked out with the point of a knife. Singe off any remaining hair, also cut out shot-damaged flesh.

Cutting Up Rabbits and Squirrels: Cut off head, tail, and feet and discard. The

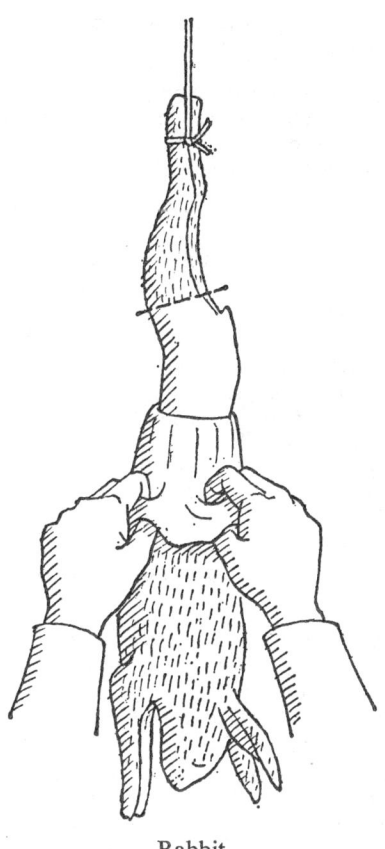
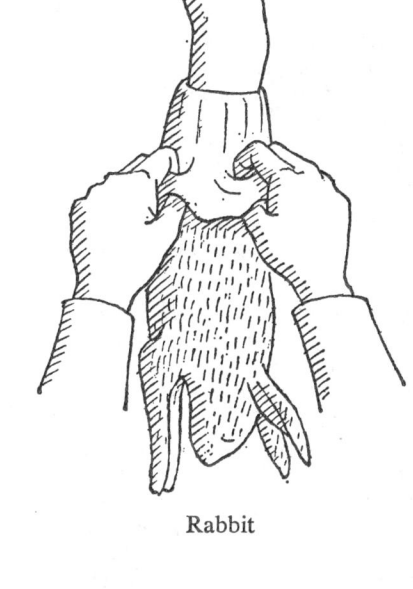

Rabbit

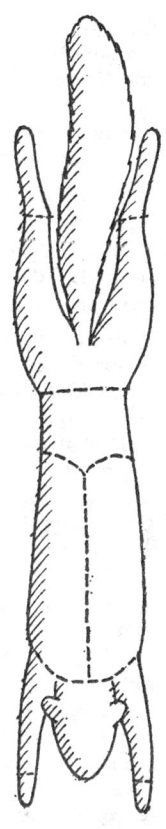

Squirrel

animal can be stuffed whole and pot roasted or cut up and fried, braised, or stewed. Simply sever at the joints and cut back and breast into 3 or 4 pieces.

How Much Game Per Person? When the animal or cut is unusually bony, allow ¾–1 pound per person, otherwise ⅓–½ pound.

About Frozen Game: Much of the game sold today is frozen. Thaw thoroughly before cooking, then prepare as you would fresh game. The best way to thaw game is in its original wrapper in the refrigerator; 1″ steaks will take about 12 hours, small roasts 3–4 hours

per pound, and large roasts 4–6 hours per pound.

⚖ ROAST SADDLE OF VENISON

Rack and loin of venison are excellent roasts, but the saddle (double loin) is choicest of all. If young and tender, it can be roasted like lamb; if of doubtful age, it should be marinated before roasting, and if mature it should be pot roasted like beef. The best way to tell an animal's age is to look at the bones. The bones of a young animal will be spongy and red inside, those of an older animal will appear flinty. Because venison is lean, it should be larded *and*

barded to keep it from drying out, and it should not be roasted beyond medium rare. Though some cooks sear venison at a high temperature, then finish roasting at a low heat, it seems juiciest when roasted at 350° F. throughout.
Makes 8 servings

½–¾ pound fat back or salt pork
1 (5–6-pound) saddle of venison
½ pound suet, cut in ½" cubes

Cut ½ the fat back into lardoons ¼" wide and 2"–3" long and cut the rest into thin slices for barding.* Pique* ends of roast with lardoons, then bard outer curved side. Let roast come to room temperature; meanwhile, preheat oven to 350° F. Stand saddle fat side up in a shallow roasting pan and insert a meat thermometer in largest lean muscle, not touching bone. Scatter suet in bottom of pan. Roast, uncovered, 15–20 minutes per pound for rare (125–30° F.) and 25 minutes per pound for medium rare (140–45° F.), basting frequently with pan drippings and removing suet cubes as they brown. About 15 minutes before roast is done, remove barding fat. When done, lift saddle to a hot platter and let "rest" 10 minutes before carving. If you like, make Pan Gravy. Carve in long slices the length of saddle—and don't forget choice morsels of tenderloin tucked underneath the ribs. About 200 calories per serving.

VARIATION:

⚔ **Marinated Roast Saddle of Venison:** Lard roast as above, cover with a marinade made by boiling 2 cups each red Burgundy and water 5 minutes with 1 peeled, bruised clove garlic, 4–6 juniper berries, and 1 *bouquet garni** tied in cheesecloth. Pour over venison, cover and refrigerate 1–2 days, turning meat occasionally. Lift from marinade, pat dry, bard, and roast as directed. If you like, strain marinade and use as the liquid when making Pan Gravy. About 210 calories per serving.

SMOTHERED VENISON STEAKS OR CHOPS

Steaks and chops from very young venison can be brushed with butter or oil and broiled or panbroiled like beefsteaks. Older steaks and chops should be prepared this way.
Makes 4 servings

3 pounds venison sirloin or round steak, cut 1½" thick, or 4 loin or rib chops, cut 1½" thick
⅓ cup unsifted flour
1½ teaspoons salt
¼ teaspoon pepper
3 tablespoons bacon or beef drippings or cooking oil
1 large yellow onion, peeled and minced
2 stalks celery, minced
2 small carrots, peeled and minced
2 cups hot beef broth or water
¾ cup sour cream at room temperature (optional)

Dredge steaks in a mixture of flour, salt, and pepper, then brown on both sides in drippings in a large, heavy skillet over moderately high heat or in an electric skillet set at 400° F. Remove meat and set aside. Stir-fry onion, celery, and carrots in drippings 8 minutes until golden. Return meat to pan, spoon vegetables on top, sprinkle with 1 tablespoon flour dredging mixture, and pour in broth. Turn heat to low (325° F. on electric skillet), cover, and simmer 30–40 minutes until tender—chops will take 30–40 minutes, steaks 1–1½ hours. Baste 1 or 2 times during cooking. Serve steaks topped with vegetables and pan juices, which will have thickened into gravy. If you like, smooth sour cream into gravy just before serving.

VARIATION:

Oven-Braised Venison Steak: Brown venison and vegetables as directed, transfer to an ungreased 3-quart casserole, cover, and bake 1½–2 hours at 300° F. until tender.

Both versions: About 400 calories per serving (without sour cream).

RAGOUT OF VENISON

Makes 4–6 servings

2 pounds boned venison shoulder, neck,
or shank, cut in 1"–1½" cubes
½ cup unsifted flour
1½ teaspoons salt
¼ teaspoon pepper
2 tablespoons cooking oil
8 scallions, minced (include green tops)
¾ pound mushrooms, wiped clean and
sliced thin
2 (10½-ounce) cans beef bouillon
1 teaspoon prepared mild yellow mustard
1 tablespoon Worcestershire sauce
2 tablespoons flour blended with ¼ cup
cold water

Dredge venison by shaking in a bag with
flour, salt, and pepper. Brown in oil in a
large, heavy kettle over moderately high
heat; remove and set aside. Stir-fry
scallions and mushrooms in drippings
3–5 minutes until mushrooms are golden,
add meat to kettle, also all but the final
ingredient. Stir well, cover, and simmer
1½–2 hours until venison is fork tender.
Mix in flour paste and heat, stirring,
until thickened and no raw starch taste
remains. Serve with wild rice or buttered
noodles. About 425 calories for each of
4 servings (without wild rice or noodles),
285 calories for each of 6 servings.

⊠ VENISONBURGERS

Venison shank, neck, shoulder, and
scraps make excellent burgers mixed
with sausage meat or fat pork. They
must be cooked well done.
Makes 3–4 servings

⅔ pound venison, ground once
⅓ pound fat pork (cheek, jowl,
trimmings), ground once, or ⅓ pound
sausage meat
2 tablespoons cooking oil, butter,
margarine, or bacon drippings
1 teaspoon salt
⅛ teaspoon pepper

Lightly mix venison and pork and
shape into 3 plump patties or 4 slim
ones. Brown in oil in a large, heavy
skillet over moderately high heat 6–7
minutes on each side until well done.

Season with salt and pepper just before
serving. About 355 calories for each of
3 servings, 265 calories for each of 4
servings.

VARIATIONS:

⊲⊳ **Rare Venisonburgers:** Mix 4 parts
ground venison with 1 part ground suet,
shape and cook as directed, allowing
4–5 minutes per side. About 240 calories
for each of 3 servings, 180 calories for
each of 4 servings.

Venison Loaf: Mix 4 parts ground
venison with 1 part ground suet and
substitute for beef in meat loaves.

BROILED BUFFALO STEAKS

The buffalo being raised for the table is
surprisingly delicate and tender, rather
like lean beef. The cuts of buffalo are
similar to beef (see Beef Chart) and
similarly prepared, the not-so-tender
shoulder, rump, flank, and shanks being
best for stews and the tender rib and
loin perfect for steaks and roasts. Where
do you buy buffalo? From a gourmet
meat market. How do you cook it?
Here are two ways (for other ideas, use
recipes for beef, substituting comparable
cuts of buffalo).
Makes 4 servings

4 buffalo rib or loin steaks, cut about 1"
thick
Cooking oil (optional)
4–6 crushed juniper berries (optional)
Salt
Pepper

Preheat broiler. If steaks seem extra
lean, brush well with oil. For a woodsy
flavor, also rub with juniper berries. Let
stand at room temperature 1–1½ hours
if convenient. Place steaks on a well-
greased broiler pan and broil 2" from
the heat about 3 minutes on a side for
very rare, 4 for rare, and 5 for medium
rare. (*Note:* Because of its leanness,
buffalo will toughen and dry if cooked
beyond medium rare.) Season with salt
and pepper and serve. About 350–450
calories per serving, depending upon
how well marbled with fat the meat is.

VARIATION:

Charcoal-Broiled Buffalo Steaks: Prepare a hot charcoal fire.* Prepare steak for cooking as above, then broil 4″ from the coals about 3 minutes on a side for very rare, 4–5 for rare, and 6 for medium rare. Calorie counts the same as for Broiled Buffalo Steaks.

BEAR OR WILD BOAR POT ROAST

Loin of young bear or wild boar, also wild boar hams, can be roasted like pork, and like it must be served well done because of the danger of trichinosis. When in doubt about age or tenderness of a cut, pot roast. Always trim fat from bear meat—it has a strong, gamy flavor.
Makes 8–10 servings

1 (5–7-pound) bear rump roast or wild
    boar ham
2 tablespoons bacon or beef drippings
1 teaspoon salt
¼ teaspoon pepper
1 tart apple, peeled and cored
1 medium-size yellow onion, peeled
1½ cups apple cider or beef broth

Gravy:

1 large carrot, peeled and grated fine
1 stalk celery, minced
2 tablespoons butter, margarine, bacon
    or beef drippings
¼ cup unsifted flour
1 cup beef broth
½ teaspoon salt
⅛ teaspoon pepper
⅛ teaspoon liquid gravy browner

Trim bear of fat; if using boar, remove skin and trim fat to ½″. Heat drippings in a large, heavy kettle over moderate heat and brown meat on all sides, about 15 minutes. Add all but gravy ingredients, cover, and simmer 3½–4 hours until tender. Transfer to a hot platter and keep warm while making gravy; strain kettle liquid and reserve. Stir-fry carrot and celery in butter in a large skillet over moderate heat 8–10 minutes until carrot is tender; sprinkle with flour and brown lightly, stirring. Add kettle liquid and remaining gravy ingredients and heat, stirring, until thickened. Slice meat, not too thin, and serve with plenty of gravy. About 500 calories for each of 8 servings, 400 calories for each of 10 servings.

ROAST WHOLE RABBIT

Makes 4 servings

1 (3-pound) young, tender rabbit,
    cleaned and dressed (reserve liver,
    heart, and kidneys)
1 teaspoon salt
¼ teaspoon pepper
6 slices bacon or salt pork
½ cup water

Preheat oven to 350° F. Rub rabbit inside and out with salt and pepper; close cavity with poultry pins. Arrange rabbit breast side down in a crouching position on a rack in a large, heavy kettle. Drape with bacon, add water, cover, and bake ¾ hour; uncover and bake ½ hour. Remove bacon, baste with drippings, and bake 15 minutes longer until browned and fork tender. While rabbit roasts, make giblet stock* from liver, heart, and kidneys. When rabbit is done, remove to a hot platter, remove poultry pins, and let "rest" 10 minutes; make Pan Gravy using giblet stock. *To carve:* Cut off fore and hind legs and sever at each joint; split rabbit down center back, using poultry shears if necessary, then carve down along ribs. About 420 calories per serving.

VARIATIONS:

Roast Stuffed Rabbit: Loosely stuff rabbit with 1–1½ cups savory stuffing (see Some Sauces, Gravies, and Seasonings for Game and Game Birds). Sew cavity shut and roast as directed. About 515 calories per serving.

Roast Cut-Up Rabbit: Have rabbit disjointed; rub with salt and pepper, arrange on a rack in a heavy kettle, and drape with bacon or brush lavishly with melted butter, margarine, or bacon drippings. Add water and roast as directed, basting often with additional butter during last 15 minutes if bacon is not used. About 420 calories per serving.

Crisp Oven-"Fried" Rabbit: Have rabbit disjointed; dip in melted butter, then in seasoned bread crumbs to coat. Arrange in a greased shallow baking pan, cover with foil, and bake 1 hour. Uncover and bake 30 minutes longer without turning but basting often with melted butter, until crumbs are crisp and brown. About 460 calories per serving.

Oven-Barbecued Rabbit: Have rabbit disjointed and marinate in 1–1½ cups favorite barbecue sauce 3–4 hours in refrigerator. Lift rabbit from sauce, arrange on a rack in a shallow baking pan, add ½ cup water, cover with foil, and bake 45 minutes; uncover and bake 45 minutes longer, brushing often with barbecue sauce. About 460 calories per serving.

¢ FRIED RABBIT WITH PLANTATION GRAVY

Makes 4 servings

1 (3-pound) rabbit, cleaned, dressed, and disjointed
½ cup unsifted flour
1½ teaspoons salt
¼ teaspoon pepper
½ cup butter or margarine

Gravy:

3 tablespoons flour
1 cup chicken broth
1 cup milk
½ teaspoon salt
⅛ teaspoon pepper
⅛ teaspoon thyme
⅛ teaspoon marjoram

Dredge rabbit by shaking in a bag with flour, salt, and pepper. Melt butter in a large skillet over moderate heat and brown rabbit evenly on all sides, about 5 minutes. Turn heat to low, cover, and cook 1–1½ hours until fork tender, turning once or twice. For a crispy coating, cook uncovered the last 15 minutes. Transfer rabbit to a hot platter and keep warm. For the gravy,

blend flour into pan drippings but do not brown. Add broth and milk, then seasonings; heat, stirring, until thickened. Pass gravy separately. About 400 calories per serving.

VARIATION:

Rabbit with Tarragon and White Wine: Brown rabbit as directed, sprinkle with 2 tablespoons minced fresh tarragon or 1 teaspoon dried tarragon, cover, and cook as above. When making gravy, substitute 1 cup dry white wine for milk, omit the herbs, and stir in ¼ cup heavy cream just before serving. About 440 calories per serving.

¢ RABBIT STEW

Makes 4 servings

1 (3-pound) rabbit, cleaned, dressed, and disjointed
1 large yellow onion, peeled and coarsely chopped
4–5 medium-size carrots, peeled and cut in 1″ chunks
1½ teaspoons salt
⅛ teaspoon white pepper
½ teaspoon grated lemon rind
⅛ teaspoon mace (optional)
1½ cups water
½ cup milk
2 tablespoons butter or margarine
2 tablespoons flour blended with ¼ cup milk
1 tablespoon minced parsley

Place all but last 2 ingredients in a heavy kettle, cover, and simmer about 1½ hours until rabbit is fork tender. Blend in flour mixture and heat, stirring, until slightly thickened and no raw starch taste remains. Sprinkle with parsley and serve. About 450 calories per serving.

VARIATIONS:

¢ **Rabbit Stew with Dumplings:** Prepare stew as directed. Prepare 1 recipe Dumplings, drop on top of stew and cook as dumpling recipe directs. Sprinkle with parsley and serve. About 625 calories per serving.

¢ **Rabbit Pie:** Prepare stew as directed but omit carrots; spoon into an ungreased 2"–3" deep 2-quart casserole and place a pie funnel in center. Preheat oven to 425° F. Prepare 1 recipe Flaky Pastry I and roll into a circle 3" larger than casserole. Dampen casserole rim, lay pastry over rabbit, fold edges under, and crimp to seal. Brush with 1 egg yolk mixed with 1 tablespoon cold water; make a hole in pastry over pie funnel. Bake 30–40 minutes until golden brown. About 795 calories per serving.

¢ HASENPFEFFER (PEPPERY RABBIT STEW)

Germans prepare *Hasenpfeffer* many ways. In farm homes it's simply done as in the recipe below, in restaurants (and in Pennsylvania Dutch country) it's more highly spiced.
Makes 4 servings

1 (3-pound) rabbit, cleaned, dressed, and disjointed (save liver, heart, and kidneys)
¼ teaspoon peppercorns
¼ teaspoon mustard seeds
4 cloves
3 bay leaves
1 cup cider vinegar
1 cup water
1 large yellow onion, peeled and sliced very thin
½ cup plus 2 tablespoons unsifted flour
¼ cup butter, margarine, or bacon drippings
½ cup dry red wine or water
1 teaspoon salt
1 teaspoon sugar

Remove all fat from rabbit; place rabbit in a deep bowl with liver, heart, and kidneys. Tie spices and bay leaves in cheesecloth and simmer, covered, with vinegar, water, and onion 5 minutes; pour over rabbit, cover, and refrigerate 1–2 days, turning rabbit occasionally. Lift rabbit from marinade (do not dry) and dredge in ½ cup flour; brown in butter in a large, heavy skillet over moderate heat 4–5 minutes. Transfer to a 3-quart kettle. Brown remaining flour in drippings; strain marinade, add, and heat, stirring, until thickened. Pour over rabbit, add onion and cheesecloth

bag, also remaining ingredients, cover, and simmer 1–1½ hours until rabbit is tender. Shake kettle occasionally and check liquid level, adding a little extra water if mixture thickens too much. Serve with Potato Dumplings or noodles. About 370 calories per serving (without dumplings or noodles).

VARIATION:

¢ **Pennsylvania Dutch Hasenpfeffer:** When making marinade, substitute 1 teaspoon mixed pickling spice for the peppercorns, mustard seeds, and cloves. Proceed as directed, using ½ cup water instead of wine when cooking rabbit. Just before serving, stir in 2–3 crushed gingersnaps and 1 cup sour cream. Heat 1–2 minutes but do not boil. Good with mashed potatoes and boiled rutabaga. About 490 calories per serving (without potatoes and rutabaga).

JUGGED HARE OR RABBIT

Hare is European, jack rabbit the American counterpart; either can be "jugged" and so can any rabbits. The best jug is a deep brown earthenware pot, but a heavy casserole will do. Hare's blood used to be used to thicken the gravy, but few hunters today bother to save the blood of game (it must be caught in a clean plastic bag, then mixed with a little vinegar to keep it liquid).
Makes 8 servings

1 (5–6-pound) hare or jack rabbit or 2 (2½–3-pound) rabbits, cleaned, dressed, and disjointed
1 cup unsifted flour
4 slices bacon
2 tablespoons butter or margarine
1½ teaspoons salt
¼ teaspoon pepper
2 bay leaves
½ teaspoon thyme
½ teaspoon sage
1 tablespoon minced parsley
1 large yellow onion, peeled and stuck with 4 cloves
1 (2") strip lemon rind
⅛ teaspoon cayenne pepper
2 cups beef broth

2 cups dry port or red Bordeaux wine
2 tablespoons red currant jelly
Blood from hare or rabbits or ¼ cup
    unsifted flour blended with ½ cup cold
    water

Preheat oven to 325° F. Dredge hare by
shaking in flour in a bag. Brown bacon
in a large skillet over moderate heat,
crumble, and reserve. Brown hare in
drippings and butter, a few pieces at a
time, then transfer to an ungreased
6-quart bean pot or deep casserole. Add
bacon and all but last 2 ingredients,
cover tightly, and bake until tender, 2–3
hours for hare or jack rabbit, 1–1½
hours for rabbit. Discard lemon peel
and onion. Stir jelly and blood into liquid, return to oven, and bake uncovered
5 minutes; do not boil or mixture will
curdle. Or ladle about ½ cup hot liquid
into flour paste, blend in jelly, and stir
into pot. Bake uncovered about 5 minutes, stirring once, until thickened. Serve
hare from the pot. Good with Forcemeat Balls—they can be fried or simmered on top of jugged hare (see Forcemeat Ball recipe). Pass red currant jelly.
About 340 calories per serving (without
Forcemeat Balls).

¢ SQUIRREL FRICASSEE

Gray squirrels are better eating than the
red. Prepare by either of the following
recipes, cook like a rabbit, or use in
place of chicken in Brunswick Stew
(the original Brunswick Stew was made
with small furred game).
Makes 2 servings

1 squirrel, cleaned, dressed, and
    disjointed
⅓ cup unsifted flour
1 teaspoon salt
¼ teaspoon pepper
3 tablespoons butter or margarine
1 medium-size yellow onion, peeled
    and minced
1 clove garlic, peeled and crushed
    (optional)
¼ cup julienne strips of lean ham
¾ cup chicken broth
¼ cup milk or light cream

1 tablespoon flour blended with ¼ cup
    milk or light cream

Dredge squirrel in a mixture of flour,
salt, and pepper, then brown in a heavy
saucepan in butter over moderately high
heat. Add all but last ingredient, cover,
and simmer about 1 hour until tender.
Blend in flour paste and heat, stirring,
until thickened. Taste for salt and pepper
and adjust as needed. Serve with hot
biscuits. About 500 calories per serving
(without biscuits).

¢ CASSEROLE OF SQUIRRELS AND RICE

Makes 4–6 servings

¼ pound salt pork, cut in small dice
2 squirrels, cleaned, dressed, and
    disjointed
2 medium-size yellow onions, peeled and
    minced
¾ cup uncooked rice
1 medium-size sweet green pepper,
    cored, seeded, and minced
1 (1-pound) can tomatoes (do not drain)
1 cup chicken broth
½ teaspoon salt
¼ teaspoon pepper

Preheat oven to 325° F. Brown salt
pork in a 3-quart flameproof casserole
over moderately low heat; remove with
a slotted spoon and reserve. Pour off all
but 2 tablespoons drippings, raise heat
to moderate, and brown squirrels lightly
all over, 5–7 minutes; lift out and set
aside. Stir-fry onions, rice, and green
pepper in drippings 2–3 minutes until
rice is straw colored, return meat and
salt pork to casserole, add remaining
ingredients, breaking tomatoes up.
Cover and bake ½ hour, stir mixture,
re-cover, and bake about ½ hour longer
until squirrels are tender. About 510 calories for each of 4 servings, 340 calories
for each of 6 servings.

¢ BRAISED RACCOON, WOODCHUCK, OPOSSUM, OR MUSKRAT

Very young raccoon, opossum, woodchuck, and muskrat are tender enough

to roast like rabbit, but the average animals aren't. Braising is the way to make them tender. The fat of these animals is strong-flavored, so remove it before cooking.

Makes 4–6 servings

*1 raccoon, woodchuck, or opossum or
    2 medium-size muskrats, cleaned,
    dressed, and disjointed*
1 cup unsifted flour
3 teaspoons salt
¼ teaspoon pepper
¼ cup bacon or beef drippings
1 pound small white onions, peeled
*3 cups water or a ½ and ½ mixture of
    beef broth and water*
*6–8 medium-size carrots, peeled and cut
    in 2" chunks*
*½ small rutabaga, peeled and cut in
    1–1½" cubes*

Discard any fat from animal, then dredge in flour mixed with 2 teaspoons salt and the pepper. Brown in drippings in a large, heavy kettle over high heat, 5–7 minutes; lift out and set aside. Brown onions in drippings 10–12 minutes over moderate heat; add water and stir, scraping up browned bits. Return meat to kettle, add remaining ingredients, including remaining salt. Cover and simmer until tender, 3–4 hours depending on age and size of animal. If you prefer, transfer kettle to a 325° F. oven and bake, covered, 30–40 minutes per pound of animal. Lift meat and vegetables to a hot deep platter, top with a little cooking liquid, and pass the rest. Good with applesauce. Calorie counts unavailable for raccoon, woodchuck, opossum and muskrat.

GAME BIRDS

America has about a dozen different families of game birds—everything from dark-fleshed ducks and geese to delicate white-meated pheasants. With one or two exceptions, game birds can be prepared by the same basic methods. Be-cause these methods are determined more by the size of the bird than by the kind or color of its flesh, birds are grouped here by size.

America's Popular Game Birds

Giant Game Birds (8–16 pounds):

Wild Turkey: These huge, often sinewy birds are in a category by themselves.

Large Game Birds (4–9 pounds):

Wild Goose: Wild goose usually means *Canada Goose,* but good, too, is the smaller (3–4 pounds) *Brant.*

Medium-Size Game Birds (1–4 pounds):

Wild Duck: The best table ducks are *Mallards, Pintails, Canvasbacks, Ring-Necks, Redheads, Gadwalls, Wood Ducks, Black Ducks, Ruddy Ducks, Scaups,* and the small (usually about ¾ pound) *Teals (Green-Winged, Blue-Winged, Cinnamon).* All feed upon grasses, seeds, and grains and usually (though not invariably) have fine flavor. Not so fine are the fish-eating ducks: *Mergansers, Scoters, Harlequins, Goldeneyes, Buffleheads, Old Squaws,* and *Shovelers.*

Other Waterfowl: Coots (Mud Hens) and *Gallinules.* These plump, chicken-like birds may or may not have good flavor—depends upon what they've been eating and how brackish their habitat.

Upland Birds: Pheasant, all large *Grouse (Ruffed, Sage, Blue, Sharp-Tailed, Prairie Chicken).* (*Note:* In America, grouse are often called partridge. There are, however, two true partridges in America [see Small Game Birds]).

Small Game Birds (¼–1 pound):

Quail, especially *Bobwhite;* small *Grouse (Spruce* and *Ptarmigan); Partridge (Gray* and *Chukar); Dove, Pigeon,* and *Squab* (young pigeon); *Woodcock, Snipe.* Plovers were popular once, but they have been overkilled and are now protected.

About Frozen and Canned Game Birds:
Gourmet markets sell most of the popular game birds frozen, also canned small birds. Always prepare frozen birds by wrapper directions, if any. If not, thaw in the refrigerator in the original wrapper before cooking; allow about 24 hours for small- or medium-size birds, 1½–2 days for a wild goose or turkey up to 12 pounds. Giblets are usually tucked inside the body cavity and should be removed as soon as possible; thaw separately. Once thawed, prepare frozen birds as you would the fresh; never refreeze. Canned birds are already cooked and need only be heated before serving (follow can directions). Those that have been smoked may have strong flavor; to tone it down, simmer in water to cover about 10 minutes, drain, pat dry, and then follow label instructions.

How Much Game Bird Per Serving?
Allow about 1 pound dressed bird per serving; if birds are very small, this may mean 2–3 birds per person.

How to Clean and Dress Game Birds

The procedure is similar for all birds, though downy ducks and geese require an extra plucking. In days past, birds were bled after being shot, but newer bullets eliminate the need. When birds are eviscerated depends upon weather and whether or not they're to be hung. In cold weather, they needn't be gutted immediately, and, of course, if they are to be hung, they should not be drawn until after hanging.

To Hang: Nowadays, birds are hung only until cold or, at most, 24 hours. If you prefer a gamier flavor, however, by all means hang the bird longer. Pick a cool, dry, shady, well-ventilated spot away from insects and pets and hang undressed, undrawn birds by their feet. How long? Depends on weather (birds ripen faster in warm weather, the bird's age (old birds need to hang longer than young), and the sophistication of your palate. Usually, 2–3 days' hanging will produce a pretty "high" bird. Best tests: Pluck a feather from just above the tail; if it pulls out easily, the bird has hung long enough. Or ruffle abdomen feathers; if the skin has a blue-green tinge, the bird is ready for cooking.

To Remove Feathers: All but the smallest birds with superfragile skin should be plucked and if possible, dry plucked (dunking a bird in hot water affects flavor). Chill bird 24 hours, then, starting at the neck, pull out feathers, a few at a time, in quick gentle jerks against the grain. Use a light touch over the breast, where skin is tender. When bird is plucked, tweeze out pinfeathers. *Tip:* The neatest way to pluck is outdoors, directly into a paper bag. Never burn feathers—the smell is horrendous. If a bird won't dry pluck, dunk head first into a large kettle of simmering water and let stand about 15 seconds; repeat 3–4 times. Shake off excess moisture and pluck as above.

To Remove Duck and Goose Down: Pluck outer feathers. Melt paraffin in boiling water in a large pot (for each bird you'll need 1 cake paraffin and 2 quarts water). Dip birds head first into pot to coat, remove, and cool until paraffin hardens. Peel off paraffin and the down will come away with it. Redip and peel as needed.

To Singe: After birds are plucked, burn off any hair, using long wooden matches, a candle, or spill, taking care not to scorch the flesh.

To Skin: Tiny game birds (especially woodcock, snipe, pigeon, and dove) have such tender skin they can't be plucked. To remove feathers, slit neck skin lengthwise, then carefully work skin free from breast and back, wings, and legs with fingers—it's rather like taking off coveralls.

To Eviscerate:
(1) Cut off head, peel neck skin down around shoulders, then cut off neck as close to body as possible, leaving windpipe and esophagus intact. Reach under

flap of breast skin and pull out crop and attached tubes.

(2) Make a cut below breastbone, just big enough to admit your hand, reach in, feel around for firm, round gizzard and gently ease it out of bird (intestines, liver, and heart should come away with it).

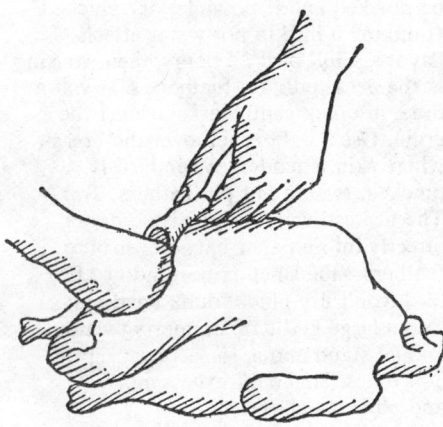

Also scoop out kidneys, lungs, and any lumps of fat. Discard all organs except gizzard, liver, and heart.

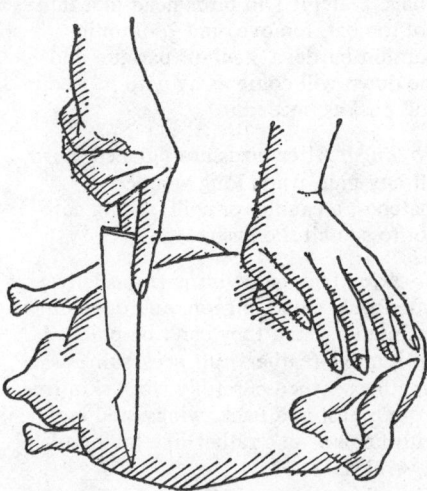

(3) Cut out oil sac at base of tail.
(4) Wipe bird inside and out with a damp cloth, then pat dry.

To Prepare Giblets:

Liver: Separate gall bladder from liver —carefully so it doesn't rupture, spilling the bitter juices inside; trim away any greenish spots on liver.

Gizzard: Cut away fat and any bits of intestine; also scrape off outer membrane. Cut gizzard open, peel away inner membrane, bringing with it contents of gizzard.

Heart: Trim off veins and arteries, peel away membrane.

To Make Giblet Stock: (*Note:* Method may also be used for making stock from the hearts and livers of rabbits, squirrels, and other small furred game.) Wash giblets well in cool water, cover with cold salted water (1 teaspoon salt per pint water), cover, and simmer about 1 hour, replenishing water as needed. If you plan to use giblets in recipes, reduce cooking time so that they don't toughen and dry; liver, gizzard, and heart will be tender in 20 minutes, neck in 30. (*Note:* The liver of a large wild goose or turkey will need about ½ hour, the heart, gizzard, and neck 1½–2 hours.) Taste stock for salt and pepper and add as needed. Use as is for making soups, sauces, and stews or, if you like, strain first through a fine sieve lined with a double thickness of cheesecloth.

To Cut Up Birds: Using poultry shears or a sharp knife, cut as follows:

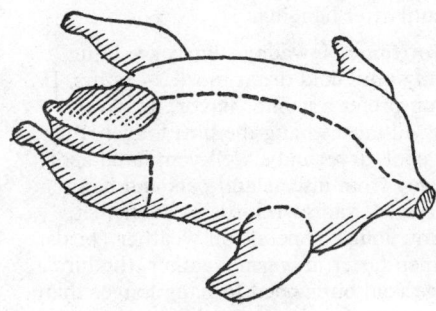

To Halve (Split)

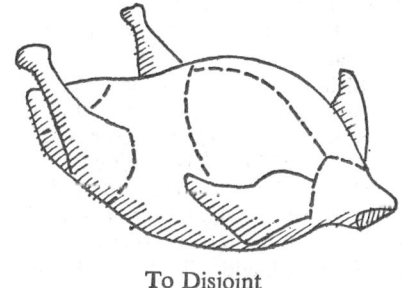

To Disjoint

How to Cook Game Birds

The principles of cooking game birds are essentially the same as for domestic fowl —with two differences. Game birds have little or no fat and must be barded (wrapped in bacon or sheets of salt pork or other fat) and/or heavily basted to keep them from drying out. Second, dark-meated game birds like wild duck are often served rare (some people want them only passed through the oven). Otherwise, the basics are similar. Tough old birds, obviously, roast poorly and should be steamed, stewed, or braised. Young tender birds, like young tender chickens, are gloriously adaptable. (*Note:* Always try to bring game birds to room temperature before cooking.)

To Roast (best for young small- or medium-size birds; wild goose and turkey should be roasted only if very young and small—less than 8 pounds). (*Note:* This method is for well-done birds; for rare wild duck, see the separate recipe that follows.)

General Preparation: Have birds cleaned and dressed; sprinkle cavities with salt and pepper.

Basic Method: Preheat oven to 350° F. Place ½ small peeled, cored apple and/or ½ small peeled yellow onion inside each bird, also 1 bay leaf, a sprig of fresh sage, thyme, or marjoram or a small *bouquet garni** tied in cheesecloth, and 1–2 tablespoons medium-dry sherry or port. Skewer or sew openings shut, then fold wings back and under and tie legs together. Arrange birds breast side up on a rack in a shallow roasting pan. Cover breast of each with a double thickness of cheesecloth saturated with melted butter, margarine, bacon drippings, or lard. Roast uncovered, basting often with additional melted fat, until leg joints move easily and breast meat feels tender. Use the following times as a guide:

Wild Turkey or Goose: 25–30 minutes per pound

Medium-Size (1–4 pounds) Birds: 30–40 minutes per pound

Small (under 1 pound) Birds: 50–60 minutes per pound

If birds have been skinned, leave cheesecloth cover on until last 5 minutes so they will not dry out; otherwise, remove during last 15 minutes so birds will brown. Never try to brown skinned birds. Transfer birds to a hot platter, remove strings and stuffing, and let "rest" 10 minutes before serving. Serve small birds whole, carve larger birds as you would chicken or turkey.* *For Extra Flavor:* Baste birds throughout roasting with Herb, Parsley, Tarragon, Shallot, or Garlic Butter or with a ½ and ½ mixture of melted butter and dry red or white wine, beer, or fruit juice. Stuff birds with fresh berries or cherries, brandied peaches, dates or figs, or sultana raisins sprinkled with brandy instead of apple, onion, and herbs. *To Flambé Small Birds:* Arrange roasted birds in a deep platter, pour ¼–⅓ cup warmed brandy or rum over all, blaze with a match, and baste with flaming liquid until flames die.

VARIATIONS:

Game Birds Baked in Vine Leaves: Tie fresh or brined grape leaves around each bird, cover with buttered cheesecloth, and roast as directed, removing cheesecloth and vine leaves toward end of cooking. Drain off pan drippings, pour ¼ cup port or Madeira over each bird, and finish roasting, basting often. Remove birds to platter, add peeled seedless green grapes to pan (allow ¼ cup grapes for each bird) and warm gently while birds "rest." Pour over birds and serve.

Game Birds with Calvados, Cream, and Truffles: Roast birds as directed through point of removing cheesecloth; drain off all but 1–2 tablespoons drippings. Pour ¼ cup each calvados (or brandy or champagne) and heavy cream over each bird if medium size, 2 tablespoons if small, and finish roasting as directed, basting 1–2 times. Lift birds to platter; to pan liquid add 1–2 minced truffles, warm briefly, and pour over birds.

Game Birds Smitane: Roast birds as directed and transfer to platter. Make Pan Gravy from drippings, then for each cup gravy, mix in ⅓ cup sour cream, ¼ cup sautéed sliced mushrooms, and 5–6 sliced ripe or stuffed green olives. Spoon some sauce over the birds and pass the rest. For a glamorous dinner, serve only the boned breasts Smitane style. Arrange them, slightly overlapping, on a platter, smother with sauce, and surround with artichoke bottoms filled with buttered green peas.

Virginia-Style Game Birds: Roast birds as directed; if tiny, leave whole, otherwise halve or quarter according to size. Arrange on slices of sautéed, baked ham (Smithfield is best) and keep warm. Make Pan Gravy from drippings and for each cup gravy whisk in 2 tablespoons red currant jelly and ¼ teaspoon finely grated orange rind. Pour over all and serve.

Regency-Style Game Birds: Roast birds as directed; if tiny, leave whole, otherwise halve or quarter according to size. Serve on slices of toast spread with pâté and pass Victoria Sauce.

Roast Stuffed Game Birds (best for young birds weighing 3–8 pounds):

General Preparation: Same as for roasting.

Basic Method: Stuff bird loosely with any favorite stuffing (see Some Sauces, Gravies, and Seasonings for Game and Game Birds), allowing ¾–1 cup per pound of bird. Skewer openings shut, tie legs together, and fold wings back and under. Cover with butter-saturated cheesecloth and roast as for unstuffed birds, increasing cooking times about 10 minutes per pound. (*Note:* For an extra-moist bird, add a little extra liquid to stuffing.)

To Braise (best for not-so-young small- and medium-size whole birds):

General Preparation: Same as for roasting.

Basic Method: Preheat oven to 350° F. Tie a 2″–3″ strip of lemon or orange rind in cheesecloth with a *bouquet garni** and tuck inside each bird. Tie legs together, fold wings back and under. If birds have been skinned, dredge lightly in flour. Brown birds lightly all over in 2 tablespoons butter and set aside. Make a bed of butter-sautéed, minced vegetables in an ungreased Dutch oven (for each bird allow ¼ cup each onion, carrot, mushrooms, and celery, also 1 tablespoon minced parsley). Place birds on vegetables and pour in just enough beef or chicken broth (or a ½ and ½ mixture of chicken broth and dry red or white wine, beer, grape or orange juice) to moisten. If you like, add a peeled clove garlic. Cover and braise until leg joints move easily: Medium-size birds will take 35–45 minutes per pound, small birds 50–60. Baste 1 or 2 times with pan juices. Lift birds to a hot deep platter and keep warm. Skim fat from liquid, remove garlic clove. Purée vegetables and liquid in an electric blender at low speed or put through a fine sieve. Pour into a saucepan, and for each 1 cup purée add ¼ cup heavy cream or 1 tablespoon flour blended with 1 tablespoon cold water; heat, stirring, until thickened; do not boil. Pour some sauce over birds and pass the remainder. (*Note:* Birds can be halved or quartered before braising. Brown in butter as directed and arrange on vegetables. Add 1 bouquet garni, tied in cheesecloth, to casserole, also 1 strip lemon or orange rind. Cover and braise as directed, allowing ¾ hour for quartered medium-size birds and 30–40 minutes for small halved birds.)

VARIATIONS:

Curried Game Birds: Prepare by basic method above but rub birds well with curry powder before browning and refrigerate 4–6 hours. Also mix 1 teaspoon curry powder into each cup sautéed vegetables. Otherwise, proceed as directed. Serve birds on a bed of Rice Pilaf mixed with chopped pistachio nuts and topped with sauce.

Game Birds Braised with Cabbage: Prepare by basic recipe but braise on a 1½" bed of shredded red or green cabbage instead of sautéed vegetables. Add garlic and liquid called for, also 2 fresh link sausages, sliced ½" thick. When birds are done, remove garlic and serve on bed of cabbage.

Game Birds with Caraway, Sauerkraut, and Raisins: Brown birds as in basic method, place in a buttered casserole on a 1" bed of drained sauerkraut sprinkled with 1 tablespoon caraway seeds and ½ cup each minced yellow onion and seedless raisins. Add 1 cup beef broth, cover, and braise until tender. Good with tall, cool glasses of beer.

Norman Game Birds: Brown birds as in basic method, place in a buttered casserole on a 1" bed of chopped, peeled apples that have been lightly sprinkled with nutmeg and sugar and liberally dotted with butter. Add no liquid, cover, and braise as directed. When tender, lift birds to a platter, stir 2–3 tablespoons heavy cream into apples and, if you like, 2–3 tablespoons calvados, brandy, or apple cider. Spoon mixture around birds or pass separately.

To Oven Broil (best for very young tender small- or medium-size birds):

General Preparation: Have birds cleaned and dressed but not skinned. Large pheasant or duck should be halved or quartered. Tiny birds will broil more evenly if left whole, then flattened slightly with the heel of your hand.

Basic Method: Preheat broiler, setting oven temperature at 350° F. Place whole birds breast side down, pieces skin side down, on a buttered rack on a foil-lined broiler pan, sprinkle lightly with salt and pepper, and brush well with melted butter. Broil as far from heat as possible, 15–20 minutes, turn, and broil 15–20 minutes longer until evenly browned and juices run clear when thigh is pricked. (*Note:* For rare duck, broil 5" from heat 8–10 minutes per side.)
For Extra Flavor: Brush birds with Tarragon, Parsley, or Shallot Butter instead of plain butter.

To Charcoal Broil (best for very young tender small- or medium-size birds):

General Preparation: Same as for oven broiling.

Basic Method: Prepare a moderately hot charcoal fire.* Lay birds breast side up, pieces skin side up, on a well-oiled grill and broil 6" from heat 30–45 minutes until fork tender, turning often and brushing frequently with melted unsalted butter or a ½ and ½ mixture of melted butter and lemon juice. Season just before serving.

VARIATIONS:

Barbecued Game Birds: Marinate birds 2–3 hours in refrigerator in a favorite barbecue sauce, then broil as directed, basting often with a ½ and ½ mixture of sauce and melted butter.

Game Birds in Foil: Halve or quarter birds, brush with melted butter, and sprinkle with salt and pepper; wrap each piece in well-greased foil and cook 4" from coals 30–40 minutes until fork tender; turn packages after 15 minutes. Unwrap, place pieces skin side down, and grill 4–5 minutes to brown.

To Spit Roast (best for young small- or medium-size birds):

General Preparation: Same as for oven broiling.

In Oven or Rotisserie: Preheat unit. Skewer neck skin and wings of each bird to body, tie legs together, pulling close to body. Bard* (wrap) birds with bacon or salt pork. (*Note:* Butchers will often do this for you.) Spit birds lengthwise without crowding, adjust balance as needed, and lock tines in place. Roast 5"–6" from heat, allowing ¾–1 hour for small birds, 1–1½ hours for the medium size, basting frequently with melted unsalted butter. Remove barding fat during last 10–15 minutes so birds will brown. Take from spit, remove strings and skewers, season, and serve.

Over Charcoal: Prepare a moderately hot charcoal fire.* Prepare birds as for oven spit roasting, roast 5" from coals using above times as a guide.

To Panfry (Sauté; best for young small birds):

General Preparation: Have birds cleaned, dressed, and halved.

Basic Method: Lightly sprinkle birds with salt and pepper and dust with flour. Brown 2–3 minutes on a side in ¼ cup butter, margarine, or cooking oil over moderate heat. Turn heat to low and continue cooking 10 minutes, turning frequently. Serve as is or smothered with Pan Gravy made from drippings. *For Extra Flavor:* Rub birds with garlic before dusting with flour, also, if you like, with thyme, sage, or marjoram.

VARIATIONS:

Game Birds Américaine: Dip birds in flour, then eaten egg, then toasted bread crumbs and panfry as directed. Serve on a bed of wild rice garnished with broiled, bacon-wrapped giblets and sautéed button mushrooms and cherry tomatoes.

Deviled Game Birds: Panfry birds as directed, transfer to a hot platter and keep warm; drain all but 2 tablespoons drippings from pan, add 2 tablespoons each beef broth and minced gherkins, 1 tablespoon each lemon juice and Worcestershire sauce, and 2 teaspoons Dijon-style mustard. Warm briefly, pour over birds, and serve.

Game Birds Lucullus: Panfry birds as directed and transfer to platter. Drain all but 2 tablespoons drippings from pan; for each bird sauté 1 (½") slice pâté that has been lightly dredged in flour until golden brown. Place pâté on unbuttered toast cut to fit, top with a slice or 2 of truffle and arrange around birds. Pass Madeira Sauce.

Spiced and Spiked Game Birds: Dredge game birds in ¼ cup unsifted flour mixed with 1 teaspoon nutmeg, ¾ teaspoon each salt and cinnamon, ¼ teaspoon each ginger and cloves and a pinch pepper. Panfry as directed and transfer to platter. Stir ¼ cup each heavy cream and rum, brandy or sherry into drippings, warm briefly and pour over birds.

To Stew (best for large birds or birds of questionable age and tenderness): Follow directions for stewing a hen or capon (see Chicken).

To Steam (best for large birds or those of questionable tenderness): Follow directions for stewing a hen or capon (see Chicken). Also see Potted Wild Goose or Turkey, a method of oven steaming.

About Pressure Cooking Game Birds

Don't. It's a sacrilege to pressure cook any succulent young bird (it will disintegrate). As for big old birds, they suffer too, becoming tougher and drier. Better to steam or stew them.

POTTED WILD GOOSE OR TURKEY

Wild goose or turkey weighing more than 8 pounds is of questionable age and tenderness. "Potting," which used to be done in huge brown earthenware casseroles, makes it succulent. Save giblets for gravy or soup.
Makes 6–10 servings

1 (8–16-pound) wild goose or turkey, cleaned and dressed
1 tablespoon salt

¼ teaspoon pepper
6–8 slices salt pork or fat bacon
2 large yellow onions, peeled and
    quartered
2 large carrots, peeled and cut in 1"
    chunks
2 bay leaves
1 bouquet garni,* tied in cheesecloth
1 quart chicken or beef broth or water
½ cup melted butter, margarine, or
    bacon drippings

Preheat oven to 325° F. Rub bird inside
and out with salt and pepper; tie legs
together and to body, fold wings back
and under. Place bird breast side up on a
rack in a large Dutch oven and drape
with salt pork. Add all but last ingredient,
cover, and bake about 25 minutes per
pound, basting with pan juices every 30
minutes. About ½ hour before bird is
done, drain off liquid with a bulb baster,
remove vegetables and seasonings and
discard. Raise oven to 425° F., and pour
melted butter over bird. Roast uncovered,
basting often, until golden brown and
legs move easily in sockets. Transfer to a
hot large platter, remove strings, and let
"rest" 10 minutes. Make Giblet Gravy if
you like. About 330 calories for each of
6 servings (from an 8-pound bird), 445
calories for each of 10 servings (from a
16-pound bird). (Note: 16 pounds may
seem too big a bird for just 10 servings.
It isn't because a mature wild goose or
turkey has so little edible meat. The legs
and wings are too tough and sinewy to be
good.)

⚔ RARE ROAST WILD DUCK

For crisp brown skin and rare meat,
wild duck must be roasted fast at high
heat. It should not be stuffed, so if you
want stuffing, bake it separately
beforehand.
Makes 2 servings

1 (2–2½-pound) wild duck, cleaned and
    dressed
1 teaspoon salt
¼ teaspoon pepper
1 bouquet garni,* tied in cheesecloth
2 tablespoons melted butter, margarine,
    or bacon drippings

Gravy:

½ cup medium-dry red wine, chicken or
    beef broth, or giblet stock*
2 tablespoons minced shallots or scallions
1 bay leaf
4 peppercorns
⅛ teaspoon nutmeg (optional)

Set a shallow roasting pan and rack in
oven while it preheats to 450° F. Rub
duck inside and out with salt and pepper
and tuck bouquet garni in cavity. Tie legs
together, fold wings back, and brush bird
with butter. Roast uncovered, breast side
up, about 15 minutes for very rare, 25
minutes for medium rare. Meanwhile,
simmer gravy ingredients, uncovered, 8–
10 minutes; strain and keep warm.
Transfer duck to a carving board with
well, remove strings and let "rest" 5
minutes. Carve meat from duck and
arrange on a hot serving platter. Drain
blood and juices into gravy and warm
briefly, stirring; do not boil or mixture
will curdle. Taste for salt and adjust as
needed. Spoon some gravy over duck and
pass the rest. About 260 calories per
serving.

VARIATIONS:

⚔ **Spit-Roasted Rare Wild Duck:**
Preheat oven or rotisserie; season and
truss bird as above, also skewer neck flap
and wings to body. Balance lengthwise
on spit, and roast 5" from heat 20
minutes for very rare and 30 for medium
rare, basting frequently with melted
butter. Make gravy and serve as directed.
About 260 calories per serving.

⚔ **Charcoal Spit-Roasted Rare Wild
Duck:** Build a very hot charcoal fire.*
Prepare, spit and roast duck 5" from
heat as above. Be prepared to douse
flare-ups. About 260 calories per serving.

⚔ **Tyrolean-Style Roast Wild Duck:**
Omit bouquet garni and spoon ¾ cup hot
applesauce mixed with 1 teaspoon each
cinnamon and nutmeg into duck cavity;
sew or close with poultry pins. Brush
duck with ½ cup hot red wine vinegar
mixed with 2 tablespoons each sugar and
olive or other cooking oil. Roast as
above, basting 1 or 2 times with vinegar

mixture. Prepare gravy and serve as directed. About 285 calories per serving.

⚔ **Pressed Wild Duck:** Roast duck very rare and prepare gravy. Meanwhile, warm a chafing dish over simmering water. Slice off both duck breasts and place in chafing dish; if leg meat is tender, add (if not, save for soup). Pour blood and juices over meat and adjust heat so water barely simmers. Cut up carcass and put all but leg bones in well of a duck press. Pour gravy over bones and press, forcing gravy and juices into a hot bowl; repress twice. Stir in 2 tablespoons warm brandy and pour into chafing dish. Serve with wild rice or bulgur wheat. (*Note:* If you don't have a duck press, put bones through fine blade of meat grinder or break up with a mallet. Warm 1–2 minutes in gravy, strain, and pour into chafing dish.) About 225 calories per serving.

⚔ **ROAST MERGANSER**

Mergansers, scoters, and other fish-eating ducks need special attention to rid them of their fishy flavor. They're best not stuffed and cooked fairly well done.
Makes 2 servings

1 (2–2½-pound) *merganser or other fish-eating duck, cleaned and dressed*
1 *tablespoon salt*
½ *lemon*
½ *cup cider vinegar*
1 *yellow onion, peeled*
1 *stick cinnamon*
1 *tart apple, peeled and cored*
Boiling water
2 *tablespoons melted butter or margarine*

Rub duck inside and out with salt and lemon; pour vinegar into cavity, add onion, cover loosely, and let stand at room temperature 1–2 hours. Preheat oven to 350° F. Drain vinegar from duck and remove onion; wash inside and out with tepid water and pat dry on paper toweling. Poke cinnamon stick into apple hollow, and tuck inside bird. Tie legs together, fold wings back and under, and place breast side up in a shallow

roasting pan. Pour in boiling water to a depth of ½″ and roast, uncovered, 15 minutes, basting twice; drain off water. Brush duck with butter and roast, uncovered, 1 hour or until legs move easily in sockets. If breast browns too fast, cover with cheesecloth dipped in butter or, if bird is fat, with foil. Let bird "rest" 5–10 minutes before serving. Remove strings and discard apple and cinnamon. Instead of making Pan Gravy (drippings may taste fishy), serve with a suitable sauce (see some Sauces, Gravies, and Seasonings for Game and Game Birds). About 210 calories per serving (without sauce).

SUPRÊMES OF PHEASANT À LA CRÈME

When pheasants have sinewy legs, use them for soup and prepare the breasts this way.
Makes 4 servings

2 (2½–3-pound) *pheasants, guinea fowl, grouse, or partridges, cleaned and dressed*
2 *cups chicken broth*
1 *cup water*
1 *small yellow onion, peeled*
1 *carrot, peeled*
1 *stalk celery, cut in 1″ lengths*
4 *peppercorns*
3 *tablespoons butter or margarine*
¼ *cup unsifted flour*
¾ *cup heavy cream*
½ *teaspoon salt*
⅛ *teaspoon nutmeg*
⅛ *teaspoon paprika*

Place birds breast side up, side by side, on a rack in a large kettle; add broth, water, vegetables, and peppercorns. Cover and simmer ¾–1 hour until breasts are tender; cool birds in broth ½ hour, lift out, and carefully remove breasts so halves are intact. Skin breasts (save skin and remainder of birds for soup). Strain broth, then boil uncovered to reduce to 1½ cups. Melt butter in a large skillet over moderate heat, blend in flour, slowly add broth, cream, salt, and nutmeg, and heat, stirring, until thickened and no raw starch taste

SOME SAUCES, GRAVIES AND SEASONINGS FOR GAME AND GAME BIRDS

	Sauces and Gravies	Stuffings	Herbs, Spices, Seasonings	Condiments
Venison, Bear, Wild Boar	Bordelaise Brown Sauce Fines Herbes Bourguignonne Charcutière (wild boar) Chevreuil (venison) Cumberland Grand Veneur (venison) Madeira Pan Gravy Périgueux Poivrade Romaine Victoria		Bay leaves Cinnamon Cloves Garlic Ginger Juniper berries Mustard Onion Paprika Parsley Rosemary Sage Thyme	Applesauce Chutney Cranberry sauce Currant jelly Gooseberry jam Rosemary jelly Wine jelly
Small furred game (Rabbit, Squirrel, Muskrat, Raccoon)	Barbecue Bordelaise Brown Sauce Fines Herbes Bourguignonne Chasseur Madeira Marchands de Vin Pan Gravy Périgueux Poivrade Robert Victoria	Basic Bread Chestnut Sage and Onion Wild Rice	Basil Bay leaves Cinnamon Cloves Garlic Ginger Juniper berries Lemon Mace Marjoram Mustard Nutmeg Onion Orange Oregano Parsley Sage Tarragon Thyme	Same as for venison
Game Birds	Bercy Bigarade Chasseur Chaud-Froid Diable Espagnole Giblet Gravy Madeira Pan Gravy Périgueux Poivrade Robert Rouennaise (duck) Suprême Victoria	Apple-Pecan Basic Bread Chestnut Chestnut-Mushroom Corn Bread and Sausage Giblet Sage and Onion Wild Rice	Bay leaves Caraway Cinnamon Cloves Coriander Dill Garlic Ginger Juniper berries Lemon Nutmeg Onion Orange Oregano Paprika Parsley Rosemary Sage Tarragon Thyme Truffles	Applesauce Cranberry sauce Currant jelly Gooseberry jam Pickled or Brandied peaches Rosemary jelly Wine jelly

remains. Add breasts and warm slowly (do not boil), basting with sauce; lift to a hot platter, coat generously with sauce and dust with paprika. Pass remaining sauce. About 475 calories per serving.

VARIATIONS:

⚖️ **Breasts of Pheasant in Aspic:** Simmer birds as directed, omitting carrot. Remove breasts, skin, and chill 3–4 hours. Save 2 cups strained cooking liquid, mix in 1 envelope unflavored gelatin, 1 egg white beaten to soft peaks, and 1 crushed eggshell. Heat, stirring with a whisk, until mixture foams up. Remove from heat, stir once, and let stand undisturbed 5 minutes. Line a sieve with a fine dish towel wrung out in cold water, set over a deep bowl, pour in hot liquid (egg, shell, and all), and let drip through to clarify. *Do not stir.* Chill clarified aspic until syrupy. Set breasts on a rack over a tray and spoon a thin, even layer of aspic over each. Chill until tacky, then decorate with truffle and pimiento cutouts and sprigs of fresh parsley or tarragon. Chill briefly to set; keep remaining aspic over warm water. Add another thin aspic layer to seal in designs; chill until firm. Also chill remaining aspic, then dice and use to garnish platter along with radish roses and watercress sprigs. About 210 calories per serving.

Breasts of Pheasant Chaud-Froid: Simmer birds as directed, omitting carrot. Remove breasts, skin, and chill. Make sauce as in Suprêmes of Pheasant (above), reducing flour to 3 tablespoons. Mix 1 envelope unflavored gelatin with ⅓ cup water and heat, stirring to dissolve; mix into sauce and chill until mixture will coat a metal spoon. Set breasts on a rack over a tray and cover with a thin, even layer of gelatin mixture. Chill until tacky, then continue building up layers until no meat shows through. While final layer is still tacky, decorate as above. If you like, seal in designs with clear aspic made using 2 cups canned chicken broth. About 475 calories per serving.

FRICASSEE OF GAME BIRDS

A delicious way to prepare not so young and tender birds.
Makes 6 servings

2 (3-pound) game birds, cleaned, dressed, and disjointed
Giblets from birds
1 yellow onion, peeled and sliced thin
1 stalk celery, cut in 1" lengths
2 (10½-ounce) cans chicken broth
2 tablespoons butter or margarine
½ teaspoon rosemary
1 tablespoon lemon juice
1 cup light cream (about)
⅓ cup unsifted flour blended with ⅓ cup milk
1 teaspoon salt (about)
⅛ teaspoon white pepper (about)
1 tablespoon minced parsley

Place birds, giblets, onion, celery, broth, butter, rosemary, and lemon juice in a kettle, cover, and simmer 1½–2 hours until meat is fork tender but not falling off bones; cool birds in broth ½ hour. Strain broth, measure, and add enough light cream to total 3 cups. Skin birds and, if you like, bone, keeping meat in as large pieces as possible. Pour broth mixture into a clean saucepan, blend in flour paste and heat, stirring, until thickened. Add salt and pepper, taste and adjust as needed. Add meat, mix gently, and heat, shaking pan now and then, 5 minutes. Sprinkle with parsley and serve with boiled noodles or rice. About 340 calories per serving (without noodles or rice).

SALMI OF GAME BIRDS

Salmi is a spectacular do-ahead ragout of fowl finished at the table.
Makes 4–6 servings

2 (2–2½-pound) pheasants, guinea hens or ducks, cleaned and dressed
⅓ cup minced scallions
2 tablespoons butter or margarine
1½ cups dry white wine
4 peppercorns
4 juniper berries
Giblets from birds

III. QUICK AND EASY RECIPES

Quick Fish Stew – Spaghetti with Butter – Confetti Corn, Baked Eggs,
and Broccoli – Baked Alaska

Quick Fish Stew (page 572)

Spaghetti with Butter, Cream, Parmesan, and Mushrooms (pages 702-03)

Confetti Corn (page 825); Baked Eggs in Tomatoes (pages 659-60); and Osaka
Skillet Broccoli (page 798)

Baked Alaska (page 1057); and Cherries Jubilee (page 1026)

1½ cups hot Espagnole Sauce
½ pound sautéed button mushrooms
1–2 truffles, sliced thin

Early in the day, roast birds by basic method until barely tender; cool until easy to handle. Carefully remove breasts so halves are intact, and cut meat from legs; discard all skin, wrap, and refrigerate meat. Also wrap and chill carcass, wings and leg bones. About 1 hour before serving, place carcass, wings, and leg bones in a saucepan, add scallions, butter, wine, seasonings, and giblets, partially cover, and simmer ¾ hour. Strain into Espagnole Sauce and mix well. Place reserved meat in a chafing dish, add sauce, and carry to table. Set over simmering water and heat, basting meat with sauce, until piping hot. Scatter mushrooms and truffles on top and serve from chafing dish. About 580 calories for each of 4 servings, 390 calories for each of 6 servings.

PIGEON PIE

Makes 6 servings

1 pound lean boiled ham, cut in ½"
  cubes
6 pigeons, doves, or other very small
  game birds, cleaned, dressed, and
  halved lengthwise
Pigeon livers or 2–3 chicken livers
2 tablespoons butter or margarine
2 tablespoons minced parsley
1 teaspoon salt
¼ teaspoon pepper
1½–2 cups chicken broth or Chicken
  Gravy
1 recipe Flaky Pastry I
1 egg yolk beaten with 1 tablespoon
  cold water (glaze)

Preheat oven to 425° F. Stand a pie funnel in the center of an ungreased 1½-quart 2" deep casserole; layer ham into casserole. Arrange birds breast side down on ham. Sauté livers in butter 2–3 minutes over moderate heat, then mince and mix with parsley; scatter mixture over birds, sprinkle with salt and pepper and pour in 1½ cups broth. Mix pastry and roll into a circle 3" larger than casserole; dampen rim of casserole, top with pastry, roll pastry edges under even with rim, and crimp to seal. Make a hole in middle of pastry to expose funnel so steam can escape. Brush with glaze and bake, uncovered, ½ hour; lower heat to 350° F. and bake 20–30 minutes longer until pastry is golden and birds are tender (test by poking a skewer through steam hole around funnel). If casserole seems to be baking dry, funnel a little extra broth in through hole. Serve hot or cold. About 580 calories for each of 4 servings, 390 calories for each of 6 servings.

CHAPTER 10

POULTRY

Of man's many meats, poultry has always been the aristocrat. The ancient
Chinese domesticated a variety of exotic birds, fattened them for the table, and
lavished upon them the wizardry of Oriental cuisine. From the East the birds
were brought West, into Asia Minor, Greece, and Rome. It was the Romans who
produced the first capon, not because they believed its flesh would be superior,
but because Roman law restricted the number of hens and cocks that could be
eaten. By castrating the cock, they circumvented the law and continued to feast
with abandon. Thanks to today's streamlined poultry industry, there is no
shortage of poultry. Birds are bred and pampered to plump succulence, most are
sold dressed and ready-to-cook (sometimes even prestuffed and frozen), many
are available year round, often at bargain prices. And all are unusually versatile.

The Food Value of Poultry

All poultry is a nourishing high protein
food, and much of it (ducks and geese
excepted) fairly low-calorie.

The Kinds of Poultry

Chicken:

Squab Chicken: An infant weighing
about 1 pound.

Broiler-Fryer: The all-purpose chicken, a
1½–4 pounder that can be broiled, fried,
roasted, braised, or poached with equal
success. The term "broiler-fryer," coined
by the poultry industry, is replacing the
older terminology of "broiler" or
"broiling chicken," "fryer," or "frying
chicken."

Roaster or Roasting Chicken: A plump
(3½–5 pound), young (about 12 weeks)
chicken perfect for roasting.

Capon: A cock castrated while young; it

is full breasted, meaty, and tender,
weighs 4–7 pounds, and is superb
roasted. It is also the bird to use when an
especially succulent cooked chicken meat
is required for a recipe.

Bro-Hen: Another of the poultry
industry's coined terms, this one meaning
a plump, meaty laying hen weighing 4½–
6 pounds. Best when stewed.

Fowl: A stewing hen.

Stewing Hen: A tough old bird weighing
3–6½ pounds. Use for stock, soups, or
recipes calling for ground or minced
cooked chicken.

Turkey (America's gift to the world of
poultry):

Fryer-Roaster: A small (4–9 pound),
young (usually under 16 weeks) turkey
of either sex. It has tender meat, soft
smooth skin, and flexible breastbone

cartilage and can be broiled or oven fried as well as roasted.

Young Hen and Young Tom: Young (5–7 months) female and male with tender meat and skin. Best when roasted. Weights (see note below) vary considerably according to age and breed.

Yearling Hen and Yearling Tom: Mature female and male just over 1 year old. They have reasonably tender meat and can be roasted. Again, weights vary according to breed and age.

Mature Hen and Mature Tom: Female and male more than 15 months old; they have coarse skin, tough meat and are rarely seen in stores today.

Note About Turkey Weights: Turkeys are also categorized by size (ready-to-cook weight): *small* (4–10 pounds), *medium* (10–19 pounds), and *large* (20 pounds or more).

Other Kinds of Poultry:

Rock Cornish Game Hen: A relatively new breed produced by crossing a Cornish chicken and a White Rock. The baby of the chicken family, it weighs 1–2 pounds but averages 1¼. The breast is meaty and plump and the bird especially suited to roasting. It can also be braised or prepared like medium-size game birds (see How to Cook Game Birds). Marketed frozen and ready-to-cook.

Squab: A young domesticated pigeon especially raised for the table. It weighs 1 pound or less and may be prepared like Rock Cornish game hen.

Guinea Fowl: A raucous West African exotic now popular in barnyard flocks. It is a cousin to the pheasant and has rather dry, delicately gamy meat. Guinea hens are preferable to cocks; they weigh 2–4 pounds and may be prepared like chicken.

Pheasant (Farm-Raised): A plump (2–4-pound) bird with superbly flavored though somewhat dry meat. It is the wild pheasant (see game birds) raised in captivity for greater tenderness. Marketed frozen.

Duck: (*Duckling* is a better word because commercially raised ducks are marketed while still young and tender. Most famous is Long Island duckling).

Broiler or Fryer Duckling: A very young duckling weighing about 3 pounds.

Roaster Duckling: A slightly older bird (8–16 weeks) weighing 3–5 pounds.

Goose: Geese raised for the table go to market while still *goslings;* they weigh 4–14 pounds, are fat birds, and are best when roasted.

About Buying Poultry

All poultry moved in interstate commerce is federally inspected to ensure wholesomeness. Some birds, at the packer's request, are graded for quality:

USDA GRADE A: The choicest bird, full fleshed and well finished.

USDA GRADE B: Secondbest, slightly less meaty and attractive.

USDA GRADE C: A grade used mostly for turkeys. These birds are scrawnier, may have torn skin, broken bones and bruises. They are not handsome but, properly prepared, are good eating.

Frequently used today is the *combination tag* that carries not only the *inspection stamp* but also the *grade* and *type of bird* (i.e., roaster, stewing hen).

Characteristics of Quality and Freshness: Home-grown, locally marketed birds are often uninspected and ungraded, so the buyer must rely on her own judgment. To be sure of good poultry, look for:
– Well-fleshed breasts and short, plump legs; ducks should have broad, flat, and meaty breasts and backs well padded with fat.
– Soft, moist (but not wet), smooth, creamy, or yellow skin with a minimum of pinfeathers.

– Youthfulness—flexible breastbones in chickens and turkeys, pliable bills in ducks and geese.

Note: Reject birds with dry or purplish skin, hard scaly legs, and an "off" odor; also pass over those that have been sloppily dressed.

Popular Market Forms of Fresh Poultry:

Chicken:

Whole, Ready-To-Cook: Such birds are cleaned and dressed inside and out, free of pinfeathers. Head, feet, and entrails were removed before weighing and pricing. The giblets have been washed, trimmed, and wrapped (they're usually tucked inside the body cavity).

Halved or Quartered: Popular supermarket forms.

Cut Up or Disjointed: Separated at the joints into breasts, backs, drumsticks, thighs, wings, etc.

Chicken Parts: It is now possible to buy just the parts of chicken you want—2 pounds of drumsticks, say, or a pound of breasts. Chicken livers are also available by the pound.

Turkey:

Whole, Ready-To-Cook: Fully cleaned and dressed birds. Some packer descriptions meaning the same thing: "Pan-Ready," "Oven-Ready," "Table-Dressed."

Quarter or Half Roast: Ready-to-cook large birds sold by the half or quarter.

Cut-Up Turkey or Turkey by the Piece: Specific parts of the bird sold separately by the pound.

Other Kinds of Poultry:

Rock Cornish Game Hen and Squab: If you live near a game hen or squab farm, you may be able to buy fresh, whole, ready-to-cook birds; otherwise, you'll have to settle for the frozen.

Guinea Fowl and Farm-Raised Pheasant: Fresh, whole, ready-to-cook birds are sometimes available at gourmet butchers; the frozen are far more plentiful.

Duck and Goose: These are available fresh, whole, and ready-to-cook but usually only at the source—the New York City area for duck, Wisconsin or North Dakota for goose. Most ducks and geese come to market frozen. In the New York City area it is also sometimes possible to buy duck parts.

How Much Poultry Should You Buy? Allow ¾–1 pound ready-to-cook bird per person; in the case of Rock Cornish game hens and squabs, this will mean 1 bird per person (if appetites are hearty). (*Note:* If a turkey weighs 20 pounds or more, figure about ½ pound ready-to-cook bird per person.)

About Cleaning and Dressing Poultry

The days of chasing, catching, killing, and cleaning one's own poultry belong to history. In fact, rare is the American woman who will have to do more than unwrap (and perhaps thaw) a ready-to-cook bird. *If* you're the exception follow the steps outlined under Game Birds for plucking, singeing, and eviscerating. Domesticated birds, of course, should not be hung.

About Cutting Up Poultry

The best way is to have the butcher do it for you—and most will gladly. Turkey and goose are too cumbersome to tackle at home, but chicken, duck, pheasant, guinea fowl, game hen, and squab can easily be cut up:

To Halve or Quarter (for all but duck; game hen and squab should be no more than halved; they're too small to quarter): Cut closely along each side of backbone and remove (1). Cut out oil sac at base of tail. Nick breast cartilage, cut through flesh and skin; pull halves apart and remove keel bone. For quarters, cut diagonally along bottom rib (2).

directed for halving and quartering, then cut up each side of body from leg joint to wing joint, using poultry shears. Halve breast and remove keel bone as directed for halving chicken.

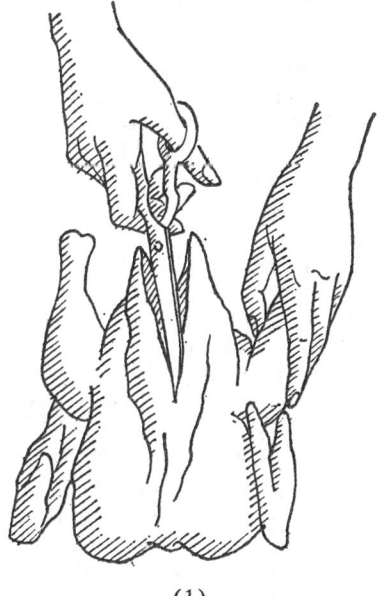

(1)

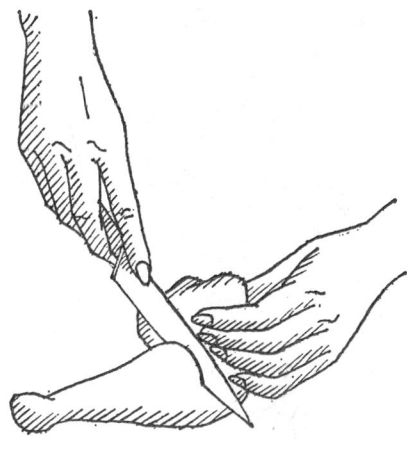

To Halve or Quarter Duck:
Place breast down and with a boning knife cut from neck down each side of backbone (1). Lift backbone out. Turn breast side up, bend carcass backward so that breastbone pops up (2). Pull out breastbone. Spread duck flat and split down center to halve. To quarter, cut each half in two as shown (3).

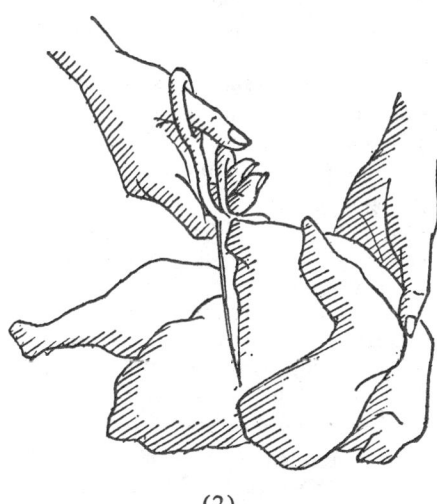

(2)

To Cut Up or Disjoint Chicken:
Remove wings, then legs, rolling knife along curves of ball joints. Sever legs at "knee" joints, separating into drumsticks and thighs.
Remove backbone and oil sac as

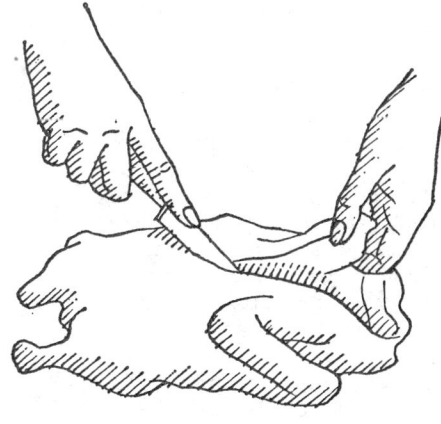

(1)

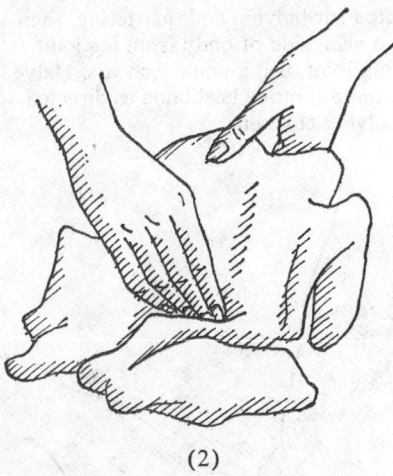

(2)

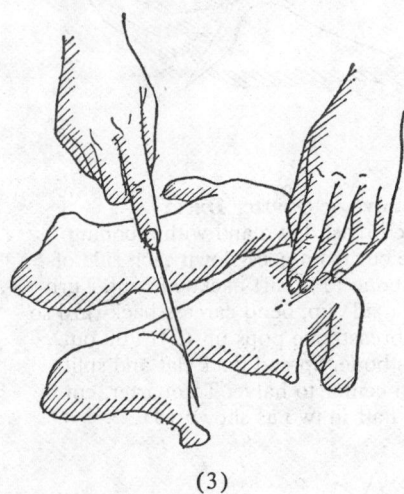

(3)

About Frozen Poultry

All of America's popular birds come frozen and in the same market forms as fresh birds. Certain of them—Rock Cornish game hens, squabs, pheasant, duck, and goose—are more readily available frozen than fresh. Among specialty items are frozen stuffed turkeys, frozen turkey rolls, and boneless roasts, frozen breaded turkey steaks (to be butter-browned like minute steaks) and countless precooked frozen chicken and turkey dinners.

To Be Sure of Top Quality: Buy solidly frozen birds with no discoloration or signs of freezer burn and no signs of having thawed and refrozen (a block of frozen juices at the bottom of the package).

How to Cook Frozen Poultry: Thaw birds thoroughly, then cook as you would fresh poultry. *Exception:* Frozen stuffed turkeys that must be cooked from the solidly frozen state (follow package directions carefully).

Best Ways to Thaw Frozen Poultry:

Refrigerator Method: This is the safest but also the slowest. Place wrapped bird on a tray in the refrigerator. Ducks and geese will thaw in 2–3 days, chickens in 12–16 hours, chicken parts in 4–9 hours. Small birds will thaw somewhat faster.

Quick Method: Place wrapped birds in a large kettle, cover with cold water, and let stand at room temperature, changing water often. Ducks, geese, and large chickens will thaw in 2–4 hours, small chickens in about 1 hour, game hens in ½ hour.

Special Techniques for Turkeys: Latest recommendations from the Poultry and Egg National Board are based upon how soon you want to cook the bird:

If You Want to Cook the Turkey Immediately: Unwrap frozen turkey and place on a rack in a shallow roasting pan; roast uncovered 1 hour at 325° F. Take turkey from oven and remove neck and giblets from body cavity and neck area; cook these immediately. Return turkey to oven *at once* and roast until done. Cook the stuffing separately.

If You Want to Cook the Turkey Later in the Day: Place wrapped turkey in a large kettle and cover with cold water; let stand at room temperature, changing water very often; or let stand in sink under a slow stream of cold water. A 5–9-pound turkey will thaw in 3–4 hours; a larger bird in 4–7. Roast the turkey as soon as it is thawed.

If You Want to Cook the Turkey Tomorrow: Leave turkey in its original wrapper, then place in a large brown paper bag or wrap in 2–3 layers of newspaper. Set on a tray or in a baking pan and let thaw at room temperature.

THAWING TIME

WEIGHT	TIME
4–10 pounds	6 10 hours
10–16 pounds	10–14 hours
16–24 pounds	14–18 hours

If You Want to Cook the Turkey the Day After Tomorrow: Use the refrigerator method described above.

Notes of Caution: Never let a thawed bird stand at room temperature. Refrigerate at once or, better still, roast. Never stuff a thawed bird until just before you pop it into the oven.

About Canned Poultry

Frozen and fresh poultry have all but eclipsed the canned. Most readily available are canned chicken meat (wonderful for sandwiches, salads, and casseroles), whole chicken, and an assortment of ready-to-heat dishes (fricassees, stews, à la kings, etc.). In gourmet shops you'll also find such canned delicacies as preserved goose and smoked quail or pheasant.

Other Forms of Poultry

There is smoked turkey, some of which is ready to eat, some of which requires further cooking (read labels carefully). And in Oriental groceries you'll find such exotics as dried duck feet and preserved duck.

Some Special Terms and Techniques Applying to Poultry

Ballotine: A fully or partially boned bird (usually chicken or turkey), stuffed with forcemeat, reshaped, and roasted or steamed. Ballotines are usually served hot but can be served cold.

To Bard: To cover or wrap in thin sheets of fat back, salt pork, or bacon before roasting to keep a bird moist and juicy. Most poultry has enough fat of its own to ensure succulence, but guinea fowl, pheasant, and game hens may not.

To Bone: To remove all major bones; wing tips and lower leg bones are sometimes left in a bird to give it shape. Because birds are anatomically similar, all can be boned by the basic techniques below (always save bones for making stock). Large birds are easier to bone than small ones (it's easier to see what you're doing); tiny birds like squabs or game hens are rarely boned—too tedious.

How to Bone a Whole Bird: Wipe bird with a damp cloth and pat dry; remove loose fat from body cavity. If bird is a turkey, duck, or goose, cut off wings; otherwise cut off tips at "elbow" joint. Lay bird breast side down on a board and slit center back from neck to tail (1) with a sharp knife; cut out tail and oil sac. Working down and around one side toward breast, peel flesh away from bones (2), freeing stubborn parts with the knife (it's rather like taking off a jacket). Sever ball joints at hips and shoulders (3). When you reach the ridge of the breastbone (keel bone), repeat operation on the other side, again working flesh free around back and toward breast. Lift carcass with 1 hand and very carefully cut against ridge, taking care not to pierce skin. Lay bird skin side down, cut and scrape all meat from leg and wing bones, turning meat and skin inside out as you go. (*Note:* If you plan to stuff and reshape the bird, leave drumstick and wingtips in; otherwise remove.) Use pliers to pull out leg tendons of turkey, goose, hen, or capon. Feel boned bird carefully for any hidden bones (the wishbone is often overlooked) and remove.

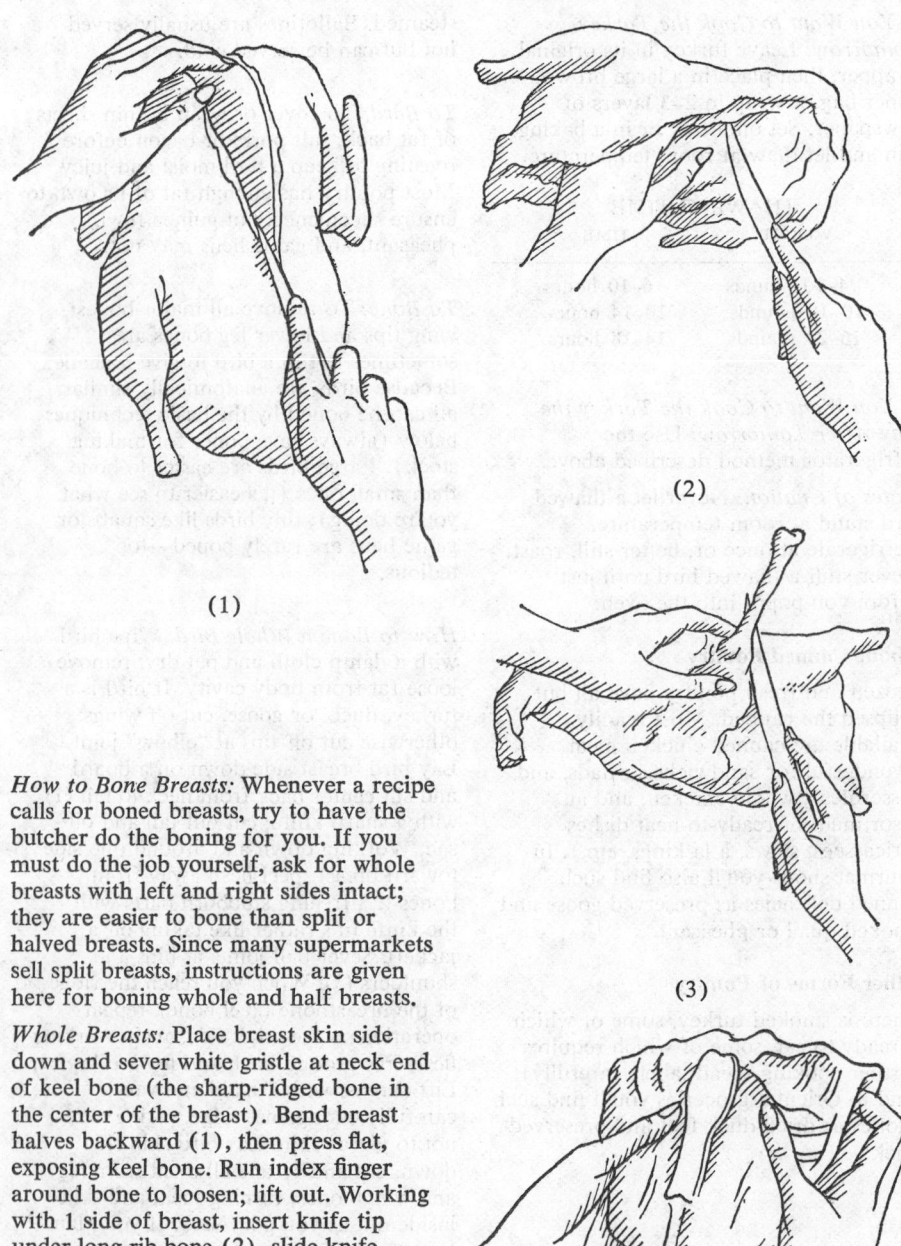

(1)

(2)

(3)

How to Bone Breasts: Whenever a recipe calls for boned breasts, try to have the butcher do the boning for you. If you must do the job yourself, ask for whole breasts with left and right sides intact; they are easier to bone than split or halved breasts. Since many supermarkets sell split breasts, instructions are given here for boning whole and half breasts.

Whole Breasts: Place breast skin side down and sever white gristle at neck end of keel bone (the sharp-ridged bone in the center of the breast). Bend breast halves backward (1), then press flat, exposing keel bone. Run index finger around bone to loosen; lift out. Working with 1 side of breast, insert knife tip under long rib bone (2), slide knife underneath bone, cutting meat free. Work flesh free of ribs, cutting as needed around outer edge of breast up to shoulder; lift out rib cage; repeat on other side. Remove wishbone and white tendons on either side of it (3). Skin, if you like (it easily peels off).

(1)

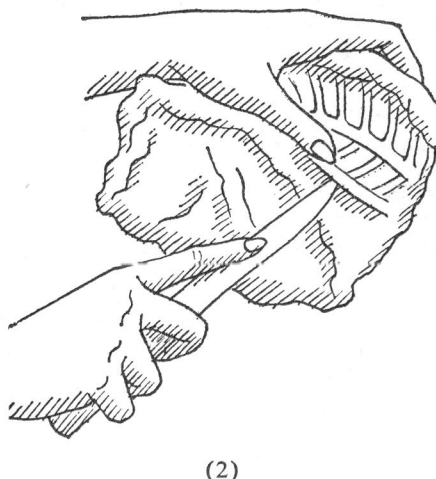

(2)

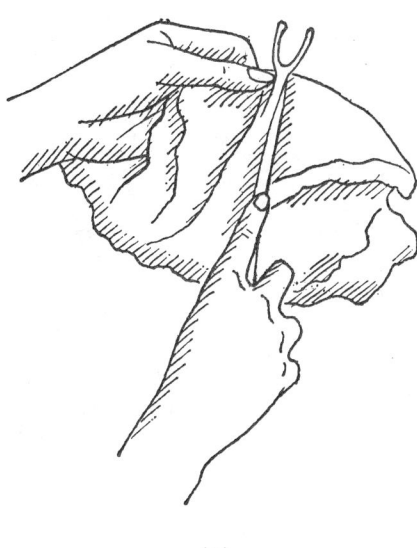

(3)

Deep Basted: A commercial technique of injecting butter underneath the skin of turkeys to make them buttery and juicy.

To Disjoint: To cut up a bird (usually chicken) by severing at the joints (see About Cutting Up Poultry).

To Draw: To eviscerate.

Galantine: A bird, usually chicken or turkey, completely boned, then stuffed with forcemeat and shaped into a plump sausage-like roll. It is poached, then chilled and served cold, often elaborately decorated and glazed with aspic.

Giblets: The gizzard, heart, and liver of a bird (see What to Do with Giblets).

Keel or Keel Bone: The longitudinal breastbone, sharp and ridged. In young birds it is pliable; in old birds rigid.

Oysters: The choice nuggets of dark meat found in the cavities of the hip bone.

Pinfeathers: The coarse, quill-like feathers of a bird. The easiest way to remove them is with tweezers.

To Pluck: To pick feathers from a bird.

Rack: The carcass of a bird.

To Singe: To burn off fine hairs remaining on a bird after plucking.

To Stuff: To fill the body and neck cavities of a bird with a savory dressing, with forcemeat, fruit, or vegetables. Always stuff a bird loosely—so the stuffing has room to expand—and always stuff *just before cooking*, never earlier or you're flirting with food poisoning. Also, remove stuffing from leftover bird and refrigerate separately.

Suprêmes: Boned breasts of poultry (see Suprêmes of Chicken in recipe section).

To Truss: To fold a bird's wings back and under and tie its legs close to the body so it will roast more evenly (see How to Roast Poultry).

Tucked Bird: A bird (usually turkey) made more compact by having its drumsticks tucked under a flap of breast skin.

Half Breasts: Place breast skin side up, slide knife point between flesh and bottom rib, then, keeping cutting edge against rib cage, peel back flesh, using knife as needed to free stubborn bits. Lift out ribs and cut out white tendons. Skin if you like.

To Bone Drumsticks and Thighs: Cut length of drumstick or thigh on under-side to bone and peel away flesh.

Turken or Churkey: A large, bareheaded breed of chicken, *not*, as sometimes proclaimed, a cross between a turkey and a chicken.

Vent: The opening at the base of the tail of a drawn bird.

Volaille: The French word for poultry.

Wishbone: The breastbone.

Should Poultry Be Brought to Room Temperature Before Cooking? Some cooks like to do so, but it is often not practical—or even advisable—to let birds stand several hours at room temperature. Stuffed birds or those that

have been thawed should never be left out on a kitchen counter—too much danger of food poisoning.

About Using Meat Thermometers: Thermometers can be used when roasting large, fleshy birds, but because of the shape and boniness of poultry, the readings are not a completely reliable indicator of doneness. There are two ways to insert a thermometer in birds: in the large meaty muscle on the *inside* of the thigh so that the thermometer does not touch bone (when a chicken is done, the reading will be 190° F.; for a turkey it will be 180–85° F.); or, if a bird is stuffed, through the carcass into the

HOW TO COOK POULTRY

The basic principles of cooking meat apply to cooking poultry (see the Ways of Cooking Meat). To determine the best ways to cook specific birds, use the following quick reference table.

Bird	Weight in Pounds	Roast	Spit-Roast	Broil	Charcoal Broil	Panfry (Sauté)	Deep Fat Fry	Oven Fry	Braise	Simmer (Poach)	Stew	Steam
Chicken:												
Squab chicken	1			X		X	X					
Broiler-fryer	1½-4	X	X	X	X	X	X	X	X	X	X	X
Roaster	3½-5	X	X					X	X	X	X	X
Capon	4-7	X	X						X	X	X	X
Bro-hen, stewing hen	3-6½									X		
Turkey:												
Fryer-roaster	4-9	X	X	X	X			X	X			
Young or yearling hens and toms	10-24	X	X									
Rock Cornish game hens, squabs:	1-2	X	X						X			
Guinea fowl, pheasant:	2-4	X	X						X			
Duck:												
Broiler or fryer duckling	3	X	X	X	X				X			
Roaster duckling	3-5	X	X						X			
Goose:	4-14	X	X						X			

center of the stuffing, again with thermometer tip not touching bone (when a bird is done, the thermometer should read 165° F.).

Tests for Doneness: The old-fashioned finger tests are probably the most accurate ways to tell if a bird is done: Cover thumb and forefinger with a bit of paper towel and pinch the thickest part of the thigh; if the meat feels very soft, the bird is done. Or, grasp drumstick; if it moves easily in the hip socket, the bird is done. This last test is best for birds being stewed or steamed until very well done.

How to Roast Poultry

Best Birds: See the table under How to Cook Poultry.

Basic Preparation for Cooking: Remove paper of giblets from body (save giblets for gravy or use in stuffing; see What to Do with Giblets). Also remove any loose fat from body cavity. Wipe bird with a damp cloth but do not wash (most birds coming to market today are beautifully cleaned and dressed; washing them merely destroys some of their flavor). Singe off any hairs and remove pinfeathers. Sprinkle neck and body cavities with salt.

To Stuff a Bird: You'll need about ½ cup stuffing per pound of bird. Choose a stuffing that complements the bird you're roasting (see Some Sauces, Gravies, and Seasonings for Poultry), then spoon stuffing *loosely* into both body and neck cavities. If you pack stuffing into a bird, it will become tough and rubbery in cooking. If a particular recipe makes more stuffing than a bird will hold, simply wrap the leftover in foil and bake alongside the bird in the pan. (*Note:* Do not stuff a bird until *just* before roasting; and do not let a stuffed bird stand at room temperature. Ever.)

To Truss a Bird: After stuffing bird, skewer or sew openings shut as shown, then truss by folding the wings back and

underneath body and tying drumsticks close to body so bird will have a more compact shape and roast more evenly.

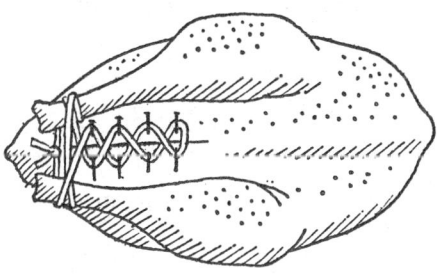

Basic Roasting Method

Chicken:

Whole Birds: Preheat oven to 400° F. if bird weighs 2 pounds or less, to 375° F. if between 2½ and 4 pounds, and to 325° F. if more than 4 pounds. Prepare bird for roasting as directed, place breast side up on a rack in a shallow roasting pan and brush, if you like, with melted butter or margarine or cooking oil. Insert meat thermometer in thigh or stuffing,* not touching bone. Roast uncovered, using times given in Poultry Roasting Chart as a guide. (*Note:* For extra flavor, baste often during cooking with seasoned butter or, if you prefer, glaze,* during last ½ hour of roasting—see Some Marinades and Glazes for Poultry.)

Chicken Halves or Quarters: Preheat oven to 400° F. Wipe pieces of chicken with a damp cloth and place skin side up in a lightly greased shallow roasting pan. Brush with melted butter or cooking oil and sprinkle with salt and pepper. Roast uncovered, without turning, until tender and browned, brushing, if needed to keep chicken moist, with additional butter or oil. Use times in roasting chart as a guide.

VARIATION:

Oven-Barbecued Chicken: Marinate pieces of chicken in any favorite barbecue sauce 1 hour at room temperature. Preheat oven to 350° F. Place chicken skin side down in a foil-lined shallow baking pan and roast, uncovered, ½ hour. Turn, brush with barbecue sauce, and roast ½ hour longer. Brush again with sauce and roast 15 minutes longer, basting frequently with sauce.

Turkey:

Breast-Up Method for a Whole Bird: This is the preferred way today; it produces an exquisitely brown bird. Preheat oven to 325° F. Prepare turkey for roasting as directed and place breast side up on a rack in a shallow roasting pan. Insert meat thermometer in thigh or stuffing,* not touching bone, and roast uncovered, according to times given in Poultry Roasting Chart. Baste, if you like, with melted butter or margarine every ½–¾ hour. If bird browns too fast, tent breast loosely with foil.

VARIATION:

Beer and Butter Basted Turkey: Rub turkey well with softened butter, then roast as directed, rubbing with additional softened butter every ½ hour and basting with about ½ cup beer. You'll need about ¼ pound butter and 2–3 (12-ounce) cans of beer.

Breast-Down Method for a Whole Bird: Though this method produces juicier breast meat, it has disadvantages: The breast skin is apt to stick to the rack and tear as the turkey is being turned and the act of turning a hot, hefty turkey is both difficult and dangerous. Preheat oven to 325° F. Prepare turkey for roasting as directed and place breast side down in a V rack in a shallow roasting pan. Roast, uncovered, until half done according to roasting chart, turn breast side up, insert meat thermometer in thickest part of inside thigh,* not touching bone, and continue roasting, uncovered, until done. Baste, if you like, during cooking with drippings or melted butter.

Fast Foil Method for a Whole Bird: This is the method to use for birds, especially big ones, that must be cooked in a "hurry." Turkeys cooked this way will have more of a steamed than roasted

flavor. Preheat oven to 450° F. Prepare turkey for roasting as directed and place in the center of a large sheet of heavy foil; brush well with softened butter, margarine, or shortening. Bring foil up on both sides of breast and make a simple overlapping fold at the top, smooth down around turkey, then crumple ends of foil up to hold in juices. Place turkey breast side up in a shallow roasting pan and roast as follows:

Ready-to-Cook Weight	Total Roasting Time
6–8 pounds	1½–2 hours
8–12 pounds	2–2½ hours
12–16 pounds	2½–3 hours
16–20 pounds	3–3½ hours
20–24 pounds	3½–4 hours

About 30–40 minutes before turkey is done, open tent of foil and fold back and away from bird so it will brown nicely.

(*Note:* When roasting turkey by any of the three preceding methods, it's a good idea to cut string holding drumsticks to tail about 1 hour before bird is done so that inner legs and thighs will brown.)

Turkey Halves or Quarters: Preheat oven to 325° F. Wipe pieces of turkey with a damp cloth and pat dry; skewer skin to meat around edges to prevent it from shrinking during cooking; tie leg to tail, lay wing flat over breast meat, and tie string around to hold in place. Place pieces of turkey skin side up on a rack in a shallow roasting pan and brush well with melted butter or margarine; sprinkle with salt and pepper. Insert meat thermometer in center of inside thigh muscle. Roast uncovered, basting occasionally with drippings or additional melted butter, using times in Poultry Roasting Chart as a guide.

Cut-Up Turkey: Preheat oven to 325° F. Wipe pieces with a damp cloth and pat dry, place skin side up on a rack in a shallow roasting pan, brush well with melted butter or margarine, and sprinkle with salt and pepper. Roast uncovered, basting occasionally with drippings or extra melted butter, using times in Poultry Roasting Chart as a guide.

Rock Cornish Game Hens and Squabs: Preheat oven to 400° F. Prepare birds for roasting as directed. Rub well with softened butter or margarine or drape with strips of bacon or fat back. Place breast side up on a rack in a shallow roasting pan and roast uncovered, basting often with drippings or melted butter, according to times given in Poultry Roasting Chart.

VARIATIONS:

Napa Valley Roast Rock Cornish Game Hens or Squabs: Stuff each bird with ¼ cup seedless green grapes that have been tossed with 1 teaspoon sugar. Brush generously with a hot mixture of ¼ cup melted butter, 1 tablespoon honey, 1 teaspoon seasoned salt, and ⅛ teaspoon pepper. Place breast side up on a rack in a shallow roasting pan, add ½ cup each sauterne and water to pan, and roast as directed, basting often.

Mustardy Rock Cornish Game Hens or Squabs in Lemon Cream Sauce: Spread each hen with 1 teaspoon Dijon mustard, then roast as directed. Halve birds and set aside. For each bird, heat 1 cup heavy cream and 1 teaspoon finely grated lemon rind in a double boiler over simmering water 10 minutes; for each bird, lightly beat 1 egg yolk. Blend a little hot mixture into yolks, return to pan, and heat and stir over simmering water until slightly thickened. Pour off all but 1 tablespoon drippings from roasting pan, add cream sauce, stirring to scrape up browned bits. Add salt, pepper, and, if you like, lemon juice to taste. Return hens to pan and set in oven turned to lowest heat; let warm 10 minutes. Serve in a deep platter smothered with sauce.

Guinea Fowl and Farm-Raised Pheasant: Preheat oven to 350° F. Prepare bird for roasting as directed. Brush well with melted butter or margarine or, if bird

seems especially lean, bard.* Place breast side up on a rack in a shallow roasting pan and roast uncovered, basting often with drippings or brushing with additional melted butter, using times in Poultry Roasting Chart as a guide.

Duck or Goose:

Whole Birds: Preheat oven to 325° F. Prepare bird for roasting as directed. Also rub inside well with half a lemon before stuffing. Prick skin well all over with a sharp fork so fat underneath will drain off during cooking. Rub skin well with salt (this helps to crispen skin). Place bird breast side up on a rack in a shallow roasting pan and roast uncovered, draining off drippings as they accumulate and pricking as needed. Use times in Poultry Roasting Chart as a guide. (*Note:* For a particularly crisp skin, raise oven temperature to 450° F. during last ½ hour of roasting. Also drain all drippings from pan and spoon ¼–½ cup ice water over bird. Or, if you prefer, glaze* bird during last part of roasting—see Some Marinades and Glazes for Poultry.

Some Notes About Goose Stuffings: In Europe, very simple stuffings are popular: quartered, cored tart apples sprinkled with cinnamon or nutmeg and sometimes mixed with plumped raisins; drained sauerkraut mixed with caraway seeds; or equal parts minced apples, celery, and cranberries or pitted dried prunes or apricots.

VARIATIONS:

Roast Duck or Goose with Sauerkraut and Applesauce: Roast bird as directed and ½ hour before it is done remove rack and drain off all drippings. Place a 1″ bed drained sauerkraut in bottom of pan, add ½ cup applesauce or whole cranberry sauce, and toss well to mix. Place bird breast side up on sauerkraut and finish roasting as directed. Serve wreathed with the sauerkraut.

Orange-Tea-Glazed Roast Duck or Goose: Roast bird as directed, basting every 20 minutes with the following mixture: 2 cups hot strong tea blended with ¼ cup honey and the slivered rind

POULTRY ROASTING CHART

Note: Times given are for birds taken from the refrigerator and stuffed. Reduce total roasting times by about 15 minutes if birds are unstuffed. Times are approximate at best, so test often for doneness toward end of cooking.

Bird	Oven Temperature	Total Cooking Time in Hours	Special Treatment Needed	Internal Temperature When Done
Chicken				
2 pounds	400° F.	1-1½	Tent bird loosely with	190° F.
2½-4 pounds	375° F.	1½-2¼	foil if it browns too	190° F.
4-7 pounds	325° F.	3-5	fast.	190° F.
Halves or quarters	400° F.	3/4-1		190° F.
Turkey (whole)				
4-8 pounds	325° F.	2½-3½	Tent bird loosely with	180-85° F.
8-12 pounds	325° F.	3½-4½	foil or cover breast with	180-85° F.
12-16 pounds	325° F.	4½-5½	butter-soaked cheese-	180-85° F.
16-20 pounds	325° F.	5½-6½	cloth if it browns too	180-85° F.
20-24 pounds	325° F.	6½-7	fast.	180-85° F.
Turkey halves or quarters				
5-8 pounds	325° F.	2½-3	Tent loosely with foil	180-85° F.
8-10 pounds	325° F.	3-3½	if browning too fast.	180-85° F.
10-12 pounds	325° F.	3½-4		180-85° F.
Boneless turkey rolls and roasts (unstuffed)				
3-5 pounds	325° F.	2½-3	Tent loosely with foil	170-75° F.
5-7 pounds	325° F.	3-3½	if browning too fast.	170-75° F.
7-9 pounds	325° F.	3½-4		170-75° F.
Turkey breasts (unstuffed)				
4-6 pounds	325° F.	2¼-3	Tent loosely with foil	180-85° F.
6-8 pounds	325° F.	3-3½	if browning too fast.	180-85° F.
8-10 pounds	325° F.	3½-4		180-85° F.
10-12 pounds	325° F.	4-4¼		180-85° F.
12-14 pounds	325° F.	4¼-4½		180-85° F.
Rock Cornish game hens and squabs				
3/4-1½ pounds	400° F.	3/4-1	Brush often with melted butter or drippings.	—
Guinea fowl and farm-raised pheasant				
2-4 pounds	350° F.	1½-2½	Brush or baste often with melted butter or drippings.	—

POULTRY ROASTING CHART (continued)

Bird	Oven Temperature	Total Cooking Time in Hours	Special Treatment Needed	Internal Temperature When Done
Duck (whole)				
4-5½ pounds	325° F.	2½-3	Prick often with a sharp fork throughout cooking and drain off drippings as they collect.	—
Duckling halves and quarters	450° F. for 1/2 hour THEN 350° F. for 1½ hours	2		
Goose				
4-6 pounds	325° F.	2¾-3	Prick goose often with a sharp fork during cooking and drain off drippings as they collect. Also allow about 1/2 hour margin in cooking times at left according to breed of goose; some cook faster than others.	—
6-8 pounds	325° F.	3-3½		—
8-12 pounds	325° F.	3½-4½		—
12-14 pounds	325° F.	4½-5		—

Note: If meat thermometer is inserted in center of stuffing (not touching bone) instead of in thigh, bird should be done when thermometer reads 165° F. The legs of all birds except chicken and turkeys are too skimpy to hold a meat thermometer, so if a thermometer is used, it must be inserted in the stuffing.

of 1 orange. Sprinkle with a little extra grated rind just before serving. (*Note:* For distinctive flavor, add ½ teaspoon Formosa Oolong tea to the regular when brewing.)

Duckling Halves or Quarters: Preheat oven to 450° F. Wipe pieces of duckling with a damp cloth and pat dry; prick skin well all over with a sharp fork. Place skin side up on a rack in a shallow roasting pan and roast, uncovered, ½ hour; lower oven temperature to 350° F. and roast 1½ hours longer until tender. Drain off drippings as they accumulate. Glaze,* if you like, during last ½ hour of cooking (see Some Marinades and Glazes for Poultry).

How to Spit-Roast Poultry

Best Birds: See the table under How to Cook Poultry.

Basic Preparation for Cooking: The same as for roasting. *Do not stuff bird.* Tie drumsticks firmly to tail; skewer neck skin to back, flatten wings against sides of breast, and tie string around breast to hold wings in. Insert spit lengthwise, slightly on the diagonal, through bird from vent to the top of the breastbone; tighten holding forks. Test balance of bird on spit and readjust, if necessary, so bird will turn smoothly. If bird is large enough to do so, insert meat thermometer in center of plump inside thigh muscle and make sure thermometer will clear unit as spit turns. (*Note:* If spitting several small birds, allow about ½" between birds so heat will circulate freely.)

To Spit-Roast in Oven or Rotisserie: Preheat unit. Prepare and spit bird as directed, attach spit to rotisserie, and roast, using table below as a guide.

Note: Below times are for birds taken straight from the refrigerator; they can be used as a guide only. Chicken, turkey, and boneless turkey roasts only are of a size and shape to make use of meat thermometer practical. Test birds for doneness often after minimum cooking time is up. When spit-roasting fat birds like duck or goose, watch carefully and drain off drippings as they accumulate.

To Spit-Roast over Charcoal: Build a moderately hot charcoal fire.* Prepare

and spit bird as directed. Attach spit to motor, adjust spit height so it is 5" from coals, and place a drip pan where it will catch the drippings (especially important with duck and goose). Roast, increasing times given for oven spit-roasting by ¼–½ hour, depending on size of bird and the weather (on a cool, windy day, over-all cooking times may need to be increased by as much as ¾ hour for large birds). Watch birds carefully toward end of cooking and test often for doneness.

VARIATION:

Spit-Barbecued Birds: Prepare and spit-roast as directed, brushing often during last ½ hour of cooking with any barbecue sauce.

How to Broil Poultry

Best Birds: See the table under How to Cook Poultry.

Bird	Total Roasting Time	Internal Temperature When Done
Chicken		
2–3 pounds	1–1¼ hours	190° F.
4–5 pounds	1½–2 hours	190° F.
6–7 pounds	2½–3 hours	190° F.
Turkey		
4–6 pounds	2–3 hours	180–85° F.
6–8 pounds	3–3½ hours	180–85° F.
8–10 pounds	3½–4 hours	180–85° F.
10–12 pounds	4–5 hours	180–85° F.
Boneless Turkey Roasts (If there are wrapper directions for spit roasting, follow them; otherwise, use times below. Let roast "rest" ½ hour at room temperature before carving.)		
3–5 pounds	2–3 hours	170–75° F.
5–7 pounds	3–3½ hours	170–75° F.
7–9 pounds	3½–4 hours	170–75° F.
Cornish Game Hens and Squabs		
¾–1½ pounds	40–45 minutes	————
Guinea Fowl and Farm-Raised		
Pheasant		
2–4 pounds	1–2 hours	————
Duck		
4–5 pounds	1½–2½ hours	————
Goose		
4–6 pounds	2–3 hours	————

Bird	Best Weight for Broiling	Distance from Heat	Minutes on First Side	Minutes on Second Side
Chicken	1½–3 pounds	6″	20–25	15–20
Turkey	4–6 pounds	9″	40	40–50
Duckling	3 pounds or less	7″–8″	30	30–45

Basic Preparation for Cooking: Have small chickens and ducklings halved, larger ones quartered; turkeys should be cut up. Wipe the birds with a damp cloth.

To Broil in the Oven: Preheat broiler. Place bird skin side down on a lightly greased broiler rack. Brush chicken or turkey with melted butter or margarine or cooking oil, but not duckling. Duckling should be pricked well all over so that the fat underneath skin can drain off during broiling. Broil according to table above, brushing chicken or turkey well with additional melted butter after turning and throughout cooking as needed. Duckling should be pricked throughout cooking and its drippings drained off as they accumulate.

Note: These times can be used only as a guide; test often for doneness toward end of minimum cooking time: twist a drumstick in its socket; if it pulls loose, bird is done. Or make a tiny slit down to bone; if no pink meat remains, bird is done. Livers of birds can be broiled too. Toward end of cooking, brush well with melted butter or margarine, place on broiler rack, and broil 3–5 minutes per side, depending on size.

To Charcoal Broil: Build a moderately hot charcoal fire.* Adjust height of grill so it is 6″–8″ from coals. Prepare bird as directed; brush chicken and turkey well with cooking oil, melted butter or margarine; prick duck skin all over with a sharp fork. Place bird skin side up on a lightly greased grill and broil, turning often, until tender. Chicken will need 50–60 minutes altogether, depending on size; turkey 1½–1¾ hours and duck 1–1½ hours. Brush chicken and turkey throughout broiling with additional oil or melted butter; prick duck often (also be prepared to douse flare-ups). (*Note:* If day is cool and gusty, you'll have to increase cooking times somewhat.)

VARIATIONS:

⚖ **Low-Calorie Broiled Chicken or Turkey:** Broil or charcoal-broil as directed, brushing with low-calorie garlic, herb, or Italian dressing instead of oil, butter, or margarine. About 225 calories per average portion of turkey and 250 per average portion of chicken. White meat pieces will be slightly lower.

Marinated or Barbecued Birds: Marinate birds in any marinade or barbecue sauce 3–4 hours in refrigerator before cooking; broil or charcoal-broil as directed, brushing often with marinade or sauce during last ½ hour of cooking.

Lemon-Broiled Chicken or Turkey: Mix ½ cup melted butter or margarine with the juice of 1 lemon and ½ teaspoon rosemary. (*Note:* For turkey, double quantities.) Brush liberally over bird and broil or charcoal-broil as directed, brushing often.

Portuguese-Style Charcoal-Broiled Chicken or Turkey: Mix ¼ cup olive oil with 2 peeled and crushed cloves garlic, 1 tablespoon paprika, 1 teaspoon salt, and ⅛ teaspoon pepper. (*Note:* Double amounts for turkey.) Brush bird well with mixture and let stand at room temperature ½ hour. Broil or charcoal-broil as directed, brushing often with mixture.

Chicken in a Basket over Charcoal: Place cut-up chicken in a metal rotisserie basket, balance basket in center of spit, and tighten screws. Attach spit to motor and position so center of basket is 5″–6″ from coals. Broil chicken 1½–1¾ hours or until fork tender and golden. (*Note:* Keep an eye on wings because tips sometimes catch in basket and brown unevenly. *Stop basket* before adjusting.) When chicken is done, remove from basket and sprinkle with salt and pepper. (*Note:* Chicken can be marinated 3–4 hours in any barbecue sauce in refrigerator before cooking.)

Chicken in Foil over Charcoal: Butter 4 (12″) squares heavy foil well; lay 1 chicken quarter in the center of each, sprinkle with salt and pepper, and wrap tight. Grill 3″–4″ from glowing coals 1–1¼ hours until tender, turning packages halfway through cooking. Unwrap chicken, place skin side down on grill, cover loosely with foil, and brown 4–5 minutes. (*Note:* Chicken can be marinated 3–4 hours in any barbecue sauce or marinade [see Some Marinades and Glazes for Poultry] in refrigerator before cooking. Include 1–2 tablespoons marinade in each foil package and brush with marinade during final browning.)

How to Fry Poultry

Best Birds: Chicken and very small, young turkey.

Basic Preparation for Cooking: Have birds cut up; wipe with a damp cloth but do not pat dry.

To Panfry (Sauté) Chicken: Dredge by shaking 1–2 pieces at a time in a bag in seasoned flour (⅔ cup unsifted flour, 1 teaspoon salt, ¼ teaspoon pepper, and, if you like, ¼ teaspoon paprika for 1 bird). Pour ½″ cooking oil or melted shortening in a large, heavy skillet and heat over moderately high heat until a cube of bread will sizzle. Put larger, meatier pieces of chicken skin side down in hot fat; add remaining chicken and fry, uncovered, 15–25 minutes on each side, adjusting heat as needed so chicken does not brown too fast. Turn chicken only once during cooking. Add liver and heart during last few minutes. Drain chicken on paper toweling and serve.

VARIATIONS:

Chili-Fried Chicken: Prepare as directed, adding 1 tablespoon chili powder and ¼ teaspoon each garlic and onion powder to seasoned flour.

Curry-Fried Chicken: Prepare as directed, adding 2–3 teaspoons curry powder and ¼ teaspoon each ginger and garlic powder to seasoned flour.

Cheesy-Fried Chicken: Prepare as directed, reducing flour in seasoned flour to ½ cup and adding ½ cup finely grated Parmesan cheese and 1 teaspoon oregano or marjoram.

Crisp-Fried Chicken: Dip pieces of chicken in evaporated milk or light cream, then dredge and fry as directed.

To Panfry (Sauté) Turkey: This is really a combination of frying and braising. Have a small (4–9-pound) turkey cut up. For each 5 pounds of turkey, blend together ¾ cup unsifted flour, 2 teaspoons each salt and paprika, and ¼ teaspoon pepper. Dredge turkey in seasoned flour by shaking in a paper bag. Pour enough cooking oil or melted shortening in a large, heavy skillet to cover bottom; heat over moderately high heat until a cube of bread will sizzle. Begin browning turkey, biggest pieces first. Slip smaller pieces in and around the large ones. Brown about 20 minutes, turning as needed with tongs so pieces brown evenly. Add 2–4 tablespoons water, cover, and cook over low heat ¾– 1 hour until turkey is tender. Turn pieces 2 or 3 times as they cook. Uncover and cook 10 minutes longer to crispen. (*Note:* The liver may be added during the last 15 minutes.)

To Pan- and Oven-Fry Chicken (Combination Method): Preheat oven to 350° F. Dredge and brown chicken as for panfrying; transfer to an ungreased shallow baking pan, arranging pieces skin side up in a single layer. Bake, uncovered, 35–45 minutes until tender.

To Deep-Fat Fry Chicken: Prepare a small (1½–2½ pound) broiler-fryer for frying as directed above. Beat 1 egg with ¼ cup cold milk; also mix 1 cup unsifted flour with 1 teaspoon salt and ¼ teaspoon pepper. Dip chicken in egg, roll in flour to coat evenly, and fry, 3–4 pieces at a time, in 350° F. deep fat 15–17 minutes until richly browned all over. Drain on paper toweling.

VARIATIONS:

Southern Fried Chicken: Let chicken marinate in milk to cover 1 hour at room temperature. Dip in egg mixture as directed, then dredge in ½ cup unsifted flour mixed with ¾ cup cracker meal, 1 tablespoon paprika, 1½ teaspoons salt, and ¼ teaspoon pepper. Fry in deep fat as directed.

Batter-Fried Chicken: Prepare 1 recipe Basic Batter for Fried Foods. Dip a 1–1½-pound cut-up chicken in batter, then fry, 3–4 pieces at a time, in 350° F. deep fat 15–17 minutes until nut brown. Drain on paper toweling. (*Note:* Because the batter acts as an insulator and slows cooking, use only the very smallest chickens for batter-frying.)

To Oven-Fry Chicken: Preheat oven to 350° F. Place a large, shallow roasting pan in oven, add ¼ pound butter or margarine and let melt as oven preheats. Meanwhile, dredge chicken pieces in seasoned flour as for panfrying. Roll chicken in the melted butter, then arrange skin side up 1 layer deep and bake, uncovered, 1–1¼ hours until fork tender and browned.

VARIATIONS:

Chicken Italiano: Lightly beat 1 egg with the juice of 1 lemon. Dip chicken pieces in egg, then in 1 cup Italian-style seasoned bread crumbs. Place in a single layer in a greased large, shallow baking pan, drizzle with ½ cup melted butter or margarine, and bake as directed.

Chicken Parmesan: Dip chicken pieces in ⅔ cup melted butter or margarine, then roll in 1 cup soft white bread crumbs mixed with ⅓ cup finely grated Parmesan, 2 tablespoons minced parsley, ½ crushed clove garlic, 1 teaspoon salt, and ⅛ teaspoon pepper to coat evenly. Arrange 1 layer deep in a greased large, shallow baking pan and drizzle evenly with remaining melted butter. Bake as directed.

Crispy Oven-Fried Chicken: Dredge chicken pieces in ⅔ cup unsifted flour mixed with 1 teaspoon each salt and paprika, ½ teaspoon each onion powder and savory, and ¼ teaspoon each garlic powder and pepper. Dip in 1 egg that has been lightly beaten with ¼ cup cold milk, then roll in ⅔ cup cracker meal mixed with 3 tablespoons minced parsley to coat evenly. Arrange 1 layer deep in a greased large, shallow baking pan and drizzle with ½ cup melted butter or margarine. Bake as directed.

To Oven-Fry Turkey: Preheat oven to 400° F. Place 1 cup butter (for each 5 pounds turkey) in a large, shallow roasting pan and let melt in preheating oven. Dredge a small (4–9-pound) cut-up turkey in seasoned flour (1½ cups unsifted flour, 1 tablespoon salt, ½ teaspoon pepper), roll in melted butter in pan, then arrange skin side down 1 layer deep in pan. Bake uncovered ¾ hour, turn skin side up, and bake ¾ hour longer until fork tender and nicely browned.

VARIATION:

Chili or Curry-Flavored Oven-Fried Turkey: Prepare as directed but add 1–2 tablespoons chili or curry powder and ½ teaspoon garlic powder to the seasoned flour.

How to Braise Poultry

Braising is an all-encompassing word used to describe foods that are browned in fat, then cooked, covered, with some additional liquid. Fricasseeing is a way of braising, so is cooking birds en casserole. Any bird can be braised, but it's an especially good way to deal with those that are a bit too tough to roast, broil, or fry. See the collection of recipes that follow.

How to Simmer Poultry

Birds can be *poached* in a small amount of liquid or *stewed* in quantities of it. Disjointed young chickens or parts of them (especially the breasts) are frequently poached before being used in recipes. Stewing is usually reserved for tough, over-the-hill birds that need long and slow simmering to make them tender.

Best Birds: Any birds can be stewed, though chickens are the ones that most often end up in the kettle. The methods given below can be used for other birds as well as for chicken.

To Poach: (Also see Suprêmes of Chicken).

Basic Preparation for Cooking: Have bird disjointed; wipe pieces with a damp cloth.

Basic Method: Place chicken pieces in a single layer in a large, heavy skillet (not iron), add water, chicken broth, or a ½ and ½ mixture of broth and dry white wine almost to cover. Also add, if you like, a *bouquet garni** tied in cheesecloth. Cover and simmer 30–35 minutes until tender. Remove and use in any recipes calling for cooked or poached chicken. Or cover with a suitable sauce and serve (see Some Sauces, Gravies, and Seasonings for Chicken).

To Stew:
Basic Preparation for Cooking: If bird is whole, remove paper of giblets from body cavity; also pull out any loose fat and discard. Wipe bird or pieces of bird with a damp cloth.

Basic Method: Place bird or pieces in a large, heavy kettle and add water almost to cover—a large hen or capon will require about 3 quarts. Add 1 teaspoon salt and, if you like, a small onion peeled and quartered or stuck with

3–4 cloves, 2–3 stalks celery and/or parsley, 2 bay leaves, and 6 peppercorns. Or, if you prefer, add a *bouquet garni** tied in cheesecloth. Cover and simmer slowly until tender. Times vary enormously according to the size and age of the bird. An old hen can take 2–3 hours to become tender, but a capon of the same or slightly larger size may be nearly falling off the bones after only 1 hour. So watch the pot closely. Plump broiler-fryers will be done in 40–55 minutes and a cut-up broiler-fryer or capon in about 25–40. Some parts (wings and backs), of course, cook more quickly than others; remove individual pieces from the kettle as they become tender. (*Note:* Neck, heart, and gizzard can be cooked along with the other parts of the chicken and will probably need the full cooking time. The liver [and sometimes heart] will cook in 10–15 minutes, so cook at the beginning, remove and reserve, or add at the end of cooking.)

How to Steam Poultry

Best Birds: Moderately young and tender chickens or capons.

Basic Preparation for Cooking: Same as for stewing.

Basic Method: Place whole or cut-up bird on a rack in a large kettle, pour in water to a depth of 1″, cover, and bring to a boil. Reduce heat so water just simmers and steam, adding additional water if kettle threatens to boil dry, until bird is tender. A cut-up bird will cook in about ¾ hour, a whole bird in 1–1½. Use steamed chicken in recipes calling for cooked chicken.

About Pressure Cooking Poultry

Only tough old birds should be pressure cooked; young tender ones will fall to pieces. Because cooker techniques differ from model to model, follow manufacturer's instructions. Place chicken, liquid and, if you like, a few chunks of celery, onion, and carrot in cooker, cover, and cook at 15 pounds pressure 25–35 minutes or as manufacturer advises. Lower pressure slowly.

What to Do with the Giblets

You can freeze giblets separately in small plastic bags and save them until you have enough to use in a recipe (see recipes for chicken livers that follow). Or the giblets can be used immediately in stuffings or gravies or slipped into any of the recipes calling for cooked poultry. But first they must be cooked.

To Cook Giblets: Wash giblets carefully in cool water; if liver is green, discard— the gall bladder has ruptured, spilling its bitter gall and ruining the liver. Place giblets in a small saucepan and, if you like, the neck. Add *just* enough cold water to cover, cover pan, and simmer over low heat 10–15 minutes. Remove liver and reserve, also remove heart if it is tender. Re-cover and simmer remaining giblets until tender, 1–2 hours —time will depend on size and age of bird; add additional water during cooking as needed. Remove giblets, mince, and use in recipes calling for cooked poultry meat; also reserve cooking liquid to use in soups and gravies.

To Make Giblet Stock: Cook as directed above, but increase amount of water to 2–3 cups, depending on size of giblets, and add 1 teaspoon salt; replenish water as needed during cooking. Taste stock for seasoning and adjust; if you wish, strain through a fine sieve lined with a double thickness of cheesecloth before using in recipes. Mince giblets and use in any recipes calling for cooked poultry meat.

About Poultry Stocks

Any liquid used for poaching or stewing a bird is stock and should be saved to use in cooking vegetables, making sauces and gravies. Specific recipes for chicken and turkey broths can be found in the chapter on soups.

How to Render Chicken or Goose Fat

"Duck fat," someone once said, "isn't fit for anything but greasing your boots." Perhaps. But chicken and goose fat are excellent for browning poultry, potatoes, and other vegetables (turkey fat is good too, but today's birds have almost none). Carefully rendered raw chicken or goose fat can be used as the shortening in biscuits and other hot breads. Jewish women render chicken fat with an apple and onion into *schmaltz,* which they use as a butter substitute. Goose fat has an especially delicate flavor and is an essential ingredient of fine pâtés and *confit d'oie* (preserved goose). The best fats to render are those pulled raw from the body cavity of a bird. But pan drippings from a roasting bird can be saved, clarified* (see To Clarify Meat Drippings in the meat chapter), and used for gravies or browning meats and vegetables.

General Preparation of Fat: Pull fat from body cavity of bird, rinse in cold water, and cut in ½″ cubes.

Stove-Top Method of Rendering: (*Note:* This method also clarifies the fat.)

Place prepared fat in a large, heavy saucepan and add enough cold water to come about halfway up fat. Heat uncovered over moderately low heat, stirring frequently, until all fat is melted. Continue heating and stirring until nearly all water has evaporated; liquid will become clear and golden and bubbles will almost subside; strain through a double thickness of cheesecloth, cool, and chill. Carefully lift off fat and discard any liquid that has settled to the bottom; also scrape off any milky, semiliquid layer on bottom of fat. Pack fat in containers, cover, and refrigerate or freeze.

VARIATION:

Seasoned Fat: Render as directed but add 1 peeled and minced onion and 1 peeled and cored tart green apple, cut in wedges, to the pan; remove apple the instant it becomes tender, but leave onion in until almost all water evaporates unless it browns too much. Strain, cool, and store as directed.

Oven Method of Rendering: Preheat oven to 250° F. Spread prepared fat in the bottom of a shallow baking pan and add about ½ cup cold water. Heat uncovered, stirring occasionally, until fat is melted and most of the water evaporated. Strain, cool, and store as above. To clarify, follow directions for clarifying rendered fat in the meat chapter.

How to Carve Poultry

Except for minor variations, the technique of carving is the same for all birds:
1. *Separate and Remove Leg:* Pull leg away from body and cut off, following contour of bird. Place on a separate plate.

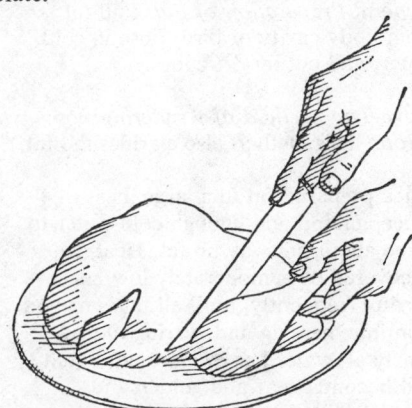

2. *Cut Meat from Leg:* Sever "knee" joint, separating drumstick and thigh. Hold drumstick with a napkin, tilt to a convenient angle, and slice meat parallel to bone.
3. *Cut Meat from Thigh:* Hold thigh firmly to plate with fork and slice

parallel to the bone. (*Note:* If a large group is being served, remove other drumstick and thigh and slice.)
4. *Remove Wing:* Place knife parallel with and as close to breast as possible, cut through joint, and remove wing.

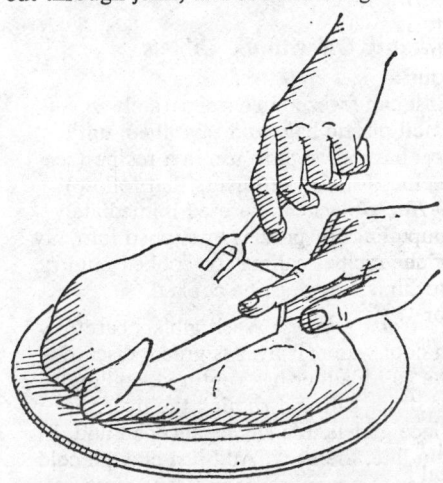

5. *Carve Breast:* Beginning halfway up breast, carve down, ending at cut made to remove wing. Begin each new slice a little higher on the breast, keeping slices as thin and even as possible.

Slice only what meat is needed at a time. Make fresh slices for "seconds."
(*Note:* Ducks are more difficult to carve than chicken or turkey, and if they are small, you may prefer to quarter them —see How to Cut Up Poultry—in the kitchen before serving.)

Some Marinades and Glazes for Poultry

Marinades: To enrich flavor of whole or cut-up poultry, marinate in refrigerator 3–4 hours before cooking, turning occasionally in marinade, then brush or baste often with marinade during last 20–30 minutes of cooking. Use any of the following, allowing about 1 cup marinade per chicken, 2–3 cups per large bird, and ½ cup per small bird.

— *Herbed or Spiced Wine or Cider* (½ cup dry red, white, or rosé wine or cider mixed with ¼ cup boiling water and 1 teaspoon sage, savory, or thyme or ¼ teaspoon cinnamon, nutmeg, or mace).
— *Juniper Wine* (½ cup dry red, white, or rosé wine mixed with ¼ cup each olive oil and boiling water and 1 teaspoon bruised juniper berries; omit oil if using for duck or goose).
— *Garlic Wine* (½ cup dry red, white, or rosé wine mixed with ¼ cup each olive oil and boiling water and 2 crushed cloves garlic; omit oil if using for duck or goose).
— Any herb, garlic, or Italian salad dressing.
— Any of the following:
Beer Marinade
Poultry Marinade
Buttermilk Marinade
All-Purpose Barbecue Sauce
Japanese Steak Sauce
California Orange-Ginger Barbecue Sauce
Chinese Barbecue Sauce
South American Hot Barbecue Sauce

Glazes: For a gorgeously glistening brown bird, brush with one of the following glazes during the last 20–30 minutes of broiling or roasting. You'll need about ½ cup glaze for a chicken, about 1 cup for a bigger bird, and ¼ cup for a tiny bird:
— A ½ and ½ mixture of melted apple and currant or quince jelly.
— A ½ and ½ mixture of hot apple juice and minced chutney.
— Melted orange, lime, or ginger marmalade.
— Warm wine, beer, cider, orange, grape, or pineapple juice mixed with dark brown sugar (2 tablespoons sugar to each ½ cup liquid).

Butters: Instead of being marinated or glazed, chicken, turkey, and other dry-meated birds can be brushed or basted often during roasting or broiling with one of these seasoned butters: Chili, Chive, Curry, Garlic, Herb, Lemon, Maître d'Hôtel, Mustard, Paprika, or Shallot (see chapter on sauces and gravies for recipes).

Some Ways to Garnish Poultry

Any of the garnishes suggested for pork are suitable for poultry (see Some Garnishes for Roast Pork Platters). Choose small garnishes for small birds, larger ones for larger birds, emphasizing a contrast of colors, textures, and shapes. The point is to enhance the bird, not to overwhelm. Some other garnishing ideas to try:

— A chain of baby link sausages, cooked until brown and glistening, draped over a plump roast turkey or goose.
— Lemon or lime cups filled with cranberry sauce, tart jelly, chutney, or mincemeat.
— Red Cabbage and Chestnuts, Sweet and Sour Red Cabbage, Shredded Ruby Cabbage, or sauerkraut wreathed around roast duck or goose.
— Clusters of Braised Chestnuts or Braised Onions and tiny bundles of buttered asparagus tips bound with strips of pimiento.
— Clusters of tangerine or orange and grapefruit sections.
— Chicken Quenelles or Mousselines sprinkled with minced truffles (for poached chicken).

SOME SAUCES, GRAVIES, AND SEASONINGS FOR POULTRY

	Sauces and Gravies for		Stuffings for	Herbs and Spices	Condiments
	Roasted, Broiled, Sautéed Birds	Simmered, Steamed Birds	Birds to Be Roasted	for Cooking Poultry	
Chicken, turkey, game hen, squab, guinea fowl, pheasant	All-purpose barbecue	Allemande	Basic bread and variations	Basil	Applesauce
	Bordelaise	Aurore	Basic rice and variations	Bay leaves	Bread sauce
	Brown sauce fines herbes	Béchamel	Basic wild rice and variations	Caraway seeds	Chutney
	Chasseur	Caper	Brandied wild rice, corn bread, and chestnut	Chervil	Cranberry sauce
	Diable	Chaud-froid (cold)	Bulgur wheat-pecan	Chili powder	Gingered pears
	Espagnole	Mornay	Chestnut mushroom	Chives	*Jellies:* apple, crab apple, currant, rosemary, wine
	Giblet gravy	Mushroom	Corn and pepper	Cinnamon	Pickled or brandied peaches
	Madeira	Mustard	Corn bread and sausage and variations	Cloves	*Relishes:* corn, cranberry-orange, fruit and nut, peach
	Mushroom	Parsley	Giblet	Coriander	Spiced apricots or crab apples
	Mushroom gravy	Poulette	Mincemeat	Curry powder	
	Pan gravy	Quick mushroom	Orange-sweet potato	Dill	
	Plum	Quick mustard	Prune, apple, and cranberry	Garlic	
	Portugaise	Soubise	Sage and onion dressing	Ginger	
	Quick mushroom	Suprême	Tangerine cracker (small birds)	Juniper berries	
	Robert	Velouté		Lemon	
	Tomato			Mace	
	Victoria			Marjoram	
				Mustard	
				Nutmeg	
				Onion	
				Orange	
				Oregano	
				Paprika	
				Parsley	
				Poultry seasoning	
				Rosemary	
				Saffron	
				Sage	
				Savory	
				Sesame seeds	
				Shallots	
				Tarragon	
				Thyme	

	Sauces and Gravies	Stuffings for Duck or Goose to Be Roasted	Herbs and Spices to Use in Cooking	Condiments
Roast duck or goose, broiled duckling	Bigarade Bordelaise Bourguignonne Brown sauce fines herbes Chasseur Espagnole Giblet gravy Madeira Madeira mushroom Mushroom gravy Pan gravy Plum Port wine Poivrade Victoria	Amish potato Basic bread and variations Bulgur wheat-pecan Chestnut Giblet Herbed fruit Prune, apple, and cranberry Sage and onion dressing Sauerkraut	Bay leaves Caraway seeds Chives Cinnamon Cloves Curry powder Garlic Ginger Juniper berries Lemon Mace Marjoram Nutmeg Onion Orange Paprika Parsley Sage Thyme	Same as for chicken Pickled red cabbage Sauerkraut

CHICKEN FRICASSEE

Makes 4 servings

1 (3–3½-pound) broiler-fryer, cut up
¼ cup butter or margarine
3 cups water
*1 medium-size yellow onion, peeled
　and stuck with 6 cloves*
*1 medium-size carrot, peeled and cut in
　1" chunks*
1 stalk celery, cut in 1" chunks
1 bouquet garni, tied in cheesecloth
　with 6 peppercorns*
1 teaspoon salt

Sauce:

3 tablespoons butter or margarine
¼ cup unsifted flour
*2 cups chicken broth, reserved from
　cooking chicken*
*1 egg yolk, lightly beaten with ½ cup
　light or heavy cream*
1 teaspoon lemon juice
¼ teaspoon sugar
1 teaspoon salt (about)
1 tablespoon minced parsley (garnish)
4 thin lemon slices (garnish)

Brown chicken in butter in a large,
heavy kettle over moderately high heat;
add all but sauce ingredients, cover, and
simmer 30–40 minutes until chicken is
tender. Lift chicken from kettle and
keep warm; strain broth, skim off fat
and measure 2 cups to use in sauce.
Melt butter in a large saucepan over
moderate heat, blend in flour, slowly
stir in broth, and heat, stirring, until
thickened. Mix a little hot sauce into
yolk mixture, return to pan, and heat
and stir over lowest heat 1 minute; do
not boil. Blend in lemon juice, sugar,
and salt to taste. Add chicken to sauce
and warm over lowest heat 1–2 minutes.
Serve in a deep platter sprinkled with
parsley and garnished with lemon. Good
with boiled noodles or rice, mashed
potatoes or hot biscuits. About 470
calories per serving.

VARIATIONS:

Georgian Chicken Fricassee: Prepare
as directed but when making sauce use 1
cup each broth and dry white wine.

Just before serving, mix in ½ pound
Pan-Braised Onions and ½ pound
sautéed button mushrooms. About 490
calories per serving.

Chicken and Vegetable Fricassee: Prepare as directed; just before serving, mix
in 1 (10-ounce) package frozen mixed
vegetables cooked and drained by package directions. Omit parsley and lemon
and garnish instead with hot buttered
asparagus tips. About 520 calories per
serving.

Blanquette of Chicken or Turkey (good
for leftovers): Prepare sauce as directed,
mix with 3 cups large chunks cooked
chicken or turkey meat (preferably
white). Bring to serving temperature in
the top of a double boiler. About 470
calories per serving.

PORTUGUESE-STYLE ROAST CAPON WITH OLIVE AND EGG STUFFING

Lisbon is one of the few European
capitals where one can be wakened at
5 A.M. by a rooster crowing. Not
surprisingly, Lisbon cooks specialize in
chicken. Here is a slightly streamlined
version of one of their best dishes.
Makes 6 servings

*1 (5–6-pound) capon, cleaned and
　dressed*
1 fifth Portuguese vinho verde *or other
　dry white wine*
1 tablespoon olive oil

Stuffing:

*4 medium-size yellow onions, peeled
　and coarsely chopped*
3 cloves garlic, peeled and crushed
⅔ cup olive oil
Cooked capon giblets, minced
1 (8-ounce) package poultry stuffing mix
*2 (5½-ounce) jars unpitted green olives,
　drained, pitted, and minced*
6 hard-cooked eggs, peeled and diced
¼ teaspoon pepper
¼ teaspoon cinnamon
½ cup giblet stock*
¼ cup dry port wine

The day before you roast the bird, take

giblets from body cavity and refrigerate. Place bird in a large bowl, add wine, cover, and marinate overnight in refrigerator. Next day, prepare giblet stock,* mince cooked giblets and reserve for stuffing along with ½ cup stock. Preheat oven to 325° F. For the stuffing, stir-fry onions and garlic in oil in a large, heavy skillet 10–12 minutes over moderate heat until lightly browned. Remove from heat, mix in giblets and remaining stuffing ingredients. Remove bird from marinade, drain, then loosely stuff neck and body cavities. Skewer openings shut and truss.* Wrap any remaining stuffing in foil. Rub bird well with 1 tablespoon oil, place breast side up on a rack in a large, shallow roasting pan; lay foil-wrapped stuffing in pan beside bird. Pour about 1½ cups wine marinade over bird and roast uncovered about 40 minutes per pound, basting every 20 minutes with marinade, until bird is golden brown and leg joints move easily. Lift bird to a large platter, remove skewers and string, garnish with watercress, cherry tomatoes, and black olives, and serve. Spoon extra stuffing into a separate bowl and pan drippings into a gravy boat. About 985 calories per serving.

COQ AU VIN (CHICKEN IN WINE)

Makes 4 servings

2 ounces lean salt pork, cut in small dice
3–4 tablespoons butter or margarine
1 (3–3½-pound) broiler-fryer, cut up
1 pound small white onions, peeled, parboiled, and drained
1 clove garlic, peeled and crushed
½ pound button mushrooms, wiped clean
¼ cup warm cognac or brandy
1 bouquet garni, tied in cheesecloth*
¼ teaspoon pepper
½–1 teaspoon salt
1½ cups Burgundy or other dry red wine
3 tablespoons Beurre Manié

Brown salt pork in a large, heavy kettle over moderate heat; remove with a slotted spoon and reserve. Add 3 tablespoons butter to kettle and brown

chicken, a few pieces at a time; remove and reserve. Add onions and brown well all over, about 10 minutes, adding more butter if necessary. Push onions to side of kettle, add garlic and mushrooms, and stir-fry 3–5 minutes until lightly browned. Return salt pork and chicken to kettle, pour cognac over chicken and blaze. When flames die, add all but final ingredient, cover, and simmer about ¾ hour until chicken is tender. Lift chicken and vegetables to a deep casserole and keep warm. Stir small pieces of *Beurre Manié* into kettle liquid and heat, stirring, until thickened and smooth. Taste for salt and add remainder if needed. Strain gravy over chicken and serve. Good with boiled new potatoes or rice.

VARIATION:

Coq au Vin au Casserole: Prepare as directed, but instead of cooking on the top stove, bake in a covered casserole 30–40 minutes at 350° F. until chicken is tender.

Both versions: About 625 calories per serving (without potatoes or rice).

POULET BASQUAIS (BASQUE-STYLE CHICKEN)

Good with buttered noodles.
Makes 4 servings

1 (3-pound) broiler-fryer, cut up
3 tablespoons olive oil
2 large ripe tomatoes, peeled, cored, seeded, and chopped
4 sweet green peppers, cored, seeded, and quartered
¼ pound mushrooms, wiped clean and sliced thin
¼ pound lean cooked ham, diced
1½ teaspoons salt
¼ teaspoon pepper
½ cup dry white wine or chicken broth
2 tablespoons tomato paste
1 tablespoon minced parsley
2 pimientos, drained and cut in thin strips

Brown chicken in oil in a heavy kettle over moderately high heat. Add tomatoes, green peppers, mushrooms, ham, salt, pepper, and wine, cover, and simmer slowly ¾ hour until chicken is fork tender. Remove chicken to a serving platter with a slotted spoon and keep warm. Blend tomato paste into kettle liquid and boil rapidly, uncovered, 1 minute. Pour some sauce over chicken, sprinkle with parsley, and decorate with pimiento. Pass remaining sauce. About 485 calories per serving.

¢ CHICKEN CACCIATORE

Makes 4 servings

¼ cup olive oil
1 (3–3½-pound) broiler-fryer, cut up
2 medium-size yellow onions, peeled and minced
1 clove garlic, peeled and crushed
¼ pound mushrooms, wiped clean and sliced thin
1 small sweet green pepper, cored, seeded, and coarsely chopped
1 (1-pound) can tomatoes (do not drain)
¾ cup dry white or red wine
¼ cup tomato paste
½ teaspoon rosemary
1 teaspoon salt
¼ teaspoon pepper

Heat oil in a heavy kettle over moderately high heat 1 minute, then brown chicken well; remove and reserve. Stir-fry onions 5 minutes, add garlic, mushrooms, and green pepper, and stir-fry 3–4 minutes longer until onions are golden. Add tomatoes, breaking up clumps, blend wine and tomato paste and stir in along with rosemary. Return chicken to kettle, sprinkle with salt and pepper, cover, and simmer, stirring now and then, about ¾ hour until tender. Serve with spaghetti. About 475 calories per serving (without spaghetti).

¢ CHICKEN MARENGO

Now a classic, this was originally an odds-and-ends dish made for Napoleon at the Battle of Marengo.
Makes 4 servings

2 tablespoons olive oil
1 (3-pound) broiler-fryer, cut up

½ pound button mushrooms, wiped clean
2 cloves garlic, peeled and crushed
1 large ripe tomato, peeled, cored, seeded, and chopped, or ⅔ cup coarsely chopped canned tomatoes
½ cup dry white wine
2 tablespoons tomato paste
1 teaspoon salt
⅛ teaspoon pepper
1 tablespoon minced parsley

Heat oil in a large, flameproof casserole over moderate heat or in a deep electric skillet set at 350° F. Brown chicken well on all sides, then remove and set aside. Sauté mushrooms in casserole 3–5 minutes until golden; add garlic and stir-fry 1 minute. Stir in all remaining ingredients except parsley and return chicken to casserole. Cover and simmer about ¾ hour until tender. Sprinkle with parsley and serve. About 360 calories per serving.

CHICKEN ZINGARA

Makes 4 servings

2 medium-size yellow onions, peeled and sliced thin
3 tablespoons bacon drippings, butter, or margarine
1 (3-pound) broiler-fryer, cut up
1 teaspoon salt
1 tablespoon paprika
⅓ cup dry red wine
¼ cup sweet Madeira wine
1 cup Rich Brown Sauce
1 tablespoon tomato paste
1 tablespoon minced cooked ham
1 tablespoon minced boiled tongue
1 tablespoon minced mushrooms
1 tablespoon minced black truffles

Stir-fry onions in drippings in a large, heavy skillet or electric frying pan over moderate heat 8–10 minutes until golden. Push onions to side of pan, add chicken, and sauté about 10 minutes until browned; reduce heat to low. Turn chicken skin side up, add salt, and sprinkle evenly with paprika. Add red wine, cover, and simmer about ¾ hour until chicken is tender. (Note: Recipe may be prepared to this point early in the day, then reheated slowly before proceeding.) Arrange chicken on a serving platter and keep warm. Mix Madeira and remaining ingredients into skillet with onions and simmer, uncovered, 5 minutes. Pour over chicken and serve. Good with boiled rice or buttered noodles. About 495 calories per serving (without rice or noodles).

MAGYAR CHICKEN PAPRIKA
Makes 4 servings

2 medium-size yellow onions, peeled and sliced thin
3 tablespoons bacon drippings or 1½ tablespoons each butter and cooking oil
1 (3–3½-pound) broiler-fryer, cut up
1 teaspoon salt
1 tablespoon paprika (the Hungarian sweet rose paprika is best)
⅓ cup chicken broth or dry red wine
1 cup sour cream

Stir-fry onions in drippings in a large, heavy skillet or electric frying pan over moderate heat 8–10 minutes until golden. Push to side of pan, add chicken, and fry about 10 minutes until lightly browned; turn heat to low. Arrange chicken skin side up, add salt, and sprinkle paprika evenly over all. Add broth, cover, and simmer ¾ hour until chicken is tender. (Note: You may prepare recipe to this point early in the day, then reheat slowly before serving.) Arrange chicken on a platter and keep warm. Mix sour cream into onions, heat 1–2 minutes but do not boil, then pour over chicken. Good with buttered noodles, kasha, or boiled potatoes. About 460 calories per serving (without noodles, kasha, or boiled potatoes).

ROMANIAN CHICKEN AND APRICOTS
Makes 4 servings

1 (3½–4-pound) broiler-fryer, cut up
3 tablespoons olive oil
1 medium-size yellow onion, peeled and minced
2 tablespoons flour
1 (1-pound) can apricots, drained (reserve liquid)
Apricot liquid plus enough chicken broth to total 2 cups
1 large sprig sage or rosemary or ¼ teaspoon dried sage or rosemary
1 teaspoon salt
⅛ teaspoon pepper

Brown chicken well in oil in a large, heavy kettle over moderately high heat; drain on paper toweling. Drain all but 2 tablespoons drippings from skillet, add onion, turn heat to moderate, and stir-fry 8–10 minutes until golden; blend in flour. Add apricot liquid mixture and heat, stirring, until slightly thickened. Return chicken to skillet; add sage, salt, and pepper, cover, and simmer slowly about ¾ hour until chicken is tender. Meanwhile, halve and pit apricots. Uncover chicken, add apricots, and simmer 5–10 minutes longer. Serve over boiled rice. About 460 calories per serving (without rice).

PAELLA
This paella is geared to American rice, pans, and palates.
Makes 6 servings

¼ cup olive oil
3 (6–8-ounce) frozen rock lobster tails, cut crosswise in 1" chunks
½ pound raw shrimp, shelled and deveined
1 (2½–3-pound) broiler-fryer, cut up
1 large yellow onion, peeled and minced
2 cloves garlic, peeled and crushed
1 large sweet green pepper, cored, seeded, and minced
½ cup diced cooked ham or 1 chorizo (Spanish sausage), sliced ½" thick
1½ cups uncooked rice
2¾ cups chicken broth or water
2 teaspoons salt
¼ teaspoon pepper
¼–½ teaspoon powdered saffron
¼ cup tomato paste
1 (10-ounce) package frozen green peas
1½ dozen clams or mussels in the shell, prepared for cooking
1 pimiento, slivered (garnish)

Heat oil in a large (at least 5-quart) burner-to-table kettle over moderately high heat 1 minute, add lobster and shrimp, and stir-fry 3–4 minutes until pink; remove with a slotted spoon and reserve. Brown chicken well, remove, and reserve. Stir-fry onion in drippings 5 minutes, then add garlic, green pepper, and ham and stir-fry 3–4 minutes. Add rice, broth, 1½ teaspoons salt, ⅛ teaspoon pepper, the saffron and tomato paste. Return chicken to kettle, sprinkle with remaining salt and pepper, cover, and simmer ½ hour. Add lobster, shrimp, and peas (break them up when adding), cover, and simmer 10–15 minutes until chicken and peas are tender. Arrange clams on top, cover, and simmer 5 minutes until clams partially open. Sprinkle with pimiento and serve. About 610 calories per serving.

¢ ARROZ CON POLLO

Makes 4 servings

1 (3–3½-pound) broiler-fryer, cut up
⅓ cup unsifted flour
3 tablespoons olive oil
1 medium-size yellow onion, peeled and minced
1 clove garlic, peeled and crushed
½ cup julienne strips cooked ham
1 cup uncooked rice
1 cup chicken broth
1 (1-pound) can tomatoes (do not drain)
2 teaspoons salt
¼ teaspoon pepper
¼ teaspoon powdered saffron
1 bay leaf, crumbled
1 (4-ounce) can pimientos, drained and cut in 1" pieces
1 (10-ounce) package frozen green peas, cooked by package directions

Preheat oven to 350° F. Dredge chicken by shaking with flour in a bag. Heat oil in a large, heavy skillet over moderately high heat 1 minute, then brown chicken well, a few pieces at a time; drain on paper toweling. Reduce heat to moderate and stir-fry onion and garlic 5 minutes, add ham and stir-fry 3–4 minutes longer until onion is golden. Add rice, stir-fry 1 minute, then add broth, tomatoes, breaking up clumps, 1 teaspoon salt, ⅛ teaspoon pepper, the saffron and bay leaf; mix well. Spoon into an ungreased 2½-quart casserole about 2" deep, arrange chicken on top and sprinkle with remaining salt and pepper. Cover tightly and bake about 1 hour until chicken is fork tender. Uncover, scatter pimientos on top, and bake uncovered 10 minutes longer. Spoon peas around edge of casserole and serve. About 655 calories per serving.

VARIATION:

¢ **Mexican-Style Arroz Con Pollo:** Brown chicken as directed; stir-fry 1 minced, cored, and seeded hot green chili pepper along with onion and garlic. Proceed as directed, substituting 1–2 browned, thickly sliced, *chorizos* (Spanish sausages) for the ham and adding ¼ teaspoon cumin seeds along with other seasonings. About 665 calories per serving.

PUEBLA-STYLE CHICKEN MOLE

There are *moles* and *moles.* This one is rich, dark, and peppery like that served at Puebla, Mexico (chocolate is the key ingredient). The dried *ancho* and *pasilla* chilis called for can be bought at most gourmet, Spanish, or Latin American groceries.

Makes 4 servings

1 (3½–4-pound) broiler-fryer, cut up
1 quart water
2 teaspoons salt (about)
3 dried ancho chili peppers, washed, cored, and seeded
3 dried pasilla chili peppers, washed, cored, and seeded
1½ cups boiling water
2 tablespoons lard
1 medium-size yellow onion, peeled and minced
1 clove garlic, peeled and crushed
½ cup blanched slivered almonds or piñon nuts
1 tablespoon sesame seeds
⅛ teaspoon cloves
⅛ teaspoon cinnamon
¼ teaspoon coriander

1–1½ teaspoons crushed dried red chili peppers (depending on how hot you like things)

⅓ cup seedless raisins

2 medium-size tomatoes, peeled, cored, seeded, and coarsely chopped

1 (1-ounce) square unsweetened chocolate, coarsely grated

1 cup chicken broth (reserved from poaching chicken)

1 teaspoon light brown sugar

Place chicken in a large, heavy skillet (not iron), add water and salt, cover, and simmer about ¾ hour until tender; remove to paper toweling and pat dry; reserve broth. While chicken simmers, break dried ancho and pasilla chilis into small pieces, discard seeds, cover with boiling water, and let stand until chicken is done; purée chilis and their soaking water in an electric blender at high speed. Wipe skillet dry, add lard, and brown chicken well over moderately high heat; drain on paper toweling. Stir-fry onion and garlic in drippings over moderate heat 8–10 minutes until golden; add puréed chilis, nuts, sesame seeds, spices, raisins, and tomatoes and stir-fry 3–5 minutes to blend flavors. Purée skillet mixture, a little at a time, in an electric blender at high speed. Return to skillet, add chocolate, broth, and sugar, and heat, stirring, until chocolate is melted; taste for salt and adjust as needed. Return chicken to skillet, cover, set over lowest heat, and let "mellow" ½–¾ hour, basting chicken occasionally with sauce in skillet. Serve over boiled rice. About 565 calories per serving (without rice).

VARIATION:

Turkey Mole: Prepare as directed, substituting 4 pounds turkey parts for the chicken. About 600 calories per serving (without rice).

BURMESE SPICED CHICKEN IN PEANUT-COCONUT SAUCE

Makes 4 servings

1 (3½–4-pound) broiler-fryer, cut up

3 tablespoons peanut oil

2 (3-ounce) cans flaked coconut

2½ cups milk

2 medium-size yellow onions, peeled and minced

1 clove garlic, peeled and crushed

1 tablespoon minced fresh mint or mint flakes

¼ teaspoon cinnamon

¼ teaspoon ginger

¼ teaspoon cayenne pepper

¼ teaspoon black pepper

⅛ teaspoon cloves

½ teaspoon salt

3 tablespoons soy sauce

½ cup minced, roasted, blanched peanuts

Brown chicken well on all sides in oil in a large, heavy skillet over moderately high heat; drain on paper toweling. Meanwhile, simmer coconut in milk 5 minutes; strain milk and reserve. (*Note:* Coconut can be dried out by spreading on a baking sheet and letting stand, uncovered, 2½–3 hours in a 200° F. oven. Use to decorate cakes, cookies, or candies.) Pour all but 2 tablespoons drippings from skillet, add onions and garlic, and stir-fry 8–10 minutes until golden. Mix in mint, spices, salt, soy sauce, and reserved milk, return chicken to skillet, cover, and simmer slowly ½ hour. Lift chicken from sauce and set aside. Purée skillet mixture, a very little bit at a time, in an electric blender at high speed. Wipe out skillet, pour in purée, add chicken and peanuts, cover, and simmer 15–20 minutes longer, stirring occasionally, until chicken is tender. Serve over boiled rice. About 840 calories per serving (without rice).

⚖ CHICKEN TERIYAKI

Makes 6 servings

Breasts of 3 large broiler-fryers, boned,* halved, and skinned

½ cup soy sauce

¼ cup mirin (sweet rice wine) or medium or dry sherry

1 tablespoon sugar

2 teaspoons finely grated fresh gingerroot

Place breasts between wax paper and

pound to flatten slightly. Marinate 1–2 hours in refrigerator in a mixture of soy sauce, *mirin*, sugar, and ginger, turning once or twice. Preheat broiler. Remove chicken from marinade and arrange on lightly oiled rack in broiler pan. Broil 5″–6″ from heat about 4 minutes on each side; brush with marinade when turning. Serve with tiny bowls of remaining marinade (sake cups are a good size) or pour a little marinade over each portion. Good with Japanese Rice with Toasted Seaweed and a spinach salad. About 230 calories per serving (without rice).

VARIATION:

⚖ **Yakitori:** Flatten breasts, then cut in 1″ cubes and marinate as directed. Thread on bamboo or thin metal skewers alternating with chunks of scallion and halved chicken livers. Broil about 8 minutes, giving skewers a quarter turn every 2 minutes; brush frequently with marinade. (*Note:* Miniatures may be served as appetizers; use 1″ chicken cubes and quartered livers.) About 255 calories per serving.

¢ COUNTRY CAPTAIN

A very mild curry popular in the South.
Makes 6–8 servings

1 (5½–6-pound) stewing hen or capon, cleaned and dressed
2 bay leaves
2 stalks celery (include tops)
2 quarts water
2 large yellow onions, peeled and coarsely chopped
2 large sweet green peppers, cored, seeded, and coarsely chopped
2 cloves garlic, peeled and crushed
¼ cup olive or other cooking oil
⅓ cup minced parsley
1 cup dried currants or seedless raisins
1 tablespoon curry powder
1 teaspoon cayenne pepper
¼ teaspoon black pepper
½ teaspoon thyme
¼ teaspoon cloves
2 teaspoons salt

2 (1-pound 12-ounce) cans tomatoes (do not drain)
3 cups reserved chicken stock
1 cup toasted, blanched almonds (topping)

Remove fat from body cavity of bird, then place bird and giblets in a large kettle, add bay leaves, celery, and water, cover, and simmer 10–15 minutes; remove liver and reserve. Re-cover chicken and simmer about 1–1½ hours longer until tender; lift chicken from kettle and cool; strain stock and reserve. In the same kettle stir-fry onions, green peppers, and garlic in oil 8–10 minutes over moderate heat until onion is golden. Add all but last ingredient and simmer, uncovered, 45 minutes, stirring now and then. Meanwhile, skin chicken, remove meat from bones, and cut in bite-size pieces. Add chicken, reserved liver, and giblets to sauce and simmer, uncovered, 15 minutes. Serve with or over fluffy boiled rice, topped with almonds. (*Note:* Recipe can be made several days ahead and kept refrigerated until shortly before serving; it also freezes well.) About 605 calories for each of 6 servings (without rice or almonds), 455 calories for each of 8 servings.

CHICKEN JAIPUR

A spicy chicken curry.
Makes 4–6 servings

1 (4–5-pound) stewing hen, cleaned and dressed
1 quart water
1 large yellow onion, peeled and stuck with 4 cloves
1 large carrot, peeled and quartered
2½ teaspoons salt
4 peppercorns
1½ cups simmering milk
1 (3½-ounce) can flaked coconut
1 large yellow onion, peeled and minced
1 clove garlic, peeled and crushed
3 tablespoons butter or margarine
⅓ cup curry powder
3 tablespoons minced crystallized ginger
¼–½ teaspoon cayenne pepper

⅛ teaspoon black pepper
1 teaspoon minced fresh mint or ½
   teaspoon mint flakes
⅛ teaspoon cloves
1½ cups reserved chicken stock
Juice of 1 lime
1 cup heavy cream

Remove fat from body cavity of bird, then place bird and giblets in a large kettle, add water, onion, carrot, salt, and peppercorns, cover, and simmer 15–20 minutes; remove liver and reserve. Re-cover chicken and simmer 1–1½ hours longer until tender; lift chicken and giblets from kettle and cool; strain stock and reserve. Pour milk over coconut and let steep until lukewarm; strain, reserving milk and discarding coconut. Stir-fry minced onion and garlic in butter in a very large, heavy skillet 8–10 minutes until golden; blend in curry powder, ginger, and all herbs and spices. Add reserved milk and chicken stock, cover and simmer ½ hour. Meanwhile, remove and discard chicken skin, take meat from bones, and cut in bite-size pieces. Add chicken and, if you like, liver and giblets to curry, cover, and simmer ½ hour. Mix in lime juice and cream and heat, stirring, 5–10 minutes. Serve with boiled rice. Good condiments: chutney, flaked coconut, chopped roasted peanuts, seedless raisins. About 800 calories for each of 4 servings (without rice or condiments), about 530 calories for each of 6 servings.

¢ ◲ ⚔ **CHICKEN CHOP SUEY**

Makes 4–6 servings

3 tablespoons cooking oil
2 medium-size yellow onions, peeled and
   minced
3 stalks celery, cut in thin diagonal slices
2 cups shredded Chinese cabbage
2 cups diced or julienne strips cooked
   chicken
1 (5-ounce) can bamboo shoots, drained
   and cut in thin strips
2 cups chicken broth
2 tablespoons soy sauce
2 tablespoons cornstarch blended with ¼
   cup cold water

1 (3-ounce) can water chestnuts,
   drained and sliced thin
1 (1-pound) can bean sprouts, drained

Heat oil in a wok or large, heavy skillet over moderately high heat 1 minute, add onions, celery, and cabbage, and stir-fry 3–4 minutes (do not brown). Add chicken and bamboo shoots and stir-fry 1 minute; add broth, soy sauce, and cornstarch paste and cook and stir until thickened. Add chestnuts and bean sprouts and toss 1–2 minutes. Taste for salt and add more if needed. Serve over boiled rice. About 355 calories for each of 4 servings, 235 for each of 6 servings (without rice).

¢ ◲ ⚔ **CHICKEN CHOW MEIN**

Makes 6 servings

½ pound mushrooms, wiped clean and
   sliced thin
6 scallions, minced (include some tops)
2 small sweet green peppers, cored,
   seeded, and minced
4 stalks celery, minced
2 tablespoons cooking oil
2½ cups chicken broth
2 tablespoons soy sauce
¼ cup cornstarch blended with ¼ cup
   cold water
½ teaspoon salt
⅛ teaspoon pepper
3 cups bite-size pieces cooked chicken
   meat, preferably white meat
1 (1-pound) can bean sprouts, drained
1 (3-ounce) can water chestnuts, drained
   and sliced thin

Stir-fry mushrooms, scallions, green peppers, and celery in oil in a large, heavy skillet over moderately high heat 8–10 minutes until golden brown. Add broth and soy sauce, turn heat to low, cover, and simmer 10 minutes. Mix in cornstarch paste, salt, and pepper and heat, stirring constantly, until thickened and clear. Add chicken, bean sprouts, and water chestnuts and heat and stir about 5 minutes, just to heat through. Taste for salt and adjust if needed. Serve over boiled rice. About 255 calories per serving (without rice).

⚖ **MOO GOO GAI PEEN (CHICKEN WITH MUSHROOMS)**

Makes 2 servings

Breast of 1 large broiler-fryer, boned,* halved, and skinned
2 tablespoons peanut oil
½ cup thinly sliced mushrooms
1 cup finely shredded Chinese cabbage
⅓ cup thinly sliced bamboo shoots
2 (½") cubes fresh gingerroot, peeled and crushed
⅓ cup chicken broth
1 tablespoon dry sherry (optional)
½ (7-ounce) package frozen snow pea pods, slightly thawed
3 water chestnuts, sliced thin
2 teaspoons cornstarch blended with 1 tablespoon cold water
¾ teaspoon salt (about)
⅛ teaspoon sugar

Cut chicken across the grain into strips about 2" long and ¼" wide; set aside. Heat 1 tablespoon oil in a large, heavy skillet over moderately high heat about 1 minute, add mushrooms, cabbage, bamboo shoots, and ginger, and stir-fry 2 minutes. Add broth, cover, and simmer 2–3 minutes. Pour all into a bowl and set aside. Wipe out skillet, heat remaining oil, and stir-fry chicken 2–3 minutes; if you like sprinkle with sherry and stir a few seconds longer. Return vegetables and broth to skillet, add snow peas and chestnuts, and heat, stirring until bubbling. Mix in cornstarch paste, salt, and sugar and heat, stirring until clear and slightly thickened; taste for salt and adjust as needed. Serve with boiled rice. About 250 calories per serving (without sherry or rice).

CHICKEN WITH SNOW PEAS AND WATER CHESTNUTS

Makes 4 servings

1 (3½-pound) broiler-fryer, cut up, skinned, and boned*
¼ cup soy sauce
¼ cup dry sherry or port
1 clove garlic, peeled and crushed
2 (½") cubes fresh gingerroot, peeled and crushed
¾ cup unsifted flour
⅓ cup peanut oil
1 (5-ounce) can water chestnuts, drained and sliced thin
1 (7-ounce) package frozen snow pea pods (do not thaw)
½ cup water

Cut chicken in bite-size pieces and marinate 2–3 hours in refrigerator in a mixture of soy sauce, sherry, garlic, and ginger. Remove from marinade and dredge in flour; save marinade. Heat oil in a large, heavy skillet over moderately high heat about 1 minute, add chicken, and stir-fry 2–3 minutes to brown lightly. Add marinade and remaining ingredients and stir-fry 2–3 minutes until peas are crisp-tender. Serve with or over boiled rice. About 525 calories per serving (without rice).

⊠ **CHAFING DISH CHICKEN AND SHRIMP IN SOUR CREAM-SHERRY SAUCE**

Makes 4 servings

3 tablespoons butter or margarine
3 tablespoons flour
1 cup chicken broth
¾ teaspoon garlic salt
⅛ teaspoon white pepper
Pinch nutmeg
1 cup sour cream
¼–⅓ cup medium-dry sherry
1½ cups diced cooked white chicken meat
1½ cups coarsely chopped large (or whole small) shelled and deveined boiled shrimp
1 recipe Rice Pilaf

Melt butter in a chafing dish over simmering water. Blend in flour, slowly add broth, and heat, stirring constantly, until thickened and smooth. Mix in seasonings, sour cream, and sherry; add chicken and shrimp and heat, stirring, 4–5 minutes. Ladle over pilaf and serve. About 800 calories per serving.

¢ ⊠ COMPANY CHICKEN CASSEROLE

Makes 4 servings

1 (3–3½-pound) broiler-fryer, cut up
¼ cup unsifted flour
½ teaspoon salt
¼ teaspoon pepper
¼ cup melted butter or margarine
1 (10½-ounce) can condensed cream of mushroom soup
⅔ cup milk
Pinch thyme
1 (1-pound) can small white onions, drained
1 (4-ounce) can sliced mushrooms, drained
2 pimientos, drained and cut in julienne strips

Preheat oven to 425° F. Dredge chicken in a mixture of flour, salt, and pepper. Pour butter in a shallow 2½-quart casserole and arrange chicken skin side down in butter, in a single layer. Bake, uncovered, ½ hour. Turn chicken skin side up and bake 15 minutes longer; remove drippings with a bulb baster. Blend soup, milk, and thyme until smooth and pour into casserole; arrange onions, mushrooms, and pimientos around chicken. Reduce oven to 325° F., cover casserole, and bake 15–20 minutes until bubbly. About 525 calories per serving.

OVEN-GLAZED CHICKEN

Makes 4 servings

⅓ cup fine toasted bread crumbs
½ teaspoon thyme
½ teaspoon sage
1 teaspoon salt
⅛ teaspoon pepper
¼ teaspoon garlic powder
1 (2½–3-pound) broiler-fryer, cut up
¼ cup milk
⅓ cup mayonnaise

Preheat oven to 425° F. Mix crumbs, herbs, salt, pepper, and garlic powder. Dip chicken in milk, then in crumb mixture to coat evenly and arrange skin side up, 1 layer deep, in a heavily greased shallow roasting pan. Bake, uncovered, 15 minutes to set crumbs, then gently spread chicken with mayonnaise (don't turn—do only the top side). Reduce oven to 350° F. and bake, uncovered, 45–50 minutes longer until chicken is fork tender, glazed, and golden brown. About 425 calories per serving.

CHICKEN TETRAZZINI

This luscious dish deserves the bravos heaped on its famous namesake, Italian coloratura Luisa Tetrazzini.
Makes 6–8 servings

1 (5–6-pound) stewing hen, cleaned and dressed
1 quart water
1½ teaspoons salt
1 small yellow onion, peeled
1 medium-size carrot, peeled
1 stalk celery
1 bay leaf
3–4 peppercorns
1 pound spaghettini or linguine
½ pound mushrooms, wiped clean, sliced and lightly sautéed in butter

Sauce:

¼ cup butter or margarine
¼ cup sifted flour
2 cups reserved chicken stock
1½ cups milk or ¾ cup each milk and dry white wine
1 cup heavy cream
2 teaspoons salt
⅛ teaspoon white pepper
1–2 tablespoons lemon juice (optional)
⅛ teaspoon nutmeg (optional)

Topping:

¾ cup soft, fine bread crumbs mixed with ¾ cup grated Parmesan cheese

Remove fat from body cavity of hen, then place hen, giblets, water, salt, onion, carrot, celery, bay leaf, and peppercorns in a large, heavy kettle, cover, and simmer about 2 hours until tender. (*Note:* Chicken liver should be removed after 10–15 minutes, cooled, and reserved.) Cool hen in stock, then skin and cut meat from bones in bite-size chunks; also dice all giblets; skim stock of fat, strain, and reserve. For sauce, melt butter over moderate heat, blend in flour, add stock and remaining sauce ingredients, and heat, stirring, until thickened. Preheat oven to 350° F. Cook pasta by package directions, drain and combine with sauce, mushrooms, chicken, and giblets, including liver. Place in a buttered shallow 3-quart casserole, sprinkle with topping and bake, uncovered, 30–40 minutes until bubbly. Brown quickly under broiler and serve. About 875 calories for each of 6 servings, 655 calories for each of 8 servings.

VARIATIONS:

Turkey Tetrazzini: Prepare as directed, substituting a 6-pound turkey for the chicken. About 875 calories for each of 6 servings, 655 calories for each of 8 servings.

Ham Tetrazzini: Prepare sauce as directed; also cook pasta. Toss with 3 cups diced cooked ham and the mushrooms called for, then top and bake as directed. About 755 calories for each of 6 servings, 565 calories for each of 8 servings.

¢ **CHICKEN JAMBALAYA BAKE**

An easy, economical chicken, rice, and tomato casserole.
Makes 4–6 servings

1 (3–3½-pound) broiler-fryer, cut up
⅔ cup unsifted flour
2 tablespoons chili powder
3½ teaspoons salt
⅓ cup olive oil
1 large yellow onion, peeled and coarsely chopped
1 clove garlic, peeled and crushed
⅔ cup uncooked rice
1 (1-pound 12-ounce) can tomatoes (do not drain)
¼ cup water
⅛–¼ teaspoon cayenne pepper (depending on how hot you like things)

Preheat oven to 350° F. Dredge chicken by shaking in a bag with flour, chili powder, and 3 teaspoons salt; brown in oil in a large, heavy kettle and drain on paper toweling; pour off all but 3 tablespoons drippings. Stir-fry onion, garlic, and rice in drippings 3–5 minutes over moderate heat until rice is golden. Mix in tomatoes, water, cayenne, and remaining salt and heat, stirring, until mixture simmers. Return chicken to kettle, pushing down into liquid, cover, and bake 1 hour until chicken and rice are tender. About 535 calories for each of 4 servings, 360 calories for each of 6 servings.

CIRCASSIAN CHICKEN

An unusual Turkish cold chicken and walnut dish that's perfect for a buffet. It's rich, needs only a green salad and rolls to accompany.
Makes 6 servings

1 (6–6½-pound) capon, cleaned and dressed (save giblets for a gravy or other recipe)
3 quarts water
1 onion, peeled and stuck with 3 cloves
2 bay leaves
1 stalk celery, cut in large chunks
1 medium-size carrot, peeled and cut in large chunks
6 peppercorns
1½ teaspoons salt

Sauce:
1 pound shelled walnuts
3 slices white bread, trimmed of crusts and soaked in ¼ cup milk
1 teaspoon salt
⅛ teaspoon pepper
2⅓ cups reserved chicken broth (about)

Topping:
2 tablespoons olive oil mixed with 1 teaspoon paprika

Place chicken, water, onion, bay leaves, celery, carrot, peppercorns, and salt in a large, heavy kettle, cover, and simmer about 1 hour until chicken is tender; lift chicken from broth and cool; strain broth and reserve. For sauce, purée walnuts, a few at a time, in an electric blender at high speed; mix with bread, salt, pepper, and enough broth to make a sauce about the consistency of thick gravy; again purée, a little bit at a time, in blender at high speed. Skin chicken, remove meat, and cut in strips about 1½" long and ¼" wide. Mound about half the chicken on a large platter and spread with half the walnut sauce; arrange remaining chicken on top and spread with remaining sauce. Cover and chill several hours. Remove from refrigerator and let stand at room temperature 1 hour. Just before serving, drizzle paprika mixture over top in a crisscross design. About 960 calories per serving.

CHICKEN MOUSSELINES OR QUENELLES

Fragile poached chicken dumplings.
Makes 2–4 servings

Breast of 1 medium-size broiler-fryer, boned* and skinned
1 egg white
⅔ cup heavy cream
1 teaspoon salt
Pinch white pepper
1 teaspoon lemon juice
1 quart boiling water

Grind chicken very fine and mix with egg white. Press mixture through a fine sieve and place in a bowl over cracked ice. Beat with a wooden spoon 2–3 minutes until mixture thickens and will cling to a spoon turned upside down. Add cream, 2 tablespoons at a time, beating ½ minute after each addition; mixture will be soft but should hold a shape. Stir in ½ teaspoon salt, the pepper, and ½ teaspoon lemon juice. Pour water into a large skillet (not iron), add remaining salt and lemon juice, and adjust heat so liquid just trembles. Using 2 wet teaspoons, shape chicken mixture into egg-size balls and slide into poaching liquid (liquid should just cover mousselines; if not add a little extra simmering water). Poach, uncovered, 6–8 mousselines at a time, 3–5 minutes until just firm. Lift out with a slotted spoon and drain on paper toweling. Loosely cover poached mousselines and keep warm. Shape and poach the rest (wet the spoons often).

Use to garnish Chicken Breasts in Champagne Sauce, Suprêmes de Volaille à Blanc, or any poached or baked chicken suprêmes. Or top with Mushroom, Suprême, or Aurore Sauce and serve as a main course. About 490 calories for each of 2 servings, 245 calories for each of 4 servings (without sauce).

CHICKEN MAYONNAISE

Cool and creamy, a wise choice for a hot weather party buffet.
Makes 12 servings

1 (6–6½-pound) stewing hen, cleaned and dressed (save giblets for soup or gravy)
2½ quarts water
5 teaspoons salt
1 medium-size yellow onion, peeled and stuck with 3 cloves
1 cup diced celery
1 cup finely chopped walnuts or blanched almonds
4 hard-cooked eggs, peeled and finely chopped
1 small yellow onion, peeled and finely grated
1 (10-ounce) package frozen tiny green peas, cooked by package directions and drained but not seasoned
2 envelopes unflavored gelatin
2 cups reserved chicken stock
1 cup heavy cream
1 pint thick mayonnaise
¼ teaspoon pepper

Place hen in a large, heavy kettle with water, 3 teaspoons salt, and the onion, cover, and simmer about 2 hours until tender. Lift hen from stock and cool; strain and reserve stock. Skin chicken, separate meat from bones, and mince; place in a large mixing bowl with celery, nuts, eggs, grated onion, and peas, toss well to mix, and set aside. Heat gelatin in reserved stock and cream over moderate heat, stirring until dissolved; do not boil. Off heat, blend in mayonnaise, remaining salt, and the pepper. Pour over chicken mixture and stir well to mix. Pour into a 2½-quart decorative round mold, cover with saran and chill several hours or overnight until firm. Unmold on a large platter, garnish as desired (stuffed eggs, marinated artichoke hearts, and sprigs of cress are especially pretty). Slice into thin wedges and serve. About 675 calories per serving.

CHICKEN GALANTINE

Start this recipe the day before you plan to serve it.
Makes 4–6 servings

1 (3–3½-pound) broiler-fryer, boned*
   (reserve bones and carcass)

Stuffing:

½ pound veal, ground twice
½ cup soft white bread crumbs
¼ cup minced mushrooms
2 scallions, minced
1 teaspoon minced parsley
¼ teaspoon sage
¼ teaspoon thyme
½ teaspoon salt
¼ teaspoon pepper
1 egg, lightly beaten
2 tablespoons dry sherry, Madeira, or
   water
¼ pound boiled ham, sliced ¼" thick
¼ pound boiled tongue, sliced ¼" thick
2 truffles, minced

Poaching Liquid:

2 quarts water
1 veal knuckle, cracked (optional)
2 teaspoons salt
1 medium-size yellow onion, peeled
   and stuck with 4 cloves
1 carrot, peeled and cut in large chunks
2 stalks celery, cut in large chunks
1 bouquet garni,* tied in cheesecloth

Open chicken flat and lay skin side down on a large board; turn legs and wings inside out so chicken is nearly rectangular. In places where meat is more than ½" thick, trim off and use to "pad" skimpy places or grind and add to stuffing. Lightly knead together all but last 3 stuffing ingredients and spread ½ down center of chicken, leaving wide margins all around. Cut ham and tongue slices into strips ¼" wide and lay across stuffing, alternating

flavors; sprinkle with truffles and top with remaining stuffing. Pull sides of chicken up over stuffing, enclosing it

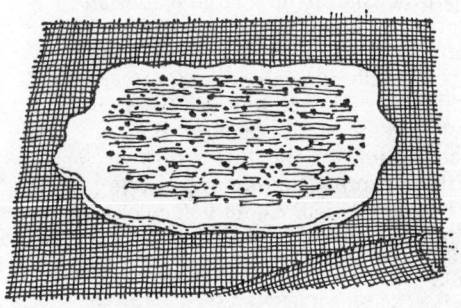

and forming a fat sausage-like roll. Secure seam with toothpicks or small poultry pins; gather skin at ends

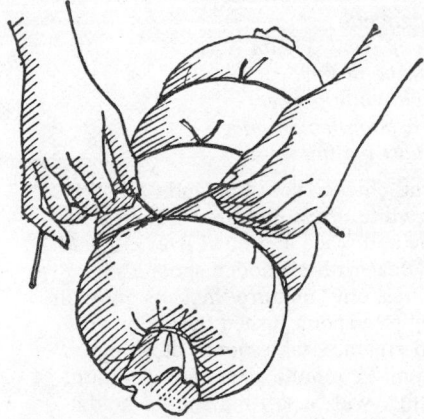

together and tie firmly or sew together. Wrap chicken in a triple thickness of cheesecloth wrung out in cold water, pulling cloth as tight as possible to shape chicken in a plump, firm roll. Tie around with string in several places, twist ends and tie also. Place roll in a large kettle, add reserved bones and all poaching liquid ingredients. Cover and simmer 1 hour, turning roll after ½ hour. Cool roll, still wrapped, in broth 1 hour, then lift to a deep bowl, top with a small cutting board or heavy plate, and weight down to force out as much liquid and air as possible; let stand

1 hour. Remove cheesecloth, cover roll with foil, and chill overnight. Slice—not too thin—and arrange slices, slightly overlapping, on a platter. Garnish as desired and serve.

To Decorate Galantine: Strain poaching liquid, clarify, and use to make aspic.* Chill aspic until very cold but still liquid. Chill galantine well too; then set on a rack over a tray. Spoon several thin layers of aspic over galantine to glaze evenly. Decorate as desired with sprigs of chervil or tarragon and cutouts of truffle, hard-cooked egg white, pimiento, and radish or carrot. Cutouts will stick better if dipped in aspic, then lightly pressed onto roll. Seal in designs with additional layers of aspic. Chill until firm; also chill remaining aspic. Set aspic on a platter, wreathe with chopped aspic, and sprig with watercress.

VARIATIONS:

Capon Galantine: Prepare as directed, using a 5–6-pound boned capon. Double stuffing recipe and use 3 quarts water in poaching liquid. Increase simmering time to 1½ hours.

Turkey Galantine: Prepare as directed, using an 8–10-pound boned turkey. Triple stuffing recipe and double poaching liquid ingredients. Increase simmering time to 2½–3 hours.

Chicken Ballotine: Prepare roll and simmer as directed; lift from broth, sprinkle with parsley, and serve hot with Chicken Gravy or Poulette Sauce. (*Note:* When making *ballotines,* the French often do not bone chicken completely but leave drumsticks and wing bones in to give bird character. The bird is then stuffed, sewn, or skewered up the back and reshaped to look as much like an unboned chicken as possible. It is then roasted* like any stuffed chicken. When carved, it is sliced straight across like the boneless rolls.)

Chicken galantine and all variations: about 550 calories for each of 4 servings, 370 calories for each of 6 servings.

CHICKEN KIEV

Traditionally, Kiev is seasoned only with butter, salt, and pepper, though chefs nowadays often add garlic, parsley, or chives. The trick in preparing Kiev is to seal the butter inside the chicken breast so that when the meat is cut it gushes out.
Makes 4–6 servings

Breasts of 3 large broiler-fryers, boned, halved, skinned, and pounded flat*
½ teaspoon salt
⅛ teaspoon pepper
6 finger-size slivers ice cold butter (Note: The best way to make these is to halve 1 stick butter crosswise, then quarter each half lengthwise.)
½ cup cooking oil

Coating:
2 eggs, lightly beaten
2 tablespoons milk
2 tablespoons water
½ teaspoon salt
⅛ teaspoon pepper
1 cup unsifted flour
1½ cups fine dry bread crumbs

Chill chicken breasts several hours, then spread flat on a cutting board and sprinkle with salt and pepper; lay a finger of butter in the center of each, then fold top and bottom margins over butter, tightly roll jelly-roll style and secure with poultry pins; chill rolls 15 minutes. Meanwhile, for coating mix eggs with milk, water, salt, and pepper. Dip rolls in flour, then egg, then in crumbs to coat evenly; pay particular attention to the ends, making sure they're well coated; chill rolls 1 hour. Preheat oven to 350° F. Heat oil in a large, heavy skillet over moderately high heat until a cube of bread will sizzle; add rolls and fry, turning gently with a slotted spoon, until nut brown all over; drain on paper toweling. Arrange 1 layer deep in an ungreased shallow baking pan and bake, uncovered, 15 minutes. Serve at once.

VARIATIONS:

Herbed Kiev: Prepare as directed, sprinkling about ½ teaspoon minced parsley and/or minced chives over each finger of butter and adding a dab of crushed garlic (use only 1 clove for the whole recipe). Roll breasts and proceed as directed.

Deep-Fried Kiev: Prepare as directed, then brown rolls in a deep fat fryer in 360° F. fat instead of in skillet. Drain, transfer to oven, and bake as directed.

All versions: about 525 calories for each of 4 servings, 350 calories for each of 6 servings.

STUFFED CHICKEN BREASTS

Any favorite stuffing can be used for stuffing chicken breasts instead of those given below. For 4 servings, you will need ½ cup stuffing.
Makes 4 servings

Breasts of 2 large broiler-fryers, boned,*
  halved, skinned, and pounded flat
¼ teaspoon salt
⅛ teaspoon white pepper
⅓ cup liver pâté or deviled ham
¼ cup soft white bread crumbs
2 scallions, minced
¼ cup unsifted flour
2 tablespoons butter or margarine
½ cup chicken broth

Preheat oven to 350° F. Spread breasts flat and sprinkle with salt and pepper. Mix pâté, crumbs, and scallions, place 2 tablespoons on each breast, roll up, and secure with poultry pins. Dredge rolls with flour and brown in butter in a heavy skillet over moderately high heat about 5 minutes. Transfer to an ungreased shallow casserole, add broth, cover, and bake 20 minutes until tender. Remove poultry pins and serve. About 385 calories per serving.

VARIATIONS:

Chicken Breasts with Spicy Ham Stuffing: Prepare as directed, stuffing breasts with ½ cup ground boiled ham mixed with 1 lightly beaten egg yolk, 1 teaspoon prepared yellow mustard,

and the bread crumbs and scallions called for. Good with Madeira Sauce. About 340 calories per serving (without sauce).

Chicken Breasts Stuffed with Wild Rice and Mushrooms: Prepare as directed, stuffing breasts with ½ cup cooked wild rice mixed with ¼ cup minced sautéed mushrooms, 2 minced scallions, and 1 lightly beaten egg yolk. About 345 calories per serving.

Ham and Cheese Stuffed Chicken Breasts: Spread breasts flat, sprinkle with salt, pepper, and 2 minced scallions. Lay 1 slice cut-to-fit boiled ham and Swiss cheese on each breast, roll, and cook as directed. About 350 calories per serving.

Chicken Breasts Stuffed with Chicken Livers and Walnuts: Prepare as directed, stuffing breasts with 4 minced sautéed chicken livers mixed with ¼ cup finely chopped walnuts and the crumbs and scallions called for. About 360 calories per serving.

⚖ **Chicken Breasts Stuffed with Oysters:** Prepare as directed, stuffing breasts with ⅓ cup minced, drained raw oysters or clams mixed with ⅓ cup bread crumbs and 2 minced scallions. About 300 calories per serving.

CHAUD-FROID OF CHICKEN BREASTS

Preparing a *chaud-froid* is not difficult if the sauce is quite cold—but still liquid—and the food to be coated is well chilled. The chaud-froid sauce will then set almost immediately.
Makes 4 servings

Breasts of 2 large broiler-fryers, boned*
  and halved
1 recipe Chaud-Froid Sauce
2 cups aspic made with chicken stock*
Cutouts of truffle and pimiento; parsley
  or tarragon sprigs (decoration)

Poach breasts by basic method* and cool in stock; remove from stock, skin, and chill. Strain stock and use in preparing chaud-froid sauce and aspic. When chaud-froid sauce is the proper consistency, set breasts on a rack over a tray and cover with a thin, even layer of sauce. Chill until tacky, then continue building up layers until no meat shows through. While final layer is still tacky, decorate with truffle and pimiento cutouts and herb sprigs. Seal in designs with a thin glaze of aspic and chill until firm. Also chill remaining aspic. Serve breasts on a platter wreathed with chopped aspic and sprigged with watercress. About 400 calories per serving.

SUPRÊMES OF CHICKEN

Suprêmes of chicken (*suprêmes de volaille* in French) are boned, skinned half breasts; if the first joints of wing are attached, they become *côtelettes.* The thin strip of meat lying next to the breastbone is called the *filet.* Perfectly cooked suprêmes are springy to the touch, creamy white with juices that run clear. They may be cooked by one of the basic methods below, seasoned with salt and pepper, and served as is; they may be topped with a suitable sauce (see Some Sauces, Gravies, and Seasonings for Poultry) or they may be given one of the lavish classic treatments that follow.

To Poach: Arrange suprêmes in a single layer in a buttered heavy skillet or shallow, flameproof casserole. Sprinkle lightly with salt and pepper, add chicken broth almost to cover and a *bouquet garni** tied in cheesecloth. Cover and simmer, either on top of the stove or in a 325° F. oven, about 20 minutes until tender.

To Bake: Preheat oven to 425° F. Allow 3–4 tablespoons butter for each 4 suprêmes and heat to bubbling in a shallow, flameproof casserole over moderate heat. Roll breasts in butter, cover loosely with foil, and bake 20 minutes until just tender.

To Sauté: Melt ¼ cup butter in a large, heavy skillet; lightly dredge suprêmes in flour, then brown over moderate heat about 8 minutes, turning often, until tender.

To Broil: Preheat broiler. Flatten suprêmes slightly and arrange on oiled rack in broiler pan. Brush well with melted butter (or Herb or Lemon Butter) and broil 5″–6″ from heat 4–5 minutes on a side, brushing often with additional butter.

Some Classic Ways to Serve Suprêmes of Chicken

Suprêmes de Volaille à Blanc (in Wine and Cream Sauce): Bake 4 suprêmes as directed, transfer to a hot platter and keep warm. To pan drippings add ¼ cup each dry white wine and chicken broth and boil, uncovered, until reduced by half. Turn heat to low and blend in 1 cup heavy cream, ¾ teaspoon salt, ⅛ teaspoon white pepper and 1–2 teaspoons lemon juice. Warm 1–2 minutes but do not boil; pour over suprêmes and serve sprinkled with minced parsley.

Suprêmes de Volaille Amandine: Sauté 4 suprêmes as directed and keep warm. Stir-fry ¼ cup blanched slivered almonds in drippings over moderate heat until golden, blend in 1 tablespoon flour and 1 cup heavy cream, and heat, stirring, until thickened. Season with salt and pepper, let mellow several minutes over low heat, add 1 teaspoon lemon juice, pour over suprêmes, and serve.

Suprêmes de Volaille en Papillote: Poach 4 suprêmes as directed and cool slightly in poaching liquid. Mix 1 cup hot Béchamel or Medium White Sauce, ¼ cup minced raw mushrooms, 2 tablespoons minced, pitted ripe olives, 1 teaspoon each minced chives and parsley and ½ crushed clove garlic. Butter 4 large squares foil, spread each with ¼ of the sauce, top with a suprême, wrap tightly, arrange on a baking sheet, and bake 10–12 minutes at 425° F. Serve in foil packages.

Virginia-Style Suprêmes: Flatten 4 suprêmes slightly; cut 4 thin slices Virginia ham to fit suprêmes, dip in beaten egg, and lay on suprêmes, pressing lightly. Dip each "package" in beaten egg, then in toasted, seasoned bread crumbs. Brown slowly on both sides in ¼ cup melted butter in a heavy skillet over moderate heat; cover, reduce heat to low, and cook 5 minutes. Uncover and cook 2–3 minutes longer to crispen.

Chicken Breasts in Champagne Sauce: Poach suprêmes as directed, using a ½ and ½ mixture of chicken broth and champagne, dry white wine, or cider. Drain off poaching liquid and measure; for each cup, lightly beat 2 egg yolks. Heat cooking liquid in the top of a double boiler directly over moderate heat until simmering, spoon a little into yolks, return to pan, set over simmering water, and heat and stir until thickened and no raw taste of egg remains. Season to taste, pour over suprêmes and serve.

Suprêmes Véronique: Bake 4 suprêmes as directed but add ½ cup dry white wine to the pan. Drain off cooking liquid, to it add 1 cup light cream, and use to make 1½ cups Medium White Sauce. Pour sauce over suprêmes, garnish with peeled seedless green grapes, and serve. If you like, brown quickly under broiler before serving.

☒ ⚖ SAUTÉED CHICKEN LIVERS
Makes 6 servings

1½ pounds chicken livers
½ cup unsifted flour
1 teaspoon salt
¼ teaspoon pepper
3–4 tablespoons bacon drippings, butter, or margarine

Halve each chicken liver at the natural separation and dredge in a mixture of flour, salt, and pepper. Stir-fry in drippings in a large, heavy skillet over moderately high heat about 5 minutes until browned all over. (*Note:* Livers will be medium rare. If you prefer them rarer, cook about 1 minute less, if more well done, turn heat to moderately low and cook 1–2 minutes longer.)

Serve on buttered toast triangles for breakfast, lunch, or supper. About 250 calories per serving (without toast).

☒ ⚖ BRAISED CHICKEN LIVERS WITH PARSLEY GRAVY
Makes 4–6 servings

1½ pounds chicken livers
3 tablespoons bacon drippings, butter, or margarine
1 teaspoon salt
⅛ teaspoon pepper
4 teaspoons flour
1 cup chicken broth
¼ teaspoon liquid gravy browner
2 tablespoons minced parsley
2–3 tablespoons medium-dry sherry (optional)

Halve each chicken liver at the natural separation, pat dry on paper toweling, and stir-fry in drippings in a large, heavy skillet over moderately high heat about 5 minutes until brown. Turn heat to moderately low and sprinkle livers with salt and pepper. Blend flour with ¼ cup chicken broth, add remaining broth and gravy browner and pour into skillet. Cook and stir gently until slightly thickened. Add parsley and, if you like, the sherry and serve. About 315 calories for each of 4 servings (without sherry), 210 for each of 6 (without sherry).

☒ CHICKEN LIVERS IN SOUR CREAM
A good chafing dish recipe.
Makes 4 servings

1 pound chicken livers
2 tablespoons bacon drippings, butter, or margarine
1 cup minced scallions (include some tops)
¼ pound mushrooms, wiped clean and coarsely chopped
⅛ teaspoon rosemary
¼ teaspoon basil
1 teaspoon salt
⅛ teaspoon pepper
1 clove garlic, peeled and crushed
1 teaspoon Worcestershire sauce

1 cup chicken broth
1 cup sour cream

Cut livers in two at the natural separation and pat dry on paper toweling. Stir-fry in drippings in a large, heavy skillet over moderately high heat until browned all over, about 5 minutes. Push livers to one side of skillet, add scallions, and sauté 2–3 minutes until golden. Turn heat to moderately low, mix in all remaining ingredients except sour cream, and simmer uncovered 7–10 minutes, stirring occasionally. If you like, transfer at this point to a chafing dish. Mix in sour cream and simmer 2–3 minutes until hot but not boiling. Serve over boiled rice, buttered noodles, or toast triangles. About 340 calories per serving (without rice, noodles, or toast).

⊠ OLD-FASHIONED CREAMED CHICKEN OR TURKEY

Makes 4 servings

¼ pound mushrooms, wiped clean and
   sliced thin (include stems)
¼ cup butter or margarine
¼ cup unsifted flour
1 cup chicken broth
1 cup light cream
¾ teaspoon salt (about)
⅛ teaspoon white pepper
2 cups cooked chicken or turkey meat,
   cut in bite-size pieces
2 tablespoons dry sherry (optional)

Sauté mushrooms in butter in the top of a double boiler directly over moderately high heat 2–3 minutes until golden. Blend in flour, slowly stir in broth and cream, and heat, stirring, until thickened. Set over just simmering water, mix in remaining ingredients, cover, and let mellow 10–15 minutes. Serve over hot buttered toast, biscuits, corn bread, toasted English muffins, pancakes, or waffles. Also good over mashed potatoes, boiled rice, or noodles or used as a filling for pancakes, crepes, or baked frozen patty shells. About 430 calories per serving made with chicken (without bread, potatoes, rice, or noodles), about

450 calories per serving if made with turkey.

VARIATIONS:

Creamed Chicken or Turkey and Eggs: Prepare as directed, but just before setting mixture over water to mellow, mix in 2 peeled, hard-cooked eggs cut in wedges. About 470 calories per serving if made with chicken, 490 calories per serving if made with turkey.

Creamed Chicken or Turkey and Ham: Prepare as directed, using a ½ and ½ mixture of chicken or turkey and ham. About 490 calories per serving if made with chicken, about 510 calories per serving if made with turkey.

CHICKEN OR TURKEY AND MUSHROOM CREPES

Makes 4 servings

1 recipe Crepes for Savory Fillings

Filling:

1 (10½-ounce) can condensed cream of
   mushroom soup (do not dilute)
1 cup light cream
Pinch nutmeg
¾ teaspoon salt (about)
⅛ teaspoon pepper
2 cups minced cooked chicken or
   turkey meat
1 (4-ounce) can mushroom stems and
   pieces, drained and minced
1 pimiento, drained and minced
Paprika

Preheat oven to 350° F. Prepare crepes as recipe directs and spread flat with most attractive sides face down. Mix soup and cream until smooth, add nutmeg, salt, and pepper. Mix ¾ cup soup mixture with chicken, mushrooms, and pimiento, taste for salt and adjust as needed. Spoon a little chicken mixture down center of each crepe, then roll up. Place crepes seam side down in a single layer in an ungreased shallow au gratin dish, top with remaining soup mixture, and bake uncovered 30–40 minutes until bubbly. Dust with paprika and serve. About 520 calories per serving if made with chicken, 540 calories per serving made with turkey.

VARIATIONS:

Ham and Chicken Crepes: Prepare as directed, substituting 1 cup diced cooked ham for 1 cup chicken. About 580 calories per serving.

Chicken Crepes au Gratin: Prepare and bake crepes as directed; sprinkle ½ cup finely grated Cheddar or Parmesan cheese on top, and broil 3″–4″ from heat 2–3 minutes until flecked with brown. About 575 calories per serving.

⊠ QUICK CHICKEN OR TURKEY À LA KING

Makes 4 servings

1 (10½-ounce) can condensed cream of mushroom soup (do not dilute)
½ cup milk
1½ cups diced cooked chicken or turkey meat
2 tablespoons minced pimiento
4 English muffins, split, toasted, and lightly buttered, or 4 frozen waffles, toasted

Blend soup and milk until smooth in a saucepan, cover, and heat over moderate heat 5 minutes, stirring occasionally. Add chicken, heat, and stir 3–5 minutes. Mix in pimiento, spoon over muffins, and serve. About 400 calories per serving.

VARIATION:

Eggs à la King: Prepare as directed, substituting 5–6 diced, hard-cooked eggs for the chicken. About 370 calories per serving.

⊠ QUICK CHICKEN OR TURKEY STEW

Makes 4–6 servings

2 (10½-ounce) cans condensed cream of mushroom soup
½ cup light cream or evaporated milk
1 (1-pound) can mixed vegetables, drained
1 (1-pound) can small whole white potatoes, drained

1 (1-pound) can whole white onions (do not drain)
1 (4-ounce) can sliced mushrooms (do not drain)
2 cups bite-size pieces cooked chicken or turkey meat
½ teaspoon salt (about)
¼ teaspoon pepper
2 tablespoons minced parsley

Mix mushroom soup and cream in a very large saucepan, add remaining ingredients except parsley, cover, and simmer 10–15 minutes. Taste for salt and adjust if needed. Ladle into bowls, sprinkle with parsley, and serve. If made with chicken, about 565 calories for each of 4 servings, 375 calories for each of 6 servings. If made with turkey, about 585 calories for each of 4 servings, 390 calories for each of 6 servings.

¢ MOTHER'S CHICKEN OR TURKEY STEW

Makes 6 servings

1 (5–6-pound) stewing hen or turkey, cut up
1 medium-size yellow onion, peeled and stuck with 4 cloves
5–6 medium-size carrots, peeled and cut in 2″ chunks
2 stalks celery, minced
2 sprigs parsley
2½ teaspoons salt (about)
¼ teaspoon pepper
1 quart water
1 cup milk
6 tablespoons flour blended with ⅓ cup cold milk

Place all but last ingredient in a heavy burner-to-table kettle or electric skillet set at 225° F., cover, and simmer about 2–2½ hours until chicken is tender. (Note: Remove chicken liver after 10–15 minutes, cool, and reserve.) Discard onion and parsley. Drain off liquid, reserving 3 cups, then skim off fat. (Note: If there is not enough liquid to total 3 cups, add water as needed.) Pour liquid into a saucepan, blend in flour paste, and heat, stirring, until thickened. Pour sauce over chicken, taste for salt and adjust as needed. Return chicken liver to stew, cover all, and let stand over low heat 5–10 minutes to mellow flavors. Good with boiled noodles or rice, Polenta or mashed potatoes. About 445 calories per serving made with chicken (without noodles, rice, Polenta, or potatoes), about 460 calories per serving if made with turkey.

VARIATIONS:

Chicken or Turkey Stew with Dumplings: Prepare stew as directed; also prepare a favorite dumpling recipe. Drop dumplings on top of stew and cook as dumpling recipe directs. Recipe too flexible for a meaningful calorie count.

Chicken or Turkey Stew with Biscuits: Prepare stew as directed and transfer to a hot, ungreased 3-quart casserole. Mix 1 recipe Baking Powder Biscuits, then cut and arrange biscuits, almost touching, on top of stew. Bake, uncovered, 15–20 minutes at 375° F. until lightly browned. About 695 calories per serving made with chicken, 710 calories made with turkey.

Chicken or Turkey and Vegetable Stew: Prepare stew as directed, then stir in any of the following: 1 (10-ounce) package frozen green peas, cut green beans, whole kernel corn, or baby lima beans, cooked and drained by package directions. Cover and let mellow 10 minutes over low heat before serving. Recipe too flexible for calorie count.

⊿⊳ ¢ BRUNSWICK STEW

American Indian women, who invented Brunswick Stew, used to make it with squirrel or rabbit. If you have a hunter in the family, try it their way.
Makes 12–15 servings

1 (6-pound) stewing hen or capon, cleaned and dressed
1 gallon cold water
2 stalks celery (include tops)
1 tablespoon sugar
5 medium-size potatoes, peeled and cut in ½" cubes
3 medium-size yellow onions, peeled and coarsely chopped

6 large ripe tomatoes, peeled, cored, seeded, and coarsely chopped
2 (10-ounce) packages frozen baby lima beans (do not thaw)
2 (10-ounce) packages frozen whole kernel corn (do not thaw)
1 medium-size sweet green pepper, cored and cut in short, thin slivers
2 tablespoons salt (about)
¼ teaspoon pepper

Remove fat from body cavity of bird, then place bird and giblets in a very large kettle. Add water and celery, cover, and simmer 1–2 hours until *just* tender. Remove bird and giblets from broth and cool. Strain broth and skim off fat. Rinse kettle, pour in broth, add sugar, all vegetables but corn and green pepper, cover, and simmer 1 hour. Meanwhile, skin chicken, cut meat in 1" chunks and dice giblets. Return chicken and giblets to kettle, add remaining ingredients, cover, and simmer 40–45 minutes, stirring occasionally. Taste for salt, adding more if needed. Serve piping hot in soup bowls as a main dish. Particularly good with coleslaw and Hushpuppies or crisp corn sticks. (*Note:* This stew freezes well.) About 310 calories for each of 12 servings, about 250 calories for each of 15 servings.

⊿⊳ ¢ CHICKEN OR TURKEY HASH

Makes 4 servings

1 medium-size yellow onion, peeled and minced
½ medium-size sweet green or red pepper, cored, seeded, and minced (optional)
2 tablespoons bacon drippings, butter, or margarine
2 cups diced cooked chicken or turkey meat
2 cups diced cooked cold peeled potatoes
¼ cup applesauce
1 tablespoon minced parsley
1 teaspoon salt
⅛ teaspoon pepper
½ teaspoon poultry seasoning
4 poached or fried eggs (optional)

Stir-fry onion and, if you like, green pepper in drippings in a large, heavy skillet over moderate heat 5–8 minutes until onion is pale golden. Mix in all remaining ingredients except eggs, pat down with a broad spatula, and cook, uncovered, without stirring about 10 minutes until a brown crust forms on the bottom. Using 2 broad spatulas, turn hash and brown flip side 8–10 minutes. Cut into 4 portions and serve. If you like, top each serving with a poached or fried egg. About 290 calories per serving made with chicken (without egg), about 310 calories per serving if made with turkey.

VARIATIONS:

¢	**Chicken or Turkey and Sweet Potato Hash:** Prepare as directed but substitute 2 cups diced cooked or drained canned sweet potatoes or yams for the potatoes. About 305 calories per serving if made with chicken, 325 calories per serving if made with turkey.

¢	**Chicken or Turkey 'n' Stuffing Hash:** Prepare as directed but use 1 cup any leftover bread stuffing and 1 cup diced cooked or mashed potatoes instead of 2 cups potatoes. Omit poultry seasoning. About 330 calories per serving if made with chicken, 350 calories per serving if made with turkey.

Cheesy Chicken or Turkey Hash: Prepare as directed but substitute mashed potatoes for the diced and grated Parmesan cheese for the applesauce; add ¼ teaspoon garlic powder. Fry 1 side as directed, turn, sprinkle with 2–3 tablespoons grated Parmesan or Cheddar cheese, and brown under broiler. About 330 calories per serving if made with chicken, 350 calories per serving if made with turkey.

CHICKEN OR TURKEY CROQUETTES

Makes 4 servings

¼ cup butter or margarine
¼ cup sifted flour
1 cup milk
1 chicken bouillon cube

1 tablespoon minced parsley
¼ teaspoon poultry seasoning
1 teaspoon finely grated lemon rind (optional)
2 tablespoons dry sherry (optional)
½ teaspoon salt (about)
⅛ teaspoon pepper
1 egg, lightly beaten
1½ cups coarsely ground cooked chicken or turkey meat
½ cup soft white bread crumbs
Shortening or cooking oil for deep fat frying

Coating:
1 egg, lightly beaten with 1 tablespoon cold water
¼ cup cracker crumbs mixed with ¼ cup minced blanched almonds

Melt butter in a large saucepan over moderate heat and blend in flour; slowly stir in milk, add bouillon cube, parsley, and all seasonings, and heat, stirring, until mixture thickens. Blend a little hot sauce into egg, return to pan, set over lowest heat, and heat, stirring, 1 minute; do not boil. Off heat, mix in chicken and bread crumbs; taste for salt and adjust. Cool, then chill until easy to shape. Shape into 8 patties or sausage-shaped rolls, dip in egg mixture, then roll in crumbs to coat. Let dry on a rack at room temperature while heating fat. Place shortening in a deep fat fryer and heat to 375° F. Fry the croquettes, ½ at a time, 2–3 minutes until golden brown and crisp; drain on paper toweling, then keep warm by setting, uncovered, in oven turned to lowest heat while you fry the rest. Good with Tomato or Parsley Sauce. About 435 calories per serving if made with chicken, about 455 calories per serving if made with turkey.

VARIATIONS:

Curried Chicken or Turkey Croquettes: Prepare croquette mixture as directed but omit poultry seasoning and add 1–2 teaspoons curry powder and ¼ cup well-drained, minced chutney. Fry as directed and serve with Chicken or Turkey Gravy or Light Curry Sauce.

About 435 calories per serving made with chicken, 455 calories per serving made with turkey (without gravy).

Chicken and Shellfish Croquettes: Prepare croquette mixture as directed but use a ½ and ½ mixture of chicken and finely ground cooked shrimp, lobster, or crab meat; omit poultry seasoning. Fry as directed. About 405 calories per serving if made with shrimp, 395 calories per serving if made with lobster or crab.

Chicken and Ham or Tongue Croquettes: Prepare croquette mixture as directed but use a ½ and ½ mixture of chicken and finely ground cooked lean ham or tongue; omit poultry seasoning and add 1 teaspoon prepared mild yellow mustard. Fry as directed. About 460 calories per serving whether made with ham or tongue.

CHICKEN OR TURKEY DIVAN

A luscious way to use up leftovers.
Makes 6 servings

¼ cup butter or margarine
¼ cup sifted flour
1 cup chicken broth
1 cup milk
¾ teaspoon salt
⅛ teaspoon white pepper
⅛ teaspoon nutmeg
¼ cup plus 2 tablespoons grated Parmesan cheese
3 tablespoons dry sherry
2 (10-ounce) packages frozen broccoli or asparagus spears, cooked by package directions and drained
10–12 slices cooked chicken or turkey meat
½ cup heavy cream

Preheat oven to 350° F. Melt butter in a saucepan over moderate heat, blend in flour, slowly add broth and milk, and heat, stirring until thickened; mix in salt, pepper, nutmeg, ¼ cup cheese, and the sherry. Arrange broccoli in a single layer in a buttered 2-quart *au gratin* dish or shallow casserole and sprinkle with remaining cheese. Top with chicken slices. Beat cream until soft peaks will form and fold into sauce; pour evenly over chicken and bake, uncovered, about ½ hour until bubbly. Broil quickly to brown and serve. About 375 calories per serving if made with chicken, 385 calories if made with turkey.

VARIATIONS:

Chicken Divan Hollandaise: Prepare as directed but mix ½ cup Hollandaise Sauce and 1 teaspoon Worcestershire sauce into cheese sauce before adding cream. About 415 calories per serving.

Chicken Breasts Divan: Prepare as directed, substituting 6 poached chicken breasts for the sliced chicken and arranging them slightly overlapping on the broccoli. About 415 calories per serving.

¢ CHICKEN OR TURKEY-NOODLE CASSEROLE

Makes 4 servings

¼ cup butter or margarine
¼ cup sifted flour
1 cup chicken broth
1 cup milk
1 chicken bouillon cube
1 teaspoon salt
¼ teaspoon pepper
¼ cup minced pimiento (optional)
2 cups bite-size pieces cooked chicken or turkey meat
1 (8-ounce) box thin noodles, cooked by package directions and drained

Topping:
1 cup soft white bread crumbs mixed with 3 tablespoons melted butter or margarine

Preheat oven to 350° F. Melt butter in a large saucepan over moderate heat and blend in flour; slowly stir in broth and milk, add bouillon cube, salt, and pepper, and heat, stirring, until mixture thickens. Off heat, mix in all remaining ingredients except topping. Spoon into a buttered 2-quart casserole, sprinkle with topping, and bake uncovered ½ hour. About 555 calories per serving made with chicken, 575 per serving made with turkey.

VARIATION:

Chicken or Turkey-Noodle Casserole with Vegetables: Prepare chicken mixture as directed, then stir in 1 (10-ounce) package frozen mixed vegetables, cooked by package directions, 1 (4-ounce) undrained can sliced mushrooms, and 3 minced scallions. Spoon into a buttered 2½-quart casserole, top, and bake as directed. Or, if you prefer, omit topping and scatter 1 cup chow mein noodles over casserole for last 5 minutes of baking. With bread crumb or chow mein noodle topping: about 610 calories per serving if made with chicken, 630 calories per serving if made with turkey.

¢ **CHICKEN OR TURKEY POT PIE**

Makes 6 servings

¼ cup butter or margarine
6 tablespoons flour
1 cup milk
2 cups chicken broth or a ½ and ½
    mixture of broth and apple cider or
    dry white wine
3 cups bite-size pieces cooked chicken or
    turkey meat
¼ teaspoon rosemary
¼ teaspoon savory
1 tablespoon minced parsley
1 teaspoon salt
¼ teaspoon white pepper
2 cups thinly sliced cooked carrots
2 cups cooked green peas
1 recipe Flaky Pastry I
1 egg yolk mixed with 1 tablespoon
    cold water (glaze)

Preheat oven to 425° F. Melt butter in a large saucepan over moderate heat, blend in flour, add milk and broth, and heat, stirring, until thickened. Add chicken and all seasonings, cover, and simmer 5–10 minutes, stirring occasionally. Cool to room temperature. Mix in carrots and peas and spoon into an ungreased 2½-quart casserole about 9″ in diameter. Prepare pastry and roll into a circle 3″ larger than casserole; make 3 V-shaped steam slits near center.

Dampen casserole rim, fit pastry on top, roll pastry edges under even with rim, and crimp to seal. Brush with glaze, being careful not to cover slits. Bake 30–40 minutes until browned and bubbly (place a sheet of foil on rack under casserole to catch drips). To serve, cut wedges of pastry and ladle chicken mixture on top. About 455 calories per serving if made with chicken, 470 per serving if made with turkey.

VARIATION:

Homestead Chicken or Turkey Pie: Stir-fry 1 peeled and minced yellow onion and ½ pound thinly sliced mushrooms in the butter 5 minutes; blend in flour and finish sauce as directed above. Do not cool and do not add carrots and peas. Transfer to casserole. Prepare 1 recipe Baking Powder Biscuits and roll into a circle ¼″ thick and about 1″ larger than casserole; cut V-slits in center. Dampen casserole rim, fit pastry on top, and press edges to seal. (*Note:* Scraps can be rerolled and cut into biscuits.) Brush topping with glaze and bake, uncovered, 15–20 minutes until lightly browned. Serve as directed. About 720 calories per serving if made with chicken, 735 calories per serving if made with turkey.

BASIC CHICKEN OR TURKEY SOUFFLÉ

Makes 4 servings

¼ cup butter or margarine
¼ cup sifted flour
1 cup milk
1 chicken bouillon cube
½ teaspoon salt
⅛ teaspoon white pepper
4 eggs, separated (at room temperature)
1 cup finely ground cooked chicken or
    turkey meat
2 teaspoons minced chives (optional)
¼ teaspoon cream of tartar

Melt butter in a small saucepan over moderate heat and blend in flour; slowly stir in milk. Add bouillon cube, salt, and pepper and heat and stir until mixture thickens. Lightly beat yolks, blend in a little hot sauce, then return to pan; set over lowest heat and heat, stirring, 1–2 minutes; do not boil. Off heat, mix in chicken and, if you like, chives. Lay a piece of wax paper flat on top of sauce and cool to room temperature. Preheat oven to 350° F. Beat egg whites until frothy, add cream of tartar, and beat until stiff but not dry. Stir about ¼ cup egg whites into sauce, then carefully fold in the rest, taking care not to break down volume. Spoon into an ungreased 1½-quart soufflé dish and bake, uncovered, 45–50 minutes until puffy and tinged with brown. Serve at once. Good with Tomato, Shrimp, Parsley, or Mushroom Sauce. About 335 calories per serving if made with chicken, 355 per serving if made with turkey.

VARIATIONS:

Herbed Chicken or Turkey Soufflé: Prepare as directed, including chives and adding 1 tablespoon each minced parsley and minced fresh dill, tarragon, chervil, or basil. About 335 calories per serving if made with chicken, 355 per serving if made with turkey.

Chicken or Turkey and Ham or Tongue Soufflé: Prepare as directed, using ¾ cup ground chicken and ½ cup ground cooked lean ham or tongue. About 385 calories per serving if made with chicken, 405 calories per serving if made with turkey.

Curried Chicken or Turkey Soufflé: Melt butter, blend in flour and 1 tablespoon each curry powder and finely grated onion. Add milk slowly and proceed as directed. About 335 calories per serving if made with chicken, 355 calories per serving if made with turkey.

⚔ ¢ CHICKEN OR TURKEY TIMBALES

Makes 4 servings

1 cup milk
1 cup soft white bread crumbs
2 tablespoons butter or margarine
1 tablespoon finely grated yellow onion
1 chicken bouillon cube
½ teaspoon salt

⅛ teaspoon pepper
⅛ teaspoon sage
⅛ teaspoon thyme
2 eggs, lightly beaten
1 cup finely ground cooked chicken or turkey meat

Preheat oven to 325° F. Mix all but last 2 ingredients in a saucepan and bring to a boil, stirring constantly. Remove from heat. Stir a little hot mixture into eggs, then return to pan and mix well. Mix in chicken. Spoon into 4 well-buttered custard cups and set in a shallow baking pan; pour enough water into pan to come halfway up cups. Bake, uncovered, about 35 minutes until just set. Loosen edges of timbales and invert gently on a hot platter. Serve with Chicken Gravy, Tomato or Mushroom Sauce. About 265 calories per serving if made with chicken (without gravy or sauce), about 285 calories per serving if made with turkey.

⚔ ¢ HOT CHICKEN OR TURKEY LOAF

Makes 8 servings

3 cups finely chopped cooked chicken or turkey meat
2 cups dry white bread crumbs
½ cup minced celery
2 pimientos, drained and coarsely chopped
1½ teaspoons salt
¼ teaspoon pepper
1 tablespoon finely grated yellow onion
1 tablespoon lemon juice
2 teaspoons Worcestershire sauce
1 tablespoon minced parsley
2 cups chicken broth
3 eggs, lightly beaten

Preheat oven to 350° F. Mix together all but last 2 ingredients. Stir broth into eggs, then pour over chicken mixture and mix well. Lightly pack mixture into a greased 9″×5″×3″ loaf pan, set in a large baking pan, and pour in enough boiling water to come about halfway up loaf pan. Bake, uncovered, about 1 hour until loaf begins to pull away from sides of pan. Lift loaf pan from water bath and cool upright 5–10 minutes; loosen loaf, invert on a hot platter and ease out. Serve hot with Chicken or Mushroom Gravy. Good cold, sliced thin and accompanied by salad. About 200 calories per serving if made with chicken (without gravy), 220 calories per serving if made with turkey.

VARIATIONS:

¢ ⚖ **Surprise Chicken Loaf:** Prepare chicken mixture as directed and pack half into loaf pan. Arrange 3 peeled hard-cooked eggs lengthwise down center of mixture, place rows of pimiento, stuffed green or pitted ripe olives on either side of eggs, cover with remaining chicken mixture and bake as directed. About 245 calories per serving.

¢ ⚖ **Chicken and Rice Loaf:** Prepare chicken mixture as directed but reduce bread crumbs to 1½ cups and add 1½ cups boiled rice. About 210 calories per serving.

⚖ **HOT CHICKEN OR TURKEY MOUSSE**

Makes 6 servings

¼ cup butter or margarine
5 tablespoons flour
1 cup milk
1 chicken bouillon cube
1 teaspoon salt
Pinch nutmeg
3 eggs, separated (at room temperature)
½ cup light cream
1½ cups finely ground cooked white meat of chicken or turkey

Preheat oven to 350° F. Melt butter in a saucepan over moderate heat and blend in flour; slowly stir in milk. Add bouillon cube, salt, and nutmeg and heat, stirring, until mixture thickens. Remove from heat. Lightly beat yolks and briskly blend in a little hot sauce. Return to pan and mix well; stir in cream and chicken. Beat egg whites until soft peaks form, then fold into chicken mixture. Spoon into a well-oiled 5-cup ring mold, set in a large baking pan, and pour enough boiling water into pan to come

⅔ of the way up mold. Bake, uncovered, ¾–1 hour until just set. Lift mousse from water bath and cool upright 5–10 minutes. Loosen with a spatula, invert on a hot platter, and *ease* out. Serve as is or fill center with Creamed Mushrooms, Saffron Rice, or hot mixed vegetables. Good with Mushroom or Aurore Sauce.

VARIATION:

⚖ **Cold Chicken or Turkey Mousse:** Prepare mousse mixture as directed, but before folding in egg whites stir in 1 tablespoon each finely grated yellow onion and lemon juice, ¼ teaspoon powdered rosemary, and a pinch cayenne pepper. If you like, also add ⅓ cup each minced celery and water chestnuts. Fold in egg whites and bake as directed. Cool slightly, then unmold. Cool to room temperature, cover, and chill 2–3 hours. When serving, garnish with lettuce, watercress, and cherry tomatoes. Serve with mayonnaise, thinned slightly with cream.

Both versions: about 280 calories per serving if made with chicken (without mushrooms, rice, mixed vegetables, or sauce), about 300 calories per serving if made with turkey.

LYONNAISE TURKEY ROLL EN CASSEROLE

There are frozen white meat turkey rolls (both plain and smoked), white and dark meat rolls, even ham and turkey rolls. All are good prepared this way.
Makes 6 servings

1 (3-pound) frozen boneless turkey roll, thawed
¼ cup butter or margarine
2 large yellow onions, peeled and sliced thin
½ cup beef broth
1 tablespoon tomato paste
1 cup chicken broth
1 bay leaf
½ teaspoon salt
⅛ teaspoon pepper
½ pound button mushrooms, wiped clean

*2 tablespoons flour blended with 2
tablespoons cold water*

Preheat oven to 350° F. Brown turkey
in butter in a heavy skillet over moderate
heat and transfer to an ungreased deep
flameproof 2½-quart casserole. Stir-fry
onions in butter remaining in skillet 8–
10 minutes until golden, then remove
with a slotted spoon and spread over
turkey; save skillet drippings. Mix beef
broth and tomato paste and add to
casserole along with all but last 2
ingredients. Cover and bake 2–2½ hours
until tender. Lift turkey to a hot platter
and keep warm. Sauté mushrooms in
skillet drippings over moderately high
heat 2–3 minutes until golden; add to
casserole. Blend flour paste into casserole
liquid and stir until thickened over low
heat. Remove strings from roll, carve
into fairly thick slices, cutting almost—
but not quite—through at the bottom.
Return turkey to casserole, spoon some
sauce in between slices, carry to the
table, and serve. About 380 calories per
serving.

ROAST STUFFED TURKEY ROLL WITH CAFÉ AU LAIT SAUCE

Makes 6–10 servings

*1 (3–5-pound) frozen boneless turkey
roll, thawed
1 recipe Chicken Liver and Mushroom
Stuffing
3 strips fat bacon*

Sauce:
*1 cup chicken broth
½ cup milk
1 cup hot strong black coffee
1 teaspoon salt
⅛ teaspoon pepper
2 tablespoons brandy (optional)
¼ cup unsifted flour blended with ¼ cup
cold water*

Preheat oven to 325° F. Untie turkey
roll and lay flat, skin side down. Spread
stuffing on meat, leaving a wide margin,
then roll up and tie around in several
places. Place on a rack in a roasting pan
and drape bacon on top. Insert meat
thermometer in center of roll. Bake,
uncovered, 2½–3 hours until
thermometer registers 170–75° F.
Remove bacon for last ½ hour so roll
browns evenly. Lift roll to hot platter and
let rest while making sauce. Pour all but
2 tablespoons drippings from pan, add
broth, milk and coffee, and stir to scrape
up brown bits; pour into a saucepan.
Mix in remaining ingredients and heat,
stirring until thickened. To serve, slice
roll not too thin, removing strings as you
go. Pass sauce separately. About 610
calories for each of 6 servings, 475
calories for each of 10 servings.

EASY TURKEY WELLINGTON

Boneless turkey roast baked in a flaky
pastry.
Makes 4 servings

*1 (2-pound) frozen boneless turkey roast,
thawed
1 (8-ounce) package refrigerated dough
for crescent rolls
1 (8-ounce) can liver pâté
2 tablespoons dry sherry or Madeira
1 egg lightly beaten with 1 tablespoon
cold water (glaze)*

Roast turkey roast by package
directions; cool to room temperature.
Preheat oven to 425° F. Meanwhile,
open package of dough, spread dough
flat, and halve crosswise but do not
separate into individual rolls. Fit halves
together on an ungreased baking sheet
so you have a rectangle about 9″ × 14″;
pinch edges together to seal; also press
perforations shut so you have an
unbroken sheet of dough. Remove string
on turkey roast and lay roll across center
of dough. Mix pâté and sherry and
spread on top of turkey roast. Bring
dough sides up to meet on top of roast
and crimp to seal; close dough over ends
of roast. Make 3 steam slits on each side
of roll, then brush pastry with glaze,
taking care not to seal vents. Bake,
uncovered, on center rack 20–25
minutes until golden. Ease onto a hot
platter. To serve, slice straight across
with a very sharp knife, making slices
fairly thick. Also good served cold.
About 695 calories per serving.

¢ DEVILED TURKEY DRUMSTICKS

Makes 4 servings

2 frozen turkey drumsticks and 2 thighs,
   thawed

Sauce:

¼ cup butter or margarine
1 tablespoon powdered mustard
1 teaspoon grated yellow onion
4 teaspoons cider vinegar or lemon juice
Pinch cayenne pepper

Make 3–4 tiny lengthwise slits in each
piece of turkey. Melt butter in a
saucepan, stir in remaining sauce
ingredients, and pour into an ungreased
shallow roasting pan. Roll turkey in
sauce and let stand at room temperature
1 hour. Preheat oven to 350° F. Roast
turkey, uncovered, about 2 hours until
tender, basting occasionally with pan
drippings or a little melted butter. Turn
turkey as needed to brown evenly. Tent
with foil if it browns too fast. About
380 calories per serving.

VARIATIONS:

¢ **Deviled Turkey Wings:** Substitute 6
turkey wings for the legs and proceed as
directed, allowing about 1½ hours'
roasting time. About 380 calories per
serving.

¢ **Deviled Leftover Turkey:** Cut thick
slices from cooked drumsticks and
thighs, roll in sauce, and coat with dry
white bread crumbs. Place in a greased
baking pan and bake, uncovered, ½ hour
at 400° F. Brown under broiler and
serve. Recipe too flexible for a
meaningful calorie count.

¢ CREOLE-STYLE TURKEY DRUMSTICKS

Makes 4 servings

2 frozen turkey drumsticks and 2 thighs,
   thawed
⅓ cup unsifted flour
3 tablespoons olive or other cooking oil
1 large yellow onion, peeled and minced
1 medium-size sweet green pepper,
   cored, seeded, and minced

2 stalks celery, minced
1 clove garlic, peeled and crushed
1 teaspoon salt
¼ teaspoon pepper
1 tablespoon minced parsley
½ teaspoon thyme
1 bay leaf, crumbled
1 (1-pound 3-ounce) can tomatoes (do
   not drain)

Dredge turkey in flour and brown in oil
in a very large, heavy skillet over
moderate heat; drain on paper toweling.
Stir-fry onion, green pepper, celery, and
garlic in drippings 8 minutes until onion
is pale golden. Mix in remaining
ingredients, breaking up tomatoes; return
turkey to skillet, cover, and simmer 1½–
2 hours until tender, basting now and
then and adding a little water if pan
seems dry. Or, if you prefer, transfer
mixture to an ungreased 3-quart casserole, cover, and bake 1½–2 hours at
350° F. Or do the whole thing in an
electric skillet, set at 350° F. Serve with
boiled or Saffron Rice. About 340 calories
per serving (without rice).

VARIATION:

¢ **Creole-Style Turkey Parts:** Prepare
as directed, substituting 6 turkey wings
or a 2-pound thawed boneless turkey roll
for drumsticks. Or use a 4-pound frozen
whole turkey breast, thawed and split;
use a larger can of tomatoes (1-pound
12-ounce size) but cook for the same
length of time. About 355 calories per
serving if made with turkey breast, 430
calories per serving if made with turkey
wings or a boneless turkey roll.

ROCK CORNISH GAME HENS NORMANDY STYLE

Especially attractive when garnished with
clusters of red and green grapes.

Makes 8 servings

4 (1–1¼-pound) Rock Cornish game
   hens, thawed and halved lengthwise
¼ cup cooking oil
¼ cup butter or margarine
½ pound mushrooms, wiped clean and
   sliced thin

2 cups apple cider or a ½ and ½ mixture
    of cider and dry white wine
½ clove garlic, peeled and crushed
1½ teaspoons salt
¼ teaspoon white pepper
¼ teaspoon thyme
2 tablespoons cornstarch blended with 2
    tablespoons cold water
½ cup heavy cream

Preheat oven to 325° F. Pat hens dry
on paper toweling and brown, 2 or 3
halves at a time, in a mixture of oil and
butter in a large, heavy skillet over
moderate heat. Drain hens on paper
toweling, then arrange in a large,
shallow roasting pan without crowding.
Stir-fry mushrooms in skillet drippings
3–5 minutes over moderate heat and
spoon over hens. Mix cider and garlic
and pour over all; sprinkle in salt,
pepper, and thyme. Cover with foil and
bake ½ hour; uncover and bake 15
minutes longer. Lift hens to a serving
platter, spoon mushrooms on top and
keep warm. Pour pan liquid into a
saucepan and bring to a simmer. Smooth
in cornstarch paste and heat, stirring,
until thickened and clear. Add cream,
taste for salt and adjust as needed.
Spoon some sauce over birds and pass
the remainder. About 365 calories per
serving.

HERBED ROCK CORNISH GAME HENS OR SQUABS WITH MUSHROOMS AND WINE

Makes 4 servings

2 (1–1¼-pound) Rock Cornish game
    hens or squabs, thawed
Herb Butter (see below)
3 tablespoons melted butter or
    margarine
1 cup dry white wine
½ cup chicken broth
1 tablespoon lemon juice
1 dozen button mushrooms, wiped clean
    and fluted*

Herb Butter:

¼ cup butter or margarine, softened to
    room temperature
2 tablespoons minced scallions

2 tablespoons minced parsley
½ teaspoon poultry seasoning
1 teaspoon Worcestershire sauce
½ teaspoon garlic salt

Preheat oven to 425° F. Make a small
slit in the skin on each side of the breast
of each hen. Mix herb butter and, using
a small, thin-bladed knife, spread evenly
over breasts underneath skin. Skewer
openings shut and truss* birds; place
breast side up on a rack in a shallow
roasting pan and roast, uncovered, 20
minutes, brushing 1–2 times with melted
butter. Reduce oven to 325° F.; remove
rack and place birds directly in pan. Pour
wine, broth, and lemon juice over birds
and roast, uncovered, basting frequently
with drippings, about ½ hour until just
tender. Add fluted mushrooms and roast
10 minutes longer. Lift hens and
mushrooms to a hot platter; if pan juices
seem skimpy, stir in a little more wine or
broth. Pour some pan juices over the
birds and pass the rest. About 400
calories per serving.

HAWAIIAN-STYLE ROCK CORNISH GAME HENS OR SQUABS

Makes 4 servings

2 (1–1¼-pound) Rock Cornish game
    hens or squabs, thawed and halved
    lengthwise
Marinade (see below)
2 tablespoons cooking oil
1 large yellow onion, peeled and sliced
    thin
2 teaspoons sugar
4 pineapple rings
2 tablespoons butter or margarine
2 cups hot boiled rice
½ cup minced macadamia nuts or
    toasted slivered almonds
4 preserved kumquats, sliced thin
1 pimiento, slivered
⅓ cup mandarin orange sections

Marinade:

¼ cup soy sauce
¼ cup pineapple juice
1 tablespoon lime juice
1 clove garlic, peeled and crushed

¼ teaspoon ginger
¼ teaspoon oregano
¼ teaspoon pepper

Lay hens in a shallow dish; warm marinade over low heat, stirring, about 5 minutes; pour over birds, cover, and refrigerate 4–6 hours, turning birds occasionally. Pat birds dry on paper toweling and brown in oil in a large, heavy skillet; lift out and set aside. Sauté onion in drippings 8–10 minutes over moderate heat, sprinkle with sugar, and sauté until lightly browned. Return hens to skillet, pour in marinade, cover, and simmer about ¾ hour until tender. Meanwhile, dry pineapple well on paper toweling and brown lightly in butter over moderate heat. To serve, toss rice with nuts, kumquats, pimiento, and orange sections and mound on a hot large platter. Arrange birds and pineapple rings on top and drizzle with some of the pan drippings.

VARIATION:
Prepare as directed but substitute canned lichee nuts for the pineapple and the syrup from the can for the pineapple juice in the marinade; do not brown the lichee nuts.

Both versions: about 615 calories per serving if made with macadamia nuts, 640 calories per serving if made with almonds.

DUCKLING WITH ORANGE SAUCE (DUCKLING À L'ORANGE, DUCKLING À LA BIGARADE)

To be strictly authentic, this recipe should be made with bitter Seville oranges. Any clear-skinned orange will do, however, if you add lemon juice for tartness.
Makes 6 servings

2 (4-pound) ducklings, cleaned, dressed, and quartered
1 tablespoon salt
¼ teaspoon pepper
1 cup chicken broth
1 cup dry white wine

Finely slivered rind of 4 oranges (use orange part only and slice oranges to use as a garnish)
1½ cups water
½ cup sugar
1 cup orange juice
2 tablespoons lemon juice
¼ cup brandy
2 tablespoons butter or margarine
2 tablespoons flour
1 cup giblet stock*

Preheat oven to 450° F. Rub ducklings with 2 teaspoons salt and the pepper; place skin side up on a rack in a large shallow roasting pan and prick skin well all over. Roast, uncovered, 20–25 minutes, turning and pricking frequently; drain off fat. Pour broth and wine over ducklings, reduce oven to 350° F., and roast about 1 hour longer, basting frequently, until golden brown and leg joints move easily. Meanwhile, place rind and 1 cup water in a small saucepan and boil, uncovered, 3 minutes; drain and reserve rind. Boil remaining water and sugar, uncovered, 10–15 minutes until amber; add rind, orange and lemon juices, and brandy, cover, and keep warm over lowest heat. When ducklings are done, transfer to a heated platter and keep warm. Strain pan juices into a shallow bowl, scraping browned bits from bottom, and skim off fat. Melt butter in a saucepan, blend in flour, add pan juices, giblet stock, rind mixture, and remaining salt, and cook, stirring, until slightly thickened. Pour some sauce over the ducklings and pass the rest. Garnish platter with orange slices and sprigs of watercress or rose geranium. About 500 calories per serving.

DUCKLING WITH BING CHERRY SAUCE (DUCKLING MORELLO)
Makes 6 servings

2 (4-pound) ducklings, cleaned, dressed, and quartered
3 teaspoons salt
¼ teaspoon pepper
1 (1-pound 1-ounce) can pitted Bing cherries (do not drain)
1½ cups giblet stock*

1¾ cups chicken broth
1 teaspoon lemon juice
¼ cup cornstarch blended with ½ cup cold water
¼–⅓ cup dry Madeira wine

Preheat oven to 450° F. Rub ducklings with 2 teaspoons salt and ⅛ teaspoon pepper. Place skin side up on a rack in a large, shallow roasting pan and prick skin all over with a sharp fork. Roast, uncovered, 20–25 minutes, turning and pricking frequently; drain off all drippings. Reduce oven to 350° F. and roast 1 hour longer; again drain off drippings. Drain liquid from cherries into roasting pan, baste ducklings, and roast 15–30 minutes until golden brown and leg joints move easily. Transfer to a heated platter and keep warm while you make the sauce. Pour giblet stock and broth into roasting pan and stir, scraping browned bits from bottom; transfer all to a saucepan. Add lemon juice, remaining salt and pepper and heat, uncovered, over moderate heat 1–2 minutes. Blend in cornstarch paste and heat, stirring constantly, until thickened and clear. Add cherries and wine and heat 2–3 minutes longer. Spoon some sauce over ducklings and pass the rest. About 410 calories per serving.

WOR SHEW OPP (BRAISED BONELESS DUCKLING)

Makes 3–4 servings

1 (5-pound) duckling, cleaned and dressed
1 quart water
½ cup soy sauce
2 tablespoons dark brown sugar or Chinese bead molasses (obtainable in Chinese groceries)
1 star anise (also available in Chinese groceries)
3 tablespoons cornstarch
Shortening or cooking oil for deep fat frying
½ cup giblet stock*
1 tablespoon cornstarch blended with 1 tablespoon cold water
2 tablespoons minced toasted almonds

Preheat oven to 450° F. Remove fat from cavity of duckling and discard. Also remove giblets, cook,* mince, and reserve along with stock. Meanwhile, pat duckling dry, skewer openings shut, truss,* and prick body all over with a sharp fork. Place breast side up on a rack in a shallow roasting pan and roast, uncovered, ½ hour. Transfer to a deep kettle, add water, soy sauce, sugar, and anise, cover, and simmer 1½–1¾ hours until very tender; cool in liquid until easy to handle. Cut meat from bones in bite-size pieces. Reserve liquid and skim off fat. Heat shortening in a deep fat fryer to 375° F. Dredge pieces of duck in cornstarch, shake off excess, and fry, a few pieces at a time, 1–2 minutes until golden; drain on paper toweling and keep warm while you fry the rest. Heat ½ cup duck cooking liquid with the giblet stock and giblets in a small saucepan, blend in cornstarch paste, and heat, stirring, until thickened and clear. Mound duckling in a shallow dish, pour sauce over all, and sprinkle with almonds. Serve with hot boiled rice. About 520 calories for each of 3 servings (without rice), 390 calories for each of 4 servings.

CHINESE-STYLE ROAST DUCKLING

Duckling cooked this way is good at a buffet; simply slice thin and serve between small, fresh hot rolls.
Makes 3–4 servings

1 medium-size yellow onion, peeled and minced
2 stalks celery, minced
4 dried mushrooms
1 star anise
1 clove garlic, peeled and crushed
2 teaspoons sugar
¼ cup soy sauce
¼ cup dry sherry
1 (5-pound) duckling, cleaned and dressed
1 teaspoon salt

Basting Sauce:

¼ cup honey
2 tablespoons cider vinegar
1 tablespoon soy sauce

Preheat oven to 450° F. Place onion, celery, mushrooms, anise, garlic, sugar, soy sauce, and sherry in a small saucepan and cook and stir 2–3 minutes over moderate heat. Skewer neck flap of duckling to back, then pour hot mixture into body cavity. (*Note:* If liquid tends to flow out through vent, prop lower part of duckling up with a ball of foil.) Sew up vent and tie legs together. Place duckling breast side up on a rack in a shallow roasting pan and rub well with salt. Roast, uncovered, ½ hour. Meanwhile, mix basting sauce and keep warm over low heat. Reduce heat to 350° F. and roast about 1½ hours longer, basting every 20 minutes with sauce, until leg joints move easily. Transfer duckling to a heated platter and serve. About 535 calories for each of 3 servings, 400 calories for each of 4 servings.

DUCKLING OR GOSLING EN DAUBE

Makes 6–8 servings

2 (4–5-pound) ducklings or goslings, cleaned and dressed
1 tablespoon bacon drippings or clarified butter*
1 large yellow onion, peeled and minced
2 stalks celery, minced
1 teaspoon allspice
2 teaspoons salt
¼ teaspoon pepper
6–8 medium-size carrots, peeled and cut in 1" chunks
4 leeks, washed, trimmed, and cut in 1" chunks (include some tops)
6 turnips, peeled and halved
1 bouquet garni,* tied in cheesecloth
1 fifth dry red wine

Gravy:

⅓ cup unsifted flour
¼ cup butter or margarine
1 cup giblet stock*
½ teaspoon salt (about)
⅛ teaspoon pepper

Cook giblets* and reserve along with stock. Dry birds well, remove loose fat in body cavities, skewer openings shut, and truss; prick birds well all over with a sharp fork, then brown, 1 at a time, using bacon drippings at first, in a heavy skillet over moderately low heat 20–30 minutes; turn as needed to brown evenly and drain off drippings as they accumulate. Meanwhile, preheat oven to 325° F. Set browned birds aside, drain all but 1 tablespoon drippings from skillet, add onion and celery, and stir-fry 8–10 minutes over moderate heat until golden; spoon into a large Dutch oven. Lay birds breast side up on onion mixture, sprinkle each with ½ teaspoon allspice, ½ teaspoon salt, and ⅛ teaspoon pepper. Tuck vegetables around birds and sprinkle them with remaining salt. Add *bouquet garni* and wine, cover, and bake 1½–1¾ hours until leg joints move easily; baste with pan liquid every ½ hour. Meanwhile, mince giblets and reserve. Also brown flour in butter in a heavy saucepan over moderate heat and set aside. When birds are done, drain off liquid and skim off fat. Blend pan liquid and giblet stock into flour and heat, stirring, until thickened. Add giblets, salt, and pepper, taste, and adjust seasoning as needed. Serve birds in a deep platter wreathed with vegetables and topped with some of the gravy. Pass remaining gravy. About 395 calories for each of 6 servings, 300 calories for each of 8 servings.

GERMAN-STYLE POTATO STUFFED ROAST GOOSE

Excellent with Sweet and Sour Red Cabbage or Shredded Ruby Cabbage.
Makes 10 servings

1 (10–12-pound) goose, cleaned and dressed
2 large yellow onions, peeled and sliced thin
¼ cup butter or margarine
6 large potatoes, parboiled, peeled, and cut in ½" cubes
2 cloves garlic, peeled and crushed

Raw goose liver, minced
1 teaspoon sage
1½ teaspoons salt
¼ teaspoon pepper

Preheat oven to 325° F. Remove fat
from body cavity of goose and save if
you like to render and use in cooking.
Remove giblets, hold out liver, but save
the rest for soup or giblet stock.* Prick
goose well all over with a sharp fork.
Sauté onions in butter in a large, heavy
kettle over moderately high heat
5 minutes, add potatoes and garlic, and
sauté 5 minutes. Off heat, mix in
remaining ingredients. Spoon loosely
into cavity of goose, skewer openings
shut, and truss.* Place goose breast side
up on a rack in a shallow roasting pan
and roast 20–22 minutes per pound
until leg joints move easily; prick every
½ hour and drain off drippings as they
collect. If you like a crisp skin, spoon
all drippings from pan, pour ¼ cup cold
water over bird, and roast 10 minutes
longer. Lift bird to a hot platter, remove
skewers and strings, and let "rest" about
10 minutes. Make gravy from drippings
if you like. Garnish as desired and serve.
About 490 calories per serving.

BRAISED GOOSE WITH
CHESTNUTS AND ONIONS

Young (4–8-pound) geese can be
cooked in any of the ways suitable for
duckling. The average supermarket size
(10–12 pounds) is good prepared this
way.
Makes 10 servings

1 (10–12-pound) goose, cleaned, dressed,
    and cut up
1 tablespoon bacon drippings or
    rendered goose fat*
1 medium-size carrot, peeled and
    minced
1 medium-size yellow onion, peeled and
    minced
2 cloves garlic, peeled and crushed
1 teaspoon sugar
1 tablespoon flour

1 quart giblet stock* or part stock and
    part chicken broth
½ cup tomato purée
1 teaspoon salt
¼ teaspoon pepper
1 pound small white onions, peeled
2 tablespoons rendered goose fat or
    clarified butter*
1½ pounds chestnuts, shelled, peeled,
    and quartered

If breasts of goose are large, have
butcher halve them crosswise as well
as lengthwise. Early in the day, take fat
from body of goose and render.* Also
remove giblets and cook*; mince
giblets and reserve along with stock.
Preheat oven to 325° F. Prick goose
well all over with a sharp fork and
brown, a few pieces at a time, in a
large, heavy kettle, using bacon drippings at first, about 20 minutes over
moderately low heat; pour off drippings
as they collect and save; also prick goose
often during browning. Drain goose on
paper toweling and set aside. Drain all
but 2 tablespoons drippings from kettle,
add carrot, onion, and garlic, and stir-fry
8–10 minutes over moderate heat until
golden; sprinkle with sugar and brown
2 minutes. Blend in flour, add stock,
purée, salt, and pepper and heat, stirring,
until mixture boils. Return goose to
kettle, cover, transfer to oven, and bake
2 hours. Meanwhile, brown whole
onions in goose fat in a heavy skillet
over moderate heat about 10 minutes;
drain on paper toweling. When goose
has cooked 2 hours, add onions, cover,
and bake ½ hour; add chestnuts, cover,
and bake ¼–½ hour longer until goose
is very tender. Lift goose to a hot
deep platter, wreathe with onions and
chestnuts, cover, and keep warm. Strain
cooking liquid through a fine sieve,
pressing vegetables to extract all liquid;
skim off as much fat as possible. Reduce
sauce to about 2 cups by boiling rapidly
uncovered, add giblets, taste for salt and
pepper and adjust as needed. Ladle over
goose and serve. About 540 calories per
serving.

Some Ways to Use Poultry Leftovers

There aren't apt to be leftovers from
small birds unless you've misjudged.
Quarters, halves, and parts reheat well,
wrapped in foil, in about ½ hour at
350° F. Leftover turkey, goose, duck,
and chicken can be used in any recipe
calling for cooked poultry meat (if
recipe calls for more meat than you
have, round out with canned chicken).
Or they can be used as follows:

Sliced Hot Poultry: Slice meat, not too
thin, remove skin, and layer into an
ungreased casserole. Add just enough
hot sauce or gravy to cover (see Sauces,
Gravies, and Seasonings for Poultry),
cover with foil, and heat 20 minutes at
350° F.

**Hot Roast Chicken or Turkey Sand-
wiches:** Heat slices in sauce or gravy as
above and serve on toast or bread
spread, if you like, with cranberry sauce,
chutney, or relish. Or serve on hot
leftover stuffing. To reheat stuffing,
spread in a greased piepan and bake,

uncovered, at 350° F., brushing
occasionally with melted butter until
lightly browned.

To Make the Most of Small Amounts:
– Cube, dice, or cut in julienne strips and
toss into hearty salads or add to
casseroles, broths, or vegetable soups.
– Add scraps and bones to stock pot.
– Grind and add to savory stuffings.
– Grind, mix with mayonnaise, a little
softened cream cheese, and mustard,
and use as a sandwich spread. For extra
zip, add a little applesauce or minced
chutney.
– Grind, mix with any seasoned butter,
a little minced scallions or capers,
mustard, or other spicy condiment,
and use as a cocktail spread.
– Dice or slice thin, layer in custard
cups, fill to the brim with Quick Aspic
or Madrilène Aspic, chill until firm,
unmold, and serve with mayonnaise.
– Stretch with an equal quantity of hot
Medium White Sauce, Mornay or
Parsley Sauce and serve over crepes,
toast, waffles, hot biscuits, or corn
bread.

CHAPTER 11

SEAFOOD

Few nations are more blessed with the sea's bounty than America, yet few do more poorly by it. A fish is to fry, we think. So we slosh it with batter or jacket it in bread crumbs and plunk it into bubbling oil. There's nothing wrong with fried fish—especially if it's catfish served with hushpuppies—but there are far too many kinds of fish to lump in the same kettle.

From a catch far less impressive than our own, the French have built an inspired repertoire of recipes. The Scandinavians know dozens of ways to prepare salmon and herring; the Greeks do exciting things with squid and octopus; the Italians—well, it was *they* who taught the French to cook; the Chinese whisk shrimp in and out of a *wok* with a crunch of green vegetables so that it's irresistibly succulent; the Japanese have made an art and ritual of *sushi*—thinly sliced raw fish arrayed with fancily cut vegetables.

This isn't to say we haven't some classics of our own. It's hard to top a boiled Maine lobster, for example. Or Maryland crab or Louisiana shrimp gumbo. But we *can* do better by most of our catch. If we lavished half as much love on the cooking of fish as we do on the catching, we would do very well indeed.

The Kinds of Seafood

Basically, there are two—*fish* and *shellfish*. Fish, for the sake of simplicity, have fins, backbones, and gills. Shellfish subdivide into two categories: *crustaceans* (crabs, crayfish, lobsters, shrimp, and other footed sea animals with armorlike shells) and *mollusks* (clams, mussels, oysters, scallops, and other soft, spineless creatures living inside hard shells).

In addition to fish and shellfish, there are mavericks that defy easy classification: squid and octopus (technically mollusks that carry their shells internally); turtles, terrapins, frogs, and snails (amphibians). Because all require special preparation, they will be discussed individually.

The Food Value of Seafood

All seafood is high in protein; most of it is also high in minerals (notably calcium, phosphorous, copper, and iron) but low in calories. Food values vary from fish to fish, however.

¢ SIMPLE COURT BOUILLON FOR FISH AND SHELLFISH

The simplest court bouillon is salt water (1–1½ teaspoons salt to 1 quart cold water). It is used to poach or steam very delicate white fish because it never masks the true flavor of the fish. The following recipe, although simple, has a touch of piquance. It is suitable for poaching any fish or shellfish. Makes 1 quart

1 large sprig parsley
1 bay leaf
1 (3"–4") sprig fresh thyme or ¼ teaspoon dried thyme
3 peppercorns
1 quart cold water
¼ cup white vinegar
1 medium-size yellow onion, peeled and stuck with 3 cloves
1 carrot, peeled and cut in small dice
1 stalk celery, chopped fine
1 teaspoon salt

Tie parsley, bay leaf, thyme, and peppercorns in cheesecloth. Place in a saucepan, add remaining ingredients, cover, and simmer 1 hour; strain through a fine sieve. Calories negligible.

WHITE WINE COURT BOUILLON

Especially good for shellfish.
Makes about 2 quarts

½ pound fishbones, heads, and trimmings (from any delicate white fish)
1 quart water
1 quart dry white wine
2 small yellow onions, each peeled and stuck with 1 clove
2 bay leaves
2 cloves garlic, peeled
1 teaspoon thyme
1 teaspoon salt
6 bruised peppercorns

Place fishbones and water in a large saucepan, cover, and simmer 20 minutes; strain broth through a fine sieve lined with a double thickness of cheesecloth; discard bones. Rinse out pan, add strained broth and remaining ingredients, and simmer, uncovered, 20 minutes. Again strain broth through a double thickness of cheesecloth. Calories negligible.

RED WINE COURT BOUILLON

A good base for fish sauces and aspics.
Makes about 2 quarts

1 pound fishbones, heads, and trimmings (from any delicate white fish)
1½ quarts water
2 cups dry red wine
2 small yellow onions, each peeled and stuck with 2 cloves
1 carrot, peeled and cut in 1" chunks
1 celery stalk, cut in 1" chunks
1 clove garlic, peeled
2 parsley sprigs
½ teaspoon thyme
1 teaspoon salt
6 bruised peppercorns

Place fishbones and water in a large saucepan, cover, and simmer 20 minutes; add remaining ingredients, cover, and cook ½ hour longer. Strain broth through a fine sieve lined with a double thickness of cheesecloth. Calories negligible.

¢ HERBED COURT BOUILLON FOR FISH AND SHELLFISH

More fragrant than Simple Court Bouillon for Fish and Shellfish.
Makes about 2 quarts

1 stalk celery
2 sprigs parsley
2 sprigs fresh dill
2 sprigs fresh thyme or a pinch dried thyme
2 bay leaves
6 bruised peppercorns
2 quarts water
1½ cups dry white wine
1 medium-size yellow onion, peeled and stuck with 1 clove
1 teaspoon salt
½ pound fishbones, heads, and trimmings (from any delicate white fish)

Tie celery, parsley, dill, thyme, bay leaves, and peppercorns in a double thickness of cheesecloth. Place in a large, heavy kettle with remaining ingredients and simmer, uncovered, 20 minutes. Strain through a fine sieve lined with a double thickness of cheesecloth. Calories negligible.

RICH COURT BOUILLON FOR FISH AND SHELLFISH

An excellent base for soups, sauces, and elaborate seafood dishes.
Makes about 3 quarts

*2 pounds fishbones, heads, and trimmings
    (from any delicate white fish)*
3 quarts cold water
½ cup white vinegar
*1 medium-size yellow onion, peeled and
    quartered*
1 stalk celery, coarsely chopped
1 bouquet garni,* tied in cheesecloth
1 teaspoon salt.

Place all ingredients in a large kettle, cover, and simmer 1 hour. Strain through a large sieve lined with a double thickness of cheesecloth.

VARIATIONS:

Rich Wine Court Bouillon: Prepare as directed, substituting 1 quart dry or medium-dry white or red wine for 1 quart of the water and ¼ cup lemon juice for the vinegar.

Court Bouillon for Aspics: Prepare as directed, reducing water to 2 quarts and increasing simmering time to 2 hours. Skim off any froth and strain liquid through a cheesecloth-lined sieve; do not press solids. Measure liquid and, if needed, add cold water to make 2 quarts. To see if liquid will jell, chill 1 cup. If it sets up as firm as commercial gelatin, you need not add gelatin. If it doesn't, mix in 1 envelope unflavored gelatin softened in ¼ cup cold water and heat, stirring, until dissolved. *To clarify court bouillon:* Place all liquid (including chilled portion) in a large, deep saucepan. Add 2 egg whites, beaten to soft peaks, also 2 eggshells, crushed. Bring to a boil, stirring constantly with a wire whisk, and as soon as mixture foams up, remove from heat. Stir 1 or 2 times, then let stand *undisturbed* 5 minutes. Meanwhile, line a large, fine sieve with a fine linen towel or napkin wrung out in cold water and set over a deep bowl so bottom of sieve will be clear of aspic collecting in bowl. Pour aspic into sieve, egg whites, shells, and all, and let drip through undisturbed.

Aspic is now ready to use as recipes direct.

Calories negligble for all versions.

Some Garnishes for Fish and Shellfish

Parsley, paprika, radish roses, and lemon slices are the usual fish platter garnishes. For more originality, try any or a colorful combination of two of the following artistically grouped around the fish or shellfish.

— Hollowed-out cherry tomatoes, cucumber chunks, or lemon halves filled with tartar or other sauce.
— Artichoke bottoms filled with puréed peas or spinach.
— Artichoke bottoms filled with red or black caviar, topped with a dab of sour cream and sprigged with dill or fennel.
— Sautéed mushroom caps filled with cocktail shrimp or buttered green peas.
— Tiny bundles of buttered asparagus tips bound together with strips of pimiento.
— Stuffed hard-cooked eggs.
— Cherry tomatoes set in artichoke bottoms or on lemon slices.
— Lemon slices sprinkled with capers or minced celery or paprika and topped with a rolled anchovy fillet.
— Lemon flowers, pickle fans, or celery frills (see About Sandwich Garnishes).
— Celery tops or sprigs of fresh dill, fennel, or watercress.

Some Ways to Use Up Leftover Fish and Shellfish

It is unlikely that you'll be faced with much leftover fish unless you'd planned on eight for dinner and only four came. Here are some recipes (all can be found in the recipe section) particularly suited to leftovers, also some suggestions for using up small amounts.

Recipes Good for Leftovers:
Crisp-Crusted Fish and Green Pepper Pie

Potato-Fish Pie
Basic Fish Soufflé (and all variations)
Fish Loaf
Fish Croquettes
Fish Cakes (or use recipe for Codfish
   Cakes, substituting leftover fish for
   salt cod)
Kedgeree
Basic Shellfish Croquettes
Basic Shellfish Soufflé

To Make the Most of Very Small Amounts:

– Combine with canned fish or shellfish,
mayonnaise to bind, and seasonings to
taste and use as a sandwich filling or to
stuff eggs, tomatoes, or avocados.
– Stretch with an equal quantity of hot
Medium White Sauce, Mornay, Parsley,
or Egg Sauce and spoon over crepes,
puff pastry shells, hot toast, or biscuits.
– Stretch with an equal quantity of hot
Medium White Sauce, Mornay, Velouté
or Parsley Sauce, layer into buttered
ramekins with hot boiled rice or thin
noodles, top with grated cheese or
buttered crumbs, and broil quickly to
brown.
– Marinate any leftover cold fried fish à
la Dalmatian Marinated Fish, reducing
amount of marinade as needed.
– Use in making Easy Fish Stock or any
court bouillon.

FISH

All fish, whether salt or fresh water, fall
into two categories: the *lean* (delicate,
low-calorie fish whose oils are concentrated in the liver) and the *oily or fat*
whose oils are distributed throughout the
flesh. Oily fish are usually darker fleshed
and stronger flavored than lean fish
(tuna, for example, is darker and
stronger than flounder). To determine
which fish are which, see the charts of
America's popular salt and fresh water
fish included in this chapter.

About Buying Fresh Fish

Find a good fish market and make
friends with the owner—it's the surest
way of getting absolutely fresh, top
quality seafood. If you live inland in the
land of supermarkets and must always
be your own judge, look for these
characteristics of quality and freshness:

– Sparkling, clear, bulging eyes.
– Rosy, sweet-smelling gills.
– Bright, shimmery, tightly clinging
scales.
– Firm, springy, translucent, lifelike
flesh.
– An over-all fresh, clean smell.

Popular Market Forms of Fresh Fish:

Whole or Round: Fish as they're
taken from the water. Before cooking
they must be drawn or cleaned
(eviscerated) and scaled.

Drawn or Cleaned: Whole fish that have
been eviscerated. Scales must be
removed before cooking.

Cleaned and Dressed or Pan-Dressed:
Ready-to-cook fish that have been
cleaned and scaled. Usually head, tail
and fins have been removed, too.
Dressed refers to fish weighing 1 pound
or more, *pan-dressed* to those weighing
less.

Steaks: Cross-section cuts of large,
cleaned, and dressed fish; they contain
backbone.

Fillets: The boneless sides of fish or,
more recently, any thin, long boneless
piece of fish.

Butterfly Fillets: Both sides of the fish,
boned but still attached on one side so
that they can be opened flat like a book.

Chunks: Thick, cross-cut slices of large,
cleaned, and dressed fish. Like steaks,
they contain a cross-section of the
backbone.

SOME HERBS AND SPICES COMPLIMENTARY TO SEAFOOD

Herb or Spice	Lean White Fish	Oily or Gamy Fish	Shellfish
Bay Leaves	X	X	X
Chervil	X	X	X
Chives	X	X	X
Crab boil			X crab and shrimp
Curry powder	X except delicate fish	X	X
Dill	X	X	X
Fennel	X	X	X
Filé powder		X	X
Fines herbes	X	X	X
Ginger	X	X	X
Juniper berries		X	X
Mace	X	X	X
Marjoram		X	X
Oregano		X	X
Paprika	X	X	X
Parsley	X	X	X
Rosemary		X	X
Saffron			X
Sage		X	
Savory		X	
Tarragon	X	X	X
Thyme	X	X	X

SOME SAUCES, BUTTERS, AND SEASONINGS FOR SEAFOOD

Note: To determine which specific fish fit which category below, see following charts of popular salt and fresh water fish.

Sauces	Very Delicate Lean White Fish (Flounder, Sole, Fluke, etc.)					Lean White Fish (Cod, Haddock, Pike, Whiting, Bass, etc.)					Delicate Oily Fish (Salmon, Eel, Trout, Mackerel, Butterfish, etc.)			
	Broiled, Sautéed	Deep Fat Fried	Baked	Poached, Steamed	Cold	Broiled, Sautéed	Deep Fat Fried	Baked	Poached, Steamed	Cold	Broiled, Sautéed	Baked	Poached, Steamed	Cold
Allemande			X	X				X	X			X	X	
Américaine			X	X				X	X			X	X	
Aoli										X				
Aurore	X					X					X			
Barbecue						X					X	X		
Béarnaise	X	X				X	X				X	X	X	
Béchamel			X	X				X	X			X	X	
Bercy			X	X				X	X					
Bordelaise											X			
Bourguignonne												X		
Caper	X		X	X		X		X	X		X	X		
Cardinal				X					X					
Cheese			X	X				X	X					
Chiffon					X					X				X
Chivry			X	X				X	X					
Cocktail														
Colbert						X		X	X		X	X		
Creole								X	X			X		
Curry								X	X			X		
Diplomate				X				X	X					
Duxelles								X	X			X		
Egg			X	X				X	X					
Espagnole								X	X		X	X	X	
Figaro											X	X		
Fines Herbes			X	X				X	X					
Gribiche											X			X
Hollandaise	X		X	X		X		X	X		X	X	X	
Hot Horseradish														
Joinville			X	X				X	X					
Lobster			X	X				X	X				X	
Louis														
Marinière			X	X				X	X				X	
Mayonnaise					X					X			X	X
Mornay			X	X				X	X			X	X	
Mousseline			X	X				X	X			X	X	
Mustard									X		X	X	X	
Nantua			X	X				X	X				X	
Normande			X	X				X	X					
Oyster									X				X	
Parsley	X		X	X		X		X	X		X	X	X	
Portugaise				X				X	X			X	X	
Poulette				X					X				X	

528

Gamy Fish (Barracuda, Shark, Swordfish, Tuna, etc.)				Clams			Crab				Lobster			Oysters			Scallops				Shrimp			
Broiled	Baked	Poached, Steamed	Cold	Sautéed	Deep Fat Fried	Steamed	Boiled, Steamed	Cold	Sautéed Soft Shell	Deep-Fat-Fried Soft Shell	Boiled, Steamed	Broiled	Cold	Sautéed	Deep Fat Fried	Roasted, Steamed	Broiled, Sautéed	Deep Fat Fried	Poached	Cold	Broiled, Sautéed	Deep Fat Fried	Boiled	Cold
							X				X								X				X	
																			X				X	
												X					X							
X	X																X				X			
X	X	X										X					X				X			
																			X				X	
X																								
X																								
X	X	X		X						X				X	X		X	X			X	X		
											X								X				X	
			X					X					X							X				
					X		X	X							X		X			X	X	X		X
	X	X																	X				X	
	X	X																	X				X	
X	X																		X					
																			X					
X	X																							
X	X	X										X								X	X	X		X
X	X																							
			X					X					X							X				X
X	X										X													
	X				X		X	X					X						X				X	X
		X					X	X											X				X	X
							X				X								X					
X	X	X		X										X			X				X			
	X																	X						
					X									X	X		X	X			X	X		
X	X				X										X		X	X			X	X		
															X			X						

SOME SAUCES, BUTTERS, AND SEASONINGS FOR SEAFOOD (continued)

	Very Delicate Lean White Fish (Flounder, Sole, Fluke, etc.)					Lean White Fish (Cod, Haddock, Pike, Whiting, Bass, etc.)					Delicate Oily Fish (Salmon, Eel, Trout, Mackerel, Butterfish, etc.)			
Sauces	Broiled, Sautéed	Deep Fat Fried	Baked	Poached, Steamed	Cold	Broiled, Sautéed	Deep Fat Fried	Baked	Poached, Steamed	Cold	Broiled, Sautéed	Baked	Poached, Steamed	Cold
Provençale				X				X	X		X	X	X	
Ravigote								X	X		X	X	X	
Rémoulade		X			X	X				X	X			X
Rosy			X	X				X	X					
Sauce verte (green mayonnaise)					X					X				X
Shrimp			X	X				X	X					
Soubise								X	X			X	X	
Sour cream cucumber				X	X	X		X		X		X	X	X
Tartar	X	X			X	X	X			X	X			X
Tempura											X			
Tomato			X	X		X		X	X		X	X	X	
Velouté			X	X				X	X			X	X	
Vinaigrette					X								X	X
Vincent					X								X	X
Butters														
Anchovy	X	X				X		X			X	X		
Beurre noir						X					X			
Caper	X	X				X		X	X		X	X		
Chive	X	X				X		X			X	X		
Garlic						X								
Herb	X	X	X					X	X		X	X	X	
Lemon	X	X	X			X		X	X		X	X	X	
Lobster	X	X				X		X			X			
Maître d'hôtel	X	X	X			X		X	X		X	X	X	
Noisette	X	X				X		X			X	X		
Shallot	X	X				X		X			X	X		
Shrimp	X	X				X		X	X		X			
Stuffings														
Basic bread stuffing			X					X				X		
Crab or shrimp			X					X				X		
Easy almond			X					X				X		
Fruit												X		
Lemon bread			X					X				X		
Oyster			X					X				X		
Quick mushroom			X					X				X		
Tomato and green pepper			X					X				X		
Vegetable			X					X				X		

Gamy Fish (Barracuda, Shark, Swordfish, Tuna, etc.)				Clams			Crab				Lobster			Oysters			Scallops				Shrimp			
Broiled	Baked	Poached, Steamed	Cold	Sautéed	Deep Fat Fried	Steamed	Boiled, Steamed	Cold	Sautéed Soft Shell	Deep-Fat-Fried Soft Shell	Boiled, Steamed	Broiled	Cold	Sautéed	Deep Fat Fried	Roasted, Steamed	Broiled, Sautéed	Deep Fat Fried	Poached	Cold	Broiled, Sautéed	Deep Fat Fried	Boiled	Cold
X	X																X	X			X			
X	X	X					X															X		
X			X		X			X		X			X		X			X		X		X		X
			X					X					X							X				X
																			X					
X			X		X					X					X			X		X		X		X
			X																	X				X
X																		X			X	X		
X	X	X														X			X				X	
X														X	X		X				X			
X				X	X				X	X							X				X			
X														X	X		X				X			
X				X	X						X	X					X	X			X	X		
X											X	X					X				X			
X	X	X		X	X						X	X		X	X		X	X			X	X		
X				X	X		X	X			X	X		X	X		X	X			X	X		
X				X	X		X	X			X	X		X	X		X	X			X	X		
X				X	X						X	X		X	X		X	X			X	X		
X				X	X						X	X		X	X		X	X			X	X		
X							X	X			X	X		X	X		X	X			X	X		
	X											X												
	X											X												
	X											X												
	X											X												
	X											X												
	X																							

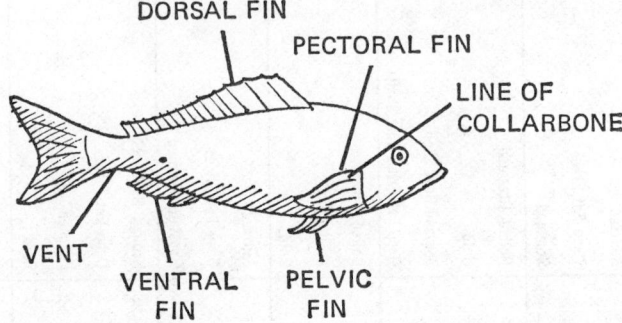

DORSAL FIN

PECTORAL FIN

LINE OF
COLLARBONE

VENT

VENTRAL
FIN

PELVIC
FIN

How Much Fish Should You Buy?

Market Form	Amount per Serving
Whole, drawn	¾–1 pound
Whole, dressed	½ pound
Fillets, Steaks, Chunks	⅓ pound

How to Clean Fresh Fish

If you buy fish, you can have the store clean and dress it. But if there are sportsmen in your family or neighborhood, you may have to cope with an uncleaned, undressed catch. The job isn't fun, but fortunately it *is* fast. Here's the procedure:

1. *Scaling:* Wash fish, place on cutting board, and with one hand hold head firmly (if you salt your hands, you'll get a better grip). With knife blade held almost vertical, scrape from tail to head, against grain of scales. Pay special attention to area around fins. A second technique is to nail fish to board through the tail with an ice pick or long, thin nail, then to scrape briskly toward head (there's less danger of slipping and cutting yourself). There are scalers to make the job easier; but many fishermen prefer a homemade gadget: a slim block of wood with bottle caps nailed upside-down on one side of it.

2. *Cleaning:* Split belly from vent to head and scoop out viscera. Cut around pelvic fins and lift them out.

3. *Removing Head and Tail:* Cut just behind collarbone so head and pectoral fins will come off in one operation. If fish is large and backbone tough, move fish to edge of cutting board so head overhangs, then snap off. Trim to even up cut; slice off tail.

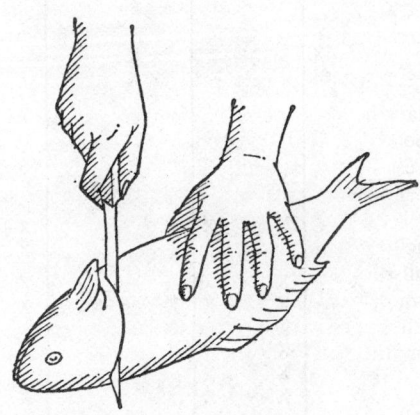

4. *Finning:* Cut along each side of dorsal fin, then yank forward to remove (root bones will come away too). Remove ventral fin the same way.

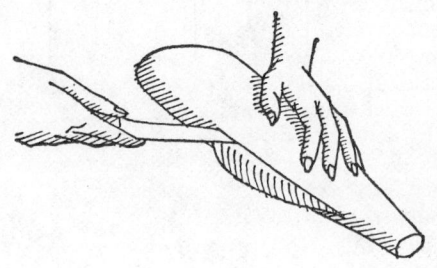

(*Note:* Simply snipping off fins leaves many little bones inside the fish. Rinse fish under cold running water.)

To Cut into Steaks: Slice fish crosswise, making cuts ½"–1" or more apart, depending on how thick you like your steaks.

To Fillet: With an extra-sharp knife (or fillet knife), cut along back of fish from one end to the other, then with knife blade held parallel to backbone, slide it along backbone, separating meat from bones; lift off boneless piece. Turn fish over and repeat on the other side. If you want to skin the fillet, place skin side down on cutting board, hold firmly by tail end (again salt your hands for a better grip), slip knife through flesh just to skin, turn and flatten against skin, then slide length of fillet.

To Fillet Herring (a slightly different technique): Clean and dress herring, then split entire length of stomach. Place herring cut side down, like an open book with 2 halves out to the side. Press fingertips firmly up and down backbone several times. Turn fish over, grab tail end of backbone with one hand, anchor fish to board with the other, and pull backbone up toward head. It should come away in 1 piece, bringing all the little bones with it. Now cut herring down the back into 2 fillets.

About Frozen Fish

Many of America's popular fish are available frozen in one or more of the following forms: whole, dressed, steaks, fillets, chunks, portions, and sticks.

To Be Sure of Top Quality: Buy only solidly frozen fish that shows no discoloration or freezer burn, no signs of having thawed and refrozen (a block of frozen juices at the bottom of the package); reject any fish with a strong or "off" odor. Unfortunately, much frozen fish can't be seen until the package is opened, but if you have doubts on examining the fish, return it to the market.

How to Cook Frozen Fish: Should frozen fish be thawed before cooking? It depends, on the size of the fish and how it's to be cooked. Here are some guidelines:

Fish Portions and Sticks: Cook solidly frozen.

Fillets and Steaks: Most authorities agree that it's best to thaw these 1–2 hours in the refrigerator until they're easy to separate and handle. They must be thawed (at least until soft on the outside) if they are to be breaded or the breading won't stick. If there are package directions for thawing and cooking, follow them.

Whole Fish, Dressed Fish, and Large Chunks: Whole fish must be thawed so that they can be cleaned and dressed. Dressed fish and large chunks must be thawed if they're to be stuffed. And, many experts believe, whole fish and large pieces will poach and steam more evenly if thawed before cooking. As for baking, it seems to make little difference, *except* that solidly frozen fish will take approximately twice as long to cook as the thawed.

Best Ways to Thaw Frozen Fish: Always thaw just before cooking and, once thawed, never refreeze; thawed fish can be held in refrigerator about one day, but no longer. Don't unwrap fish before thawing; simply set in refrigerator and thaw, allowing about twenty-four hours for a one-pound package. Don't thaw at room temperature to hasten things— the danger of spoilage is too great. Instead, thaw wrapped fish under a slow steam of *cold* running water, allowing 1–2 hours per pound. Never use warm water.

About Canned Fish

The list of canned fish is long and getting longer. Here are some of the most popular items:

Anchovies: Fillets are available either flat or rolled around capers; paste comes in tubes.

Bonito: See Tuna.

Mackerel: Canned chunks are available, either plain or in sauce (tomato or wine). Mackerel roe is also canned.

Salmon: The five kinds available, from expensive to inexpensive are: red or sockeye; chinook or king; coho or silver (also sometimes called medium red); pink or humpback; and, finally, chum.

Sardines: These are packed whole in oil, also boned and skinned. The most highly prized are the Portuguese, packed in a top grade olive oil; next best are the herbed and spiced French sardines.

Tuna: The choicest is *albacore* or *white meat tuna.* *Light meat* tuna ranges from pink to red-brown and comes from bluefin, skipjack or bonito, or yellowfin. Three packs are available: *fancy or solid* (expensive), best used when appearance is important; *chunk* (moderate), good for salads and casseroles; and *flaked* (relatively inexpensive), good for sandwich spreads and canapés.

Some Gourmet Items: Red (salmon) and black (sturgeon) caviar (see discussion in chapter on appetizers and hors d'oeuvre); eel; smoked and pickled herring; shad roe.

Other Forms of Fish

In addition to being sold fresh, frozen, and canned, many fish are also available in brine, dried, salted, and/or smoked (kippered). Consult charts of popular salt and fresh water fish to determine which are available in which forms. Directions for preparing them are in the recipe section.

How to Cook Fresh Fish

Fish is as fragile as a soufflé; cooking can never make it more tender than it already is, only more attractive and flavorful. The greatest crime committed against fish is overcooking. When is fish done—and not overdone? The instant the flesh turns from translucent to opaque and flakes (falls easily into natural divisions) when probed with a fork. Flaking is the test of doneness for all fish, regardless of how it's cooked. Keep the fork handy, test often, take fish from the heat the second it flakes.

To Bake (best for whole fish, large chunks, steaks, and fillets; for names of fish that are "good bakers," consult the fish charts that follow).

To Bake Whole Fish:

General Preparation: Have fish cleaned but leave head and tail on. If you're squeamish about looking a baked fish in the eye, take the head off before transferring to platter, *but not before—* a headless fish will lose juices during cooking. Lightly sprinkle cavity of fish with salt and pepper. Do not slash skin.

Basic Method: Preheat oven to 400° F. Line a large, shallow baking pan with foil and grease well (so fish will be easier to transfer to platter and pan will be quicker to clean). Lay fish in pan (if you are baking more than 1 fish at a time, make sure they do not touch one another). If fish are lean, brush well with melted butter or margarine or drape with bacon strips. Bake, uncovered, 10–15 minutes per pound, basting as needed with additional melted butter. It is difficult to be more specific about baking times because fish vary so in shape. Keep the testing fork handy and begin probing gently after minimum baking time is up. (*Note:* Small fish take proportionately longer to cook than large ones.) When fish is done, carefully transfer to a heated platter, top with some of the pan juices, and serve as is or with a compatible sauce (see chart Some Sauces, Butters, and Seasonings for Seafood). *For Extra Flavor:* Baste fish with a seasoned butter, a ½ and ½ mixture of melted butter and dry white wine, with light cream or with herb, French, or Italian dressing. *For Low-Calorie Baked Fish:* Choose a lean, low-calorie fish and baste with a low-calorie French, Italian, herb, or garlic dressing during cooking instead of butter.

Continental Method (also called *Braising*): Preheat oven to 400° F. Line pan with foil and grease, then make a ½″ bed of finely chopped vegetables in pan (equal parts minced onions, celery, and carrots; minced onions and mushrooms; or minced onions, tomatoes, and sweet red or green peppers); mix in 2–3 tablespoons minced fresh parsley and about 2 tablespoons melted butter or margarine. Lay fish on vegetables and proceed as in Basic Method above.

To Bake a Whole, Stuffed Fish: (Bluefish, cod, haddock, mackerel, red snapper, salmon, shad, and trout are particularly elegant when stuffed.) For other fish to stuff and bake, see charts of salt and fresh water fish.

General Preparation: Should fish be boned before stuffing? Yes, if possible. A boned fish is easier and pleasanter to eat; unfortunately, all fish are not easy to bone without filleting. Try to have your fish market bone the fish and prepare it for stuffing. If you must prepare it yourself, here are two ways. For each it's best to have fish that has not been cleaned and dressed.

Method 1. Slit fish down the back, slide a sharp, thin-bladed knife down along backbone, first on 1 side, then on the other, to separate meat from bone. With poultry shears, cut through backbone at both ends and lift backbone out. Remove all viscera through this opening. Scale the fish, remove fins, then rinse well in cool water and pat dry.

Method 2. Slit fish down belly and eviscerate, following Method 1. Deepen cut to backbone, separating meat from bones as you go. Cut through backbone at head and tail ends using poultry shears and pull backbone out through the stomach opening; vertebrae and other small bones should come away with the backbone, but examine cavity carefully for any "missed bones" and pull out. Rinse fish in cool water and pat dry.

Basic Method of Baking: Preheat oven to 400° F. Line a large, shallow baking pan with foil, then grease the foil. Loosely stuff fish with a bread or other suitable stuffing (see Some Sauces, Butters, and Seasonings for Fish for suggestions); you'll need about 2 cups stuffing for a 3–4-pound fish, 1 quart for a 6–7-pounder. Wrap any remaining stuffing in foil and place in baking pan. Toothpick cavity of fish shut or, if skin is tough, loosely sew up. Brush fish well with melted butter or margarine and bake, uncovered, 12–15 minutes per pound (*this is per pound of dressed weight, not stuffed weight*). While fish bakes, baste as needed with additional melted butter; remove fish from oven as soon as it will flake at the touch of a fork. *For Extra Flavor:* Use any of the suggestions given in the Basic Method above. When fish is done, carefully transfer to a hot platter and remove toothpicks or thread.

To Plank a Whole Fish: Oil a large hardwood plank generously and set in preheating oven to warm; it should be heated to 400° F. as for other baked fish. Center a whole, cleaned 3–4-pound fish on the hot plank, brush with 1–2 tablespoons melted butter, margarine, or cooking oil, and sprinkle with ½ teaspoon salt and ⅛ teaspoon pepper. Bake, uncovered, without basting 10–15 minutes per pound until fish will flake. Remove from oven, pipe a border of Duchess Potatoes around edge of plank, and broil 2–3 minutes, 4″ from heat, until touched with brown. Garnish plank by filling any empty spaces with clusters of buttered green peas and cherry tomatoes. (*Note:* For details on the selection and care of the plank, see Planked Steak.)

To Bake Fish Fillets, Steaks, and Chunks:

General Preparation: Pat fish dry on paper toweling. Leave fillets whole or fold envelope style, ends toward center.

Basic Method: Preheat oven to 350° F. Line a large, shallow baking pan with foil and grease well. Arrange fish pieces in a single layer, not touching. Sprinkle lightly with salt and pepper. If fish is lean, drizzle with ¼–⅓ cup melted butter or margarine; otherwise, brush lightly with melted butter. Bake, uncovered, 20–30 minutes, basting once or twice, until fish flakes. Lift fish to a heated platter with a pancake turner, top with some of the pan juices, sprinkle with paprika and/or parsley, and serve. *For Extra Flavor:* Substitute Lemon, Parsley, or Herb Butter for the plain. *For Low-Calorie Baked Fillets, Steaks, and Chunks:* Choose a lean, low-calorie fish and baste with a low-calorie French, Italian, herb, or garlic dressing instead of butter.

To Oven Broil (best for steaks, fillets, and small whole or split fish):

General Preparation: If fish are whole, have cleaned or cleaned and dressed; if you like, split in half lengthwise. Pat fish, steaks, or fillets dry on paper toweling and, if you want, dredge lightly in flour.

Basic Method: Preheat broiler. Line broiler pan and rack with foil. Arrange fish on rack in a single layer, not touching each other, brush with melted butter or margarine, and sprinkle with salt and pepper. Just how long fish should be broiled can only be estimated at best because size, shape, and delicacy of fish vary greatly. The flaking test is the only true test of doneness. Use the following tables as a guide:

FISH BROILING CHART

Cut	Thickness	Distance from Heat	Minutes on First Side	Minutes on Second Side
Steaks	½"	2"	3	3–5
Steaks	1"	2"	3–5	4–5

(*Note:* Lean fish like cod, halibut, and bass should be basted once during cooking with melted butter or margarine or cooking oil.)

Fillets	¼"–½"	2"	4–5 minutes (do not turn)	
Fillets	¾"–1"	2"	7–10 minutes (do not turn)	

(*Note:* All fillets should be basted at least once during cooking; very lean ones [cod, fluke, flounder, sole, etc.] twice. If fillets have not been skinned, broil skin side down.)

Split (halved) fish	½"–1"	3"	7–10 minutes (do not turn)	
Split (halved) fish	1"–1½"	3"	10–14 minutes (do not turn)	

	Weight			
Whole fish (small)	1–2 lbs.	3"	3–5	5–6
Whole fish (medium)	3–5 lbs.	5"–6"	5–7	7–10
Whole flat fish (fluke, flounder, etc.)	————	3"	8–10 minutes (do not turn)	

(*Note:* Broil split fish skin side down and baste once during cooking, twice if very lean. Whole fish should be basted at least once during cooking, 2–3 times if lean.)

For Extra Flavor: Use a seasoned butter for basting or a ½ and ½ mixture of melted butter and lemon juice or dry white wine. *For Low-Calorie Broiled Fish:* Select a lean fish and baste with low-calorie herb or garlic dressing instead of butter.

To Charcoal Broil (best for thick [1″] fillets, small to medium whole or split fish):

General Preparation: Same as for oven broiling.

Basic Method: Prepare a moderately hot charcoal fire.* Grease a long-handled, hinged wire grill well. Brush fish generously with a ½ and ½ mixture of melted butter and lemon juice, place in grill, and broil 4″ from coals 5–8 minutes on one side, basting frequently with butter mixture. Turn and grill other side 5–8 minutes, basting often, until fish flakes when touched with a fork.

VARIATION:

Barbecued Fish: (best for 1″ fillets and steaks): Marinate fish 1–2 hours in a favorite barbecue sauce before cooking. Charcoal broil as above but baste with barbecue sauce instead of butter.

To Panfry (Sauté) (best for fillets, steaks, and small whole fish):

General Preparation: Have whole fish cleaned and, if you like, dressed. Pat fish very dry between several thicknesses of paper toweling.

Basic Method: Lightly sprinkle both sides of fish with salt and pepper, then dust with flour. Sauté in 3–4 tablespoons butter or margarine or cooking oil or, if you prefer, a ½ and ½ mixture of butter and cooking oil in a large, heavy skillet over moderate heat or in an electric skillet set at 350° F. Thin fillets or steaks will take 2–3 minutes per side, thicker pieces 4–5 minutes on a side, and small whole fish 3–5 minutes per side. As fish are done, drain on paper toweling, then keep warm by setting uncovered in oven turned to lowest heat.

VARIATIONS:

Fillets or Steaks Amandine: Sauté as in Basic Method, using butter, transfer to a hot platter and keep warm. Add 2 tablespoons butter to skillet and ¼–⅓ cup thinly sliced blanched almonds and stir-fry 2–3 minutes until bubbly and brown. Pour over fish and serve.

Fillets or Steaks à la Meunière: Dip fish in milk, then in flour lightly seasoned with salt and pepper. Sauté as above in butter, transfer to a hot platter, and sprinkle with lemon juice and a little minced parsley. Add 2 tablespoons butter to skillet and heat, stirring up any browned bits from bottom of skillet, about 2 minutes until lightly browned. Pour over fish and serve.

Breaded Fried Fish: Lightly sprinkle both sides of whole fish, fillets, or steaks with salt and pepper and dust with flour. Dip in a mixture of beaten egg and water (2 tablespoons water for each egg) and fine dry bread crumbs, cracker meal, or a ½ and ½ mixture of flour and corn meal. Sauté by Basic Method above. *For a dry, crisp crust,* let fish dry 10–15 minutes on a wire rack after breading; then sauté. *For extra flavor,* mix 1–2 tablespoons grated Parmesan or minced parsley into crumbs, or ½ teaspoon sage or thyme.

To Oven "Fry" (best for steaks, fillets, and small whole fish):

General Preparation: Have whole fish cleaned and, if you like, dressed. Pat fish very dry on paper toweling.

Basic Method: Preheat oven to 500° F. Mix ½ cup milk with 1 teaspoon salt and ⅛ teaspoon white pepper. Dip fish in milk, then in fine dry bread crumbs, cracker meal, or crushed cornflakes. Place in a well-greased shallow baking pan and drizzle with melted butter or margarine. Bake, uncovered, without turning or basting 10–15 minutes until golden brown and fish just flakes.

To Deep-Fat-Fry (best for fillets cut in sticks or squares or very small fish, such as smelt):

General Preparation: If using whole fish, clean but do not dress. Pat fish very dry on paper toweling.

Basic Method: Bread fish as for Breaded Fried Fish (above), arrange in a single layer in a deep fat basket, and fry 3–4 minutes in 375° F. fat until golden brown; drain on paper toweling before serving. Scoop any bits of fish or breading from fat before adding a fresh batch of fish and keep fat as nearly at 375° F. as possible. Never let the fat smoke—the whole house will reek of fish for days.

VARIATIONS:

Batter-Fried Fish: See recipe for Fish and Chips.

Shallow-Fried Fish: This method is good for fillets as well as for fish sticks and small whole fish. Bread fish as for Breaded Fried Fish or dip in batter as for Fish and Chips. Pour 1"–1½" cooking oil or melted shortening in a large, heavy skillet or electric skillet set at 375° F. When fat reaches 375° F. on deep fat thermometer, lower pieces of fish, one at a time, into fat using a pancake turner and arrange in a single layer; fish should not touch each other. Fry 2–3 minutes on each side until lightly browned. Drain on paper toweling before serving.

To Poach (best for whole fish, chunks, steaks, and fillets): See charts of popular salt and fresh water fish for names of those that poach well. Also see special recipes for Poached Salmon and Truite au Bleu.

General Preparation: Have whole fish cleaned and, if you like, dressed.

Fillets, Steaks, Chunks, and Small Whole Fish: Arrange fish barely touching in a single layer in a large, heavy skillet (not iron); if using fragile fish, use a burner-to-table skillet to avoid excessive handling. Add Easy Fish Stock or a court bouillon to cover or, if you prefer, boiling water plus ¼ cup lemon juice or white wine vinegar, 1 minced scallion, 1 sprig parsley, 1 teaspoon salt, 3–4 peppercorns, and ½ bay leaf. Cover and simmer gently until fish will flake: 5–10 minutes for steaks and fillets, 6–8 minutes per pound for small whole fish and chunks. (*Note:* It's important to keep water trembling, *not* boiling, so that fish will be moist and tender but firm.) Using a large pancake turner, transfer fish to a heated serving platter. Serve hot with a suitable sauce (see Some Sauces, Butters, and Seasonings for Seafood) or cool to room temperature, chill well, and serve with mayonnaise or a cold sauce. (*Note:* Save poaching liquid to use as a base for soups and sauces.)

Large Whole Fish and Chunks: Wrap fish in a double thickness of cheesecloth and place on a rack in a large, heavy kettle. Add Easy Fish Stock or a court bouillon to cover or, if you prefer, the water and seasonings called for in poaching fillets. (*Note:* If more than 3 cups water are needed for poaching the fish, double the amount of lemon juice and seasonings.) Cover and bring slowly to a simmer, adjust heat so water stays at a tremble, then poach 8–10 minutes per pound until fish will flake. Carefully lift fish from kettle using 2 pancake turners; remove cheesecloth and peel away fish skin. Serve hot with a compatible sauce or chill and serve cold.

To Steam (best for whole fish, chunks, steaks, thick fillets or rolled-up thin fillets):

General Preparation: Have whole fish cleaned or cleaned and dressed; whole fish or large chunks should be wrapped in a double thickness of cheesecloth as directed for poaching.

Basic Method: Use a fish or vegetable steamer or deep kettle fitted with a rack. Grease rack well, pour in boiling water to a depth of 1" (or as kettle manufacturer directs), place fish on rack, sprinkle lightly with salt and white pepper, cover, and steam over boiling water as follows: 5–10 minutes for steaks and fillets; 6–8 minutes per pound for large chunks or whole fish. Lift to a heated platter and serve with an appropriate sauce or butter; or cool to room temperature, then chill well and serve cold. *For Extra Flavor:* Add a *bouquet garni** tied in cheesecloth to water in kettle or use a court bouillon, white wine, cider, or beer in place of water. *For Low-Calorie Steamed Fish:* Choose a lean fish and dress with a low-calorie Italian, garlic, or herb dressing instead of a butter or sauce.

About Pressure Cooking Fish: Don't! The fish will disintegrate.

How to Serve Whole Fish and Large Chunks

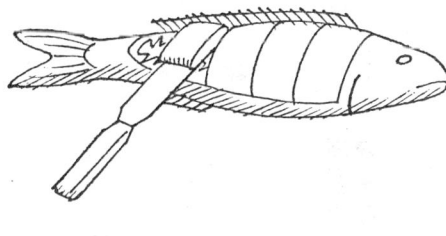

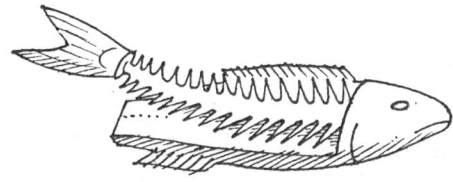

Turn platter so back of fish is away from you; beginning near head, make a cut the length of fish along backbone and loosen flesh from bone. Slice 1″–2″ wide, cutting only to bones, and lift out each slice, using a fish or pie server. Lift out backbone, pulling away vertebrae; continue slicing as before.

¢ ☒ FISH CAKES

A half-and-half combination of fish and mashed potatoes that is both easy and economical.
Makes 4 servings

1½ cups skinned, boned, cooked flaked fish (any kind)
1½ cups seasoned mashed potatoes
1 egg, lightly beaten
2 tablespoons minced parsley
⅛ teaspoon pepper
½ teaspoon salt (about)
1 egg, lightly beaten with 1 tablespoon cold water
½ cup toasted bread crumbs
⅓ cup cooking oil

Mix fish with potatoes, egg, parsley, pepper, and salt; taste for salt and add more if needed. Shape mixture into 4 flat cakes, dip in egg mixture, then in crumbs to coat. Heat oil in a large, heavy skillet over moderate heat until a cube of bread will sizzle. Add fish cakes and brown 3–5 minutes on each side. Drain on paper toweling and serve. Pass Parsley Sauce or Tomato Sauce if you like. About 320 calories per serving.

FISH CROQUETTES

A perfect way to use up any leftover fish.
Makes 4 servings

2 tablespoons butter or margarine
3 tablespoons flour
1 cup milk
½ teaspoon salt (about)
⅛ teaspoon white pepper
2 teaspoons Worcestershire sauce
1 egg yolk, lightly beaten
1½ cups soft white bread crumbs
1½ cups skinned, boned, cooked, finely ground fish (any kind)
1 tablespoon lemon juice
Shortening or cooking oil for deep fat frying

Coating:
1 egg, lightly beaten
1 cup fine dry bread crumbs

Melt butter in a saucepan over moderate heat, blend in flour, slowly add milk, and heat, stirring, until thickened. Off heat, mix in seasonings, egg yolk, crumbs, fish, and lemon juice; taste for salt and adjust if needed. Cover and chill 3–4 hours. Shape mixture into 8 patties or sausage-shaped rolls, dip in egg and roll in crumbs to coat. Let stand at room temperature on a wire rack while heating fat. Place shortening in a deep fat fryer and heat to 375° F.; use a deep fat thermometer. Place 3 or 4 croquettes in fryer basket, lower into hot fat, and fry 2–3 minutes until golden brown and crisp; drain on paper toweling, then keep warm by setting, uncovered, in oven turned to lowest heat while you fry the rest. Serve hot with Tartar Sauce. About 380 calories per serving (without sauce).

AMERICA'S POPULAR SALT WATER FISH

Market Name	Size	Type of Fish	Description	Season	Where Available	Best Ways to Cook
Amberjack	10-12 pounds	Lean	Fine-fleshed, mild. *Market Forms:* whole (more often caught than bought).	Winter, spring	South Atlantic coast	Bake (stuffed or unstuffed), broil, panfry
Barracuda	10-15 pounds	Oily	Strong, dark-fleshed; Pacific barracuda is smaller, leaner. *Market Forms:* whole, occasionally fresh and frozen steaks (more often caught than bought).	Year round	Atlantic and Gulf coasts, California	Bake, broil, charcoal broil
Bluefish	3-10 pounds	Lean	Delicate, fine-grained white to silvery gray meat. *Market Forms:* whole.	Spring, summer, fall	Atlantic and Gulf coasts	Bake (stuffed or unstuffed), broil
Butterfish	Average 1/2 pound	Oily	Also called dollarfish, pumpkinseed. Rich, tender, sweet white meat. *Market Forms:* whole.	Spring, summer, fall	Atlantic and Gulf coasts	Broil, panfry
Cobia	Average 10 pounds	Oily	Firm, light flesh of good but not strong flavor. *Market Forms:* whole, steaks, chunks (more often caught than bought).	Spring	South Atlantic and Gulf coasts	Bake (stuffed or unstuffed), broil, or charcoal broil
Cod	Average 10 pounds but can reach 100 pounds	Lean	Bland snowy meat; poorly cooked, it can be watery or woolly. Young (1½-2½-pound) cod are called scrod (so are young haddock and pollack). *Market Forms:* whole, fresh, and frozen steaks and fillets; smoked, salted, dried. Special delicacies: cod cheeks (sounds) and tongues:	Year round	North Atlantic and Pacific	*Whole or large pieces:* bake (stuffed or unstuffed), braise, poach. *Steaks:* panfry, broil, charcoal broil. *Fillets:* panfry, poach, broil

540

Market Name	Size	Type of Fish	Description	Season	Where Available	Best Ways to Cook
Croaker	Average 1 pound	Lean	Delicate, often underrated little fish. *Market Forms:* whole.	Year round	Middle and South Atlantic coasts	Broil, panfry
Drum (red and black)	8-10 pounds	Lean	The red drum, also called Channel bass or redfish, is choicer; black drum is bony. *Market Forms:* whole (if small), fillets, steaks; 5-pounders are called "puppy drums."	Summer, fall	New York to Texas	Bake (stuffed or unstuffed), broil or panfry steaks, fillets
Eel	Average 1-4 pounds	Oily	Surprisingly mellow-flavored meat. *Market Forms:* live; also smoked, canned.	Year round	Maine to Texas	Bake, broil, panfry, deep fry, poach
Flounder	Average 2-3 pounds	Lean	A family of flat fish often sold as lemon or gray sole; America has no true sole (other than that imported from Europe). Flounder is related to sole and similarly fine, white, and delicate. *Market Forms:* whole, fresh and frozen fillets.	Year round	Atlantic, Gulf, and Pacific coasts	Bake, broil, charcoal broil, panfry, deep fry, poach
Fluke	1-5 pounds	Lean	A flounderlike fish with delicate white meat; also called plaice. *Market Forms:* whole, fresh and frozen fillets.	Spring, summer	North Atlantic	Same as for Flounder
Haddock	2-5 pounds	Lean	A fine-grained codlike fish. *Market Forms:* whole, fresh and frozen fillets; smoked (finnan haddie), salted, flaked.	Year round	North Atlantic	Bake (stuffed or unstuffed), broil, panfry, deep fry, poach
Hake (see Whiting)						

AMERICA'S POPULAR SALT WATER FISH (continued)

Market Name	Size	Type of Fish	Description	Season	Where Available	Best Ways to Cook
Halibut	1½-50 pounds or more	Lean	A large, moderately strong flat fish; badly cooked, it becomes dry and woolly. *Market Forms:* small (1½ pounds) fish are sold whole as "chicken halibut"; large halibut are cut into steaks and fillets and available fresh, frozen, and smoked.	Year round but best in spring	Atlantic and Pacific coasts	Bake (stuffed or unstuffed), broil, panfry, poach, steam
Herring	1/2-3/4 pound	Oily	An enormous family that includes alewives, shad, and sardines (sardines are young herring 3"-6" long; sprats are smoked sardines; brislings are European sardines). *Market Forms:* whole; brined, salted, pickled, smoked (kippered), canned.	Spring	Atlantic and Pacific coasts	Bake (stuffed or unstuffed), broil, charcoal broil, panfry; brine, marinate, pickle
Jack crevalle	2-20 pounds	Oily	This fish and its little cousin, the blue runner, are popular game fish; their meat is too gamy and bloody for most palates. *Market Forms:* whole (more often caught than bought).	Late fall, early winter	Southern Atlantic and Gulf coasts	Marinate steaks and broil or barbecue
Kingfish	Average 3 pounds	Oily	Rich, firm-fleshed fish much like mackerel; a California cousin is the corbina. *Market Forms:* whole, steaks, fillets.	Late fall, winter	Southern Atlantic and Gulf coasts	Bake (stuffed or unstuffed), broil, panfry, stew

Market Name	Size	Type of Fish	Description	Season	Where Available	Best Ways to Cook
Lemon sole (see Flounder)						
Lingcod	5-20 pounds	Lean	Not a cod, despite its name, but a sleek delicate white fish. *Market Forms:* whole, steaks, fillets.	Year round	West Coast	Bake (stuffed or unstuffed), broil, panfry
Mackerel (Atlantic)	1-2 pounds	Oily	The huge mackerel family includes wahoo, chub, king, and Spanish mackerel, but the best is the small, rich, firm-fleshed Atlantic mackerel. *Market Forms:* whole, fresh and frozen fillets; smoked, salted, canned.	Spring and summer	Virginia north	Bake (stuffed or unstuffed), broil, panfry, poach
Mullet	2-3 pounds	Oily	Often called "poor man's meat," mullet has firm flesh and robust flavor. *Market Forms:* whole, fresh and frozen fillets; smoked, salted.	Year round	Atlantic and Gulf coasts	Bake, broil, panfry, stew
Ocean perch	3/4-1 pound	Lean	A rather firm, coarse white fish that flakes nicely when properly cooked; flavor is delicate. *Market Forms:* frozen fillets and fish sticks.	Year round	North Atlantic	Bake, broil, panfry, deep fry, poach
Pacific mackerel	1-2 pounds	Oily	Fine, firm, dark fish of good strong flavor. *Market Forms:* whole, fillets.	All year but best in fall	California	Bake, broil, barbecue
Pacific sole	3/4-7 pounds	Lean	A family of delicate, white flat fish that includes petrale and rex sole, sand dabs, flounder, and turbot. *Market Forms:* whole, fillets.	Year round	West Coast	Bake, broil, charcoal broil, panfry, deep fry, poach

543

Market Name	Size	Type of Fish	Description	Season	Where Available	Best Ways to Cook
Pollock	4-12 pounds	Lean	A cousin to cod, pollock is firmer, and slightly stronger flavored. *Market Forms:* whole, steaks, fresh and frozen fillets; smoked.	Year round	North Atlantic	Bake (stuffed or unstuffed), broil, panfry, deep fry, poach
Pompano	1½-3 pounds	Oily	Often considered to be America's finest fish because of its exceptionally fine, succulent flesh and delicate flavor. *Market Forms:* whole, fresh and frozen fillets.	Year round	Southern Atlantic and Gulf coasts	Bake *en papillote*, broil, panfry
Porgies	Scup: 1-2 pounds; Sheepshead: 2-6 pounds	Lean	Scup and sheepshead both have fine flavor and white meat. *Market Forms:* whole, occasionally fillets.	Spring, early summer	Scup: North Atlantic; Sheepshead: Atlantic and Gulf coasts	Broil, panfry; Sheepshead may be stuffed and baked
Red snapper	Up to 50 pounds but 5-10-pounders are best	Lean	A beautiful fish with meaty, moist, mildly flavored flesh. *Market Forms:* whole, steaks, fresh and frozen fillets.	Year round	South Atlantic and Gulf coasts	Bake (stuffed or unstuffed), broil, panfry, poach
Rockfish	2-5 pounds	Lean	Mild fish with pinkish-white meat. *Market Forms:* whole, fillets.	Year round	West Coast	Bake (stuffed or unstuffed), broil, panfry, poach
Sablefish	4-20 pounds	Oily	Mild but buttery white fish. *Market Forms:* whole, steaks, fillets.	Year round	West Coast	Bake (stuffed or unstuffed), broil, barbecue

Market Name	Size	Type of Fish	Description	Season	Where Available	Best Ways to Cook
Salmon	6-30 pounds	Oily	Luscious, mellow meat ranging from pale to dark pink. The 5 Pacific varieties: Chinook (biggest); chum; pink or humpback; coho or silver; sockeye or red (the smallest and finest). Eastern salmon is Atlantic or Kennebec. *Market Forms:* whole, chunks, fresh and frozen steaks; smoked (lox), salted, canned, potted.	Spring and summer	Pacific Northwest, North Atlantic	*Whole Salmon or Large Chunks:* Stuff and bake, plank, poach, steam; *Steaks:* Bake, broil, charcoal broil, panfry, poach
Sardines (see Herring)						
Sea bass	1/2-5 pounds	Lean	A moist white fish of good flavor but many bones. *Market Forms:* whole.	Year round	Atlantic Coast	Bake (stuffed or unstuffed), broil, charcoal broil, poach
Sea squab	4-6 ounces	Lean	This is the blowfish; when dressed, it looks like a skinless drumstick; the meat is juicy and mild. *Market Forms:* dressed.	Spring, summer, early fall	North and mid-Atlantic coast	Broil, panfry, deep fry
Sea trout (see Weakfish)						
Shad	Average 3-5 pounds	Fairly oily	The king of the herring family because of its delicate, snowy meat. *Market Forms:* whole, fillets. Also available: fresh and canned shad roe.	Early spring	Atlantic and Pacific coasts	Bake (stuffed or unstuffed), broil, panfry fillets
Shark	25-40 pounds	Oily	Firm, chewy meat similar to swordfish. *Market Forms:* fresh and frozen steaks and fillets; salted, smoked.	Year round	Atlantic and Pacific coasts	Bake, broil, barbecue

545

AMERICA'S POPULAR SALT WATER FISH (continued)

Market Name	Size	Type of Fish	Description	Season	Where Available	Best Ways to Cook
Skate	10 pounds up	Lean	This is the sting ray; only the "wings" are edible. The strangely gelatinous meat is scraped from the bones, not cut. *Market Forms:* dressed wings.	Year round	Atlantic and Pacific coasts	Poach
Smelt	2-8 ounces	Oily	Two different types of fish are called smelt: silversides (which include grunion) and true smelt (whitebait, silver, and surf smelt). All are small, all have firm, well-flavored meat. *Market Forms:* whole.	Year round but best in spring and summer	Atlantic and Pacific coasts, also Great Lakes, where smelt have been transplanted	Bake, broil, panfry, deep fry
Striped bass	Average 1-10 pounds	Lean	These large white-meated sea bass are becoming more popular as a food fish. *Market Forms:* whole, fresh and frozen fillets.	Year round	Atlantic, Gulf, and Pacific coasts	Bake (stuffed or unstuffed), broil, charcoal broil, poach; panfry fillets
Sturgeon	15-300 pounds	Lean	Flavorful, firm-fleshed fish. *Market Forms:* boned chunks, steaks; smoked.	Year round but best in spring, summer	North Atlantic and Pacific	Bake, panfry, poach
Swordfish	200-600 pounds	Oily	Firm, salmon-colored flesh. *(Note:* Swordfish is now considered risky because of its high mercury content.)	Spring and summer	South Atlantic and Pacific	Bake, plank, broil, charcoal broil, barbecue
Tautog	2-5 pounds	Lean	Also called blackfish, this one is popular in New England; flesh is lean and juicy. *Market Forms:* whole (more often caught than bought).	Spring, summer, and fall	Mid- and North Atlantic coasts	Bake (stuffed or unstuffed), broil, panfry

Market Name	Type of Fish	Size	Description	Season	Where Available	Best Ways to Cook
Tuna	Oily	10 to several hundred pounds	All tuna belong to the mackerel family: albacore or white-meat tuna, also the three light-meat tunas — bluefin or horse mackerel, yellowfin, and skipjack or bonito. All have firm meat with pronounced flavor. *Market Forms:* fresh and frozen steaks, large chunks and occasionally fillets; also available canned and smoked.	Spring, summer, fall	Atlantic and Pacific coasts	Bake, broil, charcoal broil, barbecue, panfry, poach
Weakfish	Lean	Sea Trout: 12 pounds; Speckled Trout: 8 pounds	These are sea trouts, specifically the one called sea trout and the one called spotted or speckled trout. Both have lean, mild flesh. *Market Forms:* whole, fillets.	Year round	Atlantic and Gulf coasts	Bake (stuffed or unstuffed), broil, charcoal broil, panfry
White sea bass	Lean	12-20 pounds	This California cousin of the weakfish also has delicate white meat. *Market Forms:* whole (when small), steaks, fillets.	All year; best in summer and fall	Southern California, Mexico	Bake (stuffed or unstuffed), broil, panfry, poach
Whiting	Lean	2-5 pounds	Also called silver hake, this fine-grained, mild-fleshed white fish is extremely versatile and popular. *Market Forms:* whole, fresh and frozen fillets; also salted.	Spring, summer, fall	North Atlantic	Bake (stuffed or unstuffed), broil, charcoal broil, panfry, deep-fry, poach
Wolffish	Lean	Average 10 pounds	Sometimes called ocean catfish, this fish has delicate white flesh like that of haddock. *Market Forms:* whole, steaks, fillets.	Fall, winter, spring	North Atlantic	Bake (stuffed or unstuffed), broil, panfry, deep-fry, poach

AMERICA'S POPULAR FRESH WATER FISH

SEASONS: These vary from state to state and year to year, so inquire locally.

Market Name	Size	Type of Fish	Description	Where Available	Best Ways to Cook
Bass	Average 3-5 pounds	Lean	One of the finest fresh water fish; most popular species: largemouth, smallmouth, rock, and spotted bass. *Market Forms:* whole (more often caught than bought).	One or another species found throughout most of U.S.	Bake (stuffed or unstuffed), broil, charcoal broil, panfry
Buffalo fish	2-20 pounds	Lean	Fairly coarse-fleshed, bony family of fish. *Market Forms:* whole, steaks, fillets; also smoked.	East, Midwest	Bake, poach
Burbot	3 pounds	Lean	A fresh water cod with delicate white meat. *Market Forms:* whole.	East, Midwest, Northeast	Bake (stuffed or unstuffed), broil, panfry, poach, steam
Carp	2-7 pounds	Lean	A firm, musky fish that is a best eaten in winter and spring. *Market Forms:* whole, fillets, chunks.	Entire U.S.	Bake (stuffed or unstuffed), poach
Catfish	1-20 pounds	Oily	There are many kinds of catfish from the whopping blue to the medium-size Channel cat to the baby bullhead. All have cat-like chin "whiskers," tough scaleless skins (which must be removed), and firm, strong-flavored flesh.	All but the Pacific states	Panfry, deep fry, poach
Crappies	Average 2 pounds	Lean	Large sunfish that are winter favorites; there are two species: black and white. *Market Forms:* whole (more often caught than bought).	Great Lakes, Mississippi Valley	Broil, panfry
Grayling and lake herring or cisco (see *Whitefish*)					

548

Market Name	Size	Type of Fish	Description	Where Available	Best Ways to Cook
Pickerel, pike, and muskallunge	1-10 pounds or more	Lean	These three form a small but famous family, a challenge to fishermen and delight to cooks. Meat is extra delicate and tender, though bony. *Market Forms:* whole, occasionally as fillets.	Most Eastern and Central states	Bake (stuffed or unstuffed), broil, poach
Sheepshead	1-3 pounds	Lean	These are fresh water drums and have tender white meat of excellent flavor. *Market Forms:* whole, fillets.	Primarily Midwest and South	Bake (stuffed or unstuffed), broil, panfry
Salmon (landlocked)	2-8 pounds	Oily	Similar to salt water salmon except smaller; also called Sebago salmon. *Market Forms:* whole, steaks.	New England, primarily Maine	See *Salt Water Salmon*
Suckers	1-5 pounds	Lean	Firm, sweet-fleshed but bony fish family; best is probably the white sucker. *Market Forms:* whole, fresh and frozen fillets; salted, smoked.	Most states but abundant in Mississippi Basin	Bake, broil, panfry, poach
Sunfish	1/4-1 pound	Lean	Also called bream, this large family includes the bluegill and pumpkinseed, small fish of superior flavor. *Market Forms:* whole.	Primarily Midwest and Gulf states	Broil, panfry
Trout	Best size: 1-6 pounds	Midway between lean and oily	Unquestionably the royal family of fresh water fish. Best known are Dolly Varden, brook, brown, lake, and rainbow trout. All are superb. *Market Forms:* fresh and frozen whole.	One or another species found in most of U.S. except in very warm climates	Bake (stuffed or unstuffed), broil, charcoal broil, panfry, poach
Whitefish	1-6 pounds	Fairly oily	A distinguished group, all related to salmon. Best known: lake herring (cisco), lake whitefish, arctic and American grayling, pilotfish. Meat is firm but creamy, flavor excellent. *Market Forms:* whole, fillets; smoked. Roe is choice.	New England, Great Lakes area	Bake (stuffed or unstuffed), broil, panfry, poach, steam
Yellow perch	Average 1 pound	Lean	Small fish of particularly fine flavor. *Market Forms:* whole.	New England, Great Lakes area, some parts of West and South	Bake, broil, panfry

FISH AND CHIPS

Ideally, you should have two deep fat fryers set up so fish and chips can fry at the same time. But if you can't manage that, do the potatoes first and set in a slow oven to keep warm while you fry the fish.
Makes 4 servings

Batter:

1 cup sifted flour
1 teaspoon salt
¾ cup cold water
¼ teaspoon baking powder

Chips:

1 recipe French Fried Potatoes
1¾–2 pounds haddock fillets, cut in 4"×3" strips
Shortening or cooking oil for deep fat frying

Begin batter first: Mix flour, salt, and water until smooth, cover, and let stand at room temperature 20–30 minutes. Meanwhile, prepare potatoes for frying as recipe directs; also pat fish dry on paper toweling. Place shortening or oil in a deep fat fryer, insert thermometer, and begin heating over high heat. When fat reaches 375° F., fry potatoes as directed, removing to a paper-towel-lined baking sheet and setting, uncovered, in oven set at lowest temperature to keep warm while you fry fish. Stir baking powder into batter. Dip 2–3 pieces fish into batter, allowing excess to drain off. Fry 5–6 minutes in 375° F. fat, turning as needed to brown evenly. Drain on paper toweling and set, uncovered, in oven to keep warm while you fry remaining fish. Serve with salt, pepper, and cider or malt vinegar. About 460 calories per serving.

¢ ⊠ EASY SCALLOPED FISH

Makes 4 servings

1½ pounds delicate white fish fillets (cod, haddock, fluke, flounder, halibut, etc.)
1 teaspoon salt
¼ teaspoon pepper
½ cup cracker meal
2 tablespoons butter or margarine
1 cup boiling milk

Preheat oven to 400° F. Arrange fish in a single layer in a buttered shallow 2-quart casserole. Sprinkle with half the salt and pepper. Mix remaining salt and pepper with cracker meal and scatter evenly over fish. Melt butter in milk and pour over fish. Bake, uncovered, in top ⅓ of oven 20 minutes until fish just flakes when touched with a fork. About 300 calories per serving.

VARIATIONS:
– Prepare as directed but mix ¼ cup grated Parmesan or ⅓ cup grated sharp Cheddar cheese into cracker meal. About 325 calories per serving.
– Sprinkle fish with ¼–½ teaspoon thyme, tarragon, marjoram, chervil, basil, or dill before adding meal. About 300 calories per serving.
– Sprinkle fish with 1–2 tablespoons lemon juice and, if you like, 1–2 tablespoons minced parsley before adding meal. About 300 calories per serving.

⚖ ¢ FISH LOAF

A moist, delicate fish loaf flavored with lemon and parsley.
Makes 8 servings

4 cups skinned, boned, cooked, flaked fish (any kind)
3 cups soft white bread crumbs or coarse cracker crumbs
1½ cups milk or, if you prefer, ¾ cup milk and ¾ cup either Easy Fish Stock or bottled clam juice
2 eggs, lightly beaten
1 medium-size yellow onion, peeled and grated
2 stalks celery, minced
1–2 teaspoons salt
¼ teaspoon pepper
2 tablespoons lemon juice
2 tablespoons minced parsley

Preheat oven to 350° F. Mix fish and crumbs; combine milk and eggs and mix into fish along with remaining ingredients. Taste for salt and adjust as needed. Spoon into a greased 9"×5×3" loaf pan and bake, uncovered, 45–55 minutes until just firm. Cool upright in pan on wire cake rack 5 minutes, invert on a hot platter, and garnish with lemon wedges. If you like, pass hot Tomato Sauce or Parsley Sauce. About 235 calories per serving (without sauce).

VARIATIONS:

☒ ⚔ ¢ **Quick Salmon or Tuna Loaf:** Substitute 2 (1-pound) cans salmon or 4 (7-ounce) cans tuna for the flaked fish. Drain cans, measure liquid, and add enough milk to measure 1½ cups. Flake fish, then proceed as recipe directs. About 220 calories per serving if made with tuna, 255 calories per serving if made with salmon.

⚔ ¢ **Herbed Fish Loaf:** Prepare as directed, adding any one of the following: 1 tablespoon minced fresh dill, tarragon, or chervil; 2 teaspoons minced fresh basil or marjoram. If fresh herbs are unavailable, substitute ½ teaspoon of the dried. About 235 calories per serving.

¢ **CRISP-CRUSTED FISH AND GREEN PEPPER PIE**

Makes 6 servings

1 recipe Flaky Pastry II
1½ cups skinned, boned, cooked, flaked fish (any kind)
3 hard-cooked eggs, shelled and sliced thin
¼ cup butter or margarine
1 medium-size yellow onion, peeled and minced
1 small sweet green pepper, cored, seeded, and minced
1 stalk celery, minced
¼ cup unsifted flour
1½ cups milk
1 teaspoon salt
¼ teaspoon pepper

Preheat oven to 425° F. Prepare pastry and roll half into a 12″ circle; fit into a 9″ piepan but do not trim edge. Layer fish and eggs into pie shell. Roll remaining pastry into a 12″ circle, cut 3 V-shaped steam slits near center, and cover loosely with wax paper while you proceed with recipe. Melt butter in a saucepan over moderate heat, add onion, green pepper, and celery, and stir-fry 3–5 minutes until onion is very pale golden. Blend in flour, slowly add milk, and heat, stirring, until thickened; mix in salt and pepper. Pour sauce over fish, top with pastry, press edges to seal, then trim and crimp. Bake, uncovered, ½ hour until lightly browned. About 550 calories per serving.

VARIATION:

⚔ **Potato-Fish Pie:** Omit pastry. Layer fish into a buttered 9″ piepan and top with sauce. Spoon 3 cups hot seasoned mashed potatoes over surface and roughen with a fork. Brush lightly with beaten egg and bake 25–30 minutes as directed. Cut potato "crust" into pie-shaped wedges and top with fish mixture. About 290 calories per serving.

BASIC FISH SOUFFLÉ

Makes 4 servings

¼ cup butter or margarine
¼ cup sifted flour
1 cup milk or ½ cup each milk and Easy Fish Stock
½ teaspoon salt
⅛ teaspoon white pepper
4 eggs, separated (at room temperature)
1 cup skinned, boned, cooked, flaked fish (any kind)
2 teaspoons minced parsley
¼ teaspoon cream of tartar

Melt butter in a small saucepan over moderate heat, blend in flour, slowly add milk, and heat, stirring, until thickened; turn heat to low and mix in salt and pepper. Beat egg yolks lightly, blend in a little hot sauce, then return to saucepan; heat and stir 1–2 minutes but do not boil. Off heat, mix in fish and parsley. Lay a piece of wax paper directly on sauce and cool to room temperature. Preheat oven to 350° F. Beat egg whites until frothy, add cream of tartar, and continue beating until stiff but not dry. Stir about ¼ cup egg white into sauce, then carefully fold in remainder, taking care not to break down volume.

Spoon into an ungreased 1½-quart soufflé dish and bake, uncovered, 45–50 minutes until puffy and tinged with brown. Serve at once. Good with Caper, Tomato, Parsley, or Shrimp Sauce. About 305 calories per serving (without sauce).

VARIATIONS:

Herbed Fish Soufflé: Prepare as directed but increase minced parsley to 1 tablespoon and add 1 tablespoon minced fresh dill, tarragon, or chervil. About 305 calories per serving.

Curried Fish Soufflé: Prepare as directed but smooth 1 tablespoon each curry powder and finely grated onion into melted butter just after blending flour. About 305 calories per serving.

Rosy Fish Soufflé: Prepare as directed, but mix 2 tablespoons tomato paste and ¼ teaspoon each oregano and basil into hot sauce just before adding fish. About 315 calories per serving.

Lemon Fish Soufflé: Make sauce as directed but for the liquid use the juice of ½ lemon, ½ cup Easy Fish Stock, and then enough heavy cream to total 1 cup. Proceed as directed, adding 1 teaspoon grated lemon rind to sauce along with fish. About 410 calories per serving.

⚖ **VELVETY FISH MOUSSE**

Makes 6 servings

¾ pound delicate white fish fillets (cod,
*   flounder, halibut, hake, turbot, etc.)*
¼ cup butter or margarine
6 tablespoons flour
1 cup milk or a ½ and ½ mixture of
*   milk and Easy Fish Stock*
3 eggs, separated
½ cup heavy cream
1 teaspoon salt
⅛ teaspoon pepper
Pinch nutmeg
½ teaspoon anchovy paste
1 teaspoon lemon juice

Preheat oven to 350° F. Put fish through finest blade of meat grinder. Melt butter in a saucepan over moderate heat, blend in flour, slowly add milk, and heat, stir-ring, until thickened. Turn heat to low. Beat egg yolks lightly, blend in a little sauce, then return to saucepan. Heat, stirring, 1–2 minutes, but do not allow to boil. Off heat, mix in fish and all remaining ingredients except egg whites. Beat egg whites until soft peaks form, then fold into fish mixture. Spoon into a well-oiled 5-cup ring mold, set in a large baking pan, and pour in boiling water to come ⅔ of the way up mold. Bake, uncovered, 45–55 minutes or until just set. Lift mold from water bath and cool 5–10 minutes, loosen mousse with a spatula, invert on hot platter, and *ease* out. Serve as is, or fill center with Creamed Shrimp, Creamed Mushrooms, or buttered asparagus tips and drizzle with Sauce Américaine or other suitable sauce (see Sauces, Butters, and Seasonings for Seafood). About 280 calories per serving (without sauce of any sort).

VARIATIONS:

Salmon or Tuna Mousse: Substitute 1½ cups finely ground salmon or tuna for white fish and proceed as directed. About 320 calories per serving if made with salmon, 310 calories per serving if made with tuna.

⚖ **Lobster, Shrimp, or Crab Mousse:** Substitute 1½ cups finely ground cooked lobster, shrimp, or crab meat and proceed as directed. About 295 calories per serving.

⚖ **Mousse Baked in a Fish Mold** (4 servings): Use an easy-to-handle fish-shaped mold of about 1-quart capacity (fish will not cook evenly in larger molds). Butter mold well and make sure it will not tip in water bath (use crumpled foil as needed to prop). Prepare recipe as directed and fill mold to within ½″ of top; spoon any remaining mixture into buttered ramekins. Bake mold as directed in water bath 1 hour; ramekins will take about 15 minutes. Cool and unmold as directed, outline "scales" with slivers of pimiento or tissue-thin cucumber slices, and serve. About 280 calories per serving.

⚖ **Cold Fish Mousse:** Prepare and unmold mousse as directed; cool to room temperature, and chill 2–3 hours. When serving, garnish with watercress, cucumber slices, and lemon "baskets" filled with mayonnaise. About 280 calories per serving (without mayonnaise).

Turban of Fish: Butter a 6-cup mold well and line with 8 small fillets of flounder or other delicate white fish, placing snowiest sides against mold and overlapping edges. Sprinkle with a little salt and pepper. Prepare mousse mixture as directed and pour into mold, filling to within ½″ of top; lap any trailing ends of fillets over surface of mousse. Bake in water bath as directed, unmold, and serve with Sauce Américaine or other suitable sauce (see Sauces, Butters, and Seasonings for Seafood). About 330 calories per serving without sauce.

⚖ **QUENELLES**

Quenelles are soufflé-light fish balls poached in delicate broth; they may be used to garnish fish platters or served as a light entree. The mixture may also be used as a fish stuffing.
Makes 4 servings

¾ pound delicate white fish fillets (pike, pickerel, hake, turbot, flounder, etc.)
1 egg white
⅔ cup heavy cream
1 teaspoon salt
Pinch white pepper
Pinch nutmeg
1 quart boiling water
½ teaspoon lemon juice

Grind fish very fine and place in a bowl over cracked ice. Add egg white and beat with a wooden spoon 2–3 minutes until mixture thickens and will cling to a spoon turned upside-down. Add cream, 2 tablespoons at a time, beating ½ minute after each addition; mixture will be soft but should hold a shape. Stir in ½ teaspoon salt, pepper, and nutmeg. Pour water into a large skillet (not iron), add remaining salt and lemon juice, and adjust heat so liquid just trembles. Using 2 wet teaspoons, shape fish mixture into egg-size balls and slide into poaching liquid (liquid should just cover quenelles; if not, add a little extra water). Poach, uncovered, 6–8 quenelles at a time, 3–5 minutes until just firm. Lift out with a slotted spoon and drain on paper toweling. Loosely cover poached quenelles and keep warm in oven set at lowest heat. Shape and poach remaining mixture (you'll have to wet spoons often). Use quenelles to garnish a fish platter or top with Mushroom, Portugaise, or Normande Sauce and serve as a main course. About 150 calories per serving (without sauce).

VARIATIONS:

Gratinéed Quenelles: Poach and drain quenelles; transfer to a buttered 1½-quart *au gratin* dish. Coat lightly with Mornay Sauce, sprinkle lightly with finely grated Parmesan or Gruyère cheese, and broil quickly to brown. Recipe too flexible for a meaningful calorie count.

Quenelles à la Florentine: Poach and drain quenelles and arrange on a bed of hot buttered, chopped spinach in a 2-quart au gratin dish. Gratinée as directed above. Recipe too flexible for a meaningful calorie count.

About Sole and Flounder

Unless you live in a large Eastern metropolis where English, Channel, or Dover Sole is imported, it is unlikely that you will be able to buy true sole. America has no true sole, only flounder, fluke, and other related flatfish that masquerade as sole (they're usually advertised as lemon or gray sole). These flatfish all have delicate white meat, but they lack the elegance of sole. If you can buy imported sole, by all means use it in the recipes that follow. If not use flounder, sand dabs, or any other flounder-like flatfish (see chart of America's Popular Salt Water Fish).

Some Classic Ways to Serve Fillets of Sole, Flounder, or Other Delicate White Fish

All amounts based on 1½–2 pounds fillets or enough for 4–6 servings

À l'Anglaise: Sauté, broil, or poach fillets by basic method and top with Maître d'Hôtel or melted butter.

À l'Arlésienne: Poach fillets by basic method and arrange on a hot platter with sautéed peeled cherry tomatoes and sautéed sliced artichoke bottoms. Strain poaching liquid and quickly reduce to 1 cup; smooth in 2 tablespoons tomato paste, 1 tablespoon butter, and ¼ crushed clove garlic. Pour over fish and serve.

À la Bonne Femme: Arrange fillets 1 layer deep in a buttered, large, shallow casserole, sprinkle lightly with salt and white pepper, top with ¼ cup each minced shallots and mushrooms stems. Add ½ cup each dry white wine and Easy Fish Stock, cover, and bake 20 minutes at 350° F. Draw liquid off fillets with a bulb baster and quickly reduce to 1 cup. Meanwhile, melt 3 tablespoons butter in a small saucepan and blend in 3 tablespoons flour. Add reduced liquid and heat, stirring, until thickened. Top each fillet with 4 sautéed mushroom caps, smother with sauce, and broil quickly to brown.

À la Bordelaise: Sauté 1 minced yellow onion and 1 minced carrot in 2 tablespoons butter in a large skillet 3–4 minutes over moderate heat; lay fillets on top and poach in dry red wine by basic method. Lift fish to a hot platter, surround with sautéed button mushrooms and Pan-Braised Onions. Strain poaching liquid and quickly reduce to 1 cup; blend in ¼ cup Rich Brown Sauce, pour over fish, and serve.

À la Florentine: Poach fillets by basic method and arrange flat or rolled up on a bed of hot buttered, chopped spinach. Pour enough Mornay Sauce over fish to coat evenly, sprinkle lightly with grated Parmesan cheese, and broil just until flecked with brown.

À la Marinière: Poach fillets by basic method and arrange on a hot platter. Wreathe with Mussels à la Marinière and drizzle with a little Marinière Sauce. Pass extra sauce.

À la Nantua: Poach fillets by basic method and serve topped with Nantua Sauce and a scattering of diced or sliced truffles. Pass extra sauce.

À la Niçoise: Poach fillets by basic method, arrange on a hot platter, and lay anchovy fillets on top in a crisscross pattern; top each fillet with 2 overlapping slices lemon. Wreathe platter with clusters of peeled cherry tomatoes sautéed lightly in Anchovy Butter and pitted black olives, sprinkle with capers and a little minced fresh tarragon.

À la Normande: Poach fillets by basic method and arrange on a hot platter; surround with small poached shucked oysters, steamed shucked mussels, boiled, shelled, and deveined shrimp, tiny fried smelts, and sautéed button mushrooms. Pour some Normande Sauce over fillets and dot with truffle slices. Pass extra sauce.

À la Portugaise: Sauté 2–3 peeled, sliced tomatoes, 1 minced yellow onion, and 1 crushed clove garlic in 2 tablespoons olive oil 3–4 minutes over moderate heat in a shallow, flameproof casserole. Lay fillets on top of vegetables and bake, uncovered, 20 minutes at 350° F., basting 1 or 2 times. Sprinkle with buttered bread crumbs and broil lightly to brown.

Amandine: Sauté fillets by basic method and arrange on a hot platter. In the same skillet, lightly brown ⅓ cup slivered blanched almonds in ¼ cup butter and pour over fish. Garnish with lemon and parsley and serve.

Aux Fines Herbes: Sauté or poach fillets by basic method. Meanwhile, melt ¼ cup butter in a small saucepan over low heat, mix in 1 tablespoon each minced fresh chives, chervil, shallots or scallion, and parsley. Let steep until fish is done. Arrange fish on a hot platter, smother with herbed butter, and serve.

Crécy: Poach fillets by basic method in Easy Fish Stock, transfer to a hot platter, and surround with boiled buttered baby carrots. Quickly reduce poaching liquid to 1 cup, smooth in ¼ cup each Béchamel Sauce and puréed cooked carrots; pour over fish and serve.

Joinville: Poach fillets by basic method and arrange spoke-fashion on a hot circular platter. Mound ½ pound boiled, shelled, and deveined shrimp and ½ pound sautéed button mushrooms in center. Sprinkle with 2 tablespoons minced truffles and top with a little Joinville Sauce. Pass extra sauce.

Marguery: Fold fillets envelope fashion, ends toward center, and poach by basic method in Easy Fish Stock. Arrange on a hot platter, surround with shucked, steamed mussels and boiled, shelled, and deveined shrimp. Quickly reduce poaching liquid in the top of a double boiler over direct heat to 1½ cups; beat in 3 tablespoons butter, 1 at a time. Add a little hot liquid to 3 lightly beaten egg yolks, set over simmering water, and heat, stirring, until thickened. Pour over fish and serve.

Mornay: Poach fillets by basic method and lift to a shallow *au gratin* dish. Cover with Mornay Sauce, sprinkle lightly with grated Parmesan cheese, and broil quickly to brown.

Princesse: Poach or sauté fillets by basic method and arrange on a hot platter. Surround with clusters of boiled buttered asparagus tips and serve with Browned Butter.

Saint-Germain: Sauté fillets by basic method, arrange on a hot platter, wreathe with Château Potatoes, and serve with Béarnaise Sauce.

Véronique: Poach fillets in white wine by basic method but add 1 teaspoon lemon juice. Arrange fish on a hot platter and keep warm. Quickly reduce poaching liquid to ½ cup; smooth in 1 cup Béchamel or Thick White Sauce and 3 tablespoons whipped cream. Pour over fish and broil quickly to brown. Garnish with clusters of seedless green grapes

and serve. If you prefer, simmer 1 cup peeled grapes 3 minutes in water to cover, drain, then add to sauce along with whipped cream. Pour over fish and broil to brown.

⚞ SOLE OR FLOUNDER À L'AMÉRICAINE

Makes 6 servings

2 pounds sole or flounder fillets
1 teaspoon salt
⅛ teaspoon white pepper
1 cup dry white wine
1 cup boiling water

Sauce Américaine:

1 small yellow onion, peeled and minced
1 carrot, peeled and cut in small dice
3 tablespoons minced shallots or scallions
1 clove garlic, peeled and crushed
2 tablespoons cooking oil
¼ cup brandy
2 large tomatoes, peeled, cored, seeded, and coarsely chopped
2 tablespoons tomato paste
1 cup Easy Fish Stock
1 cup dry white wine
1 teaspoon tarragon
1 teaspoon minced parsley
1 (4–5-ounce) frozen rock lobster tail
1 tablespoon butter or margarine
¼ teaspoon sugar
Pinch cayenne pepper

Prepare sauce early in the day to allow flavors to blend: Sauté onion, carrot, shallots, and garlic in oil in a saucepan over moderate heat 3–5 minutes until onion is very pale golden. Add brandy, warm briefly, remove from heat, and blaze with a match. Add all but last 3 sauce ingredients, cover, and simmer 10 minutes; remove lobster, take meat from shell, slice crosswise ¼″ thick, and refrigerate. Continue simmering sauce, *uncovered,* about 1 hour, stirring occasionally. Liquid should be reduced by half; if not, boil rapidly to reduce. Strain liquid through a fine sieve into a small saucepan, pressing vegetables lightly. Heat 1–2 minutes over low heat, whisk in butter, sugar, and cayenne, taste for salt and adjust as needed. Cover and set aside. About 10 minutes before serving, fold fillets envelope fashion, ends toward middle, and arrange in a large skillet (not iron); sprinkle with salt and pepper. Pour in wine and water, cover and simmer slowly 7–10 minutes until fish will just flake. Meanwhile, add lobster to sauce and reheat slowly until bubbly. Using a slotted spoon, lift fish to a hot deep platter, smother with sauce, and serve. About 295 calories per serving.

SOLE OR FLOUNDER BERCY

Makes 4 servings

1 large yellow onion, peeled and minced
½ pound mushrooms, wiped clean and sliced thin
¼ cup butter or margarine
1½ pounds fillets of sole, flounder, or other delicate white fish (cod, haddock, fluke, halibut, etc.)
½ cup red Burgundy wine
1 teaspoon salt
⅛ teaspoon white pepper
1 tablespoon flour blended with 2 tablespoons cold water

Preheat oven to 350° F. Sauté onion and mushrooms in butter in a skillet over moderate heat 3–5 minutes until onion is very pale golden; spoon into an ungreased shallow 2-quart casserole. Fold fillets envelope fashion, ends toward middle, and arrange in a single layer on top of vegetables. Pour in wine, sprinkle fish with salt and pepper, and bake uncovered 20–30 minutes until fish will just flake. Using a bulb baster, drain liquid from fish into a small saucepan, mix in flour paste, and heat, stirring until slightly thickened. Pour sauce over fish and serve. About 310 calories per serving.

FILLETS OF SOLE OR FLOUNDER CARDINAL

Genuine Sole Cardinal is sprinkled with minced lobster coral just before serving, but since that means buying a whole lobster, we've made the coral optional. Makes 6 servings

8 fillets of sole or flounder (about 2 pounds)
1 teaspoon salt
⅛ teaspoon white pepper
1 cup dry white wine
1 cup boiling water

Stuffing:

1 cup cooked, minced delicate white fish (haddock, cod, fluke, halibut, etc.)
1 cup soft white bread crumbs
1 tablespoon milk
1 egg, lightly beaten
1 teaspoon minced chives
1 teaspoon minced parsley
½ teaspoon salt
⅛ teaspoon pepper
Pinch nutmeg

Cardinal Sauce:

3 tablespoons butter or margarine
3 tablespoons flour
½ cup milk
½ cup Easy Fish Stock
½ cup heavy cream
Meat of 1 (4–5-ounce) boiled rock lobster tail or 1 (1-pound) lobster coarsely chopped
½ teaspoon salt
Pinch cayenne pepper
1 tablespoon minced truffle

Optional Topping:

Minced coral of 1 small boiled lobster

Sprinkle fillets with salt and pepper and set aside. Pour wine and water into a large skillet (not iron) and set aside. Now prepare stuffing: Beat all ingredients together until smooth. Place about 1 tablespoon stuffing on each fillet, roll up, and secure with toothpicks. Arrange fillets seam side down in skillet, cover, and simmer slowly 7–10 minutes until fish will just flake. Meanwhile, make the sauce: Melt butter in a saucepan, blend in flour, slowly stir in milk, stock, and cream, then heat, stirring, until thickened. Mix in lobster, salt, cayenne, and truffle. With a slotted spoon lift fish to a deep platter, top with sauce and, if you like, minced coral. About 350 calories per serving (without topping).

FILLETS OF SOLE OR FLOUNDER WITH CRAB SAUCE

Makes 4 servings

1½ pounds sole or flounder fillets
½ teaspoon salt
⅛ teaspoon white pepper

Sauce:

2 tablespoons butter or margarine
2 tablespoons flour
½ cup milk
½ cup light cream
½ teaspoon salt
⅛ teaspoon white pepper
2 teaspoons lemon juice
¼ pound fresh lump or backfin crab meat, well picked over

Preheat oven to 350° F. Fold fillets envelope fashion by lapping each end over toward center and arrange 1 layer deep in a buttered shallow 2-quart casserole or *au gratin* dish; sprinkle with salt and pepper. Bake, uncovered, 15 minutes. Meanwhile, prepare sauce: Melt butter in a saucepan over moderately low heat, blend in flour, slowly add milk and cream, and heat, stirring, until thickened. Lightly mix in salt, pepper, lemon juice, and crab, cover, and keep warm. Remove liquid from fish, using a bulb baster, then cover fish with sauce. Bake, uncovered, 10–15 minutes longer until fish flakes when touched with a fork. About 325 calories per serving.

⚖ FISH FILLETS IN WHITE WINE AND HERBS

Makes 6 servings

2 pounds delicate white fish fillets (cod, haddock, fluke, flounder, halibut, etc.)
1 teaspoon salt
⅛ teaspoon white pepper
2 teaspoons minced fresh dill or 1 teaspoon dried dill
1 teaspoon minced chives (fresh, frozen, or freeze-dried)
1 teaspoon minced parsley
2 tablespoons butter or margarine
1½ cups dry white wine

½ cup heavy cream
3 egg yolks, lightly beaten

Preheat oven to 350° F. Fold fillets envelope fashion, ends toward middle, and arrange in a single layer in a buttered shallow 2½-quart casserole or *au gratin* dish; sprinkle with salt, pepper, and herbs and dot with butter. Pour in wine and bake, uncovered, 20–30 minutes until fish flakes when touched with a fork. Using pancake turner, transfer fillets to hot platter and keep warm. Pour cooking liquid into the top of a double boiler, set over direct heat, and boil rapidly, uncovered, until liquid reduces to about 1 cup. Mix cream and egg yolks, add a little hot liquid, mix well, and return to double boiler. Set over simmering water and heat, stirring, until thickened. Taste for salt and adjust if needed. Pour sauce over fish and serve. About 285 calories per serving.

CRUMB-TOPPED BAKED FLOUNDER

Makes 4 servings

1½ pounds flounder or other delicate white fish fillets (cod, haddock, fluke, halibut, etc.)
1 teaspoon salt
⅛ teaspoon white pepper
2 cups soft white bread crumbs
1 tablespoon minced parsley
⅓ cup melted butter or margarine

Preheat oven to 350° F. Arrange fillets in a single layer in a buttered shallow 2-quart casserole; sprinkle with ½ teaspoon salt and the pepper. Toss bread crumbs with remaining salt, the parsley, and butter and scatter evenly over fish. Bake, uncovered, 25–30 minutes until fish flakes, then broil 4″ from the heat 2–3 minutes to brown. Garnish with lemon wedges and serve. About 365 calories per serving.

VARIATIONS:

Almond-Crumb-Topped Baked Flounder: Prepare as directed but add ½ cup coarsely chopped, blanched, toasted almonds to bread crumb mixture. About 470 calories per serving.

Sesame Baked Flounder: Prepare as directed but add ¼ cup toasted sesame seeds to crumb mixture. About 390 calories per serving.

CHEESE STUFFED FLOUNDER IN MARINARA SAUCE

Makes 4 servings

8 small flounder fillets (about 1½ pounds)
½ teaspoon salt
⅛ teaspoon white pepper
⅓ cup grated Parmesan cheese
2 tablespoons minced parsley
4 slices processed sharp cheese, halved
1 (1-pound) jar marinara sauce

Preheat oven to 350° F. Sprinkle fillets with salt, pepper, Parmesan cheese, and 1 tablespoon parsley; lay a half slice of cheese on each and roll up. Arrange rolls, seam side down, in a single layer in a buttered shallow 2-quart casserole or *au gratin* dish and top with sauce. Bake, uncovered, 20–30 minutes. Sprinkle with remaining parsley and serve. About 365 calories per serving.

⚕ LOW-CALORIE FILLETS OF FLOUNDER EN PAPILLOTE

Makes 4 servings

4 large flounder fillets (about 1½ pounds)
1½ teaspoons salt
½ cup minced scallions
1 tablespoon butter or margarine
1 tablespoon flour
2 ripe tomatoes, peeled, cored, seeded, and chopped fine
1 teaspoon red or white wine vinegar
½ teaspoon basil or oregano
⅛ teaspoon pepper

Preheat oven to 350° F. Cut 4 large squares of cooking parchment (available at gourmet shops) or heavy duty foil (large enough to wrap fillets); lay a fillet on each and sprinkle with 1 teaspoon salt. Sauté scallions in butter in a small skillet over moderate heat 3–5 minutes until limp; sprinkle in flour, add remaining salt and all other ingredients, and heat, stirring, over low heat 3–5 minutes to blend flavors. Spoon a little sauce over each fillet and wrap tightly drugstore style. Place packages on a baking sheet and bake 30–40 minutes; unwrap 1 package and check to see if fish flakes; if not, rewrap and bake a little longer. Serve in foil to retain all juices. About 180 calories per serving.

PAUPIETTES OF SOLE OR FLOUNDER WITH ROSY SAUCE

Paupiettes are stuffed and rolled fillets of meat or fish. They're unusually versatile because a change of stuffing or sauce creates a whole new dish.

Makes 6 servings

2 pounds sole or flounder fillets
1 teaspoon salt
⅛ teaspoon white pepper
2 cups Basic Bread Stuffing for Fish
½ cup milk
½ cup water

Rosy Sauce:

2 tablespoons butter or margarine
2 tablespoons flour
Fish cooking liquid
¼ cup heavy cream
2 tablespoons tomato paste
Pinch nutmeg

Lay fillets flat, more attractive side down, and sprinkle with salt and pepper. Place about ¼ cup stuffing on each fillet and roll up from widest end; secure with toothpicks. (*Note:* If paupiettes are very wide, halve crosswise.) Arrange seam side down in a large skillet (not iron), add milk and water, cover, and simmer 7–10 minutes until fish will just flake. *Or* arrange in a buttered shallow casserole, add milk and water, cover loosely, and bake 20–30 minutes at 350° F. Lift rolls to a heated deep platter with a slotted spoon, cover, and keep warm. Strain cooking liquid and reserve. For the sauce, melt butter in a small saucepan over moderate heat, blend in flour, slowly stir in cooking liquid and remaining ingredients. Heat, stirring, until thickened. Taste for salt and pepper and adjust as needed. Pour over paupiettes and serve. About 385 calories per serving.

VARIATIONS:

⚔ **Mushroom Stuffed Paupiettes:** Stuff fillets with 1 pound minced sautéed mushrooms mixed with 2 minced scallions, 1 cup soft white bread crumbs, ½ teaspoon salt, and ¼ teaspoon pepper. Roll and cook as directed. Serve with Mushroom Sauce. About 295 calories per serving (with ¼ cup Mushroom Sauce).

Shrimp Stuffed Paupiettes: Stuff fillets with 1 cup minced cooked shrimp mixed with ¾ cup soft white bread crumbs, 2 tablespoons mayonnaise, and 2 teaspoons lemon juice. Roll and cook as directed; serve with Shrimp Sauce. About 470 calories per serving (with ¼ cup Shrimp Sauce).

Anchovy and Caper Stuffed Paupiettes: Drain and mince 1 (2-ounce) can anchovy fillets, mix with ¼ cup minced capers, spread on *unsalted* fish fillets, roll, and cook as directed. Serve with Caper Sauce. About 415 calories per serving (with ¼ cup Caper Sauce).

Paupiettes Stuffed with Quenelles: Mix 1 recipe Quenelles but do not poach. Place 1 large shaped quenelle on each fillet, roll up loosely, secure with toothpicks, and cook paupiettes as directed. Serve with Rosy, Tomato, or Shrimp Sauce. About 350 calories per serving (with ¼ cup any of the suggested sauces).

COD À LA LISBOA (LISBON-STYLE COD)

Makes 4 servings

1 (2-pound) center-cut slice cod
2½ cups water
1 small yellow onion, peeled and stuck with 1 clove
1 clove garlic, peeled and quartered
2 bay leaves
1 teaspoon salt
6 peppercorns
4 medium-size potatoes, boiled, peeled, and quartered

1 (9-ounce) package whole green beans, cooked by package directions and drained well
Red or white wine vinegar

Dressing:

1½ cups olive oil
2 cloves garlic, peeled and quartered
1 bay leaf crumbled
2 teaspoons salt

Wipe cod with a damp cloth. Bring water, onion, garlic, bay leaves, salt, and peppercorns to a boil in a large saucepan over moderate heat and simmer, uncovered, 5 minutes. Add cod, cover, and simmer 10 minutes, just until fish will flake. Cool in broth until easy to handle, then drain cod well; remove skin and bones and divide into large chunks. Place chunks of cod in a large, shallow bowl and carefully lay potatoes and beans on top. Mix dressing and pour over all, cover, and marinate in refrigerator 3–4 hours before serving, turning beans, potatoes and fish occasionally in marinade. Arrange cod and vegetables on plates, top with a little marinade, and serve with a carafe of wine vinegar. About 425 calories per serving.

VARIATION:

Omit dressing altogether; as soon as cod is done, drain, bone, skin, and divide into large chunks. Serve hot with hot potatoes and beans, top all with Hollandaise Sauce or serve with oil, vinegar, salt, and pepper. About 410 calories per serving (with 3 tablespoons Hollandaise Sauce).

¢ CREAMED SALT COD

Makes 4 servings

1½ pounds filleted salt cod
2 cups hot Medium White Sauce, prepared without salt
⅛ teaspoon pepper
2 hard-cooked eggs, peeled and sliced

Soak cod overnight in cold water to cover; drain and rinse. Place in a saucepan with enough cold water to cover and simmer, covered, 10–15 minutes until fish will flake. Drain, cool slightly, and coarsely flake, removing any bones and skin. Mix fish gently into sauce, add pepper, cover, and let stand over lowest heat 10 minutes to blend flavors. Taste for salt and adjust as needed. Using eggs to garnish, serve as is or over hot boiled potatoes or buttered toast. About 470 calories per serving.

BRANDADE DE MORUE (SALT COD WITH GARLIC, OIL, AND CREAM)

This rich cod purée can be served hot or cold, as a luncheon entree or a cocktail spread. The best way to make it is in an electric blender.
Makes 3–4 entree servings, enough cocktail spread for 12

1 pound filleted salt cod
½ cup heavy cream (about)
½ cup olive oil (about)
1 clove garlic, peeled and crushed
⅛ teaspoon pepper
4 slices French bread or 8 small triangles white bread
2–3 tablespoons olive oil or butter

Soak cod overnight in cold water to cover; drain and rinse. Place in a saucepan with just enough cold water to cover and simmer, covered, 10–15 minutes until fish will flake. Drain, cool slightly, and coarsely flake, removing any bones or skin. Purée fish with ¼ cup each cream and oil, the garlic and pepper in an electric blender at high speed. Add remaining cream and oil alternately, 1 tablespoon at a time, puréeing until the texture of mashed potatoes; if too stiff, blend in a little additional cream and oil. If you don't have a blender, put fish through finest blade of meat grinder twice; add cream and oil alternately, a little at a time, beating well after each addition; beat in garlic and pepper. Heat to serving temperature in the top of a double boiler over simmering water, stirring occasionally. Meanwhile, fry bread in oil in a skillet over moderately high heat until golden. Mound fish in the center of a hot platter and surround with bread.

VARIATION:

To Serve Cold: Instead of warming fish, chill slightly, taste for pepper and add more if needed; also, if you like, add ½ teaspoon grated lemon rind and 1–2 teaspoons lemon juice. Serve with melba toast.

About 835 calories for each of 3 entree servings, 625 calories for each of 4 entree servings, and 210 calories for each of 12 appetizer servings (without Melba toast).

⚖ ¢ CODFISH CAKES
Makes 4 servings

1 (2-ounce) package dried, shredded salt cod
1½ cups cold water
1½ cups hot, unseasoned mashed potatoes
⅛ teaspoon pepper
1 tablespoon Worcestershire sauce (optional)
2 tablespoons minced fresh parsley (optional)
2 tablespoons melted butter or margarine
1 egg, lightly beaten
⅓ cup cooking oil

Soften cod in cold water 4–5 minutes; drain and squeeze dry in a strainer. Mix with all remaining ingredients except oil, shape into 4–6 flat patties, cover, and chill 1 hour. Heat oil in a large, heavy skillet over moderate heat until a cube of bread will sizzle, add fish cakes, and brown 3–5 minutes on each side. Drain on paper toweling and serve. About 220 calories per serving.

VARIATION:

⚖ **Codfish Balls:** Prepare cod mixture as directed, but instead of shaping into cakes, drop from a tablespoon into hot deep fat (375° F.) and fry 1–2 minutes until golden brown. Fry only a few balls at a time and drain well on paper toweling before serving. About 220 calories per serving, 55 calories per codfish ball.

BAKED HADDOCK IN CREAM SAUCE

Makes 6 servings

2 pounds haddock or flounder fillets
2 tablespoons lemon juice
1 teaspoon salt
⅛ teaspoon white pepper
2 tablespoons butter or margarine

Sauce:

3 tablespoons butter or margarine
¼ cup unsifted flour
1 cup light cream
1 teaspoon salt
¼ teaspoon paprika

Preheat oven to 350° F. Fold fillets envelope fashion, ends toward middle, and arrange in a single layer in a buttered shallow 2-quart casserole; sprinkle with lemon juice, salt, and pepper and dot with butter. Bake, uncovered, 20–30 minutes or until fish just flakes. Meanwhile, prepare sauce: Melt butter in a saucepan over moderate heat, blend in flour, slowly add cream, and heat, stirring, until thickened; add salt, cover, and keep warm. When fish is done, drain off liquid with a bulb baster and reserve. Beat 1 cup fish liquid into sauce, pour evenly over fish, and bake uncovered 5–7 minutes. Dust with paprika and serve. About 300 calories per serving.

VARIATIONS:

Baked Haddock au Gratin: Prepare recipe as directed but, before final 5–7-minute baking, top with 1 cup soft white bread crumbs mixed with 3 tablespoons melted butter or margarine and, if you like, 2 tablespoons minced parsley. Finish baking as directed, then broil 1–2 minutes to brown. About 375 calories per serving.

Baked Haddock in Cheese Sauce: Prepare as directed but, when making sauce, add 1 teaspoon Worcestershire sauce, ⅛ teaspoon powdered mustard, a pinch cayenne pepper, and 1 cup coarsely grated sharp Cheddar cheese. Pour sauce over fish as directed, top with ¼ cup grated cheese, bake 5–7 minutes, then broil 1–2 minutes to brown. About 400 calories per serving.

Baked Haddock in Shrimp Sauce: Prepare as directed, but when making sauce add 1 cup coarsely chopped cooked shrimp, 1 tablespoon tomato paste, and, if you like, 2–3 tablespoons dry sherry. Proceed as basic recipe directs, garnish with 12 cooked, shelled, and deveined small shrimp, and serve. About 350 calories per serving.

Baked Haddock and Mushrooms: Stir-fry ½ pound thinly sliced mushrooms and ½ cup each minced onion and sweet green pepper in 2 tablespoons butter or margarine 5–8 minutes over moderate heat until onion is pale golden. Sprinkle fish with lemon juice, salt, and pepper as directed in basic recipe but omit butter; top with sautéed vegetables, then complete recipe as directed. About 350 calories per serving.

⚖ FINNAN HADDIE

Once upon a time, fire swept the little town of Findon, Scotland, smoking tons of haddock that had been hung to dry. Fortunately someone thought to taste the fish before it was dumped. Result: smoked haddock or finnan (Findon) haddie. Today it comes filleted or split (with backbone in). Often it is supersalty, but a half hour of soaking in tepid water will take care of that.
Makes 4–6 servings

2 pounds smoked haddock fillets, rinsed and cut in serving-size pieces
1 cup milk or ½ cup milk and ½ cup water
⅛ teaspoon white pepper
2 tablespoons butter or margarine

Place haddock in a large, heavy skillet, add milk, sprinkle with pepper, and dot with butter; heat, uncovered, over moderate heat until almost boiling, turn heat to low, baste well, then cover and simmer 10 minutes until fish flakes when touched with a fork. Serve as is or, if you like, topped with plump pats of butter. About 255 calories for each of 4 servings (without pats of butter), 180 calories for each of 6 servings.

VARIATIONS:

Creamed Finnan Haddie: Poach haddock as directed above and drain, reserving cooking liquid. Make 2 cups Medium White Sauce, using 1 cup poaching liquid and 1 cup light cream. Add haddock, 1 tablespoon minced parsley and serve over hot buttered toast or in puff pastry shells. About 420 calories for each of 4 servings, 280 calories for each of 6 servings.

⚖ **Scottish Nips:** Poach haddock as directed above, drain, flake, and measure. To each cup haddock, add ½ cup heavy cream and a pinch cayenne pepper. Slowly bring to a simmer, spread on unbuttered small toast triangles, and serve as cocktail appetizers. About 45 calories for each Scottish nip.

⚖ **Baked Finnan Haddie:** Preheat oven to 350° F. Do not poach haddock; place instead in a single layer in a buttered shallow 2-quart casserole. Add ½ cup each milk and light cream, sprinkle with pepper and dot with butter. Cover and bake 20–25 minutes, basting occasionally, until fish flakes. Lift haddock to a hot platter, top with a little of the pan juices, then dot with 2 tablespoons butter and serve. About 265 calories for each of 4 servings, 175 calories for each of 6 servings.

⚖ **Baked Finnan Haddie with Egg Sauce:** Bake finnan haddie as directed and, as soon as fish is done, drain pan juices into a saucepan; keep fish warm. Blend 2 tablespoons flour with 2 tablespoons water, stir into pan juices, and heat, stirring, until thickened and smooth. Mix in 1 minced, hard-cooked egg and a pinch white pepper. Serve sauce over fish. About 295 calories for each of 4 servings, 195 calories for each of 6 servings.

CREAMY SMOKED HADDOCK AND POTATO CASSEROLE

Makes 4–6 servings

1 pound smoked haddock or cod fillets, rinsed
1½ cups water
2 cups hot unseasoned mashed potatoes
2 tablespoons minced parsley
½ cup minced scallion tops (green part only)
2 tablespoons olive or other cooking oil
⅛ teaspoon pepper
1 cup heavy cream
Salt
2 tablespoons butter or margarine

Place haddock and water in a saucepan, cover, and quickly bring to a boil. Turn heat to low and simmer 10 minutes until fish is cooked through; drain, then flake with a fork. (*Note:* Haddock fillets occasionally have a few bones, so check and discard any you find.) Mix fish, potatoes, parsley, scallions, oil, and pepper; cool to room temperature. Meanwhile, preheat oven to 350° F. Beat cream until soft peaks form and fold into fish. Taste for salt and add as needed. Spoon into a buttered 1½-quart casserole and dot with butter. Bake, uncovered, 30 minutes. To brown, run quickly under broiler. About 440 calories for each of 4 servings, 295 calories for each of 6 servings.

⚖ KEDGEREE

An English breakfast dish by way of India. Kedgeree doesn't have to have curry powder; in fact it's better without it if you use smoked fish in the recipe. Makes 4–6 servings

¼ cup butter or margarine
3 cups flaked cooked haddock or cod or 1½ cups each flaked cooked smoked haddock and cod
2 cups boiled rice
1 teaspoon salt (about)
⅛ teaspoon white pepper
½ teaspoon curry powder (optional)
3 hard-cooked eggs, shelled

Melt butter in the top of a double boiler over simmering water. Add fish and mix well. Add rice, salt, pepper, and curry powder if you like. Dice 2 eggs and cut the third into wedges. Mix in diced eggs, cover, and heat 10–15 minutes until heated through. Taste for salt and adjust. Mound mixture on a hot platter and garnish with egg wedges. If made with fresh haddock or cod: about 285 calories for each of 4 servings, 190 calories for each of 6 servings. If made with smoked haddock and cod: about 325 calories for each of 4 servings, 220 calories for each of 6 servings.

⊠ HERRING IN OATMEAL

A Scottish favorite.
Makes 4 servings

⅓ cup uncooked oatmeal
½ teaspoon salt
¼ teaspoon pepper
4 herring, cleaned and dressed
1 egg, lightly beaten
3 tablespoons butter or margarine

Buzz oatmeal in an electric blender at high speed a few seconds until fairly fine; mix with salt and pepper. Dip herring in egg, then in oatmeal to coat evenly. Melt butter in a large skillet over moderate heat and sauté herring about 3 minutes on each side until golden brown. (*Note:* Any small fish may be prepared this way). About 365 calories per serving.

IRISH HERRING IN ALE

Makes 6 servings

2 medium-size yellow onions, peeled and minced
2 carrots, peeled and cut in small dice
1 clove garlic, peeled and crushed
4 peppercorns
1 teaspoon salt
1 bay leaf
2 cloves
2 (12-ounce) bottles ale
6 herring, cleaned and dressed
2 medium-size yellow onions, peeled and sliced thin

Preheat oven to 350° F. Place minced onions, carrots, garlic, seasonings, and 1 bottle ale in an ungreased deep 3-quart casserole. Cover and bake 30 minutes. Add herring, cover with sliced onions, and pour in remaining ale. Bake, uncovered, 20–30 minutes until fish will flake. Cool herring in broth to lukewarm, then transfer with sliced onions to a deep serving platter; top with a little broth. Serve lukewarm or slightly chilled with

Irish Soda Bread. About 340 calories per serving (without Irish Soda Bread).

SALT HERRING AND BEETS À LA RUSSE

Makes 4 servings

3 herring in brine
1 (1-pound) can sliced beets (do not drain)
2 tablespoons butter or margarine
2 tablespoons flour
1 tablespoon prepared horseradish
1 tablespoon lemon juice
⅛ teaspoon pepper
1 cup sour cream

Soak herring in cold water 24 hours, changing water several times. Remove heads, fillet, and skin* herring and cut in serving-size pieces. Drain beet liquid into a 1-cup measure and add enough cold water to round out measure. Melt butter in a saucepan over moderate heat, blend in flour, slowly stir in beet liquid, and heat, stirring, until thickened. Meanwhile, preheat oven to 350° F. Off heat, mix remaining ingredients into sauce, add herring, and toss to mix. Spoon into a buttered 1½-quart casserole, cover loosely, and bake 20–30 minutes. Serve with boiled potatoes. About 585 calories per serving (without boiled potatoes).

⚖ ROLLMOPS

Makes 6 servings

6 herring in brine
3 dill pickles, quartered lengthwise
2 medium-size yellow onions, peeled, sliced thin, and separated into rings
1 cup cider vinegar
1 cup water
6 peppercorns
1 bay leaf
1 clove garlic, peeled and halved
3 cloves
⅛ teaspoon crushed hot red chili peppers

Soak herring in cold water 24 hours, changing water several times. Remove heads and fillet* herring. Place a piece of dill pickle and some onion on each piece of herring, roll up, and secure with a toothpick. Arrange rolls seam side down in a heatproof glass bowl. Bring vinegar, water, and spices to a boil, cool slightly, and pour over herring. Add any remaining onion, cover tightly, and chill 3–4 days before serving. About 245 calories per serving.

HERRING IN SOUR CREAM

Makes 4 entree servings, enough appetizers for 10–12

4 herring in brine
1 cup sour cream
3 tablespoons white wine or white wine vinegar
1 large yellow or red onion, peeled, sliced thin, and separated into rings
¼ teaspoon powdered mustard
Pinch cayenne pepper

Soak herring in cold water 24 hours, changing water several times. Remove heads, fillet and skin* herring, and cut into bite-size pieces. Mix remaining ingredients, add herring, and pack in a 1-quart jar or glass bowl. Cover tightly and chill 1–2 days before serving. About 340 calories for each of 4 entree servings, 135 calories for each of 10 appetizer servings, and 115 calories for each of 12 appetizer servings.

⚔ PICKLED HERRING

Makes 6 servings

6 herring in brine
2 medium-size yellow onions, peeled, sliced thin, and separated into rings
1 lemon, sliced thin
1½ cups cider vinegar
6 peppercorns
1 teaspoon mustard seeds
1 teaspoon mixed pickling spices
1 teaspoon sugar

Soak herring in cold water 24 hours, changing water several times. Remove heads, fillet* each herring, and, if you like, skin the fillets. If herring is to be served as an appetizer, cut into bite-size pieces. Place half the herring in a single layer in a large shallow heatproof bowl (not metal), top with half the onions and lemon; add remaining herring, onion and

lemon. Bring vinegar, spices, and sugar to a boil and pour over herring. Cover and chill 3–5 days before serving. About 215 calories per serving.

KIPPERED HERRING

Also called *kippers* or *bloaters,* these salted and smoked herring are usually sold as fillets by the pound (allow 1 kipper per person). They also come canned. When buying, avoid any that seem leathery or dry, also any with an overpowering smell. Cook any of the following ways, and serve for breakfast (the English way), lunch, or supper.

To Bake: Preheat oven to 350° F. Line a shallow baking pan with foil and grease lightly; spread kippers flat and arrange skin side down in pan, brush lightly with melted butter or margarine, drizzle, if you like, with a very little Worcestershire sauce, and bake uncovered 8–10 minutes.

To Broil: Preheat broiler. Spread kippers flat and arrange skin side down on broiler pan. Spread each with 1 tablespoon butter or margarine and, if you like, sprinkle with 1 teaspoon lemon juice. Broil 3″–4″ from the heat 2–3 minutes—just long enough to heat through.

To Panfry (Sauté): Spread kippers flat. Allowing about 1 tablespoon butter or margarine for each kipper, sauté gently over moderately low heat about 2 minutes on a side.

To Poach: Spread kippers flat and arrange skin side down in a single layer in a large skillet (not iron); add boiling water or milk just to cover, cover skillet, and bring liquid just to a simmer over moderate heat. Lift kippers to a hot platter, dot with butter, and serve. Especially good with scrambled eggs.

To Steam: Spread kippers flat and arrange skin side down in a single layer on a steamer rack over about 1″ boiling water. Cover and steam 5 minutes.

Some Ways to Use Kippered Herring
Cook by any of the methods above, then

remove skin and any bones, flake, and use as follows:
— Fold into scrambled eggs or omelets, allowing about ½ cup flaked kippers for 4–6 eggs.
— Mix equal quantities flaked kippers and Medium White Sauce and serve on toast, split toasted muffins, in patty shells or Crepes or over buttered noodles.
— Substitute for half the fish called for in Kedgeree.
— Spoon onto melba rounds, drizzle with lemon juice, and serve as cocktail snacks.

BAKED BLUEFISH SMOTHERED WITH HERBS AND CREAM

Makes 2–4 servings

1 (2–3-pound) bluefish, cleaned and dressed
1 teaspoon salt
⅛ teaspoon pepper
½ cup butter or margarine
5 shallots, peeled and minced
1 medium-size yellow onion, peeled and coarsely chopped
⅓ cup minced parsley
2 tablespoons minced fresh dill
1 cup light cream

Preheat oven to 375° F. Sprinkle fish inside and out with salt and pepper and place in an ungreased shallow oval casserole large enough to accommodate it. Dot fish inside and out with ¼ cup butter. Mix shallots, onions, parsley, and dill and scatter over fish. Bake, uncovered, 15 minutes; dot with remaining butter and bake 10 minutes longer. Pour in cream and bake, uncovered, 15–20 minutes and serve. About 1075 calories for each of 2 servings, 540 calories for each of 4 servings.

CHINESE SWEET-AND-SOUR CARP

Carp, the lucky fish of the Chinese, is said to bring wealth and well-being to those who eat it.
Makes 4–6 servings

1 (4–5-pound) carp, cleaned

Sauce:

2 tablespoons peanut or other cooking oil
1 clove garlic, peeled and crushed
1 medium-size sweet green pepper, cored, seeded, and cut in ½" squares
1 medium-size carrot, peeled and cut in julienne strips
1 cup Easy Fish Stock or ½ cup each water and pineapple juice
¼ cup cider vinegar
3 tablespoons sugar
2 tablespoons soy sauce
2 teaspoons cornstarch blended with 2 tablespoons cold water
2 pineapple rings, cut in ¾" chunks

Bend fish into an "S" shape and run 2 long skewers through from head to tail to hold in shape. Place on a rack in a fish steamer or large oval kettle over gently boiling water, cover, and steam about 25 minutes until fish will just flake. About 10 minutes before fish is done, begin sauce: Heat oil in a wok or heavy skillet over moderate heat 1 minute, add garlic, pepper, and carrot, and stir-fry 2–3 minutes; do not brown. Mix in stock, vinegar, sugar and soy sauce, cover, and simmer 2–3 minutes. Add cornstarch paste and pineapple and heat, stirring, until slightly thickened and clear. Lift fish to a hot deep platter and remove skewers. Pour sauce on top and serve with boiled rice. About 335 calories for each of 4 servings (without rice), about 225 calories for each of 6 servings.

CARP IN BEER

A Bavarian specialty.
Makes 4 servings

1 (3–4-pound) carp, cleaned
1 quart beer or ale
1 large yellow onion, peeled and minced
1 stalk celery, chopped fine
1 lemon, sliced thin
1 bay leaf
1½ teaspoons salt
6 peppercorns
6 gingersnaps, crumbled

Place carp and all remaining ingredients except gingersnaps in a fish poacher or large kettle, cover, and simmer 15–20 minutes until fish just flakes when touched with a fork. Lift fish from liquid, arrange on a hot platter and keep warm. Boil kettle liquid, uncovered, until reduced to about 2 cups, stir in gingersnaps, and simmer 2–3 minutes. Strain liquid, pour some over fish, and pass the rest. About 326 calories per serving.

VARIATION:

Carp in Creamy Beer Sauce: Poach fish and reduce kettle liquid as directed above. Instead of adding gingersnaps, strain liquid. Stir in 3 tablespoons flour blended with ¼ cup heavy cream and heat, stirring, until thickened and smooth. Mix in 2 tablespoons butter and 1 tablespoon minced parsley. Spoon some sauce over fish and pass the remainder. About 415 calories per serving.

⚖ **BAKED STUFFED SHAD**

If possible, have fish market bone and prepare fish for stuffing.
Makes 6 servings

1 (4-pound) shad, prepared for stuffing*
1 teaspoon salt
¼ teaspoon pepper
2 cups Quick Mushroom or other
*   stuffing for fish*
¼ cup butter or margarine
½ cup dry white wine

Preheat oven to 400° F. Wipe shad inside and out with damp paper toweling. Sprinkle cavity with half the salt and pepper. Spoon stuffing loosely into cavity and sew up; wrap any remaining stuffing in foil. Place fish and extra stuffing in a well-buttered oven-to-table roasting pan or large casserole. Sprinkle shad with remaining salt and pepper, dot with butter, and add wine. Bake uncovered, basting often, about 40 minutes until fish flakes easily. Remove threads and serve. (*Note:* The shad can be transferred to a hot platter, but, since it's extra fragile, the less handling the better.) About 280 calories per serving.

VARIATIONS:

Portuguese-Style Stuffed Shad: Prepare shad for stuffing as directed above. Make 2 cups Quick Mushroom Stuffing for Fish, then mix in 2 thinly sliced yellow onions and ½ crushed clove garlic that have been sautéed until golden in 2 tablespoons olive oil, also ½ cup coarsely chopped, peeled, and seeded ripe tomato. Stuff fish as directed and begin baking; after 25 minutes, baste with 1 cup hot tomato sauce. Serve with pan juices. About 440 calories per serving.

Empress Stuffed Shad: Prepare shad for stuffing, then stuff with the following: 1 pair blanched shad roe, broken up and mixed with ¾ cup soft white bread crumbs, 2 tablespoons each melted butter and minced chives, 1 teaspoon minced fresh tarragon or ¼ teaspoon dried tarragon, ½ teaspoon salt, and ⅛ teaspoon pepper. Bake as directed. About 410 calories per serving.

POACHED SALMON

Makes 6–8 servings

2 quarts water
1½ cups dry white wine
2 bay leaves
1 sprig parsley
1 stalk celery
3 sprigs fresh dill or ¼ teaspoon dill seed
1 sprig fresh thyme or a pinch dried
*   thyme*
1 small yellow onion, peeled and
*   quartered*
10 peppercorns, bruised
1 teaspoon salt
1 (5-pound) center cut piece fresh
*   salmon, cleaned and dressed*

Boil all ingredients except salmon, uncovered, 25 minutes and strain through a double thickness of cheesecloth. Wipe salmon with damp cloth and wrap in a double thickness of cheesecloth. Place in a large oval kettle on a rack so that loose cheesecloth ends are on top. Pour in strained liquid, cover, and simmer 40 minutes (liquid should never boil). Lift rack and salmon from kettle, remove cheesecloth, peel off skin and carefully scrape away any darkened flesh. Serve hot with Hollandaise Sauce or cool to room temperature, chill 8–10 hours and serve with Green Mayonnaise. About 430 calories for each of 6 servings (without Hollandaise or mayonnaise), 320 calories for each of 8 servings.

VARIATIONS:

Salmon in Aspic: Poach and chill salmon as directed; reserve 2 cups cooking liquid. Transfer chilled salmon to platter and keep cold. Mix 1 envelope unflavored gelatin into reserved liquid, add 1 egg white, beaten to soft peaks, and 1 eggshell, and heat, stirring with a whisk, until mixture foams up. Remove from heat, stir once, then let stand undisturbed 5 minutes. Line a sieve with a fine dish towel wrung out in cold water, set over a deep bowl, pour in hot liquid (egg, shells and all) and let drip through to clarify. Chill clarified aspic until syrupy and spoon a thin, even layer over salmon; chill until tacky, then decorate with cutouts of truffle and pimiento, sliced stuffed green olives, and sprigs of fresh tarragon or chervil; chill briefly to set but keep remaining aspic over warm water. Seal designs with another layer of aspic and chill until firm. Also chill remaining aspic, then dice and use to garnish platter along with lemon wedges and parsley fluffs. Serve with mayonnaise or other suitable cold sauce (see Sauces, Butters, and Seasonings for Seafood). About 435 calories for each of 6 servings (without sauce), 325 for each of 8 servings.

Whole Salmon in Aspic (Makes 10 servings): Substitute a whole small salmon (8 pounds) for center cut piece and poach as directed. Peel skin from body of fish but leave it on head and tail. Glaze salmon with aspic and decorate as directed. About 300 calories per serving.

Salmon in Mayonnaise Gelatin: Poach and chill salmon as directed; also make and clarify aspic as for Salmon in Aspic. In addition, prepare a mayonnaise gelatin: Heat 1 cup chicken broth, skimmed of all fat, with 1 envelope un-flavored gelatin, stirring until gelatin dissolves. Smooth in 1 cup mayonnaise and chill until mixture will coat a metal spoon. Spoon a thin, even layer of mayonnaise gelatin over salmon, chill until tacky, and, if necessary, continue adding thin layers until no pink shows through. While mayonnaise gelatin is still tacky, decorate as above. Chill clear aspic until syrupy and use to seal in design. About 735 calories for each of 6 servings, 555 calories for each of 8 servings.

CRISPY CUCUMBER STUFFED SALMON STEAKS

Makes 4 servings

4 salmon steaks, cut 1¼" thick

Stuffing:

3 tablespoons minced yellow onion
2 tablespoons butter or margarine
1 chicken bouillon cube, crumbled
½ cup hot water
⅓ cup diced, peeled cucumber
1 tablespoon minced parsley
1 tablespoon minced chives (fresh, frozen, or freeze-dried)
1 tablespoon minced fresh dill or ½ teaspoon dried dill
¼ teaspoon salt
⅛ teaspoon pepper
2 cups coarse soda cracker crumbs
¼ cup melted butter or margarine

Preheat oven to 375° F. Arrange salmon steaks in a greased large, shallow baking pan. Stir-fry onion in butter in a large, heavy skillet 3–5 minutes over moderate heat until limp. Mix in bouillon cube and water and heat, stirring, until dissolved. Off heat, add remaining ingredients and toss lightly to mix. Mound stuffing in hollow of each steak, bring ends around to enclose and secure with toothpicks. Drizzle with melted butter and bake, uncovered, 20–25 minutes until fish will just flake. Serve as is or with Lemon Sauce or Parsley Sauce. About 615 calories per serving (without sauce).

⚖ SALMON STEAKS EN CASSEROLE

The Irish say that salmon is best baked in a sealed casserole so that none of the flavor escapes.
Makes 4 servings

4 small salmon steaks, cut ¾"–1" thick
2 tablespoons butter or margarine,
softened to room temperature
¼ teaspoon salt
2–3 sprigs fresh tarragon, lemon balm,
thyme, or dill
1 lemon, sliced thin
⅓ cup simmering apple cider, Easy Fish
Stock, or water

Preheat oven to 325° F. Place steaks in a well-buttered large, shallow casserole that has a tight-fitting lid. Spread steaks with butter and sprinkle with salt. Lay herb on top and cover with lemon slices. Add cider, cover casserole with foil, then with lid and bake 20–30 minutes just until fish flakes when touched with a fork. Remove lemon and herb, carefully lift steaks to platter, drizzle with a little pan liquid, garnish with parsley fluffs, and serve. Tiny new potatoes, buttered green peas, and homemade mayonnaise are the perfect accompaniments. About 295 calories per serving.

VARIATIONS:

Liffey Salmon Steak Platter (6 servings): Cook salmon as directed, transfer to a large platter, and surround with clusters of the following: ½ pound hot shrimp boiled in cider, then shelled and deveined; 1–2 dozen Fried Oysters and ½ pound button mushrooms simmered 5–7 minutes in 2 tablespoons butter and ¼ cup heavy cream. Pass Tomato Sauce. About 510 calories per serving (without sauce).

Tara Salmon: Prepare steaks as directed, but use milk as the cooking liquid instead of cider. Serve on a bed of Colcannon. About 315 calories per serving (without Colcannon).

▧ TRUITE AU BLEU (BLUE TROUT)

For this classic recipe it's best if the fish are still alive or at least just out of the water. The vinegar turns their skin silvery blue, hence the name.
Makes 4 servings

4 (1-pound) fresh trout, cleaned
3 cups cold water
1 cup white vinegar
1 bouquet garni,* tied in cheesecloth
1 teaspoon salt
4 peppercorns

Sauce:

Melted butter or Hollandaise Sauce

Wipe trout with damp paper toweling. Boil remaining ingredients in a fish poacher or large kettle 2–3 minutes, add trout, cover, reduce heat, and simmer 4–5 minutes until fish just flakes when touched with a fork. Using a slotted spoon and pancake turner, carefully lift trout from water and serve at once with sauce. About 330 calories per serving (with 1 tablespoon butter or sauce). *To Serve Cold:* Cool trout in cooking liquid, lift out, chill well, and serve with Ravigote Sauce or Tartar Sauce. About 310 calories per serving (with 2 tablespoons Ravigote Sauce), 385 calories per serving (with 2 tablespoons Tartar Sauce).

VARIATION:

⚖ **Carp au Bleu:** Substitute 1 (3–4-pound) cleaned carp for the trout; simmer as recipe directs 15–20 minutes. About 165 calories per serving (without sauce).

▧ GILLIES' SKILLET TROUT

Gillies are Scottish hunting and fishing guides whose duties include cooking as well as directing sportsmen through the Highlands. Their simple way of preparing trout is delicious at home but unbeatable by a rippling mountain stream.
Makes 4 servings

4 slices bacon
4 (1-pound) trout, cleaned
1 cup unsifted flour

1½ teaspoon salt
¼ teaspoon pepper
1 cup light cream or milk

Fry bacon in a large skillet until crisp and brown; remove, drain on paper toweling, and crumble. Set aside. Dredge trout in a mixture of flour, salt, and pepper and panfry in drippings 3–5 minutes on each side until golden brown. Add cream and simmer 2 minutes, just until bubbly. Toss in bacon and serve at once with Scottish Bannock or thick chunks of bread. About 485 calories per serving if made with cream, 400 calories per serving if made with milk.

BAKED MUSHROOM-SMOTHERED TROUT

Makes 4 servings

4 (1-pound) trout, cleaned
1 teaspoon salt
¼ teaspoon pepper
½ pound mushrooms, wiped clean and sliced thin
2 tablespoons butter or margarine
1 cup heavy cream
½ cup croutons* (optional)
1 tablespoon minced parsley

Preheat oven to 400° F. Rub cavity of each trout with salt and pepper, then arrange in a single layer in a buttered, large, shallow casserole. Sauté mushrooms in butter in a skillet 3–5 minutes over moderately high heat until golden; off heat stir in cream and pour over trout. Cover loosely with foil and bake 15–20 minutes, just until trout flakes when touched with a fork. Scatter croutons and parsley on top and serve. (Note: If you prefer, remove heads and tails before adding croutons and parsley.) About 510 calories per serving (without croutons).

TROUT BAKED EN PAPILLOTE WITH JUNIPER BERRIES AND FENNEL

Makes 2 servings

2 (1-pound) trout, cleaned
4 tablespoons butter (no substitute)
½ teaspoon crushed juniper berries

¼ teaspoon fennel seeds
2 tablespoons minced scallions
1 teaspoon grated lemon rind
½ teaspoon salt
¼ teaspoon pepper
¼ cup dry white wine

Preheat oven to 400°F. Cut 2 pieces of foil large enough to wrap around trout and spread one side of each with about 1 tablespoon butter. Lay trout on foil, mix all remaining ingredients except wine, and sprinkle inside each trout. Dot trout with remaining butter, drizzle with wine, and wrap tightly. Lay packages side by side on a baking sheet and bake about 15–20 minutes just until trout flakes when touched with a fork. Serve trout in foil or transfer to a heated platter and top with drippings in foil. (Note: If you prefer, remove heads and tails before serving.) About 460 calories per serving.

POMPANO EN PAPILLOTE

Makes 4 servings

¼ pound button mushrooms, wiped clean
4 tablespoons butter or margarine
4 pompano fillets or 4 small pompano (about 1 pound each), cleaned and dressed
1 teaspoon salt
¼ teaspoon pepper

Sauce:

½ pound mushrooms, wiped clean and minced
3 scallions, minced
2 tablespoons butter or margarine
1 cup Thick White Sauce
1 tablespoon minced parsley

Preheat oven to 425° F. Prepare sauce first: Stir-fry mushrooms and scallions in butter over moderately high heat 3–5 minutes to brown lightly; mix with remaining sauce ingredients and set aside. Sauté button mushrooms in 2 tablespoons butter over moderately high heat 3–5 minutes until lightly browned, lift out, and reserve. Butter 4 large squares of foil and in the center of each spread 2–3 tablespoons sauce. Place a fillet on each, dot with remaining butter, and sprinkle with salt and pepper. Top each fillet with 2–3 tablespoons sauce, and a few button mushrooms, then wrap tightly, using drugstore wrap. Place packets on a baking sheet and bake 20 minutes until fish just flakes (open 1 package to check and, if not done, bake a few minutes longer). Serve fish in packets. About 685 calories per serving.

VARIATION:

Tampa Pompano en Papillote: Instead of using the sauce above, mix 1 cup Thick White Sauce with 2 minced scallions, 1 tablespoon minced parsley, a pinch nutmeg, and 1 cup minced cooked shrimp or crayfish. Proceed as recipe directs. About 720 calories per serving.

⚖ **PIQUANT FISH EN PAPILLOTE**

Makes 6 servings

1 (4–5-pound) whole or center cut fish, cleaned and dressed
  (any lean or oily fish of suitable size)
1½ teaspoons salt
¼ teaspoon pepper
⅓ cup lemon juice, tarragon, red or white wine vinegar
¼ cup capers

Preheat oven to 400° F. Brush a large piece of heavy duty foil lightly with cooking oil and lay fish on top. Sprinkle with salt and pepper, bring sides of foil up slightly, pour lemon juice over fish, and scatter with capers. Wrap tightly, drugstore style, set on a baking sheet, and bake 40 minutes. Unwrap, test for flaking, and if not done rewrap and bake a little longer. Cool 5 minutes in foil, slide onto a hot platter, top with cooking juices, and serve.

VARIATION:

Fish en Papillote Cooked over Charcoal: Build a moderately hot charcoal fire.* Season and wrap fish as directed, place on grill 5″ from coals, and cook 45 minutes. Unwrap, test for flaking, and if not done rewrap and cook a little longer. Serve as directed.

Both versions: about 195 calories per serving if made with lean fish, 290 calories per serving if made with oily fish.

LEMONY BAKED STUFFED HALIBUT STEAKS

Makes 4–6 servings

2 large halibut steaks of equal size, cut ½″–¾″ thick
½ teaspoon salt
⅛ teaspoon pepper
¼ cup melted butter or margarine
Juice of 1 lemon
1 recipe Lemon Bread Stuffing for Fish

Preheat oven to 350° F. Sprinkle both sides of steaks with salt and pepper; mix butter and lemon juice and brush lightly over both sides of steaks. Place 1 steak in a well-greased shallow baking pan, cover with stuffing, and top with second steak; fasten loosely with toothpicks. Brush with butter mixture and bake, uncovered, 30–40 minutes, brushing often with remaining butter, until fish just flakes when touched with a fork. Remove toothpicks and serve hot with Parsley Sauce or Lemon Sauce or top each portion with a generous pat Maître d'Hôtel Butter. About 420 calories for each of 4 servings (without butter or sauce), about 280 calories for each of 6 servings.

⊠ **CURRIED FISH STEAKS WITH SOUR CREAM SAUCE**

Makes 4 servings

⅓ cup unsifted flour
1 teaspoon salt
⅛ teaspoon white pepper
3 teaspoons curry powder
4 small halibut or salmon steaks, cut ¾″–1″ thick
⅓ cup milk
¼ cup butter or margarine
1 small yellow onion, peeled and minced
½ medium-size sweet green pepper, cored, seeded, and minced
1 cup sour cream

Mix flour, salt, pepper, and 2 teaspoons curry powder. Dip steaks in milk, then in seasoned flour. Melt butter in a large, heavy skillet over moderate heat and sauté steaks 4–5 minutes on each side until golden. Transfer to a hot platter and keep warm. Stir-fry onion and pepper in drippings 3–4 minutes until limp; smooth in remaining curry powder and sour cream, and heat, stirring, 1–2 minutes; do not boil. Pour over fish and serve. About 465 calories per serving if made with halibut and 510 calories per serving if made with salmon.

FISH STEAKS DUGLÈRE

Makes 4 servings

1 small yellow onion, peeled and minced
4 medium-size tomatoes, peeled, cored, seeded, and chopped fine
1 clove garlic, peeled and crushed
¼ cup butter or margarine
4 small delicate white fish steaks (cod, halibut, pollock, sea bass, etc.), cut ¾"–1" thick
1 teaspoon salt
⅛ teaspoon white pepper
2 tablespoons minced parsley
⅛ teaspoon thyme
1 bay leaf
½ cup dry white wine
2 tablespoons flour blended with ¼ cup milk

In a large skillet sauté onion, tomatoes, and garlic in butter over moderate heat 4–5 minutes until onion is limp. Turn heat to moderately low, lay fish on vegetables, sprinkle with salt, pepper, 1 tablespoon parsley, and the thyme. Add bay leaf and wine, cover, and simmer 10 minutes until fish flakes when touched with a fork. Lift fish to a hot deep platter and keep warm. Remove bay leaf from sauce, mix in flour-milk paste, and heat, stirring constantly, until thickened and no raw starch taste remains. Taste for salt and adjust as needed. Pour sauce over fish, sprinkle with remaining parsley, and serve. About 360 calories per serving.

DALMATIAN MARINATED FISH

Makes 4 servings

½ cup unsifted flour
1 teaspoon salt
½ teaspoon pepper
1 large tuna or halibut steak, cut 1" thick (about 2 pounds)
¼ cup olive oil

Marinade:

2 tablespoons olive oil
1 large yellow onion, peeled, sliced thin, and separated into rings
2 carrots, peeled and sliced thin
1 large dill pickle or 2 gherkins, sliced thin
1 cup dry red or white wine
6 peppercorns
3 bay leaves
1 tablespoon capers
2 tablespoons tomato paste
¼ cup minced pitted green olives

Mix flour with salt and pepper and set aside. Cut steaks into 1½" chunks, removing any bones and skin as you go; dredge chunks in seasoned flour. Heat oil in a large, heavy skillet over moderately high heat until a cube of bread will sizzle, and brown fish chunks well on all sides, about 5 minutes; drain on paper toweling. To the same skillet, add oil for marinade and stir-fry onion and carrots 5–8 minutes over moderate heat until golden. Mix in remaining marinade ingredients and simmer, stirring occasionally, 10 minutes. Place fish in a bowl, top with hot marinade, cool to room temperature, and serve. About 610 calories per serving.

TAVIRA TUNA STEAK

The men of Tavira, a small port on Portugal's Algarve coast, are tuna fishermen, and their wives are superb cooks, as this mint-flavored tuna recipe quickly proves.

Makes 4 servings

1 large tuna steak, cut 1½" thick (about 2 pounds)
½ teaspoon salt
¼ teaspoon pepper

Marinade:

¼ cup olive oil
¼ cup dry port or sherry
2 cloves garlic, peeled and crushed
2 tablespoons minced fresh mint
2 tablespoons minced parsley
Juice of ½ lemon

Rub both sides of steak with salt and pepper; place tuna in an ungreased large, shallow baking dish or casserole. Mix marinade and pour on top; cover and marinate in refrigerator 3–4 hours, basting several times with marinade. Preheat oven to 350° F. Bake tuna, covered, 15 minutes, uncover, and bake 15–18 minutes longer, basting often with marinade, until fish will just flake. Serve from casserole, topping each portion with some of the marinade. About 465 calories per serving.

⊠ QUICK FISH STEW

Makes 4–6 servings

1 medium-size yellow onion, peeled
  and minced
2 scallions, minced
2 cloves garlic, peeled and crushed
¼ cup butter or margarine
2 pounds fish fillets (use any 2 of the
  following: cod, flounder, haddock,
  red snapper, sea bass)
1 (9-ounce) package frozen rock lobster
  tails
2 cups Easy Fish Stock or 2 (10½-
  ounce) cans chicken broth or 1 cup
  each bottled clam juice and water
1 (1-pound 12-ounce) can tomatoes
  (do not drain)
1 cup dry white wine
1 teaspoon salt (about)
¼ teaspoon pepper
18 mussels or little neck clams in the
  shell, well scrubbed (mussels should
  also be bearded)
1 (10-ounce) package frozen green peas
1–2 tablespoons minced parsley

In a large kettle over moderate heat, sauté onion, scallions, and garlic in butter 3–5 minutes until very pale golden. Meanwhile, cut fish in 2″ chunks and slice lobster tails crosswise through the shell into 1″ chunks. Add to kettle with all remaining ingredients except mussels, peas, and parsley. Break up any large clumps of tomato, cover, and simmer 10 minutes. Add peas and mussels, cover, and simmer 10 minutes longer. Sprinkle with parsley, taste for salt and adjust as needed. Ladle into soup bowls and serve with hot buttered French bread. About 505 calories for each of 4 servings (without bread), 335 calories for each of 6 servings.

BOUILLABAISSE

There are those who say you can't make Bouillabaisse unless you're from Marseille and use the local catch (especially an ugly fish called *rascasse*). But there are excellent adaptations of the classic recipe made with American fish. Here's one of them. Makes 6 servings

1 cup minced yellow onions or scallions
½ cup minced leeks (include green tops)
2–3 cloves garlic, peeled and crushed
½ cup olive oil
1 (1-pound 12-ounce) can tomatoes
  (do not drain)
1½ quarts Easy Fish Stock or a ½ and ½
  mixture of water and bottled clam
  juice
1 large bouquet garni,* tied in cheese-
  cloth
½ teaspoon thyme
¼ teaspoon fennel seeds
½ teaspoon saffron
1 (2″) strip orange rind (orange part
  only)
1 teaspoon salt
¼ teaspoon pepper
2 (1¼-pound) live lobsters or 2½
  pounds frozen Alaska king crab legs,
  cut in serving-size pieces (include
  shells)
1 pound eel, cleaned, dressed, and cut
  in 1″ chunks, or 1 pound scallops,
  washed well
1 pound halibut, haddock, sea bass, or
  wolffish, cleaned, dressed, and cut in
  2″ chunks
1 pound mackerel, tuna, or mullet,
  cleaned, dressed, and cut in 2″ chunks

1 pound flounder fillets, cut in 2″
chunks
2 dozen mussels or little neck clams in
the shell, well scrubbed (mussels
should also be bearded)
1 tablespoon minced parsley

In a 3-gallon oven-to-table kettle sauté onions, leeks, and garlic in oil over moderate heat 3–5 minutes until very pale golden. Add tomatoes, breaking up clumps, stock, all herbs and seasonings, cover, and simmer ½ hour. Add lobsters, eel, halibut, and mackerel, cover, and simmer 5 minutes. Add flounder and mussels, cover, and simmer 7–10 minutes until mussels open. Remove *bouquet garni* and orange rind, taste for salt and pepper and adjust as needed. Ladle into hot soup plates, sprinkle with parsley, and serve with plenty of hot Garlic Bread. Set out lobster crackers and picks, also plenty of napkins. (*Note:* This recipe is best made with live lobster. If you can't get your fish market to cut the live lobsters into serving-size pieces and are squeamish about doing it yourself, parboil the lobsters 5 minutes, then cut them up.) About 535 calories per serving.

CACCIUCCO (ITALIAN SEAFOOD STEW)

Italians don't bone the fish for this stew. The flavor is better with the bones in, but the eating is more tedious so we've called for fillet. If you prefer, substitute equal quantities of cleaned and dressed fish.
Makes 8 servings

1 medium-size yellow onion, peeled and
minced
1 clove garlic, peeled and crushed
¼ cup olive oil
1 pound squid, prepared for cooking and
cut in 2″ pieces
2 cups Easy Fish Stock or water
2 anchovy fillets, minced
⅛ teaspoon crushed hot red chili peppers
2 tablespoons minced parsley
3 ripe plum tomatoes, peeled, seeded,
and chopped fine

2 tablespoons tomato paste
1 pound halibut or striped bass fillets,
cut in 2″ pieces
1 pound bluefish or red snapper fillets,
cut in 2″ pieces
½ pound bay or sea scallops (halve sea
scallops if extra large)
1 pound shelled and deveined raw
shrimp
1 (9-ounce) package frozen rock lobster
tails, thawed and cut in 1″ chunks
1 cup dry white wine
4 slices Italian bread, toasted and lightly
rubbed with garlic

Stir-fry onion and garlic in oil in a very large, heavy kettle 3–5 minutes over moderate heat until limp. Add squid, stock, anchovies, chili peppers, parsley, tomatoes, and tomato paste; mix well, cover, and simmer ½ hour. Add all remaining ingredients except toast, cover, and simmer 15 minutes. Taste for salt and adjust as needed. Arrange toast in bottom of a large soup tureen, ladle fish and liquid on top. (*Note:* Mixture should be quite thick; if not, lift fish to tureen with a slotted spoon and boil liquid, uncovered, to reduce.) About 410 calories per serving.

⚖ ¢ SEAFOOD PROVENÇAL

Makes 6 servings

2 pounds fillets or steaks of delicate
white fish (cod, haddock, flounder,
fluke, halibut, etc.)
1½ teaspoons salt
¼ teaspoon pepper
1 clove garlic, peeled and crushed
1 cup Easy Fish Stock
3 firm tomatoes, halved but not peeled
2 tablespoons olive or other cooking oil
⅛ teaspoon thyme
½ cup soft white bread crumbs
2 tablespoons melted butter or margarine

Preheat oven to 350° F. Fold fillets envelope fashion, ends toward center, and arrange in a single layer in a well-buttered shallow 2½-quart casserole. Sprinkle with 1 teaspoon salt and ⅛ teaspoon pepper. Stir garlic into stock and pour over fish. Bake uncovered,

basting 2 or 3 times, 20–30 minutes until
fish will flake. Meanwhile, sauté tomatoes
in oil in a skillet over moderate heat 4–5
minutes until lightly browned; keep
warm. When fish is done, draw liquid off
with a bulb baster. Arrange tomatoes
around fish, sprinkle with thyme and
remaining salt and pepper. Top with
crumbs, drizzle with butter, and broil
3″–4″ from heat 1–2 minutes to brown.
About 210 calories per serving.

⚖ **COULIBIAC**

This rich Russian fish dish is usually
wrapped in brioche but it's just as good
—and good-looking—made this
superquick way with packaged,
refrigerated dough. Much lower calorie,
too.
Makes 12–14 servings

2 (8-ounce) packages refrigerated dough
  for crescent rolls
2 cups cooked seasoned kasha or rice
2 cups skinned, boned, flaked cooked
  salmon
3 hard-cooked eggs, shelled and sliced
  thin

Sauce:

4 scallions, minced
½ pound mushrooms, wiped clean and
  coarsely chopped
2 tablespoons butter or margarine
2 tablespoons flour
1 cup Easy Fish Stock or water
2 tablespoons tomato purée
1 teaspoon salt
⅛ teaspoon pepper
1 teaspoon chervil
1 teaspoon tarragon
1 tablespoon minced parsley

Glaze:

1 egg, lightly beaten with 1 tablespoon
  water

Preheat oven to 375° F. Make sauce
first: Stir-fry scallions and mushrooms in
butter in a large saucepan over moderate
heat 3–5 minutes until limp; blend in
flour, slowly add stock, and heat, stirring,
until thickened. Off heat, mix in

remaining ingredients; cool 10 minutes.
Meanwhile, open 1 package of dough,
spread flat, halve crosswise but do not
separate into individual rolls. Fit halves
together on an ungreased baking sheet
so you have a rectangle about 9″×14″;
pinch edges together to seal, also press
all perforations closed so you have an
unbroken sheet of dough. Spread 1½
cups kasha over dough, leaving ½″ margins all around, cover with fish, spread
with sauce, then top with eggs and remaining kasha. Shape second roll of
dough into an unbroken sheet just like
the first and lay on top of filling, letting
edges hang over. Brush edges of bottom
dough lightly with egg glaze, bring up
over top edges and pinch together to
seal. Make 6 steam slits in top of coulibiac. Brush glaze over dough and bake,
uncovered, on center rack ½ hour. Carefully ease onto a hot serving platter. To
serve, cut straight across in thick slices.
About 290 calories for each of 12 servings, 245 calories for each of 14 servings.

⚖ **GEFILTE FISH**
Makes 6 servings

1½ pounds delicate white fish (carp, pike,
  or haddock, etc.), cleaned, dressed,
  and filleted (save head, skin, and
  bones)
1½ pounds oily fish (whitefish or
  mackerel, etc.), cleaned, dressed, and
  filleted (save head, skin, and bones)
2 large onions, peeled and sliced thin
2 large carrots, peeled and sliced ½″
  thick
2 stalks celery, coarsely chopped (include
  tops)
1½ quarts cold water
3½ teaspoons salt (about)
½ teaspoon pepper
1 large yellow onion, peeled and minced
2 eggs, lightly beaten
½ cup soft white bread crumbs or matzo
  meal
¼ cup ice water

Place fish heads, skin, and bones in a
6-quart kettle, add onion slices, carrots,
celery, water, 2 teaspoons salt, and ¼
teaspoon pepper. Cover and simmer

while preparing fish. Put fish through finest blade of meat grinder with minced onion, or place in a large chopping bowl and chop until fine or purée, a little at a time, in an electric blender at low speed. Mix with remaining salt and pepper, eggs, crumbs, and ice water. Wet hands and shape into egg-sized balls. Lower into simmering broth with a wet spoon, cover, and simmer 1½ hours. Cool balls to room temperature in broth, lift to a bowl with a slotted spoon. Strain broth over balls, then add carrot slices. Cover and chill overnight. Serve gefilte fish with some of the jellied broth and carrots, also with white or red prepared horseradish. About 180 calories per serving.

VARIATION:

⚖ Prepare as directed, adding 1 finely grated carrot to fish mixture just before shaping. About 185 calories per serving.

ESCABECHE DE PESCADO (MEXICAN PICKLED FISH)

Makes 4–6 entree servings, enough appetizers for 10

2 pounds red snapper or other delicate white fish fillets, cut in 2″ squares
1 teaspoon salt
¼ teaspoon pepper
⅓ cup unsifted flour
¼ cup cooking oil

Marinade:

1 medium-size yellow onion, peeled, sliced thin, and separated into rings
1 carrot, peeled and sliced ¼″ thick
5 cloves garlic, peeled and minced
1 cup olive oil
1 cup cider vinegar
Juice of 1 lime
⅓ cup hot water
1 teaspoon salt
¼ teaspoon pepper
1 teaspoon thyme
2 bay leaves
1 tablespoon minced parsley
2 pimientos, seeded and coarsely chopped
¼ teaspoon crushed hot red chili peppers

Sprinkle fish with salt and pepper and dredge lightly in flour. Heat oil in a large, heavy skillet over moderately high heat and brown fish quickly, about 2 minutes on a side; drain on paper toweling. In a separate skillet, begin marinade: Stir-fry onion, carrot, and garlic in ¼ cup olive oil over moderate heat 3–5 minutes until limp. Mix in remaining marinade ingredients including remaining olive oil, and simmer, uncovered, 10–15 minutes. Arrange fish 2 or 3 layers deep in a large glass, porcelain, or stainless-steel bowl. Pour in marinade, cool to room temperature, then cover and chill 24 hours. Toss mixture gently and serve, topping fish with some of the marinade. About 340 calories for each of 4 entree servings, 225 calories for each of 6 entree servings (add 65 calories for each tablespoon of marinade used). About 135 calories for each of 10 appetizer servings.

VARIATIONS:

Pickled Tuna: Substitute 2 pounds boneless tuna for white fish and prepare as directed. About 425 calories for each of 4 servings, 285 for each of 6, 170 for each of 10.

⚖ **Shellfish Escabeche:** Substitute 2 pounds cooked lobster meat; boiled, shelled, and deveined shrimp; lump or backfin crab meat or *raw* bay scallops for the fish. Do not fry; place in bowl, top with hot marinade, and proceed as directed. If made with scallops: about 185 calories for each of 4 servings, 125 for each of 6, 75 for each of 10. If made with lobster or crab: about 220 calories for each of 4 servings, 145 calories for each of 6, 90 for each of 10 servings. If made with shrimp: 265 calories for each of 4 servings, 175 for each of 6, 105 for each of 10.

CEVICHE (PERUVIAN RAW PICKLED FISH)

To be really authentic, serve as a main course with hot boiled sweet potatoes, peeled and sliced in thick rounds, and chunks of fresh corn on the cob.

Makes 2–3 main course servings, enough appetizers for 6

1 pound flounder, fluke, halibut, or other firm-fleshed, delicate white fish fillets
3 medium-size yellow onions, peeled, sliced thin, and separated into rings
3 medium-size hot red chili peppers, cored, seeded, and cut in thin strips
3 medium-size Italian sweet peppers or 1 sweet green pepper, cored, seeded, and cut in thin strips
¾ cup lime juice
¾ cup lemon juice
1 tablespoon olive oil
½ clove garlic, peeled and crushed
½ teaspoon salt
2 tablespoons minced parsley

Cut raw fillets into strips about 3″ long and ½″ wide and place in a large glass, porcelain, or stainless-steel bowl. Add all remaining ingredients except parsley and toss well to mix. Cover and chill 24 hours, turning mixture often. When ready to serve, toss again and sprinkle with parsley. Lift out fish and top each portion with some of the vegetables and 1–2 spoonfuls of marinade. About 315 calories for each of 2 entree servings, 210 calories for each of 3, and 105 for each of 6 appetizer servings.

VARIATION:

Scallops Ceviche: Prepare as directed, substituting 2 pounds whole raw bay scallops for the fish. About 510 calories for each of 2 entree servings, 340 calories for each of 3 entree servings, and 170 calories for each of 6 appetizer servings.

⚛ SASHIMI (JAPANESE-STYLE RAW FISH AND VEGETABLES)

If you're squeamish about eating raw fish, skip this recipe. If not, prepare as the Japanese do, paying great attention to the artistic arrangement of fish and garnishes on small colored plates. Serve as an appetizer or main course with *sake*.
Makes 6 main course servings, enough appetizers for 10

2 pounds fresh pompano, red snapper, or tuna fillets
1 cucumber, sliced paper thin (do not peel)
Watercress sprigs

Condiments:

Soy sauce
½ cup minced white radishes
⅓ cup minced fresh gingerroot
¼ cup prepared horseradish
Powdered mustard
Mirin or dry sherry

Insist that the fish is *ocean*-fresh; chill well, then with an extra-sharp knife, slice ⅛″ thick across the grain and slightly on the bias. Cut slices into strips about 1″×2″ and arrange slightly overlapping on 6 individual plates. Cover and chill until near serving time.

Setting Up the Sashimi: At each place set out a small bowl of soy sauce and, in the center of the table, group colorful bowls of minced radishes, gingerroot, horseradish, and mustard, each with its own spoon, around a bottle of *mirin* or sherry.

Serving the Sashimi: Arrange cucumber slices and watercress sprigs on plates with raw fish and set on larger plates filled with crushed ice.

Eating Sashimi: Before anyone eats anything, he mixes a dip by adding a little of the condiments in the center of the table to his bowl of soy sauce. The procedure is then simply to pick up slices of raw fish or cucumber, one at a time, with chopsticks or fork, dip in sauce, and eat. If made with red snapper: about 160 calories for each of 6 entree servings, 95 for each of 10 appetizer servings. If made with pompano: 270 calories for each of 6 servings, 160 for each of 10 appetizer servings. If made with tuna: 215 calories for each of 6 entree servings and 130 for each of 10 appetizer servings.

VARIATION:

⚛ **Scallops Sashimi:** Instead of using thin slices of raw fish, substitute 2 pounds tiny whole raw bay scallops, well washed and chilled. About 140 calories for each of 6 entree servings and 85 calories for each of 10 appetizer servings.

⊠ SALMON CHEDDAR CASSEROLE

Makes 4 servings

1 (1-pound) can salmon, drained
1 cup cooked rice (leftover is perfect)
1 (4-ounce) can sliced mushrooms, drained
1 (11-ounce) can Cheddar cheese soup (do not dilute)
2 tablespoons onion flakes
2 tablespoons dry white wine
¼ teaspoon thyme
¼ teaspoon salt
⅛ teaspoon pepper

Topping:

⅓ cup cracker meal mixed with 2 tablespoons melted butter or margarine

Preheat oven to 375°F. Pick over salmon, removing any dark skin or coarse bones; mix with remaining ingredients except topping and spoon into a lightly buttered shallow 1½-quart casserole. Sprinkle topping over surface and bake, uncovered, 1 hour until lightly browned and bubbly. About 350 calories per serving.

DILLY SALMON LOAF

Makes 6–8 servings

2 (1-pound) cans salmon (do not drain)
2 cups coarse soda cracker crumbs
⅓ cup minced yellow onion
¼ cup minced sweet green pepper
2 tablespoons minced fresh dill or 1 teaspoon dried dill
3 eggs
1 tablespoon lemon juice
1 teaspoon Worcestershire sauce
½ cup evaporated milk
⅛ teaspoon white pepper

Preheat oven to 325° F. Pick over salmon, removing any coarse bones and dark skin, then flake. Add remaining ingredients and mix well, using your hands. Pack into a well-greased 9″×5″×3″ loaf pan and bake, uncovered, about 1 hour and 20 minutes until lightly browned and firm to the touch. Let loaf stand upright in pan 5 minutes before turning out. Serve hot or cold. Particularly good with Sour Cream Cucumber Sauce. About 365 calories for each of 6 servings, 275 calories for each of 8 servings (without sauce).

TUNA AND CAPER SOUFFLÉ

Makes 4 servings

¼ cup butter or margarine
2 tablespoons minced yellow onion
¼ cup unsifted flour
1 cup milk or evaporated milk
½ teaspoon salt
⅛ teaspoon white pepper
4 eggs, separated (at room temperature)
1 (7-ounce) can tuna, drained and flaked
1 tablespoon minced parsley
1 tablespoon minced drained capers
½ teaspoon dill
¼ teaspoon cream of tartar

Melt butter in a small saucepan over moderate heat, add onion, and stir-fry 3–5 minutes until limp; blend in flour, slowly add milk, and heat, stirring, until thickened; turn heat to low and mix in salt and pepper. Beat egg yolks lightly, blend in a little hot sauce, then return to pan. Heat and stir 1–2 minutes but do not boil. Off heat, mix in tuna, parsley, capers, and dill. Place a piece of wax paper flat on the surface of the sauce to prevent a "skin" from forming, and cool to room temperature. Preheat oven to 350° F. Beat egg whites until foamy, add cream of tartar, and continue beating until stiff but not dry. Stir about ¼ cup egg whites into sauce, then fold in remainder. Spoon into an ungreased 1½-quart soufflé dish and bake, uncovered, 45–50 minutes until puffy and browned. Serve at once. Good with Caper or Parsley Sauce. About 310 calories per serving.

VARIATION:

Salmon Soufflé: Prepare as directed, substituting 1 cup flaked cooked or canned salmon for the tuna. About 330 calories per serving.

⊠ MADRAS TUNA

A spicy, sweet-sour curry.
Makes 4 servings

1 medium-size yellow onion, peeled and
*   minced*
½ clove garlic, peeled and crushed
6 tablespoons butter or margarine
6 tablespoons flour
3 tablespoons curry powder
½ teaspoon salt
¼ teaspoon cayenne pepper
1 (13-ounce) can evaporated milk
1¼ cups milk
¼ cup minced, drained chutney
1 (7-ounce) can tuna, drained and flaked

Stir-fry onion and garlic in butter in a
large, heavy skillet 5–8 minutes over
moderate heat until golden; blend in
flour, curry powder, salt, and pepper.
Add evaporated milk and milk and heat,
stirring constantly, until thickened and
smooth. Stir in chutney and tuna and
heat, stirring, 3–5 minutes. Serve over
boiled rice accompanied, if you like, with
chutney, flaked coconut, and chopped
toasted peanuts. About 480 calories per
serving.

⊠ QUICK TUNA SURPRISE

Makes 6 servings

2 (10½-ounce) cans condensed cream of
*   mushroom soup (do not dilute)*
½ cup milk
1 (8-ounce) jar Cheddar cheese spread
1 teaspoon prepared mild yellow mustard
2 (7-ounce) cans tuna, drained well and
*   flaked*
1 (10-ounce) package frozen green peas

Blend soup and milk in a saucepan until
smooth; add cheese. Heat over moderate
heat, stirring constantly, until cheese
melts. Lightly mix in all remaining ingredients except peas, cover, and simmer
6–7 minutes until heated through; stir
occasionally. Meanwhile, cook peas by
package directions but add no salt; drain
well. Mix peas into creamed tuna and
serve over hot biscuits, toast, waffles,
boiled noodles or rice, or in baked
frozen puff pastry shells. About 410

calories per serving (without biscuits,
toast, waffles, noodles, rice, or puff
pastry shells).

⚖ TUNA NIÇOISE

A cooling summer luncheon entree made
with tuna, ripe olives, and tomatoes.
Makes 6 servings

2 (7-ounce) cans white meat tuna,
*   drained and flaked*
1 yellow onion, peeled and chopped fine
½ clove garlic, peeled and crushed
2 tablespoons capers
¼ cup coarsely chopped ripe olives
1 stalk celery, chopped fine
1 tablespoon minced parsley
1 tablespoon minced fresh basil or
*   tarragon or ½ teaspoon of the dried*
1 tablespoon minced fresh chives
3 tablespoons olive oil
⅓ cup mayonnaise
⅛ teaspoon pepper
6 large, crisped lettuce cups or 6 large
*   ripe tomatoes, hollowed out*

Mix together all ingredients except
lettuce cups or tomatoes, cover, and chill
several hours. Mound into lettuce cups
or tomatoes and serve. About 260
calories per serving if served in lettuce
cups, 290 calories per serving if served in
tomatoes.

EELS

Though eels are fish, they aren't treated
exactly like fish because of their unusual
shape. Their meat is surprisingly tender
and much less "fishy" than you would
expect. There is no season on eels, and in
addition to being sold fresh they are also
available smoked, canned, and frozen.
Frozen eels should be thawed before
cooking, then prepared like fresh eels.
The canned and smoked are best used in
casseroles or salads or marinated and
served cold as appetizers.

Amount Needed: About ⅓–½ pound eel
per serving. Eels sometimes weigh as

much as 25 or 30 pounds, but those sold in fish markets range from 1 to 4.

For Top Quality: Buy eel live from a tank *but* make sure the market skins and cleans it before you take it home.

How to Skin and Clean Eel: This is hard work, so brace yourself (which is why you should have the job done for you if at all possible). First, score neck skin just behind head and tie a strong string around it. Nail or fasten string to a wall or post and peel back a bit of the skin, just enough to get a grip on (sprinkle salt or sand on your hands so eel won't slip through them so easily). Peel skin back toward tail, using pliers if necessary to get a stronger grip. Cut off head, slit belly from neck to vent, remove stomach and intestines. Rinse eel under cool running water.

How to Cook Eels

Most of the basic methods of cooking fish are suitable for eels *except* that they need slight adaptation because of the eels' shape.

General Preparation (for all cooking methods): Wash eel well. If eel has a black covering membrane (this in addition to the skin, which has been removed), it's advisable to remove it by blanching so eel will be more attractive. Blanching is especially recommended if eel is to be sautéed, deep fat fried, or mixed into a casserole or salad.

To Blanch: Coil eel in a large saucepan or, if extra large, cut in 2″ chunks. Cover with cold water, add 1 tablespoon lemon juice for each quart, cover, and boil 5 minutes. Drain and cool under cold running water until easy to handle, then peel off membrane.

To Oven Broil: Preheat broiler. Cut eel in 2″–4″ lengths, blanch, and pat dry on paper toweling. Broil 4″–5″ from the heat 5–6 minutes, brushing with melted butter or margarine and turning often so eel browns evenly. Serve with Maître

d'Hôtel Butter or any suitable sauce (see Sauces, Butters, and Seasonings for Seafood).

To Panfry (Sauté): Cut eel in 2″ chunks, blanch, and pat dry on paper toweling. Dip in milk, then dredge in flour lightly seasoned with salt and pepper and sauté in 3–4 tablespoons butter, margarine, or cooking oil 5–7 minutes, turning occasionally, until lightly browned. Drain on paper toweling and serve as is or with Parsley Sauce or Tartar Sauce.

VARIATIONS:

Eel à la Meunière: Sauté eel as directed, transfer to a hot platter, sprinkle with lemon juice and minced parsley and keep warm. Add 1–2 tablespoons butter to skillet, heat until lightly browned and bubbly, pour over eel, and serve.

Breaded Fried Eel: Cut eel in 2″ chunks, blanch, and pat dry on paper toweling. Dip in seasoned flour and a mixture of beaten egg and milk (2 tablespoons milk for each egg), then roll in fine dry crumbs or cracker meal. Sauté as directed.

To Deep-Fat-Fry: Blanch and bread eel as for panfrying, then deep-fry 3–4 minutes in 375° F. fat until crisply browned. Drain on paper toweling before serving.

VARIATION:

Batter-Fried Eel: Prepare batter given in Fish and Chips recipe. Cut eel in 2″ chunks, blanch, and pat dry on paper toweling. Dip in batter, then deep fry in 375° F. fat 3–4 minutes until golden brown. Drain and serve.

To Poach: Cut eel in 2″ lengths, cover with lightly salted water (1 teaspoon salt to 2 cups water) or Simple Court Bouillon, and simmer covered 15–20 minutes until flesh will just flake. Drain and serve hot with Parsley Sauce or Velouté Sauce or, if you prefer, chill and serve cold with Sauce Verte.

JELLIED EELS

Makes 4 entree servings, enough
appetizers for 8–10

2 (1½-pound) eels, skinned, cleaned, and
   dressed and cut in 2" lengths
1 cup each dry white wine and water or
   2 cups Easy Fish Stock
1 medium-size yellow onion, peeled and
   coarsely chopped
1 small carrot, peeled and sliced thick
2 tablespoons lemon juice
1 bay leaf
1 sprig parsley
4 peppercorns
1 clove garlic, peeled (optional)
1 teaspoon salt
1 envelope unflavored gelatin

Place all ingredients except gelatin in a
large saucepan, cover, and simmer 15–
20 minutes until eels are tender; cool eels
in broth until easy to handle. Strain
broth into a clean saucepan, sprinkle in
gelatin, and heat, stirring, over moderate
heat until gelatin dissolves. Take eel
meat from bones, place in a bowl, and
pour in broth. Cover and chill until firm.
Unmold on a platter or break up with a
fork and serve chunks of jelly with eel.
Good with mayonnaise. About 620
calories for each of 4 entree servings
(without mayonnaise), 310 calories for
each of 8 appetizer servings, and 250
calories for each of 10 appetizers.

NORMANDY-STYLE EEL STEW

Eels cooked in apple cider.
Makes 4 servings

2 (1½-pound) eels, skinned, cleaned,
   dressed, and cut in 2" lengths
1 medium-size yellow onion, peeled and
   minced
1 carrot, peeled and cut in small dice
1 stalk celery, chopped fine
1 teaspoon salt (about)
⅛ teaspoon pepper
¼ teaspoon thyme
1 bay leaf
2 cups apple cider
¼ cup butter or margarine
¼ cup unsifted flour
½ cup heavy cream

1 egg yolk, lightly beaten

Garnishes:

1 tablespoon minced parsley
½ recipe Pan-Braised Onions
1 recipe Sautéed Mushrooms (use button
   mushrooms)

Place eels, onion, carrot, celery,
seasonings, and cider in a large saucepan
over moderate heat, cover, and simmer
15–20 minutes until eels are fork tender;
pour off liquid, strain, and reserve. Melt
butter in a saucepan over moderate heat,
blend in flour, slowly mix in reserved
broth and cream, and heat, stirring, until
thickened. Spoon a little hot sauce into
egg yolk, then return to pan; add eels
and heat, stirring, over lowest heat just
long enough to warm eels. Serve in a
tureen sprinkled with parsley and garnished with clusters of onions and mushrooms. Pass hot French bread. About
1,095 calories per serving (without
French bread).

ENGLISH EEL AND EGG PIE

Makes 6 servings

2 (1½-pound) eels, skinned, cleaned,
   dressed, and cut in 2" lengths
1 teaspoon salt
⅛ teaspoon pepper
1 cup hot Thin White Sauce
Pinch nutmeg
1 teaspoon lemon juice
3 hard-cooked eggs, shelled and sliced
   thin
1 recipe Flaky Pastry I
1 egg, lightly beaten (optional glaze)

Preheat oven to 425° F. Blanch eels and
peel off thin black membrane*; arrange
in a buttered 1½-quart casserole, sprinkle
with salt and pepper. Mix sauce with
nutmeg and lemon juice, spoon over
eels, and top with eggs. Prepare pastry
and roll into a circle about 3" larger in
diameter than the casserole; cut steam
vents in the center, fit over casserole, and
crimp edge to seal. If you like, brush
pastry with beaten egg to glaze. Bake ½
hour until pastry is golden. To serve, cut
pastry into wedges and top with eel
mixture. About 685 calories per serving.

ROE

There are two types of roe: *hard* (female eggs inside a delicate membrane) and the less familiar *soft roe* (milt or sperm, also wrapped in a tissue-thin membrane). Shad roe is the most highly prized (possibly because of its short season and scarcity), though that of herring, cod, mackerel, mullet, flounder, and whitefish are all delicious. Sizes of roe vary enormously, from the bite-size herring roe to the medium-size shad roe (5"–6" long and 3" across) to the huge cod roe (it weighs from 1 pound to 3 or more). All hard roe has a slightly gritty texture when cooked but delicate flavor; all is a high protein food rich in B vitamins. Soft roe is paler (almost white), blander, and creamier than hard roe. The choicest comes from carp, herring, and mackerel, in that order. Like hard roe, it is highly nutritious.

Season: Spring, *early* spring for shad roe, usually March and April or, as New Englanders say, "When the shad bush blooms."

Amount Needed: Allow ¼–⅓ pound per person. If the roe is very small, you will need several pair per person; with shad roe, 1 pair per person is ample. Larger roe will serve more than 1 person.

For Top Quality: Look for moist, firm, unbroken roe with a clean, fresh smell.

About Frozen and Canned Roe

In addition to being marketed fresh, hard roe is also available frozen and canned. When salted, it becomes *caviar* (see discussion in chapter on Appetizers and Hors d'Oeuvre). Not every roe becomes caviar, however. The most delectable (black, but sometimes gray or gold) is from sturgeon, the next best (red) is from salmon. Three great pretenders are roe of lumpfish, paddlefish, and white-fish, cleverly salted and colored black.

How to Cook Frozen Roe: Thaw completely in the refrigerator, then prepare like fresh roe.

How to Prepare Canned Roe: Brown gently in butter and serve.

How to Cook Fresh Roe

Easy does it! All roe is fragile and must be given kid-glove care. Too much heat will shatter it or dry it out, too much seasoning will mask its subtle flavor. The more simply roe is cooked, the better it will be.

General Preparation:

Hard Roe: Wash *very* gently in a bowl of cool water and pat dry on paper toweling. Some cooks recommend pricking the covering membrane several places with a needle to keep it from bursting during cooking. But if the roe is cooked *gently*—as it should be—the membrane isn't likely to burst.

Soft Roe: Wash carefully in a bowl of cool water, using the lightest possible touch; pull away the blue vein running along one side of roe. Lift roe from water and pat dry on paper toweling.

To Oven Broil (for hard roe of medium size only): This is a pretty risky way to cook roe; broiler heat is simply too intense for delicate roe and tends to shatter and shrink it. But, there are people who dote upon broiled roe, so . . . Preheat broiler. Have roe at or near room temperature to reduce chances of shattering and slather with melted butter or margarine. Place in a well-buttered piepan and broil 4" from the heat, 4–5 minutes on a side, basting often with additional melted butter. Turn roe only once and use a pancake turner, handling lightly so membrane doesn't break. (*Note:* Some books recommend parboiling roe 10 minutes in lightly salted boiling water before broiling to reduce chances of bursting. Try it, if you like, but don't expect the roe to have much flavor.)

To Panfry (*Sauté*): Here's the best method for hard and soft roe. Have roe at or near room temperature. Dip in milk, then dredge in flour lightly seasoned with salt and pepper. Place in a *cold* skillet with melted butter (allow ¼ cup butter for each 1 pound roe) and sauté slowly over moderate heat until lightly browned. Small roe will take about 2 minutes on a side, medium-size roe 3½–4 minutes per side. Turn roe one time only and handle very carefully. (*Note:* Large roe, that of cod, for example, should be poached by the method below, patted dry on paper toweling, then just browned lightly, about 5 minutes on each side in the butter.) Serve the sautéed roe as is, topped with some of the pan juices. Or serve on lightly buttered toast, drizzled with Lemon Butter. (*Note:* Large roe is usually broken into smaller pieces, then served in the same way as smaller roe.)

VARIATIONS:

Roe à la Meunière: Sauté as directed, transfer to a hot platter, and sprinkle with lemon juice and a little minced parsley. Add 1–2 tablespoons butter to skillet, heat until bubbly and the color of topaz, pour over roe and serve.

Breaded Fried Roe: Dredge roe in flour lightly seasoned with salt and pepper, dip in a mixture of beaten egg and milk (2 tablespoons milk for each egg), then roll in fine dry crumbs or cracker meal to coat. Sauté as directed.

To Poach: Arrange roe in a large, heavy skillet (not iron), add cold water barely to cover; for each 2 cups water, add ½ teaspoon salt and 1 tablespoon lemon juice. Cover skillet and simmer roe over moderately low heat (water should just tremble) as follows: 5 minutes for small roe, 10 minutes for medium-size roe or large roe that is to be sautéed after poaching, and 15–20 minutes for large roe that is to be poached only. When done, roe will be white and firm (but not hard). Drizzle with Parsley or Herb Butter and serve. Large roe can be broken into chunks and smothered with Béchamel, Poulette, or Shrimp Sauce or drizzled with seasoned melted butter.

SHELLFISH

BASIC SHELLFISH CROQUETTES

If croquettes are to be light and crisp, and not the least bit greasy, the deep fat must be good and hot—in this case, 375° F.
Makes 4 servings

3 tablespoons butter or margarine
3 tablespoons flour
1 cup milk or light cream
½ teaspoon salt
⅛ teaspoon liquid hot red pepper seasoning
1 tablespoon minced parsley
1 tablespoon minced fresh dill or ½ teaspoon dried dill
1 egg, lightly beaten
1½ cups soft white bread crumbs
1½ cups minced, cooked lobster, shrimp, crab meat, scallops, clams, mussels, or oysters
1 tablespoon lemon or lime juice
Shortening or cooking oil for deep fat frying

Coating:

1 egg, lightly beaten
1 cup cracker meal or toasted, packaged, seasoned bread crumbs

Melt butter in a saucepan over moderate heat and blend in flour; slowly add milk and heat, stirring, until thickened. Off heat, mix in seasonings, egg, crumbs, shellfish, and lemon juice; cover and chill 3–4 hours. Shape into 8 patties or small balls, dip in egg, and roll in cracker meal to coat. Let stand at room temperature on a wire rack while heating fat. Place shortening in a deep fat fryer and heat to 375° F.; use a deep fat thermometer. Place 3 or 4 croquettes in fryer basket, lower into hot fat, and fry 2–3 minutes until golden brown and crisp; drain on paper toweling, then keep warm while you fry the rest by setting uncovered in oven turned to lowest heat. Serve hot with Tartar Sauce. If made with scallops, clams, mussels, or oysters: About 405 calories per serving (without Tartar Sauce). If made with lobster, shrimp, or crab: about 425 calories per serving.

BASIC SHELLFISH SOUFFLÉ

Delicate but not difficult to make. Makes 4 servings

¼ cup butter or margarine
¼ cup unsifted flour
1 cup light cream
½ teaspoon salt
⅛ teaspoon white pepper
⅛ teaspoon nutmeg or mace
4 eggs, separated (at room temperature)
1 cup finely chopped cooked shrimp, lobster, or crab meat
¼ teaspoon cream of tartar ·

Melt butter in a small saucepan over moderate heat, blend in flour, slowly add cream, and heat, stirring, until thickened and smooth; mix in salt, pepper and nutmeg and turn heat to low. Beat egg yolks lightly, blend in a little hot sauce, then return to saucepan. Heat and stir 1–2 minutes but do not allow to boil. Off heat, mix in shellfish; lay a piece of wax paper flat on surface of sauce to prevent a "skin" from forming, and cool to room temperature. Preheat oven to 350° F. Beat egg whites until foamy, add cream of tartar, and continue beating until stiff but not dry. Stir about ¼ cup egg white into sauce, then carefully fold in remainder. Spoon into an ungreased 1½-quart soufflé dish and bake, uncovered, about 45 minutes until puffy and tinged with brown. Rush to the table and serve. Good with Shrimp Sauce or Sauce Américaine.

VARIATION:

Herbed Shellfish Soufflé: Prepare as directed but add 1 tablespoon minced parsley and 1 tablespoon minced fresh dill, tarragon, or chervil to sauce along with shellfish.

Both versions: About 385 calories per serving (without sauce).

ABALONE

You must go to California to find fresh abalone, and even then you may not succeed because the supply is scarce. Laws now limit the number and size of abalone that can be taken, also the season for taking them. These giant mollusks are "fished" by skin divers who pry them off rocks with crowbars. Not everyone likes abalone; in fact, many people consider them more trouble than they're worth (badly cooked, they can be very tough). Frozen abalone steaks from Japan and Mexico are sold in gourmet markets; canned minced abalone is also available.

Amount to Buy: 1 pound abalone in the shell per person; about ⅓ pound abalone meat.

For Top Quality: Buy only abalone with shells clamped shut or, better yet, go after your own and bring them home alive.

How to Open and Clean Abalone: If you've caught, bought, or been given a live abalone, here's what to do with it. Force a wooden or metal wedge between the meat and the shell and move around the rim of the shell until the abalone gives up and drops from the shell. Cut off the end that was next to the shell, taking care not to break the sack. Wash meat well in cool water, then trim away all tough, dark portions around the edges (these can be used in soups or stews if you like).

How to Cook Abalone

The classic dish is abalone steak, sometimes breaded, sometimes not, but always sautéed quickly in butter. The meat can also be minced or ground for use in soups, stews, and fritters.

General Preparation for Steaks: If abalone is in 1 large piece, slice across the grain into steaks, making each slightly more than ¼″ thick. To tenderize, pound each steak with a wooden mallet or edge of a plate, using a light, rhythmic motion until muscles relax and abalone is limp and velvety. (*Note:* Most frozen steaks have already been tenderized and are ready to cook [read label carefully].)

SAVORY ABALONE STEW

Makes 4 servings

2 abalone steaks, cut a little more than
 ¼″ thick and pounded until tender
1 large yellow onion, peeled and minced
1 clove garlic, peeled and crushed
⅓ cup minced sweet green pepper
¼ cup butter or margarine
1 bay leaf, crumbled
½ teaspoon oregano
¼ teaspoon basil
1 (8-ounce) can tomato sauce
2 cups water
2 large potatoes, peeled and cut in ½″
 cubes
½ teaspoon salt
¼ teaspoon cayenne pepper

Cut abalone in ¼″–½″ cubes and set aside. Stir-fry onion, garlic, and green pepper in butter in a large saucepan 5–8 minutes over moderate heat until onion is pale golden; mix in all remaining ingredients except abalone, cover, and simmer 10–12 minutes until potatoes are almost tender. Add abalone and simmer 5–8 minutes longer until abalone and potatoes are tender. Ladle into hot soup bowls and serve as a main course with chunks of Italian bread and a crisp green salad. About 350 calories per serving.

⚖ ⊠ ABALONE STEAKS

Makes 4 servings

¼ cup butter or margarine
4 abalone steaks, cut a little more than
 ¼″ thick and pounded until tender
Salt
Pepper

Melt butter in a large, heavy skillet over moderately high heat, and when it begins to bubble, add abalone steaks and sauté just 1 minute on each side.

Sprinkle with salt and pepper and serve. About 220 calories per serving.

VARIATION:

⚖ **Breaded Abalone Steaks:** Mix ⅔ cup unsifted flour with 1 teaspoon salt and ¼ teaspoon pepper; beat 2 eggs with 2 tablespoons cold water until frothy. Dredge steaks in flour, dip in egg, then in fine dry bread crumbs to coat evenly. Sauté as above, allowing just enough time on each side to brown crumbs lightly. About 250 calories per serving.

CLAMS

Clams were probably the first New World food sampled by Pilgrims. They arrived ravenous after weeks at sea, fell upon the New England beaches in search of food and found hard and soft clams by the bucketful. Later, they learned from the Indians how to roast clams over open fires, to simmer them into soups and stews, and to layer them into pits with corn, potatoes, and lobsters in that most convivial of picnics, the clambake.

The Kinds of Clams

The terminology is confusing because there are so many different kinds of clams, also because each has several names. Here's a quick roundup:

East Coast Clams: There are two types, the hard and soft shell.

Hard Shell Clams: These are also called by the Indian name, *quahog,* and come in three sizes: *large or chowder* (at least 3″ in diameter and best for chowders or stuffed clams); *cherrystones* or medium (about 2″ across and good for steaming or eating on the half shell), and *littlenecks* or small (1½″ across and usually reserved for eating on the half shell).

Frosted Tomatoes; Belgian Style Tomatoes; and Tomatoes Finlandia (All three recipes page 903)

Roast Beef Leftovers: Yukon Stew with biscuits baked on top (pages 217 and 944); Beef-stuffed Vegetables (page 216); and Beef Curry (page 216)

Butterscotch Parfait (pages 1063 and 1053-55); Chocolate Ice Cream and Hot Fudge Sauce (pages 1054 and 1062); and Strawberry Ice Cream Soda (pages 120-21)

Soft Clams or Steamers: The shells are long, thin, and oval and the clams inside are long, too, and stick long black necks outside their shells (explaining their nickname, *longneck*). These are the clams harvested along beaches and mud flats, the lightning-quick burrowers.

West Coast Clams: Most famous of the 35-plus varieties are:

Butter Clams: Sweet-meated little clams from the Puget Sound area that are best eaten on the half shell. Indians used them as money, so they're also called *moneyshells.*

Geoduck (pronounced gooey-duck): These long-necked monsters are fun to dig at low tide but rarely appear in markets.

Mud Clams: Popular, large oval clams found along the Northern California and Oregon coasts; only the white flesh is eaten.

Pismo Clams: One of the choicest Pacific clams; it is big, tender and sweet—and becoming scarce. Only clams measuring 5″ across or more may be taken. The tender adductor muscle is often served on the half shell, the body meat is usually fried, hashed, or minced into chowders. The name Pismo comes from Pismo Beach, California, where these clams were first found.

Razor Clams: These, so named because their long slender shells resemble the old-fashioned barber's razor, are so delectable many gourmets rate them higher than the Eastern soft clams.

About Buying Fresh Clams

Season:

East Coast Varieties: Year round.

West Coast Varieties: Year round in the Pacific Northwest. In California the season is shorter, usually November through April. Spring and summer are the time of the dread "red tide" when microscopic organisms fill the sea, mak-

ing clams and certain other shellfish unsafe to eat. At such times, many clamming beaches are closed.

Popular Market Forms: Atlantic and Pacific clams are both sold live and in the shell either by the dozen or pound; they are also sold shucked by the pint or quart. In addition, many markets, if asked, will remove the top shells and prepare clams for serving or cooking on the half shell.

Amount Needed: The quantity varies tremendously according to the size of the clams, how they are cooked and served, not to mention appetites. Here's a general guide:

Clams on the Half Shell: Allow 6–8 small- or medium-size clams per person.

Steamed or Stewed Clams: Allow 1–1½ dozen clams per serving, depending on size of clams and richness of broth.

Shucked Clams: 1 pint will serve 3–4, more if stretched with other ingredients.

For Top Quality:

Clams in the Shell: Look for tightly closed clams, or at least those that "clam up" when their shells are tapped. Any that remain open are dead and should be rejected.

Shucked Clams: Choose clams that are plump and sweet-smelling with clear liquor and no shell fragments.

About Frozen and Canned Clams

Quick-frozen shucked clams are available, as are frozen, ready-to-heat-and-eat clam fritters and patties. Canned clams, both whole and minced, chowders, and clam juice are all widely marketed. *To Cook Frozen Clams:* Thaw quick-frozen shucked clams completely in refrigerator, then prepare as you would fresh clams. Once clams have thawed, cook immediately; never refreeze. Clam fritters, patties, and other frozen prepared clam dishes should be heated or cooked by package directions.

How to Use Canned Clams: These are already cooked and ideal for quick soups, salads, canapés, and casseroles.

About Preparing Fresh Clams in the Shell

How to Cleanse Clams of Grit: The easiest way is to let the clams do the job themselves. Here's how: Scrub clams well to remove surface grit and mud, then place in a large, deep enamel kettle and cover with cold salted water (1 tablespoon salt to each quart water). Toss in a handful of corn meal, set kettle in a cool place and let stand several hours or overnight. Lift clams from water and rinse well in cool water; discard any that are open or do not clamp shut when thumped.

How to Open Clams: There are two ways, one difficult, one easy. If the clams are to be served or broiled on the half shell, you'll have to use brute force. If they're to be removed from the shell and used in chowders, patties, or casseroles, they can quickly be steamed open. (*Note:* Geoducks require special attention [see method that follows].)

(1) *To Pry Open:* Holding a clam in the palm of one hand, insert clam knife between upper and lower shells, then move it along rim, twisting slightly to break "seal" and force clam open (the job is much easier with soft clams than with hard). Cut clam free of shell and remove any grit or bits of shell. Do the opening over a bowl so none of the clam juice is lost; also strain juice through a sieve lined with a double thickness of cheesecloth before using.

(2) *To Steam Open:* Place clams in a large, deep kettle, pour in about ¾ cup boiling water, cover, and steam over moderate heat about 5–8 minutes until shells partially open. Drain and remove meat from shells—it will come away zip-quick if you work under a gentle stream of cool water.

How to Cook Clams

Clams can be cooked simply or glamorized in a variety of ways. Purists insist nothing surpasses a steamed clam, dunked in melted butter, but then everyone is not a purist. . . .

General Preparation: If clams are in the shell, cleanse of grit and shuck or not as recipes specify. Check extra-heavy clams carefully; they may be full of sand or mud. This is all the preparation Eastern hard and soft clams need, also the West Coast butter clam. Other Pacific varieties, however, require further attention:

Geoduck: Plunge clam into boiling water and let stand until shell opens. Drain and cut body meat from shell. Skin the clam, discard the stomach (the dark portion) and separate neck from body. Put neck through coarse blade of meat grinder and slice body into thin steaks (about ¼″ thick). The neck meat is best used in chowders, the steaks quickly panfried in butter.

Mud Clams: When clams are shucked, trim away all black portions; split the necks lengthwise and rinse away any grit. Cook as you would hard clams.

Pismo Clams: Cut hinge or adductor muscle from body meat; it is tender enough to serve raw on the half shell. Remove stomach (the dark part) from the body, rinse clam, then lightly pound any firm parts to "tenderize." These clams are particularly good fried or deep-fat-fried.

Razor Clams: Cut off tip of the neck, cut clam from shell, and split from the base of the foot (that part next to the shell) to the top of the neck. Trim off all dark parts (the gills and digestive organs). Leave clam whole and fry or deep-fry, or grind and use for chowders or patties.

To Charcoal Broil: This is a bit of a fuss. Build a moderately hot charcoal fire.* Pat shucked clams dry on paper toweling, then wrap each in a ½ slice bacon and thread on long thin skewers;

or secure bacon slices with toothpicks and place clams in a well-greased hinged, long-handled wire grill. Broil 4″ from heat 3–4 minutes on a side until bacon is golden and crisp.

To Panfry (Sauté): Pat shucked clams dry on paper toweling. Dredge in flour lightly seasoned with salt and pepper and sauté in butter (about ⅓ cup butter for 1 pint clams) about 3 minutes over moderate heat, turning once, until clams are lightly browned. Serve with lemon wedges.

VARIATIONS:

Pan-"Roasted" Clams: These aren't roasted but sautéed. Pat clams dry on paper toweling but do not dredge. Sauté in butter (about ½ cup butter for 1 pint clams) 2–3 minutes, turning once, just until clams plump up and are heated through. Serve with lemon.

Breaded Fried Clams: Pat clams dry, dredge in flour lightly seasoned with salt and pepper, dip in a mixture of beaten egg and milk (2 tablespoons milk for each egg), and roll in fine dry crumbs, cracker meal, or a ½ and ½ mixture of flour and corn meal. Sauté as directed until golden and drain on paper toweling before serving.

To Deep-Fat-Fry: Pat shucked clams dry on paper toweling, then bread as above. Heat cooking oil or shortening in a deep fat fryer to 375° F., place a single layer of clams in fryer basket, lower into fat, and fry 1–2 minutes until golden brown. Drain on paper toweling and serve with lemon.

VARIATION:

Batter-Fried Clams (Clam Fritters): Make up batter given in Fish and Chips recipe. Pat clams dry on paper toweling, dip in batter, then fry, 6–8 at a time, in 375° F. fat about 2 minutes until golden brown. Drain on paper toweling and serve.

To Oven Roast: Scrub clams well and cleanse of grit but do not shuck. Preheat oven to 450° F. Place clams in a shallow baking pan and roast, uncovered,

12–15 minutes until they open; reject any that do not. Serve clams in the shell with plenty of melted butter and lemon wedges.

To Roast over Charcoal: Scrub clams and cleanse but do not shuck. Build a moderately hot charcoal fire.* Wrap clams, about 6 to a package, in heavy foil. Place packages directly on coals and roast 4–6 minutes until clams open. Serve with lemon and melted butter.

To Steam: Steamers or soft clams are best, though small hard clams may also be steamed. Scrub clams well and cleanse of grit but do not shuck. Place clams in a large, deep kettle, add ⅔ cup boiling water, cover, and steam 5 minutes over moderate heat until clams open; discard any that don't. Serve in the shell with melted butter, a bowl of broth, and lemon wedges. When eating, peel black skin from neck and hold by the neck when dunking in broth and butter.

To Serve Clams on the Half Shell

Allow 6–8 cherrystone, littleneck, or butter clams per serving. If possible, have your fish market open clams and discard top shells. If you must do the job yourself, follow directions given earlier for cleansing and prying open clams. Fill large, shallow bowls or soup plates with crushed ice and arrange clams in ice. Garnish with lemon wedges and parsley fluffs. Set out the pepper mill (but *not* cocktail sauce unless guests insist). After eating clams on the half shell, be sure to drink the juice from each shell.

CLAMS CASINO

Makes 2 entree servings, enough appetizers for 4

Rock salt
6 slices bacon
2 dozen cherrystone clams on the half shell
¼ cup butter or margarine, softened to room temperature
2 teaspoons anchovy paste
¼ cup minced sweet green pepper
¼ cup minced pimiento

Preheat oven to 450° F. Make beds of rock salt in 4 piepans (the 8″ or 9″ size is best and the jiffy foil pans work perfectly), dampen slightly with water and heat, uncovered, in oven 5 minutes. Meanwhile, cut each bacon slice into 4 equal pieces and stir-fry over moderate heat until limp; drain on paper toweling and reserve. Arrange 6 clams in each pan, pushing down into hot salt so they won't tip. Mix butter and anchovy paste until smooth and tuck about ½ teaspoonful under each clam. Sprinkle a little sweet green pepper and pimiento on each clam, top with a piece of bacon, and bake, uncovered, 5–7 minutes until bacon is crisp. Serve clams from pans. About 540 calories for each of 2 entree servings, 270 calories for each of 4 appetizer servings.

VARIATION:

Oysters Casino: Prepare as directed, substituting oysters on the half shell for clams. About 540 calories for each of 2 entree servings, 270 calories for each of 4 appetizer servings.

CLAMS ORIGANATA

Whenever possible, make crumbs from stale Italian bread; the recipe will have much better flavor.
Makes 2 entree servings, enough appetizers for 4

Rock salt
2 dozen littleneck or cherrystone clams
  on the half shell
1½ cups fine dry bread crumbs
2 cloves garlic, peeled and crushed
2 tablespoons minced parsley
2 teaspoons minced fresh oregano or 1
  teaspoon dried oregano
3 tablespoons olive or other cooking oil
⅛ teaspoon pepper

Preheat broiler. Make beds of rock salt in 4 (8″ or 9″) piepans and dampen slightly with water; heat, uncovered, in oven 5 minutes while broiler preheats. Arrange 6 clams in each pan, pushing down into hot salt so they won't tip. Mix remaining ingredients and spoon enough on each clam to cover. Broil 5″ from

the heat 3–4 minutes until lightly browned. About 430 calories for each of 2 entree servings, 215 calories for each of 4 appetizer servings.

BOSTON-STYLE STUFFED CLAMS

The stuffing is a delicate blend of minced clams, onion, parsley, and soft bread crumbs.
Makes 2–4 servings

Rock salt
1 dozen large clams on the half shell
¾ cup soft white bread crumbs
1 tablespoon minced yellow onion
1 tablespoon minced parsley
2 teaspoons lemon juice
¼ teaspoon pepper
½ cup fine dry or toasted seasoned bread
  crumbs mixed with 2 tablespoons
  melted butter or margarine

Preheat oven to 425° F. Make a bed of rock salt in a large, shallow baking pan and dampen slightly with water; heat, uncovered, in oven 5 minutes. Drain juice from clams, reserving ¼ cup; mince clams and combine with juice; butter clam shells well. Mix clams and juice with all remaining ingredients except buttered crumbs and spoon into shells. Anchor shells in hot salt so they won't tip, top clams with buttered crumbs, and bake, uncovered, 10 minutes until lightly browned. About 310 calories for each of 2 servings, 155 calories for each of 4 servings.

VARIATIONS:

⚖ **Stuffed Clams au Gratin:** Prepare clam mixture as directed, adding ⅓ cup crisp crumbled bacon. Omit buttered crumb topping and top instead with ¼ cup cracker meal mixed with ¼ cup grated Parmesan. Bake as directed. About 285 calories for each of 2 servings, 145 calories for each of 4 servings.

Creamed, Stuffed Clams: Prepare clam mixture as directed but for the liquid ingredients use ⅓ cup Thick White Sauce and 2 tablespoons medium-dry sherry instead of clam juice and lemon juice. Fill shells, top with buttered crumbs, and bake as directed. About 400 calories for each of 2 servings, 200 calories for each of 4 servings.

CLAMS BULHAO PATO

Bulhão Pato was a Portuguese poet whose recipe for garlic- and coriander-flavored clams is better remembered than his poetry.
Makes 4 servings

5–6 dozen soft clams in the shell,
  prepared for cooking
1½ cups boiling water
⅓ cup olive oil
3 cloves garlic, peeled and crushed
½ cup minced parsley
½ cup minced fresh coriander leaves or
  2 tablespoons minced carrot tops
⅛ teaspoon pepper
½ teaspoon salt

Place clams in a very large, deep kettle, add all remaining ingredients, cover, and steam over moderate heat 5–10 minutes just until shells open; discard any that do not open. Serve clams in shells in soup bowls topped with some of the broth. (*Note:* Tip kettle when ladling out liquid to avoid any sediment in the bottom.) Serve with hot crusty bread. About 315 calories per serving (without bread).

SCALLOPED CLAMS

Makes 4 servings

1 pint shucked clams or 2 (8-ounce) cans
  minced clams (do not drain)
½ cup light cream or milk (about)
2 cups coarse soda cracker crumbs
½ cup melted butter or margarine
2 tablespoons minced parsley
½ teaspoon salt
⅛ teaspoon pepper
½ teaspoon Worcestershire sauce
2 tablespoons dry sherry (optional)

Preheat oven to 350° F. Drain liquid from clams, measure, and add enough cream to total 1 cup; set aside. If using fresh clams, mince. Mix crumbs with butter, parsley, salt and pepper and spoon about ⅓ into a buttered 1-quart casserole. Cover with half the clams, add another ⅓ crumbs, then remaining

clams. Stir Worcestershire sauce and, if you like, sherry into clam liquid mixture; pour over clams and top with remaining crumbs. Bake, uncovered, about ½ hour until lightly browned. About 515 calories per serving.

¢ ☒ CLAM HASH

Makes 4 servings

3 slices bacon
1 (10½-ounce) can minced clams,
  drained
¼ cup minced yellow onion
3 cups diced cooked potatoes
3 eggs, lightly beaten
¼ cup milk or light cream
1 teaspoon salt
⅛ teaspoon pepper
Pinch nutmeg

Fry bacon in a skillet over moderate heat until crisp; drain, crumble, and reserve. Mix clams, onion, and potatoes and add to drippings in skillet, pressing down with a spatula to form a large "pancake." Fry over moderately low heat without stirring 7–10 minutes until brown on the bottom; flip mixture over, press down. Mix eggs with all remaining ingredients and pour over clams. Cook just until eggs are set, tilting pan as needed to let uncooked eggs run underneath. Sprinkle with bacon, cut in wedges, and serve. About 445 calories per serving.

CLAM SOUFFLÉ

So very delicate!
Makes 4–6 servings

¼ cup butter or margarine
¼ cup unsifted flour
1 cup milk or a ½ and ½ mixture of
  milk and liquid drained from clams
¼ teaspoon salt
⅛ teaspoon pepper
4 eggs, separated (at room tempera-
  ture)
1 pint shucked clams, drained and
  minced or 2 (8-ounce) cans minced
  clams, drained
¼ teaspoon cream of tartar

Melt butter in a small saucepan over moderate heat, blend in flour, slowly add milk, and heat, stirring, until thickened. Turn heat to low, stir in salt and pepper. Beat egg yolks lightly, blend in a little hot sauce, then return all to pan. Heat, stirring, 1–2 minutes but do not boil. Off heat mix in clams; lay a piece of wax paper flat on surface of sauce and cool to room temperature. Meanwhile, preheat oven to 350° F. Beat egg whites until foamy, add cream of tartar and continue to beat until stiff but not dry. Stir about ¼ cup egg whites into clam mixture, then fold in remainder. Spoon into an ungreased 1½-quart soufflé dish and bake, uncovered, ¾ hour until puffy and brown. Serve at once. About 325 calories for each of 4 servings, 215 calories for each of 6 servings.

NEW ENGLAND CLAM PIE

A two-crusted pie filled with clams, diced salt pork, and potatoes.
Makes 6 servings

1 recipe Flaky Pastry II
1 pint shucked clams or 2 (8-ounce) cans minced clams (do not drain)
¼ pound salt pork or bacon, cut in small dice
1 small yellow onion, peeled and minced
1 tablespoon flour
2 medium-size potatoes, boiled, drained, and cubed
1 tablespoon minced parsley
⅛ teaspoon pepper

Preheat oven to 425° F. Prepare pastry according to recipe and roll out half to form a 12″ circle. Fit into a 9″ piepan but do not trim edge. Roll remaining pastry into a 12″ circle, cut 3 V-shaped slits near center, and cover with wax paper while preparing filling. Drain clams, reserving ⅓ cup liquor (if necessary, add milk to round out measure); mince clams. Lightly brown salt pork in a small skillet over moderately low heat; remove and reserve. Pour off all but 2 tablespoons drippings, add onion, and sauté over moderate heat 3–5 minutes until limp.

Blend in flour and clam liquid and heat, stirring, until thickened. Off heat, mix in potatoes, clams, parsley, and pepper. Spoon into prepared pie shell, fit reserved pastry on top, press 2 crusts together, trim and crimp edges. Bake about ½ hour until pastry is lightly browned. About 330 calories per serving.

INDOOR CLAMBAKE

The usual order of building a clambake is clams on the bottom, then lobsters and vegetables, but the following upside-down arrangement has an advantage. The clams can be enjoyed as a first course while the slower-cooking items finish "baking." To do the indoor clambake, you'll need a giant kettle or "clambaker," obtainable in hardware and kitchen shops.
Makes 6–8 servings

8 ears sweet corn in the husk
2 gallons cold water mixed with ½ cup salt
Seaweed
6 (1–1¼-pound) live lobsters
8 medium-size potatoes, scrubbed but not peeled
6 dozen soft clams in the shell, prepared for cooking, or 2 dozen each clams, oysters, and mussels in the shell, prepared for cooking

Condiments:

2 cups melted butter or margarine
1 bottle liquid hot red pepper seasoning

Remove outer husks of corn but not tightly clinging inner husks; pull off tassels. Soak corn 1 hour in 6 quarts salt water. Meanwhile, pour remaining salt water in a very large deep kettle, add a rack and cover with a thin layer of seaweed or, if unavailable, outer corn husks which have been soaked well in salt water. Drain soaked ears and arrange on rack. Add lobsters and potatoes, then top with clams and more seaweed or husks. Cover tightly and bring to a boil; reduce heat so water stays at a slow simmer and steam ¾–1 hour. Lift out clams and serve with condiments as a first course. Meanwhile, clambake should be re-covered and allowed to steam until potatoes are tender. They will be done by the time everyone has finished with the clams. Pile lobsters, potatoes, and corn on huge platters and serve at once with the condiments. Set out bibs, lobster crackers and picks, and plenty of napkins. About 570 calories for each of 6 servings, 430 calories for each of 8 servings.

CONCH

Conch (pronounced *konk*) isn't everyone's dish—too tough, too strong. But those who live where it's caught— Florida, the Gulf Coast, and West Indies—consider it something special. It's available year round, live and in the shell; also frozen (cooked or uncooked) and canned.

Amount to Buy: 1 pound conch in the shell per person; ¼–⅓ pound conch meat.

For Top Quality: Buy the conch right off the boat or from a market whose word you trust.

How to Cook Conch

Because of its rubbery texture and strong ocean flavor, conch is best stewed or ground into fritters or patties. It can also be sautéed, *if* first parboiled until tender. Frozen conch need not be thawed before using.

General Preparation (for all cooking methods): Everyone familiar with conch has a pet way to tenderize it. The most effective ways seem to be parboiling or pounding with a mallet. But first: scrub conch shell well under cold running water, place in a large heavy kettle, add boiling water to cover, 1 tablespoon salt, and ¼ cup lemon juice. Cover and boil 3 minutes; drain in a colander under cold running water until easy to handle. Pry

meat from shell with a strong, long-tined fork, cut off hard black "foot" and tightly curled tip. Wash again in cold water. Conch is now ready to simmer into soups or stews. If it is to be panfried or made into fritters, it should be parboiled.

To Parboil: Leave conch meat whole or slice thin; place in a saucepan, add water to cover, and for each pint water add 1 tablespoon lemon juice. Cover and simmer until tender, about 1½–2 hours for sliced conch, 2–4 hours for the whole. Drain well.

BAHAMIAN CONCH CHOWDER

A hearty main dish containing conch, carrots, tomatoes, and potatoes.
Makes 4 servings

1 pound conch meat, prepared for cooking
3 tablespoons butter, margarine, or cooking oil
1 large yellow onion, peeled and minced
2 cloves garlic, peeled and crushed
2 carrots, peeled and cut in small dice
2 tomatoes, peeled, cored, seeded, and chopped fine
⅛ teaspoon crushed hot red chili peppers
⅛ teaspoon curry powder
1 (6-ounce) can tomato paste
1 quart water (about)
1½ teaspoons salt (about)
3 small potatoes, peeled and cut in ½" cubes

Cut conch meat into ½" cubes. Melt butter in a large saucepan over moderate heat and stir-fry onion, garlic, carrots, tomatoes, peppers and curry powder 3–5 minutes. Add conch and stir 1 minute. Add tomato paste, water, and salt, cover, and simmer 1½–2 hours until conch is very tender; replenish water as needed to keep chowder from getting too thick. Add potatoes and simmer 10–15 minutes longer until tender. Serve piping hot. About 340 calories per serving.

VARIATION:

Omit potatoes and stir 1½ cups boiled rice into chowder just before serving. About 335 calories per serving.

⚖ SCUNGILLI MARINARA

Scungilli is the Italian word for conch, and *marinara* is a favorite Italian way of preparing it—with tomatoes, garlic, and onion.
Makes 4 servings

½ cup minced yellow onion
1 clove garlic, peeled and crushed
2 tablespoons olive oil
1 (1-pound) can Italian plum tomatoes (*do not drain*)
¼ cup tomato paste
½ cup dry red wine
½ teaspoon sugar
1 teaspoon salt
1 teaspoon oregano
⅛ teaspoon pepper
1 pound sliced parboiled conch meat
2 tablespoons finely grated Parmesan cheese

Sauté onion and garlic in oil in a large saucepan over moderate heat 8–10 minutes until golden. Turn heat to low, add all remaining ingredients except conch and cheese, cover, and simmer 1 hour, stirring occasionally. If mixture becomes too thick, thin with a little water. Cool sauce slightly and purée in an electric blender at low speed or put through a food mill. Return to pan, add conch, cover, and simmer 3–5 minutes. Mix in cheese and serve hot over spaghetti or other pasta. About 280 calories per serving.

⚖ PANFRIED CONCH AND ONIONS

Makes 4–6 servings

1½ pounds sliced parboiled conch meat
2 large yellow onions, peeled, sliced thin, and separated into rings
¼ cup butter, margarine, or cooking oil
½ teaspoon salt
⅛ teaspoon pepper

Pat conch slices very dry on paper toweling. Stir-fry onions in butter in a large, heavy skillet 3–5 minutes over moderately high heat until limp. Add conch and stir-fry 3–5 minutes longer until lightly browned. Season and serve.

About 275 calories for each of 4 servings, 180 calories for each of 6 servings.

VARIATION:

⚖ **Breaded Fried Conch:** Omit onions. Dredge conch slices in flour, dip in lightly beaten egg, and roll in fine dry bread crumbs or cracker meal to coat. Use cooking oil for the frying and increase amount to 1 cup. Heat oil in a deep, heavy skillet until a cube of bread will sizzle, add breaded conch slices, and fry 3–4 minutes until nicely crisp and brown. Drain on paper toweling and serve with Tartar Sauce. About 305 calories for each of 4 servings (without Tartar Sauce), 200 calories for each of 6 servings.

⚖ CONCH BURGERS

Makes 4–6 servings

2 cups finely ground parboiled conch meat
2 cups soft white bread crumbs
2 eggs, lightly beaten
1 tablespoon Worcestershire sauce
¼ teaspoon liquid hot red pepper seasoning
½ teaspoon minced garlic
1 tablespoon grated yellow onion
¼ cup unsifted flour
3 tablespoons butter, margarine, bacon drippings, or cooking oil

Mix conch with all remaining ingredients except flour and butter. Shape into 6 patties and dredge with flour. Heat butter in a large skillet over moderate heat and brown patties 3–4 minutes on each side. Serve hot with Tartar Sauce or Tomato Sauce. About 280 calories for each of 4 servings, 185 calories for each of 6 servings.

CRABS

After shrimp, crab rates as America's favorite shellfish. Easterners insist nothing beats blue crabs for succulence, flavor, and versatility but they get an argument from Westerners, to whom Dungeness is *the* crab. Fortunately, both coasts are blessed with an abundance of crabs. And fortunately, modern packing and shipping have brought fresh and frozen crabs to every state.

The Kinds of Crabs

There are five popular crabs in America; three are widely known, two are local specialties.

Blue Crabs: Far and away the biggest seller. Blue crabs come from Atlantic and Gulf coasts but are at their best in Chesapeake Bay. Depending upon season, they are *hard* or *soft shell.* Soft-shell crabs are nothing more than hard-shell crabs that have molted or shucked their hard shells. Choicest crab meat is that from the back—snowy, white, and sweet; claw meat has tinges of brown.

Dungeness: The king of the West Coast, 2–3 times the size of the blue crab. Meat is pinkish-white and delectably sweet.

Alaska King Crab: A giant sometimes measuring 6 feet across and weighing 20 pounds. Only the scarlet-skinned white leg meat is eaten.

Rock Crab: Taken from both New England and California coasts, these crabs are not well known elsewhere. Their meat has excellent flavor but is tan to brown in color.

Stone Crab: This Miami-Florida Keys favorite is practically all claw. It is rarely available outside Florida.

The Season for Fresh Crabs

Blue Crabs:

Hard Shell: Year round though supply is limited in cold weather.

Soft Shell: July and August.

Dungeness: Mid-November to late July in California, year round in the Pacific Northwest.

Alaska King Crab: Year round, but only available frozen.

Rock Crabs: Year round with supplies limited in winter.

Stone Crabs: Mid-October to June.

About Buying Fresh Crabs

Popular Market Forms:

Blue Crabs:

Hard Shell: Live in the shell; iced tins of fresh-cooked crab meat: choicest is *lump* or *backfin,* solid chunks from the back containing little shell or cartilage; *flake* is less expensive and contains bits and pieces of meat and considerably more shell (good for ramekins and casseroles where appearance doesn't matter so much); also sometimes available are reasonably priced *mixtures of flake and dark claw meat.*

Soft Shell: Live.

Alaska King Crab: Not available fresh.

Dungeness: Live or cooked in the shell; cooked meat.

Rock Crabs: Live in the shell.

Stone Crabs: Live in the shell.

Amount Needed: Allow about 1 pound crab in the shell per person, ¼–⅓ pound crab meat, depending upon how it is to be prepared. Hard-shell blue crabs weigh from ¼–1 pound, the soft shell considerably less. Though some people can easily eat half a dozen soft-shell crabs, 3–4 make a respectable portion. Dungeness crabs weigh 1¾ to 3½ pounds and Alaska king crabs from 6–20. Rock crabs are small, about ⅓–½ pound apiece. Weight matters less with stone crabs since it's the claw that's eaten; allow about 4 claws per person.

For Top Quality: If crabs are alive, make sure they are also *lively.* When buying fresh-cooked crab meat, look for that with a sweet-clean smell.

About Frozen and Canned Crab

The best known frozen crab is the Alaska king; it is precooked, then frozen in or out of the shell. Cooked Dungeness and blue crab meat is also frozen; so, too, are uncooked soft-shell crabs and stone crab claws. All of the popular American crabs are canned.

How to Use Frozen Crab: Always thaw or not as package directions or recipes direct; when crab is to be thawed, always do so in the refrigerator. *How to Use Canned Crab:* This is fully cooked and particularly suited to crab cakes, deviled crab, casseroles—whenever appearance is not the first consideration.

How to Clean and Cook Crabs

With the exception of soft-shell crabs, which can be sautéed or deep-fat-fried, live crabs are best simply boiled or steamed. They may be eaten as is with a suitable sauce or butter or the meat may be taken from the shell and used in a variety of ways (see recipes that follow).

Hard-Shell Crabs:

Blue Crabs, Rock Crabs: Cook, then clean.

To Boil: Bring a large kettle of sea water or lightly salted water to a boil (allow 1 tablespoon salt to 1 quart water), grab crabs, 1 at a time, across center back of shell and drop into water. As soon as water returns to a boil, cover and simmer 8 minutes per pound of crabs. Drain, rinse under cool running water, and when cool enough to handle clean as directed below.

To Steam: Plunge live crabs in a kettle of hot tap water—it should not be steaming hot, just a bit too hot for your hands. When crabs stop kicking, drain and, if necessary, scrub in warm water with a soft brush to remove bits of mud and sand. Old salts from crab country pooh-pooh the idea of scrubbing, but it does make the crabs more pleasant to eat. Place a rack in a large, deep kettle and pour in about 1½" boiling water or, better yet, boiling sea water. Pile crabs up on rack so that they are well out of the water, cover and steam 25–30 minutes, just until crabs turn bright orange and their shells rise

slightly. Lift crabs from kettle with tongs, drain briefly on paper toweling, and serve hot. Set out lobster or nut crackers and picks and lots of melted butter.

To Clean: Break off claws as close to body as possible, then cut or break off legs. Get a firm grip on top shell and pull off. Scrape all feathery, spongy material from center of body, also the soft, yellowish stomach and digestive tract. Encasing the choice lump crab meat now is a thin inner skeleton; pull or slice off either the left or right half,

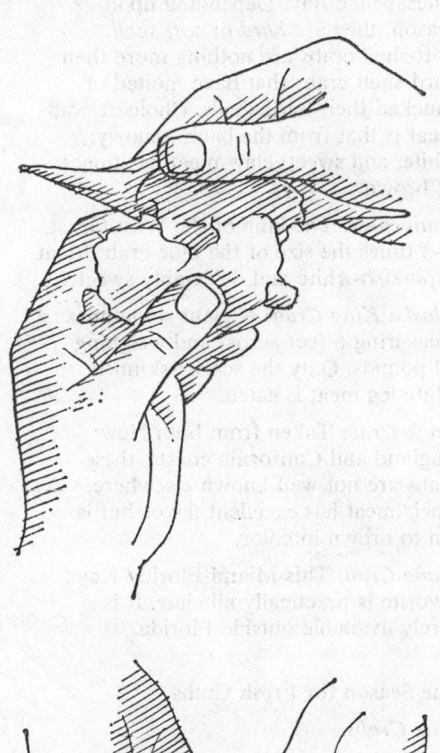

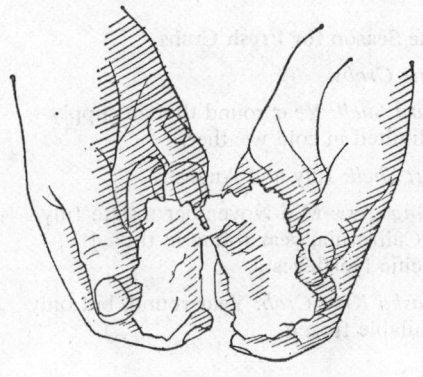

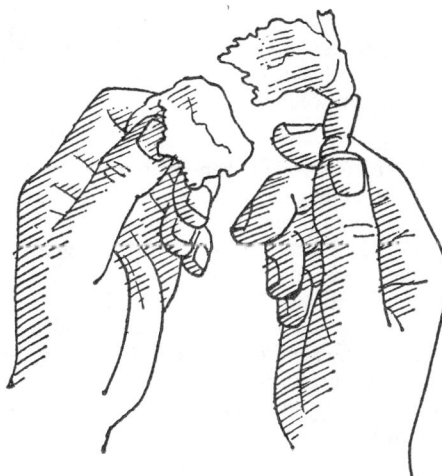

scrape any meat from cut-off piece and reserve, then scoop out chunks of meat in body pockets and reserve. Repeat with other half of body. Crack claws and legs and pull or pick out meat, using a lobster or nut pick for stubborn bits.

Dungeness Crabs: People disagree as to whether live Dungeness crabs should be cooked and then cleaned or vice versa. Take your choice.

To Clean: Wear rubber gloves to protect your hands from jagged pieces of shell. Grab crab from behind, getting a good grip on its body and two hind legs. Lay crab on its back on a large cutting board, place a sharp knife along midline and hit hard with a mallet to kill crab instantly. Twist off front claws, 1 at a time, where they join body; also twist off legs. Scrub claws and legs well and set aside. Pry off shell, using a knife if necessary, and scrape out spongy gills; save creamy "crab butter" underneath to use in sauces. Crack each segment of claws and legs and rinse well. Split crab body down midline, then cut each half into manageable (about 1½″) chunks and rinse well.

To Boil: Bring a large kettle of sea water or lightly salted water (1 tablespoon salt to each quart water) to a boil, drop in crab, and when water returns to a boil, cover and simmer 10–12 minutes for cracked crab, 15–20 for whole crab, depending on size. Drain and serve hot with melted butter. If crab has been boiled whole, clean and crack as described above before eating.

VARIATION:

California Cold Cracked Crab: Clean and crack crab and boil as directed. Drain, cool, then chill several hours. Serve on beds of cracked ice with freshly made Mayonnaise.

Stone Crabs: Only the claw meat is eaten, so little cleaning is needed. Twist off claws, scrub well, then drop in lightly salted boiling water to cover, cover, and boil 15–20 minutes. Drain and serve hot with melted butter or cool and serve with mayonnaise or Sauce Verte. Set out lobster crackers and picks.

Soft-Shell Blue Crabs:

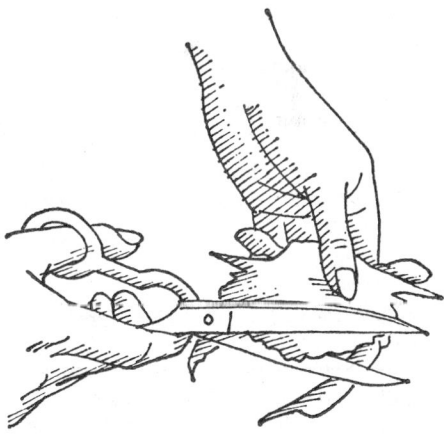

To Clean: With scissors, cut off "face" portion just behind eyes. Lift up shell by the points and cut out feathery, spongy gills; also scoop or cut out yellowish digestive organs. Rinse crabs well under cool running water to remove any yellow traces and pat dry on paper toweling.

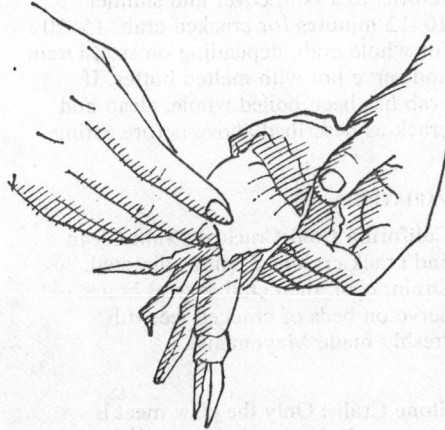

Turn crab on its back and cut off apron or tail flap folded underneath body; smooth soft shell back in place. Crab is now ready to cook. Everything remaining is edible—legs, claws, soft shell, body.

To Panfry (*Sauté*): Clean crabs as directed. Dredge lightly in seasoned flour. Melt ¼–⅓ cup butter or margarine in a large, heavy skillet over moderate heat and, when beginning to foam, add crabs and sauté about 3 minutes on a side until crisp and golden brown. (*Note:* Work carefully because crabs will sputter in the hot butter.) Do only 3–4 at a time, drain well on paper toweling, and set uncovered in an oven turned to lowest heat to keep warm while you fry the rest.

VARIATIONS:

Soft-Shell Crabs à la Meunière: Dredge and sauté crabs as above. When all are done, melt 1–2 tablespoons fresh butter in skillet and squeeze in the juice of ½ lemon. Pour over crabs, sprinkle with minced parsley, and serve.

Breaded Soft-Shell Crabs: Clean crabs as directed. Dip in lightly beaten egg, then in fine dry bread crumbs or cracker meal to coat. Heat about ⅛″ cooking oil or a ½ and ½ mixture of cooking oil and butter in a large, heavy skillet over moderate heat, add 3–4 crabs, and

sauté 3 minutes on each side until crisply golden. Drain on paper toweling, sprinkle with salt and pepper, and serve with lemon wedges.

To Deep-Fat-Fry: Clean crabs as directed and bread as above. Meanwhile, heat oil or shortening in a deep fat fryer to 375° F. Place 2–3 crabs in fryer basket, lower into fat, and fry 3–4 minutes until nicely browned and crisp. Drain on paper toweling and keep warm while frying remaining crabs. Always scoop any browned crumbs from fat before adding more crabs. Serve with lemon wedges.

To Broil: Clean crabs as directed and dredge in flour or, if you prefer, bread as for panfrying. Preheat broiler. Arrange crabs on their backs on a lightly oiled broiler rack. Drizzle with melted butter or margarine and broil 4″–5″ from the heat about 3 minutes until lightly browned. Turn, drizzle again with melted butter, and broil 3 minutes longer until crisp and golden brown. Watch closely toward the end.

VARIATION:

Lemon-Broiled Soft-Shell Crabs: Broil as directed, using Lemon Butter for basting instead of plain butter.

How to Eat Crabs in the Shell

Blue Crabs, Rock Crabs:
(1) Twist off claws and legs and set aside.
(2) Pull off top shell, scrape out and discard feathery gray-white gills and yellowish digestive organs.
(3) Peel or cut away thin inner "shell" covering body; underneath is the best part of the crab. Pull out the plump chunks of meat with a small fork or pick, dipping each morsel in accompanying sauce or butter.
(4) Crack each segment of claws and twist out meat with a small fork or pick.
(5) Treat legs like soda straws, sucking one end to get out any bits of meat inside.

Dungeness: Because of their size, these crabs are nearly always cleaned and cracked before they are served. If for some reason a whole crab comes to the table, attack it following directions for cleaning Dungeness crab.

Stone Crabs: Only the claws are served in the shell; crack with lobster crackers and twist out meat with a small fork or pick.

Alaska King Crab Legs: These present no problem because enough meat is exposed to make eating easy. Simply pull it out with a fork and cut as needed into bite-size chunks and eat, first dunking into any accompanying butter or sauce.

⚖ ⬚ **SPICED BLUE CRABS**

Makes 4–6 servings

1 quart cider vinegar
⅓ cup salt
1 celery stalk
¼ cup powdered mustard
¼ cup whole cloves
3 tablespoons cayenne pepper
2 tablespoons ginger
1 tablespoon mace
1½ gallons boiling water
2 dozen medium-size live blue crabs

Place all ingredients except crabs in a 3-gallon enamel or stainless-steel kettle, bring to a boil, cover, and simmer 5 minutes. Add crabs, cover, and simmer 15 minutes. Drain and serve hot or cool, chill, and serve cold. Set out several sets of lobster crackers and picks. About 105 calories for each of 4 servings, 70 calories for each of 6 servings.

⬚ **BAKED ALASKA KING CRAB LEGS**

Since Alaska king crab legs are always packaged fully cooked, they only need to be heated through before eating. Makes 2 servings

1 (12-ounce) package frozen ready split Alaska king crab legs (do not thaw)

½ cup melted butter or margarine
½ clove garlic, peeled and crushed (optional)
Juice of ½ lemon

Preheat oven to 400° F. Place crab legs, flesh side up, in an ungreased shallow baking pan. Mix butter, garlic, and lemon juice and brush over crab legs. Bake, uncovered, 15 minutes until bubbly, brushing often with butter mixture. About 300 calories per serving.

VARIATIONS:

⚖ **Low-Calorie Baked King Crab Legs:** Prepare as directed, substituting low-calorie Italian, garlic, or herb dressing for the butter mixture. About 125 calories per serving.

Baked Herbed King Crab Legs: Prepare as directed but omit garlic from melted butter. Add instead 2 teaspoons each minced parsley and fresh tarragon, chervil, or dill or 1 teaspoon parsley flakes and ¼ teaspoon dried tarragon, chervil, or dill. About 300 calories per serving.

Baked Italian-Style King Crab Legs: Prepare as directed, substituting olive oil for butter and adding ¼ teaspoon oregano. About 350 calories per serving.

Barbecued King Crab Legs: Prepare as directed, substituting any barbecue sauce for the melted butter mixture. About 355 calories per serving.

Baked Sherried King Crab Legs: Prepare as directed, but omit garlic from butter mixture and substitute 3 tablespoons dry sherry for the lemon juice. About 315 calories per serving.

Broiled King Crab Legs: Prepare any of the above recipes but, instead of baking, broil 4″–5″ from the heat about 10–12 minutes until bubbly and lightly browned. About 300 calories per serving.

⚔ ☒ **HERBED CRAB SAUTÉ**

Makes 4 servings

⅓ cup unsalted butter
1 pound fresh lump or backfin crab
    meat, well picked over, or 1 pound
    cooked stone crab meat, well picked
    over, or 3 (6-ounce) packages frozen
    Alaska king crab meat, thawed and
    drained
1 tablespoon minced parsley
1 tablespoon minced fresh chives
½ teaspoon minced fresh tarragon or
    chervil
⅓ cup dry white wine
Juice of ½ lemon
1 tablespoon minced capers
½ teaspoon salt
Pinch pepper

Melt butter in a large, heavy skillet
over moderate heat, add crab and herbs,
and sauté 2–3 minutes. Add remaining
ingredients, sauté 5 minutes longer, and
serve. Particularly good over hot
buttered toast. About 260 calories per
serving (without toast).

CRAB CIOPPINO

A favorite California crab stew filled
with tomatoes and studded with shrimp
and clams.
Makes 4–6 servings

1 medium-sized yellow onion, peeled and
    minced
1 stalk celery, minced
½ sweet green pepper, cored, seeded,
    and minced
1 clove garlic, peeled and crushed
⅓ cup olive oil
6 large ripe tomatoes, peeled, cored, and
    coarsely chopped
¼ cup tomato paste
1 bay leaf, crumbled
1 teaspoon salt
½ teaspoon oregano
½ teaspoon basil
½ teaspoon pepper
1 cup dry red wine
1½ cups water (about)
1 (3–3½-pound) Dungeness crab,
    cleaned and cracked

1 pound raw shrimp in the shell
1½ dozen littleneck clams in the shell,
    well scrubbed

Stir-fry onion, celery, green pepper, and
garlic in the oil in a large, heavy kettle
8–10 minutes over moderate heat until
golden; add all remaining ingredients
except seafood, cover, and simmer
1½–2 hours until flavors are well
blended. If sauce becomes too thick (it
should be about the consistency of a
medium white sauce), thin with a little
water or wine. Taste for salt and pepper
and adjust as needed. Add all seafood to
sauce, cover, and simmer 12–15 minutes
longer or until shrimp and crab turn
orange and clams open. Serve from a
giant tureen with buttery crusts of
Italian bread and a dry red wine. About
600 calories for each of 4 servings
(without bread), about 400 calories for
each of 6 servings.

☒ **QUICK CRAB NEWBURG**

Makes 6 servings

⅓ cup butter or margarine
1 pound crab meat (fresh, thawed
    frozen, or drained canned), well
    picked over
¼ teaspoon seasoned pepper
1 pint sour cream, at room temperature
2 tablespoons tomato paste
2 tablespoons dry sherry
2 tablespoons finely grated Parmesan
    cheese

Melt butter in a large skillet over
moderately low heat. Add crab and
stir-fry 2–3 minutes. Mix in remaining
ingredients and heat 2–3 minutes,
stirring gently (do not boil). Serve over
boiled rice or lightly buttered hot toast.
About 350 calories per serving (without
rice or toast).

⚔ ☒ **CRAB MEAT NORFOLK**

One of the easiest ways to prepare crab
and one of the most delicately seasoned.
Makes 4 servings

1 pound fresh lump or backfin crab
    meat, well picked over
4 teaspoons white wine vinegar

¼ teaspoon salt
⅛ teaspoon cayenne pepper
Pinch black pepper
⅓ cup butter or margarine

Preheat oven to 375° F. Mix crab
lightly with vinegar, salt, and pepper.
Place in an ungreased 1-quart *au gratin*
dish or shallow casserole and dot evenly
with butter. Bake, uncovered, 15–20
minutes until bubbly. About 240 calories
per serving.

⊠ CRAB MORNAY

Crab baked in a rich cheese sauce.
Makes 4 servings

*1 pound fresh lump or backfin crab
    meat, well picked over
1¾ cups Mornay Sauce
¼ cup finely grated Gruyère or
    Parmesan cheese*

Preheat oven to 375° F. Toss crab with
Mornay sauce to mix, spoon into an
ungreased 1-quart *au gratin* dish or
shallow casserole, and scatter cheese on
top. Bake, uncovered 15–20 minutes
until bubbly, then broil quickly to brown
About 390 calories per serving.

VARIATION:

Crab à la Florentine: Butter a 1½-
quart *au gratin* dish and cover bottom
with a layer of chopped, buttered
spinach. Mix crab and Mornay sauce as
directed and spoon over spinach. Top
with ½ cup soft white bread crumbs
mixed with 2 tablespoons melted butter,
sprinkle lightly with paprika, and bake
as directed. About 500 calories per
serving.

CRAB IMPERIAL NEWBURG

Good with fluffy boiled rice, a crisp
green salad, and a well-chilled dry white
wine.
Makes 4–6 servings

*1 pound fresh lump or backfin crab
    meat, well picked over
3 tablespoons butter or margarine
2 tablespoons flour
1½ cups light cream*

*3 egg yolks, lightly beaten
1 teaspoon salt
2 teaspoons prepared horseradish
1 teaspoon powdered mustard
¼ teaspoon cayenne pepper
1 tablespoon paprika
3 tablespoons dry sherry*

Preheat oven to 350° F. Place crab in
an ungreased 1½-quart *au gratin* dish or
shallow casserole. Melt butter in a small
saucepan over moderate heat and blend
in flour. Add cream and heat, stirring,
until thickened and smooth. Spoon a
little hot sauce into yolks, then return
all to saucepan; turn heat to low and
warm, stirring, 1 minute—no longer.
Off heat mix in remaining ingredients;
pour sauce evenly over crab and bake,
uncovered, ½–¾ hour until bubbly.
About 435 calories for each of 4
servings, 290 calories for each of
6 servings.

DEVILED CRAB I

A delicate deviled crab.
Makes 4 servings

*4 hard-cooked eggs
2 tablespoons butter or margarine
2 tablespoons flour
1¼ cups milk
1 teaspoon paprika
½ teaspoon powdered mustard
¼ teaspoon cayenne pepper
1 tablespoon Worcestershire sauce
Juice of ½ lemon
2 tablespoons minced parsley
½ teaspoon salt
1 pound fresh lump or backfin crab
    meat, well picked over*

Topping:

*⅓ cup fine dry bread crumbs mixed
    with 2 tablespoons melted butter or
    margarine*

Preheat oven to 375° F. Chop egg
whites fine; sieve the yolks and set
aside. Melt butter in a small saucepan
over moderate heat and blend in flour.
Add milk and heat, stirring, until
thickened and smooth. Off heat mix in
sieved yolks and all remaining
ingredients except egg whites, crab, and

topping. Place crab and egg whites in a
buttered shallow 1½-quart casserole, add
sauce, and stir well to mix. Sprinkle
topping over surface and bake,
uncovered, 1 hour until browned and
bubbly. About 380 calories per serving.

DEVILED CRAB II

A richer, spicier recipe.
Makes 6 servings

1½ pounds fresh lump or backfin crab
  meat, well picked over
¼ cup butter or margarine
2 tablespoons minced shallots or
  scallions
¼ cup unsifted flour
½ teaspoon powdered mustard
1 cup light cream
½ cup milk
½ cup dry sherry
Juice of ½ lemon
2 tablespoons prepared spicy brown
  mustard
2 tablespoons prepared mild yellow
  mustard
2 teaspoons ketchup
1 teaspoon Worcestershire sauce
1 tablespoon minced parsley
¼ teaspoon salt
⅛ teaspoon cayenne pepper

Topping:

½ cup cracker meal mixed with
  2 tablespoons melted butter or
  margarine

Preheat oven to 375° F. Place crab in
an ungreased shallow 2-quart casserole
or au gratin dish. Melt butter in a large
saucepan over moderate heat and sauté
shallots 5–8 minutes or until pale
golden. Blend in flour and powdered
mustard then add cream and milk and
heat, stirring constantly, until thickened
and smooth. Off heat mix in all
remaining ingredients except topping.
Pour over crab and toss lightly. Sprinkle
topping over surface and bake,
uncovered, 1 hour until browned and
bubbly. About 415 calories per serving.

BAKED CRAB-STUFFED AVOCADOS

Makes 6 servings

3 tablespoons butter or margarine
2 tablespoons flour
½ cup light cream
½ cup milk
½ teaspoon salt
⅛ teaspoon white pepper
1 tablespoon minced chives
1 tablespoon capers
½ pound crab meat (fresh, thawed
  frozen, or drained canned), well
  picked over
3 medium-size ripe avocados
2 tablespoons lemon juice

Preheat oven to 350° F. Melt butter in
a saucepan over moderate heat. Blend
in flour, slowly add cream and milk, and
cook, stirring, until thickened and
smooth. Off heat mix in salt, pepper,
chives, capers, and crab. Peel, halve, and
pit avocados; brush well with lemon
juice and place in a well-buttered
shallow baking pan. Fill with crab
mixture and bake, uncovered, 25–30
minutes until avocados are heated
through. About 335 calories per serving.

⊠ ROSY KING CRAB BAKE

Makes 2 servings

2 tablespoons minced shallots or yellow
  onion
3 tablespoons butter or margarine
3 tablespoons flour
1 cup light cream
2 tablespoons chili sauce
2 tablespoons dry white wine
½ teaspoon salt
¼ teaspoon celery salt
¼ teaspoon paprika
⅛ teaspoon cayenne pepper
1 (6-ounce) package frozen Alaska king
  crab meat, thawed and drained

Preheat oven to 400° F. Stir-fry shallots
in butter in a small saucepan 3–5
minutes over moderate heat until limp.
Blend in flour, add cream, and heat,
stirring, until thickened and smooth.
Blend in all remaining ingredients except

crab and heat 1–2 minutes. Fold in crab, spoon into a buttered 1-quart *au gratin* dish or shallow casserole, and bake, uncovered, 15–20 minutes until bubbly. Serve over boiled rice. About 550 calories per serving (without rice).

BAKED STUFFED DUNGENESS CRAB

Makes 2 servings

1 (2-pound) Dungeness crab, boiled in the shell and cooled
2 tablespoons butter or margarine
2 teaspoons minced chives
⅛ teaspoon pepper
1 hard-cooked egg, shelled and chopped fine
1 tablespoon capers, drained and minced
¼ cup fine dry bread crumbs mixed with 1 tablespoon melted butter or margarine

Preheat oven to 450° F. Clean crab and remove meat from body, claws, and legs*; leave large back shell intact. Pick over crab meat, discarding bits of shell and cartilage, and flake. Melt butter in a skillet over moderately low heat, add crab, and stir-fry 2–3 minutes; mix in chives, pepper, egg, and capers. Spoon into shell, top with buttered crumbs, and place in a shallow baking pan. Bake, uncovered, 10 minutes, then broil 4" from the heat 2–3 minutes to brown lightly. Serve in the shell. About 450 calories per serving.

VARIATIONS:

Pilaf Stuffed Dungeness Crab: Prepare crab mixture as directed, but when stir-frying crab meat in butter, add ½ cup cold cooked rice. Proceed as directed. About 495 calories per serving.

Frisco-Style Stuffed Dungeness Crab: Prepare crab mixture as directed but omit capers. Off heat, stir in ½ cup Medium White Sauce, ¼ cup sautéed minced mushrooms, and 2 tablespoons dry sherry. Spoon into shell, top with buttered crumbs, and bake as directed. About 650 calories per serving.

⚖ ⊠ MARYLAND CRAB CAKES

Spicily seasoned.
Makes 4 servings

1 pound fresh lump or backfin crab meat, well picked over
2 eggs, lightly beaten
2 tablespoons mayonnaise
1 tablespoon prepared horseradish
1 tablespoon prepared spicy brown mustard
1 tablespoon minced parsley
¼ teaspoon salt
¼ teaspoon liquid hot red pepper seasoning
Pinch pepper
⅔ cup cracker meal
⅓ cup cooking oil

Mix crab well with all but last 2 ingredients and shape into cakes about 3" across and ½" thick; dip in cracker meal to coat well. Heat oil in a large, heavy skillet over moderately high heat until a cube of bread will sizzle, add cakes, and brown 3–4 minutes on a side. Drain well on paper toweling and serve with Tartar Sauce. About 255 calories per serving (without tartar sauce).

⊠ HOT CRAB BURGERS

Makes 4–6 servings

¾ cup butter or margarine
2 (7½-ounce) cans crab meat, drained and well picked over
2 tablespoons cider vinegar
2 tablespoons minced pimiento
¼ cup minced celery
1 tablespoon minced parsley
½ teaspoon salt
⅛ teaspoon pepper
½ cup heavy cream
4–6 hamburger or hot dog buns, split and toasted

Melt butter in a skillet over moderately low heat. Add crab and stir-fry 2–3 minutes. Add all remaining ingredients except buns and simmer uncovered, stirring occasionally, 15 minutes. Fill buns with crab mixture and serve. About 570 calories for each of 4 servings, 400 calories for each of 6 servings.

CRAB LOUIS

Makes 4 servings

1 quart crisp, coarsely shredded lettuce
*1 pound fresh-cooked crab meat, well
 picked over (Dungeness, lump, or
 backfin) or thawed frozen Alaska king
 crab*
4 tomatoes, quartered
*4 hard-cooked eggs, peeled and
 quartered*

Dressing:

1 cup mayonnaise
⅓ cup ketchup
¼ cup heavy cream, whipped
2 tablespoons finely grated scallions
2 tablespoons minced parsley
2 tablespoons minced sweet green pepper
2 teaspoons lemon juice
1 teaspoon prepared horseradish
Pinch salt

On 4 luncheon size plates, make beds of
lettuce. Mound crab on top. Mix dressing
and spoon over crab, then garnish each
plate with tomatoes and hard-cooked
eggs. About 800 calories per serving.

COOL CRAB CUP

Makes 4 servings

*1 pound fresh lump or backfin crab
 meat, well picked over*
1 cup shredded lettuce

Dressing:

2 teaspoons prepared horseradish
2 tablespoons chili sauce
2 tablespoons minced sweet green pepper
2 tablespoons minced dill pickle
1 tablespoon minced scallion
2 tablespoons lemon juice
½ teaspoon salt
⅛ teaspoon pepper
⅔ cup mayonnaise

Place crab in a mixing bowl. Mix
dressing, pour over crab, and toss lightly
to mix. Cover and chill several hours.
Serve on beds of shredded lettuce as a
first or main course. About 415 calories
per serving.

VARIATIONS:

Lobster Cup: Prepare as directed,
substituting 2 cups diced boiled lobster
for the crab. About 420 calories per
serving.

Shrimp Cup: Prepare as directed,
substituting 2 cups diced boiled shrimp
for the crab. If you prefer, use the
tiny Danish shrimp. About 445 calories
per serving.

Crab Stuffed Tomatoes or Avocados:
Prepare as directed but serve in
hollowed-out ripe tomatoes or in
avocado halves instead of on lettuce.
About 425 calories per serving if served
in tomatoes, about 600 calories per
serving if served in avocado halves.

CRAYFISH

Crawfish, crawdads, *écrevisse*—these are
the sweet-tender little fresh water cousins
of the lobster. To Europeans they are a
delicacy unsurpassed, and in Finland,
where the season begins at midnight on
July 15 and lasts a short two months, the
whole country rollicks with crayfish fests
(by tradition, every crayfish tail must be
followed by a swig of iced schnapps).
The American crayfish, at six inches, is
nearly twice as long as the European but
no less succulent. It is found in creeks
around Lake Michigan, in the Pacific
Northwest, and in Gulf Coast bayous.
The season varies from area to area but
is usually at its peak in mid or late
summer. Occasionally, crayfish are
shipped live to metropolitan areas; more
often they are canned.

Amount to Buy: Allow about 1 dozen
crayfish in the shell per person, more if
appetites are large (in Finland, 20 are
considered a "decent" portion) or about
⅓ pound crayfish meat per person.

For Top Quality: Buy crayfish that are
live and kicking.

How to Cook Crayfish

There is really only one way, experts will tell you—*boiling*—but the flavor of boiled crayfish varies markedly according to the seasonings used.

General Preparation: Wash crayfish carefully under cold running water; tear off the thin shell-like fin on the center-top of the tail (the dark, threadlike intestinal vein should come away with it).

To Boil: For each dozen crayfish, you will need 1 quart sea water (or 1 quart tap water mixed with 1 tablespoon salt) or 1 quart Simple Court Bouillon. Bring to a boil in a large, deep kettle, drop in live crayfish, cover, and simmer 5 minutes, just until crayfish turn scarlet. Drain and serve hot with melted butter or cool in broth and serve at room temperature.

VARIATION:

Finnish-Style Crayfish: Boil crayfish as directed in sea or salt water but add 1 large bunch fresh dill, preferably that which is beginning to flower, separated into stalks. Cool crayfish in cooking liquid to room temperature before serving. If you like, marinate crayfish in liquid 1–2 days in refrigerator, then bring to room temperature before serving.

How to Eat Crayfish

This is messy work, so give every guest a large bib and plenty of paper napkins. Also set out lots of ice cold beer.

(1) Twist off claws, snip off pointed tips, then separate claws at "elbow" joint. Slice off broad base of claws and suck meat out.
(2) Separate body of crayfish from tail and suck any meat from body (there will not be much).
(3) With the point of a knife, lift top shell from tail, take out tail meat, and remove dark vein, if any. Slosh meat in melted butter or place on lightly buttered toast and eat. This is the *pièce de résistance.*

LOBSTER

Of all America's seafoods, lobster is king. Steamed simply over sea water, or boiled in it with perhaps a sprig or two of seaweed, lobster is a thing of beauty (and a joy as long as it lasts). Underneath that scarlet armor, fat snowy chunks wait to be twisted out and sloshed in melted butter. What can top that? According to Down Easters (and all lobster lovers), nothing. Not the most glorious French soufflé, not the lordliest English sirloin.

The Kinds of Lobster

The best known—and best—is the giant clawed *American or Maine Lobster.* But there is another, the *rock or spiny lobster,* which swims in the Gulf of Mexico and in the warm waters off the coast of Southern California. It has no claws to speak of, but its tail is big and broad and full of delectable meat. Unfortunately, these lobsters are rarely available outside their immediate areas except as frozen tails.

About Buying Fresh Lobster

Season: Year round.

Popular Market Forms: Live in the shell; cooked in the shell; iced cooked lobster meat. It's no longer necessary to live in the East to buy live Maine lobsters; a number of firms will pack them in seaweed and airmail them to you.

Amount Needed: Allow a 1–3-pound lobster per person, depending on appetites, and about ¼–⅓ pound lobster meat. Maine lobsters are graded in 4 sizes: chickens (¾–1 pound), quarters (1¼ pounds), large (1½–2¼ pounds), jumbo (2½ pounds up).

For Top Quality: Live lobsters should be thrashing about (be sure to have the claws pegged so you won't get nipped);

cooked whole lobsters should have a fresh "seashore" odor and their tails, when straightened out, should spring right back. Cooked, iced lobster meat should be firm and sweet smelling.

About Frozen and Canned Lobster

Frozen uncooked rock lobster tails are widely available; the plumpest and choicest come from South Africa and Australia. Also marketed are tins of frozen, cooked lobster meat, and in the gourmet line such classics as Lobster Newburg. Canned lobster meat and tails are generally stocked by groceries, as are canned lobster bisques, Newburgs, and thermidors. *To Cook Frozen Lobsters:* The tails are usually cooked solidly frozen (but read package directions); cooked frozen meat should be thawed before using. *How to Use Canned Lobster:* Because this meat is fully cooked, it is a good choice for salads and casseroles.

How to Cook Lobster

Lobster is marvelously adaptable, but it is at its best simply steamed, boiled, or baked. Broiling tends to dry it out (though lovers of broiled lobster will forever argue the point).

General Preparation: How lobster is prepared depends upon how it is to be cooked. For steaming or boiling it needs no preparation at all. For baking and broiling, however, it must be split live and, for certain other recipes, cut in large chunks.

To Split Live Lobsters: Don't be squeamish about cutting into a live lobster; it has little feeling. Place lobster

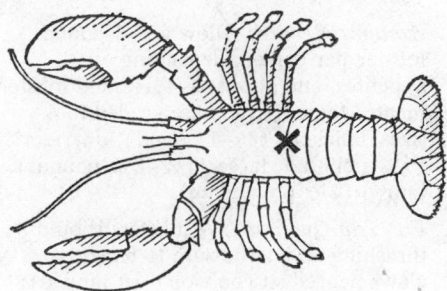

on its stomach with claws up over the head. Drive the point of a sharp sturdy knife into center back (X) where body meets tail (this kills lobster), and turn lobster on its back and quickly cut down through the body and head to split.

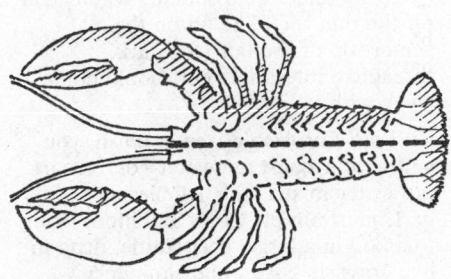

Now cut through tail (don't be alarmed if legs twitch a bit; these are simple muscular spasms and do not mean lobster is suffering). Spread halves flat, meat side up, and pull soft, beige intestinal vein from tail; discard papery stomach sac located just behind the eyes. Lift out coral (ovary and undeveloped roe) and buttery gray-green tomalley (liver) and save if they are to be used in sauces or stuffings; otherwise leave in place in the body cavity (they're great delicacies). Once in a great while, though law forbids their being taken, you may come upon a female just ready to lay eggs. These appear as a dark caviar-like mass in the body and upper tail and are considered the choicest of delicacies. Serve separately or mix into stuffings along with coral and tomalley.

To Clean and Crack Live Lobsters:

Follow all steps for splitting live lobsters; twist off claws and crack each section; cut body and tail into large or small chunks as individual recipes specify. Do not remove meat from shells unless directed otherwise. *Note to the Faint of Heart:* If you simply cannot bring yourself to cut into a live lobster, there is an alternative (although the finished lobster may not be quite so succulent). Bring a huge kettle of lightly salted water to a boil, drop in live lobsters, cover, and simmer 3–5 minutes just until they stop squirming. Drain, cool in a colander under cold running water until easy to handle, then split or clean and crack as directed.

To Boil: The best possible medium for boiling lobsters is sea water. If you haven't got it, you can fake it by adding 1 tablespoon salt to each quart water. Unless you have an absolutely colossal kettle, don't try to cook more than 2 lobsters in a pot. Bring 3–4 quarts sea or salt water to a boil, grasp lobsters, 1 at a time, by cupping your hand around back and plunge head first into boiling water. Cover and, from time water returns to a boil, cook 5–6 minutes per pound (1½-pound lobsters will take 8–9 minutes, 2-pound lobsters, 10–12). If lobsters are extra large, cook 5 minutes for the first pound and 4 minutes for each additional pound. *Simple Test for Doneness:* Pull one of the antennae on the head; if it comes easily from socket, lobster is done. Color of lobsters is important, too; when cooked they will be a dazzling scarlet. Drain lobsters and serve hot, either whole or split and cracked, with melted butter and lemon wedges. Or cook, chill, and serve with Sauce Verte.

VARIATIONS:

Savory Boiled Lobster: Prepare as directed, using a court bouillon instead of salt water.

Lobster Boiled in Beer: Boil as directed, using 2–2½ quarts beer or ale and 1–1½ quarts water instead of salt water. The beer gives the lobster extra-rich, slightly malty flavor.

To Steam: Pour 1″ sea or salt water into a large, heavy kettle and bring to a boil over moderately high heat. Add lobsters, cover, and steam 15 minutes. Serve hot or cold as you would boiled lobster.

To Bake: Preheat oven to 350° F. Split and clean live lobsters the (1½–2½-pound size is best) and arrange side by side, cut side up, in a large, shallow roasting pan. Cover exposed meat with pats of butter (each lobster will take ⅓–½ stick) and squeeze the juice of ½ lemon over each lobster. Bake, uncovered, 25–30 minutes, basting often with pan juices. Sprinkle with salt and freshly ground black pepper and serve at once.

To Oven Broil: Preheat broiler. Split and clean live lobster. Lay lobsters flesh side up as flat as possible on a foil-lined broiler pan, brush generously with melted butter or margarine, and broil 4″ from the heat 12–15 minutes, brushing often with melted butter, until lightly browned. Sprinkle with salt, pepper, and lemon juice and serve piping hot.

How to Eat Lobster

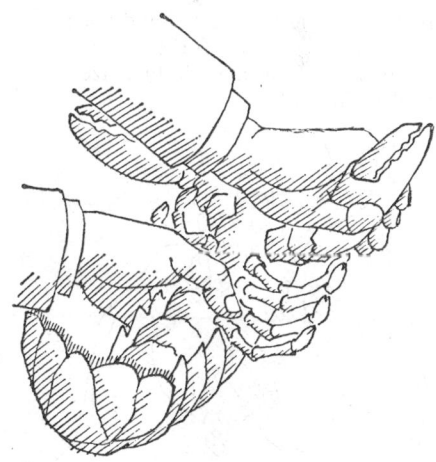

(1) Twist off claws, crack each in several places with lobster or nut crackers, and twist out meat with a fork.

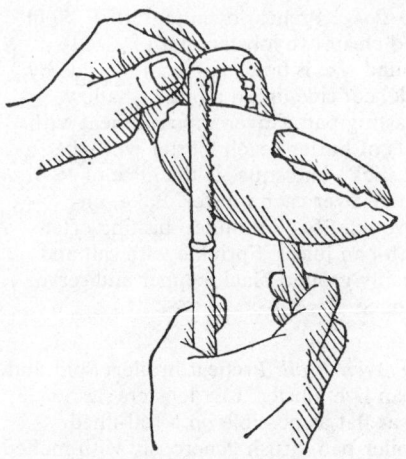

and arch left and right sides backward to split in two.

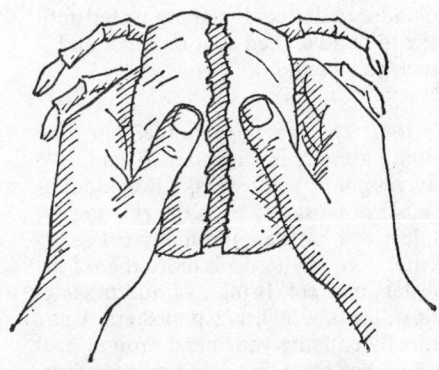

(2) Separate tail from body by arching lobster backward until it cracks.

The green tomalley and red coral are both in this part. Avoid grayish, feathery portions.

(4) Pull off lobster legs and suck each as you would a straw to get out any meat or juices inside.

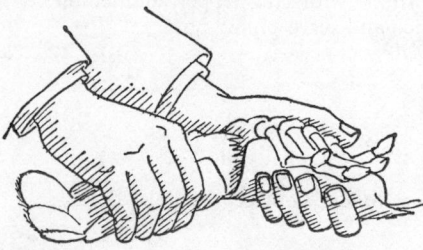

Break off fins at base of tail and push meat from shell with a fork; remove intestinal vein. Cut meat in bite-size chunks with fork.

LOBSTER NEWBURG I

The simple, classic version—perfect for a chafing dish.
Makes 4 servings

1 pound cooked lobster meat, cut in
  small chunks
¼ cup butter or margarine
½ cup medium-dry sherry
¼ teaspoon paprika
¾ teaspoon salt
1½ cups hot Velouté Sauce
¼ cup heavy cream

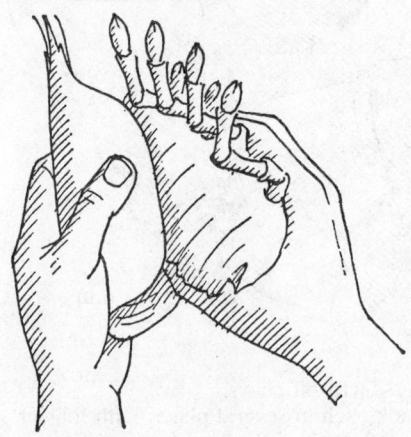

(3) Pull body from shell

Pick over lobster meat, separating out any bits of coral; sieve coral and reserve to use as a garnish. Stir-fry lobster meat in butter in a chafing dish skillet over direct, moderate heat 2–3 minutes; add sherry, paprika, and salt and simmer, uncovered, 2–3 minutes. Blend in sauce and cream, set over chafing dish warmer, and simmer, but do not boil 2–3 minutes. Sprinkle with coral, if any, or with a little paprika. Serve from chafing dish, ladling over boiled rice or into crisp pastry shells. About 480 calories per serving (without rice or pastry shells).

LOBSTER NEWBURG II

Delicately flavored but far richer than
Lobster Newburg I.
Makes 4 servings

*1 pound cooked lobster meat, cut in
    small chunks*
¼ cup butter or margarine
½ cup dry vermouth
¼ cup brandy
1¾ cups heavy cream
¾ teaspoon salt
Pinch pepper
Pinch nutmeg or mace
2 egg yolks, lightly beaten

Stir-fry lobster in butter in a large, heavy
skillet 2–3 minutes over moderate heat;
lift to a plate with a slotted spoon. Add
vermouth and brandy to skillet and boil
rapidly, stirring, until mixture just
covers bottom of skillet. Add cream and
simmer, stirring, until reduced by about
⅓. Mix in salt, pepper, and nutmeg; also
add lobster. Transfer to the top of a
double boiler and set over simmering
water. Mix a little hot sauce into yolks,
return to pan, and heat, stirring, 2–3
minutes until slightly thickened. Ladle
over boiled rice or into crisp pastry
shells or, if you prefer, transfer to a
chafing dish and serve at the table. About
695 calories per serving (without rice or
pastry shells).

BROILED LOBSTERS WITH HERB AND CRUMB STUFFING

Makes 4 servings

4 (1¼-pound) live lobsters
½ cup melted butter or margarine

Stuffing:

1 quart soft white bread crumbs
1 clove garlic, peeled and crushed
½ cup butter or margarine
¼ teaspoon salt
⅛ teaspoon pepper
2 tablespoons minced chives
2 tablespoons minced parsley

Preheat broiler. Split lobsters in half
lengthwise, remove stomach and
intestinal vein,* reserve any tomalley or
coral. Make stuffing by sautéing crumbs
and garlic in butter in a large, heavy
skillet over moderate heat 2–3 minutes
until pale golden; off heat mix in
remaining ingredients, also any tomalley
and chopped coral. Lay lobsters as flat as
possible, shell side down, on a foil-lined
broiler pan and brush generously with
melted butter. Broil 4″ from heat 12–15
minutes until lightly browned, brushing
often with butter. Remove from broiler,
mound stuffing into body cavity of each
lobster, return to broiler, and broil 2–3
minutes to brown lightly. Serve with
melted butter and lemon wedges. About
690 calories per serving.

VARIATION:

Prepare as directed, reducing bread
crumbs in stuffing to 3 cups and adding
1 cup finely chopped toasted blanched
almonds. About 870 calories per serving.

LOBSTER FRA DIAVOLO

Lobster prepared the Italian way in a
garlic-scented tomato sauce. It is flamed
with brandy just before serving.
Makes 4 servings

2 (1½-pound) live lobsters, cleaned,
    cracked, and cut in 2″ chunks
½ cup olive oil
*1 medium-size yellow onion, peeled and
    coarsely chopped*
1 clove garlic, peeled and crushed
1 teaspoon oregano
¼ teaspoon nutmeg
⅛ teaspoon cloves
½ teaspoon salt
⅛ teaspoon pepper
4 sprigs parsley
2 cups canned tomatoes
4 cups hot boiled rice
¼ cup brandy, warmed slightly

Sauté lobsters in oil in a large, heavy
kettle, turning often, about 5 minutes
until they turn a rich scarlet. Add onion,
garlic and seasonings and heat, stirring,
3–5 minutes. Add parsley and tomatoes,
cover, and simmer 15–20 minutes.
Arrange lobster in center of a large
platter, surround with rice and top with
kettle sauce. Pour brandy over lobster,

blaze with a match, and carry flaming to the table. About 575 calories per serving.

LOBSTER CARDINAL

Makes 2 servings

2 (1½-pound) lobsters, boiled, drained, split lengthwise, and cleaned
½ pound mushrooms, wiped clean and coarsely chopped
1 truffle, minced
3 tablespoons butter or margarine
1 tablespoon grated Parmesan cheese

Sauce:

1 cup hot Béchamel Sauce
½ cup boiled, minced lobster meat
⅓ cup heavy cream
½ teaspoon anchovy paste
Pinch cayenne pepper

Preheat broiler. Remove meat from lobsters; dice claw and body meat and slice tail ¼″–½″ thick. Mince enough tail meat to total ½ cup; reserve for sauce. Spread shells as flat as possible on a baking sheet and set aside. Sauté diced claw and body meat with mushrooms and truffle in butter about 5 minutes until mushrooms are limp; set aside while you prepare the sauce. Place Béchamel sauce in the top of a double boiler, add reserved minced lobster and remaining sauce ingredients; set over simmering water and heat, stirring, about 2–3 minutes. Mix a little sauce into mushroom mixture, just enough to bind. Make a bed of this mixture in each lobster shell, arrange tail slices on top and spoon enough sauce over all to coat. Sprinkle with Parmesan and broil 4″–5″ from the heat 3–4 minutes until browned and bubbly. About 710 calories per serving.

LOBSTER À L'AMÉRICAINE

Makes 4 servings

2 (1¼–1½-pound) live lobsters or 4 (8-ounce) frozen South African rock lobster tails
⅓ cup olive oil
¼ cup brandy

Sauce:

2 tablespoons butter or margarine
1 small yellow onion, peeled and minced
3 tablespoons minced shallots or scallions
1 clove garlic, peeled and crushed
2 large tomatoes, peeled, cored, seeded, and coarsely chopped
2 tablespoons tomato paste
2 cups dry white wine
2 tablespoons minced parsley
1 tablespoon minced fresh tarragon or 1 teaspoon dried tarragon
1 (4″) sprig fresh thyme or ½ teaspoon dried thyme
½ bay leaf
½ teaspoon salt
⅛ teaspoon cayenne pepper

If lobsters are live, clean*; twist off claws, crack, and reserve; cut tails crosswise into chunks at segmented divisions and cut body into 2″ chunks. Leave meat in shell and save any coral or tomalley for the sauce. If using frozen tails, simply cut crosswise into 1″ chunks while still solidly frozen. Stir-fry lobster in oil in a large, heavy skillet over moderate heat 3–5 minutes until shells turn scarlet; lift out lobster and set aside; do not drain off oil. In the same skillet, begin sauce: Melt butter and stir-fry onion, shallots, and garlic 3–5 minutes over moderate heat until limp. Mix in remaining sauce ingredients and simmer uncovered, stirring occasionally, about 1 hour. Sauce should have reduced by half; if not, boil rapidly to reduce. Strain sauce through a fine sieve into a large saucepan and set over low heat. Pour brandy over lobster and blaze with a match; when flames die, add lobster to sauce, cover, and simmer 12–15 minutes just to blend flavors. Mix in any tomalley and chopped coral, heat 1–2 minutes longer, and serve with boiled rice or Rice Pilaf. About 495 calories per serving (without rice or Rice Pilaf).

LOBSTER CANTONESE

Makes 4 servings

½ pound ground lean pork
1 clove garlic, peeled and crushed

3 tablespoons peanut or other cooking oil
2 cups chicken broth
¼ cup soy sauce
1 teaspoon sugar
1 teaspoon monosodium glutamate
  (MSG)
2 (1¼–1½-pound) live lobsters,
  cleaned,* cracked, and cut into 2"
  chunks
2 tablespoons cornstarch blended with ¼
  cup cold water
¼ cup scallions, minced (include green
  tops)
1 egg, lightly beaten

Stir-fry pork and garlic in oil in a *wok* or large, heavy skillet over moderate heat until pork is no longer pink. Mix in broth, soy sauce, sugar, and MSG; add lobsters, cover, and simmer 10 minutes. Add cornstarch mixture and heat, stirring, until thickened and clear. Stir in scallions, drizzle in egg, and cook, stirring, 2–3 minutes until egg is just set. Serve with boiled rice. About 395 calories per serving (without rice).

⊠ BROILED ROCK LOBSTER TAILS

Makes 4 servings

4 (8–12-ounce) thawed frozen rock
  lobster tails
2 tablespoons lemon juice
⅓ cup melted butter or margarine
⅛ teaspoon pepper

Preheat broiler. With kitchen shears, cut away thin undershell, exposing meat; bend tails backward until they crack and will almost lie flat. Arrange on a foil-lined broiler pan, shell side down, sprinkle with lemon juice, and brush liberally with butter. Broil 4"–5" from the heat, brushing with any remaining butter, 10–15 minutes, depending on size, until lightly browned. (*Note:* If large tails are unavailable, use the smaller, adjusting cooking times as follows: 5–6 minutes for 3–5-ounce tails, 7–9 minutes for 6–8 ounce tails.) Sprinkle with pepper, and serve with lemon wedges and additional melted butter. About 300 calories per serving.

VARIATION:

⚖ **Low-Calorie Broiled Rock Lobster Tails:** Use the 8-ounce tails and broil as directed, substituting low-calorie Italian, garlic, or herb dressing for the butter. About 170 calories per serving.

COLD CURRIED LOBSTER

Makes 4 servings

1½ pounds cooked lobster meat, well
  picked over and cut in bite-size chunks

Dressing:

⅔ cup mayonnaise
⅓ cup sour cream
2 tablespoons minced parsley
2 tablespoons minced fresh dill
1 tablespoon minced fresh tarragon
2 tablespoons capers
1 tablespoon curry powder
2 tablespoons finely grated yellow onion
Juice of ½ lime
3–4 dashes liquid hot red pepper
  seasoning

Place lobster in a large bowl. Mix dressing ingredients until well blended, pour over lobster, and toss to mix. Cover and chill several hours. Serve as is, in lettuce cups, hollowed-out tomatoes, or avocado halves. About 500 calories per serving (without lettuce, tomatoes, or avocado halves).

LOBSTER THERMIDOR

A showy way to prepare frozen rock lobster tails.
Makes 4 servings

4 (8–10-ounce) frozen rock lobster tails,
  boiled by package directions and
  drained
3 tablespoons minced scallions (white
  part only)
2 tablespoons butter or margarine
⅓ cup dry white wine
1 teaspoon powdered mustard
2 cups hot Mornay Sauce
4 teaspoons grated Parmesan cheese

Preheat broiler. Remove lobster meat from shells, cut in ½" chunks, and set aside; reserve shells. Stir-fry scallions in butter in a small saucepan over moderate

heat 2–3 minutes until limp. Add wine
and boil, uncovered, until reduced to ¼
cup. Blend in mustard, then stir into
Mornay sauce. Mix a little hot sauce into
lobster meat, just enough to bind. Place
lobster shells in a shallow baking pan, fill
with lobster mixture, then cover with
remaining Mornay sauce, and sprinkle
each lobster with 1 teaspoon grated
Parmesan. Broil 4″–5″ from heat 3–4
minutes until browned and bubbly.
About 475 calories per serving.

MUSSELS

Someday, if there's a shortage of clams
and oysters, we may be driven to eat
mussels. Fishermen tell us there are
millions of them along both coasts, but
we seem to feel, as long as we've loads of
clams and oysters, why bother?
Mussels are stronger flavored than
clams or oysters, slightly tougher, too (or
is that because we don't know how to
cook them?). In Europe, especially
Mediterranean Europe, people do
delectable things with mussels—stuff
them with rice and currants and piñon
nuts; simmer them, shell and all, in
tomato sauces heady with garlic. We
would do well to follow their lead.

The Kinds of Mussels

There is only one of importance, the
blue edible mussel, which lives in dense
colonies on wharf pilings and along
rocky shores.

About Buying Fresh Mussels

Season:

East Coast: Year round.

West Coast: November through April
(because of the dangerous, warm
weather "red tide," see Clams).

Popular Market Forms: Alive, in the
shell; they are sold either by the dozen
or the pound.

Amount Needed: Allow about ½–1
dozen mussels per person, depending on
size of mussels and appetites.

For Top Quality: Look for mussels with
tightly closed shells that will not slip or
budge when pressed.

Other Forms of Mussels

To date, mussels are only available
canned, not frozen. These are already
cooked and best used for quick soups,
fritters, patties, or casseroles.

How to Cleanse Mussels of Grit: Scrub
mussels hard with a stiff brush under cold
running water, pull or cut off the long
beard, and scrape away any small
barnacles or incrustations on the shells.
Submerge mussels in a kettle of cool
water and let stand 2–3 hours so they
will purge themselves of sand. Discard
any that float, also any with shells not
tightly clamped shut.

How to Open Mussels: As with clams,
there are two ways, prying and
steaming. How mussels are to be
prepared determines which to use.

(1) *To Pry Open* (for mussels to be
stuffed): Insert a paring knife into back
of mussel to the right of the hinge and
with blunt edge facing hinge. Move knife
clockwise around crevice, twisting
slightly to force shell open; take care not
to cut hinge. Open mussels over a bowl
so that none of their juice is lost. Once
mussel is open, trim away any stray
whiskers.

(2) *To Steam Open and Shuck* (for
mussels to be cut from shell and used in
fritters, chowders, etc.): Place mussels in
a large kettle, pour in about ¾ cup
boiling water, cover, and steam over
moderate heat 3 minutes, just until shells
open. Discard any that do not open; they
are dead and full of mud. Drain
mussels, remove meat from shells, and
trim off any tag ends of beard. (*Note:*
Before using mussel liquid, strain through
a fine sieve lined with a double thickness
of cheesecloth.)

How to Cook Mussels

Because of their robust flavor, mussels are better cooked in the company of vegetables, herbs, and spices than by the utterly basic methods. Even when they are steamed, they benefit from a little lily-gilding (recipes follow).

General Preparation: Cleanse as directed above and, if recipes so specify, open.

⚛ COQUILLES OF MUSSELS

Makes 6 servings

3 dozen mussels in the shell, prepared for cooking
1¼ cups hot Thick White Sauce
3 tablespoons melted butter or margarine
2 cups hot seasoned mashed potatoes
⅓ cup fine dry bread crumbs mixed with 1 tablespoon melted butter or margarine

Steam mussels open and shuck*; reserve ¼ cup of liquid from mussels and strain, then mix with white sauce, 1 tablespoon butter, and the mussels. Spoon into 6–8 buttered large scallop shells and arrange on a baking sheet. Place potatoes in a pastry bag fitted with a small rosette tube and pipe a decorative border around edge of each shell; brush with 1 tablespoon melted butter. Scatter buttered crumbs on top of mussels and bake, uncovered, 5–7 minutes until lightly browned. About 285 calories per serving.

VARIATIONS:

Creamed Mussels: Mix white sauce, mussels liquid, mussels, and butter as directed, then heat in the top of a double boiler over simmering water 4–5 minutes, stirring occasionally until piping hot. Spoon over hot buttered toast, sprinkle with parsley, and serve. About 315 calories per serving.

⚛ Creamed Mussels au Gratin: Mix white sauce, mussels liquid, mussels, and butter as directed, stir in 2 tablespoons minced chives, spoon into an ungreased 1½-quart *au gratin* dish, and top with ⅔ cup fine dry bread crumbs mixed with 2 tablespoons melted butter and ⅓ cup

grated Parmesan cheese. Bake, uncovered, 10–15 minutes until bubbly and lightly browned. About 295 calories per serving.

⚛ FILEY BAY MUSSELS

Rather like "deviled" mussels on the half shell.

Makes 4 servings

Rock salt
3 dozen mussels in the shell, prepared for cooking
½ cup butter (no substitute), softened to room temperature
2 tablespoons minced shallots or chives
1 clove garlic, peeled and crushed
2 tablespoons minced parsley
1 tablespoon prepared mild yellow mustard
2 teaspoons steak sauce

Preheat broiler. Make a bed of rock salt in a very large, shallow baking pan, dampen slightly with water, and heat uncovered in oven 5 minutes while broiler preheats. Meanwhile, steam mussels open,* lift off top shells and discard. Arrange mussels in hot salt, pushing shells down well so they won't tip. Cream butter with remaining ingredients and place about 1 teaspoonful on each mussel. Broil 3"–4" from the heat 2–3 minutes until bubbly. Transfer to a hot platter or individual plates and serve. About 280 calories per serving.

MUSSELS MARINIÈRE

Makes 4 servings

⅓ cup minced shallots or ½ cup minced yellow onion
½ cup butter (no substitute)
3 dozen mussels in the shell, prepared for cooking
4 sprigs parsley
2 (4") sprigs fresh thyme or ½ teaspoon dried thyme
1 bay leaf
2 cups dry white wine
2 tablespoons minced parsley

Stir-fry shallots in ¼ cup butter 5–8 minutes in a large, heavy kettle over moderate heat until golden. Add mussels, herbs, and wine, cover, bring to a boil, then reduce heat and simmer 3 minutes until mussels open. Discard any unopened mussels, also empty half shells. Transfer mussels, still in their shells, to a heated tureen and keep warm. Strain cooking liquid through a double thickness of cheesecloth, add remaining butter and minced parsley, and heat, stirring, just until butter melts. Taste for salt and add if needed. Pour sauce over mussels and serve with hot French bread. About 385 calories per serving (without bread).

VARIATION:

Clams Marinière: Prepare as directed, substituting steamer or cherrystone clams for mussels. About 375 calories per serving.

MARSEILLE-STYLE MUSSELS WITH GARLIC AND TOMATO

Makes 4 servings

1 large yellow onion, peeled and minced
3–4 cloves garlic, peeled and crushed
3 stalks celery, chopped fine
¼ cup olive oil
6 large ripe tomatoes, peeled, cored, seeded, and chopped fine or
1 (1-pound 12-ounce) can tomatoes
2 cups dry white wine
3 dozen mussels in the shell, prepared for cooking
1 tablespoon minced parsley

Stir-fry onion, garlic, and celery in oil in a large, heavy kettle 5–8 minutes over moderate heat until golden; add tomatoes and wine, cover and simmer 15 minutes. Add mussels and simmer 3 minutes longer. Off heat, discard any mussels that have not opened along with any empty half shells. Transfer mussels, still in their shells, to a heated tureen and keep warm. Strain cooking liquid through a double thickness of cheesecloth. Return to heat, bring to a simmer, and stir in parsley. Taste for salt and add if needed. Pour sauce over mussels and serve with hot buttered French bread. About 420 calories per serving (without bread).

ARMENIAN MUSSELS STUFFED WITH RICE, CURRANTS, AND PIÑON NUTS

Makes 4–6 servings

⅓ cup olive oil
1 large yellow onion, peeled and minced
3 dozen mussels in the shell, prepared for cooking
⅓ cup dried currants
⅓ cup piñon nuts
½ teaspoon salt
¼ teaspoon cinnamon
¼ teaspoon allspice
⅛ teaspoon pepper
½ cup dry white wine
1¾ cups water
1 cup uncooked rice

Heat oil in a large, heavy kettle over moderate heat about 1 minute, add onion, and stir-fry 3–5 minutes until limp. Add mussels, currants, piñon nuts, salt, and spices and heat, stirring, 2–3 minutes until mussels begin to open. Add wine and water, cover, and simmer 3–5 minutes until mussels open wide. Lift out all mussels; discard any that do not open, and reserve the rest; trim off any stray bits of beard. Bring kettle mixture to a rapid boil, stir in rice, and boil gently, uncovered, 12–15 minutes until rice is done and all liquid absorbed. Stir rice well to mix ingredients, then spoon into mussels, filling shells full and packing ever so lightly so mixture will not fall out. Cool to room temperature before serving. About 525 calories for each of 4 servings, 350 calories for each of 6 servings.

OYSTERS

Oysters have a long and well-documented history. The Greeks served them at cocktail parties as "provocatives to drinking," the Romans imported oysters from England, packed in snow, then parked them in salt water ponds until they could be fattened up on a diet of wine and pastry. American Indians were great oyster eaters, too, judging from the middens of shells found up and down both coasts. Colonists were enthusiasts from the beginning, and by the early eighteenth century, when trains began rushing fresh seafood into the Midwest, oysters became the rage. Soon every town of consequence had its own oyster parlor, and newspaper society pages devoted columns to oyster parties. The Abraham Lincolns, while still in Illinois, gave oyster suppers at which nothing but oysters was served. Oysters continue to be popular, so much so that, even though they are now "grown" commercially, the supply doesn't meet the demand.

The Kinds of Oysters

There are three popular American species, one taken from the Atlantic and Gulf of Mexico, two from the Pacific.

Eastern Oyster: Found along the east coast from Massachusetts to Texas, this oyster accounts for 89 per cent of America's catch. It includes the famous *blue points,* named for Blue Point, Long Island, where they were first found (but now simply a term referring to any oyster from 2"–4" long), also the choice Virginia *Chincoteagues,* considered by many to be America's finest oyster. The subtle flavor differences among Eastern oysters depends on the oysters' diet and upon the composition of the waters in which they live.

Olympias: These sweet miniatures (it takes 300–500 to make a quart) are the pearls among oysters (and very nearly as expensive). Originally found all along the West Coast, they now come primarily from Puget Sound "farms."

Japanese or Pacific: This giant transplant from Japan is the West Coast's most popular oyster. Too large to eat on the half shell, it is usually cut up and fried, hashed or stewed.

About Buying Fresh Oysters

Season: There is some truth to the old

R month theory. Though oysters are edible between May and August, they aren't very plump or tasty because this is their season to spawn. Few markets sell oysters in summer.

Popular Market Forms:

Eastern Oysters: Live and in the shell by the dozen; shucked by the pint or quart.

Olympias: Shucked and packed in small bottles.

Japanese: Shucked and packed in 10- or 12-ounce jars.

Amount Needed: It depends—on the size of the oysters (and appetites), on how the oysters are prepared and served. But here's a guide:

Oysters on the Half Shell: Allow about ½ dozen blue points per person, ½–1 dozen Chincoteagues, depending on size. If you splurge on Olympias, you'll have to order them especially and allow 3–4 dozen per person.

Oysters to Be Cooked in the Shell: Allow ½–1 dozen small or medium oysters per person, depending on richness of recipe.

Shucked Oysters: 1 pint will serve about 3, more if stretched with other ingredients.

For Top Quality:

Oysters in the Shell: Choose only those that are tightly shut or those that clamp shut when handled.

Shucked Oysters: Select plump, sweet-smelling oysters with clear liquor free of shell particles and grit.

About Frozen and Canned Oysters

Shucked, raw Eastern oysters are now available frozen; they are also canned (either plain or smoked). Japanese or Pacific oysters are also canned. *To Cook Frozen Oysters:* Thaw in the refrigerator, then prepare as you would fresh oysters; cook immediately after thawing and never refreeze. *How to Use Canned*

Oysters: Because these are fully cooked, they're best used in quick soups, stews, fritters, and casseroles. The smoked variety is usually served as cocktail snacks, though they, too, can be used in soups and stews.

How to Shuck Fresh Oysters: Wash and rinse oysters well in cool water. Place oysters on counter, flat side up, and knock off thin edge (bill) with a hammer. Insert an oyster knife into broken edge and slip it around to back of oyster; sever hinge as close to flat upper shell as possible, lift off top shell and discard. Cut muscle from lower shell; carefully feel oyster for bits of shell and grit, paying particular attention to the hinge. If oysters are to be served or cooked on the half shell, replace in deep lower shells. (*Note:* Open oysters over a small bowl to catch any spilled juice and strain juice through a double thickness of cheesecloth before using.)

How to Cook Oysters

There are those who say oysters should never be cooked, that the only way to savor them is on the half shell with a squirt of lemon and a grinding of black pepper. Maybe so. But just as many people insist that an oyster's true glory emerges only in the cooking. Here are the best methods.

General Preparation: Shuck oysters or not as recipes direct. Obviously, if a recipe calls for oysters to be shucked, the best plan is to buy them already out of the shell.

To Panfry (*Sauté*): Pat shucked oysters dry on paper toweling. Dredge in flour delicately seasoned with salt and pepper and sauté in butter or margarine (about ⅓ cup butter for 1 pint oysters) 3–4 minutes over moderate heat, turning once, just until oysters plump up and brown lightly. Serve with lemon.

VARIATIONS:

Pan-"Roasted" Oysters: Pat oysters dry but do not dredge. Sauté in butter or margarine (½ cup per pint of oysters) 3–4 minutes over moderate heat, turning once, just until they plump up and their edges ruffle. Serve with lemon.

Spicy Pan-"Roasted" Oysters: Pan roast oysters as above but reduce amount of butter to ¼ cup for each pint oysters. With a slotted spoon, ladle cooked oysters over slices of hot buttered toast. To pan add 2 tablespoons ketchup and 1 teaspoon Worcestershire sauce; heat and stir 1 minute, spoon over oysters and serve.

Pepper Pan Roast: Stir-fry ¼ cup each minced yellow onion and sweet green pepper in ⅓ cup butter or margarine 3–5 minutes over moderate heat until limp. Add 1 pint shucked oysters and pan roast as above.

Breaded Fried Oysters: Pat shucked oysters dry and dredge in flour lightly seasoned with salt and pepper. Dip in a mixture of beaten egg and water (1 tablespoon cold water to each egg), then roll in cracker meal, fine dry crumbs, or a ½ and ½ mixture of flour and corn meal. Sauté in butter or margarine (½ cup for 1 pint oysters) 3–4 minutes over moderately high heat, turning once, until golden brown. Drain on paper toweling and serve with lemon.

To Deep-Fat-Fry: Pat shucked oysters dry on paper toweling and bread as above. Heat cooking oil or shortening in a deep fat fryer to 375° F., place a single layer of oysters in fryer basket, lower into fat, and fry 2–3 minutes until lightly browned. Drain on paper toweling and set uncovered in an oven turned to lowest heat to keep warm while you fry the rest. Serve with lemon and, if you like, Tartar Sauce or Rémoulade Sauce.

VARIATION:

Batter-Fried Oysters (Oyster Fritters): Make up batter given in Fish and Chips recipe. Pat shucked oysters dry on paper toweling, dip in batter, and fry, 6–8 at a time, as directed above.

To Oven Roast: Preheat oven to 500° F. Scrub oysters but do not shuck. Place flat side up in a large, shallow baking pan and bake, uncovered, 12–15 minutes until shells open. Serve in the shell or, if you prefer, on the half shell (simply cut hinge and lift off shallow top shell).

To Roast over Charcoal: Prepare a moderately hot charcoal fire.* Scrub oysters but don't shuck. Wrap, 4–6 to a package, in heavy foil, place directly on coals, and roast, without turning, 6 minutes. Serve with lemon.

VARIATION: Do not wrap oysters; instead, place flat side up on grill 4″ from coals and roast 10–15 minutes until shells open.

To Steam: Scrub oysters but do not shuck. Place in a deep kettle, add ⅔ cup boiling water, cover, and steam over moderate heat 10–12 minutes until shells open. Serve with melted butter and lemon wedges and, if you like Worcestershire and liquid hot red pepper seasoning.

To Serve Oysters on the Half Shell

Allow 6–8 blue point oysters per person; have fish market open them and prepare for serving on the half shell. If you have to do this job yourself, see directions given earlier for opening oysters. Fill large, shallow bowls or soup plates with crushed ice and arrange oysters in ice. Garnish with lemon wedges and ruffs of parsley. Set out the pepper mill and pass thinly sliced, buttered pumpernickel or crisp thin crackers. When eating, to savor every last drop, drink the oyster liquor from each shell after eating the oyster.

VARIATION:

Oysters on the Half Shell with Caviar: Prepare as directed, then top each oyster with about ½ teaspoon red or black caviar and a few shreds of grated

fresh horseradish. Serve with lemon wedges.

⊠ GRAND CENTRAL OYSTER STEW

The Oyster Bar in New York's Grand Central Terminal still makes oyster stew the way it did on opening day in 1912. People say the recipe can't be duplicated at home because Oyster Bar chefs never measure anything. Perhaps not, but here's a recipe that comes close. Make it fast and serve in hot, hot bowls. Makes 4 servings

1 cup milk
1 cup light cream
1 pint shucked oysters (do not drain)
2 tablespoons butter
¼ teaspoon salt
¼ teaspoon celery salt
Pinch pepper
Pinch paprika

Heat soup bowls. Scald milk and cream in a large, heavy saucepan over moderately high heat. Drain oyster liquor into a separate saucepan and bring to a boil. Spoon 2 tablespoons hot liquor into a third saucepan, add oysters and butter, and heat, uncovered, over moderate heat, swirling oysters around 3–4 minutes until edges just begin to curl; add oysters at once to hot milk, mix in hot oyster liquor, salt, celery salt, pepper, and paprika. Ladle into heated bowls and serve piping hot with oyster crackers. About 300 calories per serving.

CREAMED OYSTERS

Makes 4 servings

1 pint shucked oysters (do not drain)
3 tablespoons butter or margarine
3 tablespoons flour
1 cup light cream
1 teaspoon lemon juice
Pinch nutmeg
⅛ teaspoon paprika
4 slices lightly buttered toast (optional)

Drain oysters and reserve ¼ cup liquor. Melt butter in a saucepan over moderate heat, blend in flour, slowly add cream, and heat, stirring, until thickened. Add reserved liquor, lemon juice, nutmeg and paprika, reduce heat, and simmer, stirring, 1 minute. Add oysters and cook, swirling pan occasionally, 4–5 minutes just until edges begin to curl. Serve as is or spooned over buttered toast. About 300 calories per serving (without toast).

VARIATIONS:

Oyster Shortcake: Prepare recipe as directed and ladle over hot, split, buttered biscuits. Sprinkle with minced parsley and serve. About 360 calories per serving.

Creamed Oysters à la Ritz: Prepare recipe as directed but just before serving stir in ¼ cup medium-dry sherry or Marsala and 2 tablespoons minced pimiento. Serve in individual ramekins or small casseroles and surround with toast points spread with Anchovy Butter. About 415 calories per serving.

Oyster Pie: (Makes 4–6 servings). Prepare 1 recipe Flaky Pastry I, roll into a 12″ circle, and cut 3 steam vents in center. Prepare Creamed Oysters as directed and pour into an ungreased 9″ piepan; place a pie funnel in center of pan. Cover oysters with pastry, trim and crimp edges, and brush pastry with beaten egg. Bake ½ hour at 425° F. until pastry is golden. About 575 calories per serving.

Oyster and Mushroom Pie: (Makes 4–6 servings). Prepare pastry as for Oyster Pie. Also prepare Creamed Oysters as directed but sauté ½ pound thinly sliced mushrooms in the butter 3–4 minutes until golden before adding flour. Proceed as for Oyster Pie. About 615 calories per serving.

⊠ CHAFING DISH OYSTERS

Makes 4 servings

¼ cup butter or margarine
1 pint shucked oysters, drained
½ cup heavy cream
Pinch cayenne pepper
Pinch mace
¼ cup medium-dry sherry or brandy
4 hot waffles

Melt butter in a chafing dish over direct heat, add oysters, and heat, swirling oysters round, 4–5 minutes just until edges start to curl. Place chafing dish on stand, add cream, seasonings, and sherry, and heat, stirring, until piping hot but not boiling. Ladle over waffles and serve. About 480 calories per serving.

⚖ OYSTERS POULETTE

Two ingredients only and so very elegant. Low calorie, too.
Makes 4 servings

1 pint shucked oysters (do not drain)
1½ cups hot Poulette Sauce

Simmer oysters in their liquor in the top of a double boiler over simmering water 3–4 minutes just until their edges begin to curl. Drain off liquor, add sauce, and mix gently. Heat 3–4 minutes and serve in puff pastry shells or over triangles of buttered toast or black bread. About 185 calories per serving.

⚖ ⊠ BROILED CRUMBED OYSTERS ON THE HALF SHELL

Makes 4 servings

2 dozen oysters on the half shell
½ teaspoon salt
⅛ teaspoon pepper
½ cup soft white bread crumbs mixed with 2 tablespoons melted butter or margarine

Preheat broiler. Sprinkle oysters with salt, pepper, and buttered crumbs and arrange on foil-lined broiler pan. Broil 3″ from the heat 4–5 minutes until lightly browned. About 160 calories per serving.

OYSTERS ROCKEFELLER

There are dozens of variations of this New Orleans classic. This one may be no more original than the others, but it *is* good.
Makes 4 entree servings, enough appetizers for 6

Rock salt
¼ cup minced scallions or shallots
¼ cup minced celery
½ clove garlic, peeled and crushed
1 cup butter or margarine
2 cups finely chopped watercress leaves
⅓ cup soft white bread crumbs
⅓ cup minced parsley
⅓ cup minced fresh fennel
¼ cup Pernod or anisette
Pinch cayenne pepper
2 dozen oysters on the half shell

Preheat oven to 450° F. Make beds of rock salt in 4 piepans (the 8" or 9" size is best), dampen slightly with water, and heat uncovered in oven 5 minutes. Meanwhile, stir-fry scallions, celery, and garlic in butter over moderate heat 3–5 minutes until limp. Add watercress and stir-fry 1 minute, just until wilted. Pour skillet mixture into an electric blender cup, add remaining ingredients except oysters, and purée at high speed. Arrange 6 oysters in shells in each pan of hot salt, pushing shells down into salt so they cannot tip. Cover each oyster with 1 tablespoon purée and bake, uncovered, 5–7 minutes until bubbly. Serve at once in pans of salt. About 525 calories for each of 4 entree servings, 350 calories for each of 6 appetizer servings.

OYSTERS REMICK

"Deviled" oysters on the half shell.
Makes 4 entree servings, enough
appetizers for 6

Rock salt
6 slices bacon
2 dozen oysters on the half shell
¾ cup mayonnaise
3 tablespoons chili sauce
¾ teaspoon prepared Dijon-style
*   mustard*
1 teaspoon lemon juice
2–3 drops liquid hot red pepper
*   seasoning*

Preheat oven to 450° F. Make beds of rock salt in 4 piepans (the 8" or 9" size), dampen slightly with water, and heat uncovered in oven 5 minutes.

Meanwhile, cut each bacon strip into 4 equal-size pieces and stir-fry over moderate heat until limp. Drain on paper toweling and reserve. Arrange 6 oysters in shells in each pan, pushing shells down in hot salt so they won't tip. Blend mayonnaise with chili sauce, mustard, lemon juice, and pepper seasoning and cover each oyster with a heaping teaspoonful. Top with a piece of bacon and bake, uncovered, about 5–7 minutes until bacon is crisp. Serve from pans. About 500 calories for each of 4 entree servings, 335 calories for each of 6 appetizer servings.

OYSTERS FLORENTINE

Oysters and spinach on the half shell
topped with cheese sauce.
Makes 2 entree servings, enough
appetizers for 4

Rock salt
1½ dozen oysters on the half shell
1 (10-ounce) package frozen chopped
*   spinach, cooked by package directions*
*   and drained well*
2–3 scallions, trimmed and sliced thin
1 cup hot Mornay Sauce
⅓ cup grated Parmesan cheese

Preheat broiler. Make beds of rock salt in 2 (8" or 9") piepans, dampen slightly with water, and let heat, uncovered, in oven 5 minutes while broiler preheats. Scoop oysters and their liquor from shells into a saucepan; reserve shells. Poach oysters 3–4 minutes over moderately low heat just until edges begin to curl; drain. Purée spinach and scallions in an electric blender at high speed or put through a food mill. Arrange oyster shells, 9 to a pan, in hot salt. Spoon a little spinach mixture into each shell, add an oyster, top with Mornay sauce, then sprinkle with cheese. Broil 5" from the heat 1–2 minutes just until flecked with brown. About 500 calories for each of 2 entree servings, 250 calories for each of 4 appetizer servings.

DEVILED OYSTERS

Makes 4 servings

2 dozen oysters on the half shell
2 tablespoons minced yellow onion
2 tablespoons butter or margarine
3 tablespoons flour
1 cup light cream
1 tablespoon spicy brown prepared
  mustard
1 tablespoon Worcestershire sauce
⅛ teaspoon salt
⅛ teaspoon cayenne pepper
⅛ teaspoon nutmeg
1 tablespoon minced parsley
1 egg, lightly beaten
⅓ cup soft white bread crumbs mixed
  with 2 tablespoons melted butter or
  margarine

Preheat oven to 400° F. Remove
oysters from shells and chop coarsely;
reserve liquid and shells. Stir-fry onion
in butter in a saucepan over moderate
heat 3–5 minutes until limp, blend in
flour, then add cream and reserved
oyster liquid and heat, stirring, until
thickened and smooth. Off heat, mix
in all seasonings, also parsley, egg, and
chopped oysters. Spoon into oyster shells
and top with buttered crumbs. Place on
baking sheets and bake, uncovered,
10 minutes until bubbly. About 360
calories per serving.

OYSTERS BAKED IN MUSHROOM
CAPS

Makes 2–3 entree servings, enough
appetizers for 6

2 dozen large mushroom caps, wiped
  clean
¼ cup butter or margarine
2 dozen shucked oysters, drained
2 dozen rounds white bread cut to fit
  mushroom caps and fried until crisp
  in butter

Preheat oven to 425° F. Sauté
mushroom caps in butter over
moderately high heat 3–5 minutes until
golden. Arrange cup side up on greased
baking sheet and fill each with an oyster.
Bake, uncovered, 5–7 minutes until

oyster edges start to curl. Serve on fried
bread rounds. About 570 calories for
each of 2 entree servings, 380 calories
for each of 3 entree servings, and 190
calories for each of 6 appetizer servings.

⚖ ⊠ OYSTERS EN BROCHETTE

Makes 4 servings

8 slices bacon
2 dozen mushroom caps
2 dozen shucked oysters, drained
½ cup melted butter or margarine
Juice of 1 lemon
Pepper

Preheat broiler. Fry bacon slices in a
heavy skillet over moderately high heat
2–3 minutes until limp; drain on paper
toweling. On each of 4 long skewers
alternate mushroom caps and oysters,
interweaving 2 bacon strips. Mix melted
butter with lemon juice and brush
generously over each skewer; sprinkle
with pepper. Place on a foil-lined
broiler pan and broil 3″ from the heat
5–7 minutes, turning and brushing often
with remaining butter mixture, until
lightly browned. Serve at once. About
230 calories per serving.

VARIATIONS:

**Oriental-Style Skewered Steak and
Oysters:** Marinate oysters and 2 dozen
1″ raw beef tenderloin cubes in ½ cup
peanut oil mixed with ¼ cup each soy
sauce and *sake* or dry sherry, ½ crushed
clove garlic, and 2 teaspoons grated
fresh gingerroot 2–3 hours in refrigerator. Lift from marinade and skewer alternately on 4 long skewers as above,
interweaving bacon strips. Broil as
directed, brushing often with marinade.
About 415 calories per serving.

Charcoal-Broiled Oysters en Brochette:
Prepare a moderately hot charcoal fire.*
Skewer oysters by either of the recipes
above and broil 4″ from the coals
5–6 minutes, turning often and brushing
with butter or marinade. The same
calorie counts as for the two recipes
above.

ANGELS ON HORSEBACK

Makes 2 servings

1 dozen shucked oysters, drained
6 slices bacon, halved, or 6 thin strips
boiled ham the size of half bacon
strips
2 slices hot buttered toast
1 cup Hollandaise Sauce

Preheat broiler. Pat oysters dry on paper toweling, wrap each in a piece of bacon, and secure with a toothpick. Arrange on a foil-lined broiler pan and broil 3″ from the heat, about 5 minutes, turning often so bacon browns evenly. Remove toothpicks, pile oysters on toast and smother with Hollandaise. About 565 calories per serving.

VARIATIONS:

Tipsy Angels on Horseback: Marinate oysters in 1½ cups dry white wine mixed with ½ crushed clove garlic and 1 tablespoon minced parsley 2–3 hours in the refrigerator. Lift from marinade and proceed as directed. About 565 calories per serving.

Devils on Horseback: Sprinkle oysters lightly with lemon juice and liquid hot red pepper seasoning. Wrap in bacon and broil as directed. Serve on toast but omit Hollandaise. About 325 calories per serving.

⚖ ☒ SCALLOPED OYSTERS

Makes 4 servings

1 pint shucked oysters (do not drain)
1 cup light cream
2 cups coarse soda cracker crumbs
½ cup melted butter
½ teaspoon salt
¼ teaspoon pepper

Preheat oven to 375° F. Drain oysters, reserving ¼ cup liquor; mix liquor and cream and set aside. Mix crumbs with butter, salt, and pepper and sprinkle ⅓ of mixture in a buttered 1-quart casserole. Arrange half of oysters on top and pour in half of cream mixture. Cover with another ⅓ crumb mixture, add remaining oysters and cream. Top

with remaining crumbs and bake, uncovered, 30–35 minutes until bubbly and lightly browned. About 570 calories per serving.

⚖ ☒ CONFEDERATE OYSTER BAKE

Couldn't be easier, couldn't be better.
Makes 6 servings

1 quart shucked oysters, drained
2 tablespoons minced parsley
2 tablespoons minced shallots or
scallions
¼ teaspoon pepper
1 tablespoon lemon juice
¾ cup milk
1¼ cups fine dry bread crumbs
6 tablespoons butter or margarine

Preheat oven to 325° F. Layer oysters in a greased 8″ × 8″ × 2″ baking dish or 1½-quart casserole, sprinkling as you go with parsley, shallots, pepper, and lemon juice. Pour in milk, top with crumbs, and dot generously with butter. Bake, uncovered, about 30 minutes until crumbs are golden. Serve at once. About 260 calories per serving.

OYSTER LOAF

Oyster loaves, popular in nineteenth-century San Francisco and New Orleans, were nicknamed "squarers" because errant night-owl husbands would pick them up on the way home to "square" things with their wives.
Makes 4–6 servings

1 small round loaf Italian bread or
1 (1-pound) loaf unsliced firm white
bread
⅓ cup melted butter or margarine
1 pint shucked oysters, drained

Preheat oven to 350° F. Slice off top ¼ of loaf and set aside; hollow out loaf, leaving walls about ¾″ thick. Brush inside of loaf generously with butter, also the cut side of "lid." Place loaf and lid (cut side up) on an ungreased baking sheet and bake 20–30 minutes until lightly toasted (lid will toast in about 10). Meanwhile, sauté oysters, following basic method.* Fill loaf with oysters, top with lid and serve. Round loaves should be cut in wedges, rectangular loaves in thick slices. About 300 calories for each of 4 servings, 200 calories for each of 6 servings.

VARIATIONS:

⚖ **Individual Oyster Loaves:** Substitute 4–6 hard French rolls for the single loaf and hollow out, making shells about ½" thick. Butter and toast, allowing 5–10 minutes, fill with hot oysters, and serve. About 295 calories for each of 4 servings, 195 calories for each of 6 servings.

⚖ **Creamed Oyster Loaves** (Makes 6 servings): Hollow out, butter, and toast 6 hard French rolls as above. Meanwhile, simmer oysters in their liquor 4–5 minutes just until edges ruffle. Drain oysters, stir in ½ cup hot cream, 1 teaspoon lemon juice, ½ teaspoon anchovy paste, ⅛ teaspoon each cayenne pepper and nutmeg. Spoon mixture into rolls and serve. About 295 calories per serving.

Clam Loaf: Prepare as directed, substituting clams for oysters. About 310 calories for each of 4 servings, 205 calories for each of 6 servings.

Crab, Lobster, or Shrimp Loaf: Prepare loaf or rolls as above and fill with hot Herbed Crab Sauté or Quick Crab Newburg; Creamed Scallops; Shrimp and Mushrooms Gruyère; Shrimp in Dill Sauce, Shrimp or Lobster Newburg. Recipe too flexible for meaningful calorie counts.

HANGTOWN FRY

The story goes that this oyster omelet was the last meal requested by a man about to be hanged in Hangtown (now Placerville), California. Whatever its origin, Hangtown Fry is a California classic.
Makes 2 servings

8 shucked oysters, well drained
1 egg beaten with 1 tablespoon cold water

⅓ cup fine soda cracker crumbs
3 tablespoons butter or margarine
4 eggs
¼ teaspoon salt
⅛ teaspoon pepper
4 slices crisply fried bacon

Optional Garnish:

1 (7-ounce) package French-fried onion rings, prepared by package directions
OR
½ cup minced sweet green pepper stir-fried in 2 tablespoons butter 3–5 minutes over moderate heat until limp

Pat oysters dry on paper toweling, dip in beaten egg, then crumbs and brown in butter in a 9" skillet over moderate heat, allowing only 1–2 minutes per side. While oysters fry, quickly beat eggs with salt and pepper. Pour over browned oysters, turn heat to low, and cook, pulling mixture from outer edge toward center as you would for an omelet so uncooked portions run underneath; keep oysters as evenly spaced in eggs as possible. When eggs are just set but still quivery, invert on a hot platter. Garnish with bacon and, if you like, smother with French-fried onion rings or minced sweet green pepper. About 545 calories per serving (without garnish).

⚖ ⊠ OYSTER AND CORN "OYSTERS"

Makes 4 servings

¼ cup sifted flour
¼ teaspoon salt
¼ teaspoon baking powder
2 tablespoons milk
1 egg, lightly beaten
1 cup whole kernel corn, well drained
⅓ cup cooking oil
1½ dozen shucked oysters, drained

Mix flour, salt, and baking powder in a bowl, slowly add milk, and beat until smooth. Beat in egg and stir in corn. Heat oil in a large, heavy skillet over moderate heat 1 minute. Using a large serving spoon, scoop up an oyster, dip into corn mixture, filling spoon, then drop into hot fat. Fry, 3–4 "oysters" at a time, 3–4 minutes until browned on both sides.

Drain on paper toweling and keep hot while you fry the rest by setting, uncovered, in oven turned to lowest heat. About 200 calories per serving.

⚖️ PICKLED OYSTERS

Makes 4 first course servings

1 pint shucked oysters (do not drain)
1 medium-size yellow onion, peeled and sliced paper thin
1 lemon, sliced paper thin
½ cup white wine vinegar
1 teaspoon mixed pickling spices
⅛ teaspoon pepper
2 tablespoons olive or other cooking oil
2 tablespoons minced parsley

Simmer oysters in their liquor over moderately low heat 4–5 minutes just until edges begin to curl. Drain, reserve liquor, and cover oysters with ice water. Cool oysters 5 minutes in water, drain again, and arrange in a single layer in an ungreased large, shallow casserole. Cover with onion and lemon slices. Bring vinegar, reserved cooking liquor, spices, and oil to a boil, reduce heat, and simmer uncovered 5 minutes. Strain liquid over oysters, cool to room temperature, then cover and chill overnight. Serve sprinkled with parsley. About 100 calories per serving.

PERIWINKLES

These miniature sea snails are a great French favorite, especially in Brittany, where steaming mountains of them are served alongside platters of *langoustines*. Occasionally, fancy American fish markets have them for sale; more often they are gathered locally along the East Coast from Delaware north.

Season: Year round.

Amount Needed: About 1½ dozen periwinkles per serving.

For Top Quality: When gathering your own, pick only those tightly clinging to pilings or rocks well below the tide mark. When buying, select those that "clam up" when handled.

How to Cook Periwinkles

General Preparation: Rinse well in cold water.

To Boil: Place periwinkles in a large saucepan and cover with sea water or salt water (1 tablespoon salt for each quart water), cover, and simmer 15–25 minutes until the operculum (tiny trap-door sealing opening) opens. Drain periwinkles and serve hot with melted butter, Lemon or Garlic Butter.

To Bake: Rinse periwinkles and boil as directed above. Using a nut pick or long straight pin, twist meat from each shell. Now proceed as for Escargots à la Bourguignonne, tucking 3 periwinkles into each empty snail shell. Close snail shell openings with the Bourguignonne Butter and bake as directed.

How to Eat Periwinkles

Eating periwinkles from the shell is no more difficult than eating snails—except that they're so much smaller. Pick them up one at a time and, using a nut pick, toothpick, or long straight pin, twist meat from shell. Peel off operculum, transfer meat to a small fork and dip in accompanying butter.

SCALLOPS

Down the centuries, scallop shells have been as cherished as the tiny sea animals inside them. It is from a scallop shell that Botticelli's Venus rises; it is the scallop shell that became the emblem of St. James, patron saint of Spain; it is the scallop shell that chefs found the perfect size and shape for baking creamed seafood (hence the term "scalloped," meaning "creamed"). Scallops were so rare, in fact, that fish markets sometimes counterfeited them out of haddock and cod. They were little known in this country until vast beds of them were found off the coast of New England in the 1930's. Although Europeans eat everything inside the scallop shell and relish particularly the bean-shaped coral of the female, we eat only the "eye" or firm, marshmallow-shaped muscle hinging top and bottom shells together.

The Kinds of Scallops

There are two: *ocean or sea scallops,* dredged from deep in the North Atlantic, and *bay scallops,* harvested in tidewater bays and sheltered inlets up and down the East Coast. Scallops are also found on the West Coast, especially around Puget Sound, but these are not as good as the Eastern variety.

Sea Scallops: Measuring from 1″–1½″ across, these are tannish, firm, and nutty. They can be tough, however, and are best sliced across the grain or diced and used in casseroles.

Bay Scallops: These are tiny, sometimes only ½″ across, creamy pink, and so sweet and delicate they can be eaten raw with only a drizzling of lemon or lime juice. The most delectable of all are those dipped from the chilly inshore waters of Long Island, New England, and Canada. Some gourmets rank them gastronomically with the finest caviar. Because of their extreme tenderness, they should be cooked as quickly and carefully as possible.

About Buying Fresh Scallops

Season:

Sea Scallops: September to April.

Bay Scallops: Autumn and winter.

Popular Market Forms: Bay and sea scallops are sold whole, out of the shell, by the pound.

Amount Needed: ⅓–½ pound per person.

For Top Quality: Look for sweet-smelling scallops packed in little or no liquid.

About Frozen Scallops

Sea scallops are available fresh frozen, frozen breaded, and frozen precooked. Bay scallops, unfortunately, are almost never frozen. *To Cook Frozen Scallops:* Thaw uncooked scallops in refrigerator just until they can be separated or, if you prefer, thaw completely (1 pound will take 3–4 hours to thaw), then cook as you would fresh scallops. Breaded or precooked frozen scallops should be prepared by package directions.

How to Open Fresh Scallops: Occasionally you may find scallops in the shell (or perhaps dip them up yourself). If so, here are two ways to open them.

1. *To Pry Open:* Hold scallop in one hand, dark side of shell down, slip a sharp knife into hinge and slip underneath large muscle, severing it as close to shell as possible. Cut muscle just underneath top shell the same way, open, and remove scallop. Wash well in cold water to remove grit or bits of shell.

2. *To Roast Open:* Scrub scallops in cold water, place dark side down in a large, shallow roasting pan, set in a 300° F. oven, and let stand uncovered about 5 minutes until shells open; discard any that don't. Remove from oven, cut out meat, and wash well in cool water.

How to Cook Scallops

Scallops are wonderfully adaptable— superb when cooked simply, sensational when dressed up. Here are the best basic ways to prepare them.

General Preparation (for all cooking methods): Wash well in cold water to remove bits of shell and grit.

To Oven Broil: Preheat broiler. Pat scallops dry on paper toweling, dip in melted butter, margarine, or cooking oil, arrange in a single layer in a shallow baking pan, and broil 3″–4″ from the heat 5–7 minutes, without turning or basting, until lightly browned. Sprinkle with salt and pepper and serve with lemon. For extra flavor, dip scallops in Lemon, Parsley, or Herb Butter instead of plain butter.

VARIATIONS:

⚖ **Low-Calorie Broiled Scallops:** Substitute low-calorie French, Italian, garlic, or herb dressing for the butter and broil as directed. About 125 calories per ⅓ pound serving.

Breaded Scallops: After dipping scallops in melted butter, roll in fine dry bread crumbs or cracker meal and broil as directed, turning and basting once so scallops brown evenly.

To Charcoal Broil: Build a moderately hot charcoal fire.* Wrap each scallop in a half slice bacon and thread on skewers so bacon won't unwrap; or secure bacon slices with toothpicks and arrange scallops in a well-greased, hinged, long-handled wire grill. Broil 4″ from heat 5–6 minutes on a side until bacon is brown and crisp.

To Panfry (*Sauté*): Pat scallops dry on paper toweling, then sauté in butter (about ¼ cup for 1 pound scallops) in a large, heavy skillet over moderately high heat 4–5 minutes until lightly browned. Sprinkle with salt and pepper and serve with lemon.

VARIATIONS:

Scallops Amandine: Pat scallops dry, dredge in flour lightly seasoned with salt and pepper, then sauté as above. Remove to a hot platter and keep warm. To skillet add 2–3 tablespoons butter or margarine and ½ cup slivered almonds and stir-fry 2–3 minutes until lightly browned. Pour over scallops and serve.

Scallops à la Meunière: Dip scallops in milk, then in flour lightly seasoned with salt and pepper. Sauté in butter as directed above, transfer to a hot platter, sprinkle with lemon juice and a little minced parsley, and keep warm. Add 1–2 tablespoons butter to skillet, heat until lightly browned and bubbly, pour over scallops, and serve.

Breaded Fried Scallops: Pat scallops dry, dip in a mixture of beaten egg and milk (2 tablespoons milk to each egg), then roll in fine dry bread crumbs or cracker meal to coat evenly. Pour ¼″ cooking oil or a ½ and ½ mixture of cooking oil and melted butter or margarine in a large heavy skillet and heat over moderately high heat until a cube of bread will sizzle. Brown scallops, turning as necessary, 4–6 minutes until golden brown all over. Drain on paper toweling and serve with lemon wedges.

To Oven "Fry": Preheat oven to 500° F. Mix ¼ cup milk with ½ teaspoon salt and a pinch white pepper; also mix ⅓ cup fine dry bread crumbs or cracker meal with ¼ teaspoon paprika. Dip scallops in milk, then in crumbs to coat evenly. Arrange in a single layer in a buttered shallow baking pan, drizzle with melted butter, and bake uncovered, without turning or basting, 7–9 minutes until golden.

To Deep-Fat-Fry: Pat scallops dry on paper toweling and bread as for Breaded Fried Scallops (above). Heat cooking oil or shortening in a deep fat fryer to 375° F., place a single layer of scallops in deep fat basket, lower into fat, and fry 2–3 minutes until golden brown. Drain on paper toweling and serve with lemon.

VARIATION:

Batter-Fried Scallops: Make up batter given in Fish and Chips recipe. Pat scallops dry on paper toweling, dip in flour, then in batter, then fry, a few at a time, in 375° F. fat 2–3 minutes until golden brown. Drain on paper toweling and serve with lemon and Tartar Sauce.

To Poach: Place scallops in a large, heavy skillet (not iron), add lightly salted boiling water to cover, *or* dry white wine brought just to a simmer *or,* if you prefer, a boiling court bouillon. If using water or wine, add a *bouquet garni** tied in cheesecloth. Cover and simmer 3–4 minutes until scallops turn milky white. Drain (cooking liquid can be used for making soups or sauces) and serve with Parsley, Caper, Mornay, or other suitable sauce (see Sauces, Butters, and Seasonings for Seafood) or use in recipes calling for poached scallops.

COQUILLES ST. JACQUES À LA PARISIENNE (SCALLOPS AND MUSHROOMS IN WINE CREAM SAUCE)

This is the classic *coquilles St. Jacques.* It can be served as a first course or light luncheon dish.
Makes 6–8 servings

1½ cups dry white wine
3 tablespoons minced shallots
1 bay leaf
1 parsley sprig
½ teaspoon salt
Pinch pepper
1½ pounds bay scallops, washed
½ pound mushrooms, wiped clean and minced
1½ cups water (about)

Sauce:

4 tablespoons butter or margarine
5 tablespoons flour
¾ cup reduced scallops' cooking liquid
⅔ cup heavy cream
2 egg yolks, lightly beaten
2 teaspoons lemon juice
¼ teaspoon salt
Pinch white pepper

Topping:

1¼ cups soft white bread crumbs
⅓ cup finely grated Gruyère cheese
¼ cup melted butter or margarine

Simmer wine, shallots, bay leaf, parsley, salt, and pepper, uncovered, 5 minutes in a large enamel or stainless-steel saucepan. Add scallops, mushrooms, and enough water to cover, and simmer, covered, 3–4 minutes until scallops turn milky white. Drain, reserving cooking liquid. Set scallops and mushrooms aside to cool, return liquid, bay leaf, and parsley to saucepan and boil rapidly uncovered until reduced to ¾ cup. Meanwhile, slice scallops across the grain

⅛" thick. For the sauce, melt butter in a small saucepan and blend in flour. Strain reduced cooking liquid and add along with cream. Heat, stirring constantly, until thickened and smooth. Spoon a little hot sauce into yolks, then return to pan; set over lowest heat and cook and stir 1 minute; do not allow to boil. Mix in lemon juice, salt, and pepper. Pour over scallops and mushrooms and toss to mix. Spoon into 6 to 8 well-buttered very large scallop shells or into individual *au gratin* dishes; mix topping and sprinkle evenly over each. Set coquilles on a large baking sheet. (*Note:* Recipe may be prepared to this point early in the day, covered and chilled until just before serving.) Preheat broiler. If you have not made coquilles ahead and chilled them, broil 5" from heat 4–5 minutes until bubbly and dappled with brown. If they have been chilled, set far below broiler unit (lowest oven shelf) and let warm 5–6 minutes, then move up and broil 5" from heat 3–4 minutes until bubbly and browned. About 470 calories for each of 6 servings, 350 calories for each of 8 servings.

COQUILLES ST. JACQUES À LA PROVENÇALE (SCALLOPS AU GRATIN)

Spicier than the classic *coquilles St. Jacques,* this Provençal version is also easier to make.
Makes 4 servings

1 pound bay scallops, washed
1 medium-size yellow onion, peeled and minced
1 tablespoon minced shallots
1 clove garlic, peeled and crushed
3 tablespoons butter or margarine
½ cup unsifted flour
1½ teaspoons salt
¼ teaspoon pepper
2 tablespoons olive oil
¾ cup dry white wine
2 bay leaves
⅛ teaspoon thyme
⅓ cup finely grated Gruyère cheese

Pat scallops dry on paper toweling and slice crosswise ¼" thick. Stir-fry onion, shallots, and garlic in 2 tablespoons butter in a large, heavy skillet over moderate heat 5–8 minutes until golden; remove from skillet and reserve. Dredge scallops lightly in a mixture of flour, salt, and pepper. Heat olive oil in the same skillet over high heat about 1 minute, add scallops, and stir-fry 2–3 minutes. Reduce heat to low, return onion mixture to skillet, add wine, bay leaves, and thyme, cover, and simmer 2–3 minutes; remove bay leaves. Spoon into 4 buttered large scallop shells and set on a baking sheet. Top with grated cheese and dot with remaining butter. (*Note:* Recipe may be prepared to this point early in the day, covered, and chilled until just before serving.) Preheat broiler. If you have not made coquilles ahead, broil 5″ from heat 4–5 minutes until bubbly and browned. If they have been chilled, set far below broiler unit (lowest oven shelf) and let warm 5–6 minutes; then move up and broil 5″ from heat 3–4 minutes until bubbly and touched with brown. About 370 calories per serving.

SEA SCALLOPS BAKED IN WINE AND CHEESE SAUCE

Makes 4 servings

1⅔ cups dry white wine
1 scallion, minced
1 bay leaf
2 parsley sprigs
1 stalk celery
½ teaspoon salt
Pinch pepper
1½ pounds sea scallops, washed
1⅓ cups water (about)
1 medium-size yellow onion, peeled and minced
1 clove garlic, peeled and crushed
¾ pound mushrooms, wiped clean and sliced thin
3 tablespoons butter or margarine

Sauce:

4 tablespoons butter or margarine
4 tablespoons flour
1 cup reduced scallops' cooking liquid
1 cup light cream
⅓ cup coarsely grated Gruyère cheese

Juice of ½ lemon or lime
¼ teaspoon salt
4–5 dashes liquid hot red pepper seasoning

Topping:

1 cup soft white bread crumbs mixed with 3 tablespoons melted butter or margarine

Preheat oven to 375° F. Bring wine, scallion, bay leaf, parsley, celery, salt, and pepper to a simmer in a large enamel or stainless-steel saucepan; add scallops and enough water to cover and simmer, covered, 4–5 minutes until milky white. Drain scallops and set aside to cool; return cooking liquid, bay leaf, parsley, and celery to saucepan and boil, uncovered, until reduced to 1 cup; strain and reserve. Meanwhile, stir-fry onion, garlic, and mushrooms in butter in a large, heavy skillet 5–8 minutes over moderate heat until onion is pale golden. Cut scallops in ½″ cubes and add to skillet. For the sauce, melt butter in a small saucepan and blend in flour; stir in reduced cooking liquid and cream and heat, stirring, until thickened and smooth. Add remaining sauce ingredients and heat and stir until cheese is melted; pour into skillet and toss to mix. Transfer to a buttered 1½-quart *au gratin* dish or shallow casserole and sprinkle with topping. Bake, uncovered, 20–25 minutes until bubbly, then broil quickly to brown. About 740 calories per serving.

⊠ HERBED SKILLET SCALLOPS

Makes 4 servings

1½ pounds bay scallops, washed
⅓ cup butter or margarine
1 tablespoon minced shallot or scallion
1 tablespoon minced parsley
1 tablespoon minced fresh dill
⅓ cup dry vermouth
Juice of ½ lemon or lime
½ teaspoon salt
4–5 dashes liquid hot red pepper seasoning

Pat scallops very dry on paper toweling. Melt butter in a large, heavy skillet over moderate heat, add shallot, and stir-fry 3–5 minutes until limp; add herbs and warm 1 minute. Turn heat to moderately high, add scallops, and stir-fry 3–5 minutes until lightly browned. Remove scallops with a slotted spoon to a heated platter and keep warm. Add remaining ingredients to skillet and heat and stir 2 minutes to blend flavors. Pour over scallops and serve. About 335 calories per serving.

⊠ SKILLET SCALLOPS RIVIERA

Scallops "greened" with minced parsley, green olives, and capers.
Makes 4 servings

1½ pounds bay scallops, washed
1 cup flour mixed with ¼ teaspoon
  pepper
⅓ cup olive oil
1 clove garlic, peeled and crushed
¼ cup minced parsley
⅓ cup minced pimiento-stuffed green
  olives
2 tablespoons minced capers

Pat scallops very dry on paper toweling and dredge in seasoned flour. Heat oil in a large, heavy skillet over moderately high heat until a cube of bread will sizzle, add scallops and garlic, and stir-fry 4–5 minutes until lightly browned. Add remaining ingredients, toss quickly to mix, and serve. About 380 calories per serving.

SCALLOPS MARINARA

Makes 4 servings

2 medium-size yellow onions, peeled and
  coarsely chopped
2 cloves garlic, peeled and crushed
¼ cup olive oil
1 bay leaf, crumbled
½ teaspoon basil
½ teaspoon oregano
1 tablespoon light brown sugar
½ teaspoon salt
⅛ teaspoon pepper
½ cup dry white wine
1 (6-ounce) can tomato paste
1 (1-pound 12-ounce) can tomatoes

1½ pounds bay scallops or sea scallops,
  washed and, if large, sliced
1 tablespoon minced parsley

Stir-fry onions and garlic in olive oil in a large, heavy skillet 8–10 minutes over moderate heat until golden. Add herbs, brown sugar, salt, pepper, and wine and cook and stir 2–3 minutes. Add tomato paste and tomatoes, breaking up any large clumps, and simmer, uncovered, 40–45 minutes, stirring often, until flavors are well blended. Add scallops, cover, and simmer 4–5 minutes until milky white. Sprinkle with parsley and serve over spaghetti or boiled rice. Pass grated Parmesan cheese. About 450 calories per serving (without rice or spaghetti or Parmesan).

CURRIED SCALLOPS

Makes 4 servings

1 cup dry white wine
2 cups water
1 large yellow onion, peeled and stuck
  with 4 cloves
1 cinnamon stick
1 carrot, peeled and cut in large chunks
2 parsley sprigs
1 stalk celery
½ teaspoon salt
¼ teaspoon pepper
1½ pounds sea scallops, washed
1 large yellow onion, peeled and minced
1 clove garlic, peeled and crushed
3 tablespoons butter or margarine
¼ cup curry powder
¼ teaspoon cayenne pepper
2 tablespoons minced crystallized ginger
1 cup Coconut Milk
1½ cups reduced scallops' cooking liquid
Juice of 1 lime
½ cup heavy cream

Bring wine, water, onion, cinnamon stick, carrot, parsley, celery, salt, and pepper to a simmer in a large enamel or stainless-steel saucepan; add scallops and simmer, covered, 4–5 minutes until milky white. Drain scallops and cool; return cooking liquid and all of its seasonings to pan and boil, uncovered, until reduced to 1½ cups. Meanwhile, stir-fry onion and garlic in butter in a very large, heavy skillet over moderate heat 8–10 minutes until golden. Cut scallops in ½″ cubes, cover, and keep cool. Blend curry powder and cayenne into onion, add ginger, coconut milk, and strained scallops' cooking liquid. Cover and simmer slowly ¾–1 hour until flavors are well blended. Mix in lime juice and cream, taste for salt and adjust as needed. Bring to a simmer, add scallops, and warm 2–3 minutes. Serve over boiled rice with chutney. About 405 calories per serving (without rice or chutney).

⚖ ⊠ SCALLOPS EN BROCHETTE
Makes 4 servings

*1½ pounds bay scallops or small sea
    scallops, washed*
⅓ cup French, Italian, or Herb Dressing

Pat scallops dry on paper toweling, mix with dressing, and let stand 30 minutes at room temperature. Preheat broiler. Arrange on small skewers, not too close together, and broil 3″ from heat 5–6 minutes, turning often and brushing with dressing, until evenly browned. About 240 calories per serving if made with French dressing, 260 calories per serving if made with Italian or herb dressing.

VARIATIONS:

⚖ **Low-Calorie Scallops en Brochette:** Prepare as directed, substituting low-calorie dressing for the regular. About 180 calories per serving.

Mushrooms and Scallops en Brochette: Wipe 1½ pound mushrooms clean with a damp cloth, then skewer alternately with scallops. If you like, interweave bacon strips. Brush with dressing or melted butter and broil as directed. About 285 calories per serving if made with French dressing, 305 calories per serving if made with Italian or herb dressing.

Sweet-Sour Scallop Kebabs: Alternate scallops on skewers with chunks of pineapple, interweaving strips of bacon, and place 1 layer deep in a shallow pan. Mix ¼ cup each melted butter, pineapple juice, light brown sugar, and grated onion, 2 teaspoons powdered mustard, 2 tablespoons lemon juice, ½ teaspoon salt, and a pinch pepper. Pour over kebabs, cover, and let stand at room temperature ½ hour. Remove kebabs from marinade and broil as directed, brushing often with marinade. Recipe too flexible for a meaningful calorie count.

CHILLED SCALLOPS IN GREEN DRESSING
An unusual summer luncheon entree.
Makes 4 servings

1½ pounds bay scallops, washed
⅔ cup dry white wine
2 bay leaves
*1 (4″) sprig fresh thyme or ¼ teaspoon
    dried thyme*
*1 small yellow onion, peeled and coarsely
    chopped*
Crisp lettuce cups

Green Dressing:

1 tablespoon minced fresh chives
1 tablespoon minced fresh tarragon
1 tablespoon minced fresh dill
⅓ cup minced parsley
⅓ cup minced raw spinach
1 cup mayonnaise
2 teaspoons scallops' cooking liquid
¼ teaspoon salt

Pat scallops dry on paper toweling and halve any that seem extra large. Place scallops, wine, bay leaves, thyme, and onion in a small saucepan, cover, and simmer over moderate heat 3–4 minutes until scallops turn milky white. Drain, saving 2 teaspoons cooking liquid. Mix together all dressing ingredients, add scallops, and toss lightly to mix. Cover and chill several hours. Serve in lettuce cups. About 620 calories per serving.

SHRIMP

In just fifty short years, shrimp have zoomed ahead of other shellfish to become America's favorite, all because refrigeration and quick shipping have made them as available in Nebraska as in New Orleans (also because the supply appears to be endless). Time was when the only thing most of us knew to do with shrimp was to make them into cocktails. But as Deep South shrimp reached the heartlands, so, too, did some of the great shrimp country recipes— pies, patties, puddings, not to mention gumbos and jambalayas. Then came the international specialties—from the Orient and Mediterranean, from Latin and South America—and in the process

of trying them all we're putting away better than a quarter *billion* pounds of shrimp a year.

The Kinds of Shrimp

There are several kinds of shrimp—the *common gray-green;* the *brownish-pink Brazilian;* the *Gulf Coast pink;* the rare, *deep sea "royal red,"* and the *cold water miniatures* from Alaska and Denmark. In addition, there are *prawns,* not just a large shrimp, as many people believe, but a bright pink European species (the French call it *langoustine* and the Italians *scampi*). Further complicating the terminology is the fact that *scampi* now means a way of cooking shrimp (broiled with lots of oil and garlic) as well as the animal itself. Actually, the varieties of shrimp matter little because all can be used interchangeably. What matters more are the sizes:

Size	Number per Pound	Best Used for
Colossal	10 or less	Scampi, stuffed shrimp
Jumbo	12–15	Broiling, butterflying and deep fat frying, stuffed shrimp
Medium	16–20	Casseroles, creamed dishes, cocktails
Medium-Small	21–25	Casseroles, creamed dishes
Small	31–42	Casseroles, creamed dishes, salads
Miniatures (Danish or cocktail shrimp)	200 or more	Open face sandwiches, canapés, soups, salads

As might be expected, the larger the shrimp, the more expensive.

About Buying Fresh Shrimp

Season: Year round.

Popular Market Forms: Unless you live in a shrimping area, the shrimp you buy will be the tail part only. These are available raw and·in the shell ("green shrimp," the markets call them), or shelled and deveined. In addition, you can buy fresh-cooked shrimp in the shell or shelled and deveined. A specialty

item: refrigerated, ready-to-serve shrimp cocktails.

Amount Needed: Allow ⅓–½ pound shelled shrimp per person, about ¾ pound unshelled shrimp, depending, of course, on appetites and richness of the dish.

For Top Quality: Raw shrimp should be firm but moist and sweet-smelling; cooked shrimp should also be firm and sweet-smelling and there should be a lot of "spring" or resilience to the tail; if the cooked shrimp have been shelled and deveined, they should look succulent, neither too moist nor too dry.

About Frozen, Canned, and Dried Shrimp

You can buy frozen raw shrimp in or out of the shell, deveined or undeveined, also breaded and ready to deep-fry. Frozen cooked shrimp come shelled and deveined, also breaded and in a variety of precooked dinners. On the horizon: freeze-dried shrimp. Canned shrimp have lost considerable ground since the arrival of frozen shrimp, but they are still available, deveined, or in the standard pack (not deveined). The most popular canned shrimp are probably the tiny Danish ones. Two specialty items: shrimp paste (in tubes) and dried shrimp; both should be used according to label instructions. *How to Use Frozen Shrimp:* With the exception of frozen, uncooked breaded shrimp, frozen shrimp are better if thawed before cooking (leave shrimp in their package and thaw in the refrigerator or under a gentle stream of cold running water). Once shrimp are thawed, drain well, then prepare as you would fresh shrimp; never refreeze. Most brands of frozen shrimp are accompanied by directions; follow them. *How to Use Canned Shrimp:* Because these shrimp are fully cooked, they're particularly suited for use in soups, salads, and casseroles; the tiny Danish shrimp are good for sandwich fillings, canapé spreads, and cocktail dips.

How to Cook Shrimp

Boiling is the most popular way to cook shrimp, with deep fat frying close behind. But, they may also be broiled in the oven or over charcoal and, of course, added to soups, sauces, skillet dinners, and casseroles. The greatest difficulty most people have with shrimp is overcooking them. They really only need to heat through. How can you tell if they are done and not overdone? By color. As soon as shrimp turn pink, they are done.

General Preparation: Sooner or later, all shrimp must be shelled and deveined. Sometimes it's done before cooking, sometimes afterwards, and sometimes at the table, with everyone attacking his own portion.

To Shell and Devein Shrimp: The process is the same whether shrimp are raw or cooked. Starting at the large end, peel away the thin shell, unwinding it from around tail. If shrimp are to be deep fat fried, or if recipes so specify, leave tail fins on; otherwise, remove. To devein, make a shallow incision (about ⅛″ deep) down center back (outer curved side) with a small, sharp knife and pull out dark vein running length of tail. Rinse away any broken bits of vein under cool running water. (*Note:* Not every shrimp will have the dark vein, but the majority will.)

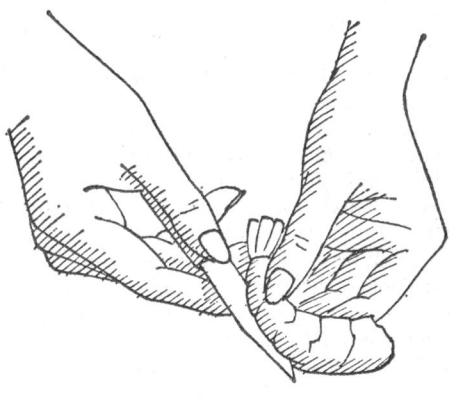

To Butterfly Shrimp: This is most often done when shrimp are to be dipped in batter and deep fat fried. Deepen incision made for deveining, cutting almost but not quite through to underside; spread shrimp as flat as possible (like an open book) and pat dry on paper toweling.

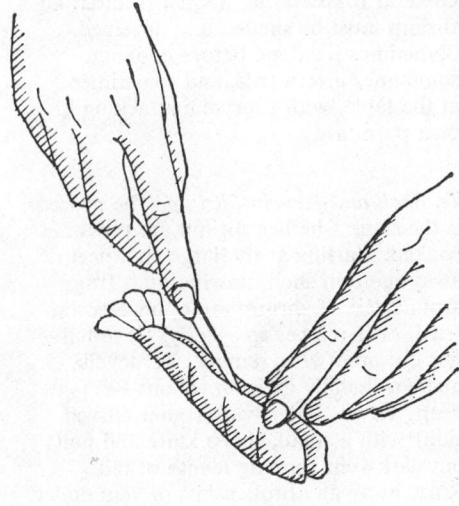

To Boil: The only real difference
between boiling shrimp in the shell or
out is the amount of salt needed
(unshelled shrimp take twice as much).
Allow 1 quart water for each pound
shrimp, 2 tablespoons salt for unshelled
shrimp and 1 tablespoon for the shelled.
Bring salt water to a boil, add shrimp,
cover, and simmer 3–5 minutes,
depending on size, just until shrimp turn
pink. Drain and, if in the shell, shell and
devein. Serve hot with Lemon, Garlic, or
Herb Butter, chill and use for shrimp
cocktail; or use in any recipes calling
for cooked shrimp. (*Note:* If you live
near the ocean, use sea water for boiling
the shrimp, adding 1 teaspoon salt if the
shrimp are being cooked in the shell.)

VARIATIONS:

Savory Boiled Shrimp: Boil shrimp as
directed, substituting a court bouillon for
salt water.

Shrimp Boiled in Beer: Boil shrimp as
directed, using a ½ and ½ mixture of
beer or ale and water instead of salt
water.

To Oven Broil: Select large shrimp,
shell and devein. Preheat broiler. Place
shrimp on a foil-lined broiler pan or in a
large piepan. Brush generously with
melted butter or margarine or a ½ and
½ mixture of melted butter and lemon
juice, dry white wine, or sherry. Broil 3″
from the heat 3–5 minutes on a side,
brushing often with butter. Sprinkle with
salt and pepper and serve.

VARIATION:

⚖ **Low-Calorie Broiled Shrimp:** Broil
as directed, using low-calorie Italian,
herb, or garlic dressing in place of
butter. About 150 calories per ⅓ pound
serving.

To Charcoal Broil: Select large shrimp
and shell and devein. Build a moderately
hot charcoal fire.* Thread shrimp on
large, thin skewers or place in a well-
greased, hinged, long-handled wire grill.
Brush shrimp generously with melted
butter or margarine and broil 4″ from
coals about 5 minutes on a side until pink
and delicately browned.

To Panfry (Sauté): Shell and devein
shrimp. Sauté in butter, margarine, or
cooking oil (about ¼ cup for each
pound of shrimp), stirring briskly, 3–5
minutes over moderate heat, just until
pink. Sprinkle with lemon juice, salt, and
pepper and serve.

VARIATION:

Shrimp à la Meunière: Shell and devein
shrimp, dip in milk, then in flour lightly
seasoned with salt and pepper. Sauté in
butter as above, transfer to a hot platter,
sprinkle with lemon juice and minced
parsley, and keep warm. Add 1–2
tablespoons butter to skillet, heat quickly
until bubbly and faintly brown, pour
over shrimp and serve.

To Deep-Fat-Fry: Shell and devein
shrimp and, if extra large, butterfly.*
Heat shortening or cooking oil in a deep
fat fryer to 375° F. Dip shrimp in flour
lightly seasoned with salt and pepper,
then in a mixture of beaten egg and milk
(2 tablespoons milk to each egg), and
then in fine dry bread crumbs, cracker
meal, or a ½ and ½ mixture of flour and
corn meal. Place in a single layer in
fryer basket, lower into hot fat, and fry

3–5 minutes until golden. Drain on paper toweling and serve with lemon wedges and Tartar Sauce.

VARIATION:

Batter-Fried Shrimp: See recipes for Hawaiian Sweet-and-Sour Shrimp and Japanese Butterfly Shrimp.

SHRIMP NEWBURG

Makes 4 servings

3 tablespoons butter or margarine
3 tablespoons flour
¾ teaspoon salt
⅛ teaspoon cayenne pepper
⅛ teaspoon nutmeg or mace
1 pint light cream
2 egg yolks, lightly beaten
1 pound shrimp, boiled, shelled, and
    deveined
2 tablespoons dry sherry
4 slices hot buttered toast, halved
    diagonally

Melt butter in the top of a double boiler directly over moderate heat, blend in flour, salt, pepper and nutmeg, add cream and heat, stirring constantly, until thickened and smooth. Blend a little hot sauce into yolks, return to pan, and set over simmering water. Add shrimp and heat, stirring occasionally, 3–5 minutes until a good serving temperature. Stir in sherry and serve over toast. About 605 calories per serving.

SHRIMP IN DILL SAUCE

Makes 6 servings

2 tablespoons butter or margarine
2 tablespoons minced shallots
1¼ cups dry white wine
½ cup water
1 bay leaf
2 pounds shelled and deveined raw
    shrimp
¼ cup unsalted butter
5 tablespoons flour
1 cup heavy cream
2 tablespoons minced fresh dill
½ teaspoon salt
⅛ teaspoon white pepper

Melt butter in a large saucepan over moderate heat, add shallots, and sauté 5 minutes until golden. Add wine, water, bay leaf, and shrimp and simmer, uncovered, stirring occasionally, 3–5 minutes until shrimp just turn pink. Remove from heat and set aside. Melt unsalted butter in a small saucepan over moderate heat and blend in flour. Add cream and heat, stirring constantly, until thickened and smooth; mix in dill, salt, and pepper. Stir cream sauce into shrimp, return to a moderate heat, and cook, stirring constantly, 3–5 minutes until heated through (do not allow to boil); remove bay leaf. Serve over boiled rice or hot buttered toast. About 440 calories per serving (without rice or toast).

SHRIMP WIGGLE

A good chafing dish choice.
Makes 4 servings

1 (10-ounce) package frozen baby green
    peas, cooked and seasoned by package
    directions
1 pound fresh or frozen thawed, shelled,
    and deveined cooked small shrimp
2 cups hot Velouté Sauce, Béchamel
    Sauce, or Medium White Sauce
2 teaspoons finely grated yellow onion
4 slices hot buttered toast or 4 frozen
    puff pastry shells, baked by package
    directions

Mix peas, shrimp, sauce, and onion and heat and stir 3–5 minutes over low heat to blend flavors. Spoon over toast or into baked pastry shells and serve. If made with Velouté Sauce: About 460 calories per serving if served over toast and 625 calories per serving if served in puff pastry shells. If made with Béchamel Sauce: about 500 calories per serving if served over toast and 665 calories per serving if served in puff pastry shells. If made with Medium White Sauce: about 420 calories per serving if served over toast and 585 calories per serving if served in puff pastry shells.

SHRIMP CURRY I

A mellow, sweet-sour curry
Makes 6 servings

3 medium-size yellow onions, peeled and
  coarsely chopped
3 cloves garlic, peeled and crushed
6 tablespoons butter or margarine
⅔ cup coarsely chopped celery
3 tart apples, peeled, cored, and diced
2 large tomatoes, peeled, cored, seeded,
  and coarsely chopped
3 (½") cubes fresh gingerroot, peeled
  and crushed (use garlic crusher)
2 tablespoons curry powder
½ teaspoon turmeric
½ teaspoon coriander
¼ teaspoon cumin
¼ teaspoon cinnamon
¼ teaspoon crushed hot red chili peppers
⅛ teaspoon mace
1 (3½-ounce) can flaked coconut
1½ cups water
⅔ cup dry white wine
1 pint yogurt
1 teaspoon salt
2 pounds shelled and deveined raw
  shrimp

Stir-fry onions and garlic in butter in a
large, heavy skillet over moderate heat
10–12 minutes until golden brown; mix
in celery, apples, tomatoes, and all
spices, cover, and simmer 25–30 minutes.
Meanwhile, place coconut and water in
an electric blender and purée at high
speed. When sauce has simmered allotted
time, stir in puréed coconut, wine,
yogurt, and salt and heat, uncovered,
stirring now and then, 10 minutes. Add
shrimp and simmer, uncovered, stirring
occasionally, about 5 minutes until just
pink. Serve hot over boiled rice. (*Note:*
This curry will be even better if made a
day ahead, cooled to room temperature,
then refrigerated until just before
serving. Reheat slowly.) About 495
calories per serving (without rice).

SHRIMP CURRY II

A fiery curry that freezes well. It's
lower in calories than Shrimp Curry I.
Makes 8 servings

4 medium-size yellow onions, peeled
  and minced
4 cloves garlic, peeled and crushed
6 tablespoons peanut oil
3 teaspoons turmeric
4 teaspoons mustard seeds
1 teaspoon fenugreek
3 teaspoons cumin
2–3 teaspoons crushed hot red chili
  peppers
4 teaspoons coriander
2 teaspoons ginger
1½ teaspoons cinnamon
¼ teaspoon cloves
½ teaspoon chili powder
1 quart Coconut Milk
4 (½") cubes fresh gingerroot, peeled
  and crushed (use garlic crusher)
2 large tomatoes, peeled, cored, seeded,
  and coarsely chopped
Juice of 2 lemons
¼ teaspoon salt
4 pounds shelled and deveined raw
  shrimp
1 cup light cream

Stir-fry onions and garlic in ¼ cup
peanut oil in a large, heavy kettle over
moderate heat 8–10 minutes until
golden. Meanwhile, place all dried
spices in an electric blender cup, cover
with plastic food wrap, then lid and
purée at high speed until fine and
smooth. Mix blended spices into kettle,
turn heat to low, and let "mellow" 10
minutes. Add all but last 2 ingredients
and simmer, uncovered, stirring
occasionally, 25–30 minutes until
flavors are well blended. Stir-fry shrimp
in a large, heavy skillet in remaining oil
3–5 minutes over moderately high heat,
just until no longer pink. Add to sauce
along with cream and simmer,
uncovered, stirring occasionally, 5–10
minutes to blend flavors. Serve over
boiled rice with chutney and, if you
like, minced roasted peanuts, flaked
coconut, and raisins. (*Note:* Like
Shrimp Curry I, this one will be better
if made a day ahead.) About 380
calories per serving (without rice and
condiments).

SHRIMP GUMBO

Makes 4 servings

3/4 pound small okra pods, washed,
  trimmed, and sliced 1/4" thick, or
  1 (10-ounce) package frozen sliced
  okra (do not thaw)
1/4 cup shortening or cooking oil
2/3 cup minced scallions (include some
  green tops)
2 cloves garlic, peeled and crushed
1 (1-pound 12-ounce) can tomatoes (do
  not drain)
1/2 cup boiling water
2 bay leaves
1 teaspoon salt
1/4 teaspoon liquid hot red pepper
  seasoning
1 pound shelled and deveined raw
  shrimp
1/8 teaspoon filé powder

Sauté okra 2 minutes on a side in
shortening in a large, heavy saucepan
over moderate heat until golden brown;
drain on paper toweling and reserve.
Add scallions and garlic to pan and
stir-fry 3–5 minutes until limp. Add all
remaining ingredients except okra,
shrimp, and filé powder and simmer,
uncovered, 20–25 minutes, stirring
occasionally, until slightly thickened and
flavors are well blended. Add okra and
shrimp and cook 3–5 minutes, just until
shrimp turn pink. Remove bay leaves,
stir in filé powder, and serve over boiled
rice. About 300 calories per serving
(without rice).

SHRIMP JAMBALAYA

A Creole favorite—shrimp with ham,
rice, and tomatoes.
Makes 4–6 servings

2 onions, peeled and coarsely chopped
1 clove garlic, peeled and crushed
1/3 cup olive oil
1 cup diced cooked ham
1 1/4 cups uncooked rice
1 (1-pound 12-ounce) can tomatoes
  (do not drain)
1 1/2 teaspoons salt
1/2 teaspoon cayenne pepper
1 tablespoon minced parsley

1 3/4 cups boiling water or chicken broth
1 pound shelled and deveined small raw
  shrimp

Stir-fry onions and garlic in oil in a
large, heavy kettle 5–8 minutes over
moderate heat until golden; add ham
and rice and stir-fry 5 minutes until
rice is very lightly browned. Add all
remaining ingredients except shrimp
and bring to a boil, stirring. Adjust heat
so mixture stays at a simmer, cover, and
simmer 20 minutes until rice is very
nearly done. Add shrimp, pushing well
down into mixture, cover, and simmer
3–5 minutes just until pink. Serve with
hot buttered French bread and a crisp
green salad. About 645 calories for each
of 4 servings, 430 calories for each of
6 servings.

SHRIMP CREOLE

Makes 4 servings

2 medium-size yellow onions, peeled and
  minced
2 medium-size sweet green peppers,
  cored, seeded, and minced
2 cloves garlic, peeled and crushed
2 stalks celery, minced
2 tablespoons olive or other cooking oil
2 tablespoons butter or margarine
1 (1-pound 12-ounce) can tomatoes
  (do not drain)
1/2 teaspoon paprika
1/8 teaspoon cayenne pepper
1 teaspoon salt
1 teaspoon filé powder
1 1/2 pounds shelled and deveined raw
  shrimp

Stir-fry onions, green peppers, garlic,
and celery in oil and butter in a large
saucepan 5–8 minutes over moderately
low heat until onions are golden. Stir in
tomatoes, breaking up any large pieces,
paprika, pepper, and salt; cover and
simmer 35–45 minutes, stirring
occasionally. If sauce seems thin, boil,
uncovered, 2–3 minutes to reduce. Add
filé powder and shrimp and simmer,
uncovered, 3–5 minutes until shrimp
are just cooked through. Serve over
boiled rice. About 340 calories per
serving (without rice).

SHRIMP THERMIDOR

Makes 6 servings

2 pounds shelled and deveined raw
  shrimp
3 tablespoons minced shallots or
  scallions
6 tablespoons butter or margarine
6 tablespoons flour
¾ teaspoon salt
½ teaspoon powdered mustard
Pinch cayenne pepper
1 cup milk
1 cup shrimp cooking water
3 egg yolks, lightly beaten
⅓ cup grated Parmesan cheese

Preheat oven to 425° F. Boil shrimp
according to basic method,* then drain,
reserving 1 cup cooking water; set
shrimp aside while you prepare sauce.
Stir-fry shallots in butter in the top of a
large double boiler directly over
moderate heat 3–5 minutes until limp;
blend in flour, salt, mustard and pepper,
slowly add milk and shrimp cooking
water, and heat, stirring, until thickened
and smooth. Briskly mix 1 cup sauce
into yolks, then return to pan. Set over
simmering water and stir 1–2 minutes
until no taste of raw egg remains. Spoon
½–¾ cup sauce into an ungreased
2-quart au gratin dish or shallow
casserole. Arrange shrimp in sauce and
top with remaining sauce. Sprinkle with
Parmesan. Bake, uncovered, 10–15
minutes until hot but not boiling, then
broil 5"–6" from heat about 2 minutes
to brown. Serve with boiled rice. About
340 calories per serving (without rice).

VARIATION:

Thermidor Ramekins: Prepare shrimp
and sauce as directed and divide among
6 ungreased individual ramekins. Bake
10 minutes and broil 1–2 to brown.
About 340 calories per serving.

⚖ SCAMPI

Broiled shrimp redolent of garlic and
olive oil.
Makes 2 servings

1 pound raw jumbo shrimp in the shell
1 cup olive oil

2 tablespoons minced parsley
1 clove garlic, peeled and crushed
1 teaspoon salt
¼ teaspoon pepper

Shell shrimp, leaving tail ends on, then
devein.* Rinse in cool water, pat dry,
and place in a shallow bowl. Mix
remaining ingredients and pour over
shrimp; cover and chill 2–3 hours in
refrigerator, turning 1 or 2 times in
marinade. Preheat broiler. Place shrimp
on a foil-lined broiler pan and brush
generously with marinade. Broil 5"–6"
from heat 3 minutes on a side, basting
often with marinade. About 170 calories
per serving.

VARIATIONS:

⚖ **Wine Scampi:** Prepare as directed
but add 3 tablespoons dry vermouth or
sherry to the marinade. About 175
calories per serving.

⚖ **Scampi Italian Style:** Do not shell
the shrimp; mix marinade as directed but
increase garlic to 2 cloves. Cover
shrimp with marinade and chill 2–3
hours, turning often. Broil 3–5 minutes
on a side, basting often with marinade.
Serve shrimp in the shell with plenty of
paper napkins. Any remaining marinade
or pan drippings can be used as a dip.
About 170 calories per serving.

SHRIMP RUMAKI

Soy-marinated, bacon-wrapped broiled
shrimp.
Makes 4 main course servings, enough
hors d'oeuvre for 8

1½ pounds shelled and deveined raw
  jumbo shrimp
1 cup soy sauce
1 cup medium-sweet sherry
1 teaspoon finely grated fresh gingerroot
  or ¼ teaspoon dried ginger
12 slices bacon, halved crosswise

Marinate shrimp in a mixture of soy
sauce, sherry, and ginger 2–3 hours in
refrigerator, turning occasionally.
Preheat oven to 400° F. Drain marinade
from shrimp and reserve. Wrap a piece
of bacon around each shrimp and secure

with a toothpick. Arrange shrimp on a rack in a large, shallow roasting pan and bake, uncovered, 10 minutes, basting 1 or 2 times with marinade. Turn shrimp and bake 10 minutes longer, basting once or twice, until bacon is nicely browned. Remove toothpicks and serve as a main course, or leave toothpicks in and serve as an hors d'oeuvre. About 315 calories per entree serving, 155 calories for each of 8 hors d'oeuvre servings.

PEPPERY SZECHUAN SHRIMP

Szechuan, a province in south central China, produces a cuisine as peppery as that of our own Southwest. By comparison, Cantonese cooking, the cuisine most familiar to Americans, seems bland. The following recipe is "hot." If you are not fond of fiery dishes, reduce the amount of hot red chili peppers. If, on the other hand, you like hot dishes truly hot, increase slightly the amount of chilis.
Makes 6 servings

2 pounds shelled and deveined raw shrimp
1 cup peanut oil (about)
½ cup thinly sliced scallions (include green tops)
2 cloves garlic, peeled and crushed
3 tablespoons finely grated fresh gingerroot
½ cup sake or dry sherry
¼ cup soy sauce
1 tablespoon sugar
1 tablespoon rice or cider vinegar
½ cup ketchup
½ cup chili sauce
¼ teaspoon crushed hot red chili peppers
¼ teaspoon salt (about)

Pat shrimp dry on paper toweling. Heat oil in a *wok* or large, heavy skillet over moderately high heat. Add shrimp, about half at a time, and stir-fry 3–4 minutes until pink. Drain on paper toweling. Pour all but about 2 tablespoons oil from wok or skillet, add scallions and garlic, and stir-fry 3–5 minutes over moderate heat until limp. Add remaining ingredients except shrimp and heat and stir 5 minutes. Add shrimp and heat, tossing in sauce, 3–4 minutes. Taste for salt and adjust if needed. Serve with boiled rice. About 330 calories per serving without rice.

CANTONESE-STYLE SHRIMP WITH VEGETABLES
Makes 4–6 servings

1½ pounds shelled and deveined raw shrimp
¼ cup peanut or other cooking oil
½ pound mushrooms, wiped clean and sliced thin
1 (5-ounce) can water chestnuts, drained and sliced thin
2 cups diced celery
2 cups finely shredded Chinese cabbage
8 scallions, trimmed and minced (include tops)
1 medium-size sweet green pepper, cored, seeded, and minced
1 tablespoon minced fresh gingerroot
1 clove garlic, peeled and crushed (optional)
2 tablespoons cornstarch blended with ¼ cup cold chicken broth
1¾ cups chicken broth
2 teaspoons salt
1 teaspoon sugar

Stir-fry shrimp in 2 tablespoons oil in a large, heavy skillet or *wok* over moderately high heat 2–3 minutes until just turning pink; drain on paper toweling and reserve. Add remaining oil to skillet, also mushrooms, water chestnuts, vegetables, ginger, and, if you wish, garlic; stir-fry 2–3 minutes until crisp tender. Add shrimp and remaining ingredients and cook and stir until slightly thickened. Serve over boiled rice or thin noodles. About 365 calories for each of 4 servings (without rice or noodles), 245 calories for each of 6 servings.

VARIATION:

Loong Ha Peen (Chicken, Shrimp, and Vegetables): Reduce amount of shrimp to 1 pound and add 1 cup coarsely chopped, cooked chicken meat. Prepare as directed, stirring chicken into sautéed vegetables along with sautéed shrimp. About 395 calories for each of 4 servings, 265 calories for each of 6 servings.

⚖️ GINGERY CHINESE SHRIMP

Makes 2–3 main course servings, enough hors d'oeuvre for 4–6

1 pound shelled and deveined raw
   shrimp
1½ teaspoons cornstarch
2 teaspoons dry vermouth or sherry
1 teaspoon salt
¼ teaspoon monosodium glutamate
   (MSG)
2 scallions, sliced ¼″ thick (include
   some tops)
2 (¼″) cubes fresh gingerroot, peeled
   and crushed (use garlic crusher)
¾ cup cooking oil

If shrimp are very large, halve crosswise; place in a bowl, add cornstarch, vermouth, salt, MSG, scallions, and ginger, and toss to mix. Cover and chill 2 hours. Heat oil in a large, heavy skillet over moderately high heat until a cube of bread will sizzle, add shrimp and stir-fry 2–3 minutes or just until shrimp turn pink. Drain on paper toweling and serve with boiled rice as a main course, or spear each shrimp with a toothpick and serve hot as an hors d'oeuvre. About 270 calories for each of 2 entree servings, 180 calories for each of 3 entree servings. About 135 calories for each of 4 hors d'oeuvre servings and 90 calories for each of 6 hors d'oeuvre servings.

JAPANESE BUTTERFLY SHRIMP

Makes 6–8 entree servings, enough hors d'oeuvre for 10–12

3 pounds large raw shrimp in the shell
Shortening or cooking oil for deep fat
   frying
½ cup rice flour
1 recipe Tempura Batter
1 recipe Tempura Sauce

Shell shrimp, leaving tail ends on, then devein.* To butterfly, cut down center back of each shrimp to within ⅛″ of underside and spread flat. Rinse shrimp in cool water, pat dry on paper toweling, cover, and chill several hours. About ½ hour before serving, begin heating shortening in a deep fat fryer; insert deep fat thermometer. Also make *tempura* batter and sauce. When fat reaches 380° F., quickly dredge shrimp in rice flour, dip in batter, and fry, 5 or 6 at a time, 3–5 minutes until golden brown. Drain on paper toweling and set, uncovered, in oven turned to lowest heat to keep warm and crisp while you fry remaining shrimp. Scoop any crumbs of batter from fat before each new batch of shrimp and keep fat temperature as near 380° F. as possible. Serve shrimp as an entree or hors d'oeuvre, using tempura sauce as a dip. About 350 calories for each of 6 entree servings, 260 calories for each of 8 entree servings. About 210 calories for each of 10 hors d'oeuvre servings and 175 calories for each of 12 hors d'oeuvre servings.

HAWAIIAN SWEET-AND-SOUR SHRIMP

Makes 6 servings

2 pounds large raw shrimp in the shell
Shortening or cooking oil for deep fat
   frying (for best flavor, use part peanut
   oil)

Sweet-Sour Sauce:

1 large yellow onion, peeled and cut in
   thin wedges
1 large sweet green pepper, cored,
   seeded, and cut in 2″ × ¾″ strips
¼ cup peanut oil
⅔ cup firmly packed light brown sugar
½ cup rice vinegar or cider vinegar
¼ cup tomato paste
1 (13¼-ounce) can pineapple chunks
   (do not drain)
⅓ cup water or dry white wine
¼ cup soy sauce
⅛ teaspoon cayenne pepper
1 tablespoon cornstarch blended with
   ¼ cup cold water

Shrimp Batter:

1 egg
1 cup unsifted rice flour
1 tablespoon sugar
1 teaspoon salt
¾ cup ice water

Shell shrimp, leaving tail ends on, then devein* and butterfly by cutting down center back of each shrimp to within ⅛″ of underside and spreading flat. Rinse shrimp in cool water and pat dry on paper toweling. Begin heating shortening in a deep fat fryer; insert deep fat thermometer. Also make sweet-sour sauce: Stir-fry onion and green pepper in peanut oil 5–8 minutes until onion is golden; add all remaining sauce ingredients except cornstarch paste and simmer, uncovered, stirring occasionally, 10 minutes. Mix in cornstarch paste and heat, stirring constantly, until thickened and clear. Turn heat to lowest point and let sauce cook slowly while you prepare shrimp. For the batter, beat egg until foamy, mix in remaining ingredients, and beat well until the consistency of heavy cream. When fat reaches 375° F., dip shrimp in batter, then fry, about 5 or 6 at a time, 3–5 minutes until golden. Drain on paper toweling. When all shrimp are done, mound on a heated large platter, smother with sweet-sour sauce, and serve. About 710 calories per serving.

CHARLESTON SHRIMP PIE

A delicate, Deep South favorite that's easy to make.
Makes 6 servings

2 pounds shrimp, boiled, shelled, and deveined
8 slices firm-texured white bread
1 pint light cream
1 pint milk
1 tablespoon melted butter or margarine
½ cup dry sherry
2 teaspoons salt
¼ teaspoon mace or nutmeg
¼ teaspoon cayenne pepper

Preheat oven to 375° F. Place shrimp in a buttered 2½-quart casserole or soufflé dish. Soak bread in cream and milk 15 minutes in a large bowl, add remaining ingredients, and beat until smooth with a wooden spoon. Pour over shrimp and toss well to mix. Bake, uncovered, 1 hour and 15 minutes or until lightly browned and bubbly. About 380 calories per serving.

⊠ BAKED SHRIMP AND RED RICE

This Louisiana classic couldn't be easier.
Makes 4 servings

¼ cup olive or other cooking oil
1 medium-size yellow onion, peeled and minced
1 clove garlic, peeled and crushed
½ cup minced green pepper
½ cup uncooked rice
1 (1-pound) can tomatoes (do not drain)
½ cup water
1½ teaspoons salt
¼ teaspoon pepper
¼ teaspoon oregano
1 bay leaf, crumbled
1½ pounds shelled and deveined raw shrimp

Preheat oven to 350° F. In a buttered 2-quart casserole, mix all ingredients except shrimp. Cover and bake 1 hour, stirring 2 or 3 times. Add shrimp, pushing well down into mixture, re-cover, and bake ½ hour longer or until rice is done. About 415 calories per serving.

VARIATION:

Baked Scallops and Red Rice: Prepare as directed, substituting 1½ pounds bay scallops for the shrimp. About 365 calories per serving.

⚖ PICKLED SHRIMP À LA LORNA

Serve as a summer luncheon entree or as hors d'oeuvre on crisp crackers with bits of sliced onion.
Makes 8 main course servings, enough hors d'oeuvre for 12

3 pounds shrimp, boiled, shelled,
    deveined, and cooled
3 medium-sized yellow onions, peeled
    and sliced very thin
1 (3/16-ounce) box bay leaves
1½ cups olive or other cooking oil
1½ cups French dressing
1½ cloves garlic, peeled and halved

Place a layer of shrimp in a deep
enamel kettle, top with a layer of sliced
onions and a layer of bay leaves.
Continue building up layers as long as
shrimp last. Mix oil and French dressing
and pour over all. Drop in garlic, cover,
and marinate in refrigerator at least
4 hours before serving. (*Note:* These
pickled shrimp will keep in the
refrigerator about 1 week.) About 110
calories for each of 8 entree servings,
75 calories for each of 12 hors d'oeuvre
servings.

⊠ SHRIMP DE JONGHE

Easy but impressive.
Makes 8 servings

1 cup unsalted butter (no substitute),
    softened to room temperature
2 cloves garlic, peeled and crushed
2 shallots, peeled and minced, or
    1 scallion, minced
1 tablespoon minced parsley
1 tablespoon minced chives
¼ teaspoon tarragon
¼ teaspoon marjoram
¼ teaspoon chervil
⅛ teaspoon nutmeg
3 cups soft white bread crumbs
2 tablespoons lemon juice
⅓ cup dry sherry
3 pounds shelled and deveined boiled
    small shrimp

Preheat oven to 375° F. Cream butter
with garlic, shallots, herbs, and nutmeg
until well blended; mix in crumbs, lemon
juice, and sherry. Layer shrimp and
crumbs into 8 well-buttered individual
ramekins, ending with a layer of crumbs.
Bake, uncovered, 20 minutes until
topping is lightly browned and mixture
heated through. About 425 calories per
serving.

FROGS' LEGS

Though people do still go frogging, most
of the frogs' legs served today are from
especially raised and pampered frogs.
Only the hind legs are eaten. They are
plump and tender and taste much like
young chicken.

About Buying Fresh Frogs' Legs

Season: Year round.

Popular Market Forms: Dressed and
ready to cook.

Amount Needed: About ½ pound or
2–4 pairs of frogs' legs per serving,
depending on size; the smaller the legs,
the more tender they'll be.

For Top Quality: Look for resilient,
pale pink frogs' legs with a good fresh
odor.

About Frozen Frogs' Legs

Frozen frogs' legs are more readily
available in most parts of the country
than the fresh; they are dressed and
ready to cook but should be thawed first
in the refrigerator. Use immediately
after thawing, never refreeze, and
prepare as you would fresh frogs' legs.

How to Dress Fresh Frogs' Legs: It's
doubtful that you'll have to do this yourself, but just in case, here's the technique:
Cut off hind legs as close to the body as
possible; wash well under running cold
water. Cut off feet, then, starting at the
top of the legs, peel off skin just as
though you were removing a glove.

How to Cook Frogs' Legs

Because of their delicacy, frogs' legs
should be treated simply: poached,
sautéed, or deep fat fried. Like fish, they
do not become more tender in cooking,
only more appetizing.

General Preparation: Separate pairs of
legs by severing at the crotch; wipe well
with damp paper toweling, then pat dry.

Some people like to soak frogs' legs 1–2 hours in milk before cooking, but it seems to make little difference in their tenderness or flavor.

To Panfry (*Sauté*): Make sure legs are very dry. Dip in milk, then in flour lightly seasoned with salt and pepper and sauté in a ½ and ½ mixture of butter and olive or other cooking oil (for 6–8 pairs of legs, you'll need about 2 tablespoons butter, 2 tablespoons oil.) Cook 5–6 minutes over moderate heat, turning often so legs brown evenly. Serve topped with some of the pan juices and with lemon.

VARIATION:

Breaded Fried Frogs' Legs: Dip legs in seasoned flour, then in lightly beaten egg and finally in fine dry bread crumbs (seasoned or plain) or cracker meal. Sauté as above.

To Deep-Fat-Fry: Select very young, tender frogs' legs, pat very dry, dip in seasoned flour, then in beaten egg, then in fine dry bread crumbs or cracker meal to coat evenly. Fry 2–3 minutes in 375° F. deep fat until golden brown. Drain on paper toweling and serve with lemon wedges and Tartar Sauce. (*Note:* If you prefer a crisp crumb coating, let breaded legs dry 10–15 minutes on a rack at room temperature before frying.)

To Poach: Place prepared legs in a large, heavy skillet (not iron), add liquid just to cover (a ½ and ½ mixture of milk and water or dry white wine); for each pint liquid, add 1 teaspoon salt and a pinch pepper. Cover and simmer 10–15 minutes, depending on size, just to cook through. Lift out legs, sprinkle with minced parsley or *fines herbes,** and drizzle with melted butter or Béchamel Sauce.

SOME CLASSIC WAYS TO SERVE FROGS' LEGS

All amounts based on 6 pairs medium-size frogs' legs, enough for 4 servings

À la Lyonnaise: Sauté frogs' legs by basic method. At the same time, stir-fry 2 thinly sliced large yellow onions, separated into rings, in 2 tablespoons butter 5–8 minutes until pale golden. Add onions to frogs' legs, toss very gently, transfer to a hot platter, and keep warm. Pour all but 2 tablespoons drippings from skillet in which frogs' legs were cooked, add 2 tablespoons cider vinegar, heat 1–2 minutes, scraping up any browned bits, and pour over legs. Sprinkle with parsley and serve.

À la Meunière: Sauté frogs' legs by basic method, transfer to a hot platter, and keep warm. Drain all but 2 tablespoons drippings from skillet, add ¼ cup lemon juice, and heat 1–2 minutes, stirring up browned bits. Pour over frogs' legs, sprinkle with parsley, and serve.

À la Provençale: Sauté frogs' legs by basic method. At the same time, stir-fry 2 peeled and minced medium-size yellow onions and 2 peeled and crushed cloves garlic in 2 tablespoons olive oil 5–8 minutes until pale golden. Add 3 peeled, cored, seeded, and finely chopped tomatoes, ¼ cup dry red wine, and ¼ teaspoon each salt and sugar and heat, stirring, 2–3 minutes. Pour over frogs' legs, toss very gently, sprinkle with minced parsley and serve.

Au Gratin: Sauté frogs' legs by basic method and transfer to a buttered 1½-quart *au gratin* dish. Cover with 2 cups hot Medium White Sauce, sprinkle with ⅓ cup buttered bread crumbs, and broil 3″–4″ from heat 2–3 minutes to brown.

Deviled: Sauté frogs' legs by basic method, transfer to a hot platter and keep warm. Drain all but 2 tablespoons drippings from skillet, add 1 tablespoon each prepared mild yellow mustard, Worcestershire sauce, lemon juice, and brandy. Heat and stir 1–2 minutes, scraping up any browned bits, pour over frogs' legs, and serve.

Mornay: Sauté frogs' legs by basic method and transfer to a buttered 1½-quart *au gratin* dish. Smother with 2 cups hot Mornay Sauce, sprinkle with ¼ cup grated Parmesan cheese, and broil 3″–4″ from heat 2–3 minutes to brown.

Poulette: Poach frogs' legs by basic method, using part white wine and a *bouquet garni.** Drain legs, transfer to a hot deep platter, and keep warm. Mix 1½ cups heavy cream with 3 lightly beaten egg yolks in the top of a double boiler; set over simmering water and heat, stirring, until slightly thickened. Off heat mix in 1 tablespoon each butter and lemon juice and 2 tablespoons minced parsley. Pour over legs, garnish, if you like, with ½ pound sautéed button mushrooms, and serve.

Vinaigrette: Poach frogs' legs by basic method, using part white wine and a *bouquet garni.** Drain, cool, and chill several hours. Serve on lettuce, topped with Vinaigrette Dressing. If you prefer, cut meat from frogs' legs, toss with just enough vinaigrette to coat lightly, and marinate several hours in refrigerator.

SNAILS (ESCARGOTS)

Snails have long been a European favorite (the Romans were so fond of them they kept whole vineyards for them to feed upon), but until recently, we've been squeamish about trying them. American snails are smaller than the European (it takes about 50 of ours to make a pound). Fortunately, the fresh are relatively inexpensive (about the same price as hamburger) and, equally fortunately, they are raised under strict supervision and do not need the "purifying" starvation period required for European snails. Canned snails are sold in gourmet shops along with bags of polished shells, but their flavor cannot compare with that of the fresh.

Amount Needed: Allow about 1 dozen snails per person.

For Top Quality: Just make sure the snails are still alive.

How to Prepare Fresh Snails for Cooking: Place snails in a large, shallow pan, cover with lukewarm water, and let stand 10 minutes; snails should partially emerge from shells, discard any that don't. Cover "selects" with cold water, add about 1 teaspoon salt, then dampen edge of bowl and coat with salt so snails can't crawl out. Let stand at room temperature 1 hour, rinse well in cold water, then scrub shells well and rinse again. Place snails in a saucepan, cover with boiling water, cover, and simmer 5 minutes; drain and cool under cold running water, washing off the white material that looks like partially cooked egg white (it's edible, just not very attractive). Remove snails from shells by twisting out with a small skewer or snail fork; reserve shells. Remove bits of green gall from snails, also snip off heads and tiny curled black tails.

To Poach (necessary before fresh snails can be used in recipes): Place prepared snails in a saucepan, cover with water (you'll need about 1½ cups for 1 pound snails), or a ½ and ½ mixture of white wine and water or beef broth; add a peeled and quartered carrot, a celery stalk cut in chunks, a minced scallion or shallot, a *bouquet garni** tied in cheesecloth, and a few bruised peppercorns. Cover and simmer 1½–2 hours until tender. Cool snails in broth to room temperature.

To Clean Shells: It's best to do this while snails are poaching so that both will be ready at the same time. Place scrubbed shells in a saucepan, add 1 quart boiling water mixed with 2 tablespoons baking soda and 2 teaspoons salt, cover, and simmer ½ hour. Drain, rinse in cold water, and let dry thoroughly before using. (*Note:* If carefully washed after using, the shells may be kept and used over and over again. In addition to being used for various snail recipes, they are the perfect container for baking periwinkles.)

How to Eat Snails: Whenever snails are served in the shell, eating them requires special implements: *escargotières* (snail plates), snail pincers, and snail forks.

To eat snails gracefully, pick them up, 1 at a time, with snail pincer and twist out snail as shown with the special fork. Dip in sauce, then eat.

ESCARGOTS À LA BOURGUIGNONNE

If you've never eaten snails, this is a good way to begin, because the seasonings are superb. This particular dish is often served as a first course, but it can also be the entree.
Makes 4 servings

*1 pound fresh snails or 4 dozen canned
   snails with shells*
*½ cup butter, softened to room
   temperature*
1 clove garlic, peeled and crushed
2 tablespoons minced shallots or scallions
1½ teaspoons minced parsley
¼ teaspoon salt
Pinch pepper
⅓ cup fine soft white bread crumbs

Prepare fresh snails for cooking and

poach,* also clean shells.* If using canned snails, drain well and pat dry on paper toweling. Preheat oven to 350° F. Mix butter with garlic, shallots, parsley, salt, and pepper. Replace each snail in a shell and close openings with generous dabs of butter; dip buttered ends into crumbs. Arrange snails in snail plates and bake, uncovered, 10–12 minutes until piping hot. About 320 calories per serving.

VARIATION:

Escargots in Chablis: Poach snails and clean shells as directed. Meanwhile, boil 1½ cups chablis with 2 teaspoons minced shallots until reduced to ¾ cup; strain through a double thickness of cheesecloth, then mix in ½ teaspoon beef extract. Before returning snails to shells, pour a little wine mixture into each shell. Replace snail and close with dabs of butter as above but omit crumbs. Arrange snails in snail plates and bake as directed. About 315 calories per serving.

⚔ BAKED ESCARGOTS CORSICAN STYLE

Especially good as a first course. Anchovy fillets, spinach, and lemon add piquancy.
Makes 4 servings

*1 pound fresh snails or 4 dozen canned
   snails*
6–8 anchovy fillets, minced
1 cup finely shredded raw spinach
1 teaspoon lemon juice
2 tablespoons fine dry bread crumbs
¼ cup butter

Prepare fresh snails for cooking and poach.* If using canned snails, drain well. Preheat oven to 450° F. Coarsely chop snails and mix with anchovies, spinach, and lemon juice. Butter 4 large scallop shells or individual ramekins and fill with snail mixture. Sprinkle with crumbs and dot with butter. Place shells or ramekins on a baking sheet and bake, uncovered, 5–7 minutes until crumbs are lightly browned. About 240 calories per serving.

⚖ **ESCARGOTS À LA PROVENÇALE**

Unlike many Provençal recipes, this one contains no tomatoes. But the other traditional flavorings are there—garlic, onion, olive oil, and parsley.
Makes 4 servings

1 pound fresh snails or 4 dozen canned snails
1 medium-size yellow onion, peeled and minced
2 cloves garlic, peeled and crushed
2 tablespoons olive oil
¼ pound mushrooms, wiped clean and minced
¼ cup dry red wine
4 slices hot buttered toast, trimmed of crusts
2 tablespoons minced parsley

Prepare fresh snails for cooking and poach.* If using canned snails, drain well and pat dry on paper toweling. Stir-fry onion and garlic in oil in a skillet 8–10 minutes over moderate heat until golden; add mushrooms and stir-fry 1–2 minutes longer. Add wine and simmer, uncovered, stirring occasionally, 5 minutes. Add snails and heat, uncovered, 5 minutes. Spoon over toast, sprinkle with parsley, and serve. About 290 calories per serving.

MARINATED SNAILS WITH MAYONNAISE OR RÉMOULADE SAUCE

Good as a first course or light entree.
Makes 4 servings

1 pound fresh snails or 4 dozen canned snails with shells
2 tablespoons olive oil
2 tablespoons white wine vinegar
2 tablespoons minced chives
2 tablespoons minced parsley
1 cup Homemade Mayonnaise or Rémoulade Sauce

Prepare fresh snails for cooking and poach,* also clean shells.* If using canned snails, drain well and pat dry on paper toweling. Before returning snails to shells, toss with oil, vinegar, chives, and parsley. Return snails to shells, wrap airtight, and chill 2–3 hours. Arrange in snail plates and serve cold with mayonnaise or *rémoulade* as a dip. About 685 calories per serving if served with Homemade Mayonnaise, about 690 calories per serving if served with Rémoulade Sauce.

SQUID AND OCTOPUS

If young, tender, and properly prepared, these two can be exquisite; abused they are rubbery and tough. Squid and octopus are both inkfish, both are tentacled, and both are prepared more or less the same way. Of the two, squid is the more delicate. Most come from the North Atlantic, and the smaller they are the better. Octopus are fished from the Atlantic, too, but farther south. They may reach awesome size (about seven feet with tentacles extended), but again, the smaller the better. Canned and dried squid are sometimes available in gourmet or ethnic groceries; some squid is also being frozen, but most of it goes to restaurants.

Season: Year round.

Amount Needed: About ⅓–½ pound per person. The choicest squid weigh only a few ounces apiece. Octopus run larger, and even the smallest may weigh about 1 pound.

For Top Quality: Choose squid or octopus that are firm-tender and sweet-smelling with little or no liquid.

How to Prepare Squid and Octopus for Cooking: If possible, have your fish market clean squid or octopus for you. If you must do it yourself:

1. Lay squid or octopus, back side up on a counter with tentacles fully extended (the back is the side on which the eyes are most visible).

2. With a sharp knife, cut down center back, exposing cuttlebone (this is the

cuttlebone used as canary food); lift it out and discard.

3. Grasp head and tentacles and pull toward you, turning octopus or squid inside out; take care not to rupture ink sac. Save sac, if you like, and use ink in broths or stews. Discard all other internal organs. The only parts you want are the meaty body covering and the tentacles.

4. Remove heads from squid; remove eyes, mouth, and parrot-like beak from octopus.

5. Cut off tentacles close to head, push out and discard bead of flesh at root of each tentacle.

6. Wash body and tentacles several times in cool water. Squid are now ready to use as recipes direct, *but octopus, unless very small and tender, must be beaten until tender.*

7. Place octopus flat on a cutting board and pound rhythmically with the blunt edge of a meat cleaver or edge of a heavy plate until meat is soft and velvety.

8. If you object to the octopus' purple skin, here's how to remove. Place octopus in a large kettle, cover with salted boiling water (about 1 teaspoon salt to 1 quart water), cover, and boil 20 minutes. Drain, plunge in ice water, and, using a stiff brush, scrub away purple skin.

About Using the Ink: Europeans often use squid or octopus ink to color and enrich soups and stews. But taste first, to see if you like the flavor. To collect the ink, hold sac over a small bowl, puncture with the point of a knife and squeeze ink out. If used in soups or stews, it should be added along with other liquid ingredients.

⚖ FRIED SQUID

Makes 4 servings

2 pounds small squid, prepared for cooking
⅓ cup unsifted flour
1 egg, lightly beaten with 1 tablespoon cold water
¾ cup toasted seasoned bread crumbs (about)
⅓ cup cooking oil

Cut squid in 2″ pieces (if tentacles are very small, leave whole); pat very dry on paper toweling. Dip in flour, then egg, and then in crumbs to coat evenly. Let dry on a rack at room temperature 10–15 minutes. Heat oil in a large, heavy skillet over moderate heat 1 minute. Sauté body pieces first, a few at a time, 4–5 minutes until browned on both sides; drain on paper toweling and keep warm. Sauté tentacles about 2 minutes (stand back from the pan because they sputter the way chicken livers do). Serve with lemon wedges. If you like, pass Tartar Sauce or any well-seasoned seafood sauce. About 290 calories per serving.

SQUID À LA MARSEILLAISE

Squid stuffed with onion, tomatoes, and crumbs, then simmered in dry white wine.
Makes 4–6 servings

2 pounds squid, prepared for cooking
1 large yellow onion, peeled and minced
4 tablespoons olive oil
2 cloves garlic, peeled and crushed
2 ripe tomatoes, peeled, cored, seeded, and chopped fine
1½ cups soft white bread crumbs
1 tablespoon minced parsley
¼ teaspoon salt
⅛ teaspoon pepper
1 cup dry white wine
1 cup water
1 bay leaf

Mince squid tentacles and set aside. Stir-fry onion in 2 tablespoons oil in a skillet over moderate heat 5–8 minutes until pale golden; add tentacles, garlic, and tomatoes and stir-fry 2–3 minutes. Off heat, mix in crumbs, parsley, salt, and pepper; loosely stuff into body cavities of squid and close with toothpicks. Brown squid lightly on both sides in remaining oil in a flameproof casserole over moderately high heat, add wine, water, and bay leaf; stir in any remaining stuffing. Cover and simmer 20–30 minutes until squid is tender. Check consistency of liquid occasionally and, if too thick, thin with a little water or wine. Remove bay leaf and toothpicks and serve in shallow bowls with French bread or over hot boiled rice. About 405 calories for each of 4 servings (without bread or rice), about 270 calories for each of 6 servings.

GREEK-STYLE SQUID STUFFED WITH SAVORY RICE

Makes 4 servings

2 pounds squid, prepared for cooking
2 medium-size yellow onions, peeled and minced
2 tablespoons olive oil
2 cloves garlic, peeled and crushed
2 teaspoons minced parsley
½ teaspoon dried dill
2 cups hot cooked seasoned rice
⅓ cup dried currants (optional)
1 (1-pound) can Spanish-style tomato sauce

Preheat oven to 350° F. Chop tentacles fine and set aside. Stir-fry onions in oil in a large, heavy skillet over moderate heat 8–10 minutes until golden; add garlic and tentacles and stir-fry 1 minute. Off heat, mix in parsley, dill, rice, and, if you like, currants; stuff into body cavities of squid and close with toothpicks. Arrange squid in a single layer in a greased large casserole, pile any leftover stuffing on top, and pour in tomato sauce. Cover and bake 25 minutes until squid is tender. Remove toothpicks and serve with some sauce spooned over each portion. About 360 calories per serving.

MEDITERRANEAN-STYLE SQUID OR OCTOPUS

Squid in a rich tomato-wine sauce.
Makes 4–6 servings

2 pounds squid or octopus, prepared for cooking
2 medium-size yellow onions, peeled and minced
¼ cup olive or other cooking oil
2–3 cloves garlic, peeled and crushed
1 (6-ounce) can tomato paste
1 cup dry white wine or dry vermouth
1 cup water
⅛ teaspoon crushed hot red chili peppers
1 tablespoon minced parsley
¼–½ teaspoon salt

Cut squid or octopus in 2″ chunks and set aside. Sauté onions in oil 8–10 minutes until golden, add garlic, and stir-fry 1 minute. Add squid or octopus and all remaining ingredients except salt, mix well, cover, and simmer ¾–1 hour, stirring occasionally, until tender (the best way to tell if squid or octopus is tender is to eat a piece). Taste for salt and add as needed. Serve over hot boiled rice. If made with squid: About 385 calories for each of 4 servings, 260 calories for each of 6 servings. If made with octopus: About 365 calories for each of 4 servings, 245 calories for each of 6 servings (without rice).

TURTLE, TORTOISE, AND TERRAPIN

These are all turtles; the word turtle usually refers to sea turtles (or to snappers), tortoise to land turtles, and terrapin to habitués of bogs and swamps. But there aren't any hard and fast rules, and terminology varies from species to species and area to area. Turtle sizes vary tremendously—from the giant sea turtles weighing a thousand pounds or more to tortoises and terrapins weighing as little as five. Choicest sea turtle (and the most readily available) is the green turtle from the South Atlantic and Caribbean. As for land turtles, it's entirely a matter of personal preference. Some people like snapping turtles, others diamondback terrapins, still others "cooters" or "gophers."

Season: Year round for sea turtles; spring, summer, and fall for tortoises and terrapins.

Popular Market Forms: In areas where they are caught, sea turtles are dressed and sold as steaks or as diced or cubed meat. Land turtles, though found throughout most of the United States, don't often come to market. To enjoy them, you must catch your own.

Amount Needed: Allow ¼–½ pound turtle meat per serving. A 4–5-pound turtle will yield 3–4 cups meat.

For Top Quality: Look for moist, resilient meat with good fresh odor. Color will vary from almost white to gray or green, depending on variety of turtle and whether meat is from the leg, neck, or back (back meat is considered the best).

About Frozen and Canned Turtle Meat

Diced sea turtle meat is available frozen cooked and canned; occasionally frozen cooked snapping turtle meat is also available. Both frozen and canned turtle meat can be used interchangeably for parboiled fresh meat; it is not necessary to thaw the frozen meat before using unless pieces need to be separated and cooked quickly.

How to Dress a Live Tortoise or Terrapin

1. Poke a stick in turtle's mouth and, when he grabs hold, pull, stretching head away from body; chop off head with a meat cleaver or hatchet and discard.

2. Hang turtle upside-down by its tail in a cool, airy place and let bleed 24 hours.

3. Drop turtle upside-down in a kettle of boiling water and blanch 1–2 minutes to loosen tough outer covering; drain. Peel outer covering from legs, neck, and tail, also from around shell to loosen. This is slow work, so have patience. Do not remove tender inner skin—when cooked, it's good.

4. Cut off each leg as close to body as possible and snip off claws, using wire clippers; reserve legs. Also cut off tail and reserve; if turtle is male, remove genitals on underside of tail.

5. Pull top and bottom shells apart, first cutting through soft bridges joining them if necessary. Near the front end of the shell you will find the liver; lift it out and separate from gall bladder, working gently so bladder doesn't rupture. Discard bladder, also "sandbags" and digestive organs (some people like to mince the small intestines and add to stews and broths). Save top shell (there is choice meat on the underside); also save cross-shaped breastbone and meat attached to it, but discard all other inner parts of turtle.

6. Sprinkle all pieces except liver with salt and chill several hours. Cover with cold water, return to refrigerator, and let stand 24 hours, changing water 2 or 3 times. Liver should be loosely wrapped and refrigerated or, if you prefer, cooked right away. Simply slice thin and sauté in butter as you would calf's liver.

7. When turtle meat has soaked 24 hours, drain and rinse well in cold water.

To Parboil (necessary before fresh turtle can be used in recipes): Place dressed turtle pieces in a large kettle, lay shell on top, outer side up. Add 2–3 celery stalks and peeled carrots, cut in thick chunks, 2 bay leaves, 6–8 parsley sprigs, 1 teaspoon thyme, a dozen bruised peppercorns, 1 tablespoon salt and 2 medium-size peeled yellow onions each stuck with 2 cloves. Pour in enough cold water to cover and bring to a boil. Reduce heat so water just simmers, cover kettle, and simmer 1–1½ hours until meat can be cut with a fork. Drain off broth, strain, and use for making soups and stews. Cut turtle meat from bones, also cut meat from underside of shell; dice or cube meat as recipes direct. The turtle is now ready to use in recipes.

SEA TURTLE STEAKS
Makes 4 servings

1½ pounds sea turtle steaks, cut ⅛″ thick
1 cup unsifted flour
1 teaspoon salt
1 teaspoon paprika

¼ teaspoon pepper
⅓ cup butter or margarine
½ cup dry vermouth
1 cup heavy cream
1 tablespoon minced fresh dill or parsley

Dredge steaks in a mixture of flour, salt, paprika, and pepper and brown quickly in butter in a large, heavy skillet over moderately high heat. Add vermouth, turn heat to low, cover, and simmer ¾–1 hour until tender. Lift steaks to a hot platter and keep warm. Smooth cream into skillet and boil rapidly, stirring, until reduced by about ⅓. Pour over steaks, sprinkle with dill, and serve. About 545 calories per serving.

TURTLE HASH

Makes 4 servings

2 pounds turtle meat, parboiled and cut in 1" cubes
3 cups water (about)
¼ pound salt pork, cut in small dice
1 medium-size yellow onion, peeled and minced
2 pounds potatoes, peeled and cut in ½" cubes
¼ teaspoon pepper

Place turtle meat and just enough water to cover in a saucepan; simmer, covered, ¾–1 hour until very tender. Meanwhile, slowly brown salt pork in a heavy skillet over moderate heat; remove with a slotted spoon to paper toweling to drain. Stir-fry onion in drippings 5–8 minutes until pale golden, add potatoes, 1 cup water, and the pepper. Cover and simmer about 10 minutes until potatoes are just tender. Drain turtle meat, mix gently into potatoes along with salt pork, and heat, stirring, 3–5 minutes until very hot. Serve with hot buttered biscuits or corn bread. About 470 calories per serving.

TURTLE STEW

Delicious made with either sea or land turtle.
Makes 4–6 servings

2 medium-size yellow onions, peeled and coarsely chopped
1 medium-size sweet green pepper, cored, seeded, and minced
4 carrots, peeled and cut in small dice
1 cup minced celery
½ cup olive oil
2 pounds turtle meat, parboiled and cut in ½"–1" cubes
½ teaspoon thyme
½ teaspoon oregano
⅛ teaspoon cloves
1 bay leaf, crumbled
1 teaspoon salt (about)
¼ teaspoon pepper
1 (1-pound) can tomatoes (do not drain)
2 cups turtle broth,* Easy Fish Stock, or chicken broth
4 hard-cooked eggs, shelled
½ cup dry sherry or Madeira wine

Stir-fry onions, green pepper, carrots, and celery in oil 10–12 minutes until lightly browned. Add turtle and all but last 2 ingredients, cover, and simmer about 1 hour until turtle is very tender. Check stew now and then and, if it seems thin, uncover during last 15–20 minutes of cooking. Meanwhile, dice egg whites and sieve the yolks. Stir eggs and sherry into stew and heat, stirring now and then, 5 minutes. Taste for salt and adjust as needed. Serve in soup bowls with hot corn bread and a crisp green salad. About 510 calories for each of 4 servings, 340 calories for each of 6 servings.

CHAPTER 12

EGGS AND CHEESE

"They know, in France, 685 different ways of dressing eggs, without counting those which our savants invent every day." *De la Reynière*

Add to those 685 the dozens of ways other countries know to prepare eggs and the total staggers. No food is more versatile. Eggs can be cooked in the shell or out, simply or lavishly, solo or with something sweet or savory. They leaven angel-food cakes and soufflés, color and thicken sauces, bind croquettes, emulsify mayonnaise, clarify aspics, give batter-fried food crisp fragile crusts, glaze baked goods, smooth ice creams and candies, and enrich the flavor and food value of everything. Eggs have been called nature's "nutritional bombshells" because of their near-perfect protein and high vitamin and mineral content. Yet they are low in calories, about 80 per large egg.

About Buying Eggs

Quality: There are three federal grades for eggs, marked on the carton or tape sealing it: USDA AA (the very top quality), USDA A (second best) and USDA B. All are widely available. Choose top grades when appearance counts (as in poached or hard-cooked eggs); these eggs have excellent shape, firm whites, and high-standing yolks. Grade B eggs have thinner whites, flatter yolks, cost less, and are good "cooking eggs" to use in making cakes and cookies, pies and puddings.

Size: Size has nothing to do with grade; weight determines. The four most common sizes, usually included in the grade stamp (see opposite):

Color: The breed of hen determines shell color and personal preference which you buy; white and brown eggs are equally flavorful and nutritious. Yolk color is affected by the hen's diet. Cloudy whites mean extra-fresh eggs.

Freshness: The fresher the better— *except* if eggs are to be hard-cooked. Shells cling to fresh eggs, making them difficult to peel, so use eggs several days or a week old. To determine if an egg is fresh, cover with cold water; if it floats, it's old. Beware of cracked eggs—they spoil rapidly. If you should accidentally crack an egg, use as soon as possible.

Egg Size	Weight per Dozen
Extra Large	27 ounces
Large	24 ounces
Medium	21 ounces
Small	18 ounces

Note: Recipes in this book are based on large eggs.

Blood Specks: Bloody eggs are removed during grading, but occasionally flecks of blood show in the yolk. They're harmless, do not mean an egg is fertile or bad. Remove with a piece of shell or paper toweling.

Fertile Eggs: These contain no magical properties, as some health faddists insist, and are no more nutritious than infertile eggs. They are overpriced and quick to spoil.

Other Kinds of Eggs

Because "eggs" so automatically mean hen eggs, we tend to overlook those of other fowl. Duck eggs are delicious (especially if ducks have swum in unbrackish ponds) and can be used interchangeably with large hen eggs (try them in custard). Eggs of geese and other domestic fowl may also be used. Simply multiply the number of hen's eggs in a recipe by 2 ounces, then substitute an equivalent weight of other fowl eggs.

Other Forms of Eggs

Commercially frozen egg products (whole mixed eggs, egg whites, and yolks), are available, but almost altogether on the wholesale level. Dried egg solids (whole eggs, whites, and yolks) are sometimes available in 5- or 8-ounce cartons. They are prey to bacteria, however, and should be used only for baking or in other thoroughly cooked dishes. To simplify measuring and using:

1 ounce dried whole egg=2 large eggs
1 ounce dried egg yolk =3½ fresh yolks
1 ounce dried egg white=6¼ fresh whites

About Storing and Freezing Eggs
See separate chapters on Freezing and Storage.

Some Special Terms and Techniques of Egg Cookery

To Break an Egg: Rap center of egg sharply against the edge of a counter or bowl, pull halves apart, letting egg fall into bowl. If using many eggs, break each

separately into a small dish so that 1 bad egg won't destroy the lot. Here's a quick table of equivalents:

4–6 whole raw eggs=1 cup
10–12 raw whites =1 cup
13–14 raw yolks =1 cup

To Separate an Egg: Break egg, catch yolk in half shell, and let white fall into a small bowl; transfer yolk to empty shell, again letting white drain into bowl. Place yolk in a separate bowl.

To remove a speck of Yolk from White: The merest dot of yolk will keep whites from whipping. To remove, scoop up with a piece of shell or paper toweling.

To Remove Shell Fragments: Scoop out with a piece of shell.

To Beat Whole Eggs: The point is to blend whites and yolks so that eggs will mix more quickly with other ingredients or to make the eggs fluffy and of uniform color.

To Beat Whites: For best results, bring whites to room temperature and beat just before using; beaten egg whites quickly break down on standing. French chefs use unlined copper bowls and balloon whisks for greatest volume. Next best, a whisk and conventional bowl. Rotary beaters work well, electric mixers less so because they tend to break down the beaten whites. The greatest danger in beating whites is *overbeating*. For most recipes, whites are beaten either to *soft peaks* (as shown opposite), or to *stiff peaks* (also described as *stiff but not dry*). Peaks can be very soft; firm but too soft to "peak"; or stiff enough to stand straight up when beater is withdrawn. But the beaten whites should never look dry. If so, they've been overbeaten and their volume is lost forever. Volume is the point of beating egg whites, because the air incorporated into them is what leavens a soufflé or omelet or angel-food cake (overbeating causes more flops than underbeating). (*Note:* Whites beaten with a pinch of salt, sugar, or cream of tartar or a drop

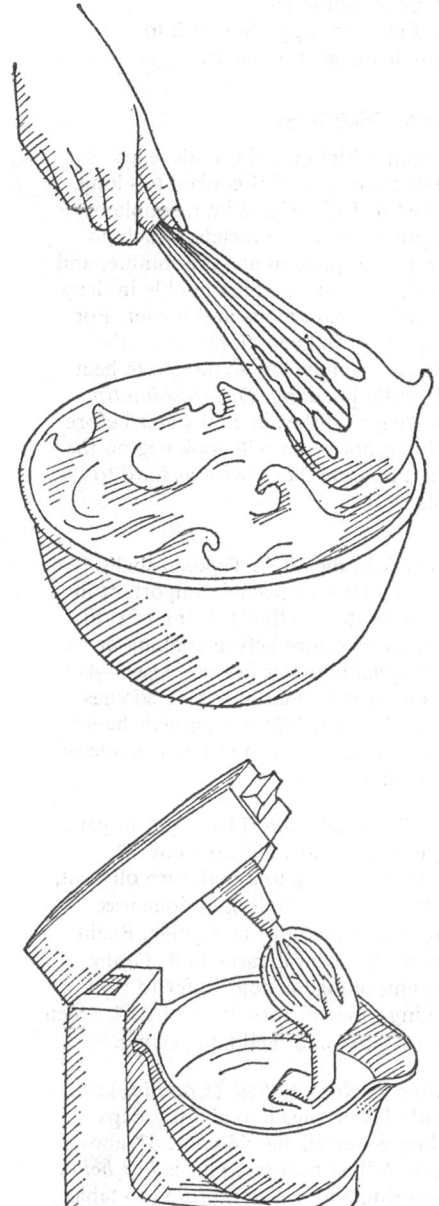

sauces or custards, yolks should be beaten *lightly,* just to blend; further beating weakens their thickening power. Cake recipes often call for beating yolks until *thick and lemon-colored* (not the best description because yolks are more nearly the color of mayonnaise) or if beaten with sugar, until mixture *makes a ribbon* (drops from beater in a thin flat ribbon that doubles back on itself in bowl).

About Folding In Beaten Egg Whites:
Easy does it! Once whites are beaten, they must be combined with a base mixture so that very little volume is lost. The gentle, over-and-over folding motion shown

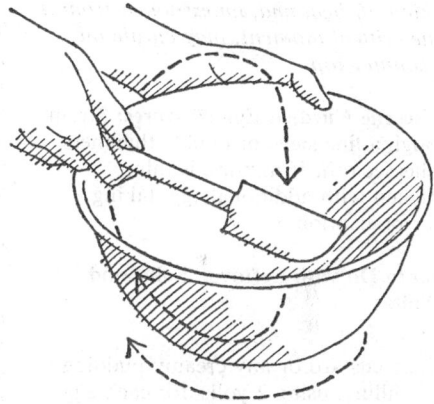

is the technique and a rubber spatula or flat whisk the best implement. If base mixture is thick, *stir in* ¼–½ cup of whites to lighten it, then *fold in* the rest.

About Adding Eggs to Hot Mixtures:
Eggs or yolks are often blended into soups, sauces, or cream dishes shortly before serving—to thicken them, add flavor and color. Not a difficult technique, except that eggs curdle easily.

To Prevent Curdling: Beat eggs lightly, quickly blend in a little hot mixture (about ½ cup), then return to pan, stirring briskly. Burner should be at lowest

of lemon juice or vinegar will have greater volume and stability than those beaten without.)

To Beat Yolks: These need not be at room temperature. When used to thicken point or, better still, topped with an asbestos "flame tamer." Cook, stirring constantly, about 2 minutes, *just* until mixture coats a metal spoon (leaves a thin, even, custard-like film).

About Cooking Egg-Thickened Mixtures:
The old theory was that all egg mixtures had to be cooked in the top of a double boiler over simmering, not boiling, water. And there are times when they still should be—if the cooking is prolonged, for example, as with Stirred Custard or Zabaglione, if the cook is a beginner. But most cooks can deal with simple eggthickened mixtures over direct low heat if they stir constantly, watch closely, and take the mixture from the heat the instant it thickens. *An important point to remember: Egg mixtures continue cooking off heat and, unless taken from it at the critical moment, may curdle on the counter top.*

To Rescue Curdled Egg Mixtures: Strain through a fine sieve or double thickness of cheesecloth. If mixture is thin, rethicken with additional egg, taking every precaution.

What to Do with Leftover Yolks and Whites

Yolks:
– Make custard or any creamy pudding or pie filling, using 2 yolks for each egg.
– Make Mayonnaise, Hollandaise, Zabaglione, or other egg yolk sauce.
– Add yolks to creamed soups, seafood, meats, or vegetables (about 1 yolk per cup).
– Add an extra yolk or 2 to scrambled eggs.
– Hard-cook yolks,* sieve, and use in making cocktail spreads or as a garnish.

Whites:
– Make a soufflé, adding 3–4 extra whites.
– Make an angel-food cake.
– Make meringues or a meringue-topped pie.
– Make divinity or seafoam candy.
– Make Prune or Apricot Whip.

– Make a chiffon pie.
– Add an extra egg white or 2 to scrambled eggs or omelets.

How to Cook Eggs

Like other high-protein foods, eggs toughen and shrivel if cooked too long, too fast or furiously. With a couple of exceptions: French omelets, which go from pan to plate in about a minute, and French-fried eggs, which bubble in deep fat. Both remain moist and tender. For egg cookery in general, however, the basic rule stands: low to moderate heat and gentle handling. *Dishwashing tip:* Soak "eggy" dishes in cold water before washing; hot water will cook egg on the dishes, making them twice as hard to wash.

To Cook in the Shell: To keep shells from cracking (especially important in Boiling Water Method), bring eggs to room temperature before cooking or warm quickly under hot tap. Use 3–4-day-old eggs for hard-cooking so eggs will peel easily. (*Note:* Eggshells badly discolor aluminum, so use pans made of other materials.)

Cold Water Method: Place eggs in pan, add enough cold water to come 1″ above eggs, bring to a boil, turn off heat, cover, and cook to desired doneness, using following table as a guide. Begin timing *after* heat is turned off. Drain eggs and plunge in cold water to stop cooking, prevent formation of dark green around yolk, and facilitate peeling.

Boiling Water Method (Coddling): Gently lower eggs into about 6 cups boiling water (it should come 1″ above eggs). Adjust heat so water is *just below* simmering and cook according to table. Drain and chill eggs as in Cold Water Method.

To Peel: Soft-cooked eggs are usually sliced in half and scooped into small dishes or served large end up in egg cups; to eat, slice off top, sprinkle in seasonings, and eat from shell. *Oeufs mollets*

Degree of Doneness	Description	Approximate Cooking Time (in Minutes)	
		Cold Water Method	Boiling Water Method
Very soft-cooked	Jelly-like white, runny yolk	1	3
Soft-cooked	Just-set white, runny yolk	2	4
Medium-soft	Firm-tender white, soft yolk	3	5
Oeufs Mollets (a French favorite)	Firm-tender white, yolk beginning to set around the edges	—	6
Hard-cooked	Firm-tender white *and* yolk	15	10–12

and hard-cooked eggs are peeled: Crack gently on a flat surface, roll egg over surface or between hands to craze and loosen shell. Starting at the large end where there is an air space, peel off shell and membrane, dipping as needed in cold water to make the going easier. Take care not to tear white.

To Keep Peeled Eggs Warm: Immerse in hot water, *not* on the stove.

To Hard-Cook Egg Yolks: Place yolks in individual ramekins, set in 1–1½″ simmering water, cover, and cook 5–7 minutes until firm. Use in salads or spreads or as a garnish.

To Tell if an Egg Is Hard-Cooked or Raw: Spin egg on counter. If it wobbles, it's cooked; if it spins neatly, it's raw.

To Poach: Pour about 2″ water into a shallow saucepan or skillet (not iron) and bring to a boil; adjust heat so water simmers, break eggs, 1 at a time, into a small dish. Stir water into a whirlpool, slip egg in, stirring in the same direction. Repeat with other eggs and cook 3–5 minutes to desired firmness. Lift out with a slotted spoon and serve. (*Note:* It's not necessary, as once thought, to add salt or vinegar to the water.)

VARIATION: Poach as directed, but use milk or broth instead of water.

To Steam-Poach: Break eggs into buttered cups of an egg poacher, set over simmering water, cover, and steam 3–4 minutes.

To Fry:

Method I: Heat 1–2 tablespoons butter, margarine, or bacon drippings for each egg in a large, heavy skillet over moderate heat about 1 minute, break eggs into skillet, spacing so they don't run together, reduce heat slightly, and cook, basting with fat or turning, to desired firmness. Soft-fried eggs "sunny side up" will take 2–3 minutes; "over easy" eggs about 2 minutes on the the first side and 1–2 minutes on the second.

Method II: Lightly grease a large, heavy skillet (not iron) and heat over moderate heat just until a drop of water will dance. Break eggs into skillet, turn heat to low, and cook just until edges turn milky, about 1 minute. Add ½ teaspoon water for each egg, cover, and steam to desired firmness.

To French-Fry: Pour about 3″ cooking oil into a small deep saucepan and heat over moderately high heat until almost smoking. Break egg into a small dish, slide into fat, roll over with 2 wooden spoons until nearly round. Fry until puffed and golden, 2–2½ minutes; drain on paper toweling and serve. (*Note:* These eggs should be cooked 1 at a time.)

To Scramble (*Note:* Never try to scramble just 1 egg; allow 2 per person or, if scrambling many eggs, 1½ per person):

Method I: Beat eggs just enough to blend whites and yolks, season lightly with salt and pepper. Pour into a heavy skillet (not iron) lightly coated with melted butter, margarine, or bacon drippings and cook and stir over low heat 2–3 minutes until creamy-firm.

Method II: Break eggs into a bowl, for each egg add 1 tablespoon cream, milk, or water; season lightly with salt and pepper. Beat until frothy, pour into a heavy skillet (not iron) lightly coated with melted butter, margarine, or bacon drippings, and cook and stir over low heat 2–3 minutes until creamy-firm.

Method III: Prepare eggs as for Method II. Melt 2–3 tablespoons butter in the top of a double boiler, pour in eggs, and cook and stir over simmering water 3–4 minutes to desired firmness. These eggs are super-creamy.

Some Variations on Scrambled Eggs: Prepare 6–8 eggs by any of the above methods and, about 1 minute before they're done, mix in any of the following:
– ⅓ cup minced sautéed chicken livers or pâté
– ⅓ cup minced cooked sausages or frankfurters
– ⅓ cup minced cooked ham, tongue, luncheon meat, or salami
– ⅓ cup minced cooked fish, shellfish, chicken, or turkey
–⅓ cup minced sautéed mushrooms, yellow onions, sweet red or green peppers
– ⅓ cup coarsely grated sharp Cheddar, Swiss, or Gruyère cheese
– ⅓ cup cooked asparagus tips, minced cooked cauliflower or broccoli
– ⅓ cup crisp, crumbled bacon
– ⅓ cup minced cooked artichoke hearts
– ⅓ cup sour cream and 2 tablespoons minced chives
– ⅓ cup sour cream and 2 tablespoons red or black caviar
– ⅓ cup peeled, seeded, minced tomato
– 1 tablespoon fresh minced herb (parsley, chives, dill, tarragon, chervil, marjoram)

To Bake or Shirr (Oeufs en Cocottes):

These two techniques are similar, the only difference being that shirred eggs are started on the top of the stove and finished in the oven and baked eggs are cooked altogether in the oven. Break eggs into buttered ramekins or custard cups and top each, if you like, with 1 tablespoon light cream. Set cups in a shallow baking pan, pour in enough warm water to come halfway up cups. *To Shirr:* Cook over low heat just until whites begin to set, then transfer to a 325° F. oven and bake, uncovered, about 5 minutes until whites are milky and yolks soft but not runny. *To Bake:* Place eggs in ramekins, set in water bath, and bake uncovered 15–20 minutes at 325° F. (*Note:* Do not sprinkle eggs with salt and pepper until after they are done, otherwise, the yolks will be spotted.)

VARIATIONS:

– Place about 2 tablespoons minced cooked ham, chicken, chicken livers, fish, or shellfish into the bottom of each ramekin before adding eggs.
– Place 1 cooked artichoke bottom into each ramekin before adding eggs or, if you prefer, 2–3 tablespoons minced sautéed mushrooms, onions, or sweet peppers.
– Before baking eggs, top with a little crumbled bacon or grated cheese.
– Before baking eggs, sprinkle with a little minced parsley, fresh dill, tarragon, chervil, or chives.
– Before baking eggs, top with 2–3 tablespoons tomato, mushroom, or cheese sauce.

A Note About Serving Eggs: Have plates or platter warm, *not hot,* or eggs may cook beyond the point of desired doneness—especially important for omelets, scrambled eggs, and other simple egg dishes that quickly overcook.

Some Garnishes for Eggs

Almost anything savory and colorful is appropriate: crisp bacon strips, frizzled ham or Canadian bacon slices, glistening sausage links or patties, kippered herring, anchovy strips or rolls, sautéed chicken livers, tomato wedges or cherry tomatoes, clusters of green or black olives. And, of course, the old standbys —parsley, paprika, and watercress.

SKILLET EGG AND POTATO BREAKFAST

Makes 4 servings

8 slices bacon
2 cups diced cooked potatoes
¼ cup minced yellow onion
½ teaspoon salt
¼ teaspoon pepper
4 eggs
*¾ cup coarsely grated sharp Cheddar
cheese*

Fry bacon until crisp in a large, heavy skillet; drain on paper toweling and crumble. Pour off all but 2 tablespoons drippings and brown potatoes and onions 10–12 minutes over moderate heat. Sprinkle with half the salt and pepper. Break eggs over potatoes, spacing evenly. Turn heat to low, cover, and cook 3–4 minutes or until eggs are done to your liking. Sprinkle with remaining salt and pepper, cheese, and crumbled bacon and serve. About 285 calories per serving.

SCOTCH WOODCOCK

There are two ways to make Scotch Woodcock; the easiest is simply to spread hot buttered toast with anchovy paste and top with softly scrambled eggs. This is a more elaborate version.
Makes 6 entree servings, 2 dozen appetizers

*6 slices hot buttered toast, trimmed of
crusts*
*2 (2-ounce) cans anchovy fillets, drained
and mashed*
Freshly ground pepper
1 tablespoon minced parsley

Sauce:

1 cup heavy or light cream
4 egg yolks, lightly beaten
2 tablespoons butter (no substitute)

Make sauce first: Heat cream in the top of a double boiler over simmering water, mix a little into yolks, return to pan, and heat, stirring constantly, 7–10 minutes until smooth and thickened. (*Note:* Do not let water underneath boil or mixture will be scrambled eggs, not sauce.) Drop in butter and beat well; remove top of

double boiler from bottom. Spread toast with anchovies, and halve diagonally, or, if to be served as appetizers, cut in "fingers." Arrange on hot plates, spoon or spread sauce over each piece, and top with a hearty grinding of pepper and sprinkling of parsley. About 285 or 340 calories per entree serving, depending upon whether made with light or heavy cream; 70 or 85 calories per appetizer.

⚖ EGG IN A NEST

Makes 1 serving

1 slice firm-textured white bread
1 tablespoon butter or margarine
1 egg
⅛ teaspoon salt
Pinch pepper

Spread both sides of bread with butter, then, using a 2½″ round cutter, cut out center of slice. Place both slice and cutout circle in a small skillet and brown lightly on both sides over moderate heat, 2–3 minutes. Remove bread circle and keep warm. Break egg into hole in slice, cover, and cook about 4 minutes until white is firm. Transfer to a heated plate, taking care not to break the yolk. Season with salt and pepper. Top with bread circle and serve. About 245 calories per serving.

VARIATION:

⚖ Spread sautéed circle with ketchup, deviled ham, or cheese spread and place, spread side down, on egg. About 250 calories per serving made with ketchup, 260 if made with deviled ham or cheese spread.

EGGS BENEDICT

Makes 4 servings

*4 thin slices boiled ham or Canadian
bacon*
1 tablespoon butter or margarine
*2 hot, split, toasted, and buttered English
muffins*
4 poached eggs
1 cup hot Hollandaise Sauce

Lightly brown ham in butter over moderate heat; arrange on muffins, trimming to fit. Top with eggs, cover with sauce, and serve. About 300 calories per serving.

VARIATION:

⊠ ⚖ **Benedict-Style Eggs:** Prepare as directed but instead of Hollandaise use 1 (10½-ounce) can cream of celery, mushroom, tomato, or cheese soup, heated and thinned with ⅓ cup milk. Calories per serving: About 240 if made with tomato soup, about 270 if made with celery or mushroom soup, and about 285 if made with cheese soup.

⚖ **EGGS FLORENTINE**

Makes 6 servings

2 (10½-ounce) packages frozen chopped spinach, cooked by package directions and drained
6 poached eggs
1½ cups hot Mornay Sauce
¼ cup finely grated Parmesan cheese

Preheat oven to 350° F. Spoon spinach into a buttered 1 quart *au gratin* dish or shallow casserole or into 6 buttered custard cups set on a baking sheet. Make 6 depressions in spinach and slip a poached egg into each. Spoon sauce evenly over eggs, covering completely, and sprinkle with cheese. Bake uncovered, 15 minutes, then broil 5" from heat until speckled with brown. About 160 calories per serving.

⊠ **EGGS AMERICANO**

Poached eggs on toast topped with a mild curry sauce.
Makes 4 servings

2 tablespoons minced yellow onion
2 tablespoons cooking oil
1 (10½-ounce) can condensed cream of celery soup blended with ¼ cup milk
Dash liquid hot red pepper seasoning
¼ teaspoon curry powder
¼ teaspoon rosemary
¼ teaspoon oregano
4 slices hot lightly buttered toast
¼ cup finely grated Parmesan cheese
8 poached eggs

Sauté onion in oil in a saucepan over moderate heat 5–8 minutes until pale golden. Stir in soup mixture and all seasonings, reduce heat to moderately low, cover, and simmer about 5 minutes, stirring occasionally. Arrange toast on 4 individual heated plates, sprinkle 1 tablespoon cheese over each slice and top with a poached egg. Spoon sauce over eggs and serve. About 380 calories per serving.

HUEVOS RANCHEROS

Fried eggs on tortillas smothered with a chili-flavored tomato sauce. A Mexican classic.
Makes 2–4 servings

4 tortillas (homemade or packaged)
3 tablespoons lard or cooking oil
4 eggs
1 small yellow onion, peeled and minced
¼ cup minced sweet green pepper or 2 tablespoons minced hot green chili pepper
½ clove garlic, peeled and crushed
¾ cup canned tomato sauce
1½ teaspoons chili powder
¼ teaspoon salt
⅛ teaspoon sage
Pinch crushed dried hot red chili peppers (optional)

Preheat oven to 200° F. Fry tortillas on 1 side in 2 tablespoons lard in a large, heavy skillet over moderately low heat about 1 minute until pliable; drain on paper toweling, arrange on heatproof plates and set in oven. Fry eggs in drippings *just* until whites are set, then arrange on tortillas and keep warm in oven. Stir-fry onion and pepper in remaining lard 3–4 minutes, add remaining ingredients, and heat and stir until bubbling; turn heat to low and simmer, uncovered, 1–2 minutes. Spoon sauce over eggs and serve. About 370 calories for each of 2 servings, about 190 for each of 4.

EGGS FOO YOUNG

Eggs Foo Young are a good way to use leftovers, which explains the many

variations served in Chinese restaurants.
Makes 4 servings

6 eggs, lightly beaten
1 cup well-drained bean sprouts
¼ cup minced scallions (include some
tops)
¼ cup minced bamboo shoots, celery, or
shredded Chinese cabbage
4 water chestnuts, minced
⅓–½ cup slivered cooked ham, chicken,
or lean roast pork or minced cooked
shrimp
1 teaspoon soy sauce
2–3 tablespoons peanut or other cooking
oil

Sauce:

1 cup chicken broth
1 teaspoon soy sauce
½ teaspoon sugar
2 teaspoons cornstarch blended with 1
tablespoon cold water

Prepare sauce first: Heat and stir all
ingredients in a small saucepan over
moderate heat until slightly thickened;
keep warm until needed. Mix eggs with
all vegetables, meat, and soy sauce. Heat
2 teaspoons oil in a heavy 4″–6″ skillet
over moderate heat ½ minute, add ⅓
cup egg mixture and fry as you would a
pancake until lightly browned on bottom;
turn and brown flip side. Keep warm (but
do not stack) while you fry remaining
"pancakes," adding more oil as needed
and stirring egg mixture before each new
"pancake." Serve hot topped with sauce.
About 300 calories per serving if made
with chicken or shrimp; about 330 per
serving if made with pork or ham.

About Omelets

Omelets aren't as temperamental as
they're rumored to be. Still, people
approach them with trembling. By
heeding the tips below, you should be
able to make an acceptable omelet (the
perfect one will take practice).

There are two kinds of omelets: *the plain
or French,* made on top of the stove,
and *the soufflé or puffed,* begun on the
stove top but finished in the oven. For
plain omelets, yolks and whites are
beaten together just to mix; for soufflé
omelets, the whites are whipped
separately and folded in at the last.

Tips for Making Better Omelets

– Assemble all ingredients and
implements beforehand. If omelet is to
be filled, have filling ready.
– Use the freshest eggs possible and have
them at room temperature (you'll get
better volume). For an extra-tender
omelet, add 1 teaspoon cold water per
egg—*not* milk or cream, which will
toughen it.
– Do not overbeat eggs. For a plain
omelet, 20–30 seconds with a fork or
whisk will do it. For a soufflé omelet,
yolks should be briskly beaten with a
fork and the whites beaten with a whisk
until soft but firm peaks form.
– Use unsalted butter for cooking
omelets.
– *Use a proper omelet pan* (without it,
even an expert would have trouble). If
the pan is too heavy, it cannot be
manipulated easily as the omelet cooks; if
too light, eggs may scorch. It should be
round bottomed with sides that flare at
the top, no more than 6″–8″ in
diameter, of medium weight and made of
cast aluminum, tin-lined copper, thick
stainless steel, enameled cast iron, or
teflon-lined aluminum. It should be well
seasoned and used exclusively for making
omelets. *To season an omelet pan:* Half
fill with cooking oil, set over lowest heat,
and warm uncovered 1 hour. Turn off
heat and let oil cool in pan to room
temperature; pour out (save for cooking,
if you like) and wipe pan with paper
toweling. *To care for an omelet pan:*
Wipe after each use with paper toweling
but do not wash. If something burns on
the bottom, scour with salt and fine steel
wool (not soap-filled). Rinse, dry, and
reseason if necessary.
– Make only 1 small omelet at a time;
large ones are difficult to handle and
cook unevenly.
– Once eggs are in the pan, raise burner
heat to moderately high—or as high as

your proficiency allows without scorching eggs. Omelets are an exception to the low-heat rule of egg cookery. If they are to be lightly browned on the bottom, creamy inside and moist on top, the heat must be high and the handling deft.
– Serve an omelet the second it comes from the pan on a *warm*—not hot— plate.

About Filled Omelets

Plain omelets are easier to fill than the puffy, which are too bulky to fold well; these should be filled either by mixing filling with uncooked eggs or, better still, by ladling it over finished omelets before they are turned out. Plain omelets can be filled with almost any meat, fish, poultry, cheese, vegetable, fruit, preserve, or nut. Meat and vegetable fillings are usually warmed in butter in the omelet pan, then topped with the eggs (by the time the omelet is cooked, the filling will be in the center). Cheese, fruit, nuts, and other delicate fillings can be scattered over the omelet just before it's folded. Most fillings (cheese and nuts excepted) should be warm so that they do not cool the omelet.

Some Fillings for Savory Omelets

Cheese: Hard cheeses (Parmesan, romano, sapsago) can be mixed with the uncooked eggs; grate fine and allow 2–3 tablespoons cheese per 3-egg omelet. Softer cheeses (Cheddars, Gruyère, Roquefort, mozzarella, cottage or cream cheese) should be added in small dabs just before omelet is folded; again allow 2–3 tablespoons cheese per 3-egg omelet.

Meat: Any cooked, minced meat can be used. Allow ¼–⅓ cup per 3-egg omelet and warm in butter in omelet pan before adding eggs.

Seafood: Any drained canned, thawed frozen, or cooked fish or shellfish can be used. Bone and flake, allow ¼–⅓ cup per 3-egg omelet, and warm in butter in omelet pan before adding eggs.

Vegetable: Raw and cooked vegetables both make good fillings. In either case, they should be minced or diced; allow ¼–⅓ cup per 3-egg omelet. *Best vegetables to use raw:* tomato, avocado, finocchio, spinach, sweet red or green pepper. *Best cooked vegetables:* asparagus, broccoli, cauliflower, zucchini, yellow squash, carrots, green peas, potatoes, mushrooms, spinach, onions, artichokes.

Combination Fillings: Leftover meats seafoods, and vegetables can be minced, mixed, and used to fill omelets. Allow ¼–⅓ cup per 3-egg omelet and warm in butter in omelet pan before adding eggs. *Some good combinations:* ham and asparagus or spinach; corned beef and potatoes; franks and baked beans; beef and potatoes or onion; pork and apples or sweet potatoes; chicken and rice; rice and minced ripe or green olives; chicken liver and crumbled bacon; sautéed sausages and onions, potatoes or apples.

Dessert Omelet Fillings

Fruit: Well-drained canned, thawed frozen, or fresh fruits are suitable. Small berries can be added whole, but larger fruits should be sliced thin, minced, or puréed. Allow about ⅓–½ cup fruit per 3-egg omelet and add just before folding. If fruits are cold, warm slightly before adding.

Jelly, Jam, or Preserves: Use ⅓ cup warmed jelly, jam, or preserves per 3-egg omelet; pour over omelet just before folding.

Nut: Use ⅓ cup minced, ground, or thinly sliced nuts per 3-egg omelet (thinly sliced *marrons glacés* are especially good). Scatter over omelet just before folding.

Liquor or Liqueur: Drizzle 1–2 table-spoons warmed liquor or liqueur (rum, cognac, kirsch, calvados, etc.) over ome-let just before folding. Fold, drizzle with 2–3 tablespoons more liquor or liqueur. Blaze with a match, if you like, and serve flaming.

PLAIN OR FRENCH OMELET

Omelets should be made to order, one at a time.
Makes 1 serving

1 tablespoon unsalted butter or
*   margarine*
3 eggs, at room temperature
1 tablespoon cold water
½ teaspoon salt
⅛ teaspoon white pepper

Warm butter in an 6"–8" omelet pan over low heat while you mix eggs. Beat eggs, water, salt, and pepper vigorously with a fork or whisk 20–30 seconds until blended and frothy. When butter is bubbly but not brown, tip to coat sides of pan and pour in eggs. Turn heat to moderately high and, using a fork, draw edges of eggs as they cook in toward center, at the same time tilting and gently shaking pan so uncooked portions flow underneath. Continue until omelet is just set and top creamy and moist. Take pan from heat at once, loosen omelet edges with fork, shaking gently. If omelet should stick, slide a dab of butter underneath and tilt pan so it runs over bottom. Fold omelet in ½ or, if you prefer, let fold over as shown as you turn onto a warmed plate. Serve as is or topped with Tomato, Mornay, Mushroom, or other savory sauce. About 345 calories per serving.

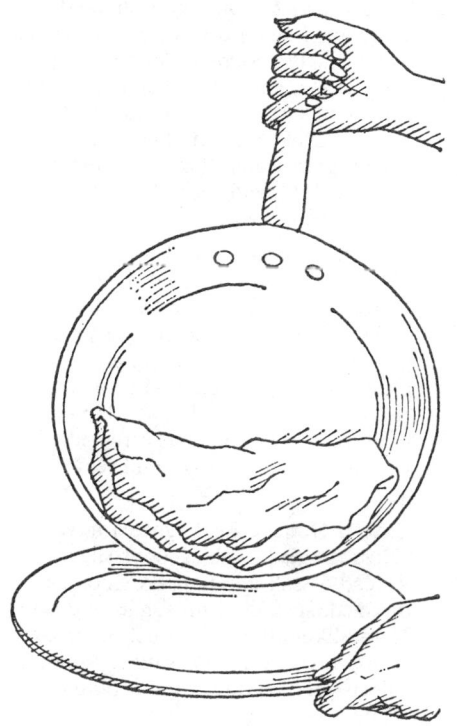

To Glaze: Fold omelet in pan, brush with melted butter, and brown quickly under broiler.

To Fill: There are 2 techniques (for filling ideas, see Some Fillings for Omelets):
– Lightly sauté filling in pan, add eggs, and cook as directed; when omelet is done, filling will be in center.
– Sprinkle filling over omelet just before folding.

VARIATIONS:

Fines Herbes Omelet: Gently warm 1 teaspoon minced chives, ½ teaspoon minced fresh chervil, and ¼ teaspoon minced fresh tarragon (or ½ teaspoon dried *fines herbes*) in melting butter. Add eggs and cooked as directed. About 345 calories per serving.

Lorraine Omelet: Prepare omelet as directed and, just before folding, top with 2 tablespoons coarsely grated Gruyère cheese, 1 tablespoon minced parsley, and 2 crisp brown slices of bacon. Fold and serve. About 490 calories per serving.

Lyonnaise Omelet: Prepare omelet as directed and, just before folding, top with 1 thinly sliced, sautéed yellow onion. Fold and serve. For extra zip, top with a drizzling of vinegar and browned butter. About 415 calories per serving.

Caviar Omelet: Prepare omelet as directed and, just before folding, top with ¼ cup caviar (red or black) and 2 tablespoons each sour cream and minced Spanish or Bermuda onion. Fold and serve. About 555 calories per serving.

Spanish Omelet: Stir-fry 1 slivered pimiento, 1 small peeled, cored, seeded, and coarsely chopped tomato, 1 crushed clove garlic, and 1 tablespoon minced parsley in 1 tablespoon butter 5–7 minutes over moderate heat. Cook omelet as directed, top with tomato mixture, fold, and serve. About 390 calories per serving.

Ham, Mushroom, and Tomato Omelet: Sauté ½ cup thinly sliced mushrooms in 1 tablespoon butter over moderate heat 3–5 minutes until golden; add ¼ cup julienne strips cooked ham, and 1 small peeled, cored, seeded, and coarsely chopped tomato; cook and stir 5–7 minutes. Cook omelet as directed, top with ham mixture, fold, and serve. About 420 calories per serving.

Dessert Omelet: Beat eggs with water called for and 2 tablespoons sugar instead of salt and pepper. Cook as directed, sprinkle with sugar, and serve. If you like, fill with a sweet filling or top with a favorite dessert sauce. About 435 calories per serving without filling or topping.

Note: You can put almost anything you want into an omelet—pâté and truffles if you're rich, minced luncheon meat if you're not. Once you get the feel of omelet making, improvise with the fillings. One New York City restaurant prepares 553 different omelets, so the sky is really the limit.

⚔ PUFFED OR SOUFFLÉ OMELET

Makes 2 servings

4 eggs, separated (at room temperature)
¼ cup cold water
½ teaspoon salt
⅛ teaspoon white pepper
1 tablespoon butter or margarine

Preheat oven to 350° F. Beat yolks briskly with a fork. In a separate bowl beat whites until frothy; add water, salt, and pepper and beat until soft peaks form; fold gently into yolks. Heat butter in an 8″ omelet pan with a heatproof handle over moderate heat until bubbly

but not brown; tip pan so butter coats bottom and sides. Pour in eggs and cook, uncovered, without stirring 5 minutes until underside is pale golden. Transfer to oven and bake, uncovered, 12–15 minutes until puffy and delicately browned. Loosen omelet with a spatula, divide in half, using 2 forks, invert on a heated platter, and turn out. Or crease center with a spatula and fold omelet in half as you tip out of pan. About 215 calories per serving.

VARIATIONS:

Filled Soufflé Omelet: When omelet comes from oven, sprinkle filling over ½ nearest pan handle and fold as above. Or, fold filling into eggs *just before* cooking. (See Some Fillings for Omelets.)

Sweet Soufflé Omelet: Prepare as directed but omit salt and pepper, and beat ¼ cup sugar into egg whites. Cook as directed, sprinkle with sugar, and top with a favorite dessert sauce. About 310 calories per serving without sauce.

GREEK SHEPHERD'S OMELET

Makes 1 serving

1 tablespoon olive oil
1 clove garlic, peeled and halved
* lengthwise*
2 bay leaves
3 eggs, at room temperature
1 tablespoon cold water
3 tablespoons crumbled feta cheese

Warm oil, garlic, and bay leaves in an 8″ omelet pan over lowest heat 3–4 minutes. Meanwhile, beat eggs and water briskly with a fork to blend. Remove garlic and bay leaves from pan, raise burner heat to moderately high, and heat 1–2 minutes, tilting pan so that oil coats bottom and sides. When oil is hot but not smoking, pour in eggs and, using a fork, draw curling edges in toward center. Keep tilting and gently shaking pan so uncooked eggs flow underneath. After 1–1½ minutes (eggs should still be creamy), sprinkle feta over half the omelet, fold as directed for plain omelet. Gently slide omelet onto a heated plate and serve. About 405 calories per serving.

⊠ ONION FRITTATA

An Italian omelet that is browned on both sides.
Makes 2–4 servings

1 medium-size Bermuda onion, peeled
and sliced paper thin
3 tablespoons olive or other cooking oil
1 clove garlic, peeled and crushed
4 eggs, lightly beaten
¾ teaspoon salt
⅛ teaspoon pepper
1 teaspoon basil
2 tablespoons grated Parmesan cheese

Sauté onion in half the oil over moderately low heat 5–8 minutes until limp, not brown; add garlic and stir-fry 1 minute. Mix onion and garlic with eggs, seasonings, and cheese. Heat remaining oil in a heavy 9″ or 10″ skillet over moderate heat ½ minute, add egg mixture, and cook without stirring 3–4 minutes until browned underneath and just set on top. Cut in quarters, turn, and brown flip side 2–3 minutes. About 390 calories for each of 2 servings, 195 for each of 4.

VARIATIONS:

Ham and Tomato Frittata: Omit onion; sauté ½ cup slivered prosciutto or cooked ham and 1 coarsely chopped, peeled, and seeded tomato in oil 5 minutes, then proceed as directed. About 425 calories for each of 2 servings, 215 for each of 4.

Artichoke Frittata: Omit onion; sauté ½ cup thinly sliced parboiled or drained canned artichoke hearts in oil 3–4 minutes, add garlic, and proceed as directed. About 390 calories for each of 2 servings, 195 for each of 4.

PIPERADE

This Basque "omelet" is closer to scrambled eggs, cooked until soft and creamy and topped with onions, tomatoes, sweet peppers, and ham.
Makes 4–6 servings

3 medium-size yellow onions, peeled and
sliced thin
2 sweet green peppers, cored, seeded,
and cut in strips ¼″ wide
1 sweet red pepper, cored, seeded, and
cut in strips ¼″ wide
2 tablespoons lard, olive or other
cooking oil
3 tablespoons butter or margarine
1 clove garlic, peeled and crushed
4 medium-size ripe tomatoes, peeled,
cored, seeded, and coarsely chopped
1½ teaspoons salt
⅛ teaspoon pepper
½ cup cooked ham strips cut ¼″ wide
and 2″ long
8 eggs, lightly beaten

Stir-fry onions and pepper in lard and 1 tablespoon butter in a large, heavy skillet over moderately low heat about 10 minutes until limp, not brown. Add garlic and tomatoes and stir-fry 5–8 minutes until almost all liquid has evaporated. Add seasonings and ham and keep warm. Melt remaining butter in a heavy 10″ skillet over moderately low heat, add eggs, and scramble *just* until set. Remove from heat, spread with ham mixture, and stir lightly into *surface* of eggs. Cut in wedges and serve. Good with crusty French bread and a crisp green salad. About 420 calories for each of 4 servings, 280 for each of 6.

VARIATION:

Prepare as directed but just before spreading with ham mixture sprinkle with ¼–⅓ cup coarsely grated Gruyère cheese. About 450 calories for each of 4 servings, 300 for each of 6.

⚖ ⊠ BAKED EGGS IN TOMATOES

Nutritious diet fare.
Makes 4 servings

2 large firm ripe tomatoes, halved
crosswise
4 eggs
¼ cup soft white bread crumbs
¼ cup coarsely grated sharp Cheddar
1 tablespoon minced parsley
¼ teaspoon salt
⅛ teaspoon pepper
2 tablespoons melted butter or margarine

Preheat oven to 425° F. Scoop pulp from tomatoes, then stand cut sides up in a greased 9" piepan and bake, uncovered, 5–7 minutes. Break eggs, 1 at a time, into a custard cup and slide into a tomato. Mix crumbs, cheese, parsley, salt, and pepper, sprinkle over eggs, and drizzle with butter. Bake, uncovered, about 15 minutes until eggs are just set and topping golden. About 205 calories per serving.

VARIATIONS:

⚖ **Low-Calorie Baked Eggs in Tomatoes:** Prepare as directed but omit drizzling of butter. About 160 calories per serving.

⚖ **Baked Eggs in Toast Cups:** Prepare 4 toast cups.* Slide an egg into each cup, sprinkle with topping, drizzle with butter, and bake 15–20 minutes at 350° F. until eggs are set. Good with hot Cheese or Mushroom Sauce. About 220 calories per serving.

STUFFED EGGS BAKED IN CHEESE SAUCE

Makes 4 servings

1 recipe Basic Stuffed Eggs or Deviled Eggs
2 tablespoons butter or margarine
2 tablespoons flour
1 cup milk
½ teaspoon salt
⅛ teaspoon pepper
1 teaspoon Worcestershire sauce
½ teaspoon prepared mild yellow mustard
1 cup coarsely grated sharp Cheddar cheese

Preheat oven to 350° F. Arrange eggs 1 layer deep in a buttered 9" piepan or *au gratin* dish. Melt butter over moderate heat in a small saucepan; blend in flour, slowly add milk and seasonings, and heat and stir until thickened; add cheese, stirring until melted. Pour over eggs and bake, uncovered, 20–30 minutes until bubbly; if you like, brown lightly under broiler. About 455 calories per serving.

VARIATIONS:

Stuffed Eggs in Mushroom Sauce: Prepare as directed but substitute 1½

cups Mushroom Sauce for the cheese sauce; if you like, sprinkle with ¼ cup grated Cheddar just before baking. About 400 calories per serving (with cheese).

Baked Stuffed Eggs the French Way: Prepare as directed, but substitute 1½ cups Béchamel, Velouté, Suprême, or Mornay Sauce for the cheese sauce. About 455 calories per serving for Suprême or Mornay Sauce, 340 if made with Béchamel or Velouté.

Rosy Baked Stuffed Eggs: Prepare as directed but substitute 1½ cups Tomato Sauce for cheese sauce. About 375 calories per serving.

EGGS AND BROCCOLI AU GRATIN

Makes 4 servings

1 (2-pound) bunch broccoli, parboiled
4 hard-cooked eggs, peeled and quartered
3 tablespoons butter or margarine
3 tablespoons flour
¼ teaspoon powdered mustard
¼ teaspoon salt
⅛ teaspoon white pepper
1½ cups milk
1½ teaspoons Worcestershire sauce
2 cups coarsely grated sharp Cheddar cheese

Preheat oven to 350° F. Drain broccoli well and arrange in an ungreased shallow 2-quart casserole; distribute eggs evenly over broccoli. Melt butter in a saucepan over moderately low heat, blend in flour, mustard, salt, and pepper; slowly stir in milk and cook and stir until thickened and smooth. Mix in Worcestershire sauce and 1½ cups cheese. Pour sauce evenly over broccoli and eggs, top with remaining cheese, and bake uncovered 20–30 minutes until lightly browned and bubbly. Serve hot as a main dish. About 490 calories per serving.

BACON AND EGG PIE

Makes 6–8 servings

1 recipe Flaky Pastry II
1 egg, lightly beaten (glaze)

Filling:

12 slices crisply cooked bacon
6 eggs
¼ teaspoon salt
⅛ teaspoon pepper

Preheat oven to 425° F. Prepare pastry as directed, roll out into 2 (12") circles and fit 1 in a 9" piepan. Lay 6 slices bacon over bottom crust. Break eggs, 1 at a time, into a cup and gently slide on top of bacon, spacing evenly. Top with remaining bacon. Dampen rim of bottom crust; cut steam slits in top crust and fit over filling. Press edges of pastry together, trim, and crimp to seal. Brush with glaze, being careful not to cover steam slits, and bake 25–30 minutes until golden. Serve hot or cold. About 475 calories for each of 6 servings, 355 for each of 8.

RANCH-STYLE EGG AND POTATO "PIE"

Makes 4 servings

4 medium-size potatoes, peeled
¼ cup cooking oil
1 teaspoon salt
⅛ teaspoon pepper
2 tablespoons minced chives
1 cup coarsely grated Cheddar cheese
8 eggs

Slice potatoes paper thin into a bowl of cold water; drain and pat dry on paper toweling. Heat oil 1–2 minutes over moderately low heat in a large, heavy skillet or flameproof casserole, spread potato slices over bottom and press down with a pancake turner. Sauté about 30 minutes, without stirring, until a crisp brown crust forms on bottom and potatoes are tender. Meanwhile, preheat oven to 350° F. Sprinkle salt, pepper, chives, and cheese over potatoes. Break eggs, 1 at a time, into a cup and gently slide on top of cheese, spacing evenly. Bake, uncovered, 5–8 minutes until eggs are cooked to your liking. Cut into portions, including an egg with each, and serve. About 480 calories per serving.

✠ BASIC CREAMED EGGS

Makes 4 servings

2 cups hot Medium White Sauce
1 teaspoon Worcestershire sauce (optional)
1 tablespoon minced parsley
6 hard-cooked eggs, peeled and quartered or sliced thin
Salt to taste

Mix all ingredients and serve over hot buttered toast or English muffins, boiled rice or frizzled ham, cooked asparagus or broccoli, or in puff pastry shells. About 325 calories per serving (without toast, etc.).

VARIATIONS:

Eggs in Cheese Sauce: Mix 1 cup coarsely grated sharp Cheddar cheese and 1 teaspoon prepared mild yellow mustard into sauce along with above seasonings, heat and stir until cheese melts, fold in eggs, and serve. About 440 calories per serving.

Scalloped Eggs: Prepare as directed, then layer into a buttered 1½-quart casserole with 1½ cups soft buttered bread crumbs, beginning and ending with eggs. Top with ⅓ cup fine buttered crumbs and bake, uncovered, ½ hour at 350° F. until browned and bubbly. About 450 calories per serving.

Eggs Goldenrod: Mix sauce with seasonings and coarsely chopped egg whites. Spoon over toast and top with sieved egg yolks. About 390 calories per serving.

Curried Eggs: Prepare as directed but omit parsley; add 2 teaspoons curry powder warmed 3–5 minutes in 2 tablespoons butter over low heat, and, if you like, ¼ cup toasted slivered almonds. Serve over rice. About 470 calories per serving without rice.

Deviled Creamed Eggs: Prepare as directed but substitute 6 deviled eggs (12 halves) for the hard-cooked. Arrange in an ungreased shallow *au gratin* dish, cover with sauce (made without parsley), and bake uncovered 15 minutes at 350° F. About 545 calories per serving.

Eggs à la King: Prepare as directed, then fold in 1 cup sautéed sliced mushrooms, ½ cup cooked green peas, and 2 tablespoons minced pimiento. About 360 calories per serving.

Creamed Eggs, Bacon, and Onion: Prepare as directed but omit parsley and add ½ cup each minced sautéed onion and crisp crumbled bacon. About 400 calories per serving.

Some Additional Ways to Vary Basic Creamed Eggs: Prepare recipe as directed, then just before serving mix in any of the following:
– ¾–1 cup diced cooked ham, tongue, luncheon meat, or sliced cooked sausages
– ¾–1 cup chipped beef
– 6–8 coarsely chopped sautéed chicken livers or 3–4 sautéed lamb kidneys
– ¾–1 cup tiny whole shelled and deveined boiled shrimp, or minced cooked crab meat or lobster
– ¾–1 cup flaked tuna or salmon
– 1 peeled and diced ripe avocado
– ¾–1 cup leftover cooked vegetables (peas, diced carrots, corn, lima beans, asparagus tips, cauliflower or broccoli flowerets)
– 1–1½ cups diced boiled potatoes

⎩⎫ **DEVILED EGGS**

Makes 4 servings

6 hard-cooked eggs, peeled and halved
    lengthwise
¼ cup mayonnaise
2 teaspoons lemon juice
¼ teaspoon powdered mustard or
    1 teaspoon prepared spicy brown
    mustard
1 teaspoon grated yellow onion
    (optional)
1 teaspoon Worcestershire sauce
¼ teaspoon salt
Pinch white pepper

Some Suggested Garnishes:

Parsley, watercress, tarragon, dill, or
    chervil sprigs
Minced chives, dill, or parsley
Pimiento strips
Sliced pitted ripe or green olives
Capers

Rolled anchovy fillets
Paprika

Mash yolks well, mix in remaining ingredients, mound into whites, and chill ½ hour. Garnish as desired and serve. About 225 calories per serving without garnish.

VARIATIONS:

Deviled Eggs with Cheese: Prepare yolk mixture as directed, then beat in ⅓ cup finely grated sharp Cheddar, Parmesan, or Gruyère cheese or crumbled blue cheese. About 310 calories per serving.

⎩⎫ **Anchovy Eggs:** Prepare yolk mixture as directed but omit mustard; mix in instead 2 tablespoons anchovy paste. About 230 calories per serving.

⎩⎫ **Mexican Deviled Eggs:** When preparing yolk mixture, omit mustard, reduce mayonnaise to 2 tablespoons, and add 2 tablespoons chili sauce and 1 teaspoon chili powder. About 185 calories per serving.

⎩⎫ **Curried Deviled Eggs:** Prepare yolk mixture as directed but increase grated onion to 2 teaspoons and add 2 teaspoons curry powder. About 230 calories per serving.

⊠ ⎩⎫ **JIFFY DEVILED EGGS**

Makes 4–6 servings

8 hard-cooked eggs
½ cup relish-type sandwich spread
1 tablespoon milk
1 teaspoon prepared spicy brown
    mustard
¼ teaspoon salt
Pinch pepper

Chill eggs, then peel and halve lengthwise. Mash yolks with a fork and blend in remaining ingredients; stuff into whites, mounding mixture up, and serve. (*Note:* Flavor will be better if eggs are chilled about 1 hour before serving.) About 280 calories for each of 4 servings, 185 for each of 6.

⚖ BASIC STUFFED EGGS

Makes 4 servings

6 hard-cooked eggs, peeled and halved
  lengthwise
¼–⅓ cup milk, heavy, light, or sour
  cream
¼ teaspoon salt
Pinch white pepper

Mash yolks well, blend in remaining
ingredients, and mound into whites,
using a pastry bag fitted with a large
decorative tip if you like. Chill ½ hour,
garnish as desired (see Some Suggested
Garnishes for Deviled Eggs), and serve.
Calories per serving: about 130 if made
with milk, 160 if made with light or sour
cream, 190 if made with heavy cream.

Some Quick Stuffing Variations: Blend
any of the following into yolk mixture,
adjusting liquid as needed to make a
creamy consistency:
– 1 (2¼–2½-ounce) can deviled ham,
meat, or chicken spread or pâté
– ¼ cup ground cooked ham, tongue,
luncheon meat, chicken, or chicken
livers
– ¼ cup crisp crumbled bacon
– ¼ cup minced cooked fish or shellfish
– ¼ cup red caviar and 2 teaspoons
lemon juice
– 2 tablespoons anchovy paste and
1 tablespoon minced capers
– ¼ cup minced pitted ripe or green
olives
– 2 tablespoons each minced scallions
and celery and 1 tablespoon finely
grated onion
– ¼ cup grated sharp cheese (any kind)
and 2 tablespoons minced chutney or
nuts
– ¼ cup cottage or cream cheese,
1 tablespoon each minced chives and
pimiento and 2–3 dashes liquid hot red
pepper seasoning
– ¼ cup puréed cooked spinach,
asparagus, beets, peas, or carrots

⚖ ROSEMARY EGGS

Makes 4 servings

6 hard-cooked eggs
2 tablespoons mayonnaise
1 tablespoon light cream
1 teaspoon white wine vinegar
1 tablespoon minced shallots or yellow
  onion
¼ teaspoon minced fresh rosemary or
  ⅛ teaspoon dried rosemary
⅛ teaspoon powdered mustard
½ teaspoon salt
Pinch white pepper

Chill eggs well, then peel and halve
lengthwise. Scoop yolks into a small
mixing bowl and mash with a fork. Add
remaining ingredients to yolks and beat
with a fork until creamy. Stuff whites
with yolk mixture, mounding it up well.
Chill at least 1 hour before serving.
About 180 calories per serving.

EGG CROQUETTES

Makes 4 servings

4 hard-cooked eggs, peeled and minced
⅔ cup cold Thick White Sauce
½ cup soft white bread crumbs
½ teaspoon salt
⅛ teaspoon pepper
1 egg, lightly beaten
½ cup toasted fine bread crumbs
Shortening or cooking oil for deep fat
  frying

Mix hard-cooked eggs, sauce, soft
crumbs, salt, and pepper. Using about
¼ cup for each, shape into 6 logs about
3″ long and 1″ across. Dip in beaten
egg, then crumbs to coat well. Cover and
chill ½ hour. Meanwhile, heat fat in a
deep fat fryer with basket and deep fat
thermometer over moderate heat to
375° F. Fry rolls, a few at a time, about
1½ minutes until golden. Drain on paper
toweling and serve. Good with Tomato
Sauce. About 325 calories per serving.

VARIATION:

Cheese Croquettes: Omit hard-cooked
eggs; while sauce is still hot, stir in
1 cup coarsely grated sharp Cheddar
cheese. Cool, add crumbs and seasonings,
and proceed as directed. About 355
calories per serving.

⚖ EGGS IN ASPIC

Makes 4 servings

2 cups aspic made with beef or
  chicken broth*
2–3 tablespoons Madeira or cognac
Truffle or pimiento cutouts
4 firm poached eggs, chilled

Mix aspic and Madeira, chill until syrupy, then spoon 2–3 tablespoons into each of 4 ungreased custard cups or ramekins, swirling round to coat sides and bottom; chill until firm. Keep remaining aspic syrupy. Decorate chilled aspic with cutouts, trim poached eggs to fit cups and arrange on aspic, attractive side down. Fill cups with aspic and chill until firm. Unmold and sprig with watercress. Serve with mayonnaise as a light main course or salad. About 120 calories per serving (without mayonnaise).

VARIATIONS:

⚖ **Stuffed or Deviled Eggs in Aspic:** Prepare as directed but substitute 2 stuffed or deviled eggs (4 halves) for the poached, arranging stuffed sides down on aspic. About 150 calories per serving.

⚖ **Eggs in Madrilène Aspic:** Prepare as directed but substitute madrilène for aspic; heat and stir madrilène with 1 envelope unflavored gelatin until gelatin dissolves, cool, and mix in 3 tablespoons dry sherry or port. Chill until syrupy and proceed as directed. About 140 calories per serving.

⚖ **Tarragon Eggs in Aspic:** Begin as directed, chilling a layer of aspic in ramekins; decorate with fresh tarragon leaves and truffle diamonds, add 2 paper thin slices boiled ham cut to fit, top with a little aspic, and chill until tacky. Add a poached or hard-cooked egg (with end sliced off so yolk shows), fill with aspic, and chill until firm. About 130 calories per serving.

⚖ **Hard-Cooked Eggs in Aspic:** Prepare as directed, substituting medium-size hard-cooked eggs for the poached. Cut off about ⅓ of ends and place cut sides down in cups so yolks show when eggs are unmolded. About 125 calories per serving.

⚖ ¢ PICKLED EGGS

Good picnic fare.
Makes 4–6 servings

1½ cups white vinegar
1 teaspoon mixed pickling spices
1 clove garlic, peeled and bruised
1 bay leaf
6 hard-cooked eggs, peeled

Simmer vinegar and spices, uncovered, 10 minutes; cool slightly, add garlic and bay leaf. Pack eggs into a screw-top jar, add vinegar mixture, cover, and cool to room temperature. Refrigerate 7–10 days before serving—longer for stronger flavor. Serve as an appetizer or with cold cuts and salad. About 135 calories for each of 4 servings, 90 for each of 6.

VARIATION:

⚖ **Pickled Eggs and Beets:** Prepare as directed but add 6–8 small whole boiled and peeled beets to eggs before adding vinegar. Marinate 2–3 days before serving. About 150 calories for each of 4 servings, 100 for each of 6.

CHEESE

No one knows who first made cheese, though legend credits an early wayfarer whose milk ration, carried in a skin pouch, turned to curds and whey. That ancient cheese would have been much like our cottage cheese. Pungent ripened cheeses arrived later, again by accident. A shepherd boy, the story goes, found that a cheese he'd left in a cave was covered with mold. He tried it, liked it, and blue cheese came into being.

Cheese is made from the milk or cream of many animals; some is unripened (cottage and cream cheese), some is mold-ripened (the whole family of blues), some bacteria-ripened

(Limburger, Liederkranz). Cheeses range from hard to soft, bland to overpowering, white to dark brown. All are excellent meat substitutes because of their high quality protein, vitamin, and mineral content. Depending upon whether cheese is made from skim or whole milk or cream, it can be low in calories or loaded.

The kinds of cheese available today are bewildering. France alone produces hundreds, including most of the great classics. Italy, Holland, England, Switzerland, Scandinavia, America, and Canada are also major producers. America's appetite for cheese has become so insatiable that cheese shops are proliferating and supermarket dairy counters are offering obscure imported varieties as well as the familiar domestics.

Confronted with dozens of cheeses, the buyer wonders which to try. Which to use in cooking, which to serve with cocktails, which to offer as dessert. The best way to bring order to the confusion is to group cheeses by type and use. But first, some oft-used terms defined:

Pasteurized Cheese: America's cheese, like its other dairy products, is pasteurized. This means, of course, that the cheese is wholesome; but it also means that the organisms responsible for the cheese's character have been destroyed and that the color, texture, and flavor won't change much as the cheese ages.

Process Cheese: Watered-down cheese; preservatives, emulsifiers, artificial coloring, and flavoring are often added.

Process Cheese Food: Further watered-down and adulterated cheese, which in some instances isn't cheese at all.

Some Popular Cheeses Grouped by Type and Use

Soft, Unripened Cheeses (highly perishable): Serve slightly chilled; curd cheeses can be served anytime or used in cooking. The cream cheeses, teamed with fresh berries or tart preserves, make elegant desserts, especially if accompanied by chilled champagne or moderately sweet white wine.

Cheese	Country of Origin	Description
Cottage, pot, and farmer's cheese	U.S.A.	Bland but sour curd cheeses; cottage cheese is moistest (especially cream style, which has fresh cream added), pot cheese is next, and farmer's cheese driest; it is often shaped.
Cream cheese	U.S.A.	Rich, bland, and buttery
Gervais	France	Sour, doubly rich cream cheese
Petit-Suisse	France	Mild, doubly rich cream cheese
Neufchâtel	France, U.S.A.	Soft cream cheese, pungent if ripe
Ricotta	Italy	Fine-cured cousin of cottage cheese

Soft, Ripened Cheeses: Serve at room temperature. Excellent with fruit, wine, and French bread between the main course and dessert; also good before dinner with cocktails. (*Note:* Cheese crusts are not cut away but eaten.) *Compatible Fruits:* Apples, pears, peaches, grapes. *Compatible Wines:* Dry reds, *except* for Liederkranz and Limburger, which are better with beer.

Cheese	Country of Origin	Description
Brie	France	The cheese that sends gourmets into ecstasy; perfectly ripened, it is golden and creamy throughout, neither too bland nor pungent.
Camembert	France	France's favorite and a rival of Brie. It should be ivory-hued, butter-soft but not runny. Mild to strong.
Crema Dania	Denmark	Rich, creamy, and zippy when ripe
Liederkranz	U.S.A.	Strong and creamy
Limburger	Belgium	Creamy-firm and strong enough "to blow a safe"; not for the meek

Semisoft Cheeses: Serve at room temperature. Excellent between the main course and dessert, accompanied by fruit and wine. Also good as anytime snacks and as cocktail party fare. (*Note:* Cut away any rind before eating; cheeses are usually served in the rind, unless it's unsightly.) Fontina, mozzarella, and Monterey Jack are excellent cooking cheeses because they melt smoothly; feta is delicious crumbled into salads or omelets. *Compatible Fruits:* Tart apples, crisp pears, grapes; feta is especially good with dried figs or apricots and pistachio nuts. *Compatible Wines:* Dry, full-bodied reds except for feta, which is better with a white retsina.

Cheese	Country of Origin	Description
Bel Paese	Italy	Smooth, mellow, and nutty
Feta	Greece	Snowy, salty, crumbly sheep's milk cheese preserved in brine
Fontina	Italy	Pale, mild, and nutty
Monterey Jack	U.S.A.	Pale, mild to sharp Cheddar type
Mozzarella	Italy	The pizza cheese—white and delicate
Muenster	France (Alsace), U.S.A.	American Muenster is pale and bland; the European is sharper and darker. Sometimes has caraway seeds.
Oka	Canada	Smooth, mellow, and mild
Pont l'Évêque	France	France's fourth most important cheese (after Brie, Camembert, and Roquefort). Soft, pale yellow, and piquant; shot through with tiny "eyes"
Port du Salut	France	Pale, butter smooth, but robust
Reblochon	France	Ivory-colored under its russet skin; soft but authoritative
Tilsit	Germany	The color of cream, full of small "eyes," fairly sharp
Wensleydale	England	Pale yellow, sharp, butter-flavored; there is also a blue Wensleydale.

Firm Cheeses: Serve at room temperature. Good anytime as snacks, also between the main course and dessert with fruit and wine. These are cooking favorites because of their robust flavor and smooth-melting quality. *Compatible Fruits:* Apples, pears, grapes, plums. *Compatible Wines:* Full-bodied dry reds except for the Cheddar types, which are better with beer, ale, or stout.

Cheese	Country of Origin	Description
Caerphilly	Wales	Smooth, white, and salty
Cheddar	England, U.S.A., Canada	Huge family ranging from sharp to mild, white to orange. Good U.S. Cheddars: Colby, Coon, Herkimer, Pineapple, Vermont, Wisconsin
Cheshire	England	Rich, zesty red or white Cheddar type; popular for Welsh Rabbit
Edam	Netherlands	Mild, golden "cannonball" cheese, coated with red wax
Gjetost	Norway	Curious, sweet-salty, fudge-textured brown cheese made of caramelized goat's milk. Norwegians like it for breakfast, sliced paper thin, on buttered rye bread; also for dessert.
Gloucester	England	There are two—single and double, or mild and sharp; both are velvety.
Gouda	Netherlands	Mild, creamy cheese much like Edam; well aged, it is crumbly and piquant.
Gruyère	Switzerland	Rich, nutty-sweet, cream colored, shot with small "eyes"; superb for cooking
Kashkaval	Bulgaria	Salty, crumbly, white sheep cheese
Lancashire	England	White with lots of bite; when young, cheese is mellow and butter-smooth.
Leicester	England	Bright orange-rose, crumbly, sharp, and lemony
Provolone	Italy	Smoky-mellow pale yellow giant trussed with rope and swung from rafters
Swiss or Emmentaler	Switzerland	Pale cream to tan cheese with big holes; nutty-sharp with a sweet aftertaste

The "Blues": Serve at room temperature. Good with cocktails before dinner; delicious with fruit, rough bread, and wine between the entree and dessert; excellent crumbled into salads, salad dressings, casseroles, and omelets. *Compatible Fruits:* Apples and pears. *Compatible Wines:* Robust dry reds except for Stilton, which is committed to vintage port.

Cheese	Country of Origin	Description
Danish blue	Denmark	Creamy-white with blue-green marbling; salty with lots of bite
Gorgonzola	Italy	Pale green-veined, soft cheese; pungent
Roquefort	France	Made of sheep's milk and "Queen of the Blues"; crumbly, creamy-white with deep blue-green mottling; extra strong
Stilton	England	Oyster white, blue-green-veined cheese, mellower than other blues because of a vaguely Cheddarish flavor

Hard ("Grating") Cheeses: Except for Parmesan, good eaten out of hand, these are used almost altogether as toppings (soup and pasta) or to heighten the flavor of sauces, salads, and casseroles. Use sparingly.

Cheese	Country of Origin	Description
Parmesan	Italy	Sharp, grainy, and golden; the foundation of Italian cuisine
Romano	Italy	Sheep's milk cheese, similar to but more pungent than Parmesan
Sapsago	Switzerland	Hard, conical green cheese, sour and pungent with dried Alpine clover

Some Tips on Cooking with Cheese

– Use low to moderate heat. Cheese becomes rubbery, tough, and indigestible when cooked too long or at too high a heat.
– Use well-aged cheeses for cooking— especially for sauces and fondues, where smoothness counts. Badly aged cheeses will clump and separate and nothing can be done to bring them back together. Should this happen, it's best to discard the rubbery clumps and thicken the sauce with a flour paste.
– When cheeses are to be melted into a sauce, coarsely grate or dice.
– Use strong cheeses sparingly so their flavors don't dominate.
– If a particular cheese called for in a recipe is unavailable, substitute a similar one from the same group (see Some Popular Cheeses Grouped by Type and Use).

Some Tips on Serving Cheese

In General:
– Serve soft, unripened cheeses cold, *but all others at room temperature.* Bringing cheese to room temperature can take from ½–3 hours, depending on the cheese and the weather. Soft cheeses

warm faster than hard, small cheeses faster than large. All, of course, come to room temperature faster in hot weather than in cold.
– Serve cheeses in their rinds or crusts unless unsightly. Crusts are usually edible; rinds are not.
– Present cheese on a simple board, wooden tray, or marble slab, not on crystal, china, or silver, which are incompatible with its earthiness.
– Put out only what cheese you expect to be eaten.
– Allow plenty of space between cheeses on a board and don't group the strongs with the milds. Provide a separate knife for each cheese.
– Don't clutter a cheese board with garnishes, which will only wilt and get smeared with cheese. The best garnish is no garnish.
– Choose simple rough breads (French or Italian) and unseasoned, unsalted crackers for cheese. Highly seasoned ones overpower the cheese.
– Serve breads and crackers separately, not on the cheese board.

Before Dinner:
– Serve 1 or, at most, 2 cheeses—rich or sharp ones (blue or Brie, perhaps) that guests aren't apt to overeat. It's easy to nibble away at bland cheeses until the appetite's gone.

At Cocktail Parties:
– Vary the cheeses, striking a balance between hard and soft, sharp and bland. A good practice is to choose one from each of the following categories: Soft, Ripened; Semisoft; Firm; Blue.
– Avoid the superstrong Limburger and Liederkranz. In a hot crowded room, they'll soon smell to high heaven.
– Put out plenty of cheese (¼–½ pound per guest is a good estimate) and in whole wheels or 2–3-pound slabs so there will be enough to go around.

At the End of a Meal:
– Suit the cheese to the meal. If dinner has been rich, cheese is out of order. It is also inappropriate following an

Oriental or Indian meal. But after a French, Italian, Viennese, or Scandinavian meal, it is perfect. Elegant menus deserve queenly cheeses, rougher fare, coarser cheeses. As a general rule, French cheeses are best with French wines, Italian cheeses with Italian wines, and English or Nordic cheeses with beer or ale.
– Set out a single tray of cheese and bowl of fruit from which everyone can help themselves.

About Keeping and Storing Cheese
See the chapter on storage.

WELSH RABBIT

Makes 4 servings

1 tablespoon butter or margarine
½ cup milk, ale, or beer
½ teaspoon powdered mustard
Pinch cayenne pepper
1 tablespoon Worcestershire sauce
¾ pound sharp Cheddar cheese, coarsely grated

Heat butter, milk, mustard, cayenne, and Worcestershire sauce in the top of a double boiler or chafing dish over *just* simmering water 7–10 minutes. Add cheese, a little at a time, stirring constantly until smooth and quite thick. Remove from heat immediately and serve over hot buttered toast. About 365 calories per serving if made with milk, 355 if made with ale or beer, not including toast. Add about 120 calories for each slice buttered toast.

⚖ TOMATO-CHEESE RABBIT

Makes 6 servings

2 tablespoons butter or margarine
¼ cup unsifted flour
¼ teaspoon oregano
¼ teaspoon basil
½ teaspoon salt
¼ teaspoon cayenne pepper
1 cup light cream
1 tablespoon onion juice
½ cup coarsely grated sharp Cheddar cheese
1 cup tomato juice
⅛ teaspoon baking soda

Melt butter in a small saucepan over moderate heat and blend in flour, herbs, salt, and pepper. Mix in cream and heat, stirring, until thickened and smooth. Turn heat to low, add onion juice and Cheddar, and heat, stirring, until cheese is melted. Meanwhile, in a separate small saucepan, bring tomato juice to a boil over high heat; off heat, stir in soda. Add tomato juice slowly to cheese sauce, stirring constantly. Serve over hot buttered toast. About 185 calories per serving not including toast. Add about 120 calories for each slice buttered toast.

CHEESE FONDUE

Sometimes, despite all precautions, a fondue will "lump." The cheese, not the cook, is usually to blame. If the cheese is poorly aged or not *Swiss* Gruyère or Emmentaler, it may never melt smoothly. The Swiss like to drink kirsch with fondue (usually a pony halfway through the proceedings) and to follow with broiled sausage and crisp apples or pears.
Makes 4 servings

⅔ *pound well-aged imported Gruyère*
   cheese, cut in ¼" cubes
⅓ *pound well-aged imported*
   Emmentaler cheese, cut in ¼" cubes
3 *tablespoons flour*
½ *teaspoon paprika*
¼ *teaspoon nutmeg or mace*
⅛ *teaspoon white pepper*
1 *clove garlic, peeled and halved*
1¾ *cups Neuchâtel, Chablis, or Riesling*
   wine
1 *tablespoon lemon juice*
2 *tablespoons kirsch*
¼ *teaspoon baking soda (optional)*
1½ *loaves day-old French bread, cut in*
   1½" cubes (each should have crust on
   1 side)

Toss cheeses in a bowl with flour, paprika, nutmeg, and pepper. Rub a 2-quart fondue *caquelon* or heavy round flameproof earthenware pot well with garlic. Add wine and heat, uncovered, over low heat until bubbles dot bottom of pot. Begin adding dredged

cheeses (and any loose bits of flour and spices) by the handful, stirring with a wooden spoon in a figure 8 motion. Raise heat to moderate, continue stirring and adding cheese, flour, and spices a little at a time until all are in. Mix in lemon juice. At first, cheese will clump, but keep stirring. After 15–20 minutes, fondue should begin to "cream up." When fondue is smooth and bubbling gently, stir in kirsch and, for a lighter fondue, the soda. Set caquelon over its warmer and adjust flame so fondue bubbles *gently*—too much heat will make it rubbery. Serve with bread cubes and long-handled fondue forks. (*Note:* If fondue should separate and lump, return to moderately low stove heat and beat gently with a whisk; blend ½ teaspoon cornstarch with ¼ cup wine (same kind as in recipe) and blend into fondue. If fondue becomes too thick, thin with a little warmed wine.) About 990 calories per serving

CHEDDAR-BEER FONDUE

Much easier and almost as good as Swiss fondue. Somewhat lower in calories, too.
Makes 4 appetizer servings; 2 entree servings

1 *clove garlic, peeled and halved*
1 *tablespoon butter or margarine*
2 *cups coarsely grated sharp Cheddar*
   cheese or ½ pound American cheese,
   finely diced
1 *tablespoon flour*
⅓ *cup beer*
1–2 *tablespoons aquavit (optional)*
1 *small loaf day-old French or Italian*
   bread, cut in 1" cubes (each should
   have crust on 1 side)

Rub inside of the top of a double boiler with garlic. Add butter and melt over simmering water. Toss cheese and flour together, add to butter along with beer and, if you like, aquavit. Heat, stirring rapidly, until smooth. Transfer to a chafing dish, set over simmering water, and serve with crusts of bread, long-handled fondue forks, and plenty of napkins. About 855 calories for each of 2 servings, 425 for each of 4.

⚖ HOMEMADE COTTAGE CHEESE

Rennet tablets, necessary for making cottage cheese, have disappeared from grocery shelves but are still available at drugstores.
Makes about 1 quart

1 gallon skim milk
½ cup sour cream
¼ penny-size rennet tablet, crushed in 2 tablespoons cold water
1–1½ teaspoons salt
⅓ cup heavy cream (optional)

Warm milk over lowest heat in a large stainless-steel or enamel kettle to 70° F. (a household thermometer can be used to test temperature) or let stand covered at room temperature 2–3 hours. Blend ½ cup of this milk with sour cream, return to kettle, and mix well. Stir in rennet, cover with a dry towel, and let stand undisturbed at room temperature (about 70° F.) 12–18 hours until a firm curd forms (mixture will look set with whey visible around edges). With a long stainless-steel knife, cut curd in kettle into ½″ cubes; set kettle on a large, heavy rack *over* simmering water in a larger kettle and heat, uncovered, to 110–15° F. (use a candy thermometer), stirring every 2–3 minutes. Maintain 110–15° F. temperature for ½ hour, stirring every 5 minutes. Ladle into a colander lined with a double thickness of cheesecloth and let whey drain 2–3 minutes, lifting corners of cheesecloth occasionally, to move curd. Lift cheesecloth and curd, twisting top to form a bag, and plunge into cold water; move cloth gently to rinse curd. Drain and plunge into ice water; let stand 1–2 minutes. Lay bag of curd in a colander and drain well. Remove curd from cloth, season to taste with salt, and, if you like, mix in cream. Cover and chill before serving. Use within 2–3 days. About 95 calories per ½ cup serving (without heavy cream).

⚖ ☒ CURDS AND SOUR CREAM

A Slavic specialty eaten on pumpernickel.
Makes 4 servings

1 pound cottage or pot cheese
1 cup sour cream
½ cup minced scallions (include some tops)
½ cup minced cucumber
½ cup minced radishes
1 teaspoon salt
Freshly ground pepper

Mix all but last ingredient and chill well. Sprinkle with pepper and serve on lettuce or, as the Slavs do, with buttered pumpernickel. Also good spooned over buckwheat kasha or hot boiled new potatoes. About 230 calories per serving (on lettuce).

VARIATION:

⚖ **Calorie Counter's Curds:** Prepare as directed but substitute yogurt for sour cream. Serve in lettuce. About 140 calories per serving.

¢ SWISS CHEESE PUFF

Makes 4 servings

8 slices firm-textured white bread, trimmed of crusts
3 cups coarsely grated Swiss cheese
3 eggs, lightly beaten
2 cups milk
1 teaspoon salt
⅛ teaspoon white pepper
2 tablespoons minced scallions
⅛ teaspoon paprika

Preheat oven to 300° F. Alternate layers of bread and cheese in a buttered shallow 1½-quart casserole, beginning with bread and ending with cheese. Mix all remaining ingredients except paprika and pour into casserole. Sprinkle with paprika and bake, uncovered, 35–40 minutes until puffed, golden, and *just* set (a silver knife inserted midway between center and rim should come out clean). Serve immediately. About 575 calories per serving.

VARIATION:

Cheddar Bake: Prepare as directed but substitute sharp or mild Cheddar for the Swiss cheese and omit scallions. About 600 calories per serving.

About Soufflés

Like omelets, soufflés have a reputation for being difficult. They aren't, once the basic technique is learned. Soufflés are nothing more than sauces into which beaten egg whites are folded. It is the air, whipped into the whites, that leavens soufflés, so the point is to achieve the greatest possible volume of whites and to maintain it. This is done by using a balloon whip or wire whisk (and, if you have one, an unlined copper bowl), also by lightening the base sauce a bit by *stirring in* ¼–½ cup beaten whites before *folding in* the balance (see To Beat Egg Whites and About Folding In Beaten Egg Whites at the beginning of this chapter).

To Grease or Not to Grease the Soufflé Dish: Opinions are sharply divided. Some insist that soufflés climb to greater heights in greased and crumbed dishes; others say not, that it's like making a monkey climb a greased pole. Recipes in this book call for ungreased dishes and have produced cloud-high soufflés. But by all means, try both methods.

To Make a Top Hat Soufflé: Just before baking soufflé, insert a table knife into soufflé mixture about 1″–1½″ from rim of dish and draw a circle concentric with dish. When baked, soufflé center will puff way up, forming the top hat.

Note: Other soufflé recipes are included in the meat, poultry, seafood, vegetable and dessert chapters.

⚖ BASIC CHEESE SOUFFLÉ

Makes 4 servings

3 tablespoons butter or margarine
3 tablespoons flour
1 cup milk
1¼ cups coarsely grated Cheddar cheese

or ¾ cup coarsely grated Swiss or Gruyère cheese
3 eggs, separated
1 teaspoon salt
⅛ teaspoon pepper

Melt butter in a saucepan over moderate heat, blend in flour, slowly stir in milk, and heat, stirring, until thickened. Add cheese and stir until melted. Beat yolks lightly, blend in a little hot sauce and return to pan; heat and stir 1–2 minutes over lowest heat. Off heat, mix in salt and pepper; lay a piece of wax paper flat on surface of sauce and cool to room temperature. Meanwhile, preheat oven to 350° F. Beat egg whites until stiff but not dry, stir about ¼ cup into sauce, then fold in remaining whites. Spoon into an ungreased 5-cup soufflé dish and bake, uncovered, 35–40 minutes until puffy and browned. Serve at once, accompanied, if you like, with Mushroom Sauce or Tomato Sauce. About 335 calories per serving if made with Cheddar, 285 if made with Swiss cheese.

⚖ **To Make with Process Cheese:** Prepare as directed but use only ⅓ cup process cheese; it is gummy and will make soufflé heavy. About 260 calories per serving.

VARIATIONS:

⚖ **Herbed Cheese Soufflé:** Prepare as directed, but add any of the following to cheese sauce: 1 tablespoon minced fresh dill or parsley; 1 teaspoon oregano, basil, sage, thyme, tarragon, or marjoram. Same calorie counts as for Basic Cheese Soufflé.

Deviled Cheese Soufflé: Prepare as directed but to cheese sauce add: 1 teaspoon each Worcestershire sauce and prepared spicy brown mustard, 1 tablespoon ketchup, ¼ teaspoon garlic powder, and ⅛ teaspoon cayenne pepper. About 345 calories per serving if made with Cheddar, 295 if made with Swiss cheese.

⚖ **Wine and Cheese Soufflé:** Prepare as directed but substitute ½ cup dry white wine for ½ cup of the milk. Serve, if you like, with hot Mornay Sauce (lightly laced with white wine). Same calorie counts as Basic Cheese Soufflé, not including sauce.

Cheese and Onion Soufflé: Prepare sauce as directed but before cooling mix in ½ cup thinly sliced Bermuda onion rings sautéed until limp, not brown. Cool sauce, fold in whites, and bake as directed. About 340 calories if made with Cheddar, 290 if made with Swiss cheese.

Some Additional Ways to Vary Cheese Soufflé: Prepare basic recipe as directed but before cooling cheese sauce mix in any of the following:
– ¼–⅓ cup minced cooked ham, crisp crumbled bacon, or minced sautéed chicken livers
– ¼ cup deviled ham or pâté
– ¼ cup minced sautéed mushrooms and 2 tablespoons minced pimiento
– ⅓ cup minced cooked vegetable (asparagus, spinach, broccoli, cauliflower, cabbage, or Brussels sprouts)
– ¼ cup each sautéed minced yellow onion and sweet green or red peppers
– ¼ cup minced ripe or green olives
– ¼ cup minced cooked fish or shellfish

⊠ TOP-OF-THE-STOVE SOUFFLÉED CHEESE

Makes 4 servings

4 eggs, lightly beaten
1 cup cottage cheese
¼ cup milk
¾ teaspoon salt
⅛ teaspoon white pepper
1½ cups hot Tomato Sauce or Mushroom Sauce

Mix all ingredients except sauce in the top of a double boiler set over simmering water. Beat with a whisk or rotary beater until mixture thickens, 2–3 minutes. Cover, pull pan from heat, but leave over hot water, undisturbed, 5–10 minutes. Spoon onto warm plates and top with sauce. About 320 calories per serving.

VARIATION:

⚖ **Low-Calorie Souffléed Cheese:** Prepare as directed but serve topped with minced chives instead of sauce. About 140 calories per serving.

QUICHE LORRAINE

Makes 10 appetizer servings; 6 entree servings

Pastry:

1 recipe Flaky Pastry I

Filling:

½ pound crisply cooked bacon, crumbled
½ pound Gruyère or Swiss cheese, coarsely grated
4 eggs, lightly beaten
1 teaspoon salt
⅛ teaspoon white pepper
Pinch cayenne pepper
⅛ teaspoon nutmeg (optional)
1¾ cups light cream
1 tablespoon melted butter

Preheat oven to 425° F. Prepare pastry, roll into a 12″ circle, and fit into a 9″ piepan, making a high, fluted edge. Prick bottom and sides of pastry well with a fork; cover with wax paper and fill with uncooked rice or dried beans. Bake 5–7 minutes until firm but not brown, then cool slightly on a wire rack. Remove paper and rice. Sprinkle bacon and cheese evenly over pie shell. Mix together remaining ingredients and strain through a fine sieve. Place pie shell on partly pulled-out oven rack, then pour in egg mixture. Bake, uncovered, 15 minutes at 425° F., reduce heat to 350° F., and bake 10–15 minutes longer or until a knife inserted halfway between center and rim comes out clean. Cool on a wire rack 8–10 minutes before cutting into wedges. Serve as an appetizer or luncheon entree. About 620 calories for each of 6 servings, 375 calories for each of 10.

VARIATIONS:

Roquefort Quiche: Prepare as directed, using ¼ pound each Roquefort and Gruyère. Approximately the same calories per serving as *quiche Lorraine*.

Quiche Bourbonnaise: Prepare as directed but substitute ½ pound slivered cooked ham for the bacon and reduce cheese to ¼ pound. About 550 calories for each of 6 servings, 335 for each of 10.

Onion Quiche: Prepare as directed but substitute 1 thinly sliced, lightly sautéed Bermuda onion for the bacon; separate into rings and arrange over crust. Reduce cream to 1½ cups. About 475 calories for each of 6 servings, 285 for each of 10.

Quiche Niçoise: Prepare as directed but omit bacon; arrange thinly sliced tomatoes over crust, overlapping slices slightly; scatter with ⅓ cup thinly sliced ripe olives and sprinkle with ¼ teaspoon garlic powder. Reduce amount of cheese to ¼ pound and cream to 1½ cups. About 465 calories for each of 6 servings, 280 for each of 10.

Clam Quiche: Prepare as directed but substitute 1 cup well-drained minced clams for the bacon. Make egg mixture using 1 cup heavy cream and ½ cup clam liquid instead of 1¾ cups cream. About 545 calories for each of 6 servings, 330 for each of 10.

CHEDDAR ONION TART

Makes 6 servings

1 recipe Flaky Pastry I
1 medium-size Bermuda onion, peeled, sliced paper thin, and separated into rings
1½ cups milk
1½ cups coarsely grated sharp Cheddar cheese
3 eggs, lightly beaten
¾ teaspoon salt
⅛ teaspoon pepper
⅛ teaspoon paprika

Preheat oven to 425° F. Prepare pastry, roll into a 12″ circle, and fit into a 9″ piepan, making a high, fluted edge; prick bottom and sides well with a fork. Cover with wax paper and fill with uncooked rice or dried beans. Bake 5–7 minutes until firm, not brown; cool

briefly on a wire rack. Remove paper and rice and scatter onion evenly into pie shell. Scald milk, add cheese, and stir until melted. Off heat, stir a little hot mixture into eggs, return to pan, and mix well. Add salt and pepper and pour over onion. Sprinkle with paprika and bake, uncovered, 15 minutes, lower heat to 350° F., and bake 15 minutes longer until knife inserted midway between center and rim comes out clean. Cool 10 minutes on a wire rack before cutting. About 390 calories per serving.

CROQUE-MONSIEUR

An egg-dipped, fried cheese and ham "sandwich" to be eaten with knife and fork.
Makes 2 servings

4 thin slices firm-textured white bread, trimmed of crusts and buttered on 1 side
3 (1-ounce) packages Gruyère or Swiss cheese, coarsely grated
2 thin slices boiled ham, cut to fit bread
2 eggs lightly beaten with 2 tablespoons cold water
2–3 tablespoons butter or margarine
½ cup hot Medium White Sauce blended with 2 tablespoons finely grated Parmesan cheese

Sandwich cheese and ham between slices of bread pressing lightly, dip in egg, making sure edges are well coated, and brown on both sides in butter over moderate heat. Lift to warm plates and top with sauce. About 695 calories per serving.

VARIATION:

Croque-Madame: Prepare as directed but substitute very thinly sliced white meat of chicken or turkey for the ham. About 690 calories per serving.

⟐ CROSTINI ALLA MOZZARELLA (BREADED, FRIED MOZZARELLA CHEESE)

Don't cut cheese cubes any larger than ¾″ or they won't cook properly.
Makes 6 entree servings or 36 appetizers

Shortening or cooking oil for deep fat
frying
½ pound mozzarella cheese (low
moisture type is best), cut in ¾"
cubes
¼ cup unsifted flour
2 eggs, lightly beaten
3 cups soft white bread crumbs

Begin heating shortening over moderate
heat; insert deep fat thermometer.
Dredge cheese in flour, dip in eggs, then
in crumbs, then in eggs and crumbs
again; press crumbs lightly so they stick.
When fat reaches 375° F., fry cheese, a
few cubes at a time, 30–40 seconds
until well browned. (*Note:* Timing and
temperature are important; cheese
should be slightly runny just underneath
the crumbs but firm in the center.) Lift
out with slotted spoon, drain on paper
toweling, and keep warm while you fry
the rest. Serve as soon as possible, as
entree, if you like, with hot Tomato
Sauce, or with toothpicks as an appetizer.
About 225 calories for each of 6
servings, about 40 calories per appetizer.

CHEESE BLINTZES

Makes 1 dozen

½ cup sifted flour
¼ teaspoon salt
2 eggs, lightly beaten
¾ cup milk or a ½ and ½ mixture of
milk and cold water
1 tablespoon melted butter or margarine
1–2 tablespoons butter or margarine

Filling:

1 pound cottage or pot cheese
2 egg yolks, lightly beaten
3–4 tablespoons sugar
⅛ teaspoon salt
⅛ teaspoon cinnamon
1–2 tablespoons milk (optional)

Topping:

1 cup sour cream

Sift flour and salt into a bowl; mix eggs,
milk, and melted butter, slowly add to
flour, and beat until smooth. Butter
bottom and sides of a heavy 6" skillet
and heat over moderately high heat until

a drop of water will dance. Using about
2 tablespoons batter for each blintze,
add to skillet and tip back and forth until
bottom is evenly coated. Brown lightly
on 1 side, about ½ minute, turn out,
browned side up, on a kitchen towel or
paper toweling. Cook remaining blintzes
the same way. Mix filling ingredients,
adding milk to moisten if needed. Place
about 1½ tablespoons filling in center of
each blintze, fold bottom up and sides in
over filling, then roll up. Brown in
remaining butter over moderate heat
and serve with sour cream. About 175
calories per blintze if made with cottage
cheese, 165 if made with pot cheese.

VARIATION:

Season filling to taste with finely grated
lemon or orange rind and top with
stewed fruit instead of sour cream.

UKRAINIAN CHEESE TURNOVERS

Makes about 10

1 recipe Sour Cream Pastry or Flaky
Pastry I
1 egg, lightly beaten with 1 tablespoon
cold water (glaze)

Filling:

1 cup minced scallions (include some
tops)
¼ cup butter or margarine
¼ cup minced parsley
2 cups coarsely grated Swiss cheese

Prepare pastry, wrap in wax paper, and
chill while you make the filling. Preheat
oven to 450° F. Stir-fry scallions in
butter over moderately low heat 5–7
minutes until limp; off heat, mix in
parsley and cheese. Roll pastry, ½ at a
time, and cut in rounds using a 4" saucer
as a guide. Brush edges with glaze,
spoon a little filling onto lower halves of
rounds, fold over, and crimp edges with
a fork. Brush with glaze and bake,
uncovered, on ungreased baking sheets
15 minutes; lower heat to 350° F. and
bake 15 minutes longer until golden.
Serve hot. About 340 calories per
turnover if made with sour cream pastry,
250 per turnover if made with flaky
pastry.

CHAPTER 13

CEREALS, RICE, AND PASTA

When man discovered that seeds of certain grasses were edible, that they could be planted to provide food for himself and his family, he emerged from savagery. It was no longer necessary to kill in order to survive. Such life-giving foods, inevitably, were held sacred and became the basis of much mythology. Our word *cereal,* in fact, derives from Ceres, Roman goddess of grain and harvest.

The family of cereals is vast. All, to greater or lesser degrees, are high energy foods with B vitamins in abundance. The more refined or polished the cereal, the less nutritious because most of the nutrients are contained in the husk. Enrichment programs, however, are replacing vitamins and minerals lost in the milling. A cereal marked *"restored"* has had the nutritive content restored to the level of whole grain. *"Enriched cereal"* has been given the added boost of nutrients not present in the whole grain (usually vitamins A or D).

The Kinds and Forms of Cereals

The vast array of cereals available today can be divided into three basic categories: the *regular cooking,* the *quick cooking,* and the *ready to eat.* Briefly, here are the kinds of grains and forms in which they're sold:

Barley: One of man's first foods but not commonly used today except for making beer. The polished grain, or *pearl,* comes in three sizes—coarse, medium, and fine —and is a good extender of soups and stews. *Scotch barley,* sold primarily in health food stores, is husked and coarsely ground. It must be soaked overnight before using.

Bran: Not a single grain but the husk of any grain separated out in the milling.

Buckwheat: No relation to wheat but another species altogether; it is Siberian and the foundation of many Russian dishes, notably *kasha,* a pilaf-like dish of braised buckwheat groats. Kasha has become something of a generic term today, meaning any braised or baked cracked cereal and, in fact, some bulgur wheat is marketed as kasha. True kasha, however, is a particular recipe made of buckwheat.

Bulgur: (see Wheat).

Corn: America's gift to the world and the grain upon which much of Latin America lives yet. Both yellow and white meal are available, enriched and the old-fashioned unbolted (unsifted) stone or water ground (ground on millstones), which Southerners prefer to all others.

Hominy is white flint corn, the kernels of which have been skinned either mechanically or in a lye bath. It is available dry (cracked or whole) or canned (whole). *Hominy grits* are simply dried hominy ground to meal; they can be prepared like corn meal.

Couscous: The Arabic word for semolina (see Wheat).

Farina: Broadly speaking, any ground grain. Today, however, farina usually means ground wheat, either the whole grain (*dark farina*) or the refined (*light farina* or *cream of wheat*).

Grits: Finely ground grain, now almost always meaning *hominy grits* (see Corn).

Groats: Coarsely ground grain, usually buckwheat.

Kasha: (see Buckwheat).

Masa Harina: A special corn flour popular throughout Mexico and Latin America; it is what gives tortillas their characteristic nutty-sweet flavor.

Millet: An Asian grain little used in this country except as forage. Health food stores sell millet flour, also millet seeds, which can be cooked like other whole grains.

Oats: One of the most nutritious and important grains. Most are rolled into oatmeal, ground into flour or puffed into breakfast cereal.

Rice: The "bread" of the Orient and a grain once so revered only emperors were permitted to plant it. There are dozens of varieties of rice, but, to simplify, there are the *long grain* and the *short grain*. Long grain rice is best for serving solo or using in casseroles because the grains remain separate; short grain rice cooks down into a softness more suitable for puddings. *Brown rice* is simply unpolished rice (only the husks have been removed). It is more nutritious than polished rice, cheaper, and, some people think, of better flavor. *Wild rice* is not rice (see description that follows). Polished rice is available in three popular forms: *regular, converted* (also known as

processed or parboiled), and *quick cooking* (fully cooked, dehydrated rice that needs only stand in boiling water a few minutes). (*Note:* Recipes in this book, unless otherwise noted, were tested using converted rice). This rice has been steam-treated so that its grains become tender without gumming up or losing their identity.

Rye: The bulk of rye grown goes either into whiskey or flour. Rye groats are sometimes available, however, and should be cooked like buckwheat or other groats.

Semolina: (see Wheat).

Wheat: The staff of life for much of the world, source of flours, myriad breakfast cereals, also such ethnic exotics as *cracked wheat;* that Middle Eastern favorite called *bulgur* (parched, cracked wheat from which some of the bran has been removed); and *semolina* (the hard heart of durum wheat, ground either into the flour from which pasta is made or into granules, cooked much like farina and known to Arabs as *couscous*). Other wheat products include *wheat germ,* the tender, perishable embryo; it can be scattered over cereals, mixed into meat loaves and croquettes, slipped into casseroles and salads, or used as a topping.

Wild Rice: A luxurious, nut-flavored, long grain marsh grass of the northern Lake States, so expensive still that Indians of the area (by law the only persons allowed to harvest it) carry small pouches of it in place of money. The longer the grain, the greater the price.

How to Cook Cereals

Except for rice and wild rice, which will be discussed separately, all cereals are cooked more or less the same way. The only variable is the proportion of liquid to cereal, determined by size of grain (whether whole, cracked, or ground) rather than by species. It's always best to cook cereal by package directions because each manufacturer knows his

PROPORTIONS FOR 4 SERVINGS

Cereal	Quantity	Water	Salt
Rolled oats or wheat	1 cup	2 cups	½ teaspoon
Buckwheat or other groats, bulgur and cracked wheat, other cracked or coarsely ground cereals	1 cup	2 cups	1 teaspoon
Farina, corn meal, grits, and other granular cereals	1 cup	5 cups	1 teaspoon

product best. As a general rule, however, the following methods work for all cereals (except for the quick-cooking, which should be prepared strictly as the label directs).

Direct Heat Method: Bring water and salt to a full rolling boil in a heavy saucepan. Gradually sprinkle in cereal, stirring all the while. Turn heat to low and cook uncovered, stirring often, 15–20 minutes until tender and no raw taste of starch remains. Toward end of cooking, use an asbestos flame-tamer, if possible, to keep cereal from scorching.

Double Boiler Method (slower but surer): Place water and salt in top part of a double boiler and bring quickly to a boil over direct heat. Sprinkle cereal in gradually, stirring constantly. When cereal begins to thicken, set over simmering water and cook uncovered, stirring occasionally, 20–30 minutes until done.

Some Ways to Dress Up Cooked Cereals

– Cook in milk or a ½ and ½ mixture of cream and water instead of in water.
– To the cooking water, add 1 tablespoon sugar mixed with 1 teaspoon cinnamon and, if you like, a pinch nutmeg, allspice, or cloves.
– About 5 minutes before cereal is done, stir in ½–1 cup seedless raisins, dried

currants, diced dates, dried apricots, figs, or prunes.
– About 5 minutes before cereal is done, stir in ¾ cup coarsely chopped pecans, walnuts, roasted almonds, or peanuts.
– When serving, mound into a Baked Apple or on top of baked or fried bananas.
– When serving, make a well in the center of each portion and fill with Melba Sauce or any fruit jam, jelly, or preserves.

– When serving, top with any of the following:
– Maple or brown sugar and, if you like, a pinch of cinnamon or nutmeg
– Maple syrup, honey, or molasses and heavy cream
– A ½ and ½ mixture of brown sugar and wheat germ
– Brown sugar, minced fresh mint, and yogurt or sour cream
– Heavy or sour cream and thawed frozen berries or peaches

Note: Chicken or beef broth can be used for cooking rice instead of water, but salt should be reduced accordingly.

Basic Method (for fluffy, tender rice): Bring water and salt to a rapid boil over high heat in a heavy saucepan, add rice, cover, reduce heat so rice bubbles gently, and cook until rice is tender and all water absorbed. Regular and converted

HOW TO COOK RICE

Kind of Rice	Quantity of Uncooked Rice	Water	Salt	Yield of Cooked Rice	Number of Servings
White (regular)	1 cup	2 cups	1 teaspoon	3 cups	4
White (converted)	1 cup	2–2½ cups	1 teaspoon	4 cups	4–6
White (quick-cooking)	1 cup	(cook by package directions)		2 cups	2–3
Brown	1 cup	2½ cups	1 teaspoon	4 cups	4–6

rice will take 20–25 minutes, brown rice 40–45. If you like, uncover and let dry out 3–5 minutes before serving. Fluff with a fork.

Open Pan Method (for firm, tender white rice; especially good to use if rice is to be added to casseroles or stuffings): Bring water and salt to a rapid boil over high heat in an extra-heavy saucepan, stir in rice, reduce heat slightly, and cook, uncovered, *without stirring* until water is barely visible, about 10 minutes. Turn heat to low and continue cooking, uncovered, until all moisture is absorbed, about 8–10 minutes. Fluff with a fork.

Oven Method (for mellow, nutty flavor): Preheat oven to 400° F. In a heavy flameproof casserole, melt 2 tablespoons butter or margarine over direct moderate heat. Add rice and stir-fry about ½ minute. Add water and salt, cover tightly, and bake until rice is tender and all liquid absorbed. White rice will take about 20 minutes, brown about 45. Fluff with a fork and serve.

VARIATION:

Stir-fry 2 tablespoons minced yellow onion in butter 2–3 minutes, then add rice and proceed as directed. For added zip, add a parsley sprig or celery top and 2–3 dashes liquid hot red pepper seasoning. Remove parsley or celery before serving.

Tips for Making Better Rice

– Be sure to use a large enough pan; rice will quadruple or triple in bulk during cooking. Also make sure pan is heavy so there is little danger of scorching.

– Once rice comes to a boil, stir as little as possible, and use a fork if you must stir —less chance of mashing or breaking the rice.

– To help keep rice grains beautifully distinct, add 1 or 2 drops cooking oil or a dab of butter or margarine to the cooking water. Also gives rice a lovely glisten.

– If rice must be held before serving, transfer to a colander and set over simmering water; keep covered. Rice will keep hot without overcooking. *Or* transfer rice to a heavy casserole and set in oven turned to lowest heat. Keep tightly covered.

What to Do with Leftover Rice

To Reheat: Place rice in a large, fine sieve and with moistened hands break up any clumps. Set sieve over simmering water, cover, and steam about 10 minutes. Rice will be almost as good as it was the first time around. *Or* place rice in a buttered casserole and break up clumps with moistened hands. Dot well with butter, cover, and bake ½ hour at 325° F.

To Use Up Small Amounts:
– Mix into meat loaves, croquettes, or stuffings.
– Combine with leftover meat and vegetables in a casserole or soup.
– Add to any creamed meat or vegetable mixture.
– Marinate in Garlic or Herb Dressing and serve in hollowed-out tomatoes.
– Toss with mixed greens in a salad.
– Add to pancake batter.

– Scramble with eggs.
– Team with custard sauce and/or fresh fruit as a dessert.

Some Quick Ways to Dress Up Rice

During Cooking (amounts based on 1 cup uncooked rice and basic method of cooking):

Saffron Rice: Add ⅛ teaspoon powdered saffron to cooking liquid or soak ¼ teaspoon saffron in ¼ cup cooking liquid about 10 minutes, then cook as directed. Season to taste with salt and pepper.

Arroz Amarillo (Yellow Mexican Rice): Stir-fry rice in 3 tablespoons olive oil with 1 small minced yellow onion and 1 crushed clove garlic about 5 minutes over moderate heat until pale golden; mix in ⅔ cup canned tomato sauce and 2 cups chicken broth and cook by basic method. Season to taste with salt and freshly ground pepper.

Pineapple Rice: Cook rice in a ½ and ½ mixture of pineapple juice and chicken broth. Just before serving, mix in 1 (8-ounce) drained can pineapple tidbits and, if you like, 1 cup coarsely chopped cashew nuts. Omit salt and pepper.

Orange Rice: Cook rice in a ½ and ½ mixture of orange juice and chicken broth with 2 teaspoons grated orange rind and ⅛ teaspoon nutmeg. Just before serving, mix in ½ cup diced, seeded orange sections. Add a pinch of salt but omit pepper.

Raisin, Currant, Date, Apricot, or Fig Rice: Cook as directed but add ¼ cup seedless raisins or dried currants, diced dates, dried apricots, or figs to the pot. Season to taste with salt and pepper. Especially good with curry.

Onion Rice: Stir-fry 1 minced Bermuda onion and the rice in 3 tablespoons butter about 5 minutes over moderate heat until pale golden; then cook as directed and season to taste.

Garlic Rice: Stir-fry 1 minced clove garlic in 2 tablespoons butter 2 minutes over moderate heat; add rice and stir-fry 3 minutes longer, then cook as directed. Season to taste.

Savory Rice: Stir-fry ¼ cup each minced yellow onion and celery and 1 crushed clove garlic in 2 tablespoons butter over moderate heat 8–10 minutes until golden. Add rice and cook as directed, using beef broth. Season to taste with salt and pepper and, if you like, Worcestershire sauce.

Green Rice: Stir-fry ½ cup minced scallions (include tops) in 2 tablespoons butter 3–4 minutes over moderate heat until limp; add rice and cook as directed, using chicken broth. Season to taste and mix in 1 cup minced parsley.

Confetti Rice: Stir-fry ⅓ cup each minced yellow onion, sweet red and green pepper in 3 tablespoons butter or olive oil; add rice and cook as directed, using chicken broth. Season to taste with salt and liquid hot red pepper seasoning.

Curried Rice: Warm 2 teaspoons curry powder in 1 tablespoon butter 1–2 minutes over moderate heat; add rice and cook as directed, using chicken broth. Season to taste.

Chili Rice: Warm 2 teaspoons curry powder and ½ teaspoon each garlic and onion powder in 2 tablespoons olive oil 2 minutes over moderate heat; add rice and cook as directed, using beef or chicken broth. Season to taste with salt and crushed dried hot red chili peppers. Just before serving, mix in ⅓ cup crisp crumbled bacon.

Herbed Rice: Warm 2 tablespoons minced fresh dill, basil, chives, or parsley or 1 tablespoon minced fresh sage or thyme in 2 tablespoons butter 2 minutes over moderate heat; add rice and cook as directed, using chicken broth. Season to taste. (*Note:* 1 teaspoon of the dried herb may be substituted for the fresh, but the flavor will not be as good.)

Mushroom Rice: Stir-fry ½ pound thinly sliced or coarsely chopped mushrooms in 3 tablespoons butter over moderately high heat 2–3 minutes until golden; add rice and cook as directed, using beef or chicken broth. Season to taste.

Just Before Serving: Cook 1 cup rice by basic method, season with salt and pepper, then mix in any of the following:

Poppy or Caraway Seed Rice: 2 tablespoons each poppy or caraway seeds and melted butter.

Rice Amandine: ⅓ cup butter-browned slivered blanched almonds.

Nut Rice: 2 tablespoons melted butter and ⅓ cup coarsely chopped pecans, walnuts, macadamia, piñon, or pistachio nuts or toasted peanuts or cashews.

Olive Rice: ½ cup minced pitted ripe or pimiento-stuffed green olives and 1–2 tablespoons olive oil.

Avocado-Tomato Rice: 1 coarsely chopped small firm-ripe avocado and ½ cup coarsely chopped, peeled, seeded tomato.

Minted Rice (delicious with lamb): ¼ cup minced fresh mint warmed 2–3 minutes in 2 tablespoons butter.

Soy Rice: ¼ cup minced scallions sautéed in 2 tablespoons peanut oil 2–3 minutes over moderate heat, 2 tablespoons each soy sauce and minced pimiento and ½ teaspoon sugar; reduce salt as needed. Cover and let stand off heat 2–3 minutes; toss and serve.

Sour Cream Rice: ¾–1 cup warmed sour cream; cover rice and let stand off heat 5 minutes. Sprinkle with 1–2 tablespoons minced chives, toss lightly and serve.

Cheesy Rice: ⅓–½ cup grated sharp Cheddar, Parmesan, Swiss, or mozzarella cheese; cover rice and let stand off heat 4–5 minutes to melt cheese; toss lightly and serve.

⚖ ☒ ¢ **TOASTED RICE**

If you like the nutty flavor of toasted rice, toast a pound, store airtight, and use as needed.
Makes 4 servings

1 cup uncooked rice

Preheat oven to 350° F. Spread rice out in a shallow baking pan and toast, stirring now and then, 8–10 minutes until golden. Cook as you would regular rice. About 180 calories per serving.

VARIATION:

Toasted Rice and Vegetable Casserole: In a greased 2-quart casserole, mix 1 cup toasted rice, 1 (10-ounce) package frozen mixed vegetables thawed just enough to separate, 1 (4-ounce) can drained sliced mushrooms, 2 cups chicken or beef broth, and ½ teaspoon salt. Cover and bake about 20 minutes at 350° F. until rice is tender. About 245 calories per serving.

⚖ ¢ ☒ **RICE RING**

White, brown, and wild rice can all be molded by the following method. So can cracked or bulgur wheat, buckwheat groats, and all of the flavored rices (Curried, Herbed, etc.) except for very soft ones containing sauce. For variety, mold in individual ramekins or 1½-quart fluted or decorative molds instead of a ring mold.
Makes 8 servings

6 cups hot seasoned cooked rice
¼ cup melted butter or margarine

Mix rice and butter with a fork and pack lightly into a *well-buttered* or oiled 1½-quart ring mold. Let stand 1 minute, then invert on a hot platter. Fill center with any creamed mixture, stew, or curry. (*Note:* If dinner must be held, don't mold rice until the very last minute; it will keep hot in the pan far better than in the mold.) About 190 calories per serving.

RICE PILAF

Makes 4 servings

¼ cup butter or margarine
1 cup uncooked rice
2 cups hot chicken or beef broth
½ teaspoon salt (about)
⅛ teaspoon pepper

Melt butter in a heavy saucepan over moderately low heat, add rice, and stir-fry about 5 minutes until straw-colored. Add broth, salt, and pepper, cover, and cook over lowest heat without stirring 18–20 minutes until all liquid is absorbed. Uncover and cook 3–5 minutes longer to dry out. Fluff with a fork, taste for salt and adjust as needed. About 305 calories per serving.

VARIATIONS:

Baked Pilaf (a good way to make pilaf in quantity): Stir-fry rice as directed in a flameproof casserole or Dutch oven-type kettle, add broth and seasonings, cover, and bake about ½ hour at 350° F. until all liquid is absorbed. For drier rice, uncover and bake 5 minutes longer. About 305 calories per serving.

Middle East Pilaf: Stir-fry 1 small minced yellow onion in butter along with rice, add broth and seasonings, also ¼ cup seedless raisins or dried currants, ¼ teaspoon each cinnamon and allspice, ⅛ teaspoon each turmeric and cardamom. Cover and cook as directed. About 330 calories per serving.

Indian Pilaf: Stir-fry 1 medium-size minced yellow onion in butter along with rice, add 2 teaspoons curry powder, and stir-fry ½ minute. Add broth and seasonings, also ¼ cup sultana or seedless raisins. Cover and cook as directed. Add ¼ cup coarsely chopped toasted blanched almonds, then fluff with a fork. About 390 calories per serving.

Bulgur Pilaf: Prepare any of the preceding pilafs as directed, but substitute 1 cup uncooked bulgur or cracked wheat for rice. Calorie counts approximately the same as for any of the pilafs made with rice.

Main Dish Pilaf: Prepare rice or bulgur pilaf as directed; just before serving, add 1½ cups diced cooked meat, chicken, fish, or shellfish and toss lightly to mix. Recipe too flexible for a meaningful calorie count.

BROWN RICE PILAF

Makes 4–6 servings

¼ cup butter or margarine
1 cup uncooked brown rice
1 (10½-ounce) can condensed beef broth
1 cup water
⅛ teaspoon pepper

Preheat oven to 325° F. Melt butter in a flameproof 2-quart casserole over moderately low heat, add rice, and cook, stirring constantly, 3–4 minutes; do not brown. Off heat, stir in remaining ingredients. Cover and bake 1–1¼ hours until rice is tender. Fluff with a fork and serve. About 310 calories for each of 4 servings, 205 calories for each of 6 servings.

VARIATION:

Just before serving, toss in any of the following: ½ cup chopped, cooked chicken livers, shrimp, ham, sweetbreads, poultry, game, or leftover meat. (*Note:* By adding as much as 2 cups of any of these, you can serve pilaf as a main dish.) Recipe too flexible for a meaningful calorie count.

ARMENIAN RICE

Delicious with roast lamb or shish kebabs.
Makes 6 servings

6 tablespoons butter or margarine
⅔ cup fine egg noodles
1½ cups uncooked rice
3 cups boiling water
1 tablespoon salt

Melt butter in a large, heavy kettle over moderately high heat, toss in noodles and stir-fry 3–5 minutes until pale brown. Add rice and stir-fry 5 minutes until tweedy and golden. Add water and salt, stir well, cover, and boil gently over moderate heat about 20 minutes until rice is tender and all water absorbed. About 300 calories per serving.

RISOTTO ALLA MILANESE

There are dozens of *risotti* (soft rice mixtures that are to the north of Italy what pasta is to the south). This one is a classic. Delicious with veal or chicken. Makes 4 servings

2 tablespoons each butter and beef
  marrow or ¼ cup butter or margarine
1 small yellow onion, peeled and minced
1 cup uncooked rice
2 cups hot chicken or beef broth
Pinch powdered saffron or ⅛ teaspoon
  saffron, soaked in ¼ cup of the hot
  broth (strain and reserve broth)
½ teaspoon salt (about)
⅛ teaspoon pepper
¼ cup grated Parmesan cheese

Melt butter and marrow in a heavy saucepan over moderately low heat, add onion and rice, and stir-fry about 5 minutes until rice is straw-colored. Add broth, saffron, salt, and pepper, cover, and cook over lowest heat 18–20 minutes until all liquid is absorbed. Uncover and dry out 3–5 minutes. Add Parmesan and fluff with a fork; taste for salt and adjust as needed. About 330 calories per serving.

VARIATIONS:

Mushroom Risotto: Stir-fry ½ pound minced mushrooms along with onion and rice; proceed as directed and toss in ¼ cup piñon nuts along with the Parmesan. About 405 calories per serving.

Savoy Risotto: Omit onion, but stir-fry rice as directed, adding 1 crushed clove garlic during last 2 minutes. Add 1 cup each dry white wine and chicken broth, the seasonings, and proceed as directed. Substitute ⅓ cup grated Emmentaler or Gruyère cheese for the Parmesan, fork into rice, cover, and let stand off heat 5 minutes to melt cheese. About 375 calories per serving.

Risi e Bisi (Makes 6 servings): Prepare as directed, omitting saffron if you like. When rice has cooked in liquid 10 minutes, add 1 (10-ounce) package frozen green peas (break up in package before adding). Cover and proceed as directed. About 380 calories per serving.

CHICKEN LIVER RISOTTO

Makes 4 servings

1 pound chicken livers
6 tablespoons butter or margarine
1 large yellow onion, peeled and minced
½ cup thinly sliced mushrooms
1 cup uncooked rice
2½ cups hot chicken broth
½ teaspoon salt
⅛ teaspoon pepper
2 tablespoons minced parsley
¼ cup grated Parmesan cheese

Halve livers at the natural separation and pat dry on paper toweling. Melt ¼ cup butter in a large skillet or flameproof casserole that has a tight fitting lid over moderately high heat. Add livers and sauté 3–4 minutes, stirring, until lightly browned; remove with a slotted spoon to a heated plate, cover, and keep warm. Melt remaining butter in the same skillet, add onion, and stir-fry 4–5 minutes. Add mushrooms and stir-fry 5 minutes longer until onion and mushrooms are brown. Add rice, broth, salt, and pepper, mix well, and heat uncovered until just boiling. Turn heat to low, cover, and simmer 15–20 minutes until rice is tender. Add livers, parsley, and Parmesan, toss lightly with 2 forks, and serve. About 555 calories per serving.

VARIATION:

Calf's Liver Risotto: Prepare as directed, substituting 1 pound calf's liver, cut in bite-size pieces, for the chicken livers. About 565 calories per serving.

¢ ⚖ **SPANISH RICE**

Makes 4 servings

1 large yellow onion, peeled and minced
2 tablespoons cooking oil
1 small sweet green pepper, cored,
  seeded, and minced
½ cup uncooked rice
¼ teaspoon chili powder
1 (1-pound) can tomatoes (do not drain)
½ cup water
1 bay leaf, crumbled
¾ teaspoon salt
⅛ teaspoon pepper
¼ teaspoon sugar

Sauté onion in oil in a heavy saucepan over moderate heat 5–8 minutes until limp. Add green pepper and stir-fry 5 minutes. Stir in rice and chili powder and brown rice lightly. Add remaining ingredients, chopping up tomatoes, cover, and simmer 20 minutes. Uncover and cook 5 minutes longer. About 195 calories per serving.

VARIATIONS:

¢ ⚖ **Baked Spanish Rice with Cheese:** Brown vegetables and rice in a flameproof casserole, add remaining ingredients and ½ cup grated sharp Cheddar cheese. Mix lightly, cover, and bake ½ hour at 350° F.; uncover and bake 5 minutes longer. Serve as a main dish. About 250 calories per serving.

⚖ **Spanish Rice with Olives and Saffron:** Soak ¼ teaspoon saffron in the ½ cup water called for, 10 minutes, then strain, reserving liquid. Prepare recipe as directed, using saffron water and adding ½ cup thinly sliced pimiento-stuffed green or ripe olives along with tomatoes. About 210 calories per serving.

¢ **JAMBALAYA**

Jambalaya is a Creole rice classic. Originally made with ham (its name comes from *jamón*, the Spanish word for ham), it is as likely to be made today with sausage, shrimp, or chicken. But the method remains the same, which means making a *roux*, browned flour and fat mixture. A roux is such an integral part of Creole cooking that many recipes begin simply, "First, you make a roux." It's assumed everyone knows how. Old-time Creole cooks will "work a roux" 4 or 5 times as long as the recipe below calls for to obtain a rich caramel flavor. But it really isn't necessary.

Makes 6 servings

1¼ pounds pork sausage meat or diced
  cooked ham
¼ cup bacon drippings (optional)
3 tablespoons flour
2 medium-size yellow onions, peeled and
  coarsely chopped
12 scallions, sliced ½" thick (include
  tops)
2 cloves garlic, peeled and crushed
¼ cup minced parsley
2 teaspoons salt (slightly less if ham is
  used)
1 teaspoon cayenne pepper
2 cups uncooked rice
2⅔ cups chicken broth or water

Stir-fry sausage in a large, heavy kettle over moderately high heat 5 minutes, remove to a bowl with a slotted spoon. (*Note:* If using ham, stir-fry in bacon drippings. Measure drippings and add additional bacon drippings as needed to make ¼ cup.) Blend in flour and heat and stir 1–2 minutes to make a rich brown roux. Add onions, scallions, and garlic and stir-fry 10–12 minutes over moderate heat until golden brown and well worked into roux. Return sausage to kettle, add all remaining ingredients except broth and stir-fry 1–2 minutes. Add broth, bring to a boil, then turn heat to lowest point, cover, and simmer 45 minutes. Uncover, stir well, and heat 10 minutes, stirring occasionally, until rice dries out a bit. Serve hot as a budget main dish or potato substitute. About 770 calories per serving if made with sausage, 625 calories per serving if made with diced cooked ham.

¢ **CAJUN "DIRTY RICE"**

Makes 4 servings

½ cup minced red onion
3 tablespoons bacon drippings

2 chicken livers, minced
2 scallions, minced (include tops)
1 clove garlic, peeled and crushed
2 tablespoons minced parsley
½ cup water
½ teaspoon salt (about)
⅛–¼ teaspoon crushed dried hot red
   chili peppers
4 cups hot boiled rice

Stir-fry onion in drippings in a large, heavy skillet over moderate heat 10–12 minutes until lightly browned. Add livers and brown. Add scallions, garlic, and parsley and stir-fry about 5 minutes until limp. Add water, salt, and peppers to taste and cook and stir 5–10 minutes over low heat to blend flavors. Pour over rice, toss lightly to mix, and serve. About 310 calories per serving.

VARIATION:

¢ **Baked Cajun Rice:** Prepare as directed, spoon into a greased 1½-quart casserole, dot liberally with butter, and bake uncovered about 20 minutes at 350° F. to brown lightly. About 350 calories per serving.

¢ LOUISIANA RED BEANS AND RICE

Makes 4 servings

1 cup dried red kidney beans, washed
   and sorted
1 quart cold water
1 (⅛-pound) chunk salt pork
1 medium-size yellow onion, peeled and
   coarsely chopped
1 clove garlic, peeled and crushed
1 stalk celery, coarsely chopped
1 bay leaf, crumbled
¼ teaspoon cumin
⅛ teaspoon pepper
1 tablespoon light brown sugar
½ teaspoon salt (about)
4 cups hot boiled rice
2 tablespoons minced parsley

Soak beans overnight in 2 cups water or use the quick method.* Drain, measure soaking water, and add enough cold water to make 2 cups. Place beans, water, and salt pork in a large, heavy

saucepan, cover, and simmer ¾ hour. Add all but last 3 ingredients, cover, and simmer ½–¾ hour longer until tender. Discard salt pork; season to taste with salt. Ladle over rice, sprinkle with parsley, and serve. About 480 calories per serving.

¢ JAMAICAN-STYLE RICE

A spicy mixture of rice, onions, and kidney beans
Makes 6 servings

3 cups water
1 teaspoon butter or margarine
1⅓ cups uncooked rice
2 medium-size yellow onions, peeled and
   minced
3 tablespoons olive oil
1 (1-pound 4-ounce) can red kidney
   beans, drained
1 teaspoon salt
⅛ teaspoon pepper
⅛ teaspoon allspice

Place water in a large saucepan and bring to a boil; stir in butter and rice and boil rapidly, uncovered, 10–15 minutes, without stirring, until most of the water is absorbed. Turn heat to low and cook, uncovered, 5 minutes longer until all water is absorbed. While rice cooks, stir-fry onions in oil in a large, heavy skillet 8–10 minutes over moderate heat until golden; stir in beans, salt, pepper, and allspice, turn heat to low, and sauté, stirring occasionally, 10–15 minutes. When rice is done, add to bean mixture and toss lightly to mix. Serve hot. About 320 calories per serving.

☒ CHINESE FRIED RICE

Makes 4 servings

3 cups cold cooked rice
3 tablespoons peanut or other cooking
   oil
½ cup julienne strips of lean cooked
   roast pork or ham
4 scallions, minced (white part only)
¼ cup chicken broth
1 tablespoon soy sauce
¼ teaspoon sugar
⅛ teaspoon pepper

Stir-fry rice in oil in a large, heavy skillet over moderate heat, pressing out any lumps, until pale golden. Add pork and scallions and stir-fry 1 minute. Add remaining ingredients, cover, and heat 1 minute. Serve very hot. About 295 calories per serving.

VARIATION:

Chinese Fried Eggs and Rice: Stir-fry rice, pork, and scallions as directed, then push to side of skillet; omit broth but add 1 or 2 lightly beaten eggs; scramble lightly, then mix into rice along with soy sauce, sugar, and pepper. About 330 calories per serving.

JAPANESE GINGER RICE WITH TOASTED SEAWEED

The Japanese like short grain rice because it cooks down to pudding softness. They're also fond of dried seaweed (available in pressed sheets at gourmet shops and Oriental groceries; separate sheets before measuring). The two are delicious together.
Makes 4 servings

1 cup uncooked short grain rice
2 cups boiling chicken broth or weak tea
1 (1") piece fresh gingerroot, peeled and minced
¼ teaspoon salt
2 teaspoons soy sauce
1 cup crumbled dried seaweed

Preheat oven to 350° F. Mix rice, broth, ginger, salt, and soy sauce in a heavy saucepan, cover, and bring to a boil over high heat; turn heat to low, stir once, then cover and cook 15 minutes. Meanwhile spread seaweed on an ungreased baking sheet and toast, uncovered, 12–15 minutes until slightly crisp. When rice has cooked 15 minutes, uncover and cook 3–5 minutes longer. Fluff with a fork and serve sprinkled with seaweed. About 225 calories per serving.

¢ **KHICHIRI (EAST INDIAN RICE AND LENTILS)**

Good topped with yogurt or chutney and especially good with curry.
Makes 4–6 servings

½ cup dried lentils, washed and sorted
1 medium-size yellow onion, peeled and minced
2½ cups chicken broth or water
½ cup uncooked rice
¾ teaspoon salt (about)
Pinch crushed dried hot red chili peppers
2 tablespoons margarine
2 teaspoons cumin seeds

Simmer lentils and onion in broth in a covered heavy saucepan 25 minutes, stirring occasionally. Add rice, salt, and chili peppers, cover, and simmer 20 minutes until rice is tender and all liquid absorbed. Uncover and cook 2–3 minutes to dry out. Meanwhile, melt margarine in a small skillet over moderately low heat, add cumin seeds, and stir-fry ½ minute until they begin to pop. Pour over rice and toss with a fork. Taste for salt and adjust as needed. Calories per serving: about 230 for each of 4 servings if made with water and 260 if made with chicken broth; about 155 for each of 6 servings if made with water and 170 if made with chicken broth.

¢ **BAKED RICE IRANIAN STYLE (CHELOU)**

It takes long cooking and a heavy casserole to make this Middle Eastern favorite. The aim is to get a crusty bottom layer of rice (use a flameproof glass dish so you can tell at a glance) that can be broken up and sprinkled over the softer rice on top.
Makes 4 servings

4 tablespoons melted butter or margarine
4 cups hot cooked rice
1 egg yolk, lightly beaten

Preheat oven to 400° F. Pour 2 tablespoons butter into a heavy 1½-quart casserole and swirl to coat bottom and sides. Mix ½ cup rice with the egg yolk and spread evenly over bottom of casserole, packing lightly. Spoon remaining rice on top, mounding it up. With a spoon handle, make a hole down through center of rice, then cover and bake 15 minutes. Uncover, sprinkle with remaining butter, re-cover, and bake 40–50 minutes until crusty and brown on the bottom. Remove from oven and cool on a wire rack 10 minutes. Fluff rice with a fork, turn onto a hot platter, then scrape out crusty layer and scatter evenly over all. About 300 calories per serving.

RICE CROQUETTES

Makes 6–8 servings

2 tablespoons butter or margarine
2 tablespoons flour
½ cup milk
1 egg, lightly beaten
3 cups cooked rice (leftover is fine)
¼ teaspoon salt (about)
⅛ teaspoon pepper
Shortening or cooking oil for deep fat frying
¼ cup unsifted flour
1 egg, lightly beaten with 1 tablespoon cold water
½ cup toasted fine bread crumbs

Melt butter in a small saucepan over moderate heat, blend in flour, slowly stir in milk, and heat, stirring until thickened. Off heat, beat in egg; mix in rice, salt, and pepper, taste for seasoning and adjust. Cool to room temperature; shape into logs about 3″ long and 1″ wide and chill 1 hour. Begin heating shortening in a deep fat fryer with basket and deep fat thermometer over moderately high heat. Dredge logs in flour, dip in egg mixture, and roll in crumbs to coat well. When fat reaches 375° F., fry croquettes, a few at a time, 2–3 minutes until golden. Drain on paper toweling and keep warm while frying the rest. Serve hot as a potato substitute. About 270 calories for each of 6 servings, 200 for each of 8 servings.

VARIATIONS:

Savory Rice Croquettes: Prepare as directed but substitute Curried, Herbed, Mushroom or Amandine Rice for the plain. About 270 calories for each of 6 servings if made with Curried or Herbed Rice, 330 if made with Mushroom Rice, and 365 if made with Amandine Rice. About 200 calories for each of 8 servings if made with Curried or Herbed Rice, 250 if made with Mushroom Rice, and 275 if made with Amandine Rice.

Main Dish Rice Croquettes: Prepare as directed but use 2 cups rice and 1 cup any minced leftover meat, poultry, or seafood. Good topped with Mushroom or Tomato Sauce. Recipe too flexible for a meaningful calorie count.

Bulgur or Kasha Croquettes: Prepare as directed but substitute cooked bulgur wheat or buckwheat groats for rice. Approximately the same number of calories per serving as for croquettes made with rice.

EASY RICE AND CHEESE CROQUETTES

Makes 4 servings

Shortening or cooking oil for deep fat frying
2 cups cold cooked rice
2 egg yolks, lightly beaten
⅓ cup grated Parmesan, Gruyère, or mozzarella cheese
1 tablespoon minced parsley
1 teaspoon prepared spicy brown mustard
¼ cup unsifted flour
2 egg whites, lightly beaten
½ cup toasted fine bread crumbs

Begin heating fat in a deep fat fryer with basket and deep fat thermometer over moderately high heat. Mix rice, egg yolks, cheese, parsley, and mustard and shape into logs 3″ long and 1″ wide. Dredge in flour, dip in egg whites, and roll in crumbs to coat. When fat reaches 375° F., fry croquettes, a few at a time, 2–3 minutes until golden. Drain on paper toweling and keep warm while frying the rest. Serve hot as a potato substitute. About 300 calories per serving if made with Parmesan or Gruyère cheese, about 290 per serving if made with mozzarella cheese.

¢ ⚖️ **RICE PANCAKES**

Good for breakfast with ham or bacon. And a good way to use up leftover rice. Makes 4 servings

1 cup cooked rice
1 tablespoon finely grated yellow onion
⅓ cup plus 2 tablespoons milk
1 egg, lightly beaten

Simmer rice, onion, and ⅓ cup milk in a covered saucepan over lowest possible heat (a flame-tamer is good) 15–20 minutes until all milk is absorbed and rice very soft. Off heat, mix in remaining milk and the egg. Heat an oiled griddle over moderate heat until a drop of water will dance (or to 350° F. if using an electric griddle). Drop mixture by rounded tablespoonfuls, spread to about 3″ in diameter, and brown lightly on both sides. Keep warm while browning the rest. Pass syrup or warm honey. About 95 calories per serving (without syrup).

¢ ⚖️ **Dessert Rice Pancakes:** Prepare as directed but omit onion and add 2 tablespoons each sugar and seedless raisins. About 135 calories per serving.

¢ **Savory Rice Pancakes:** Prepare as directed but use Curried, Herbed, Mushroom, or other flavored rice instead of plain. Recipe too flexible for a meaningful calorie count.

BASIC BOILED WILD RICE

Wild rice is expensive, but it's richer than regular rice and goes further— 1 cup uncooked rice equals 3⅓ cups cooked rice, enough for 4–6 servings. To extend, mix ½-and-½ with cooked brown rice or bulgur wheat. Makes 4–6 servings

1 cup wild rice
3 cups water

1 teaspoon salt
2–3 tablespoons melted butter or margarine

Wash rice well in a strainer under cold running water. Place in a heavy saucepan with water and salt, cover, and bring to a boil over moderate heat. Uncover and boil gently, without stirring, about 35 minutes until *just* tender. Drain, set uncovered over lowest possible heat (an asbestos flame-tamer is handy), and dry 5 minutes, shaking pan occasionally. Mix in butter with a fork and serve. (*Note:* To keep hot, transfer to the top of a double boiler, cover, and set over simmering water. Don't try to keep warm more than 20 minutes or lovely crisp texture will be lost.) About 220 calories for each of 4 servings, 150 calories for each of 6 servings.

VARIATIONS:

Wild Rice for Game and Poultry: Sauté 1 minced yellow onion in 2 tablespoons butter 5–8 minutes until limp, add rice, 3 cups giblet stock or chicken broth, the salt, and ¼ teaspoon each sage, thyme, and marjoram. Cook as directed but do not add butter at the end. About 240 calories for each of 4 servings, 160 calories for each of 6 servings.

Wild Rice with Ham: Stir-fry ¼ pound finely diced cooked ham in 2 tablespoons bacon drippings over moderate heat 3–5 minutes until golden, add rice, water, and salt and proceed as directed but omit butter at the end. About 270 calories for each of 4 servings, 180 calories for each of 6 servings.

Wild Rice with Mushrooms and Bacon: Brown 6 slices bacon until crisp, remove to paper toweling, and crumble. In drippings, sauté ½ pound coarsely chopped mushrooms 3–5 minutes until golden. Add rice, 3 cups chicken broth, and ½ teaspoon salt and cook as directed. Add crumbled bacon (but not butter) and toss lightly to mix. About 275 calories for each of 4 servings, 185 calories for each of 6 servings.

Herbed Wild Rice: Cook rice in 3 cups chicken broth with 2 tablespoons minced chives or scallions, 1 tablespoon minced parsley, 1 teaspoon basil or savory, and ½ teaspoon salt. Mix in butter and serve. About 255 calories for each of 4 servings, 170 calories for each of 6 servings.

Wild Rice with Sour Cream and Chives: Cook rice as directed but omit butter. Transfer to the top of a double boiler, set over simmering water, and fork in ¾ cup sour cream, 3 tablespoons minced chives, and, if you like, ¼ cup cooked crumbled bacon. Cover and heat 10 minutes, fluff with a fork, and serve. About 290 calories for each of 4 servings, 195 calories for each of 6 servings.

WILD RICE AMANDINE

Makes 6 servings

6 scallions, minced (include some tops)
¼ cup unsalted butter
1 clove garlic, peeled and crushed
1 cup wild rice, washed in cold water
2 cups chicken broth
½ cup dry white wine
½ teaspoon salt (about)
⅛ teaspoon pepper
⅓ cup slivered toasted blanched
  almonds

Preheat oven to 325° F. Stir-fry scallions in butter in a 1-quart flameproof casserole over moderately low heat 3–5 minutes until limp. Add garlic and rice and stir-fry 1–2 minutes, add remaining ingredients except almonds, and boil gently, uncovered, without stirring 20 minutes. With a fork, mix in almonds and bake, uncovered, 15–20 minutes until all liquid is absorbed. About 240 calories per serving.

VARIATION:

Brandied Wild Rice: Cook as directed but use 2¼ cups chicken or beef broth instead of broth and wine and mix in 4–6 tablespoons brandy along with

almonds. Bake as directed. About 265 calories per serving.

☒ WILD RICE CAKES

Makes 6 servings

1 recipe Basic Boiled Wild Rice (do not
  drain)
3 tablespoons white corn meal
¼ cup bacon drippings or cooking oil

While rice is still hot, mix in corn meal, 1 tablespoon at a time, and cool to room temperature. Shape into 3″ patties, brown in drippings in a heavy skillet over moderate heat, drain on paper toweling, and serve. Good with ham, Canadian bacon, or sausages. About 240 calories per serving.

CASSEROLE OF WILD RICE, CHICKEN LIVERS, AND SAUSAGE

A festive accompaniment for poultry or game birds.
Makes 12 servings

1 pound pork sausage meat
¾ pound chicken livers, halved at the
  natural separation
2 large yellow onions, peeled and
  minced
1 pound mushrooms, wiped clean and
  sliced thin
2 cups wild rice, washed in cold water
1 quart chicken broth
1½ teaspoons salt
¼ teaspoon pepper
1 teaspoon poultry seasoning
1 cup light cream

Break up sausage meat in a large, heavy kettle and brown lightly over moderate heat, stirring now and then. Lift out with slotted spoon and reserve; drain off all but ¼ cup drippings and reserve. Sauté chicken livers in drippings over moderately high heat 3–4 minutes until lightly browned, remove, coarsely chop, and add to sausage. Add 2 tablespoons reserved drippings to kettle and sauté onions over moderate heat 5–8 minutes until pale golden; add mushrooms and sauté 2–3 minutes longer. Stir in rice, broth, and all seasonings and boil gently, uncovered, 20 minutes. Meanwhile, preheat oven to 325° F. With a fork mix in sausage, chicken livers, and cream. Spoon into a greased 3-quart casserole and bake, uncovered, 20–30 minutes until all liquid is absorbed. Fluff with a fork before serving. About 350 calories per serving.

BASIC BUCKWHEAT KASHA

To be strictly accurate, *kasha* is braised buckwheat groats. But the word has become a generic meaning for any braised, cracked cereal. Serve in place of potatoes.
Makes 4–6 servings

1 cup buckwheat groats
1 egg, lightly beaten
¼ cup butter or margarine
2 cups chicken or beef broth or water
1 teaspoon salt (about)
¼ teaspoon pepper

Mix groats and egg in a large, heavy skillet or saucepan set over moderate heat and cook and stir until dry, not brown. Add remaining ingredients, cover, and simmer 15 minutes until liquid is absorbed and groats are tender. Fluff with a fork, taste for salt and adjust if needed. About 355 calories for each of 4 servings, 240 calories for each of 6 servings.

VARIATIONS:

Old World Buckwheat Kasha: Sauté 1 large minced yellow onion in the butter 8–10 minutes until golden, add groats mixed with egg and ⅓ cup minced celery, and stir-fry 1–2 minutes. Add chicken broth, salt, pepper, 1 teaspoon poultry seasoning, and ⅛ teaspoon curry powder. Cover and cook as directed. About 375 calories for each of 4 servings, 250 calories for each of 6 servings.

Buckwheat-Mushroom Kasha: Sauté 1 cup coarsely chopped mushrooms in the butter 3–4 minutes until golden, add groats mixed with egg, and stir-fry 1–2 minutes. Cook as directed. Just before serving, mix in ⅓ cup minced toasted almonds, pecans, walnuts, or

piñon nuts. About 445 calories for each of 4 servings, 295 calories for each of 6 servings.

Kasha Varnishkas (Makes 6 servings): Cook the groats as directed and while they cook boil ½ pound broad noodles by package directions; also stir-fry 1 large peeled and minced yellow onion in the ¼ cup butter 8–10 minutes until golden. Mix groats with drained noodles, onion, and 1 tablespoon poppy seeds. Place in a buttered 2½-quart casserole and bake, uncovered, 15 minutes at 350° F. About 405 calories per serving.

BULGUR WHEAT KASHA

Makes 4–6 servings

1 large yellow onion, peeled and minced
¼ cup butter or margarine
1 cup bulgur wheat
2 cups chicken or beef broth
1 teaspoon salt
¼ teaspoon pepper

Preheat oven to 350° F. Sauté onion in butter in a flameproof casserole over moderate heat 5–8 minutes until pale golden. Add bulgur wheat and stir-fry 2–3 minutes until golden. Add remaining ingredients, cover, and bake ½ hour until liquid is absorbed and bulgur tender. Fluff with a fork and serve as a potato substitute. About 335 calories for each of 4 servings, 225 calories for each of 6 servings.

VARIATIONS:

Apple-Almond Kasha: Prepare as directed but stir-fry 1½ cups peeled, minced tart apples along with bulgur wheat. Also add ¼ teaspoon each thyme, sage, and celery seeds and 1 tablespoon minced parsley. Cover and bake as directed; just before serving top with ½ cup slivered blanched almonds sautéed in ¼ cup butter. About 560 calories for each of 4 servings, 375 calories for each of 6 servings.

Bulgur-Mushroom Kasha: Prepare as directed but stir-fry 1 cup thinly sliced mushrooms along with bulgur wheat; add 1 teaspoon poultry seasoning along with salt, and just before serving mix in ⅓ cup warmed heavy cream or sour cream. About 410 calories for each of 4 servings if made with heavy cream, 385 if made with sour cream; about 275 calories for each of 6 servings if made with heavy cream, 255 if made with sour cream.

BAKED KASHA WITH WALNUTS

Especially good with roast lamb.
Makes 4 servings

1 medium-size yellow onion, peeled and
*   minced*
3 tablespoons bacon drippings, butter, or
*   margarine*
2 cups cooked buckwheat groats, bulgur,
*   or cracked wheat*
½ teaspoon salt
⅛ teaspoon pepper
½ cup coarsely chopped walnuts

Preheat oven to 350° F. Brown onion in 2 tablespoons drippings in a small skillet over moderate heat 10–12 minutes; mix into *kasha* along with salt, pepper, and walnuts and toss well. Spoon into a greased 1½-quart casserole, sprinkle with remaining drippings, cover, and bake ½ hour. Serve in place of potatoes. About 320 calories per serving.

⚔ ¢ STEWED BARLEY AND VEGETABLES

Makes 4–6 servings

1 cup medium pearl barley
1 large yellow onion, peeled and minced
3 carrots, peeled and cut in small dice
2 stalks celery, cut in small dice
1 cup diced rutabaga
2 tablespoons minced parsley
2 teaspoons salt (about)
¼ teaspoon pepper
1 quart beef broth

Mix all ingredients in a large, heavy saucepan, cover, and simmer 1–1¼ hours until barley is tender. Taste for salt and adjust. Serve as a vegetable. About 225 calories for each of 4 servings, 150 for each of 6 servings.

BAKED BARLEY AND MUSHROOM CASSEROLE

4–6 servings

1 cup medium pearl barley
4 tablespoons butter or margarine
1 large yellow onion, peeled and minced
1 cup coarsely chopped mushrooms
3 cups chicken or beef broth
2 teaspoons salt
¼ teaspoon pepper

Preheat oven to 350° F. Stir-fry barley in 2 tablespoons butter in a skillet over moderate heat about 2 minutes until lightly browned; transfer to an ungreased 1½-quart casserole. Sauté onion in remaining butter 5–8 minutes until pale golden, add mushrooms, if you like, and sauté 3–5 minutes longer; add to casserole. Mix in all remaining ingredients, cover, and bake about 1¼ hours until barley is tender, stirring now and then. Fluff with a fork and serve as a potato substitute. About 330 calories for each of 4 servings, 220 for each of 6 servings.

CHEESE GNOCCHI

Serve hot as a luncheon entree or as a potato substitute with veal or chicken.
Makes 4 servings

Gnocchi:

½ pound ricotta cheese
½ cup sifted flour
6 tablespoons grated Parmesan cheese
2 tablespoons melted butter or
*   margarine*
½ teaspoon salt
Pinch nutmeg
2 eggs, lightly beaten

Topping:

⅓ cup melted butter or margarine
⅓ cup grated Parmesan cheese

Preheat oven to 350° F. Mix *gnocchi* ingredients and spoon about half into a pastry bag fitted with a large plain tube (opening should be about ½″ across). Heat about 5 quarts salted water to boiling in a large kettle; adjust heat so water bubbles *very gently*.

Squeeze out gnocchi over water, cutting with a knife at 1" intervals and letting drop into water. Simmer, uncovered, 2–3 minutes until gnocchi float, then remove with a slotted spoon and drain in a colander. Arrange gnocchi 1 layer deep in a buttered 1½-quart *au gratin* dish or shallow casserole, drizzle with melted butter, and sprinkle with cheese. Bake, uncovered, 10 minutes, then broil about 2 minutes to brown lightly. About 400 calories per serving.

POTATO GNOCCHI

Serve as an accompaniment to veal or chicken.
Makes 4 servings

Gnocchi:

2 cups hot mashed potatoes (without milk or seasoning)
1 cup sifted flour
2 eggs, lightly beaten
1½ teaspoons salt
⅛ teaspoon white pepper
Pinch nutmeg

Topping:

1½ cups hot Italian Tomato Sauce
¼ cup grated Parmesan cheese

Mix all *gnocchi* ingredients and spoon about half into a pastry bag fitted with a large, plain tube (opening should be about ½" in diameter). Bring about 5 quarts salted water to a boil in a large kettle, then adjust heat so water bubbles *very gently*. Squeeze out gnocchi over water, cutting with a knife at 1" intervals and letting drop into water. Simmer, uncovered, until gnocchi float, then simmer 1 minute longer. Lift out with slotted spoon, drain in a colander, and keep hot in a shallow serving dish. When all gnocchi are done, cover with sauce and sprinkle with cheese. If you like, pass extra Parmesan. About 310 calories per serving.

VARIATION:

Cool uncooked gnocchi mixture to room temperature, then roll on a lightly floured board into a rope about ½"

thick. Cut in 1" lengths and imprint lightly with the back of a fork. Cook and serve as directed. About 310 calories per serving.

FARINA GNOCCHI PARMIGIANA

Makes 6 servings

3 cups milk
2 teaspoons salt
Pinch nutmeg
1 cup quick-cooking farina
2 tablespoons melted butter or margarine
3 egg yolks, lightly beaten
½ cup butter
½ cup finely grated Parmesan cheese

Heat milk, salt, and nutmeg, covered, in the top of a double boiler over just boiling water until steaming. Add farina slowly, stirring with a wooden spoon; cook and stir until smooth and very thick, about 10 minutes. Set double boiler top on a damp cloth, mix in melted butter and yolks. Brush a large, shallow pan or casserole with cold water.

Add farina mixture, spreading to a thickness of ½", cover, and chill 1–2 hours. Cut into strips ¾" wide, turn out on a board, and roll under your palms into ropes; cut in 1" lengths. (*Note:* Dip knife in cold water to prevent sticking.) Preheat oven to 400° F.

Arrange half of *gnocchi*, slightly overlapping, over bottom of a buttered 1½-quart *au gratin* dish or shallow casserole. Dot with ¼ cup butter and ¼ cup Parmesan; repeat to make a second layer. Bake, uncovered, 10–15 minutes, then broil 4"–5" from heat 2–3 minutes until lightly browned. Serve hot as a potato substitute with veal scaloppine, veal chops, or chicken, or as a luncheon entree with soup and salad. About 380 calories per serving.

BOILED COUSCOUS (SEMOLINA)

Couscous is the Arabic word for finely ground semolina. It is also the name of the North African lamb stew served

over it (see the chapter on lamb).
Boiled couscous can be served in place
of rice or potatoes.
Makes 6 servings

1 quart beef or chicken broth or water
2 cups uncooked couscous (available in
gourmet shops and Middle Eastern
groceries)
¼ cup butter or margarine
1 teaspoon salt (about)

Bring broth to a rapid boil in a large,
heavy saucepan, gradually add
couscous, stirring briskly to prevent
lumping. Cook and stir 2–3 minutes, add
butter and salt, and mix lightly.
Remove from heat, cover, and let stand
10–15 minutes until all moisture is
absorbed and no raw taste remains.

Fluff with a fork and serve smothered
with gravy. (*Note:* If using to make the
lamb stew called Couscous, place cooked
couscous in a large colander lined with
a triple thickness of dampened
cheesecloth, set over kettle of stew,
cover, and let steam while stew cooks.

Prepared this way, the couscous will be
light and moist and delicately lamb-
flavored.) About 295 calories per
serving.

⚖️ POLENTA

Polenta, or corn meal mush Italian style,
often takes the place of bread in
Northern Italy. The mush is cooked until
very thick, turned out, cut in chunks,
and eaten with chicken, rabbit, or fish
stew. Sometimes polenta is topped with
the stew, sometimes with Italian sausages
and Tomato Sauce. Leftovers are good
fried or baked with cheese and sauce. If
you have the time and patience, cook
polenta the Italian way in a very heavy
kettle, *stirring constantly.* Otherwise, use
the more foolproof double boiler.
Makes 6 servings

1 cup yellow corn meal
1 cup cold water

1½ pints boiling water
1 teaspoon salt

Mix meal and cold water in the top of a
double boiler set over simmering water
or in a heavy 4-quart kettle over
moderately low heat (if you have one,
use the unlined copper polenta pot). Stir
in boiling water and salt and cook about
45 minutes until very thick; stir every 5
minutes if using double boiler, constantly
if using the kettle to avoid lumping.
Mixture is ready to serve when a crust
forms on sides of pan. Scrape polenta
onto a hot buttered platter, cool 2–3
minutes, then slice as you would bread or
cut in squares and serve. (*Note:* To cut
more cleanly, use string and a sawing
motion.) About 85 calories per serving.

VARIATIONS:

⚖️ **Fried Polenta:** Cut cold leftover
polenta in 2″ squares ½″–¾″ thick,
brown lightly, 2–3 minutes on each side,
in 2 tablespoons olive oil or bacon
drippings over moderately low heat.
About 130 calories per serving.

⚖️ **Polenta Parmigiana:** Prepare polenta
as directed and, while hot, spoon into a
buttered 8″ or 9″ square pan; smooth
top and cool. Cut in 2″ or 3″ squares,
arrange in a single layer in a buttered *au
gratin* dish or shallow casserole. Drizzle
with ⅓ cup each melted butter and
grated Parmesan cheese. Bake,
uncovered, ½ hour at 400° F., then
brown lightly under broiler. Serve as
potato substitute. About 190 calories per
serving.

Baked Polenta with Italian Sausages:
Arrange 2″ squares cold cooked
polenta in a single layer in a buttered
2-quart *au gratin* dish or shallow
casserole. Top with 6 cooked sweet
Italian sausages, split lengthwise, and 2
cups Tomato Sauce; sprinkle with ¼ cup
grated Parmesan cheese. Bake,
uncovered, ½ hour at 400° F. Serve as
an entree. About 390 calories per
serving.

⚖ ¢ BAKED HOMINY CASSEROLE

Makes 6 servings

1 (1-pound 12-ounce) can hominy
Liquid drained from hominy plus
    enough milk to measure 1⅓ cups
3 eggs, lightly beaten
1 cup soft white bread crumbs
1½ teaspoons salt
⅛ teaspoon white pepper
2 tablespoons minced parsley

Preheat oven to 350° F. Mix all
ingredients and spoon into a buttered
2-quart casserole. Set casserole in a
larger pan half full of hot water and
bake, uncovered, about 1 hour until just
firm. Serve hot as a potato substitute.
About 150 calories per serving.

VARIATIONS:

Baked Hominy and Cheese Casserole:
Prepare as directed but reduce eggs to
2 and add ½ pound grated sharp
Cheddar cheese. Serve as a luncheon
entree. About 265 calories per serving.

**Baked Hominy Casserole with Sausages
or Franks:** Prepare casserole as directed
and bake ½ hour; arrange 6 browned
link sausages or frankfurters spoke
fashion on top and bake ½ hour longer.
About 270 calories per serving if made
with sausages, 290 calories per serving if
made with frankfurters.

⚖ ▨ HOMINY, BACON, AND EGG SCRAMBLE

A simple dish that is suitable for
breakfast, lunch, or supper.
Makes 4 servings

8 slices bacon
1 (1-pound) can hominy, drained
2 eggs, lightly beaten with ¼ cup milk
2 tablespoons grated Parmesan cheese
⅛ teaspoon pepper

Brown bacon in a large, heavy skillet,
lift to paper toweling, crumble, and
reserve. Drain off all but ¼ cup
drippings, add hominy, and stir-fry over
moderate heat 2–3 minutes. Add eggs
and scramble until soft; mix in cheese
and pepper. Spoon onto warm plates and

top with bacon. About 220 calories per
serving.

¢ ▨ HOMINY, BEANS, AND SALT PORK

Makes 4–6 servings

½ pound salt pork, trimmed of rind and
    cut in small dice
1 (1-pound) can hominy, drained
2 cups boiled dried or drained canned
    white or lima beans
½ teaspoon salt (about)
¼ teaspoon pepper

Stir-fry salt pork 8–10 minutes in a
heavy kettle over moderate heat until
lightly browned. Pour off all but ¼ cup
drippings, mix in remaining ingredients,
cover, and heat until piping hot, stirring
now and then. Taste for salt and adjust
as needed. Serve for breakfast (with
eggs) or as a potato substitute. About
505 calories for each of 4 servings,
340 calories for each of 6 servings.

GRITS AND GRUYÈRE FRITTERS

Makes 6 servings

Shortening or cooking oil for deep fat
    frying
2 cups cooked hominy grits, chilled
¾ cup coarsely grated Gruyère cheese
¼ teaspoon pepper
⅛ teaspoon nutmeg
1 egg, lightly beaten with 1 tablespoon
    cold water
¾ cup fine dry bread crumbs

Begin heating shortening in a deep fat
fryer with a deep fat thermometer. Mash
grits with a fork, mix in cheese, pepper,
and nutmeg. Shape into logs about 2½"
long and 1" across. Dip in egg, then in
bread crumbs. When fat reaches 375° F.,
fry, a few at a time, 2–3 minutes until
golden brown. Drain on paper toweling
and serve hot as a potato substitute.
About 230 calories per serving.

VARIATION:

Grits and Gruyère Appetizers (Makes
about 2½ dozen): Prepare as directed
but shape into small balls (about 1")
instead of logs. Deep-fry, spear with

toothpicks, and serve hot. About 45 calories each.

GRITS AND SMITHFIELD HAM PATTIES

Makes 6 servings

2 cups cooked hominy grits, chilled
1 cup minced Smithfield ham
¼ teaspoon black pepper
⅛ teaspoon cayenne pepper
1 egg, lightly beaten with 1 tablespoon cold water
¾ cup fine dry bread crumbs
⅓ cup peanut or other cooking oil
2 cups hot Mushroom or Cheese Sauce

Mash grits with a fork, mix in ham and peppers. Shape into patties about the size of small hamburgers. Dip in egg, then in crumbs to coat evenly. Heat oil in a large, heavy skillet over moderately high heat until very hot but not smoking. Add patties and brown about 2 minutes on a side. Drain on paper toweling and serve topped with sauce. About 335 calories per serving.

PASTA

There are dozens of stories about how pasta came to Italy from China, probably none of them true. It's now thought noodles may have originated in both places, quite independently of the other. The Chinese noodles would have been first, and they would have been made in those ancient days as they are today, of rice or soy flour. First mention of spaghetti in Italy occurred early in the Middle Ages, well before Marco Polo is said to have brought it back from the Orient. But this was pasta made of wheat flour, particularly semolina, ground from the hard golden heart of durum flour. Pasta rapidly became an Italian staple. It was cheap, satisfying, quick to prepare, and so versatile it combined equally well with harvests of land and sea. Why so many shapes and sizes? No one knows, though perhaps it was a way of adding variety to what might have become a boring routine.

Basically, there are two types of Italian pasta: *macaroni and spaghetti*, made of semolina and water and just enough egg to bind them, and *egg pasta or noodles*, containing a high proportion of egg. Green noodles have simply had spinach added. There is other European pasta, notably the German *Spätzle* and Middle European *Nockerln*, both soft noodle-like dumplings used to extend the main dish and catch the gravy or sauce.

Some Popular Kinds of Pasta

Spaghettis (String Shapes):
Fedeline
Capellini
Spaghettini
Vermicelli
Spaghetti
Fusilli

Flat and Ribbon Shapes:
Linguine (egg pasta)
Taglierini (egg pasta)
Fettuccine (egg pasta)
Lasagne
Mafalde

Noodles:
Tagliatelle
Fine Noodles
Medium Noodles
Wide or Broad Noodles

Stuffed Pasta:
Ravioli
Cappelletti Tortellini

Macaronis (Tubular or Hollow Shapes):
Bucatini
Tubetti
Tufoli
Rigatoni
Ziti
Ditalini
Ditali
Cannelloni
Manicotti
Elbow Macaroni

Fancy Shapes:
Farfalline (little bows)
Farfalle (bows)
Conchiglie (seashell macaroni)

Soup Pasta:
Stellette (little stars)
Semini (little seeds)
Alphabet
Peperini (pepper seeds)
Anelli Campanelline (small rings)
Quadruccini (little squares)
Conchigliette (little seashells)

Oriental Noodles:
Chow Mein Noodles (crisp-fried and
ready to use)
Celophane Noodles (also called bean
thread and Chinese vermicelli)
Harusame (Japanese noodles made of soy
flour)
Soba (Japanese buckwheat noodle)
Rice Stick (fine rice flour noodles)

How to Use Pasta

Generally speaking, long, thin pasta and
small tubes are boiled and sauced. Broad
flat pasta, also the larger fancy shapes,
are boiled, then baked *en casserole* with
cheese, meat, seafood, or vegetable and
sauce. Large tubes are boiled, stuffed,
sauced, and baked. Soup pasta is added
to soups or thin stews minutes before
serving so that the rawness cooks out
but not the firm-tenderness.

Italians intensely dislike soft or mushy
pasta and eat it *al dente* (to the tooth,
meaning there's still a bit of resilience).
They are also likely to eat it before the
main course or as an accompaniment to
meat, which is why Italian cookbooks
often state that a pound of pasta will
serve 8 to 10. It won't the way we eat it.

How Much Pasta per Person: Figure 4
servings per pound if the pasta is to be
eaten as the main dish, 6–8 if it is an
accompaniment.

How to Cook Pasta

Spaghetti and Macaroni: For each 1
pound pasta, bring 6–7 quarts water
and 2 tablespoons salt to a full rolling
boil in a large, heavy kettle over high
heat. To keep pasta from clumping, add
about a teaspoon olive or other cooking
oil. Do not break strands of pasta, even
if very long, but ease into the kettle,
pushing farther in as ends soften, until
completely submerged. Water should be
boiling rapidly all the while, so if
necessary add pasta a little at a time.
As soon as all pasta is in the pot, begin
timing it; do not cover but *do* move pasta
occasionally with a long-handled fork.
Depending on size and shape, pasta will
take 5–10 minutes to become *al dente;*
very large pasta may take 15–20 minutes.
Begin testing after 4 minutes, and test
regularly thereafter, pulling out a strand
and biting it. There should be no raw
starch taste but pasta should be firm-
tender. The second it's done, pull off the
fire. If you've cooked a small amount,
fork out or lift with tongs to serving
platter, letting excess moisture run back
into kettle. This method won't work,
however, for more than a pound of
pasta, becuase you can only lift out a bit
at a time and that left in the pot goes
mushy. So drain in a colander—fast—
and return to kettle. *Do not rinse.* Set
kettle over low heat and shake about ½
minute, then serve pasta immediately.
Mound on a hot platter or individual
serving plates (wide-rimmed soup plates
are best), top, if you like, with a hearty
lump of softened butter, then with sauce.
If sauce is mixed into pasta before
serving, do so with a lifting and turning
motion, as though tossing salad; never
stir.

If Pasta Must Wait: As soon as pasta is
drained, return to kettle and dot well
with butter. Cover and set in oven turned
to lowest heat. Pasta will hold about ½
hour this way. If dinner is delayed longer
than that, cook a new batch (the old can
be used in stuffings, meat loaves, or
casseroles).

To Reheat Leftover Pasta: Sauced pasta
is no problem; simply heat slowly in a
covered saucepan to serving temperature.
Unsauced pasta should be covered with

boiling water and allowed to stand about 2 minutes, then drained well.

Noodles and Egg Pasta: These are softer than spaghetti and cook faster. They're also slightly saltier. Follow procedure for spaghetti but use half the amount of salt. Add noodles by handfuls to rapidly boiling water and cook uncovered. Fine noodles will be done in about 3 minutes, larger ones in 5–7. (*Note:* Homemade noodles will cook faster than the commercial, so watch carefully and taste often.) When noodles taste done, they are done. Drain quickly in a colander, again do not rinse, mound in serving dish, mix in a few dabs of butter, then sauce. Noodles do not wait well, so serve as soon as they're done.

Oriental Noodles: All of these hair-fine, translucent noodles are prepared more or less the same way. Soak in warm water about 10 minutes to soften, then drain well and use as recipes direct. They may also be deep-fat-fried without being soaked. Heat oil (preferably peanut oil) to 380° F., crumble noodles into fat a little at a time, and fry, stirring gently with a slotted spoon, ½–1 minute until frizzled and pale golden. Drain on paper toweling and use as a crunchy topping for Chinese dishes.

How to Eat Pasta

It's the long slithery strands that intimidate. With practice, however, eating spaghetti is as easy as eating scrambled eggs. Simply catch a few strands on the ends of your fork, then twirl round and round against your plate (the Italian way) or against the bowl of a large spoon (the American way) until the pasta is wound into a neat mouthful. That's all there is to it.

About Sauces for Pasta

In addition to the recipes that follow, there are a number of sauces suitable for pasta in the chapter on sauces and gravies.

¢ HOMEMADE PASTA DOUGH

Makes about 1½ pounds

4 cups sifted flour
1½ teaspoons salt
4 eggs, lightly beaten
¼ cup lukewarm water
2 teaspoons olive or other cooking oil

Sift flour with salt; make a well in center and pour in eggs, water, and oil. Gradually draw dry ingredients from edges of bowl into liquid to form a fairly stiff dough (you may need to use hands at the end). Or mix with a dough hook on an electric mixer (hold a dry towel over bowl so flour doesn't fly). Knead dough on lightly floured board about 10 minutes until smooth and elastic. Cover with dry cloth and let rest ½ hour. Quarter dough and roll paper thin, one piece at a time, into a 13"–14" square on a lightly floured board, using as little additional flour as possible and keeping edges straight.

For Noodles (including lasagne noodles): Roll dough up loosely, jelly-roll fashion, cut crosswise in strips of desired width, and unroll. Cover with dry cloth and let dry at room temperature 1 hour. Cook by basic recipe but remember that homemade noodles will cook faster than the commercial. (*Note:* Noodles may be dried overnight [turn now and then] and stored airtight; use within 1 week.)

For Cannelloni, Manicotti, or Ravioli: Cut rolled dough into squares of desired size.

To Use a Pasta Machine: Prepare as directed up to point of rolling. Flatten each piece of dough into a rectangle and feed into machine following manufacturer's instructions. For the first rolling, set dial at widest opening (No. 10), then decrease for each successive rolling until desired thickness is reached. No. 3 or 4 is good for noodles, No. 2 for cannelloni, manicotti, and ravioli. If strips become unwieldy in the rolling, halve crosswise. (*Note:* Keep remaining dough covered while rolling each piece.) About 360 calories per ¼-pound serving.

VARIATION:

Pasta Verde (Green Pasta): Sift the flour with 1 teaspoon salt; add 2 lightly beaten eggs, 2 tablespoons lukewarm water, 2 teaspoons olive oil, and 1 cup well-drained, puréed, cooked spinach; proceed as directed. About 370 calories per ¼-pound serving.

¢ NOODLE RING

A festive way to serve plain buttered noodles.
Makes 4 servings

½ pound noodles, cooked and drained by package directions
¼ cup melted butter
1 teaspoon salt
⅛ teaspoon white pepper

Preheat oven to 375° F. Toss noodles with butter, salt, and pepper then *pack* into a *well-buttered* 1½-quart ring mold. Place mold in a larger pan half filled with water and bake, uncovered, 20–30 minutes. Lift mold from water bath, loosen edges, and invert on a hot platter. Ring is now ready to fill with any creamed meat, fish, or vegetable. About 320 calories per serving (without filling of any sort).

VARIATIONS:

Egg-Noodle Ring: Prepare noodle mixture as directed but add 2 lightly beaten eggs and ½ cup heavy cream. Bake as directed, allowing 35–40 minutes until ring is firm. Unmold and fill with something delicate—Creamed Sweetbreads, perhaps, or asparagus tips. About 465 calories per serving (without filling).

Cheese-Noodle Ring: Prepare noodle mixture as directed but add 2 lightly beaten eggs, ½ cup milk, and 1 cup coarsely grated sharp Cheddar cheese. Butter ring mold and coat with fine dry bread crumbs; pack in noodle mixture and bake as directed about 40 minutes. Fill with creamed spinach, broccoli, cauliflower, chicken, or turkey. About 535 calories per serving (without filling).

Some Quick Ways to Dress Up Noodles

The following amounts are for 1 pound noodles, cooked and drained by package directions. Depending upon richness of sauce, each will serve 6–8 if noodles are used as a potato substitute, 4–6 if a main course.

Savory Noodles: Dress noodles with ⅓–½ cup seasoned butter: Browned, Garlic, Dill, Herb, or Parsley-Lemon.

Noodles Noisette: Toss noodles with ⅓ cup minced, blanched, toasted almonds or peanuts, pecans, cashews, walnuts, piñon, or pistachio nuts and ⅓–½ cup melted butter.

Noodles Amandine: Sauté ½ cup slivered, blanched almonds in ½ cup butter until golden; off heat mix in 2 teaspoons lemon juice, pour over noodles, and toss to mix.

Fried Noodles: Slowly brown cooked noodles in ½ cup melted butter (you'll probably have to do 2 batches), stirring occasionally, about 15 minutes.

Herbed Noodles: Toss noodles with ½ cup melted butter and ¼ cup minced chives or parsley, or 1–2 tablespoons minced fresh or 1 teaspoon dried basil, oregano, savory, marjoram, dill, or chervil.

Poppy Seed Noodles: Toss noodles with ½ cup melted butter and 2 tablespoons poppy seeds. (*Note:* Toasted sesame seeds and caraway seeds are equally good.)

Garlic Noodles: Toss noodles with 1 cup coarse dry bread crumbs browned in ½ cup Garlic Butter.

Creamed Noodles: Toss noodles with 1–1½ cups hot Thin White Sauce and, if you like, ⅓ cup sautéed sliced mushrooms, ⅓ cup minced pimiento or scallions, or ½ cup mixed cooked vegetables (diced carrots, green beans, and peas).

Sauced Noodles: Toss noodles with ½ cup hot milk and 1 cup hot Parsley, Mushroom-Cheese, Velouté, Curry,

Mornay, or Egg Sauce. Or toss with 1½ cups hot Tomato Sauce, Sauce Verte, or any gravy.

Noodles Florentine: Toss noodles with 1 cup minced, well-drained, cooked spinach and ⅓ cup melted butter.

Noodles Smetana: Toss noodles with ½ cup melted butter, 1 pint sour cream, 1½ teaspoons garlic salt, ¼ cup minced chives, and ⅛ teaspoon pepper.

Noodles Hungarian: Return drained noodles to pan, add 1 pound cottage cheese, ½ cup melted butter or bacon drippings, and pepper to taste. Toss gently over lowest heat to warm cheese. Serve topped with crisp, crumbled bacon or crisply browned, diced salt pork.

Cheese Noodles: Return drained noodles to pan, add ⅔ cup hot milk, 1 cup grated sharp Cheddar or Swiss cheese or ½ cup grated Parmesan or crumbled blue cheese. Toss lightly over lowest heat until cheese melts.

Creamed Noodles and Onions: Return drained noodles to pan, add 1 cup coarsely chopped, boiled white onions and a little cooking liquid, ⅔ cup heavy cream, and 2 tablespoons butter. Toss over lowest heat just until heated through.

Noodles Lyonnaise: Stir-fry 1 thinly sliced large Bermuda onion in ½ cup butter over moderate heat until pale golden, 5–8 minutes. Serve on top of buttered noodles.

Noodles Polonaise: Lightly brown 1 cup coarse white bread crumbs in ⅓ cup butter. Off heat, mix in the sieved yolks of 4 hard-cooked eggs and 2 tablespoons minced parsley. Serve on top of buttered noodles.

¢ SPÄTZLE

These tiny teardrop-shaped German noodles are served as a potato substitute (though in Germany often *in addition* to potatoes). They're good with all kinds of meats, also as a soup garnish.

Makes 4 servings

1 cup sifted flour
½ teaspoon salt
Pinch nutmeg (optional)
Pinch paprika (optional)
1 egg, lightly beaten
⅓ cup cold water
2 tablespoons melted butter or margarine

Sift flour with salt and, if you like, spices. Mix egg and water and add slowly to dry mixture; beat hard until smooth (batter will be quite thick). Bring about 2 quarts well-salted water (or chicken or beef broth) to a slow boil in a large, heavy saucepan. Balance a colander on rim of saucepan so that it is well *above* water. Spoon about ⅓ of batter into colander, then carefully press through holes, letting *spätzle* fall into water. Cook 3–4 minutes, lift out with a slotted spoon and keep warm while cooking remaining spätzle. Toss spätzle with melted butter and serve hot. About 170 calories per serving.

¢ NOCKERLN

These delicate little Middle European dumplings are made to be smothered with the sauces and gravies of goulash and *paprikash.*

Makes 6 servings

¼ cup butter or margarine
1 egg, lightly beaten
6 tablespoons milk
½ teaspoon salt
1 cup sifted flour

Cream butter until light; mix egg with milk and salt. Add flour alternately to butter with egg mixture, beginning and ending with flour, then beat until smooth. Bring 4 quarts well-salted water to a slow boil. Drop in *nockerln* from a ½ teaspoon and cook, uncovered, a few at a time, 4–5 minutes. (*Note:* Cook no more than 1 layer of nockerln at a time and wet each spoon each time you dip it in the batter.) Lift cooked dumplings from kettle with a slotted spoon and keep warm while you cook the rest. About 160 calories per serving.

VARIATION:

Swirl cooked nockerln in ¼ cup melted butter in a large, heavy kettle over moderately low heat, just to coat, then serve. About 230 calories per serving.

¢ **DELUXE MACARONI AND CHEESE**

Makes 6 servings

¼ cup butter or margarine
¼ cup unsifted flour
1 teaspoon powdered mustard
2½ cups milk
3 cups coarsely grated sharp Cheddar cheese
¼ teaspoon salt (about)
⅛ teaspoon white pepper
1 tablespoon Worcestershire sauce
1 tablespoon finely grated yellow onion (optional)
½ pound elbow macaroni, cooked and drained by package directions

Preheat oven to 350° F. Melt butter in a saucepan over moderate heat, blend in flour and mustard, slowly stir in milk, and cook, stirring until thickened. Mix in 2 cups grated cheese and all remaining ingredients except macaroni. Taste for salt and add a little more if needed. Cook and stir until cheese melts. Off heat, mix in macaroni; turn into a buttered 2-quart casserole, sprinkle with remaining cheese, and bake uncovered about ½ hour until bubbly and lightly browned. About 515 calories per serving.

¢ **ITALIAN MACARONI, PIMIENTO, AND CHEESE LOAF**

Makes 6–8 servings

½ pound elbow macaroni, cooked and drained by package directions
2 cups milk, scalded
3 eggs, lightly beaten
2 cups soft white bread crumbs
1 cup coarsely grated mozzarella cheese
1 cup finely grated Parmesan cheese
1 cup coarsely grated provolone cheese
¼ cup minced scallions (include some tops)
2 tablespoons minced parsley
¼ cup minced pimiento

1 teaspoon salt (about)
¼ teaspoon white pepper
2–3 cups hot Tomato or Mushroom Sauce (optional)

Preheat oven to 350° F. Mix all ingredients but sauce, taste for salt and adjust. Spoon into a well-buttered 9"×5"×3" loaf pan and bake, uncovered, about 1 hour until firm in the center. Let stand upright 5 minutes; loosen and invert on a hot platter. If you like, spoon some sauce over each serving and pass the rest. Slice, not too thin, as you would a meat loaf. About 475 calories for each of 6 servings (without sauce), about 355 calories for each of 8 servings.

VARIATION:

Macaroni and Cheddar Loaf: Prepare as directed but substitute ¾ pound coarsely grated sharp Cheddar for the 3 Italian cheeses. About 500 calories for each of 6 servings (without sauce), about 370 calories for each of 8 servings.

¢ **FISHERMAN'S BAKED SHELLS**

You can vary this next recipe by varying the fish. Use mussels, for example, instead of clams (but don't mince—they're nicer left whole). Or use tiny squid instead of shrimp, salmon instead of tuna.

Makes 6 servings

1 medium-size yellow onion, peeled and minced
1 clove garlic, peeled and crushed
1 medium-size carrot, peeled and cut in fine dice
1 stalk celery, cut in fine dice
2 tablespoons butter or margarine
2 tablespoons flour
1 (7½-ounce) can minced clams, drained (reserve liquid)
Liquid drained from clams plus enough bottled clam juice to make 2 cups
1 cup dry white wine or water
¼ teaspoon basil
¼ teaspoon savory
¾ pound raw shrimp, shelled and deveined
2 tablespoons cooking oil

1 (7-ounce) can tuna, drained and flaked
½ pound seashell macaroni, cooked and
    drained by package directions
2 tablespoons minced parsley

Stir-fry onion, garlic, carrot, and celery
in butter in a 2-quart saucepan over
moderate heat 3–5 minutes until limp.
Mix in flour, add clam juice, wine, and
herbs, cover, and simmer 30 minutes,
stirring now and then. Meanwhile,
stir-fry shrimp in oil over moderate heat
3–5 minutes until pink; remove and
reserve. Preheat oven to 350° F. When
sauce is ready, mix in clams, shrimp, and
tuna. Layer macaroni and sauce in a
buttered 3-quart casserole, cover, and
bake 30 minutes. Sprinkle with parsley
and serve. About 385 calories per
serving.

¢ SPAGHETTI AND MEAT BALLS
IN TOMATO SAUCE

Makes 4 servings

Sauce:

1 (1-pound) can tomatoes (do not drain)
1 (6-ounce) can tomato paste
1 cup water
1 teaspoon salt
¼ teaspoon pepper
2 teaspoons sugar
2 teaspoons basil
1 tablespoon minced onion
½ teaspoon garlic juice

Meat Balls:

1 pound ground beef
1 cup soft white bread crumbs
¼ cup water
¼ cup milk
1 small yellow onion, peeled and minced
1 tablespoon Worcestershire sauce
1 teaspoon salt
¼ teaspoon pepper
2 tablespoons cooking oil (for browning)

Pasta:

1 pound spaghetti

Place all sauce ingredients in a large
saucepan, cover, and simmer 1 hour,
stirring occasionally and breaking up
tomatoes. Meanwhile, mix meat ball

ingredients except oil and shape into 1″
balls. Brown 4–5 minutes in the oil in a
large, heavy skillet over moderate heat,
doing only ⅓ of balls at a time and
draining on paper toweling. Pour all but
2 tablespoons drippings from skillet, mix
in a little sauce, scraping up browned
bits, and return to saucepan. Add meat
balls, cover, and simmer 15 minutes.
Cook spaghetti by package directions,
drain, and arrange on a large, deep
platter. Place meat balls on top, spoon a
little sauce over all, and pass the rest.
About 860 calories per serving.

SPAGHETTI AL PESTO
(GENOESE-STYLE SPAGHETTI
WITH FRESH BASIL SAUCE)

In Italy, women laboriously pound garlic,
piñon nuts, basil, and spinach into pesto
sauce using a mortar and pestle. The
electric blender does a faster, better job.
Makes 4 servings

Sauce:

2 cloves garlic, peeled and crushed
⅓ cup piñon nuts
1¾ cups fresh basil leaves, minced
1 cup fresh spinach leaves, washed well
    and minced
1 cup olive oil
½ cup finely grated Parmesan cheese

Pasta:

1 pound thin spaghetti
¼ cup olive oil

Purée garlic, nuts, basil, and spinach
with ½ cup oil in an electric blender at
low speed. (Note: Because mixture is
thick, you'll have to stop blender often
and stir.) Pour purée into a small bowl
and add remaining oil, a little at a time,
beating well with a fork after each
addition; mix in cheese and let sauce
"mellow" at room temperature at least
1 hour. Cook spaghetti by package
directions, adding 1 tablespoon olive oil
to the cooking water; meanwhile, warm
remaining oil over low heat. When
spaghetti is al dente (just tender), drain
quickly and return to kettle; add hot oil
and toss well. To serve, divide spaghetti
among 4 plates and top each portion

with a generous ladling of pesto sauce. Set out more freshly grated Parmesan. About 1165 calories per serving (without additional Parmesan).

¢ **SPAGHETTI WITH WHITE CLAM SAUCE**

Makes 2–4 servings

Sauce:

2 cloves garlic, peeled and minced
¼ cup olive or other cooking oil
2 tablespoons flour
2 cups clam juice (use liquid drained from clams, rounding out measure as needed with bottled clam juice)
1½ cups finely chopped fresh clams or 2 (10½-ounce) cans minced clams, drained (save liquid)
1 tablespoon minced parsley
⅛ teaspoon pepper

Pasta:

½ pound thin spaghetti, cooked by package directions and drained
¼ cup coarsely chopped parsley (garnish)

Stir-fry garlic in oil in a saucepan about 1 minute over low heat; do not brown. Blend in flour, add clam juice, and heat, stirring constantly, until mixture thickens slightly; cover and simmer 10–15 minutes. Add clams, minced parsley, and pepper, cover, and simmer 3–5 minutes. Pour sauce over hot spaghetti and toss with 2 forks to mix well. Sprinkle with coarsely chopped parsley and serve. About 885 calories for each of 2 servings, 445 calories for each of 4 servings.

¢ **SPAGHETTI ALL'AMATRICIANA**

Spaghetti topped with a peppy salt-pork and tomato sauce.
Makes 4 servings

Sauce:

½ pound salt pork, trimmed of rind and cut in small dice
Salt pork drippings plus enough bacon drippings to total ¼ cup
1 small yellow onion, peeled and minced

1 clove garlic peeled and stuck on a toothpick
1 (1-pound 12-ounce) can Italian plum tomatoes (do not drain)
1 small chili pepper, cored, seeded, and minced (optional)

Pasta:

1 pound thin spaghetti, cooked and drained by package directions

Topping:

⅓ cup grated Romano cheese mixed with ⅓ cup grated Parmesan cheese
Freshly ground pepper

Brown salt pork 8–10 minutes in a large, heavy skillet over moderate heat; drain on paper toweling and reserve. In ¼ cup drippings, sauté onion 8–10 minutes until golden. Add remaining ingredients, breaking up tomatoes, and reserved salt pork and simmer, uncovered, ½ hour, stirring now and then. Discard garlic. Heap pasta in 4 large bowls, top with sauce, a generous sprinkling of cheese, and a grinding of pepper. Pass remaining cheese. About 1075 calories per serving.

⊠ **SPAGHETTI WITH BUTTER, CREAM, AND PARMESAN**

A refreshing change from potatoes. Also makes a nice light entree.
Makes 8 servings

½ cup butter (no substitute)
½ cup heavy cream
1 pound thin spaghetti, cooked and drained by package directions
½ cup grated Parmesan cheese
Salt and pepper to taste

Heat butter and cream in a small saucepan but do not boil. Mound pasta in a buttered warm large bowl, pour in cream, sprinkle with cheese, and toss thoroughly but lightly. Season to taste and serve. About 390 calories per serving.

VARIATIONS:

Spaghetti with Butter, Cream, Parmesan, and Piñon Nuts: Toss in ⅓ cup minced piñon nuts (or minced, blanched almonds) along with cream and cheese. About 425 calories per serving.

Spaghetti with Butter, Cream, Parmesan, and Truffles: Toss in 2–3 minced truffles along with cream and cheese. About 430 calories per serving.

Spaghetti with Butter, Cream, Parmesan, and Mushrooms: Toss in ½ cup minced, sautéed mushrooms along with cream and cheese. About 420 calories per serving.

Spaghetti with Herbs: Heat ½ teaspoon each basil and oregano along with butter and cream. Pour sauce over pasta; omit cheese but add 2 tablespoons each minced chives and parsley, and toss to mix. About 365 calories per serving.

SPAGHETTI CARBONARA

Spaghetti dressed with cream, cheese, bacon, and eggs.
Makes 4 servings

1 pound thin spaghetti
¼ cup bacon drippings
6 eggs, lightly beaten
½ teaspoon salt
⅛ teaspoon white pepper
¾ cup light cream
½ pound crisply cooked bacon, crumbled
½ cup finely grated Parmesan cheese

Cook spaghetti by package directions, timing carefully so it is done just as you begin cooking the eggs. The spaghetti must be *very hot* when the eggs are poured over it so they will cling and continue to cook a bit. Heat drippings in a large, heavy skillet over moderate heat 1–2 minutes. Mix eggs, salt, pepper, and cream, pour into drippings, cook and stir 2–3 minutes until eggs just *begin* to thicken—they should be creamy but *not set;* remove from heat. Quickly drain spaghetti and arrange on a heated platter, pour eggs on top and toss to mix. Sprinkle with bacon and Parmesan and toss again. Serve at once.

VARIATION:

Prepare as directed, substituting linguine, macaroni, or fusilli for the spaghetti.

Both versions: About 875 calories per serving.

⊠ NOODLES ALFREDO

If you prepare this recipe with homemade noodles, so much the better.
Makes 4 servings

1 pound hot thin or medium-wide
   noodles, cooked by package directions
1 pound unsalted butter, sliced ¼" thick
   and softened to room temperature
1 pound Parmesan cheese, grated fine

Quickly drain noodles and return to kettle. Add butter and cheese and toss lightly but rapidly until noodles are evenly coated. Serve on heated plates. About 1700 calories per serving.

VARIATION:

Creamed Noodles Alfredo (not as authentic but almost as good, and certainly less caloric): Toss hot drained noodles with 1 cup melted butter, 2 cups finely grated Parmesan cheese, and 1 cup warm heavy cream. About 1255 calories per serving.

¢ ⊠ LINGUINE ALLA ROMANA

Makes 4 servings

½ pound ricotta cheese
½ cup unsalted butter (no substitute)
1 pound linguine or spaghetti, cooked
   and drained by package directions
½ cup grated Parmesan cheese
½ teaspoon salt (about)
Freshly ground pepper

Mix ricotta and butter in a heavy saucepan and simmer, uncovered, over lowest heat 5–7 minutes, stirring now and then. Place linguine in 4 large bowls, top with sauce, sprinkle with cheese and salt and, finally, a grinding of pepper. Toss to mix and serve. About 755 calories per serving.

¢ FETTUCCINE AND FISH

Makes 4 servings

Sauce:

1 medium-size yellow onion, peeled, sliced thin, and separated into rings
1 medium-size sweet green or red pepper, cored, seeded, and minced
2 tablespoons olive or other cooking oil
1 (1-pound) can Italian plum tomatoes (do not drain)
2 tablespoons tomato paste
½ cup water
¾–1 pound haddock or any lean fish fillets, cut in 1" cubes
1 (2-ounce) can anchovy fillets, drained and minced (optional)

Pasta:

1 pound fettuccine; cooked and drained by package directions

Topping:

1 tablespoon minced fresh basil or parsley

Stir-fry onion and pepper in oil in a large skillet over moderate heat 3–5 minutes until limp. Add tomatoes, chopping as you add, tomato paste, and water; simmer, uncovered, 15 minutes. Scatter fish on top, cover, and simmer 10 minutes. Place pasta in a hot deep serving dish, top with sauce, and toss lightly. Sprinkle with basil and serve with grated Parmesan. (*Note:* If not using anchovies, taste for salt and adjust.) About 670 calories per serving.

VARIATION:

¢ **Fettuccine and Dried Salt Cod (Fettuccine con Baccalà):** Use ¾ pound filleted salt cod instead of haddock; soak in cold water to cover for 4 hours, drain, pat dry, and cube. Make sauce as directed, omitting anchovies. If you like, add ¼ cup each piñon nuts and sultana raisins just before pouring over pasta. About 645 calories per serving (without piñon nuts and raisins).

¢ BEEF AND SAUSAGE STUFFED RIGATONI OR TUFOLI

Makes 6 servings

½ pound rigatoni or tufoli, cooked by package directions until barely al dente, then drained and rinsed in cool water

Filling:

½ pound ground beef chuck
½ pound sweet or hot Italian sausages, removed from casings and minced
¼ pound mushrooms, wiped clean and minced
¾ cup hot Italian Tomato Sauce
⅓ cup diced mozzarella cheese

Topping:

2½ cups hot Italian Tomato Sauce
¼ cup grated Parmesan cheese

Preheat oven to 350° F. While rigatoni cool, prepare filling: Stir-fry beef and sausages in a large, heavy skillet over moderate heat 4–5 minutes until no longer pink; add mushrooms and stir-fry 2–3 minutes. Mix in sauce and simmer, uncovered, 5 minutes; cool slightly and stir in cheese. Using a small teaspoon, stuff into rigatoni; layer in an oiled 2½-quart casserole or *au gratin* dish, topping with some of the 2½ cups sauce as you go. Add remaining sauce, sprinkle with cheese, and bake uncovered 30 minutes until bubbly. About 520 calories per serving.

VARIATIONS:

Prepare as directed but substitute one of the following fillings for that above: Chicken and Prosciutto, Spinach and Ricotta, or Cheese Stuffing for Ravioli. About 320 calories per serving if made with Spinach and Ricotta Filling, 430 calories per serving if made with Chicken and Prosciutto Filling, and 525 calories per serving if made with Cheese Stuffing.

¢ MEAT-FILLED RAVIOLI

Ravioli, plump little pasta pillows stuffed with meat, eggs, vegetables, or cheese, can be made ahead, then baked in sauce just before serving. If you like, make a quantity and freeze *uncooked* (simply place 1 layer deep on foil-lined trays, roll up inside foil, and freeze until needed).

Makes 6 servings

½ *recipe Homemade Pasta Dough*

Filling:

1 pound beef chuck, ground twice
1 small yellow onion, peeled and minced
1 clove garlic, peeled and crushed
1 tablespoon olive or other cooking oil
2 tablespoons flour
¾ cup beef broth
¼ cup tomato paste
1 teaspoon salt
⅛ teaspoon pepper

Topping:

1 cup grated Parmesan cheese
3 cups hot Italian Tomato or Marinara Sauce

Prepare dough as directed and let rest while making filling. Stir-fry beef, onion, and garlic in oil in a saucepan over moderate heat 4–5 minutes until no longer pink; put through finest blade of meat grinder. Return to pan, set over moderate heat, sprinkle in flour, and slowly mix in remaining filling ingredients. Cook and stir until thickened, reduce heat, and simmer uncovered 5 minutes; cool to room temperature. Meanwhile, roll half of the dough on a lightly floured board into a paper thin 14″ square. Drop rounded teaspoonfuls of filling over dough, spacing 2″ apart in neat rows. Roll remaining dough into a square of the same size and lay over the first. Press lightly around mounds of filling, then cut in 2″ squares with a ravioli cutter or pastry wheel forming "pillows." (*Note:* If you have ravioli pans [trays with 12 depressions and sharp raised edges], lay 1 sheet of rolled dough on pan, drop filling into depressions, cover with second dough sheet, and roll with a rolling pin to separate squares. Make sure edges are sealed so filling won't ooze out.) Place ravioli 1 layer deep on a lightly floured tray, dust with flour, and let stand uncovered ½ hour; turn and let stand ½ hour longer. Bring about 5 quarts salted water to a boil in a large kettle (to keep ravioli from sticking, add 1 teaspoon cooking oil). Drop in about a dozen ravioli and cook 7–10 minutes, moving them around so they don't stick. Lift to a hot, buttered large platter with a slotted spoon, top with 2 tablespoons cheese and 3–4 tablespoons sauce, and keep warm. Continue cooking ravioli, adding to dish and topping with cheese and sauce. Serve very hot with remaining cheese and sauce. About 570 calories per serving.

VARIATIONS:

¢ **Mushroom, Eggplant, or Cheese Ravioli:** Prepare as directed but use Italian Mushroom-Eggplant or Italian Cheese Sauce instead of tomato sauce. About 585 calories per serving if made with Mushroom-Eggplant Sauce, 600 if made with Italian Cheese Sauce.

¢ **Sausage Stuffed Ravioli:** Prepare as directed but substitute ¾ pound sweet Italian sausages and ¼ pound salami, removed from casings and minced, for the beef. About 665 calories per serving.

Chicken and Prosciutto Stuffed Ravioli: Prepare as directed but use the following filling: 1 cup each ground cooked chicken and prosciutto ham mixed with 2 lightly beaten egg yolks, ⅛ teaspoon each nutmeg and pepper, and 2 tablespoons each melted butter and grated Parmesan cheese. About 545 calories per serving.

¢ **Spinach and Ricotta Stuffed Ravioli:** Prepare as directed but for the meat filling substitute: 1 cup each ricotta cheese and well-drained, puréed, cooked spinach mixed with 1 lightly beaten egg yolk and a pinch nutmeg. About 435 calories per serving.

¢ **Cheese Stuffed Ravioli:** Prepare as directed but fill with the following mixture: 1 pound ricotta cheese mixed with ½ cup grated Parmesan or mozzarella cheese, 1 lightly beaten egg,

1 teaspoon each minced parsley and basil, and ¾ teaspoon salt. Omit sauce and sprinkle layers with 2–3 tablespoons each melted butter and grated Parmesan. About 640 calories per serving.

¢ **LASAGNE**

Makes 8–10 servings

1 pound sweet Italian sausages
2 quarts (about) hot Savory Beef and
  Tomato Sauce for Pasta, or Marinara
  Sauce
1 pound lasagne, cooked and drained
  by package directions
1 pound ricotta cheese
⅔ cup finely grated Parmesan cheese
¾ pound mozzarella cheese, coarsely
  grated

Preheat oven to 350° F. Sauté sausages 15–20 minutes over moderate heat or until cooked through, drain on paper toweling, and slice ½″ thick. Spoon a thin layer of sauce into an ungreased 13″×9″×2″ baking pan and arrange a single layer of lasagne (about ¼ of the total) on top, slightly overlapping. Add another thin layer of sauce, top with ⅓ of the sausage and ricotta, and sprinkle with ¼ of the Parmesan and mozzarella. Continue building up layers until all ingredients are in the pan, ending with Parmesan and mozzarella. (*Note:* Recipe can be prepared to this point early in the day or days ahead. Cool, cover, and refrigerate or freeze until needed. Bring to room temperature before proceeding.) Bake, uncovered, 35–45 minutes until lightly browned and bubbling. Cut into squares and serve. If made with Savory Beef and Tomato Sauce, about 1115 calories for each of 8 servings, 890 for each of 10 servings. If made with Marinara Sauce, about 870 calories for each of 8 servings, 695 for each of 10.

VARIATION:

Meat Ball Lasagne: Prepare 1 recipe Savory Meat Balls as directed but omit the gravy. Simmer the meat balls 10–15 minutes in 2 quarts Marinara Sauce, then prepare the lasagne as above, substituting the meat balls, sliced ¼″ thick, for the Italian sausages. About 865 calories for each of 8 servings, 690 calories for each of 10 servings.

¢ **CANNELLONI OR MANICOTTI SQUARES**

Cannelloni and manicotti are large pasta squares (or, if bought, tubes). In this country the larger tube or square (usually 5″) is manicotti, the smaller (4″) one, cannelloni. Tufoli may be substituted for either.

Makes 1½ dozen 4″ squares

½ recipe Homemade Pasta Dough
5 quarts water
2 tablespoons salt
1 teaspoon cooking oil

Prepare and roll dough as directed; cut in 4″ squares, cover with cloth, and let dry 1 hour at room temperature. Bring water, salt, and oil to a boil in a large kettle and cook, uncovered, about 6 squares at a time, in rapidly boiling water 7–10 minutes until tender. Lift with a slotted spoon to a dampened dish towel. Squares are now ready to fill. About 60 calories per manicotti or cannelloni square.

¢ **CANNELLONI WITH MEAT FILLING**

Makes 6 servings

1 recipe Cannelloni Squares

Filling:

1 teaspoon cooking oil
1 pound ground beef chuck
2 tablespoons minced yellow onion
2 teaspoons salt
¼ teaspoon pepper
1 teaspoon savory
2 tablespoons flour
¾ cup beef consommé
Few drops liquid gravy browner

Sauce:

3 cups Italian Tomato Sauce or Marinara
  Sauce or canned meatless spaghetti
  sauce

Topping:

½ pound mozzarella cheese, coarsely grated

Prepare and cook cannelloni squares as recipe directs, then reserve. Preheat oven to 375° F. Brush a large skillet with oil and heat 1–2 minutes over moderately high heat. Add beef and brown well 4–5 minutes, stirring constantly. Add onion, salt, pepper, and savory. Sprinkle flour over beef, then slowly stir in consommé. Cook and stir until thickened; mix in gravy browner, reduce heat to low, cover, and simmer 15–20 minutes, stirring now and then. Remove from heat and cool 10 minutes. Drop 1½ tablespoons filling in center of each cannelloni square, fold bottom edge up over filling, then roll up jelly-roll style and arrange seam side down in a single layer in a buttered shallow 3-quart casserole. Cover with sauce, sprinkle with mozzarella, and bake uncovered 25–30 minutes until bubbling and lightly browned. (*Note:* If not brown enough, broil 4″ from heat 1–2 minutes.) About 585 calories per serving if made with Italian Tomato Sauce, 590 calories per serving if made with Marinara Sauce, and 520 calories per serving if made with canned meatless spaghetti sauce.

CANNELLONI ALLA NERONE

A classic chicken liver, chicken and ham stuffing rolled up in homemade cannelloni, but good, too, in Manicotti Pancakes or boiled tufoli.
Makes 6 servings

1 recipe Cannelloni Squares

Filling:

4 chicken livers, halved at the natural separation
1 tablespoon butter or margarine
2 small cooked chicken breasts, boned and skinned
4 slices prosciutto ham
½ cup grated Parmesan cheese
1½ pints hot Béchamel Sauce

Prepare and cook cannelloni squares as directed. Preheat oven to 375° F. For

the filling: Sauté chicken livers in butter 2–3 minutes over moderate heat, just until firm, then put through finest blade of meat grinder along with chicken and ham. Mix in ¼ cup cheese and ⅓ cup sauce, taste for salt and adjust. Place about 1½ tablespoons filling on each cannelloni square, roll up tightly, and arrange seam side down in a single layer in a buttered 3-quart shallow casserole. Sprinkle with remaining cheese and pour sauce over all. (*Note:* Recipe can be prepared to this point early in the day, covered, and chilled until ready to bake.) Bake, uncovered, about ½ hour until bubbling; if you like, brown lightly under broiler. About 625 calories per serving.

¢ CANNELLONI GARIBALDI

Cannelloni filled with sweet Italian sausages, chopped spinach, and grated Parmesan cheese.
Makes 6 servings

1 recipe Cannelloni Squares

Filling:

1 pound sweet Italian sausages
1 (10-ounce) package frozen chopped spinach, cooked by package directions but not seasoned
¼ cup finely grated Parmesan cheese
1 egg, lightly beaten

Sauce:

3 cups Mushroom Marinara Sauce

Topping:

¼ cup finely grated Parmesan cheese

Prepare and cook cannelloni squares as recipe directs, then reserve. Preheat oven to 375° F. Remove sausage meat from casings and brown in a large, heavy skillet over moderately low heat 10–15 minutes, stirring occasionally and breaking up large clumps with a spoon; transfer with a slotted spoon to a bowl. Drain spinach in a sieve, pressing out as much water as possible with a spoon. Add spinach, cheese, and egg to sausage and toss well to mix. Divide filling evenly among cannelloni squares, roll up, and arrange seam side down in a single layer in a buttered shallow 3-quart casserole. Spoon sauce evenly over all and top with cheese. Bake, uncovered, about 30 minutes until bubbling. About 625 calories per serving.

¢ BAKED MEATLESS "MANICOTTI"

A cheese-rich meat substitute. Makes 6 servings

Manicotti Pancakes:

2 eggs, lightly beaten
¾ cup milk
½ teaspoon salt
1 cup sifted flour

Filling:

1 pound ricotta cheese
3 tablespoons grated Parmesan cheese
2 tablespoons minced parsley
1 teaspoon salt
1 egg, lightly beaten

Topping:

1½ pints hot Marinara or Italian Tomato Sauce

Preheat oven to 350° F. For the pancakes, mix eggs, milk, and salt; slowly add flour and beat until smooth. Using 1 tablespoon batter for each pancake, drop onto a greased griddle set over moderate heat and spread into 4″ circles. Brown lightly, turn, and brown flip side. Lay most attractive side *down* on paper toweling while you cook the rest. Mix filling ingredients, spoon about 1½ tablespoons on center of each pancake, then fold top and bottom toward center, envelope fashion. Arrange seam side down in a buttered 13″×9½″×2″ baking pan and top with sauce. Bake, uncovered, ½ hour until bubbling. Serve hot with extra grated Parmesan. About 355 calories per serving if made with Italian Tomato Sauce (without extra Parmesan), 365 if made with Marinara Sauce.

VARIATION:

⚖ **Meatless Cannelloni:** Substitute 1 recipe Cannelloni Squares or ¾ pound packaged cannelloni or tufoli for Manicotti Pancakes. Cook, drain, and fill; top with sauce and bake as directed. About 285 calories per serving if made with Italian Tomato Sauce and Manicotti Pancakes, about 255 calories per serving if made with Italian Tomato Sauce and packaged cannelloni or tufoli. About 295 calories per serving if made with Marinara Sauce and Manicotti Pancakes, 265 calories per serving if made with Marinara Sauce and packaged cannelloni or tufoli.

CHICKEN AND MUSHROOM STUFFED MANICOTTI

1 recipe Manicotti Pancakes or Manicotti Squares

Filling:

½ pound mushrooms, wiped clean and minced (include stems)
2 tablespoons butter or margarine
2 cups cooked minced chicken (preferably white meat)
1 teaspoon grated lemon rind
½ teaspoon salt
⅛ teaspoon pepper

Sauce:

2 cups Thick White Sauce
1 cup heavy cream
⅓ cup grated Parmesan cheese

Prepare manicotti as directed. Preheat oven to 375° F. For the filling: Sauté mushrooms in butter over moderate heat 3–4 minutes until golden; off heat, mix in remaining ingredients. Mix sauce and cream and blend ⅓ cup into chicken mixture. Spoon about 1½ tablespoons filling on each manicotti, roll up, and arrange seam side down in a buttered 3-quart casserole. Sprinkle with cheese and top with remaining sauce. Bake, uncovered, ½ hour, then brown lightly under broiler. About 645 calories per serving.

CHAPTER 14

SAUCES, GRAVIES, AND BUTTERS

Sauce cookery is neither mysterious nor complicated if you consider that there are five, perhaps six, "mother" sauces from which most of the others descend: *White Sauce* (and its richer cousin Béchamel), *Velouté* (similar to White Sauce except that the liquid is light stock instead of milk), *Espagnole* (rich brown stock-based sauce), *Hollandaise* (cooked, egg-thickened sauce), *Mayonnaise* (an uncooked oil and egg emulsion), and *Vinaigrette* (oil and vinegar–it and mayonnaise are included in the salad chapter). No sauce is difficult to make (though some are tedious) and none requires more than learning a few basic techniques. The time required to prepare certain sauces may seem overlong. In some cases, slow simmering is needed to boil down liquids and concentrate flavors. In others, it is needed to give the sauce a particular finish or finesse.

In addition to the classic sauce families, there are a few orphan sauces that defy categorization: flavored butters, purées, barbecue sauces, sweet-sour sauces, not to mention the myriad sauce mixes crowding supermarket shelves and the jiffy sauces that can be made from canned soups. All sauces, however, the thick and the thin, the hot, the cold, the quick, and the classic, serve the same purpose: to enhance the food they accompany. They should never dominate, never inundate the food with which they are served.

Some Terms and Techniques of Sauce Making

Beurre Manié: Butter-flour mixture, pinched off, a bit at a time, or rolled into small balls and beaten into hot sauces to thicken them. A wire whisk is the best tool to use when adding *beurre manié*.

Beurre Noir: Literally "black butter"; but actually, butter heated to an even nut brown.

Beurres Composés: The French term for flavored butters.

Brunoise: Finely shredded or diced vegetables, poached in stock and used in making sauces. The most often used are leeks, onions, and carrots.

Caramel: Liquid melted sugar, used to color and flavor sauces. See soup chapter for recipe for Caramelized Sugar.

Clarified Butter: Melted butter, skimmed

of milk solids; it is clear and golden and much less likely to burn than unclarified butter. *To Make:* Melt butter over low heat, watching that it does not brown. Remove from heat and let stand 2–3 minutes until solids settle. Skim off clear liquid butter and discard sediment. (*Note:* ½ cup butter=about ⅓ cup clarified butter.)

Cream: To mix a white or light sauce with coarsely chopped or diced meat, fish, fowl, or vegetables. A good ratio: 1 cup sauce to 2 cups solids.

Deglaze: To scrape up browned bits in a pan in which meat, fowl, or fish has browned, usually by adding a small amount of liquid and bringing to a boil. These pan scrapings enrich the color and flavor of brown sauces and gravies.

Degrease: To remove grease. The easiest —but slowest—way is to chill a mixture until fat rises to the top and hardens so that it can be lifted off. Liquid fat may be skimmed off hot sauces, or, if quantity is small, blotted up with paper toweling.

Drawn Butter: The same as clarified butter.

Fond: The French word for stock used as a base for soups and sauces. *Fond blanc* is white stock, *fond brun,* brown stock.

Fumet: A concentrated stock used to give body to sauces.

Ghee: The East Indian version of clarified butter.

Glace de Viande: A meat glaze made by greatly reducing brown beef stock. It is used to color and flavor sauces and gravies. Commercial beef extract makes a good substitute.

Liaison: The French term for "thickener." The ways of thickening sauces are many, each requiring a different technique:

Starch Thickeners: Starches such as flour, cornstarch, or arrowroot, when heated in liquid, swell and coagulate, thickening the liquid. Whether the liquid thickens smoothly depends upon whether the

starch particles were kept separate during cooking. And that depends on the cook. Raw flour, cornstarch, or other powdery thickener tossed into a bubbling liquid will lump, but if blended first with fat or a small amount of cold liquid, then blended into the hot liquid and stirred until after thickening, each will produce a silky-smooth sauce. (*Note:* The easiest way to blend starch and cold liquid is with the fingers or, if there is slightly more liquid than starch, in a shaker jar. Not all starches have the same thickening power, not all produce the same results, i.e., some will make a sauce opaque, some translucent, and others sparklingly clear. Here's a quick table (opposite).

A Note about Flours: The new nonlumping "sauce" flours ensure satiny sauces, even for the haphazard cook who forgets to stir; but they are more expensive than conventional all-purpose flours.

Eggs as Thickeners: Egg yolks are more commonly used than whole eggs; they not only thicken a sauce but enrich its color and flavor as well. Generally speaking, it will take 2 egg yolks to make 1 cup liquid about the consistency of Medium White Sauce. The egg yolks should be beaten briskly with a fork, just until uniformly liquid, then blended with a little cold liquid or beaten hard with a small amount of a hot sauce before being added to that sauce. Otherwise, the eggs will curdle. For best results, cook and stir egg-thickened sauces over lowest heat (insulated by an asbestos flame-tamer) or in the top of a double boiler over *simmering,* not boiling, water. Cook and stir only until sauce is thickened (about the consistency of stirred custard) and no raw taste of egg remains. If, despite all care, a sauce should curdle, strain through a fine sieve or double thickness of cheesecloth. If mixture is thin, rethicken with egg, taking every precaution. If sauce is Hollandaise or one of its descendants, you can salvage by following directions in the Hollandaise recipe.

Thickener	Thickening Power	Use to Thicken	Special Techniques	Sauce Appearance
Flour	1 T. will slightly thicken 1 cup liquid (see White Sauce chart)	Gravies, sweet and savory sauces	Blend with an equal quantity fat or cold liquid before adding. Cook several minutes *after thickening* to remove raw taste.	Opaque
Brown Flour	½ that of flour	Gravies, brown sauces	Same as flour	Opaque

(*Note: To Make Brown Flour:* Heat and stir flour in a dry heavy skillet over low heat until a pale amber color.)

Thickener	Thickening Power	Use to Thicken	Special Techniques	Sauce Appearance
Cornstarch	Twice that of flour	Sweet-sour or sweet sauces	Same as flour. Do not cook more than 3 minutes or sauce may thin.	Almost transparent
Rice Flour (available in Oriental groceries)	1–1½ times that of flour	Sweet-sour or sweet sauces; also gravies	Same as flour	Translucent
Potato Flour or Starch (available in specialty shops)	2–2½ times that of flour	Gravies, savory sauces	Same as flour but do not boil or cook after thickening—the sauce will thin out.	Translucent
Arrowroot (available in specialty shops)	2–2½ times that of flour	Sweet sauces and glazes	Mix with equal amount of sugar or about twice as much cold liquid; do not boil or reheat—sauce will thin.	Sparkling, clear

Blood as a Thickener: Game sauces and gravies are sometimes thickened with blood. It should be absolutely fresh (mixing with a little vinegar helps keep it liquid), strained, then added to the sauce shortly before serving. Swirl it in slowly, as you would an egg yolk mixture, and cook and stir over low heat just until sauce thickens. Never boil a blood-thickened sauce or it will curdle.

Marinade: A spicy or piquant mixture in which food is soaked so that it absorbs some of the flavors.

Marinate: To soak in a marinade.

Mirepoix: A mixture of diced, sautéed vegetables (usually carrots, onions, shallots, celery) used as a base for sauces.

Paste: A blend of starch and cold liquid, usually 1 part starch to 2 parts liquid, used to thicken sauces.

Reduce: To boil a liquid uncovered so that it reduces in volume. The purpose is to thicken a sauce and concentrate the flavors.

Roux: A smooth blend of melted butter and flour used in thickening sauces. When the butter and flour are not browned, the roux is a *roux blanc* (white roux); when the roux is worked over low heat until pale tan it is a *roux blond,* and when it is browned still further, it becomes a *roux brun.*

Salpicon: Diced ingredients (vegetables, meats, fish, or a mixture) served in a sauce.

Skim: To scoop fat from the top of a sauce with a skimmer or large, flat spoon.

Thickener: See Liaison.

Some Tips for Making Better Sauces

– Use heavy, flat-bottom pans of enamel, tin-lined copper, stainless steel, porcelain, or flameproof glass. Aluminum is apt to turn white sauces gray and discolor those made with egg or vinegar.
– Use a comfortable wooden spoon for stirring or, if you prefer, a wire whisk.
– When making a thick or moderately thick sauce, keep burner heat low and stir often to prevent sauce from scorching (especially important if starch is the thickener).
– If doubling or tripling a sauce recipe, allow more cooking time so that sauce can thicken and mellow properly.
– To enrich color of gravies and brown sauces, add Caramelized Sugar or liquid gravy browner.
– To enrich flavor of gravies and brown sauces, add bouillon cubes, Glace de Viande, or beef extract.
– Taste sauces often as they cook, adjusting seasonings as needed. Remember that cold sauces can take more seasoning than hot ones—cold numbs the palate.
– To prevent a skin from forming on a sauce as it cools, place a circle of wax paper *flat on sauce.*
– To smooth out a lumpy sauce, strain. Whirling in an electric blender can turn a starch-thickened sauce gluey.

About Keeping and Holding Sauces

Egg- or starch-thickened sauces, as a rule, keep poorly. About 4–5 days in the refrigerator is a maximum. Place wax paper flat on surface of sauce, then add a cover so that sauce will not absorb refrigerator odors. *Health Tip:* Never try to hold these sauces at room (or more than room) temperature for more than 20–30 minutes. You invite food poisoning. And when making creamed dishes, do not mix the sauce and the minced foods until shortly before serving unless each is cooled separately, refrigerated, and reheated. At buffets, creamed foods should be kept bubbly-hot in chafing dishes, again to reduce the risk of food poisoning.

Acid sauces are less perishable, especially tomato or other puréed vegetable sauces. Properly refrigerated, they should keep well about 2 weeks.

About Freezing Sauces

Egg- and starch-thickened sauces do not freeze successfully. Many of the pasta sauces do, however, For details, see chapter on freezing.

WHITE SAUCES

⊠ BASIC WHITE SAUCE

Makes 1 cup

Melt fat in a small saucepan (not aluminum) over low heat and blend in flour to form a smooth paste. Gradually stir in milk and heat, stirring constantly, until thickened and smooth. (*Note:* Don't be alarmed if sauce seems to "curdle" as milk is added—it's merely the fat hardening on contact with the cold milk; sauce will soon smooth out.) Add seasonings, then let mellow about 5 minutes, stirring occasionally over lowest heat. (*Note:* If sauce must be held a short while—up to 20–25 minutes—transfer to the top of a double boiler, set over simmering water, and cover. To hold longer, remove from heat, place a circle of wax paper flat on sauce [to prevent a skin from forming], and cool to room temperature; refrigerate until needed.

Type	Fat (Butter, Margarine, or Drippings)	Flour	Milk	Seasonings	Use
Very thin	1 tablespoon	½ tablespoon	1 cup	¼ teaspoon salt, pinch pepper	For thickening thin cream soups
Thin	1 tablespoon	1 tablespoon	1 cup	¼ teaspoon salt, pinch pepper	For thickening standard cream soups
Medium	2 tablespoons	2 tablespoons	1 cup	¼ teaspoon salt, pinch pepper	As a base for sauces and creamed dishes
Thick	3 tablespoons	3 tablespoons	1 cup	¼ teaspoon salt, pinch pepper	For binding casserole ingredients
Very thick	¼ cup	¼ cup	1 cup	¼ teaspoon salt, pinch pepper	For binding croquettes

Reheat in the top of a double boiler. Calories for each 1 cup: About 275 for Very Thin White Sauce, 285 for Thin White Sauce, 410 for Medium White Sauce, 535 for Thick White Sauce, and 660 for Very Thick White Sauce.

VARIATIONS:

Parsley Sauce: To each cup Medium White Sauce, add 2 tablespoons minced parsley and let mellow, stirring, about 5 minutes. Good with fish, carrots, or beets. About 25 calories per tablespoon.

Mint Sauce: To each cup Medium White Sauce, add 1 tablespoon minced mint and let mellow, stirring, about 5 minutes. Good with boiled onions. About 25 calories per tablespoon.

Cheese Sauce: To each cup Medium White Sauce, add ¾–1 cup coarsely grated Cheddar, American, or Gruyère cheese, 1 teaspoon Worcestershire sauce, and a pinch each powdered mustard and cayenne. For a peppier sauce, increase mustard and cayenne slightly and add 1 teaspoon grated onion and ¼ minced clove garlic. Heat and stir sauce until cheese is melted and flavors blended. Thin, if needed, with a little milk. About 35 calories per tablespoon.

Quick Mushroom Sauce: To each cup Thick White Sauce, add 1 undrained (3-ounce) can sliced or chopped mushrooms; heat and stir 3–5 minutes to blend flavors. About 40 calories per tablespoon.

Mushroom Sauce: Begin 1 recipe Medium White Sauce as directed, but before blending in flour stir-fry 1 cup minced mushrooms in the butter 3–5 minutes. Blend in flour and proceed as directed. If you like, spike sauce with a little dry sherry or vermouth. About 30 calories per tablespoon.

Mushroom and Cheese Sauce: Begin 1 recipe Medium White Sauce as directed, but before blending in flour stir-fry 2 tablespoons minced yellow onion 3–5 minutes until limp; add ½ pound button mushrooms, cover, and simmer 7–8 minutes, stirring once or twice. Blend in flour, add 1 cup light cream or milk, ¾ cup coarsely grated sharp Cheddar cheese, and the seasonings called for. Heat and stir until thickened and smooth, then let mellow about 5 minutes longer over lowest heat, stirring occasionally. Good over boiled potatoes or summer squash. About 35 calories per tablespoon if made with milk, 50 calories per tablespoon if made with cream.

Mustard Sauce: Into each cup Medium White Sauce blend ¼ cup prepared mild yellow or spicy brown mustard and 1–2 teaspoons cider vinegar; let mellow over lowest heat 3–5 minutes before serving. Good with ham. About 30 calories per tablespoon.

Hot Mustard Sauce: Begin 1 recipe Medium White Sauce as directed but blend ½ teaspoon powdered mustard into butter along with flour. Proceed as for Mustard Sauce (above), adding 1 teaspoon Worcestershire sauce and 2 or 3 drops liquid hot red pepper seasoning. Good with ham. About 30 calories per tablespoon.

Chiffon Sauce: Prepare 1 recipe Medium White Sauce in the top of a double boiler, omitting pepper and reducing salt to ⅛ teaspoon; blend a little hot sauce into 1 lightly beaten egg yolk, return to pan, set over simmering water, and cook and stir 2–3 minutes. Place a circle of wax paper flat on sauce and cool 20–30 minutes. Beat 2 tablespoons tarragon vinegar into sauce in a slow steady stream. Whip 1 egg white to soft peaks and fold into sauce; cover and chill 1–2 hours. Good with cold shellfish. About 30 calories per tablespoon.

⊠ BEURRE MANIÉ

Makes about 3 tablespoons, enough to thicken slightly 1½ cups liquid

3 tablespoons butter, softened slightly
2 tablespoons flour

Blend butter and flour until smooth. Pinch off small pieces and add, 1 at a time, stirring constantly, to hot liquids, gravies, and sauces to thicken. About 120 calories per tablespoon.

BÉCHAMEL SAUCE

A French white sauce from which many other sauces descend. Depending upon the food to be sauced, make with part milk, part broth (chicken broth for meat or poultry, fish stock for seafood, vegetable cooking water for eggs, cheese, or vegetables).
Makes 1⅔ cups

4 tablespoons butter (no substitute)
¼ cup unsifted flour
2 cups milk or 1 cup each milk and chicken broth, Easy Fish Stock, or vegetable cooking water
½ teaspoon salt (about)
⅛ teaspoon white pepper
2 tablespoons minced yellow onion
2 ounces ground veal (use only if sauce is for meat or poultry)
1 small sprig fresh thyme or a pinch dried thyme
¼ bay leaf
Pinch nutmeg

Melt 3 tablespoons butter in a double boiler top over direct moderate heat; blend in flour, slowly add milk, and heat, stirring, until thickened. Mix in salt and pepper. Set over simmering water. Stir-fry onion in remaining butter 3–5 minutes over moderate heat until limp, add veal if sauce is for meat or poultry, and stir-fry until no longer pink; add to sauce along with remaining ingredients, cover and cook 1 hour over simmering water, beating now and then with a whisk and scraping bottom and sides of pan with a rubber spatula. (*Note:* Be careful when removing lid not to let water condensed there drop in sauce.) Strain sauce, taste for salt and adjust. Serve hot or use as a base for other sauces. From about 20 to 35 calories per tablespoon depending upon whether made with milk, a combination of milk and broth, and whether made with or without meat.

VARIATIONS:

Anchovy Sauce (Makes 1⅔ cups): Prepare Béchamel using milk and fish stock and omitting salt; before setting to simmer, blend in 4 teaspoons anchovy paste and a pinch cayenne. Proceed as above. Good with fish. About 30 calories per tablespoon.

Caper Sauce (Makes 2 cups): Prepare Béchamel using milk and fish stock and omitting salt; just before serving, mix in ⅓ cup coarsely chopped capers and 1 tablespoon lemon juice. Serve with fish. About 20 calories per tablespoon.

Caper and Horseradish Sauce (Makes 2 cups): Prepare Caper Sauce and mix in 2 tablespoons prepared horseradish. Good with boiled beef brisket. About 22 calories per tablespoon.

Hot Horseradish Sauce (Makes 2 cups): Prepare Béchamel, mix in ¼–⅓ cup drained prepared horseradish, ⅛ teaspoon powdered mustard blended with 2 tablespoons light cream, and heat 2–3 minutes. Good with corned or boiled beef. About 35 calories per tablespoon.

Mornay Sauce (Makes 2½ cups): (*Note:* This delicate cheese sauce can be used with seafood, poultry, eggs, or vegetables; let recipe decide which stock you use in making it.) Prepare Béchamel, add ½ cup of the same stock used in the Béchamel, and heat uncovered in the top of a double boiler until sauce reduces to 2 cups. Add ¼ cup each grated Parmesan and Gruyère and heat and stir until melted. Off heat, beat in 2 tablespoons butter, 1 teaspoon at a time. (*Note:* If Mornay is to be used for a gratiné, use half as much cheese and butter.) About 35 calories per tablespoon.

Nantua Sauce (Makes about 3 cups): Prepare Béchamel using milk and fish stock, mix in ⅓ cup heavy cream, and keep warm. Boil ¼–⅓ pound crayfish or shrimp in 1½ cups water with ½ teaspoon salt 3–5 minutes; shell, devein, and mince. Boil cooking liquid, uncovered, until reduced to ¼ cup; mix into sauce along with crayfish; add a pinch cayenne and, if you like, 1 tablespoon brandy. Off heat, beat in 2 tablespoons Shrimp Butter, 1 teaspoon at a time. Good with seafood or eggs. About 26 calories per tablespoon.

Soubise Sauce (Makes about 1 quart): Prepare Béchamel and keep warm. Meanwhile, simmer 4 coarsely chopped yellow onions, covered, with 1½ cups water (or a ½-and-½ mixture of water and chicken or beef broth) and 3 tablespoons butter about ¾ hour until mushy. Uncover and boil until liquid reduces to 1 cup. Purée onions and liquid at low speed in an electric blender or put through a food mill. Mix into sauce, season to taste with salt, pepper, and nutmeg. Good with poultry, fish, brains, and sweetbreads. About 20 calories per tablespoon.

VELOUTÉ SAUCE

If a velouté is used to sauce poultry, egg, or vegetable dishes, make with chicken broth; if to sauce meat, use veal stock; if seafood, fish stock.
Makes about 1⅔ cups

6 tablespoons butter (no substitute)
6 tablespoons flour
2 cups chicken broth, Veal (White) Stock or Easy Fish Stock
¼ teaspoon salt (about)
Pinch white pepper
2–3 tablespoons coarsely chopped mushrooms (optional)

Melt butter in a heavy saucepan over moderate heat. Blend in flour, gradually stir in broth, and heat, stirring constantly, until thickened and smooth. Add seasonings, mushrooms, if you like, reduce heat, and simmer uncovered ½ hour, stirring often and skimming light scum from sides of pan as it collects. Turn heat to lowest point, cover, and simmer ½ hour, stirring now and then. (*Note:* When uncovering sauce, don't let moisture on lid drop into sauce.) Strain sauce through a fine sieve and serve hot. About 30 calories per tablespoon (with or without mushrooms).

VARIATIONS:

⚔ **Allemande Sauce** (Makes 1 quart): Prepare Velouté with chicken broth and keep warm. Heat 2 cups chicken broth in the top of a double boiler and blend ½ cup into 4 lightly beaten egg yolks; return to pan, set over simmering water, and cook and stir 3–4 minutes until thickened and no raw egg taste remains. Blend in Velouté and, if you like, 3–4 teaspoons lemon juice. Strain and serve with chicken, fish, brains, or sweetbreads. About 18 calories per tablespoon.

⚔ **Poulette Sauce** (Makes 1 quart): Prepare Allemande Sauce, using lemon juice, and keep warm in double boiler. Meanwhile, boil 1½ cups chicken broth and ¼ pound minced mushrooms, uncovered, 20 minutes, stirring occasionally, until liquid is reduced to ½ cup. Strain liquid into Allemande Sauce and heat and stir 2–3 minutes. Mix in 2–3 tablespoons minced parsley and serve with vegetables, sweetbreads, or brains. About 15 calories per tablespoon.

Aurore Sauce (Makes 2 cups): Make Velouté with chicken broth or fish stock, blend in ½ cup tomato purée, cover, and simmer 5–7 minutes. Beat in 2 tablespoons butter, 1 teaspoon at a time. Taste and, if tart, add ¼ teaspoon sugar. Good over eggs, poultry, or sweetbreads. About 35 calories per tablespoon.

Bercy Sauce (Makes 2 cups): Make Velouté with fish stock and keep warm. Stir-fry 2 tablespoons minced shallots or scallions (white part) in 2 tablespoons butter over moderate heat 3–4 minutes until limp. Add ½ cup each dry white wine and fish stock and boil slowly, uncovered, until liquid reduces to ½ cup; mix into sauce along with 1 tablespoon minced parsley. Good with fish. About 35 calories per tablespoon.

Marinière Sauce (Makes 2½ cups): Begin Bercy Sauce as directed, using strained liquid from Steamed Mussels in the Velouté and in the wine-shallot mixture instead of fish stock. When wine-shallot mixture is reduced, blend into 2 lightly beaten egg yolks, mix into sauce, set over simmering water, and cook and stir 3–4 minutes until no raw egg taste remains. Beat in 2 tablespoons butter, 1 teaspoon at a time; add salt and pepper to taste, strain, mix in the parsley, and serve with seafood. About 28 calories per tablespoon.

Bontemps Sauce (Makes 3 cups): Prepare Velouté with chicken broth or veal stock and keep warm. Stir-fry 1 small minced yellow onion in 2 tablespoons butter 3–5 minutes until limp, add 2 cups apple cider, ¾ teaspoon salt, and ⅛ teaspoon

paprika, and boil slowly uncovered until reduced to 1 cup. Mix into Velouté, add 2 teaspoons Dijon mustard, and simmer uncovered 10 minutes. Beat in 2–3 tablespoons butter, 1 teaspoon at a time. Serve with broiled meat. About 29 calories per tablespoon.

Chivry Sauce (Makes 2 cups): Prepare Velouté with chicken broth or fish stock and keep warm. Boil 1 cup dry white wine, uncovered, with 1 tablespoon each minced fresh (or 1 teaspoon each dried) tarragon and chervil until reduced to ½ cup; strain liquid into sauce. Beat in 2 tablespoons Green Butter and 1 tablespoon Tarragon Butter, 1 teaspoon at a time. Serve with eggs or seafood. About 35 calories per tablespoon.

Egg Sauce (Makes 2 cups): Prepare Velouté with fish stock, mix in 2 minced hard-cooked eggs and, if you like, 1 teaspoon minced parsley. Serve with white fish. About 30 calories per tablespoon.

Indienne (Indian) Sauce (Makes 2 cups): Before beginning Velouté, stir-fry 1 minced large yellow onion, 1 minced stalk celery, and 2 tablespoons minced celery root in butter called for 5–8 minutes over moderate heat until limp. Blend in 2 teaspoons curry powder, the flour called for, and proceed with Velouté as directed, adding ¼ teaspoon thyme, ⅛ teaspoon mace and ½ bay leaf along with other seasonings. Strain sauce, mix in ½ cup heavy cream and 1 tablespoon lemon juice. Good with cold roast lamb. About 40 calories per tablespoon.

Lobster Sauce (Makes 2 cups): Prepare Velouté with fish stock, add 1 cup dry white wine, and simmer uncovered until sauce reduces to 2 cups; beat in, 1 teaspoon at a time, ¼ cup Lobster Butter or 1 tablespoon anchovy paste and 2 tablespoons butter. Mix in ⅓ cup minced cooked lobster and a pinch cayenne. Serve with seafood. About 43 calories per tablespoon.

Normande (Normandy) Sauce (Makes 2 cups): Prepare Velouté with fish stock and keep warm. Boil 1½ cups chicken broth, uncovered, with ¼ pound minced mushrooms until reduced to ½ cup, stirring occasionally; strain liquid into sauce, add ½ cup fish stock, and simmer uncovered about ½ hour until reduced to 2 cups. Lightly beat 2 egg yolks with ¼ cup heavy cream, blend in ⅓ cup hot sauce, return to pan, and cook and stir about 3 minutes over lowest heat until no raw egg taste remains; do not boil. Mix in a pinch cayenne. Good with fish, especially sole. About 39 calories per tablespoon.

Diplomate Sauce (Makes 2½ cups): Prepare Normande Sauce and pour into a double boiler top set over simmering water. Beat in ¼ cup Lobster Butter, 1 tablespoon at a time. Mix in ¼ cup minced cooked lobster, 2 tablespoons brandy, and, if you like, 2 tablespoons minced truffles. Good over white fish. About 43 calories per tablespoon.

Joinville Sauce (Makes 2½ cups): Prepare Normande Sauce and pour into a double boiler top set over simmering water. Beat in ¼ cup each Lobster Butter and Shrimp Butter, 1 tablespoon at a time. Good with fish. About 43 calories per tablespoon.

Oyster Sauce (Makes about 3 cups): Prepare Normande Sauce and keep warm in a double boiler top set over simmering water. Poach ½ pint small shucked oysters in their liquor over moderately low heat 3–4 minutes until edges ruffle; remove and reserve oysters; boil liquor, uncovered, until reduced to ¼ cup, strain through a cheesecloth-lined sieve, mix into sauce, and heat 2–3 minutes. Mix in oysters and serve with white fish fillets. About 30 calories per tablespoon.

Ravigote Sauce (Makes 2 cups): Prepare Velouté (use mushrooms) and keep warm. Boil ¼ cup each dry white wine and white wine vinegar, uncovered, with 1 teaspoon each minced fresh (or ¼ teaspoon each dried) tarragon and chervil, 1 tablespoon each minced chives and shallots or scallions, and 1 parsley sprig until reduced to ⅓ cup; strain

liquid into sauce. Blend in ¼ cup heavy cream and a pinch cayenne pepper. Good with seafood. About 39 calories per tablespoon.

Suprême Sauce (Makes 3 cups): Prepare Velouté, using chicken broth, and keep warm. Boil 1½ cups chicken broth and ¼ pound minced mushrooms, uncovered, about 20 minutes until liquid reduces to ½ cup; strain liquid into sauce and simmer, uncovered, ½ hour, skimming scum from pan's sides as it collects. Slowly blend in 1 cup heavy cream, then serve with poultry, sweetbreads, or brains. About 37 calories per tablespoon.

Albuféra Sauce (Makes 3 cups): Prepare Suprême Sauce (above) using no salt in the Velouté, mix in ⅓ cup Glace de Viande or 2 teaspoons beef extract, then beat in 3 tablespoons Pimiento Butter, 1 tablespoon at a time. Good with sweetbreads or brains. About 44 calories per tablespoon.

Talleyrand Sauce (Makes about 3½ cups): Prepare Velouté with chicken broth, mix in 2 cups chicken broth, and simmer uncovered until sauce reduces to 2 cups. Turn heat to low, mix in ½ cup each heavy cream and dry Madeira; beat in 2 tablespoons butter, one at a time, then strain sauce. Mix in 2 tablespoons each minced truffles, pickled tongue, and 1 tablespoon each butter-sautéed minced onion, celery, and carrot seasoned with a pinch of thyme. About 32 calories per tablespoon.

✕ ITALIAN CHEESE SAUCE

In Italy, cheese sauce is made with any available cheese and sometimes with a mixture of them. Try ½ cup Parmesan mixed with ¼ cup finely grated, aged provolone or Romano. Serve over pasta, accompanied, if you like, by separate bowls of grated Parmesan and minced Italian parsley.
Makes about 2½ cups, enough for 4 servings

¼ cup butter or margarine
2 tablespoons flour
1 cup milk
1 cup light cream
1 clove garlic, peeled, bruised, and stuck
   on a toothpick
¾ cup finely grated Parmesan cheese
Freshly ground black pepper

Melt butter in a saucepan over moderate heat, blend in flour, slowly stir in milk and cream, add garlic, and heat, stirring constantly, until thickened. Turn heat to low, add cheese, a little at a time, and heat, stirring, until melted. Partially cover and simmer 2–3 minutes. Remove garlic, add a grating of pepper, and serve hot over pasta. (*Note:* If well-aged cheese is used, no salt is needed in this sauce.) About 35 calories per tablespoon. About 355 calories for each of 4 servings.

LIGHT CURRY SAUCE

Makes 2 cups

2 medium-size yellow onions, peeled
   and minced
1 stalk celery, minced
1 clove garlic, peeled and crushed
   (optional)
¼ cup butter or margarine
1 tablespoon curry powder
¼ cup unsifted flour
2 cups chicken broth, Veal (White)
   Stock, or water
1 teaspoon salt
⅛ teaspoon black pepper
Pinch cayenne pepper

Stir-fry onions, celery, and, if you like, garlic in butter in a saucepan over moderate heat 5–8 minutes until limp, not brown. Add curry powder and stir-fry 1 minute. Blend in flour, slowly add broth, salt, pepper, and cayenne pepper, and heat, stirring, until thickened. Cover and simmer ½ hour, stirring now and then.

VARIATION:

Brown Curry Sauce: Prepare as directed but brown flour in the fat. Sub-stitute beef broth for chicken broth, also stir in 1 tablespoon each tomato paste and lemon juice and ⅛ teaspoon crushed dried hot red chili peppers.

Both versions: About 21 calories per tablespoon.

⚖ LEMON SAUCE

Serve with veal loaf or fish.
Makes 2 cups

2 cups Veal (White) Stock, chicken
   broth, or Easy Fish Stock (depending
   upon dish to be sauced)
2 tablespoons cornstarch mixed with 2
   tablespoons cold water
¼ cup butter
1 egg yolk, lightly beaten with 1
   tablespoon cold water
3 tablespoons lemon juice
Salt
White pepper
1 teaspoon minced parsley (optional)

Heat stock, mix in cornstarch, and cook, stirring constantly, until thickened. Add butter and beat to blend. Reduce heat, cover, and simmer 2–3 minutes. Blend a little hot sauce into egg yolk, return to pan, and heat and stir 1–2 minutes; do not boil. Off heat, mix in remaining ingredients, adding salt and pepper to taste. About 18 calories per tablespoon.

▨ SHRIMP SAUCE

Makes about 2 cups

2 tablespoons butter or margarine
2 tablespoons flour
1 cup milk or light cream
2 teaspoons tomato paste
½ teaspoon salt
⅛ teaspoon paprika
1 cup coarsely chopped cooked shrimp
2 tablespoons dry sherry (optional)

Melt butter in a saucepan over low heat, blend in flour, gradually stir in milk and heat, stirring constantly, until thickened and smooth. Mix in remaining ingredients and cook and stir about 5 minutes to blend flavors. Serve hot as a sauce for poached, baked, or broiled white fish, for seafood soufflés or mousses. About 18 calories per tablespoon if made with milk, 29 calories per tablespoon if made with cream.

CHAUD-FROID SAUCE

Chaud-froid sauce is used to glaze cooked foods that are served cold, usually whole chickens, small game birds, or chicken breasts.
Makes about 2 cups

3 tablespoons butter or margarine
3 tablespoons flour
2 cups clear chicken broth
1 envelope unflavored gelatin
1 egg yolk, lightly beaten with ¼ cup
  heavy cream
Salt
White pepper

Melt butter over moderate heat, blend in flour, gradually stir in 1½ cups chicken broth, and heat, stirring constantly, until thickened. Mix gelatin and remaining broth, add to sauce, and stir until dissolved. Reduce heat, cover, and simmer 3–4 minutes. Blend a little hot sauce into egg yolk, return to pan, and cook and stir 1–2 minutes; do not boil. Season to taste with salt and pepper, bearing in mind that cold sauces need slightly more seasoning. Place a circle of wax paper flat on sauce and cool to room temperature. Uncover, stir well, and chill until sauce coats the back of a metal spoon thickly but is still of pouring consistency. Use as recipes direct. (*Note:* If sauce becomes too thick, set over a bowl of hot water and stir until sauce thins.) About 23 calories per tablespoon.

VARIATION:

Omit butter, flour, and broth; use instead 1 recipe hot Velouté Sauce and proceed as directed, adding gelatin, egg yolk mixture, and salt and pepper to season. About 33 calories per tablespoon.

BROWN SAUCES AND GRAVIES

⊿⊳ ⊠ PAN GRAVY

While a roast "rests," make gravy of your choice.
Makes about 2 cups

¼ cup roasting pan drippings (round out
  amount as needed with bacon
  drippings or butter)
2 cups hot water, vegetable cooking
  water, or beef broth or any
  combination of the 3
¼ cup unsifted flour
Liquid gravy browner (optional)
Salt
Pepper

Drain drippings from roasting pan and reserve ¼ cup. Pour water into roasting pan and stir, scraping up browned bits (heat, if necessary, to loosen bits). Pour drippings into a large skillet, blend in flour, and cook and stir over moderate heat until light brown. Add water mixture and heat, stirring, until thickened; reduce heat and simmer 3–5 minutes. Add gravy browner to color, if you like, salt and pepper to taste. For a silken gravy, strain through a fine sieve. About 16 calories per tablespoon.

For Thin Gravy: Reduce flour to 2 tablespoons. About 14 calories per tablespoon.

For Thick Gravy: Increase flour to 5–6 tablespoons. About 18 calories per tablespoon.

For Stronger Flavor: Dissolve 1 or 2 beef bouillon cubes in the hot water.

For Extra-Large Roasts: Double the recipe. About 16 calories per tablespoon.

VARIATIONS:

⊠ ⊿⊳ **Au Jus Gravy:** Drain all but 1 tablespoon clear drippings from roasting pan, add water, and heat and stir, scraping up browned bits, 2–3 minutes until slightly reduced. If you like, add a touch of gravy browner and/or dry red wine. Season to taste and ladle over each portion. About 3 calories per tablespoon.

⚖ ☒ **Chicken (or Turkey) Gravy:** Prepare as directed using Chicken or Turkey Broth. (*Note:* If turkey is a big one, double the recipe.) About 17 calories per tablespoon.

☒ **Chicken (or Turkey) Cream Gravy:** Prepare as directed using 1½ cups Chicken or Turkey Broth and ½ cup light cream. About 25 calories per tablespoon.

⚖ ☒ **Giblet Gravy:** Prepare as directed using Giblet Stock. Mix in minced cooked giblets and neck meat just before serving. About 17 calories per tablespoon.

⚖ ☒ **Herb Gravy:** Prepare as directed, warming any of the following herbs in drippings before blending in flour: ½ teaspoon savory, thyme, or marjoram (good with beef), 1 teaspoon tarragon or mint, or ¼ teaspoon rosemary (lamb or veal), ½ teaspoon sage and/or thyme (pork or poultry). About 16 calories per tablespoon.

⚖ **Jus Lié:** Drain all drippings from roasting pan; pour 2 cups hot Veal (White) Stock or chicken broth into pan and heat, stirring, to scrape up browned bits. Stir in 2 tablespoons cornstarch blended with 2 tablespoons cold water and heat and stir until thickened and clear. Season to taste. Good with veal and chicken. About 4 calories per tablespoon.

☒ **Milk Gravy:** Prepare Pan Gravy as directed but use 1 cup each milk and broth. Add no gravy browner. Especially good with poultry. About 21 calories per tablespoon.

Mushroom Gravy: Prepare Pan Gravy and mix in ½ pound thinly sliced mushrooms and 1 minced yellow onion that have been sautéed 3–5 minutes in 2 tablespoons butter. Cover and simmer 4–5 minutes; taste for seasoning and

adjust as needed. About 25 calories per tablespoon.

⚖ **Onion Gravy:** Stir-fry 2 thinly sliced medium-size yellow onions in pan drippings 8–10 minutes over moderate heat until golden, blend in flour, and proceed as Pan Gravy recipe directs. About 18 calories per tablespoon.

⚖ ☒ **Quick Mushroom Gravy:** Drain all drippings from roasting pan; pour 1 cup beef broth and 1 (10½-ounce) can condensed cream of mushroom soup into pan and heat and stir about 5 minutes, scraping up browned bits. Mix in 1 (4-ounce) can drained mushroom stems and pieces and 1 teaspoon Worcestershire sauce. About 13 calories per tablespoon.

☒ **Sour Cream Gravy** (Makes 2½ cups): Prepare Pan Gravy as directed, smooth in 1 cup sour cream, and adjust seasonings as needed. Heat briefly but do not allow to boil. About 25 calories per tablespoon.

⚖ ☒ **Wine Gravy:** Make Pan Gravy using 1 cup each dry red wine and beef broth (for beef), 1 cup each rosé and water (for lamb or veal), or 1 cup each dry white wine and chicken broth (for poultry). About 18 calories per tablespoon.

⚖ ☒ MADEIRA-MUSHROOM SAUCE
Makes about 1¾ cups

2 tablespoons butter or margarine
½ pound button mushrooms, wiped clean and halved
4 teaspoons flour
1 cup condensed beef broth
1 teaspoon Worcestershire sauce
1 tablespoon minced chives
3 tablespoons sweet Madeira wine

Melt butter in a heavy skillet over moderately high heat, add mushrooms, and sauté 3–4 minutes until golden. Push to side of pan, blend in flour, slowly stir in broth and cook, and stir until thickened. Add remaining ingredients and cook and stir 3–5 minutes.

Serve with steaks, London Broil, or sautéed kidneys. About 15 calories per tablespoon.

ESPAGNOLE SAUCE

Serve with broiled meats, poultry, or fish or use as a base for the variations that follow. Makes about 2⅔ cups

4 slices bacon, minced
1 medium-size yellow onion, peeled and
  minced
1 medium-size carrot, peeled and minced
1 stalk celery, minced
6 tablespoons butter (no substitute)
6 tablespoons flour
5 cups beef broth or Easy Fish Stock
  (depending upon whether sauce is for
  meat or seafood)
Pinch minced fresh or dried thyme
½ bay leaf
¼ cup tomato purée

Stir-fry bacon over moderate heat 3–4 minutes until crisp; drain on paper toweling. Sauté onion, carrot, and celery in drippings 8–10 minutes until golden; drain on paper toweling. Melt butter in a saucepan over moderate heat, blend in flour, then cook and stir 1–2 minutes until lightly browned. Gradually mix in broth and cook, stirring constantly, until slightly thickened. Add bacon, sautéed vegetables, and herbs. Reduce heat and boil, uncovered, very slowly ½ hour, skimming light scum from pan sides as it collects. Strain sauce through a fine sieve into a clean saucepan, pressing vegetables lightly to extract juices. Mix in tomato purée, set lid on askew, and simmer 20–30 minutes until sauce coats a metal spoon. Skim or blot off any fat, then serve hot. About 28 calories per tablespoon.

VARIATIONS:

Bigarade (Orange) Sauce (Makes about 1 quart): Prepare Espagnole with beef broth and keep warm. Add 1 cup dry white wine to pan drippings from roast duck or goose, heat, and stir, scraping up brown bits, then boil uncovered until reduced to ½ cup. Strain, skim off fat, and mix into sauce along with 1 cup

orange juice and 1 tablespoon lemon juice. Boil ½ cup sugar and ½ cup water 15 minutes until amber colored and blend into sauce. Also boil finely slivered rind (orange part only) of 4 oranges in 1 cup water 3–4 minutes; drain rind, then add rind to sauce. If you like, add 2 tablespoons curaçao. Serve with roast duck or goose. About 29 calories per tablespoon.

Diable Sauce (Makes about 3½ cups): Prepare Espagnole with beef broth and keep warm. Boil 1 cup red or white wine vinegar, uncovered, with 2 tablespoons minced shallots or scallions until reduced to ½ cup. Mix into sauce along with 2 tablespoons each Worcestershire and tomato purée and ¼ teaspoon cayenne. Good with broiled poultry, also sweetbreads, brains, and tongue. About 23 calories per tablespoon.

Piquante Sauce: (Makes about 1 quart): Prepare Diable and mix in ¼ cup minced gherkins and 2 tablespoons minced parsley. Good with liver, tongue, and tripe. About 20 calories per tablespoon.

Poivrade (Pepper) Sauce (Makes about 3½ cups): Prepare Espagnole with beef broth and keep warm. Boil ¾ cup dry white wine with ¾ cup white wine vinegar until reduced by half; mix into sauce along with 6–8 crushed peppercorns, ½ bay leaf, and a pinch fresh or dried thyme. Cover and simmer 5 minutes, strain through a cheesecloth-lined sieve, and serve with broiled steaks or chops. About 21 calories per tablespoon.

Chevreuil (Roebuck) Sauce (Makes about 1 quart): Prepare Poivrade, add ½ cup dry red wine and a good pinch cayenne; simmer, uncovered, 10 minutes. Good with meat and game. About 19 calories per tablespoon.

Grand Veneur Sauce (Makes about 1 quart): Prepare Poivrade, stir in ¾ cup gooseberry jelly or strained gooseberry jam, and simmer uncovered 10 minutes. If you like, mix in ⅓ cup heavy cream.

Serve with venison. About 36 calories per tablespoon without heavy cream, 41 calories per tablespoon with heavy cream.

Réforme (Reform) Sauce (Makes about 1 quart): Prepare Poivrade and keep warm. Sauté ¼ pound minced mushrooms in 2 tablespoons butter 3–4 minutes, then add to sauce along with ¼ cup diced cooked smoked tongue, 2 tablespoons minced gherkins, and 2 minced truffles. Simmer, uncovered, 5 minutes, mix in 2 minced hard-cooked egg whites, and serve with lamb or mutton chops. About 25 calories per tablespoon.

Rich Brown Sauce (Demi-Glace): See separate recipe that follows.

Victoria Sauce (Makes about 1 quart): Prepare Espagnole with beef broth, add 1½ cups tawny port wine, ⅓ cup red currant jelly, 3 cloves, ¼ teaspoon pepper, and 2 tablespoons finely grated orange rind. Boil slowly, uncovered, stirring now and then, until reduced to about 3½ cups. Remove cloves, mix in ⅓ cup orange juice and ⅛ teaspoon cayenne. Serve with roast poultry, game, or game birds. About 27 calories per tablespoon.

Yorkshire Sauce (Makes about 3 cups): Prepare ½ recipe Espagnole and keep warm. Simmer 2 cups tawny port wine, uncovered, with 2 tablespoons finely slivered orange rind 10 minutes; mix into sauce along with 2 tablespoons red currant jelly, ¼ cup orange juice, and a good pinch cinnamon and cayenne pepper. Simmer, uncovered, 5 minutes. Good with ham or roast duck. About 26 calories per tablespoon.

RICH BROWN SAUCE (DEMI-GLACE, OR HALF GLAZE)

Makes 3¼ cups

1 recipe Espagnole Sauce
1 cup beef broth or Easy Fish Stock
(depending upon whether sauce is to be used with meat or fish)
¼ cup dry Madeira or sherry

Mix Espagnole and broth and boil slowly, uncovered, until reduced to 3 cups (sauce should coat a metal spoon). Mix in wine and serve or use as a base for other sauces. About 25 calories per tablespoon.

VARIATIONS:

Bordelaise Sauce (Makes about 1 quart): Prepare Rich Brown Sauce and keep warm. Boil 2 cups dry red wine, uncovered, with 2 tablespoons minced shallots or scallions, a small sprig fresh thyme (or ¼ teaspoon dried thyme), and 1 small bay leaf until reduced to 1⅓ cups. Strain wine into sauce and simmer, uncovered, until reduced to 1 quart. Mix in ½ cup minced marrow from Marrowbones and 1 tablespoon minced parsley. Adjust salt, if needed, and serve with broiled or roasted meat, poultry, or game. About 25 calories per tablespoon.

Rouennaise Sauce (Makes 1 cup): Mince 1 raw duck liver (or 2 chicken livers) and mix with 1 cup Bordelaise. Add a pinch allspice and simmer, uncovered, ½ hour. Strain and serve with duck. About 31 calories per tablespoon.

Bourguignonne (Burgundy) Sauce (Makes about 1 quart): Prepare Rich Brown Sauce and keep warm. Stir-fry ¼ cup minced yellow onion in 2 tablespoons butter 3–5 minutes over moderate heat until limp, add 3 cups red Burgundy and 1 *bouquet garni** tied in cheesecloth and boil, uncovered, until reduced by half. Stir into sauce, reduce to about 1 quart, strain, season to taste with salt and pepper, and serve with roasts, steaks, chops, or fish. (*Note:* For extra flavor, reduce wine in pan meat was cooked in.) About 30 calories per tablespoon.

Brown Sauce Fines Herbes (Makes 1 cup): Mix 1 cup Rich Brown Sauce with ¼ teaspoon lemon juice and 1 tablespoon each minced fresh (or 1 teaspoon each dried) parsley, tarragon, and chervil; let stand about a minute to blend flavors. Serve with broiled meats or poultry, baked or poached fish. About 25 calories per tablespoon.

Charcutière Sauce (Makes about 1 quart): Prepare Rich Brown Sauce with beef broth and keep warm. Stir-fry ⅓ cup minced yellow onion in 2 tablespoons butter 5–8 minutes over moderate heat until pale golden; mix into sauce along with ⅓ cup minced gherkins and serve with pork. About 24 calories per tablespoon.

Chasseur Sauce (Makes about 3 cups): Prepare ½ recipe Rich Brown Sauce with beef broth and keep warm. Sauté ½ pound minced mushrooms in 2 tablespoons each olive oil and butter over moderate heat 2–3 minutes until pale golden; add 2 tablespoons minced shallots and sauté 2 minutes. Add 1 cup dry white wine and boil until reduced by half. Mix into sauce along with 1 cup hot Tomato Sauce and 1 tablespoon each minced fresh (or 1 teaspoon each dried) parsley, tarragon, and chervil. Adjust salt as needed and serve with roasts, steaks or chops, poultry or game. About 26 calories per tablespoon.

Chateaubriand Sauce (Makes about 1 quart): Prepare Rich Brown Sauce with beef broth and keep warm. Boil 2 cups dry white wine with 2 tablespoons minced shallots or scallions, a small sprig fresh thyme (or ¼ teaspoon dried thyme), and ½ bay leaf until reduced to 1⅓ cups; strain into sauce and boil until reduced to 1 quart. Stir in 2 tablespoons minced fresh (or 1½ teaspoons dried) tarragon, 1 tablespoon lemon juice, ¼ teaspoon salt, and ⅛ teaspoon cayenne. Serve with chateaubriand or other broiled steak. About 19 calories per tablespoon.

Duxelles Sauce (Makes about 5 cups): Prepare Rich Brown Sauce and keep warm. Sauté ½ pound minced mushrooms, 1 minced small yellow onion, and 2 minced shallots or scallions in 3 tablespoons butter 5 minutes over moderate heat until limp; add 1 cup dry white wine, ½ teaspoon salt, and ⅛ teaspoon each pepper and nutmeg and boil, uncovered, until liquid is reduced to ½ cup. Stir into sauce along with 1 cup tomato purée and 2 tablespoons minced parsley and simmer 5 minutes.

Good with meat or game fish. About 22 calories per tablespoon.

Italienne (Italian) Sauce (Makes about 5 cups): Prepare Duxelles, mix in ⅓ cup minced lean cooked ham and 2 tablespoons each minced fresh (or 2 teaspoons each dried) tarragon and chervil. Serve with brains, sweetbreads, or liver. About 24 calories per tablespoon.

Lyonnaise Sauce (Makes about 3½ cups): Prepare Rich Brown Sauce with beef broth and keep warm. Stir-fry 2 minced large yellow onions in 2 tablespoons butter 8–10 minutes over moderate heat until golden. Stir into sauce along with ⅓ cup dry white wine, 3 tablespoons white or red wine vinegar, and, if you like, 2 tablespoons tomato paste. Simmer, uncovered, ½ hour. Serve with steaks and chops. About 28 calories per tablespoon.

Madeira Sauce (Makes 1¼ cups): Simmer 1 cup Rich Brown Sauce with ¼ cup dry Madeira wine 2–3 minutes. Good with broiled poultry or steaks, ham, sweetbreads, brains, heart, or kidneys. About 28 calories per tablespoon.

Financière Sauce (Makes 1¼ cups): Prepare Madeira Sauce and mix in 2 tablespoons minced truffles. Serve with sweetbreads or brains. About 28 calories per tablespoon.

Port Wine Sauce (Makes 1¼ cups): Prepare like Madeira Sauce but use tawny port wine instead of Madeira. Good with ham. About 28 calories per tablespoon.

Raisin Sauce (Makes 1½ cups): Prepare Madeira or Port Wine Sauce as directed and mix in ¼–⅓ cup seedless raisins; simmer slowly about 10 minutes to plump raisins. Good with ham and tongue. About 35 calories per tablespoon.

Marchands de Vin Sauce (Makes about 1 quart): Prepare Rich Brown Sauce with beef broth and keep warm. Stir-fry 2 minced bunches scallions (white part) and ½ pound minced mushrooms in ⅓ cup butter 3–4 minutes over moderate heat; add 1½ cups dry red wine and boil, uncovered, until reduced by half. Stir into sauce along with 1 tablespoon lemon juice. Good with steaks. About 31 calories per tablespoon.

Périgueux Sauce (Makes 1 cup): Mix 2 tablespoons minced truffles into 1 cup Rich Brown Sauce. Good with steak, game, and game birds. About 25 calories per tablespoon.

Périgourdine Sauce (Makes 1 cup): Mix 2 thinly sliced truffles into 1 cup Rich Brown Sauce. Good with steak, game, and game birds. About 25 calories per tablespoon.

Régence (Regency) Sauce (Makes about 1 quart): Prepare Rich Brown Sauce with beef broth and keep warm. Stir-fry 1 cup minced lean cooked ham and 2 peeled and quartered yellow onions in 2 tablespoons butter 5 minutes over moderate heat until onions are pale golden. Add 1 cup chicken broth and ½ cup dry white wine, cover, and simmer until onions are mushy, about ¾ hour. Uncover and boil until liquid reduces to about 1 cup, then purée at low speed in an electric blender or put through a food mill. Mix into sauce and simmer 5 minutes. Good with brains and sweetbreads. About 29 calories per tablespoon.

Robert Sauce (Makes about 1 quart): Prepare Rich Brown Sauce with beef broth and keep warm. Sauté 1 minced large yellow onion in 2 tablespoons butter 5–8 minutes over moderate heat until pale golden, add 1 cup dry white wine and boil, uncovered, until reduced to ½ cup. Stir into sauce along with ¼ teaspoon sugar and 1½ teaspoons powdered mustard blended with 1 teaspoon cold water. Simmer, uncovered, 20 minutes and serve with pork or ham, veal chops, sweetbreads, or brains. About 24 calories per tablespoon.

Romaine Sauce (Makes about 1 quart): Prepare Rich Brown Sauce with beef broth and keep warm. Boil ¼ cup sugar with ¼ cup water, uncovered, 8–10

minutes until amber colored. Off heat, stir in 2 tablespoons white wine vinegar and ½ cup chicken broth; boil until reduced to ½ cup, add ¼ cup toasted piñon nuts and 2 tablespoons each dried currants and seedless raisins, cover, and simmer 10 minutes. Stir into sauce and serve with game, lamb chops, or steaks. About 28 calories per tablespoon.

Tarragon Sauce (Makes about 3½ cups): Prepare Rich Brown Sauce with beef broth and keep warm. Boil 1 cup dry white wine, uncovered, with 3 tablespoons minced fresh (or 2 teaspoons dried) tarragon until reduced to ¼ cup. Mix into sauce, simmer uncovered 5 minutes, then strain and mix in 1–2 tablespoons minced fresh tarragon. Good with roast veal. About 25 calories per tablespoon.

Tortue Sauce (Makes about 1 quart): Prepare Rich Brown Sauce with beef broth and keep warm. Simmer 1 cup dry white wine, uncovered, with 2 sprigs fresh thyme (or ¼ teaspoon dried thyme), ½ bay leaf, 1 sprig each parsley, fresh sage, and rosemary (or ¼ teaspoon of the dried), 3 fresh basil leaves (or ¼ teaspoon dried basil) 15–20 minutes; strain liquid into sauce, add ¼ cup minced mushrooms, ½ cup tomato purée, ½ cup Veal (White) Stock, and simmer uncovered until reduced to 1 quart. Mix in ¼ cup dry Madeira and ⅛ teaspoon each allspice and cayenne. Serve with kidneys or tongue. About 22 calories per tablespoon.

Zingara Sauce (Makes about 1 quart): Prepare Rich Brown Sauce with beef broth, mix in ½ cup tomato purée, 2 tablespoons each julienne strips cooked ham and boiled tongue, minced mushrooms and truffles, and 1 teaspoon paprika. Good with roast veal. About 23 calories per tablespoon.

⚖ ☒ GLACE DE VIANDE

Never salt a sauce until after *glace de viande* is added; then taste and salt as needed. Use sparingly to add flavor to sauces, soups, and gravies.
Makes ⅓ cup

1 cup Brown Beef Stock or canned
condensed beef broth

Boil stock, uncovered, over high heat
until reduced to ⅓ cup. (*Note:* A similar
flavor can be obtained by dissolving 1
tablespoon beef extract in ¼ cup cold
water.) About 6 calories per tablespoon.

COLBERT SAUCE

Makes about 1 cup

¼ cup Glace de Viande or 1 tablespoon
beef extract
1 tablespoon hot water
½ cup butter, softened to room
temperature (no substitute)
2 tablespoons lemon juice
1 tablespoon minced parsley
Pinch nutmeg
Pinch cayenne pepper
2 tablespoons dry Madeira wine

Heat *glace de viande* with hot water in a
small saucepan. Slowly beat in butter, 1
tablespoon at a time, then mix in
remaining ingredients. Drizzle sparingly
over broiled meat or fish. About 55
calories per tablespoon.

⚔ ⊠ SHALLOT SAUCE

Makes about ¾ cup

3 tablespoons minced shallots
2 tablespoons butter or drippings from
· broiled or panfried steak
½ cup beef broth
2 tablespoons dry red wine or red wine
vinegar
1 teaspoon minced parsley (optional)

Sauté shallots in butter (preferably in
pan steak was cooked in) over moderate
heat 3–5 minutes until limp. Add
remaining ingredients, heat, stirring, to
boiling, then pour over steaks. About 15
calories per tablespoon.

⚔ GARLIC SAUCE

Makes about 2 cups

1 cup beef broth
1 cup water
1 clove garlic, peeled and bruised

1 medium-size yellow onion, peeled and
minced
1 bay leaf
2 tablespoons minced celery leaves
¼ teaspoon salt (about)
⅛ teaspoon pepper
¼ cup heavy cream
3 thin slices lemon

Simmer all but last 2 ingredients,
covered, 20 minutes, then strain into a
clean saucepan. Add cream and heat
over lowest heat 3–5 minutes; taste for
salt and pepper and adjust. Serve hot
with lemon slices floating on top. Good
with roast lamb or veal. About 10
calories per tablespoon.

HERB SAUCE

Delicious with steaks and chops.
Makes 2 cups

2 cups beef broth
4 scallions, peeled and minced
1 tablespoon minced chives
¼ teaspoon each marjoram, thyme,
savory, sage, and basil
⅛ teaspoon nutmeg
⅛ teaspoon pepper
¼ cup butter or margarine
¼ cup unsifted flour
¼ teaspoon salt (about)
1 tablespoon lemon juice
1 teaspoon minced fresh tarragon or ¼
teaspoon dried tarragon
1 teaspoon minced fresh chervil or ¼
teaspoon dried chervil

Simmer broth, scallions, chives, herbs,
nutmeg, and pepper covered 15 minutes;
strain broth through a cheesecloth-
lined sieve and reserve. Melt butter in a
saucepan over moderate heat, blend in
flour, and cook and stir 1–2 minutes
until light brown. Slowly mix in reserved
broth and heat, stirring, until thickened.
Lower heat and simmer 5 minutes. Mix
in salt, lemon juice, tarragon, and chervil
and serve. About 20 calories per
tablespoon.

HOLLANDAISE AND OTHER EGG-THICKENED SAUCES

HOLLANDAISE SAUCE

If you remember one basic rule—that too much heat will curdle an egg-thickened sauce—you should have little difficulty making Hollandaise. Cook over *simmering*, not boiling, water, take from the heat the minute sauce thickens, and remember that all is not lost if the sauce does curdle. It can be rescued. Hollandaise should be served warm, not hot, not cold.

Makes about 1⅓ cups

4 egg yolks
1 tablespoon cold water
½ cup butter, softened to room
temperature (no substitute)
¼ teaspoon salt
Pinch white pepper
1–2 tablespoons lemon juice

Beat yolks until thick and lemon colored, mix in water and transfer to the top of a double boiler set over barely simmering water. Heat and stir 2–3 minutes until warm, not hot. Add butter, 2 tablespoons at a time, stirring continuously and not adding more butter until previous addition is well blended in. When all butter is in, cook and stir 2–3 minutes until sauce thickens enough to coat the back of a metal spoon. Set double boiler top on counter, mix in salt, pepper, and lemon juice and stir 1–2 minutes. Serve with vegetables or seafood. About 50 calories per tablespoon.

To Salvage Curdled Hollandaise: Add 2 tablespoons boiling water and beat vigorously until smooth. *Or* set pan in an ice bath, beat hard until smooth, then warm very gently over just simmering water, stirring constantly.

To Make Hollandaise Ahead of Time: Prepare as directed, then transfer to a small bowl; place a circle of wax paper flat on sauce to prevent a skin from forming. About 15 minutes before serving, set bowl of sauce in very hot—not boiling—water and stir now and then as sauce warms; replenish hot water as needed. If sauce seems thick, beat in 1–2 tablespoons hot water.

VARIATIONS:

Béarnaise Sauce (Makes about 1⅓ cups): Before beginning sauce, boil ¼ cup dry white wine, uncovered, with ¼ cup white wine vinegar, 1 tablespoon each minced fresh (or 1 teaspoon each dried) tarragon and chervil, 1 tablespoon minced shallots or scallions (white part), ⅛ teaspoon salt, and a pinch white pepper until liquid reduces to 2 tablespoons; strain liquid and cool to room temperature. Prepare Hollandaise as directed, substituting reduced liquid for lemon juice. Just before serving, mix in ½ teaspoon each minced fresh tarragon and chervil and a pinch cayenne. Good with broiled meats. About 50 calories per tablespoon.

Choron Sauce (Makes about 1⅓ cups): Prepare Béarnaise and blend in 2 tablespoons tomato paste. Good with steak. About 51 calories per tablespoon.

Paloise Sauce (Makes about 1⅓ cups): Prepare Béarnaise as directed but substitute 2 tablespoons minced fresh mint for the tarragon and chervil in the vinegar mixture; also mix in 1 teaspoon minced mint instead of tarragon and chervil at the end. Good with roast veal or lamb. About 50 calories per tablespoon.

Mousseline (Chantilly) Sauce (Makes 2 cups): Prepare Hollandaise, then fold in ½ cup heavy cream beaten to soft peaks. Add extra salt and pepper if needed. Good with seafood and vegetables. About 69 calories per tablespoon.

Figaro Sauce (Makes 1⅔ cups): Prepare Hollandaise, blend in ⅓ cup tomato purée and 1 tablespoon minced parsley, and heat and stir over barely simmering water 2–3 minutes. Good with seafood. About 51 calories per tablespoon.

Maltaise (Maltese) Sauce (Makes 1⅔ cups): Prepare Hollandaise, then blend in the juice of 1 orange, heated to lukewarm, and ¼ teaspoon finely grated orange rind. Good with boiled vegetables, especially asparagus, green beans, and broccoli. About 51 calories per tablespoon.

Mustard Hollandaise (Makes about 1⅓ cups): Prepare Hollandaise as directed but blend ½ teaspoon powdered mustard with lemon juice before adding to sauce. Good with boiled vegetables and fish. About 50 calories per tablespoon.

⊠ BLENDER HOLLANDAISE

Quicker and easier than old-fashioned Hollandaise.
Makes about 1⅓ cups

4 egg yolks
2 tablespoons lemon juice
¼ teaspoon salt
Pinch white pepper
½ cup hot melted butter

Blend yolks, lemon juice, salt, and pepper in an electric blender at high speed ½ minute; uncover and continue blending at high speed, at the same time adding butter drop by drop. As mixture thickens, add butter in a thin slow stream. When about half the butter is in, you can pour a little faster. Continue blending until thick and satiny, then serve. About 50 calories per tablespoon.

VARIATIONS:

Blender Béarnaise: Prepare reduced vinegar-herb mixture as for regular Béarnaise, then prepare recipe above, substituting vinegar mixture for lemon juice. Just before serving, mix in ½ teaspoon each minced fresh tarragon and chervil. About 50 calories per tablespoon.

Note: Any of the variations on standard Hollandaise can be made with the blender variety.

⚖ AVGOLEMONO SAUCE

A favorite Greek sauce, thickened with egg and lightly flavored with lemon. Serve with asparagus, broccoli, or globe artichokes. Also good with roast veal. Makes 1½ cups

1¼ cups chicken broth
Pinch nutmeg
3 egg yolks, lightly beaten
3–4 tablespoons lemon juice
Salt
Pepper

Heat broth and nutmeg in the top of a double boiler over simmering water. Blend about ½ cup broth into egg yolks, return to pan, and cook, stirring constantly, until thickened. Off heat, mix in lemon juice, 1 tablespoon at a time; season to taste with salt and pepper. About 10 calories per tablespoon.

BATARDE SAUCE

An imitation Hollandaise, less caloric than the real thing.
Makes about 1⅔ cups

2 tablespoons butter (no substitute)
2 tablespoons flour
1¼ cups water, vegetable cooking water or Easy Fish Stock (depending upon dish to be sauced)
1 egg yolk, lightly beaten with 1 tablespoon cold water
⅓ cup butter, softened to room temperature
½ teaspoon salt
⅛ teaspoon white pepper
1–2 tablespoons lemon juice

Melt butter over moderate heat, blend in flour, gradually mix in water, and cook, stirring, until thickened. Blend ¼ cup hot sauce into egg yolk, return to pan, and cook and stir over lowest heat 2 minutes until no raw taste of egg remains; do not boil. Off heat, beat in softened butter, 1 tablespoon at a time. Season with salt, pepper, and lemon juice. Serve warm—not hot—with fish or vegetables. About 32 calories per tablespoon.

MAYONNAISE SAUCES

Note: Other mayonnaise sauces can be found in the chapter on salads and salad dressings.

⊠ SOME EASY MAYONNAISE SAUCES

To make any of the following sauces of pouring consistency, use ½ cup milk or cream and ½ cup mayonnaise instead of 1 cup mayonnaise. The cold mayonnaises will be more flavorful if allowed to stand 15–20 minutes at room temperature before serving. ·

Aioli Sauce (Makes 1 cup): Blend 1 cup mayonnaise with 4 crushed garlic cloves and a pinch each sugar and cayenne. Serve slightly chilled or at room temperature with hot or cold seafood or meat, cold poultry or vegetables. Also good floated on Gazpacho. About 110 calories per tablespoon.

Anchovy Mayonnaise (Makes 1 cup): Blend 1 cup mayonnaise with 7–8 minced anchovies (or 2 tablespoons anchovy paste) and ½ crushed clove garlic. Let mellow 1 hour before serving. (*Note:* If preparing homemade mayonnaise, omit salt.) Serve with cold seafood. About 115 calories per tablespoon.

Andalouse Mayonnaise (Makes 1½ cups): Blend 1 cup mayonnaise with ⅓ cup tomato purée, 2 diced pimientos, and ½ crushed clove garlic. Good with cold meat or fish. About 75 calories per tablespoon.

Applesauce Mayonnaise (Makes 2 cups): Blend 1 cup each mayonnaise and applesauce, season with ⅛ teaspoon each cinnamon and nutmeg, and serve with cold pork, ham, or tongue. About 60 calories per tablespoon.

Avocado Mayonnaise (Makes 1½ cups): Blend 1 cup mayonnaise with 1 puréed ripe avocado, 1 minced pimiento, 1 tablespoon lemon juice, and salt to taste. Good with cold shellfish. About 90 calories per tablespoon.

Buttermilk Mayonnaise (Makes 1½ cups): Blend 1 cup mayonnaise, ½ cup buttermilk, 2 tablespoons minced chives, and a few drops liquid hot red pepper seasoning. Serve over cold vegetables. About 75 calories per tablespoon.

Caviar Mayonnaise (Makes 1 cup): Mix ¼ cup red or black caviar into 1 cup mayonnaise. (*Note:* Reduce salt if preparing homemade mayonnaise.) Serve with seafood. About 120 calories per tablespoon.

Chutney Mayonnaise (Makes 1¼ cups): Mix 1 cup mayonnaise with ¼ cup minced chutney. Serve with cold meat or poultry. About 100 calories per tablespoon.

Cranberry Mayonnaise (Makes 1½ cups): Mix 1 cup mayonnaise with ½ cup whole or jellied cranberry sauce and 1 teaspoon finely grated orange rind. Serve with cold pork, ham, or poultry. About 75 calories per tablespoon.

Dill Mayonnaise (Makes 1 cup): Blend 1 cup mayonnaise with 1–2 tablespoons minced fresh dill. Serve with seafood. About 110 calories per tablespoon.

French Mayonnaise (Makes 1⅓ cups): Blend 1 cup mayonnaise with ⅓ cup French dressing, 1 teaspoon finely grated onion, and ½ crushed clove garlic. Heat and stir over lowest heat 2–3 minutes; do not boil. Serve over broccoli, asparagus, or green beans. About 100 calories per tablespoon.

Grenache Mayonnaise (Makes 1¾ cups): Blend 1 cup mayonnaise with ½ cup warm red currant jelly and 2 tablespoons each prepared horseradish and Madeira wine. Chill and serve with cold meat, poultry, or game. About 85 calories per tablespoon.

Herb Mayonnaise (Makes 1 cup): Blend 1 cup mayonnaise with 1 teaspoon each minced fresh tarragon, chervil, chives,

V. HOMESPUN AMERICAN FAVORITES

Indoor Clambake – Baked Country Cured Ham – Caesar Salad –
The home pantry

Indoor Clambake (pages 590-91)

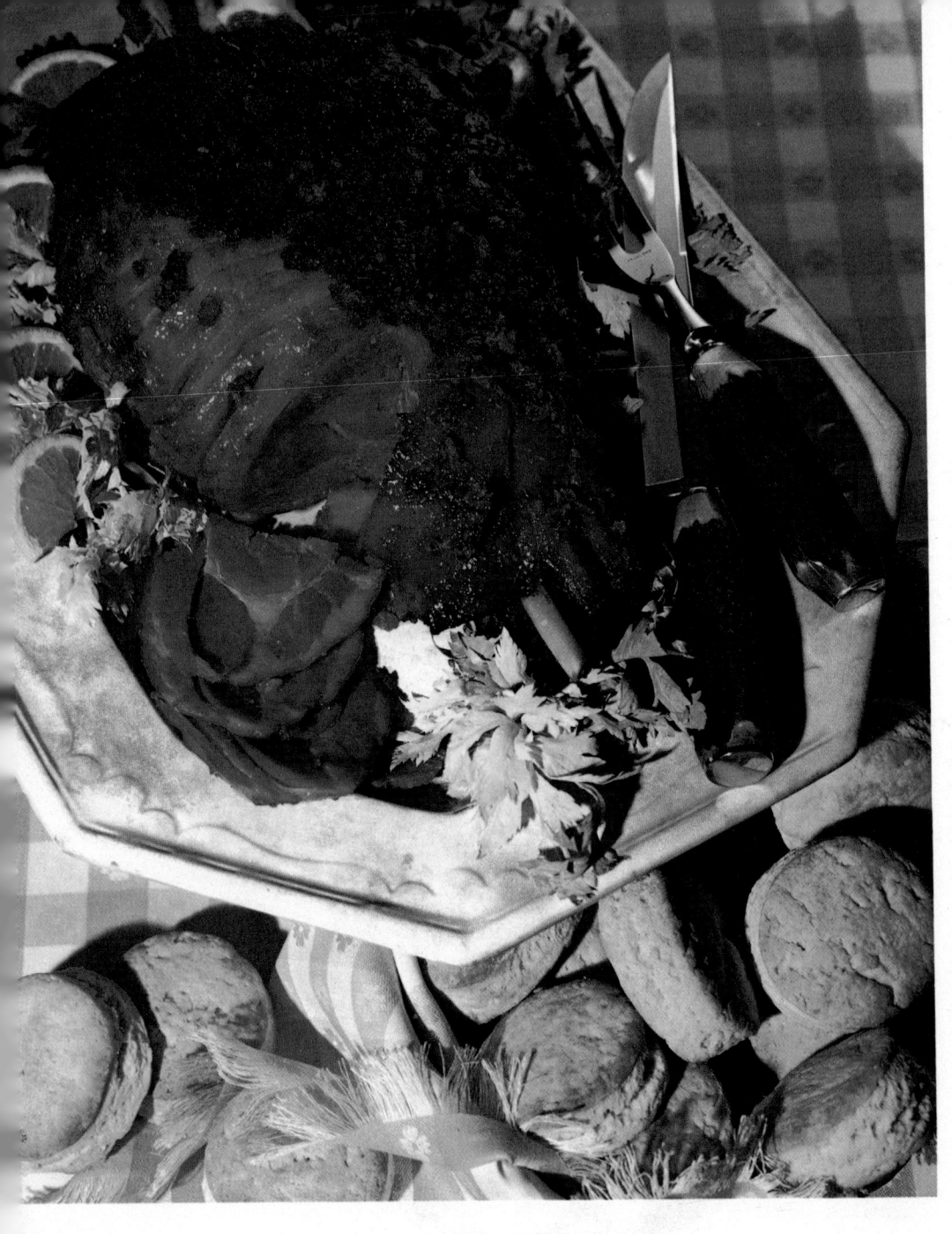

Baked Country Cured Ham (pages 378-79); and Baking Powder Biscuits (page 944)

Caesar Salad (page 904)

The **Home** Pantry (pages 1216-33 and 1244-59)

and parsley. Serve with seafood or cold meat or poultry. About 110 calories per tablespoon.

Mint Mayonnaise (Makes 1 cup): Blend 1 cup mayonnaise with 2–3 teaspoons minced fresh mint or ¼ cup mint jelly. Serve with cold lamb or veal. About 110 calories per tablespoon made with fresh mint, 115 calories made with mint jelly.

Perfection Mayonnaise (Makes 1¾ cups): Blend 1 cup mayonnaise with ½ cup sour cream and 2 tablespoons each ketchup, steak sauce, tarragon vinegar, and minced parsley. Serve with seafood. About 75 calories per tablespoon.

Pimiento and Olive Mayonnaise (Makes 1½ cups): Mix 1 cup mayonnaise with ½ cup minced pimiento-stuffed green olives or ¼ cup each minced pimiento and pitted ripe olives. Serve with cold meat or seafood. About 75 calories per tablespoon.

Quick Lemon-Caper Sauce (Makes 1½ cups): Mix 1 cup mayonnaise with 3 tablespoons lemon juice and 2 tablespoons each minced capers and parsley. Serve with seafood. About 75 calories per tablespoon.

Mustard Mayonnaise Sauce (Makes 1¼ cups): Blend 1 cup mayonnaise with ¼ cup milk, 3 tablespoons prepared spicy brown mustard, and 1 tablespoon cider vinegar. Warm 2–3 minutes, stirring, over lowest heat; do not boil. Serve with ham, pork, tongue, boiled beef, or poached chicken. Also good with hot green vegetables. About 90 calories per tablespoon.

Shellfish Cocktail Mayonnaise (Makes 1¼ cups): Mix 1 cup mayonnaise with ¼ cup each chili sauce and minced mustard pickles and 1 tablespoon each cider vinegar and Worcestershire sauce. Serve with shellfish. About 100 calories per tablespoon.

Tuna Mayonnaise (See Vitello Tonnato).

Vincent Sauce (Makes 1½ cups): Mix 1 cup mayonnaise with 2 tablespoons each minced chives, parsley, and watercress, 1 minced hard-cooked egg, and 1 teaspoon Worcestershire sauce. Serve with cold meat or seafood. About 80 calories per tablespoon.

Watercress Mayonnaise (Makes 1¼ cups): Mix 1 cup mayonnaise with ¼ cup minced watercress leaves and 2 tablespoons minced scallions. Serve with cold poultry or seafood. About 80 calories per tablespoon.

⊠ MOCK HOLLANDAISE SAUCE

A good quick substitute for real Hollandaise.
Makes about 1½ cups

¼ cup butter or margarine
Juice of ½ lemon
1¼ cups mayonnaise

Melt butter in a small saucepan over low heat. Beat in lemon juice and mayonnaise, then heat and beat about 2 minutes. Serve as a sauce for broccoli, cauliflower, asparagus, or globe artichokes. About 110 calories per tablespoon.

TARTAR SAUCE I

Nice and tart.
Makes about 1¼ cups

1 cup mayonnaise
3 shallots, peeled and minced, or 3 scallions, minced
1 tablespoon minced parsley
1 tablespoon minced fresh tarragon
¼ cup minced gherkins or dill pickle
2 tablespoons capers
1 teaspoon prepared Dijon-style mustard
½ teaspoon sugar
2 tablespoons red wine vinegar

Mix all ingredients, cover, and chill 2–3 hours. Serve with any seafood. (*Note:* If sauce seems thick, thin with red wine vinegar.) About 90 calories per tablespoon.

TARTAR SAUCE II

Olives give this version special character.
Makes about 1 cup

1 cup mayonnaise
1 tablespoon drained sweet pickle relish
1 tablespoon minced green olives
1 tablespoon minced parsley
1 tablespoon minced scallion
2 teaspoons drained, minced capers
1 teaspoon prepared Dijon-style mustard

Mix all ingredients and let stand at room
temperature 10–15 minutes. Serve with
any seafood. About 113 calories per
tablespoon.

HORSERADISH CREAM SAUCE

Makes about 1 cup

½ cup heavy cream
½ cup mayonnaise or mayonnaise-type
  salad dressing
2 tablespoons prepared horseradish
1–2 tablespoons lemon juice
1 tablespoon finely grated lemon rind
Pinch cayenne pepper

Gradually beat cream into mayonnaise
and, when smooth, stir in remaining
ingredients. Chill ½ hour and serve with
cold roast beef, ham, tongue, or poultry.
About 80 calories per tablespoon.

VARIATION:

Whipped Horseradish Sauce: Beat cream
to soft peaks, omit mayonnaise, and fold
in remaining ingredients; season to taste
with salt and pepper. About 30 calories
per tablespoon.

TAPENADE

Makes about 1½ cups

1 cup mayonnaise
1 (2-ounce) can anchovy fillets, drained
  and minced
⅓ cup capers, minced
1 clove garlic, peeled and crushed
1 teaspoon finely grated lemon rind
1 tablespoon minced parsley

Mix all ingredients, cover, and chill 1–2
hours. Serve as a dunk for chilled raw
vegetables. About 75 calories per
tablespoon.

OIL AND VINEGAR SAUCES

Note: Other oil and vinegar sauces can
be found in the chapter on salads and
salad dressings.

DIJONNAISE SAUCE

Makes ¾ cup

2 hard-cooked eggs, shelled
½ cup olive or other cooking oil
2 tablespoons white or red wine vinegar
1–2 tablespoons Dijon mustard
¼ teaspoon salt
⅛ teaspoon white pepper

Press egg yolks through a fine sieve (save
whites for sandwiches or salads). Beat in
¼ cup oil, drop by drop; beat in 1
tablespoon vinegar. Add remaining oil in
a fine steady stream, beating vigorously
all the while. (Note: If mixture curdles,
beat in 1–2 tablespoons boiling water.)
Mix in mustard, salt, and pepper. Serve
with steak or ham. About 100 calories
per tablespoon.

GRIBICHE SAUCE

A rich tartar-like sauce that is superb
with cold fish or shellfish.
Makes 1 cup

2 hard-cooked eggs, shelled
½ cup olive or other cooking oil
2 tablespoons white vinegar
2 tablespoons minced gherkins
2 tablespoons minced capers
1 tablespoon minced parsley
1 teaspoon minced fresh chervil or ¼
  teaspoon dried chervil
1 teaspoon minced fresh tarragon or ¼
  teaspoon dried tarragon
¼ teaspoon salt

Press egg yolks through a fine sieve and
beat in ¼ cup oil, drop by drop. Beat in
1 tablespoon vinegar, then add remaining oil in a fine, steady stream, beating
vigorously all the while. (Note: If mixture

curdles, beat in 1–2 tablespoons boiling water.) Add remaining vinegar along with other ingredients and the finely chopped egg whites. Chill slightly before serving. About 75 calories per tablespoon.

COLD RAVIGOTE SAUCE

Makes about 1⅓ cups

¾ cup olive or other cooking oil
¼ cup white or red wine vinegar
¼ teaspoon salt
⅛ teaspoon pepper
2 tablespoons minced capers
2 tablespoons minced yellow onion
2 tablespoons minced chives
1 tablespoon minced parsley
1 teaspoon minced fresh tarragon or ¼ teaspoon dried tarragon
1 teaspoon minced fresh chervil or ¼ teaspoon dried chervil

Beat oil, vinegar, salt, and pepper until slightly thickened. Mix in remaining ingredients and let stand at room temperature ½ hour. Beat lightly with a fork and use to dress seafood or chicken salad. About 70 calories per tablespoon.

GREEN SAUCE (SALSA VERDE)

Makes about 1 cup

¼ cup red or white wine vinegar
¼ teaspoon salt
⅛ teaspoon white pepper
¼ teaspoon powdered mustard
1 tablespoon minced parsley
1 tablespoon minced chives
1 tablespoon minced watercress or spinach
2 shallots, peeled and minced, or 2 scallions, minced (include tops)
¾ cup olive oil

Mix vinegar, salt, pepper, and mustard in a bowl with a fork. Mix in parsley, chives, watercress, and shallots. Add oil and beat vigorously until blended and slightly thickened. Chill slightly and beat again before serving. Good with Bollito Misto, boiled beef, or boiled tongue. About 88 calories per tablespoon.

⊠ SOME EASY SOUR CREAM SAUCES

All but the first sauce can be served hot or cold. For best results, bring sour cream to room temperature before mixing sauce. Heat gently, preferably in the top of a double boiler so sour cream doesn't curdle. As a general rule, serve hot with hot food, cold with cold food.

Sour Cream-Almond Sauce (Makes 1¼ cups): Mix ¼ cup minced toasted almonds (or piñon, pistachio, or peanuts) with 1 cup sour cream; salt to taste. Good with baked potatoes and broiled fish. About 35 calories per tablespoon.

Sour Cream-Anchovy Sauce (Makes 1¼ cups): Blend 1 cup sour cream with 3 tablespoons each milk and anchovy paste and 1 tablespoon lemon juice. Serve with fish. About 30 calories per tablespoon.

Sour Cream-Bacon Sauce Makes 1¼ cups): Mix 1 cup sour cream with ¼ cup crisp crumbled bacon and 2 tablespoons melted bacon drippings. Good with baked potatoes, seafood, and green vegetables. About 40 calories per tablespoon.

Sour Cream-Blue Cheese Sauce (Makes 2 cups): Blend 1 cup sour cream with 1 (3-ounce) package softened cream cheese, ⅓ cup crumbled blue cheese, and 3 tablespoons evaporated milk. Good with green vegetables. About 35 calories per tablespoon.

Sour Cream-Caper Sauce (Makes 1⅓ cups): Mix 1 cup sour cream with 3 tablespoons each lemon juice (or white vinegar) and minced capers and 2 tablespoons minced chives. Serve with seafood. About 30 calories per tablespoon.

Sour Cream-Cheese Sauce (Makes 1¾ cups): Melt 1 cup finely grated sharp Cheddar cheese with ¼ cup milk and 1 teaspoon steak sauce in the top of a double boiler over simmering water. Blend in 1 cup sour cream. Good with fish, baked potatoes, and green vegetables. About 35 calories per tablespoon.

Sour Cream-Chive Sauce (Makes 1¼ cups): Mix 1 cup sour cream with 3–4 tablespoons minced chives and salt and pepper to taste. If you like, add ½ crushed clove garlic or ¼ teaspoon garlic powder. Good with baked potatoes, carrots, and seafood. About 25 calories per tablespoon.

Sour Cream-Chutney Sauce (Makes 1¼ cups): Mix 1 cup sour cream with ¼ cup minced chutney and 2 tablespoons Worcestershire sauce. Good with cold meat or poultry. About 35 calories per tablespoon.

⚖ **Sour Cream-Cucumber Sauce** (Makes 2 cups): Mix 1 cup each sour cream and peeled, diced, seeded cucumber with 2 tablespoons white wine vinegar, 1 tablespoon minced fresh dill, and salt and pepper to taste. Good with fish or ham. About 17 calories per tablespoon.

Sour Cream-Curry Sauce (Makes 1 cup): Blend 1 cup sour cream with 1 teaspoon curry powder warmed 2–3 minutes with 1 tablespoon each butter and finely grated onion; add salt and pepper to taste. Good with meat or fish. About 35 calories per tablespoon.

Sour Cream-Dill Sauce (Makes 1¼ cups): Mix 2 tablespoons each minced fresh dill and mayonnaise with 1 cup sour cream; add salt and pepper to taste. Good with seafood. About 35 calories per tablespoon.

Sour Cream-Herb Sauce (Makes 1 cup): Mix 1 tablespoon each minced fresh tarragon, chervil, and parsley with 1 cup sour cream; add salt and pepper to taste. Good with meat, seafood, or vegetables. About 25 calories per tablespoon.

Sour Cream Hollandaise (Makes 1½ cups): Heat and stir 1 cup sour cream, 6 lightly beaten egg yolks, ¾ teaspoon salt, and ⅛ teaspoon white pepper in the top of a double boiler over simmering water 2–3 minutes until no raw taste of egg remains. Off heat, mix in 4–5 teaspoons lemon juice. Good with green vegetables, seafood, or poultry. About 35 calories per tablespoon.

Sour Cream-Horseradish Sauce (Makes 1¼ cups): Blend 2 tablespoons each cider vinegar and prepared horseradish with 1 cup sour cream. Good with beef, ham, or pork. About 30 calories per tablespoon.

Sour Cream-Mustard Sauce (Makes 1 cup): Blend 2–3 tablespoons any prepared mustard and 1 tablespoon cider vinegar with 1 cup sour cream. Good with beef, ham, or pork. About 30 calories per tablespoon.

Sour Cream-Red Currant Sauce (Makes 1½ cups): Blend 1 cup sour cream with ½ cup warmed red currant jelly (or apple, guava, or cranberry jelly) and a pinch allspice. Good with game and game birds. About 45 calories per tablespoon.

Sour Cream Sauce (Makes 1¼ cups): Blend 1 cup sour cream with ¼ cup mayonnaise and salt and pepper to taste. Good with boiled red or green cabbage. About 45 calories per tablespoon.

Sour Cream-Sesame Sauce (Makes 1 cup): Mix 2 tablespoons toasted sesame seeds (or poppy or caraway seeds) with 1 cup sour cream. Good with green vegetables. About 30 calories per tablespoon.

Sour Cream-Sherry Sauce (Makes 1¼ cups): Blend 3–4 tablespoons dry sherry and a pinch nutmeg with 1 cup sour cream. Good with poultry or shrimp. About 30 calories per tablespoon.

Sour Cream-Soup Sauce (Makes 2 cups): Heat and stir 1 (10-ounce) can condensed cream of chicken, mushroom, or celery soup with 1 cup sour cream over low heat until smooth. Add 1 tablespoon each minced parsley and chives and serve hot over meat, poultry, or vegetables. About 25 calories per tablespoon.

Sour Cream-Tomato Sauce (Makes 1¼ cups): Mix ¼ cup tomato paste, chili sauce, or ketchup and 1 tablespoon lemon juice with 1 cup sour cream. If you like, add 1 tablespoon minced parsley or dill. Good with seafood. About 30 calories per tablespoon.

⚖ LOW-CALORIE VARIATIONS

The following "sour cream" sauces will be low-calorie if made with yogurt instead of sour cream:

Sour Cream-Caper: 8 calories per tablespoon

Sour Cream-Chive: 8 calories per tablespoon

Sour Cream-Chutney: 15 calories per tablespoon

Sour Cream-Cucumber: 6 calories per tablespoon

Sour Cream-Curry: 15 calories per tablespoon

Sour Cream-Dill: 8 calories per tablespoon

Sour Cream-Herb: 8 calories per tablespoon

Sour Cream-Horseradish: 8 calories per tablespoon

Sour Cream-Mustard: 10 calories per tablespoon

SMITANE SAUCE

Serve with steaks and chops. Also good as a topping for baked potatoes and green vegetables.
Makes about 1 cup

1 large yellow onion, peeled and minced
2 tablespoons butter or margarine
½ cup dry white wine
1 cup sour cream
¼ teaspoon salt
Paprika

Stir-fry onion in butter over moderate heat 3–5 minutes until limp, not brown. Add wine and simmer, uncovered, until liquid reduces to about 2 tablespoons. Turn heat to low, gradually stir in sour cream and salt, and heat gently; do not boil. Dust with paprika and serve warm. About 50 calories per tablespoon.

⊠ DRAWN BUTTER SAUCE

Makes 1 cup

¼ cup clarified butter* or melted
*   margarine*

2 tablespoons flour
1 cup any warm fish or vegetable stock
*   or water*
½ teaspoon salt
⅛ teaspoon paprika
½–1 teaspoon lemon juice

Warm butter in a small saucepan over low heat and blend in flour. Add stock and heat, stirring constantly, until thickened and smooth. Mix in salt, paprika, and lemon juice to taste. Good with broiled fish or steamed green vegetables. (*Note:* Traditionalists strain this sauce before serving, but doing so is unnecessary if the sauce is correctly made and satin-smooth.) About 30 calories per tablespoon.

⊠ SOME FLAVORED BUTTERS

Each makes enough to dress 6 servings of meat, fish, or vegetables

Anchovy Butter: Cream ½ cup butter until light; mix in 4 teaspoons anchovy paste (or 4–5 minced anchovy fillets), ½ teaspoon lemon juice, and 2–3 drops liquid hot red pepper seasoning. Let stand 15 minutes before using. Spread on fish before or after broiling, on broiled steaks, or use as a sandwich spread with seafood fillings. About 140 calories per serving.

Bercy Butter: Boil ½ cup dry white wine with 1 tablespoon minced shallots until reduced to 3 tablespoons; cool. Mix in ½ cup melted butter, ¼ cup diced poached marrow from Marrowbones (optional), 1 tablespoon lemon juice, 2 teaspoons minced parsley, ¼ teaspoon salt, and a pinch pepper. Serve warm with broiled meat or fish. About 135 calories per serving (without marrow).

Beurre Noir ("Black" Butter): Melt ½ cup butter over moderate heat and cook until nut brown. Off heat, mix in 1 tablespoon each minced parsley, capers, and cider vinegar. Serve with fish, vegetables, sweetbreads, or brains. About 135 calories per serving.

Browned Butter: Mix ½ cup lightly browned butter and 4 teaspoons Worcestershire sauce; use to dress steaks, chops, fish, or vegetables (especially good with cauliflower). About 140 calories per serving.

Caper Butter: Mix ½ cup melted butter, ¼ cup small capers, 1 tablespoon lemon juice, and a pinch cayenne pepper; serve with fish, brains, sweetbreads, or vegetables. About 140 calories per serving.

Chili Butter: Mix ½ cup melted butter and 1 teaspoon chili powder; warm gently 5 minutes and use to baste broiled tomatoes, meat, fish, or poultry. About 135 calories per serving.

Chive Butter: Mix ½ cup melted butter, 2 tablespoons minced chives, ¼ teaspoon salt, and a pinch pepper. *Or,* cream butter until light, blend in remaining ingredients, spoon into a small crock, and chill until firm. Serve poured or dotted over steak, chops, fish, or vegetables. About 135 calories per serving.

Curry Butter: Warm ½ cup melted butter and 1 teaspoon curry powder gently 5 minutes; serve with broiled meat, poultry, fish, or tomatoes. Also good with boiled broccoli or cauliflower. About 135 calories per serving.

Dill Butter: Let ½ cup melted butter, 3–4 tablespoons minced fresh dill, and ⅛ teaspoon nutmeg stand in warm place 1 hour; use to dress fish or vegetables. About 135 calories per serving.

Garlic Butter: Mix ½ cup melted butter, 1 or 2 crushed cloves garlic, ¼ teaspoon salt, and a pinch pepper; warm 5 minutes and strain if you like. *Or,* cream butter until light and blend in remaining ingredients. Serve on broiled meat or fish, with steamed lobster, or use to make Garlic Bread. About 135 calories per serving.

Green Butter: Simmer ¼ cup minced fresh spinach leaves with 2 tablespoons each minced parsley, chives, and water 2–3 minutes; press through a fine sieve, drain, and mix into ½ cup creamed butter along with a pinch each of salt

and pepper. Chill and serve with fish or vegetables. About 135 calories per serving.

Herb Butter: Mix ½ cup creamed unsalted butter with ½ teaspoon each minced fresh sweet marjoram and thyme (or substitute ½ teaspoon minced fresh rosemary). Cover and chill until firm. Serve with fish or vegetables. (*Note:* With rosemary it's delicious with lamb chops and green peas.) About 135 calories per serving.

Horseradish Butter: Mix ½ cup creamed butter and 1 tablespoon prepared horseradish; cover and chill 1 hour. Serve with steaks and chops. About 140 calories per serving.

Lemon Butter: Warm ½ cup melted butter, 2 tablespoons lemon juice, and a pinch pepper 2–3 minutes. Serve with fish or vegetables. *Parsley-Lemon Butter:* Add 2–3 tablespoons minced parsley to Lemon Butter. Each version: about 135 calories per serving.

Lobster Butter: Finely grind 1 cup mixed cooked lobster meat, coral, and some shell. Mix with ½ cup melted butter and blend at high speed in an electric blender. Heat until butter melts, then blend again at high speed. Rub through a fine sieve, cool, beat with a fork, season to taste with salt and pepper, and chill until firm. Serve with fish. About 160 calories per serving.

Maître d'Hôtel Butter (Parsley Butter): Mix ½ cup creamed butter with 2 tablespoons each minced parsley and lemon juice, ¼ teaspoon salt, and ⅛ teaspoon white pepper. On foil shape into a roll about 1¼″ in diameter, wrap, and chill until firm. Or roll into balls about ½″ in diameter, place in a piepan, cover, and chill until firm. Use to season broiled steaks, chops, chicken, or fish by topping each serving with 2 or 3 balls or ¼″ thick pats. About 135 calories per serving.

Marchands de Vin Butter: Boil ½ cup dry red wine with 2 tablespoons minced shallots until reduced to ¼ cup. Beat in

½ cup soft butter, 2 tablespoons at a time, add 1 tablespoon Glace de Viande or 1 teaspoon beef extract, 1 tablespoon each minced parsley and lemon juice, and a pinch pepper. Serve on steaks and chops. About 135 calories per serving.

Mushroom Butter: Sauté ¼ pound minced mushrooms in 2 tablespoons butter 3–5 minutes until browned and tender; press through a fine sieve and cool slightly. Mix in 6 tablespoons creamed butter, 1 tablespoon sherry, ¼ teaspoon salt, and a pinch pepper. Cover and chill; spread on steaks and chops. About 145 calories per serving.

Mustard Butter: Cream ½ cup softened butter with ½ teaspoon powdered mustard and 1–2 tablespoons any prepared mustard. Use to dress broiled meats and fish or boiled vegetables (especially good with broccoli and asparagus). About 135 calories per serving.

Noisette Butter: Lightly brown ½ cup butter over moderate heat; stir in 3 tablespoons lemon juice and pour sizzling hot over vegetables or fish. About 135 calories per serving.

Orange Butter: Let ½ cup melted butter and 1 tablespoon finely slivered orange rind (orange part only) steep in a warm place ½ hour. Warm gently and serve with boiled beets, carrots, parsnips, peas, winter squash, turnips, or ruta-bagas. About 135 calories per serving.

Paprika Butter: Blend ½ cup creamed butter with 1–2 teaspoons paprika (Hungarian rose, preferably), cover, and chill. Use to dress fish and vegetables. About 135 calories per serving.

Pimiento Butter: Pound 2 seeded canned pimientos to a smooth paste in a mortar and pestle. Blend into ½ cup creamed butter along with ¼ teaspoon salt. Cover, chill, and serve with meat, fish, or vegetables. About 140 calories per serving.

Seasoned Butter: Mix ½ cup melted butter, 1 teaspoon salt, and ¼ teaspoon freshly ground black pepper. Use to dress seafood or vegetables. About 135 calories per serving.

Shallot Butter: Crush 6–8 peeled shallots in a garlic press, mix into ½ cup creamed butter along with ¼ teaspoon salt and a pinch pepper. Cover and chill 1 hour; serve with steaks, chops, and seafood. About 135 calories per serving.

Shrimp Butter: Mince ¼ pound cooked, shelled, and deveined shrimp, add 1 tablespoon lemon juice, then pound to a paste in a mortar and pestle. Blend into ½ cup creamed butter, add a pinch each salt and paprika, cover, and chill 2 hours. *Or,* mix 1–2 tablespoons shrimp paste into ½ cup melted butter, season, and let stand in a warm place 1 hour. Serve with seafood. About 155 calories per serving.

Tarragon Butter: Let ½ cup melted butter steep with 1 tablespoon each minced fresh tarragon and tarragon vinegar 1 hour in a warm place. *Or,* mix tarragon and vinegar into creamed butter and chill. Serve with meat, fish, poultry, and vegetables. About 135 calories per serving.

Tomato Butter: Blend ½ cup creamed butter with ¼ cup tomato paste, ¼ teaspoon salt and a pinch pepper; cover and chill until firm. Serve with fish. About 145 calories per serving.

Tuna Butter: Pound ¼ cup drained canned tuna with 1 tablespoon lemon juice to a paste in a mortar and pestle. Blend in ½ cup creamed butter and ⅛ teaspoon pepper. Cover and chill until firm. Serve with seafood. About 155 calories per serving.

Watercress Butter: Mix ¼ cup minced watercress leaves and ¼ cup soft butter to a paste in a mortar and pestle. Blend in ¼ cup creamed butter and add ¼ teaspoon salt and a pinch pepper. Serve with meat, seafood, poultry, or vegetables. Good as a sandwich spread, especially with egg salad or cheese. About 135 calories per serving.

TOMATO AND PASTA SAUCES

Note: Other pasta sauces can be found in the chapter on cereals, rice, and pasta.

⚖ TOMATO SAUCE

Makes about 1 quart

2 tablespoons diced salt pork or bacon
1 tablespoon butter or cooking oil
2 medium-size yellow onions, peeled and minced
1 medium-size carrot, peeled and minced
1 tablespoon flour
1 (1-pound 13-ounce) can tomato purée
1 cup Veal (White) Stock or water
1 bouquet garni,* tied in cheesecloth
1 clove garlic, peeled and stuck on a toothpick
1½ teaspoons salt (about)
¼ teaspoon pepper
1 teaspoon sugar

Stir-fry pork in a large, heavy saucepan over moderate heat 3–4 minutes until pale golden. Add butter, onions, and carrot and sauté 5–8 minutes until limp, not brown. Blend in flour, mix in purée and stock, then add remaining ingredients. Cover and simmer, stirring occasionally, 1 hour; remove *bouquet garni* and garlic. Purée, a little at a time, at low speed in an electric blender or put through a food mill. Reheat, taste for salt and adjust as needed. About 10 calories per tablespoon.

VARIATIONS:

⚖ **Creole Sauce:** Prepare as directed, using oil instead of butter; also sauté 2 minced and seeded sweet green peppers and 2 stalks minced celery along with onions and carrot; use 2 cloves garlic and add 1 teaspoon paprika and ⅛ teaspoon cayenne pepper along with other seasonings. Simmer, purée, then stir in 1 teaspoon filé powder, reheat

briefly, and serve. Good with seafood. About 15 calories per tablespoon.

⚖ **Portugaise (Portuguese) Sauce** (Makes 1½ quarts): Prepare as directed but omit salt pork and use 3 tablespoons olive oil for sautéing vegetables. Simmer and purée as directed; mix in 2 cups Rich Brown Sauce (or rich brown gravy), cover, and simmer 10 minutes. Stir in 3 tablespoons minced parsley and serve. Good with poultry and seafood. About 15 calories per tablespoon.

Provençal Sauce: Prepare as directed, using ¾ cup each dry white wine and veal stock instead of 1 cup stock. Just before serving, stir in 1 tablespoon minced parsley. Good with seafood. About 20 calories per serving.

ITALIAN TOMATO SAUCE

Good with any pasta. This sauce freezes well.
Makes about 1 quart, enough for 4 servings

2 cloves garlic, peeled and crushed
¼ cup olive or other cooking oil
1 (1-pound 12-ounce) can tomato purée
½ cup water
1½ teaspoons salt
1 teaspoon sugar
1 teaspoon basil
1 bay leaf, crumbled
⅛ teaspoon crushed dried hot red chili peppers

Sauté garlic in oil in a saucepan over moderate heat 1–2 minutes until golden. Add remaining ingredients, cover, and simmer 30–40 minutes, stirring now and then. (*Note:* If doubling recipe, use 3 cloves garlic; if tripling, 4 cloves.) About 215 calories for each of 4 servings.

VARIATIONS:

Bolognese Tomato Sauce (Makes 5 cups): Stir-fry ½ pound ground beef chuck with garlic, breaking beef up with a spoon, 8–10 minutes until browned. Proceed as directed, adding 1 teaspoon oregano along with other herbs. About 335 calories per serving.

Italian Mushroom-Eggplant Sauce
(Makes 5 cups): Stir-fry ½ pound thinly
sliced mushrooms and 1 peeled and
diced medium-size eggplant with garlic
4–5 minutes until lightly browned.
Proceed as directed but simmer sauce 1
hour. About 260 calories per serving.

Red Clam Sauce (Makes 6 cups): Prepare as directed but substitute liquid
drained from 2 (7½-ounce) cans
minced clams for the water. About 5
minutes before serving, mix in clams.
About 295 calories per serving.

MARINARA SAUCE

Makes about 1½ quarts

1 cup minced yellow onion
2 cloves garlic, peeled and crushed
¼ cup olive or other cooking oil
1 (2-pound 3-ounce) can Italian plum
  tomatoes (do not drain)
1 (6-ounce) can tomato paste
½ cup dry red wine
½ cup water
2 teaspoons salt
1½ teaspoons sugar
¼ teaspoon pepper
1 tablespoon minced fresh oregano or 1
  teaspoon dried oregano
¼ cup finely grated Romano cheese
  (optional)

Sauté onion and garlic in oil in a large,
heavy saucepan over moderate heat 8–10
minutes until golden. Add remaining
ingredients except cheese, cover, and
simmer 1 hour, stirring occasionally.
Press sauce through a sieve or purée, a
little at a time, in an electric blender at
low speed. Reheat to simmering, add
cheese if you wish, and serve hot with
any pasta. About 225 calories per 1-cup
serving (without cheese).

VARIATIONS:

Mushroom-Marinara Sauce: Prepare as
directed but mix in ¾–1 pound sautéed
sliced mushrooms just before serving.
About 275 calories per 1-cup serving.

Anchovy-Marinara Sauce: Prepare as
directed but omit salt; just before serving, mix in 2 (2-ounce) cans anchovy
fillets, drained and minced. About 285
calories per 1-cup serving.

MOLE SAUCE

Makes about 2 cups

3 ripe tomatoes, peeled, cored, seeded,
  and coarsely chopped
½ cup ground blanched almonds or
  unsalted peanuts
1 (4-ounce) can peeled green chilies,
  drained, or 1 tablespoon chili powder
2 cloves garlic, peeled and crushed
2 tablespoons grated yellow onion
1 tablespoon sesame seeds
¼ teaspoon coriander
¼ teaspoon salt
⅛ teaspoon cinnamon
1 cup chicken broth
1 (1-ounce) square unsweetened
  chocolate, coarsely grated

Purée all ingredients in an electric
blender at high speed 1 minute. Transfer to a saucepan and simmer, uncovered,
stirring now and then, ½ hour. Sauce is
now ready to add to braised chicken or
turkey. About 370 calories per 1-cup
serving, 25 calories per tablespoon.

⚖ SALSA FRÍA

Mexican green tomatoes (*tomatillos*),
available canned in Latin-American
groceries, make a good addition to
salsa fría. Chop 2 or 3 fine and add
along with the other tomatoes.
Makes about 2 cups

4 ripe tomatoes, peeled, cored, seeded,
  and coarsely chopped
1 large red onion, peeled and minced
1 medium-size sweet green pepper,
  cored, seeded, and minced
½ small hot red chili pepper, cored and
  seeded, or 1 (4-ounce) can peeled
  green chilies, drained and minced very
  fine
1 clove garlic, peeled and crushed
1 tablespoon red wine vinegar
1 tablespoon olive oil
1 teaspoon salt (about)
¼ teaspoon coriander or 1 teaspoon
  minced fresh coriander leaves
Pinch cloves

Mix all ingredients and chill well; taste for salt and adjust as needed. Serve cold with steaks or fish either on the side of the plate or in individual bowls. About 10 calories per tablespoon.

VARIATION:

⚖ Prepare as directed but substitute 1 (1-pound) can tomatoes, drained and coarsely chopped, for fresh tomatoes, and ⅛–¼ teaspoon crushed dried hot red chili peppers for the fresh or canned. About 10 calories per serving.

BEEF, SAUSAGE, AND MUSHROOM SAUCE FOR PASTA

Here's a versatile sauce that freezes beautifully and can be used for making lasagne or ladled over steaming spaghetti, linguine, or macaroni.
Makes about 1 gallon, enough for 16–18 servings

1 pound sweet Italian sausages
1½ pounds ground beef chuck
3 large yellow onions, peeled and minced
4 cloves garlic, peeled and crushed
4 teaspoons salt
2 tablespoons oregano
1 tablespoon basil
1 teaspoon chili powder
⅛ teaspoon crushed dried hot red chili peppers
1 (8-ounce) can mushrooms (do not drain)
1 (1-quart 14-ounce) can tomato juice
4 (6-ounce) cans tomato paste
1 cup water

Slit sausage casings and remove meat; sauté over moderate heat in a large, heavy skillet, breaking meat up with a fork, about 10 minutes until golden brown. Transfer to a large kettle with a slotted spoon. Drain all but 3 tablespoons drippings from skillet, add beef and brown over moderate heat; transfer to kettle, using a slotted spoon. Again drain all but 3 tablespoons drippings from skillet; add onions and garlic and sauté, stirring occasionally, 8–10 minutes until golden. Transfer to kettle. Mix remaining ingredients into kettle,

cover, and simmer 2 hours over moderate heat, stirring occasionally. Serve hot over pasta, or cool to room temperature and freeze for use later. About 195 calories for each of 16 servings, 175 calories for each of 18 servings.

SAVORY BEEF AND TOMATO SAUCE FOR PASTA

Makes about 1 quart, enough for 4 servings

2 medium-size yellow onions, peeled and coarsely chopped
1 clove garlic, peeled and crushed
2 tablespoons olive oil
1 pound ground beef chuck
1 large bay leaf, crumbled
½ teaspoon oregano
¼ teaspoon summer savory
¼ teaspoon nutmeg
1½ teaspoons salt
⅛ teaspoon pepper
2 tablespoons bourbon (optional)
1 tablespoon light brown sugar
1 (1-pound 12-ounce) can tomatoes (do not drain)
1 (6-ounce) can tomato paste
⅔ cup water

Sauté onions and garlic in oil in a large, heavy skillet over moderate heat, stirring occasionally, 10 minutes, until golden. Add beef, breaking it up with a spoon, and sauté 8–10 minutes until just pink. Stir in bay leaf, oregano, savory, nutmeg, salt, pepper, bourbon, if you like, and brown sugar and heat, stirring, 5 minutes. Reduce heat to low, stir in remaining ingredients, and simmer uncovered, stirring occasionally, 1½ hours. Serve hot over pasta. About 470 calories for each of 4 servings.

⌧ WHITE CLAM SAUCE FOR SPAGHETTI

Makes about 3 cups, enough for 4 servings

2 cloves garlic, peeled and crushed
1 medium-size yellow onion, peeled and minced
2 tablespoons olive or other cooking oil

2 (10½-ounce) cans minced clams,
    drained (reserve liquid)
¼ teaspoon basil
¼ teaspoon oregano
1 tablespoon minced parsley
⅛ teaspoon white pepper
¼ teaspoon salt

Stir-fry onion and garlic in oil in a heavy
saucepan over moderate heat 8–10
minutes until golden. Add clam liquid
(but not clams) and all remaining ingredients; cover and simmer 15 minutes. Add clams, cover, and simmer 5–7
minutes. Serve over hot spaghetti or
linguine. About 140 calories for each of
4 servings.

☒ TUNA SAUCE FOR PASTA

Makes about 1 cup, enough for 2
servings

1 clove garlic, peeled and crushed
2 tablespoons olive oil
2 tablespoons butter or margarine
1 (7½-ounce) can tuna in olive oil (do
    not drain)
2 anchovy fillets, minced
1 teaspoon minced parsley
⅛ teaspoon freshly ground black pepper

Sauté garlic in oil and butter in a saucepan 1–2 minutes over moderate heat
until golden. Mix in tuna and anchovies,
turn heat to low, and warm, breaking up
tuna chunks. Cover and simmer 5 minutes. Ladle into a sauceboat, sprinkle
with parsley and pepper, and serve with
spaghetti or linguine. About 360
calories for each of 2 servings.

VARIATION:

☒ **Anchovy-Olive Sauce for Pasta:**
Sauté garlic in ¼ cup each olive oil and
butter. Add 2 (2-ounce) cans anchovy
fillets, drained and minced, instead of
tuna and anchovies called for and cook
and stir until anchovies disintegrate.
Mix in ¼ cup coarsely chopped pitted
ripe olives, the parsley and pepper and
serve. About 630 calories for each of 2
servings.

BARBECUE SAUCES AND MARINADES

Note: Other barbecue sauces and
marinades can be found in the individual
meat, poultry, and seafood sections.

¢ ALL-PURPOSE BARBECUE SAUCE

Makes about 1¼ cups

¼ cup cider vinegar
½ cup water
2 tablespoons sugar
1 tablespoon prepared mild yellow
    mustard
½ teaspoon pepper
1½ teaspoons salt
¼ teaspoon paprika
1 thick slice lemon
½ medium-size yellow onion, peeled and
    sliced thin
¼ cup butter or margarine
½ cup ketchup
2 tablespoons Worcestershire sauce

Simmer all but last 2 ingredients,
uncovered, 20 minutes, stirring
occasionally; off heat, mix in ketchup
and Worcestershire sauce. Use in making
any barbecued dish. About 585 calories
per cup, 37 calories per tablespoon.

☒ BARBECUE SAUCE FOR BEEF

Makes 2 cups

½ cup cooking oil
½ cup dry red wine or red wine vinegar
2 tablespoons Worcestershire sauce
1 clove garlic, peeled and crushed
¼ teaspoon seasoned pepper
1 cup tomato juice

Shake all ingredients in a shaker jar to
blend; use as a marinade for beef or as a
brush-on basting. About 575 calories per
cup, 36 calories per tablespoon.

⚖ ⊠ BARBECUE GRAVY FOR BEEF

Makes about 2½ cups

½ cup Barbecue Sauce for Beef
1 cup tomato juice
1 cup condensed beef broth
2 tablespoons cornstarch blended with 2 tablespoons cold water

Heat and stir all ingredients over moderate heat until thickened and clear. Reduce heat and let mellow 3–5 minutes. Serve with any barbecued beef. About 11 calories per tablespoon.

SOUTH AMERICAN HOT BARBECUE SAUCE

Hot and spicy. Especially good for basting charcoal-broiled meats.
Makes about 3 cups

½ cup minced yellow onion
½ cup minced sweet green pepper
2 cloves garlic, peeled and crushed
¼ cup olive oil
2 teaspoons chili powder
2 cups tomato purée
½ cup red wine vinegar
⅓ cup firmly packed dark brown sugar
¼ teaspoon crushed dried hot red chili peppers
1½ teaspoons salt

Stir-fry onion, green pepper, and garlic in oil in a saucepan over moderate heat 5–8 minutes until onion is pale golden. Add chili powder and stir-fry 1–2 minutes. Add remaining ingredients, cover, and simmer ½ hour. Use as a basting sauce for spareribs, beef, or poultry. About 320 calories per cup, 20 calories per tablespoon.

⊠ CALIFORNIA ORANGE-GINGER BARBECUE SAUCE

Makes about 3 cups

1 cup orange juice
1 cup ginger ale
½ cup ketchup
¼ cup cooking oil
¼ cup honey or light corn syrup
¼ cup sweet sherry
2 tablespoons frozen orange juice concentrate
1 teaspoon ginger
1 teaspoon salt
Pinch cayenne pepper

Mix all ingredients and use to baste poultry, lamb, or pork. About 427 calories per cup, 27 calories per tablespoon.

⊠ CHINESE BARBECUE SAUCE

Makes about ½ cup

⅔ cup firmly packed dark brown sugar
2 tablespoons cider vinegar
2 tablespoons soy sauce
⅛ teaspoon curry powder
¼ teaspoon garlic powder

Mix together all ingredients until sugar dissolves. Use for brushing barbecued spareribs, loin of pork, leg of lamb, or lamb shanks. About 70 calories per tablespoon.

⊠ ⚖ TERIYAKI SAUCE

A strong sauce best added with a light hand.
Makes about ¾ cup

½ cup soy sauce
¼ cup mirin (sweet rice wine), sake, or medium-dry sherry
1 tablespoon sugar (if sake or sherry is used)
2 teaspoons finely grated fresh gingerroot or 1 tablespoon minced preserved ginger
¼ clove garlic, peeled and crushed (optional)

Mix all ingredients and use as a marinade or basting sauce for broiled beef or chicken or roast pork. About 11 calories per tablespoon if made with *mirin,* 15 calories per tablespoon if made with *sake* and sugar or with sherry and sugar.

⊠ POULTRY MARINADE

Suit the wine or vinegar in the marinade to the bird—white for chicken, Cornish game hens, or turkey; red for duckling, goose, or game birds.
Makes 2 cups

*1 cup medium-dry white or red wine,
   sweet or dry Vermouth, or ½ cup each
   wine vinegar and water*
1 cup olive or other cooking oil
*1 clove garlic, peeled and crushed
   (optional)*
*Few crushed sprigs fresh rosemary,
   tarragon, or thyme*
¼ teaspoon crushed juniper berries

Place all ingredients in a large jar, cover, and shake vigorously. Use to marinate and/or baste poultry. If made with wine: About 1100 calories per cup, 69 calories per tablespoon. If made with water and vinegar: About 1012 calories per cup, 63 calories per tablespoon.

⚖ ⊠ BUTTERMILK MARINADE

Makes 1 quart

1 quart buttermilk
2 tablespoons white vinegar
*1 large yellow onion, peeled and sliced
   thin*
2 teaspoons prepared horseradish
½ teaspoon sage
1 teaspoon salt
⅛ teaspoon pepper

Mix all ingredients and use to marinate poultry, game, or lamb. About 105 calories per cup, 6 calories per tablespoon.

⊠ BEER MARINADE

Makes 2 cups

1 (12-ounce) can beer
½ cup French dressing
1 clove garlic, peeled and crushed
1 teaspoon powdered mustard
½ teaspoon salt
¼ teaspoon pepper

Mix all ingredients and use to marinate poultry, beef, game, or shrimp. About 315 calories per cup, 20 calories per tablespoon.

OTHER SAUCES

⚖ ⊠ QUICK AND EASY CHILI SAUCE

Makes about 5½ cups

1 (1-pound) can tomatoes (do not drain)
1 (1-pound 12-ounce) can tomato purée
*1 large yellow onion, peeled and grated
   fine*
2 cloves garlic, peeled and crushed
¼ cup cider vinegar
1 tablespoon chili powder
1½ teaspoons salt
1 teaspoon sugar
*⅛ teaspoon crushed dried hot red chili
   peppers*
⅛ teaspoon allspice
*2 tablespoons cornstarch mixed with 2
   tablespoons cider vinegar.*

Purée tomatoes in an electric blender or put through a food mill. Mix with all but last ingredient and heat in a large saucepan until bubbling. Stir in cornstarch paste and heat, stirring constantly, 2–3 minutes. Reduce heat and simmer, uncovered, 10 minutes. Cool, ladle into sterilized jars, and seal. Sauce will keep in a cool place without refrigeration 2–3 weeks, longer in refrigerator. About 5 calories per tablespoon.

⊠ COCKTAIL SAUCE

Makes 1 cup

1 cup ketchup or chili sauce
1–2 tablespoons prepared horseradish
1 tablespoon lemon juice
*2–3 dashes liquid hot red pepper
   seasoning*

Mix all ingredients and let stand ½ hour for flavors to blend. Serve with seafood. About 20 calories per tablespoon.

VARIATION:

⊠ Fin and Claw Cocktail Sauce:
Prepare as directed but use ½ cup mayonnaise and ½ cup chili sauce instead of all ketchup. About 75 calories per tablespoon.

BREAD SAUCE

Traditional with game birds but good, too, with any poultry.
Makes 2 cups

1 large yellow onion, peeled and stuck with 6 cloves
2 cups milk
2 tablespoons butter
1 teaspoon salt (about)
¼ teaspoon white pepper
Pinch mace (optional)
Pinch cayenne pepper
1 cup fine dry bread crumbs
2 tablespoons light or heavy cream

Simmer onion, covered, in milk with butter and seasonings ¾ hour until mushy; remove onion, pick out cloves and discard. If you like mince onion and return to milk. Mix in crumbs and heat, stirring constantly, over low heat until the consistency of oatmeal. Taste for salt and adjust, blend in cream, and serve. About 20 calories per tablespoon.

CUMBERLAND SAUCE

Serve with venison.
Makes about 2 cups

2 tablespoons finely slivered orange rind (orange part only)
1 tablespoon finely slivered lemon rind (yellow part only)
1 shallot, peeled and minced, or 1 scallion, minced (white part only)
⅓ cup water
1 cup red currant jelly
1 cup tawny port wine
½ teaspoon powdered mustard mixed with 1 teaspoon water
¼ cup orange juice
2 tablespoons lemon juice
½ teaspoon salt
⅛ teaspoon ginger
Pinch cayenne pepper

Boil orange and lemon rind and shallot in water 3–4 minutes; drain off water. Simmer remaining ingredients, covered, stirring now and then, 10 minutes. Add rinds and shallots, cover, and simmer 5 minutes. About 45 calories per tablespoon.

⊠ ⚖ SWEET-SOUR SAUCE

Makes 1⅔ cups

1 cup water or pineapple juice or a ½ and ½ mixture of water and beef or chicken broth
¼ cup cider vinegar
¼ cup soy sauce
⅓ cup firmly packed light brown sugar
1 teaspoon finely grated fresh gingerroot or ⅛ teaspoon powdered ginger
½ clove garlic, peeled and crushed
2 tablespoons cornstarch blended with 2 tablespoons cold water

Heat together all but last ingredient; when steaming, mix in cornstarch paste and cook and stir until thickened and clear. Lower heat, cover, and simmer 5 minutes. Serve with roast pork, spareribs, broiled shrimp, or Chinese-style vegetables. About 15 calories per tablespoon.

VARIATIONS:

Pineapple-Pepper Sweet-Sour Sauce: Drain liquid from 1 (8¾-ounce) can pineapple tidbits and add enough pineapple juice to total 1 cup. Prepare sauce as directed, using the pineapple juice and adding ½ cup minced sweet green pepper before simmering. Just before serving, stir in pineapple tidbits. About 20 calories per tablespoon.

Chinese-Style Sweet-Sour Sauce: Stir-fry 1 medium-size sweet green pepper, cored, seeded, and cut in ½" squares, with 1 carrot, peeled and cut in julienne strips, in 2 tablespoons peanut or other cooking oil 2–3 minutes over moderate heat; do not brown. Mix in liquid and proceed as recipe directs, reducing soy sauce to 2 tablespoons. Before serving, mix in 1 tablespoon dry sherry and, if you like, ½ cup pineapple tidbits. About 25 calories per tablespoon (without pineapple tidbits).

⊠ JAPANESE STEAK SAUCE

Makes about 1 cup

¼ cup minced yellow onion
2 tablespoons butter or margarine
½ cup Japanese soy or teriyaki sauce

1 tablespoon chili sauce or ketchup
2 tablespoons dry sherry or sake
2 teaspoons powdered mustard
½ teaspoon pepper

Stir-fry onion in butter in a small saucepan over moderate heat 8–10 minutes until golden. Mix in remaining ingredients and simmer, uncovered, 5 minutes. Serve hot over any broiled steak. Good, too, with lamb and pork chops. About 20 calories per tablespoon.

⚖ ▧ TEMPURA SAUCE

Makes about 1½ cups

¼ cup Japanese soy sauce
1 cup hot beef broth
1 teaspoon light brown sugar
2 tablespoons dry sherry or sake
1 medium-size radish, grated fine
¼ teaspoon monosodium glutamate
¼ teaspoon finely grated fresh gingerroot

Mix all ingredients and let stand at room temperature 10 minutes. Mix well again and serve with Japanese Butterfly Shrimp or tempura. About 5 calories per tablespoon.

⚖ ¢ ▧ HOT CHINESE MUSTARD SAUCE

Very hot. Use sparingly.
Makes ¼ cup

2 tablespoons powdered mustard
1 tablespoon cold water
1 tablespoon white vinegar
¼ teaspoon salt
¼ teaspoon sugar
2 or 3 drops liquid hot red pepper seasoning
Pinch turmeric
Pinch ginger

Blend mustard with water and vinegar until smooth, mix in remaining ingredients, and let stand 10 minutes to develop and blend flavors. Serve as a dip for spareribs or Chinese egg rolls. About 5 calories per tablespoon.

▧ FRESH MINT SAUCE

Makes about 1 quart

1½ cups cider or white vinegar
1½ cups sugar
1 cup minced fresh mint leaves (measure loosely packed)

Wash and sterilize enough preserving jars and closures to hold 1 quart (baby food jars are ideal). Stir vinegar and sugar together in a large bowl until sugar dissolves. Add mint and mix well; ladle into jars, distributing mint evenly. Screw lids on and store in a dark, cool place (sauce will keep 2–3 months). Serve with hot or cold roast lamb, lamb chops, or tiny boiled new potatoes. About 20 calories per tablespoon.

▧ EASY RAISIN SAUCE

Makes about 2½ cups

3 tablespoons cornstarch
2 cups apple cider
1 tablespoon orange juice
1 teaspoon finely grated orange rind
2 tablespoons butter or margarine
1 cup seedless raisins

In a closed shaker jar, blend cornstarch with ½ cup apple cider until smooth. Pour into a small saucepan, add all remaining ingredients, and heat, stirring constantly over moderate heat, until thickened and clear and no raw starch taste remains. Turn heat to low and let sauce mellow 2–3 minutes, stirring occasionally. Serve warm with ham or tongue. About 25 calories per tablespoon.

PLUM SAUCE

Makes about 1½ cups

½ cup mango chutney
1 cup red plum jelly
2 teaspoons light brown sugar
2 teaspoons red wine vinegar

Drain and reserve liquid from chutney; chop solids fine. Mix chutney liquid and chopped chutney with remaining ingredients, cover, and let stand at room temperature 1 hour. Serve with Barbecued or Chinese-Style Spareribs. About 30 calories per tablespoon.

⊠ WHOLE CRANBERRY SAUCE

Makes about 1 quart

2 cups water
2 cups sugar
1 pound fresh or frozen cranberries,
washed and stemmed

Bring water and sugar to a boil in a large, heavy saucepan over moderate heat, stirring constantly; boil, uncovered, 5 minutes without stirring. Add cranberries, cover, and simmer 5–7 minutes until skins pop open. Serve warm or chilled with poultry or pork. About 30 calories per tablespoon.

VARIATIONS:

⊠ **Spicy Whole Cranberry Sauce:** Prepare as directed but add 1 stick cinnamon and 18 whole cloves tied in cheesecloth along with cranberries, remove before serving. About 30 calories per tablespoon.

⊠ **Orange-Cranberry Sauce:** Prepare as directed but substitute light brown sugar for the granulated and the juice of 3 oranges and ¼ cup water for the 2 cups water. If you like, add a cinnamon stick. About 30 calories per tablespoon.

CHAPTER 15

STUFFINGS AND FORCEMEATS

Many a routine dish has been transformed into something unique by the addition of a stuffing or forcemeat (*farce,* the French call these savory mixtures of finely minced meat and vegetables). Most are easy to make (if not quick), most are economical and a good way to stretch the number of servings. The varieties of stuffings are as broad as the imagination. They can be made wholly or partly from scratch or they can be stirred up in minutes, using any of the package mixes available. Stuffings and forcemeats, by the way, are an excellent way to use up odds and ends of meats, vegetables, and breads.

Some Tips on Making and Using Stuffings and Forcemeats

– Mix stuffings and forcemeats just before using—there is danger of food poisoning if they are made far ahead of time.

– To save last minute frenzy, have all ingredients chopped or minced beforehand, but do not mix. Keep ingredients in separate containers in the refrigerator and put together just before using.

– Never put stuffing into a bird, roast, or fish until just before cooking.

– Never stuff anything that is to be frozen, either before or after cooking. It is true that prestuffed frozen turkeys are available, but commercial packers have access to preservatives the housewife doesn't.

– Always remove stuffing from leftover bird, roast or fish, wrap and refrigerate separately—again to reduce risk of food poisoning.

– Team rich stuffings with not so rich poultry, meat, or fish, light stuffings with heavier poultry, meat, or fish. (*Note:*

Best stuffings for specific seafoods and poultry are named in the charts of Sauces, Gravies, and Seasonings in each of those sections.)

– Never use raw pork or pork sausage in a stuffing or forcemeat; always sauté first in a skillet until no pink color remains.

– To mellow flavor of minced onions, garlic, celery, and mushrooms, sauté lightly before mixing into stuffing.

– When using soft white commercial bread in stuffings, reduce amount of moisture in recipe slightly. These breads are already oversoft and if mixed with additional liquid may produce a soggy stuffing. (*Note:* At holiday time, many supermarkets sell special "stuffing" breads.)

– Always mix stuffings with a light hand. Never pack them into a bird, fish, or roast—just drop or spoon in lightly. Stuffings expand on heating and, if too tightly packed, may become leaden. Moreover, they may rupture the bird, fish, or roast.

– Mix forcemeats with a deft hand from start to finish. Properly made, they should be moist, velvety, and airy.

How Much Stuffing Is Enough?

For stuffing lovers, there is never enough. For practical purposes, however, figure ½–¾ cup stuffing per pound of food to be stuffed. It is unlikely that you will be able to get the full amount into the bird, fish, or roast—don't try. Wrap any extra stuffing in heavy foil, then add to roasting pan about 1 hour before bird, fish, or roast is done. Or, if there is as much as 4 cups, spoon into a lightly greased casserole and bake, uncovered, during the last ¾–1 hour of cooking, just until touched with brown. Use the following chart as a guide in determining quantity of stuffing needed.

Quantity of Stuffing	Size Bird It Will Stuff	Number of Servings
1 pint	3–4 pounds	2–3
1½ pints	5–6 pounds	4–5
1 quart	6–8 pounds	6
1½ quarts	8–10 pounds	8
2 quarts	10–12 pounds	10
3 quarts	12–15 pounds	12–14
4 quarts (1 gallon)	15–20 pounds	18–20

What to Do with Stuffing Leftovers

– Slice and serve cold with roast poultry or meat.
– Fluff with a fork, place on a heavy piece of foil, dot with softened butter, wrap, and heat 15–20 minutes at 350° F.
– Fluff with a fork, place in a well-greased small casserole or shallow baking pan, drizzle with melted butter or smother with sliced sautéed mushrooms, and bake about 20 minutes at 375° F. until heated through.
– Fluff with a fork and spoon into hollowed-out tomatoes or parboiled onions or parboiled, scooped-out halves of summer squash. Dot well with butter and bake 20–30 minutes at 375° F. until vegetables are tender and stuffing lightly browned.

¢ ⊠ BASIC BREAD STUFFING

Makes about 2 quarts, enough to stuff a 10–12-pound turkey

1 cup minced yellow onion
¾ cup minced celery (include some leaves)
½ cup butter or margarine or bacon drippings
2 quarts (½″) stale bread cubes or 2 quarts soft white bread crumbs
2 teaspoons poultry seasoning or ¾ teaspoon each sage, thyme, and marjoram
1½ teaspoons salt
½ teaspoon pepper
¼ cup minced parsley
1–2 eggs, lightly beaten (optional)

Sauté onion and celery in butter in a skillet over moderate heat 5 minutes until pale golden. Mix with remaining ingredients, tossing with 2 forks. (*Note:* For moister stuffing, mix in ⅓ cup chicken broth.) Use to stuff poultry or pork. Or, if you prefer, bake uncovered in a well-greased 2½-quart casserole at 325° F. about 1 hour until lightly browned. About 235 calories per cup if made without eggs, 255 calories per cup if made with 2 eggs.

VARIATIONS:

Stuffing Balls (Makes 1 dozen): Prepare as directed using 2 lightly beaten eggs or 1 egg and ⅓ cup chicken broth. Shape into 1 dozen balls and arrange 1″ apart on a well-greased baking sheet. Bake, uncovered, 35–40 minutes at 325° F. until golden brown. About 165 calories per stuffing ball if made without eggs, 170 per stuffing ball if made with 2 eggs.

Chestnut Stuffing: Prepare as directed but reduce bread cubes to 1½ quarts and poultry seasoning to 1½ teaspoons. Mix in 1 pound coarsely chopped Boiled, Sautéed, or peeled Roasted Chestnuts. About 300 calories per cup if made without eggs, 320 calories per cup if made with 2 eggs.

Pecan Stuffing: Prepare as directed but reduce bread cubes to 1½ quarts and add 1½ cups coarsely chopped pecans (or walnuts, filberts, almonds, or Brazil nuts); toast nuts first if you like. About 330 calories per cup if made without eggs, 350 per cup if made with 2 eggs.

Water Chestnut Stuffing (nice for Cornish game hens or fish): Reduce bread cubes to 1½ quarts, omit poultry seasoning but add 1 teaspoon thyme; also mix in 2 cups coarsely chopped or thinly sliced water chestnuts and 2 minced pimientos. About 230 calories per cup if made without eggs, 250 calories per cup if made with 2 eggs.

Sage and Mushroom Stuffing: Sauté 1½ pounds thinly sliced mushrooms (include stems) along with onion and celery in ⅔ cup butter. Add 1½ quarts bread cubes, 1 teaspoon sage, ½ teaspoon marjoram, and the salt and pepper called for; omit poultry seasoning and parsley. Excellent with veal. About 215 calories per cup if made without eggs, 235 per cup if made with 2 eggs.

Oyster Stuffing: Prepare recipe using 3 cups bread cubes and 3 cups coarsely crushed crackers; reduce poultry seasoning to 1½ teaspoons and add 1 pint oysters, drained and minced. About 290 calories per cup if made without eggs, 310 per cup if made with 2 eggs.

Ham and Pepper Stuffing: Sauté 1 large cored, seeded, and minced sweet green or red pepper along with onion and celery. Reduce bread cubes to 7 cups and add 1½ cups diced cooked ham. About 270 calories per cup if made without eggs, 290 per cup if made with 2 eggs.

Apple-Raisin Stuffing: Reduce minced onion to ½ cup, bread cubes to 1½ quarts, and poultry seasoning to 1 teaspoon. Add 3 cups coarsely chopped, peeled, tart apple and ¾ cup seedless raisins. Good with pork. About 255 calories per cup if made without eggs, 275 per cup if made with 2 eggs.

Corn Bread Stuffing: Prepare as directed but sauté vegetables in bacon drippings and use 3 cups bread cubes and 5 cups corn bread crumbs (preferably from corn bread made without sugar). About 285 calories per cup if made without eggs, 305 per cup if made with 2 eggs.

Amish Potato Stuffing: Prepare as directed, using 1 quart bread cubes and 3 cups unseasoned mashed potatoes (or sweet potatoes); reduce poultry seasoning to 1½ teaspoons and add ¼ teaspoon nutmeg. About 235 calories per cup if made without eggs, 255 per cup if made with 2 eggs.

Savory Sausage Stuffing: Sauté 1 pound sausage meat slowly in a heavy skillet, breaking up with a fork, until lightly browned and cooked through, about 20 minutes; transfer to a bowl with slotted spoon. Proceed as directed, using ½ cup drippings for sautéing vegetables and reducing bread cubes to 7 cups. About 370 calories per cup if made without eggs, 390 per cup if made with 2 eggs.

Bread and Apricot Stuffing: Cover 1½ cups dried apricots with boiling water and soak 10 minutes; drain and coarsely chop. Reduce onion to ½ cup, bread cubes to 1½ quarts, and poultry seasoning to ½ teaspoon. Prepare as directed, adding apricots along with bread and mixing in ½ teaspoon cinnamon and ¼ teaspoon nutmeg. About 315 calories per cup if made without eggs, 335 per cup if made with 2 eggs.

Black Olive and Onion Stuffing: Reduce onion to ½ cup and sauté with 2 minced, seeded pimientos and the celery. Reduce bread cubes to 1½ quarts and poultry seasoning to 1 teaspoon; add 2 cups coarsely chopped pitted ripe olives. About 260 calories per cup if made without eggs, 280 per cup if made with 2 eggs.

BASIC RICE STUFFING

Makes about 1 quart, enough to stuff a 6–8-pound bird

1 medium-size yellow onion, peeled and minced
¼ cup minced celery
¼ cup butter or margarine
1 cup uncooked rice
2 cups chicken broth
¾ teaspoon salt (about)
¼ teaspoon pepper
¼ teaspoon each sage, thyme, and marjoram

Sauté onion and celery in butter in a heavy saucepan over moderate heat 5 minutes until pale golden. Add rice and stir-fry 1–2 minutes; add remaining ingredients, cover, reduce heat so rice bubbles gently, and cook 20–25 minutes until all liquid is absorbed. Uncover and fluff with a fork. Taste for salt and adjust as needed. Cool and use as a stuffing. About 265 calories per cup.

VARIATIONS:

Rice and Kidney Stuffing (Makes 5 cups): Sauté ¾ pound lamb kidneys in the butter called for 3–5 minutes over moderately high heat; remove and mince. Stir-fry vegetables in drippings and proceed as directed, adding kidneys along with seasonings. About 290 calories per cup.

Rice and Chicken Liver Stuffing (Makes 5 cups): Prepare like Rice and Kidney Stuffing, but substitute ½ pound chicken livers for kidneys. About 270 calories per cup.

Sherried Rice with Raisins and Almonds (Makes 5 cups): Prepare Basic Rice Stuffing as directed but omit celery and herbs, use 1½ cups beef broth and ½ cup dry sherry instead of chicken broth, and add ½ cup each seedless raisins and toasted slivered almonds and ¼ teaspoon each nutmeg and allspice along with broth. About 360 calories per cup.

Rice and Mushroom Stuffing (Makes 5 cups): Sauté ½ pound minced mushrooms (include stems) along with onion and celery in ⅓ cup butter; proceed as directed for Basic Rice Stuffing. About 245 calories per cup.

Avocado-Rice Stuffing (Makes 5 cups): Prepare basic recipe as directed but omit herbs; cool and mix in 2 firm-ripe, coarsely chopped, pitted, and peeled avocados tossed with 2 tablespoons lemon juice. About 360 calories per cup.

BASIC WILD RICE STUFFING

Expensive as wild rice is, putting it in a stuffing is not a waste of money, because only it can provide a certain crunch and nuttiness. Use for elegant birds—game birds or a plump young turkey. If 1 cup wild rice seems an extravagance, use ½ cup wild rice and ½ cup rice, brown rice, or bulgur wheat.
Makes about 1 quart, enough to stuff a 6–8-pound bird

1 medium-size yellow onion, peeled and minced
⅓ cup celery
¼ cup bacon drippings
¼ cup minced cooked ham
1 cup wild rice, washed well
½ teaspoon rosemary
3 cups chicken broth or water
1 teaspoon salt (about)
⅛ teaspoon pepper

Sauté onion and celery in drippings in a large, heavy saucepan over moderate heat 5–8 minutes until pale golden; add ham and stir-fry 1 minute; add rice and rosemary and stir-fry ½ minute. Add broth, salt, and pepper, cover, and bring to a boil; uncover and boil gently, without stirring, about 30 minutes until barely tender. Drain and set, uncovered, over lowest heat to dry 2–3 minutes, shaking pan now and then. Taste for salt and adjust as needed. About 250 calories per cup.

VARIATIONS:

Wild Rice and Grape Stuffing: Prepare stuffing as directed, then mix in 1–1½ cups halved, seedless green grapes. About 275 calories per cup.

Wild Rice and Cranberry Stuffing: Let 1 (8-ounce) can whole cranberry sauce drain in a fine sieve while preparing stuffing as directed; then mix in cranberries and 1 teaspoon finely grated lemon rind. About 270 calories per cup.

Wild Rice and Mushroom Stuffing: Sauté ½ pound minced mushrooms along with onion and celery, then proceed as directed. About 265 calories per cup.

Wild Rice and Liver Pâté Stuffing: Prepare stuffing as directed. Blend ¼ pound liver pâté, liverwurst, or *pâté de foie gras* with ¼ cup brandy, then mix into stuffing. About 400 calories per cup.

BRANDIED WILD RICE, CORN BREAD, AND CHESTNUT STUFFING

Makes 1 gallon or enough to stuff a 15–20-pound turkey or suckling pig

1 (½-pound) piece lean bacon, cut in ¼″ cubes
4 medium-size yellow onions, peeled and coarsely chopped
3 cloves garlic, peeled and crushed
1½ cups finely diced celery
1½ pounds mushrooms, wiped clean and sliced thin
½ cup minced parsley
¼ cup minced fresh sage or 1½ tablespoons dried sage
1 (8-ounce) box wild rice, cooked by package directions
8 cups crumbled corn bread or 2 (8-ounce) packages corn bread stuffing mix
1½ pounds chestnuts, shelled, peeled, and quartered
1¼ cups melted butter or margarine
1 cup chicken broth or water
½ cup brandy
¼ teaspoon pepper

Brown bacon in a large, heavy skillet over moderately high heat and drain on paper toweling. Stir-fry onions, garlic, and celery in drippings 8–10 minutes until golden. Add mushrooms, parsley, and sage and sauté, stirring occasionally, 8–10 minutes. Mix with all remaining ingredients (you'll have to use a very large kettle for this job) and use for stuffing a large turkey or suckling pig. Wrap any leftover stuffing in heavy foil and chill until about 1 hour before serving; place foil package in roasting pan alongside turkey or pig and let heat as turkey or pig finishes roasting. About 470 calories per cup.

CORN BREAD AND SAUSAGE STUFFING

Makes about 2 quarts, enough to stuff a 10–12-pound turkey

1½ pounds sausage meat
1 cup minced yellow onions
1 cup minced celery
2 (8-ounce) packages corn bread stuffing mix
½ teaspoon sage
½ teaspoon thyme
1 teaspoon poultry seasoning
2½ teaspoons salt
½ teaspoon pepper
1 cup melted butter or margarine

Sauté sausage slowly in a heavy skillet, breaking up with a fork, until lightly browned and thoroughly cooked, about 20 minutes; transfer to a large bowl with a slotted spoon. Drain all but ¼ cup drippings from skillet; add onions and celery and stir-fry over moderate heat 8–10 minutes until golden. Add to sausage along with remaining ingredients and toss lightly to blend. Use to stuff turkey, any poultry or game bird. About 690 calories per cup.

VARIATIONS:

Corn Bread and Oyster Stuffing: Omit sausage and sauté onion and celery in ¼ cup bacon drippings as directed. Toss with stuffing mix, seasonings, and butter, then mix in 1 pint minced, well-drained oysters. About 465 calories per cup.

Corn Bread, Ham, and Olive Stuffing: Omit sage and sauté onion and celery in in ¼ cup bacon drippings as directed;

add ½ pound finely diced cooked ham and stir-fry 2 minutes. Toss with stuffing mix, seasonings, and butter, then mix in ½ cup minced ripe or green olives. About 500 calories per cup.

Corn Bread and Cranberry Stuffing:
Omit sage and sauté onion and celery in ¼ cup butter in a large saucepan as directed; add 1 pint washed and stemmed cranberries and ½ cup water, cover, and simmer until berries pop. Cool slightly and toss with stuffing mix, seasonings, and ¼ cup melted butter. About 440 calories per cup.

¢ SAGE AND ONION DRESSING

Makes about 2 quarts, enough to stuff a 10–12-pound bird

4 medium-size yellow onions, peeled and minced
1 cup water
6 cups soft white bread cubes
2 teaspoons sage
½ cup melted butter or margarine
2 teaspoons salt
¼ teaspoon pepper

Simmer onions and water, covered, 20 minutes. Off heat, mix in remaining ingredients. Use to stuff poultry or spoon lightly into a well-greased 2½-quart casserole. Bake, uncovered, 1 hour at 325° F. and serve with roast pork, ham, chicken, turkey, duckling, or goose. About 215 calories per cup.

PECAN-BULGUR WHEAT STUFFING

Makes about 1 quart, enough to stuff a crown roast or 6–8-pound bird

1 medium-size yellow onion, peeled and minced
½ cup minced celery
½ pound mushrooms, wiped clean and minced
½ cup butter or margarine
1 cup bulgur wheat
1¾ cups chicken broth
1 teaspoon salt (about)
1 teaspoon sage
1 teaspoon thyme

¼ teaspoon pepper
½ cup minced pecans

Sauté onion, celery, and mushrooms in butter in a saucepan over moderate heat 5–8 minutes until pale golden. Add bulgur wheat and stir fry 2–3 minutes. Add remaining ingredients except pecans, cover, and simmer ½ hour until liquid is absorbed and bulgur wheat tender. Mix in pecans, taste for salt and adjust as needed. (*Note:* If you wish to bake stuffing separately, spoon into a well-greased casserole and bake 20 minutes at 350° F.) About 310 calories per cup.

CHESTNUT MUSHROOM STUFFING

Makes 3 quarts or enough to stuff a 12–15-pound turkey or suckling pig

4 medium-size yellow onions, peeled and coarsely chopped
2 cloves garlic, peeled and crushed
4 large stalks celery, coarsely chopped (do not include tops)
¼ cup butter or margarine
1 pound fresh mushrooms, wiped clean and sliced thin
¼ cup minced parsley
½ teaspoon sage
½ teaspoon thyme
1 tablespoon salt
¼ teaspoon pepper
¾ cup melted butter or margarine
8 cups soft bread crumbs or 2 (8-ounce) packages poultry stuffing mix
1 pound chestnuts, shelled, peeled, and quartered
¼ cup dry sherry

Stir-fry onions, garlic, and celery in butter in a large, heavy skillet over moderate heat 8–10 minutes until golden; add mushrooms, parsley, sage, thyme, salt, and pepper and heat, stirring occasionally, 8–10 minutes. Mix with all remaining ingredients (use a 6-quart kettle) and use to stuff turkey or suckling pig. Wrap any leftover stuffing in heavy foil and chill until about an hour before serving; place foil package in roasting pan and let heat while turkey or pig finishes roasting. About 465 calories per cup.

ORANGE-SWEET POTATO STUFFING

Makes about 1½ quarts, enough to stuff an 8–10-pound bird

½ cup minced yellow onion
1 medium-size carrot, peeled and cut in small dice
¼ cup butter or margarine
2 cups hot mashed sweet potatoes
2 eggs, lightly beaten
2 cups stale bread crumbs
¼ cup minced celery leaves
3 oranges, peeled, seeded, sectioned, and coarsely cut up
1 teaspoon finely grated orange rind
½ teaspoon salt (about)
¼ teaspoon rosemary
¼ teaspoon pepper

Sauté onion and carrot in butter in a skillet over moderate heat 5 minutes until onion is pale golden, reduce heat, and stir fry 2–3 minutes longer until carrot is crisp tender. Beat sweet potatoes and eggs together until light and fluffy, mix in onion and carrot and all remaining ingredients. Taste for salt and adjust as needed. About 250 calories per cup.

⊠ TANGERINE CRACKER STUFFING

Makes about 3 cups, enough to stuff a 5-pound bird

4 slices bacon
⅓ cup minced scallions (include tops)
⅓ cup minced celery
2 cups coarsely crushed soda crackers
1 (8-ounce) can tangerine (mandarin orange) sections, drained and coarsely cut up
⅓ cup coarsely chopped toasted almonds
1 teaspoon finely grated orange rind

Fry bacon in a skillet over moderate heat until crisp, drain on paper toweling, and crumble. Sauté scallions and celery in drippings 3–5 minutes until

limp, not brown. Toss with remaining ingredients including bacon. Taste for salt and pepper and adjust as needed. About 370 calories per cup

SAUERKRAUT STUFFING

Makes about 1½ quarts, enough to stuff a 10-pound goose

1 large Spanish onion, peeled and minced
1 clove garlic peeled and minced
⅓ cup butter, margarine, or bacon drippings
2 tart cooking apples, peeled, cored, and coarsely chopped
¼ cup firmly packed light brown sugar
2 (1-pound 4-ounce) cans sauerkraut drained and chopped moderately fine
½ teaspoon thyme or celery seed

Sauté onion and garlic in butter in a large skillet over moderately low heat about 5 minutes until onion is limp not brown. Add apples and sugar and stir until sugar is dissolved, then mix in sauerkraut and thyme. About 175 calories per cup.

SOME EASY WAYS TO SPICE UP STUFFINGS MADE FROM PACKAGE MIXES

Each variation makes about 1½ quarts, enough to stuff an 8–10-pound bird

Prepare 1 (8-ounce) package poultry stuffing mix by package directions, then vary any of the following ways. To bake separately, spoon into a well-greased 1½-quart casserole and bake, uncovered, about 35 minutes at 325° F. until lightly browned.

Apple and Pecan Stuffing: Mix in ¾ cup moderately finely chopped pecans and 2 peeled, cored, and coarsely chopped tart cooking apples. About 255 calories per cup.

Herbed Bread Stuffing: Mix in ½ cup minced yellow onion sautéed in ¼ cup butter over moderate heat 5 minutes until pale golden; also mix in ½ teaspoon each sage, thyme, chervil, and savory and 2 tablespoons minced parsley. About 215 calories per cup.

Sausage and Mushroom Stuffing:
Prepare Herbed Bread Stuffing as
directed. Also sauté ½ pound sausage
meat or thinly sliced link sausages in a
skillet over moderately low heat about
15 minutes until cooked through.
Remove with a slotted spoon to paper
toweling, pour off all but ⅓ cup
drippings, then stir-fry ½ cup minced
yellow onion and ½ pound thinly sliced
mushrooms (include stems) 5 minutes
until pale golden. Toss into stuffing
along with sausage and 1 tablespoon
Worcestershire sauce. About 270
calories per cup.

Herbed Fruit Stuffing: Prepare Herbed
Bread Stuffing as directed, then mix in ½
cup each seedless raisins and halved
seedless green or seeded red grapes, 2
peeled, seeded, and sectioned oranges, ¼
cup minced celery, and, if you like, ¼
cup minced walnuts. About 315 calories
per cup if made with walnuts, about 280
calories per cup if made without walnuts.

Giblet Stuffing: To the prepared stuffing
mix, add the cooked and minced giblets
from the bird to be stuffed; if you like,
use giblet stock in stuffing instead of
liquid called for and add an extra 2–3
sautéed minced chicken livers. About
200 calories per cup.

Oyster and Almond Stuffing: Add ½ cup
minced yellow onion sautéed in ¼ cup
butter until pale golden, also 1 cup
minced, drained oysters, ¼ cup oyster
liquor, and 1 cup coarsely chopped
toasted almonds. About 380 calories per
cup.

Chicken Liver and Mushroom Stuffing:
Dredge ½ pound chicken livers in flour
and sauté in ¼ cup butter or bacon
drippings over moderately high heat
about 5 minutes until browned. Remove
with slotted spoon and mince. Sauté
¼ pound sliced mushrooms in drippings
2–3 minutes until golden. Mix livers,
mushrooms, and 1 tablespoon minced
parsley into stuffing. About 270 calories
per cup.

Corn and Pepper Stuffing: Sauté ½ cup
minced yellow onion and 6 minced
yellow-green sweet Italian peppers in
¼ cup cooking oil over moderate heat
5 minutes until pale golden; reduce heat
and simmer 2–3 minutes until peppers
are tender. Mix into stuffing along with
1 cup drained canned whole kernel corn.
(*Note:* This recipe is also good made
with corn bread stuffing mix.) About
270 calories per cup.

Mincemeat Stuffing: Add ½ cup each
minced yellow onion and celery sautéed
in ¼ cup butter until pale golden. Also
mix in 1 cup well-drained prepared
mincemeat. About 330 calories per cup.

Prune, Apple, and Cranberry Stuffing:
Prepare fruit before stuffing. Simmer
1 cup fresh cranberries with ¼ cup sugar
and ½ cup water until berries pop. Off
heat, mix in 1 cup diced, pitted prunes
and let stand 10 minutes. Drain off
liquid and use as part of liquid called
for in stuffing. Prepare mix, toss in
prepared fruit, 1 diced, peeled, and
cored tart cooking apple, and ¼
teaspoon allspice. About 290 calories
per cup.

VEAL AND PORK FORCEMEAT

Pounding is necessary for a smooth
forcemeat, though vigorous beating with
a wooden spoon or electric mixer works
fairly well. Any meat can be used for
forcemeat, but this combination is
unusually good. Use for Galantine or
Ballottine or to stuff chicken or game
birds. For a 10-pound turkey, double
recipe. Forcemeat balls can be used to
garnish soup, a poultry or pork platter,
leftovers can be cooked like hamburgers.
Small panfried patties or balls make
excellent hors d'oeuvre.
Makes about 1½ pints, enough to stuff
a 5-pound bird

½ cup finely minced yellow onion
2 tablespoons butter or margarine
⅓ cup scalded milk
1 cup dry bread crumbs
½ pound veal, ground twice
½ pound lean pork, ground twice

¼ pound ground pork fat
1 turkey liver, 2–3 chicken livers, or
  livers from bird to be stuffed, ground
  fine (optional)
1 egg, lightly beaten
¼ cup brandy
1 teaspoon finely grated lemon rind
¾ teaspoon salt
½ teaspoon thyme
Pinch mace
⅛ teaspoon white pepper

Sauté onion in butter in a skillet
5 minutes over moderate heat until pale
golden; set aside. Pour milk over crumbs,
mix until smooth, and cool. Pound
onion, all meats and fat, a little at a
time, in a mortar and pestle until very
smooth. Mix in remaining ingredients,
including crumb paste, and knead until
well blended. Use as a stuffing. About
795 calories per cup if made without
turkey or chicken livers, about 815
calories per cup if made with livers.

VARIATIONS:

Veal and Ham Forcemeat: Prepare as
directed but substitute ½ pound twice-
ground lean cooked ham for the pork.
(*Note:* Forcemeat may also be made
with veal.) About 745 calories per cup
if made without turkey or chicken
livers, about 775 calories per cup if
made with livers.

Veal and Pork Forcemeat Balls (Makes
about 4 dozen): Prepare as directed but
omit onion and liver, also substitute ¼
cup light cream for the brandy. Shape
into marble-size balls. *To Use as a Soup
Garnish:* Poach balls, a few at a time,
in salted simmering water, chicken or
beef broth 4–5 minutes until just cooked
through. Remove with a slotted spoon
and add to hot soup just before serving.
(*Note:* Recipe can be halved for small
amounts of soup; use all veal and serve
in a delicately flavored soup.) About
50 calories per ball.

To Use as a Garnish: Brown balls, a
few at a time, in about ½" hot lard or
vegetable shortening over moderate

heat 3–4 minutes, turning often. Drain
on paper toweling and mound at one
end of a poultry platter or use to fill
center of a pork crown roast. About
65 calories per ball.

¢ BASIC BREAD STUFFING
FOR FISH

Makes about 2 cups, enough to stuff a
3–4-pound fish

1 medium-size yellow onion, peeled and
  minced
½ cup minced celery
¼ cup butter or margarine
2 cups soft white bread crumbs or
  2 cups (½") stale bread cubes
½ teaspoon salt
⅛ teaspoon pepper
1 tablespoon minced parsley
¼ teaspoon each thyme and sage or
  ½ teaspoon poultry seasoning
1 egg, lightly beaten

Sauté onion and celery in butter in a
large, heavy skillet over moderate heat
5 minutes until pale golden. Add all
remaining ingredients and toss well to
mix. About 410 calories per cup.

LEMON BREAD STUFFING FOR
FISH

Makes about 1½ cups, enough to stuff
a 3-pound fish

¼ cup minced yellow onion
¼ cup minced celery
2 tablespoons butter or margarine
1¼ cups toasted ½" bread cubes
1½ teaspoons finely grated lemon rind
1 tablespoon lemon juice
1 tablespoon minced parsley
¼ teaspoon salt
¼ teaspoon sage
⅛ teaspoon pepper
2 tablespoons milk

Stir-fry onion and celery in butter in a
large, heavy skillet over moderate heat
5–8 minutes until golden. Pour over
bread crumbs, add remaining ingredients,
and toss lightly to mix. About 175
calories per cup.

VEGETABLE STUFFING FOR FISH

Makes about 2 cups, enough to stuff a 3–4-pound fish

⅓ cup minced scallions
½ cup minced celery
1 small sweet green pepper, cored, seeded, and minced
1 medium-size carrot, peeled and cut in small dice
½ pound mushrooms, wiped clean and minced (include stems)
½ clove garlic, peeled and crushed (optional)
2 tablespoons olive or other cooking oil
2 tomatoes, peeled, seeded, and coarsely chopped
1 pimiento, seeded and minced
¼ cup minced ripe olives
¾ teaspoon salt
⅛ teaspoon pepper

Stir-fry scallions, celery, green pepper, carrot, mushrooms, and, if you like, the garlic in oil in a large, heavy skillet over moderate heat 5–8 minutes until pepper and carrot are crisp tender. Off heat, mix in remaining ingredients. About 230 calories per cup.

TOMATO AND GREEN PEPPER STUFFING FOR FISH

Makes about 2 cups, enough to stuff a 3–4-pound fish

1 small yellow onion, peeled and minced
1 medium-size sweet green pepper, cored, seeded, and minced
¼ cup butter or margarine
1½ cups dry bread crumbs or coarse cracker crumbs
½ cup coarsely peeled, seeded, and chopped tomato
1 hard-cooked egg, peeled and minced
1 teaspoon minced parsley
½ clove garlic, peeled and minced
½ teaspoon salt
⅛ teaspoon pepper

Sauté onion and green pepper in butter in a skillet over moderate heat 5 minutes until onion is pale golden. Off heat, mix

in remaining ingredients. About 430 calories per cup.

⊠ QUICK MUSHROOM STUFFING FOR FISH

Especially good for stuffed, baked shad. Makes about 2 cups, enough to stuff a 3–4-pound fish

1½ cups soft white bread crumbs
2 tablespoons minced chives
2 tablespoons minced parsley
½ teaspoon dried tarragon or marjoram
1 (4-ounce) can mushroom stems and pieces, drained and minced
½ teaspoon salt
⅛ teaspoon white pepper
3 tablespoons melted butter or margarine
1 egg, lightly beaten

Place all ingredients in a bowl and toss lightly to mix. About 315 calories per cup.

⊠ FRUIT STUFFING FOR FISH

Makes about 2 cups, enough to stuff a 3–4-pound fish

1 cup cold cooked rice
1 cup well-drained crushed pineapple
1 orange, peeled, sectioned, seeded, and coarsely cut up
¼ cup sultana raisins
2 tablespoons melted butter
1 teaspoon finely grated lemon rind

Place all ingredients in a bowl and toss lightly to mix. About 360 calories per cup.

CRAB OR SHRIMP STUFFING FOR FISH

Makes about 3 cups, enough to stuff a 5–6-pound fish

¼ cup minced scallions (include some tops)
¼ cup minced celery
⅓ cup butter or margarine
2 cups (½″) soft bread cubes
1 cup flaked cooked or canned crab meat or minced cooked, shelled, and deveined shrimp
1 tablespoon lemon juice

Pinch nutmeg
Pinch cayenne pepper

Stir-fry scallions and celery in butter in a skillet over moderate heat 2–3 minutes. Add bread cubes and stir-fry until lightly browned. Off heat, add remaining ingredients and toss lightly to mix. About 305 calories per cup.

VARIATION:

Clam Stuffing for Fish: Prepare as directed but substitute 1 (7½-ounce) can drained minced clams for crab meat. About 315 calories per cup.

⊠ EASY ALMOND STUFFING FOR FISH

Especially good for trout.
Makes about 2 cups, enough to stuff a 3–4-pound fish

1 cup poultry stuffing mix
3 tablespoons melted butter
¼ cup minced celery
2 tablespoons minced parsley
¾ cup finely chopped, toasted, blanched almonds

Toss all ingredients together to mix. About 565 calories per cup.

CHAPTER 16

VEGETABLES

Of all the world's foods, none has greater color or variety than vegetables. None can lift a meal more quickly from the humdrum to the dramatic. And few offer cooks greater challenge.

It takes experience to whip potatoes into snowy drifts without cooling them down, to lift asparagus from the pot the second it's turning from crisp to tender, to build a soufflé out of spinach. Few people understand the art of vegetable cookery better than the Chinese and Japanese, to whom every leaf, stalk, and root is a living thing to be cooked as quickly and kindly as possible. They use practically no water, preferring to cut vegetables into delicate shapes and stir-fry them in a smidgen of oil (there are few better ways, incidentally, of preserving vitamins).

The French, too, have a talent with vegetables, particularly green vegetables, which they blanch in boiling salted water, then "refresh" in ice water. This sets the color, crunch, and flavor, meaning that a vegetable can be held several hours if necessary. It then needs only a warming in butter, broth, or sauce. Americans, strangely, have been cool toward vegetables until recently. Something—travel, perhaps, or the proliferation of ethnic restaurants–has glamorized vegetables, given them an importance long overdue.

How to Bring Out the Best in Vegetables

– The quicker vegetables go from plot to pot, the better. If you grow your own, you're lucky. If not, shop on days fresh shipments arrive.
– Buy only what perishable vegetables you can use within a day or two.
– Wash vegetables before cooking, *not* before refrigerating.
– Slice or dice vegetables as you're ready to cook them; never soak in water (except for potatoes and artichokes, which will darken if not soaked).
– Boil vegetables whole and unpeeled whenever possible. The smaller the pieces, the greater the nutrient loss.
– Boil vegetables quickly in a minimum of water (potatoes and artichokes excepted) and use any "pot likker" in soups and sauces. The French method may seem to contradict this rule but doesn't because the final heating is the cooking.

– Cook only as much of a vegetable as you need (leftovers fade fast). The best way to reheat vegetables is in the top of a double boiler with enough broth, water, milk, or sauce to moisten and revitalize them.

Basic Ways of Cooking Vegetables

Boiling: Cooking *in* boiling or simmering liquid. Start vegetables in boiling liquid, then time after liquid returns to a boil. Adjust heat so liquid boils gently throughout cooking. Cover pot or not as individual recipes recommend.

Parboiling: Partial cooking; often called for when vegetables are to be added to stews, casseroles, or other recipes.

Poaching: A variation of boiling in which asparagus or broccoli is simmered flat in a skillet in an inch or so of water.

Steaming: Cooking in a covered pot on a rack over boiling water. Though standing in some water, artichokes and stalked vegetables are technically steamed; only those parts *in* water are boiled.

Frying (Sautéing): Cooking, uncovered, in a small amount of fat until tender and/or brown. Use a skillet or French sauté pan and moderately high heat.

Stir-Frying: The Oriental technique of tossing finely cut foods as they fry.

French or Deep Fat Frying: Cooking immersed in hot fat, 360–400° F. You'll need 3 pounds shortening or 2 quarts oil to do a proper job, also a deep fat fryer and thermometer. Vegetables to be deep fat fried should be cut in small pieces if they're to cook through by the time they brown.

Braising (Panning): A combination of sautéing and boiling. A popular method is to brown a vegetable lightly in butter, then add broth or wine and simmer, covered, until tender—either on top of the stove or in a 325–350° F. oven.

Pressure Cooking: High speed steaming in a pressure cooker.

Baking: Cooking uncovered without liquid or fat in the oven (this refers to baking potatoes and other vegetables solo, not *en casserole*).

Roasting: Oven cooking, usually uncovered in some fat, often in tandem with a roast.

Broiling: Quick cooking under or over intense heat. Only a few vegetables—tomatoes, eggplant—broil well; they must be sliced thick and brushed with oil or marinade.

Charcoal Broiling: Cooking over hot coals; again tomatoes and eggplant are best.

About Storing, Canning, and Freezing Vegetables

(See chapters on the larder, canning, and freezing)

How to Dress Up Canned Vegetables
Because canned vegetables are already cooked, they should only be heated through. Two ways to do it:
– Drain can liquid into saucepan and boil, uncovered, until reduced by half. Add vegetable, a fat chunk of butter, and heat and stir 2–3 minutes. For seasoning ideas, see the Vegetable Seasoning Chart.
– Pick a sauce compatible with the vegetable (see Vegetable Seasoning Chart), then prepare, using can liquid. Add ⅓–½ cup sauce to each cup of vegetable, warm and stir until heated through, about 5 minutes.

Some Ways to Glamorize Frozen Vegetables

With so many specialty frozen vegetables available, we tend to neglect the plain-frozen standbys. Almost any of them improve when cooked in chicken or beef broth instead of water, also with the simplest additions to the pot. For example (amounts for a 9- or 10-ounce package unless otherwise indicated):

Artichoke hearts and asparagus:
  – To the pot add a sprig fresh tarragon or dill or a pinch of the dried.
  – Cook in ¼ cup each butter and water with a strip of lemon rind.
  – Cook artichokes in a ½-and-½ mixture of tarragon vinegar and water.

Beans (green, wax, or Italian):
  – To the pot add 1 peeled clove garlic, 1 bay leaf, and 2 tablespoons olive oil.
  – Cook in Italian or herb dressing instead of water; omit seasonings called for.
  – Cook with 1 (4-ounce) can undrained sliced mushrooms; add no water.
  – Cook 2 packages beans with 1 (1-pound) can undrained white onions; add no water.
  – Cook in ¼ cup each dry white wine and water with a little mint or fennel.
  – Cook in ¼ cup each wine vinegar, and water with 2 tablespoons sugar.
  – Cook with 1 cup minced celery, using water called for.

Beans (Lima):
  – To the pot add ⅓ cup minced scallions.
  – To the pot add a *bouquet garni** or rosemary sprig.
  – Cook in milk (or evaporated milk) instead of water (simmer, don't boil).

Broccoli, Brussels sprouts and cauliflower:
  – Place frozen vegetable in a shallow casserole, top with 1 (10½-ounce) can condensed cream of mushroom, chicken, or celery soup mixed with ½ cup milk. Cover and bake 40–50 minutes at 350° F. (The cheese soup works well too.)
  – Cook broccoli in a skillet with 2 tablespoons each cooking oil, vinegar, and water with a peeled clove of garlic.

Carrots:
  – To the pot add 1 thick orange or lemon slice or 2 tablespoons orange marmalade.
  – To the pot add a *bouquet garni** or rosemary sprig.
  – Cook with 1 bunch small scallions (white part only), using water called for.
  – Cook with 2 tablespoons butter and a small piece peeled fresh gingerroot, using water called for.

Corn:
  – Cook frozen ears in ginger ale or a ½-and-½ mixture of milk and water.
  – Cook cut corn in milk or light cream instead of water; add 1 teaspoon sugar.
  – Cook cut corn in light cream instead of water with 1 tablespoon minced chives.
  – Cook cut corn with ¼ cup frozen chopped sweet green pepper and 2 tablespoons butter; add no water.

Green peas—Use *no water;* cook instead in any of the following:
  – 2 tablespoons butter with a mint sprig or small peeled white onion.
  – 2 tablespoons butter with 1 teaspoon each grated orange rind and chopped mint.
  – 2 tablespoons each butter and small cocktail onions.
  – ¼ cup heavy cream and 2 shredded lettuce leaves.

Squash (butternut):
  – Sprinkle with a little nutmeg, cinnamon, and cloves, bake as directed, and stir before serving.
  – Drizzle with a little maple syrup or honey before baking; stir before serving.
  – Dot with Herb Butter before baking; stir before serving.

Squash (zucchini and summer)—Use *no water;* cook instead with:
  – 1 large peeled and chopped tomato and 1 tablespoon each olive oil and minced fresh basil.
  – 1 large, peeled and sliced onion that has been sautéed in 2 tablespoons butter or olive oil. Simply add squash to skillet after sautéeing onion, and cook covered, until tender. Season with a little summer savory or oregano.

Spinach—Use *no water;* instead, cover and cook with:
  – 2 tablespoons olive oil and 1 peeled clove garlic.
  – 2 tablespoons butter and ¼ cup minced scallions.
  – 3 tablespoons heavy cream, a pinch nutmeg or mace.
  – 2 tablespoons butter and ¼ cup chopped mushrooms.

Handy as pressure cookers are, they shouldn't be used for all vegetables. Delicate ones will overcook and become mushy or slimy, dried ones may break apart, clog the safety valve, and threaten to blow the lid off the cooker.

Vegetables That Pressure Cook Poorly:

Jerusalem artichokes	Corn (on the cob or off)	Eggplant	Mushrooms
Asparagus	Cucumbers	Endive	Okra
Celery	Dried beans, peas, or lentils	Ferns	Peppers
Chestnuts		Fennel	Tomatoes
Chinese cabbage		Leeks	Zucchini

Vegetables That Pressure Cook Well: Most other vegetables pressure cook nicely in jig time, particularly such slow boilers as potatoes, parsnips, rutabagas, and turnips. Always add water to a pressure cooker as its manufacturer directs, and use his instructions for sealing, building up, and reducing pressures. Use the chart below as a guide for vegetable preparation, seasoning, and approximate cooking times (count time *after* 15 pounds pressure is reached).

Vegetable	Preparation	For Better Flavor Cook With	Time at 15 Pounds Pressure
Globe artichokes	Wash and trim as for steaming; leave whole.	1/4 teaspoon salt	6-10 minutes depending on size
Beans (green or wax)	Prepare as for boiling; leave whole, snap or French.	—	1-2 minutes for Frenched beans 2-3 minutes for whole or snapped
Beans (lima)	Shell.	—	2 minutes for baby limas 3-5 minutes for Fordhooks
Beets	Prepare as for boiling; leave whole.	—	10-20 minutes depending on size and age
Beet greens	Prepare as for steaming.	—	2-3 minutes
Broccoli	Prepare as for steaming.	1/4 teaspoon salt	1½-2 minutes
Brussels sprouts	Prepare as for boiling.	1/4 teaspoon salt	2 minutes
Cabbage (green)	Cut into thin wedges or shred medium fine.	1/4 teaspoon salt	5-6 minutes for wedges 3 minutes for shredded cabbage
Cabbage (red)	Shred medium fine.	1-2 tablespoons lemon juice or vinegar	3-4 minutes

759

ABOUT PRESSURE COOKING VEGETABLES (continued)

Vegetable	Preparation	For Better Flavor Cook With	Time at 15 Pounds Pressure
Cardoons	Prepare as for boiling.	1/4 teaspoon salt	15 minutes
Carrots	Prepare as for boiling; leave whole, slice, or sliver.	1/2 teaspoon sugar	2-3 minutes for sliced or slivered carrots 4-6 minutes for whole carrots
Cauliflower	Wash and divide into large flowerets of equal size.	—	3-4 minutes
Celeriac	Trim, wash, peel, and slice or dice.	1/2 teaspoon salt	5 minutes
Chard, collards, kale, mustard	Prepare as for boiling.	—	3-5 minutes
Dandelion greens	Prepare as for cooking.	—	4 minutes
Kohlrabi	Prepare as for boiling.	1/4 teaspoon salt	4-5 minutes
Onions (white)	Peel but leave whole.	—	5-6 minutes
Onions (yellow)	Peel but leave whole.	—	6-8 minutes
Parsnips	Prepare as for boiling. If young, leave whole; otherwise slice or dice.	1 teaspoon light brown sugar	2 minutes for sliced or diced parsnips 6-8 minutes for whole young parsnips
Green peas	Shell.	A few pea pods	1 minute
Irish potatoes (use boiling varieties only)	Scrub but do not peel.	—	10-15 minutes for new potatoes 15-20 minutes for mature boiling potatoes
Sweet potatoes	Scrub but do not peel.	—	8-10 minutes

760

Vegetable	Preparation	For Better Flavor Cook With	Time at 15 Pounds Pressure
Pumpkin	Cut in chunks 4" long and 2" wide but do not peel.	—	15 minutes
Rutabaga	Peel and cut in 1" cubes.	—	10-12 minutes
Salsify	Prepare as for boiling; cut in 2" chunks, slice, or sliver.	1/4 teaspoon salt	4-8 minutes for slices or slivers 10-12 minutes for chunks
Spinach	Prepare as for steaming.	1/2 teaspoon salt	1 minute
Summer squash (yellow and pattypan only)	Prepare as for boiling or steaming and cut in slices 1/4" thick.	1/4 teaspoon salt	2 minutes
Winter squash Acorn	Halve, remove seeds and stringy portions.	—	8-10 minutes
Butternut	Peel and cut in 2"-3" chunks.	—	5-9 minutes
Hubbard and other thick-fleshed varieties	Peel and cut in 2"-3" chunks.	—	12-15 minutes
Turnip greens	Prepare as for boiling.	—	3-5 minutes
Turnips	Peel and cut in 1/2" cubes.	—	3-5 minutes

VEGETABLE SEASONING CHART

If vegetables are really fresh, they need only the simplest seasoning. But when they've stood too long in the bin, are canned or must be reheated, they profit by a bit of dressing up. Picking combinations from the chart below, add to each cup of cooked vegetables: 2-3 tablespoons sauce, butter, or topping; or 1/2 teaspoon minced fresh herbs (1/4 teaspoon of the dried); and/or a pinch of spice. If vegetables are to be warmed in the sauce, use 1/3-1/2 cup for each cup of vegetables.

Vegetable	For Hot Vegetables			For Hot or Cold Vegetables	For Cold Vegetables
	Sauces	Butters	Toppings	Herbs and Spices	Sauces and Dressings
Globe Artichokes	Béchamel	Browned	Chopped, hard-cooked egg	Basil	Aioli
Asparagus	Hollandaise	Lemon	Crisp bacon bits	Chervil	Chiffon
	Mock Hollandaise	Seasoned	Crushed cheese crackers	Chives	French
	Mornay		Grated Cheddar or Parmesan	Curry	Oil and Vinegar
	Mousseline		Minced pimiento	Dill	Rémoulade
	Poulette			Oregano	Russian
	Velouté			Parsley	
				Toasted sesame seeds	
				Artichokes only:	
				Bay leaves	
				Coriander	
				Garlic	
Beans:	Béchamel	Browned	Chopped toasted almonds	Basil	Blue Cheese
Green	Cheese	Garlic	or pecans	Bay leaves	French
Wax	Hollandaise	Herb	Crumbled French-fried	Celery seeds	Garlic
Lima	Mock Hollandaise	Lemon	onions	Chervil	Green Goddess
	Mornay		Crumbled Roquefort	Dill	Mayonnaise
	Mustard		Grated Cheddar, Swiss, or	Garlic	Spanish Vinaigrette
	Poulette		Parmesan cheese	Marjoram	
	Velouté		Minced scallions	Mustard	
				Oregano	
				Parsley	
				Savory	
				Tarragon	
				Thyme	

762

	Sauces	Butters	Toppings	Seeds/Spices	Herbs/Spices	Special
Beets *Carrots* *Parsnips*	Béchamel Medium White Mousseline Parsley Poulette Velouté	Herb Lemon Maître d'Hôtel Orange Seasoned	Buttered, browned bread crumbs Currant jelly or orange marmalade Light brown sugar Maple sugar or syrup *Carrots only:* seedless green grapes	Caraway seeds Cardamom Celery seeds Chervil Chives Cinnamon Coriander Cumin Dill Fennel Ginger	Horseradish Mace Marjoram Mint Nutmeg Oregano Parsley Rosemary Savory Tarragon Thyme	*Beets and Carrots only:* Oil and Vinegar Ravigote Sour Cream Horseradish
Broccoli *Brussels sprouts* *Cauliflower* *Collards* *Green cabbage* *Kale*	Béchamel Cheese Hollandaise Mock Hollandaise Mousseline Poulette	Browned Lemon Maître d'Hôtel	Buttered bread crumbs Capers Crisp bacon bits Fried parsley Grated Cheddar or Parmesan cheese Toasted, chopped almonds, pecans, or peanuts	Basil Caraway seeds Cardamom Celery seeds Chervil Chives Cumin seeds Curry powder Dill Ginger	Mustard Paprika Saffron Savory Tarragon Thyme Turmeric *Cabbage only:* Horseradish Juniper berries	*Broccoli and cauliflower only:* Aïoli Chiffon Ravigote Spanish Vinaigrette
Red cabbage	Medium White Parsley Velouté	Lemon Maître d'Hôtel	Apple cider Red wine vinegar Sour cream	Anise seeds Caraway seeds Celery seeds Chervil Coriander Cumin seeds Dill	Fennel Horseradish Juniper berries Mace Nutmeg Savory Tarragon	

VEGETABLE SEASONING CHART (continued)

Vegetable	For Hot Vegetables			For Hot or Cold Vegetables	For Cold Vegetables
	Sauces	Butters	Toppings	Herbs and Spices	Sauces and Dressings
Celeriac *Celery* *Cucumbers* *Endive* *Fennel*	Béchamel Cheese Medium White Mornay Parsley Poulette Velouté	Browned Herb Lemon Seasoned	Buttered bread crumbs Chopped, toasted almonds, pecans, or piñon nuts; Brazil nut slivers Grated Cheddar, Parmesan, or Swiss cheese Minced pimiento	Basil Bay leaves Chervil Chives Cumin seeds Dill Fennel Mace Marjoram Mint Oregano Paprika Parsley Savory Tarragon Thyme	Aïoli French Mayonnaise Rémoulade Russian Thousand Island
Corn	*Whole kernel only:* Cheese Medium White Parsley	Browned Chili Curry Herb Maître d'Hôtel Seasoned	*Whole kernel only:* Crisp bacon bits Crumbled French-fried onions Minced green pepper or pimiento Minced ripe or green olives Minced scallions or red onion	Chervil Chives Dill Parsley Savory Thyme *Whole kernel only:* Celery seeds	
Greens: *Beet* *Chard* *Mustard* *Spinach* *Turnip*	Béchamel Cheese Hollandaise Italian dressing Mock Hollandaise Mornay Mustard	Browned Lemon	Chopped, toasted almonds, pecans or peanuts Crisp bacon bits Crumbled corn bread Crushed cheese crackers Minced hard-cooked egg Minced onion	Basil Bay leaves Curry powder Mustard Oregano Parsley Tarragon Thyme	Oil and Vinegar

	Sauces	Seasoned Butters	Toppings & Additions	Herbs & Spices	Herbs & Spices	Salad Dressings
Mushrooms	Cheese Mousseline Parsley	Browned Garlic Maître d'Hôtel	Crisp bacon bits Cognac (try flaming) Medium sweet sherry Medium sweet Madeira Sour cream	Basil Bay leaves Chervil Chives Curry powder Dill	Fennel Marjoram Oregano Savory Tarragon Thyme	Herb Oil and Vinegar
Okra	Cheese Mushroom Tomato Velouté	Browned Lemon	Crisp bacon bits Grated Parmesan Sour cream	Basil Bay leaves Chervil Chives	Dill Fennel Savory Thyme	
Onions *Leeks* *Scallions*	Béchamel Cheese Medium White Mornay Parsley Velouté	Browned Herb Orange	Buttered bread crumbs Chopped, toasted pecans or peanuts Crisp bacon bits Medium dry sherry Medium dry Madeira	Basil Bay leaves Chervil Chili powder Curry powder Dill Fennel Mace	Mustard Nutmeg Paprika Parsley Sage Savory Tarragon Thyme	French Herb Oil and Vinegar
Green peas	Béchamel Cheese Mint Mustard Mushroom and Cheese	Herb Maître d'Hôtel Orange Seasoned	Buttered bread crumbs or poultry stuffing mix Chopped, toasted almonds, pecans, or peanuts Crumbled French-fried onions Sliced scallions Sliced water chestnuts	Basil Chervil Fennel Ginger Mint Mace	Parsley Rosemary Savory Tarragon Thyme Turmeric	

VEGETABLE SEASONING CHART (continued)

	For Hot Vegetables			For Hot or Cold Vegetables	For Cold Vegetables
Vegetable	Sauces	Butters	Toppings	Herbs and Spices	Sauces and Dressings
Irish potatoes	Cheese Medium White Mushroom and Cheese Parsley	Browned Herb Lemon Maître d'Hôtel	Crumbled French-fried onions Grated Cheddar or Gruyère cheese Minced dill pickle Sour cream	Basil Bay leaves Caraway seeds Celery seeds Chervil Chives Cumin Curry powder Dill	Marjoram Mint Oregano Parsley Rosemary Sage Savory Tarragon Thyme	Herb Mayonnaise Oil and Vinegar Spanish Vinaigrette
Summer squash *Eggplant*	Béchamel Cheese Mornay Mushroom and Cheese Parsley	Herb Maître d'Hôtel Seasoned	Buttered bread crumbs or poultry stuffing mix Chopped, toasted almonds or pecans Crumbled French-fried onions Grated Parmesan or Cheddar cheese Minced sautéed green or red pepper	Basil Bay leaves Chervil Chives Cinnamon Cumin seeds Curry powder Dill Mace Mayonnaise	Mint Nutmeg Oregano Parsley Rosemary Sage Savory Tarragon Thyme	French Herb Italian Oil and Vinegar Spanish Vinaigrette
Winter squash *Pumpkin* *Sweet potatoes* *Yams*	Medium White Parsley	Herb Lemon Orange	Dark or light brown sugar Maple sugar or syrup Molasses Sweet sherry Sweet Madeira	Allspice Cinnamon Cloves Ginger Mace	Nutmeg Parsley Savory Thyme	

766

	For baked, broiled, or fried slices only:					

Tomatoes	Béarnaise
	Béchamel
	Cheese
	Hollandaise
	Mock Hollandaise
	Mustard
	Mushroom and
	  Cheese
	Parsley
		Chili
		Curry
		Garlic
		Herb
		Maître
		  d'Hôtel
		Seasoned
			Buttered bread crumbs or
			  poultry stuffing mix
			Deviled or minced ham
			Duxelles or sautéed,
			  minced mushrooms
			Crumbled French-fried onions
			Grated Cheddar, Parmesan, or
			  Swiss cheese
			Puréed peas or spinach
			Mustard (especially Dijon)
			Any seafood salad
				Basil
				Bay leaves
				Chervil
				Chili powder
				Chives
				Cumin seeds
				Curry powder
				Dill
				Horseradish
					Marjoram
					Mint
					Mustard
					Oregano
					Paprika
					Parsley
					Sage
					Tarragon
					Thyme
						French
						Herb
						Italian
						Oil and Vinegar
						Russian
						Spanish Vinaigrette
						Thousand Island

Turnips **Rutabaga**	Béchamel Cheese Medium White Parsley	Browned Herb Lemon Orange	Crisp bacon bits Crumbled French-fried onions Grated Cheddar or Parmesan cheese	Cardamom Chervil Cinnamon Cumin Dill Fennel	Ginger Mace Nutmeg Paprika Savory Tarragon	

Use fresh, frozen, canned, or leftover vegetables in soufflés, but drain them *very well* before puréeing or chopping and measuring so that they will not thin the sauce too much. The chart below indicates which liquid ingredients and seasonings are most compatible with which vegetable, and notes any modifications that should be made in the *Basic Vegetable Soufflé* recipe. Choose the type of soufflé you want to make from the chart, then prepare according to the *Basic Vegetable Soufflé* recipe that precedes. *NOTE:* T = tablespoon, t = teaspoon.

BASIC VEGETABLE SOUFFLÉ CHART

Vegetable	Liquid	Seasonings	Special Instructions
Artichoke (globe) About 240 calories per serving if made with milk, 280 per serving if made with cream.	1/2 cup milk or light cream + 1/2 cup chicken broth	1 t. grated onion, 1/4 cup minced mushrooms, and 1 T. grated Parmesan	Use artichoke hearts or bottoms. Stir-fry onion and mushrooms in butter called for, then blend in flour. Mix in cheese along with egg yolks.
Asparagus About 235 calories per serving if made with milk, 275 if made with cream.	1/2 cup milk or light cream + 1/2 cup chicken broth	1 T. grated Parmesan and 2 T. minced pimiento	—
Broccoli About 230 calories per serving.	1/2 cup milk + 1/2 cup chicken broth	1 t. finely grated lemon rind or 2 T. minced capers	Purée stems and flowerets together or use flowerets only.
Carrot About 230 calories per serving if made with milk, 275 per serving if made with cream.	1/2 cup milk or light cream + 1/2 cup chicken broth	1 T. grated onion, 1 T. minced parsley, and a pinch of thyme OR 1 t. each finely grated orange rind and mint flakes and a pinch nutmeg or mace	Purée carrots for a full-flavored soufflé.
Cauliflower About 230 calories per serving if made with milk, 275 if made with cream.	1/2 cup milk or light cream + 1/2 cup cooking water or chicken broth	1 T. grated Parmesan, 1/4 t. minced chives, chervil, or dill, and 1/8 t. nutmeg	Purée stems and flowerets together or use flowerets only.
Celery About 250 calories per serving if made with milk, 290 if made with cream.	1/2 cup milk or light cream + 1/2 cup cooking water or chicken broth	1 minced small yellow onion, 3 T. grated Parmesan, and a pinch of thyme	Cook onion with celery. Add cheese and thyme to hot sauce.

Corn (whole-kernel) About 315 calories per serving if made with milk, 360 if made with cream.	1/2 cup milk or light cream + 1/2 cup cooking water or chicken broth	2 T. minced onion and 2 T. each minced green pepper and pimiento	Stir-fry onion in butter called for, mix remaining seasonings into hot sauce.
Green pea About 315 calories per serving.	1/2 cup light cream + 1/2 cup cooking water or chicken broth	1 T. grated onion, 1 t. finely grated orange rind, 1 T. mint flakes, and a pinch each of rosemary and nutmeg	Stir-fry onion and orange rind in butter called for, then blend in flour. Mix remaining seasonings into hot sauce.
Mushroom About 255 calories per serving.	1/2 cup light cream + 1/2 cup beef broth	2 T. minced onion and a pinch each of thyme and mace	Stir-fry 1⅓ cups minced raw mushrooms with onion, thyme, and mace in butter called for, then blend in flour.
Onion About 295 calories per serving.	1/2 cup light cream + 1/2 cup beef broth	1/2 small minced clove of garlic, 1/2 t. thyme, pinch of nutmeg, and 3 T. grated Parmesan	Use 2 cups chopped raw onion instead of 1⅓ cups cooked vegetable called for in basic vegetable soufflé. Stir-fry in butter with garlic, thyme, and nutmeg. Blend in flour; add cheese to hot sauce.
Potato About 290 calories per serving if made with milk, 330 if made with cream.	1/2 cup milk or light cream + 1/2 cup beef or chicken broth	1/4 cup minced onion, 2 T. minced parsley, 1/4 t. each sage and thyme, and a pinch of mace	Use hot, unseasoned mashed potatoes. Stir-fry all seasonings in butter called for; blend in flour.
Pumpkin, yam, sweet potato, winter squash About 255 calories per serving for pumpkin or winter squash soufflé, 300 per serving for yam or sweet potato soufflé.	1/2 cup milk + 1/2 cup chicken broth	2 T. minced onion, 1 T. light brown sugar, 1 t. each apple-pie spice and finely grated orange rind	Use hot, unseasoned mashed pumpkin, yams, sweet potatoes, or winter squash. Stir-fry all seasonings in butter called for, then blend in flour.
Spinach About 275 calories per serving.	1/2 cup light cream + 1/2 cup beef broth	1 minced small yellow onion and 1/4 t. nutmeg	Brown butter called for, add onion and stir-fry until limp; blend in flour and nutmeg.
Summer squash About 230 calories per serving if made with milk, 275 per serving if made with cream.	1/2 cup milk or light cream + 1/2 cup chicken broth	1 minced small yellow onion and 1/4 t. each rosemary and nutmeg	Stir-fry all seasonings in butter called for, then blend in flour.

BASIC VEGETABLE SOUFFLÉ

Because the basic proportions and methods of preparing any vegetable soufflé are very much the same, you can, by using the master recipe below, make a variety of different vegetable soufflés. If, for example, you choose to make a Mushroom Soufflé, turn first to the Basic Vegetable Soufflé Chart that precedes to determine what liquid ingredient you should use, what seasonings, what special instructions you should note, then prepare the Mushroom Soufflé following the recipe below.
Makes 4 servings

3 tablespoons butter or margarine
3 tablespoons flour
1 cup liquid (see Basic Vegetable
   Soufflé Chart)
4 eggs, separated
1 teaspoon salt
Pinch white pepper
Seasonings (see Basic Vegetable Soufflé
   Chart)
1⅓ cups puréed, mashed, or finely
   chopped cooked vegetable (see Basic
   Vegetable Soufflé Chart)
Pinch cream of tartar

Melt butter in a saucepan over moderate heat, blend in flour, slowly stir in liquid, and heat, stirring, until thickened and no raw taste of flour remains. Beat egg yolks lightly, blend in a little hot sauce, then stir back into pan; heat and stir 1–2 minutes over lowest heat. Off heat, mix in salt, pepper, seasonings, and vegetable. Lay a piece of wax paper flat on sauce and cool to room temperature. (*Note:* You can make recipe up to this point ahead of time, then cover and chill until about 2 hours before serving. Let mixture come to room temperature before proceeding.) Preheat oven to 350° F. Beat egg whites until frothy, add cream of tartar, and continue beating until stiff but not dry. Fold whites into vegetable mixture, spoon into an ungreased 5-cup soufflé dish. Bake, uncovered, on center rack of oven 35–45 minutes until puffy and browned. Serve at once, accompanied, if you like, with an appropriate sauce (see Some Sauces, Butters, and Toppings for Vegetables).

VEGETABLE FRITTERS

A variety of vegetables lend themselves to batter frying. Some should be parboiled first; others need not be. But all should be cut in small—about bite-size—pieces and all should be thoroughly dry before being dipped in batter and deep fried.
Makes 4 servings

Suitable Vegetables:
Artichoke Hearts (2 9-ounce packages frozen artichoke hearts, parboiled, drained, and patted dry on paper toweling)
Carrots (1 pound carrots, peeled, sliced ½″ thick, parboiled, drained, and patted dry on paper toweling)
Cauliflowerets (flowerets from 1 large head, parboiled, drained, and patted dry on paper toweling)
Parsley Fluffs (3 cups, washed and patted dry on paper toweling)
Parsnips (1 pound parsnips, peeled, sliced ½″ thick, parboiled, drained, and patted dry on paper toweling)
Sweet Potatoes (4 medium-size potatoes, parboiled, peeled, sliced ¼″ thick, and patted dry on paper toweling)
Turnips or Rutabaga (2 cups 1″ cubes, parboiled, drained, and patted dry on paper toweling)
Zucchini or Yellow Squash (4 medium-size squash, scrubbed and sliced ½″ thick)

Shortening or cooking oil for deep fat
   frying
1 recipe Basic Batter for Fried Foods

Prepare vegetable as directed and set aside. Heat shortening or oil in a deep fat fryer over moderately high heat to 380° F. on a deep fat thermometer. Dip vegetable, a few pieces at a time, into batter, allowing excess to drain off. Drop into fat and fry 2–5 minutes until golden brown (time will vary according to vegetable). Drain on paper toweling, then keep warm in a 250° F. oven while you fry the rest (don't cover or fritters will become soggy). Serve piping hot with lemon wedges or, if you prefer, with soy sauce. Recipe too flexible for a meaningful calorie count.

VEGETABLES À LA GRECQUE

Certain vegetables—summer squash, mushrooms, leeks, to name three—are delicious served cold in a fragrant lemon and oil dressing. Here's how to prepare them.
Makes 4 servings

Suitable Vegetables:
Artichoke Hearts (2 9-ounce packages frozen artichoke hearts boiled 10 minutes and drained)
Asparagus (2 pounds asparagus, washed, trimmed, parboiled, and drained)
Celery Hearts (6 medium-size celery hearts, parboiled and drained)
Cucumbers (8 small cucumbers, peeled, quartered, seeded, parboiled, and drained)
Endives (6 medium-size endives, parboiled, drained, and halved)
Fennel (4 bulbs of fennel, parboiled and drained)
Green or Wax Beans (1 pound green or wax beans, tipped, parboiled, and drained)
Hearts of Palm (one 14-ounce can hearts of palm, drained and sliced ½" thick)
Leeks (2 bunches leeks, trimmed, parboiled, and drained)
Mushrooms (1 pound medium-size mushrooms, stemmed and peeled)
Zucchini or Yellow Squash (2 pounds zucchini or yellow squash, scrubbed, sliced ½" thick, parboiled, and drained)

1 recipe À la Grecque Marinade

Prepare vegetable as directed above, cover with marinade, and chill 2–3 hours, turning occasionally. Serve cold as a vegetable, salad, or first course, spooning a little marinade over each portion.

VARIATION:

Vegetables à la Dijonnaise: Prepare vegetable as directed. Blend 1 tablespoon Dijon mustard into À la Grecque Marinade, pour over vegetable, and marinate as directed. Recipes too flexible for meaningful calorie counts.

GLOBE ARTICHOKES

(Also known as French or Italian Artichokes)
These large, green flowerlike buds are possibly the most beautiful of the world's vegetables; certainly they are one of the most delicate and elegant. Native to Mediterranean Europe, artichokes were brought first to America by the French who settled in Louisiana in the eighteenth century. But it was the Spaniards, settling in California, who first grew them with success. The mild California climate proved ideal for artichokes, and the fertile Salinas Valley below San Francisco particularly favorable (the Salinas Valley is today the "artichoke capital of the world"). With millions of artichokes now being harvested each year, we can all enjoy a luxury once reserved for the rich and the royal.

Season	For Top Quality	Amount to Buy	Nutritive Value	Calories (unseasoned)
October–June; peak months: April, May	Pick tight, plump green buds heavy for their size.	1 (⅓–¾ pound) artichoke per person.	Poor	Low: 30–50 per steamed artichoke; 80 per cup of hearts

To Prepare Artichokes for Cooking:
Snap off stems, pulling any tough fibers
from bottom of artichokes. Cut off
ragged stem edges, remove blemished
outer petals, then snip off prickly petal
tips. Wash under cold running water
and rub cut edges with lemon to prevent
darkening.

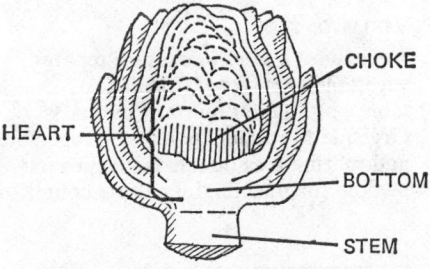

To Remove Choke (this can be done
before or after cooking), spread petals
and reach down into the center, pulling
out thistly pieces. With a teaspoon,
scoop out any remaining prickly bits.
(*Note:* Dechoked artichokes will cook
twice as fast as those with chokes in.)
If artichokes are not to be cooked
immediately, keep covered with cold
acidulated water (1 tablespoon lemon
juice or white vinegar to 1 quart water).

To Prepare Artichoke Hearts: Break off
stems and trim away ragged edges.
Remove all but inner cone of petals, lay
each heart on its side and slice off
prickly tips. Rub cut edges with lemon
and drop into acidulated water. To keep
creamy-white, don't dechoke until after
cooking.

To Prepare Artichoke Bottoms: These
can be made before or after cooking. In
either case, begin with the hearts,
remove all petals and chokes. If raw, rub
with lemon and soak in acidulated
water; boil as you would artichoke
hearts.

To Slice an Artichoke: Cut off stem and
top ⅓ of artichoke and discard; remove
choke. Lay artichoke on its side and cut
horizontally straight across the bud in
¼″ slices, letting them fall in acidulated
water. Pat dry before sautéing or
frying.

Cooking Tip: Cook artichokes in an
enamel, stainless-steel, or teflon-lined
pan so they won't discolor or taste of
metal.

Serving Tip: Don't serve artichokes with
wine or tea—for some reason, the
flavors cancel one another out.

How to Eat an Artichoke: Eating an
artichoke is like playing "he-loves-me,
he-loves-me-not" with a daisy. Pluck off
one petal at a time, dip base in
accompanying sauce, then nibble off
flesh. If the choke hasn't been removed,
lift out or loosen with knife and fork.
Cut bottom into bite-sized chunks and
eat with a fork, first dunking each into
sauce.

BASIC STEAMED GLOBE
ARTICHOKES

Steaming is the preferred method for
cooking artichokes because there is less
chance of their overcooking. Steamed
artichokes, moreover, are easier to
drain than boiled artichokes because
they have not been submerged in
cooking water.
Makes 4 servings

*4 large globe artichokes, prepared for
  cooking*
Boiling water (about 3 cups)
¼ cup cider vinegar
1 teaspoon salt
*1 clove garlic, peeled and quartered
  (optional)*

Stand artichokes stem down in a deep
enamel, stainless-steel, or teflon-lined
kettle just big enough to hold them
snugly. (You can stand them on a trivet,
if you like, but it's not necessary.) Pour
in boiling water to a depth of 1″, add
remaining ingredients, cover, and steam
45 minutes over moderate heat or until
you can pull a leaf off easily (remember
that dechoked artichokes will cook
twice as fast). Lift artichokes from
kettle with tongs and drain upside down
in a colander. Serve hot as a first course
or vegetable with melted butter or hot
sauce (see Vegetable Seasoning Chart
for ideas). Or chill and serve as a first

course or salad. About 140 calories per serving topped with 1 tablespoon melted butter.

To Boil Artichokes: Follow above recipe but add enough boiling water to cover.

To Boil Artichoke Hearts: For 4 servings you will need 8 artichokes. Prepare hearts* as directed. Bring 1 quart water, 2 tablespoons lemon juice, and 1½ teaspoons salt to a boil in a large, deep saucepan, add hearts, cover, and simmer 30–40 minutes until tender (liquid should cover hearts at all times, so add additional water if necessary). Drain upside down in a colander, remove chokes,* season with melted butter or margarine, and serve. About 140 calories per serving topped with 1 tablespoon melted butter.

To Parboil Artichokes or Artichoke Hearts for Use in Other Recipes: Boil as directed above, but reduce cooking time to 25 minutes. Omit butter. (*Note:* Dechoked artichokes will parboil in 15 minutes.)

VARIATIONS:

To Serve Cold: Cool artichokes or artichoke hearts in cooking liquid, then cover and chill until ready to use. Drain, pat dry on paper toweling, and remove chokes. Serve cold as a first course or salad with Italian or French Dressing. About 110 calories per serving with 1 tablespoon Italian dressing, 135 with 1 tablespoon French dressing.

⚖ **Low-Calorie Artichokes or Artichoke Hearts:** Instead of serving with butter or sauce, sprinkle artichokes with seasoned salt or drizzle with low-calorie herb or Italian dressing. About 48 calories per serving.

Artichoke Hearts DuBarry: Boil and drain artichoke hearts as directed. Return to pan, add 2 tablespoons butter, 8 sautéed button mushrooms, 8 boiled baby carrots, and/or 8 braised small white onions. About 100 calories per serving.

ARTICHOKE BOTTOMS STUFFED WITH VEGETABLES
Makes 4 servings

8 globe artichoke hearts, boiled and drained
¼ cup butter or margarine
1½ cups hot seasoned vegetables (asparagus tips or cauliflowerets; chopped spinach; peas and diced carrots; or sautéed chopped mushrooms)
2 tablespoons minced parsley

Strip all leaves from the hearts and remove chokes.* Melt butter in a large skillet over moderately low heat and sauté bottoms 3–4 minutes, basting all the while. Fill with vegetables and sprinkle with parsley. For extra glamour, top with Lemon Butter. About 160 calories per serving if stuffed with asparagus, cauliflower, or spinach, 180 per serving if stuffed with peas and carrots, 200 per serving if stuffed with sautéed chopped mushrooms.

VARIATIONS:

To Serve Cold: Instead of sautéing bottoms in butter, marinate 2–3 hours in the refrigerator in French dressing. Fill with cold, seasoned, cooked vegetables.

Florentine Style: Fill with chopped buttered spinach, top with Mornay Sauce and grated Parmesan, and brown quickly under the broiler.

Lyonnaise Style: Fill with a mixture of sautéed sausage and minced onion.

Piedmontese Style: Fill with Risotto, top with grated Parmesan, and broil quickly to brown.

Argenteuil Style: Fill with puréed, cooked, seasoned white asparagus.

Brittany Style: Fill with puréed, cooked, seasoned white haricot beans.

Artichoke Bottoms Soubise: Fill with puréed, creamed onions.

Artichoke Bottoms Princesse: Fill with puréed, cooked, seasoned green peas.

All variation recipes too flexible for meaningful calorie counts.

STUFFED ARTICHOKE BOTTOMS À LA PARISIENNE

Here's an excellent dish for a ladies' lunch.
Makes 4 servings

8 globe artichoke hearts, boiled and drained
1½ cups creamed chicken, ham, or shellfish
¼ cup soft white bread crumbs
¼ cup grated Parmesan cheese

Preheat oven to 375° F. Strip all leaves from hearts and remove chokes.* Arrange in a buttered shallow casserole and fill with one of the creamed mixtures. Mix crumbs with Parmesan and sprinkle over filling. Bake, uncovered, in top half of the oven 20–25 minutes until browned and bubbly. Serve as a light entree. About 150 calories per serving if stuffed with creamed chicken or shellfish, 175 calories per serving if stuffed with ham.

ROMAN ARTICHOKES STUFFED WITH ANCHOVIES

Stuffed artichokes are eaten like the steamed: pluck off petals, one at a time, then finish by eating the heart and stuffing with knife and fork.
Makes 4 servings

4 large globe artichokes, prepared for cooking
½ cup soft white bread crumbs
4 anchovy fillets, chopped fine
2 tablespoons minced parsley
¼ teaspoon pepper
½ cup olive oil
2 cups boiling water

Remove chokes from artichokes.* Mix crumbs, anchovies, parsley, pepper, and 2 tablespoons olive oil and spoon into centers of artichokes. Place remaining oil and the water in a large kettle and stand artichokes in the liquid stem end down. (The liquid should only half cover artichokes, so ladle from—or add to—the pot as needed.) Cover and simmer 35–45 minutes until a leaf will pull off

easily. Serve hot as a first course or vegetable with Drawn Butter Sauce or Lemon Butter. About 150 calories per serving (without Drawn Butter Sauce or Lemon Butter). Add about 30 calories per serving for each tablespoon of Drawn Butter Sauce added, 135 calories for each tablespoon of Lemon Butter added.

BRAISED ARTICHOKES PROVENÇAL

Makes 6 servings

6 large globe artichokes, parboiled and drained
1 medium-size yellow onion, peeled and sliced thin
1 carrot, peeled and sliced thin
1 clove garlic, peeled and crushed
2 tablespoons butter or margarine
2 tablespoons olive oil
½ teaspoon salt
⅛ teaspoon white pepper
1 sprig parsley
½ bay leaf
1 cup dry white wine
1 cup chicken broth
2 tablespoons lemon juice
1 tablespoon minced parsley (garnish)

Preheat oven to 325° F. Cut off top ⅓ of each artichoke and discard, then quarter remaining ⅔ lengthwise and remove chokes.* In a large flameproof casserole over moderately low heat, stir-fry onion, carrot, and garlic in butter and oil 5 minutes (don't allow to brown). Lay artichokes over onion mixture and sprinkle with salt and pepper. Add all remaining ingredients except garnish and cover. When casserole begins to boil, set in oven and bake, covered, 1¼–1½ hours until most of the liquid has bubbled away and artichokes are tender. To serve, strain cooking liquid, spoon over artichokes, and sprinkle with minced parsley. Provide a fork and spoon for scraping flesh from artichoke petals—they are too messy to eat with your fingers. About 125 calories per serving.

Season	For Top Quality	Amount to Buy	Nutritive Value	Calories (unseasoned)
October–March	Pick firm, unscarred tubers with tender beige-to-brown skins.	3–4 artichokes (about ¼ pound) per person.	Poor	Fairly low—about 60 per average serving

⚖ ITALIAN-STYLE MARINATED ARTICHOKE HEARTS

Makes 4–6 servings

½ cup low-calorie Italian dressing
1 clove garlic, peeled and crushed
Juice of ½ lemon
Pinch pepper
2 (9-ounce) packages frozen artichoke
  hearts, boiled and drained

Mix dressing, garlic, lemon juice, and pepper and pour over artichoke hearts. Cover and marinate in the refrigerator 2–3 hours, turning hearts occasionally. Toss well and serve cold as a vegetable or salad. About 75 calories for each of 4 servings, 50 calories for each of 6.

JERUSALEM ARTICHOKES

There's no reason why Jerusalem artichokes should be called Jerusalem artichokes. They aren't from Jerusalem and they aren't artichokes. Nut-brown and potato-flavored, they're actually tubers of a sunflower that grows wild in the Eastern United States. Eat them out of hand like a radish, or, better still, boil, bake, mash, hash, or pickle.

To Prepare for Cooking: Scrub well in cool water with a vegetable brush, cut away eyes, small knobs, or blemishes but do not peel unless the skins seem tough and inedible (because of their knobbiness, Jerusalem artichokes are the very dickens to peel).

BOILED JERUSALEM ARTICHOKES

Makes 4 servings

1 pound Jerusalem artichokes, prepared
  for cooking
2 cups boiling water
½ teaspoon salt
Butter or margarine
Salt
Pepper

Place artichokes in a large saucepan, add water and the ½ teaspoon salt, and simmer, covered, 8–10 minutes until just tender (artichokes will seem quite crisp and raw throughout most of the cooking, then quite suddenly become soft). Drain well and serve with plenty of butter, salt, and pepper. About 160 calories per serving with 1 tablespoon of butter or margarine.

VARIATIONS:

⚖ **Low-Calorie Jerusalem Artichokes:** Instead of serving with butter, sprinkle with seasoned salt or drizzle with a little low-calorie Italian salad dressing. About 70 calories per serving.

Jerusalem Artichoke Purée: Follow above recipe, increasing cooking time to 10–12 minutes so artichokes are very soft. Press flesh from skins and mash or whip until creamy with an electric mixer. Beat in 2 tablespoons each butter and heavy cream (just enough to give artichokes a good consistency), then season to taste with salt, pepper and nutmeg. Warm 1–2 minutes, stirring over lowest heat, and serve. About 135 calories per serving.

BAKED JERUSALEM ARTICHOKES

Makes 4 servings

1 pound uniformly large Jerusalem
  artichokes (they should be about 2"
  long and 1½" across), prepared for
  cooking
Butter or margarine
Salt
Pepper

Preheat oven to 400° F. Place artichokes
in a shallow roasting pan and bake,
uncovered, 15–20 minutes until tender.
(As with boiled artichokes, they'll seem
quite crisp until 1–2 minutes before
they're done, so watch carefully.) Serve
oven-hot with lots of butter, salt and
freshly ground pepper. About 160
calories per serving with 1 tablespoon
of butter.

HASHED BROWN JERUSALEM ARTICHOKES

Makes 4 servings

1 pound Jerusalem artichokes, prepared
  for cooking
2 tablespoons butter or margarine
¼ teaspoon salt
Pepper

Peel artichokes and slice thin. Melt
butter in a large skillet over moderate
heat, add artichokes, and fry 5–7
minutes, stirring now and then, until
tender and lightly tinged with brown.
Season with salt and pepper and serve.
About 110 calories per serving.

CREAMED JERUSALEM ARTICHOKES

It's best to make the cream sauce while
the artichokes cook so the two are done
at the same time.
Makes 4–6 servings

1½ pounds Jerusalem artichokes,
  prepared for cooking
2 cups boiling water
1 tablespoon lemon juice
2 tablespoons butter or margarine
2 tablespoons flour
½ teaspoon salt

Pinch white pepper
Pinch mace
1 cup light cream
1 egg yolk
1 tablespoon minced parsley or
  chives

Peel artichokes and cut in ½" cubes.
Place in a large saucepan, add water and
lemon juice, cover, and simmer 5–7
minutes until just tender; drain.
Meanwhile, melt butter over moderate
heat in a small saucepan and blend in
flour, salt, pepper and mace. Add cream,
then cook, stirring constantly, until
thickened. Beat egg yolk with a fork,
mix in a little of the hot sauce, then
stir back into sauce in pan. Mix parsley
or chives into sauce, pour over
artichokes, toss lightly, and serve. About
295 calories for each of 4 servings, 195
calories for each of 6 servings.

ASPARAGUS

Spring's first asparagus begins coming
to market about the end of February
with slim young stalks the color of
budding leaves and snug, pointed tips
faintly tinged with lavender. This is the
asparagus Americans know best, but
Europeans prefer the chunky, butter-
smooth white varieties, particularly the
French Argenteuil asparagus and the
German Stangenspargel. Both of these
are sometimes available in big-city
American markets. Try them, if you
should find them in your market, and
prepare them as you would green
asparagus—their flavor is slightly more
delicate, their texture somewhat softer.
Both the green and the white asparagus
are fragile vegetables, best when cooked
gently and quickly (the greatest crime
perpetrated against asparagus is
overcooking—when properly cooked,
the stalks will be bright green, tender
but crisp, never soft, never mushy).

To Prepare for Cooking: Snap off tough
stem ends, wash asparagus well in tepid
water, remove scales (they harbor grit),
and, if skins seem coarse, peel with a
vegetable peeler.

Season	For Top Quality	Amount to Buy	Nutritive Value	Calories (unseasoned)
Late February–July; peak months: April, May	Choose straight, bright green (or pale ivory) stalks of uniform size with tight tips and moist bases.	Allow 8–10 stalks (about ½ pound) per person; bundles average 2–2½ pounds, contain 3–4 dozen stalks.	Green has some Vitamin C and A, the white far less.	Low—35–40 per average serving

Serving Tip: Serve steamed asparagus, drizzled with melted butter or sauced with Hollandaise, as a separate course before or after the entree.

How to Eat: Use a fork whenever stalks are tender, limp or drippy. It's proper, however, to eat crisp spears with your fingers (except at formal dinners).

STEAMED ASPARAGUS

Makes 4 servings

2 pounds asparagus, prepared for cooking
½ cup boiling water
¼ cup melted butter or margarine
1 teaspoon salt
⅛ teaspoon pepper

Tie stalks in serving-size bunches, keeping strings loose so asparagus does not bruise. Stand stems down in a deep saucepan or double boiler bottom (by inverting top over bottom, you can improvise a steamer). Add water, cover, and simmer 15–20 minutes until stems are tender. Drain, remove strings, and season with butter, salt, and pepper. *Or* omit butter and top with Hollandaise or other appropriate sauce (see Vegetable Seasoning Chart). About 85 calories per serving (with butter).

To Poach: Lay individual asparagus stalks flat in a large, heavy skillet, preferably in 1 layer but never more than 2. Add 1 teaspoon salt, enough boiling water to cover (about 2 cups), then cover skillet and simmer 15–20 minutes until crisp-tender. Drain well and season with butter and pepper.

To Parboil for Use in Other Recipes: Prepare as directed but reduce cooking time to 12 minutes; omit seasonings.

VARIATIONS:

To Serve Cold: Lay steamed asparagus flat in a large bowl and cover with ice water. When cold, drain well, cover, and chill until ready to use. (See Vegetable Seasoning Chart for sauce suggestions.)

Low-Calorie Asparagus: Omit butter; dress with 2 tablespoons lemon juice or ¼ cup low-calorie Italian or Roquefort dressing. About 40 calories per serving.

Asparagus with Dill: Add 1 tablespoon minced fresh dill to the melted butter. About 85 calories per serving.

Asparagus with Capers: Reduce salt to ½ teaspoon and mix 1 tablespoon minced capers with the melted butter. About 90 calories per serving.

Buttered Asparagus Tips: Use the top 2″ of each stalk only, prepare as for Steamed Asparagus, but cook just 5–8 minutes. Season as directed. About 80 calories per serving.

Creamed Asparagus Tips: Prepare Buttered Asparagus Tips but omit *all* seasonings. To each cup asparagus, add ½ cup hot Medium White Sauce, mix lightly, heat through, and serve. (*Note:* The Cheese, Mushroom, and Mustard variations of Basic White Sauce are equally good with asparagus tips.) About 85 calories per serving.

ASPARAGUS POLONAISE

Makes 4 servings

2 pounds hot steamed asparagus or
   2 (10-ounce) packages boiled frozen
   asparagus
3 hard-cooked egg yolks
1 tablespoon minced parsley
⅓ cup soft white bread crumbs
3 tablespoons Browned Butter

Preheat broiler. Drain asparagus well and arrange in rows in a shallow buttered casserole. Press egg yolks through a fine sieve, mix with parsley, and sprinkle over asparagus. Toss crumbs in butter and sprinkle on top. Broil 4″–5″ from the heat 2–3 minutes until lightly browned. About 170 calories per serving.

⊠ CHEESE AND ASPARAGUS CASSEROLE

Makes 4 servings

2 (15-ounce) cans asparagus or 2
   (10-ounce) packages boiled frozen
   asparagus (do not drain either one)
1 pint light cream (about)
6 tablespoons butter or margarine
6 tablespoons flour
¾ teaspoon salt
⅛ teaspoon white pepper
2 cups coarsely grated sharp Cheddar
   cheese
1 cup poultry stuffing mix

Preheat oven to 400° F. Drain canned asparagus liquid or asparagus cooking water into a quart measure and add enough light cream to measure 3 cups. Melt 4 tablespoons butter over moderate heat and blend in flour. Add the 3 cups liquid and heat, stirring constantly, until thickened. Add salt, pepper, and 1 cup cheese; cook and stir until cheese is melted. Arrange asparagus in a buttered shallow 2-quart casserole and top with cheese sauce. Toss remaining cheese with stuffing mix, sprinkle over sauce and dot with remaining butter. Bake,

uncovered, 10–12 minutes until bubbly and touched with brown. About 645 calories per serving.

ASPARAGUS DIVAN

Makes 6 servings

2 pounds cooked Buttered Asparagus
   Tips
6 slices hot buttered white toast
2 tablespoons sweet Madeira or sherry
2 cups hot Cheese Sauce
¼ cup grated Parmesan cheese

Preheat broiler. Arrange hot asparagus tips on toast in an ungreased shallow roasting pan. Stir wine into sauce, pour evenly over asparagus, and sprinkle with Parmesan. Broil 4″ from the heat 3–4 minutes until sauce is speckled with brown and bubbly. About 375 calories per serving.

VARIATIONS:

Asparagus Divan on Ham: Substitute a thick slice of cooked ham for each piece of toast. Serve as an entree. About 390 calories per serving.

Asparagus and Egg Divan: Top asparagus with 6 very soft poached eggs before adding sauce and Parmesan. Serve as an entree. About 455 calories per serving.

CHINESE ASPARAGUS

Makes 4–6 servings

2 pounds asparagus, prepared for
   cooking
1 tablespoon cornstarch
2 tablespoons cold water
1 cup chicken broth
2 teaspoons soy sauce
1 tablespoon dry sherry
¼ teaspoon sugar
¼ teaspoon MSG (monosodium
   glutamate)
3 tablespoons peanut or other vegetable
   oil
¼ cup thinly sliced water chestnuts or
   bamboo shoots

Cut each asparagus stalk diagonally into slices ¼″ thick. Blend cornstarch with water in a small saucepan, add broth, soy sauce, sherry, sugar, and MSG, and heat, stirring, over moderate heat until slightly thickened. Remove from burner but keep warm. Heat oil in a large, heavy skillet or *wok* over moderate heat 1 minute. Add asparagus and stir-fry 3 minutes until crisp-tender. Slowly stir in sauce and heat 2 minutes longer, stirring constantly. Add water chestnuts or bamboo shoots and serve. About 155 calories for each of 4 servings, 105 calories for each of 6 servings.

SPANISH-STYLE ASPARAGUS BAKE

Makes 4 servings

2 pounds asparagus, steamed or poached, or 1 (1-pound) can cut asparagus
2 hard-cooked eggs, peeled and halved
2 pimientos, cut in small dice
2 tablespoons lemon juice
2 tablespoons cooking oil
2 tablespoons light cream
1 tablespoon minced chives
¼ teaspoon salt
⅛ teaspoon white pepper

Preheat oven to 350° F. Drain asparagus well; if using the fresh, halve crosswise. Arrange in an ungreased shallow 1-quart casserole. Scoop egg yolks from whites and set aside. Mince egg whites, mix with pimientos, and scatter over asparagus. Press yolks through a fine sieve, then beat in the lemon juice, oil, and cream, one at a time. Mix in remaining ingredients, pour over asparagus, and bake uncovered ½ hour. Serve at once. About 165 calories per serving.

BEANS

Of all vegetable families, none is quite so big or bountiful as the bean family. There are big beans and little beans, delicate and hearty beans, black beans and white (and every color in between). There are foreign exotics and American favorites: limas, green beans, and kidney beans. These three, nutritionists maintain, are America's most valuable contribution to the world table, more so than potatoes or tomatoes because, as a protein-rich food, beans, down the ages, have nourished people unable to afford meat. The easiest way to learn the many kinds of beans is to subdivide them by type: the *fresh* and the *dried*.

The Varieties of Beans Cooked Fresh

Green Beans (also known as *snap, string,* and *haricot beans*): A kidney bean tender enough to eat pod and all.

Wax Beans: Yellow "green" beans.

Italian Green Beans: Broader, flatter than green beans, brighter, too. Most often available frozen.

Lima Beans (the *"butter beans"* of the South): There are large limas (Fordhooks) and baby limas, better all-round beans because they are less starchy and do not cook down to mush.

Cranberry Beans (also called *shellouts* and *shell beans*): These pods look like outsize, splotchy red wax beans. The pods are tough but the inner cream-colored beans are nutty and tender.

Black-Eyed Peas: A Deep South favorite, small, pale green beans with black eyes. Pods are misshapen, russeted green, inedible.

To Prepare for Cooking:

Green, Wax, or Italian Green Beans: There are few "strings" today because science has bred them out. Wash in cool water and snap off ends. If beans are tender, leave whole; if not, snap in 2″ lengths. Green and wax beans may be Frenched for variety (slivered the long way); most vegetable peelers have Frenchers at one end. Frenched beans will cook faster than the snapped.

Limas, Cranberry Beans, Black-Eyed Peas: Shell. To hasten the job, peel a strip from outer curved edge with a vegetable peeler or snip seam open with scissors.

Cooking Tip: Never add soda to the cooking water to brighten green beans—makes them soapy and destroys vitamin C.

Season	For Top Quality	Amount to Buy	Nutritive Value	Calories (unseasoned)
Summer for Italian green beans, black-eyed peas. Year round for all others.	Choose firm, well-filled pods with lots of snap; wax and green beans should also be of uniform size and fairly straight.	1 pound green or wax beans will serve 4; 1 pound un-shelled limas, cranberry beans, or black-eyed peas 1–2 persons.	All but wax beans are fairly high in vitamin A and contain some C.	Low for green and wax beans, 30–40 per serving; high for shelled types: limas 180 per serv-ing.

An Alphabet of Dried Beans

Black Beans (also called *turtle beans*): Black skinned, creamy fleshed; the staple of South American soups and stews.

Black-Eyed and *Yellow-Eyed Peas:* Southern favorites called "peas" because their flavor resembles that of field peas. They differ only in the color of their "eyes." Black-eyed peas are available fresh in summer. Yellow-eyed peas are also known as yellow-eyed beans in some parts of the country.

Cannellini: White Italian kidney beans, available dry in Italian groceries, canned in supermarkets. Good *en casserole* with tomatoes and sausages.

Chick-Peas (also called *garbanzo beans* and *cece*): Chick-peas resemble withered filberts and are, in fact, the most nutlike of beans. They work equally well in soups, salads, and casseroles.

Cowpeas: A sort of baby black-eyed pea used in much the same way.

Cranberry Beans: (See Fresh Beans.)

Fava Beans (also called *horse beans* and *English broad beans*): Wrinkled, beige-skinned, strong-flavored giants as big as your thumb.

Flageolets: In France green beans are grown just for the tender, pale green inner beans known as *flageolets*. Though they're available fresh abroad, we must be content with the dried or canned.

Kidney Beans: Old friends, these, the red-brown beans of chili and the basis of many a Mexican recipe. They are also a popular "baking" bean in New England.

Lima Beans: Baby limas are more often dried than Fordhooks because they hold their shape better.

Pink Beans: A kissing cousin of the kidney bean, this is the bean of refried beans and other Southwestern favorites.

Pinto Beans: Another kidney bean, this one pink with brown freckles.

Red Beans: Yet another kidney bean, a smaller, redder variety that's Mexico's favorite.

White Beans: This isn't a single bean but a family of four: the big *marrowfat*, the medium sized *Great Northern*, and the smaller *navy* (or *Yankee*) and *pea beans*.

To Prepare for Cooking: Place beans in a colander or large sieve and rinse well in cool water. Sort carefully, removing withered or broken beans and any bits of stone. Soak, using one of the following methods:

Basic Method: Allowing 1 quart cold water for 1 pound dried beans, soak overnight or for 6–8 hours (discard any beans that float). If your kitchen is very warm, soak beans, covered, in the refrigerator so they don't sour.

For Top Quality	Amount to Buy	Nutritive Value	Calories (unseasoned)
Most dried beans are boxed, so buy brands you know and trust; if buying from a bin, choose clean, unwithered, unbuggy beans.	1 pound dried beans will serve 4–6 persons.	All dried beans are high in iron, most B vitamins and protein (incomplete protein, but valuable in rounding out meals).	High—from 230 per cup (white beans, black-eyed peas, red or pinto beans) to 260 (limas)

Quick Method: Allow 1 quart cold water for 1 pound of beans. Place beans and water in a large kettle, cover, and bring to a boil over high heat. Reduce heat to moderate and let beans boil gently 2 minutes. Remove from heat and let stand 1 hour with the lid on.

Cooking Tips:

(1) Always use some soaking water for cooking beans (it contains vitamins).
(2) Don't salt beans (or add tomatoes or other acid foods) until toward the end of cooking because they toughen the beans.
(3) To keep the pot from boiling over, add 1 tablespoon margarine, drippings, or cooking oil. A chunk of bacon or salt pork will do the trick too. So will a ham bone.

Some Special Beans and Bean Products

Mung Beans: We don't often see these dark, bb-sized Oriental beans, though we're thoroughly familiar with their sprouts. Many Americans today, in fact, are growing their own bean sprouts.

Soybeans: "Superbeans" might have been a better name because these beans provide oil for our margarines, a high protein flour, soy sauce, bean pastes and curds, and a yellow sprout prized by the Chinese.

Bean Powders: These are relatively new, flours, really, that can be used for thickening gravies and sauces, dredging foods to be fried, enriching breads, croquettes, and meat loaves.

BOILED FRESH GREEN OR WAX BEANS

Because beans can so easily cook dry and burn it's best to cook them covered. Makes 4 servings

1 pound green or wax beans, prepared for cooking
1 teaspoon salt
1 cup boiling water
2 tablespoons butter or margarine
⅛ teaspoon pepper

Place beans in a large saucepan, add salt and water, cover, and simmer until crisp-tender, about 15 minutes for Frenched beans, 20–25 for the snapped or whole. Drain, season with butter and pepper, and serve. About 80 calories per serving of green beans, 90 per serving of wax beans.

To Parboil for Use in Other Recipes: Follow method above, reducing cooking time to 10 minutes. Omit seasonings.

VARIATIONS:

To Serve Cold: Omit seasonings. Chill beans in ice water, drain, pat dry on paper toweling, wrap in Saran, and refrigerate until ready to use. Dress with a tart oil and vinegar dressing and serve as a salad.

⚖️ **Low-Calorie Beans:** Dress with ¼ cup low-calorie Italian dressing instead of butter. About 35 calories per serving of green beans, 45 for the wax.

Green Beans Amandine: Increase butter to ⅓ cup, melt in a small skillet, add ⅓ cup slivered blanched almonds, and stir-fry 3–5 minutes until golden. Toss with beans and serve. About 175 calories per serving.

Green Beans with Mushrooms: Stir ½ cup sautéed sliced mushrooms or 1 (3-ounce) can drained sliced mushrooms into beans along with butter. About 85 calories per serving.

Beans with Bacon and Dill: Just before serving, stir in ⅓ cup crisp cooked bacon and 1 tablespoon minced fresh dill. About 120 calories per serving of green beans, 130 per serving of wax beans.

Beans with Oil and Vinegar: Omit butter and dress beans with 3 tablespoons olive oil and 2 tablespoons tarragon-flavored white wine vinegar. About 125 calories per serving of green beans, 135 calories per serving of wax beans.

⚖ **Sweet-Sour Beans:** Omit butter and toss beans with ¼ cup cider vinegar and 1–1½ tablespoons sugar. Serve hot or chill and serve cold. About 45 calories per serving of green beans, 55 calories per serving of wax beans.

¢ ⚖ **GREEN BEANS IN MUSTARD SAUCE**

Makes 4 servings

1 pound green beans, boiled and drained (reserve cooking water)
1 tablespoon butter or margarine
1 tablespoon flour
Green bean cooking water plus enough milk to total ¾ cup
3 tablespoons prepared mild yellow mustard
1 tablespoon Worcestershire sauce
½ teaspoon salt
¼ teaspoon cayenne pepper

Keep beans warm. Melt butter over moderate heat and blend in flour. Add the ¾ cup liquid and heat, stirring constantly, until thickened. Mix in remaining ingredients and heat, stirring, 2–3 minutes to blend flavors. Pour sauce over beans, toss lightly to mix, and serve. About 75 calories per serving.

GREEN BEANS AND ONIONS IN SOUR CREAM

Makes 6–8 servings

2 pounds green beans, prepared for cooking
1 (1⅜-ounce) package dry onion soup mix
1½ cups boiling water
2 tablespoons butter or margarine
½ cup sour cream
⅛ teaspoon pepper

Place beans in a large saucepan with onion soup mix and water, cover, and boil gently 20–25 minutes until tender and most of the cooking liquid has evaporated. Mix in butter, sour cream, and pepper and serve. About 130 calories for each of 6 servings, 100 calories for each of 8 servings.

GREEN OR WAX BEANS AU GRATIN

Makes 4 servings

1 pound green or wax beans or 2 (10-ounce) packages frozen green, wax, or Italian beans, boiled and drained
1½ cups hot Cheese Sauce or Mornay Sauce
⅓ cup coarsely grated sharp Cheddar cheese
1 tablespoon melted butter or margarine

Preheat broiler. Arrange beans in an ungreased 2-quart *au gratin* dish or shallow casserole, cover with sauce, sprinkle with cheese, and dot with butter. Broil 5″ from heat 3–4 minutes until cheese melts and is nicely browned. Green beans: about 280 calories per serving made with Mornay Sauce, 320 made with Cheese Sauce. Wax beans: about 290 calories per serving with Mornay Sauce, 330 with Cheese Sauce.

VARIATION:

Lima Beans au Gratin: Substitute boiled baby lima beans (you'll need 3 pounds in the pod) or 2 (10-ounce) packages frozen limas for the green beans. About 430 calories per serving made with Mornay Sauce, 470 calories per serving made with Cheese Sauce.

¢ **BEANS LYONNAISE**

Makes 4 servings

1 pound green or wax beans, Frenched and parboiled
3 tablespoons butter or margarine
1 large yellow onion, peeled and sliced thin
1 teaspoon salt
⅛ teaspoon white pepper
1 teaspoon minced parsley
1 teaspoon white wine vinegar

Drain beans well and pat dry between paper toweling. Melt butter in a large, heavy skillet over moderate heat 1 minute. Add onion and sauté 5–8 minutes until pale golden. Add beans and stir-fry 3–4 minutes until *just* tender. Add remaining ingredients, toss lightly to mix, and serve. About 115 calories per serving if made with green beans, 125 calories per serving if made with wax beans.

¢ **GREEN BEANS PROVENÇAL**

Don't try to stir-fry more than this amount of beans in one skillet; if you double the recipe, use two.
Makes 4 servings

1 pound green beans, parboiled
2 tablespoons olive oil
1 small clove garlic, peeled and crushed
2 teaspoons minced parsley
¾ teaspoon salt
⅛ teaspoon pepper

Drain beans well and pat dry between paper toweling. Heat oil in a large, heavy skillet over moderate heat 1 minute. Add beans and stir-fry 3–4 minutes, until crisp-tender and *very lightly* browned. Add garlic and stir-fry 1 minute. Off heat, mix in parsley, salt, and pepper and serve. About 90 calories per serving.

BEANS FROM POMPEII

Makes 4 servings

1 pound young green or wax beans, prepared for cooking
1½ cups canned Italian-style plum tomatoes (include some liquid)
½ cup beef bouillon
1 teaspoon salt
⅛ teaspoon pepper
1 teaspoon minced parsley

Place beans in a large, heavy skillet, add tomatoes, breaking them up, then add all remaining ingredients except parsley. Cover and boil slowly 25–30 minutes until beans are tender. Add parsley and serve with plenty of "sauce." For extra savor, sprinkle each serving with a little grated Parmesan. About 110 calories per serving if made with green beans (without Parmesan), 120 calories per serving if made with wax beans.

SOFRITO WAX BEANS

Makes 6 servings

Sofrito Sauce:
3 slices bacon, diced
2 tablespoons lard
1 medium-size yellow onion, peeled and chopped fine
1 clove garlic, peeled and crushed
1 small sweet green pepper, cored, seeded, and chopped fine
1 sweet red pepper, cored, seeded, and chopped fine
1 large ripe tomato, peeled, seeded, and coarsely chopped
Pinch coriander or 2 leaves fresh coriander
4 pitted green olives, chopped fine
¼ teaspoon capers, chopped fine (optional)
1 teaspoon oregano
⅓ cup water
½ teaspoon salt

1½ pounds hot wax beans, boiled and drained

Fry bacon 2–3 minutes over moderate heat in a large, heavy skillet, add lard, onion, garlic, green and red peppers, and sauté 7–8 minutes until onion is pale golden. Add remaining sauce ingredients, cover, and simmer slowly 7–10 minutes, stirring once or twice. Pour sauce over beans, toss lightly to mix, and serve. About 225 calories per serving.

ORIENTAL-STYLE BEANS WITH WATER CHESTNUTS

Makes 4 servings

1 pound green beans
3 tablespoons peanut or other cooking oil
12 small scallions, trimmed of green tops
¼ cup chicken broth
1 teaspoon salt
⅛ teaspoon pepper
1 (5-ounce) can water chestnuts, drained and sliced paper thin

Cut beans diagonally, into ¼″ slices or sliver lengthwise into matchstick strips. Heat oil in a large, heavy skillet or *wok* over moderate heat, add beans and scallions, and stir-fry 5–7 minutes. Add chicken broth, cover tightly, reduce heat to low, and simmer 4–5 minutes until beans are tender. Off heat, mix in salt, pepper, and water chestnuts and serve. About 145 calories per serving.

BOILED FRESH BABY LIMA BEANS

The basic way to cook lima beans and a handy beginning for a number of flavor variations.
Makes 4 servings.

3 pounds baby lima beans, shelled
1 teaspoon salt
2 cups boiling water
2 tablespoons butter or margarine
⅛ teaspoon pepper

Place limas in a large saucepan, add salt and water, cover, and simmer 20–30 minutes until tender. Drain, season with butter and pepper, and serve. About 230 calories per serving.

To Parboil for Use in Other Recipes: Use above method but reduce cooking time to 10–15 minutes; omit seasonings.

VARIATIONS:

To Serve Cold: Omit seasonings; chill beans in ice water, drain, pat dry between paper toweling, wrap in saran, and refrigerate until ready to use. (See Vegetable Seasoning Chart for Sauce Suggestions.)

Lima Beans with Cheese: Reduce butter to 1 tablespoon, add ¼ cup Cheddar or blue cheese spread or 1 (3-ounce) package cream cheese with chives to beans and warm over lowest heat, stirring, until cheese melts. About 230 calories per serving with Cheddar or blue cheese, 280 per serving with cream cheese.

Lima Beans with Bacon and Sour Cream: Reduce butter to 1 tablespoon and stir in ½ cup sour cream and ¼ cup crisp, crumbled bacon just before serving. About 290 calories per serving.

Lima Beans with Parsley and Paprika: Toss in 2 tablespoons minced parsley and 1 teaspoon paprika just before serving. About 230 calories per serving.

Lima Beans with Dill: Reduce butter to 1 tablespoon and stir in ½ cup sour cream and 1 tablespoon minced fresh dill just before serving. About 265 calories per serving.

⊠ BABY LIMAS WITH PECANS

Makes 2–4 servings

1 (10-ounce) package frozen baby lima beans (do not thaw)
¼ cup boiling water
2 tablespoons butter or margarine
¼ cup sour cream
1 cup pecan halves
½ teaspoon salt
Pinch pepper

Place beans, water, and butter in a small saucepan, cover, and boil gently 15–20 minutes until tender. Uncover and cook 2–3 minutes longer or until most of the liquid has evaporated. Watch the beans closely at this point, as they're apt to scorch. Mix in remaining ingredients, reduce heat to low, warm 3–5 minutes to blend flavors, and serve. About 680 calories for each of 2 servings, 340 calories for each of 4 servings.

LIMA BEANS WITH CARROTS AND BACON
Makes 4–6 servings

1 (¼-pound) piece bacon, diced
2 medium-size carrots, peeled and sliced thin
1 medium-size yellow onion, peeled and sliced thin
3 pounds baby lima beans, shelled
¾ cup boiling water
1 teaspoon salt
1 teaspoon paprika
Pinch pepper
¼ cup dry white wine
¾ cup sour cream
3 tablespoons minced fresh dill

Brown the bacon in a large, heavy skillet over moderately high heat, then drain on paper toweling. Sauté carrots and onion in the drippings over moderate heat about 8 minutes until onion is golden. Add beans to skillet along with water, salt, paprika, and pepper. Cover, reduce heat to moderately low, and simmer 20–25 minutes until beans are tender. Mix in bacon, wine, sour cream, and dill, heat, stirring, 1–2 minutes longer, and serve. About 370 calories for each of 4 servings, 250 calories for each of 6 servings.

⊠ QUICK SUCCOTASH
Makes 4 servings

1 (10-ounce) package frozen baby lima beans (do not thaw)
½ cup boiling water
1 teaspoon salt
2 tablespoons butter or margarine
1 tablespoon onion flakes
1 (10-ounce) package frozen whole kernel corn (do not thaw)
½ teaspoon paprika
⅛ teaspoon pepper
½ cup heavy cream

Place limas, water, salt, butter, and onion flakes in a saucepan, cover, and simmer 8–10 minutes. Add corn, re-cover, and simmer 10 minutes longer, stirring occasionally, until vegetables are tender. Mix in remaining ingredients and heat, uncovered, 1–2 minutes more. Ladle into soup bowls and serve. About 285 calories per serving.

VARIATION:

New England Succotash: Substitute raw shelled cranberry beans (1½ pounds in the pod should be enough) for the frozen limas and fresh corn cut from the cob for the frozen (about 2 ears will be sufficient). Also substitute 1 minced onion for the onion flakes and increase amount of boiling water to 1 cup. Proceed as directed, increasing cooking time slightly so that both beans and corn are crisp-tender. About 285 calories per serving.

¢ BOILED FRESH CRANBERRY BEANS

These beans can be used in place of limas in recipes.
Makes 4 servings

3 pounds cranberry beans in the pod
1 teaspoon salt
2 cups boiling water
2 tablespoons butter or margarine
⅛ teaspoon pepper

Shell beans just before you're ready to use them and place in a saucepan. Add salt and water, cover, and boil slowly 10–12 minutes until tender. Drain, season with butter and pepper, and serve. About 230 calories per serving.

¢ BOILED FRESH BLACK-EYED PEAS

Makes 4 servings

3 pounds black-eyed peas in the pod
1 teaspoon salt
1½ quarts boiling water
1 (¼-pound) piece lean bacon, cut in large chunks
⅛ teaspoon pepper

Shell peas, place in a saucepan, add salt, water, and bacon, cover, and boil slowly 1–1½ hours or until of desired tenderness. Check pot occasionally and add more water if necessary. Season with pepper, taste for salt and adjust as needed. Serve peas and "pot likker" in small bowls. About 415 calories per serving.

VARIATION:

¢ **Carolina-Style Black-Eyed Peas:** Prepare as directed but increase water to 2 quarts, omit salt, and substitute 1 (¼-pound) chunk salt pork or fat back for the bacon. Simmer slowly 2½–3 hours until soft-tender, adding water as needed to keep mixture soupy. Taste for salt and adjust as needed. Season with pepper. Serve peas in cooking liquid with freshly baked corn bread to accompany. About 430 calories per serving.

¢ BOILED DRIED BEANS

This method works for the whole family of dried beans—only the cooking time varies.
Makes 6 servings

1 pound dried beans, washed and sorted
2 quarts cold water (about)
1 tablespoon margarine, roast drippings, or cooking oil

Soak beans in 1 quart water overnight or use the quick method.* Drain, measure soaking water, and add enough cold water to make 1 quart. Simmer beans, covered, in the water with margarine, drippings, or oil, stirring now and then, as follows:

30–40 minutes	for black-eyed peas, cow-peas
50 minutes–1 hour	for lima beans
1–1½ hours	for chick-peas (garbanzos), flageolets, cannellini, pink or red kidney beans
1½–2 hours	for pea, navy, Great Northern, marrowfat, black or pinto beans

Use the beans in other recipes or add salt and pepper to taste and serve. To dress them up, season with a fat chunk of Herb Butter or top with Parsley Sauce or Cheese Sauce. From 250 to 280

calories per serving depending on kind of beans (Limas are the most caloric).

VARIATIONS:

¢ **To Serve Cold** (for all but black beans): Cool beans in their cooking water, drain, then rinse under cold running water. Cover and chill until ready to use. Serve cold as a vegetable, dressed with oil, vinegar, and garlic, or toss into salads.

¢ **Savory Beans** (for white or light beans): Simmer a ham bone or pig's knuckle with the beans, a chunk of bacon or salt pork, leftover beef bones, even bouillon cubes. Other good additions to the pot: parsley sprigs, young carrots, a clove of garlic, a yellow onion stuck with a clove or two, almost any leftover vegetable. Recipe too flexible for a meaningful calorie count.

Black Beans and Sour Cream: Simmer beans with a ham bone, a medium-size onion, chopped fine, and a crushed clove of garlic. Top each serving with a dollop of sour cream. About 300 calories per serving with 1 tablespoon of sour cream.

CREAMED PURÉE OF DRIED BEANS

Makes 4 servings

½ pound dried white or lima beans, boiled and drained
¼ cup milk
¼ cup light cream
2–4 tablespoons melted butter or margarine
½ clove garlic, peeled and crushed
Pinch white pepper
2 tablespoons grated Parmesan cheese (optional)

Preheat oven to 350° F. Mash beans with a potato masher. (If you want to remove bean skins, do not drain; press beans *and* their liquid through a coarse sieve.) Beat in remaining ingredients, spoon into a buttered shallow 1½-quart casserole, roughen surface with a fork and bake, uncovered, 25–30 minutes. To brown, broil 5″ from the heat about 4 minutes. About 220 calories per serving made with white beans, 235 per serving made with limas.

VARIATIONS:

Purée of Beans au Gratin: Omit Parmesan. Just before broiling, sprinkle purée with ⅓ cup grated sharp Cheddar cheese and 2 tablespoons melted butter. About 360 calories per serving with white beans, 375 per serving with limas.

Purée of Vegetables au Gratin: Combine equal quantities of puréed beans and carrots or rutabaga, then proceed as for Purée of Beans au Gratin. Recipe too flexible for a meaningful calorie count.

¢ BOSTON BAKED BEANS

A good meat substitute, although in New England, Boston Baked Beans are traditionally accompanied by ham, hot dogs, sausages, or meat loaf.
Makes 4–6 servings

2 cups dried pea beans, washed and sorted
2 quarts cold water (about)
2 teaspoons salt
½ teaspoon powdered mustard
3 tablespoons dark brown sugar
3 tablespoons molasses
1 medium-size yellow onion, peeled and coarsely chopped (optional)
1 (¼-pound) piece salt pork

Soak beans overnight in 1 quart water or use the quick method.* Drain, measure soaking water, and add cold water to make 1 quart. Place beans in a large kettle, add the water, cover, and simmer, stirring occasionally, 1 hour. Drain, reserving 2 cups cooking water. Meanwhile, preheat oven to 400° F. Place beans in an ungreased 2-quart bean pot. Mix reserved cooking water with salt, mustard, sugar, and molasses and stir into beans; add onion if you like. Score rind of salt pork at ½″ intervals, then push into beans so only the rind shows. Cover and bake 1 hour; reduce temperature to 250° F. and bake 4 hours; uncover pot and bake 1 hour longer. Stir about every hour. Serve bubbling hot from the pot. About 530

calories for each of 4 servings, 355 calories for each of 6 servings.

RUMMY BAKED BEANS

Makes 6 servings

1 pound dried pea beans, washed and sorted
2½ quarts cold water
1 (¼-pound) piece bacon, diced
2 medium-size yellow onions, peeled and cut in thin wedges
⅓ cup molasses
¼ cup firmly packed light brown sugar
1 teaspoon powdered mustard
¼ teaspoon baking soda
2½ teaspoons salt
⅛ teaspoon pepper
¼ cup rum

Soak beans overnight in 1 quart water or use the quick method.* Drain and rinse in cold water. Place beans in a large kettle, add bacon and remaining water, cover, and simmer very slowly 40 minutes. Drain, reserving 1 cup cooking water. Meanwhile, preheat oven to 275° F. Place beans and bacon in an ungreased 2½-quart bean pot. Add onion wedges, pushing them well down into beans. Mix reserved water with remaining ingredients and stir into beans. Cover and bake 6½ hours until beans are richly amber brown. Serve hot as a meat substitute. About 430 calories per serving.

⊠ EASY BRANDIED BEANS

Makes 8 servings

4 (1-pound 2-ounce) jars "oven"-baked beans (do not drain)
¼ cup molasses
⅓ cup brandy
2 tablespoons light brown sugar
1½ teaspoons powdered mustard
2 tablespoons onion flakes
2 tablespoons ketchup
½ teaspoon ginger

Preheat oven to 350° F. Place beans in an ungreased shallow 3-quart casserole and stir in all remaining ingredients. Bake, uncovered, about 1 hour, stirring now and then, until bubbly. About 485 calories per serving.

⊠ ¢ THREE BEAN CASSEROLE

Makes 8–10 servings

1 (1-pound) can pork and beans (do not drain)
1 (1-pound) can small lima beans, drained
1 (1-pound) can red kidney beans (do not drain)
1 (10½-ounce) can condensed onion soup (do not dilute)
¼ cup chili sauce
1 tablespoon prepared hot spicy mustard
¼ cup molasses

Preheat oven to 350° F. Empty beans into an ungreased 2-quart casserole. Mix all remaining ingredients together, then stir into beans. Bake, uncovered, 45 minutes to 1 hour, stirring once or twice. Serve as a vegetable or meat substitute. About 245 calories for each of 8 servings, 195 calories for each of 10 servings.

¢ ESTOUFFAT (WHITE BEAN STEW)

In France, *estouffade* means "stew," and this hearty white bean dish *is* a stew. Its name probably comes from the way people in the southern province of Languedoc pronounce *estouffade* (like Southern Americans, they've *quite* an accent).

Makes 6 servings

1 pound dried white beans, flageolets, or limas, boiled just 1 hour but not drained
½ pound salt pork, cut into slices ¼" thick
1 large yellow onion, peeled and chopped fine
3 large ripe tomatoes, peeled, seeded, and coarsely chopped
2 cloves garlic, peeled and crushed
1 bouquet garni,* tied in cheesecloth
Salt to taste

Keep beans warm in their cooking water. Brown salt pork in a large, heavy skillet over moderate heat and drain on paper toweling. Sauté onion in the drippings 6–8 minutes until pale golden;

add tomatoes and garlic and sauté 1–2 minutes longer. Add sautéed mixture to beans, also salt pork and *bouquet garni*. Cover and simmer 1 hour, stirring occasionally. Add salt to taste and serve. About 575 calories per serving.

¢ BEAN AND CABBAGE HOT POT (OUILLADE)

Here's a traditional dish from the French Pyrenees, where the vegetables grow big and beautiful on the terraced hillsides.

Makes 6–8 servings

½ pound dried white beans, flageolets, or limas, boiled but not drained
2 cups boiling water
2 teaspoons salt
6 small potatoes, peeled
1 large yellow onion, peeled and sliced thin
1 pound small young carrots, peeled
1 small rutabaga, peeled and cut in ½" cubes
1 small cabbage, cored and cut in 8 wedges
¼ teaspoon pepper

Keep beans warm in their cooking liquid. Place all remaining ingredients in a second kettle, cover, and boil gently 25–30 minutes or until potatoes and rutabaga are tender. Drain beans and add to other vegetables. Stir *gently*, then simmer, covered, about 10 minutes. Serve hot with pot roast, boiled tongue, or corned beef. Or serve in place of meat. If made with white beans, about 265 calories for each of 6 servings and 200 calories for each of 8 servings. If made with limas, about 280 calories for each of 6 servings and 210 calories for each of 8 servings.

¢ BEANS IN ONION SAUCE

A husky French country dish that is both easy and economical to make.

Makes 4 servings

4 large yellow onions, peeled and quartered
¾ cup water
3 tablespoons butter or margarine
¾ cup hot Medium White Sauce

½ teaspoon salt (about)
⅛ teaspoon white pepper
3 cups hot boiled dried white or lima
  beans

Place onions, water, and butter in a
saucepan, cover, and simmer 45 minutes
or until onions are mushy. Uncover, boil
slowly until liquid reduces to about ½
cup, then purée in an electric blender at
slow speed or put through a food mill.
Mix in white sauce, salt, and pepper.
Taste for salt and add a little more if
needed. Pour onion sauce over hot,
drained beans, mix gently, and serve.
About 365 calories per serving.

TURKISH "FRIED" WHITE BEANS AND CARROTS

Makes 6–8 servings

1 pound dried white beans, boiled just
  1 hour but not drained
3 large yellow onions, peeled and
  chopped fine
2 cloves garlic, peeled and minced
1 cup olive oil
4 medium-size carrots, peeled and cut
  into rounds ¼" thick
1 tablespoon salt (about)
¼ teaspoon pepper

Keep beans warm in their cooking
liquid. Meanwhile, sauté onions and
garlic in the oil in a large skillet over
moderately low heat 5–8 minutes until
pale golden; stir into beans (include all
olive oil). Add carrots, salt, and pepper,
cover, and simmer 45 minutes, stirring
occasionally, until vegetables are tender.
About 600 calories for each of 6
servings, 450 calories for each of 8
servings.

NEAPOLITAN BEANS WITH PARMESAN

Makes 6 servings

1 pound dried cannellini beans, boiled
  but not drained
2 tablespoons bacon drippings
¼ teaspoon sage
½ cup tomato paste

4 Italian plum tomatoes, peeled, seeded,
  and coarsely chopped, or 4 canned
  tomatoes, drained and coarsely
  chopped
2½ teaspoons salt
¼ teaspoon pepper
½ cup grated Parmesan cheese
1 tablespoon minced parsley
Grated Parmesan cheese (topping)

To the beans add all remaining
ingredients except parsley and cheese
topping, cover, and simmer 1 hour,
stirring now and then. Mix in parsley
and serve with a sprinkling of Parmesan.
About 340 calories per serving.

¢ SAVORY LIMA BEANS WITH WINE

If the pork hock is meaty enough, this
can double as a main dish.
Makes 6–8 servings

1 pound dried large lima beans, washed
  and soaked
Soaking water plus enough cold water
  to measure 3 cups
1 pork hock or pig's foot
1 medium-size yellow onion, peeled and
  stuck with 6 cloves
1 bay leaf, crumbled
1 tablespoon salt
⅛ teaspoon pepper
1 cup dry white wine

Place beans, water, pork hock, onion,
and bay leaf in a large kettle, cover, and
simmer 1 hour. Add remaining
ingredients, cover, and simmer 45
minutes longer. Remove onion and pork
hock. Cut meat from bones, add to
beans, and serve. About 335 calories
for each of 6 servings, 275 calories for
each of 8 servings.

¢ MEXICAN FRIED BEANS (FRIJOLES FRITOS)

Makes 4 servings

¼ cup lard
1 recipe Mexican Beans (below)

Melt lard in a large, heavy skillet over
moderate heat. Ladle in a few of the
beans and mash, adding a tablespoon

790 THE DOUBLEDAY COOKBOOK

or so of the bean liquid. Continue to add beans, mashing with bean liquid, until all are used up (you'll need about ½ cup liquid to give the beans the right consistency). (*Note:* You can mash all the beans, or leave about half of them whole.) Heat, stirring, until piping hot. To be really Mexican, serve with ham and Huevos Rancheros. About 320 calories per serving.

VARIATIONS:

¢ **Fried Beans with Cheese:** Just before serving add ½ cup coarsely grated Monterey Jack or sharp Cheddar cheese to beans and heat, stirring, about ½ minute until cheese melts. About 375 calories per serving.

¢ **Fried Beans with Tomato:** After mashing beans, mix in ½ cup tomato paste, ¼–½ teaspoon chili powder, and, if you like, a touch of garlic. Heat and serve. About 355 calories per serving.

¢ **Refried Beans (Frijoles Refritos):** As the title suggests, simply refry leftover fried beans in more lard until heated through and crisp here and there. Recipe too flexible for a meaningful calorie count.

¢ MEXICAN BEANS (FRIJOLES MEXICANOS)

Makes 4 servings

1 cup dried pinto or red kidney beans, washed and soaked
Soaking water plus enough cold water to measure 3 cups
1 tablespoon lard
1 large yellow onion, peeled and coarsely chopped (optional)
4 slices bacon, diced (optional)
1½ teaspoons salt

Place all ingredients except salt in a large saucepan, cover, and simmer until tender: 1–1½ hours for red kidney beans, 1½–2 hours for pinto beans. Mix in salt and serve. The cooking liquid should be quite thick; if not, simmer uncovered until the consistency of gravy (don't boil, however, or beans may break up). About 195 calories per serving (without

onion and bacon), 255 calories per serving (with onion and bacon).

¢ BARBECUED BEANS

This casserole improves on standing, so bake the day before and refrigerate until needed. About ½ hour before serving, pop, covered, into a 350° F. oven.
Makes 6–8 servings

1 pound dried red kidney beans, washed and soaked
2 large yellow onions, peeled and chopped fine
2 cloves garlic, peeled and crushed
2 tablespoons bacon drippings
½ cup ketchup
½ cup chili sauce
½ cup cider vinegar
½ cup firmly packed dark brown sugar
½ teaspoon powdered mustard
½ teaspoon chili powder
2 teaspoons salt (about)
½ teaspoon pepper
5 cups water (about)

Preheat oven to 350° F. Drain beans, place in an ungreased 3-quart bean pot or casserole, and mix in all remaining ingredients. Cover tightly (use a double thickness of foil if casserole has no lid) and bake 5–6 hours, stirring occasionally, until beans are tender and sauce thick. If mixture gets too dry before beans are done, stir in a little warm water. About 400 calories for each of 6 servings, 300 calories for each of 8 servings.

¢ SOUTH-OF-THE-BORDER BEAN POT

A robust Mexican main dish filled with kidney beans, green pepper, and tomatoes. It's peppery, so if you are unaccustomed to hot dishes, reduce the amount of chili peppers to suit you.
Makes 4–6 servings

1 pound dried red kidney beans, washed and soaked
1 medium-size yellow onion, peeled and coarsely chopped
1 clove garlic, peeled and crushed

½ cup minced sweet green pepper
1 (1-pound 12-ounce) can tomatoes (do not drain)
3 tablespoons olive oil
½ teaspoon oregano
1 teaspoon crushed coriander
1¼ teaspoons salt
⅛ teaspoon black pepper
2 teaspoons minced parsley
1 tablespoon honey or light corn syrup
2 teaspoons red wine vinegar
¼ teaspoon crushed hot red chili peppers (optional)

Preheat oven to 275° F. Drain beans, rinse under cold running water, and place in an ungreased 2½-quart bean pot. Mix in all remaining ingredients. Bake, uncovered, 2½ hours, stirring well every hour. Cover and bake 2–2½ hours longer or until beans are tender yet still firm, again stirring every hour. If beans seem to be drying out before they're tender, mix in a little hot water. Serve bubbling hot from the pot. About 510 calories for each of 4 servings, 340 calories for each of 6 servings.

¢ SWEDISH BAKED BEANS

Somewhat like Boston Baked Beans, but more spicily flavored. These beans are popular at smorgasbords.
Makes 6–8 servings

1 pound dried red kidney, cranberry, or pinto beans, boiled but not drained
1 medium-size yellow onion, peeled and chopped fine
1 clove garlic, peeled and crushed
½ cup ketchup or tomato sauce
1 tablespoon Worcestershire sauce
⅔ cup firmly packed light brown sugar
2 tablespoons molasses
¼ cup cider vinegar
¼ teaspoon powdered mustard
1½ teaspoons cornstarch
2 tablespoons cold water
6 slices bacon

Preheat oven to 325°F. Transfer beans and their cooking liquid to an ungreased 3-quart casserole and mix in onion and garlic. Blend ketchup, Worcestershire sauce, sugar, molasses, vinegar, and mustard and stir into beans. Blend

cornstarch and water until smooth and mix in well. Lay bacon on top of beans, cover, and bake 1½ hours. Raise oven temperature to 400° F., uncover, and bake 10 minutes to crisp bacon. About 485 calories for each of 6 servings, 360 calories for each of 8 servings.

¢ SPANISH BEAN POT

Richly glazed, rum-and-coffee-flavored baked beans.
Makes 6 servings

1 pound dried pinto beans, boiled but not drained
1 clove garlic, peeled and crushed
¼ teaspoon thyme
⅛ teaspoon crushed hot red chili peppers
1 large Spanish onion, peeled and sliced thin
2 tablespoons olive oil or other cooking oil
2 tablespoons cider vinegar
2 tablespoons prepared mild yellow mustard
2 tablespoons sugar
½ cup hot strong coffee
1 jigger dark Jamaica rum (optional)

Preheat oven to 350° F. Transfer beans and their cooking liquid to an ungreased 3-quart casserole and mix in all remaining ingredients except coffee and rum. Cover and bake 1 hour. Mix in coffee and, if you like, the rum, re-cover, and bake 15 minutes longer. Taste for salt and adjust if needed. About 300 calories per serving.

¢ SOUTHERN-STYLE BLACK-EYED PEAS

Makes 4–6 servings

1 pound dried black-eyed peas, washed
1 (¼-pound) piece bacon or salt pork, cut in 1" cubes
1½ quarts water
1 tablespoon salt
¼ teaspoon cayenne pepper

Place peas, bacon, and water in a large, heavy kettle, cover, and simmer very slowly 2–2½ hours until tender. Season with salt and pepper and serve.

About 545 calories for each of 4 servings, 365 calories for each of 6 servings.

¢ HOPPING JOHN

Makes 6 servings

2 (10-ounce) packages frozen black-eyed peas (do not thaw)
3 cups boiling water
1 (¼-pound) piece lean bacon
1 yellow onion, peeled and coarsely chopped
3 cups hot fluffy cooked rice
2 tablespoons bacon drippings, butter, or margarine
2 teaspoons salt
⅛–¼ teaspoon crushed hot red chili peppers
⅛ teaspoon black pepper

Place peas, water, bacon, and onion in a large saucepan, cover, and simmer 30–35 minutes until peas are tender. Remove bacon, lightly mix in remaining ingredients, and serve in place of potatoes. About 360 calories per serving.

¢ BAKED CHICK-PEA PILAF

Makes 6 servings

½ medium-size Spanish onion, peeled and chopped fine
3 tablespoons olive or other cooking oil
1 (1-pound 4-ounce) can chick-peas (do not drain)
½ cup uncooked rice
1 beef or chicken bouillon cube
¼ cup boiling water
1 pimiento, seeded and coarsely chopped
1 teaspoon salt

Preheat oven to 325° F. Sauté onion in oil over moderate heat 5–8 minutes until pale golden. Place chick-peas and rice in an ungreased 1½-quart casserole and mix lightly. Dissolve bouillon cube in boiling water, add to casserole along with onion and remaining ingredients, and stir to mix. Cover and bake 1–1¼ hours, stirring occasionally, until rice is tender. About 215 calories per serving.

CHICK-PEAS AND KASHA

To be really authentic, each serving of this Syrian dish should be topped with a dollop of yogurt.
Makes 4–6 servings

2 cups canned or boiled dried chick-peas
2 cups cooked buckwheat groats
½ cup beef bouillon
2 tablespoons butter or margarine

Preheat oven to 350° F. Drain peas, then remove skins by rubbing each pea between your thumb and forefinger. Coarsely chop peas, add buckwheat, and toss to mix. Spoon into a buttered 1½-quart casserole, pour bouillon over all, and dot with butter. Cover and bake 30 minutes. About 275 calories for each of 4 servings, 180 calories for each of 6 servings.

¢ GREEK-STYLE CHICK-PEAS AND TOMATOES

This dish has the consistency of a good, rich "spoon soup" and is easiest to eat out of soup bowls. It can also be served over spaghetti as a pasta sauce.
Makes 6 servings

¼ cup olive or other cooking oil
1 medium-size Spanish onion, peeled and sliced thin
2 cloves garlic, peeled and crushed
2 (1-pound 4-ounce) cans chick-peas, drained, or 1 pound dried chick-peas, boiled and drained
2 cups tomato or marinara sauce
1 tablespoon minced parsley
¼ teaspoon finely chopped mint

Heat oil in a large saucepan over moderate heat 1 minute. Add onion and garlic and stir-fry 5 minutes, then mix in chick-peas and tomato sauce. Reduce heat to low, cover, and simmer 30 minutes. Mix in parsley and mint and serve. About 310 calories per serving.

¢ FLORIDA BLACK BEANS AND PEPPERS

If you like black bean soup, you will also like black beans prepared this way

with minced green and red peppers.
Makes 6 servings

1 pound dried black beans, boiled but
   not drained
½ cup olive or other cooking oil
1 large Spanish onion, peeled and sliced
   thin
2 large sweet green peppers, cored,
   seeded, and chopped fine
1 large sweet red pepper, cored, seeded,
   and chopped fine
1 clove garlic, peeled and crushed
1 teaspoon salt (about)
⅛ teaspoon pepper
½ cup cider vinegar
2 tablespoons sugar

Keep beans warm in their cooking
liquid. Heat oil in a large skillet over
moderate heat 1 minute. Add onion,
peppers, and garlic, sauté 5–8 minutes
until onion is pale golden, then stir into
beans. Add salt and pepper, cover, and
simmer 45 minutes. Mix in vinegar and
sugar, re-cover, and simmer 5–10
minutes longer. About 435 calories per
serving.

⊠ BRAZILIAN BLACK BEANS

Makes 4 servings

6 slices bacon, cut crosswise in julienne
   strips
1 medium-size yellow onion, peeled and
   coarsely chopped
1 clove garlic, peeled and crushed
2 bay leaves
2 (1-pound) cans black beans (drain
   1 can)
1 tablespoon white corn meal
1 tablespoon cider vinegar
⅛ teaspoon crushed hot red chili
   peppers

Brown bacon in a large, heavy skillet
over moderate heat and drain on paper
toweling. Pour off all but 2 tablespoons
drippings, add onion and garlic to skillet,
and stir-fry 8 minutes until golden. Add
remaining ingredients, turn heat to low,
and simmer uncovered, stirring
occasionally, about 15 minutes. Serve,
topping each portion with bacon. About
375 calories per serving.

BEETS

To the ancient Greeks, the beet was a
food fit for the gods (it was, in fact, the
one vegetable considered worthy enough
to offer the god Apollo). The first beet
recipes come to us from Apicius, the
first-century Roman epicure whose
cookbook is still sold today. These
ancients, however, ate the greens and
threw away the beet (it remained for
the Russians and Germans to discover
how delicious the roots were). Today
we have learned to enjoy both the
sweet crimson beet root and the crinkly-
tart green tops.

To Prepare for Cooking:
Beets: Cut off all but 1″ of the tops and
leave root ends on so beets won't fade.
Scrub in cold water, taking care not to
break skins. Do not peel.

Greens: Sort, discarding coarse stems
and blemished leaves, then wash by

Season	For Top Quality	Amount To Buy	Nutritive Value	Calories (unseasoned)
Year round; peak months for greens and beets: June–October	Pick crisp-tender greens; firm, un-scarred beets of equal size, 1½–2″ in diameter.	½ pound beets or greens per person.	Greens are rich in vitamins A and C, beets are considerably less nutritious.	Low for greens about 25 per serving; Moderate for beets— about 50 a serving

plunging up and down in cool water. To perk up limp leaves, soak briefly in ice water.

¢ BOILED BEETS

Makes 4 servings

2 pounds beets, prepared for cooking
1½ teaspoons salt
1 quart boiling water
2 tablespoons butter or margarine
Pinch pepper

Place beets, salt, and boiling water in a large saucepan, cover, and boil 35–45 minutes until tender. Drain, plunge in cold water 1–2 minutes, then peel and remove any stem or root ends. If beets are small, leave whole; if not, slice thin. Return to pan, add butter and pepper, and warm uncovered, shaking pan gently, until butter melts and gilds beets. About 125 calories per serving.

To Parboil for Use in Other Recipes: Boil as directed but reduce cooking time to 20–25 minutes.

VARIATIONS:

¢ **To Serve Cold:** Cook, drain, and plunge in cold water as directed. When cool, peel, remove root and stem ends, and, if you like, slice. Toss with about 1 cup good tart dressing (see Vegetable Seasoning Chart) and chill 2–3 hours.

¢ **Orange-Glazed Beets:** Boil, drain, and peel as directed; stir ¼ cup orange marmalade into beets with butter and warm, uncovered, shaking pan gently, about 5 minutes until beets are glazed. About 185 calories per serving.

¢ **Beets with Sour Cream and Dill:** Boil, drain, and peel; reduce butter to 1 tablespoon and stir in ⅓ cup sour cream and 1 tablespoon minced dill. Warm 2–3 minutes (but do not boil) and serve. About 140 calories per serving.

¢ **Beets with Horseradish:** Cook, drain, and peel; mix 2 tablespoons each prepared horseradish and white wine vinegar into beets along with butter. Warm and serve. About 125 calories per serving.

¢ BAKED BEETS

Baked beets are mellower, sweeter, nuttier than the boiled.
Makes 4 servings

2 pounds beets, prepared for cooking
1 teaspoon salt
Pinch pepper
2 tablespoons butter or margarine

Preheat oven to 350° F. Place beets in a roasting pan, cover with foil, and bake 2–2½ hours until tender. Cool until easy to handle (if you're in a hurry, plunge in ice water), then peel. If the beets are small, leave whole; otherwise slice, dice, or cut in julienne strips. Place in a saucepan with salt, pepper, and butter and warm, uncovered, over low heat, shaking pan gently, 2–3 minutes. About 125 calories per serving.

¢ HARVARD BEETS

Makes 4–6 servings

½ cup sugar
2 tablespoons cornstarch
1 teaspoon salt
¼ teaspoon pepper
1 cup cider vinegar
¼ cup water
¼ cup butter or margarine
2 pounds boiled fresh beets, peeled and diced or cut in julienne strips, or 2 (1-pound) cans julienne beets, drained

Mix sugar, cornstarch, salt, and pepper in a large saucepan and slowly stir in vinegar. Add water and butter and cook, stirring, over moderate heat until thickened and clear. Reduce heat to low, add beets, cover, and simmer 15 minutes. About 295 calories for each of 4 servings, 200 calories for each of 6 servings.

HOT SPICY SHREDDED BEETS

Particularly good with pork, poultry, or ham.
Makes 4 servings

2 pounds beets, trimmed, peeled, and coarsely grated

½ cup coarsely grated onion
3 tablespoons butter or margarine
½ cup water
¼ cup dry red wine
Juice of ½ lemon
¼ teaspoon cinnamon
¼ teaspoon nutmeg
⅓ teaspoon salt
⅛ teaspoon pepper

Simmer all ingredients, covered, 25–30 minutes until beets are tender and flavors well blended. Stir once or twice during cooking. About 175 calories per serving.

BEETS IN ORANGE-LEMON SAUCE

Makes 4–6 servings

1 tablespoon cornstarch
2 tablespoons sugar
1 cup orange juice
2 tablespoons lemon juice
2 pounds boiled fresh beets, peeled, or 2 (1 pound) cans small whole beets, drained
2 tablespoons butter or margarine
1–2 teaspoons grated orange rind

Mix cornstarch and sugar, slowly add fruit juices, then cook and stir over moderate heat until thickened and clear. Add beets and butter, turn heat to low, cover, and simmer 10–15 minutes to blend flavors. Add rind to taste and serve. About 180 calories for each of 4 servings, 120 calories for each of 6 servings.

BEETS BAKED WITH SOUR CREAM AND CARAWAY SEEDS

Makes 4–6 servings

2 pounds fresh beets, boiled, peeled, and diced, or 2 (1-pound) cans julienne beets, drained
1½ cups sour cream
1 teaspoon caraway seeds
Pinch nutmeg or mace

Preheat oven to 350° F. Mix beets with remaining ingredients and spoon into an ungreased small casserole. Bake, uncovered, 20–25 minutes to heat through. About 255 calories for each of 4 servings, 170 calories for each of 6 servings.

⊠ BEETS TOKAY

Beets and grapes in a smooth white sauce. Delicious!
Makes 4–6 servings

2 pounds fresh beets, boiled, peeled, and sliced, or 2 (1-pound) cans sliced beets, drained
1½ cups hot Medium White Sauce
½ cup diced celery
1 cup halved, seeded Tokay grapes

Preheat oven to 350° F. Mix all ingredients, place in a buttered 1½-quart casserole, cover, and bake 25 minutes. Stir and serve. About 255 calories for each of 4 servings, 170 calories for each of 6 servings.

⊠ BEETS IN BURGUNDY

Spicy, finely cut beets in dry red wine.
Makes 3 servings

1 (1-pound) can julienne beets (do not drain)
1 tablespoon cornstarch
⅓ cup sugar
⅛ teaspoon cloves
Pinch salt
¼ cup red wine vinegar
½ cup red burgundy wine
2 tablespoons butter or margarine

Drain beets, saving ¼ cup liquid. Mix cornstarch, sugar, cloves, and salt in a saucepan, slowly add beet liquid, vinegar, and wine, and cook, stirring, over moderate heat until thickened and clear. Add beets and butter, turn heat to low, cover, and simmer 15 minutes to blend flavors. About 250 calories per serving.

STEAMED BEET GREENS

(See recipe for Steamed Spinach.)

BREADFRUIT

In Florida, California, and large metropolitan areas, these big pebbly green-brown fruits are not unfamiliar. Their flesh is the color and texture of

Season	For Top Quality	Amount To Buy	Nutritive Value	Calories (unseasoned)
July–August	Choose plump, firm but not too hard breadfruit with fairly clean skins.	1 breadfruit serves 2–4	Some vitamin C	Moderate —about 85 per average serving

bread, tastes something like globe artichokes, and is best when boiled, mashed, creamed, or baked and stuffed.

To Prepare for Cooking: Scrub well, halve, and peel deep enough that no green shows. Cut around hard, stringy core and pull out. Leave as halves or cut in 1–1½" chunks.

To Boil: Cover with lightly salted boiling water and boil, covered, until tender: about 2–2½ hours for halves, 1½–1¾ hours for chunks. Drain, season with butter, salt, and pepper, and serve.

To Parboil for Use in Other Recipes: Boil as directed, reducing cooking time to 1¼ hours for halves, 1 hour for chunks.

To Mash: Boil chunks as directed, increasing time to 2 hours so they are very soft. Drain, mash with a potato masher, and mix with a little cream, butter, salt, and pepper.

To Cream: Boil chunks as directed, drain, and mix with 1½ cups hot Medium White Sauce.

To Bake and Stuff: Parboil halves and drain; fill with any mixture you would use for stuffing yellow squash, wrap halves in foil, and bake 30–40 minutes at 350° F. Unwrap and serve, allowing a half for each person.

BROCCOLI

First cousin to cauliflower, second cousin to cabbage, broccoli was almost unknown in this country until the late 1920's, when an enterprising Italian farmer in California began advertising his broccoli crop over the radio.

To Prepare for Cooking: Discard coarse stem ends and leaves. Wash broccoli in cold water; separate into stalks of about the same size and make deep X-cuts in the base of each so they'll cook as quickly as the tender heads.

STEAMED BROCCOLI

Makes 4 servings

1 (2-pound) head broccoli, prepared for
   cooking
1¼ cups boiling water

Season	For Top Quality	Amount To Buy	Nutritive Value	Calories (unseasoned)
Year round with supplies at their best in spring and again in fall	Look for crisp, moist stalks and dark green or purplish heads. Reject any that are yellowed or flowering.	½ pound per person	High in vitamins A and C, fairly high in calcium	Low—about 40 per average serving

½ teaspoon salt
⅛ teaspoon pepper
3 tablespoons butter or margarine

Stand stalks stem end down in a deep saucepan (the top of a double boiler is perfect). Add water and salt, cover (or invert double boiler bottom over top), and simmer 15–20 minutes until crisp-tender. Drain, return to pan, season with pepper and butter, and warm over low heat just until butter is melted. Taste for salt and add more if needed. About 125 calories per serving.

To Parboil for Use in Other Recipes: Steam as directed, reducing cooking time to 10 minutes. Omit seasonings.

VARIATIONS:

To Serve Cold: Steam as directed, then chill in ice water. Drain, pat dry on paper toweling, cover, and refrigerate until ready to use (see Vegetable Seasoning Chart for sauce and dressing ideas). Serve as an appetizer, vegetable, or salad.

⟁ **Low-Calorie Steamed Broccoli:** Dress with seasoned salt or low-calorie Italian dressing instead of butter. About 50 calories per serving.

Broccoli Amandine: Increase butter to ⅓ cup, melt over moderate heat, and in it sauté ⅓ cup slivered blanched almonds, stirring, 3–5 minutes until golden brown. Add 1 tablespoon lemon juice, the pepper and pour over drained broccoli. About 280 calories per serving.

BROCCOLI PARMIGIANA

Makes 4 servings

1 (2-pound) head broccoli, steamed, or 2 (10-ounce) packages frozen broccoli spears, boiled and drained

Sauce:

3 tablespoons butter or margarine
3 tablespoons flour
1½ cups milk
1 egg yolk, lightly beaten
¾ teaspoon salt
⅛ teaspoon white pepper
¾ cup grated Parmesan cheese

Topping:

¾ cup soft white bread crumbs mixed with 2 tablespoons grated Parmesan cheese

Prepare sauce while broccoli cooks: melt butter over moderate heat and blend in flour. Add milk and heat, stirring, until thickened. Mix a little sauce into yolk, stir back into sauce in pan, and mix in remaining sauce ingredients. Cook and stir 1 minute but do not boil. Preheat broiler. Spoon a little sauce into an unbuttered shallow 1½-quart casserole, add broccoli, pour in remaining sauce and sprinkle with topping. Broil 4″ from the heat 2–3 minutes until flecked with brown. About 335 calories per serving.

VARIATION:

Eggs and Broccoli Parmigiana: For a light entree, arrange 4 soft poached eggs on broccoli before adding sauce and topping. About 415 calories per serving.

BROCCOLI WITH ANCHOVIES ROMAN STYLE

Makes 6 servings

2 (2-pound) heads broccoli, prepared for cooking
¼ cup olive oil
2 cloves garlic, peeled
¼ cup boiling water
1 tablespoon anchovy paste
½ cup dry white wine
⅛ teaspoon pepper

Divide broccoli into flowerets of equal size (save stalks for soup). Heat oil in a large, heavy skillet over moderate heat 1 minute, add garlic, sauté 1–2 minutes, and discard. Reduce heat to moderately low and stir-fry broccoli in the oil 4–5 minutes. Add water, cover, and simmer 5–7 minutes until crisp-tender. Lift broccoli to a heated vegetable dish and keep warm. Mix anchovy paste, wine, and pepper into cooking liquid and heat, stirring, 1–2 minutes. Pour over broccoli and serve. About 180 calories per serving.

BROCCOLI IN WHITE WINE SAUCE

Makes 4 servings

2 tablespoons butter or margarine
¼ cup dry white wine
1 (2-pound) head broccoli, parboiled and drained
¼ teaspoon salt
⅛ teaspoon pepper
Pinch nutmeg

Add butter and wine to broccoli, cover, and simmer 5 minutes over low heat. Uncover and simmer 5–10 minutes longer, basting with pan liquid, until tender. Season with salt, pepper, and nutmeg and serve. About 115 calories per serving.

CASTILIAN SAUTÉED BROCCOLI WITH RIPE OLIVES

Makes 4 servings

1 (2-pound) head broccoli, parboiled and drained
1 small clove garlic, peeled and crushed
2 tablespoons olive oil
1 tablespoon butter or margarine
¾ cup thinly sliced, pitted ripe olives
¼ teaspoon salt (about)

Cut broccoli in 2″ lengths. Sauté garlic in oil and butter in a large skillet over moderate heat 1 minute, add broccoli, and stir-fry 5–7 minutes. Add olives, stir gently, cover, and let steam 3–4 minutes. Add salt to taste and serve. About 150 calories per serving.

VARIATION:

Sautéed Broccoli with Parmesan: Cook broccoli by the recipe above, leaving out olives. Just before serving, squeeze a lemon wedge over broccoli and sprinkle with about ⅓ cup grated Parmesan cheese. About 125 calories per serving.

⊠ BROCCOLI WITH PEANUT BUTTER SAUCE

Peanut butter may sound an odd seasoning for broccoli, but when smoothed into a golden brown sauce, it brings out the best in the broccoli.
Makes 4 servings

1 (2-pound) head broccoli, steamed, or 2 (10-ounce) packages frozen broccoli spears, boiled
⅓ cup butter or margarine
2 tablespoons chopped, toasted, blanched peanuts
2 tablespoons cream-style peanut butter

Drain broccoli, place in a heated serving dish, and keep warm. Melt butter over moderately low heat, add peanuts, and sauté 2–3 minutes. Blend in peanut butter, reduce heat to low, and heat, stirring, about 2 minutes. Pour over broccoli and serve. About 295 calories per serving.

⊠ OSAKA SKILLET BROCCOLI

Chilled, this makes an unusually good hors d'oeuvre.
Makes 2–4 servings

1 (2-pound) head broccoli, prepared for cooking
¼ cup peanut oil
1 clove garlic, peeled and crushed
2 (½″) cubes fresh gingerroot, peeled and crushed
¼ cup water
2 tablespoons Japanese soy or teriyaki sauce

Divide broccoli into small flowerets (save stalks for soup). Heat oil in a large heavy skillet over moderate heat 1 minute, add garlic and ginger, and stir-fry 1 minute. Add broccoli and remaining ingredients, cover, and simmer 8–10 minutes until crisp-tender. Serve, topping each portion with a little pan liquid. About 355 calories for each of 2 servings, 180 calories for each of 4 servings.

BROCCOLI BAKED IN MUSTARD SAUCE

Makes 8 servings

2 (2-pound) heads broccoli, parboiled and drained (reserve cooking liquid)

Sauce:

¼ cup butter or margarine
¼ cup unsifted flour
Broccoli cooking liquid plus enough
   milk to measure 2¼ cups
¼ cup dry vermouth
1 cup coarsely grated Gruyère cheese
2 tablespoons prepared mild yellow
   mustard
2 tablespoons prepared spicy brown
   mustard
¼ teaspoon salt
⅛ teaspoon cayenne pepper

Topping:

¼ cup fine dry bread crumbs mixed with
   1 tablespoon melted butter or
   margarine

Preheat oven to 375° F. Cut broccoli in
2″ lengths and place in a buttered
shallow 2½-quart casserole. Melt butter
over moderate heat and blend in flour.
Add broccoli cooking liquid-milk mixture and heat, stirring, until thickened.
Mix in remaining sauce ingredients and
pour over broccoli. Sprinkle with topping and bake, uncovered, 35–40 minutes until browned and bubbling. About
170 calories per serving.

BROCCOLI, EGG, AND SOUR CREAM CASSEROLE

Makes 4 servings

1 (2-pound) head broccoli, steamed,
   drained, and coarsely chopped, or 2
   (10-ounce) packages frozen chopped
   broccoli, boiled and drained
2 hard-cooked eggs, peeled and sliced
1 cup sour cream
½ cup mayonnaise
2 tablespoons tarragon vinegar
⅛ teaspoon paprika

Preheat oven to 350° F. Arrange broccoli in an ungreased shallow 1½-quart
casserole, top with egg slices, and set
aside. Over lowest heat warm sour
cream with mayonnaise and vinegar,
stirring, 4–5 minutes (do not boil); pour
over broccoli. Bake, uncovered, 10
minutes, sprinkle with paprika, and
serve. About 430 calories per serving.

BROCCOLI CREPES AU GRATIN

For a small luncheon an elegant entree
that's not difficult to make.
Makes 4 servings

1 (10-ounce) package frozen chopped
   broccoli, boiled and drained
8 (6″) thin pancakes made from any
   pancake mix
1 teaspoon salt
⅛ teaspoon pepper
1 hard-cooked egg, sliced thin
1 (10½-ounce) can condensed cream of
   asparagus or celery soup (do not
   dilute)
¼ cup light cream
½ cup coarsely grated sharp Cheddar
   cheese

Preheat oven to 350° F. Spoon a little
broccoli in the center of each pancake,
sprinkle with salt and pepper, and top
with a slice of egg. Roll pancakes up and
place, seam side down, in a buttered 1½-
quart au gratin dish or shallow casserole.
Blend soup with cream, spoon over
crepes, and sprinkle with cheese. Bake,
uncovered, 20–25 minutes until bubbly,
then broil 3″ from the heat 2–3
minutes to brown. About 325 calories
per serving.

VARIATION:

Asparagus Crepes au Gratin (4
servings): Prepare as directed, substituting 2 (10-ounce) packages frozen asparagus spears for broccoli. Lay 2 or 3
stalks across center of each crepe, then
season, roll, and proceed as directed.
About 335 calories per serving.

BRUSSELS SPROUTS

Little more than a curiosity in this
country until frozen foods made them
widely available, these baby cabbages
have long been popular abroad. French
royalty used to reject any larger than a
pea, Belgians insist yet that they be the
size of a grape.

To Prepare for Cooking: Since most
sprouts are washed and trimmed before
they're packed, about all that's needed
is a quick sorting to remove withered

Season	For Top Quality	Amount To Buy	Nutritive Value	Calories (unseasoned)
September–March; peak months: October and November	Choose firm, clean compact heads of a crisp green color.	A 1-pint carton will serve 2–3 persons.	Very high in vitamin C, fairly high in vitamin A	Low—about 45 per average serving

leaves. Trim off stems (but not too close or sprouts will fall apart). To ensure even cooking, make an X-cut in the base of each sprout with the point of a knife. Rinse sprouts in cold, lightly salted water, then drain well.

BOILED BRUSSELS SPROUTS

Makes 4–6 servings

1 quart Brussels sprouts, prepared for cooking
1½ cups boiling water
1 teaspoon salt
¼ teaspoon pepper
2 tablespoons butter or margarine

Place sprouts in a saucepan with water and salt, cover, and boil gently 15–20 minutes until crisp tender. Drain, season with pepper and butter and serve. About 95 calories for each of 4 servings, 65 calories for each of 6 servings.

To Parboil for Use in Other Recipes: Follow recipe above but cut cooking time in half. Omit seasonings.

VARIATIONS:

⚖ Low-Calorie Brussels Sprouts: Season with 1–2 tablespoons lemon juice or tarragon vinegar and a pinch of nutmeg instead of butter. About 45 calories for each of 4 servings, 30 calories for each of 6.

Brussels Sprouts Véronique: Boil and season sprouts as directed, then toss in ¾ cup seedless green grapes and a pinch of nutmeg or mace. About 115 calories for each of 4 servings. 75 calories for each of 6 servings.

Brussels Sprouts Parmigiana: Boil and drain as directed but do not season. Place sprouts in a buttered 2-quart casserole, top with ½ cup melted butter and ⅓ cup grated Parmesan. Bake, uncovered, 15 minutes at 350° F. About 115 calories for each of 4 servings, 75 calories for each of 6 servings.

Dilled Sprouts in Sour Cream: Boil and drain as directed but do not season. Quarter each sprout or, if small, halve. Return to pan and stir in 1½ cups sour cream, 4 minced scallions, 2 teaspoons minced fresh dill (or ½ teaspoon of the dried), ½ teaspoon salt, and a pinch each garlic salt and white pepper. Set over lowest heat, cover, and warm 5–7 minutes, taking care cream doesn't boil. About 275 calories for each of 4 servings, 185 calories for each of 6 servings.

BRUSSELS SPROUTS AU GRATIN

Makes 6 servings

1 quart fresh Brussels sprouts or 2 (10-ounce) packages frozen sprouts, boiled and drained
1½ cups hot Cheese Sauce or Mornay Sauce
⅓ cup coarsely grated sharp Cheddar cheese
1 tablespoon melted butter or margarine

Preheat broiler. Arrange sprouts in an ungreased 1½-quart au gratin dish or shallow casserole. Cover with sauce, sprinkle with cheese, and drizzle with butter. Broil 4″–5″ from the heat 3–4 minutes until lightly browned. About 195 calories per serving if made with Mornay Sauce, 220 per serving if made with Cheese Sauce.

BRUSSELS SPROUTS WITH CHESTNUTS

Makes 6 servings

*1 quart fresh Brussels sprouts or 2
(10-ounce) packages frozen sprouts,
boiled and drained*
2 tablespoons butter or margarine
1 tablespoon flour
½ cup chicken broth
Pinch salt
Pinch pepper
1 teaspoon lemon juice
*1 cup coarsely chopped cooked or
canned chestnuts*

Return sprouts to pan and keep warm.
Melt butter over moderate heat and
blend in flour. Add chicken broth
slowly and cook, stirring until slightly
thickened. Mix in remaining ingredients,
pour over sprouts, toss lightly, and serve.
About 140 calories per serving.

BRUSSELS SPROUTS IN ONION SAUCE (SOUBISE)

Makes 6 servings

*3 large yellow onions, peeled and
quartered*
½ cup boiling water
2 tablespoons butter or margarine
*½ cup hot Béchamel Sauce or Medium
White Sauce*
¼ teaspoon salt (about)
Pinch white pepper
*1 quart Brussels sprouts, boiled and
drained*

Simmer onions, covered, in water and
butter 45 minutes until mushy. Uncover,
boil slowly to reduce liquid to ¼ cup,
then purée all in an electric blender at
low speed or put through a food mill.
Mix butter or margarine, Béchamel or
White Sauce, salt, and pepper into onion
purée; taste for salt and add more if
needed. Place sprouts in an ungreased
shallow 1½-quart casserole, top with
onion purée mixture, cover, and bake
15–20 minutes, stirring once or twice.
About 125 calories per serving.

VARIATION:
Just before serving, sprinkle casserole
with ½ cup finely grated sharp Cheddar
cheese and broil 4″–5″ from the heat
2–3 minutes to brown. About 170
calories per serving.

CREAMED BRUSSELS SPROUTS AND CELERY

Makes 4–6 servings

*2 (10-ounce) packages frozen Brussels
sprouts (do not thaw)*
1 cup diced celery
1 cup boiling water
¼ teaspoon salt
½ cup light cream
Pinch white pepper
2 tablespoons butter or margarine
*2 tablespoons flour blended with 2
tablespoons cold water*

Place sprouts, celery, water, and salt in
a saucepan, cover, and boil 10 minutes
until sprouts are *barely* tender. Mix in
cream, pepper, and butter and turn heat
to low. Blend in flour-water paste and
heat, stirring, until thickened and smooth.
Cover, simmer 10 minutes longer to
blend flavors, and serve. About 175
calories for each of 4 servings, 115
calories for each of 6 servings.

CABBAGE

Few vegetables are surrounded by more
legends than cabbage. According to
Greek myth, the first cabbage sprang
from the tears of a prince whom
Dionysus, god of wine, punished for
trampling grapes. From this legend
arose another—that cabbage could prevent drunkenness. Aristotle, it's said,
dined well upon cabbage before setting
out for a night on the town. And the
Romans preceded their orgies by consuming quantities of cabbage. The
cabbages of myth, however, were
sprawling varieties, not the firm round
heads we know today. These were
brought to America by English colonists
and thrived so well in the New World
they soon rivaled potatoes as "the most
popular vegetable." Available to us
today are not only the smooth green

Season	For Top Quality	Amount To Buy	Nutritive Value	Calories (unseasoned)
Year round for all cabbages	Buy firm, heavy heads with crisp, unblem- ished leaves. Green cabbages fade in storage, so a white head may be old.	A medium size head (3–3½ pounds) will serve 4–6.	All raw cabbage is fairly high in vitamin C, the cooked somewhat less so.	Low—from 30–60 per cup, Savoy being lowest, red cab- bage highest

cabbage but also the crinkly green Savoy, the red and the long slim Chinese, or celery, cabbage.

To Prepare for Cooking: Strip away coarse or soiled outer leaves, halve head, and core. Slice, shred, or cut in thin wedges as individual recipes specify.

Serving Tip: Instead of discarding cabbage cores, trim off woody bits, par- boil 10–15 minutes in lightly salted water, cool, and slice into salads.

¢ STEAMED GREEN OR RED CABBAGE

Though many recipes recommend steaming cabbage 7 to 11 minutes, we've found it's really quite raw unless cooked for 25. If you like yours crisp and pungent, by all means use the shorter time. To make red cabbage really red, add a little lemon juice, vinegar (any flavor), or dry red wine to the cooking water.
Makes 4–6 servings

1 medium-size cabbage, cored and cut
    in thin wedges or 1″ slices
1 cup boiling water
3 tablespoons butter or margarine
1 teaspoon salt
Pinch pepper

Place cabbage in a large pot, add water, cover, and steam over moderate heat 20–25 minutes, stirring occasionally. Drain, add butter, salt, and pepper, return to heat, and warm, uncovered, tossing cabbage occasionally, 2–3 min- utes. Green cabbage: About 110 calories

for each of 4 servings, 75 calories for each of 6. Red cabbage: about 135 calories for each of 4 servings, 90 calories for each of 6.

To Parboil for Use in Other Recipes: Use method above but steam only 15 minutes; omit seasonings.

VARIATIONS:

¢ ⚖ **Low-Calorie Cabbage:** *For the green,* reduce butter to 1 tablespoon. About 45 calories for each of 6 servings, 60 for each of 4. *For the red,* omit butter and dress with 2 tablespoons vinegar. About 50 calories for each of 6 servings, 70 for each of 4.

Austrian Cabbage: Steam and season green cabbage as directed above, then chop coarsely and mix in 1 cup sour cream and 2 teaspoons poppy seeds. Spoon into a buttered 3-quart casserole, cover, and bake 15–20 minutes at 350° F. About 230 calories for each of 4 servings, 155 calories for each of 6 servings.

Creamy Cabbage: Steam green cabbage by recipe above, adding butter to cook- ing water. Do not drain. Stir in salt, pepper, 1 (6-ounce) can evaporated milk, and ¼ teaspoon nutmeg. Heat, stirring, 5 minutes (do not boil). Serve in soup bowls with lots of the cooking liquid. About 175 calories for each of 4 servings, 115 calories for each of 6 servings.

CREOLE CABBAGE

Makes 4 servings

1 large yellow onion, peeled and minced
1 small sweet green pepper, cored, seeded, and minced
1 small sweet red pepper, cored, seeded, and minced
1 stalk celery, minced (do not include top)
1 clove garlic, peeled and crushed
2 tablespoons cooking oil
3–4 ripe tomatoes, peeled, seeded, and coarsely chopped
1 small cabbage, shredded medium fine
1½ teaspoons salt
⅛ teaspoon pepper

Stir-fry onion, sweet peppers, celery, and garlic in the oil in a large kettle 5–8 minutes until onion is pale golden. Add tomatoes and stir-fry 2 minutes; add cabbage, salt, and pepper, cover, turn heat to low, and simmer 15–20 minutes until cabbage is tender. About 135 calories per serving.

SAFFRON CABBAGE

Makes 4–6 servings

3 slices bacon
1 medium-size yellow onion, peeled and sliced thin
1 medium-size cabbage, shredded medium fine
½ teaspoon salt
⅛ teaspoon powdered saffron
½ cup beef bouillon
Pinch pepper

Brown bacon in a large kettle over moderate heat; drain on paper toweling, crumble, and reserve. Sauté onion in the drippings 5–8 minutes until pale golden; add cabbage, sprinkle with salt and saffron, and mix in bouillon. Cover and boil slowly 10–15 minutes until cabbage is tender. Drain and season with pepper. Serve topped with bacon. About 125 calories for each of 4 servings, 85 calories for each of 6 servings.

¢ PENNSYLVANIA DUTCH CABBAGE KNABRUS

Makes 4 servings

¼ cup bacon drippings, butter, or margarine
1 small cabbage, shredded medium fine
3 medium-size yellow onions, peeled and sliced thin
1–2 teaspoons salt
¼ teaspoon pepper

Melt fat in a large kettle over moderate heat, layer cabbage and onions into kettle, sprinkling each with salt (use 1 teaspoon in all). Cover and simmer 15–20 minutes, stirring once or twice, until cabbage is tender. Season with pepper, taste for salt and add more if needed. About 160 calories per serving.

¢ COLCANNON

Originally, Colcannon was a leftover dish, the mashed potatoes and cabbage or kale being stirred up and set in the oven to warm while the supper cooked.

Makes 4 servings

1 small cabbage, steamed and chopped fine
2 cups hot seasoned mashed potatoes
2 tablespoons bacon drippings, butter, or margarine
¼ teaspoon salt
Pinch white pepper

Preheat oven to 400° F. Mix cabbage with remaining ingredients, spoon into a well-buttered 1½-quart casserole, and roughen surface with a fork. Bake, uncovered, 35–45 minutes until lightly browned. About 140 calories per serving.

VARIATIONS:

– Follow recipe above, substituting 1½ pounds kale, steamed and finely chopped, for the cabbage. About 140 calories per serving.
– Follow recipe above, stirring 1–2 tablespoons minced parsley into colcannon before baking. About 140 calories per serving.
– Follow recipe above, adding 1–2 finely chopped, steamed leeks (they can be steamed in the same pot with the

cabbage). About 145 calories per serving.

¢ BAKED CABBAGE

Makes 6 servings

*1 medium-size cabbage, cut in 8
    wedges and parboiled
1 medium-size yellow onion, peeled and
    coarsely chopped
¼ cup butter or margarine
1 cup coarse dry bread crumbs
2 tablespoons minced parsley
1 tablespoon minced fresh dill or ½
    teaspoon dried dill
½ cup canned condensed beef consommé
1 teaspoon salt
⅛ teaspoon pepper*

Preheat oven to 350° F. Drain cabbage and arrange in a buttered 2½-quart casserole. Sauté onion in butter over moderate heat 10–12 minutes, stirring until browned; mix in crumbs, parsley, and dill. Pour consommé over cabbage, sprinkle with salt and pepper, and top with sautéed mixture. Cover and bake 45–50 minutes until cabbage is tender. Uncover and bake 15–20 minutes longer to brown. About 125 calories per serving.

¢ SCALLOPED CABBAGE

The perfect companion for roast pork or ham.
Makes 6 servings

*1 medium-size cabbage, cut in ½"
    slices, parboiled, and drained (save
    cooking water)*

Sauce:

*¼ cup butter or margarine
¼ cup unsifted flour
1 teaspoon salt
⅛ teaspoon mace
Pinch cayenne pepper
Pinch black pepper
Cabbage cooking water plus enough
    milk to total 2 cups*

Topping:

*1 cup toasted fine bread crumbs mixed
    with 3 tablespoons melted butter or
    margarine*

Preheat oven to 350° F. Place cabbage in an ungreased 2-quart *au gratin* dish or shallow casserole and set aside. Melt butter and blend in flour, salt, mace, and peppers. Add the 2 cups liquid and heat, stirring, over moderate heat until thickened. Pour over cabbage, sprinkle with topping, and bake uncovered 30 minutes until bubbly. About 275 calories per serving.

SPICY EAST INDIAN BAKED CABBAGE

Here's an unusual vegetable to serve with curry.
Makes 4 servings

*4 cups finely chopped cabbage
1 medium-size yellow onion, peeled and
    minced
1 teaspoon salt
¼ cup flaked coconut
½ teaspoon chili powder
¼ teaspoon turmeric
Very small pinch crushed hot red chili
    peppers
2 eggs, lightly beaten
¼ cup cold water*

Preheat oven to 350° F. Mix all ingredients and spoon into a buttered 1½-quart casserole. Cover and bake about 50 minutes until cabbage is tender; uncover and bake 10 minutes longer to crispen surface slightly. About 105 calories per serving.

¢ SWEET AND SOUR RED CABBAGE

Makes 4–6 servings

*1 medium-size red cabbage, sliced very
    thin
⅔ cup boiling water
3 tablespoons butter or margarine
¼ cup red wine vinegar
½ teaspoon caraway seeds
⅛ teaspoon salt
⅛ teaspoon pepper
2 teaspoons light brown sugar
⅛ teaspoon nutmeg*

Place all ingredients in a large pot, toss to mix, cover, and simmer, stirring once or twice, 15–20 minutes until cabbage is crisp-tender. Serve hot in soup bowls with plenty of the cooking liquid. About 145 calories for each of 4 servings, 100 calories for each of 6 servings.

SHREDDED RUBY CABBAGE

Makes 4–6 servings

1 cup water
3 tablespoons sugar
1 teaspoon salt
¼ cup red currant jelly
1 medium-size red cabbage, coarsely grated
1½ cups finely chopped yellow onion
2 tablespoons cider vinegar

Heat water, sugar, salt, and jelly in a very large saucepan over moderate heat 2–3 minutes, stirring until sugar dissolves. Stir in cabbage and onion, cover, and simmer 20 minutes until cabbage is crisp-tender. Uncover and boil, stirring constantly, 4–5 minutes until liquid evaporates. Add vinegar, toss to mix, and serve. About 195 calories for each of 4 servings, 130 calories for each of 6 servings.

RED CABBAGE AND CHESTNUTS

This combination of cabbage and chestnuts goes particularly well with game.
Makes 6 servings

1 medium-size red cabbage, shredded medium fine
¾ cup beef bouillon
2 teaspoons cider vinegar
½ teaspoon salt
¼ teaspoon pepper
18–20 chestnuts, boiled, peeled, and coarsely chopped
2 tablespoons bacon drippings

Place cabbage, bouillon, vinegar, salt, and pepper in a large pot, cover, and simmer 20–25 minutes until cabbage is barely tender. Mix in chestnuts and drippings and boil, uncovered, 5–7 minutes until most of the liquid has evaporated. About 150 calories per serving.

VARIATION:

Savoy Cabbage and Chestnuts: Follow recipe above, substituting Savoy cabbage for the red and reducing simmering time to 15 minutes. About 145 calories per serving.

FLEMISH RED CABBAGE AND APPLES

If you make this recipe a day or so ahead, then reheat slowly in a covered kettle, it will taste even better.
Makes 4–6 servings

1 small red cabbage, shredded medium fine
½ large Spanish onion, peeled and sliced thin
4 apples (Baldwin, McIntosh, or Jonathan), peeled, cored, and sliced thin
¼ cup firmly packed dark brown sugar
1½–2 teaspoons salt
½ cup dry red wine or red wine vinegar
2 tablespoons butter or margarine
Pinch pepper

Place cabbage, onion, apples, sugar, 1½ teaspoons salt, and wine in a large, heavy kettle, toss to mix, cover, and boil slowly, stirring once or twice, 20–25 minutes until cabbage is just tender. Mix in butter and pepper; taste for salt and add more if needed. About 255 calories for each of 4 servings, 170 calories for each of 6 servings.

STEAMED CHINESE CABBAGE

Makes 4 servings

2–3 heads Chinese cabbage, cut crosswise into fine shreds
½ cup boiling water
¾ teaspoon salt
Pinch pepper
2 tablespoons butter or margarine

Place cabbage, water, and salt in a large saucepan, cover, and boil slowly 7–9 minutes until crisp-tender. Drain, add pepper and butter, and shake pan uncovered over low heat 1–2 minutes until butter melts and gilds cabbage. About 85 calories per serving.

To Parboil for Use in Other Recipes:
Steam as directed above, reducing cooking time to 5 minutes; omit seasonings.

VARIATION:

⚖ **Low-Calorie Chinese Cabbage:**
Omit salt and butter and dress with a sprinkling of seasoned salt or drizzling of low-calorie Italian or herb dressing. About 32 calories per serving.

SAUTÉED CHINESE CABBAGE WITH SESAME SEEDS

Makes 4 servings

3 tablespoons peanut or other cooking oil
2–3 heads Chinese cabbage, shredded fine
1 teaspoon sesame seeds
2 teaspoons Japanese soy sauce

Heat oil in a large, heavy skillet or *wok* over moderately low heat 1 minute, add cabbage, and stir-fry 4 minutes. Add sesame seeds and stir-fry 1 minute. Mix in soy sauce. Cabbage should be crisp-tender; if not, stir-fry 1–2 minutes longer. About 115 calories per serving.

VARIATION:

Follow recipe above, stir-frying 6–8 minced scallions (include green tops) along with the cabbage. About 120 calories per serving.

SAUERKRAUT

Sauerkraut isn't, as most of us think, a German invention. The Chinese stumbled upon the recipe centuries ago while the Great Wall was being built. Among the coolies' rations was a mixture of shredded cabbage and rice wine which, over the weeks, softened and soured into the world's first kraut. If you want to try making your own sauerkraut, you'll find the recipe in the chapter Pickles, Preserves, Jams, and Jellies.

To Prepare for Cooking: Always taste sauerkraut before cooking or heating. If it seems too salty (the fresh often is), soak 15 minutes in cold water, rinse, and drain.

To Cook Fresh Sauerkraut: Drain kraut, place in large saucepan, add just enough water, beef or chicken broth, or dry white wine to cover, and simmer, covered, 30–40 minutes until tender. Drain and serve (sauerkraut needs no additional seasoning).

To Heat Precooked Sauerkraut: Heat sauerkraut, covered, in its own liquid or, if salty, in ¾–1 cup water or dry white wine 5–10 minutes. Drain and serve.

⚖ ¢ CARAWAY SAUERKRAUT

Makes 6–8 servings

1 large yellow onion, peeled and chopped fine
2 tablespoons butter or margarine
2 (1-pound) cans sauerkraut (do not drain)
2–3 tablespoons caraway seeds

Sauté onion in butter in a large, heavy kettle over moderate heat 5–8 minutes until pale golden. Add sauerkraut, cover, and simmer slowly 20 minutes. Drain, mix in caraway seeds, cover, and let stand over lowest heat 5–7 minutes to blend flavors. About 70 calories for

For Top Quality	Amount To Buy	Nutritive Value	Calories (unseasoned)
Buy brands you know and like. Precooked kraut is sold in cans and, more recently, in refrigerated plastic bags. Fresh kraut is sold by delicatessens, specialty groceries.	¼–⅓ pound per person	Fairly high in vitamin C	Low—about 45 per cup

each of 6 servings, 50 calories for each of 8 servings.

BRAISED SAUERKRAUT WITH JUNIPER BERRIES

Makes 4 servings

1 (1-pound 4-ounce) can sauerkraut, drained
¼ pound salt pork, cut in small dice
3 small white onions, each peeled and stuck with 2 cloves
1 carrot, peeled and quartered
1 bouquet garni* and 1 tablespoon juniper berries tied in cheesecloth
½ cup beef broth
½ cup water

Preheat oven to 350° F. Squeeze sauerkraut as dry as possible. Brown salt pork in a heavy kettle over moderate heat; add sauerkraut and all remaining ingredients, cover, and bring to a boil. Transfer kettle to oven and bake, covered, 45–50 minutes, until onions are very tender. (*Note:* Check kettle occasionally and add a little hot water, if necessary, to keep it from boiling dry.) Discard carrot, cheesecloth bag, and cloves. Chop onions coarsely into sauerkraut and serve. About 245 calories per serving.

CARDOONS

Few of us know these giant prickly green stalks, although in France and Italy they're as common as cauliflower. Cardoons are related to artichokes and, according to some botanists, they're the *original* artichoke. They are available, occasionally, in big-city specialty food shops and are a delicacy worth trying.

To Prepare for Cooking: Discard tough stalks and all leaves. Wash each stalk well, cut in 3″ lengths, remove stringy parts, and rub cut edges with lemon. Like celery stalks, cardoons have a heart; trim and quarter it.

To Cook Cardoons: Whether they're to be served in a salad or as a vegetable, cardoons must be cooked. Cover with lightly salted boiling water or chicken broth and simmer, covered, about 2 hours until tender. Drain. Chill and slice into salads, marinate in Vinaigrette or Italian Dressing, or use hot to prepare:

Herbed Cardoons: Toss cardoons with a little melted butter, minced chives, tarragon, or chervil, and salt and pepper to taste.

Sautéed Cardoons: Pat cardoons dry on paper toweling, then sauté 8–10 minutes in butter or olive oil until golden. Season with salt, pepper, and mace.

Breaded Cardoons: Dry cardoons on paper toweling, dip in beaten egg, roll in fine dry crumbs, and fry in deep fat (380° F.) 3–4 minutes until golden.

Sauced Cardoons: Warm cardoons in hot Béchamel or Mornay Sauce (1 cup sauce to 2 cups cardoons) 3–5 minutes, stirring.

CARROTS

When carrots first appeared in England some 350 years ago, ladies were so enchanted by the lacy tops they wore garlands of them in their hair. It was the English who brought carrots to America, the Indians who carried them cross country. Southwestern tribes grow much of today's crop, and to visit these areas at

Season	For Top Quality	Amount To Buy	Nutritive Value	Calories (unseasoned)
Winter	Look for crisp, unblemished stalks	1 pound cardoons serves 2–4.	Not determined	Not determined

Season	For Top Quality	Amount To Buy	Nutritive Value	Calories (unseasoned)
Year round	Look for firm, bright orange carrots of equal size without cracks or splits. If buying by the bunch, make sure tops are not wilted.	1 pound carrots serves 3–4. There are 6–8 medium-size carrots per pound, 12–14 slim ones, 2–3 dozen babies.	High in vitamin A	Low—about 25 per raw, medium-size carrot

harvest time is to see miles of flatlands herringboned with the orange and green of freshly pulled carrots.

To Prepare for Cooking: Mature carrots should be peeled and trimmed of stem and root ends; young tender carrots need only be trimmed and scrubbed. Always try to cook carrots whole; if they seem too large, halve or quarter; if tough, slice, dice, or cut into julienne strips.

¢ **BOILED CARROTS**

Makes 3–4 servings

6–8 medium-size carrots, prepared for cooking
1½ cups boiling water, ginger ale, beef or chicken broth
½ teaspoon salt
Pinch pepper
2 tablespoons butter or margarine

Boil carrots, covered, in lightly salted boiling water (or one of the alternate cooking liquids) as follows: 35–45 minutes for whole carrots; 20–25 for the halved or quartered; 10–15 for the thickly sliced; 5–10 for the thinly sliced, diced, or julienne. Drain, add seasonings, and warm uncovered over low heat 1–2 minutes until butter melts. (*Note:* When boiling cut carrots, reduce cooking liquid to 1 cup.) About 120 calories for each of 3 servings, 90 calories for each of 4 servings.

Boiled Baby Carrots: Follow method above and boil 10–15 minutes.

To Parboil for Use in Other Recipes: Use recipe above but boil whole carrots only 20–25 minutes; the halved or quartered 10; thickly sliced or whole baby carrots 7; thinly sliced, diced, or julienne carrots 3–4. Omit seasonings.

VARIATIONS:

¢ **To Serve Cold:** Boil and drain as directed, then chill in ice water. Drain, cover, and refrigerate. See Vegetable Seasoning Chart for appropriate cold dressings.

⚖ ¢ **Low-Calorie Carrots:** Omit butter; dress with lemon or orange juice and/or 1 tablespoon minced chives. About 50 calories for each of 3 servings, 40 for each of 4.

¢ **Lemon-Glazed Carrots:** Boil and drain carrots by above recipe and keep warm. Melt butter, mix in pepper, ¼ cup light brown sugar, and ½ teaspoon grated lemon rind, and warm, stirring, 3–5 minutes until sugar dissolves. Pour over carrots and serve. About 190 calories for each of 3 servings, 140 calories for each of 4 servings.

¢ **Carrots Rosemary:** Boil and drain carrots as directed above. Return to heat, add pepper and butter, ½ teaspoon each minced fresh rosemary and summer savory (or ¼ teaspoon of the dried), 1 tablespoon each lemon juice and light brown sugar. Warm over lowest heat, turning carrots now and then, about 5 minutes to glaze. About 140 calories for each of 3 servings, 105 calories for each of 4 servings.

MASHED CARROTS

Makes 4 servings

6–8 medium-size hot boiled carrots
¼ teaspoon salt
2 tablespoons butter or margarine,
*   softened to room temperature*
2 tablespoons heavy cream
Pinch nutmeg or mace (optional)

Mash carrots with a potato masher, beat with an electric mixer or purée in an electric blender at high speed. Add all remaining ingredients and beat well with a fork. About 115 calories per serving.

VARIATIONS:

Mashed Carrots and Potatoes: Add 1½ cups hot mashed potatoes to mashed carrots, mix in all seasonings, and beat until light. About 160 calories per serving.

Mashed Carrots and Yams: Add 1½ cups hot mashed yams or sweet potatoes, 2 tablespoons honey or maple syrup, and a pinch cinnamon to mashed carrots. Mix in the salt, butter, cream, and nutmeg and beat until light. About 205 calories per serving.

Mashed Carrots and Rutabagas: Mix 1½ cups hot mashed rutabagas into carrots, add all seasonings, and beat until light. About 145 calories per serving.

Mashed Carrots and Turnips: Mix 1½ cups hot mashed turnips into carrots, add seasonings, and beat until fluffy. About 130 calories per serving.

Mashed Carrots and Parsnips: Mix 1½ cups hot mashed parsnips into carrots, add seasonings, and beat until light. About 185 calories per serving.

CARROTS VICHY

If you have a bottle of Vichy water, try cooking young carrots in it for particularly rich flavor. If not, use the following recipe, which substitutes tap

water and a pinch of soda but tastes like the real thing.
Makes 4 servings

12–14 small young carrots, peeled
2 tablespoons sugar
½ teaspoon salt
½ cup boiling water
2 tablespoons butter or margarine
Pinch baking soda
Pinch white pepper
1 tablespoon minced parsley

Place carrots, sugar, salt, water, butter, and soda in a saucepan. Cover and boil gently 10–15 minutes until carrots are fork tender. Uncover and boil until almost all liquid is gone, shaking pan frequently so carrots become lightly glazed. Sprinkle with pepper and parsley and serve. About 110 calories per serving.

HOT MACÉDOINE OF VEGETABLES

A macédoine of vegeables is a mixture of cooked vegetables of similar size and shape. Usually they're diced, sometimes cut in diamonds or small balls. Almost any mixture can be used if the colors and flavors go well together (avoid using beets because their color runs).
Makes 4–6 servings

1 cup diced cooked carrots
1 cup diced cooked turnips
1 cup diced cooked celery
1 cup cooked green peas
1 cup baby limas
1 cup cooked green or wax beans, cut in
*   ½" lengths*
3–4 tablespoons butter or margarine
Salt
Pepper

Drain all vegetables well and place in a saucepan with butter and salt and pepper to taste. Warm over low heat 2–3 minutes, shaking pan, until butter melts and serve. About 180 calories for each of 4 servings, 120 calories for each of 6 servings.

VARIATION:

Cold Macédoine of Vegetables: Chill cooked vegetables in ice water, drain, pat dry on paper toweling, and refrigerate until ready to use. Instead of seasoning with butter, salt, and pepper, dress with Spanish Vinaigrette Dressing or thin mayonnaise. Serve as a salad, cold vegetable, or hors d'oeuvre. About 180 calories for each of 4 servings, 120 calories for each of 6 servings (with 4 tablespoons dressing).

VENETIAN CARROTS IN CREAM

Carrots prepared this way go well with roast fresh ham or spring lamb.
Makes 4 servings

12–14 small young carrots, peeled
½ cup chicken broth
¼ teaspoon salt
Pinch white pepper
Pinch nutmeg
⅓ cup heavy cream

Place carrots and broth in a saucepan, cover, and simmer 10–15 minutes until tender. (*Note:* There should be very little liquid left, so uncover and boil rapidly to reduce, if necessary.) Add remaining ingredients and simmer, uncovered, 2–3 minutes longer, basting carrots occasionally. Do not allow to boil. About 115 calories per serving.

FLEMISH-STYLE CARROTS

Belgians have a particular talent with vegetables. Flemish-style carrots are sautéed in butter until faintly caramel, then seasoned with lemon so that they aren't too sweet.
Makes 4 servings

¼ cup butter or margarine
6–8 medium-size carrots, peeled and cut in matchstick strips
⅓ cup boiling water
1 tablespoon light brown sugar
1 teaspoon salt
⅛ teaspoon mace
2 egg yolks
½ cup light cream
1 tablespoon lemon juice

Melt butter in a large, heavy skillet over moderate heat, add carrots, and sauté, stirring, 12–15 minutes until lightly glazed. Add water, brown sugar, salt, and mace, cover, and simmer 8–10 minutes until carrots are crisp-tender. Uncover and cook 2 minutes longer. Beat egg yolks with cream, mix into carrots, season with lemon juice, and serve. About 245 calories per serving.

CARROTS PROVENÇAL

An unusual combination of carrots, onion, garlic, and tomatoes.
Makes 4 servings

2 tablespoons olive or other cooking oil
1 medium-size yellow onion, peeled and chopped fine
1 clove garlic, peeled and crushed
2 ripe tomatoes, peeled, seeded, and coarsely chopped
6–8 medium-size carrots, cut in julienne strips and parboiled
½ teaspoon salt
⅛ teaspoon pepper

Heat oil in a large, heavy skillet over moderate heat 1 minute. Add onion and garlic and sauté 5–8 minutes until onion is pale golden. Add tomatoes, sauté 1–2 minutes, then add drained carrots, cover, reduce heat to low, and simmer 5 minutes until carrots are tender. Uncover and simmer 2–3 minutes longer, stirring. Season with salt and pepper and serve. About 130 calories per serving.

CANTONESE CARROTS WITH GREEN PEPPER AND CELERY

Makes 4 servings

12–14 small young carrots, peeled
3 stalks celery
½ medium-size sweet green pepper, cored and seeded
2 tablespoons peanut or other cooking oil
1 scallion, chopped fine (include tops)
Pinch MSG (monosodium glutamate)
¾ teaspoon salt

Cut carrots on the bias into diagonal slices about ¼″ thick. Cut celery the same way, making slices ⅛″ thick. Cut green pepper into matchstick strips. Heat oil in a large, heavy skillet over moderately low heat 1 minute. Add carrots and celery and stir-fry 4 minutes. Add green pepper and scallion and stir-fry 5 minutes or until carrots are crisp tender. Sprinkle vegetables with MSG and salt, toss, and serve. About 105 calories per serving.

CARROT AND ONION "PIE"

Makes 4 servings

6–8 medium-size carrots, peeled and
　halved or quartered
1 large yellow onion, peeled and coarsely
　chopped
1½ cups boiling water
2 tablespoons melted butter or margarine
1 teaspoon salt (about)
⅛ teaspoon pepper
2 tablespoons butter or margarine
1 teaspoon minced parsley
1 teaspoon minced chervil (optional)

Preheat oven to 350° F. Boil carrots and onion in the water, covered, about 20 minutes until tender. Drain and put through a food mill or purée in an electric blender at high speed. Beat melted butter, salt, and pepper into carrot purée, taste for salt and add more if needed. Spoon into a well-buttered 9″ or 10″ piepan and dot with remaining butter. Bake, uncovered, 15–20 minutes. Sprinkle with parsley and, if you like, the chervil and serve. About 150 calories per serving.

BAKED CARROTS AND RICE

A mellow, crunchy combination of shredded carrots and rice that makes an unusual potato substitute.
Makes 6 servings

¼ cup butter or margarine
3 cups coarsely grated raw carrots
½ cup minced onion
1 teaspoon minced parsley
1½ teaspoons salt
¼ teaspoon summer savory
¼ teaspoon mace
Pinch rosemary
Pinch pepper
3 tablespoons dry sherry
3 cups cooked rice
1 cup milk
2 eggs, lightly beaten

Preheat oven to 325° F. Melt butter in a large, heavy skillet over moderate heat, add carrots and onion, and sauté, stirring occasionally, about 15 minutes until carrots are crisp-tender. Mix in parsley, salt, savory, mace, rosemary, pepper and sherry and heat, stirring, 1–2 minutes. Off heat, mix in rice. Beat milk with eggs, add to carrots, and stir until well blended. Spoon into a buttered 9″×9″×2″ baking dish, cover with foil, and set in a shallow pan; pour ½″ water into pan. Bake 45 minutes, remove foil, and bake 30 minutes longer. About 245 calories per serving.

CAULIFLOWER

Snowy . . . succulent . . . a little bit sweet, a little bit nutty . . . that's cauliflower. "Cabbage with a college

Season	For Top Quality	Amount To Buy	Nutritive Value	Calories (unseasoned)
Year round; peak months: September–December	Choose snowy, compact heads with crisp green leaves and few or no dark spots. Reject any open, spongy heads.	1 large (3–3½-pound) cauliflower will serve 4.	High in vitamin C	Low—25–30 per average serving

education," Mark Twain called it.
Certainly it's the most elegant cabbage, a
vegetable grown only for emperors and
kings until twentieth-century farming
made it available to all.

To Prepare for Cooking: Remove green
leaves, cut off heavy stem close to base,
and wash head well in cool water,
holding it upside down. Leave head
whole, making a deep X-cut in the base
of the heavy stem to hasten cooking; or
divide into bite-size flowerets, trimming
each stem to a length of 1".

Serving Tip: Try serving raw
cauliflowerets with seasoned salt or
Curry Dip as a cocktail hors d'oeuvre.

BOILED CAULIFLOWER

Some say cauliflower should be cooked
uncovered, some say it should be
uncovered the first 5 minutes only, some
say it should be covered at all times.
We've tried all three ways and prefer the
third because it minimizes the
"cabbage-y" cooking odor. The same
technique works for all members of the
cabbage family.
Makes 4 servings

*1 large cauliflower, prepared for
  cooking*
1½ cups boiling water
*1 slice lemon (to keep cauliflower
  snowy)*
½ teaspoon salt
⅛ teaspoon white pepper

Place cauliflower stem down in a large
saucepan, add all but last ingredient,
cover, and boil until crisp-tender: 20–30
minutes for a head, 5–7 for flowerets.
Drain well. To keep head intact while
transferring to serving dish, tilt pan and
ease it out. Sprinkle with pepper, dress
with Browned Butter or one of the
sauces listed in the Vegetable Seasoning
Chart. About 30 calories per serving
without Browned Butter or sauce.

To Steam Cauliflower: Place cauliflower
on a rack in a steamer, pour in boiling
water to a depth of 1", cover, and steam
head 30–40 minutes, flowerets 10–15.

To Parboil for Use in Other Recipes: Use
either method above, reducing cooking
times thus: boil heads 10 minutes,
flowerets 3–5; steam heads 20 minutes,
flowerets 7–10. Omit seasonings.

VARIATIONS:

To Serve Cold: Chill boiled or steamed
cauliflower in ice water, drain, and pat
dry on paper toweling; refrigerate until
ready to use. Serve as a salad or cold
vegetable dressed with one of the sauces
listed in the Vegetable Seasoning Chart.

⚖ **Low-Calorie Cauliflower:** Boil or
steam as directed, drain and dress with
low-calorie herb or Italian dressing
instead of butter or sauce. If you like,
add a sprinkling of minced chives,
parsley, or dill. About 35 calories per
serving.

CAULIFLOWER POLONAISE

Makes 4–6 servings

1 large cauliflower, steamed and drained
2 tablespoons butter or margarine
1 cup soft white bread crumbs
*2 hard-cooked eggs, peeled and chopped
  fine*
1 tablespoon minced parsley

Transfer cauliflower to a vegetable dish
and keep warm. Melt butter in a small
skillet over moderate heat, add crumbs,
and stir-fry 4–5 minutes until lightly
browned. (*Note:* Crumbs brown slowly at
first, quickly toward the end, so watch
carefully.) Off heat, mix in eggs and
parsley. Sprinkle crumb mixture over
cauliflower and serve. About 155
calories for each of 4 servings, 105
calories for each of 6 servings.

CAULIFLOWER IN CIDER AND
CREAM

Makes 4–6 servings

2 tablespoons butter or margarine
2 tablespoons flour
1 cup heavy cream
½ cup apple cider
½ teaspoon salt

Pinch white pepper
1 large cauliflower, divided into
   flowerets, parboiled, and drained

Melt butter in the top of a double boiler
over simmering water and blend in flour;
slowly mix in cream and cider. Heat,
stirring, until thickened. Season with salt
and pepper, add cauliflowerets, and toss
gently to mix. Cover and warm, still over
simmering water, 10–15 minutes to blend
flavors. About 315 calories for each of 4
servings, 210 calories for each of 6
servings.

DEVILED CAULIFLOWER

To give this dish special zip, add a beef
bouillon cube to the cooking water.
Makes 4 servings

1 large cauliflower, divided into
   flowerets, boiled and drained (save
   cooking water)
1/4 cup butter or margarine
3 tablespoons flour
1 teaspoon powdered mustard
Cauliflower cooking water plus enough
   milk to total 1 2/3 cups
1 tablespoon Worcestershire sauce
1 tablespoon prepared spicy brown
   mustard
1/2 teaspoon salt
1 teaspoon ketchup
1/8 teaspoon pepper

Keep cauliflower warm. Melt butter over
moderate heat and blend in flour and
powdered mustard. Mix in the 1 2/3 cups
liquid and heat, stirring, until thickened.
Mix in remaining ingredients and heat,
stirring, 2–3 minutes. Pour sauce over
cauliflower, toss lightly to mix, and
serve. About 180 calories per serving.

CAULIFLOWER CARUSO

A piquant dish that goes well with veal
cutlets, scaloppine, or broiled chicken.
Makes 4–6 servings

1 large cauliflower, divided into
   flowerets, boiled and drained
1 small yellow onion, peeled and chopped
   fine
2 tablespoons olive or other cooking oil

1 tablespoon minced anchovies
1/4 cup dry white wine or chicken broth
1 tablespoon lemon juice
1 teaspoon minced parsley
1 teaspoon minced fresh chervil or 1/2
   teaspoon dried chervil
1/2 teaspoon minced fresh basil or 1/4
   teaspoon dried basil
Pinch pepper

Keep cauliflower warm. Sauté onion in
oil in a large skillet over moderate heat
5–8 minutes until pale golden. Add
anchovies and sauté 1 minute. Stir in
wine or broth and lemon juice, reduce
heat to low, cover, and simmer 10
minutes. Add cauliflower, mix gently,
sprinkle with parsley, herbs, and pepper.
Cover and simmer 5–7 minutes until
heated through, basting cauliflower once
or twice with sauce. About 120 calories
for each of 4 servings, 80 calories for
each of 6 servings.

PURÉED CAULIFLOWER À LA
DU BARRY

Makes 4 servings

1 large cauliflower, boiled until very
   tender and drained
1 cup hot, seasoned mashed potatoes
1/4 cup heavy cream
2 tablespoons melted butter or margarine
1 teaspoon salt
1/8 teaspoon white pepper
Pinch mace
2 tablespoons butter or margarine

Preheat oven to 350° F. Purée
cauliflower in an electric blender at high
speed or put through a food mill. With a
wooden spoon or wire whisk, beat purée
with potatoes and cream until fluffy. Mix
in melted butter, salt, pepper, and mace.
Spoon into a buttered shallow 1 1/2-quart
casserole and dot with butter. Bake,
uncovered, 1 hour until golden brown.
About 215 calories per serving.

VARIATION:

Mix in any of the following just before
baking: 1/4 cup minced scallions (include
some tops); 1/2 cup coarsely chopped
toasted almonds; 1/4 cup finely chopped
pecans. About 215 calories per serving if

made with scallions, 320 calories per serving if made with almonds, and 245 calories per serving if made with pecans.

CAULIFLOWER SOUFFLÉ

Topped with Cheese Sauce or Mornay Sauce, this makes a luscious luncheon entree.
Makes 4 servings

¼ cup butter or margarine
¼ cup sifted flour
½ cup cauliflower cooking water
½ cup light cream
4 eggs, separated
¾ teaspoon salt
Pinch white pepper
2 cups puréed, cooked cauliflower
Pinch cream of tartar

Preheat oven to 350° F. Melt butter over moderate heat and blend in flour. Mix in cauliflower cooking water and cream and heat, stirring, until thickened and smooth. Beat egg yolks lightly, mix in a little hot sauce, then stir back into sauce in pan. Cook, stirring, 1–2 minutes, but do not boil. Mix sauce, salt, and pepper into cauliflower purée. (*Note:* You can make recipe up to this point well ahead of time, then cool, cover, and chill until about 2 hours before serving. Let sauce come to room temperature before proceeding.) Beat egg whites until frothy, add cream of tartar, and continue beating until fairly stiff peaks form. Fold whites into sauce, then spoon into an ungreased 5-cup soufflé dish. Bake, uncovered, on center rack about 45 minutes or until puffed and golden. Rush to the table and serve. About 280 calories per serving (without sauce).

CAULIFLOWER PUDDING

A rich cauliflower custard aromatic of savory and mace.
Makes 4–6 servings

2 medium-size cauliflowers, divided into flowerets and parboiled
1 (13-ounce) can evaporated milk
2 tablespoons melted butter or margarine
2 eggs

2 teaspoons salt
¼ teaspoon pepper
¼ teaspoon summer savory
⅛ teaspoon mace

Preheat oven to 300° F. Drain cauliflower thoroughly and chop coarsely. Place all remaining ingredients in a large bowl and beat with an electric mixer or rotary beater until frothy. Mix in cauliflower. Transfer to a lightly buttered 2-quart casserole or soufflé dish and bake, uncovered, 1–1½ hours until no longer liquid. Stir mixture 1 or 2 times from the bottom as it cooks. About 280 calories for each of 4 servings, 185 calories for each of 6 servings.

CAULIFLOWER AU GRATIN

Such an easy, elegant recipe.
Makes 4–6 servings

1 large cauliflower, divided into flowerets, boiled, and drained
½ teaspoon salt
⅛ teaspoon white pepper
1½ cups hot Cheese Sauce or Mornay Sauce
⅓ cup coarsely grated sharp Cheddar cheese
1 tablespoon melted butter or margarine

Preheat broiler. Arrange flowerets in an ungreased *au gratin* dish or shallow casserole. Season with salt and pepper and cover evenly with sauce. Sprinkle with cheese and drizzle with butter. Broil 5″ from heat 3–4 minutes until cheese melts and is dappled with brown. About 280 calories for each of 4 servings and 185 calories for each of 6 if made with Mornay Sauce. About 320 calories for each of 4 servings and 210 for each of 6 if made with Cheese Sauce.

VARIATION:

After browning, top with ½ cup toasted, slivered almonds. About 385 calories for each of 4 servings and 255 calories for each of 6 if made with Mornay Sauce. About 425 calories for each of 4 servings and 280 for each of 6 if made with Cheese Sauce.

CAULIFLOWER BAKED IN WINE AND CREAM SAUCE

Makes 4–6 servings

1½ cups chicken broth
1 large cauliflower, divided into flowerets
⅔ cup heavy cream (about)
¼ cup butter or margarine
¼ cup unsifted flour
Pinch mace
2 tablespoons dry white wine
½ cup finely grated Parmesan cheese
⅛ teaspoon salt
Pinch pepper

Topping:

⅔ cup cracker meal
3 tablespoons melted butter or margarine
1 tablespoon finely grated Parmesan cheese

Bring broth to a boil in a large saucepan, add cauliflower, cover, and simmer 20–25 minutes until crisp-tender. Drain, reserving broth. Measure broth and add cream to make 2 cups. Melt butter over moderate heat and blend in flour and mace. Add broth mixture and heat, stirring, until thickened. Off heat, mix in wine, Parmesan, salt, and pepper. Arrange flowerets in an ungreased 2-quart au gratin dish and top with sauce. Mix topping and sprinkle over surface. Preheat broiler, then broil 5″ from heat 3–4 minutes until browned and bubbly. About 520 calories for each of 4 servings, 345 calories for each of 6 servings.

CELERIAC

(Also called Knob Celery, Turnip Celery, and German Celery)

Long treasured in Europe, this plump root celery has never become popular in this country. It tastes like strong celery, has the texture of a turnip, and is best when creamed, puréed, or prepared au gratin.

To Prepare for Cooking: Cut off all stalks and root ends and discard; scrub knob well in cool water, then peel (the skin is very tough and stringy). Slice, cube, or cut into julienne strips.

Cooking Tip: Substitute celeriac for celery in soups and stews.

Serving Tip: Marinate raw julienne strips of celeriac 2–3 hours in the refrigerator in a good tart dressing and serve in—or as—a salad.

BOILED CELERIAC

If you've never tasted celeriac, try it one of these easy ways. You may discover that you like it very much.
Makes 4 servings

3 knobs celeriac, prepared for cooking
1½ cups boiling water or chicken broth
1 teaspoon salt (about)
⅛ teaspoon white pepper
2 tablespoons melted butter or margarine

Place celeriac, water or broth, and salt (reduce to taste if you use broth) in a saucepan, cover, and boil until crisp-tender: 15 minutes for julienne strips, 20–30 for cubes and slices. Drain, add pepper and butter, and toss to mix. About 95 calories per serving.

To Parboil for Use in Other Recipes: Use method above but reduce cooking time to 10 minutes for julienne strips, to 15 for cubes and slices. Omit seasonings.

Season	For Top Quality	Amount To Buy	Nutritive Value	Calories (unseasoned)
August–May	Look for firm, crisp knobs 2–4″ in diameter with few scars or blemishes.	A 2–4″ knob serves 1–2.	Low	Low—about 45 per average serving

VARIATIONS:

To Serve Cold: Cook and drain as recipe directs; chill in ice water. Drain, pat dry on paper toweling, and refrigerate until needed. Serve as a cold vegetable or salad, with one of the dressings recommended in the Vegetable Seasoning Chart.

⚖ **Low-Calorie Celeriac:** Season with lemon juice instead of butter, use seasoned salt for ordinary salt, and sprinkle with 2 tablespoons minced chives. About 45 calories per serving.

Creamed Celeriac: Omit butter and mix boiled, drained celeriac with 1½ cups hot Medium White Sauce. About 195 calories per serving.

Puréed Celeriac: Cook 1 small peeled cubed Irish potato with celeriac. Purée vegetables with ¼ cup cooking liquid in an electric blender at low speed or put through a food mill. Mix in ⅛ teaspoon white pepper, 2 tablespoons heavy cream, a pinch of nutmeg, and, for a rich purée, 2 tablespoons melted butter. If mixture has cooled, warm over low heat, stirring. About 145 calories per serving (without additional butter), 195 calories per serving (with additional butter).

CELERIAC AU GRATIN

An especially good casserole. Easy, too.
Makes 4 servings

*3 knobs celeriac, cut in julienne strips,
  boiled and drained*
1½ cups hot Cheese Sauce
½ cup soft white bread crumbs

¼ cup finely grated Parmesan cheese
1 tablespoon minced parsley
2 tablespoons melted butter or margarine

Preheat oven to 400° F. Arrange celeriac in an ungreased 1½-quart *au gratin* dish or shallow casserole and top with sauce. Toss remaining ingredients together and sprinkle over sauce. Bake, uncovered, 20 minutes until crumbs are lightly browned. About 370 calories per serving.

CELERY

Celery is a Mediterranean vegetable, which ancients looked upon as medicine rather than food (it was said to purify the blood). When the French began to cultivate wild celery, it was the seed they prized (and used as an herb), not the stalk. No one knows who first thought to eat the crisp, succulent stalks—odd considering how much we rely on them today to give crunch to salads and stuffings, delicate savor to soups and stews.

To Prepare for Cooking: Cut root end and green leafy tops from celery (save for stock pot); separate head into individual stalks. Wash well in cool water, slice or chop as individual recipes specify.

To Prepare Celery Hearts: Peel away all but inner 4 or 5 stalks (save for salads, soups, or stews), halve lengthwise, then trim off root ends and leafy tops so each heart is about 5″ long. Soak hearts ½ hour in ice water; rinse.

Season	For Top Quality	Amount To Buy	Nutritive Value	Calories (unseasoned)
Year round	Whether buying white or green (Pascal) celery, choose crunchy stalks, neither cracked nor bruised, with crisp green leaves.	1 large head (1½ pounds), cooked, will serve 4.	Some minerals; rather low in vitamins	Very Low—about 5 per stalk

Serving Tip: To make raw stalks supercrisp, pull threads from outer side of each; soak stalks 20–30 minutes in 1 gallon ice water mixed with ¼ cup sugar.

¢ ⚖ BOILED CELERY

Cooked celery makes a delicious, low-calorie vegetable.
Makes 4 servings

1 large bunch celery, prepared for
cooking
1½ cups boiling water
½ teaspoon salt
Pinch pepper
2 tablespoons melted butter or margarine

Cut stalks in 1½″ lengths or dice. Boil, covered, in lightly salted water 20–30 minutes if cut in lengths, 10–15 if diced. Drain, add pepper and butter, and serve. About 65 calories per serving.

To Parboil for Use in Other Recipes: Use recipe above but reduce cooking time to 10 minutes for celery cut in lengths, to 5 minutes for the diced. Omit seasonings.

VARIATIONS:

¢ **To Serve Cold:** Boil and drain as directed; chill in ice water, drain, pat dry on paper toweling, and refrigerate until needed. Serve as a salad or cold vegetable with one of the dressings recommended in the Vegetable Seasoning Chart.

⚖ ¢ **Low-Calorie Celery:** Instead of seasoning with butter, dress with 2 tablespoons low-calorie herb or Italian dressing, 2 tablespoons minced chives, and a dash of Worcestershire sauce. About 15 calories per serving.

Celery Amandine: Boil and drain celery as directed and sprinkle with pepper. Omit butter and top instead with 1–1½ cups hot Medium White Sauce. Mix lightly, sprinkle with 2–3 tablespoons toasted slivered almonds, and serve. About 145 calories per serving.

Celery au Gratin: Cut celery in 1½″ lengths, boil and drain as directed. Sprinkle with pepper but omit butter.

Mix with 1½ cups hot Mornay Sauce, spoon into an ungreased 1-quart *au gratin* dish, sprinkle with ⅓ cup grated sharp Cheddar cheese, and broil 5″ from the heat 3–4 minutes until lightly browned. About 240 calories per serving.

BRAISED CELERY HEARTS

Makes 4 servings

4 celery hearts, parboiled and drained
2 tablespoons butter or margarine
1 cup water, chicken or beef broth or ¾
cup water or broth and ¼ cup dry
vermouth
⅛ teaspoon pepper
½ teaspoon salt (optional)

Pat celery dry between several layers of paper toweling. Heat butter until bubbly in a heavy skillet over moderately low heat, add celery and cook gently, turning frequently until pale golden. Add water, sprinkle with pepper and salt (omit salt if using broth), cover, and simmer about ½ hour until fork tender. When serving, top each portion with a little cooking liquid. About 65 calories per serving if cooked in water, 75 calories per serving if cooked in broth or in broth and vermouth.

CELERY AND CARROT CURRY

Good with ham, pork, lamb, or chicken.
Makes 4–6 servings

6–8 medium-size carrots, peeled and cut
in matchstick strips
¾ cup boiling water
2 beef bouillon cubes
4 large stalks celery, cut in matchstick
strips
1¼ cups milk (about)
2 tablespoons butter or margarine
1 small yellow onion, peeled and minced
2 tablespoons flour
1 tablespoon curry powder
¼ teaspoon ginger
Pinch nutmeg

Place carrots in a large saucepan, add water and bouillon cubes, cover, and simmer 8–10 minutes. Add celery, re-cover, and simmer 10 minutes longer until vegetables are crisp-tender. Drain cooking liquid into a measuring cup and add enough milk to total 1½ cups. In a separate saucepan, melt butter over moderate heat and sauté onion, stirring, 5–8 minutes until pale golden. Blend in flour and spices, add milk mixture, and heat, stirring, until thickened. Pour sauce over vegetables, toss to mix, and let "season," uncovered, over lowest heat 5–10 minutes, stirring occasionally. About 170 calories for each of 4 servings, 110 for each of 6 servings.

SCALLOPED CELERY WITH ALMONDS

Makes 4–6 servings

1 large bunch celery, prepared for cooking
1½ cups boiling water
1–1¼ teaspoons salt
3 tablespoons butter or margarine
3 tablespoons flour
½ cup light cream
⅛ teaspoon white pepper
½ cup finely chopped blanched almonds
½ cup fine dry bread crumbs

Preheat oven to 350° F. Cut celery stalks in 3″ lengths; arrange in an ungreased shallow 2-quart flameproof casserole, add water and 1 teaspoon salt. Cover and simmer 20–25 minutes over moderate heat until crisp-tender. Drain off cooking water, reserving 1 cup. Melt butter over moderate heat and blend in flour. Mix in cooking water and cream and cook and stir about 5 minutes until thickened. Season with pepper, taste for salt and add remaining ¼ teaspoon if needed. Pour sauce over celery. Mix almonds with crumbs and sprinkle on top. Bake, uncovered, 30 minutes until browned and bubbly. About 295 calories for each of 4 servings, 200 calories for each of 6 servings.

BLUE CHEESE-CELERY CASSEROLE

Makes 4 servings

4 cups coarsely chopped celery (you'll need about 1 bunch)

1 cup chicken broth
1 cup hot seasoned mashed potatoes
½ teaspoon salt
⅛ teaspoon pepper
¼ cup crumbled blue cheese

Topping:
1 cup soft white bread crumbs mixed with 2 tablespoons melted butter or margarine

Simmer celery, covered, in broth 1 hour until mushy (when celery is about ⅔ done, begin preheating oven to 400° F.). Purée celery with cooking liquid in an electric blender at low speed or put through a food mill. Mix in remaining ingredients except topping and spoon into a buttered 1-quart casserole. Sprinkle with topping and bake, uncovered, 35–45 minutes until lightly browned. About 190 calories per serving.

⊠ ¢ CHINESE STIR-FRIED CELERY

Makes 4 servings

1 large bunch celery, prepared for cooking
¼ cup peanut or other cooking oil

Cut each stalk diagonally into slices ⅛″ thick, discarding any strings. Heat oil in a *wok* or large, heavy skillet over moderate heat, add celery, and stir-fry 5–7 minutes until crisp-tender but not brown. About 140 calories per serving.

VARIATIONS:

⊠ ¢ **Chinese Celery with Soy and Sesame Seeds:** Stir-fry as directed; just before serving toss in 1 tablespoon each soy sauce and sesame seeds. About 145 calories per serving.

¢ **Stir-Fried Celery, Pepper, and Scallions:** Stir-fry ½ thinly slivered sweet red pepper and 3–4 minced scallions along with the celery. About 145 calories per serving.

Stir-Fried Celery and Mushrooms: Stir-fry ⅔ cup thinly sliced mushrooms along with the celery. About 145 calories per serving.

Season	For Top Quality	Amount To Buy	Nutritive Value	Calories (unseasoned)
June–November	Look for crisp leaves and fleshy stalks free of insect injury.	A 1-pound bunch serves 2 amply.	Very high in vitamin A	Low—less than 40 per ½-pound serving

CHARD

(Also called Swiss Chard)

Chard is a bonus vegetable: the crinkly green leaves can be steamed much like spinach, the silvery stalks can be simmered like asparagus, or the two can be chopped and cooked together.

To Prepare for Cooking: Discard root ends and separate stalks from leaves. Wash leaves 2 or 3 times in cool water to remove all grit; trim stalks of tough or woody ribs and wash well in cool water. Keep stalks and leaves separate.

BOILED CHARD

Makes 4 servings

2 pounds chard, prepared for cooking
½ cup boiling water
½ teaspoon salt
Pinch pepper
2 tablespoons melted butter or
*   margarine*

Coarsely chop stalks and leaves but keep the two separate. Place stalks in a large pot, add water and salt, cover, and boil 5 minutes. Add leaves, cover, and boil 5–10 minutes longer until

tender. Drain, toss with pepper and butter, and serve. About 90 calories per serving.

To Boil Stalks Alone: Prepare stalks for cooking, leave whole or cut in 2–3″ lengths. Place in a pot with 1 cup boiling water and ½ teaspoon salt and boil, covered, 10–15 minutes until tender. Drain, season with pepper and butter, and serve.

Steamed Chard Leaves: Prepare leaves for cooking, place in a large pot with ½ cup boiling water and ½ teaspoon salt, cover, and steam 5–10 minutes until tender. Drain and season with butter and pepper or oil and vinegar. About 90 calories per serving.

To Parboil for Use in Other Recipes: Boil stalks by method above but reduce cooking time to 5–7 minutes; omit seasonings. The leaves don't need parboiling.

VARIATIONS:

To Serve Cold: Boil or steam as directed and drain; chill stalks and/or leaves in ice water. Drain, toss with a good tart dressing, and refrigerate several hours.

⚖ **Low-Calorie Chard:** Season with red or white wine vinegar instead of butter. About 40 calories per serving.

Season	For Top Quality	Amount To Buy	Nutritive Value	Calories (unseasoned)
Year round	Choose plump, firm, clean chayotes with few nicks, blemishes.	1 chayote serves 2.	Not determined	Thought to be low

Puréed Chard: Boil and drain as directed; purée in an electric blender at high speed or put through a food mill. Mix in 2 tablespoons each butter and heavy cream, a pinch pepper and warm 1–2 minutes, stirring, over low heat. About 115 calories per serving.

CHAYOTES

(Also called Christophene, Cho-Cho, Mango Squash, Mirliton, and Vegetable Pear)

These Caribbean squashes, fairly common in the Gulf States, are beginning to appear elsewhere. The size and shape of an avocado, they have deeply furrowed, waxy, pale yellow skins. They taste like summer squash and can be substituted for it in recipes.

To Prepare for Cooking: Scrub well in cool water, then peel unless chayotes are to be stuffed and baked (you'll notice a sticky substance on your hands—it's harmless and washes right off). Halve chayotes and with a table knife pry out long, slender seed. Leave as halves, cut each in two lengthwise, or slice crosswise ¾″ thick.

To Boil: Cover with lightly salted boiling water and simmer, covered, until firm but tender: about 45 minutes for halves, 30 for quarters, 20 for slices. Drain, season with butter, salt, and pepper or top with Mornay, Basic Cheese, or Medium White Sauce.

To Parboil for Use in Other Recipes: Use method above but reduce cooking time to 30 minutes for halves, 20 for quarters, and 10–15 for slices.

To Bake and Stuff: Fill parboiled, *unpeeled,* scooped-out halves with any mixture you would use for stuffing summer squash. Bake, uncovered, at 350° F. about 30–40 minutes.

To Serve as Salad: Cool and chill boiled chayote halves or slices. Fill halves with any meat or fish salad;

marinate slices in a tart dressing and toss into green salad.

CHESTNUTS

(Also called Marrons)

To us chestnuts are a luxury, something to savor before the fire with a glass of fine sherry, something to save for that special Thanksgiving stuffing. To Europeans, however, they're commonplace, a popular potato substitute. Try them their way in place of potatoes.

To Shell and Peel Chestnuts: This is a tedious job, so have patience. Make an X-cut into shell on flat side of each nut. Cover nuts with cold water, bring to a boil, cover, and boil 1–2 minutes. Remove from heat but do not drain. Using a slotted spoon, scoop 2–3 nuts from the pan at a time and peel off both the hard outer shell and the inner brown skin (use a small knife to loosen skins if necessary). Keep chestnuts in hot water until you're ready to peel them. If any seem unduly stubborn, simply reheat briefly in boiling water and try again to peel.

BOILED CHESTNUTS

Serve in place of potatoes with poultry, pork, game, or game birds.
Makes 4 servings

1 pound shelled, peeled chestnuts
2 cups boiling water or chicken broth
3 tablespoons butter or margarine
Salt
Pepper

Simmer chestnuts, covered, in water or broth 15–20 minutes until tender but not mushy. Drain, add butter, salt, and pepper to taste, and warm uncovered over low heat, shaking pan gently, until butter melts and gilds nuts. About 295 calories per serving (if cooked in water), 310 per serving (if cooked in broth).

Season	For Top Quality	Amount To Buy	Nutritive Value	Calories (unseasoned)
Fall and winter	Choose plump, unshriveled nuts with unscarred, uncracked shells.	1½ pounds unshelled nuts will yield 1 pound shelled nuts and serve about 4.	Some incomplete protein, iron and B vitamins	Very high —about 20 per fresh nut, 40 per dried nut

To Boil Dried Chestnuts: Wash and sort, carefully removing any that are withered, discolored, or buggy. Cover with cold water, remove any that float, then soak overnight. Drain, rinse several times, and scrape off bits of brown skin remaining. Cover with fresh cold water and simmer, covered, 1–1½ hours until plump and tender. Drain and use cup-for-cup in place of fresh boiled chestnuts.

VARIATIONS:

Sautéed Chestnuts: Boil and drain chestnuts by recipe above, add salt and pepper but omit butter. Sauté instead in ¼ cup butter 4–5 minutes until lightly browned. About 320 calories per serving (if cooked in water), 335 per serving (cooked in broth).

Creamed Chestnuts: Boil and drain chestnuts as recipe directs, then halve. Add butter, salt, and pepper called for, also ½ cup heavy cream. Warm, uncovered, over lowest heat until just simmering. Stir occasionally. About 400 calories per serving (if cooked in water), 415 per serving (if cooked in broth).

Riced Chestnut Pyramid: Boil and drain chestnuts as directed, season with salt and pepper but omit butter. Put chestnuts through a potato ricer, letting them mound into a pyramid on a heated plate. Serve with melted butter. About 220 calories per serving (if cooked in water), 235 per serving (if cooked in broth)—without butter.

Puréed Chestnuts: Boil as directed in chicken broth; drain and purée in an electric blender at high speed or put through a food mill. Beat in 2 tablespoons each butter and light cream; add salt and pepper to taste. About 310 calories per serving.

ROASTED CHESTNUTS

Makes 4 servings

1½ pounds chestnuts in the shell
¼ cup cooking oil

Preheat oven to 400° F. With a sharp knife, make an X-shaped cut on the flat side of each shell. Arrange nuts in a roasting pan, sprinkle with oil, and toss lightly. Roast, uncovered, 10–15 minutes. Cool just until easy to handle, then shell and remove inner brown skins. The chestnuts are now ready to use in recipes or to eat out of hand. About 245 calories per serving.

VARIATION:

Hearth-Roasted Chestnuts: Do not make X-cuts on chestnuts, do not use oil. Lay chestnuts at edge of fire near glowing coals (you don't need a pan) and roast about 10 minutes, turning frequently, until nuts "pop." Shell and eat. About 220 calories per serving.

BRAISED CHESTNUTS

These chestnuts can be served as a vegetable, alone, or mixed with creamed onions, boiled cabbage, Brussels sprouts, or broccoli. They can also be used to garnish roast chicken, turkey, or game platters.

Makes 4 servings

¼ cup melted butter or margarine
1 small yellow onion, peeled and
  minced
1 stalk celery, minced (include green
  tops)
1 pound shelled, peeled chestnuts, whole
  or halved
⅛ teaspoon white pepper
1½ cups chicken broth or ¾ cup each
  beef consommé and water
1 star anise (optional)

Preheat oven to 350° F. Pour butter into
a 1½-quart casserole, add onion and
celery, and top with chestnuts. Sprinkle
with pepper, pour in broth, and, if you
like, add anise. Cover and bake 35–45
minutes until chestnuts are very tender.
When serving, top each portion with
some of the pan juices. About 340
calories per serving.

COLLARDS

Nearly every Southern farm has its
collard patch, every kitchen its "mess o'
greens" simmering on the back of the
stove with a chunk of streaky bacon or
salt pork. There's always lots of "pot
likker" and oven-fresh corn bread for
sopping it up.

To Prepare for Cooking: Wash well in
cool water to remove grit and sand.
Discard tough stems and leaf midribs;
cut large leaves into bite-size pieces.

Cooking Tip: Try stir-frying finely
shredded young collard leaves in bacon
drippings 8–10 minutes over moderately
high heat until crisp-tender.

¢ BOILED COLLARDS, TURNIP GREENS, OR MUSTARD GREENS

Makes 4 servings

2 pounds collards, turnip greens, or
  mustard greens, prepared for
  cooking
½ cup boiling water
¾ teaspoon salt
Pinch pepper
2 tablespoons bacon drippings, melted
  butter or margarine

Break leaves into bite-size pieces or
chop fine. Place in a large pot, add
water and salt, cover, and simmer until
tender: 10–15 minutes for turnip or
mustard greens, 15–20 for collards.
(*Note:* Very young leaves may cook in
5–7 minutes.) Drain, add pepper and
drippings, and toss to mix. About 105
calories per serving.

VARIATION:

⚖ ¢ **Low-Calorie Boiled Greens:**
Omit drippings and dress with a sprinkling of white wine vinegar and a pinch
nutmeg. About 55–60 calories per
serving.

CORN

(Also called Maize)

One of the joys of summer is feasting
upon sugary ears of sweet corn, dripping
with butter and so hot you can hardly
hold them. A gift from the American
Indian, corn provides not only kernels
to nibble off the cob but also corn meal,
cornstarch, corn syrup, hominy, hominy
grits, and bourbon. There are hundreds

Season	For Top Quality	Amount To Buy	Nutritive Value	Calories (unseasoned)
Year round; supply short only in April, May.	Choose crisp, clean frosty blue-green leaves free of insect injury.	1 pound serves 2.	Very high in vitamins A and C, also calcium	Moderately low—55 per cup of cooked collards

Season	For Top Quality	Amount To Buy	Nutritive Value	Calories (unseasoned)
May–October; in big cities corn is available year round, but best only in summer.	Buy ears in the husk preferably from iced bins; husks should be bright green and snug-fitting; kernels bright, plump, and milky.	2 ears per person	Fair source of vitamin A and certain of the B complex	High—70 for quite a small ear; 170 per cup of whole kernel corn

of varieties of corn, but those we like best are sweet—truly sweet, unfortunately, only when rushed from stalk to pot. If you live in a corn-growing area, try to befriend a farmer who will let you pick your own.

To Prepare for Cooking: Just before cooking—*no earlier*—peel away husks, remove tassels and silks. Break off tip and stem end. Do not wash.

To Cut Corn off the Cob: For *cream-style,* cut down the center of each row

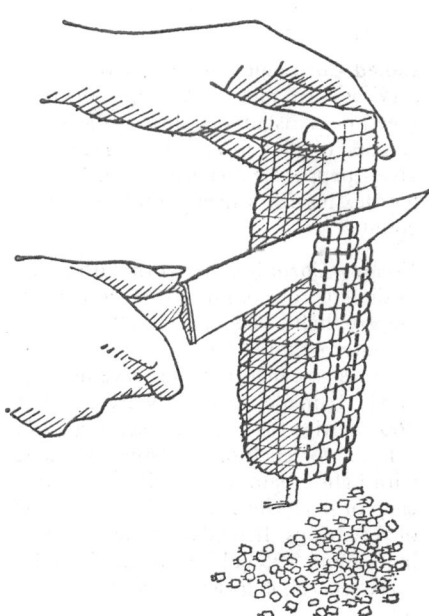

of kernels, then, using the back of the knife, scrape corn into a bowl. For *whole kernel corn,* simply cut kernels from cob, doing 3 or 4 rows at a time.

Cooking Tip: To give not so fresh corn a just-picked flavor, add 1–2 tablespoons sugar to the cooking water. Never cook corn in salted water.

⊠ BOILED FRESH CORN ON THE COB

For truly sweet and tender corn, don't salt the cooking water. Add a teaspoon of sugar, if you like, but *no* salt. Allow 2 ears per person

Fresh ears sweet corn, prepared for cooking
4–5 quarts boiling water
Salt
Pepper .
Butter or margarine

Place water in a 1½-gallon kettle over high heat and, when boiling vigorously, drop in corn. Cover and boil 5–8 minutes, depending on the size of the ears. Lift ears from water with tongs and serve with salt, pepper, and plenty of butter. About 70 calories per ear of corn (without butter).

VARIATION:

Substitute 1 quart milk for 1 quart water and boil as directed. About 70 calories per ear of corn (without butter).

CHARCOAL-ROASTED FRESH EARS OF CORN

Allow 2 ears per person

Prepare a moderately hot charcoal fire.* Pull back husks to expose kernels but do not tear off. Remove silks, then smooth husks back over ears and tie at tips. Lay ears on a grill 3–4" from coals and roast 12–15 minutes, turning frequently. Husk while piping hot (wear gloves) and serve at once with salt, pepper, and butter. About 70 calories per ear of corn (without butter).

VARIATIONS:

– After removing silks and tying husks at the tips as directed above, soak ears 10–15 minutes in ice water. Drain, shake off excess water, and roast as directed. If you want to roast directly in coals, soak 30 minutes. Bury in coals and roast 10 minutes. About 70 calories per ear of corn (without butter).
– Husk ears, wrap in buttered squares of aluminum foil, and roast 3" from coals 20–30 minutes, turning frequently. About 75 calories per ear of corn (without additional butter).

OVEN ROASTING EARS

An unusually good way to prepare frozen corn on the cob is to roast in the oven—it's firm yet tender and has a delightful nutty flavor.
Makes 2–4 servings

2 (2-ear) packages frozen corn on the cob (do not thaw)
Butter or margarine
Salt
Pepper

Preheat oven to 400° F. Wrap each solidly frozen ear in several thicknesses heavy foil, twisting ends to seal. Place on lowest oven rack and roast 1 hour. Unwrap and serve with butter, salt, and pepper. About 70 calories per ear of corn (without butter).

VARIATION:

Charcoal-Roasted Frozen Ears: Prepare a moderate charcoal fire.* Wrap frozen ears as directed above and roast 3–4" from coals 1 hour, giving them a quarter turn every 15 minutes. Unwrap and serve with butter, salt, and pepper. About 70 calories per ear of corn (without butter).

BOILED FRESH WHOLE KERNEL CORN

Makes 4–6 servings

6–8 ears sweet corn, prepared for cooking
1 cup boiling water or skim milk
½ teaspoon sugar
½ teaspoon salt
Pinch white pepper
2 tablespoons butter or margarine

Cut corn from cob.* Place in a saucepan with water or milk and sugar, cover, and simmer 5–8 minutes until tender. Drain and season with salt, pepper, and butter. About 155 calories for each of 4 servings, 105 calories for each of 6 servings.

VARIATIONS:

Boiled Corn and Vegetables: Just before serving corn, mix in 1½ cups boiled green peas, asparagus tips, or diced carrots; or ½ cup sautéed minced red or green pepper or Spanish onion. Recipe too flexible for a meaningful calorie count.

Creamy Corn: Simmer corn with sugar as directed above but use ½ cup cream (heavy, light, or half-and-half) instead of water or milk. Do not drain. Add all seasonings called for and serve in soup bowls. If made with heavy cream, about 260 calories for each of 4 servings, 175 calories for each of 6 servings. If made with light cream, about 210 calories for each of 4 servings, 140 calories for each of 6 servings. If made with half-and-half, about 195 calories for each of 4 servings, 130 calories for each of 6 servings.

⊠ HERBED CORN IN CREAM

Makes 4–6 servings

*4 cups fresh whole kernel sweet corn or
2 (1-pound) cans whole kernel corn,
drained*
¾ cup heavy cream
2 tablespoons butter or margarine
*2 tablespoons minced chives (fresh,
frozen, or freeze-dried)*
*¼ teaspoon minced fresh basil or ⅛
teaspoon dried basil*
*¼ teaspoon minced fresh chervil or ⅛
teaspoon dried chervil*
Salt
Pepper
Pinch paprika

Place all but last 3 ingredients in the top
of a double boiler over simmering water,
cover, and cook 10 minutes until corn is
tender. Add salt and pepper to taste,
ladle into soup bowls, and sprinkle with
paprika. About 380 calories for each of
4 servings, 255 calories for each of 6
servings.

OLD-FASHIONED SUCCOTASH

Makes 4–6 servings

2 cups fresh whole kernel sweet corn
*2 cups fresh baby lima or cranberry
beans, parboiled*
1 cup light cream
*2 tablespoons butter, margarine, or
bacon drippings*
2 teaspoons sugar
Pinch white pepper
1 teaspoon salt

Place all ingredients but salt in a saucepan and simmer, uncovered, stirring occasionally, 10–12 minutes until beans
are tender. Mix in salt; ladle into soup
bowls. About 360 calories for each of 4
servings, 240 calories for each of 6
servings.

VARIATIONS:

Green Bean Succotash: Substitute ½
pound parboiled cut green beans for the
lima beans and prepare as recipe directs.
About 290 calories for each of 4
servings, 195 calories for each of 6
servings.

Hominy-Green Bean Succotash: Instead of using recipe above, place 2 cups
each of boiled, drained hominy and
boiled, drained cut green beans in a
large saucepan, add ½ cup heavy
cream, 3 tablespoons bacon drippings,
and salt and pepper to taste. Warm,
stirring, 3–4 minutes just to blend flavors.
Serve in soup bowls, topped, if you like,
with crisp bacon bits. About 245
calories for each of 4 servings, 165
calories for each of 6 servings.

⊠ CONFETTI CORN

Makes 4 servings

*1 large sweet green pepper, cored,
seeded, and chopped fine*
*1 (3½-ounce) can pimiento, drained and
chopped fine*
*1 small yellow onion, peeled and
chopped fine*
¼ cup butter or margarine
*1 (1-pound 1-ounce) can whole kernel
corn, drained*
¼ teaspoon salt
Pinch pepper

Stir-fry green pepper, pimiento, and
onion in butter 8–10 minutes until onion
is golden. Add corn, salt, and pepper,
cover, and simmer 3–4 minutes, just
long enough to heat through. About 210
calories per serving.

SCALLOPED CORN

A marvelously mellow corn casserole.
Makes 4 servings

2 tablespoons butter or margarine
2 tablespoons flour
1¼ cups milk
1 teaspoon salt
⅛ teaspoon pepper
1 egg, lightly beaten
*¼ teaspoon prepared mild yellow
mustard*
*2 cups whole kernel corn (fresh; drained
frozen cooked or canned)*
1 cup coarse soda cracker crumbs
*2 tablespoons melted butter or
margarine*

Preheat oven to 350° F. Melt butter
over moderate heat, blend in flour, then

add milk and heat, stirring, until thickened and smooth. Off heat mix in salt, pepper, egg, mustard, and corn. Pour into a lightly buttered 1½-quart casserole, sprinkle with crumbs, and drizzle with melted butter. Bake, uncovered, 30 minutes until lightly browned. About 350 calories per serving.

CORN GUMBO

Makes 4–6 servings

1 medium-size yellow onion, peeled and minced
½ medium-size sweet green pepper, cored, seeded, and chopped fine
1 stalk celery, chopped fine
2 tablespoons bacon drippings
1½ cups coarsely chopped, seeded, peeled tomatoes
2 cups fresh, thawed frozen, or canned whole kernel corn (drain the frozen or canned)
4–6 baby okra pods, sliced ½" thick
1 teaspoon salt
¼ teaspoon gumbo filé
⅛ teaspoon pepper

Sauté onion, green pepper, and celery in drippings in a large saucepan 8–10 minutes over moderate heat until onion is golden. Add all remaining ingredients except salt, gumbo filé, and pepper, cover, and simmer slowly 10–15 minutes, stirring occasionally. Mix in salt, gumbo filé, and pepper. Ladle into soup bowls and serve. About 175 calories for each of 4 servings, 115 calories for each of 6 servings.

CORN PUDDING

Everyone's favorite.
Makes 6 servings

3 tablespoons butter or margarine
2 (10-ounce) packages frozen whole kernel corn (do not thaw)
¼ teaspoon nutmeg
4 eggs
¼ cup unsifted flour
½ teaspoon baking powder
1 tablespoon sugar
1 teaspoon salt
⅛ teaspoon white pepper

1 (13-ounce) can evaporated milk
⅓ cup light cream

Preheat oven to 325° F. Melt butter in a large saucepan over moderate heat, add corn, and simmer, uncovered, stirring occasionally, 8–10 minutes until heated through. Do not drain; stir in nutmeg. Beat eggs until foamy in a large mixing bowl. Mix flour with baking powder, sugar, salt, and pepper, add to eggs, and beat until smooth. Mix in corn, then milk and cream. Pour into a buttered, shallow 1½-quart casserole, set in a shallow roasting pan, and pour in enough cold water to come about halfway up casserole. Bake, uncovered, about 1 hour and 20 minutes or until a knife inserted in center of pudding comes out clean. About 355 calories per serving.

CORN PIE

Makes 6 servings

Pastry:
1 recipe Flaky Pastry I

Filling:
4 eggs, lightly beaten
1¼ cups milk or light cream
1¼ teaspoons salt
Pinch white pepper
1 tablespoon grated yellow onion
1½ cups whole kernel corn (fresh or drained canned)

Preheat oven to 425° F. Prepare pastry and fit into a 9" piepan, making a high, fluted edge. Prick bottom and sides of pastry with a fork, cover with wax paper, and fill with uncooked rice or dried beans. Bake 5–7 minutes until firm but not brown, remove rice or beans. Stir together all filling ingredients and pour into pie shell. Bake 10 minutes at 425° F., reduce heat to 350° F., and bake 30 minutes longer or until center is almost firm. Cool about 10 minutes before cutting. About 310 calories per serving (if made with milk), 380 per serving (if made with cream).

VARIATIONS:

Bacon and Corn Pie: Add ½–¾ cup crumbled cooked bacon to filling and bake as directed. About 360 calories per serving (if made with milk), 430 calories per serving (if made with cream).

Corn Quiche: Add ¾ cup coarsely grated Gruyère or Swiss cheese to filling and bake as directed. About 380 calories per serving (if made with milk), 450 calories per serving (if made with cream).

CORN OYSTERS

These corn cakes are delicious for breakfast, lunch, or supper. Top, if you like, with maple syrup.
Makes 6 servings

½ cup sifted flour
¾ teaspoon salt
½ teaspoon baking powder
¼ cup milk
1 egg, lightly beaten
2 cups whole kernel corn (fresh or drained canned)
⅓ cup cooking oil

Sift flour with salt and baking powder into a bowl. Slowly add milk and beat until smooth. Beat in egg and mix in corn. Heat oil in a large, heavy skillet over moderate heat 1 minute. Drop batter by tablespoonfuls into skillet and fry, a few "oysters" at a time, 3–4 minutes until browned on both sides. Drain on paper toweling and set, uncovered, in a 250° F. oven to keep warm while you fry the rest. About 160 calories per serving (without syrup).

CORN FRITTERS

Makes 6 servings

Lard, shortening, or cooking oil for deep fat frying

Fritters:
1½ cups sifted flour
1½ teaspoons salt
2 teaspoons baking powder
2 eggs, lightly beaten
½ cup milk
2 cups cooked whole kernel corn, drained well

Begin heating fat in a deep fat fryer over moderately high heat; insert deep fat thermometer. Meanwhile, sift flour, salt, and baking powder together into a bowl. Add eggs, a little of the milk and beat until smooth. Add remaining milk and beat again. Stir in corn. When fat reaches 375° F., drop in batter from a measuring tablespoon. Do only 5 or 6 fritters at a time, frying each until crisply golden and turning as needed to brown evenly. Drain on paper toweling and set, uncovered, in a 250° F. oven to keep warm while you fry the rest. About 250 calories per serving.

VARIATION:

Corn-Cheese Fritters: Add 1 cup coarsely grated sharp Cheddar cheese to batter. (If mixture seems thick, stir in 1–2 tablespoons cold water.) Fry as directed. About 325 calories per serving.

CUCUMBERS

It was cucumbers the Israelites craved in the Wilderness, cucumbers the Emperor Tiberius ate daily, and cucumbers

Season	For Top Quality	Amount To Buy	Nutritive Value	Calories (unseasoned)
Year round	Choose uniformly firm green cucumbers with no dark, soft spots.	1 medium-size cucumber will serve 1–2.	Poor	Low—about 30 per medium-size cucumber

Charlemagne ordered grown lest he run out of pickles. Delicious raw, cucumbers are equally so baked in butter, stir-fried in peanut oil, or smothered in cream sauce. The French and Chinese are the masters of cucumber cooking, and we include some of their favorite recipes here.

To Prepare for Cooking: Most cucumbers today are dipped in wax to keep them crisp and fresh, so it's a good idea to peel before using. Cut up and seed as individual recipes specify. The easiest way to seed cucumbers is simply to scoop them out with a teaspoon.

BOILED CUCUMBERS

Makes 4 servings

3 medium-size cucumbers, peeled, halved, and seeded
½ cup boiling water
¼ teaspoon salt
Pinch white pepper
2 tablespoons butter or margarine

Leave cucumbers as halves or cut in 1″ cubes. Place in a saucepan with water and salt, cover, and simmer until crisp-tender: 8–10 minutes for cubes, 10–12 for halves. Drain, add pepper and butter, set over low heat, and warm uncovered until butter melts. About 70 calories per serving.

To Steam Cucumbers: Place halves or cubes in a steamer over rapidly boiling water, cover, and steam 8–10 minutes for cubes, 10–12 for halves. Season as above and serve. About 70 calories per serving.

To Parboil for Use in Other Recipes: Boil or steam as directed above, reducing cooking times as follows: to 5 minutes for cubes, to 8 for halves. Omit seasonings.

VARIATIONS:

◁▷ **Low-Calorie Cucumbers:** Omit butter and dress with 1–2 tablespoons lemon juice and/or a sprinkling minced chives, parsley, or dill. For additional savor, substitute seasoned salt for salt. About 25 calories per serving.

Cucumbers au Gratin: Boil by recipe above, drain, season with pepper, and place in a buttered 1½-quart *au gratin* dish. Top with ½ cup grated Parmesan mixed with ½ cup soft white bread crumbs and drizzle with 2 tablespoons melted butter. Broil 5″ from heat 2 minutes until browned (watch closely so cucumbers don't burn). About 190 calories per serving.

SAUTÉED CUCUMBERS

Makes 4 servings

3 medium-size cucumbers, peeled, seeded, and cut in 1½″ cubes, parboiled and drained
2 tablespoons butter or margarine
1 tablespoon cooking oil
1 egg, lightly beaten
½ cup toasted seasoned bread crumbs

Pat cucumbers dry on paper toweling. Melt butter in a heavy skillet over moderate heat, add oil and heat ½ minute. Dip cucumber in egg, then in crumbs to coat evenly. Sauté, a few cubes at a time, 4–5 minutes, until golden brown and crisp. Drain on paper toweling, set, uncovered, in a 250° F. oven to keep warm while you sauté the rest. Good with lemon wedges or Tartar Sauce. About 120 calories per serving.

◁▷ **CHINESE-STYLE CUCUMBERS IN SOY SAUCE**

Makes 4 servings

3 medium-size cucumbers, peeled, quartered lengthwise, and seeded
2 tablespoons peanut oil
1 tablespoon Japanese soy sauce
1 tablespoon minced chives (fresh, frozen, or freeze-dried)

Cut each cucumber quarter into slices ¼″ thick and pat dry on paper toweling. Heat oil in a large, heavy skillet or *wok* over moderate heat 1 minute. Add cucumbers and stir-fry 3–4 minutes, until crisp-tender. Add soy sauce and toss to mix; sprinkle with chives and serve. About 60 calories per serving.

CUCUMBERS BRAISED IN WHITE WINE AND CHICKEN BROTH

Makes 4 servings

3 medium-size cucumbers, peeled, halved, and seeded
¼ cup melted butter or margarine
½ cup medium-dry white wine
½ cup chicken broth

Preheat oven to 350° F. Place cucumbers in an ungreased shallow 1½-quart casserole and pour butter evenly over all. Bake, uncovered, 10 minutes. Pour wine and broth into casserole, cover, and bake 30 minutes longer until fork tender. About 150 calories per serving.

VARIATION:

Braised Vegetable-Stuffed Cucumbers: Prepare and bake as directed, then fill hollow of each cucumber with cooked, seasoned peas, cauliflowerets, diced carrots, or creamed spinach. Recipe too flexible for a meaningful calorie count.

CUCUMBERS PROVENÇAL

Makes 4 servings

3 medium-size cucumbers, peeled, seeded, cut in 1" cubes, parboiled, and drained
2 tablespoons butter or margarine
2 tablespoons olive or other cooking oil
1 clove garlic, peeled and crushed
2 medium-size ripe tomatoes, peeled, seeded, and coarsely chopped
1 tablespoon minced parsley
½ teaspoon salt
⅛ teaspoon pepper

Pat cucumbers dry on paper toweling. Melt butter in a large, heavy skillet over moderate heat, add oil and heat ½ minute. Sauté garlic ½ minute until pale golden, add cucumbers and tomatoes, and sauté 4–5 minutes until tender, stirring constantly. Off heat, add remaining ingredients, toss lightly to mix, and serve. About 150 calories per serving.

BAKED STUFFED CUCUMBERS

Makes 4 servings

2 medium-size cucumbers, peeled and halved
5–6 tablespoons melted butter or margarine
2 cups soft white bread crumbs
¼ teaspoon salt
⅛ teaspoon pepper
1 teaspoon dried chervil
½ cup coarsely chopped, peeled, seeded tomatoes
3 tablespoons sliced blanched almonds

Preheat oven to 350° F. Scoop seeds and center pulp from cucumbers so they are boat-shaped. Coarsely chop pulp and reserve ¼ cup. Parboil cucumbers 5 minutes, then drain and arrange in a well-buttered shallow baking pan. (*Note:* Use a pancake turner for handling cucumbers because they're delicate and break easily.) Brush cucumbers lightly all over with a little melted butter. Toss crumbs with reserved cucumber pulp, ¼ cup melted butter, and all remaining ingredients except almonds and stuff cucumbers. Top with almonds and drizzle with melted butter. Bake, uncovered, 35 minutes until cucumbers are fork tender and almonds lightly browned. About 260 calories per serving.

DANDELIONS

Ever wonder how dandelions got their name? It's a corruption of *dent de lion* ("tooth of the lion"), which is the way the French described the dandelion's jagged leaves. It is these leaves that are good to eat, particularly if cooked gently like spinach in a small amount of water, then tossed with butter or dressed with oil and lemon. These are the same dandelions that blight our lawns, though those sold in groceries have been especially grown for the table.

To Prepare for Cooking: Trim away roots and sort, removing yellowed or wilted leaves. Wash well in cool water and tear into bite-size pieces.

Serving Tip: Add crisped dandelion

Season	For Top Quality	Amount To Buy	Nutritive Value	Calories (unseasoned)
Spring	Choose clean, tender leaves with stems and roots attached.	1 pound serves 2.	High in vitamin A and iron	Low—about 50 per average serving

greens to tossed salads for special bite and zest.

WILTED DANDELIONS OR NETTLES

Makes 4 servings

4 slices bacon
2 pounds (3–4 quarts) dandelion or nettle leaves, prepared for cooking
¼ cup red wine vinegar
1–2 tablespoons sugar
½ teaspoon salt
Pinch pepper

Brown bacon in a large, heavy kettle over moderate heat and drain on paper toweling. Add leaves to kettle along with all remaining ingredients, cover, and simmer 10–15 minutes until tender. Remove leaves from kettle and chop fine. Serve topped with any cooking liquid and crumbled bacon. About 160 calories per serving.

DASHEENS

(Also known as Taro)

Cooked, mashed, and fermented, dasheens are the *poi* of Hawaii; boiled or baked, they are the "potatoes" of Jamaica. Like potatoes, dasheens are mealy and nutty; unlike them, they are gray-lavender inside. Some are no bigger than pullet eggs, but coconut-size dasheens are more common.

To Prepare for Cooking: Scrub in cool water with a vegetable brush. Peel and cut in 1½" chunks if dasheens are to be boiled; leave whole and do not peel if they are to be baked.

To Boil: Cover dasheens with lightly salted boiling water, cover, and simmer about 1 hour until tender. Drain and mash as you would potatoes, seasoning with butter, salt, and pepper; or instead of mashing, mix cubes with hot Medium White Sauce (about 1 cup sauce to 2 cups dasheens).

To Bake: Parboil whole, unpeeled dasheens 30 minutes. Drain and bake, uncovered, in a shallow roasting pan 1–1½ hours at 375° F. until a fork pierces them easily. Halve or quarter dasheens, also peel, if you like, and season as you would baked potatoes.

EGGPLANT

(Sometimes called by the French name *aubergine*)

For centuries eggplant stood high on Europe's list of "dangerous and immoral foods," the rumor being it drove men mad. Fortunately, Arabs and Orientals knew better; they ate eggplant with relish

Season	For Top Quality	Amount To Buy	Nutritive Value	Calories (unseasoned)
Year round	Choose clean, unscarred tubers of uniform size.	1 average dasheen serves 2–4.	Some minerals but generally poor	Moderate–high—110 per serving

Season	For Top Quality	Amount To Buy	Nutritive Value	Calories (unseasoned)
Year round	Choose firm, evenly purple eggplants, without cuts or scars, that weigh heavy for their size.	1 medium-size eggplant will serve 4; allow 1–2 "frying" eggplants per person.	Poor	Low—about 40 per average serving

and created many of the recipes we consider classics. Today we appreciate eggplant for what it is—one of the most versatile of vegetables.

To Prepare for Cooking: Wash well in tepid water; peel or not as individual recipes specify (the skin is often left on to give dishes color, flavor, and texture).

Serving Tip: Salt thin strips of raw peeled eggplant, pat dry on paper toweling, toss with Vinaigrette Dressing and minced tarragon or chervil, and serve as a salad.

FRIED EGGPLANT

Eggplant cooks so quickly that, when fried, it need only be browned on both sides. Use, if possible, the slim, drier "frying" variety that doesn't have to be salted and blotted on paper toweling. Makes 4–6 servings

*1 medium-size eggplant or 6 slim
    "frying" eggplants cut in ½" rounds
    (do not peel)*
2 teaspoons salt (about)
1 egg, lightly beaten
⅛ teaspoon mace
⅛ teaspoon pepper
⅓ cup olive or other cooking oil
½ cup cracker meal

If using the large eggplant, sprinkle about 1 teaspoon salt over rounds and weight down between paper toweling 1 hour. Mix egg with 1 teaspoon salt, the mace, and pepper. Heat 3–4 tablespoons oil 1–2 minutes in a large, heavy skillet over moderately high heat. Dip rounds in egg, a few at a time, then in crumbs and brown on both sides, adding more oil to skillet as needed. Drain browned rounds on paper toweling and set, uncovered, in a 250° F. oven to keep warm while you fry the rest. About 280 calories for each of 4 servings, 190 calories for each of 6 servings.

⊠ BROILED EGGPLANT

Makes 4 servings

*1 medium-size eggplant, cut in rounds
    ½" thick (do not peel)*
⅓ cup olive or other cooking oil (about)
1 teaspoon salt
⅛ teaspoon pepper

Preheat broiler. Brush eggplant rounds generously with oil and broil 4–5" from heat about 5 minutes until speckled with brown. Turn, brush again with oil, and broil 5 minutes longer. Sprinkle with salt and pepper and serve. For extra dash, top with chopped parsley, grated Parmesan cheese, or Tomato Sauce. About 190 calories per serving (without grated Parmesan or Tomato Sauce).

VARIATION:

◁▷ **Low-Calorie Broiled Eggplant:** Brush rounds with lemon juice or low-calorie Italian dressing instead of oil and broil as directed. About 40–45 calories per serving.

BASQUE-STYLE EGGPLANT, PEPPERS, AND TOMATOES
Makes 6–8 servings

*1 medium-size eggplant, peeled and cut
 in ¾" cubes*
2 tablespoons flour
¼ cup olive or other cooking oil
*3 large sweet green peppers, cored,
 seeded, and cut in ½" squares*
*3 cups coarsely chopped, seeded, peeled
 ripe tomatoes*
1 teaspoon salt
1 tablespoon minced parsley

Dredge eggplant in flour and stir-fry in
oil in a large, heavy skillet over
moderately high heat 7–8 minutes until
browned. Add peppers and sauté 3–4
minutes, then add tomatoes and cook 2–3
minutes longer, stirring. Cover, reduce
heat to low, and simmer 15 minutes. Mix
in salt and parsley and, if mixture seems
too liquid, turn up heat and boil,
uncovered, stirring, until the consistency
of stew. Serve with garlic bread. About
160 calories for each of 6 servings, 120
calories for each of 8 servings.

IZMIR EGGPLANT
Want an unusual—unusually good—
vegetable to go with roast lamb? Then
try this Turkish way of preparing
eggplant.
Makes 4–6 servings

*1 medium-size eggplant, cut in ½" cubes
 (do not peel)*
*2 medium-size yellow onions, peeled and
 coarsely chopped*
2 cloves garlic, peeled and crushed
2 bay leaves
⅓ cup olive oil
1 (8-ounce) can tomato sauce
Juice of ½ lemon
¼ teaspoon oregano
¼ teaspoon salt
⅛ teaspoon pepper

Stir-fry eggplant, onions, garlic, and bay
leaves in the oil in a large, heavy skillet
over moderate heat 12–15 minutes until
eggplant is tender. Mix in remaining
ingredients, reduce heat to low, and
simmer uncovered, stirring now and then,

10 minutes longer. About 250 calories
for each of 4 servings, 165 calories for
each of 6 servings.

RATATOUILLE (EGGPLANT, ZUCCHINI, AND TOMATO STEW À LA PROVENÇALE)
Ratatouille takes some doing, but once
the pot's on, perfuming the air, the effort
seems worthwhile. This dish keeps well,
is even better the second time around.
Makes 4–6 servings

*1 medium-size eggplant, peeled and
 sliced in ¼" rounds*
*3 medium-size zucchini, cut in ¼"
 rounds*
1 tablespoon salt (about)
¾ cup olive oil (about)
*2 medium-size yellow onions, peeled and
 sliced thin*
*2 medium-size sweet green peppers,
 cored, seeded, and sliced thin*
2 cloves garlic, peeled and crushed
*4 medium-size tomatoes, peeled, juiced,
 seeded, and coarsely chopped*
⅛ teaspoon pepper
3 tablespoons minced parsley

Sprinkle eggplant and zucchini with 1
teaspoon salt and weight down between
paper toweling 1 hour. Cut eggplant in
¼" strips and stir-fry, about ¼ at a
time, 3–5 minutes in 2–3 tablespoons
oil over moderately high heat. Drain on
paper toweling. (Eggplant soaks up oil,
but don't use more than 2–3 tablespoons
for each batch or the ratatouille will be
greasy). Brown all zucchini in 2
tablespoons oil and drain. Stir-fry onions
with peppers and garlic in remaining oil
10 minutes over moderate heat until
golden, lay tomatoes on top, add 1½
teaspoons salt and the pepper, cover, and
simmer 8–10 minutes. Uncover and
simmer 10 minutes longer. In an
ungreased shallow 2½-quart flameproof
casserole, build up alternate layers as
follows: onion mixture (sprinkle with
parsley), eggplant-zucchini (sprinkle
with salt), onions (parsley), eggplant-
zucchini (salt), onions (parsley). (*Note:*
At this point ratatouille can be cooled,
covered, and held in the refrigerator

1–2 days. Bring to room temperature before proceeding.) Simmer, covered, over low heat 35–40 minutes until vegetables are tender—don't stir. Uncover and simmer 40 minutes longer, also without stirring, until almost all juices are gone. Serve hot or cold as a vegetable or use for filling Crepes. About 500 calories for each of 4 servings, 335 calories for each of 6 servings.

¢ PISTO (SPANISH VEGETABLE STEW)

Pisto, Spanish cousin to *ratatouille,* can be eaten hot or cold, as an appetizer, vegetable, or main dish, depending on how much meat goes into it.
Makes enough appetizers for 50, vegetable servings for 16

1 cup diced lean cooked ham
½ cup olive oil
4 large yellow onions, peeled and sliced thin
2 medium-size sweet red peppers, cored, seeded, and coarsely chopped
1 (7½-ounce) can pimientos, drained and cut in ¼″ strips
4 cloves garlic, peeled and crushed
1 medium-size eggplant, washed and cut in ½″ cubes (do not peel)
½ pound mushrooms, wiped clean and sliced thin
2–3 teaspoons salt
2 (9-ounce) packages frozen artichoke hearts (do not thaw)
2 (1-pound) cans tomatoes (do not drain)

Brown ham in the oil in a large kettle over moderate heat. Add onions, peppers, pimientos, garlic, eggplant, and mushrooms, cover, and simmer slowly, stirring occasionally, 15 minutes until onions are golden. Add remaining ingredients and simmer, covered, 30–40 minutes until artichokes are tender. Cool, cover, and chill 4–5 hours. Serve cold or reheat and serve hot. About 45 calories for each of 50 appetizer servings, 135 calories for each of 16 vegetable servings.

VARIATIONS:

Main Dish Ham Pisto: Make as directed, increasing ham to 4 cups. Serve hot with fluffy cooked rice. Makes 12–14 servings. About 250 calories for each of 12 servings, 215 calories for each of 14 servings (without rice).

Main Dish Beef Pisto: Substitute 2 pounds ground beef chuck for the ham, brown lightly in the oil, then proceed as recipe directs and serve hot with rice. Makes 12–14 servings. About 320 calories for each of 12 servings, 275 calories for each of 14 servings (without rice).

SULTAN'S EGGPLANT

Makes 4 servings

1 large eggplant
½ teaspoon lemon juice
¼ cup light cream
¼ cup soft white bread crumbs
½ teaspoon salt (about)
2 teaspoons grated Parmesan cheese
⅛ teaspoon white pepper
2 tablespoons butter or margarine
1 tablespoon minced parsley

Preheat oven to 400° F. Prick eggplant all over with a sharp fork and bake, uncovered, about 1 hour until soft. Cool until easy to handle and slip off skin. Beat eggplant briskly with a fork or rotary beater, mix in lemon juice, and heat slowly, stirring, just until warm. Add all remaining ingredients except parsley and heat, stirring, 3–5 minutes. Sprinkle with parsley and serve. About 140 calories per serving.

VARIATION:

Roasting the eggplant over charcoal will give the dish a woodsy flavor. Simply place well-pricked eggplant on a grill over a moderate charcoal fire and roast 5″ from the coals, turning frequently, about 45 minutes. Peel, mix with remaining ingredients, heat, and serve as directed. About 140 calories per serving.

EGGPLANT PARMIGIANA

When making a *parmigiana*, do as the Italians do—use a light hand with the garlic and a heavy one with Parmesan.

Makes 6–8 servings

2 small eggplants, cut in ¼″ rounds (do not peel)
2 eggs, lightly beaten
1½ cups dry bread crumbs mixed with ½ teaspoon salt and ⅛ teaspoon pepper
1 clove garlic, peeled and halved
¾ cup olive oil (about)
1 (1-pound 4-ounce) can Italian plum tomatoes (do not drain)
⅓ cup tomato paste
2 tablespoons minced fresh basil or 2 teaspoons dried basil
1 teaspoon salt
⅛ teaspoon pepper
1 cup grated Parmesan cheese
½ pound mozzarella cheese, sliced very thin

Dip eggplant rounds in eggs, then in seasoned crumbs. Cover loosely and chill 20 minutes. Sauté garlic in 2 tablespoons olive oil 1–2 minutes in a large saucepan over moderate heat, then remove. Add tomatoes, tomato paste, basil, salt, and pepper, cover, and simmer, stirring occasionally, 30 minutes. Preheat oven to 350° F. Pour oil in a large, heavy skillet to a depth of ¼″ and brown eggplant over moderately high heat, doing a few rounds at a time and adding more oil as needed. Drain on paper toweling. Spoon a thin layer of tomato sauce into an ungreased, shallow 2½-quart casserole, then build up alternate layers of eggplant, tomato sauce, Parmesan, and mozzarella, dividing ingredients equally and ending with mozzarella. Bake, uncovered, 30 minutes until bubbly. Serve as a vegetable or, for an Italian dinner, as a main dish following a hearty soup or pasta. About 590 calories for each of 6 servings, 440 calories for each of 8 servings.

EGGPLANT STUFFED WITH PILAF AND RAISINS

Makes 4 servings

1 medium-size eggplant
1–1½ teaspoons salt
1 medium-size yellow onion, peeled and chopped fine
2 tablespoons olive oil
2 tablespoons water
1¼ cups Rice Pilaf
¼ cup seedless raisins
⅛ teaspoon pepper
1 teaspoon minced fresh dill or ½ teaspoon dried dill
1 teaspoon minced parsley

Slice 1″ off stem end of eggplant to make a lid, then, using a sharp knife, hollow out eggplant, leaving a shell ½″ thick; sprinkle inside lightly with salt. Chop flesh medium fine. Sauté onion in the oil 8–10 minutes over moderately high heat until golden, add chopped eggplant, and stir-fry 2–3 minutes. Add water, cover, and simmer over lowest heat 10–15 minutes until eggplant is tender. Mix with pilaf and remaining ingredients, fill eggplant shell, and cover with stem lid. Stand eggplant upright in a deep kettle, pour in water to a depth of 3″, cover, and simmer about 45 minutes until fork tender. Check pot occasionally to see that eggplant isn't slipping from its upright position. Lift eggplant from water, cut into wedges, and serve. About 185 calories per serving.

BAKED EGGPLANT STUFFED WITH MUSHROOMS AND CHICK-PEAS

Makes 4 servings

1 medium-size eggplant, halved lengthwise (do not peel)
2 teaspoons salt
1 large yellow onion, peeled and chopped fine
1 clove garlic, peeled and crushed
3 tablespoons cooking oil
1 cup finely chopped mushrooms
1 cup cooked chick-peas, chopped fine
⅛ teaspoon pepper
1½ cups tomato sauce
½ cup water

Score eggplant halves in a crisscross pattern and sprinkle each with ½ teaspoon salt. Let stand 1 hour, then press out as much liquid as possible. Rinse in cold water and pat dry on paper toweling. Scoop out centers, leaving shells ½″ thick; chop centers fine. Preheat oven to 375° F. Sauté onion and garlic in 2 tablespoons oil in a large skillet over moderate heat 6–8 minutes until pale golden. Add remaining oil, mushrooms, and chopped eggplant and sauté 4–5 minutes until mushrooms brown. Off heat, stir in chick-peas, remaining salt, and the pepper. Brush rims of eggplant shells with oil and fill with sautéed mixture. Place halves in an ungreased shallow casserole and spread ¼ cup tomato sauce over each. Mix remaining tomato sauce with water and pour into casserole. Bake, uncovered, 1 hour until shells are fork tender. Serve, topped with some of the sauce. About 235 calories per serving.

TURKISH STUFFED EGGPLANT (IMAM BAYILDI)

A Turkish imam's wife once served her husband an eggplant dish so delicious he swooned. Here's the recipe, appropriately named Imam Bayildi, meaning "the parson fainted." Serve it hot as a vegetable, cold as an appetizer.
Makes 4 servings

1 medium-size eggplant, halved
  lengthwise (do not peel)
2 teaspoons salt
1 large yellow onion, peeled and minced
2 cloves garlic, peeled and crushed
½ cup olive oil
3 medium-size tomatoes, peeled, seeded,
  and coarsely chopped
⅛ teaspoon pepper

Score cut surfaces of eggplant halves in a crisscross pattern, sprinkle each with ½ teaspoon salt, and let stand 1 hour. Press out as much liquid as possible, rinse in cold water and pat dry on paper toweling. Scoop out centers, leaving shells ½″ thick, and brush rims with oil. Cut centers in ½″ cubes. Preheat oven to 350° F. Sauté onion and garlic in ¼ cup oil over moderate heat 8–10 minutes until golden; drain on paper toweling and reserve. Sauté tomatoes in 2 tablespoons oil 5 minutes and mix with onion; brown eggplant cubes in remaining oil, add to onion, and season with pepper and remaining salt. Taste and, if too tart, mix in a little sugar. Place eggplant shells in a lightly greased shallow casserole, cutting a slice off the bottoms, if necessary, to make them stand. Fill and bake, uncovered, 45–50 minutes until tender. About 330 calories per serving.

BELGIAN ENDIVE

(Also known as French Endive, Witloof, and Chicory)

Endive was one of the "bitter herbs" God commanded the Israelites to eat with lamb at the Feast of Passover. Earlier, it was a favorite of the Egyptians, who tossed the leaves into salads and brewed the roots into a bitter drink. The recipes we prize today, however, come from the Belgians and French.

To Prepare for Cooking: Pull off any wilted or discolored outer leaves and cut a thin slice from the root end of each stalk; wash well in cool water.

Season	For Top Quality	Amount To Buy	Nutritive Value	Calories (unseasoned)
October–May	Choose crisp, clean stalks with tightly clinging leaves.	1 stalk per person	Poor	Very low— about 20 per stalk

Serving Tip: Crispen individual endive leaves in ice water and serve with seasoned salt as a low-calorie cocktail snack.

BOILED BELGIAN ENDIVES

Makes 4 servings

4 medium-size Belgian endives, prepared for cooking
1 cup boiling water or chicken broth
1 tablespoon lemon juice
¼ teaspoon salt
Pinch white pepper
2 tablespoons melted butter or margarine

Leave endives whole, halve lengthwise, or cut in rounds ⅛″ thick. Boil, covered, in water or broth with lemon juice and salt until tender: 5 minutes for rounds, 14 for halves, 20 for stalks. Drain, add pepper and butter, and toss gently to mix. About 70 calories per serving (if made with water), 80 per serving (if made with broth).

To Parboil for Use in Other Recipes: Use method above but reduce cooking time to 2–3 minutes for rounds, 5–8 for halves, and 10 for whole stalks. Omit seasonings.

VARIATIONS:

To Serve Cold: Boil and drain as directed but do not season. Chill stalks in ice water, drain, and marinate in the refrigerator several hours in a good tart dressing (see Vegetable Seasoning Chart). Serve as a salad or cold vegetable.

⚖ **Low-Calorie Endives:** Boil and drain as directed; omit butter and dress with low-calorie herb, Italian, or French dressing. About 25 calories per serving.

Belgian Endives au Gratin: Boil, drain, and season endives by recipe above; place in an ungreased 1-quart *au gratin* dish, top with 1½ cups hot Cheese Sauce and ¼ cup grated Cheddar cheese. Broil 5″ from heat 3–4 minutes to brown. About 270 calories per serving.

Endives and Ham au Gratin: For additional elegance, roll each endive in 2 thin slices boiled ham before arranging in au gratin dish. Cover with sauce and cheese and broil as directed. About 340 calories per serving.

Swiss-Style Endives: Boil, drain, and season endives by recipe above; place in a buttered 1-quart au gratin dish, sprinkle with about 1 teaspoon sugar and ⅓ cup grated Gruyère or Swiss cheese; broil 5″ from heat 2–3 minutes until browned. About 120 calories per serving.

BRAISED BELGIAN ENDIVES

This recipe brings out the delicate flavor of endives.
Makes 4 servings

4 medium-size Belgian endives, prepared for cooking
2 tablespoons butter
¼ cup chicken broth
¼ teaspoon salt
1 teaspoon lemon juice
Minced parsley or chives (optional garnish)

Sauté endives in butter in a heavy skillet over moderately low heat 7–12 minutes, turning frequently so they become an even nut-brown. Add all remaining ingredients except garnish, cover, and simmer 10–12 minutes until tender. Serve topped with cooking liquid and, if you like, a little minced parsley or chives. About 75 calories per serving.

FENNEL

(Also called Finochio)

This aromatic Mediterranean vegetable deserves more recognition. It looks like bulbous celery, tastes faintly of licorice, and is delicious raw in salads or cooked in a variety of ways.

To Prepare for Cooking: Discard coarse or blemished outer stalks, trim off feathery tops (save to use as a seasoning) and tough base. Wash well in cool water, using a vegetable brush if necessary to remove stubborn grit.

Season	For Top Quality	Amount To Buy	Nutritive Value	Calories (unseasoned)
Summer	Choose crisp, plump, un-scarred bulbs with fresh, feathery tops.	1 bulb will serve 1–2.	Some vitamin A and C	Low—about 35 per average serving

Leave whole or cut up as individual recipes specify.

To Prepare Fennel Hearts: Peel away all heavy outer stalks (save for soups). Quarter bulbs lengthwise and wash in cool water.

Cooking Tip: Mince feathery fennel tops and use as an herb to season salads, boiled carrots, beets, parsnips, or cabbage. Fennel also adds delicate fragrance to broiled chicken and white fish.

BOILED FENNEL

Makes 4 servings

4 bulbs fennel, prepared for cooking
1½ cups boiling water or chicken broth
1 teaspoon salt (about)
Pinch white pepper
2 tablespoons butter or margarine

Prepare hearts* or cut stalks in 1″ slices. Bring water or broth to a boil, add salt (reducing amount if broth is salty) and fennel, cover, and boil until crisp-tender: 7–10 minutes for slices, 12–15 for hearts. Drain, add pepper and butter, and toss. About 85 calories per serving (if made with water), 95 per serving (made with broth).

To Parboil for Use in Other Recipes: Use recipe above but reduce cooking time to 5 minutes for slices, 10 for hearts. Omit seasonings.

VARIATIONS:

To Serve Cold: Boil and drain hearts as directed but do not season. Chill in ice water, drain, top with dressing (see Vegetable Seasoning Chart), and chill

several hours. Serve as an appetizer, a salad, or cold vegetable.

⚖ **Low-Calorie Fennel:** Boil and drain as directed. Omit butter and dress with low-calorie French or Italian dressing. About 35 calories per serving.

Butter-Braised Fennel: Parboil and drain hearts but do not season. Sauté in 3 tablespoons butter 3–4 minutes, turning constantly. Add 2 tablespoons water, cover, and simmer 5–7 minutes until hearts are glazed and golden brown. Add pepper and serve. About 110 calories per serving (cooked in water), 120 per serving (cooked in broth).

Fennel Parmigiana: Parboil hearts, drain and place in an ungreased 1-quart au gratin dish. Drizzle with ¼ cup melted butter, sprinkle with ¼ cup grated Parmesan, and broil 4″ from heat 3–4 minutes until lightly browned. About 170 calories per serving (if fennel is cooked in water), 180 per serving (if cooked in broth).

FERNS

(Also called Fiddleheads)

The tender shoots of ferns that grow along mossy creek banks are one of spring's rare treats. Most highly prized is the cinnamon fern, which tastes of both asparagus and artichoke. Bracken and ostrich ferns are good too, though tougher and saltier. Canned ferns are available in speciality shops, but the best are those you pick fresh yourself.

Season	For Top Quality	Amount Needed	Nutritive Value	Calories (unseasoned)
May	Pick young, silvery green shoots no more than 2″ above the ground and tightly curled like the scroll at the top of a fiddle.	Allow ½ cup per person.	Not determined	Not determined but probably low

To Prepare for Cooking: Sort, discarding any ferns that are discolored. Cut off stems—you want only the tightly curled "heads." Wash carefully in cool water to remove all traces of sand.

BUTTERED FERNS

Makes 4 servings

2 cups ferns, prepared for cooking
½ teaspoon salt
⅛ teaspoon white pepper
½ cup boiling water
¼ cup melted butter or margarine

Place ferns in a saucepan along with salt, pepper, and boiling water. Cover and simmer 20–30 minutes until tender. Drain well, add butter, and toss lightly to mix. Calorie counts for ferns unavailable.

HEARTS OF PALM

(Also called Swamp Cabbage, Cabbage Palm, and Palmetto Cabbage)

These smooth ivory palmetto shoots are rarely seen fresh, though once in a great while they appear in gourmet markets. Canned hearts of palm, cooked and ready to eat, are widely available.

To Prepare for Cooking: Fresh hearts are bitter and must be soaked and sometimes blanched before cooking. Peel away coarse outer layers, cut off fibrous tops, then wash well in tepid water. Leave whole or slice into rounds ½″ thick; soak 1 hour in cool water. Drain and taste for bitterness. If still bitter, boil 5 minutes in acidulated water to cover (1 tablespoon lemon juice to 1 quart water) and drain.

To Boil: Place prepared hearts in a saucepan, add lightly salted boiling water to cover, and simmer, covered, until tender: about 45 minutes for slices, 1½–2 hours for whole hearts (when cooking whole hearts, change water at least 3 times to extract as much bitterness as possible). Drain well, drizzle

Season	For Top Quality	Amount To Buy	Nutritive Value	Calories (unseasoned)
Spring	Choose firm, moist, fairly clean hearts with few cuts, scars or blemishes.	1 heart, trimmed, will weigh 1½–2½ pounds and serve 2–3. Canned hearts are smaller and will serve 1.	Not determined	Not determined

with melted butter, or serve as you would asparagus with Hollandaise Sauce. Or chill in ice water, drain, and use in salads.

HEARTS OF PALM BRAISED IN WHITE WINE

Makes 3–4 servings

1 (14-ounce) can hearts of palm, drained
2 tablespoons butter or margarine
¼ cup sauterne
1 tablespoon finely chopped pimiento (garnish)
1 hard-cooked egg yolk, sieved (garnish)

Slice hearts crosswise into ½″ rounds and sauté in butter 5 minutes over low heat, stirring once or twice. Add wine, cover, and simmer 10 minutes, basting now and then. Transfer hearts to a heated vegetable dish and keep warm; reduce cooking liquid to about 2 tablespoons by boiling rapidly, uncovered. Spoon over hearts, sprinkle with pimiento and egg, and serve. Calorie counts for hearts of palm unavailable.

HEARTS OF PALM IN CREAM CHEESE SAUCE

Makes 4 servings

1 (14-ounce) can hearts of palm, drained (reserve liquid)

Sauce:
1 tablespoon butter or margarine
1 tablespoon flour
¾ cup milk
1 (3-ounce) package cream cheese, softened to room temperature
¼ teaspoon salt
Pinch white pepper

Slice hearts crosswise into rounds ½″ thick; simmer, covered, in reserved liquid 10 minutes. Meanwhile prepare sauce: melt butter over moderate heat and blend in flour. Slowly add ½ cup milk and reserved can liquid and heat, stirring, until thickened. Reduce heat to

low and simmer, uncovered, 2–3 minutes. Blend remaining milk with cheese, mix into sauce, and simmer, stirring, 2–3 minutes. Drain hearts, top with sauce, and serve. Calorie counts for hearts of palm unavailable.

SAUTÉED HEARTS OF PALM MEDALLIONS

Makes 4 servings

1 (14-ounce) can hearts of palm, drained
1 egg, lightly beaten with 1 tablespoon cold water
⅔ cup toasted seasoned bread crumbs
3 tablespoons butter or margarine

Slice hearts crosswise into rounds ½″ thick and pat very dry on paper toweling. Dip rounds in egg, then in crumbs to coat evenly; place on a wire rack and let dry 15 minutes. Melt butter in a large skillet over moderate heat, add rounds, a few at a time, and brown lightly about 1 minute on a side. Drain on paper toweling and set, uncovered, in a 250° F. oven to keep warm while you brown the rest. Calorie counts for hearts of palm unavailable.

KALE

(Also known as Borecole and Colewort)

This sprawling, crinkly cousin of cabbage is so ancient no one knows where it originated. It is from "keal," the Scottish word for the vegetable, that we get "kale." It was also from the Scots that we obtained our first kale plants.

To Prepare for Cooking: Discard woody stems and coarse leaf midribs, then wash thoroughly in cool water. Tear large leaves into bite-size pieces.

Serving Tip: Toss tender young kale leaves into green salads for refreshing crunch.

Season	For Top Quality	Amount To Buy	Nutritive Value	Calories (unseasoned)
Fall, winter	Choose clean, crisp green leaves whether kale is sold loose or pre-washed, pre-trimmed, and bagged in plastic.	1 pound serves 2.	Very high in vitamin A; high in vitamin C and calcium	Low—about 30 per average serving

BOILED KALE

To minimize the strong cooking odor of kale, keep the pot tightly covered.
Makes 4 servings

2 pounds kale, prepared for cooking
3 cups boiling water
1 teaspoon salt
⅛ teaspoon pepper
2 tablespoons butter, margarine, or
* bacon drippings*

Coarsely chop kale and place in a large saucepan along with water and salt. Cover and boil slowly 15–20 minutes until tender (to keep kale as green as possible, lift lid once or twice during cooking). Drain well and, if you like, chop kale more finely. Season with pepper and butter or drippings and serve. About 80 calories per serving.

VARIATIONS:

⚖ **Low-Calorie Kale:** Boil and drain as directed; omit salt and butter or drippings, and dress with seasoned salt and lemon juice. About 30 calories per serving.

Kale 'n' Cabbage: Combine equal amounts boiled kale and hot Steamed Green Cabbage, dress with Lemon Butter, and toss to mix. About 80 calories per serving.

KOHLRABI

(Also known as Cabbage Turnip)

Kohlrabi is the most unusual member of the cabbage family. It looks more like a large pale green turnip than a cabbage and has a delicate, nutlike flavor all its own. It is delicious simply boiled and buttered, mashed, creamed, or baked in a casserole with a grated cheese topping.

To Prepare for Cooking: Remove leaves and stems and discard (if they're very young and tender, they can be cooked with other greens or tossed into salads). Wash bulbs, peel, and cut up as individual recipes specify.

Serving Tip: If you should find really young delicate kohlrabi, peel and slice raw into a green salad.

Season	For Top Quality	Amount To Buy	Nutritive Value	Calories (unseasoned)
May–December; peak months: June, July	Choose firm, crisp bulbs about 3″ in diameter with fresh green leaves.	Allow 1–2 bulbs per person.	High in vitamin C	Low—about 35 per average serving

BOILED KOHLRABI

Makes 4–6 servings

8 bulbs kohlrabi, prepared for cooking
1½ cups boiling water
1 teaspoon salt
⅛ teaspoon pepper
2 tablespoons butter or margarine

Cut kohlrabi in ½″ cubes, place in a saucepan with water and salt, cover, and boil gently 20–25 minutes until fork tender. Drain, add pepper and butter, and shake pan, uncovered, over low heat until butter melts. About 85 calories for each of 4 servings, 60 calories for each of 6 servings.

To Parboil for Use in Other Recipes: Use recipe above but reduce cooking time to 15 minutes; omit seasonings.

VARIATIONS:

⚖ **Low-Calorie Kohlrabi:** Boil and drain as directed; omit butter and sprinkle with minced chives and lemon juice. About 35 calories per serving.

Mashed Kohlrabi: Boil and drain as directed, then mash with a potato masher before seasoning. Sprinkle with pepper, add 2 tablespoons butter and 1 tablespoon heavy cream, and mix well. About 100 calories for each of 4 servings, 70 calories for each of 6 servings.

Kohlrabi au Gratin: Boil, drain, and season kohlrabi by recipe above. Place in an unbuttered 1½-quart *au gratin* dish, top with 1½ cups hot Cheese Sauce and ¼ cup grated Cheddar cheese, and broil 5″ from heat 3–4 minutes to brown. About 290 calories for each of 4 servings, 190 calories for each of 6 servings.

Creamed Kohlrabi: Boil and drain as directed but do not season; mix with 1½ cups hot Medium White Sauce or Béchamel Sauce, add a pinch of mace, and serve. If made with White Sauce: about 190 calories for each of 4 servings, 125 for each of 6. If made with Béchamel Sauce: about 220 calories for each of 4 servings, 145 for each of 6.

LEEKS

Leeks, of course, are onions, but they are so special and so elegant they deserve a section to themselves. Strangely, though peasant food abroad, they've never been widely grown in this country and have thus remained a luxury.

To Prepare for Cooking: Cut off roots and tough green tops, peel away coarse outer layers of stalk, and wash thoroughly in tepid water to remove all sand and grit.

BOILED LEEKS

Makes 4 servings

2 bunches leeks, prepared for cooking
1 cup boiling water, chicken or beef broth
2 tablespoons butter or margarine
½ teaspoon salt (about)
Pinch pepper

Lay leeks in a large skillet, add water or broth, cover, and simmer 12–15 minutes until crisp-tender. Drain, add butter, salt, and pepper to taste, and warm uncovered, shaking skillet gently, 1–2 minutes until butter is melted. About 85 calories per serving (if cooked in water), 95 per serving (if cooked in broth).

Season	For Top Quality	Amount To Buy	Nutritive Value	Calories (unseasoned)
Year round; two peak seasons: September–December and April–July	Look for fresh green tops and crisp, white clean stalks.	A bunch weighs about 1 pound and serves 2.	Some minerals and vitamin C, otherwise poor	Low—about 35 per leek

To Parboil for Use in Other Recipes:
Use method above but reduce cooking
time to 8–10 minutes; omit seasonings.

VARIATIONS:

To Serve Cold: Boil and drain as
directed; chill in ice water, and drain.
Cover with a fragrant dressing (see
Vegetable Seasoning Chart) and
refrigerate several hours.

⚖ **Low-Calorie Leeks:** Boil and
drain leeks; omit butter and dress with 2
tablespoons lemon juice or tarragon
vinegar or 3 tablespoons low-calorie
Italian or garlic dressing. About 60
calories per serving.

Leeks au Gratin: Parboil and drain
leeks; place in an ungreased 1½-quart
au gratin dish and add 1 cup beef
bouillon. Cover and bake 20 minutes at
350° F.; uncover and bake 10 minutes
longer. Mix 1½ cups soft white bread
crumbs with ¼ cup each grated
Parmesan and melted butter. Sprinkle
over leeks and broil 4″ from heat 2–3
minutes until lightly browned. About
275 calories per serving.

LEEK PIE

Delicious as a first course or as a
luncheon or light supper entree.
Makes 6–8 servings

1 recipe Torte Pastry
6 medium-size leeks, washed, trimmed,
  and sliced thin
1 cup boiling water
1½ teaspoons salt
1 (13-ounce) can evaporated milk
⅓ cup milk

2 (3-ounce) packages cream cheese,
  softened to room temperature
2 eggs, lightly beaten
⅛ teaspoon white pepper
Pinch mace

Preheat oven to 325° F. Make pastry
according to the recipe and fit into a
9″ piepan, making a high, fluted edge;
do not bake. Place leeks, boiling water,
and ½ teaspoon salt in a small saucepan,
cover, and simmer 10–12 minutes; drain
leeks well and reserve. In a separate
saucepan, heat evaporated milk, milk,
cream cheese, and remaining salt over
moderate heat about 10 minutes, beating
with a whisk until cheese is melted and
mixture smooth. Mix a little hot sauce
into yolks, then return to pan; stir in
leeks, pepper, and mace. Pour into crust
and bake, uncovered, 45–50 minutes
until filling is set and crust lightly
browned. Cool 15–20 minutes on a wire
rack, then cut into wedges and serve
warm. About 540 calories for each of 6
servings, 405 calories for each of 8
servings.

LENTILS

The pottage Esau sold his birthright for
was made of lentils, probably the red
lentils of Egypt. Those we know better
are the khaki-colored French lentils,
although the smaller Egyptian red lentils
are sometimes available in big city
Armenian or Turkish groceries. Both
the red lentils and the green are only
available dried.

For Top Quality	Amount To Buy	Nutritive Value	Calories (unseasoned)
Buy brands you know or, if buying in bulk, choose lentils that are clean, firm, and un-shriveled.	1 pound dried lentils will serve 4 persons.	High protein food rich in vitamin A, most of the B complex, and minerals	Very high— about 350 per cup of cooked lentils

To Prepare for Cooking: Place lentils in a colander and rinse under cool water, sorting to remove any bits of gravel or shriveled lentils.

¢ BOILED LENTILS

A good topping for lentils is crisply browned croutons or salt pork cubes.
Makes 4 servings

1 pound dried lentils, washed and sorted
3 cups cold water, chicken or beef broth
½ teaspoon salt (about)
⅛ teaspoon pepper

Place all ingredients except pepper in a heavy saucepan, cover, and bring to a boil over high heat. Reduce heat to low and simmer about 45 minutes, stirring occasionally, until lentils are tender but not mushy. (*Note:* Most of the water will be absorbed during cooking, so keep a close eye on the pot to make sure lentils don't stick.) Mix in pepper, taste for salt and add more if needed. About 350 calories per serving (if cooked in water), 370 per serving (if cooked in broth).

VARIATIONS:

Lentils and Ham: Add a ham bone or pork hock and boil as directed in water. Cut meat from bone and mix into lentils before serving. About 420 calories per serving.

Savory Lentils: Cook lentils in chicken or beef broth with 1 peeled and chopped large yellow onion, 1 bay leaf, ¼ teaspoon dried thyme or rosemary, or a *bouquet garni.** About 380 calories per serving.

DHAL

Dhal is the Indian word for lentils, the "meat" of vegetarian sects. This dhal *can* double as meat, although you may prefer it as a potato substitute, a side dish for curry, or even a spaghetti sauce.
Makes 4–6 servings

1 cup dried lentils, washed and sorted
1 quart cold water
¾ teaspoon salt
½ teaspoon chili powder

¼ teaspoon turmeric
2 large yellow onions, peeled and chopped fine
2 tablespoons Clarified Butter
3 medium-size ripe tomatoes, peeled, cored, seeded, and coarsely chopped

Place lentils, water, salt, chili powder, and turmeric in a heavy saucepan, cover, and bring to a boil over high heat. Reduce heat to low and simmer 45 minutes, stirring occasionally, until lentils are tender, not mushy. Meanwhile, sauté onions in butter over moderate heat 8–10 minutes until golden. Add tomatoes and stir-fry 4–5 minutes. Set aside. When lentils are tender, stir in onions and tomatoes, cover, and simmer 5 minutes. If you plan to serve the dhal over rice or pasta, thin with about 1 cup boiling water until the consistency of a spaghetti sauce. About 445 calories for each of 4 servings, 300 calories for each of 6 servings.

RED LENTILS AND RICE

Red lentils and rice are popular throughout the Middle East. Sometimes they're curried, sometimes reinforced with bits of meat, fish, hard-cooked eggs, or cheese (a good way to stretch the meat budget). Lebanese women top lentils and rice with salad greens—it's unusual but good.
Makes 6 servings

1 cup red lentils, washed and sorted
1 quart cold water, beef or chicken broth (about)
2 teaspoons salt (about)
2 medium-size yellow onions, peeled and sliced thin
¼ cup olive or other cooking oil
¼ teaspoon pepper
½ cup uncooked rice
1 teaspoon curry powder (optional)
1 tablespoon minced parsley

Place lentils, water, and salt (reduce amount to taste if using broth) in a large, heavy saucepan, cover, and bring to a boil; adjust heat so mixture simmers gently and cook 20 minutes. Meanwhile, sauté onions in oil 5–8 minutes until pale golden. Set aside. When lentils have cooked 20 minutes, stir in onions and all remaining ingredients except parsley. Simmer, covered, 20–25 minutes until rice is tender. (*Note:* Watch pot carefully so mixture doesn't stick; add a little water if necessary to give it the consistency of thick applesauce.) Sprinkle with parsley and serve. About 370 calories per serving (if made with water), 400 per serving (if made with broth).

LETTUCES

(See chapter on salads for descriptions of the different varieties.)

Romaine . . . iceberg lettuce . . . watercress . . . escarole . . . all can be cooked and served as vegetables, either by themselves or in tandem with other vegetables. Because of their delicacy, lettuces should be cooked a few minutes only so that they lose none of their fresh green color.

PANNED LETTUCE, ONIONS AND CAPERS

Makes 4 servings

2 tablespoons butter or margarine
4 small white onions, peeled and chopped fine
2 heads iceberg lettuce, romaine, or escarole or 4 heads Boston lettuce, washed and shredded medium fine
¼ cup water
¾ teaspoon salt
2–3 tablespoons capers
Pinch white pepper

Melt butter in a large, heavy saucepan over moderate heat, add onions and sauté 5–8 minutes until pale golden. Add lettuce, water, and salt, cover, turn heat to low, and steam 4–5 minutes. Add capers and pepper, toss to mix, and serve. About 95 calories per serving.

BUTTER-BRAISED HEARTS OF LETTUCE

Makes 4 servings

2 heads romaine or 4 heads Boston lettuce, trimmed of stems and coarse leaves and washed
2 tablespoons butter or margarine
¼ cup chicken or beef broth
¾ teaspoon salt (about)
Pinch pepper

If using romaine, slice off tops so hearts are 8″ or 9″ long. Place butter and broth in a large skillet, cover, and bring to a simmer. Add lettuce, cover, and simmer 10 minutes until just tender. Halve hearts lengthwise, transfer to serving dish, and salt to taste. Boil remaining cooking liquid, uncovered, until reduced to about 2 tablespoons. Mix in pepper, pour over lettuce, and serve. About 80 calories per serving.

VARIATIONS:

Braised Lettuce with Sour Cream: Braise as directed; mix ¾ cup sour cream into reduced cooking liquid along with pepper. Warm (but do not boil) 1–2 minutes, pour over lettuce, and serve. About 170 calories per serving.

Butter-Braised Iceberg Lettuce: Core and quarter a large (about 2 pounds) trimmed head iceberg lettuce and braise by method above. Serve with Hollandaise Sauce, Herb or Lemon Butter. About 80 calories per serving (without sauce).

BUTTERED WATERCRESS

Being naturally salty, watercress needs no salt.
Makes 4 servings

3 bunches watercress
⅔ cup boiling water
Pinch pepper
3 tablespoons butter or margarine

Trim stalks of watercress so they're 1″ long, then wash cress in cold water, discarding any yellowed or wilted leaves. Place cress in a saucepan with water, cover, and simmer 8–10 minutes until just tender. Drain, add pepper and butter, and shake pan uncovered over low heat until butter melts. If you like, chop watercress before serving. About 105 calories per serving.

MUSHROOMS

To ancient Egyptians, mushrooms were "sons of gods" sent to earth on thunderbolts; to the medieval Irish they were leprechaun umbrellas, and to the English they were food, edible only if gathered under a full moon. During Louis XIV's reign, the French began growing mushrooms in caves near Paris. They're grown that way yet. Because gathering wild mushrooms is risky, we concentrate here on the commercially grown and edible wild species sometimes available in groceries: the beige *morel*, the yellow *chanterelle*, and the creamy *shaggy mane*. You can buy the strong French *crêpes* canned and the Oriental black mushrooms and wood ears dried.

To Prepare for Cooking: Discard woody stem ends and wipe mushrooms clean with a damp cloth; never wash or soak—you'll send the delicate flavor down the drain.

To Peel: With a paring knife, catch a bit of loose skin on underside of cap and pull up toward top of cap. Repeat until all skin is removed. It isn't necessary to peel mushrooms unless they're to be served raw (try them in salads or stuffed with a salty spread as an hors d'oeuvre).

To Prepare Dried Mushrooms for Cooking: Black mushrooms and wood ears should be soaked in boiling water to cover 15 minutes. Drain and squeeze as dry as possible before cooking.

⊠ SAUTÉED MUSHROOMS

So simple and yet so elegant.
Makes 2 servings

½ pound small- to medium-size mushrooms, wiped clean
3 tablespoons butter or margarine
¼ teaspoon salt
⅛ teaspoon pepper

If mushrooms are small and tender, trim stems to within ½" of the caps. Otherwise, pull stems out of caps and save for soups, stuffings, or meat loaves. Sauté mushrooms rapidly in butter over moderately high heat, stirring or shaking skillet, until lightly browned, about 3 minutes. Drain on paper toweling, season with salt and pepper, and serve. About 180 calories per serving.

VARIATIONS:

Sautéed Sliced Mushrooms: Thinly slice mushrooms and sauté by method above but reduce cooking time to 2 minutes. About 180 calories per serving.

BROILED MUSHROOMS

Makes 4 servings

1 pound medium-size mushrooms, wiped clean and stemmed
¾ cup melted butter or margarine or cooking oil
1 teaspoon salt
⅛ teaspoon pepper

Season	For Top Quality	Amount To Buy	Nutritive Value	Calories (unseasoned)
Year round though supplies may be short in summer.	Choose clean, snowy, plump mushrooms of equal size; the veil that joins cap to stem should be intact, hiding brown gills.	1 pound will serve 2–4.	Poor except for being fairly high in niacin	Low—about 40 per cup

Using your hands, toss mushrooms in butter or oil until well coated. Cover loosely and let stand at room temperature 30 minutes, tossing once or twice. Preheat broiler. Arrange caps, cup side down, on a broiler rack and brush lightly with butter or oil. Broil 5″ from heat 5 minutes until lightly browned; turn caps, brush again with butter or oil, and broil 3 minutes longer until fork tender. Sprinkle with salt and pepper. About 335 calories per serving.

SKILLET MUSHROOMS

Makes 4 servings

1 teaspoon salt
1 pound mushrooms, wiped clean and sliced ¼″ thick (include stems)
2 tablespoons water
Pinch pepper
4 pats Maître d'Hôtel Butter (optional)

Heat a large, heavy skillet over high heat 1 minute. Sprinkle in salt, add mushrooms and stir-fry 2–3 minutes, until golden. Keep mushrooms moving constantly to avoid burning. Add water and pepper, turn heat to low, and cook 1 minute. Serve topped, if you like, with pats of Maître d'Hôtel butter. About 30 calories per serving (without butter), 135 calories per serving (with butter).

VARIATION:

⚖ **Low-Calorie Skillet Mushrooms:** Omit butter pats and dress with a few drops onion, garlic, or lemon juice. About 30 calories per serving.

CREAMED MUSHROOMS

Ladled over hot buttered toast or used to fill puff pastry shells, Carolines, or hollowed-out rolls, these mushrooms can be served as a luncheon entree.
Makes 4 servings

1 pound medium-size mushrooms, wiped clean and sliced ¼″ thick (include stems)
¼ cup butter or margarine
2 tablespoons flour
1¼ cups milk or ½ light cream and ½ chicken broth

¾ teaspoon salt
Pinch white pepper
½ teaspoon Worcestershire sauce

Stir-fry mushrooms in butter in a large skillet over moderately high heat 2–3 minutes until golden. Blend flour with milk (or cream and broth) until smooth, then slowly stir into mushrooms. Reduce heat to low and cook and stir until thickened. Mix in salt, pepper, and Worcestershire sauce and serve. About 190 calories per serving (if made with milk), 240 calories per serving (if made with cream and broth).

VARIATION:

Mushrooms in Madeira Sauce: Prepare recipe above and just before serving stir in 2 tablespoons sweet Madeira wine. About 200 calories per serving (if made with milk), 250 calories per serving (if made with cream and broth).

MUSHROOMS, ONIONS AND GREEN PEPPERS

Delicious over broiled steak.
Makes 6 servings

1 medium-size Spanish onion, peeled and chopped fine
3 tablespoons cooking oil
1 pound mushrooms, wiped clean and sliced thin (include stems)
1 large sweet green pepper, cored, seeded, and thinly slivered
1 teaspoon salt
⅛ teaspoon pepper
Pinch mace

Sauté onion in oil in a large, heavy skillet over moderately high heat 8 minutes until golden. Add mushrooms and green pepper and sauté 4–5 minutes until lightly browned. Reduce heat to low and stir-fry 2–3 minutes until pepper is tender. Season with salt, pepper, and mace and serve. About 95 calories per serving.

BAKED MUSHROOM CAPS STUFFED WITH HAZELNUTS

A luscious garnish for a roast platter.
Makes 4–6 servings

24 perfect small- to medium-size
mushrooms, wiped clean
½ cup unsalted butter, softened to room
temperature
⅔ cup finely chopped unblanched
hazelnuts or pecans
2 tablespoons minced chives
2 tablespoons minced parsley
1 teaspoon salt
⅛ teaspoon pepper
2 tablespoons cognac
¼ cup cracker meal
1½ cups milk (about)

Preheat oven to 300° F. Carefully
remove mushroom stems from caps; set
caps aside and chop stems fine. Mix
chopped stems with all remaining
ingredients except milk and stuff each
mushroom cap, mounding mixture in the
center. Place stuffed caps in an ungreased
9"×9"×2" baking pan and pour in
milk to a depth of ¾". Bake, uncovered,
basting every 15 minutes with milk, 1
hour or until tender. Lift mushrooms
from milk and use to garnish a roast or
steak platter or serve hot as a vegetable
with a little of the milk spooned over
each serving. About 505 calories for each
of 4 servings, 335 calories for each of 6
servings.

MUSTARD GREENS

(Also called Chinese Mustard and
Mustard Spinach)

It's said that Aesclepius, god of medicine,
gave mustard to man. He intended that
the plant be used medicinally, but man
soon learned how delicious the greens
were if gathered young and cooked like
spinach. They still are.

To Prepare for Cooking: Pick over
greens carefully, removing any roots,

woody stems or blemished leaves. Wash
2–3 times in cool water to remove all
grit and sand.

To Boil: See recipe for Boiled Collards,
Turnip Greens or Mustard Greens under
Collards.

OKRA

(Also sometimes called Gumbo)

People are generally of two minds about
okra—they either adore it or abhor it.
It's not the flavor they dislike (that is
delicate, rather like eggplant) but the
texture (too often slimy). The best
preventive: don't overcook.

To Prepare for Cooking: Cut off stems
(but not stem ends of pods); scrub okra
well in cool water. Leave whole or slice
as individual recipes specify.

Cooking Tip: Never cook okra in iron or
tin pans because it will turn black (it's
edible, just unattractive).

⊠ BOILED OKRA

Makes 4 servings

1 pound okra, prepared for cooking
¾ cup boiling water
1 teaspoon salt
⅛ teaspoon pepper
2 tablespoons butter or margarine

Leave pods whole if small; if large, slice
1" thick. Place okra in a saucepan with
water and salt, cover, and boil gently
until just tender: 6–10 minutes for whole
pods, 3–4 minutes for slices. Drain, add
pepper and butter, and set uncovered
over low heat, shaking pan gently, until
butter melts. About 85 calories per
serving.

Season	For Top Quality	Amount To Buy	Nutritive Value	Calories (unseasoned)
Year round; peak season: June–October	Choose crisp, tender leaves without holes or blemishes.	1 pound greens will serve 2.	High in vita-mins A and C, also in calcium	Low—about 40 per average serving

Season	For Top Quality	Amount To Buy	Nutritive Value	Calories (unseasoned)
Year round; peak months: July–October	Choose young, tender clean pods 2–4″ long; reject any with bruises or punctures.	1 pound will serve 2–4.	Some vitamin C and A	Low—about 35 per average serving

To Steam Okra: Place okra in a steamer over boiling water, cover, and steam until tender: 3–5 minutes for slices, 8–10 minutes for whole pods. About 85 calories per serving.

To Parboil for Use in Other Recipes: Boil or steam as directed but reduce cooking time to 2 minutes for slices, 5 minutes for pods.

VARIATIONS:

⚖ **Low-Calorie Boiled Okra:** Omit butter and dress with low-calorie herb dressing. About 35 calories per serving.

⚖ **Combo:** Mix drained, parboiled okra with 1 cup coarsely chopped canned tomatoes (do not drain), ⅛ teaspoon garlic powder, 2 tablespoons chili sauce, and 1 tablespoon minced parsley. Cover and simmer 3–5 minutes until okra is tender. Serve over (or with) hot Garlic Bread. About 60 calories per serving (without bread).

SOUTHERN FRIED OKRA

One of the very best ways to cook okra because little of the original crispness is lost.
Makes 4 servings

1 pound small okra pods, prepared for cooking
¼ cup unsifted flour
1 egg, lightly beaten with 1 tablespoon cold water
1 cup white or yellow corn meal, fine dry bread crumbs, or cracker meal
3 tablespoons butter or margarine, lard, or bacon drippings
¾ teaspoon salt
Pinch pepper

Cut off okra stem ends and tips and slice pods crosswise into rounds ¼″ thick. Pat dry on paper toweling. Dip rounds in flour, then in egg, then roll in meal or crumbs to coat evenly. Set on paper toweling. Heat butter, lard, or drippings in a large, heavy skillet 1 minute over moderate heat. Add okra and sauté about 2 minutes on a side until golden brown. Drain on paper toweling, sprinkle with salt and pepper. About 215 calories per serving.

BATTER-FRIED OKRA

Makes 4 servings

1 pound small okra pods, parboiled and drained
Lard, shortening, or cooking oil for deep fat frying

Batter:
1 cup sifted flour
1 teaspoon salt
1 cup milk
1 egg, lightly beaten

Pat okra dry on paper toweling. Begin heating fat in a deep fat fryer over moderately high heat; insert deep fat thermometer. Sift flour and salt together into a bowl, slowly add milk and beat until smooth. Beat in egg. When fat reaches 375° F., dip okra, a few pieces at a time, into batter, allowing excess to drain off, then drop into fat. Fry 1–2 minutes until golden brown. Using a slotted spoon, remove to paper toweling to drain. Set uncovered in a 250° F. oven to keep warm while you fry the rest. About 150 calories per serving.

VI. NEW FLAVOR COMBINATIONS

Raw Zucchini Salad — Fillets of Sole — Poulet Basquais

Raw Zucchini Salad (page 907)

Fillets of Sole à la Marinière; Fillets of Sole à la Niçoise; and Fillets of Sole à la Florentine (All three recipes page 554)

Poulet Basquais (pages 491-92); and Buttered Noodles (page 697)

VEGETABLE GUMBO

A Creole vegetable stew.
Makes 4 servings

3 slices bacon, diced
¼ cup finely chopped yellow onion
¼ cup finely chopped celery
1 (1-pound) can tomatoes (do not drain)
1 (10-ounce) package frozen whole baby okra (thaw only to separate pods, then slice in 1" rounds)
1 (10-ounce) package frozen whole kernel corn (do not thaw)
1 teaspoon salt
⅛ teaspoon pepper
Pinch powdered saffron
Pinch filé powder
2 cups hot cooked rice

Fry bacon in a large skillet over moderate heat 2–3 minutes; add onion and celery and sauté 8–10 minutes until golden. Add tomatoes and okra, cover, and boil gently 3–4 minutes. Add corn, salt, pepper, and saffron, re-cover, and boil 3–4 minutes longer until okra is tender. Stir in filé powder, ladle over rice, and serve. About 270 calories per serving.

ONIONS

During the Civil War, General Grant notified the War Department, "I will not move my army without onions." He got them; moreover, no one thought the request odd, because armies had always traveled with onions. Originally, they were said to make men valiant, later they were used to enliven dull army food. There are many kinds of onions, each a specialist. The best way to distinguish them is to categorize as follows: *dry onions, green or fresh onions, specialty onions.*

Dry Onions

These are dry-skinned, not very perishable onions that keep well unrefrigerated.

Bermuda Onions: These large flat onions can be white, tan, even red skinned; all are mild and sweet, perfect for slicing into salads or onto hamburgers. About 2–3 per pound.

Spanish Onions: Often mistakenly called Bermudas, these fawn-colored jumbos average ½ pound apiece. They're mild, sweet, and juicy, good raw, French-fried, or stuffed and baked.

White Onions: Mild, shimmery little silverskins about the size of a walnut (there are 18–24 per pound) that are best creamed or simmered in stews. Those less than 1" in diameter are *pickling onions;* those smaller still, *cocktail onions.*

Yellow Onions: The strongest of the dry onions, these are the round, golden skinned "cooking" onions we chop or slice and stir into everything from chili to chop suey. About 3–5 per pound.

Red or Italian Onions: Strong, purple-red onions that are best eaten raw in antipasti or salads. About 3–4 per pound.

Season	For Top Quality	Amount To Buy	Nutritive Value	Calories (unseasoned)
Year round for red, white, and yellow onions; March–June for Bermudas; and August–May for Spanish onions	Choose firm, well-shaped onions with dry, clean, bright skins. Reject any that are sprouting.	1 pound will serve 2–4.	Poor	Low—about 30 per ¼ pound of cooked onions; 40 per ¼ pound raw onions

To Prepare for Cooking: Peel. A quick
and tearless way to do small white onions
is to let stand 1 minute in boiling water
until skins begin to shrivel, then to drain
and plunge in ice water. The skins will
slip off neatly as peach skins.

Green or Fresh Onions

These are perishable, freshly pulled
onions that should be kept in the
refrigerator.

Spring or Green Onions: Long, strong,
slim onions with green tops and slightly
bulbous stems.

Scallions: A sister to the spring onion but
slimmer and sweeter.

Leeks: (see the special section on leeks).

Chives: These fragrant wispy green
"tops" are the most delicate of all
onions. Buy by the pot if possible, set
on a sunny window sill, and use as an
herb.

To Prepare for Cooking: Scallions and
spring onions must be trimmed of roots,
wilted tops, and any coarse outer stem
coverings. Leave whole or cut up as
individual recipes specify. Chives should
be washed in cool water, patted dry on
paper toweling gathered into a bunch,
and minced or snipped with scissors.

Specialty Onions

There are only two, both available year
round, both used sparingly as seasonings.

Garlic: An average bulb, composed of
cloves that fit together rather like
sections of a tangerine, is about the size
of a tangerine. Individual cloves can be
small as a lima bean or big as a walnut.
When a recipe calls for a clove of
garlic, use one about the size of the
end of your little finger (or the
equivalent). Buy only one bulb of garlic
at a time (they quickly dry out) and
choose one that is plump and firm.
Always peel garlic before using; leave
whole, mince, or crush as individual
recipes specify, but bear in mind that
crushed garlic has about 3 times the
impact of the minced.

Shallots: Copper skinned and about the
size of hazelnuts, shallots are milder
than garlic but stronger than most
onions. Buy about ¼ pound at a time
(shallots quickly dry up) and select ones
that are plump and firm. Peel before
using and cut as individual recipes
specify.

In addition to the onions described
above, there is an ever-widening array
of *convenience onions*—powders, juices,
flakes, salts, and dry soup mixes that
save much in time and tears but cannot
compare with fresh onions for flavor.

Season	For Top Quality	Amount To Buy	Nutritive Value	Calories (unseasoned)
Year round for all fresh onions	Choose spring onions and scallions with succulent white stems 2–3″ long and crisp green tops. If potted chives are unavailable, choose those with a "just-cut" look.	1 bunch scallions or spring onions contains 5–6 stalks and will serve 1–2.	Poor	Very low—about 4 per spring onion or scallion

BOILED ONIONS

Makes 4 servings

1½ pounds small white onions, peeled
1½ cups boiling water, chicken or beef
  broth
1½ teaspoons salt (about)
3 tablespoons butter or margarine
¼ teaspoon paprika
Pinch mace
Pinch pepper

Place onions in a saucepan with water
or broth and 1 teaspoon salt, cover, and
boil 20 minutes until tender. Drain, add
remaining salt if onions were boiled in
water, the butter, paprika, mace, and
pepper and warm, shaking pan gently,
1–2 minutes until butter melts. About
115 calories per serving (cooked in
water), 125 per serving (cooked in
broth).

To Parboil for Use in Other Recipes:
Use recipe above but reduce cooking
time to 15 minutes; omit all seasonings.

VARIATIONS:

⚖ **Low-Calorie Boiled Onions:** Cook
onions as directed in water. Omit butter
and spices and dress with low-calorie
Italian or herb dressing. About 40
calories per serving.

Creamed Onions: Boil and drain onions
as directed but do not season; combine
with 1½ cups hot Medium White Sauce,
1 tablespoon light brown sugar, and a
pinch nutmeg and cayenne pepper.
Warm, stirring, 2–3 minutes to blend
flavors. About 200 calories per serving
(cooked in water), 210 calories per
serving (cooked in broth).

Glazed Onions: Boil and drain onions as
directed (reserve 1 tablespoon cooking
liquid). Do not season. Melt ¼ cup
butter in a large skillet, add reserved
cooking liquid, ⅓ cup light brown sugar,
a pinch each mace and pepper, and
simmer, stirring, 3–4 minutes until
syrupy. Add onions and heat 5–8
minutes, turning frequently, until evenly
glazed. Serve hot as a vegetable or use

to garnish a roast platter. About 210
calories per serving (cooked in water),
220 calories per serving (cooked in
broth).

PAN-BRAISED ONIONS

Makes 4–6 servings

2 pounds small white onions, peeled
¼ cup unsalted butter
½ cup dry vermouth
¼ teaspoon salt
Pinch pepper

Sauté onions in butter in a large, heavy
skillet over moderately high heat,
turning frequently, 10 minutes until
golden. Add vermouth, reduce heat to
moderately low, cover, and simmer
15 minutes until crisp-tender. Sprinkle
with salt and pepper and turn onions in
pan juices to glaze evenly. Serve hot as
a vegetable or use in making such stews
as Boeuf à la Bourguignonne. About
185 calories for each of 4 servings,
125 calories for each of 6 servings.

SAUTÉED ONIONS

Makes 4 servings

6 medium-size yellow onions, peeled
2–3 tablespoons flour (optional)
¼ cup butter, margarine, or cooking oil
Salt
Pepper

Thinly slice onions and separate into
rings or chop medium fine. Dredge, if
you like, in flour (onions will be a bit
browner). Heat butter or oil in a large,
heavy skillet over moderate heat
1 minute (or use an electric skillet with
temperature control set at 350° F.).
Sauté onions, turning frequently,
8–10 minutes for golden, 10–12 minutes
for well browned. If you like them
slightly crisp, raise heat to moderately
high at the end of cooking and stir-fry
1 minute. Drain quickly on paper
toweling, sprinkle with salt and pepper,
and serve. About 160 calories per
serving (made without flour).

FRENCH-FRIED ONION RINGS

Crisp and sweet.
Makes 4 servings

1 large Spanish onion, peeled and sliced
    ¼" thick
Lard, shortening, or cooking oil for
    deep fat frying

Batter:
⅔ cup sifted flour
¾ teaspoon salt
¼ teaspoon baking powder
⅔ cup milk

Begin heating fat in a deep fat fryer
over moderately high heat; insert deep
fat thermometer. Separate onion slices
into rings. Sift flour, salt, and baking
powder together into a bowl. Slowly add
milk and beat until bubbles appear on
surface of batter. When fat reaches
375° F., dip onion rings, 4 or 5 at a
time, into batter, allowing excess to
drain off, then drop into fat. Fry
1 minute until golden brown; turn rings
to brown evenly if they don't flip on
their own. Remove to a paper-towel-
lined baking sheet and set uncovered in
a 250° F. oven while you fry the rest.
(Note: Skim bits of batter from fat
between fryings before they burn.)
About 160 calories per serving.

VARIATION:

Shallow Fried Onion Rings: Pour 1½"
cooking oil into an electric skillet
(temperature control set at 375° F.)
or large, heavy skillet set over
moderately high heat. When hot, not
smoking, dip onion rings into batter and
fry as recipe directs. About 160 calories
per serving.

BAKED ONIONS

Baked onions are mellower and sweeter
than boiled onions. They are delicious
with roast meats or fowl.
Makes 4 servings

4 medium-size Spanish onions (do not
    peel)
⅓ cup water
1 teaspoon salt

⅛ teaspoon pepper
¼ cup melted butter or margarine

Preheat oven to 400° F. Trim root end
from onions and arrange in a buttered
shallow casserole. Pour in water. Bake,
uncovered, 1½ hours until fork tender.
Using a small piece of paper toweling
as a pot holder, grasp skin of onion at
the top and pull off. Sprinkle onions with
salt and pepper, drizzle with butter,
and serve. About 160 calories per
serving.

ROASTED ONIONS

Oven-roasted onions glazed with
drippings.
Makes 4 servings

8 medium-size yellow or Bermuda
    onions or 4 medium-size Spanish
    onions, peeled
½ cup bacon drippings, shortening, or
    lard
Salt
Pepper

Preheat oven to 400° F. Place onions in
a roasting pan or casserole, add
drippings, shortening, or lard. Roast,
uncovered, until fork tender: 45–50
minutes for yellow or Bermuda onions;
1¼–1½ hours for Spanish onions. Turn
onions halfway through cooking so
they'll brown evenly. Drain on paper
toweling, sprinkle with salt and pepper,
and serve. About 180 calories per
serving.

CREAMED SCALLIONS

Scallions are a good substitute for the
more expensive, less available leeks,
especially when creamed.
Makes 4 servings

4 bunches scallions, washed and trimmed
    of roots and tops
1 cup boiling water
1 teaspoon salt
½ cup heavy cream
2 tablespoons butter or margarine
2 tablespoons flour blended with
    2 tablespoons cold water
⅛ teaspoon white pepper

Place scallions, water and salt in a saucepan, cover, and boil gently 5–7 minutes until just tender. Lift scallions from liquid and keep warm. Add cream and butter to scallion liquid, then stir in flour-water paste. Heat, stirring, until thickened and smooth. Add pepper, taste for salt and add more if needed. Pour sauce over scallions, mix lightly, and serve. About 190 calories per serving.

ONIONS IN CHEDDAR SAUCE

Makes 4 servings

1½ pounds small white onions, boiled
and drained (reserve cooking water)
2 tablespoons butter or margarine
2 tablespoons flour
⅛ teaspoon cinnamon
⅛ teaspoon mace
Onion cooking water plus enough
evaporated milk to total 1½ cups
1¼ cups coarsely grated sharp Cheddar
cheese
1 teaspoon prepared spicy brown
mustard
1 teaspoon ketchup
½ teaspoon Worcestershire sauce
¼ teaspoon cayenne pepper
1 tablespoon cream sherry

Keep onions warm. In a separate saucepan melt butter over moderate heat and blend in flour, cinnamon, and mace. Add the 1½ cups liquid and heat, stirring constantly, until thickened. Mix in cheese and all remaining ingredients and heat, stirring, 1–2 minutes until smooth. Pour sauce over onions, heat 1–2 minutes longer, and serve. About 280 calories per serving.

¢ ONION STEW

Makes 4 servings

4–5 medium-size yellow onions, peeled
1 quart water
1 teaspoon salt (about)
Pinch white pepper
¼ cup butter or margarine
Croutons (optional garnish)

Place onions, water, and salt in a saucepan, cover, and boil gently

30 minutes until very soft. Remove from heat and let stand, covered, 1 hour. Quarter each onion and return to liquid. Stir in pepper, cover, and heat slowly until piping hot. Taste for salt and adjust as needed. Ladle into heated soup bowls, add 1 tablespoon butter to each, and serve. Pass croutons to be sprinkled on top if you like. About 140 calories per serving (without croutons).

CHAMP

Champ is a traditional dish from Northern Ireland made with scallions and mashed potatoes.
Makes 4 servings

3 bunches scallions, prepared for
cooking and coarsely chopped
(include tops)
½ cup boiling water
½ teaspoon salt
3 cups hot seasoned mashed potatoes
2 tablespoons butter or margarine

Place scallions, water, and salt in a small saucepan, cover, and boil 4–5 minutes until scallions are very tender. Drain well and briskly beat scallions into potatoes with a fork. Spoon into a heated vegetable dish, dot with butter, and serve. About 160 calories per serving.

VARIATION:

Baked Champ: Spoon mixture into a buttered 1½-quart casserole, roughen surface with a fork, and drizzle with melted butter. Bake, uncovered, 20 minutes at 400° F., then broil 4″ from the heat 1–2 minutes to brown. About 160 calories per serving.

STUFFED ONIONS

Boiled Spanish or yellow onions, hollowed out, can be filled with many vegetables: buttered peas and mushrooms; creamed diced carrots and peas; puréed spinach; mashed sweet potatoes; Harvard Beets; Mexican-Style Corn and Peppers.

Makes 4 servings

4 medium-size Spanish onions, peeled
2⅓ cups water
1 teaspoon salt
1 tablespoon cooking oil

Stuffing:

2 tablespoons butter or margarine
¾ cup soft white bread crumbs
1 teaspoon salt
⅛ teaspoon pepper
¼ cup finely grated sharp Cheddar
   cheese
Minced parsley (garnish)

Preheat oven to 400° F. Cut a ½″ slice
from the top of each onion (save for
other recipes). Place onions, 2 cups
water, and salt in a large saucepan,
cover, and simmer 20–25 minutes.
Drain well. With a spoon, scoop out
center of each onion, leaving a shell
½″ thick, place shells in a buttered
shallow 1-quart casserole, and brush
with oil. Pour remaining water into
casserole. Chop onion centers fine and
sauté 5 minutes in butter over moderate
heat. Mix in all remaining stuffing
ingredients except parsley, spoon into
onion shells, and bake uncovered 30–40
minutes until lightly browned. Sprinkle
with parsley and serve. About 200
calories per serving.

Some Additional Stuffings for Onions

To the chopped sautéed onion centers,
add any of the following:
– ¾ cup hot cooked rice, ¼ cup chopped
peeled tomatoes, and a pinch each garlic
salt and powdered saffron.
– ½ cup each hot cooked rice and
slivered boiled ham and 2 tablespoons
grated Parmesan cheese.
– ¾ cup minced ripe olives, ¼ cup finely
chopped toasted almonds, and
1 tablespoon heavy cream.
– 1 cup poultry stuffing mix and
2 tablespoons melted butter.
– 1 cup seasoned mashed potatoes and
2 tablespoons melted butter. Fill onion
shells and bake as directed in basic
recipe above.

FINNISH ONION FRY IN SOUR CREAM

Makes 4 servings

¼ cup butter or margarine
1 pound Spanish onions, peeled and
   chopped fine
½ pound mushrooms, wiped clean and
   sliced thin
2 pimientos, seeded and slivered
1 cup sour cream
½ teaspoon salt
⅛ teaspoon paprika

Melt butter in a very large, heavy skillet
over moderately low heat, add onions,
and cook, stirring occasionally, 10–12
minutes until tender but not browned;
lift from skillet and reserve. Raise heat
to moderately high and sauté mushrooms
2–3 minutes until golden. Return onions
to skillet, add pimientos, and mix well.
Reduce heat to low, mix in sour cream
and salt, and heat, stirring, 1–2 minutes
(do not boil). Sprinkle with paprika and
serve. About 280 calories per serving.

PISSALADIÈRE (ONION TART À LA NIÇOISE)

Nearly every French town has an onion
tart, but only in Nice, where the cooking
is as much Italian as French, does
it resemble pizza (it's called
pissaladière).

Makes 6 servings

1 recipe Pizza Dough (see Pizza in the
   bread chapter)
6 medium-size yellow onions, peeled
   and sliced thin
1 clove garlic, peeled and crushed
1 bay leaf
¼ cup olive oil
1 teaspoon salt
⅛ teaspoon pepper
1 (2-ounce) can anchovy fillets, drained
1 cup brined, pitted ripe Italian olives

Make pastry according to recipe and fit
into a 12″ pizza pan. Preheat oven to
450° F. Sauté onions, garlic, and bay
leaf in oil in a large, heavy skillet over
moderate heat 8–10 minutes until onions
are golden. Stir in salt; remove bay leaf.
Spread onions evenly over pastry and

sprinkle with pepper. Arrange anchovies, spoke fashion, over onions and dot olives here and there. Bake, uncovered, 15 minutes until pastry is browned. Cut into wedges and serve as a light entree or cut into smaller wedges and serve as an appetizer. About 480 calories per serving.

PARSNIPS

The Roman Emperor Tiberius was so fond of parsnips he sent to the Rhine country each year for his supply because in that climate they grew to plump and sugary perfection. His cooks were ordered to treat the parsnips with reverence, to boil them gently and sauce them with honey wine. Parsnips later fell from favor and they have never regained their popularity. In Tudor England they were used primarily for making bread, in Ireland for brewing beer. Even today, few people relish parsnips, possibly because they have been eclipsed by their cousin, the carrot, whose sweeter, nuttier flavor most of us prefer. Parsnips are worth trying, however, because they are economical and make a welcome change of pace.

To Prepare for Cooking: Remove root ends and tops; scrub well in cool water and peel. If parsnips seem large, halve and remove woody central cores. Otherwise leave whole or cut as individual recipes specify.

Cooking Tip: To improve the flavor of parsnips, add a little brown sugar to the cooking water and, if you like, a peeled 1″ cube gingerroot or blade of mace.

¢ BOILED PARSNIPS

Makes 2–4 servings

1 pound parsnips, prepared for cooking
1½ cups boiling water
2 tablespoons butter or margarine
1 teaspoon salt
⅛ teaspoon pepper

Place parsnips in a large saucepan, add water, cover, and boil 30–35 minutes until tender; drain. Cut into thin slices or small cubes and return to pan. Add remaining ingredients and warm, uncovered, over low heat, shaking pan gently, 2–3 minutes until butter is melted and parsnips lightly glazed. About 250 calories for each of 2 servings, 125 calories for each of 4 servings.

To Parboil for Use in Other Recipes: Boil as directed above but reduce cooking time to 10 minutes; omit seasonings.

VARIATIONS:

¢ **Mashed Parsnips:** Quarter and core parsnips, boil as directed, but reduce cooking time to 15–20 minutes. Drain and mash with a potato masher. Beat in butter, salt, and pepper called for, also, if you like, 1–2 tablespoons heavy cream. About 250 calories for each of 2 servings (without heavy cream), 125 calories for each of 4.

¢ **Currant-Glazed Parsnips:** Add 2 tablespoons currant jelly to parsnips along with butter, salt, and pepper and warm as directed to glaze. About 320 calories for each of 2 servings, 160 calories for each of 4 servings.

Season	For Top Quality	Amount To Buy	Nutritive Value	Calories (unseasoned)
Year round; peak seasons: fall, winter, and spring	Look for clean, firm, well-shaped roots of medium size (large parsnips may be woody).	A 1-pound bunch will serve 2–4.	Poor	Moderate— about 74 per ¼ pound serving

¢ **Orange-Glazed Parsnips:** Add 2 tablespoons orange marmalade to parsnips along with butter and seasonings and warm as directed to glaze. About 320 calories for each of 2 servings, 160 calories for each of 4 servings.

¢ **Caramel-Glazed Parsnips:** To drained parsnips add ¼ cup each butter and light brown sugar, 1 tablespoon lemon juice, ⅛ teaspoon nutmeg, and the salt and pepper called for. Warm, uncovered, over lowest heat 10 minutes, stirring occasionally, until evenly glazed. About 450 calories for each of 2 servings, 225 calories for each of 4.

¢ **Gingery Parsnips:** Add 2 tablespoons minced preserved ginger and ⅛ teaspoon mace to parsnips along with butter, salt, and pepper and warm as directed to glaze. About 300 calories for each of 2 servings, 150 calories for each of 4.

¢ ROASTED PARSNIPS

Makes 4 servings

½ cup melted bacon or beef drippings or
    shortening
1½ pounds medium-size parsnips,
    prepared for cooking and halved
½ teaspoon salt

Preheat oven to 400° F. Pour drippings or shortening into a 10″ flameproof glass piepan, add parsnips, turning in drippings to coat. Roast, uncovered, 40–45 minutes until lightly browned and fork tender, turning once or twice so they brown evenly. Drain on paper toweling, sprinkle with salt, and serve. About 210 calories per serving.

¢ PARSNIP CAKES

Makes 4–6 servings

1 egg, lightly beaten
Pinch nutmeg
Salt
Pepper
2 pounds parsnips, boiled and mashed
1 egg lightly beaten with 1 tablespoon
    cold water

¾ cup toasted seasoned bread crumbs
¼ cup butter or margarine

Mix egg, nutmeg, salt, and pepper to taste into parsnips. Cool to room temperature, cover, and chill 1 hour. Using ⅓ cup as a measure, shape mixture into 8 cakes and flatten; dip in egg, then in crumbs to coat evenly, cover, and chill ½ hour. Melt butter in a large skillet over moderate heat, add half the cakes, and brown well on both sides, about 3–4 minutes. Drain on paper toweling and set, uncovered, in a 250° F. oven to keep warm while you brown the rest. About 365 calories for each of 4 servings, 245 calories for each of 6 servings.

FRENCH-FRIED PARSNIPS

Makes 4 servings

1½ pounds parsnips, parboiled and cut
    in ⅜″ strips as for French fries
Lard, shortening, or cooking oil for deep
    fat frying
Salt

Pat parsnip strips dry on paper toweling. Meanwhile, begin heating fat in a deep fat fryer over moderately high heat; insert wire basket and deep fat thermometer. When fat reaches 375° F., drop in about half the parsnips and fry 1–2 minutes until golden brown and crisp. Transfer to a paper-towel-lined baking sheet and set, uncovered, in a 250° F. oven to keep warm while you fry the rest. Sprinkle with salt and serve. About 160 calories per serving.

VARIATION:

Batter-Fried Parsnips: Parboil parsnips and cut into strips as directed above; also heat fat for deep frying. Prepare a batter: sift together 1 cup flour and 1 teaspoon salt, slowly add 1 cup milk, then beat well. Add 1 lightly beaten egg and beat again. Dip parsnip strips, a few at a time, into batter, allowing excess to drain off, then fry as recipe directs. About 210 calories per serving.

Season	For Top Quality	Amount To Buy	Nutritive Value	Calories (unseasoned)
Year round for all peas; peak season: April–August	Choose bright green, tender, slightly velvety pods. Green pea pods should be well filled, snow pea pods slender and crisp. Cook as soon after buying as possible.	1 pound green peas in the pod serves 1–2; 1 pound snow peas 4–6; 1 pound dried peas 4–6.	Green and snow peas have fair amounts of vitamins A, C, and niacin; dried peas are high in protein and iron.	High—about 115 per cup of green peas; 290 per cup of dried peas. Not known for snow peas.

PEAS

"This subject of peas continues to absorb all others," wrote Madame de Maintenon of the new fad at Louis XIV's court. "Some ladies, after having supped at the Royal Table and well supped, too, returning to their own homes, at the risk of suffering from indigestion, will again eat peas before going to bed. It is both a fashion and a madness." These were *petits pois,* a tiny variety of today's green peas and a far cry from the mealy, unsweet field peas of old (these are now almost unavailable except as dried whole or split yellow peas). The newest member of the pea family (at least the newest to Americans) is the tender snow or sugar pea of Chinese cooking.

To Prepare for Cooking:
Green Peas: Shell *just* before cooking, no sooner.

Snow or Sugar Peas: Trim off stem ends; wash pods (but don't soak) in cool water.

Dried Whole Peas: Wash, sort, and soak overnight in 1 quart cold water. Or use the quick method* recommended for soaking dried beans.

Dried Split Peas: Wash and sort.

Cooking Tip: Add a pea pod to the pot when cooking green peas—gives them a just-picked flavor.

BOILED FRESH GREEN PEAS

Makes 4 servings

3 pounds green peas in the pod
½ cup boiling water
1 teaspoon sugar
1 teaspoon salt
Pinch pepper
2 tablespoons butter or margarine

Shell peas, place in a saucepan with water and sugar, cover, and boil 8–10 minutes until tender. Drain, add salt, pepper, and butter, and toss lightly to mix. About 110 calories per serving.

To Parboil for Use in Other Recipes: Boil as directed but reduce cooking time to 5 minutes; omit seasonings.

VARIATIONS:

To Serve Cold: Boil and drain as directed, then chill in ice water. Drain and refrigerate until needed. Use in salads or other recipes calling for cold peas.

Minted Green Peas: Boil as directed, adding a mint sprig to the pot. About 110 calories per serving.

Green Peas with Rosemary: Tuck a sprig fresh rosemary into the pot, letting it perfume the peas as they boil, or add a pinch dried rosemary to peas before serving. About 110 calories per serving.

Green Peas in Cream: Boil and drain peas by method above, stir in ¼ cup heavy cream and a pinch mace or nutmeg along with seasonings called for; serve in soup bowls. About 160 calories per serving.

Puréed Green Peas: Purée boiled, drained peas in an electric blender at high speed or put through a food mill. Mix in 2 tablespoons heavy cream along with seasonings called for and beat until light. (*Note:* Makes 2–3 servings.) About 275 calories for each of 2 servings, 185 calories for each of 3 servings.

Some Vegetables to Team with Green Peas: Diced, cooked carrots or celery; boiled tiny new potatoes; sautéed, sliced mushrooms; cooked or canned whole kernel or cream-style corn; boiled cauliflowerets; canned pearl onions or sautéed, sliced scallions.

GREEN PEAS WITH MINT AND ORANGE

Makes 4 servings

3 pounds green peas, shelled and boiled, or 2 (10-ounce) packages frozen peas, cooked by package directions
¼ cup butter or margarine
2 tablespoons finely slivered orange rind (use only the orange part)
2 tablespoons minced fresh mint or 1 teaspoon mint flakes
½ teaspoon salt
Pinch pepper

While peas are cooking, melt butter in a small saucepan over low heat. Add orange rind and heat, uncovered, 2–3 minutes, stirring occasionally. Drain peas well. Add butter and rind, also mint, salt, and pepper. Toss lightly to mix and serve. About 160 calories per serving.

GREEN PEAS AND DUMPLINGS

Makes 4 servings

3 pounds green peas, shelled
1¼ cups boiling water
1 cup light cream
2 tablespoons butter or margarine
1 tablespoon sugar
1 mint sprig
1 teaspoon salt
Pinch pepper
Dumplings:
1 cup sifted flour
1 tablespoon sugar
1½ teaspoons baking powder
½ teaspoon salt
1 tablespoon butter or margarine
½ cup milk

Place peas, boiling water, cream, butter, sugar, mint, salt, and pepper in a large saucepan, cover, set over moderate heat, and let come to a full boil. Meanwhile, quickly sift flour with sugar, baking powder, and salt into a small bowl and cut in butter with a pastry blender until mixture is the texture of coarse meal. Pour in milk and stir briskly with a fork *just* to mix, no longer. Drop dumplings from a tablespoon on top of *boiling* pea liquid, covering surface. Cover and simmer exactly 15 minutes (don't peek or dumplings won't be light). Remove mint and serve in soup bowls, spooning lots of cooking liquid over each portion. About 400 calories per serving.

⊠ SOY GREEN PEAS

The Chinese usually prepare snow peas this way, but the recipe works equally well with green peas.

Makes 4 servings

2 (10-ounce) packages frozen green peas (do not thaw)
2 tablespoons peanut oil
1½ teaspoons sugar
3 tablespoons soy sauce
½ teaspoon ginger

Hit packages of frozen peas against the edge of a counter to break up the solid mass. Heat peanut oil in a large, heavy skillet over moderately high heat about 1 minute. Add peas and stir-fry 5–7 minutes until heated through. Add remaining ingredients, stir-fry 1 minute longer, and serve. About 130 calories per serving.

PEAS À LA FRANÇAISE

Makes 4 servings

3 pounds green peas, shelled
1 cup finely shredded romaine or iceberg
*   lettuce*
12 scallions, trimmed and cut in rounds
*   ¼" thick*
1 bouquet garni
¼ teaspoon sugar
¼ cup boiling water
¼ cup butter or margarine
1 teaspoon salt
Pinch pepper

Place all ingredients except butter, salt, and pepper in a saucepan, cover, and boil 8–10 minutes, stirring once or twice, until peas are tender. Drain and remove *bouquet garni*. Add butter, salt, and pepper, cover, and shake pan gently over low heat until butter melts. Toss lightly and serve. About 175 calories per serving.

VARIATION:

Substitute 2 (10-ounce) packages frozen green peas for the fresh, reducing amount of boiling water to 2 tablespoons. Add butter to saucepan before cooking, then boil peas, covered, 5–7 minutes, breaking up any large chunks after 2 minutes of cooking. Season and serve. About 175 calories per serving.

PEAS À LA BONNE FEMME

Peas and onions cooked in chicken broth.
Makes 6 servings

2 tablespoons butter or margarine
12 very small white onions, peeled
2 slices bacon, diced
4 teaspoons flour
1 cup chicken broth
3 pounds green peas, shelled, or 2
*   (10-ounce) packages frozen peas (do*
*   not thaw)*
Salt
Pepper

Melt butter in a large skillet over moderately high heat. Brown onions slowly all over, 6–8 minutes, then push to one side of skillet. Add bacon and sauté 2–3 minutes until crisp and golden. Stir in flour, slowly add chicken broth, and mix until smooth. Cook, stirring constantly, until thickened. Reduce heat to moderately low, cover, and simmer 10 minutes until onions are crisp-tender. Add peas, cover, and simmer 8–10 minutes for the fresh, 5–7 for the frozen (break these up after 2 minutes of cooking). Season to taste with salt and pepper. About 140 calories per serving.

FARM-STYLE GREEN PEAS

Carrots, onion, lettuce, and green peas cooked in apple cider and lightly flavored with bacon.
Makes 6 servings

2 tablespoons bacon drippings, butter, or
*   margarine*
2 medium-size carrots, peeled and diced
1 medium-size yellow onion, peeled and
*   sliced thin*
2 leaves romaine or iceberg lettuce
3 pounds green peas, shelled, or 2
*   (10-ounce) packages frozen peas (do*
*   not thaw)*
¼ teaspoon sugar
1 teaspoon salt
⅛ teaspoon pepper
1 teaspoon minced parsley
¾ cup apple cider or juice
1 teaspoon minced fresh chervil or ½
*   teaspoon dried chervil*

Melt drippings or butter in a saucepan over moderate heat, add carrots and onion, and stir-fry 2–3 minutes. Lay lettuce leaves on top of carrots and onion and add all remaining ingredients except chervil. Cover and simmer 10 minutes for fresh peas, 5–7 for the frozen (break these up after 2 minutes of cooking). Drain, reserving cooking liquid; discard lettuce. Sprinkle chervil over vegetables and toss gently to mix. Spoon into a heated vegetable dish and keep warm. Boil cooking liquid, uncovered, until reduced to ¼ cup, pour over vegetables, and serve. About 100 calories per serving.

⊠ BOILED FRESH SNOW PEA PODS

Makes 4–6 servings

1 pound small snow pea pods, prepared for cooking
2 cups boiling water
½ teaspoon salt
Pinch pepper
2–4 tablespoons melted butter or margarine

Place pea pods in a large saucepan, pour in boiling water, and set over high heat. The instant water returns to a full rolling boil, time peas and boil, uncovered, exactly 2 minutes. Drain in a colander, transfer to a heated vegetable dish, sprinkle with salt and pepper, and drizzle with butter. Toss very gently and serve. About 70 calories for each of 4 servings (with 2 tablespoons butter), 80 for each of 6 (with 4 tablespoons butter).

VARIATIONS:

Snow Peas and Water Chestnuts: Add 3–4 thinly sliced water chestnuts to peas just before serving. About 75 calories for each of 4 servings, 85 calories for each of 6.

Snow Peas and Scallions: Add 8 finely chopped scallions (white part only) to peas just before serving. About 75 calories for each of 4 servings, 85 calories for each of 6.

⊠ CHINESE-STYLE SNOW PEAS

Makes 4–6 servings

1 pound small snow pea pods, prepared for cooking
3 tablespoons peanut or sesame oil
¾ teaspoon salt
Pinch pepper
Pinch MSG (monosodium glutamate)

Pat pods dry on paper toweling. Heat oil in a large, heavy skillet or *wok* over moderately high heat 1 minute. Add pea pods, reduce heat to moderate, and stir-fry 2 minutes. Cover skillet and cook 1–2 minutes longer, shaking pan frequently, until peas are crisp-tender. Toss in remaining ingredients and serve.

About 115 calories for each of 4 servings, 75 calories for each of 6 servings.

VARIATION:

Substitute 2 (7-ounce) packages frozen snow peas for the fresh. Plunge solidly frozen pods into boiling water for 1 minute or just long enough to separate them. Drain, pat dry on paper toweling, then proceed as recipe directs. About 115 calories for each of 4 servings, 75 calories for each of 6.

¢ BOILED DRIED WHOLE PEAS

For special piquancy, drizzle a little vinegar over these peas before serving. Makes 4–6 servings

1 pound dried whole green or yellow peas, washed and sorted
2½ quarts cold water (about)
2 tablespoons butter, margarine, bacon or roast drippings
2–3 teaspoons salt
⅛ teaspoon pepper

Soak peas in 1 quart water overnight or use the quick method.* Drain, measure soaking water, and add enough cold water to total 1½ quarts. Simmer peas, covered, in the water 1¾–2 hours, stirring occasionally, until tender and almost all water has evaporated. If mixture seems soupy, simmer uncovered a few minutes. Stir in butter or drippings, salt to taste, and pepper and serve. About 340 calories for each of 4 servings, 230 calories for each of 6 servings.

¢ SPLIT PEA PURÉE

Makes 4 servings

1 cup dried split green or yellow peas, washed and sorted
2 cups cold water
¾ teaspoon salt
1 small yellow onion, peeled and chopped fine
2 tablespoons butter or margarine

Place all ingredients in a heavy saucepan, cover, and bring to a boil over high heat. Reduce heat to moderately low and simmer 35–40 minutes, stirring occasionally, until peas are mushy. (*Note*: If lid does not fit tightly, you may have to add an extra ¼ cup boiling water toward the end of cooking so peas don't stick.) Remove from heat and beat peas with a wooden spoon or, if you prefer, purée in an electric blender at high speed or press through a fine sieve. Reheat, if necessary, and serve hot. About 235 calories per serving.

VARIATION:

Savory Split Pea Purée: Use 2 cups chicken or beef broth for cooking peas instead of water. Add all seasonings called for above, also 1 minced carrot, 2 stalks celery, chopped fine, 1 crushed clove garlic, and 1 bay leaf. Cover and simmer as recipe directs. Remove bay leaf and purée in an electric blender at high speed. Top, if you wish, with crisp crumbled bacon or Croutons. About 255 calories per serving (without bacon or croutons).

PEPPERS

When Columbus discovered the West Indies, he found island natives eating scarlet and emerald pods that contained all the fire of costly East Indian black pepper. He called these pods "peppers" and "peppers" they have remained, although botanically they are not peppers but members of a large family that also includes tomatoes and potatoes. Old World cooks applauded the New World peppers, found them " more pungent than the peppers of the Caucasus," and devised delightful new ways of using them. The peppers we know today can be lumped into two large categories— the sweet and the hot. Either may be green or red because peppers, like tomatoes, turn red (or in some instances, sunny yellow) as they ripen.

To Prepare for Cooking: Wash in cool water; cut up as individual recipes specify. Always wash your hands well after cutting or working with hot peppers.

To Prepare for Stuffing: Using a small sharp knife, cut a wide circle around stem of pepper and lift off (save if stem-lids are to be used to cover stuffing during baking). Scoop out core and seeds and discard.

To Parboil Before Stuffing: Because peppers will not always cook as fast as their stuffing, they must sometimes be parboiled. To do so, prepare for stuffing by method above, then lay peppers on their sides in a large kettle and add lightly salted boiling water to cover. If tops are to be used, add to kettle. Cover and boil 6–8 minutes until crisp-tender (remove tops after 4 minutes). Pour off water and drain peppers upside-down on paper toweling.

PEPPERS STUFFED WITH SPANISH RICE

Makes 4 servings

4 large sweet green or red peppers, washed
4 cups Spanish Rice
¼ cup coarsely grated Monterey Jack or sharp Cheddar cheese
1 cup water (about)

Preheat oven to 375° F. Prepare peppers for stuffing and parboil.* Stand close

Season	For Top Quality	Amount To Buy	Nutritive Value	Calories (unseasoned)
Year round for all; Peak season: June–October	Choose bright, firm fleshy pods. Pimientos are available only canned.	1 sweet pepper per person; 2–3 Italian peppers	The red are high in vitamins A and C, the green in vitamin C.	Very low— 15–20 per pepper, the red being the higher

together in an ungreased shallow 1-quart casserole, fill with Spanish rice, and sprinkle with cheese. Pour water around peppers. Bake, uncovered, 45 minutes until peppers are tender, checking occasionally to make sure water hasn't boiled away—there should be a little in the bottom of the casserole at all times. Using 2 large spoons, lift peppers to a heated dish and serve. About 290 calories per serving.

VARIATIONS:

Peppers Stuffed with Spanish Rice and Meat: Reduce amount of Spanish rice to 2½ cups and mix with 1½ cups chopped, cooked meat, poultry, or seafood (this is a splendid way to use up leftover cold cuts, ham, or hot dogs). Stuff and bake peppers as directed. Serve hot, topped if you like, with Tomato Sauce. About 305 calories per serving (without Tomato Sauce).

Peppers Stuffed with Macaroni Marinara: Instead of stuffing peppers with Spanish rice, stuff with 3 cups boiled macaroni shells mixed with 2 cups Marinara Sauce. Sprinkle peppers with cheese. Pour 1½ cups Marinara Sauce into kettle with peppers and bake as directed above. Serve from casserole, spooning some of the sauce over each portion. About 215 calories per serving.

Some Other Stuffings for Peppers (allow 1 cup per pepper and bake as directed above): Macaroni and cheese, chili con carne, corned beef hash, franks or pork and beans, Izmir Eggplant, Rice Pilaf, Saffron Rice, Ratatouille, Pisto, Jambalaya, any *risotto*.

SAUTÉED SWEET GREEN OR RED PEPPERS

Serve these peppers as a vegetable or use to garnish meat or egg platters. They're also good mixed with sautéed sliced mushrooms, hashed brown potatoes, boiled whole kernel corn, or buttered baby limas.
Makes 2–4 servings

2 tablespoons cooking oil
2 large sweet green or red peppers, washed, cored, seeded, and cut in long, thin strips
¼ teaspoon salt
Pepper

Heat oil in a heavy skillet over moderate heat 1 minute. Add peppers and sauté, stirring frequently, 4–6 minutes until lightly browned. Turn heat to low, cover, and simmer 2–3 minutes until crisp-tender. Using a slotted spoon, transfer to a heated vegetable dish, sprinkle with salt, a grinding or two of the pepper mill, and serve. About 125 calories for each of 2 servings, 65 calories for each of 4 servings.

ITALIAN PEPPERS AND ONIONS

Makes 4 servings

3 tablespoons olive oil
3 large sweet red or green peppers or 8 Italian sweet green peppers, washed, cored, seeded, and cut in long, thin strips
1 medium-size Spanish onion, peeled and sliced thin
1 clove garlic, peeled and crushed
½ teaspoon salt
Pinch pepper

Heat oil in a large, heavy skillet over moderate heat. Add peppers, onion, and garlic and stir-fry 8 minutes until onion is golden. Cover, turn heat to low, and simmer 5 minutes, shaking pan occasionally. Uncover, cook, stirring, 1–2 minutes to drive off excess moisture; add salt and pepper and serve. Especially good with veal or chicken or in a hero sandwich with hot Italian sausages. About 125 calories per serving.

⚖ MARINATED ROASTED PEPPERS

An elegant cold appetizer or salad.
Makes 2–4 servings

4 medium-size sweet green peppers, washed
1 tablespoon olive oil
1 tablespoon red wine vinegar
1 clove garlic, peeled and quartered

VEGETABLES

4 bay leaves
¼ teaspoon salt
Pinch pepper

Preheat broiler. Lay peppers on their sides on broiler pan and broil 2″ from the heat, turning frequently, 15–20 minutes until skins are blackened all over. Cool under running cold water and slake off blackened skin. Core peppers, seed, and cut into 1″×2″ strips. Place in a small bowl, add remaining ingredients and toss gently to mix. Cover and marinate at room temperature several hours, turning occasionally. Remove garlic and bay leaves and serve. About 90 calories for each of 2 servings, 45 calories for each of 4 servings.

PEPPERS IN SWISS CHEESE SAUCE

Makes 4 servings

5 large sweet green peppers, washed

Sauce:

2 tablespoons butter or margarine
2 tablespoons flour
1¼ cups milk
¼ pound Swiss cheese, coarsely grated
½ teaspoon salt
Pinch white pepper

Preheat broiler. Lay peppers on their sides on broiler pan and broil 2″ from heat, turning frequently, 15–20 minutes until black all over. Turn oven control from broil to 375° F. Cool peppers under cold running water and rub off blackened skins; core, seed, and cut into 2″ squares. Place peppers in an ungreased 1-quart casserole and set aside while you make the sauce. Melt butter in a saucepan over moderate heat,

blend in flour, then slowly stir in milk. Heat, stirring constantly, until thickened. Add cheese, salt, and pepper, cook, and stir 1–2 minutes longer until cheese melts and sauce is smooth. Pour over peppers and mix lightly. Cover and bake 20–25 minutes until peppers are very tender. About 160 calories per serving.

PLANTAIN

Wherever explorers sailed in warm waters, they found plantains, starchy banana-shaped fruits for which natives knew as many ways to cook as we do potatoes. Plantains taste rather like yams and, like them, are best when baked, sautéed, or candied.

To Prepare for Cooking: Peel (just as you would a banana) unless plantains are to be baked in their skins.

To Bake: Choose ripe plantains; do not peel but slit skins lengthwise down one side. Place on a baking sheet and bake, uncovered, 20 minutes at 350° F. Turn and bake 25–30 minutes longer until tender. Serve hot with lots of butter, salt and pepper.

To Sauté: Use ripe plantains; peel and quarter lengthwise. Sauté in ¼ cup butter over moderate heat, turning often, 15–20 minutes until tender. Roll in sugar and serve.

To Deep-Fry: Peel hard green plantains and slice very thin on the bias so slices are oval. Soak 1 hour in lightly salted water, drain, and pat dry on paper toweling. Fry, a few chips at a time, in 2″ cooking oil over high heat 2–3 minutes until golden. Drain on paper

Season	For Top Quality	Amount To Buy	Nutritive Value	Calories (unseasoned)
Year round	Choose ripe black-skinned plantains unless they are to be deep-fat-fried.	1 plantain will serve 1–3 depending on size.	Some vitamin A, also some of the B group	Very high— about 125 per ¼ pound serving

toweling, sprinkle with salt, and serve at room temperature.

To Candy: Peel ripe plantains, quarter lengthwise, and soak ½ hour in lightly salted water. Drain, place in a buttered 9″×9″×2″ baking dish, dot well with butter, and sprinkle heavily with light brown sugar. Bake, uncovered, 20–25 minutes at 350° F., turn, dot again with butter, and sprinkle with sugar. Bake 25–30 minutes longer until tender.

IRISH POTATOES

The Irish potato isn't Irish. It's South American, one of the New World foods brought to Europe by the conquistadors. Europe wasn't impressed and potatoes might never have been accepted if they hadn't had boosters like Sir Francis Drake, Sir Walter Raleigh, Frederick the Great, even Marie Antoinette, who wore potato flowers in her hair. The real credit for establishing potatoes, however, belongs to the poor of Ireland and Germany, who proved that they were *enjoyable* as well as edible. There are so many kinds of potatoes even experts can't keep them straight. Grocers usually classify them simply as *all-purpose, baking* or *boiling potatoes.* New potatoes, often billed separately, are boiling potatoes (*new* refers both to immature potatoes and to those that haven't been in storage; they are in best supply between mid-May and mid-September). Here are *America's Top Potatoes and How to Use Them:*

For Top Quality: Regardless of type, choose firm, well shaped, clean, blemish-free potatoes. Reject any with large green "sunburn spots" and those that are sprouting.

Calories: MODERATE—90–100 per medium-size potato. *Nutritive Value:* Some vitamin C.

Potato	Best Uses	Season	Amount To Buy
Round Whites, also marketed as Maine, Eastern, or All-purpose potatoes.	Boiling, frying, and, if a mealy type, baking	Year round but supplies may be short in late summer and early fall.	1 potato per person; there are 3–4 per pound.
Round Reds, which include the luscious little New Potatoes.	Boiling	Year round but best in the spring	2–4 potatoes per person, depending on size; there are 4–8 per pound, depending on size
California Long Whites or White Rose; also sometimes marketed as California News	Boiling	Mid-May to Mid-September; Mid-December to Mid-March	1 potato per person; there are 3–5 per pound.
Russet Burbank, more often sold as Idaho Potatoes or Bakers	Baking, frying; if closely watched, can be boiled.	Year round but supplies may be short in summer.	1 potato per person; there are 2–3 per pound

To Prepare for Cooking: Scrub and remove eyes. To preserve nutrients, do not peel.

¢ BOILED POTATOES

Makes 4–6 servings

6 medium-size potatoes, scrubbed
2 cups boiling water, chicken or beef
  broth
1 teaspoon salt

Peel potatoes only if they're to be boiled in broth or a stew, at the same time cutting out eyes and green "sunburned" spots; drop in cold water to prevent darkening. Place potatoes, water or broth, and salt (reduce amount if broth is salty) in a large saucepan, cover, and boil slowly about 30 minutes until tender. Drain and peel (if not already done). Return to pan, set uncovered over lowest heat, and shake briskly 1–2 minutes to drive off steam. Serve piping hot with butter, salt, and pepper. About 150 calories for each of 4 servings (without butter), 100 calories for each of 6 servings.

To Parboil for Use in Other Recipes: Peel potatoes and leave whole or halve. Boil halves 10 minutes in lightly salted water, whole potatoes 15–20 minutes. Do not season.

VARIATIONS:

¢ **Parsleyed Potatoes:** Roll boiled, peeled potatoes in ¼ cup each melted butter and minced parsley (or for special fragrance, ½-and-½ minced parsley and mint or basil). About 250 calories for each of 4 servings, 170 calories for each of 6 servings.

¢ **Potato Balls:** With a melon baller, cut raw, peeled potatoes into 1″ balls. (*Note:* Because of waste, you'll need 9–12 potatoes for 4–6 servings; scraps can be cooked separately and used for mashed potatoes.) Boil potato balls 15–20 minutes until just tender; drain and serve with salt, pepper, and butter or, if you like, sprinkled with minced parsley. Recipe too flexible for a meaningful calorie count.

¢ **Riced Potatoes:** Force boiled, peeled potatoes through a ricer or fine sieve, letting them mound in a serving dish. Drizzle with ¼ cup melted butter and sprinkle with 1 tablespoon minced parsley, basil, or chives. About 250 calories for each of 4 servings, 170 calories for each of 6 servings.

¢ **Mashed Potatoes:** Boil potatoes in skins as directed, drain, and dry out over low heat but do not season. Mash or beat with an electric mixer. Add ⅓ cup softened butter, salt and pepper to taste, and, depending on how creamy you like your potatoes, ¼–⅓ cup hot milk, evaporated milk, or cream. Beat briskly with whisk or mixer *just* until light. If potatoes grow cold, or if dinner is delayed, spoon into a buttered casserole, cover, and warm 8–10 minutes in a 250° F. oven. About 295 calories for each of 4 servings, 200 calories for each of 6 servings (if made with cream).

¢ BAKED POTATOES

Allow 1 large Idaho or other mealy type
  potato per person (always choose
  those of uniform size with few eyes
  and no green spots).

Preheat oven to 425° F. (Potatoes *can* be baked at any temperature between 300° F. and 450° F., but they'll be flakiest done at 425° F. They can also be baked along with other foods, but again, won't be so nice and dry.) Scrub potatoes well, then pierce almost to the center with a sharp fork so steam can escape. Bake directly on oven racks about 1 hour until tender (those baked at lower temperatures will take longer, of course, sometimes as much as ½ hour). Make an X-shaped cut in the top of each potato, press sides gently to open, then push a fat chunk of butter down inside each and sprinkle with salt and pepper.

To Oil (or Not to Oil) the Skins: If you like a soft-skinned potato, oil.

To Wrap (or Not to Wrap) in Foil: Again it's a matter of choice. Foil-wrapped potatoes will be soft skinned and moist inside. They'll also bake about 15 minutes faster.

To Speed Baking: Insert aluminum potato nails and potatoes will cook twice as fast.

To Charcoal Bake: Wrap each potato in foil and bake at edge of a moderate charcoal fire ¾–1 hour, turning 2 or 3 times. If you like crisp, charred skins, bake without wrapping (test for doneness after ½ hour).

About 100 calories per baked potato (without butter or other topping).

To Give Baked Potatoes Special Flair, top with any of the following:
Sour cream (or, for fewer calories, cottage cheese) and minced chives
Melted butter and minced chives, dill, basil, parsley, or marjoram
Melted butter, minced dill pickle, and crisp bacon bits
Melted butter and minced onion or scallions

¢ FRANCONIA POTATOES (OVEN-ROASTED POTATOES)

Makes 4 servings

½ cup melted beef or bacon drippings or cooking oil
6 medium-size potatoes, peeled, halved, parboiled, and drained
Salt

Preheat oven to 400° F. Pour drippings in a shallow roasting pan, add potatoes, turning in fat to coat. Roast uncovered, turning occasionally, about 40 minutes until tender and nut brown. Drain on paper toweling, sprinkle with salt, and serve. About 200 calories per serving.

VARIATIONS:

¢ **Potatoes Roasted with Meat:** When roast has about 1 hour longer to cook, add peeled, halved, parboiled potatoes to pan and roast uncovered, turning occasionally, until meat is done. If there are few pan drippings, add 2–3 tablespoons cooking oil. About 200 calories per serving.

¢ **Château Potatoes:** Peel 6 *raw* potatoes, quarter, and then trim each quarter until it is the size and shape of a jumbo olive. Roast as directed above, reducing cooking time to 30 minutes. Drain, season, and, if you like, sprinkle with minced parsley. About 175 calories per serving.

¢ **Parisienne Potatoes:** With a melon baller, cut raw, peeled potatoes into 1" balls. Roast and season as for Château Potatoes. About 150 calories per serving.

¢ **Sautéed Château or Parisienne Potatoes:** Cut potatoes as directed but, instead of roasting, sauté in ¼ cup clarified butter* 15–20 minutes over moderately low heat, turning frequently. About 175 calories per serving for Château Potatoes, 150 per serving for Parisienne Potatoes.

SOME WAYS TO USE LEFTOVER POTATOES

About 2–4 servings

MASHED:

Potato Casserole: Mix 2 cups mashed potatoes with ¼ cup heavy cream and 1 teaspoon onion flakes. Spoon into a buttered 1-quart casserole, top with ¼ cup grated sharp Cheddar or Swiss cheese, and bake uncovered 30 minutes at 350° F. About 345 calories for each of 2 servings, 170 calories for each of 4 servings.

Potato Cups: Beat 1 egg into 2 cups mashed potatoes and spoon into 4 buttered custard cups. Press a ½" cube Camembert, Port du Salut, or Brie cheese into the center of each, top with cracker meal, and bake 10–15 minutes at 425° F. About 300 calories for each of 2 servings, 150 calories for each of 4 servings.

Potato Patties or Croquettes: Shape into patties, roll in flour, dip in lightly beaten egg, then in toasted bread crumbs. Brown 1–2 minutes on a side in 2 tablespoons butter. *For additional flavor, mix in any of the following before* shaping (1 tablespoon to 1 cup mashed potatoes): grated or fried chopped onion; minced parsley, dill, or chives; cooked crumbled bacon; finely chopped toasted peanuts, almonds, pecans, or piñon nuts. Recipe too flexible for a meaningful calorie count.

Substitute for freshly mashed potatoes when making Farmhouse Potato Topping, Cottage Potato Casserole, or Easy Potato Soufflé-Pudding.

BOILED OR BAKED (peel before using):

Creamed Potatoes: Slice or dice potatoes. Measure, place in a saucepan, add ¼ cup heavy cream for each 1 cup potatoes, and simmer uncovered over low heat, stirring now and then, until cream has reduced by ½. Season with salt and white pepper to taste, sprinkle with minced chives, parsley, or dill, and serve. Recipe too flexible for a meaningful calorie count.

Potatoes au Gratin: Mix 2 cups sliced, diced, or coarsely grated potatoes with 1 cup Medium White Sauce or Parsley Sauce. Spoon into a buttered 1-quart *au gratin* dish, top with cracker meal or grated Cheddar cheese, and bake uncovered 20 minutes at 350° F. Brown under the broiler and serve. *Variation:* If you like, mix in any leftover peas, beans, corn, chopped asparagus, broccoli, or cauliflower and bake as directed. Recipe too flexible for a meaningful calorie count.

Potato-Onion Pie: Mix 2 cups thinly sliced potatoes with 1 thinly sliced sautéed yellow onion. Place in a buttered 9″ piepan, spread with ½ cup sour cream, and bake uncovered 20 minutes at 350° F. Sprinkle with paprika and serve. About 400 calories for each of 2 servings, 200 calories for each of 4 servings.

Substitute for freshly cooked potatoes when making any potato salad (if potatoes are firm), Hashed Brown Potatoes, O'Brien Potatoes, or Lyonnaise Potatoes.

SOME WAYS TO GLAMORIZE INSTANT MASHED POTATOES

For 4 servings

—Prepare by package directions but substitute milk, beef or chicken broth for the water and heat with 2 tablespoons each butter and Cheddar cheese spread. When potatoes are fluffy, beat in a pinch each savory and mace.
—Prepare by package directions, adding 2 tablespoons onion, celery, parsley, or mint flakes to the cooking liquid.
—Prepare by package directions, reducing amount of liquid by 2–3 tablespoons. Stir in ¼ cup sour cream and ½ teaspoon paprika before serving.
—Prepare by package directions, reducing amount of liquid by 2–3 tablespoons. Omit salt. Beat in ½ (2-ounce) tube anchovy paste, ¼ cup sour cream, and 2 tablespoons each grated yellow onion, minced fresh parsley, and tarragon.
—Prepare by package directions but omit butter and salt. Mix in ¼ cup minced stuffed green olives and 2 tablespoons each olive oil and grated yellow onion.
—Prepare by package directions and, just before serving, stir in 2 tablespoons of any of the following: prepared horseradish or spicy brown mustard; minced fresh basil, chives, dill, parsley, or scallions.
—Prepare by package directions and, just before serving, mix in ¼ cup of any of the following: any cheese spread; chopped toasted almonds, pecans, or peanuts; chopped French-fried onion rings.

STUFFED BAKED POTATOES

Makes 4 servings

4 large, hot baked potatoes
½ cup hot milk
¼ cup butter or margarine, softened to
  room temperature
1 teaspoon salt
⅛ teaspoon white pepper
Melted butter or margarine

Preheat broiler. Cut a ¼″ lengthwise

slice from top of each potato, then scoop flesh into a bowl, taking care not to break skins. Mash potatoes and beat in milk, butter, salt, and pepper. Spoon into skins, roughen surface with a fork, and brush with melted butter. Place on a lightly greased baking sheet and broil 3"–4" from heat 2–3 minutes until lightly browned. About 245 calories per serving.

VARIATION:

Add any of the following to the mashed potato mixture: 1 cup grated sharp Cheddar cheese; ½ cup crumbled blue cheese; ¼ cup minced onion, scallions, or chives; 1 (7-ounce) can drained, flaked tuna or salmon; 1 cup cooked sausage meat. Recipe too flexible for a meaningful calorie count.

¢ HASHED BROWN POTATOES

Makes 4 servings

6 large potatoes, boiled, peeled, and cut in ½" cubes
1 medium-size yellow onion, peeled and minced
3 tablespoons bacon drippings, butter, margarine, or cooking oil
1 teaspoon salt
⅛ teaspoon pepper

Brown potatoes and onion 5–7 minutes in fat in a heavy skillet over moderate heat, pressing into a pancake. Shake pan often so mixture doesn't stick. Sprinkle with salt and pepper, cut in 4 wedges, turn, brown other sides, and serve. About 235 calories per serving.

VARIATIONS:

¢ **O'Brien Potatoes:** Follow recipe above, frying ½ minced sweet green pepper and 2 tablespoons coarsely chopped pimiento with onion and potatoes. Fry 10–15 minutes, turning often, until potatoes are lightly crisp. Add salt and pepper. About 240 calories per serving.

¢ **Lyonnaise Potatoes:** Slice potatoes ¼" thick instead of cubing; omit onion. Fry potatoes in fat 10–12 minutes until golden. In a separate skillet, sauté 2

thinly sliced, peeled yellow onions in 2 tablespoons butter 8–10 minutes until golden; add to potatoes, fry 1–2 minutes longer, sprinkle with salt, pepper, and minced parsley. About 295 calories per serving.

¢ **Country Fried Potatoes:** Cut *raw*, peeled potatoes in ½" slices; omit onion. Place potatoes in a skillet with drippings called for, cover, and cook 10 minutes. Uncover and fry 10–12 minutes, stirring, until browned. Add salt and pepper and serve. About 225 calories per serving.

¢ **Oven-Fried Potatoes for a Crowd:** Peel 9 pounds potatoes and cut in ½" cubes. Place in 2 large roasting pans and drizzle each with ½ cup melted drippings or oil. Cover with foil and bake 15 minutes at 400° F.; uncover, stir, and bake 30 minutes. Raise heat to 500° F., stir, and bake 10–15 minutes until brown. Sprinkle well with salt and pepper and serve, using a slotted spoon. Makes about 20 servings. About 200 calories per serving.

FRENCH-FRIED POTATOES

Makes 4–6 servings

3 pounds Idaho or all-purpose potatoes
Shortening or oil for deep fat frying
Salt
Pepper

Peel potatoes, 1 at a time, cut into strips the length of the potato and ⅜" wide, letting each fall into cold water. When all strips are cut, soak 10 minutes in cold water. Drain and pat dry on paper toweling. Meanwhile, heat shortening or oil in a deep fat fryer over high heat (use a deep fat thermometer). When fat reaches 375° F., place ⅓ of the potatoes in frying basket and fry 8–10 minutes until golden brown. Drain on paper toweling and keep warm in a 250° F. oven while you fry the rest. Sprinkle with salt and pepper and serve very hot. About 230 calories for each of 4 servings, 155 calories for each of 6 servings.

VARIATIONS:

Twice-Fried French Fries: Prepare potatoes as directed. Heat shortening or oil to 330° F., add potatoes, about 1 cup at a time, and fry 2 minutes until lightly golden and all sputtering stops. Drain on paper toweling. Potatoes can now be held until just before serving. For the second trying, heat fat to 375° F. and fry, ⅓ of the potatoes at a time, 5 minutes until crisply golden. About 230 calories for each of 4 servings, 155 calories for each of 6 servings.

Shoestring Potatoes: Cut potatoes into matchstick strips about 2″ long and ⅛″ thick. Soak in cold water as for French fries, drain, and pat dry. Fry about ⅓ of the potatoes at a time in deep fat (375° F.) 3–5 minutes until crisp and golden. Drain on paper toweling and serve. About 230 calories for each of 4 servings, 155 calories for each of 6 servings.

SOUFFLÉ POTATOES

For this tricky recipe, you *must* have mature storage potatoes with plenty of starch. If you can't find them, don't even try to make Soufflé Potatoes. Even when the potatoes are perfect, a few slices may refuse to "puff."
Makes 4 servings

6 large mature Idaho potatoes
Cooking oil, shortening, or lard for deep fat frying
Salt

Peel potatoes, trimming so they're uniformly oval. Cut *lengthwise* into slices ⅛″ thick (they must be of uniform thickness) and soak 20 minutes in ice water. Meanwhile, heat fat in a deep fat fryer over moderately high heat; insert wire basket and deep fat thermometer. Drain potatoes and pat dry on paper toweling. When fat reaches 300° F., lift pan from heat and drop in enough slices to form a single layer. As they rise to surface, agitate basket to keep them covered with fat. When fat temperature drops to 200° F. (after

about 4 minutes), remove slices to paper toweling to drain. Repeat with remaining slices. (*Note:* You can prepare recipe to this point early in the day; cool potatoes and cover until shortly before serving. No need to refrigerate.) Reheat fat to 400° F. Drop in slices 1 at a time. They should bob to the surface at once and puff. Cook 1–2 minutes, turning as needed to brown puffs evenly. Drain on paper toweling, sprinkle with salt, and serve. Puffs will deflate on standing but may be repuffed by dropping in 400° F. fat (*Note:* If you have 2 deep fat fryers, use one for the partial cooking, the other for the puffing.) About 150 calories per serving.

SCALLOPED POTATOES

Makes 4–6 servings

1 quart very thinly sliced, peeled potatoes (you'll need 4–5 medium-size potatoes)
2 small yellow onions, peeled and sliced paper thin
¼ cup butter or margarine
2 tablespoons flour
1 tablespoon minced fresh dill or ¼ teaspoon dried dill
¼ teaspoon summer savory (optional)
1 teaspoon salt
⅛ teaspoon pepper
1½ cups milk

Preheat oven to 325° F. In a buttered 2-quart casserole build up alternate layers of potatoes and onions, beginning and ending with potatoes. Dot each onion layer with butter and sprinkle with flour, herbs, salt and pepper. Pour in milk, cover, and bake 45 minutes. Uncover and bake 30–40 minutes until potatoes are tender and almost all liquid is absorbed. Broil, if you like, to brown and serve. About 290 calories for each of 4 servings, 195 calories for each of 6 servings.

VARIATIONS:

Cream-Scalloped Potatoes: Follow recipe above, substituting light or heavy cream for milk and omitting flour. Bake as directed. If made with light cream:

about 420 calories for each of 4 servings, 285 for each of 6. If made with heavy cream: 545 calories for each of 4 servings, 365 calories for each of 6 servings.

¢ **Budget-Scalloped Potatoes:** Follow recipe above, substituting bacon drippings for butter and water for milk. Bake as directed. About 315 calories for each of 4 servings, 210 calories for each of 6 servings.

Scalloped Potatoes with Ham: Use a 2½-quart casserole. Layer 2 cups diced cooked ham in with other ingredients but omit flour. Mix 1 (10½-ounce) can condensed cream of celery or mushroom soup with ¾ cup milk and pour into casserole in place of milk. Bake as directed. About 695 calories for each of 4 servings, 465 calories for each of 6 servings.

Scalloped Potatoes with Cheese: Use a 2½-quart casserole. Layer 1½ cups grated Gruyère or sharp Cheddar cheese in with other ingredients, omitting flour. Pour 2 cups milk over all and bake as directed. About 465 calories for each of 4 servings, 310 calories for each of 6 servings.

STE. MICHELE SCALLOPED POTATOES

Potatoes scalloped the French way, with scallions, Gruyère cheese, plenty of butter and cream.
Makes 4 servings

3–4 large potatoes
½ cup thinly sliced scallions (include tops)
1 (6-ounce) package Gruyère cheese, grated
1 teaspoon salt
¼ teaspoon white pepper
½ teaspoon minced garlic
¼ cup butter or margarine
⅓ cup light cream

Preheat oven to 400° F. Peel potatoes and slice ⅛" thick, letting them drop into cold water. Drain and pat dry on paper toweling. Layer ⅓ of the potatoes in a buttered 1½-quart *au gratin* dish or shallow casserole. Add half the scallions and cheese and sprinkle with ⅓ of the salt, pepper, and minced garlic. Dot with ⅓ of the butter. Add a second layer of potatoes, scallions, and cheese and season as before. Top with remaining potatoes, seasonings, and butter. Pour cream over all and bake, uncovered, ½ hour. Reduce oven to 350° F. and bake 20–25 minutes longer until potatoes are crusty golden and fork tender. About 375 calories per serving.

EASY POTATO SOUFFLÉ-PUDDING

Makes 4 servings

2 cups hot seasoned mashed potatoes
½ cup milk
3 eggs, separated
¼ teaspoon dill
½ teaspoon salt
⅛ teaspoon white pepper

Preheat oven to 375° F. Mix potatoes and milk. Beat egg yolks lightly, then stir into potatoes along with dill, salt, and pepper. Cover loosely and cool to room temperature. Beat egg whites until soft peaks form and fold into potato mixture. Spoon into an ungreased 5-cup soufflé dish and bake, uncovered, on center rack about 35 minutes until puffed and golden. About 145 calories per serving.

FARMHOUSE POTATO TOPPING

Makes 4 servings

3 cups hot unseasoned mashed potatoes
1 egg, lightly beaten
2 tablespoons softened butter or margarine
¾ cup sour cream
⅛ teaspoon white pepper
1 teaspoon salt
¼ teaspoon nutmeg

Mix together all ingredients and use as a topping for oven-baked stews. Or spoon into a buttered shallow 1-quart casserole and broil 4" from heat 3–4 minutes. About 255 calories per serving.

COTTAGE POTATO CASSEROLE

Makes 6 servings

3 cups cream-style cottage cheese
4 cups hot unseasoned mashed potatoes
¾ cup sour cream
2 tablespoons finely chopped scallions
  (include tops)
2 teaspoons salt
⅛ teaspoon white pepper
1–2 tablespoons melted butter or
  margarine

Preheat oven to 350° F. Sieve cottage
cheese or purée in an electric blender at
medium speed. Mix with potatoes and
all remaining ingredients except butter.
Spoon into a buttered 2-quart casserole,
roughen surface with a fork, and brush
with melted butter. Bake, uncovered,
30 minutes until lightly browned. About
360 calories per serving.

DUCHESS POTATOES

Makes 6 servings

6 medium-size potatoes, boiled and
  drained
¼ cup butter or margarine
Pinch nutmeg
⅛ teaspoon white pepper
1 teaspoon salt
2 tablespoons milk
1 egg, lightly beaten
1 egg yolk, lightly beaten
1 egg beaten with 1 tablespoon cold
  water (glaze)

Peel potatoes, mash, and measure
4 cups. Beat butter, nutmeg, pepper, salt,
milk, egg and egg yolk into potatoes.
Meanwhile, preheat broiler. Fill a
pastry bag fitted with a large rosette tip
with potatoes and press out onto a
lightly greased baking sheet, forming
12 spiral cones about 2½″ in diameter.
Or simply spoon potatoes into 12
mounds. Brush lightly with egg glaze.
Broil 5″ from heat 3–5 minutes until
lightly browned and serve. About 210
calories per serving.

VARIATIONS:

– Bake 10 minutes at 450° F. instead of
broiling.

– Beat any one of the following into the
potatoes: ¼ teaspoon minced garlic,
1 tablespoon minced parsley or chives,
1 teaspoon minced basil, dill, or chervil.
Broil or bake as directed. About 210
calories per serving.

Planked Potatoes: These usually
accompany planked steak, chops, or fish.
When meat has browned on one side,
turn and transfer to oiled plank. Pipe a
ruffled border of potatoes around edge
of plank, brush with egg glaze, and broil
until meat is done. If potatoes brown
too fast, cover loosely with foil. About
210 calories per serving.

DAUPHINE POTATOES

These deep-fried potatoes, admittedly,
are somewhat tedious to make. But
they're puffy and light and so very worth
the trouble.
Makes 4–6 servings

2 cups hot unseasoned mashed potatoes
  (add no milk or cream)
¼ the recipe for Choux Pastry (do not
  cook)
1 teaspoon salt
Pinch pepper
Pinch nutmeg or mace
Cooking oil, shortening, or lard for deep
  fat frying
Flour

Mix potatoes, pastry mixture, salt,
pepper and nutmeg until smooth and
chill 1 hour. Begin heating fat in a deep
fat fryer over moderately high heat;
insert deep fat thermometer. Using a
rounded teaspoon as a measure, shape
potato mixture into small balls, logs, or
cork shapes, then roll in flour. When fat
reaches 375° F., fry potatoes, a few at
a time, 2–3 minutes until golden. Drain
on paper toweling and keep warm while
you fry the rest by setting, uncovered, in
a 250° F. oven. Serve piping hot. About
260 calories for each of 4 servings, 175
calories for each of 6 servings.

VARIATIONS:

Breaded Dauphine Potatoes: Mix and
shape potatoes by recipe above. Roll in
flour as directed, then dip in 1 egg

beaten with 1 tablespoon cold water and roll in fine dry bread crumbs. Let dry on a rack 10 minutes, then fry as above. About 320 calories for each of 4 servings, 215 calories for each of 6 servings.

Lorette Potatoes: Add ¼ cup grated Gruyère cheese to potato mixture, shape into small crescents, roll gently in flour, dip in egg mixture, then roll in crumbs as for Breaded Dauphine Potatoes (above). Fry as directed. About 370 calories for each of 4 servings, 245 calories for each of 6 servings.

¢ POTATO PANCAKES

Makes 4 servings

2 large Idaho potatoes, peeled
1 egg, lightly beaten
2 tablespoons flour
1 small yellow onion, peeled and finely
  grated
¼ teaspoon baking powder
1 teaspoon salt
2 tablespoons cooking oil

Coarsely grate potatoes into a bowl of cold water and let stand 15–20 minutes. Meanwhile mix egg and flour until smooth and stir in all remaining ingredients except oil. Drain potatoes, squeeze as dry as possible, and stir into batter. Heat oil in a large, heavy skillet over high heat 1–2 minutes. Drop potato mixture by spoonfuls into oil, shaping into 4 or 5 large cakes and flattening slightly with a spatula. Brown 1–2 minutes on each side, turn heat down low, and cook pancakes 20–25 minutes, turning frequently, so they're cooked through. Drain on paper toweling and serve piping hot. Good with sour cream or applesauce. About 150 calories per serving (without sour cream or applesauce).

RÖSTI

In German Switzerland this pie-sized potato pancake is served almost every day.
Makes 4 servings

3 large Idaho potatoes

¼ cup lard, butter, or margarine
1½ teaspoons salt
⅛ teaspoon pepper

Peel potatoes, 1 at a time, and grate moderately coarsely, letting shreds fall into cold water. When all are grated, drain well and pat dry on paper toweling. Heat fat in a heavy 9″ skillet over moderate heat 1 minute, add potatoes, salt, and pepper, toss lightly in the fat, then press down gently with a pancake turner to level the surface. Turn heat to moderately low and fry slowly about 15 minutes, without stirring, until a golden-brown crust forms on the bottom. Loosen "pancake" with a spatula and turn by easing out onto a plate. Invert onto a second plate, then slide back into skillet and brown the other side. To serve, slide onto platter and cut in wedges. About 160 calories per serving.

VARIATION:

Mix a little finely grated yellow onion into potatoes before frying. About 165 calories per serving.

POTATOES ANNA

One of the great classic potato recipes, this one is said to have been created by a lovesick French chef in honor of a beautiful lady named Anna.
Makes 6 servings

⅓ cup clarified butter*
5 large potatoes (the baking varieties
  won't work)
1½ teaspoons salt mixed with ¼
  teaspoon pepper

Preheat oven to 450° F. Brush a 9″ ovenproof glass pie dish or shallow 1½-quart casserole with butter. (Glass is better because you can check on the final browning.) Peel potatoes and slice very thin, letting slices drop into cold water. Drain and measure potatoes (you should have 6 cups); pat dry on paper toweling. Arrange the most perfect slices in slightly overlapping concentric circles over the bottom of the pie dish, then add a row around the sides. Brush generously with butter and sprinkle with salt and pepper. Layer remaining slices the same way, brushing with butter and sprinkling with salt and pepper. You needn't be so artistic about the middle layers, but do make sure potatoes are well packed. Cover dish with foil, weight down with a heavy lid, and bake on center rack 50–55 minutes until potatoes are *just* tender. Uncover, reduce heat to 425° F., move dish to lowest rack, and bake 15–20 minutes until bottom slices turn amber-brown. Take from oven, let stand 4–5 minutes, then loosen sides and bottom with a spatula, trying not to disturb the design. Invert on a heated platter and ease out potatoes. (If any should stick to the dish, simply lift out and replace in design.) Cut in wedges and serve. About 180 calories per serving.

VARIATIONS:

– Sprinkle a little finely grated Parmesan cheese between potato layers. About 195 calories per serving.

– Sprinkle a little minced fresh basil or chives between potato layers. About 180 calories per serving.

– Spread sautéed chopped onions between potatoes, using ½ cup in all. About 190 calories per serving.

¢ BOILED NEW POTATOES

Really fresh new potatoes, those dug in the spring or early summer, will cook faster than those that have been in storage. The not so new sometimes take as long as an hour to become tender.
Makes 4 servings

12 medium-size new potatoes, scrubbed
3 cups boiling water
1 or 2 sprigs mint (optional)

Place all ingredients in a large saucepan, cover, and boil gently 30–45 minutes until fork tender. Drain, discarding mint, if used, and serve potatoes in or out of their skins with butter, salt, and freshly ground pepper. About 90 calories per serving (without butter).

VARIATIONS:

¢ **Parsleyed New Potatoes:** Just before serving, peel potatoes, roll in ¼ cup melted butter, then in ¼ cup minced parsley. About 190 calories per serving.

¢ **Herbed New Potatoes:** Certain fresh herbs—chives, dill, basil, marjoram—go beautifully with new potatoes. Simply roll the boiled, peeled potatoes in ¼ cup melted butter, then in 2 tablespoons minced herbs. About 190 calories per serving.

¢ **Lemon-Glazed New Potatoes:** When potatoes are tender, peel, then warm 10–12 minutes in a heavy skillet over low heat with ¼ cup firmly packed light brown sugar and 2 tablespoons each butter, water, and lemon juice, basting constantly to glaze. About 190 calories per serving.

NEW POTATOES IN DILL SAUCE

Makes 4 servings

16 small new potatoes, boiled in their skins

Sauce:
3 tablespoons unsalted butter
2 tablespoons minced fresh dill
2 tablespoons flour
1 cup light cream
¾ teaspoon salt
⅛ teaspoon white pepper

Drain potatoes, peel, return to pan, and keep warm. Melt butter in a small saucepan over moderate heat, add dill, and heat, stirring, 1–2 minutes. Blend in flour, then add cream, salt, and pepper and heat, stirring constantly, about 5 minutes until thickened and smooth. Pour sauce over potatoes, set over lowest heat, and warm uncovered, stirring occasionally, 10–12 minutes. About 305 calories per serving.

DANISH-STYLE NEW POTATOES

Delectable! Young new potatoes in a buttery, brown sugar glaze.
Makes 6–8 servings

18 medium-size new potatoes, boiled in their skins

Glaze:

½ cup firmly packed light brown sugar
¼ cup water
2 tablespoons butter or margarine
1 teaspoon salt
2 tablespoons minced fresh dill

Drain potatoes and let cool 10 minutes. Meanwhile, heat all glaze ingredients except dill in a large, heavy skillet over moderate heat, stirring, 5–8 minutes until slightly thickened and bubbly. Reduce heat to low and stir in dill. Peel potatoes, add to skillet, and warm 10–15 minutes, rolling in glaze, until they glisten and are the color of topaz. About 255 calories for each of 6 servings, 190 calories for each of 8 servings.

SWEET POTATOES

It was Columbus who introduced America's sunny, honey sweet yams to Europe. Europeans apparently liked them from the start, because they were well established by the time Irish potatoes became acceptable.

To Prepare for Cooking: Scrub well; to preserve vitamins, cook in the skins.

¢ BOILED SWEET POTATOES OR YAMS

Makes 4 servings

4 medium-size sweet potatoes or yams
2 cups boiling water
1 teaspoon salt

Scrub potatoes well in cold water, cut off root end, and remove any bruised spots. Place in a large saucepan with water and salt, cover and boil 35–40 minutes until *just* tender (sweet potatoes tend to be mushy, so watch closely during the last 5–10 minutes). Drain and serve in or out of the skins with plenty of butter, salt, and pepper. About 150 calories per serving (without butter).

To Parboil for Use in Other Recipes: Boil as directed but reduce cooking time to 20 minutes.

VARIATIONS:

¢ **Mashed Sweet Potatoes:** Boil and drain by method above and peel. Mash with a potato masher or whip in an electric mixer. Beat in ¼ cup softened butter, 3 tablespoons honey, ¼ teaspoon each salt and mace, and a pinch pepper. About 270 calories per serving.

¢ **Orange-Flavored Mashed Sweet Potatoes:** Prepare mashed potatoes as directed above and beat in 2 tablespoons orange juice and 1 teaspoon grated orange rind along with other seasonings. About 270 calories per serving.

¢ **Maple-Flavored Mashed Sweet Potatoes:** Prepare and season mashed potatoes by basic method above, substituting maple syrup for honey and adding ¼ teaspoon vanilla. About 265 calories per serving.

¢ BAKED SWEET POTATOES OR YAMS

Makes 4 servings

4 medium-size sweet potatoes or yams

Preheat oven to 400° F. Scrub potatoes well in cold water but do not peel. Bake directly on oven rack or in a shallow baking pan 45 minutes to 1 hour or until tender. Serve piping hot with lots of butter, salt, and pepper. About 150 calories per serving (without butter).

Season	For Top Quality	Amount To Buy	Nutritive Value	Calories (unseasoned)
Year round	Choose firm, clean scar-free potatoes of uniform size.	1 potato per person; there are 2–3 per pound	Very high in vitamin A, some vitamin C	Very high— 150–70 per medium-size potato

VARIATION:

To Charcoal Bake: Wrap in foil and bake as directed for Irish potatoes.* About 150 calories per serving (without butter).

ORANGE-CANDIED SWEET POTATOES OR YAMS

Makes 4 servings

2 tablespoons butter or margarine
½ cup firmly packed dark brown sugar
¼ cup orange juice
1 teaspoon finely grated orange rind
4 medium-size sweet potatoes or yams, parboiled, peeled, and halved
1 navel orange, peeled and sectioned (garnish)

Heat butter, sugar, orange juice and rind, uncovered, in a very large, heavy skillet over moderately low heat, stirring occasionally, until sugar dissolves. Add potatoes and simmer, uncovered, 10–15 minutes, basting and turning to glaze evenly. Transfer to serving dish and keep warm. Warm orange sections in skillet 2–3 minutes, garnish potatoes, and serve. About 330 calories per serving.

VARIATION:

Substitute 1 (1-pound 8-ounce) can sweet potatoes or yams, drained, for the fresh and simmer 8–10 minutes to glaze. About 330 calories per serving.

SWEET POTATO CAKES

Nice and spicy. Delicious with baked ham.
Makes 6 servings

3 medium-size sweet potatoes, boiled and peeled
¼ cup milk
¼ cup melted butter or margarine
3 eggs
1 teaspoon baking powder
½ teaspoon ginger
¼ teaspoon cinnamon
⅛ teaspoon mace
½ teaspoon salt
Pinch pepper
¼ cup cooking oil

Mash potatoes, mix in all remaining ingredients except oil, and beat until fluffy. Heat 2 tablespoons oil in a large, heavy skillet 1–2 minutes over moderately high heat, then drop in potato mixture by the tablespoon and brown 2–3 minutes (don't try to do more than 4 or 5 cakes at a time). Using a pancake turner, turn cakes gently, flatten slightly, and brown the flip side 2–3 minutes. Keep warm in a 250° F. oven while you do the rest. Fry remaining cakes in the same way, adding more oil to the skillet as needed. Serve piping hot. About 225 calories per serving.

SWEET POTATO PUFF

Makes 6–8 servings

4 medium-size sweet potatoes, boiled and peeled
½ cup melted butter or margarine
⅓ cup milk
3 tablespoons honey or maple syrup
4 eggs
Juice and grated rind of 1 orange
1 teaspoon baking powder
½ teaspoon cinnamon
½ teaspoon cardamom
¼ teaspoon mace
¼ teaspoon salt

Preheat oven to 350° F. Mash potatoes well, mix in all remaining ingredients, and beat until fluffy. Spoon into a lightly buttered 2-quart casserole and bake, uncovered, about 45 minutes until puffy and lightly browned. About 330 calories for each of 6 servings, 250 calories for each of 8 servings.

VARIATION:

Marshmallow-Frosted Sweet Potato Puff: Stud casserole with marshmallows, then bake as directed, reducing cooking time to about 30 minutes so marshmallows are just nicely tinged with brown. About 350 calories for each of 6 servings, 265 calories for each of 8 servings.

YAM, APPLE, AND RAISIN CASSEROLE

Makes 4–6 servings

4 medium-size yams, peeled and sliced
    ½″ thick
2 apples (McIntosh, Baldwin, or
    Jonathan), peeled, cored, and cut in
    ¼″ rings
½ cup seedless raisins
½ teaspoon salt
½ cup firmly packed light or dark brown
    sugar
¼ cup butter or margarine
1 cup soft white bread crumbs
2 tablespoons melted butter or
    margarine

Preheat oven to 375° F. Layer yams,
apples, and raisins into a buttered
2-quart casserole, sprinkling with salt
as you go. Top with sugar and dot with
butter. Cover and bake 50 minutes until
yams are tender, basting once or twice.
Mix crumbs and melted butter and
scatter over yams. Bake, uncovered, 10
minutes to brown lightly. About 530
calories for each of 4 servings, 355
calories for each of 6 servings.

YAM-PECAN SOUFFLÉ

Makes 6 servings

2 teaspoons cornstarch
⅔ cup pineapple or orange juice
¼ cup firmly packed light brown sugar
4 eggs, separated
1 (1-pound 8-ounce) can yams, drained
    and mashed
1 teaspoon salt
⅛ teaspoon pepper
¼ cup finely chopped pecans

Preheat oven to 375° F. Blend
cornstarch with ⅓ cup fruit juice in a
small saucepan, add remaining juice and
the brown sugar. Cook and stir 2–3
minutes over moderate heat until
mixture boils and thickens. Beat egg
yolks lightly, mix in a little of the hot
fruit sauce, then return all to pan. Heat,
stirring, 1–2 minutes but do not allow
to boil. Mix sauce into yams, then add
salt, pepper, and pecans. Beat egg whites

until firm peaks form and fold into
yams. Spoon into an ungreased 1½-quart
soufflé dish and bake, uncovered, on
center oven rack 40–45 minutes until
puffed and golden. Rush to the table and
serve. About 235 calories per serving.

VARIATION:

Dessert Yam-Pecan Soufflé: Double the
amount of light brown sugar, omit salt
and pepper, then proceed as recipe
directs. Top with sweetened whipped
cream flavored with a little grated
orange rind or slivered crystallized
ginger. About 320 calories per serving
(including 2 tablespoons sweetened
whipped cream to top).

PUMPKIN

When baked or boiled and served with
butter or smoky-flavored bacon
drippings, pumpkin fills that need for a
different vegetable.

To Prepare for Cooking: How you plan
to cook the pumpkin determines what
should be done with it. Small pumpkins,
for example, can be baked whole, in
which case you need only cut a circle
around the stem, making a "lid," and
scoop out seeds and pulp. Pumpkins to
be boiled should be cut into 2–3″
chunks or strips and peeled.

BOILED PUMPKIN

Makes 4 servings

1 (3–4-pound) ripe pumpkin, cut in
    2–3″ chunks or strips and peeled
1 quart boiling water
1½ teaspoons salt
Pinch pepper
2–3 tablespoons butter or margarine

Place pumpkin, water, and salt in a
saucepan, cover, and boil gently 25–30
minutes until fork tender. Drain, add
pepper and butter, and serve. About 110
calories per serving.

To Parboil for Use in Other Recipes:
Boil as directed but reduce cooking time
to 15 minutes; omit seasonings.

To Steam: Place pumpkin chunks or
strips in a steamer over rapidly boiling

Season	For Top Quality	Amount To Buy	Nutritive Value	Calories (unseasoned)
Autumn	Choose small, firm, bright orange pumpkins, 6–7″ in diameter, that seem heavy for their size.	1 pound raw pumpkin yields 1 cup cooked pumpkin or 1 serving.	High in vitamin A	Moderate —about 75 per cup

water, cover, and steam 30–35 minutes until fork tender. Season and serve. About 110 calories per serving.

VARIATIONS:

Mashed Pumpkin: Boil and drain as directed, then mash. Heat, uncovered, over low heat, shaking pan now and then, 3–5 minutes to drive off excess moisture. Add pepper and butter and, if you like, 2–3 tablespoons heavy cream; mix well or beat until fluffy with an electric mixer. Also good with a little brown sugar or honey added. About 135 calories per serving (without cream, brown sugar or honey).

Pumpkin au Gratin: Prepare Mashed Pumpkin as directed, spoon into a buttered 1½-quart casserole, and top with ½ cup grated Parmesan cheese mixed with ½ cup dry white bread crumbs; drizzle with 2–3 tablespoons melted butter. Bake, uncovered, 25–30 minutes at 400° F. until golden. About 255 calories per serving.

Pumpkin and Potatoes: Mix equal parts seasoned mashed pumpkin and seasoned mashed potatoes, spoon into a buttered casserole, roughen top with a fork, and broil 5″ from heat 2 minutes until browned. Recipe too flexible for a meaningful calorie count.

BAKED WHOLE PUMPKIN

Makes 4–6 servings

1 (4-pound) ripe pumpkin
1 teaspoon salt
⅛ teaspoon pepper

3 tablespoons melted butter or margarine

Preheat oven to 375° F. Cut a 3″ circle around stem, remove and save to use as a "lid." Scoop out seeds and strings and sprinkle inside of pumpkin evenly with salt and pepper. Place pumpkin on an ungreased baking sheet and set lid on tray skin side down. Bake, uncovered, 1–1½ hours until fork tender; test lid for doneness after ¾ hour, remove if tender and set aside, otherwise continue cooking. When pumpkin is tender, remove liquid inside with a bulb baster. Using a pancake turner, lift to a large platter, pour in butter, and cover with lid. Carry to table and carve in wedges, serving skin and all. About 160 calories for each of 4 servings, 105 calories for each of 6 servings.

VARIATIONS:

Foil-Baked Pumpkin: Cut pumpkin into pieces about 4″ square; remove strings and seeds but do not peel. Sprinkle each piece with salt and pepper, dot with butter, and wrap in foil. Place on a baking sheet and bake 1–1½ hours at 375° F. until fork tender. Partially unwrap and serve each portion as you would a baked potato with extra butter, salt, and pepper. Recipe too flexible for a meaningful calorie count.

New England Baked Pumpkin: Prepare Foil-Baked Pumpkin as directed, substituting bacon drippings for butter and sprinkling each piece with 1–2 teaspoons maple or dark brown sugar and, if you like, a little cinnamon, nutmeg, and/or orange juice. Serve topped with crisply cooked crumbled bacon or diced salt pork. Recipe too flexible for a meaningful calorie count.

PUMPKIN PURÉE

Use in Pumpkin Pie or any recipe calling for pumpkin purée.
Makes about 1 quart

1 (6–7-pound) ripe pumpkin
¼ teaspoon salt

Preheat oven to 375° F. Halve pumpkin crosswise and scoop out seeds and strings. Place halves in a large baking pan, hollow side down, and bake uncovered 1½–2 hours until fork tender. Remove from oven and cool. Scrape pulp from shells and purée in an electric blender, a little at a time, or put through a food mill. Mix in salt. About 75 calories per cup.

PUMPKIN AND ONION CASSEROLE

Makes 4–6 servings

3 medium-size yellow onions, peeled, sliced thin, and separated into rings
3 tablespoons bacon drippings
1 (3–4-pound) ripe pumpkin, cut in 1″ cubes, peeled, parboiled, and drained
½ teaspoon salt
⅛ teaspoon pepper
2 teaspoons minced parsley

Preheat oven to 375° F. Stir-fry onions in drippings over moderate heat 3–5 minutes until limp, not brown. Layer pumpkin and onions (include drippings) in an ungreased 1½-quart casserole,

seasoning with salt and pepper as you go. Cover and bake 1 hour. Uncover, sprinkle with parsley, and serve. About 195 calories for each of 4 servings, 130 calories for each of 6 servings.

RUTABAGA

Rutabagas aren't just big yellow turnips but a distinct species altogether. Botanists believe they're a hybrid of turnips and cabbage and that they originated in Russia only about 250 years ago.

To Prepare for Cooking: Peel (rutabagas are dipped in melted paraffin before shipping so they'll stay fresh longer), then cut in 1″ cubes or strips for easier handling. Rutabagas are often extremely hard, so use your sharpest knife and cut carefully.

¢ BOILED RUTABAGA

Makes 4 servings

1 medium-size rutabaga, prepared for cooking
1½ cups boiling water
1½ teaspoons salt
⅛ teaspoon pepper
3–4 tablespoons butter or margarine

Place rutabaga in a large saucepan with water and salt, cover, and boil 20–30 minutes until tender. Drain well, add pepper and butter, set over low heat, and warm, shaking pan, until butter melts. Toss to mix and serve. About 150 calories per serving.

Season	For Top Quality	Amount To Buy	Nutritive Value	Calories (unseasoned)
Year round; peak months: October and November	Choose firm, fairly smooth, 2- or 3-pound rutabagas with few leaf scars around the crown.	Figure ½ pound rutabaga per serving.	High in vitamin C, fairly high in vitamin A and iron	Moderate —about 75 per ½ pound serving

To Parboil for Use in Other Recipes:
Boil by method above but reduce
cooking time to 12–15 minutes; omit
seasonings.

VARIATIONS:

⟳ ¢ **Low-Calorie Rutabaga:** Boil and
drain as directed but substitute seasoned
salt for salt. Omit butter and sprinkle
with mace. About 75 calories per serving.

¢ **Mashed Rutabaga:** Boil, drain, and
season as directed, then mash with a
potato masher. Heat, stirring, 2–3
minutes to dry off excess moisture and
serve. About 150 calories per serving.

¢ **Cottage-Style Rutabaga:** Boil 1
peeled, cubed potato and 1 peeled, sliced
carrot with rutabaga. Drain, season as
directed, and mash. About 180 calories
per serving.

Rutabaga au Gratin: Boil and drain but
do not season. Mix with 1½ cups hot
Cheese Sauce and spoon into an ungreased 2-quart *au gratin* dish. Top with
⅓ cup grated sharp Cheddar cheese
and broil 5″ from heat 3–4 minutes
until bubbly. About 335 calories per
serving.

Rutabaga with Bacon and Sour Cream:
Boil, drain, and season as directed. Stir
in ½ cup sour cream and 4 slices cooked,
crumbled bacon and serve. About 260
calories per serving.

¢ HASHED BROWN RUTABAGA

Makes 6–8 servings

3 tablespoons butter or margarine
1 medium-size rutabaga, boiled and
  mashed
2 cups hot seasoned mashed potatoes
2 tablespoons grated yellow onion

Melt butter in a large, heavy skillet over
moderate heat. Mix rutabaga, potatoes,
and onion, spoon into skillet, and pat
down with a pancake turner. Brown
bottom slowly about 5–7 minutes. Stir to
distribute brown bits throughout, pat
down again, and brown as before. Using
a pancake turner, scoop into a heated
vegetable dish, turning so that browned

parts are on top. About 160 calories for
each of 6 servings, 120 calories for each
of 8 servings.

SCALLOPED RUTABAGA AND APPLES

Makes 6 servings

1 medium-size rutabaga, quartered and
  peeled
3 apples (Baldwin, McIntosh, or
  Jonathan), peeled, cored, and sliced
  thin
¼ cup butter or margarine
1½ teaspoons salt
⅛ teaspoon pepper
¼ cup firmly packed light brown sugar
1½ cups water

Preheat oven to 400° F. Halve rutabaga
quarters lengthwise, then cut crosswise
into slices ⅛″ thick. Arrange ½ the
slices in a buttered 2-quart flameproof
casserole and top with apples. Dot with
½ the butter and sprinkle with ½ the salt,
pepper, and sugar. Top with remaining
rutabaga, butter, salt, pepper, and sugar.
Pour water over all, cover, set over high
heat until mixture boils, then transfer
to oven and bake 1 hour. Stir gently
and bake, uncovered, 20–30 minutes
longer until almost all liquid is gone.
About 185 calories per serving.

SALSIFY
(Also called Oyster Plant)

Once fairly popular, salsify now falls
into the category of "forgotten
vegetables." Too bad, because it has a
pleasing, delicate flavor. Some people
think it tastes like oysters (hence its
nickname), others insist it's more like
artichokes. Actually, there are two kinds
of salsify, the common, or white skinned,
and the rarer, more delicate black
salsify. Both are prepared exactly the
same way.

To Prepare for Cooking: Remove tops
and upper part of roots that look to
have been wound with cord. Scrub
roots with a vegetable brush in cold
water. Peel roots, 1 at a time, and cut

Season	For Top Quality	Amount To Buy	Nutritive Value	Calories (unseasoned)
Summer, fall, and winter	Choose firm roots the size and shape of small carrots.	Allow 3 roots (⅓–½ pound) per person.	Some minerals	Moderate —85–90 per average serving

into 2″ chunks, letting them fall into acidulated water (1 quart cold water mixed with the juice of 1 lemon) to keep them from turning brown. When all roots are prepared, soak 10 minutes longer in acidulated water.

BOILED SALSIFY

Makes 4 servings

2 bunches salsify, prepared for cooking
1½ cups boiling water
2 tablespoons butter or margarine
½ teaspoon salt
Pinch pepper

Place salsify in a saucepan with water, cover, and boil 20–25 minutes until tender. Drain, add butter, salt, and pepper, set over low heat, and warm uncovered, shaking pan gently, 2–3 minutes until butter melts. About 140 calories per serving.

To Parboil for Use in Other Recipes: Boil as directed but reduce cooking time to 15 minutes; omit seasonings.

VARIATIONS:

Herbed Salsify: Prepare as directed, adding 1 tablespoon each minced parsley and chives along with butter, salt, and pepper. About 140 calories per serving.

Salsify with Dill and Sour Cream: Prepare as directed, adding ¼ cup sour cream and 2 tablespoons minced dill along with butter, salt, and pepper. About 195 calories per serving.

Creamed Salsify: Boil and drain as directed but do not season; mix with 1½ cups hot Medium White Sauce, season to taste with salt and white pepper, and warm uncovered over low heat, stirring occasionally, 5 minutes to blend flavors. About 245 calories per serving.

SORREL

(Also called Sour Dock and Patience)

Most of us find these crisp leaves too bitter to eat alone (except when puréed into sorrel soup), so we toss the youngest leaves into salads to add refreshing bite and steam the older with spinach—just a handful—to add character.

To Prepare: Wash by plunging up and down in a sinkful of tepid water; drain.

To Steam: Place sorrel in an enamel, stainless-steel, or teflon-lined pot, add

Season	For Top Quality	Amount To Buy	Nutritive Value	Calories (unseasoned)
Year round	Choose young, tender, crisp leaves about 2–3″ long.	¼–½ pound per person, depending on whether sorrel is to be served alone or mixed with other greens.	High in vitamins A and C	Low—about 40 per cup

no water, cover, and steam over moderate heat 10–15 minutes until tender. Toss with melted butter or bacon drippings, season to taste with salt and pepper.

To Steam with Sorrel: Use 1 part sorrel to 3 parts spinach and steam following the recipe for Steamed Spinach.

SPINACH

"Many English people that have learned it of the Dutch," wrote a seventeenth-century British herbalist, "doe stew the herbe in a pot without any other moisture than its owne and after the moisture is a little pressed from it, they put butter and a little spice unto it, and make therewith a dish that many delight to eate of." The "herbe" was spinach and we haven't found a better way to cook it today, whether it's crinkly or plain leafed or that supermarket newcomer, New Zealand spinach. It, by the way, isn't spinach at all; we include it here because it's best when cooked like spinach.

To Prepare for Cooking:

Bulk Spinach: Sort, removing any blemished leaves; trim off roots and coarse stems. Wash leaves by plunging up and down in a sinkful of tepid water (this helps float out sand) and rinse several times in cool water. Lift from rinse water, shake lightly, and place directly in cooking pot.

Bagged Spinach: Remove coarse stems and deteriorating leaves; rinse well.

Cooking Tip: Always cook spinach in an enamel, stainless-steel, or teflon-lined pot so it will not darken or taste of metal.

STEAMED SPINACH

Makes 4 servings

2 pounds bulk spinach or 2 (10-ounce) bags prewashed spinach, prepared for cooking
3 tablespoons melted butter or margarine
1 teaspoon salt
⅛ teaspoon pepper

Place spinach in a large pot, add no water, cover, and steam 3–5 minutes over moderate heat until slightly wilted but still bright green. Drain, add seasonings, and toss to mix. About 115 calories per serving.

VARIATIONS:

To Serve Cold: Steam as directed but do not drain or season; cool, then cover and chill (see Vegetable Seasoning Chart for dressing ideas). Drain before dressing.

Season	For Top Quality	Amount To Buy	Nutritive Value	Calories (unseasoned)
Year round for spinach; peak months: March –July; spring and early summer for New Zealand spinach	Buy loose or bulk spinach if possible and choose crisp, dark green moist leaves with roots attached. If buying prewashed, bagged spinach, make sure it's not wilted, slimy, or dry.	½ pound bulk spinach per person; 1 (10-ounce) bag serves 2.	Very high in vitamin A; high in iron and vitamin C	Low—about 40 per cup

⚖️ **Low-Calorie Spinach:** Steam and drain as directed but omit butter. Dress with 3 tablespoons lemon juice or low-calorie Italian dressing. About 40 calories per serving.

Chopped Spinach: Chop steamed, drained spinach and toss with butter, salt, and pepper. About 115 calories per serving.

Puréed Spinach: Purée steamed, *undrained* spinach in an electric blender at high speed or put through a food mill. Return to pan, add seasonings, cover, and warm, stirring occasionally, 3–4 minutes. About 115 calories per serving.

Italian-Style Spinach: Steam and drain as directed; omit butter and dress with 3 tablespoons olive oil; if you like, toss in ¼ crushed clove garlic. About 135 calories per serving.

Spinach with Bacon: Steam and drain as directed; omit butter and toss with 2 tablespoons bacon drippings and ¼ cup crisp crumbled bacon. About 115 calories per serving.

Creamed Spinach: Steam as directed; drain in a fine sieve, pressing as dry as possible, chop fine, and return to pan. Add 1 cup hot Medium White Sauce and warm, uncovered, over low heat, stirring occasionally, 3–5 minutes. About 140 calories per serving.

Spinach au Gratin: Steam as directed; drain in a fine sieve, pressing as dry as possible, chop fine, and return to pan. Mix with 1 cup hot Cheese Sauce, place in an ungreased 1-quart casserole, top with ½ cup grated Cheddar cheese mixed with ½ cup coarse dry bread crumbs, and broil 4–5″ from heat 2–3 minutes to brown. About 280 calories per serving.

SPINACH RING

A showy way to shape spinach for a special dinner.
Makes 6 servings

7 (*10-ounce*) *packages frozen chopped spinach, cooked by package directions*
3 *tablespoons butter or margarine*

1 *teaspoon salt*
⅛ *teaspoon pepper*
⅛ *teaspoon nutmeg*

Drain spinach in a strainer, pressing as dry as possible. Mix with remaining ingredients. Pack *tightly* in a lightly buttered 1-quart ring mold, then invert at once on a hot platter. If you like, fill center with hot Creamed Mushrooms or a small bowl of sauce (see Vegetable Seasoning Chart). About 110 calories per serving (unfilled).

VARIATION:

Baked Spinach Ring: Drain spinach as directed, mix in 2 lightly beaten eggs and all seasonings called for. Pack into mold and bake, uncovered, in a water bath at 350° F. 30–40 minutes until firm. Loosen edges, invert, and serve. About 140 calories per serving.

⊠ CURRIED SPINACH

Exotic and easy.
Makes 4 servings

2 (*10-ounce*) *packages frozen chopped spinach, cooked by package directions and drained well*
1 *tablespoon butter or margarine*
2 *tablespoons sour cream*
2 *teaspoons curry powder*
⅛ *teaspoon nutmeg*
½ *teaspoon salt*
Pinch pepper

Keep spinach warm. In a separate small saucepan, melt butter over low heat. Blend in remaining ingredients, pour over spinach, toss well to mix, and serve. About 80 calories per serving.

⊠ SPINACH DRESSED WITH OIL AND VINEGAR

The Italian way to season spinach. And very good, too.
Makes 4 servings

¼ *cup olive oil*
2 (*10-ounce*) *packages frozen leaf spinach (do not thaw)*
1 *clove garlic, peeled and crushed*

3 tablespoons cider vinegar
½ teaspoon salt
Pinch pepper

Place olive oil, spinach, and garlic in a saucepan and simmer, uncovered, about 15 minutes until spinach is heated through. Stir from time to time, breaking up any frozen chunks. Remove from heat, add remaining ingredients, and toss well to mix. Serve hot or at room temperature. About 165 calories per serving.

SPINACH BAKED WITH MUSHROOMS

Makes 4–6 servings

2 pounds fresh spinach, steamed, or 2 (10-ounce) packages frozen chopped spinach, cooked by package directions
⅔ cup light cream
½ teaspoon salt
Pinch pepper
3 tablespoons butter or margarine
½ pound mushrooms, wiped clean and sliced thin

Topping:
2 tablespoons butter or margarine
1 cup coarse dry white bread crumbs
¼ cup coarsely chopped toasted, blanched almonds

Preheat oven to 375° F. Drain spinach in a sieve, pressing as dry as possible. If using fresh spinach, chop fine. Mix spinach with cream, salt, and pepper. Melt butter in a skillet over moderately high heat, add mushrooms, and sauté 2–3 minutes until golden. Mix mushrooms and spinach, then spoon into a buttered 1-quart casserole. For the topping, melt butter in a small saucepan over moderate heat, stir in crumbs, and brown lightly 1–2 minutes. Add almonds, toss to mix, and sprinkle over spinach. Bake, uncovered, 20–30 minutes until lightly browned. About 355 calories for each of 4 servings, 235 calories for each of 6 servings.

SPINACH-ONION-SOUR CREAM BAKE

Makes 4 servings

2 tablespoons butter or margarine
1 medium-size yellow onion, peeled and minced
2 (10-ounce) packages frozen chopped spinach (do not thaw)
¼ teaspoon mace
1 teaspoon salt
⅛ teaspoon pepper
1 cup sour cream

Preheat oven to 325° F. Melt butter in a large saucepan over moderate heat, add onion, and stir-fry 5–8 minutes until pale golden. Add spinach, mace, salt, and pepper, cover, and simmer 15 minutes. Uncover, break up any frozen chunks, and simmer uncovered 10 minutes longer until all moisture has evaporated. Mix in sour cream. Spoon into an unbuttered 9" piepan, bake uncovered ½ hour, and serve. About 220 calories per serving.

SPINACH CUSTARDS

These custards are especially good with cold baked ham.

Makes 2 servings

1 (10-ounce) package frozen chopped spinach, cooked by package directions
¼ teaspoon cornstarch
½ cup milk
½ teaspoon salt
2 eggs, lightly beaten
1 tablespoon finely grated yellow onion
1 tablespoon finely chopped pimiento (optional)

Preheat oven to 375° F. Drain spinach in a fine sieve, pressing as dry as possible. Chop very fine, then return to saucepan and set over low heat to dry, 1–2 minutes. Remove from heat and set aside. Blend cornstarch with 1 tablespoon milk and mix into spinach along with all remaining ingredients including remaining milk. Ladle into 2 well-buttered custard cups, set in a shallow baking pan, and pour hot water into pan to a depth of about 1". Bake, uncovered, on center oven rack 30–35

Season	For Top Quality	Amount To Buy	Nutritive Value	Calories (unseasoned)
Year round for all three types	Choose firm, tender skinned, blemish-free squash that are heavy for their size.	½ pound per person	Some vitamins A and C	Very low— about 30 per cup

minutes until a knife inserted near the center of a custard comes out clean. Remove cups from water bath and cool 3–5 minutes. Serve in cups or, if you prefer, loosen edges with a spatula and invert to unmold. About 165 calories per serving.

SQUASH

No American Indian food seems to have impressed Europeans more than squash, perhaps because there are so many varieties of it. Fortunately they can be classified as either *summer* or *winter* *squash*. Our word "squash," incidentally, comes from the Indian *"askutasquash,"* meaning "green thing eaten green."

The Three Kinds of Summer Squash

These tender skinned, delicately flavored squash take equally well to saucepan, skillet, or oven. Most can be used interchangeably for one another.

Yellow Squash: There are two types, the *crookneck* and the slightly plumper *straightneck*. Both are sunny yellow outside, pale and succulent inside. About 2–4 per pound.

Pattypan (also called *cymling*): Flat, round, pale green squash with scalloped edges. They can be small as a biscuit or big as a pie. The large may weigh 1–2

pounds; the small a fraction of that.

Zucchini (also called *courgette*): *This* isn't one squash but three, all green skinned and white fleshed. The one called *zucchini* is cucumber-sized with dark lacy stripes. The other two are the slimmer yellow and green striped *cocozelle,* and the more rounded *caserta* with two-tone green stripes. About 2–4 per pound.

To Prepare for Cooking:

Yellow Squash and Zucchini: Cut off ends and scrub well; peel only if skins are old. If young and tender leave whole; otherwise cut in ½" slices, or halve and seed.

Pattypan: Wash in cool water, peel, seed, and cut in ½" cubes.

Four Favorite Winter Squash

These hard-skinned varieties are best when boiled and mashed or baked in the skins.

Acorn Squash: Not much bigger than a large avocado, these are small enough to handle easily. Usually green, but sometimes orange, they're moist and tender. About 1–2 pounds each.

Butternut: A large pear-shaped squash with thin, fawn-colored skin and fine,

Season	For Top Quality	Amount To Buy	Nutritive Value	Calories (unseasoned)
Year round for acorn squash; fall and winter for the others	Choose heavy squash with hard, clean un-blemished skins.	½ pound per person	Very high in vitamin A, some vitamin C and iron	Very high— about 130 per cup

bright orange flesh. About 2–3 pounds each.

Buttercup: Smallish, turban-shaped, green- and gray-striped squash with faintly sweet orange flesh. About 2 pounds each.

Hubbard: A rough, tough, green or orange skinned giant often sold by the chunk. It is drier and stringier than smaller squash.

To Prepare for Boiling: Halve, scoop out seeds and pulp; peel and cut in 1–2″ chunks. Work slowly and carefully because squash are hard and their skins slippery. *To Prepare for Baking:* If very small, leave whole; otherwise halve lengthwise and remove seeds and pulp. If extra large, quarter or cut in sixths or eighths. Do not peel. When squash are baked whole, halve and seed before serving.

Some Lesser Lights: In addition to the winter squash above, there are others, most of them used as decoration because they're not very moist or tender. Still, if cooked like Hubbard squash, they can be palatable. These varieties are:
 Warren Turban, Delicious, Marblehead, Boston Marrow, Cushaw

BOILED SUMMER SQUASH

Makes 4 servings

2 pounds summer squash (yellow, pattypan, or zucchini), prepared for cooking
1 teaspoon salt
½ cup boiling water
⅛ teaspoon pepper
3 tablespoons butter or margarine

Place squash in a large saucepan, add salt and water, cover, and boil until crisp tender—10–15 minutes for slices or cubes, 20–25 for halves, 30–40 for whole squash. Drain well, return to pan, and warm uncovered, shaking pan occasionally, 2–3 minutes to drive off moisture. Season with pepper and butter and serve. About 105 calories per serving.

To Steam: Place prepared squash in a steamer over boiling water, cover, and steam, using times above as a guide. Remove from steamer and season with salt, pepper, and butter. About 105 calories per serving.

To Parboil for Use in Other Recipes: Boil or steam as directed, reducing cooking time to 5 minutes for slices or cubes, 10–15 for halves, 15–20 for whole squash. Omit seasonings.

VARIATIONS:

To Serve Cold: Slice or cube; boil and drain as directed. Chill in ice water, drain, mix with dressing (see Vegetable Seasoning Chart for ideas), and chill until ready to serve.

⚖ **Low-Calorie Squash:** Boil and drain as directed but omit butter. Dress with low-calorie herb, garlic, or Italian dressing. About 35 calories per serving.

Squash and Carrots: Combine equal amounts sliced boiled carrots and squash, season as directed, then stir in 1 teaspoon minced fresh mint or basil. About 120 calories per serving.

Squash and Scallions: Cook 4–6 minced scallions with squash and season as directed. About 110 calories per serving.

Italian-Style Zucchini: Cook 1 clove peeled, halved garlic with zucchini and dress with 2 tablespoons olive oil and 1 tablespoon red wine vinegar instead of butter. About 95 calories per serving.

SKILLET SQUASH AND ONIONS

Makes 4 servings

3 tablespoons butter, margarine, or olive oil
2 pounds yellow squash or zucchini, scrubbed and sliced ½″ thick
3 medium-size yellow onions, peeled and sliced ¼″ thick
1 teaspoon salt
¼ teaspoon summer savory
¼ teaspoon oregano
⅛ teaspoon nutmeg
⅛ teaspoon pepper

Heat butter or oil over low heat in a

large skillet 1–2 minutes. Add remaining ingredients and stir gently to mix. Cover and cook over low heat, stirring occasionally, 30–35 minutes until squash is fork tender. About 135 calories per serving.

SCALLOPED SUMMER SQUASH

Makes 4 servings

2 pounds summer squash, boiled
3 tablespoons butter or margarine
3 tablespoons grated yellow onion
¾ teaspoon salt
⅛ teaspoon pepper

Topping:

½ cup fine cracker crumbs mixed with 1
  tablespoon melted butter or margarine

Preheat oven to 350° F. Drain squash well and mash with a potato masher. Mix in all remaining ingredients except topping. Spoon into a buttered shallow 1½-quart casserole and top with buttered crumbs. Bake, uncovered, 25–30 minutes until lightly browned. About 170 calories per serving.

PARMESAN STUFFED SQUASH

Good for a party because the squash can be prepared well ahead of time.
Makes 4–6 servings

6 medium-size zucchini or yellow
  squash, halved and parboiled
1½ teaspoons salt
¼ teaspoon pepper
¼ cup butter or margarine
½ cup finely chopped yellow onion
3 cups soft bread crumbs
⅛ teaspoon paprika
½ cup grated Parmesan cheese
1 tablespoon minced parsley

Scoop out squash halves, leaving shells ¼″ thick; discard seedy centers. Sprinkle with 1 teaspoon salt and the pepper; arrange in a lightly buttered 13″× 9″×2″ pan. Preheat oven to 425° F. Melt butter in a skillet over moderate heat, add onion, and sauté 8 minutes until golden. Remove from heat and mix in all remaining ingredients including remaining ½ teaspoon salt.

Stuff shells with crumb mixture. (*Note:* You may prepare recipe to this point early in the day; cool, cover, and chill. Bring to room temperature before proceeding.) Bake, uncovered, 20–30 minutes until crumbs are lightly browned and squash tender. About 300 calories for each of 4 servings, 200 calories for each of 6 servings.

BAKED YELLOW SQUASH PUDDING

Makes 6–8 servings

4 pounds yellow squash, scrubbed and
  sliced ¼″ thick
3 medium-size yellow onions, peeled and
  cut in thin wedges
¼ cup boiling water
¼ cup butter or margarine
¼ teaspoon thyme
⅛ teaspoon rosemary
⅛ teaspoon nutmeg
1 teaspoon salt
⅛ teaspoon pepper
1 tablespoon light brown sugar
¼ cup minced parsley

Preheat oven to 350° F. Place squash, onions, water, and butter in a large kettle, cover, and simmer 25–30 minutes until squash is mushy. Uncover and simmer 10 minutes longer, mashing large pieces with a fork. Stir in all remaining ingredients. Transfer to a buttered 3-quart *au gratin* dish and bake, uncovered, 2½ hours until light caramel in color. About 135 calories for each of 6 servings, 100 calories for each of 8 servings.

YELLOW SQUASH AND CHIVE CHEESE AU GRATIN

Makes 6–8 servings

4 pounds yellow squash, scrubbed and
  sliced 1″ thick
1 (10½-ounce) can condensed beef
  consommé
2 tablespoons minced onion
¼ cup butter or margarine
6 (3-ounce) packages cream cheese with
  chives, softened to room temperature
2 tablespoons minced parsley

2 tablespoons minced fresh dill or
½ teaspoon dried dill

Topping:

½ cup cracker meal mixed with
2 tablespoons melted butter or
margarine

Preheat oven to 375° F. Place squash,
consommé, and minced onion in a large
saucepan, cover, and simmer 15 minutes
until squash is crisp-tender. Meanwhile,
in a separate saucepan, heat butter and
cheese over lowest heat, stirring, until
melted and smooth. Stir in parsley and
dill. When squash is done, drain
consommé into cheese sauce and beat
until smooth. Place squash in a buttered
shallow 3-quart casserole and pour
cheese sauce over all. Sprinkle topping
over squash and bake, uncovered, 40
minutes until browned. About 450
calories for each of 6 servings, 335
calories for each of 8 servings.

BAKED ZUCCHINI WITH ROSEMARY

Makes 4–6 servings

2 pounds zucchini, scrubbed
2 cups boiling water
1 medium-size yellow onion peeled and
chopped fine
1 clove garlic, peeled and crushed
¼ cup olive oil
Juice of ½ lemon
3 tablespoons flour mixed with ¼ cup
cold water
⅛ teaspoon rosemary
⅛ teaspoon summer savory
⅛ teaspoon nutmeg
1 teaspoon salt
⅛ teaspoon pepper
¼ cup grated Parmesan cheese
¼ cup minced parsley

Topping:

1½ cups soft white bread crumbs
2 tablespoons grated Parmesan cheese
⅓ cup melted butter or margarine

Preheat oven to 325° F. Quarter each
zucchini by cutting in half lengthwise,
then in half crosswise. Place in a large
saucepan with boiling water, cover, and

boil 15–20 minutes until crisp-tender.
Drain, reserving 1 cup cooking water.
Sauté onion and garlic in oil in a heavy
skillet over moderate heat 8 minutes
until onion is golden. Stir in cooking
water and all remaining ingredients
except cheese, parsley, and topping.
Heat, stirring constantly, until thickened
and smooth. Off heat, mix in cheese and
parsley. Arrange half the zucchini in a
buttered 8" × 8" × 2" baking dish. Cover
with half the sauce. Add remaining
zucchini and sauce. Mix topping
and sprinkle over surface. Bake, uncovered, about 1 hour until browned
and bubbly. About 455 calories for each
of 4 servings, 305 calories for each of 6
servings.

ZUCCHINI AND LEEK PUDDING-SOUFFLÉ

Half soufflé, half pudding, and one of
the best ways we know to prepare
zucchini.

Makes 4 servings

4 medium-size zucchini, scrubbed and
coarsely grated
2 leeks or scallions, trimmed and sliced
3 shallots, peeled and minced
1 tablespoon olive oil
1½ teaspoons salt
¼ teaspoon marjoram
Pinch nutmeg
⅛ teaspoon freshly ground black pepper
2 tablespoons margarine
3 tablespoons flour
1 cup condensed beef consommé
2 tablespoons grated Parmesan cheese
2 egg yolks, lightly beaten
6 egg whites
⅛ teaspoon cream of tartar

Stir-fry zucchini, leeks, and shallots in
olive oil with 1 teaspoon of the salt, the
marjoram, nutmeg, and pepper in a
large, heavy skillet over moderately
high heat about 5 minutes until lightly
golden. Reduce heat to lowest point and
keep warm. Meanwhile, melt margarine
in a small saucepan over moderate heat
and blend in flour. Off heat, whisk in
consommé, return to heat, and cook,
stirring, 3–5 minutes until thickened and

no raw flour taste remains. Remove from heat and mix in 1 tablespoon of the Parmesan, ¼ teaspoon of salt, and zucchini mixture. Whisk in egg yolks, place plastic wrap flat on top, and cool to room temperature. (*Note:* You may prepare recipe up to this point ahead of time and chill until about 2 hours before serving. Let sauce come to room temperature before proceeding.) Preheat oven to 375°. Butter a 1-quart soufflé dish, add remaining tablespoon of Parmesan, and tilt dish round and round to coat. Tap out excess cheese. Beat egg whites until frothy, add cream of tartar and remaining ¼ teaspoon salt, and beat until fairly stiff peaks form. Whisk about ¼ of the beaten whites into the zucchini mixture, then fold in remaining whites with a rubber spatula. Pour into prepared soufflé dish and bake, uncovered, on center oven rack 40–45 minutes until puffed and touched with brown. Serve at once. About 215 calories per serving.

ARMENIAN ZUCCHINI CUSTARD

Makes 4–6 servings

2 pounds zucchini, scrubbed and
*   coarsely grated*
1 medium-size yellow onion, peeled and
*   minced*
1 clove garlic, peeled and crushed
3 tablespoons olive oil
⅓ cup minced parsley
⅛ teaspoon thyme
⅛ teaspoon rosemary
1 teaspoon salt
⅛ teaspoon pepper
5 eggs
½ cup sifted flour
¾ cup grated Parmesan cheese

Preheat oven to 300° F. Stir-fry zucchini, onion, and garlic in oil in a large, heavy skillet over moderate heat 10–12 minutes until zucchini is tender. Mix in parsley, thyme, rosemary, salt, and pepper. Beat eggs until frothy, then mix in flour and Parmesan. Stir zucchini mixture into eggs, spoon into a buttered 1½-quart casserole, and bake uncovered 1–1¼ hours until a silver knife inserted

in the center comes out clean. About 360 calories for each of 4 servings, 240 calories for each of 6 servings.

BOILED WINTER SQUASH

Makes 4 servings

2 pounds winter squash (butternut,
*   acorn, buttercup, or Hubbard),*
*   prepared for boiling*
1½ cups boiling water
1 teaspoon salt
Pinch pepper
2 tablespoons butter or margarine

Place squash, water, and salt in a saucepan, cover, and boil gently 15–20 minutes until fork tender. Drain, add pepper and butter, and serve. About 180 calories per serving.

To Parboil for Use in Other Recipes: Boil as directed, reducing cooking time to 10 minutes; omit seasonings.

VARIATIONS:

Mashed Winter Squash: Boil and drain as directed and mash with a potato masher. Add pepper and butter and, if you like, 2 tablespoons cream. Mix or beat with an electric mixer until fluffy. About 180 calories per serving (without cream).

Spicy Mashed Squash in Orange Cups: Fill 4–6 large orange cups* with hot mashed squash, sprinkle each with cinnamon sugar, and top with a marshmallow. Broil 4–5″ from heat 2 minutes until marshmallow is lightly browned. About 220 calories per serving (with 1 teaspoon cinnamon sugar to top each orange cup).

BAKED BUTTERNUT OR ACORN SQUASH

Makes 4 servings

1 (2-pound) butternut or acorn squash,
*   halved lengthwise and seeded*
1 teaspoon salt
¼ teaspoon pepper
2 tablespoons butter or margarine

Preheat oven to 375° F. Place each piece of squash hollow side up on a square of foil large enough to wrap it; sprinkle with salt and pepper and dot with butter. Wrap tightly. Place squash on a baking sheet and bake 45 minutes until fork tender. Unwrap and serve with extra butter if you like. About 180 calories per serving.

To Charcoal Bake: Season and wrap each piece of squash as directed. Bake on a grill set 3–4″ above a moderately hot charcoal fire ¾–1 hour, turning 2 or 3 times. About 180 calories per serving.

VARIATION:

Before wrapping add a little honey or maple syrup, brown, maple, or cinnamon sugar, or orange marmalade to squash along with butter, salt, and pepper (about 2 tablespoons in all will be enough). Wrap and bake as directed. About 210 calories per serving.

BAKED HUBBARD SQUASH

Because this is such a giant squash, it requires special baking instructions. Makes 8 servings

4–5 pounds Hubbard squash (try to get a whole small squash rather than a chunk of a giant one), prepared for baking*
1½ teaspoons salt
¼ teaspoon pepper
¼ cup butter or margarine

Preheat oven to 400° F. Place each piece of squash hollow side up on a piece of foil large enough to wrap it, sprinkle evenly with salt and pepper, and dot with butter; wrap tightly and place in a roasting pan. Bake about 1 hour until fork tender. Unwrap and serve with extra butter if you like. About 180 calories per serving.

VARIATIONS:

Mashed Hubbard Squash: Bake as directed, then scoop flesh from skin and mash with a potato masher; taste for salt and pepper and adjust. Add 2 tablespoons melted butter and beat until fluffy. About 205 calories per serving.

"Candied" Hubbard Squash: Just before wrapping squash pieces, sprinkle with

¼ cup light brown sugar, or drizzle with ¼ cup maple syrup or honey. Wrap and bake as directed. About 205 calories per serving.

FRUIT-GLAZED BUTTERNUT OR ACORN SQUASH

Makes 4 servings

1 (2-pound) butternut or acorn squash, halved, seeded, peeled, and sliced ½″ thick
1½ cups pineapple or orange juice
¼ cup firmly packed light brown sugar
½ teaspoon salt
3 tablespoons melted butter or margarine

Preheat oven to 350° F. Arrange squash in an ungreased 1½-quart casserole. Mix remaining ingredients and pour over squash. Cover and bake about 45 minutes, basting 2 or 3 times, until fork tender. Uncover, baste, and bake 10 minutes longer to glaze lightly. About 310 calories per serving.

VARIATION:

Substitute Hubbard squash for the butternut or acorn and increase baking time to about 1 hour. About 310 calories per serving.

BUTTERNUT SQUASH PARMIGIANA

An unusual way to prepare butternut squash, but the butter, cheese, and bread crumbs enhance its mellow flavor. Makes 4 servings

1 (2-pound) butternut or acorn squash, halved, seeded, peeled, cut in 1″ chunks, and parboiled
1 teaspoon salt
Pinch pepper
2 tablespoons butter or margarine
¼ cup toasted fine bread crumbs
¼ cup grated Parmesan cheese

Preheat oven to 350° F. Arrange squash in an ungreased shallow 1½-quart casserole, sprinkle evenly with salt and pepper, and dot with butter. Mix crumbs and cheese and sprinkle on top. Cover and bake 25–30 minutes until fork tender. Raise oven temperature to 400° F., uncover, and bake 10 minutes longer to brown. About 230 calories per serving.

VARIATION:

Substitute Hubbard squash for the butternut or acorn and prepare as directed. About 230 calories per serving.

TOMATOES

The astonishing truth about tomatoes is that for centuries people considered them poisonous. They weren't eaten in this country until about 150 years ago, when a New Jersey farmer stood on the Salem County Courthouse lawn and ate one publicly to prove he would neither sicken nor die. He made his point and soon the most doubting Thomases were eating tomatoes. Today, of course, it's difficult to imagine life without them. Here are the most popular types and how to use them:

Red Globe Tomatoes: These are the juicy, everyday tomatoes, good either raw or cooked. There are 3–4 per pound.

Beefsteak Tomatoes: These large, firm tomatoes are perfect for broiling or slicing into sandwiches. About 1–2 per pound.

Cherry Tomatoes: Juicy, bite-size tomatoes ideal for picnics or cocktail snacks. About 30 in a 1-pint carton.

Plum Tomatoes: Sometimes red, sometimes golden, these plump, mellow Italian tomatoes cook superbly. About 5–6 per pound.

Cranberry Tomatoes: These are the tiny, tart "wild" tomatoes occasionally carried by gourmet groceries. Toss into salads or serve as a cocktail snack to be eaten like nuts. About 100 per pint.

Green Tomatoes: There are two types: the small *immature green* that are used in pickles and relishes and the larger *mature green* that are excellent for frying or broiling. From 3–8 per pound.

To Ripen: Do not (repeat DO NOT) stand green tomatoes on a sunny window sill, because they'll ripen unevenly and become pithy. Instead, place in a perforated bag or box with a ripe apple and set in a cool (65–75° F.) spot.

To Peel: Do not core. Spear stem end with a long-handled fork and twirl slowly over an open flame just until skin splits. Or, if you prefer, twirl slowly in boiling water about ½ minute. Plunge into ice water, core, and slip off skin.

To Seed and Juice: Halve tomatoes crosswise and squeeze gently in your hand—seeds and juices will spurt out. To save juice, squeeze over a strainer set in a bowl. The strainer catches the seeds, which can be tossed out.

Serving Tip: If tomatoes are to go into a sandwich, slice from top to bottom instead of crosswise. There'll be much less juice to make the bread soggy.

Season	For Top Quality	Amount To Buy	Nutritive Value	Calories (unseasoned)
Year round but the best are summer tomatoes	Choose firm, well-formed tomatoes of good strong color (whether red, green, or yellow) with smooth, unblemished skins.	1 medium-size tomato per person; 1 pound will serve 4.	Fairly high in vitamins A and C	Very low—about 35 per medium-size tomato

⊠ FRIED TOMATOES

Makes 4 servings

*3 tablespoons butter, margarine, bacon
  drippings, or cooking oil*
*4 large, firm, ripe beefsteak tomatoes,
  washed and sliced ¾" thick (do not
  peel)*
½ teaspoon salt
⅛ teaspoon pepper

Heat butter 1 minute in a large, heavy
skillet over moderate heat. Add
tomatoes and fry 3–4 minutes on a side
until golden brown. Sprinkle with salt
and pepper and serve. About 110
calories per serving.

VARIATIONS:

⊠ **Fried Tomatoes with Sour Cream:**
Transfer fried tomatoes to platter and
keep warm. Blend 2 teaspoons flour into
skillet drippings, mix in ½ cup milk, and
heat, stirring 1–2 minutes until
thickened. Off heat, mix in ½ cup sour
cream, ⅛ teaspoon paprika, and ¼
teaspoon salt. Pour over tomatoes and
serve. About 185 calories per serving.

⊠ **Fried Green Tomatoes:** Use green
tomatoes instead of ripe, fry as directed,
but sprinkle slices with sugar halfway
through cooking. About 150 calories per
serving.

⊠ **Fried Tomatoes Lyonnaise:** Spread
½ cup sautéed minced onions on serving
plate, arrange fried tomatoes on top,
then add ½ cup more sautéed onions.
About 185 calories per serving.

⊠ **Fried Tomatoes Provençal:** Fry
tomatoes in 3 tablespoons olive oil with
1 crushed clove garlic. Season with salt
and pepper and serve. About 130
calories per serving.

⊠ PENNSYLVANIA DUTCH
   FRIED TOMATOES

These tomatoes, unlike plain fried
tomatoes, are lightly sugared and topped
with heavy cream.
Makes 4 servings

*4 large firm, ripe tomatoes or 4 large
  green tomatoes, washed and sliced
  ¾" thick (do not peel)*
¼ cup unsifted flour
3 tablespoons bacon drippings
¼ cup firmly packed light brown sugar
½ teaspoon salt
1 cup heavy cream

Dip tomato slices in flour to dredge
lightly. Heat drippings, in a large, heavy
skillet over moderate heat 1 minute, add
tomatoes, and fry 3–4 minutes on a side
until lightly browned; sprinkle with
brown sugar and salt. Pour cream into
skillet and heat 1–2 minutes, basting
tomatoes once. Transfer tomatoes to a
heated platter, pour cream over all,
and serve. About 395 calories per
serving.

⊠ BROILED TOMATOES

For an Italian touch, brush the tomatoes
lightly with olive oil before sprinkling in
the seasonings. And omit the butter.
Makes 4 servings

*4 large firm, ripe tomatoes, washed and
  halved crosswise (do not peel)*
½ teaspoon salt
⅛ teaspoon pepper
*1 tablespoon minced fresh chervil or
  1 teaspoon dried chervil (optional)*
*1 tablespoon minced fresh basil or
  1 teaspoon dried basil (optional)*
¼ cup butter or margarine

Preheat broiler. Arrange tomatoes cut
side up in a lightly greased shallow pan.
Mix salt, pepper, and, if you like, the
herbs and sprinkle over tomatoes; dot
with butter. Broil 5–6" from heat 10–12
minutes until lightly browned. About 135
calories per serving.

VARIATIONS:

Deviled Tomatoes: Mix ¼ cup cracker
meal, 2 tablespoons melted butter,
1 tablespoon each grated Parmesan and
minced chives, 1 teaspoon prepared mild
yellow mustard, and a pinch pepper. Pat
on tomato halves instead of seasonings
called for above and broil 5" from heat
about 3 minutes until browned. About
130 calories per serving.

Broiled Tomatoes with Anchovies and Cheese: Place each tomato half cut side up on a 3–4″ circle of buttered toast spread with anchovy paste. Sprinkle lightly with minced fresh basil and grated Cheddar cheese and broil 5–6″ from heat 3–4 minutes until bubbly and browned. About 205 calories per serving.

▧ BAKED TOMATOES

Serve at breakfast or brunch accompanied by ham, bacon or sausage, and eggs.
Makes 4 servings

4 large firm, ripe beefsteak tomatoes, washed and halved crosswise (do not peel)
1 teaspoon salt
⅛ teaspoon pepper
¼ cup butter or margarine

Preheat oven to 375° F. Place tomatoes cut side up in a buttered roasting pan or shallow casserole. Sprinkle with salt and pepper and dot with butter. Bake, uncovered, 15–20 minutes until fork tender. (*Note:* Winter tomatoes, being drier, will take longer to bake than summer tomatoes.) About 135 calories per serving.

STUFFED TOMATOES

A good basic recipe to vary as you wish. Experiment with some of the stuffing variations given below or concoct one of your own.
Makes 4 servings

4 large firm, ripe tomatoes, washed
½ teaspoon salt
⅛ teaspoon pepper
Stuffing:
1 tablespoon butter or margarine
¼ cup finely chopped yellow onion
2 cups soft white bread crumbs
¾ teaspoon salt
⅛ teaspoon pepper
1 cup chopped tomato pulp (saved from tomato centers)
¼ cup grated Parmesan cheese

Preheat oven to 375° F. Cut a thin slice from top of each tomato and reserve. Using a teaspoon, scoop out pulp and seeds. Coarsely chop pulp and reserve 1 cup (use the rest in soups or stews). Sprinkle inside of tomatoes with salt and pepper. Melt butter in a small skillet over moderate heat, add onion, and sauté 8–10 minutes until golden. Mix onion with all remaining stuffing ingredients except Parmesan. Stuff tomatoes, sprinkle with Parmesan, and, if you like, replace reserved tops. Stand tomatoes in a buttered shallow casserole and bake, uncovered, ½ hour until tender. About 160 calories per serving.

Some Other Ideas for Stuffing Tomatoes:

– Substitute any of the following combinations for the recipe given above, allowing ½ cup stuffing per tomato and using chopped tomato pulp to moisten as needed:
• 1¾ cups poultry stuffing mix or cooked rice mixed with ¼ cup each sautéed chopped onion and celery. About 185 calories per tomato stuffed with stuffing mix, 110 per tomato stuffed with rice.
• 1 cup browned sausage meat mixed with 1 cup cooked rice and 1 tablespoon minced parsley. About 200 calories per serving.
• 1 cup coarsely chopped sautéed mushrooms mixed with 1 cup Savoy Risotto. About 195 calories per serving.
• ½ cup finely chopped hard-cooked eggs mixed with ¼ cup crisp crumbled bacon, ¼ cup minced pitted green olives, and 1 cup soft white bread crumbs. About 145 calories per serving.

– Instead of making stuffing, mix 1 cup reserved tomato pulp with 1 cup cooked vegetables: small cauliflowerets, whole kernel or cream-style corn, green peas, baby limas, cut green beans, or sautéed diced eggplant. Recipe too flexible for a meaningful calorie count.
– Drain hollowed-out tomatoes upside-down on paper toweling and fill with any of the following: macaroni and cheese; creamed spinach, mushrooms or celery; creamed chicken, ham, brains, sweetbreads, shrimp, crab, or lobster. Top with buttered crumbs before baking.

(*Note:* If filling is very delicate [like sweetbreads or brains], bake empty tomato shells right side up 20 minutes at 375° F., fill, and bake 10 minutes longer. Otherwise, fill and bake ½ hour as directed in basic recipe.) Recipe too flexible for a meaningful calorie count.

⚔ ☒ ¢ STEWED TOMATOES

Another basic recipe that invites improvisation.
Makes 4 servings

4 large ripe tomatoes, peeled, cored, and
  quartered, or 1½ pounds Italian plum
  tomatoes, peeled
1 tablespoon water (optional)
¾ teaspoon salt
¼ teaspoon sugar
Pinch pepper

Place tomatoes in a heavy saucepan, add water (if they seem dry) and remaining ingredients. Cover and simmer 5–7 minutes until *just* soft; uncover and simmer ½ minute longer. Serve in small bowls as a vegetable. About 35 calories per serving.

VARIATIONS:

⚔ ☒ ¢ **Savory Stewed Tomatoes:** Cook any of the following with the tomatoes: 2 tablespoons minced yellow onion or scallions and ½ crushed clove garlic; ¼ cup minced celery or sweet green pepper; 1 bay leaf; 1 teaspoon minced fresh basil, oregano, or marjoram, or ½ teaspoon of the dried. About 40 calories per serving.

☒ ¢ **Dressed-Up Stewed Tomatoes:** Just before serving add any one of the following: 2 tablespoons butter or grated Parmesan; 1–2 tablespoons maple syrup; 1 tablespoon minced parsley; ⅓ cup soft white bread crumbs or croutons. Recipe too flexible for a meaningful calorie count.

☒ ¢ **Stewed Vegetables:** Just before serving, stir in any of the following: 1 cup hot cooked whole kernel corn or cream-style corn; 1 cup sautéed sliced mushrooms; 1½ cups hot cooked green beans; 2 cups hot cooked baby okra pods. Recipe too flexible for a meaningful calorie count.

☒ EASY SCALLOPED TOMATOES

Makes 3–4 servings

1 (1-pound) can whole tomatoes (do not
  drain)
1 cup poultry stuffing mix
¼ cup finely chopped scallions (include
  green tops)
¼ teaspoon tarragon or chervil
⅛ teaspoon crushed fennel seeds
  (optional)
2 tablespoons butter or margarine

Preheat oven to 375° F. Empty tomatoes into a buttered 9″ piepan and cut them into quarters. Toss together all remaining ingredients except butter and scatter evenly over tomatoes. Dot with butter and bake, uncovered, 20 minutes. About 205 calories for each of 3 servings, 155 calories for each of 4 servings.

TOMATO-CHEESE-CORN PIE

A vegetable dish hearty enough to serve as an entree.
Makes 6 servings

Pastry:

1 recipe Flaky Pastry I

Filling:

2 tablespoons butter or margarine
1 large yellow onion, peeled and sliced
  thin
2 cups coarsely grated sharp Cheddar
  cheese
2 medium-size, firm ripe tomatoes,
  peeled and sliced ½″ thick
½ teaspoon salt
⅛ teaspoon pepper
1 (1-pound) can cream-style corn

Preheat oven to 425° F. Make pastry and roll to a diameter of 9½″. Cut 3 V-shaped slits or decorative holes near the center. Cover with cloth while you make the filling. Melt butter in a small skillet over moderate heat, add onion, and stir-fry 5–8 minutes until pale golden; set aside. Sprinkle ½ cup cheese over bottom of an ungreased 9″ piepan and top with tomato slices. Sprinkle with salt, pepper, and onion. Spread corn evenly over tomatoes and top with remaining cheese. Brush rim of pan lightly with cold water. Cover pie with pastry, roll overhang under even with rim, and crimp. Bake 25 minutes until lightly browned. (*Note:* Put a piece of foil on the rack below pie to catch any drips.) About 440 calories per serving.

TRUFFLES

Truffles grow only at the roots of certain trees and only in a few areas of the world; they're dug once a year by especially trained pigs or dogs and bring about $60 a pound. Oddly, though gourmets rave about truffles, they cannot agree on the flavor. Some say that truffles taste like oysters, others like mild garlic, still others like well-ripened Brie. It is flavor for which truffles are cherished, not nutritive value or beauty. Truffles are wrinkled, warty, black, brown or beige fungi usually about the size of chestnuts or golf balls. The choicest are the black Périgord truffles of Southern France; second best are the white (actually beige) truffles from Northern Italy. Though fresh truffles make rare appearances in New York specialty markets, most of us must be content with the canned. And even these are a great luxury.

How to Heighten the Flavor of Canned Truffles: Open can but do not drain; add 1–2 tablespoons Madeira and let truffles stand 30–45 minutes before using.

How to Use Canned Truffles (1 truffle is usually enough for any recipe):
– Mince and stir into meat stuffing, an omelet, or potato salad (use a light hand

with herbs or omit them altogether so you don't overpower the truffle).
– Slice tissue thin, cut into fancy shapes with truffle cutters, and use to decorate pâté, ham or fowl in aspic, or canapés.
– Save can liquid and use to season sauces and meat stuffings.

How to Save Leftover Canned Truffles: Wrap in foil and freeze. Or leave in the can, cover with melted bacon drippings, and refrigerate (they'll keep several weeks).

TURNIPS AND TURNIP GREENS

(The greens are often called Turnip Salad)

Most vegetables as ancient as turnips (more than 4,000 years old) have been in and out of favor half a dozen times. Not so turnips. They've never been particularly popular and only today are we beginning to appreciate their gingery piquancy.

To Prepare for Cooking:

Turnips: Trim off any stems and root ends and discard. Very tiny tender turnips can be scrubbed and cooked whole in their skins; larger turnips should be peeled and quartered or cut in ½" cubes.

Turnip Greens: Discard coarse stems and leaf midribs; sort greens, rejecting any that are wilted, blemished, or yellow. Wash by plunging up and down in tepid water, rinse several times, then lift from water, shake lightly, and place directly in pot.

Season	For Top Quality	Amount To Buy	Nutritive Value	Calories (unseasoned)
Year round for turnips; peak season: fall. January–April for greens	Choose firm, smooth turnips 2–3" across with few leaf scars or roots; clean, tender, crisp greens.	¼ pound turnips per person; ½ pound greens	Greens are very high in vitamins A and C; turnips contain some vitamin C.	Very low— about 30 per cup of greens; 35 per cup of turnips

To Boil Turnip Greens: See recipe for Boiled Collards, Turnip Greens, or Mustard Greens.

Cooking Tips:
– Always cook turnip greens in enamel, stainless-steel, or teflon-lined pots so they don't darken or taste of metal.
– Toss young greens or thin strips of raw turnip into salads for refreshing zing.

Serving Tip: Don't serve turnips with seafood because they overpower it. They're best with pork, ham, or pot roasts.

¢ BOILED TURNIPS

To give turnips richer flavor, boil in beef or chicken broth instead of water.
Makes 4 servings

1¼ pounds turnips, prepared for cooking
1½ cups boiling water, beef or chicken broth
1 teaspoon salt (about)
2 tablespoons butter or margarine
⅛ teaspoon pepper

Place turnips, water or broth, and salt (reduce amount if broth is salty) in a saucepan, cover, and boil until tender: 35–40 minutes for whole small turnips, 25–30 for quarters, and 15–20 for cubes. Drain, then shake pan, uncovered, over low heat to drive off steam. Add butter and continue to shake over low heat until butter melts. Add pepper and serve. About 85 calories per serving (if cooked in water), 95 per serving (cooked in broth).

To Parboil for Use in Other Recipes: Boil as directed, reducing cooking time to 25 minutes for small whole turnips, 15–20 for quarters, and 10 for cubes. Omit seasonings.

VARIATIONS:

⚖ ¢ **Low-Calorie Turnips:** Boil in water and drain as directed; omit butter and sprinkle with 2 tablespoons minced chives, dill, or fennel. About 35 calories per serving.

¢ **Parsleyed Turnips:** Boil in broth and season as directed; just before serving stir in 1 tablespoon lemon juice and 1 tablespoon minced parsley. About 95 calories per serving.

¢ **Mashed Turnips:** Boil and drain as directed; mash with a potato masher or, if stringy, press through a fine sieve. Beat in butter and pepper and warm 2–3 minutes over low heat, stirring. Sprinkle with minced parsley and serve. About 85 calories per serving (if cooked in water), 95 calories per serving (if cooked in broth).

¢ **Glazed Turnips:** Parboil quartered turnips in beef broth as directed; drain, reserving broth, but do not season. Brown turnips in a heavy skillet 3–5 minutes in 3 tablespoons oil over moderately high heat. Add broth, 2 tablespoons each sugar and butter, cover, and simmer 15–20 minutes until tender. If cooking liquid hasn't become syrupy, boil uncovered to reduce, turning turnips until well glazed. Sprinkle with pepper and minced parsley and serve. About 260 calories per serving.

TURNIPS AU GRATIN

Those who don't like turnips will probably like them prepared this way.
Makes 4 servings

1¼ pounds turnips, peeled, cubed, boiled, and drained
2 tablespoons butter or margarine
2 tablespoons flour
1 cup milk
½ teaspoon salt
⅛ teaspoon pepper
Pinch powdered mustard
¾ cup coarsely grated sharp Cheddar cheese

Preheat oven to 400° F. Arrange turnips in an ungreased 1½-quart *au gratin* dish or shallow casserole. Melt butter over moderate heat, blend in flour, and slowly stir in milk. Heat, stirring constantly, until thickened; mix in salt, pepper, mustard, and ½ cup cheese. Pour sauce over turnips and mix lightly; sprinkle remaining cheese on top. Bake, uncovered, 20 minutes until bubbly. About 220 calories per serving.

¢ ROASTED TURNIPS

Sweeter than boiled turnips, less watery, too.
Makes 4 servings

1¼ pounds medium-size turnips, peeled
½ cup lard, bacon drippings, or cooking oil
1 teaspoon salt

Preheat oven to 375° F. Place turnips in an ungreased shallow casserole and add lard, drippings, or oil. Bake, uncovered, 50 minutes, turning turnips after ½ hour. Raise oven temperature to 400° F. and bake 10–15 minutes longer until lightly browned and tender. Drain on paper toweling, sprinkle with salt, and serve. About 135 calories per serving.

¢ SKILLET TURNIPS AND RED ONIONS

Makes 4 servings

1¼ pounds medium-size turnips, peeled and cubed
1 large red onion, peeled and sliced thin
⅓ cup water
3 tablespoons butter or margarine
¾ teaspoon salt

Place all ingredients in a large, heavy skillet, cover, and simmer 15–20 minutes, shaking skillet frequently. Uncover toward end of cooking and stir gently so turnips become nicely glazed. If mixture seems dry, add 1 tablespoon water. About 125 calories per serving.

TURNIPS STUFFED WITH MUSHROOM RISOTTO

Makes 4 servings

8 medium-size turnips, parboiled and drained
1½ cups Mushroom Risotto
¼ cup grated Parmesan cheese
1½ cups chicken broth

Preheat oven to 350° F. Hollow out turnips to form "cups" (save centers for soup or stew). Stuff with risotto, sprinkle with cheese, and arrange in an ungreased shallow casserole. Pour broth around turnips, cover, and bake 20 minutes. Uncover, bake 15 minutes longer, basting 2 or 3 times. About 215 calories per serving.

WILD GREENS

Milkweed . . . nettles . . . pokeweed . . . purslane. They're yours for the picking, and very good they are. Like other greens, they're low in calories and high in vitamins A and C. All should be cooked in enamel, stainless-steel, or teflon-lined pots so that they don't darken or taste of metal.

Milkweed
Milkweed grows throughout the Eastern United States and almost every part of it is edible—the fragile young shoots and leaves, the flower buds and small, tender seed pods. All are naturally bitter and need special treatment to remove the astringency. Allow about ½ pound per person.

To Prepare: Whether cooking shoots, leaves, buds, or pods, wash well in cool water. Place in a large pot, cover with boiling water, and boil 1 minute. Drain and cover with fresh boiling water. Repeat boiling and draining process 3 or 4 times until all bitterness is gone, then boil 5–10 minutes longer until crisp-tender. Drain, season with butter, salt, and pepper, and serve.

Nettles
"Baby" nettle leaves are delicious. Look for them in early spring (wear thick gloves). Allow about 1½ pints per person.

To Prepare: Wash as you would spinach by plunging up and down in tepid water. Rinse, lift from water, shake lightly, and place in a pot. Add no water, cover, and steam over moderate heat until tender: about 10 minutes for youngest leaves, 20–30 for the not so young. Drain and purée in an electric blender at high speed or put through a food mill. Season with butter, salt, and pepper and serve on hot buttered toast or in pastry shells. *Or,* follow the recipe for Wilted Dandelions or Nettles.

Pokeweed

Although the mature stems, roots, and berries are mildly poisonous, the first shoots of spring are good to eat. Look in open fields for the tall, silvery stalks of last year's crop; at their base you'll find plump new shoots. Choose those no more than 6″ to 8″ high and allow 3 to 4 per person.

To Prepare: Wash well in tepid water, peeling off any coarse outer layers of stalk. Place shoots in a large pan, cover with boiling water, and boil covered 10 minutes. Drain, cover with fresh boiling water, and boil covered 8–10 minutes longer until tender. Drain, dress with butter or heavy cream, salt, and pepper. *Or,* chill and serve cold with oil and vinegar.

Purslane

(Also called Portulaca)

If gardeners knew how savory purslane is, they wouldn't work so hard to weed it out of their flower beds. The stems, leaves, and flower buds are all good to eat, but the young shoots are the most succulent of all. Allow about 1 cup per person.

To Prepare: Wash in tepid water and discard any tough or blemished portions. Place in a saucepan, add lightly salted water to cover, and boil covered about 10 minutes until tender. Drain, season with butter, salt, and pepper, and serve. *Or,* sauté young shoots in 2–3 tablespoons bacon drippings over moderate heat 2–3 minutes, then cover and steam 6–8 minutes until tender. Drizzle with white wine vinegar, season with salt and pepper, and serve. *Or,* use in gumbos and other Creole dishes in place of okra.

CHAPTER 17

SALADS AND SALAD DRESSINGS

The Romans, who liked most things twice-gilded, took their salads straight—lettuce sprinkled with salt. It is, in fact, from their word for salt (*sal*) that our word salad derives. Our salads are a good deal more complex than the Roman and may appear at almost any point in a meal. Californians begin dinner with crisp green salads, simply dressed, and Southerners often end it with frozen fruit salads. The French prefer salad either before or after the main course (so that the dressing doesn't overpower the wine) and Swedes construct whole smorgasbords out of cold marinated fish and vegetables.

Salads can be nothing more than greens tossed with oil and vinegar, or they can be elaborate concoctions of meat, seafood, poultry, vegetables, pasta, or fruit. They may be bland or tart, savory or sweet, light or lavish, and they may be served hot or cold, jellied or frozen.

The Salad Greens

Most salads are built around—or upon—greens. Time was when green salad was a wedge of iceberg lettuce drenched with French or Thousand Island dressing. No more, thanks to the variety of greens now available year round. Nutritionally, salad greens are low in calories and relatively high in vitamins C and A (the darker the green, the greater the vitamin content), iron, and calcium. Here, then, are the varieties of greens available:

Lettuces:

Crisphead or Iceberg: The old standby, tightly packed, crunchy, pale green heads. Sweet, succulent, and bland.

Leaf or Simpson: Loose-leafed, medium to bronzy green, depending on variety (Salad Bowl, Garden, Bronze, Ivy, and Oak are popular leaf lettuces). Coarser textured and stronger flavored than iceberg.

Boston or Butterhead: Smallish, loose, medium green heads with buttery, easily bruised leaves. Exceptionally good flavor.

Bibb or Limestone: Loveliest of lettuces. Tulip-shaped, tiny, crinkly-crisp heads of medium to pale yellow-green. Not widely available but worth hunting up. These need extra-careful washing to float out hidden caches of soil. Delicate, mellow flavor.

Romaine or Cos: Supercrisp, green, elongated heads from the Aegean island of Cos. Essential to tossed green salads for crunch and a certain amount of tang.

Other Salad Greens:

Chicory or Curly Endive: Frilly, sprawling heads, bright green around the edges, pale in the center. Bitter, somewhat coarse, and best when teamed with more delicate greens.

Escarole: A coarse cousin of chicory with fairly broad, bitter, flat green leaves.

Field Salad (also known as *Corn Salad, Lamb's Lettuce,* and *Lamb's Quarter*): Small, dark, spoon-shaped leaves, loosely clustered into rosettes. A rarity in most markets and available only in fall and winter. Flavor is biting, radish-like.

Garden Cress or Peppergrass: Small, spicy-hot plants of the mustard family gathered when barely out of the ground. Not often marketed in this country but worth growing from seed. A handful of leaves will revitalize a listless salad.

Nasturtium: Leaves of this sunny flower have lots of dash and bite. They're good alone or tossed with other greens. The blossoms are edible, too, and contribute color and pungency.

Rugula (Arugula) or Rocket: Rugula is the Italian name and the one most often used, since these dark, bitter-sharp greens are an Italian favorite. Use sparingly in green salads.

Sorrel or Dock: Crisp, sour, tongue-shaped leaves with a fresh, spring green color. Add with a light hand.

Watercress: Deep green, succulent, tart, and burning. The leaves and tender young stems provide welcome crunch and piquancy.

Belgian Endive, Cabbage, Chinese Cabbage, Dandelions, and Spinach, all popular additions to the salad bowl, are described in detail in the vegetable chapter. So are *Beet, Mustard, and Turnip Greens,* which, if young, fresh, and tender, team well with other greens.

About Buying Salad Greens

Choose crisp greens free of blemishes, bruises or soft spots, nicks or cuts. Also avoid those with "rust spots" (these may go clear through the head), wilted or yellow leaves. If you are buying a head of lettuce, be sure the head is firm and compact. Whenever possible, buy unpackaged greens that you can inspect closely.

How to Wash and Crisp Salad Greens

There are two schools of thought. One insists that greens will keep longer if they are not washed until shortly before using. The second (to which we belong) maintains just the opposite, that greens should be attended to as soon as they come home from garden or grocery. Peel off and discard any wilted or damaged outer leaves, then *wash* carefully (never allow to soak).

Headed Lettuces: With point of paring knife, cut out stem end, then hold head under a stream of cold water; it will force leaves apart and cleanse them. Drain well and wrap head in paper or cloth toweling, then pop into a plastic bag and place in hydrator compartment of refrigerator. If salad is to be made fairly soon, separate leaves, blot on toweling, and roll up; refrigerate until needed. *To Make Lettuce Cups:* Carefully pull off outer leaves (they will be nicely cup-shaped) and place on a towel-lined tray. Top with another towel and crisp in refrigerator until needed.

Loose-Leafed Lettuces: Cut out stem end, pull off leaves, and slosh up and down several times in a sinkful of cool water. Repeat, changing water as needed, to float out grit and soil. Blot leaves dry on paper toweling, roll loosely in cloth or paper toweling, then store in hydrator until needed. If greens are not to be used within a day or so, slip into a plastic bag, towel and all.

Watercress, Field Salad, and Other Stemmed Greens: Open bunch and discard roots and coarse stems. Swish leaves and tender young stems up and down in several changes of cool water until free of dirt. Rinse in cold water, blot on several thicknesses of paper toweling, then roll up in dry cloth and store in hydrator. (*Note:* If watercress is not to be used right away, open bunch but do not trim; stand in a glass of cold water, cover with a plastic bag, and store in refrigerator.)

A Word About Wire Salad Baskets: Many cooks wash greens in wire baskets, then whirl them dry by swinging the baskets through the air. An all-right method for sturdy greens, but not for fragile ones because the wire mesh will bruise them.

About Making Tossed Green Salads

The Bowl: Wooden salad bowls have become absurdly sacrosanct, hallowed things never to be rinsed, let alone washed. So they go on and on, gathering oils, essence of garlic, and rancidity. "Wash" does not mean "soak"—which would indeed ruin a wooden bowl—but a quick sudsing, rinsing, and drying after each use is good practice. Better still, choose a non-porous, washable ceramic, glass, or metal bowl, a *big* one (it's impossible to toss salad in a small bowl).

Choosing the Greens: The best green salads provide contrasts—of color (greens range from near-white to near-black), texture, shape, and flavor. But the contrasts must be subtle lest one flavor or texture overshadow the others. Salad artists devote years to their art, experimenting with combinations of greens, dressings, and herbs until they achieve a delectable balance. Consider the whole meal when constructing the salad, and select greens that will complement it—strong entrees demand delicate salads, light ones something substantial.

Good Salad Herbs: Because a handful of herbs have become known as "salad herbs," we tend to slight a number of others that work very well with tossed greens. The best herbs to use are fresh herbs (if you have a sunny window and a halfway green thumb, try growing your own; it isn't difficult). Don't load a salad with herbs, but settle upon one or two (and no more than three) that are compatible with one another and your choice of greens (tasting is the best way to tell). As a rule, two tablespoons of minced fresh herbs are sufficient for one quart prepared greens. Sprinkle the herbs into the greens, or mix into the oil. If you use dried herbs, crush between your fingers, add to the oil, and let stand twenty to thirty minutes at room temperature so they will gain fragrance. Dried herbs are stronger than the fresh, so use only one-third to one-fourth as much.

Favorite Salad Herbs:

Basil	Tarragon
Chervil	Fines Herbes (a mix
Chives	of chervil, chives,
Dill	parsley, and
Parsley	tarragon)

Others to Try:

Borage } Both are cool, cucumber-flavored
Burnet }
Coriander Leaves (flavor is a cross between carrots and parsley)
Fennel
Marjoram
Mint
Oregano
Rosemary
Summer Savory
Thyme

Good Vegetable Additions to Green Salads: Raw cucumbers, carrots, and radishes are naturals for tossed salads, but so are a lot of other raw vegetables. As for cooked vegetables, nearly any vegetable that can be served cold can be tossed into a green salad. Here are some suggestions (all vegetables should be cut in bite-size or at least easy-to-eat pieces):

Raw Vegetables: Carrots, cauliflowerets, celeriac, celery, cucumbers (these are often coated with wax to retard spoilage; if so, peel before using), fennel, kale, and kohlrabi (if young and tender), mushrooms, onions (the whole huge family), radishes, sweet peppers, turnips, and zucchini. (*Note:* Tomatoes are not particularly suitable because of their juiciness. To keep them from watering down the salad: Slice tomatoes vertically instead of horizontally; marinate tomato wedges in dressing and add at the very last minute as a garnish, or best of all, use whole cherry tomatoes.)

Cooked Vegetables: Artichoke hearts and bottoms, asparagus, beans (the whole family of fresh and dried), beets, broccoli, carrots, celeriac, celery, cucumbers, eggplant, hearts of palm, leeks, lentils, green peas and snow pea pods, sweet green or red peppers (especially Marinated Roasted Peppers), and Irish potatoes.

Good Fruit Additions to Green Salads: Grapefruit, orange, mandarin orange, and tangerine sections (make sure all seeds and white pith are removed); diced or sliced avocados or apples (dip in lemon juice to prevent darkening); peeled seeded grapes.

Other Flavorful Additions to Green Salads:
– Cheese: Cubes of Cheddar, Swiss, or Gruyère cheese, crumbles of Roquefort or blue cheese
– Croutons (plain or seasoned)
– Capers, sweet or sour pickles, ripe or green olives, slivered pimiento
– Bacon crumbles, slivered prosciutto or boiled ham
– Truffles—especially good with delicate greens and French dressing
– Nuts: toasted slivered almonds, piñon nuts, peanuts, water chestnuts
– Seeds: celery, caraway, and toasted sesame seeds
– Flower petals: chrysanthemums, marigolds, roses, nasturtiums, violets, pumpkin or squash blossoms

About Adding Garlic: Someone once said there was no such thing as "a touch of garlic." Perhaps not, but that doesn't mean you have to add enough to blow a safe. For fairly subtle garlic flavor, use one of the following techniques:
– Rub salad bowl with a cut clove of garlic before adding greens; or for slightly stronger flavor, sprinkle a little salt in bowl, then rub with garlic.
– Toss a *chapon* with salad, then remove before serving. A *chapon* is a stale chunk of French bread rubbed well with a cut or crushed clove of garlic.
– Slice garlic into salad oil, then warm briefly over lowest heat. Cool oil to room temperature and remove garlic before dressing salad. (*Note:* Never let garlic stand long in oil; it will become bitter.)

Choosing the Dressing: Salad greens team happily with a huge variety of dressings—any oil and vinegar type (except very sweet ones), any tart creamy dressing, any savory cheese dressing. Consider the make-up of the salad—and the entire meal—then pick a dressing compatible with both. If there are dieters, also consider the calories (there is a good selection of low-calorie dressings in the recipe section that follows).

Putting Tossed Green Salads Together

Prepare the Dressing—at least a half hour ahead of time so that flavors will mellow. If you are going to make an oil and vinegar dressing, combine herbs and other seasonings with oil and let stand a half hour at room temperature. (*Note:* It's best to make dressings in small quantities; few keep well. If adding cooked or raw vegetables to salad, let marinate in a little of the dressing for about a half hour at room temperature.)

Prepare the Greens—just before making the salad. Use only those that have been well washed and crisped in the refrigerator. If greens still show drops of water, blot gently on paper toweling. Break, tear, or cut greens into bite-size or easy-to-eat pieces and drop into salad bowl. (*Note:* Until recently, people thought cutting greens bruised them, destroyed the food value. But that theory is being questioned. The best way today seems to be whichever is easiest, most efficient. Endive, for example, is simpler to cut than tear; iceberg lettuce just the opposite.) *How many greens for a salad?* Allow one to two cups prepared greens per person (depending on appetites).

Dress and Toss the Salad: Place all salad ingredients in a large bowl and drizzle with a small amount of dressing; toss lightly, lifting greens from the bottom to the top, until leaves glisten. Taste, add more dressing if needed, also salt and pepper. (*Note:* If you are dressing salad with oil and vinegar, drizzle oil in first and toss until leaves are lightly coated. Then sprinkle vinegar on top and toss again, tasting as you go and adding extra vinegar as needed.) Vinegar and salt should always be added to tossed greens at the very last minute because they will quickly wilt a salad. The best way to avoid overdressing a salad is to underdress, then to add more dressing if necessary. As a rule, three to four tablespoons dressing per quart of prepared greens is sufficient.

Other Kinds of Salads

There are dozens of different salads in addition to the tossed, which may be grouped roughly as follows: *Vegetable* (both cooked and raw), *Fruit* (both raw and cooked), *Main Dish* (meat, poultry, seafood, egg, and pasta salads), *Molded,* and *Frozen.* Main dish, molded, and frozen salads are treated fully in the accompanying recipe section (and there are additional recipes in the meat, poultry, seafood, and egg chapters). Vegetable and fruit salads, however, are less a matter of specific recipes than of improvisation. Here is the place to let your imagination run

wild, mixing and matching flavors, combining tints and textures, tasting as you go. These salads can be presented as *platter salads*—fruits and/or vegetables grouped on a platter rather than tossed.

Some Good Vegetable Salad Combinations: (*Note:* To shave calories, substitute a low-calorie dressing for that recommended below.)

– Diced cooked potatoes, carrots, green peas, baby limas, and minced red onion; add enough mayonnaise to bind.
– Diced cooked beets, hard-cooked eggs, elbow macaroni, minced sweet green pepper, and yellow onion; add enough mayonnaise to bind.
– Cooked asparagus tips and halved cherry tomatoes marinated in French Dressing.
– Cooked artichoke bottoms filled with Russian Salad.
– Drained sauerkraut mixed with minced raw celery, yellow onion, and sweet green or red pepper. Dress with French, Shallot, or Wine Dressing.

Some Good Fruit Salad Combinations: *Note:* Apples, peaches, bananas, and avocados must be dipped in lemon or other citrus juice to prevent darkening. They should be added to the salad just before serving. Slice, dice, or cube fruits, keeping each in proportion to the other. Dress with any dressing suitable for fruit salads.

– Oranges or tangerines, apples, grapes, and pecans or toasted almonds
– Bananas, oranges or tangerines, and dates
– Bananas, oranges, pineapple, and mango or papaya
– Pineapple and strawberries and/or grapes
– Melon balls, grapes, and pineapple
– Melon balls and lemon-dipped avocado cubes
– Cooked plums, peaches, and figs

About Garnishing Salads

Tossed Salads should look casual, so the simpler the garnish the better—strategically placed radish roses or carrot curls, clusters of ripe or green olives, crumbles of bacon or French-fried onions, shreds of fresh horseradish, Cheddar cubes, or paprika-dusted cream cheese balls.

Vegetable and Main Dish Salads: These are best dressed up by serving in hollowed-out tomatoes, vegetable cases, or avocado halves (these must be well brushed with lemon juice to keep them from darkening).

Savory Aspics, Molded Vegetable, Meat, or Fish Salads: Trim with ruffs of greenery (parsley, watercress, chicory), clusters of ripe or green olives, plain or fancily cut radishes, carrot or celery curls, pickle fans, clusters of tiny cooked shrimp, cherry tomatoes.

Fruit and Molded Fruit Salads: Decorate with clusters of green and red grapes, preserved kumquats, melon balls, lemon-dipped unpeeled red apple cubes, and avocado cubes or crescents, mandarin oranges, orange or grapefruit sections, any fresh berries or any compatible combinations of these. For greenery: mint or fennel sprigs, rose geranium or lemon verbena leaves. A touch of color is all that's needed.

About Salads to Go

Most salads are poor travelers. Best choices—*if* they can be kept well chilled in transit—are cooked vegetable, meat, or seafood salads. Salad greens are apt to wilt or crush, but if wrapped in several thicknesses of *damp* paper toweling, then tied in a plastic bag and kept cool, they should arrive on location crisp and fresh. The dressing should travel separately and be added at the very last minute.

Some Ways to Serve Tomatoes

French-Style: Arrange ripe tomato slices on a large plate, alternating, if you like, with cucumber slices and overlapping slightly. Sprinkle with salt and freshly ground pepper, drizzle with olive oil and red wine vinegar, and let stand at room temperature about a half hour before serving.

Belgian-Style: Alternate slices of tomato and Bermuda onion rings on a large plate, overlapping slightly. Sprinkle with salt, sugar, freshly minced chives and chervil. Sprinkle lightly with celery seeds, drizzle with French Dressing, cover, and marinate one to two hours in refrigerator.

Italian-Style: Arrange ripe tomato slices, slightly overlapping, on a large plate, alternating, if you like, with thin slices of mozzarella cheese. Sprinkle with salt and freshly ground pepper, drizzle with olive oil and red wine vinegar or lemon juice, and scatter lavishly with minced fresh basil. Let stand at room temperature about one hour before serving.

Mediterranean-Style: Arrange ripe tomato slices on a large plate but do not overlap. Sprinkle with salt and freshly ground pepper, olive oil and lemon juice. Mound with Caponata, garnish with ripe olives and watercress, and serve.

Tomatoes Finlandia: Mix equal parts minced cooked shrimp or pickled herring and hard-cooked eggs, add mayonnaise to bind, salt, pepper, and minced fresh dill to taste. Mound on tomato slices and serve.

"Frosted" Tomatoes: Spread tomato slices with thick layers of cottage cheese, sprinkle with minced chives and dill, and serve.

Marinated Tomatoes and Artichokes: Marinate equal parts tomato wedges and cooked artichoke hearts in French or other tart dressing two to three hours in the refrigerator. Toss and serve.

Roquefort Tomatoes and Avocados:
Marinate equal parts slim tomato
wedges and lemon-dipped avocado
slices in any Roquefort or blue cheese
dressing about 1 hour in refrigerator.

Provençal Tomato Hash: Mix equal
quantities diced, peeled, seeded tomatoes, diced cucumber, and pitted ripe or
green olives. Dress with olive oil and red
wine vinegar, season with minced fresh
parsley and dill or fennel, and let stand
at room temperature about 1 hour.
Sprinkle with freshly ground pepper and
serve in lettuce cups.

CAESAR SALAD

Makes 6 servings

1 clove garlic, peeled
⅔ cup olive oil (about)
2 cups ½″ bread cubes made from stale
French or Italian bread
1 large head romaine, washed and
crisped
½ teaspoon salt
¼ teaspoon pepper
1 egg (either raw or boiled in the shell 1
minute)
3–4 tablespoons lemon juice
6 anchovy fillets, drained and minced
⅓ cup grated Parmesan cheese

Crush garlic into oil, cover, and let
stand overnight at room temperature.
Next day, drain oil from garlic; discard
garlic. Heat ⅓ cup of the oil in a heavy
skillet over moderately high heat 1–2
minutes. When hot but not smoking,
add bread cubes and brown on all sides,
tossing constantly. Drain on paper
toweling and reserve. (*Note:* You can do
these well ahead of time to avoid a last
minute rush.) Break romaine in bite-size
pieces into a salad bowl. Sprinkle with
remaining oil, the salt and pepper and
toss; add a few extra drops oil if needed
to coat all leaves lightly. Break egg into
a cup and slide onto salad, pour lemon
juice directly on egg, and toss lightly.
Add anchovies, Parmesan, and bread
cubes, toss again, and serve. About 295
calories per serving.

VARIATION:

⊠ **Jiffy Caesar Salad:** Rub a large salad
bowl with a cut clove garlic; break romaine into bowl, top with the egg and
anchovy fillets. Toss, add 1–1½ cups
packaged plain or seasoned croutons, ⅓
cup grated Parmesan, and ⅓ cup French
dressing, and toss again. About 205
calories per serving.

⚖ WINTER HEALTH SALAD

A brilliant combination of vegetables.
Makes 4–6 servings

2 cups finely shredded cabbage
1 sweet green pepper, cored, seeded, and
cut in julienne strips
1 pimiento, seeded and cut in julienne
strips
1 medium-size carrot, coarsely grated
(scrub but do not peel)
1 small red onion, peeled and minced,
or ¼ cup minced scallions (include
tops)
½ cup minced celery (include tops)
½ cup minced cucumber (do not peel
unless cucumbers are waxed)
½ small white turnip, peeled and finely
grated
⅓ cup tiny cauliflowerets or broccoli
flowerets (optional)
4 radishes, thinly sliced
¼–⅓ cup French dressing

Chill all vegetables well; add just enough
dressing to coat all lightly, toss, and
serve. For lunch, top with a scoop of
cottage cheese or cubed sharp Cheddar.
About 65 calories for each of 4 servings,
45 calories for each of 6 (without
cheese).

VARIATION:

⚖ **Extra-Low-Calorie Winter Health
Salad:** Prepare as directed but dress with
Tangy Low-Calorie Salad Dressing.
About 45 calories for each of 4 servings,
30 calories for each of 6 (without
cheese).

NASTURTIUM SALAD

Nasturtium leaves make a sharp and pungent salad.
Makes 4–6 servings

1 pint young nasturtium leaves, washed and patted dry on paper toweling
1 quart prepared mixed salad greens

Dressing:

⅓ cup olive oil
½ clove garlic, peeled and crushed
1 tablespoon minced parsley
½ teaspoon minced fresh marjoram or ¼ teaspoon dried marjoram
¼ teaspoon salt
⅛ teaspoon pepper
¼ cup sour cream
2 tablespoons tarragon vinegar

Place nasturtium leaves and greens in a salad bowl. Beat dressing ingredients until creamy, pour over greens, toss lightly to mix, and serve. About 220 calories for each of 4 servings, 150 calories for each of 6 servings.

WILTED SPINACH SALAD WITH HOT BACON DRESSING

Makes 4–6 servings

1 (10-ounce) bag fresh spinach

Dressing:

6 slices bacon, cut crosswise in julienne strips
2 scallions, washed and sliced thin (include some tops)
½ cup red wine vinegar
2 tablespoons ketchup
½ teaspoon salt
⅛ teaspoon pepper

Sort spinach carefully, removing blemished leaves and coarse stems; wash in a colander under cold running water. Pat dry on paper toweling, then place in a large salad bowl. Brown bacon in a skillet and drain on paper toweling. Stir-fry scallions in drippings 5–8 minutes until tender, mix in remaining dressing ingredients, and heat, stirring, about 5 minutes. Pour hot dressing over spinach and toss well. Sprinkle in bacon crumbles, toss again, and serve. About 180 calories for each of 4 servings, 120 calories for each of 6 servings.

WILTED LETTUCE

An old Southern salad, slightly sweet-sour.
Makes 4 servings

4 slices bacon
2 tablespoons cider vinegar
1 teaspoon sugar
¼ teaspoon salt
⅛ teaspoon pepper
1 quart prepared mixed salad greens
¼ cup minced scallions (optional)

Fry bacon until crisp, drain on paper toweling, crumble, and reserve. Drain all but 3 tablespoons drippings from skillet; mix in vinegar, sugar, salt, and pepper and heat and stir just until simmering. Pour over greens and, if you like, scallions, add bacon, toss, and serve. About 165 calories per serving.

VARIATION:

Carolina-Style Wilted Lettuce: Heat ¼ cup bacon or ham drippings in a small skillet; mix in ½ cup boiling water, the vinegar, sugar, salt, and pepper and bring to a boil. Pour over 1 quart prepared iceberg lettuce, toss, and garnish with sliced hard-cooked eggs and scallions. Delicious with fried country ham. About 185 calories per serving.

STUFFED LETTUCE

Makes 6 servings

1 medium-size head iceberg lettuce

Stuffing:

1 (8-ounce) package cream cheese, softened to room temperature
1 tablespoon mayonnaise
1 teaspoon finely grated yellow onion
¼ cup finely grated carrot
¼ cup minced sweet red or green pepper
¼ cup peeled, minced, well-drained tomato
Few drops liquid hot red pepper seasoning
¼ teaspoon salt

Core lettuce and make a small hollow (save scraps for another salad). Mix stuffing ingredients and pack firmly into hollow. Wrap lettuce in foil or saran and chill well. Slice crosswise about ¾" thick and serve with French or Thousand Island Dressing. About 155 calories per serving.

VARIATION:

Fruit-Stuffed Lettuce: Core and hollow out lettuce as directed. Instead of the stuffing above, mix 1 (8-ounce) package softened cream cheese with 1 tablespoon each mayonnaise and lemon juice, ½ cup well-drained crushed pineapple, fruit salad, or chopped raw apple, and ¼ cup minced toasted almonds, pecans, or walnuts. Stuff and chill as directed. About 220 calories per serving.

JAPANESE VEGETABLE SALAD WITH TOASTED SESAME SEED DRESSING

Toasted sesame seeds provide a rich nutty flavor.
Makes 4 servings

2 cups prepared mixed salad greens
1 cup finely shredded or sliced red cabbage
1 cup fine julienne strips of peeled, seeded cucumber
½ cup finely shredded radishes
½ cup finely shredded carrot or raw broccoli stalks
½ cup minced cooked shrimp, scallops, or delicate white fish (optional)

Dressing:

3 tablespoons peanut or other salad oil
2 tablespoons sesame seeds
¼ cup rice vinegar or 2 tablespoons cider vinegar
2 tablespoons mirin or cream sherry
1 tablespoon lemon juice
1 tablespoon soy sauce

Place greens, vegetables, and, if you like, shrimp in a large salad bowl. Heat and stir oil and sesame seeds in a small, heavy skillet over moderately high heat about 1 minute until pale caramel colored; remove from heat and stir 1 minute longer. (*Note:* Be careful not to overbrown seeds—they'll be bitter.) Mix in remaining dressing ingredients,

pour over salad mixture, toss lightly, and serve. About 165 calories per serving (with shrimp).

CREAMY SWEET-SOUR COLESLAW

This coleslaw is even better the second day.
Makes 6–8 servings

2 quarts moderately finely grated cabbage
¼ cup finely grated Bermuda or Spanish onion
2 medium-size carrots, peeled and grated moderately fine
2 tablespoons minced sweet green pepper
½ cup relish-type sandwich spread
½ cup sour cream
2 tablespoons tarragon vinegar
1 teaspoon salt
⅛ teaspoon pepper

Place all ingredients in a large bowl and toss thoroughly to mix. Cover and chill 2–3 hours. Stir well and serve. About 165 calories for each of 6 servings, 125 calories for each of 8 servings.

CARAWAY COLESLAW WITH CREAMY OIL AND VINEGAR DRESSING

A fragrant sweet-sour slaw. Olive oil makes the difference.
Makes 6–8 servings

2 quarts moderately finely grated cabbage
1 medium-size yellow onion, peeled and grated fine

Dressing:

⅓ cup olive oil
⅓ cup tarragon vinegar
2 tablespoons superfine sugar
1 tablespoon caraway seeds
1 teaspoon salt
⅛ teaspoon pepper
1 cup sour cream

Place cabbage and onion in a large bowl. Mix all dressing ingredients except sour cream and stir until sugar dissolves; blend in sour cream. Pour dressing over cabbage and toss well to mix. Cover and chill several hours before serving. About 250 calories for each of 6 servings, 185 calories for each of 8 servings.

VARIATION:

Red and Green Slaw: Prepare as directed, using a ½ and ½ mixture of moderately finely grated red and green cabbage. About 260 calories for each of 6 servings, 195 calories for each of 8 servings.

OLD-FASHIONED CAROLINA COLESLAW WITH CELERY SEED DRESSING

The mustardy dressing has plenty of bite.
Makes 6 servings

1 medium-size cabbage, trimmed, cored, and quartered

Dressing:

2 eggs
1½ teaspoons powdered mustard
3 tablespoons sugar
½ teaspoon salt
¾ cup heavy cream
⅓ cup boiling cider vinegar
1 tablespoon butter or margarine
1½ teaspoons celery seeds

Slice cabbage quarters paper thin and place in a large mixing bowl. Lightly beat eggs in the top of a double boiler and mix in mustard, sugar, and salt. Beat in cream, then add vinegar in a slow stream, stirring constantly. Heat and stir over simmering water 3–5 minutes until the consistency of stirred custard. Off heat, mix in butter and celery seeds; pour dressing over cabbage and toss well to mix. Cover and chill 2–3 hours. Just before serving, toss well again. About 230 calories per serving.

MARINATED HEARTS OF PALM

Makes 3–4 servings

1 (14-ounce) can hearts of palm, drained
3 tablespoons olive oil

1–2 tablespoons red wine vinegar or lemon juice
Freshly ground black pepper
1 tablespoon minced fresh tarragon, chervil, dill, chives, or parsley
1 pimiento, slivered

Halve hearts of palm lengthwise and arrange in a large flat-bottomed bowl. Drizzle evenly with olive oil and vinegar, add a couple of grindings of pepper, sprinkle with tarragon, cover, and marinate in refrigerator 2–3 hours, turning occasionally. Garnish with pimiento and serve as is or on a bed of dark crisp greens. Calorie counts unavailable for hearts of palm.

VARIATION:

Prepare as directed but substitute ¼–⅓ cup French or Garlic Dressing (or any favorite tart dressing) for the oil and vinegar. Calorie counts unavailable for hearts of palm.

RAW ZUCCHINI SALAD

Use only the tenderest young zucchini for making this salad. Otherwise it may be too bitter.
Makes 4–6 servings

2 cups thinly sliced unpeeled baby zucchini, chilled
2 medium-size firm-ripe tomatoes, cored and thinly sliced
1 medium-size red onion, peeled, sliced paper thin, and separated into rings
¾ cup thinly sliced raw, peeled mushrooms (optional)
⅓ cup French dressing
2 cups prepared mixed salad greens

Mix all ingredients except greens, cover, and chill 1 hour, turning now and then. Line a salad bowl with the greens, mound zucchini mixture on top, and toss at the table (there should be enough dressing for the greens, too; if not add a little more). About 185 calories for each of 4 servings, 125 calories for each of 6 servings.

VARIATION:

Okra Salad: Prepare as directed but substitute baby okra for zucchini. About 205 calories for each of 4 servings, 140 calories for each of 6 servings.

¢ RADISH SALAD

Makes 4 servings

¾ cup very thinly sliced red radishes
¾ cup very thinly sliced white radishes
1 small sweet green pepper, cored, seeded, and cut in julienne strips
¼ cup minced celery root
¼ cup French dressing
1 teaspoon sugar

Toss all ingredients together, chill ½ hour, and serve on crisp greens. About 110 calories per serving.

RAW MUSHROOM SALAD

A perfectly elegant salad aromatic of tarragon. Plan it for a special dinner. Delicious with poultry or seafood.
Makes 4 servings

1 pound medium-size mushrooms, rinsed in cold water, patted dry, and sliced thin
2 tablespoons minced fresh tarragon or 1 teaspoon dried tarragon
1 tablespoon minced chives
⅔ cup olive oil
2 tablespoons tarragon vinegar
Juice of ½ lemon
¼ teaspoon salt
⅛ teaspoon pepper

Place all ingredients in a mixing bowl and toss well to mix. Cover and marinate 1–3 hours at room temperature. Drain and serve as is or on crisp lettuce leaves. About 185 calories per serving.

RAW CAULIFLOWER SALAD WITH SOUR CREAM-PARMESAN DRESSING

Makes 4–6 servings

1 medium-size cauliflower, trimmed, divided into flowerets, and sliced paper thin
1 cup thinly sliced radishes

½ cup minced watercress leaves
2 tablespoons minced scallions
Dressing:
1 cup sour cream
½ clove garlic, peeled and crushed
Juice of ½ lemon
2 tablespoons olive or other salad oil
1 tablespoon finely grated Parmesan cheese
½ teaspoon salt
⅛ teaspoon black pepper
Pinch cayenne pepper

Toss cauliflower with radishes, watercress, and scallions and chill about ½ hour. Meanwhile, blend together dressing ingredients. Pour dressing over salad mixture, toss well, and serve. About 215 calories for each of 4 servings, 145 calories for each of 6 servings.

¢ ⚖ WILTED CUCUMBERS

Makes 4 servings

2 medium-size cucumbers, peeled or not (as you like) and sliced paper thin
1½ teaspoons salt
2 tablespoons boiling water
2 tablespoons sugar
⅓ cup white, tarragon, or cider vinegar
Grinding of pepper

Layer cucumbers in a bowl, salting as you go, weight down, cover, and let stand at room temperature 1–2 hours. Drain, wash in a colander under cold running water, then drain and press out as much liquid as possible; pat dry on paper toweling. Mix water and sugar until sugar dissolves, add vinegar, pour over cucumbers, and toss well. Cover and chill 1–2 hours, mixing now and then. Top with a grinding of pepper and serve as is or in lettuce cups. About 40 calories per serving.

CUCUMBERS IN SOUR CREAM

Good with fish, shellfish, or ham.
Makes 4 servings

¾ cup sour cream
1 tablespoon tarragon vinegar
1 tablespoon lemon juice
1 tablespoon minced fresh dill

¼ teaspoon salt
⅛ teaspoon pepper
2 medium-size cucumbers, peeled and
    sliced ¼" thick

Blend all ingredients but cucumbers, add
cucumbers, and toss to mix. Cover and
chill 1–2 hours. Toss again and serve.
About 110 calories per serving.

TURKISH CUCUMBER SALAD (CACIK)

A cooling salad dressed with yogurt and
seasoned with fresh mint and dill.
Makes 6–8 servings

4 medium-size cucumbers, peeled and
    quartered lengthwise

Dressing:
1 pint yogurt
1 clove garlic, peeled and crushed
2 tablespoons olive oil
Juice of ½ lemon
1 tablespoon minced fresh mint
2 tablespoons minced fresh dill
½ teaspoon salt
⅛ teaspoon white pepper

Slice cucumber quarters ⅛" thick and
drain on paper toweling. Beat dressing
ingredients until creamy, add cucumbers,
and toss well to mix. Cover and chill
several hours. Toss again, serve in small
bowls or, if you prefer, crisp lettuce cups.
About 105 calories for each of 6
servings, 80 calories for each of 8
servings.

⚖ ¢ ORIENTAL CUCUMBER SALAD

Sliced cucumbers in an unusual soy-red
wine vinegar dressing.
Makes 6 servings

3 large cucumbers, scrubbed well and
    sliced thin
3 tablespoons soy sauce
3 tablespoons red wine vinegar
3 tablespoons peanut oil
⅛ teaspoon pepper

Place cucumber slices in a large, shallow
bowl. Mix remaining ingredients and
pour over cucumbers. Toss well, cover,
and chill several hours, tossing

occasionally so all cucumber slices are
marinated. Serve cold. About 85 calories
per serving.

SALADE NIÇOISE

When served as a luncheon entree, this
classic salad usually contains tuna (see
seafood chapter for recipe).
Makes 4 servings

1 clove garlic, peeled and halved
1 head Boston lettuce, trimmed, broken
    in bite-size pieces, and chilled
½ cup French dressing
2 cups cold diced cooked potatoes
2 cups cold cooked cut green beans
½ cup ripe olives
2 tomatoes, cored and cut in wedges
1 (2-ounce) can rolled anchovies,
    drained
1 tablespoon capers
1 teaspoon minced fresh chervil
1 teaspoon minced fresh tarragon

Rub a salad bowl with garlic, add
lettuce, 2–3 tablespoons dressing, and
toss. Mix ¼ cup dressing with potatoes
and beans, then pile on lettuce. Garnish
with olives, tomatoes, and anchovies,
sprinkle with capers, herbs, and
remaining salad dressing. Do not toss.
About 340 calories per serving.

RUSSIAN SALAD

Makes 6 servings

1 cup cold diced cooked potatoes
1 cup cold cooked cut green beans
1 cup cold diced cooked carrots
1 cup cold cooked green peas
⅓ cup French dressing
⅓ cup mayonnaise
1 cup cold diced cooked beets
1 head Boston or romaine lettuce,
    trimmed, and chilled
1 tablespoon capers

Mix all vegetables except beets with
French dressing, cover, and chill 2–3
hours. Drain and save dressing; mix 1
tablespoon with mayonnaise, add to
vegetables along with beets, and toss
well. Mound on lettuce and top with
capers. About 245 calories per serving.

MOLDED COTTAGE CHEESE AND SPINACH SALAD

Makes 6–8 servings

1 quart lightly packed prepared fresh
  spinach leaves, minced
3 hard-cooked eggs, peeled and diced
1½ cups cottage cheese
1 medium-size sweet green pepper,
  cored, seeded, and minced
½ cup minced celery
½ cup mayonnaise
1¼ teaspoons salt
⅛ teaspoon pepper

Mix all ingredients and pack into a
lightly oiled 5-cup ring mold. Cover and
chill 3–4 hours. Unmold and garnish, if
you like, with tomato wedges and
parsley or watercress sprigs. About 300
calories for each of 6 servings, 225
calories for each of 8 servings.

OLD-FASHIONED POTATO SALAD

Nothing fancy but unusually good.
Makes 6 servings

6 medium-size boiled potatoes, chilled,
  peeled, and cubed
4 hard-cooked eggs, chilled, peeled, and
  diced
½ medium-size sweet green pepper,
  cored, seeded, and minced
1 medium-size yellow onion, peeled and
  minced
2 stalks celery, diced
1 cup mayonnaise
¼ cup sweet pickle relish
1½ teaspoons salt
⅛ teaspoon pepper

Stir all ingredients together to mix,
cover, and chill several hours before
serving. Serve as is or in crisp lettuce
cups. About 480 calories per serving.

HERBED POTATO SALAD

Dill and marjoram make this salad
especially fragrant.
Makes 6–8 servings

6 medium-size boiled potatoes, chilled,
  peeled, and cubed
6 hard-cooked eggs, chilled, peeled, and
  diced

1 medium-size yellow onion, peeled and
  minced
4 stalks celery, diced
½ cup minced sweet green pepper
  (optional)
½ cup minced dill pickle
1 cup mayonnaise
½ cup light cream
2 tablespoons white wine vinegar
2 tablespoons minced fresh dill or ¼
  teaspoon dried dill
½ teaspoon minced fresh marjoram or ¼
  teaspoon dried marjoram
1½ teaspoons salt
⅛ teaspoon pepper

Mix all ingredients in a very large bowl,
cover, and chill several hours before
serving. About 545 calories for each of
6 servings, 410 calories for each of 8
servings.

GERMAN POTATO SALAD

Nice and tart.
Makes 6 servings

1 tablespoon flour
¾ cup cold water
¼ cup cider vinegar
2 tablespoons sugar
¼ teaspoon white pepper
2–3 teaspoons salt
6 medium-size warm boiled potatoes,
  peeled and cubed
½ cup minced yellow onion
½ cup minced sweet green pepper
1 cup coarsely chopped celery
3–4 slices crisp cooked bacon, crumbled
6 hard-cooked eggs, peeled and diced

Blend flour and 2 tablespoons water in a
small saucepan, add remaining water,
vinegar, sugar, pepper, and 2 teaspoons
salt, and cook, stirring, until mixture
boils. Place potatoes, onion, green pepper
and celery in a large bowl and toss
lightly. Pour in hot dressing and mix
well. Cool to room temperature, add
bacon and eggs, and toss again. Taste for
salt and add more if needed. Serve at
room temperature. About 250 calories
per serving.

VARIATION:

Hot German Potato Salad: Cut 4 strips bacon crosswise in julienne strips, brown in a large skillet, and drain on paper toweling. In drippings stir-fry ⅔ cup minced onion until golden, 5–8 minutes. Blend in 1 tablespoon flour, add ¾ cup water or beef broth and the vinegar, sugar, salt, and pepper called for above. Heat and stir until mixture boils; keep warm. While potatoes are still hot, slice thin into a large bowl; scatter with bacon, omit green pepper, celery, and eggs. Pour hot dressing over potatoes, toss gently to mix, sprinkle with 1 tablespoon minced parsley, and serve. About 195 calories per serving.

SPANISH POTATO SALAD

What makes it Spanish are the green olives and olive oil dressing.
Makes 6 servings

6 medium-size boiled potatoes, chilled, peeled, and sliced thin
¾ cup minced pimiento-stuffed green olives
2 tablespoons finely grated Spanish or Bermuda onion
⅓ cup olive oil
2 teaspoons white wine vinegar
⅛ teaspoon pepper

Mix all ingredients in a large bowl, cover, and chill several hours before serving. About 240 calories per serving.

CELERY VICTOR

This cool American classic was created by Victor Hirtzler, for years chef at San Francisco's stately old St. Francis Hotel.
Makes 4 servings

1 large bunch celery, prepared for cooking
1½ cups boiling beef bouillon
1 cup French dressing
1 small bunch watercress or 1½ cups finely shredded iceberg lettuce
¼ teaspoon salt
⅛ teaspoon pepper
1 tablespoon minced parsley
8 anchovy fillets
1 large ripe tomato, cut in 8 wedges
8–12 ripe olives

Cut celery in 3″ lengths and simmer, covered, in bouillon 30 minutes until tender. Drain celery, toss with dressing, cover, and marinate in the refrigerator 4–6 hours or overnight. To serve, arrange watercress or lettuce on individual salad plates. Lift celery from dressing and arrange on top. Sprinkle each portion with salt, pepper, and parsley and decorate with anchovies, tomato wedges, and olives. Serve as an appetizer or salad. About 175 calories per serving.

ASPARAGUS VINAIGRETTE

Makes 4 servings

2 pounds asparagus, steamed or poached, or 2 (10-ounce) packages frozen asparagus spears, cooked by package directions
⅔ cup French Dressing or Spanish Vinaigrette

Drain asparagus well. Arrange in a large, shallow bowl, pour in dressing, cover, and marinate in refrigerator several hours, turning now and then. Serve on a bed of lettuce as a salad or first course. About 135 calories per serving (if made with French Dressing), 140 per serving (if made with Spanish Vinaigrette).

VARIATION:

Other Vegetables to Serve Vinaigrette: Artichoke hearts and bottoms, beans (green, wax, and lima), broccoli, carrots, cauliflower, celeriac, celery (especially the hearts), cucumbers, endive, fennel, hearts of palm, leeks, green peas, zucchini. Simply cook by basic method, drain well, add enough French Dressing to coat lightly, and marinate several hours in the refrigerator. Recipe too flexible for a meaningful calorie count.

CURRIED ASPARAGUS SALAD

Makes 3–4 servings

1 pound hot steamed asparagus or 1 (1-pound) can asparagus, drained
½ cup French Dressing
6–8 lettuce leaves, washed and crisped
1 pimiento, drained and cut in ¼″ strips

Curry Dressing:
½ cup mayonnaise
1 tablespoon sour cream
½ teaspoon curry powder
½ teaspoon lemon juice

Marinate asparagus in French Dressing 3–4 hours in refrigerator, turning occasionally. Shortly before serving, mix Curry Dressing. Drain asparagus (reserve French Dressing for other salads later) and arrange on lettuce. Top with Curry Dressing, garnish with pimiento, and serve. About 375 calories for each of 3 servings, 280 calories for each of 4 servings.

GREEN BEAN SALAD

Cooked green beans in a spicy red dressing. Especially good with pork, ham, or lamb.
Makes 6 servings

1½ pounds green beans, boiled and drained, or 2 (9-ounce) packages frozen cut green beans, cooked and drained by package directions
1 medium-size red onion, peeled and sliced thin

Dressing:
2 tablespoons minced fresh tarragon or ½ teaspoon dried tarragon
1 clove garlic, peeled and crushed
2 teaspoons prepared spicy brown mustard
1 tablespoon ketchup
½ teaspoon salt
Pinch pepper
½ cup olive oil
3 tablespoons red or white wine vinegar

Place beans and onion in a large bowl. Blend together dressing ingredients, pour over beans and onion, and toss to mix. Cover and let stand at room temperature about 1 hour. Toss again and serve. About 200 calories per serving.

THREE BEAN SALAD

Green, wax, and kidney beans marinated in a sweet-sour dressing.
Makes 6 servings

1 (1-pound) can cut green beans, drained
1 (1-pound) can wax beans, drained
1 (1-pound) can red kidney beans, drained
1 cup minced celery
1 cup minced sweet green pepper
1 cup minced yellow onion
½ cup minced sweet or dill pickle (optional)
½ cup olive oil
6 tablespoons cider vinegar
3 tablespoons sugar
1 teaspoon salt
⅛ teaspoon pepper

Mix all ingredients, cover, and chill several hours before serving. About 355 calories per serving.

HOT SWEET-SOUR BEAN SPROUT SALAD

Delicious with roast pork, ham, chicken, or turkey.
Makes 4 servings

1 pound fresh bean sprouts (readily available in Oriental groceries and occasionally in supermarkets)

Dressing:
6 slices bacon, cut crosswise in julienne strips
1 small yellow onion, peeled and coarsely chopped
½ small sweet green pepper, cored, seeded, and coarsely chopped
1 tablespoon ketchup
¼ cup tarragon vinegar
¼ teaspoon salt
Pinch pepper

Wash sprouts several times in cool water, discard any that are dark or blemished, and drain the rest in a colander. Brown bacon in a small skillet and drain on paper toweling. Stir-fry onion and green pepper in drippings over moderate heat 8–10 minutes until onion is golden. Mix in remaining dressing ingredients and simmer, uncovered, 5 minutes. Just before serving, set colander of sprouts in sink and turn on hot water full blast. Move colander about so all sprouts are heated—this will take 3–4 minutes.

Quickly drain sprouts and place in a salad bowl. Pour in hot dressing, add bacon, toss to mix, and serve. About 210 calories per serving.

DRIED BEAN SALAD

Makes 4 servings

2 cups any cold boiled dried beans
⅓ cup minced celery
⅓ cup minced sweet green pepper
⅓ cup minced yellow onion
3 tablespoons olive or other salad oil
2 tablespoons cider vinegar
1–2 tablespoons sugar
½ teaspoon salt (about)
⅛ teaspoon pepper
2 tablespoons minced parsley

Mix all ingredients, cover, and chill several hours or overnight, tossing now and then. Taste for salt and adjust. About 235 calories per serving.

VARIATIONS:

Creamy Dried Bean Salad: Prepare as directed but omit oil and add ⅓ cup mayonnaise and 2–3 tablespoons chili sauce. About 300 calories per serving.

Parmesan Bean Salad: Prepare and chill salad as directed. Just before serving toss in ¼ cup finely grated Parmesan cheese. About 260 calories per serving.

Bean and Beet Salad (Makes 6 servings): Prepare as directed but add 1 (1-pound) can pickled beets, drained and diced, and 2 extra tablespoons olive oil. About 325 calories per serving.

CHICK-PEA AND TOMATO SALAD

Keeps well in the refrigerator and is actually better after 1 or 2 days.
Makes 6–8 servings

2 medium-size ripe tomatoes, peeled, cored, seeded, and cubed
½ cup minced sweet green pepper
½ cup minced Bermuda or Spanish onion
1 clove garlic, peeled and crushed
3 (1-pound 4-ounce) cans chick-peas, drained well
¼ cup minced parsley
1 tablespoon minced chives

1 teaspoon minced fresh marjoram or
½ teaspoon dried marjoram or oregano
½ teaspoon salt
⅛ teaspoon pepper
¼ cup olive oil
3 tablespoons red wine vinegar

Place all ingredients in a large bowl and toss well to mix. Cover and marinate at room temperature at least 1 hour. Toss well again and serve. About 200 calories for each of 6 servings, 150 calories for each of 8 servings.

RICE AND BLACK-EYED PEA SALAD

Makes 6 servings

1 quart hot boiled rice
1 (10-ounce) package frozen black-eyed peas, cooked and drained by package directions
1 medium-size yellow onion, peeled and minced
1 clove garlic, peeled and crushed
1 large carrot, peeled and coarsely grated
¼ cup minced parsley
1½ teaspoons salt
⅛ teaspoon black or cayenne pepper
3–4 tablespoons olive oil

Mix all ingredients together, adding just enough oil to coat all lightly. Serve warm or at room temperature as a main dish salad. Good mounded in hollowed-out tomatoes. About 240 calories per serving.

BASIC MACARONI SALAD

Makes 6 servings

½ pound elbow macaroni, cooked and drained by package directions and chilled
1 cup diced celery
½ cup minced scallions or 1 small yellow onion, peeled and minced
⅓ cup minced sweet green and/or red pepper
1 cup mayonnaise or mayonnaise-type salad dressing
2 tablespoons white vinegar or lemon juice
2 teaspoons prepared mild yellow mustard
1½ teaspoons salt (about)
⅛ teaspoon pepper

Mix all ingredients, cover, and chill several hours; taste for salt and adjust. Serve garnished with tomato wedges and quartered hard-cooked egg. About 465 calories per serving.

VARIATIONS:

Cheese-Macaroni Salad: Prepare as directed but add 1 cup diced sharp Cheddar, Swiss, or Gruyère cheese and use ½ cup each mayonnaise and Roquefort or blue cheese dressing. About 540 calories per serving.

Macaroni and Meat, Chicken or Shellfish Salad: Prepare as directed but add 3 cups cubed cooked ham, tongue, chicken, turkey or shellfish and an extra ⅓ cup mayonnaise or ¼ cup French dressing. Serve as an entree. About 705 calories per serving (made with ham or tongue), 655 per serving (made with chicken or turkey), 630 (made with shellfish).

German Macaroni Salad: Omit mayonnaise and vinegar; dress instead with ½ cup olive oil and ¼ cup white wine vinegar; also add 1 large minced dill pickle. About 345 calories per serving.

"Deli" Salad: Mix 2 cups Basic Macaroni Salad with 2–2½ cups mixed cubed salami, bologna, corned beef, ham, tongue, luncheon meat, or chicken roll— whatever combination pleases you; chill well and serve as an entree. About 575 calories per serving (if made with any of the meats), 545 calories per serving (made with chicken).

RICE-STUFFED TOMATOES AL PESTO

Makes 8 servings

8 large ripe beefsteak tomatoes

Stuffing:

2 cups water
¼ cup olive oil
1 cup uncooked rice
1 medium-size yellow onion, peeled and minced
1 clove garlic, peeled and crushed
2 tablespoons minced parsley

2 tablespoons minced fresh basil
½ cup piñon nuts
2 tablespoons finely grated Parmesan cheese
¾ teaspoon salt
Pinch pepper

Core tomatoes, scoop out seeds and pulp, leaving only firm outer walls; drain upside down on several thicknesses paper toweling. Bring water and 1 tablespoon olive oil to a boil in a small saucepan, stir in rice, and boil rapidly uncovered, stirring occasionally, 10–12 minutes until almost all water is absorbed; turn heat to low and let rice dry out. Meanwhile, stir-fry onion and garlic in remaining oil in a large, heavy skillet over moderate 8–10 minutes until golden. Mix in rice and remaining stuffing ingredients, turn heat to low, and heat, stirring occasionally, 5 minutes; cool to room temperature. Stuff tomatoes with mixture and serve as an entree. About 245 calories per serving.

TABBOULEH

A Middle Eastern salad that can also be served as a first course.
Makes 4–6 servings

1 cup uncooked bulgur wheat
2 cups boiling chicken broth or water
1 cup minced parsley
¼ cup minced fresh mint or 2 tablespoons dried mint
1 medium-size yellow onion, peeled and minced
2 ripe tomatoes, peeled, cored, and coarsely chopped
¼ cup olive oil
¼ cup lemon juice
½ teaspoon salt (about)
⅛ teaspoon pepper
½ head romaine lettuce, trimmed and chilled

Mix bulgur wheat and broth, cover, and let stand at room temperature 2 hours. Fluff with a fork, add parsley, mint, onion, and tomatoes, and toss to mix. Beat oil, lemon juice, salt, and pepper until well blended, add to salad, and toss again. Cover and chill well. Taste for salt and adjust if needed. Arrange romaine leaves spoke fashion on a platter or in a shallow bowl and mound salad in center. Diners can serve themselves by scooping up salad with romaine leaves, or individual portions can be served on leaves. About 310 calories for each of 4 servings, 210 calories for each of 6 servings.

CHEF'S SALAD

Makes 4 servings

3 cups prepared mixed salad greens (include watercress if possible)
½ medium-size cucumber, peeled and cut in ¼" cubes
½ medium-size Spanish onion, peeled and sliced thin
1 cup julienne strips boiled ham, chilled
½ cup julienne strips cooked smoked tongue, chilled
1 cup julienne strips cooked white meat of chicken or turkey, chilled
½ cup julienne strips Swiss cheese, chilled
4 radishes, washed and sliced thin
½–¾ cup French dressing

Toss greens lightly with cucumber and onion in a large salad bowl. Group ham, tongue, chicken, and cheese on greens in a spoke fashion; fill center with radishes. Cover and chill until serving time. Dress at the table by adding about ½ cup dressing and tossing gently. About 410 calories per serving.

VARIATIONS:

– Use any combination of meat and cheese instead of those listed—luncheon meat, salami, headcheese, Cheddar cheese, etc.
– Substitute boneless sardines, flaked tuna, or cooked, smoked, flaked haddock for the ham and/or tongue.
– Use washed, crisped spinach leaves as part of the greens.
– Use any favorite salad dressing instead of French—Russian, Thousand Island, Italian, Green Goddess, etc.

Recipe variations all too flexible for meaningful calorie counts.

CHICKEN OR TURKEY SALAD

A good basic salad to vary according to whim.
Makes 6 servings

3 cups diced cold cooked chicken or turkey meat
1 cup diced celery
¼ cup minced yellow onion or scallions
¼ cup minced sweet green pepper (optional)
2 tablespoons minced pimiento
¾ cup mayonnaise
2 tablespoons French dressing, lemon juice, or milk
¼ teaspoon salt (about)
⅛ teaspoon pepper
1 tablespoon minced parsley (garnish)

Mix all ingredients except parsley, cover, and chill 2–3 hours. Taste for salt and adjust. Sprinkle with parsley and serve. For a party, mound in avocado halves or hollowed-out tomatoes. About 425 calories per serving (if made with French dressing), 395 calories per serving (if made with lemon juice or milk).

To Use for Sandwiches: Mince chicken instead of dicing, then proceed as directed.

VARIATIONS:

Chicken, Egg, and Caper Salad: Prepare as directed using French dressing, but mix in 3 diced, peeled, hard-cooked eggs and 2 tablespoons each capers and minced sweet or dill pickle. About 470 calories per serving.

Chicken and Vegetable Salad: Reduce celery to ½ cup and mix in 1–1½ cups any of the following combinations: mixed cooked peas and diced carrots; diced avocado and cucumber; diced cooked potatoes and cooked cut green beans; cooked asparagus tips and diced radishes; diced unpeeled raw baby zucchini and diced, peeled, cored, and seeded tomatoes; drained canned bean sprouts, shredded Chinese cabbage, and slivered water chestnuts. Recipe too flexible for a meaningful calorie count.

Chicken, Olive, and Walnut Salad: Reduce celery to ½ cup and add ½ cup each sliced pitted ripe or green olives and ½ cup coarsely chopped walnuts. About 500 calories per serving (if made with French dressing), 470 per serving (if made with milk or lemon juice).

Chicken and Ham Salad: Prepare as directed, using 1½ cups each diced, cooked ham (or tongue, luncheon meat, corned beef, cooked veal or lamb) and chicken. Recipe too flexible for a meaningful calorie count.

Chicken and Seafood Salad: Prepare as directed, using 1½ cups each diced, cooked fish or shellfish and chicken. About 425 calories per serving (if made with French dressing), 395 calories per serving (if made with lemon juice or milk).

Some Quick Ways to Vary the Flavor: Mix any of the following into mayonnaise before adding to salad:
– 2 teaspoons curry or chili powder
– ¼ cup minced hot chutney, hot mustard pickle, or hot pepper relish
– 1 tablespoon prepared spicy brown mustard or prepared horseradish
– 2 tablespoons soy sauce and 1 tablespoon Worcestershire sauce (omit salt)
– ¼ cup chili sauce or any thick bottled salad dressing (Roquefort, Russian, Thousand Island, etc.)
– 2 tablespoons minced fresh dill, basil, or chives (or 1 teaspoon dried).

Flavor variations too flexible for meaningful calorie counts.

CHICKEN WALDORF SALAD

Makes 4 servings

3 cups ½" cubes of cold cooked chicken meat
2 medium-size tart apples, peeled, cored, and diced
⅔ cup minced celery
¼ cup coarsely chopped pecans
2 tablespoons toasted, blanched, slivered almonds
1½ cups mayonnaise
1 teaspoon salt
⅛ teaspoon white pepper

Mix all ingredients well, cover, and chill 2–3 hours. Stir, taste for salt and add more if needed. Serve in lettuce cups, avocado halves, or hollowed-out tomatoes. About 875 calories per serving (in lettuce cups).

CHOW CHOW CHICKEN OR TURKEY SALAD

Makes 4 servings

1½–1¾ cups cold diced, cooked chicken or turkey meat (preferably white meat)
1 cup finely chopped celery
⅓ cup coarsely chopped mustard pickles
1 pimiento, drained and minced
¼ cup coarsely chopped, blanched almonds
1 teaspoon finely grated yellow onion
½–1 teaspoon salt
⅛ teaspoon white pepper
¼ cup French dressing
⅓ cup mayonnaise

Mix together all ingredients, cover, and chill 2–3 hours to blend flavors. Serve as is or in lettuce cups, hollowed-out tomatoes, or avocado halves. For a touch of the exotic, serve in mango or small papaya halves. About 380 calories per serving.

EGG SALAD

Makes about 3 cups, enough for 4 salads, 6–8 sandwiches

12 hard-cooked eggs, chilled, peeled, and coarsely chopped
1 tablespoon minced yellow onion
¼ cup minced celery (optional)
1 tablespoon minced parsley (optional)
1 teaspoon salt
⅛ teaspoon pepper
¼–⅓ cup mayonnaise or mayonnaise-type salad dressing
3–4 tablespoons milk

Mix all ingredients together, adding just enough mayonnaise and milk to give salad a good consistency. Cover and chill several hours. Stir well and use as a main course salad—in lettuce cups or hollowed-out tomatoes—or as a sandwich spread. About 480 calories per cup, 30 calories per tablespoon.

VARIATIONS:

Pickle-Egg Salad: Prepare as directed but add 2 tablespoons minced dill or sweet pickle and substitute 1–2 tablespoons pickle juice for 1–2 tablespoons milk. About 490 calories per cup, 31 calories per tablespoon.

Dilly Egg Salad: Prepare as directed, adding 1 tablespoon each minced fresh dill and capers. About 490 calories per cup, 31 calories per tablespoon.

Herbed Egg Salad: Prepare as directed, adding 1 tablespoon each minced parsley and chives and 1 teaspoon minced fresh or ¼ teaspoon dried tarragon, chervil, marjoram, or rosemary. About 480 calories per cup, 30 calories per tablespoon.

Anchovy-Egg Salad: Prepare as directed, adding 2 tablespoons anchovy paste and omitting salt. About 510 calories per cup, 32 calories per tablespoon.

Curried Egg Salad: Prepare as directed, adding 2–3 teaspoons curry powder and 1–2 tablespoons minced chutney. About 500 calories per cup, 31 calories per tablespoon.

Olive-Egg Salad: Prepare as directed, but omit salt and add ⅓ cup minced green or ripe olives. About 510 calories per cup, 32 calories per tablespoon.

Caviar-Egg Salad: Prepare as directed but mix in 1 (1-ounce) jar black caviar and omit salt. About 525 calories per cup, 33 calories per tablespoon.

Mustard-Egg Salad: Prepare as directed, but add 1 tablespoon prepared spicy brown mustard and 3–4 dashes liquid hot red pepper seasoning. Use 2 tablespoons tarragon vinegar for 2 tablespoons milk. About 480 calories per cup, 30 calories per tablespoon.

Deviled Egg Salad: Prepare as Mustard-Egg Salad directs, but substitute relish-type sandwich spread for the mayonnaise. About 480 calories per cup, 30 calories per tablespoon.

BASIC HAM OR TONGUE SALAD

Makes 4–6 servings

2 cups cubed, cooked ham or tongue or 1 cup of each
3 hard-cooked eggs, peeled and coarsely chopped
½ medium-size sweet green pepper, cored, seeded, and cut in julienne strips
2 tablespoons minced yellow onion (optional)
1 large dill pickle, minced
½ cup mayonnaise or mayonnaise-type salad dressing
1 tablespoon lemon juice
1 tablespoon light cream
1 teaspoon Worcestershire sauce
½ teaspoon prepared mild yellow mustard

Mix all ingredients, cover, and chill 2–3 hours. Serve mounded in lettuce cups or in the center hollow of a tomato aspic or jellied vegetable salad ring. About 435 calories for each of 4 servings (served in lettuce), 290 calories for each of 6.

VARIATION:

Ham and Cheese Salad: Prepare as directed, using 1½ cups cubed ham and 1 cup cubed sharp Cheddar, Swiss, or Gruyère cheese. About 510 calories for each of 4 servings, 340 calories for each of 6 servings.

EASY TUNA SALAD

Makes about 3 cups, enough for 4 salads or 6–8 sandwiches

2 (7-ounce) cans tuna, drained and flaked
½ cup minced Bermuda onion
Juice of ½ lemon
¾–1 cup mayonnaise (depending on how creamy a mixture you want)
2 tablespoons minced parsley
Pinch salt
⅛ teaspoon pepper

Mix all ingredients and chill several hours before serving. Serve as a salad in hollowed-out tomatoes or on crisp lettuce leaves or as a sandwich spread. About 600 calories per cup, 38 calories per tablespoon.

VARIATIONS:

Tart Tuna Salad: Prepare as directed but add 2 tablespoons minced capers and 1 tablespoon minced fresh dill or ½ teaspoon dried dill. About 600 calories per cup, 38 calories per tablespoon.

Herbed Tuna Salad: Prepare as directed but increase parsley to 3 tablespoons and add 1 tablespoon minced fresh marjoram or ½ teaspoon dried marjoram. About 600 calories per cup, 38 calories per tablespoon.

Tuna-Cheese Salad: Prepare as directed but reduce mayonnaise to ½ cup and add ¼ cup sour cream; also add ¾ cup coarsely grated Cheddar cheese and 1 tablespoon capers. About 600 calories per cup, 38 calories per tablespoon.

Tuna-Cucumber Salad: Prepare as directed but add ⅓ cup minced cucumber or, if you prefer, diced celery. About 600 calories per cup, 38 calories per tablespoon.

Tuna-Anchovy Salad: Prepare as directed but omit salt and add 3–4 minced, drained anchovy fillets. About 605 calories per cup, 38 calories per tablespoon.

Tuna-Olive Salad: Prepare as directed but omit salt and lemon juice and add ½ cup minced green or ripe olives. About 610 calories per cup, 38 calories per tablespoon.

SCANDINAVIAN HERRING SALAD (SILDESALAT)

Serve as an appetizer or entree.
Makes 4 entree servings, enough appetizers for 6–8

3 herring in brine
2 cups cold diced, boiled potatoes
2 cups cold diced, boiled beets
1 small yellow onion, peeled and minced
½ teaspoon powdered mustard blended with 1 tablespoon cider vinegar
1 teaspoon sugar
¾ cup heavy cream, whipped to soft peaks
⅛ teaspoon pepper

Soak herring in cold water 24 hours,

changing water several times. Remove heads, fillet and skin* herring, and cut in 1″ cubes. Mix herring with vegetables; add remaining ingredients and mix again. Chill well before serving. About 390 calories for each of 4 entree servings, 260 calories for each of 6 appetizer servings, and 195 calories for each of 8 appetizer servings.

BASIC SHELLFISH SALAD

The flavor will be best if shellfish is freshly cooked and still slightly warm when mixed into salad.
Makes 4 servings

1 pound cooked, shelled, and deveined shrimp, diced, cooked lobster, crab meat, or scallops
½ cup mayonnaise
2 tablespoons lemon juice or French dressing
Pinch cayenne pepper
½ teaspoon anchovy paste (optional)
1 tablespoon minced chives
½ cup diced celery, chilled
½ cup diced cucumber, chilled

Mix all but last 2 ingredients, cover, and chill 2–3 hours. Add celery and cucumber, mix well, and taste for salt if anchovy paste is not used. Serve mounded in lettuce cups, hollowed-out tomatoes, halved avocados, or in the center of a tomato aspic or jellied vegetable salad ring. About 350 calories per serving (made with lemon juice), 395 (made with French dressing).

VARIATIONS:

Shellfish, Egg, and Avocado Salad: Prepare as directed but add 3 coarsely chopped hard-cooked eggs and 1 diced, peeled avocado along with celery and cucumber; toss very gently. About 500 calories per serving (made with lemon juice), 545 calories per serving (made with French dressing).

Shellfish Salad Louisiana: Prepare as directed, using 2 cups mixed, cooked shrimp, lobster, and crab meat and adding ¼ cup chili sauce and ¼ teaspoon prepared horseradish. About 405 calories per serving (made with lemon juice), 450 (made with French dressing).

Spanish Shellfish Salad: Prepare as directed but blend ⅛ teaspoon powdered saffron into lemon juice before mixing into salad; omit celery and cucumber and add 1 cup cubed, cooked potatoes, ½ cup cooked green peas, ⅓ cup coarsely chopped, pitted ripe olives, and 1 cup shredded Boston lettuce or romaine. Add a little extra mayonnaise if needed. About 470 calories per serving (without extra mayonnaise).

Shellfish and Saffron Rice Salad: Prepare as directed, adding 1½ cups cold Saffron Rice, ¼ cup minced sweet green pepper, and 1 tablespoon each olive oil and cider vinegar along with celery and cucumber. About 450 calories per serving (if made with lemon juice), 495 calories per serving (if made with French dressing).

⊠ QUICK CURRIED SHRIMP SALAD

Makes 4 servings

⅓ cup mayonnaise
3 tablespoons sour cream
1 teaspoon curry powder
1 teaspoon lemon juice
1 teaspoon minced chives
⅛ teaspoon pepper
1 pound cooked, shelled, and deveined shrimp, chilled
Crisp lettuce cups

Mix all ingredients except shrimp and lettuce; add shrimp and toss to mix well. Cover and chill 30 minutes or longer. Serve in lettuce cups. Or divide in 6 smaller portions and serve as an appetizer. About 300 calories per entree serving, 200 calories for each of 6 appetizers.

VARIATION:

Quick Curried Chicken or Turkey: Prepare as directed, substituting 3 cups ½″ cubes cooked chicken or turkey meat for shrimp and adding, if you like, ½ cup diced celery and/or apple. About 310 calories per entree serving (made with ½ cup each diced celery and apple).

CRAB RAVIGOTE

Makes 6 servings

1½ pounds fresh lump or backfin crab meat, well picked over, or 4 (6-ounce) packages frozen Alaska king crab meat, thawed and drained
¼ cup tarragon vinegar
¾ cup mayonnaise
½ medium-size yellow onion, peeled and minced
2 tablespoons capers, minced
1 tablespoon minced chives
1 teaspoon minced parsley
1 teaspoon minced fresh chervil
1 teaspoon minced fresh tarragon
1 tablespoon slivered pimiento

Mix crab meat and vinegar, cover, and marinate in refrigerator 2 hours, turning now and then. Drain off vinegar and mix it with all but last ingredient, pour over crab, toss well, and arrange on lettuce or in avocado halves. Garnish with pimiento and serve. About 210 calories per serving (in lettuce).

GRAPEFRUIT AND AVOCADO SALAD

Makes 6 servings

2 grapefruit, peeled and sectioned
2 medium-size ripe avocados
Juice of 1 lemon
½ cup French, Roquefort French, or Sweet French Dressing

Make sure all white pith is removed from grapefruit sections. Halve, pit, and peel avocados; slice into thin crescents and dip in lemon juice to prevent darkening. Place in a large bowl with grapefruit, add dressing, and toss to mix. Serve as is or on a bed of crisp mixed greens. About 290 calories per serving (with French Dressing), 305 (with Roquefort French Dressing), and 325 (with Sweet French Dressing).

VARIATIONS:

Orange and Avocado Salad: Prepare as directed but substitute 4 navel oranges for the grapefruit. Calorie counts the same as for Grapefruit and Avocado Salad.

Papaya and Avocado Salad: Prepare as directed but substitute 1 large, ripe papaya, pitted, peeled, and thinly sliced, for the grapefruit. Use Sweet French Dressing. About 300 calories per serving.

Tomato and Avocado Salad: Prepare as directed but use 3 large, ripe beefsteak tomatoes, peeled, cored, and cut in slim wedges, instead of grapefruit. Use French or Roquefort French Dressing. About 280 calories per serving (with French Dressing), 295 (with Roquefort French Dressing).

Avocado and Endive Salad: Prepare as directed but substitute 4–6 Belgian endives, cut in 1″ chunks and separated into individual leaves, for the grapefruit. Use French or Roquefort French Dressing. About 275 calories per serving (with French Dressing), 290 (with Roquefort French Dressing).

WALDORF SALAD

Makes 4 servings

4 medium-size tart red apples, cored and
*   diced (do not peel)*
¾ cup finely chopped celery
⅓ cup coarsely chopped walnuts
⅔–1 cup mayonnaise

Stir all ingredients together, adding just enough mayonnaise for good consistency. Cover and chill 2–3 hours. Stir well and serve on lettuce leaves. About 425 calories per serving.

VARIATIONS:

Date-Marshmallow Waldorf Salad: Prepare as directed but reduce celery to ⅓ cup and add ½ cup diced, pitted dates and 16 miniature marshmallows. About 545 calories per serving.

Red Grape Waldorf Salad: Prepare as directed but add 1 cup halved, seeded red grapes. About 440 calories per serving.

Pear Waldorf Salad: Prepare as directed but substitute 4 ripe pears for apples. About 455 calories per serving.

Banana Waldorf Salad: Prepare as directed but add 2 peeled, thinly sliced bananas. About 465 calories per serving.

Sour Cream Waldorf Salad: Prepare as directed, but add 1 tablespoon honey and substitute ½ cup sour cream for ½ cup mayonnaise. About 305 calories per serving.

AMBROSIA SALAD

A Southern favorite served both as salad and dessert.
Makes 4–6 servings

1 cup well-drained mandarin oranges
1 cup miniature marshmallows
1 cup well-drained pineapple chunks
1 cup flaked coconut
1 cup coarsely chopped pecans (optional)
1 cup sour cream

Mix all ingredients, cover, and chill about 1 hour. Serve as is, on pineapple rings, or in lettuce cups. About 535 calories for each of 4 servings, 355 calories for each of 6 servings.

FIVE FRUIT SALAD

A more elaborate ambrosia.
Makes 6 servings

1½ cups well-drained pineapple chunks
*   or diced apricot halves*
2 bananas, peeled and diced
2 oranges or tangerines, peeled,
*   sectioned, seeded, diced, and drained*
2 apples or pears, peeled, cored, and
*   diced*
1 cup diced, pitted dates
1 cup miniature marshmallows
*   (optional)*
1¼ cups mayonnaise or Fruit
*   Mayonnaise*

Mix all ingredients, cover, and chill several hours. Stir well and serve as is or mounded in lettuce cups. About 560 calories per serving (without marshmallows).

About Gelatins and Molded Salads

Cool, shimmering, jewel-bright, these are the glamour salads. They're good party choices because they're showy, also because they can be made hours, even days, ahead of time. The vital ingredient, of course, is gelatin, either unflavored or fruit-flavored. Unflavored gelatin is 85 per cent protein and low in calories. Flavored gelatins are sweetened either with sugar or one of the non-caloric artificial sweeteners. Depending upon the calorie value of the foods being molded, gelatin salads are excellent choices for dieters.

How Much Gelatin? The perfect molded salad is tender yet strong enough to stand on its own. Too much gelatin makes the salad rubbery, too little makes it collapse. Here is the standard ratio:

To Mold 2 cups of Liquid, Use: 1 envelope (1 tablespoon) unflavored gelatin *or* 1 (3-ounce) package fruit-flavored gelatin.

Note: Very sweet mixtures will "set up" softer than tart or savory ones. *Do not attempt to mold fresh or frozen pineapple or pineapple juice; they contain an enzyme that breaks down the gelatin and keeps it from setting.* Canned pineapple, however, can be used.

To Dissolve Gelatin:

Unflavored Gelatin: There are 4 techniques; which you use is determined by the individual recipe.

Over Direct Heat: Sprinkle gelatin over cold liquid, then heat and stir constantly over low heat until dissolved. (*Note:* If cream or milk is used, gelatin will take about twice as long to dissolve.)

By Adding Hot Liquid: Soften gelatin in a small amount of cold liquid, then pour in simmering-hot liquid and stir until dissolved.

By Mixing with Sugar: Mix sugar with dry gelatin, add cold liquid, and heat and stir over low heat until dissolved, or pour boiling liquid over sugar-gelatin mixture and stir until dissolved.

Over Boiling Water: Soften gelatin in a small amount of cold liquid, set over boiling water (or place in a ramekin and stand in a small amount of boiling water), and heat and stir until dissolved. Combine with remaining liquid.

Flavored Gelatins: One simple method: Pour boiling or simmering-hot liquid over gelatin and stir until dissolved.

About Combining Solid Foods with Gelatin: If minced fruits, meats, or vegetables are added to gelatin while it is still liquid, they will sink or float, depending upon whether they're lighter or heavier than the gelatin. Celery, apples, pears, bananas, avocados, and peaches are all floaters. Grapes, most citrus and canned fruits, most cooked meats and vegetables are sinkers. To distribute foods evenly throughout gelatin, chill gelatin mixture until thick and syrupy (it should be about the consistency of raw egg white), then fold in foods and chill until firm.

(*Note:* Always drain all foods well before adding so that they do not water down gelatin. For 2 cups of gelatin mixture, allow 1–2 cups solids, either minced, cubed, or cut in small pieces.)

Gelatin Setting Times: These will vary somewhat even in standard gelatin mixtures, depending upon sweetness or tartness of mixture, shape and size of mold (large molds take proportionately longer to set up than small ones), temperature and humidity of refrigerator. The following times, however, are average *minimums:*

Clear Gelatin (with no foods mixed in): about 2 hours

Gelatins with Foods Mixed in: about 4 hours

Layered Gelatins: about 12 hours (*Note:* A detailed discussion of layered gelatins and ribbon loaves follows.)

To Hasten Jelling: Dissolve 1 package gelatin in 1 cup boiling liquid, then add 7–10 ice cubes and stir until mixture is syrupy; remove any unmelted ice cubes. Or, prepare gelatin mixture as recipe directs, then set in an ice water bath or in a large bowl of crushed ice and stir until syrupy. (*Note:* It's generally bad practice to quick-jell a mixture in the freezer—except for mousses and chiffon-type molds—because the gelatin may freeze and break down.)

About Molds: Clear gelatins can be molded in deeply sculptured molds (and come out as sparkling and faceted as jewels), but mixtures containing solids should be molded in something simpler; if not, they will be difficult to unmold and the intricacy of the design will be lost. Recipes occasionally call for oiled or greased molds (to facilitate unmolding), but oil leaves an unpleasant film on the gelatin. A better method is simply to rinse mold quickly in cold water, then to add gelatin mixture to the wet mold.

How to Unmold Gelatin Salads: Keep mold refrigerated and do not unmold until ready to serve.
– Dip mold in *warm* (not hot) water to depth of gelatin mixture.
– Remove from water, loosen edges with tip of a paring knife.
– Place a serving plate, quickly rinsed in cold water but not dried, flat on top of mold, then invert so plate is on the bottom and shake gently. Gelatin should ease right out. By having serving plate moist, you can easily center mold.
– Wipe up any drops of liquid, garnish as desired, and serve.

⚖ **TOMATO ASPIC**

Plenty of variations here to try, some simple, some sophisticated.
Makes 4–6 servings

1 quart tomato juice
2 sprigs parsley
1 stalk celery, coarsely chopped
  (include tops)
2 tablespoons minced onion
1 bay leaf, crushed
1½ teaspoons salt
1½ teaspoons sugar
¼ teaspoon basil
1–2 drops liquid hot red pepper
  seasoning

2 envelopes unflavored gelatin
2 tablespoons lemon juice
1 pint prepared mixed salad greens

Simmer 2 cups tomato juice, covered, 20 minutes with parsley, celery, onion, bay leaf, salt, sugar, basil, and pepper seasoning, stirring occasionally; strain tomato juice, discarding the solids, mix in gelatin, and stir to dissolve. Mix in remaining tomato juice and lemon juice. Pour into an ungreased 1-quart ring mold and chill until firm, at least 4 hours. To serve, unmold on a flat round platter, fill center, and decorate base with greens. Pass French dressing or mayonnaise. About 75 calories for each of 4 servings (without dressing), 50 for each of 6 servings.

VARIATIONS:

Tomato, Cream Cheese, and Olive Aspic: Begin aspic as directed and smooth 2 (3-ounce) packages softened cream cheese into hot tomato juice-gelatin mixture. Stir in remaining tomato juice and lemon juice and chill until syrupy. Mix in ¼ cup thinly sliced pimiento-stuffed green olives, pour into a 5-cup mold, and chill until firm. About 245 calories for each of 4 servings, 165 calories for each of 6 servings.

Egg-Tomato Aspic: Prepare aspic, chill until syrupy, and divide in 3 equal parts; pour ⅓ into a 1-quart mold and arrange 1 sliced hard-cooked egg on top (it will sink about halfway), chill until tacky; keep remaining aspic syrupy. Arrange another sliced hard-cooked egg on tacky layer, pour in another ⅓ of aspic and chill until tacky. Top with a third sliced hard-cooked egg and remaining aspic. Chill until firm. About 135 calories for each of 4 servings, 90 calories for each of 6 servings.

Vegetable Aspic (Makes 6 servings): Prepare aspic as directed and chill until syrupy; fold in 1½–2 cups mixed, diced raw or cooked vegetables (any combination you fancy). Spoon into a 1½-quart mold and chill until firm. Recipe too flexible for a meaningful calorie count.

Tomato-Cheese Aspic (Makes 6 servings): Prepare aspic and chill until syrupy; fold in 1 cup cottage cheese and ¼ cup each minced sweet green pepper and celery. Mold as directed in a 1½-quart mold. *For a 2-Layer Aspic:* Pour half of syrupy aspic into mold and chill until tacky. Mix remaining aspic with the cheese and vegetables, spoon on top, and chill until firm. About 120 calories per serving.

⚖ **Seafood Aspic** (Makes 6 servings): Prepare aspic and chill until syrupy; fold in 1 teaspoon anchovy paste and 1½ cups coarsely chopped cooked fish or shellfish; mold as directed in a 1½-quart mold. About 95 calories per serving.

Ham or Tongue Aspic (Makes 6 servings): Prepare aspic and chill until syrupy; fold in 1½ cups diced, cooked ham or tongue and ¼ cup minced mustard pickle; mold as directed in a 1½-quart mold. About 185 calories per serving.

Chicken or Turkey Aspic (Makes 6 servings): Prepare aspic and chill until syrupy; fold in 1½ cups diced cooked chicken or turkey and ¼ cup applesauce. Mold as directed in a 1½-quart mold. About 145 calories per serving.

⚖ **CUCUMBER ASPIC**

Makes 6–8 servings

4 small cucumbers, peeled
2 cups water
1 teaspoon salt
2 envelopes unflavored gelatin
1 tablespoon finely grated yellow onion
4 teaspoons lemon juice
½ teaspoon Worcestershire sauce
Pinch cayenne pepper
2 or 3 drops green food coloring

Coarsely chop 2 cucumbers and simmer, covered, with water and salt about 20 minutes until mushy; drain liquid into gelatin, set over low heat, and heat and stir until dissolved. Press cooked cucumbers through a fine sieve, then mix into gelatin along with onion, lemon juice, Worcestershire, cayenne, and coloring.

Cover and chill until syrupy. Meanwhile, halve and seed remaining cucumbers and coarsely grate. Mix into gelatin, spoon into an ungreased 5-cup mold, and chill until firm. Unmold and serve on crisp greens. Pass mayonnaise, if you like, or Old-Fashioned Cooked Dressing. About 25 calories for each of 6 servings (without mayonnaise), 20 for each of 8.

LEMON-AVOCADO ASPIC

Makes 4–6 servings

1 (3-ounce) package lemon-flavored gelatin
1 teaspoon salt
1¾ cups boiling water
1 teaspoon lemon juice
Few drops liquid hot red pepper seasoning
1 teaspoon finely grated yellow onion
1½ cups thinly sliced avocado
¼ cup finely shredded red cabbage

Mix gelatin and salt with boiling water, stirring until dissolved; mix in lemon juice, pepper seasoning, and onion and chill until syrupy. Fold in avocado and cabbage, spoon into an ungreased 1-quart mold, and chill until firm. Unmold and serve with mayonnaise. About 180 calories for each of 4 servings (without mayonnaise), 120 calories for each of 6 servings.

VARIATIONS:

Creamy Lemon and Avocado Mold: Mix gelatin and salt with 1 cup boiling water, blend in ¾ cup sour cream, and proceed as directed. About 260 for each of 4 servings, 175 calories for each of 6 servings.

Lime-Avocado Mousse: Mix 1 (3-ounce) package lime-flavored gelatin with the salt and 1 cup boiling water, stirring until dissolved. Cool but do not chill. Mix in ¾ cup mayonnaise or sour cream, the seasonings called for above, and 1½ cups puréed avocado; omit cabbage. Mold as directed. Good topped with cold marinated shellfish. If made with mayonnaise: About 325 calories for each of 4 servings, 215 for each of 6.

If made with sour cream: About 260
calories for each of 4 servings, 175 for
each of 6 servings.

MOLDED COTTAGE AND CREAM CHEESE SALAD

Makes 14–16 servings

1 envelope unflavored gelatin
1 cup cold water
*1 (3-ounce) package lemon-flavored
   gelatin*
2 cups boiling water
¼ cup cider vinegar
¼ cup canned pineapple juice
1 teaspoon finely grated yellow onion
½ teaspoon prepared horseradish
1 teaspoon salt
1 cup cottage cheese
*1 (3-ounce) package cream cheese,
   softened to room temperature*
⅔ cup evaporated milk or light cream
*½ cup coarsely chopped
   pimiento-stuffed green olives*
1 cup minced celery
¼ cup minced sweet green pepper
*2 canned pineapple rings, coarsely
   chopped*
⅓ cup toasted, slivered almonds

Sprinkle unflavored gelatin over cold
water, then heat and stir until dissolved;
pour over lemon gelatin along with
boiling water and stir until dissolved.
Stir in vinegar, canned pineapple juice,
onion, horseradish, and salt, then cover
and chill until syrupy; beat with a rotary
beater or electric mixer until frothy.
Blend cheeses and milk and fold into
gelatin along with remaining ingredients.
Spoon into an ungreased 2-quart mold
and chill several hours or overnight until
firm. Unmold and serve with mayonnaise
or Old-Fashioned Cooked Dressing.
About 135 calories for each of 14
servings (without mayonnaise or
dressing), 120 calories for each of 16
servings.

AVOCADO MOUSSE

If an avocado seems green, you can
"ripen" by letting stand ¾–1 hour in an
oven turned to lowest possible temperature (150–200° F.). Cool and chill before
using.
Makes 6 servings

1 envelope unflavored gelatin
1 cup cold water
1 tablespoon minced yellow onion
½ teaspoon salt
Pinch cayenne pepper
*1 cup puréed ripe avocado (about 2
   small ones)*
¼ cup mayonnaise or sour cream

Sprinkle gelatin over water, then heat
and stir until dissolved. Mix in remaining
ingredients, spoon into an ungreased
3-cup mold, cover tightly, and chill
until firm. Unmold (especially pretty on
a bed of watercress) and serve at once
(the mousse discolors rapidly on standing); wrap any leftovers airtight. About
195 calories per serving (if made with
mayonnaise), 145 calories per serving
(if made with sour cream).

JELLIED GARDEN VEGETABLE SALAD

Makes 8 servings

3 envelopes unflavored gelatin
½ cup sugar
3½ cups water
½ cup white vinegar
1 teaspoon salt
1 tablespoon minced parsley
1 tablespoon minced chives
½ cup cooked green peas
*½ cup diced, cooked carrots or finely
   grated raw carrots*
1 cup finely shredded cabbage
¼ cup thinly sliced radishes
½ cup diced celery
½ cup diced cucumber
¼ cup minced sweet green or red pepper
1 small red onion, peeled and minced
*2 medium-size firm-ripe tomatoes,
   peeled, cored, seeded, and coarsely
   chopped*

Heat and stir gelatin, sugar and 1 cup
water until dissolved. Add remaining
water, vinegar, salt, parsley, and chives
and chill until syrupy. Mix in remaining
ingredients and spoon into an ungreased
2-quart ring mold or 9″×5″×3″ loaf

pan; cover and chill until firm. Unmold and top, if you like, with a thin mayonnaise-type dressing. About 90 calories per serving (without mayonnaise).

To Use Other Vegetables: Substitute any compatible combination of cooked and raw vegetables for those listed above. You'll need 1 quart minced vegetables, total.

VARIATION:

Vegetable Ribbon Salad: Prepare gelatin mixture as directed and divide into 4 equal parts. Chill 1 part until syrupy, mix in peas and carrots, spoon into an ungreased decorative 2-quart mold, cover and chill until tacky. Meanwhile, chill second part of gelatin until syrupy, mix in cabbage and radishes, spoon into mold, cover, and chill until tacky. Chill third part of gelatin until syrupy, mix in celery, cucumber, and green pepper, add to mold, cover, and chill until tacky. Chill remaining gelatin until syrupy *but do not add onion and tomatoes;* pour into mold, cover, and chill until firm. Unmold and serve as directed. About 90 calories per serving.

◁|△ **PERFECTION SALAD**

Makes 6 servings

1 envelope unflavored gelatin
¼ cup sugar
1¼ cups water
2 tablespoons lemon juice
1 tablespoon cider vinegar
¾ teaspoon salt
1½ cups finely shredded green, red, or Chinese cabbage or ½ cup of each
½ cup diced celery
¼ cup coarsely chopped pimiento-stuffed green olives
¼ cup minced sweet red or green pepper
2 tablespoons finely grated carrot

Sprinkle gelatin and sugar over water and heat, stirring, over moderately low heat until dissolved. Off heat, stir in lemon juice, vinegar, and salt; chill until

syrupy. Fold in remaining ingredients, spoon into an ungreased 1-quart mold, and chill until firm. Unmold on lettuce leaves and serve with mayonnaise. About 55 calories per serving (without mayonnaise).

VARIATION:

△|△ **Perfection Salad for a Crowd:** (Makes 12 servings.) Double recipe and spoon into an ungreased 13"×9"×2" baking pan. Chill until firm and cut in large squares. About 55 calories per serving.

SOUFFLÉ SALAD

No need for salad dressing—it's built in. Makes 4–6 servings

1 cup boiling water
1 (3-ounce) package lemon, lime, or apple-flavored gelatin
½ cup cold ginger ale
½ cup mayonnaise or mayonnaise-type salad dressing
½ teaspoon salt (about)
Few drops liquid hot red pepper seasoning
1 tablespoon minced yellow onion
1½ cups mixed diced cooked vegetables or finely shredded cabbage or thinly sliced avocado

Pour boiling water over gelatin and stir until dissolved. Add all but last ingredient and mix well, using a rotary beater or wire whisk. Pour into a shallow pan and chill in freezer about 15–20 minutes until there's a 1" frozen border all round (mixture should still be liquid in center). Scrape into a bowl and whip until fluffy. Fold in vegetables, spoon into an ungreased 1-quart mold, and chill until firm. Unmold and serve on a bed of greens. If made with diced cooked vegetables: about 335 calories for each of 4 servings, 225 calories for each of 6 servings. If made with shredded cabbage: about 310 calories for each of 4 servings, 205 calories for each of 6. If made with sliced avocado: about 395 calories for each of 4 servings, 265 calories for each of 6.

JELLIED CHICKEN OR TURKEY SALAD

For small families, this recipe may be halved and molded in a 1-quart mold or 4 custard cups.
Makes 8 servings

2 envelopes unflavored gelatin
½ cup cold water
3 cups chicken broth
2 tablespoons lemon juice
½ teaspoon salt
3 cups minced cold cooked chicken or turkey meat (preferably white meat)
¼ cup minced celery
¼ cup minced sweet green pepper
¼ cup minced scallions
2 tablespoons minced pimiento

Heat and stir gelatin with water and broth until dissolved; mix in lemon juice and salt. Chill until thick and syrupy, mix in remaining ingredients, spoon into an ungreased 9″×5″×3″ loaf pan, cover, and chill until firm. Loosen edges and unmold. If you like, pass a thin mayonnaise-type dressing. About 110 calories per serving (without mayonnaise).

VARIATIONS:

Jellied Meat Salad: Prepare as directed, substituting 1½ cups each water and beef broth for chicken broth and 3 cups minced cooked lean beef, lamb, or veal for chicken. If you like, reduce lemon juice to 1 tablespoon and add 1 teaspoon Worcestershire sauce. About 180 calories per serving.

Jellied Ham or Tongue Salad: Prepare as directed, using 1½ cups each beef and chicken broth and 3 cups minced, cooked ham or tongue instead of chicken. About 160 calories per serving.

Jellied Shellfish Salad: Prepare as directed, using 1½ cups each chicken broth and water or tomato juice and 3 cups minced, cooked shellfish instead of chicken. About 90 calories per serving.

Jellied Meat, Poultry, or Shellfish and Vegetable Salad: Prepare any of the above salads as directed but omit celery and green pepper and add ¾–1 cup any leftover mixed cooked vegetables. Recipe too flexible for a meaningful calorie count.

Creamy Jellied Meat, Poultry, or Shellfish Salad: Heat and stir gelatin in ½ cup cold water until dissolved; blend in 1 pint mayonnaise and 1 cup water, tomato juice, chicken or beef broth; add lemon juice called for above and salt to taste. Chill until syrupy, mix in 3 cups minced, cooked meat, poultry, or shellfish, ¼ cup minced scallions, and 1 cup any leftover mixed cooked vegetables. Mold as directed. Recipe too flexible for a meaningful calorie count, but because of the mayonnaise used, approximately 5 times the calorie count of Jellied Chicken or Turkey Salad.

MOLDED GRAPEFRUIT AND PINEAPPLE SALAD

Makes 4–6 servings

1 (3-ounce) package lime or lemon-flavored gelatin
1 cup boiling water
1 cup fresh or canned grapefruit sections, cut up (include juice)
1 (13½-ounce) can pineapple chunks, drained
¼ cup quartered maraschino or candied cherries
¼ cup coarsely chopped pecans

Mix gelatin with boiling water, stirring until dissolved; cool, then chill until syrupy and stir in remaining ingredients. Spoon into an ungreased 3-cup mold or 4–6 individual molds. Chill until firm, unmold, and serve with mayonnaise or Cream Cheese and Fruit Dressing. About 240 calories for each of 4 servings, 160 calories for each of 6 servings (without mayonnaise or dressing).

APRICOT-PINEAPPLE SALAD

Good as dessert or salad.
Makes 6–8 servings

½ cup boiling water
1 (3-ounce) package orange-flavored gelatin
1 (8¾-ounce) can pitted apricots (drain and save liquid)

1 (8½-ounce) can crushed pineapple (drain and save liquid)
Canned fruit liquid plus enough cold water to total 1 cup
1 tablespoon lemon juice
½ cup heavy cream, whipped to soft peaks

Pour boiling water over gelatin and stir until dissolved; add fruit liquid and lemon juice, pour into a shallow pan, and chill in freezer 15–20 minutes until there is a 1" frozen border all round. Meanwhile, dice apricots. Scrape gelatin mixture into a bowl and whip until fluffy. Fold in remaining ingredients, spoon into an ungreased 5-cup mold, and chill until firm. Unmold and serve as is or on greens. No dressing needed. About 195 calories for each of 6 servings, 145 calories for each of 8 servings.

MOLDED CHERRY-PECAN SALAD

Makes 8 servings

1 (1-pound) can pitted sour red cherries (do not drain)
1 cup sugar
½ cup water
1 (3-ounce) package cherry-flavored gelatin
1 envelope unflavored gelatin
Grated rind of 1 orange
2 oranges, peeled, seeded, and diced
1 (8½-ounce) can crushed pineapple (do not drain)
½ cup coarsely chopped pecans

Heat cherries, sugar, and water to boiling, stirring occasionally. Off heat, mix in gelatins and stir until dissolved. Cool, then chill until syrupy; mix in remaining ingredients, spoon into an ungreased 5-cup mold or 8 individual molds. Chill until firm. Unmold and, if you wish, serve with a thin mayonnaise-type dressing. About 285 calories per serving (without mayonnaise).

MOLDED SPICY CRANBERRY SALAD

Makes 8 servings

1 pound fresh or frozen cranberries, washed

2 cups water
2 cinnamon sticks and 24 cloves, tied in cheesecloth
1 cup sugar
½ teaspoon salt
2 envelopes unflavored gelatin
⅔ cup minced celery
1 cup canned crushed pineapple, drained
1 cup minced walnuts

Simmer cranberries, water, and spices covered until cranberry skins pop, 5–7 minutes; discard spice bag. Purée cranberries and cooking liquid, a little at a time, in an electric blender at low speed or put through a food mill. Return to pan, stir in sugar, salt, and gelatin, and simmer, stirring, until gelatin dissolves. Cool, then chill, stirring occasionally, until thick and syrupy. Mix in remaining ingredients, ladle into an ungreased 5-cup mold or 8 individual molds, and chill until firm. To serve, unmold and garnish with chicory or other crisp greens. About 255 calories per serving.

MOLDED CRANBERRY-PECAN SALAD

Makes 10–12 servings

1 (3-ounce) package cherry-flavored gelatin
2 (3-ounce) packages black raspberry-flavored gelatin
1 teaspoon unflavored gelatin
1 cup sugar
1 quart boiling water
1 pound fresh or frozen cranberries, put through fine blade of food grinder
2 small tart red apples, cored and ground fine (do not peel)
1 large seedless orange, ground fine (do not peel or seed)
1¾ cups coarsely chopped pecans
1¼ cups finely diced celery

Dissolve gelatins and sugar in boiling water; cool to room temperature, cover, and chill just until syrupy. Mix in remaining ingredients, pour into an ungreased 2½-quart decorative mold, and chill 6–8 hours until firm. To serve, unmold and cut into slim wedges. No dressing is needed. About 315 calories for each of 10 servings, 260 calories for each of 12 servings.

About Making Gelatin Ribbon Loaves

Any compatible gelatin mixtures can be layered—jellied meat and vegetables, jellied poultry and tart fruit or vegetables, aspic with almost anything savory. Bear in mind *combined yield* of gelatin mixtures and use a mold large enough to accommodate both. For best results:
– Keep thickness of layers in proportion to each other.
– Do not try to mold more than 3 or 4 layers in a 1- or 2-quart mold or 9"×5"×3" loaf pan (it holds 2 quarts).
– Always chill 1 layer until *tacky-firm* before adding another. If gelatin is too firm, layers will not stick together; if too liquid, they will run together.
– Have gelatin mixtures at room temperature or, better still, chilled *just* until syrupy before adding to mold.
– Add heaviest layers last (those containing minced foods) so that when loaf is unmolded, they will be on the bottom; otherwise they may topple or slide off.
– Give a ribbon loaf plenty of time to set up before unmolding—at least 12 hours.

TOMATO AND CHEESE RIBBON LOAF

Makes 8–10 servings

1 recipe Tomato Aspic
2 envelopes unflavored gelatin
¾ cup water
3 cups sieved cottage cheese
⅔ cup sour cream
2 tablespoons minced parsley
2 tablespoons minced scallions (include some tops)
1 teaspoon salt
⅛ teaspoon white pepper

Prepare aspic as directed and pour half

into an ungreased 9"×5"×3" loaf pan; chill until tacky-firm; keep remaining aspic syrupy over tepid water. Meanwhile, sprinkle gelatin over water and heat and stir over moderately low heat until dissolved. Mix with remaining ingredients and chill quickly until syrupy either by setting in freezer or in a bowl of cracked ice. Pour half of cheese gelatin on molded tomato aspic and chill until tacky; keep remaining cheese mixture syrupy over tepid water. Add remaining tomato aspic to mold, chill until tacky, then top with remaining cheese gelatin. Chill overnight until firm. Slice about ½" thick and serve on crisp greens. Good with a thin mayonnaise-type dressing. About 355 calories for each of 8 servings (without mayonnaise), 285 calories for each of 10 servings.

VARIATIONS:

Tomato-Avocado Ribbon Aspic: Prepare 1 recipe each Tomato Aspic and Lemon-Avocado Aspic; beginning with Tomato Aspic, layer into a loaf pan following technique above. About 250 calories for each of 8 servings, 200 calories for each of 10.

Tomato-Chicken Ribbon Loaf: Prepare 1 recipe Tomato Aspic and ½ recipe Jellied Chicken Salad. Starting with Tomato Aspic, layer into loaf pan. About 270 calories for each of 8 servings, 215 calories for each of 10 servings.

FROZEN FRUIT SALAD

More dessert than salad. It's rich but not too sweet.
Makes 6–8 servings

1 tablespoon water mixed with 1 tablespoon lemon juice
1 teaspoon unflavored gelatin
1 tablespoon confectioners' sugar
1 (3-ounce) package cream cheese, softened to room temperature
⅓ cup mayonnaise
½ cup heavy cream
1 (1-pound) can fruit cocktail, drained, or 1½ cups mixed diced fresh fruit

Place water mixture in a custard cup, sprinkle in gelatin and sugar, and set in a small pan of simmering water; heat and stir until gelatin dissolves. Beat cream cheese and mayonnaise until blended and stir in gelatin mixture; whip cream to soft peaks and fold in along with fruit. Spoon into a 9″ square pan and freeze just until firm. Cut in squares and serve on lettuce. About 275 calories for each of 6 servings, 205 calories for each of 8 servings.

VARIATION:

Frozen Fruit and Nut Salad: Prepare as directed but omit cream cheese and increase mayonnaise to ½ cup. Add ¼ cup minced nuts (pistachios are especially good) and 6 minced maraschino cherries along with fruit. (*Note:* To keep cherries from coloring mixture, rinse briefly in cold water and pat dry.) About 325 calories for each of 6 servings, 245 calories for each of 8 servings.

⊠ FROZEN CRANBERRY RIBBON SALAD

Makes 6–8 servings
1 (1-pound) can whole or jellied
  cranberry sauce
¼ cup lemon juice
½ cup mayonnaise
⅓ cup sugar
1 cup heavy cream
¼ cup minced pecans, walnuts, or
  toasted almonds (optional)

If using jellied cranberry sauce, soften by standing unopened can in very hot water; mix lemon juice into sauce, spoon into a refrigerator tray, and freeze until firm. Mix mayonnaise and sugar; beat cream to soft peaks and fold in. Spread on top of cranberry layer, sprinkle, if you like, with nuts, and freeze until firm. Cut in squares and serve on lettuce. About 500 calories for each of 6 servings and 375 calories for each of 8 servings (if made with nuts); about 470 calories for each of 6 servings and 350 calories for each of 8 servings (if made without nuts).

⊠ FROZEN MARSHMALLOW AND PINEAPPLE SALAD

Really a dessert.
Makes 6–8 servings

2 (3-ounce) packages cream cheese,
  softened to room temperature
1 cup drained crushed pineapple
2 cups miniature marshmallows
¼ cup coarsely chopped maraschino
  cherries
1 teaspoon lemon juice
½ cup coarsely chopped pecans or
  walnuts

Blend cheese and pineapple; mix in remaining ingredients and spoon into a refrigerator tray. Freeze until firm, cut in squares, and serve. About 285 calories for each of 6 servings, 215 calories for each of 8 servings.

SALAD DRESSINGS

The parade of bottled dressings along supermarket shelves is so long it may seem foolish to make a dressing from scratch. It isn't. Good as some commercial dressings are, they can never match the delicacy and bouquet of those made at home from first quality oils, vinegars, and seasonings.

The Salad Oils: Keep a selection of oils on hand—on a cool, dark shelf, never in the refrigerator (cold turns oils cloudy). Unless you use oils frequently, buy in small amounts so that you can use up a bottle before it becomes rancid. Oils give salads a special mellowness and are the medium in which all flavors mingle. They are also, alas, what add calories to salads (1 tablespoon salad oil averages about 115). So if you are dieting, use one of the low-calorie types. A more detailed discussion of oils is included in the chapter The Larder.

The Vinegars: Nearly every supermarket stocks a good variety of plain and flavored vinegars. Keep an assortment on hand on a cool, dark shelf. It's best to buy in fairly small bottles because vinegars do mold and produce sediment. The sediment can be strained out, but a moldy vinegar should be discarded.

Cider Vinegar: The all-purpose, golden brown vinegar made from apples. It is good for cooked or highly seasoned dressings but too rough and coarse to use solo with oil.

Distilled Vinegar: White vinegar, acid and sour and better for pickles than salads.

Malt Vinegar: An English favorite, tart but mellow; use interchangeably with cider vinegar.

Wine Vinegars: These are simply wines that have gone a step too far, which explains why there are white, red, and rosé wine vinegars. (*Note:* Save any tag ends of the wine bottle; when the wine sours into vinegar, use to dress salads.)

Flavored Vinegars: These, usually made from cider or white wine vinegar, include all the herb vinegars, also garlic, onion, and shallot vinegars. You can buy them at any grocery or, if you have an herb garden, make your own (recipes follow).

Rice Vinegar: A delicate white Japanese vinegar, about half as acid as cider vinegar. To achieve a proper salad tartness, you'll have to use about twice as much.

Pear Vinegar: A fairly new item with a fresh flowery bouquet.

Tips on Making Salad Dressings

– Most dressings do not keep well, so make in small quantities.
– For best flavor, dressings should be made at least a half hour ahead of time, sometimes even longer. Oil and vinegar types should stand at room temperature so flavors marry, but cream or mayonnaise dressings should be kept refrigerated.

– Do not use garlic or onion powders and salts; they rapidly become stale and can ruin an otherwise excellent salad. It's far better to mince fresh garlic and onion; more effort, true. But worth it.
– Use fresh herbs in preference to the dry. And when using the dry, make sure they haven't been sitting on the shelf for months. An old herb adds about as much character to salad as dried grass.
– Use the finest quality oils, vinegars, and seasonings.
– Use coarse salt or kosher salt if possible and, of course, freshly ground black pepper.
– When dressing salads with oil and vinegar, use a heavy hand with the oil and a light one with the vinegar. *The classic proportion is 3 or 4 parts oil to 1 part vinegar.* For variety, try substituting lemon or lime juice (or part lemon or lime juice) for the vinegar.

⚖ GARLIC VINEGAR

Makes 1 pint

1 pint boiling cider vinegar
6 cloves garlic, peeled and halved

Pour vinegar into a jar, drop in garlic, cover, and let stand 24 hours at room temperature. Discard garlic, strain vinegar through a double thickness of cheesecloth into a fresh pint jar. Use for making salad dressings and sauces. About 3 calories per tablespoon.

⚖ HERB VINEGAR

Herbs will be at their peak of flavor if picked just before they bloom.
Makes 1 pint

2 cups tender fresh herb leaves or sprigs
  (tarragon, chervil, dill, basil, or thyme)
  washed gently in cool water and
  patted dry on paper toweling
1 pint boiling vinegar (cider or white
  wine)

Place herbs in a wide-mouthed heatproof jar and crush lightly with the handle of a wooden spoon. Pour in vinegar and cool to room temperature. Screw on lid and let stand in a cool spot (not refrigerator)

10 days to 2 weeks; once every day, turn jar upside down, then right side up again. Taste vinegar after 10 days and, if strong enough, strain through several thicknesses of cheesecloth into a fresh pint jar. If too weak, let stand the full 2 weeks. If still too weak, strain off vinegar and bring to a boil; fill a fresh jar with freshly picked herbs, cover with boiling vinegar, and let stand a week to 10 days, turning once a day. Strain vinegar and use for making salad dressings and sauces. About 3 calories per tablespoon.

À LA GRECQUE MARINADE

Leeks, zucchini, and certain other cooked vegetables are delicious when marinated in this delicate lemon and oil dressing. They may be served as a first course, a salad, or a vegetable.
Makes about 3 cups

⅓ cup lemon juice
½ cup olive oil
1 pint hot water
½ teaspoon salt
⅛ teaspoon each fennel and coriander seeds tied in cheesecloth
1 bay leaf
1 (4″) sprig fresh thyme or ⅛ teaspoon dried thyme
Pinch white pepper

Mix all ingredients together and use in preparing vegetables that are to be served *à la grecque*. About 20 calories per tablespoon.

⊠ FRENCH DRESSING (VINAIGRETTE)

Called *vinaigrette* in France, French dressing is simply 3–4 parts olive oil to 1 part vinegar, seasoned with salt and pepper.
Makes 1 cup

¼ cup red or white wine vinegar
¼ teaspoon salt
⅛ teaspoon white pepper
¾ cup olive oil

In a bowl mix vinegar, salt, and pepper with a fork. Add oil and mix vigorously until well blended and slightly thickened. (*Note:* For a creamier dressing, beat over ice 1–2 minutes.) Use to dress green or vegetable salads. (*Note:* If you prefer, substitute any good salad oil for the olive oil and cider or malt vinegar for the wine vinegar.) About 95 calories per tablespoon.

VARIATIONS:

Garlic French Dressing: Drop 1 peeled, bruised clove garlic into dressing and let stand 2–3 days at room temperature; remove garlic before using dressing. About 95 calories per tablespoon.

Tarragon French Dressing: Make dressing with tarragon vinegar and add 1 tablespoon minced fresh or ½ teaspoon dried tarragon. About 95 calories per tablespoon.

Roquefort French Dressing: Prepare dressing as directed and crumble in 3 tablespoons Roquefort cheese. Cover and let stand several hours at room temperature before using. About 105 calories per tablespoon.

Spanish Vinaigrette: Prepare dressing as directed and place in a shaker jar with 1 tablespoon minced green olives and 1 teaspoon each minced chives, capers, parsley, and gherkin, and 1 sieved hard-cooked egg yolk. Shake, let stand at room temperature ½ hour; shake again before using. About 100 calories per tablespoon.

Lorenzo Dressing: Prepare dressing as directed and blend in 2 tablespoons chili sauce or ketchup. About 100 calories per tablespoon.

Chiffonade Dressing: Prepare dressing as directed, then mix in 2 tablespoons each minced ripe olives, chives, and sweet green pepper and 1 minced hard-cooked egg. About 105 calories per tablespoon.

Sweet French Dressing: Prepare dressing as directed, then mix in ¼ cup each orange juice and honey or superfine sugar. Use to dress fruit salads. About 110 calories per tablespoon if made with sugar, 115 calories per tablespoon if made with honey.

FRESH HERB DRESSING

Makes ¾ cup

½ cup olive oil
1 tablespoon minced fresh dill, tarragon,
   chervil, or fennel
1 tablespoon minced chives
¼ teaspoon minced fresh marjoram
   (optional)
½ teaspoon salt
⅛ teaspoon pepper
¼ cup tarragon vinegar

Place oil, herbs, salt, and pepper in a
shaker bottle or large glass measuring
cup and let stand at room temperature
3–4 hours. Add vinegar and shake or stir
well to blend. Use to dress any crisp
green salad, using only enough to coat
each leaf lightly. Save leftover dressing
to use for other salads later (dressing will
keep about 1 week). About 85 calories
per tablespoon.

FRESH BASIL-MINT DRESSING

Makes about ½ cup

⅓ cup olive oil
1 tablespoon minced fresh basil
1 teaspoon minced fresh mint
1 teaspoon minced chives
3 tablespoons red wine vinegar
¼ teaspoon salt
Pinch pepper

Place oil in a small bowl, add herbs, and
let stand at room temperature at least 1
hour. Mix in remaining ingredients and
use to dress sliced tomatoes or crisp salad
greens. About 85 calories per tablespoon.

GARLIC-HERB DRESSING

Makes about ⅓ cup

1 clove garlic, peeled and crushed
½ teaspoon tarragon
½ teaspoon marjoram
½ teaspoon powdered mustard
¼ teaspoon salt
⅛ teaspoon pepper
¼ cup olive oil
2 tablespoons red wine vinegar

Shake all ingredients in a small jar with a
tight-fitting lid and let stand at room

temperature at least 1 hour. Shake again
and use to dress any crisp green salad.
About 95 calories per tablespoon.

SHALLOT DRESSING

Makes about ½ cup

1 tablespoon minced shallots
½ teaspoon paprika
½ teaspoon powdered mustard
¼ teaspoon tarragon or chervil
½ teaspoon salt
Pinch pepper
⅓ cup olive oil
3 tablespoons tarragon vinegar

Place all ingredients except vinegar in a
small bowl, stir well to mix, cover, and
let stand at room temperature about 1
hour. Stir again, mix in vinegar, and use
to dress crisp green salads. About 85
calories per tablespoon.

SWEET-SOUR DRESSING

Makes about 1¾ cups

1 cup salad oil
⅓ cup red wine vinegar
¼ cup mayonnaise or mayonnaise-type
   salad dressing
¼ cup chili sauce
¼ teaspoon salt
2 tablespoons sugar
Pinch cayenne pepper
1 clove garlic, peeled and crushed

Shake all ingredients in a large, wide-
mouthed jar with a tight-fitting lid. Cover
and chill several hours. Before using,
shake well. Use to dress crisp green
salads. About 95 calories per tablespoon.

⚖ ⊠ BUTTERMILK DRESSING

Dieters, note just how low the calories
are.
Makes about 1½ cups

½ cup cider vinegar
1 tablespoon salad oil
1 teaspoon salt
⅛ teaspoon white pepper
1 cup buttermilk

Shake all ingredients in a jar with a tight-
fitting lid and use to dress cabbage or

crisp green salads. (*Note:* Dressing will keep about a week in the refrigerator.) About 10 calories per tablespoon.

⊠ LEMON-LIME DRESSING

Makes about 1 cup

Juice of 1 lemon
Juice of ½ lime
2 tablespoons honey
⅔ cup olive oil
1 tablespoon minced chives
1 tablespoon minced fresh basil or dill
Pinch salt
Pinch pepper

Shake all ingredients in a jar and use to dress sliced tomatoes or crisp green salads. About 95 calories per tablespoon.

WINE DRESSING

A good way to use up any tag ends of wine.
Makes 1¼ cups

⅓ cup dry red or white wine
¼ cup red or white wine vinegar
1 clove garlic, peeled, bruised, and stuck
  on a toothpick
¼ teaspoon salt
¼ teaspoon powdered mustard
⅛ teaspoon white pepper
⅔ cup olive or other salad oil

Mix wine, vinegar, and garlic, cover, and let stand at room temperature 2 hours; remove garlic. Beat in salt, mustard, and pepper, then drizzle in oil, beating constantly. Shake well and use to dress green salads. About 70 calories per tablespoon.

⊠ SOUR CREAM DRESSING

Makes 1¼ cups

1 cup sour cream
3 tablespoons white or cider vinegar
2 tablespoons sugar
½ teaspoon salt
Pinch cayenne pepper

Mix all ingredients, cover, and chill well. Use to dress fruit or green salads. For a thinner dressing, blend in a little milk or French dressing. About 30 calories per tablespoon.

VARIATIONS:

⚖ **Low-Calorie Yogurt Dressing:**
Prepare as directed but substitute yogurt for sour cream, reduce vinegar to 2 tablespoons and sugar to ½ teaspoon; also add ¼ cup skim milk and 2 tablespoons minced chives or 1 tablespoon finely grated yellow onion. About 10 calories per tablespoon.

California Sour Cream Dressing:
Prepare as directed but use 2 tablespoons lemon juice instead of the vinegar; add 2 sieved hard-cooked egg yolks and, if you like, 1 tablespoon minced fresh dill. About 35 calories per tablespoon.

Fruity Sour Cream Dressing: Prepare as directed but use 2 tablespoons lemon juice instead of the vinegar; increase sugar to 3 tablespoons and add 2 tablespoons orange juice and 1 teaspoon finely grated orange rind. Thin, if needed, with a little extra orange juice. About 35 calories per tablespoon.

Sour Cream-Roquefort Dressing:
Prepare as directed, then mix in 2 tablespoons finely crumbled Roquefort cheese. About 35 calories per tablespoon.

CREAMY ROQUEFORT DRESSING

Makes about 2½ cups

1 (8-ounce) jar mayonnaise-type salad
  dressing
1 tablespoon sugar
1 teaspoon prepared mild yellow mustard
½ teaspoon prepared horseradish
½ teaspoon Worcestershire sauce
½ teaspoon minced garlic
1 tablespoon grated onion
½ pound Roquefort cheese
3–4 tablespoons cider vinegar

Blend salad dressing with sugar, mustard, horseradish, Worcestershire sauce, garlic and onion. Crumble in Roquefort and stir well. Mix in 3–4 tablespoons vinegar, depending upon how thick a dressing you want, and use to dress green salads. (*Note:* Dressing keeps well in refrigerator several days.) About 65 calories per tablespoon.

⊠ BLENDER GARLIC-ROQUEFORT DRESSING

Makes about 1½ cups

¾ cup olive oil
⅓ cup tarragon or red wine vinegar
2 tablespoons honey
½ (3-ounce) package Roquefort cheese,
  softened to room temperature
1 clove garlic, peeled and crushed
½ teaspoon powdered mustard
1 teaspoon paprika
⅛ teaspoon salt
⅛ teaspoon pepper

Buzz all ingredients in an electric blender at high speed 1–2 minutes until creamy. Pour into a jar, cover, and chill until ready to use. Shake well, then use to dress crisp green salads. (*Note:* Dressing keeps well about 2 weeks in refrigerator, so make a double batch if you like.) About 80 calories per tablespoon.

CAMEMBERT CREAM DRESSING

Makes about 1 pint

4 ounces Camembert cheese, trimmed
  of rind and softened to room
  temperature
1 (8-ounce) package cream cheese,
  softened to room temperature
⅓ cup buttermilk
⅓ cup tarragon vinegar
½ teaspoon sugar
⅛ teaspoon pepper

Cream cheeses together, add remaining ingredients, and beat well; cover and chill 1–2 hours. Beat well just before serving. Use to dress any crisp green salad. (*Note:* Dressing keeps well about a week in refrigerator.) About 40 calories per tablespoon.

AVOCADO DRESSING

It's best to make this dressing just before using, because it darkens on standing. If it must be made in advance, spread with a thin film of mayonnaise, then cover and refrigerate until needed (this will minimize discoloration). Stir mayonnaise in before serving.
Makes about 1 cup

2 fully ripe medium-size avocados,
  halved and pitted
3 tablespoons lemon juice
1 tablespoon finely grated yellow onion
½ teaspoon salt
¼ teaspoon sugar
Few drops liquid hot red pepper
  seasoning

Scoop flesh from avocados and press through a fine sieve; beat in remaining ingredients. Serve over wedges of lettuce, halved endive spears, or in hollowed-out tomatoes. Or use to dress any seafood salad instead of mayonnaise. About 50 calories per tablespoon.

⊠ CREAM CHEESE AND FRUIT DRESSING

Makes 1 cup

1 (3-ounce) package cream cheese,
  softened to room temperature
½ cup orange or pineapple juice
2 tablespoons lemon juice
2 tablespoons sugar
Pinch cayenne pepper

Whip cheese until fluffy, then beat in remaining ingredients; cover and chill. Serve over fruit salads, avocado halves, or lettuce wedges. About 30 calories per tablespoon.

VARIATIONS:

Cream Cheese and Nut Dressing:
Prepare as directed, then mix in ¼ cup minced pecans or toasted almonds. About 40 calories per tablespoon.

Cream Cheese and Chutney Dressing:
Prepare as directed but use ⅓ cup milk in place of orange juice and add ¼ cup minced chutney (include some liquid). About 40 calories per tablespoon.

⚖ LOW-CALORIE FRUIT DRESSING

Makes 1⅓ cups

1 clove garlic, peeled, bruised, and stuck
  on a toothpick
5 tablespoons lemon juice
1 cup pineapple, orange, or tangerine
  juice

1 tablespoon light corn syrup or honey
½ teaspoon salt
¼ teaspoon paprika

Let garlic stand in lemon juice at room temperature 2 hours, then remove. Beat in remaining ingredients, cover, and chill. Shake well and use to dress fruit salads. About 20 calories per tablespoon.

About Making Mayonnaise

Mayonnaise isn't tricky to make—*if* you follow these basic rules:
– Have all ingredients at room temperature before beginning.
– Measure oil accurately into a wide-mouthed container so you can dip it out by spoonfuls during early stages of mixing.
– If mixing by hand, place a damp cloth under bowl to keep it from sliding around as you mix. Use a fork or wire whisk for beating.
– Add oil in the beginning *by the drop* so that it will emulsify with the egg yolks.
– If you substitute vinegar for lemon juice, use the very finest quality so mayonnaise will have a delicate flavor.
– *If mayonnaise separates, use 1 of the following remedies:*
– Beat in 1–2 teaspoons hot water.
– Beat 1 egg yolk with 2 or 3 drops oil until very thick, then beat in curdled mayonnaise *drop by drop.*
– Buzz in an electric blender at high speed.

HOMEMADE MAYONNAISE

Makes 1½ cups

2 egg yolks
¾ teaspoon salt
½ teaspoon powdered mustard
⅛ teaspoon sugar
Pinch cayenne pepper
4–5 teaspoons lemon juice or white
   vinegar
1½ cups olive or other salad oil
4 teaspoons hot water

Beat yolks, salt, mustard, sugar, pepper, and 1 teaspoon lemon juice in a small bowl until very thick and pale yellow.

(*Note:* If using electric mixer, beat at medium speed.) Add about ¼ cup oil, *drop by drop,* beating vigorously all the while. Beat in 1 teaspoon each lemon juice and hot water. Add another ¼ cup oil, a few drops at a time, beating vigorously all the while. Beat in another teaspoon each lemon juice and water. Add ½ cup oil in a very fine steady stream, beating constantly, then mix in remaining lemon juice and water; slowly beat in remaining oil. If you like, thin mayonnaise with a little additional hot water. Cover and refrigerate until needed. (*Note:* Store in warmest part of refrigerator—less chance of the mayonnaise's separating—and do not keep longer than one week.) About 130 calories per tablespoon.

VARIATIONS:

Blender Mayonnaise: Place yolks, salt, mustard, sugar, pepper, and 3 teaspoons lemon juice in blender cup and buzz at low speed 15 seconds. Increase speed to moderately high and slowly drizzle in ¼ cup oil. As mixture begins to thicken, continue adding oil in a fine steady stream, alternating with hot water and remaining lemon juice. Stop blender and scrape mixture down from sides as needed. About 130 calories per tablespoon.

Sauce Verte: Prepare mayonnaise as directed and set aside. Place ¼ cup each minced fresh spinach, watercress leaves, and parsley in a small pan, add 2 tablespoons each minced chives and water and 1 teaspoon minced fresh or ½ teaspoon dried tarragon, cover, and simmer 2 minutes. Press mixture through a fine sieve, drain briefly and blend into mayonnaise. Serve with cold cooked seafood or use to dress green salads. About 130 calories per tablespoon.

Rémoulade Dressing: Prepare mayonnaise as directed, then mix in 1 tablespoon each minced capers and gherkins, 2 teaspoons each anchovy paste and Dijon mustard, and 1 teaspoon each minced parsley and fresh chervil. Serve with seafood or use to dress cold vegetable salads or sliced tomatoes. About 130 calories per tablespoon.

Sauce Niçoise: Prepare mayonnaise as directed and set aside. Mix 2 tablespoons tomato purée with 2 minced pimientos and ½ crushed clove garlic; press through a fine sieve and blend into mayonnaise. About 135 calories per tablespoon.

Russian Mayonnaise: Prepare mayonnaise, then mix in ¼ cup black or red caviar, ½ cup sour cream, and 1 tablespoon minced fresh dill. About 145 calories per tablespoon.

Mustard Mayonnaise: Prepare mayonnaise, then mix in 4 teaspoons Dijon mustard. About 130 calories per tablespoon.

Curry Mayonnaise: Prepare mayonnaise, then blend in 1–2 teaspoons curry powder. About 130 calories per tablespoon.

Chantilly Mayonnaise: Prepare mayonnaise, then fold in ½ cup heavy cream, beaten to soft peaks. About 150 calories per tablespoon.

Fruit Mayonnaise: Prepare mayonnaise, then beat in 3 tablespoons each orange juice and superfine sugar, 1 teaspoon finely grated orange rind, and a pinch nutmeg. For added zip, mix in 1 tablespoon Grand Marnier or other fruit liqueur. Serve with fruit salads. About 140 calories per tablespoon.

Thin Mayonnaise: Prepare mayonnaise, then thin to desired consistency by beating in hot water, a tablespoon at a time. About 130 calories per tablespoon.

COOKED SALAD DRESSING

Note to cholesterol counters: this dressing contains only a third as many egg yolks as old-fashioned cooked dressing.
Makes about 1¼ cups

2 tablespoons flour
2 tablespoons sugar
1 teaspoon powdered mustard
¾ teaspoon salt
Pinch cayenne pepper
¾ cup cold water, or ½ cup milk and ¼ cup water
2 egg yolks, lightly beaten
¼ cup lemon juice or white wine vinegar
2 tablespoons salad oil

Mix flour, sugar, mustard, salt, cayenne, and water in the top of a double boiler over simmering water; beat egg yolks and lemon juice just to blend, then mix in. Heat, stirring constantly, until thickened. Beat in oil, 1 tablespoon at a time. Place a piece of wax paper flat on dressing and cool to room temperature; chill before serving. If you like, thin with a little water or milk. About 25 calories per tablespoon if made with water, 30 calories per tablespoon if made with milk and water.

VARIATIONS:

Cooked Salad Dressing à la Crème: Prepare dressing as directed, then fold in ½ cup heavy cream, beaten to soft peaks. About 45 calories per tablespoon if made with water, 50 calories per tablespoon if made with milk and water.

Piquant Cooked Dressing: Prepare dressing, cool, and mix in ½ cup sour cream, 1 teaspoon each prepared horseradish, grated yellow onion, and Worcestershire sauce. Bruise a peeled clove garlic, stick on a toothpick, and chill in dressing; remove before serving. About 35 calories per tablespoon if made with water, about 40 calories per tablespoon if made with milk and water.

Cooked Fruit Salad Dressing: Prepare dressing as directed but substitute 1 tablespoon cornstarch for the flour and use ½ cup orange juce and ¼ cup pineapple juice for the water; reduce lemon juice to 2 tablespoons. If you like, fold in ¼ teaspoon bruised celery, dill, or caraway seeds, also ½ cup heavy cream, whipped to soft peaks. About 30 calories per tablespoon (without whipped cream), 50 calories per tablespoon (with whipped cream).

OLD-FASHIONED COOKED DRESSING

This is such a versatile dressing. Make without seeds and serve over cold poached salmon. Or use in any of the ways that you would use mayonnaise. Makes 1 pint

6 egg yolks, lightly beaten
½ teaspoon powdered mustard
½ cup sugar
½ cup heavy cream
1 teaspoon salt
½ cup melted butter or margarine
1 cup warm cider vinegar
1½ teaspoons celery or poppy seeds (optional)

Mix yolks, mustard, sugar, cream, salt, and butter in the top of a double boiler; slowly beat in vinegar, set over simmering water, and heat and stir until the consistency of custard sauce. Remove from heat and stir 1 minute; mix in seeds if you like. Place a piece of wax paper flat on dressing and cool to room temperature. Cover and chill well. Stir before using. About 60 calories per tablespoon.

⚖ TANGY LOW-CALORIE SALAD DRESSING

Good with any green salad.
Makes 1½ cups

1 tablespoon cornstarch
1 cup cold water
3 tablespoons salad oil
¼ cup cider vinegar
1 teaspoon salt
1 teaspoon sugar
2 tablespoons ketchup
1 teaspoon prepared mild yellow mustard
½ teaspoon paprika
½ teaspoon prepared horseradish
½ teaspoon Worcestershire sauce
½ teaspoon oregano

Blend cornstarch and water and heat and stir over moderate heat until thickened and clear. Off heat, beat in remaining ingredients with a rotary beater or electric mixer. Cover and chill well. Shake before using. About 20 calories per tablespoon.

⚖ MUSTARD SALAD DRESSING

Makes about 1½ cups

2 tablespoons butter or margarine
2 tablespoons flour
1 cup milk
1 teaspoon salt
1½ teaspoons sugar
2 teaspoons powdered mustard blended with 2 tablespoons cold water
⅓ cup cider vinegar

Melt butter in a small saucepan over moderately low heat, blend in flour, add milk slowly, and cook and stir until thickened and smooth. Mix in salt, sugar, and mustard paste. Add vinegar, 1 tablespoon at a time, beating well after each addition. Cool dressing, then cover and chill 2–3 hours. Beat well before using. Use to dress any cooked vegetable or seafood salad. (Note: Dressing keeps well about a week in refrigerator.) About 20 calories per tablespoon.

VARIATION:

⚖ **Extra-Low-Calorie Mustard Dressing:** Prepare as directed but use skim milk instead of regular. About 15 calories per tablespoon.

THOUSAND ISLAND DRESSING

Makes about 1½ cups

1 cup mayonnaise
1 hard-cooked egg, peeled and chopped fine
1 tablespoon minced onion, scallion or chives
¼ cup chili sauce
¼ cup minced pimiento-stuffed green olives
1 tablespoon minced sweet green pepper
2–3 drops liquid hot red pepper seasoning

Mix all ingredients well, cover, and chill about 2 hours. Use to dress crisp wedges of lettuce. (Note: This dressing keeps well in the refrigerator for several days.) About 80 calories per tablespoon.

VARIATIONS:

⚖ **Low-Calorie Thousand Island Dressing** (Makes about 1 cup): Substitute yogurt for mayonnaise and 2 tablespoons minced parsley for the olives; use minced egg white only and reduce chili sauce to 1 tablespoon. About 10 calories per tablespoon.

Extra-Creamy Thousand Island Dressing (Makes about 2½ cups): Prepare as directed but substitute minced parsley for the green pepper; mix in ¼ cup minced dill pickle, 1 tablespoon Worcestershire sauce, and ¼ teaspoon paprika; finally, fold in ½ cup heavy cream beaten until glossy but not stiff. About 100 calories per tablespoon.

⊠ RUSSIAN DRESSING (AMERICAN STYLE)

Makes about 1¾ cups

1 cup mayonnaise or mayonnaise-type salad dressing
¼ cup French Dressing
¼ cup chili sauce
2 tablespoons minced sweet green pepper
2 tablespoons minced pimiento
1 tablespoon minced yellow onion
1 teaspoon prepared horseradish

Blend all ingredients together and use to dress green salads. About 80 calories per tablespoon.

VARIATION:

Russian Dressing (Russian Style): Prepare dressing as directed and mix in 2–3 tablespoons black caviar. About 85 calories per tablespoon.

GREEN GODDESS DRESSING I

Years ago when George Arliss was opening in San Francisco in *The Green Goddess,* the Palace Hotel chef created a salad dressing in his honor. Of the two versions below, the first is the most like the original, the second a popular, easy variation.
Makes about 1 quart

1 clove garlic, peeled and halved
⅓ cup minced parsley
⅓ cup minced chives
1 tablespoon minced scallions
¼ cup minced fresh tarragon
8 anchovy fillets, rinsed, drained, and minced

3 cups mayonnaise
⅓ cup tarragon vinegar

Rub a small bowl well with cut sides of garlic; discard garlic. Add remaining ingredients and mix well; cover and chill 1–2 hours. Use to dress crisp green salads. (*Note:* Dressing keeps well in refrigerator about 1 week.) About 85 calories per tablespoon.

VARIATION:

Green Goddess Dressing II: Prepare as directed but substitute ½ (2-ounce) tube anchovy paste for the minced anchovies and 1 cup sour cream for 1 cup of the mayonnaise. About 70 calories per tablespoon.

GREEN MAYONNAISE I

Green Mayonnaise I is nippier than Green Mayonnaise II, which substitutes spinach for watercress.
Makes about 1½ cups

½ cup minced parsley
⅓ cup minced watercress
2 tablespoons minced chives
1 tablespoon minced fresh dill
1¼ cups mayonnaise
1 teaspoon lemon juice
¼ teaspoon salt
2–3 drops liquid hot red pepper seasoning

Mix all ingredients well, cover, and chill several hours. Serve with cold boiled shellfish (especially lobster) or use to dress fish or vegetable salads. About 50 calories per tablespoon.

VARIATION:

Green Mayonnaise II: Prepare as directed, substituting minced raw spinach for the watercress and minced fresh tarragon or chervil for the dill. Omit chives if you like. About 50 calories per tablespoon.

WATERCRESS DRESSING

Makes 1½ cups

½ bunch watercress, washed
½ teaspoon celery salt

1 cup mayonnaise
1 tablespoon lemon juice

Pick leaves from watercress and mince; mix with remaining ingredients, cover, and chill 30 minutes. Good over wedges of lettuce, Belgian endives, halved lengthwise, or a mixture of avocado, orange, and grapefruit sections. About 75 calories per tablespoon.

CAVIAR DRESSING

Makes about 1 pint

1 hard-cooked egg, peeled and halved
1 cup mayonnaise
1 cup sour cream
Juice of ½ lemon
1 tablespoon prepared spicy brown
  mustard
1 scallion, minced (do not include tops)
1 (1-ounce) jar black caviar

Rub egg yolk through a fine sieve and mince the white; mix with remaining ingredients, cover, and chill about 1 hour. Stir well and use to dress tossed green salads or tomato aspic. Good, too, with cold boiled shrimp or lobster. (*Note:* Dressing keeps well several days in refrigerator.) About 75 calories per tablespoon.

CREAMY BUTTERMILK-CHIVE DRESSING

Makes 1½ cups

½ cup buttermilk
1 cup mayonnaise or mayonnaise-type
  salad dressing
2 tablespoons minced chives
¼ teaspoon salt
Pinch white pepper

Blend all ingredients together, cover, and chill 2 hours. Mix well again and use to dress green salads. (*Note:* Dressing keeps well about 1 week in refrigerator.) About 75 calories per tablespoon.

CHAPTER 18

BREADS

Making bread is one of cooking's true joys, yet many of us have lost that joy, if indeed we ever knew it. Every woman should make bread once, at least, if only to feel the warm dough responding to her touch, if only to fill her house with the promise of fresh loaves and the memories of her children with happiness.

Basically, there are two kinds of bread: *quick breads* (biscuits, muffins, pancakes, etc.), which can be cooked as soon as they're mixed, and *yeast breads,* which require more time and attention.

The Ways of Mixing Breads

Different breads require different techniques in handling; all are basic, most are easy:

Muffin Method (for muffins, popovers, waffles, pancakes, most corn breads): Dry ingredients are sifted together into a mixing bowl, liquid ingredients are combined, added all at once, and mixed in *just* enough to dampen the dry ingredients. There is great temptation to overbeat these batters, but if the bread—especially the muffin—is to be light and meltingly tender, the batter must be lumpy. If flecks of flour show, no harm done. Too much mixing makes the muffin tough.

Biscuit or Pastry Method (for biscuits and dumplings): Dry ingredients are sifted together into a bowl, the fat is cut in with a pastry blender or 2 knives until the texture of coarse meal, then the liquid is sprinkled over the mixture and stirred briskly. Kneading follows, usually about 20 seconds on a lightly floured board. It is the distribution of small fat particles throughout the dough that produces a flaky biscuit.

Cake Method (for most quick fruit and/or nut loaves): The shortening is creamed with the sugar and eggs, then the sifted dry ingredients added alternately with the liquid; nuts and fruit are folded in at the end.

Yeast Bread: Not one method but several; see Yeast Breads.

Tips for Making Better Breads

About Pans and Preparing Pans:

– Always use pan sizes recipes specify.
– Use baking sheets for biscuits and individually shaped rolls; if you have none, use a turned-upside-down large baking pan.
– For richly browned loaves (especially yeast loaves), use heatproof glass or dull finish, dark metal pans.
– For greasing pans, use cooking oil, shortening, or clarified* unsalted butter. Brush over bottom and sides of pans, applying in a thin, even film with a crumple of paper toweling or a pastry brush.
– If bread contains sticky fruit or filling, grease *and* flour pans (sprinkle a little

flour into greased pans, tilt from one side to the other to coat with a thin film, then tap out excess flour).
– When using muffin tins, grease only those cups that will be used; if you've greased more cups than you need, wipe grease from those not to be used.

About Mixing Breads:

– Read recipe carefully before beginning.
– Assemble all utensils and measure ingredients before beginning.
– Use as light a hand as possible in mixing breads. Muffins, especially, need a delicate touch.
– Unless recipes indicate otherwise, mix breads by hand, using a comfortable long-handled wooden spoon.
– To avoid last minute confusion, measure all ingredients for quick breads well ahead of time, then mix shortly before time to serve.

About Rolling Doughs:

– Use a lightly floured surface and rolling pin (experienced cooks prefer a pastry cloth and stockinette-covered pin), adding only what flour is needed to keep dough from sticking to board. Too much flour will toughen the dough.
– Roll doughs with quick, firm strokes from the center outward, keeping in mind the ultimate shape you want— circle, rectangle, square—and adjusting position of dough as needed to achieve that shape with a minimum of handling.
– Use floured cutters when cutting dough, floured scissors or knives for snipping or slicing it.

About Placing Breads and Rolls in Pans:

– Never fill muffin pan cups more than two-thirds full when making muffins or popovers; to make popover batter go farther, half fill cups.
– For soft-sided biscuits or rolls, place close together; for crusty sides, space about 1″ apart.
– Always brush any loose topping or wipe any spilled glaze from baking sheets before baking breads.

About Baking Breads (also see About Baking Yeast Breads for special techniques applying to yeast breads only):

– Let oven preheat a full 15 minutes before baking.
– Bake breads as near center of oven as possible unless recipes direct otherwise.
– When baking several pans of bread at once, stagger carefully so heat will circulate as evenly as possible; never let pans touch each other or oven walls.
– Check bread after minimum cooking time, then bake full time if needed.

To Tell if Breads Are Done:

Biscuits, Muffins, Rolls, and other Small Breads: They should be dappled with brown, firm and springy to the touch, and, if baked in muffin tins, slightly pulled from sides of cups.

Quick Loaves: They should have pulled slightly from sides of pans, be golden brown and springy to the touch.

Yeast Loaves: They should have pulled slightly from sides of pans, be richly browned and sound hollow when tapped.

About Cooling Breads:

– Unless recipes direct to the contrary, always remove breads from pans as soon as they come from the oven.
– Cool breads on wire racks and allow plenty of space around loaves for air to circulate. This keeps moisture from condensing on breads and spoiling them.

About Serving Breads:

– Serve muffins, biscuits, corn breads, popovers, and yeast rolls oven hot; cool yeast breads and fruit or nut loaves to room temperature before serving.
– Nestle hot breads in napkin-lined baskets so they will stay hot.
– If muffins or rolls should be done before the rest of the meal, tip each slightly in its muffin cup, turn off heat, and let stand in oven until ready to serve.
– To slice fresh loaves more easily, use a hot serrated bread knife (run quickly

under hot water, then dry). Or use a fine strong thread in a sawing motion.

About Reheating Breads:

Biscuits: Wrap in foil, not individually but en masse, and heat 15–20 minutes at 375° F. *Or* set unwrapped on a trivet in a large skillet, add 2–3 tablespoons water, cover and let steam over moderate heat 5–8 minutes.

Rolls, Muffins, Corn Breads: Bundle in foil and heat 8–10 minutes at 350° F. Or use the steaming method described for biscuits.

About Keeping Breads: Breads do not keep well; in damp weather they mold, in fair weather they harden and dry. Wrap tightly in foil, plastic bags, or wax paper and store in a breadbox in a cool, dry place. Or, if weather is unusually damp or muggy, in the refrigerator. The refrigerator, contrary to what many people believe, is not a good place to store bread because it *hastens* staling.

About Freezing Breads: See chapter on freezing.

QUICK BREADS AND BATTERS

Note: Unless recipes specify otherwise, use all-purpose flour in the recipes that follow and double-acting baking powder.

¢ ⊠ BASIC MUFFINS

Makes about 1¼ dozen

2 cups plus 2 tablespoons sifted flour
1 tablespoon baking powder
2 tablespoons sugar
1 teaspoon salt
1 egg, beaten until frothy
1 cup milk
3 tablespoons cooking oil, melted butter or margarine

Preheat oven to 425° F. Sift all dry ingredients together into a mixing bowl.

Mix egg, milk, and oil. Make a well in center of dry ingredients and pour in egg mixture all at once; stir lightly and quickly just to mix; *batter should be lumpy.* Spoon into muffin pans—bottoms of cups should be greased but *not* sides —filling each cup two-thirds. Bake about 20 minutes until lightly browned. Serve oven hot with plenty of butter. About 105 calories per muffin (without butter).

VARIATIONS:

Bacon Muffins: Sift dry ingredients as directed but reduce salt to ½ teaspoon; add ¼ cup minced crisp bacon and toss to dredge. Lightly beat egg and milk with 2 tablespoons each cooking oil and melted bacon drippings; mix into dry ingredients by basic method and bake as directed. About 115 calories per muffin (without butter).

Date, Raisin, or Currant Muffins: Sift 2¼ cups flour, 3 tablespoons sugar, 1 tablespoon baking powder, and ½ teaspoon salt into mixing bowl; add 1 teaspoon finely grated lemon rind and 1 cup diced, pitted dates, seedless raisins, or dried currants; toss to dredge. Lightly beat egg and milk with ¼ cup cooking oil, mix into dry ingredients by basic method, and bake as directed. About 130 calories per muffin (without butter).

Nut Muffins: Sift 2¼ cups flour, ¼ cup light brown sugar, 1 tablespoon baking powder, and ½ teaspoon salt into bowl; add ¾ cup minced nuts (any kind) and toss to dredge. Lightly beat egg and milk with ¼ cup oil or melted butter; mix into dry ingredients by basic method and bake as directed. About 140 calories per muffin (without butter).

Blueberry Muffins: Sift 2¼ cups flour, ¼ cup sugar, 1 tablespoon baking powder, and ¼ teaspoon salt into mixing bowl. Add 1 cup washed and dried blueberries and toss to mix. Beat egg and milk with ¼ cup melted butter; mix into dry ingredients by basic method and bake as directed. About 130 calories per muffin (without butter).

Orange Muffins: Sift 2¼ cups flour, ¼ cup sugar, 2½ teaspoons baking powder, ½ teaspoon baking soda, and ¼ teaspoon salt into mixing bowl. Add finely grated rind of 1 orange and toss to dredge. Lightly beat egg with ½ cup each milk and orange juice and ¼ cup melted butter (no substitute). Mix egg mixture into dry ingredients by basic method and bake as directed. About 120 calories per muffin (without butter).

¢ WHOLE WHEAT MUFFINS

Makes 1 dozen

¾ cup unsifted whole wheat flour
1 cup sifted all-purpose flour
3 tablespoons sugar
1 tablespoon baking powder
1 teaspoon salt
1 egg
1 cup milk
¼ cup cooking oil
1 tablespoon molasses

Preheat oven to 425° F. Place whole wheat flour in a large mixing bowl, then sift all-purpose flour with sugar, baking powder, and salt directly into bowl; toss well to mix. Beat egg with milk, oil, and molasses until foamy. Make a well in the center of the dry ingredients, pour in liquid all at once and stir lightly and quickly just to mix; batter should be quite lumpy. Spoon into greased muffin pans, three-fourths filling each cup. (*Note:* For best results, only bottoms of cups should be greased, not sides.) Bake 20–22 minutes until lightly browned. Serve hot with plenty of butter. About 135 calories per muffin (without butter).

¢ BRAN MUFFINS

Makes 1 dozen

1¼ cups ready-to-eat bran cereal
1 cup milk
1¼ cups sifted flour
1 tablespoon baking powder
½ teaspoon salt
¼ cup sugar
1 egg
¼ cup cooking oil, melted butter or
  margarine

Preheat oven to 425° F. Soak bran in milk 2–3 minutes. Sift dry ingredients together into a mixing bowl. Beat egg and oil until blended, then stir into bran and milk. Make a well in center of dry ingredients and pour in bran mixture all at once. Stir lightly and quickly just to mix (batter should be lumpy). Spoon into muffin pans—bottoms of cups should be greased but not sides—filling each cup two-thirds. Bake about 25 minutes until lightly browned and springy to the touch. Serve hot with lots of butter. About 140 calories per muffin (without butter).

VARIATIONS:

Raisin-Bran Muffins: Prepare as directed, adding ¾ cup seedless raisins to the sifted dry ingredients; toss well to dredge before combining with liquid ingredients. About 170 calories per muffin (without butter).

Nut-Bran Muffins: Prepare as directed, adding ¾ cup minced pecans or walnuts to the sifted dry ingredients; toss well to dredge before mixing with liquid ingredients. About 185 calories per muffin (without butter).

¢ RYE MUFFINS

Not unlike pumpernickel.
Makes 1 dozen

1 tablespoon caraway seeds
2 tablespoons boiling water
¾ cup unsifted rye flour
3 tablespoons light brown sugar
1 cup sifted all-purpose flour
1 tablespoon baking powder
1 teaspoon salt
1 egg
1 tablespoon dark molasses
¾ cup milk
¼ cup cooking oil

Preheat oven to 425° F. Soak caraway seeds in boiling water 15–20 minutes. Place rye flour and sugar in a bowl and rub well between your fingers, breaking up any lumps of sugar. Sift all-purpose flour, baking powder, and salt directly into another bowl and toss well to mix. Beat egg with molasses, milk, and oil until foamy, then stir in caraway seeds and water. Make a well in center of dry ingredients and pour in milk mixture all at once. Stir quickly and lightly just enough to mix; batter should be lumpy. Spoon into muffin pans—bottoms of cups should be greased but not sides—filling each cup two-thirds. Bake about 20 minutes until lightly browned. Serve hot with lots of butter. About 135 calories per muffin (without butter).

¢ BAKING POWDER BISCUITS

These will be light and feathery if you follow the directions exactly.
Makes 1½ dozen

2 cups sifted flour
1 teaspoon salt
1 tablespoon baking powder
⅓ cup chilled shortening
¾ cup milk
Milk, melted butter or margarine
* (optional glaze)*

Preheat oven to 450° F. Sift flour with salt and baking powder into a bowl and cut in shortening with a pastry blender until the texture of very coarse meal; make a well in center, pour in milk, and stir briskly with a fork just until dough holds together. Knead gently on a lightly floured board 7 or 8 times. Roll ½" thick and cut in rounds with a floured biscuit cutter; reroll and cut scraps. Place on ungreased baking sheets —1" apart for crusty-sided biscuits, almost touching for soft. For glistening brown tops, brush with glaze. Bake 12–15 minutes until lightly browned. Serve oven hot with lots of butter. (*Note:* For hot-hot-hot biscuits, bake in piepans that can come to the table. To reheat leftover biscuits, wrap together in a large foil package and warm 15–20 minutes at 350° F.) About 85 calories per biscuit (without butter).

VARIATIONS:

¢ **Drop Biscuits:** Prepare basic recipe but increase milk to 1 cup. Do not knead or roll but drop by tablespoonfuls 1" apart on greased baking sheets. Bake as directed. About 85 calories per biscuit (without butter).

¢ **Biscuit Topping for Casseroles:**
Prepare 1 recipe Drop Biscuits (above) and drop by rounded tablespoonfuls, almost touching, on top of hot casserole mixture. (*Note:* Bake any leftover dough as basic recipe directs.) Bake casserole, uncovered, as recipe directs or 15–20 minutes at 425° F. until lightly browned. *To serve:* Cut through biscuit topping as you would piecrust. About 250 calories for each of 6 pie-shaped wedges, 190 calories for each of 8 wedges.

¢ **Quick Biscuit Topping for Casseroles:**
For Drop Biscuits (above), substitute packaged biscuit mix prepared by label directions or canned refrigerated biscuits; drop onto casserole and bake as directed. About 80 calories per biscuit.

¢ **Stir-and-Roll Biscuits:** Sift dry ingredients into bowl as directed. Pour ⅓ cup cooking oil into a measuring cup, and add ⅔ cup milk; *do not stir* but pour all at once into well in dry ingredients. Mix briskly with a fork until dough holds together. Knead in bowl 10 times without adding more flour. Turn onto an *unfloured* board, top with a sheet of wax paper and roll ½" thick. Cut and bake on ungreased baking sheets 12–14 minutes at 475° F. About 85 calories per biscuit (without butter).

☒ **Extra-Quick Biscuits:** Prepare basic dough as directed, pat into a rectangle ½" thick and cut in 1½" squares or 2" triangles. Bake as directed. About 85 calories per biscuit (without butter).

Extra-Rich Biscuits: Prepare basic dough as directed but add 2 tablespoons sugar to dry ingredients and increase shortening to ½ cup. About 90 calories per biscuit (without butter).

¢ **Buttermilk Biscuits:** Prepare basic or stir-and-roll dough as directed but reduce baking powder to 2 teaspoons, add ¼ teaspoon baking soda, and substitute cold buttermilk for milk. About 85 calories per biscuit (without butter).

Sweet Pinwheel Biscuits: Prepare basic dough and roll into a rectangle about

12" long, 6"–7" wide, and ¼" thick. Spread with softened butter, sprinkle with ¼ cup light brown sugar, 1 teaspoon cinnamon, ⅛ teaspoon nutmeg, and ¼–⅓ cup seedless raisins, dried currants, or coarsely chopped pecans or walnuts. Or, if you prefer, top butter with marmalade, jam, or a drizzling of honey. Roll the short way, jelly roll style, pinch seam to seal, then slice 1" thick. Lay pinwheels flat in greased muffin pans, brush lightly with milk, and bake 12–15 minutes at 425° F. Recipe too flexible for a meaningful calorie count.

Savory Pinwheel Biscuits: Prepare like Sweet Pinwheel Biscuits (above) but spread with deviled ham or any cheese or meat spread instead of sugar and spices. About 105–115 calories per serving depending on filling (cheese would tend to run higher than meat).

Party Biscuits: Prepare and roll basic dough as directed; cut with a 1½" cutter and bake 10–12 minutes at 450° F. Split biscuits, fill with slices of Smithfield ham, roast chicken, or turkey, and serve as buffet food. About 95 calories per biscuit.

¢ **Herb Biscuits:** Prepare basic recipe as directed, but before adding milk lightly toss in any of the following: ½ teaspoon each sage and thyme (nice with pork), ½ teaspoon each basil and oregano (good with veal), ¼ cup minced chives or parsley (delicious with chicken), 2 teaspoons dill or 1½ teaspoons caraway seeds. About 85 calories per biscuit (without butter).

¢ **Onion Biscuits:** Prepare basic recipe as directed, but before adding milk toss in 1–2 tablespoons instant minced onion or ¼ cup crumbled French-fried onion rings. About 85 calories per biscuit (without butter).

Bacon Biscuits: Prepare basic recipe as directed, but before adding milk toss in ⅓–½ cup finely crumbled, crisp bacon. About 100 calories per biscuit (without butter).

¢ **Cheese Biscuits:** Prepare basic recipe as directed, but before adding milk toss in ½ cup coarsely grated sharp Cheddar cheese. About 100 calories per biscuit (without butter).

¢ **Orange or Lemon Biscuits:** Prepare extra rich dough as directed, but before adding milk toss in the finely grated rind of 1 orange or ½ lemon. About 90 calories per biscuit (without butter).

Berry Biscuits: Mix drop biscuits as directed, then stir in 1 cup washed, well-dried blueberries, raspberries, or very small strawberries. Sprinkle biscuits with sugar before baking. About 90 calories per biscuit (without butter).

¢ **Make-Ahead Biscuits:** Prepare any biscuit recipe as directed, then bake 7–8 minutes at 450° F. until risen but not browned. Cool, wrap, and freeze. To serve, arrange solidly frozen biscuits on ungreased baking sheets and bake in top ⅓ of a 450° F. oven 8–10 minutes until browned.

Some Quick Toppings to Jazz Up Biscuits: Before baking, brush tops of biscuits with a little milk, melted butter or margarine, then sprinkle with any of the following:
– Cinnamon sugar
– Poppy, caraway, or sesame seeds
– Finely ground pecans, walnuts, almonds, or peanuts
– Grated Parmesan cheese
– Corn meal
– Seasoned salt

¢ **CHEESE-CORN MEAL BISCUITS**

Makes about 1½ dozen

½ cup corn meal
¾ cup milk, scalded
1 cup sifted flour
1 tablespoon baking powder
¾ teaspoon salt
3 tablespoons butter, margarine, or lard
¾ cup coarsely grated mild Cheddar
  cheese
1 egg yolk, lightly beaten (glaze)

Preheat oven to 450° F. Briskly mix corn meal into hot milk, cover, and set aside. Sift flour with baking powder and salt into a bowl. Using a pastry blender, cut in butter until mixture resembles coarse meal. Add corn meal mixture and cheese and stir lightly to blend. Turn onto a lightly floured board, knead gently about ½ minute. Roll ½" thick and cut into rounds with a biscuit cutter. Arrange 1½" apart on an ungreased baking sheet and brush tops with glaze. Bake 12–15 minutes or until well risen and golden. About 85 calories per biscuit.

¢ ⊠ **BANNOCKS**
A husky Scottish griddlecake made with oatmeal.
Makes 2 dozen

4¼ cups uncooked oatmeal (not quick-cooking)
2 teaspoons salt
1 teaspoon baking soda
¼ cup melted bacon drippings or lard
1 cup very hot water

Preheat griddle over moderately high heat while you mix bannocks, or, if using an electric griddle, preheat to 400° F. Place 4 cups oatmeal in a mixing bowl; buzz the rest in an electric blender at high speed until moderately fine, then reserve to use in rolling out dough. Add remaining ingredients to bowl and mix well. Knead on a board lightly dusted with the fine oatmeal 1 minute, roll ¼" thick, and cut into rounds with a 3" cutter. Cook on an *ungreased* griddle 5–6 minutes per side until lightly browned and cooked through. Serve hot with plenty of butter. About 110 calories per bannock (without butter).

¢ **IRISH SODA BREAD**
In Ireland this bread is made as often with whole wheat flour as with white, and usually without shortening. It's a close-textured loaf. When serving, cut straight across the loaf into thin slices instead of dividing into wedges.
Makes a 6" round loaf

1 cup sifted all-purpose flour
2 teaspoons baking soda
1½ teaspoons salt
¼ cup shortening or margarine
3 cups unsifted whole wheat flour
1⅔ cups buttermilk or sour milk

Preheat oven to 400° F. Sift all-purpose flour, soda, and salt together into a large bowl. With a pastry blender cut in shortening until the texture of coarse meal. Mix in whole wheat flour. Pour in buttermilk all at once and mix well to blend (you may have to use your hands). Turn out on a lightly floured board and knead until fairly smooth, about 5 minutes. Shape into a round loaf about 6" across, with a sharp knife cut a cross ¼" deep in top and sprinkle with a very little flour. Place cross side up in a well-greased round 2-quart casserole about 2½" deep. Bake, uncovered, about 40 minutes until crusty brown and hollow sounding when tapped. Turn loaf out on wire rack and cool before cutting. About 110 calories for each of 20 slices.

VARIATION:

¢ **White Irish Soda Bread:** Sift 4 cups all-purpose flour with soda and salt and cut in shortening; omit whole wheat flour and reduce buttermilk to 1½ cups; otherwise proceed as directed. About 110 calories for each of 20 slices.

¢ **HILDA'S YORKSHIRE SCONES**
Makes about 10

1½ cups sifted flour
¼ cup sugar
¼ teaspoon salt
1½ teaspoons baking powder
¼ cup margarine
⅓ cup seedless raisins
1 egg, lightly beaten
2 tablespoons milk

Preheat oven to 425° F. Sift flour, sugar, salt, and baking powder into a bowl. Using a pastry blender or 2 knives, cut in margarine until the texture of coarse meal. Add raisins and toss to mix. Add egg and milk and mix with a fork until mixture forms a soft dough. Roll on a floured board or pat into a circle about ½″ thick, adding only enough flour to keep dough from sticking. Cut into rounds with a floured 2″ cutter; reroll and cut scraps. Bake 2″ apart on a greased baking sheet 12–15 minutes until golden. Let cool 1–2 minutes on a wire rack. Scones are best eaten warm, not hot—split in half and slathered with butter. About 145 calories per scone (without butter).

¢ POPOVERS

Makes about 6 popovers

1 cup sifted flour
½ teaspoon salt
¾ cup milk
¼ cup cold water
2 eggs

Preheat oven to 450° F. Beat all ingredients in a small bowl with a rotary beater until just smooth. Scrape bottom of bowl with rubber spatula once or twice during beating. Spoon into a well-greased muffin tin, filling each cup two-thirds. Bake 40 minutes until well browned, puffed, and firm. (*Note:* For dry, crisp popovers, bake 35 minutes, quickly cut a small slit in the side of each popover so steam can escape, and bake 5–10 minutes longer.) Serve immediately with plenty of butter. About 115 calories per popover (without butter).

¢ YORKSHIRE PUDDING

A 100-year-old Yorkshire recipe adapted for today's silken flours. Like a soufflé, Yorkshire pudding will not wait, so serve straight from the oven.
Makes 6 servings

½ cup sifted flour
½ teaspoon salt
½ cup milk
¼ cup cold water
2 eggs, lightly beaten
1 tablespoon melted roast beef drippings

Mix flour and salt in a small bowl, add milk, a little at a time, beating with a rotary beater or electric mixer until smooth. Add water and eggs and beat until bubbly. Cover loosely and let stand in a cool place (not refrigerator) about ½ hour. Meanwhile, preheat oven to 500° F. (*Note:* If you've been doing a roast, shove temperature up after roast comes from oven.) Beat batter 1–2 minutes until bubbles appear on surface. Pour ½ teaspoon drippings into each of 6 muffin pan cups and heat in the oven 1–2 minutes until almost smoking hot. Spoon 3 tablespoons batter into each cup and bake 8 minutes *without opening oven door.* Reduce temperature to 400° F. and bake 8–10 minutes longer until well browned, risen, and crisp. (*Note:* Do not pierce with a fork or puddings will collapse.) Arrange puddings around roast and serve at once, allowing 1 pudding with each portion of meat and topping with plenty of hot gravy. About 80 calories per serving (without gravy).

VARIATION:

¢ **Old-Fashioned Yorkshire Pudding:** Prepare batter and preheat oven to 500° F. Pour 3 tablespoons melted roast beef drippings into a 13″×9″×2″ baking pan (or similar-size pan in which beef was roasted) and heat in oven 2 minutes. Meanwhile beat batter until bubbles appear. Pour batter into pan and bake 10 minutes, reduce temperature to 450° F., and bake 12–15 minutes longer until well browned and crisp. Cut in large squares and serve. About 80 calories per serving (without gravy).

CHEESE CRACKERS

Makes about 6 dozen

1½ cups sifted flour
1 teaspoon salt
⅛ teaspoon paprika
⅛ teaspoon cayenne pepper
½ cup chilled margarine (no substitute)
½ pound sharp Cheddar cheese, coarsely grated
2½–3 tablespoons ice water

Mix flour, salt, paprika and cayenne in a shallow bowl and cut in margarine with a pastry blender until mixture resembles coarse meal. Add cheese and toss to mix. Sprinkle ice water evenly over surface, 1 tablespoon at a time, mixing lightly with a fork; dough should just hold together. Divide dough into 2 parts, turn out on a lightly floured board, and shape each into a roll about 9″ long and 1½″ in diameter; wrap in foil and chill well. About 10 minutes before crackers are to be baked, preheat oven to 375° F. Slice rolls ¼″ thick and space crackers 1″ apart on ungreased baking sheets. Bake 10 minutes until golden, then transfer at once to wire racks to cool. Store airtight. Serve at room temperature or, if you prefer, reheat about 5 minutes at 350° F. About 30 calories per cracker.

¢ BASIC CORN BREAD

Makes an 8″×8″×2″ loaf

1 cup sifted flour
1 cup sifted corn meal
1 tablespoon baking powder
¾ teaspoon salt
1 tablespoon sugar (optional)
1 egg
1 cup milk
¼ cup cooking oil, melted shortening,
* or bacon drippings*

Preheat oven to 400° F. Sift flour, corn meal, baking powder, salt, and, if you like, sugar into a bowl; beat egg with milk and oil just to blend. Make a well in dry ingredients, pour in egg mixture, and stir until well blended. Pour into a well-greased 8″×8″×2″ baking pan and bake 20–25 minutes until bread pulls slightly from edges of pan, is lightly browned and springy to the touch. Cut in large squares and serve oven hot with lots of butter. About 110 calories for each of 16 squares (without butter), 145 calories for each of 12 squares.

VARIATIONS:

¢ **Corn Sticks** (Makes 14): Preheat oven to 425° F. Grease corn stick pans, set in oven, and let heat while oven preheats. Mix batter as directed, spoon into hot pans, and bake 15–20 minutes until nicely browned and springy to the

touch. Serve at once. About 125 calories per corn stick.

¢ **Corn Muffins** (Makes 1 dozen): Preheat oven to 425° F. Mix batter as directed, spoon into greased muffin pans, filling each cup two-thirds. Bake 15–20 minutes until lightly browned and springy to the touch. Serve hot. About 145 calories per muffin.

¢ CRACKLING BREAD

Cracklings are the crunchy brown bits left over after rendering pork fat into lard. In the old days there were plenty of cracklings at hog butchering time. Today, unless you raise hogs, you'll have to buy fresh pork fat from your butcher (some will give it to you) and make your own cracklings. Here's how. Makes 8 small patties

Cracklings:
2 cups diced fresh pork fat

Bread:
¾ cup sifted flour
1½ cups corn meal
½ teaspoon baking soda
¾ teaspoon salt
1 cup diced cracklings
2 tablespoons drippings from cracklings
1 cup plus 2 tablespoons buttermilk

Render pork fat in a large iron skillet over moderately low heat, stirring now and then, until all fat is melted and cracklings are crisp and golden brown; this will take about 45 minutes. Watch carefully and reduce heat if fat threatens to smoke and burn. Drain cracklings on paper toweling and cut up any big pieces; save drippings to use in cooking. Preheat oven to 400° F. Mix flour with corn meal, soda, and salt; add cracklings and toss to mix. Combine drippings and buttermilk, pour into meal mixture, and stir to mix. Shape into hamburger-size patties or oblong cakes and bake on a greased baking sheet about 25 minutes until lightly browned and firm. Serve hot—no butter needed. About 200 calories per piece.

¢ BAKED JOHNNYCAKE

Makes an 8″×8″×2″ loaf

1 cup sifted flour
1 cup corn meal, preferably white
1 teaspoon salt
1 tablespoon baking powder
1 egg, lightly beaten
¼ cup melted butter or margarine
2 tablespoons dark molasses
1⅓ cups milk

Preheat oven to 375° F. Sift flour, meal, salt, and baking powder together into a bowl. Add remaining ingredients and beat just until blended. Spoon into a greased 8″×8″×2″ pan and bake 25–30 minutes until pale golden and springy to the touch. Turn out on a wire rack and cool 1–2 minutes; turn upright, cut in 2″ squares, and serve hot with plenty of butter. About 110 calories for each of 16 squares (without butter).

⊠ ¢ RHODE ISLAND JONNYCAKES

There are Rhode Island jonnycakes and Rhode Island jonnycakes (*not* spelled johnnycake, by the way). If you come from "South County," Rhode Island, you like your jonnycakes thick—the batter should be about the consistency of a soft drop-cookie dough so that it mounds on a spoon and stands up on the griddle. And the cakes themselves will be thick, ½–¾ inch, and cooked at least 10 minutes on each side until crispy-brown. "You can't hurry jonnycakes," they say in "South County." But if, on the other hand, you're from Northern Rhode Island, you like your jonnycakes thin—almost as thin as a crepe. The recipe below is a basic one, and you can experiment with batter thickness until you determine just the consistency you like. It's best to cook jonnycakes on an old-fashioned iron griddle, but you can use an electric skillet or griddle set at a low temperature.
Makes 4 servings

1 cup fine water-ground white corn meal
½ teaspoon salt

1 tablespoon sugar
1 cup boiling water (about)
Milk (to thin batter)
3–4 tablespoons bacon drippings or shortening

Mix together corn meal, salt, and sugar. Pour in boiling water and toss with a fork just to mix. There should be enough water just to dampen the ingredients so that no dry particles show. Next, add enough milk to thin batter to the consistency you like. Heat 2 tablespoons bacon drippings or shortening on a heavy griddle over moderate heat until a drop of water will dance about. Then drop batter by rounded tablespoonfuls onto griddle, reduce heat, and brown slowly, a few at a time, 5–10 minutes on a side, depending on thickness, until crispy and brown. Jonnycakes should be about 2½″ in diameter. Lift to paper toweling and keep warm while frying the remainder (add more bacon drippings or shortening as needed). Serve hot with butter or, if you prefer, with butter and maple syrup. If the cakes are thick, try splitting and tucking in a slice of sharp Cheddar cheese—delicious! About 225 calories per serving (without butter, syrup, or cheese).

OLD-FASHIONED DEEP SOUTH SPOON BREAD

This custard-like corn meal pudding makes a good potato substitute.
Makes 4–6 servings

1 pint light cream
⅓ cup milk
¼ cup unsalted butter
2 tablespoons sugar
1 teaspoon salt
1 cup sifted stone- or water-ground white corn meal
4 eggs, separated
1 teaspoon baking powder

Preheat oven to 375° F. Heat cream, milk, butter, sugar, and salt uncovered, stirring occasionally, until scalding; off heat, mix in corn meal, beating until smooth and thick. Lightly beat yolks and stir in baking powder. Stir a little of the hot mixture into yolks, then return to pan and blend well. Beat whites until soft peaks form and fold in. Bake, uncovered, in a lightly buttered 2-quart casserole or soufflé dish 30–35 minutes until puffy and lightly browned. Serve oven hot with lots of butter, salt, and freshly ground black pepper. About 625 calories for each of 4 servings (without butter), 420 calories for each of 6 servings.

¢ CORN MEAL MUSH

A Southern breakfast favorite.
Makes 4 servings

½ cup corn meal, preferably enriched yellow meal
2½ cups boiling water
¾ teaspoon salt

Sprinkle meal into rapidly boiling water, add salt, and heat, stirring, over very low heat about ½ hour until quite thick. Ladle into bowls, top with pats of butter, and serve hot for breakfast. About 60 calories per serving (without butter).

VARIATION:

Fried Mush: Prepare mush as directed and pour into heatproof water glasses or small tin cans (the soup size is perfect) that have been rinsed out in cold water. Cool until firm. Unmold, slice mush ½"–¾" thick and brown in hot bacon drippings, butter, or margarine. Serve with hot syrup in place of pancakes or waffles. About 135 calories per serving (without syrup).

HUSHPUPPIES

For this recipe you *must* use old-fashioned, stone- or water-ground white corn meal—enriched yellow meal flies to pieces in the hot fat. Hushpuppies, it's said, were originally tag ends of corn bread dough, deep fat fried and tossed to dogs at mealtime to "hush them up." Serve hushpuppies with seafood, especially breaded or batter-fried fish.
Makes about 2 dozen

Shortening or cooking oil for deep fat frying

2 cups sifted fine stone- or water-ground white corn meal
1 tablespoon sugar
¾ teaspoon baking soda
2 teaspoons salt
1 tablespoon minced yellow onion
1 egg
1 cup buttermilk
4–5 tablespoons cold water

Begin heating fat in a deep fat fryer; use a deep fat thermometer. Stir corn meal, sugar, soda, and salt together to mix. Place onion in a small bowl, add egg and buttermilk, and beat until frothy; pour all at once into meal and stir lightly to mix. Add just enough water to make dough a good dropping consistency—it should be about the same as drop biscuit dough. When fat reaches 375° F., scoop up rounded ½ tablespoons of dough, shape lightly on end of spoon to smooth out rough edges, drop into fat, and fry about 2 minutes until evenly browned. Drain quickly on paper toweling and serve—hushpuppies should be sizzling hot. About 70 calories each.

¢ TORTILLAS

Masa harina is a special corn flour used to make tortillas and other Mexican breads. It's available in gourmet food shops, Latin American and Spanish groceries.
Makes 15

2 cups masa harina
1 teaspoon salt
1¼ cups very hot water

Mix masa and salt, stir in water, and blend well. Pinch off a piece of dough and roll into a ball about 1½" in diameter; flatten in a tortilla press or, if you have none, between 2 dampened 6" double thickness squares of cheesecloth, pressing as hard as possible with a cutting board. Remove board and roll with a rolling pin until about 5" across. Lift off top cheesecloth, very gently invert tortilla on palm of hand, and peel off bottom cheesecloth. Cook in an ungreased, heavy skillet over moderately high heat or on an electric griddle set at 400° F. ½–1 minute on each side, just until tortilla begins to color. It should not brown. Keep warm in a napkin or linen towel while you shape and cook remaining tortillas. Serve hot. About 70 calories each.

VARIATION:

Chili Tostados: Prepare and cook tortillas as directed, then fry, a few at a time, in ½" cooking oil over moderate heat until lightly browned. Drain on paper toweling, spread with hot chili con carne, top with shredded lettuce, a drizzling of French dressing, and a sprinkling of grated Parmesan or Cheddar cheese. Fold tortilla over filling and serve. About 200 calories each.

EASY DATE-NUT BREAD

Start this recipe the day before you bake it.
Makes 2 9"×5"×3" loaves

2 cups coarsely cut-up pitted dates
2 cups boiling water
2 teaspoons baking soda
1 cup sugar
1 tablespoon melted butter or margarine
1 egg, lightly beaten
2¾ cups sifted flour
1 cup coarsely chopped pecans or
    walnuts
1 teaspoon vanilla

Mix dates, water, and soda; cool, cover, and let stand at room temperature overnight. Next day preheat oven to 325° F. Add sugar, butter, and egg to date mixture and stir until sugar dissolves. Add flour, a few spoonfuls at a time, mixing after each addition until smooth. Stir in nuts and vanilla. Spoon into 2 greased and floured 9"×5"×3" loaf pans and bake about 1 hour, until loaves shrink slightly from sides of pan and are springy to the touch. Cool upright in pans on wire rack 10 minutes, turn out, and cool completely. Wrap airtight and store overnight before cutting. (*Note:* These loaves freeze well.) About 90 calories for each of 20 slices.

PRUNE AND WALNUT BREAD

This loaf tastes better and cuts more easily if wrapped airtight and "seasoned" about a day.
Makes a 9"×5"×3" loaf

2 cups sifted flour
1 teaspoon baking powder
½ teaspoon salt
1 cup boiling water
1 teaspoon baking soda
1 cup coarsely chopped pitted prunes
⅔ cup sugar
1 egg
2 tablespoons melted butter or
    margarine
½ teaspoon vanilla
⅔ cup coarsely chopped walnuts

Preheat oven to 300° F. Sift flour with baking powder and salt and set aside. Mix boiling water, soda, and prunes and cool to lukewarm; drain off liquid and reserve. Beat sugar, egg, butter, and vanilla until well blended. Add flour mixture, about ⅓ at a time, alternately with reserved prune liquid, beginning and ending with flour; beat just until smooth. Mix in prunes and walnuts. Spoon into a greased 9"×5"×3" loaf pan and bake 1 hour until loaf shrinks slightly from sides of pan and is springy to the touch. Cool upright in pan on a wire rack 20 minutes before turning out. Cool thoroughly, slice, and serve. About 135 calories for each of 20 slices.

VARIATIONS:

Apricot-Pecan Bread: Prepare as directed, substituting dried apricots for the prunes and pecans or blanched almonds for the walnuts. About 130 calories for each of 20 slices.

Raisin or Currant and Nut Bread: Prepare as directed, substituting seedless raisins or dried currants for the prunes. For the nuts use walnuts, pecans, filberts, or blanched almonds. About 135 calories for each of 20 slices.

ORANGE NUT BREAD

Delicious spread with cream cheese.
Makes a 9"×5"×3" loaf

2¾ cups sifted flour
2½ teaspoons baking powder
½ teaspoon baking soda
½ teaspoon salt
2 tablespoons butter or margarine,
　softened to room temperature
1 cup strained honey
1 egg, lightly beaten
1½ teaspoons finely grated orange rind
¾ cup orange juice
¾ cup coarsely chopped pecans, walnuts,
　or blanched almonds

Preheat oven to 325° F. Sift flour with
baking powder, soda, and salt and set
aside. Blend butter with honey until
creamy; add egg and orange rind and
mix well. Add sifted ingredients
alternately with orange juice, beginning
and ending with the sifted. Fold in nuts.
Spoon into a greased 9"×5"×3" loaf
pan and bake 1–1¼ hours until loaf
pulls slightly from sides of pan and is
springy to the touch. Let cool upright in
pan 10 minutes, then turn out and cool
on a wire rack. About 155 calories for
each of 20 slices.

CRANBERRY NUT BREAD

Makes a 9"×5"×3" loaf

1 cup cranberries (fresh or frozen)
1 cup sugar
3 cups sifted flour
4 teaspoons baking powder
½ teaspoon salt
½ cup coarsely chopped walnuts or
　pecans
Grated rind of 1 orange
1 egg, lightly beaten
1 cup milk
2 teaspoons melted butter or margarine

Preheat oven to 350° F. Put cranberries
through coarse blade of meat grinder
and mix with ¼ cup sugar. Sift remaining
sugar with flour, baking powder, and
salt; mix in nuts and orange rind. Lightly
beat egg with milk and melted butter
and stir into flour mixture. Fold in
cranberries. Spoon into a buttered

9"×5"×3" loaf pan and bake about
1 hour until loaf pulls slightly from sides
of pan and is springy to the touch. Cool
upright in pan 10 minutes, then turn out
on a wire rack and cool before slicing.
About 140 calories for each of 20 slices.

BANANA TEA BREAD

Makes a 9"×5"×3" loaf

1¾ cups sifted flour
2 teaspoons baking powder
¼ teaspoon baking soda
½ teaspoon salt
⅓ cup shortening
⅔ cup sugar
2 eggs, well beaten
1 cup mashed ripe bananas

Preheat oven to 350° F. Sift flour with
baking powder, soda, and salt and set
aside. Cream shortening until light, add
sugar gradually, continuing to cream
until fluffy. Beat in eggs. Add flour
mixture alternately with bananas,
beginning and ending with flour. Spoon
into a well-greased 9"×5"×3" loaf
pan and bake about 1 hour and 10
minutes until loaf pulls slightly from
sides of pan and is springy to the touch.
Cool upright in pan 10 minutes, then
turn out on a wire rack and cool before
slicing. About 110 calories for each of
20 slices.

CINNAMON COFFEE CAKE

Makes 2 9"×5"×3" loaves

2½ cups sifted flour
2½ teaspoons baking powder
1 cup butter or margarine
1 cup sugar
3 eggs
1 teaspoon vanilla
1 cup sour cream
½ cup coarsely chopped pitted dates
½ cup finely chopped pecans or walnuts
½ cup firmly packed light brown sugar
　mixed with 2 teaspoons cinnamon

Preheat oven to 350° F. Sift flour with
baking powder and set aside. Cream
butter and sugar until light, then beat
in eggs, 1 at a time; mix in vanilla. Add
flour, a few spoonfuls at a time,

alternately with sour cream, beginning and ending with flour. Stir in dates and nuts. Spoon about half the batter into 2 greased and floured 9"×5"×3" loaf pans and sprinkle with half the brown sugar mixture. Add remaining batter and sprinkle with remaining sugar mixture. Bake about 1 hour until loaves pull slightly from sides of pan and are springy to the touch. Cool upright in pans on a wire rack 10 minutes, then turn out and cool completely. Slice and serve with butter. (*Note:* These loaves freeze well.) About 130 calories for each of 20 slices.

¢ BOSTON BROWN BREAD

A rich, dark steamed bread, which New Englanders eat with baked beans.
Makes 3 small round loaves

1 cup sifted all-purpose flour
1 teaspoon salt
1 teaspoon baking powder
1 teaspoon baking soda
1½ cups unsifted whole wheat flour
½ cup corn meal
¾ cup dark molasses
2 cups sour milk or buttermilk
1 cup seedless raisins

Grease 3 clean small shortening tins (the 14-ounce size) and line bottoms with greased circles of wax paper. Sift all-purpose flour with salt, baking powder, and soda into a large bowl, stir in whole wheat flour and corn meal, then mix in molasses and sour milk. Stir in raisins. Spoon into cans, filling no more than two-thirds, cover with a *greased* double thickness of foil and tie or tape securely. Place on a rack in a large kettle, pour in enough boiling water to come halfway up cans, cover, and steam about 1 hour until well risen and a metal skewer inserted in center of bread comes out clean. Lift cans from water, cool upright 1–2 minutes on a wire rack, then invert and ease loaves out. Cool slightly on racks before cutting or cool to room temperature. Slice ¼" thick. (*Note:* The best way to cut this bread is with fine strong thread, using a sawing motion.) The bread can be steamed in any well-greased molds instead of shortening tins. Just make sure to fill no more than two-thirds and to cover with greased foil. 1–1½-pint molds will take 1–1½ hours, 1-quart molds 2–2½ hours, and 1½-quart molds about 3 hours. About 85 calories per slice.

SPICY BAKING POWDER DOUGHNUTS

Children love these.
Makes 2 dozen

3½ cups sifted flour
½ teaspoon salt
2 teaspoons baking powder
1 teaspoon baking soda
½ teaspoon cinnamon
½ teaspoon nutmeg
2 eggs
1 cup sugar
2 tablespoons cooking oil or shortening
¾ cup buttermilk or sour milk
Shortening or cooking oil for deep fat
  frying

Topping:
½ cup superfine sugar mixed with
  1 teaspoon cinnamon

Sift flour with salt, baking powder, soda, and spices and set aside. In a large mixer bowl, beat eggs, sugar, and oil at medium speed; add buttermilk. Add dry ingredients all at once and beat just until smooth. Cover and chill 1 hour. Meanwhile, begin heating fat in a deep fat fryer; insert deep fat thermometer. Roll dough ½" thick on a lightly floured surface and cut with a doughnut cutter; reroll and cut scraps. When fat reaches 375° F., slide 4 doughnuts into fat. (*Note:* To transfer doughnuts without pushing them out of shape, use a slotted pancake turner dipped in the hot fat.) Fry doughnuts 2–3 minutes until brown all over, using tongs to turn. Drain on paper toweling; roll in topping while still warm or dip in Easy White Icing. About 150 calories each.

VARIATIONS:

Chocolate Doughnuts: Prepare as
directed but omit spices; increase sugar
to 1⅓ cups and add along with it
2 squares melted unsweetened chocolate.
After frying, dust doughnuts with sifted
confectioners' sugar. About 190 calories
each.

Orange or Lemon Doughnuts: Prepare
as directed, mixing 4 teaspoons finely
grated orange or lemon rind and ¼
teaspoon orange or lemon extract into
egg mixture. About 150 calories each.

Sugar Puffs (Makes about 3½ dozen):
Prepare as directed but reduce flour to
2 cups, eggs to 1, and sugar to ⅓ cup.
Do not chill. Fry scant tablespoonfuls in
deep fat as directed and roll in superfine
sugar while warm. About 40 calories
each.

⚖️ **ROSETTES (SWEDISH PATTY
SHELLS) FOR SAVORY
FILLINGS**

Rosette irons with patty shell attachments can be bought in housewares
departments of many large stores. Read
accompanying instructions before
beginning this recipe.
Makes about 4 dozen

*Shortening or cooking oil for deep fat
    frying*
2 eggs
1 cup milk
1 teaspoon sugar
½ teaspoon salt
1 cup sifted flour

Begin heating fat in a deep fat fryer;
use a deep fat thermometer. Beat eggs,
milk, sugar, and salt just to blend,
sprinkle in flour, a little at a time, and
beat until smooth. When fat reaches
355–65° F., heat iron by submerging
in hot fat 10 seconds. Lift out, shake off
excess fat, and dip iron carefully into
batter so top is *exactly level* with surface
of batter—any deeper and patty shell
will not come off the iron. Plunge
coated iron into fat and, as soon as
batter begins to puff, gradually ease
iron out—patty shell should slip back

into fat. When lightly browned, lift out
with a slotted spoon and drain on paper
toweling. (*Note:* You'll have to work
fast, the whole procedure takes only a
few seconds.) Heat iron and repeat with
remaining batter, never frying more than
2 patty shells at a time and keeping fat
as near 365° F. as possible. Cool patty
shells in a single layer on paper toweling.
When ready to use, warm, uncovered,
7–10 minutes in a 325° F. oven, then
fill with hot creamed chicken, seafood,
or vegetables. Stored airtight, patty
shells will keep well about 1 week. About
20 calories each (unfilled).

¢ ⊠ **BASIC PANCAKES**

Electric griddles or skillets are ideal for
cooking pancakes because they maintain
a constant heat. Follow manufacturer's
directions for greasing and preheating.
Batters containing fat or oil can usually
be cooked in an ungreased skillet.
Makes 1 dozen

1 cup sifted flour
½ teaspoon salt
2 tablespoons sugar
2 teaspoons baking powder
1 egg, lightly beaten
¾ cup milk
*2 tablespoons cooking oil, melted butter
    or margarine*

Preheat griddle over moderate heat
while you mix batter or, if using an
electric griddle, preheat as manufacturer
directs. Sift flour, salt, sugar, and baking
powder into a bowl or wide-mouthed
pitcher. Combine egg, milk, and oil,
slowly stir into dry ingredients, and mix
only until dampened—batter should be
lumpy. When a drop of cold water will
dance on the griddle, begin cooking
pancakes, using about 3 tablespoons
batter for each, allowing plenty of
space between them and spreading each
until about 4″ across. Cook until
bubbles form over surface, turn gently,
and brown flip side. (*Note:* For extra-
light and tender pancakes, turn *before*
bubbles break and turn 1 time only.)
Stack 3–4 deep on heated plates and
keep warm while cooking the rest. Serve

as soon as possible with butter, maple syrup, or other topping (see Some Toppings for Waffles and Pancakes). About 80 calories per pancake (without butter, syrup, or topping).

For Thinner Pancakes: Add 2–3 extra tablespoons milk.

If Batter Has Stood a While: Mix in about ¼ teaspoon additional baking powder before cooking.

VARIATIONS:

Nut Pancakes: Prepare batter as directed and just before cooking fold in ½ cup coarsely chopped pecans, walnuts, almonds, or roasted peanuts. About 115 calories per pancake (without butter or syrup).

Berry Pancakes: Prepare batter as directed and just before cooking fold in ½ cup fresh, slightly thawed frozen or drained canned berries (any kind as long as they're small). About 85 calories per pancake (without butter or syrup).

¢ **Apple Pancakes:** Prepare as directed, sifting ¼ teaspoon each cinnamon and nutmeg along with dry ingredients; just before cooking, fold in ½–¾ cup minced, peeled tart apple. About 90 calories per pancake (without butter or syrup).

¢ **Rice Pancakes:** Prepare as directed but increase eggs to 2 and milk to 1 cup; just before cooking, fold in ½ cup cooked rice or wild rice. About 90 calories per pancake (without butter or syrup).

¢ **Buttermilk Pancakes:** Prepare as directed but reduce baking powder to 1 teaspoon, add ¾ teaspoon baking soda, and use 1 cup buttermilk or sour milk instead of sweet milk. About 75 calories per pancake (without butter or syrup).

¢ **Whole Wheat Pancakes:** Prepare as directed, using ½ cup each unsifted whole wheat flour and sifted all-purpose flour; increase milk to 1 cup. About 85 calories per pancake (without butter or syrup).

¢ **Buckwheat Pancakes:** Prepare as directed, using ½ cup each unsifted buckwheat flour and sifted all-purpose flour, increase milk to 1 cup. About 85 calories per pancake (without butter or syrup).

Sausage Pancakes: Prepare as directed but reduce sugar to 1 teaspoon. Cook pancakes until bubbles break, dot with thin slices of cooked sausages or frankfurters, turn, and brown. Serve for lunch or supper. About 115 calories per pancake.

Cheese Pancakes: Prepare as directed but reduce sugar to 1 teaspoon. Just before cooking, mix in ½ cup grated sharp Cheddar or processed cheese. Cook as directed and serve for lunch or supper, topped with any creamed meat or vegetable. About 100 calories per pancake (without topping).

Onion Pancakes: Prepare as directed but reduce sugar to 1 teaspoon. Just before cooking, mix in ½ cup sautéed minced onion and a pinch each sage and thyme. Cook as directed and serve for lunch or supper, topped with Welsh Rabbit or any creamed or curried meat or vegetable. About 80 calories per pancake (without topping).

Corn and Pepper Pancakes: Prepare as directed but reduce sugar to 1 teaspoon. Just before cooking, mix in ½ cup well-drained canned whole kernel corn and ¼ cup minced sweet red or green pepper. Cook as directed and serve as is in place of potatoes or topped with chili as a main course. About 90 calories per pancake (without topping).

SOUFFLÉ PANCAKES

Don't stack these rich, puffy pancakes. They will flatten out.
Makes 8

¼ cup packaged biscuit mix
1 tablespoon sugar
¼ cup sour cream
4 eggs, separated

Preheat griddle over moderate heat while you mix the batter or, if using an electric griddle, preheat to 375° F. Stir biscuit mix, sugar, sour cream, and egg yolks, together until well blended. Beat egg whites until soft peaks form, stir half of whites into batter, and fold in the rest. When a drop of cold water will dance across the griddle, grease lightly and add pancakes, using about 3 tablespoons batter for each and spacing far apart. Spread pancakes so they are about 4″ across and cook about 1 minute until 1 or 2 bubbles appear on surface and undersides are brown; turn and brown flip sides. Lift to hot plates and serve with maple syrup (no butter needed because these pancakes are rich). About 90 calories per serving (without syrup).

¢ YEAST-RAISED PANCAKES

Makes 1½ dozen

1¾ cups scalded milk
2 tablespoons sugar
½ teaspoon salt
¼ cup warm water (105–15° F.)
1 package active dry yeast
1 egg, lightly beaten
2 tablespoons cooking oil, melted butter
*   or margarine*
2 cups sifted flour

Mix milk, sugar, and salt and cool to lukewarm. Pour water into a warm mixing bowl, sprinkle in yeast and stir to dissolve; mix in cooled mixture, also egg and oil. Slowly add flour and beat until smooth. Cover and let rise in a warm draft-free place until doubled in bulk, about 35 minutes. Toward end of rising, preheat griddle over moderate heat, or, if using an electric one, by manufacturer's instructions. When batter is fully risen, stir down and pour about ¼ cup onto griddle for each pancake; allow plenty of space between pancakes, then spread each until about 4″ across. Cook until bubbles form on surface and underside is brown, turn, and brown flip side. Keep warm while cooking the rest. Serve hot with butter and syrup or other suitable topping (see Some Toppings for Waffles and Pancakes). About 85 calories per pancake (without butter, syrup, or topping).

VARIATIONS:

Blini: Prepare and cook pancakes as directed; fill each with 1 tablespoon red or black caviar, fold in half, and serve with sour cream. About 85 calories per pancake (without sour cream).

¢ **English Crumpets** (Makes 14): Prepare batter as directed but reduce flour to 1⅓ cups. Cook as directed, but until bubbles on pancakes *break;* brown flip side very lightly only. Cool pancakes. When ready to serve, toast, smother "holey" sides with butter, quarter crumpets, and serve hot as a teatime snack. About 75 calories per crumpet (without butter).

¢ **Yeast-Raised Waffles** (Makes 8): Prepare as directed but reduce flour to 1½ cups. Bake in a preheated waffle iron. About 160 calories per waffle (without butter or syrup).

About Using Waffle Irons

Automatic waffle irons take the frustrations out of waffle baking. But, old irons, properly used, produce exquisitely crisp, nut-brown waffles. Here are a few tips for using them:
– Heat iron until a drop of water will dance over the grids.
– Pour batter in center of iron until ½–⅔ full, then close and bake until all steaming stops. Open iron gently. If top sticks, waffle probably needs to bake longer. The first waffle often sticks to an old iron, so bake it a little browner than you like and discard. Doing so will temper the iron nicely for the waffles to follow.
– Never wash or grease an iron once it has been seasoned.

¢ BASIC WAFFLES

More than a half-dozen variations here to try.
Makes 8

2 cups sifted flour
2 tablespoons sugar
1 tablespoon baking powder

1 teaspoon salt
2 eggs, separated
1¾ cups milk
6 tablespoons cooking oil, melted butter,
   margarine, or bacon drippings

Preheat waffle iron according to manufacturer's directions. Sift flour, sugar, baking powder, and salt into a bowl. Combine egg yolks, milk, and oil, pour into flour mixture, and beat with a rotary beater or electric mixer just until smooth. Beat egg whites until soft peaks form and fold into batter. Pour batter into waffle iron as manufacturer directs and bake at medium heat until steaming stops and waffle is golden. Serve with plenty of butter and warm syrup or other topping. About 260 calories per waffle (without butter or syrup).

VARIATIONS:

Extra-Rich Waffles: Prepare as directed but reduce flour to 1¾ cups and milk to 1½ cups; increase eggs to 3 and oil to ½ cup. About 285 calories per waffle (without butter or syrup).

¢ **Buttermilk Waffles:** Prepare as directed, substituting buttermilk or sour milk for sweet; reduce baking powder to 2 teaspoons and add 1 teaspoon baking soda. About 245 per waffle (without butter or syrup).

Ham Waffles: Prepare as directed but omit sugar; add 1 cup finely diced lean boiled ham to batter before folding in egg whites. About 310 calories per waffle (without butter).

Cheese Waffles: Prepare as directed but omit sugar; add ½ cup finely grated sharp Cheddar or Parmesan cheese to batter before folding in egg whites. About 275 calories per waffle (without butter).

Nut Waffles: Prepare as directed and add ⅓–½ cup coarsely chopped walnuts, pecans, almonds, hazelnuts, peanuts, or piñon nuts to batter before folding in egg whites. About 295 calories per waffle (without butter or syrup).

Blueberry Waffles: Prepare as directed; scatter a few (about 2 tablespoons) washed and dried blueberries over batter in iron before baking. About 260 calories per waffle (without butter or syrup).

Savory Waffles: Prepare as directed but omit sugar; serve topped with creamed chicken or turkey, tuna or chipped beef, Welsh Rabbit or Shrimp Newburg. About 385 calories per serving (with topping).

Dessert Waffles: Prepare extra-rich waffles and top with ice cream or sweetened sliced peaches or berries and whipped cream. About 340 calories per serving (topped with a scoop of ice cream).

¢ **CREPES FOR SAVORY FILLINGS**

Makes 10 crepes

½ cup sifted flour
¼ teaspoon salt
2 eggs, lightly beaten
½ cup milk
1 tablespoon cold water
1 tablespoon melted butter or margarine

Sift flour and salt together into a bowl; mix all remaining ingredients and add slowly to dry ingredients, beating until smooth. Let stand at room temperature 15 minutes. Brush bottom and sides of a heavy 6" skillet with cooking oil and set over moderate heat ½ minute. Stir batter, then add 2 tablespoonfuls to skillet, tipping it back and forth so batter *just* coats bottom (crepe should be *very thin*). Brown lightly on 1 side, about 30 seconds, turn and brown other side. Place on a paper-towel-lined baking sheet, most attractive side down so that when crepe is rolled it will be on the outside. Cook remaining crepes the same way; they are now ready to be filled. About 55 calories per crepe (unfilled).

VARIATION:

¢ **Simple Dessert Crepes:** Add 1 tablespoon sugar to dry ingredients, then mix and cook crepes as directed; keep warm in a 250° F. oven until all are done. To serve, spread with jam, honey, or marmalade, fill with crushed berries, or simply drizzle with melted butter and sprinkle with sugar. Roll and top with dollops of sour cream. About 105 calories for each crepe (filled with ¼ cup unsweetened crushed berries and topped with 1 tablespoon sour cream).

Some Toppings for Waffles and Pancakes

For Breakfast:
Butter and
– Any syrup or honey
– A sprinkling of sugar—granulated, brown, maple, or raw
– Any tart jam, preserves, or marmalade
Whipped cream cheese and
– Any tart jam, preserves, jelly, or marmalade
– Any syrup or honey
– Applesauce
– Any sliced fresh fruit
– Stewed prunes, apricots, or figs

For Lunch or Supper (make basic pancakes or waffles as directed but reduce sugar to 1 teaspoon):
– Any creamed meat, seafood, or vegetable
– Any curried meat, eggs, or seafood
– Welsh Rabbit
– Chop Suey
– Chili con Carne and sprinklings of minced onion, grated sharp Cheddar, and shredded lettuce

For Dessert:
– Sour cream and any fruit preserves
– Sour cream and a thick sprinkling of brown or maple sugar (a dusting of cinnamon or nutmeg adds zip)
– Vanilla ice cream or sweetened whipped cream and fresh sliced or thawed frozen berries or peaches
– Vanilla ice cream and any dessert sauce
– Chocolate ice cream and Fudge or Butterscotch Sauce
– Fruit cocktail or crushed pineapple and sweetened whipped cream

¢ DUMPLINGS (BASIC RECIPE)

The new way to cook dumplings is uncovered for 10 minutes, then tightly covered for another 10 so that the steam will fluff up the dumplings.
Makes 7–8 dumplings

1 cup sifted flour
1½ teaspoons baking powder
½ teaspoon salt
2 tablespoons chilled shortening
½ cup milk

Sift flour, baking powder, and salt together into a bowl; cut in shortening with a pastry blender until mixture resembles coarse meal. Add milk all at once and mix lightly *just* until dough holds together. Drop by rounded tablespoonfuls on top of gently bubbling soup or stew. Adjust burner so liquid just simmers, then simmer *uncovered* 10 minutes; cover and simmer 10 minutes longer. (*Note:* If soup or stew needs thickening, do so *after* removing dumplings.) About 100 calories for each of 7 dumplings, 90 calories for each of 8 dumplings.

VARIATIONS:

¢ **Parsley or Chive Dumplings:** Prepare as directed, mixing 2 tablespoons minced parsley or chives into dry ingredients. About 100 calories for each of 7 dumplings, 90 calories for each of 8.

¢ **Sage, Thyme, and Onion Dumplings:** Prepare as directed, mixing ¼ teaspoon each sage and thyme and 1 teaspoon instant minced onion into dry ingredients. About 100 calories for each of 7 dumplings, 90 calories for each of 8.

¢ **Caraway Dumplings** (especially good with goulash): Prepare as directed, mixing 1½ teaspoons caraway seeds into dry ingredients. About 100 calories for each of 7 dumplings, 90 calories for each of 8.

Saffron Dumplings: Prepare as directed, mixing ⅛ teaspoon each powdered saffron and sage or thyme into dry ingredients. About 100 calories for each of 7 dumplings, 90 calories for each of 8.

¢ **Cheese Dumplings:** Prepare as directed, mixing 2–3 tablespoons coarsely grated sharp Cheddar cheese to dry ingredients. About 115 calories for each of 7 dumplings, 100 calories for each of 8.

⊠ QUICK DUMPLINGS

Makes about 1 dozen

2 cups packaged biscuit mix
½ teaspoon salt
1 egg, lightly beaten
½ cup milk

Mix biscuit mix and salt. Combine egg and milk, add to dry ingredients all at once, and stir lightly and quickly with a fork to form a soft dough. Drop by rounded tablespoonfuls on top of just boiling stew or soup. Simmer, uncovered, over low heat 10 minutes, then cover and simmer 10 minutes longer. About 60 calories per dumpling.

VARIATION:

⊠ **Biscuit Dumplings:** Separate biscuits from a can of refrigerated biscuits and arrange on top of bubbling stew or soup. Cover and simmer 15–20 minutes. Sprinkle with minced parsley just before serving. About 60 calories per dumpling.

¢ BREAD DUMPLINGS

A delicious way to use up stale bread. These dumplings are good in soups or stews.
Makes 14–16

3 cups ½″ cubes stale bread, trimmed of
  crusts
¼ cup unsifted flour
1 teaspoon salt
⅛ teaspoon pepper
¼ teaspoon baking powder
⅛ teaspoon nutmeg (optional)
1 tablespoon minced parsley
2 tablespoons minced yellow onion
¼ cup milk
1 egg, lightly beaten
1 tablespoon melted butter or margarine

Mix all ingredients together, let stand 5 minutes, and mix again. Drop by rounded teaspoonfuls into a little flour, then roll into balls. Drop into *just* boiling soup or stew, simmer uncovered 5 minutes, cover, and simmer 2–3 minutes longer. Do not cook more than 1 layer deep at a time. Serve in soup or stew, allowing 3–4 per serving. (*Note:* For stew, the dumplings can be made twice as large; simmer uncovered 7–10 minutes, cover, and simmer 5–7 minutes longer.) About 65 calories for each of 14 dumplings, 55 calories for each of 16 dumplings.

BASIC BATTER FOR FRIED FOODS

An all-purpose batter that can be used for almost any foods to be fried: chicken, fish fillets, shellfish, vegetables, fruit.
Makes about 1½ cups

1 cup sifted flour
1 teaspoon baking powder
½ teaspoon salt
1 egg, lightly beaten
1 cup milk
2 tablespoons cooking oil

Sift flour with baking powder and salt. Mix egg, milk, and oil, slowly add to dry ingredients, and beat until smooth. Pat food to be fried very dry and, if you like, dredge lightly in flour. Dip pieces, 1 at a time, in batter, then fry in deep fat as individual recipes direct. About 890 calories for the 1½ cups, about 37 calories per tablespoon (about what it would take to coat a shrimp or small piece of fruit or vegetable).

TEMPURA BATTER

Beer is what gives this batter its exceptional lightness.
Makes about 1 pint

3 eggs
1⅔ cups rice flour
1½ teaspoons salt
1 teaspoon baking powder
1 (12-ounce) can beer

Beat eggs until frothy. Sift rice flour with salt and baking powder and add to eggs alternately with beer. Use for Japanese Butterfly Shrimp or for coating bite-size chunks of cucumber, carrot, cauliflower, and zucchini or parsley fluffs to be fried in deep fat. About 1060 calories for the 1 pint, about 32 calories per tablespoon.

To Halve Recipe: Use 1 extra-large egg, ¾ cup plus 2 tablespoons rice flour, ¾ teaspoon salt, ½ teaspoon baking powder, and ¾ cup beer. About 500 calories for 1 cup, about 31 calories per tablespoon.

VEGETABLE FRITTER BATTER

Makes about 1½ cups

¾ cup sifted flour
1 teaspoon baking powder
1 teaspoon salt
¾ cup milk
1 egg, lightly beaten

Sift flour, baking powder, and salt together into a bowl. Slowly add milk and beat until smooth. Add egg and beat well. Use for dipping vegetables that are to be deep-fat-fried. About 605 calories for the 1½ cups, about 25 calories per tablespoon.

⊠ GARLIC FRENCH BREAD

Everyone's favorite. And so easy to prepare.
Makes 6 servings

¼ pound butter or margarine, softened to room temperature
1 clove garlic, peeled and crushed
1 loaf French bread about 18″ long

Blend garlic with butter and let stand at room temperature about 1 hour. About ½ hour before serving, preheat oven to 375° F. Meanwhile, slice bread 1″ thick, cutting *to* but not *through* the bottom and holding knife at a slight angle. Spread both sides of each slice with garlic butter and wrap loaf snugly in heavy foil. Place on a baking sheet and warm 20–25 minutes. Unwrap and serve in a long napkin-lined bread basket or break into chunks and serve in a round napkin-lined basket. About 250 calories per serving, 83 calories per slice.

VARIATIONS:

Herbed Garlic Bread: Mix 1 teaspoon minced parsley and ¼ teaspoon each thyme and oregano or marjoram into garlic butter; proceed as directed. About 250 calories per serving, 83 calories per slice.

Cheese-Garlic Bread: Mix 1 tablespoon grated Parmesan, ¼ teaspoon salt, ⅛ teaspoon pepper, and ¼ teaspoon each savory and oregano or thyme into garlic butter; proceed as directed. About 255 calories per serving, 85 calories per slice.

Curry or Chili-Garlic Bread: Mix 1–2 teaspoons curry or chili powder into garlic butter and proceed as directed. About 250 calories per serving, 83 calories per slice.

⊠ SOME FLAVORED TOASTS

Enough for 4 slices

Cinnamon Toast: Mix 4 teaspoons sugar with 1 teaspoon cinnamon, sprinkle on well-buttered toast, and heat 3–5 minutes at 350° F. About 125 calories per slice.

Honey Toast: Toast bread on 1 side. Butter untoasted sides, then drizzle with honey (about 2 teaspoons in all) and sprinkle lightly with nutmeg or mace. Broil honey side up 4–5″ from heat 3–4 minutes until golden brown. About 155 calories per slice.

Maple Toast: Prepare like honey toast, substituting maple syrup for honey. About 145 calories per slice.

Marmalade Toast: Toast bread on 1 side. Brush untoasted sides with a ½ and ½ mixture of softened butter and orange or other fruit marmalade (1 tablespoon each is enough for 4 slices). Broil spread side up 4–5″ from heat 2–3 minutes until lightly browned. About 105 calories per slice.

Orange-Raisin Toast: Mix 1 teaspoon finely grated orange rind with 1 tablespoon each softened butter or margarine and orange juice, 2 tablespoons light brown sugar, and a pinch each cinnamon and nutmeg. Spread on toasted raisin bread and broil spread side up 4–5″ from heat 2–3 minutes until bubbly. About 150 calories per slice.

Butterscotch Toast: Blend 2 tablespoons softened butter or margarine with ¼ cup light brown sugar and spread on toast. Sprinkle each slice with about 1 tablespoon minced pecans or walnuts, then broil spread side up 4–5″ from heat 3–4 minutes until bubbly and browned. About 210 calories per slice.

Chive Toast: Blend 2 tablespoons softened butter or marjoram with 1 teaspoon minced chives, spread on day-old bread (1 side only), then toast about 45 minutes at 300° F. until golden brown and crisp. About 110 calories per slice.

Herb Toast: Prepare like chive toast, substituting 1 teaspoon minced fresh herb (dill, chervil, tarragon, savory, marjoram, or parsley) for the chives. About 110 calories per slice.

Curry Toast: Prepare like chive toast, substituting ½–1 teaspoon curry powder for the chives and adding a pinch each garlic and onion salt. About 110 calories per slice.

Garlic Toast: Blend 2 tablespoons softened butter with ¼ crushed clove garlic, spread on day-old bread, and toast as for chive toast. About 110 calories per slice.

Cheese Toast: Blend 2 tablespoons softened butter or margarine with 1 teaspoon grated Parmesan and, if you like, a pinch garlic or onion powder. Toast as for chive toast. About 112 calories per slice.

How to Make Melba Toast

Slice white or any other bread ⅛″ thick, trim off crusts, and halve slices diagonally or cut in small rounds; bake, uncovered, on ungreased baking sheets 10–12 minutes at 300° F. until crisp and lightly browned. Cool and store airtight.

How to Make Rusks

Trim crusts from an unsliced loaf of firm-textured white bread, then slice ½″ thick; cut in "fingers" 3″ long and 1–1½″ wide and bake, uncovered, on ungreased baking sheets 30–40 minutes at 300° F. until nicely browned.

How to Make Toast Cups

Trim crusts from thinly sliced, firm-textured white bread and brush 1 side of each slice with melted butter or margarine; press slices, buttered sides down, into muffin cups and brush insides with melted butter. Bake, uncovered, 10–12 minutes at 350° F. until golden brown. Remove from pans and use as patty shells for creamed meats or vegetables.

How to Make Croustades

Trim crusts from an unsliced loaf of firm-textured white bread, then slice 2½″ thick; cut each slice into a large cube, rectangle, or round and hollow out centers, leaving walls and bottoms ½″ thick (use centers for making bread crumbs). Brush inside and out with melted butter or margarine and bake, uncovered, on ungreased baking sheets 12–15 minutes at 350° F. until golden. Use as patty shells for creamed meats or vegetables.

How to Make Bread Cubes and Crumbs

Bread cubes and crumbs have dozens of uses. Mix into stuffings, toss into salads or casseroles, use as crunchy toppings or coatings.

For Soft Bread Cubes: Stack 2–3 slices bread on a board and cut into strips of desired width, then cut crosswise to form cubes of even size.

For Toasted Bread Cubes: Arrange soft bread cubes on an ungreased baking sheet 1 layer deep and toast in a 300° F. oven, turning occasionally, until evenly golden brown. Or broil 5"–6" from heat, turning often and watching closely.

For Soft Bread Crumbs: Tear fresh slices of bread into small pieces, or buzz bread at high speed in a blender. The job is done zip-quick.

For Dry Bread Crumbs: Put slices of dry bread through fine blade of meat grinder. A neat trick is to tie or rubber band a paper or plastic bag to end of grinder so crumbs drop directly into it. For extra-fine crumbs, sift, then store fine and coarse crumbs separately.

For Buttered Crumbs:

Soft: Toss 1 cup soft bread crumbs with ¼–⅓ cup melted butter or margarine.

Dry: Melt 3–4 tablespoons butter or margarine in a skillet over moderate heat, add 1–1½ cups dry crumbs, and heat, stirring, until golden brown.

For Seasoned Crumbs:

Garlic: Mix ¼ crushed clove garlic with ¼–⅓ cup melted butter or margarine, then toss with 1 cup soft or dry bread crumbs.

Cheese: Toss ¼ cup grated Parmesan cheese with 1 cup dry bread crumbs and 3–4 tablespoons melted butter or margarine.

Herb: Toss 1 cup dry bread crumbs with ¼ cup melted butter, margarine, or olive oil and ¼ teaspoon oregano, marjoram, or thyme.

Yields:

1 standard slice fresh bread	{	about 1 cup soft bread cubes
		about ¾ cup toasted bread cubes
		about 1 cup soft bread crumbs

1 standard slice dry bread	{	about ⅓ cup dry bread cubes
		about ¾ cup dry bread crumbs

CROUTONS

Croutons add flavor and crunch to soups, salads, and casseroles. The ½" size are best for soups and salads, the ¼" for casserole toppings. Croutons needn't be cubes, however; cut in triangles, diamonds or discs or into fancy shapes with truffle cutters. Make up a quantity, store airtight, or freeze, then reheat uncovered a few minutes at 425° F. to crispen. Packaged croutons, both plain and seasoned, are also available.
Makes 1 pint

Shortening or cooking oil for deep fat frying
8 slices day-old or stale bread, trimmed of crusts and cut in ¼" or ½" cubes

Heat shortening in a deep fat fryer until deep fat thermometer reaches 350° F. Place about ½ cup cubes in fryer basket, lower into fat and fry 10–15 seconds, turning, as needed, until evenly golden brown. Lift out, drain on paper toweling, and fry remaining cubes the same way. (*Note*: Skim crumbs from fat before adding each fresh batch.)

To Skillet Fry: Heat 1" cooking oil or a ½ and ½ mixture of melted butter or margarine and cooking oil in a large, heavy skillet over moderately high heat until a cube of bread will sizzle. Fry cubes about ½ cup at a time, 15–20 seconds, turning, as needed, until evenly golden brown. Drain on paper toweling.

To Oven "Fry": Preheat oven to 300° F. Butter both sides of bread or brush with melted butter and cut into cubes. Spread out on an ungreased baking sheet and bake, uncovered, 15 minutes; turn croutons and bake about 10 minutes longer until evenly browned.

VARIATIONS:

Garlic Croutons: Shake hot croutons in a bag with 1 teaspoon garlic salt. *Or* spread bread with Garlic Butter, cut in cubes, and oven fry as above.

Italian Croutons: Mix ½ cup each softened butter and grated Parmesan, ½ teaspoon each crushed garlic, basil, and oregano. Spread on bread, cut in cubes, and oven fry.

Herbed Croutons: Mix ⅔ cup softened butter with 2 teaspoons minced chives and ½ teaspoon each minced parsley, basil and chervil. Spread on bread, cut in cubes, and oven fry.

Recipes all too flexible for meaningful calorie counts.

☒ ¢ FRENCH TOAST

If you have stale bread on hand, by all means use it for making French toast.
Makes 4 servings

2 eggs, lightly beaten
⅔ cup milk
¼ teaspoon salt
¼ cup butter, margarine, shortening, or cooking oil
8 slices firm-textured white bread

Beat egg with milk and salt just to blend and place in a piepan. Melt about ¼ the butter in a large, heavy skillet. Quickly dip bread in egg mixture, turning to coat both sides well, then brown on each side in butter (add more butter to skillet as needed). Serve hot with honey, syrup, preserves, or tart jelly and a sprinkling of confectioners' sugar. About 290 calories per serving (without topping).

VARIATION:

Prepare as directed, using raisin or whole wheat bread instead of white. About 330 calories per serving (without topping).

¢ ☒ MILK TOAST

Makes 1 serving

1 (¾″ thick) slice hot buttered toast or cinnamon toast
1 cup hot milk
Brown sugar (optional)
Nutmeg (optional)

Place toast in a hot shallow soup bowl, pour in milk, sprinkle lightly, if you like, with brown sugar and nutmeg, and serve. About 300 calories per serving if made with buttered toast (without brown

sugar topping), about 355 calories per serving if made with cinnamon toast (without brown sugar topping).

YEAST BREADS

Yeast is a delicate living thing that needs food, warmth, moisture, and air if it is to grow and leaven dough. The ingredients mixed with yeast all help provide the proper environment.

Essential Ingredients of Yeast Breads:

Wheat Flour: Flour provides the framework of bread; its skeins of protein (gluten), developed in kneading, stretched as the yeast grows, and set during baking, give bread its characteristic texture. *All-purpose flour* (called for in all the following recipes unless otherwise specified) makes excellent yeast bread; so does *bread flour,* which contains an even higher percentage of protein. But it is not so easily available today. *Cake or pastry flour* is too soft to make good bread. Wheat flour alone may be used in making bread, or it may be mixed with rye flour, oatmeal, corn meal, or other grains.

Sugar: This is the food yeast needs; sugar also helps breads brown.

Salt: Salt isn't just for flavor. It controls the action of the yeast and keeps dough from rising too fast. Too much salt slows rising.

Fat: Lard, shortening, butter, margarine, or cooking oil can be used in making bread. Their functions: to make bread tender, give it fine texture, improve the keeping quality, and aid in browning.

Liquid: Either milk or water can be used to make bread. Milk increases the food value and keeping quality; water gives bread nuttier flavor, chewier texture, and crisper crust.

Yeast: The "life" and leavening of yeast

breads. In the old days, women saved bits of yeast sponge from one baking, often mixing in leftover potato cooking water, to use as starters for the next batch. Popular, too, was sour dough—raw dough left to ferment in stone crocks, which could be used in place of yeast. And when there was no yeast, women made "salt" or "self-rising" bread by using soured corn meal batter as the leavening. Modern yeasts have made the old-fashioned ways unnecessary, though some women still make these rough breads for the joy of it.

Active Dry Yeast: The most widely available form of yeast; it comes in ¼-ounce packets or 4-ounce jars. Kept in a cool, dry spot, it keeps fresh several months. When dissolved in warm water, it does the work of one (⅗-ounce) cake compressed yeast. All of the following recipes call for active dry yeast; if unavailable, substitute one cake compressed yeast for each ¼-ounce package.

Compressed Yeast: Not often seen today, this was the standard before World War II (dry yeast was developed during the war). It must be refrigerated and used within 1–2 weeks, or frozen and used within 6 months. Thaw at room temperature, then use at once. To determine if compressed yeast is still viable, crumble; if it crumbles easily, it's good.

The Care and Handling of Yeast: For most recipes (refrigerator doughs and the new cool-rise method excepted), yeast doughs must be kept warm from start to finish. And that means beginning with a warm bowl (simply rinse a bowl with warm water and dry). As you work with yeast dough, you'll learn what temperature is just right. If you are *aware* that the dough feels cool or warm, then it *is*. At the proper temperature, the dough should be so near your own body temperature that you scarcely feel it.

To Dissolve Yeast: Water (or potato cooking water) is best. It should be

warm, between 105° F and 115° F. Test using a candy thermometer or, if you have none, by the old baby's formula way of letting a drop fall on your forearm. It should feel warm, *not* hot.

About Combining Dissolved Yeast with Other Liquids: A critical step, for a too hot liquid can kill the yeast, a too cold one slows its growth. The perfect temperature is lukewarm, 90–95° F.

Nonessential (but Popular) Ingredients of Yeast Breads: Eggs, fruit, nuts, herbs, and spices are added purely for variety.

Ways to Mix Yeast Breads

Standard Method: Dissolve yeast in warm (105–15° F.) water. Scald milk, mix in sugar, salt, and shortening, and cool to lukewarm; combine with yeast, work in flour, and knead until satiny and elastic. Place in a greased, large warm bowl, turn dough to grease all over, cover with cloth (some people prefer a damp cloth, others a dry one), and set in a warm (80–85° F.) place to rise.

Batter Method: The same as the standard method except that the mixture is much thinner and beaten to blend rather than kneaded.

New Rapid-Mix: A modern refinement in which dry yeast is mixed directly with the dry ingredients (see recipe for Rapid-Mix White Bread).

Sponge Method: The old-fashioned way. Dissolve yeast in water and mix in enough flour to make a soft batter. Set in a warm, dry spot overnight or until mixture becomes "spongy." Next day prepare bread following standard method, mixing sponge into lukewarm milk mixture, then proceeding as directed.

About Kneading

This is the fun part of making bread. The technique isn't difficult, though at first it may seem so. Once you get the rhythm, however, you won't want to stop. Most doughs are kneaded on a lightly floured surface (board or pastry cloth), though extra-soft doughs should be done right in the mixing bowl. (*Note:* If you're lucky enough to have one of the heavy-duty electric mixers with a dough hook, you can knead any dough in the bowl—follow manufacturer's directions.)

To Knead Average Doughs: Shape dough into a large, round ball on a lightly floured bread board and fold over toward you; push down with heels of hands, give dough a quarter turn, and repeat the folding, pushing and turning until dough is satiny, smooth, and elastic, usually 8–10 minutes. Use very little flour on your hands or board, only enough to keep dough from sticking.

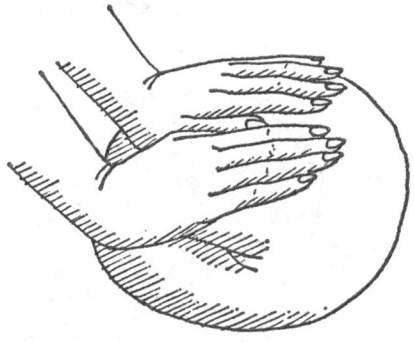

To Knead Very Soft Doughs: Use one hand only; these doughs are supersticky, and if you get both hands involved, you'll be sorry. The technique isn't so much kneading as stretching the dough right in the bowl, pulling it up again and again from the sides of the bowl. Use a large, heavy, shallow bowl, held firmly in place with your free hand. In the beginning, the dough will seem utterly unmanageable, but before long (8–10 minutes) it will begin to blister and to cling to itself, leaving your hand and the bowl relatively clean. It is now ready to rise.

About the Rising Period

This is when the yeast goes to work, leavening the bread. Most breads and rolls get two risings, one before shaping, one after. Some may require three risings, others one only. For the first

rising, dough should be allowed to double in bulk; for the second, to double or not as individual recipes direct. Successive risings usually take somewhat less time than the first, so watch carefully. (*Note:* Braids and other intricately shaped breads should be allowed to rise fully after shaping, otherwise they may split during baking. No shaped bread, however, should more than double; if it overrises, it will be coarse and dry and have poor volume.)

Optimum Rising Conditions: A warm (80–85° F.), dry, and draftless spot. Sometimes a turned-off oven can be used (unless pilot light makes oven too hot); sometimes dough can be set over a bowl of warm water. Never, however, use the top of a refrigerator—too much uneven heat.

If Kitchen Is Cool: Use an extra package of yeast in making the dough; it will not make the bread taste too yeasty.

To Hasten Rising: Use an extra package of yeast in making dough and/or set bowl of dough over a large bowl of warm water, changing water as it cools.

Approximate Rising Times: (first rising):

Soft Doughs: ¾–1 hour to double in bulk

Average Doughs: 1–1½ hours to double in bulk

Heavy Doughs: 1½–2 hours to double in bulk

(*Note:* Times can be approximate at best, since warmth of kitchen and vitality of yeast both affect speed of rising.)

When Is Dough Doubled in Bulk?

Soft Doughs and Batter Breads: Dough or batter should look spongy, puffed, and moist. Press lightly near edge; if imprint remains, dough is doubled in bulk.

Average or Heavy Doughs: Stick two fingers into dough about ½"; if depressions remain, dough is doubled in bulk. If they disappear, give dough another 15–20 minutes to rise, then test again.

About Refrigerator Doughs: The cold of a refrigerator does not kill yeast, merely retards or stops its growth. Once out of the refrigerator, the yeast will begin to work again. Refrigerator doughs usually contain more yeast than standard doughs, also slightly more sugar. Any dough, thus, can be refrigerated if you up the amount of yeast by half or, better still, double it and add an extra tablespoon or so of sugar. How long dough will keep in the refrigerator depends both upon the dough and the temperature inside the refrigerator. Most doughs keep well under refrigeration 3–4 days.

Doughs can be refrigerated as soon as they're mixed or after the first rising; they must be well greased and well covered so that they remain moist and pliable.

When you're ready to bake, take dough from refrigerator. If it has not risen at all, let stand at room temperature 2–3 hours until doubled in bulk; then punch down, shape, and proceed as for unrefrigerated doughs. If the dough has had one rising before going into cold storage, shape as soon as you take it from the refrigerator, let rise until light, about 1 hour, then bake.

About Punching Dough Down

There's a reason for this. Collapsing raised dough evens the texture by breaking up any large bubbles of gas.

Batters: Stir down with a spoon until batter is its original size.

Doughs: Shove a fist deep into the center of the dough so it collapses like a balloon, then fold edges of dough into center.

About Shaping Breads and Rolls

Like sculptor's clay, yeast dough can be fashioned into dozens of shapes, and in European countries it is, especially for holidays and festivals. Some sculpted loaves are museum pieces.

How to Shape Loaves:

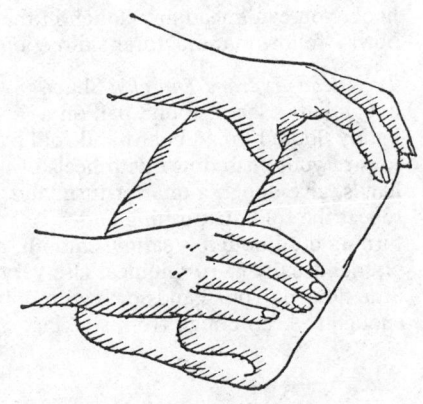

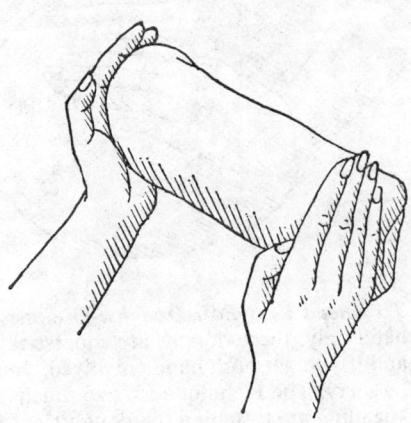

Standard Loaf

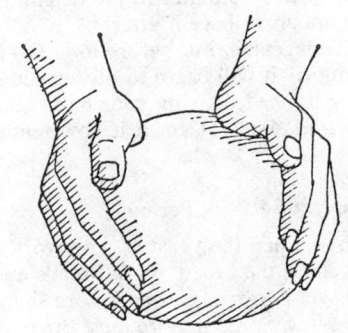

Round Loaf

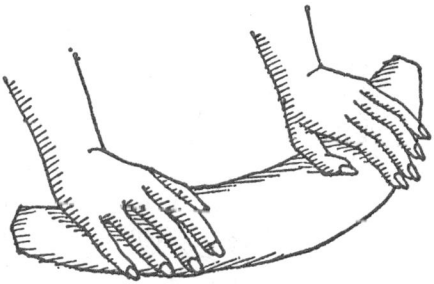

French Loaf

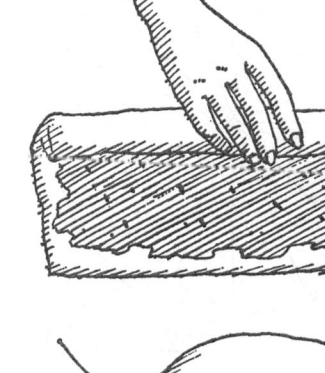

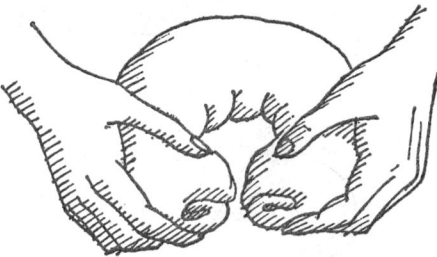

Rings

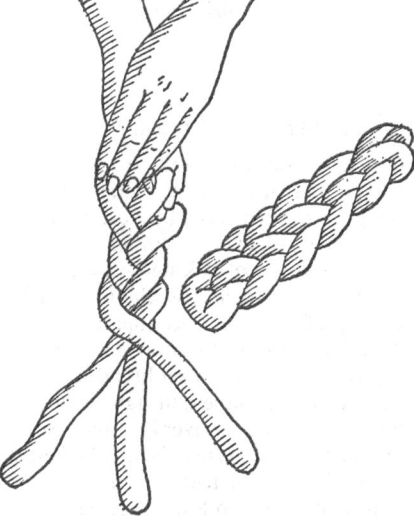

How to Shape Rolls: For rolls of uniform size, divide dough into equal parts before shaping.

Braids

Pan Rolls

Cloverleaf Rolls
Quick Cloverleaf Rolls

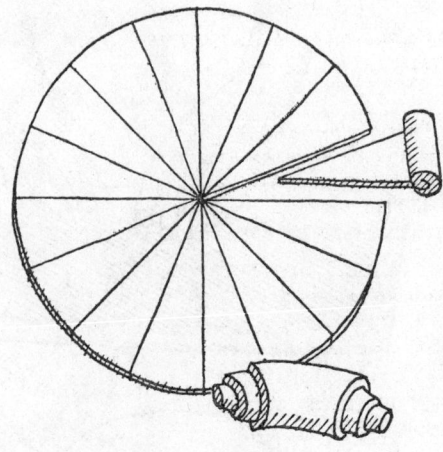

Croissants

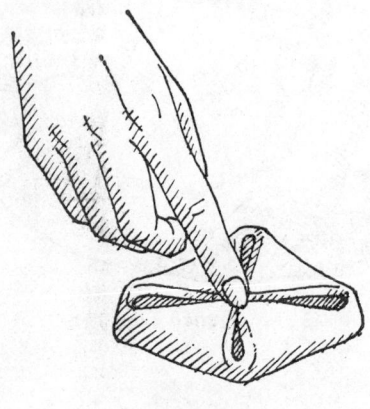

Danish Pastry

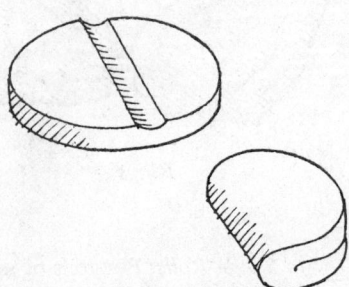

Parker House Rolls

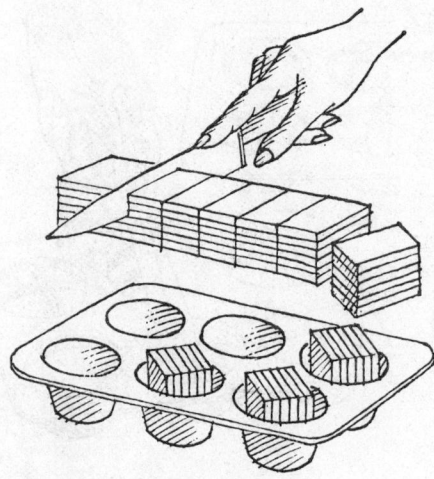

Fan Tans

About Baking Yeast Breads

Best temperatures are from 350–450° F., the lower heats being better for richer, sweeter breads because there's less danger of overbrowning. The first 10–15 minutes of baking—called "oven spring"—is critical; it is the time when the top of the loaf rises quickly, "breaking" or "shredding" around the edges of the pan, giving bread its characteristic shape and light texture. A perfect loaf has an evenly shredded break. If bread hasn't risen sufficiently before baking, or if the oven temperature is too low, there will be poor volume and little break. If the dough has overrisen, the strands of protein will be stretched to breaking during "oven spring" and the loaf will collapse.

To Give Crusts a Professional Finish

For Soft Brown Crusts: Brush bread or rolls before or after baking with melted butter or margarine, milk, or cream.

For Hard Crusts: Brush bread or rolls before baking with lightly beaten egg white or salty water and bake with a shallow pan of water set on rack underneath.

For Shiny Light Brown Crusts: Brush bread or rolls before baking with 1 egg

VII. ENTERTAINING

Planked Steak – Rice à l'Impératrice and Crown Roast of Pork –
Home candy kitchen

Planked Steak with Vegetables (pages 229-30 and 871)

Rice à la Imperatrice (page 1041); and Crown Roast of Pork (page 352)

Gifts from the home candy kitchen: fondants and fudges, pralines and brittles, marzipan fruits and mints, hand-dipped chocolates and fruit jellies (pages 1195-1211)

white lightly beaten with 1 tablespoon cold water; or, if you prefer, brush with mixture during last 10–15 minutes of baking.

For Shiny Dark Brown Crusts: Brush bread or rolls before baking with 1 egg or 1 egg yolk lightly beaten with 1 tablespoon water, milk, or cream (the egg yolk will produce the brownest crust).

For Seed Crusts: Brush bread or rolls before baking with 1 egg or egg white lightly beaten with 1 tablespoon water and sprinkle with poppy, caraway, or seasame seeds.

For Sweet Glazes: See individual recipes for sweet breads that follow.

Why Things Sometimes Go Wrong with Yeast Breads

Small Doughy Loaves: Too much or too little heat during rising *or* too long or too short rising.

Sour or Too Yeasty Bread: Too much heat during rising.

Lopsided Loaves: An unlevel oven or pans touching one another and/or oven walls.

Crumbly Bread: Too long in the rising, especially after shaping.

Coarse or "Holey" Bread: Insufficient kneading; also too long in the rising.

Heavy, Dry Bread: Too much flour.

¢ **BASIC WHITE BREAD**

If you've never made yeast bread, this is a good recipe to begin with. The recipe isn't difficult and the results are delicious. Makes 2 9″×5″×3″ loaves

½ cup scalded milk
3 tablespoons sugar
2 teaspoons salt
3 tablespoons butter, margarine or lard
1½ cups warm water (105–15° F.)
1 package active dry yeast
6 cups sifted flour (about)
1–2 tablespoons melted butter or margarine (optional)

Mix milk, sugar, salt and butter in a small bowl, stirring until sugar dissolves; cool to lukewarm. Pour warm water into a large warm bowl, sprinkle in yeast, and stir until dissolved. Stir in milk mixture, add 3 cups flour, and beat with a wooden spoon until smooth. Mix in enough additional flour, a little at a time, to make a soft dough (you will have to use your hands toward the end). Mixture will be sticky but should leave sides of bowl reasonably clean. Knead on a lightly floured board until satiny and elastic, 8–10 minutes, adding as little extra flour as possible. Shape into a smooth ball, place in a greased large bowl, turning dough to grease all over. Cover with cloth and let rise in a warm draft-free spot until doubled in bulk, about 1 hour. Punch down, turn onto lightly floured board and let rest 5 minutes; knead lightly 2 minutes. Halve piece of dough and shape* each into a loaf about 7″ long and 4″ wide; place in greased 9″×5″×3″ loaf pans, cover, and let rise about 1 hour in a warm spot until doubled in bulk. About 15 minutes before baking, preheat oven to 400° F. When loaves have risen, brush tops with melted butter if you like a soft crust. Bake 35–40 minutes until golden brown and loaves sound hollow when tapped. Turn out immediately and cool on wire racks. About 80 calories per slice.

VARIATIONS:

¢ **Cornell Bread** (a supernutritious bread): Prepare as directed, substituting 6 tablespoons *each* nonfat dry milk powder and soya flour and 2 tablespoons wheat germ for 1 cup of the flour. Mix in at the beginning with the first addition of flour. About 80 calories per slice.

¢ **Raisin Bread:** Prepare as directed, increasing butter and sugar each to ¼ cup and mixing 1¼ cups seedless raisins in after first 3 cups of flour. About 100 calories per slice.

¢ **Bran Bread:** Prepare as directed, substituting ¼ cup molasses for the sugar and 1 cup bran for 1 cup of the flour. About 80 calories per slice.

¢ ⊠ **RAPID-MIX WHITE BREAD**

Here is the new streamlined way to make yeast bread.

Makes 2 9"×5"×3" loaves

5½–6½ cups unsifted flour
3 tablespoons sugar
2 teaspoons salt
1 package active dry yeast
1½ cups water
½ cup milk
3 tablespoons butter, margarine, or
* shortening at room temperature*

Mix 2 cups flour, sugar, salt, and undissolved yeast in large electric mixer bowl. Heat water, milk, and butter over low heat just until warm, not hot. Gradually add to dry ingredients and beat 2 minutes at medium mixer speed. Add about ¾ cup more flour or enough to make a thick batter and beat 2 minutes at high speed, scraping sides of bowl frequently. Stir in enough additional flour to make a soft dough. Knead dough on a lightly floured board until satiny and elastic, 8–10 minutes; place in a greased large bowl, turning to grease all over, cover, and let rise in a warm, draft-free place until doubled in bulk, about 1 hour. Punch dough down, turn onto board, cover, and let rest 15 minutes. Divide in half and shape* into 2 loaves. Place in greased 9"×5"×3" pans, cover, and let rise until doubled in bulk. Toward end of rising, preheat oven to 400° F. Bake loaves 25–30 minutes until nicely browned and hollow sounding when tapped. Remove from pans and cool on racks. About 75 calories per slice.

VARIATION:

¢ **Cool-Rise Loaves:** Mix dough and knead as directed; leave on board, cover, and let rest 20 minutes. Divide in half, shape* into 2 loaves, and place in greased pans. Brush tops with oil, cover with oiled wax paper, then saran. Refrigerate 2–24 hours. When ready to bake, preheat oven to 400° F. Uncover loaves and let stand at room temperature 10 minutes; prick any surface bubbles with a greased toothpick. Bake 30–40 minutes until nicely browned and hollow sounding when tapped. Cool as above. About 75 calories per slice.

¢ **POTATO BREAD**

Potato gives the bread extra flavor and softer texture.

Makes 2 9"×5"×3" loaves

½ cup scalded milk
¼ cup shortening, butter, or margarine
2 tablespoons sugar
2 teaspoons salt
⅓ cup warm water (105–15° F.)
2 packages active dry yeast
1½ cups lukewarm, riced, cooked,
* unseasoned potatoes*
½ cup lukewarm potato cooking water
5¼–5½ cups sifted flour

Mix milk, shortening, sugar, and salt; cool to lukewarm. Pour water into a warm large bowl, sprinkle in yeast, and stir to dissolve. Add cooled mixture, potatoes, potato cooking water, and about 2 cups flour; beat until smooth. Mix in enough remaining flour to make a firm dough that leaves the sides of bowl clean. Knead on a lightly floured board until elastic, about 10 minutes. Shape into a ball, place in a greased bowl, turning to grease all over. Cover with cloth and let rise in a warm, draft-free place until double in bulk, about 1 hour. Punch down, cover, and let rise again. Punch down once more and knead lightly 1–2 minutes. Divide dough in half, shape* into 2 loaves, and place in greased 9"×5"×3" loaf pans. Cover and let rise until almost doubled in bulk. Toward end of rising, preheat oven to 400° F. Bake loaves 10 minutes, reduce heat to 350° F., and bake 30–35 minutes longer until well browned and hollow sounding when tapped. Turn out and cool upright on a wire rack before cutting. About 75 calories per slice.

¢ **BATTER BREAD**

This recipe makes smallish loaves with an old-fashioned yeasty flavor and firm, chewy texture.

Makes 2 9"×5"×3" loaves

1 cup milk, scalded
3 tablespoons sugar
1 tablespoon salt
2 tablespoons butter or margarine,
  softened to room temperature
1 cup warm water (105–15° F.)
2 packages active dry yeast
4¼ cups unsifted flour

Mix milk with sugar, salt, and butter, stirring until sugar dissolves; cool to lukewarm. Place warm water in a large warm bowl, sprinkle in yeast, and stir to dissolve; add milk mixture. Stir in flour and beat vigorously until well blended, about 2 minutes. Batter will be shiny and smooth and leave sides of bowl fairly clean. Use an electric mixer at low speed, if you wish, adding flour a little at a time. When all flour is in, beat at medium speed 2 minutes. Cover dough with cloth and let rise in a warm, draft-free place 40 minutes until slightly more than doubled in bulk. About 15 minutes before batter is fully risen, preheat oven to 375° F. Stir batter down and beat vigorously ½ minute by hand. Divide batter between 2 well-greased 9″×5″×3″ loaf pans. Bake 40–50 minutes or until loaves are well browned and sound hollow when tapped. Turn loaves out on wire cake racks to cool. About 55 calories per slice.

SALLY LUNN

A high-rising Southern bread that is almost as rich as sponge cake.
Makes 6–8 servings

2 packages active dry yeast
⅓ cup warm water (105–15° F.)
⅔ cup milk, scalded and cooled to
  lukewarm
½ cup butter (no substitute), softened to
  room temperature
⅓ cup sugar
4 eggs
1 teaspoon salt
4 cups sifted flour

Sprinkle yeast over warm water and stir lightly to mix; let stand 5 minutes, then mix in milk and set aside. Cream butter until light, add sugar, and continue creaming until fluffy. Add eggs, one at a

time, beating well after each addition; mix in salt. Add flour alternately with yeast mixture, beginning and ending with flour. Beat vigorously with a wooden spoon until smooth and elastic. Place in a well-buttered bowl, cover with cloth, and let rise in a warm, draft-free place until doubled in bulk, about 1 hour. Beat dough hard with a wooden spoon 100 strokes. Transfer to a buttered and floured 3-quart crown mold or bundt pan, cover, and let rise in a warm place 25–30 minutes until doubled in bulk. Meanwhile, preheat oven to 350° F. When dough has risen, bake about ½ hour until well browned and hollow sounding when tapped. Unmold, cut into thick wedges, and serve steaming hot with lots of butter. About 515 calories for each of 6 servings (without butter), 390 calories for each of 8 servings.

¢ SOUR DOUGH BREAD

For those who *truly* want to make bread "from scratch."
Makes 2 round or long, narrow loaves

Sour Dough Starter:
1 cup sifted flour
1 cup cold water
1 tablespoon sugar

Bread:
5 cups sifted flour
1 tablespoon salt
1 tablespoon sugar
1 cup warm water (105–15° F.)
1 package active dry yeast
1 cup sour dough starter

Prepare starter at least 2 days before you plan to use it. Mix flour and water until smooth in a 1-quart bowl or glass jar; add sugar and stir until dissolved. Cover loosely and let stand in a warm (about 80° F.), draft-free place until fermented (mixture will be bubbly and smell sour); stir from time to time during fermentation. For the bread, sift flour with salt and sugar and set aside. Pour warm water into a warm large bowl, sprinkle in yeast, and stir to dissolve. Mix in starter, then flour, a little at a time, working last bit in with your hands. Knead on a lightly floured board until elastic, 8–10 minutes. Shape into a ball, place in a greased bowl, and turn to grease all over. Cover with cloth and let rise in a warm, draft-free place until doubled in bulk, about 1 hour. Punch down, knead lightly 1–2 minutes, and divide in half. Shape* into 2 round or long, tapering loaves and arrange 3″ apart on a lightly floured baking sheet. Cover and let rise until nearly doubled in bulk. Toward end of rising, preheat oven to 400° F. Brush tops of loaves with cold water and, if you like, make a diagonal ¼″ deep slash the length of loaf with a sharp knife. Bake with a shallow pan half full of hot water on shelf below loaves 35–40 minutes until well browned and hollow sounding when tapped. Cool on wire racks before cutting. About 65 calories per slice.

RICH FRENCH BREAD

A softer, sweeter bread than Pain Ordinaire.
Makes 2 12″ loaves

¾ cup scalded milk
2 tablespoons butter or margarine, softened to room temperature
1 tablespoon sugar
2 teaspoons salt
1¼ cups warm water (105–15° F.)
1 package active dry yeast
5¼–5½ cups sifted flour
1 egg yolk lightly beaten with 1 tablespoon cold water (glaze)

Mix milk, butter, sugar, and salt until sugar dissolves; cool to lukewarm. Pour warm water into a warm large bowl, sprinkle in yeast, and stir to dissolve. Add cooled mixture, then mix in 5 cups flour, a little at a time; work in enough extra flour to form a fairly stiff dough. Knead on a lightly floured board until elastic, about 8 minutes. Shape into a ball, place in a greased bowl, turning to grease all over. Cover with cloth and let rise in a warm, draft-free place until doubled in bulk, about 1 hour. Punch down, knead lightly 1–2 minutes, and divide in half. Shape* into 2 loaves about 12″ long and 4″ wide, tapering ends;

arrange 3″ apart on a baking sheet sprinkled with corn meal. Cover and let rise until doubled in bulk. Toward end of rising, preheat oven to 425° F. Brush loaves with glaze and make 3 diagonal slashes about ¼″ deep across each with a sharp knife. Bake ½ hour, reduce oven to 350° F., and bake 15 minutes longer until golden brown and loaves sound hollow when tapped. Cool on racks before cutting. About 70 calories per slice.

¢ PAIN ORDINAIRE (CRUSTY FRENCH BREAD)

Makes 2 12″ loaves

1 package active dry yeast
1¾ cups warm water (105–15° F.)
2 teaspoons salt
5¼–5½ cups sifted flour
1 egg white mixed with 1 tablespoon cold water (glaze)

Sprinkle yeast over warm water and stir to dissolve. Mix salt with flour, then add to yeast mixture, a little at a time, working in enough at the end to form a fairly stiff dough. Knead on a lightly floured board until elastic, about 8 minutes. Shape into a ball, place in a greased bowl, turning to grease all over. Cover with cloth and let rise in a warm, draft-free place until doubled in bulk, about 1 hour. Punch dough down, knead lightly 1–2 minutes and divide in half. Shape* into 2 loaves about 12″ long and 4″ wide, tapering ends; arrange 3″ apart on a baking sheet sprinkled with corn meal. Cover and let rise until doubled in bulk. Toward end of rising, preheat oven to 425° F. Brush loaves with glaze and make 3 diagonal slashes about ¼″ deep across each with a sharp knife. Bake ½ hour with a shallow baking pan half full of water on rack underneath bread, reduce heat to 350°, and bake 20–25 minutes longer until golden brown and hollow sounding when tapped. Cool on racks before cutting. About 55 calories per slice.

VARIATION:

Hard Rolls (Makes about 2 dozen):

Prepare dough and let rise as directed; punch down, knead 1 minute, and shape into 1½" balls. Place 2" apart on baking sheets sprinkled with corn meal. Cover and let rise until doubled in bulk, about ½ hour. Brush with glaze and slash each roll across the top; bake 15–20 minutes at 425° F. Cool before serving. About 95 calories per roll.

¢ WHOLE WHEAT BREAD

This hearty, wholesome bread needs no kneading and toasts beautifully.
Makes 2 9"×5" loaves

1 cup milk
1½ cups cold water
¼ cup molasses
2 tablespoons light brown sugar
1 tablespoon butter or margarine
1 tablespoon salt
½ cup warm water (105–15° F.)
2 packages active dry yeast
4 cups sifted all-purpose flour
5 cups unsifted whole wheat flour
2 tablespoons milk (glaze)

Bring milk and cold water to a boil in a small saucepan. Off heat, mix in molasses, sugar, butter, and salt; cool to lukewarm. Place lukewarm water in a warm large mixing bowl and sprinkle in yeast. Stir cooled mixture into yeast, then beat in all-purpose flour, 1 cup at a time. Finally, mix in whole wheat flour, 1 cup at a time. Place dough in a buttered large bowl, cover with cloth, and let rise about 1 hour in a warm draft-free place until doubled in bulk. Punch dough down and stir briefly (it will be stiff). Divide dough in half and pat firmly into 2 well-greased 9"×5"×3" loaf pans, rounding tops a little; brush tops with milk to glaze. Cover and let rise 45–50 minutes until almost doubled in bulk. About 15 minutes before you're ready to bake, preheat oven to 400° F. When loaves are risen, bake 20 minutes, reduce oven to 375°F., and bake 45–50 minutes longer or until richly browned and hollow sounding when tapped. Turn loaves out immediately and cool on wire racks. About 105 calories per slice.

¢ RYE BREAD

Dark, light, and medium rye flours are all available; use the medium (its the most widely available) unless you want a particularly dark or light bread.
Makes 2 7" round loaves

2 tablespoons dark brown sugar
2 tablespoons shortening
1 tablespoon salt
1 cup boiling water
½ cup cold water
½ cup warm water (105–15° F.)
1 package active dry yeast
2½ cups unsifted rye flour
3¼–3½ cups sifted all-purpose flour

Mix sugar, shortening, salt, and boiling water in a small bowl, add cold water, and cool to lukewarm. Pour warm water into a warm large bowl, sprinkle in yeast, and stir to dissolve. Add cooled mixture and rye flour and beat well. Mix in 3 cups all-purpose flour, a little at a time, then work in enough additional flour to make a fairly stiff dough that leaves sides of bowl reasonably clean. Knead until fairly smooth and elastic, 8–10 minutes, on a lightly floured board, adding as little extra flour as possible. Shape into a ball, place in a well-greased 3-quart bowl, and turn dough to grease all over. Cover with cloth and let rise in a warm, draft-free place until doubled in bulk, 1½–2 hours. Punch down, knead lightly 1–2 minutes, and divide dough in half. Shape* each into a round loaf about 5½" across and place 3" apart on a baking sheet sprinkled with corn meal. Cover and let rise until doubled in bulk, about 1½ hours. Toward end of rising, preheat oven to 400° F. Bake loaves 30–35 minutes until brown and hollow sounding when tapped. Cool on a wire rack before cutting. About 70 calories per slice.

VARIATIONS:

¢ **Pumpernickel Bread:** Prepare as directed, substituting ⅓ cup dark molasses for the sugar, increasing shortening to ⅓ cup, and omitting cold water. Increase rye flour to 3 cups, reduce white flour to 1⅔ cups, and add

1 cup whole wheat flour. Proceed as directed, allowing extra rising time because the dough is heavier. About 80 calories per slice.

¢ **Swedish Limpa Bread:** Prepare as directed, increasing brown sugar to ⅓ cup and adding ⅓ cup dark molasses, 2 teaspoons each anise seeds, and finely grated lemon or orange rind to shortening, salt, and boiling water; omit cold water. Otherwise, proceed as directed. For a soft crust, brush loaves with milk or melted butter before baking. About 80 calories per slice.

¢ OATMEAL BREAD

If you want a lighter, sweeter bread, use a ½ and ½ mixture of molasses and honey or molasses and maple syrup instead of molasses alone.
Makes 2 9″×5″×3″ loaves

1 cup scalded milk
2 tablespoons shortening or margarine
2 teaspoons salt
1 cup dark molasses or a ½ and ½
  mixture of molasses and honey or
  maple syrup
1 cup cold water
¼ cup warm water (105–15° F.)
1 package active dry yeast
1½ cups uncooked oatmeal
6 cups sifted flour

Mix milk, shortening, salt, and molasses, stir in cold water, and cool to lukewarm. Pour warm water into a warm very large bowl, sprinkle in yeast, and stir to dissolve. Add cooled mixture, oatmeal, and 4 cups flour and mix well. Mix in remaining flour and knead on a lightly floured board until elastic, 5–8 minutes. Shape into a ball, place in a greased bowl, turning to grease all over. Cover with cloth and let rise in a warm, draft-free place until doubled in bulk, about 1½ hours. Punch down and knead lightly 1–2 minutes. Divide dough in half, shape* into 2 loaves, and place in greased 9″×5″×3″ loaf pans. Cover and let rise until almost doubled in bulk. Toward end of rising, preheat oven to 375° F. Bake loaves 40 minutes until browned and hollow sounding when

tapped. Turn out and cool upright on a wire rack before cutting. About 110 calories per slice.

¢ ANADAMA BREAD

Anadama ("Anna, damn her") was a fisherman's attempt to make something "different" out of his lazy wife Anna's same old dinner (corn meal and molasses).
Makes a 9″×5″×3″ loaf

½ cup corn meal
3 tablespoons shortening
¼ cup dark molasses
2 teaspoons salt
¾ cup boiling water
¼ cup warm water (105–15° F.)
1 package active dry yeast
1 egg, lightly beaten
3 cups sifted flour

Stir corn meal, shortening, molasses, salt, and boiling water in a small bowl until shortening melts; cool to lukewarm. Pour warm water into a warm large bowl, sprinkle in yeast, and stir to dissolve. Add egg, corn meal mixture, and about half the flour. Beat 300 strokes by hand or 2 minutes at medium electric mixer speed. Stir in remaining flour, using hands at the end to mix well. Spoon into a well-greased 9″×5″×3″ loaf pan; flour hands and smooth surface. Cover and let rise in a warm, draft-free place until dough is within 1″ of top of pan. Toward end of rising, preheat oven to 375° F. If you like, sprinkle top of loaf with a little corn meal; bake 30–35 minutes until well browned and hollow sounding when tapped. Turn loaf out on a wire rack and cool before cutting. About 100 calories per slice.

VARIATION:

¢ **Easy Oatmeal Bread:** Substitute ½ cup uncooked oatmeal for corn meal, reduce flour to 2¾ cups, and proceed as recipe directs. About 100 calories per slice.

CHEESE BREAD

Especially good toasted.
Makes 2 9"×5"×3" loaves

1½ cups milk
2 cups finely grated sharp Cheddar
  cheese
2 tablespoons shortening
2 tablespoons sugar
2 teaspoons salt
⅓ cup warm water (105–15° F.)
2 packages active dry yeast
1 egg, lightly beaten
6½ cups sifted flour (about)
1 egg yolk, lightly beaten with 1
  tablespoon cold water (glaze)
1–2 teaspoons caraway, poppy, or
  toasted sesame seeds (optional)

Heat milk, cheese, shortening, sugar, and
salt over moderate heat, stirring, until
cheese is melted; cool to lukewarm.
Pour warm water into a warm large
bowl, sprinkle in yeast, and stir to
dissolve. Add cooled mixture, egg and
about 3 cups flour; beat until smooth.
Mix in enough remaining flour to make
a firm dough. Knead on a lightly floured
board until elastic, 5–8 minutes. Shape
into a ball, turn in a greased bowl to
grease all over, cover with cloth, and
let rise in a warm, draft-free place until
doubled in bulk, about 1 hour. Punch
down and knead 1–2 minutes; divide
dough in half, shape* into 2 loaves, and
place in greased 9"×5"×3" loaf
pans. Cover and let rise until nearly
doubled in bulk, about 1 hour. Toward
end of rising, preheat oven to 375° F.
Brush loaves with glaze and, if you like,
sprinkle with seeds. Bake 30–40 minutes
until well browned and hollow sounding
when tapped. Turn out and cool
upright on wire rack before cutting.
About 120 calories per slice.

VARIATIONS:

Cheese-Herb Bread: Prepare as directed,
adding ¾ teaspoon each marjoram and
thyme or 1½ teaspoons oregano to yeast
mixture. About 120 calories per slice.

Cheese-Onion Bread: Prepare as
directed, adding ¼ cup minced onion

to scalded milk. About 120 calories
per slice.

Pimiento-Cheese Bread: Prepare as
directed but, when shaping loaves, roll
into rectangles about 14"×9",
sprinkle evenly with ¼–⅓ cup minced
pimiento, and roll up from the short side.
Bake as directed. About 120 calories per
slice.

PIZZA

Makes 2 14" pies

Pizza Dough:

¼ cup warm water (105–15° F.)
1 package active dry yeast
4¼ cups sifted flour
1 teaspoon salt
1 teaspoon sugar
1¼ cups lukewarm water
2 tablespoons olive or other cooking oil

Pizza Sauce:

1 (8-ounce) can tomato sauce
1 (6-ounce) can tomato paste
1 tablespoon olive or other cooking oil
2 tablespoons water
1 clove garlic, peeled and crushed
1 teaspoon oregano
½ teaspoon salt
½ teaspoon sugar
⅛ teaspoon crushed dried hot red chili
  peppers

Topping:

¾ pound mozzarella cheese, thinly
  sliced or coarsely grated
⅓–½ cup grated Parmesan cheese
1 teaspoon oregano

Pour warm water into a warm large
bowl, sprinkle in yeast, and stir to
dissolve. Mix in 2 cups flour, the salt
and sugar. Add lukewarm water and oil
and beat until smooth. Mix in remaining
flour and knead on a lightly floured
board until elastic. Shape into a ball,
turn in greased bowl to grease all over,
cover, and let rise in a warm, draft-free
place until doubled in bulk, about 1 hour.
Meanwhile, warm all sauce ingredients
together in a covered saucepan over
lowest heat, stirring now and then,
20 minutes; keep warm until ready to

use. Preheat oven to 450° F. Punch dough down, divide in half, refrigerate 1 piece, and roll the other into a circle about 15″ across. Place on a greased 14″ pizza pan, roll edges under even with rim, and brush with a little oil. Spread half the sauce evenly over dough, sprinkle with half the mozzarella, Parmesan, and oregano. Prepare remaining dough the same way. (*Note:* Dough may be rolled to fit a 15½″× 12″ baking sheet if a pizza pan is unavailable.) Bake, uncovered, 20–25 minutes until edges are well browned and cheese bubbly. Cut each pie in 6 wedges and serve hot. Pass extra Parmesan, oregano, and chili peppers if you like. About 300 calories per pie-shaped wedge (6 wedges for each pie).

VARIATIONS:

– The ways to vary pizza topping are as endless as your imagination. Some favorites (to be added between the mozzarella and Parmesan): sliced *fully cooked* sweet or hot Italian sausages; sliced sautéed mushrooms; lightly sautéed strips of green and/or red peppers; lightly sautéed onion rings; drained anchovies; sliced green or ripe olives or any combination of these.

▨ **Quick Pizza** (Makes a 14″ pie): Prepare 1 (13¼-ounce) package hot-roll mix by package directions but increase water to 1 cup and omit egg. *Do not let rise.* Roll out to fit a 14″ pizza pan and brush with oil. Halve sauce recipe above and mix, substituting ½ teaspoon garlic powder for the garlic; do not heat. Spread on dough and top with half the cheeses and oregano called for. Bake as directed. About 300 calories per pie-shaped wedge (6 wedges per pie).

▨ **Individual Muffin Pizzas** (Makes 6): Split and toast 3 English muffins; arrange on an ungreased baking sheet. Spread with 1 (8-ounce) can meatless spaghetti sauce. Top with thin slices of mozzarella, sprinkle with Parmesan and oregano. Broil 4″–5″ from the heat about 3 minutes until bubbly. About 165 calories per pizza.

⚖ ¢ **BREAD STICKS**

Makes about 5 dozen

¾ cup boiling water
2 tablespoons shortening
2 teaspoons sugar
1 teaspoon salt
¼ cup warm water (105–15° F.)
1 package active dry yeast
3½ cups sifted flour
2 egg whites, beaten to soft peaks
1–2 tablespoons milk

Mix boiling water, shortening, sugar, and salt and cool to lukewarm. Pour warm water into a warm mixing bowl, sprinkle in yeast, and stir to dissolve. Add cooled mixture and 1½ cups flour and beat well. Mix in egg whites, then remaining flour. Knead on a lightly floured board until elastic, about 8 minutes. Shape into a ball, place in a greased bowl, turning to grease all over. Cover and let rise in a warm, draft-free place until doubled in bulk, about 1 hour. Punch dough down, knead lightly 1–2 minutes, and divide in half. Roll out 1 portion into a rectangle about 15″ long, 8″ wide, and ⅓″ thick, keeping edges as straight as possible. Cut into strips 8″ long and ½″ wide and roll lightly with floured palms, just enough to round cut edges. Place sticks ½″ apart on greased baking sheets; repeat with remaining dough. Cover and let rise until doubled in bulk, about ½ hour. Meanwhile, preheat oven to 400° F. Brush sticks with milk and bake with a shallow baking pan, half full of water set on rack underneath, 12–15 minutes until lightly browned. Cool on wire racks and store airtight. About 15 calories per bread stick.

VARIATIONS:

⚖ ¢ **Herb Bread Sticks:** Prepare as directed, adding 1 teaspoon each basil and oregano or marjoram to boiling water mixture. About 15 calories per bread stick.

⚖ ¢ **Salt Bread Sticks:** Prepare and shape as directed; after brushing sticks with milk, sprinkle heavily with coarse (kosher-style) salt. Bake as directed. About 15 calories per bread stick.

⚎ ¢ **Poppy or Sesame Seed Bread Sticks:** Prepare and shape as directed; after brushing sticks with milk, sprinkle heavily with poppy or sesame seeds. Brush seeds from baking sheets and bake as directed. About 17 calories per bread stick.

¢ RICH DINNER ROLLS

Makes about 2½ dozen

1 cup scalded milk
¼ cup sugar
1 teaspoon salt
¼ cup butter or margarine
½ cup warm water (105–15° F.)
2 packages active dry yeast
2 eggs, lightly beaten
5½ cups sifted flour (about)
1–2 tablespoons melted butter or
* margarine*

Mix milk, sugar, salt, and butter in a small bowl, stirring until sugar dissolves; cool to lukewarm. Pour warm water into a warm large bowl, sprinkle in yeast, and stir until dissolved. Stir in milk mixture, eggs, and 2 cups flour, beating with a wooden spoon until smooth. Mix in enough additional flour, a little at a time, to make a soft dough (it will be sticky but should leave sides of bowl clean). Knead on a lightly floured board 8–10 minutes until smooth and elastic; shape into a ball, place in a greased large bowl, turning to grease all over. Cover with cloth and let rise in a warm, draft-free spot until doubled in bulk, 30–40 minutes. Punch dough down. Shape* as desired, place rolls in greased pans, cover, and let rise about ½ hour until doubled in bulk. About 15 minutes before baking, preheat oven to 375° F. Brush tops of rolls with melted butter and bake 15–20 minutes until lightly browned and hollow sounding when tapped. Serve hot. About 110 calories per roll.

¢ BUTTERMILK ROLLS

These are unusually light and feathery. Makes 2 dozen

3 cups sifted flour
1 tablespoon sugar
1 teaspoon salt
¼ teaspoon baking soda
¼ cup chilled lard, butter, or
* margarine*
1 package active dry yeast
¼ cup warm water (105–15° F.)
⅔ cup lukewarm huttermilk
1–2 tablespoons melted butter or
* margarine*

Sift dry ingredients into a bowl and cut in lard until the texture of coarse meal. Sprinkle yeast over warm water and stir to dissolve; add buttermilk, pour into a well in flour mixture, and stir until dough comes together. Knead on a lightly floured board until elastic, about 5 minutes. Let rise in a buttered bowl, covered with cloth, in a warm, draft-free spot about ¾ hour until doubled in bulk. Punch dough down, turn onto board, and knead 1 minute. Shape into 1½″ balls, place 2″ apart on greased baking sheets, cover, and let rise until doubled, about ½ hour. Meanwhile, preheat oven to 425° F. Brush rolls with melted butter and bake 15–20 minutes until browned. About 80 calories per roll.

VARIATION:

¢ **Crusty Buttermilk Rolls:** After brushing rolls with butter, sprinkle with corn meal; bake as directed. About 80 calories per roll.

POTATO PUFF ROLLS

People rave about these. Makes about 3 dozen

¾ cup scalded milk
3 tablespoons shortening
2 tablespoons sugar
2 teaspoons salt
¼ cup warm water (105–15° F.)
1 package active dry yeast
1 egg, lightly beaten
1 cup lukewarm, unseasoned mashed
* potatoes*
4 cups sifted flour
2 tablespoons melted butter or
* margarine*

Mix milk, shortening, sugar, and salt

and cool to lukewarm. Pour warm water into a warm mixing bowl, sprinkle in yeast and stir to dissolve. Add cooled mixture, egg, potatoes, and 2 cups flour and beat well. Mix in remaining flour and knead on a lightly floured board until satiny and elastic. Shape into a ball, place in a greased bowl, turning to grease all over. Cover and chill in refrigerator at least 3 hours or overnight. Knead dough lightly 1 minute, then divide in half. Roll 1 portion on lightly floured board to a thickness of ½″ and cut in rounds with a 2″ cutter. Brush tops lightly with butter and fold in half, pressing edges together lightly. Arrange rolls 1″ apart on greased baking sheets. Repeat with remaining dough. Cover rolls and let rise in a warm, draft-free place until almost doubled in bulk, about ½ hour. Meanwhile preheat oven to 400° F. Bake rolls 15–17 minutes until golden brown. Serve hot. About 70 calories per roll.

CROISSANTS

Makes about 2–2½ dozen

¾ cup scalded milk
2 teaspoons sugar
1 teaspoon salt
¼ cup warm water (105–15° F.)
1 package active dry yeast
2¼–2½ cups sifted flour
½ cup butter (no substitute)
1 egg yolk lightly beaten with
  1 tablespoon cold water (glaze)

Mix milk, sugar, and salt and cool to lukewarm. Pour warm water into a warm mixing bowl, sprinkle in yeast, and stir to dissolve. Add cooled mixture, then mix in flour, a little at a time, to make a soft dough. Knead on a lightly floured board until satiny and elastic, about 5 minutes. Shape into a ball, place in a greased bowl, turning to grease all over. Cover with cloth and let rise in a warm, draft-free place until doubled in bulk, about 1 hour. Punch down, wrap in wax paper, and chill 20 minutes. Meanwhile work butter with your hands until pliable but still cold. Roll

dough on a lightly floured board into a rectangle about 12″×16″. Dab ½ the butter over ⅔ of dough and fold letter style,

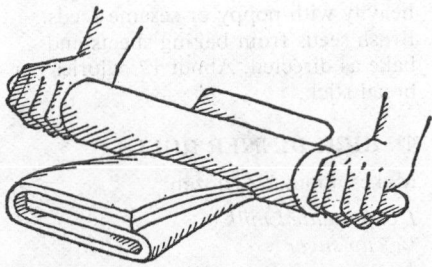

bringing unbuttered ⅓ in first. Pinch all edges to seal. Give dough ¼ turn and roll quickly with short, even strokes into a 12″×16″ rectangle. Butter the same way, fold and roll again using remaining butter. Roll and fold twice more (without adding any more butter), then wrap and chill 2–3 hours or overnight. (*Note:* If kitchen is warm, chill dough as needed between rollings.) Halve dough, and keep 1 piece cold while shaping the other: Roll into a 15″ circle and cut into 12 or 16 equal-size wedges.

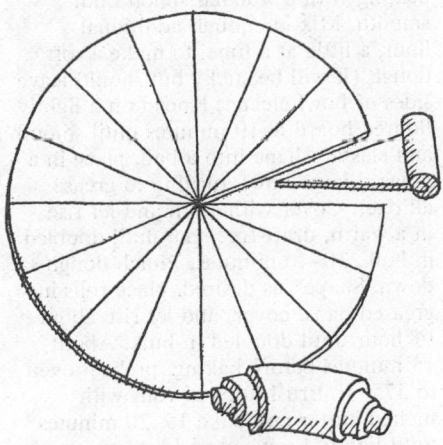

Croissants

Roll up loosely from the wide side and place, triangle points down, 2″ apart on ungreased baking sheets. Cover and let rise until almost doubled in size, about 1 hour. Toward end of rising, preheat oven to 375° F. Brush rolls with glaze and bake 15–20 minutes until well browned. Cool slightly before serving or serve at room temperature. About 90 calories for each of 2 dozen croissants, 75 for each of 2½ dozen.

¢ NO-KNEAD REFRIGERATOR ROLLS

Makes about 4 dozen

1 cup boiling water
¼ cup butter or margarine
½ cup sugar
2 teaspoons salt
1 cup warm water (105–15° F.)
2 packages active dry yeast
1 egg, lightly beaten
7 cups sifted flour (about)
1 egg yolk, lightly beaten with
* 1 tablespoon cold water (glaze)*

Mix boiling water, butter, sugar, and salt in a small bowl, stirring until sugar dissolves; cool to lukewarm. Pour warm water into a warm large bowl, sprinkle in yeast, and stir until dissolved. Stir in cooled mixture, egg, and about 4 cups flour; beat well with a wooden spoon until smooth. Mix in enough of the remaining flour to make a fairly soft dough, using your hands toward the end. Place dough in a greased large bowl, turn to grease all over, cover with wax paper, then a damp cloth. Refrigerate until doubled in bulk or until 2 hours before needed. (*Note:* Dough will keep 4–5 days in refrigerator and should be punched down occasionally as it rises; keep covering cloth damp.) To use, punch dough down and cut off amount needed. Shape* as desired, place rolls in greased pans, spacing 2″ apart, cover with a dry cloth, and let rise in a warm, draft-free spot 1½–2 hours (size of rolls and coldness of dough will determine). About 15 minutes before baking, preheat oven to 400° F. Brush tops of rolls with glaze and bake about 15 minutes until lightly browned and hollow sounding when tapped. Serve warm. About 80 calories per roll.

⊠ QUICK YEAST-RAISED DINNER ROLLS

Makes 16 rolls

¾ cup warm water (105–15° F.)
1 package active dry yeast
2½ cups packaged biscuit mix
1 egg yolk, lightly beaten with 1
* tablespoon cold water (glaze)*

Pour warm water into a warm bowl, sprinkle in yeast, and stir until dissolved. Stir in about ⅔ of the biscuit mix and beat vigorously with a wooden spoon. Mix in remaining biscuit mix. Sprinkle a board lightly with biscuit mix, turn out dough, and knead until smooth, 1–2 minutes. Cover with a cloth and let rest 10 minutes. Divide dough into 16 equal pieces, shape into smooth balls, space 2″ apart on greased baking sheets, and cover with a cloth. Let rise in a warm, draft-free place ¾–1 hour until doubled in bulk. About 15 minutes before baking, preheat oven to 400° F. Brush tops of rolls with glaze and bake about 15 minutes until lightly browned and hollow sounding when tapped. About 65 calories per roll.

VARIATION:

Sprinkle rolls with sesame or poppy seeds after brushing with glaze; bake as directed. About 65 calories per roll.

¢ BASIC SWEET DOUGH

A good all-round dough to use in making fancy yeast breads.
Makes enough for 2 10″ rings or 2 9″×5″×3″ loaves or 4 dozen rolls

1 cup scalded milk
¼ cup butter or margarine
½ cup sugar
1 teaspoon salt
¼ cup warm water (105–15° F.)
2 packages active dry yeast
2 eggs, lightly beaten
5 cups sifted flour

Mix milk, butter, sugar, and salt and cool to lukewarm. Pour warm water into a warm large bowl, sprinkle in yeast, and stir to dissolve. Add cooled mixture, eggs, and 3 cups flour and beat well. Mix in remaining flour and knead lightly on a lightly floured board until elastic. Shape into a ball, turn in a greased bowl to grease all over, cover with cloth, and let rise in a warm, draft-free place until doubled in bulk, about 1 hour. Dough is now ready to shape and use as individual recipes direct. About 95 calories per wedge (equal to ⅛ of 1 ring-shaped loaf), 85 calories per 1-inch slice of loaf, and 65 calories per roll.

HOT CROSS BUNS

Makes 4 dozen

1 recipe Basic Sweet Dough
1 cup seedless raisins or dried currants
1 teaspoon allspice
½ cup minced candied citron (optional)
2 egg yolks, lightly beaten with
* 2 tablespoons cold water (glaze)*
2 times the recipe for Easy White Icing

Prepare dough as directed, but add raisins, allspice, and, if you like, citron to yeast along with cooled mixture; proceed as directed and let rise. Divide dough in half and shape into 1½″ balls. Arrange 2″ apart on greased baking sheets and flatten slightly with palm of hand. Cover and let rise in a warm, draft-free place until doubled in bulk, about ¾ hour. Meanwhile, preheat oven to 400° F. Brush buns with glaze and bake 12–15 minutes until golden brown. Lift to wire racks and, while still warm, draw a cross on top of each with icing. About 110 calories per bun.

BASIC TEA RING

Makes a 10″ ring

½ recipe Basic Sweet Dough

Filling:

2 tablespoons melted butter or margarine
¾ cup minced pecans, walnuts, or
* blanched almonds*
½ cup sugar
1½ teaspoons cinnamon

Topping:

1 recipe Easy White Icing

Prepare dough and let rise as directed; punch down and roll on a lightly floured board into a rectangle about 12″ × 17″. Brush with melted butter. Mix nuts, sugar, and cinnamon and sprinkle evenly over dough; roll up from longest side

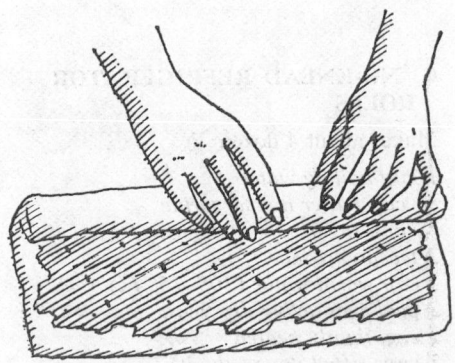

jelly-roll fashion and place seam side down on a greased baking sheet. Bring ends around to form a ring and pinch edges to seal.

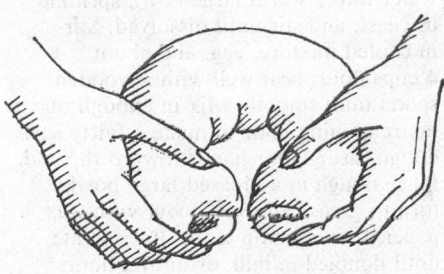

With scissors, snip into ring every 1″ and twist slices so cut sides are up. Cover and let rise in a warm, draft-free place until doubled in bulk, about 1 hour. Toward end of rising, preheat oven to 350° F. Bake 35–40 minutes until golden brown. Lift ring to a wire rack set over wax paper and drizzle with icing while still warm. About 160 calories for each of 20 slices.

VARIATIONS:

– Substitute any favorite filling for the one above (see Some Fillings for Coffee Cakes).

Chelsea Buns (Makes 1½ dozen): Prepare and roll dough as directed. For the filling, substitute dried currants for the nuts. Roll up as directed but do not shape into a ring; instead, slice 1" thick and arrange cut sides up 1½" apart on greased baking sheets. Let rise, then bake 15–20 minutes until golden. Lift to racks and drizzle with icing while still warm. About 175 calories per bun.

Caramel Sticky Buns (Makes 1½ dozen): Prepare Basic Tea Ring (above) as directed, but do not shape into a ring; instead, slice 1" thick. Mix 1 cup firmly packed light or dark brown sugar with ½ cup melted butter and 2 tablespoons light corn syrup and spread over the bottom of a greased 13"×9"×2" baking pan. Arrange rolls cut sides up and ½" apart on top, cover, and let rise. Bake 25–30 minutes at 375° F. Let stand in pan 5 minutes, then invert on a wire rack set over wax paper. Serve while still warm. About 275 calories per bun.

¢ BUBBLE LOAF

Makes a 9"×5"×3" or 9" tube loaf

½ recipe Basic Sweet Dough

Caramel Glaze:

¼ cup dark corn syrup
1 tablespoon melted butter or margarine
¼ teaspoon lemon extract
¼ teaspoon vanilla or maple extract

Prepare dough and let rise as directed. Punch down and let rest 10 minutes. Pinch off bits of dough and roll into 1" balls. Arrange 1 layer deep, ¼" apart, in the bottom of a greased 9"× 5"×3" loaf pan or 9" tube pan. Layer in remaining balls, fitting them into spaces in layer below. Cover and let rise in a warm, draft-free place until doubled in bulk, about ¾ hour. Meanwhile, mix glaze ingredients and preheat oven to 350° F. When dough is fully risen, pour glaze evenly over all. Bake 40–45 minutes, cool upright in pan on a wire rack 5 minutes, then invert and cool. There are 2 ways to serve: slicing or pulling off the "individual bubbles." About 90 calories for each of 20 slices.

CHERRY KOLACHE

Makes about 3½ dozen rolls

1 recipe Basic Sweet Dough
2 cups cherry preserves
3 tablespoons melted butter or margarine
Confectioners' or granulated sugar

Prepare dough and let rise as directed. Punch down, roll ½" thick on a lightly floured board, and cut in rounds with a 3" cutter. Arrange 1½" apart on greased baking sheets, cover, and let rise in a warm, draft-free place until doubled in bulk, about ½ hour. With thumb, make a depression in center of each roll and fill with about 2 teaspoons cherry preserves. Let rise 15 minutes; meanwhile, preheat oven to 400° F. Bake 12–15 minutes until golden brown. Transfer to wire racks, brush with melted butter, and dust with sugar. About 135 calories per roll.

Note: Dainty tea-size *kolache* can be made by rolling dough into ¾" balls; let rise as directed, make thumbprints in center, and fill with preserves; bake as directed. *Or* dough can be rolled into a 12"×15" rectangle, cut in 3" squares and spread with preserves, leaving ¼"– ½" margins all round; fold 4 corners in toward center until points touch, then pinch to seal. Let rise and bake as directed. About 35 calories per tea-size roll.

VARIATIONS:

Prune Kolache: Prepare as directed, filling with the following mixture instead of cherry preserves: Mix 2 cups minced pitted cooked prunes (or apricots or figs), ½ cup sugar, 1 tablespoon grated orange or lemon rind, and 1 tablespoon orange or lemon juice. If you like, add ¼–½ teaspoon cinnamon or allspice. About 135 calories per roll.

Poppy Seed-Nut Kolache: Prepare as directed, filling with the following mixture: 1½ cups minced blanched almonds, hazelnuts, or other nuts mixed with ½ cup poppy seeds and ¼ cup warm honey. About 120 calories per roll.

KUGELHUPF

A fruit-filled, sweet yeast bread good with afternoon tea or coffee or as dessert.
Makes a 10″ tube loaf

1 recipe Basic Sweet Dough (reduce amount of flour to 4 cups)
2 egg yolks
½ cup seedless raisins
½ cup dried currants
½ cup minced mixed candied fruits (optional)
20 blanched almonds, halved
Confectioners' sugar

Prepare dough as directed, adding extra egg yolks and fruits to yeast along with cooled mixture and 3 cups flour; beat well and add remaining 1 cup flour to makes a very soft dough. Do not knead. Grease and flour a 10″ tube pan or 3½-quart Turk's-head mold and arrange almonds in bottom. Spoon in dough, cover, and let rise in a warm, draft-free place until doubled in bulk, about 1 hour. Toward end of rising, preheat oven to 400° F. Bake 10 minutes, reduce oven to 350° F., and bake 50–60 minutes longer until lightly browned and springy to the touch. Turn out at once on a wire rack set over wax paper and dust with sifted confectioners' sugar. Slice and serve. About 195 calories for each of 20 slices.

VARIATION:

Instead of using halved almonds, sprinkle prepared mold with ⅓–½ cup minced almonds; spoon in dough and proceed as directed. About 195 calories for each of 20 slices.

DANISH PASTRY

Makes about 3½ dozen

1 recipe Basic Sweet Dough
1 teaspoon cardamom
1 cup butter (no substitute)

2 egg yolks, lightly beaten with 2 tablespoons cold water (glaze)

Filling:

1 cup (about) jelly, jam, almond paste, applesauce, Cheese, Nut, or Prune Filling

Prepare basic dough as directed, mixing cardamom into scalded milk mixture. When dough is fully risen, punch down, cover, and chill 20 minutes. Meanwhile, knead butter until pliable but still cold. Roll dough on a lightly floured board into a rectangle about 12″ × 10″. Dot ½ the butter over ⅔ of dough, leaving ½″ margins all round. Fold unbuttered ⅓ in toward center, then far ⅓ on top as though folding a letter; pinch edges to seal.

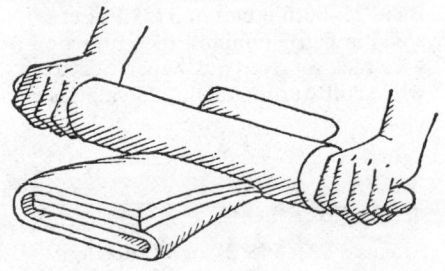

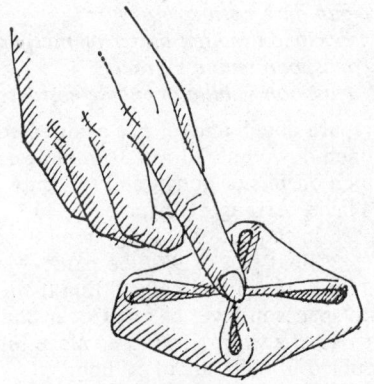

Give package a ¼ turn and roll with short, even strokes into a rectangle about 12″ × 16″. Dot with remaining butter, fold, and roll as before. Roll and fold twice more, lightly flouring board and pin as needed to keep dough from sticking. Wrap and chill 1 hour. (*Note:* If kitchen is warm, you may need to chill dough between rollings.) Divide dough in half, chill 1 piece while shaping the other. Roll out ⅓" thick and cut in 3" or 4" squares; place 1–2 teaspoons filling in center of each square, moisten edges and fold 2 opposite corners in toward center; press edges to seal. Arrange 2" apart on greased baking sheets, chill 2 hours, or let rise in a warm place until about half doubled in bulk. Preheat oven to 425° F. Brush with glaze, set in oven, and reduce heat at once to 375° F. Bake 15 minutes until browned. Cool on wire racks before serving. About 145 calories per pastry (filled with jelly or jam).

VARIATIONS:

Danish Twists: Prepare dough as directed, let rise, then punch down and roll the butter in as above. Divide in half, chill 1 piece while shaping the other. Roll into a rectangle about 12" × 16", brush well with melted butter, and sprinkle with ¼ cup sugar mixed with 1 teaspoon cinnamon. Fold dough in half the long way so you have a strip 6" × 16". Cut crosswise into strips ¾" wide. Twist ends of each in opposite directions, arrange on greased baking sheets, let rise, and bake as directed. Shape and bake remaining dough the same way. About 145 calories each.

Danish Ring: Prepare dough as directed, let rise, then punch down and roll butter into dough as above. Divide in half and chill 1 piece while shaping the other. Roll into a rectangle about 12" × 16", brush with melted butter, then sprinkle or spread with any of the fillings above. Roll up from the longest side jelly-roll fashion, place seam side down on a greased baking sheet, and bring ends around to form a ring, pressing edges to seal. Or, if you prefer, coil snail fashion. Let rise in a warm place until about half doubled in bulk, glaze, and sprinkle with sliced blanched

almonds and granulated sugar. Bake 25–30 minutes at 375° F. until golden brown and hollow sounding when tapped. Shape and bake remaining pastry the same way. About 145 calories per 1-inch slice (filled with jelly or jam).

PANETTONE (ITALIAN CHRISTMAS BREAD)

Makes a tall 9" loaf

1 recipe Basic Sweet Dough (reduce amount of scalded milk to ¾ cup)
¼ cup butter or margarine
3 egg yolks, lightly beaten
1 cup sultana raisins
1 cup minced candied citron or mixed candied fruits
½ cup piñon nuts (optional)
2 tablespoons melted butter or margarine
Confectioners' sugar

Prepare basic recipe as directed, adding the ¼ cup butter above to the scalded milk along with the butter, sugar, and salt called for in basic recipe; cool to lukewarm and stir into yeast mixture along with all but last ingredient above. Proceed as basic recipe directs. While dough is rising, prepare pan: Tear off a 30" piece of heavy duty foil and fold over and over again until you have a strip 30" long and 4" wide. Grease 1 side of strip and stand greased side around the inside edge of a greased 9" layer cake pan; secure with a paper clip to form a collar. Punch dough down, knead lightly 1–2 minutes, and shape into a smooth round loaf about 9" across. Place in pan, cover, and let rise in a warm, draft-free place until doubled in bulk, about 1 hour. Toward end of rising, preheat oven to 400° F. Bake 10 minutes, reduce oven to 350° F., and bake 40–50 minutes longer until golden brown and hollow sounding when tapped. Turn out on a wire rack, dust with confectioners' sugar and cool. To serve, cut in thin wedges. About 330 calories for each of 16 wedges.

STOLLEN

Makes 2 large loaves

1 recipe Basic Sweet Dough
1 cup seedless raisins
1 cup minced blanched almonds
¾ cup minced candied fruits or a
  ½ and ½ mixture of citron and
  candied cherries
1 tablespoon finely grated lemon rind
3 tablespoons melted butter or
  margarine
1 recipe Easy White Icing

Prepare dough as directed, adding raisins, almonds, candied fruit, and lemon rind to yeast along with lukewarm mixture. Add remaining flour, knead, and let rise as directed. Divide dough in half and roll or pat out half on a lightly floured board to form an oval about 12″×8″. Brush with melted butter, fold in half the long way, and bend ends in slightly to form a crescent; press edges firmly to seal. Transfer to a greased baking sheet and brush with melted butter. Shape remaining dough the same way and place on a baking sheet. Cover loaves and let rise in a warm, draft-free place until doubled in bulk, about ¾ hour. Toward end of rising, preheat oven to 375° F. Bake 35–40 minutes until golden brown. Lift to wire racks set over wax paper and, while still warm, drizzle with icing. For a festive touch, decorate with "flowers" made with blanched almond halves, candied cherries, and slivered angelica. About 140 calories for each of 20 slices.

VARIATION:

Christmas Bread: Prepare dough as directed, using ½ cup each sultana and seedless raisins and adding 1 teaspoon cinnamon and ½ teaspoon nutmeg along with the fruit. Shape into 2 round loaves and place in greased 9″ piepans. Or, if you prefer, make 2 braids.* Let rise, bake, and ice as directed. For a shiny crust, brush dough before baking with 1 egg lightly beaten with 1 tablespoon cold water; omit icing. About 140 calories for each of 20 slices.

CINNAMON-RAISIN PINWHEELS

Makes 20 rolls

½ cup sugar
3 tablespoons butter or margarine
1 teaspoon salt
¾ cup boiling water
1 package active dry yeast
¼ cup warm water (105–15° F.)
1 egg, lightly beaten
4½ cups sifted flour

Filling:
¼ cup light corn syrup
¼ cup melted butter or margarine
⅓ cup sugar or firmly packed light
  brown sugar
1½ teaspoons cinnamon
1½ cups seedless raisins

Stir sugar, butter, and salt into boiling water and cool to lukewarm. Dissolve yeast in the warm water in a warm large bowl; add cooled mixture, egg, and 3 cups flour and beat until smooth. Mix in remaining flour, a little at a time. Knead dough on a lightly floured board until elastic, about 5 minutes; place in a greased bowl, and let rise in a warm, draft-free spot 1 hour or until doubled in bulk. Punch dough down, turn onto board, and divide in half. Roll each into a rectangle about 15″×9″, brush with corn syrup and melted butter, sprinkle with sugar, cinnamon, and raisins. Roll each jelly-roll style the short way and cut into 10 slices. Lay slices flat, almost touching, in greased layer cake pans, cover, and let rise about ½ hour until doubled in bulk. Meanwhile, preheat oven to 350° F. Brush with melted butter and bake 30–35 minutes until lightly browned. About 210 calories per roll.

SWEDISH CINNAMON RINGS

This is a rich coffee cake, so cut each ring in small wedges. You should be able to get about 20 wedge-shaped slices out of each ring.
Makes 3 12″ or 4 10″ rings

Dough:
2 packages active dry yeast

½ cup warm water (105–15° F.)
1 cup butter or margarine
¾ cup sugar
1 tablespoon crushed cardamom seeds
  (it's easy to crush them in an electric
  blender)
1 teaspoon salt
1½ cups light cream, scalded
2 eggs
8 cups sifted flour

Filling:

½ cup butter or margarine, softened to
  room temperature
1 cup firmly packed light brown sugar
2 teaspoons cinnamon

Decorations (optional):

2 recipes Lemon Sugar Glaze
Diced candied red or green cherries

Sprinkle yeast over warm water in a warm large bowl and stir to dissolve. Mix butter, sugar, cardamom and salt with cream and cool to lukewarm. Stir into yeast, then beat in eggs, 1 at a time. Add flour, 1 cup at a time, beating well after each addition. You will probably have to turn dough onto a board and knead in the final cup. Knead dough about 5 minutes until smooth and elastic. Place in a greased large bowl, turn so dough is greased all over, cover with cloth, and let rise in a warm, draft-free place 1½–1¾ hours until doubled in bulk. Punch dough down, turn onto a lightly floured board, and knead 1–2 minutes. Divide dough into 3 or 4 equal parts, depending upon whether you want large- or medium-size rings. Roll each piece of dough into a rectangle (about 14″×18″ for medium-size rings, 18″×22″ for large). Spread lightly with butter; mix brown sugar and cinnamon and sprinkle over butter, then roll up jelly-roll style and shape into a ring. Using sharp scissors, make diagonal snips deep into each ring every 2″ and turn cut-side up. Place rings on lightly greased baking sheets, cover with cloth, and let rise in a warm place until doubled in bulk, 30–40 minutes. Meanwhile, preheat oven to 375° F. When rings have risen, bake 20–30 minutes until nicely browned and hollow sounding when tapped. Transfer to wire racks to cool and, if you like, glaze and decorate. Serve warm or at room temperature. To reheat, wrap in foil and heat 10 minutes at 350° F. If you do not decorate rings, and cut each ring into 20 thin wedge-shaped slices, each slice will be about 140 calories.

PUMPKIN COFFEE CAKE

Makes 8 servings

Dough:

¼ cup milk, scalded
¼ cup sugar
½ teaspoon salt
3 tablespoons butter or margarine
1 package active dry yeast
¼ cup warm water (105–15° F.)
1 egg, lightly beaten
2¼ cups unsifted flour (about)
1 egg yolk, beaten with 1 tablespoon
  cold water (glaze)

Filling:

¾ cup cooked, mashed pumpkin
½ cup sugar
1 teaspoon cinnamon
½ teaspoon ginger
½ teaspoon salt
1 cup chopped walnuts or pecans
¼ cup seedless raisins

Frosting:

½ cup sifted confectioners' sugar
1 teaspoon milk or light cream
⅛ teaspoon vanilla

Mix milk with sugar, salt, and butter, stirring until sugar dissolves; cool to lukewarm. Sprinkle yeast over warm water and stir until dissolved. Combine milk and yeast mixtures, add egg and half the flour, and beat until smooth. Stir in remaining flour (dough will be fairly soft). Turn onto a lightly floured board and knead 7–8 minutes until smooth and elastic, adding only enough extra flour to keep dough from sticking. Place dough in a greased bowl, turn to grease all sides, cover with cloth, set in a warm, draft-free place, and let rise about 1 hour until doubled in bulk. Punch dough down, turn onto a lightly floured board, and roll into a rectangle about 22" × 10". Mix pumpkin with sugar, spices, and salt and spread evenly over dough, not quite to edges. Sprinkle with ½ cup walnuts and the raisins. Roll up jelly-roll fashion from the wide side, lift to a greased baking sheet, and coil into a ring. Cover and let rise in a warm place about 1 hour until doubled in bulk. Meanwhile, preheat oven to 350° F. Brush ring with egg glaze and bake 30–35 minutes until well browned and hollow sounding when tapped. Mix frosting ingredients together until smooth and frost ring while still warm; sprinkle with remaining nuts. Serve warm or at room temperature. About 400 calories per serving.

Some Fillings for Coffee Cakes and Sweet Breads

Substitute any of the following for fillings called for in Basic Tea Ring, Danish Pastry, Pumpkin Coffee Cake, or other filled yeast bread.

Almond Paste: Cream together until light ⅓ cup each butter and sugar; add 1 egg, ¼ teaspoon almond extract, and ½ cup almond paste and beat until smooth.

Nut: Cream together until light ¼ cup butter and ⅓ cup sugar; mix in 1 tablespoon grated orange or lemon rind. Spread on dough, then sprinkle with 1 cup minced blanched almonds, pecans, or walnuts.

Prune: Heat together over low heat, stirring constantly until thickened, 1 cup coarsely chopped pitted prunes (or dates, dried apricots, or figs), ¼ cup sugar, 2 tablespoons lemon juice, 1 teaspoon grated lemon rind, and 1 tablespoon butter.

Spiced Apple: Mix 2 tablespoons melted butter with ½ cup firmly packed light brown sugar, 1 teaspoon cinnamon, ¼ teaspoon nutmeg, and 1–1½ cups well-drained canned sliced apples. If you like, also mix in ½ cup seedless raisins.

Cottage Cheese: Mix together 1 cup cottage cheese, 1 lightly beaten egg yolk, ⅓ cup superfine sugar, ½ teaspoon vanilla, and 1 teaspoon finely grated lemon or orange rind.

Custard: Mix 1 cup Custard Sauce and ½ cup poppy seeds.

▨ *Some Quickies:*
– 1 cup any jelly, jam, preserves, or marmalade
– 1 cup mincemeat
– 1 cup canned apple, cherry, or pumpkin pie filling
– 1 cup whipped cream cheese mixed with ¼ cup poppy seeds and 1 teaspoon finely grated lemon or orange rind

BRIOCHE I (TRADITIONAL METHOD)

A difficult recipe, not for beginners. Makes 2 dozen

1 package active dry yeast
2¼ cups warm water (105–15° F.)
4½ cups sifted flour
1 teaspoon salt
3 tablespoons sugar
6 eggs
1½ cups butter (no substitute), softened to room temperature
1 egg yolk, lightly beaten with 1 tablespoon cold water (glaze)

Beat yeast with ¼ cup warm water and ½ cup flour until smooth and sticky. Pour remaining water into a warm bowl; with a rubber spatula, scrape yeast mixture into water, trying to keep in 1 piece, and let sink to the bottom. Let rise in a warm, draft-free spot until yeast mixture floats and is doubled in bulk, 7–10 minutes. Meanwhile, mix remaining flour with salt and sugar on a pastry board and make a large well in the center. Break 3 eggs into a bowl and set aside. Break remaining eggs into well in flour and, using 1 hand, gradually work flour from edges of well into eggs. Add remaining eggs and continue mixing until dough holds together (it will be very sticky). Keeping a metal spatula in 1 hand to help scrape dough from board, scoop up as much dough as possible with other hand and throw or slap hard against board. You won't be able to get all the dough at once and it will stick like glue to your fingers. But keep throwing as much as possible against board, scraping up a little more each time with the spatula.

Continue throwing dough against board until it is smooth, shiny and leaves board and your fingers almost clean, about 100 times. Squeeze ⅓ of butter into dough with your fingers; repeat until all butter is incorporated and dough smooth. Also squeeze in yeast sponge, but not water it was floating in (dough will be soft).

Scoop into a lightly buttered 3-quart bowl, cover with cloth, and let rise in a warm, draft-free place until doubled in bulk, about 2 hours. Stir dough down, cover with foil, and refrigerate 6–8 hours or overnight. Open refrigerator as little as possible during this period.

Dough will rise slightly and become quite firm. Scrape dough onto a lightly floured board, knead lightly with floured hands, and shape quickly into a ball. Cut ball in 4 equal pieces with a floured knife and cut 3 of the quarters into 8 pieces, totaling 24. Roll into smooth balls and place in greased brioche or muffin pans, 1 ball per cup. With dampened index finger, make a deep depression in center of each ball. Roll remaining dough into 24 small balls and place 1 in each depression to form the "topknot." Cover brioches, set in a warm spot and let rise until doubled in bulk, about 1 hour.

About 15 minutes before you're ready to bake, preheat oven to 425° F.; set rack in lower ⅓ of oven. Gently brush brioches with glaze, taking care not to let it run into cracks around topknots (an artist's brush is best). Set pans on baking sheets and bake 12–15 minutes until well browned. (Note: You probably won't be able to bake all the brioches at once, so refrigerate 1 batch while baking the other.) Remove from pans at once after baking and serve hot or, if you prefer, cool on wire racks to room

temperature. (Note: To reheat leftover brioches, bundle loosely in foil and warm 10 minutes at 350° F. These brioches freeze well; thaw before reheating.) About 205 calories per brioche.

BRIOCHE II (EASY METHOD)

So much less complicated than Brioche I and almost as good.
Makes 2 dozen

1 package active dry yeast
¼ cup warm water (105–15°F.)
4 cups sifted flour
3 tablespoons sugar
1 teaspoon salt
1½ cups butter or margarine, softened to room temperature
6 eggs, lightly beaten
1 egg yolk, lightly beaten with 1 tablespoon cold water (glaze)

Mix yeast, warm water, and ¼ cup flour until smooth in a small bowl; set in a pan of lukewarm water (water should come ⅓ of way up bowl) and let stand in a warm spot until bubbles form on yeast mixture, 5–10 minutes. Meanwhile, sift 3 cups flour with the sugar and salt and set aside. Cream butter in a large bowl with an electric mixer until fluffy. Add flour mixture, a little at a time, alternately with eggs. Beat 2 minutes at medium speed. Add yeast mixture, beat ½ minute at low speed, then 2 minutes at medium speed. Add remaining ¾ cup flour by hand, a little at a time, beating with a wooden spoon after each addition. Cover dough with cloth, set in a warm, draft-free spot, and let rise until doubled in bulk, 2½–3 hours. Stir dough down, cover with foil, and refrigerate 6–8 hours or overnight. Now divide dough, shape into 24 brioches, allow to rise, glaze, and bake as directed in Brioche I. About 200 calories per brioche.

BRIOCHE FRUIT LOAVES

Delicious toasted and buttered!
Makes 2 9"×5"×3" loaves

1 recipe Brioche I or II
2 cups mixed dried or candied fruits (seedless raisins, currants, coarsely

chopped candied red cherries or citron)
⅓–½ cup slivered or sliced blanched almonds (optional)
1 egg yolk, lightly beaten with 1 tablespoon cold water (glaze)

Prepare brioche up to point of shaping dough; instead of making individual brioches, halve dough. Roll each piece on a lightly floured board into a rectangle 9″×12″. Sprinkle with fruit and press in lightly. Roll up the short way, jelly-roll style, and pinch seams together. Place each loaf seam-side down in a greased 9″×5″×3″ loaf pan. Slash tops lengthwise down center with a sharp knife and, if you like, sprinkle almonds into slits. Cover with cloth and let rise in a warm, draft-free spot until doubled in bulk, 1–1½ hours. About 15 minutes before you're ready to bake, preheat oven to 350° F. Brush loaves with glaze and bake 35–40 minutes until well browned and hollow sounding when tapped. If tops or almonds brown too fast, cover loosely with foil. Turn loaves out immediately and cool upright on a wire rack. Slice and serve with plenty of butter. (Note: These loaves freeze well.) About 155 calories for each of 20 slices (with almonds).

OLD-FASHIONED YEAST-RAISED DOUGHNUTS

Stored airtight, these doughnuts keep fairly well. They're best, of course, eaten straight from the deep fat fryer.
Makes about 3 dozen

¼ cup butter or margarine
⅔ cup scalded milk
⅔ cup warm water (105–15° F.)
2 packages active dry yeast
¾ cup sugar
5 cups sifted flour (about)
2 eggs, lightly beaten
1 teaspoon salt
1 teaspoon cardamom
½ teaspoon cinnamon
½ teaspoon mace
Shortening or cooking oil for deep fat frying

Topping:
½ cup superfine sugar mixed with 1 teaspoon cinnamon

Melt butter in milk and cool to lukewarm. Place water in a warm large mixing bowl, sprinkle in yeast, and stir until dissolved; add milk mixture and sugar. By hand, beat 2½ cups flour in until smooth; mix in eggs, salt, and spices. Mix in remaining flour, adding a little extra, if needed, to form a soft but manageable dough. Knead lightly 1 minute on a floured pastry cloth; shape into a ball, place in a greased large bowl, cover, and let rise in a warm, draft-free spot until doubled in bulk, about 1 hour. Punch dough down, roll ½″ thick on pastry cloth, using a floured, stockinette-covered rolling pin. Cut with a floured doughnut cutter and place 1½″ apart on ungreased baking sheets. Reroll and cut scraps. Cover with cloth and let rise in a warm spot about 25 minutes until doubled in bulk. Meanwhile, begin heating fat in a deep fat fryer. When doughnuts have risen and fat reached 375° F., ease 4 doughnuts into fat, 1 at a time. Fry about 2 minutes until golden brown all over, using tongs to turn. Drain on paper toweling. (Note: Never fry more than 4 doughnuts at a time and keep fat as near 375° F. as possible; if too hot, doughnuts will brown before they cook inside.) While doughnuts are warm, roll in topping. About 130 calories per doughnut.

VARIATIONS:

Jelly Doughnuts: Prepare as directed, but roll dough ¼″ thick instead of ½″. Cut in 2½″ rounds and put 1 teaspoonful tart jelly in the center of ½ the rounds. Top with remaining rounds, moisten touching edges slightly and pinch to seal. Let rise, then fry as directed. Roll in confectioners' sugar while still warm. About 150 calories per doughnut.

Crullers: Prepare as directed, but instead of cutting into doughnuts, cut in strips 8″ long and ½″–¾″ wide; let rise, then twist strips several times and pinch ends. Fry at once and roll in topping while still warm. About 130 calories per cruller.

CHAPTER 19

SANDWICHES

Sandwiches are named for the Earl of Sandwich, an eighteenth-century Englishman who was so fond of gambling he had meat or other savory served between slices of bread so that he needn't interrupt his game. Open-face sandwiches are even older, dating to medieval Scandinavia when slices of bread served as plates. Open *or* shut, sandwiches have become universal favorites. And who in those early days could have predicted it?

About Breads

Any bread can be used in making sandwiches, but certain breads and fillings team more happily than others. Here's a quick table of compatibles:

Bread	Suitable Fillings
White bread	Any filling (*Note:* Use day-old bread if filling is soft or runny)
Whole or cracked wheat, oatmeal, rye, or pumpernickel, cheese bread	Cold cuts and cheeses, smoked fish
Fruit or nut breads	Cream cheese, jams, jellies
French or Italian bread	Hero sandwiches, also any meat, egg, or seafood salad
Hard rolls, hamburger, and hot dog buns	Heroes, hamburgers, hot dogs, sloppy Joes, barbecued meat

About Butters and Mayonnaises

These help bind fillings to bread and, at the same time, keep runny fillings from soaking into bread. They can be used straight from the wrapper or jar or flavored any of the following ways (all amounts based on ¼ cup mayonnaise or butter):

Especially Good with:

Mustard: Blend 1–2 teaspoons mild or spicy prepared mustard with butter or mayonnaise.

Ham, tongue, and other cold cuts

Horseradish: Blend 1 teaspoon prepared horseradish with butter or mayonnaise.

Roast beef

Garlic or Onion: Blend ¼ crushed clove garlic or 1 teaspoon finely grated onion into butter or mayonnaise.	Cold cuts or cheese
Lemon: Blend 1 teaspoon lemon juice and ¼ teaspoon finely grated lemon rind into butter or mayonnaise.	Seafood, chicken, or turkey
Anchovy or Shrimp: Blend 1 teaspoon shrimp or anchovy paste into butter or mayonnaise.	Seafood
Dill: Blend 2–3 teaspoons minced fresh dill or 1 tablespoon minced dill pickle into butter or mayonnaise.	Salami, seafood, egg salad, chicken, or turkey
Parsley or Watercress: Blend 2–3 teaspoons minced parsley or cress into butter or mayonnaise.	Cold cuts, cheese, seafood, chicken, or turkey
Chutney: Blend 1 tablespoon minced chutney into butter or mayonnaise.	Cold sliced chicken, turkey, or lamb
Curry: Blend 1 teaspoon each curry powder, finely minced onion, and chutney into butter or mayonnaise.	Cold sliced chicken, turkey, or lamb; also seafood

Tips for Making Better Sandwiches

Sandwiches in General:

– Leave crusts on all but dainty tea sandwiches; they help keep sandwiches fresh.
– Assemble components, then put sandwiches together just before serving, particularly important if fillings are drippy.
– Soften butter to room temperature so it spreads more easily.
– If filling is creamy, butter 1 slice of bread only.
– Be generous—but not lavish—with butter or mayonnaise; 1 teaspoon per slice is ample.
– Spread butter or mayonnaise *and* filling to edges of bread.
– Use several thin slices of meat or cheese rather than a single thick one.
– Make sure salad-type fillings are creamy, *not soupy.*
– Make toasted sandwiches at the very last minute and do not stack toast—it will become soggy.

Sandwiches to Go:

– Choose sandwich fillings that won't soak into bread.

– Spread bread with butter, then chill before adding filling so that butter will harden and help keep filling from seeping into bread.
– Pack lettuce leaves, pickles, tomatoes, etc., separately and slip into sandwiches just before serving.
– Keep all salad-type fillings well chilled (especially in transit) and make sandwiches on location.
– Choose less perishable fillings for lunch box sandwiches cold cuts, sliced cheese, peanut butter, jelly, etc.—instead of quick-to-spoil creamy salad types.
– Keep lunch box sandwiches refrigerated until ready to go and eat within 4 hours.
– Halve sandwiches before wrapping— makes for easier eating.
– Wrap sandwiches individually in wax paper or plastic sandwich bags.

Sandwiches in Quantity:

To Help Compute Quantities:

– 1 (1-pound) loaf averages 20 slices; 1 pullman or sandwich loaf 33–34.
– Allowing a rounded teaspoon per slice, 1 pound butter will spread 50–60 slices or 2½–3 (1-pound) loaves.

– Allowing a rounded teaspoon per slice, 1 pint mayonnaise will spread 50–60 slices or 2½–3 (1-pound) loaves.
– Allowing ¼ cup per sandwich, 1 quart filling will make 16 sandwiches.

To Stretch Butter: Add ½ cup milk to each 1 pound butter and cream until fluffy.

For Quickest Assembly:

– Choose the simplest sandwiches possible.
– Line bread up in rows, pairing slices so they'll match.
– Whip butter or cheese spreads until fluffy so they'll spread zip-quick.
– Place dabs of butter or mayonnaise on alternate rows of slices, then mounds of filling on remaining rows. Spread well to edges, put slices together, and press lightly.
– Use a No. 24 ice cream scoop or ¼ cup measure for apportioning fillings.

Party Sandwiches

– Use a firm, fine-textured bread to avoid ragged edges; if unavailable, use day-old bread and chill well before cutting.
– For attractiveness, slice bread thin and trim off crusts.
– Be sparing about fillings so they don't seep through the bread or ooze out the edges.
– When making sandwiches ahead, cover with wax paper or saran, never a damp towel. Refrigerate until ready to serve.
– Add garnishes and decorations at the last minute.

How to Cut and Shape Party Sandwiches

(*Note:* Spreads included in the hors d'oeuvre chapter are perfect for party sandwiches).

Fancy Cutouts: Trim crusts from an unsliced loaf, slice thin lengthwise, spread with filling, then cut, using a sharp bread knife or cookie cutters.

Double Deckers: Make cutouts and mix or match breads and shapes.

Ribbon Loaf: Trim crusts from an unsliced loaf, slice lengthwise about ½″ thick, spread, and reassemble. Frost with softened cream cheese, tinted pastel, if you like. Chill well before slicing. For variety, alternate slices of dark and light breads and 2 or more compatible fillings of contrasting color.

Ribbon Sandwiches: Prepare ribbon loaf, chill well, then slice thin. Cut slices into small squares or rectangles.

Round Ribbon Loaf: Trim crusts from unsliced bread, slice and cut slices in circles of the same size. Spread and assemble as for Ribbon Loaf (above). Frost if you like. To serve, cut in thin wedges.

Checkerboards: Prepare 2 ribbon loaves, beginning one with dark bread and the other with light.

Chill well, slice, spread, and restack slices as shown into checkerboards. Chill and slice.

Roll-Ups: Slice extra-fresh bread, spread with a soft filling, roll, and use toothpick to secure. For interest, roll around a sprig of watercress or dill, a carrot or celery stick, cooked asparagus spear, or finger of ham, tongue, or cheese.

Pinwheels: Trim crusts from an unsliced loaf and slice thin lengthwise. Spread each slice with a colorful filling and roll up, jelly-roll style, from the short side. Wrap in dry toweling, chill several hours, then slice thin. (*Note:* If you use extra-fresh, soft bread, it should roll without cracking. Some cooks recommend flattening the bread with a rolling pin, but it shouldn't be necessary if the bread itself is soft. Besides, flattened bread tastes like damp cardboard.)

Decorated Open-Face Sandwiches: Trimmings can be as simple or lavish as time and talent permit: a sprig of dill or a tarragon leaf laid across the filling, an olive slice or fancy truffle cutout, or a showy piped-on design of cream cheese.

About Sandwich Garnishes

Party sandwiches demand garnishes, dainty doll-like ones; Danish sandwiches require something flashier than everyday lunch or supper sandwiches. They don't need trimmings, but how much handsomer they are when garnished. Some trimmings to try (these same garnishes can also be used to decorate meat, fish, and fowl platters):

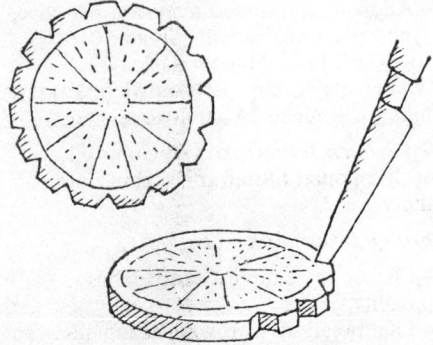

Cartwheels
Best for slices of cucumber, lemon, lime, or orange.

Radish Roses

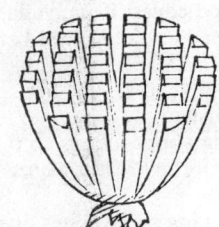

Radish Pompons
Cut, then crisp in ice water.

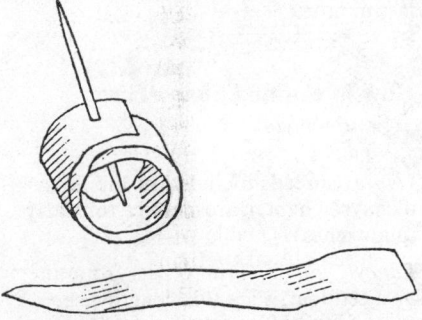

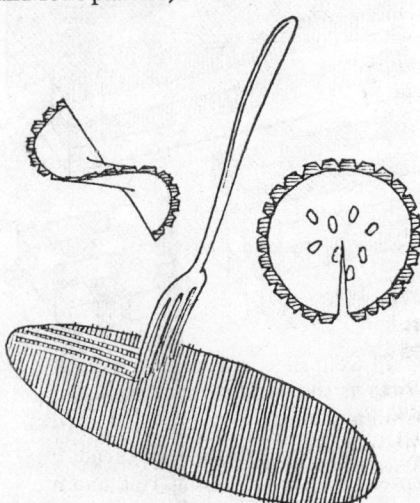

Twists or Butterflies
Thin slices of tomato, cucumber, beet, lemon, lime, and orange can all be shaped this way.

Carrot Curls
Bacon curls are rolled the same way. After cutting and rolling carrots, crisp in ice water.

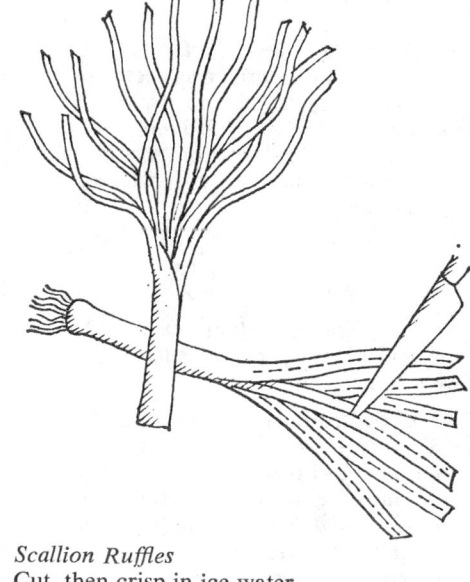

Celery Frills
Cut as shown above, then crisp in ice
water.

Hard-Cooked Egg (Slices, Wedges, and
Strips)

Anchovy Rolls and Strips

Onion Rings (Raw and French-Fried)

Herb Sprigs (Chervil, Chives, Dill,
Fennel, Cress, Parsley, Tarragon)

Scallion Ruffles
Cut, then crisp in ice water.

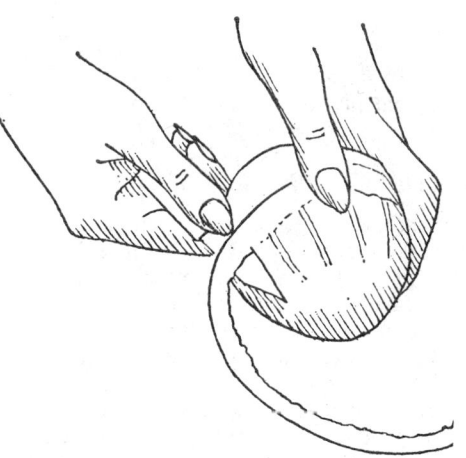

Pickle Fans

Rind Roses
With knife or vegetable peeler, peel a
long, continuous strip of rind, then roll
into a rose.

Cutouts (Truffle, Pimiento, Aspic,
Cooked Beet or Carrot, Hard-Cooked
Egg White work best. Cut out with
decorative truffle cutters.)

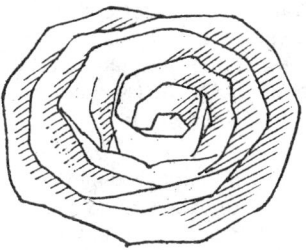

About Toasted Sandwiches

Any filling can be served on toasted bread, but favorites are bacon, lettuce and tomato, cheese, and creamy salad types—tuna salad, egg salad, chicken salad. Toast bread just before making sandwiches and don't stack, lest toast become soggy.

About Grilled Sandwiches

Best sandwiches to grill are those with fairly thick meat or cheese fillings that won't ooze out in the grilling.

How to Grill: Prepare sandwich as directed, then brown lightly 2–3 minutes on a side in 2–3 teaspoons butter or margarine over moderate heat. (*Note:* If you like, sandwich can be dipped in egg —1 egg lightly beaten with ¼ cup milk and a pinch each salt and pepper— then browned as directed. Increase amount of butter slightly if needed.)

About Freezing Sandwiches
(See chapter on freezing.)

Some Sandwiches to Try

What goes into a sandwich can be as exotic or basic as you like because there aren't any hard and fast rules. There are old favorites, of course—and the following list includes them as well as some less familiar combinations. Unless directions specify to the contrary, use any buttered bread or rolls, season fillings to taste with salt and pepper, and serve with a suitable garnish (see About Sandwich Garnishes).

Meat: (*Note:* Sliced hot or cold roast meat sandwiches, Hot Steak Sandwiches, Hamburgers, Sloppy Joes, and Frankfurters are all included elsewhere; see Index for page numbers.)

Basic Meat Salad: Mix any minced cooked meat with enough mayonnaise or salad dressing to make a good spreading consistency. For additional flavor, add any or a combination of the following (tasting as you mix): minced onion, celery, sweet or dill pickles, chives, or parsley; prepared mustard or horseradish; ketchup or chili sauce.

Meat Loaf: Slice any cold meat loaf, not too thin; spread with cold gravy or any of the following: prepared mustard or horseradish, mustard pickle or sweet pickle relish, chili sauce or ketchup. *Optionals:* Lettuce and sliced tomato. *Variations:* Team meat loaf with any of the following: sautéed sliced onions, pickled red cabbage, fried apple or pineapple rings, applesauce, minced chutney.

Hot Corned Beef or Pastrami: Slice thin and serve on rye bread spread with mustard.

Cold Corned Beef: Slice thin and serve on rye spread with mustard, topped with lettuce, sliced tomato, and mayonnaise. *Variations:* For the lettuce and tomato, substitute any of the following: egg salad, coleslaw, minced Harvard Beets, any sliced cheese or cheese spread.

Ham and Cheese: Sandwich thin slices boiled or baked ham and Swiss, American, or Cheddar cheese between bread spread with mustard and/or mayonnaise. Lettuce optional.

Cold Ham and Egg: Mix equal parts ground cooked ham and minced hard-cooked egg with enough mayonnaise and mustard to bind. Use as a spread. *Or* layer sliced ham and hard-cooked egg between bread spread with mayonnaise and mustard.

Hot Ham and Egg: Sandwich slices of fried ham and a fried egg (cooked until firm) between slices of buttered toast spread with mustard.

B.L.T.: Layer crisp bacon strips, sliced tomato, and lettuce between slices of toast spread with mayonnaise.

Bacon and Beans: Sandwich drained, mashed baked beans between slices of buttered toast with crisp bacon strips and, if you like, thin slices of Bermuda onion.

Poultry: (*Note:* Hot roast chicken or turkey sandwiches are included in the poultry chapter; see Index for page numbers.)

Basic Chicken or Turkey Salad: Follow directions for Basic Meat Salad; also see chapter on salads for specific recipes.

Curried Chicken or Turkey and Nuts: Mix minced or ground cooked chicken or turkey with minced toasted almonds, peanuts, or cashews, curry powder and grated onion to taste, and mayonnaise to bind. Use as a spread.

Chicken or Turkey and Apple: Mix minced or ground cooked chicken or turkey with minced apple, celery, and walnuts and enough mayonnaise to bind; use as a spread.

Chicken or Turkey and Cheese: Mix minced or ground cooked chicken or turkey with grated Swiss or Cheddar cheese, sweet pickle relish to taste, and mayonnaise to bind. Use as a spread.

Chicken or Turkey and Ham: Mix equal parts minced or ground cooked chicken or turkey with minced cooked ham (or tongue, bologna, or other cold cuts), minced scallions or onion to taste, and mayonnaise to bind. Use as a spread.

Sliced Cold Chicken or Turkey: Layer between slices of buttered bread or toast with sliced tomato, lettuce, and mayonnaise. *Optionals:* Any cold cuts or sliced cheese.

Chicken and Avocado: Sandwich slices of cold chicken between slices of bread lavishly spread with Guacamole.

Chopped Chicken Liver: Mince sautéed chicken livers, mix with enough melted butter or mayonnaise to bind, and season, if you like, with a little minced onion. Use as a spread. *Optional:* Mix in a little crisp, crumbled bacon.

Seafood: (*Note:* Hot Crab Burgers, Angels on Horseback, Individual Oyster Loaves, and other specific seafood sandwiches are included in the seafood chapter; see Index for page numbers.)

Basic Seafood Salad: Mix any flaked cooked fish (tuna, salmon, haddock, or other delicate white fish) or minced cooked shellfish (shrimp, lobster, crab, etc.) with enough mayonnaise, Tartar Sauce, or Rémoulade Sauce to bind. *Some Good Additions:* Minced hard-cooked egg; minced onion and celery; minced parsley, tarragon, chervil, or dill; lemon juice; capers; curry powder. (Also see Salads for specific recipes.)

Hot Seafood Sandwiches: Sandwich any fish sticks or cakes, any breaded or batter-fried fish or shellfish between slices of bread or into buns spread with Tartar Sauce or Rémoulade Sauce.

Egg:

Basic Egg Salad: Mix minced hard-cooked eggs with enough mayonnaise or relish-type sandwich spread to bind. *Some Good Additions:* Minced onion and celery; minced dill or sweet pickle; minced parsley, tarragon, chervil, dill, or marjoram; grated Cheddar or Swiss cheese; crisp crumbled bacon; minced ripe or pimiento-stuffed olives; prepared mustard or horseradish. Taste as you mix until flavors seem "just right." (Also see salad chapter for specific recipes.)

Fried Egg: Sandwich a fried egg (cooked until firm) between slices of buttered toast. *Optionals:* Sliced tomato, lettuce, minced scallions, grated Parmesan cheese.

Scrambled Egg or Omelet: Sandwich firmly cooked scrambled eggs or any small omelet between buttered toast or buns. *Optionals:* Hollandaise Sauce and/ or minced, buttered spinach.

Cheese:

Plain Cheese: Sandwich any thinly sliced cheese between slices of bread spread with butter or mayonnaise and, if you like, mustard. *Optionals:* Lettuce and sliced tomato; any cold cuts.

Grilled Cheese Sandwich: Make a Plain Cheese Sandwich and grill (see How to Grill Sandwiches).

Toasted Cheese Sandwich: (see Cheese Dreams).

Some Spreads to Make with Grated Cheese: Mix coarsely grated Cheddar, American, or Swiss cheese with enough mayonnaise or salad dressing to bind, then add any of the following for flavor: minced pickles, grated onion, crumbled bacon, minced, cooked ham or cold cuts, minced chutney and ground almonds or peanuts. For piquancy, add prepared mustard or horseradish, ketchup or Worcestershire, tasting as you mix.

Cream Cheese and Jelly: Spread any bread with cream cheese, then any jam, jelly, preserves, or marmalade. *Optionals:* Any minced nuts; raisins or minced, pitted dates, prunes, dried figs or apricots.

Cream Cheese and Bacon: Sandwich toast together with cream cheese and crisp crumbled bacon. *Optionals:* Minced ripe or pimiento-stuffed olives; minced, sautéed chicken livers; deviled ham; shrimp or anchovy paste; sliced tomatoes or cucumbers.

Peanut Butter:

Peanut Butter and Jelly: Sandwich buttered bread together with creamy or crunchy peanut butter and any tart jelly, jam, or preserves.

Peanut Butter and Bacon: Sandwich buttered toast together with creamy or crunchy peanut butter and crisp, crumbled bacon. *Optionals:* Lettuce and sliced tomato.

Some Other Things to Team with Peanut Butter: Minced ripe or pimiento-stuffed olives mixed with minced celery and sweet pickle; mashed or sliced ripe bananas; crushed pineapple and flaked coconut; chutney and minced hard-cooked egg or grated Cheddar; seedless raisins and mayonnaise; applesauce and marshmallow cream (children love this one); grated carrot and raisins.

Vegetables:

Lettuce: Sandwich any crisp lettuce leaves between slices of bread spread with mayonnaise or other salad dressing.

Lettuce and Tomato: Layer sliced tomatoes and crisp lettuce leaves between slices of bread spread with mayonnaise or other salad dressing.

Cucumber: Layer thinly sliced cucumbers (sprinkled lightly with vinegar if you like) between buttered slices of bread.

Tomato and Onion: Layer thinly sliced tomatoes and Bermuda onion between slices of bread or toast spread with butter or mayonnaise.

Potato and Pepper: Layer thinly sliced, boiled new potatoes, Bermuda onion, and sweet green or red pepper between slices of bread spread with mayonnaise or relish-type sandwich spread. *Variation:* Substitute Roquefort or Thousand Island Dressing or sour cream for the mayonnaise.

Baked Bean: Spread slices of Boston Brown Bread with cream cheese, mound with cold baked beans, top with a bacon slice, and serve open face.

Mushroom: Sandwich sautéed, sliced mushrooms between slices of bread or toast spread with chive cheese.

Carrot and Raisin: Combine grated carrots and seedless raisins with enough mayonnaise to bind and use as a spread. *Optionals:* A little minced, cooked chicken, turkey, or ham; minced apple.

Club Sandwiches

Whole meals sandwiched between 2 or 3 slices of bread or toast. Junior clubs have similar, though abbreviated, fillings and 2 slices of bread only. Here are some popular combinations with ingredients listed *in order from the bottom up.* Simply build up layers, salting and peppering as you go. When sandwiches are assembled, toothpick layers together at all 4 corners, then halve or quarter diagonally. Cover toothpick ends with olives, cocktail onions, or chunks of pickle.

Simple Club
Buttered slice of white toast
Slice of roast chicken or turkey
Slice of white toast spread with
mayonnaise (both sides)
Lettuce leaves
Sliced tomato
Crisp bacon strips
Buttered slice of white toast

Country Club
Slice of cracked wheat toast spread with
relish-type sandwich spread
Slice of Swiss cheese
Slice of boiled ham spread with mustard
Buttered slice of white toast (both sides)
Slice of roast chicken or turkey
Thin slice of cranberry jelly
Crisp romaine leaves
Crisp bacon strips
Buttered slice of cracked wheat toast

Pink Lady Club
Slice of white toast spread with tartar
sauce
Minced, cooked shrimp or lobster
Buttered (both sides) rye toast trimmed
of crusts
Sliced chicken roll or roast chicken
Sliced tomato and watercress sprigs
Slice of white toast spread with
mayonnaise

King Club
Slice of buttered rye bread
Sour cream mixed with horseradish
Slice of roast beef
Crumbled French fried onion rings
Buttered slice of rye bread (both sides)
Slice of Roquefort or blue cheese
Potato salad
Slice of rye bread

Italian Double Decker
Buttered slice of Italian bread
Anchovy fillets
Sliced hard-cooked egg
Sliced pimiento-stuffed olives drizzled
with Italian dressing
Buttered slice of Italian bread (both
sides)
Slice of mozzarella or provolone cheese

Slice of salami or prosciutto ham
Minced hot red pepper
Slice of Italian bread spread with
mayonnaise

Deli Double Decker
Slice of pumpernickel spread with pâté,
chopped liver, or liverwurst
Slice of Bermuda onion
Sliced dill pickles
Slice of pumpernickel buttered (both
sides)
Slice of roast turkey spread with Russian
dressing
Slice of pumpernickel

Alligator Triple Decker
Buttered slice of whole wheat toast
Boneless sardines sprinkled with capers
Slice of buttered whole wheat toast
(both sides)
Sliced avocado
Sliced tomato spread with Green
Goddess Dressing
Slice of whole wheat toast
Tuna salad
Slice of whole wheat toast

Barney's Triple Decker
Buttered slice of rye bread
Slice of corned beef spread with mustard
Drained sauerkraut
Slice of pumpernickel spread with
mayonnaise (both sides)
Sliced hard-cooked egg
Minced scallions
Sliced cucumber
Slice of buttered rye bread (both sides)
Slice of pastrami
Shredded lettuce
Slice of pumpernickel spread with
mayonnaise

Opera Club
Slice of party rye bread spread with
cream cheese
Red caviar
Slice of party rye bread with chive
cheese
Slice of smoked salmon or smoked
sturgeon
Wilted cucumbers sprinkled with minced
fresh dill
Slice of party rye spread with
mayonnaise

Heroes or Submarines

Sandwiches Italian-style, whoppers filled to overflowing with sausages, cheeses, peppers—and any of a dozen other things. Begin with split and buttered small Italian loaves or hard rolls, then build up layers, adding anything you fancy. Here are some good combinations, some Italian, some American:

– Slices of prosciutto, provolone cheese, and fried eggplant spread with mustard and chili sauce.
– Slices of Cheddar cheese, dill pickles, Spanish or Italian onion, boiled ham, salami, or liverwurst and tomato, green pepper rings, and shredded lettuce spread with mayonnaise or drizzled with Italian dressing.
– Slices of chicken roll or roast chicken spread with deviled ham; slices of Muenster cheese, cucumbers, and bologna spread with mayonnaise and sprinkled with minced scallions.
– Egg salad, slices of tomato and corned beef.
– Instead of buttering bread or rolls, brush with olive oil and sprinkle with garlic salt; add slices of mozzarella cheese, tomato, and salami, then anchovy fillets and Caponata or hot, sautéed, sliced sweet red peppers. Serve as is or, if you like, wrap in foil and bake 20 minutes at 400° F.

Danish Sandwiches

Lovely to look at and fun to construct. Nearly any combination of bread, meat, filling, and garnish can be used in making these open-face works of art. Here are half a dozen popular combinations, all to be eaten with knife and fork.

– Butter a slice of rye bread and top with a slice of pâté. Mound a few sautéed, sliced mushrooms in the center and lay a crisp bacon strip diagonally across. Place a gherkin fan to one side, tuck a small lettuce leaf underneath, and garnish with a twisted slice of tomato.
– Butter a slice of white bread and top with 2–3 paper thin slices rare roast beef, crumpling slightly instead of laying flat. Add a small lettuce leaf, top with a dollop of Béarnaise, lay a twisted slice of tomato in the center, and add a few shreds of grated horseradish and crumbles of French-fried onions. Garnish with a pickle fan.
– Spread a slice of white or brown bread with unsalted butter or mayonnaise, mound with tiny Danish shrimp, top with cucumber and lemon slices.
– Spread a slice of rye or pumpernickel with butter, mound tissue-thin slices of corned beef on top. Add a twisted slice of tomato, a dill pickle fan, and a few shreds of grated horseradish.
– Spread the bottom half of a soft round bun with butter, top with thin circles of boiled ham, then mound with shrimp or other seafood salad. Garnish with twisted slices of tomato and cucumber, a frill of crinkly lettuce, and slices of hard-cooked egg.
– Spread a slice of pumpernickel with unsalted butter, top with pickled herring, small crisp onion rings, and slices of cherry tomato. Tuck a lettuce leaf to one side and add a sprig of watercress.

PIMIENTO CHEESE SPREAD

Makes about 1¾ cups, enough for 6–8 sandwiches

3 cups coarsely grated sharp Cheddar
  cheese
2 tablespoons finely grated onion
⅓ cup minced pimiento
½ cup mayonnaise
1 teaspoon prepared spicy brown
  mustard
1 tablespoon milk or light cream

Mix all ingredients, then beat with a fork until creamy. Cover and let "ripen" in the refrigerator several hours or, better still, overnight. Use as a spread for any bread. About 495 calories for each of 6 sandwiches (2 slices white bread, no butter or mayonnaise), 390 for each of 8 sandwiches.

CREAM CHEESE AND OLIVE SPREAD

Makes about 1 cup, enough for 4 sandwiches

1 (8-ounce) package cream cheese, softened to room temperature
½ cup minced pimiento-stuffed green olives
2 tablespoons milk or light cream
1 teaspoon prepared spicy brown mustard

Beat all ingredients with a fork until creamy, cover, and chill 2–3 hours. Let stand at room temperature 15–20 minutes and use as a spread for any bread. About 355 calories per sandwich (2 slices white bread, no butter or mayonnaise).

⊠ CREAM CHEESE AND WATERCRESS SPREAD

Makes about 1½ cups, enough for 4–6 sandwiches

1 (8-ounce) package cream cheese, softened to room temperature
½ cup minced watercress leaves
1 tablespoon grated onion
⅛ teaspoon white pepper

Cream all ingredients together until light and use as a sandwich spread. Especially good for dainty afternoon tea sandwiches. This recipe makes enough filling for 2–2½ dozen tea sandwiches. About 335 calories for each of 4 sandwiches (2 slices bread, no butter or mayonnaise), 265 calories for each of 6 sandwiches, and 35 calories for each tea sandwich.

⊠ EGG AND PARMESAN SANDWICH SPREAD

Makes about 1½ cups, enough for 4–6 sandwiches

4 hard-cooked eggs, peeled and coarsely chopped
¼ cup mayonnaise
¼ cup grated Parmesan cheese
½ teaspoon salt
⅛ teaspoon pepper

Blend all ingredients together and use as a spread for any type of bread. About 370 calories for each of 4 sandwiches (2 slices bread, no butter or mayonnaise), 285 calories for each of 6 sandwiches.

BEEF AND CHEESE SPREAD

Makes about 1 cup, enough for 4 sandwiches

1 (8-ounce) package cream cheese, softened to room temperature
1 (3-ounce) package chipped beef, minced
2 tablespoons minced onion

Mix all ingredients well with a fork and use as a spread for any bread. (Note: This spread will be more flavorful if "ripened" in the refrigerator several hours or, better still, overnight.) About 380 calories per sandwich (2 slices bread, no butter or mayonnaise).

⊠ TONGUE AND CHUTNEY SPREAD

Makes about 2 cups, enough for 6–8 sandwiches

1 (1-pound) can tongue, chilled and cut in ¼″ cubes
½ cup minced chutney
1 small sweet apple, peeled, cored, and minced

Mix all ingredients and use as a spread for white, whole wheat, or rye bread. About 395 calories for each of 6 sandwiches (2 slices bread, no butter or mayonnaise), 325 calories for each of 8 sandwiches.

⊠ SALMON-CAPER SPREAD

Makes about 1½ cups, enough for 6 sandwiches

1 (1-pound) can salmon, drained
3 tablespoons mayonnaise
2 teaspoons tarragon vinegar
2 teaspoons minced capers
2 tablespoons minced chives

Pick over salmon, discarding any coarse bones and dark skin; mash well. Blend in remaining ingredients and use as a spread for white or brown bread. About 300 calories per sandwich (2 slices bread, no butter or mayonnaise).

WHITSTABLE SANDWICH SPREAD

Whitstable is a little fishing village east of London famous for its tiny shrimp. Women here make lovely tea sandwiches filled with Whitstable shrimp, minced watercress, scallions, and hard-cooked eggs.
Makes about 2 cups, enough for 6–8 sandwiches

1 cup cooked, shelled, and deveined
* shrimp, coarsely chopped*
½ cup minced watercress
¼ cup minced scallions (include some
* tops)*
2 hard-cooked eggs, peeled and coarsely
* chopped*
2 tablespoons French dressing

Toss all ingredients together lightly and use as a sandwich spread for white or brown bread. About 205 calories for each of 6 sandwiches (2 slices bread, no butter or mayonnaise), 185 calories for each of 8 sandwiches.

DATE FILLING

Good with moist, sweet breads spread with cream cheese.
Makes 1½ cups, enough for 1½ dozen small sandwiches

1 (8-ounce) package pitted dates,
* coarsely chopped*
½ cup water
¼ cup sugar
2 tablespoons lemon juice
. ⅓ cup minced pecans, walnuts, or
* blanched almonds*

Simmer dates, water, sugar, and lemon juice, uncovered, about 15 minutes, stirring now and then, until thick. Cool, mix in nuts, and use as a spread for tea sandwiches. About 65 calories per small tea sandwich (2 slices bread, no butter or cream cheese).

VARIATION:

Fig, Apricot, or Prune Filling: Prepare as directed, substituting pitted prunes, dried figs or apricots for the dates. About 65 calories per small tea sandwich (2 slices bread, no butter or cream cheese).

⊠ CHEESE DREAMS

Makes 2 servings

4 strips bacon, halved crosswise
4 slices white or whole wheat bread
4 teaspoons butter or margarine
4 sandwich-size slices American cheese
⅛ teaspoon oregano

Preheat broiler. Fry bacon until it begins to curl and turn golden; drain on paper toweling. Toast bread in broiler 4–5" from heat 3–4 minutes until golden brown; turn and toast 1 minute on second side. Butter lightly toasted sides, top with cheese, a sprinkling of oregano, and bacon. Broil 4–5" from heat 3–4 minutes until bacon is crisp and cheese melted. Serve piping hot. About 250 calories per serving.

HAWAIIAN CHICKEN SANDWICHES

Makes 6 servings

2 cups minced, cooked chicken meat
⅓ cup minced celery
⅓ cup mayonnaise
½–1 teaspoon salt
¼ teaspoon white pepper
¼ cup finely chopped pecans
6 large round hard rolls
6 pineapple rings, drained well
⅓ cup grated mild Cheddar cheese

Preheat broiler. Mix chicken, celery, mayonnaise, ½ teaspoon salt, pepper, and pecans. Taste for salt and add more if needed. Slice tops off rolls and pull out soft centers—hollows should be large enough to hold about ½ cup chicken mixture. (Save centers for bread crumbs.) Fill rolls with chicken mixture, top with pineapple, and sprinkle with cheese. Broil 3–4" from heat 2–3 minutes until cheese melts. About 430 calories per serving.

DIVAN SANDWICHES

Makes 4 sandwiches

4 slices hot buttered toast
1 (1-pound) can white asparagus spears,
*   drained*
4 slices cold roast turkey, chicken, or
*   ham*
½ cup mayonnaise
1 pimiento, minced
1 tablespoon lemon juice
2 egg whites, beaten to soft peaks

Preheat broiler. Lay toast, buttered sides
up, on rack in broiler pan; top with
asparagus and turkey. Mix mayonnaise,
lemon juice, and pimiento; fold in egg
whites and spread evenly over turkey,
right to edges of toast. Broil 6–7″
from heat about 5 minutes until flecked
with brown and puffy. Or, if you prefer,
bake 3–5 minutes at 450° F. instead of
broiling. About 410 calories per
sandwich.

WESTERN SANDWICHES

Makes 2 sandwiches

¼ cup minced cooked ham
¼ cup minced yellow onion
¼ cup minced sweet green pepper
1 tablespoon butter or margarine
2 eggs, lightly beaten
2 tablespoons cold water
⅛ teaspoon salt
Pinch pepper
4 slices hot buttered toast, buttered
*   bread, or 2 hard rolls, split in half.*

Stir-fry ham, onion, and green pepper in
butter in a heavy 9″ skillet over
moderate heat 2–3 minutes until onion is
limp. Mix eggs, water, salt, and pepper,
pour into skillet and fry like a pancake
until firm and lightly browned
underneath; turn and brown flip side.
Halve and sandwich between toast,
folding as needed to fit. About 295
calories per sandwich.

POTTED SALMON SANDWICHES

Makes about 1¼ cups filling, enough for
4–6 sandwiches

1 (7¾-ounce) can salmon, drained

1 tablespoon anchovy paste
1 tablespoon lemon juice
Pinch cayenne pepper
⅛ teaspoon cloves
¼ cup butter or margarine, softened to
*   room temperature*
8–12 slices firm-textured white or brown
*   bread*
½ medium-size cucumber, peeled and
*   sliced paper thin*

Pick over salmon, discarding any coarse
bones and dark skin; mash with a fork.
Add all remaining ingredients except
bread and cucumber, mix well to form a
smooth paste. Spread *each* slice of
bread with salmon, cover half the slices
with cucumber, and top with remaining
bread. (*Note:* Make these sandwiches
shortly before serving—they become
soggy on standing.) About 310 calories
for each of 4 sandwiches (2 slices bread,
no butter or mayonnaise), 245 calories
for each of 6 sandwiches.

MONTE CRISTO SANDWICHES

Crisply grilled chicken (or turkey) and
cheese sandwiches.
Makes 1 sandwich

4 tablespoons butter or margarine
*   (about), softened to room temperature*
3 slices firm-textured white bread
2 slices cold roast chicken or turkey
2 slices Monterey Jack, Swiss, or
*   Cheddar cheese*
1 egg, lightly beaten
¼ cup milk
⅛ teaspoon salt

Butter bread, 2 slices on 1 side only, 1
slice on both sides. Lay chicken on a
buttered slice, top with doubly buttered
slice, cheese, and last slice, buttered side
down. Press together lightly; if you like,
trim off crusts. Mix egg, milk, and salt,
dip in sandwich, coating edges as well as
sides. Heat 2 tablespoons butter in a
skillet or griddle and brown sandwich
over moderately low heat about 2
minutes on each side. About 935 calories
per sandwich.

VARIATIONS:

Monte Carlo: Prepare as directed but

substitute boiled smoked tongue or ham for the chicken. About 940 calories per sandwich.

Cocktail Monte Cristos: Prepare sandwich as directed, cut in 1″ cubes, dip in egg, and fry. Serve with toothpicks as a cocktail snack. About 100 calories each cocktail sandwich.

MOZZARELLA IN CARROZZA (MOZZARELLA IN A CARRIAGE)

Hearty enough for lunch or supper.
Makes 6 servings

Sauce:

½ cup butter or margarine
¼ cup lemon juice
2 tablespoons minced, drained capers
2 tablespoons minced parsley
6 anchovy fillets, finely chopped

Sandwiches:

6 (¼ inch) slices mozzarella cheese
12 slices Italian-style or firm-textured, day-old white bread, trimmed of crusts
⅓ cup milk or evaporated milk
⅓ cup toasted bread crumbs
¾ cup olive or other cooking oil (about)
¼ cup butter or margarine
3 eggs, lightly beaten

Heat all sauce ingredients, uncovered, over low heat 15 minutes. Cover and keep warm at the back of the stove. Sandwich each slice of mozzarella between 2 slices of bread, then trim so edges of bread are even with cheese. Or, using a large round cookie cutter, cut bread and cheese so they are the same size. Dip edges of each sandwich in milk, then in crumbs to coat evenly. Heat oil and butter in a large, heavy skillet over moderately high heat about 1 minute. (*Note:* Oil should be about 1″ deep in skillet, so add more if necessary.) Dip sandwiches in beaten eggs to coat well, then fry, a few at a time, in oil about 1 minute on each side until golden brown. Drain on paper toweling. Serve hot, topped with some of the sauce. About 460 calories per serving.

VARIATION:

Prepare as directed, adding a cut-to-fit slice cooked ham to each sandwich. About 530 calories per serving.

⊠ HAM AND CHEESE CRESCENTS

A quick, hearty lunch or snack.
Makes 4 servings

1 (8-ounce) package refrigerated dough for crescent rolls
4 teaspoons prepared mild yellow mustard
3 thin sandwich-size slices lean boiled ham, each cut in 3 equal-size pieces
½ cup coarsely grated sharp Cheddar cheese

Preheat oven to 375° F. Spread each triangle of dough with mustard, top with ham, and sprinkle with cheese; roll up jelly-roll fashion and make into crescent shapes following package directions. Arrange on an ungreased baking sheet and bake 15–20 minutes until lightly browned. About 315 calories per serving.

CHEESE TACOS

Makes 6 servings

¼ cup lard or shortening
6 Tortillas (homemade or packaged)

Filling:

6 slices American, Cheddar, or Monterey Jack cheese, coarsely cut up
¼ cup minced yellow onion
1 teaspoon chili powder

Heat lard in a large, heavy skillet over moderate heat and dip in each tortilla 1 or 2 seconds just to soften; spread flat on a baking sheet. Top with cheese and onion and sprinkle with chili powder. Fold in half and fasten with toothpicks. Fry in lard over moderately high heat about 1 minute per side until dappled with brown; drain on paper toweling, and serve. Or, if you prefer, instead of frying, bake uncovered 15 minutes at 400° F. until brown and crisp. About 200 calories per serving.

VARIATIONS:

Chicken Tacos: Omit filling above; fill tortillas with minced, cooked chicken (or pork or beef) moistened with canned enchilada or taco sauce; fold and fry as directed. Serve with sliced radishes, avocado, and shredded lettuce. About 250 calories per serving.

Sausage Tacos: Omit filling above; fill tortillas with minced sautéed chorizo sausage mixed with a little minced onion; fold and fry as directed. About 270 calories per serving.

Bean Tacos: Omit filling above; fill tortillas with Fried or Refried Beans, fold and fry as directed. About 275 calories per serving.

CHAPTER 20

DESSERTS AND DESSERT SAUCES

The category of desserts includes everything from lavish architectural confections to humble bread puddings. There are fruit desserts, puddings hot and cold, ice creams and sherbets, sweet omelets and crepes.

When choosing a dessert, consider the balance of the menu. The richer the main course, the simpler the dessert should be. Cold weather calls for something hot and hearty, summer something cool and light. If the entree contains little protein, add a dessert made with milk, cream, eggs, or cheese. Remember, too, that all desserts don't zoom off the upper limits of the calorie scale. A number included here are well below 100 calories per serving.

Some Ways to Garnish Desserts

Desserts do not demand garnishes, but for a dinner party you may want to glamorize them a bit (opposite).

FRUIT DESSERTS

Once highly seasonal and available primarily where grown, fresh fruits are abundant today around most of the country and much of the calendar. Moreover, such tropical exotics as mangoes, papayas, and passion fruits are beginning to appear in supermarket fruit bins alongside apples and oranges.

Fruits are unusually adaptable; they team well with one another, many can be poached, baked, broiled, or sautéed as well as served *au naturel*. A fruit dessert may be as unpretentious as a pear, crisp and tart, served with a chunk of

Cheddar, or as theatrical as Cherries Jubilee, carried flaming into a darkened room. It may be low-calorie (sliced oranges sprinkled with freshly minced mint) or high (strawberry shortcake drifted with whipped cream). Whatever the dessert, the fruit should look luscious, fresh, and plump, never fussed over—or left over.

The following directory describes favorite fruits (and a few not so well known), recommends which to cook (and how to cook them), which to serve raw, offers calorie counts and shopping tips.

Some Simple, Basic Ways of Preparing and Serving Fruit

About Peeling, Coring, and Seeding Fruit: Use a stainless-steel knife to prevent fruit from darkening and prepare fruit as you need it, not ahead of time.

Garnish	Appropriate Desserts
Mint, rose geranium, or lemon verbena sprigs	Fruit cups, compotes, ices, sherbets
Lemon or orange wedges, slices or twists, mandarin orange sections	Fruit cups and compotes, lemon or orange puddings, ices, sherbets
Clusters of grapes or berries. (*Note:* for a festive touch, frost by dipping in beaten egg white, then in sugar; let dry thoroughly before using.)	Fruit cups and compotes, steamed fruit puddings
Mini Fruit Kebabs (small pineapple cubes, any firm-ripe grapes, cherries, or berries alternated on toothpicks)	Fruit compotes, steamed fruit puddings, fruit ice cream mousses and bombes
Preserved kumquats	Hot or cold fruit compotes, stewed fruits
Minced crystallized ginger or candied fruits	Vanilla or fruit custards or stirred puddings, fruit sherbets, or ice creams
Flaked or toasted coconut	Fruit cups or compotes, also chocolate, vanilla, or caramel puddings
Minced nuts	Chocolate, vanilla, or caramel puddings
Chocolate curls*	Chocolate, vanilla, caramel, mocha, or coffee puddings or ice creams
Clusters or wreaths of minced or cubed fruit-flavored gelatin	Molded gelatin desserts

Apples, Pears, Figs, and Other Thin, Hard-Skinned Fruits: Use a vegetable peeler or paring knife, paring as thinly as possible. If apples are to be left whole, core with an apple corer, then peel. Otherwise, halve or quarter and cut out core with a paring knife. Pears should be treated the same way; be sure to trim away all gritty flesh surrounding core.

Peaches, Apricots, Nectarines: Plunge fruit in boiling water, let stand about 1 minute, then plunge in cold water and slip off skins. If fruits are to be used whole, do not pit; otherwise, halve and lift pit out.

Citrus Fruits: Cut a thin slice off stem end, then with a paring knife or grapefruit knife cut away rind in an unbroken spiral, taking as much bitter white pith with it as possible.

Grapes: Slit skins lengthwise and "pop" grapes out. To seed, halve and scoop seeds out.

Pineapple: Slice off top and bottom; stand pineapple on counter, and peel straight down from top to bottom.

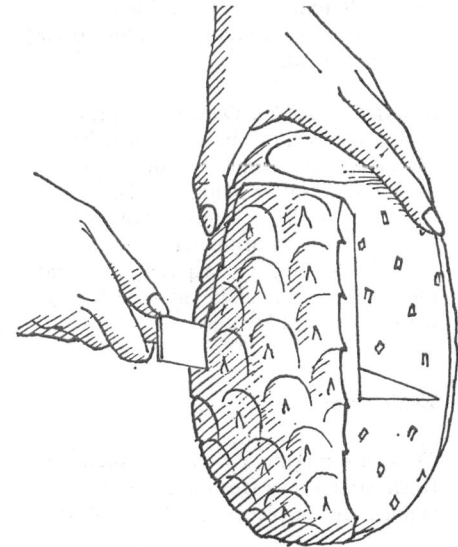

To get the "eyes" out, either (1) make spiral, grooved cuts as shown,

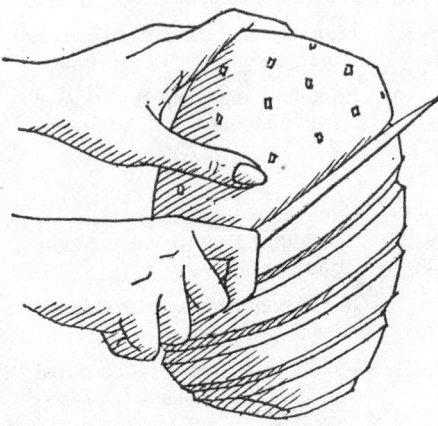

following line of eyes, or (2) peel fruit and dig eyes out with the point of a vegetable peeler or knife. *To core:* If pineapple is to be cut in rings, peel and slice, then cut core from each. Otherwise, quarter pineapple lengthwise, then slice off cores—they will be at the point of each quarter.

Avocados: If really ripe, skin can be pulled off with the hands. If firm, halve avocado lengthwise, twist out seed, halve each half lengthwise, and pull or cut skin from each quarter.

Others: Bananas are no problem. Cherries, berries, plums, etc., are usually eaten unpeeled.

About Fruits That Darken: Apples, apricots, avocados, bananas, peaches, nectarines, and some varieties of pear and plum darken after being cut. To keep them bright, dip in lemon or other citrus juice or in an ascorbic acid solution made by mixing ½ teaspoon powdered ascorbic acid (available at drugstores) with ½ cup cold water.

Fruit Cups

These are mixtures of fruit, sometimes fresh, sometimes fresh and frozen or canned, cut in pieces small enough to eat in one bite. For especially pretty fruit cups, team 3–4 fruits of contrasting color, size, shape, and texture: oranges, pineapple, strawberries, and grapes, for example: bananas, tangerines, peaches, and cherries or melon balls; avocado, grapefruit, pears, and plums. For added flavor, mix in a little orange, apple, or pineapple juice, slivered crystallized ginger, grated coconut, minced mint, rose geranium, or lemon verbena. Or, if you prefer, spike with sweet sherry, port or Madeira, or with a fruit liqueur.

Macédoine of Fruit

Named after ancient Macedonia, where fruit desserts were popular, macédoines are mixtures of prettily cut fruits marinated in wine or liqueur. Choose any fresh plump ripe fruits, pare, core, and slice or cube. Layer into a large bowl, sprinkling as you go with superfine sugar, then drizzle with kirsch, Cointreau, Grand Marnier, curaçao, maraschino, other fruit liqueur, or, if you prefer, a fine cognac or brandy. Cover and chill 2–3 hours before serving. Some appealing mixtures:

– Thinly sliced strawberries, pineapple, seedless green grapes with Cointreau.
– Thinly sliced pineapple, pears, and peaches with Grand Marnier or white crème de menthe.
– Sliced oranges with cognac, Grand Marnier, or curaçao.
– Thinly sliced apricots, bananas, and strawberries with kirsch or Cointreau.

Serve macédoines cold, set in a large bowl of crushed ice, or flame.

To Flame: First of all, arrange fruits in a flameproof bowl. After chilling, bring macédoine to room temperature. Warm about ¼ cup brandy, rum, or cognac over low heat about 1 minute, pour over fruit and blaze with a match—stand back, mixture will burst into flames. Serve at once.

Fruit Fools

Wonderfully easy old-fashioned desserts, the kind Grandma served when she had sun-ripened fruits and lots of thick country cream. They are equal parts sweetened fruits and heavy cream, sometimes whipped, sometimes not. Sweet berries make glorious fruit fools; so do soft-ripe peaches and apricots, stewed apples and rhubarb. Fruit purées, if really thick, can be mixed ½ and ½ with whipped cream. A mock but very good fool can be made by combining equal parts fruit and mushy vanilla ice cream. Serve fruit fools unadorned or, for a company touch, scattered with minced pistachios or toasted almonds, slivered preserved ginger, crumbled sugar cookies, gingersnaps, or macaroons.

Fruit Purées

Any soft fruit, raw or stewed, purées well. Force through a fine sieve, a food mill or whirl in an electric blender at high speed (berry purées should be sieved to remove seeds). Serve as is or as a sauce over ice creams or puddings.

Broiled and Sautéed (Fried) Fruits
(See separate recipes that follow.)

Fruit Kebabs

Choose fairly firm but fleshy raw or canned fruits—1″ cubes of apricot, peach, pear, or pineapple, thick banana slices, seedless grapes, sweet cherries— and alternate colorful combinations on short metal skewers. Drizzle with honey or light corn syrup (or Heavy Poaching Syrup) and melted butter. Broil about 4″ from the heat 3–5 minutes, turning and brushing often with additional honey and melted butter. Serve sizzling hot.

About Serving Fruit with Cheese
(See chapter on eggs and cheese.)

About Canned and Frozen Fruits

Nearly all popular fruits—and a number of unusual ones like lichees and papayas —are canned and/or frozen. Some are packed in syrup, others in water for the diet conscious. These are most suitable for compotes and fruit cups, for serving over or under ice creams and puddings. Canned peach, apricot, and pear halves bake and broil well (follow directions for fresh fruits, reducing times slightly).

About Dried Fruits

In the dim days of history, man learned that fruits dried under the sun kept well many months. Today the drying is done mechanically, producing plump, moist, ready-to-use fruits: prunes (dried plums), dates, apricots, raisins (dried grapes). Other commonly dried fruits are apples, currants, peaches, pears, nectarines, and figs.

Dates, raisins, and currants are not cooked except as they are used in breads, cakes, puddings, and pies. Prunes, figs, apricots, and peaches (especially the extra-soft "tenderized" ones) can be used straight from the package or they may be stewed. Dried apples and pears, being a good deal drier, must be cooked.

About Soaking Dried Fruits: Modern techniques have very nearly made soaking a thing of the past. Read and follow label directions carefully. Soaking too long or in too much water makes fruits mushy and flavorless.

About Stewing Dried Fruits:

Apples and Pears: Soak or not as package label directs. Place in a large saucepan, add cold water to cover, set over moderate heat, cover, and simmer about 40 minutes until tender. Sweeten, if you like, adding ¼–⅓ cup sugar per cup of fruit. *For Extra Flavor:* Tuck a couple of lemon slices down into fruit, or a cinnamon stick, or several mint or rose geranium sprigs.

Apricots, Peaches, and Nectarines: Soak or not as directed. Place in a large saucepan, cover with cold water, cover pan, and simmer 40–45 minutes until tender. Sweeten, if you like, using 3–4 tablespoons sugar per cup of fruit.

(continued on page 1021)

Fruit	Description and Season	Buying Tips	Nutritive Value	Best Uses / Preparation Tips
Apples (all-purpose varieties):	*The following pie apples: Jonathan, McIntosh, Northern Spy, Stayman, Winesap, Yellow Transparent, York Imperial* (see About Pie Apples, chapter on pies and pastries, for descriptions)	Regardless of type, select firm, fragrant, bruise- and blemish-free apples. Suit variety to use. As a rule, tart crisp apples are best for cooking, sweet, juicy ones are best for eating raw. "Windfalls," often offered as bargains, are perfect for applesauce, apple butter, jams, and jellies.	All apples contain some vitamin A, calcium, and phosphorous, large amounts of potassium. About 70 calories per medium-size apple.	Eating out-of-hand; raw in salads, desserts; general cooking. *Tip:* Unless dipped in lemon or other tart fruit juice, apples will turn brown after being cut open.
	Baldwin: Round, mottled red; juicy, tart-sweet. SEASON: November-April			
	Cortland: Round, red, carmine-striped; tart, snowy flesh that doesn't brown after cutting. SEASON: October-December			
	Gravenstein: Round, red-flecked yellow-green; tart, juicy. SEASON: July-September			
	Grimes Golden: Round, gold with brown flecks; juicy, sweet, crisp-tender. SEASON: October-February			
	Wealthy: Round, bright red; sweet, juicy. SEASON: August-December			
Apples (cooking varieties):	*All pie apples* (see Pies and Pastries)			
	Rome Beauty: Plump, round, red, tart; hold shape in cooking. SEASON: November-May			Baked apples
Apples (eating varieties):	*Delicious (Golden and Red):* Big, long, yellow or red; juicy-sweet. SEASON: September-April			*Tips:* Vegetable peelers speed apple peeling; corers and corer-wedgers handy.

Apricots: Smallish, oval, orange-yellow; flesh smooth, fragrant, sweet. Varietal names unimportant. SEASON: May-September	Choose plump, firm, evenly golden fruit. Allow 1-2 per serving.	High in vitamin A, some C. About 20 calories per apricot.	Eating out-of-hand; raw in desserts, salads; simmered; in pies, puddings. *Tip:* To speed peeling, dip in boiling water.
Avocados: Pear-shaped, smooth green or pebbly black skinned; flesh bland, buttery, nutty. Weigh 1/2-3 pounds each. SEASON: Year round	Choose heavy, medium-size fruit, firm but resilient. Allow 1/4-1/2 avocado per person.	High in B vitamins. Calories vary with maturity, variety; average about 185 per 3½-ounce serving.	Raw in fruit salads, desserts; in ice creams; as container for meat or fish salads. *Tip:* Dip flesh in lemon or other tart juice to prevent darkening. When halving, cut lengthwise.
Bananas: "Seedless," butter-smooth, fragrant tropical fruits. Varietal names unimportant to shopper. SEASON: Year round	Buy firm bananas by the bunch; use as they soften, fleck with brown. Allow 1 banana per person.	Some vitamin A and C; low sodium, low fat; about 85 calories per medium fruit.	Eating out-of-hand; raw in salads, desserts; general cooking. *Tip:* Dip flesh in lemon juice to stop browning.
Berries:			
Blackberries, Dewberries: Plump, glossy, sweet-tart, purple-black; many seeds. *Boysenberries* are large, long Dewberries, *Loganberries* dark red ones. SEASON: Summer	Choose full, lustrous, mold- and bruise-free berries. Allow about 1/4 pound per person.	Some iron, vitamin C. About 60 calories per 1/4 pound portion.	Raw with cream, sugar; in pies, puddings, ice cream, jams, preserves, cordials.
Blueberries: Small, round, dusty blue; tart; tiny seeds. SEASON: Summer	Choose plump, unbroken berries of even size. Allow 1/4 pound per person.	Some iron, vitamin C. About 65 calories per 1/4 pound.	Raw with cream, sugar; in pies, puddings, pancakes, muffins.
Cranberries: Hard, acid, ruby hued. SEASON: September-February	Choose bright, plump berries. Allow 1/4 pound per person.	High in vitamin C. 50 calories per 1/4 pound (unsweetened).	In sauces, relishes, pies, puddings. *Tip:* Be sure to remove wiry stems.
Currants: Small tart red, white or black cousin of gooseberries. SEASON: Summer	Select bright, plump berries with stems attached. Allow 1/4 pound per person.	Some vitamins A, C. About 60 calories per 1/4 pound (unsweetened).	In pies, puddings, jellies, jams, preserves.

FRESH FRUITS — WHEN AND HOW TO USE THEM (continued)

Fruit	Description and Season	Buying Tips	Nutritive Value	Best Uses Preparation Tips
Gooseberries: Silver-green berries the size of small grapes; tart. SEASON: Summer	Choose full, evenly sized and colored berries. Allow 1/4 pound per person.	Some vitamins A, C. 45 calories per 1/4 pound (unsweetened).	In pies, puddings, jams. *Tip:* Remove both stem and blossom ends before using.
Lingonberries: Tart red cranberry-like Northern berry. SEASON: Summer	Same as for cranberries. Allow 1/4 pound per person.	Undetermined.	In pancakes, omelets, fruit sauces.
Raspberries: Fragile, cup-shaped, red, black, or golden; juicy-sweet. SEASON: May-December	Choose bright, plump, uncrushed, unmoldy fruit. Allow 1 cup per serving.	Some vitamin C. 70 calories per cup.	Raw with sugar, cream; in pies, puddings, ice cream.
Strawberries: Plump, sweet, juicy, heart-shaped, bright red; gritty external seeds. SEASON: Year round, most plentiful from May-August	Choose clean, solid, well-shaped and colored berries with caps attached; reject leaky boxes. Allow 1 cup per person.	High in vitamin C. 55 calories per cup.	Raw with sugar, cream; in fruit cups, desserts, pies, puddings, ice cream. *Tip:* Remove stems and caps.
Cherries (sweet): Popular varieties: *Bing* (maroon, heart-shaped), *Chapman* (big, round, purple), *Royal Ann Lambert* (big, round, red-brown), *Tartarian* (big, heart-shaped, salmon colored), (heart-shaped, deep purple). SEASON: May-September	Choose plump; bright cherries; firm, if a sweet variety, less so if sour. Allow 1 cup per serving.	Some vitamin A. Calories: about 80 per cup sweet cherries, 60 per cup sour cherries (unsweetened).	In pies, puddings, ice cream, gelatin salads. Sweet cherries also good mixed into fruit desserts. *Tips:* Stem, then scoop out pits using a cherry pitter or point of a vegetable peeler.
Cherries (sour): Popular types: *Early Richmond* (dark red, plump, round), *Montmorency* (round, red, juicy), *Morello* (round, black, juicy). SEASON: June-mid-August			

1010

Fruit / Description	How to Select	Food Value	Uses
Coconuts: Hard-shelled, snowy, nutty-fleshed fruits of a tropical palm. SEASON: Year round	Buy heavy fruit in which milk sloshes. "Eyes" should not be wet or moldy.	Poor. About 400 calories per 1/4 pound.	In pies, cakes, puddings, fruit desserts, candies (see candy chapter for preparation tips).
Crab Apples: Small, hard, wild apples. SEASON: Fall	Choose those as unblemished as possible.	Poor. About 75 calories per 1/4 pound.	For pickling, spicing; in jellies, jams; as garnishes.
Figs: Popular varieties: *Black Mission* (purple, rich, honey-sweet), *Calimyrna* (white, juicy), *Kadota* (green, sweet, fragrant). SEASON: June-October	Choose soft-ripe, plump, unbruised figs; overripe ones smell sour. Allow 3-4 figs per person.	Some vitamin A, minerals. About 30 calories per small fig.	Eating out-of-hand, raw with cream; stewed, in puddings, preserves.
Grapefruit: Type (i.e., pink, seedless, Florida, which has many seeds but is luscious) more important than botanical variety. SEASON: Year round	Choose heavy, firm fruit, not puffy or coarse skinned. Allow 1/2 per person.	High in vitamin C. 55 calories per medium-size 1/2 grapefruit.	Raw as halves, in fruit desserts, salads. *To peel:* Slice off top, cut rind away in spiral. *To section:* Cut down both sides of divider membranes.
Grapes (table varieties): *Red Grapes:* *Cardinal:* Dark red California hybrid of Tokay and Ribier. Few seeds. SEASON: June-August *Catawba:* Oval, maroon, sweet Eastern grape. SEASON: September-November *Delaware:* Small, sweet red Eastern grape. One of the best. SEASON: September-November *Emperor:* Rosy, egg-shaped California grape; bland, some seeds. SEASON: November-May *Red Malaga:* Tender-skinned, firm maroon California grape; delicate. SEASON: July-October	Regardless of type, select plump, clean, unshriveled grapes firmly attached to stems. Bright color, especially with red or black grapes, indicates ripeness. Fully ripe green grapes have an amber cast. Allow 1/4-1/3 pound per person.	All grapes contain some vitamin A and C, calcium and phosphorous. About 75 calories per 1/4 pound, sour grapes somewhat less.	Eating out-of-hand; in table arrangements. Sweet varieties with few seeds (Thompson Seedless) are best for fruit salads, fruit cups, and desserts. Tart strong varieties (Concord) are best for jams and jellies. All grapes make beautiful garnishes.

FRESH FRUITS — WHEN AND HOW TO USE THEM (continued)

Fruit	Description and Season	Buying Tips	Nutritive Value	Best Uses Preparation Tips
	Tokay: Thick-skinned, red California grape; bland; seeds. SEASON: August-October	Regardless of type, select plump, clean, unshriveled grapes firmly attached to stems. Bright color, especially with red or black grapes, indicates ripeness. Fully ripe green grapes have an amber cast. Allow 1/4-1/3 pound per person.	All grapes contain some vitamin A and C, calcium and phosphorous. About 75 calories per 1/4 pound, sour grapes somewhat less.	Eating out-of-hand; in table arrangements. Sweet varieties with few seeds (Thompson Seedless) are best for fruit salads, fruit cups, and desserts. Tart strong varieties (Concord) are best for jams and jellies. All grapes make beautiful garnishes.
	Black Grapes:			
	Concord: Tart, blue-black Eastern grape; some seeds. SEASON: September-October			
	Ribier: Large, oblong, jet black, tough-skinned California grape; tart, some seeds. SEASON: July-February			
	Green/White Grapes:			
	Almeria: Tough-skinned California grape; not tart, not sweet. SEASON: October-April			
	Muscadine: Large family of Southern grapes, green, russet, or black; includes Scuppernong. Juicy and sweet. SEASON: September-October			
	Niagara: Strong, foxy Eastern grape. SEASON: September-November			
	Thompson Seedless: Luscious, sweet, seedless green California grape. SEASON: June-January			
	White Malaga: Bland California grape being replaced by Thompson Seedless. SEASON: September-November			

1012

Fruit	Buying	Nutrition	Uses
Guavas: Small, oval, thick-fleshed, perfumy tropical fruit. Flesh red or golden; many seeds. SEASON: Year round in Deep South, Florida, California	Choose firm-ripe fruit beginning to soften. Allow 1/4 pound per person.	High in vitamins C, A. About 70 calories per 1/4 pound.	Eating out-of-hand, raw in fruit salads; in jellies and pastes. *Tip:* Peel as thinly as possible.
Kumquats: Tiny, tart, orange citrus fruits eaten skin and all. SEASON: November-February	Buy heavy, unshriveled fruit, 2-3 per person.	High in vitamin A. 70 calories per 1/4 pound.	Eating out-of-hand, raw in desserts; in preserves. *To seed:* Halve lengthwise and scrape out seeds.
Lemons: Sunny, sour citrus fruits. SEASON: Year round	Buy heavy, soft-skinned fruit; green tinges indicate super-sourness.	High in vitamin C, low in calories.	As a flavoring and garnish.
Lichees: Scarlet, cherry-size, leathery shelled Chinese fruits; snowy, juicy, perfumy flesh. Dried lichees, eaten like raisins, are called lichee nuts. SEASON: Summer	Buy unshriveled fruit, 1/3 pound per person.	Some vitamin C. 75 calories per 1/3 pound.	Eating out-of-hand, peeled, raw in fruit desserts. *Tip:* Pit as you would cherries.
Limes: Sour, green citrus fruit. SEASON: Year round	Same as for lemons.	Same as for lemons.	Same as for lemons.
Loquats: Yellow-orange, tart-sweet, downy Chinese plums; many seeds. SEASON: Summer	Buy firm-ripe, bright fruit, 2-3 per person.	Some vitamin A. 25 calories per loquat.	Eating out-of-hand, peeled, raw in fruit salads, dessert. *Tip:* Rub down from skin to remove fuzz before eating.
Mangoes: Large, kidney-shaped, tropical fruits, red-orange and green skinned; flesh orange, peach-like flavor with a hint of pine; one huge seed. SEASON: May-September	Choose fresh, firm fruit. Allow about 1/2 mango per person.	High in vitamins A and C. About 85 calories per 1/2 mango.	Raw in fruit desserts, salads; in pickles, chutney. *To seed:* Halve lengthwise, pry out seed. *Tip:* Peel as thinly as possible.

1013

FRESH FRUITS — WHEN AND HOW TO USE THEM (continued)

Fruit	Description and Season	Buying Tips	Nutritive Value	Best Uses Preparation Tips
Melons:		Regardless of type, select clean, firm, plump melons with clean scars at the stem ends. Ripe cantaloupes will soften slightly at blossom end, honeydews will yield slightly when pressed. Sniffing the stem or blossom end for fragrance is a test for ripeness. Good ripe watermelons will sound hollow when thumped. Allow 1/2 small melon per person, slices or wedges of larger melons.	Orange-fleshed melons are high in vitamin A, all contain some vitamin C. Calories vary according to type: 1/2 small cantaloupe runs about 60 calories, 1/4 pound watermelon about 40.	All melons can be served more or less the same way — raw, in slices, halves, cubes, or balls; mixed into fruit salads and desserts; puréed into sherbet and ice cream; as garnishes.
	Cantaloupe: Plump round melon, buff rind with green netting; sweet, juicy, orange flesh. SEASON: March-December			
	Casaba: Large yellow melon, pointed at stem end, ridged rind; sweet, ivory-hued flesh. SEASON: August-November; a Christmas variety available in December			
	Crenshaw: Large oval melon with pointed ends, green and yellow rind, sweet salmon flesh. SEASON: July-October			
	Honeyball: Round melon, lightly webbed, buff-pink rind; pink, sweet flesh. SEASON: June-November			
	Honeydew: Large, round pale green melon with honey-sweet green flesh. SEASON: June-October			
	Persian Melon: Like cantaloupe but bigger. SEASON: July-October			
	Spanish Melon: Large oblong melon with pointed ends, ridged green skin, pale green, sweet flesh. SEASON: June-October			
	Watermelon: Dozens of varieties, some round, some long, some light, some dark green. Newest are midgets with few seeds. SEASON: June-September			

How To Make Melon Baskets

1014

	Buying	Nutrition	Uses
Nectarines: Small, smooth-skinned peaches; richer, sweeter than other types. SEASON: June-September	Buy plump, firm, unblemished, unbruised fruit, 1-2 per person.	High in vitamin A. About 75 calories per nectarine.	Same as for peaches. *Tip:* Dip in citrus juice after cutting to prevent browning.
Oranges (juice types): *Hamlin:* Early Florida-Texas orange, smooth rind; tart, few seeds. SEASON: October-January *Parson Brown:* Heavily seeded Florida orange; coarse flesh; tart. SEASON: October-December *Pineapple:* Midseason Florida orange; tart-sweet, many seeds. SEASON: January-March *Valencia:* Popular variety grown in Florida, Texas, Arizona, and California; deep golden rind, sweet, juicy, few seeds. SEASON: January-November	Regardless of type, oranges should weigh heavy for their size, be plump and firm. Rind color has little to do with quality — many oranges are dyed; those with greenish casts may be fully ripe. Allow 1 orange per person. It takes 2-3 to make 1 cup juice.	High in vitamin C; about 60 calories per medium-size orange, 100-110 calories per cup of juice, depending on sweetness.	Squeezed into juice. Sweeter, less seedy types can be sectioned and mixed into fruit cups, salads, desserts. *To section:* Same as for grapefruit.
Oranges (eating types): *Navel:* Large, thick-skinned, seedless Florida-California orange with navel on blossom end. Sweet, easily peeled and sectioned. SEASON: November-mid-June *Temple:* Popular, large oval Florida orange, thought to be a hybrid of tangerine and orange. Deep orange rind, sweet, rich, and juicy. Many seeds. SEASON: December-April		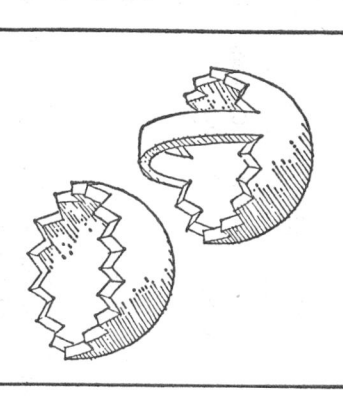 How To Make Orange Baskets	Eating oranges are best eaten out-of-hand, sectioned or sliced raw into desserts, salads. Temples also juice well.
Oranges (exotic types): *Mandarin:* A variety of tangerine. *Seville or Bigarade:* Sour, bitter Mediterranean oranges, occasionally available in gourmet markets.			In marmalade; for making candied orange rind.

FRESH FRUITS — WHEN AND HOW TO USE THEM (continued)

Fruit	Description and Season	Buying Tips	Nutritive Value	Best Uses / Preparation Tips
Papayas: Tropical melon-like fruit; sweet-musky orange flesh; large cluster of dark seeds in the center; its juice contains an enzyme used in meat tenderizers. SEASON: Year round		Choose yellow fruit, soft but not mushy. Green fruit won't ripen. Sizes: 1-20 pounds. 2-3-pound size best. Allow 1/4 pound per person.	High in vitamins A and C. About 50 calories per 1/4 pound.	Raw in fruit salads, desserts. Also in wedges like melon with lemon or lime. Use seeds as garnishes. *Tip:* Juice can cause skin rash, so wear gloves while peeling and preparing papayas.
Passion fruits (granadillas): Subtropical, purple, egg-shaped, sweet-tart fruits about 3" long; flesh golden. SEASON: Autumn		Select plump, firm-soft, blemish-free fruits, 1-2 per person.	Undetermined. About 50 calories per 1/4 pound.	Eating out-of-hand, peeled; in pies, puddings; also raw in fruit desserts. Juice delicious in punch.
Peaches: Varieties matter less than types: *clingstone* (most are canned commercially) and *freestone* (*Elberta* is a favorite), best for eating, cooking because pits remove easily. Peach flesh may be white, yellow, orange. SEASON: mid-May-October		Choose firm-tender, fragrant, blemish-free fruit showing little green. Allow 1 peach per person.	High in vitamin A, some C. About 35 calories per medium-size peach.	Eating out-of-hand; raw in fruit salads, desserts; in pies, puddings, upside-down cakes, shortcakes. *Tips:* Dip peaches in boiling water and skins will slip off. Dip cut peaches in citrus juice to prevent browning.
Pears (all-purpose varieties): *Anjou:* Big, yellow-russet; crisp, vinous flavor. SEASON: October-May *Bosc:* Large, thin-necked, cinnamon pear; tart. SEASON: October-April Allow		Regardless of type, buy firm-ripe — not hard — pears of good color and shape. Reject unclean, bruised, blemished ones. Allow	Poor for all varieties. About 100 calories per medium-size pear.	Eating out-of-hand; poaching; canning; preserving; in upside-down cakes; sliced raw into fruit salads, cups, and desserts.

Fruit / Variety	Buying	Nutrition / Calories	Uses / Tips
Clapp Favorite: Almost round, red-yellow, sweet, smooth, juicy. SEASON: August-November			
Seckel: Small russet pear; flesh gritty at core; spicy flavor. SEASON: August-December			*Tip:* Some types darken after cutting, so dip in citrus juice to be safe. Also trim away any gritty areas surrounding core.
Winter Nelis: Large, roundish, russeted dark green pear; buttery, spicy. SEASON: October-May			
Pears (eating varieties):			
Bartlett: Big, bell-shaped, yellow-green pear; smooth, sweet-musky. SEASON: July-mid-October	1 pear per person.		Eating out-of-hand; raw in fruit cups, desserts, salads. Bartletts also good for canning.
Comice: Large, roundish, chartreuse; fine, juicy-sweet flesh. SEASON: October-March			

How To Make Pineapple Boats

Fruit / Variety	Buying	Nutrition / Calories	Uses / Tips
Persimmons: Two principal types: *wild American* (small, puckery, good only after first frost) and *Oriental* (plump, vermilion fruits big as apples; flesh soft and sweet). SEASON: October-February	Choose plump, glossy, firm-tender fruit with stems and caps attached. Allow 1 per person.	High in vitamin A, some C. About 80 calories per medium-size Oriental persimmon.	Eating out-of-hand (wild varieties only if squishy-ripe); raw in fruit cups, desserts; in puddings, pies. *Tip:* Peel as thinly as possible.
Pineapples: Large prickly tropical fruits, pale to deep yellow; flesh tart and juicy. SEASON: Year round	Buy fresh, clean fruit, heavy for its size with flat "eyes" and strong bouquet. Allow about 1/4 pound per serving.	Some vitamin C; about 60 calories per 1/4 pound serving.	Raw in fruit salads, desserts; in pies, puddings, ice creams, upside-down cake. *Tip:* Do not use with gelatin (an enzyme in pineapple keeps it from thickening).

FRESH FRUITS — WHEN AND HOW TO USE THEM (continued)

Fruit	Description and Season	Buying Tips	Nutritive Value	Best Uses Preparation Tips
Plums (European types): These are fairly small, tart, blue, green, or black skinned. Popular varieties: *Damson* (small, acid, black), *Green Gage* (green, mild, and sweet), *Prune-Plum* (dark purple, firm, tart). SEASON: Early summer	Regardless of type, buy clean, plump, fresh plums, soft enough to yield when pressed. Reject bruised, sunburned (browned) ones. Allow 1-2 plums per person.	All plums are high in vitamin A and contain some C. Calories vary with sweetness; a medium-size, not too sweet plum averages about 25 calories.	Eating out-of-hand; poaching; in fruit cups, compotes, salads, desserts; in puddings, preserves.
Plums (Japanese types): These are large, lush, scarlet, yellow, or magenta. Popular ones: *Burbank* (maroon-skinned, sweet), *Duarte* (maroon-skinned, scarlet-fleshed, sweet), *Santa Rosa* (red-purple, tart-sweet, juicy). SEASON: August-October			Eating out-of-hand; raw in fruit desserts.
Pomegranates: Curious red Persian fruits, about the size of oranges with fleshy, ruby clusters of kernels, each encasing a dark seed. These are eaten much like grapes, the flesh being sucked from the seeds. SEASON: September-January	Choose medium to large fruits, bright pink or red. Allow about 1/2 fruit per person.	Undetermined. About 40 calories per 1/4 pound.	Eating out-of-hand; pulp good in sherbet, ice cream. *To eat:* Halve lengthwise, remove rind and membrane. Eat ruby kernels, discarding seeds. *To juice:* Halve crosswise and ream as you would an orange. Juice good in punch.

	Choosing	Food value	Uses
Prickly pears: Fruits of *Opuntia* cactus of the Southwest; flesh may be yellow, red, purple; sweet and watery with little flavor. SEASON: Early autumn	Choose plump, unshriveled fruits about the size of pears with few barbs. Allow 1 per person.	Poor. About 30 calories per medium-size fruit.	Eating out-of-hand; raw in fruit cups and desserts; in jellies. *Tip:* Barbs must be singed off before fruit is peeled.
Pumpkins (see vegetable chapter)			
Quinces: Hard golden fruits; not edible raw. SEASON: October-December	Buy as unblemished fruits as possible.	High in vitamin C. About 50 calories per medium-size fruit.	In jellies, jams, preserves.
Rhubarb: Succulent scarlet stalks; not eaten raw. SEASON: February-August	Choose crisp, straight, bright red stalks. A 1-pound bunch serves 2-4.	Poor. Calories vary according to cooking method.	Stewed; in pies, jams. *Tip:* Roots are poisonous, so trim stalks carefully.
Tangelos: Grapefruit-tangerine hybrids that taste like tart oranges. SEASON: November-March	Buy plump fruit, heavy for its size. Allow 1 per person.	High in vitamin C. About 50 calories per medium-size fruit.	Use as you would oranges or tangerines.
Tangerines: Small, flat, loose-skinned oranges of the mandarin type, easily peeled and sectioned. Puffiness, flabby skins indicate poor quality. Allow 1 tangerine per person. SEASON: November-May	Choose plump, heavy fruits.	High in vitamin C. About 40 calories per medium-size fruit.	Eating out-of-hand; sectioned in fruit desserts and salads.

POACHED (STEWED) FRUITS

Note: For best results, fruits should be firm, not mushy. Quantities are enough for 4 ample servings.

Fruit	Quantity and Preparation	Poaching Syrup	Method	Optional Flavorings (Choose One)
Apples (Rome Beauties are best)	1 quart peeled, cored quarters or eighths OR 4 whole peeled and cored apples	3 cups Thin	Simmer apples, uncovered, in syrup 8-10 minutes until firm-tender. Serve in some syrup.	Cinnamon stick 3-4 cloves Piece crystallized ginger Strip lemon or orange rind Mint, rose geranium sprigs
Apricots, Pears, Oranges	4 peeled whole or halved apricots or pears, 4 peeled whole oranges	2 cups Medium	Simmer, uncovered, in syrup until heated through, about 5 minutes for apricots, 10-15 for pears and oranges. Serve in some syrup.	Cinnamon stick 1 teaspoon curry powder Strip lemon or orange rind Piece crystallized ginger 1" vanilla bean
Cherries	1 quart whole, pitted or unpitted	2 cups Medium	Simmer, uncovered, in syrup 3-5 minutes. Serve in some syrup.	Cinnamon stick 2-3 cloves Strip lemon or orange rind
Berries, Peaches, Plums	1 quart whole berries, 4 whole peeled or halved peaches, 8 whole unpeeled plums	1 cup Heavy	Simmer, uncovered, in syrup until heated through — 2-3 minutes for berries, 5 for plums, peaches about 10. Serve in syrup.	1 cinnamon stick and 1 teaspoon curry powder (for peaches only) 1" vanilla bean 2 lemon or orange slices
Rhubarb	1 quart 1" chunks	1 cup Heavy	Simmer, uncovered, in syrup about 15 minutes until crisp tender. Serve in syrup.	1 teaspoon finely grated orange or lemon rind

VARIATION: Prepare as directed but substitute 1/4-1/3 cup fruit liqueur, rum, brandy, sherry, Porto, or Madeira for 1/4-1/3 cup syrup. (*Note:* Also see separate recipes that follow.)

1020

POACHING SYRUPS

Type	Sugar	Water	Method	Yield
Thin	1 cup	3 cups	Boil sugar and water uncovered 3-5	3 cups
Medium	1 cup	2 cups	minutes until sugar is dissolved.	2 cups
Heavy	1 cup	1 cup		1 cup

BAKED FRUITS

Fruit	Preparation and Method	Cooking Time and Temperature
Apples (see separate recipes that follow)		
Apricots, pears, peaches	Peel, core, or pit and halve; drizzle with lemon juice, sprinkle with sugar and, if you like, nutmeg and cinnamon. Dot with butter and cover.	15-20 minutes at 425°F. (canned fruit bakes in 10 minutes)
Bananas (see separate recipes that follow)		
Grapefruit, oranges (use Temple or Navel)	Halve grapefruit; peel oranges but leave whole. Sprinkle with sugar or honey and dot with butter. Do not cover.	30-40 minutes at 350°F. Baste occasionally with pan drippings.
Pineapple	Quarter lengthwise, prickly crown and all; do not peel. Cut out core, then score flesh in cubes and loosen. Sprinkle with sugar or honey, dot with butter. Do not cover.	30-40 minutes at 350°F. Baste now and then with pan drippings.
Rhubarb	Cut 2 pounds rhubarb in 1" lengths. Place in a shallow baking dish, sprinkle with 3 tablespoons water and 1½ cups superfine sugar. Also sprinkle lightly with nutmeg and cinnamon, if you like, or drizzle with lemon or orange juice. Cover.	1/2-3/4 hour at 350°F.

For Extra Flavor: Simmer a few slices lemon, orange, or preserved ginger or a small piece of vanilla bean along with fruit.

Figs: Soak or not as directed. Place in a large saucepan, add cold water to cover, and simmer covered 20–30 minutes until tender. Sweeten, if you like, using about 1 tablespoon sugar or honey per cup of fruit. *For Added Flavor:* Simmer with a few slices lemon or crystallized ginger.

Prunes: Soak or not as label directs. Pit if you like. (*Note:* Pitted prunes are now available.) Place in a large pan, add cold water just to cover, and simmer covered about ¾ hour until tender. (*Note:* "Tenderized" prunes will take only 20 minutes. No need to add sugar.) *For Extra Flavor:* Simmer 2–3 slices lemon studded with cloves along with prunes.

(*Note:* Stewed dried fruits will be

plumper, mellower, richer if allowed to stand overnight at room temperature in their cooking liquid before being served.)

To "Plump" Raisins and Dried Currants: If hard and dry, raisins and currants will sink to the bottom of breads and puddings. To prevent this, cover with boiling water and let stand about 5 minutes until they grow plump and soft. Drain well before using. Instead, if you like, soak 5–10 minutes in rum or brandy.

About Cutting and Mincing Dried Fruits: These are sticky and difficult to cut with a knife. Snip with scissors.

⚖ ⊠ AMBROSIA

A vitamin-C-rich dessert that everyone likes.
Makes 6 servings

4 large navel oranges, peeled
⅓ cup sifted confectioners' sugar
1 cup finely grated fresh coconut or 1 (3½-ounce) can flaked coconut
¼ cup orange juice

Remove all outer white membrane from oranges and slice thin crosswise. Layer oranges into a serving bowl, sprinkling with sugar, coconut, and orange juice as you go. Cover and chill 2–3 hours. Mix lightly and serve. About 130 calories per serving.

VARIATION:

⚖ Reduce oranges to 2 or 3 and add 2–3 peeled, thinly sliced bananas or 1 small fresh pineapple, peeled, cored, and cut in thin wedges. About 140 calories per serving.

CARIBBEAN COMPOTE

Tropical fruits in port wine.
Makes 8–10 servings

1 medium-size pineapple, peeled, cored, and cut in thin wedges
3 navel oranges, peeled and sectioned
1 small honeydew melon, halved, seeded, peeled, and cut in bite-size chunks
⅔ cup superfine sugar
⅓ cup tawny port wine

Juice of 2 limes
2 medium-size bananas
1 large ripe avocado

Place pineapple, oranges, melon, sugar, and wine in a very large bowl and toss well to mix. Cover and chill 2–3 hours. Place lime juice in a small mixing bowl. Peel bananas and slice about ½" thick, letting slices fall into lime juice; toss lightly. Halve avocado, remove pit, then peel and cut in bite-size cubes, letting these fall into bowl with bananas; toss lightly. Add bananas, avocado, and lime juice to chilled fruits and toss lightly. Re-cover and chill about 30 minutes. Toss lightly and serve in stemmed goblets. About 230 calories for each of 8 servings, 185 calories for each of 10 servings.

HOT FRUIT COMPOTE

A good basic recipe that can be varied a number of ways.
Makes 6–8 servings

1 (1-pound) can peach or apricot halves
1 (1-pound) can pear halves
1 (1-pound) can purple or greengage plums
1 cup firmly packed light brown sugar
¼ cup lemon juice
1 tablespoon finely slivered orange rind
2 tablespoons butter or margarine

Preheat oven to 350° F. Drain and measure 1 cup syrup from canned fruits and mix with sugar, lemon juice, and orange rind. Arrange fruits in a large casserole, add sugar mixture, and dot with butter. Bake, uncovered, ½ hour; serve hot with cream or cool and ladle over ice cream or pound cake. About 370 calories for each of 6 servings, 280 calories for each of 8 servings.

VARIATIONS:

Spiced Hot Fruit Compote: Add ½ teaspoon cinnamon and ¼ teaspoon each ginger, nutmeg, and allspice to sugar mixture and proceed as directed. Or omit ginger and substitute ¼ cup ginger marmalade for the lemon juice. About 370 calories for each of 6 servings, 280 calories for each of 8 servings.

Brandied Hot Fruit Compote: Prepare fruit compote as directed, using ½ cup each brandy and syrup drained from fruit; also reduce lemon juice to 2 tablespoons. About 460 calories for each of 6 servings, 350 calories for each of 8 servings.

Curried Hot Fruit Compote: First, heat and stir 1½ teaspoons curry powder in the butter called for in a flameproof casserole 1–2 minutes over moderate heat. Add fruits, substituting 1 (1-pound) can pineapple chunks for the plums, pour in sugar mixture, mix well, and bake as directed. Serve hot with meat or poultry. About 370 calories for each of 6 servings, 280 calories for each of 8 servings.

⚖ **MINTY PINEAPPLE FANS IN COINTREAU**

A cooling summer dessert. Low-calorie, too.
Makes 4 servings

1 medium-size ripe pineapple
⅓ cup sugar
8 sprigs mint, washed
⅓ cup Cointreau

Cut off top and stem end of pineapple, then halve, core, and peel. Divide each half lengthwise into 4 wedges, then cut in paper-thin, fan-shaped pieces. Place pineapple fans in a large bowl, add remaining ingredients, and toss well to mix. Cover and marinate in the refrigerator 2–3 hours. Remove mint sprigs and serve. About 160 calories per serving and, if you drain pineapple before serving, about half that.

⚖ **GINGERED HONEYDEW MELON**

Makes 4–6 servings

1 medium-size ripe honeydew melon (about 3½–4 pounds)
1½ cups water
½ cup sugar
6 (1-inch) squares crystallized ginger
½ lemon, quartered

Halve melon lengthwise and scoop out

seeds; remove rind and cut melon in bite-size cubes; place in a large mixing bowl. Simmer water, uncovered, with sugar and ginger about 30 minutes, stirring occasionally. Off heat, add lemon and cool to lukewarm. Pour syrup and lemon over melon, toss to mix, cover, and chill 3–4 hours. Remove lemon, spoon melon into stemmed goblets, and top with a little of the syrup. About 65 calories for each of 6 servings, 100 for each of 4.

⚖ ⊠ **GREEN GRAPES AND SOUR CREAM**

One of the easiest elegant desserts.
Makes 4 servings

3 cups seedless green grapes, stemmed, washed, dried, and chilled
½ cup sour cream or unflavored yogurt
¼ cup dark brown sugar

Mix grapes and sour cream, spoon into dessert bowls, sprinkle with sugar, and serve. About 135 calories per serving if made with yogurt.

STRAWBERRIES ROMANOFF

A glamorized version of strawberries and cream.
Makes 4–6 servings

1 quart fresh strawberries, washed, stemmed, and, if large, halved lengthwise
2–3 tablespoons superfine sugar (optional)
⅓ cup orange juice
¼ cup curaçao
¾ cup heavy cream
2 tablespoons confectioners' sugar
¼ teaspoon vanilla

Taste berries and, if tart, sprinkle with sugar. Let stand 10 minutes at room temperature, then toss lightly to mix. Add orange juice and curaçao and toss again; cover and chill several hours, turning berries occasionally. Spoon into a shallow serving dish. Whip cream with sugar and vanilla until soft peaks form, spoon into a pastry bag fitted with a large, fluted tube, and pipe cream over berries, covering completely. About 325 calories for each of 4 servings, 220 calories for each of 6 servings.

⚖ STRAWBERRIES GRAND MARNIER

Dieters won't feel deprived if served this dessert.
Makes 4 servings

1 quart fresh strawberries, washed, stemmed, and halved lengthwise
2–3 tablespoons superfine sugar (optional)
⅓ cup Grand Marnier

Taste berries and, if too tart, sprinkle with sugar. Let stand 10 minutes at room temperature, then toss lightly to mix. Pour Grand Marnier over berries and toss again; cover and chill several hours, turning berries occasionally. Serve topped with some of the Grand Marnier and, if you like, sprigged with mint. About 100 calories per serving (without sugar).

⚖ LICHEES IN PORT WINE

A refreshing and unique summer dessert.
Makes 4–6 servings

2 pounds fresh lichees, peeled, seeded, and halved, or 3 cups halved, drained, canned lichees (both are available in Chinese groceries)
½ cup ruby port wine

Place lichees and port in a small bowl and toss well to mix; cover and chill several hours. Serve in stemmed goblets. About 100 calories for each of 6 servings, 150 for each of 4.

¢ OLD-FASHIONED APPLESAUCE

The kind Grandmother used to make.
Makes 4–6 servings

3 pounds greenings or other tart cooking apples, peeled, cored, and quartered
1 cup sugar
⅔ cup water

Simmer all ingredients uncovered in a large saucepan, stirring frequently, 20–25 minutes until mushy. Serve hot or cold. About 210 calories for each of 4 servings, 140 calories for each of 6 servings.

VARIATION:

¢ **Spicy Applesauce:** Prepare as directed, using light brown sugar instead of granulated, reducing water to ⅔ cup, and adding the juice of ½ lemon, ¼ teaspoon cinnamon, ⅛ teaspoon nutmeg, and 1 tablespoon butter or margarine. About 235 calories for each of 4 servings, 160 calories for each of 6 servings.

GOLDEN SAFFRON APPLES

Makes 4 servings

⅛ teaspoon saffron
½ cup plus 1 tablespoon water
¾ cup sugar
4 large tart cooking apples, peeled, cored, and cut in thick wedges
1 teaspoon lemon juice
1 teaspoon grated orange rind
2 tablespoons toasted, blanched, slivered almonds

Crush saffron and soak in 1 tablespoon water 10 minutes; boil sugar with remaining water, uncovered, stirring occasionally, 4–5 minutes to make a thin syrup. Turn heat to low, strain saffron water into syrup, add apples, lemon juice, and orange rind, cover, and simmer 7–10 minutes until apples are tender but not mushy. Cool apples in their syrup, then chill well. Serve topped with almonds. About 240 calories per serving.

¢ BAKED APPLES

Makes 4 servings

4 large cooking apples (Rome Beauties are best)
⅔ cup sugar
⅔ cup water
1 tablespoon butter or margarine
Pinch cinnamon and/or nutmeg
2–3 drops red food coloring

Preheat oven to 350° F. Core apples, then peel about ⅓ of the way down from the stem end, or, if you prefer, peel entirely. Arrange in an ungreased shallow baking pan. Boil remaining ingredients about 5 minutes to form a clear syrup, pour over apples, and bake uncovered ¾–1 hour, basting often with syrup, until crisp-tender. Serve hot or cold, topped if you like with Custard sauce or whipped cream. About 225 calories per serving (without sauce or whipped cream).

VARIATIONS:

¢ **"Red Hot" Apples:** Core and peel apples as directed; place in pan and in the hollow of each place 2 tablespoons sugar and 1 tablespoon butter or margarine. Prepare syrup as directed but add 1 (1¾-ounce) container red cinnamon candies. Bake as directed, basting often. Fill centers with vanilla ice cream and serve. About 285 calories per serving.

¢ **Brown Sugar Glazed Apples:** Bake apples as directed, remove from oven, baste with syrup, then sprinkle each with 1 tablespoon dark brown sugar mixed with a pinch of cinnamon. Broil 4" from the heat 1–2 minutes until sugar melts. About 270 calories per serving.

¢ **Baked Stuffed Apples:** Core and peel apples as directed, place in pan and half fill hollows with chopped pitted dates, prunes, or other dried fruit; sprinkle 2 tablespoons sugar into each hollow, finish filling with chopped fruit, and dot with butter or margarine. Omit syrup; instead, pour ½ cup water around apples and bake as directed, but without basting. About 265 calories per serving.

⚶ ¢ ⊠ FRIED APPLE RINGS

Good as dessert or as a garnish for a roast pork platter.
Makes 6 servings

⅓ cup butter or margarine
4 medium-size cooking apples, cored but
*   not peeled and sliced ½" thick*
Unsifted flour

Heat butter in a large, heavy skillet over moderate heat 1 minute. Dredge apples in flour, shake off excess, and sauté, a few at a time, in butter about 10 minutes, turning often until lightly browned. Drain on paper toweling and serve hot. About 155 calories per serving.

VARIATIONS:

⚶ ¢ **Cinnamon Apple Rings:** Fry apple rings as directed, sprinkle with cinnamon sugar, and serve as an accompaniment to meats. Topped with sweetened whipped cream, these make a delicious dessert. About 170 calories per serving (without cream).

⚶ ¢ **Curried Apple Rings:** Prepare as directed but sprinkle with 1–1½ teaspoons curry powder halfway through sautéing. (*Note:* Any of the following sautéed fruits may be curried the same way.) About 155 calories per serving.

Sautéed Pineapple Rings: Pat 6–8 well-drained pineapple rings dry on paper toweling, then dredge and sauté as directed about 5–8 minutes. About 175 calories per serving.

⚶ **Sautéed Peaches or Apricots:** Pat 6 fresh or drained canned peach or apricot halves dry on paper toweling, then dredge and sauté 5–6 minutes as directed. About 130 calories per serving.

Sautéed Halved Bananas: Peel 6 underripe bananas and halve lengthwise. Dredge and sauté in butter about 5 minutes. Sprinkle lightly with salt and serve with meat or poultry. About 170 calories per serving.

⊠ BAKED BANANAS

Makes 4 servings

4 slightly underripe bananas
¼ cup melted butter or margarine
Sugar, dark brown sugar, or salt

Preheat oven to 350°F. Peel bananas and arrange whole or split lengthwise in a buttered 1-quart *au gratin* dish or shallow casserole; brush well with butter. Bake uncovered 15–20 minutes until soft and pale golden. Sprinkle with sugar and serve as dessert or sprinkle with salt and serve as an accompaniment to roast loin of pork or chicken. About 200 calories per serving.

⊠ BANANAS FLAMBÉ

A showy but *easy* dessert you can prepare at the table.
Makes 4 servings

½ cup butter (*no substitute*)
¾ cup firmly packed light brown sugar
2 tablespoons lemon juice
4 slightly underripe bananas, peeled and halved lengthwise
⅓ cup brandy or light rum

Melt butter in a chafing dish or flameproof casserole (burner-to-table type) over moderately low heat, mix in sugar and lemon juice and heat, stirring until sugar dissolves. Add bananas and simmer, uncovered, about 10 minutes, turning gently with a slotted spatula now and then, to glaze evenly. Warm brandy in a small saucepan, pour over bananas, blaze, and spoon over bananas until flames die. Serve at once. About 440 calories per serving.

VARIATIONS:

Peaches, Pears, or Nectarines Flambé: Substitute 4 large firm peaches, pears, or nectarines for bananas. Peel fruit and leave whole (but core the pears). Proceed as directed. About 420 calories per serving.

Baked Glazed Fruit: Bake any of the above fruits, uncovered, in sugar mixture about ½ hour at 350° F., turning now and then in syrup to glaze. Omit brandy. Recipe too flexible for a meaningful calorie count.

⊠ CHERRIES JUBILEE

More culinary pyrotechnics. Bound to impress dinner guests if you bring flaming into a darkened room.
Makes 4–6 servings

1 (1-pound 13-ounce) can pitted Bing cherries
¼ cup sugar
1 tablespoon cornstarch
1 tablespoon lemon juice

1 tablespoon butter (*no substitute*)
⅓ cup kirsch or brandy

Drain and reserve liquid from cherries. Mix sugar and cornstarch in a saucepan, gradually mix in cherry liquid, and heat, stirring constantly, over moderate heat until boiling. Reduce heat and simmer, uncovered, 3 minutes, stirring now and then. Add lemon juice, butter, and cherries and simmer, uncovered, 2–3 minutes. Meanwhile, warm kirsch in a small saucepan. Transfer cherry mixture to a chafing dish or flameproof serving dish, pour in kirsch, blaze with a match, and carry flaming to the table. Serve as is or spooned over vanilla ice cream. About 255 calories for each of 4 servings (without ice cream), 170 calories for each of 6 servings.

STEWED FRESH FIGS

Makes 6 servings

1 quart firm-ripe figs, peeled
2 cups water
1½ cups sugar
2 tablespoons lemon juice

Place all ingredients in a saucepan and simmer, uncovered, 15–30 minutes until figs are clear and tender; cover and cool in liquid. Serve at room temperature with a little liquid poured over each serving. If you like, pass heavy or light cream. About 225 calories per serving.

VARIATIONS:

Stewed Dried Figs: Substitute 1 pound dried figs for the fresh and simmer as directed until figs are plump and soft. About 355 calories per serving.

Gingered Figs: Simmer 1 (2-inch) piece bruised, peeled gingerroot along with figs; remove before serving. Or use 2 tablespoons minced crystallized ginger and serve along with figs. About 225 calories per serving if made with fresh figs, 355 calories per serving if made with dried figs.

Spiced Figs: Tie 1 stick cinnamon and 4 cloves in cheesecloth and simmer along with figs; remove just before serving. About 225 calories per serving if made with fresh figs, 355 calories per serving if made with dried figs.

Honeyed Figs: Quarter fresh figs and simmer with 1 cup each water and honey and the lemon juice called for. Serve as is or as a sauce over ice cream. About 335 calories per serving (without ice cream).

⊠ ⚖ BROILED GRAPEFRUIT

Good for breakfast or dessert.
Makes 4 servings

2 medium-size grapefruits, halved
4 teaspoons light brown sugar
1 tablespoon melted butter or margarine
4 maraschino cherries

Preheat broiler. Cut around grapefruit sections to loosen, then sprinkle each ½ grapefruit with 1 teaspoon brown sugar and drizzle with ¾ teaspoon melted butter. Broil 5″ from heat 5–7 minutes until golden. Top each ½ grapefruit with a cherry and serve hot. About 100 calories per serving.

VARIATIONS:

⊠ ⚖ **Broiled Sherried Grapefruit:** Just before serving, pour 1 teaspoon sweet sherry over each ½ grapefruit. About 110 calories per serving.

⊠ **Honey-Broiled Grapefruit:** Substitute 1 tablespoon honey or maple syrup for each teaspoon of brown sugar and proceed as directed. About 175 calories per serving.

⊠ ⚖ **Spicy Broiled Grapefruit:** Prepare as directed, adding a pinch cinnamon, nutmeg, or allspice to each ½ grapefruit just before broiling. About 100 calories per serving.

⊠ **Broiled Oranges, Peaches, Apricots, Pears, or Pineapples:** Halved oranges, peaches, and apricots and pineapple rings can all be broiled. Sprinkle cut sides slightly with sugar and butter and broil 3–5 minutes until delicately browned. Recipe too flexible for a meaningful calorie count.

PEARS HÉLÈNE (POIRES HÉLÈNE)

A restaurant classic easily prepared at home.
Makes 4 servings

2 cups water
¾ cup sugar
2 large firm-ripe pears, peeled, halved, and cored
1 teaspoon vanilla
1 pint vanilla ice cream
1 recipe hot Basic Chocolate Sauce

Mix water and sugar in a large skillet (not iron) and heat over moderate heat, stirring until sugar dissolves. Add pears, cover, and simmer 10–12 minutes, turning once in the liquid, until tender but not mushy. Mix in vanilla, then cool pears in liquid. Spoon ice cream into 4 dessert dishes, mounding it slightly. Top each with a pear half, hollow side down. Drizzle some chocolate sauce over pears and pass the rest in a sauceboat. About 605 calories per serving.

BAKED PEARS AU GRATIN

Makes 4 servings

Juice of ½ lemon
3 large firm ripe pears, peeled, cored, and sliced ¼″ thick
¼ cup firmly packed light brown sugar
¼ cup light rum
2 tablespoons unsalted butter

Topping:

⅓ cup fine dry bread crumbs
¼ cup sugar
1 tablespoon finely grated Parmesan cheese
3 tablespoons melted unsalted butter

Preheat oven to 400° F. Place lemon juice in a 9″ piepan, add pears, and toss lightly to mix; sprinkle with sugar, drizzle with rum, and dot with butter. Mix topping ingredients and sprinkle evenly over pears. Bake, uncovered, 20–25 minutes until lightly browned and bubbly. Serve hot or warm, topped, if you like, with a hearty scoop of vanilla ice cream. About 400 calories per serving (without ice cream).

⊠ PEACH COUPE CHAMPAGNE

Makes 4 servings

2 large ripe peaches
¼ teaspoon lemon juice
1 pint peach, strawberry, or raspberry
  ice cream
1 pint white or pink champagne, well
  chilled

Peel peaches, halve, pit, and place in a bowl; sprinkle with lemon juice to prevent darkening. Place a peach half, hollow up, in each of 4 chilled champagne glasses. Mound a generous scoop of ice cream in each peach hollow, fill glasses to the brim with champagne, and serve. About 190 calories per serving.

PEACHES POACHED IN PORT WINE

Makes 4 servings

2 cups dry port wine
1 cup water
½ cup sugar
2 (1-inch×2-inch) pieces crystallized
  ginger
1 (2-inch) piece vanilla bean
½ lemon, sliced
4 large ripe peaches, peeled

Boil port, water, sugar, ginger, vanilla bean, and lemon in a large uncovered saucepan 10 minutes; remove lemon. Reduce heat to moderately low, add peaches, and simmer uncovered, turning occasionally, 10–15 minutes. Transfer all to a large bowl, cover, and let stand at room temperature 2–3 hours. Serve peaches topped with some of the cooking liquid. About 270 calories per serving.

PEACH MELBA (PÊCHE MELBA)

Also delicious this way are nectarines and pears.
Makes 6 servings

1 cup water
1 cup sugar
3 large firm-ripe peaches, peeled, halved,
  and pitted
2 tablespoons lemon juice
1½ pints vanilla ice cream
1 recipe Melba Sauce

Mix water and sugar in a large skillet (not iron) over moderate heat and heat and stir until sugar dissolves; boil, uncovered, 2 minutes. Add peaches and simmer, uncovered, 10–15 minutes, turning once, until tender but not mushy. Mix in lemon juice and cool peaches in syrup. Place scoops of ice cream in individual dessert dishes, top each with a peach half, hollow side down, and add 2–3 tablespoons Melba Sauce. About 360 calories per serving.

PEACH CARDINAL (PÊCHE CARDINAL)

Pears and nectarines are also excellent prepared this way.
Makes 8 servings

1 cup water
1 cup sugar
4 large firm-ripe peaches, peeled,
  halved, and pitted
1 teaspoon vanilla
2 tablespoons lemon juice
1 quart strawberry ice cream
½ recipe Dessert Cardinal Sauce

Mix water and sugar in a very large skillet (not iron) over moderate heat and stir until sugar dissolves; boil, uncovered, 2 minutes. Add peaches and simmer, uncovered, 10–15 minutes, turning once, until tender but not mushy. Mix in vanilla and lemon juice, and cool peaches in syrup. Place scoops of ice cream in individual dessert dishes, top each with a peach half, hollow side down, and add 2–3 tablespoons Cardinal Sauce. About 245 calories per serving.

BERRY COBBLER

Try this when plump sweet berries are in season.
Makes 6 servings

Filling:

2 quarts fresh berries (any kind),
  washed and stemmed
6 tablespoons cornstarch
2 cups sugar (about)
2 tablespoons butter or margarine

Topping:

1½ cups sifted flour

2 teaspoons baking powder
¼ cup sugar
½ teaspoon salt
¼ cup butter or margarine
½ cup milk

Preheat oven to 400° F. Place berries in an ungreased 3-quart casserole; mix cornstarch and sugar and stir into berries. Taste and, if too tart, add more sugar. Dot with butter and let stand 20 minutes; stir well. Meanwhile, prepare topping: Sift flour, baking powder, sugar, and salt into a bowl, then cut in butter with a pastry blender until mixture resembles coarse meal. Mix in milk with a fork to form a stiff dough. Drop from a tablespoon on top of berries, spacing evenly. Bake, uncovered, 30 minutes until lightly browned and bubbly. Cool to room temperature before serving. Good topped with whipped cream or vanilla ice cream. About 640 calories per serving (without whipped cream or ice cream).

VARIATION:

Peach Cobbler: Prepare as directed, substituting 6–8 peeled, pitted, thinly sliced ripe peaches for the berries— enough to fill casserole ⅔ —and reducing sugar if peaches are very sweet. About 560 calories per serving.

¢ APPLE BROWN BETTY

Always popular. But try the variations, too.
Makes 4–6 servings

1 quart (½-inch) bread cubes or 3 cups
    soft bread crumbs (made from day-old
    bread trimmed of crusts)
⅓ cup melted butter or margarine
1 quart thinly sliced, peeled, and cored
    tart cooking apples
1 cup firmly packed light brown sugar
1 teaspoon cinnamon or ½ teaspoon
    nutmeg
1 teaspoon finely grated lemon rind
2 tablespoons lemon juice
¼ cup water

Preheat oven to 400° F. Toss bread cubes with butter; set aside. Toss apples with remaining ingredients except

water. Beginning and ending with bread cubes, layer bread and apples into a buttered 2-quart casserole. Sprinkle with water, cover, and bake ½ hour. Uncover and bake ½ hour longer until lightly browned. Serve warm with cream, whipped cream, ice cream, or any suitable sauce. About 545 calories for each of 4 servings (without cream or ice cream), 365 calories for each of 6.

VARIATIONS:

Peach or Apricot Brown Betty: Prepare as directed but substitute 2 (1-pound) cans drained sliced peaches or pitted quartered apricots or 3 cups thinly sliced peeled and pitted fresh peaches or apricots for the apples. If you like, substitute ¼ cup syrup drained from canned fruit for the water. About 550 calories for each of 4 servings, 370 calories for each of 6 servings.

Berry-Apple Brown Betty: Prepare as directed, using 2 cups each sliced apples and stemmed blueberries or blackberries. About 545 calories for each of 4 servings, 365 calories for each of 6 servings.

SWISS APPLE CHARLOTTE

Makes 6 servings

6 cups thinly sliced peeled and cored
    tart cooking apples
1½ cups sugar
1 tablespoon lemon juice
⅛–¼ teaspoon nutmeg
¼ cup butter or margarine
1¾–2 cups fine dry bread crumbs
Heavy cream or sweetened whipped
    cream (topping)

Preheat oven to 350° F. Mix apples with sugar, lemon juice, and nutmeg to taste and arrange in a buttered 2-quart casserole about 2″ deep, scattering small pieces of butter through the apples as you fill the dish. Top with crumbs, cover, and bake 35–45 minutes until apples are tender; uncover and bake 10 minutes longer to brown crumbs lightly. Cool about 5 minutes, then serve with cream. About 380 calories per serving (without cream topping).

⊠ QUICK APPLE CRISP

The dessert to serve when time is short.
Makes 4 servings

1 (1-pound 6-ounce) can apple pie filling
1 (5-ounce) stick pastry mix
½ cup firmly packed light brown sugar
¼ teaspoon nutmeg
¼ teaspoon cinnamon

Preheat oven to 375° F. Empty apple
pie filling into a greased 8" round layer
cake pan. Crumble pastry mix into a
bowl, add sugar, nutmeg, and cinnamon,
and mix lightly with a fork. Sprinkle
pastry mixture evenly over filling and
bake, uncovered, 25–30 minutes until
golden. Serve hot, topping, if you like,
with a dollop of vanilla ice cream or
whipped cream. About 460 calories per
serving (without ice cream or whipped
cream).

VARIATION:

⊠ **Quick Peach Crisp:** Prepare as
directed, substituting 2 thawed (10-
ounce) packages frozen peaches for the
apple pie filling and using a 9" pan
instead of an 8". About 440 calories per
serving (without ice cream or whipped
cream).

FRESH PEACH CRISP

The spicy topping makes this Peach Crisp
special.
Makes 4–6 servings

4 large peaches, peeled, pitted, and
*   sliced thin*
Juice of ½ lemon
¼ cup sugar

Topping:

⅔ cup unsifted flour
1 cup firmly packed light brown sugar
1 teaspoon cinnamon
½ teaspoon ginger
⅛ teaspoon mace
¼ teaspoon salt
½ cup butter or margarine, softened to
*   room temperature*

Preheat oven to 350° F. Arrange
peaches in an ungreased 9" piepan;
sprinkle with lemon juice and sugar.
Mix topping ingredients and pat on top
of peaches. Bake, uncovered, about 45
minutes until lightly browned and
bubbly. (*Note:* It's a good idea to place
a piece of aluminum foil under the piepan to catch any drips.) Cool to room
temperature and serve as is or topped
with whipped cream or vanilla ice
cream. About 560 calories for each of
4 servings (without whipped cream or
ice cream), 375 calories for each of 6
servings.

VARIATION:

Fresh Apple Crisp: Prepare as directed,
substituting 5–6 peeled, cored, and
thinly sliced greenings or other tart
cooking apples for the peaches. About
630 calories for each of 4 servings, 425
calories for each of 6 servings (without
whipped cream or ice cream).

⊠ EASY PINEAPPLE CRISP

Couldn't be easier!
Makes 10 servings

1 (1-pound) can crushed pineapple (do
*   not drain)*
1 (14-ounce) package butter pecan cake
*   mix*
½ cup butter or margarine

Preheat oven to 350° F. Spread pineapple over the bottom of a lightly
greased 13"×9"×2" baking pan.
Scatter cake mix evenly over pineapple,
then dot with butter. Bake, uncovered,
about 1 hour until pale golden and
slightly crisp. Serve warm with vanilla
ice cream or heavy cream. About 425
calories per serving (without ice cream
or cream).

SPICY PERSIMMON PUDDING

Makes 12 servings

1⅓ cups sifted flour
1 cup sugar
½ teaspoon baking soda
Pinch salt
½ teaspoon ginger
½ teaspoon cinnamon
½ teaspoon nutmeg
1 cup puréed ripe persimmons

3 eggs, lightly beaten
1 quart milk
½ cup melted butter or margarine

Preheat oven to 300° F. Sift flour with sugar, soda, salt, and spices into a large bowl. Mix persimmons with eggs, milk, and butter and add to dry ingredients, a little at a time, mixing well after each addition. Pour into a greased 13″×9″× 2″ pan and bake, uncovered, about 1 hour until a silver knife inserted near center comes out clean. Serve warm, topped, if you like, with whipped cream. About 270 calories per serving (without whipped cream).

OLD-FASHIONED STRAWBERRY SHORTCAKE

Makes 6–8 servings

3 pints strawberries, washed and
*   stemmed*
½ cup superfine sugar
1 recipe Extra-Rich Biscuits
Butter
Sweetened whipped cream (optional)

Mash strawberries lightly with a potato masher or fork, mix with sugar, and let stand at room temperature while you make the biscuits. Prepare biscuits as directed and, while still hot, split and butter. Smother with strawberries and, if you like, top with whipped cream. For particularly pretty shortcake, save out 8–10 large perfect berries and use to garnish. About 580 calories for each of 6 servings (without whipped cream), 435 calories for each of 8 servings.

VARIATIONS:

Other Fruit Shortcakes: Prepare as directed but substitute 4–5 cups any prepared sweetened berries or other fruit for the strawberries. Recipe too flexible for a meaningful calorie count.

Southern-Style Shortcake: Serve berries or other fruit on rounds or squares of sponge cake instead of on buttered biscuits. Top with whipped cream. Recipe too flexible for a meaningful calorie count.

PUDDINGS

"Pudding," says Webster, "is a dessert of a soft, spongy or thick creamy consistency." Custard is pudding. So are mousses and Bavarians and creams, dessert soufflés, both hot and cold, gelatin fluffs and sponges. To bring order to the category, puddings are arranged here by type of thickener: Custards and other egg-thickened mixtures, starch puddings, gelatin desserts, etc.

About Custards

When they are good—silky-smooth and tender—they are very, very good, but when they are bad . . . well, the less said the better. What makes custards curdle and weep? Too much heat, invariably, or overcooking (which amounts to the same thing). Custards cannot be hurried. Like all egg dishes, they must be cooked gently and slowly (read about the techniques of egg cookery in the chapter on eggs and cheese).

Stirred custards should always be cooked in the top of a double boiler *over simmering* water and stirred throughout cooking. Baked custards should bake slowly in moderate or moderately slow ovens and, as an added safeguard against curdling, in a hot water bath.

Should the milk used in custards be scalded? It isn't necessary if the milk is pasteurized; scalding dates to the days of raw milk, which needed heating to destroy microorganisms. Scalding does, however, seem to mellow the flavor of custards, particularly stirred custards, and to shorten cooking time somewhat.

To Test Custards for Doneness:

Stirred Custard: The standard test is to cook until mixture will "coat the back of a metal spoon," not as easy to determine as it sounds because uncooked custard will also leave a film on a spoon. The difference is that cooked custard should leave a thick, translucent, almost jellylike coat about the consistency of gravy. If you suspect that custard is on the verge of curdling, plunge pan into ice water to stop cooking.

Baked Custard: Insert a table knife into custard midway between rim and center (*not* in the middle as cookbooks once instructed). If knife comes out clean, custard is done. Remove at once from water bath and cool. To chill quickly, set custard in ice water—but only if baking dish is one that can take abrupt changes of temperature without breaking.

What to Do About Curdled Custard: If it's baked custard, the best idea is to turn it into a Trifle by mixing with small hunks of cake; if stirred custard, strain out the lumps and serve as a sauce over cake, fruit, or gelatin dessert.

Caution: Keep custards refrigerated; they spoil easily, often without giving a clue.

¢ ⚖ BAKED CUSTARD

Makes 10 servings

5 eggs (6 if you plan to bake custard in a single large dish)
⅔ cup sugar
¼ teaspoon salt
1 teaspoon vanilla
1 quart milk, scalded
Nutmeg or mace

Preheat oven to 325° F. Beat eggs lightly with sugar, salt, and vanilla; gradually stir in hot milk. Pour into 10 custard cups or a 2-quart baking dish (buttered if you want to unmold custards). Sprinkle with nutmeg, set in a large shallow pan, and pour in warm water to a depth of 1". Bake, uncovered, about 1 hour until a knife inserted midway between center and rim comes out clean. Remove custards from water bath and cool to room temperature. Chill slightly before serving. About 160 calories per serving.

By making custard with skim milk, you can reduce calories to about 125 per serving.

VARIATIONS:

Egg Yolk Custard: Prepare as directed, using 2 egg yolks for each whole egg. About 180 calories per serving.

⚖ **Vanilla Bean Custard:** Prepare as directed, substituting a 2" piece vanilla bean for the extract; heat bean in milk as it scalds; remove before mixing milk into eggs. About 160 calories per serving.

¢ **Butterscotch Custard:** Prepare as directed, using light brown sugar and a ½ and ½ mixture of milk and evaporated milk. About 210 calories per serving.

¢ **Chocolate Custard:** Prepare as directed, melting 2 (1-ounce) grated squares unsweetened chocolate in scalding milk. For a richer custard, use a ½ and ½ mixture of milk and evaporated milk. Omit nutmeg. About 190 calories per serving (made with milk, not evaporated milk).

¢ **Crème Caramel:** Mix custard as directed. Spoon about 1 tablespoon caramelized sugar* into each custard cup, add custard, and bake as directed. Chill, then unmold by dipping custards quickly in warm water and inverting. About 210 calories per serving.

STIRRED CUSTARD OR CUSTARD SAUCE

A good basic recipe with nearly a dozen flavor variations.
Makes 4 servings, about 2 cups sauce

2 cups milk, scalded
5 tablespoons sugar
Pinch salt
4 egg yolks, lightly beaten
1 teaspoon vanilla

Heat milk, sugar, and salt in the top of a double boiler over direct, moderate heat, stirring until sugar dissolves. Spoon a little hot mixture into yolks, return to pan, set over *simmering* water, and cook and stir 2–3 minutes until thickened and no raw egg taste remains. Mix in vanilla and serve hot or cool quickly by setting pan in ice water and stirring briskly. Serve as is or over cake, fruit, or pudding. About 200 calories per serving.

VARIATIONS:

¢ ⚖️ **Low-Calorie Stirred Custard:** Prepare as directed but use skim milk instead of whole, reduce sugar to ¼ cup, and use 2 lightly beaten eggs instead of all yolks. About 125 calories per ½ cup serving.

¢ **Thin Custard Sauce:** Prepare as directed but increase milk to 2½ cups. About 350 calories per cup. About 22 calories per tablespoon.

¢ **Thick Custard Sauce:** Scald 1½ cups milk; blend remaining ½ cup milk with ¼ cup cornstarch. Mix sugar and salt with hot milk, blend in cornstarch paste and heat and stir over direct, moderate heat until thickened. Mix a little hot sauce into 3 lightly beaten eggs, return to pan, set over simmering water, and heat, stirring constantly, 2–3 minutes until no raw taste of egg remains. Mix in vanilla or, if you prefer, ⅛ teaspoon almond extract. Serve hot, or cool as directed and use in making Trifle or other dessert where a thick custard sauce is called for. About 420 calories per cup, 26 calories per tablespoon.

¢ **Lemon Custard Sauce:** Prepare as directed, substituting ¼ teaspoon lemon extract and 2 teaspoons finely grated lemon rind for vanilla. About 400 calories per cup, 25 calories per tablespoon.

Orange Custard Sauce: Prepare as directed, using 1 cup each orange juice and milk and 1 tablespoon finely grated orange rind instead of vanilla. About 380 calories per cup, 24 calories per tablespoon.

¢ **Chocolate Custard Sauce:** Prepare as directed, blending 1 (1-ounce) coarsely grated square unsweetened chocolate into the scalding milk. About

470 calories per cup, 30 calories per tablespoon.

¢ **Coffee Custard Sauce:** Prepare, using 1 cup each hot strong black coffee and milk; reduce vanilla to ¼ teaspoon. About 320 calories per cup, 20 calories per tablespoon.

¢ **Mocha Custard Sauce:** Prepare Coffee Custard Sauce (above), blending 1 (1-ounce) coarsely grated square unsweetened chocolate into scalding liquid. About 400 calories per cup, 25 calories per tablespoon.

¢ **Maple Custard Sauce:** Prepare as directed, substituting ⅓ cup firmly packed light brown sugar for the granulated and ½ teaspoon maple flavoring for vanilla. About 410 calories per cup, 26 calories per tablespoon.

¢ **Molasses Custard Sauce:** Prepare as directed, using ¼ cup molasses and 2 tablespoons sugar instead of the 5 tablespoons sugar. About 420 calories per cup, 26 calories per tablespoon.

¢ **Caramel Custard Sauce:** Increase sugar to ⅓ cup, caramelize,* then add scalded milk and proceed as directed. About 400 calories per cup, 25 calories per tablespoon.

¢ **Spicy Custard Sauce:** Prepare as directed but reduce vanilla to ¼ teaspoon and add ½ teaspoon cinnamon *or* ¼ teaspoon each cinnamon and nutmeg *or* ¼ teaspoon ginger and a pinch cardamom. About 400 calories per cup, 25 calories per tablespoon.

Coconut Custard Sauce: Prepare as directed but flavor with ¼ teaspoon each vanilla and almond extract; mix in ⅓ cup flaked or toasted coconut. About 460 calories per cup, 29 calories per tablespoon.

Sour Cream Custard Sauce: (Makes about 3 cups): Prepare and cool as directed, then blend in, a little at a time, 1 cup sour cream. About 420 calories per cup, 26 calories per tablespoon.

CRÈME BRÛLÈE

This extra-rich custard with a crackly, broiled-on sugar topping is showy, yet simple to make.
Makes 6 servings

3 cups heavy cream
⅓ cup superfine sugar
½ teaspoon vanilla
6 egg yolks, lightly beaten
¾–1 cup light brown sugar (not *firmly packed*)

Cook and stir cream, sugar, vanilla, and yolks in the top of a double boiler over simmering water 7–10 minutes until mixture coats a *wooden* spoon. Pour into an ungreased shallow 1½-quart casserole and stir 1–2 minutes. Place wax paper directly on surface of crème, cool to room temperature, then chill 1–2 hours. Preheat broiler. Sprinkle a ¼″ layer of brown sugar evenly over crème, set casserole in a shallow bed of crushed ice, and broil 6″–8″ from heat about 3 minutes until sugar melts and bubbles (watch so it doesn't burn). Remove from ice, chill 10–15 minutes, then serve, including some of the crackly topping with each portion. About 680 calories per serving.

FLAN

A popular Spanish custard dessert, unusually smooth because it is made with egg yolks only.
Makes 6–8 servings

*⅓ cup caramelized sugar**
8 egg yolks
½ cup sugar
¼ teaspoon salt
½ teaspoon vanilla
3 cups milk, scalded

Preheat oven to 325° F. Pour caramelized sugar into a well-buttered 9″ layer cake pan. Beat egg yolks lightly with sugar, salt, and vanilla; gradually mix in hot milk. Pour into pan, set in a large, shallow pan, and pour in hot water to a depth of ½″. Bake, uncovered, about 1 hour until a knife inserted in the *center* comes out clean. Remove custard from water bath and cool to room temperature. Chill 2–3 hours. Dip pan quickly in very hot water, then invert on serving dish. Cut in wedges and serve. About 270 calories for each of 6 servings, 200 calories for each of 8 servings.

VARIATIONS:

Rum Flan: Prepare as directed, using ½ cup light rum and 2½ cups milk. About 340 calories for each of 6 servings, 255 calories for each of 8 servings.

Pineapple Flan: Prepare as directed, using 2 cups pineapple juice and 1 cup milk; reduce vanilla to ¼ teaspoon and add ¼ teaspoon almond extract. About 270 calories for each 6 servings, 200 calories for each of 8 servings.

FLOATING ISLAND

Makes 4 servings

1 recipe Stirred Custard

Meringue:

2 egg whites
⅛ teaspoon salt
¼ cup sugar

Preheat broiler. Pour custard into 4 custard cups. Beat egg whites with salt until frothy, gradually beat in sugar, a little at a time, and continue to beat until stiff peaks form. Using a serving spoon dipped in cold water, float a large spoonful of meringue on each custard. Set custard cups in a large pan of ice water and broil 4″ from heat until tinged with brown. Serve at once. About 255 calories per serving.

VARIATION:

Oeufs à la Neige: Before making custard, prepare meringue as directed. Heat 2 cups milk to simmering in a large skillet (not iron), drop meringue by spoonfuls on milk, and poach 2–3 minutes, turning once with a spoon dipped in hot water. Using a slotted spoon, transfer meringues to a wet plate and cool. Prepare Stirred Custard as directed, using poaching milk. Cool custard. Float poached meringues on custard and chill 2–3 hours before serving. About 255 calories per serving.

TRIFLE OR TIPSY CAKE

Makes 8 servings

*1 recipe Easy Sponge Loaf or 1 small
  sponge or yellow cake*
¾ cup strawberry jam
*1 (1-pound 14-ounce) can pitted
  apricots, drained and puréed*
*1 (11-ounce) can mandarin oranges,
  drained (optional)*
½ cup Marsala or cream sherry
1 recipe Thick Custard Sauce
1 cup heavy cream
¼ cup superfine sugar
¼ teaspoon vanilla
Candied cherries or fruit (garnish)

Split cake into thin layers, spread with
jam and about half of the apricot purée,
and sandwich back together. Cut in bars
about 1″×2″ and pack into a 2-quart
serving dish; arrange oranges in and
around cake if you like. Prick cake well
all over and pour Marsala on top; spread
with remaining purée and smother with
custard sauce. Cover and chill 2 hours.
Shortly before serving, whip cream with
sugar until stiff; fold in vanilla. Frost on
top of Trifle and decorate with candied
cherries. About 600 calories per serving.

ZABAGLIONE

Serve this fluffy wine custard hot or cold
as a dessert or dessert sauce. Especially
good over fresh sliced peaches, strawberries, or homemade Angel Food Cake
(a luscious way to use up the yolks).
Makes 6 servings

6 egg yolks
⅔ cup superfine sugar
Pinch salt
⅔ cup Marsala wine

Beat egg yolks in top of a double boiler
(set on a counter) with a rotary or
electric beater until cream colored. Add
sugar, a little at a time, beating hard
after each addition. Beat in salt and
Marsala. Set *over* simmering water
(should not touch bottom of pan) and
heat and beat constantly with a wire
whisk until thick and foamy, about 5–7
minutes. Set double boiler top on counter

and continue beating 2–3 minutes. Serve
warm or cool further, continuing to
beat so mixture does not separate. About
170 calories per serving (without fruit or
cake).

¢ ⚖ RENNET CUSTARD

Perfect for those allergic to eggs.
Makes 4 servings

*2 cups whole or skim milk (fresh milk
  only)*
3 tablespoons sugar
1 teaspoon vanilla
*1 rennet tablet (obtainable at most
  drugstores)*
1 tablespoon cold water

Warm milk with sugar until about
110° F. Off heat, mix in vanilla. Crush
rennet tablet in the cold water, add to
milk and stir 2–3 seconds, no longer.
Pour into 4 custard cups and let stand
undisturbed 15 minutes. Chill 2 hours
and serve. If you like, garnish with
preserves, toasted coconut, whipped
cream, chopped nuts, or fresh berries.
About 115 calories per serving made
with whole milk, 80 calories with skim
milk (without garnish).

VARIATIONS:

⚖ ¢ **Lemon or Orange Rennet
Custard:** Prepare as directed but flavor
with ½ teaspoon lemon or orange extract
or 1 tablespoon finely grated lemon or
orange rind instead of vanilla. Tint
yellow or pale orange, if you like, with
food coloring. About 115 calories per
serving.

Rum-Cream Rennet Custard: Prepare as
directed but substitute 1 cup light or
heavy cream for 1 cup milk; also
substitute 2 tablespoons light rum for the
cold water. About 195 calories per
serving.

⚖ **Fruit and Rennet Custard:** Arrange
2–3 slices fresh peach, pear, or banana
or a few berries in the bottom of each
custard cup, then fill with any of the
rennet custards. About 130 calories per
serving.

VANILLA POTS DE CRÈME

Makes 6–7 servings

6 egg yolks
⅓ cup sugar
1 pint heavy cream
1 (1-inch) piece vanilla bean or 1
  teaspoon vanilla

Preheat oven to 325° F. Beat egg yolks with sugar until cream colored. Scald cream with vanilla bean or scald, then add vanilla extract. Remove vanilla bean if used. Gradually stir cream into yolks and strain through a small, fine sieve into 6–7 *pots de crème.* Set pots in a large, shallow pan and pour in warm water to a depth of 1". Bake, uncovered, 25–30 minutes until a knife inserted midway between center and rim comes out clean. Remove pots from water bath, cool, cover, and chill. Serve cold, topped, if you like, with swirls of whipped cream. About 385 calories for each of 6 servings (without whipped cream), 330 calories for each of 7 servings.

VARIATIONS:

Coffee Pots de Crème: Prepare as directed but add 1½ teaspoons instant coffee powder to yolk mixture along with scalded cream and stir until dissolved. If you like, flavor with 1–2 tablespoons coffee liqueur. About 385 calories for each of 6 servings, 330 calories for each of 7 servings.

Brandy (or Rum) Pots de Crème: Prepare as directed but add 3 tablespoons dark rum or brandy to yolk mixture along with scalded cream. About 415 calories for each of 6 servings, 360 calories for each of 7 servings.

CLASSIC POTS DE CRÈME AU CHOCOLAT

A dark chocolate French custard. Very rich!
Makes 4 servings

1 pint heavy cream
1 (1-ounce) square unsweetened
  chocolate, coarsely grated
6 tablespoons sugar

4 egg yolks, lightly beaten
¼ teaspoon vanilla

Mix cream, chocolate, and sugar in the top of a double boiler, set over simmering water, and heat, beating with a wire whisk, until sugar dissolves and chocolate is blended in. Stir a little hot mixture into egg yolks, then return to pan and cook and stir 2–3 minutes until thickened. Pour mixture into a bowl at once, stir in vanilla, and cool slightly, stirring now and then. Pour into 4 *pots de crème* or custard cups. Cool to room temperature, then chill 2 hours. Serve cold, topped, if you like, with swirls of whipped cream or a few toasted, slivered almonds. About 585 calories per serving (without whipped cream or nuts).

¢ OLD-FASHIONED BREAD AND BUTTER PUDDING

A perfectly delicious way to use up stale bread.
Makes 6–8 servings

4 slices day-old or stale bread
2 tablespoons butter or margarine
½ cup seedless or sultana raisins
¼ teaspoon each cinnamon and nutmeg,
  mixed together
3 eggs, lightly beaten
⅓ cup sugar
2¼ cups milk

If you like, trim crusts from bread, then butter each slice and quarter. Arrange 2 quartered slices in the bottom of a buttered 1½-quart casserole, sprinkle with half the raisins and half the spice mixture. Top with remaining bread, raisins, and spice mixture. Beat eggs with sugar until cream colored, add milk, and pour over bread. Let stand at room temperature 1 hour. Preheat oven to 350° F. Set casserole in a large, shallow pan and pour in hot water to a depth of 1". Bake, uncovered, about 1 hour until a knife inserted midway between center and rim comes out clean. Cool slightly and serve. If you like, pass cinnamon-sugar to sprinkle on top. About 260 calories for each of 6 servings, 200 calories for each of 8 servings (without cinnamon sugar sprinkled on top).

¢ QUEEN OF PUDDINGS

This lemon-flavored bread pudding is
spread with jam, then topped with
meringue.
Makes 6 servings

2 cups day-old bread crumbs
1 quart milk, scalded
2 eggs plus 2 egg yolks, lightly beaten
⅓ cup sugar
¼ teaspoon salt
¼ cup melted butter or margarine
Finely grated rind of 1 lemon
½ cup raspberry or strawberry jam or
red currant jelly

Meringue:

2 egg whites
¼ cup superfine sugar

Preheat oven to 350° F. Place bread
crumbs in a buttered 1½-quart casserole.
Slowly mix milk into eggs, then stir in
sugar, salt, butter, and lemon rind; pour
over bread and let stand ½ hour at room
temperature. Mix lightly, set casserole in
a shallow pan, pour warm water into pan
to a depth of 1″, and bake, uncovered,
about 1 hour or until a knife inserted
midway between center and rim comes
out clean. Remove from oven but leave
in water bath; spread jam over pudding.
Beat egg whites until frothy, slowly beat
in sugar, and continue to beat until soft
peaks form. Cover jam with meringue;
return pudding to oven (same temperature) and bake about 15 minutes until
meringue is lightly browned. Cool
slightly and serve. About 465 calories per
serving.

EXTRA DARK AND RICH CHOCOLATE MOUSSE

Makes 4 servings

4 (1-ounce) squares unsweetened
chocolate
⅔ cup sugar
¼ cup heavy cream
⅛ teaspoon salt
2 tablespoons hot water
5 eggs, separated
1 teaspoon vanilla
1 tablespoon cognac or coffee liqueur
Whipped cream (optional topping)

Place chocolate, sugar, cream, and salt
in the top of a double boiler, set over
simmering water, and heat, stirring
occasionally, until chocolate is melted
and sugar thoroughly dissolved, about 20
minutes. Add hot water and heat,
stirring, until smooth and satiny. Beat in
egg yolks, 1 at a time, and remove at
once from heat. Beat egg whites to soft
peaks; mix about ½ cup whites into
chocolate mixture, then lightly fold in the
rest, taking care not to break down the
volume. Mix in vanilla and cognac,
cover, and chill 12 hours before serving.
Top, if you like, with fluffs of whipped
cream. About 445 calories per serving
(without whipped cream).

CHOCOLATE MOUSSE

Not as rich or as difficult to make as
Extra Dark and Rich Chocolate
Mousse.
Makes 8 servings

6 (1-ounce) squares semisweet chocolate
or 1 (6-ounce) package semisweet
chocolate bits
2 tablespoons hot water or strong black
coffee
5 eggs, separated
1½ teaspoons vanilla
1½ cups heavy cream
Chocolate curls* (optional decoration)

Place chocolate and hot water in the top
of a double boiler, set over simmering
water, and heat and stir until chocolate
is melted. Lightly beat yolks, add a little
hot mixture, then stir back into pan and
heat and stir over simmering water 1–2
minutes until no raw taste of egg
remains. Off heat, mix in vanilla. Beat
cream until very thick and glossy (it
should almost form soft peaks) and fold
into chocolate mixture. Beat egg whites
until soft peaks form and fold in, a little
at a time, until no flecks of white show.
Spoon into a serving dish, cover, and
chill at least 12 hours. Scatter with
chocolate curls, if you like, just before
serving. About 315 calories per serving.

⚖ FRUIT WHIP

Fruit whip will have richer flavor if the
dried fruit is stewed the day before and

soaked overnight in its stewing liquid. Drain before puréeing.
Makes 6 servings

3 egg whites
¼ teaspoon salt
Pinch cream of tartar
½ cup sugar
1 cup cold puréed stewed prunes, dried apricots, peaches, or figs
⅛ teaspoon cinnamon or nutmeg
1 tablespoon lemon juice

Beat egg whites, salt, and cream of tartar until frothy, gradually beat in sugar, then continue beating until stiff peaks form. Fold remaining ingredients into egg whites, spoon into goblets, and chill well. Serve with Custard Sauce or sweetened whipped cream. About 120 calories per serving (without sauce or whipped cream).

VARIATIONS:

⚖ **Fruit and Nut Whip:** Prepare as directed, then fold in ¼ cup minced pecans, walnuts, or toasted almonds. About 150 calories per serving.

⚖ **Baked Fruit Whip:** Prepare as directed but do not chill. Spoon into an ungreased 5-cup soufflé dish or casserole, set in a large, shallow baking pan, pour in hot water to a depth of 1″, and bake uncovered 30–35 minutes at 350° F. until puffy and just firm. Serve warm with cream. About 120 calories per serving (without cream).

About Dessert Soufflés

Dessert soufflés are neither as fragile nor temperamental as reputation would have them. Their biggest shortcoming is that they must be baked at the last minute. They may, however, be partially made ahead of time to avoid last-minute scurrying around. They are prepared exactly like savory soufflés (see About Soufflés in the chapter on eggs and cheese). They can be baked in unbuttered soufflé dishes or straightsided casseroles or, for glistening brown crusts, in *well-buttered and sugared* ones

(butter dish well, spoon in a little granulated sugar, then tilt from one side to the other until evenly coated with sugar; tap out excess).

BASIC HOT DESSERT SOUFFLÉ

From this one basic recipe, you can make seven different soufflés.
Makes 4 servings

2 tablespoons cornstarch
½ cup sugar
1 cup milk
4 egg yolks
2 teaspoons vanilla or the finely grated rind of 1 lemon
4 egg whites
¼ teaspoon cream of tartar

Preheat oven to 350° F. Mix cornstarch and sugar in a heavy saucepan, gradually mix in milk, and heat, stirring constantly over moderate heat, until boiling. Boil and stir 1 minute; mixture will be quite thick. Off heat, beat in egg yolks, 1 at a time; mix in vanilla. Lay a piece of wax paper flat on sauce and cool to room temperature. (*Note:* Soufflé can be made up to this point well ahead of time to avoid last-minute rush.) Beat egg whites with cream of tartar until stiff but not dry, stir about ¼ cup into sauce, then fold in remaining whites. Spoon into a buttered and sugared 6-cup soufflé dish and bake, uncovered, 35–45 minutes until puffy and browned. Serve at once, accompanied, if you like, with Custard Sauce or sweetened whipped cream. About 225 calories per serving (without sauce or whipped cream).

VARIATIONS:

Hot Coffee Soufflé: Prepare as directed, substituting 1 cup cold, very strong black coffee for the milk. About 190 calories for each of 4 servings.

Hot Orange Soufflé: Prepare as directed but use 3 tablespoons cornstarch and substitute 1¼ cups orange juice for the milk; substitute 2 teaspoons finely grated orange rind and 1 teaspoon finely grated lemon rind for the vanilla. About 225 calories per serving.

Hot Chocolate Soufflé: Prepare sauce as directed, increasing sugar to ¾ cup. Before adding yolks, blend in 2 (1-ounce) squares grated unsweetened chocolate or 2 (1-ounce) envelopes no-melt unsweetened chocolate. Proceed as directed, reducing vanilla to 1 teaspoon. About 345 calories per serving.

Hot Nut Soufflé: Prepare sauce as directed but flavor with ½ teaspoon each vanilla and almond extract. Before folding in egg whites, mix in ½ cup minced, toasted, blanched almonds (or minced pecans, walnuts, Brazil nuts, or hazelnuts). Proceed as directed. About 320 calories per serving.

Hot Fruit Soufflé: Prepare sauce as directed but use 3 tablespoons cornstarch, ⅔ cup sugar, ½ cup milk, and 1 cup sieved fruit purée (peach or berry is particularly good). Proceed as directed but bake in a 7-cup soufflé dish. About 300 calories per serving.

Hot Grand Marnier Soufflé: Prepare sauce as directed, using ¾ cup milk and flavoring with the grated rinds of 1 orange and 1 lemon. After adding yolks, beat in ¼–⅓ cup Grand Marnier (or curaçao, Cointreau, or rum). Proceed as directed. About 250 calories per serving.

About Starch-Thickened Puddings

These are really thick sweet sauces, and the techniques of preparing them are the same as for savory starch-thickened sauces (see About Starch Thickeners and Some Tips for Making Better Sauces in the chapter on sauces, gravies, and butters).

The most important points to remember when making starch-thickened pudding are to use a pan heavy enough and a heat low enough to prevent scorching, also to stir constantly as mixture thickens to prevent lumping. Once thickened, starch puddings should mellow several minutes over low heat to remove all raw starch flavor. Like custards, they spoil easily and must be kept refrigerated.

¢ BASIC STIRRED VANILLA PUDDING

Makes 4 servings

2 tablespoons cornstarch
½ cup sugar
2 cups milk
1 egg, lightly beaten
1 teaspoon vanilla
1 tablespoon butter or margarine

Mix cornstarch and sugar in a heavy saucepan. Gradually mix in milk and heat, stirring constantly over moderate heat, until mixture boils. Boil and stir 1 minute. Turn heat to very low, mix a little hot sauce into egg, return to pan, and cook and stir 2–3 minutes until no raw taste of egg remains. Do not boil. Off heat, mix in vanilla and butter; cool slightly, pour into serving dishes and serve warm. Or place a circle of wax paper directly on surface of pudding and cool completely; chill and serve cold. If you like decorate with swirls of whipped cream. About 235 calories per serving (without whipped cream).

VARIATIONS:

¢ **Caramel Pudding:** Prepare as directed but substitute ¾ cup firmly packed dark brown sugar for the granulated. If you like, flavor with maple extract instead of vanilla. About 245 calories per serving.

¢ **Chocolate Pudding:** Prepare as directed but increase sugar to ¾ cup and add 1 square coarsely grated unsweetened chocolate along with egg. Reduce vanilla to ½ teaspoon, omit butter, and beat pudding briefly with a rotary beater after removing from heat. About 295 calories per serving.

¢ **Mocha Pudding:** Prepare Chocolate Pudding (above) and add 1 teaspoon instant coffee powder along with chocolate. If you like, serve cold sprinkled with slivered, blanched almonds. About 295 calories per serving (without almonds).

Surprise Fruit Pudding: Slice stale white or yellow cake thin, spread with any jam, cut in small cubes, and place about ¼ cup into each of 6 custard cups. Top with thinly sliced bananas, oranges, or peaches and fill with Vanilla Pudding. Cool and serve. About 340 calories per serving.

¢ ⚖ **VANILLA BLANCMANGE (CORNSTARCH PUDDING)**

Slightly thicker than Basic Stirred Vanilla Pudding and not quite so sweet. Try the flavor variations, too.
Makes 8 servings

⅔ cup sugar
6 tablespoons cornstarch
¼ teaspoon salt
1 quart milk
2 teaspoons vanilla

Mix sugar, cornstarch, and salt in the top of a double boiler, then gradually blend in milk. Set over just boiling water and heat, stirring constantly, until thickened. Cook 5–7 minutes, stirring now and then. Remove from heat, add vanilla, and cool 10 minutes, stirring now and then. Pour into a 5-cup mold that has been rinsed in cold water, or into 8 individual molds. Chill until firm, 3–4 hours for large mold, 1–2 hours for small ones. Unmold and serve with any dessert sauce, fresh or stewed fruit. About 165 calories per serving (without sauce or fruit).

VARIATIONS:

Chocolate Blancmange: Prepare as directed, using 1⅓ cups sugar and 7 tablespoons cornstarch; when thickened, add 3 (1-ounce) squares coarsely grated unsweetened chocolate, stirring until melted, then cook 5 minutes longer. Off heat, beat in 1 teaspoon vanilla. Beat occasionally with a wire whip as mixture cools. Pour into molds and chill as directed. Good with whipped cream. About 290 calories per serving (without whipped cream).

Fruit Blancmange: Prepare as directed, using 2 cups each milk and sieved fruit purée (berries, peaches, pineapple, and banana are good) instead of all milk. Adjust sugar according to sweetness of fruit and tint, if you like, an appropriate color. About 170 calories per serving.

⚖ **Lemon Blancmange:** Prepare as directed, using 7 tablespoons cornstarch, ½ cup lemon juice, 3½ cups milk, and the finely grated rind of 1 lemon. Tint pale yellow. About 165 calories per serving.

⚖ **Orange Blancmange:** Prepare as directed, using 7 tablespoons cornstarch, 2 cups each milk and orange juice, and the finely grated rind of 1 orange. Tint orange if you like. About 160 calories per serving.

¢ **TAPIOCA PUDDING**

Tapioca, starch from cassava roots, can be used to thicken soups, sauces, and puddings. It is made into flakes and flour, but more popular are the granules called *quick cooking tapioca* (available plain and in various flavors) and "fisheye" tapioca in medium and large pearl sizes.
Makes 4 servings

⅓ cup medium or large pearl tapioca
1 cup cold water
2 cups milk
⅓ cup sugar
⅛ teaspoon salt
¼ teaspoon vanilla

Soak tapioca in cold water at least 3 hours or overnight if you prefer; do not drain. Transfer to a large, heavy saucepan, add remaining ingredients except vanilla, and simmer over lowest heat, stirring now and then, 1 hour. Off heat, mix in vanilla; serve warm or chilled. If you like, top with cream or stewed fruit. About 215 calories per serving (without cream or fruit).

VARIATIONS:

Baked Tapioca Pudding: Prepare pudding as directed, but simmer only ½ hour. Mix in vanilla, pour into a buttered 1-quart casserole, dot with 1 tablespoon butter, and bake, uncov- ered, 1 hour at 325° F. until lightly browned. About 240 calories per serving.

Chocolate Tapioca Pudding: Prepare as directed but increase sugar to ½ cup and add 1 (1-ounce) square unsweetened chocolate during last half hour of simmering; stir frequently until chocolate melts. About 285 calories per serving.

Butterscotch Tapioca Pudding: Soak tapioca as directed. Warm ¾ cup firmly packed dark brown sugar in 2 tablespoons butter in a large saucepan over moderate heat, stirring frequently, until melted. Mix in tapioca, milk, and salt and proceed as directed. About 235 calories per serving.

¢ BAKED RICE PUDDING

Short grain rice, *not* converted, makes the best pudding.
Makes 4–6 servings

⅓ cup uncooked short grain rice
1 quart milk
½ cup sugar
*⅛ teaspoon nutmeg or 1 teaspoon
  vanilla*
2–3 tablespoons butter or margarine

Preheat oven to 300° F. Sprinkle rice evenly over the bottom of a buttered 1½-quart casserole. Mix milk and sugar, pour over rice, sprinkle with nutmeg, and dot with butter. Bake, uncovered, 2½ hours, stirring every 15 minutes for the first 1½ hours, until lightly browned. Serve warm, topped, if you like, with cream. About 375 calories for each of 4 servings (without cream), 250 calories for each of 6 servings.

VARIATIONS:

¢ **Raisin Rice Pudding:** Prepare as directed and bake 1½ hours; stir in ⅔–1 cup seedless or sultana raisins and bake 1 hour longer. About 490 calories for each of 4 servings, 325 calories for each of 6 servings.

Creamy Rice Pudding: Prepare pudding as directed and bake 2 hours; mix in ½ cup heavy cream and bake ½ hour longer. About 480 calories for each of 4 servings, 320 calories for each of 6 servings.

¢ **Cold Rice Pudding:** Reduce rice to ¼ cup and proceed as directed. Chill pudding and serve with fresh fruit or whipped cream. About 360 calories for each of 4 servings (without whipped cream or fruit), 240 calories for each of 6 servings.

⊠ ¢ **"Quick" Baked Rice Pudding:** Heat milk, sugar, nutmeg, and butter in the top of a double boiler over direct heat until just boiling. Mix in rice, set over boiling water, and cook, stirring now and then, 40 minutes. Transfer to a buttered 1-quart casserole and bake 20 minutes at 350° F. until lightly browned. About 375 calories for each of 4 servings, 250 calories for each of 6 servings.

¢ **Lemon or Orange Rice Pudding:** Prepare as directed but omit nutmeg; mix in 1 tablespoon finely grated lemon rind or 2 tablespoons finely grated orange rind and ½ teaspoon lemon or orange extract. About 375 calories for each of 4 servings, 250 calories for each of 6 servings.

RICE À L'IMPÉRATRICE

An impressive cold rice pudding studded with candied fruit and molded in a decorative mold.
Makes 8 servings

1⅓ cups milk
½ cup uncooked long grain rice
*⅓ cup minced mixed candied fruit
  soaked in 1 tablespoon kirsch*
1 cup heavy cream
*½ cup sweetened whipped cream
  (garnish)*
*Quartered candied cherries and angelica
  strips (garnish)*

Custard:

1 envelope unflavored gelatin
1 cup milk
½ cup sugar
4 egg yolks, lightly beaten
1 teaspoon vanilla

Heat milk to boiling in a small, heavy saucepan, stir in rice, cover, and simmer over lowest heat, stirring now and then, 20–30 minutes until rice is just tender. Fluff rice with a fork and cool. Meanwhile, make the custard: Sprinkle gelatin over milk, let stand 2–3 minutes, mix, and pour into the top of a double boiler. Add sugar, set over simmering water, and heat and stir until steaming. Mix a little milk into egg yolks, return to pan, and cook and stir 2–3 minutes until custard will coat the back of a metal spoon. Remove from heat, mix in vanilla, cool slightly, then stir into rice along with candied fruit; cool to room temperature. Beat cream until soft peaks form, fold into rice, spoon into an unbuttered 1½-quart decorative mold, cover, and chill several hours or overnight. Unmold and decorate with fluffs of whipped cream, cherries, and angelica. About 320 calories per serving.

VARIATION:

Pears or Peaches à l'Impératrice: Unmold Rice à l'Impératrice in the center of a large, shallow crystal bowl; surround with cold poached or canned pear or peach halves, hollows filled with red currant jelly. Sprig with mint. About 420 calories per serving.

¢ **INDIAN PUDDING**

This New England corn meal pudding is traditionally very soft and may even "weep" (separate) slightly when served. No matter, it's spicy and good.
Makes 6 servings

¼ *cup corn meal*
1 quart milk
¾ *cup molasses*
⅓ *cup firmly packed light brown sugar*
¼ *cup butter or margarine*
¼ *teaspoon salt*
½ *teaspoon cinnamon*
½ *teaspoon ginger*
½ *cup seedless raisins (optional)*

Preheat oven to 325° F. Mix corn meal and 1 cup milk. Heat 2 cups milk in the top of a double boiler over simmering water until steaming. Mix in corn meal mixture and cook 15–20 minutes, stirring now and then. Stir in molasses and sugar and cook 2–3 minutes longer. Off heat, mix in butter, salt, spices, and, if you like, raisins. Spoon into a buttered 1-quart casserole and pour remaining milk evenly over top. Bake, uncovered, about 1½ hours until a

table knife inserted midway between center and rim comes out clean. Serve warm with whipped cream or ice cream dusted with nutmeg. About 375 calories per serving (without whipped cream or ice cream).

For a Firmer Pudding: Prepare corn meal mixture as directed; instead of pouring final cup milk over pudding, mix with 2 lightly beaten eggs and blend into pudding. Bake 2 hours at 300° F. just until firm. About 405 calories per serving.

VARIATION:

Apple Indian Pudding: When preparing corn meal mixture, increase meal to ⅓ cup. Toss 1½–2 cups thinly sliced, peeled, and cored tart cooking apples with ⅓ cup sugar, scatter over the bottom of a buttered 2-quart casserole, top with pudding mixture, and bake as directed. About 440 calories per serving.

About Steamed Puddings

These rich, moist puddings aren't often made today. Too troublesome, perhaps. There's no denying they require time and effort. But served on a frosty day, they add such a warm, nostalgic touch, making the bother seem supremely worthwhile.

About Pudding Molds: Unless you make steamed puddings often, you probably won't want to buy proper pudding molds. You can get by using metal cooking bowls, coffee tins, ice-cream bombe molds (if you have them), even custard cups.

About Preparing and Filling Pudding Molds: Butter molds well, then pour in enough pudding batter to fill mold two-thirds—no more; steamed puddings must have plenty of room to expand. Cover mold snugly, either with a lid or a well-greased double thickness of aluminum foil tied securely in place.

About Steaming Puddings: Any deep, heavy kettle fitted with a rack can be used for steaming puddings (if the kettle has no rack of its own, use a cake rack).

Stand molds upright on rack, pour in enough boiling water to reach halfway up the sides of the molds. Tightly cover kettle and adjust burner so water simmers or boils gently. Check kettle occasionally, adding boiling water as needed to keep molds half submerged throughout steaming. (*Note:* Puddings may be steamed in pressure cookers; follow manufacturer's instructions carefully.)

About Unmolding Steamed Puddings: Remove puddings from steamer and uncover. Let stand a few minutes, then loosen, if necessary with a thin spatula and invert on serving plate. Or, if you prefer, before uncovering mold, dip it quickly in cold water to loosen pudding. Uncover and turn out. If you like a slightly drier pudding, warm 3–5 minutes in a 350° F. oven after unmolding.

To Serve Steamed Puddings: Cut in wedges as you would cake and top with Hard Sauce or other sauce of compatible flavor.

BASIC STEAMED LEMON PUDDING

To avoid a cracked pudding, uncover and let stand 2–3 minutes so that steam can escape, then unmold. There are, by the way, more than a half-dozen different ways to vary the flavor of this basic recipe.
Makes 8 servings

1½ cups sifted flour
2 teaspoons baking powder
¼ teaspoon salt
½ cup butter, margarine, or shortening
½ cup sugar
2 eggs
Finely grated rind of 1 lemon
2 tablespoons lemon juice
½ cup milk

Sift flour with baking powder and salt and set aside. Cream butter and sugar until light, add eggs, one at a time, beating well after each addition. Beat in lemon rind and juice. Add flour alternately with milk, beginning and ending with flour; beat well after each addition. Spoon into a well-greased 1½-quart mold or metal bowl, cover with a greased double thickness of foil, and tie around with string. Set on a rack in a large kettle and pour in enough boiling water to come halfway up mold. Cover and steam 1–1½ hours or until metal skewer inserted in center of pudding comes out clean. Keep water simmering throughout, replenishing as needed with boiling water. Uncover mold and let stand 2–3 minutes, then invert on serving dish. Cut in wedges and serve warm with hot Lemon Sauce or Custard Sauce. Leftover pudding may be wrapped in foil and reheated in a 350° F. oven for 20–30 minutes. About 255 calories per serving (without sauce).

VARIATIONS:

Steamed Orange Pudding: Substitute the grated rind of 1 large orange for the lemon; omit lemon juice and use ¼ cup each orange juice and milk instead of all milk. Otherwise, prepare as directed. About 255 calories per serving.

Steamed Chocolate Pudding: Increase sugar to ¾ cup, beat in 3 (1-ounce) envelopes no-melt unsweetened chocolate after eggs and substitute 1 teaspoon vanilla for lemon rind and juice. About 335 calories per serving.

Steamed Ginger Pudding: Substitute ½ cup firmly packed light brown sugar for the granulated; omit lemon rind and juice and add 1½ teaspoons ginger. About 260 calories per serving.

Steamed College Pudding: Prepare batter and mix in ⅓ cup each sultana raisins and dried currants and ¼ cup minced mixed candied fruit and 1 teaspoon allspice. About 300 calories per serving.

Jam or Marmalade Topped Steamed Pudding: Spoon ¼ cup strawberry, raspberry, or black currant jam or orange marmalade into bottom of pudding mold, then add batter and steam as directed. Unmold and top with an additional ⅓ cup hot jam or marmalade.

Serve with hot Custard Sauce. About 335 calories per serving (without sauce).

Steamed Date Pudding: Prepare batter as directed and mix in ½ pound finely cut-up pitted dates. About 315 calories per serving.

Individual Steamed Puddings: Prepare any batter as directed and fill greased custard cups two-thirds full, cover with foil, and tie as directed; steam ½ hour.

PLUM PUDDING

The English plum pudding served at Christmas doesn't contain plums; it resembles steamed fruit cake, is made weeks ahead and mellowed in a cool, dry place. If you have no cool spot (about 50° F.), freeze the pudding or make only 1 week ahead and refrigerate. The English hide silver charms or coins in the pudding batter—and lucky the child who finds one.
Makes 12 servings

1½ cups seedless raisins
½ cup dried currants
½ cup finely chopped mixed candied fruit
1 tart apple, peeled, cored, and grated fine
Finely grated rind of 1 lemon
Finely grated rind of 1 orange
¾ cup ale or orange juice or ½ cup ale and ¼ cup brandy or rum
1 cup sifted flour
1 teaspoon baking powder
½ teaspoon salt
1 teaspoon cinnamon
½ teaspoon allspice
¼ teaspoon nutmeg
1 cup fine dry bread crumbs
1 cup firmly packed dark brown sugar
⅓ cup molasses
1 cup finely ground suet
3 eggs, lightly beaten
½ cup minced, toasted, blanched almonds

Mix fruits, rinds, and ale and let stand ½ hour. Sift flour with baking powder, salt and spices, stir in remaining ingredients, add fruit mixture, and mix well. Spoon into 2 well-buttered 1-quart

molds or metal bowls, cover with double thicknesses of foil, and tie firmly in place. Set on a rack in a large kettle, add boiling water to come halfway up puddings, cover, and steam 4 hours; keep water simmering slowly and add more boiling water as needed to maintain level. Cool puddings on racks with foil still intact, then store in a cool place, freeze, or refrigerate. To reheat, steam 1 hour exactly the same way you cooked them. Unmold puddings on a hot platter and decorate with holly. If you like, pour ¼ cup warm brandy over each pudding and blaze. Cut in wedges and serve with Hard Sauce. Also good with Brandy or Rum Sauce or Stirred Custard. About 440 calories per serving (without sauce).

ABOUT GELATIN DESSERTS

The beauty of gelatins is that they are both versatile *and* reliable—easy enough for the most inexperienced beginner. A gelatin dessert may be nothing fancier than fruit gelatin, prepared by package directions, chopped or diced, perhaps, then topped with sliced fruit or whipped cream. Or it may be a sparkling mold, jeweled with berries or chunks of fruit, a cool custard-smooth cream, a fluffy sponge, or silky mousse.

Some Basic Ways to Use Gelatins in Dessert

(Also see About Gelatins in the chapter on salads.)

To Whip Gelatin: Dissolve fruit-flavored gelatin as label directs, then cool and chill until just beginning to thicken. Beat hard with a rotary or electric beater until light and fluffy and the consistency of whipped cream. Use in preparing gelatin sponges and mousses. (*Note:* Any gelatin mixture of normal consistency *not* containing solid bits of food may be whipped.)

To Mold Fruits (Makes 4–6 servings): The standard (3-ounce) package of fruit-flavored gelatin will set 2 cups liquid and 2 cups prepared, cut-up, drained fruits. For variety and extra flavor, dissolve gelatin in hot ginger ale or fruit juice instead of water, or a ½ and ½ mixture. Cool, then chill until syrupy before adding fruits so that they won't sink to the bottom or rise to the top. Mix or match fruits and gelatin flavors, putting together any combination that appeals. *Caution: Do not try to congeal fresh or frozen pineapple or pineapple juice. They destroy gelatin's jelling power.*

To Make Your Own Fruit Gelatin (Makes 4 servings): Mix 1 envelope unflavored gelatin and ⅓–½ cup sugar in a heavy saucepan; gradually mix in ½ cup fruit juice and heat and stir over moderately low heat until gelatin and sugar dissolve. Off heat, mix in 1 cup additional fruit juice, cool, chill until syrupy, then fold in 1½ cups prepared berries or cut-up fruit. Spoon into mold and chill until firm.

To Mold Fruit Purée (Makes 4 servings): Mix 1 envelope unflavored gelatin and ⅓ cup cold fruit juice in a small saucepan and heat and stir over moderately low heat until dissolved. Cool slightly, mix in 2 cups fruit purée sweetened to taste and tint an appropriate color if you like. Pour into mold and chill until firm. Good topped with fruit sauce or whipped cream.

To Make Fruit Velvet (Makes 4 servings): Prepare 1 (3-ounce) package fruit-flavored gelatin as label instructs, then cool and chill until syrupy. Beat hard with a rotary or electric beater until foamy, then fold in 1 cup well-drained, prepared, cut-up fruit and 1 cup heavy cream, whipped to soft peaks. Pour into mold and chill until firm.

To Jell Ice Cream (Makes 4–6 servings): Dissolve 1 (3-ounce) package fruit gelatin in boiling water as label directs, cool to room temperature, then beat in 1 pint mushy ice cream of a compatible flavor. Pour into mold and chill until firm. Serve from the bowl—do not unmold.

IMPERIAL PEACH MOLD

Makes 6 servings

1 (3-ounce) package lemon-flavored gelatin
1 (3-ounce) package peach-flavored gelatin
2½ cups peach nectar
1¾ cups ginger ale
4 ripe peaches or 8 canned peach halves, drained
Lemon juice (optional)
2 tablespoons apple or red currant jelly
½ cup heavy cream
6 maraschino cherries

Mix gelatins in a bowl. Heat peach nectar to boiling, pour over gelatins, stirring until they dissolve; add ginger ale and pour into a 1-quart mold. Cool, then chill until firm. Unmold on a large platter. Surround with peeled and pitted peach halves, hollow sides up (dip fresh ones in lemon juice to prevent darkening) and fill hollows with jelly. Whip cream to soft peaks, drop by spoonfuls onto jelly, and top with cherries. About 340 calories per serving.

PORT WINE JELLY

Both simple and sophisticated.
Makes 4–6 servings

1⅓ cups water
2 envelopes unflavored gelatin (3 envelopes if you want to mold the jelly in a decorative mold)
⅔ cup sugar
Juice of 1 lemon, strained through a fine sieve
Juice of 1 orange, strained through a fine sieve
2 cups dark ruby port wine

Place water, gelatin, and sugar in a small saucepan, stir well to mix, then heat, stirring, over moderate heat about 5 minutes until sugar and gelatin are dissolved. Remove from heat and cool slightly. Mix in fruit juices and port. Pour into an ungreased 1-quart bowl or decorative mold, cover, and chill several hours until firm. To serve, spoon jelly into dessert glasses and top, if you like, with sweetened whipped cream. Or, if you have used the decorative mold, unmold on a platter and garnish with fluffs of sweetened whipped cream. About 240 calories for each of 4 servings (without whipped cream), 160 calories for each of 6 servings.

LEMON FLUFF

Tart and lemony, light and billowy.
Makes 5–6 servings

4 eggs, separated
⅔ cup superfine sugar
1½ teaspoons unflavored gelatin
¼ cup cold water
½ teaspoon grated lemon rind
¼ cup lemon juice

Beat egg yolks until very thick and light; add sugar, a little at a time, beating well after each addition, then continue beating until thick and the color of cream. Heat gelatin and water, uncovered, in a small saucepan, stirring occasionally, over low heat until gelatin dissolves; mix in lemon rind and juice and stir into egg mixture. Chill until mixture mounds when dropped from a spoon. Beat egg whites until they form stiff peaks and fold into yolk mixture. Spoon into 5 or 6 parfait glasses or into a 1-quart serving bowl. Cover and chill until serving time. Serve as is or topped with sugared fresh or thawed frozen fruit. (*Note:* Do not spoon from serving bowl into individual dishes until a few minutes before serving or mixture may liquefy.) About 175 calories for each of 5 servings, 145 calories for each of 6 servings.

⚖ LOW-CALORIE GINGERED ORANGE FLUFF

Makes 4 servings

1 cup boiling water
1 envelope low-calorie orange-flavored gelatin (there are 2 envelopes in a ¾-ounce package)
½ cup orange or tangerine juice
½ cup low-calorie ginger ale
Pinch ginger

Mix boiling water and gelatin dessert until dissolved; stir in remaining ingredients. Chill until mixture mounds when dropped from a spoon, then beat with a rotary beater until foamy. Spoon into serving dishes and chill until firm. Serve cold, topped, if you like, with any low-calorie topping. About 25 calories per serving (without topping).

VARIATIONS:
Substitute any other flavor of low-calorie fruit gelatin for the orange, mixing with an appropriate fruit juice: apple and apple juice (26 calories per serving), peach and peach nectar (26 calories per serving), raspberry or strawberry and cranberry juice (30 calories per serving), grape and grape juice (31 calories per serving), pineapple and pineapple juice (28 calories per serving).

MOLDED RASPBERRY MOUSSE

Makes 6–8 servings

2 (10-ounce) packages frozen raspberries, thawed
1 cup water
2 envelopes unflavored gelatin
⅓ cup sugar
⅓ cup rosé wine
¼ cup Cherry Heering
1 pint heavy cream

Topping:

2 (10-ounce) packages frozen raspberries, thawed
2 tablespoons Cherry Heering

Put raspberries through a food mill or purée in an electric blender at high speed; strain and set aside. Heat and stir water, gelatin, and sugar in a small saucepan 4–5 minutes over moderate heat until gelatin and sugar are dissolved. Off heat, mix in purée, wine, and Cherry Heering. Cover and chill until thick and syrupy, about 20–30 minutes, then beat until fluffy; whip cream until soft, glossy peaks form and fold in. Pour into a decorative 2-quart mold, cover, and chill several hours until firm. Meanwhile, purée berries for topping, strain, and mix in Cherry Heering. Chill until ready to use. To serve, loosen mold by dipping quickly in warm water; invert on a large platter. Top with a little of the sauce and pass the rest. About 570 calories for each of 6 servings, 430 calories for each of 8 servings.

VARIATION:

Molded Strawberry Mousse: Prepare as directed, substituting strawberries for raspberries. About 570 calories for each of 6 servings, 430 calories for each of 8 servings.

BASIC COLD SOUFFLÉ (VANILLA)

Makes 4 servings

1 envelope unflavored gelatin
½ cup sugar
1 cup milk
2 eggs, separated
1½ teaspoons vanilla
¾ cup heavy cream

Mix gelatin and sugar in the top of a double boiler, gradually stir in milk, set over simmering water, and heat and stir until sugar dissolves; mix a little hot mixture into lightly beaten egg yolks, return to pan, and cook and stir 2–3 minutes until slightly thickened. Pour into a large bowl and mix in vanilla; cool to room temperature, stirring occasionally, then chill until mixture mounds when dropped from a spoon. Whip cream to soft peaks and fold in. With a separate beater (or the same one well washed), beat egg whites to stiff peaks and fold in. Spoon into a 1-quart soufflé dish and chill until firm. Top, if you like, with whipped cream fluffs, toasted slivered almonds, and/or fresh berries before serving. About 345 calories per serving (without topping).

For a Top Hat Soufflé (Makes 8 servings): Extend height of a 1-quart soufflé dish by wrapping a 4"-wide, double thickness foil strip around outside so it stands 2" above rim; fasten with cellophane tape. Double any of the cold soufflé recipes, pour into dish, and chill until firm. Remove collar carefully before serving.

VARIATIONS:

Cold Lemon Soufflé: Prepare as directed, substituting ½ cup each lemon juice and water for the milk and ½ teaspoon finely grated lemon rind for the vanilla. About 315 calories per serving.

Cold Orange Soufflé: Prepare as directed, substituting 1 cup orange juice for milk and 1 teaspoon finely grated orange rind for vanilla. About 330 calories per serving.

Cold Fruit Soufflé: Prepare as directed but substitute 1¼ cups any fruit purée for the milk and use 1 egg *yolk* only. Flavor with ¼ teaspoon almond extract instead of vanilla. Otherwise, proceed as directed, folding in whipped cream and beaten egg whites. About 315 calories per serving.

Cold Chocolate Soufflé: Prepare as directed and, while gelatin mixture is still hot, mix in 2½ (1-ounce) coarsely grated squares unsweetened chocolate, stirring until melted. Garnish with chocolate curls* and fluffs of whipped cream. About 435 calories per serving (without chocolate curls and whipped cream).

COLD COFFEE SOUFFLÉ

Makes 10–12 servings

2 envelopes unflavored gelatin
1 cup sugar
¼ teaspoon salt
2½ cups milk
4 eggs, separated
¼ cup plus 1 teaspoon instant coffee
   powder
1 teaspoon vanilla
1 pint heavy cream
Chocolate curls* and blanched almond
   halves (optional garnishes)

Heat and stir gelatin, ½ cup sugar, salt, and 2 cups milk in the top of a double boiler directly over moderate heat

5–6 minutes until sugar and gelatin are dissolved. Beat egg yolks lightly with remaining milk, mix in a little of the hot mixture, then return all to pan. Set over simmering water and cook and stir 5–6 minutes until slightly thickened and no raw egg taste remains. Off heat, mix in coffee and vanilla. Place a piece of wax paper flat on sauce and cool to room temperature, then chill, stirring occasionally, until mixture mounds slightly. Meanwhile, wrap a double thickness strip of foil about 4" wide tightly around top of a 1½-quart soufflé dish to form a collar extending 2" above rim; fasten with cellophane tape. Beat egg whites until foamy, add remaining sugar, and beat until stiff; fold into coffee mixture. Beat cream until soft peaks form and fold in. Spoon into soufflé dish, leveling surface. Chill until firm, at least 2 hours. Remove collar and decorate, if you like, with chocolate curls and almond "daisies." About 325 calories for each of 10 servings, 270 calories for each of 12 servings (without garnish).

¢ SPANISH CREAM

This silky cool dessert is thickened both with eggs and gelatin.
Makes 6 servings

1 envelope unflavored gelatin
⅔ cup sugar
2½ cups milk
3 eggs, separated
1 teaspoon vanilla

Mix gelatin and ⅓ cup sugar in the top of a double boiler, slowly stir in milk, set over simmering water, and heat and stir until sugar dissolves. Blend a little hot mixture into lightly beaten egg yolks, return to pan, and cook and stir 2–3 minutes until slightly thickened. Pour into a large bowl, mix in vanilla, cool, then chill until mixture mounds slightly when dropped from a spoon. Beat egg whites until frothy, gradually beat in remaining sugar, and continue beating until stiff peaks form. Fold custard mixture into meringue, spoon into a 1-quart mold or 6 goblets and chill until

firm. If molded, unmold on a dessert platter. Top, if you like, with fruit, chocolate, or butterscotch sauce. About 200 calories per serving (without fruit or sauce).

VARIATIONS:

¢ **Chocolate Spanish Cream:** Prepare as directed and, while custard is still hot, blend in 1 (1-ounce) coarsely grated square unsweetened chocolate or 1 (1-ounce) square no-melt unsweetened chocolate. About 225 calories per serving.

¢ **Layered Spanish Cream:** Prepare as directed but cool custard mixture only slightly. While still warm, fold into meringue and spoon into a crystal bowl. Chill until firm. Mixture will separate into 2 layers—custard on top, a jellylike mixture underneath. About 200 calories per serving.

BASIC BAVARIAN CREAM (VANILLA)

Bavarian Cream is a cousin of mousses; it has a custard base, which mousses haven't, also whipped cream, which mousses may or may not contain.
Makes 6–8 servings

½ cup sugar
1 envelope unflavored gelatin
1½ cups milk
3 egg yolks, lightly beaten
1½ teaspoons vanilla
¾ cup heavy cream
2 tablespoons confectioners' sugar
3 egg whites (optional)

Mix sugar, gelatin, and milk in the top of a double boiler and heat over simmering water until steaming hot. Mix a little hot mixture into yolks, return to double boiler top, and cook and stir 3–5 minutes until mixture coats the back of a metal spoon. Off heat, mix in vanilla; cool, then chill, stirring occasionally, until mixture mounds when dropped from a spoon. Whip cream with confectioners' sugar until stiff peaks form, then fold into custard mixture. If you like, also beat egg whites to soft peaks and fold in. Spoon into a 1½-quart mold or 6–8 custard cups or parfait glasses and chill 3–4 hours until firm. If molded, unmold on a dessert platter and wreathe, if you like, with crushed sweetened berries, sliced fresh peaches, or any stewed fruit. About 265 calories for each of 6 servings (without fruit), 200 calories for each of 8 servings.

VARIATIONS:

Rum Bavarian Cream: Prepare as directed but use ½ cup light rum and 1 cup milk in the custard mixture instead of all milk and reduce vanilla to ½ teaspoon. (*Note:* Brandy, crème de menthe, or any fruit liqueur may be used in place of rum; tint an appropriate color.) About 340 calories for each of 6 servings, 255 calories for each of 8 servings.

Chocolate Bavarian Cream: Prepare as directed but add 1 (6-ounce) package semisweet chocolate bits to the hot custard mixture, stirring until melted. About 395 calories for each of 6 servings, 300 calories for each of 8 servings.

Mocha Bavarian Cream: Prepare Chocolate Bavarian Cream (above) as directed, using 1 cup milk and ½ cup very strong hot black coffee in the custard mixture. About 395 calories for each of 6 servings, 300 calories for each of 8 servings.

Fruit Bavarian Cream: Prepare as directed, using ½ cup milk and 1 cup puréed berries, peaches, apricots, bananas, or other fruit in the custard mixture; flavor with 1 tablespoon lemon juice instead of vanilla and tint, if you like, an appropriate pastel color. About 395 calories for each of 6 servings, 300 calories for each of 8 servings.

Charlotte Russe (Makes 12–15 servings): Line the bottom and sides of a 9″ spring-form pan with split ladyfingers (you'll need about 20), then sprinkle with ¼ cup light rum. Chill while you prepare 2 recipes Basic Bavarian Cream (omit egg whites); spoon into pan and chill 4–6 hours or overnight. Unmold by removing spring form sides and inverting on chilled platter. Garnish with fluffs of whipped cream and maraschino cherries. To serve, cut in wedges as you would a layer cake. About 450 calories for each of 12 servings, 360 calories for each of 15 servings.

SWEDISH CREAM

So rich and smooth it never fails to impress.
Makes 4 servings

1 pint light cream
1 envelope unflavored gelatin
⅔ cup sugar
1 pint sour cream
1 teaspoon vanilla
2 cups sliced fresh or frozen thawed peaches or berries

Heat cream, gelatin, and sugar in a small saucepan over lowest heat, stirring constantly, 15–20 minutes until all sugar and gelatin are dissolved; do not allow to boil. Remove from heat and cool 5 minutes; beat in sour cream with a wire whisk or rotary beater. Stir in vanilla, cover, and chill 2–3 hours until firm. To serve, spoon into individual dessert dishes and top with fruit. About 700 calories per serving.

LOW-CALORIE POTS DE CRÈME AU CHOCOLAT

Makes 4 servings

1 (½-ounce) envelope low-calorie chocolate pudding mix
1 cup skim milk
1 teaspoon instant coffee powder
1 (1-ounce) square semisweet chocolate, grated
1 teaspoon vanilla

Mix pudding mix and ¼ cup milk in a small saucepan; stir in remaining ingredients. Heat, uncovered, over low heat, stirring constantly, until smooth and thickened; do not boil. Remove from heat, place a piece of wax paper directly on surface of mixture, and cool to lukewarm. Pour into 4 *pots de crème* or ramekins, cover, and chill 2–3 hours until set. Serve cold. About 100 calories per serving.

FROZEN DESSERTS

Ices and ice creams are thought to have originated in ancient China, then traveled the trade routes west to the Mediterranean. Romans served them, but it was sixteenth-century Florentine chefs who glorified them. For the wedding feasts of Catherine de Médicis and Henry II of France, they prepared a new flavor every day. Soon Italian ices and "iced creams" were fashionable throughout Western Europe and their popularity never waned. While abroad, Thomas Jefferson sampled ice cream, copied down a recipe, and on returning to America introduced it at a state dinner at the White House. Today there are many kinds of frozen desserts. Here's a quick lexicon.

The Kinds of Frozen Desserts

Bombe: Ice cream and/or sherbet or ice, frozen in a decorative mold, often in layers of contrasting color and flavor.

Coupe: Ice cream or sherbet served in a broad-bowled goblet topped with fruit and/or whipped cream and *marrons glacés* (glazed chestnuts).

Frappé: Sherbet or ice frozen to the mushy stage.

Granité: A granular Italian ice frozen without stirring. When served, it is scraped into fluffy, snow-like crystals instead of being spooned.

Ice: A watery frozen dessert made of sugar, water, and flavoring (usually fruit juice).

Ice Cream: Originally, frozen sweetened and flavored cream but today almost any creamy frozen dessert. *French ice cream* has an egg custard base.

Mousse: An extra-rich ice cream frozen without being stirred. It often contains whipped cream.

Parfait: Ice cream or whipped cream layered into a tall footed glass with a topping—fruit, chocolate, nut—then frozen.

Sherbet: Fine-textured frozen fruit dessert, originally water-based but today more often made with milk. Gelatin and/or egg white is frequently added to make sherbets smoother.

Sorbet: The French word for *sherbet;* it has come to mean a mushy frozen fruit ice or sherbet, a frappé. It may be served between courses or as dessert.

About Freezing Ice Creams, Sherbets, and Ices

To Freeze in a Crank-Type Freezer (*Hand or Electric*): Prepare mix according to recipe, cover, and chill 1–2 hours. Meanwhile, wash and scald all freezer parts, then rinse in cold water and dry thoroughly. Set freezer can into freezer, fit dasher into place, and pour in chilled ice cream mix. (*Note:* Mixture will expand as it freezes so never fill freezer can more than two-thirds.) Put lid on can, attach crank top, and lock into place. Add enough crushed ice to fill freezer one-third, distributing evenly around can. Then, using 1 part rock or kosher salt to 8 parts ice (1 to 6 if you want mixture to freeze faster), layer salt and ice into freezer until filled. Let stand 3–5 minutes, then begin turning. If freezer is the hand-crank variety, turn smoothly and slowly, always in the same direction. Stop turning only when mixture is too stiff to crank (electric freezers will shut off or begin to labor heavily). Drain water from freezer and, if necessary, scoop out enough ice to expose top ⅓ of can. Wipe away any salt, paying particular attention to seam around lid. Uncover can, lift out dasher, and scrape all frozen mixture back into can; pack down with a large spoon. Plug hole in can top with a cork (some freezers have an additional solid cover), cover can, then repack freezer, using 1 part salt to

4 parts crushed ice. Cover with heavy paper, cloth, or newspapers and let season ½ hour. Or, if you prefer, pack ice cream into plastic freezer containers and let stand ½ hour in freezer. (*Note:* Don't *store* ice cream in freezer, however. It will become brick hard.)

To Freeze in Refrigerator: Turn temperature setting to coldest point. (*Note:* If you make ice cream often, it's a good idea to have a special set of ice cube trays for just this purpose. Frequently washed ice cube trays lose their finish, causing ice cubes to stick.) Any small excess amounts of ice-cream mix can be frozen in custard cups.

Bombes: Chill a melon or brick bombe mold well in freezer. (*Note:* If you have no mold, use a metal mixing bowl.) Meanwhile soften commercial ice cream or sherbet until workable or, if making your own, freeze only until mushy. Pack into mold, smoothing with a large spoon so that you have an even layer about 1″ thick over bottom and sides; freeze until firm. Add a second layer of contrasting color and flavor, packing tightly against the first layer, and freeze until firm. Fill center with soft ice or ice cream of yet another flavor and freeze until firm. *To Unmold:* Wipe mold with a cloth wrung out in hot water, then invert on a serving platter. (*Note:* Bombes can be frozen by packing them in a mixture of crushed ice and rock or kosher salt — 1 part salt to 4 parts ice—but it seems an unnecessary lot of work unless you have no freezer.)

Ice Creams: Prepare base mix as recipe directs and freeze until mushy. Remove from tray and beat at high speed until fluffy. Also whip cream until soft peaks form, fold into base, and freeze until firm. (*Note:* For extra creaminess, beat once again before freezing until firm.)

Mousses: Prepare mix, spoon into shallow trays or mold, cover with foil or wax paper (because of their high cream content, mousses are more apt to pick

up refrigerator odors), and freeze until firm without beating or stirring.

Parfaits: Layer ice cream or sherbet into parfait glasses with a topping of your choice, then freeze until firm. Some combinations to try:
– Vanilla ice cream with Melba Sauce or Chocolate Sauce or any puréed fruit
– Vanilla ice cream and orange sherbet with Melba Sauce or any puréed berries or peaches
– Chocolate ice cream and whipped cream or Marshmallow Sauce
– Pistachio ice cream, chocolate ice cream, and Chocolate Sauce or Fudge Sauce

Sherbets and Ices: Prepare as recipe directs, spoon into refrigerator trays, and freeze until mushy. Remove from trays, beat until light, then freeze until firm. (*Note:* An extra beating before freezing until firm will make the mixture more velvety.)

⚖ BASIC FRUIT ICE

An easy recipe you can experiment with. Mix two or more fruit juice flavors, if you like, or use one flavor only.
Makes about 1½ quarts

1 envelope unflavored gelatin
½–1 cup sugar (depending upon sweetness of fruit juice)
1 quart sweet fruit juice (any berry, peach or apricot nectar, pineapple or orange juice) or 1 pint each crushed fruit and water
2 tablespoons lemon juice
Few drops food coloring (optional)
2 egg whites

Mix gelatin and ½ cup sugar in a saucepan, add juice, and heat and stir over low heat until gelatin and sugar dissolve. (*Note:* If using crushed fruit, heat gelatin and sugar with the water and, when dissolved, mix in fruit.) Taste for sugar and adjust as needed. Mix in lemon juice, tint an appropriate color, if you like, pour into 2 refrigerator trays, and freeze until mushy. Spoon into a large bowl and beat hard until fluffy. Beat egg whites to very soft peaks, fold into fruit mixture, spoon into 3 refrigerator trays, cover, and freeze until firm. About 80 calories per ½-cup serving if made with a tart fruit juice and ½ cup sugar.

VARIATIONS:

⚔ **Lemon or Lime Ice:** Prepare as directed, using 1½ cups sugar, 3 cups water, and 1 cup lemon or lime juice. About 150 calories per ½-cup serving.

⚔ **Wine Ice:** Mix gelatin with ½ cup sugar and 1 cup each orange juice and water and heat and stir until gelatin and sugar dissolve. Mix in 2 cups dry or sweet white, red, or rosé wine or champagne and proceed as directed. When serving, drizzle a little wine over each portion. About 80 calories per ½-cup serving if made with dry wine.

⚔ **Spiked Ice:** Prepare Basic Fruit Ice as directed but add ¼–½ cup any compatible fruit liqueur along with the beaten egg whites (orange juice and curaçao, for example, pineapple and crème de menthe, berry juice and crème de cassis, fraise, or framboise). About 100 calories per ½-cup serving.

🔲 ⚔ **LEMON OR LIME GRANITÉ**

Granité is a granular ice frozen without being stirred. It can be served at the mush stage or frozen hard, then scraped up in fine, feathery shavings. Particularly good topped with a little fruit liqueur or rum.
Makes about 1½ quarts

1 quart water
2 cups sugar
1 cup lemon or lime juice
1 tablespoon finely grated lemon or lime rind
Few drops yellow and/or green food coloring

Bring water and sugar to a boil in a saucepan, stirring, then reduce heat and simmer, uncovered, 5 minutes. Cool, mix in juice and rind, and tint pale yellow or green. Pour into 3 refrigerator trays, cover, and freeze to a mush without stirring. Spoon into goblets and serve or freeze hard, scrape up with a spoon, and

pile into goblets. About 130 calories per ½-cup serving.

VARIATIONS:

⚔ **Orange Granité:** Prepare as directed, substituting 1 quart orange juice for the water, reducing sugar to ¾ cup and lemon juice to 2 tablespoons; also use orange rind instead of lemon. About 85 calories per ½-cup serving.

⚔ **Fruit Granité:** Boil 3 cups water and 1½ cups sugar into syrup as directed. Cool, add 2 tablespoons lemon juice and 2 cups puréed fruit (any berries, peaches, pineapple, sweet cherries); omit rind. Freeze and serve as directed. About 140–50 calories per ½-cup serving depending upon fruit used.

⚔ **Coffee or Tea Granité:** Boil 1 cup each water and sugar into syrup as directed; cool, add 3 cups strong black coffee or tea and to tea mixture, add ¼ cup lemon juice. Freeze and serve as directed. About 65 calories per ½-cup serving.

⚔ **Melon Granité:** Mix 1 quart puréed ripe melon (any kind) with ½–1 cup sugar (depending on sweetness of melon) and 2 tablespoons lemon juice; let stand 1 hour at room temperature, stirring now and then, until sugar is dissolved. Freeze as directed. About 65 calories per ½-cup serving *if* made with ½ cup sugar, 135 calories if made with 1 cup sugar.

⚔ **LEMON OR LIME MILK SHERBET**

Makes about 1½ quarts

1 envelope unflavored gelatin
1⅓ cups sugar
1 quart milk
¾ cup lemon or lime juice
2 teaspoons finely grated lemon or lime rind
Few drops yellow or green food coloring (optional)
2 egg whites

Mix gelatin and sugar in a saucepan, gradually add milk, and heat and stir over low heat until sugar and gelatin dissolve. Cool, add juice and rind, and, if you like, tint pale yellow or green. Pour into 2 refrigerator trays and freeze until mushy. Remove from trays and beat until fluffy. Beat egg whites to very soft peaks and fold into fruit mixture. Spoon into 3 refrigerator trays and freeze until firm. About 150 calories per ½-cup serving.

VARIATIONS:

⚖ **Orange Milk Sherbet:** Heat and stir gelatin with ¾ cup sugar and 2 cups milk until dissolved; cool, add 2 tablespoons lemon juice, 2 cups orange juice, and 1 tablespoon finely grated orange rind. Proceed as directed. About 110 calories per ½-cup serving.

⚖ **Fruit Milk Sherbet:** Heat and stir gelatin with ¾ cup sugar and 2 cups milk until dissolved; cool, add 2 tablespoons lemon juice, ½ cup water, and 1½ cups puréed fruit (berries, sweet cherries, peaches, apricots, pineapple, etc.). Taste for sugar, adding a bit more if needed, then proceed as directed. About 125 calories per ½-cup serving.

⚖ **Extra-Low-Calorie Sherbets:** Prepare any of the above sherbets as directed but use skim milk instead of whole, reduce sugar to ½ cup, and use 1 egg white only. About 65 calories per ½-cup serving.

⊠ **EASY STRAWBERRY OR RASPBERRY LEMON CREAM SHERBET**

Makes about 6 servings

2 (10-ounce) packages frozen strawberries or raspberries, thawed
1 (6-ounce) can frozen lemonade concentrate, thawed
1 pint heavy cream

Purée strawberries in an electric blender at low speed, then strain to remove seeds. Add lemonade concentrate and mix well. Beat cream until soft peaks form and fold in. Spoon into 2 refrigerator trays and freeze until firm. About 370 calories per serving.

BASIC REFRIGERATOR ICE CREAM

Turn freezer to coldest setting before beginning this recipe. From this one basic recipe, you can make 14 different flavors of ice cream.
Makes 1½ quarts

1 cup sugar
2 teaspoons cornstarch
1 quart milk
3 eggs, separated
2 teaspoons vanilla
1 cup heavy cream, whipped

Mix sugar and cornstarch in top of a double boiler and gradually stir in milk. Add egg yolks and beat until frothy. Set over simmering water and heat 15 minutes, stirring now and then at first, constantly toward the end. Cool and stir in vanilla. Beat egg whites to soft peaks and fold in. Pour into 2 refrigerator trays and freeze until mushy. Spoon into a large bowl, beat hard until fluffy, then beat in cream. Spoon into 3 trays and freeze until firm. (*Note:* For extra smoothness, beat once more before freezing until firm.) About 215 calories per ½-cup serving.

VARIATIONS:

Berry Ice Cream: Prepare as directed but reduce vanilla to 1 teaspoon and add 2 cups any crushed, sweetened-to-taste berries (fresh, frozen, or canned) along with beaten egg whites. About 235 calories per ½-cup serving.

Banana Ice Cream: Prepare as directed but reduce vanilla to 1 teaspoon and add 2 cups puréed ripe bananas (about 6 medium-size bananas) along with egg whites. About 260 calories per ½-cup serving.

Pineapple Ice Cream: Prepare as directed but reduce vanilla to 1 teaspoon and add 1 (1-pound 14-ounce) can crushed pineapple (undrained) along with egg whites. About 280 calories per ½-cup serving.

Peach or Apricot Ice Cream: Prepare as directed but reduce vanilla to ½ teaspoon and add ½ teaspoon almond extract; mix in 2 cups peach or apricot purée along with beaten egg whites. About 250 calories per ½-cup serving.

Orange Ice Cream: Prepare custard mixture as directed, using ¾ cup sugar and 3 cups milk. Add 1 (6-ounce) can thawed frozen orange juice concentrate and 1 cup freshly squeezed orange juice; omit vanilla. Proceed as directed. About 250 calories per ½-cup serving.

Chocolate Ice Cream: Add 2 (1-ounce) squares coarsely grated unsweetened chocolate to hot custard mixture and stir until melted. Reduce vanilla to 1 teaspoon and proceed as directed. About 240 calories per ½-cup serving.

Coffee Ice Cream: Sprinkle ⅓ cup instant coffee powder over hot custard mixture and stir until blended. Reduce vanilla to ½ teaspoon and proceed as directed. About 220 calories per ½-cup serving.

Burnt Almond Ice Cream: Prepare custard mixture as directed, using ½ cup sugar; caramelize* ½ cup sugar and mix in along with vanilla called for. Proceed as directed, mixing 1 cup coarsely chopped toasted, blanched almonds into beaten frozen mixture along with whipped cream. About 285 calories per ½-cup serving.

Butter Pecan Ice Cream: Prepare as directed, mixing 1 cup coarsely chopped, butter-browned pecans into beaten frozen mixture along with whipped cream. About 295 calories per ½-cup serving.

Pistachio Ice Cream: Prepare as directed but reduce vanilla to 1 teaspoon and add ½ teaspoon almond extract. Tint mixture pale green before freezing. Mix ¾ cup coarsely chopped pistachio nuts into beaten frozen mixture along with whipped cream. About 260 calories per ½-cup serving.

Peppermint Ice Cream: Prepare as directed but omit vanilla and add ¼ teaspoon peppermint extract; also mix 1½ cups finely crushed peppermint candy into beaten frozen mixture along with whipped cream. About 270 calories per ½-cup serving.

Rum-Raisin Ice Cream: Soak ⅔ cup minced seedless raisins in ⅓ cup dark rum while preparing recipe; fold into beaten frozen mixture along with whipped cream. About 270 calories per ½-cup serving.

Eggnog Ice Cream: Prepare basic recipe as directed and mix ¼ cup rum or brandy into beaten frozen mixture along with whipped cream. About 240 calories per ½-cup serving.

BASIC FREEZER ICE CREAM (VANILLA)

The principal difference between freezer-cranked and refrigerator ice cream is that, with the former, the cream goes into the freezer mix in the beginning. Avoid using extra-thick or clotted cream—the freezer's churning action may turn it to butter. (*Note:* Any of the refrigerator ice creams can be frozen in a crank freezer. Simply mix in heavy cream—do not whip—at the start.)
Makes about 2 quarts

1 quart light cream
1½ cups superfine sugar
2 tablespoons vanilla or 1 (3-inch)
 piece vanilla bean, split lengthwise
1 pint heavy cream

Heat and stir light cream and sugar over moderate heat until sugar dissolves thoroughly. If using vanilla bean, heat along with mixture; remove vanilla bean (but not tiny seeds). Cool mixture, mix in vanilla extract (if bean wasn't used) and the heavy cream. Chill 1–2 hours, then freeze in a crank-type freezer* (hand or electric) following manufacturer's directions. About 300 calories per ½-cup serving.

VARIATIONS:

Chocolate Freezer Ice Cream: Prepare as directed but heat 3 squares unsweetened chocolate along with the light cream and 2 cups superfine sugar, stirring until melted. About 325 calories per ½-cup serving.

Coffee Freezer Ice Cream: Prepare as directed but heat ⅓ cup instant coffee powder along with light cream and sugar. If you like, stir in ¼ cup coffee liqueur along with vanilla. About 300 calories per ½-cup serving.

Mocha Freezer Ice Cream: Prepare as directed but heat 1 square unsweetened chocolate and ¼ cup instant coffee powder along with light cream and sugar. About 315 calories per ½-cup serving.

Fruit Freezer Ice Cream: Heat 1 pint cream and the sugar as directed. Cool, omit vanilla, but mix in 2 cups any fruit purée (sieved berry, fresh peach, mango, papaya, pineapple, banana, apricot) and the heavy cream. Add ¼ cup lemon or orange juice, and, if flavor is peach, apricot, or pineapple, 1 teaspoon almond extract. Proceed as directed. About 310 calories per ½-cup serving.

Ginger Freezer Ice Cream: Prepare vanilla mix as directed but reduce vanilla to 1 tablespoon. Add 1½ cups minced preserved ginger, 1 cup syrup drained from bottles of ginger, and 2 tablespoons lemon juice. Freeze as directed. About 315 calories per ½-cup serving.

FRENCH VANILLA ICE CREAM

An extra-smooth ice cream made with egg yolks.
Makes 1½ quarts

2 cups milk
1 cup sugar
6 egg yolks, lightly beaten
1 tablespoon vanilla
1 pint heavy cream

Beat milk, sugar, and egg yolks in the top of a double boiler until frothy. Set over simmering water and heat 15 minutes, stirring now and then at first, constantly toward the end. Cool, add vanilla and cream. Freeze in a crank-type freezer* (hand or electric), following manufacturer's directions. About 270 calories per ½-cup serving.

To Freeze in Refrigerator: Prepare custard mixture as directed, cool, and mix in vanilla; pour into 2 refrigerator trays and freeze until mushy. Spoon into a large bowl and beat hard until fluffy. Whip cream until thick and satiny and fold in. Spoon into 3 refrigerator trays, cover, and freeze until firm, stirring twice during the first hour.

VARIATIONS:

French Chocolate Ice Cream: Prepare custard mixture as directed and, while still hot, mix in 3 (1-ounce) coarsely grated squares semisweet chocolate, stirring until well blended. Cool, add 2 teaspoons vanilla, and proceed as directed, freezing either in freezer or refrigerator. About 305 calories per ½-cup serving.

(*Note:* Any of the variations given for Basic Refrigerator Ice Cream can be used for French Vanilla Ice Cream. Simply follow basic recipe above, adding amounts of fruits, flavorings, or nuts called for in the variations.)

⊠ DARK CHOCOLATE ICE CREAM

Smooth and dark and super-rich. But so very easy.
Makes 4 servings

1 (6-ounce) package semisweet chocolate bits
1 (7½-ounce) jar marshmallow cream
1 (13-ounce) can evaporated milk
1 teaspoon vanilla
1 cup heavy cream

Melt chocolate bits in the top of a double boiler over simmering water; add marshmallow cream and heat, stirring occasionally, until melted. Pour in milk, a little at a time, mixing well after each addition, then mix in vanilla. Remove from heat and set aside. Whip cream until soft peaks form and fold into chocolate mixture. Pour into a 9″×5″×3″ loaf pan and freeze until mushy. Remove from pan and beat until fluffy. (*Note:* With a portable mixer, you can do this *in* the pan. Return to pan and freeze until firm.) When serving, make the portions small. About 700 calories per serving.

⊠ BANANA-ORANGE ICE CREAM

Makes 4 servings

3 large ripe bananas, peeled and mashed
1½ cups orange juice (preferably fresh)
Juice of 2 lemons
1 (13-ounce) can evaporated milk
½ cup light corn syrup
½ cup superfine sugar

Mix all ingredients together, pour into 2 refrigerator trays, and freeze until mushy. Remove from trays and beat until fluffy; return to trays and freeze until firm. About 460 calories per serving.

TUTTI-FRUTTI ICE CREAM

Makes 8 servings

1 (1-pound 14-ounce) can crushed
*   pineapple, drained (save juice for*
*   drinks)*
¼ cup coarsely chopped candied red and
*   green cherries*
¼ cup finely chopped citron
⅓ cup coarsely chopped, pitted dates
3–4 tablespoons dark rum (optional)
3 pints vanilla ice cream, softened
*   slightly*

Mix together all ingredients, spoon into 3 refrigerator trays or a 9″×5″×3″ loaf pan, and freeze until firm. Allow to soften slightly before serving. About 280 calories per serving.

VARIATION:

Tutti-Frutti Party Bombe: Mix as directed, pack in a chilled 2-quart melon mold, and freeze until firm. Unmold and decorate with rum-flavored, sweetened whipped cream put through a pastry bag fitted with a fluted tip. About 280 calories per serving (without whipped cream).

FROZEN COFFEE CREAM

When serving, make the portions small —this is a *very* rich dessert.
Makes 6–8 servings

1 (13-ounce) can evaporated milk
1 cup light cream
1 envelope unflavored gelatin
⅓ cup instant coffee powder
⅔ cup sugar
2 tablespoons coffee liqueur
1 teaspoon vanilla
1 pint heavy cream

Place milk and light cream in a small saucepan and sprinkle gelatin over surface; let stand at room temperature 10 minutes. Mix in coffee powder and sugar, set over lowest heat, and heat, stirring, 20–25 minutes until gelatin, coffee, and sugar are dissolved; do not boil. Remove from heat and cool to room temperature. Stir in coffee liqueur and vanilla. Pour into a refrigerator tray and freeze until mushy; remove from pan and beat until fluffy. Whip heavy cream until thick and satiny, then beat into coffee mixture. Divide between 2 refrigerator trays and freeze until firm. About 565 calories for each of 6 servings, 425 calories for each of 8 servings.

⊠ BISCUIT TORTONI

You can buy the little paper cups used for *tortoni* in Italian delicatessens, also in some gourmet shops. If unavailable, substitute cupcake papers but set in muffin tins to give them extra support. Once tortoni are frozen, lift from tins.
Makes 6 servings

1 cup heavy cream
⅓ cup confectioners' sugar
½ teaspoon vanilla
1 egg white
2 tablespoons light rum
⅓ cup crushed dry macaroons
¼ cup minced, toasted, blanched
*   almonds*

Whip cream with sugar and vanilla until soft peaks form. Beat egg white to soft peaks and fold into cream along with rum and macaroons. Spoon into paper cups, sprinkle with almonds, cover with foil circles, and freeze until firm. About 280 calories per serving.

SPUMONI

This Italian ice-cream bombe comes in
many flavors, textures, and colors. To
vary recipe below, substitute raspberry
or chocolate ice cream for the Vanilla-
Almond and leave the filling white.
Makes about 1½ quarts

Vanilla-Almond Ice Cream:

2 cups milk
4 egg yolks, lightly beaten
¾ cup sugar
1½ teaspoons vanilla
⅓ cup minced, toasted, blanched
  almonds

Cream-Fruit Filling:

1 cup heavy cream, tinted pale pink if
  you like
½ cup sifted confectioners' sugar
1 egg white
¼ cup minced maraschino cherries
2 tablespoons each candied citron,
  lemon peel, orange peel, and angelica
2 tablespoons light rum or brandy

Set a 2-quart melon mold to chill in
freezer. Beat milk, egg yolks, and sugar
in the top of a double boiler until
frothy. Set over simmering water and
heat and stir until mixture will coat a
metal spoon and no raw egg taste
remains; cool, mix in vanilla and
almonds. Pour into a refrigerator tray
and freeze until mushy; spoon into a
bowl and beat hard until fluffy; return
to tray, cover, and freeze until creamy-
firm but not hard. Pack firmly into
melon mold, smoothing with the back
of a spoon to form a thick, even lining.
Cover and freeze ½ hour. Meanwhile,
prepare filling: Whip cream with sugar
until soft peaks form; beat egg white
to soft peaks and fold into cream along
with remaining ingredients. Spoon into
center of melon mold, cover, and freeze
overnight. Unmold on a serving platter,
loosening, if necessary, by rubbing a
cloth wrung out in hot water over
bottom of mold. Decorate, if you like,
with candied cherries and angelica strips.
To serve, cut in wedges. About 250
calories per ½-cup serving.

☒ BAKED ALASKA

A spectacular dessert easy enough for
beginners.
Makes 8 servings

1 (9″) square firm white or yellow cake,
  homemade or bought
1 half-gallon brick ice cream (any
  flavor)

Meringue:

3 egg whites
⅛ teaspoon salt
¼ teaspoon cream of tartar
⅓ cup superfine sugar

Preheat oven to 500° F. Cut cake into
a rectangle 5″×7″ and place on a foil-
lined baking sheet (save scraps for
snacks). Halve ice cream lengthwise,
place half on cake, and set in freezer
while you prepare meringue (also
returning remaining ice cream to
freezer). Beat egg whites with salt and
cream of tartar until foamy, gradually
beat in sugar, then continue beating
until very stiff peaks form. Remove cake
from freezer and quickly frost with
meringue, making sure it covers cake and
ice cream entirely and touches baking
sheet all around; swirl meringue into
peaks. Bake uncovered on center oven
rack about 3 minutes until tan all over.
Serve immediately, slicing with a large
sharp knife. About 435 calories per
serving.

ABOUT DESSERT OMELETS

A favorite with the French, the dessert
omelet has never become very popular
in this country except among gourmet
cooks. Like savory omelets, dessert
omelets must be made to order, one at
a time. For small dinners, however, they
are both practical and impressive if the
hostess is skilled in the art of omelet
making. Before trying the sweet omelet
recipe included here, read About
Omelets in the chapter on eggs and
cheese.

APPLE AND BRANDY OMELET

Makes 2 servings

1 sweet crisp apple, peeled, cored, and
  sliced thin
2 tablespoons butter
3–4 tablespoons warm Calvados or
  brandy, warmed slightly
1 Sweet Soufflé Omelet
1 tablespoon sugar

Sauté apple in butter in a small skillet
over moderately low heat 8–10 minutes
until tender, lightly glazed, and golden.
Add 1 tablespoon Calvados and keep
warm. Prepare omelet as directed and
cover with apples just before folding
and turning out. Crease omelet lightly
through center, fold, and ease onto a hot
platter. Sprinkle with sugar, pour
remaining Calvados over surface, and,
if you wish, flame before serving. About
465 calories per serving.

SOME SPECIALTY
DESSERTS

CREPES SUZETTE

Not as complicated to make as you
might think.
Makes 6 servings

1 recipe Simple Dessert Crepes with
  1 tablespoon orange juice added to
  batter
6 sugar lumps
1 orange
1 lemon
½ cup orange juice
½ cup butter (no substitute)
2 tablespoons superfine sugar
¼ cup Cointreau or curaçao
2 tablespoons light rum or Benedictine
¼ cup brandy or Grand Marnier

Mix and cook crepes as recipe directs,
then fold each in half and then in half
again; keep warm in a 250° F. oven
until all are done. Rub sugar lumps on
rind of orange and lemon, drop into
orange juice, and crush to dissolve. Melt
butter in a chafing dish over moderately

low heat, add superfine sugar and orange
juice, and heat, stirring constantly, until
mixture reduces slightly. Doing 1 crepe
at a time, lift to chafing dish, unfold in
sauce, coating well, then fold as before
and push to side of chafing dish. Pour
remaining ingredients over crepes—do
not stir—and heat, moving pan gently
over flame so crepes don't burn. Tilt pan
until liqueurs ignite and spoon flaming
over crepes. Serve on hot dessert plates
topped with some of the sauce. About
435 calories per serving.

⚖ POACHED MERINGUE RING

A beautiful base for sliced fresh berries
or any dessert sauce.
Makes 6 servings

6 egg whites
⅛ teaspoon cream of tartar
¼ teaspoon salt
¾ cup superfine sugar
1 teaspoon vanilla
1 teaspoon lemon juice
¼ teaspoon almond extract

Preheat oven to 325° F. Beat egg
whites, cream of tartar, and salt with
a rotary egg beater until foamy. Add
sugar, a little at a time, beating well
after each addition. Continue to beat
until whites stand in stiff peaks. Fold in
vanilla, lemon juice, and almond extract.
Pack mixture in an ungreased 6-cup
ring mold. Set mold in a shallow pan of
cold water and bake, uncovered, 1 hour
until meringue is lightly browned and
pulls from the sides of mold. Remove
meringue from oven and water bath and
let cool upright in mold to room
temperature. Loosen edges carefully
with a spatula and unmold by inverting
on a dessert platter. Cut into wedges and
serve as is or with a generous ladling
of dessert sauce (Algarve Apricot Sauce
is especially good) or with sliced fresh
berries. About 110 calories per serving
(without sauce or fruit).

COEUR À LA CRÈME

For this dessert you will need a heart-
shaped basket or perforated metal mold

so that the cheese mixture can drain properly. They are stocked by housewares sections of many department stores, also by gourmet food shops.
Makes 8 servings

1 pound cottage cheese
1 pound cream cheese, softened to
room temperature
⅛ teaspoon salt
1 pint heavy cream
1 quart fresh strawberries, washed and
stemmed, or 2 (10-ounce) packages
frozen strawberries, thawed
Sugar (optional)

Press cottage cheese through a fine sieve. Mix with cream cheese and salt and beat until smooth with a rotary beater. Using a wooden spoon, beat in cream, a little at a time. Line a 1½-quart heart-shaped basket or perforated mold with a double thickness of cheesecloth that has been wrung out in cold water; let ends overlap mold, and smooth out as many wrinkles as possible. Spoon cheese mixture into mold, cover with overlapping ends of cloth, and set on a tray deep enough to contain draining whey. Cover loosely with foil and refrigerate overnight; check occasionally to see that whey is not overflowing. To serve: Turn ends of cheesecloth back and invert mold on a large, shallow dish. Garnish with 10–12 large perfect berries; sweeten the rest to taste, crush slightly, and pass as a sauce. About 500 calories per serving.

MONT BLANC AUX MARRONS

An Alp of riced chestnuts snowcapped with sweetened whipped cream. *Not* for calorie counters.
Makes 8 servings

1 pound shelled, peeled chestnuts
(you'll need about 1½ pounds
unshelled chestnuts)
3 cups milk
⅔ cup sugar
2 teaspoons vanilla
1 pint heavy cream
¼ cup sifted confectioners' sugar

Simmer chestnuts, milk, sugar, and

1 teaspoon vanilla in the top of a double boiler over just boiling water 30–40 minutes until very tender. Drain (save milk for pudding or custard). Force chestnuts through a potato ricer or coarse sieve, mounding into a high, fluffy pyramid on a large platter. Chill 2–3 hours. Whip cream with confectioners' sugar and remaining vanilla until very soft peaks form, and gently frost pyramid, letting a bit of the base show. Serve at once. About 465 calories per serving.

¢ COTTAGE PUDDING

As much cake as pudding and buttery-rich.
Makes 8 servings

2 cups sifted flour
1 tablespoon baking powder
¼ teaspoon salt
½ cup butter or margarine
½ cup sugar
1 egg, lightly beaten
1 teaspoon vanilla or the finely grated
rind of 1 lemon
¾ cup milk

Preheat oven to 350° F. Sift flour with baking powder and salt; set aside. Cream butter and sugar until light, add egg, and beat well. Mix vanilla and milk. Add flour and milk alternately to egg mixture, beginning and ending with flour and beating after each addition. Spoon into a buttered 8″×8″×2″ baking pan and bake, uncovered, about 50 minutes until top springs back when touched. Cut in squares and serve warm with hot Custard Sauce or whipped cream. About 245 calories per serving (without sauce or whipped cream).

VARIATIONS:

Apple or Cherry Cottage Pudding:
Prepare batter as directed and mix in 2 cups very thinly sliced, peeled, and cored tart apples or well-drained, canned pitted red cherries. Bake as directed in a buttered 9″×9″×2″ pan. About 260 calories per serving.

Eve's Pudding: Spread 1½ cups applesauce in the bottom of a greased

9"×9"×2" pan, cover with batter, and bake as directed. About 275 calories per serving.

¢ **Raisin Cottage Pudding:** Prepare as directed, using grated lemon rind and adding 2 tablespoons lemon juice and ¾ cup seedless or sultana raisins. About 285 calories per serving.

Castle Pudding: Put 2 tablespoons maple syrup, jam, or jelly into each of 8 buttered custard cups then fill two-thirds with Cottage Pudding batter. Bake 25 minutes at 350° F., then invert on serving plates. About 300 calories per serving.

CHOCOLATE CHIP PUDDING

Makes 4 servings

2½ cups cubed stale cake (any flavor)
2 eggs, lightly beaten
¼ cup sugar
⅛ teaspoon salt
2 cups milk, scalded
¼ cup coarsely chopped pecans or
    walnuts
½ teaspoon vanilla
¼ teaspoon nutmeg
½ cup semisweet chocolate bits
1 cup light cream (optional)

Preheat oven to 350° F. Put cake in a lightly buttered 2-quart casserole; mix together all remaining ingredients except chocolate bits and cream, pour over cake, and mix lightly. Bake, uncovered, 30–35 minutes until barely firm. Sprinkle chocolate bits over surface and bake, uncovered, 10 minutes longer until pudding is firm and chocolate melted. Serve hot, topped, if you like, with cream. About 445 calories per serving (without cream).

EASY DATE AND WALNUT PUDDING

Use scissors dipped in hot water to snip dates quickly.
Makes 20 servings

2 cups boiling water
2 teaspoons baking soda
1 pound pitted dates, coarsely cut up
¼ cup butter or margarine

2 cups sugar
2 cups sifted flour
1 teaspoon vanilla
1 cup coarsely chopped walnuts

Preheat oven to 325° F. Pour water over soda, mix well, and pour over dates. Add butter and stir until melted; cool slightly. Mix sugar and flour in a large bowl, add about ½ date mixture and beat well. Add remaining date mixture and vanilla and beat again. Stir in nuts. Spoon into a well-greased 13"×9"×2" baking pan and bake 50 minutes until springy to the touch. Cut into squares and serve warm or cold with whipped cream or vanilla ice cream. About 240 calories per serving (without whipped cream or ice cream).

DESSERT SAUCES

VANILLA SAUCE

A good basic sauce suited to a variety of desserts.
Makes about 2½ cups

2 tablespoons cornstarch
½ cup sugar
2 cups water or milk
¼ cup butter or margarine
1½ teaspoons vanilla
Pinch nutmeg

Mix cornstarch and sugar in a heavy saucepan, gradually add water, and heat, stirring constantly, until mixture boils. Reduce heat and simmer, uncovered, 2–3 minutes, stirring now and then. Add butter, vanilla, and nutmeg and stir until butter melts and is blended. Serve hot. About 20 calories per tablespoon if made with water, 30 calories per tablespoon if made with milk.

VARIATIONS:

Vanilla Bean Sauce: Scald 2 cups milk, add ½ vanilla bean, split lengthwise, cover, and let steep 20 minutes; discard bean (but not the tiny black seeds).

Combine cornstarch and sugar as directed, gradually add milk, and heat and stir until mixture boils. Proceed as directed, omitting vanilla extract and nutmeg. About 20 calories per tablespoon if made with water, 30 calories per tablespoon if made with milk.

French Vanilla Sauce: Prepare Vanilla Bean Sauce (above) as directed, spoon a little hot sauce into 2 lightly beaten egg yolks, return to pan, and heat and stir 1 minute over lowest heat; do not boil. About 35 calories per tablespoon.

Vanilla Sauce Mousseline: Prepare any of the above vanilla sauces as directed; place a circle of wax paper flat on sauce and cool to room temperature. Whip ½ cup heavy cream to soft peaks, fold into sauce, and serve. About 40 to 45 calories per tablespoon, depending upon base sauce used.

⊠ **EGGNOG SAUCE**

Makes about 2 cups

2 egg yolks
½ cup sifted confectioners' sugar
1 teaspoon vanilla
1 cup heavy cream

Beat egg yolks, sugar, and vanilla until thick and creamy. Whip cream to soft peaks, then fold in yolk mixture. Serve with fruit. About 40 calories per tablespoon.

VARIATION:

Orange or Lemon Eggnog Sauce: Just before serving fold in 1 tablespoon finely grated orange or lemon rind and/or 1–2 tablespoons brandy, light rum, or Marsala. About 40 calories per tablespoon (without brandy, rum, or Marsala).

NESSELRODE SAUCE

Serve cold over pudding, fruit, or ice cream.
Makes about 1 quart

1 recipe Stirred Custard
¼ cup Málaga or Marsala wine
¼ cup sultana raisins
¼ cup dried currants

2 tablespoons minced candied red cherries
2 tablespoons minced candied orange peel
2 tablespoons minced candied citron
½ cup shelled, peeled chestnuts, boiled and drained
½ cup heavy cream

Prepare and cool custard as directed. Meanwhile, pour wine over fruits and let stand 1 hour; also purée chestnuts. Mix fruits and chestnuts into custard. Whip cream to soft peaks and fold in. Cover and chill ½ hour before serving. About 30 calories per tablespoon.

⊠ **BASIC CHOCOLATE SAUCE**

Seven sauces from one easy recipe.
Makes about 1 cup

2 (1-ounce) squares unsweetened chocolate
½ cup water
½ cup sugar
½ cup light corn syrup
2 tablespoons butter or margarine
½ teaspoon vanilla

Place chocolate, water, sugar, and syrup in a small, heavy saucepan, set over low heat, and heat, stirring now and then, until chocolate melts. Beat in butter and vanilla. Serve hot or at room temperature. About 85 calories per tablespoon.

VARIATIONS:

Creamy Chocolate Sauce: Substitute ½ cup light cream or evaporated milk for the water. About 100 calories per tablespoon.

Chocolate-Marshmallow Sauce: Omit sugar and add 16 large marshmallows; stir frequently as chocolate and marshmallows melt. About 90 calories per tablespoon.

Chocolate-Peppermint Sauce: Substitute ½ teaspoon peppermint extract for the vanilla. About 85 calories per tablespoon.

Chocolate-Nut Sauce: Prepare sauce as directed and mix in ⅓ cup chopped pecans, walnuts, toasted, blanched almonds, or peanuts. About 110 calories per tablespoon.

Chocolate-Cherry Sauce: Prepare sauce as directed and mix in ¼ cup quartered maraschino cherries before serving. About 90 calories per tablespoon.

Bittersweet Chocolate Sauce: Melt 1 (6-ounce) package semisweet chocolate bits with ½ cup light corn syrup in the top of a double boiler over simmering water. Beat in 1 (5⅓-ounce) can evaporated milk, 2 tablespoons hot water, and ½ teaspoon vanilla; heat and stir until creamy. About 90 calories per tablespoon.

⊠ HOT FUDGE SAUCE

Makes 1¼ cups

1½ cups sugar
2 tablespoons flour
¾ cup cold water
3 (1-ounce) squares unsweetened chocolate or 3 (1-ounce) envelopes unsweetened no-melt chocolate
3 tablespoons butter or margarine
1 teaspoon vanilla

Mix sugar and flour in a heavy saucepan, blend in water, and heat, stirring constantly over moderate heat, until boiling and thickened. Reduce heat to low, add chocolate, and heat and stir until chocolate melts. Beat in butter and vanilla. Cool slightly, beating now and then. Serve warm. About 95 calories per tablespoon.

⊠ QUICK MOCHA SAUCE

Makes 1¼ cups

2 (6-ounce) packages semisweet chocolate bits
6 tablespoons very hot strong black coffee
1 teaspoon vanilla

Purée chocolate bits, coffee, and vanilla in an electric blender at medium speed until chocolate melts and sauce is smooth. Serve at once over vanilla ice cream or sliced pound cake. This sauce can be stored, covered, in the refrigerator for several days. If too thick, thin with 1–2 tablespoons boiling water. About 82 calories per tablespoon.

⊠ MARSHMALLOW CREAM SAUCE

Makes about 1 cup

4–5 tablespoons cold water
1 cup marshmallow cream
¼ teaspoon vanilla

Mix water with marshmallow cream, adding a little at a time, then blend until smooth. Stir in vanilla and serve cold with pudding or fruit. *Or* heat, stirring constantly, over moderately low heat and serve warm. About 50 calories per tablespoon.

VARIATIONS:

Chocolate Marshmallow Cream: Prepare as directed, set over low heat, and beat in 1 (1-ounce) square coarsely grated unsweetened chocolate or 1 (1-ounce) envelope no-melt unsweetened chocolate. Heat and stir until blended. About 55 calories per tablespoon.

Fruit Marshmallow Cream (About 1½ cups): Prepare as directed and beat in ½ cup strawberry, raspberry, peach, or apricot jam, black or red currant, or grape jelly, and 1 teaspoon lemon juice. Omit vanilla. About 50 calories per tablespoon.

Spicy Marshmallow Cream: Prepare as directed and beat in ¼ teaspoon each cinnamon and nutmeg and 1 teaspoon finely grated lemon rind. Omit vanilla. About 50 calories per tablespoon.

Peppermint Marshmallow Cream: Prepare as directed, substituting ⅛ teaspoon peppermint extract for the vanilla and, if you like, adding a few drops green or red food coloring. About 50 calories per tablespoon.

Liqueur Marshmallow Cream: Prepare as directed, using 2 tablespoons each water and crème de menthe or fruit liqueur instead of all water. Omit vanilla. About 55 calories per tablespoon.

BUTTERSCOTCH SAUCE

Makes about 2 cups

1 cup firmly packed dark brown sugar
1 cup maple syrup
¼ cup butter or margarine
1 teaspoon salt
2 teaspoons vanilla
¾ cup light cream

Heat sugar and syrup in a heavy saucepan over moderately low heat, stirring constantly until sugar dissolves. Raise heat to moderately high and boil uncovered 5 minutes. Off heat, add butter, salt, and vanilla. *Do not stir.* Let stand, uncovered, 5 minutes. Add cream, then beat about 1 minute until creamy, blond, and well blended. Serve warm. About 75 calories per tablespoon.

VARIATION:

Butterscotch Syrup (About 3 cups): Prepare as directed but increase light cream to 1½ cups. Serve over waffles, pancakes, or ice cream. About 60 calories per tablespoon.

⊠ CARAMEL SYRUP

Makes 2 cups

1 (1-pound) box dark brown sugar
1½ cups water
2 teaspoons vanilla
¼ teaspoon salt

Heat and stir sugar in a heavy saucepan over low heat until liquid. Off heat, gradually stir in water. Return to low heat and heat and stir until smooth. Cool 5 minutes, mix in vanilla and salt. Pour into a jar, cool, cover, and refrigerate. Use as an ice-cream topping or milk flavoring. About 53 calories per tablespoon.

BASIC NUT SYRUP

Makes about 2 cups

2 cups sugar
1 cup water
¼ cup dark corn syrup
½ teaspoon vanilla
1 cup coarsely chopped walnuts, pecans, toasted almonds, hazelnuts, or blanched, roasted, unsalted peanuts

Mix sugar, water, and syrup in a 1-quart heavy saucepan, set over moderately low heat, and heat and stir until sugar dissolves. Raise heat and boil gently, uncovered, *without stirring* 3 minutes; stir once and, if the consistency of maple syrup, remove from heat; if not, boil 1 minute longer. Cool slightly and add vanilla and nuts. Stir just to mix and serve warm or cool over ice cream. About 80 calories per tablespoon.

VARIATIONS:

Orange-Nut Syrup: Prepare as directed, substituting orange juice for water and the grated rind of 1 orange for vanilla. About 85 calories per tablespoon.

Pistachio Syrup: Prepare as directed, substituting light corn syrup for the dark. Add ⅛ teaspoon almond extract, tint pale green, if you like, and stir in ½ cup shelled and peeled pistachio nuts. About 70 calories per tablespoon.

⊠ LEMON OR LIME SAUCE

Spoon over ice cream or yellow cake.
Makes about 2½ cups

2 tablespoons cornstarch
1 cup sugar
1½ cups water
½ cup lemon or lime juice
¼ cup butter or margarine
2 teaspoons finely grated lemon or lime rind

Mix cornstarch and sugar in a heavy saucepan, gradually add water and fruit juice, and heat, stirring constantly, until mixture boils. Reduce heat and simmer, uncovered, 2–3 minutes, stirring now and then. Add butter and rind and stir until butter is melted and well blended. Serve hot. About 30 calories per tablespoon.

VARIATION:

Orange Sauce: Prepare as directed, using 2 cups orange juice instead of water and lemon juice, and grated orange rind instead of lemon. For tartness, add 1–2 tablespoons lemon juice. About 35 calories per tablespoon.

⊠ BRANDY OR RUM SAUCE

Delicious over steamed puddings or ice cream.
Makes about 2½ cups

2 tablespoons cornstarch
½ cup sugar
1¾ cups milk
¼–⅓ cup brandy or light rum
¼ cup butter or margarine
½ teaspoon vanilla
Pinch nutmeg

Mix cornstarch and sugar in a heavy saucepan, gradually add milk and brandy, and heat, stirring constantly, until mixture boils. Reduce heat and simmer, uncovered, 2–3 minutes, stirring now and then. Add butter, vanilla, and nutmeg and stir until butter melts and is well blended. Serve hot. About 35 calories per tablespoon.

LEMON-RAISIN SAUCE

Good over gingerbread.
Makes 2⅔ cups

1 cup sugar
2 tablespoons cornstarch
1½ cups cold water
½ cup lemon juice
2 teaspoons finely grated lemon rind
1 egg yolk
2 tablespoons butter or margarine
¼ cup sultana raisins

Mix sugar and cornstarch in a heavy saucepan, blend in water and lemon juice, and heat, stirring constantly over moderate heat, until mixture boils. Reduce heat and simmer 2–3 minutes, stirring now and then. Mix lemon rind and egg yolk, blend a little hot sauce into egg, return to pan, and beat and stir 1–2 minutes; do not boil. Off heat, add butter and raisins and let stand 2 minutes. Serve warm. About 30 calories per tablespoon.

RED CHERRY SAUCE

Delicious over vanilla ice cream or pound cake.
Makes about 2 cups

1 (1-pound) can pitted sour red cherries (do not drain)
⅔ cup sugar
2 tablespoons cornstarch
¼ teaspoon almond extract
Few drops red food coloring

Drain liquid from cherries and reserve. Mix sugar and cornstarch in a heavy saucepan, blend in cherry liquid, and heat over moderate heat, stirring constantly, until mixture boils. Reduce heat and simmer 2–3 minutes, stirring now and then. Add cherries and almond extract and heat 2 minutes. Off heat, mix in food coloring. Serve hot or cold (thin with a little water if sauce seems thick). About 35 calories per tablespoon.

VARIATION:

Pineapple Sauce: Mix ½ cup sugar with the cornstarch, blend in 1 cup pineapple juice, and proceed as recipe directs, adding 1 (8½-ounce) undrained can crushed pineapple at the end instead of cherries. Omit almond extract and add 1 tablespoon lemon juice. Tint pale yellow if you like. About 35 calories per tablespoon.

⊠ JAM OR JELLY SAUCE

Makes about 1½ cups

1 cup jam or jelly (any kind)
2 teaspoons cornstarch
⅔ cup cold water
2 teaspoons lemon juice

Heat jam or jelly in a small, heavy saucepan over moderately low heat. Mix cornstarch and water, blend into jam, and heat and stir until mixture boils. Reduce heat and simmer, stirring now and then, 2–3 minutes. Off heat, mix in lemon juice. Serve warm over pudding. About 30 calories per tablespoon.

VARIATIONS:

Jam and Nut Sauce: Prepare sauce as directed, cool slightly, and mix in ¼–⅓ cup minced pecans, walnuts, or toasted almonds. About 40 calories per tablespoon.

Sultana Jam Sauce: Prepare sauce as directed and mix in ¼ cup sultana raisins; let stand 5 minutes to plump raisins. About 35 calories per tablespoon.

Ginger-Jam Sauce: Prepare sauce as directed, using peach, apricot, or pineapple jam, then mix in ¼ cup minced crystallized ginger. About 35 calories per tablespoon.

Marmalade Sauce: Substitute orange, lemon, or grapefruit marmalade for jam and prepare as directed; omit lemon juice. About 30 calories per tablespoon.

Sherried Peach or Apricot Jam Sauce: Prepare as directed, using ½ cup water and ¼ cup dry sherry (or brandy) instead of the ⅔ cup water; omit lemon juice. About 40 calories per tablespoon.

⊠ MELBA SAUCE

Serve as a sauce for Peach Melba, ice cream, or fruit or use to flavor milk shakes and sodas.
Makes about 1½ cups

1 pint fresh raspberries, washed, or 2 (10-ounce) packages frozen raspberries, thawed
⅓ cup red currant jelly
⅓–½ cup sugar
1 tablespoon cornstarch blended with 2 tablespoons water

Purée raspberries in an electric blender at high speed and strain. Pour into a saucepan, mix in jelly, sugar, and cornstarch paste, and cook and stir over moderate heat until thickened and clear. Cool, taste for sweetness, and add more sugar if needed. About 40 calories per tablespoon if made with fresh berries, 55 calories per tablespoon if made with frozen berries.

VARIATIONS:

Strawberry Sauce: Prepare as directed, substituting 1 pint fresh strawberries or 2 (10-ounce) packages thawed frozen strawberries for the raspberries. About 40 calories per tablespoon if made with fresh berries, 50 if made with frozen berries.

Currant Sauce: Substitute 1 pint very ripe red or black currants for the raspberries

and omit the currant jelly. If you like, mix the cornstarch with port wine or blackberry liqueur instead of water. Proceed as directed. About 25 calories per tablespoon.

⚖ DESSERT CARDINAL SAUCE

Use as a dessert sauce for ice cream, sherbet, or fresh fruit.
Makes about 5 cups

1 (10-ounce) package frozen raspberries, thawed
½ cup superfine sugar
1 tablespoon lemon juice
2–3 tablespoons kirsch (optional)
2 pints fresh strawberries, washed, stemmed, and sliced thin

Purée raspberries in an electric blender at high speed or put through a food mill, then strain. Add ¼ cup sugar, lemon juice, and, if you like, the kirsch; stir well. Mix strawberries with remaining sugar. Gently stir raspberry sauce into strawberries. About 10 calories per tablespoon made without kirsch, 12 calories per tablespoon made with kirsch.

ALGARVE APRICOT SAUCE

In the south of Portugal lies the Algarve, where figs, peaches, and apricots grow. Women make them into a variety of sweets, among them this tart apricot sauce, luscious over a poached meringue.
Makes about 2¼ cups

1 (1-pound 14-ounce) can peeled whole apricots (do not drain)
Juice and grated rind of 1 lemon
1 cup firmly packed light brown sugar
¼ cup butter

Pit apricots and purée in an electric blender at high speed or put through a food mill. Place in a small saucepan, add lemon juice, rind, and sugar, and simmer uncovered, stirring occasionally, 1 hour until thick and caramel colored. Remove from heat, stir in butter, and cool to room temperature. Serve over Poached Meringue Ring or as a dessert sauce for ice cream, sliced oranges or peaches. About 55 calories per tablespoon.

⊠ HONEY SAUCE

Serve warm or cool over pudding, fruit, or ice cream.
Makes 1½ cups

1 cup honey
1 tablespoon cornstarch blended with 1
   tablespoon cold water
¼ cup butter or margarine
2 teaspoons lemon juice

Heat honey in a small, heavy saucepan over moderate heat. Stir in cornstarch mixture and heat and stir until boiling; reduce heat and simmer 2–3 minutes. Beat in butter and lemon juice. About 60 calories per tablespoon.

VARIATION:

Honey-Nut Sauce: Prepare sauce as directed, cool, and mix in ½ cup coarsely chopped pecans, walnuts, or toasted almonds. About 80 calories per tablespoon.

⊠ EASY PEPPERMINT SAUCE

To save yourself the job of crushing peppermint sticks, buy the small peppermint candies. Best over chocolate ice cream.
Makes 1½ cups

½ pound red-striped peppermint candies
   or 2 cups coarsely crushed peppermint
   sticks
1 cup water
½ cup sugar

Heat candy and water in a heavy saucepan over moderate heat, stirring often until candy begins to dissolve, then boil slowly, uncovered, until completely dissolved, stirring now and then. Add sugar and heat and stir 2–3 minutes. Cool and serve over ice cream. About 50 calories per tablespoon.

⊠ HARD SAUCE

The perfect sauce for steamed puddings.
Makes about 1 cup

½ cup butter (no substitute), softened to
   room temperature
2 cups sifted confectioners' sugar
⅛ teaspoon salt

1 tablespoon hot water
1 teaspoon vanilla

Beat butter until creamy; gradually beat in sugar, a little at a time. Beat in remaining ingredients and continue to beat until fluffy. Serve chilled or at room temperature. About 115 calories per tablespoon.

VARIATIONS:

Brandy or Rum Hard Sauce: Omit hot water and vanilla; add 2 tablespoons brandy or rum or 2 teaspoons brandy or rum extract. About 120 calories per tablespoon.

Lemon or Orange Hard Sauce: Omit water and vanilla; instead, beat in 2 tablespoons lemon or orange juice and 1 tablespoon finely grated lemon rind or 2 tablespoons finely grated orange rind. About 115 calories per tablespoon.

Mocha Hard Sauce: Increase hot water to 2 tablespoons and beat in 1 tablespoon instant coffee powder and 2 tablespoons cocoa. About 120 calories per tablespoon.

Cream Fluff Hard Sauce: Prepare sauce as directed but omit water; at the end gradually beat in ¼ cup heavy cream. About 130 calories per tablespoon.

⊠ MOCK DEVONSHIRE CREAM

Serve as a topping for fresh fruit, fruit pies, and cobblers.
Makes about 1 pint

1 cup heavy cream
3 tablespoons sifted confectioners'
   sugar
1 cup sour cream

Whip cream with the sugar until soft peaks form, then blend in sour cream. About 45 calories per tablespoon.

⊠ SWEETENED WHIPPED CREAM

For best results, whip cream by hand just before needed, using a chilled bowl and beater.
Makes about 2 cups

1 cup very cold heavy cream

*2 tablespoons sugar or ¼ cup sifted
confectioners' sugar*
*½ teaspoon vanilla or ¼ teaspoon
almond, maple, or peppermint extract*

Beat cream in a chilled bowl until frothy; slowly beat in sugar and flavoring and continue beating until soft, glossy peaks form, scraping bowl often. (*Note:* If you should slightly overbeat cream, stir in 1–2 tablespoons cold milk.) If you must delay using it, refrigerate, then beat lightly with a wire whisk just before using. About 30 calories per tablespoon.

VARIATIONS:

Plain Whipped Cream: Whip cream as directed but omit sugar and flavoring. About 28 calories per tablespoon.

Decorative Whipped Cream: Whip cream with ⅓ cup sifted confectioners' sugar, flavor, then tint, if you like, a pastel color. Pipe through a pastry tube fitted with a decorative tip. *To Freeze:* Do not color whipped cream; pipe onto wax-paper-lined baking sheets and freeze until hard; wrap frozen fluffs individually, then group in plastic freezer bags. Use within 2 months. Nice on warm pies. About 35 calories per tablespoon.

Chocolate Whipped Cream: Whip as directed, beating in 3 tablespoons sugar blended with 3 tablespoons cocoa; reduce vanilla to ¼ teaspoon. About 40 calories per tablespoon.

Coffee Whipped Cream: Prepare as directed but add 1 teaspoon instant coffee powder. About 30 calories per tablespoon.

Mocha Whipped Cream: Blend 2 tablespoons sugar, 1 tablespoon cocoa, and 1 teaspoon instant coffee powder. Whip into cream as directed. About 35 calories per tablespoon.

Orange or Lemon Whipped Cream: Whip as directed, flavoring with ¼ teaspoon orange or lemon extract and 2 teaspoons finely grated rind instead of vanilla. About 30 calories per tablespoon.

Spiced Whipped Cream: Whip as directed, adding ¼ teaspoon each nutmeg and cinnamon. About 30 calories per tablespoon.

Nutty Whipped Cream: Whip as directed, then fold in ¼–⅓ cup any minced nuts. About 40 calories per tablespoon.

Fruity Whipped Cream: Whip as directed, omitting vanilla, then fold in ⅓ cup any sweetened fruit purée. About 45 calories per tablespoon.

Coconut Whipped Cream: Whip as directed, then fold in ⅓ cup flaked coconut. About 35 calories per tablespoon.

Spiked Whipped Cream: Whip as directed, but flavor with 2–3 tablespoons brandy, rum, bourbon, crème de menthe, or fruit liqueur instead of vanilla. About 35 calories per tablespoon.

Party Whipped Cream (Makes about 2 quarts): Warm 2 teaspoons unflavored gelatin and ¼ cup cold water until gelatin dissolves; cool slightly and gradually mix in 1 quart heavy cream; chill ½ hour. Whip cream, beating in 1 cup sifted confectioners' sugar and 2 teaspoons vanilla. (*Note:* If you use an electric mixer, hold out ⅓ cup cream and stir in after the rest is whipped.) This cream will hold well in the refrigerator about 1 hour. About 30 calories per tablespoon.

⚶ WHIPPED EVAPORATED MILK TOPPING

Makes about 1½ cups

½ cup evaporated milk (do not dilute)
1 tablespoon lemon juice
½ cup sifted confectioners' sugar
*½ teaspoon vanilla or ¼ teaspoon
almond extract*

Chill evaporated milk in an ice cube tray in freezer until ice crystals form around edge, 20–30 minutes. Meanwhile, chill bowl and beater. Whip milk until soft peaks form; add remaining ingredients and beat until stiff peaks form. If not to be used at once, refrigerate and use within 1 hour. About 15 calories per tablespoon.

VARIATIONS:

Any of the Sweetened Whipped Cream flavor variations work well with this topping.

◻ ⚖ **LOW-CALORIE DESSERT TOPPING**

Makes 4 servings

3 tablespoons ice water
3 tablespoons nonfat dry milk powder
2 teaspoons lemon juice
Few drops liquid noncaloric sweetener or 2 teaspoons low-calorie granulated sugar substitute
¼ teaspoon vanilla or almond extract

Pour ice water into a chilled bowl, sprinkle powdered milk on surface, and beat with a rotary or electric beater until soft peaks form. Add lemon juice, sweeten to taste, add vanilla, and beat until stiff peaks form. Use at once. About 14 calories per serving.

VARIATIONS:

◻ ⚖ **Low-Calorie Coffee Dessert Topping:** Substitute 3 tablespoons very strong iced coffee for ice water and omit vanilla. About 14 calories per serving.

◻ ⚖ **Low-Calorie Orange Dessert Topping:** Substitute 1 tablespoon frozen, slightly thawed orange juice concentrate diluted with 2 tablespoons ice water for the ice water, omit vanilla, and after whipping fold in 1 tablespoon finely grated orange rind. About 20 calories per serving.

HOMEMADE SOUR CREAM

Makes about 1 cup

1 cup heavy cream, at room temperature
¼ cup sour cream or buttermilk

Mix creams in a screw-top jar, cover, and let stand at room temperature about 24 hours until very thick. Chill well before using and keep refrigerated. About 60 calories per tablespoon if made with sour cream, 55 calories per tablespoon if made with buttermilk.

CHAPTER 21

PIES AND PASTRIES

More than any other dessert, pies are typically American. Our speech ("as easy as pie"), our songs ("I'm as normal as blueberry pie . . ."), our literature (to eat "humble pie") are strewn with references. Apple pies, traditionally, usher in autumn, pumpkin pies belong to Thanksgiving, mince pies to Christmas, and cherry pies to George Washington's birthday. Foreign countries have specialties too—if not pies, flaky pastries, honey-drenched or filled with meltingly smooth creams: the éclairs, cream puffs, and Napoleons of France, the tortes of Germany and Austria, the cheese cakes of Italy, the wispy honey-laden pastries of the Middle East. Many can be made at home, some with less effort than seems possible.

The Kinds of Pastry and How to Mix Them

Conventional Pastry: The piecrust pastry, tender and flaky when properly made. The secret is to cut the fat into the flour until it is the texture of coarse meal so that in baking, these flecks of fat melt, leaving the pastry flaky. There are a number of variations on the standard method (see recipes that follow).

Puff Pastry (Pâte Feuilletée): The feathery, many-layered French pastry used for Napoleons, Cream Horns, and dozens of lavish pastries. It is made by rolling and folding chilled butter (or sometimes lard if the pastry is a savory one) into a simple dough so that it separates into tissue-thin "leaves" when baked. A less tedious variation is *Rough Puff Pastry.*

Sweet Short Pastry (also called *Tart* or *Sweet Torte Pastry* and in French, *Pâte Brisée;* the German *Mürbteig* is of this type): Rather like a cookie dough, this egg-rich, sweet pastry is most often used for fruit flans and tarts.

Choux Pastry (Pâte à Choux): A paste containing a high proportion of eggs that is beaten until smooth and elastic enough to "puff" during baking. This is the pastry of cream puffs and éclairs.

Phyllo Pastry (pronounced FEE-lo): The tissue-thin, crisp pastry used for Greek and Middle Eastern pastries. It requires a special hard flour, a special technique, and years of practice. Phyllo leaves, ready to fill and bake, are available in many gourmet markets and Greek groceries.

Strudel Pastry: An elastic dough that is kneaded, rolled, and stretched until big as a table and "thin enough to read a newspaper through." It is filled with fruit, cheese, or poppy seeds, rolled up jelly-roll style, and baked until golden brown and crisp. Strudel dough sheets can be bought at gourmet groceries.

Crumb "Pastries": These aren't pastries but crumbs, crushed dried cereals, nuts, coconut, etc., mixed with sugar or syrup and melted butter and pressed into piepans.

Essential Ingredients of Pastries

Flour: Experts use *pastry flour* for piecrusts because it makes them unusually tender. Available at gourmet groceries (and occasionally through local bakeries), it is softer than all-purpose flour but not so delicate as cake flour. It is not suitable for pastries where elasticity is needed (choux and strudel).

IMPORTANT NOTE:
USE ALL-PURPOSE FLOUR FOR
PASTRIES IN THIS BOOK UNLESS
RECIPES SPECIFY OTHERWISE.

Fat: For most piecrusts, a solid fat is used. It may be vegetable shortening or lard, which many cooks prefer because of its mellow flavor and brittle texture. Mixtures of shortening and butter or margarine may be used, but the proportion of butter (do not use the whipped variety) should be kept low (about 1 to 3) if the pastry is to be flaky. For best results, chill the fat before using. Some pastries are made with cooking oil; it produces a tender (though not very flaky) crust. (*Note:* Use cooking oil only if recipes call for it; do not use interchangeably with shortening or lard.)

Liquid: Water (but occasionally fruit juice, milk, or cream) is used to bind the fat and flour, making pastry workable. For flaky pastry, use cold water; for a denser, mealier texture, warm or hot water.

Salt: Added strictly for flavor; without it, pastries would taste flat.

Extra Ingredients of Pastries

Sugar: Added to tart or torte pastries for sweetness, tenderness, and better browning.

Eggs: Added for richness of flavor and color. Usually egg yolks, rather than whole eggs, are used.

Leavening: Used in cookie dough-type pastries when a certain lightness and sponginess are wanted.

Flavorings: These are merely embellishments—grated cheese or nuts, spices, seeds, grated orange or lemon rind, sometimes vanilla or other extracts —added for variety and interest.

Some Pastry-Making Terms and Techniques

To Brush: To apply a thin coating of liquid, usually glaze or melted butter, with a pastry brush to give pastry a satiny or glistening finish. Bottom crusts are sometimes brushed with beaten egg white to "waterproof" them and keep juices from soaking in.

To Crimp: To pinch or crease edges of pastry in a zigzag or fluted pattern. Crimped edges seal top and bottom crusts together and also act like dams, holding fillings in.

Croûte: The French word for *crust; en croûte* refers to something baked in a pastry.

To Cut In: To work fat into flour with a pastry blender, 2 knives, or the fingertips. The motion is literally a cutting one (except when fingers are used), the fat particles being broken up and coated with flour.

To Dot: To dab bits of butter or other solid over the surface of something, usually before baking. In pies, fruit fillings are often dotted with butter.

To Dust: To cover with a thin film of flour.

To Fill: To put filling in a pie shell or other pastry.

To Fit: To press pastry against the contours of a pan.

Flan: The French word for a flat, open-face pie usually filled with fruit or cream filling or a combination of the two; it may be larger than American-style pies or smaller. For baking flan, a *flan ring* (bottomless round metal ring with straight sides) is placed on a baking sheet and the pastry pressed into it.

To Glaze: To coat with glaze. In pastry making, both crusts and fillings may be glazed, crusts with beaten egg or milk and sugar, fillings with syrup, thin gelatin, or clear sweet sauce.

To Line: To cover a pan with a thin layer of pastry, crumb crust, or other material.

Meringue: A stiffly beaten mixture of egg whites and sugar used as a pie topping or dropped from a spoon and baked like cookies.

"Mixture Forms a Ball": The term used to describe pastry when just the right amount of liquid has been added to the flour-shortening mixture. The pastry will just hang together in a ball but be neither sticky (too much liquid) nor crumbly (too little).

Pastry Blender: A gadget indispensable to every pastry cook, 6–8 arched blades or wires, mounted on a wooden handle, that cut fat into flour in record time. If you have none, use 2 table knives instead, cutting back and forth through the fat and flour or, if you prefer, rub fat and flour together with your fingertips. The difficulty of the finger method is that the heat of the hands may melt the shortening and make the pastry tough.

Pastry Cloth: A heavy square of canvas that makes rolling pastry easier because the fabric gives up only a small amount of flour to the pastry yet keeps it from sticking.

Pastry Wheel: A handy cutting wheel with either a plain or zigzag blade mounted on a wooden handle.

To Patch: To fill in cracks, holes, uneven edges of pastry by pressing in small scraps. Sometimes it is necessary to dampen the pastry scraps so they will stick.

Pie Funnel: A heatproof ceramic funnel about 3″ high, often with a decorative top, used in deep-dish pies to help prop up the crust and keep the pie from boiling over. It stands in the center of the pie, its top poking through the pastry.

Pie Shell: Crust fitted into a piepan; it may be baked or unbaked.

To Prick: To pierce pastry, usually a bottom crust, at intervals with a fork so it will lie flat during baking.

To Roll Out: To roll pastry with a rolling pin.

To Roll Up: To roll a pastry over and over, jelly-roll style. The technique is used for making Palmiers and Strudel.

To Seal: To pinch pastry edges together, sealing in filling.

Short: Containing a high proportion of shortening; a short crust is tender and crumbly.

Spring Form Pan: A fairly deep, straight-sided round pan with removable bottom and a side seam that locks and unlocks to facilitate removing pastry. It is most often used for cheese cakes.

Steam Slits or Vents: Decorative slits or holes cut in a top crust to allow steam to escape during baking; these also help keep pies from boiling over.

Stockinette: A knitted cotton "stocking" fitted over a rolling pin to make rolling pastry easier. It works like a pastry cloth, giving up very little flour to the pastry but at the same time keeping it from sticking. Stockinettes are inexpensive and available in nearly every dime store. Wash and dry after each use.

Tart: A small pastry, usually open-face, often with a short sweet crust. It may be bite-size or big enough for one ample dessert portion. Tart shells may be baked in muffin tins or fluted tart tins (see About Making Tarts).

"Texture of Coarse Meal": The term used to describe the consistency of fat when properly cut into flour. In making pastry, the fat should be cut in only until pebbly and coarse. Some cooks prefer the particles even coarser, about the size of small beans, because these solid flecks of fat, scattered throughout the flour, are what make the pastry flaky and crisp.

To Toss: To mix quickly and lightly with a fork, using a tossing motion. This is the technique used in mixing liquid into pastries, the object being to handle as gently as possible so that the fat particles aren't mashed. When the pastry holds together, the mixing's done.

How to Make Better Pies and Pastries

About Pans:

– For richly browned bottom crusts, use heatproof glass, dark metal, or heavy teflon-lined pans. Bright shiny pans deflect the heat, producing pale crusts.
– For best results, use types and sizes of pans recipes call for.
– When making a juicy fruit pie, use a pan with a trough around the rim to catch "boil-ups."
– Do not grease or flour piepan; do, however, make sure it is spotless and dry.

About Mixing Pastries:

– Read recipe before beginning and make sure you have all ingredients and implements on hand.
– For mixing, use a large, heavy, round-bottomed bowl.
– Measure all ingredients before beginning.
– For extra-flaky pastry, chill shortening and water 15–20 minutes before using.
– Use the lightest possible touch in mixing pastries. Cut fat into flour until "the texture of coarse meal" or for a superflaky crust, until "the size of small beans." Scatter liquid over mixture, one tablespoon at a time, tossing with a fork until it just "forms a ball."
– Do not knead pastry unless recipe calls for it (strudel dough, for example, must be kneaded). But piecrusts, never.

About Rolling Pastries:

– Lightly gather pastry together with hands and shape loosely into a ball.
– Chill pastry, if you like, about ½ hour before rolling. Some cooks insist that the chilling step is vital if the pastry is to be flaky and tender. But many tests have proved that, if the pastry is properly handled throughout mixing and rolling, the chilling makes little difference.
– Place pastry on a lightly floured pastry cloth or board, flatten lightly into a small circle (or rectangle or square, depending on shape needed), then with lightly floured, stockinette-covered rolling pin, flatten until about ½″ thick. Even up any ragged edges.
– Roll pastry from the center outward, using short, firm strokes and changing direction as needed to keep pastry as nearly circular (or rectangular or square) as possible. Always bear in mind the ultimate size and shape you want when rolling and roll toward that end. For most piecrusts, ⅛″ is a good thickness. As for diameter, pastry should be about 3″ larger in diameter than the pan you plan to use.
– Use as little flour in rolling as possible; it's the extra flour that toughens the pastry.
– If edges crack or pastry is rolled too thin in spots, patch with scraps. Dampen, then press in place and roll. The patchwork should be invisible.
– To transfer pastry easily to pan, place rolling pin across center of pastry, lop half of pastry over rolling pin, and lift gently into pan.

About Fitting Pastries into Pans:

– Center pastry circle in pan so that overhang is equal all around.
– Press gently, fitting against contours of pan.
– *If a single crust pie:* Trim overhang all around with scissors so it is about 1″ larger than pan. Roll under, even with rim, and crimp as desired.
– *If a double crust pie:* Do not trim overhang. Brush bottom and sides well with beaten egg white if filling is extra juicy and let air-dry 15–20 minutes. Roll top crust as you did the bottom, making it slightly thinner if you like. Cut decorative steam slits in the center. Add filling to pie shell, mounding it up in the center. Fit top crust over filling, trim both crusts evenly all around so they overhang about ½–1″. Roll up and over

even with rim, then seal and crimp.

About Baking Pastries:

– Let oven preheat a full 15 minutes before baking.
– Unless recipes direct to the contrary, bake pies as near the center of the oven as possible so they will brown evenly.
– When baking more than one pie at a time, stagger pans on rack or racks, leaving plenty of room between them for heat to circulate. Do not let pans touch oven walls.
– If crust should brown too fast, cover with a piece of foil or dampened piece of cloth. (*Note:* Crimped edges, in particular, brown faster than the rest of the crust.)

To Tell When Pies Are Done:

Double Crust Pies: The crust should be tan and crisp, the filling bubbly.

Single Crust Pies: The crimped edges should be nicely browned and crisp. The filling, if a custard type, should be set (a table knife inserted midway between center and rim should come out clean).

Meringue Pies: Meringue should look "set," be very faint tan with peaks of darker brown.

About Cooling Pies: Follow individual recipes carefully. Most pies should cool a few minutes on a wire rack before being cut; some should be brought to room temperature and others well chilled.

About Storing and Keeping Pies: Pies with custard or cream fillings, also those with whipped cream toppings, should be kept refrigerated (let stand at room temperature about 20 minutes before serving). Other kinds of pie may simply be kept in a cool corner of the kitchen.

About Reheating Pies: Fruit and mince pies are about the only ones that benefit from reheating. They will taste freshly baked if heated about 15 minutes at 325° F. and served hot.

About Freezing Pies: See chapter on freezing.

About Cutting Pies:

In General: Mentally divide pie into the needed number of pieces before making the first cut, then cut, using a pie server to transfer pieces to plates.

Double Crust Pies: Use a very sharp knife with a thin blade.

Single Crust Pies: Cut as you would a double crust pie, but dip knife often in hot water if filling is sticky.

Meringue Pies: Use a sharp knife, dipping into warm water after every cut to keep meringue from sticking.

How to Crimp or Flute a Piecrust

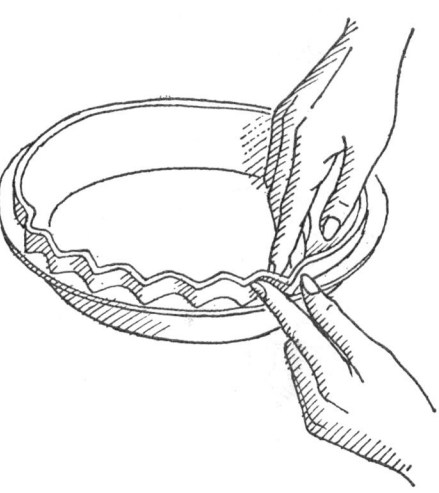

Crimped Crust

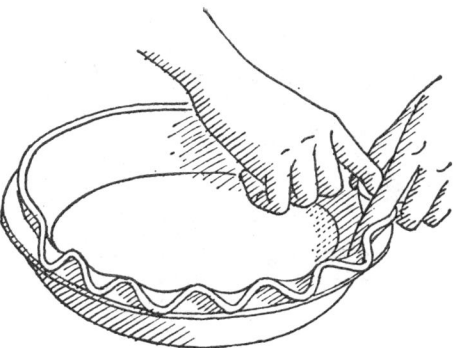

Fluted Crust

How to Make Lattice-Top Crusts

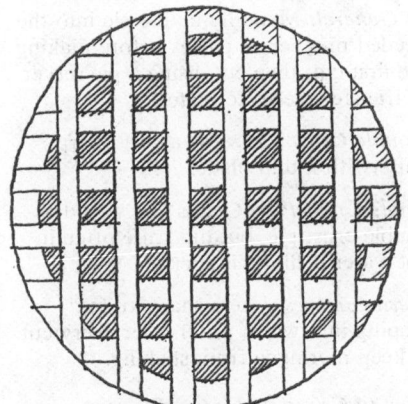

Plain Lattice

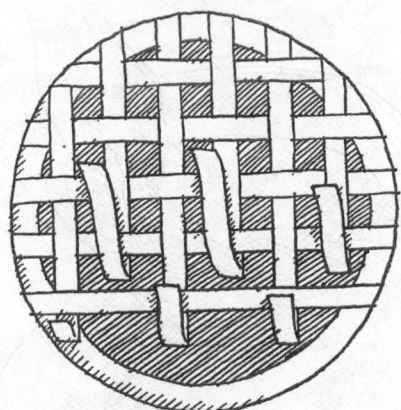

Woven Lattice

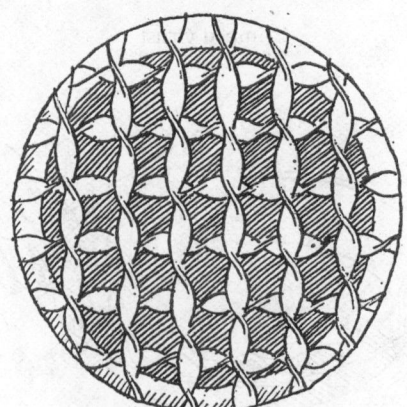

Twisted Lattice

Some Decorative Tricks with Pastry

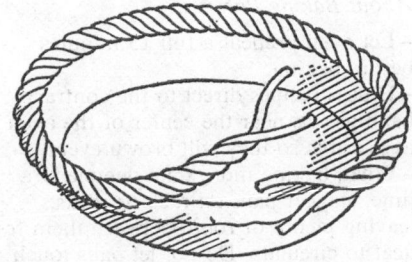

Spiral or Twist

Cut long strips of pastry about ½″ wide and twist together, tightly for a spiral, loosely for a twist. Dampen pastry rim and attach by pressing lightly.

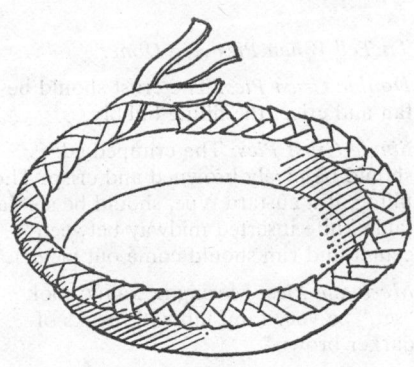

Braid

A variation on the twist made by braiding 3 long thin strips of pastry and attaching to dampened rim.

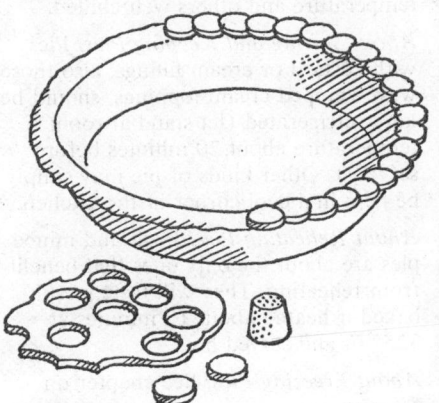

Coin

Cut out tiny pastry circles with a
thimble and arrange, overlapping, on
dampened rim. To make a button trim,
simply perforate centers of circles with a
needle so they resemble buttons.

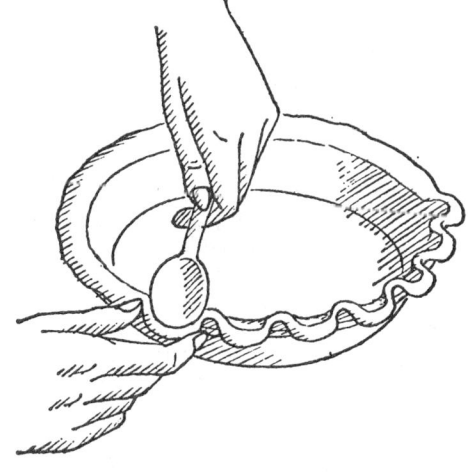

Ruffle

Simply scallop pastry edge using a
measuring teaspoon.

Some Fancy Cutouts for Top Crusts:

Fruit Cutouts	Wedge Cutouts	
Circle in the Square	Christmas Tree Cutouts	Sunburst
Hatchet Cutouts	Star Burst	

¢ FLAKY PASTRY I

For 1 single crust 8″, 9″, or 10″ pie

1¼ cups sifted flour
½ teaspoon salt
⅓ cup chilled vegetable shortening or
  lard
¼ cup ice water

Place flour and salt in a shallow mixing bowl and cut in shortening with a pastry blender until mixture resembles coarse meal. Sprinkle water over surface, 1 tablespoon at a time, and mix in lightly and quickly with a fork, just until pastry holds together. Shape gently into a ball on a lightly floured pastry cloth, then flatten into a circle about 1″ thick, evening up rough edges. Using a lightly floured, stockinette-covered rolling pin and short, firm strokes, roll into a circle about 3″ larger than the pan you plan to use. To transfer pastry to pan, lay rolling pin across center of pastry circle, fold half of pastry over pin and ease into pan; press lightly. Seal any cracks or holes by pressing dampened scraps of pastry on top. Trim pastry so it hangs evenly 1″ over rim, roll overhang under even with rim and crimp or flute as shown.

To Bake an Unfilled Pie Shell: Preheat oven to 425° F. Prick bottom and sides of pastry well with a fork. To minimize shrinkage, lay a large square of wax paper over crust and fill with uncooked rice or dried beans (experienced cooks keep a jar on hand, using beans or rice over and over). Bake pastry 10–12 minutes, just until tan. Lift out paper of rice. Cool before filling unless recipes direct otherwise.

To Bake a Filled Pie Shell: Follow directions given in individual recipes. About 1090 calories total, 136 for each of 8 wedges and 180 for each of 6 wedges.

VARIATIONS:

Cheese Pastry I: Prepare as directed but toss ½ cup finely grated Cheddar cheese into flour-shortening mixture before adding water. Especially good with apple pie. About 1315 calories total, 165 for each of 8 wedges and 220 for each of 6 wedges.

Orange Pastry I: Prepare as directed but substitute ¼ cup cold orange juice for the water and add 1–2 teaspoons finely grated lemon or orange rind to the flour-shortening mixture. Especially good with fruit or fruit-flavored chiffon pies.

Nut Pastry I: Prepare as directed but toss ¼ cup finely ground nuts (pecans, walnuts, black walnuts, hazelnuts) into flour-shortening mixture before adding water. Especially good with chocolate or other cream or chiffon-type pies. About 1300 calories total, 160 for each of 8 wedges and 215 for each of 6.

¢ Spicy Pastry I: Mix ¼ teaspoon each cinnamon, cloves, and allspice and a pinch nutmeg, mace, or ginger with flour; proceed as directed. Good with pumpkin, apple, peach, or other spicy fruit pies.

¢ Seed Pastry I: Prepare as directed but toss 1–2 tablespoons poppy, caraway, or toasted sesame seeds with flour-shortening mixture before adding water. The poppy seed crust is good with custard or vanilla cream pies, the caraway with apple, pear, or peach, and the toasted sesame with chocolate or butterscotch cream pies.

The calorie counts for Orange Pastry I, Spicy Pastry I, and Seed Pastry I are all approximately the same as for Flaky Pastry I.

¢ FLAKY PASTRY II

For 1 double crust 8″ or 9″ pie

2 cups sifted flour
1 teaspoon salt
⅔ cup chilled vegetable shortening or
  lard
4–6 tablespoons ice water

Mix exactly like Flaky Pastry I. Roll half the pastry as directed and fit into pan. Cover loosely and chill while you prepare filling; also wrap and chill unrolled portion. (*Note:* If filling is intricate, make it *before* the pastry.) Just before filling pie shell, roll remaining pastry as you did the first and cut 3 V-shaped slits or decorative holes near center for steam to escape. Fill pie shell and brush rim with cold water. Cover with top crust. For a high fluted edge (best for juicy pies), roll crusts over and even with rim, then crimp. For a flat edge, trim crusts even with rim and press with tines of a fork to seal. Bake according to times given in individual recipes that follow. About 1980 calories total, about 250 calories for each of 8 wedges and 330 calories for each of 6 wedges.

VARIATIONS:

Cheese Pastry II: Prepare as directed but toss 1 cup finely grated Cheddar cheese into flour-shortening mixture before adding water. If necessary, add an extra tablespoon ice water. About 2425 calories total, about 304 calories for each of 8 wedges and about 405 calories for each of 6 wedges.

Orange Pastry II: Prepare as directed but substitute ¼–⅓ cup cold orange juice for the water and add 1 tablespoon finely grated orange or lemon rind. Good with berry or other fruit pies.

¢ **Spicy Pastry II:** Mix ½ teaspoon each cinnamon and allspice and a pinch each ginger, cloves, and nutmeg with flour; then proceed as directed. Good with apple, peach, or other spicy fruit pies.

¢ **Seed Pastry II:** Prepare as directed but toss 2–3 tablespoons poppy, caraway, or toasted sesame seeds with flour-shortening mixture before adding water. The poppy seed crust is good with apple or peach pies, the caraway with apple or pear, and the sesame with apple, peach, or pear.

The calorie counts for Orange Pastry II, Spicy Pastry II, and Seed Pastry II are all approximately the same as for Flaky Pastry II.

¢ HOT WATER PASTRY

A tender crust but not as flaky as Flaky Pastry.
For 1 single crust 8″ or 9″ pie

1¼ cups sifted flour
½ teaspoon salt
¼ teaspoon baking powder
⅓ cup vegetable shortening or lard
3 tablespoons boiling water

Sift flour with salt and baking powder and set aside. With a fork, beat shortening and water until smooth and creamy; chill 20 minutes, then sprinkle in flour, a little at a time, mixing with a fork until pastry begins to hold together. Gather together with fingers and shape into a ball on a lightly floured pastry cloth. Roll and fit into piepan as directed for Flaky Pastry I. To bake an unfilled pie shell, follow directions for Flaky Pastry I; to bake a filled shell, follow instructions given in individual recipes. About 1090 calories total, 136 for each of 8 wedges and 180 for each of 6 wedges.

VARIATION:

Hot Water Pastry for 1 Double Crust 8″ or 9″ Pie: Use 2 cups sifted flour, double all remaining ingredients, and proceed as directed. Roll pastry into top and bottom crusts as directed for Flaky Pastry II. About 1980 calories total, about 250 calories for each of 8 wedges and 330 calories for each of 6 wedges.

OIL PASTRY

Can be used interchangeably with the more conventional Flaky Pastry II.
For 1 double crust 8″ or 9″ pie

2 cups sifted flour
1 teaspoon salt
½ cup cooking oil
¼ cup ice water

Sift flour and salt into a bowl; beat oil and water with a fork until slightly thickened and creamy, pour all at once over flour and toss with fork to blend. Gather pastry together (it should just hold together) and, if too dry, add a few additional drops oil and toss again.

Shape gently into a ball. Place half of pastry on a 12″ square of wax paper and flatten until about 1″ thick; even up rough edges. Top with a second square of wax paper and roll from center outward into a circle about 3″ larger in diameter than pan you plan to use. (*Note:* If you wipe counter with a damp cloth before rolling, wax paper won't slide around.) Peel off top paper and invert pastry on pan; peel off remaining paper and fit pastry in pan; do not trim overhang. Roll remaining pastry the same way, peel off top paper, and cut 3 V-shaped slits or decorative holes near center for steam to escape. Fill pie shell with desired filling, brush rim with cold water, and invert pastry on filling. Peel off paper and, if pie is juicy, make a high fluted edge. If not, trim crusts even with rim and seal with tines of a fork. Bake according to times given in individual recipes. About 1800 calories total, about 225 calories for each of 8 wedges and 300 calories for each of 6 wedges.

For a Single Crust 8″ or 9″ Pie: Prepare and roll as directed, using the following quantities: 1¼ cups flour, ½ teaspoon salt, ⅓ cup cooking oil, and 2–3 tablespoons ice water. Fit into pan, crimp, and bake as directed for Flaky Pastry I. About 1170 calories total, about 146 calories for each of 8 wedges and 195 calories for each of 6 wedges.

SOUR CREAM PASTRY

Rich and tender and more flavorful than Flaky Pastry.
For 1 double crust 8″ or 9″ pie

2 cups sifted flour
½ teaspoon salt
½ teaspoon baking powder
½ cup chilled vegetable shortening
¼ cup sour cream
1 egg, lightly beaten

Sift flour with salt and baking powder, then cut in shortening until mixture resembles coarse meal. Blend sour cream and egg, pour all at once into flour, and mix briskly with a fork until

pastry *just* holds together. Wrap in wax paper and chill while you prepare filling. Divide pastry in half, shape into 2 balls, then roll, 1 at a time, on a lightly floured board into a circle 3″ larger in diameter than the piepan you're using. Fit 1 circle into pan, pressing gently to smooth out any air bubbles underneath. Fill pie, brush rim of pastry lightly with cold water, top with second pastry circle (it should have steam vents cut in center), and press edges to seal. Roll overhang over until even with rim, and crimp. Bake according to directions given in filling recipe. About 1885 calories total, about 235 calories for each of 8 wedges and 315 calories for each of 6 wedges.

EXTRA-SHORT PASTRY

This short pastry puts the finishing touch on very special pies, whether sweet or savory. It's also perfect for tarts and turnovers, sausage rolls, or tiny meat- or fish-filled appetizers.
For 1 single crust 8″ or 9″ pie

1½ cups sifted flour
½ teaspoon salt
¼ cup butter or margarine, chilled
¼ cup lard or vegetable shortening, chilled
2 teaspoons lemon juice
3 tablespoons ice water (about)

Mix flour and salt in a shallow bowl and, using a pastry blender, cut in butter and lard until the texture of very coarse meal. Sprinkle lemon juice evenly over surface, then water, 1 tablespoon at a time, mixing lightly with a fork after each addition. Pastry should *just* hold together. Shape into a "brick" on a lightly floured pastry cloth and flatten until about 1″ thick; even up rough edges. Place pastry so short side faces you and, using a lightly floured, stockinette-covered rolling pin, roll with short firm strokes to a rectangle 5″×15″. Fold near ⅓ of pastry in toward center, then far ⅓. Press edges lightly with rolling pin to seal. Give pastry a ¼ turn and roll again into a rectangle; fold and seal as before. Wrap and chill ½ hour. Roll, fold, and seal 2 more times, flouring board as little as possible, then wrap and chill ½ hour. (*Note:* If kitchen is hot, chill between *each* rolling.) Roll pastry into a circle 3″ larger in diameter than the piepan you plan to use if for a pie shell; ½″ larger if for a top crust. *For a pie shell,* fit, trim, and bake as directed in Flaky Pastry I. *For a top crust,* follow directions for Rough Puff Pastry. About 1450 calories total, about 180 calories for each of 8 wedges and 240 calories for each of 6 wedges.

TORTE PASTRY

A rich, sweet pastry.
For 1 single crust 8″, 9″, or 10″ pie

½ cup unsalted butter, softened to room temperature
1⅔ cups sifted flour
1½ teaspoons baking powder
1 tablespoon sugar
¾ teaspoon salt
2 egg yolks

Knead all ingredients in a bowl until thoroughly blended. Pat into piepan, pushing dough up sides and crimping edges. About 1600 calories total, about 200 calories for each of 8 wedges and 265 calories for each of 6 wedges.

To Bake an Unfilled Pie Shell: Preheat oven to 375° F. Prick crust well all over with the tines of a fork, and bake 20–25 minutes until lightly browned. Cool before filling.

To Bake a Filled Pie Shell: Follow directions given in individual recipes that follow.

VARIATION:

Sweet Torte Pastry: Increase flour to 1¾ cups and substitute ¼ cup Vanilla Sugar for the sugar; omit salt. Proceed as directed. About 1630 calories total, about 205 calories for each of 8 wedges and 270 calories for each of 6 wedges.

CHOUX PASTRY (PÂTE À CHOUX)

Makes about 1 dozen Cream Puffs or Éclairs; 4½–5 dozen Profiteroles

1 cup water
½ cup butter or margarine
¼ teaspoon salt
1 cup sifted flour
4 eggs at room temperature

Preheat oven to 400° F. Quickly bring water, butter, and salt to boiling. Pull pan almost off burner and turn heat to moderate. Add flour *all at once* and stir quickly with a wooden spoon until mixture forms a ball. Set pan on a damp cloth. Break an egg into a cup and slide into flour mixture. Beat hard with a wooden spoon to blend. Add remaining eggs, 1 at a time, beating well. Each egg *must* be blended in before the next is added; mixture will look odd at first, almost curdled, but as you beat, it will become smooth. Pastry is now ready to use in making Cream Puffs, Éclairs, Profiteroles, Carolines, and Croquembouche. About 130 calories for each Cream Puff or Éclair (unfilled), 25 calories for each of 5 dozen Profiteroles (unfilled).

MÜRBTEIG PASTRY

This German pastry is perfect for fruit flans because it doesn't get soggy. It's delicate and short, so make it on a cool day.
For 1 single crust 8″, 9″, or 10″ pie

2 cups sifted flour
½ cup superfine sugar
Finely grated rind of 1 lemon
¾ cup chilled butter or margarine
3 egg yolks, lightly beaten

Sift flour with sugar and mix in lemon rind. Cut in butter with a pastry blender until mixture resembles fine bread crumbs. Add yolks and mix with a fork until pastry forms a ball. (You may have to use your hands at the end, but handle as lightly as possible). Wrap pastry and chill 1 hour. Using short, light strokes, roll on a *lightly* floured board into a circle 3″ larger than the pan you're using; fit into pan, trimming edges to hang evenly 1″ all round. Roll overhang under until even with rim and crimp. Chill pie shell 2 hours. Preheat oven to 450° F. Prick bottom and sides of pastry with a fork, line with wax paper and fill with rice or dried beans to weight down. Bake 5 minutes, lift out paper of rice, reduce oven to 350° F., and bake 12 minutes longer until golden. Cool pie shell before filling.

VARIATION:

Spicy Mürbteig (not authentic but nice with fruit pies): Prepare as directed but sift ¼ teaspoon cinnamon and a pinch nutmeg with flour.

Both versions: About 2585 total calories, about 325 calories for each of 8 wedges and about 430 calories for each of 6 wedges.

ROUGH PUFF PASTRY

Because this pastry is so rich and flaky, it makes a better top than bottom crust. It's usually reserved for pies, casseroles, or cobblers that have no bottom crusts. It can also be used to make Patty Shells, Beef Wellington, Napoleons, and Cream Horns.
For 1 single crust 8″ or 9″ pie

1½ cups sifted flour
½ teaspoon salt
½ cup chilled butter or margarine
2 teaspoons lemon juice
5–6 tablespoons ice water

Mix flour and salt in a shallow bowl and cut in ¼ cup butter with a pastry blender until the texture of coarse meal. Sprinkle in lemon juice, then water, one tablespoon at a time, mixing lightly and quickly with a fork until pastry *just* holds together. Shape into a "brick" on a lightly floured pastry cloth and flatten until about 1″ thick. Turn so short side faces you, and even up edges. Using a lightly floured, stockinette-covered rolling pin and short, firm strokes, roll into a rectangle 5″×15″. Beginning at

far edge, dot ¼ of remaining butter evenly over ⅔ of pastry, leaving ¼″ margins all round. Fold near ⅓ of pastry in toward center, then far ⅓ until even with fold. Press edges lightly with rolling pin to seal. Give pastry a ¼ turn and roll again into a 5″×15″ rectangle. Dot with butter, fold and seal as before; wrap and chill ½ hour. Roll, fold, and seal twice more, using as little flour as possible; wrap and chill ½ hour.

To Use as a Top Crust: Roll into a circle ½″ larger than pan or casserole you plan to use, then trim off excess ½″ in a single long circular strip and reserve. Cut 3 V-shaped slits or decorative holes in center of circle. Lay strip around dampened edge of pan or casserole, center pastry circle over filling, press edges firmly to strip and crimp. Bake according to pie or casserole directions. About 1410 calories total, 175 calories for each of 8 wedges, 235 for each of 6.

To Make Patty Shells: Follow directions for making Small Patty Shells but use Rough Puff Pastry instead of regular Puff Pastry. About 235 calories for each of 6 patty shells.

PUFF PASTRY

Do not attempt this recipe on a hot day —dough will be unmanageable. Make, if possible, with some *pastry* (not cake) flour (obtainable at gourmet groceries), reducing water slightly as needed.
Makes 1 dozen Small Patty Shells or 1 large *Vol-au-Vent*

4 cups sifted flour, preferably a ½ and ½
  mixture of pastry and all-purpose
  flour
1½ teaspoons salt
1 cup plus 2 tablespoons ice water
1 tablespoon lemon juice
1 pound unsalted butter, chilled

Mix flour and salt in a bowl. Combine water and lemon juice, sprinkle evenly over flour, about ¼ cup at a time, mixing lightly and quickly with a fork after each addition (pastry should hold together, be firm yet pliable). Add a few drops more ice water if mixture seems dry. Knead on a lightly floured board about 10 minutes until smooth and elastic; cover and let stand at room temperature ½ hour. Meanwhile, knead and squeeze butter until malleable (about consistency of dough), free of lumps, but still cold. Shape into a 5" square and dust with flour. Shape dough into a "brick" on a lightly floured pastry cloth and, with a lightly floured stockinette-covered rolling pin, flatten to a thickness of 1"; even up ragged edges. Place pastry so short side faces you, and roll with short, firm strokes into a rectangle 6"×18". Place butter in center, fold near ⅓ of pastry in toward center, then far ⅓. Press edges lightly with rolling pin to seal. Give pastry a ¼ turn and roll again into a rectangle; fold and seal as before. Wrap and chill ¾ hour. Roll, fold, and seal 2 more times, then chill ¾ hour. Roll, fold, and seal twice more and chill 1 hour. Use as little flour as possible when rolling and handle pastry with fingertips. Pastry is now ready to use as recipes direct. To store, wrap and chill overnight or wrap airtight and freeze (thaw in refrigerator before using). About 4850 calories per *Vol-au-vent*, 405 calories per Patty Shell.

VOL-AU-VENT (LARGE PATTY SHELL)

A *Vol-au-vent* filled with creamed poultry or seafood may be oval or round. The oval is traditional, but you may find the round easier to cut. Simply cut 2 (8") rounds, using a layer cake pan as a guide, then remove a 5" circle from the center of 1 round.
Makes an 8" oval

1 recipe Puff Pastry

Glaze:

1 egg, lightly beaten with 1 tablespoon cold water

Make pastry as directed. Also cut an 8"×5½" oval from cardboard to use as a pattern. Roll half of pastry on a lightly floured pastry cloth into a rectangle 8"×10" and ½" thick. Place

pattern in center of rectangle and cut out oval. Carefully transfer to a baking sheet brushed with cold water. Roll and cut remaining pastry the same way, then cut a 5" oval from center, leaving an oval ring about 1½" wide. Brush ring with cold water and arrange, damp side down, on pastry oval; press seams lightly to seal. Brush ring with cold water and prick bottom of oval to prevent uneven rising. Roll the 5" oval cutout until it is the size of the bottom oval and lay on pastry shell—sort of like a "lid"; press seams lightly. Make a vertical ridged pattern around sides of pastry shell by pressing at regular intervals with the back of a knife; chill shell ½ hour. Meanwhile, preheat oven to 425° F. Brush top of shell with glaze but do not let run down sides or shell will not rise evenly. Bake on center oven rack 20 minutes, reduce oven to 350° F., and bake 30–40 minutes longer until well browned and crisp. (*Note:* Shell will rise 2–3 times its original height, so make sure second oven rack is out of the way.) Remove "lid" by sliding a knife underneath it and set on a wire rack. With a fork, scoop out soft insides of shell and discard. Return shell to oven and let dry out 5–7 minutes. Using 2 pancake turners, lift to platter. Fill with a hot filling, replace lid, and serve. For cold fillings, cool shell on a wire rack, then fill. (*Note:* Shell can be baked ahead of time and stored airtight several days; reheat 10 minutes at 400° F.) About 4850 calories total.

SMALL PATTY SHELLS (BOUCHÉES)

Small puff pastry shells to be filled with sweet or savory mixtures.
Makes 1 dozen

1 recipe Puff Pastry

Glaze:

1 egg, lightly beaten with 1 tablespoon cold water

Make pastry as directed and roll half to a thickness of ¼" on a lightly floured board. Cut into rounds with an unfloured 2½" cookie cutter (wipe cutter with a dry cloth before each cut and, to make shells rise evenly in baking, press cutter straight down through pastry). Arrange ⅓ of the rounds on a baking sheet brushed with cold water, spacing 1" apart. Cut centers from ⅓ of remaining rounds with a 1¾" round cutter. Brush tops of rings with cold water and place, tops down, on rounds. Pinch seams lightly to seal and brush rings with cold water. Press the 1¾" cutter into remaining rounds, just enough to mark with a circle, not to cut clear through. Top each shell with a marked round, marked side up, and pinch seams as before. Brush tops with glaze but do not let glaze run down sides of shells or they will not rise evenly. Roll and cut remaining pastry the same way (also any scraps). Chill shells ½ hour. Meanwhile, preheat oven to 450° F. Bake shells on center oven rack 10 minutes, reduce heat to 350° F., and bake 15–20 minutes longer until golden brown and crisp. With a sharp, pointed knife, lift off marked circle tops from patties and save to use as "lids." With a fork, scoop out and discard soft insides of shells. Return shells to oven for 3–5 minutes to dry out. Patty shells are now ready to be filled with hot creamed mixtures. Cool on wire racks before filling with cold fillings. (*Note:* Stored airtight, these will keep well several days. Reheat, uncovered, 10 minutes at 350° F.) About 405 calories per patty shell.

⊠ GRAHAM CRACKER CRUST

Crumb crusts can be substituted for baked pie shells in most recipes. They are especially good with chiffon and cream fillings. If a recipe calls for an unbaked crumb crust, prepare up to point of baking, then chill well, fill, and proceed as individual recipe directs.
For 1 single crust 9" pie

*1½ cups graham cracker crumbs
  (about 20 cracker squares)
⅓ cup butter or margarine, softened to
  room temperature
¼ cup sugar*

Preheat oven to 350° F. Blend crumbs, butter, and sugar in a bowl. Spoon into a 9" pie pan and, using the back of a spoon, press firmly against bottom and sides (but not over rim). Bake 8–10 minutes. Cool before filling. About 1440 calories total, about 180 calories for each of 8 wedges, 240 calories for each of 6.

VARIATIONS:

Vanilla Wafer Crust: Substitute vanilla wafer crumbs for the graham cracker, reduce butter to ¼ cup and sugar to 1–2 tablespoons. About 1400 calories total, about 175 calories for each of 8 wedges, 235 calories for each of 6 wedges.

Chocolate Crumb Crust: Substitute crushed chocolate wafers for cracker crumbs, reduce butter to ¼ cup and sugar to 1–2 tablespoons. About 1500 calories total, about 190 calories for each of 8 wedges, 250 calories for each of 6 wedges.

Gingersnap Crumb Crust: Prepare as directed but substitute crushed gingersnaps for the cracker crumbs and omit sugar. About 1400 calories total, about 175 calories for each of 8 wedges, 235 calories for each of 6 wedges.

Cereal Crust: Prepare as directed but substitute 1½ cups crushed cornflakes, rice cereal or wheat cereal for the cracker crumbs. About 855 calories total, about 105 calories for each of 8 wedges, 140 calories for each of 6 wedges.

Nut-Crumb Crust: Reduce crumbs to 1 cup and add ½ cup minced nuts (walnuts, pecans, hazelnuts, toasted blanched almonds, or Brazil nuts). About 1575 calories total, about 195 calories for each of 8 wedges, 265 calories for each of 6.

Marble Crumb Crust: Prepare as directed but toss 2 (1-ounce) squares finely grated semisweet chocolate with the crumbs. About 1720 calories total, 215 calories for each of 8 wedges, 285 calories for each of 6 wedges.

TOASTED COCONUT CRUST

Good with cream or chiffon fillings.
For 1 single crust 9" pie

2 cups flaked coconut
¼ cup melted butter or margarine

Preheat oven to 300° F. Mix coconut
and butter. Press firmly against the
bottom and sides of a 9" piepan. Bake
about 20 minutes until golden. Cool
before filling. About 1085 calories
total, about 135 calories for each of
8 wedges and 180 calories for each of 6
wedges.

VARIATIONS:

Chocolate-Coconut Crust: Prepare as
directed but reduce butter to 2 tablespoons and add 2 (1-ounce) squares
melted unsweetened chocolate, 2 tablespoons warm milk, and ⅓ cup sifted
confectioners' sugar; mix well. Press into
pan and chill 1–2 hours before filling.
About 1360 calories total, about 170
calories for each of 8 wedges and 225
calories for each of 6 wedges.

Easy Unbaked Coconut Crust: Substitute
2 cups packaged toasted coconut for the
flaked coconut, mix with butter, press
into piepan, and chill 1–2 hours before
filling. About 1085 calories total, about
135 calories for each of 8 wedges and
180 calories for each of 6 wedges.

⊠ TOASTED NUT CRUST

A crunchy, rich, sweet crust, ideal for
chiffon fillings.
For 1 single crust 9" pie

1½ cups ground nuts (walnuts, pecans,
  Brazil nuts, blanched almonds, or
  hazelnuts)
¼ cup sugar
2 tablespoons butter or margarine,
  softened to room temperature

Preheat oven to 400° F. Mix nuts,
sugar, and butter with your hands, press
firmly against bottom and sides of a
buttered 9" piepan. Bake 6–8 minutes.
Cool before filling. About 1580
calories total, about 195 calories for
each of 8 wedges, 265 calories for each
of 6 wedges.

VARIATION:

Substitute 1 egg white, beaten to soft
peaks, for the butter; mix with a spoon,
press into buttered pan, and bake about
10 minutes until tan. Cool before filling.
About 1390 calories total, about 175
calories for each of 8 wedges, 230
calories for each of 6 wedges.

⊠ COOKIE CRUST

Couldn't be easier!
For 1 single crust 9" pie

1 tablespoon butter or margarine,
  softened to room temperature
1 tablespoon sugar
1 roll refrigerated slice-and-bake cookie
  dough (sugar cookie, chocolate, or
  coconut)

Preheat oven to 375° F. Butter
bottom, sides, and rim of a 9" piepan,
then coat with sugar. Slice cookie
dough ⅛" thick and line sides of pan,
overlapping slices slightly and allowing
cookies to form a scalloped edge around
rim. Line bottom with slices, pressing
lightly to fill spaces. Bake 8–10 minutes
until tan. Cool before filling. Good with
cream fillings. Recipe too flexible for a
meaningful calorie count.

⊠ ICE CREAM PIE SHELL

For 1 single crust 9" pie

1 quart vanilla or other flavor ice cream
  (about), slightly softened

Chill a 9" piepan in the freezer 15–20
minutes. Spoon ice cream into pan,
smoothing bottom and sides with the
back of a spoon to make a shell. Freeze
until firm. Good filled with ice cream of
contrasting flavor and color and topped
with a cold fruit sauce. Also good filled
with fresh fruit and topped with whipped
cream. About 1180 calories total (if
made with vanilla ice cream), about 150
calories for each of 8 wedges and 195
calories for each of 6 wedges.

Ground Rules for Making Meringues

– Bring egg whites to room temperature
before beating.

— Make sure there are no flecks of yolk in the whites; if so, scoop out with a piece of shell.
— Make sure mixing bowl and beater are spotless.
— Follow recipe to the letter.
— Add sugar very slowly, beating well after each addition so it dissolves fully. If it does not, "beads" of syrup or sugar grains will form on baked meringue.
— Be careful not to overbeat egg whites (especially if using electric mixer). Meringue should be *glossy and very stiff but not dry*. If meringue clumps as it's spread, it is overbeaten. To rescue, return to mixing bowl, add 1–2 tablespoons cold water and beat briefly and briskly.
— To keep meringue from shrinking during baking, spread evenly over filling, making sure it touches pie shell all around.

(*Note:* For additional tips, read To Beat Whites in the chapter on eggs and cheese.)

BASIC MERINGUE TOPPING FOR PIES

To Top an 8″ Pie, Use:

2 egg whites, at room temperature
⅛ teaspoon cream of tartar
Pinch salt
¼ cup sugar
½ teaspoon vanilla

To Top a 9″ Pie, Use:

3 egg whites, at room temperature
¼ teaspoon cream of tartar
⅛ teaspoon salt
6 tablespoons sugar
½ teaspoon vanilla

To Top 10″ Pie, Use:

4 egg whites, at room temperature
¼ teaspoon cream of tartar
⅛ teaspoon salt
½ cup sugar
1 teaspoon vanilla

Preheat oven to 350° F. Beat egg whites until frothy, using a rotary beater or electric mixer at moderate speed; add cream of tartar and salt and continue beating, adding sugar, 1 tablespoon at a time. When all sugar is incorporated, add vanilla and beat hard (highest mixer speed) until glossy and peaks stand straight up when beaters are withdrawn. Spoon about half the meringue around edge of *warm* filling, spreading so it touches pastry all around. Pile remaining meringue in center, then spread to cover all filling, pulling into peaks with the back of a spoon or swirling round. If you prefer, pipe meringue over filling, using a pastry bag fitted with a decorative tip. Bake on center oven rack 12–15 minutes until lightly browned. Cool at least 2 hours before serving. To simplify the serving of a meringue pie, dip knife in warm water before cutting each slice.

Meringue for an 8″ pie: About 225 calories total, about 35 calories for each of 6 servings.

Meringue for a 9″ pie: About 330 calories total, about 40 calories for each of 8 servings.

Meringue for a 10″ pie: About 445 calories total, about 55 calories for each of 8 servings.

⚖ MERINGUE PIE SHELL

For 1 single crust 9″ pie

3 egg whites at room temperature
⅛ teaspoon cream of tartar
⅛ teaspoon salt
½ cup sugar
1 teaspoon vanilla or ½ teaspoon almond
  extract

Preheat oven to 250° F. Beat egg whites until foamy; mix in cream of tartar and salt. Add sugar, 1 tablespoon at a time, beating constantly, then continue to beat at highest speed until glossy and stiff enough to stand straight up when beaters are withdrawn. Spoon meringue into lightly greased 9″ piepan, then spread with the back of a spoon to cover bottom and sides but not the rim; make sides a little thicker than the bottom and

½"–¾" higher than rim of pan. Bake 1 hour until creamy white and firm, turn oven off and let meringue dry in oven without opening door until oven cools. Shell is now ready to fill as desired. About 430 calories total, about 55 calories for each of 8 wedges, 70 calories for each of 6 wedges.

VARIATION:

Nut Meringue Pie Shell: Prepare meringue as directed, fold in 1 cup ground blanched almonds or hazelnuts, a little at a time, then spoon into pan and bake as directed. About 1280 calories total, about 160 calories for each of 8 wedges, 215 calories for each of 6 wedges.

⚖ MERINGUES

Makes about 2 dozen

6 egg whites, at room temperature
¼ teaspoon cream of tartar
¼ teaspoon salt
¾ cup sugar
¾ cup superfine sugar
1 teaspoon vanilla or ½ teaspoon almond extract
1 or 2 drops any food coloring (optional)

Preheat oven to 250° F. Beat egg whites until foamy; mix in cream of tartar and salt. Mix sugars and add, 1 tablespoon at a time, beating all the while. This will take some time, perhaps 10–12 minutes. Add flavoring and if you like, tint a pastel hue; beat at highest mixer speed until glossy and stiff enough to stand straight up when beaters are withdrawn. Drop by heaping spoonfuls 2" apart on foil-lined baking sheets; smooth into mounds or, if you prefer, pipe meringue onto sheets through a pastry bag fitted with a large plain or star tip. Don't make meringues more than 2½" across or they won't bake properly. Bake 1 hour until creamy white and firm, turn oven off, and let meringues dry several hours or overnight in oven without opening door. Lift off foil and serve as is or with ice cream or fruit. Wrapped airtight, these keep well. About 50 calories each.

VARIATIONS:

⚖ **Meringue Star Shells** (Makes 1 dozen): Beat meringue as directed. Draw 6 (3") circles on 2 foil-lined baking sheets, not too close together, and spread ⅓"–½" deep with meringue. Spoon remaining meringue into a pastry bag fitted with a small star tip. Edge meringue circles with borders of small stars, 1 just touching another, then build up layers to form shells about 1½" deep. Bake and dry out as directed. To serve, fill with any ice cream or fruit. About 100 calories each.

⚖ **Meringues Glacées:** Make and bake meringues as directed, halve, and fill with ice cream. Or sandwich 2 meringues together with ice cream. Top with any dessert sauce or fruit. About 120 calories each if halved and filled with ice cream, about 170 calories each if sandwiched together with ice cream.

Meringues Chantilly: Sandwich baked meringues together with sweetened whipped cream, tinted, if you like, for a party touch. Or if you prefer, tint meringues and leave cream plain. About 200 calories each.

¢ COUNTRY-STYLE APPLE PIE

Aromatic of lemon, cinnamon and nutmeg.
Makes 8 servings

1 recipe Flaky Pastry II

Filling:

6 medium-size tart cooking apples
¾–1 cup sugar
2 teaspoons lemon juice
¼ teaspoon cinnamon
⅛ teaspoon nutmeg
¼ teaspoon salt
2 tablespoons butter or margarine

Glaze (optional):

1 tablespoon milk
1 tablespoon sugar

Preheat oven to 425° F. Prepare pastry

ABOUT PIE APPLES

There are hundreds of different kinds of apples, most coming into season during the fall and remaining plentiful throughout winter and early spring. All apples, however, do not cook well — the crisp, juicy-sweet apples we love to eat out of hand, for example, lack the tartness and texture needed for successful pies. For best results, use one of these excellent "pie" apples:

Kind of Apple	Description	Season
Jonathan	Small to medium size, deep red with creamy-colored, tart, crisp flesh. Juicy.	October-February
McIntosh	Medium size, bright red with green around stem. White, crisp-tender, juicy flesh.	October-March
Newtown Pippin	Medium size, yellow skin, tart, hard-to-crisp juicy yellowish flesh.	February-June
Northern Spy	Large, bright red with firm, tart, juicy, yellowish flesh.	October-March
Rhode Island Greening	Medium to large, green or yellow-green skin; cream-colored, tart, crisp, juicy flesh.	October-February
Stayman	Striped, dull red apple, medium to large, with tart-crisp, juicy, ivory-hued flesh.	November-April
Winesap	Deep red, small to medium, with some green around stem; firm, crisp, tart, cream-colored flesh.	January-May
Yellow Transparent	Medium, yellow-green with white, juicy, tart flesh.	July-August
York Imperial	Medium-to-large, light or purple-red over yellow; ivory-colored, hard, tart flesh.	October-April

Note: Such all-purpose cooking apples as Gravenstein, Wealthy, Rome Beauty, and Baldwin may also be used in pies, but the nine varieties above give especially fine flavor and texture.

as directed and fit half into a 9″ piepan; do not trim edge. Roll top crust, cut steam slits in center, and cover with cloth while you prepare filling. Peel, core, and thinly slice apples, taste, and sweeten as needed with sugar; add lemon juice, spices, and salt and toss gently. Pile apple mixture in pie shell and dot with butter. Brush pastry rim lightly with cold water, fit top crust over apples, trim, seal, and crimp edges. For a shiny crust, brush with milk and sprinkle with sugar. Bake 15–20 minutes with a piece of foil on rack underneath to catch drips, reduce heat to 350° F., and bake 25–30 minutes longer until crust is lightly browned. Cool 5–10 minutes before serving. Serve hot or cold with heavy cream, vanilla ice cream, or chunks of good sharp Cheddar. About 410 calories per serving (without cream, ice cream, or cheese).

DEEP DISH APPLE PIE

Makes 8 servings

1 recipe Flaky Pastry I

Filling:

12 medium-size tart cooking apples
1½ cups sugar (about)
½ teaspoon cinnamon
¼ teaspoon nutmeg
2 tablespoons flour
1 tablespoon lemon juice
2 tablespoons butter or margarine

Glaze (optional):

1 tablespoon milk
1 tablespoon sugar

Preheat oven to 425° F. Prepare
pastry as directed and roll into a 10″
square; cut steam slits in center and
cover with a cloth while you prepare the
filling. Peel, core, and thinly slice apples,
taste, and sweeten as needed with sugar;
add cinnamon, nutmeg, and flour and
toss to mix. Pile apple mixture into an
ungreased 9″×9″×2″ pan, sprinkle
with lemon juice, and dot with butter.
Fit pastry over apples, roll overhang
under even with rim and crimp edges.
For a shiny crust, brush with milk and
sprinkle with sugar. Bake 40–50
minutes (with a piece of foil on rack
below to catch drips) until crust is
browned and apples are tender. (*Note:*
If in doubt, poke a skewer through a
steam vent to test.) Cool 5–10 minutes
before serving. Serve warm or cold in
bowls with light cream or ice cream.
About 450 calories per serving (without
cream).

VARIATIONS:

Deep Dish Berry or Fruit Pie: Double
filling recipe of Basic Berry or Fresh
Fruit Pie and use to fill the 9″ square
pan; proceed as recipe directs. About 450
calories per serving (without cream).

Large Family Deep Dish Fruit Pie
(Makes 18 servings): Triple the filling
recipe of Country-Style Apple, Basic
Berry or Fresh Fruit Pie and pile into
an ungreased 13″×9″×2″ pan. Cover
with 1 recipe Flaky Pastry II rolled 1″
larger than top of pan. Make slits in

center, fit over filling, crimp edges, glaze,
and bake as directed about 50 minutes.
Recipe too flexible for a meaningful
calorie count.

¢ APPLE TURNOVERS

Makes 6 servings

1 recipe Flaky Pastry II

Filling:

2 cups peeled and diced tart cooking
  apples
⅓ cup sugar
¼ teaspoon cinnamon
¼ teaspoon nutmeg
2 tablespoons lemon juice

Glaze:

Milk
Sugar

Preheat oven to 400° F. Make pastry
as directed and roll total amount into a
rectangle 12″×18″, keeping edges as
straight as possible. Cut into 6 (6″)
squares; brush edges with cold water.
Mix filling ingredients and place about
⅓ cup in the center of each square; fold
diagonally to form triangles. Press edges
together with a floured fork and snip
steam slits in tops with kitchen shears.
Brush with milk and sprinkle with sugar.
Arrange 2″ apart on an ungreased baking sheet and bake 25–30 minutes until
golden brown. Cool a few minutes on a
wire rack. Serve warm or cold with or
without cream or ice cream. Or if you
like, cool and drizzle with Quick Glacé
Icing or Easy White Icing. About 410
calories per serving (without cream, ice
cream, or icing).

VARIATIONS:

Fruit Turnovers: Prepare as directed,
substituting 2 cups any suitable fresh,
frozen, or canned, drained fruit for the
apples and adding sugar as needed to
sweeten. Recipe too flexible for a
meaningful calorie count.

Jam Turnovers (Makes 1 dozen): Roll
out pastry and cut into 12 (4″) squares.
Place 2 tablespoons jam, preserves,
marmalade, or mincemeat in the center
of each, fold, seal, and glaze. Bake 15
minutes at 425° F. About 305 calories
per serving.

Fried Apple Pies (Makes 8 servings):
Roll pastry ⅛″ thick and cut into 8
(4″) circles. Place ¼ cup thick applesauce in the center of each, fold over and
seal edges *well*. Do not glaze. Fry in
365° F. deep fat 2–3 minutes, turning as
needed, until evenly golden brown. Drain
on paper toweling, roll in sugar, and
serve warm. About 425 calories per
serving.

FRESH FRUIT PIE

This basic recipe can be used for making
peach, apricot, plum, pear, cherry,
grape, or currant pies.
Makes 8 servings

1 recipe Flaky Pastry II

Filling:

1 quart sliced, pitted, and peeled fresh
firm-ripe peaches, apricots, or
nectarines; pitted purple or
greengage plums; peeled, cored, and
sliced pears; stemmed and pitted tart
cherries; seeded, halved Tokay or
whole seedless green grapes or
stemmed currants
¾–1½ cups sugar
¼–⅓ cup sifted flour
⅛ teaspoon salt
1 teaspoon lemon juice (optional)
¼ teaspoon almond extract or nutmeg,
cinnamon, or ginger (optional)
2 tablespoons butter or margarine

Glaze (optional):

1 tablespoon milk
1 tablespoon sugar

Preheat oven to 425° F. Make pastry as
directed and fit half into a 9″ piepan; do
not trim edge. Roll out top crust, cut
steam slits in center, and cover with a
cloth while you prepare the filling. Place
fruit in a bowl, add sugar to sweeten,
and sprinkle with flour and salt; toss
lightly. (*Note:* Cherries will need maximum amount of flour, firmer fruits
less.) If you like, sprinkle with lemon
juice and almond extract (especially
good with peaches, apricots, and
cherries). Spoon into pie shell and dot
with butter. Brush pastry rim with cold
water, fit top crust over fruit, trim, seal,

and crimp edges. For a glistening crust,
brush with milk and sprinkle with sugar.
Bake 35–45 minutes (with a piece of foil
on rack below to catch drips) until
lightly browned and bubbling. Cool 5–10
minutes before cutting. Serve warm or
cold with or without cream or ice cream.
About 400 calories per serving (made
with ¾ cup sugar and served without
cream or ice cream).

VARIATIONS:

Frozen Fruit Pie: Prepare as directed,
using 1 quart solidly frozen fruit. About
400 calories per serving (without cream
or ice cream).

Canned Fruit Pie: Prepare as directed
using 2 (1-pound) cans fruit. Drain fruit
well, reserving ½ cup liquid. Mix fruit
with enough sugar to sweeten, flour, and
seasonings and spoon into pie shell. Pour
in reserved liquid (mixed with a few
drops red food coloring if it is a cherry
pie), dot with butter, and proceed as
directed. Recipe too flexible for a
meaningful calorie count.

Tapioca Fruit Pie: Substitute 3
tablespoons quick-cooking tapioca for
the flour and proceed as recipe directs.
About 425 calories per serving.

BASIC BERRY PIE

Makes 8 servings

1 recipe Flaky Pastry II

Filling:

1 quart ripe berries (any kind), hulled,
stemmed, and drained
1–1½ cups sugar
¼ cup unsifted flour
⅛ teaspoon salt
1 teaspoon finely grated orange or
lemon rind (optional)
2 tablespoons butter or margarine

Glaze (optional):

1 tablespoon milk
1 tablespoon sugar

Preheat oven to 425° F. Make pastry as
directed and fit half into a 9″ piepan; do
not trim edge. Roll top crust, cut steam
slits in center, and cover with cloth

VIII. EATING ALFRESCO

Charcoal Broiled Shish Kebabs – "All-American" picnic – Spiced Blue Crabs – French Chocolate Ice Cream

Charcoal Broiled Shish Kebabs (page 320-321); and Spit-Roasted Leg of Lamb (page 313)

Crisp-Fried Chicken (page 482); Jiffy Deviled Eggs (page 662); Herbed Potato Salad (page 910); and Creamy Sweet-Sour Coleslaw (page 906)

Spiced Blue Crabs (page 597)

French Chocolate Ice Cream (page 1055)

while you prepare filling. Dry berries on paper toweling, place in a bowl, and sprinkle with 1 cup sugar, the flour, salt, and, if you like, rind; toss *lightly*. Taste berries and if too tart add more sugar. Spoon into pie shell, and dot with butter. Brush pastry rim with cold water. Fit top crust over berries, trim, seal, and crimp edges. For a glistening crust, brush with milk and sprinkle with sugar. Bake 35–45 minutes (with a piece of foil on rack below to catch drips) until lightly browned and bubbling. Cool 5–10 minutes before cutting. Serve hot or cold with or without cream or ice cream. About 445 calories per serving (made with 1 cup sugar and served without cream or ice cream).

VARIATIONS:

Dutch Berry Pie: Prepare and bake pie as directed. After removing from oven, funnel ⅓ cup heavy cream in through steam slits. Cool and serve. About 475 calories per serving.

Frozen Berry Pie: Prepare as directed, using 1 quart solidly frozen berries for the fresh and increasing flour to ⅓ cup. About 450 calories per serving.

Canned Berry Pie: Substitute 2 (1-pound) cans berries for the fresh; drain well, reserving ½ cup liquid. Mix berries with sugar, flour, and seasonings as directed and spoon into pie shell. Pour in the ½ cup liquid, dot with butter, and proceed as directed. About 445 calories per serving.

FRESH RHUBARB PIE

Makes 8 servings

1 recipe Flaky Pastry II

Filling:

2 pounds rhubarb, trimmed and cut in ½″ chunks
1⅓–1¾ cups sugar
⅓ cup unsifted flour
⅛ teaspoon salt
2 or 3 drops red food coloring (optional)
2 tablespoons butter or margarine

Glaze (optional):

1 tablespoon milk
1 tablespoon sugar

Preheat oven to 425° F. Make pastry as directed and fit half into a 9″ piepan; do not trim edge. Roll remaining pastry into a 12″ circle and cut steam slits in center; cover with cloth while you prepare filling. Toss rhubarb with enough sugar to sweeten, then mix in flour, salt, and food coloring if rhubarb is pale. Pile in pie shell and dot with butter. Brush pastry rim with cold water, fit top crust over rhubarb, trim, seal, and crimp edges. For a glistening crust, brush with milk and sprinkle with sugar. Bake 40–50 minutes (with foil on rack underneath to catch drips) until browned and bubbling. Cool 5–10 minutes before cutting. Good with cream, whipped cream, or vanilla ice cream. About 480 calories per serving (made with 1⅓ cups sugar and served without cream or ice cream).

VARIATION:

Rhubarb-Strawberry Pie: Prepare as directed, using 1 pound rhubarb and 1 pint stemmed, halved strawberries; omit food coloring. For a special occasion, top with a lattice crust.* About 480 calories per serving.

SOUR CREAM PEACH PIE

Peaches and cream baked in a flaky crust and topped with a buttery brown sugar mixture.
Makes 6–8 servings

1 recipe Flaky Pastry I

Filling:

5 ripe peaches
1 cup sour cream
¾ cup sugar
3 tablespoons flour
1 egg
⅛ teaspoon mace
1 tablespoon light rum
¼ teaspoon vanilla

Topping:

¼ cup melted butter or margarine
⅓ cup unsifted flour
½ cup firmly packed light brown sugar

Preheat oven to 400° F. Prepare pastry as directed and fit into a 9″ piepan, making a high fluted edge; do not bake. Peel peaches, halve, pit, and slice thin directly into pie shell. Mix remaining filling ingredients and pour over peaches. Bake 25 minutes and remove from oven. Mix topping and crumble evenly over peaches. Return to oven and bake 20 minutes longer. Cool 10–20 minutes before serving. About 550 calories for each of 6 servings, 410 calories for each of 8.

STREUSEL PEACH PIE

Makes 6–8 servings

1 recipe Flaky Pastry I

Filling:

1 quart sliced, pitted, and peeled firm-ripe peaches
½ cup sugar
Finely grated rind and juice of 1 orange

Topping:

½ cup firmly packed light brown sugar
½ cup sifted flour
⅓ cup butter or margarine

Preheat oven to 425° F. Make pastry as directed and fit into a 9″ piepan, making a high fluted edge; do not bake. Gently mix peaches, sugar, orange rind and juice and spoon into pie shell. Mix brown sugar and flour, then, using a pastry blender, cut in butter until mixture is crumbly. Sprinkle over peaches, pressing down lightly. Bake (with a piece of foil on rack below to catch drips) about 40 minutes until lightly browned. Serve warm with or without whipped cream or sour cream. About 485 calories for each of 6 servings (without cream), 365 calories for each of 8 servings.

VARIATIONS:

Streusel Pecan-Peach Pie: Make pastry and fill as directed. For the topping: Mix the sugar, ¼ cup flour, and ½ teaspoon cinnamon; cut in butter and toss with ½ cup minced pecans. Spread over peaches and bake as directed. About 535 calories for each of 6 servings, 400 calories for each of 8.

Streusel Apple, Pear, or Plum Pie: Substitute 1 quart peeled, cored, and sliced tart apples or pears or halved pitted plums for the peaches; adjust sugar in filling as needed to sweeten the fruit, then proceed as directed. Recipe too flexible for a meaningful calorie count.

EASY PUMPKIN PIE

Makes 6–8 servings

1 recipe Flaky Pastry I

Filling:

3 eggs, lightly beaten
1 (1-pound) can pumpkin purée
1 (13-ounce) can evaporated milk
1 tablespoon brandy
1 tablespoon molasses
⅔ cup firmly packed light brown sugar
½ teaspoon cinnamon
¼ teaspoon ginger
¼ teaspoon allspice
¼ teaspoon cloves

Preheat oven to 450° F. Make pastry as directed and fit into a 9″ piepan, making a high fluted edge; do not bake. Beat all filling ingredients together, using a whisk or rotary egg beater, and pour into pie shell. Bake 10 minutes, reduce temperature to 325° F., and bake 45–50 minutes longer until crust is lightly browned and filling set (a silver knife inserted midway between center and rim should come out clean). Cool to room temperature before serving. About 445 calories for each of 6 servings, 335 calories for each of 8.

OLD-FASHIONED PUMPKIN PIE

Richer and spicier than Easy Pumpkin Pie.
Makes 6–8 servings

1 recipe Flaky Pastry I
1 egg white, lightly beaten

Filling:

1½ cups pumpkin purée
⅔ cup firmly packed dark brown sugar
1¼ teaspoons cinnamon
½ teaspoon ginger
Pinch nutmeg
¼ teaspoon maple flavoring (optional)
¼ teaspoon salt

1 cup milk
1 cup light cream
3 eggs, lightly beaten

Make pastry as directed and fit into a 9″ piepan, making a high fluted edge; brush with egg white and chill 1 hour. Preheat oven to 450° F. For the filling, mix pumpkin and sugar until sugar dissolves. Add remaining ingredients, stirring well to blend. Set pie shell on pulled-out center oven shelf, then pour in filling. Bake 10 minutes, reduce heat to 350° F., and bake 30–35 minutes longer until a knife inserted midway between center and rim comes out clean. Serve warm or at room temperature. Good topped with sweetened whipped cream. About 460 calories for each of 6 servings (without whipped cream), about 345 calories for each of 8 servings.

BRANDIED MINCEMEAT IN CHEESE PASTRY

Makes 8 servings

1 recipe Cheese Pastry II

Filling:

1 (1-pound 12-ounce) jar mincemeat
3–4 tablespoons brandy

Preheat oven to 450° F. Empty mincemeat into a strainer set over a bowl and drain 10 minutes; pour off at least 3–4 tablespoons liquid and discard; save the rest. Meanwhile, make pastry as directed and fit half in a 9″ or 10″ piepan. Roll top crust and make steam slits in center. Mix drained mincemeat with brandy to taste and the reserved liquid and spoon into pie shell. Moisten pastry edges lightly with cold water. Fit top crust over filling, trim edges, seal, and crimp. Bake 10 minutes (with foil on rack underneath to catch drips), reduce heat to 350° F., and bake 20–25 minutes longer until lightly browned. Serve warm or cold with Hard Sauce or wedges of sharp Cheddar. About 590 calories per serving (without Hard Sauce or cheese).

LEMON MERINGUE PIE

Makes 6–8 servings

1 recipe Flaky Pastry I

Filling:

½ cup cornstarch
1½ cups sugar
¼ teaspoon salt
1¾ cups cold water
1 teaspoon finely grated lemon rind
4 egg yolks, lightly beaten
⅓–½ cup lemon juice
2 tablespoons butter or margarine

Meringue:

1 recipe Basic Meringue Topping for a 9″ Pie

Make pastry, fit into a 9″ piepan, and bake as directed; reduce oven to 350° F. Mix cornstarch, sugar, and salt in a heavy saucepan, slowly blend in water, and heat, stirring constantly, until thickened and smooth. Mix in lemon rind and cook, stirring, 2–3 minutes. Blend a little hot mixture into yolks, return to pan and cook and stir over lowest heat 2–3 minutes; do not boil. Off heat, stir in ⅓ cup lemon juice (½ cup for really tart flavor) and the butter. Spoon filling into pie shell. Prepare meringue as directed, spread over filling, and bake 12–15 minutes until touched with brown. Cool pie at least 2 hours before serving. (Note: Pie will cut more easily if knife is dipped in warm water before each cut is made.) About 540 calories for each of 6 servings, 405 calories for each of 8 servings.

VARIATIONS:

Lime Meringue Pie: Prepare as directed, substituting lime juice and rind for the lemon. About 540 calories for each of 6 servings, 405 calories for each of 8 servings.

Orange Meringue Pie: Prepare as directed, using ¼ cup each orange and lemon juice and grated orange rind instead of lemon. About 545 calories for each of 6 servings, 410 calories for each of 8 servings.

KEY LIME PIE

There are dozens of variations of this Florida Keys classic, some made with a graham cracker crust, some topped with

meringue. But this particular version is most like the original: a crisp piecrust filled with a creamy, tart lime filling, then crowned with whipped cream.
Makes 6–8 servings

1 recipe Flaky Pastry I

Filling:

4 egg yolks, lightly beaten
1 (14-ounce) can sweetened condensed milk
⅔ cup fresh lime juice
Few drops green food coloring

Topping:

1 cup heavy cream, whipped with 3 tablespoons superfine sugar

Make pastry as directed, fit into a 9" piepan, and bake as directed; cool while you make the filling. Beat yolks with condensed milk just to blend, add lime juice, and beat until smooth (the filling will be soft). Tint pale green and pour into baked pie shell. Chill well, then spread whipped cream topping over filling, making sure it touches pastry all around. Return to refrigerator and chill several hours before serving, or better still, overnight, so that filling will firm up somewhat (it will never really be firm). About 680 calories for each of 6 servings, 510 calories for each of 8 servings.

VANILLA CREAM PIE

Makes 6–8 servings

1 recipe Flaky Pastry I

Filling:

¼ cup cornstarch
⅔ cup sugar
¼ teaspoon salt
2½ cups milk
3 egg yolks, lightly beaten
2 teaspoons vanilla
1 tablespoon butter or margarine

Topping (optional):

1½ cups sweetened whipped cream or 1 recipe Basic Meringue Topping for a 9" Pie

Make pastry, fit into a 9" piepan, and

bake as directed. Mix cornstarch, sugar, and salt in a saucepan, slowly blend in milk, and heat, stirring, until thickened. Turn heat to lowest point and heat and stir 1–2 minutes. Blend a little hot mixture into egg yolks, return to pan, and cook and stir 1–2 minutes over lowest heat until quite thick; do not boil. Off heat, mix in vanilla and butter. Place a circle of wax paper flat on filling and cool to lukewarm. Fill shell, then chill 2 hours at least. Serve as is or topped with whipped cream. *To top with meringue:* Cool filling slightly, then fill pie shell. Prepare meringue as directed, spread over filling, and bake 12–15 minutes at 350° F. until touched with brown. Cool 2 hours before serving. About 400 calories for each of 6 servings, 300 calories for each of 8 servings (without topping).

VARIATION:

Coconut Cream Pie: Prepare filling as directed, then mix in 1 cup flaked or finely grated coconut. Reduce vanilla to 1 teaspoon and, if desired, serve topped with whipped cream. About 455 calories for each of 6 servings (without whipped cream), about 340 calories for each of 8 servings (without whipped cream).

BUTTERSCOTCH CREAM PIE

Makes 6–8 servings

1 recipe Flaky Pastry I

Filling:

1 cup firmly packed dark brown sugar
¼ cup cornstarch
¼ teaspoon salt
2⅔ cups milk
3 egg yolks, lightly beaten
¼ cup butter or margarine
1 teaspoon vanilla

Topping (optional):

1 cup heavy cream, whipped
or
1 recipe Basic Meringue Topping for a 9" Pie

Make pastry, fit into a 9" piepan, and bake as directed; cool. Mix brown sugar, cornstarch, and salt in a heavy saucepan, slowly add milk, and blend until smooth. Heat, stirring constantly, over moderate heat until almost boiling. Turn heat to low and cook and stir until thickened, about 2 minutes. (*Note:* Mixture scorches easily, so watch.) Blend a little hot mixture into yolks, return to pan, and cook and stir 1–2 minutes over lowest heat until quite thick. Do not boil. Off heat, stir in butter and vanilla. Pour into pie shell, cool to room temperature, then chill 2 hours before serving. If you wish, top with whipped cream. If you prefer to top with meringue, *do not cool and chill filling.* Make meringue, spread on *warm* filling and bake as directed in meringue recipe. About 645 calories for each of 6 servings, 485 calories for each of 8 servings (without topping).

CHOCOLATE CREAM PIE

Makes 6–8 servings

1 recipe Flaky Pastry I

Filling:

2 tablespoons flour
3 tablespoons cornstarch
1 cup sugar
¼ teaspoon salt
2½ cups milk
3 (1-ounce) squares unsweetened chocolate or 3 (1-ounce) envelopes no-melt unsweetened chocolate
3 egg yolks, lightly beaten
1 tablespoon butter or margarine
1 teaspoon vanilla

Topping:

¾ cup heavy cream
3 tablespoons confectioners' sugar (optional)
Chocolate curls* or chopped pistachio nuts (optional garnish)

Make pastry, fit into a 9″ piepan, and bake as directed. Mix flour, cornstarch, sugar, and salt in a heavy saucepan and slowly stir in milk. Heat and stir over moderate heat until thickened and smooth; blend in chocolate. Ladle about ½ cup hot mixture into egg yolks, mix well, and return to pan. Cook and stir 1

minute over lowest heat—do not boil. Off heat, stir in butter and vanilla. Place a circle of wax paper directly on filling and cool to room temperature; stir well and spoon into pie shell. Chill 1–2 hours. Whip cream, adding sugar, if you like, and spread over filling. Decorate with chocolate curls and serve. About 685 calories for each of 6 servings, 515 calories for each of 8 servings.

BLACK BOTTOM PIE

This two-toned pie is chocolate on the bottom, rum chiffon on top.
Makes 6–8 servings

1 (9″) crumb crust pie shell (Graham Cracker, Gingersnap, or Chocolate), baked and cooled

Filling:

⅔ cup sugar
2 tablespoons cornstarch
1 envelope unflavored gelatin
2½ cups milk
3 eggs, separated
2 (1-ounce) squares unsweetened chocolate
2 tablespoons light rum
¼ cup superfine sugar
¾ cup heavy cream
Chocolate curls* (garnish)

Mix sugar, cornstarch, and gelatin in the top of a double boiler, gradually mix in milk, and heat, stirring constantly, over simmering water until steaming. Beat egg yolks lightly, stir in a little hot mixture, then return to pan and cook and stir 3–5 minutes until quite thick and smooth. Place a circle of wax paper flat on sauce and cool to lukewarm. Meanwhile, melt chocolate over simmering water and cool. Measure 1½ cups custard sauce into a bowl, blend in chocolate, pour into crust, and chill ½ hour. Cool remaining mixture until it mounds when dropped from a spoon; stir in rum. Beat egg whites until foamy, gradually beat in superfine sugar, and continue to beat until soft peaks form. Fold into rum-custard mixture. Spoon lightly on top of chocolate layer and chill until firm. Whip cream to soft peaks, spread on pie, and decorate with chocolate curls. About 705 calories for each of 6 servings, 530 calories for each of 8 servings.

BANANA CREAM PIE

Makes 6–8 servings

1 recipe Flaky Pastry 1

Filling:

2 tablespoons flour
2 tablespoons cornstarch
½ cup sugar
¼ teaspoon salt
1¾ cups milk
3 egg yolks, lightly beaten
1 teaspoon vanilla
1 tablespoon butter or margarine
3 ripe bananas

Topping:

¾ cup heavy cream, whipped

Make pastry, fit into a 9″ piepan, and bake as directed. Mix flour, cornstarch, sugar, and salt in a saucepan. Slowly blend in milk and heat and stir until thickened and smooth; turn heat to lowest point and heat and stir 1–2 minutes. Blend a little hot mixture into egg yolks, return to pan, and cook and stir 1–2 minutes over lowest heat until quite thick; do not boil or mixture will curdle. Off heat, mix in vanilla and butter. Place a circle of wax paper directly on mixture and cool to room temperature. Stir filling and spoon half into pie shell. Peel bananas, slice ¼″ thick, and arrange evenly over filling. Top with remaining filling. "Frost" with whipped cream, chill 20–30 minutes and serve. (*Note:* If you know you won't eat all the pie at one sitting, top individual servings with whipped cream instead of frosting the whole pie—whipped cream breaks down in the refrigerator.) About 640 calories for each of 6 servings, 480 calories for each of 8 servings.

SOUR CREAM RAISIN PIE

Makes 6–8 servings

1 recipe Flaky Pastry 1

Filling:

3 eggs
1 cup sugar
¼ teaspoon salt
1½ teaspoons cinnamon
½ teaspoon nutmeg
1 cup sour cream
1¼ cups seedless raisins

Preheat oven to 450° F. Make pastry as directed and fit into a 9″ piepan, making a high fluted edge; do not bake. Beat eggs until thick and cream colored, add sugar gradually, beating well after each addition. Continue beating until thick and light. Blend in remaining ingredients and spoon into pie shell. Bake 10 minutes. Reduce heat to 350° F., and bake 30 minutes longer or until a knife inserted midway between center and rim comes out clean. Cool 15 minutes before cutting. Serve warm or at room temperature. About 535 calories for each of 6 servings, 400 calories for each of 8 servings.

¢ SHOOFLY PIE

In Pennsylvania Dutch country you may find this pie served for breakfast. Its original function was to distract flies from other foods.

Makes 6–8 servings

1 recipe Flaky Pastry 1

Filling:

⅔ cup boiling water
½ teaspoon baking soda
½ cup molasses

Crumb Topping:

1½ cups sifted flour
¼ teaspoon salt
¾ cup firmly packed light brown sugar
⅓ cup butter, margarine, or shortening

Preheat oven to 350° F. Prepare pastry as directed and fit into a 9″ piepan, making a high fluted edge; do not bake. Mix filling. Also mix flour, salt, and sugar and cut in butter with a pastry blender until the texture of coarse meal. Sprinkle about ⅓ cup topping into pie shell, pour in filling, and sprinkle evenly with remaining topping. Bake on center oven rack 35–40 minutes until well browned. Cool on a wire rack and serve slightly warm or cold. Good with whipped cream or vanilla ice cream. About 540 calories for each of 6 servings (without whipped cream or ice cream), 405 calories for each of 8 servings.

CUSTARD PIE

For a crisp bottom crust, use the Slipped Custard Pie recipe (see Variations below).
Makes 6–8 servings

1 recipe Flaky Pastry I

Filling:

4 eggs
⅔ cup sugar
½ teaspoon salt
2½ cups milk
1 teaspoon vanilla
¼ teaspoon nutmeg

Make pastry as directed and fit into a 9″ piepan, making a high fluted edge; do not bake. Preheat oven to 425° F. With a rotary beater, beat eggs lightly, add sugar and salt, and beat until thick and cream colored. Gradually beat in milk and vanilla, then strain through a fine sieve and pour into pastry shell. Sprinkle with nutmeg and bake 15 minutes; reduce temperature to 350° F. and bake 12–15 minutes longer or until a silver knife inserted midway between center and rim comes out clean. (*Note:* Center will still be soft but will set on standing.) Do not overbake or custard will curdle. Cool on a wire rack to room temperature before serving, or serve well chilled. About 400 calories for each of 6 servings, 300 calories for each of 8 servings.

VARIATIONS:

Rich Custard Pie: Prepare as directed, substituting 1 cup heavy cream for 1 cup of the milk. About 515 calories for each of 6 servings, 385 calories for each of 8 servings.

Coconut Custard Pie: Prepare as directed but, just before pouring custard into pie shell, fold in ¾ cup flaked

coconut. Pour into shell, sprinkle with ¼ cup flaked coconut (omit nutmeg), and bake as directed. About 455 calories for each of 6 servings, 340 calories for each of 8 servings.

Egg Yolk Custard Pie: Prepare as directed, using 8 egg yolks for custard instead of 4 whole eggs. About 425 calories for each of 6 servings, 320 calories for each of 8 servings.

Slipped Custard Pie: Make and bake a 9″ pie shell as directed in Flaky Pastry I. Prepare and strain custard mixture, pour into a well-buttered 9″ piepan, and sprinkle with nutmeg. Set piepan in a larger pan, add enough hot water to come halfway up piepan. Bake at 350° F. 30–35 minutes or until custard tests done; cool on a wire rack to room temperature. Gently loosen custard from sides of piepan with a spatula, hold level, and shake to loosen bottom. Now tilt and carefully slide into pie shell; hold pans close together and coax custard along. Let custard settle a few minutes before serving. About 400 calories for each of 6 servings, 300 calories for each of 8 servings.

RICH COCONUT PIE

For a truly exquisite pie, use freshly grated coconut.
Makes 6–8 servings

1 recipe Flaky Pastry I

Filling:

¼ cup butter or margarine, softened to room temperature
1 cup superfine sugar
2 eggs
2 tablespoons flour
½ cup milk
¼ teaspoon almond extract
2 cups finely grated coconut

Preheat oven to 350° F. Make pastry as directed and fit into a 9″ piepan, making a high fluted edge; do not bake. Cream butter and sugar until light, beat in eggs, 1 at a time. Sprinkle in flour and blend until smooth. Mix in remaining ingredients and spoon into pastry shell. Bake 45 minutes until browned and springy to the touch. Cool on a wire rack and serve at room temperature. About 540 calories for each of 6 servings, 405 calories for each of 8 servings.

VANILLA CHIFFON PIE

Plenty of flavor variations here to try. Makes 6–8 servings

*1 (9") pie shell, baked and cooled
  (Flaky Pastry I or a crumb crust)*

Filling:

*¾ cup sugar
1 envelope unflavored gelatin
1 cup milk
4 eggs, separated
2 teaspoons vanilla
⅓ cup heavy cream (optional)
¼ teaspoon nutmeg*

Mix ½ cup sugar and the gelatin in the top of a double boiler, gradually mix in milk, and heat and stir over simmering water until steaming hot. Beat egg yolks lightly, blend in a little hot milk mixture, and return to pan. Cook and stir 3–5 minutes until thickened and no raw taste of egg remains. Mix in vanilla, set pan over cold water, and place a circle of wax paper flat on sauce. Cool, stirring now and then, until mixture mounds slightly on a spoon. Whip cream, if you like, and fold into sauce. Beat egg whites until foamy, gradually beat in remaining sugar, and beat to soft peaks; fold into sauce. Spoon into pie shell and chill until firm, at least 3–4 hours. Sprinkle with nutmeg and serve. (*Note:* If you prefer, use cream to garnish pie instead of mixing into filling.) About 405 calories for each of 6 servings, 305 calories for each of 8 servings (with pastry crust and without optional heavy cream).

VARIATIONS:

Chocolate Chiffon Pie: Prepare as directed but use only 3 egg yolks and add 2 (1-ounce) squares unsweetened chocolate. Beat ½ cup sugar with 3 egg whites and fold into sauce; reduce vanilla to 1 teaspoon and omit nutmeg.

Decorate with chocolate curls.* About 525 calories for each of 6 servings, 395 calories for each of 8 servings.

Coffee Chiffon Pie: Prepare as directed but add 2 tablespoons instant coffee powder or freeze-dried coffee along with egg yolks; reduce vanilla to 1 teaspoon. About 405 calories for each of 6 servings, 305 calories for each of 8 servings.

Coconut Chiffon Pie: Prepare as directed but reduce vanilla to ½ teaspoon and add ½ teaspoon almond extract. Fold in ¾ cup finely grated coconut along with beaten egg whites. Chill, then serve topped with toasted, flaked coconut. About 460 calories for each of 6 servings, 345 calories for each of 8 servings.

Lemon, Lime, or Orange Chiffon Pie: Prepare as directed but use ⅓ cup lemon or lime juice or ⅓ cup thawed frozen orange juice concentrate and ⅔ cup water instead of milk; also use 2 tablespoons finely grated lemon, lime, or orange rind instead of vanilla. Tint filling an appropriate color, if you like, before spooning into pie shell. Omit nutmeg. About 415 calories for each of 6 servings, 310 calories for each of 8 servings.

Berry Chiffon Pie: Prepare as directed but substitute 1 cup crushed, sieved ripe berries for the milk, omit egg yolks, and flavor with 1 tablespoon finely grated lemon rind instead of vanilla. (*Note:* If you use frozen berries, reduce sugar to ½ cup—¼ cup in the sauce, ¼ cup in the beaten egg whites.) Fold in the whipped cream, then the beaten egg whites. Cover pie shell, if you like, with ½ cup sliced berries before pouring in filling. Chill until firm; omit nutmeg. About 435 calories for each of 6 servings, 325 calories for each of 8 servings.

Peach or Apricot Chiffon Pie: Prepare like Berry Chiffon Pie (above) but use 1 cup peach or apricot purée instead of berries. If you like, cover bottom of pie shell with a layer of sliced peaches or apricots before pouring in filling. About

435 calories for each of 6 servings, 325 calories for each of 8 servings.

Pumpkin Chiffon Pie: Mix 1¼ cups pumpkin purée with ¾ cup firmly packed light brown sugar and the gelatin called for; proceed as recipe directs but use only 2 egg yolks. Omit vanilla and add ½ teaspoon each cinnamon and nutmeg. Cool, fold in 2 egg whites beaten with ¼ cup sugar, fill pie shell, chill well, then serve topped with fluffs of whipped cream. About 420 calories for each of 6 servings (without whipped cream), 315 calories for each of 8 servings.

STRAWBERRY BAVARIAN PIE

Strictly speaking, a Bavarian does *not* contain egg whites. If you hate having leftover whites, however, beat to soft peaks and fold into filling at the end. Makes 6–8 servings

1 (9") pie shell (Flaky Pastry I, Sweet Torte, or Graham Cracker Crust), baked and cooled

Filling:

½ cup sugar
1 envelope unflavored gelatin
½ cup milk
3 egg yolks, lightly beaten
1 tablespoon lemon juice
1 cup puréed strawberries
Few drops red food coloring
¾ cup heavy cream
2 tablespoons confectioners' sugar
3 egg whites (optional)

Mix sugar, gelatin, and milk in the top of a double boiler and heat over simmering water until steaming hot. Mix a little hot milk mixture into yolks, return to pan, and cook and stir 3–5 minutes until thickened and no raw taste of egg remains. Off heat, mix in lemon juice, berries, and food coloring; cool, stirring occasionally, until mixture mounds when dropped from a spoon. Whip cream with confectioners' sugar until firm peaks form, then fold into strawberry mixture. If you like, also beat egg whites to soft peaks and fold in. Spoon into pie shell and chill at least 4

hours before serving. About 435 calories for each of 6 servings (made with pastry crust and optional egg whites), 325 calories for each of 8 servings.

VARIATIONS:

Rum Bavarian Pie: Prepare filling as directed, using 1 cup milk and omitting lemon juice, berries, and food coloring; flavor with ½ cup light rum. About 520 calories for each of 6 servings, 390 calories for each of 8 servings.

Chocolate Bavarian Pie: Prepare filling as directed but use 1½ cups milk and 1 (6-ounce) package semisweet chocolate bits; omit lemon juice, berries, and coloring and flavor with 1 teaspoon vanilla. About 655 calories for each of 6 servings, 490 calories for each of 8 servings.

Mocha Bavarian Pie: Prepare Chocolate Bavarian Pie (above) as directed, using 1 cup milk and ½ cup very strong hot black coffee. About 640 calories for each of 6 servings, 480 calories for each of 8 servings.

Almond Bavarian Pie: Prepare filling as directed, using 1¼ cups milk; omit lemon juice, berries, and coloring and mix in ¾ cup finely ground blanched almonds and ½ teaspoon almond extract. About 540 calories for each of 6 servings, 405 calories for each of 8 servings.

Nesselrode Pie: Prepare filling as directed, using 1¼ cups milk; omit lemon juice, berries, and coloring and add 2 tablespoons light rum. Just before adding whipped cream, fold in ¼ cup finely chopped mixed candied fruits and 3 egg whites, beaten to soft peaks. Proceed as directed, and just before serving decorate with candied fruits. About 515 calories for each of 6 servings, 385 calories for each of 8 servings.

GRASSHOPPER PIE

This tastes very much like the Grasshopper cocktail—a mixture of crème de menthe and crème de cacao. Makes 6–8 servings

1 (9") pie shell (Graham Cracker Crust, Flaky Pastry I, or Mürbteig), baked and cooled

Filling:

¾ cup sugar
1 envelope unflavored gelatin
½ cup cold water
3 eggs, separated
⅓ cup green crème de menthe
¼ cup crème de cacao
½ cup heavy cream
Few drops green food coloring (optional)

Topping:

½ cup heavy cream, whipped to soft peaks
Chocolate curls*

Heat and stir ½ cup sugar, gelatin, and water in the top of a double boiler over simmering water until gelatin dissolves. Lightly beat egg yolks, blend in a little hot mixture, then return to pan. Cook and stir 3–5 minutes until thickened and no raw taste of egg remains. Off heat, mix in liqueurs; place a circle of wax paper flat on sauce and cool until mixture mounds when dropped from a spoon. Whip cream to soft peaks, fold into sauce, and, if you like, tint pale green. Beat egg whites until foamy, gradually beat in remaining sugar, and continue to beat until soft peaks form; fold into sauce. Spoon into pie shell and chill until firm, at least 3–4 hours. Top with swirls of whipped cream and sprinkle with chocolate curls. About 675 calories for each of 6 servings, 505 calories for each of 8 servings.

VARIATION:

Brandy Alexander Pie: Prepare as directed but substitute ⅓ cup brandy for the crème de menthe. About 675 calories for each of 6 servings, 505 calories for each of 8 servings.

OLD-FASHIONED SOUTHERN PECAN PIE

Almost too good to be true.
Makes 6–8 servings

1 recipe Flaky Pastry I

Filling:

1 cup pecan halves
1 (1-pound) box light brown sugar
¼ cup unsifted flour
½ teaspoon salt
½ cup milk
1½ teaspoons vanilla
3 eggs
½ cup melted butter or margarine

Preheat oven to 325° F. Make pastry as directed and fit into a 9" piepan; do not bake. Arrange pecans in concentric rings over bottom of pastry. Blend sugar, flour, and salt, then mix in milk and vanilla. Beat in eggs, 1 at a time, using a wire whisk or rotary beater; mix in butter, a little at a time. Pour filling over pecans. Bake pie 1 hour and 15 minutes or until filling is puffy and crust golden. Serve at room temperature. And cut the pieces small—the pie is *rich*. About 695 calories for each of 6 servings, 520 calories for each of 8 servings.

LEMON CHESS PIE

The South's favorite pie is "chess" (probably a corruption of "cheese" from the English "lemon cheese"). Lemon is a popular chess flavor, but there are others —so many no one knows which is the original. Here are three especially good ones.
Makes 6–8 servings

1 recipe Flaky Pastry I

Filling:

1½ cups sugar
2 tablespoons flour
Finely grated rind of 2 lemons
5 eggs
Juice of 2 lemons
⅓ cup melted butter or margarine

Preheat oven to 325° F. Make pastry as directed and fit into a 9" piepan; do not bake. Mix sugar, flour, and rind, then, beat in eggs, 1 at a time. Stir in lemon juice and finally the melted butter, adding a bit at a time and beating well after each addition. Pour filling into pie shell and bake about 1 hour until puffy and golden (filling will seem unset). Cool pie to room temperature (filling will settle and thicken). Serve at room temperature. About 545 calories for each of 6 servings, 410 calories for each of 8 servings.

BROWN SUGAR CHESS PIE

Rich, rich, *rich!*
Makes 6 8 servings

1 recipe Flaky Pastry I

Filling:

1 (1-pound) box light brown sugar
4 eggs
¼ cup milk
1½ teaspoons vanilla
½ teaspoon salt
½ cup melted butter or margarine

Preheat oven to 325° F. Make pastry as directed and fit into a 9″ piepan; do not bake. Blend together all filling ingredients except butter, then mix in butter, a little at a time; pour into pie shell and bake about 1 hour until puffy and golden. Cool pie to room temperature before serving (filling will settle and thicken). Cut the pieces small. About 560 calories for each of 6 servings, 420 calories for each of 8 servings.

COLONIAL CHESS PIE

This chess pie, unlike the others, contains raisins and walnuts. And is it RICH! Makes 6–8 servings

1 recipe Flaky Pastry I

Filling:

½ cup unsalted butter
1⅔ cups sugar
1 cup light cream
1⅓ cups seedless raisins
6 egg yolks, lightly beaten
1½ cups coarsely chopped walnuts
½ teaspoon vanilla
½ teaspoon salt

Preheat oven to 425° F. Make pastry as directed and fit into a 9″ piepan; do not bake. Heat and stir butter, sugar, cream, and raisins over moderate heat just until boiling; remove from heat.

Blend a little hot mixture into yolks, return to pan, and stir in remaining ingredients. Pour into pie shell and bake 15 minutes, reduce oven to 375° F. and bake 45–50 minutes longer until puffy and golden. Cool to room temperature before serving. About 970 calories for each of 6 servings, 730 calories for each of 8 servings.

THE VERY BEST CHEESE PIE

Unbelievably smooth.
Makes 10 servings

Crust:

18 graham crackers rolled to crumbs
(there should be 1½ cups)
¼ cup sugar
5 tablespoons melted butter or margarine

Filling:

2 (8-ounce) packages cream cheese,
softened to room temperature
2 eggs
½ cup sugar
1 teaspoon vanilla

Topping:

1 cup sour cream
¼ cup sugar
1 teaspoon vanilla

Preheat oven to 375° F. Mix crust ingredients and pat firmly into the bottom and ⅓ of the way up the sides of a 9″ spring form pan. Beat filling ingredients with a rotary beater or electric mixer until satiny and pour into crust. Bake 20 minutes, remove from oven, and cool 15 minutes. Meanwhile, raise oven to 475° F. Blend topping ingredients and spread gently over cheese filling. Return pie to oven and bake 10 minutes longer. Cool in pan to room temperature, then cover with foil and chill 10–12 hours before serving. Cut in *slim* wedges. About 430 calories per serving.

CHERRY TOPPING FOR CHEESE CAKE

The following toppings can be spread over Cottage Cheese Cake or the Very Best Cheese Pie after they have been

baked and thoroughly cooled.
Makes enough to top a 9″ cheese cake

½ cup sugar
2 tablespoons cornstarch
1 (1-pound) can sour red cherries,
 drained (reserve liquid)
Cherry liquid plus enough water to total
 ¾ cup
1 teaspoon lemon juice
Few drops red food coloring

Mix sugar and cornstarch in a saucepan,
gradually blend in cherry liquid, and
heat, stirring, until boiling. Reduce heat
and simmer 5 minutes, stirring occasionally. Off heat, mix in lemon juice, cherries, and food coloring. Cool 5 minutes,
spread on top of cooled cheese cake, and
chill several hours. About 850 calories
total, about 85 calories for each of 10
servings and 70 calories for each of 12.

VARIATIONS:

Blueberry Topping: Prepare as directed
but substitute 1 (1-pound) can blueberries for cherries and reduce sugar to
¼ cup; omit food coloring. About 660
calories total, about 66 calories for
each of 10 servings and 55 calories for
each of 12.

Cranberry Topping: Substitute 1 (1-
pound) can whole cranberry sauce (do
not drain) for cherries. Mix sauce with
⅓ cup sugar, 1 tablespoon cornstarch
blended with ¼ cup orange juice and
proceed as directed. About 1100 calories
total, about 110 calories for each of 10
servings and 90 calories for each of 12.

Pineapple Topping: Drain liquid from
1 (8-ounce) can crushed pineapple and
add enough canned pineapple juice to
total ½ cup. Blend ¼ cup sugar and 1
tablespoon cornstarch, mix into pineapple juice, and heat and stir as above
until thickened and clear. Mix in lemon
juice and pineapple (but not food
coloring), cool, and spread over cheese
cake as directed. About 450 calories
total, about 45 calories for each of 10
servings and 40 calories for each of 12.

COTTAGE CHEESE CAKE

Makes 12 servings

Crust:

2½ cups graham cracker crumbs
⅓ cup sugar
⅓ cup melted butter or margarine

Filling:

2 pounds cottage cheese
4 eggs, separated
½ cup sugar
¼ cup sifted flour
2 tablespoons lemon juice
1 teaspoon finely grated lemon rind

Preheat oven to 325° F. Mix crust
ingredients and pat firmly over the
bottom and up the sides of a 9″ spring
form pan. Purée cottage cheese in an
electric blender 1–2 minutes at high
speed until smooth or press through a
fine sieve; set aside. Beat egg yolks until
thick, slowly add sugar, and beat until
the color of cream. Beat in flour, lemon
juice and rind, and cottage cheese. In a
separate bowl, beat egg whites to soft
peaks; with a wire whisk mix into cheese
mixture until completely blended. Spoon
into crust and bake 1 hour on center
oven rack until lightly browned. Turn
off oven, open door, and let cake cool in
oven ½ hour. Lift to a wire rack and
cool in pan to room temperature,
remove spring form, cover cake with
foil, and chill well before serving. About
340 calories per serving.

STRAWBERRY TOPPING FOR CHEESE CAKE

Makes enough to top a 9″ cheese cake

1 quart strawberries, washed and
 stemmed
⅓ cup sugar
1 tablespoon cornstarch
¼ cup water
Few drops red food coloring

Crush enough small berries to make 1
cup and press through a fine sieve. Mix
sugar and cornstarch in a saucepan,
blend in sieved berries and water, and
heat and stir over moderate heat until

boiling; lower heat and simmer 2–3 minutes, stirring until thickened and clear. Add coloring and cool slightly. Arrange whole berries, points up, on a baked, cooled cheese cake, spoon sauce over all, and chill 2 hours. About 500 calories total, about 50 calories for each of 10 servings and 40 calories for each of 12.

LEMON ANGEL PIE

A shattery meringue crust billowing with a creamy lemon filling.
Makes 6–8 servings

1 (9") Meringue Pie Shell, baked and
cooled

Filling:

4 egg yolks
½ cup sugar
¼ cup lemon juice
2 tablespoons finely grated lemon rind
1 cup heavy cream

Beat egg yolks in the top of a double boiler until thick and cream colored. Gradually beat in sugar, then lemon juice and rind. Set over simmering water and cook, stirring constantly, about 5–8 minutes until thick. Remove from heat, place a circle of wax paper flat on mixture, and cool to room temperature. Whip cream until soft peaks form, and spread half in bottom of pie shell. Cover with filling and top with remaining whipped cream. Or fold lemon mixture into whipped cream, then fill pie shell. Chill overnight. About 320 calories for each of 6 servings, 230 calories for each of 8 servings.

VARIATIONS:

Lime Angel Pie: Prepare as directed but substitute ¼ cup lime juice and 1 tablespoon grated lime rind for the lemon juice and rind. About 320 calories for each of 6 servings, 240 calories for each of 8 servings.

Orange Angel Pie: Prepare as directed but substitute ¼ cup thawed, frozen orange juice concentrate and 2 tablespoons finely grated orange rind for the lemon juice and rind. About 340 calories for

each of 6 servings, 255 calories for each of 8 servings.

CHOCOLATE ANGEL PIE

If chocolate is your choice, you'll prefer this angel pie to the lemon.
Makes 6–8 servings

1 (9") Meringue Pie Shell, baked and
cooled

Filling:

¼ cup hot water
1 (12-ounce) package semisweet
chocolate bits, melted
1 cup heavy cream
½ cup sifted confectioners' sugar
1 teaspoon vanilla

Blend water and chocolate bits until smooth and cool to room temperature. Beat cream and sugar to stiff peaks, fold into chocolate mixture, flavor with vanilla, and spoon into meringue shell. Chill well before serving. About 535 calories for each of 6 servings, 400 calories for each of 8 servings.

VARIATION:

Mocha Angel Pie: Prepare as directed but use ¼ cup strong hot black coffee instead of water. About 535 calories for each of 6 servings, 400 calories for each of 8 servings.

PEACH SUNDAE PIE

Makes 8 servings

1 (9") pie shell (Graham Cracker,
Nut-Crumb, Toasted Coconut, Flaky
Pastry I, or Sweet Torte Pastry), baked
and cooled

Filling:

1 quart peach or vanilla ice cream
3 ripe peaches, peeled, pitted, and sliced
thin
¼ cup Melba Sauce
¾ cup heavy cream, whipped to soft
peaks (optional)
¼ cup minced nuts (walnuts, pecans,
pistachios, toasted almonds)

Soften ice cream slightly, spread in pie shell, making edges a little higher than center, and freeze until firm. Top with peaches, drizzle with sauce, "frost," if you like with whipped cream, and sprinkle with nuts. Serve at once. About 400 calories per serving (made with graham cracker crust and with whipped cream).

VARIATIONS:

Other Flavors: Prepare as directed, using any favorite combinations of ice cream and fruit—strawberry and raspberry, lemon and strawberry, orange and blueberry, etc. Or, if you prefer, omit the fruit and whipped cream and spread ice cream with any favorite sundae topping. Recipe too flexible for a meaningful calorie count.

Alaska Pie: Fill pie shell with ice cream (not sherbet or ice milk, which will melt too fast) and freeze until hard. Omit peaches, sauce, and whipped cream. Cover ice cream *completely* with 1 recipe Basic Meringue Topping for a 9" Pie and bake 3–5 minutes at 500° F. until touched with brown. Serve at once. About 350 calories per serving.

STRAWBERRY ICE CREAM PARFAIT PIE

Makes 8 servings

1 (9") pie shell (any kind), baked and cooled

Filling:

1 (3-ounce) package strawberry-flavored gelatin
1¼ cups boiling water
1 pint strawberry ice cream
1½ cups sliced strawberries
¾ cup heavy cream, whipped to soft peaks

Mix gelatin and water in a large bowl. Add ice cream by spoonfuls and stir until melted and well blended. Chill until mixture mounds when dropped from a spoon, then fold in berries. Spoon into pie shell and chill until firm. Garnish with whipped cream. About 340 calories per serving (made with standard piecrust).

VARIATIONS:

Prepare as directed but use any of the following combinations of gelatin, ice cream, and fruit instead of that given above: raspberry-flavored gelatin, raspberry ice cream, and raspberries; orange-flavored gelatin, vanilla ice cream, and orange sections; lemon-flavored gelatin, peach ice cream, and sliced peaches; mixed fruit-flavored gelatin, pistachio ice cream, and sliced bananas. Recipe too flexible for a meaningful calorie count.

ABOUT MAKING TARTS

Tarts, in classical cuisine, are short cookie-like pastry shells filled with raw or cooked fruit, often accompanied with custard or cream filling. They are usually open face (at least they are never sealed under a top crust) and may be small, medium, or large. The most beautiful are arrangements of fruit jeweled under a clear sweet glaze.

In America, tarts are simply little pies, single or double crusted, sometimes enough for one serving, sometimes no more than a mouthful. Almost any pie recipe can be used for tarts. (*Note:* You will probably need 1½–2 times the amount of pastry because it takes more to line several little pans than a single large one.)

Some Ways to Shape Tart Shells: Prepare pastry, roll out ⅛" thick, then cut in circles about 1" larger all around than tin you plan to use. Fluted tart tins, available in many housewares departments, make especially dainty tarts, but tarts can also be fitted into muffin pans or over upside-down custard cups or gelatin molds.

About Baking Tarts: Follow individual pie recipes, making the following adjustments in baking times and temperatures:

Unfilled Tart Shells: Preheat oven to 450° F. Roll and fit pastry into tins, prick well all over, and bake 10–15 minutes until crisp and tan. Cool in pans on wire racks a few minutes, then ease out, using a metal skewer to free stubborn spots. Cool thoroughly before filling. (*Note:* Preserves or jams may be used to fill small tarts instead of pie fillings.)

Filled Tarts: Preheat oven to 425° F. Roll and fit pastry into tins; do not prick. Add filling, enough to fill each tart ½–⅔, no more. Add top crust, if any, crimp edges, and seal. Bake 15–20 minutes until pastry is crisp and tan and filling bubbly. Cool or not as individual recipes direct. (*Note:* To minimize breakage, keep tarts in tins until just before serving.)

Some Ways to Decorate Tarts: Keep decorations simple, in proportion to the tart and appropriate to the occasion. Here are a few suggestions:

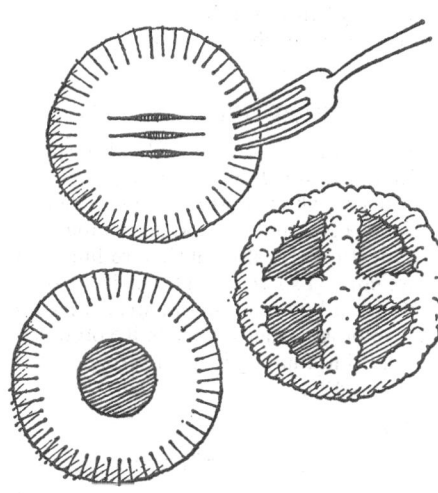

SWISS STRAWBERRY TART

Makes 6–8 servings

1 recipe Flaky Pastry I

Filling:

3 tablespoons flour
¼ cup sugar
⅛ teaspoon salt
1 cup milk
½ teaspoon vanilla

2 egg yolks, lightly beaten
⅓ cup heavy cream
3 cups ripe strawberries, washed, stemmed, and dried

Glaze:

¾ cup red currant jelly

Make pastry, fit into a 9″ piepan, and bake as directed; cool. Mix flour, sugar, and salt in the top of a double boiler, add milk slowly, stirring until smooth, then cook and stir over direct moderate heat until thickened and smooth; stir in vanilla. Blend a little hot mixture into yolks, return to top of double boiler, set over simmering water, and cook and stir 3–4 minutes until thick and no taste of raw egg remains. Remove from heat, place a circle of wax paper flat on sauce and cool to room temperature. Whip cream and fold into sauce. Spread over bottom of pie shell and arrange strawberries, points up, on top. To glaze, melt jelly over low heat, cool to barely lukewarm, then spoon evenly over berries. Cover and chill until serving time (but no longer than 1–2 hours or pastry will become soggy). About 485 calories for each of 6 servings, 365 calories for each of 8 servings.

VIENNESE FRUIT FLAN

Cut the pieces small—this one's rich! Makes 8–10 servings

1 (9″) Sweet Torte or Mürbteig pie shell, baked and cooled

Filling:

1 cup heavy cream
¼ cup superfine sugar
1 teaspoon vanilla
1 quart stemmed strawberries or a mixture of sliced peaches, seedless green or seeded black grapes, and any stemmed berries

Glaze:

1 cup water
2 tablespoons sugar
4 teaspoons arrowroot or cornstarch blended with 2 tablespoons cold water
1 teaspoon lemon juice
Few drops red food coloring

Beat cream with sugar and vanilla until soft peaks form; spread over bottom of pie shell and arrange fruit artistically on top. Mix glaze (omitting coloring) and heat, stirring, over low heat until thickened and *clear*. Tint pale pink, cool to lukewarm, then spoon evenly over fruit. Keep in a cool place (not the refrigerator) and serve within 2–3 hours. About 380 calories for each of 8 servings, 305 calories for each of 10 servings.

TRUDY'S VIENNESE LINZERTORTE

Makes an 8″ torte

Pastry:

1½ cups sifted flour
¼ cup sugar
½ teaspoon baking powder
½ teaspoon salt
1 teaspoon cinnamon
½ cup firmly packed dark brown sugar
½ cup butter, chilled (no substitute)
1 egg, lightly beaten
½ cup finely ground unblanched almonds

Cream Filling:

1 egg
⅓ cup sugar
¼ cup sifted flour
¼ teaspoon salt
1½ cups scalding hot milk
1 teaspoon vanilla

Raspberry Topping:

1 (10-ounce) package thawed frozen raspberries (do not drain)
2 tablespoons sugar
2 tablespoons cornstarch
1 tablespoon lemon juice

Sift flour with sugar, baking powder, salt, and cinnamon, then, using a pastry blender, cut in brown sugar and butter until mixture resembles coarse meal. Add egg and almonds and blend with a fork until mixture forms a ball. Wrap half the pastry and chill. Press remaining pastry into the bottom and up the sides of an 8″ piepan, cover, and chill. To prepare filling, beat egg until frothy, add sugar gradually, and beat 2–3 minutes until thick. Add flour and salt slowly and blend until smooth. Gradually add milk, stirring constantly. Transfer to the top of a double boiler, set over simmering water, and cook, stirring, 2–3 minutes until thickened and smooth. Reduce heat, cover, and cook 5 minutes, stirring frequently. Off heat, mix in vanilla; place a piece of wax paper directly on surface and cool to room temperature. Meanwhile, prepare topping: Mix all ingredients in a saucepan and bring to a boil, stirring; reduce heat and simmer, uncovered, 5–7 minutes, stirring occasionally, until thick; cool to room temperature. Preheat oven to 375° F. Spoon filling into pastry shell and carefully spread with topping. Roll remaining pastry into an 8″ circle and cut in strips ½″ wide; arrange lattice-fashion over filling. Lay 1–2 long strips around rim to cover lattice ends and press gently to seal. Bake 30–35 minutes until lightly browned. Cool several minutes before serving. About 300 calories for each of 12 servings.

APPLE STRUDEL

You can make strudel with all-purpose flour, but bread flour will produce a thinner, flakier pastry. Remove your rings before pulling and stretching strudel pastry; also make sure fingernails are clipped so you don't tear it. (*Note:* You can buy ready-to-fill strudel pastry at some gourmet groceries if you don't feel up to making it from scratch.) Makes 12 servings

Pastry:

1½ cups sifted flour (preferably bread flour)
¼ teaspoon salt
1 egg, lightly beaten
1 tablespoon cooking oil
⅓ cup lukewarm water
Cooking oil (for brushing pastry)

Filling:

¾ cup (about) melted butter (no substitute)
1 cup toasted fine bread crumbs
5 medium-size tart cooking apples, peeled, cored, and minced

⅔ cup sugar, mixed with 1 teaspoon
  cinnamon
¾ cup seedless raisins
½ cup minced, blanched almonds
2 teaspoons finely grated lemon rind

Topping:

Sifted confectioners' sugar

Mix flour and salt and make a well in
the center. Combine egg, oil, and water,
pour into well, and, using a fork, pull
dry ingredients into liquid; mix to form a
soft dough. Knead on a lightly floured
board 3–4 minutes until smooth and
elastic. Place dough in an oiled bowl, turn
to grease all over, cover, and let stand
in a warm place ½ hour. Meanwhile,
cover a table about 3 feet square with
an old tablecloth or sheet, smooth out,
pull taut and fasten underneath with
tape. Sprinkle all over with flour, adding
a little extra in the center. With a lightly
floured rolling pin, roll dough into an 18″
circle. Brush all over with oil. Slip
floured hands, backs up, underneath
pastry, then gently and evenly stretch
dough, working from the center toward
edges and moving hands around circle to
stretch all areas as evenly and thinly as
possible. The fully stretched dough should
be semitransparent and cover the table.
Work carefully to avoid tearing holes,
but if small ones appear, ignore or pinch
together (don't try to patch). Let pastry
hang over edge of table and let stand,
uncovered, 10 minutes (no longer or it
may become brittle). Preheat oven to
400° F. Brush pastry generously with
butter and with kitchen shears cut off
thick edges and square up sides. Sprinkle
crumbs over top half of pastry, leaving
2″ margins at the top and both sides.
Cover crumbs with apples, sprinkle with
sugar, raisins, almonds, and lemon rind;
drizzle with 2–3 tablespoons melted butter. Fold top margin down and side
margins in over filling. Grasping cloth at
the top, tilting and holding taut with both
hands, let strudel roll itself up, jelly-roll
fashion. Ease strudel onto a buttered
baking sheet and curve into a horseshoe.
Brush with butter and bake on center
rack 20 minutes; reduce oven to 350° F.,

brush again with butter, and bake 20–25
minutes longer, brushing once more with
butter after 10 minutes or so. When
strudel is richly browned, transfer to a
wire rack and cool. Dust with confectioners' sugar and slice 2″ thick. Serve
slightly warm or cool, with or without
whipped cream. About 365 calories per
serving (without cream).

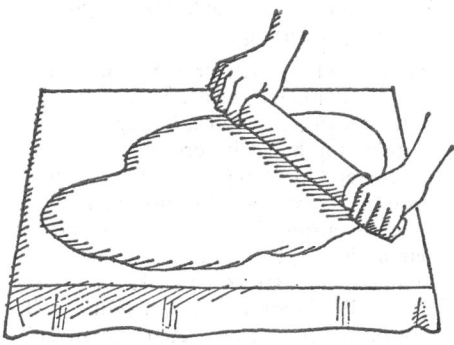

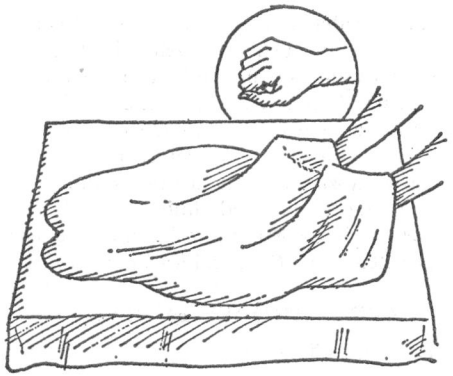

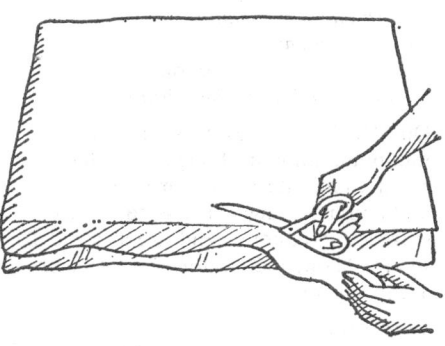

How to Roll and Stretch Strudel

VARIATIONS:

Cherry Strudel: Prepare as directed, using Cherry Strudel Filling instead of apple. About 390 calories per serving.

Cheese Strudel: Use Cheese Strudel Filling instead of apple and place on stretched pastry in a row at the top, leaving 2″ margins at top and sides. Fold the margins in over filling, roll, and bake strudel as directed. About 420 calories per serving.

Poppy Seed Strudel: Prepare and stretch pastry as directed; brush with melted butter and ½ cup warm honey, then sprinkle top half with crumbs. Across the top end in a single row place 2 cups ground poppy seeds, ½ cup sugar, 1 cup seedless raisins, the finely grated rind of 1 lemon, leaving a 2″ margin at the top and each side. Drizzle with ½ cup heavy cream. Fold margins in over filling, roll, and bake strudel as directed. About 380 calories per serving..

Jam Strudel: Prepare and stretch pastry as directed; brush with melted butter, scatter crumbs over top half of pastry, leaving 2″ margins as above. Spread 1½–2 cups warmed strawberry, raspberry, or apricot jam over crumbs, top with ¾ cup sultana raisins and ½ cup minced blanched almonds. Fold margins in over filling, roll, and bake as directed. About 435 calories per serving.

CHERRY STRUDEL FILLING

Enough to fill 1 strudel

2 (1-pound) cans pitted tart red or sweet dark cherries, drained
½–1 cup sugar
¼ teaspoon almond extract
1 cup minced, blanched almonds

Quarter the cherries, toss with the minimum amount of sugar, and let stand 10 minutes; taste for sweetness and add more sugar if needed. Mix in extract and almonds and use as strudel filling. About 1925 calories total (with 1 cup sugar).

VARIATION:

Fresh Cherry Strudel Filling: Simmer 1 quart stemmed, pitted, ripe tart red or dark sweet cherries with ½–1 cup sugar and ¼ cup water 5 minutes until softened. Cool in liquid and drain; taste for sugar and adjust, then mix with extract and almonds. About 1555 calories total (with 1 cup sugar).

CHEESE STRUDEL FILLING

Enough to fill 1 strudel

1 pound cottage cheese
⅓ cup sugar
1 egg plus 1 egg white, lightly beaten
¼ cup heavy cream
1 cup seedless raisins
1 cup minced walnuts
Finely grated rind and juice of 1 lemon

Purée cottage cheese in an electric blender 1–2 minutes at high speed until smooth or press through a fine sieve. Mix with remaining ingredients and use as strudel filling. About 2290 calories total.

PALMIERS

Makes about 5 dozen

1 recipe Puff Pastry
½ cup sugar (about)

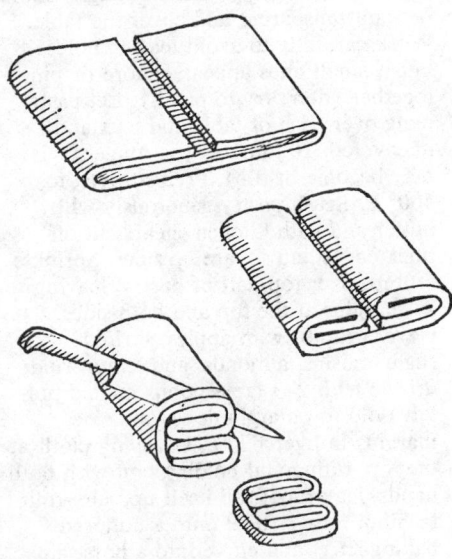

How to Fold and Cut Palmiers

Make pastry as directed, divide in 3 equal parts, and roll, one at a time, into a 12½″ square about ⅛″ thick. With a sharp knife, cut ¼″ off all margins, making edges ruler straight. Brush square with cold water, sprinkle evenly with about 2 tablespoons sugar. Make a light mark down center of square and fold each side in toward center as shown so folds meet exactly; fold again through center of each half, then fold 1 roll over on top of the other. Wrap and chill 1 hour. Preheat oven to 450° F. With a very sharp knife, slice rolls crosswise every ½″, dip both cut sides of slices in sugar, arrange 1½″ apart on ungreased baking sheets, and bake 5–7 minutes until browned on the bottom; turn, using a pancake turner, reduce heat to 375° F. and bake 5 minutes longer until browned underneath. Cool on wire racks. Serve as is or, if you like, sandwiched together with sweetened stiffly whipped cream. About 90 calories each (unfilled, unsandwiched).

NAPOLEONS

Napoleons are best eaten the day they're made. If you must prepare them ahead of time, spread pastry thinly with hot sieved apricot preserves before filling to keep Napoleons crisp. Also refrigerate until about 20 minutes before serving. Makes about 1 dozen

1 recipe Puff Pastry
2 recipes Pastry Cream or 1 quart sweetened stiffly whipped cream
Sifted confectioners' sugar

Prepare pastry as directed, divide in 3 equal parts, and roll out 1 piece on a lightly floured board into a rectangle 12½″ × 14½″ and ⅛″ thick, keeping edges as straight as possible. With a sharp knife, trim ⅛″ off all margins. Roll pastry over a lightly floured rolling pin and unroll on a baking sheet brushed with cold water; prick well all over, cover, and chill ½ hour. Meanwhile, preheat oven to 450° F. Roll remaining 2 pieces the same way, transfer to baking sheets and chill. (*Note:* If you do

not have 3 baking sheets, keep pastry chilled and roll when a sheet is free— make sure it is cool.) Bake pastry, 1 sheet at a time, on center oven rack 10 minutes until golden brown and crisp. Ease onto an extra-large wire rack (or 2 racks tied together) and cool thoroughly. Place pastry sheets on a large, flat surface and even up margins (all 3 pieces should be about the same size). Cut each the long way into strips 4″ wide and, as though making triple decker sandwiches, sandwich strips together, 3 deep, with filling (do not spread filling on top layer). Chill 1 hour. Using a sharp knife held vertically and a sawing motion, cut strips crosswise at 2″ intervals. Dust with confectioners' sugar and serve as soon as possible. About 400 calories each.

VARIATION:

Prepare and bake 3 pastry sheets as directed. Cut 2 into strips as above; spread the third uncut sheet with 2 recipes Quick Glacé Icing. Melt 4 (1-ounce) squares semisweet chocolate and drizzle in parallel lines over icing; before it hardens, draw a toothpick across lines every ½″ or so to make a crisscross design; when icing hardens, cut sheet into strips as you did the other two. Assemble Napoleons as above, using glazed strips as the top ones. About 550 calories each.

CREAM HORNS

For this recipe, you will need cream horn tubes, obtainable at gourmet shops or confectionary supply houses. Makes about 2½ dozen

1 recipe Puff Pastry

Glaze:

1 egg, lightly beaten with 1 tablespoon cold water
Sugar

Make pastry as directed and roll out half at a time on a lightly floured pastry cloth to a thickness of ⅛″, keeping sides as straight as possible. You will need long strips, so roll for length rather than width (it will take a 30" strip to wrap a cream horn tube 5" long). Cut pastry in strips ½" wide. Brush cream horn tubes with cold water and, starting at the point, wind with pastry strips, overlapping edges slightly but taking care not to stretch pastry. If it is necessary to piece pastry (when one strip is not long enough for the tube), make seams as smooth as possible. Cover pastry horns and chill ½ hour. Meanwhile, preheat oven to 450° F. Arrange horns 1" apart on baking sheets brushed with cold water. Brush horns with glaze, then sprinkle with sugar. Brush any spilled sugar from baking sheets and bake horns 10 minutes; reduce oven to 350° F. and bake 3–5 minutes longer or until golden brown and crisp. Remove tubes from horns by twisting free. Cool pastry horns on wire racks and serve filled with sweetened whipped cream or Pastry Cream. About 240 calories each (filled with sweetened whipped cream).

CREAM PUFFS

Makes 1 dozen

1 recipe Choux Pastry
1 egg yolk, mixed with 1 tablespoon cold water (glaze)
2 recipes Pastry Cream or 1 quart ice cream or any suitable cream filling
¼ cup sifted confectioners' sugar

Preheat oven to 400° F. Make pastry as directed and drop by rounded table-spoonfuls 3" apart on an ungreased baking sheet to form 12 puffs, or put through a pastry bag fitted with a large, plain tip. Brush tops with glaze and bake 45–50 minutes until puffed, golden brown, and hollow sounding when tapped. (*Note:* Do not open oven door during first quarter hour.) Cool puffs on wire racks away from drafts. To fill, cut a ¾" slice off the top of each puff and pull out any soft dough inside. Fill, replace tops, cover, and chill until serving time. Dust with confectioners' sugar and serve. About 240 calories each (filled with pastry cream).

VARIATIONS:
– Frost tops of filled puffs with any favorite icing.
– Top with hot or cold chocolate or butterscotch sauce.
– Fill with fresh, canned, or frozen fruit mixed with whipped cream instead of pastry cream.
– Fill with softened ice cream (any flavor); wrap airtight and freeze. Thaw 5–10 minutes before serving. These will keep about 1 month in the freezer.

All variations too flexible for meaningful calorie counts.

CHOCOLATE ÉCLAIRS

Makes 1 dozen

1 recipe Choux Pastry
1 egg yolk, mixed with 1 tablespoon cold water (glaze)
2 recipes Pastry Cream
1 recipe Chocolate Glacé Icing

Preheat oven to 400° F. Make pastry as directed and drop by rounded table-spoonfuls 2" apart in rows that are 6" apart on an ungreased baking sheet to form 12 equal-sized mounds. Using a spoon and a spatula, shape each mound into an oval about 4" long, 1½" wide, and 1" high. Or put mixture through a pastry bag fitted with a large, plain tip. Brush tops with glaze and bake 40–45 minutes until puffed, golden brown, and hollow sounding when tapped. Cool away from drafts on wire racks. Halve éclairs lengthwise and gently pull out any soft dough inside. Fill with pastry cream and replace tops. Arrange on a wire rack with a piece of wax paper underneath. Spoon icing evenly over each and allow to harden. Serve within 1–2 hours. Do not refrigerate. About 280 calories each.

PROFITEROLES

Bite-size Cream Puffs. Perfect for a tea if served plain without sauce.
Makes about 4½ dozen

1 recipe Choux Pastry
1 egg yolk, mixed with 1 tablespoon cold water (glaze)

3 recipes Pastry Cream or 7 cups
   sweetened whipped cream (about)
⅓ cup sifted confectioners' sugar

Preheat oven to 400° F. Prepare pastry as directed and drop by rounded teaspoonfuls 2″ apart on ungreased baking sheets or put through a pastry bag fitted with a medium-size plain tip. Smooth into little round "pillows" about 1″ high and brush tops lightly with glaze. Bake 20–25 minutes until puffed, golden brown, and crisp. Cool on wire racks away from drafts. Just before serving make a small slit in the side of each Profiterole and squirt in filling with a pastry bag fitted with a small, plain tip. Dust with confectioners' sugar and serve. Good with chocolate sauce. About 100 calories each (without chocolate sauce).

VARIATIONS:

Profiteroles au Chocolat: Fill with Chocolate Cream Filling, arrange in a large bowl, or pile in a small pyramid and pour Dark Chocolate Sauce over all. (*Note:* Pyramid will be easier to shape if you use chocolate sauce as a "glue" to stick profiteroles together.) About 150 calories each.

Ice Cream Profiteroles: Fill with any softened ice cream; wrap airtight and freeze. Thaw 10 minutes before serving. Top with Butterscotch or Fudge Sauce. These keep about 1 month in the freezer. About 160 calories each (without sauce).

Carolines: Make profiteroles as directed but fill with a cold savory mixture instead of a sweet one (creamed meat, seafood, or eggs are all suitable). To serve Carolines hot, reheat pastries *before filling*— 5–7 minutes at 325° F. Split, fill with hot savory mixture, and serve. Hot or cold, these make good cocktail or buffet food. Recipe too flexible for a meaningful calorie count.

CROQUEMBOUCHE

This pastry pyramid must be made on a dry day so that the glaze will harden properly. It can be made with Meringue

Kisses as well as Profiteroles and, for a really showy dessert, wreathed in spun sugar.*
Makes 15–18 servings

1 recipe Profiteroles

Glaze:

1 cup water
1½ cups sugar

Base:

1 (9″) cardboard circle covered with foil

Topping:

¼ cup sifted confectioners' sugar

Prepare *profiteroles* as directed. Heat and stir glaze ingredients until sugar dissolves, then boil uncovered, stirring occasionally, 10–15 minutes until the color of amber; keep warm over lowest heat. Place base on a large round platter and set near range. Using glaze as a "glue," stick a ring of profiteroles, browned sides up, around edge of base. Form a second, slightly smaller ring on top by sticking profiteroles in spaces of first row and slanting slightly toward center. Fill middle with unglazed Profiteroles to support "walls." Continue building pyramid

and top with a single Profiterole. (*Note:* If syrup should harden, add 1–2 tablespoons boiling water and heat until again syrupy.) Dust confectioners' sugar over Croquembouche. To serve, start at the top and pull off Profiteroles with 2 forks; allow 3–4 per person. About 190 calories for each of 15 servings, 160 calories for each of 18 servings.

BAKLAVA

A terrific (and calorific) Greek-Middle Eastern pastry, dripping with honey syrup. Packages of phyllo pastry leaves (sheets) are available in Middle Eastern groceries and bakeries.

Makes 30 servings

1 (1-pound) package phyllo pastry leaves at room temperature
1½ cups (about) melted unsalted butter (no substitute)

Filling:

1 pound walnuts or toasted, blanched almonds, chopped fine
½ cup sugar
1 teaspoon cinnamon

Syrup:

1 cup honey
1 cup sugar
1 cup water
2 tablespoons lemon juice
2 (1") strips lemon rind

Preheat oven to 350° F. Unroll pastry leaves and separate into 3 stacks of equal height; place 1 stack in a buttered 17"×12"×2" baking pan and brush every second sheet with melted butter. Mix filling and scatter ⅓ of it over pastry stack in pan; top with half of the leaves from the second stack, brushing every other one with butter. Sprinkle with another ⅓ filling, top with remaining leaves from second stack, again brushing with butter. Sprinkle with remaining filling and top with third stack of pastry leaves, again brushing every second leaf with butter. With a sharp knife, cut Baklava into 30 squares. Measure remaining butter and add a little extra, if needed, to total ½ cup; brown lightly over low heat, then pour evenly over pastry. Bake on center rack ½ hour, reduce oven to 300° F., and bake ½ hour longer. Meanwhile, prepare syrup: Heat and stir all ingredients in a heavy saucepan over moderate heat until sugar dissolves, then boil slowly 20 minutes. Strain syrup and pour over Baklava as soon as it comes from the oven. Serve warm or cold. About 310 calories per serving.

CHAPTER 22

CAKES, FILLINGS,
AND FROSTINGS

The old-fashioned art of cake making is being threatened by the dozens of excellent mixes on the market, also by a growing calorie consciousness. Consequently, this chapter is somewhat slimmer than cake chapters of other basic cookbooks. Still, there are plenty of recipes—some easy, some involved— for those who love to make cakes from "scratch" and those who want to learn how.

The Kinds of Cakes and How to Mix Them

There are dozens of different kinds of cakes, descended from three basic types: *the butter or creamed cakes* (those containing butter or some fat, also baking powder or soda to leaven), *the sponge cakes* (air-leavened cakes made with a great many eggs or egg whites) and *the chiffon* (a combination of the butter and sponge, containing some fat —usually cooking oil—and a high proportion of eggs). The type of cake determines the method of mixing:

Butter Cakes:

Conventional Method of Mixing (this can be done either by hand or electric mixer): Have butter, margarine, or shortening at room temperature (except in sultry summer weather, when butter or margarine is best used straight from the refrigerator); cream (moderate mixer speed) until light, gradually add sugar, and cream until fluffy. Add eggs (or egg yolks), one at a time, beating well after each addition. Add sifted dry ingredients (lowest mixer speed) alternately with the liquid, beginning and ending with the dry and adding ¼ to ⅓ at a time. Finally, if eggs have been separated, beat whites to soft peaks and fold in by hand. (*Note:* If cake contains minced fruits and/or nuts, gently fold in at the end. To keep them from sinking to the bottom of the cake during baking, hold out a bit [about ¼–⅓] of the dry ingredients, toss with the minced fruits or nuts and fold in along with them.)

Quick or One-Bowl Method: This streamlined way of mixing cakes more or less arrived with electric mixers and should not be used for old-fashioned butter cakes. It is closer to the muffin method of mixing than the conventional cake method in that the sifted dry ingredients go into the bowl first, the combined liquids are added all at once, and the two beaten just enough to blend (use low, then moderate mixer speed and scrape down beaters and sides of bowl as needed). Sometimes the eggs are separated, the yolks being added along with the other liquid ingredients and the whites folded in at the last.

Sponge Cakes (these include Angel Food as well as the different types of sponge):

True Sponge: Have egg yolks at room temperature and beat until frothy; add sugar gradually and beat until very thick and the color of cream (use moderate to high mixer speed or lots of elbow grease if beating by hand). Add sifted dry ingredients a little at a time and mix well after each addition (low mixer speed). Beat egg whites (also at room temperature) to soft peaks and fold in by hand.

Angel Food: These cakes can be made by electric mixer, but you'll get better volume if you do the beating by hand, preferably with a balloon whip in an unlined copper bowl. The trouble with mixers is that they overbeat and break down the egg whites. Even with hand beating there is great temptation to whip the whites into tall stiff peaks. Properly beaten, however, the peaks should be soft and the whites flow, not run, when the bowl is tipped. For greatest stability, they should be beaten with a little of the sugar; the remainder is sifted and added with the flour, a little at a time.

Chiffon Cakes: These are best made with an electric mixer. Flour, sugar, and other dry ingredients go into the bowl first; oil, egg yolks, liquids, and flavorings are added to a well in the dry ingredients and the mixture beaten at slow, then moderate speed, until batter is smooth and satiny. Egg whites, beaten to very stiff peaks, are then folded in just enough to blend.

About Essential Ingredients for Cakes

A cake will be no better than what goes into it. Choose ingredients of top quality; do not improvise, substituting one ingredient for another, but use the types of sugars, flours, shortenings, and leavenings recipes specify.

Fat: Essential to butter cakes for texture, tenderness, and flavor. Butter adds the best flavor, but vegetable shortening, some cooks believe, produces a higher, more tender cake. By combining the two, you can produce a cake of exceptionally fine flavor and volume. Do not use margarine interchangeably for butter unless recipe gives it as an alternate; margarine has somewhat greater shortening power than butter, and in a cake of delicate balance it may make the cake fall or split. Do not use hard fats like lard for making cakes and do not use cooking oil unless recipes call for it.

Sugar: This, of course, means granulated sugar unless recipe specifies light or dark brown sugar. When using brown sugar, make sure it is fresh and soft and moist (it is virtually impossible to remove or beat out hard lumps from old, dried sugar). And when measuring brown sugar, *pack* the sugar into the measuring cup.

Eggs: Egg sizes vary enormously (see chapter on eggs and cheese); those used in developing these recipes were large. For greater cake volume, have eggs at room temperature.

Flour: Cake and all-purpose flour can both be used in making cakes but should not be used interchangeably for one another, at least, not measure for measure. To use one in place of the other, make the following adjustments:

1 cup sifted cake flour=⅞ cup sifted all-purpose flour
1 cup sifted all-purpose flour=1 cup plus 2 tablespoons sifted cake flour

Cake flour produces an exceptionally fine-textured, tender cake, and experts prefer it, especially for butter cakes. All-purpose flour, with slightly more body, is more reliable and a better choice for beginners. Self-rising flour, which contains both baking powder and salt, can be used in recipes calling for both baking powder and salt. To use, simply sift and measure the amount of flour called for and omit baking powder and salt. A word of caution: Self-rising flour should be absolutely fresh, otherwise it may not do a proper job of leavening. No matter what kind of flour you're using, always sift before measuring, spoon into the measure lightly, and level off top with the edge, not the flat side, of a knife or spatula. *A note about the presifted flours:* Though excellent for sauces and gravies, they do not produce as fine-grained cakes as the old-fashioned sift-yourself flours.

IMPORTANT NOTE: *All cake recipes in this book should be made with all-purpose flour unless recipe specifies cake flour.*

Leavenings: Air can leaven a cake and so can steam, but when we speak of leavenings, we usually mean baking soda (if cake contains sour milk or other acid ingredient) or baking powder. There are three basic kinds of baking powders: *double-acting,* which releases leavening gases on contact with moisture and again during baking; *tartrate,* a single-acting powder that releases a volume of gas the instant it's dampened, and *phosphate,* a slightly slower-to-react single-acting powder. Read can labels carefully to determine which type of baking powder you're dealing with. Do not substitute one type for another unless you bear in mind that 1 teaspoon double-acting powder has the leavening power of 1½ teaspoons phosphate powder and 2 teaspoons tartrate powder. Tartrate powder is particularly tricky and should not be used unless the cake is mixed zip-quick and popped straight into the oven; it does, however, produce cakes of unusually fine grain. All baking powders lose potency on standing, so it's best to buy in small quantities and store tightly covered. *To test a baking powder's effectiveness:* Mix 1 teaspoon baking powder with ⅓ cup warm water; if it fizzes, the baking powder's good; if it doesn't, better buy a new supply. If you're in the middle of a cake and discover that your can of baking powder is inactive or empty, you can get by using this *emergency homemade baking powder:*

2 teaspoons cream of tartar ⎫ to leaven
1 teaspoon baking soda ⎬ each 1 cup
½ teaspoon salt ⎭ flour

IMPORTANT NOTE: *Baking powder in the cake recipes that follow is double-acting baking powder.*

Milk: Milk, in a cake recipe, means sweet whole milk.

Flavorings: Always use finest quality true extracts or flavorings, not perfumy imitations that can spoil an otherwise fine cake. Also make sure nuts are strictly fresh.

Some Cake-Making Terms and Techniques

To Beat: This refers to vigorous mixing with a spoon (use a comfortable, long-handled wooden spoon for best results) in a round and round motion, also to beating with a rotary or electric mixer.

To Blend: To combine one ingredient with another until absolutely homogeneous, as in blending chocolate into a batter.

To Cream: To work one or more ingredients, usually fat or fat and sugar, by beating with an electric mixer or by pressing over and over against the side of a bowl with the back of a spoon until soft and creamy. Properly creamed for a cake, butter (or butter and sugar) will be very pale yellow, fluffy, and neither greasy nor sugary. This will take 3–4 minutes in an electric mixer, sometimes, when eggs are added, mixture will seem to curdle; this will not affect the cake.

To Dredge: To toss chopped nuts, dried or candied fruits with flour, sugar, or other dry ingredients to prevent their sinking to the bottom of a cake during baking.

Dry Ingredients: Flour, baking powder or other leavening, salt (and sometimes cocoa or other dry ingredients) sifted together.

To Fill: To put layers of a cake together with filling (usually a softer mixture than frosting).

To Fold In: To incorporate one mixture into another, usually a light one such as beaten egg whites, into a batter using a very gentle over and over motion with minimum loss of lightness and air.

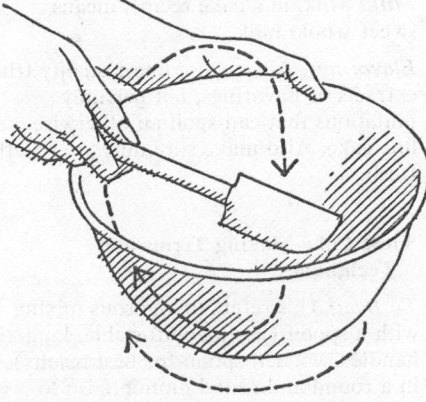

A rubber spatula is the best implement to use, though spoons, even portable electric mixers set at lowest speed and drawn through the mixture with a folding motion, work well.

To Frost: To spread with frosting.

To Glaze: To cover thinly with hard icing, fruit purée, or other shiny mixture.

To Ice: To frost.

To Mix: To blend a number of ingredients together by stirring or beating.

To Sift: To separate fine from coarse particles or to blend dry ingredients by passing them through a fine sieve or flour sifter.

To Stir: To mix in a circular motion, gently without beating.

To Whip: To beat rapidly with a whisk, rotary or electric beater to incorporate as much air as possible as in whipping cream or beating egg whites to stiff peaks.

To Work: To soften or blend by kneading or creaming.

How to Make Better Cakes

About Pans and Preparing Pans:

– For lightly, evenly browned cakes, use shiny baking pans rather than dark or discolored ones, which will overbrown— even burn—the cake. Do not use glass baking dishes unless you compensate for their slow heat conduction by raising oven temperature 25° F. They bake cakes too slowly, may dry them out, or form a thick hard crust all round. When using the new nonstick pans, follow manufacturer's directions closely, also watch baking cakes carefully until you learn how fast or slow pans conduct heat.

– Grease or grease and flour pans or not as recipes direct. As a general rule, any batter containing butter or other fat must be baked in a greased pan and, if extra rich, in a greased and floured pan. Grease bottoms of pans only unless recipes direct to the contrary. Cakes will rise more evenly all round if they can cling to ungreased pan sides.

– For greasing, use melted clarified butter* (unsalted) if you aren't on a budget, and shortening or cooking oil if you are. Apply thinly and evenly with a pastry brush or wad of paper toweling.

(*Note:* If batter is extra rich or contains sticky fruit, you may even need to grease the new nonstick pans.) To grease and flour, simply shake a small amount of flour into a greased pan, tilt back and forth until there is a thin, even layer of flour over bottom, then tap out excess.

– To simplify dishwashing, line pan bottoms with wax paper cut to fit or with packaged cake pan liners, available in most large department stores, then grease or not, as directed.

– *For best results, always use pan sizes recipes specify.* There are occasions, however, when a different shape is needed, and there are a number of batters that will bake successfully in pan shapes or sizes other than those recommended: all of the simple butter cakes, Real Sponge Cake, Devil's Food Cake,

Recommended Pan Size	Alternate Pan Size
2 (8") Layers	1½–2 dozen cupcakes
3 (8") Layers	2 (9"×9"×2") pans
1 (9") layer	1 (8"×8"×2") pan
2 (9") layers	1 (13"×9"×2") pan 1 (15½"×10½"×1") jelly-roll pan 2 (8"×8"×2") pans 1 (9") tube pan 2½ dozen cupcakes
1 (13"×9"×2") pan	2 (8"×8"×2") pans 1 (10") tube pan 2 (9") layers 2 (15½"×10½"×1") jelly-roll pans 2 (9"×5"×3") loaves
1 (9"×5"×3") pan	1 (9"×9"×2") pan 2 dozen cupcakes

Nut Cake, Spice Cake, White Wedding Cake, Burnt Sugar Cake, Basic White Cake. Avoid changing pans for Pound Cake, any of the chiffons, other sponges and loaf cakes. Use the table above as a guide and, unless recipe specifies to the contrary, fill pans no more than half full. Bake any leftover batter as cupcakes.

About Mixing Cakes:

– Read recipe through before beginning it and make sure you have all ingredients on hand.
– Have all utensils out, pans prepared, and ingredients measured and sifted before beginning.
– Have all ingredients at room temperature (except in very hot weather) before beginning. In summer, simply take straight from refrigerator.
– When using an electric mixer, use a medium speed for the creaming but a low speed for working in dry and liquid ingredients unless recipes direct to the contrary.
– When mixing by hand, use a comfortable, long-handled wooden spoon.
– Always cream fat and sugar thoroughly—it's virtually impossible to

overbeat at this point. *But* mix in dry ingredients with a light touch, just enough to blend. Overbeating at this point will make the cake tough.
– Fold in beaten egg whites last, *very gently,* so you don't break down the volume.

About Placing Batter in Pans:

– Always put batter in cool pans and never fill more than ½–⅔ full.
– Spread batter well to edges of pan.
– When making a layer cake, apportion batter evenly between pans so layers will be of equal size. Using an ice cream ball scoop and filling pans by adding a scoopful of batter first to one pan and then the other is a trick experts use.
– Once pans are filled, tap gently to break any large air bubbles.

About Baking:

– Have oven checked and regulated often by a local serviceman so it is as accurate as possible. Also make sure it stands level on the floor, otherwise cakes may be lopsided.
– Let oven preheat a full 15 minutes before baking.

– Unless recipes direct otherwise, bake cakes as near the center of the oven as possible. Those placed too low may burn on the bottom, those placed too high on top.

– When baking several cakes or layers at once, stagger on shelves, leaving plenty of room around them so heat can circulate evenly. Never let pans touch each other or oven walls.

– Cake baking time breaks down into 4 quarters, the first 2 being the most critical (don't open oven door during this time or jar oven in any way).

First Quarter of Baking . . . cake begins to rise
Second Quarter of Baking . . . cake continues to rise and browns slightly
Third Quarter of Baking . . . cake continues browning
Fourth Quarter of Baking . . . cake finishes browning and shrinks from sides of pan

To tell when cakes are done, use the following tests:
– Insert cake tester or toothpick in center of cake; if it comes out clean with no crumbs adhering, cake is done.
– Gently press top of cake; if it is springy to the touch and finger leaves no imprint, cake is done.
– Examine edges of pan; if cake has pulled away from pan, it is done.

About Cooling Cakes and Removing from Pans:

Butter Cakes:
– Cool upright in pans on a wire rack about 10 minutes before turning out.
– Loosen edges of cake with a spatula, invert cake on rack, then turn right side up and cool thoroughly before frosting.

Sponge and Chiffon Cakes:
– Cool cake thoroughly upside down in pan. If pan does not have "feet" so that it will stand upside down, simply "hang" on a 1-quart soft drink bottle by inserting bottle neck into pan tube.
– Loosen cake edges (and around center

tube) and invert on cake plate. Do not turn right side up.

About Storing and Keeping Cakes: Any cake with a custard or whipped cream filling or frosting should be kept refrigerated. Others last longest kept in a cake keeper in a cool spot. Fruit cakes should be wrapped in rum- or fruit-juice-soaked cheesecloth, then in foil and stored airtight in a cool, dark place.

About Freezing Cakes: Nearly all cakes freeze well; for details, see the chapter on freezing.

About Cutting Cakes (solid lines indicate cuts that should be made first, dotted lines successive cuts). Use a thin, sharp-pointed knife for butter cakes, a serrated knife or fine thread and a seesaw motion for sponge, angel, and chiffon cakes.

Layer Cakes:

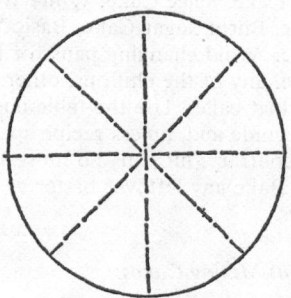

Conventional Way

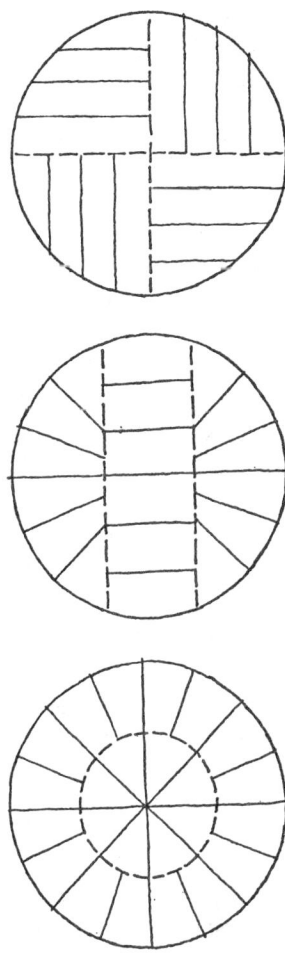

For More Servings

Loaf Cakes:

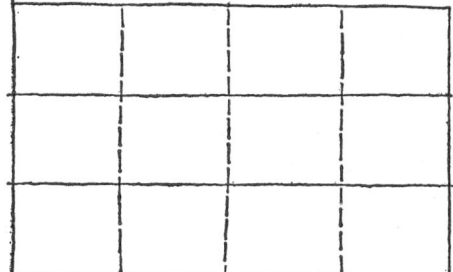

Conventional Way

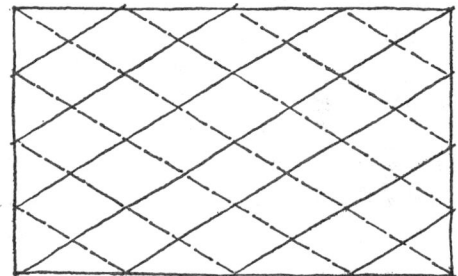

For More Servings

Tiered Wedding Cakes:

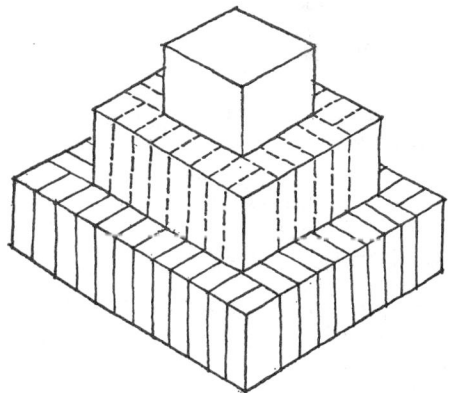

The cutting procedure for tiered cakes, whether round or square, is essentially the same. Cut bottom tier all around, then cut middle tier, again cut bottom tier, lift off top tier and present to bride, finally, cut remaining middle tier.

Why Things Sometimes Go Wrong With Cakes

Occasionally, despite all care and pre-caution, a cake will fail. Here are some common causes of cake failures, how to recognize and remedy them.

Description	Cause
Collapsed Center	Too much sugar or shortening; too little baking powder; underbaking
Fallen Cake	Same as collapsed center; also too little flour
Lopsided Cake	Unlevel oven shelves; also, sometimes, cake pans touching one another or oven walls
Cake Overflowing Pan	Using too small a pan
Heavy Cake	Too much sugar or too little baking powder
Dry Cake	Too much flour or too little shortening; also overbaking
Coarse Texture	Too much shortening or baking powder; undermixing; too low an oven heat
Uneven Texture	Undermixing
Cracked or Uneven Top	Too much flour or too hot an oven
Sticky Top or Crust	Too much sugar
Uneven Browning	Crowding oven rack; using dark pans; baking at too high a temperature

Note: For tips on baking cakes at high altitudes, see section High Altitude Cooking.

¢ BASIC TWO-EGG BUTTER CAKE

An economical all-purpose cake.
Makes two 8″ layers

1¾ cups sifted cake flour
2 teaspoons baking powder
¼ teaspoon salt
½ cup milk
1 teaspoon vanilla
½ cup butter or margarine, softened to room temperature
1 cup sugar
2 eggs

Preheat oven to 375° F. Sift flour with baking powder and salt and set aside; combine milk and vanilla. Cream butter until light, add sugar gradually, continuing to cream until fluffy. Add eggs, one at a time, beating well after each addi-tion. Add dry ingredients alternately with milk, beginning and ending with the dry and adding about ⅓ of total at a time. Beat *just* until smooth. Spoon into 2 greased and floured 8″ layer cake pans and bake 25–30 minutes until cakes shrink slightly from sides of pans and are springy to the touch; cool upright in pans on wire racks 5–7 minutes, then invert on racks. Turn layers right side up and cool completely. Fill and frost as desired. About 175 calories for each of 12 servings (unfrosted).

BASIC THREE-EGG BUTTER CAKE

Slightly richer than the Two-Egg Butter Cake (above).
Makes 2 9″ layers

2 cups sifted cake flour

2 teaspoons baking powder
¼ teaspoon salt
½ cup milk
1 teaspoon vanilla
½ cup butter or magarine, softened to
    room temperature
1 cup sugar
3 eggs, separated

Preheat oven to 375° F. Sift flour with
baking powder and salt and set aside;
combine milk and vanilla. Cream butter
until light, add sugar gradually, continuing to cream until fluffy. Add egg
yolks, one at a time, beating well after
each addition. Add dry ingredients
alternately with milk, beginning and
ending with the dry and adding about
⅓ of total at a time; beat *just* until
smooth. Beat egg whites until soft peaks
form, and gently fold into batter. Spoon
into 2 greased and floured 9″ layer
cake pans and bake 25–30 minutes until
cakes shrink slightly from sides of pans
and are springy to the touch; cool upright in pans on wire racks 5–7 minutes;
then invert on racks. Turn right side up
and cool completely. Fill and frost as
desired. About 165 calories for each of
16 servings (unfrosted).

VARIATION:

Poppy Seed Cake: Pour milk called for
over ⅓ cup poppy seeds and let stand at
room temperature 3–4 hours, then
proceed as recipe directs. Fill with Poppy
Seed Cream Filling and frost with a
butter cream frosting. About 165
calories for each of 16 servings
(unfrosted).

SWEET LEMON LOAF

This cake is very tender, so slice it thick.
Makes a 9″ × 5″ × 3″ loaf

1½ cups sifted flour
1½ teaspoons baking powder
¼ teaspoon salt
½ cup butter or margarine, softened to
    room temperature
1 cup sugar
2 eggs
½ cup milk
Finely grated rind and juice of 1 lemon

½ cup coarsely chopped pecans or
    walnuts (optional)

Glaze:

Juice of 1 lemon
¼ cup sugar

Preheat oven to 350° F. Sift flour with
baking powder and salt and set aside.
Cream butter until light, slowly add
sugar and beat until fluffy. Add eggs, one
at a time, beating well after each addition. Add dry ingredients alternately with
milk, beginning and ending with the dry
and adding about ⅓ of the total at a
time. Add lemon rind and juice and beat
just until smooth. Stir in nuts, if you like,
and spoon into a greased and floured
9″ × 5″ × 3″ loaf pan. Bake about 1
hour until cake pulls from sides of pan
and is springy to the touch. Let cool
upright in pan on a wire rack while you
make the glaze. Heat lemon juice and
sugar over low heat, stirring until sugar
dissolves. Pour evenly over top of cake
and let cake cool thoroughly in pan
before turning out. Wrap tightly and
store overnight before cutting. About
450 calories for each of 8 servings
(without optional nuts).

BASIC WHITE OR SILVER CAKE

For a really silvery cake, use vegetable
shortening.
Makes 2 9″ layers

2½ cups sifted cake flour
1 tablespoon baking powder
½ teaspoon salt
⅔ cup butter, margarine, or vegetable
    shortening
1½ cups sugar
1 teaspoon vanilla
½ teaspoon almond extract
¾ cup milk
4 egg whites, at room temperature

Preheat oven to 375° F. Sift flour with
baking powder and salt and set aside.
Cream butter until light, gradually add
1¼ cups sugar, continuing to cream until
fluffy. Add vanilla and almond extract
and at low speed, mix in dry ingredients
alternately with the milk, beginning and
ending with the dry and adding about

⅓ of the total at a time. In a separate bowl beat egg whites until frothy, slowly add remaining sugar, and beat to very soft peaks. Fold into batter just until blended. Spoon into 2 greased and floured 9″ layer cake pans and bake 20–25 minutes until cakes shrink slightly from sides of pans and are springy to the touch. Cool upright in pans on wire racks 5 minutes, then invert on racks, turn right side up, and cool completely. Fill and frost as desired. About 200 calories for each of 16 servings (unfrosted).

VARIATIONS:

Marble Cake: Prepare batter as directed and divide in half. Blend 3 tablespoons cocoa with 3 tablespoons hot water and mix into half the batter. Drop alternate spoonfuls of white and chocolate batter into pans, dividing amounts equally; zigzag a knife through batter to marbleize and bake as directed. About 210 calories for each of 16 servings (unfrosted).

Rainbow Cake: Prepare batter as directed and divide in 3 equal parts. Tint one pink, one yellow, and one green (or, if you prefer, leave one plain). Layer equal amounts of each color in each pan and bake as directed. When cool, put layers together with any white or pastel frosting (7-Minute is particularly good). Divide remaining frosting in 3 parts and tint as you did cake batter. Put alternate spoonfuls of each color on top and sides of cake, then swirl with a broad spatula to marbleize. If you like, scatter crushed peppermint candy on top. About 200 calories for each of 16 servings (unfrosted).

Lady Baltimore Cake: Prepare cake as directed; also prepare 1 recipe 7-Minute Frosting. To about ⅓ of the frosting, add ¾ cup coarsely chopped pecans or walnuts, ½ cup seedless raisins, ⅓ cup diced dried figs, and ¼ teaspoon almond extract; put cake layers together with the fruit frosting, then ice with remaining 7-Minute Frosting. About 270 calories for each of 16 servings (frosted and filled).

Coconut Cream Cake: Prepare cake as directed; also prepare a double recipe of Basic Vanilla Cream Filling; divide in half and mix ½ cup flaked coconut into one part. Put cake layers together with coconut filling. Spread remaining filling over top and sides of cake, then coat thickly with flaked coconut (about 1½ cups). About 250 calories for each of 16 servings (frosted and filled).

BOSTON CREAM PIE

Makes a 9″ 2-layer cake

2 9″ layers Basic Three-Egg Butter Cake, Real Sponge Cake, or layers made from a yellow cake mix
1 recipe Basic Vanilla Cream Filling, Double Cream Filling, or 1½ cups sweetened whipped cream
1 recipe Chocolate Glaze

Sandwich cake layers together with filling, spread glaze on top, and let stand until glaze hardens. Store in refrigerator. About 250 calories for each of 16 servings (made with Basic Three-Egg Butter Cake and Basic Vanilla Cream Filling).

WHITE WEDDING CAKE

Begin recipe about 3–4 days before the wedding. For a 3-tier cake, each 2 cake layers thick, you will need to triple the batter recipe given below. Make 3 separate lots rather than a giant unmanageable one. You will need: 1 (13″) round cake pan about 2½″ deep, 2 (10″), and 2 (7″) round cake pans of similar depth (these special wedding cake pans can be bought at specialty shops and confectionery supply houses); a heavy 16″ circle of plywood neatly covered with heavy foil; 1 (10″) and 1 (7″) white cardboard cake divider; a large lazy Susan to simplify decorating and a pastry bag and decorative star tip.

Makes a 3-tier cake, about 100 servings

Batter (Make Up 3 Separate Batches):

6 cups sifted flour
2 tablespoons baking powder
2 teaspoons salt
2 cups milk, at room temperature

2 teaspoons vanilla
1 pound butter or margarine or 1⅓
  cups margarine and ⅔ cup vegetable
  shortening
4 cups sugar
8 eggs, at room temperature
2 teaspoons lemon extract
2 tablespoons finely grated lemon rind

Filling:

1 recipe Pineapple-Coconut Filling

Frosting:

4 times the recipe Basic Lemon or Orange
  Butter Cream Frosting, tinted pale
  pink or yellow if you like

Decorations:

About 4 yards narrow white satin ribbon
Small sprays of artificial or real flowers
  matching bride's bouquet

Preheat oven to 325° F. Sift flour with
baking powder and salt and set aside.
Combine milk and vanilla. Cream butter
until light, add sugar gradually, continue
to cream until fluffy. Add eggs, one at a
time, beating well after each addition.
Mix in lemon extract and rind. Add dry
ingredients alternately with milk, beginning and ending with the dry and adding about ⅙ of the total at a time.
Beat just until smooth. Spoon into one
ungreased 13″ and one ungreased 7″
round cake pan lined on the bottom
with wax paper, filling no more than half
full (this is a high-rising batter). Cover
small pan with wax paper and refrigerate; bake large layer 60–65 minutes
until it pulls from sides of pan and is
springy to the touch. Cool upright
in pan on wire rack 10 minutes, then
loosen and invert on rack; peel off paper,
turn right side up, and cool thoroughly.

Meanwhile, mix a second batch of
batter, cover bowl, and refrigerate until
needed. Wash, dry, and reline 13″ pan
with wax paper, half fill with batter;
also half fill second 7″ pan, cover, and
refrigerate. Bake 13″ layer as before,
turn out and cool. Mix a third batch of
batter, spoon into the 2 (10″) pans,
ungreased but lined on the bottom with
wax paper, filling no more than half full;

cover with wax paper and refrigerate.
When both large layers are baked, raise
oven to 350° F. and bake the 2 small-
and 2 medium-size layers, staggering on
oven shelves and allowing plenty of
space between pans. Small layers will
bake in 40–45 minutes, the medium in
about 50. Cool and turn out as you did
the large layers. When all cakes are
thoroughly cool, wrap airtight in foil and
store in a cool place, not refrigerator.
(Note: Any leftover batter can be baked
as cupcakes—do not more than half fill
muffin cups.)

To Assemble and Frost Cake: Center
foil-covered plywood circle on lazy
Susan and cover outer rim with wax
paper triangles, letting points hang over
(these are to catch frosting drips). Center
1 (13″) layer on board, spread with
filling and top with second (13″) layer,
bottom side up. Spread lightly with
frosting, just to seal in crumbs. Place a
10″ layer on a 10″ divider, spread with
filling, and center on 13″ tier; top with
second (10″) layer, bottom side up, and
frost top lightly. Set 7″ layer on 7″
divider, spread with filling, and center
on 10″ tier; top with final 7″ layer.
Beginning at the top, lightly frost sides
of each tier to seal in crumbs and let dry
at room temperature 1–2 hours. Starting
again at the top, frost entire cake.

(Note: If you plan to decorate with
frosting, make surface as smooth as
possible.) For a simple finish, swirl
frosting into waves with a wide metal
spatula. Let dry 2 hours before decorating further.

To Decorate: Beginning at the top, pipe
decorative borders around base of top
and middle tiers, then add rosettes,
scrolls, any designs you fancy (see Tips
on Decorating Cakes). Pull out wax
paper triangles around base of cake and
pipe a decorative border around base of
cake. Keep in a cool, dust-free place or
invert a very large cardboard carton
over cake, making sure top and sides do
not touch.

Final Trimmings: On the day of the wedding, make rosettes from the ribbon and arrange with tiny flower sprays between the tiers, "gluing" to cake with a little frosting. Decorate top with small posies wreathed in ribbon or any suitable commercial decorations. Keep cool until serving time.

To Serve: See About Cutting Cakes. About 140 calories for each of 100 servings.

POUND CAKE

Here is a truly old-fashioned pound cake made without baking powder so the texture will be firm, fine, and moist. Makes a 9"×5"×3" loaf

2¼ cups sifted cake flour
¼ teaspoon salt
⅛ teaspoon nutmeg or mace
1 cup butter (no substitute), softened to room temperature
1 cup sugar
5 eggs, separated
1 teaspoon vanilla or orange extract or 1 tablespoon finely grated lemon rind

Preheat oven to 350° F. Line a 9"×5"×3" loaf pan with greased wax paper (let paper lop over rim about ½" to make removing cake easier). Sift flour, salt, and nutmeg together and set aside. Cream butter until light, then add sugar slowly, creaming until fluffy. Beat egg yolks until thick and light, add to butter mixture, a little at a time, beating well after each addition. Blend flour in gradually, then mix in vanilla and beat *just* until smooth. Beat egg whites until soft peaks form and fold gently into batter. Spoon into pan and bake 65–70 minutes until cake pulls slightly from sides of pan. Cool upright in pan on a wire cake rack 30 minutes before slicing. About 360 calories for each of 10 servings.

THELMA'S 1, 2, 3, 4 CAKE

This cake keeps well if wrapped airtight; it also freezes well.
Makes a 9" tube cake

3 cups sifted flour

2 teaspoons baking powder
¼ teaspoon salt
1 cup milk
1 teaspoon vanilla or almond, lemon or orange extract
1 cup butter or margarine, softened to room temperature, or vegetable shortening
2 cups sugar
4 eggs, separated

Preheat oven to 350° F. Sift flour with baking powder and salt and set aside; combine milk and vanilla. Cream butter until light; add sugar gradually, continuing to cream until fluffy. Beat egg yolks until thick and pale yellow; mix into creamed mixture. Add dry ingredients alternately with milk, beginning and ending with the dry and adding about ⅓ of the total at a time. Beat *just* until smooth. Beat egg whites until soft peaks form and gently fold into batter. Spoon into a greased and floured 9" tube pan and bake about 1 hour until cake shrinks slightly from sides of pan and is springy to the touch. Cool cake upright in its pan on a wire rack 25–30 minutes; loosen edges, invert on rack, and cool thoroughly. Serve plain or frost with a butter cream frosting. About 305 calories for each of 16 servings (unfrosted).

BASIC CHOCOLATE BUTTER CAKE

Makes 2 9" layers

2 cups sifted cake flour
¾ teaspoon baking soda
½ teaspoon salt
¾ cup buttermilk or sour milk
1 teaspoon vanilla
½ cup butter or margarine, softened to room temperature
1⅓ cups sugar
3 eggs
3 (1-ounce) squares unsweetened chocolate, melted or 3 (1-ounce) envelopes no-melt unsweetened chocolate

Preheat oven to 350° F. Sift flour with baking soda and salt and set aside. Combine buttermilk and vanilla. Cream butter until light, add sugar gradually, beating until fluffy. Add eggs, one at a time, beating well after each addition; mix in chocolate. Add dry ingredients alternately with milk, beginning and ending with the dry and adding about ⅓ of the total at a time. Beat *just* until smooth. Spoon into 2 greased and floured 9″ layer cake pans and bake 30–35 minutes until cakes shrink slightly from sides of pans and are springy to the touch. Cool upright in pans on wire racks 5–7 minutes, then invert on racks. Turn cakes right side up and cool thoroughly. Fill and frost as desired. About 220 calories for each of 16 servings (unfrosted).

VARIATION:

Mocha Butter Cake: Prepare as directed but blend 1 tablespoon instant coffee powder with buttermilk and vanilla. Fill and frost with Mocha Butter Cream Frosting. About 220 calories for each of 16 servings (unfrosted).

☒ CRAZY CHOCOLATE CAKE

"Crazy" in that the method of mixing is wholly unconventional. The cake, however, is unusually fine-grained.
Makes 2 9″ layers

Group I:

2 cups sugar
1 cup sour milk
1 cup butter, softened to room
  temperature (no substitute)
1½ teaspoons vanilla
3 cups sifted cake flour

Group II:

2 eggs
¾ cup unsifted cocoa
2 teaspoons baking soda
¼ teaspoon salt
1 cup boiling strong coffee

Preheat oven to 325° F. Add ingredients to a large mixing bowl by alternating between Groups I and II. For example, first into bowl would be sugar, second eggs, third sour milk, fourth cocoa, and so on. Do not mix. When all ingredients

are in the bowl, beat 1 minute with an electric mixer at moderate speed or 3 minutes by hand. Pour into 2 well-greased 9″ layer cake pans and bake 45–50 minutes until cakes shrink slightly from sides of pans and are springy to the touch. Cool upright in pans on wire racks 5–7 minutes, then invert to remove. Turn cakes right side up and cool thoroughly. Fill and frost as desired (good with 7-Minute Frosting). About 300 calories for each of 16 servings (unfrosted).

¢ DEVIL'S FOOD CAKE

Dark and rich.
Makes 2 9″ layers

2 cups sifted cake flour
2 cups sugar
½ cup cocoa
1 teaspoon baking soda
½ teaspoon salt
½ cup vegetable shortening
1¼ cups milk
1 teaspoon vanilla
3 eggs
1 teaspoon baking powder

Preheat oven to 350° F. Sift flour, sugar, cocoa, baking soda, and salt into large electric mixer bowl. Drop in shortening and add ¾ cup milk and the vanilla. Mix at lowest speed 15 seconds just to blend. (*Note:* Hold a towel over bowl to catch splatters.) Beat 2 minutes at medium speed, scraping bowl and beaters once or twice. Add remaining ingredients and beat 2 minutes longer. Spoon into 2 ungreased (9″) layer cake pans lined with wax paper and bake 40–45 minutes until cakes shrink slightly from sides of pan and are springy to the touch. Cool upright in pans on wire racks 5 minutes, then invert on racks, peel off paper, turn right side up, and cool completely. Fill and frost as desired. About 250 calories for each of 16 servings (unfrosted).

VARIATIONS:

¢ **Devil's Food Loaf:** Prepare as directed and bake in an ungreased 13″×9″×2″ pan lined with wax paper. Same time, same temperature. About

165 calories for each of 24 servings (unfrosted).

Mocha Fudge Cake: Prepare as directed but substitute 3 melted (1-ounce) squares unsweetened chocolate or 3 (1-ounce) envelopes no-melt unsweetened chocolate for the cocoa, add 1 tablespoon instant coffee powder and mix in with the shortening. About 260 calories for each of 16 servings (unfrosted).

SACHERTORTE

Sachertorte, Vienna's famous chocolate cake, is densely dark and rich. It was invented 150 years or so ago by Franz Sacher for Prince Metternich when calories meant nothing.
Makes a 9″ cake

1 cup sifted cake flour
¼ teaspoon salt
6 (1-ounce) squares unsweetened or semisweet chocolate
¾ cup butter, softened to room temperature (no substitute)
1 cup sugar
6 egg yolks
8 egg whites
1 cup apricot preserves
1 recipe Chocolate Glaze
1 cup heavy cream, whipped to soft peaks (optional topping)

Preheat oven to 350° F. Sift flour with salt and set aside. Melt chocolate over simmering water, then cool. Cream butter until light, gradually add ¾ cup sugar and cream until fluffy. Add egg yolks, one at a time, beating well after each addition. Beat in chocolate, scraping bowl often until thoroughly blended. In a separate bowl, beat egg whites until frothy; gradually add remaining sugar and beat until soft peaks form. Stir about ½ cup egg whites into creamed mixture. Sift and fold in flour alternately with remaining egg whites, beginning and ending with flour and adding about ¼ at a time. Spoon into a 9″ spring form pan lined on the bottom with wax paper, then greased and floured on bottom *and* sides. Tap pan lightly on counter to break any large bubbles.

Bake on center oven rack 45–55 minutes, until top is springy to the touch. Cool upright in pan on a wire rack 10 minutes, loosen cake, and remove spring form; invert cake on rack, remove pan bottom, and carefully peel off paper. Turn right side up and cool completely on rack. Halve cake horizontally, spread with preserves, put layers together and spread top thinly with preserves. Spoon chocolate glaze on top and let stand until set. Cut in small pieces and serve topped with whipped cream. About 365 calories for each of 16 servings (without cream).

BÛCHE DE NOËL (CHRISTMAS LOG)

A rich chocolate log traditionally served on Christmas Eve in France.
Makes 1 roll

½ cup sifted cake flour
¾ teaspoon baking powder
¼ teaspoon salt
4 eggs, at room temperature
¾ cup sugar
1 teaspoon vanilla
3 (1-ounce) squares unsweetened chocolate, melted, or 3 (1-ounce) envelopes no-melt unsweetened chocolate
2 tablespoons very strong warm black coffee
Sifted cocoa
2 recipes Mocha or Chocolate Butter Cream Frosting

Preheat oven to 400° F. Line the bottom of a 15½″×10½″×1″ jelly-roll pan with wax paper. Sift flour with baking powder and salt and set aside. With electric or rotary beater, beat eggs at high speed until foamy; slowly add sugar, a little at a time, and beat until very thick and cream colored. Mix in vanilla, blend chocolate with coffee and mix into batter. Fold in dry ingredients just until blended. Spoon into pan, spreading batter evenly. Bake 12–14 minutes until springy to the touch. Loosen edges of cake and invert on a clean dish towel heavily sprinkled with sifted cocoa. Peel off paper and cut off crisp edges with a sharp knife. Beginning at the short side, roll cake and towel up; cool completely on a wire rack. Unroll, remove towel, spread about 1 cup mocha frosting to within ½″ of edges and carefully reroll. Wrap loosely in foil and chill 1 hour. With a sharp knife, cut a small piece from each end on the diagonal and reserve to make "branches." Place roll seam side down on serving plate and tuck a strip of wax paper under each side. Spread with remaining frosting, then draw fork tines in a wavy pattern the length of log to resemble bark or use a serrated ribbon tip and a pastry bag to force frosting out in a ridged bark effect. Lay trimmed-off ends on roll cut side down at an angle, off center. Press into frosting lightly, then frost edges. If you wish, sprinkle log with minced pistachio nuts and write "Noel" in white decorative icing. About 680 calories for each of 12 servings.

BURNT SUGAR CAKE

Makes 2 9″ layers

Burnt Sugar Syrup:

¾ cup sugar
¾ cup boiling water

Cake:

3 cups sifted cake flour
1 tablespoon baking powder
½ teaspoon salt
½ cup milk
1 teaspoon vanilla
1 teaspoon maple flavoring (optional)
½ cup burnt sugar syrup
¾ cup butter or margarine
1⅓ cups sugar
3 eggs

Frosting:

⅓ cup butter or margarine
1 (1-pound) box confectioners' sugar, sifted
¼ cup burnt sugar syrup
1 teaspoon vanilla
¼ teaspoon salt

For syrup: Melt sugar in a heavy skillet or saucepan over low heat, stirring now and then. Heat, stirring constantly, until amber colored. Off heat, gradually stir in boiling water (it will foam up), return to low heat, and stir until sugar dissolves. Cool to room temperature. Preheat oven to 350° F. Sift flour with baking powder and salt and set aside. Mix milk with flavorings and ½ cup burnt sugar syrup. Cream butter until light, add sugar gradually, creaming until fluffy. Add eggs, one at a time, beating well after each addition. Add dry ingredients alternately with milk mixture, beginning and ending with the dry and adding about ⅓ of the total at a time. Beat just until smooth. Spoon into 2 ungreased 9″ layer pans lined with wax paper. Bake about ½ hour until cakes pull from sides of pan and are springy to the touch. Cool upright in pans on wire racks 5 minutes, loosen, and invert on racks; peel off paper, turn right side up, and cool. For the frosting: Cream butter until fluffy, beat in sugar, a little at a time, adding alternately with the syrup. Mix in vanilla and salt and beat until satiny and of good spreading consistency. If mixture seems stiff, thin with a little additional syrup. Put cake layers together with some frosting, then frost with the remainder. About 445 calories for each of 16 servings.

NUT CAKE

Use the nuts you like best for making this cake.
Makes a 13″×9″×2″ cake

2 cups sifted cake flour
1½ teaspoons baking powder
½ teaspoon salt
⅓ cup milk, at room temperature
1 teaspoon vanilla
½ teaspoon almond extract
1 cup butter or margarine
1 cup sugar
3 eggs
1¼ cups finely chopped toasted nuts (pecans, walnuts or black walnuts, filberts, or almonds)
Few untoasted nut halves (garnish)

Preheat oven to 350° F. Sift flour with baking powder and salt and set aside. Mix milk, vanilla and almond extract. Cream butter until light, add sugar gradually, continuing to cream until fluffy. Add eggs, one at a time, beating well after each addition. Add flour alternately with milk, beginning and ending with flour. Stir in chopped nuts. Spoon into an ungreased 13″×9″×2″ pan lined on the bottom with wax paper and scatter nut halves on top. Bake about ½ hour until cake pulls from sides of pan and is springy to the touch. Cool upright in pan on a wire rack 10 minutes, loosen edges of cake, invert on rack, peel off paper, turn right side up, and cool thoroughly. (*Note:* If you prefer, omit garnish and, when cake is cool, frost as desired.) About 140 calories for each of 24 servings (unfrosted).

VARIATIONS:

Nut Layer Cake: Prepare batter as directed, spoon into 2 ungreased (9″) layer cake pans lined on the bottom with wax paper and bake 25–30 minutes at 350° F. until cakes test done. Cool as directed; fill and frost as desired. About 210 calories for each of 16 servings (unfrosted).

Nut-Seed Cake: Add 2 tablespoons caraway or poppy seeds to cake batter along with flour. About 140 calories for each of 24 servings (unfrosted).

Nut-Candied Fruit Cake: Add ½ cup minced mixed candied fruit to cake batter along with flour. About 160 calories for each of 24 servings (unfrosted).

Orange-Nut Cake: Prepare as directed but add the finely grated rind of 2 oranges to creamed mixture before adding eggs. About 140 calories for each of 24 servings (unfrosted).

Chocolate-Nut Cake: Prepare as directed but add 4 melted (1-ounce) squares semisweet chocolate to creamed mixture before adding eggs. About 175 calories for each of 24 servings (unfrosted).

ORANGE, DATE, AND NUT LOAF

Makes a 13″×9″×2″ cake

4 cups sifted flour
1 teaspoon salt
1 teaspoon baking soda
1 cup butter or margarine, softened to room temperature
2 cups sugar
4 eggs
1 teaspoon vanilla
2 tablespoons finely grated orange rind
1½ cups buttermilk
1½ cups coarsely chopped pecans or walnuts
1 cup minced, pitted dates or ½ cup each minced dates and sultana raisins

Preheat oven to 350° F. Sift flour with salt and baking soda and set aside. Cream butter until light, add sugar gradually and cream until fluffy. Add eggs, one at a time, beating well after each addition. Blend in vanilla and orange rind. Add dry ingredients, about ⅓ at a time, alternately with buttermilk, beginning and ending with the dry. Stir in nuts and dates and spoon into a greased and floured 13″×9″×2″ pan. Bake about 1 hour and 10 minutes or until cake shrinks slightly from sides of pan and top is springy to the touch. Cool cake upright in its pan on a wire rack. Cut in squares and serve. About 285 calories for each of 24 servings.

WALNUT TORTE

No flour needed in this *torte;* the nuts and bread crumbs give it body.
Makes a 9″ 2-layer cake

1 cup lightly packed, finely ground walnuts or black walnuts
½ cup fine dry bread crumbs
6 eggs, separated
1 cup sugar
¼ teaspoon almond extract
2 teaspoons finely grated orange or lemon rind

Preheat oven to 350° F. Mix nuts and crumbs and set aside. Beat egg yolks until thick and pale yellow, slowly add ¾ cup sugar, and beat until very thick and the color of cream. In a separate bowl, beat egg whites until frothy, gradually add remaining sugar, and beat until soft peaks form. Fold egg whites into yolk mixture alternately with nut mixture, beginning and ending with whites. Stir in almond extract and grated orange or lemon rind. Spoon into 2 ungreased (9″) round pans lined on the bottom with wax paper. Bake about 20 minutes or until a faint imprint remains when top is touched. Cool upright in pans on wire racks 5–7 minutes, carefully loosen cakes with a spatula, invert on racks, peel off paper, turn right side up, and cool thoroughly. Fill and frost as desired—especially good with Mocha or Nut Butter Cream Frosting. About 140 calories for each of 16 servings (unfrosted).

VARIATION:

Hazelnut Torte: Prepare as directed, using finely ground, blanched hazelnuts or filberts instead of walnuts. About 140 calories for each of 16 servings (unfrosted).

APPLESAUCE CAKE

A moist old-fashioned cake. It contains no eggs, so it is suitable for those allergic to them.
Makes a 9″ cake

2 cups sifted flour
½ teaspoon baking soda
1 teaspoon baking powder
½ teaspoon salt
¾ teaspoon cinnamon
½ teaspoon nutmeg
¼ teaspoon cloves
2 tablespoons milk
1 teaspoon vanilla
1 cup applesauce
½ cup butter or margarine
1 cup firmly packed light brown sugar
¾ cup seedless raisins
¾ cup minced pecans or walnuts

Preheat oven to 350° F. Sift flour with baking soda, baking powder, salt and spices and set aside. Mix milk, vanilla, and applesauce. Cream butter until light, add sugar gradually, continuing to cream until fluffy. Add dry ingredients alternately with applesauce mixture, beginning and ending with the dry and adding about ⅓ of the total at a time. Beat just until smooth. Mix in raisins and nuts. Spoon into an ungreased 9″ pan lined with wax paper and bake 35 minutes until cake shrinks slightly from sides of pan and is springy to the touch. Cool upright in pan on a wire rack 5 minutes, then invert on rack, peel off paper, turn right side up, and cool completely. Frost or not as desired or serve slightly warm with Lemon-Raisin Sauce. About 225 calories for each of 16 servings (unfrosted).

¢ SPICE CAKE

Makes an 8″ × 8″ × 2″ cake

1½ cups sifted flour
1½ teaspoons baking powder
¼ teaspoon salt
1 teaspoon cinnamon
¾ teaspoon nutmeg
¼ teaspoon allspice
¼ teaspoon cloves
¼ teaspoon ginger
½ cup plus 2 tablespoons milk
1 teaspoon vanilla
½ cup butter or margarine
1 cup sugar
1 egg

Preheat oven to 350°F. Sift flour with baking powder, salt, and spices and set aside. Mix milk and vanilla. Cream butter until light, add sugar gradually, continuing to cream until fluffy. Add egg and beat well. Add dry ingredients alternately with milk, beginning and ending with the dry and adding about ⅓ of the total at a time. Spoon into an ungreased 8″ × 8″ × 2″ pan lined on the bottom with wax paper. Bake about 45 minutes until cake pulls from sides of pan and is springy to the touch. Cool upright in pan on a wire rack 10 minutes, loosen edges, and invert on a rack. Peel off paper, turn right side up and cool. Frost or not as desired. About 200 calories for each of 12 servings (unfrosted).

VARIATIONS:

¢ **Spice Layer Cakes:** Double the ingredients, prepare batter as directed, and bake in 2 ungreased 9″ layer cake pans lined on the bottom with wax paper about 45 minutes at 350° F. About 240 calories for each of 20 servings (unfrosted).

¢ **Lemon-Spice Cake:** Prepare as directed but add 1 teaspoon lemon extract and the finely grated rind of 1 lemon along with the egg. About 200 calories for each of 12 servings (unfrosted).

¢ **Raisin-Spice Cake:** Add ¼ cup seedless raisins to batter with final addition of flour. About 210 calories for each of 12 servings (unfrosted).

¢ GINGERBREAD

Makes a 9″×9″×2″ cake

2½ cups sifted flour
1½ teaspoons baking soda
½ teaspoon salt
1¼ teaspoons ginger
1 teaspoon cinnamon
½ teaspoon cloves
½ teaspoon allspice
½ cup vegetable shortening
½ cup sugar
1 egg
1 cup molasses
1 cup boiling water

Preheat oven to 350° F. Sift flour with soda, salt, and spices and set aside. Cream shortening until fluffy, then add sugar, a little at a time, beating well after each addition. Beat in egg. Combine molasses and boiling water and add alternately with the sifted dry ingredients, beginning and ending with the dry and beating after each addition just enough to mix. Pour into a greased, wax-paper-lined 9″×9″×2″ pan and bake 50–60 minutes until gingerbread pulls from sides of pan and is springy to the touch. Cool gingerbread upright in its pan on a wire rack. Cut in large squares and serve. About 200 calories for each of 16 servings.

¢ GRANDMOTHER'S SOFT GINGER CAKE

This thin batter bakes into an unusually soft-crumbed cake.
Makes a 9″×9″×2″ cake

2½ cups sifted cake flour
1½ teaspoons baking soda
¼ teaspoon salt
1 teaspoon cinnamon
1 teaspoon cloves
1 teaspoon ginger
¼ teaspoon nutmeg
½ cup vegetable shortening
⅔ cup sugar
1 egg
⅔ cup molasses
1¼ cups boiling water

Preheat oven to 375° F. Sift flour with soda, salt, and spices and set aside. Cream shortening until fluffy, add sugar, a little at a time, creaming well after each addition. Beat in egg. Combine molasses and boiling water and add alternately with sifted dry ingredients, beginning and ending with the dry. Beat after each addition to mix. Pour into a lightly greased 9″×9″×2″ pan and bake 40–45 minutes until cake pulls from sides of pan and is springy to the touch. Cool cake upright in its pan on a wire rack. To serve, cut in large squares and top, if you like, with whipped cream or vanilla ice cream. About 165 calories for each of 16 servings (without whipped cream or ice cream).

PINEAPPLE UPSIDE-DOWN CAKE

Makes a 10″ round or 9″ square cake

⅓ cup butter or margarine
½ cup firmly packed light or dark brown sugar
1 (1-pound 4-ounce) can sliced pineapple, drained
8 maraschino cherry halves, well drained
14–16 pecan halves

Cake:

1⅓ cups sifted flour
1 cup sugar
2 teaspoons baking powder
½ teaspoon salt

⅓ cup vegetable shortening
⅔ cup milk
1 teaspoon vanilla
½ teaspoon lemon extract
1 teaspoon finely grated lemon rind
1 egg

Preheat oven to 350° F. Melt butter in a heavy 10″ skillet (with ovenproof handle) or in a 9″×9″×2″ pan over low heat. Off heat, sprinkle brown sugar evenly over butter. Arrange pineapple in a pattern on sugar and fill spaces with cherries and pecans. Set aside while mixing cake. Sift flour, sugar, baking powder, and salt into large mixer bowl, drop in shortening and milk and beat at lowest speed just to blend. (*Note:* It's a good idea to hold a towel over bowl to prevent spills at first.) Beat 2 minutes at medium speed, scraping bowl and beaters once or twice. Add remaining ingredients and beat 2 minutes longer, scraping bowl now and then. Pour batter evenly over fruit. Bake 40–50 minutes until cake is golden brown and pulls from sides of pan. Cool upright in pan on wire rack 3–4 minutes, loosen edges of cake, invert on heatproof serving plate, and leave pan over cake 1–2 minutes. Remove pan and serve warm or cold with sweetened whipped cream. About 250 calories for each of 16 servings (without whipped cream).

VARIATIONS:

Apricot or Peach Upside-Down Cake: Substitute 1 (1-pound 4-ounce) can drained apricot or cling peach halves for pineapple rings; arrange hollow side up on sugar. Or use well-drained sliced cling peaches. Proceed as directed. About 250 calories for each of 16 servings.

Apple Upside-Down Cake: Peel, core, and thinly slice 2 large tart apples and arrange in an attractive pattern on top of sugar. If you like, dot here and there with pitted cooked prunes, seedless or sultana raisins. Proceed as directed. About 230 calories for each of 16 servings (without prunes or raisins).

Gingerbread Upside-Down Cake: Prepare fruit layer as directed. Prepare cake batter substituting ⅓ cup each dark molasses and boiling water for the milk; mix and cool before adding. Also add 1 teaspoon each ginger and nutmeg along with egg and other flavorings. Bake as directed. About 265 calories for each of 16 servings.

⚖️ REAL SPONGE CAKE

Note all the variations you can make from this one basic recipe.
Makes 2 9″ layers

6 eggs, separated, at room temperature
1 cup sifted sugar
½ teaspoon salt
2 teaspoons vanilla
1 cup sifted cake flour

Preheat oven to 350° F. Beat egg yolks until thick, slowly add sugar, salt, and vanilla, beating constantly; continue beating until very thick and the color of cream. Slowly mix in flour (lowest mixer speed). Beat egg whites to soft peaks (they should *just* flow when bowl is tipped) and fold lightly into batter, about ¼ at a time. Spoon into 2 wax-paper-lined 9″ layer cake pans and bake 25 minutes until golden and springy. Cool upright in pans on a wire rack 5 minutes, then loosen carefully with a spatula and turn out. Peel off paper, turn right side up, and cool completely. Fill and frost as desired. About 100 calories for each of 16 servings (unfrosted).

To Bake in Other Pans:

⚖️ **Tube Pan:** Spoon batter into an ungreased 10″ tube pan and bake 45 minutes at 350° F. Invert at once and cool completely in pan. (*Note:* If cut in 12 wedges and served unfrosted, each slice will total about 125 calories.)

⚖️ **Loaf Pan:** Spoon batter into a wax-paper-lined 13″×9″×2″ loaf pan and bake ½ hour at 350° F. Cool upright in pan 5 minutes, invert, peel off paper, turn right side up, and cool. 63 calories per unfrosted 2″ square.

⚖ **Muffin Pans** (Makes 2 Dozen Cupcakes): Spoon batter into muffin tins lined with cupcake papers, filling each ¾ full; bake 12–15 minutes at 350° F. Remove from pans and cool upright on wire racks. 63 calories per unfrosted cupcake.

VARIATIONS:

⚖ **Lemon Sponge Cake** (Approximately the same calorie counts as above): Prepare as directed but flavor with 1 teaspoon lemon extract and 1 tablespoon each lemon juice and finely grated rind instead of vanilla.

⚖ **Orange Sponge Cake** (Approximately the same calorie counts as above): Prepare as directed but flavor with 1 teaspoon orange extract, 1 tablespoon lemon juice, and 2 tablespoons finely grated orange rind instead of vanilla.

Nut Sponge Cake: Prepare as directed but just before folding in whites mix in ¾–1 cup minced pecans, walnuts, or toasted, blanched almonds. About 150 calories for each of 16 servings (unfrosted).

⚖ **Chocolate Sponge Cake:** Sift ¼ cup cocoa with flour and add to egg-sugar mixture alternately with vanilla and 2 tablespoons cold water, beginning and ending with flour. Proceed as directed. About 115 calories for each of 16 servings (unfrosted).

⚖ **Coffee Sponge Cake:** Beat egg yolks, sugar, salt, and vanilla as directed; add flour alternately with 1 tablespoon instant coffee powder dissolved in 2 tablespoons cold water; proceed as directed. About 100 calories for each of 16 servings (unfrosted).

⚖ **Mocha Sponge Cake:** Prepare Chocolate Sponge Cake (above) as directed but dissolve 1 tablespoon instant coffee powder in the 2 tablespoons cold water. Mix in alternately with flour as directed. About 115 calories for each of 16 servings (unfrosted).

Coconut Cream Sponge Cake: Prepare Real Sponge Cake as directed and put layers together with sweetened whipped cream mixed with ½ cup flaked coconut. Frost with sweetened whipped cream and sprinkle with flaked coconut (about 1 cup). About 185 calories for each of 16 servings (frosted).

¢ ⚖ **Economy Sponge Cake:** Sift the flour with 1½ teaspoons baking powder. Beat 3 egg yolks with the sugar as directed, then add flour alternately with ¼ cup cold water mixed with 2 teaspoons vanilla, beginning and ending with dry ingredients. Beat 3 egg whites with ¼ teaspoon cream of tartar and proceed as directed. Bake 20–25 minutes at 350° F. in the 9″ layer cake pans. Do not put layers together but serve unfrosted, each layer cut in 12 wedges. About 55 calories for each of 12 servings. (*Note:* This recipe is a good choice for persons on low-cholesterol diets.)

¢ ⚖ **Economy Chocolate Sponge Cake:** Prepare Economy Sponge Cake as directed but sift ¼ cup cocoa along with the flour. About 60 calories for each of 12 servings.

⊠ ⚖ **EASY SPONGE LOAF**
Makes an 8″×8″×2″ cake

3 eggs
¾ cup sugar
⅛ teaspoon salt
1 teaspoon vanilla
¾ cup sifted flour

Preheat oven to 350° F. Beat eggs until frothy, slowly add sugar and salt, beating constantly; continue beating until thick and the color of cream. Mix in vanilla, then flour, a little at a time. Spoon into an 8″×8″×2″ pan lined with greased wax paper and bake 35 minutes until golden and springy to the touch. Cool cake upright in its pan on a wire rack 5 minutes, then loosen carefully with a spatula and turn out. Peel off wax paper and cool before cutting or using in Trifle or other recipes. About 70 calories per 2″ square (unfrosted).

⚖ GÉNOISE

Génoise, the classic European sponge cake, is the foundation of showy *Gâteaux* and *Petits Fours*. It can be made entirely by mixer instead of the more traditional way given here. But eggs should be slightly warmed before beating, then beaten until very thick and creamy in a warm bowl about 15 minutes (beware of overheating mixer). Makes a 9″ cake

4 eggs, at room temperature
¾ cup superfine sugar
1 teaspoon vanilla
1 teaspoon finely grated lemon or
orange rind
¾ cup sifted cake flour
*3 tablespoons melted clarified butter,**
cooled to lukewarm (no substitute)

Preheat oven to 350° F. Butter a 9″ spring form pan, line bottom with wax paper, butter paper, and dust bottom and sides of pan with flour. Place eggs, sugar, vanilla, and rind in a large stainless-steel or copper mixing bowl and set *over*, not in, a large pan ⅓ filled with barely simmering water. With a large wire whisk, beat until mixture foams and is almost doubled in volume, about 5–6 minutes. Transfer to large mixer bowl and beat at moderately high speed until very thick (when beaters are raised, mixture should drop in a slowly dissolving ribbon). Set bowl on damp cloth, sift in ¼ cup flour, fold in gently, then fold in 1 tablespoon butter. Continue adding flour and butter the same way, the same amounts each time, until all are incorporated. Pour batter into pan, tap lightly on counter to break any large bubbles, and bake on center oven rack 30–35 minutes until cake shrinks slightly from sides of pan and is springy to the touch. Cool upright in pan on a wire rack 10 minutes (cake will sink a little in the middle), then loosen edges carefully with a spatula and remove spring form sides. Invert on rack, lift off pan bottom, peel off paper, turn cake right side up, and cool thoroughly. Slice into 2 or 3 layers and fill and frost as desired.

About 125 calories for each of 12 servings (unfrosted).

VARIATIONS:

Favorite Génoise: Sprinkle cut surfaces of Génoise with 2–3 tablespoons kirsch or other fruit liqueur and sandwich layers together with apricot purée and sweetened whipped cream. Frost with Basic or Coffee Butter Cream Frosting and scatter thickly with minced filberts or pistachio nuts. Recipe too flexible for a meaningful calorie count.

⚖ **Génoise for Petits Fours:** Prepare batter as directed and pour into an ungreased 13″×9″×2″ pan lined on the bottom with wax paper. Bake 25 minutes at 350° F. Cool as directed. Cake is now ready to cut and make into Petits Fours. About 30 calories for each of 48 petits fours (unfrosted).

⚖ **Génoise for a Four-Layer Cake:** Use 6 eggs, 1 cup superfine sugar, 1½ teaspoons each vanilla and grated rind, 1 cup sifted cake flour, and ¼ cup clarified butter. Prepare batter as directed and divide between 4 wax-paper-lined, greased, and floured 9″ layer cake pans. Bake 15 minutes at 350° F., then cool as directed. About 125 calories for each of 16 servings (unfrosted).

PETITS FOURS

The tricky part of petits fours is frosting them evenly. A base coat of Apricot Glaze seals in loose crumbs, makes the icing go on more smoothly, and keeps the little cakes moist. A help, too, is frosting with Quick Glacé Icing instead of dipping—the more traditional and tedious way—in melted fondant. Makes about 4 dozen

1 (1–2-day-old) Génoise for Petits Fours
or any firm-textured white or yellow
cake baked in a 13″×9″×2″ pan
1 recipe Apricot Glaze
3 recipes Quick Glacé or Chocolate
Glacé Icing (or some of each)
1 recipe Decorative Butter Cream
Frosting or Royal Icing
Silver dragées, candied violets,
chocolate shot (optional)

Cut all hard edges from cake, then even up loaf by trimming off browned top so it is uniformly 1½″ thick. Cut in 1½″ squares or rounds, small rectangles or triangles and brush off loose crumbs. Spear cakes, 1 at a time, on a fork and dip in apricot glaze to coat top and sides. Place uncoated side down about 2″ apart on wire racks set over baking sheets. Let stand uncovered 1 hour. Prepare icing as directed, then, using a large spoon, ladle over cakes, one at a time, so top and sides are evenly coated. (*Note:* Enough must be poured over all at once to create a smooth finish.) Scrape up run-over on baking sheets and remelt. Let cakes dry thoroughly before decorating. Tint decorative icing as desired and pipe on tiny flowers, leaves, stars, scrolls, any design you like. Or decorate with silver *dragées,* candied violets, chocolate shot (see Tips on Decorating Cakes). Store in a cool, dry place until serving time. (*Note:* Petits fours can be frozen but their frosting won't be quite so glossy.) About 240 calories each.

VARIATION:

⚖️ **Simple Petits Fours:** Frost top of a trimmed sheet of cake with Basic Butter Cream Frosting or any flavored butter cream frosting, then cut in desired shapes with a sharp knife, wiping blade after each cut. Decorate with bits of candied cherries, slivered almonds, strips of angelica, colored sugar, or toasted coconut. About 100 calories each.

JELLY ROLL

The filling *needn't* be jelly, as these variations prove.
Makes 1 roll

¾ cup sifted cake flour
¾ teaspoon baking powder
¼ teaspoon salt
4 eggs, at room temperature
¾ cup sugar
1 teaspoon vanilla
Confectioners' sugar
1 cup any fruit jelly or jam or 1½ cups
　sweetened whipped cream

Preheat oven to 400° F. Line the bottom of a 15½″×10½″×1″ jelly-roll pan with wax paper. Sift flour with baking powder and salt and set aside. With electric or rotary beater, beat eggs at high speed until foamy; slowly add sugar, a little at a time, and continue beating until very thick and the color of mayonnaise. Mix in vanilla. Fold in flour mixture just until blended. Spoon into pan, spreading batter evenly. Bake 12–14 minutes until golden and springy to the touch. Loosen edges of cake, invert on a clean dish towel lightly dusted with sifted confectioners' sugar. Peel off paper carefully and trim off crisp edges with a very sharp knife. Starting from short side, roll cake and towel up together and cool on a wire rack. Unroll, remove towel, spread jelly to within ½″ of edges and reroll. Place seam side down and sift confectioners' sugar on top. (*Note:* If jelly or jam is stiff, warm slightly before spreading.) When serving, make slices about 1″ thick. About 190 calories for each of 12 servings (made with jelly or jam).

VARIATIONS:

Lemon Jelly Roll: Prepare cake as directed but omit vanilla; add ½ teaspoon lemon extract and 1 tablespoon each lemon juice and finely grated lemon rind. Fill with Lemon Cheese or Lemon Filling instead of jelly. About 190 calories for each of 12 servings.

Orange Jelly Roll: Prepare as directed but omit vanilla and flavor with ½ teaspoon orange extract and 1 tablespoon finely grated orange rind. Fill with Orange Filling. About 190 calories for each of 12 servings.

Strawberry Jelly Roll: Prepare batter as directed and mix in 2 or 3 drops red food coloring; bake as directed. Spread with 1 cup heavy cream, sweetened and whipped to soft peaks, and 1½–2 cups thinly sliced strawberries and roll; or fill with Strawberry Filling. Wrap in foil and chill 1 hour. Sprinkle with confectioners' sugar before serving. About 180 calories for each of 12 servings (made with whipped cream and sliced strawberries).

Chocolate Jelly Roll: When making cake, reduce flour to ⅔ cup, add ¼ cup cocoa and sift with flour, baking powder, and salt. Add 1 tablespoon cold water along with vanilla; bake as directed. Fill with Chocolate Cream Filling or Chocolate, Mocha, or Coffee Butter Cream Frosting. Dust with confectioners' sugar before serving. About 380 calories for each of 12 servings (made with Chocolate, Mocha, or Coffee Butter Cream Frosting).

⚖ ANGEL FOOD CAKE

If you follow the directions exactly, you'll bake a tall and tender cake.
Makes a 10″ tube cake

1½ cups sifted sugar
1 cup sifted cake flour
1 teaspoon cream of tartar
¼ teaspoon salt
12 egg whites, at room temperature
1 teaspoon vanilla
½ teaspoon almond extract
1 teaspoon lemon juice

Preheat oven to 325° F. Sift ¾ cup sugar with the flour and set aside. Sprinkle cream of tartar and salt over egg whites; beat with a wire whisk or rotary beater until *very* soft peaks form (whites should *flow, not run,* when bowl is tipped). Sift a little of the remaining sugar over whites and gently fold in, using a whisk; repeat until all sugar is mixed in. Now sift a little sugar-flour mixture over whites, and fold in with the whisk; repeat until all is incorporated (it may take as many as 10 additions). Fold in vanilla, almond extract, and lemon juice. Pour batter into an *ungreased* 10″ tube pan and bake 1–1¼ hours until cake is lightly browned and has pulled from the sides of pan. Invert pan and cool cake thoroughly in pan; then loosen edges with a spatula and turn out. Leave plain or frost as desired. About 120 calories for a piece equal to 1/12 of the cake (unfrosted).

BASIC CHIFFON CAKE

For maximum volume use 1–2 more egg whites than yolks.
Makes a 10″ tube cake

2¼ cups sifted cake flour
1½ cups sugar
1 teaspoon salt
1 tablespoon baking powder
½ cup cooking oil
6 egg yolks, at room temperature
¾ cup cold water
2 teaspoons vanilla
1 teaspoon lemon juice
7–8 egg whites, at room temperature
½ teaspoon cream of tartar

Preheat oven to 325° F. Sift flour, sugar, salt, and baking powder into a bowl. Make a well in the center and add, in the order listed, the oil, egg yolks, water, vanilla, and lemon juice. Beat until smooth. Using largest bowl and electric mixer or rotary beater, beat egg whites and cream of tartar until they will form *very stiff peaks* (whites should be stiffer than for Angel Food Cake or Meringue). With a rubber spatula, gently fold into batter, ¼ at a time, just until blended. Pour into an *ungreased* 10″ tube pan and bake 55 minutes; raise oven to 350° F. and bake 10 minutes longer until cake is lightly browned and has pulled from sides of pan. Invert and cool cake thoroughly in pan; loosen edges with a spatula and turn out. Leave plain or frost as desired. About 290 calories for each of 12 servings (unfrosted).

VARIATIONS:

Lemon Chiffon Cake: Prepare as directed but reduce vanilla to 1 teaspoon and add ½ teaspoon lemon extract and 2 tablespoons finely grated lemon rind. About 290 calories for each of 12 servings (unfrosted).

Orange Chiffon Cake: Prepare as directed but reduce vanilla to 1 teaspoon, substitute ¾ cup orange juice for the cold water, and add 2 tablespoons finely grated orange rind. About 290 calories for each of 12 servings (unfrosted).

Spiced Chiffon Cake: Prepare as directed but reduce vanilla to 1 teaspoon and add 1 teaspoon cinnamon and ½ teaspoon each nutmeg, cloves, and allspice. About 290 calories for each of 12 servings (unfrosted).

Butterscotch-Maple Chiffon Cake: Prepare as directed but substitute 2 cups firmly packed light brown sugar for the granulated, reduce vanilla to 1 teaspoon, omit lemon juice, and add 1–2 teaspoons maple flavoring. If you like, fold in ¾ cup finely chopped pecans or walnuts just before folding in egg whites. About 300 calories for each of 12 servings (without nuts and unfrosted).

Chocolate Chiffon Cake: Blend ⅓ cup cocoa with ¾ cup boiling water, then cool to room temperature. Reduce flour to 1¾ cups, sift with dry ingredients as directed, then add oil, egg yolks, cocoa mixture, and 1 teaspoon vanilla (omit lemon juice) and beat until smooth. Proceed as recipe directs. About 320 calories for each of 12 servings (unfrosted).

Mocha Chiffon Cake: Prepare Chocolate Chiffon Cake (above) as directed but blend cocoa with ¾ cup very strong hot black coffee instead of boiling water. About 320 calories for each of 12 servings (unfrosted).

LIGHT FRUIT CAKE

Makes a 9″×5″×3″ loaf

1¼ cups sifted flour
½ teaspoon baking powder
½ teaspoon salt
½ teaspoon nutmeg
¼ teaspoon ginger
½ cup butter or margarine
½ cup sugar
3 eggs
1 teaspoon vanilla
½ teaspoon almond extract
1 cup sultana raisins
1 pound mixed candied fruits (pineapple, orange, and lemon peel, citron), chopped fine
¼ pound candied red cherries, coarsely chopped

1 cup toasted, slivered almonds or coarsely chopped pecans or walnuts
Blanched almond halves (garnish)
Candied cherry halves (garnish)

Preheat oven to 300° F. Grease, then line the bottom and sides of a 9″×5″×3″ loaf pan with foil; grease foil lightly. Sift flour with baking powder, salt, and spices and set aside. Cream butter until light, gradually add sugar, continuing to cream until fluffy. Add eggs, 1 at a time, beating well after each addition. Mix in vanilla and almond extract. Add dry ingredients, about ⅓ cup at a time, beating just to blend. Toss raisins with candied fruits, cherries, and nuts, and stir into batter. Spoon into pan and decorate with almond and cherry halves. Bake 1½–1¾ hours until cake shrinks slightly from sides of pan, is lightly browned, and a metal skewer inserted in center comes out clean. Cool cake upright in pan on a wire rack ½ hour. Invert on rack, peel off foil, turn right side up and cool thoroughly. Wrap in brandy-, rum-, or fruit-juice-soaked cheesecloth, then in foil and store airtight 2–3 weeks before serving. About 260 calories for each of 20 servings.

JAMAICAN RUM CAKE

A superrich dark fruit cake that takes 2 days to make and 3 weeks to ripen. Makes 2 9″×5″×3″ loaves

1 cup dried currants
1½ cups seedless raisins
1 cup seeded raisins
¾ cup coarsely chopped dried black figs
¾ cup coarsely chopped pitted dates
½ cup coarsely chopped candied cherries
1½ cups minced mixed candied fruits
1½ cups dark Jamaican rum
2 cups sifted flour
2 teaspoons baking powder
1 teaspoon cinnamon
1 teaspoon nutmeg
½ teaspoon salt
1 cup butter or margarine, softened to room temperature
2 cups firmly packed dark brown sugar

5 eggs
¾ cup blanched, toasted, sliced almonds

The day before you bake the cake, place all fruits in a large bowl, add rum, mix well, cover, and let stand overnight at room temperature. Next day grease and line the bottom and sides of 2 (9″×5″ ×3″) loaf pans with brown paper or foil; grease linings well. Preheat oven to 275° F. Sift flour, baking powder, cinnamon, nutmeg, and salt together into a bowl. Cream butter until light; add sugar gradually and cream until fluffy. Beat in eggs, one at a time. Add dry ingredients, about ½ cup at a time, alternately with fruits (including any liquid in bottom of bowl), beginning and ending with dry ingredients. Fold in almonds. Spoon batter into pans and, if you wish, decorate tops with candied cherries and/or blanched almond halves. Place on center oven rack; half fill a roasting pan with water and place on rack below. Bake 4 hours until cakes shrink slightly from sides of pan. Cool upright in pans on wire racks 1 hour. Carefully turn out and peel off paper. Turn cakes right side up and cool thoroughly. Wrap in rum-soaked cheese-cloth, then in foil and store in an airtight container about 3 weeks to ripen. About 235 calories for each of 20 servings (from 1 loaf).

ROYAL FRUIT WEDDING CAKE

The rich dark fruit cake served alongside the bride's white cake used to be called the groom's cake. Today, either may be served as the wedding cake. There are advantages to the fruit cake: It can be made well ahead and, in fact, improves on standing (it's the best choice if the top tier is to be saved for the first anniversary). Disadvantages? Its hard Royal Icing, though more durable, is difficult to cut and in humid weather may "weep." This next recipe is a hundred years old. It makes an outstanding Christmas cake (⅓ of the recipe will make a 10″ tube cake). Makes a 3-tier cake, about 150 servings

Fruit Mixture:

1½ pounds citron, chopped fine
¾ pound candied orange peel, chopped fine
¾ pound candied lemon peel, chopped fine
6 ounces candied ginger, chopped fine
3 pounds seedless raisins
1½ pounds sultana raisins
1½ pounds dried currants
¾ pound candied cherries, coarsely chopped
¾ pound shelled pecans or walnuts, minced
Finely grated rind of 6 lemons
1½ cups orange marmalade
¾ cup lemon juice
¾ cup orange juice
1½ teaspoons vanilla
1 teaspoon almond extract

Cake Mixture:

6 cups sifted flour
1 tablespoon cinnamon
1½ teaspoons nutmeg
¾ teaspoon mace
¾ teaspoon cloves
¾ teaspoon allspice
1½ teaspoons baking powder
1½ teaspoons salt
1½ pounds butter or margarine
3 cups sugar
18 eggs

Decorations:

6 times the recipe Marzipan (make in 2 or 3 batches)
Lightly beaten whites of 2 eggs
3–4 times the recipe Royal Icing (make one batch at a time, as needed)
1 recipe Sugar Bells

Make cakes at least 2 weeks before the wedding; if properly stored, they can be made 2 months ahead. Place fruit mixture in a large bowl, toss well, cover, and let stand overnight at room temperature. Grease, then line bottom and sides of a 13″, a 10″, and a 7″ round cake pan with a double thickness of brown paper; grease paper well. Preheat oven to 250° F. Sift together twice the flour, spices, baking powder, and salt and set aside. Cream butter until light, add sugar gradually, and cream until fluffy. Add eggs, 1 at a time, beating well after each addition. Add dry ingredients, about 1 cup at a time, beating just to blend. (*Note:* Unless you have an extra-large mixing bowl, you will have to transfer batter to a large kettle before all dry ingredients are incorporated.) Stir in fruit mixture. Spoon batter into pans, filling to within ½″ of tops. Cover 13″ pan with foil and refrigerate. Bake smaller 2 cakes on center oven rack with a pan of water on rack underneath 4½–5 hours until cakes pull slightly from sides of pan and a metal skewer inserted in centers comes out clean. If cakes brown too fast, cover loosely with foil. Cool upright in pans on wire racks ½ hour, invert on racks, peel off paper, turn right side up, and cool thoroughly. Bake 13″ cake the same way 5½–6 hours. When all cakes are cool, wrap in brandy-, rum-, or fruit-juice-soaked cheesecloth, then in foil and store airtight.

To Decorate: A few days before the wedding, unwrap cakes and prepare *marzipan.* Turn cakes upside-down and fill small holes with marzipan. Cut a wax paper circle the size of each cake, sprinkle lightly with confectioners' sugar, then with a stockinette-covered rolling pin, roll marzipan out on wax paper circles ⅛″ thick. Trim away ragged edges so you have perfect circles; brush tops of cakes with lightly beaten egg white and invert circles on cakes of matching size. Peel off paper. Roll remaining marzipan ⅛″ thick and, using a ruler, cut in strips exactly the depth of each cake. Brush sides of cakes with egg white, then wrap a marzipan strip around each, *not* overlapping edges but trimming so they just meet; press lightly until as smooth as possible. (*Note:* Side strips may be put on in 2 or 3 pieces if easier, but surface *must be absolutely smooth.*) Let dry 3–4 hours at room temperature. At this point, each cake should be placed on a heavy cardboard circle cut to fit or metal divider disc (obtainable from con-

fectioners' supply houses). If tiers are to be separated by pillars, the supporting posts should be inserted and interlocking ornamental pillars attached (cakes are frosted and decorated individually on their respective divider discs). Make up Royal Icing, a batch at a time as needed, and frost top and sides of each cake *thinly* (if too thick, icing will crack), making surface as smooth as possible (it will help to dip spreading spatula in hot water occasionally, also to work with tier set on a lazy Susan). Let cakes dry overnight in a cool, dry, dust-free spot. Next day, make up additional icing as needed and pipe on decorations (see Tips on Decorating Cakes).

To Assemble: If cake is a simple tiered one, center largest tier on a serving tray (or plywood circle covered with heavy foil). Top with middle tier, then small one, and pipe a fluted border of icing around base of each tier. Add Sugar Bells and any other final decorative touches you like. Keep cake cool until serving time. If cake is a towering pillared one, decorate individual tiers and put together on location shortly before the reception.

To Cut and Serve: See About Cutting Cakes.
About 340 calories for each of 150 servings.

About Cupcakes

Cupcakes can be made from almost any cake batter if you use the following guide for filling pans: fill each muffin pan cup ⅔ full for conventional butter cake batters, fill ½ full for quick-method batters like that used for Easy Yellow Cupcakes, fill ¾ full for true sponge batters, and fill ⅞ full for chiffon cake batters. Use cupcake papers to save greasing and washing pans and to give cupcakes better shape. Or, if you prefer, grease and flour unlined muffin pan cups. Bake cupcakes at 375° F., 12–25 minutes, depending on batter, until springy to the touch.

⚖ ¢ ⊠ EASY YELLOW CUPCAKES

Makes 1½ dozen

1⅓ cups sifted flour
¾ cup sugar
2 teaspoons baking powder
¼ teaspoon salt
¼ cup vegetable shortening
⅔ cup milk
1 egg
1 teaspoon vanilla

Preheat oven to 375° F. Sift flour, sugar, baking powder, and salt together into a large mixing bowl. Add shortening and milk, stir to blend, then beat slowly about 1½ minutes with an electric mixer. Add egg and vanilla and beat slowly 1½ minutes. Spoon batter into muffin tins lined with cupcake papers, filling each half full. Bake 20–25 minutes until cakes are golden brown and springy to the touch. Remove cakes from pans and cool upright on wire racks. Frost as desired. About 105 calories each (unfrosted).

VARIATIONS:

⚖ ¢ ⊠ **Easy Chocolate Cupcakes:** Prepare as directed but add 2 (1-ounce) melted squares unsweetened chocolate or 2 (1-ounce) envelopes no-melt unsweetened chocolate along with egg and vanilla. About 125 calories each (unfrosted).

⚖ ¢ ⊠ **Easy Butterscotch-Spice Cupcakes:** Substitute ¾ cup firmly packed dark brown sugar for the granulated and 1 teaspoon maple flavoring for vanilla. Also sift ½ teaspoon each cinnamon and nutmeg along with dry ingredients, then proceed as directed. About 110 calories each (unfrosted).

⊠ **Easy Raisin-Nut Cupcakes:** Prepare as directed and mix in ½ cup each seedless raisins (or dried currants, minced pitted prunes, or dates) and minced walnuts or pecans. About 155 calories each (unfrosted).

¢ ⚖ ⊠ **Easy Orange Cupcakes:** Prepare as directed but use ⅓ cup each orange juice and milk instead of all milk; omit vanilla and add 2 teaspoons finely grated orange rind. About 105 calories each (unfrosted).

¢ ⚖ ⊠ **Easy Lemon Cupcakes:** Prepare as directed but substitute ¼ teaspoon lemon extract for vanilla and add the finely grated rind of 1 lemon. About 105 calories each (unfrosted).

⊠ **Chocolate Chip Cupcakes:** Prepare as directed and fold in 1 (6-ounce) package semisweet chocolate bits. About 170 calories each (unfrosted).

⚖ SOUR CREAM PATTY CAKES

You can quickly sour fresh cream by adding a little vinegar and letting stand in a warm place about ½ hour. For the amount of cream called for below, use 5 tablespoons heavy cream and 1 tablespoon vinegar.
Makes 1 dozen

1 cup sifted flour
1 teaspoon baking powder
6 tablespoons sugar
¼ teaspoon salt
¼ cup butter or margarine, chilled
1 egg, lightly beaten
6 tablespoons soured or unsoured fresh light cream
1 teaspoon grated orange or lemon rind
½ teaspoon orange or lemon extract

Preheat oven to 425° F. Sift flour with baking powder, sugar, and salt. Cut in butter with a pastry blender until mixture resembles coarse meal. Add egg and cream and mix well. (*Note:* If you use soured cream, mix curds with whey before measuring.) Stir in rind and extract. Spoon into greased and floured muffin tins, filling each cup ⅔ full. Bake 12 minutes or until tops spring back when touched. Remove cakes from pans and cool upright on a wire rack. About 125 calories each.

VARIATION:

Fruit or Nut Patty Cakes: Prepare as directed, adding 2–3 tablespoons chopped candied cherries or nuts or ¼ cup dried currants or seedless raisins along with the rind and extract. About 140 calories each.

EASY INDIVIDUAL FRUIT CAKES

Makes about 2 dozen

1 (1-pound 1-ounce) package pound
  cake mix
¾ cup brandy or sweet white wine
⅛ teaspoon cloves
¼ teaspoon ginger
¼ teaspoon nutmeg
¼ teaspoon cinnamon
¼ teaspoon orange extract
⅛ teaspoon almond extract
1 cup minced mixed candied fruit
½ cup seedless raisins
½ cup dried currants
1 tablespoon flour
1 cup finely chopped walnuts
Candied cherries or blanched almond
  halves (garnish)

Preheat oven to 325° F. Prepare cake mix by package directions, using the eggs but substituting brandy or wine for the liquid called for. Beat in spices and extracts. Dredge fruit in flour, then mix into batter along with nuts. Spoon into muffin tins lined with cupcake papers, filling each ⅔ full. Decorate tops with candied cherries or "daisies" made of almond halves. Bake 35–45 minutes until golden and springy to the touch. Cool cakes in papers (but not in pans) on wire racks. Peel off papers, wrap cakes in brandy- or wine-soaked cheesecloth, then in foil and "season" about 1 week in an airtight container. About 205 calories each.

FILLINGS AND FROSTINGS

"The icing on the cake" . . . the finishing touch. Not every cake needs an icing; some, in fact—pound cake, angel cake, fruit cake—are better

without it. But most cakes are bare without frosting of some sort. Generally speaking, superrich cakes call for less-than-superrich icings, plain cakes for something a little showy. The same holds true for layer cakes that are filled (between the layers) as well as frosted.

Some Tips on Frosting Cakes

Preparing the Cake:
– Cool cake thoroughly before frosting unless recipe directs otherwise.
– Trim cake so that it is symmetrical.
– Brush or rub off loose crumbs and trim away ragged edges with scissors; also trim or, using a fine grater, remove any overbrown top or bottom crust.
– Choose a flat plate 2″ larger in diameter than the cake and cover plate rim, petal-fashion, with triangles of wax paper, letting points hang over edge (these are to catch drips and keep plate clean). When cake is frosted, simply pull out wax paper.
– Center cake on plate, bottom side up if a tube cake, right side up if a layer or loaf cake.
– To make the frosting easier, set cake plate on a lazy Susan or turned-upside-down bowl so that you can rotate it as you spread on frosting.

Filling the Cake:
– Place one layer bottom side up on plate as directed above.
– Prepare and cool filling before using unless recipe calls for a warm filling (warm fillings usually seep into cakes too much, making them soggy).
– Spread filling, not too thick, to within ¼″ of edge and, if extra soft, to within 1″ of edge. Add next layer, bottom side up (*unless* it is the top layer) and press lightly into filling.
– Repeat until all layers are in place, remembering that the final layer should be placed right side up.
– Wipe off any filling that has squished out from between layers onto sides of cake.

Frosting the Cake:

If Frosting Is Thick:
– Using a metal spatula, spread a thin layer over top and sides of cake to seal in crumbs. Let dry at room temperature 10 minutes.
– Refrost sides of cake, working from bottom up, to form a slight "rim" around top of cake; this helps keep sides straight and top level.
– Pile remaining frosting on top and spread out to meet edges.
– If frosting is soft, swirl into waves with spatula or draw fork tines lightly over surface.

If Frosting Is Thin:
– Avoid using glazes or hard-drying thin frostings like Royal Icing in humid weather; they may never harden.
– Spoon frosting or glaze over top of cake and let run down sides. This is a good way to ice chiffon, angel, or sponge cakes.
– To give Royal Icing a glass-smooth finish, frost top and sides as quickly as possible, dipping spatula often in hot water and shaking off excess (don't worry at this point about smoothing surface). Then hold edge of spatula blade against sides of cake, slightly at an angle, and rotate cake slowly, scraping off roughened places.
– Dip spatula in hot water and repeat process, smoothing out all rough spots.
– Smooth off top, dipping spatula in hot water as needed.

Frosting Cupcakes:
– Cool cupcakes thoroughly; meanwhile, prepare frosting.
– Holding cupcakes by the bottom, dip one at a time into frosting, then lift out with a slight twirling motion so there is a curlicue on top.
– Set on wire racks and let dry thoroughly. Or, if you like, while frosting is still soft, stud with walnut or pecan halves, chocolate bits, candied cherries, raisins, or chunks of dried fruit. Or scatter lightly with flaked coconut or minced nuts, fine cookie crumbs, or grated semisweet chocolate.

What to Do with Leftover Frosting:
– Cover and refrigerate until needed.
– Bring to room temperature and use to frost cupcakes or cookies.
– Use as a dessert topping (particularly good with steamed puddings).

Tips on Decorating Cakes

The Simplest Decorations: These require no icing and are usually nothing more than confectioners' sugar, sifted through a lace doily onto a cake; a poured-on glaze of melted semisweet chocolate or warmed preserves; a dusting of colored sugar, cocoa, or cinnamon sugar. Quick, easy, and inviting.

Easy Ways to Dress Up Frosted Cakes: Ready-made colored frostings in squirt-on cans or tubes make decorating a snap. They need no refrigeration, are quick and easy to use. Also available in some supermarkets and most gourmet shops: decorating jellies in assorted colors; colored sugars and decorettes; silver dragées; chocolate and butterscotch bits; hard candies and gumdrops; birthday candles and holders. Take whatever is available, add imagination, and create an original special occasion cake.

Flower Cakes: Dot frosted cakes with real flowers (daisies, chrysanthemums, rosebuds, violets), crystalized violets or roses (available in gourmet shops), or fashion flowers out of blanched almonds, slivers of candied fruits, or well-drained mandarin orange sections.

Marble Cakes: Frost top of cake with Snow Glaze (double recipe but add only 3 tablespoons milk to make frosting stiffer). Prepare ½ recipe Chocolate Glaze and drizzle in parallel lines over snow glaze. Before chocolate hardens, draw a toothpick across lines, creating a zigzag effect.

Simple Anytime Decorations:
– Frost a chocolate or mocha cake with Basic or Coffee Butter Cream Frosting and sprinkle top with chocolate curls.*

– Frost any yellow or white butter cake with Whipped Cream Frosting, arrange a ring of miniature meringues on top, and fill center with fresh strawberries.
– Frost sides of a chocolate cake with Basic Butter Cream Frosting, cover top with Chocolate Glaze, and coat sides with chocolate shot or minced nuts.

More Intricate Decorations:

About Cake-Decorating Equipment:

Cake-Decorating Sets: These are widely available in metal or plastic and include a slim selection of decorating tips. Good for beginners.

Pastry (or Decorating) Bags: The best are plastic-lined cotton bags and come in a variety of sizes; they are waterproof, washable, and if properly cared for will last almost indefinitely. Also available: transparent plastic bags, also washable and reusable.

To Make Your Own Decorating Bag:
– Cut an 8″ square of parchment, wax paper, or heavy typewriter bond, then halve diagonally into 2 triangles.
– Roll into a sharp-pointed cone and fold points down.

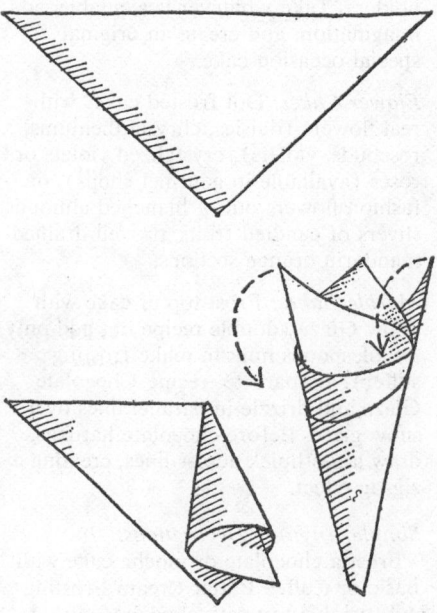

– To make fine lines (flower stems, dots, writing), snip point off to make a tiny hole.
– For broader lines, snip a little more off point.
– For making stars, scrolls, and leaves, snip still more off point and cut with a single or double notch.
– To use with decorative tips, cut ½″– ¾″ off point and drop in desired tip.
– To fill: Spoon enough frosting into cone to half fill, then fold corners in and top down. (*Note:* If bag should go limp before decorating is done, cut off directly above decorating tip, drop tip into a fresh cone, and squeeze frosting from old bag into the new.)

Decorating Tips (also called Decorating Tubes): These may be bought singly or in partial or complete sets (more than a hundred tips) from gourmet shops and confectionery supply houses. Decorating guides come with the sets.

A beginner's set might include:
Tips ⌗2 and 5 (for writing, making flower buds, scrolls)
Tips ⌗14, 18, 22 (for stars, swags, large scrolls)
Tip ⌗30 (for large stars and shells)
Tip ⌗6 (for fancy borders)
Tips ⌗66 and 90 (for small and large leaves)

To Use Pastry Bags and Decorative Tips:
– Never more than half fill bag.
– Roll or fold top down and push frosting out, using steady, gentle pressure so decorations will have crisp outlines. Practice, if you like, on a piece of wax paper or turned-upside-down cake pan until you get the hang of it.
– If you set bag aside for a while, push out a bit of frosting before resuming decoration; some of it may have hardened.
– For really intricate designs, sketch out patterns on paper and use as a guide.

Flower Nails: These look like oversized thumbtacks, are made of metal or plastic, and are useful for shaping flowers. Top nail head with a tiny square of wax paper, form flower, then lift off paper and let flower dry. Peel off paper and place flower on cake. For a make-shift flower nail, use a small jar with a lid.

Decorating Stencils: Cardboard and plastic stencils in a variety of patterns and letters are available in gourmet shops and confectionery supply houses. You can also make your own (manila folders work especially well). To use, hold stencil over frosting and fill cut-out spaces with colored sugar, decorettes, thin colored frosting or melted semi-sweet chocolate.

Decorating Combs: Available in plastic and aluminum. To use, simply draw comb through soft frosting in straight or wavy lines.

About Decorative Frostings: Use Royal Icing for intricate designs and Decora-tive Butter Cream Frosting for softer, simpler ones.

To Color Frostings: Use liquid or paste food colors (available in a wide range of colors at gourmet shops). Always add colors *gradually,* drop by drop for liquid colors, and dabbed on the end of a toothpick for the paste. Mix in thoroughly before adding more color. It's far better to undercolor than over-color (many colored frostings will darken on drying). Prepare more of each color than you think you will need so that you will not have to mix up another batch (it will be virtually impossible to match the colors exactly). (*Note:* Always keep frostings covered with damp cloth or paper toweling as you work to prevent their drying out.)

How to Mix Colors

Orange=red+yellow (more yellow than red)
Strawberry=red+yellow (more red than yellow)
Lime Green=yellow+green (more green than yellow)
Chartreuse=yellow+green (more yellow than green)

Violet=blue+red (more blue than red)
Maroon=blue+red (more red than blue)
Brown=yellow+red and a smidgen of green

About Decorating with Chocolate: Always use type of chocolate called for in a recipe and do not substitute cocoa for chocolate.

To Grate Chocolate: Chill chocolate well, then grate into a deep bowl (it tends to fly all over).

To Melt Chocolate: Break into small pieces and melt over hot, not boiling water (chocolate scorches easily, so melt very slowly). Or place chocolate in a custard cup and set in a pan of hot water. Cool melted chocolate slightly before adding to any frosting. *To Smooth Out Lumps:* If a drop of water falls into melted chocolate, the chocolate will lump. To make it smooth again, stir in ½–1 teaspoon vegetable shortening for each ounce of chocolate. It won't affect the flavor.

To Make Chocolate Curls: Warm chocolate (semisweet or German sweet) in wrapper in your hands, just enough to soften outside slightly. Unwrap and shave into thin curls over a piece of wax paper, using a vegetable peeler. Scatter onto cakes as decoration.

To Make Chocolate Cutouts: Melt 6 (1-ounce) packages semisweet chocolate over hot water and blend in 1 teaspoon vegetable shortening. Spread evenly and thinly on a baking sheet lined with wax paper and quick-chill in freezer or refrigerator until chocolate begins to harden. Cut out in desired shapes with cookie cutters (or, for very small decorations, with truffle cutters). Return to refrigerator or freezer and let harden thoroughly. Lift off decorations and use to decorate cakes. To store: Layer into a cakebox, separating layers with wax paper, cover, and keep in refrigerator or freezer.

To Write with Chocolate: Melt semi-sweet chocolate and blend with a few drops light corn syrup; cool until slightly thickened, then drizzle off the end of a spoon in a thin even stream or, if thick enough, push through a pastry bag fitted with a fine, plain tip.

To Glaze with Chocolate: Melt unsweetened or semisweet chocolate, cool slightly, then spoon or drizzle over a frosted cake. (*Note:* Let frosting harden several hours before adding chocolate. This works especially well with 7-Minute Frosting.)

Some General Decorating Hints:

– Choose a firm-textured cake that will support weight of decorations rather than a delicate sponge or angel food.
– Allow plenty of time for decorating; it is often necessary to let part of the decorations harden before adding more.
– Choose a cool, dry day for the decorating, not a hot, humid one, when icings will not harden.
– If your hands are warm, put only a small amount of frosting in pastry bag at a time, lest body heat soften it too much to be workable.
– Keep designs simple, in proportion to size of cake.
– Suit the designs to the occasion.

⊠ BASIC BUTTER CREAM FROSTING

Try the flavor variations that follow or experiment with ideas of your own. This frosting is superbly adaptable.
Makes enough to fill and frost an 8″ or 9″ 2-layer cake or 24 cupcakes

⅓ *cup butter or margarine, softened to room temperature*
1 (1-pound) box confectioners' sugar, sifted
5–6 tablespoons light cream
2 teaspoons vanilla
¼ *teaspoon salt*

Cream butter until fluffy; beat in sugar, a little at a time, adding alternately with cream. Mix in vanilla and salt and beat until satiny and of good spreading consistency. If mixture seems too stiff, thin with a little additional cream. Add 250 calories to each serving if cake is cut in 12 pieces, 190 to each serving if cake is

cut in 16 pieces, and 125 calories to each of 24 cupcakes.

VARIATIONS:

Browned Butter Cream Frosting: Brown butter lightly instead of creaming, then beat in sugar and proceed as directed. Calorie counts the same as for Basic Butter Cream Frosting.

Coffee Butter Cream Frosting: Prepare by basic method above, beating 2 teaspoons instant coffee powder into butter along with sugar. Calorie counts the same as for Basic Butter Cream Frosting.

Mocha Butter Cream Frosting: Prepare by basic method above, beating 2 teaspoons instant coffee powder and 2(1-ounce) squares melted unsweetened chocolate into creamed butter before adding sugar. Add 275 calories to each serving if cake is cut in 12 pieces, 210 calories if cut in 16 pieces, and 140 calories to each of 24 cupcakes.

Chocolate Butter Cream Frosting: Prepare by basic method but blend 3 (1-ounce) squares melted unsweetened chocolate or ½ cup sifted cocoa into creamed butter before adding sugar. Proceed as directed. Add 290 calories to each serving if cake is cut in 12 pieces, 220 calories to each serving if cake is cut in 16 pieces, and 145 calories to each of 24 cupcakes.

Maple Butter Cream Frosting: Prepare by basic method, substituting ½ cup maple syrup for the light cream and reducing vanilla to ½ teaspoon. Calorie counts approximately the same as for Mocha Butter Cream Frosting.

Nut Butter Cream Frosting: Prepare as directed and, when of good spreading consistency, mix in ⅓–½ cup minced walnuts, pecans, blanched filberts, or almonds. Calorie counts approximately the same as for Chocolate Butter Cream Frosting.

Orange or Lemon Butter Cream Frosting: Prepare by basic method, substituting 4–5 tablespoons orange or lemon juice for the cream; omit vanilla and add 3–4 teaspoons finely grated orange or lemon rind and ¼ teaspoon almond extract. Add 230 calories to each serving if cake is cut in 12 pieces, 175 to each serving if cake is cut in 16 pieces, and 115 calories to each of 24 cupcakes.

Cherry Butter Cream Frosting: Prepare by basic method, substituting 5–6 tablespoons maraschino cherry juice for the light cream; omit vanilla. When frosting is of good spreading consistency, fold in ¼ cup minced, well-drained maraschino cherries. About 10 calories more per serving than Basic Butter Cream Frosting.

Pineapple Butter Cream Frosting: Prepare by basic method, substituting ⅓ cup drained, canned crushed pineapple for the cream; reduce vanilla to ½ teaspoon and add ¼ teaspoon almond extract. Calorie counts the same as for Basic Butter Cream Frosting.

Berry Butter Cream Frosting: Prepare by basic method, substituting ⅓ cup sieved, puréed fresh or thawed frozen strawberries, raspberries, or blackberries for the cream. Omit vanilla and add 1 teaspoon lemon juice. Calorie counts the same as Basic Butter Cream Frosting.

Decorative Butter Cream Frosting: Prepare Basic Butter Cream Frosting as directed but reduce cream to 1–2 tablespoons; if you want a really snowy frosting, substitute vegetable shortening for butter and add a drop blue food coloring. (*Note:* Use only on firm frostings or decorations may sink in. On warm or humid days, add a little extra confectioners' sugar so decorations will hold their shape.) About 10 calories less per serving than Basic Butter Cream Frosting.

☒ CREAM CHEESE FROSTING

Slightly firmer than butter frosting, this one also invites improvisation.
Makes enough to fill and frost an 8" or 9" 2-layer cake

2 (*3-ounce*) *packages cream cheese, softened to room temperature*

1 (*1-pound*) *box confectioners' sugar, sifted*
1 *teaspoon vanilla*
1–2 *tablespoons milk, light cream, or evaporated milk*

Beat cream cheese until very soft, then gradually beat in confectioners' sugar. Mix in vanilla and enough milk to make a good spreading consistency. Add approximately 185 calories to each of 16 servings of cake.

VARIATIONS:

Sour Cream-Cream Cheese Frosting: Prepare as directed but substitute ¼ cup sour cream for the milk. Add approximately 190 calories to each of 16 servings of cake.

Chocolate Cream Cheese Frosting: Beat cream cheese until soft, mix in 2 (1-ounce) squares melted unsweetened chocolate and proceed as directed, increasing milk to 3 tablespoons. Add about 205 calories to each of 16 servings of cake.

Coffee Cream Cheese Frosting: Prepare as directed, adding 1 tablespoon instant coffee powder along with sugar. Add about 185 calories to each of 16 servings of cake.

Orange or Lemon Cream Cheese Frosting: Prepare as directed but omit vanilla and use orange or lemon juice instead of milk. Flavor with the finely grated rind of 1 lemon or orange. Add about 185 calories to each of 16 servings of cake.

☒ WHIPPED CREAM FROSTING

Spread on cakes shortly before they're cut and eaten.
Makes enough to fill and frost a 9" tube or 2-layer cake

1 *pint heavy cream, well chilled*
1 *cup sifted confectioners' sugar*
1 *teaspoon vanilla*

In a chilled bowl with chilled beaters, beat cream until frothy. Gradually add confectioners' sugar, then vanilla. Continue beating until thick enough to spread. Use at once. Add about 140 calories to each of 16 servings of cake.

VARIATIONS:

Chocolate Whipped Cream Frosting: Sift ½ cup cocoa with confectioners' sugar and beat into cream as directed. Add about 150 calories to each of 16 servings of cake.

Coffee Whipped Cream Frosting: Mix 1 tablespoon instant coffee powder with the cream and proceed as directed. Add about 140 calories to each of 16 servings of cake.

Fruit Whipped Cream Frosting: Prepare as directed but flavor with ½ teaspoon orange or lemon extract, instead of vanilla, and the finely grated rind of 1 lemon or orange. Add about 140 calories for each of 16 servings of cake.

Nut Whipped Cream Frosting: Prepare as directed but flavor with maple flavoring or almond extract instead of vanilla and fold in ¾ cup minced pecans, filberts, boiled chestnuts, or toasted almonds. Add about 170 calories to each of 16 servings of cake.

Tipsy Whipped Cream Frosting: Prepare as directed but flavor with brandy or rum extract instead of vanilla or 1–2 tablespoons brandy, rum, or bourbon. (*Note:* For a really Tipsy Cake, pierce unfrosted cake layers all over with a metal skewer and drizzle with a little liquor; cover loosely and let stand 1 hour before filling and frosting.) Add about 145 calories to each of 16 servings of cake.

Coconut Whipped Cream Frosting: Prepare as directed and fold in 1 cup flaked or toasted flaked coconut. Add about 160 calories to each of 16 servings of cake.

Neapolitan Fruit Cream Filling: Use this only as a filling, it's too soft for frosting. Make half the recipe and fold in ½ cup minced, well-drained peaches, pears, apricots, pineapple, or fruit salad or ½ cup thinly sliced bananas or berries. Add about 145 calories to each of 16 servings of cake.

Warm Weather Whipped Cream Frosting: Blend 1 teaspoon unflavored gelatin and 2 tablespoons cold water in a custard cup. Set in a small pan of simmering water and stir until gelatin dissolves; cool. Gradually beat into cream, then proceed as recipe directs. Add about 140 calories to each of 16 servings of cake.

7-MINUTE FROSTING

Some electric mixers will whip up 7-Minute Frosting in *less* than 7 minutes. Makes enough to fill and frost an 8″ or 9″ 2-layer cake or 24 cupcakes

2 egg whites
1½ cups sugar
¼ teaspoon cream of tartar or 1 tablespoon light corn syrup
⅓ cup cold water
1 teaspoon vanilla

Mix all ingredients except vanilla in the top of a double boiler and set over just boiling water. Beat constantly with rotary or electric beater until stiff peaks form, 4–7 minutes. Off heat, add vanilla and beat until of good spreading consistency. Add about 75 calories to each of 16 servings of cake, 50 calories to each of 24 cupcakes.

VARIATIONS:

Orange or Lemon 7-Minute Frosting: Prepare as directed but use orange or lemon juice instead of water and ½ teaspoon orange or lemon extract instead of vanilla. If you like, fold in the finely grated rind of 1 orange or lemon just before using and tint pale orange or yellow. Calorie counts approximately the same as for 7-Minute Frosting.

Peppermint 7-Minute Frosting: Prepare as directed but flavor with ½ teaspoon peppermint extract or ¼ teaspoon oil of peppermint instead of vanilla. Tint pale pink and fold in ⅓ cup crushed peppermint candy. Add about 105 calories to each of 16 servings of cake, 70 calories to each of 24 cupcakes.

Coffee 7-Minute Frosting: Prepare as directed but use ½ cup firmly packed dark brown sugar and 1 cup granulated; also dissolve 1 tablespoon instant coffee powder in the water before adding.

Calorie counts approximately the same as for 7-Minute Frosting.

Caramel 7-Minute Frosting: Prepare as directed but use 1 cup firmly packed dark brown sugar and ½ cup granulated; flavor with maple flavoring instead of vanilla. Calorie counts approximately the same as for 7-Minute Frosting.

Fruit or Nut 7-Minute Frosting: Prepare as directed, then fold in ½–¾ cup prunes, or raisins or ½–¾ cup coarsely chopped nuts. Add about 100 calories to each of 16 servings of cake, 65 calories to each of 24 cupcakes.

Chocolate 7-Minute Frosting: Prepare as directed, then fold in 2 melted and cooled (1-ounce) squares unsweetened chocolate. Do not beat, just stir to mix. Add about 95 calories to each of 16 servings of cake, 65 calories to each of 24 cupcakes.

Marshmallow 7-Minute Frosting: Prepare as directed, then fold in 1 cup snipped marshmallows. Add about 90 calories to each of 16 servings of cake, 60 calories to each of 24 cupcakes.

Coconut 7-Minute Frosting: Prepare as directed, tint pastel, if you like, then fold in ½ cup flaked coconut. After frosting cake, sprinkle with additional flaked coconut. Add about 85 calories to each of 16 servings of cake, 55 calories to each of 24 cupcakes.

WHITE MOUNTAIN FROSTING

A fluffy white frosting that you don't have to beat *on* the stove.
Makes enough to fill and frost an 8" or 9" 2-layer cake

¾ cup sugar
¼ cup light corn syrup
¼ cup water
3 egg whites, at room temperature
1 teaspoon vanilla or ½ teaspoon almond
  extract

Mix sugar, corn syrup, and water in a small, heavy saucepan, insert candy thermometer, partially cover pan, and bring to a boil over moderate heat. Remove cover and boil *without stirring* until thermometer registers 240–42° F. or until a drop on the tip of a spoon will spin a 6"–8" thread. Just before syrup reaches proper temperature, begin beating egg whites with an electric mixer until soft peaks form. When syrup reaches correct temperature, set mixer at high speed and pour syrup into whites in a slow thin stream. Continue beating until glossy and firm enough to hold a shape. Beat in vanilla. Add about 55 calories to each of 16 servings of cake.

VARIATIONS:

Pink Mountain Frosting: Prepare as directed but substitute ¼ cup maraschino cherry liquid for water and use almond extract. Calorie count the same as for White Mountain Frosting.

Lemon or Orange Mountain Frosting: Prepare as directed but substitute lemon or orange juice for water and flavor with ½ teaspoon lemon or orange extract and the finely grated rind of 1 lemon or orange. Calorie count the same as for White Mountain Frosting.

Marble Mountain Frosting: Prepare as directed and just before spreading swirl in 1 (1-ounce) square coarsely grated unsweetened chocolate or 1 (1-ounce) envelope no-melt unsweetened chocolate to create a marbleized effect. Add about 65 calories to each of 16 servings of cake.

Maple Mountain Frosting: Use ¾ cup firmly packed light brown sugar instead of granulated and substitute 1 teaspoon maple flavoring for vanilla. Calorie count the same as for White Mountain Frosting.

Rock Candy Mountain Frosting: Prepare as directed but flavor with ½ teaspoon peppermint extract instead of vanilla and, just before serving, fold in ½ cup crushed peppermint sticks. Add about 85 calories to each of 16 servings of cake.

Marshmallow Mountain Frosting: Prepare as directed up to point of adding vanilla. With scissors, snip 8 marshmallows into small bits and fold into frosting along with vanilla. Add about 70 calories to each of 16 servings of cake.

SEAFOAM FROSTING

Almost as good as seafoam candy. Delicious on chocolate or burnt sugar cakes.
Makes enough to fill and frost an 8″ or 9″ 2-layer cake

⅔ cup firmly packed light brown sugar
¼ cup light corn syrup
1 egg white
⅛ teaspoon cream of tartar
⅛ teaspoon salt
2 tablespoons water
1 teaspoon vanilla

Combine all ingredients except vanilla in the top of a double boiler, set over boiling water, and beat with a rotary beater or portable electric mixer until mixture stands in peaks. Off heat, add vanilla and continue beating until mixture will hold deep swirls. Use at once. Add about 50 calories to each of 16 servings of cake.

FUDGE FROSTING

Really fudgy.
Makes enough to frost an 8″ or 9″ round or square cake

1½ cups sugar
½ cup water or milk
1 tablespoon light corn syrup
1 tablespoon butter or margarine
2 (1-ounce) squares unsweetened chocolate, coarsely grated, or 2 (1-ounce) envelopes no-melt unsweetened chocolate
1 teaspoon vanilla

Place all ingredients except vanilla in a heavy saucepan with a candy thermometer, set over moderate heat, and stir once or twice as chocolate melts. Boil *without stirring* until thermometer reaches 234° F. or until a little mixture dropped into cold water forms a very soft ball. Remove from heat at once and cool without stirring to 120° F. (lukewarm); mix in vanilla and beat until thick and of good spreading

consistency. (*Note:* If frosting seems thick, add a little milk or light cream; if too thin, beat in a little sifted confectioners' sugar.) Add about 100 calories to each of 16 servings of cake (if frosting is made with water), 105 calories (if frosting is made with milk).

VARIATIONS:

Vanilla Fudge Frosting: Prepare as directed but use milk, light or sour cream instead of water and omit chocolate. Add about 90 calories to each of 16 servings (if frosting is made with milk), about 100 calories (if made with light or sour cream).

Caramel Fudge Frosting: Prepare as directed, using 1 cup firmly packed light or dark brown sugar and ½ cup granulated sugar; also use milk, dark corn syrup and, if you like, add 1 teaspoon maple flavoring in addition to vanilla. Omit chocolate. Add about 95 calories to each of 16 servings of cake.

✗ EASY FUDGE FROSTING

Makes enough to fill and frost an 8″ or 9″ 2-layer cake

2 cups sugar
¼ cup light corn syrup
½ cup butter or margarine
½ cup milk
2 (1-ounce) squares unsweetened chocolate, coarsely grated, or 2 (1-ounce) envelopes no-melt unsweetened chocolate
1 teaspoon vanilla

Stir all ingredients except vanilla in a heavy saucepan over low heat until chocolate melts. Bring to a full rolling boil, stirring constantly, then boil 1 minute. Off heat, beat until lukewarm; stir in vanilla and continue stirring until a good spreading consistency. Add about 185 calories to each of 16 servings of cake.

VARIATION:

Easy Caramel Fudge Frosting: Prepare as directed but use 2 cups firmly packed light or dark brown sugar instead of granulated sugar; omit corn syrup and chocolate. Add about 160 calories to each of 16 servings of cake.

☒ BROILED PENUCHE ICING

A fast frosting for simple cakes.
Makes enough to top a 9″ square cake

⅔ cup firmly packed light or dark brown sugar
¼ cup butter or margarine, softened to room temperature
¼ cup heavy cream
½ cup finely chopped nuts

Preheat broiler. Mix all ingredients and spread evenly on warm cake. Set on wire cake rack over baking pan and broil 5″ from the heat 3–4 minutes until mixture bubbles and browns lightly. Cool slightly before cutting. Add about 100 calories to each of 16 servings of cake.

For a 13″×9″×2″ Cake: Use 1 cup sugar, ⅓ cup each butter and cream and ¾ cup nuts. Add about 90 calories to each of 24 servings of cake.

VARIATIONS:

Broiled Coconut Icing: Prepare as directed but substitute ½ cup flaked coconut for nuts. Add about 100 calories to each of 16 servings of cake.

Broiled Peanut Butter Icing: Prepare as directed but substitute ¼ cup peanut butter for butter and use ½ cup minced *unsalted* toasted, blanched peanuts. Add about 125 calories to each of 16 servings of cake.

☒ ROYAL ICING (ORNAMENTAL FROSTING)

This frosting holds its shape well, dries hard, and is ideal for making durable decorations. It also helps keep cakes moist.
Makes enough to decorate an 8″, 9″, or 10″ cake

3 egg whites, at room temperature
¼ teaspoon cream of tartar
1 (1-pound) box confectioners' sugar, sifted

Beat egg whites and cream of tartar until foamy. Gradually beat in sugar, then beat at high speed until very thick and glossy (beaters when withdrawn should leave sharp, firm peaks). Use to frost and decorate cakes. Keep bowl of frosting covered with damp cloth as you work to prevent "crusting." If frosting should lose stiffness, beat at high speed until firm again, or if necessary (sometimes true in humid weather) beat in a little additional confectioners' sugar. About 2310 calories total (amount per serving of cake depends entirely upon how lavishly the cake is decorated).

☒ QUICK GLACÉ ICING

This icing dries hard with a lovely glossy finish.
Makes enough to glaze about 1⅓ dozen Petits Fours

3 cups sifted confectioners' sugar
3 tablespoons light corn syrup
3 tablespoons water
Few drops any food coloring (optional)

Place all ingredients except food coloring in the top of a double boiler over *simmering* water and heat, stirring, until sugar dissolves and mixture is smooth. Do not allow water underneath to boil or icing will not be glossy. Tint with food coloring as desired. Spoon over Petits Fours or any small cakes set on wire racks over baking sheets. Scrape up run-over from baking sheet, return to double boiler, and warm again until of pouring consistency. If thick, add a few drops warm water. Add about 105 calories to each of the petits fours.

VARIATION:

Chocolate Glacé Icing: Prepare as directed and, when sugar is dissolved, add 1½ ounces semisweet chocolate broken into bits and heat, stirring until blended. Add 1–2 tablespoons warm water to thin to pouring consistency; do not overheat or icing will not be glossy. Add about 155 calories to each of the petits fours.

⊠ SNOW GLAZE

A quick and easy topping for any simple cake.
Makes enough to glaze a large loaf or tube cake or 24 cupcakes

1 cup sifted confectioners' sugar
2 tablespoons warm milk
¼ teaspoon almond extract

Sprinkle confectioners' sugar slowly into milk and blend smooth. Mix in almond extract, spread on cake, and let stand until glaze hardens. Add about 30 calories to each of 16 servings of cake, 20 calories to each of 24 cupcakes.

VARIATIONS:

Sugar Glaze: Prepare as directed but substitute warm water for milk. Calorie counts the same as for Snow Glaze.

Lemon or Orange Sugar Glaze: Prepare as directed but substitute warm lemon or orange juice for milk and flavor with 1 teaspoon finely grated lemon or orange rind. Calorie counts the same as for Snow Glaze.

Tutti-Frutti Glaze: Prepare as directed but substitute 1 lightly beaten egg white for milk. Spread glaze on cake and decorate with slivered mixed candied fruit peel, candied red cherries, angelica, and thinly sliced blanched almonds. Recipe too flexible for a meaningful calorie count.

Easy White Icing (perfect for icing hot sweet breads): Prepare as directed but use cold milk and reduce quantity to about 1 tablespoon. Flavor with ¼ teaspoon vanilla instead of almond extract. Calorie counts approximately the same as for Snow Glaze.

⊠ CHOCOLATE GLAZE

Makes enough to glaze an 8″ or 9″ cake or 6–8 Éclairs

2 (1-ounce) squares unsweetened chocolate
1 teaspoon butter or margarine
1 cup sifted confectioners' sugar
3 tablespoons warm water

Melt chocolate and butter in the top of a double boiler over simmering water; stir to blend well. Set top of double boiler on a damp cloth, add ½ cup confectioners' sugar and 1 tablespoon water; beat until smooth. Add remaining sugar and water and beat until glossy. Use to glaze éclairs, other pastries, or the tops of cakes. Add about 40 calories to each of 16 servings of cake, 100 calories to each of 6 éclairs and 75 calories to each of 8 éclairs.

APRICOT GLAZE

An excellent base coat for Petits Fours and other small cakes to be covered with thin, hard, smooth icings.
Makes enough to glaze 4 dozen Petits Fours

2 cups apricot preserves
½ cup water

Heat preserves and water in a saucepan over low heat, stirring constantly, until mixture bubbles; heat and stir 2–3 minutes longer, press through a fine sieve, and cool slightly before using. Add about 50 calories to each of the petits fours.

BASIC VANILLA CREAM FILLING

Makes about 1 cup, enough to fill an 8″ or 9″ 2-layer cake

2 tablespoons cornstarch
⅓ cup sugar
¾ cup milk
1 egg yolk, lightly beaten with ¼ cup milk
1 teaspoon vanilla

Blend cornstarch, sugar, and milk in a small saucepan and heat, stirring constantly, over moderate heat until mixture boils and is thick; boil and stir ½ minute longer. Off heat, beat a little hot mixture into egg yolk, return all to pan *gradually*, beating constantly. Mix in vanilla and cool to room temperature, beating now and then. Add about 30 calories to each of 16 servings of cake.

VARIATIONS:

Poppy Seed Cream Filling: Prepare as directed and mix in 2 tablespoons poppy seeds. Add about 30 calories to each of 16 servings of cake.

Double Cream Filling: Prepare as directed and fold in ⅓ cup heavy cream whipped to soft peaks. (*Note:* Also good with any of the flavor variations.) Add about 50 calories to each of 16 servings of cake.

Chocolate Cream Filling: Prepare as directed but increase sugar to ½ cup and add 2 (1-ounce) squares melted semi-sweet chocolate or 2 (1-ounce) envelopes no-melt unsweetened chocolate along with vanilla; blend well. If mixture seems thick, thin with a little milk. Add about 60 calories to each of 16 servings of cake.

Butterscotch Cream Filling: Substitute ½ cup firmly packed dark brown sugar for the granulated and, if you like, use maple flavoring instead of vanilla. Add about 30 calories to each of 16 servings of cake.

Coffee Cream Filling: Add 1½ teaspoons instant coffee powder along with the sugar. Add about 30 calories to each of 16 servings of cake.

Fruit Cream Filling: Prepare as directed but omit vanilla and add ¼ teaspoon lemon or orange extract and 2 teaspoons finely grated lemon or orange rind. Add about 30 calories to each of 16 servings of cake.

Coconut Cream Filling: Prepare as directed and mix in ½–⅔ cup flaked coconut. Add about 40 calories to each of 16 servings of cake.

PASTRY CREAM

What to put inside feathery French pastries.
Makes enough to fill a 3-layer cake or 1 dozen Cream Puffs or Éclairs

½ cup sifted flour
½ cup sugar
⅛ teaspoon salt
2 cups milk
2 eggs plus 2 egg yolks, lightly beaten
1 teaspoon vanilla

Mix flour, sugar, and salt in the top of a double boiler. Add milk slowly, blending until smooth. Heat and stir over direct moderate heat until thickened and smooth. Mix about ½ cup hot mixture into eggs, then return to pan. Set over simmering water and cook and stir 2–3 minutes until thick. Off heat, stir in vanilla. Place a piece of wax paper flat on sauce to prevent a skin from forming and cool. Stir well, cover, and chill until ready to use as a pastry filling. Add about 75 calories to each of 16 servings of cake, about 100 calories to each of 12 cream puffs or éclairs.

LEMON FILLING

Makes enough to fill an 8″ or 9″ 2-layer cake

3 tablespoons cornstarch
1 cup sugar
½ cup lemon juice
1 cup hot water
2 tablespoons butter or margarine
2 tablespoons finely grated lemon rind
Few drops yellow food coloring

Mix cornstarch and sugar in a saucepan, stir in lemon juice, and water and bring to a full boil, stirring constantly. Reduce heat slightly and heat and stir until thickened and clear. Off heat, beat in butter and lemon rind, then tint pale yellow. Place wax paper flat on sauce and cool to room temperature. Beat with a whisk or rotary beater before using. Add about 70 calories to each of 16 servings of cake.

VARIATIONS:

Lime Filling: Prepare as directed but substitute lime juice and rind for the lemon. Tint pale green. Add about 70 calories to each of 16 servings of cake.

Orange Filling: Prepare as directed, using 1 cup orange juice and ½ cup hot water; substitute orange rind for the lemon. Tint pale orange with a red and yellow food coloring. Add about 70 calories to each of 16 servings of cake.

Pineapple Filling: Mix cornstarch with sugar, add 1 cup pineapple juice, ¼ cup hot water, and ½ cup well-drained crushed pineapple. Heat and stir until thickened; off heat, beat in the butter and ¼ teaspoon lemon rind. Do not tint.

Add about 85 calories to each of 16 servings of cake.

Rich Fruit Filling: Prepare any of the preceding recipes in the top of a double boiler over direct heat. When cornstarch mixture is thickened and clear, mix a little into 2 lightly beaten egg yolks, return to pan, set over simmering water, and heat and stir 1–2 minutes. Proceed as directed but do not tint. Recipe too flexible for a meaningful calorie count.

Fruit Cream Filling: Prepare Lemon, Lime, Orange, or Pineapple Filling as directed and, just before using, mix in 1 cup softly whipped cream. For the Lemon, Lime or Orange Fillings add about 95 calories for each of 16 servings of cake. For the Pineapple Filling, add about 110 calories for each of 16 servings of cake.

STRAWBERRY FILLING

Soft and fluffy. Use to fill angel, white, or yellow cakes or jelly rolls.
Makes enough to fill a 9″ or 10″ 3-layer cake

1 (6-ounce) package strawberry-flavored
  gelatin
1 cup very hot water
1 (10-ounce) package thawed frozen,
  sliced strawberries or 1 pint fresh
  strawberries, hulled and sliced thin
1 teaspoon almond extract
½ cup heavy cream

Mix gelatin and water, stirring until gelatin dissolves. Add strawberries and almond extract and mix well. Cover and chill until thick and syrupy, but not firm. Whip cream to soft peaks, then fold into strawberry mixture. Chill 20–30 minutes until thick but not set. Use to fill Angel Food Cake, cut in 3 layers, any 3-layer white or yellow cake, or roll up inside jelly roll. Add about 55 calories to each of 16 servings of cake.

PINEAPPLE-COCONUT FILLING

Makes enough to fill a 3-tier wedding cake

2 (1-pound 4-ounce) cans crushed
  pineapple (do not drain)

1½ cups sugar
¼ cup lemon juice
¼ cup cornstarch blended with ½ cup
  cold water or pineapple juice
2 (3½-ounce) cans flaked coconut

Mix all but last ingredient in a saucepan, set over moderate heat and heat and stir until thickened and clear and no taste of cornstarch remains. Cool 10 minutes, stir in coconut, and cool to room temperature, stirring now and then. Add about 25 calories to each of 100 pieces of wedding cake.

SUGAR BELLS

For wedding cakes. You will need 1 (3¼″), 1 (2″), and 1 (1¼″) plastic bell molds (obtainable from confectioners' supply houses and sometimes local bakeries).
Makes 3 large, 10 medium, and 16 small bells

2½ pounds superfine sugar
1 egg white
Cornstarch
1 recipe Royal Icing (optional)

Place sugar and egg white in a bowl and rub between your palms until evenly moist and mixed. Dust each mold inside with cornstarch, tapping out excess. Pack sugar firmly into molds, level off bottoms, and invert on wax paper; carefully lift off molds. Repeat until all sugar is molded. Let bells dry 1–2 hours until hard about ¼″ in from the outside. With a small spoon or spoon handle, scoop out soft insides, leaving shells ⅛″–¼″ thick. Cover scooped-out sugar with damp cloth and use for molding more bells. Let bells dry overnight at room temperature. Pipe icing around edges, if you like, to give a more finished look. Use to decorate any wedding or anniversary cake. Calorie counts will vary considerably according to how much each sugar bell is hollowed out and how lavishly it is decorated with royal icing. As a very rough estimate, figure about 130 calories per medium-size bell.

CHAPTER 23

COOKIES

Take a wintry afternoon, add an oven full of cookies scenting the air with their warm, sugary promise and you have one of the memories dear to most of us. Cookies are where most of us begin our cooking lessons because they're fast, fun, and practically disaster-proof–a little too much liquid or flour won't destroy them *or* the cook's enthusiasm.

Basically, there are six different types of cookies: *Drop, Rolled, Molded or Pressed, Refrigerator, Bar,* and *No-Bake.* We'll discuss them one by one, but first, some tips that apply to them all.

How to Make Better Cookies

About Pans and Preparing Pans:

– For delicately browned cookies, choose shiny baking sheets rather than dark ones. Dark surfaces absorb heat more quickly and cookies tend to overbrown on the bottom. When using the new non-stick pans, keep a close eye out until you learn how fast they bake.
– For uniform baking, make sure baking sheets are 1"–2" smaller all round than the oven (heat must circulate freely). Also make certain pans do not touch oven walls at any point.
– Grease pans only when recipes specify doing so.
– For greasing, use melted clarified butter* (unsalted) if you can afford it and shortening or cooking oil if you can't. Apply evenly and thinly with a pastry brush or small crumple of paper toweling, coating *bottoms of pans only.* To simplify dishwashing, grease only those areas cookies will actually touch.

(*Note:* Even the new nonstick pans need greasing if the cookies contain much sugar or fruit.)

– When baking cookies in quantity, line baking sheets with foil or, better still, with baking pan liner paper, a silicone-coated parchment that eliminates greasing altogether. It is available in kitchen departments of large department stores. Have several sheets of foil or paper cut to size, then as each batch of cookies comes from the oven, lift them off, paper and all, and slide a fresh sheet into place.
– If you have no baking sheets, use a turned-upside-down roasting pan—turned upside down because cookies bake poorly in high-sided pans.

About Mixing Cookies:

– Read recipe through carefully before beginning it.
– Have all utensils out, pans prepared, and ingredients measured before beginning.
– When using an electric mixer, use a medium speed for creaming shortening, sugar, and eggs and low speed for working in dry ingredients unless recipes specify otherwise.
– When mixing by hand, use a spoon with a long, comfortable handle—

wooden spoons are especially good.
— Always mix in dry ingredients with a light hand and only enough to blend. Overbeating at this point tends to make the cookies tough.

About Placing Cookies on Pans:

— Always put cookies on *cool* baking sheets; if sheets are warm, cookies will spread unnecessarily. When baking in quantity, use 2 or 3 sheets so that there is time to cool each before adding a fresh batch of cookies.
— Allow plenty of spreading room when spacing cookies on sheets (recipes specify just how much). As a rule, the thinner the dough or the higher the butter or shortening content, the more cookies will spread.
— Whenever you have less than a full sheet of cookies to bake, use a turned-upside-down pie tin or small baking pan. An unfilled sheet of cookies will bake unevenly.
— Avoid placing cookies too near edges of baking sheets; they will brown much more quickly than those in the center.
— Always scrape crumbs from a used sheet and wipe it thoroughly with paper toweling before reusing.

About Baking:

— Let oven preheat a full 15 minutes before baking cookies.
— Unless recipe states otherwise, bake cookies as near the center of oven as possible. Those placed too low tend to burn on the bottom, those placed too high will be brown on top but raw in the middle.
— Unless your oven is very large, do not attempt to bake more than one sheet, certainly no more than 2 sheets of cookies at a time. Whenever you bake 2 sheets at once, stagger them, one slightly above the other, so heat can circulate freely and reverse positions of pans halfway through baking.
— Because there is some heat build-up in even the best of ovens, you can expect second, third, and fourth sheets of cookies to bake slightly faster than the first.

— Turn baking sheets as needed during baking so that cookies will brown as evenly as possible.
— Always use a timer when baking cookies.
— Check cookies after minimum baking time and, if not done, bake maximum time.
— If, despite all precautions, some cookies are done ahead of others, simply remove from baking sheet.

— To tell when cookies are done, use the following tests:

Crisp, Thin Cookies: Check color; cookies should be firm to the touch, delicately browned or lightly ringed with brown.
Fairly Thick Dropped or Shaped Cookies: Press lightly in the center; if no imprint remains, cookies are done.
Meringue Kisses: Tap lightly; if kisses sound hollow, they are done.
Bars: Press lightly in center; mixture should feel firm yet springy. Bars should also have pulled from sides of pan.
— To rescue cookies that have burned on the bottom, grate off blackened parts with a fine lemon rind grater.

About Removing Cookies from Baking Sheets:

— Use wide spatulas or pancake turners.
— Unless recipe states otherwise, lift cookies at once to wire racks to cool. Exceptions are very soft cookies, which must be firm before a spatula can be slipped underneath them.

About Cooling Cookies:

— Never overlap cookies on racks and never arrange more than one layer deep; cookies will stick to one another.
— Remove to canisters as soon as cool.

About Storing Cookies:

Soft Cookies: Store in canisters with tight-fitting covers and, if necessary, with a chunk of apple or bread to keep them moist (replace apple or bread often). Brownies and other bars can be stored in their baking pans, tightly wrapped in foil or plastic food wrap.

Crisp Cookies: Blanket statements can't be made because much depends on weather. Crisp cookies, for example, will soon go limp if stored in a loosely covered container in a muggy climate; in such areas they *must* be stored airtight. But in dry areas, the treatment is just the opposite: Store in loosely covered containers. If cookies should soften, crispen by heating three to five minutes at 350° F.

About Freezing Cookies: (See the chapter on freezing and canning).

About Packing and Shipping Cookies:

– Choose soft, sturdy, undecorated cookies that won't crumble in transit (a list is given in the Cookie Chart).
– For shipping, pick a sturdy cardboard box and line with wax paper. Cushion bottom with a thick layer of crumpled wax paper, cellophane "excelsior" or unseasoned popcorn. For long-distance shipping, pack cookies in a metal canister and cushion it in the box.
– Wrap cookies individually in plastic food wrap or, if flat, in pairs back to back. Tape each packet shut.
– Layer cookies in rows, always putting heaviest cookies on the bottom. Before adding a second layer, fill all holes and crevices with unseasoned popcorn. Add a cushioning layer of paper toweling (several thicknesses), then another layer of cookies. You'll have better luck if you don't try to send more than two or three layers of cookies.
– Cover top layer with crushed wax paper or paper toweling.
– Tape box shut, wrap in heavy paper and tie securely in several places.
– Print address clearly and mark package "fragile."
– If cookies are to be shipped great distances, use air parcel post.

About Decorating Cookies

Cookies can be decorated either before or after baking. Simple, sprinkled, or pressed-on designs can be applied before cookies go into the oven, but intricate designs, whether painted or piped on, are best done after baking.

To Decorate Before Baking:

Most Suitable Cookies: Simple, relatively flat cookies: dropped or rolled cookies, molded or cookie press cookies, refrigerator or commercial slice-and-bake cookies.

Sprinkle-On Decorations: Brush unbaked cookies with milk, cream, or lightly beaten egg white and sprinkle with colored sugar or coconut, silver *dragées,* chocolate jimmies, decorettes, finely chopped nuts or candied fruit, cinnamon sugar (supermarket shelves are loaded with jiffy decorator items). Brush any spilled sugar or decoration from baking sheet, then bake as directed. For an extra-special touch, cut paper stencils out of heavy paper—bells, stars, initials—and color cut-out areas only.

Press-On Decorations: Brush unbaked cookies with milk or cream and press on raisins, dried currants, candied cherries, nuts, chocolate or butterscotch bits, mini-marshmallows, gumdrops, cinnamon "red hots" in desired designs.

Paint-On Decorations: These are best for light-colored rolled cookies. Make an egg paint by mixing 1 egg yolk with ¼ teaspoon cold water and 2 or 3 drops food coloring (this amount will be enough for 1 or 2 colors). Using fresh new paintbrushes, paint simple designs on unbaked cookies, then bake as directed until firm but not brown. If paint thickens on standing, thin with a few drops cold water.

To Decorate After Baking:

Most Suitable Cookies: Large, simple, flat cookies, especially rolled cookies.

Paint-On Decorations: Cool cookies and frost with a smooth, thin layer of Royal Icing. Keep bowl of icing covered with a damp cloth or paper toweling to keep it from hardening while you work. For an absolutely smooth surface, keep dipping knife or spatula in hot water and use long sweeping strokes. Let icing harden thoroughly. Paint on designs, using clean, fresh paintbrushes and paste food colors (liquid colors will soften icing too much).

Pipe-On Decorations: Cool cookies and, if you like, frost with Royal Icing as directed for Paint-On Decorations. Tint small amounts of icing desired colors and put through pastry tubes fitted with plain or decorative tips, tracing outlines of cookies or adding any decorative touches you like. Be sure to keep each container of icing covered with a damp cloth so it won't dry out.

To Make Hanging Cookies (wonderful as Christmas tree decorations):

Most Suitable Cookies: Large decorated rolled cookies, particularly fancy cutouts.

To Attach Hangers to Unbaked Cookies: "Stick" large loops of thin ribbon or thread to backs of unbaked cookies with tiny dabs of dough. Bake as directed, then decorate.

To Attach Hangers to Baked Cookies (good only for those that are not shattery-crisp): While cookies are still warm and pliable, quickly draw lengths of coarse thread through top, using a sturdy needle. Don't insert too close to edge or cookies may break. Allow 6"–8" thread for each cookie so it can easily be hung. Decorate as desired.

How to Dress Up Commercial Slice-and-Bake Cookies

The rolls of refrigerator cookie dough in supermarket coolers needn't just be sliced and baked. You can mix the flavors (as in Bullseyes and Checkerboards), roll the dough into balls or bake into chewy bars. You can crown the cookies with frosting or sandwich them together with cream fillings. Here are some quickies to try. (All, incidentally, are easy enough for children to make.)

Bullseyes: Take 1 light and 1 dark roll refrigerated slice-and-bake cookie dough and slice each ¼" thick (some good combinations: sugar cookie and choco-

late or butterscotch, butterscotch and chocolate). Cut center from each slice with a 1½" round cutter, then remove small circles from the "centers" with a 1" round cutter. Reassemble cookies, mixing dark and light to form bullseyes. Lift to ungreased baking sheets with a pancake turner and bake 6–8 minutes at 375° F. until just firm. Cool 1 minute on sheets before transferring to wire racks to cool.

Checkerboards: Take 1 light and 1 dark roll refrigerated slice-and-bake cookie dough and quarter each lengthwise. Roll slightly with hands to round edges of each quarter. Reassemble rolls, checkerboard style as shown, and press lightly

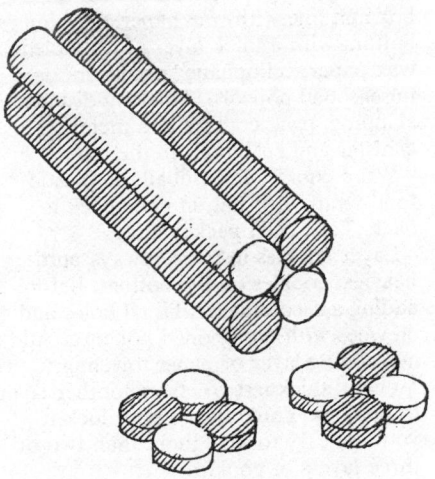

together. Slice ¼" thick, bake and cool by package directions.

Cutouts: Slice 1 roll sugar or coconut cookie dough ¼" thick. With tiny decorative cutters (truffle cutters are perfect), cut out centers of half the slices (save scraps, pinch together, and use for Nut Balls). Bake all and cool by package directions. Sandwich plain and cut-out rounds together with any frosting, jelly or preserves, marshmallow cream or bottled ice-cream sundae topping.

Nut Balls: Slice 1 roll any flavor slice-and-bake cookie dough ¼" thick and shape each slice into a small ball; roll in finely chopped nuts. Arrange 1″ apart on ungreased baking sheets and flatten slightly; top each with a nut half. Bake about 8 minutes at 375° F. until pale tan. Cool 1 minute on sheets, then transfer to wire racks.

Coconut Balls: Prepare like Nut Balls, substituting flaked coconut for nuts.

Snow-Capped Fudgies: Slice 1 roll chocolate slice-and-bake cookie dough ¼″ thick and bake as package directs— but only for 5 minutes. Top each cookie with 5–6 miniature marshmallows, grouping them close together. Bake 2–3 minutes longer until marshmallows are lightly browned and slightly melted. Cool on wire racks.

Quick Marguerites: Slice and bake 1 roll sugar cookie dough as directed; cool cookies and spread with peach, apricot, or berry preserves; top with marsh-mallow cream and serve. Or, if you prefer, top cookies with preserves, then miniature marshmallows and return to oven 2–3 minutes to brown lightly.

Butterscotch or Chocolate Dot Cookies: Slice 1 roll sugar cookie, butterscotch, or chocolate cookie dough ¼″ thick, arrange on baking sheets and lightly press 10–12 butterscotch, semisweet, or milk chocolate bits onto each cookie. Bake and cool as directed.

Coconut or Raisin Cookies: Slice 1 roll sugar cookie, coconut, or butterscotch cookie dough ¼″ thick and bake 5 minutes. Sprinkle each cookie with 1–2 teaspoons flaked coconut or dot with seedless raisins and press in lightly. Bake 2–3 minutes longer until cookies are pale tan. Cool as package directs.

Cherry Twinks: Slice 1 roll sugar or coconut cookie dough ¼″ thick and shape around well-drained maraschino cherries (you'll need 2 slices for each cherry). Bake on ungreased sheets about 8 minutes at 375° F. until light tan. Cool cookies on wire racks, then dip tops in vanilla frosting mix, prepared by package directions.

VARIATION:

Prepare as directed, substituting ½ dried fig, pitted date, or prune for each cherry.

Chocolate-Nut Thins (delightful thin bars): Halve 1 roll sugar or coconut cookie dough crosswise, then slice each piece *lengthwise* ¼″ thick. Arrange 2 rows of 8 slices on an ungreased baking sheet, allowing ¼″ between slices (this will be only half the slices). Bake 8 minutes at 375° F. Remove from oven, and while still on baking sheet, spread with 2 (1½-ounce) bars melted milk chocolate or ½ (5¾-ounce) package melted milk chocolate bits and sprinkle with ⅓ cup minced pecans, walnuts, or blanched almonds. Cool on sheet 15 minutes, then halve each slice crosswise. Bake and frost remaining slices the same way.

Coconut-Chip Chews: Slice 1 roll chocolate chip slice-and-bake cookie dough 1″ thick and quarter each piece; space evenly over bottom of an un-greased 9″×9″×2″ baking pan. Bake 5 minutes at 375° F., remove from oven, and spread partially baked pieces lightly to make an even layer. Cover with 2 cups flaked coconut mixed with 1 lightly beaten egg. Bake 25 minutes longer until coconut is delicately browned. Cool upright in pan on a rack about 15 minutes and cut into bars.

Chewy Slice-and-Bake Bars: Slice 1 roll any flavor slice-and-bake cookie dough 1″ thick and quarter each piece; space evenly over the bottom of an ungreased 9″×9″×2″ baking pan and bake 5 minutes at 375° F. Remove from oven and spread partially baked pieces, making an even layer. Bake 15–20 minutes longer until top is just firm and mixture pulls slightly from edges of pan. Cool upright in pan on a wire rack 15 minutes, then cut into bars.

Streusel-Topped Bars: Prepare Chewy Slice-and-Bake Bars (above) through point of spreading partially baked dough into a single layer. For *streusel* topping: Mix ⅓ cup each sifted flour and firmly packed light brown sugar, then cut in 3 tablespoons butter with a pastry blender until the size of small peas. Scatter mixture evenly over bars and proceed as directed.

Praline Bars: Using nut or butterscotch cookie dough, prepare Chewy Slice-and-Bake Bars (above) through point of spreading partially baked dough into a single layer. Quickly cream ¼ cup softened butter and ½ cup firmly packed light or dark brown sugar, dot evenly over all, and sprinkle with 1 cup finely chopped pecans. Proceed as directed.

⊠ ¢ **BASIC COOKIE MIX**

A good mix to have on hand because there are ten different quick cookies you can make from it.
Makes about 9 cups

4 cups sifted flour
4 cups sugar
1½ cups nonfat dry milk powder
1½ tablespoons baking powder
1½ teaspoons salt

Place all ingredients in a large bowl and mix well with a spoon; sift mixture twice. Store in a tightly covered container. Keeps several weeks at room temperature.

10 Quick Cookies to Make from the Basic Mix

Sugar Cookies (Makes 3 dozen): With a spoon, mix 2 cups Basic Cookie Mix, ½ cup melted butter or margarine, 1 lightly beaten egg, and 1 teaspoon vanilla. Lightly flour hands and shape in 1″ balls; arrange 2″ apart on well-greased baking sheets. Bake 12–15 minutes at 350° F. until golden. Cool 1–2 minutes on sheets, then transfer to wire racks to cool. About 60 calories per cookie.

Raisin Cookies (Makes 3 dozen): Prepare Sugar Cookie dough as directed, mix in ½ cup seedless raisins or sultanas, shape and bake as directed. About 70 calories per cookie.

Coconut Cookies (Makes 3 dozen): Prepare Sugar Cookie dough as directed, mix in ½ cup flaked coconut, shape and bake as directed. About 65 calories per cookie.

Chocolate Chip Cookies (Makes 3 dozen): Prepare Sugar Cookie dough as directed, mix in ½ cup semisweet chocolate bits, shape and bake as directed. About 70 calories per cookie.

Nut Cookies (Makes 3 dozen): Prepare Sugar Cookie dough as directed, mix in ½ cup chopped walnuts, pecans, or blanched almonds, shape and bake as directed. About 70 calories per cookie.

Spice Drops (Makes 3 dozen): Mix 2 cups Basic Cookie Mix with 1 teaspoon cinnamon, ¼ teaspoon each ginger and allspice, and ⅛ teaspoon nutmeg. Stir in 1 lightly beaten egg, ½ cup melted butter or margarine, and 1–2 tablespoons water, just enough to make mixture a good consistency for dropping from a spoon. Drop from a teaspoon onto well-greased baking sheets, spacing cookies 2″ apart, and bake 12–15 minutes at 350° F. until golden. Cool 1–2 minutes on sheets, then transfer to wire racks to cool. About 60 calories per cookie.

Chocolate Drops (Makes 3 dozen): Mix 2 cups Basic Cookie Mix with ¼ cup sifted cocoa. Stir in 1 lightly beaten egg, ½ cup melted butter, ¼ cup water, and 1 teaspoon vanilla. Drop from a teaspoon onto well-greased baking sheets, spacing cookies 2″ apart, and bake 12–15 minutes at 350° F. until lightly browned around edges. Let cool 1–2 minutes on sheets, then lift to wire racks to cool. About 70 calories per cookie.

Peanut Butter Balls (Makes 3 dozen): Mix 2 cups Basic Cookie Mix with 1 lightly beaten egg, ¼ cup melted butter or margarine, ½ cup crunchy or creamy peanut butter, and 1 teaspoon vanilla. With lightly floured hands, shape into 1″ balls and space 2″ apart on lightly greased baking sheets. Bake 12 minutes at 350° F. or until the color of sand. Transfer to wire racks to cool. About 70 calories per cookie.

Brownies (Makes 16): With a spoon mix 2 cups Basic Cookie Mix, 1 lightly beaten egg, ⅓ cup each cold water and melted butter or margarine, 1 teaspoon vanilla, and 2 (1-ounce) envelopes no-melt unsweetened chocolate or ¼ cup sifted cocoa. Fold in ½–¾ cup chopped pecans or walnuts. Beat by hand 1 minute, spoon into a greased 9″×9″×2″ baking pan, and bake 25 minutes at 375° F. or until top springs back when touched. Cool upright in pan on rack, then cut into large squares. About 150 calories per brownie.

Oatmeal Bars (Makes 32): With a spoon mix 2 cups Basic Cookie Mix, 1½ cups uncooked quick-cooking oatmeal, 1 lightly beaten egg, ¾ cup melted butter or margarine, ¼ cup cold water, 1 teaspoon vanilla, and ½ teaspoon almond extract. Spoon into a greased 13″×9″×2″ baking pan and bake 30–35 minutes at 350° F. until top is golden and sides shrink slightly from sides of pan. Cool upright in pan 10 minutes, then cut into small bars. About 120 calories per bar.

DROP COOKIES

These are old favorites because they're so quick to mix and bake. They can be plain or studded with nuts, chocolate, or fruit; they can be crisp or chewy, thick or thin, rich or slimming (well, at least fairly low in calories). Best of all, they do not have to be rolled or shaped or pushed through a cookie press—simply dropped from a spoon and popped in the oven.

Some Tips:
– To minimize spreading during baking, chill dough slightly, then mound in center when dropping onto cookie sheets.
– Space cookies on sheets carefully, remembering that the thinner the dough, the more the cookies will spread (recipes specify just how much room to leave between cookies).
– For more interesting or uniform size cookies, put dough through a pastry bag fitted with a large, plain round tube, piping directly onto baking sheets. Cookies without nuts, fruit, or other obstructive bits can be pressed through a large open star tip. (*Note:* Don't fill pastry bag more than ⅔ full because the heat of your hands will soften the dough and make cookies spread more than usual.)

⊠ CREAM CHEESE FLAKES

Being egg-free, these cookies are good for those with an allergy to eggs.
Makes 5 dozen

1 cup butter or margarine
1 (3-ounce) package cream cheese, softened to room temperature
1 cup sugar
½ teaspoon salt
1 tablespoon light cream or milk
1 tablespoon finely grated lemon or orange rind
2½ cups sifted flour

Preheat oven to 350° F. Cream butter and cheese, add sugar and salt, and continue creaming until light and fluffy. Add cream and lemon rind; slowly blend in flour. Drop from a teaspoon onto ungreased baking sheets, spacing cookies 2″ apart; flatten cookies slightly and bake 15 minutes until lightly ringed with brown. Transfer at once to wire racks to cool. About 60 calories per cookie.

⊠ LEMON WAFERS

Nice and tart.
Makes about 4½ dozen

½ cup butter or margarine, softened to room temperature
1⅓ cups sugar
3 eggs
3 tablespoons lemon juice
Grated rind of 1 lemon
2 cups unsifted flour
¼ teaspoon mace
¼ teaspoon salt

Preheat oven to 375° F. Cream butter

until light and fluffy, then beat in sugar. Mix in eggs, one at a time, beating well after each addition. Stir in lemon juice and rind; mix in flour, mace, and salt. Drop from a teaspoon onto lightly greased baking sheets, spacing cookies 2″ apart. Bake about 15 minutes until cookies are lightly ringed with brown. While still warm, transfer to wire racks to cool. About 55 calories per cookie.

⊠ ¢ BROWN SUGAR DROPS

Try the variations as well as the basic recipe.
Makes 6 dozen

3½ cups sifted flour
1 teaspoon baking soda
1 teaspoon salt
1 cup butter or margarine or ½ cup each
 vegetable shortening and butter,
 softened to room temperature
2 cups firmly packed light or dark brown
 sugar
2 eggs
½ cup sour milk or buttermilk
2 teaspoons maple flavoring (optional)

Preheat oven to 400° F. Sift flour with soda and salt and set aside. With a rotary beater or electric mixer cream butter, sugar, and eggs until well blended. Mix in sour milk and maple flavoring. Slowly mix in dry ingredients. Drop by rounded teaspoonfuls 2″ apart on greased baking sheets and bake 8–10 minutes until nearly firm (cookie should barely retain fingerprint when lightly touched). Transfer cookies to wire racks to cool. About 70 calories per cookie.

VARIATIONS:

Coconut Drops: Prepare as directed, mixing 1½ cups flaked coconut into dough at the end. Bake as above. About 80 calories per cookie.

Filled Brown Sugar Drops: Prepare as directed and drop by level teaspoonfuls; make a thumbprint or small well in center of each cookie and fill with dabs of jam, marmalade, peanut butter, or Fig Filling. Cover with a dab of cookie dough and bake 10–12 minutes. About 100 calories per cookie.

Hermits (Makes about 8 dozen): Prepare as directed but substitute ½ cup cold coffee for the sour milk. Mix 1½ teaspoons cinnamon and ½ teaspoon nutmeg into dough, then 1½ cups minced walnuts or pecans and 2 cups chopped seedless raisins. Bake as directed. About 80 calories per cookie.

Rocks (Makes 8 dozen): Prepare as directed, then stir in 2 cups seedless or sultana raisins, 1½ teaspoons nutmeg, and ½ cup finely chopped candied citron. Bake as directed. About 80 calories per cookie.

Fruit Drops (Makes 8 dozen): Prepare as directed, then stir in 2 cups of any of the following: dried currants, minced dates, prunes, dried apricots or figs, candied cherries, or mixed candied fruits. Bake as directed. About 80 calories per cookie.

⊠ TOLL HOUSE COOKIES

Makes about 4 dozen

1 cup plus 2 tablespoons sifted flour
½ teaspoon baking soda
½ teaspoon salt
½ cup butter or vegetable shortening,
 softened to room temperature
⅓ cup plus 1 tablespoon sugar
⅓ cup plus 1 tablespoon firmly packed
 light brown sugar
1 teaspoon vanilla
1 egg
1 (6-ounce) package semisweet chocolate
 bits
½ cup coarsely chopped pecans

Preheat oven to 375° F. Sift flour with baking soda and salt and set aside. Cream butter, sugars, and vanilla until light and fluffy. Beat in egg. Mix in dry ingredients; stir in chocolate bits and pecans. Drop by well-rounded ½ teaspoonfuls on lightly greased baking sheets, spacing cookies 2″ apart. Bake 10–12 minutes until lightly edged with brown. Transfer immediately to wire racks to cool. About 65 calories per cookie.

COOKIE CHART*
OR WHICH COOKIE RECIPES TO

	Halve	Double	Let Children Try	Pack and Ship
Drop Cookies:				
Applesauce Cookies		X	X	
Benne Wafers	X			
Brandy Snaps		X		
Brown Sugar Drops	X		X	X
Carrot Cookies		X		X
Chocolate Drops			X	X
Chocolate Macaroons	X			X
Chocolate Pecan Wafers				X
Coconut Discs		X	X	X
Coconut Drops	X		X	X
Cream Cheese Flakes	X			
Dropped Oatmeal Chippies	X	X	X	X
Filled Brown Sugar Drops	X		X	
Florentines		X		
Fruit Drops	X		X	X
Hermits	X		X	X
Maude's Cookies		X	X	X
Mincemeat Discs		X	X	X
Mincemeat Hermits	X		X	X
Old-Fashioned Ginger Biscuits		X	X	X
Orange-Almond Lace Cookies	X			
Pecan Crisps	X	X	X	X
Rocks	X		X	X
Spice Drops			X	X
Sugarless Oatmeal Drops	X	X		
Sugar Pillows	X		X	X
Toll House Cookies		X	X	X
Rolled Cookies:				
Butterscotch Sugar Cookies	X			
Chocolate Sugar Cookies	X			
Coconut Sugar Cookies	X			
Decorative Cookies	X		X	
Fig Newtons	X			X
Gingerbread Boys	X	X	X	
Golden Cheddar Rings	X			
Moravian Christmas Cookies	X			
Nut Sugar Cookies	X			
Pepparkakor	X		X	

*Those cookies not listed are not very well suited to any category.

	Halve	Double	Let Children Try	Pack and Ship
Rolled Cookies (continued)				
Soft Sugar Cookies	X			
Spitzbuben	X			
Springerle	X			
Sugar Cookies	X			
Molded or Pressed Cookies:				
Almond Butterballs	X	X		X
Butterballs	X	X		X
Chocolate Chip Cookies			X	X
Chocolate Spritz	X		X	X
Coconut Butterballs	X			
Coconut Cookies			X	X
Nut Cookies			X	X
Old-Fashioned Butter "S" Cookies	X			
Orange-Almond Balls			X	X
Peanut Butter Balls			X	X
Peanut Butter Cookies	X		X	X
Pressed Molasses Spice Cookies			X	X
Raisin Cookies			X	X
Snickerdoodles	X		X	X
Spritz	X		X	X
Sugar Marbles			X	X
Thumbprint Cookies	X	X·		X
Refrigerator Cookies:				
Almond-Orange Icebox Cookies		X		X
Basic Refrigerator Cookies		X		X
Chocolate Checkerboards		X		X
Chocolate Refrigerator Cookies		X		X
Fig and Almond Pinwheels				X
Filled Refrigerator Cookies		X		
Nut Refrigerator Cookies		X		X
Oatmeal Icebox Cookies		X		X
Orange-Chocolate Jewels				X
Bars:				
Apple-Oatmeal Bars				X
Basic Brownies		X	X	X
Black Walnut and Coconut Bars				X
Brownies			X	X
Brown Sugar Brownies		X	X	X
Butterscotch Brownies		X	X	X
Chewy Pecan-Cinnamon Bars				X·
Coconut Brownies		X	X	X

COOKIE CHART
OR WHICH COOKIE RECIPES TO (continued)

	Halve	Double	Let Children Try	Pack and Ship
Bars (continued)				
Coconut Topped Brownies		X		X
Congo Squares			X	X
Currant and Raisin Bars				X
Date-Oatmeal Bars				X
Fig-Oatmeal Bars				X
Fruit Bars				X
Fruit and Nut Bars				X
Fudgey Saucepan Brownies			X	X
German Date Squares				X
Layered Apricot Bars				X
Marble Brownies				X
Minted Double Chocolate Tea Brownies		X		X
Mocha Brownies		X		X
Oatmeal Bars			X	X
Scottish Shortbread	X			X
Snowy Coconut Chews		X	X	X
Toll House Brownies		X	X	X
Two-Tone Brownies				X
Wheat and Milk-Free Brownies			X	X
No-Bake Cookies:				
Butterscotch Haystacks		X	X	X
Chocolate Haystacks		X	X	X
Fruit Balls	X	X	X	X
Fudge Nuggets			X	X
No-Bake Chocolate Bon-Bons	X	X	X	X
No-Bake Rum Balls	X	X		X
Peanut Butter Bars			X	X
Porcupines	X		X	X

Note: All of the suggestions given in How to Dress Up Commercial Slice-and-Bake Cookies are easy enough for children to do.

⊠ PECAN CRISPS

Rather like a praline cookie.
Makes about 5 dozen

1 cup butter (no substitute)
1 (1-pound) box light brown sugar
2 eggs
2½ cups unsifted flour
½ teaspoon baking soda
½ teaspoon salt
1 teaspoon vanilla
1½ cups coarsely chopped pecans

Preheat oven to 350° F. Cream butter
until light, add sugar, and continue
creaming until fluffy. Beat in eggs, one
at a time. Mix in flour, soda, and salt,
then remaining ingredients. Drop from a
teaspoon onto lightly greased baking
sheets, spacing cookies about 2"
apart, and bake 12–15 minutes until
lightly browned. Remove at once to
wire racks to cool. About 100 calories
per cookie.

⚔ ⊠ MAUDE'S COOKIES

A centuries-old Quaker recipe. The
cookies are buttery and bland but the
crystallized ginger decoration adds bite.
Moreover, they are fairly low-calorie.
Makes 3½–4 dozen small cookies

½ cup butter (no substitute), softened to
room temperature
⅓ cup sugar
1 egg, well beaten
¾ cup sifted flour
½ teaspoon vanilla
3½–4 dozen pieces crystallized ginger
about the size of raisins

Preheat oven to 350° F. Cream butter
until fluffy, add sugar, and continue
creaming until light. Beat in egg, then
mix in flour and vanilla. Drop from a
half teaspoon onto *lightly* greased baking
sheets, spacing cookies 2" apart—they
spread quite a bit. Press a piece of
candied ginger into the center of each
cookie and bake 8–10 minutes until
ringed with tan. Transfer at once to
wire racks to cool. About 35 calories per
cookie.

FROSTED ORANGE DROPS

Makes about 4 dozen

½ cup vegetable shortening
1 cup sugar
½ teaspoon salt
4 egg yolks
1 tablespoon finely grated orange rind
½ cup orange juice
2½ cups sifted flour
1½ teaspoons baking powder
½ cup coarsely chopped black walnuts

Frosting:

1 tablespoon butter or margarine
1 tablespoon orange juice
1 teaspoon finely grated orange rind
1 cup sifted confectioners' sugar
¼ teaspoon salt

Preheat oven to 375° F. Cream shortening with sugar, salt, and egg yolks until
light; mix in orange rind and juice. Sift
flour with baking powder, and stir into
creamed mixture; mix in nuts. Drop
from a teaspoon onto greased baking
sheets, spacing 2" apart. Bake 12–15
minutes until touched with brown.
Meanwhile, prepare frosting: Cream
butter, orange juice, and rind until light,
stir in confectioners' sugar and salt, and
beat until smooth. Cool cookies slightly
on wire racks, then frost. About 80
calories per cookie.

CHOCOLATE PECAN WAFERS

Dark and chewy.
Makes 4 dozen

½ cup butter or margarine
1 cup sugar
¼ teaspoon salt
1 teaspoon vanilla
2 eggs
¾ cup sifted flour
4 (1-ounce) squares semisweet
chocolate, melted
¾ cup finely chopped pecans

Cream butter, sugar and salt until light
and fluffy, add vanilla and eggs, and
beat well. Slowly mix in flour and
remaining ingredients. Chill mixture in
bowl ½ hour. Meanwhile, preheat oven
to 350° F. Drop by rounded teaspoon-

fuls 2″ apart on greased baking sheets
and flatten with bottom of a glass dipped
in sugar (resugar glass for each cookie).
Bake 15 minutes until tops retain almost
no impression when touched. Transfer
immediately to wire racks to cool. About
65 calories per cookie.

BENNE WAFERS

In the South, sesame seeds are called
"benne." This recipe is a Charleston
favorite.
Makes about 4 dozen

1 cup sifted flour
¼ teaspoon salt
½ teaspoon baking powder
2 cups firmly packed dark brown sugar
½ cup butter or margarine
2 eggs, lightly beaten
1 teaspoon vanilla
⅔ cup toasted sesame seeds

Preheat oven to 325° F. Sift flour with
salt and baking powder and set aside.
Cream sugar and butter until thoroughly
mixed; beat in eggs and vanilla. Slowly
mix in flour, then sesame seeds, mixing
just to blend. Drop mixture by level
teaspoonfuls 5″ apart on well-greased
baking sheets. Bake 10 minutes until
lightly browned; cool on sheets about ½
minute, then lift to wire racks with a
pancake turner. Store airtight when
cool. About 80 calories per cookie.

⚖ ¢ CARROT COOKIES

A cookie somewhat more nutritious than
most.
Makes about 5 dozen

½ cup butter or margarine
1 cup sugar
1 cup cooled, mashed, cooked carrots
(unseasoned)
1 egg
½ teaspoon vanilla
½ teaspoon cinnamon
¼ teaspoon ginger
¼ teaspoon allspice
1 tablespoon finely grated orange rind
2 cups sifted flour
2 teaspoons baking powder
¼ teaspoon salt

Preheat oven to 350° F. Cream butter
until fluffy; add sugar gradually, beating
well after each addition. Mix in carrots,
egg, vanilla, spices, and orange rind.
Sift flour with baking powder and salt
and beat in gradually. Drop from a
teaspoon 1½″ apart onto lightly greased
baking sheets and bake 12–15 minutes
until firm but not brown. Let cool about
1 minute on baking sheets, then transfer
to wire racks to cool. About 40 calories
per cookie.

PUMPKIN COOKIES

Because the cookies are made with
pumpkin, raisins, and nuts, they provide
a little more than just "empty calories."
Makes 4 dozen

2 cups sifted flour
1 teaspoon baking soda
¼ teaspoon salt
1 teaspoon cinnamon
¼ teaspoon nutmeg
½ cup butter or margarine
1 cup sugar
1 teaspoon vanilla
1 cup canned pumpkin
1 cup seedless raisins
1 cup chopped pecans or walnuts

Preheat oven to 375° F. Sift flour with
soda, salt, and spices and set aside.
Cream butter with sugar until light, add
vanilla and pumpkin, and mix well.
Slowly add dry ingredients, then stir in
raisins and nuts. Drop by rounded
teaspoonfuls 2″ apart on greased baking
sheets and bake 15 minutes until lightly
browned. Transfer to wire racks to
cool. About 95 calories per cookie.

⊠ COCONUT DISCS

Try making these cookies with freshly
grated coconut instead of canned flaked
coconut. They will taste nuttier and not
quite so sweet.
Makes 2 dozen

2 tablespoons butter or margarine,
  softened to room temperature
½ cup sugar
1 egg, lightly beaten
¼ teaspoon almond extract
1 cup packaged biscuit mix
2 tablespoons milk
⅔ cup flaked coconut

Preheat oven to 375° F. Mix butter
with sugar, egg, and almond extract.
Add biscuit mix and milk and blend until
smooth. Stir in coconut. Drop by
rounded teaspoonfuls 2" apart on
greased baking sheets and bake 10
minutes until lightly browned. Transfer
to wire racks to cool. About 70 calories
per cookie.

VARIATION:

Mincemeat Discs (Makes 2 dozen):
Substitute firmly packed light brown
sugar for the granulated, omit almond
extract, milk, and coconut. Prepare as
directed, blending in ⅔ cup mincemeat
at the end. Drop and bake as directed.
About 85 calories per cookie.

⊠ **APPLESAUCE COOKIES**

If you like caraway seeds, by all means
stir them into the cookie dough. They
give the cookies quite a different flavor.
Makes 2½ dozen

2 tablespoons butter or margarine,
  softened to room temperature
½ cup sugar
1 egg, lightly beaten
1 cup packaged biscuit mix
½ cup applesauce
1 teaspoon finely grated lemon rind
1½ teaspoons caraway seeds (optional)

Preheat oven to 375° F. Cream butter
well with sugar and egg; mix in
remaining ingredients until smooth.
Drop from a teaspoon 2" apart on well-
greased baking sheets and bake 8
minutes until golden around the edges.
Transfer at once to wire racks to cool.
(Note: Since these cookies brown nicely
on the underside but not on top, they're
more attractive served bottom side up.)
About 50 calories per cookie.

**OLD-FASHIONED GINGER
BISCUITS**

For crisp cookies, store airtight; for
softer ones, store loosely covered. To
crispen again in humid weather, heat
3–5 minutes at 350° F., then cool.
Makes 4½ dozen

2 cups sifted flour
½ teaspoon salt
2 teaspoons ginger
½ teaspoon cloves
2 teaspoons baking soda
¾ cup butter or margarine
1¼ cups sugar
1 egg, lightly beaten
¼ cup molasses

Preheat oven to 350° F. Sift flour with
salt, spices, and baking soda and set
aside. Cream butter and sugar until light
and fluffy. Add egg and molasses, beating
well after each addition. Mix in dry
ingredients just until blended. Drop by
rounded teaspoonfuls 3" apart on
greased baking sheets and bake 15
minutes until golden brown. (Note: Keep
unused dough chilled until ready to
bake.) Cool cookies on sheets 1–2 minutes, then transfer to wire racks to cool.
About 60 calories per cookie.

⊠ **DROPPED OATMEAL
CHIPPIES**

Makes 3½ dozen

1 cup sifted flour
2 teaspoons baking powder
½ teaspoon salt
½ cup butter or margarine, softened to
  room temperature
1 cup firmly packed light brown sugar
1½ cups uncooked quick-cooking
  oatmeal
2 eggs, lightly beaten
1 teaspoon vanilla
1 cup chopped pitted dates or seedless
  raisins

Preheat oven to 350° F. Sift flour with
baking powder and salt. Stir butter and
sugar together until just mixed; blend in
flour, oatmeal, eggs, and vanilla. Stir in
dates. Drop by rounded teaspoonfuls

2″ apart on greased baking sheets and bake 15–18 minutes until lightly browned and tops spring back when touched. Transfer at once to wire racks to cool. About 75 calories per cookie.

⚖ ☒ SUGARLESS OATMEAL DROPS

Makes 2½ dozen

1 cup sifted flour
2 teaspoons baking powder
¼ teaspoon salt
½ cup butter or margarine, softened to room temperature
1 cup low-calorie granulated sugar substitute
2 eggs, lightly beaten
1½ teaspoons vanilla
1⅓ cups uncooked oatmeal
½ teaspoon cinnamon (optional)

Preheat oven to 350° F. Sift flour with baking powder and salt. Cream butter until light and blend in sugar substitute. Mix in remaining ingredients. Drop by level teaspoonfuls 1″ apart on greased baking sheets and bake 15 minutes or until edges are lightly browned and cookies just firm to the touch. Transfer to wire racks to cool. About 50 calories per cookie.

⚖ ☒ MONTROSE DROP CAKES

These little rose-flavored Scottish cakes are usually baked in tiny tart tins, but they can be dropped from a spoon directly onto baking sheets. Because the cakes are so small, they are fairly low-calorie. Rose water, used to flavor these cookies, is available at specialty food shops.
Makes about 5 dozen

½ cup butter (no substitute)
⅔ cup sugar
3 eggs
1 tablespoon brandy
1 teaspoon rose water
¼ teaspoon nutmeg
1 cup sifted flour
½ teaspoon baking powder
¼ teaspoon salt
⅔ cup dried currants

Preheat oven to 375° F. Cream butter until fluffy, add sugar gradually, beating well after each addition. Beat in eggs, one at a time, then brandy, rose water, and nutmeg. Sift flour with baking powder and salt and mix in a little bit at a time. Stir in currants. Drop from a teaspoon onto greased baking sheets, spacing cookies 3″ apart. Bake 8–10 minutes until ringed with tan. Let cool on baking sheets about 1 minute, then transfer to wire racks to cool. About 40 calories per cookie.

⚖ MACAROONS

These cookies are milk- and wheat-free, good for anyone with those specific allergies.
Makes about 4½ dozen

1 (½-pound) can almond paste
3 egg whites
1 cup sugar
½ cup sifted confectioners' sugar

Preheat oven to 300° F. Using a sharp knife, slice almond paste ¼″ thick, then chop until the consistency of coarse meal. Place in a large mixing bowl, add egg whites, and mix using your hands. Knead in the sugar, a little bit at a time, then work in the confectioners' sugar until smooth. Line 2 baking sheets with heavy brown paper, then drop macaroons onto paper from a teaspoon, making each about 1″ in diameter and spacing about 2″ apart. Bake on lowest oven shelf 25–30 minutes until crazed and faintly tan. Remove from oven and let cool on paper to room temperature. Dampen paper by setting on top of moist towels, then peel off macaroons. Let cookies dry on wire racks at room temperature 1 hour, then store airtight. About 45 calories per cookie.

⚖ CHOCOLATE "MACAROONS"

Makes 4 dozen

4 egg whites
2 cups sifted confectioners' sugar
2 cups fine vanilla wafer crumbs
2 (1-ounce) squares semisweet chocolate, grated
1½ teaspoons cinnamon

Preheat oven to 325° F. Beat egg whites until foamy, slowly add confectioners' sugar, and continue beating until firm peaks form. Stir in crumbs, chocolate, and cinnamon. Drop by level teaspoonfuls 2″ apart on well-greased baking sheets and bake 20 minutes. Transfer at once to wire racks to cool. About 40 calories per cookie.

COCONUT MACAROONS

Makes about 3 dozen

4 egg whites
¼ teaspoon salt
¾ teaspoon vanilla
¼ teaspoon almond extract
1⅓ cups sugar
2 (3½-ounce) cans flaked coconut

Preheat oven to 325° F. Beat egg whites with salt, vanilla, and almond extract until soft peaks form. Add sugar gradually, about 2 tablespoons at a time, and continue beating until stiff peaks form. Fold in coconut. Drop by rounded teaspoonfuls onto greased baking sheets, spacing cookies about 2″ apart. Bake 18–20 minutes until very delicately browned and firm to the touch. Cool briefly on sheets (just until macaroons can be lifted without losing their shape), then transfer to wire racks to cool. About 60 calories per cookie.

⚖ MERINGUE KISSES

It's said that Marie Antoinette loved meringue kisses so she often made them herself. If you've never made them, see Ground Rules for Making Meringue in the chapter on pies and pastries before beginning this recipe.
Makes about 3½ dozen

4 egg whites, at room temperature
¼ teaspoon salt
¼ teaspoon cream of tartar
1 cup sugar
¾ teaspoon vanilla or ¼ teaspoon almond extract
1 or 2 drops red or green food coloring (optional)

Preheat oven to 250° F. Line baking sheets with foil. Beat egg whites with a rotary beater or electric mixer at moderate speed until foamy; stir in salt and cream of tartar. Add sugar, 1 tablespoon at a time, beating well after each addition. Add vanilla and food coloring, if you wish, to tint meringue a pastel color. Beat hard at highest mixer speed until meringue is glossy and forms peaks that stand straight up when beater is withdrawn. Drop by rounded teaspoonfuls 2″ apart on prepared baking sheets; leave surface peaked or smooth into rounded caps. If you prefer, pipe meringue through a pastry bag fitted with a medium-size plain or star tip making each kiss about 1½″ in diameter. Bake 35–45 minutes until creamy-white and firm. For crisp kisses: Turn off oven and let kisses cool in oven 2–3 hours without opening door. For chewier kisses, lift foil and kisses to wire rack and cool. Peel kisses from foil, using a spatula to help loosen them if necessary. Store airtight. About 20 calories per cookie.

VARIATIONS: (With the exception of Filled Kisses and Rainbow Kisses, all are low-calorie.)

Frosted Kisses: Dip tops of baked, cooled kisses in Chocolate or Fudge Frosting; let dry on wire racks. About 30 calories per cookie.

Filled Kisses: Sandwich 2 kisses together with a favorite filling or frosting. Recipe too flexible for a meaningful calorie count.

Rainbow Kisses: Before baking, divide meringue into 3 equal parts and tint pastel yellow, green, and pink. Bake as directed and cool. Sandwich different colors together with plain or tinted sweetened whipped cream. About 65 calories per cookie.

Meringue Chews: Preheat oven to 325° F. Prepare kisses as directed, then bake 10–12 minutes until tops are just firm to the touch. Cool on foil on wire racks. About 20 calories per cookie.

Candied Kisses: Prepare meringue mixture as directed, then fold in ⅔ cup very finely chopped candied fruits or mixed candied red and green cherries; shape and bake as directed. About 30 calories per cookie.

Nut Kisses: Prepare meringue mixture as directed, then fold in 1 cup finely chopped nuts: pecans, walnuts, blanched almonds, filberts, pistachios. Shape, sprinkle tops with a few additional nuts, and bake as directed. About 45 calories per cookie.

Chocolate Kisses: Prepare meringue mixture as directed, then fold in 2 melted and cooled (1-ounce) squares unsweetened or semisweet chocolate, leaving a marbled effect if you like. About 30 calories per cookie.

Coconut Kisses: Prepare meringue mixture as directed, fold in 1½ cups flaked coconut, shape and bake as directed. About 30 calories per cookie.

Brown Sugar Kisses: When making meringue, substitute 1 cup light brown sugar for the granulated and proceed as recipe directs. (*Note:* For especially good flavor, use 1 teaspoon maple flavoring instead of vanilla, or ½ teaspoon each vanilla and maple flavoring.) About 20 calories per cookie.

Coffee Kisses: Prepare meringue mixture as directed, then beat in 1 teaspoon vanilla and 4 teaspoons instant coffee powder dissolved in 1 tablespoon boiling water. Shape and bake as directed, then let stand in turned-off oven at least 4 hours or until crisp and dry. About 25 calories per cookie.

Fruit Kisses: Prepare meringue mixture as directed, then beat in ⅓ cup sieved, *thick* berry preserves (strawberry, raspberry, black raspberry, etc.), adding 1 rounded teaspoonful at a time and beating well after each addition. Omit vanilla and almond extract. Shape and bake 3½ hours at 200° F., then let stand at least 4 hours in turned-off oven. About 30 calories per cookie.

⚖ HAZELNUT KISSES

Makes about 5 dozen

2 egg whites
⅛ teaspoon salt
1 cup sifted confectioners' sugar
1 cup finely ground unblanched hazelnuts or filberts
1 (1-ounce) square unsweetened chocolate, grated fine
½ teaspoon cinnamon
¼ teaspoon finely grated lemon rind (optional)
Candied red cherry slices (optional garnish)

Preheat oven to 300° F. Beat egg whites with salt until stiff peaks form; mix in remaining ingredients except cherries and drop from a half teaspoon onto ungreased, foil-lined baking sheets, spacing cookies about 1½″ apart. Decorate each, if you like, with a slice of candied cherry. Bake 20 minutes until faintly browned, remove from oven, and cool about 2 minutes before removing from foil. Cool on wire racks. About 25 calories per cookie.

BRANDY SNAPS

Don't attempt these on a wet or humid day; they won't be crisp.
Makes 1½ dozen

¼ cup molasses
¼ cup butter or margarine, softened to room temperature
⅓ cup sugar
½ cup sifted flour
½ teaspoon ginger
1–2 teaspoons brandy

Brandy Cream (optional filling):

½ cup heavy cream
¼ cup sifted confectioners' sugar
1–2 tablespoons brandy

Preheat oven to 325° F. Bring molasses just to a boil over moderate heat, add butter and sugar, and stir until melted. Off heat mix in flour, ginger, and brandy. Stand pan in a bowl of very hot water to keep mixture soft as you work, replenishing hot water as needed. Drop mixture from level teaspoons onto greased baking sheet, spacing 3″ apart. Bake one sheet at a time, 5 minutes in top ⅓ of oven, then 2–3 minutes on middle rack. Cool cookies on sheet about 1 minute or until they can be lifted with a pancake turner; while still warm and pliable, bend into a tube around the handle of a wooden spoon. Cool on wire racks. If cookies harden too soon, return quickly to oven to soften. If you like, fill just before serving with Brandy Cream. To make, whip cream and confectioners' sugar until soft peaks form; fold in brandy. (*Note:* the easiest way to fill cookies is with a pastry bag fitted with a plain or rosette tip.) About 100 calories per cookie if unfilled, about 140 per cookie if filled.

To Serve as Flat Wafers: Let cookies stand a little longer on baking sheets so they won't curl between rack rungs as they cool.

⚜ ORANGE-ALMOND LACE COOKIES

Makes 4 dozen

½ cup butter (no substitute)
½ cup sugar
½ teaspoon finely grated orange rind
½ cup ground blanched almonds
2 tablespoons flour
2 tablespoons milk

Preheat oven to 350° F. Mix all ingredients in a saucepan and heat and stir over moderate heat just until mixture bubbles; remove from heat at once. Drop by half teaspoonfuls 4″ apart on ungreased baking sheets (you will only get 4 or 5 cookies on each sheet). Bake 6–7 minutes until golden brown and bubbly. Let stand 1 minute, just until cookies are firm enough to lift off sheet with a pancake turner. Cool on wire racks, then store airtight. About 30 calories per cookie.

To Curl Cookies: As you lift each cookie from baking sheet, curl around handle of wooden spoon to form a cornucopia or "cigarette"; cool seam side down. If cookies cool too quickly to curl, return to oven briefly to soften.

FLORENTINES

Makes 2 dozen

¼ cup butter or margarine
⅓ cup firmly packed light brown sugar
¼ cup sifted flour
¼ cup plus 1 tablespoon heavy cream
¾ cup finely chopped or slivered blanched almonds
⅓ cup minced candied orange peel or mixed candied peel and candied cherries
4 (1-ounce) squares semisweet chocolate
3 tablespoons butter or margarine

Preheat oven to 350° F. Cream butter and sugar until light and fluffy. Stir in flour alternately with cream; then stir in almonds and peel. Drop mixture by level teaspoonfuls 3″ apart on greased and floured baking sheets; with a knife dipped in cold water, spread into 2″ rounds. Bake about 12 minutes until lacy and golden brown, watching carefully toward the end. Cool 1–2 minutes on sheets, then, using a pancake turner, carefully transfer to wire racks to cool. If cookies cool too much to remove easily, return to oven 1–2 minutes to soften. Melt chocolate and butter together in a double boiler over simmering water, stirring frequently; cool slightly. Arrange cookies flat side up on wax paper and spread with chocolate. When chocolate hardens, store cookies airtight. About 120 calories per cookie.

⚜ LADYFINGERS

If you've never tasted homemade ladyfingers, you don't know what you're missing.
Makes 1½ dozen

3 eggs, separated
⅔ cup sifted confectioners' sugar
½ teaspoon vanilla
Pinch salt
½ cup sifted cake flour

Preheat oven to 325° F. Beat egg yolks until pale lemon colored, slowly add ⅓ cup confectioners' sugar and continue beating until thick and the color of mayonnaise. Beat in vanilla. Beat egg whites until soft peaks form, add salt and 2 tablespoons confectioners' sugar, and continue beating until stiff. Mix flour with remaining confectioners' sugar. Fold egg whites into yolk mixture, about ¼ at a time and alternately with flour, beginning and ending with whites. (*Note:* Sift flour onto yolk mixture for more even distribution and don't try to fold in every speck of egg white each time before adding more.) Spoon mixture into a pastry bag (no tube necessary because the bag opening is the perfect size) and press out evenly but lightly into strips 4″ long, spacing them 2″ apart on buttered and floured baking sheets. (*Note:* You can shape ladyfingers with 2 tablespoons or simply drop mixture by rounded teaspoonfuls without shaping.) Bake in center or upper ⅓ of oven 12–15 minutes until pale golden. Cool on sheets 1 minute, then, using a wide spatula, transfer to wire racks to cool. Serve as is, sprinkled with confectioners' sugar or sandwiched together with jam, chocolate frosting, or sweetened whipped cream. About 50 calories per cookie.

For a Crisper Crust (nice for Charlotte Russe): Sprinkle ladyfingers with confectioners' sugar just before baking.

¢ ⚖ **MADELEINES**

Madeleines are spongy little cakes baked in small individual molds. The molds come in sets of a dozen and are available in kitchen departments of large department stores, also at gourmet shops. You'll need two dozen molds for this recipe because the batter is unusually light and must be baked the minute it's mixed.
Makes 2 dozen

*2 tablespoons clarified butter**
½ cup sifted cake flour
⅛ teaspoon salt
2 eggs
⅓ cup sugar
½ teaspoon finely grated lemon rind
¼ cup butter (no substitute), melted
Confectioners' sugar

Preheat oven to 350° F. Brush madeleine molds with clarified butter and refrigerate until needed. Sift together flour and salt. Beat eggs until frothy, add sugar, 2 tablespoons at a time, beating well after each addition, then continue beating at high mixer speed until very thick and lemon colored. Fold in flour, ⅓ at a time. Mix lemon rind and butter; fold into batter, 1 tablespoon at a time, working quickly with a rubber spatula. (*Note:* Make very sure spatula reaches bottom of bowl when folding in butter.) Fill molds ⅔ full, place on baking sheets, and bake 15–17 minutes until golden and tops spring back when touched. Cool in molds 1–2 minutes, then lift out with a spatula. Cool fluted side up on wire rack. Dust generously with confectioners' sugar before serving. About 40 calories per cookie.

ROLLED COOKIES

Children adore these cookies—as much to make as to eat. They love the feel of the dough, they love rolling it out, cutting it into plain and fancy shapes. But most of all, they delight in decorating the cookies—strewing them with colored sugar, frosting them, and "squirting" or painting on designs (the aerosol cans of decorator frostings are perfect for children, as are the spillproof paste colors available in gourmet shops; they're as easy to use as poster paints).

All rolled cookie doughs, of course, aren't suitable for children. Many are so tender and rich even skillful cooks find them a challenge (for a list of rolled cookies children *can* make with relative ease, see the Cookie Chart).

Temperature is all-important when it comes to rolling dough—temperature of the day, of the kitchen, of the dough, and of your hands. All should be cool if you're to succeed.

Some Tips:

– Chill dough until firm but not hard; if dough is too cold and hard, especially a butter-rich dough, it will crack and split and be difficult to roll. The perfect temperature for rolling is when dough yields slightly when pressed but does not stick to your fingers.

– If dough is unusually soft or sticky, chill board and rolling pin as well as the dough.

– If your hands are warm, keep a bowl of ice water handy and cool them from time to time by dipping into the water. Rolling dough is especially difficult for women with warm hands because the heat of their hands oversoftens the dough, making it stick to everything.

– Roll only a small amount of dough at a time (about 1 cup) and keep the rest in the refrigerator until needed.

– Before rolling, shape dough roughly into the form you want—circle, rectangle, or square—and when rolling, shift position of dough on board and direct rolling pin strokes as needed to achieve that shape.

– When rolling, bear down on pin *lightly*, only enough to stretch and move dough in the direction you want.

– Resist the temptation of adding flour whenever the dough threatens to stick. Flour does make the dough easier to work, but it also makes the cookies tough and dry. The secret of crisp-tender rolled cookies is using little or no flour in the rolling. Here are two ways:

(1) Use a pastry cloth and stockinette-covered rolling pin. Both need only the lightest flouring because the porousness of the cloth holds the flour and releases very little into the dough.

(2) Roll dough between 2 sheets of wax paper. This method is particularly good for soft, butter-rich doughs and for cookies that must be rolled tissue-thin. The process is a bit tricky, but it does work. Place a small amount of dough between 2 sheets of wax paper (no flour needed) and roll quickly and lightly until dough is ¼"–½" thick; peel off top sheet of paper and invert it on board so used side is down. Flop dough over onto sheet, peel off top sheet, and reverse it also so that fresh side touches dough. Continue rolling to desired thickness, reversing or replenishing wax paper as needed. If dough threatens to stick despite frequent changes of paper, simply pop into refrigerator in its semirolled state, paper and all. A few minutes' chilling will firm up the dough and make the paper peel off like magic. When dough is desired thickness, remove top sheet and cut cookies (bottom sheet should still be in place). Chill cookies briefly on wax paper so they can be lifted with ease to baking sheets. With this method, you should be able to roll dough without using any additional flour. But if at the end dough tends to stick despite all precautions, dust *very* lightly with flour (with an exceedingly soft dough, this may be necessary to keep top sheet of wax paper from sticking after final rolling).

– Flour cutters *only* if dough is soft and sticky and then only *lightly*. A quick way to do it is to sift a little flour into a shallow bowl, then simply dip cutter into it, shaking off any excess.

– When cutting cookies, cut as close together as possible so there will be few scraps to reroll. Unless you've used very little flour in rolling, the rerolls will be tough.

– If dough is unusually soft, cut into the simplest shapes—circles, diamonds, squares—to reduce breakage.

– Use a wide spatula or pancake turner for transferring cookies to baking sheets. The spatula need not be floured unless dough is supersoft.

– Space cookies ¾"–1" apart on baking sheets unless recipes specify otherwise; most rolled cookies spread very little during baking.

About Cookie Cutters

Lucky the woman who owns a set of old-fashioned tin cookie cutters. They do really cut (unlike the plastic and aluminum cutters made today) and their designs are enchanting. It is still possible to find these old cutters, but it requires a bit of sleuthing in antique shops both at home and abroad. The best of the contemporary cutters are European, best in design, best in cutting ability. They're available at most gourmet shops as single cutters, cutter blocks, and cutter wheels.

You can, of course, design your own cutters. All you have to do is make a pattern, take it to a tinsmith and let him worry about the rest. Failing a handy tinsmith, you can still make cookies from your own designs. Simply sketch your designs on heavy paper (Manila file folders are the perfect weight and grease resistant to boot), cut them out, lay on rolled-out dough, and "trace" around them with a very sharp knife.

¢ SUGAR COOKIES

A good basic cookie with plenty of flavor variations to try.
Makes about 7 dozen

3¾ cups sifted flour
1½ teaspoons baking powder
1 teaspoon salt
1 cup butter or margarine
1½ cups sugar
2 teaspoons vanilla
2 eggs

Preheat oven to 375° F. Sift flour with baking powder and salt and set aside. Cream butter, sugar, and vanilla until light and fluffy. Add eggs, 1 at a time, beating well after each addition. Slowly mix in dry ingredients until just blended (lowest speed if you use mixer). If your kitchen is very hot, wrap dough in wax paper and chill about 1 hour so it will roll more easily. Roll ¼ of dough at a time on a lightly floured board to $\frac{1}{16}$"–⅛" thickness and cut with plain or fluted cutters (a 2" or 3" size is good). Transfer to lightly greased baking sheets with a pancake turner, spacing cookies 2" apart. If you like, brush with milk and sprinkle lightly with sugar. Bake in top ⅓ of oven 8–9 minutes until pale tan. Transfer to wire racks to cool. Reroll and cut trimmings.

For Softer Cookies: Roll dough ⅛"–¼" thick and cut with a 3" cutter; bake as directed 10–12 minutes until edges are just golden.

For Slice-and-Bake Cookies: Shape dough into a log about 2" in diameter, then chill several hours until firm or freeze. Slice ¼" thick and bake about 10 minutes until firm but not brown. About 55 calories per cookie.

VARIATIONS:

Sugar Pillows: Reduce flour to 3 cups and prepare dough as directed. Drop by rounded teaspoonfuls on lightly greased baking sheets, spacing cookies 2" apart. Lightly butter the bottom of a water glass, dip in sugar, then flatten cookies until ¼" thick (you'll have to resugar the glass about every other cookie). Bake 10–12 minutes until firm but not browned. Cool on wire racks. About 55 calories per cookie.

Chocolate Sugar Cookies: Add 4 (1-ounce) squares melted and cooled semisweet chocolate or 4 (1-ounce) envelopes no-melt semisweet chocolate to creamed mixture after adding eggs. Proceed as recipe directs. About 70 calories per cookie.

Pinwheels: Prepare dough as directed; mix half of it with 2 (1-ounce) envelopes no-melt semisweet chocolate. Roll ⅓ of the plain dough into a rectangle 6" × 8" and ¼" thick. Roll ⅓ of chocolate dough into a rectangle the same size, and, using a pancake turner, carefully place on top of plain dough. Roll the 2 together to a thickness of ⅛", keeping shape as nearly rectangular as possible, then roll up jelly-roll style, from the short side. Repeat with remaining dough. Wrap and chill rolls ½ hour, then slice

¼" thick and bake 10–12 minutes until cookies barely show a print when lightly pressed. Cool as directed. About 65 calories per cookie.

Sugar Marbles: Reduce amount of flour to 3 cups and prepare dough as directed. Into half mix 2 (1-ounce) envelopes no-melt semisweet chocolate. Pinch off about ½ teaspoon each plain and chocolate dough, then roll the 2 together into a small ball, squeezing slightly, to achieve a marbled effect. Repeat until dough is used up. Space marbles 2" apart on greased cookie sheets and bake about 10 minutes. About 55 calories per cookie.

Butterscotch Sugar Cookies: Substitute 2 cups firmly packed light or dark brown sugar for the 1½ cups sugar and proceed as directed. About 65 calories per cookie.

Nut Sugar Cookies: Work 1 cup finely chopped pecans, walnuts, filberts, pistachios, Brazil nuts, or toasted, blanched almonds into dough after dry ingredients. Roll and bake as directed. About 75 calories per cookie.

Coconut Sugar Cookies: Chop 1½ cups flaked coconut fairly fine and mix into dough after dry ingredients. Substitute 1½ teaspoons almond extract for the vanilla. Roll and bake as directed. About 75 calories per cookie.

Lemon or Orange Sugar Cookies: Substitute 1 teaspoon lemon or orange extract for vanilla and add 2–3 tablespoons finely grated lemon or orange rind along with eggs. Roll and bake as directed. About 55 calories per cookie.

Decorative Cookies: If fancy cutouts are to be made, increase amount of flour in basic recipe by about ½ cup (there'll be less breakage while you decorate cookies). Roll and cut cookies. For ideas on decorating, see About Decorating Cookies. About 60 calories per cookie.

SAND TARTS

This dough lends itself to all kinds of quick variations that will delight children. Makes 4 dozen

⅔ cup butter or margarine
1 cup sugar
¼ teaspoon salt
1 egg
1 teaspoon vanilla
2¾ cups sifted flour

Glaze:

1 egg white, lightly beaten
¼ cup sugar
Blanched, halved almonds (optional decoration)

Cream butter, sugar, and salt until light and fluffy; beat in egg, then vanilla. Mix in flour, ⅓ at a time, beating just to blend. Wrap dough and chill 1 hour. Preheat oven to 375° F. Roll, a small amount of dough at a time, ⅛" thick and cut with a 2" round cutter. Arrange 1" apart on greased baking sheets, brush with egg white and sprinkle with sugar. If you like, top each with an almond half. Bake 8–10 minutes until pale golden. Cool on wire racks. About 80 calories per cookie.

VARIATIONS:

Slice-and-Bake Sandies: Prepare dough as directed and chill 1 hour; shape into a 2" roll, wrap in foil, and chill overnight. Slice ⅛" thick, glaze and bake as directed. About 80 calories per cookie.

Jumbles: Prepare and roll cookies as directed; cut with a 2½" fluted round cutter, and in the center of half the cookies put ½ teaspoon tart jam or jelly, marmalade or mincemeat, semisweet chocolate bits or chopped mixed candied fruits. Top with remaining cookies, press edges together and snip tiny steam vents in centers with scissors. Do not glaze. Bake about 12 minutes until pale golden and cool on wire racks. About 155 calories per cookie.

Jelly Cutouts: Prepare, roll, and cut cookies as directed in basic recipe, then cut out centers of half the cookies, using a 1″ round cutter or decorative truffle cutters. Glaze cutout cookies only. Bake all as directed, then sandwich together with jelly, using cutout cookies as the top layer. (*Note:* Centers can be rerolled and cut, or baked—2–3 minutes will do it.) About 150 calories per cookie.

Turnovers: Prepare and roll cookies as directed but cut with a 3″ round cutter. Drop ½ teaspoon any jam or preserves on half of each cookie, fold over, and seal edges. Glaze and bake 12 minutes. Cool on wire racks. About 90 calories per cookie.

ROSE TREE COOKIES

A buttery-crisp old Quaker cookie that's tricky to make (don't attempt it in warm weather or in a warm kitchen). The secret is to cream the butter and sugar until fluffy and white and to roll the dough paper thin, using as little flour as possible.
Makes about 5 dozen

1 cup butter (no substitute)
1½ cups sugar
1 egg
*1¼ teaspoons baking soda, dissolved in
   2 teaspoons hot water*
2 teaspoons vanilla
2½ cups sifted flour

Cream butter and sugar until fluffy and white (about 10 minutes with an electric mixer at low speed). Beat in egg, then soda mixture and vanilla. Work in flour slowly. Divide dough in half and spoon each onto a large sheet of wax paper; flatten into large circles or rectangles about 1″ thick, wrap, and chill 1–2 hours until firm enough to roll but not brittle. When you're ready to roll dough, preheat oven to 375° F. Roll about ¼ of each package at a time between 2 sheets of wax paper. (*Note:* You should be able to roll the dough paper thin with very little additional flour if you change sheets of paper when dough begins to stick—the wax paper will peel off zip-quick if you chill all briefly.) Cut with a 2½″–3″ round cutter, chill 5–10 minutes more so circles can be lifted off

paper easily, then space 1½″ apart on an ungreased baking sheet. Bake cookies 5–7 minutes until pale tan, cool on sheet about 1 minute, then lift to wire rack to cool. Store airtight. About 60 calories per cookie.

GINGERBREAD BOYS

Let the children help make and decorate these.
Makes 2 dozen

2½ cups sifted flour
½ teaspoon salt
2 teaspoons ginger
½ cup butter or margarine
½ cup sugar
½ cup molasses
½ teaspoon baking soda
¼ cup hot water

Decorations:

Cinnamon candies ("red-hots")
Seedless raisins

Easy Icing:

1 cup sifted confectioners' sugar
¼ teaspoon salt
½ teaspoon vanilla
1 tablespoon heavy cream (about)

Sift flour with salt and ginger and set aside. Melt butter in a large saucepan over low heat, remove from heat and mix in sugar, then molasses. Dissolve soda in hot water. Add dry ingredients to molasses mixture alternately with soda-water, beginning and ending with dry ingredients. Chill dough 2–3 hours. Preheat oven to 350° F. Roll out dough, a small portion at a time, ⅛″ thick. Cut with gingerbread boy cutter, handling dough carefully, and transfer cookies to ungreased baking sheets (they should be spaced about 2″ apart). Press on cinnamon candies for buttons and raisins for eyes and bake 10–12 minutes until lightly browned. Cool 2–3 minutes on sheets, then lift to wire racks. While cookies cool, prepare icing: Mix sugar, salt, and vanilla; add cream, a few drops at a time, mixing well after each addition until icing is smooth and will hold a shape. Using a decorating tube, pipe outlines for collars, boots, cuffs, and belts. If you like, make a little extra icing, tint yellow, and use to pipe in hair. When frosting has hardened, store airtight. (*Note:* Gingerbread boys can be made several days ahead and piped with icing shortly before serving. If they soften in storage, warm 3–5 minutes at 350° F. to crispen, then cool on racks.) About 130 calories each.

⚖ GOLDEN CHEDDAR RINGS

Serve as a cookie or as an appetizer with cocktails.
Makes about 7½ dozen

¾ cup butter (no substitute), softened to room temperature
2 cups sifted flour
1 teaspoon paprika
½ teaspoon salt
¼ teaspoon cayenne pepper
1 pound sharp Cheddar cheese, coarsely grated
2 tablespoons superfine sugar

Preheat oven to 400° F. Rub butter, flour, paprika, salt, and cayenne together, using your hands, until smooth and creamy. Add cheese and knead on a piece of foil 3–4 minutes until smooth and thoroughly blended. Roll dough thin, half at a time, on a lightly floured pastry cloth (it should be about as thin as piecrust). Cut into rings with doughnut cutter and bake on ungreased baking sheets 4–6 minutes until *faintly* browned. Remove at once to wire racks to cool and, while still hot, sprinkle lightly with sugar. Scraps and "holes" can be rerolled and cut. About 45 calories each.

¢ MORAVIAN CHRISTMAS COOKIES

These dark ginger-molasses cookies store beautifully, so you can make them well ahead of the Christmas rush. The Moravian women of Old Salem, North Carolina, roll them paper thin and cut in fancy shapes.
Makes 4½ dozen

4 cups sifted flour
1 teaspoon ginger
1 teaspoon cinnamon
1 teaspoon mace
½ teaspoon cloves
¼ cup butter or margarine
¼ cup lard
½ cup firmly packed dark brown sugar
1 cup molasses
1½ teaspoons baking soda
1 tablespoon very hot water

Sift flour with spices. Cream butter, lard, and sugar until light and fluffy; add molasses and beat well. Dissolve soda in water. Mix ¼ of dry ingredients into creamed mixture, then stir in soda-water. Work in remaining dry ingredients, ⅓ at a time. Wrap dough and chill 4–6 hours. Preheat oven to 350° F. Roll dough, a little at a time, as thin as possible (⅛" is maximum thickness, ¹⁄₁₆" far better). Cut with Christmas cutters, space cookies 1½" apart on lightly greased baking sheets, and bake about 8 minutes until lightly browned. Cool 1–2 minutes on sheets, then transfer to wire racks. When completely cool, store airtight. About 70 calories per cookie.

To Decorate: Make an icing by mixing 1 cup sifted confectioners' sugar with 2–3 teaspoons heavy cream. Trace outlines of cookies with icing by putting through a pastry tube fitted with a fine tip. About 80 calories per cookie.

MARGUERITES

The rose water flavoring is what makes these cookies distinctive. It is available at many drugstores, also at specialty food shops.
Makes 4 dozen

3¼ cups sifted flour
½ teaspoon salt
½ teaspoon cinnamon
½ teaspoon nutmeg
¼ teaspoon mace
1 cup butter or margarine
1 cup sugar
3 egg yolks
¼ cup rose water

Topping:

3 egg whites

4 cups sifted confectioners' sugar
2 tablespoons lemon juice
½ (1-pound) jar peach or apricot
  preserves or marmalade

Sift flour with salt and spices. Cream butter and sugar until light and fluffy; beat in yolks, 1 at a time. Mix in dry ingredients alternately with rose water, beginning and ending with dry ingredients and beating only enough to blend. Chill dough 1–2 hours. Preheat oven to 350° F. Roll dough, a small amount at a time, ¼″ thick and cut in rounds with a 2½″ cutter. Space cookies 2″ apart on greased baking sheets and bake 10–12 minutes until light tan. Cool cookies on sheets 2–3 minutes, then transfer to wire racks. When all cookies are done, reduce oven temperature to 325° F. and prepare topping: Beat egg whites until frothy, add confectioners' sugar, ¼ cup at a time, beating well after each addition. Add lemon juice and beat until stiff peaks form. Spread each cookie, not quite to edge, with 1 teaspoon preserves, top with a rounded teaspoon meringue and spread to cover. Arrange 1″ apart on ungreased baking sheets and bake 15 minutes until topping is creamy white and firm. Cool on wire racks. About 140 calories each.

VARIATION:

⚖ ☒ **Jiffy Marguerites:** Instead of making cookies, spread soda crackers with preserves and meringue and bake as directed. For 1½ dozen crackers, use the following meringue proportions: 1 egg white, 1⅓ cups sifted confectioners' sugar, and 2 teaspoons lemon juice. About 50 calories each.

CHOCOLATE-FILLED PECAN DREAMS

Makes about 4 dozen

¾ cup butter or margarine
⅔ cup sifted confectioners' sugar
1 egg yolk
¾ cup very finely chopped pecans
1⅔ cups sifted flour

Filling:

¼ cup butter or margarine
1 cup sifted confectioners' sugar
1 egg white
¼ teaspoon vanilla
2 (1-ounce) envelopes no-melt
  semisweet chocolate

Cream butter and sugar until light and fluffy; add egg yolk and mix well. Mix in nuts and flour just until blended. Chill dough 1–2 hours. Preheat oven to 350° F. Roll out dough, a small amount at a time, ¼″ thick and cut with a 2″ round cookie cutter. Space 2″ apart on ungreased baking sheets and bake 10–12 minutes until pale tan. Transfer to wire racks to cool. For the filling: Cream butter and sugar until light and fluffy, add egg white and vanilla and beat well; blend in chocolate. When cookies are cold, sandwich together with filling. (*Note:* If cookies are not to be served the same day, do not fill; store airtight, then assemble shortly before serving.) About 85 calories per cookie.

CREAM-FILLED MOLASSES COOKIES

Makes about 5 dozen

¾ cup vegetable shortening
1 teaspoon salt
1 cup molasses
¾ cup sugar
1 egg
4½ cups sifted flour
2 teaspoons ginger
1 teaspoon soda

Cream Filling:

1 tablespoon butter
1 cup sifted confectioners' sugar
⅛ teaspoon salt
¼ teaspoon ginger
⅛ teaspoon cinnamon
1 tablespoon boiling water

Preheat oven to 350° F. Cream shortening with salt, molasses, sugar, and egg until light; sift flour with ginger and soda and add, 1 cup at a time, to creamed mixture, beating smooth after each addition. If dough seems very soft, chill until firm enough to roll. Roll, about ¼ of dough at a time, on a lightly floured board to a thickness of ⅛"–¼". Cut half of dough with a doughnut cutter, other half with round cookie cutter of the same diameter. Repeat until all dough is rolled and cut. Bake on greased baking sheets 10–12 minutes, remove to wire racks to cool. Meanwhile, prepare filling: Cream butter, sugar, salt, ginger and cinnamon until light, then beat in boiling water. To assemble cookies, spread rounds with filling, top with doughnut-shaped cookies, and press lightly into place. About 105 calories per cookie.

FIG NEWTONS

Not as difficult to make as you might think and so much better than the store-bought.
Makes 3 dozen

3 cups sifted flour
½ teaspoon salt
½ teaspoon cinnamon (optional)
⅔ cup butter or margarine
½ cup firmly packed dark brown sugar
½ cup firmly packed light brown sugar
2 egg whites
1 teaspoon vanilla

Fig Filling:

2 cups finely chopped dried golden figs
1 cup water
2 tablespoons sugar
2 tablespoons lemon juice

Sift flour with salt and, if you like, cinnamon. Cream butter and sugars until very fluffy; beat in egg whites and vanilla. Slowly work in flour; wrap dough and chill 2–3 hours. Meanwhile, prepare filling: Simmer all ingredients together, stirring frequently, 5–7 minutes until thick. Cool but do not chill. When dough has chilled long enough, preheat oven to 350° F. Roll out dough, a small portion at a time, ¼" thick and cut in pieces about 2½" wide and 3" long. Place a level teaspoon fig mixture in center of each, fold dough around filling as though folding a business letter. Flatten cookies slightly

and place seam side down 1" apart on ungreased baking sheets; bake about 12 minutes until lightly browned and just firm. Cool on racks. About 100 calories each.

SPITZBUBEN

Delicate almond cookies sandwiched together with jelly or jam (vary their flavors if you like).
Makes 2½ dozen

2 cups sifted flour
½ teaspoon salt
1 cup sugar
½ cup finely chopped blanched almonds
⅔ cup butter (no substitute), softened to room temperature
1 teaspoon vanilla
2 tablespoons heavy cream
1 (1-pound) jar red currant jelly or raspberry jam
Vanilla Sugar or sifted confectioners' sugar

Preheat oven to 350° F. Sift flour with salt and sugar; mix in nuts. Using your hands, work in butter until thoroughly blended. Mix vanilla and cream and add, a few drops at a time, mixing with a fork until mixture holds together. (*Note:* If kitchen is warm, chill dough about 1 hour or until a good consistency for rolling.) Roll out, a small amount at a time, ⅛" thick and cut with a 2" scalloped round cookie cutter. Space cookies 2" apart on ungreased baking sheets and bake about 12 minutes until golden brown. Cool on sheets 3–4 minutes, then transfer to wire racks. When cool, sandwich cookies together with jelly and dust with vanilla sugar or confectioners' sugar. (*Note:* Being egg-free, these cookies are good for those with egg allergies.) About 170 calories per cookie.

PFEFFERNÜSSE (GERMAN PEPPERNUTS)

The secret of good "peppernuts" is to ripen the dough 2–3 days before baking and to store the cookies 1–2 weeks with a piece of apple before eating.
Makes 3½ dozen

3 cups sifted flour
1 teaspoon cinnamon
⅛ teaspoon cloves
¼ teaspoon white pepper
3 eggs
1 cup sugar
⅓ cup very finely chopped blanched
  almonds
⅓ cup very finely chopped mixed
  candied orange peel and citron
Vanilla Sugar or confectioners' sugar
  (optional)

Sift flour with spices and set aside. Beat
eggs until frothy, slowly add sugar, and
continue beating until thick and lemon
colored. Slowly mix in flour, then
almonds and fruit peel. Wrap in foil and
refrigerate 2–3 days. When ready to
bake, preheat oven to 350° F. Roll,
about ⅓ of dough at a time, ¼"–½"
thick and cut with a 1¾" round
cutter. Space cookies 1" apart on
greased baking sheets and bake 15–18
minutes until light brown. Cool on wire
racks and store with ½ an apple in a
covered container 1–2 weeks before
eating. If you like, dredge in vanilla sugar
or dust with confectioners' sugar before
serving. About 70 calories per cookie if
not dredged in sugar, 80 calories if
dredged in sugar.

PEPPARKAKOR (CHRISTMAS GINGER SNAPS)

These gingery brown cookies are
Sweden's favorite at Christmas time.
They are rolled very thin, cut into stars,
bells, angels, and Santa Clauses, and
hung upon either the Christmas tree or
the small wooden *pepparkakor* tree.
Makes about 5 dozen

3½ cups sifted flour
1 teaspoon baking soda
½ teaspoon salt
1½ teaspoons ginger
1½ teaspoons cinnamon
1½ teaspoons cloves
1 cup butter or margarine
1 cup firmly packed dark brown sugar
2 egg whites

Icing:

4 cups sifted confectioners' sugar
2 egg whites

Sift flour with soda, salt, and spices.
Cream butter and sugar until very fluffy;
beat in egg whites. Slowly work in dry
ingredients. Wrap and chill 12 hours.
Preheat oven to 350° F. Roll out dough,
a small portion at a time, ⅛" thick on
a lightly floured board and cut in
decorative shapes; space cookies about
1" apart on ungreased baking sheets
and bake 10–12 minutes until lightly
browned around the edges. Transfer to
wire racks to cool. While cookies cool,
prepare icing: Slowly blend confectioners' sugar into egg whites and
beat until smooth. Fit pastry bag with a
fine, plain tip and pipe icing onto
cookies, tracing outlines, filling in details, or adding any decorative touches
you wish. (*Note:* To make hanging
cookies, see directions given in About
Decorating Cookies.) About 100
calories per cookie.

LEBKUCHEN

A spicy German cookie studded with
candied fruits.
Makes about 4½ dozen

3 cups sifted flour
½ teaspoon baking soda
1 teaspoon cinnamon
½ teaspoon nutmeg
½ teaspoon cloves
1 cup firmly packed dark brown sugar
1 cup honey, at room temperature
1 egg
1 teaspoon finely grated lemon rind
1 tablespoon lemon juice
½ cup finely chopped blanched almonds
½ cup finely chopped mixed candied
  orange peel and citron

Frosting:

1 cup sifted confectioners' sugar
4–5 teaspoons milk

Decoration:

Blanched halved almonds
Slivered or halved candied cherries

Sift flour with baking soda and spices.

Beat sugar, honey and egg until well blended; add lemon rind and juice. Slowly mix in dry ingredients just until blended; stir in almonds and fruit peel. Wrap and chill 12 hours. Preheat oven to 400° F. Roll out ⅓ of dough at a time ¼" thick and cut with a 2" round cookie cutter *or* cut in rectangles 2½" × 1½". Arrange 2" apart on lightly greased baking sheets and bake 8 minutes until edges are lightly browned and tops spring back when touched. Cool on wire racks. For the frosting: Mix sugar and milk until smooth; spread a little on top of each cookie or dip cookie tops in frosting. Decorate with almonds and cherries. Let frosting harden before storing cookies. About 80 calories per cookie.

For Drop Cookies: Reduce flour to 2½ cups; drop by rounded teaspoonfuls and bake as directed. About 75 calories per cookie.

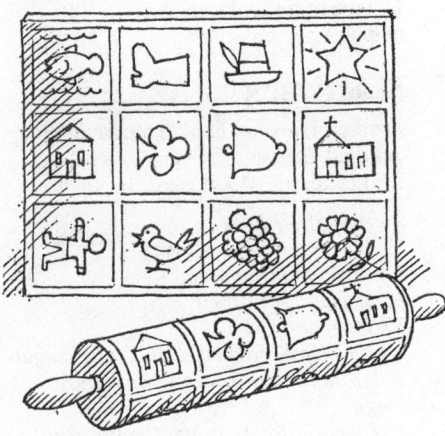

SPRINGERLE

The original 3-D cookies, *Springerle* date to pagan Germany when the poor, having no animals to sacrifice at the Winter Festival, made effigies of them out of cookie dough. Today, springerle are square or rectangular cookies with pressed-in designs, made either by rolling dough on a springerle board or with a springerle rolling pin (available in

gourmet shops). Sometimes used, too, are individual wooden cookie blocks called *Spekulatius* blocks.
Makes about 5 dozen

4 cups sifted flour
1 teaspoon baking powder
½ teaspoon salt
4 eggs
2 cups sugar
2 teaspoons finely grated lemon rind
　(optional)
Anise seeds

Sift flour with baking powder and salt. Beat eggs until lemon colored, slowly add sugar, ½ cup at a time, beating well after each addition; continue beating until very thick and pale, about 10 minutes with a mixer. Slowly mix in lemon rind and dry ingredients, beating just to blend. Wrap and chill dough 3–4 hours. Roll, ⅓ at a time, slightly less than ½" thick, keeping shape as nearly rectangular as possible and about the width of the rolling pin. Roll a lightly floured springerle rolling pin over dough 1 time, pressing firmly so dough is about ¼" thick and evenly so imprint is clear. If using springerle board, roll dough ¼" thick on lightly floured board, using regular rolling pin, then invert on lightly floured surface. If using spekulatius block, roll dough ¼" thick, then press firmly and evenly, using block like a stamp. (*Note:* In warm weather, chill springerle pin or board along with dough to make rolling easier.) Cut on imprint lines to separate individual cookies, transfer to a lightly floured surface, and let stand uncovered overnight. Preheat oven to 325° F. Sprinkle greased baking sheets generously with anise seeds, lift cookies to sheets, and bake 15 minutes until golden but not brown. Cool 1 minute on sheets before transferring to racks to cool. (*Note:* Some people like to mellow springerle about a week in an airtight canister before serving.) About 110 calories per cookie.

MOLDED OR PRESSED COOKIES

These three-dimensional cookies are great favorites everywhere, but especially in Europe, where women are artists at shaping dough (Scandinavian museums exhibit cookie masterpieces alongside other folk art). Almost as soon as a little girl can toddle into the kitchen, she is given a dab of dough to shape. By the time she reaches her teens, she knows how to fashion wreaths and rings, rosettes and ribbons, pinwheels and pretzels and checker-boards. She has learned to use the cookie press with speed and skill and has built up a delectable cookie repertoire (the better to catch a husband).

The dough for molded and pressed cookies is quite short (rich in butter or shortening) and has the look and feel of shortbread. There are three basic ways to handle it:
(1) Roll into chunky logs (à la refrigerator cookies), chill until firm, slice thin, and bake.
(2) Hand-shape into little balls, pillows, crescents, or logs.
(3) Push through a pastry bag or cookie press. (*Note:* Only the softer doughs are suitable for pressing.)
There are a number of kinds of cookie presses. Before buying, shop around, talk with friends, and if possible borrow a press to try.

Some Tips:
—Choose a cool day for making molded or pressed cookies. Heat makes the dough too soft to hold a shape.
—When using cookie press, always follow manufacturer's instructions.
—Never fill cookie press or pastry bag more than ½ to ⅔ full; the heat of your hands will soften dough faster than you can press it. Invariably the last of the dough must be removed from the press, chilled, and then *re*-pressed.

—Never try to press a dough containing bits of fruit or nuts that may clog the works.
—Always press cookies onto cool or cold baking sheets.
—If dough seems too soft to press or mold, chill slightly.
—When shaping cookies, flour hands only when absolutely necessary and then *very* lightly. Most doughs can be shaped with unfloured hands.

BUTTERBALLS
They will melt in your mouth.
Makes 4 dozen

2 cups sifted flour
½ teaspoon salt
1 cup butter (no substitute)
½ cup superfine sugar
2 teaspoons vanilla or 1½ teaspoons vanilla and ½ teaspoon almond extract
½ cup sifted confectioners' sugar or Vanilla Sugar (optional)

Sift together flour and salt and set aside. Cream butter and sugar until light and fluffy; add flavoring. Slowly mix in flour, ½ cup at a time, until just blended. Chill dough 1–2 hours. Preheat oven to 325° F. Shape dough into 1″ balls, handling quickly and lightly, space 2″ apart on ungreased baking sheets, and bake about 15 minutes until the color of pale sand. Transfer to wire racks to cool. If you like, roll in confectioners' sugar before serving. About 65 calories per cookie.

VARIATIONS:

Coconut Butterballs: Stir 1 cup flaked coconut into prepared dough, then proceed as directed. If you like, brush cooled, baked cookies with beaten egg white and roll in plain or colored flaked coconut before serving. About 70 calories per cookie.

Almond Butterballs: Prepare as directed, using vanilla-almond extract combination and mixing in ½ cup finely chopped toasted blanched almonds after flour. Chill, shape into balls, roll in finely chopped toasted blanched almonds (you'll need about ¾ cup altogether), then bake as directed. (*Note:* Other nuts may be used instead of almonds; particularly good are pecans, walnuts, hazelnuts, piñons, pistachio nuts, or unsalted peanuts.) About 85 calories per cookie.

Thumbprint Cookies: Mix, chill, and shape cookies as directed. Make a deep thumbprint in center of each, fill with tart jam or jelly, and bake as directed. About 80 calories per cookie.

OLD-FASHIONED BUTTER "S" COOKIES

Makes 4 dozen

1 cup butter (no substitute)
1 cup sugar
6 egg yolks, lightly beaten
2 tablespoons finely grated lemon rind (optional)
3 cups sifted flour

Preheat oven to 325° F. Cream butter and sugar until light and fluffy, add egg yolks 1 at a time, beating well after each addition; if desired, add lemon rind. With a spoon, mix in flour. Refrigerate half the dough while shaping the rest. Pinch off a piece of dough and roll between lightly floured hands into a rope ½″ in diameter; cut in 4″ lengths and shape into *s*'s on ungreased baking sheets. Cookies should be spaced 2″ apart. Bake 18–20 minutes or until lightly browned at the edges. Cool a few minutes on sheets, then carefully transfer to wire racks. When cool, store airtight. About 80 calories per cookie.

VARIATIONS:

Other flavorings may be substituted for the lemon rind: 2 teaspoons vanilla, 1 teaspoon almond extract, or 2 tablespoons finely grated orange rind. About 80 calories per cookie.

ALMOND CRUNCHIES

Makes about 8 dozen

4 cups sifted flour
1¼ cups sugar

1½ teaspoons baking powder
¼ teaspoon nutmeg
1½ cups butter (no substitute), softened to room temperature
1 egg
1 teaspoon vanilla
¼ teaspoon almond extract

Topping:

1 egg, lightly beaten
⅓ cup finely chopped blanched almonds
½ cup coarsely crushed sugar cubes

Preheat oven to 350° F. Sift flour, sugar, baking powder, and nutmeg together into a large bowl. Blend in butter, egg, vanilla, and almond extract. Shape into 1″ balls and place, 2″ apart, on lightly greased baking sheets. To apply the topping, press each ball down to a thickness of about ¼″, using a fork dipped in the beaten egg. Sprinkle with almonds and crushed sugar and bake 10–12 minutes until delicately browned. Cool on wire racks. About 60 calories per cookie.

PEANUT BUTTER COOKIES

Makes 6 dozen

2½ cups sifted flour
1 teaspoon baking powder
½ teaspoon salt
1 cup butter or margarine or ½ cup each vegetable shortening and butter
1 cup sugar
1 cup firmly packed light brown sugar
2 eggs
1 cup crunchy peanut butter

Sift flour with baking powder and salt and set aside. Cream butter and sugars until light and fluffy; add eggs, 1 at a time, beating well after each addition. Beat in peanut butter. Slowly mix in dry ingredients, about ⅓ at a time, until just blended. Chill dough 2 hours. Preheat oven to 375° F. Shape dough into 1″ balls, arrange 3″ apart on greased baking sheets, and flatten by pressing lightly with a floured fork in a crisscross fashion. Bake 10–12 minutes until golden. Transfer to wire rack to cool. (*Note:* Dough freezes well.) About 80 calories per cookie.

⊠ SNICKERDOODLES

Children will have fun making these.
Makes about 6 dozen

2¾ cups sifted flour
¼ teaspoon salt
1 teaspoon baking soda
2 teaspoons cream of tartar
1 cup butter or margarine, softened to
  room temperature
1½ cups sugar

Topping:

2 tablespoons sugar, mixed with 2
  tablespoons cinnamon

Preheat oven to 350° F. Sift flour with
salt, baking soda, and cream of tartar.
Cream butter until light, add sugar
gradually, continuing to cream until
fluffy. Work in dry ingredients slowly
and beat *just* until smooth. Shape into
1″ balls and roll in topping. Arrange
2″ apart on ungreased baking sheets
and bake 18–20 minutes or until light
tan. Transfer at once to wire racks to
cool. Store airtight. About 55 calories
per cookie.

MEXICAN WEDDING CAKES

Meltingly tender filbert cookies.
Makes about 5 dozen

1 cup butter or margarine, softened to
  room temperature
⅔ cup plus 3 tablespoons unsifted
  confectioners' sugar
1 tablespoon vanilla
¼ teaspoon salt
2⅓ cups sifted flour
1½ cups finely ground, toasted,
  unblanched filberts

Cream butter until light and fluffy. Add
⅔ cup confectioners' sugar and continue
creaming until smooth; beat in vanilla
and salt. Mix in flour, then the filberts.
Wrap dough in foil and chill several
hours until firm. Preheat oven to 350° F.
Pinch off bits of dough and roll into 1″
balls. Place 2″ apart on ungreased
baking sheets and flatten each ball with
the palm of your hand until ¼″ thick;
even up any ragged edges. Bake 12–15
minutes until edged with brown. Trans-

fer to wire racks to cool, then sift
remaining 3 tablespoons confectioners'
sugar over cookies to dust lightly. About
65 calories per cookie.

KOURABIEDES

These butter-rich Greek cookies are
traditionally served on saints' days and
at Christmas.
Makes about 3½ dozen

1 cup unsalted butter (no substitute)
⅓ cup sifted confectioners' sugar
1 egg yolk
2¼ cups sifted flour
2 tablespoons brandy
½ cup very finely chopped walnuts or
  blanched almonds (optional)
Confectioners' sugar

Cream butter until light, slowly add
confectioners' sugar, and continue
creaming until light and fluffy; beat in
egg yolk. Slowly mix in flour, adding
alternately with brandy. If you like, mix
in nuts. Wrap dough in wax paper and
chill 1 hour. Preheat oven to 350° F.
Using a rounded teaspoon as a measure,
scoop up bits of dough and with lightly
floured hands roll into strips 3″ long.
Bend into crescents and arrange 2″
apart on ungreased baking sheets. Bake
15 minutes or until the color of sand.
Cool 2–3 minutes on sheets, then carefully transfer to wire racks. Cool and
roll in confectioners' sugar. About 80
calories per cookie (with nuts).

VARIATION:

Instead of shaping into crescents, roll
dough into 1¼″ balls and, if you like,
stud each with a clove. Bake 17–18
minutes. About 80 calories per cookie.

ALMOND TARTS (SWEDISH
  SANDBAKELSEN)

Makes 2½ dozen

½ cup butter (no substitute), softened to
  room temperature
⅓ cup sugar
1 egg yolk, lightly beaten
½ teaspoon almond extract
1 cup plus 2 tablespoons sifted flour
½ cup finely ground blanched almonds

With a wooden spoon, mix butter, sugar, egg yolk, and almond extract until well blended. Mix in flour and almonds; wrap and chill 1 hour. Preheat oven to 325° F. Press ¼" layers of dough into buttered and floured 1½"–2" tartlet tins. Stand tins on a baking sheet and bake 18–20 minutes until tarts are pale golden (watch closely toward the end). Transfer tins to a wire rack and cool until easy to handle. To remove tarts from tins, tap bottoms of tins lightly and ease tarts out. You may need to squeeze tins lightly to loosen tarts or use a large, sturdy needle to help pry them out. Cool tarts thoroughly, then store airtight. Just before serving, fill with sweetened whipped cream or invert and dot with crystallized fruit or dabs of red currant jelly. About 70 calories per cookie.

SPRITZ

From the German word meaning "to squirt," *Spritz* are cookies "squirted" through a cookie press into delicate designs.
Makes about 5 dozen

1 cup butter or margarine, softened to
    room temperature
⅔ cup sugar
2 egg yolks, lightly beaten
1 teaspoon vanilla
2½ cups sifted flour

Optional Decorative Frostings:

Plain: *Blend 1 cup sifted confectioners'*
    sugar until smooth with 2 tablespoons
    each softened butter and heavy cream.
Chocolate: *In a double boiler over hot,*
    not boiling, water, heat and stir 1 cup
    semisweet chocolate bits with 2
    tablespoons each light corn syrup and
    hot water until smooth. Keep over
    hot water but remove from stove,
    while frosting cookies.

Preheat oven to 375° F. With a wooden spoon, beat butter, sugar, egg yolks and vanilla until well mixed. Add flour, ½ cup at a time, mixing well after each addition. Press dough in desired designs through a cookie press onto ungreased baking sheets, spacing cookies 1" apart.

Bake 7–9 minutes or until cookies are almost firm but not brown. Cool on sheets 2–3 minutes, then carefully transfer to wire racks. Store airtight. About 55 calories per cookie.

To Decorate: Dip baked, cooled cookies in either of the frostings above, then sprinkle with colored sugar or decorettes, silver dragées, chocolate sprinkles, flaked coconut, shaved Brazil nuts, chopped, toasted almonds, pistachio nuts, walnuts or pecans, minced candied cherries or crystallized fruit. About 70 calories per cookie.

VARIATION:

Chocolate Spritz: Follow basic recipe above but before adding flour mix 2 (1-ounce) envelopes no-melt semisweet or unsweetened chocolate into batter. Proceed as directed. Frost and decorate if you wish. About 60 calories per cookie if unfrosted and undecorated, 75 calories per cookie if frosted and decorated.

BUTTER STARS

Makes 4½ dozen

⅔ cup butter (no substitute)
1 cup sugar
1 egg
1 teaspoon vanilla or ½ teaspoon almond
    extract
2¼ cups sifted flour
Colored sugar

Preheat oven to 350° F. Cream butter and sugar until light and fluffy; add egg and vanilla and beat well. Mix in flour just until blended. Put through cookie press fitted with a star design onto ungreased baking sheets, spacing cookies 1½" apart. Sprinkle lightly with colored sugar. Bake 10–12 minutes until firm and golden at the edges, not brown. Transfer immediately to wire racks to cool. About 70 calories per cookie.

VARIATIONS:

Butter Planks: Prepare dough as directed above and put through cookie press fitted with serrated ribbon tip, making each plank about 3" long. Bake 8 minutes at 350° F. Sandwich baked cookies together with Chocolate or Mocha Butter Cream Frosting. About 155 calories per cookie.

Almond Pretzels: Prepare dough as directed but use almond extract for flavor instead of vanilla and blend in ½ cup very finely chopped, toasted, blanched almonds after the flour. Use fluted tube attachment for cookie press and form into pretzels about 3″ in diameter. Bake as directed. About 80 calories per cookie.

Peanut Butter Stars: Prepare dough as directed, but reduce amount of butter to ½ cup and blend well with ½ cup creamy peanut butter. Omit vanilla from recipe and reduce flour to 2 cups. Press and bake as directed. About 70 calories per cookie.

Scotch Orange Crisps: When making dough, substitute ½ cup firmly packed dark brown sugar for ½ cup of the granulated; omit vanilla and add 1 tablespoon finely grated orange rind. Put through cookie press fitted with desired design and bake as directed. About 70 calories per cookie.

SUGAR PRETZELS

Christmas favorites in Germany and Scandinavia.
Makes 2½ dozen

1 cup butter (no substitute)
⅔ cup sugar
2 egg yolks, lightly beaten
1 teaspoon vanilla
2 cups plus 2 tablespoons sifted flour

Decoration:

1 egg white, lightly beaten
¼ cup green, red, or plain sugar

Preheat oven to 375° F. Cream butter until white, slowly add sugar, and continue beating until light and fluffy. Add egg yolks and vanilla and beat well. By hand mix in flour just until blended. Spoon mixture into a pastry bag fitted with a rosette tube and pipe pretzel-shaped cookies on greased and floured baking sheets. Make the cookies about 2½″ in diameter and space them 2″

apart. Brush lightly with egg white and sprinkle with colored or plain sugar. Bake 10–12 minutes until just firm but not brown. Cool 1–2 minutes, then lift to racks with a spatula. When cool, store airtight. About 110 calories per cookie.

VARIATIONS:

Berliner Kränze (Wreaths): Pipe dough into 1½″–2″ wreaths, brush with egg white, and decorate with green sugar and slivers of candied red cherries. Bake as directed. About 110 calories per cookie.

Nut Rings: Pipe dough into 1″–1½″ rings, brush with egg white, and sprinkle with ground pecans, walnuts, filberts, or flaked coconut instead of colored sugar. Bake as directed. About 110 calories per cookie.

⚖ ¢ PRESSED MOLASSES SPICE COOKIES

Makes 4 dozen

2 cups sifted flour
½ teaspoon cinnamon
½ teaspoon nutmeg
¼ teaspoon ginger
¼ teaspoon salt
¼ teaspoon baking soda
½ cup butter or margarine
½ cup sugar
¼ cup molasses
1 egg

Preheat oven to 375° F. Sift flour with spices, salt, and soda. Cream butter and sugar until light and fluffy; beat in molasses and egg. Slowly add dry ingredients, mixing just to blend. (*Note:* If weather is cool, you may need to soften dough with 2–3 teaspoons milk to make it a good consistency for the cookie press.) Press dough through cookie press in desired designs onto ungreased baking sheets, spacing cookies 1″ apart. Bake 10 minutes until firm. Cool 2 minutes on baking sheets, then transfer to wire racks. About 50 calories per cookie.

REFRIGERATOR COOKIES

In this day of extra-large freezers and refrigerators, refrigerator cookies are a hostess's best friend; a roll of cookie dough "on ice" is excellent insurance against drop-in guests. It's there whenever you need it, ready to slice and bake.

Most refrigerator cookie doughs are soft and butter-rich, much like molded or pressed cookie doughs (*these*, too, can be shaped into rolls, chilled, sliced, and baked). Extra-soft refrigerator cookie doughs need not be chilled if you're in a rush; simply drop from a spoon and bake as you would drop cookies.

Some Tips:
— If dough is extra soft, chill briefly in bowl until firm enough to shape.
— For "square" cookies, line an empty carton in which wax paper or plastic food wrap came with foil and pack dough in firmly. Chill until firm.
— For cookies with colored or flavored borders, roll chilled dough in colored or cinnamon sugar, ground nuts, or flaked coconut before slicing and baking.
— Always use your sharpest knife for slicing refrigerator cookies.
— When slicing dough, give roll a quarter turn every now and then so that it doesn't lose its round shape.
— Remember that refrigerator cookie dough freezes especially well and can be sliced and baked while still solidly frozen.

⚖ ¢ BASIC REFRIGERATOR COOKIES

Makes about 6 dozen

2 cups sifted flour
½ teaspoon salt
½ teaspoon baking soda
½ cup butter or margarine
1 cup granulated, light or dark brown sugar
1 egg
2 teaspoons vanilla

Sift flour with salt and baking soda and set aside. With rotary beater or electric mixer cream butter, sugar, egg, and vanilla until light and fluffy. Slowly mix in dry ingredients; shape dough into a roll about 2″ in diameter; wrap in foil or plastic food wrap and chill several hours or overnight. Preheat oven to 400° F. Slice roll ⅛″ thick and arrange slices ½″ apart on ungreased baking sheets. Bake 8–10 minutes until pale tan. Cool cookies on wire racks. About 35 calories per cookie.

VARIATIONS:

⚖ **Nut Refrigerator Cookies:** Prepare as directed, mixing in 1½ cups minced nuts (pecans, walnuts, filberts, Brazil, pistachio, or blanched, toasted almonds) along with dry ingredients. Proceed as directed. About 50 calories per cookie.

⚖ ¢ **Chocolate Refrigerator Cookies:** Add 2 (1-ounce) envelopes no-melt semisweet chocolate to creamed mixture, add dry ingredients, and proceed as directed. About 40 calories per cookie.

Filled Refrigerator Cookies: Prepare and slice cookies as directed. Make "sandwiches" by putting 2 slices together with 1 teaspoon jam, jelly, or preserves; snip a cross in center of each top cookie to expose filling. Bake about 10 minutes. About 90 calories per cookie.

⚖ ¢ **Chocolate Checkerboards:** Prepare dough as directed; into half mix 1

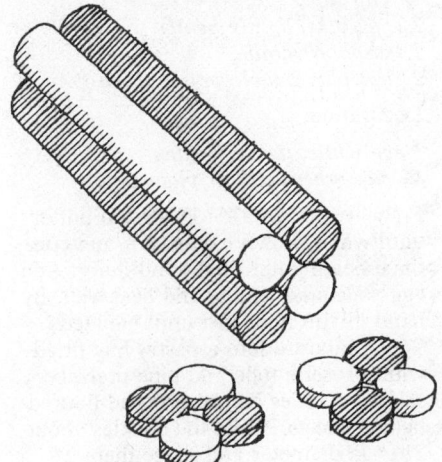

(1-ounce) envelope no-melt semisweet chocolate. Divide plain and chocolate doughs in half and roll each into a rope about ½″–¾″ in diameter. Lay 1 chocolate and 1 plain rope side by side and touching each other on counter and top with remaining 2 ropes, reversing colors as shown to form checkerboard. Press together lightly, then wrap and chill overnight. Slice and bake as directed. About 40 calories per cookie.

⚖️ ¢ **Chocolate Pinwheels:** Prepare dough as directed; into half mix 1 (1-ounce) envelope no-melt semisweet chocolate. Flatten chocolate dough on a large piece of wax paper into a rectangle roughly 12″×9″×¼″. On another piece of wax paper, flatten vanilla dough into a rectangle the same size. Carefully invert vanilla dough on the chocolate, aligning edges as well as possible; peel off wax paper, roll up like a jelly roll, wrap, and chill overnight. Slice and bake as directed. (*Note:* To reverse colors in pinwheels, simply invert chocolate dough on vanilla instead of vice-versa.) About 40 calories per cookie.

⚖️ **BUTTERSCOTCH ICEBOX COOKIES**

Makes 8 dozen

3½ cups sifted flour
2 teaspoons baking powder
½ teaspoon salt
1 cup butter, margarine, or vegetable shortening
2 cups firmly packed light brown sugar
1 egg
1½ teaspoons vanilla
3 tablespoons heavy cream

Sift flour with baking powder and salt and set aside. Cream butter and sugar until light; add egg and vanilla and beat well. Slowly add dry ingredients and cream. Shape dough into rolls about 2″ in diameter; wrap and chill several hours until firm. Preheat oven to 400° F. Slice rolls ⅛″–¼″ thick and arrange 1″ apart on ungreased baking sheets. Bake 6–10 minutes until lightly browned.

Transfer to wire racks to cool. About 50 calories per cookie.

MOLASSES ICEBOX COOKIES

Makes about 6 dozen

3¼ cups sifted flour
½ teaspoon baking soda
¼ teaspoon salt
1 tablespoon ginger
½ teaspoon cinnamon
¼ teaspoon allspice
1 cup butter, margarine, or shortening
1 cup firmly packed light brown sugar
½ cup molasses

Sift flour with soda, salt, and spices and set aside. Cream butter and sugar until very light and fluffy. Work dry ingredients in alternately with molasses, beginning and ending with dry ingredients. Divide dough in half and shape into 2 rolls about 2″ in diameter. Wrap and chill several hours until firm. Preheat oven to 350° F. Slice rolls ⅛″ thick, space cookies about 1½″ apart on ungreased baking sheets and bake 8–10 minutes until just firm to the touch. Let cool about 1 minute on baking sheets before transferring to wire racks to cool. About 60 calories per cookie.

⚖️ **ALMOND-ORANGE ICEBOX COOKIES**

Makes 8 dozen

2¾ cups sifted flour
¼ teaspoon salt
¼ teaspoon baking soda
1 cup butter or shortening
½ cup sugar
½ cup firmly packed light brown sugar
2 tablespoons orange juice
1 tablespoon finely grated orange rind
1 egg
½ cup blanched, slivered almonds

Sift flour, salt, and soda together and set aside. Cream butter until fluffy and beat in sugars. Mix in orange juice, rind and egg and beat well. Gradually stir in dry ingredients, then almonds. Shape into rolls about 1½″ in diameter, wrap and chill several hours until firm. Preheat oven to 375° F. Using a very sharp knife (because of almonds in dough), slice ⅛″ thick and place 1½″ apart on greased baking sheets. Bake 10–12 minutes until lightly ringed with brown. Transfer to wire racks to cool. About 40 calories per cookie.

VARIATION:

⚖ **Orange-Chocolate Jewels:** Prepare as directed but omit almonds; instead, stir in 2 (1-ounce) squares finely grated semisweet chocolate. Shape, chill, slice, and bake as directed. About 40 calories per cookie.

OATMEAL ICEBOX COOKIES

Makes 6 dozen

¾ cup sifted flour
½ teaspoon salt
½ teaspoon baking soda
½ cup butter or margarine
½ cup firmly packed light brown sugar
½ cup sugar
1 egg, lightly beaten
1 teaspoon vanilla
1½ cups uncooked quick-cooking
　　oatmeal
½ cup finely chopped pecans, walnuts, or
　　blanched, toasted almonds

Sift together flour, salt, and baking soda and set aside. Cream butter and sugars until light and fluffy. Beat in egg and vanilla; mix in dry ingredients, oatmeal, and nuts. Divide dough in half, turn out on lightly floured board, and shape into 2 rolls about 10″ long and 1½″ in diameter. Wrap in foil or plastic food wrap and chill well or freeze. About 10 minutes before cookies are to be baked, preheat oven to 375° F. Slice rolls ¼″ thick and arrange cookies 2″ apart on lightly greased baking sheets. Bake about 10 minutes until tan. Cool 5 minutes on baking sheet, then transfer to wire rack and cool completely. About 55 calories per cookie.

PEANUT BUTTER
REFRIGERATOR COOKIES

Children especially like these.
Makes about 5 dozen

2 cups sifted flour
¾ teaspoon baking powder
½ teaspoon cinnamon
⅓ cup butter, margarine, or vegetable
　　shortening
¼ cup creamy or crunchy peanut butter
¾ cup sugar
1 egg
½ cup finely chopped, roasted, blanched
　　peanuts

Sift flour with baking powder and cinnamon and set aside. Cream butter, peanut butter, and sugar until light; add egg and beat well. Slowly add dry ingredients; stir in nuts. Shape dough into a roll 2″–2½″ in diameter; wrap and chill several hours until firm. Preheat oven to 400° F. Slice roll ⅛″ thick, arrange 1″ apart on ungreased baking sheets, and bake 6–8 minutes until pale tan. Cool 1 minute on sheets before transferring to wire racks. About 55 calories per cookie.

FIG AND ALMOND PINWHEELS

Wrapped in foil, rolls of dough can be kept in the freezer several months. Simply slice and bake as needed.
Makes about 6 dozen

2 cups sifted flour
½ teaspoon baking powder
⅛ teaspoon baking soda
½ teaspoon salt
½ cup butter or margarine
2 tablespoons vegetable shortening
½ cup sugar
⅓ cup firmly packed light brown sugar
1 egg, lightly beaten
¾ teaspoon vanilla

Fig and Almond Filling:

1¼ cups finely chopped dried figs (about
　　½ pound)
¼ cup sugar
¾ cup water
2 teaspoons lemon juice
½ cup very finely chopped, blanched
　　almonds

Sift flour with baking powder, soda, and salt and set aside. Cream butter, shortening, sugar, and brown sugar until light and fluffy. Add egg and vanilla and beat well. Slowly mix in dry ingredients just to blend. Chill dough 6–8 hours. Meanwhile, make the filling: Mix figs, sugar, and water in a saucepan and simmer 8–10 minutes, stirring constantly, until thickened. Off heat, add lemon juice; cool and stir in nuts. Divide dough in half; roll out 1 portion to measure 9″×11″ (it should be about ¼″ thick). Spread with half the filling, leaving ½″ margins all around. Roll up from longest side jelly-roll fashion; pinch seam together, wrap in foil or wax paper, and freeze until firm. Repeat with remaining dough and filling. To bake: Preheat oven to 400° F. Slice rolls ⅛″ thick, arrange cookies 2″ apart on ungreased baking sheets, and bake about 8 minutes until lightly browned. Cool 2–3 minutes on sheets before transferring to wire racks to cool. About 70 calories per cookie.

BAR COOKIES

Here's the fastest way to fill the cookie jar. Simply stir up a batter, bake in one pan, then cool and cut in bars or squares. Most bars are as much cake as cookie, though some, the superrich, are half cookie, half candy. The advantages of bar cookies, in addition to how fast they can be made, are that they store well and are adored by nearly everyone.

Some Tips:
– If batter is very rich or contains much fruit, grease *and* flour pan.
– Always use the pan sizes given in recipes; an incorrect size can give bars an altogether different (and often unpleasant) texture.
– When placing batter in pan, spread well to corners.
– Always let bars cool upright in their pan on a wire rack several minutes before cutting (recipes specify how long).
– Use a very sharp knife for cutting bars, and if mixture is hard or sticky, dip knife in hot water.
– If your hand is unsteady, use a metal-edged ruler to guide you when cutting bars.

BASIC BROWNIES

Chewy chocolate brownies. But try the variations, too.
Makes 16 brownies

⅓ cup butter or margarine
2 (1-ounce) squares unsweetened chocolate
¾ cup sifted flour
½ teaspoon baking powder
¼ teaspoon salt
1 cup sugar
2 eggs
1 teaspoon vanilla
¾ cup coarsely chopped pecans or walnuts

Preheat oven to 350° F. Melt butter and chocolate in a small, heavy saucepan over lowest heat; cool to room temperature. Sift flour with baking powder and salt and set aside. Beat sugar, eggs, and vanilla until light and fluffy; slowly mix in chocolate mixture, then dry ingredients. Stir in nuts. Spoon into a greased 8″×8″×2″ pan and bake 30–35 minutes until brownies just begin to pull from sides of pan. Cool to room temperature upright in pan on a wire rack. Cut into 16 squares and serve. About 165 calories per brownie.

To Make with Cocoa: Increase amount of butter to ½ cup and, instead of melting, cream with sugar until fluffy. Beat in eggs and vanilla. Sift ⅓ cup sifted cocoa with flour, baking powder, and salt and work into creamed mixture. Stir in nuts and bake as directed. About 170 calories per brownie.

To Make with No-Melt Chocolate: Instead of melting butter, soften to room temperature and mix with 2 (1-ounce) envelopes no-melt unsweetened chocolate. Beat into creamed mixture and proceed as directed. About 170 calories per brownie.

VARIATIONS:

Mocha Brownies: Stir 2 tablespoons instant coffee powder into melted butter and chocolate and proceed as directed. About 165 calories per brownie.

Brown Sugar Brownies: Prepare as directed, substituting 1 cup firmly packed light brown sugar for the sugar. About 165 calories per brownie.

Minted Double Chocolate Tea Brownies: Prepare recipe as directed, but chop nuts fine. Stir ½ cup mint-flavored semisweet chocolate bits into batter along with nuts and spread in a greased 13"×9"×2" pan. Bake 20–25 minutes, cool as directed, and cut into 40 bars. About 70 calories per brownie.

Frosted Brownies: Prepare, bake, and cool brownies as directed; before cutting, spread with Chocolate Butter Cream Frosting (you'll need half the recipe). About 275 calories per brownie.

Filled and Frosted Tea Brownies: Prepare recipe as directed and bake in a greased 13"×9"×2" pan 20–25 minutes; cool and spread half of surface with Chocolate Butter Cream Frosting and other half with Coffee, Maple, or Orange Butter Cream Frosting (you'll need about ½ recipe of each). Cut each half into 24 equal-size bars and sandwich together in pairs with chocolate frosting on top. About 245 calories per brownie.

Two-Tone Brownies: Prepare recipe as directed but omit chocolate. Spoon half the batter into a greased 8"×8"×2" pan; mix 1 (1-ounce) envelope no-melt unsweetened chocolate into remaining batter and carefully spread on top. Bake as directed. About 155 calories per brownie.

Coconut Brownies: Prepare as directed, substituting ⅔ cup flaked coconut for nuts. About 145 calories per brownie.

Coconut Topped Brownies: Prepare Coconut Brownies; before baking spread with ⅔ cup flaked coconut mixed with 1 tablespoon each sugar and melted butter. Bake as directed. About 175 calories per brownie.

Snowy Coconut Chews: Omit chocolate and stir 1 cup flaked coconut into batter along with nuts. Spread in a greased 13"×9"×2" pan, bake 20–25 minutes, cool, and cut in 2" squares. About 100 calories each.

⊠ FUDGY SAUCEPAN BROWNIES

Truly dark and chewy. "The best," brownie lovers say.
Makes 16 large brownies

¾ cup butter or margarine
4 (1-ounce) squares unsweetened chocolate
2 cups sugar
4 eggs
1½ cups unsifted flour
½ teaspoon salt
1½ teaspoons vanilla
1¾ cups coarsely chopped pecans

Preheat oven to 375° F. Melt butter and chocolate in a large, heavy saucepan over lowest heat. Off heat, mix in remaining ingredients in order listed, beating well after each addition. Pour batter into a greased 9"×9"×2" pan and bake 40 minutes until brownies just begin to pull from sides of pan. Cool pan of brownies upright on a wire rack to room temperature, then cut in 16 squares. About 350 calories per brownie.

⊠ WHEAT- AND MILK-FREE BROWNIES

Most children adore brownies. For those with wheat and/or milk allergies, here's a special recipe.
Makes 2 dozen

⅓ cup margarine, softened to room temperature
1 cup firmly packed light brown sugar
2 eggs, lightly beaten
2 (1-ounce) envelopes no-melt semisweet chocolate or 2 (1-ounce) squares semisweet chocolate, melted
1 teaspoon vanilla
⅔ cup unsifted rice flour
½ teaspoon baking powder
¼ teaspoon salt
½ cup coarsely chopped pecans or walnuts

Preheat oven to 350° F. With a spoon, mix margarine and sugar well; add all remaining ingredients except nuts and blend until smooth. Stir in nuts and pour into a greased 8"×8"×2" or 9"×9"×2" pan. Bake 30 minutes or until sides shrink slightly from pan and top springs back when touched. Cool upright in pan on a wire rack, then cut into squares. About 105 calories per brownie.

MARBLE BROWNIES

Makes 16 brownies

Chocolate Layer:

1 (4-ounce) package sweet chocolate
3 tablespoons butter or margarine
2 eggs
¾ cup sugar
½ cup unsifted flour
½ teaspoon baking powder
Pinch salt
1 teaspoon vanilla
⅔ cup chopped pecans or walnuts

Vanilla Layer:

1 (3-ounce) package cream cheese
2 tablespoons butter or margarine
¼ cup sugar
1 egg
1 tablespoon flour
¾ teaspoon vanilla

Preheat oven to 350° F. Begin chocolate layer: Melt chocolate with butter over lowest heat, stirring to mix; cool to room temperature. Meanwhile, prepare vanilla layer: Beat cheese and butter until fluffy, gradually add sugar, creaming until fluffy. Beat in egg, flour, and vanilla; set aside while you finish chocolate layer. Beat 2 eggs until pale in color, add sugar slowly, and beat until mixture is quite thick. Stir in flour, baking powder, and salt, then cooled chocolate mixture, vanilla, and nuts. Spread half the chocolate layer in a greased 9"×9"×2" baking pan, top with vanilla layer, then remaining chocolate layer. Zigzag a knife through batter to create marbled effect. Bake 35–40 minutes until brownies pull from sides of pan. Cool upright in pan on a wire rack, then cut in large squares. About 165 calories per brownie.

BUTTERSCOTCH BROWNIES

Makes 16 brownies

⅔ cup sifted flour

1 teaspoon baking powder
¼ teaspoon salt
¼ cup butter or margarine
1 cup firmly packed light or dark brown sugar
1 egg
1 teaspoon vanilla
¾ cup coarsely chopped walnuts or pecans

Preheat oven to 350° F. Sift flour with baking powder and salt and set aside. Melt butter in a saucepan over low heat, add sugar, and stir until dissolved; cool 5 minutes. Beat in egg and vanilla, mix in dry ingredients and nuts. Spoon into a greased 8"×8"×2" baking pan and bake 30–35 minutes until brownies just begin to pull from sides of pan. Cool upright in pan on a wire rack to room temperature, then cut in 16 squares. About 135 calories per brownie.

VARIATION:

Toll House Brownies: Prepare as directed but reduce amount of nuts to ½ cup; stir ½ cup semisweet chocolate bits into batter along with nuts and bake as directed. About 155 calories per brownie.

SCOTTISH SHORTBREAD

The secret of good shortbread lies in the kneading. The dough *must* feel satin-smooth, and getting it that way may take as long as 15 minutes.

Makes 2 dozen slim, pie-shaped pieces

3¼ cups sifted flour
¼ cup sifted rice flour
¼ teaspoon salt
1 cup butter (no substitute), softened to room temperature
½ cup sugar

Preheat oven to 350° F. Sift flour with rice flour and salt. Using your hand or a wooden spoon, work butter and sugar together until light in color; blend in dry ingredients. Keeping dough in bowl, knead vigorously until satin-smooth and no sugar grains remain. Divide dough in half, place each on an ungreased baking sheet or 9" pie tin, and press flat into 9" circles, using palms of hands. Crimp edges as you would piecrust and cut each circle into 12 wedges (but don't separate). Bake 25 minutes until pale golden, not brown. Cool in pans on wire rack 10 minutes, then carefully recut to separate wedges; cool thoroughly. If you like, sprinkle shortbread lightly with sugar as soon as it comes from oven. About 145 calories per piece.

VARIATION:

Shortbread for Those with Milk Allergies: Make as directed, substituting ¾ cup margarine or vegetable shortening for the butter. About 125 calories per piece.

LEMON SPONGE SQUARES

Makes about 2½ dozen

Cake:

1½ cups sifted flour
½ teaspoon salt
¼ teaspoon baking powder
½ cup butter or margarine
1 cup sugar
3 eggs, separated
⅓ cup lemon juice
1 tablespoon finely grated lemon rind
1 cup sifted confectioners' sugar

Frosting:

1 cup sifted confectioners' sugar
1 tablespoon heavy cream or evaporated milk
2 tablespoons butter or margarine, softened to room temperature

Preheat oven to 350° F. Sift flour with salt and baking powder and set aside. Cream butter and sugar until light and fluffy; add egg yolks, one at a time, beating well after each addition. Mix in dry ingredients alternately with lemon juice, beginning and ending with dry ingredients. Mix in lemon rind. In a separate bowl beat egg whites until soft peaks form. Add confectioners' sugar, ¼ cup at a time, beating well after each addition, then continue to beat until stiff peaks will form. Fold egg white mixture into batter and pour into a well-greased and floured 13″×9″×2″ baking pan. Bake 35–40 minutes on

center oven rack until top springs back when lightly touched. Cool upright in pan on a rack 3–5 minutes. Meanwhile, mix frosting ingredients together until smooth. While cake is still warm, spread top evenly with frosting. Cool in pan, then cut into squares. About 130 calories per piece.

CHINESE CHEWS

The easiest way to "chop" dates is to snip them into small pieces with kitchen shears. To simplify the job, chill dates slightly before cutting.
Makes about 3 dozen

¾ cup sifted flour
1 cup sugar
1 teaspoon baking powder
Pinch salt
1 cup coarsely chopped dates
1 cup coarsely chopped walnuts
3 eggs, beaten until fluffy
½ teaspoon vanilla (optional)
⅔ cup sifted confectioners' sugar

Preheat oven to 350° F. Sift dry ingredients together and mix in dates and walnuts. Fold in eggs and, if you like, add vanilla. Spread evenly in a greased and floured 15½″×10½″×1″ jelly-roll pan (it will seem at first as though there isn't enough batter, but keep spreading it toward the corners; layer will be *very* thin). Bake 20 minutes until lightly browned and top springs back when touched. Cool upright in pan on a wire rack 10–12 minutes, then cut in 1¼″–1½″ squares. Roll in confectioners' sugar while still warm, then cool before serving. About 80 calories each.

MERINGUE NUT BARS

These cookies are wheat- and milk-free, good for those with either or both of these allergies.
Makes 4 dozen

2 egg whites
1⅓ cups sugar
1 tablespoon lemon juice
4 cups very finely chopped nuts (pecans, walnuts, or filberts)
1 teaspoon vanilla

Preheat oven to 325° F. Beat egg whites until frothy. Add sugar, 1 tablespoon at a time, beating well after each addition. Add lemon juice, then beat hard (highest mixer speed) 2–3 minutes. (*Note:* All sugar won't dissolve as it does in regular meringues, but mixture should be stiff and glossy.) Measure out 1 cup of the meringue mixture and set aside. Mix nuts and vanilla into remaining mixture; roll half of it out on a well-floured board into a rectangle about 6″ wide and ¼″ thick (the length doesn't matter, but the width should be 6″ so that bars of uniform size can be cut easily). Spread ½ cup reserved plain meringue on top. With a floured knife, cut into bars 3″ long and 1½″ wide and arrange 2″ apart on a greased and floured baking sheet. Roll, spread, and cut remaining nut meringue mixture the same way. Bake 25 minutes or until topping is creamy white and firm. Cool on wire racks. About 80 calories each.

CHEWY PECAN-CINNAMON BARS

Makes about 5 dozen

1 cup sifted flour
½ teaspoon baking powder
1 tablespoon cinnamon
¼ teaspoon salt
1 cup butter or margarine
1 cup plus 1 tablespoon sugar
2 eggs, separated
1 cup finely chopped pecans

Preheat oven to 300° F. Sift flour with baking powder, cinnamon, and salt. Cream butter with 1 cup sugar until light and fluffy; add egg yolks one at a time, beating well after each addition. Mix in dry ingredients. Spread mixture in an ungreased 14″×17″ baking sheet with a slightly raised edge. Beat egg whites until frothy, add remaining sugar and continue beating until stiff; spread evenly over mixture on sheet; sprinkle with nuts. Bake 40–45 minutes until golden. Cool upright in pan on a rack 10 minutes, cut in bars, and cool. About 65 calories each.

⊠ CONGO SQUARES

Filled with nuts and chocolate bits. And so quick to make.
Makes 4 dozen

½ cup butter or margarine, softened to room temperature
1 (1-pound) box dark brown sugar
3 eggs, lightly beaten
2½ cups sifted flour
½ teaspoon salt
1 teaspoon vanilla
1 (6-ounce) package semisweet or 1 (5¾-ounce) package milk chocolate bits
1 cup coarsely chopped walnuts or pecans

Preheat oven to 350° F. Cream butter with sugar and eggs until well blended; mix in remaining ingredients in the order listed. Spread in a greased 15½″×10½″×1″ jelly-roll pan and bake 30–35 minutes until top springs back when touched. Cool upright in pan on a wire rack, then cut into squares. About 110 calories each.

GREEK WHEAT AND WALNUT BARS (KARYDATA)

Makes 16

¾ cup butter or margarine
¾ cup sugar
3 eggs, separated
1 cup uncooked farina or wheatina
1 teaspoon cinnamon
1½ cups finely chopped walnuts
¼ teaspoon salt

Syrup:

¼ cup sugar
2 tablespoons warm water

Topping:

Sifted confectioners' sugar

Preheat oven to 375° F. Cream butter until fluffy and add sugar, a little at a time, beating well after each addition. Beat egg yolks in, one at a time. Stir in farina, cinnamon, and nuts. Beat egg whites with salt until soft peaks form and fold into batter. Spread in a greased and floured 9″×9″×2″ baking pan and bake 20–25 minutes until just firm to the touch. Meanwhile, prepare syrup: Boil sugar and water in a very small, heavy saucepan until clear and slightly thickened, about 3–5 minutes. Remove pan from oven, spoon syrup over top, distributing it as evenly as possible; return to oven and bake 5–10 minutes longer until mixture pulls from sides of pan. Cool upright in pan 5 minutes on a wire rack, then loosen and turn out. When cold, dust *lightly* with confectioners' sugar and cut into 16 bars. About 230 calories each.

BISHOP'S BARS

Like dates, candied cherries are more easily snipped into small pieces than chopped.
Makes 20

2 eggs
⅔ cup sugar
⅔ cup sifted flour
½ teaspoon baking powder
¼ teaspoon salt
1 (6-ounce) package semisweet chocolate bits
1 cup coarsely chopped pecans or walnuts
¾ cup coarsely chopped dates
⅔ cup coarsely chopped candied red cherries
½ teaspoon vanilla

Preheat oven to 375° F. Beat eggs until fluffy and pale; gradually beat in sugar and continue beating until about the color and consistency of mayonnaise. Sift flour with baking powder and salt, add chocolate bits, nuts, dates, and candied cherries, and toss well to dredge; stir into egg mixture, then mix in vanilla. Spread in a greased and floured 9″× 9″×2″ baking pan and bake 30–35 minutes until lightly browned and mixture begins to pull from sides of pan. Cool upright in pan 10–15 minutes on a wire rack, then cut in large bars (make 5 cuts one way and 4 the other). About 165 calories each.

GERMAN DATE SQUARES
Makes about 3 dozen

½ cup butter
1 cup sugar
3 eggs
½ cup sifted flour
2 teaspoons baking powder
¼ teaspoon salt
1 cup finely chopped walnuts
1 cup finely chopped, pitted dates
1 teaspoon vanilla

Preheat oven to 250° F. Cream butter until light, add sugar and continue creaming until fluffy. Add eggs, one at a time, beating well after each addition. Sift flour with baking powder and salt and mix into batter. Stir in walnuts, dates, and vanilla. Spoon into a lightly greased 9″×9″×2″ baking pan and bake, uncovered, 3 hours (mixture should be quite firm and tan and crackly on top). Cool upright in pan on a wire rack several hours, then cut into 1½″ squares (no larger because these cookies are rich). About 90 calories each.

LAYERED APRICOT BARS
Makes 2 dozen

⅔ cup dried apricots
1 cup water
½ cup butter or margarine, softened to room temperature
¼ cup sugar
1⅓ cups sifted flour
½ teaspoon baking powder
¼ teaspoon salt
1 cup firmly packed light brown sugar
2 eggs, lightly beaten
1½ teaspoons brandy flavoring or 1 teaspoon vanilla
½ cup finely chopped walnuts

Preheat oven to 350° F. Place apricots and water in a small saucepan, cover, and simmer 10 minutes; drain, cool, and chop fine; set aside. Stir butter and sugar together until well mixed; blend in 1 cup flour. Spread mixture in a greased 9″×9″×2″ pan and bake 25 minutes. Meanwhile, sift remaining flour with baking powder and salt. Beat brown sugar and eggs until thick; add flavoring.

Slowly mix in dry ingredients, apricots, and walnuts. Spread lightly and evenly over baked layer and bake ½ hour longer. Cool upright in pan on a wire rack, then cut into bars, using a knife dipped in warm water. About 130 calories each.

¢ **APPLE-OATMEAL BARS**

Makes 2 dozen

1 cup sifted flour
½ teaspoon salt
½ cup firmly packed light brown sugar
⅓ cup plus 2 tablespoons butter or margarine
1 cup uncooked quick-cooking oatmeal

Filling:

2½ cups finely chopped or thinly sliced, peeled apples
¼ cup sugar
¼ teaspoon nutmeg

Preheat oven to 400° F. Sift flour with salt and add brown sugar. Using a pastry blender, cut in ⅓ cup butter until the size of small peas; mix in oatmeal. Pack half the mixture into a well-greased 9″×9″×2″ pan; top with apples and sprinkle with sugar and nutmeg. Dot with remaining butter and cover with remaining oatmeal mixture, pressing down lightly. Bake 45–50 minutes until tan on top. Cool upright in pan on a wire rack and cut into bars. About 100 calories each.

VARIATIONS:

Date-Oatmeal Bars: Prepare oatmeal mixture as directed but, instead of preparing filling, simmer 2 cups chopped, pitted dates, uncovered, with 1 cup water and 2 tablespoons sugar 7–10 minutes until thick; cool to room temperature. Spread evenly over bottom oatmeal layer; do not dot with butter as above. Top with remaining oatmeal mixture and bake as directed. About 140 calories each.

Fig-Oatmeal Bars: Prepare like Date-Oatmeal Bars, substituting 1 cup chopped dried figs for 1 cup of the dates. About 140 calories each.

Prune-Oatmeal Bars: Prepare like Date-Oatmeal Bars, substituting 1 cup chopped, pitted prunes for 1 cup of the dates. About 140 calories each.

CURRANT AND RAISIN BARS

Makes 32 bars

1 cup sifted flour
1 teaspoon baking powder
½ teaspoon salt
2 eggs
1 teaspoon lemon extract
1 cup sugar
¾ cup seedless raisins
¾ cup dried currants

Optional Topping:

Confectioners' sugar or Lemon Sugar Glaze

Preheat oven to 350° F. Sift flour with baking powder and salt and set aside. Beat eggs until thick and lemon colored, add lemon extract, then gradually add sugar, ¼ cup at a time, beating well after each addition. Slowly mix in dry ingredients until just blended. Stir in raisins and currants. Spread mixture in a well-greased 13″×9″×2″ baking pan and bake 30 minutes until top springs back when lightly touched. Cool upright in pan on wire rack 10 minutes, cut into 32 bars, and cool completely in pan. If you like, sift confectioners' sugar over bars before serving or frost with Lemon Sugar Glaze. About 70 calories each if unglazed, 85 calories if glazed.

VARIATIONS:

Fruit Bars: Prepare as directed, substituting 1½ cups finely diced, pitted dates, prunes, dried apricots, or figs for currants and raisins. About 70 calories each.

Fruit and Nut Bars: Stir ¾–1 cup coarsely chopped walnuts, pecans, almonds, or hazelnuts into batter after adding fruit; bake as directed. Or scatter nuts evenly on top of batter after spreading in pan and bake as directed. About 90 calories each.

Black Walnut and Coconut Bars: Omit raisins and currants; stir 1½ cups flaked coconut and 1 cup coarsely chopped black walnuts into batter; bake as directed. About 95 calories each.

NO-BAKE COOKIES

These are an American invention and a good one, too. They require very little time, effort, or expertise to make and, when properly stored, will keep longer than any other type of cookie. Many, especially those rich in fruit or flavored with liquor, will actually improve on standing.

⊠ NO-BAKE RUM BALLS

Makes about 2½ dozen

1¾ cups fine vanilla wafer crumbs
1 cup finely ground pecans
1 cup unsifted confectioners' sugar
¼ cup cocoa
3 tablespoons light corn syrup
¼ cup light rum or bourbon
⅓ cup sifted confectioners' sugar (for dredging)

Place all but last ingredient in a bowl and mix well, using your hands. Roll into 1" balls and dredge in confectioners' sugar. (*Note:* These cookies keep well up to 10 days when stored in airtight canisters.) About 100 calories each.

FOUR-FRUIT BALLS

These cookies are milk-, egg-, and wheat-free, good for those with any or all of these allergies.
Makes 5 dozen

½ pound pitted dates
1 (12-ounce) package dried figs
1½ cups seedless raisins
12 pitted prunes
2 ounces crystallized ginger
1½ cups walnuts or pecans
Juice of ½ lemon
2 tablespoons pineapple or other fruit juice or rum or brandy
½ teaspoon cinnamon
Confectioners' sugar

Put dates, figs, raisins, prunes, ginger, and nuts through fine blade of meat grinder. Mix well, using your hands, sprinkle in fruit juices and cinnamon and mix again. Shape into 1" balls and roll in confectioners' sugar to coat. Let stand at room temperature 3–4 hours, then store airtight. About 100 calories each.

ORANGE-ALMOND BALLS

Makes 5 dozen

½ cup butter or margarine
1 (6-ounce) can frozen orange juice concentrate, thawed
1 (1-pound) box confectioners' sugar, sifted
1 (12-ounce) box vanilla wafers
1 cup sliced, blanched almonds
1 cup toasted, blanched almonds, chopped fine, or 1 cup toasted or colored* flaked coconut, chocolate jimmies, colored sugar, or decorettes

Heat butter and orange concentrate in a large saucepan over low heat, stirring until butter melts. Off heat, mix in confectioners' sugar. Crush vanilla wafers in an electric blender at high speed or with a rolling pin; add to mixture along with sliced almonds and mix well. Shape into 1" balls and roll in toasted almonds. Arrange on a tray or baking sheet and chill 2–3 hours before serving. Store airtight and, if weather is warm, in refrigerator. About 100 calories each.

⊠ PORCUPINES

Makes 3 dozen

2 eggs, lightly beaten
1 cup finely chopped, pitted dates
¾ cup sugar
1 cup finely chopped pecans or walnuts
2 cups toasted rice cereal
2 cups flaked coconut (about)

In a saucepan over moderate heat, heat eggs, dates, and sugar, stirring constantly about 10 minutes until mixture thickens. Cool 5 minutes and stir in nuts and cereal. Cool 10 minutes longer, then drop by rounded teaspoonfuls into flaked coconut; roll in coconut and shape into balls. About 85 calories each.

NO-BAKE CHOCOLATE BONBONS

Makes 2 dozen

¼ pound sweet chocolate
1 cup sifted confectioners' sugar
1 cup finely crushed vanilla wafer
  crumbs
¼ cup light corn syrup
2 tablespoons honey
½ cup finely chopped walnuts or pecans
sifted confectioners' sugar (for dredging)

Melt chocolate in top of double boiler over simmering water. Off heat stir in remaining ingredients except dredging sugar in order listed; as mixture stiffens, use hands to blend well. Shape into 1″ balls and roll in confectioners' sugar. Let ripen 1–2 days before serving. About 95 calories each.

⊠ CHOCOLATE HAYSTACKS

Makes 2 dozen

1 (6-ounce) package semisweet chocolate bits
1 (6-ounce) package butterscotch bits
½ cup coarsely chopped pecans, walnuts, or almonds
1 (3-ounce) can chow mein noodles

Melt chocolate and butterscotch bits in a double boiler over simmering water. Off heat mix in nuts and noodles. Drop by tablespoonfuls on wax paper and cool to room temperature. About 85 calories each.

VARIATION:

Butterscotch Haystacks: Prepare as directed, using 2 (6-ounce) packages butterscotch bits instead of 1 chocolate and 1 butterscotch. About 85 calories each.

FUDGE NUGGETS

Not as high-calorie as you might think.
Makes 3 dozen

2 cups sugar
1 cup milk
2 (1-ounce) squares semisweet chocolate

½ teaspoon instant coffee powder
2 tablespoons butter or margarine
1 teaspoon vanilla
1¾ cups graham cracker crumbs

Mix sugar and milk in a large, heavy saucepan; insert candy thermometer. Boil over moderate heat without stirring until thermometer registers 230° F.; mixture will foam up, so adjust heat as needed to prevent its boiling over. Off heat, stir in chocolate, coffee, butter and vanilla; mix until chocolate melts. Stir in crumbs and, working quickly, drop by rounded teaspoonfuls on wax paper. Cool thoroughly and serve. About 80 calories each.

MRS. BOULDIN'S DATE-NUT FINGERS

Makes about 4 dozen

½ cup margarine
1 cup sugar
1 egg, lightly beaten
1 (8-ounce) package pitted dates, chopped fine
1¼ cups toasted rice cereal
1 cup finely chopped pecans or walnuts
1 cup finely shredded coconut (about)

Melt margarine in the top of a double boiler over simmering water. Stir in sugar and egg. Heat, stirring every 5 minutes, for 20–30 minutes over simmering—not boiling—water until mixture is thick and will coat the back of a wooden spoon. Pour over dates, add cereal and nuts, and mix well. Cool to room temperature, then shape into "fingers" about 2″ long and 1″ wide and roll in coconut to coat evenly. Store airtight. About 125 calories each.

⊠ PEANUT BUTTER BARS

Crunchy and sweet.
Makes 4 dozen

1 cup sugar
1 cup light corn syrup
1 (12-ounce) jar crunchy peanut butter
4 cups toasted rice cereal
1 cup coarsely chopped unsalted peanuts (optional)

Heat and stir sugar, syrup, and peanut

butter in a very large saucepan over moderate heat until mixture boils. Off heat mix in remaining ingredients. Pack into a well-greased 9″×13″×2″ baking pan and cool. Cut into bars. About 90 calories each (without peanuts), 110 calories (with peanuts).

SPECIAL COOKIES

The two following recipes don't fit any of the basic cookie categories. Both are deep-fat-fried, both are Continental classics. And neither, surprisingly, is very high in calories.

SWEDISH ROSETTES (STRUVOR)

For these you will need a special rosette iron, available in housewares sections of many large department stores. Read instructions accompanying iron carefully before beginning this recipe.
Makes 4 dozen

Shortening or cooking oil for deep fat
 frying
2 eggs plus 1 egg yolk
¾ cup light cream
⅓ cup sugar
1 cup sifted flour
¼ teaspoon salt
Sifted confectioners' sugar

Begin heating fat in a deep fryer over moderate heat; insert deep fat thermometer. Beat eggs, cream, and sugar just to blend; sprinkle in flour and salt, a little at a time, and beat until smooth. When fat reaches 355–65° F., heat rosette iron by submerging in the hot fat about 10 seconds. Lift out, shake off excess fat, and dip iron carefully into batter so that its top is *exactly level* with that of the batter—any deeper and you won't be able to get the rosette off the iron. Plunge batter-coated iron into fat and, as soon as batter starts to "puff," gradually lift out iron so that rosette will slip back into fat. When lightly brown on one side, flip gently with a fork to brown other side. (*Note:* The whole

procedure takes only a few seconds so you'll have to work fast.) Lift rosette out with a fork or slotted spoon and drain on paper toweling. Repeat with remaining batter, reheating iron for each rosette and never frying more than 2 rosettes at a time and keeping fat as near to 355–65° F. as possible. Spread rosettes out in a single layer on several thicknesses of paper toweling to cool. Dust with confectioners' sugar and serve. These are best eaten the day they're made, but if stored airtight, they will keep fairly well about a week. About 60 calories each.

¢ ⬧ PORTUGUESE FILHOS

These crisp, wine-flavored, fried cookies are best served the day they are made and are especially good with a glass of port or Madeira.
Makes 3½ dozen

Shortening or cooking oil for deep fat
 frying
1 egg, lightly beaten
1 tablespoon port wine
3 tablespoons cold water
¼ teaspoon vanilla
2 teaspoons melted butter
2 tablespoons sugar
¼ teaspoon salt
1½ cups plus 2 tablespoons sifted flour
Confectioners' sugar

Begin heating shortening in a deep fat fryer over low heat; insert deep fat thermometer. Mix egg, port, water, vanilla, butter, sugar, and salt; sprinkle in flour and mix well. Turn out on lightly floured board and knead 1 minute just until smooth. Divide dough in half and roll, one piece at a time, *paper thin*. Cut in 2½″ squares; make a slit in one corner and pull opposite corner through. When fat reaches 375 F., drop in *filhos*, 4 or 5 at a time, and fry about 2 minutes until golden; turn them over to brown evenly if they don't flip on their own. Lift out with a slotted spoon and drain on paper toweling. Cool, then dredge with confectioners' sugar. About 50 calories per cookie.

CHAPTER 24

CANDIES AND NUTS

How many good cooks' love of food began with a batch of fudge? Dozens, probably, because nothing draws children to the kitchen faster than candy making. And nothing *involves* them more quickly in cooking. It's fun to beat divinity, pull taffy or mints, shape marzipan. Fun, too, to lick the spoon. As long as everyone's had a good time, it doesn't matter if the candy isn't perfect. The next batch will be better and the next batch better still.

Tips for Making Better Candies

– First, the weather. It does make a difference, with cooked candies especially. So choose a dry, cool, clear day. If you must make candy on a damp day, cook 2° higher on the candy thermometer than recipe specifies so that candy will harden.
– Measure ingredients precisely.
– Do not double or halve recipes for cooked candies and do not make substitutions in ingredients.
– Follow recipes to the letter; candies are critical (apt to fail) and do not take to improvisation.
– Use a heavy, deep, straight-sided pan about four times the volume of combined recipe ingredients so that candy has plenty of room to boil up without boiling over. Also choose pan with an insulated handle so you won't burn yourself.
– Use a wooden spoon for stirring— less chance of the candy's turning to sugar and less chance of burning yourself. And make sure spoon is clean and dry each time it is put into the candy.
– *Use a candy thermometer.* Clip to side of pan, making sure bulb is immersed but does not touch bottom. Some cooks recommend inserting thermometer after

candy boils (to reduce risk of crystallization), but the wait isn't necessary except for fondant. Moreover, a cold thermometer may break if shoved into boiling syrup. Keep an eye on the mercury; it will climb to 220° F. at a snail's pace, but race on thereafter and, unless watched, overshoot its mark. Read thermometer at eye level and, if in doubt about its accuracy, also use one of the tests described below. *To test accuracy of thermometer:* Insert in a pan of cold water and bring gradually to a boil; boil 10 minutes. Temperature should be 212° F. If not, note difference and adjust recipe temperatures accordingly. For example, if thermometer reads 210° F. at the boiling point, cook candy 2° lower than recipes suggest; if it registers 214° F., cook 2° higher.
– Use a marble slab for working candy or, failing that, a large ironstone platter or heavy metal tray.
– To simplify beating at the end, use a portable electric mixer.
– *To help keep creamy candies from turning to sugar:* There's no guarantee, but the following precautions should all help:
– If candy contains butter, cook in a buttered pan; also butter end of thermometer.

CANDY-MAKING TEMPERATURES AND TESTS

Thermometer Reading	Candy Stage	Test (use fresh water for each test)
230–34° F.	Thread	Syrup dropped from a spoon will form a 2″ thread.
234–40° F.	Soft Ball	A drop of syrup forms a soft ball in cold water that flattens on removal.
244–48° F.	Firm Ball	A drop of syrup forms a firm, pliable ball in cold water that holds its shape on removal.
250–65° F.	Hard Ball	A drop of syrup forms a hard but still pliable ball in cold water.
270–90° F.	Soft Crack	Syrup dropped in cold water forms pliable strands.
300–10° F.	Hard Crack	Syrup dropped in cold water forms brittle strands.

Note: These thermometer readings are slightly higher than those marked on standard candy thermometers, but they have proved more reliable.

– Brush down crystals that collect on sides of pan and thermometer with a damp pastry brush (just one crystal can turn a whole batch of candy gritty).
– When making fondant or other simple water-sugar candies, cover and boil about three minutes after sugar is dissolved; steam will wash away crystals that have gathered on sides of pan.
– Do not stir candy after sugar has dissolved.
– Do not hurry the cooking or the cooling; let syrup cool to 110° F. before beating. If speed is important, cool in a larger pan of cold water.
– Do not scrape pan when turning candy out.
– Knead cooled, cooked candy to reduce size of sugar crystals and work in any nuts afterward.
– Do not overcook candy; use a clean, dry spoon each time you make a test.
– Do not overbeat candy before turning out; it should be about the consistency of a butter frosting and just losing its gloss. Once candies begin turning, they turn fast, so you must work quickly. If candy becomes too hard, pick up and knead until soft again, then pat into a pan with your hands or shape into a roll and slice.

Some Special Candy-Making Techniques

To Color Sugar: Put about ½ cup sugar (granulated) in a small bowl and add food color, 1 drop at a time; rub sugar quickly between fingers after each addition to distribute color evenly. Be careful not to overcolor.

To Make Vanilla Sugar: Place 1 pound sugar in a canister with an airtight lid and push 2 vanilla beans deep down in. Cover and let stand at least one week before using. If you want a supply of vanilla sugar on hand, replenish sugar as needed and add a fresh vanilla bean every 6 months. Use vanilla sugar wherever vanilla extract is called for— in making candies, cookies, custards, dessert soufflés, and sauces. Allow 1 tablespoon vanilla sugar for each ¼ teaspoon vanilla and decrease recipe's total quantity of sugar accordingly. Thus, in a recipe calling for 2 cups sugar and 1 teaspoon vanilla, you would use 4 tablespoons vanilla sugar and 1¾ cups sugar.

To Spin Sugar: Pastry cooks love to frame their masterpieces with clouds of spun sugar, and frankly, the spinning's a sticky business best left to the pros.

Attempted at home without the proper technique or utensils, it can quickly wreck both cook and kitchen. However, for those who want to try their luck, here is a method that has worked fairly well at home. Pick a dry, crisp day. Place 1 cup sugar, ½ cup hot water, and ⅛ teaspoon cream of tartar in a small, heavy pan; insert candy thermometer. Heat, stirring until sugar dissolves, then boil slowly, uncovered, without stirring until thermometer reaches 310° F. While syrup cooks, cover counter near stove (and floor beneath it) with newspapers. Stand 2 clean quart-size soda bottles on counter about 2 feet apart. When syrup reaches 310° F., turn heat off; let cool a few minutes, then dip in a wooden spoon and pull out. If syrup spins a long, fine hair, temperature is right for spinning. Dip in a wire whisk, then spin by drawing threads from one bottle to the other, using a quick whipping motion. Continue dipping and spinning until you have an inch-wide skein of threads, then carefully lift off and set on wax paper. Continue spinning, reheating syrup if it should harden too much. *How to Use Spun Sugar:* Use as soon as possible—to wreathe a compote of fruits, a showy pastry or cake or shape into a nest on a circle of cardboard, fill with delicate candies, and use as a *bonbonnière*-centerpiece.

To Toast Grated Coconut: Spread coconut out in an ungreased shallow baking pan and toast uncovered, stirring often, 30–40 minutes at 300° F. until golden.

To Color Grated Coconut: Dip a toothpick in food color, stir through coconut, then rub with your fingers to distribute. Repeat until color is the intensity you want.

To Dip Candies in Fondant: (see Fondant).

To Dip Candies in Chocolate: This isn't just a matter of melting chocolate and sloshing candy through it. It's a tricky technique requiring years to master, so don't be discouraged if your chocolates are streaked or ragged around the edges.

For best results:
– Choose a cool, crisp day and have kitchen cool.
– Choose dippable candies—fondant balls, firm caramels, candied cherries.
– Have both chocolate and candies to be dipped at room temperature.
– Use semisweet chocolate (once called dot or dipping chocolate) and work with no more than 2 pounds at a time and no less than 1.
– Holding chocolate by wrapper, grate fine into the top of a double boiler, handling as little as possible; insert a candy thermometer.
– Melt very slowly over hot—*not boiling*—water, stirring until chocolate reaches 130° F. Do not add any water to chocolate. Set chocolate over—not in— cold water and cool to 85° F. Also cool water in double boiler bottom to 85° F. Replace chocolate over warm water and keep there throughout dipping.
– Using a dipping fork or 2-pronged kitchen fork, dip candies one at a time into chocolate to coat evenly; set on wax-paper-covered wire racks, twirling tail end of chocolate into curlicues on top of candies.
– Let chocolates harden 5–10 minutes before removing from paper. Trim off any ragged edges and store airtight (not in the refrigerator, which will cause chocolate to whiten and streak). (*Note:* You must work quickly with chocolate. If it hardens before candies are dipped, remelt and cool as before. Semisweet chocolate bits can be used for dipping but are stiffer and lack the finish of semisweet chocolate.)

About Special Candy Flavorings

Essences and oils are used to flavor candies as well as the familiar extracts available at supermarkets. Gourmet shops usually carry a full line of essences (butterscotch, peppermint, spearmint, etc.), also such exotics as rose, violet, and orange flower water. Drugstores are the best places to buy oils—peppermint, wintergreen, clove, etc.—because all are used in pharmacy. These are potent and must be added drop by drop.

About Decorating Candies

Candies need little decoration and, in fact, are extremely difficult to decorate because of their small size. Bar candies are best left alone, but won't be over-decorated if topped by nut halves or candied cherries. Fondant and uncooked fruit balls can be rolled in finely ground nuts, grated coconut (plain, colored, or toasted), in sugar (plain or colored), in chocolate shot or decorettes. Fondant-dipped candies can be adorned with piped-on icing designs (the same decorative icings used for cakes). But keep designs simple—a tiny star or flower or leaf. When tinting icings, use a light touch, remembering that colors often darken as icing dries. Liquid food colors work well, but the number of colors is limited. For a broader palette, investigate paste colors sold in specialty shops.

About Wrapping and Keeping Candies

When it comes to wrapping and storing, candies fall into two groups: those that dry on standing and those that absorb moisture from the air. Fudges, fondants, and other creamy candies are the drying kind; caramels and hard candies just the opposite. Always store the two kinds separately so that one doesn't give up moisture to the other. Caramels and hard candies should be individually wrapped as soon as they've cooled in wax paper, cellophane, plastic food wrap, or foil, then placed in airtight canisters. The drying kind needn't be wrapped unless you hope to keep it some time, but it *should* be stored airtight.

About Packing and Shipping Candies

Sturdy, undecorated candies are the best travelers—fudge, fondant, caramels, nougats, fruit balls, etc. Wrap each piece separately, then pack and ship as you would cookies (see About Packing and Shipping Cookies).

COOKED CANDIES

¢ ⚖ FONDANT

Fondant is more a base for other confections than a candy to be eaten by itself.
Makes about 1 pound

2 cups sugar
1½ cups hot water
⅛ teaspoon cream of tartar or ¼ teaspoon lemon juice

Heat and stir all ingredients in a large, heavy saucepan over moderate heat until sugar dissolves; cover and boil 3 minutes. Uncover, insert candy thermometer that has been heated under hot tap, and cook *without stirring* to 238° F. or until a drop of fondant forms a soft ball in cold water. (*Note:* Wipe crystals from sides of pan with a damp pastry brush as they collect—fondant will be less apt to turn grainy.) Remove fondant from heat and let stand 1–2 minutes until bubbles subside; pour— *without scraping pan*—onto a marble slab or large, heavy platter rubbed lightly with a damp cloth; cool undisturbed until barely warm. (*Note:* If you have an extra candy thermometer, insert as soon as fondant is poured.) When fondant has cooled to 110° F., scrape from edges with a broad spatula in toward center again and again until it thickens and whitens; pick up and knead until velvety. Wrap fondant in cloth wrung out in cold water and "season" ½ hour before using. (*Note:* Covered with damp cloth and stored in an airtight jar, fondant will keep 3–4 days.) About 25 calories per 1″ ball.

To Flavor Fondant: Knead in about ½ teaspoon extract (vanilla, almond, rum, spearmint, rose or orange water) or a few drops oil of peppermint or wintergreen. Add these *by the drop,* tasting as you go so you don't *overflavor.*

To Color Fondant: Dip a toothpick in desired food color, then pierce fondant in several places. Knead to distribute color; if too pale, repeat—but keep colors pastel.

To Use Fondant for Dipping: Melt fondant (either plain or flavored) in the top of a double boiler over simmering water, stirring until smooth. Drop in candy center, nut or fruit to be dipped, turn with a long-handled, two-tined fork to coat evenly, lift to wax paper, and for a professional touch twirl tag end of fondant into a curlicue on top of each piece when removing fork. Let harden, then lift from paper.

VARIATIONS:

⚖ **Coffee Fondant:** Prepare as directed, substituting 1½ cups strong black coffee for the water and 2 tablespoons light corn syrup for the cream of tartar. About 25 calories per 1″ ball.

⚖ **Honey Fondant:** Prepare as directed but add 2 tablespoons honey and omit the cream of tartar. About 25 calories per 1″ ball.

⚖ **Butter Fondant:** Prepare as directed, using the following ingredients: 2 cups sugar, 1 cup milk, 1 tablespoon light corn syrup, and 1 tablespoon butter. About 30 calories per 1″ ball.

⚖ **Opera Creams:** Prepare as directed, using the following ingredients: 2 cups sugar, 1 cup heavy cream, and ⅛ teaspoon cream of tartar. Do not boil covered; instead, after sugar dissolves, cook without stirring to 238° F. (*Note:* This fondant takes longer to cream up on the marble slab than regular fondant.) About 35 calories per 1″ ball.

Confections to Make with Fondant

Stuffed Fruits: Shape fondant into small balls and stuff into pitted dates, prunes, or dried apricots. Roll in granulated sugar. About 50 calories each.

Nut Bonbons: Sandwich large walnut or pecan halves together with small fondant balls. About 50 calories each.

Frosted Nuts or Fruits: Dip large walnut or pecan halves, whole blanched almonds, candied cherries, pitted dates, or dried apricots into melted fondant. About 50 calories each.

Snow-Capped Fudge Balls: Prepare Best Chocolate Fudge as directed but omit nuts; instead of pouring into pan, pour onto a damp marble slab or heavy platter and, when cool enough to handle, knead until soft and velvety. Shape into small balls and dip in melted fondant. About 100 calories each.

Pinwheels: Take equal parts fondant and fudge (without nuts) or two flavors and colors of fondant and knead separately until smooth. Flatten one piece into a rectangle about 6″×8″ and ⅛″ thick. Pat remaining candy on top to fit, then roll jelly-roll fashion and slice ¼″ thick. About 60 calories each.

⚖ **Thin Mints:** Flavor fondant with peppermint, tint pale green and flavor with spearmint, or tint pale pink and flavor with wintergreen. Melt in the top of a double boiler over simmering water, stirring until smooth; drop from a teaspoon onto wax paper and let harden. About 25 calories each.

Sugarplums: Roll fondant around small pieces of fruit—candied cherries, small pitted dates, cubes of preserved ginger, pieces of dried apricots. About 60 calories each.

⚖ **Snowballs:** Shape fondant into small balls and roll in flaked coconut. About 35 calories each.

Nut Balls: Shape fondant into small balls and roll in ground nuts—pecans, walnuts, almonds, pistachios, Brazil nuts, hazelnuts. About 40 calories each.

Christmas Balls: Shape fondant into small balls and roll in chocolate or silver shot, colored sugar, or decorettes. About 40 calories each.

⚖ **Coffee Drops:** Shape fondant into small balls and roll in instant coffee powder. About 25 calories each.

DIVINITY

Makes about 1½ pounds

2½ cups sugar
½ cup light corn syrup
½ cup water
2 egg whites
1 teaspoon vanilla
1½ cups coarsely chopped walnuts or
  pecans

Place sugar, syrup, and water in a large, heavy saucepan; insert candy thermometer. Heat and stir over moderate heat until sugar dissolves; lower heat slightly and cook uncovered *without stirring* to 260° F. Toward end of cooking, beat egg whites until soft peaks form. When syrup reaches 260° F., add to egg whites in a very slow, fine stream, beating hard all the while. Continue adding, more quickly toward the end, until all syrup is in. Add vanilla and beat until stiff peaks form; fold in nuts. Drop from rounded teaspoons onto wax-paper-lined baking sheets and cool thoroughly. About 40 calories per piece.

VARIATIONS:

Seafoam: Prepare as directed but use firmly packed light brown sugar instead of granulated. About 40 calories per piece.

⚖ **Confetti Divinity:** Prepare as directed but omit nuts; instead, stir in 1 cup minced mixed candied fruit. About 35 calories per piece.

⚖ **Fruit Divinity:** Prepare as directed but omit nuts; instead, stir in 1 cup minced pitted dates, prunes, or dried apricots. About 30 calories per piece.

Christmas Divinity: Prepare as directed but reduce nuts to ¾ cup; also stir in ¾ cup minced mixed red and green candied cherries. About 40 calories per piece.

⚖ **Pistachio Divinity:** Prepare as directed but reduce vanilla to ½ teaspoon and add ¼ teaspoon almond extract. Tint pale green if you like, beat until stiff, and fold in 1½ cups minced pistachio nuts. About 40 calories per piece.

BEST CHOCOLATE FUDGE

Makes about 2 pounds

4 cups sugar
1 cup milk
3 (1-ounce) squares unsweetened
  chocolate
¼ teaspoon salt
¼ cup light corn syrup
¼ cup butter or margarine
1 teaspoon vanilla
1–1½ cups coarsely chopped pecans or
  walnuts (optional)

Heat sugar, milk, chocolate, salt, and corn syrup, uncovered, in a large, heavy saucepan with a candy thermometer over moderate heat, stirring constantly, until sugar dissolves. Continue cooking, uncovered, *without stirring* but occasionally moving a wooden spoon back and forth over bottom of pan until thermometer reaches 236–38° F. or mixture forms a soft ball in cold water. Remove from heat, drop in butter, and cool, without stirring, to 110° F. Add vanilla and beat until fudge is quite thick and begins to lose its gloss. Quickly mix in nuts, if you like, and spread in a well-buttered 8″×8″×2″ baking pan. Cool until firm and cut into 1″ squares. For better flavor, store airtight and ripen 24 hours. About 80 calories per piece (with 1 cup nuts).

BLOND FUDGE

A good choice for those allergic to chocolate.
Makes about 1 pound

2 cups sugar
¼ cup light corn syrup
1⅓ cups milk
⅓ cup light cream
1 teaspoon vanilla
1 tablespoon butter
1¼ cups coarsely chopped pecans or
  walnuts (optional)

Place sugar, syrup, milk, and cream in a large, heavy saucepan (mixture tends to boil up, so pan should be at least 4 times combined volume of ingredients); insert candy thermometer. Heat and stir over moderate heat until sugar dissolves, reduce heat slightly and cook, uncovered, stirring only if mixture threatens to boil over, until thermometer reaches 238° F. or a drop of candy forms a soft ball in cold water. Toward end of cooking, mixture will be very thick, so watch closely and move spoon gently across bottom of pan occasionally to keep it from scorching. Remove from heat, add vanilla and butter *without stirring,* and cool to 110° F. Beat until thick and no longer glossy, quickly mix in nuts, if you like, and turn into a buttered 8″×8″×2″ pan, spreading to edges. Cool until firm and cut in 1″ squares. About 50 calories per piece (with nuts).

VARIATIONS:

Coconut Fudge: Prepare as directed but omit nuts; instead, stir in 1¼ cups flaked coconut. Turn out, cool, and cut as directed. About 45 calories per piece.

Toll House Fudge: Prepare as directed but reduce nuts to ¾ cup; at the same time, mix in 1 cup semisweet chocolate bits. Turn out, cool, and cut as directed. About 65 calories per piece.

PENUCHE

Makes about 1 pound

1 (1-pound) box light brown sugar
¾ cup milk
2 tablespoons butter or margarine
1 teaspoon vanilla

Heat sugar, milk, and butter in a large, heavy saucepan with a candy thermometer over moderate heat, stirring until sugar dissolves. Lower heat slightly and cook, uncovered, *without stirring* to 240° F. or until mixture forms a soft ball in cold water. Off heat, add vanilla —do not stir—and cool to 110° F. Beat until thick and no longer shiny, pour into a buttered 8″×8″×2″ pan, spreading to edges. Score in 1″ squares and cool to room temperature. Cut into 1″ squares and serve. About 40 calories per piece.

VARIATIONS:

Nut Penuche: Prepare as directed but mix in ⅔ cup coarsely chopped pecans or walnuts just before pouring into pan. About 50 calories per piece.

Coconut Penuche: Prepare as directed but mix in ⅔ cup flaked coconut just before pouring into pan. About 45 calories per piece.

Maple Penuche: Prepare as directed but use maple flavoring instead of vanilla. For a more delicate flavor, use 1 cup granulated sugar and 1¼ cups firmly packed light brown sugar instead of all brown sugar. About 40 calories per piece.

Coffee Penuche: Prepare as directed but use ¼ cup heavy cream and ½ cup very strong black coffee instead of milk. About 45 calories per piece.

PRALINES

A friend said of these, "Best I ever ate!"
Makes about 2 dozen

2 cups sugar
½ cup firmly packed light brown sugar
1 teaspoon baking soda
¼ teaspoon salt
⅛ teaspoon cinnamon
1 cup buttermilk
¼ cup butter or margarine
2 cups pecan halves

Mix sugars, soda, salt, cinnamon, and buttermilk in a large, heavy saucepan; drop in butter. Insert candy thermometer. Heat, uncovered, and without stirring over moderately high heat until candy thermometer registers 238° F. or mixture forms a soft ball in cold water. Remove from heat at once and stir in pecans. Beat briskly with a wooden spoon about 1 minute, then drop onto wax-paper-lined baking sheets, making each praline 2″–2½″ in diameter. Let harden thoroughly before serving. About 165 calories each.

CARAMELS

Cook very slowly in your heaviest saucepan. This mixture is sweet and thick—apt to scorch.
Makes about 1 pound

1 cup sugar
⅔ cup light corn syrup
1½ cups light cream
⅛ teaspoon salt
1 teaspoon vanilla

Place sugar, syrup, and ½ cup cream in a large, heavy saucepan; insert candy thermometer. Heat and stir over moderate heat until sugar dissolves. Turn heat to low and cook, uncovered, stirring occasionally, to 238° F. Mix in ½ cup cream and cook, stirring as needed to keep from sticking, to about 236° F. or until mixture forms a soft ball in cold water. Mix in remaining ½ cup cream and heat, stirring constantly, until very thick and a drop firms up quickly in cold water. Thermometer may register only 230° F., but if mixture firms up, take from heat. Mix in salt and vanilla and pour into a buttered 8″×8″×2″ pan. Cool until just warm and score in 1″ squares. Cool thoroughly, cut in squares, and wrap individually in wax paper or cellophane. About 40 calories per piece.

VARIATIONS:

Nut Caramels: Prepare as directed but just before pouring into pan stir in ⅔ cup minced walnuts or pecans. About 45 calories per piece.

Chocolate Caramels: Prepare as directed but add 1½ (1-ounce) squares melted unsweetened chocolate along with final ½ cup cream. Watch closely to see that mixture doesn't scorch during final cooking. About 45 calories per piece.

ALMOND NOUGAT

For best results, use 2 candy thermometers, one in each syrup.
Makes 1 pound

First Syrup:

½ cup sugar
½ cup light corn syrup
2 tablespoons water

Second Syrup:

1½ cups sugar
½ cup light corn syrup
¼ cup water

2 egg whites
¼ cup butter or margarine, softened to room temperature
¼ teaspoon almond extract
1 cup minced blanched almonds or ½ cup each minced almonds and minced candied red cherries

Mix first syrup in a small, heavy saucepan, insert candy thermometer, and heat over moderately high heat until sugar dissolves; cook, uncovered, *without stirring* to 246° F. Combine second syrup ingredients in a larger, heavy saucepan meanwhile, insert candy thermometer, and heat and stir over moderate heat until sugar dissolves; pull pan to side of burner. Beat egg whites to stiff peaks in large mixer bowl; add first syrup in a slow, *thin* stream, beating at moderate speed. At the same time, heat second syrup, uncovered, *without stirring* to 285° F. or until a drop forms pliable strands in cold water. Continue to beat whites at slow speed. Add second syrup in a fine, slow stream, beating at moderate speed. Add almond extract and beat until very thick; stir in nuts and, using buttered hands, press into a well-buttered 8″×8″×2″ pan. Cover loosely with wax paper and let stand in a cool place (not refrigerator) overnight. Cut in 1″ squares and let ripen 2–3 days before eating. Wrap pieces individually and store airtight. About 60 calories per piece.

OLD ENGLISH TOFFEE

Makes 1 pound

1 cup butter (no substitute)
¼ cup light cream or evaporated milk
2 cups firmly packed light brown sugar
1 teaspoon vanilla

Melt butter in a large, heavy saucepan over moderate heat; mix in cream and sugar, insert candy thermometer, and heat uncovered, stirring occasionally, until sugar dissolves. Continue cooking uncovered, moving a wooden spoon across bottom of pan *occasionally* (but not actually stirring) until thermometer reaches 280° F. or a little mixture dropped in ice water separates into firm but not brittle strands. Remove from heat, let bubbling subside, add vanilla, and stir only to blend. Pour into a well-buttered 8"×8"×2" pan and cool 10 minutes—candy should be hardening but still plastic. Turn onto a foil-lined board and score in 1" squares. Cool to room temperature, break into squares, and wrap each in foil, cellophane, or wax paper. Store airtight. About 55 calories per piece.

PEANUT BRITTLE

Makes about 1¾ pounds

2 cups roasted, blanched peanuts
2 cups sugar
½ cup water
½ cup light corn syrup
¼ cup butter or margarine
¼ teaspoon baking soda
½ teaspoon vanilla

Warm peanuts in a large, heavy skillet over low heat 5–7 minutes, shaking skillet occasionally; keep warm while making brittle. Mix sugar, water, and corn syrup in a large, heavy saucepan; insert candy thermometer. Set over high heat and heat, stirring, until sugar dissolves, then heat, uncovered, *without stirring* but moving a wooden spoon back and forth across bottom of pan occasionally to prevent scorching. When thermometer reaches 310° F. or a little hot syrup dropped in ice water turns brittle, remove from heat, add butter, peanuts, soda, and vanilla, and mix just to blend. Let bubbles subside, pour out as thin as possible on buttered baking sheets, spreading mixture with a buttered spatula. *For extra-thin brittle:* Cool until easy to handle, then pull out and stretch with buttered fingers. When brittle is cold, crack into bite-sized pieces. (*Note:* Flavor will be best if brittle ripens 24 hours in an airtight canister.) About 80 calories per piece.

VARIATIONS:

Lacy Brittle: Prepare as directed, heating ¼ teaspoon cream of tartar with sugar mixture and increasing soda to ½ teaspoon. About 80 calories per piece.

Pecan Brittle: Prepare as directed, substituting roasted pecan halves for peanuts. About 80 calories per piece.

Walnut Brittle: Prepare as directed, substituting walnut halves for peanuts. About 80 calories per piece.

Almond Brittle: Prepare as directed, substituting toasted, blanched whole almonds for peanuts. About 80 calories per piece.

BLACK WALNUT-MOLASSES CANDY

Makes about 1 pound

1½ cups molasses
1 cup sugar
1 cup light cream or evaporated milk
2 tablespoons butter or margarine
½ teaspoon baking soda
½–¾ cup finely chopped black walnuts

Mix molasses, sugar, and cream in a large, heavy saucepan, drop in butter and insert candy thermometer; heat, stirring constantly, over moderately low heat until sugar dissolves. Cook uncovered, moving a wooden spoon across bottom of pan *occasionally* (but not actually stirring) to 250° F. or until a drop of candy forms a hard ball in cold water. Off heat, add soda, then nuts and stir *just to blend*. Pour into a well-buttered 9"×9"×2" pan; do not scrape pan. Cool 15 minutes, score in 1" squares and, when hardening but still pliable, turn out on a baking sheet. Cool to room temperature and cut in 1" squares. Wrap each piece and store airtight. About 40 calories per piece.

Some Pointers on Pulled Candies

– Don't attempt to make pulled candies in a cool kitchen; candies will harden too fast.

– Rally the troops; pulling candy calls for teamwork and young strong arms.
– Remove rings—candy can pull the settings out.
– Make sure counter underneath platter or tray of hot candy is heat resistant; if not, it may get scorched.
– While candy is still too hot to handle, begin the pulling with a buttered spatula by lifting and stretching.
– Use buttered bare hands for the pulling (gloves are hopeless) and keep rebuttering them as needed to keep candy from sticking.

¢ VANILLA TAFFY

Makes 1 pound

2 cups sugar
⅔ cup light corn syrup
⅓ cup water
3 tablespoons butter or margarine
½ teaspoon vanilla

Mix sugar, syrup, and water in a heavy saucepan, drop in butter, and insert candy thermometer. Heat, stirring constantly, over moderately high heat until sugar dissolves, then cook, uncovered, *without stirring* to 270° F. or until a drop of candy forms firm, pliable strands in cold water. Pour at once onto a buttered marble slab, large ironstone platter, or heavy metal tray; do not scrape pan. Cool 1–2 minutes, then sprinkle with vanilla and, using a buttered spatula, fold edges in toward center to distribute heat evenly. When candy is cool enough to handle, pull and stretch with buttered hands until light and no longer shiny. When too stiff to pull further, stretch into a rope about ½″ in diameter, and with buttered kitchen shears cut across the grain every 1″. Separate pieces, dry thoroughly, then wrap and store airtight. About 40 calories per piece.

VARIATION:

¢ **Peppermint Taffy:** Prepare as directed but omit vanilla; sprinkle taffy instead with 8 drops oil of peppermint and, if you like, a few drops green coloring. Proceed as above. About 40 calories per piece.

¢ MOLASSES TAFFY

Makes 1¼ pounds

2 cups sugar
1 cup dark molasses
1 cup water
¼ cup butter or margarine

Mix sugar, molasses, and water in a heavy saucepan, drop in butter, and insert candy thermometer. Heat, stirring constantly, over moderately high heat until sugar dissolves, then cook, uncovered, *without stirring* to 270° F. or until a drop of the mixture forms firm, pliable strands in cold water. Pour onto a buttered marble slab at once, or large ironstone platter or heavy metal tray. Cool 1–2 minutes, then fold edges toward center to distribute heat. When cool enough to handle, pull and stretch with buttered hands until light and no longer shiny. When too stiff to pull further, stretch into a rope about ½″ in diameter and with buttered kitchen shears cut across the grain every 1″. Separate pieces as you cut, cool thoroughly, then wrap individually and store airtight. About 40 calories per piece.

MRS. B's PULLED MINTS

A difficult recipe, not for beginners. At first these mints are chewy and taffy-like, but after several days of "ripening," they soften magically and will melt in your mouth.
Makes 1½ pounds

4 cups sugar
2 cups boiling water
½ cup unsalted butter (no substitute)
6–8 drops oil of peppermint
4–5 drops green food coloring (optional)

Mix sugar and water in a heavy saucepan, drop in butter, and insert candy thermometer. Heat, stirring constantly, over moderately high heat until sugar dissolves, then cook, uncovered, *without stirring* to 258° F. or until a drop of mixture forms a hard ball in cold water. Immediately pour onto a buttered marble slab, large ironstone platter, or heavy metal tray; do not scrape out pan. Sprinkle with oil of peppermint and, if you like, coloring. Cool slightly but as soon as possible begin pulling and stretching with buttered hands. When candy pales and begins to lose its gloss, pull and twist into a rope ¾"–1" in diameter and cut across the grain with buttered kitchen shears every ½"–¾". Spread pieces out on wax paper and, when thoroughly cool, store airtight. Let "ripen" 2–3 days—mints will cream up. About 50 calories per piece.

⚖ ¢ FRUIT JELLIES

This mixture froths up, so use an extra-large pan.
Makes about 1 pound

2 envelopes unflavored gelatin
1½ cups sugar
1½ cups cold water
1 cup light corn syrup
½ teaspoon lemon juice
¼ teaspoon lemon, orange, mint, or
*   strawberry flavoring*
Few drops food coloring
Sugar or cornstarch for dredging

Mix gelatin and sugar in a large, heavy saucepan, slowly mix in water, then syrup; insert candy thermometer. Heat over moderate heat, stirring constantly, until sugar dissolves, then cook *without stirring* to 222° F. Gently set pan in a larger pan half full of cold water and cool jelly to 160° F. Mix in lemon juice, flavoring, and appropriate color. Pour into an oiled 9"×9"×2" pan and cool to room temperature. Refrigerate overnight, turn out on wax paper sprinkled with sugar or cornstarch, ease jelly out and sprinkle top with sugar or cornstarch. Cut in 1" squares with a knife dipped in hot water. Let dry 2–3 hours and store airtight. About 35 calories per 1" square if dredged in cornstarch.

APRICOT-ALMOND BALLS

An old-fashioned sweetmeat.
Makes 4 dozen

1 pound dried apricots
1½ cups sugar
¼ cup orange juice
Finely grated rind of 1 orange
1 cup minced, blanched almonds
Sifted confectioners' sugar for dredging

Put apricots through fine blade of meat grinder. Place in the top of a double boiler, set over just boiling water, and mix in sugar, orange juice, and rind. Cook, stirring now and then, ½ hour; mix in nuts and cook 5 minutes longer. Cool in pan until just slightly warm, then drop from a teaspoon into confectioners' sugar and shape into 1" balls. When all balls have been shaped, roll again in confectioners' sugar. Store airtight. About 65 calories per piece.

CANDIED APPLES

Prepare a batch for Halloween.
Makes 6

6 wooden skewers or lollipop sticks
6 medium-size red apples, washed, dried,
*   and stemmed*
2 cups sugar
2 cups light corn syrup
1 cup water
¼ cup red cinnamon candies
½ teaspoon red food coloring

Insert skewers in stem ends of apples. Place all remaining ingredients except food coloring in a heavy saucepan; insert candy thermometer and heat over moderate heat, stirring constantly, until sugar and candies dissolve; do not boil. Mix in coloring, then boil *without stirring* until thermometer reaches 300° F. or a drop of syrup turns brittle in cold water. Remove from heat. Working quickly, dip apples, one at a time, in syrup to coat evenly, twirling so excess drains off. Cool on wax-paper-lined baking sheet. About 360 calories each.

VARIATION:

Caramel Apples: Instead of preparing

syrup above, melt 1½ pounds vanilla caramels with 3 tablespoons water in the top of a double boiler, stirring until smooth. Dip apples as directed, scraping excess caramel off on rim of pan. Cool until caramel hardens. About 500 calories each.

¢ CANDIED CITRUS PEEL

Some grapefruits have excessively bitter peel. To overcome it, soak peel overnight in heavily salted water (weight peel so it stays submerged).
Makes about 1 pound

Peel from 2 grapefruits, 3 large
 thick-skinned oranges (navel are
 good), or 4 large lemons or limes
5 quarts cold water
3 cups sugar
½ cup hot water
1 teaspoon gelatin mixed with 1
 tablespoon cold water

Cover peel with 1 quart cold water, bring to a boil, then drain. Repeat process 4 times until peel is tender. If peel has thick pith, scoop out excess. Cut peel in thin strips or petal shapes. Heat 2 cups sugar and hot water in a heavy saucepan over moderately low heat, stirring constantly until sugar dissolves. Add peel and boil slowly until clear and candy-like, about 25 minutes, moving a wooden spoon occasionally over bottom of pan to keep peel from sticking. Add gelatin, cook and stir 5 minutes longer. Remove from heat and let stand 3–5 minutes; remove peel, a few pieces at a time, allowing excess syrup to drain off, then roll in remaining sugar to coat thickly. (*Note:* Toothpicks are handy for doing this messy job. Dry peel on wire racks and store airtight.) About 70 calories per piece.

For Brightly Colored Peel: Tint syrup color of fruit used or roll candied peel in colored sugar.

¢ LOLLIPOPS

Makes 1½ dozen

2 cups sugar

½ cup light corn syrup
½ cup water
⅛–¼ teaspoon oil of orange, lime,
 peppermint, or spearmint
 (obtainable at drugstores)
Few drops food coloring
1½ dozen lollipop sticks or wooden
 skewers

Mix sugar, corn syrup, and water in a heavy saucepan, insert candy thermometer, and heat, stirring constantly, over moderately high heat until sugar dissolves; cook, uncovered, *without stirring* to 300° F. or until a drop of syrup turns brittle in cold water. Cool 2–3 minutes. Meanwhile, lay lollipop sticks 3″ apart on buttered baking sheets. Add flavoring and coloring to syrup, mix gently, creating as few bubbles as possible, then drop from a teaspoon onto sticks forming lollipops about 2½″ in diameter. Cool, lift off sheets—not by sticks, but by loosening with the point of a knife. About 60 calories each.

VARIATIONS:

Licorice Lollipops: Flavor syrup with ¼ teaspoon oil of anise and color black with 1 teaspoon paste food coloring. About 60 calories each.

Butterscotch Lollipops: Prepare as directed but heat ½ cup firmly packed light brown sugar and 2 tablespoons butter along with other ingredients. Flavor with ¼ teaspoon vanilla or butterscotch extract; do not color. About 90 calories each.

UNCOOKED CANDIES

⊠ UNCOOKED FONDANT

Makes about 1 pound

¼ cup butter (no substitute), softened to
 room temperature
2 tablespoons light corn syrup
3 tablespoons heavy cream
1 (1-pound) box confectioners' sugar,
 sifted
½ teaspoon vanilla

Cream butter with corn syrup and heavy cream until smooth; slowly add sugar, a little at a time, beating well after each addition and kneading in the last bit if necessary. Work in vanilla. Roll into 1″ balls or use to stuff pitted dates, prunes, or dried apricots or to sandwich together large pecan or walnut halves. About 40 calories per piece, 90 if used to sandwich together nut halves.

VARIATION:

Citrus-Rum Fondant: Prepare as directed, substituting 3 tablespoons dark rum for the cream and 1 teaspoon grated fresh orange or tangerine rind and ⅛ teaspoon orange extract for the vanilla. About 40 calories per piece.

▨ QUICK RAISIN-PECAN FONDANT

Makes about 2 pounds

⅔ cup sweetened condensed milk
1 teaspoon vanilla or maple flavoring
4 cups sifted confectioners' sugar
½ cup seedless raisins
1 cup coarsely chopped pecans

Mix milk and vanilla, add confectioners' sugar about ½ cup at a time, stirring constantly; before adding final ½ cup, work in raisins and pecans with your hands. Knead in remaining sugar, press mixture into an ungreased 8″×8″×2″ baking pan, cover loosely with foil, and chill 2–3 hours until firm. Cut in 1″ squares and let ripen 24 hours in an airtight canister before serving. About 60 calories per piece.

VARIATION:

Chocolate-Covered Fondant Squares: Dip* fondant squares in melted semi-sweet chocolate to coat evenly. Arrange on wax paper, decorate tops with pecan halves or candied cherries, and let stand in a cool place until chocolate hardens. Wrap airtight. About 110 calories per piece.

KENTUCKY COLONELS

Bourbon-filled, chocolate-covered, butter-cream balls.
Makes 3½ dozen

½ cup butter (*no substitute*)
1 (*1-pound*) box confectioners' sugar, sifted
1 tablespoon evaporated milk or heavy cream
2 tablespoons bourbon (*about*)
1 (*6-ounce*) package semisweet chocolate bits
¼ cup hot water
42 pecan halves

Cream butter until light and fluffy, slowly blend in sugar and evaporated milk, and beat until smooth. Scoop up by rounded measuring teaspoonfuls, shape into balls and arrange 1½″ apart on ungreased baking sheets. With little finger, make deep dents in tops of balls and, using an eyedropper, add a few drops bourbon; pinch tops to seal. Chill ½ hour. Melt chocolate bits in the top of a double boiler over simmering water, add water a little at a time and beat until smooth. Keeping chocolate warm over hot water so it doesn't harden, spoon over balls, coating evenly. Top each ball with a pecan. Chill 2–3 hours before serving. Store airtight in refrigerator or other cool place. About 115 calories per piece.

▨ UNCOOKED FUDGE

As velvety and chocolaty as old-fashioned cooked fudge.
Makes about 1½ pounds

2 (*3-ounce*) packages cream cheese, softened to room temperature
4 cups sifted confectioners' sugar
2 tablespoons evaporated milk
1 (*6-ounce*) package semisweet chocolate bits
½ teaspoon vanilla
⅛ teaspoon salt
1 cup coarsely chopped pecans

Beat cream cheese until smooth, slowly blend in sugar and evaporated milk, and beat until creamy. Melt chocolate bits in the top of a double boiler over simmering water, add to cheese mixture along with vanilla and salt, and beat until smooth. Stir in pecans, press into a well-buttered 9″×9″×2″ pan, cover, and chill overnight. Cut in 1″

squares and store in refrigerator or other cool place. About 45 calories per piece.

VARIATIONS:

Uncooked Almond Fudge: Prepare as directed but substitute ½ teaspoon almond extract for vanilla and 1 cup coarsely chopped blanched almonds for pecans. About 45 calories per piece.

Uncooked Cocoa Fudge: Prepare as directed but use ½ cup cocoa instead of chocolate bits and add 2 extra teaspoons milk. About 40 calories per piece.

Uncooked Coconut Fudge: Prepare as directed but stir in 1 cup shredded or flaked coconut instead of pecans. About 45 calories per piece.

Uncooked Peanut Butter Fudge: Prepare as directed but omit chocolate; mix in 1 cup creamy peanut butter and 1 cup coarsely chopped unsalted roasted peanuts instead of pecans. About 55 calories per piece.

Uncooked Maple Fudge: Prepare as directed but omit chocolate and use maple flavoring instead of vanilla. After turning candy into pan, sprinkle with 1 cup finely grated maple sugar and press in lightly. About 42 calories per piece.

⊠ MARZIPAN

Delicately shaped and tinted marzipan fruits, flowers, vegetables, and animals are ancient Christmas confections. Special molds, used for the shaping, are sold in housewares departments of many large stores, also by candy supply houses. Pure almond paste can be bought at gourmet shops.
Makes about ½ pound

½ pound pure almond paste
1 egg white, lightly beaten
1½ cups sifted confectioners' sugar

Break up almond paste in a bowl, add egg white and about ½ cup confectioners' sugar, and mix well. Knead in remaining sugar until mixture is smooth and malleable. Marzipan is now ready to color and shape or use in other recipes. About 80 calories per 1″ ball.

To Make Fruits and Vegetables: Knead in appropriate food color, drop by drop, until marzipan is the right color. Pinch off small pieces and shape as desired. To tint or shade, dilute coloring with water and paint on with an artist's brush. Pipe on stems and leaves of green Basic Butter Cream Frosting. To give texture to citrus fruits and strawberries, dust a thimble with confectioners' sugar, then press over surface of candy. (*Note:* Beginners may find it helpful to work from real life fruit.) Stored airtight in refrigerator, candy keeps well several weeks.

VARIATIONS:

Cocoa Marzipan: Prepare marzipan, then knead in 2 tablespoons cocoa. Use to make "mushrooms" or "potatoes" (roll in cocoa after shaping and make "eyes" with a toothpick or skewer). If you prefer, roll into small (about 1″) balls and dip* in melted semisweet chocolate. About 85 calories per piece (undipped).

Chocolate-Dipped Marzipan: Prepare marzipan, then knead in ½ teaspoon vanilla, rum or brandy flavoring, and 1 tablespoon instant coffee powder. Sprinkle hands and board with confectioners' sugar, then roll marzipan, a little at a time, into ropes 1″ in diameter. Cut in ½″ lengths, flatten into ovals, and dip* in melted semisweet chocolate. Before chocolate hardens, top with almond halves. Store airtight. About 125 calories per piece.

SPICY UNCOOKED FRUIT-NUT BARS

Makes about 1½ pounds

1 cup pitted prunes
½ cup dried figs
1 cup seedless raisins
1 cup pitted dates
½ cup coarsely chopped pecans, walnuts, or blanched almonds
¼ teaspoon cloves
¼ teaspoon cinnamon
¼ teaspoon salt
Few drops orange juice (just to moisten)
Sifted confectioners' sugar (for dredging)

Put fruits and nuts through fine blade of meat grinder, mix in seasonings and just enough orange juice to make mixture hold together. Roll or pat out ¼″ thick, cut in squares or small circles, and dredge in confectioners' sugar. If you prefer, roll into small balls and dredge. About 40 calories per piece.

⊠ DOUBLE PEANUT CLUSTERS

Makes about 3½ dozen

½ cup sugar
½ cup light corn syrup
¾ cup creamy peanut butter
1 cup roasted, blanched peanuts
1 cup ready-to-eat, concentrated
  protein cereal

Bring sugar and corn syrup to a boil in a saucepan over moderately low heat, stirring constantly; remove from heat, add peanut butter, and blend until smooth. Quickly mix in remaining ingredients, then drop from a teaspoon onto wax paper, or cool until easy to handle and shape into 1″ balls. Let stand in a cool place (not the refrigerator) until firm. Store airtight. About 80 calories per piece.

NUTS

Any nuts can be used in making candies, most can be toasted and eaten out of hand, but the favorites are almonds, walnuts, pecans, peanuts, and pistachios. For variety, try some of the less familiar: Brazil nuts, cashews, chestnuts, hazelnuts and their European cousin, filberts, macadamias, piñons (pine nuts), or if you're lucky enough to live where you can gather your own, hickory, beech, and butternuts. Nuts *do* run to calories, but fortunately not "empty calories" because they are a high protein food with impressive vitamin and mineral content.

About Buying Nuts

Supermarkets carry all the popular nuts in a variety of forms. Which you buy depends on your budget and time schedule. You'll save money by buying nuts in the shell or unblanched, but you'll spend considerable time preparing them. Obviously, the more nearly ready to use nuts are (toasted, chopped, ground, etc.), the more expensive they will be.

Nuts in the Shell (1 pound unshelled nuts = ½ pound shelled nuts): This is the way to buy nuts if they must be kept some time (some unshelled nuts will keep as long as a year). Choose nuts without splits, scars, holes, or mold. Nuts commonly available in the shell: almonds, Brazil nuts, chestnuts, filberts or hazelnuts, pecans, peanuts, pistachios, and walnuts.

Shelled, Unblanched Nuts: Recipes sometimes call for unblanched nuts (skins add color, flavor, and texture). Those often available this way: almonds, filberts and hazelnuts, peanuts, pistachios. (*Note:* Pecans and walnuts are never blanched.)

Shelled, Blanched Nuts: Almonds, Brazil nuts, filberts, hazelnuts, peanuts, piñons, and pistachio nuts are frequently sold this way.

Shelled, Blanched, Roasted, or Toasted Nuts: Almonds, pecans, peanuts, cashews, hazelnuts, filberts, and macadamias are all available; also mixed roasted nuts. The newest entries are the dry-roasted nuts—lower in calories than the regular roasted nuts. For candies, it's best to use unsalted nuts unless recipes specify to the contrary.

Nut Halves and Meats: A handy form of almonds, pecans, and walnuts. If packaged in plastic bags, sniff for signs of rancidity (these nuts don't stay fresh long). If you are particular about your cooking, you'd do well to prepare your own nuts.

About Preparing Nuts

To Crack:

Thin- or Soft-Shelled Nuts (peanuts and almonds): Crack with your hands and pull out kernels. (*Note:* Chestnuts are soft-shelled but need special techniques —see Vegetables.)

Thick- or Hard-Shelled Nuts: Crack with a nutcracker, pull off shells, and with a nut pick extract kernels. (*Note:* Pecans have a bitter red-brown inner partition that must also be removed.)

To Blanch:

Almonds, Peanuts, Pistachios: Shell, cover with boiling water, and let stand 2 minutes; drain, cool slightly and slip off skins.

Chestnuts: (see vegetable chapter).

Filberts, Hazelnuts: These nuts are so tedious to blanch you'll probably want to pay a little more and buy them already blanched. But if you're counting pennies: Shell nuts, cover with boiling water, and boil 6 minutes; drain and cover with hot tap water. Lift nuts from water, one at a time, and slip and scrape off skins, using a paring knife. The skins are stubborn, will cling to the nuts and your fingers. An easier although not a 100-per-cent-successful method is to drain the blanched nuts, bundle in a turkish towel and rub together briskly.

To Chop Nuts: Do only about ½ cup at a time, using a chopping board and heavy chopping knife. Or, if a quantity must be done, use a chopping bowl and curved chopper.

To Shave Nuts (almonds and Brazil nuts, either blanched or unblanched, are the most suitable): Peel off thin slivers using a vegetable peeler.

To Grate Nuts: The quickest way is to use a rotary grater.

To Grind Nuts: Buzz a few nuts at a time in an electric blender at high speed, stopping and stirring as needed to keep nuts from clumping. Do not use a meat grinder.

To Toast or Roast Nuts: Blanch or not, as you like. Spread out in an ungreased shallow baking pan and roast uncovered, stirring often, ½–1½ hours at 300° F. until lightly browned (size and kind of nut will determine, so watch closely). If you like (and if nuts are blanched), drizzle with melted butter and sprinkle with salt. Toss well to mix and store airtight.

To Deep Fry (best for almonds and peanuts): Blanch nuts. Pour about 2″ corn or peanut oil in a large, heavy skillet and heat to 360° F. Fry nuts, about 1 cup at a time, stirring often, until pale golden. Lift to paper-towel-lined baking sheets with a slotted spoon and cool. (*Note:* Nuts will continue cooking slightly as they cool, so don't fry more than *pale* golden.) Sprinkle with salt and toss to mix. Store airtight.

About Fresh Coconut

Coconuts have double, hard shells, but most sold today wear the inner monkey-faced shell only. Choose those that are heavy for their size and full of liquid (you can tell by shaking them).

To Open: Pierce "eyes" with a screwdriver and drain liquid into a bowl (it can be used in recipes). Break coconut open with a hammer and chisel *or* place coconut on a baking sheet and heat 20 minutes at 400° F. Tap all over to loosen meat, then crack with a hammer or mallet. Pry chunks of white meat from shell and peel off brown skin with a knife or vegetable peeler.

To Grate: Grate coarse or fine with a flat or rotary grater, or cut in small cubes and buzz, a few at a time, in an electric blender at high speed. From 1 medium-size coconut, you'll get 3–4 cups grated coconut and 1 cup liquid. (*Note:* When measuring grated coconut, do not pack the measure.)

How to Color or Toast Coconut: (see Some Special Candy-Making Techniques).

COCONUT MILK OR CREAM

Makes about 1 quart

1 medium-size coconut
Liquid from coconut plus enough water,
*   milk, or light cream to total 1 quart*

Open coconut,* reserving liquid; grate meat moderately fine and place in a large, heavy saucepan with liquid mixture. Heat slowly, stirring constantly, just until mixture boils. Remove from heat, cover, and cool to room temperature. Press through a double thickness of cheesecloth or a fine sieve, forcing out as much liquid as possible. Discard coconut pulp. Use milk in making curries, confections, desserts, and beverages. Store in refrigerator.

To Make with Canned Coconut: Prepare as directed, substituting 3 (4-ounce) cans flaked or shredded coconut for the fresh and using 1 quart milk or light cream. (*Note:* If your Scottish nature rebels at discarding the coconut, spread out in a large, shallow baking pan, drizzle lightly with melted butter, and toast, stirring often, ¾–1 hour until crisp and golden. Flavor will be bland, but coconut can be used to garnish candies and fruit desserts or as a condiment for curry.)

About 10 calories per cup (fresh or canned coconut) if made with water, 110 calories per cup if made with milk, and 315 calories per cup if made with light cream.

CHINESE COCONUT CANDY

Sugared strips of fresh coconut.
Makes about 1 pound

1 medium-size coconut
Coconut liquid plus enough cold water
*   to total 1 cup*
2 cups sugar

Open coconut,* reserving liquid. Remove coconut meat in as large pieces as possible and trim off brown skin with a vegetable peeler. Cut in strips about 2″ long and ⅜″ wide. Mix sugar and coconut liquid in a large, heavy sauce-pan, insert candy thermometer, and

heat, stirring constantly, over moderate heat until sugar dissolves. Add coconut and boil, uncovered, to 240° F. or until a drop of candy forms a soft ball in cold water; stir once or twice just to keep coconut from sticking. Remove from heat and stir gently until mixture sugars and coats coconut. Using 2 forks, lift strips to wax-paper-lined baking sheets, separate into individual pieces, and cool. Store airtight. About 50 calories per piece.

SUGARED NUTS

Such a dainty sweetmeat. Easy to make, too.
Makes about 1 pound

1¼ cups sugar
⅔ cup water
2 tablespoons light corn syrup
Pinch salt
2 cups pecan or walnut halves, whole
*   blanched pistachio nuts, or toasted,*
*   blanched almonds or filberts*

Place sugar, water, syrup, and salt in a heavy saucepan; insert candy thermometer. Heat and stir over moderate heat until sugar dissolves, reduce heat slightly, and cook uncovered *without stirring* to 240° F. Remove from heat, stir in nuts, and pour onto a wax-paper-lined baking sheet. Spread out as thin as possible and let cool until hard. Break apart, separating into individual nuts. About 40 calories per nut.

VARIATIONS:

Sugared and Spiced Nuts: Prepare as directed but mix 1 teaspoon vanilla, ½ teaspoon cinnamon, and a pinch nutmeg into syrup just before adding nuts. Pour out, cool, and separate as directed. About 40 calories per nut.

Orange-Sugared Nuts: Prepare as directed but substitute strained orange juice for the water and add the finely grated rind of 1 orange. Proceed as above. About 40 calories per nut.

GLAZED NUTS

These must be made on a cool, dry day if they're to harden properly.
Makes about 1 pound

2 cups sugar
1 cup hot water
⅛ teaspoon cream of tartar
1 pound whole blanched almonds or filberts, pecan or walnut halves

Mix sugar, water, and cream of tartar in a heavy saucepan; insert candy thermometer. Heat and stir over moderate heat until sugar dissolves, reduce heat slightly, and cook, uncovered, *without stirring* until syrup is 310° F. and the color of straw. Remove from heat and set very gently in a large pan of boiling water (be careful because water will sputter). Using tongs, dip nuts into syrup, one at a time; dry on wax-paper-lined baking sheets. When thoroughly cool, store airtight. (*Note:* These candies quickly pick up moisture from the air and become sticky, so serve as soon after making as possible. If syrup should harden before all nuts are dipped reheat slowly to soften.) About 35 calories per nut.

VARIATION:

⚖ **Glazed Fruits:** Prepare syrup as directed and use for dipping dried apricot halves, pitted dates, firm, fresh, well-dried strawberries or grapes, well-dried orange or tangerine sections, candied cherries. Handle fruit carefully so you don't puncture it. From 20 to 35 calories per fruit, depending upon whether fresh or dried fruits are used. The dried fruits are higher in calories.

GARLICKY COCKTAIL ALMONDS

Makes 1 pound

1 pound whole blanched almonds
2 tablespoons melted butter or margarine
1 clove garlic, peeled and crushed
¾ teaspoon salt

Preheat oven to 275° F. Spread almonds out in a large, shallow roasting pan. Mix butter with garlic and drizzle over nuts; stir well. Roast uncovered, stirring occasionally, about 2 hours until golden brown. Drain on paper toweling. When cool, sprinkle with salt and toss to mix. About 235 calories per ¼ cup.

TOASTED CURRIED ALMONDS

Makes 1 pound

1 pound whole blanched almonds
3 tablespoons melted butter or margarine
1 tablespoon curry powder
½ teaspoon Worcestershire sauce
¼ teaspoon liquid hot red pepper seasoning
1 teaspoon salt mixed with 1 teaspoon curry powder

Preheat oven to 275° F. Spread almonds out in a large, shallow roasting pan. Mix butter with curry powder, Worcestershire sauce, and liquid hot red pepper seasoning, drizzle over nuts and stir well. Roast uncovered, stirring every 20 minutes, about 2 hours until golden brown. Drain on paper toweling. When cool, sprinkle with salt-curry powder mixture and toss well to mix. Drain on fresh paper toweling before serving. About 250 calories per ¼ cup.

HOT BUTTERED POPCORN

Makes about 4 servings

⅓ cup cooking oil
⅔ cup unpopped popcorn
3 tablespoons butter or margarine
½ teaspoon salt

Heat oil in a large, heavy saucepan over high heat about 1 minute until a kernel of corn will sizzle. Add corn, cover saucepan, and once corn begins to pop, shake pan vigorously just above burner until all corn is popped—it will take only 2–3 minutes. Pour corn into a very large bowl. Drop butter into pan and heat until it melts and bubbles up, drizzle over popcorn, and toss lightly to mix. Sprinkle with salt and toss again. About 160 calories per serving.

POPCORN BALLS

Makes 9 3″ balls or 1½ dozen 1½″ balls

1 cup sugar
1 cup light corn syrup
1 teaspoon cider vinegar
3 tablespoons butter or margarine
1 teaspoon vanilla
2 quarts popped, unseasoned popcorn

Place sugar, corn syrup, and vinegar in a heavy saucepan; insert candy thermometer and heat and stir over moderately high heat until sugar dissolves. Cook uncovered *without stirring* to 260° F. or until a drop of syrup forms a hard ball in cold water. Off heat, mix in butter and vanilla. Pour over popcorn in a large bowl and stir quickly so all pieces are coated. With buttered hands, scoop up and shape into large or small balls. Cool on wax paper. Wrap individually in wax paper or plastic food wrap. About 255 calories per large popcorn ball, 130 per small popcorn ball.

VARIATIONS:

Molasses Popcorn Balls: Prepare as directed but substitute 1 cup dark molasses for the sugar. Same calorie counts as for popcorn balls.

Colored Popcorn Balls: Prepare as directed but tint syrup desired color after sugar dissolves. Same calorie counts as for popcorn balls.

Cereal and Popcorn Balls: Prepare as directed but use a ½ and ½ mixture of popcorn and puffed rice or wheat cereal. Same calorie counts as for popcorn balls.

Popcorn and Peanut Balls: Prepare as directed, but substitute ¼ cup creamy peanut butter for the butter and add 1 cup roasted peanuts to the popcorn. About 360 calories per large ball, 180 per small ball.

Caramel Popcorn Balls: Instead of making syrup above, melt ¾ pound vanilla or chocolate caramels with 3 tablespoons water in the top of a double boiler, stirring until smooth. Pour over popcorn and shape into balls. About 200 calories per large ball, 100 calories per small ball.

CHAPTER 25

PICKLES, PRESERVES, JAMS, AND JELLIES

Pickling and preserving are two of the oldest forms of food conservation because man learned early that overly acid, sweet, or salty foods did not spoil readily. Cleopatra adored pickles, gave them credit for her beauty, and Caesar, something of a health faddist, insisted that his legions eat pickles to stave off scurvy. In the more recent past, women pickled and preserved foods so that their families would eat well throughout the winter. Today, with the winter's food supply at the supermarket, pickling and preserving have become labors of love. Odd as it may seem, a number of sophisticated New York City women look forward each summer to the "preserving season." They enjoy the homeliness of putting up a dozen or so jars of pickles and another of fruit preserves. Needless to add, family and friends welcome the fruits of their labor —reason enough for getting down the big kettles and cartons of jars.

Note: Because there is not space here to do more than cover the basics, we recommend the excellent and detailed booklets prepared by the U. S. Department of Agriculture, state agricultural extension services, manufacturers of preserving jars, and processors of liquid and powdered pectins.

The Ways of Pickling and Preserving

Brining: This is the old-fashioned slow cure in which vegetables are submerged for weeks in heavy brine ("heavy enough to float an egg," recipes used to read). Not often used today, except for making Sauerkraut (see recipe), because there are shorter, surer methods.

Fresh-Pack or Quick Process: This is the modern way of pickling—easy, efficient, and reliable. Foods—usually vegetables or fruits—are heated in vinegar, brine, or a mixture of vinegar and salt, often with sugar and spices, then packed hot into hot sterilized jars and sealed; or they may be packed cold into jars, covered with boiling hot pickling liquid and processed in a hot water bath to prevent spoilage. (*Note:* For pickles, the water bath should be hot (180–85° F.), not boiling. Hot pack pickles and relishes, if sufficiently acid or salty, usually need no processing.

Open Kettle Preserving: The method recommended for preserves, jams, jellies, fruit butters, chutneys, ketchups, and conserves, which involves nothing more complicated than cooking all ingredients in a large, open kettle until of desired consistency. Very tart or sweet mixtures, ladled boiling hot into hot sterilized jars, do not need to be processed in a hot water bath; cooler or less concentrated mixtures may (as for pickles, the water bath should be 180–85° F., not boiling).

The Equipment of Pickling and Preserving

All of the paraphernalia of canning (which see) is needed for pickling and preserving. Kettles, however, should be extra large (1½–2 gallons or more), providing plenty of boil-up room. They should be made of enameled metal, stainless steel, or other inert material, never copper, tin, zinc, or galvanized metals that can react with the acid of pickles or preserves to produce poisonous salts. Aluminum kettles are safe but sometimes darken pickles and preserves, giving them a metallic taste. Additional equipment you'll find useful: wide-mouth stone crocks for brining, large sieves, a food mill and meat grinder and for making jellies, cheese-cloth or, better still, a jelly bag (French-seamed flannel bag for straining fruit juices) and a jelmeter (calibrated glass tube used to determine jelling power of fruit juices); both of these items are stocked by good housewares depart-ments or can be ordered by them. A candy thermometer is handy to have, also a potato masher. Jelly glasses, lids, and paraffin are also essential.

PICKLES AND RELISHES

Any food almost can be pickled—pre-served in brine or vinegar. But certain vegetables and fruits pickle better than other foods—cucumbers, sweet peppers, green tomatoes, cauliflower, corn, and green beans, to name a few. The

difference between a pickle and a relish? It's merely a matter of size. When foods are left whole or in large chunks or slices, they are pickles. When minced or chopped, they become relishes. (*Dieters Note:* Most tart pickles and relishes are low-calorie.)

Essential Ingredients of Pickling

Salt: Pickling salt (fine-grained pure salt) is best, dairy or kosher salts (coarse, flaked pure salts) next best; table salt contains adulterants that will cloud the brine. (*Note:* Because of their coarseness, dairy and kosher salts, measure for measure, are not equal to pickling salt. When substituting either one for pickling salt, use 1½ times the amount of pickling salt called for.) The recipes that follow specify which salt to use.

Vinegar: Vinegars should be plain, unflavored, of top grade and 4–6 per cent acid strength (this information is included on the label). They may be cider (brown) or distilled (white) but must be clear and free of sediment. White vinegars are best for white or delicately colored vegetables; brown vinegars will darken them. Never use a vinegar of unknown acid strength; a too weak vinegar can cause pickles to soften and spoil.

Sugar: Granulated sugar is the standard, though occasionally, when a mellower, darker product is wanted, light or dark brown sugar will be called for.

Spices: Whole dried spices, freshly bought, are preferable because they can be neatly tied in cheesecloth, simmered along with the pickles, then quickly fished out of the kettle. Powdered spices darken pickles and so will whole spices if left in too long.

Water: It should be soft—either naturally or artificially so. Hard water can produce ugly white scum on pickles or, if high in iron, turn them black. To soften water: Boil hard 15 minutes, let stand 24 hours, then skim scum from top.

Carefully ladle water into a clean container, leaving any sediment behind.

Fruit and Vegetables: These should be garden fresh (never picked more than a day ahead of time), a shade underripe, free of blemishes, soft or decayed spots, and for especially pretty pickles, of small-to-medium, uniform size.

Slaked Lime (Calcium Hydroxide) and Alum: These aren't essential to pickling except when supercrisp pickles are wanted. They're used with unfermented pickles only, most often watermelon rind or green tomato. Both can be bought in drugstores and hardwares specializing in canning equipment.

Tips for Making Better Pickles and Relishes

– Read recipe through carefully before beginning and follow directions to the letter.
– Have all ingredients and equipment assembled before beginning. Make sure preserving jars are the proper type (those made specifically for preserving) and in perfect condition (no cracks or chips), spotless and sterilized (directions for sterilizing jars and closures are included in the chapter on canning). Lids should be perfect too—not warped, dented, or bent. If using closures requiring rubber rings, buy new ones of the proper size.
– Do not attempt to pickle vast quantities at a time; work instead with amounts you can handle comfortably in your kitchen.
– Use highest quality fruits and vegetables, picked, if possible, just before pickling.
– Use freshly bought vinegars, spices, salts, and sugars, never those that have been sitting around on the shelf.
– Never add chemicals to pickles or relishes to heighten their color—copper sulfate, for example, or vitriol. And do not, as Grandmother did, pickle green vegetables in copper kettles to brighten the green—vinegar, coming in contact with copper, produces a poison.
– Measure or weigh ingredients carefully.

– Pack jars, one at a time, as recipes direct, allowing amount of head space (room at the top of the jar) recommended. Jars to be processed in a hot water bath should have about ¼" of head space so that there is room for expansion of food as it sterilizes; jars requiring no processing should be filled to within ⅛" of tops. Jars processed in a pressure cooker need the most head space of all—usually 1", but follow recipe and manufacturer's directions.
– As you pack jars, run a small spatula around inside of jar to remove air bubbles.
– Make sure pickling liquid covers solids; if there is not enough, pour in a little additional vinegar or brine (same strength as that in the recipe).
– Before sealing jars, wipe tops and threading with a clean, damp cloth.
– When packing hot pickles, make sure that they *and* the pickling liquid are *boiling hot.*
– If pickles have been packed cold, do not remove metal screw bands after sealing and processing. Leave intact until jars are opened.
– When cooling sealed jars, stand several inches apart and away from drafts so that air will circulate evenly.
– Test seals after jars have cooled 12 hours. If a jar has not sealed, refrigerate and serve within the week. *Or* empty contents into a saucepan, bring slowly to a boil, and pack into a hot sterilized jar. Reseal and cool.
– Store pickles and relishes in a dark, cool, dry place and let stand some weeks before serving so that flavors will mellow and mingle.
– To keep pickles from fading, wrap jars in newspaper before storing.

Why Things Sometimes Go Wrong with Pickles

Soft or Slippery Pickles: Vinegar too weak or pickles not kept submerged in brine or pickling liquid.

Hollow Pickles ("Floaters"): Cucumbers picked too long before pickling.

Dark Pickles: Iron in the water used.

Shriveled Pickles: Pickling solution too acid, too salty, or too sweet.

Faded Pickles: Pickles kept too long on the shelf or stored in too bright a spot.

¢ ⚖ **DILL PICKLES**

Because cucumbers brined in barrels need controlled conditions not always attainable at home, these recipes use the newer, easier fresh-pack method.
Makes about 8 pints

3–3½ dozen small- to medium-size cucumbers (about 4″ long), washed and left whole or halved lengthwise (do not peel)
1 gallon cold water mixed with ¾ cup pickling salt (brine)
16 sprigs fresh dill or pickling dill or 8 tablespoons dill seeds
8 teaspoons mustard seeds
1 quart white vinegar
1 quart water
½ cup pickling salt
½ cup sugar
3 tablespoons mixed pickling spices, tied in cheesecloth

Let cucumbers stand in brine overnight. Wash and sterilize 8 (1-pint) jars and closures. Drain cucumbers and pack into hot jars, leaving ¼″ head space. To each jar add 2 sprigs dill (or 1 tablespoon dill seeds) and 1 teaspoon mustard seeds, poking halfway down in jar. Set uncovered jars on a baking sheet and keep hot in a 250° F. oven. Simmer vinegar, water, salt, sugar, and pickling spices, uncovered, 15 minutes in an enamel or stainless-steel saucepan, stirring now and then. Pour boiling hot into jars, filling to within ⅛″ of tops. Wipe rims and seal. *Or,* if you prefer, fill jars to within ¼″ of top, seal, and process in a hot water bath* 10 minutes. Take from water bath and secure seals if necessary. Cool, check seals, label, and store in a cool, dark, dry place. Let unprocessed pickles stand 4–6 weeks before using, processed ones 3 weeks. About 20–30 calories per pickle, depending on size.

VARIATIONS:

⚖ **"Kosher" Dill Pickles:** When packing cucumbers, add to each jar 1 peeled and bruised clove garlic, 1 bay leaf, and 1 (3″ × ½″) strip hot red chili pepper in addition to seasonings above. Proceed as directed. Same calorie counts as for dill pickles.

¢ **Sweet Dill Pickles:** Prepare as directed but, instead of vinegar mixture called for, simmer 5 cups vinegar and 5 cups sugar with the 3 tablespoons spices. Pour into jars as directed, leaving ¼″ head space at the top, and process in a hot water bath* 10 minutes. About 50–60 calories per pickle, depending on size.

AUNT FLORRIE'S BREAD AND BUTTER PICKLES

Makes about 6 quarts

4 quarts paper-thin unpeeled cucumber slices
8 medium-size white onions, peeled and sliced paper thin
2 medium-size sweet green peppers (or 1 green and 1 red), washed, cored, seeded, and coarsely chopped
½ cup pickling salt
1 quart cracked ice
5 cups sugar
1½ teaspoons turmeric
½ teaspoon cloves
2 tablespoons mustard seeds
1 teaspoon celery seeds
5 cups cider or white vinegar

Mix all vegetables, salt, and ice in a very large colander, weight down, pressing out liquid, set over a large kettle, and let stand 3 hours (in refrigerator if possible). (*Note:* If kitchen is warm and you haven't refrigerator space, add more cracked ice after 1½ hours.) Meanwhile, wash and sterilize 6 (1-quart) jars and closures, stand on a baking sheet, and keep hot in a 250° F. oven until needed. Mix sugar, spices, and vinegar in a very large enamel or stainless-steel kettle. Drain vegetables well and add to kettle. Heat, uncovered, over moderate heat *just* to the boiling point, moving a wooden spoon through mixture occasionally but not actually stirring. Ladle boiling hot into jars, filling to within ⅛″ of tops, wipe rims, and seal. Cool, check seals, label, and store in a cool, dark, dry place. Let stand 4–6 weeks before serving. About 100 calories per ¼ cup.

MUSTARD PICKLES

Makes 4 pints

1 medium-size cauliflower, washed, trimmed, and divided into small flowerets
2 medium-size cucumbers, peeled, seeded, and cut in ¼″ cubes
3 medium-size sweet green peppers, washed, cored, seeded, and coarsely chopped
1 medium-size sweet red pepper, washed, cored, seeded, and coarsely chopped
1 pint tiny white onions or shallots, peeled
1 quart cold water mixed with ⅓ cup pickling salt
½ cup sifted flour
1 cup sugar
3 tablespoons powdered mustard
1½ teaspoons turmeric
1 quart white vinegar

Place all vegetables and salt water in a large bowl, cover, and refrigerate overnight. Wash and sterilize 4 (1-pint) jars and their closures; stand on a baking sheet and keep hot in a 250° F. oven until needed. Transfer vegetables and brine to a large enamel or stainless-steel kettle, cover, bring to a boil over high heat, then boil 1 minute; drain in a colander and set aside. In the same kettle, mix flour, sugar, and spices; slowly blend in vinegar and heat, stirring constantly, over moderate heat until thickened. Add vegetables, cover, and heat, stirring occasionally, 8–10 minutes, just until boiling. Ladle into jars, filling to within ¼″ of tops, wipe rims, and seal. Process 10 minutes in a hot water bath.* Cool, check seals, label, and store in a cool, dark, dry place. Let stand 4–6 weeks before serving. About 45 calories per ¼ cup.

¢ ⚖ **EASY ICE WATER CUCUMBER PICKLES**

Gherkins may be substituted for cucumbers in this next recipe.
Makes 6 quarts

6–6½ dozen small cucumbers (do not peel)
Ice water
6 tablespoons pickling salt
6 tablespoons mixed pickling spices
12 tablespoons sugar
2–3 white onions, peeled and sliced thin
3 quarts boiling white vinegar

Cover cucumbers with ice water and let stand 3–4 hours, replenishing ice as needed. Wash and sterilize 6 (1-quart) jars and closures, stand on a baking sheet, and keep warm in a 250° F. oven until needed. Drain cucumbers and pack into hot jars, filling to within ¼″ of the top. Add 1 tablespoon salt, 1 tablespoon pickling spice, and 2 tablespoons sugar to each jar, top with 1–2 slices onion, and fill to within ¼″ of the top with vinegar. Wipe rims and seal. Process in a hot water bath* 10 minutes. Remove jars and secure seals if needed. Cool, check seals, label, and store in a cool, dark, dry place 4–6 weeks before serving. About 2 calories per pickle.

⚖ **GREEN TOMATO PICKLES**

Makes about 5 pints

2 quarts sliced, unpeeled green tomatoes (slices should be about ½″ thick)
2 tablespoons pickling salt
1 cup granulated sugar
1 cup dark brown sugar
1 pint cider vinegar
2 tablespoons mustard seeds
1 teaspoon celery seeds
2 bay leaves, crumbled
2 large yellow onions, peeled and sliced thin
2 large sweet green peppers, cored, seeded, and minced
1 large sweet red pepper or 1 small hot chili pepper, cored, seeded, and minced

Mix tomatoes and salt, cover, and

refrigerate overnight; drain well. Wash and sterilize 5 (1-pint) jars and closures, stand on a baking sheet, and keep hot in a 250° F. oven until needed. Mix sugars, vinegar, spices, and onions in a very large enamel or stainless-steel kettle, cover, and boil slowly 10 minutes. Add tomatoes and peppers and simmer, uncovered, stirring now and then, 5 minutes. Ladle boiling hot into jars filling to within ⅛″ of tops and making sure liquid covers vegetables. Wipe rims and seal; cool, check seals, label, and store in a cool, dark, dry place 4–6 weeks before using. About 25 calories per pickle.

⊲⊳ **DILLED GREEN TOMATOES**

Makes 4 pints

3 pounds small, firm green tomatoes, washed and stemmed
4 sweet green peppers, washed, cored, and seeded
8 cloves garlic, peeled
1 teaspoon celery seeds
1 quart water
1 pint cider or white vinegar
½ cup pickling or kosher salt
2 tablespoons pickling dill

Wash and sterilize 4 wide-mouth (1-pint) preserving jars and closures. Blanch tomatoes and peppers but do not skin; cut peppers in strips ½″ wide. Place 2 garlic cloves and ¼ teaspoon celery seeds in each jar, then fill to within ½″ of top with tomatoes and pepper strips, distributing as evenly as possible. Boil water, vinegar, salt, and dill, uncovered, 5 minutes and pour over tomatoes, filling jars to within ⅛″ of tops. Seal jars, cool, label, and store in a cool, dark, dry place. Let stand 4–6 weeks before serving. About 25 calories per ¼ cup.

⊲⊳ **DILLED GREEN BEANS**

Choose the straightest beans for this recipe—makes packing jars easier.
Makes 6 pints

3 pounds green beans
6 cloves garlic, peeled and halved
3 teaspoons mustard seeds
1½ teaspoons peppercorns

12 large sprigs fresh dill or 3 teaspoons dill seeds
3 cups cider vinegar
3 cups water
¼ cup pickling salt

Wash and sterilize 6 (1-pint) jars and closures. Snap ends off beans, cut in 4½″ lengths, and pack vertically in jars, filling centers with odd lengths. Add 2 halves garlic, ½ teaspoon mustard seeds, ¼ teaspoon peppercorns, and 2 sprigs fresh dill (or ½ teaspoon dill seeds) to each jar. Heat vinegar, water, and salt to boiling, then pour in jars, filling to within ¼″ of the top. Wipe rims and seal. Process in a hot water bath* 5 minutes. Tighten seals if necessary, cool, check seals, label, and store in a cool, dark, dry place 4–6 weeks before serving. About 10 calories per ¼ cup.

VARIATIONS:

⊲⊳ **Dilled Carrots:** Prepare as directed but substitute 3 quarts parboiled (4″) carrot sticks for beans. About 15 calories per ¼ cup.

⊲⊳ **Dilled Zucchini:** Prepare as directed but substitute 3 quarts unpeeled (4″) zucchini strips for beans. (*Note:* Baby zucchini are best.) About 10 calories per ¼ cup.

⊲⊳ ¢ **SAUERKRAUT**

Makes about 7 quarts

7–8 medium-size firm green cabbages, quartered, cored, and shredded fine
1 cup pickling salt

Wash and scald a 4-gallon crock. Mix 5 pounds of the shredded cabbage thoroughly with ¼ cup salt and pack firmly into crock, pressing down with a potato masher. Continue filling crock, adding 5 pounds shredded cabbage mixed with ¼ cup salt each time and pressing down well to extract enough liquid to cover cabbage. Cover with 4 thicknesses of cheesecloth, tucking ends down in jar. Weight down with a sterilized heavy plate topped with a sterilized large jar full of water (plate should be submerged in cabbage liquid). Set crock on a tray (it may bubble over during fermentation), drape more cheesecloth on top, and let stand at room temperature (70° F.) until fermentation stops, 2–3 weeks in warm weather, 4 weeks in cool. Fermentation will begin the day after packing; for best results, keep temperature as near 70° F. as possible. Skim scum from crock each day, covering with fresh cheesecloth if necessary. When bubbling stops, tap jar gently; if no bubbles rise, fermentation is completed (sauerkraut should be cream colored with no white spots). Wash and sterilize 7 (1-quart) jars and closures and keep hot in a 250° F. oven. Pack, one at a time, with sauerkraut, filling to within ½″ of tops and making sure kraut is covered with liquid. (*Note:* If there is insufficient liquid, fill with brine made by dissolving 2 tablespoons pickling salt in 1 quart boiling water.) Wipe rims and seal. Process in a boiling water bath* ½ hour. Tighten lids if needed, cool, check seals, label, and store in a cool, dark, dry place. (*Note:* If you have a cool cellar—55° F. or less—kraut can be stored there in the crock through the winter. Just be sure kraut is weighted down in its juices and crock loosely covered.) About 15 calories per ½ cup.

¢ PICKLED RED CABBAGE

Because this cabbage is packed cold, store with screw bands tightly screwed down.
Makes about 3 pints

2 *quarts moderately finely shredded red cabbage* (*about 1 large head*)
1 *quart cold water mixed with ¼ cup pickling salt* (*brine*)
1 *quart cider vinegar*
1 *cup sugar*
2 *tablespoons mixed pickling spices, tied in cheesecloth*

Mix cabbage and brine, cover, and let stand overnight; drain well. Wash and sterilize 3 (1-pint) jars and closures. Pack cabbage into jars, filling to within ½″ of tops. Boil vinegar, sugar and spices in an enamel or stainless-steel saucepan 10 minutes, then fill jars to within ⅛″ of tops. Wipe rims and seal.

Cool, label, and store in a cool, dark, dry place 4–6 weeks before serving. About 45 calories per ¼ cup.

⚖ PICKLED WHOLE BEETS

Makes 4 pints

4 *pounds small beets, boiled and peeled* (*they should be hot*)
2 *teaspoons pickling salt*
1 *pint white vinegar*
2 *cups sugar*
1 *tablespoon mixed pickling spices* (*optional*)

Wash and sterilize 4 (1-pint) jars and closures. Pack beets in hot jars, filling to within ½″ of the top, halving some to fill gaps; add ½ teaspoon salt to each jar. Meanwhile, bring remaining ingredients to a boil, pour over beets, filling jars to within ¼″ of the top. Wipe rims and seal. Process in a hot water bath* ½ hour. Remove jars from bath and secure seals if necessary. Cool, check seals, label, and store in a cool, dark place. Let stand 2–3 weeks before serving. About 20 calories per beet.

VARIATION:

⚖ **Pickled Sliced Beets** (Makes 3 pints): Prepare as directed but slice cooked beets ¼″ thick. (*Note:* You can use larger beets for this recipe.) About 35 calories per ¼ cup.

⚖ PICKLED ONIONS

Makes 8 pints

7 *pounds small white onions, peeled and parboiled 2 minutes*
1 *cup pickling salt*
2 *quarts cider or white vinegar*
½ *cup sugar*
4 *teaspoons mustard seeds, lightly crushed*
8 *bay leaves*

Place onions in a large bowl, cover with cold water, add salt and stir to dissolve; cover and let stand at room temperature 24 hours. Next day, wash and sterilize 8 (1-pint) jars and closures; stand on a baking sheet and keep hot in a 250° F.

oven until needed. Rinse onions under cold running water and drain well. Bring vinegar, sugar, and spices to a boil in an enamel or stainless-steel saucepan, stirring occasionally. Meanwhile, pack onions into jars; pour in boiling vinegar, filling jars to within ⅛" of tops and distributing mustard seeds and bay leaves evenly. Wipe rims and seal. Cool, check seals, label jars, and store in a cool, dark, dry place. Let stand 1 week before using. About 15 calories per onion.

⚖ PICKLED MUSHROOMS

Makes 4 pints

3 pounds mushrooms (button to medium size), wiped clean
1 quart water mixed with 3 tablespoons pickling salt (brine)
4 cloves garlic, peeled and bruised
4 bay leaves
1 teaspoon whole cloves
1 teaspoon peppercorns
4 chili pequins (tiny hot dried red peppers)
1 quart white vinegar
¼ cup olive oil

Wash and sterilize 4 (1-pint) jars and closures, stand on a baking sheet, and keep hot in a 250° F. oven until needed. Simmer mushrooms in brine, covered, 5 minutes, then drain. Into each hot jar place 1 clove garlic, 1 bay leaf, ¼ teaspoon each cloves and peppercorns, and 1 chili pequin. Heat vinegar and oil to boiling in an enamel or stainless-steel saucepan, add mushrooms and simmer, uncovered, 5 minutes. Remove mushrooms with a slotted spoon and pack into jars, then pour in boiling vinegar mixture, filling to within ⅛" of tops. Wipe rims and seal. Cool, check seals, label, and store in a cool, dark, dry place 2–3 weeks before serving. About 30 calories per ¼ cup.

¢ WATERMELON RIND PICKLES

Makes 4 pints

1 (15–16-pound) slightly underripe watermelon with thick, firm rind
2 quarts cold water mixed with ½ cup pickling salt (brine)

Syrup:

4 pounds sugar
1 quart cider vinegar
1 quart water
2 lemons, sliced thin
2 teaspoons whole cloves
2 teaspoons whole allspice
4 cinnamon sticks, broken up

Quarter melon, remove green skin and pink flesh, and cut rind in 1" cubes; measure 4 quarts cubed rind, cover with brine, and soak overnight. Drain rind, rinse with cold water, place in a very large kettle, cover with water, and simmer covered about ½ hour until barely tender and translucent. Meanwhile, prepare syrup: Mix sugar, vinegar, and water in a very large enamel or stainless-steel kettle, add lemon and spices, tied in cheesecloth, and slowly boil uncovered 20 minutes. Also wash and sterilize 4 (1-pint) jars and closures, stand on a baking sheet in a 250° F. oven until needed. Drain rind, add to syrup, and simmer uncovered until rind is clear, about ½ hour. Remove spice bag. Using a slotted spoon, pack rind into jars, then pour in boiling syrup, filling to within ⅛" of tops. Wipe rims and seal. Cool, check seals, label, and store in a cool, dark, dry place several weeks before serving. About 40 calories per ¼ cup.

SPICED CANTALOUPE

Makes 3 pints

1 (3½–4-pound) underripe cantaloupe
2 quarts cold water mixed with ½ cup pickling salt (brine)

Syrup:

6 cups sugar
2 quarts water
2 cinnamon sticks, broken up
1 tablespoon whole cloves
1 tablespoon whole allspice
1 (2") piece gingerroot, peeled and bruised
1 pint cider vinegar

Quarter melon, remove seeds, peeling, and rind, then cut flesh in ½" cubes; measure out 3 quarts, cover with brine, and soak 3 hours. Meanwhile, prepare syrup: Slowly boil 4 cups sugar and the water, uncovered, in a very large enamel or stainless-steel kettle 5 minutes. Drain and rinse cantaloupe, add to syrup, and boil, uncovered, ½ hour. Remove from heat, set lid on kettle askew, and let stand overnight. Next day, tie spices in cheesecloth and add to kettle along with vinegar and remaining sugar. Slowly boil, uncovered, until cantaloupe is clear, about ½ hour. Meanwhile, wash and sterilize 3 (1-pint) jars and closures and keep hot on a baking sheet in a 250° F. oven until needed. Using a slotted spoon, pack cantaloupe into jars, then pour in boiling syrup, filling to within ⅛" of tops; wipe rims and seal. Cool, check seals, label, and store in a cool, dark, dry place several weeks before serving. About 40 calories per ¼ cup.

PICKLED PEACHES

Dipping peaches and apricots in boiling water makes skins slip right off. Try not only the peaches but some of the other fruits included among the variations.
Makes about 10 pints

8 pounds small, firm-ripe peaches
   (clingstone varieties are best)
1 gallon cold water mixed with 2
   tablespoons each pickling salt and
   white vinegar
2 tablespoons whole cloves (about)

Basic Pickling Syrup:

1 quart white vinegar
1 quart water
3 pounds sugar
4 cinnamon sticks, broken and tied in
   cheesecloth

Peel peaches, then drop in water-salt-vinegar mixture to prevent discoloration; leave whole or halve but do not remove pits. Stud each peach with 2 cloves. Place syrup ingredients in a large enamel or stainless-steel kettle and bring to a boil. Add peaches, a few at a time, and simmer uncovered 5–7 minutes until barely tender. Remove peaches with a slotted spoon and set aside while cooking the rest. When all are cooked, bring

syrup to a boil and pour over peaches; cover and let stand overnight (this plumps peaches and gives them better flavor). Next day, wash and sterilize 10 (1-pint) jars and their closures. At the same time, drain syrup from peaches and bring to a boil; discard spice bag. Pack peaches into hot jars, then pour in boiling syrup, filling to within ¼" of the top. Wipe rims and seal. Process in a hot water bath* 10 minutes. Remove jars from bath and secure seals if necessary. Cool, check seals, label, and store in a cool, dark, dry place 4–6 weeks before serving. About 50 calories per peach.

VARIATIONS:

Pickled Apricots: Substitute 8 pounds apricots for peaches; peel, leave whole, or halve and pit. Proceed as directed. About 50 calories per apricot.

Pickled Pears: Substitute 8 pounds small, firm-ripe pears for peaches. Leave stems on but remove blossom ends. Proceed as directed. About 80 calories per pear.

Pickled Apples: Substitute 10 pounds peeled, quartered, and cored small tart apples for peaches. Add cloves to pickling syrup instead of studding fruit, then proceed as directed. About 65 calories per apple.

Pickled Crab Apples: Substitute 8 pounds unpeeled crab apples for peaches. Remove blossom ends but not stems, then prick in several places to prevent bursting. Add cloves to pickling syrup and simmer crab apples 7–10 minutes, depending on size. Proceed as recipe directs. About 45 calories per crab apple.

Pickled Quinces: Substitute 8 pounds firm-ripe quinces for peaches. Peel, quarter, core, and slice thin. For pickling syrup use 1 pint each vinegar and water and 4 pounds sugar; add cloves and cinnamon. Simmer quinces 30–40 minutes in syrup until translucent. Proceed as directed. About 45 calories per ¼ cup.

Spiced Fruits: Prepare any of the

preceding pickled fruits as directed, but tie cinnamon and cloves in cheesecloth along with 2 tablespoons whole allspice and 2 (2″) pieces bruised, peeled ginger-root. If you like, add 1 or 2 slices lemon to each jar. Same calorie counts as the individual pickled fruits.

California Fruit Pickles: Prepare any of the preceding pickled fruits as directed but use a ½ and ½ mixture of granulated and light or dark brown sugar in the pickling syrup. Same calorie counts as the individual pickled fruits.

BRANDIED PEACHES

Makes 4 pints

4 pounds small firm-ripe peaches
(clingstone varieties are best)
2 quarts cold water mixed with 1
tablespoon each pickling salt and
lemon juice
1 quart water
4 cups sugar
1 pint brandy (about)

Wash and sterilize 4 (1-pint) jars and closures, stand them on a baking sheet, and keep hot in a 250° F. oven until needed. Peel peaches, then drop in water-salt-lemon juice mixture to prevent darkening. Bring water and sugar to a boil in an enamel or stainless-steel saucepan; reduce heat, add peaches, a few at a time, and simmer 5–7 minutes until barely tender. Remove peaches with a slotted spoon and pack in hot jars, filling to within ½″ of tops. When all peaches are cooked, return filled but uncovered jars to 250° F. oven. Insert candy thermometer in syrup and boil, uncovered, until thermometer registers 222° F. Cool syrup 5 minutes, measure out 1 pint, and stir in 1 pint brandy; pour into jars, filling to within ¼″ of the top. (*Note:* If you need more liquid, mix equal quantities of syrup and brandy.) Wipe jar rims and seal. Process in a hot water bath* 10 minutes. Remove jars and secure seals, if necessary. Cool, check seals, label, and store in a cool, dark, dry place. Let stand 4–6 weeks before serving. About 55 calories per peach.

VARIATION:

Brandied Pears: Substitute 4 pounds small firm-ripe pears for peaches. Peel and remove blossom ends but leave stems on if you wish. Proceed as recipe directs. About 120 calories per pear.

◁▷ PRESERVED CINNAMON APPLE RINGS

Delicious with ham or roast pork.
Makes 2 pints

1 pint boiling water
1 cup red cinnamon candies
8 medium-size tart apples, peeled, cored,
and sliced ½″ thick
4 cups sugar

Wash and sterilize 2 (1-pint) jars and their closures, set on a baking sheet in a 250° F. oven, and keep hot until needed. Mix water and candies in a large, heavy saucepan, stirring until candies dissolve; add apples, cover, and simmer 10 minutes until transparent. Pack apples into jars and set, uncovered, in oven. Add sugar to saucepan and boil, uncovered, 3 minutes. Pour syrup over apples, filling jars to within ¼″ of tops. Wipe rims, seal, and process in a hot water bath* 20 minutes. Remove jars and secure seals if necessary. Cool, check seals, label, and store in a cool, dark, dry place. About 20 calories per apple ring.

GINGERED PEARS

Serve with any meat.
Makes 4 pints

5 pounds firm-ripe pears, peeled,
quartered, and cored
½ cup lemon juice
5 cups sugar
1 tablespoon finely grated lemon rind
⅓ cup minced gingerroot or ½ cup
minced preserved ginger

Wash and sterilize 4 (1-pint) jars and closures, stand them on baking sheet, and keep warm in a 250° F. oven until needed. Simmer all ingredients, uncovered, in a heavy enamel or stainless-steel kettle until pears are tender and translucent, about 30–40 minutes. Ladle into hot jars, filling to within ⅛" of tops. Wipe rims and seal. Cool, check seals, label, and store in a cool, dark, dry place 2–3 weeks before using. About 50 calories per pear quarter.

TOMATO KETCHUP

Ketchup can be made from mushrooms, grapes, cranberries, green tomatoes, in fact from many fruits and vegetables. But the favorite is bright red tomato ketchup.
Makes 2 pints

8 pounds unpeeled ripe tomatoes,
* coarsely chopped*
1 cup minced yellow onions
1 teaspoon celery seeds
1 teaspoon mustard seeds
1 teaspoon whole allspice
1 cinnamon stick
½ teaspoon peppercorns
2 bay leaves
1 tablespoon salt
1 cup white vinegar
1 cup sugar

Mix tomatoes and onions in a large (at least 1 gallon) enamel or stainless-steel kettle, cover, and simmer 20–30 minutes, stirring now and then, until mushy. Purée, a little at a time, at low speed in an electric blender or put through a food mill, then press through a fine sieve. Place in a clean large kettle and cook, uncovered, at a slow boil until volume reduces by half. (*Note:* It's important that kettle be large to keep ketchup from spattering kitchen.) Meanwhile, wash and sterilize 2 (1-pint) jars and their closures, stand them on a baking sheet, and keep warm in a 250° F. oven until needed. Tie all spices and bay leaves in cheesecloth and add to kettle along with salt, set lid on askew, and simmer ½ hour. Remove spice bag, add vinegar and sugar, and cook, un-covered, at a slow boil, stirring frequently, until very thick. (*Note:* Toward the end, you will have to stir constantly to prevent scorching.) Ladle ketchup into jars, filling to within ⅛" of tops, wipe rims, and seal. Cool, check seals, and store in a cool, dark, dry place. Let stand 2 weeks before using. (*Note:* To keep ketchup bright red over a long period of time, wrap jars in foil.) About 25 calories per tablespoon.

VARIATIONS:

Easy Ketchup: Substitute 2 (1-pound 12-ounce) cans tomato purée for fresh tomatoes, omit onion, and cook down as recipe directs to about ⅓ of original volume. Add spices called for but only 1½ teaspoons salt; proceed as directed. About 25 calories per tablespoon.

Cranberry Ketchup: Substitute 2 pounds cranberries for tomatoes and simmer with 1 cup water until mushy. Proceed as recipe directs but increase sugar to 2 cups. About 50 calories per tablespoon.

Hot Chili Sauce: Peel and core tomatoes before chopping; simmer as directed with 2 cups each minced onions and minced, cored, and seeded sweet red peppers and 1–2 minced, cored, and seeded hot red peppers (or ¼–½ teaspoon crushed dried hot red chili peppers). Purée mixture but do not strain. Proceed as for Tomato Ketchup (above), adding 1 tablespoon mixed pickling spices to the spices called for and increasing vinegar to 1½ cups. About 30 calories per tablespoon.

GREEN TOMATO CHUTNEY

Makes 6–7 pints

10 pounds green tomatoes, washed,
* stemmed, and coarsely chopped*
3 tart apples, peeled, cored, and minced
1 pint cider vinegar
3 cups sugar
2 cups firmly packed dark brown sugar
2 teaspoons salt
1½ teaspoons curry powder
1 teaspoon powdered mustard
½ teaspoon cayenne pepper
½ teaspoon turmeric
½ teaspoon ginger
½ pound sultana raisins

Wash and sterilize 7 (1-pint) preserving jars and closures. Mix all ingredients in a very large enamel or stainless-steel kettle, cover, and bring slowly to a boil. Uncover and *simmer*, stirring occasionally, 1½–2 hours until thick. Ladle into jars, filling to within ⅛″ of tops. Wipe rims and seal. When cool, check seal and label. Store in a cool, dark, dry place. Let stand at least 2 weeks before serving. About 25 calories per tablespoon.

APPLE CHUTNEY

When doubling this recipe, speed up the preparation by putting fruit and vegetables through the coarse blade of a meat grinder.
Makes about 4 pints

2 quarts coarsely chopped, peeled tart apples
1 cup minced, seeded sweet red peppers
1 cup minced yellow onions
1 clove garlic, peeled and minced
1 pound seedless raisins
1 (1-pound) box dark brown sugar
1 pint cider vinegar
1 tablespoon ginger
1 tablespoon cinnamon
2 teaspoons powdered mustard
2 teaspoons salt
¼ teaspoon crushed dried hot red chili peppers

Wash and sterilize 4 (1-pint) jars and their closures and stand them on a baking sheet in a 250° F. oven until needed. Mix all ingredients in a very large enamel or stainless-steel kettle, cover, and bring slowly to a boil. Uncover and simmer, stirring occasionally, 1–1½ hours until thick. (*Note:* Stir more frequently toward the end to prevent scorching.) Ladle boiling hot into jars, filling to within ⅛″ of tops. Wipe rims and seal. When cool, check seals and label. Store in a cool, dark, dry place. Let stand 1 month before serving. About 35 calories per tablespoon.

VARIATIONS:

Pear or Peach Chutney: Prepare as directed but substitute 2 quarts coarsely chopped, peeled firm-ripe pears or peaches for apples and omit red peppers. About 35 calories per tablespoon.

Mango Chutney: Substitute 4 pounds peeled, pitted, and thinly sliced green mangoes for apples, increase sugar to 2 pounds and vinegar to 1 quart. Add 1 pound dried currants and 3 tablespoons minced fresh gingerroot. Mix all ingredients in kettle, cover, and let stand overnight. Next day, proceed as directed. About 65 calories per tablespoon.

MINCEMEAT

True mincemeat should contain ground beef; if you include it, the mincemeat must be pressure processed to prevent spoilage. Mincemeat made without meat or suet need not be processed.
Makes about 6 quarts

2 pounds ground lean beef (optional)
1 cup water (optional)
5 pounds tart apples, peeled, cored, and chopped fine
1 pound seedless raisins
1 pound sultana raisins
1 pound dried currants
½ pound citron or mixed candied fruits, minced
½ pound finely ground suet (optional)
2 (1-pound) boxes dark brown sugar
1 quart apple cider, or 3 cups cider and 1 cup brandy or rum
1 tablespoon cinnamon
1 tablespoon allspice
1 tablespoon nutmeg
¼ teaspoon ginger
2 oranges or 3 large tangerines
1 lemon

Wash and sterilize 6 (1-quart) jars and closures and keep hot on a baking sheet in a 250° F. oven until needed. If using meat, simmer in water 10 minutes, breaking up with a spoon. Mix remaining ingredients except oranges and lemon in a large enamel or stainless-steel kettle. Finely grate orange and lemon rinds; also discard white pith and seeds and finely chop oranges and lemon. Add rind and fruit to kettle, also meat and liquid if you like, and simmer uncovered

1 hour, stirring occasionally at first, more often as mixture thickens. *If mixture contains meat and/or suet:* Ladle into jars, filling to within 1″ of tops, wipe rims and seal. Process in a pressure cooker* 20 minutes at 10 pounds pressure. Remove from pressure cooker, secure seals if needed, cool, and label. *If mixture contains no meat or suet:* Ladle into jars, filling to within ⅛″ of tops. Seal, cool, and label. Store mincemeat in a cool, dark, dry place several weeks before using. About 635 calories per cup (with meat and suet), 250 calories per cup (without).

⚖ PICCALILLI

Makes about 6 pints

4 pounds green tomatoes, quartered but not peeled or cored
2 medium-size sweet green peppers, cored and seeded
2 medium-size sweet red peppers, cored and seeded
4 medium-size unpeeled cucumbers, halved and seeded
2 medium-size yellow onions, peeled and quartered
3 cups cider vinegar
2 cups firmly packed light brown sugar
2 teaspoons mustard seeds
2 teaspoons celery seeds
1 teaspoon allspice
1 tablespoon prepared horseradish

Wash and sterilize 6 (1-pint) jars and closures, stand them on baking sheet, and keep hot in a 250° F. oven until needed. Put all vegetables through the medium blade of a meat grinder, then drain well. Place in a very large enamel or stainless-steel kettle, add remaining ingredients, set lid on askew, and boil slowly ½ hour, stirring now and then. Ladle into jars, filling to within ⅛″ of tops, wipe rims, and seal. Cool, check seals, label, and store in a cool, dark, dry place 4–6 weeks before using. About 12 calories per tablespoon.

⚖ CHOW CHOW RELISH

A great way to use up garden tag ends.
Makes about 4 pints

4 medium-size green tomatoes, cored and minced but not peeled
4 medium-size sweet green peppers, cored, seeded, and minced
2 medium-size sweet red peppers, cored, seeded, and minced
2 large yellow onions, peeled and minced
1 small cabbage, shredded fine
1 medium-size cauliflower, separated into flowerets, or 3 cups cut green beans
2 quarts cold water mixed with ½ cup pickling salt (brine)
3 cups white vinegar
2 cups sugar
1 tablespoon celery seeds
1 tablespoon mustard seeds
1 teaspoon powdered mustard
1 teaspoon turmeric
1 teaspoon allspice

Mix all vegetables with brine, cover, and let stand 1 hour. Meanwhile, wash and sterilize 4 (1-pint) jars and closures, stand them on a baking sheet, and keep hot in a 250° F. oven until needed. Drain vegetables well and set aside. Mix vinegar with remaining ingredients in a very large enamel or stainless-steel kettle and simmer, uncovered, 15 minutes. Add vegetables and simmer, uncovered, 10 minutes. Ladle boiling hot into jars, filling to within ⅛″ of tops. Wipe rims and seal. Cool, check seals, label, and store in a cool, dark, dry place 1 month before serving. About 10 calories per tablespoon.

⚖ PEPPER RELISH

To save time, peppers can be put through the medium blade of a meat grinder instead of being minced.
Makes about 6 pints

1 dozen sweet green peppers, cored, seeded, and minced
1 dozen sweet red peppers, cored, seeded, and minced
2 cups minced yellow onions
1 cup minced celery

3 cups white vinegar
1½ cups sugar
1 tablespoon pickling salt
1 tablespoon mustard seeds
1 teaspoon celery seeds

Sterilize 6 (1-pint) jars and closures, stand them on a baking sheet, and keep warm in a 250° F. oven until needed. Mix all ingredients in a large, heavy enamel or stainless-steel kettle, cover, and simmer 15 minutes. Ladle into jars, filling to within ⅛″ of tops and making sure liquid covers vegetables. Wipe rims and seal. Or, if you prefer, leave ½″ head space, seal jars, and process in a hot water bath* 15 minutes. Remove jars, secure seals if necessary. Cool, check seals, label, and store in a cool, dark, dry place 3–4 weeks before using. About 10 calories per tablespoon.

VARIATIONS:

⚖ **Hot Pepper Relish:** Prepare as directed but substitute 1 dozen hot red chili peppers for the sweet red peppers. About 10 calories per tablespoon.

⚖ **Pepper Slaw** (Makes about 14 pints): Finely shred 2 large heads green cabbage, mix with ¼ cup pickling salt, cover, and refrigerate overnight. Next day, drain thoroughly, mix with Pepper Relish ingredients, increasing sugar and vinegar each to 6 cups and mustard and celery seeds each to 2 tablespoons. Simmer 20–30 minutes, then ladle into jars and seal as directed. About 15 calories per tablespoon.

⚖ **CORN RELISH**

To simplify cutting corn from cobs, boil corn 3 minutes and plunge into cold water.
Makes about 6 pints

2 quarts whole kernel corn (corn cut
    from about 1½ dozen ears)
1 cup minced yellow onions
1 cup minced sweet green pepper
1 cup minced sweet red pepper
1 cup minced celery
3 cups cider vinegar
1½ cups sugar
1 tablespoon pickling salt

1 tablespoon mustard seeds
2 teaspoons turmeric
1 teaspoon celery seeds

Sterilize 6 (1-pint) jars and closures, stand them on a baking sheet, and keep warm in a 250° F. oven until needed. Mix all ingredients in a large, heavy enamel or stainless-steel kettle, cover, and simmer 20 minutes. Ladle into jars, filling to within ⅛″ of tops and making sure liquid covers vegetables. Wipe rims and seal. Or leave ½″ head space, seal, and process in a hot water bath* 15 minutes. Remove jars and secure seals if needed. Cool, check seals, label, and store in a cool, dark, dry place 3–4 weeks before using. About 15 calories per tablespoon.

VARIATION:

⚖ **Corn-Cranberry Relish** (Makes 7½ pints): Prepare as directed but add 1 pound washed and stemmed cranberries put through the medium blade of a meat grinder and increase sugar to 3 cups. About 15 calories per tablespoon.

⚖ **JERUSALEM ARTICHOKE PICKLE RELISH**

Note how very low in calories this relish is.
Makes 6 pints

5 pounds Jerusalem artichokes
2 medium-size yellow onions, peeled
    and coarsely chopped
1 cup sugar
3 cups cider vinegar
1 tablespoon turmeric
1 tablespoon mustard seeds
1 tablespoon celery seeds
2 tablespoons pickling salt
1 cinnamon stick
½ teaspoon crushed dried hot red chili
    peppers

Wash and sterilize 6 (1-pint) jars and closures, stand them on a baking sheet, and keep hot in a 250° F. oven until needed. Using a stiff vegetable brush, scrub artichokes carefully under cold running water; scrape away any blemishes but do not peel, then put through the coarsest blade of a meat grinder. Place artichokes and remaining ingredients in a large, heavy enamel or stainless-steel kettle and simmer, uncovered, ½ hour, stirring occasionally; remove cinnamon. Ladle into jars, filling to within ¼" of tops; wipe rims and seal. Process 10 minutes in a hot water bath.* Cool, check seals, label, and store in a cool, dark, dry place. Let stand 4–6 weeks before serving. About 3 calories per tablespoon.

HAMBURGER RELISH

Makes about 8 pints

4 pounds ripe tomatoes, peeled, cored, and coarsely chopped
4 pounds unpeeled green tomatoes, cored and coarsely chopped
3 medium-size sweet green peppers, cored, seeded, and minced
3 medium-size sweet red peppers, cored, seeded, and minced
2 large yellow onions, peeled and minced
1 quart minced celery
½ cup pickling salt
1 quart cider vinegar
2 (1-pound) boxes light brown sugar
1 cup granulated sugar
1 teaspoon powdered mustard
½ teaspoon pepper

Mix all vegetables, sprinkle with salt, cover, and let stand overnight in a cool place. Drain well and mix with remaining ingredients in a very large enamel or stainless-steel kettle. Simmer, uncovered, stirring now and then, about 1½ hours until thick. Meanwhile, wash and sterilize 8 (1-pint) jars and closures, stand them on a baking sheet, and keep hot in a 250° F. oven until needed. Ladle relish boiling hot into jars, filling to within ⅛" of tops. Wipe rims and seal. Cool, check seals, label, and store in a cool, dark, dry place 3–4 weeks before using. About 25 calories per tablespoon.

PEACH RELISH

Makes 6 half pints

4 pounds firm-ripe peaches (clingstone types are best), peeled, pitted, and sliced thin

1 cup sultana raisins
1½ cups firmly packed light brown sugar
¾ cup cider vinegar
1 teaspoon cinnamon
½ teaspoon cloves
¼ teaspoon ginger
½ cup slivered almonds (optional)

Place all ingredients except nuts in an enamel or stainless-steel kettle, cover, and heat very slowly to simmering; uncover and simmer ¾ hour, stirring frequently. Meanwhile wash and sterilize 6 half-pint jars and closures, stand them on a baking sheet, and keep hot in a 250° F. oven until needed. If you like, add nuts to relish. Ladle boiling hot into jars, filling to within ⅛" of tops. Wipe rims and seal. Cool, check seals, label, and store in a cool, dark, and dry place several weeks before serving. About 30 calories per tablespoon (without almonds).

BERRY RELISH

Tart-sweet berry relishes go well with most meats and poultry.
Makes 6 half pints

2 quarts firm-ripe berries (blueberries, huckleberries, cranberries, red or black currants, elderberries, or gooseberries), washed and stemmed
4 cups sugar
¾–1 cup cider vinegar
1½ teaspoons cinnamon
½ teaspoon allspice
¼ teaspoon ginger

Wash and sterilize 6 half-pint jars and closures, stand them on a baking sheet, and keep hot in a 250° F. oven until needed. Place berries in a large enamel or stainless-steel saucepan and crush a few with a potato masher. Cover and simmer, stirring now and then, until berries are soft. Mix in remaining ingredients, insert a candy thermometer, and boil slowly, stirring now and then, until thermometer registers 218° F. Ladle into jars, filling to within ⅛" of tops. Wipe rims and seal. Cool, check seals, label, and store in a cool, dark, dry place 3–4 weeks before serving. About 40 calories per tablespoon.

⚖ ⊠ RANCH RELISH

Makes 3 cups

*3 medium-size ripe tomatoes, peeled,
  seeded, and cut in ¼" cubes*
*1 medium-size yellow onion, peeled and
  minced*
*1 large sweet green pepper, washed,
  cored, seeded, and minced*
2 teaspoons salt
½ cup chili sauce

Mix all ingredients, cover, and chill at
least 2 hours to blend flavors (overnight
is better). Serve with barbecued beef,
broiled steaks and chops. About 6
calories per tablespoon.

⊠ CRANBERRY-ORANGE RELISH

Makes 1 pint

*1 pound cranberries, stemmed, washed,
  and drained*
2 large oranges
1¾ cups sugar
⅛ teaspoon salt

Pick cranberries over, discarding any
underripe ones. Finely grate orange rinds;
remove white pith and seeds from
oranges, then coarsely chop. Put
cranberries and oranges through the
medium blade of a meat grinder. Mix
with sugar and salt, cover, and let stand
at room temperature 1 hour; mix again.
Serve as is or slightly chilled. Stored
airtight in the refrigerator, relish will
keep several weeks. About 50 calories
per tablespoon.

VARIATIONS:

Cranberry-Pear Relish: Prepare as directed but substitute 4 peeled and cored
pears (firm) for oranges and add ¼ cup
minced crystallized ginger. About 60
calories per tablespoon.

Preserved Cranberry-Orange Relish
(Makes 4 half pints): Leave cranberries
whole, add grated rind and coarsely
chopped oranges, then simmer, uncovered, with the sugar, salt, and 1 cup
orange juice about ¾ hour, stirring now
and then. Ladle boiling hot into 4 sterilized half-pint jars, filling to within ⅛"

of tops, wipe rims, and seal; cool, check
seals, label, and store. About 50 calories
per tablespoon.

Fruit-Nut Conserve (Makes 5 half
pints): Prepare Preserved Cranberry-
Orange Relish (above) as directed but
add ¾ cup seedless raisins along with
sugar and juice. After simmering, add ¾
cup toasted, slivered almonds or coarsely
chopped, blanched filberts; pack into
jars as directed. About 65 calories per
tablespoon.

⊠ SOME QUICK AND EASY RELISHES

These are jiffy relishes to mix up and
serve, not ones to can. Store in the
refrigerator.

Cran-Apple Relish (Makes about 1
pint): Mix 1 (1-pound) can undrained
whole cranberry sauce with 1 unpeeled,
cored, and diced tart cooking apple and
1 teaspoon lemon juice. Or mix
cranberry sauce with ½ cup applesauce.
About 25 calories per tablespoon.

Cranberry-Chutney Relish (Makes about
2½ cups): Mix 1 (1-pound) can undrained whole cranberry sauce with ½
cup minced chutney. About 40 calories
per tablespoon.

Cranberry-Pineapple Relish (Makes
about 3 cups): Mix 1 (1-pound) can
undrained whole cranberry sauce with 1
(8-ounce) can drained crushed pineapple
and 1 teaspoon minced mint. About 30
calories per tablespoon.

Cranberry-Walnut Relish (Makes about
3 cups): Mix 1 (1-pound) can undrained
whole cranberry sauce with ⅓ cup each
minced walnuts and celery. About 30
calories per tablespoon.

⚖ *Onion Relish* (Makes about 1 cup):
Mix 1 large peeled and minced yellow,
Bermuda, or Spanish onion with 2
tablespoons each cider vinegar and
sugar and ¼ teaspoon salt. If you like
add 1 minced pimiento. Let stand at
room temperature ½ hour before serving.
About 10 calories per tablespoon.

⚖️ *Pineapple Relish* (Makes about 3 cups): Mix 1 (1-pound 4-ounce) can drained crushed pineapple with ½ cup each minced sweet green or red pepper and celery, 3 tablespoons each firmly packed light brown sugar and cider vinegar. Let stand at room temperature ½ hour before serving. About 15 calories per tablespoon.

⚖️ *Quick Corn Relish* (Makes about 3 cups): Mix 2 cups drained canned whole kernel corn with ⅓ cup each minced yellow onion and sweet green or red pepper, ¼ cup each minced celery and sweet pickle relish, ½ teaspoon salt, and 2 tablespoons each sugar and cider vinegar. Let stand at room temperature ½ hour before serving. About 15 calories per tablespoon.

⚖️ *Quick Pickled Beets* (Makes 1 pint): Sprinkle 1 (1-pound) can sliced beets with ¼ teaspoon garlic salt. Add ⅓ cup hot cider vinegar mixed with 2 tablespoons sugar and ⅛ teaspoon cloves. Chill before serving. About 10 calories per tablespoon.

Quick Pickled Peaches (Apricots, Pears, Prunes, or Figs) (Makes 6 servings): Drain syrup from 1 (1-pound) can peach halves (apricot or pear halves, whole prunes or figs) into a saucepan, add ⅓ cup each cider vinegar and sugar, ¼ teaspoon each whole allspice and mustard seeds, and 1 stick cinnamon. Simmer, uncovered, 3–4 minutes, pour over fruit, which has been studded with cloves (3–4 for each piece). (*Note:* Omit cloves if using prunes or figs.) Cool and chill. From 40–100 calories per fruit (prunes, pears, and figs are the highest, peaches and apricots the lowest).

⚖️ *Radish, Zucchini, and Lettuce Relish* (Makes about 1½ cups): Mix ½ cup each minced, unpeeled radishes and zucchini, 1 cup finely shredded iceberg lettuce, 2 tablespoons each cider vinegar and sugar, ¼ teaspoon salt, and ⅛ teaspoon caraway seeds. Let stand 15 minutes at room temperature, mix well again, and serve. About 5 calories per tablespoon.

⊠ **HOT MUSTARD FRUITS**

Delicious with baked ham or boiled tongue.
Makes 6 servings

2 tablespoons butter or margarine
⅓ cup firmly packed light brown sugar
3 tablespoons prepared spicy brown mustard
1 cup drained canned sliced peaches
1 cup drained canned apricot halves
1 cup drained canned pineapple slices, cut in half

Preheat oven to 325° F. Melt butter in a small saucepan over low heat, add sugar and mustard, and heat and stir about 5 minutes until sugar dissolves. Place fruits in an ungreased shallow 1-quart casserole and pour in mustard mixture. Bake, uncovered, ½ hour, stirring and basting fruits once or twice. Serve as a vegetable substitute. About 200 calories per serving.

VARIATION:

Hot Curried Fruits: Prepare as directed but add 2–3 teaspoons curry powder to melted butter along with sugar and mustard. About 200 calories per serving.

⚖️ ⊠ **HOMEMADE "PREPARED" MUSTARD**

Refrigerated, this mustard keeps almost indefinitely.
Makes ½ cup

1 (1½-ounce) can powdered mustard
2 tablespoons sugar
1 teaspoon salt
3 tablespoons cider vinegar
2 tablespoons olive or other cooking oil
1 tablespoon cold water
½ teaspoon Worcestershire sauce

Mix mustard, sugar, and salt, add remaining ingredients gradually, and beat until smooth. Spoon into a sterilized jar, cover tightly, and refrigerate. About 10 calories per tablespoon.

VARIATIONS:

⚖ **Spicy Hot Mustard Spread:** Prepare
as directed but add ¼ teaspoon each
ginger and turmeric and ⅛ teaspoon
cayenne pepper. About 10 calories per
tablespoon.

⚖ **Horseradish Mustard:** Prepare as
directed but add 2 tablespoons prepared
horseradish. About 10 calories per
tablespoon.

⚖ **Mild Mustard Spread:** Substitute 1
tablespoon white wine vinegar for cider
vinegar and increase water to ¼ cup.
About 10 calories per tablespoon.

⚖ **White Wine Mustard:** Mix yellow
or brown powdered mustard (the brown
is available in oriental groceries) with
the sugar and salt called for. Blend in
2 tablespoons white wine vinegar, ¼ cup
dry white wine, 1 tablespoon olive oil,
¼ teaspoon turmeric, and ⅛ teaspoon
cayenne pepper. About 10 calories per
tablespoon.

⚖ **FRESH HORSERADISH**

Stored in the refrigerator, this will keep
almost indefinitely.
Makes 1 pint

*½ pound horseradish root, scrubbed
    and peeled*
½ cup white vinegar
2 teaspoons salt

Remove any discolored parts from root
with a vegetable peeler, then coarsely
chop root. (*Note:* If you are doing
more than this amount at one time,
drop horseradish into cold water
to prevent browning.) Chop very fine, a
little at a time, in an electric blender or
put twice through the fine blade of a
meat grinder. Mix with vinegar and salt.
Pack into sterilized jars, cover tightly,
and let ripen in refrigerator 1 week
before using. About 5 calories per
tablespoon.

JELLIES

Few cooking achievements seem more
magical than the transformation of
plump, freshly picked fruits into
sparkling, quivery jellies. Yet there is
nothing mysterious about the process.
Or difficult. Three essentials are needed
to make jelly: *pectin* (the jelling agent
found naturally in certain fruits), *acid*
(also found naturally in fruits, which
strengthens the pectin), and *sugar* (which
stretches and tenderizes the pectin; either
beet or cane sugar may be used). With
a delicate balance of the three comes
perfect jelly: one that quivers but does
not run, is firm enough to stand alone
when unmolded yet tender enough to
cut easily with a spoon.

How to Make Jelly

Suitable Fruits for Natural Jellies (those
requiring no commercial liquid or
powdered pectins): Tart apples, crab
apples, Concord grapes, currants,
quinces, blackberries, cranberries,
gooseberries, and raspberries. For best
results, fruits should be firm-ripe, when
pectin content is at its peak. Neither
green nor overripe fruits have sufficient
pectin for making jelly.

Preparing the Fruit:

Apples, Crab Apples, Quinces: Wash,
cutting away any blemishes; remove
stems and blossom ends, then slice thin,
quarter, or coarsely chop. *Do not peel,
core, or seed* (these all contain pectin).

Grapes, Currants, and Berries: Stem,
wash, and sort, discarding any soft or
blemished fruits, then crush with a
potato masher (leave skins and seeds in).

Extracting the Juice: Place prepared
fruit in a large kettle, add amount of
water called for in the following chart,
and boil uncovered, stirring occasionally,
the recommended amount of time. Pour

JUICE EXTRACTION TABLE

Kind of Fruit	Quantity of Prepared Fruit	Amount of Water Needed per Quart of Fruit	Recommended Boiling Time
Apples and crab apples	1 quart	1 cup	20 minutes
Quinces	1 quart	2 cups	25 minutes
Raspberries	1 quart	None	10 minutes
Blackberries, gooseberries, and currants	1 quart	¼ cup	10 minutes
Concord grapes	1 quart	¼ cup	15 minutes
Cranberries	1 quart	1 cup	10 minutes

Note: The extracted juice (jelly stock) can be bottled and the jelly made at a later date in small quantities as needed (makes for clearer jelly). Simply heat juice to 190° F., ladle into hot sterilized jars, filling to within ¼" of tops, seal, and process 10 minutes in a hot water bath.* Cool, check seals, and store in a cool, dark, dry place until ready to make jelly.

into a damp jelly bag suspended over a large bowl (most jelly bags come equipped with their own stands) or into a cheesecloth-lined colander set in a large bowl. Let juices drip through undisturbed; squeezing the bag to force out juices will cloud the jelly. You can, however, massage the bag *very gently* once or twice. Extracting juice is a painstaking process so don't be alarmed if it takes an hour or more. (*Note:* If extracted juice seems cloudy, strain through several thicknesses of cheese-cloth.)

Testing for Pectin: Knowing how much pectin fruit juice contains is vital to making good jelly because the pectin content determines the amount of sugar needed. There are 2 tests:

With a Jelmeter (the most reliable test): These, available in housewares departments, come with full instructions; follow them. Jelmeters are calibrated glass tubes through which the extracted juice is drained, the speed of drainage indicating the pectin content and thus the quantity of sugar needed.

With Alcohol: In a small glass mix 1 teaspoon grain (*ethyl*) alcohol (available at drugstores) with 1 teaspoon room-

temperature extracted juice; let stand one minute, then pour into a second glass. If a firm precipitate forms, juice is high in pectin and should be mixed, measure for measure, with sugar. If precipitate is curdy, use ¾ as much sugar as fruit juice and, if soft, half as much sugar as juice.

The sugar-to-juice ratios given in the table below are averages and should be used as a guide only when it is not possible to make one of the more accurate pectin tests.

Cooking the Jelly: Place juice and required amount of sugar in a very large, heavy kettle (at least 4 times the volume of fruit put into it—jellies bubble higher and higher as they thicken and, unless kettle is big enough, will boil over). Set over low heat, insert a candy thermometer, and heat and stir, using a long-handled wooden spoon, until sugar is dissolved. Raise burner heat and boil rapidly, uncovered and without stirring, until thermometer registers 8° F. higher than the boiling point of water in your area. At sea level, the jelling temperature is about 220° F. Begin testing for

BASIC PROPORTIONS FOR JELLIES

Kind of Fruit Juice	Average Amount of Sugar Needed per Cup Extracted Juice
Apple, crab apple, cranberry, and currant	1 cup
Blackberry, gooseberry, raspberry, Concord grape, and quince	¾ cup

sheeting, however, shortly after mixture boils (when thermometer reads about 215° F.).

Testing for Sheeting: This is the standard jelly test, fortunately a quick and reliable one. Take up a small amount of the hot mixture on a cold metal spoon, cool slightly, then tilt. When drops cling together, forming a jelly-like sheet, jelly is done.

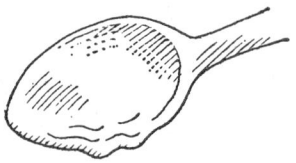

Syrupy
(not done)

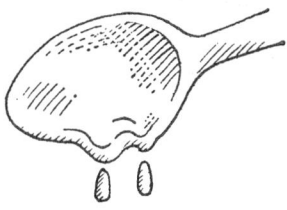

Thick Drops
(not done)

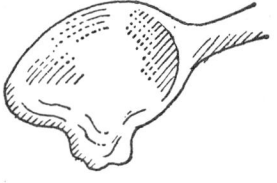

Sheeting
(done)

Preparing Jelly Glasses and Lids: These can be washed and sterilized while jelly cooks (follow directions in canning chapter). Invert sterilized glasses on paper toweling, stand lids right side up, and keep away from drafts.

Melting Paraffin: Because hot paraffin is flammable, the melting should never be done over direct heat but in the top of a double boiler. Or, better still, in a small deep coffeepot (one used exclusively for melting paraffin) set in a saucepan of boiling water (with the coffeepot, pouring's a snap). Paraffin melted slowly and kept just at the point of liquefaction will do a far better job of sealing jellies than smoking-hot paraffin which, on hardening, will shrink from the sides of the glass, split, or crack.

Filling Jelly Glasses: Place glasses on a level counter near kettle of jelly, turn right side up, one by one, as you're ready to fill them. Have jelly boiling hot, then ladle into glass, holding ladle as close to glass as possible to prevent air bubbles from forming in jelly. Fill glass to within ¼″ of the top and seal with ⅛″ melted paraffin, making sure it touches glass all round. Prick any bubbles in paraffin before it hardens so all air will be sealed out. (*Note:* A single thin layer of paraffin works better than a thick one because it remains malleable, fitting itself to the contours of the cooling jelly. Thick paraffin layers are apt to become brittle on hardening and pull from the sides of the glasses.) Cool jelly, cap glasses, label, and store in a cool, dark, dry place. (*Note:* Jelly can, if you like, be poured into small preserving jars—the half-pint size is good.) Simply pour *boiling hot* into jars, filling to within ⅛″ of tops, wipe rims with a clean damp cloth, and seal. Invert jars for about 10 seconds so hot mixture will destroy any microorganisms in the head space, then stand right side up and cool. Check seals, label, and store.

How to Rescue Runny Jelly

Sometimes jelly made with the greatest care refuses to jell, hardly a disaster because there are several ways to salvage it:

Without Adding Commercial Pectin: Empty jelly into a saucepan, bring to a boil, and continue cooking until mixture will sheet (see Testing for Sheeting). Ladle into clean sterilized glasses and reseal with paraffin.

With Commercial Powdered Pectin: Measure jelly and for each 1 quart measure ¼ cup sugar, ¼ cup water, and 4 teaspoons powdered pectin. Mix pectin and water in a large saucepan, bring to a boil, stirring constantly to prevent scorching, then mix in jelly and sugar. Boil hard for exactly ½ minute. Remove from heat, ladle into clean sterilized glasses, and reseal with paraffin.

With Commercial Liquid Pectin: Measure jelly and for each 1 quart measure ¾ cup sugar, 2 tablespoons strained lemon juice, and 2 tablespoons liquid pectin. Bring jelly to a full boil over high heat, quickly mix in sugar, lemon juice, and pectin, and heat, stirring constantly, until mixture comes to a full rolling boil. Boil hard one minute, remove from heat, ladle jelly into clean sterilized glasses, and reseal with paraffin.

About Jellies Made with Commercial Pectins

Liquid and powdered pectins, in making it possible to jell any fruit juice, have revolutionized jelly making. They must, however, be used carefully—amounts required vary considerably from juice to juice, depending on sweetness, tartness, and pectin content. No master recipe, alas, can be drawn up for the commercial pectins, so the best plan is to follow the manufacturer's recipes explicitly.

Tips for Making Better Jellies

Because so many of these tips are the same as for jams and preserves, they are included at the end of that section.

Why Things Sometimes Go Wrong with Jellies

Soft, Runny Jelly: Too little pectin or sugar or both; also undercooking.

Stiff Jelly: Too much pectin or acid or both.

Dull, Cloudy Jelly: Fruit juice not carefully extracted.

Grainy or Crystalline Jelly: Too much sugar, too little cooking.

Gummy Jelly: Overcooking.

Weepy Jelly: Fruit too acid or paraffin layer too thick.

Darkened or Off-Color Jelly: Stored at too high a temperature.

Faded Jelly: Stored in too bright a room.

JAMS, MARMALADES, FRUIT BUTTERS, PRESERVES, AND CONSERVES

These preserved fruits and fruit spreads are easy to make and foolproof enough to invite improvisation. What distinguishes one from another? Here's a fast run-down:

Jams: Crushed berries or cut-up fruits cooked with a little water and a lot of sugar until thick, slightly jelled, and of good spreading consistency.

Marmalades: Clear, tender, jelly-like spreads usually made of citrus fruits and containing shreds of rind and bits of cooked fruit.

Fruit Butters: Melba-smooth, honey-sweet spreads made by cooking strained fruit pulp with sugar and spices long and slow in an open kettle.

Preserves: Whole or cut-up fruits cooked in a sugar syrup until clear; syrup may be very thick or fairly thin.

Conserves: Jam-like spreads made of a mixture of fruits and nuts.

How to Make Jam

Suitable Fruits: Apricots, blackberries, blueberries, cherries, gooseberries, grapes, peaches, pears, plums, raspberries, rhubarb, and strawberries. Also combinations of these.

Preparing the Fruit:

Berries and Other Soft Fruits: Wash and sort fruit, removing caps, stems, and any bruised or blemished spots, then crush.

Firm Fruits: Peel, core, and pit, then quarter, dice, or coarsely chop. (*Note:* Grapes and plums will have better texture if cooked until tender with a little water—about ¼ cup for each quart prepared fruit—before being mixed with sugar.)

Cooking the Jam: Measure prepared fruit and for each quart add 3 cups sugar. Place in a very large, heavy kettle (at least 4 times volume of fruit put into it) and heat and stir over low heat until sugar dissolves. Insert a candy thermometer, then boil rapidly uncovered, stirring often, until very thick, about 218–22° F. on thermometer. Test for sheeting (see Jelly); when mixture sheets, jam is done.

Preparing Jelly Glasses, Melting Paraffin: Follow directions given for jelly.

Filling Glasses: Remove jam from heat and let stand 1–2 minutes to settle foam; skim froth from surface, then ladle into jelly glasses or preserving jars as directed for jelly. Cool, label, and store in a cool, dark, dry place.

How to Make Marmalade

(see separate recipes that follow)

How to Make Fruit Butters

Suitable Fruits: Apples and crab apples, apricots, peaches, pears and plums, grapes and quinces.

Preparing the Fruit: Prepare as directed for jam.

Making the Fruit Pulp: Measure prepared fruit and for each 1 quart add ½ cup water. Cook in a large kettle, stirring now and then, until mushy; press through a sieve or purée in a food mill.

Cooking the Fruit Butter: Measure fruit pulp and for each quart add 3 cups sugar; if you like, tie a few whole cloves, allspice, and a broken cinnamon stick in cheesecloth. Heat and stir over low heat in a large kettle until sugar dissolves, then slowly boil, uncovered, until quite thick, 1–1½ hours, stirring often to prevent scorching, especially toward the end.

Preparing Glasses, Melting Paraffin: Prepare as directed for jelly.

Filling Glasses: Remove fruit butter from heat, let stand 2 minutes, and skim off froth. Fill glasses or jars as directed for jelly. (*Note:* Many fruit butter recipes call for less sugar than this basic method; if the proportion of sugar to fruit pulp is less than 3 to 4—3 cups sugar to 4 cups pulp—there will be less chance of spoilage if the fruit butter is poured into hot sterilized preserving jars to within ¼″ of tops.) Seal and process in a hot water bath* about 10 minutes. Check seals after processing, then label jars and store in a cool, dark, dry place.

How to Make Preserves

Suitable Fruits: Cherries, figs, peaches, pears, pineapple, raspberries, and strawberries.

Preparing the Fruit:

Cherries and Berries: Wash, stem, and sort, discarding any that are bruised or blemished. Leave sweet cherries whole but halve and pit the sour.

Figs: Wash and stem, then peel carefully, trying not to cut too close to the seeds. Leave whole.

Peaches and Pears: Peel, pit or core, and slice. (*Note:* Pears are also good cut into small chips or thin pieces.)

Pineapple: Peel, core, and cube or slice thin.

Cooking the Preserves:

Soft Fruits (Berries and Peaches): Measure prepared fruit and for each 1 quart add 3 cups sugar; mix and let stand at room temperature 10 minutes to draw some of the juices from the fruit. Set over low heat and cook and stir until sugar dissolves; cover, remove from heat, and let stand overnight so fruits will plump up. Next day, bring to a boil, add a few whole cloves and a broken cinnamon stick tied in cheesecloth, if you like, and cook slowly, stirring occasionally, until fruit is clear and syrup thick. Remove spices.

Firm Fruits: Measure prepared fruit and for each 1 quart measure ½ cup water and 3 cups sugar. Mix water and sugar, bring to a boil in a large kettle, stirring until sugar dissolves. Add fruit and boil, uncovered, stirring occasionally, until fruit is clear and syrup thick. If you like, tie a few whole spices in cheesecloth—cloves, allspice, a cinnamon stick—and cook along with fruits; remove when preserves are done—the fruit clear and syrup thick.

Preparing Glasses, Melting Paraffin: Prepare as directed for jelly.

Filling Glasses: Rich jam-like preserves made of small berries or fairly finely cut fruit can be ladled into jelly glasses and sealed under paraffin. But fruits preserved whole in syrup should be packed hot in hot sterilized jars. In either case, before filling jars, let preserves stand off heat 2 minutes to settle foam; skim off froth, then pack in glasses or jars as directed for jelly. (*Note:* Preserves packed in jars should be processed 10 minutes in a hot water bath.*) Cool preserves, label, then store in a cool, dark, dry place.

How to Make Conserves

These are really simple variations on jams—mixtures of two or more fruits (use any suitable for jam) cooked with minced nuts and/or raisins. Prepare conserves like jam, teaming any combination of fruits you fancy, and using 3 cups sugar and ½ cup seedless raisins and/or chopped pecans, walnuts, or blanched almonds to each 1 quart prepared raw fruit. For better texture and flavor, add nuts during last 5 minutes of cooking.

TIPS FOR MAKING BETTER JELLIES, JAMS, PRESERVES, AND CONSERVES

In General:
– Read recipe through carefully before beginning and follow directions.
– Pick a clear, dry day for making jellies, jams, or preserves.
– Assemble equipment and ingredients before starting. Make sure jars or glasses are spotless, free of cracks and nicks.
– Make jellies, jams, and preserves in small quantities; do not double recipes.
– Measure or weigh ingredients carefully.
– Use extra-large, flat-bottomed kettles, heavy enough to reduce risk of scorching and made of an inert material, like enameled metal or stainless steel, that will not alter color or flavor of fruit.
– Use a candy thermometer to help determine doneness and check it for accuracy before using (for directions, see Candies and Nuts).
– For soft jams and preserves, slightly undercook; for stiff ones, slightly overcook.

– If you live in a hot climate or have no cool space for storing preserves, pack in preserving jars and process 10–15 minutes in a hot water bath* instead of ladling into jelly glasses and sealing with paraffin.

– When sealing with paraffin, make layer no more than ⅛″ thick, see that it touches glass all around and has no air bubbles.

– Wipe cooled, sealed glasses and jars with a clean damp cloth before storing.

– When cooling jars, allow plenty of space between them so air can circulate. Also, cool away from drafts.

– Test seals about 12 hours after cooling. If a jar has failed to seal, empty contents into a saucepan, bring to a boil, ladle into a clean, hot, sterile jar, reseal, and cool. Or, store in refrigerator and serve within 2 weeks.

– Store jams, jellies, and preserves in a dark, cool, dry place and let mellow several weeks before serving. Also, try to serve within a year, sooner if possible.

Jellies:
– Use firm-ripe fruit instead of fully ripe or, if you wish, ¼ slightly underripe fruit and ¾ ripe (but not overripe).

– Do not rush juice extraction but let it drip through jelly bag at its own snail's pace.

– If extracted juice lacks tartness (essential to making jelly jell), add 1 tablespoon strained lemon juice to each cup fruit juice.

– Do not overcook fruit when preparing for juice extraction—destroys pectin.

Jams, Marmalades, Fruit Butters, Preserves, and Conserves:
– To save money, use less-than-perfect fruits, *but* prepare carefully, trimming away all blemishes and moldy spots that might cause spoilage.

– When making preserves, have fruits of as uniform size and shape as possible.

– To keep fruit from floating to the top of jams and preserves, use fully ripe fruits and plump overnight in the sugar syrup.

– Watch all thick fruit mixtures closely

during cooking and stir as needed to prevent scorching.

– Remove any whole spices immediately after cooking to prevent fruit from darkening.

– To reduce risks of spoilage (and make jams and preserves prettier) skim off as much froth or foam as possible before ladling into jars.

¢ OLD-FASHIONED APPLE JELLY

Apples that make particularly good jelly are Rhode Island Greenings. Do not double this recipe.
Makes enough to fill 5 8-ounce jelly glasses

5 pounds Rhode Island Greenings, washed, stemmed, and sliced thin but not peeled or cored
5 cups water
½ cup plus 2 tablespoons lemon juice
3¾ cups sugar (about)

Place apples (include seeds and cores), water, and lemon juice in a very large enamel or stainless-steel kettle, cover, and boil 15–20 minutes until apples are mushy. Meanwhile, suspend 2 damp jelly bags over large, heatproof bowls or line 2 large colanders with 4 thicknesses of cheesecloth, letting ends hang over rims, and set colanders in bowls. Pour half of the apples and their juice into each bag or colander and let juice drip through. (*Note:* Cheesecloth can be tied into bags and suspended over bowls.) For sparkling, clear jelly, don't force pulp through bags. You may, however, massage bags gently, encouraging juice to trickle through. Have patience—this takes a long time. Meanwhile, sterilize 5 (8-ounce) jelly glasses and stand upside down on several thicknesses paper toweling. When juice has been extracted (you should have about 5 cups), place in a clean, large enamel or stainless-steel kettle and stir in ¾ cup sugar for each 1 cup juice; insert a candy thermometer. Boil mixture uncovered, without stirring, 20–25 minutes until thermometer registers 218–20° F.; begin testing for "sheeting" after mixture has boiled 10 minutes. Take up a little juice in a large metal spoon, cool slightly, then tilt; if drops slide together forming a jelly-like sheet, jelly is done. Remove from heat and skim off froth. Fill glasses to within ¼″ of tops and seal with ⅛″ melted paraffin. Cool, cover, label, and store in a cool, dark, dry place. About 45 calories per tablespoon.

VARIATIONS:

¢ **Old-Fashioned Rose Geranium Jelly:** Place a small rose geranium leaf in the bottom of each jelly glass, pour in apple jelly, press a second leaf into jelly, then seal with paraffin. About 45 calories per tablespoon.

¢ **Crab Apple Jelly:** Prepare as directed, substituting 5 pounds crab apples for Greenings (¼ should be slightly under-ripe, the rest ripe) and omitting lemon juice. Test extracted juice for pectin* (crab apples contain considerable pectin) and add the quantity of sugar indicated (usually 1 cup sugar for each 1 cup extracted crab apple juice is about right). Proceed as directed. About 45 calories per tablespoon.

¢ **Spiced Apple or Crab Apple Jelly:** Prepare as direced but, when cooking apples and water for juice, add 6–8 whole cloves, 1 broken cinnamon stick, and 2–3 whole allspice, tied in cheese-cloth. Remove spice bag before pouring apples into jelly bags. About 45 calories per tablespoon.

¢ **Minted Apple or Crab Apple Jelly:** Prepare as directed but when cooking apples and water for juice add 1 cup bruised mint leaves tied in cheesecloth; remove mint bag before pouring apples into jelly bags. About 45 calories per tablespoon.

Quince Jelly: Prepare as directed, sub-stituting 5 pounds coarsely chopped, unpeeled firm-ripe quinces for Greenings and omitting lemon juice; cook quinces and water (2 cups water to each quart prepared fruit) 25–30 minutes until mushy. Extract juice, test for pectin,* and add quantity of sugar indicated (usually ¾ cup sugar for each 1 cup

extracted juice). Proceed as directed. About 45 calories per tablespoon.

OLD-FASHIONED CONCORD GRAPE JELLY

Makes enough to fill 4 8-ounce jelly glasses

3 pounds Concord grapes, washed and stemmed but not peeled
¾ cup cold water
2¼ cups sugar (about)

Place grapes and water in a large enamel or stainless-steel kettle and mash well with a potato masher. Cover and bring to a boil over high heat; reduce heat slightly and boil gently 15 minutes.

Meanwhile, suspend 2 damp jelly bags over large heatproof bowls or line 2 large colanders with 4 thicknesses of cheesecloth, letting ends hang over rims; stand colanders in large bowls.

Pour half of grape mixture into each bag or colander and let juice drip through undisturbed. (*Note:* Cheesecloth can be tied into bags and suspended over bowls.) While juice is being extracted, sterilize 4 (8-ounce) jelly glasses and stand upside down on several thicknesses of paper toweling.

When most of the juice has dripped through, measure carefully—you should have about 3 cups. Place juice in a clean large enamel or stainless-steel kettle and add ¾ cup sugar for each 1 cup juice; insert a candy thermometer.

Bring mixture to a boil over high heat, reduce heat slightly, and boil uncovered, without stirring, 10–15 minutes until thermometer reaches 218–20° F. Begin testing for sheeting, however, after 5 minutes of cooking. Take up a little juice in a large metal spoon, cool slightly, then tilt; if drops run together in a jelly-like sheet, jelly is done. Remove from heat and skim off froth. Fill glasses to within ¼″ of tops and seal with ⅛″ melted paraffin. Cool, cover, label, and store in a cool, dark, dry place. About 40 calories per tablespoon.

⊠ WINE JELLY

Serve as a condiment with poultry, game, or game birds.
Makes 2½ cups

1½ cups medium-dry port, red or white
  wine, or 1 cup wine and ½ cup water
1 cup currant or grape jelly
3 whole cloves
½ stick cinnamon
1 tablespoon lemon juice
1 envelope unflavored gelatin softened
  in ¼ cup cold water

Simmer wine, jelly, spices, and lemon juice, uncovered, 10 minutes; add gelatin and heat and stir until dissolved. Strain through a cheesecloth-lined sieve, cool, then chill until firm. Break up slightly with a fork and serve cool—not straight out of the refrigerator. About 30 calories per tablespoon.

⊠ UNCOOKED BERRY JAM

This recipe can be made with a variety of berries.
Makes enough to fill 5 8-ounce jelly glasses

1 quart berries, stemmed, washed, and
  drained well
2 pounds sugar
2 tablespoons lemon juice
½ (6-ounce) bottle liquid pectin

Sterilize 5 (8-ounce) jelly glasses or, if you plan to store jam in freezer, freezer jars. Mash berries with a potato masher, then measure. You will need 1 pint mashed fruit. Strain out some of the seeds, if you like, but add extra mashed berries as needed to fill out the 1-pint measure. Mix berries and sugar well; combine lemon juice and pectin and add to berries; stir 3 minutes. (*Note:* A little undissolved sugar may remain.) Fill glasses to within ¼" of tops, cover with lids or rounds of foil, and let jam "set up" at room temperature; this may take 24 hours. Refrigerate and use within 3 weeks or freeze and use within 1 year. About 45 calories per tablespoon.

ORANGE MARMALADE

Make only small amounts of marmalade at a time so it doesn't scorch.
Makes 4 half pints

2 large thick-skinned oranges (navel or
  Valencia are best)
1 small lemon
2 cups water
4 cups sugar (about)

Peel oranges and lemon, trim away inner white part so rind is about ⅜" thick; cut in fine slivers about ½" long. Discard pith and seeds in fruit, then chop fruit fine, saving juice. Mix rind, fruit, and juice in a very large, heavy enamel, stainless-steel, or flameproof glass saucepan, add water, and simmer uncovered 10 minutes. Cover and let stand in a cool place overnight. Next day, wash and sterilize 4 half-pint jars and closures, stand them on a baking sheet, and keep hot in a 250° F. oven until needed. Measure fruit mixture and for each cup add 1 cup sugar. Return to pan, insert candy thermometer, slowly heat uncovered to boiling, stirring until sugar dissolves; boil slowly uncovered, stirring now and then, 30–40 minutes until thermometer reaches 218–20° F. Take up a little of the juice in a large metal spoon, cool slightly, then tilt; if drops slide together in a sheet, marmalade is done. Remove from heat, stir 1 minute, skim off froth, and ladle into jars, filling to within ⅛" of tops. Wipe rims and seal. Cool, check seals, label, and store in a cool, dark, dry place. About 50 calories per tablespoon.

VARIATIONS:

Bitter Orange Marmalade: Prepare as directed, using the slivered rind and chopped fruit of 4–5 Seville oranges; omit lemon. Tie seeds in cheesecloth and simmer along with rind, chopped fruit and juice, and water called for for 30–40 minutes until rind is almost tender; remove seeds and let stand overnight. Measure mixture, add enough water to total 1 quart, then proceed as

directed, using 1–1½ cups sugar per cup
of mixture, depending on how sweet a
marmalade is wanted. About 50
calories per tablespoon.

Grapefruit Marmalade: Prepare as
directed, using the rind of 2 large
grapefruits instead of oranges; after
trimming and slivering rind, measure
1½ cups to use in the marmalade;
combine with lemon rind. Bring rinds
and 1 quart water to a boil in a small
saucepan, then drain; repeat twice. Mix
rind and chopped, seeded grapefruit
sections, add the 2 cups water called for,
and proceed as directed. About 50
calories per tablespoon.

Lemon Marmalade: Prepare as directed
for Orange Marmalade (above) but use
the rind and chopped, seeded fruit of 4
large lemons; also use 1½ cups sugar for
each 1 cup fruit and rind mixture.
About 75 calories per tablespoon.

Ginger-Lime Marmalade: Prepare as
directed, using the slivered rind and
chopped fruit of 4–5 limes (you'll need
3 cups fruit and rind mixture) and the
slivered rind and chopped fruit of 1
lemon. Use 1½ cups sugar for each
cup fruit mixture and add ⅓ cup
slivered crystallized ginger. Cook and
bottle as directed. About 80 calories
per tablespoon.

Kumquat Marmalade: Prepare as
directed, using 1 quart slivered kumquat
rind and chopped fruit (you'll need
about 1¾ pounds ripe kumquats).
(*Note:* The easiest way to prepare these
small fruits is to halve lengthwise,
scrape out seeds and core, then to sliver
fruit and rind together.) Use 1½ cups
water and ½ cup lemon juice when
cooking, otherwise proceed as for
Orange Marmalade. About 52 calories
per tablespoon.

Calamondin Marmalade (Makes 5 half
pints): These supertart, tiny citrus fruits,
available in Florida and California, make
excellent marmalade. Prepare like
Kumquat Marmalade (above), substituting calamondins for kumquats,
using 2 cups water instead of water *and*
lemon juice and increasing amount of

sugar for each cup fruit mixture to 2–
2½ cups. About 83 calories per tablespoon.

GINGERED PEAR AND PINEAPPLE PRESERVES
Makes 15 half pints

Grated rind of 2 lemons
Juice of 2 lemons
10 pounds underripe pears
1 medium-size firm pineapple
1 pound crystallized ginger, coarsely
chopped
5 pounds sugar

Place lemon rind and juice in a very
large enamel or stainless-steel kettle.
Peel, quarter, and core pears, one at a
time; divide each quarter lengthwise
into 3 wedges, then slice thin, letting
pear fall into lemon juice in kettle and
tossing occasionally to mix. Peel
pineapple, quarter lengthwise, and
remove hard core; cut quarters into
long, slim wedges, then slice thin; add
to kettle along with ginger and sugar.
Set, uncovered, over moderately high
heat and bring to a boil, stirring
occasionally. Adjust heat so mixture
boils *very gently* and boil uncovered,
stirring occasionally, 1–1¼ hours until
the consistency of marmalade. Meanwhile, wash and sterilize 15 half-pint
jars and closures; stand them on a
baking sheet and keep hot in a 250° F.
oven until needed. Ladle preserves into
jars, filling to within ⅛″ of the tops;
wipe rims and seal. Cool, check seals,
label, and store in a cool, dark, dry
place. Let stand 2–3 weeks before using.
About 45 calories per tablespoon.

BLUE RIDGE APPLE BUTTER
Makes 4 half pints

4 pounds tart cooking apples, washed,
cored, and sliced but not peeled
3 cups apple cider or water
2 cups sugar (about)
1 teaspoon cinnamon
¼ teaspoon allspice
¼ teaspoon cloves
¼ teaspoon salt

Boil apples and cider, uncovered, in a large enamel or stainless-steel kettle, stirring frequently, about 20 minutes until mushy; put through a fine sieve, pressing out as much liquid as possible. Measure apple pulp and for each 1 cup add ½–¾ cup sugar, depending on how sweet you like things. Put pulp, sugar, spices, and salt in a clean enamel or stainless-steel kettle and cook, uncovered, very slowly about 1½ hours, stirring often, until very thick (spoon a little mixture on a cold saucer, if it cools into a smooth firm mass, butter is done). Meanwhile, wash and sterilize 4 half-pint jars and closures and keep hot on a baking sheet in a 250° F. oven until needed. Spoon apple butter into jars, filling to within ¼″ of tops, wipe rims, seal, and process in a hot water bath* 10 minutes. Cool, check seals, label, and store in a cool, dark, dry place several weeks before serving. About 35 calories per tablespoon.

⊠ LEMON CHEESE (LEMON CURD)

Use as a filling for cakes, pies, sweet rolls, or as a spread for hot breads. Makes about 1 quart

1 cup butter
2 cups sugar
3 tablespoons finely grated lemon rind
⅔ cup lemon juice
⅛ teaspoon salt
4 eggs

Melt butter in the top of a double boiler over simmering water. Add sugar, lemon rind, juice, and salt and stir until sugar dissolves, 2–3 minutes. Beat eggs until frothy, mix in about 1 cup lemon mixture, return to double boiler and cook and stir 7–9 minutes until thick. Ladle into small jars, cover and cool to room temperature. Store in refrigerator. About 55 calories per tablespoon.

CHAPTER 26
CANNING AND FREEZING

CANNING

Canning dates to the Napoleonic Wars, when the French Government offered twelve thousand francs to the man who could discover a way of preserving rations. The man who did was François Appert, his method being to seal food in bottles and boil them in water. Appert did not know why the process worked; Louis Pasteur would determine that half a century later.

Canned food revolutionized world eating habits by making seasonal and regional foods widely available year round. Groceries and home pantries alike towered with tins of meat, fish, fruit, and vegetables. But their popularity declined abruptly after World War II with the mass availability of commercial frozen foods, which, everyone marveled, "tasted every bit as good as the fresh."

Freezing also proved to be an easier, more economical and reliable method of conserving food at home and has since made home canning of meats, poultry, fish, and game almost obsolete. The section on freezing covers these foods fully. Because space is limited, there is room here only to cover the rudiments of canning and to concentrate upon those foods still commonly canned at home— fruits and vegetables. Those seeking fuller coverage should obtain U. S. Department of Agriculture bulletins on the canning of meat, poultry, fruits, and vegetables (available through county agricultural extension offices or by writing the Office of Information, U.S.D.A., Washington, D.C. 20250). Invaluable, too, are the excellent booklets published by manufacturers of preserving jars.

The Equipment of Canning

1½–2-Gallon Kettles, preferably stainless-steel or enamel, for sterilizing jars, blanching and precooking foods.

Water Bath Canner: Any big kettle fitted with a wire or wooden rack and tight lid will work.

Pressure Cooker for canning low-acid vegetables, meats, poultry, fish, and game.

Preserving Jars and Closures: There are a number of types, each available in half-pint, pint, quart, and half-gallon sizes, but those most suitable for home use are the half pint, pint, and quart. Most popular today are the *Standard* and *Wide-Mouth Jars with Screw Bands and Dome Caps* (use dome caps one time only but reuse screw bands if in good condition). Also available are *Jars with Porcelain-Lined Zinc Caps and Rubber Sealing Rings* (the jars and caps are reusable, but the rubber rings should be used one time only if you are to be assured of a tight vacuum seal); and finally, *Old-Fashioned Jars with Glass Lids, Clamp-Down Springs, and Rubber Sealing Rings* (again the jars and lids are reusable if in perfect condition—no chips or cracks—but the rubber rings should be used only once).

Other Useful Implements:
Wide-Mouth Funnel for easier jar filling

Colanders and Large Strainers for washing and preparing foods to be canned

Scales

Clock or Timer

Blanching or Deep-Fat-Frying Basket

Cup, Pint, and Quart Measuring Cups; Measuring Spoons

Large and Small Knives; Long-Handled Forks, Ladles, Spoons, and Slotted Spoons

Tongs or Bottle Holder

About Pressure Cookers

The most expensive single piece of equipment needed for canning, a pressure cooker should be chosen carefully. It should be sturdy, of heavy metal construction with a tightly fitting lid equipped with a *pressure gauge* (to indicate steam pressure inside cooker), a *petcock* (valve to allow air and steam to escape when opened and pressure to build up when closed), and a *safety valve* (emergency steam release that "blows" when pressure overbuilds).

Caring for a Pressure Cooker:
—Sponge (but do not scour) kettle in hot soapy water after each use and dry thoroughly. The lid should never be immersed in water; sponge off and wipe dry, paying special attention to edges, crevices, and valves. Take care not to bang or roughen rims of kettle or cover.
—Keep petcock, pressure gauge, and safety valve clean and unclogged by drawing a string through the openings. If safety valve is the ball-and-socket variety, wash well after each use.
—Have pressure gauge checked at the beginning of each canning season (county agricultural extension agents and some manufacturer's dealers can assist you). If the gauge is 5 pounds off or more, invest in a new pressure cooker. Otherwise, mark prominently on kettle or tag the lid with the test results, i.e., "pressure 1 pound high" or "pressure 2 pounds low" so that you will automatically compensate when using kettle.
—If cooker has a rubber gasket, keep clean and grease-free. Also check before using to make sure it shows no signs of age (cracking or softening). If so, replace with a new gasket.
—Never use metal brighteners in a pressure cooker; they may wear off the finish.
—Never subject a pressure cooker to abrupt temperature changes by pouring cold water into a hot cooker or plunging it in cold water. Doing so may warp or crack the cooker.
—Store cooker uncovered, stuffed with paper toweling to absorb any odors and moisture. Wrap lid separately and set on kettle askew *and* upside down.

Using a Pressure Cooker: Keep manufacturer's instructions handy and reread carefully at the beginning of each new canning season or whenever you

TO PROCESS AT 10 POUNDS PRESSURE

If Gauge Reads Low by:	*If Gauge Reads High by:*
1 pound, process at 11 pounds	1 pound, process at 9 pounds
2 pounds, process at 12 pounds	2 pounds, process at 8 pounds
3 pounds, process at 13 pounds	3 pounds, process at 7 pounds
4 pounds, process at 14 pounds	4 pounds, process at 6 pounds

have not used pressure cooker for some months.

The Care of Preserving Jars and Closures

– Carefully examine jars before using, rejecting any with nicks or cracks. Also discard warped, dented, or rusty lids or screw bands or caps with loose linings.
– Do not reuse rubber rings or dome caps; they may not seal properly.
– Wash jars and closures in hot soapy water after each use and then again *before* using. Rinse well in hot water.

– *To Sterilize Jars and Closures* (essential for foods *not processed* in a boiling water bath or pressure cooker). Stand jars on a rack in a large kettle, add water to cover, bring to a full rolling boil, cover kettle, and boil 10 minutes. Closures usually need only to be scalded, but treatment varies according to type, so follow manufacturer's instructions.
– Whether sterilized or not, jars and closures should be immersed in hot water until they are needed; for pickles, preserves, jams, and jellies, they may be kept hot in a 250° F. oven.

The Terms and Techniques of Canning

Acid and Low-Acid Foods: Any food with a high acid content—either natural, as in fruit, or artificial, as in pickles—is an acid food. Vegetables (except tomatoes), all meats and fish are low-acid foods. Acid foods are processed in a water bath, low-acid foods must be pressure processed.

To Blanch: To dip raw food in boiling water or to steam briefly to set juices, reduce bulk, intensify color, or facilitate peeling.

Botulism: A serious, often-fatal form of food poisoning that develops in low-acid foods. Sadly, it usually gives no clues. The best preventive is to can foods with the utmost care, using equipment in perfect working order. Whenever in doubt about a can of food, *boil, covered, a full 15 minutes before tasting* (corn should be boiled 20 minutes). If food should foam during heating or develop an off odor, discard immediately (where neither children nor animals will find it). Also wash and sterilize any implements that touched the food before using again.

Closure: A cap, lid, or its component parts used to seal preserving jars airtight.

Enzymes: Natural chemical agents in food which, if not destroyed in canning, will alter color, texture, and flavor of food.

Flat-Sour: A common form of spoilage among canned foods, easily detected by its sour smell. Careful canning procedures prevent it.

Head Space: The distance between the food level and the top of a jar. Pickles, jams, and jellies should have ⅛″ head space only; they are not processed and food needs no expansion room. With few exceptions, foods processed in a water bath should have ¼″–½″ head space and those in a pressure cooker 1″.

Microorganisms: The microscopic yeasts, molds, and bacteria that can cause food to spoil. The purpose of processing is to destroy them.

To Pack: To fill jars with food to be preserved. There are two methods:

Hot Pack: Packing food at or near the boiling point into hot jars. Sometimes the food is cooked or partially so, sometimes merely brought to boiling.

Cold (or Raw) Pack: Packing cold, raw food into hot jars. Food is then covered with boiling liquid (syrup, juice, or water), sealed, and processed.

To Precook: To partially or fully cook food prior to canning. The purpose is to drive out air, making food more compact.

To Process: To destroy microorganisms

in canned food by heating in a pressure cooker or water bath prescribed lengths of time. Pickles and preserves should be processed in a *hot water bath* (water temperature 180–85° F., not boiling) but fruits and tomatoes in a *boiling water bath* (212° F.).

To Sterilize: To kill microorganisms on preserving jars and lids by scalding or boiling in water.

To Seal: To make jar closures airtight.

To Vent or Exhaust: To force air or steam from a pressure cooker.

Steps to Successful Canning

Initial Preparations:
– At the beginning of the canning season, assemble all equipment and make sure it is in good working order. Have pressure cooker gauge checked for accuracy.
– Examine jars and closures, rejecting any imperfect ones. Buy whatever additional jars and fittings you need early, including spares to replace midseason casualties. At the height of the season, it may be impossible to buy the particular sizes or types you need.
– Buy fresh supplies of dome caps or rubber rings. Wash rubber rings before using and check for resilience, *not* by stretching, which may pull rings out of shape, but by folding in half or pleating. Examine folds closely and reject any rings showing cracks or softness. Also reject any that do not spring back when released.
– If in doubt about a jar or closure, test for leakage. Half fill with water, screw on cap, and stand jar upside down. If water oozes out, try lid on a jar you know to be good, also a good lid on the questionable jar. Discard all faulty jars and lids.
– Reread all instruction booklets for equipment you plan to use.
– Do not attempt to do a season's canning in one day; 1–2 canner loads are sufficient.
– Wash and sterilize jars and closures and keep covered with boiling water until needed.

– Have ready whatever canning syrups you will need.
– Never short-cut safe methods by using canning powders or aspirin.
– Never shorten processing times.
– Follow canning procedures carefully.

Selecting Fruits and Vegetables:
– Choose firm, ripe, garden fresh fruits and vegetables of highest quality. If possible gather your own (some orchards and farms encourage the practice).
– Sort food according to size and color. They will be prettier and process more evenly.
– Can food as soon after gathering as possible. If delayed, store in a cool, well-ventilated spot.

Preparing Fruits and Vegetables:
– Wash carefully, whether or not food is to be peeled. Do small amounts at a time, sloshing up and down in several changes of cool water and handling gently to avoid bruising. Lift from— rather than drain off—the final rinse water, leaving dirt and grit behind. Rinse sink or basin well between washings.
– Do not soak food in water; it will lose flavor and food value.
– Peel and cut fruits and vegetables as the Canning Guide recommends. *Tip:* Peaches, apricots, plums, tomatoes, and other thin-skinned fruits peel quickly, cleanly if plunged in boiling water, then in ice water.

Packing Jars:

In General:
– Lift jars from hot water, one at a time, as you are ready to fill them.
– If using closures requiring rubber rings, lift rings from hot water, fit on jar ledge just below rim, and press flat. Reject and use a fresh ring if first one bulges or buckles.

Cold Pack:
– Fill hot jar quickly with raw food, arranging as attractively as possible and packing all but limas, peas, and corn snugly (being starchy, these will expand during processing; other foods will shrink). Peaches and other large fruit halves will be prettiest layered into

wide-mouth jars, slightly overlapping, with hollows down. To pack berries without crushing, spoon into jar, shaking down occasionally.
– Leave ample head space (follow directions in Canning Guide).
– Pour in enough boiling syrup, water, or juice to cover food, at the same time leaving required head space. To cover food in a 1-quart jar, you will need ½–1½ cups liquid.

Hot Pack:
– Fill hot jars rapidly, one at a time, packing loosely.
– Leave recommended head space (see Canning Guide).
– If food has insufficient juices of its own to cover, add boiling syrup, water, or juice, leaving necessary head space.

Sealing Jars:

In General:
– Work air bubbles out of jar by running a knife around inside walls where bubbles congregate.
– Seal each jar as you fill it.

Jars with Screw Bands and Dome Caps:
– Wipe jar rim with a hot, damp cloth.
– Fit dome cap on with sealing ring against rim.
– Screw metal band on tight—by hand only.

Jars with Porcelain-Lined Zinc Caps:
– Wipe jar rim *and* rubber ring carefully with a hot, damp cloth (a tiny seed or bit of food can prevent a proper seal).
– Screw cap down tight, then turn back ¼″. As soon as jar is processed, cap will be screwed down tight, completing seal.

Jars with Clamp-Type (Lightning) Closures:
– Wipe jar rim *and* rubber ring well with a hot, damp cloth.
– Put glass lid on so it rests squarely on rubber ring.
– Push long wire clamp up into notch on lid; leave short wire up until after processing. Then snap down against jar shoulder to complete the seal.

Processing Jars of Food: (Caution: Never process in an oven; food will not heat through sufficiently and jars may explode.)

In a Boiling Water Bath (212° F.): For Fruits and Tomatoes.
– If food is *Cold Pack,* have water hot but not boiling lest abrupt temperature change crack jars. If food is *Hot Pack,* have water boiling.
– Using tongs or jar holder, lower jars, one at a time, into water bath, adjusting so each stands steady on rack, does not touch its neighbor or canner sides, and is not apt to tilt or tumble during processing.
– When all jars are in the water bath, make sure water level is 1″–2″ above jar tops. Add boiling water, if needed, taking care not to pour directly on jars.
– Cover water bath and, when water comes to a full rolling boil, begin timing the processing (use timetables in Canning Guide).
– Keep water boiling steadily and add boiling water to kettle as needed to keep level well above jars.

Note: Times given in Canning Guide are for altitudes near sea level. If you live at 1,000 feet above sea level or higher, adjust times as below.

– Remove jars from water bath to a wire rack as soon as processing time is up.

In a Pressure Cooker: For Vegetables except Tomatoes.
– Familiarize yourself with pressure cooker and its operation before beginning.
– Place rack in cooker and pour in boiling water to a depth of 2″–3″.
– Stand jars on rack, allowing plenty of space around them. If cooker is deep enough to accommodate 2 layers, place a rack on first layer and stagger jars so they do not stand directly above one another.
– Fasten canner cover as manufacturer directs so steam can escape only through petcock or weighted gauge opening.
– Adjust heat under cooker so that steam streams steadily out of petcock or weighted gauge opening a full 10 minutes, driving air from cooker.
– Close petcock or attach weighted gauge and begin building up pressure.

WATER BATH PROCESSING TIME ADJUSTMENTS FOR HIGH ALTITUDES

Feet above Sea Level	IF TOTAL PROCESSING TIME Is 20 Minutes or Less, Increase by:	IF TOTAL PROCESSING TIME Is More than 20 Minutes, Increase by:
1,000	1 minute	2 minutes
2,000	2 minutes	4
3,000	3	6
4,000	4	8
5,000	5	10
6,000	6	12
7,000	7	14
8,000	8	16
9,000	9	18
10,000	10	20

Note: For more detailed instructions, contact local agricultural extension office or home economics departments of local universities or utility companies.

PRESSURE ADJUSTMENTS FOR HIGH ALTITUDES

Feet above Sea Level	Pressure Needed (Equivalent to 10 Pounds at Sea Level)
2,000	11 pounds
4,000	12
6,000	13
8,000	14
10,000	15

Processing times remain constant.

— When pressure reaches 10 pounds (internal temperature will be 240° F. at altitudes near sea level), begin counting processing time.

— Keep pressure constant by adjusting burner heat and protecting cooker from drafts, *never by opening petcock.*

Note: At altitudes 2,000 feet or more above sea level, pressure greater than 10 pounds will be needed to achieve the necessary 240° F. inside cooker. Follow manufacturer's directions, or make adjustments as above.

— When processing time is up, remove cooker from heat and let stand undisturbed until *2 minutes after pressure has dropped to zero.*

— Open petcock slowly or remove weighted gauge.

— Unlock cover and open cooker, tilting cover away to deflect sudden bursts of steam.

— Lift jars to wire racks, allowing plenty of space around them.

Cooling Processed Jars:

— Complete seals on jars, if necessary, as you lift them to wire rack:

Jars with Screw Bands and Dome Caps: No adjustment needed.

Porcelain-Lined Zinc Caps: Screw down tightly.

Lightning-Type Closures: Snap short wire loop down against jar shoulder.

— Let jars cool at least 12 hours on wire racks, allowing plenty of space between them for air to circulate. Protect from drafts but do not cover with dish towels.

(*Caution:* Never set hot jars directly on a cold counter—they may break.)
– If liquid in a jar has boiled down in processing, do not open jar and add more. Leave jar sealed; food may darken but it is unlikely to spoil.

Checking Seals (*the day after canning*):

Screw Band Closures:
– Remove screw bands, wiping if necessary with a hot damp cloth to loosen.
– Press center of dome cap; if it moves, jar has not sealed. Also tap center of cap; if it makes a clear ringing sound, seal is tight. If it sounds thudding, jar may not have sealed. To test further, slowly turn jar upside down. If there is no leakage, jar is probably properly sealed. *But,* mark jar as questionable and inspect carefully for spoilage before using.

Porcelain-Lined Zinc Caps and Lightning-Type Closures:
– Turn jar halfway over. If there is no leakage, jar is sealed.

If a Jar Has Not Sealed:
– Refrigerate and use contents within 3–4 days.

– *Or* start all over again, packing into a clean, hot jar, reprocessing, and cooling.
– Check questionable jar and closure for defects before reusing.

Labeling and Storing Home-Canned Food:
– Label each jar clearly, including description of contents, canning date, and, if more than one canner load was done that day, load number.
– Include on label any remark to indicate whether seal may be faulty.
– Store jars in a cool, dark, dry place. Dampness can corrode or rust caps, inviting spoilage; warmth and light reduce quality and storage life; freezing may break jars or seals.

Using Home-Canned Foods:
– Use, if possible, within a year after canning. Though safe to eat for several years, home-canned foods lose color, texture, flavor, and food value after a year on the shelf.
– Once a jar is opened, store any unused portion in refrigerator.
– Be alert to symptoms of spoilage (see Why Things Sometimes Go Wrong with Canned Foods). Reject jars with bulging or leaky lids, off colors or odors, mold.

SUGAR SYRUP FOR CANNING AND FREEZING

Type of Syrup	Amount of Sugar or Sugar and Corn Syrup	Amount of Water	Yield
Thin	2 cup sugar *OR* ⅔ cup light corn syrup *and* 1⅓ cups sugar	1 quart	5 cups
Medium	3 cups sugar *OR* 1 cup light corn syrup *and* 2 cups sugar	1 quart	5½ cups
Heavy	4¾ cups sugar *OR* 1½ cups light corn syrup *and* 3¼ cups sugar	1 quart	6½ cups
Extra heavy	7 cups sugar *OR* 2⅓ cups light corn syrup *and* 4⅔ cups sugar	1 quart	7¾ cups

WHY THINGS SOMETIMES GO WRONG WITH CANNED FOODS

Condition	Causes	Safe to Eat?
Bulging lids or can ends	Spoilage	No
Darkened food at top of jar of fruit or pickles	Exposure to air, insufficient liquid to cover, not processed long enough to destroy enzymes.	Yes, IF there is no off odor or other sign of spoilage.
Rose or purple cast in apples, pears, peaches	Chemical reaction during processing.	Yes
Darkened or grayed vegetables	Water used in canning hard OR a reaction of vegetable acids, tanins, or sulfur with metal of cooker or canner.	Probably safe if there is no off odor or other sign of spoilage. If in doubt, discard *without* tasting.
White sediment or cloudy liquid in jar	POSSIBLE SPOILAGE. May also be caused by vegetable starches, minerals in water, or fillers in salt.	No. DO NOT TASTE. Discard.
Floating fruit	Canning syrup too heavy.	Yes
Jar unseals during storage	Spoilage	No
Jar fails to seal	Faulty jar or lid, bit of food on jar rim, failure to follow canning procedures.	Yes — IF discovered immediately after canning and *used* immediately.

NOTE: Beware of and discard — *never taste* — any food that is moldy, mushy, cloudy, soft or slimy, any that bubbles, fizzes, or spurts, any that has an off odor or color.

Also discard those that fizz or spurt when opened. With low-acid vegetables there is also the danger of botulism (see Terms and Techniques of Canning for a discussion of this serious form of food poisoning).

Boil sugar and water, stirring occasionally, until sugar dissolves. Use boiling hot for canning fruits, ice cold for freezing. (*Note:* To cover 1 pint fruit packed for freezing, you will need ½–¾ cup syrup; to cover 1 quart fruit packed for canning, 1–1½ cups.)

To Add Ascorbic Acid (to prevent fruits from darkening): Prepare any of the above syrups as directed, then add to the full amount, just before using, ½ teaspoon ascorbic acid powder or crystals mixed with 1 tablespoon cold water. (*Note:* If using the commercial solutions, add as labels direct.)

CANNING GUIDE FOR FRUITS AND ACID VEGETABLES

— *To Prevent Darkening,* dip apples, apricots, peaches, and pears after cutting in 1 gallon cold water mixed with 2 tablespoons each vinegar and salt. Do not let fruit stand in mixture longer than 20 minutes; drain well before proceeding.
— *Syrup Quantity Needed:* Depending on fruit's juiciness, use 1-1½ cups syrup per quart prepared fruit.
— *Simmering Temperature:* 185-210° F. *Boiling Temperature:* Varies with mixture; it is reached whenever mixture bubbles actively.
— *About Filling Jars:* For *Hot Pack, hot food* goes into *hot jars;* for *Cold Pack, raw food* goes into *hot jars.* Always leave 1/4″-1/2″ head space and make sure food is submerged in juices. Wipe jar rims and screw on caps before processing. *Note:* For best results, follow Steps to Successful Canning, outlined earlier.

Food	Amt. Needed per Quart Canned Food	Preparation	Method	Time in Boiling Water (212° F.) Bath	
				Pints	Quarts
Apples	2½-3 lbs.	Peel, core, cut in wedges; dip to prevent darkening.*	*Hot Pack:* Boil, uncovered, 5 minutes in Thin Syrup; fill jars, cover apples with boiling syrup, leaving 1/2″ head space.	20 min.	20 min.
Applesauce	3-4 lbs.	Prepare as recipe directs; heat to simmering.	*Hot Pack:* Fill jars to within 1/2″ of tops.	20 min.	20 min.
Berries (except strawberries), currants	1½-3 lbs.	Stem, sort, wash, and drain.	*Hot Pack* (for firm berries): Add 1/2 cup sugar to each quart prepared fruit; let stand, covered, 2 hours. Heat to boiling, fill jars to within 1/2″ of tops; if not enough syrup to cover, pour in boiling water to within 1/2″ of tops.	10 min.	15 min.
			Cold Pack (for soft berries): Pour 1/2 cup boiling Thin or Medium Syrup into each jar, add raw berries, shaking to pack without crushing, filling to 1/2″ of tops. Pour in boiling syrup to cover; leave 1/2″ head space.	15 min.	20 min.

Fruit	Amount	Preparation	Method		
Cherries	2-2½ lbs.	Stem, sort, wash, and drain. Pit or not, as you like; if not, prick cherries with sterilized pin to prevent bursting.	*Hot Pack:* Add 1/2-3/4 cup sugar per quart prepared cherries; if unpitted, also add a little water to prevent scorching; heat to simmering. Fill jars with cherries to within 1/2" of tops, cover with boiling Thin Syrup, leaving 1/2" head space.	10 min.	15 min.
			Cold Pack: Pour 1/2 cup boiling Medium or Heavy Syrup into each jar, fill to within 1/2" of tops with cherries, shaking down to pack without crushing. Cover with boiling syrup, leaving 1/2" head space.	20 min.	25 min.
Figs	1½-2½ lbs.	Use firm figs only; wash and drain but do not peel or stem.	*Hot Pack:* Cover figs with water, bring to a boil, let stand off heat 5 minutes; drain. Fill jars with figs to within 1/2" of tops, add 1 tablespoon lemon juice to each quart, cover figs with boiling Thin Syrup; leave 1/2" head space.	1 hr. and 25 min.	1½ hrs.
Fruit juices	—	Extract juice from fruit as in making jelly.* Sweeten to taste.	*Hot Pack:* Pour simmering hot into jars, leaving 1/2" head space.	5 min.	5 min.
Fruit purées	—	Use fleshy, ripe fruit. Wash, stem, and pit; do not peel. Add a little water to prevent sticking; simmer until soft. Purée in a food mill or sieve, sweeten to taste.	*Hot Pack:* Pack simmering hot in jars, leaving 1/2" head space.	10 min.	10 min.
Grapes	2-2½ lbs.	Stem, wash, and drain but do not peel or seed.	*Cold Pack:* Pour 1/2 cup boiling Medium Syrup into each jar; fill with grapes to within 1/2" of tops, add more boiling syrup; leave 1/2" head space.	15 min.	20 min.

CANNING GUIDE FOR FRUITS AND ACID VEGETABLES (continued)

Food	Amt. Needed per Quart Canned Food	Preparation	Method	Time in Boiling Water (212° F.) Bath	
				Pints	Quarts
Peaches, pears, nectarines, apricots	2-3 lbs.	Peel peaches, pears; apricots, nectarines may or may not be; halve, pit, or core, removing gritty, stringy flesh; dip to prevent darkening,* drain and rinse.	Hot Pack: Heat fruit to simmering in Medium Syrup; pack, hollows down, to within 1/2" of jar tops. Cover with boiling syrup, leaving 1/2" head space.	20 min.	25 min.
			Cold Pack (for all except pears): Pack raw fruit, hollows down, to within 1/2" of jar tops. Cover with boiling Medium Syrup; leave 1/2" head space.	25 min.	30 min.
Persimmons (wild)	—	Prepare as for Fruit Purée.	Hot Pack: Pack boiling hot in jars, leaving 1/2" head space.	15 min.	20 min.
Plums	1½-2½ lbs.	Choose firm plums; wash and peel or not; if unpeeled, prick with sterilized pin to prevent bursting.	Hot Pack: Cover plums with Heavy or Medium Syrup and heat to boiling. Cover and let stand off heat 1/2 hour. Pack plums in jars and cover with boiling syrup, leaving 1/2" head space.	20 min.	25 min.
Rhubarb	1-2 lbs.	Wash and trim stalks but do not peel; cut in 1" chunks.	Hot Pack: Mix each quart prepared rhubarb with 3/4-1 cup sugar, cover, let stand 3-4 hours. Bring slowly to boiling; boil 1/2 minute. Pack in jars, leaving 1/2" head space.	10 min.	10 min.

Tomatoes*	2½-3½ lbs.	Use perfect, firm-ripe tomatoes; peel and core but leave whole.	*Cold Pack:* Pack whole tomatoes in jars to within 1/2″ of tops; press gently to fill space. Add no liquid. Add 1/2 teaspoon salt to each pint, 1 teaspoon to each quart.	35 min. — 45 min.
		Same as above except quarter tomatoes instead of leaving whole.	*Hot Pack:* Heat and stir tomatoes until boiling. Pack into jars, leaving 1/2″ head space; add 1/2 teaspoon salt to each pint jar, 1 teaspoon salt to each quart.	10 min. — 15 min.
Tomato juice*	3-3½ lbs.	Wash, core, and dice soft-ripe tomatoes; heat and stir until mushy; strain. Add 1 teaspoon salt to each 1 quart juice.	*Hot Pack:* Pour boiling hot into jars, filling to within 1/4″ of tops.	10 min. — 15 min.

Note: For canning, use only *vine-ripened* tomatoes that are red, juicily plump, and filled with a rich tomato bouquet. Tomatoes picked green may lack the natural acids needed in order for them to can safely by the Boiling Water Bath method.

1255

CANNING GUIDE FOR LOW-ACID VEGETABLES

Note: Only those vegetables particularly suited to canning are included here, those that remain firm, colorful, flavorful.

Not Recommended for Canning: Broccoli, Brussels sprouts, cabbage, cauliflower, eggplant, leafy greens, okra, onions, rutabaga, turnips.

— Before beginning, read About Pressure Cookers and Steps to Successful Canning.
— *About Filling Jars:* The *Cold Pack* method, once thought risky for low-acid vegetables, has recently been proved safe for asparagus, carrots, green and black-eyed peas, lima, green, and wax beans, corn. It is included along with the *Hot Pack* method.

Food	Amt. Needed per Quart Canned Food	Preparation	Method	Processing Time at 10 lbs. Pressure	
				Pints	Quarts
Asparagus	2½–4½ lbs.	Use tender, tight-tipped stalks; wash, remove woody ends, scales. Rinse, leave whole or cut in 1″ lengths.	*Hot Pack:* Boil 3 minutes in water to cover; if whole, pack close together, stems down to within 1″ of jar tops. Add 1 teaspoon salt to each quart, cover with boiling cooking water, leaving 1″ head space.	25 min.	30 min.
			Cold Pack: Pack *raw* asparagus as for Hot Pack, adding salt, covering with fresh boiling water and leaving 1″ head space.	25 min.	30 min.
Beans (green and wax)	1½–2½ lbs.	Use young, tender beans. Wash, drain, string, trim off ends, and cut in 2″ lengths.	*Hot Pack:* Boil 3 minutes in water to cover; pack in jars to within 1″ of tops; add 1 teaspoon salt per quart, cover with boiling cooking water, leaving 1″ head space.	20 min.	25 min.
			Cold Pack: Pack *raw* beans as directed for Hot Pack, add salt, cover with fresh boiling water, filling to within 1″ of jar tops.	20 min.	25 min.

Vegetable	Amount	Preparation	Directions	Pints	Quarts
Beans (lima)	3-5 lbs. (unshelled)	Select young tender beans; wash, drain, and shell. Wash once more.	*Hot Pack:* Boil 3 minutes in water to cover; spoon beans in jars to within 1" of tops; add 1 teaspoon salt to each quart, cover with boiling water, leaving 1" head space. *Cold Pack:* Loosely spoon *raw* beans into jars, add salt as directed for Hot Pack and pour in fresh boiling water, leaving 1" head space.	40 min.	50 min. *Note:* If beans are large, process an extra 10 minutes.
Beets	2-3½ lbs. (minus tops)	Sort beets by size; cut off tops, leaving 1" stems on, also leave roots on. Wash well and boil in water to cover 15-25 minutes until skins slip off. Skin, trim, If small, leave whole; if not, halve, quarter, slice, or dice.	*Hot Pack:* Fill jars with hot beets to within 1" of tops, add 1 teaspoon salt to each quart; cover with fresh boiling water, leaving 1" head space.	30 min.	35 min.
Carrots	2-3 lbs. (minus tops)	Wash carrots, peel, and wash again. Leave whole, slice, or cube.	*Hot Pack:* Boil 3 minutes in water to cover; fill jars with carrots, to within 1" of tops, add 1 teaspoon salt per quart; pour in boiling cooking water, leaving 1" head space. *Cold Pack:* Pack raw carrots in jars as directed for Hot Pack, add salt, and cover with fresh boiling water, leaving 1" head space.	25 min.	30 min. 25 min. 30 min.
Celery	1½-2 lbs. (minus tops)	Discard tops; scrub well, rinse; trim stalks of coarse parts and cut in 2" lengths.	*Hot Pack:* Boil 3 minutes in water to cover; pack celery in jars to within 1" of tops, add 1 teaspoon salt to each quart, cover with boiling cooking water, leaving 1" head space.	30 min.	35 min.

CANNING GUIDE FOR LOW-ACID VEGETABLES (continued)

Food	Amt. Needed per Quart Canned Food	Preparation	Method	Processing Time at 10 lbs. Pressure	
				Pints	Quarts
Corn (cream-style)	10-16 ears	Husk corn, remove silks; following directions in vegetable chapter, cut corn from cobs as for cream-style corn.*	Hot Pack: Measure corn pulp; to each quart add 2½ cups boiling water and 1 teaspoon salt; boil together 3 minutes, ladle into pint jars, filling to within 1" of tops.	1 hr. and 25 min.	Not Recommended
			Cold Pack: Fill pint jars to within 1" of tops with raw corn pulp; add 1/2 teaspoon salt to each jar, add boiling water; leave 1" head space.	1 hr. and 35 min.	Not Recommended
Corn (whole kernel)	8-16 ears	Husk corn, remove silks; following directions in vegetable chapter, cut corn from cobs as for whole kernel corn.*	Hot Pack: Measure kernels; to each quart add 1 pint boiling water and 1 teaspoon salt; boil 3 minutes, then fill jars to within 1" of tops.	55 min.	1 hr. and 25 min.
			Cold Pack: Loosely fill jars with raw kernels to within 1" of tops; add 1 teaspoon salt to each quart, cover with boiling water, leaving 1" head space.	55 min.	1 hr. and 25 min.
Parsnips	2-3 lbs.	Scrub well, peel, and wash. Slice or leave whole.	Hot Pack: Boil 3 minutes in water to cover; pack in jars to within 1" of tops; add 1 teaspoon salt to each quart, cover with boiling cooking water, leaving 1" head space.	30 min.	35 min.
Peas (black-eyed)	3-6 lbs. (unshelled)	Shell peas, wash, and drain.	Hot Pack: Boil 3 minutes in water just to cover; pour into jars, leaving 1" head space. Add 1 teaspoon salt to each quart, also, if needed, boiling water to cover peas.	35 min.	40 min.
			Cold Pack: Pack raw peas loosely in jars to within 1" of tops; add salt as for Hot Pack, also boiling water to cover, leaving 1" head space.	35 min.	40 min.

1258

Vegetable	Amount	Preparation	Directions	Pints	Quarts
Peas (green)	3-6 lbs. (unshelled)	Shell peas and wash; drain well.	*Hot Pack:* Boil small peas 3 minutes in water just to cover, large peas 5 minutes; pour into jars, leaving 1" head space; add 1 teaspoon salt to each quart and, if needed, boiling water to cover peas.	40 min.	40 min.
			Cold Pack: Loosely pack *raw* peas in jars, leaving 1" head space; add 1 teaspoon salt to each quart. Pour in boiling water to within 1" of jar tops.	40 min.	40 min.
Potatoes (Irish)	5-6 lbs.	Use freshly dug new potatoes of uniform size; scrub, peel, and wash. Leave whole.	*Hot Pack:* Boil 10 minutes, drain well. Pack potatoes in jars to within 1" of tops; add 1 teaspoon salt per quart, add boiling water to cover potatoes, leaving 1" head space.	30 min.	40 min.
Potatoes (sweet)	2-3 lbs.	Use freshly dug, small-to-medium sweet potatoes. Scrub well, parboil 20 minutes to loosen skins. Do not prick. Skin, leave whole, halve, or quarter.	*Hot Pack (Dry):* Pack hot potatoes in jars, filling to within 1" of tops; press gently to fill spaces; add no salt or liquid.	65 min.	1 hr. and 35 min.
			Hot Pack (Wet): Fill jars to within 1" of tops with hot potatoes; add 1 teaspoon salt to each quart; cover with boiling water or Medium Syrup (see Canning Syrups), leaving 1" head space.	55 min.	1½ hrs.
Pumpkin and winter squash	1½-3 lbs.	Halve pumpkin or squash, remove seeds, cut in 2" chunks, and peel. Steam until tender, 20-25 minutes; purée in a food mill.	*Hot Pack:* Heat and stir purée to simmering; ladle into jars, filling to within 1" of tops. Add no liquid or salt.	65 min.	1 hr. and 20 min.
Summer squash	2-4 lbs.	Select, tender-skinned young squash. Wash well but do not peel. Slice 1/2" thick.	*Hot Pack:* Steam 3 minutes, pack hot in jars, leaving 1" head space. Add 1 teaspoon salt to each quart, pour in boiling water to cover squash; leave 1" head space.	30 min.	40 min.
Tomatoes	(see Canning Guide for Fruits and Acid Vegetables)				

FREEZING

Frozen food is as old as the Eskimos. Throughout history, men have sought scientific ways of freezing food, and no less a person than Sir Francis Bacon caught his death trying to freeze chickens by packing them with snow. Early in the twentieth century an American scientist named Clarence Birdseye sampled frozen venison and fish while on expedition to Labrador and found both remarkably like the fresh. He also watched fish, pulled live from the sea, freeze solid in minutes. Quick-freezing, Birdseye suspected, was the key to quality, and he set to work devising mechanical means of quick-freezing fish, meat, fruits, and vegetables. His frozen foods went on sale in the 1930's, but unfortunately few people could afford them. It was not until after World War II that the Age of Frozen Foods arrived.

Today the home freezer ranks in importance with the range and refrigerator. Nearly a third of America's families own home freezers—"mini-markets" stocked with out-of-season fruits and vegetables, meats bought "on special," the catch of fishing and hunting expeditions, brown-and-serve breads, instant dinners and party snacks. Freezing is not only the fastest, easiest, and most economical way of preserving foods at home, it is also the one that alters flavor, color, and food value the least. The intense heat of canning required to kill microorganisms and stop enzymatic action changes the character of food. Not so freezing, which does not destroy microorganisms or enzymatic action, merely stops them cold.

About Home Freezers

To freeze food successfully, a freezer must maintain a temperature of 0° F. or lower. Most refrigerator frozen food compartments average 20–32° F. and, though suitable for storing frozen foods short periods of time, are not adequate for freezing food. A home freezer is essential; which size and model you choose depends upon your individual needs and preferences.

The Equipment of Home Freezing

Most of the paraphernalia of canning is useful: large kettles (stainless-steel, enameled metal, or other material that will not react with acid foods), sieves, colanders, blanching baskets, long-handled spoons and forks, funnels, cup measures, measuring spoons, knives, etc. (see The Equipment of Canning). In addition, the following will be useful:

Hand or Electric Vegetable Shredder-Chopper-Slicer for shredding, chopping, or slicing foods to be frozen.

Food Mill or Electric Blender for puréeing foods.

Meat Grinder for grinding foods.

Potato Masher for mashing foods.

Pancake Turner for handling foods to be frozen.

Shallow Baking Pans for freezing rolls or cookies. Once foods are frozen, they can be removed from pans and bundled in plastic bags, freeing pans for use.

Freezer Thermometer for checking freezer temperature.

Freezer Packaging Materials (*Note:* To be effective, freezer wraps must be both moisture- and vaporproof).

– Aluminum Foil: Multipurpose but especially suited to wrapping meats, fish, poultry, and bulky, irregular-shaped foods and covering to-be-frozen casseroles. (*Tip:* Pad sharp bones with "wads" of foil—keeps them from piercing outer wrapper.)

– Plastic Food Wraps: Unusually soft and pliable; best for wrapping irregular shapes and soft foods.

– Plastic Bags, Pouches: Good for all but sharp or extra-large foods. *Tip:* To fill quickly, spoon food into a wide-mouth jar, invert bag over top, then turn upside down.

– Laminated Papers: Double-ply papers (cellophane, plastic, or foil bonded to heavy paper). Best for wrapping large, heavy roasts, poultry, or fish. These are reusable but must be sterilized by soaking 15 minutes in 1 quart warm water mixed with 1 teaspoon liquid chlorine bleach.

– Outer Wraps: Cloth stockinettes (available in most housewares departments) and butcher paper can both be used. They're needed to reinforce extra-large or heavy packages against freezer wear and tear.

– Freezer Tapes: A special, pliable tape that holds fast in subzero temperatures.

– Pasteboard and Plastic Containers: Sturdy and available in assorted sizes (the 1-pint size holds 3–4 vegetable or soup servings, 2–3 meat servings). Ideal for juicy or fragile foods. Reusable but, like laminated papers, these must be sterilized (use the same method).

– Freezer Jars: Wide-mouth glass jars available in half-pint, pint, and 3-cup sizes. Best for liquids, juicy or highly seasoned foods. Sterilize jars and closures before using (follow directions for sterilizing jars in canning section).

About Additives and Antibrowning Agents Used in Freezing

Sugar: Most fruits are packed in sugar or sugar syrup; use granulated sugar, not brown, which will darken fruits.

Salt: Vegetables to be frozen are sometimes washed or rinsed in salt water; use the uniodized to prevent discoloration.

Water: If hard or brackish, the water used for blanching foods may cause darkening. Soften water, if necessary, following method described in chapter on pickles, preserves, jams, and jellies.

Antibrowning Agents: Unless specially treated, apples, avocados, peaches, apricots, most varieties of pears and plums will darken during freezing. The most common preventives are:

Ascorbic Acid (Vitamin C): Available in tablet, powder, and crystalline form, also commercial solutions (usually sweetened mixtures of ascorbic and citric acid; use as labels instruct).

Citric Acid: The acid of citrus fruits and a less effective antibrowning agent than ascorbic acid; follow label directions.

Lemon Juice: Recommended only when ascorbic or citric acid is unavailable. To use, mix ¼ cup lemon juice with 1 gallon cold water and dip cut fruits; drain before packing.

Sodium Sulfite or Bisulfite: For apples only. Buy pharmaceutical grades at drugstores and use as labels direct.

Steps to Successful Freezing

Initial Preparations:
– Before starting out, assemble all ingredients and equipment.
– Make sure you have plenty of suitable packaging materials and freezer containers (sterilize if necessary).
– Check freezer space and freeze only what food it can accommodate. Most manufacturers recommend adding no more than 2–3 pounds food per cubic foot freezer space.
– Have ready whatever freezing syrups and antibrowning agents you will need.
– Reread freezer and freezer container manufacturer's instruction booklets and freezing procedures before beginning.

Food Selection and Handling:
– Choose top quality fruits, vegetables, meats, poultry, and seafood.

– Avoid foods that freeze poorly:
Avocados (except puréed)
Bananas
Cabbage, Sauerkraut
Celery
Cheese (except hard types)

Cream (except whipped)

Cucumbers

Custard or Cream Pies (or cream-filled
    pastries, cakes, cookies)

Eggs (in the shell, hard-cooked whites)

Egg or Cream-Thickened Sauces,
    Mayonnaise, Salad Dressings

Gelatins

Lettuce or Other Salad Greens

Long-Grain Rice

Irish Potatoes (except fried)

Tomatoes (except puréed and cooked)

– Wrap and quick-freeze all foods as
soon as possible after obtaining. If
necessary to postpone freezing, keep
refrigerated.

– Handle foods to be frozen as little as
possible.

– Freeze in practical meal-size portions.

– Follow freezing directions carefully;
don't take short cuts.

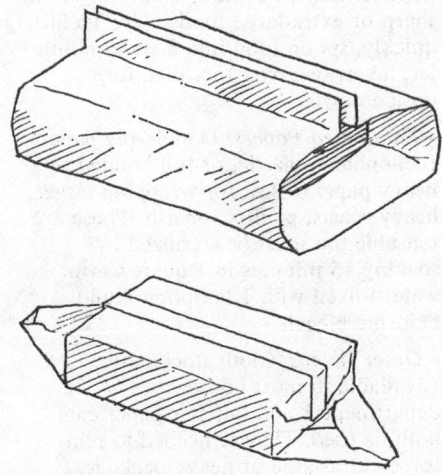

Drugstore Wrap

Packing and Wrapping:

– Pack liquid or fragile foods in sturdy,
leakproof containers.

– Use drugstore or butcher wrap for
wrapping meats, poultry, seafood,
other large, firm pieces.

– Double-wrap large, bulky, or angular
pieces as an extra precaution against
freezer wear and tear.

– Always wrap snugly, pressing out all
air pockets. Sloppy wrapping invites
"freezer burn" (streaked, faded, shriveled
spots) and spoilage.

– Use freezer tape only for sealing
packages; cellophane tape will come
unstuck.

– Wipe container rims before sealing; a
wide-mouth funnel reduces spillage.

– Wipe spills from packages before
freezing.

– Leave ½″–¾″ head space in freezer
jars, containers or bags (unless otherwise
directed) to allow for expansion of
food during freezing.

– Label packages clearly with wax pencil,
noting kind of food, weight or number
of servings, date, and any cooking or
serving tips.

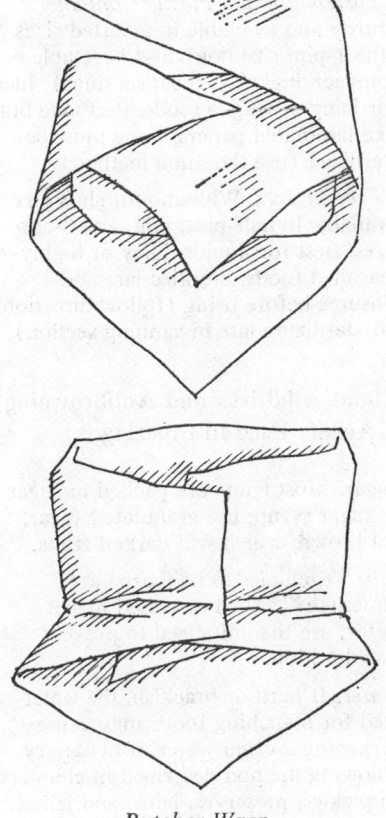

Butcher Wrap

Freezing and Storing:
– If freezer has a temperature control, turn to coldest setting 24 hours before adding food. The quicker food is frozen, the smaller the ice crystals and the better the food's texture.
– Place packages directly on freezing surfaces, leaving 1″ space around each.
– Allow 12 hours for food to freeze; if not solid in that length of time, check freezer temperature. If above 0° F., transfer unfrozen food to refrigerator and use as soon as possible.
– If you overestimate freezer capacity, refrigerate overflow packages and use within 24 hours.
– For most efficient freezer use, keep fully loaded.
– Stack frozen foods compactly in freezer and check occasionally for torn wrappers. Overwrap ripped packages or use within 1–2 weeks.
– Rotate food in freezer so that older packages are used first. Also group food by type so it will be easier to find.
– Maintain freezer temperature at 0° F. and open freezer only when necessary.
– Keep freezer inventory up to date.

– *If power should fail:* Leave freezer closed. In a fully loaded freezer, food will stay frozen up to 2 days, even in hot weather; in a half-full freezer, about 24 hours. If power will be off longer than 2 days, transfer food to a locker plant or pack in dry ice; 25 pounds dry ice will hold a fully loaded 10-cubic-foot freezer 3–4 days, a half-full freezer 2–3 days. (*Note:* Ventilate room while using dry ice.)

Thawing and Using Frozen Foods:
– Defrost foods before cooking or using only if necessary. Fruits are best thawed only enough to separate; so are minced onions or peppers and sliced mushrooms. Most vegetables should be cooked from the solidly frozen state in a minimum of water (corn on the cob is the exception; unwrap and thaw 20 minutes, then boil 5–8 minutes in plenty of unsalted water). Directions for cooking frozen meat, poultry, and seafood are included in each of those chapters.

– Unless directed to the contrary, thaw frozen foods in their wrappers. Set in a pan to catch drips (savory juices can be used in gravies, sauces, and stews).
– Thaw at room temperature or in the refrigerator (refrigerator thawing takes twice as long. A 1-pint package will thaw in 2–3 hours at room temperature, in 4–6 in the refrigerator).
– Never thaw frozen food in warm water unless directions recommend it.
– Check thawing packages frequently, also turn often, and use while still well chilled. Never allow to come to room temperature.

About Refreezing Thawed Food:
– Never refreeze any food that has reached 40° F. internal temperature (check with a freezer thermometer). That registering less than 40° F. or still showing ice crystals may be safely refrozen, though flavor, color, and texture will suffer.
– Inspect partially thawed food carefully and do not refreeze any that has an off color or aroma. Be particularly careful about seafood and poultry; they spoil more quickly than red meats.
– Never risk eating any food you suspect may be spoiled; and don't feed to pets (they get food poisoning too).

FREEZING GUIDE FOR FRUITS

– Freeze fruit varieties that freeze well; county home agents can recommend best local "freezers."
– Freeze fruits in sturdy, leakproof containers. (*Tip:* 1 quart size fills a 9″ pie.)
– Use one of the following methods of packing and treat apples, apricots, pears, peaches, plums, and other fruits that darken on exposure to air with ascorbic acid or other antibrowning agent (read About Additives and Antibrowning Agents Used in Freezing).
– Pack, seal, and freeze as fast as possible. Note type of pack on label as well as date, kind of fruit, number of servings, etc.

FREEZING GUIDE FOR FRUITS

Fruit	Amt. Needed To Fill 1 Pint	Preparation	Method, Recommended Packs
Apples (use crisp varieties)	1½ lbs.	Peel, core, slice medium thick, letting drop in 1 gal. cold water mixed with 2 T. salt; drain, rinse. If to be packed in sugar or unsweetened, soak 5 minutes in 1 gal. cold water mixed with 1 t. sodium sulfite (obtainable in drugstores). Drain.	*Syrup Pack:* Follow basic method, using Medium Syrup *with* ascorbic acid. *Sugar Pack:* Pack by basic method, using 1/2 t. ascorbic acid and 1/2 cup sugar per quart prepared fruit. *Unsweetened:* Mix 1/2 t. ascorbic acid with each quart prepared fruit; fill containers, leaving required head space.
Applesauce	1 pint	Prepare any recipe, adding 1/2 t. ascorbic acid per cup sugar used. Chill well.	Fill containers, leaving recommended head space.
Avocados	3 medium size	Peel, pit, and mash or puree.	*Sugar Pack:* Follow basic method, mixing 1/2 t. ascorbic acid and 1 cup sugar into each. quart purée. Use for desserts. *Unsweetened:* Mix 1/4 t. ascorbic acid or 2 t. lemon juice with each quart purée. Pack in containers, leaving required head space, or in avocado shells (wrap in foil).
Berries (except strawberries), *Cherries,* *Currants*	1-1⅓ pints 1-1½ lbs.	Sort, wash, drain; stem or hull; leave berries and currants whole; pit cherries but leave whole.	*Syrup Pack:* Pack as directed, using Medium or Heavy Syrup. *Sugar Pack:* Follow basic method, using 3/4 cup sugar per quart prepared fruit. *Unsweetened:* Pack dry, covering if you like, with berry juice, OR freeze spread on trays and package. (*Note:* Not recommended for cherries.)

1264

Fruit	Amt. Needed To Fill 1 Pint	Preparation	Method, Recommended Packs
Fruit purées	—	Purée fruit as directed in Canning Guide for Fruits. When sweetening, use 2/3-1½ cups sugar per quart purée, depending on tartness of fruit.	*Sugar Pack:* If fruit is type that darkens, mix 1/2 t. ascorbic acid with each quart sweetened purée. Pack as directed. *Unsweetened:* Do not sweeten purée but add ascorbic acid as for Sugar Pack. Fill containers, leaving recommended head space.
Oranges, Grapefruit	2-4 medium size	Peel, section or slice, and seed.	*Syrup Pack:* Follow basic method, using Medium Syrup with ascorbic acid. *Unsweetened:* Pack in containers, leaving required head space. Add no liquid.
Grapes	1¼ lbs.	Sort, stem, wash. If seedless, leave whole; if not, halve, seed.	*Syrup Pack:* Pack as directed, using Medium Syrup.
Melons	1½ lbs.	Halve, seed, slice, cube, or cut into balls.	*Syrup Pack:* Follow basic method, using Medium Syrup.
Peaches, Apricots, Nectarines	1-1½ lbs.	Peel, halve, and pit. Leave as halves or slice.	*Syrup Pack:* Follow basic method, using Medium Syrup *with* ascorbic acid. *Sugar Pack:* Mix 1/2-2/3 cup sugar and 1/2 t. ascorbic acid with each quart prepared fruit. Pack as directed. *Unsweetened:* Mix 1/2 t. ascorbic acid in 1 quart cold water. Pack fruit in containers, leaving required head space, cover with water mixture.
Pears	1½ lbs.	Peel, halve, and core. Leave as halves, quarter, or slice.	*Syrup Pack:* Follow basic method, using Medium Syrup *with* ascorbic acid.

Fruit	Amt. Needed To Fill 1 Pint	Preparation	Method, Recommended Packs
Persimmons (wild or cultivated)	—	Prepare like Fruit Purées, sweetening each quart purée with 1 cup sugar.	*Sugar Pack:* Mix 1/8 t. ascorbic acid with each quart sweetened purée. Pack as directed. *Unsweetened:* Do not sweeten purée. Add ascorbic acid as for Sugar Pack, fill containers, leaving recommended head space.
Pineapple	1 small	Peel, core, and remove eyes. Slice, dice, cube, or cut in wedges or sticks.	*Syrup Pack:* Pack as directed, using Medium Syrup. *Unsweetened:* Fill containers, leaving required head space; add water to cover if you like.
Plums	1 lb.	Sort and wash; do not peel. Leave whole or halve and pit.	*Syrup Pack:* Pack as directed, using Medium or Heavy Syrup *with* ascorbic acid. *Unsweetened:* Sprinkle each quart prepared fruit with 1/4 t. ascorbic acid mixed with 2 T. water. Pack in containers, leaving recommended head space.
Rhubarb	1 lb.	Wash and trim stalks; cut in 1"-2" lengths.	*Syrup Pack:* Pack as directed in Heavy Syrup. *Sugar Pack:* Mix 1 cup sugar with each quart prepared fruit. Pack as directed. *Unsweetened:* Fill containers, leaving head space; add no liquid, *OR* freeze spread on trays, then pack.
Strawberries	1½ pints	Wash, sort, and hull. Leave berries whole unless large, then halve or quarter.	*Syrup Pack:* Pack as directed in Medium or Heavy Syrup. *Sugar Pack:* Mix 3/4 cup sugar with each 1 quart prepared fruit; pack as directed. *Unsweetened:* Fill containers, leaving required head space, covering, if you like, with juice from some of the berries. Or spread on trays, freeze, then package.

FREEZING GUIDE FOR VEGETABLES

— Use mature, top quality produce; avoid vegetables that do not freeze well (charts include "good freezers" only).
— Wash in cool water (unless chart notes otherwise) and trim (for detailed preparation steps, see vegetable chapter).
— Blanch as charts recommend, about 1 quart vegetables at a time, in plenty of boiling water, using a fine mesh basket. *Tip:* For small vegetables or those cut fine, line basket with cheesecloth. (*Note:* At altitudes of more than 5,000 feet, add an extra minute to total blanching time.)
— Quick-chill blanched vegetables under cold running water or in ice water. Drain well; do not allow to soak. Pat small vegetables dry on paper toweling.
— Pack in containers (sturdy ones for fragile vegetables), leaving 1/2" head space for pints, 3/4" for larger containers *unless* chart directs otherwise.
— Seal, label, and quick-freeze.

Vegetable	Amount Needed to Fill 1 Pint	Preparation for Freezing	Recommended Blanching Time in Minutes
Asparagus	1-1½ lbs.	Use tender, tightly budded stalks; wash in tepid water, snap off woody ends, remove scales. Sort by size, cut in jar or 2" lengths, blanch, chill, pack snugly, alternating stems and tips for compactness. Leave no head space.	Slim stalks: 2 Medium stalks: 3 Thick stalks: 4
Beans (green and wax)	1 lb.	Use tender young beans; wash, drain, string if needed, trim off ends. Cut in 2" lengths, French or leave whole. Blanch, chill, and pack.	3
Beans (lima)	2-2½ lbs. (unshelled)	Wash, drain, shell, sort by size. Blanch, chill, and pack.	Small beans: 2 Medium beans: 3 Large beans: 4
Beets	1-1½ lbs.	Sort by size, cut off tops, but leave 1" stems on, also roots. Scrub, boil 35-45 minutes until tender; peel, trim, leave whole, slice, or dice. Chill, pack.	None
Broccoli	1 lb.	Remove coarse stems, leaves; peel stalks, wash, separate into stalks of equal size, halving if need be. Make X-cuts in stem ends. Blanch, chill, and pack. Leave no head space.	3
Brussels sprouts	1 lb.	Remove stem ends, coarse outer leaves, make X-cuts in stem ends. Wash in cold salted water, sort by size. Blanch, chill, and pack. Leave no head space.	Small sprouts: 3 Medium sprouts: 4 Large sprouts: 5

FREEZING GUIDE FOR VEGETABLES (continued)

Vegetable	Amount Needed to Fill 1 Pint	Preparation for Freezing	Recommended Blanching Time in Minutes
Carrots	1¼ lbs.	Wash, peel, and trim, wash again. Leave whole if small, otherwise slice, dice, or cut in julienne strips. Blanch, chill, and pack.	Whole carrots: 5 Cut carrots: 2
Cauliflower	1 small	Divide in flowerets, trim, wash, blanch, chill, pack. Leave no head space.	3
Corn on the cob		*For All Styles:* Choose tender young ears; husk and remove silks. Blanch, chill, wrap ears individually in double thickness foil.	Small ears: 3 Medium ears: 5 Large ears: 7
Whole kernel	2-2½ lbs.	Blanch and quick-chill ears, then, following directions in vegetable chapter, cut corn from cobs as for whole kernel corn.* Pack.	All ears: 4
Cream-style		Blanch and quick-chill ears, then cut from cobs as for cream-style corn* in vegetable chapter. Pack.	All ears: 4
Eggplant	1 small	*Do not freeze raw.* Prepare Fried Eggplant recipe, undercooking slightly. Drain on paper toweling; spread 1 layer deep on foil-lined trays and freeze hard. Layer in container, return to freezer. *To serve:* Heat (thawed or unthawed) uncovered in a 350°F. oven 5-10 minutes until of good serving temperature.	None
Greens (beet, chard, collards, kale, mustard, spinach, turnip greens)	1-1½ lbs.	Use young, tender greens; wash, trim off coarse stems, wash again. Blanch, chill, and pack.	Collards: 3 Other greens: 1½-2
Kohlrabi	1½ lbs.	Trim off leaves, stems; wash, peel, cut in 1/2″ cubes. Blanch, chill, pack.	1
Mushrooms	1 lb.	Cut off woody stems; wipe clean, sort by size. Leave whole if small (1″ or less across); slice if large. Blanch, adding 1/4 cup lemon juice per gallon water. Chill and pack.	Sliced or button mushrooms: 2 Whole: 3

Vegetable	Amount	Preparation	Pints per lb.
Okra	1 lb.	Choose tenderest young pods. Remove stems but not caps. Wash well, leave whole or slice 1" thick. Blanch, chill, pack.	Whole pods: 4 Sliced pods: 3
Onions	1 lb.	*Do not freeze whole.* Peel, mince, blanch, chill and pack.	1
Parsnips	1¼ lbs.	Trim, scrub, peel and cut in 1/2" cubes. Blanch, chill and pack.	2
Peas (green, black-eyed)	2-2½ lbs. (unshelled)	Shell, sort by size, blanch, chill and pack.	Baby peas: 1 Medium size: 2
Peppers (sweet green and red)	3-4 medium size	Wash, core and seed. Leave whole, halve crosswise, slice in rings or mince. Blanch, chill and pack.	Whole, halved: 3 Sliced: 2 Minced: 1
Potatoes (Irish)	3 medium	*Do not freeze raw.* Prepare Twice-Fried French Fries recipe *but fry and drain once.* Spread 1-layer deep on foil-lined trays and freeze hard. Pack in containers, return to freezer. *To serve:* Fry second time (solidly frozen) as recipe directs, allowing 1-2 minutes longer.	None
Potatoes (sweet)	3 medium	*Do not freeze raw.* Prepare Mashed Sweet Potatoes recipe, cook, pack, and freeze. Or prepare Orange-Candied Sweet Potatoes, omitting sectioned orange; cool, pack, and freeze. *To serve:* Thaw slightly and reheat slowly.	None
Pumpkin	3-4 lbs.	Prepare Pumpkin Purée recipe; cool, pack, and freeze. Thaw before using.	None
Rutabaga, turnips	1½ lbs.	Trim, peel, wash, cut in 1/2" cubes. Blanch, chill, and pack.	2
Summer squash	1 lb.	Trim, scrub; do not peel if tender; slice 1/2" thick, blanch, chill, and pack.	2
Tomatoes	2 lbs.	*Do not freeze raw.* Wash, peel, core, coarsely chop. Simmer, covered, 15-20 minutes; purée. Simmer, uncovered, until cooked down to 1 pint. Cool, pack, and freeze. *To use:* Thaw and use as you would tomato purée, seasoning to taste.	None
Winter squash	3-4 lbs.	*Do not freeze raw.* Halve, seed, cube, and peel. Steam or boil until tender, 20-25 minutes; drain and mash or purée. Cool, pack, and freeze. *To serve:* Thaw slightly and reheat slowly.	None

Basic Packing Methods

Syrup Pack: Prepare Sugar Syrup for
Canning and Freezing (recipe in canning
section) in strengths the preceding charts
specify, adding ascorbic acid if fruit is
type that darkens; chill syrup. *To Pack:*
Pour ⅓ cup syrup in container, half fill
with fruit, shaking down to pack snugly
without crushing, add fruit to fill, cover
with syrup, leaving required head space.
If fruit floats, push under syrup with a
wad of plastic food wrap or foil and put
lid on container.

Sugar Pack: Measure fruit, spread on
trays (not tin), sprinkle with amount of
sugar charts recommend (granulated,
not brown), mix gently, and let stand
until juices appear and sugar dissolves.
If fruit is type to darken, mix ½ teaspoon
ascorbic acid with each 1 cup sugar
before adding to fruit. Fill containers,
shaking fruit down and leaving necessary
head space.

Unsweetened Pack: Do not use artificial
sweeteners. If fruit is darkening type,
sprinkle each quart fruit with ¼ teaspoon
ascorbic acid dissolved in 2 tablespoons
cold water, *or* if fruit will be packed in
water or juice, add ½ teaspoon
ascorbic acid to each quart liquid. Pack
fruit dry in containers *or* pack dry, then
cover with cold water or juice made by
crushing some of the fruit, in each case
leaving required head space. *Or* spread
fruit one layer deep on foil-lined trays
and freeze solid, then fill containers to
tops.

*Head Space Recommended for All
Packs:* ½″ for pints, ¾″–1″ for larger
containers. (*Note:* Exception is fruit that
is frozen spread out, then packed; in
such instances, fill containers to the
brim.)

Notes:
– Ascorbic acid called for is powder or
crystalline form; if using commercial
solutions, add as labels instruct.
– In preceding charts, T=tablespoon,
t=teaspoon.

ABOUT FREEZING MEAT, GAME, POULTRY, AND GAME BIRDS

Nearly all uncooked, uncured meat,
variety meats, poultry, and game birds
freeze well. Use top qualities only (meat
and poultry should be federally
inspected, game and poultry fully
dressed). No meat or poultry will
improve during freezing, though ice
crystals and enzymes both work to
tenderize them (a not-so-tender steak,
for example, will be tender enough to
broil after 1–2 months in the freezer).

*General Tips for Freezing Meat, Game,
Poultry, and Game Birds:*
– Wrap and quick-freeze as soon after
obtaining as possible.
– Trim off excess fat (pull loose fat from
poultry body cavities) and, whenever
possible, remove bones to conserve
freezer space.
– Shape hamburgers, sausage patties,
meat balls and loaves before freezing.
– Package in meal-size portions or
amounts suitable for family use.
Separate chops, steaks, meat patties,
pieces of chicken with 2 layers of
freezer paper so they can be easily
separated while solidly frozen.
– Wrap snugly, fitting wrapping to
contours of food and pressing out as
much air as possible. Pad sharp bones
with wads of wrapping so they will not
pierce wrapper. Double-wrap delicate or
fragile meats (skinned game birds,
variety meats, etc.).
– Freeze liver, heart, kidneys, tongue,
pork and beef sausages uncooked;
blanch sweetbreads and brains (see
sections on sweetbreads and brains);
fully cook tripe.
– Label packages carefully, indicating
date, cut, and kind of meat or poultry,
weight, and pertinent remarks (whether
chicken is a stewing fowl or broiler-
fryer).

Special Tips for Freezing Poultry and Game Birds:
– Remove any pinfeathers and hairs, also traces of lung or windpipe in body cavity.
– Wash giblets, pack and freeze separately.
– Never stuff poultry prior to freezing.

About Thawing and Cooking Frozen Meat, Game, Poultry, and Game Birds: Roasts, steaks, chops, hamburgers, meat loaves do not need to be thawed before cooking. Most poultry and variety meats do. See chapters on meat, poultry, game and game birds for specific instructions.

ABOUT FREEZING SEAFOOD

Not all seafood freezes well; watery fish turns mushy and flavorless; oily or gamy fish becomes overly strong. Because of "flash freezing," commercial packers can freeze fish far more successfully than can the person with a home freezer. Still, freezing is a better way of preserving a fisherman's catch than canning.

Fish: Prepare fish for freezing exactly as for cooking; clean and scale, leave whole, fillet, or cut in steaks. Drugstore-wrap airtight in foil or other pliable freezer wrapping, separating steaks or fillets with 2 layers of wrapping material so they can be pulled apart while solidly frozen. Label, then store in freezer in plastic bags to seal in fishy odors.

Shrimp: Pack shelled or unshelled, raw or boiled; if boiled, quick-chill before freezing.

Hard-shell Crabs, Lobsters: Boil or steam, remove meat from shell, cool, and pack. (*Note:* If shells are needed, scrub, wrap, and freeze separately.)

Soft-shell Crabs: Prepare as for cooking, wrap individually, and freeze.

Oysters, Clams: Shuck, saving liquor. Pack in containers, cover with liquor (if insufficient, make up with brine made by mixing 1 tablespoon salt to 1 cup water).

Scallops: Wash, drain, pack in containers, and cover with brine (1 tablespoon salt to 1 cup water).

About Thawing and Cooking Frozen Seafood: Detailed instructions are included in the sections on fish, and shellfish.

About Freezing Herbs

Pick fresh herbs just before they bloom, preferably on a dry day, choosing tenderest young shoots. Wash only if dirty, rinse in cool water, and gently shake off excess moisture. Freeze by one of the following methods. (*Note:* Frozen herbs have approximately the same flavor power as fresh herbs, about ½–⅓ as much as dried herbs.)

Blanching Method: Tie herb stalks in groups of 2 or 3, blanch one minute in boiling water, then quick-chill in ice water. Remove leaves from stalks and wrap in plastic food wrap—about 5 large or 1 tablespoon small leaves to a package. Wrap each plastic packet in foil to seal in fragrance, label, and quick-freeze. Once frozen, bundle packets into a plastic bag so they won't get lost in freezer. *To Use:* Mince solidly frozen leaves and add to recipe.

Ice Cube Method: Mince herb, spoon 1 tablespoon into each compartment of an ice cube tray, add water to fill and freeze. Once frozen, empty all herb cubes of a flavor into a plastic bag (all tarragon, for example, or all dill or chives) and label bag. Bundle, if you like, in a larger plastic bag and store in freezer.

To Use: Add herb cube to soup, sauce, or stew or, if a "dry" herb is needed for a salad or other dish, thaw cube in a small strainer set over a small bowl. Add thawed herb to recipe (and liquid to soups, sauces, or stews—it will have some herb aroma).

GUIDE TO FREEZING PARTIALLY PREPARED OR FULLY COOKED FOODS

Food	Preparation for Freezing	Serving Tips
Meat, Poultry, Seafood		
Stews, casseroles	Cook until barely tender; underseason; omit potatoes, pasta, or other starchy ingredient. Cool, pack in containers or oven-to-table casseroles, and freeze.	Thaw slightly, reheat slowly as recipe directs. Add potatoes or pasta in time to cook fully.
Pies	Bake fully and freeze or cook filling only, fill pan, add top crust, and freeze without baking. (*Note:* Use an aluminum or other nonrusting piepan.)	*Large Pies:* Thaw, then reheat or bake. *Small Pies:* Bake or reheat without thawing.
Meat loaves, meat balls	Cook fully and freeze or freeze raw.	*Uncooked Loaves:* Bake without thawing, increasing time 1½ times. *Cooked Loaves:* Thaw and reheat. *Uncooked Meat Balls:* Thaw before cooking. *Cooked Meat Balls:* Reheat without thawing.
Leftovers	Freeze leftover roasts in as large pieces as possible or sliced and covered with gravy; remove all bone, fat, skin, etc. Also, remove stuffing from body cavities of poultry, bones, and shells from seafood and scrape off any sauce or gravy.	Thaw and serve cold or use in recipes calling for cooked meat, poultry, or seafood.
Breads	Bake, cool, wrap, and freeze. (*Note:* Rolls can be baked until just beginning to brown, then cooled and frozen; they will finish baking during reheating.)	Thaw in wrapper or loosened wrapper, then heat to serving temperature. (*Note:* Toast sliced bread unthawed.)

1272

Sandwiches	Butter both slices of bread; use meat spreads, savory butters as fillings, not mayonnaise mixtures, which freeze poorly. To prevent ice crystal formation, avoid contact with freezer shelves.	Thaw in wrappers.
Pies and pastries	*Pie Shells:* Freeze baked or unbaked. *Pies:* Do not freeze custard or cream pies. Double-crust fruit pies can be frozen raw or baked (increase cornstarch or other thickener in filling by 1 tablespoon.) If to be frozen raw, do not cut steam vents in top crust. Use aluminum or other nonrusting piepans.	*Pie Shells:* If raw, bake unthawed 5 minutes at 450° F., prick and bake 15 minutes longer. If baked, thaw and fill. *Pies:* If raw, cut steam vents in top crust, bake without thawing 3/4-1 hour at 425° F. If baked, heat without thawing 3/4 hour at 350° F.
Cakes	Use pure flavorings — synthetics may turn bitter. Bake cake but do not fill or frost; wrap and freeze. (*Note:* If necessary to freeze a frosted cake, freeze and then wrap.)	Thaw unfrosted, unfilled cakes in wrappers, then fill and frost. If frosted, loosen wrapper and thaw in refrigerator.
Cookies	Freeze baked or unbaked.	Refrigerator-type cookie dough can be sliced and baked while frozen; others should be thawed.
Gravies, sauces	Do not freeze egg- or cream-thickened sauces; increase starch slightly in starch-thickened sauces; when cooling, beat briskly to lessen chance of separation in freezing.	Reheat slowly without thawing, in top of a double boiler if thick, stirring or beating often.
Stocks, broths	Boil uncovered to reduce volume and save freezer space.	Reheat without thawing, diluting as needed with water.

ABOUT FREEZING DAIRY PRODUCTS

Do not try to freeze milk, and cream only if whipped (see To Freeze Decorative Whipped Cream in the dessert chapter). Butter, margarine, and lard can be frozen in their original cartons and kept about a month; to store longer, remove from cartons and wrap tightly in foil or other freezer wrap. As for cheese, only hard varieties, like Parmesan, freeze with any success; wrap snugly in foil or plastic food wrap.

ABOUT FREEZING EGGS

Note: Freeze only absolutely fresh eggs.

To Freeze Whole Eggs: Break eggs into a bowl, stir just to mix, trying not to make any bubbles. Measure eggs and for each 1 cup, mix in 1 tablespoon sugar or light corn syrup (such eggs can be used in desserts) or 1 teaspoon salt (use for savory recipes). Pack in 1-cup leakproof cartons, label, and quick-freeze. Be sure to note on label how many eggs there are in the carton and whether they have had sugar or salt added. Thaw before using.

To Freeze Yolks: Stir yolks just enough to break, measure, and for each 1 cup yolks add 1 tablespoon sugar or light corn syrup or 1 teaspoon salt. Proceed as for whole eggs.

To Freeze Whites: Do not stir whites or add sugar or salt. Break directly into ice cube trays, allowing one white per compartment. Freeze solid, then empty into plastic bags and store in freezer. Thaw before using.

ABOUT FREEZING PARTIALLY PREPARED OR FULLY COOKED FOODS

A number of recipes in this book indicate at which point preparations may be interrupted and the dish frozen. Many more can be doubled, tripled, or quadrupled and frozen for future use.

Some General Tips

—Slightly undercook foods to be frozen, particularly pasta dishes like lasagne and ravioli.
—Whenever possible, omit potatoes, pasta, rice, or other starchy foods from stews and juicy casseroles; they turn mushy and occupy unnecessary freezer space. Add to recipe when reheating.
—Underseason recipes slightly; some seasonings fade in the freezer, others gain strength. Adjust seasonings when reheating.
—Quick-chill any hot food before packing and freezing.
—Whenever practical, freeze casseroles or stews in freezer-to-oven-to-table dishes. Or freeze in foil-lined pans or casseroles and, when brick hard, lift out and wrap airtight. To reheat, unwrap and refit in pan.
—Freeze small amounts of stock, broth, and vegetable cooking water in ice cube trays; when solid, bundle cubes in plastic bags. Use in soups, sauces, stews.
—Apportion meat and vegetable leftovers in TV dinner trays, cover, label, and freeze.
—Whenever possible, reheat frozen cooked foods without thawing.

EAT WELL, KEEP WELL

Astonishing as it may seem in this age of abundance, a great many Americans (about 20 per cent, according to a recent Department of Agriculture survey) are malnourished. Not for lack of money. But for lack of understanding about how foods function in the body. We tend to eat what we like, often without restraint, and in America preferences run to carbohydrates (starches and sweets).

What we eat affects how we look, feel, and to some extent behave. The killing and crippling diseases of yesterday—scurvy, pellagra, beriberi, rickets—were all eventually traced to specific nutritional deficiencies, a vitamin C deficiency for scurvy, niacin for pellagra, thiamine for beriberi, and vitamin D for rickets. Such desperate vitamin inadequacies, fortunately, are rarely seen in America today, but poor nutrition manifests itself in bad complexions and other skin problems, in obesity, in irritability and listlessness.

Nutritionists maintain that, with rare exceptions, a person who eats moderately and wisely, selecting a variety of foods each day from The 4 Basic Food Groups, will be properly nourished.

The 4 Basic Food Groups

GROUP I—THE MILK GROUP:
Milk (all kinds), cream, cheese needed to supply calcium, high-quality protein, vitamin A, and riboflavin (a B vitamin). The *Recommended Daily Amount* varies according to age and sex:

	8-ounce glasses needed per day
Children under 9	2–3
Children 9–12	3 or more
Teen-agers	4 or more
Adults	2 or more
Pregnant Women	3 or more
Nursing Mothers	4 or more

Note: Some "milk" may be taken as cheese or ice cream:

½ cup ice cream=¼ cup milk
½ cup cottage cheese=⅓ cup milk
1 (1″) cube Cheddar cheese=½ cup milk

GROUP II—THE MEAT GROUP: All meats and organ meats, poultry and eggs, fish and shellfish, and, as occasional meat substitutes, dry beans and peas, lentils, nuts, and peanut butter. This group supplies the body with top quality protein, iron, and three important B vitamins—thiamine, riboflavin, and niacin. *Recommended Daily Amounts:* 2 or more servings from the group. Any of the following count as 1 serving: 3 ounces cooked lean meat, poultry or seafood; 2 eggs; 1 cup cooked dried beans, peas or lentils; ¼ cup peanut butter.

GROUP III—THE FRUIT AND VEGETABLE GROUP: The source of vitamin-A-rich foods (dark green and yellow vegetables such as broccoli and winter squash and such fruits as apricots, cantaloupe, mangoes, persimmons, and pumpkin); also the source of vitamin-C-rich foods (citrus fruits, cantaloupe, strawberries, sweet green and red peppers). *Recommended Amounts:* 1 serving daily of a vitamin-C-rich food, 1 serving every other day of a vitamin A food, and 2–3 additional servings daily of any other foods in the group.

GROUP IV—THE BREAD-CEREAL GROUP: All whole grains, enriched or restored breads and cereals (see chapter on cereals, rice, and pasta), necessary for B vitamins, protein, iron, and energy. *Recommended Daily Amounts:* 4 or more servings, 5 or more if breads only are eaten.

OTHER FOODS: Fats, oils, sweets, refined cereals are all important to the body as energy foods. But they are so rarely lacking in the diet it's not necessary to remind people to eat them.

About Individual Nutrients

What are proteins exactly? Carbohydrates? Vitamins? Minerals? What do they do in the body? Why are they important?

Protein: The substance of life, the body's building material. It is essential to the maintenance and repair of all bodily tissues, to the production of enzymes, hormones, and infection-fighting antibodies. Protein also provides energy to fuel the body. In truth, protein is not a single compound but many, composed of simpler compounds called *amino acids*. To date, 22 amino acids have been isolated, eight of them *essential*, meaning the body cannot manufacture them and that they must be taken in as food. The highest quality proteins are those providing the best supply of essential amino acids—animal foods, invariably, such as meat, seafood, poultry, milk, cheese, and eggs.

Carbohydrates: The energy foods—sugars and starches. The danger here is not eating too few but too many.

Fats and Oils: Complex chemical substances, controversial today because they have been implicated in circulatory and heart diseases. Their chief role in the body is to provide energy, and this they do, about twice as well as carbohydrates and proteins. But the specter of *cholesterol* looms and television commercials, hammering away at us to use this mono- or polyunsaturated fat, won't let us forget it. Cholesterol is not a fat but a related fatty substance used by the body to form vitamin D and certain hormones. Its presence in the body (particularly its accumulation in and clogging of blood vessels) is being investigated in relation to the saturation of a fat. Saturation refers, simply, to the hydrogen content of a fat and, in a far more practical sense, to the consistency. Generally speaking, the more hydrogen a fat contains, the more saturated it is and the harder or stiffer. Hydrogenated shortenings, to illustrate, are vegetable oils pumped full of hydrogen so that they become creamy and thick. The subject is far too complicated to discuss further here, not to mention unresolved. But for those who would explore it more thoroughly, we recommend an excellent free pamphlet, "Nutritional Facts About Fats," written for lay persons and available from Cornell University. Write for: Home Economics Extension Leaflet 32, New York State College of Human Ecology, Cornell University, Ithaca, New York.

Vitamins: These chemical compounds, found in minute quantities in foods, are essential to good health. The most important of them are:

Vitamin A: Helps eyes adjust to changing light intensities, helps prevent night blindness, necessary for healthy mucous membranes. *Good Sources:* Dark yellow or orange fruits, dark green and yellow vegetables, cream, butter, whole milk, fortified margarine, liver. (*Note:* Vitamin A can be stored by the body, so avoid overdoses of vitamin pills.)

The B Group: There are about a dozen B vitamins, the most important of which are *thiamine* (B_1), *riboflavin* (B_2), and *niacin.* If the body receives enough of these three, it is unlikely to be deficient in any others of the B group.

Thiamine helps keep muscles, heart, and nerves functioning properly, promotes appetite and aids carbohydrate metabolism. *Good Sources:* Meat (particularly pork), fish, poultry, enriched breads and cereals, milk, dried peas, and beans.

Riboflavin is essential for the utilization of oxygen within the body and enzyme function. *Good Sources:* The same as for thiamine.

Niacin, like riboflavin, is necessary for proper tissue use of oxygen, also for healthy skin, tongue, and digestive system. *Good Sources:* Lean meats, poultry, whole and enriched cereals, peanuts, dried peas, and beans.

Vitamin C (*Ascorbic Acid*) has literally to do with holding the body together— tissues, bones, teeth, blood vessels. It speeds healing of wounds, helps stave off infection. *Good Sources:* Citrus fruits, cantaloupe, strawberries, tomatoes, sweet green peppers, raw cabbage, collards and kale, broccoli, freshly dug Irish potatoes.

Vitamin D: Essential to calcium metabolism and the formation of sound bones and teeth. *Good Sources:* Eggs, fish liver oils, sardines, salmon, tuna, sunshine (it converts a substance on the skin to Vitamin D which can then be used by the body. *Caution:* Bathing or showering after a sunbath destroys the vitamin D). Like vitamin A, vitamin D can be stored by the body and indiscriminate use of vitamin pills may cause overdoses and illness.

Vitamin E: Despite faddists' cure-all claims for vitamin E, scientists have yet to substantiate any of them. Physicians have used vitamin E successfully to treat a certain anemia in children. Its primary role, however, seems to be as a biological antioxidant (preventing unwanted oxidation of certain fatty acids) in both the body and in foods. It is important that the diet contain adequate amounts of vitamin E, but because it is so widely found in foods we eat (vegetable oils, eggs, butter and margarine, legumes and nuts, green leafy vegetables, wheat germ), deficiencies are unlikely.

Minerals:

Calcium and Phosphorous: Necessary for strong bones and teeth, good muscle tone, sound nervous system. *Good Sources:* Milk and milk products, dark leafy greens such as kale, collards, mustard and turnip greens.

Iodine: Needed for normal thyroid function. *Good Sources:* Seafood, iodized salt.

Iron: Essential for rich, red blood. *Good Sources:* Organ meats (particularly liver), red meats, oysters, dark green leafy vegetables, eggs, dried fruits, whole or enriched cereals.

THE EFFECT OF COOKING ON VITAMINS

Vitamin	Destroyed by Heat	Leached Out in Cooking Water	Destroyed by Sunlight	Destroyed by Exposure to Air
A	not apt to be affected by cooking			
Thiamine	X	X		
Riboflavin		X	X	
Niacin		X		
C	X	X		X
D	not apt to be affected by cooking			
E	not apt to be affected by cooking			

Note: There are a number of other minerals and vitamins but they have not been included here either because they are unlikely to be missing in the diet or because their function and requirement are still undetermined.

About Water

Though not a nutrient, water is nonetheless vital. The human body, about ⅔ water, must have water in order to survive—to regulate body temperature, to aid digestion, to carry off wastes. Most foods contain water, it's true, but they may not provide the body as much water as it needs. The old rule of "6–8 glasses of liquid a day" still holds.

About Calories

Calories do count, alas, and the only way to lose weight safely and successfully is to reduce the daily calorie intake—forever if necessary. There simply is no magic pill or potion to melt away unwanted pounds. Crash diets do produce immediate results—sometimes drastic ones—but in the long run they fail because the dieter not only regains all lost weight but usually an extra few pounds as well. This sort of seesaw dieting is dangerous. So, too, are starvation diets limiting calories to less than 1,000 a day. If you have more than 5 or 10 pounds to lose, see your doctor and have him advise the reducing diet that is best for you. Most doctors discourage losing more than 2–3 pounds a week, and most agree that the only sane way to diet is to eat foods from each of the Basic 4 Food Groups, merely less of each. (A week's balanced 1,200-Calorie-a-Day Menus are included in the chapter on menu planning).

What is a calorie? Technically, a unit of heat used to measure the fuel potential of food in the body. To maintain body weight, the calorie intake (via food) must equal the outgo (via energy expended in the day's activities). When the intake exceeds the outgo, the balance is converted to fat. When the reverse is true, as in reducing diets, the body's fat reserves are tapped to provide energy.

"Middle age spread" is simply a failure to adjust eating habits to a slower life-style. We continue to stuff ourselves as we did in our teens and yet are far less active. To compound the problem, our basal metabolism is slowing down. It will continue to decline throughout life, and the woman who would keep her figure (or the man his physique) will cut daily calorie intake by about 150–200 every 10 years after the age of 25. At 35, for example, all factors remaining equal (height, weight, activity), the body will need about 150 calories less per day than it did at 25, and at 45, about 150 less than it did at 35. And so it goes throughout life.

How many calories are enough? It varies, obviously, according to age, sex, size, activity, and a number of other factors, but you can make a rough estimate. Take your *desirable body weight* (see accompanying height-weight charts), then multiply this figure by:

16 calories if you are sedentary
20 calories if you are active
24 calories if you are a woman
and very active
28 calories if you are a man and very
active

This is the number of calories you need each day to maintain *desirable body weight*. Desirable body weight is considered to be mid-20's weight. In other words, what you weighed at the age of 25 (assuming you were neither over- nor underweight). Maintaining this weight throughout life is extremely difficult for most people because excess weight comes so slowly, perhaps only 1–2 pounds a year (1 pound body fat=3,500 stored calories). The temptation is to watch the scale creep upward, reaching new plateaus, until we realize one day with a start that we are 10 or 20 pounds too heavy. Then come the remorse and the resolutions to diet.

DESIRABLE WEIGHTS FOR WOMEN, AGE 25 AND OVER*
Note: for girls between 18 and 25, subtract 1 pound for each year under 25.

Height (in shoes, 2" heels)		Weight in Pounds (in indoor clothing)		
Feet	Inches	Small Frame	Medium Frame	Large Frame
4	10	92–98	96–107	104–119
4	11	94–101	98–110	106–122
5	0	96–104	101–113	109–125
5	1	99–107	104–116	112–128
5	2	102–110	107–119	115–131
5	3	105–113	110–122	118–134
5	4	108–116	113–126	121–138
5	5	111–119	116–130	125–142
5	6	114–123	120–135	129–146
5	7	118–127	124–139	133–150
5	8	122–131	128–143	137–154
5	9	126–135	132–147	141–158
5	10	130–140	136–151	145–163
5	11	134–144	140–155	149–168
6	0	138–148	144–159	153–173

* Prepared by the Metropolitan Life Insurance Company.

DESIRABLE WEIGHTS FOR MEN, AGE 25 AND OVER*

Height (in shoes, 1" heels)		Weight in Pounds (in indoor clothing)		
Feet	Inches	Small Frame	Medium Frame	Large Frame
5	2	112–120	118–129	126–141
5	3	115–123	121–133	129–144
5	4	118–126	124–136	132–148
5	5	121–129	127–139	135–152
5	6	124–133	130–143	138–156
5	7	128–137	134–147	142–161
5	8	132–141	138–152	147–166
5	9	136–145	142–156	151–170
5	10	140–150	146–160	155–174
5	11	144–154	150–165	159–179
6	0	148–158	154–170	164–184
6	1	152–162	158–175	168–189
6	2	156–167	162–180	173–194
6	3	160–171	167–185	178–199
6	4	164–175	172–190	182–204

* Prepared by the Metropolitan Life Insurance Company.

The **Recommended Daily Dietary Allowances** chart shows several nutrients essential for maintenance of good nutrition in healthy, normally active persons in this country. They can be attained with a variety of common foods which will also provide nutrients of less defined requirements.

More detailed information may be obtained for "Recommended Dietary Allowances," publication 1146 mentioned in the Source note in the chart, page 1281.

RECOMMENDED DAILY DIETARY ALLOWANCES[1] [2]

Designed for the maintenance of good nutrition of practically all healthy persons in the U.S.A.

(Allowances are intended for persons normally active in a temperate climate)

Persons	Age in years[5] From – up to	Weight in pounds	Height in inches	Food Energy[3] Calories	Protein Grams	Calcium Grams	Iron Milligrams	Vitamin A International units	Thiamine Milligrams	Riboflavin Milligrams	Niacin Equivalent[4] Milligrams	Ascorbic Acid Milligrams	Vitamin D International units
Men	18 – 35	154	69	2,900	70	0.8	10	5,000	1.2	1.7	19	70	
	35 – 55	154	69	2,600	70	.8	10	5,000	1.0	1.6	17	70	
	55 – 75	154	69	2,200	70	.8	10	5,000	.9	1.3	15	70	
Women	18 – 35	128	64	2,100	58	.8	15	5,000	.8	1.3	14	70	
	35 – 55	128	64	1,900	58	.8	15	5,000	.8	1.2	13	70	
	55 – 75	128	64	1,600	58	.8	10	5,000	.8	1.2	13	70	
Pregnant (second and third trimester)				+200	+20	+.5	+5	+1,000	+.2	+.3	+3	+30	400
Lactating				+1,000	+40	+.5	+5	+3,000	+.4	+.6	+7	+30	400
Infants[6]	0 – 1	18	—	lb. X 52 ± 7	lb. X 1.1 ± 0.2	.7	lb. X 0.45	1,500	.4	.6	6	30	400
Children	1 – 3	29	34	1,300	32	.8	8	2,000	.5	.8	9	40	400
	3 – 6	40	42	1,600	40	.8	10	2,500	.6	1.0	11	50	400
	6 – 9	53	49	2,100	52	.8	12	3,500	.8	1.3	14	60	400
Boys	9 – 12	72	55	2,400	60	1.1	15	4,500	1.0	1.4	16	70	400
	12 – 15	98	61	3,000	75	1.4	15	5,000	1.2	1.8	20	80	400
	15 – 18	134	68	3,400	85	1.4	15	5,000	1.4	2.0	22	80	400
Girls	9 – 12	72	55	2,200	55	1.1	15	4,500	.9	1.3	15	80	400
	12 – 15	103	62	2,500	62	1.3	15	5,000	1.0	1.5	17	80.	400
	15 – 18	117	64	2,300	58	1.3	15	5,000	.9	1.3	15	70	400

[1] Source: Adapted from Recommended Dietary Allowances, Publication 1146, 59 pp., revised 1964. Published by National Academy of Sciences — National Research Council, Washington, D.C., 20418. Price $1.00. Also available in libraries.

[2] The allowance levels are intended to cover individual variations among most normal persons as they live in the United States under usual environmental stresses.

[3] Tables 1 and 2 and figures 1 and 2 in Publication 1146 (see footnote 1) show calorie adjustments for weight and age.

[4] Niacin equivalents include dietary sources of the preformed vitamin and the precursor, tryptophan. 60 milligrams tryptophan represents 1 milligram niacin.

[5] Entries on lines for age range 18 to 35 years represent the 25-year age. All other entries represent allowances for the midpoint of the specified age periods, i.e., line for children 1 to 3 is for age 2 years (24 months); 3 to 6 is for age 4½ years (54 months), etc.

[6] The calorie and protein allowances per pound for infants are considered to decrease progressively from birth. Allowances for calcium, thiamine, riboflavin, and niacin increase proportionately with calories to the maximum values shown.

Note: The Recommended Daily Dietary Allowances should not be confused with Minimum Daily Requirements. The Recommended Dietary Allowances are amounts of nutrients recommended by the Food and Nutrition Board of National Research Council, and are considered adequate for maintenance of good nutrition in healthy persons in the United States. The allowances are revised from time to time in accordance with newer knowledge of nutritional needs.

The minimum Daily Requirements are the amounts of various nutrients that have been established by the Food and Drug Administration as standards for labeling purposes of foods and pharmaceutical preparations for special dietary uses. These are the amounts regarded as necessary in the diet for the prevention of deficiency diseases and generally are less than the Recommended Dietary Allowances. The Minimum Daily Requirements are set forth in the Federal Register, vol. 6, No. 227 (Nov. 22, 1941), beginning on p. 5921, and amended as stated in the Federal Register (June 1, 1957), vol. 22, No. 106, p. 3841.

1281

ADDRESS BOOK

The following companies will fill mail order requests for specialty foods and equipment. Most have catalogues; others will answer specific inquiries.

Special Cooking Equipment
Bazaar de la Cuisine (catalogue)
1003 Second Avenue
New York, New York 10022

Bazar Français (catalogue)
666–68 Sixth Avenue
New York, New York 10010

The Bridge Company
212 East Fifty-second Street
New York, New York 10022

Dione Lucas Gourmet Center
226 East Fifty-first Street
New York, New York 10022

Hammacher Schlemmer (catalogue)
147 East Fifty-seventh Street
New York, New York 10022

Maid of Scandinavia (catalogue)
3245 Raleigh Avenue
Minneapolis, Minnesota 55416

Foreign and Specialty Foods
Byrd Mill
RFD 5
Louisa, Virginia
(Whole grain, stone-ground, flours and meals)

Casa Moneo
210 West Fourteenth Street
New York, New York 10011
(Spanish and Latin American foods, utensils; list available; catalogue)

Charles and Company
340 Madison Avenue
New York, New York 10017
(Assorted delicacies; catalogue)

Cheese-of-All-Nations
153 Chambers Street
New York, New York 10007
(Imported Cheeses)

GNL Shallot Distributors
51 DeShibe Terrace
Vineland, New Jersey 08360
(Shallots)

H. Roth and Son
Lekvar-by-the-Barrel
1577 First Avenue
New York, New York 10028
(Hungarian and Middle European foods, herbs, and spices, cooking utensils; catalogue)

Kassos Brothers
570 Ninth Avenue
New York, New York 10036
(Greek foods)

Katagiri
224 East Fifty-ninth Street
New York, New York 10022
(Japanese foods)

Maison Glass
52 East Fifty-eighth Street
New York, New York 10022
(Assorted delicacies; catalogue)

Manganaro Foods
488 Ninth Avenue
New York, New York 10018
(Italian foods and cooking utensils; catalogue)

Maryland Gourmet Mart
1072 First Avenue
New York, New York 10022
(Game, assorted delicacies; catalogue)

Paprikás Weiss Importer
1546 Second Avenue
New York, New York 10028
(Paprika, Hungarian and Middle European foods, spices, herbs, gourmet utensils; catalogue)

Schapira Coffee Company
117 West Tenth Street
New York, New York 10011
(Coffees, teas; catalogue)

Trinacria Importing Company
415 Third Avenue
New York, New York 10016
(Near and Middle Eastern foods, utensils)

Information on Foods and Cooking, Marketing, Food Conservation, and Gardening:

Superintendent of Documents
Government Printing Office
Washington, D.C. 20402
(Publication lists available)

INDEX

What It Will Mean to Cook
with Metric Measures

The metric system is a way of measuring based on the decimal system with larger measures being subdivided into units of ten. Food researchers and European cooks have always used the metric system because it is more precise than American weights and measures.

In recipes, the principal difference between our present way of measuring and the metric is that dry ingredients like flour and sugar are weighed rather than measured in a cup.

Meats, fruits, and vegetables will be sold by the kilogram instead of the pound and, in recipes, will be called for by weight rather than by cup (whether sliced, diced, or whole).

Small measures — tablespoons, teaspoons, and fractions thereof — are not likely to change.

Liquids are measured in measuring cups, but the calibrations are marked in liters, ½ liters, ¼ liters, and milliliters instead of in cups. (See opposite.) There will be no more such cumbersome measurements as ½ cup plus 1 tablespoon or 1 cup minus 3 teaspoons.

TABLE OF EQUIVALENTS OF U.S. WEIGHTS AND MEASURES

Note: All measures are level.

Pinch or dash = less than 1/8 teaspoon

3 teaspoons = 1 tablespoon

2 tablespoons = 1 fluid ounce

1 jigger = 1½ fluid ounces

4 tablespoons = ¼ cup

5 tablespoons + 1 teaspoon = 1/3 cup

8 tablespoons = ½ cup

10 tablespoons + 2 teaspoons = 2/3 cup

12 tablespoons = ¾ cup

16 tablespoons = 1 cup

1 cup = 8 fluid ounces

2 cups = 1 pint

2 pints = 1 quart

4/5 quart = 25.6 fluid ounces

1 quart = 32 fluid ounces

4 quarts = 1 gallon

2 gallons (dry measure) = 1 peck

4 pecks = 1 bushel

SOME FRACTIONAL MEASURES

½ of ¼ cup = 2 tablespoons

½ of 1/3 cup = 2 tablespoons + 2 teaspoons

½ of ½ cup = ¼ cup

½ of 2/3 cup = 1/3 cup

½ of 3/4 cup = ¼ cup + 2 tablespoons

1/3 of ¼ cup = 1 tablespoon + 1 teaspoon

1/3 of 1/3 cup = 1 tablespoon + 2 1/3 teaspoon

1/3 of ½ cup = 2 tablespoons + 2 teaspoons

1/3 of 2/3 cup = 3 tablespoons + 1 2/3 teaspoo

1/3 of 3/4 cup = ¼ cup